JAN -- 2021

WITHDRAW

REF 345.2 CALIFORNIA 2021
v.2
The standard California codes.
California.
33341005968184

S0-BMS-460

JAN -- 2021

The STANDARD
CALIFORNIA CODES
6-in-2®

VOLUME 1

CIVIL—CIVIL PROCEDURE—EVIDENCE—FAMILY—PROBATE

Selected Provisions of the Government Code

VOLUME 2

CALIFORNIA RULES OF COURT

With The

RULES OF PROFESSIONAL CONDUCT

RULES & POLICY DECLARATIONS OF THE
COMMISSION ON JUDICIAL PERFORMANCE

2021 EDITION

As revised by Legislative Enactments
up to and including the
second year of the
2019–2020 Regular Session
and Rules of Court revisions
received from the Judicial Council,
the California Supreme Court, the State Bar
of California, and the Commission
on Judicial Performance
through November 22, 2020

ALAMEDA FREE LIBRARY
1550 Oak Street
Alameda, CA 94501

LexisNexis

QUESTIONS ABOUT THIS PUBLICATION?

For questions about the **Editorial Content** appearing in these volumes or reprint permission, please call:

Katie Komer at 1-925-284-0168
Email: .... katie.komer@lexisnexis.com
or e-mail at .... CalCodes@lexisnexis.com

For assistance with replacement pages, shipments, billing or other customer service matters, please call:

Customer Services Department at .... (800) 833-9844
Outside the United States and Canada, please call .... (518) 487-3000
Fax number .... (518) 487-3584
Customer Service Website .... http://www.lexisnexis.com/custserv/

For information on other Matthew Bender Publications, please call
Your account manager .... (800) 223-1940
Outside the United States and Canada, please call .... (518) 487-3000

ISBN 978-1-5221-8542-0 (HB)
ISBN 978-1-5221-8161-3 (SB)

Copyright 1931, 1933, 1935, 1937, 1939, 1941,
1943, 1945 and 1947 by
CHASE LAW BOOK COMPANY

Copyright 1949 by
STANDARD CODES, LTD.

Copyright 1951, 1953, 1955, 1957, 1959, 1961, 1963 by
HANNA LEGAL PUBLICATIONS

Copyright © 1965–2020
By Matthew Bender & Company, Inc., a member of the LexisNexis Group.

Rules of Professional Conduct
©2020 The State Bar of California. All rights reserved. Reprinted with permission. No part of this work may be reproduced, stored in a retrieval system, or transmitted in any medium without prior written permission of The State Bar of California.

This publication is designed to provide authoritative information in regard to the subject matter covered. It is sold with the understanding that the publisher is not engaged in rendering legal, accounting, or other professional services. If legal advice or other expert assistance is required, the services of a competent professional should be sought.

LexisNexis and the Knowledge Burst logo are registered trademarks of RELX Inc. Matthew Bender and the Matthew Bender Flame Design are registered trademarks of Matthew Bender Properties Inc.

6-in-2 and SIX-IN-TWO are registered trademarks of Matthew Bender & Company, Inc.

Copyright © 2020 Matthew Bender & Company, Inc., a member of LexisNexis.
Originally published in: 1931

All Rights Reserved.

No copyright is claimed by LexisNexis or Matthew Bender & Company, Inc., in the text of statutes, regulations, and excerpts from court opinions quoted within this work. Permission to copy material may be licensed for a fee from the Copyright Clearance Center, 222 Rosewood Drive, Danvers, Mass. 01923, telephone (978) 750-8400.

MATTHEW◊BENDER

Editorial Offices
230 Park Ave., 7th Floor, New York, NY 10169 (800) 543-6862
555 Middle Creek Parkway, Colorado Springs, CO 80921 (800) 833-9844
www.lexisnexis.com

PREFACE TO VOLUME 2

This 2021 Edition of the Standard California Codes incorporates all changes required by legislative enactments up to and including ch. 372 of the second year of the 2019–2020 Regular Session, all propositions approved by the electorate at the November 3, 2020, General Election, and all changes received from the Judicial Council, the California Supreme Court, the State Bar of California, and the Commission on Judicial Performance through November 22, 2020.

This Edition gives the legislative history of each rule. Amendments made in 2020 are highlighted by printing in boldface type all matter added to a rule and indicating by a figure within brackets, such as [1], each point of deletion. The deleted matter is then shown by footnotes keyed to the corresponding figures. Where changes are extensive, the former rule may be reprinted in full.

The following reproduction of Rule 9.17, as amended effective January 1, 2019, clearly illustrates the "stressed amendment" feature:

> **Rule 9.17.   Remand with instructions.**
> [1] The Supreme Court may **at any time** remand [2] **a** matter **filed under this chapter** to the State Bar Court **or the State Bar** with instructions to **take such further actions or** conduct such further proceedings as the Supreme Court deems necessary.
> *Rule 9.17 amended effective January 1, 2019; adopted as rule 953.5 effective February 1, 1991; previously amended and renumbered effective January 1, 2007.*
> **Rule 9.17.   2019 Deletes. [1]** At any time before the final disposition of a decision of the State Bar Court filed under Business and Professions Code section 6081, **[2]** the

To read Rule 9.17 as amended, you read the section as printed, omitting the bracketed figures "[1]" and "[2]":

> **Rule 9.17.   Remand with instructions.**
> The Supreme Court may **at any time** remand **a** matter **filed under this chapter** to the State Bar Court **or the State Bar** with instructions to **take such further actions or** conduct such further proceedings as the Supreme Court deems necessary.

To reconstruct the rule as it read before being amended, you read the rule as printed, omitting the words in boldface type and inserting the words appearing in the footnote under Rule 9.17 and referred to by the bracketed figures "[1]" and "[2]" in the rule:

> **Rule 9.17.   Remand with instructions.**
> At any time before the final disposition of a decision of the State Bar Court filed under Business and Professions Code section 6081, the Supreme Court may remand the matter to the State Bar Court with instructions to conduct such further proceedings as the Supreme Court deems necessary.

In presenting this Edition of the Standard California Codes, we wish to acknowledge with gratitude the many helpful suggestions received from users of our Codes, and to express the hope that this Edition will serve effectively the needs of bench and bar alike.

THE PUBLISHER

CALIFORNIA
RULES OF COURT

2021 EDITION

Rules of practice and procedure promulgated by the Judicial Council and the Supreme Court with amendments received from November 21, 2019 through November 22, 2020.

PREFACE

The California Rules of Court includes all rules of practice and procedure adopted by the Judicial Council and the Supreme Court pursuant to the authority contained in California Constitution, Article VI, Section 6, and in various code sections. The Council originally adopted rules for the superior courts, the Supreme Court, and the courts of appeal shortly after its organization in 1926, and later adopted rules for the appellate departments of the superior court. In 1943, new rules on appeal to the Supreme Court and courts of appeal were adopted. These rules were renumbered and combined into the California Rules of Court adopted April 1, 1962. On June 30, 2006, the Judicial Council of California approved a major reorganization of the California Rules of Court, a group of more than 1,000 rules and 47 standards of judicial administration that govern state court policy and procedure. The reorganization, effective January 1, 2007, involved a major restructuring, reordering, and renumbering of the rules and standards to make them clearer, better organized, and easier to read.

Effective January 1, 2009, the Judicial Council adopted a revision of the rules relating to the superior court appellate divisions to place the rules in a more logical order, reflect current practices, fill in gaps in the rules, eliminate outdated language, and update the remaining language so it is similar to the recently revised rules for the Courts of Appeal.

THE PUBLISHER

Table Showing Changes Received From the Judicial Council
From November 21, 2019 Through November 22, 2020

Rule	Effect	Date	Rule	Effect	Date
2.251(b)	Amended	Jan. 1, 2020	5.483(f)	Relettered to (e) / Amended & Relettered from (g)	Jan. 1, 2020
2.251 Adv. Comment	Amended	Jan. 1, 2020	5.483(g)	Relettered to (f) / Relettered from (h)	Jan. 1, 2020
2.255 Hdg	Amended	Jan. 1, 2021	5.483(h)	Relettered to (g) / Relettered from (i)	Jan. 1, 2020
2.255(c)	Amended	Jan. 1, 2020	5.483(i)	Relettered to (h)	Jan. 1, 2020
2.255(g)	Adopted	Jan. 1, 2021	5.483 Adv. Comment	Amended	Jan. 1, 2020
2.257(b)–(e)	Amended	Jan. 1, 2020	5.484	Amended & Renumbered to 5.485 / Adopted	Jan. 1, 2020
2.257 Adv. Comment	Adopted	Jan. 1, 2020	5.485	Renumbered to 5.486 / Amended & Renumbered from 5.484	Jan. 1, 2020
2.540(b)	Amended	Jan. 1, 2020			
2.891	Repealed & Adopted	Jan. 1, 2020	5.486	Renumbered to 5.487 / Amended & Renumbered from 5.485	Jan. 1, 2020
2.956(a)	Amended	Jan. 1, 2021			
2.956(c)	Amended	Jan. 1, 2021	5.487	Renumbered to 5.488 / Amended & Renumbered from 5.486	Jan. 1, 2020
3.720(b)	Amended	Jan. 1, 2020			
3.720 Adv. Comment	Repealed	Jan. 1, 2020	5.488	Renumbered from 5.487	Jan. 1, 2020
3.1161(g) Hdg	Amended	Sept. 1, 2020	Ch. 3 (comm. w/Rule 5.490)	Amended	Jan. 1, 2021
3.1161(h), (i)	Amended	Sept. 1, 2020	5.493	Adopted	Jan. 1, 2021
3.1345(a), (b)	Amended	Jan. 1, 2020	5.502	Amended	Jan. 1, 2021
3.1384 Hdg	Amended	Jan. 1, 2021	5.510(c)	Amended	Jan. 1, 2021
3.1384(a)	Amended	Jan. 1, 2021	5.514(b)	Amended	Jan. 1, 2021
4.130(b), (c)	Amended	Jan. 1, 2020	5.522(c)	Amended	Jan. 1, 2021
4.130(d)	Amended	Jan. 1, 2020, Sept. 1, 2020	5.531 Hdg	Amended	Jan. 1, 2021
4.130(f)	Amended	Jan. 1, 2020	5.531(b)	Amended	Jan. 1, 2021
4.130(g)	Adopted	Jan. 1, 2020	5.550(c)	Amended	Jan. 1, 2020
	Amended	Sept. 1, 2020	5.550(d)	Adopted	Jan. 1, 2020
4.130(h)	Adopted	Jan. 1, 2020	5.552(b)–(d)	Amended	Sept. 1, 2020
4.452(a)	Amended	Jan. 1, 2021	5.555(c), (d)	Amended	Jan. 1, 2021
4.452 Adv. Comment	Amended	Jan. 1, 2021	5.570(e)	Amended	Jan. 1, 2020
4.530(g)	Amended	Jan. 1, 2021	5.570(h)	Amended	Jan. 1, 2020
5.2(b)	Amended	July 1, 2020	5.590(a)	Amended	Jan. 1, 2020
5.9(a)	Amended	Jan. 1, 2021	Ch. 7 (comm. w/Rule 5.610)	Amended	Jan. 1, 2020
5.94 Hdg	Amended	July 1, 2020	5.614 Hdg	Amended	Jan. 1, 2020
5.94(e)	Amended	July 1, 2020	5.614(b)	Amended	Jan. 1, 2020
5.94(f)	Repealed	July 1, 2020	5.614(d)–(f)	Amended	Jan. 1, 2020
5.95	Adopted	July 1, 2020	5.620(a)	Amended	Jan. 1, 2021
5.151(b), (c)	Amended	July 1, 2020	5.620(d), (e)	Amended	Jan. 1, 2021
5.165(a)	Amended	July 1, 2020	5.625(b)	Amended	Jan. 1, 2021
5.220(b)	Amended	Jan. 1, 2021	5.625(c)	Adopted	Jan. 1, 2021
5.220(e)	Amended	Jan. 1, 2021	5.635(b), (c)	Amended	Jan. 1, 2020
5.220(f)	Relettered to (h) / Adopted	Jan. 1, 2021	5.640(b), (c)	Amended	Sept. 1, 2020
5.220(g)	Relettered to (i) / Adopted	Jan. 1, 2021	5.640(e)	Amended	Sept. 1, 2020
5.220(h)	Relettered to (j) / Relettered from (f)	Jan. 1, 2021	5.640(g)	Amended	Sept. 1, 2020
5.220(i)	Repealed / Relettered from (g)	Jan. 1, 2021	5.642	Adopted	Sept. 1, 2020
			5.643	Amended	Jan. 1, 2020
5.220(j)	Relettered to (k) / Relettered from (h)	Jan. 1, 2021	5.645	Amended & Renumbered to 5.643 / Adopted	Jan. 1, 2020
5.220(k)	Relettered from (j)	Jan. 1, 2021	5.645 Adv. Comment	Repealed	Jan. 1, 2020
5.225(c)	Amended	Jan. 1, 2020	5.649	Amended	Sept. 1, 2020
5.275(b)	Amended	Jan. 1, 2020	5.668(c)	Relettered to (d) / Adopted	Jan. 1, 2020
5.275(i)	Amended	Jan. 1, 2020	5.668(d)	Relettered from (c)	Jan. 1, 2020
5.305(b)	Amended	Jan. 1, 2020	5.674(b)–(e)	Amended	Jan. 1, 2020
5.350 Hdg	Amended	Jan. 1, 2020	5.676(a)	Amended	Jan. 1, 2020
5.350(a), (b)	Amended	Jan. 1, 2020	5.676(b)	Relettered to (c) / Adopted	Jan. 1, 2020
5.350(d)–(f)	Amended	Jan. 1, 2020	5.676(c)	Relettered from (b)	Jan. 1, 2020
5.382(e)	Amended	Sept. 1, 2020	5.676(d)	Adopted	Jan. 1, 2020
5.382(h), (i)	Amended	Sept. 1, 2020	5.678	Amended	Jan. 1, 2020
Ch. 19 (comm. w/Rule 5.448)	Adopted	Jan. 1, 2020	5.682(f)	Amended	Jan. 1, 2021
Art. 1 (comm. w/Rule 5.448)	Adopted	Jan. 1, 2020	5.684(f)	Amended	Jan. 1, 2021
5.448	Adopted	Jan. 1, 2020	5.690(a)	Amended	Jan. 1, 2021
5.480	Amended	Jan. 1, 2020	5.690(d)	Adopted	Jan. 1, 2020
5.481	Amended	Jan. 1, 2020	5.695(a)	Amended	Jan. 1, 2021
5.481 Adv. Comment	Adopted	Jan. 1, 2020	5.697	Adopted	Jan. 1, 2021
5.482(a)–(d)	Amended	Jan. 1, 2020	5.706(b)	Relettered to (c) /	
5.482(f)	Amended	Jan. 1, 2020			
5.482(g)	Adopted	Jan. 1, 2021			
5.483 Hdg	Amended	Jan. 1, 2020			
5.483(a)	Amended	Jan. 1, 2020			
5.483(c), (d)	Amended	Jan. 1, 2020			
5.483(e)	Repealed / Amended & Relettered from (f)	Jan. 1, 2020			

Rule	Effect	Date
	Adopted	Sept. 1, 2020
5.706(c)	Relettered to (d) / Relettered from (b)	Sept. 1, 2020
5.706(d)	Relettered to (e) / Relettered from (c)	Sept. 1, 2020
5.706(e)	Relettered to (f) / Relettered from (d)	Sept. 1, 2020
5.706(f)	Relettered from (e)	Sept. 1, 2020
5.708(c)	Relettered to (d) / Adopted	Sept. 1, 2020
5.708(d)	Relettered to (e) / Relettered from (c)	Sept. 1, 2020
5.708(e)	Relettered to (f) / Relettered from (d)	Sept. 1, 2020
5.708(f)	Relettered to (g) / Relettered from (e)	Sept. 1, 2020
5.708(g)	Relettered to (h) / Relettered from (f)	Sept. 1, 2020
5.708(h)	Relettered to (i) / Relettered from (g)	Sept. 1, 2020
5.708(i)	Relettered to (j) / Relettered from (h)	Sept. 1, 2020
5.708(j)	Relettered to (k) / Relettered from (i)	Sept. 1, 2020
5.708(k)	Relettered from (j)	Sept. 1, 2020
5.725 Hdg	Amended	Jan. 1, 2021
5.725(a)	Amended	Jan. 1, 2021
5.725(e)	Amended	Jan. 1, 2020
5.725(f)	Repealed / Relettered from (g)	Jan. 1, 2021
5.725(g)	Relettered to (f) / Relettered from (h)	Jan. 1, 2021
5.725(h)	Relettered to (g)	Jan. 1, 2021
5.735(a)–(c)	Amended	Jan. 1, 2021
5.740 Hdg	Amended	Jan. 1, 2021
5.740(a)	Amended	Jan. 1, 2021
5.740(c)	Relettered to (d) / Adopted	Jan. 1, 2021
5.740(d)	Relettered from (c)	Jan. 1, 2021
5.785(c)	Amended	Jan. 1, 2021
5.810(c)	Amended	Jan. 1, 2021
5.810(f)	Adopted	Sept. 1, 2020
5.815 Hdg	Amended	Jan. 1, 2021
5.815(a)–(c)	Amended	Jan. 1, 2021
5.815(e)–(g)	Amended	Jan. 1, 2021
5.860	Adopted	Jan. 1, 2021
7.101(b)	Amended	Jan. 1, 2021
7.151	Repealed	Jan. 1, 2020
7.550(b)	Amended	Jan. 1, 2020
7.575	Amended	Jan. 1, 2020
7.950	Amended	Jan. 1, 2021
7.950.5	Amended	Jan. 1, 2021
7.951	Amended	Jan. 1, 2021
7.952	Amended	Jan. 1, 2021
7.955 Hdg	Amended	Jan. 1, 2021
7.955 Adv. Comment	Amended	Jan. 1, 2021
Ch. 23 Hdg (comm. w/Rule 7.1101)	Amended	Jan. 1, 2020
7.1101	Repealed / Adopted	Jan. 1, 2020
7.1102	Adopted	Jan. 1, 2020
7.1103	Adopted	Jan. 1, 2020
7.1104	Adopted	Jan. 1, 2020
7.1105	Adopted	Jan. 1, 2020
8.25(a)	Amended	Jan. 1, 2021
8.25 Adv. Comment	Amended	Jan. 1, 2021
8.40	Amended	Jan. 1, 2020
8.44(c)	Amended	Jan. 1, 2020
8.46(d)	Amended	Jan. 1, 2020
8.66	Amended	Apr. 4, 2020

Rule	Effect	Date
8.66 Adv. Comment	Amended	Apr. 4, 2020
8.71(a)	Amended	Jan. 1, 2020
8.72	Amended	Jan. 1, 2020
8.72(b)	Amended	Jan. 1, 2021
8.72 Adv. Comment	Adopted	Jan. 1, 2020
8.74	Amended	Jan. 1, 2020
8.74 Adv. Comment	Adopted	Jan. 1, 2020
8.77 Hdg	Amended	Jan. 1, 2021
8.77(a)	Amended	Jan. 1, 2020, Jan. 1, 2021
8.78(a)	Amended	Jan. 1, 2020, Jan. 1, 2021
8.78(g)	Amended	Jan. 1, 2021
8.78 Adv. Comment	Adopted	Jan. 1, 2021
8.204 Hdg	Amended	Jan. 1, 2020
8.204(b), (c)	Amended	Jan. 1, 2020
8.252(a)	Amended	Jan. 1, 2020
8.252(c)	Amended	Jan. 1, 2020
8.268(b)	Amended	Jan. 1, 2020
8.320 Adv. Comment	Amended	Jan. 1, 2020
8.380(a)	Amended	Jan. 1, 2020
8.384(a)	Amended	Jan. 1, 2020
8.401(b)	Amended	Sept. 1, 2020
8.401 Adv. Comment	Adopted	Sept. 1, 2020
8.405(b)	Amended	Jan. 1, 2021
8.450(h)	Amended	Jan. 1, 2021
8.454(h)	Amended	Jan. 1, 2021
Ch. 6 (comm. w/Rule 8.480)	Amended	Jan. 1, 2020
8.483	Adopted	Jan. 1, 2020
8.483 Adv. Comment	Adopted	Jan. 1, 2020
8.500(f)	Amended	Jan. 1, 2020
8.815	Adopted	Jan. 1, 2020
8.851(a), (b)	Amended	Sept. 1, 2020
8.851 Adv. Comment	Amended	Jan. 1, 2020, Sept. 1, 2020
8.866 Adv. Comment	Amended	Jan. 1, 2020
8.868 Adv. Comment	Amended	Jan. 1, 2020
8.830(a)	Amended	Jan. 1, 2021
8.830 Adv. Comment	Amended	Jan. 1, 2021
8.840(a)	Amended	Jan. 1, 2021
8.843(a)	Amended	Jan. 1, 2021
8.845	Adopted	Jan. 1, 2021
8.845 Adv. Comment	Adopted	Jan. 1, 2021
8.882(a)	Amended	Jan. 1, 2021
8.885(a)	Amended	Jan. 1, 2020
8.885(c), (d)	Amended	Jan. 1, 2020
8.886(a)	Amended	Jan. 1, 2020
8.917 Adv. Comment	Amended	Jan. 1, 2020
8.919 Adv. Comment	Amended	Jan. 1, 2020
9.21(a)	Amended	Jan. 1, 2021
10.10(a)	Amended	Apr. 16, 2020
10.12 Hdg	Amended	Apr. 16, 2020
10.12(a)	Amended	Apr. 16, 2020
10.13 Hdg	Amended	Apr. 16, 2020
10.13(a)	Amended	Apr. 16, 2020
10.13(c)	Amended	Apr. 16, 2020
10.16(b)	Amended	Apr. 16, 2020
10.20(b)	Amended	Apr. 16, 2020
10.21(c)	Amended	Apr. 16, 2020
10.22(c), (d)	Amended	Apr. 16, 2020
10.22(f), (g)	Amended	Apr. 16, 2020
10.34(a)	Amended	Apr. 16, 2020
10.351	Adopted	Jan. 17, 2020
10.351(d)	Amended	Apr. 16, 2020
10.469 Hdg	Amended	Jan. 1, 2021
10.469(e)	Amended	Jan. 1, 2021

Standards of Judicial Administration

Standard	Effect	Date
4.15	Adopted	Jan. 1, 2020
5.20(b)	Amended	Jan. 1, 2021
5.20(d)–(f)	Amended	Jan. 1, 2021
5.20(r)	Adopted	Jan. 1, 2021

Appendices

Appendix	Effect	Date
A	Amended	Jan. 1, 2020, Jan. 17, 2020, Mar. 24, 2020, Mar. 25, 2020, July 1, 2020, Sept. 1, 2020, Oct. 5, 2020, Jan. 1, 2021
D	Amended	Apr. 16, 2020
I	Adopted	Apr. 6, 2020
Emergency rule 1	Adopted	Apr. 6, 2020
	Amended	Aug. 13, 2020
Emergency rule 2	Adopted	Apr. 6, 2020
	Amended	Aug. 13, 2020
Emergency rule 2 Adv. Comment	Adopted	Aug. 13, 2020
Emergency rule 3	Adopted	Apr. 6, 2020
Emergency rule 4	Adopted	Apr. 6, 2020
	Repealed	June 20, 2020
Emergency rule 5	Adopted	Apr. 6, 2020
Emergency rule 6	Adopted	Apr. 6, 2020
Emergency rule 6 Adv. Comment	Adopted	Apr. 6, 2020
Emergency rule 7	Adopted	Apr. 6, 2020
Emergency rule 7 Adv. Comment	Adopted	Apr. 6, 2020
Emergency rule 8	Adopted	Apr. 6, 2020
	Amended	Apr. 20, 2020
Emergency rule 9	Adopted	Apr. 6, 2020
	Amended	May 29, 2020
Emergency rule 9 Adv. Comment	Adopted	May 29, 2020
Emergency rule 10	Adopted	Apr. 6, 2020
Emergency rule 11	Adopted	Apr. 6, 2020
	Repealed	Nov. 13, 2020
Emergency rule 12	Adopted	Apr. 17, 2020
	Repealed	Nov. 13, 2020
Emergency rule 13	Adopted	Apr. 20, 2020

Supplement to the California Rules of Court

California Code of Judicial Ethics

Canon	Effect	Date
Terminology	Amended	July 1, 2020
2B Adv. Comment	Amended	July 1, 2020
3B(9)	Amended	July 1, 2020
3B(9) Adv. Comment	Amended	July 1, 2020
3D(3)	Amended	July 1, 2020
4C(3)(d)(i)	Amended	July 1, 2020
4C(3)(d) Adv. Comment	Amended	July 1, 2020
4D(6)(d)	Amended	July 1, 2020
4E(1)	Amended	July 1, 2020
5A Adv. Comment	Amended	July 1, 2020
5B(4)	Amended	July 1, 2020
5B(4) Adv. Comment	Amended	July 1, 2020
6A Adv. Comment	Amended	July 1, 2020
6B	Amended	July 1, 2020
6C	Amended	July 1, 2020
6C Adv. Comment	Amended	July 1, 2020

Supreme Court Rules Regarding Electronic Filing

Rule	Effect	Date
2	Amended	Mar. 18, 2020

Court of Appeal—Third Appellate District

Local Rules

Rule	Effect	Date
5	Amended	Apr. 10, 2020

Court of Appeal—Sixth Appellate District

Rule	Effect	Date
4	Adopted	Oct. 26, 2020

CONTENTS

Rules

Rules

CALIFORNIA RULES OF COURT

[Approved June 30, 2006. Effective January 1, 2007.]

TITLE 1
Rules Applicable to All Courts

Chapter 1
Preliminary Rules

Rule 1.1. The California Rules of Court
Rule 1.2. Title
Rule 1.3. Authority
Rule 1.4. Contents of the rules
Rule 1.5. Construction of rules and standards
Rule 1.6. Definitions and use of terms

Rule 1.1.   The California Rules of Court

These rules are entitled the California Rules of Court.

Rule 1.1 adopted effective January 1, 2007.

Rule 1.2.   Title

The rules in this title of the California Rules of Court may be referred to as the Rules Applicable to All Courts.

Rule 1.2 adopted effective January 1, 2007.

Rule 1.3.   Authority

The rules in the California Rules of Court are adopted by the Judicial Council of California under the authority of article VI, section 6, of the Constitution of the State of California, unless otherwise indicated. The rules in division 5 of title 8 and in title 9 were adopted by the Supreme Court.

Rule 1.3 amended effective January 1, 2008; adopted effective January 1, 2007.

Rule 1.4.   Contents of the rules

(a) The titles

The California Rules of Court includes the following titles:

(1) Title 1. Rules Applicable to All Courts;
(2) Title 2. Trial Court Rules;
(3) Title 3. Civil Rules;
(4) Title 4. Criminal Rules;
(5) Title 5. Family and Juvenile Rules;
(6) Title 6. [Reserved];
(7) Title 7. Probate Rules;
(8) Title 8. Appellate Rules;
(9) Title 9. Rules on Law Practice, Attorneys, and Judges; and
(10) Title 10. Judicial Administration Rules.

(Subd (a) adopted effective January 1, 2007.)

(b) Standards of Judicial Administration

The California Rules of Court includes the Standards of Judicial Administration adopted by the Judicial Council.

(Subd (b) adopted effective January 1, 2007.)

(c) Ethics Standards for Neutral Arbitrators in Contractual Arbitrations

The California Rules of Court includes Ethics Standards for Neutral Arbitrators in Contractual Arbitrations adopted by the Judicial Council under the authority of Code of Civil Procedure section 1281.85.

(Subd (c) repealed and relettered effective January 1, 2008; adopted as subd (d) effective January 1, 2007.)

(d) The appendixes

The California Rules of Court includes the following appendixes:

(1) Appendix A. Judicial Council Legal Forms List;
(2) Appendix B. Liability Limits of a Parent or Guardian Having Custody and Control of a Minor for the Torts of a Minor;
(3) Appendix C. Guidelines for the Operation of Family Law Information Centers and Family Law Facilitator Offices;
(4) Appendix D. Judicial Council Governance Policies;
(5) Appendix E. Guidelines for Determining Financial Eligibility for County Payment of the Cost of Counsel Appointed by the Court in Proceedings Under the Guardianship-Conservatorship Law;
(6) Appendix F. Guidelines for the Juvenile Dependency Counsel Collections Program; and
(7) Appendix G. Parliamentary Procedures for the Judicial Council of California.

(Subd (d) amended effective February 26, 2013; adopted as subd (e) effective January 1, 2007; previously relettered effective January 1, 2008; previously amended effective August 14, 2009, and January 1, 2013.)

Rule 1.4 amended effective February 26, 2013; adopted effective January 1, 2007; previously amended effective January 1, 2008, August 14, 2009, and January 1, 2013.

Rule 1.5.   Construction of rules and standards

(a) Construction

The rules and standards of the California Rules of Court must be liberally construed to ensure the just and speedy determination of the proceedings that they govern.

(Subd (a) adopted effective January 1, 2007.)

(b) Terminology

As used in the rules and standards:

(1) "Must" is mandatory;
(2) "May" is permissive;
(3) "May not" means not permitted to;
(4) "Will" expresses a future contingency or predicts action by a court or person in the ordinary course of events, but does not signify a mandatory duty; and
(5) "Should" expresses a preference or a nonbinding recommendation.

(Subd (b) adopted effective January 1, 2007.)

(c) Standards

Standards are guidelines or goals recommended by the Judicial Council. The nonbinding nature of standards is indicated by the use of "should" in the standards instead of the mandatory "must" used in the rules.

(Subd (c) adopted effective January 1, 2007.)

(d) Construction of additional terms

In the rules:

(1) Each tense (past, present, or future) includes the others;
(2) Each gender (masculine, feminine, or neuter) includes the others; and
(3) Each number (singular or plural) includes the other.

(Subd (d) adopted effective January 1, 2007.)

Rule 1.5 adopted effective January 1, 2007.

Rule 1.6.   Definitions and use of terms

As used in the California Rules of Court, unless the context or subject matter otherwise requires:

(1) "Action" includes special proceeding.
(2) "Case" includes action or proceeding.
(3) "Civil case" means a case prosecuted by one party against another for the declaration, enforcement, or protection of a right or the redress or

prevention of a wrong. Civil cases include all cases except criminal cases and petitions for habeas corpus.

(4) "General civil case" means all civil cases except probate, guardianship, conservatorship, juvenile, and family law proceedings (including proceedings under divisions 6–9 of the Family Code, Uniform Parentage Act, Domestic Violence Prevention Act, and Uniform Interstate Family Support Act; freedom from parental custody and control proceedings; and adoption proceedings), small claims proceedings, unlawful detainer proceedings, and "other civil petitions" described in (5).

(5) "Civil petitions" that are not general civil cases include petitions to prevent civil harassment, elder abuse, and workplace violence; petitions for name change; election contest petitions; and petitions for relief from late claims.

(6) "Unlimited civil cases" and "limited civil cases" are defined in Code of Civil Procedure section 85 et seq.

(7) "Criminal case" means a proceeding by which a party charged with a public offense is accused and prosecuted for the offense.

(8) "Rule" means a rule of the California Rules of Court.

(9) "Local rule" means every rule, regulation, order, policy, form, or standard of general application adopted by a court to govern practice and procedure in that court or by a judge of the court to govern practice or procedure in that judge's courtroom.

(10) "Chief Justice" and "presiding justice" include the Acting Chief Justice and the acting presiding justice, respectively.

(11) "Presiding judge" includes the acting presiding judge or the judicial officer designated by the presiding judge.

(12) "Judge" includes, as applicable, a judge of the superior court, a commissioner, or a temporary judge.

(13) "Temporary judge" means an active or inactive member of the State Bar of California who, under article VI, section 21 of the California Constitution and these rules, serves or expects to serve as a judge once, sporadically, or regularly on a part-time basis under a separate court appointment for each period of service or each case heard.

(14) "Person" includes a corporation or other legal entity as well as a natural person.

(15) "Party" is a person appearing in an action. Parties include both self-represented persons and persons represented by an attorney of record. "Party," "plaintiff," "People of the State of California," "applicant," "petitioner," "defendant," "respondent," "other parent," or any other designation of a party includes the party's attorney of record.

(16) "Attorney" means a member of the State Bar of California.

(17) "Counsel" means an attorney.

(18) "Sheriff" includes marshal.

(19) "Service" means service in the manner prescribed by a statute or rule.

(20) "Memorandum" means a written document containing: a statement of facts; a concise statement of the law, evidence, and arguments relied on; and a discussion of the statutes, cases, rules, and other legal sources relied on in support of the position advanced.

(21) "Declaration" includes "affidavit."

(22) "California Courts Web Site" means the Web site established by the Judicial Council that includes news and information, reference materials, rules and forms, and a self-help center. The address is: *www.courts.ca.gov.*

Rule 1.6 amended effective January 1, 2014; adopted as rule 200.1 effective January 1, 2003; previously amended and renumbered effective January 1, 2007; previously amended effective July 1, 2007, July 1, 2008, and July 1, 2013.

Chapter 2
Timing and Holidays

Rule 1.10. Time for actions
Rule 1.11. Holiday falling on a Saturday or Sunday

Rule 1.10.　Time for actions
(a) Computation of time
The time in which any act provided by these rules is to be performed is computed by excluding the first day and including the last, unless the last day is a Saturday, Sunday, or other legal holiday, and then it is also excluded.

(Subd (a) amended effective January 1, 2007.)

(b) Holidays
Unless otherwise provided by law, if the last day for the performance of any act that is required by these rules to be performed within a specific period of time falls on a Saturday, Sunday, or other legal holiday, the period is extended to and includes the next day that is not a holiday.

(Subd (b) amended effective January 1, 2007.)

(c) Extending or shortening time
Unless otherwise provided by law, the court may extend or shorten the time within which a party must perform any act under the rules.

(Subd (c) amended effective January 1, 2007.)

Rule 1.10 amended and renumbered effective January 1, 2007; adopted as rule 200.3 effective January 1, 2003.

Rule 1.11.　Holiday falling on a Saturday or Sunday
When a judicial holiday specified by Code of Civil Procedure section 135 falls on a Saturday, the courts must observe the holiday on the preceding Friday. When a judicial holiday specified by Code of Civil Procedure section 135 falls on a Sunday, the courts must observe the holiday on the following Monday.

Rule 1.11 amended and renumbered effective January 1, 2007; adopted as rule 987 effective January 1, 1986, operative January 1, 1989.

Chapter 3
Service and Filing

Rule 1.20. Effective Date of Filing
Rule 1.21. Service

Rule 1.20.　Effective Date of Filing
Unless otherwise provided, a document is deemed filed on the date it is received by the court clerk.

Rule 1.20 amended effective January 1, 2017; adopted effective January 1, 2007; previously amended effective January 1, 2008.

Rule 1.21.　Service
(a) Service on a party or attorney
Whenever a document is required to be served on a party, the service must be made on the party's attorney if the party is represented.

(Subd (a) amended effective January 1, 2007.)

(b) "Serve and file"
As used in these rules, unless a statute or rule provides for a different method for filing or service, a requirement to "serve and file" a document means that a copy of the document must be served on the attorney for each party separately represented, on each self-represented party, and on any other person or entity when required by statute, rule, or court order, and that the document and a proof of service of the document must be filed with the court.

(Subd (b) amended effective January 1, 2007.)

(c) "Proof of service"
As used in these rules, "proof of service" means a declaration stating that service has been made as provided in (a) and (b). If the proof of service names attorneys for separately represented parties, it must also state which party or parties each of the attorneys served is representing.

(Subd (c) adopted effective January 1, 2007.)

Rule 1.21 amended effective January 1, 2007; adopted effective January 1, 2007.

Rule 1.22.　Recycled paper [Repealed]
Rule 1.22 repealed effective January 1, 2014; adopted effective January 1, 2007.

Chapter 4
Judicial Council Forms

Rule 1.30. Judicial Council forms
Rule 1.31. Mandatory forms
Rule 1.35. Optional forms
Rule 1.37. Use of forms
Rule 1.40. Statutory references on forms
Rule 1.41. Proofs of service on forms
Rule 1.42. Forms not to be rejected
Rule 1.43. Legibility
Rule 1.44. Electronically produced forms
Rule 1.45. Judicial Council pleading forms
Rule 1.51. California Law Enforcement Telecommunications System (CLETS) information form

Rule 1.30.　Judicial Council forms
(a) Application
The rules in this chapter apply to Judicial Council forms.

(Subd (a) adopted effective January 1, 2007.)

(b) Mandatory or optional forms
Judicial Council forms are either mandatory or optional.

(Subd (b) relettered effective January 1, 2007; adopted as subd (a) effective January 1, 2003.)

Rule 1.30 amended and renumbered effective January 1, 2007; adopted as rule 982 effective November 10, 1969; previously amended effective November 23, 1969, July 1, 1970, November 23, 1970, January 1, 1971, January 1, 1972, March 4, 1972, July 1, 1972, March 7, 1973, January 1, 1975, July 1, 1975, July 1, 1976, January 1, 1977, July 1, 1977, January 1, 1978, October 1, 1978, January 1, 1979, July 1, 1980, January 1, 1981, July 1, 1983, July 1, 1988, January 1, 1997, and January 1, 2006; amended and renumbered as rule 201.1 effective January 1, 2003.

Rule 1.31.   Mandatory forms

(a) Use of mandatory forms and acceptance for filing

Forms adopted by the Judicial Council for mandatory use are forms prescribed under Government Code section 68511. Wherever applicable, they must be used by all parties and must be accepted for filing by all courts. In some areas, alternative mandatory forms have been adopted.

(Subd (a) adopted effective January 1, 2007.)

(b) List of mandatory forms

Each mandatory Judicial Council form is identified as mandatory by an asterisk (*) on the list of Judicial Council forms in Appendix A to the California Rules of Court. The list is available on the California Courts website at *www.courts.ca.gov/forms*.

(Subd (b) amended effective January 1, 2015; adopted effective January 1, 2007.)

(c) Identification of mandatory forms

Forms adopted by the Judicial Council for mandatory use bear the words "Form Adopted for Mandatory Use," "Mandatory Form," or "Form Adopted for Alternative Mandatory Use" in the lower left corner of the first page.

(Subd (c) adopted effective January 1, 2007.)

(d) Words on forms

Publishers and courts reprinting a mandatory Judicial Council form in effect before July 1, 1999, must add the words "Mandatory Form" to the bottom of the first page.

(Subd (d) adopted effective January 1, 2007.)

(e) No alteration of forms

Except as provided in rule 3.52(6), concerning court fee waiver orders, and rule 5.504, concerning court orders in juvenile court proceedings, courts may not require the use of an altered mandatory Judicial Council form in place of the Judicial Council form. However, a judicial officer may modify a Judicial Council form order as necessary or appropriate to adjudicate a particular case.

(Subd (e) amended effective September 1, 2017; adopted effective January 1, 2007; previously amended effective January 1, 2007, January 1, 2009, and July 1, 2009.)

(f) No colored forms

Courts may not require that any mandatory Judicial Council form be submitted on any color of paper other than white.

(Subd (f) adopted effective January 1, 2007.)

(g) Orders not on mandatory forms

An otherwise legally sufficient court order for which there is a mandatory Judicial Council form is not invalid or unenforceable because the order is not prepared on a Judicial Council form or the correct Judicial Council form.

(Subd (g) adopted effective January 1, 2007.)

Rule 1.31 amended effective September 1, 2017; adopted effective January 1, 2007; previously amended effective January 1, 2007, January 1, 2009, July 1, 2009, and January 1, 2015.

Rule 1.35.   Optional forms

(a) Use of optional forms and acceptance for filing

Forms approved by the Judicial Council for optional use, wherever applicable, may be used by parties and must be accepted for filing by all courts.

(Subd (a) adopted effective January 1, 2007.)

(b) List of optional forms

Each optional Judicial Council form appears without an asterisk (*) on the list of Judicial Council forms in Appendix A to the California Rules of Court. The list is available on the California Courts website at *www.courts.ca.gov/forms*.

(Subd (b) amended effective January 1, 2015; adopted effective January 1, 2007.)

(c) Identification of optional forms

Forms approved by the Judicial Council for optional use bear the words "Form Approved for Optional Use" or "Optional Form" in the lower left corner of the first page.

(Subd (c) adopted effective January 1, 2007.)

(d) Words on forms

Publishers and courts reprinting an optional Judicial Council form in effect before July 1, 1999, must add the words "Optional Form" to the bottom of the first page.

(Subd (d) adopted effective January 1, 2007.)

(e) No alteration of forms

Courts may not require the use of an altered optional Judicial Council form in place of the Judicial Council form. However, a judicial officer may modify a Judicial Council form order as necessary or appropriate to adjudicate a particular case.

(Subd (e) amended effective January 1, 2009; adopted effective January 1, 2007.)

(f) No colored forms

Courts may not require that any optional Judicial Council form be submitted on any color of paper other than white.

(Subd (f) adopted effective January 1, 2007.)

Rule 1.35 amended effective January 1, 2015; adopted effective January 1, 2007; previously amended effective January 1, 2009.

Rule 1.37.   Use of forms

A person serving and filing a Judicial Council form must use the current version of the form adopted or approved by the council, unless a rule in the California Rules of Court allows the use of a different form.

Rule 1.37 adopted effective January 1, 2007.

Rule 1.40.   Statutory references on forms

The references to statutes and rules at the bottom of Judicial Council forms are advisory only. The presence or absence of a particular reference is not a ground for rejecting a form otherwise applicable in the action or proceeding for the purpose presented.

Rule 1.40 adopted effective January 1, 2007.

Rule 1.41.   Proofs of service on forms

Proofs of service are included on some Judicial Council forms solely for the convenience of the parties. A party may use an included proof of service or any other proper proof of service.

Rule 1.41 adopted effective January 1, 2007.

Rule 1.42.   Forms not to be rejected

A court must not reject for filing a Judicial Council form for any of the following reasons:

(1) The form lacks the preprinted title and address of the court;

(2) The form lacks the name of the clerk;

(3) The preprinted title and address of another court or its clerk's name is legibly modified;

(4) The form lacks the court's local form number;

(5) The form lacks any other material added by a court, unless the material is required by the Judicial Council;

(6) The form is printed by a publisher or another court;

(7) The form is imprinted with the name or symbol of the publisher, unless the name or symbol replaces or obscures any material on the printed form;

(8) The form is legibly and obviously modified to correct a code section number or to comply with the law under which the form is filed; or

(9) The form is not the latest version of the form adopted or approved by the Judicial Council.

Rule 1.42 amended effective January 1, 2007; adopted effective January 1, 2007.

Rule 1.43.   Legibility

A Judicial Council form filed must be a true copy of the original form and must be as legible as a printed form.

Rule 1.43 adopted effective January 1, 2007.

Rule 1.44.   Electronically produced forms

A party or attorney may file a duplicate of a Judicial Council form produced by a computer and a printer or similar device with a resolution of at least 300 dots per inch.

Rule 1.44 adopted effective January 1, 2007.

Rule 1.45.   Judicial Council pleading forms

(a) Pleading forms

The forms listed under the "Pleading" heading on the list of Judicial Council forms in Appendix A to the California Rules of Court are approved by the Judicial Council.

(Subd (a) amended effective July 1, 2008; previously amended effective July 1, 1999, January 1, 2005, and January 1, 2007.)

(b) Cause of action forms

Any approved cause of action form may be attached to any approved form of complaint or cross-complaint.

(Subd (b) adopted effective January 1, 1982.)

(c) Other causes of action

A cause of action for which no form has been approved may be prepared in the format prescribed by the rules in chapter 1 of division 2 of title 2 and attached to any approved form of complaint or cross-complaint. Each paragraph within a cause of action must be numbered consecutively beginning with one. Each paragraph number must be preceded with one or more identifying letters derived from the title of the cause of action.

(Subd (c) amended effective January 1, 2007; adopted effective January 1, 1982; previously amended effective January 1, 2003.)

Rule 1.45 amended effective July 1, 2008; adopted as rule 982.1 effective January 1, 1982; previously amended effective July 1, 1995, July 1, 1996, January 1, 1997, July 1, 1999, and January 1, 2005; previously amended and renumbered as rule 201.2 effective January 1, 2003; previously amended and renumbered effective January 1, 2007.

Rule 1.51. California Law Enforcement Telecommunications System (CLETS) information form

(a) Confidential CLETS Information form to be submitted to the court

A person requesting protective orders under Code of Civil Procedure section 527.6, 527.8, or 527.85; Family Code section 6320, 6404, or 6454; Penal Code sections 18100–18205; or Welfare and Institutions Code section 213.5 or 15657.03 must submit to the court with the request a completed *Confidential CLETS Information* form.

(Subd (a) amended effective January 1, 2019; adopted effective January 1, 2011.)

(b) Confidentiality of the form

The *Confidential CLETS Information* form is confidential, and access to the information on the form is limited to the persons listed in (c).

(Subd (b) adopted effective January 1, 2011.)

(c) Access to information on the form

The *Confidential CLETS Information* form must not be included in the court file. After the form is submitted to the court, only the following persons may have access to the information on the form:

(1) Authorized court personnel; and

(2) Law enforcement and other personnel authorized by the California Department of Justice to transmit or receive CLETS information.

(Subd (c) adopted effective January 1, 2011.)

(d) Amendment of the form

A person requesting protective orders or the person's attorney may submit an amended *Confidential CLETS Information* form as a matter of right to provide updated or more complete and accurate information.

(Subd (d) adopted effective January 1, 2011.)

(e) Retention and destruction of the form

(1) When a *Confidential CLETS Information* form is submitted to the court, the court, if a temporary restraining order or order after hearing is entered, may:

(A) Transmit the form to a law enforcement agency for entry into CLETS and not retain any copy; or

(B) Enter the information on the form into CLETS itself and promptly destroy the form or delete it from its records.

(2) If no temporary restraining order or order after hearing is entered, the court may promptly destroy the form or delete it from its records.

(3) Until the court has completed (1) or (2), the form must be retained in a secure manner that prevents access to the information on the form except to those persons identified in (c).

(Subd (e) adopted effective January 1, 2011.)

Rule 1.51 amended effective January 1, 2019; adopted effective January 1, 2011.

Chapter 5
Accommodations

Rule 1.100. Requests for accommodations by persons with disabilities

(a) Definitions

As used in this rule:

(1) "Persons with disabilities" means individuals covered by California Civil Code section 51 et seq.; the Americans With Disabilities Act of 1990 (42 U.S.C. §12101 et seq.); or other applicable state and federal laws. This definition includes persons who have a physical or mental medical condition that limits one or more of the major life activities, have a record of such a condition, or are regarded as having such a condition.

(2) "Applicant" means any lawyer, party, witness, juror, or other person with an interest in attending any proceeding before any court of this state.

(3) "Accommodations" means actions that result in court services, programs, or activities being readily accessible to and usable by persons with disabilities. Accommodations may include making reasonable modifications in policies, practices, and procedures; furnishing, at no charge, to persons with disabilities, auxiliary aids and services, equipment, devices, materials in alternative formats, readers, or certified interpreters for persons who are deaf or hard-of-hearing; relocating services or programs to accessible facilities; or providing services at alternative sites. Although not required where other actions are effective in providing access to court services, programs, or activities, alteration of existing facilities by the responsible entity may be an accommodation.

(Subd (a) amended effective July 1, 2017; adopted as subd (b) effective January 1, 1996; previously amended effective January 1, 2006; previously amended and relettered effective January 1, 2007.)

(b) Policy

It is the policy of the courts of this state to ensure that persons with disabilities have equal and full access to the judicial system. To ensure access to the courts for persons with disabilities, each superior and appellate court must delegate at least one person to be the ADA coordinator, also known as the access coordinator, or designee to address requests for accommodations. This rule is not intended to impose limitations or to invalidate the remedies, rights, and procedures accorded to persons with disabilities under state or federal law.

(Subd (b) adopted effective January 1, 2007.)

(c) Process for requesting accommodations

The process for requesting accommodations is as follows:

(1) Requests for accommodations under this rule may be presented ex parte on a form approved by the Judicial Council, in another written format, or orally. Requests must be forwarded to the ADA coordinator, also known as the access coordinator, or designee, within the time frame provided in (c)(3).

(2) Requests for accommodations must include a description of the accommodation sought, along with a statement of the medical condition that necessitates the accommodation. The court, in its discretion, may require the applicant to provide additional information about the medical condition.

(3) Requests for accommodations must be made as far in advance as possible, and in any event must be made no fewer than 5 court days before the requested implementation date. The court may, in its discretion, waive this requirement.

(4) The court must keep confidential all information of the applicant concerning the request for accommodation, unless confidentiality is waived in writing by the applicant or disclosure is required by law. The applicant's identity and confidential information may not be disclosed to the public or to persons other than those involved in the accommodation process. Confidential information includes all medical information pertaining to the applicant, and all oral or written communication from the applicant concerning the request for accommodation.

(Subd (c) amended effective July 1, 2017; previously amended effective January 1, 2006, and January 1, 2007.)

(d) Permitted communication

Communications under this rule must address only the accommodation requested by the applicant and must not address, in any manner, the subject matter or merits of the proceedings before the court.

(Subd (d) amended effective January 1, 2006.)

(e) Response to accommodation request

The court must respond to a request for accommodation as follows:

(1) In determining whether to grant an accommodation request or provide an appropriate alternative accommodation, the court must consider, but is not limited by, California Civil Code section 51 et seq., the provisions of the Americans With Disabilities Act of 1990 (42 U.S.C. § 12101, et seq.), and other applicable state and federal laws.

(2) The court must promptly inform the applicant of the determination to grant or deny an accommodation request. If the accommodation request is denied in whole or in part, the response must be in writing. On request of the applicant, the court may also provide an additional response in an alternative format. The response to the applicant must indicate:

(A) Whether the request for accommodation is granted or denied, in whole or in part, or an alternative accommodation is granted;

(B) If the request for accommodation is denied, in whole or in part, the reason therefor;

(C) The nature of any accommodation to be provided;

(D) The duration of any accommodation to be provided; and

(E) If the response is in writing, the date the response was delivered in person or sent to the applicant.

(Subd (e) amended effective January 1, 2010; previously amended effective January 1, 2006, and January 1, 2007.)

(f) Denial of accommodation request

A request for accommodation may be denied only when the court determines that:

(1) The applicant has failed to satisfy the requirements of this rule;

(2) The requested accommodation would create an undue financial or administrative burden on the court; or

(3) The requested accommodation would fundamentally alter the nature of the service, program, or activity.

(Subd (f) amended effective January 1, 2007; previously amended effective January 1, 2006.)

(g) Review procedure

(1) If the determination to grant or deny a request for accommodation is made by nonjudicial court personnel, an applicant or any participant in the proceeding may submit a written request for review of that determination to the presiding judge or designated judicial officer. The request for review must be submitted within 10 days of the date the response under (e)(2) was delivered in person or sent.

(2) If the determination to grant or deny a request for accommodation is made by a presiding judge or another judicial officer, an applicant or any participant in the proceeding may file a petition for a writ of mandate under rules 8.485–8.493 or 8.930–8.936 in the appropriate reviewing court. The petition must be filed within 10 days of the date the response under (e)(2) was delivered in person or sent to the petitioner. For purposes of this rule, only those participants in the proceeding who were notified by the court of the determination to grant or deny the request for accommodation are considered real parties in interest in a writ proceeding. The petition for the writ must be served on the respondent court and any real party in interest as defined in this rule.

(3) The confidentiality of all information of the applicant concerning the request for accommodation and review under (g)(1) or (2) must be maintained as required under (c)(4).

(Subd (g) amended effective January 1, 2010; previously amended effective January 1, 2006.)

(h) Duration of accommodations

The accommodation by the court must be provided for the duration indicated in the response to the request for accommodation and must remain in effect for the period specified. The court may provide an accommodation for an indefinite period of time, for a limited period of time, or for a particular matter or appearance.

(Subd (h) amended effective January 1, 2006.)

Rule 1.100 amended effective July 1, 2017; adopted as rule 989.3 effective January 1, 1996; previously amended effective January 1, 2006, and January 1, 2010; previously amended and renumbered effective January 1, 2007.

Advisory Committee Comment

Subdivision (g)(2). Which court is the "appropriate reviewing court" under this rule depends on the court in which the accommodation decision is made and the nature of the underlying case. If the accommodation decision is made by a superior court judicial officer and the underlying case is a limited civil, misdemeanor, or infraction case, the appropriate reviewing court is the appellate division of the superior court. If the accommodation decision is made by a superior court judicial officer and the case is anything other than a limited civil, misdemeanor, or infraction case, such as a family law, unlimited civil, or felony case, the appropriate reviewing court is the Court of Appeal. If the accommodation decision is made by a judicial officer of the Court of Appeal, the appropriate reviewing court is the California Supreme Court.

Chapter 6
Public Access to Court Proceedings

Rule 1.150. Photographing, recording, and broadcasting in court

(a) Introduction

The judiciary is responsible for ensuring the fair and equal administration of justice. The judiciary adjudicates controversies, both civil and criminal, in accordance with established legal procedures in the calmness and solemnity of the courtroom. Photographing, recording, and broadcasting of courtroom proceedings may be permitted as circumscribed in this rule if executed in a manner that ensures that the fairness and dignity of the proceedings are not adversely affected. This rule does not create a presumption for or against granting permission to photograph, record, or broadcast court proceedings.

(Subd (a) adopted effective January 1, 1997.)

(b) Definitions

As used in this rule:

(1) "Media coverage" means any photographing, recording, or broadcasting of court proceedings by the media using television, radio, photographic, or recording equipment.

(2) "Media" or "media agency" means any person or organization engaging in news gathering or reporting and includes any newspaper, radio or television station or network, news service, magazine, trade paper, in-house publication, professional journal, or other news-reporting or news-gathering agency.

(3) "Court" means the courtroom at issue, the courthouse, and its entrances and exits.

(4) "Judge" means the judicial officer or officers assigned to or presiding at the proceeding, except as provided in (e)(1) if no judge has been assigned.

(5) "Photographing" means recording a likeness, regardless of the method used, including by digital or photographic methods. As used in this rule, photographing does not include drawings or sketchings of the court proceedings.

(6) "Recording" means the use of any analog or digital device to aurally or visually preserve court proceedings. As used in this rule, recording does not include handwritten notes on the court record, whether by court reporter or by digital or analog preservation.

(7) "Broadcasting" means a visual or aural transmission or signal, by any method, of the court proceedings, including any electronic transmission or transmission by sound waves.

(Subd (b) amended effective January 1, 2007; adopted as subd (a) effective July 1, 1984; previously amended and relettered as subd (b) effective January 1, 1997; previously amended effective January 1, 2006.)

(c) Photographing, recording, and broadcasting prohibited

Except as provided in this rule, court proceedings may not be photographed, recorded, or broadcast. This rule does not prohibit courts from photographing or videotaping sessions for judicial education or publications and is not intended to apply to closed-circuit television broadcasts solely within the courthouse or between court facilities if the broadcasts are controlled by the court and court personnel.

(Subd (c) amended effective January 1, 2006; adopted effective January 1, 1997.)

(d) Personal recording devices

The judge may permit inconspicuous personal recording devices to be used by persons in a courtroom to make sound recordings as personal notes of the proceedings. A person proposing to use a recording device must obtain advance permission from the judge. The recordings must not be used for any purpose other than as personal notes.

(Subd (d) amended effective January 1, 2007; adopted as subd (c) effective July 1, 1984; previously amended and relettered as subd (d) effective January 1, 1997; previously amended effective January 1, 2006.)

(e) Media coverage

Media coverage may be permitted only on written order of the judge as provided in this subdivision. The judge in his or her discretion may permit, refuse, limit, or terminate media coverage. This rule does not otherwise limit or restrict the right of the media to cover and report court proceedings.

(1) *Request for order*

The media may request an order on *Media Request to Photograph, Record, or Broadcast* (form MC-500). The form must be filed at least five court days before the portion of the proceeding to be covered unless good cause is shown. A completed, proposed order on *Order on Media Request to Permit Coverage* (form MC-510) must be filed with the request. The judge assigned to the proceeding must rule on the request. If no judge has been assigned, the request will be submitted to the judge supervising the calendar department, and thereafter be ruled on by the judge assigned to the proceeding. The clerk must promptly notify the parties that a request has been filed.

(2) *Hearing on request*

The judge may hold a hearing on the request or may rule on the request without a hearing.

(3) *Factors to be considered by the judge*

In ruling on the request, the judge is to consider the following factors:

(A) The importance of maintaining public trust and confidence in the judicial system;

(B) The importance of promoting public access to the judicial system;

(C) The parties' support of or opposition to the request;

(D) The nature of the case;

(E) The privacy rights of all participants in the proceeding, including witnesses, jurors, and victims;

(F) The effect on any minor who is a party, prospective witness, victim, or other participant in the proceeding;

(G) The effect on the parties' ability to select a fair and unbiased jury;

(H) The effect on any ongoing law enforcement activity in the case;

(I) The effect on any unresolved identification issues;

(J) The effect on any subsequent proceedings in the case;

(K) The effect of coverage on the willingness of witnesses to cooperate, including the risk that coverage will engender threats to the health or safety of any witness;

(L) The effect on excluded witnesses who would have access to the televised testimony of prior witnesses;

(M) The scope of the coverage and whether partial coverage might unfairly influence or distract the jury;

(N) The difficulty of jury selection if a mistrial is declared;

(O) The security and dignity of the court;

(P) Undue administrative or financial burden to the court or participants;

(Q) The interference with neighboring courtrooms;

(R) The maintenance of the orderly conduct of the proceeding; and

(S) Any other factor the judge deems relevant.

(4) *Order permitting media coverage*

The judge ruling on the request to permit media coverage is not required to make findings or a statement of decision. The order may incorporate any local rule or order of the presiding or supervising judge regulating media activity outside of the courtroom. The judge may condition the order permitting media coverage on the media agency's agreement to pay any increased court-incurred costs resulting from the permitted media coverage (for example, for additional court security or utility service). Each media agency is responsible for ensuring that all its media personnel who cover the court proceeding know and follow the provisions of the court order and this rule.

(5) *Modified order*

The order permitting media coverage may be modified or terminated on the judge's own motion or on application to the judge without the necessity of a prior hearing or written findings. Notice of the application and any modification or termination ordered under the application must be given to the parties and each media agency permitted by the previous order to cover the proceeding.

(6) *Prohibited coverage*

The judge may not permit media coverage of the following:

(A) Proceedings held in chambers;

(B) Proceedings closed to the public;

(C) Jury selection;

(D) Jurors or spectators; or

(E) Conferences between an attorney and a client, witness, or aide; between attorneys; or between counsel and the judge at the bench.

(7) *Equipment and personnel*

The judge may require media agencies to demonstrate that proposed personnel and equipment comply with this rule. The judge may specify the placement of media personnel and equipment to permit reasonable media coverage without disruption of the proceedings.

(8) *Normal requirements for media coverage of proceedings*

Unless the judge in his or her discretion orders otherwise, the following requirements apply to media coverage of court proceedings:

(A) One television camera and one still photographer will be permitted.

(B) The equipment used may not produce distracting sound or light. Signal lights or devices to show when equipment is operating may not be visible.

(C) An order permitting or requiring modification of existing sound or lighting systems is deemed to require that the modifications be installed, maintained, and removed without public expense or disruption of proceedings.

(D) Microphones and wiring must be unobtrusively located in places approved by the judge and must be operated by one person.

(E) Operators may not move equipment or enter or leave the courtroom while the court is in session, or otherwise cause a distraction.

(F) Equipment or clothing must not bear the insignia or marking of a media agency.

(9) *Media pooling*

If two or more media agencies of the same type request media coverage of a proceeding, they must file a joint statement of agreed arrangements. If they are unable to agree, the judge may deny media coverage by that type of media agency.

(Subd (e) amended effective January 1, 2007; adopted as subd (b) effective July 1, 1984; previously amended and relettered as subd (e) effective January 1, 1997; previously amended effective January 1, 2006.)

(f) Sanctions

Any violation of this rule or an order made under this rule is an unlawful interference with the proceedings of the court and may be the basis for an order terminating media coverage, a citation for contempt of court, or an order imposing monetary or other sanctions as provided by law.

(Subd (f) amended and relettered as subd (f) effective January 1, 1997; adopted as subd (e) effective July 1, 1984.)

Rule 1.150 amended and renumbered effective January 1, 2007; adopted as rule 980 effective July 1, 1984; previously amended effective January 1, 1997, and January 1, 2006.

Chapter 7
Form and Format of Papers

Chapter 7 adopted effective January 1, 2008.

Rule 1.200. Format of citations
Rule 1.201. Protection of privacy

Rule 1.200. Format of citations

Citations to cases and other authorities in all documents filed in the courts must be in the style established by either the *California Style Manual* or *The Bluebook: A Uniform System of Citation*, at the option of the party filing the document. The same style must be used consistently throughout the document.

Rule 1.200 adopted effective January 1, 2008.

Rule 1.201. Protection of privacy

(a) Exclusion or redaction of identifiers

To protect personal privacy and other legitimate interests, parties and their attorneys must not include, or must redact where inclusion is necessary, the following identifiers from all pleadings and other papers filed in the court's public file, whether filed in paper or electronic form, unless otherwise provided by law or ordered by the court:

(1) Social security numbers. If an individual's social security number is required in a pleading or other paper filed in the public file, only the last four digits of that number may be used.

(2) Financial account numbers. If financial account numbers are required in a pleading or other paper filed in the public file, only the last four digits of these numbers may be used.

(Subd (a) adopted effective January 1, 2017.)

(b) Responsibility of the filer

The responsibility for excluding or redacting identifiers identified in (a) from all documents filed with the court rests solely with the parties and their attorneys. The court clerk will not review each pleading or other paper for compliance with this provision.

(Subd (b) adopted effective January 1, 2017.)

(c) Confidential reference list

If the court orders on a showing of good cause, a party filing a document containing identifiers listed in (a) may file, along with the redacted document that will be placed in the public file, a reference list. The reference list is confidential. A party filing a confidential reference list must use *Confidential Reference List of Identifiers* (form MC-120) for that purpose. The confidential list must identify each item of redacted information and specify an appropriate reference that uniquely corresponds to each item of redacted information listed. All references in the case to the redacted identifiers included in the confidential reference list will be understood to refer to the corresponding complete identifier. A party may amend its reference list as of right.

(Subd (c) adopted effective January 1, 2017.)

(d) Scope

The requirements of this rule do not apply to documents or records that by court order or operation of law are filed in their entirety either confidentially or under seal.

(Subd (d) adopted effective January 1, 2017.)
Rule 1.201 adopted effective January 1, 2017.

Chapter 8
Language Access Services

Chapter 8 adopted effective September 1, 2019.

Rule 1.300. Access to programs, services, and professionals

(a) Definitions

As used in this chapter, unless the context or subject matter otherwise requires, the following definitions apply:

(1) "Court-provided programs, services, and professionals" are services offered and provided by court employees or by contractors or vendors under agreement with the court.

(2) "Court litigant" is a person who is a party in a court case or other legal proceeding.

(3) "Language services" are services designed to provide access to the legal system to limited English proficient court litigants and may include in-person interpretation, telephonic interpreter services, video remote interpreting services, and services provided by assigned bilingual employees and bilingual volunteers.

(4) "Limited English proficient" describes a person who speaks English "less than very well" and who, as a result, cannot understand or participate in a court proceeding.

(5) "Private programs, services, and professionals" are services provided by outside agencies, organizations, and persons that court litigants may be required to access by court order.

(Subd (a) adopted effective September 1, 2019.)

(b) Provision of language services in court-ordered and court-provided programs, services, and professionals

As soon as feasible, each court must adopt procedures to enable limited English proficient court litigants to access court-ordered and court-provided programs, services, and professionals to the same extent as persons who are proficient in English.

(Subd (b) adopted effective September 1, 2019.)

(c) Provision of language services in private programs and services, and by private professionals

To the extent feasible, a court should avoid ordering a limited English proficient court litigant to a private program, service, or professional that is not language accessible.

(Subd (c) adopted effective September 1, 2019.)

(d) Delay in access to services

If a limited English proficient court litigant is unable to access a private program, service, or professional within the time period ordered by the court due to limitations in language service availability, the court litigant may submit a statement to the court indicating the reason for the delay, and the court may, for good cause, enter an alternative order or extend the time for completion. Court litigants may use *Service Not Available in My Language: Request to Change Court Order* (form LA-400) for this purpose. The court may respond to the request using *Service Not Available in My Language: Order* (form LA-450).

(Subd (d) adopted effective September 1, 2019.)

(e) Use of technology

Courts should seek out opportunities to collaborate with each other and with community partners in the provision of language services, and should employ technology to promote the sharing of bilingual staff and certified and registered court interpreters among courts, as appropriate.

(Subd (e) adopted effective September 1, 2019.)
Rule 1.300 adopted effective September 1, 2019.

Advisory Committee Comment

Subdivision (b). The goal of this rule is to connect limited English proficient court litigants ordered by courts to access programs or professionals with services in the languages spoken by the litigants. Recognizing that not all program providers will be willing or able to meet the language needs, the rule is intended to help courts become aware of those language services available in the community so that limited English proficient court litigants are not placed in a position where they are unable to comply with court orders because the required services are not available in a language they understand.

To facilitate equal access to justice, when courts order limited English proficient litigants to access court-provided programs, services, and professionals, to the greatest extent possible, courts should ensure that the services are language accessible.

To the extent feasible and as permitted by law, any memorandum of understanding or other written agreement for agency-referred programs, services, and professionals that trial courts enter into or amend after the implementation date of this rule should include the goals of providing language services in the languages spoken by limited English proficient court users and of notifying the court if the language needs of a limited English proficient court litigant referred to the program, service, or professional cannot be accommodated.

Subdivision (c). Courts are encouraged to offer neutral, nonendorsing information about private programs, services, and professionals providing multilingual services or language assistance to enable limited English proficient court litigants to access their programs. Private programs, services, and professionals that would like to be included on a court's informational list may confirm in writing to the court annually that they offer language services, indicating the languages covered by the program, service, or professional. Courts may require providers to use *Notice of Available Language Assistance—Service Provider* (form LA-350) for this purpose.

Subdivision (d). When a defendant is required to participate in a batterer intervention program under section 1203.097(a)(6) of the California Penal Code, the court may order "another appropriate counseling program" if a batterer's program is unavailable in the language spoken by the court litigant. In addition, a judge may, for good cause, excuse the requirement to complete the 52-week program within 18 months. The application of a similar standard to all orders to participate in noncourtroom services, whereby the unavailability of language assistance would constitute good cause to make an alternative order or to excuse delay in completion, would provide the court with flexibility to address situations in which a program or service is unavailable in the language spoken by a limited English proficient court user.

Two optional forms, *Service Not Available in My Language: Request to Change Court Order* (form LA-400) and *Service Not Available in My Language: Order* (form LA-450), were developed to facilitate communication between the court and a limited English proficient court litigant who is unable to comply with a court order because of a lack of language assistance.

Form LA-400 allows the court litigant to notify the court of the unavailability of language assistance in a court-ordered program and to request a modified order or an extension of the time for completion of the program. Form LA-450 allows the court to issue a modified order or to extend the time for completion of a court-ordered program or service. A request may be denied if the court receives information that a program is available in the language of the court litigant or that language assistance is available to help the court litigant access the program, and that the program or service may be accessed within the time mandated by the court for completion. If a request is denied on this basis, the court should provide contact information that will allow the court litigant to access the program. In addition, a request may be denied if the court finds there is good cause to believe that the request was brought for an improper purpose or that the court litigant knowingly provided false information on form LA-400.

Subdivision (e). It is the policy of the California courts to encourage the efficient and effective use of human and technological resources in the provision of language services while ensuring meaningful access for limited English proficient court users. For noncourtroom interpretation events, courts may consult the report, *Technological Options for Providing and Sharing Court Language Access Services Outside the Courtroom* (January 2018) for opportunities to collaborate with other courts and service providers to enhance language access for LEP court users.

TITLE 2
Trial Court Rules

Division 1
General Provisions

Chapter 1
Title and Application

Rule 2.1.   Title

The rules in this title may be referred to as the Trial Court Rules.
Rule 2.1 adopted effective January 1, 2007.

Rule 2.2.   Application

The Trial Court Rules apply to all cases in the superior courts unless otherwise specified by a rule or statute.
Rule 2.2 amended and renumbered effective January 1, 2007; adopted as rule 200 effective January 1, 2001; previously amended effective January 1, 2002, and January 1, 2003.

Chapter 2
Definitions and Scope of Rules

Rule 2.3.   Definitions

As used in the Trial Court Rules, unless the context or subject matter otherwise requires:

(1) "Court" means the superior court.

(2) "Papers" includes all documents, except exhibits and copies of exhibits, that are offered for filing in any case, but does not include Judicial Council and local court forms, records on appeal in limited civil cases, or briefs filed in appellate divisions. Unless the context clearly provides otherwise, "papers" need not be in a tangible or physical form but may be in an electronic form.

(3) "Written," "writing," "typewritten," and "typewriting" include other methods of printing letters and words equivalent in legibility to typewriting or printing from a word processor.
Rule 2.3 amended effective January 1, 2016; adopted effective January 1, 2007.

Rule 2.10.   Scope of rules

These rules apply to documents filed and served electronically as well as in paper form, unless otherwise provided.
Rule 2.10 amended effective January 1, 2016; adopted effective January 1, 2007.

Chapter 3
Timing

Rule 2.20.   Application for an order extending time

(a) Application—to whom made

An application for an order extending the time within which any act is required by law to be done must be heard and determined by the judge before whom the matter is pending; provided, however, that in case of the inability, death, or absence of such judge, the application may be heard and determined by another judge of the same court.
(Subd (a) amended effective January 1, 2007.)

(b) Disclosure of previous extensions

An application for an order extending time must disclose in writing the nature of the case and what extensions, if any, have previously been granted by order of court or stipulation of counsel.
(Subd (b) amended effective January 1, 2007.)

(c) Filing and service

An order extending time must be filed immediately and copies served within 24 hours after the making of the order or within such other time as may be fixed by the court.
(Subd (c) amended effective January 1, 2007.)
Rule 2.20 amended and renumbered effective January 1, 2007; adopted as rule 235 effective January 1, 1949.

Chapter 4
Sanctions

Rule 2.30.   Sanctions for rules violations in civil cases

(a) Application

This sanctions rule applies to the rules in the California Rules of Court relating to general civil cases, unlawful detainer cases, probate proceedings, civil proceedings in the appellate division of the superior court, and small claims cases.
(Subd (a) amended effective January 1, 2004; adopted effective July 1, 2001.)

(b) Sanctions

In addition to any other sanctions permitted by law, the court may order a person, after written notice and an opportunity to be heard, to pay reasonable monetary sanctions to the court or an aggrieved person, or both, for failure without good cause to comply with the applicable rules. For the purposes of this rule, "person" means a party, a party's attorney, a witness, and an insurer or any other individual or entity whose consent is necessary for the disposition of the case. If a failure to comply with an applicable rule is the responsibility of counsel and not of the party, any penalty must be imposed on counsel and must not adversely affect the party's cause of action or defense thereto.
(Subd (b) amended effective January 1, 2007; adopted as untitled subdivision effective January 1, 1985; amended and relettered effective July 1, 2001; previously amended effective January 1, 1994, and January 1, 2004.)

(c) Notice and procedure

Sanctions must not be imposed under this rule except on noticed motion by the party seeking sanctions or on the court's own motion after the court has provided notice and an opportunity to be heard. A party's motion for sanctions must (1) state the applicable rule that has been violated, (2) describe the specific conduct that is alleged to have violated the rule, and (3) identify the attorney, law firm, party, witness, or other person against whom sanctions are sought. The court on its own motion may issue an order to show cause that must (1) state the applicable rule that has been violated, (2) describe the specific conduct that appears to have violated the rule, and (3) direct the attorney, law firm, party, witness, or other person to show cause why sanctions should not be imposed against them for violation of the rule.
(Subd (c) amended effective January 1, 2007; adopted effective July 1, 2001; previously amended effective January 1, 2004.)

(d) Award of expenses

In addition to the sanctions awardable under (b), the court may order the person who has violated an applicable rule to pay to the party aggrieved by the violation that party's reasonable expenses, including reasonable attorney's fees and costs, incurred in connection with the motion for sanctions or the order to show cause.
(Subd (d) amended effective January 1, 2007; adopted effective July 1, 2001; previously amended effective January 1, 2004.)

(e) Order

An order imposing sanctions must be in writing and must recite in detail the conduct or circumstances justifying the order.

(Subd (e) amended effective January 1, 2004; adopted effective July 1, 2001.)
Rule 2.30 amended and renumbered effective January 1, 2007; adopted as rule 227 effective January 1, 1985; previously amended effective January 1, 1994, July 1, 2001, and January 1, 2004.

Division 2
Papers and Forms to Be Filed

Chapter 1
Papers

Rule 2.100. Form and format of papers presented for filing in the trial courts

(a) Preemption of local rules

The Judicial Council has preempted local rules relating to the form and format of papers to be filed in the trial courts. No trial court, or any division or branch of a trial court, may enact or enforce any local rule concerning the form or format of papers.

(Subd (a) adopted effective January 1, 2007.)

(b) Rules prescribe form and format

The rules in this chapter prescribe the form and format of papers to be filed in the trial courts.

(Subd (b) adopted effective January 1, 2007.)

(c) Electronic format of papers

Papers that are submitted or filed electronically must meet the requirements in rule 2.256(b).

(Subd (c) adopted effective January 1, 2017.)

Rule 2.100 amended effective January 1, 2017; adopted as rule 201 effective January 1, 1949; previously amended effective April 1, 1962, May 1, 1962, July 1, 1964, January 1, 1966, July 1, 1969, July 1, 1971, January 1, 1973, July 1, 1974, January 1, 1976, January 1, 1978, May 6, 1978, January 1, 1984, April 1, 1990, July 1, 1990, January 1, 1992, July 1, 1992, January 1, 1993, July 1, 1993, January 1, 1994, January 1, 1998, January 1, 1999, July 1, 1999, July 1, 2000, January 1, 2001, January 1, 2003, and January 1, 2006; previously amended and renumbered as rule 2.100 effective January 1, 2007.

Rule 2.101. Use of recycled paper; certification by attorney or party [Repealed]

Rule 2.101 repealed effective January 1, 2014; adopted effective January 1, 2007.

Rule 2.102. One-sided paper

When papers are not filed electronically, only one side of each page may be used.

Rule 2.102 amended effective January 1, 2016; adopted effective January 1, 2007.

Rule 2.103. Size, quality, and color of papers

All papers filed must be 8½ by 11 inches. All papers not filed electronically must be on opaque, unglazed paper, white or unbleached, of standard quality not less than 20-pound weight.

Rule 2.103 amended effective January 1, 2017; adopted effective January 1, 2007; previously amended effective January 1, 2016.

Rule 2.104. Font size; printing

Unless otherwise specified in these rules, all papers filed must be prepared using a font size not smaller than 12 points. All papers not filed electronically must be printed or typewritten or be prepared by a photocopying or other duplication process that will produce clear and permanent copies equally as legible as printing.

Rule 2.104 amended effective January 1, 2017; adopted effective January 1, 2007; previously amended effective January 1, 2016.

Rule 2.105. Font style

The font style must be essentially equivalent to Courier, Times New Roman, or Arial.

Rule 2.105 amended effective January 1, 2017; adopted effective January 1, 2007; previously amended effective January 1, 2016.

Rule 2.106. Font color

The font color must be black or blue-black.

Rule 2.106 amended effective January 1, 2016; adopted effective January 1, 2007.

Rule 2.107. Margins

The left margin of each page must be at least one inch from the left edge and the right margin at least ½ inch from the right edge.

Rule 2.107 amended effective January 1, 2016; adopted effective January 1, 2007.

Rule 2.108. Spacing and numbering of lines

The spacing and numbering of lines on a page must be as follows:

(1) The lines on each page must be one and one-half spaced or double-spaced and numbered consecutively.

(2) Descriptions of real property may be single-spaced.

(3) Footnotes, quotations, and printed forms of corporate surety bonds and undertakings may be single-spaced and have unnumbered lines if they comply generally with the space requirements of rule 2.111.

(4) Line numbers must be placed at the left margin and separated from the text by a vertical column of space at least ⅕ inch wide or a single or double vertical line. Each line number must be aligned with a line of type, or the line numbers must be evenly spaced vertically on the page. Line numbers must be consecutively numbered, beginning with the number 1 on each page. There must be at least three line numbers for every vertical inch on the page.

Rule 2.108 amended effective January 1, 2016; adopted effective January 1, 2007.

Rule 2.109. Page numbering

Each page must be numbered consecutively at the bottom unless a rule provides otherwise for a particular type of document. The page numbering must begin with the first page and use only Arabic numerals (e.g., 1, 2, 3). The page number may be suppressed and need not appear on the first page.

Rule 2.109 amended effective January 1, 2017; adopted effective January 1, 2007.

Rule 2.110. Footer

(a) Location

Except for exhibits, each paper filed with the court must bear a footer in the bottom margin of each page, placed below the page number and divided from the rest of the document page by a printed line.

(Subd (a) adopted effective January 1, 2007.)

(b) Contents

The footer must contain the title of the paper (examples: "Complaint," "XYZ Corp.'s Motion for Summary Judgment") or some clear and concise abbreviation.

(Subd (b) adopted effective January 1, 2007.)

(c) Font size

The title of the paper in the footer must be in at least 10-point font.

(Subd (c) amended effective January 1, 2017; adopted effective January 1, 2007.)

Rule 2.110 amended effective January 1, 2017; adopted effective January 1, 2007.

Rule 2.111. Format of first page

The first page of each paper must be in the following form:

(1) In the space commencing 1 inch from the top of the page with line 1, to the left of the center of the page, the name, office address or, if none, residence address or mailing address (if different), telephone number, fax number and e-mail address, and State Bar membership number of the attorney for the party in whose behalf the paper is presented, or of the party if he or she is appearing in person. The inclusion of a fax number or e-mail address on any document does not constitute consent to service by fax or e-mail unless otherwise provided by law.

(2) In the first 2 inches of space between lines 1 and 7 to the right of the center of the page, a blank space for the use of the clerk.

(3) On line 8, at or below 3⅓ inches from the top of the page, the title of the court.

(4) Below the title of the court, in the space to the left of the center of the page, the title of the case. In the title of the case on each initial complaint or cross-complaint, the name of each party must commence on a separate line beginning at the left margin of the page. On any subsequent pleading or paper, it is sufficient to provide a short title of the case (1) stating the name of the first party on each side, with appropriate indication of other parties, and (2) stating that a cross-action or cross-actions are involved (e.g., "and Related Cross-action"), if applicable.

(5) To the right of and opposite the title, the number of the case.

(6) Below the number of the case, the nature of the paper and, on all complaints and petitions, the character of the action or proceeding. In a case having multiple parties, any answer, response, or opposition must specifically identify the complaining, propounding, or moving party and the complaint, motion, or other matter being answered or opposed.

(7) Below the nature of the paper or the character of the action or proceeding, the name of the judge and department, if any, to which the case is assigned.

(8) Below the nature of the paper or the character of the action or proceeding, the word "Referee:" followed by the name of the referee, on any paper filed in a case pending before a referee appointed under Code of Civil Procedure section 638 or 639.

(9) On the complaint, petition, or application filed in a limited civil case, below the character of the action or proceeding, the amount demanded in the complaint, petition, or application, stated as follows: "Amount demanded exceeds $10,000" or "Amount demanded does not exceed $10,000," as required by Government Code section 70613.

(10) In the caption of every pleading and every other paper filed in a limited civil case, the words "Limited Civil Case," as required by Code of Civil Procedure section 422.30(b).

(11) If a case is reclassified by an amended complaint, cross-complaint, amended cross-complaint, or other pleading under Code of Civil Procedure section 403.020 or 403.030, the caption must indicate that the action or proceeding is reclassified by this pleading. If a case is reclassified by stipulation under Code of Civil Procedure section 403.050, the title of the stipulation must state that the action or proceeding is reclassified by this stipulation. The caption or title must state that the case is a limited civil case reclassified as an unlimited civil case, or an unlimited civil case reclassified as a limited civil case, or other words to that effect.

Rule 2.111 amended effective January 1, 2017; adopted effective January 1, 2007; previously amended effective January 1, 2008, and January 1, 2016.

Rule 2.112.   Separate causes of action, counts, and defenses

Each separately stated cause of action, count, or defense must specifically state:

(1) Its number (e.g., "first cause of action");

(2) Its nature (e.g., "for fraud");

(3) The party asserting it if more than one party is represented on the pleading (e.g., "by plaintiff Jones"); and

(4) The party or parties to whom it is directed (e.g., "against defendant Smith").

Rule 2.112 adopted effective January 1, 2007.

Rule 2.113.   Binding

Each paper not filed electronically must consist entirely of original pages without riders and must be firmly bound together at the top.

Rule 2.113 amended effective January 1, 2016; adopted effective January 1, 2007.

Rule 2.114.   Exhibits

Exhibits submitted with papers not filed electronically may be fastened to pages of the specified size and, when prepared by a machine copying process, must be equal to computer-processed materials in legibility and permanency of image. Exhibits submitted with papers filed electronically must meet the requirements in rule 2.256(b).

Rule 2.114 amended effective January 1, 2017; adopted effective January 1, 2007; previously amended effective January 1, 2016.

Rule 2.115.   Hole punching

When papers are not filed electronically, each paper presented for filing must contain two prepunched normal-sized holes, centered 2½ inches apart and ⅝ inch from the top of the paper.

Rule 2.115 amended effective January 1, 2016; adopted effective January 1, 2007.

Rule 2.116.   Changes on face of paper

Any addition, deletion, or interlineation to a paper must be initialed by the clerk or judge at the time of filing.

Rule 2.116 adopted effective January 1, 2007.

Rule 2.117.   Conformed copies of papers

All copies of papers served must conform to the original papers filed, including the numbering of lines, pagination, additions, deletions, and interlineations except that, with the agreement of the other party, a party serving papers by nonelectronic means may serve that other party with papers printed on both sides of the page.

Rule 2.117 amended effective January 1, 2016; adopted effective January 1, 2007; previously amended effective July 1, 2012.

Rule 2.118.   Acceptance of papers for filing

(a) Papers not in compliance

The clerk of the court must not accept for filing or file any papers that do not comply with the rules in this chapter, except the clerk must not reject a paper for filing solely on the ground that:

(1) It is handwritten or hand-printed;

(2) The handwriting or hand printing on the paper is in a color other than black or blue-black; or

(3) The font size is not exactly the point size required by rules 2.104 and 2.110(c) on papers submitted electronically in portable document format (PDF). Minimal variation in font size may result from converting a document created using word processing software to PDF.

(Subd (a) amended effective January 1, 2017; adopted effective January 1, 2007.)

(b) Absence of fax number or e-mail address

The clerk must not reject a paper for filing solely on the ground that it does not contain an attorney's or a party's fax number or e-mail address on the first page.

(Subd (b) adopted effective January 1, 2007.)

(c) Filing of papers for good cause

For good cause shown, the court may permit the filing of papers that do not comply with the rules in this chapter.

(Subd (c) adopted effective January 1, 2007.)

Rule 2.118 amended effective January 1, 2017; adopted effective January 1, 2007.

Rule 2.119.   Exceptions for forms

Except as provided elsewhere in the California Rules of Court, the rules in this chapter do not apply to Judicial Council forms, local court forms, or forms for juvenile dependency proceedings produced by the California State Department of Social Services Child Welfare Systems Case Management System.

Rule 2.119 adopted effective January 1, 2007.

Advisory Committee Comment

The California Department of Social Services (CDSS) has begun to distribute a new, comprehensive, computerized case management system to county welfare agencies. This system is not able to exactly conform to Judicial Council format in all instances. However, item numbering on the forms will remain the same. The changes allow CDSS computer-generated Judicial Council forms to be used in juvenile court proceedings.

Chapter 2
General Rules on Forms

Rule 2.130.   Application

The rules in this chapter apply to Judicial Council forms, local court forms, and all other official forms to be filed in the trial courts. The rules apply to forms filed both in paper form and electronically, unless otherwise specified.

Rule 2.130 amended effective January 1, 2016; adopted effective January 1, 2007.

Rule 2.131.   Recycled paper [Repealed]

Rule 2.131 repealed effective January 1, 2014; adopted effective January 1, 2007.

Rule 2.132.   True copy certified

A party or attorney who files a form certifies by filing the form that it is a true copy of the form.

Rule 2.132 adopted effective January 1, 2007.

Rule 2.133.   Hole punching

All forms not filed electronically must contain two prepunched normal-sized holes, centered 2½ inches apart and ⅝ inch from the top of the form.

Rule 2.133 amended effective January 1, 2016; adopted effective January 1, 2007.

Rule 2.134.　Forms longer than one page

(a) Single side may be used

If a form not filed electronically is longer than one page, the form may be printed on sheets printed only on one side even if the original has two sides to a sheet.

(Subd (a) amended effective January 1, 2016; adopted effective January 1, 2007.)

(b) Two-sided forms must be tumbled

If a form not filed electronically is filed on a sheet printed on two sides, the reverse side must be rotated 180 degrees (printed head to foot).

(Subd (b) amended effective January 1, 2016; adopted effective January 1, 2007.)

(c) Multiple-page forms must be bound

If a form not filed electronically is longer than one page, it must be firmly bound at the top.

(Subd (c) amended effective January 1, 2016; adopted effective January 1, 2007.)

Rule 2.134 amended effective January 1, 2016; adopted effective January 1, 2007.

Rule 2.135.　Filing of handwritten or hand-printed forms

The clerk must not reject for filing or refuse to file any Judicial Council or local court form solely on the ground that:

(1) It is completed in handwritten or hand-printed characters; or

(2) The handwriting or hand-printing is a color other than blue-black or black.

Rule 2.135 amended and renumbered effective January 1, 2007; adopted as rule 201.4 effective January 1, 2003.

Rule 2.140.　Judicial Council forms

Judicial Council forms are governed by the rules in this chapter and chapter 4 of title 1. Electronic Judicial Council forms must meet the requirements in rule 2.256.

Rule 2.140 amended effective January 1, 2017; adopted effective January 1, 2007.

Rule 2.141.　Local court forms

Local court forms are governed by the rules in this chapter and rules 10.613 and 10.614.

Rule 2.141 adopted effective January 1, 2007.

Chapter 3
Other Forms

Rule 2.150.　Authorization for computer-generated or typewritten forms for proof of service of summons and complaint

(a) Computer-generated or typewritten forms; conditions

Notwithstanding the adoption of mandatory form *Proof of Service of Summons* (form POS-010), a form for proof of service of a summons and complaint prepared entirely by word processor, typewriter, or similar process may be used for proof of service in any applicable action or proceeding if the following conditions are met:

(1) The form complies with the rules in chapter 1 of this division except as otherwise provided in this rule, but numbered lines are not required.

(2) The left, right, and bottom margins of the proof of service must be at least ½ inch. The top margin must be at least ¾ of an inch. The typeface must be Times New Roman, Courier, Arial, or an equivalent typeface not smaller than 9 points. Text must be single-spaced and a blank line must precede each main numbered item.

(3) The title and all the text of form POS-010 that is not accompanied by a check box must be copied word for word except for any instructions, which need not be copied. In addition, the optional text describing the particular method of service used must be copied word for word, except that the check boxes must not be copied. Any optional text not describing such service need not be included.

(4) The Judicial Council number of the *Proof of Service of Summons* must be typed as follows either in the left margin of the first page opposite the last line of text or at the bottom of each page: "Judicial Council form POS-010."

(5) The text of form POS-010 must be copied in the same order as it appears on form POS-010 using the same item numbers. A declaration of diligence may be attached to the proof of service or inserted as item 5b(5).

(6) Areas marked "For Court Use" must be copied in the same general locations and occupy approximately the same amount of space as on form POS-010.

(7) The telephone number of the attorney or party must appear flush with the left margin and below the attorney's or party's address.

(8) The name of the court must be flush with the left margin. The address of the court is not required.

(9) Material that would have been entered onto form POS-010 must be entered with each line indented 3 inches from the left margin.

(Subd (a) amended effective January 1, 2016; previously amended effective July 1, 1985, January 1, 1986, January 1, 1987, July 1, 1999, January 1, 2004, July 1, 2004, and January 1, 2007.)

(b) Compliance with rule

The act of filing a computer-generated or typewritten form under this rule constitutes a certification by the party or attorney filing the form that it complies with this rule and is a true and correct copy of the form to the extent required by this rule.

(Subd (b) amended effective January 1, 2004; previously amended effective July 1, 1985, January 1, 1987, January 1, 1988, and July 1, 1999; relettered effective January 1, 1986.)

Rule 2.150 amended effective January 1, 2016; adopted as rule 982.9; previously amended effective January 1, 1989, July 1, 1999, January 1, 2004, and July 1, 2004; previously amended and renumbered as rule 2.150 effective January 1, 2007.

Advisory Committee Comment

This rule is intended to permit process servers and others to prepare their own shortened versions of *Proof of Service of Summons* (form POS-010) containing only the information that is relevant to show the method of service used.

Division 3
Filing and Service

Chap. 1.　General Provisions. Rules 2.200, 2.210.
Chap. 2.　Filing and Service by Electronic Means. Rules 2.250–2.261.
Chap. 3.　Filing and Service by Fax. Rules 2.300–2.306.

Chapter 1
General Provisions

Rule 2.200. Service and filing of notice of change of address or other contact information
Rule 2.210. Drop box for filing documents

Rule 2.200.　Service and filing of notice of change of address or other contact information

An attorney or self-represented party whose mailing address, telephone number, fax number, or e-mail address (if it was provided under rule 2.111(1)) changes while an action is pending must serve on all parties and file a written notice of the change.

Rule 2.200 amended effective January 1, 2013; adopted as rule 385 effective January 1, 1984; previously amended and renumbered effective January 1, 2007.

Rule 2.210.　Drop box for filing documents

(a) Use of drop box

Whenever a clerk's office filing counter is closed at any time between 8:30 a.m. and 4:00 p.m. on a court day, the court must provide a drop box for depositing documents to be filed with the clerk. A court may provide a drop box during other times.

(b) Documents deemed filed on day of deposit

Any document deposited in a court's drop box up to and including 4:00 p.m. on a court day is deemed to have been deposited for filing on that day. A court may provide for same-day filing of a document deposited in its drop box after 4:00 p.m. on a court day. If so, the court must give notice of the deadline for same-day filing of a document deposited in its drop box.

(c) Documents deemed filed on next court day

Any document deposited in a court's drop box is deemed to have been deposited for filing on the next court day if:

(1) It is deposited on a court day after 4:00 p.m. or after the deadline for same-day filing if a court provides for a later time; or

(2) It is deposited on a judicial holiday.

(Subd (c) amended effective January 1, 2007.)

(d) Date and time documents deposited

A court must have a means of determining whether a document was deposited in the drop box by 4:00 p.m., or after the deadline for same-day filing if a court provides for a later time, on a court day.

Rule 2.210 amended and renumbered effective January 1, 2007; adopted as rule 201.6 effective January 1, 2005.

Advisory Committee Comment

The notice required by (b) may be provided by the same means a court provides notice of its clerk's office hours. The means of providing notice may include the following: information on the court's Web site, a local rule provision, a notice in a legal newspaper, a sign in the clerk's office, or a sign near the drop box.

Chapter 2
Filing and Service by Electronic Means

Rule 2.250. Construction and definitions

(a) Construction of rules

The rules in this chapter must be construed to authorize and permit filing and service by electronic means to the extent feasible.

(Subd (a) adopted effective January 1, 2011.)

(b) Definitions

As used in this chapter, unless the context otherwise requires:

(1) A "document" is a pleading, a declaration, an exhibit, or another writing submitted by a party or other person, or by an agent of a party or other person on the party's or other person's behalf. A document is also a notice, order, judgment, or other issuance by the court. A document may be in paper or electronic form.

(2) "Electronic service" has the same meaning as defined in Code of Civil Procedure section 1010.6.

(3) "Electronic transmission" has the same meaning as defined in Code of Civil Procedure section 1010.6.

(4) "Electronic notification" has the same meaning as defined in Code of Civil Procedure section 1010.6.

(5) "Electronic service address" means the electronic address at or through which the party or other person has authorized electronic service.

(6) An "electronic filer" is a party or other person filing a document in electronic form directly with the court, by an agent, or through an electronic filing service provider.

(7) "Electronic filing" is the electronic transmission to a court of a document in electronic form. For the purposes of this chapter, this definition concerns the activity of filing and does not include the processing and review of the document, and its entry into the court records, which are necessary for a document to be officially filed.

(8) An "electronic filing service provider" is a person or entity that receives an electronic filing from a party or other person for retransmission to the court or for electronic service on other parties or other persons, or both. In submission of filings, the electronic filing service provider does so on behalf of the electronic filer and not as an agent of the court.

(9) An "electronic filing manager" is a service that acts as an intermediary between a court and various electronic filing service provider solutions certified for filing into California courts.

(10) "Self-represented" means a party or other person who is unrepresented in an action by an attorney and does not include an attorney appearing in an action who represents himself or herself.

(Subd (b) amended effective January 1, 2019; adopted as unlettered subd effective January 1, 2003; previously amended and lettered effective January 1, 2011; previously amended effective July 1, 2013, and January 1, 2018.)

Rule 2.250 amended effective January 1, 2019; adopted as rule 2050 effective January 1, 2003; previously amended and renumbered effective January 1, 2007; previously amended effective January 1, 2006, January 1, 2008, January 1, 2011, July 1, 2013, and January 1, 2018.

Advisory Committee Comment

The definition of "electronic service" has been amended to provide that a party may effectuate service not only by the electronic transmission of a document, but also by providing electronic notification of where a document served electronically may be located and downloaded. This amendment is intended to modify the rules on electronic service to expressly authorize electronic notification as a legally effective alternative means of service to electronic transmission. This rules amendment is consistent with the amendment of Code of Civil Procedure section 1010.6, effective January 1, 2011, to authorize service by electronic notification. (See Stats. 2010, ch. 156 (Sen. Bill 1274).) The amendments change the law on electronic service as understood by the appellate court in *Insyst, Ltd. v. Applied Materials, Inc.* (2009) 170 Cal.App.4th 1129, which interpreted the rules as authorizing electronic transmission as the only effective means of electronic service.

Rule 2.251. Construction of rules [Repealed]

Rule 2.251 repealed effective January 1, 2011; adopted effective January 1, 2010.

Another Rule 2.251 follows.

Rule 2.251. Electronic service

(a) Authorization for electronic service

When a document may be served by mail, express mail, overnight delivery, or fax transmission, the document may be served electronically under Code of Civil Procedure section 1010.6 and the rules in this chapter.

(Subd (a) amended effective July 1, 2013; previously amended effective January 1, 2007, January 1, 2008, and January 1, 2011.)

(b) Electronic service by express consent

(1) A party or other person indicates that the party or other person agrees to accept electronic service by:

(A) Serving a notice on all parties and other persons that the party or other person accepts electronic service and filing the notice with the court. The notice must include the electronic service address at which the party or other person agrees to accept service; or

(B) Manifesting affirmative consent through electronic means with the court or the court's electronic filing service provider, and concurrently providing the party's electronic service address with that consent for the purpose of receiving electronic service. [1] A party or other person may manifest affirmative consent [2] by **serving notice of consent to all parties and other persons and either**:

(i) Agreeing to the terms of service [3] with an electronic filing service provider, which clearly [4] **state** that agreement constitutes consent to receive electronic service [5]; or

(ii) Filing *Consent to Electronic Service and Notice of Electronic Service Address* (form EFS-005-CV).

(2) A party or other person that has consented to electronic service under (1) and has used an electronic filing service provider to serve and file documents in a case consents to service on that electronic filing service provider as the designated agent for service for the party or other person in the case, until such time as the party or other person designates a different agent for service.

(Subd (b) amended effective January 1, 2020; adopted as part of subd (a); previously amended and relettered effective July 1, 2013; previously amended effective January 1, 2007, January 1, 2008, January 1, 2011, January 1, 2018, and January 1, 2019.)

Rule 2.251(b). 2019 Deletes. [1] (C) [2] under (B) [3] agreement [4] states [5] electronically

(c) Electronic service required by local rule or court order

(1) A court may require parties to serve documents electronically in specified actions by local rule or court order, as provided in Code of Civil Procedure section 1010.6 and the rules in this chapter.

(2) A court may require other persons to serve documents electronically in specified actions by local rule, as provided in Code of Civil Procedure section 1010.6 and the rules in this chapter.

(3) Except when personal service is otherwise required by statute or rule, a party or other person that is required to file documents electronically in an action must also serve documents and accept service of documents electronically from all other parties or persons, unless:

(A) The court orders otherwise, or

(B) The action includes parties or persons that are not required to file or serve documents electronically, including self-represented parties or other self-represented persons; those parties or other persons are to be served by non-electronic methods unless they affirmatively consent to electronic service.

(4) Each party or other person that is required to serve and accept service of documents electronically must provide all other parties or other persons in the action with its electronic service address and must promptly notify all other parties, other persons, and the court of any changes under (g).

(Subd (c) amended effective January 1, 2018; adopted effective July 1, 2013.)

(d) Additional provisions for electronic service required by court order

(1) If a court has adopted local rules for permissive electronic filing, then the court may, on the motion of any party or on its own motion, provided that the order would not cause undue hardship or significant prejudice to any party, order all parties in any class action, a consolidated

action, a group of actions, a coordinated action, or an action that is complex under rule 3.403 to serve all documents electronically, except when personal service is required by statute or rule.

(2) A court may combine an order for mandatory electronic service with an order for mandatory electronic filing as provided in rule 2.253(c).

(3) If the court proposes to make any order under (1) on its own motion, the court must mail notice to any parties that have not consented to receive electronic service. The court may electronically serve the notice on any party that has consented to receive electronic service. Any party may serve and file an opposition within 10 days after notice is mailed, electronically served, or such later time as the court may specify.

(4) If the court has previously ordered parties in a case to electronically serve documents and a new party is added that the court determines should also be ordered to do so under (1), the court may follow the notice procedures under (2) or may order the party to electronically serve documents and in its order state that the new party may object within 10 days after service of the order or by such later time as the court may specify.

(Subd (d) adopted effective January 1, 2018.)

(e) Maintenance of electronic service lists

A court that permits or requires electronic filing in a case must maintain and make available electronically to the parties and other persons in the case an electronic service list that contains the parties' or other persons' current electronic service addresses, as provided by the parties or other persons that have filed electronically in the case.

(Subd (e) amended and relettered effective January 1, 2018; adopted as subd (b) effective January 1, 2008; previously amended effective January 1, 2010, and January 1, 2011; previously amended and relettered as subd (d) effective July 1, 2013.)

(f) Service by the parties and other persons

(1) Notwithstanding (e), parties and other persons that have consented to or are required to serve documents electronically are responsible for electronic service on all other parties and other persons required to be served in the case. A party or other person may serve documents electronically directly, by an agent, or through a designated electronic filing service provider.

(2) A document may not be electronically served on a nonparty unless the nonparty consents to electronic service or electronic service is otherwise provided for by law or court order.

(Subd (f) amended and relettered effective January 1, 2018; adopted as subd (c) effective January 1, 2008; previously amended effective January 1, 2011; previously amended and relettered as subd (e) effective July 1, 2013.)

(g) Change of electronic service address

(1) A party or other person whose electronic service address changes while the action or proceeding is pending must promptly file a notice of change of address electronically with the court and must serve this notice electronically on all other parties and all other persons required to be served.

(2) A party's or other person's election to contract with an electronic filing service provider to electronically file and serve documents or to receive electronic service of documents on the party's or other person's behalf does not relieve the party or other person of its duties under (1).

(3) An electronic service address is presumed valid for a party or other person if the party or other person files electronic documents with the court from that address and has not filed and served notice that the address is no longer valid.

(Subd (g) amended and relettered effective January 1, 2018; adopted as subd (d) effective January 1, 2008; previously amended effective January 1, 2011; previously relettered as subd (f) effective July 1, 2013.)

(h) Reliability and integrity of documents served by electronic notification

A party or other person that serves a document by means of electronic notification must:

(1) Ensure that the documents served can be viewed and downloaded using the hyperlink provided;

(2) Preserve the document served without any change, alteration, or modification from the time the document is posted until the time the hyperlink is terminated; and

(3) Maintain the hyperlink until either:

(A) All parties in the case have settled or the case has ended and the time for appeals has expired; or

(B) If the party or other person is no longer in the case, the party or other person has provided notice to all other parties and other persons required to receive notice that it is no longer in the case and that they have

60 days to download any documents, and 60 days have passed after the notice was given.

(Subd (h) amended and relettered effective January 1, 2018; adopted as subd (e) effective January 1, 2011; previously relettered as subd (g) effective July 1, 2013.)

(i) When service is complete

(1) Electronic service of a document is complete as provided in Code of Civil Procedure section 1010.6 and the rules in this chapter.

(2) If an electronic filing service provider is used for service, the service is complete at the time that the electronic filing service provider electronically transmits the document or sends electronic notification of service.

(Subd (i) amended and relettered effective January 1, 2018; adopted as subd (b) effective January 1, 2003; previously amended effective January 1, 2007; previously relettered as subd (e) effective January 1, 2008; previously amended and relettered as subd (f) effective January 1, 2011, and as subd (h) effective July 1, 2013.)

(j) Proof of service

(1) Proof of electronic service shall be made as provided in Code of Civil Procedure section 1013b.

(2) Under rule 3.1300(c), proof of electronic service of the moving papers must be filed at least five court days before the hearing.

(3) If a person signs a printed form of a proof of electronic service, the party or other person filing the proof of electronic service must comply with the provisions of rule 2.257(a).

(Subd (j) amended and relettered effective January 1, 2018; adopted as subd (c) effective January 1, 2003; previously relettered as subd (f) effective January 1, 2008; previously amended effective January 1, 2007, January 1, 2009, July 1, 2009, January 1, 2010, and January 1, 2017; previously amended and relettered as subd (g) effective January 1, 2011; previously relettered as subd (i) effective July 1, 2013.)

(k) Electronic service by or on court

(1) The court may electronically serve documents as provided in Code of Civil Procedure section 1010.6 and the rules in this chapter.

(2) A document may be electronically served on a court if the court consents to electronic service or electronic service is otherwise provided for by law or court order. A court indicates that it agrees to accept electronic service by:

(A) Serving a notice on all parties and other persons in the case that the court accepts electronic service. The notice must include the electronic service address at which the court agrees to accept service; or

(B) Adopting a local rule stating that the court accepts electronic service. The rule must indicate where to obtain the electronic service address at which the court agrees to accept service.

(Subd (k) amended and relettered effective January 1, 2018; adopted as subd (e) effective January 1, 2003; previously amended effective January 1, 2007, and January 1, 2016; previously relettered as subd (g) effective January 1, 2008, and as subd (h) effective January 1, 2011, and as subd (j) effective July 1, 2013.)
Rule 2.251 amended effective January 1, 2020; adopted as rule 2060 effective January 1, 2003; previously amended and renumbered as rule 2.260 effective January 1, 2007, and as rule 2.251 effective January 1, 2011; previously amended effective January 1, 2008, January 1, 2009, July 1, 2009, January 1, 2010, July 1, 2013, January 1, 2016, January 1, 2017, January 1, 2018, and January 1, 2019.

Advisory Committee Comment

Subdivision (b)(1)(B). The rule does not prescribe specific language for a provision of a term of service when the filer consents to electronic service, but does require that any such provision be clear. *Consent to Electronic Service and Notice of Electronic Service Address* (form EFS-005-CV) provides an example of language for consenting to electronic service.

Subdivisions (c)–(d). Court-ordered electronic service is not subject to the provisions in Code of Civil Procedure section 1010.6 requiring that, where mandatory electronic filing and service are established by local rule, the court and the parties must have access to more than one electronic filing service provider.

Rule 2.252. General rules on electronic filing of documents

(a) In general

A court may provide for electronic filing of documents in actions and proceedings as provided under Code of Civil Procedure section 1010.6 and the rules in this chapter.

(Subd (a) amended effective July 1, 2013; previously amended effective January 1, 2007.)

(b) Direct and indirect electronic filing

Except as otherwise provided by law, a court may provide for the electronic filing of documents directly with the court, indirectly through one or more approved electronic filing service providers, or through a combination of direct and indirect means.

(Subd (b) adopted effective July 1, 2013.)

(c) No effect on filing deadline

Filing a document electronically does not alter any filing deadline.

(Subd (c) amended effective January 1, 2018; adopted effective July 1, 2013.)

(d) Filing in paper form

When it is not feasible for a party or other person to convert a document to electronic form by scanning, imaging, or another means, a court may allow that party or other person to file the document in paper form.

(Subd (d) amended effective January 1, 2018; adopted effective July 1, 2013.)

(e) Original documents

In a proceeding that requires the filing of an original document, an electronic filer may file an electronic copy of a document if the original document is then filed with the court within 10 calendar days.

(Subd (e) relettered effective July 1, 2013; adopted as subd (b) effective January 1, 2003; previously amended effective January 1, 2011.)

(f) Application for waiver of court fees and costs

The court must permit electronic filing of an application for waiver of court fees and costs in any proceeding in which the court accepts electronic filings.

(Subd (f) amended effective January 1, 2018; adopted as subd (c) effective January 1, 2003; previously amended effective January 1, 2007; previously relettered as subd (f) effective July 1, 2013.)

(g) Orders and judgments

The court may electronically file any notice, order, minute order, judgment, or other document prepared by the court.

(Subd (g) relettered effective July 1, 2013; adopted as subd (d).)

(h) Proposed orders

Proposed orders may be filed and submitted electronically as provided in rule 3.1312.

(Subd (h) relettered effective July 1, 2013; adopted as subd (e) effective January 1, 2011.)

Rule 2.252 amended effective January 1, 2018; adopted as rule 2052 effective January 1, 2003; previously amended and renumbered effective January 1, 2007; previously amended effective January 1, 2011, and July 1, 2013.

Rule 2.253. Permissive electronic filing, mandatory electronic filing, and electronic filing by court order

(a) Permissive electronic filing by local rule

A court may permit parties by local rule to file documents electronically in any types of cases subject to the conditions in Code of Civil Procedure section 1010.6 and the rules in this chapter.

(Subd (a) amended effective January 1, 2018; adopted effective July 1, 2013.)

(b) Mandatory electronic filing by local rule

A court may require parties by local rule to electronically file documents in civil actions directly with the court, or directly with the court and through one or more approved electronic filing service providers, or through more than one approved electronic filing service provider, subject to the conditions in Code of Civil Procedure section 1010.6, the rules in this chapter, and the following conditions:

(1) The court must specify the types or categories of civil actions in which parties or other persons are required to file and serve documents electronically. The court may designate any of the following as eligible for mandatory electronic filing and service:

(A) All civil cases;

(B) All civil cases of a specific category, such as unlimited or limited civil cases;

(C) All civil cases of a specific case type, including but not limited to, contract, collections, personal injury, or employment;

(D) All civil cases assigned to a judge for all purposes;

(E) All civil cases assigned to a specific department, courtroom or courthouse;

(F) Any class actions, consolidated actions, or group of actions, coordinated actions, or actions that are complex under rule 3.403; or

(G) Any combination of the cases described in subparagraphs (A) to (F), inclusive.

(2) Self-represented parties or other self-represented persons are exempt from any mandatory electronic filing and service requirements adopted by courts under this rule and Code of Civil Procedure section 1010.6.

(3) In civil cases involving both represented and self-represented parties or other persons, represented parties or other persons may be required to file and serve documents electronically; however, in these cases, each self-represented party or other person is to file, serve, and be served with documents by non-electronic means unless the self-represented party or other person affirmatively agrees otherwise.

(4) A party or other person that is required to file and serve documents electronically must be excused from the requirements if the party or other person shows undue hardship or significant prejudice. A court requiring the electronic filing and service of documents must have a process for parties or other persons, including represented parties or other represented persons, to apply for relief and a procedure for parties or other persons excused from filing documents electronically to file them by conventional means.

(5) Any fees charged by the court or an electronic filing service provider shall be consistent with the fee provisions of Code of Civil Procedure section 1010.6.

(6) The effective date of filing any document received electronically is prescribed by Code of Civil Procedure section 1010.6. This provision concerns only the effective date of filing. Any document that is received electronically must be processed and satisfy all other legal filing requirements to be filed as an official court record.

(7) A court that adopts a mandatory electronic filing program under this subdivision must report semiannually to the Judicial Council on the operation and effectiveness of the court's program.

(Subd (b) amended effective January 1, 2018; adopted effective July 1, 2013.)

(c) Electronic filing by court order

(1) If a court has adopted local rules for permissive electronic filing, then the court may, on the motion of any party or on its own motion, provided that the order would not cause undue hardship or significant prejudice to any party, order all parties in any class action, a consolidated action, a group of actions, a coordinated action, or an action that is complex under rule 3.403 to file all documents electronically.

(2) A court may combine an order for mandatory electronic filing with an order for mandatory electronic service as provided in rule 2.252(d).

(3) If the court proposes to make any order under (1) on its own motion, the court must mail notice to any parties that have not consented to receive electronic service. The court may electronically serve the notice on any party that has consented to receive electronic service. Any party may serve and file an opposition within 10 days after notice is mailed or electronically served or such later time as the court may specify.

(4) If the court has previously ordered parties in a case to electronically file documents and a new party is added that the court determines should also be ordered to do so under (1), the court may follow the notice procedures under (2) or may order the party to electronically file documents and in its order state that the new party may object within 10 days after service of the order or by such later time as the court may specify.

(5) The court's order may also provide that:

(A) Documents previously filed in paper form may be resubmitted in electronic form; and

(B) When the court sends confirmation of filing to all parties, receipt of the confirmation constitutes service of the filing if the filed document is available electronically.

(Subd (c) amended effective January 1, 2018; adopted as subd (a) and part of subd (b) effective January 1, 2003; previously amended effective January 1, 2007, January 1, 2008, and January 1, 2011; previously repealed, amended and relettered as subd (c) effective July 1, 2013.)

Rule 2.253 amended effective January 1, 2018; adopted as rule 2053 effective January 1, 2003; previously amended and renumbered effective January 1, 2007; previously amended effective January 1, 2008, January 1, 2011, and July 1, 2013.

Advisory Committee Comment

Subdivision (b)(1). This subdivision allows courts to institute mandatory electronic filing and service in any type of civil case for which the court determines that mandatory electronic filing is appropriate. The scope of this authorization is meant to be broad. It will enable courts to implement mandatory electronic filing in a flexible yet expansive manner. However, in initiating mandatory electronic filing, courts should take into account the fact that some civil case types may be easier and more cost-effective to implement at the outset while other types may require special procedures or other considerations (such as the need to preserve the confidentiality of filed records) that may make them less appropriate for inclusion in initial mandatory e-filing efforts.

Subdivision (b)(2). Although this rule exempts self-represented parties from any mandatory electronic filing and service requirements, these parties are encouraged to participate voluntarily in electronic filing and service. To the extent feasible, courts and other entities should assist self-represented parties to electronically file and serve documents.

Subdivision (c). Court-ordered electronic filing under this subdivision is not subject to the provisions in (b) and Code of Civil Procedure section 1010.6 requiring that, where mandatory electronic filing and service are established by local rule, the court and the parties must have access to more than one electronic filing service provider.

Rule 2.254.　Responsibilities of court

(a)　Publication of electronic filing requirements

Each court that permits or mandates electronic filing must publish, in both electronic and print formats, the court's electronic filing requirements.

(Subd (a) amended effective July 1, 2013; adopted as subd (b) effective January 1, 2003; previously amended effective January 1, 2007; previously relettered effective January 1, 2011.)

(b)　Problems with electronic filing

If the court is aware of a problem that impedes or precludes electronic filing, it must promptly take reasonable steps to provide notice of the problem.

(Subd (b) amended effective January 1, 2018; adopted as subd (c) effective January 1, 2003; previously amended effective January 1, 2007; previously relettered as subd (b) effective January 1, 2011.)

(c)　Public access to electronically filed documents

Except as provided in rules 2.250–2.259 and 2.500–2.506, an electronically filed document is a public document at the time it is filed unless it is sealed under rule 2.551(b) or made confidential by law.

(Subd (c) amended and relettered effective January 1, 2011; adopted as subd (d) effective January 1, 2003; previously amended effective January 1, 2007.)

Rule 2.254 amended effective January 1, 2018; adopted as rule 2054 effective January 1, 2003; previously amended and renumbered effective January 1, 2007; previously amended effective January 1, 2011, and July 1, 2013.

Rule 2.255.　Contracts with and responsibilities of electronic filing service providers and electronic filing managers

(a)　Right to contract

(1)　A court may contract with one or more electronic filing service providers to furnish and maintain an electronic filing system for the court.

(2)　If the court contracts with an electronic filing service provider, it may require electronic filers to transmit the documents to the provider.

(3)　A court may contract with one or more electronic filing managers to act as an intermediary between the court and electronic filing service providers.

(4)　If the court contracts with an electronic service provider or the court has an in-house system, the provider or system must accept filing from other electronic filing service providers to the extent the provider or system is compatible with them.

(Subd (a) amended effective January 1, 2019; previously amended effective January 1, 2007, and January 1, 2011.)

(b)　Provisions of contract

(1)　The court's contract with an electronic filing service provider may:

(A)　Allow the provider to charge electronic filers a reasonable fee in addition to the court's filing fee;

(B)　Allow the provider to make other reasonable requirements for use of the electronic filing system.

(2)　The court's contract with an electronic filing service provider must comply with the requirements of Code of Civil Procedure section 1010.6.

(3)　The court's contract with an electronic filing manager must comply with the requirements of Code of Civil Procedure section 1010.6.

(Subd (b) amended effective January 1, 2019; previously amended effective January 1, 2018.)

(c)　Transmission of filing to court

(1)　An electronic filing service provider must promptly transmit any electronic filing [1]**, any applicable filing fee, and any applicable acceptance of consent to receive electronic service** to the court directly or through the court's electronic filing manager.

(2)　An electronic filing manager must promptly transmit an electronic filing [2]**, any applicable filing fee, and any applicable acceptance of consent to receive electronic service** to the court.

(Subd (c) amended effective January 1, 2020; previously amended effective January 1, 2011, and January 1, 2019.)

> **Rule 2.255(c).　2019 Deletes. [1]** and **[2]** and

(d)　Confirmation of receipt and filing of document

(1)　An electronic filing service provider must promptly send to an electronic filer its confirmation of the receipt of any document that the filer has transmitted to the provider for filing with the court.

(2)　The electronic filing service provider must send its confirmation to the filer's electronic service address and must indicate the date and time of receipt, in accordance with rule 2.259(a).

(3)　After reviewing the documents, the court must promptly transmit to the electronic filing service provider and the electronic filer the court's confirmation of filing or notice of rejection of filing, in accordance with rule 2.259.

(Subd (d) amended effective January 1, 2011; previously amended effective January 1, 2007.)

(e)　Ownership of information

All contracts between the court and electronic filing service providers or the court and electronic filing managers must acknowledge that the court is the owner of the contents of the filing system and has the exclusive right to control the system's use.

(Subd (e) amended effective January 1, 2019; previously amended effective January 1, 2007.)

(f)　Establishing a filer account with an electronic filing service provider

(1)　An electronic filing service provider may not require a filer to provide a credit card, debit card, or bank account information to create an account with the electronic filing service provider.

(2)　This provision applies only to the creation of an account and not to the use of an electronic filing service provider's services. An electronic filing service provider may require a filer to provide a credit card, debit card, or bank account information before rendering services unless the services are within the scope of a fee waiver granted by the court to the filer.

(Subd (f) adopted effective January 1, 2019.)

(g)　Electronic filer not required to consent to electronic service

(1)　An electronic filing service provider must allow an electronic filer to proceed with an electronic filing even if the electronic filer does not consent to receive electronic service.

(2)　This provision applies only to electronic service by express consent under rule 2.251(b).

(Subd (g) adopted effective January 1, 2021.)

Rule 2.255 amended effective January 1, 2021; adopted as rule 2055 effective January 1, 2003; previously amended and renumbered effective January 1, 2007; previously amended effective January 1, 2011, January 1, 2018, January 1, 2019, and January 1, 2020.

Rule 2.256.　Responsibilities of electronic filer

(a)　Conditions of filing

Each electronic filer must:

(1)　Comply with any court requirements designed to ensure the integrity of electronic filing and to protect sensitive personal information;

(2)　Furnish information the court requires for case processing;

(3)　Take all reasonable steps to ensure that the filing does not contain computer code, including viruses, that might be harmful to the court's electronic filing system and to other users of that system;

(4)　Furnish one or more electronic service addresses in the manner specified by the court. This only applies when the electronic filer has consented to or is required to accept electronic service;

(5)　Immediately provide the court and all parties with any change to the electronic filer's electronic service address. This applies only when the electronic filer has consented to or is required to accept electronic service; and

(6)　If the electronic filer uses an electronic filing service provider, provide the electronic filing service provider with the electronic address at which the filer is to be sent all documents and immediately notify the electronic filing service provider of any change in that address.

(Subd (a) amended effective January 1, 2018; previously amended effective January 1, 2007, January 1, 2011, and July 1, 2013.)

(b)　Format of documents to be filed electronically

A document that is filed electronically with the court must be in a format specified by the court unless it cannot be created in that format. The format adopted by a court must meet the following requirements:

(1)　The software for creating and reading documents must be in the public domain or generally available at a reasonable cost.

(2)　The printing of documents must not result in the loss of document text, format, or appearance.

(3)　The document must be text searchable when technologically feasible without impairment of the document's image.

If a document is filed electronically under the rules in this chapter and cannot be formatted to be consistent with a formatting rule elsewhere in the California Rules of Court, the rules in this chapter prevail.

(Subd (b) amended effective January 1, 2017; previously amended effective January 1, 2006, January 1, 2008, and January 1, 2010.)

Rule 2.256 amended effective January 1, 2018; adopted as rule 2056 effective January 1, 2003; previously amended and renumbered effective January 1, 2007;

previously amended effective January 1, 2006, January 1, 2008, January 1, 2010, January 1, 2011, July 1, 2013, and January 1, 2017.

Advisory Committee Comment

Subdivision (b)(3). The term "technologically feasible" does not require more than the application of standard, commercially available optical character recognition (OCR) software.

Rule 2.257. Requirements for signatures on documents

(a) Electronic signature

An electronic signature is an electronic sound, symbol, or process attached to or logically associated with an electronic record and executed or adopted by a person with the intent to sign a document or record created, generated, sent, communicated, received, or stored by electronic means.

(Subd (a) adopted effective January 1, 2019.)

(b) Documents signed under penalty of perjury

When a document to be filed electronically provides for a signature under penalty of perjury of any person, the document is deemed to have been signed by that person if filed electronically provided that either of the following conditions is satisfied:

(1) The declarant has signed the document using an electronic signature, and declares under penalty of perjury under the laws of the state of California that the information submitted is true and correct. **If the declarant is not the electronic filer, the electronic signature must be unique to the declarant, capable of verification, under the sole control of the declarant, and linked to data in such a manner that if the data are changed, the electronic signature is invalidated**; or

(2) The declarant, before filing, has physically signed a printed form of the document. By electronically filing the document, the electronic filer certifies that the original, signed document is available for inspection and copying at the request of the court or any other party. In the event this second method of submitting documents electronically under penalty of perjury is used, the following conditions apply:

(A) At any time after the electronic version of the document is filed, any party may serve a demand for production of the original signed document. The demand must be served on all other parties but need not be filed with the court.

(B) Within five days of service of the demand under (A), the party or other person on whom the demand is made must make the original signed document available for inspection and copying by all other parties.

(C) At any time after the electronic version of the document is filed, the court may order the filing party or other person to produce the original signed document in court for inspection and copying by the court. The order must specify the date, time, and place for the production and must be served on all parties.

(D) Notwithstanding (A)–(C), local child support agencies may maintain original, signed pleadings by way of an electronic copy in the statewide automated child support system and must maintain them only for the period of time stated in Government Code section 68152(a). If the local child support agency maintains an electronic copy of the original, signed pleading in the statewide automated child support system, it may destroy the paper original.

(Subd (b) amended effective January 1, 2020; adopted as subd (a); previously amended effective January 1, 2007, July 1, 2016, and January 1, 2018; previously relettered and amended as subd (b) effective January 1, 2019.)

(c) Documents not signed under penalty of perjury

(1) If a document does not require a signature under penalty of perjury, the document is deemed signed by the [1] **person who** filed **it** electronically.

[2] **(2)** When a document to be filed electronically, such as a stipulation, requires the signatures of opposing parties **or persons other than the filer not under penalty of perjury**, the following [3] **procedures apply:**

(A) **The opposing party or other person has signed** a printed form of the document **before, or on the same day as, the date of filing**. [4] **The electronic filer** must maintain the original, signed document and must make it available for inspection and copying as provided in [5] **(b)(2)** of this rule and Code of Civil Procedure section 1010.6. The court and any other party may demand production of the original signed document in the manner provided in [6] **(b)(2)(A)–(C).** By electronically filing the document, the electronic filer indicates that all parties have signed the document and that the filer has the signed original in his or her possession**; or**

(B) **The opposing party or other person has signed the document using an electronic signature and that electronic signature is unique to the person using it, capable of verification, under the sole control of the person using it, and linked to data in such a manner that if the data are changed, the electronic signature is invalidated**.

(Subd (c) amended effective January 1, 2020; adopted as subd (b); previously amended effective January 1, 2007; previously relettered effective January 1, 2019.)

Rule 2.257(c). 2019 Deletes. [1] party if the document is [2] **(d) Documents requiring signatures of opposing parties** [3] procedure applies: (1) The party filing the document must obtain the signatures of all parties on [4] (2) The party filing the document [5] (a)(2) [6] (a)(2)(A)–(C). (3)

(d) Digital signature

A party **or other person** is not required to use a digital signature on an electronically filed document.

(Subd (d) amended and relettered effective January 1, 2020; adopted as subd (d); previously relettered as subd (e) effective January 1, 2019.)

(e) Judicial signatures

If a document requires a signature by a court or a judicial officer, the document may be electronically signed in any manner permitted by law.

(Subd (e) relettered effective January 1, 2020; adopted as subd (e) effective January 1, 2008; previously relettered as subd (f) effective January 1, 2019.)
Rule 2.257 amended effective January 1, 2020; adopted as rule 2057 effective January 1, 2003; previously amended and renumbered effective January 1, 2007; previously amended effective January 1, 2008, July 1, 2016, January 1, 2018, and January 1, 2019.

Advisory Committee Comment

The requirements for electronic signatures that are compliant with the rule do not impair the power of the courts to resolve disputes about the validity of a signature.

Rule 2.258. Payment of filing fees

(a) Use of credit cards and other methods

A court may permit the use of credit cards, debit cards, electronic fund transfers, or debit accounts for the payment of filing fees associated with electronic filing, as provided in Government Code section 6159, rule 10.820, and other applicable law. A court may also authorize other methods of payment.

(Subd (a) amended effective January 1, 2007.)

(b) Fee waivers

Eligible persons may seek a waiver of court fees and costs, as provided in Government Code sections 68630–68641, rule 2.252(f), and division 2 of title 3 of these rules.

(Subd (b) amended effective July 1, 2013; previously amended effective January 1, 2007, and January 1, 2010.)
Rule 2.258 amended effective July 1, 2013; adopted as rule 2058 effective January 1, 2003; previously amended and renumbered effective January 1, 2007; previously amended effective January 1, 2010.

Rule 2.259. Actions by court on receipt of electronic filing

(a) Confirmation of receipt and filing of document

(1) *Confirmation of receipt*

When a court receives an electronically submitted document, the court must promptly send the electronic filer confirmation of the court's receipt of the document, indicating the date and time of receipt. A document is considered received at the date and time the confirmation of receipt is created.

(2) *Confirmation of filing*

If the document received by the court under (1) complies with filing requirements and all required filing fees have been paid, the court must promptly send the electronic filer confirmation that the document has been filed. The filing confirmation must indicate the date and time of filing and is proof that the document was filed on the date and at the time specified. The filing confirmation must also specify:

(A) Any transaction number associated with the filing;

(B) The titles of the documents as filed by the court; and

(C) The fees assessed for the filing.

(3) *Transmission of confirmations*

The court must send receipt and filing confirmation to the electronic filer at the electronic service address the filer furnished to the court under rule 2.256(a)(4). The court must maintain a record of all receipt and filing confirmations.

(4) *Filer responsible for verification*

In the absence of the court's confirmation of receipt and filing, there is no presumption that the court received and filed the document. The electronic filer is responsible for verifying that the court received and filed any document that the electronic filer submitted to the court electronically.

(Subd (a) amended effective January 1, 2011; previously amended effective January 1, 2007, and January 1, 2008.)

(b) Notice of rejection of document for filing

If the clerk does not file a document because it does not comply with applicable filing requirements or because the required filing fee has not been paid, the court must promptly send notice of the rejection of the document for filing to the electronic filer. The notice must state the reasons that the document was rejected for filing.

(Subd (b) amended effective January 1, 2007.)

(c) Delayed delivery

If a technical problem with a court's electronic filing system prevents the court from accepting an electronic filing on a particular court day, and the electronic filer demonstrates that he or she attempted to electronically file the document on that day, the court must deem the document as filed on that day. This subdivision does not apply to the filing of a complaint or any other initial pleading in an action or proceeding.

(Subd (c) repealed, amended and relettered effective January 1, 2018; adopted as subd (d); previously amended effective January 1, 2007.)

(d) Endorsement

(1) The court's endorsement of a document electronically filed must contain the following: "Electronically filed by Superior Court of California, County of _____, on _____ (date)," followed by the name of the court clerk.

(2) The endorsement required under (1) has the same force and effect as a manually affixed endorsement stamp with the signature and initials of the court clerk.

(3) A complaint or another initial pleading in an action or proceeding that is filed and endorsed electronically may be printed and served on the defendant or respondent in the same manner as if it had been filed in paper form.

(Subd (d) relettered effective January 1, 2018; adopted as subd (e); previously amended effective January 1, 2007.)

(e) Issuance of electronic summons

(1) On the electronic filing of a complaint, a petition, or another document that must be served with a summons, the court may transmit a summons electronically to the electronic filer in accordance with this subdivision and Code of Civil Procedure section 1010.6.

(2) The electronically transmitted summons must contain an image of the court's seal and the assigned case number.

(3) Personal service of the printed form of a summons transmitted electronically to the electronic filer has the same legal effect as personal service of a copy of an original summons.

(Subd (e) amended and relettered effective January 1, 2018; adopted as subd (f); previously amended effective January 1, 2007.)

Rule 2.259 amended effective January 1, 2018; adopted as rule 2059 effective January 1, 2003; previously amended and renumbered effective January 1, 2007; previously amended effective January 1, 2008, January 1, 2011, and July 1, 2013.

Rule 2.260. Electronic service [Renumbered]

Rule 2.260 renumbered as rule 2.251 effective January 1, 2011.

Rule 2.261. Authorization for courts to continue modifying forms for the purpose of electronic filing and forms generation

Courts that participated in pilot projects for electronic filing and forms generation under former rule 981.5 are authorized to continue to modify Judicial Council forms for the purpose of accepting electronic filing or providing electronic generation of court documents provided that the modification of the forms is consistent with the rules in this chapter.

Rule 2.261 amended and renumbered effective January 1, 2007; adopted as rule 2061 effective July 1, 2004.

Chapter 3
Filing and Service by Fax

Rule 2.300. Application

(a) Proceedings to which rules apply

The rules in this chapter apply to civil, probate, and family law proceedings in all trial courts. Rule 5.386 applies to fax filing of a protective order issued by a tribal court. Rule 5.522 applies to fax filing in juvenile law proceedings.

(Subd (a) amended effective July 1, 2012; adopted as part of unlettered subd effective March 1, 1992; previously amended and lettered effective January 1, 2007.)

(b) Documents that may not be issued by fax

Notwithstanding any provision in the rules in this chapter, no will, codicil, bond, or undertaking may be filed by fax nor may a court issue by fax any document intended to carry the original seal of the court.

(Subd (b) amended and lettered effective January 1, 2007; adopted as part of unlettered subd effective March 1, 1992.)

Rule 2.300 amended effective July 1, 2012; adopted as rule 2002 effective March 1, 1992; previously amended effective January 1, 1999; previously amended and renumbered effective January 1, 2007.

Rule 2.301. Definitions

As used in this chapter, unless the context otherwise requires:

(1) "Fax" is an abbreviation for "facsimile" and refers, as indicated by the context, to facsimile transmission or to a document so transmitted.

(2) "Fax transmission" means the transmission of a document by a system that encodes a document into electrical signals, transmits these electrical signals over a telephone line, and reconstructs the signals to print a duplicate of the original document at the receiving end.

(3) "Fax machine" means a machine that can send a facsimile transmission using the international standard for scanning, coding, and transmission established for Group 3 machines by the Consultative Committee of International Telegraphy and Telephone of the International Telecommunications Union (CCITT),[1] in regular resolution. Any fax machine used to send documents to a court under rule 2.305 must send at an initial transmission speed of no less than 4800 baud and be able to generate a transmission record. "Fax machine" includes a fax modem that is connected to a personal computer.

(4) "Fax filing" means the fax transmission of a document to a court that accepts such documents.

(5) "Service by fax" means the transmission of a document to a party or the attorney for a party under the rules in this chapter.

(6) "Transmission record" means the document printed by the sending fax machine, stating the telephone number of the receiving fax machine, the number of pages sent, the transmission time and date, and an indication of any errors in transmission.

(7) "Fax filing agency" means an entity that receives documents by fax for processing and filing with the court.

Rule 2.301 amended and renumbered effective January 1, 2007; adopted as rule 2003 effective March 1, 1992.

Rule 2.302. Compliance with the rules on the form and format of papers

The document used for transmitting a fax must comply with the rules in division 2, chapter 1 of this title regarding form or format of papers. Any exhibit that exceeds 8-½ by 11 inches must be reduced in size to not more than 8-½ by 11 inches before it is transmitted. The court may require the filing party to file the original of an exhibit that the party has filed by fax.

Rule 2.302 amended and renumbered effective January 1, 2007; adopted as rule 2004 effective March 1, 1992.

Rule 2.303. Filing through fax filing agency

(a) Transmission of document for filing

A party may transmit a document by fax to a fax filing agency for filing with any trial court. The agency acts as the agent of the filing party and not as an agent of the court.

(b) Duties of fax filing agency

The fax filing agency that receives a document for filing must:

(1) Prepare the document so that it complies with the rules in division 2, chapter 1 of this title and any other requirements for filing with the court;

(2) Physically transport the document to the court; and

(3) File the document with the court, paying any applicable filing fee.

(Subd (b) amended effective January 1, 2007.)

---

[1] Recommendations T.4 and T.30, Volume VII—Facsimile VII.3, CCITT Red Book, Malaga-Torremolinos, 1984, U.N. Bookstore Code ITU 6731.

(c) Requirement of advance arrangements

A fax filing agency is not required to accept papers for filing from any party unless appropriate arrangements for payment of filing fees and service charges have been made in advance of any transmission to the agency. If an agency receives a document from a party with whom it does not have prior arrangements, the agency may discard the document without notice to the sender.

(Subd (c) amended effective January 1, 2007.)

(d) Confidentiality

A fax filing agency must keep all documents transmitted to it confidential except as provided in the rules in this chapter.

(Subd (d) amended effective January 1, 2007.)

(e) Certification

A fax filing agency, by filing a document with the court, certifies that it has complied with the rules in this chapter and that the document filed is the full and unaltered fax-produced document received by it. The agency is not required to give any additional certification.

(Subd (e) amended effective January 1, 2007.)

(f) Notation of fax filing

Each document filed by a fax filing agency must contain the phrase "By fax" immediately below the title of the document.

(Subd (f) amended effective January 1, 2007.)

Rule 2.303 amended and renumbered effective January 1, 2007; adopted as rule 2005 effective March 1, 1992.

Rule 2.304. Direct filing

(a) Courts in which applicable

A party may file by fax directly to any court that, by local rule, has provided for direct fax filing. The local rule must state that direct fax filing may be made under the rules in this chapter and must provide the fax telephone number for filings and specific telephone numbers for any departments to which fax filings should be made directly. The court must also accept agency filings under rule 2.303.

(Subd (a) amended effective January 1, 2007.)

(b) Mandatory cover sheet

A party filing a document directly by fax must use the *Facsimile Transmission Cover Sheet (Fax Filing)* (form MC-005). The cover sheet must be the first page transmitted, to be followed by any special handling instructions needed to ensure that the document will comply with local rules. Neither the cover sheet nor the special handling instructions are to be filed in the case. The court must ensure that any credit card information on the cover sheet is not publicly disclosed. The court is not required to keep a copy of the cover sheet.

(Subd (b) amended effective January 1, 2007.)

(c) Notation of fax filing

Each document transmitted for direct filing with the court must contain the phrase "By fax" immediately below the title of the document.

(Subd (c) amended effective January 1, 2007.)

(d) Presumption of filing

A party filing by fax must cause the transmitting fax machine to print a transmission record of each filing by fax. If the document transmitted to the court by fax machine is not filed with the court because of (1) an error in the transmission of the document to the court that was unknown to the sending party or (2) a failure to process the document after it has been received by the court, the sending party may move the court for an order filing the document nunc pro tunc. The motion must be accompanied by the transmission record and a proof of transmission in the following form:

"On (date) _____ at (time) _____, I transmitted to the (court name) _____ the following documents (name) _____ by fax machine, under California Rules of Court, rule 2.304. The court's fax telephone number that I used was (fax telephone number) _____. The fax machine I used complied with rule 2.301 and no error was reported by the machine. Under rule 2.304, I caused the machine to print a transmission record of the transmission, a copy of which is attached to this declaration.

"I declare under penalty of perjury under the laws of the State of California that the foregoing is true and correct."

(Subd (d) amended effective July 1, 2013; previously amended effective January 1, 2007.)

(e) Payment of fees by credit card

(1) *Credit or debit card payments*

The court may permit credit cards, debit cards, electronic funds transfers, or debit accounts to be used to pay filing fees for fax filings made directly with the court, as provided in Government Code section 6159, rule 10.820, and other applicable laws. The cover sheet for these filings must include (1) the credit or debit card account number to which the fees may be charged, (2) the signature of the cardholder authorizing the charging of the fees, and (3) the expiration date of the credit or debit card.

(2) *Rejection of charge*

If the charge is rejected by the credit or debit card issuing company, the court must proceed in the same manner as under Code of Civil Procedure section 411.20 relating to returned checks. This provision does not prevent a court from seeking authorization for the charge before the filing and rejecting the filing if the charge is not approved by the issuing company.

(3) *Amount of charge*

The amount charged is the applicable filing fee plus any fee or discount imposed by the card issuer or draft purchaser.

(Subd (e) amended effective January 1, 2007.)

(f) Filing fee accounts

If a court so provides in its local rule establishing a direct fax filing program, an account may be used to pay for documents filed by fax by an attorney or party who has established an account with the court before filing a paper by fax. The court may require the deposit in advance of an amount not to exceed $1,000, or the court may agree to bill the attorney or party not more often than monthly.

(Subd (f) amended effective January 1, 2007.)

Rule 2.304 amended effective July 1, 2013; adopted as rule 2006 effective March 1, 1992; previously amended effective July 1, 2006; previously amended and renumbered effective January 1, 2007.

Rule 2.305. Requirements for signatures on documents

(a) Possession of original document

A party who files or serves a signed document by fax under the rules in this chapter represents that the original signed document is in the party's possession or control.

(Subd (a) amended effective January 1, 2007.)

(b) Demand for original; waiver

At any time after filing or service of a signed fax document, any other party may serve a demand for production of the original physically signed document. The demand must be served on all other parties but not filed with the court.

(Subd (b) amended effective January 1, 2007.)

(c) Examination of original

If a demand for production of the original signed document is made, the parties must arrange a meeting at which the original signed document can be examined.

(Subd (c) amended effective January 1, 2007.)

(d) Fax signature as original

Notwithstanding any provision of law to the contrary, including Evidence Code sections 255 and 260, a signature produced by fax transmission is deemed to be an original.

(Subd (d) amended effective January 1, 2007.)

Rule 2.305 amended and renumbered effective January 1, 2007; adopted as rule 2007 effective March 1, 1992.

Rule 2.306. Service of papers by fax transmission

(a) Service by fax

(1) *Agreement of parties required*

Service by fax transmission is permitted only if the parties agree and a written confirmation of that agreement is made.

(2) *Service on last-given fax number*

Any notice or other document to be served must be transmitted to a fax machine maintained by the person on whom it is served at the fax machine telephone number as last given by that person on any document that the party has filed in the case and served on the party making service.

(Subd (a) amended and lettered effective January 1, 2007; adopted as part of subd (b) effective March 1, 1992.)

(b) Service lists

(1) *Duties of first-named plaintiff or petitioner*

In a case in which the parties have agreed to service by fax, the plaintiff or petitioner named first in the complaint or petition, in addition to its responsibilities under rule 3.254, must:

(A) Maintain a current list of the parties that includes their fax numbers for service of notice on each party; and

(B) Furnish a copy of the list on request to any party or the court.

(2) *Duties of each party*

In a case in which the parties have agreed to service by fax, each party, in addition to its responsibilities under rule 3.254, must:

(A) Furnish the first-named plaintiff or petitioner with the party's current fax number for service of notice when it first appears in the action; and

(B) If the party serves an order, notice, or pleading on a party that has not yet appeared in the action, serve a copy of the service list under (1) at the same time that the order, notice, or pleading is served.

(Subd (b) adopted effective January 1, 2008.)

(c) Transmission of papers by court

A court may serve any notice by fax in the same manner that parties may serve papers by fax.

(Subd (c) relettered effective January 1, 2008; adopted as subd (b) effective January 1, 2007.)

(d) Notice period extended

Except as provided in (e), any prescribed period of notice and any right or duty to do any act or make any response within any prescribed period or on a date certain after the service of a document served by fax transmission is extended by two court days.

(Subd (d) amended effective July 1, 2008; adopted as part of subd (b) effective March 1, 1992; previously amended and lettered as subd (c) effective January 1, 2007; previously relettered as subd (d) effective January 1, 2008.)

(e) Extension inapplicable to certain motions

The extension provided in (d) does not apply to extend the time for the filing of:

(1) A notice of intent to move for new trial;

(2) A notice of intent to move to vacate a judgment under Code of Civil Procedure section 663; or

(3) A notice of appeal.

(Subd (e) amended effective July 1, 2008; adopted as part of subd (b) effective March 1, 1992; previously amended and lettered as subd (d) effective January 1, 2007; previously relettered as subd (e) effective January 1, 2008.)

(f) Availability of fax

A party or attorney agreeing to accept service by fax must make his or her fax machine generally available for receipt of served documents between the hours of 9 a.m. and 5 p.m. on days that are not court holidays under Code of Civil Procedure section 136. This provision does not prevent the party or attorney from sending other documents by means of the fax machine or providing for normal repair and maintenance of the fax machine during these hours.

(Subd (f) relettered effective January 1, 2008; adopted as subd (c) effective March 1, 1992; previously amended and relettered as subd (e) effective January 1, 2007.)

(g) When service complete

Service by fax is complete on transmission of the entire document to the receiving party's fax machine. Service that is completed after 5 p.m. is deemed to have occurred on the next court day. Time is extended as provided by this rule.

(Subd (g) relettered effective January 1, 2008; adopted as subd (d) effective March 1, 1992; previously amended effective July 1, 1997; previously amended and relettered as subd (f) effective January 1, 2007.)

(h) Proof of service by fax

Proof of service by fax may be made by any of the methods provided in Code of Civil Procedure section 1013(a), except that:

(1) The date and sending fax machine telephone number must be used instead of the date and place of deposit in the mail;

(2) The name and fax machine telephone number of the person served must be used instead of the name and address of the person served as shown on the envelope;

(3) A statement that the document was sent by fax transmission and that the transmission was reported as complete and without error must be used instead of the statement that the envelope was sealed and deposited in the mail with the postage thereon fully prepaid;

(4) A copy of the transmission report must be attached to the proof of service and the proof of service must declare that the transmission report was properly issued by the sending fax machine; and

(5) Service of papers by fax is ineffective if the transmission does not fully conform to these provisions.

(Subd (h) amended effective January 1, 2017; adopted as subd (e) effective March 1, 1992; previously amended effective July 1, 1997, and May 1, 1998; previously amended and relettered as subd (g) effective January 1, 2007; previously relettered as subd (h) effective January 1, 2008.)
Rule 2.306 amended effective January 1, 2017; adopted as rule 2008 effective March 1, 1992; previously amended effective July 1, 1997, May 1, 1998, January 1, 2008, and July 1, 2008; previously amended and renumbered effective January 1, 2007.

Division 4
Court Records

Chapter 1
General Provisions

Rule 2.400. Court records

(a) Removal of records

Only the clerk may remove and replace records in the court's files. Unless otherwise provided by these rules or ordered by the court, court records may only be inspected by the public in the office of the clerk and released to authorized court personnel or an attorney of record for use in a court facility. No original court records may be used in any location other than a court facility, unless so ordered by the presiding judge or his or her designee.

(Subd (a) amended effective January 1, 2010; previously amended effective July 1, 1993, January 1, 2007, January 1, 2008, and January 1, 2009.)

(b) Original documents filed with the clerk; duplicate documents for temporary judge or referee

(1) All original documents in a case pending before a temporary judge or referee must be filed with the clerk in the same manner as would be required if the case were being heard by a judge, including filing within any time limits specified by law and paying any required fees. The filing party must provide a filed-stamped copy to the temporary judge or referee of each document relevant to the issues before the temporary judge or referee.

(2) If a document must be filed with the court before it is considered by a judge, the temporary judge or referee must not accept or consider any copy of that document unless the document has the clerk's file stamp or is accompanied by a declaration stating that the original document has been submitted to the court for filing.

(3) If a document would ordinarily be filed with the court after it is submitted to a judge or if a party submits an ex parte application, the party that submits the document or application to a temporary judge or referee must file the original with the court no later than the next court day after the document or application was submitted to the temporary judge or referee and must promptly provide a filed-stamped copy of the document or application to the temporary judge or referee.

(4) A party that has submitted a document to a temporary judge or referee must immediately notify the temporary judge or referee if the document is not accepted for filing by the court or if the filing is subsequently canceled.

(Subd (b) amended effective January 1, 2010; adopted effective July 1, 1993; previously amended effective January 1, 2007.)

(c) Return of exhibits

(1) The clerk must not release any exhibit except on order of the court. The clerk must require a signed receipt for a released exhibit.

(2) If proceedings are conducted by a temporary judge or a referee outside of court facilities, the temporary judge or referee must keep all exhibits and deliver them, properly marked, to the clerk at the conclusion of the proceedings, unless the parties file, and the court approves, a written stipulation providing for a different disposition of the exhibits. On request of the temporary judge or referee, the clerk must deliver exhibits filed or lodged with the court to the possession of the temporary judge or referee, who must not release them to any person other than the clerk, unless the court orders otherwise.

(Subd (c) amended effective January 1, 2010; adopted as subd (b) effective January 1, 1949; previously amended and relettered effective July 1, 1993; previously amended effective January 1, 2007.)

(d) Access to documents and exhibits in matters before temporary judges and referees

(1) Documents and exhibits in the possession of a temporary judge or referee that would be open to the public if filed or lodged with the court must be made available during business hours for inspection by any

person within a reasonable time after request and under reasonable conditions.

(2) Temporary judges and referees must file a statement in each case in which they are appointed that provides the name, telephone number, and mailing address of a person who may be contacted to obtain access to any documents or exhibits submitted to the temporary judge or referee that would be open to the public if filed or lodged with the court. The statement must be filed at the same time as the temporary judge's or referee's certification under rule 2.831(b), 3.904(a), or 3.924(a). If there is any change in this contact information, the temporary judge or referee must promptly file a revised statement with the court.

(Subd (d) adopted effective January 1, 2010.)

(e) Definition

For purposes of this rule, "court facility" consists of those areas within a building required or used for court functions.

(Subd (e) adopted effective January 1, 2010.)

Rule 2.400 amended effective January 1, 2010; adopted as rule 243 effective January 1, 1949; previously amended and renumbered effective January 1, 2007; previously amended effective July 1, 1993, January 1, 2008, and January 1, 2009.

Advisory Committee Comment

Subdivision (b)(1). Rules 2.810 and 2.830 provide definitions of temporary judges appointed by the court and temporary judges requested by the parties, respectively.

Subdivision (d)(1). Public access to documents and exhibits in the possession of a temporary judge or referee should be the same as if the case were being heard by a judge. Documents and exhibits are not normally available to the public during a hearing or when needed by the judge for hearing or decision preparation. A temporary judge or referee may direct that access to documents and exhibits be available by scheduled appointment.

Chapter 2
Access to Electronic Trial Court Records

Title 2, Trial Court Rules—Chapter 2, Access to Electronic Trial Court Records; amended effective January 1, 2019.

Art. 1.   General Provisions. Rules 2.500–2.502.
Art. 2.   Public Access. Rules 2.503–2.507.
Art. 3.   Remote Access by a Party, Party's Designee, Party's Attorney, Court-Appointed Person, or Authorized Person Working in a Legal Organization or Qualified Legal Services Project. Rules 2.515–2.528.
Art. 4.   Remote Access by Government Entities. Rules 2.540–2.545.

Article 1
General Provisions

Title 2, Trial Court Rules—Chapter 2, Access to Electronic Trial Court Records; Article 1, General Provisions; adopted effective January 1, 2019.

Rule 2.500. Statement of purpose
Rule 2.501. Application, scope, and information to the public
Rule 2.502. Definitions

Rule 2.500.   Statement of purpose

(a) Intent

The rules in this chapter are intended to provide the public, parties, parties' attorneys, legal organizations, court-appointed persons, and government entities with reasonable access to trial court records that are maintained in electronic form, while protecting privacy interests.

(Subd (a) amended effective January 1, 2019.)

(b) Benefits of electronic access

Improved technologies provide courts with many alternatives to the historical paper-based record receipt and retention process, including the creation and use of court records maintained in electronic form. Providing access to trial court records that are maintained in electronic form may save the courts, the public, parties, parties' attorneys, legal organizations, court-appointed persons, and government entities time, money, and effort and encourage courts to be more efficient in their operations. Improved access to trial court records may also foster in the public a more comprehensive understanding of the trial court system.

(Subd (b) amended effective January 1, 2019.)

(c) No creation of rights

The rules in this chapter are not intended to give the public, parties, parties' attorneys, legal organizations, court-appointed persons, and government entities a right of access to any record that they are not otherwise legally entitled to access.

(Subd (c) amended effective January 1, 2019; previously amended effective January 1, 2007.)

Rule 2.500 amended effective January 1, 2019; adopted as rule 2070 effective July 1, 2002; previously amended and renumbered effective January 1, 2007.

Advisory Committee Comment

The rules in this chapter acknowledge the benefits that electronic records provide but attempt to limit the potential for unjustified intrusions into the privacy of individuals involved in litigation that can occur as a result of remote access to electronic records. The proposed rules take into account the limited resources currently available in the trial courts. It is contemplated that the rules may be modified to provide greater electronic access as courts' technical capabilities improve and knowledge is gained from the experience of providing electronic access under these rules.

Rule 2.501.   Application, scope, and information to the public

(a) Application and scope

The rules in this chapter apply only to trial court records as defined in rule 2.502(3). They do not apply to statutorily mandated reporting between or within government entities, or any other documents or materials that are not court records.

(Subd (a) amended effective January 1, 2019; adopted as subd (b) effective July 1, 2002; amended and relettered effective January 1, 2007.)

(b) Information to the public

The website for each trial court must include a link to information that will inform the public of who may access their electronic records under the rules in this chapter and under what conditions they may do so. This information will be posted publicly on the California Courts website at *www.courts.ca.gov.* Each trial court may post additional information, in plain language, as necessary to inform the public about the level of access that the particular trial court is providing.

(Subd (b) amended effective January 1, 2019; adopted as subd (c) effective July 1, 2002; amended and relettered effective January 1, 2007.)

Rule 2.501 amended effective January 1, 2019; adopted as rule 2017 effective July 1, 2002; amended and renumbered effective January 1, 2007.

Advisory Committee Comment

The rules on remote access do not apply beyond court records to other types of documents, information, or data. Rule 2.502 defines a court record as "any document, paper, or exhibit filed in an action or proceeding; any order or judgment of the court; and any item listed in Government Code section 68151(a)—excluding any reporter's transcript for which the reporter is entitled to receive a fee for any copy—that is maintained by the court in the ordinary course of the judicial process. The term does not include the personal notes or preliminary memoranda of judges or other judicial branch personnel, statutorily mandated reporting between government entities, judicial administrative records, court case information, or compilations of data drawn from court records where the compilations are not themselves contained in a court record." (Cal. Rules of Court, rule 2.502(3).) Thus, courts generate and maintain many types of information that are not court records and to which access may be restricted by law. Such information is not remotely accessible as court records, even to parties and their attorneys. If parties and their attorneys are entitled to access to any such additional information, separate and independent grounds for that access must exist.

Rule 2.502.   Definitions

As used in this chapter, the following definitions apply:

(1) "Authorized person" means a person authorized by a legal organization, qualified legal services project, or government entity to access electronic records.

(2) "Brief legal services" means legal assistance provided without, or before, becoming a party's attorney. It includes giving advice, having a consultation, performing research, investigating case facts, drafting documents, and making limited third party contacts on behalf of a client.

(3) "Court record" is any document, paper, or exhibit filed in an action or proceeding; any order or judgment of the court; and any item listed in Government Code section 68151(a)—excluding any reporter's transcript for which the reporter is entitled to receive a fee for any copy—that is maintained by the court in the ordinary course of the judicial process. The term does not include the personal notes or preliminary memoranda of judges or other judicial branch personnel, statutorily mandated reporting between or within government entities, judicial administrative records, court case information, or compilations of data drawn from court records where the compilations are not themselves contained in a court record.

(4) "Court case information" refers to data that is stored in a court's case management system or case histories. This data supports the court's management or tracking of the action and is not part of the official court record for the case or cases.

(5) "Electronic access" means access by electronic means to court records available through public terminals at the courthouse and remotely, unless otherwise specified in the rules in this chapter.

(6) "Electronic record" is a court record that requires the use of an electronic device to access. The term includes both a record that has been filed electronically and an electronic copy or version of a record that was filed in paper form. The term does not include a court record that is maintained only on microfiche, paper, or any other medium that can be read without the use of an electronic device.

(7) "Government entity" means a legal entity organized to carry on some function of the State of California or a political subdivision of the State of California. Government entity also means a federally recognized Indian tribe or a reservation, department, subdivision, or court of a federally recognized Indian tribe.

(8) "Legal organization" means a licensed attorney or group of attorneys, nonprofit legal aid organization, government legal office, in-house legal office of a nongovernmental organization, or legal program organized to provide for indigent criminal, civil, or juvenile law representation.

(9) "Party" means a plaintiff, defendant, cross-complainant, cross-defendant, petitioner, respondent, intervenor, objector, or anyone expressly defined by statute as a party in a court case.

(10) "Person" means a natural human being.

(11) "The public" means a person, a group, or an entity, including print or electronic media, regardless of any legal or other interest in a particular court record.

(12) "Qualified legal services project" has the same meaning under the rules of this chapter as in Business and Professions Code section 6213(a).

(13) "Remote access" means electronic access from a location other than a public terminal at the courthouse.

(14) "User" means an individual person, a group, or an entity that accesses electronic records.

Rule 2.502 amended and renumbered effective January 1, 2019; adopted as rule 2072 effective July 1, 2002; previously amended and renumbered effective January 1, 2007.

Article 2
Public Access

Title 2, Trial Court Rules—Chapter 2, Access to Electronic Trial Court Records; Article 2, Public Access; adopted effective January 1, 2019.

Rule 2.503. Application and scope
Rule 2.504. Limitations and conditions
Rule 2.505. Contracts with vendors
Rule 2.506. Fees for electronic access
Rule 2.507. Electronic access to court calendars, indexes, and registers of actions

Rule 2.503. Application and scope

(a) General right of access by the public

(1) All electronic records must be made reasonably available to the public in some form, whether in electronic or in paper form, except those that are sealed by court order or made confidential by law.

(2) The rules in this article apply only to access to electronic records by the public.

(Subd (a) amended effective January 1, 2019; previously amended effective January 1, 2007.)

(b) Electronic access required to extent feasible

A court that maintains the following records in electronic form must provide electronic access to them, both remotely and at the courthouse, to the extent it is feasible to do so:

(1) Registers of actions (as defined in Gov. Code, § 69845), calendars, and indexes in all cases; and

(2) All court records in civil cases, except those listed in (c)(1)–(11).

(Subd (b) amended effective January 1, 2019; previously amended effective July 1, 2004, January 1, 2007, January 1, 2008, and January 1, 2010.)

(c) Courthouse electronic access only

A court that maintains the following records in electronic form must provide electronic access to them at the courthouse, to the extent it is feasible to do so, but may not provide public remote access to these records:

(1) Records in a proceeding under the Family Code, including proceedings for dissolution, legal separation, and nullity of marriage; child and spousal support proceedings; child custody proceedings; and domestic violence prevention proceedings;

(2) Records in a juvenile court proceeding;

(3) Records in a guardianship or conservatorship proceeding;

(4) Records in a mental health proceeding;

(5) Records in a criminal proceeding;

(6) Records in proceedings to compromise the claims of a minor or a person with a disability;

(7) Records in a civil harassment proceeding under Code of Civil Procedure section 527.6;

(8) Records in a workplace violence prevention proceeding under Code of Civil Procedure section 527.8;

(9) Records in a private postsecondary school violence prevention proceeding under Code of Civil Procedure section 527.85;

(10) Records in an elder or dependent adult abuse prevention proceeding under Welfare and Institutions Code section 15657.03; and

(11) Records in a gun violence prevention proceeding under Penal Code sections 18100–18205.

(Subd (c) amended effective January 1, 2019; previously amended effective July 1, 2004, January 1, 2007, January 1, 2008, January 1, 2010, and January 1, 2012.)

(d) "Feasible" defined

As used in this rule, the requirement that a court provide electronic access to its electronic records "to the extent it is feasible to do so" means that a court is required to provide electronic access to the extent it determines it has the resources and technical capacity to do so.

(Subd (d) amended effective January 1, 2007.)

(e) Remote access allowed in extraordinary criminal cases

Notwithstanding (c)(5), the presiding judge of the court, or a judge assigned by the presiding judge, may exercise discretion, subject to (e)(1), to permit remote access by the public to all or a portion of the public court records in an individual criminal case if (1) the number of requests for access to documents in the case is extraordinarily high and (2) responding to those requests would significantly burden the operations of the court. An individualized determination must be made in each case in which such remote access is provided.

(1) In exercising discretion under (e), the judge should consider the relevant factors, such as:

(A) The privacy interests of parties, victims, witnesses, and court personnel, and the ability of the court to redact sensitive personal information;

(B) The benefits to and burdens on the parties in allowing remote access, including possible impacts on jury selection; and

(C) The burdens on the court in responding to an extraordinarily high number of requests for access to documents.

(2) The court should, to the extent feasible, redact the following information from records to which it allows remote access under (e): driver license numbers; dates of birth; social security numbers; Criminal Identification and Information and National Crime Information numbers; addresses and phone numbers of parties, victims, witnesses, and court personnel; medical or psychiatric information; financial information; account numbers; and other personal identifying information. The court may order any party who files a document containing such information to provide the court with both an original unredacted version of the document for filing in the court file and a redacted version of the document for remote access. No juror names or other juror identifying information may be provided by remote access. This subdivision does not apply to any document in the original court file; it applies only to documents that are available by remote access.

(3) Five days' notice must be provided to the parties and the public before the court makes a determination to provide remote access under this rule. Notice to the public may be accomplished by posting notice on the court's website. Any person may file comments with the court for consideration, but no hearing is required.

(4) The court's order permitting remote access must specify which court records will be available by remote access and what categories of information are to be redacted. The court is not required to make findings of fact. The court's order must be posted on the court's website and a copy sent to the Judicial Council.

(Subd (e) amended effective January 1, 2019; adopted effective January 1, 2005; previously amended effective January 1, 2007.)

(f) Access only on a case-by-case basis

The court may only grant electronic access to an electronic record when the record is identified by the number of the case, the caption of the case, or the name of a party, and only on a case-by-case basis. This case-by-case limitation does not apply to the court's electronic records of a calendar, register of actions, or index.

(Subd (f) amended effective January 1, 2007; adopted as subd (e) effective July 1, 2002; previously relettered effective January 1, 2005.)

(g) Bulk distribution

The court may provide bulk distribution of only its electronic records of a calendar, register of actions, and index. "Bulk distribution" means distribution of all, or a significant subset, of the court's electronic records.

(Subd (g) amended effective January 1, 2007; adopted as subd (f) effective July 1, 2002; previously relettered effective January 1, 2005.)

(h) Records that become inaccessible

If an electronic record to which the court has provided electronic access is made inaccessible to the public by court order or by operation of law, the court is not required to take action with respect to any copy of the record that was made by the public before the record became inaccessible.

(Subd (h) relettered effective January 1, 2005; adopted as subd (g) effective July 1, 2002.)

(i) Off-site access

Courts should encourage availability of electronic access to court records at public off-site locations.

(Subd (i) relettered effective January 1, 2005; adopted as subd (h) effective July 1, 2002.)

Rule 2.503 amended effective January 1, 2019; adopted as rule 2073 effective July 1, 2002; previously amended and renumbered effective January 1, 2007; previously amended effective July 1, 2004, January 1, 2005, January 1, 2008, January 1, 2010, and January 1, 2012.

Advisory Committee Comment

The rule allows a level of access by the public to all electronic records that is at least equivalent to the access that is available for paper records and, for some types of records, is much greater. At the same time, it seeks to protect legitimate privacy concerns.

Subdivision (c). This subdivision excludes certain records (those other than the register, calendar, and indexes) in specified types of cases (notably criminal, juvenile, and family court matters) from public remote access. The committee recognized that while these case records are public records and should remain available at the courthouse, either in paper or electronic form, they often contain sensitive personal information. The court should not publish that information over the Internet. However, the committee also recognized that the use of the Internet may be appropriate in certain criminal cases of extraordinary public interest where information regarding a case will be widely disseminated through the media. In such cases, posting of selected nonconfidential court records, redacted where necessary to protect the privacy of the participants, may provide more timely and accurate information regarding the court proceedings, and may relieve substantial burdens on court staff in responding to individual requests for documents and information. Thus, under subdivision (e), if the presiding judge makes individualized determinations in a specific case, certain records in criminal cases may be made available over the Internet.

Subdivisions (f) and (g). These subdivisions limit electronic access to records (other than the register, calendars, or indexes) to a case-by-case basis and prohibit bulk distribution of those records. These limitations are based on the qualitative difference between obtaining information from a specific case file and obtaining bulk information that may be manipulated to compile personal information culled from any document, paper, or exhibit filed in a lawsuit. This type of aggregate information may be exploited for commercial or other purposes unrelated to the operations of the courts, at the expense of privacy rights of individuals.

Courts must send a copy of the order permitting remote access in extraordinary criminal cases to Criminal Justice Services, Judicial Council of California, 455 Golden Gate Avenue, San Francisco, CA 94102-3688.

Rule 2.504.   Limitations and conditions

(a) Means of access

A court that maintains records in electronic form must provide electronic access to those records by means of a network or software that is based on industry standards or is in the public domain.

(Subd (a) amended effective January 1, 2007.)

(b) Official record

Unless electronically certified by the court, a trial court record available by electronic access is not the official record of the court.

(Subd (b) amended effective January 1, 2007.)

(c) Conditions of use by persons accessing records

A court may condition electronic access to its records on:

(1) The user's consent to access the records only as instructed by the court; and

(2) The user's consent to the court's monitoring of access to its records.

The court must give notice of these conditions, in any manner it deems appropriate. The court may deny access to a member of the public for failure to comply with either of these conditions of use.

(Subd (c) amended effective January 1, 2007.)

(d) Notices to persons accessing records

The court must give notice of the following information to members of the public accessing its records electronically, in any manner it deems appropriate:

(1) The identity of the court staff member to be contacted about the requirements for accessing the court's records electronically.

(2) That copyright and other proprietary rights may apply to information in a case file, absent an express grant of additional rights by the holder of the copyright or other proprietary right. This notice must advise the public that:

(A) Use of such information in a case file is permissible only to the extent permitted by law or court order; and

(B) Any use inconsistent with proprietary rights is prohibited.

(3) Whether electronic records are the official records of the court. The notice must describe the procedure and any fee required for obtaining a certified copy of an official record of the court.

(4) That any person who willfully destroys or alters any court record maintained in electronic form is subject to the penalties imposed by Government Code section 6201.

(Subd (d) amended effective January 1, 2007.)

(e) Access policy

The court must post a privacy policy on its public-access Web site to inform members of the public accessing its electronic records of the information it collects regarding access transactions and the uses that the court may make of the collected information.

(Subd (e) amended effective January 1, 2007.)

Rule 2.504 amended and renumbered effective January 1, 2007; adopted as rule 2074 effective July 1, 2002.

Rule 2.505.   Contracts with vendors

(a) Contract must provide access consistent with rules

The court's contract with a vendor to provide public access to its electronic records must be consistent with the rules in this chapter and must require the vendor to provide public access to court records and to protect the confidentiality of court records as required by law or by court order.

(Subd (a) amended and lettered effective January 1, 2007; adopted as part of unlettered subd effective July 1, 2002.)

(b) Contract must provide that court owns the records

Any contract between the court and a vendor to provide public access to the court's electronic records must provide that the court is the owner of these records and has the exclusive right to control their use.

(Subd (b) amended and lettered effective January 1, 2007; adopted as part of unlettered subd effective July 1, 2002.)

Rule 2.505 amended and renumbered effective January 1, 2007; adopted as rule 2075 effective July 1, 2002.

Rule 2.506.   Fees for electronic access

(a) Court may impose fees

The court may impose fees for the costs of providing public access to its electronic records, under Government Code section 68150(*l*). On request, the court must provide the public with a statement of the costs on which these fees are based.

(Subd (a) amended effective July 1, 2013; adopted as part of unlettered subd effective July 1, 2002; previously amended and lettered effective January 1, 2007.)

(b) Fees of vendor must be reasonable

To the extent that public access to a court's electronic records is provided exclusively through a vendor, the court must ensure that any fees the vendor imposes for the costs of providing access are reasonable.

(Subd (b) lettered effective January 1, 2007; adopted as part of unlettered subd effective July 1, 2002.)

Rule 2.506 amended effective July 1, 2013; adopted as rule 2076 effective July 1, 2002; previously amended and renumbered effective January 1, 2007.

Rule 2.507.   Electronic access to court calendars, indexes, and registers of actions

(a) Intent

This rule specifies information to be included in and excluded from the court calendars, indexes, and registers of actions to which public access is available by electronic means under rule 2.503(b). To the extent it is feasible to do so, the court must maintain court calendars, indexes, and registers of actions available to the public by electronic means in accordance with this rule.

(Subd (a) amended effective January 1, 2007.)

(b) Minimum contents for electronically accessible court calendars, indexes, and registers of actions

(1) The electronic court calendar must include:

(A) Date of court calendar;

(B) Time of calendared event;

(C) Court department number;

(D) Case number; and

(E) Case title (unless made confidential by law).

(2) The electronic index must include:

(A) Case title (unless made confidential by law);

(B) Party names (unless made confidential by law);

(C) Party type;

(D) Date on which the case was filed; and

(E) Case number.

(3) The register of actions must be a summary of every proceeding in a case, in compliance with Government Code section 69845, and must include:

(A) Date case commenced;

(B) Case number;

(C) Case type;

(D) Case title (unless made confidential by law);

(E) Party names (unless made confidential by law);

(F) Party type;

(G) Date of each activity; and

(H) Description of each activity.

(Subd (b) amended effective January 1, 2007.)

(c) Information that must be excluded from court calendars, indexes, and registers of actions

The following information must be excluded from a court's electronic calendar, index, and register of actions:

(1) Social security number;

(2) Any financial information;

(3) Arrest warrant information;

(4) Search warrant information;

(5) Victim information;

(6) Witness information;

(7) Ethnicity;

(8) Age;

(9) Gender;

(10) Government-issued identification card numbers (i.e., military);

(11) Driver's license number; and

(12) Date of birth.

(Subd (c) amended effective January 1, 2007.)

Rule 2.507 amended and renumbered effective January 1, 2007; adopted as rule 2077 effective July 1, 2003.

Article 3
Remote Access by a Party, Party's Designee, Party's Attorney, Court-Appointed Person, or Authorized Person Working in a Legal Organization or Qualified Legal Services Project

Title 2, Trial Court Rules—Chapter 2, Access to Electronic Trial Court Records; Article 3, Remote Access by a Party, Party's Designee, Party's Attorney, Court-Appointed Person, or Authorized Person Working in a Legal Organization or Qualified Legal Services Project; adopted effective January 1, 2019.

Rule 2.515.   Application and scope

(a) No limitation on access to electronic records available under article 2

The rules in this article do not limit remote access to electronic records available under article 2. These rules govern access to electronic records where remote access by the public is not allowed.

(Subd (a) adopted effective January 1, 2019.)

(b) Who may access

The rules in this article apply to remote access to electronic records by:

(1) A person who is a party;

(2) A designee of a person who is a party;

(3) A party's attorney;

(4) An authorized person working in the same legal organization as a party's attorney;

(5) An authorized person working in a qualified legal services project providing brief legal services; and

(6) A court-appointed person.

(Subd (b) adopted effective January 1, 2019.)

Rule 2.515 adopted effective January 1, 2019.

Advisory Committee Comment

Article 2 allows remote access in most civil cases, and the rules in article 3 are not intended to limit that access. Rather, the article 3 rules allow broader remote access—by parties, parties' designees, parties' attorneys, authorized persons working in legal organizations, authorized persons working in a qualified legal services project providing brief services, and court-appointed persons—to those electronic records where remote access by the public is not allowed.

Under the rules in article 3, a party, a party's attorney, an authorized person working in the same legal organization as a party's attorney, or a person appointed by the court in the proceeding basically has the same level of access to electronic records remotely that he or she would have if he or she were to seek to inspect the records in person at the courthouse. Thus, if he or she is legally entitled to inspect certain records at the courthouse, that person could view the same records remotely; on the other hand, if he or she is restricted from inspecting certain court records at the courthouse (e.g., because the records are confidential or sealed), that person would not be permitted to view the records remotely. In some types of cases, such as unlimited civil cases, the access available to parties and their attorneys is generally similar to the public's but in other types of cases, such as juvenile cases, it is much more extensive (see Cal. Rules of Court, rule 5.552).

For authorized persons working in a qualified legal services program, the rule contemplates services offered in high-volume environments on an ad hoc basis. There are some limitations on access under the rule for qualified legal services projects. When an attorney at a qualified legal services project becomes a party's attorney and offers services beyond the scope contemplated under this rule, the access rules for a party's attorney would apply.

Rule 2.516.   Remote access to extent feasible

To the extent feasible, a court that maintains records in electronic form must provide remote access to those records to the users described in rule 2.515, subject to the conditions and limitations stated in this article and otherwise provided by law.

Rule 2.516 adopted effective January 1, 2019.

Advisory Committee Comment

This rule takes into account the limited resources currently available in some trial courts. Many courts may not have the financial means, security resources, or technical capabilities necessary to provide the full range of remote access to electronic records authorized by this article. When it is more feasible and courts have had more experience with remote access, these rules may be amended to further expand remote access.

This rule is not intended to prevent a court from moving forward with the limited remote access options outlined in this rule as such access becomes feasible. For example, if it were only feasible for a court to provide remote access to parties who are persons, it could proceed to provide remote access to those users only.

Rule 2.517.   Remote access by a party

(a) Remote access generally permitted

A person may have remote access to electronic records in actions or proceedings in which that person is a party.

(Subd (a) adopted effective January 1, 2019.)

(b) Level of remote access

(1) In any action or proceeding, a party may be provided remote access to the same electronic records that he or she would be legally entitled to inspect at the courthouse.

(2) This rule does not limit remote access to electronic records available under article 2.

(3) This rule applies only to electronic records. A person is not entitled under these rules to remote access to documents, information, data, or other materials created or maintained by the courts that are not electronic records.

(Subd (b) adopted effective January 1, 2019.)

Rule 2.517 adopted effective January 1, 2019.

Advisory Committee Comment

Because this rule permits remote access only by a party who is a person (defined under rule 2.501 as a natural human being), remote access would not apply to parties that are organizations, which would need to gain remote access under the party's attorney rule or, for certain government entities with respect to specified electronic records, the rules in article 4.

A party who is a person would need to have the legal capacity to agree to the terms and conditions of a court's remote access user agreement before using a system of remote access. The court could deny access or require additional information if the court knew the person seeking access lacked legal capacity or appeared to lack capacity—for example, if identity verification revealed the person seeking access was a minor.

Rule 2.518. Remote access by a party's designee

(a) Remote access generally permitted

A person who is a party in an action or proceeding may designate other persons to have remote access to electronic records in that action or proceeding.

(Subd (a) adopted effective January 1, 2019.)

(b) Level of remote access

(1) Except for criminal electronic records, juvenile justice electronic records, and child welfare electronic records, a party's designee may have the same access to a party's electronic records that a member of the public would be entitled to if he or she were to inspect the party's court records at the courthouse. A party's designee is not permitted remote access to criminal electronic records, juvenile justice electronic records, and child welfare electronic records.

(2) A party may limit the access to be afforded a designee to specific cases.

(3) A party may limit the access to be afforded a designee to a specific period of time.

(4) A party may modify or revoke a designee's level of access at any time.

(Subd (b) adopted effective January 1, 2019.)

(c) Terms of access

(1) A party's designee may access electronic records only for the purpose of assisting the party or the party's attorney in the action or proceeding.

(2) Any distribution for sale of electronic records obtained remotely under the rules in this article is strictly prohibited.

(3) All laws governing confidentiality and disclosure of court records apply to the records obtained under this article.

(4) Party designees must comply with any other terms of remote access required by the court.

(5) Failure to comply with these rules may result in the imposition of sanctions, including termination of access.

(Subd (c) adopted effective January 1, 2019.)
Rule 2.518 adopted effective January 1, 2019.

Advisory Committee Comment

A party must be a natural human being with the legal capacity to agree to the terms and conditions of a user agreement with the court to authorize designees for remote access. Under rule 2.501, for purposes of the rules, "person" refers to natural human beings Accordingly, the party's designee rule would not apply to parties that are organizations, which would need to gain remote access under the party's attorney rule or, for certain government entities with respect to specified electronic records, under the rules in article 4.

Rule 2.519. Remote access by a party's attorney

(a) Remote access generally permitted

(1) A party's attorney may have remote access to electronic records in the party's actions or proceedings under this rule or under rule 2.518. If a party's attorney gains remote access under rule 2.518, the requirements of rule 2.519 do not apply.

(2) If a court notifies an attorney of the court's intention to appoint the attorney to represent a party in a criminal, juvenile justice, child welfare, family law, or probate proceeding, the court may grant remote access to that attorney before an order of appointment is issued by the court.

(Subd (a) adopted effective January 1, 2019.)

(b) Level of remote access

A party's attorney may be provided remote access to the same electronic records in the party's actions or proceedings that the party's attorney would be legally entitled to view at the courthouse.

(Subd (b) adopted effective January 1, 2019.)

(c) Terms of remote access applicable to an attorney who is not the attorney of record

An attorney who represents a party, but who is not the party's attorney of record in the party's actions or proceedings, may remotely access the party's electronic records, provided that the attorney:

(1) Obtains the party's consent to remotely access the party's electronic records; and

(2) Represents to the court in the remote access system that he or she has obtained the party's consent to remotely access the party's electronic records.

(Subd (c) adopted effective January 1, 2019.)

(d) Terms of remote access applicable to all attorneys

(1) A party's attorney may remotely access the electronic records only for the purpose of assisting the party with the party's court matter.

(2) A party's attorney may not distribute for sale any electronic records obtained remotely under the rules in this article. Such sale is strictly prohibited.

(3) A party's attorney must comply with any other terms of remote access required by the court.

(4) Failure to comply with these rules may result in the imposition of sanctions, including termination of access.

(Subd (d) adopted effective January 1, 2019.)
Rule 2.519 adopted effective January 1, 2019.

Advisory Committee Comment

Subdivision (c). An attorney of record will be known to the court for purposes of remote access. However, a person may engage an attorney other than the attorney of record for assistance in an action or proceeding in which the person is a party. For example, a party may engage an attorney to (1) prepare legal documents but not appear in the party's action (e.g., provide limited-scope representation); (2) assist the party with dismissal or sealing of a criminal record when the attorney did not represent the party in the criminal proceeding; or (3) represent the party in an appellate matter when the attorney did not represent the party in the trial court. Subdivision (c) provides a mechanism for an attorney not of record to be known to the court for purposes of remote access.

Because the level of remote access is limited to the same court records that an attorney would be entitled to access if he or she were to appear at the courthouse, an attorney providing undisclosed representation would only be able to remotely access electronic records that the public could access at the courthouse. The rule essentially removes the step of the attorney having to go to the courthouse.

Rule 2.520. Remote access by persons working in the same legal organization as a party's attorney

(a) Application and scope

(1) This rule applies when a party's attorney is assisted by others working in the same legal organization.

(2) "Working in the same legal organization" under this rule includes partners, associates, employees, volunteers, and contractors.

(3) This rule does not apply when a person working in the same legal organization as a party's attorney gains remote access to records as a party's designee under rule 2.518.

(Subd (a) adopted effective January 1, 2019.)

(b) Designation and certification

(1) A party's attorney may designate that other persons working in the same legal organization as the party's attorney have remote access.

(2) A party's attorney must certify that the other persons authorized for remote access are working in the same legal organization as the party's attorney and are assisting the party's attorney in the action or proceeding.

(Subd (b) adopted effective January 1, 2019.)

(c) Level of remote access

(1) Persons designated by a party's attorney under (b) must be provided access to the same electronic records as the party.

(2) Notwithstanding (b), when a court designates a legal organization to represent parties in criminal, juvenile, family, or probate proceedings, the court may grant remote access to a person working in the organization who assigns cases to attorneys working in that legal organization.

(Subd (c) adopted effective January 1, 2019.)

(d) Terms of remote access

(1) Persons working in a legal organization may remotely access electronic records only for purposes of assigning or assisting a party's attorney.

(2) Any distribution for sale of electronic records obtained remotely under the rules in this article is strictly prohibited.

(3) All laws governing confidentiality and disclosure of court records apply to the records obtained under this article.

(4) Persons working in a legal organization must comply with any other terms of remote access required by the court.

(5) Failure to comply with these rules may result in the imposition of sanctions, including termination of access.

(Subd (d) adopted effective January 1, 2019.)
Rule 2.520 adopted effective January 1, 2019.

Advisory Committee Comment

Subdivision (b). The designation and certification outlined in this subdivision need only be done once and can be done at the time the attorney establishes his or her remote access account with the court.

Rule 2.521.   Remote access by a court-appointed person

(a) Remote access generally permitted

(1) A court may grant a court-appointed person remote access to electronic records in any action or proceeding in which the person has been appointed by the court.

(2) Court-appointed persons include an attorney appointed to represent a minor child under Family Code section 3150; a Court Appointed Special Advocate volunteer in a juvenile proceeding; an attorney appointed under Probate Code section 1470, 1471, or 1474; an investigator appointed under Probate Code section 1454; a probate referee designated under Probate Code section 8920; a fiduciary, as defined in Probate Code section 39; an attorney appointed under Welfare and Institutions Code section 5365; or a guardian ad litem appointed under Code of Civil Procedure section 372 or Probate Code section 1003.

(Subd (a) adopted effective January 1, 2019.)

(b) Level of remote access

A court-appointed person may be provided with the same level of remote access to electronic records as the court-appointed person would be legally entitled to if he or she were to appear at the courthouse to inspect the court records.

(Subd (b) adopted effective January 1, 2019.)

(c) Terms of remote access

(1) A court-appointed person may remotely access electronic records only for purposes of fulfilling the responsibilities for which he or she was appointed.

(2) Any distribution for sale of electronic records obtained remotely under the rules in this article is strictly prohibited.

(3) All laws governing confidentiality and disclosure of court records apply to the records obtained under this article.

(4) A court-appointed person must comply with any other terms of remote access required by the court.

(5) Failure to comply with these rules may result in the imposition of sanctions, including termination of access.

(Subd (c) adopted effective January 1, 2019.)
Rule 2.521 adopted effective January 1, 2019.

Rule 2.522.   Remote access by persons working in a qualified legal services project providing brief legal services

(a) Application and scope

(1) This rule applies to qualified legal services projects as defined in Business and Professions Code section 6213(a).

(2) "Working in a qualified legal services project" under this rule includes attorneys, employees, and volunteers.

(3) This rule does not apply to a person working in or otherwise associated with a qualified legal services project who gains remote access to court records as a party's designee under rule 2.518.

(Subd (a) adopted effective January 1, 2019.)

(b) Designation and certification

(1) A qualified legal services project may designate persons working in the qualified legal services project who provide brief legal services, as defined in rule 2.501, to have remote access.

(2) The qualified legal services project must certify that the authorized persons work in their organization.

(Subd (b) adopted effective January 1, 2019.)

(c) Level of remote access

Authorized persons may be provided remote access to the same electronic records that the authorized person would be legally entitled to inspect at the courthouse.

(Subd (c) adopted effective January 1, 2019.)

(d) Terms of remote access

(1) Qualified legal services projects must obtain the party's consent to remotely access the party's electronic records.

(2) Authorized persons must represent to the court in the remote access system that the qualified legal services project has obtained the party's consent to remotely access the party's electronic records.

(3) Qualified legal services projects providing services under this rule may remotely access electronic records only to provide brief legal services.

(4) Any distribution for sale of electronic records obtained under the rules in this article is strictly prohibited.

(5) All laws governing confidentiality and disclosure of court records apply to electronic records obtained under this article.

(6) Qualified legal services projects must comply with any other terms of remote access required by the court.

(7) Failure to comply with these rules may result in the imposition of sanctions, including termination of access.

(Subd (d) adopted effective January 1, 2019.)
Rule 2.522 adopted effective January 1, 2019.

Advisory Committee Comment

The rule does not prescribe any particular method for capturing the designation and certification of persons working in a qualified legal services project. Courts and qualified legal services projects have flexibility to determine what method would work for both entities. For example, the information could be captured in a remote access system if an organizational-level account could be established, or the information could be captured in a written agreement between the court and the qualified legal services project.

The rule does not prescribe any particular method for a qualified legal services project to document the consent it obtained to access a person's electronic records. Qualified legal services projects have flexibility to adapt the requirement to their regular processes for making records.

For example, the qualified legal services project could obtain a signed consent form for its records or could obtain consent over the phone and make an entry to that effect in its records, or the court and the qualified legal services project could enter into an agreement to describe how consent will be obtained and recorded.

Rule 2.523.   Identity verification, identity management, and user access

(a) Identity verification required

Except for remote access provided to a party's designee under rule 2.518, before allowing a person who is eligible under the rules in article 3 to have remote access to electronic records, a court must verify the identity of the person seeking access.

(Subd (a) adopted effective January 1, 2019.)

(b) Responsibilities of the court

A court that allows persons eligible under the rules in article 3 to have remote access to electronic records must have an identity verification method that verifies the identity of, and provides a unique credential to, each person who is permitted remote access to the electronic records. The court may authorize remote access by a person only if that person's identity has been verified, the person accesses records using the credential provided to that individual, and the person complies with the terms and conditions of access, as prescribed by the court.

(Subd (b) adopted effective January 1, 2019.)

(c) Responsibilities of persons accessing records

A person eligible to be given remote access to electronic records under the rules in article 3 may be given such access only if that person:

(1) Provides the court with all information it directs in order to identify the person to be a user;

(2) Consents to all conditions for remote access required under article 3 and by the court; and

(3) Is authorized by the court to have remote access to electronic records.

(Subd (c) adopted effective January 1, 2019.)

(d) Responsibilities of the legal organizations or qualified legal services projects

(1) If a person is accessing electronic records on behalf of a legal organization or qualified legal services project, the organization or project must approve granting access to that person, verify the person's identity, and provide the court with all the information it directs in order to authorize that person to have access to electronic records.

(2) If a person accessing electronic records on behalf of a legal organization or qualified legal services project leaves his or her position or for any other reason is no longer entitled to access, the organization or project must immediately notify the court so that it can terminate the person's access.

(Subd (d) adopted effective January 1, 2019.)

(e) Vendor contracts, statewide master agreements, and identity and access management systems

A court may enter into a contract with a vendor to provide identity verification, identity management, or user access services. Alternatively, courts may use a statewide identity verification, identity management, or access management system, if available, or a statewide master agreement for such systems, if available.

(Subd (e) adopted effective January 1, 2019.)
Rule 2.523 adopted effective January 1, 2019.

Advisory Committee Comment

Subdivisions (a) and (d). A court may verify user identities under (a) by obtaining a representation from a legal organization or qualified legal services project that the legal organization or qualified legal services project has verified the user identities under (d). No additional verification steps are required on the part of the court.

Rule 2.524.   Security of confidential information

(a) Secure access and encryption required

If any information in an electronic record that is confidential by law or sealed by court order may lawfully be provided remotely to a person or organization described in rule 2.515, any remote access to the confidential information must be provided through a secure platform and any electronic transmission of the information must be encrypted.

(Subd (a) adopted effective January 1, 2019.)

(b) Vendor contracts and statewide master agreements

A court may enter into a contract with a vendor to provide secure access and encryption services. Alternatively, if a statewide master agreement is available for secure access and encryption services, courts may use that master agreement.

(Subd (b) adopted effective January 1, 2019.)

Rule 2.524 adopted effective January 1, 2019.

Advisory Committee Comment

This rule describes security and encryption requirements; levels of access are provided for in rules 2.517–2.522.

Rule 2.525.   Searches; unauthorized access

(a) Searches by case number or caption

A user authorized under this article to remotely access a party's electronic records may search for the records by case number or case caption.

(Subd (a) adopted effective January 1, 2019.)

(b) Access level

A court providing remote access to electronic records under this article must ensure that authorized users are able to access the electronic records only at the access levels provided in this article.

(Subd (b) adopted effective January 1, 2019.)

(c) Unauthorized access

If a user gains access to an electronic record that he or she is not authorized to access under this article, the user must:

(1) Report the unauthorized access to the court as directed by the court for that purpose;

(2) Destroy all copies, in any form, of the record; and

(3) Delete from his or her web browser history all information that identifies the record.

(Subd (c) adopted effective January 1, 2019.)

Rule 2.525 adopted effective January 1, 2019.

Rule 2.526.   Audit trails

(a) Ability to generate audit trails

The court should have the ability to generate an audit trail that contains one or more of the following elements: what electronic record was remotely accessed, when it was remotely accessed, who remotely accessed it, and under whose authority the user gained access.

(Subd (a) adopted effective January 1, 2019.)

(b) Limited audit trails available to authorized users

(1) A court providing remote access to electronic records under this article should make limited audit trails available to authorized users under this article.

(2) A limited audit trail should identify the user who remotely accessed electronic records in a particular case, but must not identify which specific electronic records were accessed.

(Subd (b) adopted effective January 1, 2019.)

Rule 2.526 adopted effective January 1, 2019.

Advisory Committee Comment

The audit trail is a tool to assist the courts and users in identifying and investigating any potential issues or misuse of remote access. The user's view of the audit trail is limited to protect sensitive information.

To facilitate the use of existing remote access systems, rule 2.526 is currently not mandatory, but may be amended to be mandatory in the future.

Rule 2.527.   Additional conditions of access

To the extent consistent with these rules and other applicable law, a court must impose reasonable conditions on remote access to preserve the integrity of its records, prevent the unauthorized use of information, and limit possible legal liability. The court may choose to require each user to submit a signed, written agreement enumerating those conditions before it permits that user to remotely access electronic records. The agreements may define the terms of access, provide for compliance audits, specify the scope of liability, and provide for sanctions for misuse up to and including termination of remote access.

Rule 2.527 adopted effective January 1, 2019.

Rule 2.528.   Termination of remote access

(a) Remote access is a privilege

Remote access to electronic records under this article is a privilege and not a right.

(Subd (a) adopted effective January 1, 2019.)

(b) Termination by court

A court that provides remote access may, at any time and for any reason, terminate the permission granted to any person eligible under the rules in article 3 to remotely access electronic records.

(Subd (b) adopted effective January 1, 2019.)

Rule 2.528 adopted effective January 1, 2019.

Article 4
Remote Access by Government Entities

Title 2, Trial Court Rules—Chapter 2, Access to Electronic Trial Court Records; Article 4, Remote Access by Government Entities; adopted effective January 1, 2019.

Rule 2.540.   Application and scope

(a) Applicability to government entities

The rules in this article provide for remote access to electronic records by government entities described in (b). The access allowed under these rules is in addition to any access these entities or authorized persons working for such entities may have under the rules in articles 2 and 3.

(Subd (a) adopted effective January 1, 2019.)

(b) Level of remote access

(1) A court may provide authorized persons from government entities with remote access to electronic records as follows:

(A) Office of the Attorney General: criminal electronic records and juvenile justice electronic records.

(B) California Department of Child Support Services: family electronic records, child welfare electronic records, and parentage electronic records.

(C) Office of a district attorney: criminal electronic records and juvenile justice electronic records.

(D) Office of a public defender: criminal electronic records and juvenile justice electronic records.

(E) Office of a county counsel: criminal electronic records, mental health electronic records, child welfare electronic records, and probate electronic records.

(F) Office of a city attorney: criminal electronic records, juvenile justice electronic records, and child welfare electronic records.

(G) County department of probation: criminal electronic records, juvenile justice electronic records, and child welfare electronic records.

(H) County sheriff's department: criminal electronic records and juvenile justice electronic records.

(I) Local police department: criminal electronic records and juvenile justice electronic records.

(J) Local child support agency: family electronic records, child welfare electronic records, and parentage electronic records.

(K) County child welfare agency: child welfare electronic records.

(L) County public guardian: criminal electronic records, mental health electronic records, and probate electronic records.

(M) County agency designated by the board of supervisors to provide conservatorship investigation under chapter 3 of the Lanterman-Petris-Short Act (Welf. & Inst. Code, §§ 5350–5372): criminal electronic records, mental health electronic records, and probate electronic records.

(N) **County public conservator: criminal electronic records, mental health electronic records, and probate electronic records.**

(O) **County public administrator: probate electronic records.**

(P) Federally recognized Indian tribe (including any reservation, department, subdivision, or court of the tribe) with concurrent jurisdiction: child welfare electronic records, family electronic records, juvenile justice electronic records, and probate electronic records.

[1] **(Q)** For good cause, a court may grant remote access to electronic records in particular case types to government entities beyond those listed in [2] **(b)(1)(A)–(P)**. For purposes of this rule, "good cause" means that the government entity requires access to the electronic records in order to adequately perform its [3] **legal** duties or fulfill its responsibilities in litigation.

[4] **(R)** All other remote access for government entities is governed by articles 2 and 3.

(2) Subject to (b)(1), the court may provide a government entity with the same level of remote access to electronic records as the government entity would be legally entitled to if a person working for the government entity were to appear at the courthouse to inspect court records in that case type. If a court record is confidential by law or sealed by court order and a person working for the government entity would not be legally entitled to inspect the court record at the courthouse, the court may not provide the government entity with remote access to the confidential or sealed electronic record.

(3) This rule applies only to electronic records. A government entity is not entitled under these rules to remote access to any documents, information, data, or other types of materials created or maintained by the courts that are not electronic records.

(Subd (b) amended effective January 1, 2020; adopted effective January 1, 2019.)

Rule 2.540(b). 2019 Deletes. [1] (O) [2] (b)(1)(A)–(N) [3] statutory [4] (P)

(c) Terms of remote access

(1) Government entities may remotely access electronic records only to perform official duties and for legitimate governmental purposes.

(2) Any distribution for sale of electronic records obtained remotely under the rules in this article is strictly prohibited.

(3) All laws governing confidentiality and disclosure of court records apply to electronic records obtained under this article.

(4) Government entities must comply with any other terms of remote access required by the court.

(5) Failure to comply with these requirements may result in the imposition of sanctions, including termination of access.

(Subd (c) adopted effective January 1, 2019.)

Rule 2.540 amended effective January 1, 2020; adopted effective January 1, 2019.

Advisory Committee Comment

The rule does not restrict courts to providing remote access only to local government entities in the same county in which the court is situated. For example, a court in one county could allow remote access to electronic records by a local child support agency in a different county.

Subdivision (b)(3). As to the applicability of the rules on remote access only to electronic records, see the advisory committee comment to rule 2.501.

Rule 2.541. Identity verification, identity management, and user access

(a) Identity verification required

Before allowing a person or entity eligible under the rules in article 4 to have remote access to electronic records, a court must verify the identity of the person seeking access.

(Subd (a) adopted effective January 1, 2019.)

(b) Responsibilities of the courts

A court that allows persons eligible under the rules in article 4 to have remote access to electronic records must have an identity verification method that verifies the identity of, and provides a unique credential to, each person who is permitted remote access to the electronic records. The court may authorize remote access by a person only if that person's identity has been verified, the person accesses records using the name and password provided to that individual, and the person complies with the terms and conditions of access, as prescribed by the court.

(Subd (b) adopted effective January 1, 2019.)

(c) Responsibilities of persons accessing records

A person eligible to remotely access electronic records under the rules in article 4 may be given such access only if that person:

(1) Provides the court with all of the information it needs to identify the person to be a user;

(2) Consents to all conditions for remote access required by article 4 and the court; and

(3) Is authorized by the court to have remote access to electronic records.

(Subd (c) adopted effective January 1, 2019.)

(d) Responsibilities of government entities

(1) If a person is accessing electronic records on behalf of a government entity, the government entity must approve granting access to that person, verify the person's identity, and provide the court with all the information it needs to authorize that person to have access to electronic records.

(2) If a person accessing electronic records on behalf of a government entity leaves his or her position or for any other reason is no longer entitled to access, the government entity must immediately notify the court so that the court can terminate the person's access.

(Subd (d) adopted effective January 1, 2019.)

(e) Vendor contracts, statewide master agreements, and identity and access management systems

A court may enter into a contract with a vendor to provide identity verification, identity management, or user access services. Alternatively, courts may use a statewide identity verification, identity management, or access management system, if available, or a statewide master agreement for such systems, if available.

(Subd (e) adopted effective January 1, 2019.)

Rule 2.541 adopted effective January 1, 2019.

Rule 2.542. Security of confidential information

(a) Secure access and encryption required

If any information in an electronic record that is confidential by law or sealed by court order may lawfully be provided remotely to a government entity, any remote access to the confidential information must be provided through a secure platform, and any electronic transmission of the information must be encrypted.

(Subd (a) adopted effective January 1, 2019.)

(b) Vendor contracts and statewide master agreements

A court may enter into a contract with a vendor to provide secure access and encryption services. Alternatively, if a statewide master agreement is available for secure access and encryption services, courts may use that master agreement.

(Subd (b) adopted effective January 1, 2019.)

Rule 2.542 adopted effective January 1, 2019.

Rule 2.543. Audit trails

(a) Ability to generate audit trails

The court should have the ability to generate an audit trail that contains one or more of the following elements: what electronic record was remotely accessed, when it was accessed, who accessed it, and under whose authority the user gained access.

(Subd (a) adopted effective January 1, 2019.)

(b) Audit trails available to government entity

(1) A court providing remote access to electronic records under this article should make limited audit trails available to authorized users of the government entity.

(2) A limited audit trail should identify the user who remotely accessed electronic records in a particular case, but must not identify which specific electronic records were accessed.

(Subd (b) adopted effective January 1, 2019.)

Rule 2.543 adopted effective January 1, 2019.

Advisory Committee Comment

The audit trail is a tool to assist the courts and users in identifying and investigating any potential issues or misuse of remote access. The user's view of the audit trail is limited to protect sensitive information.

To facilitate the use of existing remote access systems, rule 2.526 is currently not mandatory, but may be amended to be mandatory in the future.

Rule 2.544. Additional conditions of access

To the extent consistent with these rules and other applicable law, a court must impose reasonable conditions on remote access to preserve the integrity of its records, prevent the unauthorized use of information, and limit possible legal liability. The court may choose to require each user to submit a signed, written agreement enumerating those conditions before it permits that user to access electronic records remotely. The agreements may define the terms of access, provide for compliance audits, specify the scope of liability, and provide for sanctions for misuse up to and including termination of remote access.

Rule 2.544 adopted effective January 1, 2019.

Rule 2.545. Termination of remote access

(a) Remote access is a privilege

Remote access to electronic records under this article is a privilege and not a right.

(Subd (a) adopted effective January 1, 2019.)

(b) Termination by court

A court that provides remote access may, at any time and for any reason, terminate the permission granted to any person or entity eligible under the rules in article 4 to remotely access electronic records

(Subd (b) adopted effective January 1, 2019.)

Rule 2.545 adopted effective January 1, 2019.

Chapter 3
Sealed Records

Rule 2.550. Sealed records
Rule 2.551. Procedures for filing records under seal

Rule 2.550.   Sealed records

(a) Application

(1) Rules 2.550–2.551 apply to records sealed or proposed to be sealed by court order.

(2) These rules do not apply to records that are required to be kept confidential by law.

(3) These rules do not apply to discovery motions and records filed or lodged in connection with discovery motions or proceedings. However, the rules do apply to discovery materials that are used at trial or submitted as a basis for adjudication of matters other than discovery motions or proceedings.

(Subd (a) amended effective January 1, 2007.)

(b) Definitions

As used in this chapter:

(1) "Record." Unless the context indicates otherwise, "record" means all or a portion of any document, paper, exhibit, transcript, or other thing filed or lodged with the court, by electronic means or otherwise.

(2) "Sealed." A "sealed" record is a record that by court order is not open to inspection by the public.

(3) "Lodged." A "lodged" record is a record that is temporarily placed or deposited with the court, but not filed.

(Subd (b) amended effective January 1, 2016; previously amended effective January 1, 2007.)

(c) Court records presumed to be open

Unless confidentiality is required by law, court records are presumed to be open.

(d) Express factual findings required to seal records

The court may order that a record be filed under seal only if it expressly finds facts that establish:

(1) There exists an overriding interest that overcomes the right of public access to the record;

(2) The overriding interest supports sealing the record;

(3) A substantial probability exists that the overriding interest will be prejudiced if the record is not sealed;

(4) The proposed sealing is narrowly tailored; and

(5) No less restrictive means exist to achieve the overriding interest.

(Subd (d) amended effective January 1, 2004.)

(e) Content and scope of the order

(1) An order sealing the record must:

(A) Specifically state the facts that support the findings; and

(B) Direct the sealing of only those documents and pages, or, if reasonably practicable, portions of those documents and pages, that contain the material that needs to be placed under seal. All other portions of each document or page must be included in the public file.

(2) Consistent with Code of Civil Procedure sections 639 and 645.1, if the records that a party is requesting be placed under seal are voluminous, the court may appoint a referee and fix and allocate the referee's fees among the parties.

(Subd (e) amended effective January 1, 2007; previously amended effective January 1, 2004.)

Rule 2.550 amended effective January 1, 2016; adopted as rule 243.1 effective January 1, 2001; previously amended effective January 1, 2004; previously amended and renumbered as rule 2.550 effective January 1, 2007.

Advisory Committee Comment

This rule and rule 2.551 provide a standard and procedures for courts to use when a request is made to seal a record. The standard is based on *NBC Subsidiary (KNBC-TV), Inc. v. Superior Court* (1999) 20 Cal.4th 1178. These rules apply to civil and criminal cases. They recognize the First Amendment right of access to documents used at trial or as a basis of adjudication. The rules do not apply to

records that courts must keep confidential by law. Examples of confidential records to which public access is restricted by law are records of the family conciliation court (Family Code, § 1818(b)), in forma pauperis applications (Cal. Rules of Court, rules 3.54 and 8.26), and search warrant affidavits sealed under *People v. Hobbs* (1994) 7 Cal.4th 948. The sealed records rules also do not apply to discovery proceedings, motions, and materials that are not used at trial or submitted to the court as a basis for adjudication. (See *NBC Subsidiary, supra,* 20 Cal.4th at pp. 1208–1209, fn. 25.)

Rule 2.550(d)–(e) is derived from *NBC Subsidiary*. That decision contains the requirements that the court, before closing a hearing or sealing a transcript, must find an "overriding interest" that supports the closure or sealing, and must make certain express findings. (*Id.* at pp. 1217–1218.) The decision notes that the First Amendment right of access applies to records filed in both civil and criminal cases as a basis for adjudication. (*Id.* at pp. 1208–1209, fn. 25.) Thus, the *NBC Subsidiary* test applies to the sealing of records.

NBC Subsidiary provides examples of various interests that courts have acknowledged may constitute "overriding interests." (See *id.* at p. 1222, fn. 46.) Courts have found that, under appropriate circumstances, various statutory privileges, trade secrets, and privacy interests, when properly asserted and not waived, may constitute "overriding interests." The rules do not attempt to define what may constitute an "overriding interest," but leave this to case law.

Rule 2.551.   Procedures for filing records under seal

(a) Court approval required

A record must not be filed under seal without a court order. The court must not permit a record to be filed under seal based solely on the agreement or stipulation of the parties.

(Subd (a) amended effective January 1, 2007.)

(b) Motion or application to seal a record

(1) *Motion or application required*

A party requesting that a record be filed under seal must file a motion or an application for an order sealing the record. The motion or application must be accompanied by a memorandum and a declaration containing facts sufficient to justify the sealing.

(2) *Service of motion or application*

A copy of the motion or application must be served on all parties that have appeared in the case. Unless the court orders otherwise, any party that already has access to the records to be placed under seal must be served with a complete, unredacted version of all papers as well as a redacted version. Other parties must be served with only the public redacted version. If a party's attorney but not the party has access to the record, only the party's attorney may be served with the complete, unredacted version.

(3) *Procedure for party not intending to file motion or application*

(A) A party that files or intends to file with the court, for the purposes of adjudication or to use at trial, records produced in discovery that are subject to a confidentiality agreement or protective order, and does not intend to request to have the records sealed, must:

(i) Lodge the unredacted records subject to the confidentiality agreement or protective order and any pleadings, memorandums, declarations, and other documents that disclose the contents of the records, in the manner stated in (d);

(ii) File copies of the documents in (i) that are redacted so that they do not disclose the contents of the records that are subject to the confidentiality agreement or protective order; and

(iii) Give written notice to the party that produced the records that the records and the other documents lodged under (i) will be placed in the public court file unless that party files a timely motion or application to seal the records under this rule.

(B) If the party that produced the documents and was served with the notice under (A)(iii) fails to file a motion or an application to seal the records within 10 days or to obtain a court order extending the time to file such a motion or an application, the clerk must promptly transfer all the documents in (A)(i) from the envelope, container, or secure electronic file to the public file. If the party files a motion or an application to seal within 10 days or such later time as the court has ordered, these documents are to remain conditionally under seal until the court rules on the motion or application and thereafter are to be filed as ordered by the court.

(4) *Lodging of record pending determination of motion or application*

The party requesting that a record be filed under seal must lodge it with the court under (d) when the motion or application is made, unless good cause exists for not lodging it or the record has previously been lodged under (3)(A)(i). Pending the determination of the motion or application, the lodged record will be conditionally under seal.

(5) *Redacted and unredacted versions*

If necessary to prevent disclosure, any motion or application, any opposition, and any supporting documents must be filed in a public redacted version and lodged in a complete, unredacted version conditionally under seal. The cover of the redacted version must identify it as "Public—Redacts materials from conditionally sealed record." The cover of the unredacted version must identify it as "May Not Be Examined Without Court Order—Contains material from conditionally sealed record."

(6) *Return of lodged record*

If the court denies the motion or application to seal, the moving party may notify the court that the lodged record is to be filed unsealed. This notification must be received within 10 days of the order denying the motion or application to seal, unless otherwise ordered by the court. On receipt of this notification, the clerk must unseal and file the record. If the moving party does not notify the court within 10 days of the order, the clerk must (1) return the lodged record to the moving party if it is in paper form or (2) permanently delete the lodged record if it is in electronic form.

(Subd (b) amended effective January 1, 2017; previously amended effective January 1, 2004, January 1, 2007, and January 1, 2016.)

(c) References to nonpublic material in public records

A record filed publicly in the court must not disclose material contained in a record that is sealed, conditionally under seal, or subject to a pending motion or an application to seal.

(Subd (c) amended effective January 1, 2004.)

(d) Procedure for lodging of records

(1) A record that may be filed under seal must be transmitted to the court in a secure manner that preserves the confidentiality of the records to be lodged. If the record is transmitted in paper form, it must be put in an envelope or other appropriate container, sealed in the envelope or container, and lodged with the court.

(2) The materials to be lodged under seal must be clearly identified as "CONDITIONALLY UNDER SEAL." If the materials are transmitted in paper form, the envelope or container lodged with the court must be labeled "CONDITIONALLY UNDER SEAL."

(3) The party submitting the lodged record must affix to the electronic transmission, the envelope, or the container a cover sheet that:

(A) Contains all the information required on a caption page under rule 2.111; and

(B) States that the enclosed record is subject to a motion or an application to file the record under seal.

(4) On receipt of a record lodged under this rule, the clerk must endorse the affixed cover sheet with the date of its receipt and must retain but not file the record unless the court orders it filed.

(Subd (d) amended effective January 1, 2016; previously amended effective January 1, 2004, and January 1, 2007.)

(e) Order

(1) If the court grants an order sealing a record and if the sealed record is in paper format, the clerk must substitute on the envelope or container for the label required by (d)(2) a label prominently stating "SEALED BY ORDER OF THE COURT ON *(DATE)*," and must replace the cover sheet required by (d)(3) with a filed-endorsed copy of the court's order. If the sealed record is in electronic form, the clerk must file the court's order, maintain the record ordered sealed in a secure manner, and clearly identify the record as sealed by court order on a specified date.

(2) The order must state whether—in addition to the sealed records—the order itself, the register of actions, any other court records, or any other records relating to the case are to be sealed.

(3) The order must state whether any person other than the court is authorized to inspect the sealed record.

(4) Unless the sealing order provides otherwise, it prohibits the parties from disclosing the contents of any materials that have been sealed in anything that is subsequently publicly filed.

(Subd (e) amended effective January 1, 2017; previously amended effective January 1, 2004, January 1, 2007, and January 1, 2016.)

(f) Custody of sealed records

Sealed records must be securely filed and kept separate from the public file in the case. If the sealed records are in electronic form, appropriate access controls must be established to ensure that only authorized persons may access the sealed records.

(Subd (f) amended effective January 1, 2017; previously amended effective January 1, 2004.)

(g) Custody of voluminous records

If the records to be placed under seal are voluminous and are in the possession of a public agency, the court may by written order direct the

agency instead of the clerk to maintain custody of the original records in a secure fashion. If the records are requested by a reviewing court, the trial court must order the public agency to deliver the records to the clerk for transmission to the reviewing court under these rules.

(h) Motion, application, or petition to unseal records

(1) A sealed record must not be unsealed except on order of the court.

(2) A party or member of the public may move, apply, or petition, or the court on its own motion may move, to unseal a record. Notice of any motion, application, or petition to unseal must be filed and served on all parties in the case. The motion, application, or petition and any opposition, reply, and supporting documents must be filed in a public redacted version and a sealed complete version if necessary to comply with (c).

(3) If the court proposes to order a record unsealed on its own motion, the court must give notice to the parties stating the reason for unsealing the record. Unless otherwise ordered by the court, any party may serve and file an opposition within 10 days after the notice is provided and any other party may file a response within 5 days after the filing of an opposition.

(4) In determining whether to unseal a record, the court must consider the matters addressed in rule 2.550(c)–(e).

(5) The order unsealing a record must state whether the record is unsealed entirely or in part. If the court's order unseals only part of the record or unseals the record only as to certain persons, the order must specify the particular records that are unsealed, the particular persons who may have access to the record, or both. If, in addition to the records in the envelope, container, or secure electronic file, the court has previously ordered the sealing order, the register of actions, or any other court records relating to the case to be sealed, the unsealing order must state whether these additional records are unsealed.

(Subd (h) amended effective January 1, 2016; previously amended effective January 1, 2004, and January 1, 2007.)

Rule 2.551 amended effective January 1, 2017; adopted as rule 243.2 effective January 1, 2001; previously amended effective January 1, 2004, and January 1, 2016; previously amended and renumbered as rule 2.551 effective January 1, 2007.

Chapter 4
Records in False Claims Act Cases

Rule 2.570. Filing False Claims Act records under seal
Rule 2.571. Procedures for filing records under seal in a False Claims Act case
Rule 2.572. Ex parte application for an extension of time
Rule 2.573. Unsealing of records and management of False Claims Act cases

Rule 2.570.   Filing False Claims Act records under seal

(a) Application

Rules 2.570–2.573 apply to records initially filed under seal pursuant to the False Claims Act, Government Code section 12650 et seq. As to these records, rules 2.550–2.551 on sealed records do not apply.

(Subd (a) amended effective January 1, 2007.)

(b) Definitions

As used in this chapter, unless the context or subject matter otherwise requires:

(1) "Attorney General" means the Attorney General of the State of California.

(2) "Prosecuting authority" means the county counsel, city attorney, or other local government official charged with investigating, filing, and conducting civil legal proceedings on behalf of or in the name of a particular political subdivision.

(3) "*Qui tam* plaintiff" means a person who files a complaint under the False Claims Act.

(4) The definitions in Government Code section 12650 apply to the rules in this chapter.

(Subd (b) amended effective January 1, 2007.)

(c) Confidentiality of records filed under the False Claims Act

Records of actions filed by a *qui tam* plaintiff must initially be filed as confidential and under seal as required by Government Code section 12652(c). Until the seal is lifted, the records in the action must remain under seal, except to the extent otherwise provided in this rule.

(d) Persons permitted access to sealed records in a False Claims Act case

(1) *Public access prohibited*

As long as the records in a False Claims Act case are under seal, public access to the records in the case is prohibited. The prohibition on public access applies not only to filed documents but also to electronic records that would disclose information about the case, including the identity of any plaintiff or defendant.

(2) *Information on register of actions*

As long as the records in a False Claims Act case are under seal, only the information concerning filed records contained on the confidential cover sheet prescribed under rule 2.571(c) may be entered into the register of actions that is accessible to the public.

(3) *Parties permitted access to the sealed court file*

As long as the records in a False Claims Act case are under seal, the only parties permitted access to the court file are:

(A) The Attorney General;

(B) A prosecuting authority for the political subdivision on whose behalf the action is brought, unless the political subdivision is named as a defendant; and

(C) A prosecuting authority for any other political subdivision interested in the matter whose identity has been provided to the court by the Attorney General.

(4) *Parties not permitted access to the sealed court file*

As long as records in a False Claims Act case are under seal, no defendant is permitted to have access to the court records or other information concerning the case. Defendants not permitted access include any political subdivision that has been named as a defendant in a False Claims Act action.

(5) Qui tam *plaintiff's limited access to sealed court file*

The *qui tam* plaintiff in a False Claims Act case may have access to all documents filed by the *qui tam* plaintiff and to such other documents as the court may order.

(Subd (d) amended effective January 1, 2007.)

Rule 2.570 amended and renumbered effective January 1, 2007; adopted as rule 243.5 effective July 1, 2002.

Rule 2.571.   Procedures for filing records under seal in a False Claims Act case

(a) No sealing order required

On the filing of an action under the False Claims Act, the complaint, motions for extensions of time, and other papers filed with the court must be kept under seal. Under Government Code section 12652, no order sealing these records is necessary.

(Subd (a) amended effective January 1, 2007.)

(b) Filing a False Claims Act case in a county where filings are accepted in multiple locations

In a county where complaints in civil cases may be filed in more than one location, the presiding judge must designate one particular location where all filings in False Claims Act cases must be made.

(Subd (b) amended effective January 1, 2007.)

(c) Special cover sheet omitting names of the parties

In a False Claims Act case, the complaint and every other paper filed while the case is under seal must have a completed *Confidential Cover Sheet—False Claims Action* (form MC-060) affixed to the first page.

(Subd (c) amended effective January 1, 2007.)

(d) Filing of papers under seal

When the complaint or other paper in a False Claims Act case is filed under seal, the clerk must stamp both the cover sheet and the caption page of the paper.

(Subd (d) amended effective January 1, 2007.)

(e) Custody of sealed records

Records in a False Claims Act case that are confidential and under seal must be securely filed and kept separate from the public file in the case.

(Subd (e) amended effective January 1, 2007.)

Rule 2.571 amended and renumbered effective January 1, 2007; adopted as rule 243.6 effective July 1, 2002.

Rule 2.572.   Ex parte application for an extension of time

A party in a False Claims Act case may apply under the ex parte rules in title 3 for an extension of time under Government Code section 12652. *Rule 2.572 amended and renumbered effective January 1, 2007; adopted as rule 243.7 effective July 1, 2002.*

Rule 2.573.   Unsealing of records and management of False Claims Act cases

(a) Expiration or lifting of seal

(1) Records in a False Claims Act case to which public access has been prohibited under Government Code section 12652(c) must remain under seal until the Attorney General and all local prosecuting authorities involved in the action have notified the court of their decision to intervene or not intervene.

(2) The Attorney General and all local prosecuting authorities involved in the action must give the notice required under (1) within 60 days of the filing of the complaint or before an order extending the time to intervene has expired, unless a new motion to extend time to intervene is pending, in which case the seal remains in effect until a ruling is made on the motion.

(Subd (a) amended effective January 1, 2007.)

(b) Coordination of state and local authorities

The Attorney General and all local prosecuting authorities must coordinate their activities to provide timely and effective notice to the court that:

(1) A political subdivision or subdivisions remain interested in the action and have not yet determined whether to intervene; or

(2) The seal has been extended by the filing or grant of a motion to extend time to intervene, and therefore the seal has not expired.

(Subd (b) amended effective January 1, 2007.)

(c) Designation of lead local prosecuting authority

In a False Claims Act case in which the Attorney General is not involved or has declined to intervene and local prosecuting authorities remain interested in the action, the court may designate a lead prosecuting authority to keep the court apprised of whether all the prosecuting authorities have either intervened or declined to intervene, and whether the seal is to be lifted.

(d) Order unsealing record

The Attorney General or other prosecuting authority filing a notice of intervention or nonintervention must submit a proposed order indicating the documents that are to be unsealed or to remain sealed.

(e) Case management

(1) *Case management conferences*

The court, at the request of the parties or on its own motion, may hold a conference at any time in a False Claims Act case to determine what case management is appropriate for the case, including the lifting or partial lifting of the seal, the scheduling of trial and other events, and any other matters that may assist in managing the case.

(2) *Exemption from case management rules*

Cases under the False Claims Act are exempt from rule 3.110 and the case management rules in title 3, division 7, but are subject to such case management orders as the court may issue.

(Subd (e) amended effective January 1, 2007.)

Rule 2.573 amended and renumbered effective January 1, 2007; adopted as rule 243.8 effective July 1, 2002.

Chapter 5
Name Change Proceedings Under Address Confidentiality Program

Title 2, Trial Court Rules—Division 4, Court Records—Chapter 5, Name Change Proceedings Under Address Confidentiality Program; adopted effective January 1, 2010.

Rule 2.575.   Confidential information in name change proceedings under address confidentiality program

(a) Definitions

As used in this chapter, unless the context or subject matter otherwise requires:

(1) "Confidential name change petitioner" means a petitioner who is a participant in the address confidentiality program created by the Secretary of State under chapter 3.1 (commencing with section 6205) of division 7 of title 1 of the Government Code.

(2) "Record" means all or a portion of any document, paper, exhibit, transcript, or other thing that is filed or lodged with the court.

(3) "Lodged" means temporarily placed or deposited with the court but not filed.

(Subd (a) adopted effective January 1, 2010.)

(b) Application of chapter

The rules in this chapter apply to records filed in a change of name proceeding under Code of Civil Procedure section 1277(b) by a confidential name change petitioner who alleges any of the following reasons or circumstances as a reason for the name change:

(1) The petitioner is seeking to avoid domestic violence, as defined in Family Code section 6211.

(2) The petitioner is seeking to avoid stalking, as defined in Penal Code section 646.9.

(3) The petitioner is, or is filing on behalf of, a victim of sexual assault, as defined in Evidence Code section 1036.2.

(Subd (b) adopted effective January 1, 2010.)

(c) Confidentiality of current name of the petitioner

The current legal name of a confidential name change petitioner must be kept confidential by the court as required by Code of Civil Procedure section 1277(b)(3) and not be published or posted in the court's calendars, indexes, or register of actions, or by any means or in any public forum. Only the information concerning filed records contained on the confidential cover sheet prescribed under (d) may be entered into the register of actions or any other forum that is accessible to the public.

(Subd (c) adopted effective January 1, 2010.)

(d) Special cover sheet omitting names of the petitioner

To maintain the confidentiality provided under Code of Civil Procedure section 1277(b) for the petitioner's current name, the petitioner must attach a completed *Confidential Cover Sheet—Name Change Proceeding Under Address Confidentiality Program (Safe at Home)* (form NC-400) to the front of the petition for name change and every other document filed in the proceedings. The name of the petitioner must not appear on that cover sheet.

(Subd (d) adopted effective January 1, 2010.)

(e) Confidentiality of proposed name of the petitioner

To maintain the confidentiality provided under Code of Civil Procedure section 1277(b) for the petitioner's proposed name, the petitioner must not include the proposed name on the petition for name change or any other record in the proceedings. In any form that requests the petitioner's proposed name, the petitioner and the court must indicate that the proposed name is confidential and on file with the Secretary of State under the provisions of the Safe at Home address confidentiality program.

(Subd (e) adopted effective January 1, 2010.)

Rule 2.575 adopted effective January 1, 2010.

Rule 2.576. Access to name of the petitioner

(a) Termination of confidentiality

The current name of a confidential name change petitioner must remain confidential until a determination is made that:

(1) Petitioner's participation in the address confidentiality program has ended under Government Code section 6206.7; or

(2) The court finds by clear and convincing evidence that the allegations of domestic violence or stalking in the petition are false.

(Subd (a) adopted effective January 1, 2010.)

(b) Procedure to obtain access

A determination under (a) must be made by noticed motion, with service by mail on the confidential name change petitioner in care of the Secretary of State's address confidentiality program as stated in Government Code section 6206(a)(5)(A).

(Subd (b) adopted effective January 1, 2010.)

Rule 2.576 adopted effective January 1, 2010.

Rule 2.577. Procedures for filing confidential name change records under seal

(a) Court approval required

Records in a name change proceeding may not be filed under seal without a court order. A request by a confidential name change petitioner to file records under seal may be made under the procedures in this chapter. A request by any other petitioner to file records under seal must be made under rules 2.550–2.573.

(Subd (a) adopted effective January 1, 2010.)

(b) Application to file records in confidential name change proceedings under seal

An application by a confidential name change petitioner to file records under seal must be filed at the time the petition for name change is submitted to the court. The application must be made on the *Application to File Documents Under Seal in Name Change Proceeding Under Address Confidentiality Program (Safe at Home)* (form NC-410) and be accompanied by a *Declaration in Support of Application to File Documents Under Seal in Name Change Proceeding Under Address Confidentiality Program (Safe at Home)* (form NC-420), containing facts sufficient to justify the sealing.

(Subd (b) amended effective January 1, 2017; adopted effective January 1, 2010.)

(c) Confidentiality

The application to file under seal must be kept confidential by the court until the court rules on it.

(Subd (c) adopted effective January 1, 2010.)

(d) Procedure for lodging of petition for name change

(1) The records that may be filed under seal must be lodged with the court. If they are transmitted on paper, they must be placed in a sealed envelope. If they are transmitted electronically, they must be transmitted to the court in a secure manner that preserves the confidentiality of the documents to be lodged.

(2) If the petitioner is transmitting the petition on paper, the petitioner must complete and affix to the envelope a completed *Confidential Cover Sheet—Name Change Proceeding Under Address Confidentiality Program (Safe at Home)* (form NC-400) and in the space under the title and case number mark it "CONDITIONALLY UNDER SEAL." If the petitioner is transmitting the petition electronically, the first page of the electronic transmission must be a completed *Confidential Cover Sheet—Name Change Proceeding Under Address Confidentiality Program (Safe at Home)* (form NC-400) with the space under the title and case number marked "CONDITIONALLY UNDER SEAL."

(3) On receipt of a petition lodged under this rule, the clerk must endorse the cover sheet with the date of its receipt and must retain but not file the record unless the court orders it filed.

(4) If the court denies the application to seal, the moving party may notify the court that the lodged record is to be filed unsealed. This notification must be received within 10 days of the order denying the motion or application to seal, unless otherwise ordered by the court. On receipt of this notification, the clerk must unseal and file the record. If the moving party does not notify the court within 10 days of the order, the clerk must (1) return the lodged record to the moving party if it is in paper form or (2) permanently delete the lodged record if it is in electronic form.

(Subd (d) amended effective January 1, 2017; adopted effective January 1, 2010; previously amended effective January 1, 2016.)

(e) Consideration of application to file under seal

The court may order that the record be filed under seal if it finds that all of the following factors apply:

(1) There exists an overriding interest that overcomes the right of public access to the record;

(2) The overriding interest supports sealing the record;

(3) A substantial probability exists that the overriding interest will be prejudiced if the record is not sealed;

(4) The proposed order to seal the record is narrowly tailored; and

(5) No less restrictive means exist to achieve the overriding interest.

(Subd (e) adopted effective January 1, 2010.)

(f) Order

(1) The order may be issued on *Order on Application to File Documents Under Seal in Name Change Proceeding Under Address Confidentiality Program (Safe at Home)* (form NC-425).

(2) Any order granting the application to seal must state whether the declaration in support of the application, the order itself, and any other record in the proceeding are to be sealed as well as the petition for name change.

(3) For petitions transmitted in paper form, if the court grants an order sealing a record, the clerk must strike out the notation required by (d)(2) on the *Confidential Cover Sheet* that the matter is filed "CONDITIONALLY UNDER SEAL," add a notation to that sheet prominently stating "SEALED BY ORDER OF THE COURT ON *(DATE)*," and file the documents under seal. For petitions transmitted electronically, the clerk must file the court's order, maintain the record ordered sealed in a secure manner, and clearly identify the record as sealed by court order on a specified date.

(4) If the court grants the application to file under seal and issues an order under (e), the petition and any associated records may be filed under seal and ruled on by the court immediately.

(5) The order must identify any person other than the court who is authorized to inspect the sealed records.

(Subd (f) amended effective January 1, 2017; adopted effective January 1, 2010; previously amended effective January 1, 2016.)

(g) Custody of sealed records

Sealed records must be securely filed and kept separate from the public file in the case. If the sealed records are in electronic form, appropriate access controls must be established to ensure that only authorized persons may access the sealed records.

(Subd (g) amended effective January 1, 2017; adopted effective January 1, 2010.)

(h) Motion, application, or petition to unseal record

(1) A sealed record may not be unsealed except by order of the court.

(2) Any member of the public seeking to unseal a record or a court proposing to do so on its own motion must follow the procedures described in rule 2.551(h).

(Subd (h) adopted effective January 1, 2010.)

Rule 2.577 amended effective January 1, 2017; adopted effective January 1, 2010; previously amended effective January 1, 2016.

Chapter 6
Other Sealed or Closed Records

Title 2, Trial Court Rules—Division 4, Court Records—Chapter 6, Other Sealed or Closed Record; adopted as Chapter 5 effective January 1, 2007; renumbered effective January 1, 2010.

Rule 2.580. Request for delayed public disclosure
Rule 2.585. Confidential in-camera proceedings

Rule 2.580. Request for delayed public disclosure

In an action in which the prejudgment attachment remedy under Code of Civil Procedure section 483.010 et seq. is sought, if the plaintiff requests at the time a complaint is filed that the records in the action or the fact of the filing of the action be made temporarily unavailable to the public under Code of Civil Procedure section 482.050, the plaintiff must file a declaration stating one of the following:

(1) "This action is on a claim for money based on contract against a defendant who is not a natural person. The claim is not secured within the meaning of Code of Civil Procedure section 483.010(b)."—or—

(2) "This action is on a claim for money based on contract against a defendant who is a natural person. The claim arises out of the defendant's conduct of a trade, business, or profession, and the money, property, or services were not used by the defendant primarily for personal, family, or household purposes. The claim is not secured within the meaning of Code of Civil Procedure section 483.010(b)."

Rule 2.580 renumbered effective January 1, 2007; adopted as rule 243.3 effective January 1, 2001.

Rule 2.585. Confidential in-camera proceedings

(a) Minutes of proceedings

If a confidential in-camera proceeding is held in which a party is excluded from being represented, the clerk must include in the minutes the nature of the hearing and only such references to writings or witnesses as will not disclose privileged information.

(b) Disposition of examined records

Records examined by the court in confidence under (a), or copies of them, must be filed with the clerk under seal and must not be disclosed without court order.

Rule 2.585 renumbered effective January 1, 2007; adopted as rule 243.4 effective January 1, 2001.

Division 5
Venue and Sessions

Chapter 1
Venue
[Reserved]

Rule 2.700. Intracounty venue
[Reserved]

Rule 2.700 adopted effective January 1, 2007.

Chapter 2
Sessions
[Reserved]

Division 6
Appointments by the Court or Agreement of the Parties

Chapter 1
Court-Appointed Temporary Judges

Rule 2.810. Temporary judges appointed by the trial courts

(a) Scope of rules

Rules 2.810–2.819 apply to attorneys who serve as court-appointed temporary judges in the trial courts. The rules do not apply to subordinate judicial officers or to attorneys designated by the courts to serve as temporary judges at the parties' request.

(Subd (a) amended effective January 1, 2009; previously amended effective January 1, 2007.)

(b) Definition of "court-appointed temporary judge"

A "court-appointed temporary judge" means an attorney who has satisfied the requirements for appointment under rule 2.812 and has been appointed by the court to serve as a temporary judge in that court.

(Subd (b) amended effective January 1, 2007.)

(c) Appointment of attorneys as temporary judges

Trial courts may appoint an attorney as a temporary judge only if the attorney has satisfied the requirements of rule 2.812.

(Subd (c) amended effective January 1, 2007.)

(d) Exception for extraordinary circumstances

A presiding judge may appoint an attorney who is qualified under rule 2.812(a), but who has not satisfied the other requirements of that rule, only in case of extraordinary circumstances. Any appointment under this subdivision based on extraordinary circumstances must be made before the attorney serves as a temporary judge and must not last more than 10 court days in a three-year period.

(Subd (d) amended effective January 1, 2017; previously amended effective January 1, 2007.)

Rule 2.810 amended effective January 1, 2017; adopted as rule 243.11 effective July 1, 2006; previously amended and renumbered effective January 1, 2007; previously amended effective January 1, 2009.

Rule 2.811. Court appointment of temporary judges

(a) Purpose of court appointment

The purpose of court appointment of attorneys as temporary judges is to assist the public by providing the court with a panel of trained, qualified, and experienced attorneys who may serve as temporary judges at the discretion of the court if the court needs judicial assistance that it cannot provide using its full-time judicial officers.

(b) Appointment and service discretionary

Court-appointed attorneys are appointed and serve as temporary judges solely at the discretion of the presiding judge.

(c) No employment relationship

Court appointment and service of an attorney as a temporary judge do not establish an employment relationship between the court and the attorney.

(d) Responsibility of the presiding judge for appointments

The appointment of attorneys to serve as temporary judges is the responsibility of the presiding judge, who may designate another judge or committee of judges to perform this responsibility. In carrying out this responsibility, the presiding judge is assisted by a Temporary Judge Administrator as prescribed by rule 10.743.

(Subd (d) amended effective January 1, 2007.)

Rule 2.811 amended and renumbered effective January 1, 2007; adopted as rule 243.12 effective July 1, 2006.

Rule 2.812. Requirements for court appointment of an attorney to serve as a temporary judge

(a) Experience required for appointment and service

The presiding judge may not appoint an attorney to serve as a temporary judge unless the attorney has been admitted to practice as a member of the State Bar of California for at least 10 years before the appointment. However, for good cause, the presiding judge may permit an attorney who has been admitted to practice for at least 5 years to serve as a temporary judge.

(b) Conditions for appointment by the court

The presiding judge may appoint an attorney to serve as a temporary judge only if the attorney:

(1) Is a member in good standing of the State Bar and has no disciplinary action pending;

(2) Has not pled guilty or no contest to a felony, or has not been convicted of a felony that has not been reversed;

(3) Has satisfied the education and training requirements in (c);

(4) Has satisfied all other general conditions that the court may establish for appointment of an attorney as a temporary judge in that court; and

(5) Has satisfied any additional conditions that the court may require for an attorney to be appointed as a temporary judge for a particular assignment or type of case in that court.

(c) Education and training requirements

The presiding judge may appoint an attorney to serve as a temporary judge only if the following minimum training requirements are satisfied:

(1) *Mandatory training on bench conduct and demeanor*

Before appointment, the attorney must have attended and successfully completed, within the previous three years, a course of at least 3 hours' duration on the subjects identified in rule 2.813(a) approved by the court in which the attorney will serve. This course must be taken in person and be taught by a qualified judicial officer.

(2) *Mandatory training in ethics*

Before appointment, the attorney must have attended and successfully completed, within the previous three years, a course of at least 3 hours' duration on the subjects identified in rule 2.813(b) approved by the court in which the attorney will serve. This course may be taken by any means approved by the court, including in-person, by broadcast with participation, or online.

(3) *Substantive training*

Before appointment, the attorney must have attended and successfully completed, within the previous three years, a course on the substantive law in each subject area in which the attorney will serve as a temporary judge. These courses may be taken by any means approved by the court, including in-person, by broadcast with participation, or online. The substantive courses have the following minimum requirements:

(A) *Small claims*

An attorney serving as a temporary judge in small claims cases must have attended and successfully completed, within the previous three years, a course of at least 3 hours' duration on the subjects identified in rule 2.813(c) approved by the court in which the attorney will serve.

(B) *Traffic*

An attorney serving as a temporary judge in traffic cases must have attended and completed, within the previous three years, a course of at least 3 hours' duration on the subjects identified in rule 2.813(d) approved by the court in which the attorney will serve.

(C) *Other subject areas*

If the court assigns attorneys to serve as temporary judges in other substantive areas such as civil law, family law, juvenile law, unlawful detainers, or case management, the court must determine what additional training is required and what additional courses are required before an attorney may serve as a temporary judge in each of those subject areas. The training required in each area must be of at least 3 hours' duration. The court may also require that an attorney possess additional years of practical experience in each substantive area before being assigned to serve as a temporary judge in that subject area.

(D) *Settlement*

An attorney need not be a temporary judge to assist the court in settlement conferences. However, an attorney assisting the court with settlement conferences who performs any judicial function, such as entering a settlement on the record under Code of Civil Procedure section 664.6, must be a qualified temporary judge who has satisfied the training requirements under (c)(1) and (c)(2) of this rule.

(E) The substantive training requirements in (3)(A)–(C) do not apply to courts in which temporary judges are used fewer than 10 times altogether in a calendar year.

(Subd (c) amended effective January 1, 2009; previously amended effective January 1, 2007.)

(d) Requirements for retired judicial officers

Commencing five years after the retired judicial officer last served in a judicial position either as a full-time judicial officer or as an assigned judge, a retired judicial officer serving as a temporary judge must satisfy all the education and training requirements of this rule. However, a retired judicial officer serving as a temporary judge in a small claims case must satisfy all the requirements of Code of Civil Procedure section 116.240(b) and the rules in this chapter before serving in the case.

(Subd (d) adopted effective January 1, 2009.)

(e) Additional requirements

The presiding judge in each court should establish additional experience and training requirements for temporary judges beyond the minimum requirements provided in this rule if it is feasible for the court to do so.

(Subd (e) relettered effective January 1, 2009; adopted as subd (d) effective July 1, 2006.)

(f) Records of attendance

A court that uses temporary judges must maintain records verifying that each attorney who serves as a temporary judge in that court has attended and successfully completed the courses required under this rule.

(Subd (f) relettered effective January 1, 2009; adopted as subd (e) effective July 1, 2006.)

(g) Application and appointment

To serve as a temporary judge, an attorney must complete the application required under rule 10.744, must satisfy the requirements prescribed in this rule, and must satisfy such other requirements as the court appointing the attorney in its discretion may determine are appropriate.

(Subd (g) relettered effective January 1, 2009; adopted as subd (f) effective July 1, 2006.)

Rule 2.812 amended effective January 1, 2009; adopted as rule 243.13 effective July 1, 2006; previously amended and renumbered effective January 1, 2007.

Advisory Committee Comment

The goal of this rule is to ensure that attorneys who serve as court-appointed temporary judges are qualified and properly trained.

Subdivision (a). If a court determines that there is good cause under (a) to appoint an attorney with less than 10 years of practice as a temporary judge, the attorney must still satisfy the other requirements of the rule before being appointed.

Subdivision (b). "Good standing" means that the attorney is currently eligible to practice law in the State of California. An attorney in good standing may be either an active or a voluntarily inactive member of the State Bar. The rule does not require that an attorney be an active member of the State Bar to serve as a court-appointed temporary judge. Voluntarily inactive members may be appointed as temporary judges if the court decides to appoint them.

Subdivision (c). A court may use attorneys who are not temporary judges to assist in the settlement of cases. For example, attorneys may work under the presiding judge or individual judges and may assist them in settling cases. However, these attorneys may not perform any judicial functions such as entering a settlement on the record under Code of Civil Procedure section 664.6. Settlement attorneys who are not temporary judges are not required to satisfy the requirements of these rules, but must satisfy any requirements established by the court for attorneys who assist in the settlement of cases.

Rule 2.813. Contents of training programs

(a) Bench conduct

Before the court may appoint an attorney to serve as a temporary judge in any type of case, the attorney must have received training under rule 2.812(c)(1) in the following subjects:

(1) Bench conduct, demeanor, and decorum;

(2) Access, fairness, and elimination of bias; and

(3) Adjudicating cases involving self-represented parties.

(Subd (a) amended effective January 1, 2007.)

(b) Ethics

Before the court may appoint an attorney to serve as a temporary judge in any type of case, the attorney must have received ethics training under rule 2.812(c)(2) in the following subjects:

(1) Judicial ethics generally;

(2) Conflicts;

(3) Disclosures, disqualifications, and limitations on appearances; and

(4) Ex parte communications.

(Subd (b) amended effective January 1, 2007.)

(c) Small claims

Before the court may appoint an attorney to serve as a temporary judge in small claims cases, the attorney must have received training under rule 2.812(c)(3)(A) in the following subjects:

(1) Small claims procedures and practices;

(2) Consumer sales;

(3) Vehicular sales, leasing, and repairs;

(4) Credit and financing transactions;

(5) Professional and occupational licensing;

(6) Tenant rent deposit law;

(7) Contract, warranty, tort, and negotiable instruments law; and

(8) Other subjects deemed appropriate by the presiding judge based on local needs and conditions.

In addition, an attorney serving as a temporary judge in small claims cases must be familiar with the publications identified in Code of Civil Procedure section 116.930.

(Subd (c) amended effective January 1, 2007.)

(d) Traffic

Before the court may appoint an attorney to serve as a temporary judge in traffic cases, the attorney must have received training under rule 2.812(c)(3)(B) in the following subjects:

(1) Traffic court procedures and practices;

(2) Correctable violations;

(3) Discovery;

(4) Driver licensing;

(5) Failure to appear;

(6) Mandatory insurance;

(7) Notice to appear citation forms;

(8) Red-light enforcement;

(9) Sentencing and court-ordered traffic school;

(10) Speed enforcement;

(11) Settlement of the record;

(12) Uniform bail and penalty schedules;

(13) Vehicle registration and licensing; and

(14) Other subjects deemed appropriate by the presiding judge based on local needs and conditions.

(Subd (d) amended effective January 1, 2007.)

Rule 2.813 amended and renumbered effective January 1, 2007; adopted as rule 243.14 effective July 1, 2006.

Advisory Committee Comment

The purpose of this rule is to ensure that all court-appointed temporary judges have proper training in bench conduct and demeanor, ethics, and each substantive area in which they adjudicate cases. Each court is responsible for approving the training and instructional materials for the temporary judges appointed by that court. The training in bench conduct and demeanor must be in person, but in other areas each court may determine the approved method or methods by which the training is provided. The methods may include in-person courses, broadcasts with participation, and online courses. Courts may offer MCLE credit for courses that they provide and may approve MCLE courses provided by others as satisfying the substantive training requirements under this rule. Courts may work together with other courts, or may cooperate on a regional basis, to develop and provide training programs for court-appointed temporary judges under this rule.

Rule 2.814.   Appointment of temporary judge

An attorney may serve as a temporary judge for the court only after the court has issued an order appointing him or her to serve. Before serving, the attorney must subscribe the oath of office and must certify that he or she is aware of and will comply with applicable provisions of canon 6 of the Code of Judicial Ethics and the California Rules of Court.

Rule 2.814 renumbered effective January 1, 2007; adopted as rule 243.15 effective July 1, 2006.

Rule 2.815.   Continuing education

(a) Continuing education required

Each attorney appointed as a temporary judge must attend and successfully complete every three years a course on bench conduct and demeanor, an ethics course, and a course in each substantive area in which the attorney will serve as a temporary judge. The courses must cover the same subjects and be of the same duration as the courses prescribed in rule 2.812(c). These courses must be approved by the court that appoints the attorney.

(Subd (a) amended effective January 1, 2007.)

(b) Records of attendance

A court that uses temporary judges must maintain records verifying that each attorney who serves as a temporary judge in that court has attended and successfully completed the courses required under this rule.

Rule 2.815 amended and renumbered effective January 1, 2007; adopted as rule 243.17 effective July 1, 2006.

Rule 2.816.   Stipulation to court-appointed temporary judge

(a) Application

This rule governs a stipulation for a matter to be heard by a temporary judge when the court has appointed and assigned an attorney to serve as a temporary judge in that court.

(Subd (a) adopted effective July 1, 2006.)

(b) Contents of notice

Before the swearing in of the first witness at a small claims hearing, before the entry of a plea by the defendant at a traffic arraignment, or before the commencement of any other proceeding, the court must give notice to each party that:

(1) A temporary judge will be hearing the matters for that calendar;

(2) The temporary judge is a qualified member of the State Bar and the name of the temporary judge is provided; and

(3) The party has a right to have the matter heard before a judge, commissioner, or referee of the court.

(Subd (b) amended and relettered effective July 1, 2006; adopted as subd (a) effective January 1, 2001.)

(c) Form of notice

The court may give the notice in (b) by either of the following methods:

(1) A conspicuous sign posted inside or just outside the courtroom, accompanied by oral notification or notification by videotape or audiotape by a court officer on the day of the hearing; or

(2) A written notice provided to each party.

(Subd (c) amended and relettered effective July 1, 2006; adopted as subd (b) effective January 1, 2001.)

(d) Methods of stipulation

After notice has been given under (a) and (b), a party stipulates to a court-appointed temporary judge by either of the following:

(1) The party is deemed to have stipulated to the attorney serving as a temporary judge if the party fails to object to the matter being heard by the temporary judge before the temporary judge begins the proceeding; or

(2) The party signs a written stipulation agreeing that the matter may be heard by the temporary judge.

(Subd (d) amended effective January 1, 2007; adopted effective July 1, 2006.)

(e) Application or motion to withdraw stipulation

An application or motion to withdraw a stipulation for the appointment of a temporary judge must be supported by a declaration of facts establishing good cause for permitting the party to withdraw the stipulation. In addition:

(1) The application or motion must be heard by the presiding judge or a judge designated by the presiding judge.

(2) A declaration that a ruling by a temporary judge is based on an error of fact or law does not establish good cause for withdrawing a stipulation.

(3) The application or motion must be served and filed, and the moving party must provide a copy to the presiding judge.

(4) If the application or motion for withdrawing the stipulation is based on grounds for the disqualification of, or limitation of the appearance by, the temporary judge first learned or arising after the temporary judge has made one or more rulings, but before the temporary judge has completed judicial action in the proceeding, the temporary judge, unless the disqualification or termination is waived, must disqualify himself or herself. But in the absence of good cause, the rulings the temporary judge has made up to that time must not be set aside by the judicial officer or temporary judge who replaces the temporary judge.

(Subd (e) amended effective January 1, 2016; adopted effective July 1, 2006; previously amended effective January 1, 2007.)

Rule 2.816 amended effective January 1, 2016; adopted as rule 1727 effective January 1, 2001; previously amended and renumbered as rule 243.18 effective July 1, 2006; previously amended and renumbered as rule 2.816 effective January 1, 2007.

Rule 2.817.   Disclosures to the parties

A temporary judge must make all disclosures required under the Code of Judicial Ethics.

Rule 2.817 renumbered effective January 1, 2007; adopted as rule 243.19 effective July 1, 2006.

Rule 2.818.   Disqualifications and limitations

(a) Code of Judicial Ethics

A temporary judge must disqualify himself or herself as a temporary judge in proceedings as provided under the Code of Judicial Ethics.

(Subd (a) lettered effective July 1, 2006; adopted as unlettered subd effective July 1, 2006.)

(b) Limitations on service

In addition to being disqualified as provided in (a), an attorney may not serve as a court-appointed temporary judge:

(1) If the attorney, in any type of case, is appearing on the same day in the same courthouse as an attorney or as a party;

(2) If the attorney, in the same type of case, is presently a party to any action or proceeding in the court; or

(3) If, in a family law or unlawful detainer case, one party is self-represented and the other party is represented by an attorney or is an attorney.

For good cause, the presiding judge may waive the limitations established in this subdivision.

(Subd (b) adopted effective July 1, 2006.)

(c) Waiver of disqualifications or limitations

(1) After a temporary judge who has determined himself or herself to be disqualified under the Code of Judicial Ethics or prohibited from serving under (b) has disclosed the basis for his or her disqualification or limitation on the record, the parties and their attorneys may agree to waive the disqualification or limitation and the temporary judge may accept the waiver. The temporary judge must not seek to induce a waiver and must avoid any effort to discover which attorneys or parties favored or opposed a waiver. The waiver must be in writing, must recite the basis for the disqualification or limitation, and must state that it was knowingly made. The waiver is effective only when signed by all parties and their attorneys and filed in the record.

(2) No waiver is permitted where the basis for the disqualification is any of the following:

(A) The temporary judge has a personal bias or prejudice concerning a party;

(B) The temporary judge has served as an attorney in the matter in controversy; or

(C) The temporary judge has been a material witness in the controversy.

(Subd (c) adopted effective July 1, 2006.)

(d) Late discovery of grounds for disqualification or limitation

In the event that grounds for disqualification or limitation are first learned of or arise after the temporary judge has made one or more rulings in a proceeding, but before the temporary judge has completed judicial action in the proceeding, the temporary judge, unless the disqualification or limitation is waived, must disqualify himself or herself. But in the absence of good cause, the rulings the temporary judge has made up to that time must not be set aside by the judicial officer or temporary judge who replaces the temporary judge.

(Subd (d) amended effective January 1, 2007; adopted effective July 1, 2006.)

(e) Notification of the court

Whenever a temporary judge determines himself or herself to be disqualified or limited from serving, the temporary judge must notify the presiding judge or the judge designated by the presiding judge of his or her withdrawal and must not further participate in the proceeding, unless his or her disqualification or limitation is waived by the parties as provided in (c).

(Subd (e) adopted effective July 1, 2006.)

(f) Requests for disqualifications

A party may request that a temporary judge withdraw on the ground that he or she is disqualified or limited from serving. If a temporary judge who should disqualify himself or herself or who is limited from serving in a case fails to withdraw, a party may apply to the presiding judge under rule 2.816(e) of the California Rules of Court for a withdrawal of the stipulation. The presiding judge or the judge designated by the presiding judge must determine whether good cause exists for granting withdrawal of the stipulation.

(Subd (f) amended effective January 1, 2007; previously adopted effective July 1, 2006.)

Rule 2.818 amended and renumbered effective January 1, 2007; adopted as rule 243.20 effective July 1, 2006; previously amended effective July 1, 2006.

Advisory Committee Comment

Subdivision (a) indicates that the rules concerning the disqualification of temporary judges are provided in the Code of Judicial Ethics. Subdivision (b) establishes additional limitations that prohibit attorneys from serving as court-appointed temporary judges under certain specified circumstances. Under subdivisions (c)–(e), the provisions of Code of Civil Procedure section 170.3 on waiver of

disqualifications, the effect of late discovery of the grounds of disqualification, and notification of disqualification of judicial officers are made applicable to temporary judges. Under subdivision (f), requests for disqualification are handled as withdrawals of the stipulation to a temporary judge and are ruled on by the presiding judge. This procedure is different from that for seeking the disqualification of a judge under Code of Civil Procedure section 170.3.

Rule 2.819.　Continuing duty to disclose and disqualify

A temporary judge has a continuing duty to make disclosures, to disqualify himself or herself, and to limit his or her service as provided under the Code of Judicial Ethics.

Rule 2.819 renumbered effective January 1, 2007; adopted as rule 243.21 effective July 1, 2006.

Chapter 2
Temporary Judges Requested by the Parties

Rule 2.830.　Temporary judges requested by the parties

(a) Application

Rules 2.830–2.834 apply to attorneys designated as temporary judges under article VI, section 21 of the California Constitution at the request of the parties rather than by prior appointment of the court, including privately compensated temporary judges and attorneys who serve as temporary judges pro bono at the request of the parties.

(Subd (a) amended effective January 1, 2007.)

(b) Definition

"Privately compensated" means that the temporary judge is paid by the parties.

(c) Limitation

These rules do not apply to subordinate judicial officers or to attorneys who are appointed by the court to serve as temporary judges for the court.

Rule 2.830 amended and renumbered effective January 1, 2007; adopted as rule 243.30 effective July 1, 2006.

Rule 2.831.　Temporary judge—stipulation, order, oath, assignment, disclosure, and disqualification

(a) Stipulation

When the parties request that an attorney be designated by the court to serve as a temporary judge on a case, the stipulation of the parties that a case may be tried by a temporary judge must be in writing and must state the name and office address of the member of the State Bar agreed on. The stipulation must be submitted for approval to the presiding judge or the judge designated by the presiding judge.

(Subd (a) amended effective July 1, 2006; previously amended and relettered effective July 1, 1993; previously amended effective January 1, 2001, and July 1, 2001.)

(b) Order, oath, and certification

The order designating the temporary judge must be signed by the presiding judge or the presiding judge's designee and refer to the stipulation. The stipulation and order must then be filed. The temporary judge must take and subscribe the oath of office and certify that he or she is aware of and will comply with applicable provisions of canon 6 of the Code of Judicial Ethics and the California Rules of Court.

(Subd (b) amended effective July 1, 2006; previously amended and relettered effective July 1, 1993; previously amended effective July 1, 2001.)

(c) When the temporary judge may proceed
The temporary judge may proceed with the hearing, trial, and determination of the cause after the stipulation, order, oath, and certification have been filed.

(Subd (c) amended and relettered effective July 1, 2006; formerly adopted as subd (b).)

(d) Disclosure to the parties

In addition to any other disclosure required by law, no later than five days after designation as a temporary judge or, if the temporary judge is not aware of his or her designation or of a matter subject to disclosure at that time, as soon as practicable thereafter, a temporary judge must disclose to the parties any matter subject to disclosure under the Code of Judicial Ethics.

(Subd (d) amended effective July 1, 2006; adopted as subd (c) effective July 1, 2001; previously amended and relettered effective July 1, 2006.)

(e) Disqualification

In addition to any other disqualification required by law, a temporary judge requested by the parties and designated by the court under this rule must disqualify himself or herself as provided under the Code of Judicial Ethics.

(Subd (e) amended and relettered effective July 1, 2006; adopted as subd (c) effective July 1, 1993; previously amended and relettered as subd (d) effective July 1, 2001.)

(f) Motion to withdraw stipulation

A motion to withdraw a stipulation for the appointment of a temporary judge must be supported by a declaration of facts establishing good cause for permitting the party to withdraw the stipulation, and must be heard by the presiding judge or a judge designated by the presiding judge. A declaration that a ruling is based on error of fact or law does not establish good cause for withdrawing a stipulation. Notice of the motion must be served and filed, and the moving party must provide a copy to the temporary judge. If the motion to withdraw the stipulation is based on grounds for the disqualification of the temporary judge first learned or arising after the temporary judge has made one or more rulings, but before the temporary judge has completed judicial action in the proceeding, the provisions of rule 2.816(e)(4) apply. If a motion to withdraw a stipulation is granted, the presiding judge must assign the case for hearing or trial as promptly as possible.

(Subd (f) amended effective January 1, 2016; adopted as subd (f) effective July 1, 1993; previously amended and relettered as subd (g) effective July 1, 2001, and as subd (f) effective July 1, 2006; previously amended effective January 1, 2007.) Rule 2.831 amended effective January 1, 2016; adopted as rule 244 effective January 1, 1999; previously amended effective April 1, 1962, July 1, 1981, July 1, 1987, July 1, 1993, July 1, 1995, January 1, 2001, and July 1, 2001; previously amended and renumbered as rule 243.31 effective July 1, 2006 and as rule 2.831 effective January 1, 2007.

Rule 2.832. Compensation

A temporary judge selected by the parties may not be compensated by the parties unless the parties agree in writing on a rate of compensation that they will pay.

Rule 2.832 renumbered effective January 1, 2007; adopted as rule 243.32 effective July 1, 2006.

Rule 2.833. Notices, use of court facilities, and order for hearing site [Renumbered]

Rule 2.833 amended and renumbered to rule 2.834 effective January 1, 2010; adopted as rule 243.33 effective July 1, 2006.

Another Rule 2.833 follows.

Rule 2.833. Documents and exhibits

All temporary judges requested by the parties and parties in proceedings before these temporary judges must comply with the applicable requirements of rule 2.400 concerning the filing and handling of documents and exhibits.

Rule 2.833 adopted effective January 1, 2010.

Rule 2.834. Motions or applications to be heard by the court [Renumbered]

Rule 2.834 amended and renumbered to rule 2.835 effective January 1, 2010; adopted as rule 243.34 effective July 1, 2006.

Another Rule 2.834 follows.

Rule 2.834. Open proceedings; notices of proceedings, use of court facilities, and order for hearing site

(a) Open proceedings

All proceedings before a temporary judge requested by the parties that would be open to the public if held before a judge must be open to the public, regardless of whether they are held in or outside a court facility.

(Subd (a) adopted effective January 1, 2010.)

(b) Notice regarding proceedings before temporary judge requested by the parties

(1) In each case in which he or she is appointed, a temporary judge requested by the parties must file a statement that provides the name, telephone number, and mailing address of a person who may be contacted to obtain information about the date, time, location, and general nature of all hearings and other proceedings scheduled in the matter that would be open to the public if held before a judge. This statement must be filed at the same time as the temporary judge's certification under rule 2.831(b). If there is any change in this contact information, the temporary judge must promptly file a revised statement with the court.

(2) In addition to providing the information required under (1), the statement filed by a temporary judge may also provide the address of a publicly accessible Web site at which the temporary judge will maintain a current calendar setting forth the date, time, location, and general nature of any hearings scheduled in the matter that would be open to the public if held before a judge.

(3) The clerk must post the information from the statement filed by the temporary judge in the court facility.

(Subd (b) amended and relettered effective January 1, 2010; adopted as subd (a) effective July 1, 2006.)

(c) Use of court facilities, court personnel, and summoned jurors

A party who has elected to use the services of a temporary judge requested by the parties is deemed to have elected to proceed outside court facilities. Court facilities, court personnel, and summoned jurors may not be used in proceedings pending before a temporary judge requested by the parties except on a finding by the presiding judge or his or her designee that their use would further the interests of justice.

(Subd (c) amended and relettered effective January 1, 2010; adopted as subd (b) effective July 1, 2006.)

(d) Appropriate hearing site

(1) The presiding judge or his or her designee, on application of any person or on the judge's own motion, may order that a case before a temporary judge requested by the parties must be heard at a site easily accessible to the public and appropriate for seating those who have made known their plan to attend hearings. The application must state facts showing good cause for granting the application, and must be served on all parties and the temporary judge and filed with the court. The proceedings are not stayed while the application is pending unless the presiding judge or his or her designee orders that they be stayed. The issuance of an order for an accessible and appropriate hearing site is not a ground for withdrawal of a stipulation that a case may be heard by a temporary judge.

(2) If a court staff mediator or evaluator is required to attend a hearing before a temporary judge requested by the parties, unless otherwise ordered by the presiding judge or his or her designee, that hearing must take place at a location requiring no more than 15 minutes' travel time from the mediator's or evaluator's work site.

(Subd (d) amended and relettered effective January 1, 2010; adopted as subd (c) effective July 1, 2006.)

Rule 2.834 amended and renumbered effective January 1, 2010; adopted as rule 243.33 effective July 1, 2006; previously renumbered as rule 2.833 effective January 1, 2007.

Rule 2.835. Motions or applications to be heard by the court

(a) Motion or application to seal records

A motion or application to seal records in a case pending before a temporary judge requested by the parties must be filed with the court and must be served on all parties that have appeared in the case and the temporary judge. The motion or application must be heard by the trial court judge to whom the case is assigned or, if the case has not been assigned, by the presiding judge or his or her designee. Rules 2.550–2.551 on sealed records apply to motions or applications filed under this rule.

(Subd (a) amended effective January 1, 2010; previously amended effective January 1, 2007.)

(b) Motion for leave to file complaint for intervention

A motion for leave to file a complaint for intervention in a case pending before a temporary judge requested by the parties must be filed with the court and served on all parties and the temporary judge. The motion must be heard by the trial court judge to whom the case is assigned or, if the case has not been assigned, by the presiding judge or his or her designee. If intervention is allowed, the case must be returned to the trial court docket unless all parties stipulate in the manner prescribed in rule 2.831(a) to proceed before the temporary judge.

(Subd (b) amended effective January 1, 2010; previously amended effective January 1, 2007.)

Rule 2.835 amended and renumbered effective January 1, 2010; adopted as rule 243.34 effective July 1, 2006; previously amended and renumbered as rule 2.834 effective January 1, 2007.

Chapter 3
Referees
[Reserved]

Chapter 4
Language Access

Title 2, Trial Court Rules—Chapter 4, Language Access; adopted effective January 1, 2018.

Art. 1.   General Provisions. Rules 2.850, 2.851.
Art. 2.   Court Interpreters. Rules 2.890–2.895.

Article 1
General Provisions

Title 2, Trial Court Rules—Chapter 4, Language Access; Article 1, General Provisions; adopted effective January 1, 2018.

Rule 2.850. Language Access Representative
Rule 2.851. Language access services complaints

Rule 2.850.   Language Access Representative

(a) Designation of Language Access Representative

The court in each county will designate a Language Access Representative. That function can be assigned to a specific job classification or office within the court.

(Subd (a) adopted effective January 1, 2018.)

(b) Duties

The Language Access Representative will serve as the court's language access resource for all court users, as well as court staff and judicial officers, and should be familiar with all the language access services the court provides; access and disseminate all of the court's multilingual written information as requested; and help limited English proficient (LEP) court users and court staff locate language access resources.

(Subd (b) adopted effective January 1, 2018.)

Rule 2.850 adopted effective January 1, 2018.

Advisory Committee Comment

Subdivision (a). See Recommendation No. 25 of the *Strategic Plan for Language Access in the California Courts*, adopted by the Judicial Council on January 22, 2015.

Rule 2.851.   Language access services complaints

(a) Purpose

The purpose of this rule is to ensure that each superior court makes available a form on which court users may submit a complaint about the provision of, or the failure to provide, language access and that each court has procedures for handling those complaints. Courts must implement this rule as soon as reasonably possible but no later than December 31, 2018.

(Subd (a) adopted effective January 1, 2018.)

(b) Complaint form and procedures required

Each superior court must adopt a language access services complaint form and complaint procedures that are consistent with this rule.

(Subd (b) adopted effective January 1, 2018.)

(c) Minimum requirement for complaint form

The language access services complaint form adopted by the court must meet the following minimum requirements:

(1) Be written in plain language;

(2) Allow court users to submit complaints about how the court provided or failed to provide language services;

(3) Allow court users to specify whether the complaint relates to court interpreters, other staff, or local translations;

(4) Include the court's mailing address and an e-mail contact to show court users how they may submit a language access complaint;

(5) Be made available for free both in hard copy at the courthouse and online on the courts' website, where court users can complete the form online and then submit to the court by hand, postal mail, or e-mail; and

(6) Be made available in the languages spoken by significant portions of the county population.

(Subd (c) adopted effective January 1, 2018.)

(d) General requirements for complaint procedures

The complaint procedures adopted by the court must provide for the following:

(1) *Submission and referral of local language access complaints*

(A) Language access complaints may be submitted anonymously.

(B) Language access complaints may be submitted orally or in other written formats; however, use of the court's local form is encouraged to ensure tracking and that complainants provide full information to the court.

(C) Language access complaints regarding local court services should be submitted to the court's designated Language Access Representative.

(D) A complaint submitted to the improper entity must immediately be forwarded to the appropriate court, if that can be determined, or, where appropriate, to the Judicial Council.

(2) *Acknowledgment of complaint*

Except where the complaint is submitted anonymously, within 30 days after the complaint is received, the court's Language Access Representative must send the complainant a written acknowledgment that the court has received the complaint.

(3) *Preliminary review and disposition of complaints*

Within 60 days after receipt of the complaint, the court's Language Access Representative should conduct a preliminary review of every complaint to determine whether the complaint can be informally resolved or closed, or whether the complaint warrants additional investigation. Court user complaints regarding denial of a court interpreter for a courtroom proceeding for pending cases should be given priority.

(4) *Procedure for complaints not resolved through the preliminary review*

If a complaint cannot be resolved through the preliminary review process within 60 days after receipt of the complaint, the court's Language Access Representative should inform the complainant (if identified) that the complaint warrants additional review.

(5) *Notice of outcome*

Except where the complaint is submitted anonymously, the court must send the complainant notice of the outcome taken on the complaint.

(6) *Promptness*

The court must process complaints promptly.

(7) *Records of complaints*

The court should maintain information about each complaint and its disposition. The court must report to the Judicial Council on an annual basis the number and kinds of complaints received, the resolution status of all complaints, and any additional information about complaints requested by Judicial Council staff to facilitate the monitoring of the *Strategic Plan for Language Access in the California Courts*.

(8) *Disagreement (Disputing) Notice of Outcome*

If a complainant disagrees with the notice of the outcome taken on his or her complaint, within 90 days of the date the court sends the notice of outcome, he or she may submit a written follow-up statement to the Language Access Representative indicating that he or she disagrees with the outcome of the complaint. The follow-up statement should be brief, specify the basis of the disagreement, and describe the reasons the complainant believes the court's action lacks merit. For example, the follow-up statement should indicate why the complainant disagrees with the notice of outcome or believes that he or she did not receive an adequate explanation in the notice of outcome. The court's response to any follow-up statement submitted by complainant after receipt of the notice of outcome will be the final action taken by the court on the complaint.

(Subd (d) adopted effective January 1, 2018.)

Rule 2.851 adopted effective January 1, 2018.

Advisory Committee Comment

Subdivision (a). Judicial Council staff have developed a model complaint form and model local complaint procedures, which are available in the Language Access Toolkit at *www.courts.ca.gov/33865.htm*. The model complaint form is posted in numerous languages. Courts are encouraged to base their complaint form and procedures on these models. If a complaint alleges action against a court employee that could lead to discipline, the court will process the complaint consistent with the court's applicable Memoranda of Understanding, personnel policies, and/or rules.

Subdivision (d)(1). Court user complaints regarding language access that relate to Judicial Council meetings, forms, or other translated material hosted on *www.courts.ca.gov*, should be submitted directly to the Judicial Council at *www.courts.ca.gov/languageaccess.htm*.

Subdivision (d)(2) and (d)(5). For noncomplicated language access-related complaints that can be resolved quickly, a written response to the complainant indicating that the complaint has been resolved will suffice as both acknowledgement of the complaint and notice of outcome.

Subdivision (d)(5). When appropriate, a written response to the complainant indicating that the language access complaint has been resolved will suffice as notice of outcome. Courts should maintain the privacy of individuals named in the complaint.

Subdivision (d)(7). Reporting to the Judicial Council regarding the overall numbers, kinds, and disposition of language access-related complaints will not include the names of individuals or any other information that may compromise an individual's privacy concerns.

Article 2
Court Interpreters

Title 2, Trial Court Rules—Chapter 4, Language Access; Article 2, Court

Interpreters; renumbered from Chapter 4 effective March 5, 2018; adopted effective January 1, 2018.

Rule 2.890. Professional conduct for interpreters
Rule 2.891. Request for court interpreter credential review
Rule 2.892. Guidelines for approval of certification programs for interpreters for deaf and hard-of-hearing persons
Rule 2.893. Appointment of interpreters in court proceedings
Rule 2.894. Reports on appointments of certified and registered interpreters and noncertified and nonregistered interpreters
Rule 2.895. Requests for interpreters

Rule 2.890. Professional conduct for interpreters

(a) Representation of qualifications

An interpreter must accurately and completely represent his or her certifications, training, and relevant experience.

(Subd (a) amended effective January 1, 2007.)

(b) Complete and accurate interpretation

An interpreter must use his or her best skills and judgment to interpret accurately without embellishing, omitting, or editing. When interpreting for a party, the interpreter must interpret everything that is said during the entire proceedings. When interpreting for a witness, the interpreter must interpret everything that is said during the witness's testimony.

(Subd (b) amended effective January 1, 2007.)

(c) Impartiality and avoidance of conflicts of interest

(1) *Impartiality*

An interpreter must be impartial and unbiased and must refrain from conduct that may give an appearance of bias.

(2) *Disclosure of conflicts*

An interpreter must disclose to the judge and to all parties any actual or apparent conflict of interest. Any condition that interferes with the objectivity of an interpreter is a conflict of interest. A conflict may exist if the interpreter is acquainted with or related to any witness or party to the action or if the interpreter has an interest in the outcome of the case.

(3) *Conduct*

An interpreter must not engage in conduct creating the appearance of bias, prejudice, or partiality.

(4) *Statements*

An interpreter must not make statements to any person about the merits of the case until the litigation has concluded.

(Subd (c) amended effective January 1, 2007.)

(d) Confidentiality of privileged communications

An interpreter must not disclose privileged communications between counsel and client to any person.

(Subd (d) amended effective January 1, 2007.)

(e) Giving legal advice

An interpreter must not give legal advice to parties and witnesses, nor recommend specific attorneys or law firms.

(Subd (e) amended effective January 1, 2007.)

(f) Impartial professional relationships

An interpreter must maintain an impartial, professional relationship with all court officers, attorneys, jurors, parties, and witnesses.

(Subd (f) amended effective January 1, 2007.)

(g) Continuing education and duty to the profession

An interpreter must, through continuing education, maintain and improve his or her interpreting skills and knowledge of procedures used by the courts. An interpreter should seek to elevate the standards of performance of the interpreting profession.

(Subd (g) amended effective January 1, 2007.)

(h) Assessing and reporting impediments to performance

An interpreter must assess at all times his or her ability to perform interpreting services. If an interpreter has any reservation about his or her ability to satisfy an assignment competently, the interpreter must immediately disclose that reservation to the court or other appropriate authority.

(Subd (h) amended effective January 1, 2007.)

(i) Duty to report ethical violations

An interpreter must report to the court or other appropriate authority any effort to impede the interpreter's compliance with the law, this rule, or any other official policy governing court interpreting and legal translating.

(Subd (i) amended effective January 1, 2007.)

Rule 2.890 amended and renumbered effective January 1, 2007; adopted as rule 984.4 effective January 1, 1999.

Rule 2.891. Periodic review of court interpreter skills and professional conduct [Repealed]

Rule 2.891 repealed effective January 1, 2020; adopted as rule 984 effective July 1, 1979; previously amended effective January 1, 1996; previously amended and renumbered effective January 1, 2007.

Another Rule 2.891 follows.

Rule 2.891. Request for court interpreter credential review

Certified and registered court interpreters are credentialed by the Judicial Council under Government Code section 68562. The council, as the credentialing body, has authority to review a credentialed interpreter's performance, skills, and adherence to the professional conduct requirements of rule 2.890, and to impose discipline on interpreters.

(a) Purpose

This rule clarifies the council's authority to adopt disciplinary procedures and to conduct a credential review, as set out in the *California Court Interpreter Credential Review Procedures*.

(Subd (a) adopted effective January 1, 2020.)

(b) Application

Under the *California Court Interpreter Credential Review Procedures*, all court interpreters certified or registered by the council may be subject to a credential review process after a request for a credential review alleging professional misconduct or malfeasance. Nothing in this rule prevents an individual California court from conducting its own review of, and disciplinary process for, interpreter employees under the court's collective bargaining agreements, personnel policies, rules, and procedures, or, for interpreter contractors, under the court's contracting and general administrative policies and procedures.

(Subd (b) adopted effective January 1, 2020.)

(c) Procedure

(1) On a request made to the council by any person, court, or other entity for the review of an interpreter's credential for alleged professional misconduct or malfeasance by an interpreter credentialed by the council, the council will respond in accordance with procedures stated in the *California Court Interpreter Credential Review Procedures*.

(2) On a request by the council in relation to allegations under investigation under the *California Court Interpreter Credential Review Procedures*, a California court is required to forward information to the council regarding a complaint or allegation of professional misconduct by a certified or registered court interpreter.

(Subd (c) adopted effective January 1, 2020.)

(d) Disciplinary action imposed

The appropriateness of disciplinary action and the degree of discipline to be imposed must depend on factors such as the seriousness of the violation, the intent of the interpreter, whether there is a pattern of improper activity, and the effect of the improper activity on others or on the judicial system.

(Subd (d) adopted effective January 1, 2020.)
Rule 2.891 adopted effective January 1, 2020.

Rule 2.892. Guidelines for approval of certification programs for interpreters for deaf and hard-of-hearing persons

Each organization, agency, or educational institution that administers tests for certification of court interpreters for deaf and hard-of-hearing persons under Evidence Code section 754 must comply with the guidelines adopted by the Judicial Council effective February 21, 1992, and any subsequent revisions, and must hold a valid, current approval by the Judicial Council to administer the tests as a certifying organization. The guidelines are stated in the *Judicial Council Guidelines for Approval of Certification Programs for Interpreters for Deaf and Hard-of-Hearing Persons,* published by the Judicial Council.

Rule 2.892 amended effective January 1, 2016; adopted as rule 984.1 effective January 1, 1994; previously amended and renumbered as rule 2.892 effective January 1, 2007.

Rule 2.893. Appointment of noncertified interpreters in criminal cases and juvenile delinquency proceedings [Repealed]

Rule 2.893 repealed effective January 1, 2018; adopted as rule 984.2 effective January 1, 1996; previously amended and renumbered effective January 1, 2007; previously amended effective January 1, 2007.

Another Rule 2.893 follows.

Rule 2.893. Appointment of interpreters in court proceedings

(a) Application

This rule applies to all trial court proceedings in which the court appoints an interpreter for a Limited English Proficient (LEP) person. This rule applies to spoken language interpreters in languages designated and not designated by the Judicial Council.

(Subd (a) adopted effective January 1, 2018.)

(b) Definitions

As used in this rule:

(1) "Designated language" means a language selected by the Judicial Council for the development of a certification program under Government Code section 68562;

(2) "Certified interpreter" means an interpreter who is certified by the Judicial Council to interpret a language designated by the Judicial Council under Government Code section 68560 et seq.;

(3) "Registered interpreter" means an interpreter in a language not designated by the Judicial Council, who is qualified by the court under the qualification procedures and guidelines adopted by the Judicial Council, and who has passed a minimum of an English fluency examination offered by a testing entity approved by the Judicial Council under Government Code section 68560 et seq.;

(4) "Noncertified interpreter" means an interpreter who is not certified by the Judicial Council to interpret a language designated by the Judicial Council under Government Code section 68560 et seq.;

(5) "Nonregistered interpreter" means an interpreter in a language not designated by the Judicial Council who has not been qualified under the qualification procedures and guidelines adopted by the Judicial Council under Government Code section 68560 et seq.;

(6) "Provisionally qualified" means an interpreter who is neither certified nor registered but has been qualified under the good cause and qualification procedures and guidelines adopted by the Judicial Council under Government Code section 68560 et seq.;

(7) "Temporary interpreter" means an interpreter who is not certified, registered, or provisionally qualified, but is used one time, in a brief, routine matter.

(Subd (b) adopted effective January 1, 2018.)

(c) Appointment of certified or registered interpreters

If a court appoints a certified or registered court interpreter, the judge in the proceeding must require the following to be stated on the record:

(1) The language to be interpreted;

(2) The name of the interpreter;

(3) The interpreter's current certification or registration number;

(4) A statement that the interpreter's identification has been verified as required by statute;

(5) A statement that the interpreter is certified or registered to interpret in the language to be interpreted; and

(6) A statement that the interpreter was administered the interpreter's oath or that he or she has an oath on file with the court.

(Subd (c) adopted effective January 1, 2018.)

(d) Appointment or use of noncertified or nonregistered interpreters

(1) *When permissible*

If after a diligent search a certified or registered interpreter is not available, the judge in the proceeding may either appoint a noncertified or nonregistered interpreter who has been provisionally qualified under (d)(3) or, in the limited circumstances specified in (d)(4), may use a noncertified or nonregistered interpreter who is not provisionally qualified.

(2) *Required record*

In all cases in which a noncertified or nonregistered interpreter is appointed or used, the judge in the proceeding must require the following to be stated on the record:

(A) The language to be interpreted;

(B) A finding that a certified or registered interpreter is not available and a statement regarding whether a *Certification of Unavailability of Certified or Registered Interpreter* (form INT-120) for the language to be interpreted is on file for this date with the court administrator;

(C) A finding that good cause exists to appoint a noncertified or nonregistered interpreter;

(D) The name of the interpreter;

(E) A statement that the interpreter is not certified or registered to interpret in the language to be interpreted;

(F) A finding that the interpreter is qualified to interpret in the proceeding as required in (d)(3) or (d)(4); and

(G) A statement that the interpreter was administered the interpreter's oath.

(3) *Provisional qualification*

(A) A noncertified or nonregistered interpreter is provisionally qualified if the presiding judge of the court or other judicial officer designated by the presiding judge:

(i) Finds the noncertified or nonregistered interpreter to be provisionally qualified following the *Procedures to Appoint a Noncertified or Nonregistered Spoken Language Interpreter as Either Provisionally Qualified or Temporary* (form INT-100-INFO); and

(ii) Signs an order allowing the interpreter to be considered for appointment on *Qualifications of a Noncertified or Nonregistered Spoken Language Interpreter* (form INT-110). The period covered by this order may not exceed a maximum of six months.

(B) To appoint a provisionally qualified interpreter, in addition to the matters that must be stated on the record under (d)(2), the judge in the proceeding must state on the record:

(i) A finding that the interpreter is qualified to interpret the proceeding, following procedures adopted by the Judicial Council (see forms INT-100-INFO, INT-110, and INT-120);

(ii) A finding, if applicable, that good cause exists under (f)(1)(B) for the court to appoint the interpreter beyond the time ordinarily allowed in (f); and

(iii) If a party has objected to the appointment of the proposed interpreter or has waived the appointment of a certified or registered interpreter.

(4) *Temporary use*

At the request of an LEP person, a temporary interpreter may be used to prevent burdensome delay or in other unusual circumstances if:

(A) The judge in the proceeding finds on the record that:

(i) The LEP person has been informed of their right to an interpreter and has waived the appointment of a certified or registered interpreter or an interpreter who could be provisionally qualified by the presiding judge as provided in 15 (d)(3);

(ii) Good cause exists to appoint an interpreter who is not certified, registered, or provisionally qualified; and

(iii) The interpreter is qualified to interpret that proceeding, following procedures adopted by the Judicial Council (see forms INT-100-INFO and INT-140).

(B) The use of an interpreter under this subdivision is limited to a single brief, routine matter before the court. The use of the interpreter in this circumstance may not be extended to subsequent proceedings without again following the procedure set forth in this subdivision.

(Subd (d) adopted effective January 1, 2018.)

(e) Appointment of intermediary interpreters working between two languages that do not include English

An interpreter who works as an intermediary between two languages that do not include English (a relay interpreter) is not eligible to become certified or registered. However, a relay interpreter can become provisionally qualified if the judge finds that he or she is qualified to interpret the proceeding following procedures adopted by the Judicial Council (see forms INT-100-INFO, INT-110, and INT-120). The limitations in (f) below do not apply to relay interpreters.

(Subd (e) adopted effective January 1, 2018.)

(f) Limit on appointment of provisionally qualified noncertified and nonregistered interpreters

(1) A noncertified or nonregistered interpreter who is provisionally qualified under (d)(3) may not interpret in any trial court for more than any four six-month periods, except in the following circumstances:

(A) A noncertified interpreter of Spanish may be allowed to interpret for no more than any two six-month periods in counties with a population greater than 80,000.

(B) A noncertified or nonregistered interpreter may be allowed to interpret more than any four six-month periods, or any two six-month periods for an interpreter of Spanish under (f)(1)(A), if the judge in the proceeding makes a specific finding on the record in each case in which the interpreter is sworn that good cause exists to appoint the interpreter, notwithstanding the interpreter's failure to achieve Judicial Council certification.

(2) Except as provided in (f)(3), each six-month period under (f)(1) begins on the date a presiding judge signs an order under (d)(3)(A)(ii) allowing the noncertified or nonregistered interpreter to be considered for appointment.

(3) If an interpreter is provisionally qualified under (d)(3) in more than one court at the same time, each six-month period runs concurrently for purposes of determining the maximum periods allowed in this subdivision.

(4) Beginning with the second six-month period under (f)(1), a noncertified or nonregistered interpreter may be appointed if he or she meets all of the following conditions:

(A) The interpreter has taken the State of California Court Interpreter Written Exam at least once during the 12 calendar months before the appointment;

(B) The interpreter has taken the State of California's court interpreter ethics course for interpreters seeking appointment as a noncertified or nonregistered interpreter, or is certified or registered in a different language from the one in which he or she is being appointed; and

(C) The interpreter has taken the State of California's online court interpreter orientation course, or is certified or registered in a different language from the one in which he or she is being appointed.

(5) Beginning with the third six-month period under (f)(1), a noncertified or nonregistered interpreter may be appointed if he or she meets all of the following conditions:

(A) The interpreter has taken and passed the State of California Court Interpreter Written Exam with such timing that he or she is eligible to take a Bilingual Interpreting Exam; and

(B) The interpreter has taken either the Bilingual Interpreting Exam or the relevant Oral Proficiency Exam(s) for his or her language pairing at least once during the 12 calendar months before the appointment.

(6) The restrictions in (f)(5)(B) do not apply to any interpreter who seeks appointment in a language pairing for which no exam is available.

(7) The restrictions in (f)(4) and (5) may be waived by the presiding judge for good cause whenever there are fewer than 25 certified or registered interpreters enrolled on the Judicial Council's statewide roster for the language requiring interpretation.

(Subd (f) adopted effective January 1, 2018.)
Rule 2.893 adopted effective January 1, 2018.

Advisory Committee Comment

Subdivisions (c) and (d)(2). When a court reporter is transcribing the proceedings, or an electronic recording is being made of the proceedings, a judge may satisfy the "on the record" requirement by stating the required details of the interpreter appointment in open court. If there is no court reporter and no electronic recording is being made, the "on the record" requirement may be satisfied by stating the required details of the interpreter appointment and documenting them in writing—such as in a minute order, the official clerk's minutes, a formal order, or even a handwritten document—that is entered in the case file.

Subdivision (d)(4). This provision is intended to allow for the one-time use of a noncertified or nonregistered interpreter who is not provisionally qualified to interpret for an LEP person in a courtroom event. This provision is not intended to be used to meet the extended or ongoing interpretation needs of LEP court users.

Subdivision (b)(7) and (d)(4). When determining whether the matter before the court is a "brief, routine matter" for which a noncertified or nonregistered interpreter who has not been provisionally qualified may be used, the judicial officer should consider the complexity of the matter at issue and likelihood of potential impacts on the LEP person's substantive rights, keeping in mind the consequences that could flow from inaccurate or incomplete interpretation of the proceedings.

Rule 2.894.   Reports on appointments of certified and registered interpreters and noncertified and nonregistered interpreters

Each superior court must report to the Judicial Council on:

(1) The appointment of certified and registered interpreters under Government Code section 71802, as required by the Judicial Council; and

(2) The appointment of noncertified interpreters of languages designated under Government Code section 68562(a), and registered and nonregistered interpreters of nondesignated languages.

Rule 2.894 amended effective January 1, 2016; adopted as rule 984.3 effective January 1, 1996; previously amended effective March 1, 2003; previously amended and renumbered as rule 2.894 effective January 1, 2007.

Rule 2.895.   Requests for interpreters

(a) Publish procedures

Each court must publish procedures for filing, processing, and responding to requests for interpreters consistent with the *Strategic Plan for Language Access in the California Courts* (adopted January 2015). Each court must publish notice of these procedures in English and up to five other languages, based on local community needs.

(Subd (a) adopted effective July 1, 2016.)

(b) Track requests

Each court must track all requests for language services and whether such services were provided. Tracking must include all requests for court interpreters in civil actions, as well as approvals and denials of such requests.

(Subd (b) adopted effective July 1, 2016.)

(c) Notify court if represented party will not be appearing

If a party who has requested an interpreter for herself or himself is represented by counsel, the attorney must notify the court in advance whenever the party will not be appearing at a noticed proceeding.

(Subd (c) adopted effective July 1, 2016.)
Rule 2.895 adopted effective July 1, 2016.

Advisory Committee Comment

The *Request for Interpreter (Civil)* (form INT-300) is concurrently adopted as a model form that will become an optional form, effective January 1, 2018. Until that time, the form can serve as a model that courts may use as part of their procedures, as required under this rule.

This rule shall not be construed in a way that conflicts with Evidence Code section 756.

Subdivision (a). "Local community needs" is described in recommendation 5 of the *Strategic Plan for Language Access in the California Courts* (adopted January 2015).

Subdivision (b). The committee recommends electronic processing of civil interpreter requests to aid the court in data collection about the provision or denial of language services.

Division 7
Proceedings

Chap. 1.   General Provisions. Rule 2.900.
Chap. 2.   Records of Proceedings. Rules 2.950–2.958.

Chapter 1
General Provisions

Rule 2.900.   Submission of a cause in a trial court

(a) Submission

A cause is deemed submitted in a trial court when either of the following first occurs:

(1) The date the court orders the matter submitted; or

(2) The date the final paper is required to be filed or the date argument is heard, whichever is later.

(Subd (a) amended effective January 1, 2007.)

(b) Vacating submission

The court may vacate submission only by issuing an order served on the parties stating reasons constituting good cause and providing for resubmission.

(c) Pendency of a submitted cause

A submitted cause is pending and undetermined unless the court has announced its tentative decision or the cause is terminated. The time required to finalize a tentative decision is not time in which the cause is pending and undetermined. For purposes of this rule only, a motion that has the effect of vacating, reconsidering, or rehearing the cause will be considered a separate and new cause and will be deemed submitted as provided in (a).

(Subd (c) amended effective January 1, 2007.)
Rule 2.900 amended and renumbered effective January 1, 2007; adopted as rule 825 effective January 1, 1989.

Chapter 2
Records of Proceedings

Rule 2.950. Sequential list of reporters
Rule 2.952. Electronic recording as official record of proceedings
Rule 2.954. Specifications for electronic recording equipment
Rule 2.956. Court reporting services in civil cases
Rule 2.958. Assessing fee for official reporter

Rule 2.950.   Sequential list of reporters

During any reported court proceeding, the clerk must keep a sequential list of all reporters working on the case, indicating the date the reporter worked and the reporter's name, business address, and Certified Short-hand Reporter license number. If more than one reporter reports a case during one day, the information pertaining to each reporter must be listed with the first reporter designated "A," the second designated "B," etc. If reporter "A" returns during the same day, that reporter will be designated as both reporter "A" and reporter "C" on the list. The list of reporters may be kept in an electronic database maintained by the clerk; however, a hard copy must be available to members of the public within one working day of a request for the list of reporters.

Rule 2.950 amended and renumbered effective January 1, 2007; adopted as rule 980.4 effective July 1, 1991.

Rule 2.952.   Electronic recording as official record of proceedings

(a) Application

This rule applies when a court has ordered proceedings to be electronically recorded on a device of a type approved by the Judicial Council or conforming to specifications adopted by the Judicial Council.

(Subd (a) amended effective January 1, 2007; previously amended effective January 1, 1990.)

(b) Definitions

As used in this rule, the following definitions apply:

(1) "Reel" means an individual reel or cassette of magnetic recording tape or a comparable unit of the medium on which an electronic recording is made.

(2) "Monitor" means any person designated by the court to operate electronic recording equipment and to make appropriate notations to identify the proceedings recorded on each reel, including the date and time of the recording. The trial judge, a courtroom clerk, or a bailiff may be the monitor, but when recording is of sound only, a separate monitor without other substantial duties is recommended.

(Subd (b) amended effective January 1, 2007; previously amended effective January 1, 1990.)

(c) Reel numbers

Each reel must be distinctively marked with the date recorded, the department number of the court, if any, and, if possible, a serial number.

(Subd (c) amended effective January 1, 2007; previously amended effective January 1, 1990.)

(d) Certificate of monitor

As soon as practicable after the close of each day's court proceedings, the monitor must execute a certificate for each reel recorded during the day, stating:

(1) That the person executing the certificate was designated by the court as monitor;

(2) The number or other identification assigned to the reel;

(3) The date of the proceedings recorded on that reel;

(4) The titles and numbers of actions and proceedings, or portions thereof, recorded on the reel, and the general nature of the proceedings; and

(5) That the recording equipment was functioning normally, and that all of the proceedings in open court between designated times of day were recorded, except for such matters as were expressly directed to be "off the record" or as otherwise specified.

(Subd (d) amended effective January 1, 2007; previously amended effective January 1, 1990.)

(e) Two or more monitors

If two or more persons acted as monitors during the recording of a single reel, each monitor must execute a certificate as to the portion of the reel that he or she monitored. The certificate of a person other than a judge, clerk, or deputy clerk of the court must be in the form of an affidavit or declaration under penalty of perjury.

(Subd (e) lettered effective January 1, 2007; adopted as part of subd (d) effective January 1, 1976.)

(f) Storage

The monitor's certificate, the recorded reel, and the monitor's notes must be retained and safely stored by the clerk in a manner that will permit their convenient retrieval and use.

(Subd (f) amended and relettered effective January 1, 2007; adopted as subd (e) effective January 1, 1976.)

(g) Transcripts

(1) Written transcripts of electronic recordings may be made by or under the direction of the clerk or a person designated by the court. The person making the transcript must execute a declaration under penalty of perjury that:

(A) Identifies the reel or reels transcribed, or the portions thereof, by reference to the numbers assigned thereto and, where only portions of a reel are transcribed, by reference to index numbers or other means of identifying the portion transcribed; and

(B) States that the transcript is a full, true, and correct transcript of the identified reel or reels or the designated portions thereof.

(2) The transcript must conform, as nearly as possible, to the requirements for a reporter's transcript as provided for in these rules.

(Subd (g) amended and relettered effective January 1, 2007; adopted as subd (f) effective January 1, 1976.)

(h) Use of transcripts

A transcript prepared and certified under (g), and accompanied by a certified copy of the monitor's certificate pertaining to each reel transcribed, is prima facie a true and complete record of the oral proceedings

it purports to cover, and satisfies any requirement in the California Rules of Court or in any statute for a reporter's transcript of oral proceedings.

(Subd (h) amended and relettered effective January 1, 2007; adopted as subd (g) effective January 1, 1976.)

(i) Original reels

A reviewing court may order the transmittal to it of the original reels containing electronic recordings of proceedings being reviewed by it, or electronic copies of them.

(Subd (i) relettered effective January 1, 2007; adopted as subd (h) effective January 1, 1976; previously amended effective January 1, 1990.)

(j) Record on appeal

(1) *Stipulation and approval of record without transcription*

On stipulation of the parties approved by the reviewing court, the original reels or electronic copies of them may be transmitted as the record of oral proceedings without being transcribed, in which case the reels or copies satisfy the requirements in the California Rules of Court or in any statute for a reporter's transcript.

(2) *Request for preparation of transcript*

In the absence of a stipulation and approval under (1), the appellant must, within 10 days after filing a notice of appeal in a civil case, serve and file with the clerk directions indicating the portions of the oral proceedings to be transcribed and must, at the same time, deposit with the clerk the approximate cost computed as specified in rule 8.130. Other steps necessary to complete preparation of the record on appeal must be taken following, as nearly as possible, the procedures in rules 8.120 and 8.130.

(3) *Preparation of transcript*

On receiving directions to have a transcript prepared, the clerk may have the material transcribed by a court employee, but should ordinarily send the reels in question to a professional recording service that has been certified by the federal court system or the Judicial Council or verified by the clerk to be skilled in producing transcripts.

(Subd (j) amended effective January 1, 2016; adopted as subd (i) effective January 1, 1990; previously amended effective January 1, 1993; previously amended and relettered as subd (j) effective January 1, 2007.)

Rule 2.952 amended effective January 1, 2016; adopted as rule 980.5 effective January 1, 1976; previously amended effective January 1, 1990, and January 1, 1993; previously amended and renumbered as rule 2.952 effective January 1, 2007.

Rule 2.954. Specifications for electronic recording equipment

(a) Specifications mandated

Electronic recording equipment used in making the official verbatim record of oral courtroom proceedings must conform to the specifications in this rule.

(Subd (a) amended effective January 1, 2007.)

(b) Sound recording only

The following specifications for electronic recording devices and appurtenant equipment apply when only sound is to be recorded:

(1) *Mandatory specifications*

(A) The device must be capable of simultaneously recording at least four separate channels or "tracks," each of which has a separate playback control so that any one channel separately or any combination of channels may be played back.

(B) The device must not have an operative erase head.

(C) The device must have a digital counter or comparable means of logging and locating the place on a reel where specific proceedings were recorded.

(D) Earphones must be provided for monitoring the recorded signal.

(E) The signal going to the earphones must come from a separate playback head, so that the monitor will hear what has actually been recorded on the tape.

(F) The device must be capable of recording at least two hours without interruption. This requirement may be satisfied by a device that automatically switches from one recording deck to another at the completion of a reel of tape of less than two hours in duration.

(G) A separate visual indicator of signal level must be provided for each recording channel.

(H) The appurtenant equipment must include at least four microphones, which should include one at the witness stand, one at the bench, and one at each counsel table. In the absence of unusual circumstances, all microphones must be directional (cardioid).

(I) A loudspeaker must be provided for courtroom playback.

(2) *Recommended features*

The following features are recommended, but not required:

(A) The recording level control should be automatic rather than manual.

(B) The device should be equipped to prevent recording over a previously recorded segment of tape.

(C) The device should give a warning signal at the end of a reel of tape.

(Subd (b) amended effective January 1, 2007.)

(c) Audio-and-video recording

The following specifications for electronic audio-video recording devices and appurtenant equipment apply when audio and video are to be recorded simultaneously.

(1) *Mandatory specifications*

The system must include:

(A) At least five charge-coupled-device color video cameras in fixed mounts, equipped with lenses appropriate to the courtroom. Cameras must conform to EIA standard, accept C-mount lenses, have 2000 lux sensitivity at f4.0 at 3200 degrees Kelvin so as to produce an adequate picture with 30 lux minimum illumination and an f1.4 lens, and be approximately 2.6″ × 2.4″ × 8.0.″

(B) At least eight phase-coherent cardioid (directional) microphones, Crown PCC-160 or equivalent, appropriately placed.

(C) At least two VHS videotape recorders with hi-fi sound on video, specially modified to record 4 channels of audio (2 linear channels with Dolby noise reduction and 2 hi-fi sound on video channels), capable of recording up to 6 hours on T-120 cassettes, modified to prevent automatic rewind at end of tape, and wired for remote control. The two recorders must simultaneously record the same audio and video signals, as selected by the audio-video mixer.

(D) A computer-controlled audio-video mixer and switching system that:

(i) Automatically selects for the VCRs the signal from the video camera that is associated with the active microphone; and

(ii) Compares microphone active signal to ambient noise signal so that microphones are recorded only when a person is speaking, and so that only the microphone nearest a speaker is active, thus minimizing recording of ambient noise.

(E) A sound system that serves both as a sound reinforcement system while recording is in progress, and as a playback amplification system, integrated with other components to minimize feedback.

(F) A time-date generator that is active and records at all times the system is recording.

(G) A color monitor.

(H) Appropriate cables, distribution amplifiers, switches, and the like.

(I) The system must produce:

(i) A signal visible to the judge, the in-court clerk, and counsel indicating that the system is recording;

(ii) An audible signal at end-of-tape or if the tape jams while the controls are set to record; and

(iii) Blanking of the judge's bench monitor when the system is not actually recording.

(2) *Recommended features*

The system should normally include:

(A) A chambers camera and microphone or microphones that, when in use, will override any signals originating in the courtroom, and that will be inactivated when not in use.

(B) Two additional videocassette recorders that will produce tapes with the same video and audio as the main two, but may have fewer channels of sound, for the use of parties in cases recorded.

(Subd (c) amended effective January 1, 2007.)

(d) Substantial compliance

A sound or video and sound system that substantially conforms to these specifications is approved if the deviation does not significantly impair a major function of the system. Subdivision (c)(1)(D)(ii) of this rule describes a specification from which deviation is permissible, if the system produces adequate sound quality.

(Subd (d) amended effective January 1, 2007.)

(e) Previous equipment

The Administrative Director is authorized to approve any electronic recording devices and equipment acquired before the adoption or amendment of this rule that has been found by the court to produce satisfactory recordings of proceedings.

(Subd (e) amended effective January 1, 2016; previously amended effective January 1, 2007.)

Rule 2.954 amended effective January 1, 2016; adopted as rule 980.6 effective January 1, 1990; previously amended and renumbered as rule 2.954 effective January 1, 2007.

Rule 2.956. Court reporting services in civil cases

(a) Statutory reference; application

This rule [1] **implements and must be applied so as to give effect to** Government Code sections [2] **68086(a)–(c).**

(Subd (a) amended effective January 1, 2021; previously amended effective January 31, 1997, and January 1, 2007.)

Rule 2.956(a). 2020 Deletes. [1] is adopted solely to effectuate the statutory mandate of **[2]** 68086(a)–(b) and must be applied so as to give effect to these sections. It applies to trial courts

(b) Notice of availability; parties' request

(1) *Local policy to be adopted and posted*

Each trial court must adopt and post in the clerk's office a local policy enumerating the departments in which the services of official court reporters are normally available, and the departments in which the services of official court reporters are not normally available during regular court hours. If the services of official court reporters are normally available in a department only for certain types of matters, those matters must be identified in the policy.

(2) *Publication of policy*

The court must publish its policy in a newspaper if one is published in the county. Instead of publishing the policy, the court may:

(A) Send each party a copy of the policy at least 10 days before any hearing is held in a case; or

(B) Adopt the policy as a local rule.

(3) *Requests for official court reporter for civil trials and notices to parties*

Unless the court's policy states that all courtrooms normally have the services of official court reporters available for civil trials, the court must require that each party file a statement before the trial date indicating whether the party requests the presence of an official court reporter. If a party requests the presence of an official court reporter and it appears that none will be available, the clerk must notify the party of that fact as soon as possible before the trial. If the services of official court reporters are normally available in all courtrooms, the clerk must notify the parties to a civil trial as soon as possible if it appears that those services will not be available.

(4) *Notice of nonavailability of court reporter for nontrial matters*

If the services of an official court reporter will not be available during a hearing on law and motion or other nontrial matters in civil cases, that fact must be noted on the court's official calendar.

(Subd (b) amended effective January 1, 2007.)

(c) Party may procure reporter or request reporter if granted fee waiver

If the services of an official court reporter are not available for a hearing or trial in a civil case, a party may:

(1) Arrange for the presence of a certified shorthand reporter to serve as an official pro tempore reporter, **whom the court must appoint unless there is good cause shown to refuse to do so**. It is that party's responsibility to pay the reporter's fee for attendance at the proceedings, but the expense may be recoverable as part of the costs, as provided by law; or

(2) [1] **If the party has been granted a fee waiver**, request that the court provide an official reporter for attendance at the proceedings [2]. **The court must provide an official reporter** if the party has been granted a fee waiver and if the court is not electronically recording the hearing or trial.

(A) **The request should be made by filing a** *Request for Court Reporter by a Party with a Fee Waiver* **(form FW-020). If the requesting party has not been granted a fee waiver, a completed** *Request to Waive Court Fees* **(form FW-001 or form FW-001-GC in guardianship or conservator cases) must be filed at the same time as the request for court reporter.**

(B) **The party should file the request 10 calendar days before the proceeding for which a court reporter is desired, or as soon as practicable if the proceeding is set with less than 10-days' notice.**

(C) **If the party has requested a court reporter for a trial, that request remains in effect if the trial is continued to a later date.**

(D) The court reporter's attendance is to be provided at no fee or cost to the fee waiver recipient.

(Subd (c) amended effective January 1, 2021; previously amended effective September 1, 2019.)

Rule 2.956(c). 2020 Deletes. [1] In compliance with any local court rules [2] ,

(d) No additional charge if party arranges for reporter

If a party arranges and pays for the attendance of a certified shorthand reporter at a hearing in a civil case because of the unavailability of the services of an official court reporter, none of the parties may be charged the reporter's attendance fee provided for in Government Code sections 68086(a)(1) or (b)(1).

(Subd (d) amended effective January 1, 2007.)

(e) Definitions

As used in this rule and in Government Code section 68086:

(1) "Civil case" includes all matters other than criminal and juvenile matters.

(2) "Official reporter" and "official reporting services" both include an official court reporter or official reporter as those phrases are used in statutes, including Code of Civil Procedure sections 269 and 274c and Government Code section 69941; and include an official reporter pro tempore as the phrase is used in Government Code section 69945 and other statutes, whose fee for attending and reporting proceedings is paid for by the court or the county, and who attends court sessions as directed by the court, and who was not employed to report specific causes at the request of a party or parties. "Official reporter" and "official reporting services" do not include official reporters pro tempore employed by the court expressly to report only criminal, or criminal and juvenile, matters. "Official reporting services" include electronic recording equipment operated by the court to make the official verbatim record of proceedings where it is permitted.

(Subd (e) amended effective January 1, 2007.)
Rule 2.956 amended effective January 1, 2021; adopted as rule 891 effective January 1, 1994; previously amended effective January 31, 1997, and September 1, 2019; previously amended and renumbered effective January 1, 2007.

Rule 2.958.   Assessing fee for official reporter

The half-day fee to be charged under Government Code section 68086 for the services of an official reporter must be established by the trial court as follows: for a proceeding or portion of a proceeding in which a certified shorthand reporter is used, the fee is equal to the average salary and benefit costs of the reporter, plus indirect costs of up to 18 percent of salary and benefits. For purposes of this rule, the daily salary is determined by dividing the average annual salary of temporary and full-time reporters by 225 workdays.

Rule 2.958 amended and renumbered effective January 1, 2007; adopted as rule 892 effective January 1, 1994; previously amended effective January 31, 1997, August 17, 2003, January 1, 2004, and July 1, 2004.

Division 8
Trials

Chapter 1
Jury Service

Rule 2.1000.   Jury service [Reserved]
Rule 2.1000 adopted effective January 1, 2007.

Rule 2.1002.   Length of juror service
(a) Purpose

This rule implements Government Code section 68550, which is intended to make jury service more convenient and alleviate the problem of potential jurors refusing to appear for jury duty by shortening the time a person would be required to serve to one day or one trial. The exemptions authorized by the rule are intended to be of limited scope and

duration, and they must be applied with the goal of achieving full compliance throughout the state as soon as possible.

(Subd (a) amended effective January 1, 2007.)

(b) Definitions

As used in this rule:

(1) "Trial court system" means all the courts of a county.

(2) "One trial" means jury service provided by a citizen after being sworn as a trial juror.

(3) "One day" means the hours of one normal court working day (the hours a court is open to the public for business).

(4) "On call" means all same-day notice procedures used to inform prospective jurors of the time they are to report for jury service.

(5) "Telephone standby" means all previous-day notice procedures used to inform prospective jurors of their date to report for service.

(Subd (b) amended effective January 1, 2007.)

(c) One-day/one-trial

Each trial court system must implement a juror management program under which a person has fulfilled his or her jury service obligation when the person has:

(1) Served on one trial until discharged;

(2) Been assigned on one day to one or more trial departments for jury selection and served through the completion of jury selection or until excused by the jury commissioner;

(3) Attended court but was not assigned to a trial department for selection of a jury before the end of that day;

(4) Served one day on call; or

(5) Served no more than five court days on telephone standby.

(Subd (c) amended effective January 1, 2007.)

(d) Exemption

(1) *Good cause*

The Judicial Council may grant an exemption from the requirements of this rule for a specified period of time if the trial court system demonstrates good cause by establishing that:

(A) The cost of implementing a one-day/one-trial system is so high that the trial court system would be unable to provide essential services to the public if required to implement such a system; or

(B) The requirements of this rule cannot be met because of the size of the population in the county compared to the number of jury trials.

(2) *Application*

Any application for exemption from the requirements of this rule must be submitted to the Judicial Council no later than September 1, 1999. The application must demonstrate good cause for the exemption sought and must include either:

(A) A plan to fully comply with this rule by a specified date; or

(B) An alternative plan that would advance the purposes of this rule to the extent possible, given the conditions in the county.

(3) *Decision*

If the council finds good cause, it may grant an exemption for a limited period of time and on such conditions as it deems appropriate to further the purposes of this rule.

(Subd (d) amended effective January 1, 2007.)
Rule 2.1002 amended and renumbered effective January 1, 2007; adopted as rule 861 effective July 1, 1999.

Rule 2.1004.   Scheduling accommodations for jurors
(a) Accommodations for all jurors

The jury commissioner should accommodate a prospective juror's schedule by granting a prospective juror's request for a one-time deferral of jury service. If the request for a deferral is made under penalty of perjury in writing or through the court's established electronic means, and in accordance with the court's local procedure, the jury commissioner should not require the prospective juror to appear at court to make the request in person.

(b) Scheduling accommodations for peace officers

If a prospective juror is a peace officer, as defined by Penal Code section 830.5, the jury commissioner must make scheduling accommodations on application of the peace officer stating the reason a scheduling accommodation is necessary. The jury commissioner must establish procedures for the form and timing of the application. If the request for special accommodations is made under penalty of perjury in writing or through the court's established electronic means, and in accordance with the court's local procedure, the jury commissioner must not require the prospective juror to appear at court to make the request in person.

(Subd (b) amended effective January 1, 2007.)

Rule 2.1004 amended and renumbered effective January 1, 2007; adopted as rule 858 effective January 1, 2005.

Rule 2.1006. Deferral of jury service

A mother who is breastfeeding a child may request that jury service be deferred for up to one year, and may renew that request as long as she is breastfeeding. If the request is made in writing, under penalty of perjury, the jury commissioner must grant it without requiring the prospective juror to appear at court.

Rule 2.1006 renumbered effective January 1, 2007; adopted as rule 859 effective July 1, 2001.

Rule 2.1008. Excuses from jury service

(a) Duty of citizenship

Jury service, unless excused by law, is a responsibility of citizenship. The court and its staff must employ all necessary and appropriate means to ensure that citizens fulfill this important civic responsibility.

(Subd (a) amended effective January 1, 2007.)

(b) Principles

The following principles govern the granting of excuses from jury service by the jury commissioner on grounds of undue hardship under Code of Civil Procedure section 204:

(1) No class or category of persons may be automatically excluded from jury duty except as provided by law.

(2) A statutory exemption from jury service must be granted only when the eligible person claims it.

(3) Deferring jury service is preferred to excusing a prospective juror for a temporary or marginal hardship.

(4) Inconvenience to a prospective juror or an employer is not an adequate reason to be excused from jury duty, although it may be considered a ground for deferral.

(Subd (b) amended effective January 1, 2007.)

(c) Requests to be excused from jury service

All requests to be excused from jury service that are granted for undue hardship must be put in writing by the prospective juror, reduced to writing, or placed on the court's record. The prospective juror must support the request with facts specifying the hardship and a statement why the circumstances constituting the undue hardship cannot be avoided by deferring the prospective juror's service.

(Subd (c) amended effective January 1, 2007.)

(d) Reasons for excusing a juror because of undue hardship

An excuse on the ground of undue hardship may be granted for any of the following reasons:

(1) The prospective juror has no reasonably available means of public or private transportation to the court.

(2) The prospective juror must travel an excessive distance. Unless otherwise established by statute or local rule, an excessive distance is reasonable travel time that exceeds one-and-one-half hours from the prospective juror's home to the court.

(3) The prospective juror will bear an extreme financial burden. In determining whether to excuse the prospective juror for this reason, consideration must be given to:

(A) The sources of the prospective juror's household income;

(B) The availability and extent of income reimbursement;

(C) The expected length of service; and

(D) Whether service can reasonably be expected to compromise the prospective juror's ability to support himself or herself or his or her dependents, or so disrupt the economic stability of any individual as to be against the interests of justice.

(4) The prospective juror will bear an undue risk of material injury to or destruction of the prospective juror's property or property entrusted to the prospective juror, and it is not feasible to make alternative arrangements to alleviate the risk. In determining whether to excuse the prospective juror for this reason, consideration must be given to:

(A) The nature of the property;

(B) The source and duration of the risk;

(C) The probability that the risk will be realized;

(D) The reason alternative arrangements to protect the property cannot be made; and

(E) Whether material injury to or destruction of the property will so disrupt the economic stability of any individual as to be against the interests of justice.

(5) The prospective juror has a physical or mental disability or impairment, not affecting that person's competence to act as a juror, that would expose the potential juror to undue risk of mental or physical harm. In any individual case, unless the person is aged 70 years or older, the prospective juror may be required to furnish verification or a method of verification of the disability or impairment, its probable duration, and the particular reasons for the person's inability to serve as a juror.

(6) The prospective juror's services are immediately needed for the protection of the public health and safety, and it is not feasible to make alternative arrangements to relieve the person of those responsibilities during the period of service as a juror without substantially reducing essential public services.

(7) The prospective juror has a personal obligation to provide actual and necessary care to another, including sick, aged, or infirm dependents, or a child who requires the prospective juror's personal care and attention, and no comparable substitute care is either available or practical without imposing an undue economic hardship on the prospective juror or person cared for. If the request to be excused is based on care provided to a sick, disabled, or infirm person, the prospective juror may be required to furnish verification or a method of verification that the person being cared for is in need of regular and personal care.

(Subd (d) amended effective January 1, 2007.)

(e) Excuse based on previous jury service

A prospective juror who has served on a grand or trial jury or was summoned and appeared for jury service in any state or federal court during the previous 12 months must be excused from service on request. The jury commissioner, in his or her discretion, may establish a longer period of repose.

(Subd (e) amended effective January 1, 2007.)

Rule 2.1008 amended and renumbered effective January 1, 2007; adopted as rule 860 effective July 1, 1997.

Rule 2.1009. Permanent medical excuse from jury service

(a) Definitions

As used in this rule:

(1) "Applicant" means a "person with a disability" or their authorized representative.

(2) "Authorized representative" means a conservator, agent under a power of attorney (attorney-in-fact), or any other individual designated by the person with a disability.

(3) "Capable of performing jury service" means a person can pay attention to evidence, testimony, and other court proceedings for up to six hours per day, with a lunch break and short breaks in the morning and afternoon, with or without disability-related accommodations, including auxiliary aids and services.

(4) "Health care provider" means a doctor of medicine or osteopathy, podiatrist, dentist, chiropractor, clinical psychologist, optometrist, nurse practitioner, nurse-midwife, clinical social worker, therapist, physician's assistant, Christian Science Practitioner, or any other medical provider, facility, or organization that is authorized and performing within the scope of the practice of their profession in accordance with state or federal law and regulations.

(5) "Permanent medical excuse" means a release from jury service granted by the jury commissioner to a person with a disability whose condition is unlikely to resolve and who, with or without disability-related accommodations, including auxiliary aids or services, is not capable of performing jury service.

(6) "Person with a disability" means an individual covered by Civil Code section 51 et seq., the Americans With Disabilities Act of 1990 (42 U.S.C. § 12101 et seq.), or other applicable state and federal laws. This definition includes a person who has a physical or mental medical condition that limits one or more of the major life activities, has a record of such a condition, or is regarded as having such a condition.

(Subd (a) adopted effective January 1, 2019.)

(b) Policy

(1) This rule is intended to allow a person with a disability whose condition is unlikely to resolve and who is unable for the foreseeable future to serve as a juror to seek a permanent medical excuse from jury service. This rule does not impose limitations on or invalidate the remedies, rights, and procedures accorded to persons with disabilities under state or federal law.

(2) It is the policy of the courts of this state to ensure that persons with disabilities have equal and full access to the judicial system, including the opportunity to serve as jurors. No eligible jurors who can perform jury service, with or without disability-related accommodations, including

auxiliary aids or services, may be excused from jury service due solely to their disability.

(Subd (b) adopted effective January 1, 2019.)

(c) Process for requesting permanent medical excuse

The process for requesting a permanent medical excuse from jury service is as follows:

(1) An applicant must submit to the jury commissioner a written request for permanent medical excuse with a supporting letter, memo, or note from a treating health care provider. The supporting letter, memo, or note must be on the treating health care provider's letterhead, state that the person has a permanent disability that makes the person incapable of performing jury service, and be signed by the provider.

(2) The applicant must submit the request and supporting letter, memo, or note to the jury commissioner on or before the date the person is required to appear for jury service.

(3) In the case of an incomplete application, the jury commissioner may require the applicant to furnish additional information in support of the request for permanent medical excuse.

(4) The jury commissioner must keep confidential all information concerning the request for permanent medical excuse, including any accompanying request for disability-related accommodation, including auxiliary aids or services, unless the applicant waives confidentiality in writing or the law requires disclosure. The applicant's identity and confidential information may not be disclosed to the public but may be disclosed to court officials and personnel involved in the permanent medical excuse process. Confidential information includes all medical information pertaining to the applicant, and all oral or written communication from the applicant concerning the request for permanent medical excuse.

(Subd (c) adopted effective January 1, 2019.)

(d) Response to request

The jury commissioner must respond to a request for a permanent medical excuse from jury service as follows:

(1) The jury commissioner must promptly inform the applicant in writing of the determination to grant or deny a permanent medical excuse request.

(2) If the request is granted, the jury commissioner must remove the person from the rolls of potential jurors as soon as it is practicable to do so.

(3) If the request is denied, the jury commissioner must provide the applicant a written response with the reason for the denial.

(Subd (d) adopted effective January 1, 2019.)

(e) Denial of request

Only when the jury commissioner determines the applicant failed to satisfy the requirements of this rule may the jury commissioner deny the permanent medical excuse request.

(Subd (e) adopted effective January 1, 2019.)

(f) Right to reapply

A person whose request for permanent medical excuse is denied may reapply at any time after receipt of the jury commissioner's denial by following the process in (c).

(Subd (f) adopted effective January 1, 2019.)

(g) Reinstatement

A person who has received a permanent medical excuse from jury service under this rule may be reinstated to the rolls of potential jurors at any time by filing a signed, written request with the jury commissioner that the permanent medical excuse be withdrawn.

(Subd (g) adopted effective January 1, 2019.)
Rule 2.1009 adopted effective January 1, 2019.

Rule 2.1010. Juror motion to set aside sanctions imposed by default

(a) Motion

A prospective juror against whom sanctions have been imposed by default under Code of Civil Procedure section 209 may move to set aside the default. The motion must be brought no later than 60 days after sanctions have been imposed.

(b) Contents of motion

A motion to set aside sanctions imposed by default must contain a short and concise statement of the reasons the prospective juror was not able to attend when summoned for jury duty and any supporting documentation.

(c) Judicial Council form may be used

A motion to set aside sanctions imposed by default may be made by completing and filing *Juror's Motion to Set Aside Sanctions and Order* (form MC-070).

(Subd (c) amended effective January 1, 2007.)

(d) Hearing

The court may decide the motion with or without a hearing.
(Subd (d) amended effective January 1, 2007.)

(e) Good cause required

If the motion demonstrates good cause, a court must set aside sanctions imposed against a prospective juror.

(f) Continuing obligation to serve

Nothing in this rule relieves a prospective juror of the obligation of jury service.

(g) Notice to juror

The court must provide a copy of this rule to the prospective juror against whom sanctions have been imposed.

Rule 2.1010 amended effective January 1, 2010; adopted as rule 862 effective January 1, 2005; previously amended and renumbered effective January 1, 2007.

2009 Note: The sunset provision was repealed to extend the provisions indefinitely.

Chapter 2
Conduct of Trial

Rule 2.1030. Communications from or with jury

(a) Preservation of written jury communications

The trial judge must preserve and deliver to the clerk for inclusion in the record all written communications, formal or informal, received from the jury or from individual jurors or sent by the judge to the jury or individual jurors, from the time the jury is sworn until it is discharged.

(Subd (a) amended and lettered effective January 1, 2007; adopted as part of unlettered subd effective January 1, 1990.)

(b) Recording of oral jury communications

The trial judge must ensure that the reporter, or any electronic recording system used instead of a reporter, records all oral communications, formal or informal, received from the jury or from individual jurors or communicated by the judge to the jury or individual jurors, from the time the jury is sworn until it is discharged.

(Subd (b) amended and lettered effective January 1, 2007; adopted as part of unlettered subd effective January 1, 1990.)
Rule 2.1030 amended and renumbered effective January 1, 2007; adopted as rule 231 effective January 1, 1990.

Rule 2.1031. Juror note-taking

Jurors must be permitted to take written notes in all civil and criminal trials. At the beginning of a trial, a trial judge must inform jurors that they may take written notes during the trial. The court must provide materials suitable for this purpose.
Rule 2.1031 adopted effective January 1, 2007.

Advisory Committee Comment

Several cautionary jury instructions address jurors' note-taking during trial and use of notes in deliberations. (See CACI Nos. 102, 5010 and CALCRIM Nos. 102, 202.)

Rule 2.1032. Juror notebooks in complex civil cases

A trial judge should encourage counsel in complex civil cases to include key documents, exhibits, and other appropriate materials in notebooks for use by jurors during trial to assist them in performing their duties.
Rule 2.1032 adopted effective January 1, 2007.

Advisory Committee Comment

While this rule is intended to apply to complex civil cases, there may be other types of civil cases in which notebooks may be appropriate or useful. Resources, including guidelines for use and recommended notebook contents, are available in *Bench Handbook: Jury Management* (CJER, rev. 2006, p. 59).

Rule 2.1033. Juror questions

A trial judge should allow jurors to submit written questions directed to witnesses. An opportunity must be given to counsel to object to such questions out of the presence of the jury.
Rule 2.1033 adopted effective January 1, 2007.

Advisory Committee Comment

See CACI No. 112 and CALCRIM No. 106. Resources, including a model admonition and a sample form for jurors to use to submit questions to the court, are available in *Bench Handbook: Jury Management* (CJER, rev. 2006, pp. 60–62).

Rule 2.1034. Statements to the jury panel [Repealed]
Rule 2.1034 repealed effective January 1, 2013; adopted effective January 1, 2007.

Rule 2.1035. Preinstruction
Immediately after the jury is sworn, the trial judge may, in his or her discretion, preinstruct the jury concerning the elements of the charges or claims, its duties, its conduct, the order of proceedings, the procedure for submitting written questions for witnesses as set forth in rule 2.1033 if questions are allowed, and the legal principles that will govern the proceeding.
Rule 2.1035 adopted effective January 1, 2007.

Rule 2.1036. Assisting the jury at impasse
(a) Determination
After a jury reports that it has reached an impasse in its deliberations, the trial judge may, in the presence of counsel, advise the jury of its duty to decide the case based on the evidence while keeping an open mind and talking about the evidence with each other. The judge should ask the jury if it has specific concerns which, if resolved, might assist the jury in reaching a verdict.
(Subd (a) adopted effective January 1, 2007.)

(b) Possible further action
If the trial judge determines that further action might assist the jury in reaching a verdict, the judge may:

(1) Give additional instructions;

(2) Clarify previous instructions;

(3) Permit attorneys to make additional closing arguments; or

(4) Employ any combination of these measures.
(Subd (b) adopted effective January 1, 2007.)
Rule 2.1036 adopted effective January 1, 2007.

Advisory Committee Comment
See Judicial Council CACI No. 5013 and Judicial Council CALCRIM No. 3550.

Chapter 3
Testimony and Evidence

Rule 2.1040. Electronic recordings presented or offered into evidence
(a) Electronic recordings of deposition or other prior testimony
(1) Before a party may present or offer into evidence an electronic sound or sound-and-video recording of deposition or other prior testimony, the party must lodge a transcript of the deposition or prior testimony with the court. At the time the recording is played, the party must identify on the record the page and line numbers where the testimony presented or offered appears in the transcript.

(2) Except as provided in (3), at the time the presentation of evidence closes or within five days after the recording in (1) is presented or offered into evidence, whichever is later, the party presenting or offering the recording into evidence must serve and file a copy of the transcript cover showing the witness name and a copy of the pages of the transcript where the testimony presented or offered appears. The transcript pages must be marked to identify the testimony that was presented or offered into evidence.

(3) If the court reporter takes down the content of all portions of the recording in (1) that were presented or offered into evidence, the party offering or presenting the recording is not required to provide a transcript of that recording under (2).
(Subd (a) adopted effective July 1, 2011.)

(b) Other electronic recordings
(1) Except as provided in (2) and (3), before a party may present or offer into evidence any electronic sound or sound-and-video recording not covered under (a), the party must provide to the court and to opposing parties a transcript of the electronic recording and provide opposing parties with a duplicate of the electronic recording, as defined in Evidence Code section 260. The transcript may be prepared by the party presenting or offering the recording into evidence; a certified transcript is not required.

(2) For good cause, the trial judge may permit the party to provide the transcript or the duplicate recording at the time the presentation of evidence closes or within five days after the recording is presented or offered into evidence, whichever is later.

(3) No transcript is required to be provided under (1):

(A) In proceedings that are uncontested or in which the responding party does not appear, unless otherwise ordered by the trial judge;

(B) If the parties stipulate in writing or on the record that the sound portion of a sound-and-video recording does not contain any words that are relevant to the issues in the case; or

(C) If, for good cause, the trial judge orders that a transcript is not required.
(Subd (b) amended and relettered effective July 1, 2011; adopted as part of unlettered subd effective July 1, 1988; amended and lettered as subd (a) effective January 1, 2003.)

(c) Clerk's duties
An electronic recording provided to the court under this rule must be marked for identification. A transcript provided under (a)(2) or (b)(1) must be filed by the clerk.
(Subd (c) amended and relettered effective July 1, 2011; adopted as part of unlettered subd effective July 1, 1988; amended and lettered as subd (a) effective January 1, 2003.)

(d) Reporting by court reporter
Unless otherwise ordered by the trial judge, the court reporter need not take down the content of an electronic recording that is presented or offered into evidence.
(Subd (d) amended and relettered effective July 1, 2011; adopted as part of unlettered subd effective July 1, 1988; amended and lettered as subd (b) effective January 1, 2003.)
Rule 2.1040 amended effective July 1, 2011; adopted as rule 203.5 effective July 1, 1988; previously amended effective January 1, 1997; previously amended and renumbered as rule 243.9 effective January 1, 2003, and as rule 2.1040 effective January 1, 2007.

Advisory Committee Comment
This rule is designed to ensure that, in the event of an appeal, there is an appropriate record of any electronic sound or sound-and-video recording that was presented or offered into evidence in the trial court. The rules on felony, misdemeanor, and infraction appeals require that any transcript provided by a party under this rule be included in the clerk's transcript on appeal (see rules 8.320, 8.861, and 8.912). In civil appeals, the parties may designate such a transcript for inclusion in the clerk's transcript (see rules 8.122(b) and 8.832(a)). The transcripts required under this rule may also assist the court or jurors during the trial court proceedings. For this purpose, it may be helpful for the trial court to request that the party offering an electronic recording provide additional copies of such transcripts for jurors to follow while the recording is played.

Subdivision (a). Note that, under Code of Civil Procedure section 2025.510(g), if the testimony at a deposition is recorded both stenographically and by audio or video technology, the stenographic transcript is the official record of that testimony for the purpose of the trial and any subsequent hearing or appeal.

Subdivision (a)(2). The party offering or presenting the electronic recording may serve and file a copy of the cover and of the relevant pages of the deposition or other transcript; a new transcript need not be prepared.

Subdivision (b). Note that, with the exception of recordings covered by Code of Civil Procedure section 2025.510(g), the recording itself, not the transcript, is the evidence that was offered or presented (see *People v. Sims* (1993) 5 Cal.4th 405, 448). Sometimes, a party may present or offer into evidence only a portion of a longer electronic recording. In such circumstances, the transcript provided to the court and opposing parties should contain only a transcription of those portions of the electronic recording that are actually presented or offered into evidence. If a party believes that a transcript provided under this subdivision is inaccurate, the party can raise an objection in the trial court.

Subdivision (b)(3)(C). Good cause to waive the requirement for a transcript may include such factors as (1) the party presenting or offering the electronic recording into evidence lacks the capacity to prepare a transcript or (2) the electronic recording is of such poor quality that preparing a useful transcript is not feasible.

Subdivision (c). The requirement to file a transcript provided to the court under (a)(2) or (b)(1) is intended to ensure that the transcript is available for inclusion in a clerk's transcript in the event of an appeal.

Subdivision (d). In some circumstances it may be helpful to have the court reporter take down the content of an electronic recording. For example, when short portions of a sound or sound-and-video recording of deposition or other testimony are played to impeach statements made by a witness on the stand, the best way to create a useful record of the proceedings may be for the court reporter to take down the portions of recorded testimony that are interspersed with the live testimony.

Chapter 4
Jury Instructions

Rule 2.1050. Judicial Council jury instructions
Rule 2.1055. Proposed jury instructions
Rule 2.1058. Use of gender-neutral language in jury instructions

Rule 2.1050. Judicial Council jury instructions
(a) Purpose
The California jury instructions approved by the Judicial Council are the official instructions for use in the state of California. The goal of these

instructions is to improve the quality of jury decision making by providing standardized instructions that accurately state the law in a way that is understandable to the average juror.

(b) Accuracy

The Judicial Council endorses these instructions for use and makes every effort to ensure that they accurately state existing law. The articulation and interpretation of California law, however, remains within the purview of the Legislature and the courts of review.

(c) Public access

The Judicial Council must provide copies and updates of the approved jury instructions to the public on the California Courts website. The Judicial Council may contract with an official publisher to publish the instructions in both paper and electronic formats. The Judicial Council intends that the instructions be freely available for use and reproduction by parties, attorneys, and the public, except as limited by this subdivision. The Judicial Council may take steps necessary to ensure that publication of the instructions by commercial publishers does not occur without its permission, including, without limitation, ensuring that commercial publishers accurately publish the Judicial Council's instructions, accurately credit the Judicial Council as the source of the instructions, and do not claim copyright of the instructions. The Judicial Council may require commercial publishers to pay fees or royalties in exchange for permission to publish the instructions. As used in this rule, "commercial publishers" means entities that publish works for sale, whether for profit or otherwise.

(Subd (c) amended effective January 1, 2016; previously amended effective August 26, 2005, and January 1, 2007.)

(d) Updating and amendments

The Judicial Council instructions will be regularly updated and maintained through its advisory committees on jury instructions. Amendments to these instructions will be circulated for public comment before publication. Trial judges and attorneys may submit for the advisory committees' consideration suggestions for improving or modifying these instructions or creating new instructions, with an explanation of why the change is proposed. Suggestions should be sent to the Judicial Council of California, Legal Services.

(Subd (d) amended effective January 1, 2016.)

(e) Use of instructions

Use of the Judicial Council instructions is strongly encouraged. If the latest edition of the jury instructions approved by the Judicial Council contains an instruction applicable to a case and the trial judge determines that the jury should be instructed on the subject, it is recommended that the judge use the Judicial Council instruction unless he or she finds that a different instruction would more accurately state the law and be understood by jurors. Whenever the latest edition of the Judicial Council jury instructions does not contain an instruction on a subject on which the trial judge determines that the jury should be instructed, or when a Judicial Council instruction cannot be modified to submit the issue properly, the instruction given on that subject should be accurate, brief, understandable, impartial, and free from argument.

(Subd (e) amended effective August 26, 2005.)

Rule 2.1050 amended effective January 1, 2016; adopted as rule 855 effective September 1, 2003; previously amended effective August 26, 2005; previously amended and renumbered as rule 2.1050 effective January 1, 2007.

Rule 2.1055. Proposed jury instructions

(a) Application

(1) This rule applies to proposed jury instructions that a party submits to the court, including:

(A) "Approved jury instructions," meaning jury instructions approved by the Judicial Council of California; and

(B) "Special jury instructions," meaning instructions from other sources, those specially prepared by the party, or approved instructions that have been substantially modified by the party.

(2) This rule does not apply to the form or format of the instructions presented to the jury, which is a matter left to the discretion of the court.

(Subd (a) amended effective August 26, 2005; previously amended effective January 1, 2003, and January 1, 2004.)

(b) Form and format of proposed instructions

(1) All proposed instructions must be submitted to the court in the form and format prescribed for papers in the rules in division 2 of this title.

(2) Each set of proposed jury instructions must have a cover page, containing the caption of the case and stating the name of the party proposing the instructions, and an index listing all the proposed instructions.

(3) In the index, approved jury instructions must be identified by their reference numbers and special jury instructions must be numbered consecutively. The index must contain a checklist that the court may use to indicate whether the instruction was:

(A) Given as proposed;

(B) Given as modified;

(C) Refused; or

(D) Withdrawn.

(4) Each set of proposed jury instructions filed on paper must be bound loosely.

(Subd (b) amended effective January 1, 2016; previously amended effective July 1, 1988, January 1, 2003, January 1, 2004, and January 1, 2007.)

(c) Format of each proposed instruction

Each proposed instruction must:

(1) Be on a separate page or pages;

(2) Include the instruction number and title of the instruction at the top of the first page of the instruction; and

(3) Be prepared without any blank lines or unused bracketed portions, so that it can be read directly to the jury.

(Subd (c) amended effective January 1, 2004; previously amended effective July 1, 1988, April 1, 1962, and January 1, 2003.)

(d) Citation of authorities

For each special instruction, a citation of authorities that support the instruction must be included at the bottom of the page. No citation is required for approved instructions.

(Subd (d) adopted effective January 1, 2004.)

(e) Form and format are exclusive

No local court form or rule for the filing or submission of proposed jury instructions may require that the instructions be submitted in any manner other than as prescribed by this rule.

(Subd (e) adopted effective January 1, 2004.)

Rule 2.1055 amended effective January 1, 2016; adopted as rule 229 effective January 1, 1949; previously amended effective April 1, 1962, July 1, 1988, January 1, 2003, January 1, 2004, and August 26, 2005; previously amended and renumbered as rule 2.1055 effective January 1, 2007.

Advisory Committee Comment

This rule does not preclude a judge from requiring the parties in an individual case to transmit the jury instructions to the court electronically.

Rule 2.1058. Use of gender-neutral language in jury instructions

All instructions submitted to the jury must be written in gender-neutral language. If standard jury instructions (*CALCRIM* and *CACI*) are to be submitted to the jury, the court or, at the court's request, counsel must recast the instructions as necessary to ensure that gender-neutral language is used in each instruction.

Rule 2.1058 amended and renumbered effective January 1, 2007; adopted as rule 989 effective January 1, 1991.

Division 9
Judgments

Rule 2.1100. Notice when statute or regulation declared unconstitutional

Within 10 days after a court has entered judgment in a contested action or special proceeding in which the court has declared unconstitutional a state statute or regulation, the prevailing party, or as otherwise ordered by the court, must serve a copy of the judgment and a notice of entry of judgment on the Attorney General and file a proof of service with the court.

Rule 2.1100 amended effective January 1, 2016; adopted as rule 826 effective January 1, 1999; previously amended and renumbered as rule 2.1100 effective January 1, 2007.

TITLE 3
Civil Rules

Division 1
General Provisions

Chapter 1
Preliminary Rules

Rule 3.1.   Title

The rules in this title may be referred to as the Civil Rules.

Rule 3.1 adopted effective January 1, 2007.

Chapter 2
Scope of the Civil Rules

Rule 3.10. Application
Rule 3.20. Preemption of local rules

Rule 3.10.   Application

The Civil Rules apply to all civil cases in the superior courts, including general civil, family, juvenile, and probate cases, unless otherwise provided by a statute or rule in the California Rules of Court.

Rule 3.10 adopted effective January 1, 2007.

Rule 3.20.   Preemption of local rules

(a) Fields occupied

The Judicial Council has preempted all local rules relating to pleadings, demurrers, ex parte applications, motions, discovery, provisional remedies, and the form and format of papers. No trial court, or any division or branch of a trial court, may enact or enforce any local rule concerning these fields. All local rules concerning these fields are null and void unless otherwise permitted or required by a statute or a rule in the California Rules of Court.

(Subd (a) amended effective January 1, 2007; adopted as untitled subd effective July 1, 1997; previously amended effective July 1, 2000.)

(b) Application

This rule applies to all matters identified in (a) except:

(1) Trial and post-trial proceedings including but not limited to motions in limine (see rule 3.1112(f));

(2) Proceedings under Code of Civil Procedure sections 527.6, 527.7, and 527.8; the Family Code; the Probate Code; the Welfare and Institutions Code; and the Penal Code and all other criminal proceedings;

(3) Eminent domain proceedings; and

(4) Local court rules adopted under the Trial Court Delay Reduction Act.

(Subd (b) amended effective January 1, 2015; adopted effective July 1, 2000; previously amended effective July 1, 2000, January 1, 2002, and January 1, 2007.)
Rule 3.20 amended effective January 1, 2015; adopted as rule 302 effective July 1, 1997; previously amended effective January 1, 2002; previously amended and renumbered as rule 981.1 effective July 1, 2000, and as rule 3.20 effective January 1, 2007.

Chapter 3
Attorneys

Rule 3.35. Definition of limited scope representation; application of rules
Rule 3.36. Notice of limited scope representation and application to be relieved as attorney
Rule 3.37. Nondisclosure of attorney assistance in preparation of court documents

Rule 3.35.   Definition of limited scope representation; application of rules

(a) Definition

"Limited scope representation" is a relationship between an attorney and a person seeking legal services in which they have agreed that the scope of the legal services will be limited to specific tasks that the attorney will perform for the person.

(Subd (a) adopted effective January 1, 2007.)

(b) Application

Rules 3.35 through 3.37 apply to limited scope representation in civil cases, except in family law cases. Rule 5.425 applies to limited scope representation in family law cases.

(Subd (b) amended effective January 1, 2016; adopted effective January 1, 2007.)

(c) Types of limited scope representation

These rules recognize two types of limited scope representation:

(1) *Noticed representation*

Rule 3.36 provides procedures for cases in which an attorney and a party notify the court and other parties of the limited scope representation.

(2) *Undisclosed representation*

Rule 3.37 applies to cases in which the limited scope representation is not disclosed.

(Subd (c) adopted effective January 1, 2007.)
Rule 3.35 amended effective January 1, 2016; adopted effective January 1, 2007.

Rule 3.36.   Notice of limited scope representation and application to be relieved as attorney

(a) Notice of limited scope representation

A party and an attorney may provide notice of their agreement to limited scope representation by serving and filing a *Notice of Limited Scope Representation* (form CIV-150).

(Subd (a) amended effective September 1, 2018; adopted effective January 1, 2007.)

(b) Notice and service of papers

After the notice in (a) is received and until either a substitution of attorney or an order to be relieved as attorney is filed and served, papers in the case must be served on both the attorney providing the limited scope representation and the client.

(Subd (b) adopted effective January 1, 2007.)

(c) Procedures to be relieved as counsel on completion of representation

Notwithstanding rule 3.1362, an attorney who has completed the tasks specified in the *Notice of Limited Scope Representation* (form CIV-150) may use the procedures in this rule to request that he or she be relieved as attorney in cases in which the attorney has appeared before the court as an attorney of record and the client has not signed a *Substitution of Attorney—Civil* (form MC-050).

(Subd (c) amended effective September 1, 2018; adopted effective January 1, 2007.)

(d) Application

An application to be relieved as attorney on completion of limited scope representation under Code of Civil Procedure section 284(2) must be directed to the client and made on the *Application to Be Relieved as Attorney on Completion of Limited Scope Representation* (form CIV-151).

(Subd (d) amended effective September 1, 2018; adopted effective January 1, 2007.)

(e) Filing and service of application

The application to be relieved as attorney must be filed with the court and served on the client and on all other parties or attorneys for parties in the case. The client must also be served with a blank *Objection to Application to Be Relieved as Attorney on Completion of Limited Scope Representation* (form CIV-152).

(Subd (e) amended effective September 1, 2018; adopted effective January 1, 2007.)

(f) No objection

If no objection is served and filed with the court within 15 days from the date that the *Application to Be Relieved as Attorney on Completion of Limited Scope Representation* (form CIV-151) is served on the client, the attorney making the application must file an updated form CIV-151 indicating the lack of objection, along with a proposed *Order on Application to Be Relieved as Attorney on Completion of Limited Scope Representation* (form CIV-153). The clerk must then forward the order for judicial signature.

(Subd (f) amended effective September 1, 2018; adopted effective January 1, 2007.)

(g) Objection

If an objection to the application is served and filed within 15 days, the clerk must set a hearing date on the *Objection to Application to Be Relieved as Attorney on Completion of Limited Scope Representation* (form CIV-152). The hearing must be scheduled no later than 25 days from the date the objection is filed. The clerk must send the notice of the hearing to the parties and the attorney.

(Subd (g) amended effective September 1, 2018; adopted effective January 1, 2007.)

(h) Service of the order

If no objection is served and filed and the proposed order is signed under (f), the attorney who filed the *Application to Be Relieved as Attorney on Completion of Limited Scope Representation* (form CIV-151) must serve a copy of the signed order on the client and on all parties or the attorneys for all parties who have appeared in the case. The court may delay the effective date of the order relieving the attorney until proof of service of a copy of the signed order on the client has been filed with the court.

(Subd (h) amended effective September 1, 2018; adopted effective January 1, 2007.)

Rule 3.36 amended effective September 1, 2018; adopted effective January 1, 2007.

Rule 3.37. Nondisclosure of attorney assistance in preparation of court documents

(a) Nondisclosure

In a civil proceeding, an attorney who contracts with a client to draft or assist in drafting legal documents, but not to make an appearance in the case, is not required to disclose within the text of the documents that he or she was involved in preparing the documents.

(Subd (a) adopted effective January 1, 2007.)

(b) Attorney's fees

If a litigant seeks a court order for attorney's fees incurred as a result of document preparation, the litigant must disclose to the court information required for a proper determination of the attorney's fees, including:

(1) The name of the attorney who assisted in the preparation of the documents;

(2) The time involved or other basis for billing;

(3) The tasks performed; and

(4) The amount billed.

(Subd (b) adopted effective January 1, 2007.)

(c) Application of rule

This rule does not apply to an attorney who has made a general appearance in a case.

(Subd (c) adopted effective January 1, 2007.)

Rule 3.37 adopted effective January 1, 2007.

Division 2
Waiver of Fees and Costs

Rule 3.50. Application of rules
Rule 3.51. Method of application
Rule 3.52. Procedure for determining application
Rule 3.53. Application granted unless acted on by the court
Rule 3.54. Confidentiality
Rule 3.55. Court fees and costs included in all initial fee waivers
Rule 3.56. Additional court fees and costs that may be included in initial fee waiver
Rule 3.57. Amount of lien for waived fees and costs
Rule 3.58. Posting notice

Rule 3.50. Application of rules

(a) Application

The rules in this division govern applications in the trial court for an initial waiver of court fees and costs because of the applicant's financial condition. As provided in Government Code sections 68631 and following, any waiver may later be ended, modified, or retroactively withdrawn if the court determines that the applicant is not eligible for the waiver. As provided in Government Code sections 68636 and 68637, the court may, at a later time, determine that the previously waived fees and costs be paid.

(Subd (a) amended and lettered effective July 1, 2009; adopted as unlettered subd effective January 1, 2007.)

(b) Definitions

For purpose of the rules in this division, "initial fee waiver" means the initial waiver of court fees and costs that may be granted at any stage of the proceedings and includes both the fees and costs specified in rule 3.55 and any additional fees and costs specified in rule 3.56.

(Subd (b) adopted effective July 1, 2009.)

(c) Probate fee waivers

Initial fee waivers in decedents' estate, probate conservatorship, and probate guardianship proceedings or involving guardians or conservators as parties on behalf of their wards or conservatees are governed by rule 7.5.

(Subd (c) adopted effective September 1, 2015.)

Rule 3.50 amended effective September 1, 2015; adopted effective January 1, 2007; previously amended effective July 1, 2009.

Rule 3.51. Method of application

(a) An application for initial fee waiver under rule 3.55 must be made on *Request to Waive Court Fees* (form FW-001). An application for initial fee waiver under rule 3.56 must be made on *Request to Waive Additional Court Fees (Superior Court)* (form FW-002). The clerk must provide the forms and the *Information Sheet on Waiver of Superior Court Fees and Costs* (form FW-001-INFO) without charge to any person who requests any fee waiver application or indicates that he or she is unable to pay any court fee or cost.

(Subd (a) lettered effective September 1, 2015; adopted as unlettered subd effective January 1, 2007.)

(b) Applications involving (proposed) wards and conservatees

An application for initial fee waiver under rules 3.55 and 7.5 by a probate guardian or probate conservator or a petitioner for the appointment of a probate guardian or probate conservator for the benefit of a (proposed) ward or conservatee, in the guardianship or conservatorship proceeding or in a civil action or proceeding in which the guardian or conservator is a party on behalf of the ward or conservatee, must be made on *Request to Waive Court Fees (Ward or Conservatee)* (form FW-001-GC). An application for initial fee waiver under rule 3.56 by a guardian or conservator or a petitioner for the appointment of a guardian or conservator for the benefit of a (proposed) ward or conservatee must be made on *Request to Waive Additional Court Fees (Superior Court) (Ward or Conservatee)* (form FW-002-GC).

(Subd (b) adopted effective September 1, 2015.)

Rule 3.51 amended effective September 1, 2015; adopted effective January 1, 2007; previously amended effective January 1, 2007, and July 1, 2009.

Rule 3.52. Eligibility [Repealed]

Rule 3.52 repealed effective July 1, 2009; adopted effective January 1, 2007.

Another Rule 3.52 follows.

Rule 3.52. Procedure for determining application

The procedure for determining an application is as follows:

(1) The trial court must consider and determine the application as required by Government Code sections 68634 and 68635.

(2) An order determining an application for an initial fee waiver without a hearing must be made on *Order on Court Fee Waiver (Superior Court)* (form FW-003) or, if the application is made for the benefit of a (proposed) ward or conservatee, on *Order on Court Fee Waiver (Superior Court) (Ward or Conservatee)* (form FW-003-GC), except as provided in (6) below.

(3) An order determining an application for an initial fee waiver after a hearing in the trial court must be made on *Order on Court Fee Waiver After Hearing (Superior Court)* (form FW-008) or, if the application is made for the benefit of a (proposed) ward or conservatee, on *Order on Court Fee Waiver After Hearing (Superior Court) (Ward or Conservatee)* (form FW-008-GC).

(4) Any order granting a fee waiver must be accompanied by a blank *Notice of Improved Financial Situation or Settlement* (form FW-010) or, if the application is made for the benefit of a (proposed) ward or conservatee, a *Notice to Court of Improved Financial Situation or Settlement (Ward or Conservatee)* (form FW-010(GC).

(5) Any order denying an application without a hearing on the ground that the information on the application conclusively establishes that the applicant is not eligible for a waiver must be accompanied by a blank *Request for Hearing About Fee Waiver Order (Superior Court)* (form FW-006) or, if the application is made for the benefit of a (proposed) ward or conservatee, a *Request for Hearing About Court Fee Waiver Order (Superior Court) (Ward or Conservatee)* (form FW-006-GC).

(6) Until January 1, 2016, a court with a computerized case management system may produce electronically generated court fee waiver orders as long as:

(A) The document is substantively identical to the mandatory Judicial Council form it is replacing;

(B) Any electronically generated form is identical in both language and legally mandated elements, including all notices and advisements, to the mandatory Judicial Council form it is replacing; and

(C) The order is an otherwise legally sufficient court order, as provided in rule 1.31(g), concerning orders not on Judicial Council mandatory forms.

Rule 3.52 amended effective September 1, 2015; adopted as rule 3.56 effective January 1, 2007; previously amended and renumbered as rule 3.52 effective July 1, 2009; previously amended effective January 1, 2007, and July 1, 2015.

Rule 3.53. Verification of financial condition [Repealed]

Rule 3.53 repealed effective July 1, 2009; adopted effective January 1, 2007.

Another Rule 3.53 follows.

Rule 3.53. Application granted unless acted on by the court

The application for initial fee waiver is deemed granted unless the court gives notice of action on the application within five court days after it is filed. If the application is deemed granted under this provision, the clerk must prepare and serve a *Notice: Waiver of Court Fees (Superior Court)* (form FW-005) or, if the application is made for the benefit of a (proposed) ward or conservatee, a *Notice: Waiver of Court Fees (Superior Court) (Ward or Conservatee)* (form FW-005-GC), five court days after the application is filed.

Rule 3.53 amended effective September 1, 2015; adopted as rule 3.57 effective January 1, 2007; previously amended effective January 1, 2007; previously amended and renumbered as rule 3.53 effective July 1, 2009.

Rule 3.54. Determination without regard to pleading or paper submitted for filing [Repealed]

Rule 3.54 repealed effective July 1, 2009; adopted effective January 1, 2007.

Another Rule 3.54 follows.

Rule 3.54. Confidentiality

(a) Confidential records

No person may have access to an application for an initial fee waiver except the court and authorized court personnel, any persons authorized by the applicant, and any persons authorized by order of the court. No person may reveal any information contained in the application except as authorized by law or order of the court.

(Subd (a) amended and lettered effective July 1, 2009; adopted as unlettered subd effective January 1, 2007.)

(b) Request for access to confidential records

Any person seeking access to an application or financial information provided to the court by an applicant must make the request by noticed motion, supported by a declaration showing good cause regarding why the confidential information should be released.

(Subd (b) adopted effective July 1, 2009.)

(c) Order

An order granting access to an application or financial information may include limitations on who may access the information and on the use of the information after it has been released.

(Subd (c) adopted effective July 1, 2009.)

Rule 3.54 amended and renumbered effective July 1, 2009; adopted as rule 3.60 effective January 1, 2007; previously amended effective January 1, 2008.

Rule 3.55. Effect of denial of application; time for payment of fees [Repealed]

Rule 3.55 repealed effective July 1, 2009; adopted effective January 1, 2007.

Another Rule 3.55 follows.

Rule 3.55. Court fees and costs included in all initial fee waivers

Court fees and costs that must be waived upon granting an application for an initial fee waiver include:

(1) Clerk's fees for filing papers;

(2) Clerk's fees for reasonably necessary certification and copying;

(3) Clerk's fees for issuance of process and certificates;

(4) Clerk's fees for transmittal of papers;

(5) Sheriff's and marshal's fees under article 7 of chapter 2 of part 3 of division 2 of title 3 of the Government Code (commencing with section 26720);

(6) Reporter's fees for attendance at hearings and trials;

(7) The court fee for a telephone appearance under Code of Civil Procedure section 367.5;

(8)4 Clerk's fees for preparing, copying, certifying, and transmitting the clerk's transcript on appeal to the reviewing court and the party. A party proceeding under an initial fee waiver must specify with particularity the documents to be included in the clerk's transcript on appeal;

(9) The fee under rule 8.130(b) or rule 8.834(b) for the court to hold in trust the deposit for a reporter's transcript on appeal; and

(10) The clerk's fee for preparing a transcript of an official electronic recording under rule 8.835 or a copy of such an electronic recording.

Rule 3.55 amended effective September 1, 2019; adopted as rule 3.61 effective January 1, 2007; previously amended effective January 1, 2009, and July 1, 2015; previously amended and renumbered as rule 3.55 effective July 1, 2009.

Advisory Committee Comment

The inclusion of court reporter's fees in the fees waived upon granting an application for an initial fee waiver is intended to provide a fee waiver recipient with an official court reporter or other valid means to create an official verbatim record, for purposes of appeal, on a request. (See *Jameson v. Desta* (2018) 5 Cal.5th 594.). It is intended to include within a waiver all fees mandated under the Government Code for the cost of court reporting services provided by a court.

Rule 3.56. Procedure for determining application [Renumbered]

Rule 3.56 renumbered as rule 3.52 effective July 1, 2009.

Another Rule 3.56 follows.

Rule 3.56. Additional court fees and costs that may be included in initial fee waiver

Necessary court fees and costs that may be waived upon granting an application for an initial fee waiver, either at the outset or upon later application, include:

(1) Jury fees and expenses;

(2) Court-appointed interpreter's fees for witnesses;

(3) Witness fees of peace officers whose attendance is reasonably necessary for prosecution or defense of the case;

(4) Witness fees of court-appointed experts; and

(5) Other fees or expenses as itemized in the application.

Rule 3.56 amended effective July 1, 2015; adopted as rule 3.62 effective January 1, 2007; previously amended and renumbered as rule 3.56 effective July 1, 2009.

Rule 3.57.   Application granted unless acted on by the court [Renumbered]

Rule 3.57 renumbered as rule 3.53 effective July 1, 2009.

Another Rule 3.57 follows.

Rule 3.57.   Amount of lien for waived fees and costs

To determine the amount of the court lien for waived fees and costs, any party to a civil action in which an initial fee waiver has been granted may ask the clerk to calculate the total amount of court fees and costs that have been waived as of the date of the request.

Rule 3.57 adopted effective July 1, 2009.

Rule 3.58.   Hearing on application [Repealed]

Rule 3.58 repealed effective July 1, 2009; adopted effective January 1, 2007; previously amended effective January 1, 2008.

Another Rule 3.58 follows.

Rule 3.58.   Posting notice

Each trial court must post in a conspicuous place near the filing window or counter a notice, 8½ by 11 inches or larger, advising litigants in English and Spanish that they may ask the court to waive court fees and costs. The notice must be substantially as follows:

"NOTICE: If you are unable to pay fees and costs, you may ask the court to permit you to proceed without paying them. Ask the clerk for the *Information Sheet on Waiver of Superior Court Fees and Costs* or *Information Sheet on Waiver of Court Fees and Costs for Appeal or Writ Proceedings* and the *Request to Waive Court Fees.*"

Rule 3.58 amended and renumbered effective July 1, 2009; adopted as rule 3.63 effective January 1, 2007.

Rule 3.59.   Changed circumstances [Repealed]

Rule 3.59 repealed effective July 1, 2009; adopted effective January 1, 2007.

Rule 3.60.   Confidentiality [Renumbered]

Rule 3.60 renumbered as rule 3.54 effective July 1, 2009.

Rule 3.61.   Court fees and costs waived by initial application [Renumbered]

Rule 3.61 renumbered as rule 3.55 effective July 1, 2009.

Rule 3.62.   Additional court fees and costs waived [Renumbered]

Rule 3.62 renumbered as rule 3.56 effective July 1, 2009.

Rule 3.63.   Posting notice [Renumbered]

Rule 3.63 renumbered as rule 3.58 effective July 1, 2009.

Division 3
Filing and Service

Chapter 1
Filing

Rule 3.100.   Payment of filing fees by credit or debit card

A party may pay a filing fee by credit or debit card provided the court is authorized to accept payment by this method under Government Code section 6159, rule 10.820, and other applicable law.

Rule 3.100 adopted effective January 1, 2007.

Chapter 2
Time for Service

Rule 3.110.   Time for service of complaint, cross-complaint, and response

(a) Application

This rule applies to the service of pleadings in civil cases except for collections cases under rule 3.740(a), unlawful detainer actions, proceedings under the Family Code, and other proceedings for which different service requirements are prescribed by law.

(Subd (a) amended effective July 1, 2007; previously amended effective January 1, 2007.)

(b) Service of complaint

The complaint must be served on all named defendants and proofs of service on those defendants must be filed with the court within 60 days after the filing of the complaint. When the complaint is amended to add a defendant, the added defendant must be served and proof of service must be filed within 30 days after the filing of the amended complaint.

(c) Service of cross-complaint

A cross-complaint against a party who has appeared in the action must be accompanied by proof of service of the cross-complaint at the time it is filed. If the cross-complaint adds new parties, the cross-complaint must be served on all parties and proofs of service on the new parties must be filed within 30 days of the filing of the cross-complaint.

(d) Timing of responsive pleadings

The parties may stipulate without leave of court to one 15-day extension beyond the 30-day time period prescribed for the response after service of the initial complaint.

(e) Modification of timing; application for order extending time

The court, on its own motion or on the application of a party, may extend or otherwise modify the times provided in (b)–(d). An application for a court order extending the time to serve a pleading must be filed before the time for service has elapsed. The application must be accompanied by a declaration showing why service has not been completed, documenting the efforts that have been made to complete service, and specifying the date by which service is proposed to be completed.

(Subd (e) amended effective January 1, 2007.)

(f) Failure to serve

If a party fails to serve and file pleadings as required under this rule, and has not obtained an order extending time to serve its pleadings, the court may issue an order to show cause why sanctions shall not be imposed.

(Subd (f) amended effective January 1, 2007.)

(g) Request for entry of default

If a responsive pleading is not served within the time limits specified in this rule and no extension of time has been granted, the plaintiff must file a request for entry of default within 10 days after the time for service has elapsed. The court may issue an order to show cause why sanctions should not be imposed if the plaintiff fails to timely file the request for the entry of default.

(Subd (g) amended effective January 1, 2007.)

(h) Default judgment

When a default is entered, the party who requested the entry of default must obtain a default judgment against the defaulting party within 45 days after the default was entered, unless the court has granted an extension of time. The court may issue an order to show cause why sanctions should not be imposed if that party fails to obtain entry of judgment against a defaulting party or to request an extension of time to apply for a default judgment within that time.

(Subd (h) amended effective January 1, 2007.)

(i) Order to show cause

Responsive papers to an order to show cause issued under this rule must be filed and served at least 5 calendar days before the hearing.

(Subd (i) amended effective January 1, 2007.)

Rule 3.110 amended effective July 1, 2007; adopted as rule 201.7 effective July 1, 2002; previously amended and renumbered effective January 1, 2007.

Chapter 3
Papers to Be Served

Rule 3.220.   Case cover sheet

(a) Cover sheet required

The first paper filed in an action or proceeding must be accompanied by a case cover sheet as required in (b). The cover sheet must be on a form prescribed by the Judicial Council and must be filed in addition to any cover sheet required by local court rule. If the plaintiff indicates on the cover sheet that the case is complex under rule 3.400 et seq. or a collections case under rule 3.740, the plaintiff must serve a copy of the cover sheet with the complaint. In all other cases, the plaintiff is not required to serve the cover sheet. The cover sheet is used for statistical purposes and may affect the assignment of a complex case.

(Subd (a) amended effective January 1, 2009; previously amended effective January 1, 2000, January 1, 2002, and January 1, 2007.)

(b) List of cover sheets

(1) *Civil Case Cover Sheet* (form CM-010) must be filed in each civil action or proceeding, except those filed in small claims court or filed under the Probate Code, Family Code, or Welfare and Institutions Code.

(2) [**Note:** Case cover sheets will be added for use in additional areas of the law as the data collection program expands.]

(Subd (b) amended effective January 1, 2007; previously amended effective July 1, 2002, and July 1, 2003.)

(c) Failure to provide cover sheet

If a party that is required to provide a cover sheet under this rule or a similar local rule fails to do so or provides a defective or incomplete cover sheet at the time the party's first paper is submitted for filing, the clerk of the court must file the paper. Failure of a party or a party's counsel to file a cover sheet as required by this rule may subject that party, its counsel, or both, to sanctions under rule 2.30.

(Subd (c) amended effective January 1, 2007; adopted effective January 1, 2002.)

Rule 3.220 amended effective January 1, 2009; adopted as rule 982.2 effective July 1, 1996; previously amended and renumbered as rule 201.8 effective July 1, 2002, and as rule 3.220 effective January 1, 2007; previously amended effective January 1, 2000, January 1, 2002, and July 1, 2003.

Rule 3.221.   Information about alternative dispute resolution

(a) Court to provide information package

Each court must make available to the plaintiff, at the time the complaint is filed in all general civil cases, an alternative dispute resolution (ADR) information package that includes, at a minimum, all of the following:

(1) General information about the potential advantages and disadvantages of ADR and descriptions of the principal ADR processes. Judicial Council staff have prepared model language that the courts may use to provide this information.

(2) Information about the ADR programs available in that court, including citations to any applicable local court rules and directions for contacting any court staff responsible for providing parties with assistance regarding ADR.

(3) In counties that are participating in the Dispute Resolution Programs Act (DRPA), information about the availability of local dispute resolution programs funded under the DRPA. This information may take the form of a list of the applicable programs or directions for contacting the county's DRPA coordinator.

(4) An ADR stipulation form that parties may use to stipulate to the use of an ADR process.

(Subd (a) amended effective January 1, 2016; previously amended effective July 1, 2002, and January 1, 2007.)

(b) Court may make package available on Web site

A court may make the ADR information package available on its Web site as long as paper copies are also made available in the clerk's office.

(Subd (b) adopted effective July 1, 2002.)

(c) Plaintiff to serve information package

In all general civil cases, the plaintiff must serve a copy of the ADR information package on each defendant together with the complaint. Cross-complainants must serve a copy of the ADR information package on any new parties to the action together with the cross-complaint.

(Subd (c) amended effective January 1, 2007; adopted as subd (b) effective January 1, 2001; previously amended and relettered effective July 1, 2002.)

Rule 3.221 amended effective January 1, 2016; adopted as rule 1590.1 effective January 1, 2001; previously amended and renumbered as rule 201.9 effective July 1, 2002, and as rule 3.221 effective January 1, 2007.

Rule 3.222.   Papers to be served on cross-defendants

A cross-complainant must serve a copy of the complaint or, if it has been amended, the most recently amended complaint and any answers thereto on cross-defendants who have not previously appeared.

Rule 3.222 amended and renumbered effective January 1, 2007; adopted as rule 202 effective January 1, 1985; previously amended effective January 1, 2003.

Chapter 4
Miscellaneous

Rule 3.250.   Limitations on the filing of papers

(a) Papers not to be filed

The following papers, whether offered separately or as attachments to other documents, may not be filed unless they are offered as relevant to the determination of an issue in a law and motion proceeding or other hearing or are ordered filed for good cause:

(1) Subpoena;

(2) Subpoena duces tecum;

(3) Deposition notice, and response;

(4) Notice to consumer or employee, and objection;

(5) Notice of intention to record testimony by audio or video tape;

(6) Notice of intention to take an oral deposition by telephone, videoconference, or other remote electronic means;

(7) Agreement to set or extend time for deposition, agreement to extend time for response to discovery requests, and notice of these agreements;

(8) Interrogatories, and responses or objections to interrogatories;

(9) Demand for production or inspection of documents, things, and places, and responses or objections to demand;

(10) Request for admissions, and responses or objections to request;

(11) Agreement for physical and mental examinations;

(12) Demand for delivery of medical reports, and response;

(13) Demand for exchange of expert witnesses;

(14) Demand for production of discoverable reports and writings of expert witnesses;

(15) List of expert witnesses whose opinion a party intends to offer in evidence at trial and declaration;

(16) Statement that a party does not presently intend to offer the testimony of any expert witness;

(17) Declaration for additional discovery;

(18) Stipulation to enlarge the scope of number of discovery requests from that specified by statute, and notice of the stipulation;

(19) Demand for bill of particulars or an accounting, and response;

(20) Request for statement of damages, and response, unless it is accompanied by a request to enter default and is the notice of special and general damages;

(21) Notice of deposit of jury fees;

(22) Notice to produce party, agent, or tangible things before a court, and response; and

(23) Offer to compromise, unless accompanied by an original proof of acceptance and a written judgment for the court's signature and entry of judgment.

(Subd (a) amended effective January 1, 2003; previously amended effective January 1, 2001.)

(b) Retaining originals of papers not filed

(1) Unless the paper served is a response, the party who serves a paper listed in (a) must retain the original with the original proof of service affixed. If served electronically under rule 2.251, the proof of electronic service must meet the requirements in rule 2.251(i).

(2) The original of a response must be served, and it must be retained by the person upon whom it is served.

(3) An original must be retained under (1) or (2) in the paper or electronic form in which it was created or received.

(4) All original papers must be retained until six months after final disposition of the case, unless the court on motion of any party and for good cause shown orders the original papers preserved for a longer period.

(Subd (b) amended effective January 1, 2017; previously amended effective January 1, 2003, and January 1, 2007.)

(c) Papers defined

As used in this rule, papers include printed forms furnished by the clerk, but do not include notices filed and served by the clerk.

Rule 3.250 amended effective January 1, 2017; adopted as rule 201.5 effective July 1, 1987; previously amended effective January 1, 2001, and January 1, 2003; previously amended and renumbered effective January 1, 2007.

Rule 3.252.   Service of papers on the clerk when a party's address is unknown

(a) Service of papers

When service is made under Code of Civil Procedure section 1011(b) and a party's residence address is unknown, the notice or papers delivered to the clerk, or to the judge if there is no clerk, must be enclosed in an envelope addressed to the party in care of the clerk or the judge.

(Subd (a) amended and lettered effective January 1, 2003.)

(b) Information on the envelope

The back of the envelope delivered under (a) must bear the following information:

"Service is being made under Code of Civil Procedure section 1011(b) on a party whose residence address is unknown."

[Name of party whose residence address is unknown]

[Case name and number]

(Subd (b) amended and lettered effective January 1, 2003.)

Rule 3.252 renumbered effective January 1, 2007; adopted as rule 202.5 effective July 1, 1997; previously amended effective January 1, 2003.

Rule 3.254.   List of parties

(a) Duties of first-named plaintiff or petitioner

Except as provided under rule 2.251 for electronic service, if more than two parties have appeared in a case and are represented by different counsel, the plaintiff or petitioner named first in the complaint or petition must:

(1) Maintain a current list of the parties and their addresses for service of notice on each party; and

(2) Furnish a copy of the list on request to any party or the court.

(Subd (a) amended effective January 1, 2016; adopted as part of unlettered subd effective July 1, 1984; previously amended and lettered as subd (a) effective January 1, 2007.)

(b) Duties of each party

Except as provided under rule 2.251 for electronic service, each party must:

(1) Furnish the first-named plaintiff or petitioner with its current address for service of notice when it first appears in the action;

(2) Furnish the first-named plaintiff or petitioner with any changes in its address for service of notice; and

(3) If it serves an order, notice, or pleading on a party who has not yet appeared in the action, serve a copy of the list required under (a) at the same time as the order, notice, or pleading is served.

(Subd (b) amended effective January 1, 2016; adopted as part of unlettered subd effective July 1, 1984; previously amended and lettered as subd (b) effective January 1, 2007.)

Rule 3.254 amended effective January 1, 2016; adopted as rule 387 effective July 1, 1984; previously amended and renumbered as rule 202.7 effective January 1, 2003, and as rule 3.254 effective January 1, 2007.

Division 4
Parties and Actions

Chapter 1
[Reserved]
Chapter 2
Joinder of Parties
[Reserved]
Chapter 3
Related Cases

Rule 3.300.   Related cases

(a) Definition of "related case"

A pending civil case is related to another pending civil case, or to a civil case that was dismissed with or without prejudice, or to a civil case that was disposed of by judgment, if the cases:

(1) Involve the same parties and are based on the same or similar claims;

(2) Arise from the same or substantially identical transactions, incidents, or events requiring the determination of the same or substantially identical questions of law or fact;

(3) Involve claims against, title to, possession of, or damages to the same property; or

(4) Are likely for other reasons to require substantial duplication of judicial resources if heard by different judges.

(Subd (a) adopted effective January 1, 2007.)

(b) Duty to provide notice

Whenever a party in a civil action knows or learns that the action or proceeding is related to another action or proceeding pending, dismissed, or disposed of by judgment in any state or federal court in California, the party must serve and file a Notice of Related Case.

(Subd (b) amended and relettered effective January 1, 2007; adopted as part of subd (a) effective January 1, 1996; previously amended effective January 1, 2007.)

(c) Contents of the notice

The Notice of Related Case must:

(1) List all civil cases that are related by court, case name, case number, and filing date;

(2) Identify the case that has the earliest filing date and the court and department in which that case is pending; and

(3) Describe the manner in which the cases are related.

(Subd (c) repealed and adopted effective January 1, 2007.)

(d) Service and filing of notice

The Notice of Related Case must be filed in all pending cases listed in the notice and must be served on all parties in those cases.

(Subd (d) adopted effective January 1, 2007.)

(e) Time for service

The Notice of Related Case must be served and filed as soon as possible, but no later than 15 days after the facts concerning the existence of related cases become known.

(Subd (e) adopted effective January 1, 2007.)

(f) Continuing duty to provide notice

The duty under (b)–(e) is a continuing duty that applies when a party files a case with knowledge of a related action or proceeding, and that applies thereafter whenever a party learns of a related action or proceeding.

(Subd (f) amended and relettered effective January 1, 2007; adopted as part of subd (a) effective January 1, 1996; previously adopted as subd (b) effective January 1, 2007.)

(g) Response

Within 5 days after service on a party of a Notice of Related Case, the party may serve and file a response supporting or opposing the notice. The response must state why one or more of the cases listed in the notice are not related or why other good cause exists for the court not to transfer the cases to or from a particular court or department. The response must be filed in all pending cases listed in the notice and must be served on all parties in those cases.

(Subd (g) amended and relettered effective January 1, 2007; adopted as subd (c) effective January 1, 1996; previously amended and relettered subd (d) effective January 1, 2007.)

(h) Judicial action

(1) *Related cases pending in one superior court*

If all the related cases have been filed in one superior court, the court, on notice to all parties, may order that the cases, including probate and family law cases, be related and may assign them to a single judge or department. In a superior court where there is a master calendar, the presiding judge may order the cases related. In a court in which cases are assigned to a single judge or department, cases may be ordered related as follows:

(A) Where all the cases listed in the notice are unlimited civil cases, or where all the cases listed in the notice are limited civil cases, the judge who has the earliest filed case must determine whether the cases must be ordered related and assigned to his or her department;

(B) Where the cases listed in the notice include both unlimited and limited civil cases, the judge who has the earliest filed unlimited civil case must determine whether the cases should be ordered related and assigned to his or her department;

(C) Where the cases listed in the notice contain a probate or family law case, the presiding judge or a judge designated by the presiding judge must determine whether the cases should be ordered related and, if so, to which judge or department they should be assigned;

(D) In the event that any of the cases listed in the notice are not ordered related under (A), (B), or (C), any party in any of the cases listed in the notice may file a motion to have the cases related. The motion must be filed with the presiding judge or the judge designated by the presiding judge; and

(E) If the procedures for relating pending cases under this rule do not apply, the procedures under Code of Civil Procedure section 1048 and rule 3.350 must be followed to consolidate cases pending in the same superior court.

(2) *Related cases pending in different superior courts*

(A) If the related cases are pending in more than one superior court on notice to all parties, the judge to whom the earliest filed case is assigned may confer informally with the parties and with the judges to whom each related case is assigned, to determine the feasibility and desirability of joint discovery orders and other informal or formal means of coordinating proceedings in the cases.

(B) If it is determined that related cases pending in different superior courts should be formally coordinated, the procedures in Code of Civil Procedure section 403 and rule 3.500 must be followed for noncomplex cases, and the procedures in Code of Civil Procedure section 404 et seq. and rules 3.501 et seq. must be followed for complex cases.

(3) *Complex cases*

The provisions in (1) of this subdivision do not apply to cases that have been designated as complex by the parties or determined to be complex by the court.

(Subd (h) amended effective January 1, 2008; adopted as subd (d) effective January 1, 1996; previously amended and relettered as subd (e) effective January 1, 2007.)

(i) Ruling on related cases

The court, department, or judge issuing an order relating cases under this rule must either:

(1) File a notice of the order in all pending cases and serve a copy of the notice on all parties listed in the Notice of Related Case; or

(2) Direct counsel for a party to file the notice in all pending cases and serve a copy on all parties.

(Subd (i) adopted effective January 1, 2007.)

(j) Cases not ordered related

If for any reason a case is not ordered related under this rule, that case will remain assigned to the court, judge, or department where it was pending at the time of the filing and service of the Notice of Related Case.

(Subd (j) adopted effective January 1, 2007.)

(k) Exception

A party is not required to serve and file Notice of Related Case under this rule if another party has already filed a notice and served all parties under this rule on the same case.

(Subd (k) adopted effective January 1, 2007.)

Rule 3.300 amended effective January 1, 2008; adopted as rule 804 effective January 1, 1996; previously amended and renumbered effective January 1, 2007.

Chapter 4
Consolidated Cases

Rule 3.350. Consolidation of cases

(a) Requirements of motion

(1) A notice of motion to consolidate must:

(A) List all named parties in each case, the names of those who have appeared, and the names of their respective attorneys of record;

(B) Contain the captions of all the cases sought to be consolidated, with the lowest numbered case shown first; and

(C) Be filed in each case sought to be consolidated.

(2) The motion to consolidate:

(A) Is deemed a single motion for the purpose of determining the appropriate filing fee, but memorandums, declarations, and other supporting papers must be filed only in the lowest numbered case;

(B) Must be served on all attorneys of record and all nonrepresented parties in all of the cases sought to be consolidated; and

(C) Must have a proof of service filed as part of the motion.

(Subd (a) amended effective January 1, 2007; adopted effective July 1, 1999.)

(b) Lead case

Unless otherwise provided in the order granting the motion to consolidate, the lowest numbered case in the consolidated case is the lead case.

(Subd (b) amended effective January 1, 2007; adopted effective July 1, 1999.)

(c) Order

An order granting or denying all or part of a motion to consolidate must be filed in each case sought to be consolidated. If the motion is granted for all purposes including trial, any subsequent document must be filed only in the lead case.

(Subd (c) amended effective January 1, 2007; adopted effective July 1, 1999.)

(d) Caption and case number

All documents filed in the consolidated case must include the caption and case number of the lead case, followed by the case numbers of all of the other consolidated cases.

(Subd (d) amended effective January 1, 2007; adopted effective July 1, 1999.)
Rule 3.350 amended and renumbered effective January 1, 2007; adopted as rule 367 effective January 1, 1984; previously amended effective July 1, 1999.

Chapter 5
Complex Cases

Rule 3.400. Definition
Rule 3.401. Complex case designation
Rule 3.402. Complex case counterdesignations
Rule 3.403. Action by court

Rule 3.400. Definition

(a) Definition

A "complex case" is an action that requires exceptional judicial management to avoid placing unnecessary burdens on the court or the litigants and to expedite the case, keep costs reasonable, and promote effective decision making by the court, the parties, and counsel.

(b) Factors

In deciding whether an action is a complex case under (a), the court must consider, among other things, whether the action is likely to involve:

(1) Numerous pretrial motions raising difficult or novel legal issues that will be time-consuming to resolve;

(2) Management of a large number of witnesses or a substantial amount of documentary evidence;

(3) Management of a large number of separately represented parties;

(4) Coordination with related actions pending in one or more courts in other counties, states, or countries, or in a federal court; or

(5) Substantial postjudgment judicial supervision.

(Subd (b) amended effective January 1, 2007.)

(c) Provisional designation

Except as provided in (d), an action is provisionally a complex case if it involves one or more of the following types of claims:

(1) Antitrust or trade regulation claims;

(2) Construction defect claims involving many parties or structures;

(3) Securities claims or investment losses involving many parties;

(4) Environmental or toxic tort claims involving many parties;

(5) Claims involving mass torts;

(6) Claims involving class actions; or

(7) Insurance coverage claims arising out of any of the claims listed in (c)(1) through (c)(6).

(Subd (c) amended effective January 1, 2007.)

(d) Court's discretion

Notwithstanding (c), an action is not provisionally complex if the court has significant experience in resolving like claims involving similar facts and the management of those claims has become routine. A court may declare by local rule that certain types of cases are or are not provisionally complex under this subdivision.

(Subd (d) amended effective January 1, 2007.)
Rule 3.400 amended and renumbered effective January 1, 2007; adopted as rule 1800 effective January 1, 2000.

Rule 3.401. Complex case designation

A plaintiff may designate an action as a complex case by filing and serving with the initial complaint the *Civil Case Cover Sheet* (form CM-010) marked to indicate that the action is a complex case.

Rule 3.401 renumbered effective January 1, 2007; adopted as rule 1810 effective January 1, 2000; previously amended effective July 1, 2002, and July 1, 2004.

Rule 3.402. Complex case counterdesignations

(a) Noncomplex counterdesignation

If a *Civil Case Cover Sheet* (form CM-010) designating an action as a complex case has been filed and served and the court has not previously declared the action to be a complex case, a defendant may file and serve no later than its first appearance a counter *Civil Case Cover Sheet* (form CM-010) designating the action as not a complex case. The court must decide, with or without a hearing, whether the action is a complex case within 30 days after the filing of the counterdesignation.

(Subd (a) amended effective January 1, 2007; previously amended effective July 1, 2004.)

(b) Complex counterdesignation

A defendant may file and serve no later than its first appearance a counter *Civil Case Cover Sheet* (form CM-010) designating the action as a complex case. The court must decide, with or without a hearing, whether the action is a complex case within 30 days after the filing of the counterdesignation.

(Subd (b) amended effective January 1, 2007; previously amended effective July 1, 2004.)

(c) Joint complex designation

A defendant may join the plaintiff in designating an action as a complex case.

Rule 3.402 amended and renumbered effective January 1, 2007; adopted as rule 1811 effective January 1, 2000; previously amended effective July 1, 2004.

Rule 3.403.   Action by court

(a) Decision on complex designation

Except as provided in rule 3.402, if a *Civil Case Cover Sheet* (form CM-010) that has been filed and served designates an action as a complex case or checks a case type described as provisionally complex civil litigation, the court must decide as soon as reasonably practicable, with or without a hearing, whether the action is a complex case.

(Subd (a) amended effective January 1, 2007; previously amended effective July 1, 2004.)

(b) Court's continuing power

With or without a hearing, the court may decide on its own motion, or on a noticed motion by any party, that a civil action is a complex case or that an action previously declared to be a complex case is not a complex case.

Rule 3.403 amended effective January 1, 2007; adopted as rule 1812 effective January 1, 2000; previously amended effective July 1, 2004; previously amended and renumbered effective January 1, 2007.

Chapter 6
Coordination of Noncomplex Actions

Rule 3.500.   Transfer and consolidation of noncomplex common-issue actions filed in different courts

(a) Application

This rule applies when a motion under Code of Civil Procedure section 403 is filed requesting transfer and consolidation of noncomplex cases involving a common issue of fact or law filed in different courts.

(Subd (a) amended and lettered effective January 1, 2007; adopted as unlettered subd effective September 21, 1996.)

(b) Preliminary step

A party that intends to file a motion under Code of Civil Procedure section 403 must first make a good-faith effort to obtain agreement of all parties to each case to the proposed transfer and consolidation.

(Subd (b) amended and relettered effective January 1, 2007; adopted as subd (a) effective September 21, 1996.)

(c) Motion and hearing

A motion to transfer an action under Code of Civil Procedure section 403 must conform to the requirements generally applicable to motions, and must be supported by a declaration stating facts showing that:

(1) The actions are not complex;

(2) The moving party has made a good-faith effort to obtain agreement to the transfer and consolidation from all parties to the actions; and

(3) The moving party has notified all parties of their obligation to disclose to the court any information they may have concerning any other motions requesting transfer of any case that would be affected by the granting of the motion before the court.

(Subd (c) amended and relettered effective January 1, 2007; adopted as subd (b) effective September 21, 1996.)

(d) Findings and order

If the court orders that the case or cases be transferred from another court, the order must specify the reasons supporting a finding that the transfer will promote the ends of justice, with reference to the following standards:

(1) The actions are not complex;

(2) Whether the common question of fact or law is predominating and significant to the litigation;

(3) The convenience of the parties, witnesses, and counsel;

(4) The relative development of the actions and the work product of counsel;

(5) The efficient utilization of judicial facilities and staff resources;

(6) The calendar of the courts;

(7) The disadvantages of duplicative and inconsistent rulings, orders, or judgments; and

(8) The likelihood of settlement of the actions without further litigation should coordination be denied.

(Subd (d) amended and relettered effective January 1, 2007; adopted as subd (c) effective September 21, 1996.)

(e) Moving party to provide copies of order

If the court orders that the case or cases be transferred from another court, the moving party must promptly serve the order on all parties to each case and send it to the Judicial Council and to the presiding judge of the court from which each case is to be transferred.

(Subd (e) amended and relettered effective January 1, 2007; adopted as subd (d) effective September 21, 1996.)

(f) Moving party to take necessary action to complete transfer and consolidation

If the court orders a case or cases transferred, the moving party must promptly take all appropriate action necessary to assure that the transfer takes place and that proceedings are initiated in the other court or courts to complete consolidation with the case pending in that court.

(Subd (f) amended and relettered effective January 1, 2007; adopted as subd (3) effective September 21, 1996.)

(g) Conflicting orders

The Judicial Council's coordination staff must review all transfer orders submitted under (e) and must promptly confer with the presiding judges of any courts that have issued conflicting orders under Code of Civil Procedure section 403. The presiding judges of those courts must confer with each other and with the judges who have issued the orders to the extent necessary to resolve the conflict. If it is determined that any party to a case has failed to disclose information concerning pending motions, the court may, after a duly noticed hearing, find that the party's failure to disclose is an unlawful interference with the processes of the court.

(Subd (g) amended effective January 1, 2016; adopted as subd (f) effective September 21, 1996; previously amended and relettered as subd (g) effective January 1, 2007.)

(h) Alternative disposition of motion

If after considering the motion the judge determines that the action or actions pending in another court should not be transferred to the judge's court but instead all the actions that are subject to the motion to transfer should be transferred and consolidated in another court, the judge may order the parties to prepare, serve, and file a motion to have the actions transferred to the appropriate court.

(Subd (h) amended and relettered effective January 1, 2007; adopted as subd (g) effective September 21, 1996.)

Rule 3.500 amended effective January 1, 2016; adopted as rule 1500 effective September 21, 1996; previously amended and renumbered as rule 3.500 effective January 1, 2007.

Chapter 7
Coordination of Complex Actions

Article 1
General Provisions

Rule 3.501.   Definitions

As used in this chapter, unless the context or subject matter otherwise requires:

(1) "Action" means any civil action or proceeding that is subject to coordination or that affects an action subject to coordination.

(2) "Add-on case" means an action that is proposed for coordination, under Code of Civil Procedure section 404.4, with actions previously ordered coordinated.

(3) "Assigned judge" means any judge assigned by the Chair of the Judicial Council or by a presiding judge authorized by the Chair of the Judicial Council to assign a judge under Code of Civil Procedure section 404 or 404.3, including a "coordination motion judge" and a "coordination trial judge."

(4) "Clerk," unless otherwise indicated, means any person designated by an assigned judge to perform any clerical duties required by the rules in this chapter.

(5) "Coordinated action" means any action that has been ordered coordinated with one or more other actions under chapter 3 (commencing with section 404) of title 4 of part 2 of the Code of Civil Procedure and the rules in this chapter.

(6) "Coordination attorney" means an attorney with the Judicial Council staff appointed by the Chair of the Judicial Council to perform such administrative functions as may be appropriate under the rules in this chapter, including but not limited to the functions described in rules 3.524 and 3.550.

(7) "Coordination motion judge" means an assigned judge designated under Code of Civil Procedure section 404 to determine whether coordination is appropriate.

(8) "Coordination proceeding" means any procedure authorized by chapter 3 (commencing with section 404) of title 4 of part 2 of the Code of Civil Procedure and by the rules in this chapter.

(9) "Coordination trial judge" means an assigned judge designated under Code of Civil Procedure section 404.3 to hear and determine coordinated actions.

(10) "Expenses" means all necessary costs that are reimbursable under Code of Civil Procedure section 404.8, including the compensation of the assigned judge and other necessary judicial officers and employees, the costs of any necessary travel and subsistence determined under rules of the State Board of Control, and all necessarily incurred costs of facilities, supplies, materials, and telephone and mailing expenses.

(11) "Included action" means any action or proceeding included in a petition for coordination.

(12) "Liaison counsel" means an attorney of record for a party to an included action or a coordinated action who has been appointed by an assigned judge to serve as representative of all parties on a side with the following powers and duties, as appropriate:

(A) To receive on behalf of and promptly distribute to the parties for whom he or she acts all notices and other documents from the court;

(B) To act as spokesperson for the side that he or she represents at all proceedings set on notice before trial, subject to the right of each party to present individual or divergent positions; and

(C) To call meetings of counsel for the purpose of proposing joint action.

(13) "Party" includes all parties to all included actions or coordinated actions, and the word "party," "petitioner," or any other designation of a party includes that party's attorney of record. When a notice or other paper is required to be given or served on a party, the notice or paper must be given to or served on the party's attorney of record, if any.

(14) "Petition for coordination" means any petition, motion, application, or request for coordination of actions submitted to the Chair of the Judicial Council or to a coordination trial judge under rule 3.544.

(15) "Remand" means to return a coordinated action or a severable claim or issue in a coordinated action from a coordination proceeding to the court in which the action was pending at the time the coordination of that action was ordered. If a remanded action or claim had been transferred by the coordination trial judge under rule 3.543 from the court in which the remanded action or claim was pending, the remand must include the retransfer of that action or claim to that court.

(16) "Serve and file" means that a paper filed in a court must be accompanied by proof of prior service of a copy of the paper on each party required to be served under the rules in this chapter.

(17) "Serve and submit" means that a paper to be submitted to an assigned judge under the rules in this chapter must be submitted to that judge at a designated court address. Every paper so submitted must be accompanied by proof of prior service on each party required to be served under the rules in this chapter. If there is no assigned judge or if the paper is of a type included in rule 3.511(a), the paper must be submitted to the Chair of the Judicial Council.

(18) "Side" means all parties to an included or a coordinated action who have a common or substantially similar interest in the issues, as determined by the assigned judge for the purpose of appointing liaison

counsel or of allotting peremptory challenges in jury selection, or for any other appropriate purpose. Except as defined in rule 3.515, a side may include less than all plaintiffs or all defendants.

(19) "Transfer" means to remove a coordinated action or severable claim in that action from the court in which it is pending to any other court under rule 3.543, without removing the action or claim from the coordination proceeding. "Transfer" includes "retransfer."

Rule 3.501 amended effective January 1, 2016; adopted as rule 1501 effective January 1, 1974; previously amended effective July 1, 1974, and January 1, 2005; previously amended and renumbered as rule 3.501 effective January 1, 2007.

Rule 3.502. Complex case—determination

The court must consider rule 3.400 et seq. in determining whether a case is or is not a complex case within the meaning of Code of Civil Procedure sections 403 and 404.

Rule 3.502 amended and renumbered effective January 1, 2007; adopted as rule 1501.1 effective September 21, 1996; previously amended effective January 1, 2000; previously amended and renumbered as rule 1502 effective January 1, 2005.

Rule 3.503. Requests for extensions of time or to shorten time

(a) Assigned judge may grant request

The assigned judge, on terms that are just, may shorten or extend the time within which any act is permitted or required to be done by a party. Unless otherwise ordered, any motion or application for an extension of time to perform an act required by these rules must be served and submitted in accordance with rule 3.501(17).

(Subd (a) amended effective January 1, 2007; adopted as part of unlettered subd effective January 1, 1974; previously amended and lettered effective January 1, 2005.)

(b) Stipulation requires consent of assigned judge

A stipulation for an extension of time for the filing and service of documents required by the rules in this chapter requires approval of the assigned judge.

(Subd (b) amended and lettered effective January 1, 2005; adopted as part of unlettered subd effective January 1, 1974.)

(c) Extension does not extend time for bringing action to trial

Nothing in this rule extends the time within which a party must bring an action to trial under Code of Civil Procedure section 583.310.

(Subd (c) adopted effective January 1, 2005.)

Rule 3.503 amended and renumbered effective January 1, 2007; adopted as rule 1503 effective January 1, 1974; previously amended effective January 1, 2005.

Rule 3.504. General law applicable

(a) General law applicable

Except as otherwise provided in the rules in this chapter, all provisions of law applicable to civil actions generally apply to an action included in a coordination proceeding.

(Subd (a) amended effective January 1, 2005.)

(b) Rules prevail over conflicting general provisions of law

To the extent that the rules in this chapter conflict with provisions of law applicable to civil actions generally, the rules in this chapter prevail, as provided by Code of Civil Procedure section 404.7.

(Subd (b) amended and lettered effective January 1, 2005; adopted as part of subd (a) effective January 1, 1974.)

(c) Manner of proceeding may be prescribed by assigned judge

If the manner of proceeding is not prescribed by chapter 3 (commencing with section 404) of title 4 of part 2 of the Code of Civil Procedure or by the rules in this chapter, or if the prescribed manner of proceeding cannot, with reasonable diligence, be followed in a particular coordination proceeding, the assigned judge may prescribe any suitable manner of proceeding that appears most consistent with those statutes and rules.

(Subd (c) amended and relettered effective January 1, 2005; adopted as subd (b) effective January 1, 1974.)

(d) Specification of applicable local rules

At the beginning of a coordination proceeding, the assigned judge must specify, subject to rule 3.20, any local court rules to be followed in that proceeding, and thereafter all parties must comply with those rules. Except as otherwise provided in the rules in this chapter or as directed by the assigned judge, the local rules of the court designated in the order appointing the assigned judge apply in all respects if they would otherwise apply without reference to the rules in this chapter.

(Subd (d) amended effective January 1, 2007; adopted as subd (c) effective January 1, 1974; previously amended and relettered effective January 1, 2005.)

Rule 3.504 amended and renumbered effective January 1, 2007; adopted as rule 1504 effective January 1, 1974; previously amended effective January 1, 2005.

Rules of Court

Rule 3.505.   Appellate review

(a) Coordination order to specify reviewing court

If the actions to be coordinated are within the jurisdiction of more than one reviewing court, the coordination motion judge must select and the order granting a petition for coordination must specify, in accordance with Code of Civil Procedure section 404.2, the court having appellate jurisdiction of the coordinated actions.

(Subd (a) amended and lettered effective January 1, 2005; adopted as part of unlettered subd effective January 1, 1974.)

(b) Court for review of order granting or denying coordination

A petition for a writ relating to an order granting or denying coordination may be filed, subject to the provisions of rule 10.1000, in any reviewing court having jurisdiction under the rules applicable to civil actions generally.

(Subd (b) amended effective January 1, 2007; adopted as part of unlettered subd effective January 1, 1974; previously amended and lettered effective January 1, 2005.)

Rule 3.505 amended and renumbered effective January 1, 2007; adopted as rule 1505 effective January 1, 1974; previously amended effective January 1, 2005.

Rule 3.506.   Liaison counsel

(a) Selection and appointment

An assigned judge may at any time request that the parties on each side of the included or coordinated actions select one or more of the attorneys of record on that side for appointment as liaison counsel, and may appoint liaison counsel if the parties are unable to agree.

(Subd (a) amended effective January 1, 2005.)

(b) Duration of appointment by coordination motion judge

Unless otherwise stipulated to or directed by an assigned judge, the appointment of a liaison counsel by a coordination motion judge terminates on the final determination of the issue whether coordination is appropriate. For good cause shown, the coordination motion judge, on the court's own motion or on the motion of any party, may remove previously appointed counsel as liaison counsel.

(Subd (b) amended and lettered effective January 1, 2005; adopted as part of subd (a) effective January 1, 1974.)

(c) Service on party that has requested special notice

Except as otherwise directed by the assigned judge, any party that has made a written request for special notice must be served with a copy of any document thereafter served on the party's liaison counsel.

(Subd (c) amended effective January 1, 2007; adopted as subd (b) effective January 1, 1974.) amended and relettered effective January 1, 2005.)

Rule 3.506 amended and renumbered effective January 1, 2007; adopted as rule 1506 effective January 1, 1974; previously amended effective January 1, 2005.)

Article 2
Procedural Rules Applicable to All Complex Coordination Proceedings

Rule 3.510. Service of papers
Rule 3.511. Papers to be submitted to the Chair of the Judicial Council
Rule 3.512. Electronic submission of documents to the Chair of the Judicial Council
Rule 3.513. Service of memorandums and declarations
Rule 3.514. Evidence presented at court hearings
Rule 3.515. Motions and orders for a stay
Rule 3.516. Motions under Code of Civil Procedure section 170.6

Rule 3.510.   Service of papers

(a) Proof of service

Except as otherwise provided in the rules in this chapter, all papers filed or submitted must be accompanied by proof of prior service on all other parties to the coordination proceeding, including all parties appearing in all included actions and coordinated actions. Service and proof of such service must be made as provided for in civil actions generally.

(Subd (a) amended and lettered effective January 1, 2005; adopted as part of unlettered subd effective January 1, 1974.)

(b) Service on liaison counsel

Except as provided in rule 3.506(c), any party for whom liaison counsel has been designated may be served by serving the liaison counsel.

(Subd (b) amended effective January 1, 2007; adopted as part of unlettered subd effective January 1, 1974; previously amended and lettered effective January 1, 2005.)

(c) Effect of failure to serve

Failure to serve any defendant with a copy of the summons and of the complaint, or failure to serve any party with any other paper or order as required by the rules in this chapter, will not preclude the coordination of the actions, but the unserved defendant or party may assert the failure to serve as a basis for appropriate relief.

(Subd (c) amended and lettered effective January 1, 2005; adopted as part of unlettered subd effective January 1, 1974.)

Rule 3.510 amended and renumbered effective January 1, 2007; adopted as rule 1510 effective January 1, 1974; previously amended effective January 1, 2005.

Rule 3.511.   Papers to be submitted to the Chair of the Judicial Council

(a) Types of papers

A copy of the following papers must be submitted to the Chair of the Judicial Council at the Judicial Council's San Francisco office:

(1) Petition for coordination, including a petition for coordination of add-on cases;

(2) Notice of submission of petition for coordination, along with the caption page of the original action;

(3) Order assigning coordination motion judge, if made by a presiding judge;

(4) Order assigning coordination trial judge, if made by a presiding judge;

(5) Notice of opposition;

(6) Response in opposition to or in support of a petition for coordination;

(7) Motion for a stay order;

(8) Notice of hearing on petition;

(9) Order granting or denying coordination, including coordination of add-on cases;

(10) Order of remand;

(11) Order of transfer;

(12) Order terminating a coordination proceeding in whole or in part;

(13) Order dismissing an included or coordinated action;

(14) Notice of appeal; and

(15) Notice of disposition of appeal.

(Subd (a) adopted effective January 1, 2005.)

(b) Obligation of party

The papers listed in (a) are to be submitted by the party that filed or submitted and served the papers or that was directed to give notice of entry of the order. Notice of submission must be filed with the court as part of the proof of service.

(Subd (b) adopted effective January 1, 2005.)

Rule 3.511 amended and renumbered effective January 1, 2007; adopted as rule 1511 effective January 1, 1974; previously amended effective January 1, 2005.

Rule 3.512.   Electronic submission of documents to the Chair of the Judicial Council

(a) Documents that may be submitted electronically

Any paper listed in rule 3.511(a) may be submitted electronically to coordination@jud.ca.gov.

(Subd (a) amended effective January 1, 2008; previously amended effective January 1, 2007.)

(b) Responsibilities of party submitting documents electronically

A party submitting a document electronically must:

(1) Take all reasonable steps to ensure that the submission does not contain computer code, including viruses, that might be harmful to the Judicial Council's electronic system and to other users of that system; and

(2) Furnish one or more electronic notification addresses and immediately provide any change to his or her electronic notification addresses.

(c) Format of documents to be submitted electronically

A document that is submitted electronically must meet the following requirements:

(1) The software for creating and reading the document must be in the public domain or generally available at a reasonable cost; and

(2) The printing of documents must not result in the loss of document text, format, or appearance.

(d) Signature on documents under penalty of perjury

(1) When a document to be submitted electronically requires a signature under penalty of perjury, the document is deemed signed by the declarant if, before submission, the declarant has signed a printed form of the document.

(2) By electronically submitting the document, the party submitting it indicates that he or she has complied with subdivision (d)(1) of this rule and that the original, signed document is available for review and copying at the request of the court or any party.

(3) At any time after the document is submitted, any other party may serve a demand for production of the original signed document. The

demand must be served on all other parties but need not be filed with the court.

(4) Within five days of service of the demand, the party on whom the demand is made must make the original signed document available for review and copying by all other parties.

(e) Signature on documents not under penalty of perjury

If a document does not require a signature under penalty of perjury, the document is deemed signed by the party if the document is submitted electronically.

(f) Digital signature

A party is not required to use a digital signature on an electronically submitted document.

Rule 3.512 amended effective January 1, 2008; adopted as rule 1511.5 effective July 1, 2005; previously amended and renumbered effective January 1, 2007.

Rule 3.513.   Service of memorandums and declarations

Unless otherwise provided in the rules in this chapter or directed by the assigned judge, all memorandums and declarations in support of or opposition to any petition, motion, or application must be served and submitted at least nine court days before any hearing on the matter at issue.

Rule 3.513 amended effective January 1, 2007; adopted as rule 1512 effective January 1, 1974; previously amended effective January 1, 2005; previously amended and renumbered effective January 1, 2007.

Rule 3.514.   Evidence presented at court hearings

All factual matters to be heard on any petition for coordination, or on any other petition, motion, or application under the rules in this chapter, must be initially presented and heard on declarations, answers to interrogatories or requests for admissions, depositions, or matters judicially noticed. Oral testimony will not be permitted at a hearing except as the assigned judge may permit to resolve factual issues shown by the declarations, responses to discovery, or matters judicially noticed to be in dispute. Only parties that have submitted a petition or motion, or a written response or opposition to a petition or motion, will be permitted to appear at the hearing, except the assigned judge may permit other parties to appear, on a showing of good cause.

Rule 3.514 renumbered effective January 1, 2007; adopted as rule 1513 effective January 1, 1974; previously amended effective January 1, 2005.

Rule 3.515.   Motions and orders for a stay

(a) Motion for stay

Any party may file a motion for an order under Code of Civil Procedure section 404.5 staying the proceedings in any action being considered for, or affecting an action being considered for, coordination, or the court may stay the proceedings on its own motion. The motion for a stay may be included with a petition for coordination or may be served and submitted to the Chair of the Judicial Council and the coordination motion judge by any party at any time prior to the determination of the petition.

(Subd (a) amended effective January 1, 2005.)

(b) Contents of motion

A motion for a stay order must:

(1) List all known pending related cases;

(2) State whether the stay order should extend to any such related case; and

(3) Be supported by a memorandum and by declarations establishing the facts relied on to show that a stay order is necessary and appropriate to effectuate the purposes of coordination.

(Subd (b) amended and lettered effective January 1, 2005; adopted as part of subd (a) effective January 1, 1974.)

(c) Service requirements for certain motions for stay orders

If the action to be stayed is not included in the petition for coordination or any response to that petition, the motion for a stay order and all supporting documents must be served on each party to the action to be stayed and any such party may serve and submit opposition to the motion for a stay order.

(Subd (c) amended and lettered effective January 1, 2005; adopted as part of subd (a) effective January 1, 1974.)

(d) Opposition to motion for stay order

Any memorandums and declarations in opposition to a motion for a stay order must be served and submitted within 10 days after service of the motion.

(Subd (d) amended and lettered effective January 1, 2005; adopted as part of subd (a) effective January 1, 1974.)

(e) Hearing on motion for stay order

A stay order may be issued with or without a hearing. A party filing a motion for a stay order or opposition thereto may request a hearing to determine whether the stay order should be granted. A request for hearing should be made at the time the requesting party files the motion or opposition. If the coordination motion judge grants the request for a hearing, the requesting party must provide notice.

(Subd (e) amended and lettered effective January 1, 2005; adopted as part of subd (a) effective January 1, 1974.)

(f) Determination of motion for stay order

In ruling on a motion for a stay order, the assigned judge must determine whether the stay will promote the ends of justice, considering the imminence of any trial or other proceeding that might materially affect the status of the action to be stayed, and whether a final judgment in that action would have a res judicata or collateral estoppel effect with regard to any common issue of the included actions.

(Subd (f) amended and relettered effective January 1, 2005; adopted as subd (e) effective January 1, 1974.)

(g) Issuance of stay order and termination of stay

If a stay order is issued, the party that requested the stay must serve and file a copy of the order in each included action that is stayed. Thirty or more days following issuance of the stay order, any party that is subject to the stay order may move to terminate the stay.

(Subd (g) amended and relettered effective January 1, 2005; adopted as subd (b) effective January 1, 1974.)

(h) Effect of stay order

Unless otherwise specified in the order, a stay order suspends all proceedings in the action to which it applies. A stay order may be limited by its terms to specified proceedings, orders, motions, or other phases of the action to which the order applies.

(Subd (h) amended and relettered effective January 1, 2005; adopted as subd (c) effective January 1, 1974.)

(i) Effect of absence of stay order

In the absence of a stay order, a court receiving an order assigning a coordination motion judge may continue to exercise jurisdiction over the included action for purposes of all pretrial and discovery proceedings, but no trial may be commenced and no judgment may be entered in that action unless trial of the action had commenced before the assignment of the coordination motion judge.

(Subd (i) amended and relettered effective January 1, 2005; adopted as subd (d) effective January 1, 1974; previously amended effective July 1, 1974.)

(j) Effect of stay order on dismissal for lack of prosecution

The time during which any stay of proceedings is in effect under the rules in this chapter must not be included in determining whether the action stayed should be dismissed for lack of prosecution under chapter 1.5 (§ 583.110 et seq.) of title 8 of part 2 of the Code of Civil Procedure.

(Subd (j) amended and relettered effective January 1, 2005; adopted as subd (f) effective January 1, 1974; previously amended effective January 1, 1986.)

Rule 3.515 renumbered effective January 1, 2007; adopted as rule 1514 effective January 1, 1974; previously amended effective July 1, 1974, January 1, 1986, and January 1, 2005.

Rule 3.516.   Motions under Code of Civil Procedure section 170.6

A party making a peremptory challenge by motion or affidavit of prejudice regarding an assigned judge must submit it in writing to the assigned judge within 20 days after service of the order assigning the judge to the coordination proceeding. All plaintiffs or similar parties in the included or coordinated actions constitute a side and all defendants or similar parties in such actions constitute a side for purposes of applying Code of Civil Procedure section 170.6.

Rule 3.516 renumbered effective January 1, 2007; adopted as rule 1515 effective January 1, 1974; previously amended effective June 19, 1982, and January 1, 2005.

Article 3
Petitions and Proceedings for Coordination of Complex Actions

Rule 3.530. Site of coordination proceedings
Rule 3.531. Potential add-on case
Rule 3.532. Petition for coordination when cases already ordered coordinated

Rule 3.520.   Motions filed in the trial court

(a) General requirements

A motion filed in the trial court under this rule must specify the matters required by rule 3.521(a) and must be made in the manner provided by law for motions in civil actions generally.

(Subd (a) amended effective January 1, 2007; previously amended effective January 1, 1983, and January 1, 2005.)

(b) Permission to submit a petition for coordination

(1) *Request for permission to submit coordination petition*

If a direct petition is not authorized by Code of Civil Procedure section 404, a party may request permission from the presiding judge of the court in which one of the included actions is pending to submit a petition for coordination to the Chair of the Judicial Council. The request must be made by noticed motion accompanied by a proposed order. The proposed order must state that the moving party has permission to submit a petition for coordination to the Chair of the Judicial Council under rules 3.521–3.523.

(2) *Order to be prepared*

If permission to submit a petition is granted, the moving party must serve and file the signed order and submit it to the Chair of the Judicial Council.

(3) *Stay permitted pending preparation of petition*

To provide sufficient time for a party to submit a petition, the presiding judge may stay all related actions pending in that court for a reasonable time not to exceed 30 calendar days.

(Subd (b) amended effective January 1, 2007; previously amended effective January 1, 1983, January 1, 2005, and July 1, 2006.)

Rule 3.520 amended and renumbered effective January 1, 2007; adopted as rule 1520 effective January 1, 1974; previously amended effective January 1, 1983, January 1, 2005, and July 1, 2006.

Rule 3.521.   Petition for coordination

(a) Contents of petition

A request submitted to the Chair of the Judicial Council for the assignment of a judge to determine whether the coordination of certain actions is appropriate, or a request that a coordination trial judge make such a determination concerning an add-on case, must be designated a "Petition for Coordination" and may be made at any time after filing of the complaint. The petition must state whether a hearing is requested and must be supported by a memorandum and declarations showing:

(1) The name of each petitioner or, when the petition is submitted by a presiding or sole judge, the name of each real party in interest, and the name and address of each party's attorney of record, if any;

(2) The names of the parties to all included actions, and the name and address of each party's attorney of record, if any;

(3) If the party seeking to submit a petition for coordination is a plaintiff, whether the party's attorney has served the summons and complaint on all parties in all included actions in which the attorney has appeared;

(4) For each included action, the complete title and case number, the date the complaint was filed, and the title of the court in which the action is pending;

(5) The complete title and case number of any other action known to the petitioner to be pending in a court of this state that shares a common question of fact or law with the included actions, and a statement of the reasons for not including the other action in the petition for coordination or a statement that the petitioner knows of no other actions sharing a common question of fact or law;

(6) The status of each included action, including the status of any pretrial or discovery motions or orders in that action, if known to petitioner;

(7) The facts relied on to show that each included action meets the coordination standards specified in Code of Civil Procedure section 404.1; and

(8) The facts relied on in support of a request that a particular site or sites be selected for a hearing on the petition for coordination.

(Subd (a) amended effective January 1, 2005.)

(b) Submit proof of filing and service

Within five court days of submitting the petition for coordination, the petitioner must submit to the Chair of the Judicial Council proof of filing of the notice of submission of petition required by rule 3.522, and proof of service of the notice of submission of petition and of the petition required by rule 3.523.

(Subd (b) amended effective January 1, 2007; previously amended effective January 1, 2005, and January 1, 2007.)

(c) Copies of pleadings in lieu of proof by declaration

In lieu of proof by declaration of any fact required by (a)(2), (4), (7), and (8), a certified or endorsed copy of the respective pleadings may be attached to the petition for coordination, provided that the petitioner specifies with particularity the portions of the pleadings that are relied on to show the fact.

(Subd (c) amended effective January 1, 2005.)

(d) Effect of imminent trial date

The imminence of a trial in any action otherwise appropriate for coordination may be a ground for summary denial of a petition for coordination, in whole or in part.

(Subd (d) amended effective January 1, 2005.)

Rule 3.521 amended effective January 1, 2007; adopted as rule 1521 effective January 1, 1974; previously amended effective January 1, 2005; previously amended and renumbered effective January 1, 2007.

Rule 3.522.   Notice of submission of petition for coordination

(a) Contents of notice of submission

In each included action, the petitioner must file a "Notice of Submission of Petition for Coordination" and the petition for coordination. Each notice must bear the title of the court in which the notice is to be filed and the title and case number of each included action that is pending in that court. Each notice must include:

(1) The date that the petition for coordination was submitted to the Chair of the Judicial Council;

(2) The name and address of the petitioner's attorney of record;

(3) The title and case number of each included action to which the petitioner is a party and the title of the court in which each action is pending; and

(4) The statement that any written opposition to the petition must be submitted and served at least nine court days before the hearing date.

(Subd (a) amended effective January 1, 2007; adopted as part of unlettered subd effective January 1, 1974; previously amended and lettered effective January 1, 2005; previously amended effective January 1, 2006.)

(b) Copies of notice

The petitioner must submit the notice and proof of filing in each included action to the Chair of the Judicial Council within five court days of submitting the petition for coordination.

(Subd (b) amended effective January 1, 2007; adopted as part of unlettered subd effective January 1, 1974; previously amended and lettered effective January 1, 2005.)

Rule 3.522 amended and renumbered effective January 1, 2007; adopted as rule 1522 effective January 1, 1974; previously amended effective January 1, 2005, and January 1, 2006.

Rule 3.523.   Service of notice of submission on party

The petitioner must serve the notice of submission of petition for coordination that was filed in each included action, the petition for coordination, and supporting documents on each party appearing in each included action and submit the notice to the Chair of the Judicial Council within five court days of submitting the petition for coordination.

Rule 3.523 amended effective January 1, 2007; adopted as rule 1523 effective January 1, 1974; previously amended effective January 1, 2005; previously amended and renumbered effective January 1, 2007.

Rule 3.524.   Order assigning coordination motion judge

(a) Contents of order

An order by the Chair of the Judicial Council assigning a coordination motion judge to determine whether coordination is appropriate, or authorizing the presiding judge of a court to assign the matter to judicial officers of the court to make the determination in the same manner as assignments are made in other civil cases, must include the following:

(1) The special title and number assigned to the coordination proceeding; and

(2) The court's address or electronic service address for submitting all subsequent documents to be considered by the coordination motion judge.

(Subd (a) amended effective January 1, 2016; adopted as part of unlettered subd effective January 1, 1974; previously amended and lettered as subd (a) effective January 1, 2005.)

(b) Service of order

The petitioner must serve the order described in (a) on each party appearing in an included action and send it to each court in which an included action is pending with directions to the clerk to file the order in the included action.

(Subd (b) amended and lettered effective January 1, 2005; adopted as part of unlettered subd effective January 1, 1974.)

Rule 3.524 amended effective January 1, 2016; adopted as rule 1524 effective January 1, 1974; previously amended effective January 1, 2005; previously renumbered as rule 3.524 effective January 1, 2007.

Rule 3.525.   Response in opposition to petition for coordination

Any party to an included action that opposes coordination may serve and submit a memorandum and declarations in opposition to the petition. Any response in opposition must be served and filed at least nine court days before the date set for hearing.

Rule 3.525 amended effective January 1, 2007; adopted as rule 1525 effective January 1, 1974; previously amended effective January 1, 2005; previously amended and renumbered effective January 1, 2007.

Rule 3.526.   Response in support of petition for coordination

Any party to an included action that supports coordination may serve and submit a written statement in support of the petition. Any response in support must be served and filed at least nine court days before the date set for hearing. If a party that supports coordination does not support the particular site or sites requested by the petitioner for the hearing on the petition for coordination, that party may request that a different site or sites be selected and include in his or her response the facts relied on in support thereof.

Rule 3.526 amended effective January 1, 2007; adopted as rule 1526 effective January 1, 1974; previously amended effective January 1, 2005; previously amended and renumbered effective January 1, 2007.

Rule 3.527.   Notice of hearing on petition for coordination

(a) Timing and notice of hearing

The coordination motion judge must set a hearing date on a petition for coordination within 30 days of the date of the order assigning the coordination motion judge. When a coordination motion judge is assigned to decide a petition for coordination that lists additional included actions sharing a common question of law or fact with included actions in a petition for coordination already pending before the judge, the judge may continue the hearing date on the first petition no more than 30 calendar days in order to hear both petitions at the same time. The petitioner must provide notice of the hearing to each party appearing in an included action. If the coordination motion judge determines that a party that should be served with notice of the petition for coordination has not been served with notice, the coordination motion judge must order the petitioner to promptly serve that party. If the coordination motion judge determines that a hearing is not required under (b), the hearing date must be vacated and notice provided to the parties.

(Subd (a) amended and relettered effective January 1, 2005; adopted as subd (b) effective January 1, 1974.)

(b) Circumstances in which hearing required

A hearing must be held to decide a petition for coordination if a party opposes coordination. A petition for coordination may not be denied unless a hearing has been held.

(Subd (b) adopted effective January 1, 2005.)

(c) Report to the Chair of the Judicial Council

If the petition for coordination has not been decided within 30 calendar days after the hearing, the coordination motion judge must promptly submit to the Chair of the Judicial Council a written report describing:

(1) The present status of the petition for coordination proceeding;

(2) Any factors or circumstances that may have caused undue or unanticipated delay in the decision on the petition for coordination; and

(3) Any stay orders that are in effect.

(Subd (c) amended effective January 1, 2005.)

Rule 3.527 renumbered effective January 1, 2007; adopted as rule 1527 effective January 1, 1974; previously amended effective January 1, 2005.

Rule 3.528.   Separate hearing on certain coordination issues

When a petition for coordination may be disposed of on the determination of a specified issue or issues, without a hearing on all issues raised by the petition and any opposition, the assigned judge may order that the specified issue or issues be heard and determined before a hearing on the remaining issues.

Rule 3.528 renumbered effective January 1, 2007; adopted as rule 1528 effective January 1, 1974; previously amended effective January 1, 2005.

Rule 3.529.   Order granting or denying coordination

(a) Filing, service, and submittal

When a petition for coordination is granted or denied, the petitioner must promptly file the order in each included action, serve it on each party appearing in an included action, and submit it to the Chair of the Judicial Council.

(Subd (a) amended effective January 1, 2007; previously amended effective January 1, 2005.)

(b) Stay of further proceedings

When an order granting coordination is filed in an included action, all further proceedings in that action are automatically stayed, except as directed by the coordination trial judge or by the coordination motion judge under (c). The stay does not preclude the court in which the included action is pending from accepting and filing papers with proof of submission of a copy to the assigned judge or from exercising jurisdiction over any severable claim that has not been ordered coordinated.

(Subd (b) amended effective January 1, 2005.)

(c) Authority of coordination motion judge pending assignment of coordination trial judge

After a petition for coordination has been granted and before a coordination trial judge has been assigned, the coordination motion judge may for good cause make any appropriate order as the ends of justice may require but may not commence a trial or enter judgment in any included action. Good cause includes a showing of an urgent need for judicial action to preserve the rights of a party pending assignment of a coordination trial judge.

(Subd (c) amended effective January 1, 2005.)

(d) Order denying coordination

The authority of a coordination motion judge over an included action terminates when an order denying a petition for coordination is filed in the included action and served on the parties to the action. A stay ordered by the coordination motion judge terminates 10 days after the order denying coordination is filed.

(Subd (d) amended effective January 1, 2005.)

Rule 3.529 amended and renumbered effective January 1, 2007; adopted as rule 1529 effective January 1, 1974; previously amended effective June 19, 1982, and January 1, 2005.

Rule 3.530.   Site of coordination proceedings

(a) Recommendation by coordination motion judge

If a petition for coordination is granted, the coordination motion judge must, in the order granting coordination, recommend to the Chair of the Judicial Council a particular superior court for the site of the coordination proceedings.

(b) Factors to consider

The coordination motion judge may consider any relevant factors in making a recommendation for the site of the coordination proceedings, including the following:

(1) The number of included actions in particular locations;

(2) Whether the litigation is at an advanced stage in a particular court;

(3) The efficient use of court facilities and judicial resources;

(4) The locations of witnesses and evidence;

(5) The convenience of the parties and witnesses;

(6) The parties' principal places of business;

(7) The office locations of counsel for the parties; and

(8) The ease of travel to and availability of accommodations in particular locations.

Rule 3.530 renumbered effective January 1, 2007; adopted as rule 1530 effective January 1, 2005.

Rule 3.531.   Potential add-on case

(a) Notice

Any party to an included action in a pending petition for coordination must promptly provide notice of any potential add-on cases in which that party is also named or in which that party's attorney has appeared. The party must submit notice to the coordination motion judge and the Chair of the Judicial Council and serve it on each party appearing in the included actions in the pending petition and each party appearing in the potential add-on cases.

(b) Stipulation or order

By stipulation of all parties or order of the coordination motion judge, each potential add-on case will be deemed an included action for purposes of the hearing on the petition for coordination.

Rule 3.531 renumbered effective January 1, 2007; adopted as rule 1531 effective January 1, 2005.

Rule 3.532. Petition for coordination when cases already ordered coordinated

(a) Assignment of coordination trial judge

If it appears that included actions in a petition for coordination share a common question of law or fact with cases already ordered coordinated, the Chair of the Judicial Council may assign the petition to the coordination trial judge for the existing coordinated cases to decide the petition as a request to coordinate an add-on case under rule 3.544.

(Subd (a) amended effective January 1, 2007.)

(b) Order

The coordination trial judge's order must specify that the request to coordinate an add-on case is either granted or denied.

(c) Filing and service

The petitioner must promptly file the order in each included action, serve it on each party appearing in an included action, and submit a copy to the Chair of the Judicial Council.

(Subd (c) amended effective January 1, 2007.)

(d) Cases added on and right to peremptory challenge

If the coordination trial judge grants the petition, the included actions will be coordinated as add-on cases and the right to file a peremptory challenge under Code of Civil Procedure section 170.6 will be limited by rule 3.516.

(Subd (d) amended effective January 1, 2007.)

(e) Assignment of coordination motion judge if cases not added on

If the coordination trial judge denies the petition as a request to coordinate an add-on case under rule 3.544, the Chair of the Judicial Council must assign a coordination motion judge to determine whether coordination is appropriate under rule 3.524.

(Subd (e) amended effective January 1, 2007.)

Rule 3.532 amended and renumbered effective January 1, 2007; adopted as rule 1532 effective January 1, 2005.

Article 4
Pretrial and Trial Rules for Complex Coordinated Actions

Rule 3.540. Order assigning coordination trial judge
Rule 3.541. Duties of the coordination trial judge
Rule 3.542. Remand of action or claim
Rule 3.543. Transfer of action or claim
Rule 3.544. Add-on cases
Rule 3.545. Termination of coordinated action

Rule 3.540. Order assigning coordination trial judge

(a) Assignment by the Chair of the Judicial Council

When a petition for coordination is granted, the Chair of the Judicial Council must either assign a coordination trial judge to hear and determine the coordinated actions or authorize the presiding judge of a court to assign the matter to judicial officers of the court in the same manner as assignments are made in other civil cases, under Code of Civil Procedure section 404.3. The order assigning a coordination trial judge must designate an address for submission of papers to that judge.

(Subd (a) amended and lettered effective January 1, 2005; adopted as part of unlettered subd effective January 1, 1974.)

(b) Powers of coordination trial judge

Immediately on assignment, the coordination trial judge may exercise all the powers over each coordinated action that are available to a judge of the court in which that action is pending.

(Subd (b) amended effective January 1, 2007; adopted as part of unlettered subd effective January 1, 1974; previously amended and lettered effective January 1, 2005.)

(c) Filing and service of copies of assignment order

The petitioner must file the assignment order in each coordinated action and serve it on each party appearing in each action, and, if the assignment was made by the presiding judge, submit it to the Chair of the Judicial Council. Every paper filed in a coordinated action must be accompanied by proof of submission of a copy of the paper to the coordination trial judge at the designated address. A copy of the assignment order must be included in any subsequent service of process on any defendant in the action.

(Subd (c) amended effective January 1, 2011; adopted as part of unlettered subd; previously amended and lettered effective January 1, 2005.)

Rule 3.540 amended effective January 1, 2011; adopted as rule 1540 effective January 1, 1974; previously amended effective January 1, 2005; previously amended and renumbered effective January 1, 2007.

Rule 3.541. Duties of the coordination trial judge

(a) Initial case management conference

The coordination trial judge must hold a case management conference within 45 days after issuance of the assignment order. Counsel and all self-represented persons must attend the conference and be prepared to discuss all matters specified in the order setting the conference. At any time following the assignment of the coordination trial judge, a party may serve and submit a proposed agenda for the conference and a proposed form of order covering such matters of procedure and discovery as may be appropriate. At the conference, the judge may:

(1) Appoint liaison counsel under rule 3.506;

(2) Establish a timetable for filing motions other than discovery motions;

(3) Establish a schedule for discovery;

(4) Provide a method and schedule for the submission of preliminary legal questions that might serve to expedite the disposition of the coordinated actions;

(5) In class actions, establish a schedule, if practicable, for the prompt determination of matters pertinent to the class action issue;

(6) Establish a central depository or depositories to receive and maintain for inspection by the parties evidentiary material and specified documents that are not required by the rules in this chapter to be served on all parties; and

(7) Schedule further conferences if appropriate.

(Subd (a) amended effective January 1, 2007; previously amended effective January 1, 2005.)

(b) Management of proceedings by coordination trial judge

The coordination trial judge must assume an active role in managing all steps of the pretrial, discovery, and trial proceedings to expedite the just determination of the coordinated actions without delay. The judge may, for the purpose of coordination and to serve the ends of justice:

(1) Order any coordinated action transferred to another court under rule 3.543;

(2) Schedule and conduct hearings, conferences, and a trial or trials at any site within this state that the judge deems appropriate with due consideration to the convenience of parties, witnesses, and counsel; to the relative development of the actions and the work product of counsel; to the efficient use of judicial facilities and resources; and to the calendar of the courts; and

(3) Order any issue or defense to be tried separately and before trial of the remaining issues when it appears that the disposition of any of the coordinated actions might thereby be expedited.

(Subd (b) amended effective January 1, 2007; previously amended effective January 1, 2005.)

Rule 3.541 amended and renumbered effective January 1, 2007; adopted as rule 1541 effective January 1, 1974; previously amended effective January 1, 2005.

Rule 3.542. Remand of action or claim

The coordination trial judge may at any time remand a coordinated action or any severable claim or issue in that action to the court in which the action was pending at the time the coordination of that action was ordered. Remand may be made on the stipulation of all parties or on the basis of evidence received at a hearing on the court's own motion or on the motion of any party to any coordinated action. No action or severable claim or issue in that action may be remanded over the objection of any party unless the evidence demonstrates a material change in the circumstances that are relevant to the criteria for coordination under Code of Civil Procedure section 404.1. If the order of remand requires that the action be transferred, the provisions of rule 3.543(c)–(e) are applicable to the transfer. A remanded action is no longer part of the coordination proceedings for purposes of the rules in this chapter.

Rule 3.542 amended and renumbered effective January 1, 2007; adopted as rule 1542 effective January 1, 1974; previously amended effective January 1, 2005, and July 1, 2006.

Rule 3.543. Transfer of action or claim

(a) Court may transfer coordinated action

The coordination trial judge may order any coordinated action or severable claim in that action transferred from the court in which it is pending to another court for a specified purpose or for all purposes. Transfer may be made by the court on its own motion or on the motion of any party to any coordinated action.

(Subd (a) amended effective January 1, 2005.)

(b) Hearing on motion to transfer

If a party objects to the transfer, the court must hold a hearing on at least 10 days' written notice served on all parties to that action. At any hearing to determine whether an action or claim should be transferred, the court must consider the convenience of parties, witnesses, and counsel; the relative development of the actions and the work product of counsel; the efficient use of judicial facilities and resources; the calendar of the courts; and any other relevant matter.

(Subd (b) amended effective January 1, 2007; adopted as part of subd (a) effective January 1, 1974; previously amended and lettered effective January 1, 2005.)

(c) Order transferring action

The order transferring the action or claim must designate the court to which the action is transferred and must direct that a copy of the order of transfer be filed in each coordinated action. The order must indicate whether the action remains part of the coordination proceedings for purposes of the rules in this chapter.

(Subd (c) amended and lettered effective January 1, 2005; adopted as part of subd (b) effective January 1, 1974.)

(d) Duties of transferor and transferee courts

(1) *Duty of transferor court*

The clerk of the court in which the action was pending must immediately prepare and transmit to the court to which the action is transferred a certified copy of the order of transfer and of the pleadings and proceedings in the transferred action and must serve a copy of the order of transfer on each party appearing in that action.

(2) *Duty of transferee court*

The court to which the action is transferred must file the action as if the action had been commenced in that court. No fees may be required for such transfer by either court.

(3) *Transmission of papers*

If it is necessary to have any of the original pleadings or other papers in the transferred action before the coordination trial judge, the clerk of the court from which the action was transferred must, on written request of a party to that action or of the coordination trial judge, transmit such papers or pleadings to the court to which the action is transferred and must retain a certified copy.

(Subd (d) amended effective January 1, 2007; adopted as part of subd (b) effective January 1, 1974; previously amended and lettered effective January 1, 2005.)

(e) Transferee court to exercise jurisdiction

On receipt of a transfer order, the court to which the action is transferred may exercise jurisdiction over the action in accordance with the orders and directions of the coordination trial judge, and no other court may exercise jurisdiction over that action except as provided in this rule.

(Subd (e) amended and lettered effective January 1, 2005; adopted as part of subd (b) effective January 1, 1974.)

Rule 3.543 amended and renumbered effective January 1, 2007; adopted as rule 1543 effective January 1, 1974; previously amended effective January 1, 2005.

Rule 3.544.   Add-on cases

(a) Request to coordinate add-on case

A request to coordinate an add-on case must comply with the requirements of rules 3.520 through 3.523, except that the request must be submitted to the coordination trial judge under Code of Civil Procedure section 404.4, with proof of service of one copy on the Chair of the Judicial Council and proof of service as required by rule 3.510.

(Subd (a) amended effective January 1, 2016; previously amended effective January 1, 2005, and January 1, 2007.)

(b) Opposition to request to coordinate an add-on case

Within 10 days after the service of a request, any party may serve and submit a notice of opposition to the request. Thereafter, within 15 days after submitting a notice of opposition, the party must serve and submit a memorandum and declarations in opposition to the request. Failure to serve and submit a memorandum and declarations in opposition may be a ground for granting the request to coordinate an add-on case.

(Subd (b) amended and lettered effective January 1, 2005; adopted as part of subd (a) effective January 1, 1974.)

(c) Hearing on request to coordinate an add-on case

The coordination trial judge may order a hearing on a request to coordinate an add-on case under rules 3.527 and 3.528 and may allow the parties to serve and submit additional written materials in support of or opposition to the request. In deciding the request to coordinate, the court must consider the relative development of the actions and the work product of counsel, in addition to any other relevant matter. An application for an order staying the add-on case must be made to the coordination trial judge under rule 3.515.

(Subd (c) amended effective January 1, 2007; adopted as subd (b) effective January 1, 1974; previously amended and relettered effective January 1, 2005.)

(d) Order on request to coordinate an add-on case

If no party has filed a notice of opposition within the time required under (b), the coordination trial judge may enter an order granting or denying the request without a hearing. An order granting or denying a request to coordinate an add-on case must be prepared and served under rule 3.529, and an order granting such request automatically stays all further proceedings in the add-on case under rule 3.529.

(Subd (d) amended effective January 1, 2007; adopted as subd (c) effective January 1, 1974; previously amended and relettered effective January 1, 2005.)

Rule 3.544 amended effective January 1, 2016; adopted as rule 1544 effective January 1, 1974; previously amended effective January 1, 2005; previously amended and renumbered as rule 3.544 effective January 1, 2007.

Rule 3.545.   Termination of coordinated action

(a) Coordination trial judge may terminate action

The coordination trial judge may terminate any coordinated action by settlement or final dismissal, summary judgment, or judgment, or may transfer the action so that it may be dismissed or otherwise terminated in the court where it was pending when coordination was ordered.

(Subd (a) amended and lettered effective January 1, 2005; adopted as part of unlettered subd effective January 1, 1974.)

(b) Copies of order dismissing or terminating action and judgment

A certified copy of the order dismissing or terminating the action and of any judgment must be transmitted to:

(1) The clerk of the court in which the action was pending when coordination was ordered, who shall promptly enter any judgment and serve notice of entry of the judgment on all parties to the action and on the Chair of the Judicial Council; and

(2) The appropriate clerks for filing in each pending coordinated action.

(Subd (b) amended and lettered effective January 1, 2005; adopted as part of unlettered subd effective January 1, 1974.)

(c) Judgment in coordinated action

The judgment entered in each coordinated action must bear the title and case number assigned to the action at the time it was filed.

(Subd (c) amended and lettered effective January 1, 2005; adopted as part of unlettered subd effective January 1, 1974.)

(d) Proceedings in trial court after judgment

Until the judgment in a coordinated action becomes final or until a coordinated action is remanded, all further proceedings in that action to be determined by the trial court must be determined by the coordination trial judge. Thereafter, unless otherwise ordered by the coordination trial judge, all such proceedings must be conducted in the court where the action was pending when coordination was ordered. The coordination trial judge must also specify the court in which any ancillary proceedings will be heard and determined. For purposes of this rule, a judgment is final when it is no longer subject to appeal.

(Subd (d) amended and lettered effective January 1, 2005; adopted as part of unlettered subd effective January 1, 1974.)

Rule 3.545 renumbered effective January 1, 2007; adopted as rule 1545 effective January 1, 1974; previously amended effective January 1, 2005.

Article 5
Administration of Coordinated Complex Actions

Rule 3.550.   General administration by Judicial Council staff

(a) Coordination attorney

Except as otherwise provided in the rules in this chapter, all necessary administrative functions under this chapter will be performed at the direction of the Chair of the Judicial Council by a coordination attorney.

(Subd (a) amended effective January 1, 2016; previously amended effective January 1, 2005, and January 1, 2007.)

(b) Duties of coordination attorney

The coordination attorney must at all times maintain:

(1) A list of active and retired judges who are qualified and currently available to conduct coordination proceedings; and

(2) A register of all coordination proceedings and a file for each proceeding, for public inspection during regular business hours at the San Francisco office of the Judicial Council.

(Subd (b) amended and lettered effective January 1, 2005; previously adopted as part of subd (a) effective January 1, 2005.)

(c) Coordination proceeding title and case number

The coordination attorney must assign each coordination proceeding a special title and coordination proceeding number. Thereafter all papers in that proceeding must bear that title and number.

(Subd (c) amended and relettered effective January 1, 2005; adopted as subd (b) effective January 1, 1974.)

Rule 3.550 amended effective January 1, 2016; adopted as rule 1550 effective January 1, 1974; previously amended effective January 1, 2005; previously amended and renumbered as rule 3.550 effective January 1, 2007.

Division 5
Venue
[Reserved]

Division 6
Proceedings

Chap. 1. General Provisions [Reserved].
Chap. 2. Stay of Proceedings. Rule 3.650.
Chap. 3. Hearings, Conferences, and Proceedings. Rule 3.670.
Chap. 4. Special Proceedings on Construction-Related Accessibility Claims. Rules 3.680, 3.682.

Chapter 1
General Provisions
[Reserved]

Chapter 2
Stay of Proceedings

Rule 3.650. Duty to notify court and others of stay

(a) Notice of stay

The party who requested or caused a stay of a proceeding must immediately serve and file a notice of the stay and attach a copy of the order or other document showing that the proceeding is stayed. If the person who requested or caused the stay has not appeared, or is not subject to the jurisdiction of the court, the plaintiff must immediately file a notice of the stay and attach a copy of the order or other document showing that the proceeding is stayed. The notice of stay must be served on all parties who have appeared in the case.

(b) When notice must be provided

The party responsible for giving notice under (a) must provide notice if the case is stayed for any of the following reasons:

(1) An order of a federal court or a higher state court;

(2) Contractual arbitration under Code of Civil Procedure section 1281.4;

(3) Arbitration of attorney fees and costs under Business and Professions Code section 6201; or

(4) Automatic stay caused by a filing in another court, including a federal bankruptcy court.

(Subd (b) amended effective January 1, 2007.)

(c) Contents of notice

The notice must state whether the case is stayed with regard to all parties or only certain parties. If it is stayed with regard to only certain parties, the notice must specifically identify those parties. The notice must also state the reason that the case is stayed.

(Subd (c) amended effective January 1, 2006.)

(d) Notice that stay is terminated or modified

When a stay is vacated, is no longer in effect, or is modified, the party who filed the notice of the stay must immediately serve and file a notice of termination or modification of stay. If that party fails to do so, any other party in the action who has knowledge of the termination or modification of the stay must serve and file a notice of termination or modification of stay. Once one party in the action has served and filed a notice of termination or modification of stay, other parties in the action are not required to do so.

(Subd (d) amended effective January 1, 2006.)

Rule 3.650 amended and renumbered effective January 1, 2007; adopted as rule 224 effective January 1, 2004; previously amended effective January 1, 2006.

Chapter 3
Hearings, Conferences, and Proceedings

Chapter 3 amended effective July 1, 2008.

Rule 3.670. Telephone appearance

(a) Policy favoring telephone appearances

The intent of this rule is to promote uniformity in the practices and procedures relating to telephone appearances in civil cases. To improve access to the courts and reduce litigation costs, courts should permit parties, to the extent feasible, to appear by telephone at appropriate conferences, hearings, and proceedings in civil cases.

(Subd (a) adopted effective January 1, 2008.)

(b) Application

This rule applies to all general civil cases as defined in rule 1.6 and to unlawful detainer and probate proceedings.

(Subd (b) relettered effective January 1, 2008; previously repealed and adopted as subd (a) effective July 1, 1998; previously amended effective January 1, 1999, January 1, 2001, January 1, 2003, and January 1, 2007.)

(c) General provision authorizing parties to appear by telephone

Except as ordered by the court under (f)(2) and subject to (d) (regarding ex parte applications) and (h) (regarding notice), all parties, including moving parties, may appear by telephone at all conferences, hearings, and proceedings other than those where personal appearances are required under (e).

(Subd (c) amended effective January 1, 2014; previously repealed and adopted as subd (b) effective July 1, 1998; previously amended effective July 1, 1999, and January 1, 2003; previously amended and relettered effective January 1, 2008.)

(d) Provisions regarding ex parte applications

(1) *Applicants*

Except as ordered by the court under (f)(2) and subject to (h), applicants seeking an ex parte order may appear by telephone provided that the moving papers have been filed and a proposed order submitted by at least 10:00 a.m. two court days before the ex parte appearance and, if required by local rule, copies have been provided directly to the department in which the matter is to be considered.

(2) *Opposing Parties*

Even if the applicant has not complied with (1), except as ordered by the court under (f)(2) and subject to the provisions in (h), parties opposing an ex parte order may appear by telephone.

(Subd (d) adopted effective January 1, 2014.)

(e) Required personal appearances

(1) Except as permitted by the court under (f)(3), a personal appearance is required for the following hearings, conferences, and proceedings:

(A) Trials, hearings, and proceedings at which witnesses are expected to testify;

(B) Hearings on temporary restraining orders;

(C) Settlement conferences;

(D) Trial management conferences;

(E) Hearings on motions in limine; and

(F) Hearings on petitions to confirm the sale of property under the Probate Code.

(2) In addition, except as permitted by the court under (f)(3), a personal appearance is required for the following persons:

(A) Persons ordered to appear to show cause why sanctions should not be imposed for violation of a court order or a rule; or

(B) Persons ordered to appear in an order or citation issued under the Probate Code.

At the proceedings described under (2), parties who are not required to appear in person under this rule may appear by telephone.

(Subd (e) amended and relettered effective January 1, 2014; adopted as subd (c) effective July 1, 1998; previously amended effective July 1, 2002, and January 1, 2003; previously amended and relettered as subd (d) effective January 1, 2008.)

(f) Court discretion to modify rule

(1) *Policy favoring telephone appearances in civil cases*

In exercising its discretion under this provision, the court should consider the general policy favoring telephone appearances in civil cases.

(2) *Court may require personal appearances*

The court may require a party to appear in person at a hearing, conference, or proceeding listed in (c) or (d) if the court determines on a hearing-by-hearing basis that a personal appearance would materially assist in the determination of the proceedings or in the effective management or resolution of the particular case.

(3) *Court may permit appearances by telephone*

The court may permit a party to appear by telephone at a hearing, conference, or proceeding under (e) if the court determines that a telephone appearance is appropriate.

(Subd (f) amended and relettered effective January 1, 2014; adopted as subd (e) effective January 1, 2008.)

(g) Need for personal appearance

If, at any time during a hearing, conference, or proceeding conducted by telephone, the court determines that a personal appearance is necessary, the court may continue the matter and require a personal appearance.

(Subd (g) relettered effective January 1, 2014; adopted as subd (f) effective January 1, 2008.)

(h) Notice by party

(1) Except as provided in (6), a party choosing to appear by telephone at a hearing, conference, or proceeding, other than on an ex parte application, under this rule must either:

(A) Place the phrase "Telephone Appearance" below the title of the moving, opposing, or reply papers; or

(B) At least two court days before the appearance, notify the court and all other parties of the party's intent to appear by telephone. If the notice is oral, it must be given either in person or by telephone. If the notice is in writing, it must be given by filing a "Notice of Intent to Appear by Telephone" with the court at least two court days before the appearance and by serving the notice by any means authorized by law and reasonably calculated to ensure delivery to the parties at least two court days before the appearance.

(2) If after receiving notice from another party as provided under (1) a party that has not given notice also decides to appear by telephone, the party may do so by notifying the court and all other parties that have appeared in the action, no later than noon on the court day before the appearance, of its intent to appear by telephone.

(3) An applicant choosing to appear by telephone at an ex parte appearance under this rule must:

(A) Place the phrase "Telephone Appearance" below the title of the application papers;

(B) File and serve the papers in such a way that they will be received by the court and all parties by no later than 10:00 a.m. two court days before the ex parte appearance; and

(C) If provided by local rule, ensure that copies of the papers are received in the department in which the matter is to be considered.

(4) Any party other than an applicant choosing to appear by telephone at an ex parte appearance under this rule must notify the court and all other parties that have appeared in the action, no later than 2:00 p.m. or the "close of business" (as that term is defined in rule 2.250(b)(10)), whichever is earlier, on the court day before the appearance, of its intent to appear by telephone. If the notice is oral, it must be given either in person or by telephone. If the notice is in writing, it must be given by filing a "Notice of Intent to Appear by Telephone" with the court and by serving the notice on all other parties by any means authorized by law reasonably calculated to ensure delivery to the parties no later than 2:00 p.m. or "the close of business" (as that term is defined in rule 2.250(b)(10)), whichever is earlier, on the court day before the appearance.

(5) If a party that has given notice that it intends to appear by telephone under (1) subsequently chooses to appear in person, the party may appear in person.

(6) A party may ask the court for leave to appear by telephone without the notice provided for under (1)–(4). The court should permit the party to appear by telephone upon a showing of good cause or unforeseen circumstances.

(Subd (h) amended effective January 1, 2016; adopted as subd (d) effective July 1, 1998; previously amended effective January 1, 1999, July 1, 1999, January 1, 2003, and January 1, 2007; previously amended and relettered subd (g) effective January 1, 2008, and subd (h) effective January 1, 2014.)

(i) Notice by court

After a party has requested a telephone appearance under (h), if the court requires the personal appearance of the party, the court must give reasonable notice to all parties before the hearing and may continue the hearing if necessary to accommodate the personal appearance. The court may direct the court clerk, a court-appointed vendor, a party, or an attorney to provide the notification. In courts using a telephonic tentative ruling system for law and motion matters, court notification that parties must appear in person may be given as part of the court's tentative ruling on a specific law and motion matter if that notification is given one court day before the hearing.

(Subd (i) amended and relettered effective January 1, 2014; adopted as subd (e) effective July 1, 1998; previously amended effective January 1, 1999, and January 1, 2003; previously amended and relettered as subd (h) effective January 1, 2008.)

(j) Provision of telephone appearance services

A court may provide for telephone appearances only through one or more of the following methods:

(1) An agreement with one or more vendors under a statewide master agreement or agreements.

(2) The direct provision by the court of telephone appearance services. If a court directly provides telephone services, it must collect the telephone appearance fees specified in (k), except as provided in (l) and (m). A judge may, at his or her discretion, waive telephone appearance fees for parties appearing directly by telephone in that judge's courtroom.

(Subd (j) amended and relettered effective January 1, 2014; adopted as subd (f) effective July 1, 1998; previously relettered as subd (i) effective January 1, 2008; previously amended effective January 1, 2003, July 1, 2011, and July 1, 2013.)

(k) Telephone appearance fee amounts; time for making requests

The telephone appearance fees specified in this subdivision are the statewide, uniform fees to be paid by parties to a vendor or court for providing telephone appearance services. Except as provided under (l) and (m), the fees to be paid to appear by telephone are as follows:

(1) The fee to appear by telephone, made by a timely request to a vendor or court providing telephone appearance services, is $94 for each appearance.

(2) An additional late request fee of $30 is to be charged for an appearance by telephone if the request to the vendor or the court providing telephone services is not made at least two days before the scheduled appearance, except:

(A) When an opposing party has provided timely notice under (h)(4) on an ex parte application or other hearing, conference, or proceeding, no late fee is to be charged to that party;

(B) When the court, on its own motion, sets a hearing or conference on shortened time, no late fee is to be charged to any party;

(C) When the matter has a tentative ruling posted within the two-day period, no late fee is to be charged to any party; and

(D) When the request to appear by telephone is made by a party that received notice of another party's intent to appear and afterward decides also to appear by telephone under (h)(2), no late fee is to be charged to that party if its request is made to the vendor or the court providing the service by noon on the court day before the hearing or conference.

(3) A fee of $5 is to be charged instead of the fees under (1) and (2) if a party cancels a telephone appearance request and no telephone appearance is made. A hearing or appearance that is taken off calendar or continued by the court is not a cancelation under this rule. If the hearing or appearance is taken off calendar by the court, there is no charge for the telephone appearance. If the hearing or appearance is continued by the court, the appearance fee must be refunded to the requesting party or, if the party agrees, be applied to the new hearing or appearance date.

(Subd (k) amended effective January 1, 2019; adopted as subd (j) effective July 1, 2011; previously amended as subd (j) effective July 1, 2013; previously amended and relettered effective January 1, 2014.)

(l) Fee waivers

(1) *Effect of fee waiver*

A party that has received a fee waiver must not be charged the fees for telephone appearances provided under (k), subject to the provisions of Code of Civil Procedure section 367.6(b).

(2) *Responsibility of requesting party*

To obtain telephone services without payment of a telephone appearance fee from a vendor or a court that provides telephone appearance services, a party must advise the vendor or the court that he or she has received a fee waiver from the court. If a vendor requests, the party must transmit a copy of the order granting the fee waiver to the vendor.

(3) *Lien on judgment*

If a party based on a fee waiver receives telephone appearance services under this rule without payment of a fee, the vendor or court that provides the telephone appearance services has a lien on any judgment, including a judgment for costs, that the party may receive, in the amount' of the fee that the party would have paid for the telephone appearance. There is no charge for filing the lien.

(Subd (l) amended and relettered effective January 1, 2014; adopted as subd (k) effective July 1, 2011.)

(m) Title IV-D proceedings

(1) *Court-provided telephone appearance services*

If a court provides telephone appearance services in a proceeding for child or family support under Title IV-D of the Social Security Act brought by or otherwise involving a local child support agency, the court must not charge a fee for those services.

(2) *Vendor-provided telephone appearance services*

If a vendor provides for telephone appearance services in a proceeding for child or family support under Title IV-D, the amount of the fee for a telephone appearance under (k)(1) is $74 instead of $94. No portion of the fee received by the vendor for a telephone appearance under this subdivision is to be transmitted to the State Treasury under Government Code section 72011.

(3) *Responsibility of requesting party*

When a party in a Title IV-D proceeding requests telephone appearance services from a court or a vendor, the party requesting the services must advise the court or the vendor that the requester is a party in a proceeding for child or family support under Title IV-D brought by or otherwise involving a local child support agency.

(4) *Fee waivers applicable*

The fee waiver provisions in (*l*) apply to a request by a party in a Title IV-D proceeding for telephone appearance services from a vendor.

(Subd (m) amended effective January 1, 2019; adopted as subd (l) effective July 1, 2011; previously amended effective July 1, 2013; previously amended and relettered effective January 1, 2014.)

(n) Audibility and procedure

The court must ensure that the statements of participants are audible to all other participants and the court staff and that the statements made by a participant are identified as being made by that participant.

(Subd (n) relettered effective January 1, 2014; adopted as subd (f); previously relettered as subd (c) effective January 1, 1989, as subd (g) effective July 1, 1998, and as subd (m) effective July 1, 2011; previously amended effective January 1, 2003, and January 1, 2007; previously amended and relettered as subd (j) effective January 1, 2008.)

(o) Reporting

All proceedings involving telephone appearances must be reported to the same extent and in the same manner as if the participants had appeared in person.

(Subd (o) relettered effective January 1, 2014; adopted as subd (h) effective July 1, 1998; previously amended effective January 1, 2003; previously relettered as subd (k) effective January 1, 2008, and as subd (n) effective July 1, 2011.)

(p) Conference call vendor or vendors

A court, by local rule, may designate the conference call vendor or vendors that must be used for telephone appearances.

(Subd (p) relettered effective January 1, 2014; adopted as subd (i) effective July 1, 1998; previously amended effective January 1, 1999, and January 1, 2003; previously relettered as subd (l) effective January 1, 2008; previously amended and relettered as subd (o) effective July 1, 2011.)

(q) Information on telephone appearances

The court must publish notice providing parties with the particular information necessary for them to appear by telephone at conferences, hearings, and proceedings in that court under this rule.

(Subd (q) relettered effective January 1, 2014; adopted as subd (j); previously amended effective January 1, 2003, and January 1, 2007; previously amended and relettered as subd (m) effective January 1, 2008; previously relettered as subd (p) effective July 1, 2011.)

Rule 3.670 amended effective January 1, 2019; adopted as rule 298 effective March 1, 1988; previously amended and renumbered as rule 3.670 effective January 1, 2007; previously amended effective January 1, 1989, July 1, 1998, January 1, 1999, July 1, 1999, January 1, 2001, July 1, 2002, January 1, 2003, January 1, 2008, July 1, 2011, July 1, 2013, January 1, 2014, and January 1, 2016.)

Advisory Committee Comment

This rule does not apply to criminal or juvenile matters, and it also does not apply to family law matters, except in certain respects as provided in rule 5.324 relating to telephone appearances in proceedings for child or family support under Title IV-D of the Social Security Act. (See Cal. Rules of Court, rule 3.670(b) [rule applies to general civil cases and unlawful detainer and probate proceedings]; rule 5.324(j) [subdivisions (j)–(q) of rule 3.670 apply to telephone appearances in Title IV-D proceedings].)

Subdivision (d). The inclusion of ex parte applications in this rule is intended to address only the way parties may appear and is not intended to alter the way courts handle ex parte applications.

Subdivision (h). Under subdivision (h)(6), good cause should be construed consistent with the policy in (a) and in Code of Civil Procedure section 367.5(a) favoring telephone appearances. Some examples of good cause to appear by telephone without notice include personal or family illness, death in the family, natural disasters, and unexpected transportation delays or interruption.

Subdivision (j). Under subdivision (j)(3) of this rule and Government Code section 72010(c), even for proceedings in which fees are authorized, the fees may be waived by a judicial officer, in his or her discretion, for parties appearing directly by telephone in that judicial officer's courtroom.

Chapter 4
Special Proceedings on Construction-Related Accessibility Claims

Title 3, Civil Rules—Division 6, Proceedings—Chapter 4, Special Proceedings on Construction-Related Accessibility Claims; adopted effective July 1, 2013.

Rule 3.680. Service of Notice of Stay and Early Evaluation Conference
Rule 3.682. Notice of Mandatory Evaluation Conferences

Rule 3.680. Service of Notice of Stay and Early Evaluation Conference

(a) Service of Application and Notice

The defendant who requested a stay and early evaluation conference on a construction-related claim under Civil Code section 55.54 must, within 10 days of issuance of the notice, serve on all other parties the application for stay and any *Notice of Stay of Proceedings and Early Evaluation Conference* (form DAL-010) issued by the court.

(Subd (a) adopted effective July 1, 2013.)

(b) Filing Proof of Service

A proof of service must be filed with the court 15 days before the date set for the early evaluation conference. *Proof of Service—Disability Access Litigation* (form DAL-012) may be used to show service of the documents.

(Subd (b) adopted effective July 1, 2013.)
Rule 3.680 adopted effective July 1, 2013.

Rule 3.682. Notice of Mandatory Evaluation Conferences

(a) Service of Application and Notice

The party who requested a mandatory evaluation conference on a construction-related accessibility claim under Civil Code section 55.545 must, within 10 days of issuance of the notice, serve on all other parties the application and any *Notice of Mandatory Evaluation Conference* (form DAL-020) issued by the court.

(Subd (a) adopted effective July 1, 2013.)

(b) Filing Proof of Service

A proof of service must be filed with the court 15 days before the date set for the early evaluation conference. *Proof of Service—Disability Access Litigation* (form DAL-012) may be used to show service of the documents.

(Subd (b) adopted effective July 1, 2013.)
Rule 3.682 adopted effective July 1, 2013.

Division 7
Civil Case Management

Chapter 1
General Provisions

Rule 3.700. Scope and purpose of the case management rules

The rules in this division are to be construed and administered to secure the fair, timely, and efficient disposition of every civil case. The rules are to be applied in a fair, practical, and flexible manner so as to achieve the ends of justice.

Rule 3.700 amended and renumbered effective January 1, 2007; adopted as rule 204 effective January 1, 2004.

Chapter 2
Differential Case Management

Rule 3.710. Authority
Rule 3.711. Local court rules
Rule 3.712. Application and exceptions
Rule 3.713. Delay reduction goals
Rule 3.714. Differentiation of cases to achieve goals
Rule 3.715. Case evaluation factors

Rule 3.710. Authority

The rules in this chapter implement Government Code section 68603(c) under the Trial Court Delay Reduction Act of 1990.

Rule 3.710 amended and renumbered effective January 1, 2007; adopted as rule 2101 effective July 1, 1991; previously amended and renumbered as rule 205 effective July 1, 2002.

Rule 3.711. Local court rules

Each court must adopt local rules on differential case management as provided in this chapter consistent with the rules on case management in chapter 3 of this division and standard 2.1 of the California Standards of Judicial Administration.

Rule 3.711 amended and renumbered effective January 1, 2007; adopted as rule 2102 effective July 1, 1991; previously amended effective January 1, 1994, and January 1, 2000; previously amended and renumbered as rule 206 effective July 1, 2002.

Rule 3.712.   Application and exceptions

(a) General application

The rules in this chapter apply to all general civil cases filed in the trial courts except those specified in (b), (c), and (d) and except those specified types or categories of general civil cases that have been exempted from the case management rules under rule 3.720(b).

(Subd (a) amended effective February 26, 2013; previously amended effective January 1, 1994, July 1, 2002, January 1, 2007, and July 1, 2007.)

(b) Uninsured motorist cases

To allow for arbitration of the plaintiff's claim, the rules in this chapter do not apply to a case designated by the court as "uninsured motorist" until 180 days after the designation.

(Subd (b) amended and relettered effective January 1, 2007; adopted as subd (c) effective July 1, 1991; previously amended effective July 1, 2002.)

(c) Coordinated cases

The rules in this chapter do not apply to any case included in a petition for coordination. If the petition is granted, the coordination trial judge may establish a case progression plan for the cases, which may be assigned for review under the case management rules in chapter 3 of this division or, after appropriate findings, for treatment as an exceptional case.

(Subd (c) amended and relettered effective January 1, 2007; adopted as subd (d) effective July 1, 1991; previously amended effective July 1, 2002.)

(d) Collections cases

The rules in this chapter do not apply to a collections case, as defined in rule 3.740(a), unless a defendant files a responsive pleading.

(Subd (d) adopted effective July 1, 2007.)

Rule 3.712 amended effective February 26, 2013; adopted as rule 2103 effective July 1, 1991; previously amended and renumbered as rule 207 effective July 1, 2002, and amended and renumbered effective January 1, 2007; previously amended effective January 1, 1994, and July 1, 2007.

Rule 3.713.   Delay reduction goals

(a) Case management goals

The rules in this chapter are adopted to advance the goals of Government Code section 68607 and standard 2.1 of the California Standards of Judicial Administration.

(Subd (a) amended effective January 1, 2007; previously amended effective July 1, 2002.)

(b) Case disposition time goals

The goal of the court is to manage general civil cases from filing to disposition as provided under standard 2.2 of the California Standards of Judicial Administration.

(Subd (b) amended effective January 1, 2007; previously amended effective January 1, 1994, July 1, 2002, and January 1, 2004.)

(c) Judges' responsibility

It is the responsibility of judges to achieve a just and effective resolution of each general civil case through active management and supervision of the pace of litigation from the date of filing to disposition.

(Subd (c) amended effective July 1, 2002.)

Rule 3.713 amended and renumbered effective January 1, 2007; adopted as rule 2104 effective July 1, 1991; previously amended and renumbered as rule 208 effective July 1, 2003; previously amended effective January 1, 1994, and January 1, 2004.

Rule 3.714.   Differentiation of cases to achieve goals

(a) Evaluation and assignment

The court must evaluate each case on its own merits as provided in rule 3.715, under procedures adopted by local court rules. After evaluation, the court must:

(1) Assign the case to the case management program for review under the case management rules in chapter 3 of this division for disposition under the case disposition time goals in (b) of this rule;

(2) Exempt the case as an exceptional case under (c) of this rule from the case disposition time goals specified in rule 3.713(b) and monitor it with the goal of disposing of it within three years; or

(3) Assign the case under (d) of this rule to a local case management plan for disposition within six to nine months after filing.

(Subd (a) amended effective January 1, 2007; previously amended effective July 1, 2002, and January 1, 2004.)

(b) Civil case disposition time goals

Civil cases assigned for review under the case management rules in chapter 3 of this division should be managed so as to achieve the following goals:

(1) *Unlimited civil cases*

The goal of each trial court should be to manage unlimited civil cases from filing so that:

(A) 75 percent are disposed of within 12 months;

(B) 85 percent are disposed of within 18 months; and

(C) 100 percent are disposed of within 24 months.

(2) *Limited civil cases*

The goal of each trial court should be to manage limited civil cases from filing so that:

(A) 90 percent are disposed of within 12 months;

(B) 98 percent are disposed of within 18 months; and

(C) 100 percent are disposed of within 24 months.

(3) *Individualized case management*

The goals in (1) and (2) are guidelines for the court's disposition of all unlimited and limited civil cases filed in that court. In managing individual civil cases, the court must consider each case on its merits. To enable the fair and efficient resolution of civil cases, each case should be set for trial as soon as appropriate for that individual case consistent with rule 3.729.

(Subd (b) amended effective January 1, 2007; previously amended effective July 1, 2002, and January 1, 2004.)

(c) Exemption of exceptional cases

(1) The court may in the interest of justice exempt a general civil case from the case disposition time goals under rule 3.713(b) if it finds the case involves exceptional circumstances that will prevent the court and the parties from meeting the goals and deadlines imposed by the program. In making the determination, the court is guided by rules 3.715 and 3.400.

(2) If the court exempts the case from the case disposition time goals, the court must establish a case progression plan and monitor the case to ensure timely disposition consistent with the exceptional circumstances, with the goal of disposing of the case within three years.

(Subd (c) amended effective January 1, 2007; adopted as subd (d) effective July 1, 1991; previously amended effective January 1, 2000, and July 1, 2002; previously amended and relettered as subd (c) effective January 1, 2004.)

(d) Local case management plan for expedited case disposition

(1) For expedited case disposition, the court may by local rule adopt a case management plan that establishes a goal for disposing of appropriate cases within six to nine months after filing. The plan must establish a procedure to identify the cases to be assigned to the plan.

(2) The plan must be used only for uncomplicated cases amenable to early disposition that do not need a case management conference or review or similar event to guide the case to early resolution.

(Subd (d) amended and relettered effective January 1, 2004; adopted as subd (e) effective July 1, 1991; previously amended effective January 1, 1994, and July 1, 2002.)

Rule 3.714 amended and renumbered effective January 1, 2007; adopted as rule 2105 effective July 1, 1991; amended and renumbered as rule 209 effective July 1, 2002; previously amended effective January 1, 1994, January 1, 2000, and January 1, 2004.

Rule 3.715.   Case evaluation factors

(a) Time estimate

In applying rule 3.714, the court must estimate the maximum time that will reasonably be required to dispose of each case in a just and effective manner. The court must consider the following factors and any other information the court deems relevant, understanding that no one factor or set of factors will be controlling and that cases may have unique characteristics incapable of precise definition:

(1) Type and subject matter of the action;

(2) Number of causes of action or affirmative defenses alleged;

(3) Number of parties with separate interests;

(4) Number of cross-complaints and the subject matter;

(5) Complexity of issues, including issues of first impression;

(6) Difficulty in identifying, locating, and serving parties;

(7) Nature and extent of discovery anticipated;

(8) Number and location of percipient and expert witnesses;

(9) Estimated length of trial;

(10) Whether some or all issues can be arbitrated or resolved through other alternative dispute resolution processes;

(11) Statutory priority for the issues;

(12) Likelihood of review by writ or appeal;

(13) Amount in controversy and the type of remedy sought, including measures of damages;

(14) Pendency of other actions or proceedings that may affect the case;

(15) Nature and extent of law and motion proceedings anticipated;

(16) Nature and extent of the injuries and damages;

(17) Pendency of underinsured claims; and

(18) Any other factor that would affect the time for disposition of the case.

(Subd (a) amended and lettered effective January 1, 2007; adopted as untitled subd effective July 1, 1991.)

Rule 3.715 amended and renumbered effective January 1, 2007; adopted as rule 2106 effective July 1, 1991; previously amended and renumbered as rule 210 effective July 1, 2002.

Chapter 3
Case Management

Rule 3.720. Application

(a) General application

The rules in this chapter prescribe the procedures for the management of all applicable court cases. These rules may be referred to as "the case management rules."

(Subd (a) amended and lettered effective February 26, 2013; adopted as unlettered subd effective January 1, 2007.)

(b) Suspension of rules

A court by local rule may exempt specified types or categories of general civil cases [1] from the case management rules in this chapter, provided that the court has in place alternative procedures for case processing and trial setting for such actions, including, without limitation, compliance with Code of Civil Procedure sections 1141.10 et seq. and 1775 et seq. The court must [2] **include** the alternative procedures [3] **in its local rules**.

(Subd (b) amended effective January 1, 2020; adopted effective February 26, 2013; previously amended effective January 1, 2016.)

Rule 3.720(b).   2019 Deletes. [1] filed before January 1, 2020, [2] post [3] on its website

(c) Rules when case management conference set

In any case in which a court sets an initial case management conference, the rules in this chapter apply.

(Subd (c) adopted effective February 26, 2013.)

Rule 3.720 amended effective January 1, 2020; adopted effective January 1, 2007; previously amended effective February 26, 2013, and January 1, 2016.

Rule 3.721. Case management review

In every general civil case except complex cases and cases exempted under rules 3.712(b)–(d), 3.714(c)–(d), 3.735(b), 2.573(e), and 3.740(c), the court must review the case no later than 180 days after the filing of the initial complaint.

Rule 3.721 amended effective July 1, 2007; adopted effective January 1, 2007.

Rule 3.722. Case management conference

(a) The initial conference

In each case, the court must set an initial case management conference to review the case. At the conference, the court must review the case comprehensively and decide whether to assign the case to an alternative dispute resolution process, whether to set the case for trial, and whether to take action regarding any of the other matters identified in rules 3.727 and 3.728. The initial case management conference should generally be the first case management event conducted by court order in each case, except for orders to show cause.

(Subd (a) adopted effective January 1, 2007.)

(b) Notice of the initial conference

Notice of the date of the initial case management conference must be given to all parties no later than 45 days before the conference, unless otherwise ordered by the court. The court may provide by local rule for the time and manner of giving notice to the parties.

(Subd (b) adopted effective January 1, 2007.)

(c) Preparation for the conference

At the conference, counsel for each party and each self-represented party must appear by telephone or personally as provided in rule 3.670; must be familiar with the case; and must be prepared to discuss and commit to the party's position on the issues listed in rules 3.724 and 3.727.

(Subd (c) amended effective January 1, 2008; adopted effective January 1, 2007.)

(d) Case management order without appearance

If, based on its review of the written submissions of the parties and such other information as is available, the court determines that appearances at the conference are not necessary, the court may issue a case management order and notify the parties that no appearance is required.

(Subd (d) adopted effective January 1, 2007.)

(e) Option to excuse attendance at initial conferences in limited civil cases

By local rule the court may provide that counsel and self-represented parties are not to attend an initial case management conference in limited civil cases unless ordered to do so by the court.

(Subd (e) adopted effective January 1, 2007.)

Rule 3.722 amended effective January 1, 2008; adopted effective January 1, 2007.

Rule 3.723.   Additional case management conferences

The court on its own motion may order, or a party or parties may request, that an additional case management conference be held at any time. A party should be required to appear at an additional conference only if an appearance is necessary for the effective management of the case. In determining whether to hold an additional conference, the court must consider each case individually on its own merits.

Rule 3.723 adopted effective January 1, 2007.

Advisory Committee Comment

Regarding additional case management conferences, in many civil cases one initial conference and one other conference before trial will be sufficient. But in other cases, including complicated or difficult cases, the court may order an additional case management conference or conferences if that would promote the fair and efficient administration of the case.

Rule 3.724.   Duty to meet and confer

Unless the court orders another time period, no later than 30 calendar days before the date set for the initial case management conference, the parties must meet and confer, in person or by telephone, to consider each of the issues identified in rule 3.727 and, in addition, to consider the following:

(1) Resolving any discovery disputes and setting a discovery schedule;

(2) Identifying and, if possible, informally resolving any anticipated motions;

(3) Identifying the facts and issues in the case that are uncontested and may be the subject of stipulation;

(4) Identifying the facts and issues in the case that are in dispute;

(5) Determining whether the issues in the case can be narrowed by eliminating any claims or defenses by means of a motion or otherwise;

(6) Determining whether settlement is possible;

(7) Identifying the dates on which all parties and their attorneys are available or not available for trial, including the reasons for unavailability;

(8) Any issues relating to the discovery of electronically stored information, including:

(A) Issues relating to the preservation of discoverable electronically stored information;

(B) The form or forms in which information will be produced;

(C) The time within which the information will be produced;

(D) The scope of discovery of the information;

(E) The method for asserting or preserving claims of privilege or attorney work product, including whether such claims may be asserted after production;

(F) The method for asserting or preserving the confidentiality, privacy, trade secrets, or proprietary status of information relating to a party or person not a party to the civil proceedings;

(G) How the cost of production of electronically stored information is to be allocated among the parties;

(H) Any other issues relating to the discovery of electronically stored information, including developing a proposed plan relating to the discovery of the information; and

(9) Other relevant matters.

Rule 3.724 amended effective August 14, 2009; adopted effective January 1, 2007.

Rule 3.725.   Case Management Statement

(a) Timing of statement

No later than 15 calendar days before the date set for the case management conference or review, each party must file a case management statement and serve it on all other parties in the case.

(b) Joint statement

In lieu of each party's filing a separate case management statement, any two or more parties may file a joint statement.

(c) Contents of statement

Parties must use the mandatory *Case Management Statement* (form CM-110). All applicable items on the form must be completed.

Rule 3.725 adopted effective January 1, 2007.

Rule 3.726.   Stipulation to alternative dispute resolution

If all parties agree to use an alternative dispute resolution (ADR) process, they must jointly complete the ADR stipulation form provided for under rule 3.221 and file it with the court.

Rule 3.726 adopted effective January 1, 2007.

Rule 3.727.   Subjects to be considered at the case management conference

In any case management conference or review conducted under this chapter, the parties must address, if applicable, and the court may take appropriate action with respect to, the following:

(1) Whether there are any related cases;

(2) Whether all parties named in the complaint or cross-complaint have been served, have appeared, or have been dismissed;

(3) Whether any additional parties may be added or the pleadings may be amended;

(4) Whether, if the case is a limited civil case, the economic litigation procedures under Code of Civil Procedure section 90 et seq. will apply to it or the party intends to bring a motion to exempt the case from these procedures;

(5) Whether any other matters (e.g., the bankruptcy of a party) may affect the court's jurisdiction or processing of the case;

(6) Whether the parties have stipulated to, or the case should be referred to, judicial arbitration in courts having a judicial arbitration program or to any other form of alternative dispute resolution (ADR) process and, if so, the date by which the judicial arbitration or other ADR process must be completed;

(7) Whether an early settlement conference should be scheduled and, if so, on what date;

(8) Whether discovery has been completed and, if not, the date by which it will be completed;

(9) What discovery issues are anticipated;

(10) Whether the case should be bifurcated or a hearing should be set for a motion to bifurcate under Code of Civil Procedure section 598;

(11) Whether there are any cross-complaints that are not ready to be set for trial and, if so, whether they should be severed;

(12) Whether the case is entitled to any statutory preference and, if so, the statute granting the preference;

(13) Whether a jury trial is demanded, and, if so, the identity of each party requesting a jury trial;

(14) If the trial date has not been previously set, the date by which the case will be ready for trial and the available trial dates;

(15) The estimated length of trial;

(16) The nature of the injuries;

(17) The amount of damages, including any special or punitive damages;

(18) Any additional relief sought;

(19) Whether there are any insurance coverage issues that may affect the resolution of the case; and

(20) Any other matters that should be considered by the court or addressed in its case management order.

Rule 3.727 adopted effective January 1, 2007.

Rule 3.728.   Case management order

The case management conference must be conducted in the manner provided by local rule. The court must enter a case management order setting a schedule for subsequent proceedings and otherwise providing for the management of the case. The order may include appropriate provisions, such as:

(1) Referral of the case to judicial arbitration or other alternative dispute resolution process;

(2) A date for completion of the judicial arbitration process or other alternative dispute resolution process if the case has been referred to such a process;

(3) In the event that a trial date has not previously been set, a date certain for trial if the case is ready to be set for trial;

(4) Whether the trial will be a jury trial or a nonjury trial;

(5) The identity of each party demanding a jury trial;

(6) The estimated length of trial;

(7) Whether all parties necessary to the disposition of the case have been served or have appeared;

(8) The dismissal or severance of unserved or not-appearing defendants from the action;

(9) The names and addresses of the attorneys who will try the case;

(10) The date, time, and place for a mandatory settlement conference as provided in rule 3.1380;

(11) The date, time, and place for the final case management conference before trial if such a conference is required by the court or the judge assigned to the case;

(12) The date, time, and place of any further case management conferences or review; and

(13) Any additional orders that may be appropriate, including orders on matters listed in rules 3.724 and 3.727.

Rule 3.728 adopted effective January 1, 2007.

Rule 3.729.   Setting the trial date

In setting a case for trial, the court, at the initial case management conference or at any other proceeding at which the case is set for trial, must consider all the facts and circumstances that are relevant. These may include:

(1) The type and subject matter of the action to be tried;

(2) Whether the case has statutory priority;

(3) The number of causes of action, cross-actions, and affirmative defenses that will be tried;

(4) Whether any significant amendments to the pleadings have been made recently or are likely to be made before trial;

(5) Whether the plaintiff intends to bring a motion to amend the complaint to seek punitive damages under Code of Civil Procedure section 425.13;

(6) The number of parties with separate interests who will be involved in the trial;

(7) The complexity of the issues to be tried, including issues of first impression;

(8) Any difficulties in identifying, locating, or serving parties;

(9) Whether all parties have been served and, if so, the date by which they were served;

(10) Whether all parties have appeared in the action and, if so, the date by which they appeared;

(11) How long the attorneys who will try the case have been involved in the action;

(12) The trial date or dates proposed by the parties and their attorneys;

(13) The professional and personal schedules of the parties and their attorneys, including any conflicts with previously assigned trial dates or other significant events;

(14) The amount of discovery, if any, that remains to be conducted in the case;

(15) The nature and extent of law and motion proceedings anticipated, including whether any motions for summary judgment will be filed;

(16) Whether any other actions or proceedings that are pending may affect the case;

(17) The amount in controversy and the type of remedy sought;

(18) The nature and extent of the injuries or damages, including whether these are ready for determination;

(19) The court's trial calendar, including the pendency of other trial dates;

(20) Whether the trial will be a jury or a nonjury trial;

(21) The anticipated length of trial;

(22) The number, availability, and locations of witnesses, including witnesses who reside outside the county, state, or country;

(23) Whether there have been any previous continuances of the trial or delays in setting the case for trial;

(24) The achievement of a fair, timely, and efficient disposition of the case; and

(25) Any other factor that would significantly affect the determination of the appropriate date of trial.

Rule 3.729 adopted effective January 1, 2007.

Rule 3.730. Case management order controls

The order issued after the case management conference or review controls the subsequent course of the action or proceeding unless it is modified by a subsequent order.

Rule 3.730 adopted effective January 1, 2007.

Rule 3.734. Assignment to one judge for all or limited purposes

The presiding judge may, on the noticed motion of a party or on the court's own motion, order the assignment of any case to one judge for all or such limited purposes as will promote the efficient administration of justice.

Rule 3.734 amended and renumbered effective January 1, 2007; adopted as rule 213 effective January 1, 1985; previously amended effective July 1, 2002.

Rule 3.735. Management of short cause cases

(a) Short cause case defined

A short cause case is a civil case in which the time estimated for trial by all parties or the court is five hours or less. All other civil cases are long cause cases.

(Subd (a) amended effective January 1, 2007.)

(b) Exemption for short cause case and setting of case for trial

The court may order, upon the stipulation of all parties or the court's own motion, that a case is a short cause case exempted from the requirements of case management review and set the case for trial.

(c) Mistrial

If a short cause case is not completely tried within five hours, the judge may declare a mistrial or, in the judge's discretion, may complete the trial. In the event of a mistrial, the case will be treated as a long cause case and must promptly be set either for a new trial or for a case management conference.

Rule 3.735 amended and renumbered effective January 1, 2007; adopted as rule 214 effective July 1, 2002.

Chapter 4
Management of Collections Cases

Chapter 4 adopted effective July 1, 2008.

Rule 3.740. Collections cases
Rule 3.741. Settlement of collections case

Rule 3.740. Collections cases

(a) Definition

"Collections case" means an action for recovery of money owed in a sum stated to be certain that is not more than $25,000, exclusive of interest and attorney fees, arising from a transaction in which property, services, or money was acquired on credit. A collections case does not include an action seeking any of the following:

(1) Tort damages;

(2) Punitive damages;

(3) Recovery of real property;

(4) Recovery of personal property; or

(5) A prejudgment writ of attachment.

(Subd (a) adopted effective July 1, 2007.)

(b) *Civil Case Cover Sheet*

If a case meets the definition in (a), a plaintiff must check the case type box on the *Civil Case Cover Sheet* (form CM-010) to indicate that the case is a collections case under rule 3.740 and serve the *Civil Case Cover Sheet* (form CM-010) with the initial complaint.

(Subd (b) amended effective January 1, 2009; adopted effective July 1, 2007.)

(c) Exemption from general time-for-service requirement and case management rules

A collections case is exempt from:

(1) The time-for-service requirement of rule 3.110(b); and

(2) The case management rules that apply to all general civil cases under rules 3.712–3.715 and 3.721–3.730, unless a defendant files a responsive pleading.

(Subd (c) adopted effective July 1, 2007.)

(d) Time for service

The complaint in a collections case must be served on all named defendants, and proofs of service on those defendants must be filed, or the plaintiff must obtain an order for publication of the summons, within 180 days after the filing of the complaint.

(Subd (d) adopted effective July 1, 2007.)

(e) Effect of failure to serve within required time

If proofs of service on all defendants are not filed or the plaintiff has not obtained an order for publication of the summons within 180 days after the filing of the complaint, the court may issue an order to show cause why reasonable monetary sanctions should not be imposed. If proofs of service on all defendants are filed or an order for publication of the summons is filed at least 10 court days before the order to show cause hearing, the court must continue the hearing to 360 days after the filing of the complaint.

(Subd (e) adopted effective July 1, 2007.)

(f) Effect of failure to obtain default judgment within required time

If proofs of service of the complaint are filed or service by publication is made and defendants do not file responsive pleadings, the plaintiff must obtain a default judgment within 360 days after the filing of the complaint. If the plaintiff has not obtained a default judgment by that time, the court must issue an order to show cause why reasonable monetary sanctions should not be imposed. The order to show cause must be vacated if the plaintiff obtains a default judgment at least 10 court days before the order to show cause hearing.

(Subd (f) adopted effective July 1, 2007.)

Rule 3.740 amended effective January 1, 2009; adopted effective July 1, 2007.

Rule 3.741. Settlement of collections case

If the plaintiff or other party seeking affirmative relief in a case meeting the definition of "collections case" in rule 3.740(a) files a notice of settlement under rule 3.1385, including a conditional settlement, the court must vacate all hearing, case management conference, and trial dates.

Rule 3.741 adopted effective July 1, 2007.

Chapter 5
Management of Complex Cases

Chapter 5 renumbered effective July 1, 2008; adopted as chapter 4 effective January 1, 2007.

Rule 3.750. Initial case management conference
Rule 3.751. Electronic service

Rule 3.750. Initial case management conference

(a) Timing of conference

The court in a complex case should hold an initial case management conference with all parties represented at the earliest practical date.

(b) Subjects for consideration

At the conference, the court should consider the following subjects:

(1) Whether all parties named in the complaint or cross-complaint have been served, have appeared, or have been dismissed;

(2) Whether any additional parties may be added or the pleadings may be amended;

(3) The deadline for the filing of any remaining pleadings and service of any additional parties;

(4) Whether severance, consolidation, or coordination with other actions is desirable;

(5) The schedule for discovery proceedings to avoid duplication and whether discovery should be stayed until all parties have been brought into the case;

(6) The schedule for settlement conferences or alternative dispute resolution;

(7) Whether to appoint liaison or lead counsel;

(8) The date for the filing of any dispositive motions;

(9) The creation of preliminary and updated lists of the persons to be deposed and the subjects to be addressed in each deposition;

(10) The exchange of documents and whether to establish an electronic document depository;

(11) Whether a special master should be appointed and the purposes for such appointment;

(12) Whether to establish a case-based Web site and other means to provide a current master list of addresses and telephone numbers of counsel; and

(13) The schedule for further conferences.

(c) Objects of conference

Principal objects of the initial case management conference are to expose at an early date the essential issues in the litigation and to avoid unnecessary and burdensome discovery procedures in the course of preparing for trial of those issues.

(d) Meet and confer requirement

The court may order counsel to meet privately before the initial case management conference to discuss the items specified in (a) and to prepare a joint statement of matters agreed upon, matters on which the court must rule at the conference, and a description of the major legal and factual issues involved in the litigation.

Rule 3.750 adopted effective January 1, 2007.

Rule 3.751. Electronic service

Parties may consent to electronic service, or the court may require electronic 36 service by local rule or court order, under rule 2.251. The court may provide in a case management order that documents filed electronically in a central electronic depository available to all parties are deemed served on all parties.

Rule 3.751 amended effective January 1, 2017; adopted as rule 1830 effective January 1, 2000; previously renumbered effective January 1, 2007.

Chapter 6
Management of Class Actions

Chapter 6 renumbered effective July 1, 2008; adopted as chapter 5 effective January 1, 2007.

Rule 3.760. Application

(a) Class actions

The rules in this chapter apply to each class action brought under Civil Code section 1750 et seq. or Code of Civil Procedure section 382 until the court finds the action is not maintainable as a class action or revokes a prior class certification.

(Subd (a) amended effective January 1, 2007.)

(b) Relief from compliance with rules

The court, on its own motion or on motion of any named party, may grant relief from compliance with the rules in this chapter in an appropriate case.

(Subd (b) amended effective January 1, 2007.)

Rule 3.760 amended and renumbered effective January 1, 2007; adopted as rule 1850 effective January 1, 2002.

Rule 3.761. Form of complaint

(a) Caption of pleadings

A complaint for or against a class party must include in the caption the designation "CLASS ACTION." This designation must be in capital letters on the first page of the complaint, immediately below the case number but above the description of the nature of the complaint.

(b) Heading and class action allegations

The complaint in a class action must contain a separate heading entitled "CLASS ACTION ALLEGATIONS," under which the plaintiff describes how the requirements for class certification are met.

Rule 3.761 renumbered effective January 1, 2007; adopted as rule 1851 effective January 1, 2002.

Rule 3.762. Case conference

(a) Purpose

One or more conferences between the court and counsel for the parties may be held to discuss class issues, conduct and scheduling of discovery, scheduling of hearings, and other matters. No evidence may be presented at the conference, but counsel must be fully prepared to discuss class issues and must possess authority to enter into stipulations.

(b) Notice by the parties

Notice of the conference may be given by any party. If notice is given by a named plaintiff, notice must be served on all named parties to the action. If notice is given by a defendant, notice must be served only on the parties who have appeared. Within 10 calendar days after receipt of the notice, the plaintiff must serve a copy on each named party who has not appeared in the action and must file a declaration of service. If the plaintiff is unable to serve any party, the plaintiff must file a declaration stating the reasons for failure of service.

(Subd (b) amended effective January 1, 2007.)

(c) Notice by the court

The court may give notice of the conference to the plaintiff. Within 10 calendar days after receipt of the notice given by the court, the plaintiff must serve a copy of the notice on all parties who have been served in the action, whether they have appeared or not, and must file a declaration of service. If the plaintiff is unable to serve any party, the plaintiff must file a declaration stating the reasons for failure of service.

(Subd (c) amended effective January 1, 2007.)

(d) Timing of notice

The notice must be filed and served on the parties at least 20 calendar days before the scheduled date of the conference.

(Subd (d) amended effective January 1, 2007.)

(e) Timing of conference

A conference may be held at any time after the first defendant has appeared. Before selecting a conference date, the party noticing the conference must:

(1) Obtain prior approval from the clerk of the department assigned to hear the class action; and

(2) Make reasonable efforts to accommodate the schedules of all parties entitled to receive notice under (b).

(Subd (e) amended effective January 1, 2007.)

Rule 3.762 amended and renumbered effective January 1, 2007; adopted as rule 1852 effective January 1, 2002.

Rule 3.763. Conference order

At the conclusion of the conference, the court may make an order:

(1) Approving any stipulations of the parties;

(2) Establishing a schedule for discovery;

(3) Setting the date for the hearing on class certification;

(4) Setting the dates for any subsequent conferences; and

(5) Addressing any other matters related to management of the case.

Rule 3.763 renumbered effective January 1, 2007; adopted as rule 1853 effective January 1, 2002.

Rule 3.764. Motion to certify or decertify a class or amend or modify an order certifying a class

(a) Purpose

Any party may file a motion to:

(1) Certify a class;

(2) Determine the existence of and certify subclasses;

(3) Amend or modify an order certifying a class; or

(4) Decertify a class.

(b) Timing of motion, hearing, extension, deferral

A motion for class certification should be filed when practicable. In its discretion, the court may establish a deadline for the filing of the motion, as part of the case conference or as part of other case management proceedings. Any such deadline must take into account discovery proceedings that may be necessary to the filing of the motion.

(c) Format and filing of motion

(1) Time for service of papers

Notice of a motion to certify or decertify a class or to amend or modify a certification order must be filed and served on all parties to the action at least 28 calendar days before the date appointed for hearing. Any opposition to the motion must be served and filed at least 14 calendar days before the noticed or continued hearing, unless the court for good cause orders otherwise. Any reply to the opposition must be served and filed at least 5 calendar days before the noticed or continued date of the hearing, unless the court for good cause orders otherwise. The provisions of Code of Civil Procedure section 1005 otherwise apply.

(2) Length of papers

An opening or responding memorandum filed in support of or in opposition to a motion for class certification must not exceed 20 pages. A reply memorandum must not exceed 15 pages. The provisions of rule 3.1113 otherwise apply.

(3) Documents in support

The documents in support of a motion for class certification consist of the notice of motion; a memorandum; evidence in support of the motion in the form of declarations of counsel, class representatives, or other appropriate declarants; and any requests for judicial notice.

(4) *Documents in opposition*

The documents in opposition to the motion consist of the opposing party's memorandum; the opposing party's evidence in opposition to the motion, including any declarations of counsel or other appropriate declarants; and any requests for judicial notice.

(Subd (c) amended effective January 1, 2007.)

(d) Presentation of evidence

Evidence to be considered at the hearing must be presented in accordance with rule 3.1306.

(Subd (d) amended effective January 1, 2007.)

(e) Stipulations

The parties should endeavor to resolve any uncontroverted issues by written stipulation before the hearing. If all class issues are resolved by stipulation of the named parties and approved by the court before the hearing, no hearing on class certification is necessary.

Rule 3.764 amended and renumbered effective January 1, 2007; adopted as rule 1854 effective January 1, 2002.

Rule 3.765.   Class action order

(a) Class described

An order certifying, amending, or modifying a class must contain a description of the class and any subclasses.

(b) Limited issues and subclasses

When appropriate, an action may be maintained as a class action limited to particular issues. A class may be divided into subclasses.

Rule 3.765 renumbered effective January 1, 2007; adopted as rule 1855 effective January 1, 2002.

Rule 3.766.   Notice to class members

(a) Party to provide notice

If the class is certified, the court may require either party to notify the class of the action in the manner specified by the court.

(b) Statement regarding class notice

The class proponent must submit a statement regarding class notice and a proposed notice to class members. The statement must include the following items:

(1) Whether notice is necessary;

(2) Whether class members may exclude themselves from the action;

(3) The time and manner in which notice should be given;

(4) A proposal for which parties should bear the costs of notice; and,

(5) If cost shifting or sharing is proposed under subdivision (4), an estimate of the cost involved in giving notice.

(c) Order

Upon certification of a class, or as soon thereafter as practicable, the court must make an order determining:

(1) Whether notice to class members is necessary;

(2) Whether class members may exclude themselves from the action;

(3) The time and manner of notice;

(4) The content of the notice; and

(5) The parties responsible for the cost of notice.

(d) Content of class notice

The content of the class notice is subject to court approval. If class members are to be given the right to request exclusion from the class, the notice must include the following:

(1) A brief explanation of the case, including the basic contentions or denials of the parties;

(2) A statement that the court will exclude the member from the class if the member so requests by a specified date;

(3) A procedure for the member to follow in requesting exclusion from the class;

(4) A statement that the judgment, whether favorable or not, will bind all members who do not request exclusion; and

(5) A statement that any member who does not request exclusion may, if the member so desires, enter an appearance through counsel.

(e) Manner of giving notice

In determining the manner of the notice, the court must consider:

(1) The interests of the class;

(2) The type of relief requested;

(3) The stake of the individual class members;

(4) The cost of notifying class members;

(5) The resources of the parties;

(6) The possible prejudice to class members who do not receive notice; and

(7) The res judicata effect on class members.

(f) Court may order means of notice

If personal notification is unreasonably expensive or the stake of individual class members is insubstantial, or if it appears that all members of the class cannot be notified personally, the court may order a means of notice reasonably calculated to apprise the class members of the pendency of the action—for example, publication in a newspaper or magazine; broadcasting on television, radio, or the Internet; or posting or distribution through a trade or professional association, union, or public interest group.

(Subd (f) lettered effective January 1, 2007; adopted as part of subd (e) effective January 1, 2002.)

Rule 3.766 amended and renumbered effective January 1, 2007; adopted as rule 1856 effective January 1, 2002.

Rule 3.767.   Orders in the conduct of class actions

(a) Court orders

In the conduct of a class action, the court may make orders that:

(1) Require that some or all of the members of the class be given notice in such manner as the court may direct of any action in the proceeding, or of their opportunity to seek to appear and indicate whether they consider the representation fair and adequate, or of the proposed extent of the judgment;

(2) Impose conditions on the representative parties or on intervenors;

(3) Require that the pleadings be amended to eliminate allegations as to representation of absent persons, and that the action proceed accordingly;

(4) Facilitate the management of class actions through consolidation, severance, coordination, bifurcation, intervention, or joinder; and

(5) Address similar procedural matters.

(Subd (a) amended effective January 1, 2007.)

(b) Altered or amended orders

The orders may be altered or amended as necessary.

(Subd (b) amended effective January 1, 2007.)

Rule 3.767 amended and renumbered effective January 1, 2007; adopted as rule 1857 effective January 1, 2002.

Rule 3.768.   Discovery from unnamed class members

(a) Types of discovery permitted

The following types of discovery may be sought, through service of a subpoena and without a court order, from a member of a class who is not a party representative or who has not appeared:

(1) An oral deposition;

(2) A written deposition; and

(3) A deposition for production of business records and things.

(b) Motion for protective order

A party representative, deponent, or other affected person may move for a protective order to preclude or limit the discovery.

(c) Interrogatories require court order

A party may not serve interrogatories on a member of a class who is not a party representative or who has not appeared, without a court order.

(d) Determination by court

In deciding whether to allow the discovery requested under (a) or (c), the court must consider, among other relevant factors:

(1) The timing of the request;

(2) The subject matter to be covered;

(3) The materiality of the information being sought;

(4) The likelihood that class members have such information;

(5) The possibility of reaching factual stipulations that eliminate the need for such discovery;

(6) Whether class representatives are seeking discovery on the subject to be covered; and

(7) Whether discovery will result in annoyance, oppression, or undue burden or expense for the members of the class.

(Subd (d) amended effective January 1, 2007.)

Rule 3.768 amended and renumbered effective January 1, 2007; adopted as rule 1858 effective January 1, 2002.

Rule 3.769.   Settlement of class actions

(a) Court approval after hearing

A settlement or compromise of an entire class action, or of a cause of action in a class action, or as to a party, requires the approval of the court after hearing.

(Subd (a) amended effective January 1, 2007.)

(b) Attorney's fees

Any agreement, express or implied, that has been entered into with respect to the payment of attorney's fees or the submission of an application for the approval of attorney's fees must be set forth in full in any application for approval of the dismissal or settlement of an action that has been certified as a class action.

(Subd (b) amended effective January 1, 2007.)

(c) Preliminary approval of settlement

Any party to a settlement agreement may serve and file a written notice of motion for preliminary approval of the settlement. The settlement agreement and proposed notice to class members must be filed with the motion, and the proposed order must be lodged with the motion.

(Subd (c) amended effective January 1, 2007.)

(d) Order certifying provisional settlement class

The court may make an order approving or denying certification of a provisional settlement class after the preliminary settlement hearing.

(e) Order for final approval hearing

If the court grants preliminary approval, its order must include the time, date, and place of the final approval hearing; the notice to be given to the class; and any other matters deemed necessary for the proper conduct of a settlement hearing.

(f) Notice to class of final approval hearing

If the court has certified the action as a class action, notice of the final approval hearing must be given to the class members in the manner specified by the court. The notice must contain an explanation of the proposed settlement and procedures for class members to follow in filing written objections to it and in arranging to appear at the settlement hearing and state any objections to the proposed settlement.

(Subd (f) amended effective January 1, 2007.)

(g) Conduct of final approval hearing

Before final approval, the court must conduct an inquiry into the fairness of the proposed settlement.

(h) Judgment and retention of jurisdiction to enforce

If the court approves the settlement agreement after the final approval hearing, the court must make and enter judgment. The judgment must include a provision for the retention of the court's jurisdiction over the parties to enforce the terms of the judgment. The court may not enter an order dismissing the action at the same time as, or after, entry of judgment.

(Subd (h) amended effective January 1, 2009.)

Rule 3.769 amended effective January 1, 2009; adopted as rule 1859 effective January 1, 2002; previously amended and renumbered effective January 1, 2007.

Rule 3.770. Dismissal of class actions

(a) Court approval of dismissal

A dismissal of an entire class action, or of any party or cause of action in a class action, requires court approval. The court may not grant a request to dismiss a class action if the court has entered judgment following final approval of a settlement. Requests for dismissal must be accompanied by a declaration setting forth the facts on which the party relies. The declaration must clearly state whether consideration, direct or indirect, is being given for the dismissal and must describe the consideration in detail.

(Subd (a) amended effective January 1, 2009; adopted as untitled subd effective January 1, 1984; previously amended and lettered as subd (a) effective January 1, 2002; previously amended effective January 1, 2007.)

(b) Hearing on request for dismissal

The court may grant the request without a hearing. If the request is disapproved, notice of tentative disapproval must be sent to the attorneys of record. Any party may seek, within 15 calendar days of the service of the notice of tentative disapproval, a hearing on the request. If no hearing is sought within that period, the request for dismissal will be deemed denied.

(Subd (b) amended effective January 1, 2007; adopted as untitled subd effective January 1, 1984; previously amended and lettered as subd (b) effective January 1, 2002.)

(c) Notice to class of dismissal

If the court has certified the class, and notice of the pendency of the action has been provided to class members, notice of the dismissal must be given to the class in the manner specified by the court. If the court has not ruled on class certification, or if notice of the pendency of the action has not been provided to class members in a case in which such notice was required, notice of the proposed dismissal may be given in the manner and to those class members specified by the court, or the action may be dismissed without notice to the class members if the court finds that the dismissal will not prejudice them.

(Subd (c) amended effective January 1, 2007; adopted effective January 1, 2002.)

Rule 3.770 amended effective January 1, 2009; adopted as rule 365 effective January 1, 1984; previously amended and renumbered as rule 1860 effective January 1, 2002, and as rule 3.770 effective January 1, 2007.

Rule 3.771. Judgment

(a) Class members to be included in judgment

The judgment in an action maintained as a class action must include and describe those whom the court finds to be members of the class.

(Subd (a) amended and lettered effective January 1, 2007; adopted as unlettered subd effective January 1, 2002.)

(b) Notice of judgment to class

Notice of the judgment must be given to the class in the manner specified by the court.

(Subd (b) amended and lettered effective January 1, 2007; adopted as unlettered subd effective January 1, 2002.)

Rule 3.771 amended and renumbered effective January 1, 2007; adopted as rule 1861 effective January 1, 2002.

Division 8
Alternative Dispute Resolution

Chapter 1
General Provisions

Rule 3.800. Definitions

As used in this division:

(1) "Alternative dispute resolution process" or "ADR process" means a process, other than formal litigation, in which a neutral person or persons resolve a dispute or assist parties in resolving their dispute.

(2) "Mediation" means a process in which a neutral person or persons facilitate communication between disputants to assist them in reaching a mutually acceptable agreement. As used in this division, mediation does not include a settlement conference under rule 3.1380.

Rule 3.800 amended and renumbered effective January 1, 2007; adopted as rule 1580 effective January 1, 2001; previously amended effective July 1, 2002.

Chapter 2
Judicial Arbitration

Rule 3.810. Application

The rules in this chapter (commencing with this rule) apply if Code of Civil Procedure, part 3, title 3, chapter 2.5 (commencing with section 1141.10) is in effect.

Rule 3.810 amended and renumbered effective January 1, 2007; adopted as rule 1600.1 effective January 1, 1988; previously amended effective July 1, 1999, and January 1, 2000; previously amended and renumbered as rule 1600 effective January 1, 2004.

Rule 3.811. Cases subject to and exempt from arbitration

(a) Cases subject to arbitration

Except as provided in (b), the following cases must be arbitrated:

(1) In each superior court with 18 or more authorized judges, all unlimited civil cases where the amount in controversy does not exceed $50,000 as to any plaintiff;

(2) In each superior court with fewer than 18 authorized judges that so provides by local rule, all unlimited civil cases where the amount in controversy does not exceed $50,000 as to any plaintiff;

(3) All limited civil cases in courts that so provide by local rule;

(4) Upon stipulation, any limited or unlimited civil case in any court, regardless of the amount in controversy; and

(5) Upon filing of an election by all plaintiffs, any limited or unlimited civil case in any court in which each plaintiff agrees that the arbitration award will not exceed $50,000 as to that plaintiff.

(Subd (a) amended effective January 1, 2004.)

(b) Cases exempt from arbitration

The following cases are exempt from arbitration:

(1) Cases that include a prayer for equitable relief that is not frivolous or insubstantial;

(2) Class actions;

(3) Small claims cases or trials de novo on appeal from the small claims court;

(4) Unlawful detainer proceedings;

(5) Family Law Act proceedings except as provided in Family Code section 2554;

(6) Any case otherwise subject to arbitration that is found by the court not to be amenable to arbitration on the ground that arbitration would not reduce the probable time and expense necessary to resolve the litigation;

(7) Any category of cases otherwise subject to arbitration but excluded by local rule as not amenable to arbitration on the ground that, under the circumstances relating to the particular court, arbitration of such cases would not reduce the probable time and expense necessary to resolve the litigation; and

(8) Cases involving multiple causes of action or a cross-complaint if the court determines that the amount in controversy as to any given cause of action or cross-complaint exceeds $50,000.

(Subd (b) adopted effective January 1, 2004.)

Rule 3.811 renumbered effective January 1, 2007; adopted as rule 1600 effective July 1, 1979; previously amended effective January 1, 1982, January 1, 1986, January 1, 1988, and July 1, 1999; previously amended and renumbered as rule 1601 effective January 1, 2004.

Rule 3.812.   Assignment to arbitration

(a) Stipulations to arbitration

When the parties stipulate to arbitration, the case must be set for arbitration forthwith. The stipulation must be filed no later than the time the initial case management statement is filed, unless the court orders otherwise.

(Subd (a) amended effective January 1, 2004; previously amended effective July 1, 1979, January 1, 1999, and January 1, 2003.)

(b) Plaintiff election for arbitration

Upon written election of all plaintiffs to submit a case to arbitration, the case must be set for arbitration forthwith, subject to a motion by defendant for good cause to delay the arbitration hearing. The election must be filed no later than the time the initial case management statement is filed, unless the court orders otherwise.

(Subd (b) amended effective January 1, 2004; adopted effective July 1, 1979; previously amended effective January 1, 1982, January 1, 1986, January 1, 1988, and January 1, 2003.)

(c) Cross-actions

A case involving a cross-complaint where all plaintiffs have elected to arbitrate must be removed from the list of cases assigned to arbitration if, upon motion of the cross-complainant made within 15 days after notice of the election to arbitrate, the court determines that the amount in controversy relating to the cross-complaint exceeds $50,000.

(Subd (c) amended effective January 1, 2004; adopted as part of subd (b) effective July 1, 1979; amended and lettered effective January 1, 2003.)

(d) Case management conference

Absent a stipulation or an election by all plaintiffs to submit to arbitration, cases must be set for arbitration when the court determines that the amount in controversy does not exceed $50,000. The amount in controversy must be determined at the first case management conference or review under the rules on case management in division 7 of this title that takes place after all named parties have appeared or defaulted.

(Subd (d) amended effective January 1, 2007; adopted as subd (c) effective July 1, 1976; previously amended effective July 1, 1979, January 1, 1982, and January 1, 2004; previously amended and relettered effective January 1, 2003.)

Rule 3.812 amended and renumbered effective January 1, 2007; adopted as rule 1601 effective July 1, 1976; previously amended effective July 1, 1979, January 1, 1982, January 1, 1985, January 1, 1986, January 1, 1988, January 1, 1991, and January 1, 2003; previously amended and renumbered as rule 1602 effective January 1, 2004.

Rule 3.813.   Arbitration program administration

(a) Arbitration administrator

The presiding judge must designate the ADR administrator selected under rule 10.783 to serve as arbitration administrator. The arbitration administrator must supervise the selection of arbitrators for the cases on the arbitration hearing list, generally supervise the operation of the arbitration program, and perform any additional duties delegated by the presiding judge.

(Subd (a) amended effective January 1, 2007; previously amended effective January 1, 2004.)

(b) Responsibilities of ADR committee

The ADR committee established under rule 10.783 is responsible for:

(1) Appointing the panels of arbitrators provided for in rule 3.814;

(2) Removing a person from a panel of arbitrators;

(3) Establishing procedures for selecting an arbitrator not inconsistent with these rules or local court rules; and

(4) Reviewing the administration and operation of the arbitration program periodically and making recommendations to the Judicial Council as the committee deems appropriate to improve the program, promote the ends of justice, and serve the needs of the community.

(Subd (b) amended effective January 1, 2007; adopted as subd (d) effective July 1, 1976; previously amended and relettered as subd (b) effective January 1, 2004.) Rule 3.813 amended and renumbered effective January 1, 2007; adopted as rule 1603 effective July 1, 1976; previously amended effective July 1, 1979, July 1, 1999, and January 1, 2004.

Rule 3.814.   Panels of arbitrators

(a) Creation of panels

Every court must have a panel of arbitrators for personal injury cases, and such additional panels as the presiding judge may, from time to time, determine are needed.

(Subd (a) amended effective January 1, 2004; previously amended effective July 1, 1979, and July 1, 2001.)

(b) Composition of panels

The panels of arbitrators must be composed of active or inactive members of the State Bar, retired court commissioners who were licensed to practice law before their appointment as commissioners, and retired judges. A former California judicial officer is not eligible for the panel of arbitrators unless he or she is an active or inactive member of the State Bar.

(Subd (b) amended effective January 1, 2007; previously amended effective July 1, 1979, January 1, 1996, July 1, 2001, and January 1, 2004.)

(c) Responsibilities of ADR committee

The ADR committee is responsible for determining the size and composition of each panel of arbitrators. The personal injury panel, to the extent feasible, must contain an equal number of those who usually represent plaintiffs and those who usually represent defendants.

(Subd (c) amended effective January 1, 2004; previously amended effective July 1, 2001.)

(d) Service on panel

Each person appointed serves as a member of a panel of arbitrators at the pleasure of the ADR committee. A person may be on arbitration panels in more than one county. An appointment to a panel is effective when the person appointed:

(1) Agrees to serve;

(2) Certifies that he or she is aware of and will comply with applicable provisions of canon 6 of the Code of Judicial Ethics and these rules; and

(3) Files an oath or affirmation to justly try all matters submitted to him or her.

(Subd (d) amended effective January 1, 2004; previously amended effective January 1, 1996, and July 1, 2001.)

(e) Panel lists

Lists showing the names of panel arbitrators available to hear cases must be available for public inspection in the ADR administrator's office.

(Subd (e) amended effective January 1, 2007; previously amended effective July 1, 2001, and January 1, 2004.)

Rule 3.814 amended and renumbered effective January 1, 2007; adopted as rule 1604 effective July 1, 1976; previously amended effective July 1, 1979, January 1, 1996, July 1, 2001, and January 1, 2004.

Rule 3.815.   Selection of the arbitrator

(a) Selection by stipulation

By stipulation, the parties may select any person to serve as arbitrator. If the parties select a person who is not on the court's arbitration panel to serve as the arbitrator, the stipulation will be effective only if:

(1) The selected person completes a written consent to serve and the oath required of panel arbitrators under these rules; and

(2) Both the consent and the oath are attached to the stipulation.

A stipulation may specify the maximum amount of the arbitrator's award. The stipulation to an arbitrator must be served and filed no later than 10 days after the case has been set for arbitration under rule 3.812.

(Subd (a) amended effective January 1, 2007; adopted effective January 1, 2004.)

(b) Selection absent stipulation or local procedures

If the arbitrator has not been selected by stipulation and the court has not adopted local rules or procedures for the selection of the arbitrator as permitted under (c), the arbitrator will be selected as follows:

(1) Within 15 days after a case is set for arbitration under rule 3.812, the administrator must determine the number of clearly adverse sides in the case; in the absence of a cross-complaint bringing in a new party, the administrator may assume there are two sides. A dispute as to the number or identity of sides must be decided by the presiding judge in the same manner as disputes in determining sides entitled to peremptory challenges of jurors.

(2) The administrator must select at random a number of names equal to the number of sides, plus one, and send the list of randomly selected names to counsel for the parties.

(3) Each side has 10 days from the date on which the list was sent to file a rejection, in writing, of no more than one name on the list; if there are two or more parties on a side, they must join in the rejection of a single name.

(4) Promptly on the expiration of the 10-day period, the administrator must appoint, at random, one of the persons on the list whose name was not rejected, if more than one name remains.

(5) The administrator must assign the case to the arbitrator appointed and must give notice of the appointment to the arbitrator and to all parties.

(Subd (b) amended effective January 1, 2016; adopted as subd (a) effective July 1, 1976; previously amended and relettered as subd (b) effective January 1, 2004; previously amended effective July 1, 1979, January 1, 1982, January 1, 1984, and January 1, 2007.)

(c) Local selection procedures

Instead of the procedure in (b), a court that has an arbitration program may, by local rule or by procedures adopted by its ADR committee, establish any fair method of selecting an arbitrator that:

(1) Affords each side an opportunity to challenge at least one listed arbitrator peremptorily; and

(2) Ensures that an arbitrator is appointed within 30 days from the submission of a case to arbitration.

The local rule or procedure may require that all steps leading to the selection of the arbitrator take place during or immediately following the case management conference or review under the rules on case management in division 7 of this title at which the court determines the amount in controversy and the suitability of the case for arbitration.

(Subd (c) amended effective January 1, 2007; adopted effective January 1, 2004.)

(d) Procedure if first arbitrator declines to serve

If the first arbitrator selected declines to serve, the administrator must vacate the appointment of the arbitrator and may either:

(1) Return the case to the top of the arbitration hearing list, restore the arbitrator's name to the list of those available for selection to hear cases, and appoint a new arbitrator; or

(2) Certify the case to the court.

(Subd (d) amended and relettered effective January 1, 2004; adopted as subd (b) effective July 1, 1976; previously amended effective January 1, 1991, and January 1, 1994.)

(e) Procedure if second arbitrator declines to serve or hearing is not timely held

If the second arbitrator selected declines to serve or if the arbitrator does not complete the hearing within 90 days after the date of the assignment of the case to him or her, including any time due to continuances granted under rule 3.818, the administrator must certify the case to the court.

(Subd (e) amended effective January 1, 2007; adopted as subd (c) effective July 1, 1976; previously amended effective January 1, 1991; previously amended and relettered effective January 1, 2004.)

(f) Cases certified to court

If a case is certified to the court under either (d) or (e), the court must hold a case management conference. If the inability to hold an arbitration hearing is due to the neglect or lack of cooperation of a party who elected or stipulated to arbitration, the court may set the case for trial and may make any other appropriate orders. In all other circumstances, the court may reassign the case to arbitration or make any other appropriate orders to expedite disposition of the case.

(Subd (f) amended effective January 1, 2007; adopted as part of subd (c) effective July 1, 1976; previously amended and relettered as subd (f) effective January 1, 2004.)

Rule 3.815 amended effective January 1, 2016; adopted as rule 1605 effective July 1, 1976; previously amended effective July 1, 1979, January 1, 1982; January 1, 1984, January 1, 1991, January 1, 1994, and January 1, 2004; previously amended and renumbered as rule 3.815 effective January 1, 2007.

Rule 3.816.   Disqualification for conflict of interest

(a) Arbitrator's duty to disqualify himself or herself

The arbitrator must determine whether any cause exists for disqualification upon any of the grounds set forth in Code of Civil Procedure section 170.1 governing the disqualification of judges. If any member of the arbitrator's law firm would be disqualified under subdivision (a)(2) of section 170.1, the arbitrator is disqualified. Unless the ground for disqualification is disclosed to the parties in writing and is expressly waived by all parties in writing, the arbitrator must promptly notify the administrator of any known ground for disqualification and another arbitrator must be selected as provided in rule 3.815.

(Subd (a) amended effective January 1, 2007; previously amended effective July 1, 1979, July 1, 1990, July 1, 2001, January 1, 2004, and July 1, 2004.)

(b) Disclosures by arbitrator

In addition to any other disclosure required by law, no later than five days before the deadline for parties to file a motion for disqualification of the arbitrator under Code of Civil Procedure section 170.6 or, if the arbitrator is not aware of his or her appointment or of a matter subject to disclosure at that time, as soon as practicable thereafter, an arbitrator must disclose to the parties:

(1) Any matter subject to disclosure under subdivisions (D)(5)(a) and (D)(5)(b) of canon 6 of the Code of Judicial Ethics; and

(2) Any significant personal or professional relationship the arbitrator has or has had with a party, attorney, or law firm in the instant case, including the number and nature of any other proceedings in the past 24 months in which the arbitrator has been privately compensated by a party, attorney, law firm, or insurance company in the instant case for any services, including service as an attorney, expert witness, or consultant or as a judge, referee, arbitrator, mediator, settlement facilitator, or other alternative dispute resolution neutral.

(Subd (b) amended effective January 1, 2008; adopted effective July 1, 2001; previously amended effective January 1, 2007.)

(c) Request for disqualification

A copy of any request by a party for the disqualification of an arbitrator under Code of Civil Procedure section 170.1 or 170.6 must be sent to the ADR administrator.

(Subd (c) amended effective January 1, 2007; adopted as subd (b) effective July 1, 1976; previously amended and relettered effective July 1, 2001; previously amended effective July 1, 1979, July 1, 1990, and January 1, 2004.)

(d) Arbitrator's failure to disqualify himself or herself

On motion of any party, made as promptly as possible under Code of Civil Procedure sections 170.1 and 1141.18(d) and before the conclusion of arbitration proceedings, the appointment of an arbitrator to a case must be vacated if the court finds that:

(1) The party has demanded that the arbitrator disqualify himself or herself;

(2) The arbitrator has failed to do so; and

(3) Any of the grounds specified in section 170.1 exists.

The ADR administrator must return the case to the top of the arbitration hearing list and appoint a new arbitrator. The disqualified arbitrator's name must be returned to the list of those available for selection to hear cases, unless the court orders that the circumstances of the disqualification be reviewed by the ADR administrator, the ADR committee, or the presiding judge for appropriate action.

(Subd (d) amended effective January 1, 2007; adopted as subd (c) effective January 1, 1994; previously amended and relettered effective July 1, 2001; previously amended effective January 1, 2004.)

Rule 3.816 amended effective January 1, 2008; adopted as rule 1606 effective July 1, 1976; previously amended effective July 1, 1979, July 1, 1990, January 1, 1994,

July 1, 2001, January 1, 2004, and July 1, 2004; previously amended and renumbered effective January 1, 2007.

Rule 3.817. Arbitration hearings; notice; when and where held

(a) Setting hearing; notice

Within 15 days after the appointment of the arbitrator, the arbitrator must set the time, date, and place of the arbitration hearing and notify each party and the administrator in writing of the time, date, and place set.

(Subd (a) amended and lettered effective January 1, 2004; adopted as part of unlettered subd effective July 1, 1976.)

(b) Date of hearing; limitations

Except upon the agreement of all parties and the arbitrator, the arbitration hearing date must not be set:

(1) Earlier than 30 days after the date the arbitrator sends the notice of the hearing under (a); or

(2) On Saturdays, Sundays, or legal holidays.

(Subd (b) amended and lettered effective January 1, 2004; adopted as part of unlettered subd effective July 1, 1976.)

(c) Hearing completion deadline

The hearing must be scheduled so as to be completed no later than 90 days from the date of the assignment of the case to the arbitrator, including any time due to continuances granted under rule 3.818.

(Subd (c) amended effective January 1, 2007; adopted as part of unlettered subd effective July 1, 1976; previously amended and relettered effective January 1, 2004.)

(d) Hearing location

The hearing must take place in appropriate facilities provided by the court or selected by the arbitrator.

(Subd (d) amended effective January 1, 2004.)

Rule 3.817 amended and renumbered effective January 1, 2007; adopted as rule 1611 effective July 1, 1976; previously amended effective July 1, 1979, and January 1, 1992; previously amended and renumbered as rule 1607 effective January 1, 2004.

Rule 3.818. Continuances

(a) Stipulation to continuance; consent of arbitrator

Except as provided in (c), the parties may stipulate to a continuance in the case, with the consent of the assigned arbitrator. An arbitrator must consent to a request for a continuance if it appears that good cause exists. Notice of the continuance must be sent to the ADR administrator.

(Subd (a) amended effective January 1, 2004; previously amended effective January 1, 1984, and January 1, 1992.)

(b) Court grant of continuance

If the arbitrator declines to give consent to a continuance, upon the motion of a party and for good cause shown, the court may grant a continuance of the arbitration hearing. In the event the court grants the motion, the party who requested the continuance must notify the arbitrator and the arbitrator must reschedule the hearing, giving notice to all parties to the arbitration proceeding.

(Subd (b) amended effective January 1, 2007; previously amended effective July 1, 1979, and January 1, 2004.)

(c) Limitation on length of continuance

An arbitration hearing must not be continued to a date later than 90 days after the assignment of the case to the arbitrator, including any time due to continuances granted under this rule, except by order of the court upon the motion of a party as provided in (b).

(Subd (c) amended effective January 1, 2004; previously amended effective January 1, 1991 and January 1, 1994.)

Rule 3.818 amended and renumbered effective January 1, 2007; adopted as rule 1607 effective July 1, 1976; previously amended effective July 1, 1979, January 1, 1984, January 1, 1991, January 1, 1992, and January 1, 1994; previously amended and renumbered as rule 1608 effective January 1, 2004.

Rule 3.819. Arbitrator's fees

(a) Filing of award required

Except as provided in (b), the arbitrator's award must be timely filed with the clerk of the court under rule 3.825(b) before a fee may be paid to the arbitrator.

(Subd (a) amended effective January 1, 2013; previously amended effective July 1, 1979, January 1, 2004, and January 1, 2007.)

(b) Exceptions for good cause

On the arbitrator's verified ex parte application, the court may for good cause authorize payment of a fee:

(1) If the arbitrator devoted a substantial amount of time to a case that was settled without a hearing or without an award being filed. For this purpose, a case is considered settled when one of the following is filed:

(A) A notice of settlement of the entire case, under rule 3.1385; or

(B) A *Request for Dismissal* (form CIV-110) of the entire case or as to all parties to the arbitration is filed; or

(2) If the award was not timely filed.

(Subd (b) amended effective January 1, 2013; previously amended effective July 1, 1979, January 1, 1987, and January 1, 2004.)

(c) Arbitrator's fee statement

The arbitrator's fee statement must be submitted to the administrator promptly upon the completion of the arbitrator's duties and must set forth the title and number of the cause arbitrated, the date of any arbitration hearing, and the date the award, notice of settlement, or request for dismissal was filed.

(Subd (c) amended effective January 1, 2013; previously amended effective July 1, 1979, January 1, 2004, and January 1, 2007.)

Rule 3.819 adopted as rule 1608 effective July 1, 1976; previously amended effective July 1, 1979, and January 1, 1987; previously amended and renumbered as rule 1609 effective January 1, 2004; previously amended and renumbered effective January 1, 2007.

Rule 3.820. Communication with the arbitrator

(a) Disclosure of settlement offers prohibited

No disclosure of any offers of settlement made by any party may be made to the arbitrator prior to the filing of the award.

(Subd (a) amended and relettered effective January 1, 2004; adopted as part of unlettered subd effective July 1, 1976.)

(b) Ex parte communication prohibited

An arbitrator must not initiate, permit, or consider any ex parte communications or consider other communications made to the arbitrator outside the presence of all of the parties concerning a pending arbitration, except as follows:

(1) An arbitrator may communicate with a party in the absence of other parties about administrative matters, such as setting the time and place of hearings or making other arrangements for the conduct of the proceedings, as long as the arbitrator reasonably believes that the communication will not result in a procedural or tactical advantage for any party. When such a discussion occurs, the arbitrator must promptly inform the other parties of the communication and must give the other parties an opportunity to respond before making any final determination concerning the matter discussed.

(2) An arbitrator may initiate or consider any ex parte communication when expressly authorized by law to do so.

(Subd (b) amended effective January 1, 2007; adopted as part of unlettered subd effective July 1, 1976; previously amended and lettered effective January 1, 2004.)

Rule 3.820 amended and renumbered effective January 1, 2007; adopted as rule 1609 effective July 1, 1976; previously amended and renumbered as rule 1610 effective January 1, 2004.

Rule 3.821. Representation by counsel; proceedings when party absent

(a) Representation by counsel

A party to the arbitration has a right to be represented by an attorney at any proceeding or hearing in arbitration, but this right may be waived. A waiver of this right may be revoked, but if revoked, the other party is entitled to a reasonable continuance for the purpose of obtaining counsel.

(Subd (a) amended effective January 1, 2004.)

(b) Proceedings when party absent

The arbitration may proceed in the absence of any party who, after due notice, fails to be present and to obtain a continuance. An award must not be based solely on the absence of a party. In the event of a default by defendant, the arbitrator must require the plaintiff to submit such evidence as may be appropriate for the making of an award.

(Subd (b) amended effective January 1, 2007; previously amended effective January 1, 2004.)

Rule 3.821 amended and renumbered effective January 1, 2007; adopted as rule 1610 effective July 1, 1976; previously amended and renumbered as rule 1611 effective January 1, 2004.

Rule 3.822. Discovery

(a) Right to discovery

The parties to the arbitration have the right to take depositions and to obtain discovery, and to that end may exercise all of the same rights, remedies, and procedures, and are subject to all of the same duties, liabilities, and obligations as provided in part 4, title 3, chapter 3 of the Code of Civil Procedure, except as provided in (b).

(Subd (a) amended and lettered effective January 1, 2007; adopted as part of unlettered subd effective July 1, 1976.)

(b) Completion of discovery

All discovery must be completed not later than 15 days before the date set for the arbitration hearing unless the court, upon a showing of good cause, makes an order granting an extension of the time within which discovery must be completed.

(Subd (b) amended and lettered effective January 1, 2007; adopted as part of unlettered subd effective July 1, 1976.)

Rule 3.822 amended and renumbered effective January 1, 2007; adopted as rule 1612 effective July 1, 1976; previously amended effective July 1, 1979, and January 1, 2004.

Rule 3.823. Rules of evidence at arbitration hearing

(a) Presence of arbitrator and parties

All evidence must be taken in the presence of the arbitrator and all parties, except where any of the parties has waived the right to be present or is absent after due notice of the hearing.

(Subd (a) amended effective January 1, 2004.)

(b) Application of civil rules of evidence

The rules of evidence governing civil cases apply to the conduct of the arbitration hearing, except:

(1) *Written reports and other documents*

Any party may offer written reports of any expert witness, medical records and bills (including physiotherapy, nursing, and prescription bills), documentary evidence of loss of income, property damage repair bills or estimates, police reports concerning an accident that gave rise to the case, other bills and invoices, purchase orders, checks, written contracts, and similar documents prepared and maintained in the ordinary course of business.

(A) The arbitrator must receive them in evidence if copies have been delivered to all opposing parties at least 20 days before the hearing.

(B) Any other party may subpoena the author or custodian of the document as a witness and examine the witness as if under cross-examination.

(C) Any repair estimate offered as an exhibit, and the copies delivered to opposing parties, must be accompanied by:

(i) A statement indicating whether or not the property was repaired, and, if it was, whether the estimated repairs were made in full or in part; and

(ii) A copy of the receipted bill showing the items of repair made and the amount paid.

(D) The arbitrator must not consider any opinion as to ultimate fault expressed in a police report.

(2) *Witness statements*

The written statements of any other witness may be offered and must be received in evidence if:

(A) They are made by declaration under penalty of perjury;

(B) Copies have been delivered to all opposing parties at least 20 days before the hearing; and

(C) No opposing party has, at least 10 days before the hearing, delivered to the proponent of the evidence a written demand that the witness be produced in person to testify at the hearing. The arbitrator must disregard any portion of a statement received under this rule that would be inadmissible if the witness were testifying in person, but the inclusion of inadmissible matter does not render the entire statement inadmissible.

(3) *Depositions*

(A) The deposition of any witness may be offered by any party and must be received in evidence, subject to objections available under Code of Civil Procedure section 2025.410, notwithstanding that the deponent is not "unavailable as a witness" within the meaning of Evidence Code section 240 and no exceptional circumstances exist, if:

(i) The deposition was taken in the manner provided for by law or by stipulation of the parties and within the time provided for in these rules; and

(ii) Not less than 20 days before the hearing the proponent of the deposition delivered to all opposing parties notice of intention to offer the deposition in evidence.

(B) The opposing party, upon receiving the notice, may subpoena the deponent and, at the discretion of the arbitrator, either the deposition may be excluded from evidence or the deposition may be admitted and the deponent may be further cross-examined by the subpoenaing party. These limitations are not applicable to a deposition admissible under the terms of Code of Civil Procedure section 2025.620.

(Subd (b) amended effective January 1, 2008; previously amended effective July 1, 1979, January 1, 1984, January 1, 1988, July 1, 1990, January 1, 2004, and January 1, 2007.)

(c) Subpoenas

(1) *Compelling witnesses to appear*

The attendance of witnesses at arbitration hearings may be compelled through the issuance of subpoenas as provided in the Code of Civil Procedure, in section 1985 and elsewhere in part 4, title 3, chapters 2 and 3. It is the duty of the party requesting the subpoena to modify the form of subpoena so as to show that the appearance is before an arbitrator and to give the time and place set for the arbitration hearing.

(2) *Adjournment or continuances*

At the discretion of the arbitrator, nonappearance of a properly subpoenaed witness may be a ground for an adjournment or continuance of the hearing.

(3) *Contempt*

If any witness properly served with a subpoena fails to appear at the arbitration hearing or, having appeared, refuses to be sworn or to answer, proceedings to compel compliance with the subpoena on penalty of contempt may be had before the superior court as provided in Code of Civil Procedure section 1991 for other instances of refusal to appear and answer before an officer or commissioner out of court.

(Subd (c) amended effective January 1, 2007; previously amended effective July 1, 1979, and January 1, 2004.)

(d) Delivery of documents

For purposes of this rule, "delivery" of a document or notice may be accomplished manually, by electronic means under Code of Civil Procedure section 1010.6 and rule 2.251, or in the manner provided by Code of Civil Procedure section 1013. If service is by electronic means, the times prescribed in this rule for delivery of documents, notices, and demands are increased as provided by Code of Civil Procedure section 1010.6. If service is in the manner provided by Code of Civil Procedure section 1013, the times prescribed in this rule are increased as provided by that section.

(Subd (d) amended effective January 1, 2017; adopted effective January 1, 1988; previously amended effective January 1, 2004, and January 1, 2016.)

Rule 3.823 amended effective January 1, 2017; adopted as rule 1613 effective July 1, 1976; previously amended and renumbered as rule 3.823 effective January 1, 2007; previously amended effective July 1, 1979, January 1, 1984, January 1, 1988, July 1, 1990, January 1, 2004, January 1, 2008, and January 1, 2016.

Rule 3.824. Conduct of the hearing

(a) Arbitrator's powers

The arbitrator has the following powers; all other questions arising out of the case are reserved to the court:

(1) To administer oaths or affirmations to witnesses;

(2) To take adjournments upon the request of a party or upon his or her own initiative when deemed necessary;

(3) To permit testimony to be offered by deposition;

(4) To permit evidence to be offered and introduced as provided in these rules;

(5) To rule upon the admissibility and relevancy of evidence offered;

(6) To invite the parties, on reasonable notice, to submit arbitration briefs;

(7) To decide the law and facts of the case and make an award accordingly;

(8) To award costs, not to exceed the statutory costs of the suit; and

(9) To examine any site or object relevant to the case.

(Subd (a) amended effective January 1, 2007; previously amended effective January 1, 2004.)

(b) Record of proceedings

(1) *Arbitrator's record*

The arbitrator may, but is not required to, make a record of the proceedings.

(2) *Record not subject to discovery*

Any records of the proceedings made by or at the direction of the arbitrator are deemed the arbitrator's personal notes and are not subject to discovery, and the arbitrator must not deliver them to any party to the case or to any other person, except to an employee using the records under the arbitrator's supervision or pursuant to a subpoena issued in a criminal investigation or prosecution for perjury.

(3) *No other record*

No other record may be made, and the arbitrator must not permit the presence of a stenographer or court reporter or the use of any recording device at the hearing, except as expressly permitted by (1).

(Subd (b) amended effective January 1, 2007; previously amended effective January 1, 2004.)

Rule 3.824 amended and renumbered effective January 1, 2007; adopted as rule 1614 effective July 1, 1976; previously amended effective January 1, 2004.

Rule 3.825. The award

(a) Form and content of the award

(1) *Award in writing*

The award must be in writing and signed by the arbitrator. It must determine all issues properly raised by the pleadings, including a determination of any damages and an award of costs if appropriate.

(2) *No findings or conclusions required*

The arbitrator is not required to make findings of fact or conclusions of law.

(Subd (a) amended effective January 1, 2007; previously amended effective January 1, 2004.)

(b) Filing the award or amended award

(1) *Time for filing the award*

Within 10 days after the conclusion of the arbitration hearing, the arbitrator must file the award with the clerk, with proof of service on each party to the arbitration. On the arbitrator's application in cases of unusual length or complexity, the court may allow up to 20 additional days for the filing and service of the award.

(2) *Amended award*

Within the time for filing the award, the arbitrator may file and serve an amended award.

(Subd (b) amended effective January 1, 2007; previously amended effective January 1, 1995, and January 1, 2004.)

Rule 3.825 amended and renumbered effective January 1, 2007; adopted as rule 1615 effective July 1, 1976; previously amended effective January 1, 1983, January 1, 1985, January 1, 1995, January 1, 2003, and January 1, 2004.

Rule 3.826. Trial after arbitration

(a) Request for trial; deadline

Within 60 days after the arbitration award is filed with the clerk of the court, a party may request a trial by filing with the clerk a request for trial, with proof of service of a copy upon all other parties appearing in the case. A request for trial filed after the parties have been served with a copy of the award by the arbitrator, but before the award has been filed with the clerk, is valid and timely filed. The 60-day period within which to request trial may not be extended.

(Subd (a) amended effective January 1, 2012; previously amended effective January 1, 1985, July 1, 1990, January 1, 2004, and January 1, 2007.)

(b) Prosecution of the case

If a party makes a timely request for a trial, the case must proceed as provided under an applicable case management order. If no pending order provides for the prosecution of the case after a request for a trial after arbitration, the court must promptly schedule a case management conference.

(Subd (b) amended effective January 1, 2007; previously amended effective January 1, 2004.)

(c) References to arbitration during trial prohibited

The case must be tried as though no arbitration proceedings had occurred. No reference may be made during the trial to the arbitration award, to the fact that there had been arbitration proceedings, to the evidence adduced at the arbitration hearing, or to any other aspect of the arbitration proceedings, and none of the foregoing may be used as affirmative evidence, or by way of impeachment, or for any other purpose at the trial.

(Subd (c) amended effective January 1, 2004.)

(d) Costs after trial

In assessing costs after the trial, the court must apply the standards specified in Code of Civil Procedure section 1141.21.

(Subd (d) amended effective January 1, 2007; previously amended effective July 1, 1979, and January 1, 2004.)

Rule 3.826 amended effective January 1, 2012; adopted as rule 1616 effective July 1, 1976; previously amended effective July 1, 1979, July 1, 1990, and January 1, 2004; previously amended and renumbered effective January 1, 2007.

Rule 3.827. Entry of award as judgment

(a) Entry of award as judgment by clerk

The clerk must enter the award as a judgment immediately upon the expiration of 60 days after the award is filed if no party has, during that period, served and filed either:

(1) A request for trial as provided in these rules; or

(2) A *Request for Dismissal* (form CIV-110) of the entire case or as to all parties to the arbitration. The *Request for Dismissal* must be fully completed. If the request is for dismissal of the entire case, it must include the signatures of all parties. If the request is for dismissal as to all parties to the arbitration, it must include the signatures of all those parties.

(Subd (a) amended effective January 1, 2013; adopted effective January 1, 2007; previously amended effective January 1, 2012.)

(b) Notice of entry of judgment

Promptly upon entry of the award as a judgment, the clerk must serve notice of entry of judgment on all parties who have appeared in the case and must execute a certificate of service and place it in the court's file in the case.

(Subd (b) amended effective January 1, 2016.)

(c) Effect of judgment

The judgment so entered has the same force and effect in all respects as, and is subject to all provisions of law relating to, a judgment in a civil case or proceeding, except that it is not subject to appeal and it may not be attacked or set aside except as provided in rule 3.828. The judgment so entered may be enforced as if it had been rendered by the court in which it is entered.

Rule 3.827 amended effective January 1, 2016; adopted effective January 1, 2007; previously amended effective January 1, 2012, and January 1, 2013.

Rule 3.828. Vacating judgment on award

(a) Motion to vacate

A party against whom a judgment is entered under an arbitration award may, within six months after its entry, move to vacate the judgment on the ground that the arbitrator was subject to a disqualification not disclosed before the hearing and of which the arbitrator was then aware, or upon one of the grounds set forth in Code of Civil Procedure sections 473 or 1286.2(a)(1), (2), and (3), and on no other grounds.

(b) Notice and grounds for granting motion

The motion must be heard upon notice to the adverse parties and to the arbitrator, and may be granted only upon clear and convincing evidence that the grounds alleged are true, and that the motion was made as soon as practicable after the moving party learned of the existence of those grounds.

Rule 3.828 adopted effective January 1, 2007.

Rule 3.829. Settlement of case

If a case is settled, each plaintiff or other party seeking affirmative relief must notify the arbitrator and the court as required in rule 3.1385.

Rule 3.829 amended and renumbered effective January 1, 2007; adopted as rule 1618 effective January 1, 1992; previously amended effective January 1, 2004.

Rule 3.830. Arbitration not pursuant to rules

These rules do not prohibit the parties to any civil case or proceeding from entering into arbitration agreements under part 3, title 9 of the Code of Civil Procedure. Neither the ADR committee nor the ADR administrator may take any part in the conduct of an arbitration under an agreement not in conformity with these rules except that the administrator may, upon joint request of the parties, furnish the parties to the agreement with a randomly selected list of at least three names of members of the appropriate panel of arbitrators.

Rule 3.830 amended and renumbered effective January 1, 2007; adopted as rule 1617 effective July 1, 1976; previously amended effective January 1, 2004.

Chapter 3
General Rules Relating to Mediation of Civil Cases

Article 1
Procedures for All Court Mediation Programs

Division 8, Alternative Dispute Resolution—Chapter 3, General Rules Relating to Mediation of Civil Cases—Article 1, Procedures for All Court Mediation Programs; adopted effective July 1, 2012.

Rule 3.835. Application

The rules in this article apply to all court mediation programs for general civil cases, as defined in rule 1.6, unless otherwise specified.

Rule 3.835 adopted effective July 1, 2012.

Rule 3.845. Form of mediator statements and reports

If a mediator is required to submit a statement or report to the court concerning the status or result of the mediation, the statement or report must be submitted on the Judicial Council *Statement of Agreement or Nonagreement* (form ADR-100). The mediator's completed form ADR-100 must not disclose the terms of any agreement or any other communications or conduct that occurred in the course of the mediation, except as allowed in Evidence Code sections 1115–1128.

Rule 3.845 adopted effective July 1, 2012.

Advisory Committee Comment

This rule does not preclude courts from asking mediators to provide other information about court-program mediations on separate forms or surveys that do not request any information that will allow identification of a specific case or mediation participant and that will not become part of the court's case file.

Article 2
Rules of Conduct for Mediators in Court-Connected Mediation Programs for Civil Cases

Rule 3.850. Purpose and function
Rule 3.851. Application
Rule 3.852. Definitions
Rule 3.853. Voluntary participation and self-determination
Rule 3.854. Confidentiality
Rule 3.855. Impartiality, conflicts of interest, disclosure, and withdrawal
Rule 3.856. Competence
Rule 3.857. Quality of mediation process
Rule 3.858. Marketing
Rule 3.859. Compensation and gifts
Rule 3.860. Attendance sheet and agreement to disclosure

Rule 3.850. Purpose and function

(a) Standards of conduct

The rules in this article establish the minimum standards of conduct for mediators in court-connected mediation programs for general civil cases. These rules are intended to guide the conduct of mediators in these programs, to inform and protect participants in these mediation programs, and to promote public confidence in the mediation process and the courts. For mediation to be effective, there must be broad public confidence in the integrity and fairness of the process. Mediators in court-connected programs are responsible to the parties, the public, and the courts for conducting themselves in a manner that merits that confidence.

(Subd (a) amended effective January 1, 2007.)

(b) Scope and limitations

These rules are not intended to:

(1) Establish a ceiling on what is considered good practice in mediation or discourage efforts by courts, mediators, or others to educate mediators about best practices;

(2) Create a basis for challenging a settlement agreement reached in connection with mediation; or

(3) Create a basis for a civil cause of action against a mediator.

(Subd (b) amended effective January 1, 2007.)

Rule 3.850 amended and renumbered effective January 1, 2007; adopted as rule 1620 effective January 1, 2003.

Rule 3.851. Application

(a) Circumstances applicable

The rules in this article apply to mediations in which a mediator:

(1) Has agreed to be included on a superior court's list or panel of mediators for general civil cases and is notified by the court or the parties that he or she has been selected to mediate a case within that court's mediation program; or

(2) Has agreed to mediate a general civil case pending in a superior court after being notified by the court or the parties that he or she was recommended, selected, or appointed by that court or will be compensated by that court to mediate a case within that court's mediation program. A mediator who is not on a superior court list or panel and who is selected by the parties is not "recommended, selected, or appointed" by the court within the meaning of this subdivision simply because the court approves the parties' agreement to use this mediator or memorializes the parties' selection in a court order.

(Subd (a) amended effective January 1, 2010; previously amended effective January 1, 2007, and January 1, 2009.)

(b) Application to listed firms

If a court's panel or list includes firms that provide mediation services, all mediators affiliated with a listed firm are required to comply with the rules in this article when they are notified by the court or the parties that the firm was selected from the court list to mediate a general civil case within that court's mediation program.

(Subd (b) amended effective July 1, 2007; previously amended effective January 1, 2007.)

(c) Time of applicability

Except as otherwise provided in these rules, the rules in this article apply from the time the mediator agrees to mediate a case until the end of the mediation in that case.

(Subd (c) amended effective January 1, 2007.)

(d) Inapplicability to judges

The rules in this article do not apply to judges or other judicial officers while they are serving in a capacity in which they are governed by the Code of Judicial Ethics.

(Subd (d) amended effective January 1, 2007.)

(e) Inapplicability to settlement conferences

The rules in this article do not apply to settlement conferences conducted under rule 3.1380.

(Subd (e) amended effective January 1, 2007.)

Rule 3.851 amended effective January 1, 2010; adopted as rule 1620.1 effective January 1, 2003; previously amended and renumbered effective January 1, 2007; previously amended effective July 1, 2007, and January 1, 2009.

Advisory Committee Comment

Subdivision (d). Although these rules do not apply to them, judicial officers who serve as mediators in their courts' mediation programs are nevertheless encouraged to be familiar with and observe these rules when mediating, particularly the rules concerning subjects not covered in the Code of Judicial Ethics such as voluntary participation and self-determination.

Rule 3.852. Definitions

As used in this article, unless the context or subject matter requires otherwise:

(1) "Mediation" means a process in which a neutral person or persons facilitate communication between the disputants to assist them in reaching a mutually acceptable agreement.

(2) "Mediator" means a neutral person who conducts a mediation.

(3) "Participant" means any individual, entity, or group, other than the mediator taking part in a mediation, including but not limited to attorneys for the parties.

(4) "Party" means any individual, entity, or group taking part in a mediation that is a plaintiff, a defendant, a cross-complainant, a cross-defendant, a petitioner, a respondent, or an intervenor in the case.

Rule 3.852 amended and renumbered effective January 1, 2007; adopted as rule 1620.2 effective January 1, 2003.

Advisory Committee Comment

The definition of "mediator" in this rule departs from the definition in Evidence Code section 1115(b) in that it does not include persons designated by the mediator to assist in the mediation or to communicate with a participant in preparation for the mediation. However, these definitions are applicable only to these rules of conduct and do not limit or expand mediation confidentiality under the Evidence Code or other law.

The definition of "participant" includes insurance adjusters, experts, and consultants as well as the parties and their attorneys.

Rule 3.853. Voluntary participation and self-determination

A mediator must conduct the mediation in a manner that supports the principles of voluntary participation and self-determination by the parties. For this purpose a mediator must:

(1) Inform the parties, at or before the outset of the first mediation session, that any resolution of the dispute in mediation requires a voluntary agreement of the parties;

(2) Respect the right of each participant to decide the extent of his or her participation in the mediation, including the right to withdraw from the mediation at any time; and

(3) Refrain from coercing any party to make a decision or to continue to participate in the mediation.

Rule 3.853 amended and renumbered effective January 1, 2007; adopted as rule 1620.3 effective January 1, 2003.

Advisory Committee Comment

Voluntary participation and self-determination are fundamental principles of mediation that apply both to mediations in which the parties voluntarily elect to mediate and to those in which the parties are required to go to mediation in a mandatory court mediation program or by court order. Although the court may order participants to attend mediation, a mediator may not mandate the extent of their participation in the mediation process or coerce any party to settle the case.

After informing the parties of their choices and the consequences of those choices, a mediator can invoke a broad range of approaches to assist the parties in reaching an agreement without offending the principles of voluntary participation and self-determination, including (1) encouraging the parties to continue participating in the mediation when it reasonably appears to the mediator that the possibility of reaching an uncoerced, consensual agreement has not been exhausted and (2) suggesting that a party consider obtaining professional advice (for example, informing an unrepresented party that he or she may consider obtaining legal advice). Conversely, examples of conduct that violate the principles of voluntary participation and self-determination include coercing a party to continue participating in the mediation after the party has told the mediator that he or she wishes to terminate the mediation, providing an opinion or evaluation of the dispute in a coercive manner or over the objection of the parties, using abusive language, and threatening to make a report to the court about a party's conduct at the mediation.

Rule 3.854.   Confidentiality

(a) Compliance with confidentiality law

A mediator must, at all times, comply with the applicable law concerning confidentiality.

(b) Informing participants of confidentiality

At or before the outset of the first mediation session, a mediator must provide the participants with a general explanation of the confidentiality of mediation proceedings.

(c) Confidentiality of separate communications; caucuses

If, after all the parties have agreed to participate in the mediation process and the mediator has agreed to mediate the case, a mediator speaks separately with one or more participants out of the presence of the other participants, the mediator must first discuss with all participants the mediator's practice regarding confidentiality for separate communications with the participants. Except as required by law, a mediator must not disclose information revealed in confidence during such separate communications unless authorized to do so by the participant or participants who revealed the information.

(d) Use of confidential information

A mediator must not use information that is acquired in confidence in the course of a mediation outside the mediation or for personal gain.

Rule 3.854 renumbered effective January 1, 2007; adopted as rule 1620.4 effective January 1, 2003.

Advisory Committee Comment

Subdivision (a). The general law concerning mediation confidentiality is found in Evidence Code sections 703.5 and 1115–1128 and in cases interpreting those sections. (See, e.g., *Foxgate Homeowners' Association, Inc. v. Bramalea California, Inc.* (2001) 26 Cal.4th 1; *Rinaker v. Superior Court* (1998) 62 Cal.App.4th 155; and *Gilbert v. National Corp. for Housing Partnerships* (1999) 71 Cal.App.4th 1240.)

Rule 3.855.   Impartiality, conflicts of interest, disclosure, and withdrawal

(a) Impartiality

A mediator must maintain impartiality toward all participants in the mediation process at all times.

(b) Disclosure of matters potentially affecting impartiality

(1) A mediator must make reasonable efforts to keep informed about matters that reasonably could raise a question about his or her ability to conduct the proceedings impartially, and must disclose these matters to the parties. These matters include:

(A) Past, present, and currently expected interests, relationships, and affiliations of a personal, professional, or financial nature; and

(B) The existence of any grounds for disqualification of a judge specified in Code of Civil Procedure section 170.1.

(2) A mediator's duty to disclose is a continuing obligation, from the inception of the mediation process through its completion. Disclosures required by this rule must be made as soon as practicable after a mediator becomes aware of a matter that must be disclosed. To the extent possible, such disclosures should be made before the first mediation session, but in any event they must be made within the time required by applicable court rules or statutes.

(Subd (b) amended effective January 1, 2007.)

(c) Proceeding if there are no objections or questions concerning impartiality

Except as provided in (f), if, after a mediator makes disclosures, no party objects to the mediator and no participant raises any question or concern about the mediator's ability to conduct the mediation impartially, the mediator may proceed.

(Subd (c) amended effective January 1, 2007.)

(d) Responding to questions or concerns concerning impartiality

If, after a mediator makes disclosures or at any other point in the mediation process, a participant raises a question or concern about the mediator's ability to conduct the mediation impartially, the mediator must address the question or concern with the participants. Except as provided in (f), if, after the question or concern is addressed, no party objects to the mediator, the mediator may proceed.

(Subd (d) amended effective January 1, 2007.)

(e) Withdrawal or continuation upon party objection concerning impartiality

In a two-party mediation, if any party objects to the mediator after the mediator makes disclosures or discusses a participant's question or concern regarding the mediator's ability to conduct the mediation impartially, the mediator must withdraw. In a mediation in which there are more than two parties, the mediator may continue the mediation with the nonobjecting parties, provided that doing so would not violate any other provision of these rules, any law, or any local court rule or program guideline.

(f) Circumstances requiring mediator recusal despite party consent

Regardless of the consent of the parties, a mediator either must decline to serve as mediator or, if already serving, must withdraw from the mediation if:

(1) The mediator cannot maintain impartiality toward all participants in the mediation process; or

(2) Proceeding with the mediation would jeopardize the integrity of the court or of the mediation process.

Rule 3.855 amended and renumbered effective January 1, 2007; adopted as rule 1620.5 effective January 1, 2003.

Advisory Committee Comment

Subdivision (b). This subdivision is intended to provide parties with information they need to help them determine whether a mediator can conduct the mediation impartially. A mediator's overarching duty under this subdivision is to make a "reasonable effort" to identify matters that, in the eyes of a reasonable person, could raise a question about the mediator's ability to conduct the mediation impartially, and to inform the parties about those matters. What constitutes a "reasonable effort" to identify such matters varies depending on the circumstances, including whether the case is scheduled in advance or received on the spot, and the information about the participants and the subject matter that is provided to the mediator by the court and the parties.

The interests, relationships, and affiliations that a mediator may need to disclose under (b)(1)(A) include: (1) prior, current, or currently expected service as a mediator in another mediation involving any of the participants in the present mediation; (2) prior, current, or currently expected business relationships or transactions between the mediator and any of the participants; and (3) the mediator's ownership of stock or any other significant financial interest involving any participant in the mediation. Currently expected interests, relationships, and affiliations may include, for example, an intention to form a partnership or to enter into a future business relationship with one of the participants in the mediation.

Although (b)(1) specifies interests, relationships, affiliations, and matters that are grounds for disqualification of a judge under Code of Civil Procedure section 170.1, these are only examples of common matters that reasonably could raise a question about a mediator's ability to conduct the mediation impartially and, thus, must be disclosed. The absence of particular interests, relationships, affiliations, and section 170.1 matters does not necessarily mean that there is no matter that could reasonably raise a question about the mediator's ability to conduct the mediation impartially. A mediator must make determinations concerning disclosure on a case-by-case basis, applying the general criteria for disclosure under (b)(1).

Attorney mediators should be aware that under the section 170.1 standard, they may need to make disclosures when an attorney in their firm is serving or has served as a lawyer for any of the parties in the mediation. Section 170.1 does not specifically address whether a mediator must disclose when another member of the mediator's dispute resolution services firm is providing or has provided services to any of the parties in the mediation. Therefore, a mediator must evaluate such circumstances under the general criteria for disclosure under (b)(1)—that is, is it a matter that, in the eyes of a reasonable person, could raise a question about the mediator's ability to conduct the mediation impartially?

If there is a conflict between the mediator's obligation to maintain confidentiality and the mediator's obligation to make a disclosure, the mediator must determine whether he or she can make a general disclosure of the circumstance without revealing any confidential information, or must decline to serve.

Rule 3.856.   Competence

(a) Compliance with court qualifications

A mediator must comply with experience, training, educational, and other requirements established by the court for appointment and retention.

(b) Truthful representation of background

A mediator has a continuing obligation to truthfully represent his or her background to the court and participants. Upon a request by any party, a mediator must provide truthful information regarding his or her experience, training, and education.

(c) Informing court of public discipline and other matters

A mediator must also inform the court if:

(1) Public discipline has been imposed on the mediator by any public disciplinary or professional licensing agency;

(2) The mediator has resigned his or her membership in the State Bar or another professional licensing agency while disciplinary or criminal charges were pending;

(3) A felony charge is pending against the mediator;

(4) The mediator has been convicted of a felony or of a misdemeanor involving moral turpitude; or

(5) There has been an entry of judgment against the mediator in any civil action for actual fraud or punitive damages.

(d) Assessment of skills; withdrawal

A mediator has a continuing obligation to assess whether or not his or her level of skill, knowledge, and ability is sufficient to conduct the mediation effectively. A mediator must decline to serve or withdraw from the mediation if the mediator determines that he or she does not have the level of skill, knowledge, or ability necessary to conduct the mediation effectively.

Rule 3.856 renumbered effective January 1, 2007; adopted as rule 1620.6 effective January 1, 2003.

Advisory Committee Comment

Subdivision (d). No particular advanced academic degree or technical or professional experience is a prerequisite for competence as a mediator. Core mediation skills include communicating clearly, listening effectively, facilitating communication among all participants, promoting exploration of mutually acceptable settlement options, and conducting oneself in a neutral manner.

A mediator must consider and weigh a variety of issues in order to assess whether his or her level of skill, knowledge, and ability is sufficient to make him or her effective in a particular mediation. Issues include whether the parties (1) were involved or had input in the selection of the mediator; (2) had access to information about the mediator's background or level of skill, knowledge, and ability; (3) have a specific expectation or perception regarding the mediator's level of skill, knowledge, and ability; (4) have expressed a preference regarding the style of mediation they would like or expect; or (5) have expressed a desire to discuss legal or other professional information, to hear a personal evaluation of or opinion on a set of facts as presented, or to be made aware of the interests of persons who are not represented in mediation.

Rule 3.857.   Quality of mediation process

(a) Diligence

A mediator must make reasonable efforts to advance the mediation in a timely manner. If a mediator schedules a mediation for a specific time period, he or she must keep that time period free of other commitments.

(b) Procedural fairness

A mediator must conduct the mediation proceedings in a procedurally fair manner. "Procedural fairness" means a balanced process in which each party is given an opportunity to participate and make uncoerced decisions. A mediator is not obligated to ensure the substantive fairness of an agreement reached by the parties.

(c) Explanation of process

In addition to the requirements of rule 3.853 (voluntary participation and self-determination), rule 3.854(a) (confidentiality), and (d) of this rule (representation and other professional services), at or before the outset of the mediation the mediator must provide all participants with a general explanation of:

(1) The nature of the mediation process;

(2) The procedures to be used; and

(3) The roles of the mediator, the parties, and the other participants.

(Subd (c) amended effective January 1, 2007.)

(d) Representation and other professional services

A mediator must inform all participants, at or before the outset of the first mediation session, that during the mediation he or she will not represent any participant as a lawyer or perform professional services in any capacity other than as an impartial mediator. Subject to the principles of impartiality and self-determination, a mediator may provide information or opinions that he or she is qualified by training or experience to provide.

(e) Recommending other services

A mediator may recommend the use of other services in connection with a mediation and may recommend particular providers of other services. However, a mediator must disclose any related personal or financial interests if recommending the services of specific individuals or organizations.

(f) Nonparticipants' interests

A mediator may bring to the attention of the parties the interests of others who are not participating in the mediation but who may be affected by agreements reached as a result of the mediation.

(g) Combining mediation with other ADR processes

A mediator must exercise caution in combining mediation with other alternative dispute resolution (ADR) processes and may do so only with the informed consent of the parties and in a manner consistent with any applicable law or court order. The mediator must inform the parties of the general natures of the different processes and the consequences of revealing information during any one process that might be used for decision making in another process, and must give the parties opportunity to select another neutral for the subsequent process. If the parties consent to a combination of processes, the mediator must clearly inform the participants when the transition from one process to another is occurring.

(h) Settlement agreements

Consistent with (d), a mediator may present possible settlement options and terms for discussion. A mediator may also assist the parties in preparing a written settlement agreement, provided that in doing so the mediator confines the assistance to stating the settlement as determined by the parties.

(Subd (h) amended effective January 1, 2007.)

(i) Discretionary termination and withdrawal

A mediator may suspend or terminate the mediation or withdraw as mediator when he or she reasonably believes the circumstances require it, including when he or she suspects that:

(1) The mediation is being used to further illegal conduct;

(2) A participant is unable to participate meaningfully in negotiations; or

(3) Continuation of the process would cause significant harm to any participant or a third party.

(j) Manner of withdrawal

When a mediator determines that it is necessary to suspend or terminate a mediation or to withdraw, the mediator must do so without violating the obligation of confidentiality and in a manner that will cause the least possible harm to the participants.

Rule 3.857 amended and renumbered effective January 1, 2007; adopted as rule 1620.7 effective January 1, 2003.

Advisory Committee Comment

Subdivision (c). The explanation of the mediation process should include a description of the mediator's style of mediation.

Subdivision (d). Subject to the principles of impartiality and self-determination, and if qualified to do so, a mediator may (1) discuss a party's options, including a range of possible outcomes in an adjudicative process; (2) offer a personal evaluation of or opinion on a set of facts as presented, which should be clearly identified as a personal evaluation or opinion; or (3) communicate the mediator's opinion or view of what the law is or how it applies to the subject of the mediation, provided that the mediator does not also advise any participant about how to adhere to the law or on what position the participant should take in light of that opinion.

One question that frequently arises is whether a mediator's assessment of claims, defenses, or possible litigation outcomes constitutes legal advice or the practice of law. Similar questions may arise when accounting, architecture, construction, counseling, medicine, real estate, or other licensed professions are relevant to a mediation. This rule does not determine what constitutes the practice of law or any other licensed profession. A mediator should be cautious when providing any information or opinion related to any field for which a professional license is required, in order to avoid doing so in a manner that may constitute the practice of a profession for which the mediator is not licensed, or in a manner that may violate the regulations of a profession that the mediator is licensed to practice. A mediator should exercise particular caution when discussing the law with unrepresented parties and should inform such parties that they may seek independent advice from a lawyer.

Subdivision (i). Subdivision (i)(2) is not intended to establish any new responsibility or diminish any existing responsibilities that a mediator may have, under the Americans With Disabilities Act or other similar law, to attempt to accommodate physical or mental disabilities of a participant in mediation.

Rule 3.858.   Marketing

(a) Truthfulness

A mediator must be truthful and accurate in marketing his or her mediation services. A mediator is responsible for ensuring that both his or her own marketing activities and any marketing activities carried out on his or her behalf by others comply with this rule.

(b) Representations concerning court approval

A mediator may indicate in his or her marketing materials that he or she is a member of a particular court's panel or list but, unless specifically permitted by the court, must not indicate that he or she is approved, endorsed, certified, or licensed by the court.

(c) Promises, guarantees, and implications of favoritism

In marketing his or her mediation services, a mediator must not:

(1) Promise or guarantee results; or

(2) Make any statement that directly or indirectly implies bias in favor of one party or participant over another.

(d) Solicitation of business

A mediator must not solicit business from a participant in a mediation proceeding while that mediation is pending.

Rule 3.858 renumbered effective January 1, 2007; adopted as rule 1620.8 effective January 1, 2003.

Advisory Committee Comment

Subdivision (d). This rule is not intended to prohibit a mediator from accepting other employment from a participant while a mediation is pending, provided that there was no express solicitation of this business by the mediator and that accepting that employment does not contravene any other provision of these rules, including the obligations to maintain impartiality, confidentiality, and the integrity of the process. If other employment is accepted from a participant while a mediation is pending, however, the mediator may be required to disclose this to the parties under rule 3.855.

This rule also is not intended to prohibit a mediator from engaging in general marketing activities. General marketing activities include, but are not limited to, running an advertisement in a newspaper and sending out a general mailing (either of which may be directed to a particular industry or market).

Rule 3.859.   Compensation and gifts

(a) Compliance with law

A mediator must comply with any applicable requirements concerning compensation established by statute or the court.

(b) Disclosure of and compliance with compensation terms

Before commencing the mediation, the mediator must disclose to the parties in writing any fees, costs, or charges to be paid to the mediator by the parties. A mediator must abide by any agreement that is reached concerning compensation.

(c) Contingent fees

The amount or nature of a mediator's fee must not be made contingent on the outcome of the mediation.

(Subd (c) amended effective January 1, 2007.)

(d) Gifts and favors

A mediator must not at any time solicit or accept from or give to any participant or affiliate of a participant any gift, bequest, or favor that might reasonably raise a question concerning the mediator's impartiality.

Rule 3.859 amended and renumbered effective January 1, 2007; adopted as rule 1620.9 effective January 1, 2003.

Advisory Committee Comment

Subdivision (b). It is good practice to put mediation fee agreements in writing, and mediators are strongly encouraged to do so; however, nothing in this rule is intended to preclude enforcement of a compensation agreement for mediation services that is not in writing.

Subdivision (d). Whether a gift, bequest, or favor "might reasonably raise a question concerning the mediator's impartiality" must be determined on a case-by-case basis. This subdivision is not intended to prohibit a mediator from accepting other employment from any of the participants, consistent with rule 3.858(d).

Rule 3.860.   Attendance sheet and agreement to disclosure

(a) Attendance sheet

In each mediation to which these rules apply under rule 3.851(a), the mediator must request that all participants in the mediation complete an attendance sheet stating their names, mailing addresses, and telephone numbers; retain the attendance sheet for at least two years; and submit it to the court on request.

(Subd (a) amended effective January 1, 2007.)

(b) Agreement to disclosure

The mediator must agree, in each mediation to which these rules apply under rule 3.851(a), that if an inquiry or a complaint is made about the conduct of the mediator, mediation communications may be disclosed solely for purposes of a complaint procedure conducted pursuant to rule 3.865 to address that complaint or inquiry.

(Subd (b) amended effective January 1, 2011; previously amended effective January 1, 2007.)

Rule 3.860 amended effective January 1, 2011; adopted as rule 1621 effective January 1, 2006; previously amended and renumbered effective January 1, 2007.

Rule 3.865.   Complaint procedure required [Renumbered]

Rule 3.865 amended and renumbered to rule 3.868 effective July 1, 2009, effective date extended to January 1, 2010; adopted as rule 1622 effective January 1, 2003; previously amended effective January 1, 2006, and January 1, 2007.

2009 Note: Another Rule 3.865 follows in Article 3.

Rule 3.866.   Designation of person to receive inquiries and complaints [Renumbered]

Rule 3.866 amended and renumbered to rule 3.867 effective July 1, 2009, effective date extended to January 1, 2010; adopted as rule 1622.1 effective January 1, 2006; previously amended and renumbered effective January 1, 2007.

2009 Note: Another Rule 3.866 follows in Article 3.

Rule 3.867.   Confidentiality of complaint procedures, information, and records [Renumbered]

Rule 3.867 amended and renumbered to rule 3.871 effective July 1, 2009, effective date extended to January 1, 2010; adopted as rule 1622.2 effective January 1, 2006; previously amended and renumbered effective January 1, 2007; previously amended effective January 1, 2008.

2009 Note: Another Rule 3.867 follows in Article 3.

Rule 3.868.   Disqualification from subsequently serving as an adjudicator [Renumbered]

Rule 3.868 amended and renumbered to rule 3.872 effective July 1, 2009, effective date extended to January 1, 2010; adopted as rule 1622.3 effective January 1, 2006; previously amended and renumbered effective January 1, 2007.

2009 Note: Another Rule 3.868 follows in Article 3.

Article 3
Requirements for Addressing Complaints About Court-Program Mediators

Title 3, Civil Rules—Division 8, Alternative Dispute Resolution—Chapter 3, General Rules Relating to Mediation of Civil Cases—Article 3, Requirements for Addressing Complaints About Court-Program Mediators adopted effective July 1, 2009, effective date extended to January 1, 2010.

Rule 3.865. Application and purpose
Rule 3.866. Definitions
Rule 3.867. Complaint coordinator
Rule 3.868. Complaint procedure required
Rule 3.869. General requirements for complaint procedures and complaint proceedings
Rule 3.870. Permissible court actions on complaints
Rule 3.871. Confidentiality of complaint proceedings, information, and records
Rule 3.872. Disqualification from subsequently serving as an adjudicator

Rule 3.865.   Application and purpose

(a) Application

The rules in this article apply to each superior court that makes a list of mediators available to litigants in general civil cases or that recommends, selects, appoints, or compensates a mediator to mediate any general civil case pending in that court. A court that approves the parties' agreement to use a mediator who is selected by the parties and who is not on the court's list of mediators or that memorializes the parties' agreement in a court order has not thereby recommended, selected, or appointed that mediator within the meaning of this rule.

(Subd (a) amended and lettered effective January 1, 2010; previously adopted as part of unlettered subd effective January 1, 2010.)

(b) Purpose

These rules are intended to promote the resolution of complaints that mediators in court-connected mediation programs for civil cases may have violated a provision of the rules of conduct for such mediators in article 2. They are intended to help courts promptly resolve any such complaints in a manner that is respectful and fair to the complainant and the mediator and consistent with the California mediation confidentiality statutes.

(Subd (b) lettered effective January 1, 2010; previously adopted as part of unlettered subd effective January 1, 2010.)

Rule 3.865 amended effective January 1, 2010; adopted effective July 1, 2009, effective date extended to January 1, 2010.

Advisory Committee Comment

As used in this article, complaint means a written communication presented to a court's complaint coordinator indicating that a mediator may have violated a provision of the rules of conduct for mediators in article 2.

Complaints about mediators are relatively rare. To ensure the quality of court mediation panels and public confidence in the mediation process and the courts, it is, nevertheless, important to ensure that any complaints that do arise are resolved through procedures that are consistent with California mediation confidentiality statutes (Evid. Code, §§ 703.5 and 1115 et seq.), as well as fair and respectful to the interested parties.

The requirements and procedures in this article do not abrogate or limit a court's inherent or other authority, in its sole and absolute discretion, to determine who may be included on or removed from a court list of mediators; to approve or revoke a mediator's eligibility to be recommended, selected, appointed, or compensated by the court; or to follow other procedures or take other actions to ensure the quality of mediators who serve in the court's mediation program in contexts other than when addressing a complaint. The failure to follow a requirement or procedure in this article will not invalidate any action taken by the court in addressing a complaint.

2009 Note: Another Rule 3.865 precedes in Article 2.

Rule 3.866.   Definitions

As used in this article, unless the context or subject matter requires otherwise:

(1) "The rules of conduct" means rules 3.850–3.860 of the California Rules of Court in article 2.

(2) "Court-program mediator" means a person subject to the rules of conduct under rule 3.851.

(3) "Inquiry" means an unwritten communication presented to the court's complaint coordinator indicating that a mediator may have violated a provision of the rules of conduct.

(4) "Complaint" means a written communication presented to the court's complaint coordinator indicating that a mediator may have violated a provision of the rules of conduct.

(5) "Complainant" means the person who makes or presents a complaint.

(6) "Complaint coordinator" means the person designated by the presiding judge under rule 3.867(a) to receive complaints and inquiries about the conduct of mediators.

(7) "Complaint committee" means a committee designated or appointed to investigate and make recommendations concerning complaints under rule 3.869(d)(2).

(8) "Complaint procedure" means a procedure for presenting, receiving, reviewing, responding to, investigating, and acting on any inquiry or complaint.

(9) "Complaint proceeding" means all of the proceedings that take place as part of a complaint procedure concerning a specific inquiry or complaint.

(10) "Mediation communication" means any statement that is made or any writing that is prepared for the purpose of, in the course of, or pursuant to a mediation or a mediation consultation, as defined in Evidence Code section 1115, and includes any communications, negotiations, and settlement discussions between participants in the course of a mediation or a mediation consultation.

Rule 3.866 adopted effective July 1, 2009, effective date extended to January 1, 2010.

Advisory Committee Comment

Paragraph (2). Under rule 3.851, the rules of conduct apply when a mediator, or a firm with which a mediator is affiliated, has agreed to be included on a superior court's list or panel of mediators for general civil cases and is notified by the court or the parties that he or she has been selected to mediate a case within that court's mediation program or when a mediator has agreed to mediate a general civil case after being notified that he or she was recommended, selected, or appointed by a court, or will be compensated by a court, to mediate a case within a court's mediation program.

Paragraphs (3) and (4). The distinction between "inquiries" and "complaints" is significant because some provisions of this article apply only to complaints (i.e., written communications presented to the court's complaint coordinator indicating that a mediator may have violated a provision of the rules of conduct) and not to inquiries.

2009 Note: Another Rule 3.866 precedes in Article 2.

Rule 3.867.   Complaint coordinator

(a) Designation of the complaint coordinator

The presiding judge must designate a person who is knowledgeable about mediation to serve as the complaint coordinator.

(Subd (a) amended and lettered effective July 1, 2009, effective date extended to January 1, 2010; adopted as unlettered subd effective January 1, 2006.)

(b) Identification of the complaint coordinator

The court must make the complaint coordinator's identity and contact information readily accessible to litigants and the public.

(Subd (b) adopted effective July 1, 2009, effective date extended to January 1, 2010.)

Rule 3.867 amended and renumbered effective July 1, 2009, effective date extended to January 1, 2010; adopted as rule 1622.1 effective January 1, 2006; previously amended and renumbered as rule 3.866 effective January 1, 2007.

Advisory Committee Comment

The alternative dispute resolution program administrator appointed under rule 10.783(a) may also be appointed as the complaint coordinator if that person is knowledgeable about mediation.

2009 Note: Another Rule 3.867 precedes in Article 2.

Rule 3.868.   Complaint procedure required

Each court to which this article applies under rule 3.865 must establish a complaint procedure by local rule of court that is consistent with this article.

(Subd amended and unlettered effective July 1, 2009, effective date extended to January 1, 2010; adopted as subd (a) effective January 1, 2003; previously amended effective January 1, 2006, and January 1, 2007.)

Rule 3.868 amended and renumbered effective July 1, 2009, effective date extended to January 1, 2010; adopted as rule 1622 effective January 1, 2003; previously amended effective January 1, 2006; previously amended and renumbered as rule 3.865 effective January 1, 2007.

2009 Note: Another Rule 3.868 precedes in Article 2.

Rule 3.869.   General requirements for complaint procedures and complaint proceedings

(a) Submission and referral of inquiries and complaints to the complaint coordinator

All inquiries and complaints should be submitted or referred to the complaint coordinator.

(Subd (a) adopted effective July 1, 2009, effective date extended to January 1, 2010.)

(b) Acknowledgment of complaint

The complaint coordinator must send the complainant a written acknowledgment that the court has received the complaint.

(Subd (b) adopted effective July 1, 2009, effective date extended to January 1, 2010.)

(c) Preliminary review and disposition of complaints

The complaint coordinator must conduct a preliminary review of all complaints to determine whether the complaint can be informally resolved or closed, or whether the complaint warrants investigation.

(Subd (c) adopted effective July 1, 2009, effective date extended to January 1, 2010.)

(d) Procedure for complaints not resolved through the preliminary review

The following procedures are required only if a complaint is not resolved or closed through the preliminary review.

(1) *Mediator's notice and opportunity to respond*

The mediator must be given notice of the complaint and an opportunity to respond.

(2) *Investigation and recommendation*

(A) Except as provided in (B), the complaint must be investigated and a recommendation concerning court action on the complaint must be made by either an individual who has experience as a mediator and who is familiar with the rules of conduct stated in article 2 or a complaint committee that has at least one such individual as a member.

(B) A court with eight or fewer authorized judges may waive the requirement in (A) for participation by an individual who has experience as a mediator in conducting the investigation and making the recommendation if the court cannot find a suitable qualified individual to perform the functions described in (A) or for other grounds of hardship.

(3) *Final decision*

The final decision on the complaint must be made by the presiding judge or his or her designee, who must not be the complaint coordinator or an individual who investigated the complaint before its submission for final decision.

(Subd (d) adopted effective July 1, 2009, effective date extended to January 1, 2010.)

(e) Notice of final action

(1) The court must send the complainant notice of the final action taken by the court on the complaint.

(2) If the complaint was not closed during the preliminary review, the court must send notice of the final action to the mediator.

(Subd (e) adopted effective July 1, 2009, effective date extended to January 1, 2010.)

(f) Promptness

The court must process complaints promptly at all stages.

(Subd (f) adopted effective July 1, 2009, effective date extended to January 1, 2010.)

(g) Records of complaints

The court should maintain sufficient information about each complaint and its disposition to identify any history or patterns of complaints submitted under these rules.

(Subd (g) adopted effective July 1, 2009, effective date extended to January 1, 2010.)

Rule 3.869 adopted effective July 1, 2009, effective date extended to January 1, 2010.

Advisory Committee Comment

Judicial Council staff have developed model local rules that satisfy the requirements of this rule. These model local rules were developed with input from judicial officers, court administrators, alternative dispute resolution (ADR) program administrators, court-program mediators, and public commentators and are designed so that they can be readily adapted to the circumstances of individual courts and specific complaints. Courts are encouraged to adopt rules that follow the model rules, to the extent feasible. Courts can obtain copies of these model rules from the Judicial Council's civil ADR program staff.

Subdivision (a). Coordination of inquiries and complaints by a person knowledgeable about mediation is important to help ensure that the requirements of this article are followed and that mediation confidentiality is preserved.

Subdivision (c). Courts are encouraged to resolve inquiries and complaints about mediators using the simplest, least formal procedures that are appropriate under the circumstances, provided that they meet the requirements stated in this article.

Most complaints can be appropriately resolved during the preliminary review stage of the complaint process, through informal discussions between or among the complaint coordinator, the complainant, and the mediator. Although complaint coordinators are not required to communicate with the mediator during the preliminary review, they are encouraged to consider doing so. For example, some complaints may arise from a misunderstanding of the mediator's role or from behavior that would not violate the standards of conduct. These types of complaints might appropriately be addressed by providing the complainant with additional information or by informing the mediator that certain behavior was upsetting to a mediation participant.

The circumstances under which a complaint coordinator might informally resolve or close a complaint include, for example, when (1) the complaint is withdrawn; (2) no violation of the rules of conduct appears to have occurred; (3) the alleged violation of the rules of conduct is very minor and the mediator has provided an acceptable explanation or response; and (4) the complainant, the mediator, and the complaint coordinator have agreed on a resolution. In determining whether to close a complaint, the complaint coordinator might also consider whether there are or have been other complaints about the mediator.

Subdivision (d). At the investigation and recommendation stage, all courts are encouraged to consider using a complaint committee comprised of members with a variety of backgrounds, including at least one person with experience as a mediator, to investigate and make recommendations concerning those rare complaints that are not resolved during the preliminary review.

Courts are also encouraged to have a judicial officer who is knowledgeable about mediation, or a committee that includes another person who is knowledgeable about mediation, make the final decision on complaints that are not resolved through the preliminary review.

Rule 3.870.   Permissible court actions on complaints

After an investigation has been conducted, the presiding judge or his or her designee may do one or more of the following:

(1) Direct that no action be taken on the complaint;

(2) Counsel, admonish, or reprimand the mediator;

(3) Impose additional training requirements as a condition of the mediator remaining on the court's panel or list;

(4) Suspend the mediator from the court's panel or list or otherwise temporarily prohibit the mediator from receiving future mediation referrals from the court; or

(5) Remove the mediator from the court's panel or list or otherwise prohibit the mediator from receiving future mediation referrals from the court.

Rule 3.870 adopted effective July 1, 2009, effective date extended to January 1, 2010.

Advisory Committee Comment

This rule does not abrogate or limit any existing legal right or duty of the court to take other actions, including interim suspension of a mediator pending final action by the court on a complaint.

2009 Note: Another Rule 3.870 follows in Chapter 4.

Rule 3.871.   Confidentiality of complaint proceedings, information, and records

(a) Intent

This rule is intended to:

(1) Preserve the confidentiality of mediation communications as required by Evidence Code sections 1115–1128;

(2) Promote cooperation in the reporting, investigation, and resolution of complaints about court-program mediators; and

(3) Protect mediators against damage to their reputations that might result from the disclosure of unfounded complaints against them.

(Subd (a) amended effective July 1, 2009, effective date extended to January 1, 2010; previously amended effective January 1, 2007.)

(b) Preserving the confidentiality of mediation communications

All complaint procedures and complaint proceedings must be designed and conducted in a manner that preserves the confidentiality of mediation communications, including but not limited to the confidentiality of any communications between the mediator and individual mediation participants or subgroups of mediation participants.

(Subd (b) amended effective July 1, 2009, effective date extended to January 1, 2010.)

(c) Confidentiality of complaint proceedings

All complaint proceedings must occur in private and must be kept confidential. No information or records concerning the receipt, investigation, or resolution of an inquiry or a complaint may be open to the public or disclosed outside the course of the complaint proceeding except as provided in (d) or as otherwise required by law.

(Subd (c) amended effective July 1, 2009, effective date extended to January 1, 2010; previously amended effective January 1, 2007.)

(d) Authorized disclosures

After the decision on a complaint, the presiding judge, or a person whom the presiding judge designates to do so, may authorize the public disclosure of information or records concerning the complaint proceeding that do not reveal any mediation communications. The disclosures that may be authorized under this subdivision include the name of a mediator against whom action has been taken under rule 3.870, the action taken, and the general basis on which the action was taken. In determining whether to authorize the disclosure of information or records under this subdivision, the presiding judge or the designee should consider the purposes of the confidentiality of complaint proceedings stated in (a)(2) and (a)(3).

(Subd (d) amended effective July 1, 2009, effective date extended to January 1, 2010; previously amended effective January 1, 2007.)

(e) Disclosures required by law

In determining whether the disclosure of information or records concerning a complaint proceeding is required by law, courts should consider the purposes of the confidentiality of complaint proceedings stated in (a). If it appears that the disclosure of information or records concerning a complaint proceeding that would reveal mediation communications is required by law, before the information or records are disclosed, notice should be given to any person whose mediation communications may thereby be revealed.

(Subd (e) amended effective July 1, 2009, effective date extended to January 1, 2010; previously amended effective January 1, 2007.)

Rule 3.871 amended and renumbered effective July 1, 2009, effective date extended to January 1, 2010; adopted as rule 1622.2 effective January 1, 2006; previously amended and renumbered as rule 3.867 effective January 1, 2007.

Advisory Committee Comment

Under rule 3.866(9), the complaint proceedings covered by this rule include proceedings to address inquiries as well as complaints (i.e., to unwritten as well as written communications indicating that a mediator may have violated a provision of the rules of conduct).

Subdivision (a). See Evidence Code sections 1115 and 1119 concerning the scope and types of mediation communications protected by mediation confidentiality. Rule 3.871 is intended to supplement the confidentiality of mediation communications established by the Evidence Code by ensuring that disclosure of information or records about a complaint proceeding does not reveal confidential mediation communications. Rule 3.871 is not intended to supersede or abrogate the confidentiality of mediation communications established by the Evidence Code.

Subdivision (b). Private meetings, or "caucuses," between a mediator and subgroups of participants are common in court-connected mediations, and it is frequently understood that these communications will not be disclosed to other participants in the mediation. (See Cal. Rules of Court, rule 3.854(c).) It is important to protect the confidentiality of these communications in complaint proceedings so that one participant in the mediation does not learn what another participant discussed in confidence with the mediator without the consent of the participants in the caucus communication.

Subdivisions (c)–(e). The provisions of (c)–(e) that authorize the disclosure of information and records related to complaint proceedings do not create any new exceptions to mediation confidentiality. Although public disclosure of information and records about complaint proceedings that do not reveal mediation communications may be authorized under (d), information and records that *would* reveal mediation communications may be publicly disclosed only as required by law (e.g., in response to a subpoena or court order) and consistent with the statutes and case law governing mediation confidentiality. A person who is knowledgeable about California's mediation confidentiality laws should determine whether the disclosure of mediation communications is required by law.

Evidence Code sections 915 and 1040 establish procedures and criteria for deciding whether information acquired in confidence by a public employee in the course of his or her duty is subject to disclosure. These sections may be applicable or helpful in determining whether the disclosure of information or records acquired by judicial officers, court staff, and other persons in the course of a complaint proceeding is required by law or should be authorized in the discretion of the presiding judge.

2009 Note: Another Rule 3.871 follows in Chapter 4.

Rule 3.872.   Disqualification from subsequently serving as an adjudicator

A person who has participated in a complaint proceeding or otherwise received information about the substance of a complaint, other than information that is publicly disclosed under rule 3.871(d), must not subsequently hear or determine any contested issue of law, fact, or procedure concerning the dispute that was the subject of the underlying mediation or any other dispute that arises from the mediation, as a judge, an arbitrator, a referee, or a juror, or in any other adjudicative capacity, in any court action or proceeding.

Rule 3.872 amended and renumbered effective July 1, 2009, effective date extended to January 1, 2010; adopted as rule 1622.3 effective January 1, 2006; previously amended and renumbered as rule 3.868 effective January 1, 2007.

Advisory Committee Comment

Persons who participated in a complaint proceeding are prohibited from subsequently adjudicating the dispute that was the subject of the underlying mediation or any other dispute that arises from the mediation because they may have learned of confidential mediation communications that were disclosed in the complaint proceeding or may have been influenced by what transpired in that proceeding. Because the information that can be disclosed publicly under rule 3.871(d) is limited and excludes mediation communications, it is unnecessary to disqualify persons who received only publicly disclosed information from subsequently adjudicating the dispute.

2009 Note: Another Rule 3.872 follows in Chapter 4.

Chapter 4
Civil Action Mediation Program Rules

Rule 3.870.   Application [Renumbered]

Rule 3.870 renumbered to rule 3.890 effective July 1, 2009; adopted as rule 1630 effective March 1, 1994; previously amended and renumbered effective January 1, 2007.

2008 Note: Another Rule 3.870 precedes in Article 3.

Rule 3.871.   Actions subject to mediation [Renumbered]

Rule 3.871 renumbered to rule 3.891 effective July 1, 2009; adopted as rule 1631 effective March 1, 1994; previously amended and renumbered effective January 1, 2007.

2008 Note: Another Rule 3.871 precedes in Article 3.

Rule 3.872.   Panels of mediators [Renumbered]

Rule 3.872 renumbered to rule 3.892 effective July 1, 2009; adopted as rule 1632 effective March 1, 1994; previously amended and renumbered effective January 1, 2007.

2008 Note: Another Rule 3.872 precedes in Article 3.

Rule 3.873.   Selection of mediators [Renumbered]

Rule 3.873 renumbered to rule 3.893 effective July 1, 2009; adopted as rule 1633 effective March 1, 1994; previously amended and renumbered effective January 1, 2007.

Rule 3.874.   Attendance, participant lists, and mediation statements [Renumbered]

Rule 3.874 renumbered to rule 3.894 effective July 1, 2009; adopted as rule 1634 effective March 1, 1994; previously amended and renumbered effective January 1, 2007; previously amended effective January 1, 2007.

Rule 3.875.   Filing of statement by mediator [Renumbered]

Rule 3.875 renumbered to rule 3.895 effective July 1, 2009; adopted as rule 1635 effective March 1, 1994; previously amended and renumbered effective January 1, 2007.

Rule 3.876.   Coordination with Trial Court Delay Reduction Act [Renumbered]

Rule 3.876 renumbered to rule 3.896 effective July 1, 2009; adopted as rule 1637 effective March 1, 1994; previously amended and renumbered effective January 1, 2007.

Rule 3.877.   Statistical information [Renumbered]

Rule 3.877 renumbered to rule 3.897 effective July 1, 2009; adopted as rule 1638 effective March 1, 1994; previously amended effective February 9, 1999; previously amended and renumbered effective January 1, 2007.

Rule 3.878.   Educational material [Renumbered]

Rule 3.878 renumbered to rule 3.898 effective July 1, 2009; adopted as rule 1639 effective March 1, 1994; amended and renumbered effective January 1, 2007.

Rule 3.890.   Application

The rules in this chapter implement the Civil Action Mediation Act, Code of Civil Procedure section 1775 et seq. Under section 1775.2, they apply in the Superior Court of California, County of Los Angeles and in other courts that elect to apply the act.

Rule 3.890 renumbered effective July 1, 2009; adopted as rule 1630 effective March 1, 1994; previously amended and renumbered as rule 3.870 effective January 1, 2007.

Rule 3.891.   Actions subject to mediation

(a) Actions that may be submitted to mediation

The following actions may be submitted to mediation under these provisions:

(1) *By court order*

Any action in which the amount in controversy, independent of the merits of liability, defenses, or comparative negligence, does not exceed $50,000 for each plaintiff. The court must determine the amount in controversy under Code of Civil Procedure section 1775.5. Determinations to send a case to mediation must be made by the court after consideration of the expressed views of the parties on the amenability of the case to mediation. The court must not require the parties or their counsel to personally appear in court for a conference held solely to determine whether to send their case to mediation.

(2) *By stipulation*

Any other action, regardless of the amount of controversy, in which all parties stipulate to such mediation. The stipulation must be filed not later than 90 days before trial unless the court permits a later time.

(Subd (a) amended effective January 1, 2007.)

(b) Case-by-case determination

Amenability of a particular action for mediation must be determined on a case-by-case basis, rather than categorically.

(Subd (b) amended effective January 1, 2007.)

Rule 3.891 renumbered effective July 1, 2009; adopted as rule 1631 effective March 1, 1994; previously amended and renumbered as rule 3.871 effective January 1, 2007.

Rule 3.892.   Panels of mediators

Each court, in consultation with local bar associations, ADR providers, and associations of providers, must identify persons who may be appointed as mediators. The court must consider the criteria in standard 10.72 of the Standards of Judicial Administration and California Code of Regulations, title 16, section 3622, relating to the Dispute Resolution Program Act.

Rule 3.892 renumbered effective July 1, 2009; adopted as rule 1632 effective March 1, 1994; previously amended and renumbered as rule 3.872 effective January 1, 2007.

Rule 3.893.   Selection of mediators

The parties may stipulate to any mediator, whether or not the person selected is among those identified under rule 3.892, within 15 days of the date an action is submitted to mediation. If the parties do not stipulate to a mediator, the court must promptly assign a mediator to the action from those identified under rule 3.892.

Rule 3.893 amended effective January 1, 2011; adopted as rule 1633 effective March 1, 1994; previously amended and renumbered as rule 3.873 effective January 1, 2007; previously renumbered effective July 1, 2009.

Rule 3.894.   Attendance, participant lists, and mediation statements

(a) Attendance

(1) All parties and attorneys of record must attend all mediation sessions in person unless excused or permitted to attend by telephone as provided in (3). If a party is not a natural person, a representative of that party with authority to resolve the dispute or, in the case of a governmental entity that requires an agreement to be approved by an elected official or a legislative body, a representative with authority to recommend such agreement, must attend all mediation sessions in person, unless excused or permitted to attend by telephone as provided in (3).

(2) If any party is insured under a policy of insurance that provides or may provide coverage for a claim that is a subject of the action, a representative of the insurer with authority to settle or recommend settlement of the claim must attend all mediation sessions in person, unless excused or permitted to attend by telephone as provided in (3).

(3) The mediator may excuse a party, attorney, or representative from the requirement to attend a mediation session under (1) or (2) or permit attendance by telephone. The party, attorney, or representative who is excused or permitted to attend by telephone must promptly send a letter or an electronic communication to the mediator and to all parties confirming the excuse or permission.

(4) Each party may have counsel present at all mediation sessions that concern the party.

(Subd (a) amended and lettered effective January 1, 2007; adopted as untitled subd effective March 1, 1994.)

(b) Participant lists and mediation statements

(1) At least five court days before the first mediation session, each party must serve a list of its mediation participants on the mediator and all other parties. The list must include the names of all parties, attorneys, representatives of a party that is not a natural person, insurance representatives, and other persons who will attend the mediation with or on behalf of that party. A party must promptly serve a supplemental list if the party subsequently determines that other persons will attend the mediation with or on behalf of the party.

(2) The mediator may request that each party submit a short mediation statement providing information about the issues in dispute and possible resolutions of those issues and other information or documents that may appear helpful to resolve the dispute.

(Subd (b) adopted effective January 1, 2007.)

Rule 3.894 renumbered effective July 1, 2009; adopted as rule 1634 effective March 1, 1994; previously amended and renumbered as rule 3.874 effective January 1, 2007.

Rule 3.895.   Filing of *Statement of Agreement or Nonagreement* by mediator

Within 10 days after conclusion of the mediation, or by another date set by the court, the mediator must complete, serve on all parties, and file a *Statement of Agreement or Nonagreement* (form ADR-100). If the mediation has not ended when the report is filed, the mediator must file a supplemental form ADR-100 within 10 days after the mediation is concluded or by another date set by the court. The completed form ADR-100 must not disclose the terms of any agreement or any other communications or conduct that occurred in the course of the mediation, except as allowed in Evidence Code sections 1115–1128.

Rule 3.895 amended effective July 1, 2012; adopted as rule 1635 effective March 1, 1994; previously amended and renumbered as rule 3.875 effective January 1, 2007; previously renumbered effective July 1, 2009.

Rule 3.896.   Coordination with Trial Court Delay Reduction Act

(a) Effect of mediation on time standards

Submission of an action to mediation under the rules in this chapter does not affect time periods specified in the Trial Court Delay Reduction Act (Gov. Code, § 68600 et seq.), except as provided in this rule.

(Subd (a) amended effective January 1, 2007.)

(b) Exception to delay reduction time standards

On written stipulation of the parties filed with the court, the court may order an exception of up to 90 days to the delay reduction time standards to permit mediation of an action. The court must coordinate the timing of the exception period with its delay reduction calendar.

(Subd (b) amended effective January 1, 2007.)

(c) Time for completion of mediation

Mediation must be completed within 60 days of a reference to a mediator, but that period may be extended by the court for up to 30 days on a showing of good cause.

(Subd (c) amended and lettered effective January 1, 2007; adopted as part of subd (b) effective March 1, 1994.)

(d) Restraint in discovery

The parties should exercise restraint in discovery while a case is in mediation. In appropriate cases to accommodate that objective, the court may issue a protective order under Code of Civil Procedure section 2017(c) and related provisions.

(Subd (d) amended and lettered effective January 1, 2007; adopted as part of subd (b) effective March 1, 1994.)

Rule 3.896 renumbered effective July 1, 2009; adopted as rule 1637 effective March 1, 1994; previously amended and renumbered as rule 3.876 effective January 1, 2007.

Rule 3.897.   Statistical information [Repealed]

Rule 3.897 repealed effective July 1, 2012; adopted as rule 1638 effective March 1, 1994; previously amended effective February 9, 1999; previously amended and renumbered as rule 3.877 effective January 1, 2007; previously renumbered effective July 1, 2009.

Rule 3.898.   Educational material

Each court must make available educational material, adopted by the Judicial Council, or from other sources, describing available ADR processes in the community.

Rule 3.898 renumbered effective July 1, 2009; adopted as rule 1639 effective March 1, 1994; previously amended and renumbered as rule 3.878 effective January 1, 2007.

Division 9
References

Chap. 1.   Reference by Agreement of the Parties Under Code of Civil Procedure Section 638. Rules 3.900–3.907.

Chap. 2.   Court-Ordered Reference Under Code of Civil Procedure Section 639. Rules 3.920–3.926.

Chap. 3.   Rules Applicable to References Under Code of Civil Procedure Section 638 or 639. Rules 3.930–3.932.

Chapter 1
Reference by Agreement of the Parties Under Code of Civil Procedure Section 638

Rule 3.900. Purposes of reference
Rule 3.901. Application for order appointing referee
Rule 3.902. Order appointing referee
Rule 3.903. Selection and qualifications of referee
Rule 3.904. Certification and disclosure by referee
Rule 3.905. Objections to the appointment
Rule 3.906. Motion to withdraw stipulation
Rule 3.907. Use of court facilities and court personnel

Rule 3.900.   Purposes of reference

A court must not use the reference procedure under Code of Civil Procedure section 638 to appoint a person to conduct a mediation.

Rule 3.900 adopted effective January 1, 2007.

Advisory Committee Comment

Rule 3.900 is not intended to prohibit a court from appointing a referee to conduct a mandatory settlement conference or, following the conclusion of a reference, from appointing a person who previously served as a referee to conduct a mediation.

Rule 3.901.   Application for order appointing referee

(a) Stipulation or motion for appointment

A written stipulation or motion for an order appointing a referee under Code of Civil Procedure section 638 must be presented to the judge to whom the case is assigned, or to the presiding judge or law and motion department if the case has not been assigned.

(b) Contents of application

The stipulation or motion for the appointment of a referee under section 638 must:

(1) Clearly state whether the scope of the requested reference includes all issues or is limited to specified issues;

(2) State whether the referee will be privately compensated;

(3) If authorization to use court facilities or court personnel is requested, describe the use requested and state the reasons that this would further the interests of justice;

(4) If the applicant is requesting or the parties have stipulated to the appointment of a particular referee, be accompanied by the proposed referee's certification as required by rule 3.904(a); and

(5) Be accompanied by a proposed order that includes the matters specified in rule 3.902.

Rule 3.901 adopted effective January 1, 2007.

Rule 3.902. Order appointing referee

An order appointing a referee under Code of Civil Procedure section 638 must be filed with the clerk or entered in the minutes and must specify:

(1) The name, business address, and telephone number of the referee and, if he or she is a member of the State Bar, the referee's State Bar number;

(2) Whether the scope of the reference covers all issues or is limited to specified issues;

(3) Whether the referee will be privately compensated; and

(4) Whether the use of court facilities and court personnel is authorized.

Rule 3.902 amended effective January 1, 2010; adopted effective January 1, 2007.

Rule 3.903. Selection and qualifications of referee

The court must appoint the referee or referees as provided in the Code of Civil Procedure section 640. If the proposed referee is a former judicial officer, he or she must be an active or an inactive member of the State Bar.

Rule 3.903 adopted effective January 1, 2007.

Rule 3.904. Certification and disclosure by referee

(a) Certification by referee

Before a referee begins to serve:

(1) The referee must certify in writing that he or she consents to serve as provided in the order of appointment and is aware of and will comply with applicable provisions of canon 6 of the Code of Judicial Ethics and with the California Rules of Court; and

(2) The referee's certification must be filed with the court.

(Subd (a) adopted effective January 1, 2007.)

(b) Disclosure by referee

In addition to any other disclosure required by law, no later than five days before the deadline for parties to file a motion for disqualification of the referee under Code of Civil Procedure section 170.6 or, if the referee is not aware of his or her appointment or of a matter subject to disclosure at that time, as soon as practicable thereafter, a referee must disclose to the parties:

(1) Any matter subject to disclosure under either canon 6D(5)(a) or 6D(5)(b) of the Code of Judicial Ethics; and

(2) Any significant personal or professional relationship the referee has or has had with a party, attorney, or law firm in the current case, including the number and nature of any other proceedings in the past 24 months in which the referee has been privately compensated by a party, attorney, law firm, or insurance company in the current case for any services. The disclosure must include privately compensated service as an attorney, expert witness, or consultant or as a judge, referee, arbitrator, mediator, settlement facilitator, or other alternative dispute resolution neutral.

(Subd (b) adopted effective January 1, 2007.)
Rule 3.904 adopted effective January 1, 2007.

Rule 3.905. Objections to the appointment

A stipulation or an agreement for an order appointing a referee does not constitute a waiver of grounds for objection to the appointment of a particular person as referee under Code of Civil Procedure section 641. Any objection to the appointment of a person as a referee must be made with reasonable diligence and in writing. The objection must be served on all parties and the referee and filed with the court. The objection must be heard by the judge to whom the case is assigned or by the presiding judge or law and motion judge if the case has not been assigned.

Rule 3.905 adopted effective January 1, 2007.

Rule 3.906. Motion to withdraw stipulation

(a) Good cause requirement

A motion to withdraw a stipulation for the appointment of a referee must be supported by a declaration of facts establishing good cause for permitting the party to withdraw the stipulation. The following do not constitute good cause for withdrawing a stipulation:

(1) A declaration that a ruling is based on an error of fact or law.

(2) The issuance of an order for an appropriate hearing site under rule 3.910.

(Subd (a) adopted effective January 1, 2007.)

(b) Service, filing and hearing of motion

Notice of the motion must be served on all parties and the referee and filed with the court. The motion must be heard by the judge to whom the case is assigned or by the presiding judge or law and motion judge. If the motion is granted, the case must be transferred to the trial court docket.

(Subd (b) adopted effective January 1, 2007.)
Rule 3.906 adopted effective January 1, 2007.

Rule 3.907. Motion or application to seal records [Repealed]

Rule 3.907 repealed effective January 1, 2010; adopted effective January 1, 2007.

Another Rule 3.907 follows.

Rule 3.907. Use of court facilities and court personnel

A party who has elected to use the services of a referee appointed under Code of Civil Procedure section 638 is deemed to have elected to proceed outside court facilities. Court facilities, court personnel, and summoned jurors may not be used in proceedings pending before such a referee except on a finding by the presiding judge or his or her designee that their use would further the interests of justice.

Rule 3.907 amended and renumbered effective January 1, 2010; adopted as rule 3.909 effective January 1, 2007.

Rule 3.908. Motion for leave to file complaint for intervention [Repealed]

Rule 3.908 repealed effective January 1, 2010; adopted effective January 1, 2007.

Rule 3.909. Proceedings before privately compensated referees [Renumbered]

Rule 3.909 amended and renumbered to rule 3.907 effective January 1, 2010; adopted as rule 3.909 effective January 1, 2007.

Rule 3.910. Request and order for appropriate and accessible hearing site [Repealed]

Rule 3.910 repealed effective January 1, 2010; adopted effective January 1, 2007.

Chapter 2
Court-Ordered Reference Under Code of Civil Procedure
Section 639

Rule 3.920. Purposes and conditions for appointment of referee

(a) Purposes prescribed by statute

A court may order the appointment of a referee under Code of Civil Procedure section 639 only for the purposes specified in that section.

(Subd (a) adopted effective January 1, 2007.)

(b) No references for mediation

A court must not use the reference procedure under Code of Civil Procedure section 639 to appoint a person to conduct a mediation.

(Subd (b) adopted effective January 1, 2007.)

(c) Conditions for appointment of discovery referee

A discovery referee must not be appointed under Code of Civil Procedure section 639(a)(5) unless the exceptional circumstances of the particular case require the appointment.

(Subd (c) adopted effective January 1, 2007.)
Rule 3.920 adopted effective January 1, 2007.

Advisory Committee Comment

Rule 3.920(b) is not intended to prohibit a court from appointing a referee to conduct a mandatory settlement conference in a complex case or, following the conclusion of a reference, from appointing a person who previously served as a referee to conduct a mediation.

Rule 3.921. Motion for appointment of a referee

(a) Filing and contents

A motion by a party for the appointment of a referee under Code of Civil Procedure section 639 must be served and filed. The motion must specify the matter or matters to be included in the requested reference. If the applicant is requesting the appointment of a particular referee, the motion must be accompanied by the proposed referee's certification as required by rule 3.924(a).

(Subd (a) adopted effective January 1, 2007.)

(b) Hearing

The motion must be heard by the judge to whom the case is assigned, or by the presiding judge or law and motion judge if the case has not been assigned.

(Subd (b) adopted effective January 1, 2007.)

Rule 3.921 adopted effective January 1, 2007.

Rule 3.922. Form and contents of order appointing referee

(a) Written order required

An order appointing a referee under Code of Civil Procedure section 639, on the motion of a party or on the court's own motion, must be in writing and must address the matters set forth in (b) through (g).

(Subd (a) amended effective January 1, 2010; adopted effective January 1, 2007.)

(b) Referee information

The order must state the name, business address, and telephone number of the referee and, if he or she is a member of the State Bar, the referee's State Bar number.

(Subd (b) adopted effective January 1, 2007.)

(c) Basis for reference

The order must specify whether the referee is appointed under paragraph (1), (2), (3), (4), or (5) of subdivision (a) of section 639 and:

(1) If the referee is appointed under section 639(a)(1)–(a)(4), the order must state the reason the referee is being appointed.

(2) If the referee is appointed under section 639(a)(5) to hear and determine discovery motions and disputes relevant to discovery, the order must state the exceptional circumstances of the particular case that require the reference.

(Subd (c) adopted effective January 1, 2007.)

(d) Subject matter and scope of reference

(1) The order must specify the subject matter or matters included in the reference.

(2) If the referee is appointed under section 639(a)(5) to hear and determine discovery motions and disputes relevant to discovery, the order must state whether the discovery referee is appointed for all purposes or only for limited purposes.

(Subd (d) adopted effective January 1, 2007.)

(e) Authority of discovery referee

If the referee is appointed under section 639(a)(5) to hear and determine discovery motions and disputes relevant to discovery, the order must state that the referee is authorized to set the date, time, and place for all hearings determined by the referee to be necessary; direct the issuance of subpoenas; preside over hearings; take evidence; and rule on objections, motions, and other requests made during the course of the hearing.

(Subd (e) adopted effective January 1, 2007.)

(f) Referee fees; apportionment

If the referee will be appointed at a cost to the parties, the order must:

(1) Specify the maximum hourly rate the referee may charge and, if any party so requests, the maximum number of hours for which the referee may charge;

(2) Include a finding that either:

(A) No party has established an economic inability to pay a pro rata share of the referee's fee; or

(B) One or more parties has established an economic inability to pay a pro rata share of the referee's fees and another party has agreed voluntarily to pay that additional share of the referee's fees.

(3) When the issue of economic hardship is raised before the referee begins performing services, the court must determine a fair and reasonable apportionment of reference costs. The court may modify its apportionment order and may consider a recommendation by the referee as a factor in determining any modification.

(Subd (f) adopted effective January 1, 2007.)

(g) Use of court facilities and court personnel

The order must specify the extent, if any, to which court facilities and court personnel may be used in connection with the reference.

(Subd (g) adopted effective January 1, 2007.)

Rule 3.922 amended effective January 1, 2010; adopted effective January 1, 2007.

Rule 3.923. Selection and qualification of referee

The court must appoint the referee or referees as provided in Code of Civil Procedure section 640. If the referee is a former California judicial officer, he or she must be an active or inactive member of the State Bar.

Rule 3.923 adopted effective January 1, 2007.

Rule 3.924. Certification and disclosure by referee

(a) Certification by referee

Before a referee begins to serve:

(1) The referee must certify in writing that he or she consents to serve as provided in the order of appointment and is aware of and will comply with applicable provisions of canon 6 of the Code of Judicial Ethics and with the California Rules of Court; and

(2) The referee's certification must be filed with the court.

(Subd (a) adopted effective January 1, 2007.)

(b) Disclosure by referee

In addition to any other disclosure required by law, no later than five days before the deadline for parties to file a motion for disqualification of the referee under Code of Civil Procedure section 170.6 or, if the referee is not aware of his or her appointment or of a matter subject to disclosure at that time, as soon as practicable thereafter, a referee must disclose to the parties:

(1) Any matter subject to disclosure under subdivisions (D)(5)(a) and (D)(5)(b) of canon 6 of the Code of Judicial Ethics; and

(2) Any significant personal or professional relationship the referee has or has had with a party, attorney, or law firm in the current case, including the number and nature of any other proceedings in the past 24 months in which the referee has been privately compensated by a party, attorney, law firm, or insurance company in the current case for any services. The disclosure must include privately compensated service as an attorney, expert witness, or consultant or as a judge, referee, arbitrator, mediator, settlement facilitator, or other alternative dispute resolution neutral.

(Subd (b) amended effective January 1, 2008; adopted effective January 1, 2007.)

Rule 3.924 amended effective January 1, 2008; adopted effective January 1, 2007.

Rule 3.925. Objection to reference

The filing of a motion for an order appointing a referee does not constitute a waiver of grounds for objection to the appointment of a particular person as referee under Code of Civil Procedure section 641, or objection to the rate or apportionment of compensation of the referee. Any objection to the appointment of a particular person as a referee must be made with reasonable diligence and in writing. The objection must be heard by the judge to whom the case is assigned, or by the presiding judge or the law and motion judge.

Rule 3.925 adopted effective January 1, 2007.

Rule 3.926. Use of court facilities

A reference ordered under Code of Civil Procedure section 639 entitles the parties to the use of court facilities and court personnel to the extent provided in the order of reference. The proceedings may be held in a private facility, but, if so, the private facility must be open to the public as provided in rule 3.931.

Rule 3.926 amended effective January 1, 2010; adopted effective January 1, 2007.

Rule 3.927. Circumstances required for appointment of discovery referee [Repealed]

Rule 3.927 repealed effective January 1, 2010; adopted effective January 1, 2007.

Chapter 3
Rules Applicable to References Under Code of Civil Procedure Section 638 or 639

Title 3, Civil Rules—Division 9, References—Chapter 3, Rules Applicable to References Under Code of Civil Procedure Section 638 or 639; adopted effective January 1, 2010.

Rule 3.930. Documents and exhibits
Rule 3.931. Open proceedings, notice of proceedings, and order for hearing site
Rule 3.932. Motions or applications to be heard by the court

Rule 3.930. Documents and exhibits

All referees and parties in proceedings before a referee appointed under Code of Civil Procedure section 638 or 639 must comply with the applicable requirements of rule 2.400 concerning the filing and handling of documents and exhibits.

Rule 3.930 adopted effective January 1, 2010.

Rule 3.931. Open proceedings, notice of proceedings, and order for hearing site

(a) Open proceedings

All proceedings before a referee that would be open to the public if held before a judge must be open to the public, regardless of whether they are held in a court facility or in another location.

(Subd (a) adopted effective January 1, 2010.)

(b) Notice regarding proceedings before referee

(1) In each case in which he or she is appointed, a referee must file a statement that provides the name, telephone number, e-mail address, and mailing address of a person who may be contacted to obtain information about the date, time, location, and general nature of all hearings scheduled in matters pending before the referee that would be open to the public if held before a judge. This statement must be filed at the same time as the referee's certification under rule 3.904(a) or 3.924(a). If there is any change in this contact information, the referee must promptly file a revised statement with the court.

(2) In addition to providing the information required under (1), the statement filed by a referee may also provide the address of a publicly accessible website at which the referee will maintain a current calendar setting forth the date, time, location, and general nature of any hearings scheduled in the matter that would be open to the public if held before a judge.

(3) The clerk must post the information from the statement filed by the referee in the court facility.

(Subd (b) amended effective January 1, 2016; adopted effective January 1, 2010.)

(c) Appropriate hearing site

(1) The presiding judge or his or her designee, on application of any person or on the judge's own motion, may order that a case before a referee must be heard at a site easily accessible to the public and appropriate for seating those who have made known their plan to attend hearings. The application must state facts showing good cause for granting the application, must be served on all parties and the referee, and filed with the court. The proceedings are not stayed while the application is pending unless the presiding judge or his or her designee orders that they be stayed. The issuance of an order for an accessible and appropriate hearing site is not grounds for withdrawal of a stipulation for the appointment of a referee.

(2) If a court staff mediator or evaluator is required to attend a hearing before a referee, unless otherwise ordered by the presiding judge or his or her designee, that hearing must take place at a location requiring no more than 15 minutes' travel time from the mediator's or evaluator's work site.

(Subd (c) adopted effective January 1, 2010.)

Rule 3.931 amended effective January 1, 2016; adopted effective January 1, 2010.

Rule 3.932. Motions or applications to be heard by the court

(a) Motion or application to seal records

A motion or application to seal records in a case pending before a referee must be filed with the court and served on all parties that have appeared in the case and the referee. The motion or application must be heard by the trial court judge to whom the case is assigned or, if the case has not been assigned, by the presiding judge or his or her designee. Rules 2.550 and 2.551 apply to the motion or application to seal the records.

(Subd (a) adopted effective January 1, 2010.)

(b) Motion for leave to file complaint for intervention

A motion for leave to file a complaint for intervention in a case pending before a referee must be filed with the court and served on all parties and the referee. The motion must be heard by the trial court judge to whom the case is assigned or, if the case has not been assigned, by the presiding judge or his or her designee. If intervention is allowed, the case must be returned to the trial court docket unless all parties stipulate in the manner prescribed in rule 3.901 to proceed before the referee.

(Subd (b) adopted effective January 1, 2010.)

Rule 3.932 adopted effective January 1, 2010.

Division 10
Discovery

Chapter 1
Format of Discovery

Rule 3.1000. Format of supplemental and further discovery

(a) Supplemental interrogatories and responses, etc.

In each set of supplemental interrogatories, supplemental responses to interrogatories, amended answers to interrogatories, and further responses to interrogatories, inspection demands, and admission requests, the following must appear in the first paragraph immediately below the title of the case:

(1) The identity of the propounding, demanding, or requesting party;

(2) The identity of the responding party;

(3) The set number being propounded or responded to; and

(4) The nature of the paper.

(Subd (a) amended effective January 1, 2007; previously amended effective January 1, 1986, and July 1, 1987.)

(b) Identification of responses

Each supplemental or further response and each amended answer must be identified by the same number or letter and be in the same sequence as the corresponding interrogatory, inspection demand, or admission request, but the text of the interrogatory, demand, or request need not be repeated.

(Subd (b) amended effective January 1, 2007; previously amended effective January 1, 1986, and July 1, 1987.)

Rule 3.1000 amended and renumbered effective January 1, 2007; adopted as rule 331 effective January 1, 1984; previously amended effective January 1, 1986, and January 1, 1987.

Chapter 2
Conduct of Discovery

Rule 3.1010. Oral depositions by telephone, videoconference, or other remote electronic means

(a) Taking depositions

Any party may take an oral deposition by telephone, videoconference, or other remote electronic means, provided:

(1) Notice is served with the notice of deposition or the subpoena;

(2) That party makes all arrangements for any other party to participate in the deposition in an equivalent manner. However, each party so appearing must pay all expenses incurred by it or properly allocated to it;

(3) Any party may be personally present at the deposition without giving prior notice.

(b) Appearing and participating in depositions

Any party may appear and participate in an oral deposition by telephone, videoconference, or other remote electronic means, provided:

(1) Written notice of such appearance is served by personal delivery, e-mail, or fax at least three court days before the deposition;

(2) The party so appearing makes all arrangements and pays all expenses incurred for the appearance.

(Subd (b) amended effective January 1, 2016; previously amended effective January 1, 2007.)

(c) Party deponent's appearance

A party deponent must appear at his or her deposition in person and be in the presence of the deposition officer.

(d) Nonparty deponent's appearance

A nonparty deponent may appear at his or her deposition by telephone, videoconference, or other remote electronic means with court approval upon a finding of good cause and no prejudice to any party. The deponent must be sworn in the presence of the deposition officer or by any other means stipulated to by the parties or ordered by the court. Any party may be personally present at the deposition.

(e) Court orders

On motion by any person, the court in a specific action may make such other orders as it deems appropriate.

(Subd (e) amended effective January 1, 2007.)

Rule 3.1010 amended effective January 1, 2016; adopted as rule 333 effective January 1, 2003; amended and renumbered as rule 3.1010 effective January 1, 2007.

Rule 3.1015. Discovery in action pending outside of California [Repealed]

Rule 3.1015 repealed on its own provisions effective January 1, 2010; adopted effective March 13, 2009.

Chapter 3
Discovery Motions
[Repealed]

Chapter 3 repealed effective January 1, 2009.

Rule 3.1020. Format of discovery motions [Renumbered]

Rule 3.1020 renumbered to rule 3.1345 effective January 1, 2009; adopted as rule 335 effective January 1, 1984; previously amended effective July 1, 1987, January 1, 1992, January 1, 1997, and July 1, 2001; previously amended and renumbered effective January 1, 2007.

Rule 3.1025. Service of motion papers on nonparty deponent [Renumbered]

Rule 3.1025 renumbered to rule 3.1346 effective January 1, 2009; adopted as rule 337 effective January 1, 1984; previously amended effective July 1, 1987; previously amended and renumbered effective January 1, 2007.

Rule 3.1030. Sanctions for failure to provide discovery [Renumbered]

Rule 3.1030 renumbered to rule 3.1348 effective January 1, 2009; adopted as rule 341 effective July 1, 2001; previously renumbered effective January 1, 2007.

Division 11
Law and Motion

Chapter 1
General Provisions

Rule 3.1100. Application

The rules in this division apply to proceedings in civil law and motion, as defined in rule 3.1103, and to discovery proceedings in family law and probate.

Rule 3.1100 amended and renumbered effective January 1, 2007; adopted as rule 301 effective January 1, 1984; previously amended effective July 1, 1984, July 1, 1997, and January 1, 2002.

Rule 3.1103. Definitions and construction

(a) Law and motion defined

"Law and motion" includes any proceedings:

(1) On application before trial for an order, except for causes arising under the Welfare and Institutions Code, the Probate Code, the Family Code, or Code of Civil Procedure sections 527.6, 527.7, 527.8, and 527.85; or

(2) On application for an order regarding the enforcement of judgment, attachment of property, appointment of a receiver, obtaining or setting aside a judgment by default, writs of review, mandate and prohibition, a petition to compel arbitration, and enforcement of an award by arbitration.

(Subd (a) amended effective January 1, 2011; previously amended effective July 1, 1997.)

(b) Application of rules on extending or shortening time

Rules 1.10(c) and 2.20 on extending or shortening time apply to proceedings under this division.

(Subd (b) amended effective January 1, 2007.)

(c) Application to demurrers

Unless the context or subject matter otherwise requires, the rules in this division apply to demurrers.

(Subd (c) amended effective January 1, 2007.)

Rule 3.1103 amended effective January 1, 2011; adopted as rule 303 effective January 1, 1984; previously amended effective July 1, 1984; previously amended and renumbered effective January 1, 2007.

Rule 3.1109. Notice of determination of submitted matters

(a) Notice by clerk

When the court rules on a motion or makes an order or renders a judgment in a matter it has taken under submission, the clerk must immediately notify the parties of the ruling, order, or judgment. The notification, which must specifically identify the matter ruled on, may be given by serving electronically or mailing the parties a copy of the ruling, order, or judgment, and it constitutes service of notice only if the clerk is required to give notice under Code of Civil Procedure section 664.5.

(Subd (a) amended effective January 1, 2016; adopted as part of untitled subd effective January 1, 1984; previously amended and lettered subd (a) effective January 1, 2007.)

(b) Notice in a case involving more than two parties

In a case involving more than two parties, a clerk's notification made under this rule, or any notice of a ruling or order served by a party, must name the moving party, and the party against whom relief was requested, and specifically identify the particular motion or other matter ruled upon.

(Subd (b) amended and lettered effective January 1, 2007; adopted as part of untitled subd effective January 1, 1984.)

(c) Time not extended by failure of clerk to give notice

The failure of the clerk to give the notice required by this rule does not extend the time provided by law for performing any act except as provided in rules 8.104(a) or 8.822(a).

(Subd (c) amended effective January 1, 2016; adopted effective January 1, 2007.)

Rule 3.1109 amended effective January 1, 2016; adopted as rule 309 effective January 1, 1984; previously amended and renumbered as rule 3.1109 effective January 1, 2007.

Chapter 2
Format of Motion Papers

Rule 3.1110. General format

(a) Notice of motion

A notice of motion must state in the opening paragraph the nature of the order being sought and the grounds for issuance of the order.

(Subd (a) amended effective January 1, 2007.)

(b) Date of hearing and other information

The first page of each paper must specify immediately below the number of the case:

(1) The date, time, and location, if ascertainable, of any scheduled hearing and the name of the hearing judge, if ascertainable;

(2) The nature or title of any attached document other than an exhibit;

(3) The date of filing of the action; and

(4) The trial date, if set.

(Subd (b) amended effective January 1, 2007; previously amended effective July 1, 1997.)

(c) Pagination of documents

Documents must be consecutively paginated. The page numbering must begin with the first page and use only Arabic numerals (e.g., 1, 2, 3). The page number may be suppressed and need not appear on the first page.

(Subd (c) amended effective January 1, 2017; adopted as part of subd (b) effective January 1, 1984; previously amended and lettered effective January 1, 2007.)

(d) Reference to previously filed papers

Any paper previously filed must be referred to by date of execution and title.

(Subd (d) amended and relettered effective January 1, 2007; adopted as subd (c) effective January 1, 1984.)

(e) Binding

For motions filed on paper, all pages of each document and exhibit must be attached together at the top by a method that permits pages to be easily turned and the entire content of each page to be read.

(Subd (e) amended effective January 1, 2016; adopted as subd (d) effective July 1, 1997; previously amended and relettered as subd (e) effective January 1, 2007.)

(f) Format of exhibits

(1) An index of exhibits must be provided. The index must briefly describe the exhibit and identify the exhibit number or letter and page number.

(2) Pages from a single deposition must be designated as a single exhibit.

(3) Each paper exhibit must be separated by a hard 8½ × 11 sheet with hard paper or plastic tabs extending below the bottom of the page, bearing the exhibit designation.

(4) Electronic exhibits must meet the requirements in rule 2.256(b). Unless they are submitted by a self-represented party, electronic exhibits must include electronic bookmarks with links to the first page of each

exhibit and with bookmark titles that identify the exhibit number or letter and briefly describe the exhibit.

(Subd (f) amended effective January 1, 2017; adopted as subd (e) effective July 1, 1997; previously amended and relettered effective January 1, 2007.)

(g) Translation of exhibits

Exhibits written in a foreign language must be accompanied by an English translation, certified under oath by a qualified interpreter.

(Subd (g) amended and lettered effective January 1, 2007; adopted as part of subd (e) effective July 1, 1997.)

Rule 3.1110 amended effective January 1, 2017; adopted as rule 311 effective January 1, 1984; previously amended effective July 1, 1997, and January 1, 2016; previously amended and renumbered as rule 3.1110 effective January 1, 2007.

Advisory Committee Comment

Subdivision (f)(4). Under current technology, software programs that allow users to apply electronic bookmarks to electronic documents are available for free.

Rule 3.1112. Motions—and other pleadings

(a) Motions required papers

Unless otherwise provided by the rules in this division, the papers filed in support of a motion must consist of at least the following:

(1) A notice of hearing on the motion;

(2) The motion itself; and

(3) A memorandum in support of the motion or demurrer.

(Subd (a) amended effective January 1, 2007.)

(b) Other papers

Other papers may be filed in support of a motion, including declarations, exhibits, appendices, and other documents or pleadings.

(Subd (b) adopted effective January 1, 2007.)

(c) Form of motion papers

The papers filed under (a) and (b) may either be filed as separate documents or combined in one or more documents if the party filing a combined pleading specifies these items separately in the caption of the combined pleading.

(Subd (c) amended and lettered effective January 1, 2007 adopted as part of subd (a) effective July 1, 1997.)

(d) Motion—required elements

A motion must:

(1) Identify the party or parties bringing the motion;

(2) Name the parties to whom it is addressed;

(3) Briefly state the basis for the motion and the relief sought; and

(4) If a pleading is challenged, state the specific portion challenged.

(Subd (d) amended and relettered effective January 1, 2007; adopted as subd (b) effective July 1, 1997.)

(e) Additional requirements for motions

In addition to the requirements of this rule, a motion relating to the subjects specified in chapter 6 of this division must comply with any additional requirements in that chapter.

(Subd (e) amended effective July 1, 2008; previously amended effective January 1, 2007.)

(f) Motion in limine

Notwithstanding (a), a motion in limine filed before or during trial need not be accompanied by a notice of hearing. The timing and place of the filing and service of the motion are at the discretion of the trial judge.

(Subd (f) adopted effective January 1, 2007.)

Rule 3.1112 amended effective July 1, 2008; adopted as rule 312 effective July 1, 1997; previously amended and renumbered effective January 1, 2007.

Rule 3.1113. Memorandum

(a) Memorandum in support of motion

A party filing a motion, except for a motion listed in rule 3.1114, must serve and file a supporting memorandum. The court may construe the absence of a memorandum as an admission that the motion or special demurrer is not meritorious and cause for its denial and, in the case of a demurrer, as a waiver of all grounds not supported.

(Subd (a) amended effective January 1, 2007; previously amended effective January 1, 2004.)

(b) Contents of memorandum

The memorandum must contain a statement of facts, a concise statement of the law, evidence and arguments relied on, and a discussion of the statutes, cases, and textbooks cited in support of the position advanced.

(Subd (b) amended effective January 1, 2004.)

(c) Case citation format

A case citation must include the official report volume and page number and year of decision. The court must not require any other form of citation.

(Subd (c) amended effective January 1, 2007; previously amended effective July 1, 1984, January 1, 1992, and January 1, 2004.)

(d) Length of memorandum

Except in a summary judgment or summary adjudication motion, no opening or responding memorandum may exceed 15 pages. In a summary judgment or summary adjudication motion, no opening or responding memorandum may exceed 20 pages. No reply or closing memorandum may exceed 10 pages. The page limit does not include the caption page, the notice of motion and motion, exhibits, declarations, attachments, the table of contents, the table of authorities, or the proof of service.

(Subd (d) amended effective January 1, 2017; adopted as part of a longer subd (d); previously amended effective July 1, 1984, January 1, 1992, and January 1, 2004.)

(e) Application to file longer memorandum

A party may apply to the court ex parte but with written notice of the application to the other parties, at least 24 hours before the memorandum is due, for permission to file a longer memorandum. The application must state reasons why the argument cannot be made within the stated limit.

(Subd (e) amended and relettered effective January 1, 2004; adopted as part of subd (d).)

(f) Format of longer memorandum

A memorandum that exceeds 10 pages must include a table of contents and a table of authorities. A memorandum that exceeds 15 pages must also include an opening summary of argument.

(Subd (f) amended and lettered effective January 1, 2007; adopted as part of subd (d); subd (d) previously amended and relettered as subd (e) effective January 1, 2004.)

(g) Effect of filing an oversized memorandum

A memorandum that exceeds the page limits of these rules must be filed and considered in the same manner as a late-filed paper.

(Subd (g) amended and lettered effective January 1, 2007; adopted as part of subd (d); previously amended and relettered as subd (e) effective January 1, 2004.)

(h) Pagination of memorandum

The pages of a memorandum must be numbered consecutively beginning with the first page and using only Arabic numerals (e.g., 1, 2, 3). The page number may be suppressed and need not appear on the first page.

(Subd (h) amended effective January 1, 2017; previously amended and relettered as subd (f) effective January 1, 2004, and as subd (h) effective January 1, 2007; adopted as subd (e) effective July 1, 2000.)

(i) Copies of authorities

(1) A judge may require that if any authority other than California cases, statutes, constitutional provisions, or state or local rules is cited, a copy of the authority must be lodged with the papers that cite the authority. If in paper form, the authority must be tabbed or separated as required by rule 3.1110(f)(3). If in electronic form, the authority must be electronically bookmarked as required by rule 3.1110(f)(4).

(2) If a California case is cited before the time it is published in the advance sheets of the Official Reports, the party must include the title, case number, date of decision, and, if from the Court of Appeal, district of the Court of Appeal in which the case was decided. A judge may require that a copy of that case must be lodged. If in paper form, the copy must be tabbed or separated as required by rule 3.1110(f)(3). If in electronic form, the copy must be electronically bookmarked as required by rule 3.1110(f)(4).

(3) Upon the request of a party to the action, any party citing any authority other than California cases, statutes, constitutional provisions, or state or local rules must promptly provide a copy of such authority to the requesting party.

(Subd (i) amended effective January 1, 2017; adopted as part of subd (e) effective January 1, 1992; previously relettered as part of subd (f) effective July 1, 2000; previously amended and relettered as subd (h) effective January 1, 2004, and as subd (j) effective January 1, 2007; repealed and relettered as subd (i) effective January 1, 2008; previously amended effective July 1, 1997, July 1, 2011, and January 1, 2016.)

(j) Attachments

To the extent practicable, all supporting memorandums and declarations must be attached to the notice of motion.

(Subd (j) relettered effective January 1, 2008; adopted as subd (f) effective July 1, 1997; previously relettered as subd (g) effective July 1, 2000; previously amended and relettered as subd (i) effective January 1, 2004, and as subd (k) effective January 1, 2007.)

(k) Exhibit references

All references to exhibits or declarations in supporting or opposing papers must reference the number or letter of the exhibit, the specific page, and, if applicable, the paragraph or line number.

(Subd (k) relettered effective January 1, 2008; adopted as subd (g) effective July 1, 1997; previously relettered as subd (h) effective July 1, 2000, and as subd (l) effective January 1, 2007; previously amended and relettered as subd (j) effective January 1, 2004.)

(l) Requests for judicial notice

Any request for judicial notice must be made in a separate document listing the specific items for which notice is requested and must comply with rule 3.1306(c).

(Subd (l) relettered effective January 1, 2008; adopted as subd (h) effective July 1, 1997; relettered as subd (i) effective July 1, 2000; previously amended effective January 1, 2003; previously amended and relettered as subd (k) effective January 1, 2004, and as subd (m) effective January 1, 2007.)

(m) Proposed orders or judgments

If a proposed order or judgment is submitted, it must be lodged and served with the moving papers but must not be attached to them. The requirements for proposed orders, including the requirements for submitting proposed orders by electronic means, are stated in rule 3.1312.

(Subd (m) amended effective January 1, 2016; adopted as subd (i) effective July 1, 1997; previously amended and relettered as subd (l) effective January 1, 2004; previously relettered as subd (j) effective July 1, 2000, as subd (n) effective January 1, 2007, and as subd (m) effective January 1, 2008.)

Rule 3.1113 amended effective January 1, 2017; adopted as rule 313 effective January 1, 1984; previously amended and renumbered as rule 3.1113 effective January 1, 2007; previously amended effective July 1, 1984, January 1, 1992, July 1, 1997, July 1, 2000, January 1, 2003, January 1, 2004, January 1, 2008, July 1, 2011, and January 1, 2016.

Advisory Committee Comment

See also rule 1.200 concerning the format of citations.

Rule 3.1114. Applications, motions, and petitions not requiring a memorandum

(a) Memorandum not required

Civil motions, applications, and petitions filed on Judicial Council forms that do not require a memorandum include the following:

(1) Application for appointment of guardian ad litem in a civil case;

(2) Application for an order extending time to serve pleading;

(3) Motion to be relieved as counsel;

(4) Motion filed in small claims case;

(5) Petition for change of name or gender;

(6) Petition for declaration of emancipation of minor;

(7) Petition for injunction prohibiting harassment;

(8) Petition for protective order to prevent elder or dependent adult abuse;

(9) Petition for order to prevent postsecondary school violence;

(10) Petition of employer for injunction prohibiting workplace violence;

(11) Petition for order prohibiting abuse (transitional housing);

(12) Petition to approve compromise of claim of a minor or a person with a disability; and

(13) Petition for withdrawal of funds from blocked account.

(Subd (a) amended effective January 1, 2011; previously amended effective January 1, 2007.)

(b) Submission of a memorandum

Notwithstanding (a), if it would further the interests of justice, a party may submit, or the court may order the submission of, a memorandum in support of any motion, application, or petition. The memorandum must comply with rule 3.1113.

(Subd (b) amended effective January 1, 2007.)

Rule 3.1114 amended effective January 1, 2011; adopted as rule 314 effective January 1, 2004; previously amended and renumbered effective January 1, 2007.

Rule 3.1115. Declarations

The caption of a declaration must state the name of the declarant and must specifically identify the motion or other proceeding that it supports or opposes.

Rule 3.1115 amended and renumbered effective January 1, 2007; adopted as rule 315 effective January 1, 1984.

Rule 3.1116. Deposition testimony as an exhibit

(a) Title page

The first page of any deposition used as an exhibit must state the name of the deponent and the date of the deposition.

(Subd (a) amended effective January 1, 2007.)

(b) Deposition pages

Other than the title page, the exhibit must contain only the relevant pages of the transcript. The original page number of any deposition page must be clearly visible.

(Subd (b) amended effective January 1, 2007.)

(c) Highlighting of testimony

The relevant portion of any testimony in the deposition must be marked in a manner that calls attention to the testimony.

(Subd (c) amended effective January 1, 2007.)

Rule 3.1116 amended and renumbered effective January 1, 2007; adopted as rule 316 effective January 1, 1992.

Chapter 3
Provisional and Injunctive Relief

Article 1
General Provisions

Rule 3.1130. Bonds and undertakings

(a) Prerequisites to acceptance of corporate sureties

A corporation must not be accepted or approved as surety on a bond or undertaking unless the following conditions are met:

(1) The Insurance Commissioner has certified the corporation as being admitted to do business in the state as a surety insurer;

(2) There is filed in the office of the clerk a copy, duly certified by the proper authority, of the transcript or record of appointment entitling or authorizing the person or persons purporting to execute the bond or undertaking for and in behalf of the corporation to act in the premises; and

(3) The bond or undertaking has been executed under penalty of perjury as provided in Code of Civil Procedure section 995.630, or the fact of execution of the bond or undertaking by the officer or agent of the corporation purporting to become surety has been duly acknowledged before an officer of this state authorized to take and certify acknowledgements.

(Subd (a) amended effective January 1, 2007.)

(b) Certain persons not eligible to act as sureties

An officer of the court or member of the State Bar may not act as a surety.

(Subd (b) amended effective January 1, 2007.)

(c) Withdrawal of bonds and undertakings

An original bond or undertaking may be withdrawn from the files and delivered to the party by whom it was filed on order of the court only if all parties interested in the obligation so stipulate, or upon a showing that the purpose for which it was filed has been abandoned without any liability having been incurred.

Rule 3.1130 amended and renumbered effective January 1, 2007; adopted as rule 381 effective January 1, 1984.

Article 2
Writs

Rule 3.1140. Lodging of record in administrative mandate cases
Rule 3.1142. Stay of driving license suspension

Rule 3.1140. Lodging of record in administrative mandate cases

The party intending to use a part of the administrative record in a case brought under Code of Civil Procedure section 1094.5 must lodge that part of the record at least five days before the hearing.

Rule 3.1140 amended and renumbered effective January 1, 2007; adopted as rule 347 effective January 1, 1984.

Rule 3.1142. Stay of driving license suspension

A request for a stay of a suspension of a driving license must be accompanied by a copy of the petitioner's driving record from the Department of Motor Vehicles.

Rule 3.1142 amended and renumbered effective January 1, 2007; adopted as rule 355 effective January 1, 1984.

Article 3
Injunctions

Rule 3.1150. Preliminary injunctions and bonds
Rule 3.1151. Requirements for injunction in certain cases

Rule 3.1150. Preliminary injunctions and bonds

(a) Manner of application and service

A party requesting a preliminary injunction may give notice of the request to the opposing or responding party either by serving a noticed motion under Code of Civil Procedure section 1005 or by obtaining and serving an order to show cause (OSC). An OSC must be used when a temporary restraining order (TRO) is sought, or if the party against whom the preliminary injunction is sought has not appeared in the action. If the responding party has not appeared, the OSC must be served in the same manner as a summons and complaint.

(Subd (a) amended effective January 1, 2007; adopted effective July 1, 1997; previously amended effective July 1, 1999.)

(b) Filing of complaint or obtaining of court file

If the action is initiated the same day a TRO or an OSC is sought, the complaint must be filed first. The moving party must provide a file-stamped copy of the complaint to the judge who will hear the application. If an application for a TRO or an OSC is made in an existing case, the moving party must request that the court file be made available to the judge hearing the application.

(Subd (b) amended effective January 1, 2007; adopted effective July 1, 1997; previously amended effective July 1, 1999.)

(c) Form of OSC and TRO

The OSC and TRO must be stated separately, with the OSC stated first. The restraining language sought in an OSC and a TRO must be separately stated in the OSC and the TRO and may not be incorporated by reference. The OSC must describe the injunction to be sought at the hearing. The TRO must describe the activities to be enjoined pending the hearing. A proposed OSC must contain blank spaces for the time and manner of service on responding parties, the date on which the proof of service must be delivered to the court hearing the OSC, a briefing schedule, and, if applicable, the expiration date of the TRO.

(Subd (c) amended effective January 1, 2007; adopted effective July 1, 1997; previously amended effective July 1, 1999.)

(d) Personal attendance

The moving party or counsel for the moving party must be personally present when the request for a TRO is made.

(Subd (d) amended effective January 1, 2007; adopted as subd (e) effective July 1, 1997; amended as [Proof of service] effective July 1, 1999; previously relettered effective July 1, 1999.)

(e) Previous applications

An application for a TRO or an OSC must state whether there has been any previous application for similar relief and, if so, the result of the application.

(Subd (e) amended effective January 1, 2007; adopted as subd (f) effective July 1, 1997; previously amended and relettered effective July 1, 1999.)

(f) Undertaking

Notwithstanding rule 3.1312, whenever an application for a preliminary injunction is granted, a proposed order must be presented to the judge for signature, with an undertaking in the amount ordered, within one court day after the granting of the application or within the time ordered. Unless otherwise ordered, any restraining order previously granted remains in effect during the time allowed for presentation for signature of the order of injunction and undertaking. If the proposed order and the undertaking required are not presented within the time allowed, the TRO may be vacated without notice. All bonds and undertakings must comply with rule 3.1130.

(Subd (f) amended effective January 1, 2007; previously amended and relettered effective July 1, 1997.)

(g) Ex parte temporary restraining orders

Applications for ex parte temporary restraining orders are governed by the ex parte rules in chapter 4 of this division.

(Subd (g) amended effective January 1, 2007; adopted effective July 1, 1999.)
Rule 3.1150 amended and renumbered effective January 1, 2007; adopted as rule 359 effective January 1, 1984; previously amended effective July 1, 1997, and July 1, 1999.

Rule 3.1151.   Requirements for injunction in certain cases

A petition for an injunction to limit picketing, restrain real property encroachments, or protect easements must depict by drawings, plot plans, photographs, or other appropriate means, or must describe in detail the premises involved, including, if applicable, the length and width of the frontage on a street or alley, the width of sidewalks, and the number, size, and location of entrances.

Rule 3.1151 amended and renumbered effective January 1, 2007; adopted as rule 361 effective January 1, 1984.

Rule 3.1152.   Requests for protective orders to prevent civil harassment, workplace violence, private postsecondary school violence, and elder or dependent adult abuse [Renumbered]

Rule 3.1152 renumbered as rule 3.1160 effective January 1, 2019; adopted as rule 363 effective January 1, 1984; previously amended effective January 1, 1993, July 1, 1995, January 1, 2000, January 1, 2002, and January 1, 2012; previously amended and renumbered effective January 1, 2007.

Rule 3.1153.   Minors may appear without counsel to seek specified restraining orders [Repealed]

Rule 3.1153 repealed effective January 1, 2012; adopted as rule 364 effective July 1, 1995; previously amended and renumbered effective January 1, 2007.

Article 4
Protective Orders

Title 3, Civil Rules—Division 11, Law and Motion—Chapter 3, Provisional and Injunctive Relief; Article 4, Protective Orders; adopted effective January 1, 2019.

Rule 3.1160. Requests for protective orders to prevent civil harassment, workplace violence, private postsecondary school violence, and elder or dependent adult abuse
Rule 3.1161. Request to make minor's information confidential in civil harassment protective order proceedings

Rule 3.1160.   Requests for protective orders to prevent civil harassment, workplace violence, private postsecondary school violence, and elder or dependent adult abuse

(a) Application

This rule applies to requests for protective orders under Code of Civil Procedure sections 527.6, 527.8, and 527.85, and Welfare and Institutions Code section 15657.03.

(Subd (a) repealed and adopted effective January 1, 2012; previously amended effective July 1, 1995, and January 1, 2007.)

(b) No memorandum required

Unless ordered by the court, no memorandum is required in support of or in opposition to a request for a protective order.

(Subd (b) repealed and adopted effective January 1, 2012; previously amended effective July 1, 1995, January 1, 2002, and January 1, 2007.)

(c) Service of requests, notices, and orders

The request for a protective order, notice of hearing, and any temporary restraining order, must be personally served on the respondent at least five days before the hearing, unless the court for good cause orders a shorter time. Service must be made in the manner provided by law for personal service of summons in civil actions.

(Subd (c) amended effective January 1, 2012; previously amended effective January 1, 1993, and January 1, 2007.)

(d) Response

The response to a request for a protective order may be written or oral, or both. If a written response is served on the petitioner or, if the petitioner is represented, on the petitioner's attorney at least two days before the hearing, the petitioner is not entitled to a continuance on account of the response.

(Subd (d) amended effective January 1, 2012; previously amended effective January 1, 2007.)

(e) Continuance

A respondent may request continuance of the hearing upon a showing of good cause. If the court in its discretion grants the continuance, any temporary restraining order that has been granted remains in effect until the end of the continued hearing unless otherwise ordered by the court.

(Subd (e) adopted effective January 1, 2012.)
Rule 3.1160 renumbered effective January 1, 2019; adopted as rule 363 effective January 1, 1984; previously amended effective January 1, 1993, July 1, 1995, January 1, 2000, January 1, 2002, and January 1, 2012; previously amended and renumbered as rule 3.1152 effective January 1, 2007.

Rule 3.1161.   Request to make minor's information confidential in civil harassment protective order proceedings

(a) Application of rule

This rule applies to requests and orders made under Code of Civil Procedure section 527.6(v) to keep a minor's information confidential in a civil harassment protective order proceeding.

Wherever used in this rule, "legal guardian" means either parent if both parents have legal custody, or the parent or person having legal custody, or the guardian, of a minor.

(Subd (a) adopted effective January 1, 2019.)

(b) Information that may be made confidential

The information that may be made confidential includes:

(1) The minor's name;

(2) The minor's address;

(3) The circumstances surrounding the protective order with respect to the minor. These include the allegations in the *Request for Civil Harassment Retraining Orders* (form CH-100) that involve conduct directed, in whole or in part, toward the minor; and

(4) Any other information that the minor or legal guardian believes should be confidential.

(Subd (b) adopted effective January 1, 2019.)

(c) Requests for confidentiality

(1) *Person making request*

A request for confidentiality may be made by a minor or legal guardian.

(2) *Number of minors*

A request for confidentiality by a legal guardian may be made for more than one minor. "Minor," as used in this rule, refers to all minors for whom a request for confidentiality is made.

(Subd (c) adopted effective January 1, 2019.)

(d) Procedures for making request

(1) *Timing of requests*

A request for confidentiality may be made at any time during the case.

(2) *Submission of request*

The person submitting a request must complete and file *Request to Keep Minor's Information Confidential* (form CH-160), a confidential form.

(3) *Ruling on request*

(A) *Ruling on request without notice*

The court must determine whether to grant a request for confidentiality without requiring that any notice of the request be given to the other party, or both parties if the minor is not a party in the proceeding. No adversarial hearing is to be held.

(B) *Request for confidentiality submitted at the same time as a request for restraining orders*

If a request for confidentiality is submitted at the same time as a request for restraining orders, the court must consider both requests consistent with Code of Civil Procedure section 527.6(e) and must consider and rule on the request for confidentiality before the request for restraining order is filed.

Documents submitted with the restraining order request must not be filed until after the court has ruled on the request for confidentiality and must be consistent with (C) below.

(C) *Withdrawal of request for restraining order*

If a request for confidentiality under (B) made by the person asking for the restraining order is denied and the requester seeks to withdraw the request for restraining orders, all of the following apply:

(i) The court must not file the request for restraining order and the accompanying proposed order forms and must return the documents to the requester personally, destroy the documents, or delete the documents from any electronic files;

(ii) The order denying confidentiality must be filed and maintained in a public file; and

(iii) The request for confidentiality must be filed and maintained in a confidential file.

(4) *Need for additional facts*

If the court finds that the request for confidentiality is insufficiently specific to meet the requirements under Code of Civil Procedure section 527.6(v)(2) for granting the request, the court may take testimony from the minor, or legal guardian, the person requesting a protective order, or other competent witness, in a closed hearing in order to determine if there are additional facts that would support granting the request.

(Subd (d) adopted effective January 1, 2019.)

(e) Orders on request for confidentiality

(1) *Rulings*

The court may grant the entire request, deny the entire request, or partially grant the request for confidentiality.

(2) *Order granting request for confidentiality*

(A) *Applicability*

An order made under Code of Civil Procedure section 527.6(v) applies in this case and in any other civil case to all registers of actions, indexes, court calendars, pleadings, discovery documents, and other documents filed or served in the action, and at hearings, trial, and other court proceedings that are open to the public.

(B) *Minor's name*

If the court grants a request for confidentiality of the minor's name and:

(i) If the minor is a party to the action, the court must use the initials of the minor or other initials, at the discretion of the court. In addition, the court must use only initials to identify both parties to the action if using the other party's name would likely reveal the identity of the minor.

(ii) If the minor is not a party to the action, the court must not include any information that would likely reveal the identity of the minor, including whether the minor lives with the person making the request for confidentiality.

(C) *Circumstances surrounding protective order (statements related to minor)*

If the court grants a request for confidentiality, the order must specifically identify the information about the minor in *Request for Civil Harassment Restraining Orders* (form CH-100) and any other applicable document that must be kept confidential. Information about the minor ordered confidential by the court must not be made available to the public.

(D) *Service*

The other party, or both parties if the person making the request for confidentiality is not a party to the action, must be served with a copy of the *Request to Keep Minor's Information Confidential* (form CH-160), *Order on Request to Keep Minor's Information Confidential* (form CH-165) and *Notice of Order Protecting Information of Minor* (form CH-170), redacted if required under (f)(4).

(3) *Order denying request for confidentiality*

(A) The order denying confidentiality must be filed and maintained in a public file. The request for confidentiality must be filed and maintained in a confidential file.

(B) Notwithstanding denial of a request to keep the minor's address confidential, the address may be confidential under other statutory provisions.

(C) *Service*

(i) If a request for confidentiality is denied and the request for restraining order has been withdrawn, and if no other action is pending before the court in the case, then the *Request to Keep Minor's Information Confidential* (form CH-160) and *Order on Request to Keep Minor's Information Confidential* (form CH-165) must not be served on the other party, or both parties if the person making the request for confidentiality is not a party to the action.

(ii) If a request for confidentiality is denied and the request for restraining order has not been withdrawn, or if an action between the same parties is pending before the court, then the *Request to Keep Minor's Information Confidential* (form CH-160) and *Order on Request to Keep Minor's Information Confidential* (form CH-165) must be served on the other party, or both parties if the person making the request for confidentiality is not a party to the action.

(Subd (e) adopted effective January 1, 2019.)

(f) Procedures to protect confidential information when request is granted

(1) If a request for confidentiality is granted in whole or in part, the court, in its discretion, and taking into consideration the factors stated in (g), must ensure that the order granting confidentiality is maintained in the most effective manner by:

(A) The judicial officer redacting all information to be kept confidential from all applicable documents;

(B) Ordering the requesting party or the requesting party's attorney to prepare a redacted copy of all applicable documents and submit all redacted copies to the court for review and filing; or

(C) Ordering any other procedure that facilitates the prompt and accurate preparation of a redacted copy of all applicable documents in compliance with the court's order granting confidentiality, provided the selected procedure is consistent with (g).

(2) The redacted copy or copies must be filed and maintained in a public file, and the unredacted copy or copies must be filed and maintained in a confidential file.

(3) Information that is made confidential from the public and the restrained person must be filed in a confidential file accessible only to the minor or minors who are subjects of the order of confidentiality, or the legal guardian who requested confidentiality, law enforcement for enforcement purposes only, and the court.

(4) Any information that is made confidential from the restrained person must be redacted from the copy that will be served on the restrained person.

(Subd (f) adopted effective January 1, 2019.)

(g) Factors in selecting redaction procedures

In determining the procedure to follow under (f), the court must consider the following factors:

(1) Whether the requesting party is represented by an attorney;

(2) Whether the requesting party has immediate access to a self-help center or other legal assistance;

(3) Whether the requesting party is capable of preparing redacted materials without assistance;

(4) Whether the redactions to the applicable documents are simple or complex; and

(5) When applicable, whether the selected procedure will ensure that the orders on the request for restraining order and the request for confidentiality are issued and redacted in an expeditious and timely manner.

(Subd (g) amended effective September 1, 2020; adopted effective January 1, 2019.)

(h) Releasing minor's confidential information

(1) [1] *To respondent*

Information about a protected minor must be **[2] released to** the respondent only as provided in Code of Civil Procedure section **[3] 527.6(v)(4)(A)(ii)**, limited to information necessary to allow the respondent to respond to the request for the protective order **[4]** and to comply with the confidentiality order and the protective order.

(2) [5] *To law enforcement*

Information about a **[6]** minor must be shared with law enforcement **[7]** as provided in Code of Civil Procedure section **[8] 527.6(v)(4)(A)(i) or by court order**.

(3) *To other persons*

If the court finds it is necessary to prevent harassment or is in the best interest of the minor, the court may release confidential information on the request of any person or entity or on the court's own motion.

(A) *Request for release of confidential information*

(i) Any person or entity may request the release of confidential information by filing *Request for Release of Minor's Confidential Information* **(form CH-176) and a proposed,** *Order on Request for Release of Minor's Confidential Information* **(form CH-179), with the court.**

(ii) Within 10 days after filing form CH-176 with the clerk, the clerk must serve, by first-class mail, the following documents on the minor or legal guardian who made the request to keep the minor's information confidential:

a. *Cover Sheet for Confidential Information* **(form CH-175);**

b. *Request for Release of Minor's Confidential Information* **(form CH-176);**

c. *Notice of Request for Release of Minor's Confidential Information* **(form CH-177);**

d. *Response to Request for Release of Minor's Confidential Information* **(form CH-178) (blank copy);**

e. *Order on Request for Release of Minor's Confidential Information* **(form CH-179).**

(B) *Opportunity to object*

(i) The person who made the request for confidentiality has the right to object by filing form CH-178 within 20 days from the date of the mailing of form CH-177, or verbally objecting at a hearing, if one is held.

(ii) The person filing a response must serve a copy of the response (form CH-178) on the person requesting release of confidential information. Service must occur before filing the response form with the court unless the response form contains confidential information. If the response form contains confidential information, service must be done as soon as possible after the response form has been redacted.

(iii) If the person who made the request for confidentiality objects to the release of information, the court may set the matter for a closed hearing.

(C) *Rulings*

The request may be granted or denied in whole or in part without a hearing. Alternatively, the court may set the matter for hearing on at least 10 days' notice to the person who made the request for release of confidential information and the person who made the request for confidential information. Any hearing must be confidential.

(i) *Order granting release of confidential information*

a. The order (form CH-179) granting the release of confidential information must be prepared in a manner consistent with the procedures outlined in (f).

b. A redacted copy of the order (form CH-179) must be filed in a public file and an unredacted copy of the order must be filed in a confidential file.

c. *Service*

If the court grants the request for release of information based on the pleadings, the court must mail a copy of form CH-179 to the person who filed form CH-176 and the person who made the request to keep the minor's information confidential. Parties may be served in court if present at the hearing.

(ii) *Order denying request to release minor's confidential information*

a. The court may deny a request to release confidential information based on the request alone.

b. The order (form CH-179) denying the release of confidential information must be filed in a public file and must not include any confidential information.

c. *Service*

If the court denies the request for release of information based on the pleadings, the court must mail a copy of form CH-179 to the person who filed form CH-176 and the person who made the request to keep the minor's information confidential. Parties may be served in court if present at the hearing.

(iii) If the court finds that the request to release confidential information is insufficiently specific to meet the requirements under Code of Civil Procedure section 527.6(v)(4)(C), the court may conduct a closed hearing to determine if there are additional facts that would support granting the request. The court may receive any relevant evidence, including testimony from the person requesting the release of a minor's confidential information, the minor, the legal guardian, the person who requested the restraining order, or other competent witness.

(Subd (h) amended effective September 1, 2020; adopted effective January 1, 2019.)

Rule 3.1161(h).　2020 Deletes. [1] *Sharing of information with the* **[2]** shared with **[3]** 527.6(v)(4)(B) **[4]** , **[5]** *Sharing of information with* **[6]** protected **[7]** only **[8]** 527.6(v)(4)(A)

(i) Protecting information in subsequent filings and other civil cases

(1) *Filings made after an order granting confidentiality*

(A) A party seeking to file a document or form after an order for confidentiality has been made must submit the *Cover Sheet for Confidential Information* (form CH-175) attached to the front of the document to be filed.

(B) Upon receipt of form CH-175 with attached documents, the court must:

(i) Order a procedure for redaction consistent with the procedures stated in (f);

(ii) File the unredacted document in the confidential file pending receipt of the redacted document if the redacted document is not prepared on the same court day; and

(iii) File the redacted document in the public file after it has been reviewed and approved by the court for accuracy.

(2) *Other civil case*

(A) Information subject to an order of confidentiality issued under Code of Civil Procedure section 527.6(v) must be kept confidential in any other civil case **with the same parties**.

(B) The minor or person making the request for confidentiality and any person who has been served with a notice of confidentiality must submit a copy of the order of confidentiality (form CH-165) in any other civil case **[1] with** the same parties.

(Subd (i) amended effective September 1, 2020; adopted effective January 1, 2019.)

Rule 3.1161(i).　2020 Deletes. [1] involving

Rule 3.1161 amended effective September 1, 2020; adopted effective January 1, 2019.

Advisory Committee Comment

Subdivisions (a)–(e). The process described in this rule need not be used for minors if the request for confidentiality is merely to keep an address confidential and a petitioning minor has a mailing address which need not be kept private that can be listed on the forms. The restraining order forms do not require the address of a nonpetitioning minor.

This rule and rule 2.551 provide a standard and procedures for courts to follow when a request is made to seal a record. The standard as reflected in Code of Civil Procedure section 527.6(v)(2) is based on *NBC Subsidiary (KNBC-TV), Inc. v. Superior Court* (1999) 20 Cal.4th 1178. The standard recognizes the First Amendment right of access to documents used at trial or as a basis of adjudication.

Article 4
Receiverships

Rule 3.1175. Ex parte application for appointment of receiver
Rule 3.1176. Confirmation of ex parte appointment of receiver
Rule 3.1177. Nomination of receivers
Rule 3.1178. Amount of undertakings
Rule 3.1179. The receiver
Rule 3.1180. Employment of attorney
Rule 3.1181. Receiver's inventory
Rule 3.1182. Monthly reports
Rule 3.1183. Interim fees and objections
Rule 3.1184. Receiver's final account and report

Rule 3.1175. Ex parte application for appointment of receiver

(a) Application

In addition to any other matters supporting an application for the ex parte appointment of a receiver, the applicant must show in detail by verified complaint or declaration:

(1) The nature of the emergency and the reasons irreparable injury would be suffered by the applicant during the time necessary for a hearing on notice;

(2) The names, addresses, and telephone numbers of the persons in actual possession of the property for which a receiver is requested, or of the president, manager, or principal agent of any corporation in possession of the property;

(3) The use being made of the property by the persons in possession; and

(4) If the property is a part of the plant, equipment, or stock in trade of any business, the nature and approximate size or extent of the business and facts sufficient to show whether the taking of the property by a receiver would stop or seriously interfere with the operation of the business.

If any of the matters listed above are unknown to the applicant and cannot be ascertained by the exercise of due diligence, the applicant's declaration or verified complaint must fully state the matters unknown and the efforts made to acquire the information.

(Subd (a) amended effective January 1, 2007; previously amended effective January 1, 2002.)

Rule 3.1175 amended and renumbered effective January 1, 2007; adopted as rule 349 effective January 1, 1984; previously amended and renumbered as rule 1900 effective January 1, 2002.

Rule 3.1176. Confirmation of ex parte appointment of receiver

(a) Order to show cause

Whenever a receiver is appointed without notice, the matter must be made returnable upon an order to show cause why the appointment should not be confirmed. The order to show cause must be made returnable on the earliest date that the business of the court will admit, but not later than 15 days or, if good cause appears to the court, 22 days from the date the order is issued.

(Subd (a) amended effective January 1, 2002.)

(b) Service of complaint, order to show cause, declarations, and memorandum

The applicant must serve on each of the adverse parties:

(1) A copy of the complaint if not previously served;

(2) The order to show cause stating the date, time, and place of the hearing;

(3) Any declarations supporting the application; and

(4) A memorandum supporting the application.

Service must be made as soon as reasonably practical, but no later than 5 days after the date on which the order to show cause is issued, unless the court orders another time for service.

(Subd (b) amended effective January 1, 2007; previously amended effective January 1, 2002.)

(c) Failure to proceed or serve adverse party

When the matter first comes on for hearing, the party that obtained the appointment must be ready to proceed. If that party is not ready to proceed or has failed to exercise diligence to effect service upon the adverse parties as provided in (b), the court may discharge the receiver.

(Subd (c) amended effective January 1, 2007; previously amended effective January 1, 2002.)

(d) Continuance

The adverse parties are entitled to one continuance to enable them to oppose the confirmation. If a continuance is granted under this subdivision, the order to show cause remains in effect until the date of the continued hearing.

(Subd (d) amended effective January 1, 2002.)

Rule 3.1176 amended and renumbered effective January 1, 2007; adopted as rule 351 effective January 1, 1984; previously amended and renumbered as rule 1901 effective January 1, 2002.

Rule 3.1177. Nomination of receivers

At the hearing of an application for appointment of a receiver on notice or at the hearing for confirmation of an ex parte appointment, each party appearing may, at the time of the hearing, suggest in writing one or more persons for appointment or substitution as receiver, stating the reasons. A party's suggestion is without prejudice to its objection to the appointment or confirmation of a receiver.

Rule 3.1177 renumbered effective January 1, 2007; adopted as rule 353 effective January 1, 1984; previously amended and renumbered as rule 1902 effective January 1, 2002.

Rule 3.1178. Amount of undertakings

At the hearing of an application for appointment of a receiver on notice or ex parte, the applicant must, and other parties may, propose and state the reasons for the specific amounts of the undertakings required from (1) the applicant by Code of Civil Procedure section 529, (2) the applicant by Code of Civil Procedure section 566(b), and (3) the receiver by Code of Civil Procedure section 567(b), for any injunction that is ordered in or with the order appointing a receiver.

Rule 3.1178 amended and renumbered effective January 1, 2007; adopted as rule 1902.5 effective January 1, 2004.

Rule 3.1179. The receiver

(a) Agent of the court

The receiver is the agent of the court and not of any party, and as such:

(1) Is neutral;

(2) Acts for the benefit of all who may have an interest in the receivership property; and

(3) Holds assets for the court and not for the plaintiff or the defendant.

(b) Prohibited contracts, agreements, arrangements, and understandings

The party seeking the appointment of the receiver may not, directly or indirectly, require any contract, agreement, arrangement, or understanding with any receiver whom it intends to nominate or recommend to the court, and the receiver may not enter into any such contract, arrangement, agreement, or understanding concerning:

(1) The role of the receiver with respect to the property following a trustee's sale or termination of a receivership, without specific court permission;

(2) How the receiver will administer the receivership or how much the receiver will charge for services or pay for services to appropriate or approved third parties hired to provide services;

(3) Who the receiver will hire, or seek approval to hire, to perform necessary services; or

(4) What capital expenditures will be made on the property.

Rule 3.1179 renumbered effective January 1, 2007; adopted as rule 1903 effective January 1, 2002.

Rule 3.1180. Employment of attorney

A receiver must not employ an attorney without the approval of the court. The application for approval to employ an attorney must be in writing and must state:

(1) The necessity for the employment;

(2) The name of the attorney whom the receiver proposes to employ; and

(3) That the attorney is not the attorney for, associated with, nor employed by an attorney for any party.

Rule 3.1180 amended and renumbered effective January 1, 2007; adopted as rule 1904 effective January 1, 2002.

Rule 3.1181. Receiver's inventory

(a) Filing of inventory

A receiver must, within 30 days after appointment, or within such other time as the court may order, file an inventory containing a complete and detailed list of all property of which the receiver has taken possession by virtue of the appointment.

(Subd (a) lettered effective January 1, 2007; adopted as part of untitled subd effective January 1, 2002.)

(b) Supplemental inventory

The receiver must promptly file a supplementary inventory of all subsequently obtained property.

(Subd (b) lettered effective January 1, 2007; adopted as part of untitled subd effective January 1, 2002.)

Rule 3.1181 amended and renumbered effective January 1, 2007; adopted as rule 1905 effective January 1, 2002.

Rule 3.1182.　Monthly reports

(a) Content of reports

The receiver must provide monthly reports to the parties and, if requested, to nonparty client lien holders. These reports must include:

(1) A narrative report of events;

(2) A financial report; and

(3) A statement of all fees paid to the receiver, employees, and professionals showing:

(A) Itemized services;

(B) A breakdown of the services by 1/10 hour increments;

(C) If the fees are hourly, the hourly fees; and

(D) If the fees are on another basis, that basis.

(Subd (a) amended effective January 1, 2007.)

(b) Reports not to be filed

The monthly reports are not to be filed with the court unless the court so orders.

Rule 3.1182 amended effective January 1, 2007; adopted as rule 1906 effective January 1, 2002; previously renumbered effective January 1, 2007.

Rule 3.1183.　Interim fees and objections

(a) Interim fees

Interim fees are subject to final review and approval by the court. The court retains jurisdiction to award a greater or lesser amount as the full, fair, and final value of the services received.

(b) Objections to interim accounts and reports

Unless good cause is shown, objections to a receiver's interim report and accounting must be made within 10 days of notice of the report and accounting, must be specific, and must be delivered to the receiver and all parties entitled to service of the interim report and accounting.

Rule 3.1183 renumbered effective January 1, 2007; adopted as rule 1907 effective January 1, 2002.

Rule 3.1184.　Receiver's final account and report

(a) Motion or stipulation

A receiver must present by noticed motion or stipulation of all parties:

(1) A final account and report;

(2) A request for the discharge; and

(3) A request for exoneration of the receiver's surety.

(Subd (a) amended and relettered effective January 1, 2004; adopted as part of unlettered subd effective January 1, 2002.)

(b) No memorandum required

No memorandum needs to be submitted in support of the motion or stipulation served and filed under (a) unless the court so orders.

(Subd (b) adopted effective January 1, 2004.)

(c) Notice

Notice of the motion or of the stipulation must be given to every person or entity known to the receiver to have a substantial, unsatisfied claim that will be affected by the order or stipulation, whether or not the person or entity is a party to the action or has appeared in it.

(Subd (c) adopted effective January 1, 2004.)

(d) Claim for compensation for receiver or attorney

If any allowance of compensation for the receiver or for an attorney employed by the receiver is claimed in an account, it must state in detail what services have been performed by the receiver or the attorney and whether previous allowances have been made to the receiver or attorney and the amounts.

(Subd (d) amended and relettered effective January 1, 2007; adopted as part of unlettered subd effective January 1, 2002; amended and lettered effective January 1, 2004.)

Rule 3.1184 amended and renumbered effective January 1, 2007; adopted as rule 1908 effective January 1, 2002; previously amended effective January 1, 2004.

Chapter 4
Ex Parte Applications

Rule 3.1200.　Application

The rules in this chapter govern ex parte applications and orders in civil cases, unless otherwise provided by a statute or a rule. These rules may be referred to as "the ex parte rules."

Rule 3.1200 adopted effective January 1, 2007.

Rule 3.1201.　Required documents

A request for ex parte relief must be in writing and must include all of the following:

(1) An application containing the case caption and stating the relief requested;

(2) A declaration in support of the application making the factual showing required under rule 3.1202(c);

(3) A declaration based on personal knowledge of the notice given under rule 3.1204;

(4) A memorandum; and

(5) A proposed order.

Rule 3.1201 adopted effective January 1, 2007.

Rule 3.1202.　Contents of application

(a) Identification of attorney or party

An ex parte application must state the name, address, e-mail address, and telephone number of any attorney known to the applicant to be an attorney for any party or, if no such attorney is known, the name, address, e-mail address, and telephone number of the party if known to the applicant.

(Subd (a) amended effective January 1, 2016.)

(b) Disclosure of previous applications

If an ex parte application has been refused in whole or in part, any subsequent application of the same character or for the same relief, although made upon an alleged different state of facts, must include a full disclosure of all previous applications and of the court's actions.

(c) Affirmative factual showing required

An applicant must make an affirmative factual showing in a declaration containing competent testimony based on personal knowledge of irreparable harm, immediate danger, or any other statutory basis for granting relief ex parte.

(Subd (c) amended effective January 1, 2007.)

Rule 3.1202 amended effective January 1, 2016; adopted effective January 1, 2007; previously amended effective January 1, 2007.

Rule 3.1203.　Time of notice to other parties

(a) Time of notice

A party seeking an ex parte order must notify all parties no later than 10:00 a.m. the court day before the ex parte appearance, absent a showing of exceptional circumstances that justify a shorter time for notice.

(Subd (a) amended effective January 1, 2008; adopted effective January 1, 2007.)

(b) Time of notice in unlawful detainer proceedings

A party seeking an ex parte order in an unlawful detainer proceeding may provide shorter notice than required under (a) provided that the notice given is reasonable.

(Subd (b) adopted effective January 1, 2007.)

Rule 3.1203 amended effective January 1, 2008; adopted effective January 1, 2007.

Rule 3.1204.　Contents of notice and declaration regarding notice

(a) Contents of notice

When notice of an ex parte application is given, the person giving notice must:

(1) State with specificity the nature of the relief to be requested and the date, time, and place for the presentation of the application; and

(2) Attempt to determine whether the opposing party will appear to oppose the application.

(Subd (a) adopted effective January 1, 2007.)

(b) Declaration regarding notice

An ex parte application must be accompanied by a declaration regarding notice stating:

(1) The notice given, including the date, time, manner, and name of the party informed, the relief sought, any response, and whether opposition is expected and that, within the applicable time under rule 3.1203, the applicant informed the opposing party where and when the application would be made;

(2) That the applicant in good faith attempted to inform the opposing party but was unable to do so, specifying the efforts made to inform the opposing party; or

(3) That, for reasons specified, the applicant should not be required to inform the opposing party.

(Subd (b) adopted effective January 1, 2007.)

(c) Explanation for shorter notice

If notice was provided later than 10:00 a.m. the court day before the ex parte appearance, the declaration regarding notice must explain:

(1) The exceptional circumstances that justify the shorter notice; or

(2) In unlawful detainer proceedings, why the notice given is reasonable.

(Subd (c) adopted effective January 1, 2007.)

Rule 3.1204 adopted effective January 1, 2007.

Rule 3.1205. Filing and presentation of the ex parte application

Notwithstanding the failure of an applicant to comply with the requirements of rule 3.1203, the clerk must not reject an ex parte application for filing and must promptly present the application to the appropriate judicial officer for consideration.

Rule 3.1205 adopted effective January 1, 2007.

Rule 3.1206. Service of papers

Parties appearing at the ex parte hearing must serve the ex parte application or any written opposition on all other appearing parties at the first reasonable opportunity. Absent exceptional circumstances, no hearing may be conducted unless such service has been made.

Rule 3.1206 adopted effective January 1, 2007.

Rule 3.1207. Appearance requirements

An applicant for an ex parte order must appear, either in person or by telephone under rule 3.670, except in the following cases:

(1) Applications to file a memorandum in excess of the applicable page limit;

(2) Applications for extensions of time to serve pleadings;

(3) Setting of hearing dates on alternative writs and orders to show cause; and

(4) Stipulations by the parties for an order.

Rule 3.1207 amended effective January 1, 2014; adopted effective January 1, 2007; previously amended effective January 1, 2008.

Chapter 5
Noticed Motions

Rule 3.1300. Time for filing and service of motion papers

(a) In general

Unless otherwise ordered or specifically provided by law, all moving and supporting papers must be served and filed in accordance with Code of Civil Procedure section 1005 and, when applicable, the statutes and rules providing for electronic filing and service.

(Subd (a) amended effective January 1, 2016; previously amended effective January 1, 2000, and January 1, 2007.)

(b) Order shortening time

The court, on its own motion or on application for an order shortening time supported by a declaration showing good cause, may prescribe shorter times for the filing and service of papers than the times specified in Code of Civil Procedure section 1005.

(Subd (b) adopted effective January 1, 2000.)

(c) Time for filing proof of service

Proof of service of the moving papers must be filed no later than five court days before the time appointed for the hearing.

(Subd (c) amended effective January 1, 2007; adopted as subd (b) effective January 1, 1984; previously relettered effective January 1, 2000.)

(d) Filing of late papers

No paper may be rejected for filing on the ground that it was untimely submitted for filing. If the court, in its discretion, refuses to consider a late filed paper, the minutes or order must so indicate.

(Subd (d) amended effective January 1, 2007; adopted as subd (c) effective January 1, 1992; previously amended and relettered effective January 1, 2000.)

(e) Computation of time

A paper submitted before the close of the clerk's office to the public on the day the paper is due is deemed timely filed. Under rules 2.253(b)(7) and 2.259(c), a court may provide by local rule that a paper that is required to be filed electronically and that is received electronically by the court before midnight on a court day is deemed filed on that court day.

(Subd (e) amended effective January 1, 2016; adopted as subd (d) effective January 1, 1992; previously relettered as subd (e) effective January 1, 2000.)

Rule 3.1300 amended effective January 1, 2016; adopted as rule 317 effective January 1, 1984; previously amended effective January 1, 1992, and January 1, 2000; previously amended and renumbered as rule 3.1300 effective January 1, 2007.

Rule 3.1302. Place and manner of filing

(a) Papers filed in clerk's office

Unless otherwise provided by local rule or specified in a court's protocol for electronic filing, all papers relating to a law and motion proceeding must be filed in the clerk's office.

(Subd (a) amended effective January 1, 2016; previously amended effective January 1, 2007.)

(b) Requirements for lodged material

Material lodged physically with the clerk must be accompanied by an addressed envelope with sufficient postage for mailing the material. Material lodged electronically must clearly specify the electronic address to which a notice of deletion may be sent. After determination of the matter, the clerk may mail or send the material if in paper form back to the party lodging it. If the lodged material is in electronic form, the clerk may permanently delete it after sending notice of the deletion to the party who lodged the material.

(Subd (b) amended effective January 1, 2017; previously amended effective January 1, 2007, and January 1, 2016.)

Rule 3.1302 amended effective January 1, 2017; adopted as rule 319 effective January 1, 1984; previously amended and renumbered as rule 3.1302 effective January 1, 2007; previously amended effective January 1, 2016.

Rule 3.1304. Time of hearing

(a) General schedule

The clerk must post electronically and at the courthouse a general schedule showing the days and departments for holding each type of law and motion hearing.

(Subd (a) amended effective January 1, 2016; previously amended effective January 1, 2003.)

(b) Duty to notify if matter not to be heard

The moving party must immediately notify the court if a matter will not be heard on the scheduled date.

(Subd (b) amended effective January 1, 2003.)

(c) Notice of nonappearance

A party may give notice that he or she will not appear at a law and motion hearing and submit the matter without an appearance unless the court orders otherwise. The court must rule on the motion as if the party had appeared.

(Subd (c) amended effective January 1, 2003; previously amended effective January 1, 1992.)

(d) Action if no party appears

If a party fails to appear at a law and motion hearing without having given notice under (c), the court may take the matter off calendar, to be reset only upon motion, or may rule on the matter.

(Subd (d) amended effective January 1, 2003; previously amended and relettered effective January 1, 1992.)

Rule 3.1304 amended effective January 1, 2016; adopted as rule 321 effective January 1, 1984; previously amended effective January 1, 1992, and January 1, 2003; amended and renumbered as rule 3.1304 effective January 1, 2007.

Rule 3.1306. Evidence at hearing

(a) Restrictions on oral testimony

Evidence received at a law and motion hearing must be by declaration or request for judicial notice without testimony or cross-examination, unless the court orders otherwise for good cause shown.

(Subd (a) amended effective January 1, 2007; previously amended effective January 1, 2003.)

(b) Request to present oral testimony

A party seeking permission to introduce oral evidence, except for oral evidence in rebuttal to oral evidence presented by the other party, must file, no later than three court days before the hearing, a written statement stating the nature and extent of the evidence proposed to be introduced and a reasonable time estimate for the hearing. When the statement is filed less than five court days before the hearing, the filing party must serve a copy on the other parties in a manner to assure delivery to the other parties no later than two days before the hearing.

(Subd (b) amended and relettered effective January 1, 2003; adopted as part of subd (a) effective January 1, 1984.)

(c) Judicial notice

A party requesting judicial notice of material under Evidence Code sections 452 or 453 must provide the court and each party with a copy of the material. If the material is part of a file in the court in which the matter is being heard, the party must:

(1) Specify in writing the part of the court file sought to be judicially noticed; and

(2) Either make arrangements with the clerk to have the file in the courtroom at the time of the hearing or confirm with the clerk that the file is electronically accessible to the court.

(Subd (c) amended effective January 1, 2017; adopted as subd (b) effective January 1, 1984; previously amended and relettered effective January 1, 2003; previously amended effective January 1, 2007.)

Rule 3.1306 amended effective January 1, 2017; adopted as rule 323 effective January 1, 1984; previously amended effective January 1, 2003; previously amended and renumbered effective January 1, 2007.

Rule 3.1308.   Tentative rulings

(a) Tentative ruling procedures

A trial court that offers a tentative ruling procedure in civil law and motion matters must follow one of the following procedures:

(1) *Notice of intent to appear required*

The court must make its tentative ruling available by telephone and also, at the option of the court, by any other method designated by the court, by no later than 3:00 p.m. the court day before the scheduled hearing. If the court desires oral argument, the tentative ruling must so direct. The tentative ruling may also note any issues on which the court wishes the parties to provide further argument. If the court has not directed argument, oral argument must be permitted only if a party notifies all other parties and the court by 4:00 p.m. on the court day before the hearing of the party's intention to appear. A party must notify all other parties by telephone or in person. The court must accept notice by telephone and, at its discretion, may also designate alternative methods by which a party may notify the court of the party's intention to appear. The tentative ruling will become the ruling of the court if the court has not directed oral argument by its tentative ruling and notice of intent to appear has not been given.

(2) *No notice of intent to appear required*

The court must make its tentative ruling available by telephone and also, at the option of the court, by any other method designated by the court, by a specified time before the hearing. The tentative ruling may note any issues on which the court wishes the parties to provide further argument at the hearing. This procedure must not require the parties to give notice of intent to appear, and the tentative ruling will not automatically become the ruling of the court if such notice is not given. The tentative ruling, or such other ruling as the court may render, will not become the final ruling of the court until the hearing.

(Subd (a) amended effective January 1, 2007; previously amended effective July 1, 2000.)

(b) No other procedures permitted

Other than following one of the tentative ruling procedures authorized in (a), courts must not issue tentative rulings except:

(1) By posting a calendar note containing tentative rulings on the day of the hearing; or

(2) By announcing the tentative ruling at the time of oral argument.

(Subd (b) amended effective January 1, 2007; previously repealed and adopted effective July 1, 2000.)

(c) Notice of procedure

A court that follows one of the procedures described in (a) must so state in its local rules. The local rule must specify the telephone number for obtaining the tentative rulings and the time by which the rulings will be available.

(Subd (c) amended effective January 1, 2007; previously amended effective July 1, 2000.)

(d) Uniform procedure within court or branch

If a court or a branch of a court adopts a tentative ruling procedure, that procedure must be used by all judges in the court or branch who issue tentative rulings.

(Subd (d) amended and lettered effective January 1, 2007; adopted as part of subd (c) effective July 1, 1992.)

(e) Tentative rulings not required

This rule does not require any judge to issue tentative rulings.

(Subd (e) amended and lettered effective January 1, 2007; adopted as part of subd (c) effective July 1, 1992.)

Rule 3.1308 amended and renumbered effective January 1, 2007; adopted as rule 324 effective July 1, 1992; previously amended effective July 1, 2000.

Rule 3.1310.   Reporting of proceedings on motions

A court that does not regularly provide for reporting or electronic recording of hearings on motions must so state in its local rules. The rules must also provide a procedure by which a party may obtain a reporter or a recording of the proceedings in order to provide an official verbatim transcript.

Rule 3.1310 amended and renumbered effective January 1, 2007; adopted as rule 324.5 effective January 1, 1992.

Rule 3.1312.   Preparation and submission of proposed order

(a) Prevailing party to prepare

Unless the parties waive notice or the court orders otherwise, the party prevailing on any motion must, within five days of the ruling, serve by any means authorized by law and reasonably calculated to ensure delivery to the other party or parties no later than the close of the next business day a proposed order for approval as conforming to the court's order. Within five days after service, the other party or parties must notify the prevailing party as to whether or not the proposed order is so approved. The opposing party or parties must state any reasons for disapproval. Failure to notify the prevailing party within the time required shall be deemed an approval. The extensions of time based on a method of service provided under any statute or rule do not apply to this rule.

(Subd (a) amended effective January 1, 2011; previously amended effective July 1, 2000, and January 1, 2007.)

(b) Submission of proposed order to court

The prevailing party must, upon expiration of the five-day period provided for approval, promptly transmit the proposed order to the court together with a summary of any responses of the other parties or a statement that no responses were received.

(Subd (b) amended effective January 1, 2007; previously amended effective July 1, 2000.)

(c) Submission of proposed order by electronic means

If a proposed order is submitted to the court electronically in a case in which the parties are electronically filing documents under rules 2.250–2.261, two versions of the proposed order must be submitted:

(1) A version of the proposed order must be attached to a completed *Proposed Order (Cover Sheet)* (form EFS-020), and the combined document in Portable Document Format (PDF) must be filed electronically; and

(2) A version of the proposed order in an editable word-processing format must also be sent electronically to the court, with a copy of the e-mail and proposed order also being sent to all parties in the action.

Each court that provides for electronic filing must provide an electronic address or addresses to which the editable versions of proposed orders are to be sent and must specify any particular requirements regarding the editable word-processing format for proposed orders.

(Subd (c) adopted effective January 1, 2011.)

(d) Failure of prevailing party to prepare proposed order

If the prevailing party fails to prepare and submit a proposed order as required by (a) and (b) above, any other party may do so.

(Subd (d) amended and relettered effective January 1, 2011; adopted as subd (c); previously amended effective July 1, 2000.)

(e) Motion unopposed

This rule does not apply if the motion was unopposed and a proposed order was submitted with the moving papers, unless otherwise ordered by the court.

(Subd (e) relettered effective January 1, 2011; adopted as subd (d) effective July 1, 2000; previously amended effective January 1, 2007.)

Rule 3.1312 amended effective January 1, 2011; adopted as rule 391 effective July 1, 1992; previously amended effective July 1, 2000; previously amended and renumbered effective January 1, 2007.

Chapter 6
Particular Motions

Article 1
Pleading and Venue Motions

Rule 3.1320. Demurrers

(a) Grounds separately stated

Each ground of demurrer must be in a separate paragraph and must state whether it applies to the entire complaint, cross-complaint, or answer, or to specified causes of action or defenses.

(Subd (a) amended effective January 1, 2007.)

(b) Demurrer not directed to all causes of action

A demurrer to a cause of action may be filed without answering other causes of action.

(Subd (b) adopted effective January 1, 2007.)

(c) Notice of hearing

A party filing a demurrer must serve and file therewith a notice of hearing that must specify a hearing date in accordance with the provisions of Code of Civil Procedure section 1005 and, if service is by electronic means, in accordance with the requirements of Code of Civil Procedure section 1010.6(a)(4) and rule 2.251(h)(2).

(Subd (c) amended effective January 1, 2016; adopted as subd (b) effective January 1, 1984; previously amended effective July 1, 2000; previously amended and relettered as subd (c) effective January 1, 2007.)

(d) Date of hearing

Demurrers must be set for hearing not more than 35 days following the filing of the demurrer or on the first date available to the court thereafter. For good cause shown, the court may order the hearing held on an earlier or later day on notice prescribed by the court.

(Subd (d) amended and lettered effective January 1, 2007; adopted as part of subd (b) effective January 1, 1984.)

(e) Caption

A demurrer must state, on the first page immediately below the number of the case, the name of the party filing the demurrer and the name of the party whose pleading is the subject of the demurrer.

(Subd (e) amended and relettered effective January 1, 2007; adopted as subd (c) effective January 1, 1984.)

(f) Failure to appear at hearing

When a demurrer is regularly called for hearing and one of the parties does not appear, the demurrer must be disposed of on the merits at the request of the party appearing unless for good cause the hearing is continued. Failure to appear in support of a special demurrer may be construed by the court as an admission that the demurrer is not meritorious and as a waiver of all grounds thereof. If neither party appears, the demurrer may be disposed of on its merits or dropped from the calendar, to be restored on notice or on terms as the court may deem proper, or the hearing may be continued to such time as the court orders.

(Subd (f) amended and relettered effective January 1, 2007; adopted as subd (d) effective January 1, 1984.)

(g) Leave to answer or amend

Following a ruling on a demurrer, unless otherwise ordered, leave to answer or amend within 10 days is deemed granted, except for actions in forcible entry, forcible detainer, or unlawful detainer in which case 5 calendar days is deemed granted.

(Subd (g) amended and relettered effective January 1, 2007; adopted as subd (e) effective January 1, 1984.)

(h) Ex parte application to dismiss following failure to amend

A motion to dismiss the entire action and for entry of judgment after expiration of the time to amend following the sustaining of a demurrer may be made by ex parte application to the court under Code of Civil Procedure section 581(f)(2).

(Subd (h) amended and relettered effective January 1, 2007; adopted as subd (f) effective January 1, 1984; previously amended effective July 1, 1995.)

(i) Motion to strike late-filed amended pleading

If an amended pleading is filed after the time allowed, an order striking the amended pleading must be obtained by noticed motion under Code of Civil Procedure section 1010.

(Subd (i) amended effective January 1, 2009; adopted as part of subd (f) effective January 1, 1984; previously amended effective July 1, 1995; previously amended and lettered effective January 1, 2007.)

(j) Time to respond after demurrer

Unless otherwise ordered, defendant has 10 days to answer or otherwise plead to the complaint or the remaining causes of action following:

(1) The overruling of the demurrer;

(2) The expiration of the time to amend if the demurrer was sustained with leave to amend; or

(3) The sustaining of the demurrer if the demurrer was sustained without leave to amend.

(Subd (j) amended effective January 1, 2011; adopted as subd (g) effective July 1, 1984; previously amended and relettered effective January 1, 2007.)

Rule 3.1320 amended effective January 1, 2016; adopted as rule 325 effective January 1, 1984; previously amended and renumbered as rule 3.1320 effective January 1, 2007; previously amended effective July 1, 1984, July 1, 1995, July 1, 2000, January 1, 2009, and January 1, 2011.

Rule 3.1322. Motions to strike

(a) Contents of notice

A notice of motion to strike a portion of a pleading must quote in full the portions sought to be stricken except where the motion is to strike an entire paragraph, cause of action, count, or defense. Specifications in a notice must be numbered consecutively.

(Subd (a) amended and lettered effective January 1, 2007; adopted as part of untitled subd effective January 1, 1984.)

(b) Timing

A notice of motion to strike must be given within the time allowed to plead, and if a demurrer is interposed, concurrently therewith, and must be noticed for hearing and heard at the same time as the demurrer.

(Subd (b) amended and lettered effective January 1, 2007; adopted as part of untitled subd effective January 1, 1984.)

Rule 3.1322 amended and renumbered effective January 1, 2007; adopted as rule 329 effective January 1, 1984.

Rule 3.1324. Amended pleadings and amendments to pleadings

(a) Contents of motion

A motion to amend a pleading before trial must:

(1) Include a copy of the proposed amendment or amended pleading, which must be serially numbered to differentiate it from previous pleadings or amendments;

(2) State what allegations in the previous pleading are proposed to be deleted, if any, and where, by page, paragraph, and line number, the deleted allegations are located; and

(3) State what allegations are proposed to be added to the previous pleading, if any, and where, by page, paragraph, and line number, the additional allegations are located.

(Subd (a) amended effective January 1, 2002.)

(b) Supporting declaration

A separate declaration must accompany the motion and must specify:

(1) The effect of the amendment;

(2) Why the amendment is necessary and proper;

(3) When the facts giving rise to the amended allegations were discovered; and

(4) The reasons why the request for amendment was not made earlier.

(Subd (b) adopted effective January 1, 2002.)

(c) Form of amendment

The court may deem a motion to file an amendment to a pleading to be a motion to file an amended pleading and require the filing of the entire previous pleading with the approved amendments incorporated into it.

(Subd (c) adopted effective January 1, 2002.)

(d) Requirements for amendment to a pleading

An amendment to a pleading must not be made by alterations on the face of a pleading except by permission of the court. All alterations must be initialed by the court or the clerk.

(Subd (d) amended and relettered effective January 1, 2002; adopted as subd (b) effective January 1, 1984.)

Rule 3.1324 renumbered effective January 1, 2007; adopted as rule 327 effective January 1, 1984; previously amended effective January 1, 2002.

Rule 3.1326.   Motions for change of venue

Following denial of a motion to transfer under Code of Civil Procedure section 396b, unless otherwise ordered, 30 calendar days are deemed granted defendant to move to strike, demur, or otherwise plead if the defendant has not previously filed a response. If a motion to transfer is granted, 30 calendar days are deemed granted from the date the receiving court sends notice of receipt of the case and its new case number.

Rule 3.1326 amended effective January 1, 2016; adopted as rule 326 effective January 1, 1984; previously amended effective July 1, 1984; previously amended and renumbered as rule 3.1326 effective January 1, 2007.

Rule 3.1327.   Motions to quash or to stay action in summary proceeding involving possession of real property

(a) Notice

In an unlawful detainer action or other action brought under chapter 4 of title 3 of part 3 of the Code of Civil Procedure (commencing with section 1159), notice of a motion to quash service of summons on the ground of lack of jurisdiction or to stay or dismiss the action on the ground of inconvenient forum must be given in compliance with Code of Civil Procedure sections 1010.6 or 1013 and 1167.4.

(Subd (a) amended effective January 1, 2016; adopted effective January 1, 2009.)

(b) Opposition and reply at hearing

Any opposition to the motion and any reply to an opposition may be made orally at the time of hearing or in writing as set forth in (c).

(Subd (b) adopted effective January 1, 2009.)

(c) Written opposition in advance of hearing

If a party seeks to have a written opposition considered in advance of the hearing, the written opposition must be filed and served on or before the court day before the hearing. Service must be by personal delivery, electronic service, fax transmission, express mail, or other means consistent with Code of Civil Procedure sections 1010, 1010.6, 1011, 1012, and 1013, and reasonably calculated to ensure delivery to the other party or parties no later than the close of business on the court day before the hearing. The court, in its discretion, may consider written opposition filed later.

(Subd (c) amended effective January 1, 2016; adopted effective January 1, 2009.)

Rule 3.1327 amended effective January 1, 2016; adopted effective January 1, 2009.

Article 2
Procedural Motions

Rule 3.1330. Motion concerning arbitration
Rule 3.1332. Motion or application for continuance of trial
Rule 3.1335. Motion or application to advance, specially set, or reset trial date

Rule 3.1330.   Motion concerning arbitration

A petition to compel arbitration or to stay proceedings pursuant to Code of Civil Procedure sections 1281.2 and 1281.4 must state, in addition to other required allegations, the provisions of the written agreement and the paragraph that provides for arbitration. The provisions must be stated verbatim or a copy must be physically or electronically attached to the petition and incorporated by reference.

Rule 3.1330 amended effective January 1, 2016; adopted as rule 371 effective January 1, 1984; previously amended and renumbered as rule 3.1330 effective January 1, 2007.

Rule 3.1332.   Motion or application for continuance of trial

(a) Trial dates are firm

To ensure the prompt disposition of civil cases, the dates assigned for a trial are firm. All parties and their counsel must regard the date set for trial as certain.

(Subd (a) repealed and adopted effective January 1, 2004; amended effective January 1, 1995.)

(b) Motion or application

A party seeking a continuance of the date set for trial, whether contested or uncontested or stipulated to by the parties, must make the request for a continuance by a noticed motion or an ex parte application under the rules in chapter 4 of this division, with supporting declarations. The party must make the motion or application as soon as reasonably practical once the necessity for the continuance is discovered.

(Subd (b) amended effective January 1, 2007; previously amended effective January 1, 1995.)

(c) Grounds for continuance

Although continuances of trials are disfavored, each request for a continuance must be considered on its own merits. The court may grant a continuance only on an affirmative showing of good cause requiring the continuance. Circumstances that may indicate good cause include:

(1) The unavailability of an essential lay or expert witness because of death, illness, or other excusable circumstances;

(2) The unavailability of a party because of death, illness, or other excusable circumstances;

(3) The unavailability of trial counsel because of death, illness, or other excusable circumstances;

(4) The substitution of trial counsel, but only where there is an affirmative showing that the substitution is required in the interests of justice;

(5) The addition of a new party if:

(A) The new party has not had a reasonable opportunity to conduct discovery and prepare for trial; or

(B) The other parties have not had a reasonable opportunity to conduct discovery and prepare for trial in regard to the new party's involvement in the case;

(6) A party's excused inability to obtain essential testimony, documents, or other material evidence despite diligent efforts; or

(7) A significant, unanticipated change in the status of the case as a result of which the case is not ready for trial.

(Subd (c) amended effective January 1, 2007; adopted effective January 1, 2004.)

(d) Other factors to be considered

In ruling on a motion or application for continuance, the court must consider all the facts and circumstances that are relevant to the determination. These may include:

(1) The proximity of the trial date;

(2) Whether there was any previous continuance, extension of time, or delay of trial due to any party;

(3) The length of the continuance requested;

(4) The availability of alternative means to address the problem that gave rise to the motion or application for a continuance;

(5) The prejudice that parties or witnesses will suffer as a result of the continuance;

(6) If the case is entitled to a preferential trial setting, the reasons for that status and whether the need for a continuance outweighs the need to avoid delay;

(7) The court's calendar and the impact of granting a continuance on other pending trials;

(8) Whether trial counsel is engaged in another trial;

(9) Whether all parties have stipulated to a continuance;

(10) Whether the interests of justice are best served by a continuance, by the trial of the matter, or by imposing conditions on the continuance; and

(11) Any other fact or circumstance relevant to the fair determination of the motion or application.

(Subd (d) adopted effective January 1, 2004.)

Rule 3.1332 amended and renumbered effective January 1, 2007; adopted as rule 375 effective January 1, 1984; previously amended effective January 1, 1985, January 1, 1995, and January 1, 2004.

Rule 3.1335.   Motion or application to advance, specially set, or reset trial date

(a) Noticed motion or application required

A party seeking to advance, specially set, or reset a case for trial must make this request by noticed motion or ex parte application under the rules in chapter 4 of this division.

(Subd (a) amended effective January 1, 2007.)

(b) Grounds for motion or application

The request may be granted only upon an affirmative showing by the moving party of good cause based on a declaration served and filed with the motion or application.

Rule 3.1335 amended and renumbered effective January 1, 2007; adopted as rule 375.1 effective January 1, 2004.

Article 3
Motions to Dismiss

Rule 3.1340. Motion for discretionary dismissal after two years for delay in prosecution
Rule 3.1342. Motion to dismiss for delay in prosecution

Rule 3.1340.   Motion for discretionary dismissal after two years for delay in prosecution

(a) Discretionary dismissal two years after filing

The court on its own motion or on motion of the defendant may dismiss an action under Code of Civil Procedure sections 583.410–583.430 for delay in prosecution if the action has not been brought to trial or conditionally settled within two years after the action was commenced against the defendant.

(Subd (a) amended effective January 1, 2007.)

(b) Notice of court's intention to dismiss

If the court intends to dismiss an action on its own motion, the clerk must set a hearing on the dismissal and send notice to all parties at least 20 days before the hearing date.

(Subd (b) amended effective January 1, 2016; adopted as part of subd (a) effective January 1, 1990; previously amended and lettered as subd (b) effective January 1, 2007.)

(c) Definition of "conditionally settled"

"Conditionally settled" means:

(1) A settlement agreement conditions dismissal on the satisfactory completion of specified terms that are not to be fully performed within two years after the filing of the case; and

(2) Notice of the settlement is filed with the court as provided in rule 3.1385.

(Subd (c) amended and lettered effective January 1, 2007; adopted as part of subd (a) effective January 1, 1990.)

Rule 3.1340 amended effective January 1, 2016; adopted as rule 372 effective January 1, 1990; previously amended and renumbered as rule 3.1340 effective January 1, 2007.

Rule 3.1342. Motion to dismiss for delay in prosecution

(a) Notice of motion

A party seeking dismissal of a case under Code of Civil Procedure sections 583.410–583.430 must serve and file a notice of motion at least 45 days before the date set for hearing of the motion. The party may, with the memorandum, serve and file a declaration stating facts in support of the motion. The filing of the notice of motion must not preclude the opposing party from further prosecution of the case to bring it to trial.

(Subd (a) amended effective January 1, 2009; previously amended effective January 1, 1986, and January 1, 2007.)

(b) Written opposition

Within 15 days after service of the notice of motion, the opposing party may serve and file a written opposition. The failure of the opposing party to serve and file a written opposition may be construed by the court as an admission that the motion is meritorious, and the court may grant the motion without a hearing on the merits.

(Subd (b) amended effective January 1, 2007.)

(c) Response to opposition

Within 15 days after service of the written opposition, if any, the moving party may serve and file a response.

(Subd (c) amended effective January 1, 2007.)

(d) Reply

Within five days after service of the response, if any, the opposing party may serve and file a reply.

(e) Relevant matters

In ruling on the motion, the court must consider all matters relevant to a proper determination of the motion, including:

(1) The court's file in the case and the declarations and supporting data submitted by the parties and, where applicable, the availability of the moving party and other essential parties for service of process;

(2) The diligence in seeking to effect service of process;

(3) The extent to which the parties engaged in any settlement negotiations or discussions;

(4) The diligence of the parties in pursuing discovery or other pretrial proceedings, including any extraordinary relief sought by either party;

(5) The nature and complexity of the case;

(6) The law applicable to the case, including the pendency of other litigation under a common set of facts or determinative of the legal or factual issues in the case;

(7) The nature of any extensions of time or other delay attributable to either party;

(8) The condition of the court's calendar and the availability of an earlier trial date if the matter was ready for trial;

(9) Whether the interests of justice are best served by dismissal or trial of the case; and

(10) Any other fact or circumstance relevant to a fair determination of the issue.

The court must be guided by the policies set forth in Code of Civil Procedure section 583.130.

(Subd (e) amended effective January 1, 2007; previously amended effective January 1, 1986.)

(f) Court action

The court may grant or deny the motion or, where the facts warrant, the court may continue or defer its ruling on the matter pending performance by either party of any conditions relating to trial or dismissal of the case that may be required by the court to effectuate substantial justice.

Rule 3.1342 amended effective January 1, 2009; adopted as rule 373 effective January 1, 1984; previously amended effective January 1, 1986; previously amended and renumbered effective January 1, 2007.

Article 4
Discovery Motions

Title 3, Civil Rules—Division 11, Law and Motion—Chapter 6, Particular Motions—Article 4, Discovery Motions adopted effective January 1, 2009.

Rule 3.1345. Format of discovery motions
Rule 3.1346. Service of motion papers on nonparty deponent
Rule 3.1347. Discovery motions in summary proceeding involving possession of real property
Rule 3.1348. Sanctions for failure to provide discovery

Rule 3.1345.   Format of discovery motions

(a) Separate statement required

Except as provided in (b), any motion involving the content of a discovery request or the responses to such a request must be accompanied by a separate statement. The motions that require a separate statement include a motion:

(1) To compel further responses to requests for admission;

(2) To compel further responses to interrogatories;

(3) To compel further responses to a demand for inspection of documents or tangible things;

(4) To compel answers at a deposition;

(5) To compel or to quash the production of documents or tangible things at a deposition;

(6) For medical examination over objection; and

(7) For issue or evidentiary sanctions.

(Subd (a) amended effective January 1, 2020; previously amended effective July 1, 1987, January 1, 1992, January 1, 1997, July 1, 2001, and January 1, 2007.)

(b) Separate statement not required

A separate statement is not required **under the following circumstances:**

(1) When no response has been provided to the request for discovery; or

(2) When a court has allowed the moving party to submit—in place of a separate statement—a concise outline of the discovery request and each response in dispute.

(Subd (b) amended effective January 1, 2020; adopted effective July 1, 2001.)

(c) Contents of separate statement

A separate statement is a separate document filed and served with the discovery motion that provides all the information necessary to understand each discovery request and all the responses to it that are at issue. The separate statement must be full and complete so that no person is required to review any other document in order to determine the full request and the full response. Material must not be incorporated into the separate statement by reference. The separate statement must include—for each discovery request (e.g., each interrogatory, request for admission, deposition question, or inspection demand) to which a further response, answer, or production is requested—the following:

(1) The text of the request, interrogatory, question, or inspection demand;

(2) The text of each response, answer, or objection, and any further responses or answers;

(3) A statement of the factual and legal reasons for compelling further responses, answers, or production as to each matter in dispute;

(4) If necessary, the text of all definitions, instructions, and other matters required to understand each discovery request and the responses to it;

(5) If the response to a particular discovery request is dependent on the response given to another discovery request, or if the reasons a further response to a particular discovery request is deemed necessary are based on the response to some other discovery request, the other request and the response to it must be set forth; and

(6) If the pleadings, other documents in the file, or other items of discovery are relevant to the motion, the party relying on them must summarize each relevant document.

(Subd (c) amended effective January 1, 2007; previously repealed and adopted effective July 1, 2001.)

(d) Identification of interrogatories, demands, or requests

A motion concerning interrogatories, inspection demands, or admission requests must identify the interrogatories, demands, or requests by set and number.

(Subd (d) amended effective January 1, 2007; adopted as subd (b) effective January 1, 1984; previously amended effective July 1, 1987; previously relettered effective July 1, 2001.)

Rule 3.1345 amended effective January 1, 2020; adopted as rule 335 effective January 1, 1984; previously amended effective July 1, 1987, January 1, 1992, January 1, 1997, and July 1, 2001; previously amended and renumbered as rule 3.1020 effective January 1, 2007; previously renumbered as rule 3.1345 effective January 1, 2009.

Rule 3.1346. Service of motion papers on nonparty deponent

A written notice and all moving papers supporting a motion to compel an answer to a deposition question or to compel production of a document or tangible thing from a nonparty deponent must be personally served on the nonparty deponent unless the nonparty deponent agrees to accept service by mail or electronic service at an address or electronic service address specified on the deposition record.

Rule 3.1346 amended effective January 1, 2016; adopted as rule 337 effective January 1, 1984; previously amended effective July 1, 1987; previously amended and renumbered as rule 3.1025 effective January 1, 2007; previously renumbered as rule 3.1346 effective January 1, 2009.

Rule 3.1347. Discovery motions in summary proceeding involving possession of real property

(a) Notice

In an unlawful detainer action or other action brought under chapter 4 of title 3 of part 3 of the Code of Civil Procedure (commencing with section 1159), notice of a discovery motion must be given in compliance with Code of Civil Procedure sections 1010.6 or 1013 and 1170.8.

(Subd (a) amended effective January 1, 2016; adopted effective January 1, 2009.)

(b) Opposition and reply at hearing

Any opposition to the motion and any reply to an opposition may be made orally at the time of hearing or in writing as set forth in (c).

(Subd (b) adopted effective January 1, 2009.)

(c) Written opposition in advance of hearing

If a party seeks to have a written opposition considered in advance of the hearing, the written opposition must be served and filed on or before the court day before the hearing. Service must be by personal delivery, electronic service, fax transmission, express mail, or other means consistent with Code of Civil Procedure sections 1010, 1010.6, 1011, 1012, and 1013, and reasonably calculated to ensure delivery to the other party or parties no later than the close of business on the court day before the hearing. The court, in its discretion, may consider written opposition filed later.

(Subd (c) amended effective January 1, 2016; adopted effective January 1, 2009.)

Rule 3.1347 amended effective January 1, 2016; adopted effective January 1, 2009.

Rule 3.1348. Sanctions for failure to provide discovery

(a) Sanctions despite no opposition

The court may award sanctions under the Discovery Act in favor of a party who files a motion to compel discovery, even though no opposition to the motion was filed, or opposition to the motion was withdrawn, or the requested discovery was provided to the moving party after the motion was filed.

(b) Failure to oppose not an admission

The failure to file a written opposition or to appear at a hearing or the voluntary provision of discovery shall not be deemed an admission that the motion was proper or that sanctions should be awarded.

Rule 3.1348 renumbered effective January 1, 2009; adopted as rule 341 effective July 1, 2001; previously renumbered as rule 3.1030 effective January 1, 2007.

Article 5
Summary Judgment Motions

Title 3, Civil Rules—Division 11, Law and Motion—Chapter 6, Particular Motions—Article 5, Summary Judgment Motions renumbered effective January 1, 2009; adopted as article 4 effective January 1, 2007.

Rule 3.1350. Motion for summary judgment or summary adjudication
Rule 3.1351. Motions for summary judgment in summary proceeding involving possession of real property

Rule 3.1352. Objections to evidence
Rule 3.1354. Written objections to evidence

Rule 3.1350. Motion for summary judgment or summary adjudication

(a) Definitions

As used in this rule:

(1) "Motion" refers to either a motion for summary judgment or a motion for summary adjudication.

(2) "Material facts" are facts that relate to the cause of action, claim for damages, issue of duty, or affirmative defense that is the subject of the motion and that could make a difference in the disposition of the motion.

(Subd (a) amended effective January 1, 2016.)

(b) Motion for summary adjudication

If made in the alternative, a motion for summary adjudication may make reference to and depend on the same evidence submitted in support of the summary judgment motion. If summary adjudication is sought, whether separately or as an alternative to the motion for summary judgment, the specific cause of action, affirmative defense, claims for damages, or issues of duty must be stated specifically in the notice of motion and be repeated, verbatim, in the separate statement of undisputed material facts.

(Subd (b) amended effective January 1, 2007; previously amended effective January 1, 2002.)

(c) Documents in support of motion

Except as provided in Code of Civil Procedure section 437c(r) and rule 3.1351, the motion must contain and be supported by the following documents:

(1) Notice of motion by *[moving party]* for summary judgment or summary adjudication or both;

(2) Separate statement of undisputed material facts in support of *[moving party's]* motion for summary judgment or summary adjudication or both;

(3) Memorandum in support of *[moving party's]* motion for summary judgment or summary adjudication or both;

(4) Evidence in support of *[moving party's]* motion for summary judgment or summary adjudication or both; and

(5) Request for judicial notice in support of *[moving party's]* motion for summary judgment or summary adjudication or both (if appropriate).

(Subd (c) amended effective January 1, 2009; previously amended effective January 1, 2002, and January 1, 2007.)

(d) Separate statement in support of motion

(1) The Separate Statement of Undisputed Material Facts in support of a motion must separately identify:

(A) Each cause of action, claim for damages, issue of duty, or affirmative defense that is the subject of the motion; and

(B) Each supporting material fact claimed to be without dispute with respect to the cause of action, claim for damages, issue of duty, or affirmative defense that is the subject of the motion.

(2) The separate statement should include only material facts and not any facts that are not pertinent to the disposition of the motion.

(3) The separate statement must be in the two-column format specified in (h). The statement must state in numerical sequence the undisputed material facts in the first column followed by the evidence that establishes those undisputed facts in that same column. Citation to the evidence in support of each material fact must include reference to the exhibit, title, page, and line numbers.

(Subd (d) amended effective January 1, 2016; previously amended effective January 1, 2002, January 1, 2007, and January 1, 2008.)

(e) Documents in opposition to motion

Except as provided in Code of Civil Procedure section 437c(r) and rule 3.1351, the opposition to a motion must consist of the following separate documents, titled as shown:

(1) *[Opposing party's]* memorandum in opposition to *[moving party's]* motion for summary judgment or summary adjudication or both;

(2) *[Opposing party's]* separate statement in opposition to *[moving party's]* motion for summary judgment or summary adjudication or both;

(3) *[Opposing party's]* evidence in opposition to *[moving party's]* motion for summary judgment or summary adjudication or both (if appropriate); and

(4) *[Opposing party's]* request for judicial notice in opposition to *[moving party's]* motion for summary judgment or summary adjudication or both (if appropriate).

Rules of Court

(Subd (e) amended effective January 1, 2016; previously amended effective January 1, 2002, January 1, 2007, and January 1, 2009.)

(f) Content of separate statement in opposition to motion

The Separate Statement in Opposition to Motion must be in the two-column format specified in (h).

(1) Each material fact claimed by the moving party to be undisputed must be set out verbatim on the left side of the page, below which must be set out the evidence said by the moving party to establish that fact, complete with the moving party's references to exhibits.

(2) On the right side of the page, directly opposite the recitation of the moving party's statement of material facts and supporting evidence, the response must unequivocally state whether that fact is "disputed" or "undisputed." An opposing party who contends that a fact is disputed must state, on the right side of the page directly opposite the fact in dispute, the nature of the dispute and describe the evidence that supports the position that the fact is controverted. Citation to the evidence in support of the position that a fact is controverted must include reference to the exhibit, title, page, and line numbers.

(3) If the opposing party contends that additional material facts are pertinent to the disposition of the motion, those facts must be set forth in the separate statement. The separate statement should include only material facts and not any facts that are not pertinent to the disposition of the motion. Each fact must be followed by the evidence that establishes the fact. Citation to the evidence in support of each material fact must include reference to the exhibit, title, page, and line numbers.

(Subd (f) amended effective January 1, 2016; previously amended effective January 1, 2002.)

(g) Documentary evidence

If evidence in support of or in opposition to a motion exceeds 25 pages, the evidence must be separately bound and must include a table of contents.

(Subd (g) amended effective January 1, 2007; previously amended effective January 1, 2002.)

(h) Format for separate statements

Supporting and opposing separate statements in a motion for summary judgment must follow this format:

Supporting statement:

Moving Party's Undisputed Material Facts and Supporting Evidence:	Opposing Party's Response and Supporting Evidence:
1. Plaintiff and defendant entered into a written contract for the sale of widgets. Jackson declaration, 2:17–21; contract, Ex. A to Jackson declaration.	
2. No widgets were ever received. Jackson declaration, 3:7–21.	

Opposing statement:

Moving Party's Undisputed Material Facts and Alleged Supporting Evidence:	Opposing Party's Response and Evidence:
1. Plaintiff and defendant entered into a written contract for the sale of widgets. Jackson declaration, 2:17–21; contract, Ex. A to Jackson declaration.	Undisputed.
2. No widgets were ever received. Jackson declaration, 3:7–21.	Disputed. The widgets were received in New Zealand on August 31, 2001. Baygi declaration, 7:2–5.

Supporting and opposing separate statements in a motion for summary adjudication must follow this format:

Supporting statement:

ISSUE 1—THE FIRST CAUSE OF ACTION FOR NEGLIGENCE IS BARRED BECAUSE PLAINTIFF EXPRESSLY ASSUMED THE RISK OF INJURY

Moving Party's Undisputed Material Facts and Supporting Evidence:	Opposing Party's Response and Supporting Evidence:
1. Plaintiff was injured while mountain climbing on a trip with Any Company USA. Plaintiff's deposition, 12:3–4.	
2. Before leaving on the mountain climbing trip, plaintiff signed a waiver of liability for acts of negligence. Smith declaration, 5:4–5; waiver of liability, Ex. A to Smith declaration.	

Opposing statement:

ISSUE 1—THE FIRST CAUSE OF ACTION FOR NEGLIGENCE IS BARRED BECAUSE PLAINTIFF EXPRESSLY ASSUMED THE RISK OF INJURY

Moving Party's Undisputed Material Facts and Alleged Supporting Evidence:	Opposing Party's Response and Evidence:
1. Plaintiff was injured while mountain climbing on a trip with Any Company USA. Plaintiff's deposition, 12:3–4.	Undisputed.
2. Before leaving on the mountain climbing trip, plaintiff signed a waiver of liability for acts of negligence. Smith declaration, 5:4–5; waiver of liability, Ex. A to Smith declaration.	Disputed. Plaintiff did not sign the waiver of liability; the signature on the waiver is forged. Jones declaration, 3:6–7.

(Subd (h) amended effective July 1, 2008; previously amended effective January 1, 1999, January 1, 2002, and January 1, 2008.)

(i) Request for electronic version of separate statement

On request, a party must within three days provide to any other party or the court an electronic version of its separate statement. The electronic version may be provided in any form on which the parties agree. If the parties are unable to agree on the form, the responding party must provide to the requesting party the electronic version of the separate statement that it used to prepare the document filed with the court. Under this subdivision, a party is not required to create an electronic version or any new version of any document for the purpose of transmission to the requesting party.

(Subd (i) amended effective January 1, 2007; adopted effective January 1, 2002.)
Rule 3.1350 amended effective January 1, 2016; adopted as rule 342 effective July 1, 1997; previously amended and renumbered as rule 3.1350 effective January 1, 2007; previously amended effective January 1, 1999, January 1, 2002, January 1, 2008, July 1, 2008, and January 1, 2009.

Advisory Committee Comment

Subdivision (a)(2). This definition is derived from statements in *L.A. Nat. Bank v. Bank of Canton* (1991) 229 Cal. App. 3d 1267, 1274 ("In order to prevent the imposition of a summary judgment, the disputed facts must be 'material,' i.e., relate to a claim or defense in issue which could make a difference in the outcome.") and *Reid v. Google, Inc.* (2010) 50 Cal.4th 512, 532-533 (Parties are encouraged "to raise only meritorious objections to items of evidence that are legitimately in dispute and pertinent to the disposition of the summary judgment motion.")

Subdivisions (d)(2) and (f)(3). Consistent with *Reid, supra*, these provisions are intended to eliminate from separate statements facts that are not material, and, thereby reduce the number of unnecessary objections to evidence.

Rule 3.1351. Motions for summary judgment in summary proceeding involving possession of real property

(a) Notice

In an unlawful detainer action or other action brought under chapter 4 of title 3 of part 3 of the Code of Civil Procedure (commencing with section 1159), notice of a motion for summary judgment must be given in compliance with Code of Civil Procedure sections 1010.6 or 1013 and 1170.7.

(Subd (a) amended effective January 1, 2016; adopted effective January 1, 2009.)

(b) Opposition and reply at hearing

Any opposition to the motion and any reply to an opposition may be made orally at the time of hearing or in writing as set forth in (c).

(Subd (b) adopted effective January 1, 2009.)

(c) Written opposition in advance of hearing

If a party seeks to have a written opposition considered in advance of the hearing, the written opposition must be filed and served on or before the court day before the hearing. Service must be by personal delivery, electronic service, fax transmission, express mail, or other means consistent with Code of Civil Procedure sections 1010, 1010.6, 1011, 1012, and 1013, and reasonably calculated to ensure delivery to the other party or parties no later than the close of business on the court day before the hearing. The court, in its discretion, may consider written opposition filed later.

(Subd (c) amended effective January 1, 2016; adopted effective January 1, 2009.)
Rule 3.1351 amended effective January 1, 2016; adopted effective January 1, 2009.

Rule 3.1352. Objections to evidence

A party desiring to make objections to evidence in the papers on a motion for summary judgment must either:

(1) Submit objections in writing under rule 3.1354; or

(2) Make arrangements for a court reporter to be present at the hearing.

Rule 3.1352 amended and renumbered effective January 1, 2007; adopted as rule 343 effective January 1, 1984; previously amended effective January 1, 2002.

Rule 3.1354. Written objections to evidence

(a) Time for filing and service of objections

Unless otherwise excused by the court on a showing of good cause, all written objections to evidence in support of or in opposition to a motion for summary judgment or summary adjudication must be served and filed at the same time as the objecting party's opposition or reply papers are served and filed.

(Subd (a) repealed, amended, and relettered effective January 1, 2007; adopted as untitled subd effective January 1, 1984; previously amended and lettered subd (b) effective January 1, 2007.)

(b) Format of objections

All written objections to evidence must be served and filed separately from the other papers in support of or in opposition to the motion. Objections to specific evidence must be referenced by the objection number in the right column of a separate statement in opposition or reply to a motion, but the objections must not be restated or reargued in the separate statement. Each written objection must be numbered consecutively and must:

(1) Identify the name of the document in which the specific material objected to is located;

(2) State the exhibit, title, page, and line number of the material objected to;

(3) Quote or set forth the objectionable statement or material; and

(4) State the grounds for each objection to that statement or material.

Written objections to evidence must follow one of the following two formats:

(First Format):

Objections to Jackson Declaration

Objection Number 1

"Johnson told me that no widgets were ever received." (Jackson declaration, page 3, lines 7–8.)

Grounds for Objection 1: Hearsay (Evid. Code, § 1200); lack of personal knowledge (Evid. Code, § 702(a)).

(Second Format):

Objections to Jackson Declaration

Material Objected to:	Grounds for Objection:
1. Jackson declaration, page 3, lines 7–8: "Johnson told me that no widgets were ever received."	Hearsay (Evid. Code, § 1200); lack of personal knowledge (Evid. Code, § 702(a)).

(Subd (b) amended effective January 1, 2016; adopted effective January 1, 2007.)

(c) Proposed order

A party submitting written objections to evidence must submit with the objections a proposed order. The proposed order must include places for the court to indicate whether it has sustained or overruled each objection. It must also include a place for the signature of the judge. The court may require that the proposed order be provided in electronic form. The proposed order must be in one of the following two formats:

(First Format):

Objections to Jackson Declaration

Objection Number 1

"Johnson told me that no widgets were ever received." (Jackson declaration, page 3, lines 7–8.)

Grounds for Objection 1: Hearsay (Evid. Code, § 1200); lack of personal knowledge (Evid. Code, § 702(a)).

Court's Ruling on Objection 1:   Sustained: _____

(Second Format):   Overruled: _____

Objections to Jackson Declaration

Material Objected to:	**Grounds for Objection:**	**Ruling on the Objection:**
1. Jackson declaration, page 3, lines 7–8: "Johnson told me that no widgets were ever received."	Hearsay (Evid. Code, §1200); lack of personal knowledge (Evid. Code, § 702(a)).	Sustained: _____ Overruled: _____

Date: _____   Judge

(Subd (c) amended effective January 1, 2016; adopted effective January 1, 2007.)

Rule 3.1354 amended effective January 1, 2016; adopted as rule 345 effective January 1, 1984; previously amended and renumbered as rule 3.1354 effective January 1, 2007; previously amended effective January 1, 2002, and January 1, 2007.

Article 6
Miscellaneous Motions

Title 3, Civil Rules—Division 11, Law and Motion—Chapter 6, Particular Motions—Article 6, Miscellaneous Motions renumbered effective January 1, 2009; adopted as article 5 effective January 1, 2007.

Rule 3.1360. Motion to grant lien on cause of action
Rule 3.1362. Motion to be relieved as counsel

Rule 3.1360.   Motion to grant lien on cause of action

A motion that a lien be granted on a cause of action, right to relief, or judgment must be accompanied by an authenticated record of the judgment on which the judgment creditor relies and a declaration as to the identity of the party involved and the amount due.

Rule 3.1360 amended and renumbered effective January 1, 2007; adopted as rule 369 effective January 1, 1984.

Rule 3.1362.   Motion to be relieved as counsel

(a) Notice

A notice of motion and motion to be relieved as counsel under Code of Civil Procedure section 284(2) must be directed to the client and must be made on the *Notice of Motion and Motion to Be Relieved as Counsel— Civil* (form MC-051).

(Subd (a) amended effective January 1, 2007; previously amended effective July 1, 2000.)

(b) Memorandum

Notwithstanding any other rule of court, no memorandum is required to be filed or served with a motion to be relieved as counsel.

(Subd (b) amended effective January 1, 2007; adopted effective July 1, 2000.)

(c) Declaration

The motion to be relieved as counsel must be accompanied by a declaration on the *Declaration in Support of Attorney's Motion to Be Relieved as Counsel—Civil* (form MC-052). The declaration must state in general terms and without compromising the confidentiality of the attorney-client relationship why a motion under Code of Civil Procedure section 284(2) is brought instead of filing a consent under Code of Civil Procedure section 284(1).

(Subd (c) amended effective January 1, 2007; adopted as subd (b) effective July 1, 1984; previously relettered and amended effective July 1, 2000.)

(d) Service

The notice of motion and motion, the declaration, and the proposed order must be served on the client and on all other parties who have appeared in the case. The notice may be by personal service, electronic service, or mail.

(1) If the notice is served on the client by mail under Code of Civil Procedure section 1013, it must be accompanied by a declaration stating facts showing that either:

(A) The service address is the current residence or business address of the client; or

(B) The service address is the last known residence or business address of the client and the attorney has been unable to locate a more current address after making reasonable efforts to do so within 30 days before the filing of the motion to be relieved.

(2) If the notice is served on the client by electronic service under Code of Civil Procedure section 1010.6 and rule 2.251, it must be accompanied by a declaration stating that the electronic service address is the client's current electronic service address.

As used in this rule, "current" means that the address was confirmed within 30 days before the filing of the motion to be relieved. Merely demonstrating that the notice was sent to the client's last known address and was not returned or no electronic delivery failure message was received is not, by itself, sufficient to demonstrate that the address is current. If the service is by mail, Code of Civil Procedure section 1011(b) applies.

(Subd (d) amended effective January 1, 2017; adopted as subd (c) effective July 1, 1984; previously amended effective July 1, 1991, January 1, 1996, January 1, 2007, and January 1, 2009; previously relettered and amended effective July 1, 2000.)

(e) Order

The proposed order relieving counsel must be prepared on the *Order Granting Attorney's Motion to Be Relieved as Counsel—Civil* (form MC-053) and must be lodged with the court with the moving papers. The order must specify all hearing dates scheduled in the action or proceeding, including the date of trial, if known. If no hearing date is presently scheduled, the court may set one and specify the date in the order. After the order is signed, a copy of the signed order must be served on the client and on all parties that have appeared in the case. The court may delay the effective date of the order relieving counsel until proof of service of a copy of the signed order on the client has been filed with the court.

(Subd (e) amended effective January 1, 2009; adopted as subd (d) effective July 1, 1984; previously amended effective January 1, 1996, and January 1, 2007; previously amended and relettered effective July 1, 2000.)

Rule 3.1362 amended effective January 1, 2017; adopted as rule 376 effective July 1, 1984; previously amended effective July 1, 1991, January 1, 1996, July 1, 2000, and January 1, 2009; previously amended and renumbered effective January 1, 2007.

Chapter 7
Civil Petitions

Title 3, Civil Rules—Division 11, Law and Motion—Chapter 7, Civil Petitions; repealed and renumbered from Chapter 8 effective July 1, 2014; adopted as Chapter 7, Petitions Under the California Environmental Quality Act, effective January 1, 2007.

Rule 3.1365. Petitions under the California Environmental Quality Act
Rule 3.1370. Emancipation of minors
Rule 3.1372. Petitions for relief from financial obligations during military service

Rule 3.1365.   Form and format of administrative record lodged in a CEQA proceeding [Renumbered]

Rule 3.1365 renumbered as rule 3.2205 effective July 1, 2014; adopted effective January 1, 2010.

Another Rule 3.1365 follows.

Rule 3.1365.   Petitions under the California Environmental Quality Act

Rules for petitions for relief brought under the California Environmental Quality Act have been renumbered and moved to division 22 of these rules, beginning with rule 3.2200.

Rule 3.1365 adopted effective July 1, 2014.

Advisory Committee Comment

Former rule 3.1365 on the form and format of administrative record lodged in a CEQA proceeding has been renumbered as rule 3.2205.

Rule 3.1366.   Lodging and service [Renumbered]

Rule 3.1366 amended and renumbered as rule 3.2206 effective July 1, 2014; adopted effective January 1, 2010.

Rule 3.1367.   Electronic format [Renumbered]

Rule 3.1367 amended and renumbered as rule 3.2207 effective July 1, 2014; adopted effective January 1, 2010.

Rule 3.1368.   Paper format [Renumbered]

Rule 3.1368 renumbered as rule 3.2208 effective July 1, 2014; adopted effective January 1, 2010; previously amended effective January 1, 2014.

Rule 3.1370.   Emancipation of minors

A petition for declaration of the emancipation of a minor must comply with rule 5.605.

Rule 3.1370 amended and renumbered effective January 1, 2007; adopted as rule 270 effective July 1, 1994.

Rule 3.1372.   Petitions for relief from financial obligations during military service

(a) Application

This rule applies to petitions for relief from financial obligations made by a servicemember under Military and Veterans Code section 409.3.

(Subd (a) adopted effective January 1, 2012.)

(b) Service of petition

Service of the petition for relief and all supporting papers must be made in the manner provided by law for service of summons in civil actions.

(Subd (b) adopted effective January 1, 2012.)

(c) No memorandum required

Unless ordered by the court, no memorandum is required in support of or opposition to a petition for relief.

(Subd (c) adopted effective January 1, 2012.)

Rule 3.1372 adopted effective January 1, 2012.

Chapter 8
Other Civil Petitions [Renumbered]

Title 3, Civil Rules—Division 11, Law and Motion—Chapter 8, Other Civil Petitions; amended and renumbered to Chapter 7 effective July 1, 2014; previously renumbered as Chapter 8 effective January 1, 2010; adopted as Chapter 7 effective January 1, 2007.

Division 12
Settlement

Rule 3.1380. Mandatory settlement conferences
Rule 3.1382. Good faith settlement and dismissal
Rule 3.1384. Petition for approval of compromise of claim of minor or person with a disability; order for deposit of funds; and petition for withdrawal
Rule 3.1385. Duty to notify court and others of settlement of entire case

Rule 3.1380.   Mandatory settlement conferences

(a) Setting conferences

On the court's own motion or at the request of any party, the court may set one or more mandatory settlement conferences.

(Subd (a) amended effective January 1, 2008; previously amended effective January 1, 1995, and July 1, 2002.)

(b) Persons attending

Trial counsel, parties, and persons with full authority to settle the case must personally attend the conference, unless excused by the court for good cause. If any consent to settle is required for any reason, the party with that consensual authority must be personally present at the conference.

(Subd (b) amended and relettered effective July 1, 2002; adopted as subd (c) effective January 1, 1985; previously amended effective January 1, 1995.)

(c) Settlement conference statement

No later than five court days before the initial date set for the settlement conference, each party must submit to the court and serve on each party a mandatory settlement conference statement containing:

(1) A good faith settlement demand;

(2) An itemization of economic and noneconomic damages by each plaintiff;

(3) A good faith offer of settlement by each defendant; and

(4) A statement identifying and discussing in detail all facts and law pertinent to the issues of liability and damages involved in the case as to that party.

The settlement conference statement must comply with any additional requirement imposed by local rule.

(Subd (c) amended effective January 1, 2008; adopted as subd (d) effective January 1, 1985; previously amended effective January 1, 1995 and January 1, 2007; previously amended and relettered effective July 1, 2002.)

(d) Restrictions on appointments

A court must not:

(1) Appoint a person to conduct a settlement conference under this rule at the same time as that person is serving as a mediator in the same action; or

(2) Appoint a person to conduct a mediation under this rule.

(Subd (d) adopted effective January 1, 2008.)

Rule 3.1380 amended effective January 1, 2008; adopted as rule 222 effective January 1, 1985; previously amended effective January 1, 1995, July 1, 2001, and July 1, 2002; previously amended and renumbered effective January 1, 2007.

Advisory Committee Comment

Subdivision (d). This provision is not intended to discourage settlement conferences or mediations. However, problems have arisen in several cases, such as *Jeld-Wen v. Superior Court of San Diego County* (2007) 146 Cal.App.4th 536, when distinctions between different ADR processes have been blurred. To prevent confusion about the confidentiality of the proceedings, it is important to clearly distinguish between settlement conferences held under this rule and mediations. The special confidentiality requirements for mediations established by Evidence Code sections 1115–1128 expressly do not apply to settlement conferences under this rule. This provision is not intended to prohibit a court from appointing a person who has previously served as a mediator in a case to conduct a settlement conference in that case following the conclusion of the mediation.

Rule 3.1382.   Good faith settlement and dismissal

A motion or application for determination of good faith settlement may include a request to dismiss a pleading or a portion of a pleading. The notice of motion or application for determination of good faith settlement must list each party and pleading or portion of pleading affected by the settlement and the date on which the affected pleading was filed.

Rule 3.1382 amended and renumbered effective January 1, 2007; adopted as rule 330 effective July 1, 1999.

Rule 3.1384.   Petition for approval of compromise of claim of minor or person with a disability; order for deposit of funds; and petition for withdrawal

(a) Petition for approval of compromise of claim

A petition for court approval of a compromise or covenant not to sue under Code of Civil Procedure section 372 must comply with rules 7.950 or 7.950.5, 7.951, and 7.952.

(Subd (a) amended effective January 1, 2021.)

(b) Order for the deposit of funds and petition for withdrawal

An order for the deposit of funds of a minor or a person with a disability, and a petition for the withdrawal of such funds, must comply with rules 7.953 and 7.954.

(Subd (b) amended effective January 1, 2007.)

Rule 3.1384 amended effective January 1, 2021; adopted as rule 378 effective January 1, 2002; previously amended and renumbered effective January 1, 2007.

Rule 3.1385.   Duty to notify court and others of settlement of entire case

(a) Notice of settlement

(1) *Court and other persons to be notified*

If an entire case is settled or otherwise disposed of, each plaintiff or other party seeking affirmative relief must immediately file written notice of the settlement or other disposition with the court and serve the notice on all parties and any arbitrator or other court-connected alternative dispute resolution (ADR) neutral involved in the case. Each plaintiff or other party seeking affirmative relief must also immediately give oral notice to all of the above if a hearing, conference, or trial is scheduled to take place within 10 days.

(2) *Compensation for failure to provide notice*

If the plaintiff or other party seeking affirmative relief does not notify an arbitrator or other court-connected ADR neutral involved in the case of a settlement at least 2 days before the scheduled hearing or session with that arbitrator or neutral, the court may order the party to compensate the arbitrator or other neutral for the scheduled hearing time. The amount of compensation ordered by the court must not exceed the maximum amount of compensation the arbitrator would be entitled to receive for service as an arbitrator under Code of Civil Procedure section 1141.18(b) or that the neutral would have been entitled to receive for service as a neutral at the scheduled hearing or session.

(Subd (a) amended effective January 1, 2007; previously amended effective January 1, 1989, July 1, 2001, July 1, 2002, January 1, 2004, and January 1, 2006.)

(b) Dismissal of case

Except as provided in (c) or (d), each plaintiff or other party seeking affirmative relief must serve and file a request for dismissal of the entire case within 45 days after the date of settlement of the case. If the plaintiff or other party required to serve and file the request for dismissal does not do so, the court must dismiss the entire case 45 days after it receives notice of settlement unless good cause is shown why the case should not be dismissed.

(Subd (b) amended effective January 1, 2009; adopted effective January 1, 1989; previously amended effective July 1, 2002, January 1, 2004, and January 1, 2006.)

(c) Conditional settlement

(1) Notice

If the settlement agreement conditions dismissal of the entire case on the satisfactory completion of specified terms that are not to be performed within 45 days of the settlement, including payment in installment payments, the notice of conditional settlement served and filed by each plaintiff or other party seeking affirmative relief must specify the date by which the dismissal is to be filed.

(2) Dismissal

If the plaintiff or other party required to serve and file a request for dismissal within 45 days after the dismissal date specified in the notice does not do so, the court must dismiss the entire case unless good cause is shown why the case should not be dismissed.

(3) Hearings vacated

(A) Except as provided in (B), on the filing of the notice of conditional settlement, the court must vacate all hearings and other proceedings requiring the appearance of a party and may not set any hearing or other proceeding requiring the appearance of a party earlier than 45 days after the dismissal date specified in the notice, unless requested by a party.

(B) The court need not vacate a hearing on an order to show cause or other proceeding relating to sanctions, or for determination of good faith settlement at the request of a party under Code of Civil Procedure section 877.6.

(4) Case disposition time

Under standard 2.2(n)(1)(A), the filing of a notice of conditional settlement removes the case from the computation of time used to determine case disposition time.

(Subd (c) amended effective July 1, 2013; adopted effective January 1, 1989; previously amended effective July 1, 2002, January 1, 2004, and January 1, 2006.)

(d) Compromise of claims of a minor or disabled person

If the settlement of the case involves the compromise of the claim of a minor or person with a disability, the court must not hold an order to show cause hearing under (b) before the court has held a hearing to approve the settlement, provided the parties have filed appropriate papers to seek court approval of the settlement.

(Subd (d) adopted effective January 1, 2009.)

(e) Request for additional time to complete settlement

If a party who has served and filed a notice of settlement under (a) determines that the case cannot be dismissed within the prescribed 45 days, that party must serve and file a notice and a supporting declaration advising the court of that party's inability to dismiss the case within the prescribed time, showing good cause for its inability to do so, and proposing an alternative date for dismissal. The notice and a supporting declaration must be served and filed at least 5 court days before the time for requesting dismissal has elapsed. If good cause is shown, the court must continue the matter to allow additional time to complete the settlement. The court may take such other actions as may be appropriate for the proper management and disposition of the case.

(Subd (e) adopted effective January 1, 2009.)

Rule 3.1385 amended effective July 1, 2013; adopted as rule 225 effective January 1, 1985; previously amended effective January 1, 1989, January 1, 1992, July 1,

2001, July 1, 2002, January 1, 2004, January 1, 2006, and January 1, 2009; previously amended and renumbered effective January 1, 2007.

Division 13
Dismissal of Actions

Rule 3.1390. Service and filing of notice of entry of dismissal

A party that requests dismissal of an action must serve on all parties and file notice of entry of the dismissal.

Rule 3.1390 amended and renumbered effective January 1, 2007; adopted as rule 383 effective January 1, 1984.

Division 14
Pretrial
[Reserved]

Division 15
Trial

Chapter 1
General Provisions
[Reserved]

Chapter 2
Consolidation or Bifurcation of Cases for Trial
[Reserved]

Chapter 3
Nonjury Trials
[Reserved]

Chapter 4
Jury Trials

Rule 3.1540. Examination of prospective jurors in civil cases

(a) Application

This rule applies to all civil jury trials.

(Subd (a) amended and lettered effective January 1, 2007; adopted as part of untitled subd effective January 1, 1949.)

(b) Examination of jurors by the trial judge

In examining prospective jurors in civil cases, the judge should consider the policies and recommendations in Standard 3.25 of the Standards of Judicial Administration.

(Subd (b) amended effective January 1, 2013; adopted as part of untitled subd effective January 1, 1949; previously amended and lettered effective January 1, 2007.)

(c) Additional questions and examination by counsel

On completion of the initial examination, the trial judge must permit counsel for each party that so requests to submit additional questions that the judge will put to the jurors.

(Subd (c) amended effective January 1, 2013; adopted as part of untitled subd effective January 1, 1949; previously amended and lettered effective January 1, 2007.)

Rule 3.1540 amended effective January 1, 2013; adopted as rule 228 effective January 1, 1949; previously amended effective January 1, 1972, January 1, 1974, January 1, 1975, January 1, 1988, January 1, 1990, June 6, 1990, and July 1, 1993; previously amended and renumbered effective January 1, 2007.

Chapter 4.5
Expedited Jury Trials

Division 15, Trial—Chapter 4.5, Expedited Jury Trials, adopted effective January 1, 2011.

Art. 1. Applicability. Rule 3.1545.

Art. 2. Rules Applicable Only to Cases with Mandatory Expedited Jury Trials. Rule 3.1546.

Art. 3. Rules Applicable Only to Cases with Voluntary Expedited Jury Trials. Rules 3.1547, 3.1548.

Art. 4. Rules Applicable to All Expedited Jury Trials. Rules 3.1549–3.1553.

Article 1
Applicability

Title 3, Civil Rules—Division 15, Trial—Chapter 4.5, Expedited Jury Trials—Article 1, Applicability; adopted effective July 1, 2016.

Rule 3.1545. Expedited jury trials

(a) Application

The rules in this chapter apply to civil actions in which the parties either:

(1) Agree to a voluntary expedited jury trial under chapter 4.5 (commencing with section 630.01) of title 8 of part 2 of the Code of Civil Procedure, or

(2) Are required to take part in an expedited jury trial under chapter 4.6 (commencing with section 630.20) of title 8 of part 2 of the Code of Civil Procedure.

(Subd (a) amended effective July 1, 2016; adopted effective January 1, 2011.)

(b) Definitions

As used in this chapter, unless the context or subject matter otherwise requires:

(1) "Consent order" means the consent order granting an expedited jury trial described in Code of Civil Procedure section 630.03.

(2) "Expedited jury trial" is a short jury trial before a reduced jury panel, and may be either a "mandatory expedited jury trial" or a "voluntary expedited jury trial".

(3) "Mandatory expedited jury trial" has the same meaning as stated in Code of Civil Procedure section 630.21.

(4) "Voluntary expedited jury trial" has the same meaning as stated for "expedited jury trial" in Code of Civil Procedure section 630.01.

(5) "High/low agreement" and "posttrial motions" have the same meanings as stated in Code of Civil Procedure section 630.01.

(Subd (b) amended effective July 1, 2016; adopted effective January 1, 2011.)

(c) Other programs

This chapter does not limit the adoption or use of other expedited trial or alternative dispute resolution programs or procedures.

(Subd (c) adopted effective January 1, 2011.)

Rule 3.1545 amended effective July 1, 2016; adopted effective January 1, 2011.

Article 2
Rules Applicable Only to Cases with Mandatory Expedited Jury Trials

Title 3, Civil Rules—Division 15, Trial—Chapter 4.5, Expedited Jury Trials—Article 2, Rules Applicable Only to Cases with Mandatory Expedited Jury Trials; adopted effective July 1, 2016.

Rule 3.1546. Assignment of judicial officers [Renumbered]

Rule 3.1546 renumbered as rule 3.1553 effective July 1, 2016; adopted effective January 1, 2011.

Another Rule 3.1546 follows.

Rule 3.1546. Pretrial procedures for mandatory expedited jury trials

(a) Pretrial procedures

The pretrial procedures for limited civil actions set out in Code of Civil Procedure sections 90–100 are applicable to all cases with mandatory expedited jury trials. The statutory procedures include limited discovery, optional case questionnaires, optional requests for pretrial statements identifying trial witnesses and exhibits, and the possibility of presenting testimony in the form of affidavits or declarations.

(Subd (a) adopted effective July 1, 2016.)

(b) Case management

The case management rules in chapter 3 of division 7 of these rules, starting at rule 3.720, are applicable to all cases with mandatory expedited jury trials, except to the extent the rules have been modified by local court rules applicable to limited civil cases.

(Subd (b) adopted effective July 1, 2016.)

(c) Opting out of mandatory expedited jury trial procedures

(1) Parties seeking to opt out of mandatory expedited jury trial procedures on grounds stated in Code of Civil Procedure section 630.20(b)

must file a *Request to Opt Out of Mandatory Expedited Jury Trial Procedures* (form EJT-003).

(2) Except on a showing of good cause, the request to opt out must be served and filed at least 45 days before the date first set for trial or, in cases in which the date first set for trial occurred before July 1, 2016, 45 days before the first trial date after July 1, 2016.

(3) Except on a showing of good cause, any objection to the request must be served and filed within 15 days after the date of service of the request, on an *Objection to Request to Opt Out of Mandatory Expedited Jury Trial Procedures* (form EJT-004).

(4) If the grounds on which a party or parties have opted out of mandatory expedited jury trial procedures no longer apply to a case, the parties must promptly inform the court, and the case may be tried as a mandatory expedited jury trial.

(Subd (c) amended effective September 1, 2017; adopted effective July 1, 2016.)

(d) Agreements regarding pretrial and trial procedures

Parties are encouraged to agree to procedures or limitations on pretrial procedures and on presentation of information at trial that could streamline the case, including but not limited to those items described in rule 3.1547(b). The parties may use *Agreement of Parties (Mandatory Expedited Jury Trial Procedures)* (form EJT-018) and the attachment (form EJT-022A) to describe such agreements.

(Subd (d) adopted effective July 1, 2016.)

Rule 3.1546 amended effective September 1, 2017; adopted effective July 1, 2016.

Advisory Committee Comment

Because Code of Civil Procedure section 630.20, which becomes operative July 1, 2016, applies to cases already on file and possibly already set for trial, as well as cases filed after the statutory provisions go into effect, the deadlines in rule 3.1546(c) for opt outs and objections may be problematic as applied to cases set for trial within the first couple of months after the rule goes into effect. It is expected that the good cause provisions within the rules regarding deadlines, along with judicious use of continuances as appropriate, will be liberally used to permit courts to manage those cases fairly, appropriately, and efficiently.

Article 3
Rules Applicable Only to Cases with Voluntary Expedited Jury Trials

Title 3, Civil Rules—Division 15, Trial—Chapter 4.5, Expedited Jury Trials—Article 3, Rules Applicable Only to Cases with Voluntary Expedited Jury Trials; adopted effective July 1, 2016.

Rule 3.1547. Consent order for voluntary expedited jury trial
Rule 3.1548. Pretrial submissions for voluntary expedited jury trials

Rule 3.1547. Consent order for voluntary expedited jury trial

(a) Submitting proposed consent order to the court

(1) Unless the court otherwise allows, to be eligible to participate in a voluntary expedited jury trial, the parties must submit to the court, no later than 30 days before any assigned trial date, a proposed consent order granting an expedited jury trial.

(2) The parties may enter into written stipulations regarding any high/low agreements or other matters. Only in the following circumstances may a high/low agreement be submitted to the court with the proposed consent order or disclosed later in the action:

(A) Upon agreement of the parties;

(B) In any case involving either

(i) A self-represented litigant, or

(ii) A minor, an incompetent person, or a person for whom a conservator has been appointed; or

(C) If necessary for entry or enforcement of the judgment.

(Subd (a) amended effective July 1, 2016; adopted effective January 1, 2011.)

(b) Optional content of proposed consent order

In addition to complying with the provisions of Code of Civil Procedure section 630.03(e), the proposed consent order may include other agreements of the parties, including the following:

(1) Modifications of the requirements or timelines for pretrial submissions required by rule 3.1548;

(2) Limitations on the number of witnesses per party, including expert witnesses;

(3) Modification of statutory or rule provisions regarding exchange of expert witness information and presentation of testimony by such witnesses;

(4) Allocation of the time periods stated in rule 3.1550 including how arguments and cross-examination may be used by each party in the five-hour time frame;

(5) Any evidentiary matters agreed to by the parties, including any stipulations or admissions regarding factual matters;

(6) Any agreements about what constitutes necessary or relevant evidence for a particular factual determination;

(7) Agreements about admissibility of particular exhibits or demonstrative evidence that are presented without the legally required authentication or foundation;

(8) Agreements about admissibility of video or written depositions and declarations;

(9) Agreements about any other evidentiary issues or the application of any of the rules of evidence;

(10) Agreements to use photographs, diagrams, slides, electronic presentations, overhead projections, notebooks of exhibits, or other methods for presenting information to the jury;

(11) Agreements concerning the time frame for filing and serving motions in limine; and

(12) Agreements concerning numbers of jurors required for jury verdicts in cases with fewer than eight jurors.

(Subd (b) amended effective July 1, 2016; adopted effective January 1, 2011.)
Rule 3.1547 amended effective July 1, 2016; adopted effective January 1, 2011.

Rule 3.1548. Pretrial submissions for voluntary expedited jury trials

(a) Service

Service under this rule must be by a means consistent with Code of Civil Procedure sections 1010.6, 1011, 1012, and 1013 or rule 2.251 and be reasonably calculated to assure delivery to the other party or parties no later than the close of business on the last allowable day for service as specified below.

(Subd (a) adopted effective January 1, 2011.)

(b) Pretrial exchange for voluntary expedited jury trials

Unless otherwise agreed by the parties, no later than 25 days before trial, each party must serve on all other parties the following:

(1) Copies of any documentary evidence that the party intends to introduce at trial (except for documentary evidence to be used solely for impeachment or rebuttal), including, but not limited to, medical bills, medical records, and lost income records;

(2) A list of all witnesses whom the party intends to call at trial, except for witnesses to be used solely for impeachment or rebuttal, and designation of whether the testimony will be in person, by video, or by deposition transcript;

(3) A list of depositions that the party intends to use at trial, except for depositions to be used solely for impeachment or rebuttal;

(4) A copy of any audiotapes, videotapes, digital video discs (DVDs), compact discs (CDs), or other similar recorded materials that the party intends to use at trial for evidentiary purposes, except recorded materials to be used solely for impeachment or rebuttal and recorded material intended to be used solely in closing argument;

(5) A copy of any proposed jury questionnaires (parties are encouraged to agree in advance on a questionnaire);

(6) A list of proposed approved introductory instructions, preinstructions, and instructions to be read by the judge to the jury;

(7) A copy of any proposed special jury instructions in the form and format described in rule 2.1055;

(8) Any proposed verdict forms;

(9) A special glossary, if the case involves technical or unusual vocabulary; and

(10) Motions in limine.

(Subd (b) amended effective July 1, 2016; adopted effective January 1, 2011.)

(c) Supplemental exchange for voluntary expedited jury trials

No later than 20 days before trial, a party may serve on any other party any additional documentary evidence and a list of any additional witnesses whom the party intends to use at trial in light of the exchange of information under subdivision (b).

(Subd (c) amended effective July 1, 2016; adopted effective January 1, 2011.)

(d) Submissions to court for voluntary expedited jury trials

No later than 20 days before trial, each party must file all motions in limine and must lodge with the court any items served under (b)(2)–(9) and (c).

(Subd (d) amended effective July 1, 2016; adopted effective January 1, 2011.)

(e) Preclusionary effect

Unless good cause is shown for any omission, failure to serve documentary evidence as required under this rule will be grounds for preclusion of the evidence at the time of trial.

(Subd (e) adopted effective January 1, 2011.)

(f) Pretrial conference for voluntary expedited jury trials

No later than 15 days before trial, unless that period is modified by the consent order, the judicial officer assigned to the case must conduct a pretrial conference, at which time objections to any documentary evidence previously submitted will be ruled on. If there are no objections at that time, counsel must stipulate in writing to the admissibility of the evidence. Matters to be addressed at the pretrial conference, in addition to the evidentiary objections, include the following:

(1) Any evidentiary matters agreed to by the parties, including any stipulations or admissions regarding factual matters;

(2) Any agreement of the parties regarding limitations on necessary or relevant evidence, including any limitations on expert witness testimony;

(3) Any agreements of the parties to use photographs, diagrams, slides, electronic presentations, overhead projections, notebooks of exhibits, or other methods of presenting information to the jury;

(4) Admissibility of any exhibits or demonstrative evidence without legally required authentication or foundation;

(5) Admissibility of video or written depositions and declarations and objections to any portions of them;

(6) Objections to and admissibility of any recorded materials that a party has designated for use at trial;

(7) Jury questionnaires;

(8) Jury instructions;

(9) Special verdict forms;

(10) Allocation of time for each party's case;

(11) Motions in limine filed before the pretrial conference; and

(12) The parties' intention on how any high/low agreement will affect an award of fees and costs.

(Subd (f) amended effective July 1, 2016; adopted effective January 1, 2011.)

(g) Expert witness documents

Any documents produced at the deposition of an expert witness are deemed to have been timely exchanged for the purpose of (c) above.

(Subd (g) adopted effective January 1, 2011.)
Rule 3.1548 amended effective July 1, 2016; adopted effective January 1, 2011.

Article 4
Rules Applicable to All Expedited Jury Trials

Title 3, Civil Rules—Division 15, Trial—Chapter 4.5, Expedited Jury Trials—Article 4, Rules Applicable to All Expedited Jury Trials; adopted effective July 1, 2016.

Rule 3.1549. Voir dire
Rule 3.1550. Time limits
Rule 3.1551. Case presentation
Rule 3.1552. Presentation of evidence
Rule 3.1553. Assignment of judicial officers

Rule 3.1549. Voir dire

Parties are encouraged to submit a joint form questionnaire to be used with prospective jurors to help expedite the voir dire process.
Rule 3.1549 amended effective July 1, 2016; adopted effective January 1, 2011.

Rule 3.1550. Time limits

Including jury voir dire, each side will be allowed five hours to present its case, including opening statements and closing arguments, unless the court, upon a finding of good cause, allows additional time. The amount of time allotted for each side includes the time that the side spends on cross-examination. The parties are encouraged to streamline the trial process by limiting the number of live witnesses. The goal is to complete an expedited jury trial within two trial days.
Rule 3.1550 amended effective July 1, 2016; adopted effective January 1, 2011.

Rule 3.1551. Case presentation

(a) Methods of presentation

Upon agreement of the parties and with the approval of the judicial officer, the parties may present summaries and may use photographs, diagrams, slides, electronic presentations, overhead projections, individual notebooks of exhibits for submission to the jurors, or other innovative methods of presentation approved at the pretrial conference.

(Subd (a) adopted effective January 1, 2011.)

(b) Exchange of items

Anything to be submitted to the jury under (a) as part of the evidentiary presentation of the case in chief must be exchanged 20 days in advance of the trial, unless that period is modified by the consent order or agreement of the parties. This rule does not apply to items to be used solely for closing argument.

(Subd (b) amended effective July 1, 2016; adopted effective January 1, 2011.)

(c) Stipulations regarding facts

The parties should stipulate to factual and evidentiary matters to the greatest extent possible.

(Subd (c) adopted effective January 1, 2011.)

Rule 3.1551 amended effective July 1, 2016; adopted effective January 1, 2011.

Rule 3.1552. Presentation of evidence

(a) Stipulations regarding rules of evidence

The parties may offer such evidence as is relevant and material to the dispute. An agreement to modify the rules of evidence for the trial made pursuant to the expedited jury trial statutes commencing with Code of Civil Procedure section 630.01 may be included in the consent order or agreement of the parties. To the extent feasible, the parties should stipulate to modes and methods of presentation that will expedite the process, either in the consent order or at the pretrial conference.

(Subd (a) amended effective July 1, 2016; adopted effective January 1, 2011.)

(b) Objections

Objections to evidence and motions to exclude evidence must be submitted in a timely manner. Except as provided in rule 3.1548(f), failure to raise an objection before trial does not preclude making an objection or motion to exclude at trial.

(Subd (b) adopted effective January 1, 2011.)

Rule 3.1552 amended effective July 1, 2016; adopted effective January 1, 2011.

Rule 3.1553. Assignment of judicial officers

The presiding judge is responsible for the assignment of a judicial officer to conduct an expedited jury trial. The presiding judge may assign a temporary judge appointed by the court under rules 2.810–2.819 to conduct an expedited jury trial. A temporary judge requested by the parties under rules 2.830–2.835, whether or not privately compensated, may not be appointed to conduct a voluntary expedited jury trial.

Rule 3.1553 amended and renumbered effective July 1, 2016; adopted as rule 3.1546 effective January 1, 2011.

Chapter 5
Testimony and Evidence
[Reserved]

Chapter 6
Expert Witness Testimony
[Reserved]

Chapter 7
Jury Instructions

Rule 3.1560. Application

The rules on jury instructions in chapter 4 of division 8 of title 2 of these rules apply to civil cases.

Rule 3.1560 adopted effective January 1, 2007.

Chapter 8
Special Verdicts

Rule 3.1580. Request for special findings by jury

Whenever a party desires special findings by a jury, the party must, before argument, unless otherwise ordered, present to the judge in writing the issues or questions of fact on which the findings are requested, in proper form for submission to the jury, and serve copies on all other parties.

Rule 3.1580 amended and renumbered effective January 1, 2007; adopted as rule 230 effective January 1, 1949.

Chapter 9
Statement of Decision

Rule 3.1590. Announcement of tentative decision, statement of decision, and judgment

(a) Announcement and service of tentative decision

On the trial of a question of fact by the court, the court must announce its tentative decision by an oral statement, entered in the minutes, or by a written statement filed with the clerk. Unless the announcement is made in open court in the presence of all parties that appeared at the trial, the clerk must immediately serve on all parties that appeared at the trial a copy of the minute entry or written tentative decision.

(Subd (a) amended effective January 1, 2010; previously amended effective January 1, 1969, July 1, 1973, January 1, 1982, January 1, 1983, and January 1, 2007.)

(b) Tentative decision not binding

The tentative decision does not constitute a judgment and is not binding on the court. If the court subsequently modifies or changes its announced tentative decision, the clerk must serve a copy of the modification or change on all parties that appeared at the trial.

(Subd (b) amended effective January 1, 2010; adopted as part of subd (a) effective January 1, 1949; previously amended and lettered effective January 1, 2007; previously amended effective January 1, 2007.)

(c) Provisions in tentative decision

The court in its tentative decision may:

(1) State that it is the court's proposed statement of decision, subject to a party's objection under (g);

(2) Indicate that the court will prepare a statement of decision;

(3) Order a party to prepare a statement of decision; or

(4) Direct that the tentative decision will become the statement of decision unless, within 10 days after announcement or service of the tentative decision, a party specifies those principal controverted issues as to which the party is requesting a statement of decision or makes proposals not included in the tentative decision.

(Subd (c) amended effective January 1, 2010; adopted as part of subd (a) effective January 1, 1949; previously amended and lettered effective January 1, 2007.)

(d) Request for statement of decision

Within 10 days after announcement or service of the tentative decision, whichever is later, any party that appeared at trial may request a statement of decision to address the principal controverted issues. The principal controverted issues must be specified in the request.

(Subd (d) adopted effective January 1, 2010.)

(e) Other party's response to request for statement of decision

If a party requests a statement of decision under (d), any other party may make proposals as to the content of the statement of decision within 10 days after the date of request for a statement of decision.

(Subd (e) amended and relettered effective January 1, 2010; adopted as subd (b) effective January 1, 1949; previously amended effective January 1, 1969, and January 1, 1982; previously amended and relettered as subd (d) effective January 1, 2007.)

(f) Preparation and service of proposed statement of decision and judgment

If a party requests a statement of decision under (d), the court must, within 30 days of announcement or service of the tentative decision, prepare and serve a proposed statement of decision and a proposed judgment on all parties that appeared at the trial, unless the court has ordered a party to prepare the statement. A party that has been ordered to prepare the statement must within 30 days after the announcement or service of the tentative decision, serve and submit to the court a proposed statement of decision and a proposed judgment. If the proposed statement of decision and judgment are not served and submitted within that time, any other party that appeared at the trial may within 10 days thereafter: (1) prepare, serve, and submit to the court a proposed statement of decision and judgment or (2) serve on all other parties and file a notice of motion for an order that a statement of decision be deemed waived.

(Subd (f) amended and relettered effective January 1, 2010; adopted as subd (c) effective January 1, 1949; previously amended effective January 1, 1969, July 1, 1973, and January 1, 1982; previously amended and relettered as subd (e) effective January 1, 2007.)

(g) Objections to proposed statement of decision

Any party may, within 15 days after the proposed statement of decision and judgment have been served, serve and file objections to the proposed statement of decision or judgment.

(Subd (g) amended and relettered effective January 1, 2010; adopted as subd (d) effective January 1, 1949; previously amended effective January 1, 1969, and January 1, 1982; previously relettered as subd (f) effective January 1, 2007.)

(h) Preparation and filing of written judgment when statement of decision not prepared

If no party requests or is ordered to prepare a statement of decision and a written judgment is required, the court must prepare and serve a proposed judgment on all parties that appeared at the trial within 20 days after the announcement or service of the tentative decision or the court may order a party to prepare, serve, and submit the proposed judgment to the court within 10 days after the date of the order.

(Subd (h) amended and relettered effective January 1, 2010; previously amended effective January 1, 1969; previously amended and relettered as subd (e) effective January 1, 1982, and as subd (g) effective January 1, 2007.)

(i) Preparation and filing of written judgment when statement of decision deemed waived

If the court orders that the statement of decision is deemed waived and a written judgment is required, the court must, within 10 days of the order deeming the statement of decision waived, either prepare and serve a proposed judgment on all parties that appeared at the trial or order a party to prepare, serve, and submit the proposed judgment to the court within 10 days.

(Subd (i) adopted effective January 1, 2010.)

(j) Objection to proposed judgment

Any party may, within 10 days after service of the proposed judgment, serve and file objections thereto.

(Subd (j) adopted effective January 1, 2010.)

(k) Hearing

The court may order a hearing on proposals or objections to a proposed statement of decision or the proposed judgment.

(Subd (k) amended and relettered effective January 1, 2010; adopted as subd (f) effective January 1, 1982; previously relettered as subd (i) effective January 1, 2007.)

(*l*) Signature and filing of judgment

If a written judgment is required, the court must sign and file the judgment within 50 days after the announcement or service of the tentative decision, whichever is later, or, if a hearing was held under (k), within 10 days after the hearing. An electronic signature by the court is as effective as an original signature. The judgment constitutes the decision on which judgment is to be entered under Code of Civil Procedure section 664.

(Subd (l) amended effective January 1, 2016; adopted as part of subd (e) effective January 1, 1949; previously amended and lettered as subd (h) effective January 1, 2007, and as subd (l) effective January 1, 2010.)

(m) Extension of time; relief from noncompliance

The court may, by written order, extend any of the times prescribed by this rule and at any time before the entry of judgment may, for good cause shown and on such terms as may be just, excuse a noncompliance with the time limits prescribed for doing any act required by this rule.

(Subd (m) relettered effective January 1, 2010; previously amended effective January 1, 1969, and July 1, 1973; previously amended and relettered as subd (g) effective January 1, 1982, and as subd (j) effective January 1, 2007.)

(n) Trial within one day

When a trial is completed within one day or in less than eight hours over more than one day, a request for statement of decision must be made before the matter is submitted for decision and the statement of decision may be made orally on the record in the presence of the parties.

(Subd (n) amended and relettered effective January 1, 2010; adopted as subd (h) effective January 1, 1983; previously amended and relettered as subd (k) effective January 1, 2007.)

Rule 3.1590 amended effective January 1, 2016; adopted as rule 232 effective January 1, 1949; previously amended and renumbered as rule 3.1590 effective January 1, 2007; previously amended effective January 1, 1969, July 1, 1973, January 1, 1982, January 1, 1983, January 1, 2007, and January 1, 2010.

Rule 3.1591. Statement of decision, judgment, and motion for new trial following bifurcated trial

(a) Separate trial of an issue

When a factual issue raised by the pleadings is tried by the court separately and before the trial of other issues, the judge conducting the separate trial must announce the tentative decision on the issue so tried and must, when requested under Code of Civil Procedure section 632, issue a statement of decision as prescribed in rule 3.1590; but the court must not prepare any proposed judgment until the other issues are tried, except when an interlocutory judgment or a separate judgment may otherwise be properly entered at that time.

(Subd (a) amended and lettered effective January 1, 2007; adopted as part of untitled subd effective January 1, 1975.)

(b) Trial of issues by a different judge

If the other issues are tried by a different judge or judges, each judge must perform all acts required by rule 3.1590 as to the issues tried by that judge and the judge trying the final issue must prepare the proposed judgment.

(Subd (b) amended and lettered effective January 1, 2007; adopted as part of untitled subd effective January 1, 1975.)

(c) Trial of subsequent issues before issuance of statement of decision

A judge may proceed with the trial of subsequent issues before the issuance of a statement of decision on previously tried issues. Any motion for a new trial following a bifurcated trial must be made after all the issues are tried and, if the issues were tried by different judges, each judge must hear and determine the motion as to the issues tried by that judge.

(Subd (c) amended and lettered effective January 1, 2007; adopted as part of untitled subd effective January 1, 1975.)

Rule 3.1591 amended and renumbered effective January 1, 2007; adopted as rule 232.5 effective January 1, 1975; previously amended effective January 1, 1982, and January 1, 1985.

Division 16
Post-trial

Rule 3.1600. Notice of intention to move for new trial

(a) Time for service of memorandum

Within 10 days after filing notice of intention to move for a new trial in a civil case, the moving party must serve and file a memorandum in support of the motion, and within 10 days thereafter any adverse party may serve and file a memorandum in reply.

(Subd (a) amended and lettered effective January 1, 2007; adopted as part of untitled subd effective January 1, 1949.)

(b) Effect of failure to serve memorandum

If the moving party fails to serve and file a memorandum within the time prescribed in (a), the court may deny the motion for a new trial without a hearing on the merits.

(Subd (b) amended and lettered effective January 1, 2007; adopted as part of untitled subd effective January 1, 1949.)

Rule 3.1600 amended and renumbered effective January 1, 2007; adopted as rule 203 effective January 1, 1949; previously amended effective April 1, 1962, January 1, 1971, January 1, 1984, and January 1, 1987; previously amended and renumbered as rule 236.5 effective January 1, 2003.

Rule 3.1602. Hearing of motion to vacate judgment

A motion to vacate judgment under Code of Civil Procedure section 663 must be heard and determined by the judge who presided at the trial; provided, however, that in case of the inability or death of such judge or if at the time noticed for the hearing thereon he is absent from the county where the trial was had, the motion may be heard and determined by another judge of the same court.

Rule 3.1602 amended and renumbered effective January 1, 2007; adopted as rule 236 effective January 1, 1949.

Division 17
Attorney's Fees and Costs

Rule 3.1700. Prejudgment costs

(a) Claiming costs

(1) *Trial costs*

A prevailing party who claims costs must serve and file a memorandum of costs within 15 days after the date of service of the notice of entry of judgment or dismissal by the clerk under Code of Civil Procedure section 664.5 or the date of service of written notice of entry of judgment or dismissal, or within 180 days after entry of judgment, whichever is first. The memorandum of costs must be verified by a statement of the party, attorney, or agent that to the best of his or her knowledge the items of cost are correct and were necessarily incurred in the case.

(2) *Costs on default*

A party seeking a default judgment who claims costs must request costs on the *Request for Entry of Default (Application to Enter Default)* (form CIV-100) at the time of applying for the judgment.

(Subd (a) amended effective January 1, 2016; previously amended effective January 1, 2007, and July 1, 2007.)

(b) Contesting costs

(1) *Striking and taxing costs*

Any notice of motion to strike or to tax costs must be served and filed 15 days after service of the cost memorandum. If the cost memorandum was served by mail, the period is extended as provided in Code of Civil Procedure section 1013. If the cost memorandum was served electronically, the period is extended as provided in Code of Civil Procedure section 1010.6(a)(4).

(2) *Form of motion*

Unless objection is made to the entire cost memorandum, the motion to strike or tax costs must refer to each item objected to by the same number and appear in the same order as the corresponding cost item claimed on the memorandum of costs and must state why the item is objectionable.

(3) *Extensions of time*

The party claiming costs and the party contesting costs may agree to extend the time for serving and filing the cost memorandum and a motion to strike or tax costs. This agreement must be confirmed in writing, specify the extended date for service, and be filed with the clerk. In the absence of an agreement, the court may extend the times for serving and filing the cost memorandum or the notice of motion to strike or tax costs for a period not to exceed 30 days.

(4) *Entry of costs*

After the time has passed for a motion to strike or tax costs or for determination of that motion, the clerk must immediately enter the costs on the judgment.

(Subd (b) amended effective January 1, 2016; previously amended effective January 1, 2007.)

Rule 3.1700 amended effective January 1, 2016; adopted as rule 870 effective January 1, 1987; previously amended and renumbered as rule 3.1700 effective January 1, 2007; previously amended effective July 1, 2007.

Rule 3.1702.   Claiming attorney's fees

(a) Application

Except as otherwise provided by statute, this rule applies in civil cases to claims for statutory attorney's fees and claims for attorney's fees provided for in a contract. Subdivisions (b) and (c) apply when the court determines entitlement to the fees, the amount of the fees, or both, whether the court makes that determination because the statute or contract refers to "reasonable" fees, because it requires a determination of the prevailing party, or for other reasons.

(Subd (a) amended effective January 1, 2007.)

(b) Attorney's fees before trial court judgment

(1) *Time for motion*

A notice of motion to claim attorney's fees for services up to and including the rendition of judgment in the trial court—including attorney's fees on an appeal before the rendition of judgment in the trial court—must be served and filed within the time for filing a notice of appeal under rules 8.104 and 8.108 in an unlimited civil case or under rules 8.822 and 8.823 in a limited civil case.

(2) *Stipulation for extension of time*

The parties may, by stipulation filed before the expiration of the time allowed under (b)(1), extend the time for filing a motion for attorney's fees:

(A) Until 60 days after the expiration of the time for filing a notice of appeal in an unlimited civil case or 30 days after the expiration of the time in a limited civil case; or

(B) If a notice of appeal is filed, until the time within which a memorandum of costs must be served and filed under rule 8.278(c) in an unlimited civil case or under rule 8.891(c)(1) in a limited civil case.

(Subd (b) amended effective July 1, 2013; previously amended effective January 1, 1999, January 1, 2006, January 1, 2007, January 1, 2009, and January 1, 2011.)

(c) Attorney's fees on appeal

(1) *Time for motion*

A notice of motion to claim attorney's fees on appeal—other than the attorney's fees on appeal claimed under (b)—under a statute or contract requiring the court to determine entitlement to the fees, the amount of the fees, or both, must be served and filed within the time for serving and filing the memorandum of costs under rule 8.278(c)(1) in an unlimited civil case or under rule 8.891(c)(1) in a limited civil case.

(2) *Stipulation for extension of time*

The parties may by stipulation filed before the expiration of the time allowed under (c)(1) extend the time for filing the motion up to an additional 60 days in an unlimited civil case or 30 days in a limited civil case.

(Subd (c) amended effective January 1, 2011; previously amended effective January 1, 1999, January 1, 2006, January 1, 2007, and July 1, 2008.)

(d) Extensions

For good cause, the trial judge may extend the time for filing a motion for attorney's fees in the absence of a stipulation or for a longer period than allowed by stipulation.

(Subd (d) amended effective January 1, 2007; adopted effective January 1, 1999.)

(e) Attorney's fees fixed by formula

If a party is entitled to statutory or contractual attorney's fees that are fixed without the necessity of a court determination, the fees must be claimed in the memorandum of costs.

(Subd (e) amended effective January 1, 2007; adopted as subd (d) effective January 1, 1994; previously relettered effective January 1, 1999.)

Rule 3.1702 amended effective July 1, 2013; adopted as rule 870.2 effective January 1, 1994; previously amended and renumbered effective January 1, 2007; previously amended effective January 1, 1999, January 1, 2006, July 1, 2008, January 1, 2009, and January 1, 2011.

Division 18
Judgments

Rule 3.1800.   Default judgments

(a) Documents to be submitted

A party seeking a default judgment on declarations must use mandatory *Request for Entry of Default (Application to Enter Default)* (form CIV-100), unless the action is subject to the Fair Debt Buying Practices Act, Civil Code section 1788.50 et seq., in which case the party must use mandatory *Request for Entry of Default (Fair Debt Buying Practices Act)* (form CIV-105). In an unlawful detainer case, a party may, in addition, use optional *Declaration for Default Judgment by Court* (form UD-116) when seeking a court judgment based on declarations. The following must be included in the documents filed with the clerk:

(1) Except in unlawful detainer cases, a brief summary of the case identifying the parties and the nature of plaintiff's claim;

(2) Declarations or other admissible evidence in support of the judgment requested;

(3) Interest computations as necessary;

(4) A memorandum of costs and disbursements;

(5) A declaration of nonmilitary status for each defendant against whom judgment is sought;

(6) A proposed form of judgment;

(7) A dismissal of all parties against whom judgment is not sought or an application for separate judgment against specified parties under Code of Civil Procedure section 579, supported by a showing of grounds for each judgment;

(8) Exhibits as necessary; and

(9) A request for attorney fees if allowed by statute or by the agreement of the parties.

(Subd (a) amended effective January 1, 2018; previously amended effective January 1, 2005, January 1, 2007, and July 1, 2007.)

(b) Fee schedule

A court may by local rule establish a schedule of attorney's fees to be used by that court in determining the reasonable amount of attorney's fees to be allowed in the case of a default judgment.

(Subd (b) amended effective January 1, 2007.)

Rule 3.1800 amended effective January 1, 2018; adopted as rule 388 effective July 1, 2000; previously amended effective January 1, 2005, and July 1, 2007; previously amended and renumbered effective January 1, 2007.

Rule 3.1802.   Inclusion of interest in judgment

The clerk must include in the judgment any interest awarded by the court.

Rule 3.1802 amended effective January 1, 2014; adopted as rule 875 effective January 1, 1987; previously amended and renumbered effective January 1, 2007.

Rule 3.1804.   Periodic payment of judgments against public entities

(a) Notice of election or hearing

A public entity electing to pay a judgment against it by periodic payments under Government Code section 984 must serve and file a notice of election stipulating to the terms of such payments, or a notice of hearing on such terms, by the earlier of:

(1) 30 days after the clerk sends, or a party serves, notice of entry of judgment; or

(2) 60 days after entry of judgment.

(b) Time for hearing

Notwithstanding any contrary local rule or practice, a hearing under (a) must be held within 30 days after service of the notice. The court must make an order for periodic payments at the hearing.

(Subd (b) amended effective January 1, 2007.)

Rule 3.1804 amended and renumbered effective January 1, 2007; adopted as rule 389 effective January 1, 2002.

Rule 3.1806.   Notation on written instrument of rendition of judgment

In all cases in which judgment is rendered upon a written obligation to pay money, the clerk must, at the time of entry of judgment, unless otherwise ordered, note over the clerk's official signature and across the face of the writing the fact of rendition of judgment with the date of the judgment and the title of the court and the case.

Rule 3.1806 amended and renumbered effective January 1, 2007; adopted as rule 234 effective January 1, 1949.

Division 19
Postjudgment and Enforcement of Judgments

Rule 3.1900.   Notice of renewal of judgment

A copy of the application for renewal of judgment must be physically or electronically attached to the notice of renewal of judgment required by Code of Civil Procedure section 683.160.

Rule 3.1900 amended effective January 1, 2016; adopted as rule 986 effective July 1, 1983; previously amended and renumbered as rule 3.1900 effective January 1, 2007.

Division 20
Unlawful Detainers

Rule 3.2000.   Unlawful detainer—supplemental costs

(a) Time for filing supplemental cost memorandum

In unlawful detainer proceedings, the plaintiff who has complied with Code of Civil Procedure section 1034.5 may, no later than 10 days after being advised by the sheriff or marshal of the exact amount necessarily used and expended to effect the eviction, file a supplemental cost memorandum claiming the additional costs and specifying the items paid and the amount.

(Subd (a) amended and lettered effective January 1, 2007; adopted as part of untitled subd effective January 1, 1987.)

(b) Motion to tax costs

The defendant may move to tax those costs within 10 days after service of the supplemental cost memorandum.

(Subd (b) amended and lettered effective January 1, 2007; adopted as part of untitled subd effective January 1, 1987.)

(c) Entry of judgment for costs and enforcement

After costs have been fixed by the court, or on failure of the defendant to file a timely notice of motion to tax costs, the clerk must immediately enter judgment for the costs. The judgment may be enforced in the same manner as a money judgment.

(Subd (c) amended and lettered effective January 1, 2007; adopted as part of untitled subd effective January 1, 1987.)

Rule 3.2000 amended and renumbered effective January 1, 2007; adopted as part of rule 870.4 effective January 1, 1987.

Division 21
Rules for Small Claims Actions

Chapter 1
Trial Rules

Rule 3.2100.   Compliance with fictitious business name laws

(a) Filing of declaration of compliance

A claimant who is required to file a declaration of compliance with the fictitious business name laws under Code of Civil Procedure section 116.430 must file the declaration in each case filed.

(Subd (a) amended and lettered effective January 1, 2007; adopted as untitled subd effective January 1, 1986.)

(b) Available methods

The clerk must make the declaration of compliance available to the claimant in any one of the following ways:

(1) The declaration of compliance may be placed on a separate form approved by the Judicial Council;

(2) The approved Judicial Council form may be placed on the reverse of the Plaintiff's Statement to the Clerk or on the back of any Judicial Council small claims form with only one side; or

(3) The precise language of the declaration of compliance that appears on the approved Judicial Council form may be incorporated into the Plaintiff's Statement to the Clerk.

(Subd (b) amended and lettered effective January 1, 2007; adopted as part of untitled subd effective January 1, 1986.)

Rule 3.2100 amended and renumbered effective January 1, 2007; adopted as rule 1701 effective January 1, 1986; previously amended effective July 1, 1991.

Rule 3.2102.   Substituted service

If substituted service is authorized by Code of Civil Procedure section 116.340 or other provisions of law, no due diligence is required in a small claims court action.

Rule 3.2102 renumbered effective January 1, 2007; adopted as rule 1702 effective July 1, 1991.

Rule 3.2104.   Defendant's claim

A defendant may file a claim against the plaintiff even if the claim does not relate to the same subject or event as the plaintiff's claim, so long as the claim is within the jurisdictional limit of the small claims court.

Rule 3.2104 renumbered effective January 1, 2007; adopted as rule 1703 effective July 1, 1991.

Rule 3.2106.   Venue challenge

A defendant may challenge venue by writing to the court. The defendant is not required to personally appear at the hearing on the venue challenge. If the court denies the challenge and the defendant is not present, the hearing must be continued to another appropriate date. The parties must be given notice of the venue determination and hearing date.

Rule 3.2106 amended and renumbered effective January 1, 2007; adopted as rule 1704 effective July 1, 1991.

Rule 3.2107.   Request for court order

(a) Request before trial

If a party files a written request for a court order before the hearing on the claim, the requesting party must mail, personally deliver, or if agreed on by the parties electronically serve a copy to all other parties in the case. The other parties must be given an opportunity to answer or respond to the request before or at the hearing. This subdivision does not apply to a request to postpone the hearing date if the plaintiff's claim has not been served.

(Subd (a) amended effective January 1, 2016; adopted effective January 1, 2007.)

(b) Request after trial

If a party files a written request for a court order after notice of entry of judgment, the clerk must send a copy of the request to all other parties in the action. A party has 10 calendar days from the date on which the clerk sent the request to file a response before the court makes an order. The court may schedule a hearing on the request, except that if the request is to vacate the judgment for lack of appearance by the plaintiff, the court must hold a hearing. The court may give notice of any scheduled hearing with notice of the request, but the hearing must be scheduled at least 11 calendar days after the clerk has sent the request.

(Subd (b) amended effective January 1, 2016; adopted effective January 1, 2007.)

Rule 3.2107 amended effective January 1, 2016; adopted effective January 1, 2007.

Rule 3.2108.   Form of judgment

The court may give judgment for damages, equitable relief, or both, and may make other orders as the court deems just and equitable for the resolution of the dispute. If specific property is referred to in the judgment, whether it be personal or real, tangible or intangible, the property must be identified with sufficient detail to permit efficient implementation or enforcement of the judgment.

Rule 3.2108 amended and renumbered effective January 1, 2007; adopted as rule 1705 effective July 1, 1991.

Rule 3.2110.   Role of clerk in assisting small claims litigants

(a) Provision of forms and pamphlets

The clerk must provide forms and pamphlets from the Judicial Council.

(Subd (a) amended and lettered effective January 1, 2007; adopted as part of untitled subd effective July 1, 1991.)

(b) Provision of Department of Consumer Affairs materials

The clerk must provide materials from the Department of Consumer Affairs when available.

(Subd (b) amended and lettered effective January 1, 2007; adopted as part of untitled subd effective July 1, 1991.)

(c) Information about small claims advisory service

The clerk must inform litigants of the small claims advisory service.

(Subd (c) amended and lettered effective January 1, 2007; adopted as part of untitled subd effective July 1, 1991.)

(d) Answering questions

The clerk may answer questions relative to filing and service of the claim, designation of the parties, scheduling of hearings, and similar matters.

(Subd (d) amended and lettered effective January 1, 2007; adopted as part of untitled subd effective July 1, 1991.)

Rule 3.2110 amended and renumbered effective January 1, 2007; adopted as rule 1706 effective July 1, 1991.

Chapter 2
Small Claims Advisors

Rule 3.2120.   Advisor assistance

(a) Notice to parties

The clerk must inform the parties, orally or in writing, about:

(1) The availability of advisors to assist small claims litigants at no additional charge as provided in Code of Civil Procedure sections 116.260 and 116.940; and

(2) The provisions of Government Code section 818.9.

(Subd (a) amended effective January 1, 2007; previously amended effective July 1, 1991.)

(b) Training

All small claims advisors must receive training sufficient to ensure competence in the areas of:

(1) Small claims court practice and procedure;

(2) Alternative dispute resolution programs;

(3) Consumer sales;

(4) Vehicular sales, leasing, and repairs;

(5) Credit and financing transactions;

(6) Professional and occupational licensing;

(7) Landlord-tenant law; and

(8) Contract, warranty, tort, and negotiable instruments law.

It is the intent of this rule that the county must provide this training.

(Subd (b) amended effective January 1, 2007; previously adopted effective January 1, 1986; previously repealed and adopted effective July 1, 1991.)

(c) Qualifications

In addition to the training required in subdivision (b), each county may establish additional qualifications for small claims advisors.

(Subd (c) adopted effective July 1, 1991.)

(d) Conflict of interest

A small claims advisor must disclose any known direct or indirect relationship the advisor may have with any party or witness in the action. An advisor must not disclose information obtained in the course of the advisor's duties or use the information for financial or other advantage.

(Subd (d) amended effective January 1, 2007; adopted as subd (c) effective January 1, 1986; previously relettered effective July 1, 1991.)

Rule 3.2120 amended and renumbered effective January 1, 2007; adopted as rule 1725 effective January 1, 1986; previously amended effective July 1, 1991.

Division 22
Petitions Under the California Environmental Quality Act

Title 3, Civil Rules—Division 22, Petitions Under the California Environmental Quality Act; adopted effective July 1, 2014.

Public Resources Code Sections 21168.6, 21178–21189.3, and 21189.50–21189.57.

Chapter 1
General Provisions

Title 3, Civil Rules—Division 22, Petitions Under the California Environmental Quality Act—Chapter 1, General Provisions; adopted effective July 1, 2014.

Rule 3.2200.   Application

Except as otherwise provided in chapter 2 of the rules in this division, which govern actions under Public Resources Code sections 21168.6.6, 21178–21189.3, and 21189.50–21189.57, the rules in this chapter apply to all actions brought under the California Environmental Quality Act (CEQA) as set forth in division 13 of the Public Resources Code.

Rule 3.2200 amended effective January 1, 2017; adopted effective July 1, 2014.

Rule 3.2205.   Form and format of administrative record lodged in a CEQA proceeding

(a) Organization

(1) *Order of documents*

Except as permitted in (a)(3), the administrative record must be organized in the following order, as applicable:

(A) The Notice of Determination;

(B) The resolutions or ordinances adopted by the lead agency approving the project;

(C) The findings required by Public Resources Code section 21081, including any statement of overriding considerations;

(D) The final environmental impact report, including the draft environmental impact report or a revision of the draft, all other matters included in the final environmental impact report, and other types of environmental impact documents prepared under the California Environmental Quality Act, such as a negative declaration, mitigated negative declaration, or addenda;

(E) The initial study;

(F) Staff reports prepared for the administrative bodies providing subordinate approvals or recommendations to the lead agency, in chronological order;

(G) Transcripts and minutes of hearings, in chronological order; and

(H) The remainder of the administrative record, in chronological order.

(2) *List not limiting*

The list of documents in (1) is not intended to limit the content of the administrative record, which is prescribed in Public Resources Code section 21167.6(e).

(3) *Different order permissible*

The documents may be organized in a different order from that set out in (1) if the court so orders on:

(A) A party's motion;

(B) The parties' stipulation; or

(C) The court's own motion.

(4) *Oversized documents*

Oversized documents included in the record must be presented in a manner that allows them to be easily unfolded and viewed.

(5) *Use of tabs or electronic bookmarks*

The administrative record must be separated by tabs or marked with electronic bookmarks that identify each part of the record listed above.

(Subd (a) adopted effective January 1, 2010.)

(b) Index

A detailed index must be placed at the beginning of the administrative record. The index must list each document in the administrative record in the order presented, or in chronological order if ordered by the court, including title, date of the document, brief description, and the volume and page where it begins. The index must list any included exhibits or appendixes and must list each document contained in the exhibit or appendix (including environmental impact report appendixes) and the volume and page where each document begins. A copy of the index must be filed in the court at the time the administrative record is lodged with the court.

(Subd (b) adopted effective January 1, 2010.)

(c) Appendix of excerpts

A court may require each party filing a brief to prepare and lodge an appendix of excerpts that contains the documents or pages of the record cited in that party's brief.

(Subd (c) adopted effective January 1, 2010.)

Rule 3.2205 renumbered effective July 1, 2014; adopted as rule 3.1365 effective January 1, 2010.

Rule 3.2206.   Lodging and service

The party preparing the administrative record must lodge it with the court and serve it on each party. A record in electronic format must comply with rule 3.2207. A record in paper format must comply with rule 3.2208. If the party preparing the administrative record elects, is required by law, or is ordered to prepare an electronic version of the record, (1) a court may require the party to lodge one copy of the record in paper format, and (2) a party may request the record in paper format and pay the reasonable cost or show good cause for a court order requiring the party preparing the administrative record to serve the requesting party with one copy of the record in paper format.

Rule 3.2206 renumbered and amended effective July 1, 2014; adopted as rule 3.1366 effective January 1, 2010.

Rule 3.2207.   Electronic format

(a) Requirements

The electronic version of the administrative record lodged in the court in a proceeding brought under the California Environmental Quality Act must be:

(1) In compliance with rule 3.2205;

(2) Created in portable document format (PDF) or other format for which the software for creating and reading documents is in the public domain or generally available at a reasonable cost;

(3) Divided into a series of electronic files and include electronic bookmarks that identify each part of the record and clearly state the volume and page numbers contained in each part of the record;

(4) Contained on a CD-ROM, DVD, or other medium in a manner that cannot be altered; and

(5) Capable of full text searching.

The electronic version of the index required under rule 3.2205(b) may include hyperlinks to the indexed documents.

(Subd (a) amended effective July 1, 2014; adopted effective January 1, 2010.)

(b) Documents not included

Unless otherwise required by law, any document that is part of the administrative record and for which it is not feasible to create an electronic version may be provided in paper format only. Not feasible means that it would be reduced in size or otherwise altered to such an extent that it would not be easily readable.

(Subd (b) amended effective July 1, 2014; adopted effective January 1, 2010.)

Rule 3.2207 renumbered and amended effective July 1, 2014; adopted as rule 3.1367 effective January 1, 2010.

Rule 3.2208.   Paper format

(a) Requirements

In the paper format of the administrative record lodged in the court in a proceeding brought under the California Environmental Quality Act:

(1) Both sides of each page must be used;

(2) The paper must be opaque, unglazed, white or unbleached, 8 ½ by 11 inches, and of standard quality no less than 20-pound weight, except that maps, charts, and other demonstrative materials may be larger; and

(3) Each page must be numbered consecutively at the bottom.

(Subd (a) amended effective January 1, 2014; adopted effective January 1, 2010.)

(b) Binding and cover

The paper format of the administrative record must be bound on the left margin or contained in three-ring binders. Bound volumes must contain no more than 300 pages, and binders must contain no more than 400 pages. If bound, each page must have an adequate margin to allow unimpaired readability. The cover of each volume must contain the information required in rule 2.111, be prominently entitled "ADMINIS-TRATIVE RECORD," and state the volume number and the page numbers included in the volume.

(Subd (b) adopted effective January 1, 2010.)

Rule 3.2208 renumbered effective July 1, 2014; adopted as rule 3.1368 effective January 1, 2010; previously amended effective January 1, 2014.

Chapter 2
California Environmental Quality Act Proceedings Under Public Resources Code Sections 21168.6, 21178–21189.3, and 21189.50–21189.57

Title 3, Civil Rules—Division 22, Petitions Under the California Environmental Quality Act—Chapter 2, California Environmental Quality Act Proceedings Under Public Resources Code Sections 21168.6, 21178–21189.3, and 21189.50–21189.57; amended effective January 1, 2017; adopted effective July 1, 2014.

Art. 1.   General Provisions. Rules 3.2220–3.2231.

Art. 2.   CEQA Challenges to Approval of Sacramento Arena Project. Rules 3.2235–3.2237.

Article 1
General Provisions

Title 3, Civil Rules—Division 22, Petitions Under the California Environmental Quality Act—Chapter 2, California Environmental Quality Act Proceedings Under Public Resources Code Sections 21168.6.6 and 21178–21189.3—Article 1, General Provisions; adopted effective July 1, 2014.

Rule 3.2220.   Definitions and application

(a) Definitions

As used in this chapter:

(1) An "environmental leadership development project" or "leadership project" means a project certified by the Governor under Public Resources Code sections 21182–21184.

(2) The "Sacramento entertainment and sports center project" or "Sacramento arena project" means an entertainment and sports center project as defined by Public Resources Code section 21168.6.6, for which the proponent provided notice of election to proceed under that statute described in section 21168.6.6(j)(1).

(3) A "capitol building annex project" means a capitol building annex project as defined by Public Resources Code section 21189.50.

(Subd (a) amended effective January 1, 2017; adopted effective July 1, 2014.)

(b) Proceedings governed

The rules in this chapter govern actions or proceedings brought to attack, review, set aside, void, or annul the certification of the environmental impact report or the grant of any project approvals for the Sacramento arena project, a leadership project, or a capitol building annex project. Except as otherwise provided in Public Resources Code sections 21168.6.6, 21178–21189.3, and 21189.50–21189.57 and these rules, the provisions of the Public Resources Code and the CEQA Guidelines adopted by the Natural Resources Agency (Cal. Code Regs., tit. 14, § 15000 et seq.) governing judicial actions or proceedings to attack, review, set aside, void, or annul acts or decisions of a public agency on the grounds of noncompliance with the California Environmental Quality Act and the rules of court generally apply in proceedings governed by this rule.

(Subd (b) amended January 1, 2017; adopted effective July 1, 2014.)

(c) Complex case rules

Any action or proceeding governed by these rules is exempted from the rules regarding complex cases.

(Subd (c) adopted effective July 1, 2014.)

Rule 3.2220 amended effective January 1, 2017; adopted effective July 1, 2014.

Rule 3.2221.   Time

(a) Extensions of time

The court may order extensions of time only for good cause and in order to promote the interests of justice.

(Subd (a) adopted effective July 1, 2014.)

(b) Extensions of time by parties

If the parties stipulate to extend the time for performing any acts in actions governed by these rules, they are deemed to have agreed that the time for resolving the action may be extended beyond 270 days by the number of days by which the performance of the act has been stipulated to be extended, and to that extent to have waived any objection to noncompliance with the deadlines for completing review stated in Public Resources Code sections 21168.6.6(c)–(d), 21185, and 21189.51. Any such stipulation must be approved by the court.

(Subd (b) amended effective January 1, 2017; adopted effective July 1, 2014.)

(c) Sanctions for failure to comply with rules

If a party fails to comply with any time requirements provided in these rules or ordered by the court, the court may issue an order to show cause as to why one of the following sanctions should not be imposed:

(1) Reduction of time otherwise permitted under these rules for the performance of other acts by that party;

(2) If the failure to comply is by petitioner or plaintiff, dismissal of the petition;

(3) If the failure to comply is by respondent or a real party in interest, removal of the action from the expedited procedures provided under Public Resources Code sections 21168.6.6(c)–(d), 21185, and 21189.51, and these rules; or

(4) Any other sanction that the court finds appropriate.

(Subd (c) amended effective January 1, 2017; adopted effective July 1, 2014.)
Rule 3.2221 amended effective January 1, 2017; adopted effective July 1, 2014.

Rule 3.2222.   Filing and service

(a) Electronic filing

All pleadings and other documents filed in actions or proceedings governed by this chapter must be filed electronically, unless the action or proceeding is in a court that does not provide for electronic filing of documents.

(Subd (a) adopted effective July 1, 2014.)

(b) Service

Other than the petition, which must be served personally, all documents that the rules in this chapter require be served on the parties must be served personally or electronically. All parties represented by counsel are deemed to have agreed to accept electronic service. All self-represented parties may agree to such service.

(Subd (b) adopted effective July 1, 2014.)

(c) Service of petition in action regarding Sacramento arena project

Service of the petition or complaint in an action governed by these rules and relating to a Sacramento arena project must be made according to the rules in article 2.

(Subd (c) adopted effective July 1, 2014.)

(d) Service of petition in action regarding leadership project and capitol building annex project

If the petition or complaint in an action governed by these rules and relating to a leadership project or a capitol building annex project is not personally served on any respondent public agency, any real party in interest, and the Attorney General within three court days following filing of the petition, the time for filing petitioner's briefs on the merits provided in rule 3.2227(a) and rule 8.702(e) will be decreased by one day for every additional two court days in which service is not completed, unless otherwise ordered by the court for good cause shown.

(Subd (d) amended effective January 1, 2017; adopted effective July 1, 2014.)

(e) Exemption from extension of time

The extension of time provided in Code of Civil Procedure section 1010.6 for service completed by electronic means does not apply to any service in actions governed by these rules.

(Subd (e) adopted effective July 1, 2014.)
Rule 3.2222 amended effective January 1, 2017; adopted effective July 1, 2014.

Advisory Committee Comment

Parties should note that, while Public Resources Code section 21167 provides the statute of limitations for filing petitions under the California Environment Quality Act, these rules provide an incentive for parties to file actions governed by these rules more quickly, in the form of extra briefing time for petitioners who file within 10 days of the issuance of a Notice of Determination. See rule 3.2227(a).

Rule 3.2223.   Petition

In addition to any other applicable requirements, the petition must:

(1) On the first page, directly below the case number, indicate that the matter is either a "Sacramento Arena CEQA Challenge," an "Environmental Leadership CEQA Challenge," or a "Capitol Building Annex Project";

(2) State one of the following:

(A) The proponent of the project at issue provided notice to the lead agency that it was proceeding under Public Resources Code section 21168.6.6 and is subject to this rule; or

(B) The project at issue was certified by the Governor as a leadership project under Public Resources Code sections 21182–21184 and is subject to this rule; or

(C) The project at issue is a capitol building annex project as defined by Public Resources Code section 21189.50 and is subject to this rule;

(3) If a leadership project, provide notice that the person or entity that applied for certification of the project as a leadership project must, if the matter goes to the Court of Appeal, make the payments required by Public Resources Code section 21183(f); and

(4) Be verified.

Rule 3.2223 amended effective January 1, 2017; adopted effective July 1, 2014.

Rule 3.2224.   Response to petition

(a) Responsive pleadings and motions

Respondent and any real party in interest must serve and file any answer to the petition; any motion challenging the sufficiency of the petition, including any motion to dismiss the petition; any other response to the petition; any motion to change venue; or any motion to intervene within 10 days after service of petition or complaint on that party or within the time ordered by the court. Any such answer, motion, or other response from the same party must be filed concurrently.

(Subd (a) adopted effective July 1, 2014.)

(b) Opposition

Any opposition or other response to a motion challenging the sufficiency of the petition or to change venue must be served and filed within 10 days after the motion is served.

(Subd (b) adopted effective July 1, 2014.)
Rule 3.2224 adopted effective July 1, 2014.

Rule 3.2225.   Administrative record

(a) Lodging and service

Within 10 days after the petition is served on the lead public agency, that agency must lodge the certified final administrative record in electronic form with the court and serve notice on petitioner and real party in interest that the record has been lodged with the court. Within that same time, the agency must serve a copy of the administrative record in electronic form on any petitioner and real party in interest who has not already been provided a copy.

(Subd (a) adopted effective July 1, 2014.)

(b) Paper copy of record

(1) On request of the court, the lead agency shall provide the court with the record in paper format.

(2) On request and payment of the reasonable cost of preparation, or on order of the court for good cause shown, the lead agency shall provide a party with the record in paper format.

(Subd (b) adopted effective July 1, 2014.)

(c) Motions regarding the record

Unless otherwise ordered by the court:

(1) Any request to augment or otherwise change the contents of the administrative record must be made by motion served and filed no later than the filing of that party's initial brief.

(2) Any opposition or other response to the motion must be served and filed within 10 days after the motion is filed.

(3) Any motion regarding the record will be heard at the time of the hearing on the merits of the petition unless the court orders otherwise.

(Subd (c) adopted effective July 1, 2014.)
Rule 3.2225 adopted effective July 1, 2014.

Rule 3.2226.   Initial case management conference

(a) Timing of conference

The court should hold an initial case management conference within 30 days of the filing of the petition or complaint.

(Subd (a) adopted effective July 1, 2014.)

(b) Notice

Petitioner must provide notice of the case management conference to respondent, real party in interest, and any responsible agency or party to the action who has been served before the case management conference, within one court day of receiving notice from the court or at time of service of the petition or complaint, whichever is later.

(Subd (b) adopted effective July 1, 2014.)

(c) Subjects for consideration

At the conference, the court should consider the following subjects:

(1) Whether all parties named in the petition or complaint have been served;

(2) Whether a list of responsible agencies has been provided, and notice provided to each;

(3) Whether all responsive pleadings have been filed, and if not, when they must be filed, and whether any hearing is required to address them;

(4) Whether severance, bifurcation, or consolidation with other actions is desirable, and if so, a relevant briefing schedule;

(5) Whether to appoint a liaison or lead counsel, and either a briefing schedule on this issue or the actual appointment of counsel;

(6) Whether the administrative record has been certified and served on all parties, whether there are any issues with it, and whether the court wants to receive a paper copy;

(7) Whether the parties anticipate any motions before the hearing on the merits concerning discovery, injunctions, or other matters, and if so, a briefing schedule for these motions;

(8) What issues the parties intend to raise in their briefs on the merits, and whether any limitation of issues to be briefed and argued is appropriate;

(9) Whether a schedule for briefs on the merits different from the schedule provided in these rules is appropriate;

(10) Whether the submission of joint briefs on the merits is appropriate, and the page limitations on all briefs, whether aggregate per side or per brief;

(11) When the hearing on the merits of the petition will be held, and the amount of time appropriate for it;

(12) The potential for settlement, and whether a schedule for settlement conferences or alternative dispute resolution should be set;

(13) Any stipulations between the parties;

(14) Whether a further case management conference should be set; and

(15) Any other matters that the court finds appropriate.

(Subd (c) adopted effective July 1, 2014.)

(d) Joint case management conference statements

At least three court days before the case management conference, petitioner and all parties that have been served with the petition must serve and file a joint case management conference statement that addresses the issues identified in (c) and any other pertinent issues.

(Subd (d) adopted effective July 1, 2014.)

(e) Preparation for the conference

At the conference, lead counsel for each party and each self-represented party must appear by telephone or personally, must be familiar with the case, and must be prepared to discuss and commit to the party's position on the issues listed in (c).

(Subd (e) adopted effective July 1, 2014.)
Rule 3.2226 adopted effective July 1, 2014.

Rule 3.2227.   Briefing and Hearing

(a) Briefing schedule

Unless otherwise ordered by the court:

(1) Within 5 days after filing its brief, each party must submit an electronic version of the brief that contains hyperlinks to material cited in the brief, including electronically searchable copies of the administrative record, cited decisions, and any other brief in the case filed electronically by the parties. Such briefs must comply with any local requirements of the reviewing court relating to e-briefs.

(2) The petitioner must serve and file its brief within 25 days after the case management conference, unless petitioner served and filed the petition within 10 days of the public agency's issuance of its Notice of Determination, in which case petitioner must file and serve its brief within 35 days after the case management conference.

(3) Within 25 days after the petitioner's brief is filed, the respondent public agency must—and any real party in interest may—serve and file a respondent's brief. Respondents and real parties must file a single joint brief, unless otherwise ordered by the court.

(4) Within 5 days after the respondent's brief is filed, the parties must jointly file an appendix of excerpts that contain the documents or pertinent excerpts of the documents cited in the parties' briefs.

(5) Within 10 days after the respondent's brief is filed, the petitioner may serve and file a reply brief.

(Subd (a) adopted effective July 1, 2014.)

(b) Hearing

(1) The hearing should be held within 80 days of the case management conference, extended by the number of days to which the parties have stipulated to extend the briefing schedule.

(2) If the court has, within 90 days of the filing of the petition or complaint, set a hearing date, the provision in Public Resources Code section 21167.4 that petitioner request a hearing date within 90 days is deemed to have been met, and no further request is required.

(Subd (b) adopted effective July 1, 2014.)
Rule 3.2227 adopted effective July 1, 2014.

Rule 3.2228.   Judgment

The court should issue its decision and final order, writ, or judgment within 30 days of the completion of the hearing in the action. The court must include a written statement of the factual and legal basis for its decision. Code of Civil Procedure section 632 does not apply to actions governed by the rules in this division.

Rule 3.2228 adopted effective July 1, 2014.

Rule 3.2229.   Notice of settlement

The petitioner or plaintiff must immediately notify the court if the case is settled.

Rule 3.2229 adopted effective July 1, 2014.

Rule 3.2230.   Settlement procedures and statement of issues

In cases governed by the rules in this chapter, unless otherwise ordered by the court, the procedures described in Public Resources Code section 21167.8, including the filing of a statement of issues, are deemed to have been met by the parties addressing the potential for settlement and narrowing of issues within the case management conference statement and discussing those points as part of the case management conference.

Rule 3.2230 adopted effective July 1, 2014.

Rule 3.2231.   Postjudgment motions

(a) Exemption from statutory provisions

In any actions governed by the rules in this article, any postjudgment motion except for a motion for attorney's fees and costs is governed by this rule. Such motions are exempt from the timing requirements otherwise applicable to postjudgment motions under Code of Civil Procedure section 1005. Motions in Sacramento arena project cases are also exempt from the timing and procedural requirements of Code of Civil Procedure sections 659 and 663.

(Subd (a) adopted effective July 1, 2014.)

(b) Time for postjudgment motions

(1) *Time for motions under Code of Civil Procedure section 473*

Moving party must serve and file any motion before the earlier of:

(A) Five days after the court clerk mails to the moving party a document entitled "Notice of Entry" of judgment or a file-stamped copy of the judgment, showing the date either was served; or

(B) Five days after the moving party is served by any party with a written notice of judgment or a file-stamped copy of the judgment, accompanied by a proof of service.

(2) *Time for motions for new trial or motions to vacate judgment*

Moving party in Sacramento arena project cases must serve and file motion before the earlier of:

(A) Five days after the court clerk mails to the moving party a document entitled "Notice of Entry" of judgment or a file-stamped copy of the judgment, showing the date either was served; or

(B) Five days after the moving party is served by any party with a written notice of judgment or a file-stamped copy of the judgment, accompanied by a proof of service.

(Subd (b) adopted effective July 1, 2014.)

(c) Memorandum

A memorandum in support of a postjudgment motion may be no longer than 15 pages.

(Subd (c) adopted effective July 1, 2014.)

(d) Opposition to motion

Any opposition to the motion must be served and filed within five days of service of the moving papers and may be no longer than 15 pages.

(Subd (d) adopted effective July 1, 2014.)

(e) Reply

Any reply brief must be served and filed within two court days of service of the opposition papers and may be no longer than 5 pages.

(Subd (e) adopted effective July 1, 2014.)

(f) Hearing and decision

The court may set a hearing on the motion at its discretion. The court should issue its decision on the motion within 15 days of the filing of the motion.

(Subd (f) adopted effective July 1, 2014.)
Rule 3.2231 adopted effective July 1, 2014.

Article 2
CEQA Challenges to Approval of Sacramento Arena Project

Title 3, Civil Rules—Division 22, Petitions Under the California Environmental Quality Act—Chapter 2, California Environmental Quality Act Proceedings Under Public Resources Code Sections 21168.6.6 and 21178–21189.3—Article 2, CEQA Challenges to Approval of Sacramento Arena Project; adopted effective July 1, 2014.

Rule 3.2235. Application
Rule 3.2236. Service of Petition
Rule 3.2237. List of responsible parties

Rule 3.2235. Application

This article governs any action or proceeding brought to attack, review, set aside, void, or annul the certification of the environmental impact report or any project approvals for the Sacramento arena project.
Rule 3.2235 adopted effective July 1, 2014.

Rule 3.2236. Service of Petition

(a) Respondent

Unless the respondent public agency has agreed to accept service of summons electronically, the petitioner or plaintiff must personally serve the petition or complaint on the respondent public agency within three court days after the date of filing.
(Subd (a) adopted effective July 1, 2014.)

(b) Real parties in interest

The petitioner or plaintiff must serve the petition or complaint on any real party in interest named in the pleading within three court days after the date of filing.
(Subd (b) adopted effective July 1, 2014.)

(c) Attorney General

The petitioner or plaintiff must serve the petition or complaint on the Attorney General within three court days after the date of filing.
(Subd (c) adopted effective July 1, 2014.)

(d) Responsible agencies

The petitioner or plaintiff must serve the petition or complaint on any responsible agencies or public agencies with jurisdiction over a natural resource affected by the project within two court days of receipt of a list of such agencies from respondent public agency.
(Subd (d) adopted effective July 1, 2014.)

(e) Proof of service

The petitioner or plaintiff must file proof of service on each respondent, real party in interest, or agency within one court day of completion of service.
(Subd (e) adopted effective July 1, 2014.)
Rule 3.2236 adopted effective July 1, 2014.

Rule 3.2237. List of responsible parties

Respondent public agency must provide the petitioner or plaintiff, not later than three court days following service of the petition or complaint on the public agency, with a list of responsible agencies and any public agency having jurisdiction over a natural resource affected by the project.
Rule 3.2237 adopted effective July 1, 2014.

Division 23
Miscellaneous

Title 3, Civil Rules—Division 23, Miscellaneous; adopted effective January 20, 2017.

Rule 3.2300. Review under Penal Code section 186.35 of law enforcement agency denial of request to remove name from shared gang database

(a) Proceedings governed

This rule applies to proceedings under Penal Code section 186.35 to seek review of a local law enforcement agency's denial of a request under Penal Code section 186.34 to remove a person's name from a shared gang database.
(Subd (a) adopted effective January 20, 2017.)

(b) Definitions

For purposes of this rule:

(1) "Request for review" or "petition" means a "notice of appeal" under Penal Code section 186.35 requesting review of a law enforcement agency's decision denying a person's request under Penal Code section 186.34 to remove a person's name from a shared gang database.

(2) "Law enforcement agency" means the local law enforcement agency that denied the request under Penal Code section 186.34 to remove a person's name from a shared gang database.
(Subd (b) adopted effective January 20, 2017.)

(c) Designated judge

The presiding judge of each superior court must designate one or more judges to handle any petitions governed by this rule that are filed in the court.
(Subd (c) adopted effective January 20, 2017.)

(d) Petition

(1) *Form*

(A) Except as provided in (i) and (ii), *Petition for Review of Denial of Request to Remove Name From Gang Database* (form MC-1000) must be used to seek review under Penal Code section 186.35 of a law enforcement agency's decision denying a request to remove a person's name from a shared gang database.

(i) A petition filed by an attorney need not be on form MC-1000. For good cause the court may also accept a petition from a nonattorney that is not on form MC-1000.

(ii) Any petition that is not on form MC-1000 must contain the information specified in form MC-1000 and must bear the name "Petition for Review of Denial of Request to Remove Name From Gang Database."

(B) The person seeking review must attach to the petition under (A) either:

(i) The law enforcement agency's written verification, if one was received, of its decision denying the person's request under Penal Code section 186.34 to remove his or her name—or, if the request was filed by a parent or guardian on behalf of a child under 18, the name of the child—from the shared gang database; or

(ii) If the law enforcement agency did not provide written verification responding to the person's request under Penal Code section 186.34 within 30 days of submission of the request, a copy of the request and written documentation submitted to the law enforcement agency contesting the designation.

(2) *Time for filing*

The petition must be filed within 90 calendar days of the date the law enforcement agency mails or personally serves the person filing the petition with written verification of the agency's decision denying that person's request under Penal Code section 186.34 to remove the name from the shared gang database.

(3) *Where to file*

The petition must be filed in either the superior court of the county in which the law enforcement agency is located or, if the person filing the petition resides in California, in the superior court of the county in which that person resides.

(4) *Fee*

The fee for filing the petition is $25, as specified in Government Code section 70615.

(5) *Service*

A copy of the petition with the attachment required under (1)(B) must be served either personally or by mail on the law enforcement agency, as provided in Code of Civil Procedure sections 1011–1013a. Proof of this service must be filed in the superior court with the petition.
(Subd (d) amended effective January 1, 2019; adopted effective January 20, 2017.)

(e) Record

(1) *Filing*

(A) The law enforcement agency must serve the record on the person filing the petition and must file the record in the superior court in which the petition was filed.

(B) The record must be served and filed within 15 days after the date the petition is served on the law enforcement agency as required by subdivision (d)(5) of this rule.

(C) If the record contains any documents that are part of a juvenile case file or are confidential under Welfare and Institutions Code section 827 or have been sealed, the law enforcement agency must include a coversheet that states "Confidential Filing – Juvenile Case File Enclosed."

(D) The procedures set out in rules 2.550 and 2.551 apply to any record sought to be filed under seal in a proceeding under this rule.

(2) *Contents*

The record is limited to the documents required by Penal Code section 186.35(c).

(3) *Format*

(A) The cover or first page of the record must:

(i) Clearly identify it as the record in the case;

(ii) Clearly indicate if the record includes any documents that are confidential under Welfare and Institutions Code section 827 or have been sealed;

(iii) State the title and court number of the case; and

(iv) Include the name, mailing address, telephone number, fax number (if available), e-mail address (if available), and California State Bar number (if applicable) of the attorney or other person filing the record on behalf of the law enforcement agency. The court will use this as the name, mailing address, telephone number, fax number, and e-mail address of record for the agency unless the agency informs the court otherwise in writing.

(B) All documents in the record must have a page size of 8.5 by 11 inches;

(C) The text must be reproduced as legibly as printed matter;

(D) The contents must be arranged chronologically;

(E) The pages must be consecutively numbered; and

(F) The record must be stapled and two-hole punched at the top of the page.

(4) *Failure to file the record*

If the law enforcement agency does not timely file the required record, the superior court clerk must serve the law enforcement agency with a notice indicating that the agency must file the record within five court days of service of the clerk's notice or the court may order the law enforcement agency to remove the name of the person from the shared gang database.

(Subd (e) amended effective January 1, 2019; adopted effective January 20, 2017.)

(f) Written argument

(1) *Contents*

(A) The person filing the petition may include in the petition or separately serve and file a written argument about why, based on the record specified in Penal Code section 186.35(c), the law enforcement agency has failed to establish by clear and convincing evidence the active gang membership, associate status, or affiliate status of the person so designated or to be so designated by the law enforcement agency in the shared gang database.

(B) The law enforcement agency may serve and file a written argument about why, based on the record specified in Penal Code section 186.35(c), it has established by clear and convincing evidence the active gang membership, associate status, or affiliate status of the person.

(C) If an argument refers to something in the record, it must provide the page number of the record where that thing appears or, if the record has not yet been filed, the page number of the relevant document.

(D) Except for any required attachment to a petition, when an argument is included in the petition, nothing may be attached to an argument and an argument must not refer to any evidence that is not in the record.

(2) *Time to serve and file*

Any written argument must be served and filed within 15 days after the date the record is served.

(3) *Format and length of argument*

(A) The cover or first page of any argument must:

(i) Clearly identify it as the argument of the person filing the petition or of the law enforcement agency;

(ii) State the title and, if assigned, court number of the case; and

(iii) Include the name, mailing address, telephone number, fax number (if available), e-mail address (if available), and California State Bar number (if applicable) of the attorney or other person filing the argument.

(B) An argument must not exceed 10 pages.

(C) The pages must be consecutively numbered.

(Subd (f) amended effective January 1, 2019; adopted effective January 20, 2017.)

(g) Oral argument

(1) *Setting oral argument*

The court may set the case for oral argument at the request of either party or on its own motion.

(2) *Requesting or waiving oral argument*

The person filing the petition or the law enforcement agency may request oral argument or inform the court that they do not want to participate in oral argument. Any such request for or waiver of oral argument must be served and filed within 15 days after the date the record is served.

(3) *Sending notice of oral argument*

If oral argument is set, the clerk must send notice at least 20 days before the oral argument date. The court may shorten the notice period for good cause; in that event, the clerk must immediately notify the parties by telephone or other expeditious method.

(4) *Sealed or confidential records*

If the responding party indicates that the record contains information from a juvenile case file or documents that are sealed or confidential under Welfare and Institutions Code section 827, the argument must be closed to the public unless the crime charged allows for public access under Welfare and Institutions Code section 676.

(Subd (g) adopted effective January 20, 2017.)

(h) Decision

As provided in Penal Code section 186.35, if, on de novo review and any arguments presented to the court, the court finds that the law enforcement agency has failed to establish by clear and convincing evidence the active gang membership, associate status, or affiliate status of the person so designated in the shared gang database, the court must order the law enforcement agency to remove the name of the person from the shared gang database.

(Subd (h) adopted effective January 20, 2017.)

(i) Service on the Attorney General

The court must serve on the Attorney General a copy of any order under (e)(4) or (h) to remove a name from a shared gang database.

(Subd (i) adopted effective January 20, 2017.)

Rule 3.2300 amended effective January 1, 2019; adopted effective January 20, 2017.

Advisory Committee Comment

Subdivision (d)(1)(B). Penal Code section 186.34(f) provides that if a person to be designated as a suspected gang member, associate, or affiliate, or his or her parent or guardian, submits written documentation to the local law enforcement agency contesting the designation, the local law enforcement agency "shall provide the person and his or her parent or guardian with written verification of the agency's decision within 30 days of submission of the written documentation contesting the designation. If the law enforcement agency denies the request for removal, the notice of its determination shall state the reason for the denial."

Subdivision (e)(2). Penal Code section 186.35(b) provides that the evidentiary record for this review proceeding "shall be limited to the agency's statement of basis of its designation made pursuant to subdivision (e) of Section 186.34, and the documentation provided to the agency by the appellant pursuant to subdivision (f) of Section 186.34."

Penal Code section 186.34(e)(1) provides that "[a] person, or, if the person is under 18 years of age, his or her parent or guardian, or an attorney working on behalf of the person may request information of any law enforcement agency as to whether the person is designated as a suspected gang member, associate, or affiliate in a shared gang database" and, if the person is so designated, "information as to the basis for the designation for the purpose of contesting the designation as described in subdivision (f)." Section 186.35(e)(2) provides that "[t]he law enforcement agency shall provide information requested under paragraph (1), unless doing so would compromise an active criminal investigation or compromise the health or safety of the person if the person is under 18 years of age."

Penal Code section 186.34(f) provides that "the person to be designated as a suspected gang member, associate, or affiliate, or his or her parent or guardian, may submit written documentation to the local law enforcement agency contesting the designation."

Penal Code section 186.34(g) also provides that "[n]othing in this section shall require a local law enforcement agency to disclose any information protected under Section 1040 or 1041 of the Evidence Code or Section 6254 of the Government Code."

TITLE 4
Criminal Rules

Division 1
General Provisions

Rule 4.1.   Title

The rules in this title may be referred to as the Criminal Rules.

Rule 4.1 adopted effective January 1, 2007.

Rule 4.2.   Application

The Criminal Rules apply to all criminal cases in the superior courts unless otherwise provided by a statute or rule in the California Rules of Court.

Rule 4.2 adopted effective January 1, 2007.

Rule 4.3.   Reference to Penal Code

All statutory references are to the Penal Code unless stated otherwise.

Rule 4.3 adopted effective January 1, 2007.

Division 2
Pretrial

Chapter 1
Pretrial Proceedings

Rule 4.100.   Arraignments

At the arraignment on the information or indictment, unless otherwise ordered for good cause, and on a plea of not guilty, including a plea of not guilty by reason of insanity;

(1) The court must set dates for:

(A) Trial, giving priority to a case entitled to it under law; and

(B) Filing and service of motions and responses and hearing thereon;

(2) A plea of not guilty must be entered if a defendant represented by counsel fails to plead or demur; and

(3) An attorney may not appear specially.

Rule 4.100 amended effective January 1, 2007; adopted as rule 227.4 effective January 1, 1985; previously amended effective June 6, 1990; previously renumbered and amended effective January 1, 2001.

Advisory Committee Comment

Cross reference: Penal Code section 987.1.

Rule 4.101.   Bail in criminal cases

The fact that a defendant in a criminal case has or has not asked for a jury trial must not be taken into consideration in fixing the amount of bail and, once set, bail may not be increased or reduced by reason of such fact.

Rule 4.101 amended effective January 1, 2007; adopted as rule 801 effective July 1, 1964; previously renumbered effective January 1, 2001.

Rule 4.102.   Uniform bail and penalty schedules—traffic, boating, fish and game, forestry, public utilities, parks and recreation, business licensing

The Judicial Council of California has established the policy of promulgating uniform bail and penalty schedules for certain offenses in order to achieve a standard of uniformity in the handling of these offenses.

In general, bail is used to ensure the presence of the defendant before the court. Under Vehicle Code sections 40512 and 13103, bail may also be forfeited and forfeiture may be ordered without the necessity of any further court proceedings and be treated as a conviction for specified Vehicle Code offenses. A penalty in the form of a monetary sum is a fine imposed as all or a portion of a sentence imposed.

To achieve substantial uniformity of bail and penalties throughout the state in traffic, boating, fish and game, forestry, public utilities, parks and recreation, and business licensing cases, the trial court judges, in performing their duty under Penal Code section 1269b to annually revise and adopt a schedule of bail and penalties for all misdemeanor and infraction offenses except Vehicle Code infractions, must give consideration to the Uniform Bail and Penalty Schedules approved by the Judicial Council. The Uniform Bail and Penalty Schedule for infraction violations of the Vehicle Code will be established by the Judicial Council in accordance with Vehicle Code section 40310. Judges must give consideration to requiring additional bail for aggravating or enhancing factors.

After a court adopts a countywide bail and penalty schedule, under Penal Code section 1269b, the court must, as soon as practicable, mail or e-mail a copy of the schedule to the Judicial Council with a report stating how the revised schedule differs from the council's uniform traffic bail and penalty schedule, uniform boating bail and penalty schedule, uniform fish and game bail and penalty schedule, uniform forestry bail and penalty schedule, uniform public utilities bail and penalty schedule, uniform parks and recreation bail and penalty schedule, or uniform business licensing bail and penalty schedule.

The purpose of this uniform bail and penalty schedule is to:

(1) Show the standard amount for bail, which for Vehicle Code offenses may also be the amount used for a bail forfeiture instead of further proceedings; and

(2) Serve as a guideline for the imposition of a fine as all or a portion of the penalty for a first conviction of a listed offense where a fine is used as all or a portion of the penalty for such offense. The amounts shown for the misdemeanors on the boating, fish and game, forestry, public utilities, parks and recreation, and business licensing bail and penalty schedules have been set with this dual purpose in mind.

Unless otherwise shown, the maximum penalties for the listed offenses are six months in the county jail or a fine of $1,000, or both. The penalty amounts are intended to be used to provide standard fine amounts for a first offense conviction of a violation shown where a fine is used as all or a portion of the sentence imposed.

Note:

Courts may obtain copies of the Uniform Bail and Penalty Schedules by contacting:

Criminal Justice Services

Judicial Council of California
455 Golden Gate Avenue
San Francisco, CA 94102-3688
or

www.courts.ca.gov/7532.htm

Rule 4.102 amended effective January 1, 2018; adopted as rule 850 effective January 1, 1965; previously renumbered as rule 4.102 and amended effective January 1, 2001; previously amended effective January 1, 1970, January 1, 1971, July 1, 1972, January 1, 1973, January 1, 1974, July 1, 1975, July 1, 1979, July 1, 1980, July 1, 1981, January 1, 1983, July 1, 1984, July 1, 1986, January 1, 1989, January 1, 1990, January 1, 1993, January 1, 1995, January 1, 1997, July 1, 2004, January 1, 2007, July 1, 2013, and January 1, 2016.

Rule 4.103. Notice to appear forms

(a) Traffic offenses

A printed or electronic notice to appear that is issued for any violation of the Vehicle Code other than a felony or for a violation of an ordinance of a city or county relating to traffic offenses must be prepared and filed with the court on *Automated Traffic Enforcement System Notice to Appear* (form TR-115), *Traffic/Nontraffic Notice to Appear* (form TR-130), *Electronic Traffic/Nontraffic Notice to Appear* (4-inch format) (form TR-135), or *Electronic Traffic/Nontraffic Notice to Appear* (3-inch format) (form TR-145), and must comply with the requirements in the current version of the Judicial Council's instructions, *Notice to Appear and Related Forms* (form TR-INST).

(Subd (a) amended effective June 26, 2015; previously amended effective January 1, 2007.)

(b) Nontraffic offenses

A notice to appear issued for a nontraffic infraction or misdemeanor offense that is prepared on *Nontraffic Notice to Appear* (form TR-120), *Traffic/Nontraffic Notice to Appear* (form TR-130), *Electronic Traffic/Nontraffic Notice to Appear* (4-inch format) (form TR-135), or *Electronic Traffic/Nontraffic Notice to Appear* (3-inch format) (form TR-145), and that complies with the requirements in the current version of the Judicial Council's instructions, *Notice to Appear and Related Forms* (form TR-INST), may be filed with the court and serve as a complaint as provided in Penal Code section 853.9 or 959.1.

(Subd (b) amended effective June 26, 2015; previously amended effective January 1, 2007.)

(c) Corrections

Corrections to citations previously issued on *Continuation of Notice to Appear* (form TR-106), *Continuation of Citation* (form TR-108), *Automated Traffic Enforcement System Notice to Appear* (form TR-115), *Nontraffic Notice to Appear* (form TR-120), *Traffic/Nontraffic Notice to Appear* (form TR-130), *Electronic Traffic/Nontraffic Notice to Appear* (4-inch format) (form TR-135), or *Electronic Traffic/Nontraffic Notice to Appear* (3-inch format) (form TR-145) must be made on a *Notice of Correction and Proof of Service* (form TR-100).

(Subd (c) amended effective June 26, 2015; previously amended effective January 1, 2007.)

(d) Electronic citation forms

A law enforcement agency that uses an electronic citation device to issue notice to appear citations on the Judicial Council's *Electronic Traffic/Nontraffic Notice to Appear* (4-inch format) (form TR-135) or *Electronic Traffic/Nontraffic Notice to Appear* (3-inch format) (form TR-145) must submit to the Judicial Council an exact printed copy of the agency's current citation form that complies with the requirements in the most recent version of the Judicial Council's instructions, *Notice to Appear and Related Forms* (form TR-INST).

(Subd (d) adopted effective June 26, 2015.)

Rule 4.103 amended effective June 26, 2015; adopted effective January 1, 2004; previously amended effective January 1, 2007.

Rule 4.104. Procedures and eligibility criteria for attending traffic violator school

(a) Purpose

The purpose of this rule is to establish uniform statewide procedures and criteria for eligibility to attend traffic violator school.

(Subd (a) amended effective January 1, 2003; previously amended effective July 1, 2001.)

(b) Authority of a court clerk to grant a request to attend traffic violator school

(1) *Eligible offenses*

Except as provided in (2), a court clerk is authorized to grant a request to attend traffic violator school when a defendant with a valid driver's license requests to attend an 8-hour traffic violator school under Vehicle Code sections 41501(a) and 42005 for any infraction under divisions 11 and 12 (rules of the road and equipment violations) of the Vehicle Code if the violation is reportable to the Department of Motor Vehicles.

(2) *Ineligible offenses*

A court clerk is not authorized to grant a request to attend traffic violator school for a misdemeanor or any of the following infractions:

(A) A violation that carries a negligent operator point count of more than one point under Vehicle Code section 12810 or one and one-half points or more under Vehicle Code section 12810.5(b)(2);

(B) A violation that occurs within 18 months after the date of a previous violation and the defendant either attended or elected to attend a traffic violator school for the previous violation (Veh. Code, §§ 1808.7 and 1808.10);

(C) A violation of Vehicle Code section 22406.5 (tank vehicles);

(D) A violation related to alcohol use or possession or drug use or possession;

(E) A violation on which the defendant failed to appear under Vehicle Code section 40508(a) unless the failure-to-appear charge has been adjudicated and any fine imposed has been paid;

(F) A violation on which the defendant has failed to appear under Penal Code section 1214.1 unless the civil monetary assessment has been paid;

(G) A speeding violation in which the speed alleged is more than 25 miles over a speed limit as stated in Chapter 7 (commencing with section 22348) of Division 11 of the Vehicle Code; and

(H) A violation that occurs in a commercial vehicle as defined in Vehicle Code section 15210(b).

(Subd (b) amended effective January 1, 2013; previously amended effective January 1, 2003, September 20, 2005, January 1, 2007, January 1, 2007, and July 1, 2011.)

(c) Judicial discretion

(1) A judicial officer may in his or her discretion order attendance at a traffic violator school in an individual case as permitted under Vehicle Code section 41501(a) or 42005 or for any other purpose permitted by law. A defendant having a class A, class B, or commercial class C driver's license may request to attend traffic violator school if the defendant was operating a vehicle requiring only a noncommercial class C or class M license. The record of conviction after completion of traffic violator school by a driver who holds a class A, class B, or commercial class C license must not be reported as confidential. A defendant charged with a violation that occurs in a commercial vehicle, as defined in Vehicle Code section 15210(b), is not eligible to attend traffic violator school under Vehicle Code sections 41501 or 42005 in lieu of adjudicating an offense, to receive a confidential conviction, or to avoid violator point counts.

(2) A defendant who is otherwise eligible for traffic violator school is not made ineligible by entering a plea other than guilty or by exercising his or her right to trial. A traffic violator school request must be considered based on the individual circumstances of the specific case. The court is not required to state on the record a reason for granting or denying a traffic violator school request.

(Subd (c) amended effective January 1, 2013; amended and relettered as part of subd (b) effective January 1, 2003; previously amended effective January 1, 1998, September 20, 2005, January 1, 2007, January 1, 2007, and July 1, 2011.)

Rule 4.104 amended effective January 1, 2013; adopted as rule 851 effective January 1, 1997; previously amended effective January 1, 1998, July 1, 2001, January 1, 2003, September 20, 2005, January 1, 2007, and July 1, 2011; previously amended and renumbered effective January 1, 2007.

Advisory Committee Comment

Subdivision (c)(1). Rule 4.104(c)(1) reflects that under Vehicle Code sections 1808.10, 41501, and 42005, the record of a driver with a class A, class B, or commercial class C license who completes a traffic violator school program is not confidential and must be reported to and disclosed by the Department of Motor Vehicles for purposes of Title 49 of the Federal Code of Regulations and to insurers for underwriting and rating purposes.

Subdivision (c)(2). Rule 4.104(c)(2) reflects court rulings in cases where defendants wished to plead not guilty and have the court order attendance of traffic violator school if found guilty after trial. A court has discretion to grant or not grant traffic violator school. (*People v. Schindler* (1993) 20 Cal.App.4th 431, 433; *People v. Levinson* (1984) 155 Cal.App.3d Supp. 13, 21.) However, the court may not arbitrarily refuse to consider a request for traffic violator school because a defendant pleads not guilty. (*Schindler, supra*, at p. 433; *People v. Wozniak* (1987) 197 Cal.App.3d Supp. 43, 44; *People v. Enochs* (1976) 62 Cal.App.3d Supp. 42, 44.) If a judicial officer believes that a defendant's circumstances indicate that a defendant would benefit from attending school, such attendance should be authorized and should not be affected by the order in which the plea, explanation, and request for traffic violator school are presented. (*Enochs, supra,* at p. 44.) A court is not required to state its reasons for granting or denying traffic violator school following a defendant's conviction for a traffic violation. (*Schindler, supra,* at p. 433.)

Rule 4.105. Appearance without deposit of bail in infraction cases

(a) Application

This rule applies to any infraction for which the defendant has received a written notice to appear.

(Subd (a) amended effective December 1, 2015; adopted effective June 8, 2015.)

(b) Appearance without deposit of bail

Except as provided in (c), courts must allow a defendant to appear for arraignment and trial without deposit of bail.

(Subd (b) adopted effective June 8, 2015.)

(c) Deposit of bail

(1) Courts must require the deposit of bail when the defendant elects a statutory procedure that requires the deposit of bail.

(2) Courts may require the deposit of bail when the defendant does not sign a written promise to appear as required by the court.

(3) Courts may require a deposit of bail before trial if the court determines that the defendant is unlikely to appear as ordered without a deposit of bail and the court expressly states the reasons for the finding.

(4) In determining the amount of bail set under (2) and (3), courts must consider the totality of the circumstances.

(Subd (c) amended effective January 1, 2017; adopted effective June 8, 2015; previously amended effective December 1, 2015.)

(d) Notice

Courts must inform defendants of the option to appear in court without the deposit of bail in any instructions or other materials courts provide for the public that relate to bail for infractions, including any website information, written instructions, courtesy notices, and forms.

(Subd (d) amended effective December 1, 2015; adopted effective June 8, 2015.)

(e) Local Website Information

The website for each trial court must include a link to the traffic self-help information posted at: *http://www.courts.ca.gov/selfhelp-traffic.htm.*

(Subd (e) adopted effective January 1, 2017.)

Rule 4.105 amended effective January 1, 2017; adopted effective June 8, 2015; previously amended effective December 1, 2015.

Advisory Committee Comment

Subdivision (a). The rule is intended to apply only to an infraction violation for which the defendant has received a written notice to appear and has appeared by the appearance date or an approved extension of that date. The rule does not apply to postconviction matters or cases in which the defendant seeks an appearance in court after a failure to appear or pay.

Subdivision (c). This subdivision takes into account the distinct statutory purposes and functions that bail and related considerations serve in infraction cases, including, for example, the posting and forfeiting of bail in uncontested cases and the use of bail to satisfy later judgments, as distinguished from felony and most misdemeanor cases.

Subdivision (c)(1). Various statutory provisions authorize infraction defendants who have received a written notice to appear to elect to deposit bail in lieu of appearing in court or in advance of the notice to appear date. (See, e.g., Veh. Code, §§ 40510 [authorizing defendants to deposit bail before the notice to appear date]; 40519(a) [authorizing defendants who have received a written notice to appear to declare the intention to plead not guilty and deposit bail before the notice to appear date for purposes of electing to schedule an arraignment and trial on the same date or on separate dates]; 40519(b) [authorizing defendants who have received a written notice to appear to deposit bail and plead not guilty in writing in lieu of appearing in person]; and 40902 [authorizing trial by written declaration].)

This rule is not intended to modify or contravene any statutorily authorized alternatives to appearing in court. (See, e.g., Pen. Code, §§ 853.5, 853.6; Veh. Code, §§ 40510, 40512, and 40512.5 [authorizing defendants to post and forfeit bail in lieu of appearing for arraignment].) The purpose of this rule is to clarify that if the defendant declines to use a statutorily authorized alternative, courts must allow the defendant to appear *without* prior deposit of bail as provided above.

Subdivision (c)(2). As used in this subdivision, the phrase "written promise to appear as required by the court" refers to a signed promise, made by a defendant who has appeared in court, to return to court on a future date and time as ordered by the court.

Subdivision (c)(3). In exercising discretion to require deposit of bail on a particular case, courts should consider, among other factors, whether previous failures to pay or appear were willful or involved adequate notice.

Subdivision (c)(4). In considering the "totality of the circumstances" under this subdivision, courts may consider whether the bail amount would impose an undue hardship on the defendant.

Rule 4.106. Failure to appear or failure to pay for a *Notice to Appear* issued for an infraction offense

(a) Application

This rule applies to infraction offenses for which the defendant has received a written notice to appear and has failed to appear or failed to pay.

(Subd (a) adopted effective January 1, 2017.)

(b) Definitions

As used in this rule, "failure to appear" and "failure to pay" mean failure to appear and failure to pay as defined in section 1214.1(a).

(Subd (b) adopted effective January 1, 2017.)

(c) Procedure for consideration of good cause for failure to appear or pay

(1) A notice of a civil assessment under section 1214.1(b) must inform the defendant of his or her right to petition that the civil assessment be vacated for good cause and must include information about the process for vacating or reducing the assessment.

(2) When a notice of civil assessment is given, a defendant may, within the time specified in the notice, move by written petition to vacate or reduce the assessment.

(3) When a court imposes a civil assessment for failure to appear or pay, the defendant may petition that the court vacate or reduce the civil assessment without paying any bail, fines, penalties, fees, or assessments.

(4) A petition to vacate an assessment does not stay the operation of any order requiring the payment of bail, fines, penalties, fees, or assessment unless specifically ordered by the court.

(5) The court must vacate the assessment upon a showing of good cause under section 1214.1(b)(1) for failure to appear or failure to pay.

(6) If the defendant does not establish good cause, the court may still exercise its discretion under section 1214.1(a) to reconsider:

(A) Whether a civil assessment should be imposed; and

(B) If so, the amount of the assessment.

(7) In exercising its discretion, the court may consider such factors as a defendant's due diligence in appearing or paying after notice of the assessment has been given under section 1214.1(b)(1) and the defendant's financial circumstances.

(Subd (c) adopted effective January 1, 2017.)

(d) Procedure for unpaid bail referred to collection as delinquent debt in unadjudicated cases

(1) When a case has not been adjudicated and a court refers it to a comprehensive collection program as provided in section 1463.007(b)(1) as delinquent debt, the defendant may schedule a hearing for adjudication of the underlying charge(s) without payment of the bail amount.

(2) The defendant may request an appearance date to adjudicate the underlying charges by written petition or alternative method provided by the court. Alternatively, the defendant may request or the court may direct a court appearance.

(3) A court may require a deposit of bail before adjudication of the underlying charges if the court finds that the defendant is unlikely to appear as ordered without a deposit of bail and the court expressly states the reasons for the finding. The court must not require payment of the civil assessment before adjudication.

(Subd (d) adopted effective January 1, 2017.)

(e) Procedure for failure to pay or make a payment under an installment payment plan

(1) When a defendant fails to pay a fine or make a payment under an installment plan as provided in section 1205 or Vehicle Code sections 40510.5, 42003, or 42007, the court must permit the defendant to appear by written petition to modify the payment terms. Alternatively, the defendant may request or the court may direct a court appearance.

(2) The court must not require payment of bail, fines, penalties, fees, or assessments to consider the petition.

(3) The petition to modify the payment terms does not stay the operation of any order requiring the payment of bail, fines, penalties, fees, or assessments unless specifically ordered by the court.

(4) If the defendant petitions to modify the payment terms based on an inability to pay, the procedures stated in rule 4.335 apply.

(5) If the petition to modify the payment terms is not based on an inability to pay, the court may deny the defendant's request to modify the

payment terms and order no further proceedings if the court determines that:

(A) An unreasonable amount of time has passed; or

(B) The defendant has made an unreasonable number of requests to modify the payment terms.

(Subd (e) adopted effective January 1, 2017.)

(f) Procedure after a trial by written declaration in absentia for a traffic infraction

When the court issues a judgment under Vehicle Code section 40903 and a defendant requests a trial de novo within the time permitted, courts may require the defendant to deposit bail.

(Subd (f) adopted effective January 1, 2017.)

(g) Procedure for referring a defendant to the Department of Motor Vehicles (DMV) for license suspension for failure to pay a fine

Before a court may notify the DMV under Vehicle Code sections 40509(b) or 40509.5(b) that a defendant has failed to pay a fine or an installment of bail, the court must provide the defendant with notice of and an opportunity to be heard on the inability to pay. This notice may be provided on the notice required in rule 4.107, the civil assessment notice, or any other notice provided to the defendant.

(Subd (g) adopted effective January 1, 2017.)
Rule 4.106 adopted effective January 1, 2017.

Advisory Committee Comment

Subdivision (a). The rule is intended to apply only to an infraction offense for which the defendant (1) has received a written notice to appear and (2) has failed to appear by the appearance date or an approved extension of that date or has failed to pay as required.

Subdivision (c)(3). Circumstances that indicate good cause may include, but are not limited to, the defendant's hospitalization, incapacitation, or incarceration; military duty required of the defendant; death or hospitalization of the defendant's dependent or immediate family member; caregiver responsibility for a sick or disabled dependent or immediate family member of the defendant; or an extraordinary reason, beyond the defendant's control, that prevented the defendant from making an appearance or payment on or before the date listed on the notice to appear.

Subdivision (e)(1). A court may exercise its discretion to deny a defendant's request to modify the payment terms. If the court chooses to grant the defendant's request, the court may modify the payment terms by reducing or suspending the base fine, lowering the payments, converting the remaining balance to community service, or otherwise modifying the payment terms as the court sees fit.

Subdivision (g). A hearing is not required unless requested by the defendant or directed by the court.

Rule 4.107. Mandatory reminder notice—traffic procedures

(a) Mandatory reminder notice

(1) Each court must send a reminder notice to the address shown on the *Notice to Appear*, unless the defendant otherwise notifies the court of a different address.

(2) The court may satisfy the requirement in paragraph (1) by sending the notice electronically, including by e-mail or text message, to the defendant. By providing an electronic address or number to the court or to a law enforcement officer at the time of signing the promise to appear, a defendant consents to receiving the reminder notice electronically at that electronic address or number.

(3) The failure to receive a reminder notice does not relieve the defendant of the obligation to appear by the date stated in the *Notice to Appear*.

(Subd (a) adopted effective January 1, 2017.)

(b) Minimum information in reminder notice

In addition to information obtained from the *Notice to Appear*, the reminder notice must contain at least the following information:

(1) An appearance date and location;

(2) Whether a court appearance is mandatory or optional;

(3) The total bail amount and payment options;

(4) The notice about traffic school required under Vehicle Code section 42007, if applicable;

(5) Notice that a traffic violator school will charge a fee in addition to the administrative fee charged by the court;

(6) The potential consequences for failure to appear, including a driver's license hold or suspension, a civil assessment of up to $300, a new charge for failure to appear, a warrant of arrest, or some combination of these consequences, if applicable;

(7) The potential consequences for failure to pay a fine, including a driver's license hold or suspension, a civil assessment of up to $300, a

new charge for failure to pay a fine, a warrant of arrest, or some combination of these consequences, if applicable;

(8) The right to request an ability-to-pay determination;

(9) Notice of the option to pay bail through community service (if available) and installment plans (if available);

(10) Contact information for the court, including the court's website;

(11) Information regarding trial by declaration, informal trial (if available), and telephone or website scheduling options (if available); and

(12) Correction requirements and procedures for correctable violations.

(Subd (b) adopted effective January 1, 2017.)
Rule 4.107 adopted effective January 1, 2017.

Advisory Committee Comment

Subdivision (a)(2). The court may provide a means for obtaining the defendant's consent and designated electronic address or number on its local website. Because notices to appear state the website address for the superior court in each county, this location may increase the number of defendants who become aware and take advantage of this option. To obtain the defendant's electronic address or number at the time of signing the promise to appear, the court may need to collaborate with local law enforcement agencies.

Subdivision (b). While not required, some local court websites may provide information about local court processes and local forms related to the information on the reminder notice. If in electronic form, the reminder notice should include direct links to any information and forms on the local court website. If in paper form, the reminder notice may include the website addresses for any information and forms on the local court website.

Rule 4.108. Installment Payment Agreements

(a) Online interface for installment payment agreements

(1) A court may use an online interface to enter into installment payment agreements with traffic infraction defendants under Vehicle Code sections 40510.5 and 42007.

(2) Before entering into an installment payment agreement, an online interface must provide defendants with the Advisement of Rights stated in Attachment 1 of *Online Agreement to Pay and Forfeit Bail in Installments* (form TR-300 (online)), and *Online Agreement to Pay Traffic Violator School Fees in Installments* (form TR-310 (online)).

(Subd (a) adopted effective January 1, 2017.)

(b) Alternative mandatory forms

(1) The Judicial Council has adopted the following alternative mandatory forms for use in entering into installment payment agreements under Vehicle Code sections 40510.5 and 42007:

(A) *Agreement to Pay and Forfeit Bail in Installments* (form TR-300); and *Online Agreement to Pay and Forfeit Bail in Installments* (form TR-300 (online)); and

(B) *Agreement to Pay Traffic Violator School Fees in Installments* (form TR-310); and *Online Agreement to Pay Traffic Violator School Fees in Installments* (form TR-310 (online)).

(2) Forms TR-300 (online) and TR-310 (online) may be used only in online interfaces for installment payment agreements as provided in subdivision (a).

(Subd (b) adopted effective January 1, 2017.)
Rule 4.108 adopted effective January 1, 2017.

Rule 4.110. Time limits for criminal proceedings on information or indictment

Time limits for criminal proceedings on information or indictment are as follows:

(1) The information must be filed within 15 days after a person has been held to answer for a public offense;

(2) The arraignment of a defendant must be held on the date the information is filed or as soon thereafter as the court directs; and

(3) A plea or notice of intent to demur on behalf of a party represented by counsel at the arraignment must be entered or made no later than seven days after the initial arraignment, unless the court lengthens time for good cause.

Rule 4.110 amended effective January 1, 2007; adopted as rule 227.3 effective January 1, 1985; previously amended effective June 6, 1990; previously renumbered and amended effective January 1, 2001.

Rule 4.111. Pretrial motions in criminal cases

(a) Time for filing papers and proof of service

Unless otherwise ordered or specifically provided by law, all pretrial motions, accompanied by a memorandum, must be served and filed at least 10 court days, all papers opposing the motion at least 5 court days, and all reply papers at least 2 court days before the time appointed for hearing. Proof of service of the moving papers must be filed no later than 5 court days before the time appointed for hearing.

(Subd (a) amended effective January 1, 2010; previously amended effective January 1, 2007.)

(b) Failure to serve and file timely points and authorities

The court may consider the failure without good cause of the moving party to serve and file a memorandum within the time permitted as an admission that the motion is without merit.

(Subd (b) amended effective January 1, 2007.)

Rule 4.111 amended effective January 1, 2010; adopted as rule 227.5 effective January 1, 1985; previously renumbered effective January 1, 2001; previously amended effective January 1, 2007.

Rule 4.112. Readiness conference

(a) Date and appearances

The court may hold a readiness conference in felony cases within 1 to 14 days before the date set for trial. At the readiness conference:

(1) All trial counsel must appear and be prepared to discuss the case and determine whether the case can be disposed of without trial;

(2) The prosecuting attorney must have authority to dispose of the case; and

(3) The defendant must be present in court.

(Subd (a) amended effective January 1, 2007; adopted as rule 227.6 effective January 1, 1985; previously amended and relettered effective January 1, 2001; previously amended effective January 1, 2005.)

(b) Motions

Except for good cause, the court should hear and decide any pretrial motion in a criminal case before or at the readiness conference.

(Subd (b) adopted effective January 1, 2001.)

Rule 4.112 amended effective January 1, 2007; subd (a) adopted as rule 227.6 effective January 1, 1985; subd (b) adopted as section 10.1 of the Standards of Judicial Administration effective January 1, 1985; previously amended and renumbered effective January 1, 2001; previously amended effective January 1, 2005.

Rule 4.113. Motions and grounds for continuance of criminal case set for trial

Motions to continue the trial of a criminal case are disfavored and will be denied unless the moving party, under Penal Code section 1050, presents affirmative proof in open court that the ends of justice require a continuance.

Rule 4.113 amended effective January 1, 2007; adopted as rule 227.7 effective January 1, 1985 previously renumbered effective January 1, 2001.

Rule 4.114. Certification under Penal Code section 859a

When a plea of guilty or no contest is entered under Penal Code section 859a, the magistrate must:

(1) Set a date for imposing sentence; and

(2) Refer the case to the probation officer for action as provided in Penal Code sections 1191 and 1203.

Rule 4.114 amended effective January 1, 2007; adopted as rule 227.9 effective January 1, 1985; previously amended and renumbered effective January 1, 2001.

Rule 4.115. Criminal case assignment

(a) Master calendar departments

To ensure that the court's policy on continuances is firm and uniformly applied, that pretrial proceedings and trial assignments are handled consistently, and that cases are tried on a date certain, each court not operating on a direct calendaring system must assign all criminal matters to one or more master calendar departments. The presiding judge of a master calendar department must conduct or supervise the conduct of all arraignments and pretrial hearings and conferences and assign to a trial department any case requiring a trial or dispositional hearing.

(Subd (a) lettered effective January 1, 2008; adopted as unlettered subd effective January 1, 1985.)

(b) Trial calendaring and continuances

Any request for a continuance, including a request to trail the trial date, must comply with rule 4.113 and the requirement in section 1050 to show good cause to continue a hearing in a criminal proceeding. Active management of trial calendars is necessary to minimize the number of statutory dismissals. Accordingly, courts should avoid calendaring or trailing criminal cases for trial to the last day permitted for trial under section 1382. Courts must implement calendar management procedures, in accordance with local conditions and needs, to ensure that criminal cases are assigned to trial departments before the last day permitted for trial under section 1382.

(Subd (b) adopted effective January 1, 2008.)

Rule 4.115 amended effective January 1, 2008; adopted as section 10 of the Standards of Judicial Administration effective January 1, 1985; amended and renumbered effective January 1, 2001; previously amended effective January 1, 2007.

Advisory Committee Comment

Subdivision (b) clarifies that the "good cause" showing for a continuance under section 1050 applies in all criminal cases, whether or not the case is in the 10-day grace period provided for in section 1382. The Trial Court Presiding Judges Advisory Committee and Criminal Law Advisory Committee observe that the "good cause" requirement for a continuance is separate and distinct from the "good cause" requirement to avoid dismissals under section 1382. There is case law stating that the prosecution is not required to show good cause to avoid a dismissal under section 1382 during the 10-day grace period because a case may not be dismissed for delay during that 10-day period. (See, e.g., *Bryant v. Superior Court* (1986) 186 Cal.App.3d 483, 488.) Yet, both the plain language of section 1050 and case law show that there must be good cause for a continuance under section 1050 during the 10-day grace period. (See, e.g., section 1050 and *People v. Henderson* (2004) 115 Cal.App.4th 922, 939–940.) Thus, a court may not dismiss a case during the 10-day grace period under section 1382, but the committees believe that the court must deny a request for a continuance during the 10-day grace period that does not comply with the good cause requirement under section 1050.

The decision in *Henderson* states that when the prosecutor seeks a continuance but fails to show good cause under section 1050, the trial court "must nevertheless postpone the hearing to another date within the statutory period." (115 Cal.App.4th at p. 940.) That conclusion, however, may be contrary to the plain language of section 1050, which requires a court to deny a continuance if the moving party fails to show good cause. The conclusion also appears to be dicta, as it was not a contested issue on appeal. Given this uncertainty, the rule is silent as to the remedy for failure to show good cause for a requested continuance during the 10-day grace period. The committees note that the remedies under section 1050.5 are available and, but for the *Henderson* dicta, a court would appear to be allowed to deny the continuance request and commence the trial on the scheduled trial date.

Rule 4.116. Certification to juvenile court

(a) Application

This rule applies to all cases not filed in juvenile court in which the person charged by an accusatory pleading appears to be under the age of 18, except when jurisdiction over the child has been transferred from the juvenile court under Welfare and Institutions Code section 707.

(Subd (a) amended effective May 22, 2017; adopted effective January 1, 2001; previously amended effective January 1, 2007.)

(b) Procedure to determine whether certification is appropriate

If an accusatory pleading is pending, and it is suggested or it appears to the court that the person charged was under the age of 18 on the date the offense is alleged to have been committed, the court must immediately suspend proceedings and conduct a hearing to determine the true age of the person charged. The burden of proof of establishing the age of the accused person is on the moving party. If, after examination, the court is satisfied by a preponderance of the evidence that the person was under the age of 18 on the date the alleged offense was committed, the court must immediately certify the matter to the juvenile court and state on the certification order:

(1) The crime with which the person named is charged;

(2) That the person was under the age of 18 on the date of the alleged offense;

(3) The date of birth of the person;

(4) The date of suspension of criminal proceedings; and

(5) The date and time of certification to juvenile court.

(Subd (b) amended effective January 1, 2007; adopted as untitled subd effective January 1, 1991; previously amended and lettered effective January 1, 2001.)

(c) Procedure on certification

If the court determines that certification to the juvenile court is appropriate under (b), copies of the certification, the accusatory pleading, and any police reports must immediately be transmitted to the clerk of the juvenile court. On receipt of the documents, the clerk of the juvenile court must immediately notify the probation officer, who must immediately investigate the matter to determine whether to commence proceedings in juvenile court.

(Subd (c) amended effective January 1, 2007; adopted as untitled subd effective January 1, 1991; previously amended and lettered effective January 1, 2001.)

(d) Procedure if child is in custody

If the person is under the age of 18 and is in custody, the person must immediately be transported to the juvenile detention facility.

(Subd (d) amended effective January 1, 2007; adopted as untitled subd effective January 1, 1991; previously amended and lettered effective January 1, 2001.)

Rule 4.116 amended effective May 22, 2017; adopted as rule 241.2 effective January 1, 1991; previously amended and renumbered effective January 1, 2001; previously amended effective July 1, 1991, and January 1, 2007.

Rule 4.117.   Qualifications for appointed trial counsel in capital cases

(a) Purpose

This rule defines minimum qualifications for attorneys appointed to represent persons charged with capital offenses in the superior courts. These minimum qualifications are designed to promote adequate representation in death penalty cases and to avoid unnecessary delay and expense by assisting the trial court in appointing qualified counsel. Nothing in this rule is intended to be used as a standard by which to measure whether the defendant received effective assistance of counsel.

(b) General qualifications

In cases in which the death penalty is sought, the court must assign qualified trial counsel to represent the defendant. The attorney may be appointed only if the court, after reviewing the attorney's background, experience, and training, determines that the attorney has demonstrated the skill, knowledge, and proficiency to diligently and competently represent the defendant. An attorney is not entitled to appointment simply because he or she meets the minimum qualifications.

(c) Designation of counsel

(1) If the court appoints more than one attorney, one must be designated lead counsel and meet the qualifications stated in (d) or (f), and at least one other must be designated associate counsel and meet the qualifications stated in (e) or (f).

(2) If the court appoints only one attorney, that attorney must meet the qualifications stated in (d) or (f).

(Subd (c) amended effective January 1, 2007.)

(d) Qualifications of lead counsel

To be eligible to serve as lead counsel, an attorney must:

(1) Be an active member of the State Bar of California;

(2) Be an active trial practitioner with at least 10 years' litigation experience in the field of criminal law;

(3) Have prior experience as lead counsel in either:

(A) At least 10 serious or violent felony jury trials, including at least 2 murder cases, tried to argument, verdict, or final judgment; or

(B) At least 5 serious or violent felony jury trials, including at least 3 murder cases, tried to argument, verdict, or final judgment;

(4) Be familiar with the practices and procedures of the California criminal courts;

(5) Be familiar with and experienced in the use of expert witnesses and evidence, including psychiatric and forensic evidence;

(6) Have completed within two years before appointment at least 15 hours of capital case defense training approved for Minimum Continuing Legal Education credit by the State Bar of California; and

(7) Have demonstrated the necessary proficiency, diligence, and quality of representation appropriate to capital cases.

(Subd (d) amended effective January 1, 2007.)

(e) Qualifications of associate counsel

To be eligible to serve as associate counsel, an attorney must:

(1) Be an active member of the State Bar of California;

(2) Be an active trial practitioner with at least three years' litigation experience in the field of criminal law;

(3) Have prior experience as:

(A) Lead counsel in at least 10 felony jury trials tried to verdict, including 3 serious or violent felony jury trials tried to argument, verdict, or final judgment; or

(B) Lead or associate counsel in at least 5 serious or violent felony jury trials, including at least 1 murder case, tried to argument, verdict, or final judgment;

(4) Be familiar with the practices and procedures of the California criminal courts;

(5) Be familiar with and experienced in the use of expert witnesses and evidence, including psychiatric and forensic evidence;

(6) Have completed within two years before appointment at least 15 hours of capital case defense training approved for Minimum Continuing Legal Education credit by the State Bar of California; and

(7) Have demonstrated the necessary proficiency, diligence, and quality of representation appropriate to capital cases.

(Subd (e) amended effective January 1, 2007.)

(f) Alternative qualifications

The court may appoint an attorney even if he or she does not meet all of the qualifications stated in (d) or (e) if the attorney demonstrates the ability to provide competent representation to the defendant. If the court appoints counsel under this subdivision, it must state on the record the basis for finding counsel qualified. In making this determination, the court must consider whether the attorney meets the following qualifications:

(1) The attorney is an active member of the State Bar of California or admitted to practice *pro hac vice* under rule 9.40;

(2) The attorney has demonstrated the necessary proficiency, diligence, and quality of representation appropriate to capital cases;

(3) The attorney has had extensive criminal or civil trial experience;

(4) Although not meeting the qualifications stated in (d) or (e), the attorney has had experience in death penalty trials other than as lead or associate counsel;

(5) The attorney is familiar with the practices and procedures of the California criminal courts;

(6) The attorney is familiar with and experienced in the use of expert witnesses and evidence, including psychiatric and forensic evidence;

(7) The attorney has had specialized training in the defense of persons accused of capital crimes, such as experience in a death penalty resource center;

(8) The attorney has ongoing consultation support from experienced death penalty counsel;

(9) The attorney has completed within the past two years before appointment at least 15 hours of capital case defense training approved for Minimum Continuing Legal Education credit by the State Bar of California; and

(10) The attorney has been certified by the State Bar of California's Board of Legal Specialization as a criminal law specialist.

(Subd (f) amended effective January 1, 2007.)

(g) Public defender appointments

When the court appoints the Public Defender under Penal Code section 987.2, the Public Defender should assign an attorney from that office or agency as lead counsel who meets the qualifications described in (d) or assign an attorney that he or she determines would qualify under (f). If associate counsel is designated, the Public Defender should assign an attorney from that office or agency who meets the qualifications described in (e) or assign an attorney he or she determines would qualify under (f).

(Subd (g) amended effective January 1, 2007.)

(h) Standby or advisory counsel

When the court appoints standby or advisory counsel to assist a self-represented defendant, the attorney must qualify under (d) or (f).

(Subd (h) amended effective January 1, 2007.)

(i) Order appointing counsel

When the court appoints counsel to a capital case, the court must complete *Order Appointing Counsel in Capital Case* (form CR-190), and counsel must complete *Declaration of Counsel for Appointment in Capital Case* (form CR-191).

(Subd (i) amended effective January 1, 2007; adopted effective January 1, 2004.)
Rule 4.117 amended effective January 1, 2007; adopted effective January 1, 2003; previously amended effective January 1, 2004.

Rule 4.119.   Additional requirements in pretrial proceedings in capital cases

(a) Application

This rule applies only in pretrial proceedings in cases in which the death penalty may be imposed.

(Subd (a) adopted effective April 25, 2019.)

(b) Checklist

Within 10 days of counsel's first appearance in court, primary counsel for each defendant and the prosecution must each acknowledge that they have reviewed *Capital Case Attorney Pretrial Checklist* (form CR-600) by signing and submitting this form to the court. Counsel are encouraged to keep a copy of this checklist.

(Subd (b) adopted effective April 25, 2019.)

(c) Lists of appearances, exhibits, and motions

(1) Primary counsel for each defendant and the prosecution must each prepare the lists identified in (A)–(C):

(A) A list of all appearances made by that party during the pretrial proceedings. *Capital Case Attorney List of Appearances* (form CR-601) must be used for this purpose. The list must include all appearances, including ex parte appearances; the date of each appearance; the department in which it was made; the name of counsel making the appearance; and a brief description of the nature of the appearance. A separate list of Penal Code section 987.9 appearances must be maintained under seal for each defendant.

(B) A list of all exhibits offered by that party during the pretrial proceedings. *Capital Case Attorney List of Exhibits* (form CR-602) must be used for this purpose. The list must indicate whether the exhibit was admitted in evidence, refused, lodged, or withdrawn.

(C) A list of all motions made by that party during the pretrial proceedings, including ex parte motions. *Capital Case Attorney List of Motions* (form CR-603) must be used for this purpose. The list must indicate if a motion is awaiting resolution.

(2) In the event of any substitution of attorney during the pretrial proceedings, the relieved attorney must provide the lists of all appearances, exhibits, and motions to substituting counsel within five days of being relieved.

(3) No later than 21 days after the clerk notifies trial counsel that it must submit the lists to the court, counsel must submit the lists to the court and serve on all parties a copy of all the lists except the list of Penal Code section 987.9 appearances. Unless otherwise provided by local rule, the lists must be submitted to the court in electronic form.

(Subd (c) adopted effective April 25, 2019.)

(d) Electronic recordings presented or offered into evidence

Counsel must comply with the requirements of rule 2.1040 regarding electronic recordings presented or offered into evidence, including any such recordings that are part of a digital or electronic presentation.

(Subd (d) adopted effective April 25, 2019.)
Rule 4.119 adopted effective April 25, 2019.

Advisory Committee Comment

Subdivision (b). *Capital Case Attorney Pretrial Checklist* (form CR-600) is designed to be a tool to assist pretrial counsel in identifying and fulfilling all their record preparation responsibilities. Counsel are therefore encouraged to keep a copy of this form and to use it to monitor their own progress.

Subdivision (c)(1). To facilitate preparation of complete and accurate lists, counsel are encouraged to add items to the lists at the time appearances or motions are made or exhibits offered.

Subdivision (c)(3). Rule 8.613(d) requires the clerk to notify counsel to submit the lists of appearances, exhibits, and motions.

Rule 4.130.   Mental competency proceedings

(a) Application

(1) This rule applies to proceedings in the superior court under Penal Code section 1367 et seq. to determine the mental competency of a criminal defendant.

(2) The requirements of subdivision (d)(2) apply only to a formal competency evaluation ordered by the court under Penal Code section 1369(a).

(3) The requirements of subdivision (d)(2) do not apply to a brief preliminary evaluation of the defendant's competency if:

(A) The parties stipulate to a brief preliminary evaluation; and

(B) The court orders the evaluation in accordance with a local rule of court that specifies the content of the evaluation and the procedure for its preparation and submission to the court.

(Subd (a) amended effective January 1, 2018; adopted effective January 1, 2007.)

(b) Initiation of mental competency proceedings

(1) The court must initiate mental competency proceedings if the judge has a reasonable doubt, based on substantial evidence, about the defendant's competence to stand trial.

(2) The opinion of counsel, without a statement of specific reasons supporting that opinion, does not constitute substantial evidence. The court may allow defense counsel to present his or her opinion regarding the defendant's mental competency in camera if the court finds there is reason to believe that attorney-client privileged information will be inappropriately revealed if the hearing is conducted in open court.

(3) In a felony case, if the judge initiates mental competency proceedings prior to the preliminary examination, counsel for the defendant may request a preliminary examination as provided in Penal Code section [1] **1368.1(a)(1), or counsel for the People may request a determination of probable cause as provided in Penal Code section 1368.1(a)(2) and rule 4.131.**

(Subd (b) amended effective January 1, 2020; adopted effective January 1, 2007.)

Rule 4.130(b). 2019 Deletes. [1] 1368.1(a)

(c) Effect of initiating mental competency proceedings

(1) If mental competency proceedings are initiated, criminal proceedings are suspended and may not be reinstated until a trial on the competency of the defendant has been concluded and the defendant [1] is found mentally competent [2] **at a trial conducted under Penal Code section 1369, at a hearing conducted under Penal Code section**

1370(a)(1)(G), or at a hearing following a certification of restoration under Penal Code section 1372.

(2) In misdemeanor cases, speedy trial requirements are tolled during the suspension of criminal proceedings for mental competency evaluation and trial. If criminal proceedings are later reinstated and time is not waived, the trial must be commenced within 30 days after the reinstatement of the criminal proceedings, as provided by Penal Code section 1382(a)(3).

(3) In felony cases, speedy trial requirements are tolled during the suspension of criminal proceedings for mental competency evaluation and trial. If criminal proceedings are reinstated, unless time is waived, time periods to commence the preliminary examination or trial are as follows:

(A) If criminal proceedings were suspended before the preliminary hearing had been conducted, the preliminary hearing must be commenced within 10 days of the reinstatement of the criminal proceedings, as provided in Penal Code section 859b.

(B) If criminal proceedings were suspended after the preliminary hearing had been conducted, the trial must be commenced within 60 days of the reinstatement of the criminal proceedings, as provided in Penal Code section 1382(a)(2).

(Subd (c) amended effective January 1, 2020; adopted effective January 1, 2007.)

Rule 4.130(c). 2019 Deletes. [1] either: (A) **[2]** ; or (B) Has his or her competency restored

(d) Examination of defendant after initiation of mental competency proceedings

(1) On initiation of mental competency proceedings, the court must inquire whether the defendant, or defendant's counsel, seeks a finding of mental incompetence.

(A) If the defense informs the court that the defendant is seeking a finding of mental incompetence, the court must appoint at least one expert to examine the defendant.

(B) If the defense informs the court that the defendant is not seeking a finding of mental incompetence, the court must appoint two experts to examine the defendant. The defense and the prosecution may each name one expert from the court's list of approved experts.

(2) Any court-appointed experts must examine the defendant and advise the court on the defendant's competency to stand trial. Experts' reports are to be submitted to the court, counsel for the defendant, and the prosecution. The report must include the following:

(A) A brief statement of the examiner's training and previous experience as it relates to examining the competence of a criminal defendant to stand trial and preparing a resulting report;

(B) A summary of the examination conducted by the examiner on the defendant, including a summary of the defendant's mental status, a diagnosis under the most recent version of the *Diagnostic and Statistical Manual of Mental Disorders*, if possible, of the defendant's current mental **health** disorder or disorders, and a statement as to whether symptoms of the mental **health** disorder or disorders which motivated the defendant's behavior would respond to mental health treatment;

(C) A detailed analysis of the competence of the defendant to stand trial using California's current legal standard, including the defendant's ability or inability to understand the nature of the criminal proceedings or assist counsel in the conduct of a defense in a rational manner as a result of a mental **health** disorder;

(D) A summary of an assessment—conducted for malingering or feigning symptoms, if clinically indicated—which may include, but need not be limited to, psychological testing;

(E) Under Penal Code section 1369, a statement on whether treatment with antipsychotic or other medication is medically appropriate for the defendant, whether the treatment is likely to restore the defendant to mental competence, a list of likely or potential side effects of the medication, the expected efficacy of the medication, possible alternative treatments, whether it is medically appropriate to administer antipsychotic or other medication in the county jail, and whether the defendant has capacity to make decisions regarding antipsychotic or other medication. If an examining psychologist is of the opinion that a referral to a psychiatrist is necessary to address these issues, the psychologist must inform the court of this opinion and his or her recommendation that a psychiatrist should examine the defendant;

(F) A list of all sources of information considered by the examiner, including legal, medical, school, military, regional center, employment, hospital, and psychiatric records; the evaluations of other experts; the results of psychological testing; police reports; criminal history; statement of the defendant; statements of any witnesses to the alleged crime; booking information, mental health screenings, and mental health records following the alleged crime; consultation with the prosecutor and defendant's attorney; and any other collateral sources considered in reaching his or her conclusion; and

(G) A recommendation, if possible, for a placement or type of placement or treatment program that is most appropriate for restoring the defendant to competency.

(3) Statements made by the defendant during the examination to experts appointed under this rule, and products of any such statements, may not be used in a trial on the issue of the defendant's guilt or in a sanity trial should defendant enter a plea of not guilty by reason of insanity.

(Subd (d) amended effective September 1, 2020; adopted effective January 1, 2007; previously amended effective January 1, 2018, and January 1, 2020.)

(e) Trial on mental competency

(1) Regardless of the conclusions or findings of the court-appointed expert, the court must conduct a trial on the mental competency of the defendant if the court has initiated mental competency proceedings under (b).

(2) At the trial, the defendant is presumed to be mentally competent, and it is the burden of the party contending that the defendant is not mentally competent to prove the defendant's mental incompetence by a preponderance of the evidence.

(3) In addition to the testimony of the experts appointed by the court under (d), either party may call additional experts or other relevant witnesses.

(4) After the presentation of the evidence and closing argument, the trier of fact is to determine whether the defendant is mentally competent or mentally incompetent.

(A) If the matter is tried by a jury, the verdict must be unanimous.

(B) If the parties have waived the right to a jury trial, the court's findings must be made in writing or placed orally in the record.

(Subd (e) adopted effective January 1, 2007.)

(f) Posttrial procedure

(1) If the defendant is found mentally competent, the court must reinstate the criminal proceedings.

(2) If the defendant is found to be mentally incompetent, the criminal proceedings remain suspended and the court must [1] **either issue an order committing the person for restoration treatment under the provisions of the governing statute, or, in the case of a person eligible for commitment under Penal Code sections 1370 or 1370.01, may consider placing the committed person on a program of diversion.**

(Subd (f) amended effective January 1, 2020; adopted effective January 1, 2007.)

Rule 4.130(f).   2019 Deletes. [1] follow the procedures stated in Penal Code section 1370 et seq.

(g) Diversion of a person eligible for commitment under section 1370 or 1370.01

(1) After the court finds that the defendant is mentally incompetent and before the defendant is transported to a facility for restoration under section 1370(a)(1)(B)(i), the court may consider whether the defendant may benefit from diversion under Penal Code section 1001.36. The court may set a hearing to determine whether the defendant is an appropriate candidate for diversion. When determining whether to exercise its discretion to grant diversion under this section, the court may consider previous records of participation in diversion under section 1001.36.

(2) The maximum period of diversion after a finding that the defendant is incompetent to stand trial is the lesser of two years or the maximum time for restoration under Penal Code section 1370(c)(1) (for felony offenses) or 1370.01(c)(1) (for misdemeanor offenses).

(3) The court may not condition a grant of diversion for defendant found to be incompetent on either:

(A) The defendant's consent to diversion, either personally, or through counsel; or

(B) A knowing and intelligent waiver of the defendant's statutory right to a speedy trial, either personally, or through counsel.

(4) A finding that the defendant suffers from a mental **health** disorder or disorders rendering the defendant eligible for diversion, any progress reports concerning the defendant's treatment in diversion, or any other records related to a mental **health** disorder or disorders that were created as a result of participation in, or completion of, diversion or for use at a hearing on the defendant's eligibility for diversion under this section, may not be used in any other proceeding without the defendant's consent,

unless that information is relevant evidence that is admissible under the standards described in article I, section 28(f)(2) of the California Constitution.

(5) If, during the period of diversion, the court determines that criminal proceedings should be reinstated under Penal Code section 1001.36(d), the court must, under Penal Code section 1369, appoint a psychiatrist, licensed psychologist, or any other expert the court may deem appropriate, to examine the defendant and return a report, opining on the defendant's competence to stand trial. The expert's report must be provided to counsel for the People and to the defendant's counsel.

(A) On receipt of the evaluation report, the court must conduct an inquiry into the defendant's current competency, under the procedures set forth in (h)(2) of this rule.

(B) If the court finds by a preponderance of the evidence that the defendant is mentally competent, the court must hold a hearing as set forth in Penal Code section 1001.36(d).

(C) If the court finds by a preponderance of the evidence that the defendant is mentally incompetent, criminal proceedings must remain suspended, and the court must order that the defendant be committed, under Penal Code section 1370 (for felonies) or 1370.01 (for misdemeanors), and placed for restoration treatment.

(D) If the court concludes, based on substantial evidence, that the defendant is mentally incompetent and is not likely to attain competency within the time remaining before the defendant's maximum date for returning to court, and has reason to believe the defendant may be gravely disabled, within the meaning of Welfare and Institutions Code section 5008(h)(1), the court may, instead of issuing a commitment order under Penal Code sections 1370 or 1370.01, refer the matter to the conservatorship investigator of the county of commitment to initiate conservatorship proceedings for the defendant under Welfare and Institutions Code section 5350 et seq.

(6) If the defendant performs satisfactorily and completes diversion, the case must be dismissed under the procedures stated in Penal Code section 1001.36, and the defendant must no longer be deemed incompetent to stand trial.

(Subd (g) amended effective September 1, 2020; adopted effective January 1, 2020.)

(h) Posttrial hearings on competence

(1) If, at any time after the court has declared a defendant incompetent to stand trial, and counsel for the defendant, or a jail medical or mental health staff provider, provides the court with substantial evidence that the defendant's psychiatric symptoms have changed to such a degree as to create a doubt in the mind of the judge as to the defendant's current mental incompetence, the court may appoint a psychiatrist or a licensed psychologist to examine the defendant and, in an examination with the court, opine as to whether the defendant has regained competence.

(2) On receipt of the evaluation report, the court must direct the clerk to serve a copy on counsel for the People and counsel for the defendant. If, in the opinion of the appointed expert, the defendant has regained competence, the court must conduct a hearing, as if a certificate of restoration of competence had been filed under Penal Code section 1372(a)(1), except that a presumption of competency does not apply. At the hearing, the court may consider any evidence, presented by any party, which is relevant to the question of the defendant's current mental competency.

(A) At the conclusion of the hearing, if the court finds that it has been established by a preponderance of the evidence that the defendant is mentally competent, the court must reinstate criminal proceedings.

(B) At the conclusion of the hearing, if the court finds that it has not been established by a preponderance of the evidence that the defendant is mentally competent, criminal proceedings must remain suspended.

(C) The court's findings on the defendant's mental competency must be stated on the record and recorded in the minutes.

(Subd (h) adopted effective January 1, 2020.)

Rule 4.130 amended effective September 1, 2020; adopted effective January 1, 2007; previously amended effective January 1, 2018, and January 1, 2020.

Advisory Committee Comment

The case law interpreting Penal Code section 1367 et seq. established a procedure for judges to follow in cases where there is a concern whether the defendant is legally competent to stand trial, but the concern does not necessarily rise to the level of a reasonable doubt based on substantial evidence. Before finding a reasonable doubt as to the defendant's competency to stand trial and initiating competency proceedings under Penal Code section 1368 et seq., the court may appoint an expert to assist the court in determining whether such a reasonable doubt exists. As noted in *People v. Visciotti* (1992) 2 Cal.4th 1, 34–36, the court may appoint an expert when it is concerned about the mental competency of the defendant, but the concern does not rise to the level of a reasonable doubt, based on substantial evidence, required by Penal Code section 1367 et seq. Should the results of this examination present substantial evidence of mental incompetency, the court must initiate competency proceedings under (b).

Once mental competency proceedings under Penal Code section 1367 et seq. have been initiated, the court is to appoint at least one expert to examine the defendant under (d). Under no circumstances is the court obligated to appoint more than two experts. (Pen. Code, § 1369(a).) The costs of the experts appointed under (d) are to be paid for by the court as the expert examinations and reports are for the benefit or use of the court in determining whether the defendant is mentally incompetent. (See Cal. Rules of Court, rule 10.810, function 10.)

Subdivision (d)(3), which provides that the defendant's statements made during the examination cannot be used in a trial on the defendant's guilt or a sanity trial in a not guilty by reason of sanity trial, is based on the California Supreme Court holdings in *People v. Arcega* (1982) 32 Cal.3d 504 and *People v. Weaver* (2001) 26 Cal.4th 876.

Although the court is not obligated to appoint additional experts, counsel may nonetheless retain their own experts to testify at a trial on the defendant's competency. (See *People v. Mayes* (1988) 202 Cal.App.4th 908, 917–918.) These experts are not for the benefit or use of the court, and their costs are not to be paid by the court. (See Cal. Rules of Court, rule 10.810, function 10.)

Both the prosecution and the defense have the right to a jury trial. (See *People v. Superior Court (McPeters)* (1995) 169 Cal.App.3d 796.) Defense counsel may waive this right, even over the objection of the defendant. (*People v. Masterson* (1994) 8 Cal.4th 965, 970.)

Either defense counsel or the prosecution (or both) may argue that the defendant is not competent to stand trial. (*People v. Stanley* (1995) 10 Cal.4th 764, 804 [defense counsel may advocate that defendant is not competent to stand trial and may present evidence of defendant's mental incompetency regardless of defendant's desire to be found competent].) If the defense declines to present evidence of the defendant's mental incompetency, the prosecution may do so. (Pen. Code, § 1369(b)(2).) If the prosecution elects to present evidence of the defendant's mental incompetency, it is the prosecution's burden to prove the incompetency by a preponderance of the evidence. (*People v. Mixon* (1990) 225 Cal.App.3d 1471, 1484, fn. 12.)

Should both parties decline to present evidence of defendant's mental incompetency, the court may do so. In those cases, the court is not to instruct the jury that a party has the burden of proof. "Rather, the proper approach would be to instruct the jury on the legal standard they are to apply to the evidence before them without allocating the burden of proof to one party or the other." (*People v. Sherik* (1991) 229 Cal.App.3d 444, 459–460.)

Rule 4.131. Probable cause determinations under section 1368.1(a)(2)

(a) Notice of a request for a determination of probable cause

The prosecuting attorney must serve and file notice of a request for a determination of probable cause on the defense at least 10 court days before the time appointed for the proceeding.

(Subd (a) adopted effective January 1, 2019.)

(b) Judge requirement

A judge must hear the determination of probable cause unless there is a stipulation by both parties to having the matter heard by a subordinate judicial officer.

(Subd (b) adopted effective January 1, 2019.)

(c) Defendant need not be present

A defendant need not be present for a determination of probable cause to proceed.

(Subd (c) adopted effective January 1, 2019.)

(d) Application of section 861

The one-session requirement of section 861 does not apply.

(Subd (d) adopted effective January 1, 2019.)

(e) Transcript

A transcript of the determination of probable cause must be provided to the prosecuting attorney and counsel for the defendant consistent with the manner in which a transcript is provided in a preliminary examination.

(Subd (e) adopted effective January 1, 2019.)

Rule 4.131 adopted effective January 1, 2019.

Chapter 2
Change of Venue

Rule 4.150. Change of venue: application and general provisions

(a) Application

Rules 4.150 to 4.155 govern the change of venue in criminal cases under Penal Code section 1033.

(Subd (a) adopted effective January 1, 2006.)

(b) General provisions

When a change of venue has been ordered, the case remains a case of the transferring court. Except on good cause to the contrary, the court must follow the provisions below:

(1) Proceedings before trial must be heard in the transferring court.

(2) Proceedings that are not to be heard by the trial judge must be heard in the transferring court.

(3) Postverdict proceedings, including sentencing, if any, must be heard in the transferring court.

(Subd (b) amended effective January 1, 2007; adopted effective January 1, 2006.)

(c) Appellate review

Review by the Court of Appeal, either by an original proceeding or by appeal, must be heard in the appellate district in which the transferring court is located.

(Subd (c) adopted effective January 1, 2006.)

Rule 4.150 amended effective January 1, 2007; adopted as rule 840 effective March 4, 1972; previously amended and renumbered effective January 1, 2001; previously amended effective January 1, 2006.

Advisory Committee Comment

Subdivision (b)(1). This subdivision is based on Penal Code section 1033(a), which provides that all proceedings before trial are to be heard in the transferring court, except when a particular proceeding must be heard by the trial judge.

Subdivision (b)(2). This subdivision addresses motions heard by a judge other than the trial judge, such as requests for funds under Penal Code section 987.9 or a challenge or disqualification under Code of Civil Procedure section 170 et seq.

Subdivision (b)(3). Reflecting the local community interest in the case, (b)(3) clarifies that after trial the case is to return to the transferring court for any posttrial proceedings. There may be situations where the local interest is outweighed, warranting the receiving court to conduct posttrial hearings. Such hearings may include motions for new trial where juror testimony is necessary and the convenience to the jurors outweighs the desire to conduct the hearings in the transferring court.

Subdivision (c). This subdivision ensures that posttrial appeals and writs are heard in the same appellate district as any writs that may have been heard before or during trial.

Rule 4.151. Motion for change of venue

(a) Motion procedure

A motion for change of venue in a criminal case under Penal Code section 1033 must be supported by a declaration stating the facts supporting the application. Except for good cause shown, the motion must be filed at least 10 days before the date set for trial, with a copy served on the adverse party at least 10 days before the hearing. At the hearing counterdeclarations may be filed.

(Subd (a) amended effective January 1, 2007; adopted effective January 1, 2006; formerly part of an unlettered subd.)

(b) Policy considerations in ruling on motion

Before ordering a change of venue in a criminal case, the transferring court should consider impaneling a jury that would give the defendant a fair and impartial trial.

(Subd (b) adopted effective January 1, 2006.)

Rule 4.151 amended effective January 1, 2008; adopted as rule 841 effective March 4, 1972; previously amended and renumbered effective January 1, 2001; previously amended effective January 1, 2006, and January 1, 2007.

Advisory Committee Comment

Rule 4.151(b) is not intended to imply that the court should attempt to impanel a jury in every case before granting a change of venue.

Rule 4.152. Selection of court and trial judge

When a judge grants a motion for change of venue, he or she must inform the presiding judge of the transferring court. The presiding judge, or his or her designee, must:

(1) Notify the Administrative Director of the change of venue. After receiving the transferring court's notification, the Administrative Director, in order to expedite judicial business and equalize the work of the judges, must advise the transferring court which courts would not be unduly burdened by the trial of the case.

(2) Select the judge to try the case, as follows:

(A) The presiding judge, or his or her designee, must select a judge from the transferring court, unless he or she concludes that the transferring court does not have adequate judicial resources to try the case.

(B) If the presiding judge, or his or her designee, concludes that the transferring court does not have adequate judicial resources to try the case, he or she must request that the Chief Justice of California determine whether to assign a judge to the transferring court. If the Chief Justice determines not to assign a judge to the transferring court, the presiding judge, or his or her designee, must select a judge from the transferring court to try the case.

Rule 4.152 amended effective January 1, 2016; adopted as rule 842 effective March 4, 1972; previously amended and renumbered as rule 4.152 effective January 1, 2001; previously amended effective January 1, 2006.

Rule 4.153. Order on change of venue

After receiving the list of courts from the Administrative Director, the presiding judge, or his or her designee, must:

(1) Determine the court in which the case is to be tried. In making that determination, the court must consider, under Penal Code section 1036.7, whether to move the jury rather than to move the pending action. In so doing, the court should give particular consideration to the convenience of the jurors.

(2) Transmit to the receiving court a certified copy of the order of transfer and any pleadings, documents, or other papers or exhibits necessary for trying the case.

(3) Enter the order for change of venue in the minutes of the transferring court. The order must include the determinations in (1).

Rule 4.153 amended effective January 1, 2016; adopted as rule 843 effective March 4, 1972; previously amended and renumbered as rule 4.153 effective January 1, 2001; previously amended effective January 1, 2006.

Advisory Committee Comment

Rules 4.152 and 4.153 recognize that, although the determination of whether to grant a motion for change of venue is judicial in nature, the selection of the receiving court and the decision whether the case should be tried by a judge of the transferring court are more administrative in nature. Thus, the rules provide that the presiding judge of the transferring court is to make the latter decisions. He or she may delegate those decisions to the trial judge, the supervising judge of the criminal division, or any other judge the presiding judge deems appropriate. If, under the particular facts of the case, the latter decisions are both judicial and administrative, those decisions may be more properly made by the judge who heard the motion for change of venue.

Rule 4.154. Proceedings in the receiving court

The receiving court must conduct the trial as if the case had been commenced in the receiving court. If it is necessary to have any of the original pleadings or other papers before the receiving court, the transferring court must transmit such papers or pleadings. If, during the trial, any original papers or pleadings are submitted to the receiving court, the receiving court is to file the original. After sentencing, all original papers and pleadings are to be retained by the transferring court.

Rule 4.154 amended effective January 1, 2006; adopted as rule 844 effective March 4, 1972; previously amended and renumbered effective January 1, 2001.

Rule 4.155. Guidelines for reimbursement of costs in change of venue cases—criminal cases

(a) General

Consistent with Penal Code section 1037, the court in which an action originated must reimburse the court receiving a case after an order for change of venue for any ordinary expenditure and any extraordinary but reasonable and necessary expenditure that would not have been incurred by the receiving court but for the change of venue.

(Subd (a) amended effective September 1, 2017; previously amended effective January 1, 2001, and January 1, 2006.)

(b) Reimbursable ordinary expenditures—court related

Court-related reimbursable ordinary expenses include:

(1) For prospective jurors on the panel from which the jury is selected and for the trial jurors and alternates seated:

(A) Normal juror per diem and mileage at the rates of the receiving court. The cost of the juror should only be charged to a change of venue case if the juror was not used in any other case on the day that juror was excused from the change of venue case.

(B) If jurors are sequestered, actual lodging, meals, mileage, and parking expenses up to state Board of Control limits.

(C) If jurors are transported to a different courthouse or county, actual mileage and parking expenses.

(2) For court reporters:

(A) The cost of pro tem reporters, even if not used on the change of venue trial, but not the salaries of regular official reporters who would have been paid in any event. The rate of compensation for pro tem reporters should be that of the receiving court.

(B) The cost of transcripts requested during trial and for any new trial or appeal, using the folio rate of the receiving court.

(C) The cost of additional reporters necessary to allow production of a daily or expedited transcript.

(3) For assigned judges: The assigned judge's per diem, travel, and other expenses, up to state Board of Control limits, if the judge is assigned to the receiving court because of the change of venue case, regardless of whether the assigned judge is hearing the change of venue case.

(4) For interpreters and translators:

(A) The cost of the services of interpreters and translators, not on the court staff, if those services are required under Evidence Code sections 750 through 754. Using the receiving court's fee schedule, this cost should be paid whether the services are used in a change of venue trial or to cover staff interpreters and translators assigned to the change of venue trial.

(B) Interpreters' and translators' actual mileage, per diem, and lodging expenses, if any, that were incurred in connection with the trial, up to state Board of Control limits.

(5) For maintenance of evidence: The cost of handling, storing, or maintaining evidence beyond the expenses normally incurred by the receiving court.

(6) For services and supplies: The cost of services and supplies incurred only because of the change of venue trial, for example, copying and printing charges (such as for juror questionnaires), long-distance telephone calls, and postage. A pro rata share of the costs of routine services and supplies should not be reimbursable.

(7) For court or county employees:

(A) Overtime expenditures and compensatory time for staff incurred because of the change of venue case.

(B) Salaries and benefit costs of extra help or temporary help incurred either because of the change of venue case or to replace staff assigned to the change of venue case.

(Subd (b) amended effective January 1, 2007; previously amended effective January 1, 1998, and January 1, 2006.)

(c) Reimbursable ordinary expenses—defendant related

Defendant-related reimbursable ordinary expenses include the actual costs incurred for guarding, keeping, and transporting the defendant, including:

(1) Expenses related to health care: Costs incurred by or on behalf of the defendant such as doctors, hospital expenses, medicines, therapists, and counseling for diagnosis, evaluation, and treatment.

(2) Cost of food and special clothing for an in-custody defendant.

(3) Transportation: Nonroutine expenses, such as transporting an in-custody defendant from the transferring court to the receiving court. Routine transportation expenses if defendant is transported by usual means used for other receiving court prisoners should not be reimbursable.

(Subd (c) amended effective January 1, 2006.)

(d) Reimbursable ordinary expenditures—defense expenses

Reimbursable ordinary expenses related to providing defense for the defendant include:

(1) Matters covered by Penal Code section 987.9 as determined by the transferring court or by a judge designated under that section.

(2) Payment of other defense costs in accordance with policies of the court in which the action originated, unless good cause to the contrary is shown to the trial court.

(3) Unless Penal Code section 987.9 applies, the receiving court may, in its sound discretion, approve all trial-related expenses including:

(A) Attorney fees for defense counsel and, if any, co-counsel and actual travel-related expenses, up to state Board of Control limits, for staying in the county of the receiving court during trial and hearings.

(B) Paralegal and extraordinary secretarial or office expenditures of defense counsel.

(C) Expert witness costs and expenses.

(D) The cost of experts assisting in preparation before trial or during trial, for example, persons preparing demonstrative evidence.

(E) Investigator expenses.

(F) Defense witness expenses, including reasonable-and-necessary witness fees and travel expenses.

(Subd (d) amended effective January 1, 2006; previously amended effective January 1, 1998.)

(e) Extraordinary but reasonable-and-necessary expenses

Except in emergencies or unless it is impracticable to do so, a receiving court should give notice before incurring any extraordinary expenditures to the transferring court, in accordance with Penal Code section 1037(d). Extraordinary but reasonable-and-necessary expenditures include:

(1) Security-related expenditures: The cost of extra security precautions taken because of the risk of escape or suicide or threats of, or the potential for, violence during the trial. These precautions might include, for example, extra bailiffs or correctional officers, special transportation to the courthouse for trial, television monitoring, and security checks of those entering the courtroom.

(2) Facility remodeling or modification: Alterations to buildings or courtrooms to accommodate the change of venue case.

(3) Renting or leasing of space or equipment: Renting or leasing of space for courtrooms, offices, and other facilities, or equipment to accommodate the change of venue case.

(Subd (e) amended effective January 1, 2006; previously amended effective January 1, 1998.)

(f) Nonreimbursable expenses

Nonreimbursable expenses include:

(1) Normal operating expenses including the overhead of the receiving court, for example:

(A) Salary and benefits of existing court staff that would have been paid even if there were no change of venue case.

(B) The cost of operating the jail, for example, detention staff costs, normal inmate clothing, utility costs, overhead costs, and jail construction costs. These expenditures would have been incurred whether or not the case was transferred to the receiving court. It is, therefore, inappropriate to seek reimbursement from the transferring court.

(2) Equipment that is purchased and then kept by the receiving court and that can be used for other purposes or cases.

(Subd (f) amended effective January 1, 2006.)

(g) Miscellaneous

(1) Documentation of costs: No expense should be submitted for reimbursement without supporting documentation, such as a claim, invoice, bill, statement, or time sheet. In unusual circumstances, a declaration under penalty of perjury may be necessary. The declaration should describe the cost and state that it was incurred because of the change of venue case. Any required court order or approval of costs also should be sent to the transferring court.

(2) Timing of reimbursement: Unless both courts agree to other terms, reimbursement of all expenses that are not questioned by the transferring court should be made within 60 days of receipt of the claim for reimbursement. Payment of disputed amounts should be made within 60 days of the resolution of the dispute.

(Subd (g) amended effective January 1, 2007; previously amended effective January 1, 2006.)

Rule 4.155 amended effective September 1, 2017; adopted as section 4.2 of the Standards of Judicial Administration effective July 1, 1989; amended and renumbered as rule 4.162 effective January 1, 2001; previously amended effective January 1, 1998, January 1, 2006, and January 1, 2007.

Division 3
Trials

Rule 4.200. Pre-voir dire conference in criminal cases
Rule 4.201. Voir dire in criminal cases
Rule 4.202. Statements to the jury panel
Rule 4.210. Traffic court—trial by written declaration
Rule 4.220. Remote video proceedings in traffic infraction cases
Rule 4.230. Additional requirements in capital cases

Rule 4.200.   Pre-voir dire conference in criminal cases

(a) The conference

Before jury selection begins in criminal cases, the court must conduct a conference with counsel to determine:

(1) A brief outline of the nature of the case, including a summary of the criminal charges;

(2) The names of persons counsel intend to call as witnesses at trial;

(3) The People's theory of culpability and the defendant's theories;

(4) The procedures for deciding requests for excuse for hardship and challenges for cause;

(5) The areas of inquiry and specific questions to be asked by the court and by counsel and any time limits on counsel's examination;

(6) The schedule for the trial and the predicted length of the trial;

(7) The number of alternate jurors to be selected and the procedure for selecting them; and

(8) The procedure for making *Wheeler/Batson* objections.

The judge must, if requested, excuse the defendant from then disclosing any defense theory.

(Subd (a) amended effective January 1, 2007; previously amended effective January 1, 2006.)

(b) Written questions

The court may require counsel to submit in writing, and before the conference, all questions that counsel requests the court to ask of prospective jurors. This rule applies to questions to be asked either orally or by written questionnaire. The *Juror Questionnaire for Criminal Cases* (form MC-002) may be used.

(Subd (b) amended effective January 1, 2006.)

Rule 4.200 amended effective January 1, 2007; adopted as rule 228.1 effective June 6, 1990; previously amended and renumbered effective January 1, 2001; previously amended effective January 1, 2006.

Advisory Committee Comment

This rule is to be used in conjunction with standard 4.30.

Rule 4.201.   Voir dire in criminal cases

To select a fair and impartial jury, the judge must conduct an initial examination of the prospective jurors orally, or by written questionnaire, or by both methods. The *Juror Questionnaire for Criminal Cases* (form MC-002) may be used. After completion of the initial examination, the court must permit counsel to conduct supplemental questioning as provided in Code of Civil Procedure section 223.

Rule 4.201 amended effective January 1, 2008; adopted as rule 228.2 effective June 6, 1990; previously amended and renumbered effective January 1, 2001; previously amended effective January 1, 2006.

Advisory Committee Comment

Although Code of Civil Procedure section 223 creates a preference for nonsequestered voir dire (*People v. Roldan* (2005) 35 Cal.4th 646, 691), a judge may conduct sequestered voir dire on questions concerning media reports of the case and on any other issue deemed advisable. (See, e.g., Cal. Stds. Jud. Admin., std. 4.30(a)(3).) To determine whether such issues are present, a judge may consider factors including the charges, the nature of the evidence that is anticipated to be presented, and any other relevant factors. To that end, a judge should always inform jurors of the possibility of sequestered voir dire if the voir dire is likely to elicit answers that the juror may believe are sensitive in nature. It should also be noted that when written questionnaires are used, jurors must be advised of the right to request a hearing in chambers on sensitive questions rather than answering them on the questionnaire. (*Copley Press Inc. v. Superior Court* (1991) 228 Cal.App.3d 77, 87.)

Rule 4.202.   Statements to the jury panel

Prior to the examination of prospective jurors, the trial judge may, in his or her discretion, permit brief opening statements by counsel to the panel.

Rule 4.202 adopted effective January 1, 2013.

Advisory Committee Comment

This statement is not a substitute for opening statements. Its purpose is to place voir dire questions in context and to generate interest in the case so that prospective jurors will be less inclined to claim marginal hardships.

Rule 4.210.   Traffic court—trial by written declaration

(a) Applicability

This rule establishes the minimum procedural requirements for trials by written declaration under Vehicle Code section 40902. The procedures established by this rule must be followed in all trials by written declaration under that section.

(Subd (a) amended effective January 1, 2007.)

(b) Procedure

(1) *Definition of due date*

As used in this subdivision, "due date" means the last date on which the defendant's appearance is timely.

(2) *Extending due date*

If the clerk receives the defendant's written request for a trial by written declaration by the appearance date indicated on the *Notice to Appear,* the clerk must, within 15 calendar days after receiving the defendant's written request, extend the appearance date 25 calendar days and must give or mail notice to the defendant of the extended due date on the *Request for Trial by Written Declaration* (form TR-205) with a copy of the *Instructions to Defendant* (form TR-200) and any other required forms.

(3) *Election*

The defendant must file a *Request for Trial by Written Declaration* (form TR-205) with the clerk by the appearance date indicated on the *Notice to Appear* or the extended due date as provided in (2). The *Request for Trial by Written Declaration* (form TR-205) must be filed in addition to the defendant's written request for a trial by written declaration, unless the defendant's request was made on the election form.

(4) *Bail*

The defendant must deposit bail with the clerk by the appearance date indicated on the *Notice to Appear* or the extended due date as provided in (2).

(5) *Instructions to arresting officer*

If the clerk receives the defendant's *Request for Trial by Written Declaration* (form TR-205) and bail by the due date, the clerk must deliver or mail to the arresting officer's agency *Notice and Instructions to Arresting Officer* (form TR-210) and *Officer's Declaration* (form TR-235) with a copy of the *Notice to Appear* and a specified return date for receiving the officer's declaration. After receipt of the officer's declaration, or at the close of the officer's return date if no officer's declaration is filed, the clerk must submit the case file with all declarations and other evidence received to the court for decision.

(6) *Court decision*

After the court decides the case and returns the file and decision, the clerk must immediately deliver or mail the *Decision and Notice of Decision* (form TR-215) to the defendant and the arresting agency.

(7) *Trial de novo*

If the defendant files a *Request for New Trial (Trial de Novo)* (form TR-220) within 20 calendar days after the date of delivery or mailing of the *Decision and Notice of Decision* (form TR-215), the clerk must set a trial date within 45 calendar days of receipt of the defendant's written request for a new trial. The clerk must deliver or mail to the defendant and to the arresting officer's agency the *Order and Notice to Defendant of New Trial (Trial de Novo)* (form TR-225). If the defendant's request is not timely received, no new trial may be held and the case must be closed.

(8) *Case and time standard*

The clerk must deliver or mail the *Decision and Notice of Decision* (form TR-215) within 90 calendar days after the due date. Acts for which no specific time is stated in this rule must be performed promptly so that the *Decision and Notice of Decision* can be timely delivered or mailed by the clerk. Failure of the clerk or the court to comply with any time limit does not void or invalidate the decision of the court, unless prejudice to the defendant is shown.

(Subd (b) amended effective January 1, 2007; previously amended effective January 1, 2000, and July 1, 2000.)

(c) Due dates and time limits

Due dates and time limits must be as stated in this rule, unless changed or extended by the court. The court may extend any date, but the court need not state the reasons for granting or denying an extension on the record or in the minutes.

(Subd (c) amended effective January 1, 2007.)

(d) Ineligible defendants

If the defendant requests a trial by written declaration and the clerk or the court determines that the defendant is not eligible for a trial by written declaration, the clerk must extend the due date 25 calendar days and notify the defendant by mail of the determination and due date.

(Subd (d) amended effective January 1, 2007.)

(e) Noncompliance

If the defendant does not comply with this rule (including submitting the required bail amount, signing and filing all required forms, and complying with all time limits and due dates), the court may deny a trial by written declaration and may proceed as otherwise provided by statute and court rules.

(Subd (e) amended effective January 1, 2007.)

(f) Evidence

Testimony and other relevant evidence may be introduced in the form of a *Notice to Appear* issued under Vehicle Code section 40500; a business record or receipt; a sworn declaration of the arresting officer; and, on behalf of the defendant, a sworn declaration of the defendant.

(Subd (f) amended effective January 1, 2007.)

(g) Fines, assessments, or penalties

The statute and the rules do not prevent or preclude the court from imposing on a defendant who is found guilty any lawful fine, assessment, or other penalty, and the court is not limited to imposing money penalties in the bail amount, unless the bail amount is the maximum and the only lawful penalty.

(Subd (g) amended effective January 1, 2007.)

(h) Additional forms and procedures

The clerk may approve and prescribe forms, time limits, and procedures that are not in conflict with or not inconsistent with the statute or this rule.

(i) Forms

The following forms are to be used to implement the procedures under this rule:

(1) *Instructions to Defendant* (form TR-200)

(2) *Request for Trial by Written Declaration* (form TR-205)

(3) *Notice and Instructions to Arresting Officer* (form TR-210)

(4) *Officer's Declaration* (form TR-235)

(5) *Decision and Notice of Decision* (form TR-215)

(6) *Request for New Trial (Trial de Novo)* (form TR-220)

(7) *Order and Notice to Defendant of New Trial (Trial de Novo)* (form TR-225)

(Subd (i) amended effective January 1, 2007; previously amended effective January 1, 2000.)

(j) Local forms

A court may adopt additional forms as may be required to implement this rule and the court's local procedures not inconsistent with this rule.

(Subd (j) amended effective January 1, 2007.)

Rule 4.210 amended and renumbered effective January 1, 2007; adopted as rule 828 effective January 1, 1999; previously amended effective January 1, 2000, and July 1, 2000.

Rule 4.220. Remote video proceedings in traffic infraction cases

(a) Authorization for remote video proceedings

A superior court may by local rule permit arraignments, trials, and related proceedings concerning the traffic infractions specified in (b) to be conducted by two-way remote video communication methods under the conditions stated below.

(Subd (a) amended effective September 1, 2015; adopted effective February 1, 2013.)

(b) Definitions

For the purposes of this rule:

(1) "Infraction" means any alleged infraction involving a violation of the Vehicle Code or any local ordinance adopted under the Vehicle Code, other than an infraction cited under article 2 (commencing with section 23152) of chapter 12 of division 11 of the Vehicle Code, except that the procedures for remote video trials authorized by this rule do not apply to any case in which an informal juvenile and traffic court exercises jurisdiction over a violation under sections 255 and 256 of the Welfare and Institutions Code.

(2) "Remote video proceeding" means an arraignment, trial, or related proceeding conducted by two-way electronic audiovisual communication between the defendant, any witnesses, and the court in lieu of the physical presence of both the defendant and any witnesses in the courtroom.

(3) "Due date" means the last date on which the defendant's appearance is timely under this rule.

(Subd (b) adopted effective February 1, 2013.)

(c) Application

This rule establishes the minimum procedural requirements and options for courts that conduct remote video proceedings for cases in which a defendant is charged with an infraction as defined in (b) and the defendant requests to proceed according to this rule.

(Subd (c) amended effective September 1, 2015; adopted effective February 1, 2013.)

(d) Designation of locations and presence of court clerk

(1) The court must designate the location or locations at which defendants may appear with any witnesses for a remote video proceeding in traffic infraction cases.

(2) The locations must be in a public place, and the remote video proceedings must be viewable by the public at the remote location as well as at the courthouse.

(3) A court clerk must be present at the remote location for all remote video proceedings.

(Subd (d) adopted effective February 1, 2013.)

(e) Required procedures and forms and request by defendant

A court that conducts remote video proceedings under this rule must comply with the following procedures and use the required forms in this section. In addition to following the standard provisions for processing traffic infraction cases, the defendant may request to proceed by remote video proceeding as provided below.

(1) *Arraignment and trial on the same date*

The following procedures apply to a remote video proceeding when the court grants a defendant's request to have an arraignment and trial on the same date:

(A) The defendant must review a copy of the *Instructions to Defendant for Remote Video Proceeding* (form TR-500-INFO).

(B) To proceed by remote video arraignment and trial, the defendant must sign and file a *Notice and Waiver of Rights and Request for Remote Video Arraignment and Trial* (form TR-505) with the clerk by the appearance date indicated on the *Notice to Appear* or a continuation of that date granted by the court and must deposit bail when filing the form.

(C) A defendant who is dissatisfied with the judgment in a remote video trial may appeal the judgment under rules 8.901–8.902.

(2) *Arraignment on a date that is separate from a trial date*

The following procedures apply to a remote video proceeding when the court grants a defendant's request to have an arraignment that is set for a date that is separate from the trial date:

(A) The defendant must review a copy of the *Instructions to Defendant for Remote Video Proceeding* (form TR-500-INFO).

(B) To proceed by remote video arraignment on a date that is separate from a trial date, the defendant must sign and file a *Notice and Waiver of Rights and Request for Remote Video Proceeding* (form TR-510) with the clerk by the appearance date indicated on the *Notice to Appear* or a continuation of that date granted by the court.

(3) *Trial on a date that is separate from the date of arraignment*

The following procedures apply to a remote video proceeding when the court grants a defendant's request at arraignment to have a trial set for a date that is separate from the date of the arraignment:

(A) The defendant must review a copy of the *Instructions to Defendant for Remote Video Proceeding* (form TR-500-INFO).

(B) To proceed by remote video trial, the defendant must sign and file a *Notice and Waiver of Rights and Request for Remote Video Proceeding* (form TR-510) with the clerk by the appearance date indicated on the *Notice to Appear* or a continuation of that date granted by the court and must deposit bail with the form as required by the court under section (f).

(C) A defendant who is dissatisfied with the judgment in a remote video trial may appeal the judgment under rules 8.901–8.902.

(4) *Judicial Council forms for remote video proceedings*

The following forms must be made available by the court and used by the defendant to implement the procedures that are required under this rule:

(A) *Instructions to Defendant for Remote Video Proceeding* (form TR-500-INFO);

(B) *Notice and Waiver of Rights and Request for Remote Video Arraignment and Trial* (form TR-505); and

(C) *Notice and Waiver of Rights and Request for Remote Video Proceeding* (form TR-510).

(Subd (e) amended effective September 1, 2015; adopted effective February 1, 2013.)

(f) Deposit of bail

Procedures for deposit of bail to process requests for remote video proceedings must follow rule 4.105.

(Subd (f) amended effective September 1, 2015; adopted effective February 1, 2013.)

(g) Appearance of witnesses

On receipt of the defendant's waiver of rights and request to appear for trial as specified in section (e)(1) or (e)(3), the court may permit law enforcement officers and other witnesses to testify at the remote location or in court and be cross-examined by the defendant from the remote location.

(Subd (g) adopted effective February 1, 2013.)

(h) Authority of court to require physical presence of defendant and witnesses

Nothing in this rule is intended to limit the authority of the court to issue an order requiring the defendant or any witnesses to be physically present in the courtroom in any proceeding or portion of a proceeding if the court finds that circumstances require the physical presence of the defendant or witness in the courtroom.

(Subd (h) adopted effective February 1, 2013.)

(i) Extending due date for remote video trial

If the clerk receives the defendant's written request for a remote video arraignment and trial on form TR-505 or remote video trial on form TR-510 by the appearance date indicated on the *Notice to Appear* and the request is granted, the clerk must, within 10 court days after receiving the defendant's request, extend the appearance date by 25 calendar days and must provide notice to the defendant of the extended due date on the *Notice and Waiver of Rights and Request for Remote Video Arraignment and Trial* (form TR-505) or *Notice and Waiver of Rights and Request for Remote Video Proceeding* (form TR-510) with a copy of any required local forms.

(Subd (i) adopted effective February 1, 2013.)

(j) Notice to arresting officer

If a court grants the defendant's request for a remote video proceeding after receipt of the defendant's *Notice and Waiver of Rights and Request for Remote Video Arraignment and Trial* (form TR-505) or *Notice and Waiver of Rights and Request for Remote Video Proceeding* (form TR-510) and bail deposit, if required, the clerk must deliver, mail, or e-mail a notice of the remote video proceedings to the arresting or citing law enforcement officer. The notice to the officer must specify the location and date for the remote video proceeding and provide an option for the officer to request at least five calendar days before the appearance date to appear in court instead of at the remote location.

(Subd (j) adopted effective February 1, 2013.)

(k) Due dates and time limits

Due dates and time limits must be as stated in this rule, unless extended by the court. The court may extend any date, and the court need not state the reasons for granting or denying an extension on the record or in the minutes.

(Subd (k) adopted effective February 1, 2013.)

(l) Ineligible defendants

If the defendant requests a remote video proceeding and the court determines that the defendant is ineligible, the clerk must extend the due date by 25 calendar days and notify the defendant of the determination and the new due date.

(Subd (l) adopted effective February 1, 2013.)

(m) Noncompliance

If the defendant fails to comply with this rule (including depositing the bail amount when required, signing and filing all required forms, and complying with all time limits and due dates), the court may deny a request for a remote video proceeding and may proceed as otherwise provided by statute.

(Subd (m) amended effective September 1, 2015; adopted effective February 1, 2013.)

(n) Fines, assessments, or penalties

This rule does not prevent or preclude the court from imposing on a defendant who is found guilty any lawful fine, assessment, or other penalty, and the court is not limited to imposing money penalties in the bail amount, unless the bail amount is the maximum and the only lawful penalty.

(Subd (n) adopted effective February 1, 2013.)

(o) Local rules and forms

A court establishing remote video proceedings under this rule may adopt such local rules and additional forms as may be necessary or appropriate to implement the rule and the court's local procedures not inconsistent with this rule.

(Subd (o) amended effective September 1, 2015; adopted effective February 1, 2013.)

(p) Notice and collection of information and reports on remote video proceedings

Each court that establishes a local rule authorizing remote video proceedings under this rule must notify the Judicial Council, institute procedures as required by the council for collecting and evaluating information about that court's program, and prepare semiannual reports to the council that include an assessment of the costs and benefits of remote video proceedings at that court.

(Subd (p) amended effective September 1, 2015; adopted effective February 1, 2013.)

Rule 4.220 amended effective September 1, 2015; adopted effective February 1, 2013.

Rule 4.230.　Additional requirements in capital cases

(a) Application

This rule applies only in trials in cases in which the death penalty may be imposed.

(Subd (a) adopted effective April 25, 2019.)

(b) Checklist

Within 10 days of counsel's first appearance in court, primary counsel for each defendant and the prosecution must each acknowledge that they have reviewed *Capital Case Attorney Trial Checklist* (form CR-605) by signing and submitting this form to the court. Counsel is encouraged to keep a copy of this checklist.

(Subd (b) adopted effective April 25, 2019.)

(c) Review of daily transcripts by counsel during trial

During trial, counsel must call the court's attention to any errors or omissions they may find in the daily transcripts. The court must periodically ask counsel for lists of any such errors or omissions and may hold hearings to verify them. Immaterial typographical errors that cannot conceivably cause confusion are not required to be brought to the court's attention.

(Subd (c) adopted effective April 25, 2019.)

(d) Lists of appearances, exhibits, motions, and jury instructions

(1) Primary counsel for each defendant and the prosecution must each prepare the lists identified in (A)–(D).

(A) A list of all appearances made by that party. *Capital Case Attorney List of Appearances* (form CR-601) must be used for this purpose. The list must include all appearances, including ex parte appearances, the date of each appearance, the department in which it was made, the name of counsel making the appearance, and a brief description of the nature of the appearance. A separate list of Penal Code section 987.9 appearances must be maintained under seal for each defendant. In the event of any substitution of attorney at any stage of the case, the relieved attorney must provide the list of all appearances to substituting counsel within five days of being relieved.

(B) A list of all exhibits offered by that party. *Capital Case Attorney List of Exhibits* (form CR-602) must be used for this purpose. The list must indicate whether the exhibit was admitted in evidence, refused, lodged, or withdrawn.

(C) A list of all motions made by that party, including ex parte motions. *Capital Case Attorney List of Motions* (form CR-603) must be used for this purpose.

(D) A list of all jury instructions submitted in writing by that party. *Capital Case Attorney List of Jury Instructions* (form CR-604) must be used for this purpose. The list must indicate whether the instruction was given, given as modified, refused, or withdrawn.

(2) No later than 21 days after the imposition of a sentence of death, counsel must submit the lists to the court and serve on all parties a copy of all the lists except the list of Penal Code section 987.9 appearances. Unless otherwise provided by local rule, the lists must be submitted to the court in electronic form.

(Subd (d) adopted effective April 25, 2019.)

(e) Electronic recordings presented or offered into evidence

Counsel must comply with the requirements of rule 2.1040 regarding electronic recordings presented or offered into evidence, including any such recordings that are part of a digital or electronic presentation.

(Subd (e) adopted effective April 25, 2019.)

(f) Copies of audio and visual aids

Primary counsel must provide the clerk with copies of any audio or visual aids not otherwise subject to the requirements of (e) that are used during jury selection or in presentations to the jury, including digital or electronic presentations. If a visual aid is oversized, a photograph of that visual aid must be provided in place of the original. For digital or electronic presentations, counsel must supply both a copy of the presentation in its native format and printouts showing the full text of each slide or image. Photographs and printouts provided under this subdivision must be on 8-1/2 by 11 inch paper.

(Subd (f) adopted effective April 25, 2019.)
Rule 4.230 adopted effective April 25, 2019.

Advisory Committee Comment

Subdivision (b). *Capital Case Attorney List of Appearances* (form CR-601), *Capital Case Attorney List of Exhibits* (form CR-602), *Capital Case Attorney List of Motions* (form CR-603), and *Capital Case Attorney List of Jury Instructions* (form CR-604) must be used to comply with the requirements in this subdivision.

Subdivision (d). To facilitate preparation of complete and accurate lists, counsel are encouraged to add items to the lists at the time appearances or motions are made, exhibits are offered, or jury instructions are submitted.

Division 4
Sentencing

Rule 4.300.　Commitments to nonpenal institutions

When a defendant is convicted of a crime for which sentence could be imposed under Penal Code section 1170 and the court orders that he or she be committed to the California Department of Corrections and Rehabilitation, Division of Juvenile Justice under Welfare and Institutions Code section 1731.5, the order of commitment must specify the term of imprisonment to which the defendant would have been sentenced. The term is determined as provided by Penal Code sections 1170 and 1170.1 and these rules, as though a sentence of imprisonment were to be imposed.

Rule 4.300 amended effective January 1, 2007; adopted as rule 453 effective July 1, 1977; previously amended and renumbered effective January 1, 2001; previously amended effective July 28, 1977, and January 1, 2006.

Advisory Committee Comment

Commitments to the California Department of Corrections and Rehabilitation, Division of Juvenile Justice (formerly Youth Authority) cannot exceed the maximum possible incarceration in an adult institution for the same crime. *People v. Olivas* (1976) 17 Cal.3d 236.

Under the indeterminate sentencing law, the receiving institution knew, as a matter of law from the record of the conviction, the maximum potential period of imprisonment for the crime of which the defendant was convicted.

Under the Uniform Determinate Sentencing Act, the court's discretion as to length of term leaves doubt as to the maximum term when only the record of convictions is present.

Rule 4.305.　Notification of appeal rights in felony cases

After imposing sentence or making an order deemed to be a final judgment in a criminal case on conviction after trial, or after imposing sentence following a revocation of probation, except where the revocation is after the defendant's admission of violation of probation, the court must advise the defendant of his or her right to appeal, of the necessary steps and time for taking an appeal, and of the right of an indigent defendant to have counsel appointed by the reviewing court.

Rule 4.305 amended effective January 1, 2013; adopted as rule 250 effective January 1, 1972; previously amended effective July 1, 1972, January 1, 1977, and January 1, 2007; previously amended and renumbered as rule 470 effective January 1, 1991; previously renumbered effective January 1, 2001.

Rule 4.306.　Notification of appeal rights in misdemeanor and infraction cases

After imposing sentence or making an order deemed to be a final judgment in a misdemeanor case on conviction after trial or following a revocation of probation, the court must orally or in writing advise a defendant not represented by counsel of the right to appeal, the time for filing a notice of appeal, and the right of an indigent defendant to have counsel appointed on appeal. This rule does not apply to infractions or when a revocation of probation is ordered after the defendant's admission of a violation of probation.

Rule 4.306 amended effective January 1, 2007; adopted as rule 535 effective July 1, 1981; previously renumbered effective January 1, 2001.

Rule 4.310.　Determination of presentence custody time credit

At the time of sentencing, the court must cause to be recorded on the judgment or commitment the total time in custody to be credited on the sentence under Penal Code sections 2900.5, 2933.1(c), and 2933.2(c). On referral of the defendant to the probation officer for an investigation and report under Penal Code section 1203(b) or 1203(g), or on setting a date for sentencing in the absence of a referral, the court must direct the sheriff, probation officer, or other appropriate person to report to the court and notify the defendant or defense counsel and prosecuting attorney within a reasonable time before the date set for sentencing as to the number of days that defendant has been in custody and for which he or she may be entitled to credit. Any challenges to the report must be heard at the time of sentencing.

Rule 4.310 amended effective January 1, 2007; adopted as rule 252 effective January 1, 1977; previously amended and renumbered as rule 472 effective January 1, 1991; previously amended and renumbered effective January 1, 2001; previously amended effective July 1, 2004.

Rule 4.315. Setting date for execution of death sentence
(a) Open session of court; notice required
A date for execution of a judgment of death under Penal Code section 1193 or 1227 must be set at a public session of the court at which the defendant and the People may be represented.

At least 10 days before the session of court at which the date will be set, the court must mail notice of the time and place of the proceeding by first-class mail, postage prepaid, to the Attorney General, the district attorney, the defendant at the prison address, the defendant's counsel or, if none is known, counsel who most recently represented the defendant on appeal or in postappeal legal proceedings, and the executive director of the California Appellate Project in San Francisco. The clerk must file a certificate of mailing copies of the notice. The court may not hold the proceeding or set an execution date unless the record contains a clerk's certificate showing that the notices required by this subdivision were timely mailed.

Unless otherwise provided by statute, the defendant does not have a right to be present in person.

(Subd (a) amended effective January 1, 2007; previously amended effective July 1, 1990.)

(b) Selection of date; notice
If, at the announced session of court, the court sets a date for execution of the judgment of death, the court must mail certified copies of the order setting the date to the warden of the state prison and to the Governor, as required by statute; and must also, within five days of the making of the order, mail by first-class mail, postage prepaid, certified copies of the order setting the date to each of the persons required to be given notice by (a). The clerk must file a certificate of mailing copies of the order.

(Subd (b) amended effective January 1, 2007.)

Rule 4.315 amended effective January 1, 2007; adopted as rule 490 effective July 1, 1989; previously amended effective July 1, 1990; previously renumbered effective January 1, 2001.

Rule 4.320. Records of criminal convictions (Gov. Code, §§ 69844.5, 71280.5)
(a) Information to be submitted
In addition to the information that the Department of Justice requires from courts under Penal Code section 13151, each trial court must also report, electronically or manually, the following information, in the form and manner specified by the Department of Justice:

(1) Whether the defendant was represented by counsel or waived the right to counsel; and

(2) In the case of a guilty or nolo contendere plea, whether:

(A) The defendant was advised of and understood the charges;

(B) The defendant was advised of, understood, and waived the right to a jury trial, the right to confront witnesses, and the privilege against self-incrimination; and

(C) The court found the plea was voluntary and intelligently made.

For purposes of this rule, a change of plea form signed by the defendant, defense counsel if the defendant was represented by counsel, and the judge, and filed with the court is a sufficient basis for the clerk or deputy clerk to report that the requirements of (2) have been met.

(Subd (a) amended effective January 1, 2007; previously amended effective January 1, 2001.)

(b) Certification required
The reporting clerk or a deputy clerk must certify that the report submitted to the Department of Justice under Penal Code section 13151 and this rule is a correct abstract of the information contained in the court's records in the case.

(Subd (b) amended effective January 1, 2007.)

Rule 4.320 amended effective January 1, 2007; adopted as rule 895 effective July 1, 1998; previously amended and renumbered effective January 1, 2001.

Rule 4.325. Ignition interlock installation orders: "interest of justice" exceptions
If the court finds that the interest of justice requires an exception to the Vehicle Code sections 14601(e), 14601.1(d), 14601.4(c), or 14601.5(g) requirements for installation of an ignition interlock device under Vehicle Code section 23575, the reasons for the finding must be stated on the record.

Rule 4.325 amended and renumbered effective January 1, 2001; adopted as rule 530 effective January 1, 1995.

Rule 4.330. Misdemeanor hate crimes
(a) Application
This rule applies to misdemeanor cases where the defendant is convicted of either (1) a substantive hate crime under section 422.6 or (2) a misdemeanor violation and the facts of the crime constitute a hate crime under section 422.55.

(Subd (a) adopted effective January 1, 2007.)

(b) Sentencing consideration
In sentencing a defendant under (a), the court must consider the goals for hate crime sentencing stated in rule 4.427(e).

(Subd (b) adopted effective January 1, 2007.)

Rule 4.330 adopted effective January 1, 2007.

Rule 4.335. Ability-to-pay determinations for infraction offenses
(a) Application
This rule applies to any infraction offense for which the defendant has received a written *Notice to Appear*.

(Subd (a) adopted effective January 1, 2017.)

(b) Required notice regarding an ability-to-pay determination
Courts must provide defendants with notice of their right to request an ability-to-pay determination and make available instructions or other materials for requesting an ability-to-pay determination.

(Subd (b) adopted effective January 1, 2017.)

(c) Procedure for determining ability to pay
(1) The court, on request of a defendant, must consider the defendant's ability to pay.

(2) A defendant may request an ability-to-pay determination at adjudication, or while the judgment remains unpaid, including when a case is delinquent or has been referred to a comprehensive collection program.

(3) The court must permit a defendant to make this request by written petition unless the court directs a court appearance. The request must include any information or documentation the defendant wishes the court to consider in connection with the determination. The judicial officer has the discretion to conduct the review on the written record or to order a hearing.

(4) Based on the ability-to-pay determination, the court may exercise its discretion to:

(A) Provide for payment on an installment plan (if available);

(B) Allow the defendant to complete community service in lieu of paying the total fine (if available);

(C) Suspend the fine in whole or in part;

(D) Offer an alternative disposition.

(5) A defendant ordered to pay on an installment plan or to complete community service may request to have an ability-to-pay determination at any time during the pendency of the judgment.

(6) If a defendant has already had an ability-to-pay determination in the case, a defendant may request a subsequent ability-to-pay determination only based on changed circumstances.

(Subd (c) adopted effective January 1, 2017.)

Rule 4.335 adopted effective January 1, 2017.

Advisory Committee Comment
Subdivision (b). This notice may be provided on the notice required by rule 4.107, the notice of any civil assessment under section 1214.1, a court's website, or any other notice provided to the defendant.

Subdivision (c)(1). In determining the defendant's ability to pay, the court should take into account factors including: (1) receipt of public benefits under Supplemental Security Income (SSI), State Supplementary Payment (SSP), California Work Opportunity and Responsibility to Kids (CalWORKS), Federal Tribal Temporary Assistance for Needy Families (Tribal TANF), Supplemental Nutrition Assistance Program, California Food Assistance Program, County Relief, General Relief (GR), General Assistance (GA), Cash Assistance Program for Aged, Blind, and Disabled Legal Immigrants (CAPI), In Home Supportive Services (IHSS), or Medi-Cal; and (2) a monthly income of 125 percent or less of the current poverty guidelines, updated periodically in the Federal Register by the U.S. Department of Health and Human Services under 42 U.S.C. § 9902(2).

Subdivision (c)(4). The amount and manner of paying the total fine must be reasonable and compatible with the defendant's financial ability. Even if the defendant has not demonstrated an inability to pay, the court may still exercise discretion. Regardless of whether the defendant has demonstrated an inability to pay, the court in exercising its discretion under this subdivision may consider the severity of the offense, among other factors. While the base fine may be suspended in whole or in part in the court's discretion, this subdivision is not intended to affect the imposition of any mandatory fees.

Rule 4.336.   Confidential Can't Afford to Pay Fine Forms

(a) Use of request and order forms

(1) A court uses the information on *Can't Afford to Pay Fine: Traffic and Other Infractions* (form TR-320/CR-320) to determine an infraction defendant's ability to pay under rule 4.335.

(2) A court may use *Can't Afford to Pay Fine: Traffic and Other Infractions (Court Order)* (form TR-321/CR-321) to issue an order in response to an infraction defendant's request for an ability-to-pay determination under rule 4.335.

(Subd (a) adopted effective April 1, 2018.)

(b) Confidential request form

Can't Afford to Pay Fine: Traffic and Other Infractions (form TR-320/CR-320), the information it contains, and any supporting documentation are confidential. The clerk's office must maintain the form and supporting documentation in a manner that will protect and preserve their confidentiality. Only the parties and the court may access the form and supporting documentation.

(Subd (b) adopted effective April 1, 2018.)

(c) Optional request and order forms

Can't Afford to Pay Fine: Traffic and Other Infractions (form TR-320/CR-320) and *Can't Afford to Pay Fine: Traffic and Other Infractions (Court Order)* (form TR-321/CR-321) are optional forms under rule 1.35.

(Subd (c) adopted effective April 1, 2018.)
Rule 4.336 adopted effective April 1, 2018.

Division 5
Felony Sentencing Law

Rule 4.401.   Authority

The rules in this division are adopted under Penal Code section 1170.3 and under the authority granted to the Judicial Council by the Constitution, article VI, section 6, to adopt rules for court administration, practice, and procedure.

Rule 4.401 amended effective January 1, 2007; adopted as rule 401 effective July 1, 1977; previously renumbered effective January 1, 2001.

Rule 4.403.   Application

These rules apply only to criminal cases in which the defendant is convicted of one or more offenses punishable as a felony by (1) a determinate sentence imposed under Penal Code part 2, title 7, chapter 4.5 (commencing with section 1170) and (2) an indeterminate sentence imposed under section 1168(b) only if it is imposed relative to other offenses with determinate terms or enhancements.

Rule 4.403 amended effective January 1, 2018; adopted as rule 403 effective July 1, 1977; previously amended and renumbered effective January 1, 2001; previously amended effective July 1, 2003, and January 1, 2007.

Advisory Committee Comment

The operative portions of section 1170 deal exclusively with prison sentences; and the mandate to the Judicial Council in section 1170.3 is limited to criteria affecting the length of prison sentences, sentences in county jail under section 1170(h), and the grant or denial of probation.

Rule 4.405.   Definitions

As used in this division, unless the context otherwise requires:

(1) "These rules" means the rules in this division.

(2) "Base term" is the determinate term in prison or county jail under section 1170(h) selected from among the three possible terms prescribed by statute; the determinate term in prison or county jail under section 1170(h) prescribed by statute if a range of three possible terms is not prescribed; or the indeterminate term in prison prescribed by statute.

(3) "Enhancement" means an additional term of imprisonment added to the base term.

(4) "Aggravation," "circumstances in aggravation," "mitigation," or "circumstances in mitigation" means factors that the court may consider in its broad discretion authorized by statute and under these rules.

(5) "Sentence choice" means the selection of any disposition of the case that does not amount to a dismissal, acquittal, or grant of a new trial.

(6) "Section" means a section of the Penal Code.

(7) "Imprisonment" means confinement in a state prison or county jail under section 1170(h).

(8) "Charged" means charged in the indictment or information.

(9) "Found" means admitted by the defendant or found to be true by the trier of fact upon trial.

(10) "Mandatory supervision" means the period of supervision defined in section 1170(h)(5)(A), (B).

(11) "Postrelease community supervision" means the period of supervision governed by section 3451 et seq.

(12) "Risk/needs assessment" means a standardized, validated evaluation tool designed to measure an offender's actuarial risk factors and specific needs that, if successfully addressed, may reduce the likelihood of future criminal activity.

(13) "Evidence-based practices" means supervision policies, procedures, programs, and practices demonstrated by scientific research to reduce recidivism among individuals under probation, parole, or postrelease supervision.

(14) "Community-based corrections program" means a program consisting of a system of services for felony offenders under local supervision dedicated to the goals stated in section 1229(c)(1)–(5).

(15) "Local supervision" means the supervision of an adult felony offender on probation, mandatory supervision, or postrelease community supervision.

(16) "County jail" means local county correctional facility.

Rule 4.405 amended effective January 1, 2018; adopted as rule 405 effective July 1, 1977; previously renumbered effective January 1, 2001; previously amended effective July 28, 1977, January 1, 1991, July 1, 2003, January 1, 2007, May 23, 2007, and January 1, 2017.

Advisory Committee Comment

Following the United States Supreme Court decision in *Cunningham v. California* (2007) 549 U.S. 270, the Legislature amended the determinate sentencing law to remove the presumption that the court is to impose the middle term on a sentencing triad, absent aggravating or mitigating circumstances. (See Sen. Bill 40; Stats. 2007, ch. 3.) It subsequently amended sections 186.22, 186.33, 1170.1, 12021.5, 12022.2, and 12022.4 to eliminate the presumptive middle term for an enhancement. (See Sen. Bill 150; Stats. 2009, ch. 171.) Instead of finding facts in support of a sentencing choice, courts are now required to state reasons for the exercise of judicial discretion in sentencing.

Rule 4.406.   Reasons

(a) How given

If the sentencing judge is required to give reasons for a sentence choice, the judge must state in simple language the primary factor or factors that support the exercise of discretion. The statement need not be in the language of the statute or these rules. It must be delivered orally on the record. The court may give a single statement explaining the reason or reasons for imposing a particular sentence or the exercise of judicial discretion, if the statement identifies the sentencing choices where discretion is exercised and there is no impermissible dual use of facts.

(Subd (a) amended effective January 1, 2018; previously amended effective January 1, 2007.)

(b) When reasons required

Sentence choices that generally require a statement of a reason include, but are not limited to:

(1) Granting probation when the defendant is presumptively ineligible for probation;

(2) Denying probation when the defendant is presumptively eligible for probation;

(3) Declining to commit an eligible juvenile found amenable to treatment to the Department of Corrections and Rehabilitation, Division of Juvenile Justice;

(4) Selecting one of the three authorized terms in prison or county jail under section 1170(h) referred to in section 1170(b) for either a base term or an enhancement;

(5) Imposing consecutive sentences;

(6) Imposing full consecutive sentences under section 667.6(c) rather than consecutive terms under section 1170.1(a), when the court has that choice;

(7) Waiving a restitution fine;

(8) Granting relief under section 1385; and

(9) Denying mandatory supervision in the interests of justice under section 1170(h)(5)(A).

(Subd (b) amended effective January 1, 2018; previously amended effective January 1, 2001, July 1, 2003, January 1, 2006, January 1, 2007, May 23, 2007, and January 1, 2017.)

Rule 4.406 amended effective January 1, 2018; adopted as rule 406 effective January 1, 1991; previously amended and renumbered effective January 1, 2001; previously amended effective July 1, 2003, January 1, 2006, January 1, 2007, May 23, 2007, and January 1, 2017.

Advisory Committee Comment

This rule is not intended to expand the statutory requirements for giving reasons, and is not an independent interpretation of the statutory requirements.

The court is not required to separately state the reasons for making each sentencing choice so long as the record reflects the court understood it had discretion on a particular issue and its reasons for making the particular choice. For example, if the court decides to deny probation and impose the upper term of punishment, the court may simply state: "I am denying probation and imposing the upper term because of the extensive losses to the victim and because the defendant's record is increasing in seriousness." It is not necessary to state a reason after exercising each decision.

The court must be mindful of impermissible dual use of facts in stating reasons for sentencing choices. For example, the court is not permitted to use a reason to impose a greater term if that reason also is either (1) the same as an enhancement that will be imposed, or (2) an element of the crime. The court should not use the same reason to impose a consecutive sentence and to impose an upper term of imprisonment. (*People v. Avalos* (1984) 37 Cal.3d 216, 233.) It is not improper to use the same reason to deny probation and to impose the upper term. (*People v. Bowen* (1992) 11 Cal.App.4th 102, 106.)

Whenever relief is *granted* under section 1385, the court's reasons for exercising that discretion must be stated orally on the record and entered in the minutes if requested by a party or if the proceedings are not recorded electronically or reported by a court reporter. (Pen. Code, § 1385(a).) Although no legal authority requires the court to state reasons for *denying* relief, such a statement may be helpful in the appellate review of the exercise of the court's discretion.

Rule 4.407.   [Repealed 2007]

Rule 4.407 repealed effective January 1, 2007; adopted as rule 407 effective July 1, 1977; previously amended effective January 1, 1991; previously renumbered effective January 1, 2001. The repealed rule related to rules of construction.

Rule 4.408.   Listing of factors not exclusive; sequence not significant

(a) The listing of factors in these rules for making discretionary sentencing decisions is not exhaustive and does not prohibit a trial judge from using additional criteria reasonably related to the decision being made. Any such additional criteria must be stated on the record by the sentencing judge.

(Subd (a) amended effective January 1, 2018; previously amended effective January 1, 2007.)

(b) The order in which criteria are listed does not indicate their relative weight or importance.

Rule 4.408 amended effective January 1, 2018; adopted as rule 408 effective July 1, 1977; previously renumbered effective January 1, 2001; previously amended effective January 1, 2007.

Advisory Committee Comment

The variety of circumstances presented in felony cases is so great that no listing of criteria could claim to be all-inclusive. (Cf. Evid. Code, § 351.)

The relative significance of various criteria will vary from case to case. This, like the question of applicability of various criteria, will be decided by the sentencing judge.

Rule 4.409.   Consideration of relevant factors

Relevant factors enumerated in these rules must be considered by the sentencing judge, and will be deemed to have been considered unless the record affirmatively reflects otherwise.

Rule 4.409 amended effective January 1, 2018; adopted as rule 409 effective July 1, 1977; previously renumbered effective January 1, 2001; previously amended effective January 1, 2007.

Advisory Committee Comment

Relevant factors are those applicable to the facts in the record of the case; not all factors will be relevant to each case. The judge's duty is similar to the duty to consider the probation officer's report. Section 1203.

In deeming the sentencing judge to have considered relevant factors, the rule applies the presumption of Evidence Code section 664 that official duty has been regularly performed. (See *People v. Moran* (1970) 1 Cal.3d 755, 762 [trial court presumed to have considered referring eligible defendant to California Youth Authority in absence of any showing to the contrary, citing Evidence Code section 664].)

Rule 4.410.   General objectives in sentencing

(a) General objectives of sentencing include:

(1) Protecting society;

(2) Punishing the defendant;

(3) Encouraging the defendant to lead a law-abiding life in the future and deterring him or her from future offenses;

(4) Deterring others from criminal conduct by demonstrating its consequences;

(5) Preventing the defendant from committing new crimes by isolating him or her for the period of incarceration;

(6) Securing restitution for the victims of crime;

(7) Achieving uniformity in sentencing; and

(8) Increasing public safety by reducing recidivism through community-based corrections programs and evidence-based practices.

(Subd (a) amended effective January 1, 2017; previously amended effective July 1, 2003, and January 1, 2007.)

(b) Because in some instances these objectives may suggest inconsistent dispositions, the sentencing judge must consider which objectives are of primary importance in the particular case. The sentencing judge should be guided by statutory statements of policy, the criteria in these rules, and any other facts and circumstances relevant to the case.

(Subd (b) amended effective January 1, 2018; adopted as part of unlettered subd effective July 1, 1977; former subd (b) amended and relettered as part of subd (a) effective July 1, 2003; lettered as subd (b) effective July 1, 2003.)

Rule 4.410 amended effective January 1, 2018; adopted as rule 410 effective July 1, 1977; previously renumbered effective January 1, 2001; previously amended effective July 1, 2003, January 1, 2007, and January 1, 2017.

Advisory Committee Comment

Statutory expressions of policy include:

Section 1170(a)(1) expresses the policies of uniformity, proportionality of terms of imprisonment to the seriousness of the offense, and the use of imprisonment as punishment. It also states that "the purpose of sentencing is public safety achieved through punishment, rehabilitation, and restorative justice."

Sections 17.5, 1228, and 3450 express the policies promoting reinvestment of criminal justice resources to support community-based corrections programs and evidence-based practices to improve public safety through a reduction in recidivism.

Rule 4.411.   Presentence investigations and reports

(a) When required

As provided in subdivision (b), the court must refer the case to the probation officer for:

(1) A presentence investigation and report if the defendant:

(A) Is statutorily eligible for probation or a term of imprisonment in county jail under section 1170(h); or

(B) Is not eligible for probation but a report is needed to assist the court with other sentencing issues, including the determination of the proper amount of restitution fine;

(2) A supplemental report if a significant period of time has passed since the original report was prepared.

(Subd (a) amended effective January 1, 2018; previously amended effective January 1, 2007, and January 1, 2015.)

(b) Waiver of the investigation and report

The parties may stipulate to the waiver of the probation officer's investigation and report in writing or in open court and entered in the minutes, and with the consent of the court. In deciding whether to consent to the waiver, the court should consider whether the information in the report would assist in the resolution of any current or future sentencing issues, or would assist in the effective supervision of the person. A waiver under this section does not affect the requirement under section 1203c that a probation report be created when the court commits a person to state prison.

(Subd (b) amended effective January 1, 2018; previously amended effective January 1, 2015.)

Rule 4.411 amended effective January 1, 2018; adopted as rule 418 effective July 1, 1977; previously amended and renumbered as rule 411 effective January 1, 1991; previously renumbered effective January 1, 2001; previously amended effective January 1, 2006, January 1, 2007, and January 1, 2015.

Advisory Committee Comment

Section 1203 requires a presentence report in every felony case in which the defendant is eligible for probation. Subdivision (a) requires a presentence report in every felony case in which the defendant is eligible for a term of imprisonment in county jail under section 1170(h).

When considering whether to waive a presentence investigation and report, courts should consider that probation officers' reports are used by (1) courts in determining the appropriate term of imprisonment in prison or county jail under section 1170(h); (2) courts in deciding whether probation is appropriate, whether a period of mandatory supervision should be denied in the interests of justice under section 1170(h)(5)(A), and the appropriate length and conditions of probation and mandatory supervision; (3) the probation department in supervising the defendant; and (4) the Department of Corrections and Rehabilitation, Division of Adult Operations, in deciding on the type of facility and program in which to place a defendant.

Subdivision (a)(2) is based on case law that generally requires a supplemental report if the defendant is to be resentenced a significant time after the original sentencing, as, for example, after a remand by an appellate court, or after the apprehension of a defendant who failed to appear at sentencing. The rule is not intended to expand on the requirements of those cases.

The rule does not require a new investigation and report if a recent report is available and can be incorporated by reference and there is no indication of changed circumstances. This is particularly true if a report is needed only for the Department of Corrections and Rehabilitation because the defendant has waived a report and agreed to a prison sentence. If a full report was prepared in another case in the same or another jurisdiction within the preceding six months, during which time the defendant was in custody, and that report is available to the Department of Corrections and Rehabilitation, it is unlikely that a new investigation is needed.

This rule does not prohibit pre-conviction, pre-plea reports as authorized by section 1203.7.

Rule 4.411.5.   Probation officer's presentence investigation report

(a) Contents

A probation officer's presentence investigation report in a felony case must include at least the following:

(1) A face sheet showing at least:

(A) The defendant's name and other identifying data;

(B) The case number;

(C) The crime of which the defendant was convicted;

(D) The date of commission of the crime, the date of conviction, and any other dates relevant to sentencing;

(E) The defendant's custody status; and

(F) The terms of any agreement on which a plea of guilty was based.

(2) The facts and circumstances of the crime and the defendant's arrest, including information concerning any co-defendants and the status or disposition of their cases. The source of all such information must be stated.

(3) A summary of the defendant's record of prior criminal conduct, including convictions as an adult and sustained petitions in juvenile delinquency proceedings. Records of an arrest or charge not leading to a conviction or the sustaining of a petition may not be included unless supported by facts concerning the arrest or charge.

(4) Any statement made by the defendant to the probation officer, or a summary thereof, including the defendant's account of the circumstances of the crime.

(5) Information concerning the victim of the crime, including:

(A) The victim's statement or a summary thereof, if available;

(B) Any physical or psychological injuries suffered by the victim;

(C) The amount of the victim's monetary loss, and whether or not it is covered by insurance; and

(D) Any information required by law.

(6) Any relevant facts concerning the defendant's social history, including those categories enumerated in section 1203.10, organized under appropriate subheadings, including, whenever applicable, "Family," "Education," "Employment and income," "Military," "Medical/psychological," "Record of substance abuse or lack thereof," and any other relevant subheadings. This includes facts relevant to whether the defendant may be suffering from sexual trauma, traumatic brain injury, post-traumatic stress disorder, substance abuse, or mental health problems as a result of his or her U. S. military service.

(7) Collateral information, including written statements from:

(A) Official sources such as defense and prosecuting attorneys, police (subsequent to any police reports used to summarize the crime), probation and parole officers who have had prior experience with the defendant, and correctional personnel who observed the defendant's behavior during any period of presentence incarceration; and

(B) Interested persons, including family members and others who have written letters concerning the defendant.

(8) The defendant's relevant risk factors and needs as identified by a risk/needs assessment, if such an assessment is performed, and such other information from the assessment as may be requested by the court.

(9) An evaluation of factors relating to disposition. This section must include:

(A) A reasoned discussion of the defendant's suitability and eligibility for probation, and, if probation is recommended, a proposed plan including recommendations for the conditions of probation and any special need for supervision;

(B) If a prison sentence or term of imprisonment in county jail under section 1170(h) is recommended or is likely to be imposed, a reasoned discussion of aggravating and mitigating factors affecting the sentence length;

(C) If denial of a period of mandatory supervision in the interests of justice is recommended, a reasoned discussion of the factors prescribed by rule 4.415(b);

(D) If a term of imprisonment in county jail under section 1170(h) is recommended, a reasoned discussion of the defendant's suitability for specific terms and length of period of mandatory supervision, including the factors prescribed by rule 4.415(c); and

(E) A reasoned discussion of the defendant's ability to make restitution, pay any fine or penalty that may be recommended, or satisfy any special conditions of probation that are proposed.

Discussions of factors (A) through (D) must refer to any sentencing rule directly relevant to the facts of the case, but no rule may be cited without a reasoned discussion of its relevance and relative importance.

(10) The probation officer's recommendation. When requested by the sentencing judge or by standing instructions to the probation department, the report must include recommendations concerning the length of any prison or county jail term under section 1170(h) that may be imposed, including the base term, the imposition of concurrent or consecutive sentences, and the imposition or striking of the additional terms for enhancements charged and found.

(11) Detailed information on presentence time spent by the defendant in custody, including the beginning and ending dates of the period or periods of custody; the existence of any other sentences imposed on the defendant during the period of custody; the amount of good behavior, work, or participation credit to which the defendant is entitled; and whether the sheriff or other officer holding custody, the prosecution, or the defense wishes that a hearing be held for the purposes of denying good behavior, work, or participation credit.

(12) A statement of mandatory and recommended restitution, restitution fines, other fines, and costs to be assessed against the defendant, including chargeable probation services and attorney fees under section 987.8 when appropriate, findings concerning the defendant's ability to pay, and a recommendation whether any restitution order should become a judgment under section 1203(j) if unpaid.

(13) Information pursuant to Penal Code section 29810(c):

(A) Whether the defendant has properly complied with Penal Code section 29810 by relinquishing all firearms identified by the probation officer's investigation or declared by the defendant on the Prohibited Persons Relinquishment Form, and

(B) Whether the defendant has timely submitted a completed Prohibited Persons Relinquishment Form.

(Subd (a) amended effective January 1, 2018; previously amended effective January 1, 1991, July 1, 2003, January 1, 2007, January 1, 2015, and January 1, 2017.)

(b) Format

The report must be on paper 8-½ by 11 inches in size and must follow the sequence set out in (a) to the extent possible.

(Subd (b) amended effective January 1, 2007; previously amended effective January 1, 1991.)

(c) Sources

The source of all information must be stated. Any person who has furnished information included in the report must be identified by name or official capacity unless a reason is given for not disclosing the person's identity.

(Subd (c) amended effective January 1, 2007; previously amended effective January 1, 1991.)

Rule 4.411.5 amended effective January 1, 2018; adopted as rule 419 effective July 1, 1981; previously amended and renumbered as rule 411.5 effective January 1, 1991; previously renumbered effective January 1, 2001; previously amended effective July 1, 2003, January 1, 2007, January 1, 2015, and January 1, 2017.

Rule 4.412. Reasons—agreement to punishment as an adequate reason and as abandonment of certain claims

(a) Defendant's agreement as reason

It is an adequate reason for a sentence or other disposition that the defendant, personally and by counsel, has expressed agreement that it be imposed and the prosecuting attorney has not expressed an objection to it. The agreement and lack of objection must be recited on the record. This section does not authorize a sentence that is not otherwise authorized by law.

(Subd (a) amended effective January 1, 2007; previously amended effective January 1, 2001.)

(b) Agreement to sentence abandons section 654 claim

By agreeing to a specified term in prison or county jail under section 1170(h) personally and by counsel, a defendant who is sentenced to that term or a shorter one abandons any claim that a component of the sentence violates section 654's prohibition of double punishment, unless that claim is asserted at the time the agreement is recited on the record.

(Subd (b) amended effective January 1, 2017; previously amended effective January 1, 2007.)

Rule 4.412 amended effective January 1, 2017; adopted as rule 412 effective January 1, 1991; previously amended and renumbered effective January 1, 2001; previously amended effective January 1, 2007.

Advisory Committee Comment

Subdivision (a). This subdivision is intended to relieve the court of an obligation to give reasons if the sentence or other disposition is one that the defendant has accepted and to which the prosecutor expresses no objection. The judge may choose to give reasons for the sentence even though not obligated to do so.

Judges should also be aware that there may be statutory limitations on "plea bargaining" or on the entry of a guilty plea on the condition that no more than a particular sentence will be imposed. Such limitations appear, for example, in sections 1192.5 and 1192.7.

Subdivision (b). This subdivision is based on the fact that a defendant who, with the advice of counsel, expresses agreement to a specified term of imprisonment normally is acknowledging that the term is appropriate for his or her total course of conduct. This subdivision applies to both determinate and indeterminate terms.

Rule 4.413. Grant of probation when defendant is presumptively ineligible for probation

(a) Consideration of eligibility

The court must determine whether the defendant is eligible for probation. In most cases, the defendant is presumptively eligible for probation; in some cases, the defendant is presumptively ineligible; and in some cases, probation is not allowed.

(Subd (a) amended effective January 1, 2018; previously amended effective January 1, 2007.)

(b) Probation in cases when defendant is presumptively ineligible

If the defendant comes under a statutory provision prohibiting probation "except in unusual cases where the interests of justice would best be served," or a substantially equivalent provision, the court should apply the criteria in (c) to evaluate whether the statutory limitation on probation is overcome; and if it is, the court should then apply the criteria in rule 4.414 to decide whether to grant probation.

(Subd (b) amended effective January 1, 2018; previously amended effective July 1, 2003, and January 1, 2007.)

(c) Factors overcoming the presumption of ineligibility

The following factors may indicate the existence of an unusual case in which probation may be granted if otherwise appropriate:

(1) *Factors relating to basis for limitation on probation*

A factor or circumstance indicating that the basis for the statutory limitation on probation, although technically present, is not fully applicable to the case, including:

(A) The factor or circumstance giving rise to the limitation on probation is, in this case, substantially less serious than the circumstances typically present in other cases involving the same probation limitation, and the defendant has no recent record of committing similar crimes or crimes of violence; and

(B) The current offense is less serious than a prior felony conviction that is the cause of the limitation on probation, and the defendant has been free from incarceration and serious violation of the law for a substantial time before the current offense.

(2) *Factors limiting defendant's culpability*

A factor or circumstance not amounting to a defense, but reducing the defendant's culpability for the offense, including:

(A) The defendant participated in the crime under circumstances of great provocation, coercion, or duress not amounting to a defense, and the defendant has no recent record of committing crimes of violence;

(B) The crime was committed because of a mental condition not amounting to a defense, and there is a high likelihood that the defendant would respond favorably to mental health care and treatment that would be required as a condition of probation; and

(C) The defendant is youthful or aged, and has no significant record of prior criminal offenses.

(3) *Results of risk/needs assessment*

Along with all other relevant information in the case, the court may consider the results of a risk/needs assessment of the defendant, if one was performed. The weight of a risk/needs assessment is for the court to consider in its sentencing discretion.

(Subd (c) amended effective January 1, 2018; previously amended effective January 1, 2007.)

Rule 4.413 amended effective January 1, 2018; adopted as rule 413 effective January 1, 1991; previously renumbered effective January 1, 2001; previously amended effective July 1, 2003, and January 1, 2007.

Advisory Committee Comment

Subdivision (c)(3). Standard 4.35 of the California Standards of Judicial Administration provides courts with additional guidance on using the results of a risk/needs assessment at sentencing.

Rule 4.414. Criteria affecting probation

Criteria affecting the decision to grant or deny probation include facts relating to the crime and facts relating to the defendant.

(a) Facts relating to the crime

Facts relating to the crime include:

(1) The nature, seriousness, and circumstances of the crime as compared to other instances of the same crime;

(2) Whether the defendant was armed with or used a weapon;

(3) The vulnerability of the victim;

(4) Whether the defendant inflicted physical or emotional injury;

(5) The degree of monetary loss to the victim;

(6) Whether the defendant was an active or a passive participant;

(7) Whether the crime was committed because of an unusual circumstance, such as great provocation, which is unlikely to recur;

(8) Whether the manner in which the crime was carried out demonstrated criminal sophistication or professionalism on the part of the defendant; and

(9) Whether the defendant took advantage of a position of trust or confidence to commit the crime.

(Subd (a) amended effective January 1, 2007; previously amended effective January 1, 1991.)

(b) Facts relating to the defendant

Facts relating to the defendant include:

(1) Prior record of criminal conduct, whether as an adult or a juvenile, including the recency and frequency of prior crimes; and whether the prior

record indicates a pattern of regular or increasingly serious criminal conduct;

(2) Prior performance and present status on probation, mandatory supervision, postrelease community supervision, or parole;

(3) Willingness to comply with the terms of probation;

(4) Ability to comply with reasonable terms of probation as indicated by the defendant's age, education, health, mental faculties, history of alcohol or other substance abuse, family background and ties, employment and military service history, and other relevant factors;

(5) The likely effect of imprisonment on the defendant and his or her dependents;

(6) The adverse collateral consequences on the defendant's life resulting from the felony conviction;

(7) Whether the defendant is remorseful; and

(8) The likelihood that if not imprisoned the defendant will be a danger to others.

(Subd (b) amended effective January 1, 2017; previously amended effective January 1, 1991, July 1, 2003, and January 1, 2007.)

Rule 4.414 amended effective January 1, 2017; adopted as rule 414 effective July 1, 1977; previously amended effective January 1, 1991; previously renumbered effective January 1, 2001; previously amended effective July 1, 2003, and January 1, 2007.

Advisory Committee Comment

The sentencing judge's discretion to grant probation is unaffected by the Uniform Determinate Sentencing Act (section 1170(a)(3)).

The decision whether to grant probation is normally based on an overall evaluation of the likelihood that the defendant will live successfully in the general community. Each criterion points to evidence that the likelihood of success is great or small. A single criterion will rarely be determinative; in most cases, the sentencing judge will have to balance favorable and unfavorable facts.

Under criteria (b)(3) and (b)(4), it is appropriate to consider the defendant's expressions of willingness to comply and his or her apparent sincerity, and whether the defendant's home and work environment and primary associates will be supportive of the defendant's efforts to comply with the terms of probation, among other factors.

Rule 4.415. Criteria affecting the imposition of mandatory supervision

(a) Presumption

Except where the defendant is statutorily ineligible for suspension of any part of the sentence, when imposing a term of imprisonment in county jail under section 1170(h), the court must suspend execution of a concluding portion of the term to be served as a period of mandatory supervision unless the court finds, in the interests of justice, that mandatory supervision is not appropriate in a particular case. Because section 1170(h)(5)(A) establishes a statutory presumption in favor of the imposition of a period of mandatory supervision in all applicable cases, denials of a period of mandatory supervision should be limited.

(Subd (a) amended effective January 1, 2017; adopted effective January 1, 2015.)

(b) Criteria for denying mandatory supervision in the interests of justice

In determining that mandatory supervision is not appropriate in the interests of justice under section 1170(h)(5)(A), the court's determination must be based on factors that are specific to a particular case or defendant. Factors the court may consider include:

(1) Consideration of the balance of custody exposure available after imposition of presentence custody credits;

(2) The defendant's present status on probation, mandatory supervision, postrelease community supervision, or parole;

(3) Specific factors related to the defendant that indicate a lack of need for treatment or supervision upon release from custody; and

(4) Whether the nature, seriousness, or circumstances of the case or the defendant's past performance on supervision substantially outweigh the benefits of supervision in promoting public safety and the defendant's successful reentry into the community upon release from custody.

(Subd (b) adopted effective January 1, 2015.)

(c) Criteria affecting conditions and length of mandatory supervision

In exercising discretion to select the appropriate period and conditions of mandatory supervision, factors the court may consider include:

(1) Availability of appropriate community corrections programs;

(2) Victim restitution, including any conditions or period of supervision necessary to promote the collection of any court-ordered restitution;

(3) Consideration of length and conditions of supervision to promote the successful reintegration of the defendant into the community upon release from custody;

(4) Public safety, including protection of any victims and witnesses;

(5) Past performance and present status on probation, mandatory supervision, postrelease community supervision, and parole;

(6) The balance of custody exposure after imposition of presentence custody credits;

(7) Consideration of the statutory accrual of post-sentence custody credits for mandatory supervision under section 1170(h)(5)(B) and sentences served in county jail under section 4019(a)(6);

(8) The defendant's specific needs and risk factors identified by a risk/needs assessment, if available; and

(9) The likely effect of extended imprisonment on the defendant and any dependents.

(Subd (c) amended effective January 1, 2018; adopted effective January 1, 2015.)

(d) Statement of reasons for denial of mandatory supervision

Notwithstanding rule 4.412(a), when a court denies a period of mandatory supervision in the interests of justice, the court must state the reasons for the denial on the record.

(Subd (d) adopted effective January 1, 2015.)

Rule 4.415 amended effective January 1, 2018; adopted effective January 1, 2015; previously amended effective January 1, 2017.

Advisory Committee Comment

Penal Code section 1170.3 requires the Judicial Council to adopt rules of court that prescribe criteria for the consideration of the court at the time of sentencing regarding the court's decision to "[d]eny a period of mandatory supervision in the interests of justice under paragraph (5) of subdivision (h) of Section 1170 or determine the appropriate period of and conditions of mandatory supervision."

Subdivision (a). Penal Code section 1170(h)(5)(A): "Unless the court finds, in the interests of justice, that it is not appropriate in a particular case, the court, when imposing a sentence pursuant to paragraph (1) or (2) of this subdivision, shall suspend execution of a concluding portion of the term for a period selected at the court's discretion." Under *People v. Borynack* (2015) 238 Cal.App.4th 958, review denied, courts may not impose mandatory supervision when the defendant is statutorily ineligible for a suspension of part of the sentence.

Subdivisions (b)(3), (b)(4), and (c)(3). The Legislature has declared that "[s]trategies supporting reentering offenders through practices and programs, such as standardized risk and needs assessments, transitional community housing, treatment, medical and mental health services, and employment, have been demonstrated to significantly reduce recidivism among offenders in other states." (Pen. Code, § 17.7(a).)

Subdivision (c)(7). Under Penal Code section 1170(h)(5)(B), defendants serving a period of mandatory supervision are entitled to day-for-day credits: "During the period when the defendant is under such supervision, unless in actual custody related to the sentence imposed by the court, the defendant shall be entitled to only actual time credit against the term of imprisonment imposed by the court." In contrast, defendants serving terms of imprisonment in county jails under Penal Code section 1170(h) are entitled to conduct credits under Penal Code section 4019(a)(6).

Subdivision (c)(8). Standard 4.35 of the California Standards of Judicial Administration provides courts with additional guidance on using the results of a risk/needs assessment at sentencing.

Rule 4.420. Selection of term of imprisonment

(a) When a sentence of imprisonment is imposed, or the execution of a sentence of imprisonment is ordered suspended, the sentencing judge must select the upper, middle, or lower term on each count for which the defendant has been convicted, as provided in section 1170(b) and these rules.

(Subd (a) amended effective May 23, 2007; previously amended effective July 28, 1977, January 1, 1991, and January 1, 2007.)

(b) In exercising his or her discretion in selecting one of the three authorized terms of imprisonment referred to in section 1170(b), the sentencing judge may consider circumstances in aggravation or mitigation, and any other factor reasonably related to the sentencing decision. The relevant circumstances may be obtained from the case record, the probation officer's report, other reports and statements properly received, statements in aggravation or mitigation, and any evidence introduced at the sentencing hearing.

(Subd (b) amended effective January 1, 2017; previously amended effective July 28, 1977, January 1, 1991, January 1, 2007, May 23, 2007, and January 1, 2008.)

(c) To comply with section 1170(b), a fact charged and found as an enhancement may be used as a reason for imposing a particular term only if the court has discretion to strike the punishment for the enhancement and does so. The use of a fact of an enhancement to impose the upper term of imprisonment is an adequate reason for striking the additional term of imprisonment, regardless of the effect on the total term.

(Subd (c) amended effective January 1, 2018; adopted effective January 1, 1991.)

(d) A fact that is an element of the crime on which punishment is being imposed may not be used to impose a particular term.

(Subd (d) amended effective January 1, 2018; adopted effective January 1, 1991; 2 previously amended effective January 1, 2007, May 23, 2007, and January 1, 2008.)

(e) The reasons for selecting one of the three authorized terms of imprisonment referred to in section 1170(b) must be stated orally on the record.

(Subd (e) amended effective January 1, 2017; previously amended and relettered effective January 1, 1991; previously amended effective July 28, 1977, January 1, 2007, and May 23, 2007.)

Rule 4.420 amended effective January 1, 2018; adopted as rule 439 effective July 1, 1977; previously amended and renumbered as rule 420 effective January 1, 1991; previously renumbered effective January 1, 2001; previously amended effective July 28, 1977, January 1, 2007, May 23, 2007, January 1, 2008, and January 1, 2017.

Advisory Committee Comment

The determinate sentencing law authorizes the court to select any of the three possible terms of imprisonment even though neither party has requested a particular term by formal motion or informal argument. Section 1170(b) vests the court with discretion to impose any of the three authorized terms of imprisonment and requires that the court state on the record the reasons for imposing that term.

It is not clear whether the reasons stated by the judge for selecting a particular term qualify as "facts" for the purposes of the rule prohibition on dual use of facts. Until the issue is clarified, judges should avoid the use of reasons that may constitute an impermissible dual use of facts. For example, the court is not permitted to use a reason to impose a greater term if that reason also is either (1) the same as an enhancement that will be imposed, or (2) an element of the crime. The court should not use the same reason to impose a consecutive sentence as to impose an upper term of imprisonment. (*People v. Avalos* (1984) 37 Cal.3d 216, 233.) It is not improper to use the same reason to deny probation and to impose the upper term. (*People v. Bowen* (1992) 11 Cal.App.4th 102, 106.)

The rule makes it clear that a fact charged and found as an enhancement may, in the alternative, be used as a factor in aggravation.

People v. Riolo (1983) 33 Cal.3d 223, 227 (and note 5 on 227) held that section 1170.1(a) does not require the judgment to state the base term (upper, middle, or lower) and enhancements, computed independently, on counts that are subject to automatic reduction under the one-third formula of section 1170.1(a).

Even when sentencing is under section 1170.1, however, it is essential to determine the base term and specific enhancements for each count independently, in order to know which is the principal term count. The principal term count must be determined before any calculation is made using the one-third formula for subordinate terms.

In addition, the base term (upper, middle, or lower) for each count must be determined to arrive at an informed decision whether to make terms consecutive or concurrent; and the base term for each count must be stated in the judgment when sentences are concurrent or are fully consecutive (i.e., not subject to the one-third rule of section 1170.1(a)).

Rule 4.421. Circumstances in aggravation

Circumstances in aggravation include factors relating to the crime and factors relating to the defendant.

(a) Factors relating to the crime

Factors relating to the crime, whether or not charged or chargeable as enhancements include that:

(1) The crime involved great violence, great bodily harm, threat of great bodily harm, or other acts disclosing a high degree of cruelty, viciousness, or callousness;

(2) The defendant was armed with or used a weapon at the time of the commission of the crime;

(3) The victim was particularly vulnerable;

(4) The defendant induced others to participate in the commission of the crime or occupied a position of leadership or dominance of other participants in its commission;

(5) The defendant induced a minor to commit or assist in the commission of the crime;

(6) The defendant threatened witnesses, unlawfully prevented or dissuaded witnesses from testifying, suborned perjury, or in any other way illegally interfered with the judicial process;

(7) The defendant was convicted of other crimes for which consecutive sentences could have been imposed but for which concurrent sentences are being imposed;

(8) The manner in which the crime was carried out indicates planning, sophistication, or professionalism;

(9) The crime involved an attempted or actual taking or damage of great monetary value;

(10) The crime involved a large quantity of contraband; and

(11) The defendant took advantage of a position of trust or confidence to commit the offense.

(12) The crime constitutes a hate crime under section 422.55 and:

(A) No hate crime enhancements under section 422.75 are imposed; and

(B) The crime is not subject to sentencing under section 1170.8.

(Subd (a) amended effective May 23, 2007; previously amended effective January 1, 1991, and January 1, 2007.)

(b) Factors relating to the defendant

Factors relating to the defendant include that:

(1) The defendant has engaged in violent conduct that indicates a serious danger to society;

(2) The defendant's prior convictions as an adult or sustained petitions in juvenile delinquency proceedings are numerous or of increasing seriousness;

(3) The defendant has served a prior term in prison or county jail under section 1170(h);

(4) The defendant was on probation, mandatory supervision, postrelease community supervision, or parole when the crime was committed; and

(5) The defendant's prior performance on probation, mandatory supervision, postrelease community supervision, or parole was unsatisfactory.

(Subd (b) amended effective January 1, 2017; previously amended effective January 1, 1991, January 1, 2007, and May 23, 2007.)

(c) Other factors

Any other factors statutorily declared to be circumstances in aggravation or that reasonably relate to the defendant or the circumstances under which the crime was committed.

(Subd (c) amended effective January 1, 2018; adopted effective January 1, 1991; previously amended effective January 1, 2007, and May 23, 2007.)

Rule 4.421 amended effective January 1, 2018; adopted as rule 421 effective July 1, 1977; previously renumbered effective January 1, 2001; previously amended effective January 1, 1991, January 1, 2007, May 23, 2007, and January 1, 2017.

Advisory Committee Comment

Circumstances in aggravation may justify imposition of the middle or upper of three possible terms of imprisonment. (Section 1170(b).)

The list of circumstances in aggravation includes some facts that, if charged and found, may be used to enhance the sentence. This rule does not deal with the dual use of the facts; the statutory prohibition against dual use is included, in part, in the comment to rule 4.420.

Conversely, such facts as infliction of bodily harm, being armed with or using a weapon, and a taking or loss of great value may be circumstances in aggravation even if not meeting the statutory definitions for enhancements or charged as an enhancement.

Facts concerning the defendant's prior record and personal history may be considered. By providing that the defendant's prior record and simultaneous convictions of other offenses may not be used both for enhancement and in aggravation, section 1170(b) indicates that these and other facts extrinsic to the commission of the crime may be considered in aggravation in appropriate cases.

Refusal to consider the personal characteristics of the defendant in imposing sentence may raise serious constitutional questions. The California Supreme Court has held that sentencing decisions must take into account "the nature of the offense and/or the offender, with particular regard to the degree of danger both present to society." (*In re Rodriguez* (1975) 14 Cal.3d 639, 654, quoting *In re Lynch* (1972) 8 Cal.3d 410, 425.) In *Rodriguez* the court released petitioner from further incarceration because "it appears that neither the circumstances of his offense *nor his personal characteristics* establish a danger to society sufficient to justify such a prolonged period of imprisonment." (*Id.* at p. 655, fn. omitted, italics added.) "For the determination of sentences, justice generally requires … that there be taken into account the circumstances of the offense together with the character and propensities of the offender." (*Pennsylvania ex rel. Sullivan v. Ashe* (1937) 302 U.S. 51, 55, quoted with approval in *Gregg v. Georgia* (1976) 428 U.S. 153, 189.)

Former subdivision (a)(4), concerning multiple victims, was deleted to avoid confusion. Some of the cases that had relied on that circumstance in aggravation were reversed on appeal because there was only a single victim in a particular count.

Old age or youth of the victim may be circumstances in aggravation; see section 1170.85(b). Other statutory circumstances in aggravation are listed, for example, in sections 422.76, 1170.7, 1170.71, 1170.8, and 1170.85.

Rule 4.423. Circumstances in mitigation

Circumstances in mitigation include factors relating to the crime and factors relating to the defendant.

(a) Factors relating to the crime

Factors relating to the crime include that:

(1) The defendant was a passive participant or played a minor role in the crime;

(2) The victim was an initiator of, willing participant in, or aggressor or provoker of the incident;

(3) The crime was committed because of an unusual circumstance, such as great provocation, that is unlikely to recur;

(4) The defendant participated in the crime under circumstances of coercion or duress, or the criminal conduct was partially excusable for some other reason not amounting to a defense;

(5) The defendant, with no apparent predisposition to do so, was induced by others to participate in the crime;

(6) The defendant exercised caution to avoid harm to persons or damage to property, or the amounts of money or property taken were deliberately small, or no harm was done or threatened against the victim;

(7) The defendant believed that he or she had a claim or right to the property taken, or for other reasons mistakenly believed that the conduct was legal;

(8) The defendant was motivated by a desire to provide necessities for his or her family or self; and

(9) The defendant suffered from repeated or continuous physical, sexual, or psychological abuse inflicted by the victim of the crime, and the victim of the crime, who inflicted the abuse, was the defendant's spouse, intimate cohabitant, or parent of the defendant's child; and the abuse does not amount to a defense.

(Subd (a) amended effective May 23, 2007; previously amended effective January 1, 1991, July 1, 1993, and January 1, 2007.)

(b) Factors relating to the defendant

Factors relating to the defendant include that:

(1) The defendant has no prior record, or has an insignificant record of criminal conduct, considering the recency and frequency of prior crimes;

(2) The defendant was suffering from a mental or physical condition that significantly reduced culpability for the crime;

(3) The defendant voluntarily acknowledged wrongdoing before arrest or at an early stage of the criminal process;

(4) The defendant is ineligible for probation and but for that ineligibility would have been granted probation;

(5) The defendant made restitution to the victim; and

(6) The defendant's prior performance on probation, mandatory supervision, postrelease community supervision, or parole was satisfactory.

(Subd (b) amended effective January 1, 2017; previously amended effective January 1, 1991, January 1, 2007, and May 23, 2007.)

(c) Other factors

Any other factors statutorily declared to be circumstances in mitigation or that reasonably relate to the defendant or the circumstances under which the crime was committed.

(Subd (c) adopted effective January 1, 2018.)

Rule 4.423 amended effective January 1, 2018; adopted as rule 423 effective July 1, 1977; previously renumbered effective January 1, 2001; previously amended effective January 1, 1991, July 1, 1993, January 1, 2007, May 23, 2007, and January 1, 2017.

Advisory Committee Comment

See comment to rule 4.421.

This rule applies both to mitigation for purposes of section 1170(b) and to circumstances in mitigation justifying the court in striking the additional punishment provided for an enhancement.

Some listed circumstances can never apply to certain enhancements; for example, "the amounts taken were deliberately small" can never apply to an excessive taking under section 12022.6, and "no harm was done" can never apply to infliction of great bodily injury under section 12022.7. In any case, only the facts present may be considered for their possible effect in mitigation.

See also rule 4.409; only relevant criteria need be considered.

Since only the fact of restitution is considered relevant to mitigation, no reference to the defendant's financial ability is needed. The omission of a comparable factor from rule 4.421 as a circumstance in aggravation is deliberate.

Rule 4.424. Consideration of applicability of section 654

Before determining whether to impose either concurrent or consecutive sentences on all counts on which the defendant was convicted, the court must determine whether the proscription in section 654 against multiple punishments for the same act or omission requires a stay of execution of the sentence imposed on some of the counts.

Rule 4.424 amended effective January 1, 2011; adopted as rule 424 effective January 1, 1991; previously renumbered effective January 1, 2001; previously amended effective January 1, 2007.

Rule 4.425. Factors affecting concurrent or consecutive sentences

Factors affecting the decision to impose consecutive rather than concurrent sentences include:

(a) Facts relating to crimes

Facts relating to the crimes, including whether or not:

(1) The crimes and their objectives were predominantly independent of each other;

(2) The crimes involved separate acts of violence or threats of violence; or

(3) The crimes were committed at different times or separate places, rather than being committed so closely in time and place as to indicate a single period of aberrant behavior.

(Subd (a) amended effective January 1, 2018; previously amended effective January 1, 1991, and January 1, 2007.)

(b) Other facts and limitations

Any circumstances in aggravation or mitigation may be considered in deciding whether to impose consecutive rather than concurrent sentences, except:

(1) A fact used to impose the upper term;

(2) A fact used to otherwise enhance the defendant's sentence in prison or county jail under section 1170(h); and

(3) A fact that is an element of the crime may not be used to impose consecutive sentences.

(Subd (b) amended effective January 1, 2018; previously amended effective January 1, 1991, January 1, 2007, and January 1, 2017.)

Rule 4.425 amended effective January 1, 2018; adopted as rule 425 effective July 1, 1977; previously amended effective January 1, 1991, January 1, 2007, and January 1, 2017; previously renumbered effective January 1, 2001.

Advisory Committee Comment

The sentencing judge should be aware that there are some cases in which the law mandates consecutive sentences.

Rule 4.426. Violent sex crimes

(a) Multiple violent sex crimes

When a defendant has been convicted of multiple violent sex offenses as defined in section 667.6, the sentencing judge must determine whether the crimes involved separate victims or the same victim on separate occasions.

(1) *Different victims*

If the crimes were committed against different victims, a full, separate, and consecutive term must be imposed for a violent sex crime as to each victim, under section 667.6(d).

(2) *Same victim, separate occasions*

If the crimes were committed against a single victim, the sentencing judge must determine whether the crimes were committed on separate occasions. In determining whether there were separate occasions, the sentencing judge must consider whether, between the commission of one sex crime and another, the defendant had a reasonable opportunity to reflect on his or her actions and nevertheless resumed sexually assaultive behavior. A full, separate, and consecutive term must be imposed for each violent sex offense committed on a separate occasion under section 667.6(d).

(Subd (a) amended effective January 1, 2007.)

(b) Same victim, same occasion; other crimes

If the defendant has been convicted of multiple crimes, including at least one violent sex crime, as defined in section 667.6, or if there have been multiple violent sex crimes against a single victim on the same occasion and the sentencing court has decided to impose consecutive sentences, the sentencing judge must then determine whether to impose a full, separate, and consecutive sentence under section 667.6(c) for the violent sex crime or crimes instead of including the violent sex crimes in the computation of the principal and subordinate terms under section 1170.1(a). A decision to impose a fully consecutive sentence under section 667.6(c) is an additional sentence choice that requires a statement of reasons separate from those given for consecutive sentences, but which may repeat the same reasons. The sentencing judge is to be guided by the criteria listed in rule 4.425, which incorporates rules 4.421 and 4.423, as well as any other reasonably related criteria as provided in rule 4.408.

(Subd (b) amended effective January 1, 2007; previously amended effective July 1, 2003.)

Rule 4.426 amended effective January 1, 2007; adopted as rule 426 effective January 1, 1991; previously renumbered effective January 1, 2001; previously amended effective July 1, 2003.

Section 667.6(d) requires a full, separate, and consecutive term for each of the enumerated violent sex crimes that involve separate victims, or the same victim on separate occasions. Therefore, if there were separate victims or the court found that there were separate occasions, no other reasons are required.

If there have been multiple convictions involving at least one of the enumerated violent sex crimes, the court may impose a full, separate, and consecutive term for each violent sex crime under section 667.6(c). (See *People v. Coleman* (1989) 48 Cal.3d 112, 161.) A fully consecutive sentence under section 667.6(c) is a sentence choice, which requires a statement of reasons. The court may not use the same fact to impose a sentence under section 667.6(c) that was used to impose an upper term. (See rule 4.425(b).) If the court selects the upper term, imposes consecutive sentences, and uses section 667.6(c), the record must reflect three sentencing choices with three separate statements of reasons, but the same reason may be used for sentencing under section 667.6(c) and to impose consecutive sentences. (See *People v. Belmontes* (1983) 34 Cal.3d 335, 347-349.)

Rule 4.427. Hate crimes

(a) Application

This rule is intended to assist judges in sentencing in felony hate crime cases. It applies to:

(1) Felony sentencing under section 422.7;

(2) Convictions of felonies with a hate crime enhancement under section 422.75; and

(3) Convictions of felonies that qualify as hate crimes under section 422.55.

(Subd (a) adopted effective January 1, 2007.)

(b) Felony sentencing under section 422.7

If one of the three factors listed in section 422.7 is pled and proved, a misdemeanor conviction that constitutes a hate crime under section 422.55 may be sentenced as a felony. The punishment is imprisonment in state prison or county jail under section 1170(h) as provided by section 422.7.

(Subd (b) amended effective January 1, 2017; adopted effective January 1, 2007.)

(c) Hate crime enhancement

If a hate crime enhancement is pled and proved, the punishment for a felony conviction must be enhanced under section 422.75 unless the conviction is sentenced as a felony under section 422.7.

(1) The following enhancements apply:

(A) An enhancement of a term in state prison as provided in section 422.75(a). Personal use of a firearm in the commission of the offense is an aggravating factor that must be considered in determining the enhancement term.

(B) An additional enhancement of one year in state prison for each prior felony conviction that constitutes a hate crime as defined in section 422.55.

(2) The court may strike enhancements under (c) if it finds mitigating circumstances under rule 4.423 and states those mitigating circumstances on the record.

(3) The punishment for any enhancement under (c) is in addition to any other punishment provided by law.

(Subd (c) adopted effective January 1, 2007.)

(d) Hate crime as aggravating factor

If the defendant is convicted of a felony, and the facts of the crime constitute a hate crime under section 422.55, that fact must be considered a circumstance in aggravation in determining the appropriate punishment under rule 4.421 unless:

(1) The court imposed a hate crime enhancement under section 422.75; or

(2) The defendant has been convicted of an offense subject to sentencing under section 1170.8.

(Subd (d) adopted effective January 1, 2007.)

(e) Hate crime sentencing goals

When sentencing a defendant under this rule, the judge must consider the principal goals for hate crime sentencing.

(1) The principal goals for hate crime sentencing, as stated in section 422.86, are:

(A) Punishment for the hate crime committed;

(B) Crime and violence prevention, including prevention of recidivism and prevention of crimes and violence in prisons and jails; and

(C) Restorative justice for the immediate victims of the hate crimes and for the classes of persons terrorized by the hate crimes.

(2) Crime and violence prevention considerations should include educational or other appropriate programs available in the community,

jail, prison, and juvenile detention facilities. The programs should address sensitivity or similar training or counseling intended to reduce violent and antisocial behavior based on one or more of the following actual or perceived characteristics of the victim:

(A) Disability;

(B) Gender;

(C) Nationality;

(D) Race or ethnicity;

(E) Religion;

(F) Sexual orientation; or

(G) Association with a person or group with one or more of these actual or perceived characteristics.

(3) Restorative justice considerations should include community service and other programs focused on hate crime prevention or diversity sensitivity. Additionally, the court should consider ordering payment or other compensation to programs that provide services to violent crime victims and reimbursement to the victim for reasonable costs of counseling and other reasonable expenses that the court finds are a direct result of the defendant's actions.

(Subd (e) adopted effective January 1, 2007.)

Rule 4.427 amended effective January 1, 2017; adopted effective January 1, 2007.

Multiple enhancements for prior convictions under subdivision (c)(1)(B) may be imposed if the prior convictions have been brought and tried separately. (Pen. Code, § 422.75(d)).

Rule 4.428. Factors affecting imposition of enhancements

(a) Enhancements punishable by one of three terms

If an enhancement is punishable by one of three terms, the court must, in its discretion, impose the term that best serves the interest of justice and state the reasons for its sentence choice on the record at the time of sentencing. In exercising its discretion in selecting the appropriate term, the court may consider factors in mitigation and aggravation as described in these rules or any other factor authorized by rule 4.408.

(Subd (a) lettered and amended effective January 1, 2018.)

(b) Striking enhancements under section 1385

If the court has discretion under section 1385(a) to strike an enhancement in the interests of justice, the court also has the authority to strike the punishment for the enhancement under section 1385(c). In determining whether to strike the entire enhancement or only the punishment for the enhancement, the court may consider the effect that striking the enhancement would have on the status of the crime as a strike, the accurate reflection of the defendant's criminal conduct on his or her record, the effect it may have on the award of custody credits, and any other relevant consideration.

(Subd (b) adopted effective January 1, 2018.)

Rule 4.428 amended effective January 1, 2018; adopted as rule 428 effective January 1, 1991; previously renumbered effective January 1, 2001; previously amended effective January 1, 1998, July 1, 2003, January 1, 2007, May 23, 2007, January 1, 2008, and January 1, 2011.

Rule 4.431. Proceedings at sentencing to be reported

All proceedings at the time of sentencing must be reported.

Rule 4.431 amended effective January 1, 2007; adopted as rule 431 effective July 1, 1977; previously renumbered effective January 1, 2001.

Reporters' transcripts of the sentencing proceedings are required on appeal (rule 8.320, except in certain cases under subdivision (d) of that rule), and when the defendant is sentenced to prison (section 1203.01).

Rule 4.433. Matters to be considered at time set for sentencing

(a) In every case, at the time set for sentencing under section 1191, the sentencing judge must hold a hearing at which the judge must:

(1) Hear and determine any matters raised by the defendant under section 1201;

(2) Determine whether a defendant who is eligible for probation should be granted or denied probation, unless consideration of probation is expressly waived by the defendant personally and by counsel; and

(3) Determine whether to deny a period of mandatory supervision in the interests of justice under section 1170(h)(5)(A).

(Subd (a) amended effective January 1, 2017; previously amended effective January 1, 2007.)

(b) If the imposition of a sentence is to be suspended during a period of probation after a conviction by trial, the trial judge must identify and state circumstances that would justify imposition of one of the three authorized terms of imprisonment referred to in section 1170(b), or any enhancement, if probation is later revoked. The circumstances identified and stated by the judge must be based on evidence admitted at the trial or other circumstances properly considered under rule 4.420(b).

(Subd (b) amended effective January 1, 2018; previously amended effective July 28, 1977, January 1, 2007, May 23, 2007, January 1, 2008, and January 1, 2017.)

(c) If a sentence of imprisonment is to be imposed, or if the execution of a sentence of imprisonment is to be suspended during a period of probation, the sentencing judge must:

(1) Determine, under section 1170(b), whether to impose one of the three authorized terms of imprisonment referred to in section 1170(b), or any enhancement, and state on the record the reasons for imposing that term;

(2) Determine whether any additional term of imprisonment provided for an enhancement charged and found will be stricken;

(3) Determine whether the sentences will be consecutive or concurrent if the defendant has been convicted of multiple crimes;

(4) Determine any issues raised by statutory prohibitions on the dual use of facts and statutory limitations on enhancements, as required in rules 4.420(c) and 4.447; and

(5) Pronounce the court's judgment and sentence, stating the terms thereof and giving reasons for those matters for which reasons are required by law.

(Subd (c) amended effective January 1, 2018; previously amended effective July 28, 1977, July 1, 2003, January 1, 2007, May 23, 2007, and January 1, 2017.)

(d) All these matters must be heard and determined at a single hearing unless the sentencing judge otherwise orders in the interests of justice.

(Subd (d) amended effective January 1, 2007.)

(e) When a sentence of imprisonment is imposed under (c) or under rule 4.435, the sentencing judge must inform the defendant:

(1) Under section 1170(c) of the parole period provided by section 3000 to be served after expiration of the sentence in addition to any period of incarceration for parole violation;

(2) Of the period of postrelease community supervision provided by section 3456 to be served after expiration of the sentence, in addition to any period of incarceration for a violation of postrelease community supervision; or

(3) Of any period of mandatory supervision imposed under section 1170(h)(5)(A) and (B), in addition to any period imprisonment for a violation of mandatory supervision.

(Subd (e) amended effective January 1, 2018; previously amended effective July 28, 1977, January 1, 1979, July 1, 2003, January 1, 2007, and January 1, 2017.)
Rule 4.433 amended effective January 1, 2018; adopted as rule 433 effective July 1, 1977; previously renumbered effective January 1, 2001; previously amended effective July 28, 1977, January 1, 1979, July 1, 2003, January 1, 2007, May 23, 2007, January 1, 2008, and January 1, 2017.

Advisory Committee Comment

This rule summarizes the questions that the court is required to consider at the time of sentencing, in their logical order.

Subdivision (a)(2) makes it clear that probation should be considered in every case, without the necessity of any application, unless the defendant is statutorily ineligible for probation.

Under subdivision (b), when imposition of sentence is to be suspended, the sentencing judge is not to make any determinations as to possible length of a term of imprisonment on violation of probation (section 1170(b)). If there was a trial, however, the judge must state on the record the circumstances that would justify imposition of one of the three authorized terms of imprisonment based on the trial evidence.

Subdivision (d) makes it clear that all sentencing matters should be disposed of at a single hearing unless strong reasons exist for a continuance.

Rule 4.435. Sentencing on revocation of probation, mandatory supervision, and postrelease community supervision

(a) When the defendant violates the terms of probation, mandatory supervision, or postrelease community supervision or is otherwise subject to revocation of supervision, the sentencing judge may make any disposition of the case authorized by statute. In deciding whether to permanently revoke supervision, the judge may consider the nature of the violation and the defendant's past performance on supervision.

(Subd (a) amended effective January 1, 2018; previously amended effective January 1, 1991.)

(b) On revocation and termination of supervision under section 1203.2, when the sentencing judge determines that the defendant will be committed to prison or county jail under section 1170(h):

(1) If the imposition of sentence was previously suspended, the judge must impose judgment and sentence after considering any findings previously made and hearing and determining the matters enumerated in rule 4.433(c).

The length of the sentence must be based on circumstances existing at the time supervision was granted, and subsequent events may not be considered in selecting the base term or in deciding whether to strike the additional punishment for enhancements charged and found.

(2) If the execution of sentence was previously suspended, the judge must order that the judgment previously pronounced be in full force and effect and that the defendant be committed to the custody of the Secretary of the Department of Corrections and Rehabilitation or local county correctional administrator or sheriff for the term prescribed in that judgment.

(Subd (b) amended effective January 1, 2018; previously amended effective July 1, 2003, January 1, 2006, January 1, 2007, and January 1, 2017.)
Rule 4.435 amended effective January 1, 2018; adopted as rule 435 effective July 1, 1977; previously renumbered effective January 1, 2001; previously amended effective January 1, 1991, July 1, 2003, January 1, 2006, January 1, 2007, and January 1, 2017.

Advisory Committee Comment

Subdivision (a) makes it clear that there is no change in the court's power, on finding cause to revoke and terminate supervision under section 1203.2(a), to continue the defendant on supervision.

The restriction of subdivision (b)(1) is based on *In re Rodriguez* (1975) 14 Cal.3d 639, 652: "[T]he primary term must reflect the circumstances existing at the time of the offense."

A judge imposing imprisonment on revocation of probation will have the power granted by section 1170(d) to recall the commitment on his or her own motion within 120 days after the date of commitment, and the power under section 1203.2(e) to set aside the revocation of probation, for good cause, within 30 days after the court has notice that execution of the sentence has commenced.

Consideration of conduct occurring after the granting of probation should be distinguished from consideration of preprobation conduct that is discovered after the granting of an order of probation and before sentencing following a revocation and termination of probation. If the preprobation conduct affects or nullifies a determination made at the time probation was granted, the preprobation conduct may properly be considered at sentencing following revocation and termination of probation. (See *People v. Griffith* (1984) 153 Cal.App.3d 796, 801.) While *People v. Griffith* refers only to probation, this rule likely will apply to any form of supervision.

Rule 4.437. Statements in aggravation and mitigation

(a) Time for filing and service

Statements in aggravation and mitigation referred to in section 1170(b) must be filed and served at least four days before the time set for sentencing under section 1191 or the time set for pronouncing judgment on revocation of probation under section 1203.2(c) if imposition of sentence was previously suspended.

(Subd (a) amended effective January 1, 2007.)

(b) Combined statement

A party seeking consideration of circumstances in aggravation or mitigation may file and serve a statement under section 1170(b) and this rule.

(Subd (b) amended effective January 1, 2007.)

(c) Contents of statement

A statement in aggravation or mitigation must include:

(1) A summary of evidence that the party relies on as circumstances justifying the imposition of a particular term; and

(2) Notice of intention to dispute facts or offer evidence in aggravation or mitigation at the sentencing hearing. The statement must generally describe the evidence to be offered, including a description of any documents and the names and expected substance of the testimony of any witnesses. No evidence in aggravation or mitigation may be introduced at the sentencing hearing unless it was described in the statement, or unless its admission is permitted by the sentencing judge in the interests of justice.

(Subd (c) amended effective May 23, 2007; previously amended effective January 1, 2007.)

(d) Support required for assertions of fact

Assertions of fact in a statement in aggravation or mitigation must be disregarded unless they are supported by the record in the case, the probation officer's report or other reports properly filed in the case, or other competent evidence.

(Subd (d) amended effective January 1, 2007.)

(e) Disputed facts

In the event the parties dispute the facts on which the conviction rested, the court must conduct a presentence hearing and make appropriate corrections, additions, or deletions in the presentence probation report or order a revised report.

(Subd (e) amended effective January 1, 2007; adopted effective January 1, 1991.)

Rule 4.437 amended effective January 1, 2008; adopted as rule 437 effective July 1, 1977; previously renumbered effective January 1, 2001; previously amended effective July 28, 1977, January 1, 1991, January 1, 2007, and May 23, 2007.

Advisory Committee Comment

Section 1170(b) states in part:

"At least four days prior to the time set for imposition of judgment, either party or the victim, or the family of the victim if the victim is deceased, may submit a statement in aggravation or mitigation to dispute facts in the record or the probation officer's report, or to present additional facts."

This provision means that the statement is a document giving notice of intention to dispute evidence in the record or the probation officer's report, or to present additional facts.

The statement itself cannot be the medium for presenting new evidence, or for rebutting competent evidence already presented, because the statement is a unilateral presentation by one party or counsel that will not necessarily have any indicia of reliability. To allow its factual assertions to be considered in the absence of corroborating evidence would, therefore, constitute a denial of due process of law in violation of the United States (14th Amend.) and California (art. I, § 7) Constitutions.

The requirement that the statement include notice of intention to rely on new evidence will enhance fairness to both sides by avoiding surprise and helping to ensure that the time limit on pronouncing sentence is met.

Rule 4.447.   Sentencing of enhancements

(a) Enhancements resulting in unlawful sentences

A court may not strike or dismiss an enhancement solely because imposition of the term is prohibited by law or exceeds limitations on the imposition of multiple enhancements. Instead, the court must:

(1) Impose a sentence for the aggregate term of imprisonment computed without reference to those prohibitions and limitations; and

(2) Stay execution of the part of the term that is prohibited or exceeds the applicable limitation. The stay will become permanent once the defendant finishes serving the part of the sentence that has not been stayed.

(Subd (a) lettered and amended effective January 1, 2018.)

(b) Multiple enhancements

If a defendant is convicted of multiple enhancements of the same type, the court must either sentence each enhancement or, if authorized, strike the enhancement or its punishment. While the court may strike an enhancement, the court may not stay an enhancement except as provided in (a) or as authorized by section 654.

(Subd (b) adopted effective January 1, 2018.)

Rule 4.447 amended effective January 1, 2018; adopted as rule 447 effective July 1, 1977; previously amended and renumbered effective January 1, 2001; previously amended effective July 28, 1977, January 1, 1991, July 1, 2003, and January 1, 2007.

Advisory Committee Comment

Subdivision (a). Statutory restrictions may prohibit or limit the imposition of an enhancement in certain situations. (See, for example, sections 186.22(b)(1), 667(a)(2), 667.61(f), 1170.1(f) and (g), 12022.53(e)(2) and (f), and Vehicle Code section 23558.)

Present practice of staying execution is followed to avoid violating a statutory prohibition or exceeding a statutory limitation, while preserving the possibility of imposition of the stayed portion should a reversal on appeal reduce the unstayed portion of the sentence. (See *People v. Gonzalez* (2008) 43 Cal.4th 1118, 1129–1130; *People v. Niles* (1964) 227 Cal.App.2d 749, 756.)

Only the portion of a sentence or component thereof that exceeds a limitation is prohibited, and this rule provides a procedure for that situation. This rule applies to both determinate and indeterminate terms.

Subdivision (b). A court may stay an enhancement if section 654 applies. (See *People v. Bradley* (1998) 64 Cal.App.4th 386; *People v. Haykel* (2002) 96 Cal.App.4th 146, 152.)

Rule 4.451.   Sentence consecutive to or concurrent with indeterminate term or term in other jurisdiction

(a) When a defendant is sentenced under section 1170 and the sentence is to run consecutively to or concurrently with a sentence imposed under section 1168(b) in the same or another proceeding, the judgment must specify the determinate term imposed under section 1170 computed without reference to the indeterminate sentence, must order that the determinate term be served consecutively to or concurrently with the sentence under section 1168(b), and must identify the proceedings in which the indeterminate sentence was imposed. The term under section 1168(b), and the date of its completion or date of parole or postrelease community supervision, and the sequence in which the sentences are deemed or served, will be determined by correctional authorities as provided by law.

(Subd (a) amended effective January 1, 2018; previously amended effective January 1, 1979, July 1, 2003, and January 1, 2007.)

(b) When a defendant is sentenced under sections 1168 or 1170 and the sentence is to run consecutively to or concurrently with a sentence imposed by a court of the United States or of another state or territory, the judgment must specify the term imposed under sections 1168(b) or 1170 computed without reference to the sentence imposed by the other jurisdiction, must identify the other jurisdiction and the proceedings in which the other sentence was imposed, and must indicate whether the sentences are imposed concurrently or consecutively. If the term imposed is to be served consecutively to the term imposed by the other jurisdiction, the court must order that the California term be served commencing on the completion of the sentence imposed by the other jurisdiction.

(Subd (b) amended effective January 1, 2018; previously amended effective January 1, 2007.)

Rule 4.451 amended effective January 1, 2018; adopted as rule 451 effective July 1, 1977; previously renumbered effective January 1, 2001; previously amended effective January 1, 1979, July 1, 2003, and January 1, 2007.

Advisory Committee Comment

Subdivision (a). The provisions of section 1170.1(a), which use a one-third formula to calculate subordinate consecutive terms, can logically be applied only when all the sentences are imposed under section 1170. Indeterminate sentences are imposed under section 1168(b). Since the duration of the indeterminate term cannot be known to the court, subdivision (a) states the only feasible mode of sentencing. (See *People v. Felix* (2000) 22 Cal.4th 651, 654–657; *People v. McGahuey* (1981) 121 Cal.App.3d 524, 530–532.)

Subdivision (b). On the authority to sentence consecutively to the sentence of another jurisdiction and the effect of such a sentence, see *In re Helpman* (1968) 267 Cal.App.2d 307 and cases cited at page 310, footnote 3. The mode of sentencing required by subdivision (b) is necessary to avoid the illogical conclusion that the total of the consecutive sentences will depend on whether the other jurisdiction or California is the first to pronounce judgment.

Rule 4.452.   Determinate sentence consecutive to prior determinate sentence

(a) If a determinate sentence is imposed under section 1170.1(a) consecutive to one or more determinate sentences imposed previously in the same court or in other courts, the court in the current case must pronounce a single aggregate term, as defined in section 1170.1(a), stating the result of combining the previous and current sentences. In those situations:

(1) The sentences on all determinately sentenced counts in all of the cases on which a sentence was or is being imposed must be combined as though they were all counts in the current case.

(2) The [1] **court** in the current case must make a new determination of which count, in the combined cases, represents the principal term, as defined in section 1170.1(a). The principal term is the term with the greatest punishment imposed including conduct enhancements. If two terms of imprisonment have the same punishment, either term may be selected as the principal term.

(3) Discretionary decisions of [2] **courts in** previous cases may not be changed by the [3] **court** in the current case. Such decisions include the decision to impose one of the three authorized terms of imprisonment referred to in section 1170(b), making counts in prior cases concurrent with or consecutive to each other, or the decision that circumstances in mitigation or in the furtherance of justice justified striking the punishment for an enhancement. However, if a previously designated principal term becomes a subordinate term after the resentencing, the subordinate term will be limited to one-third the middle base term as provided in section 1170.1(a).

(4) **If all previously imposed sentences and the current sentence being imposed by the second or subsequent court are under section 1170(h),** the second or subsequent [4] **court** has the discretion to specify whether a previous sentence is to be served in custody or on mandatory supervision and the terms of such supervision, but may not, without express consent of the defendant, modify the sentence on the earlier sentenced charges in any manner that will (i) increase the total length of the sentence imposed by the previous court; (ii) increase the total length

of the [5] **custody portion of the sentence** imposed by the previous court; (iii) increase the total length of **the** mandatory supervision **portion of the sentence** imposed by the previous court; or (iv) impose additional, more onerous, or more restrictive conditions of release for any previously imposed period of mandatory supervision.

(5) **If the second or subsequent court imposes a sentence to state prison because the defendant is ineligible for sentencing under section 1170(h), the jurisdiction of the second or subsequent court to impose a prison sentence applies solely to the current case. The defendant must be returned to the original sentencing court for potential resentencing on any previous case or cases sentenced under section 1170(h). The original sentencing court must convert all remaining custody and mandatory supervision time imposed in the previous case to state prison custody time and must determine whether its sentence is concurrent with or consecutive to the state prison term imposed by the second or subsequent court and incorporate that sentence into a single aggregate term as required by this rule. (A)(4) does not apply—and the consent of the defendant is not required—for this conversion and resentencing.**

(6) In cases in which a sentence is imposed under the provisions of section 1170(h) and the sentence has been imposed by courts in two or more counties, the second or subsequent court must determine the county or counties of incarceration or supervision, including the order of service of such incarceration or supervision. To the extent reasonably possible, the period of mandatory supervision must be served in one county and after completion of any period of incarceration. In accordance with rule 4.472, the second or subsequent court must calculate the defendant's remaining custody and supervision time.

[6] **(7)** In making the determination under [7] **(a)(6)**, the court must exercise its discretion after consideration of the following factors:

(A) The relative length of custody or supervision required for each case;

(B) Whether the cases in each county are to be served concurrently or consecutively;

(C) The nature and quality of treatment programs available in each county, if known;

(D) The nature and extent of the defendant's current enrollment and participation in any treatment program;

(E) The nature and extent of the defendant's ties to the community, including employment, duration of residence, family attachments, and property holdings;

(F) The nature and extent of supervision available in each county, if known;

(G) The factors listed in rule 4.530(f); and

(H) Any other factor relevant to such determination.

[8] **(8)** If after the court's determination in accordance with [9] **(a)(6)** the defendant is ordered to serve only a custody term without supervision in another county, the defendant must be transported at such time and under such circumstances as the court directs to the county where the custody term is to be served. The defendant must be transported with an abstract of the court's judgment as required by section 1213(a), or other suitable documentation showing the term imposed by the court and any custody credits against the sentence. The court may order the custody term to be served in another county without also transferring jurisdiction of the case in accordance with rule 4.530.

[10] **(9)** If after the court's determination in accordance with [11] **(a)(6)** the defendant is ordered to serve a period of supervision in another county, whether with or without a term of custody, the matter must be transferred for the period of supervision in accordance with provisions of rule 4.530(f), (g), and (h).

(Subd (a) amended effective January 1, 2021; previously adopted as unlettered subdivisions effective January 1, 1991; previously lettered and amended effective July 1, 2019.)

Rule 4.452(a). 2020 Deletes. [1] judge [2] the judges in the [3] judge [4] judge [5] actual custody time [6] (6) [7] subdivision (a)(5) [8] (7) [9] subdivision (a)(5) [10] (8) [11] subdivision (a)(5)

Rule 4.452 amended effective January 1, 2021; adopted as rule 452 effective January 1, 1991; previously renumbered effective January 1, 2001; previously amended effective July 1, 2003, January 1, 2007, May 23, 2007, January 1, 2017, January 1, 2018, and July 1, 2019.

Advisory Committee Comment

The restrictions of (a)(3) do not apply to circumstances where a previously imposed base term is made a consecutive term on resentencing. If the court selects a consecutive sentence structure, and since there can be only one principal term in the final aggregate sentence, if a previously imposed full base term becomes a subordinate consecutive term, the new consecutive term normally will become one-third the middle term by operation of law (section 1170.1(a)).

Rule 4.453. Commitments to nonpenal institutions

When a defendant is convicted of a crime for which sentence could be imposed under Penal Code section 1170 and the court orders that he or she be committed to the California Department of Corrections and Rehabilitation, Division of Juvenile Justice under Welfare and Institutions Code section 1731.5, the order of commitment must specify the term of imprisonment to which the defendant would have been sentenced. The term is determined as provided by Penal Code sections 1170 and 1170.1 and these rules, as though a sentence of imprisonment were to be imposed.

Rule 4.453 amended effective January 1, 2007; adopted as rule 453 effective July 1, 1977; previously amended and renumbered effective January 1, 2001; previously amended effective July 28, 1977, and January 1, 2006.

Advisory Committee Comment

Commitments to the Department of Corrections and Rehabilitation, Division of Juvenile Justice (formerly Youth Authority) cannot exceed the maximum possible incarceration in an adult institution for the same crime. (See *People v. Olivas* (1976) 17 Cal.3d 236.)

Under the indeterminate sentencing law, the receiving institution knew, as a matter of law from the record of the conviction, the maximum potential period of imprisonment for the crime of which the defendant was convicted.

Under the Uniform Determinate Sentencing Act, the court's discretion as to length of term leaves doubt as to the maximum term when only the record of convictions is present.

Rule 4.470. Notification of appeal rights in felony cases [Repealed]

Rule 4.470 repealed effective January 1, 2013; adopted as rule 250 effective January 1, 1972; previously amended effective July 1, 1972, January 1, 1977, and January 1, 2007; previously amended and renumbered as rule 470 effective January 1, 1991; previously renumbered effective January 1, 2001.

Rule 4.472. Determination of presentence custody time credit

At the time of sentencing, the court must cause to be recorded on the judgment or commitment the total time in custody to be credited on the sentence under sections 2900.5, 2933.1(c), 2933.2(c), and 4019. On referral of the defendant to the probation officer for an investigation and report under section 1203(b) or 1203(g), or on setting a date for sentencing in the absence of a referral, the court must direct the sheriff, probation officer, or other appropriate person to report to the court and notify the defendant or defense counsel and prosecuting attorney within a reasonable time before the date set for sentencing as to the number of days that defendant has been in custody and for which he or she may be entitled to credit. Any challenges to the report must be heard at the time of sentencing.

Rule 4.472 amended effective January 1, 2017; adopted as rule 252 effective January 1, 1977; previously amended and renumbered as rule 472 effective January 1, 1991; previously amended and renumbered effective January 1, 2001; previously amended effective July 1, 2003, and January 1, 2007.

Rule 4.480. Judge's statement under section 1203.01

A sentencing judge's statement of his or her views under section 1203.01 respecting a person sentenced to the Department of Corrections and Rehabilitation, Division of Adult Operations is required only in the event that no probation report is filed. Even though it is not required, however, a statement should be submitted by the judge in any case in which he or she believes that the correctional handling and the determination of term and parole should be influenced by information not contained in other court records.

The purpose of a section 1203.01 statement is to provide assistance to the Department of Corrections and Rehabilitation, Division of Adult Operations in its programming and institutional assignment and to the Board of Parole Hearings with reference to term fixing and parole release of persons sentenced indeterminately, and parole and postrelease community supervision waiver of persons sentenced determinately. It may amplify any reasons for the sentence that may bear on a possible suggestion by the Secretary of the Department of Corrections and Rehabilitation or the Board of Parole Hearings that the sentence and commitment be recalled and the defendant be resentenced. To be of maximum assistance to these agencies, a judge's statements should contain individualized comments concerning the convicted offender, any special circumstances that led to a prison sentence rather than local incarceration, and any other significant information that might not readily be available in any of the accompanying official records and reports.

If a section 1203.01 statement is prepared, it should be submitted no later than two weeks after sentencing so that it may be included in the official Department of Corrections and Rehabilitation, Division of Adult Operations case summary that is prepared during the time the offender is being processed at the Reception-Guidance Center of the Department of Corrections and Rehabilitation, Division of Adult Operations.

Rule 4.480 amended effective January 1, 2017; adopted as section 12 of the Standards of Judicial Administration effective January 1, 1973; previously amended and renumbered effective January 1, 2001; previously amended effective July 1, 1978, July 1, 2003, January 1, 2006, and January 1, 2007.

Division 6
Postconviction, Postrelease, and Writs

Title 4, Criminal Rules—Division 6, Postconviction, Postrelease, and Writs; amended effective October 28, 2011.

Chap. 1.   Postconviction. Rules 4.510, 4.530.
Chap. 2.   Postrelease. Rule 4.541.
Chap. 3.   Habeas Corpus. Rules 4.545–4.577.

Chapter 1
Postconviction

Rule 4.510. Reverse remand
Rule 4.530. Intercounty transfer of probation and mandatory supervision cases

Rule 4.510.   Reverse remand

(a) Minor prosecuted under Welfare and Institutions Code section 602(b) or 707(d) and convicted of offense listed in Welfare and Institutions Code section 602(b) or 707(d) (Penal Code, § 1170.17)

If the prosecuting attorney lawfully initiated the prosecution as a criminal case under Welfare and Institutions Code section 602(b) or 707(d), and the minor is convicted of a criminal offense listed in those sections, the minor must be sentenced as an adult.

(Subd (a) amended effective January 1, 2007.)

(b) Minor convicted of an offense not listed in Welfare and Institutions Code section 602(b) or 707(d) (Penal Code, § 1170.17)

(1) If the prosecuting attorney lawfully initiated the prosecution as a criminal case and the minor is convicted of an offense not listed in Welfare and Institutions Code section 602(b) or 707(d), but one that would have raised the presumption of unfitness under juvenile court law, the minor may move the court to conduct a postconviction fitness hearing.

(A) On the motion by the minor, the court must order the probation department to prepare a report as required in rule 5.768.

(B) The court may conduct a fitness hearing or remand the matter to the juvenile court for a determination of fitness.

(C) The minor may receive a disposition hearing under the juvenile court law only if he or she is found to be fit under rule 5.772. However, if the court and parties agree, the minor may be sentenced in adult court.

(D) If the minor is found unfit, the minor must be sentenced as an adult, unless all parties, including the court, agree that the disposition be conducted under juvenile court law.

(2) If the minor is convicted of an offense not listed in Welfare and Institutions Code section 602(b) or 707(d), but one for which the minor would have been presumed fit under the juvenile court law, the minor must have a disposition hearing under juvenile court law, and consistent with the provisions of Penal Code section 1170.19, either in the trial court or on remand to the juvenile court.

(A) If the prosecuting attorney objects to the treatment of the minor as within the juvenile court law and moves for a fitness hearing to be conducted, the court must order the probation department to prepare a report as required by rule 5.768.

(B) The court may conduct a fitness hearing or remand the matter to the juvenile court for a determination of fitness.

(C) If found to be fit under rule 5.770, the minor will be subject to a disposition hearing under juvenile court law and Penal Code section 1170.19.

(D) If the minor is found unfit, the minor must be sentenced as an adult, unless all parties, including the court, agree that the disposition be conducted under juvenile court law.

(3) If the minor is convicted of an offense that would not have permitted a fitness determination, the court must remand the matter to

juvenile court for disposition, unless the minor requests sentencing in adult court and all parties, including the court, agree.

(4) Fitness hearings held under this rule must be conducted as provided in title 5, division 3, chapter 14, article 2.

(Subd (b) amended effective January 1, 2007.)

Rule 4.510 amended effective January 1, 2007; adopted effective January 1, 2001.

Rule 4.530.   Intercounty transfer of probation and mandatory supervision cases

(a) Application

This rule applies to intercounty transfers of probation and mandatory supervision cases under Penal Code section 1203.9.

(Subd (a) amended effective February 20, 2014; adopted effective July 1, 2010; previously amended effective November 1, 2012.)

(b) Definitions

As used in this rule:

(1) "Transferring court" means the superior court of the county in which the supervised person is supervised on probation or mandatory supervision.

(2) "Receiving court" means the superior court of the county to which transfer of the case and probation or mandatory supervision is proposed.

(Subd (b) amended effective November 1, 2012; adopted effective July 1, 2010.)

(c) Motion

Transfers may be made only after noticed motion in the transferring court.

(Subd (c) adopted effective July 1, 2010.)

(d) Notice

(1) If transfer is requested by the probation officer of the transferring county, the probation officer must provide written notice of the date, time, and place set for hearing on the motion to:

(A) The presiding judge of the receiving court or his or her designee;

(B) The probation officer of the receiving county or his or her designee;

(C) The prosecutor of the transferring county;

(D) The victim (if any);

(E) The supervised person; and

(F) The supervised person's last counsel of record (if any).

(2) If transfer is requested by any other party, the party must first request in writing that the probation officer of the transferring county notice the motion. The party may make the motion to the transferring court only if the probation officer refuses to do so. The probation officer must notify the party of his or her decision within 30 days of the party's request. Failure by the probation officer to notify the party of his or her decision within 30 days is deemed a refusal to make the motion.

(3) If the party makes the motion, the motion must include a declaration that the probation officer has refused to bring the motion, and the party must provide written notice of the date, time, and place set for hearing on the motion to:

(A) The presiding judge of the receiving court or his or her designee;

(B) The probation officers of the transferring and receiving counties or their designees;

(C) The prosecutor of the transferring county;

(D) The supervised person; and

(E) The supervised person's last counsel of record (if any).

Upon receipt of notice of a motion for transfer by a party, the probation officer of the transferring county must provide notice to the victim, if any.

(4) Notice of a transfer motion must be given at least 60 days before the date set for hearing on the motion.

(5) Before deciding a transfer motion, the transferring court must confirm that notice was given to the receiving court as required by (1) and (3).

(Subd (d) amended effective November 1, 2012; adopted effective July 1, 2010.)

(e) Comment

(1) No later than 10 days before the date set for hearing on the motion, the receiving court may provide comments to the transferring court regarding the proposed transfer.

(2) Any comments provided by the receiving court must be in writing and signed by a judge and must state why transfer is or is not appropriate.

(3) Before deciding a transfer motion, the transferring court must state on the record that it has received and considered any comments provided by the receiving court.

(Subd (e) adopted effective July 1, 2010.)

(f) Factors

The transferring court must consider at least the following factors when determining whether transfer is appropriate:

(1) The permanency of the supervised person's residence. As used in this subdivision, "residence" means the place where the supervised person customarily lives exclusive of employment, school, or other special or temporary purpose. A supervised person may have only one residence. The fact that the supervised person intends to change residence to the receiving county, without further evidence of how, when, and why this is to be accomplished, is insufficient to transfer supervision;

(2) The availability of appropriate programs for the supervised person, including substance abuse, domestic violence, sex offender, and collaborative court programs;

(3) Restitution orders, including whether transfer would impair the ability of the receiving court to determine a restitution amount or impair the ability of the victim to collect court-ordered restitution; and

(4) Victim issues, including:

(A) The residence and places frequented by the victim, including school and workplace; and

(B) Whether transfer would impair the ability of the court, law enforcement, or the probation officer of the transferring county to properly enforce protective orders.

(Subd (f) amended effective November 1, 2012; adopted effective July 1, 2010.)

(g) Transfer

(1) If the transferring court determines that the permanent residence of the supervised person is in the county of the receiving court, the transferring court must transfer the case unless it determines that transfer would be inappropriate and states its reasons on the record.

(2) To the extent possible, the transferring court must establish any amount of restitution owed by the supervised person before it orders the transfer.

(3) Transfer is effective the date the transferring court orders the transfer. Upon transfer of the case, the receiving court must accept the entire jurisdiction over the case.

(4) The orders for transfer must include an order committing the supervised person to the care and custody of the probation officer of the receiving county and an order for reimbursement of reasonable costs for processing the transfer to be paid to the county of the transferring court in accordance with Penal Code section 1203.1b.

(5) Upon transfer of the case, the transferring court must transmit the entire original court file to the receiving court in all cases in which the supervisee is the sole defendant, except the transferring court shall not transfer (A) exhibits or (B) any records of payments. If transfer is ordered in a case involving more than one defendant, the transferring court must transmit certified copies of the entire original court file, except exhibits and any records of payments, to the receiving court upon transfer of the case.

(6) **A certified copy of the entire court file may be electronically transmitted if an original paper court file does not exist. Upon receipt of an electronically transmitted certified copy of the entire court file from the transferring court, the receiving court must deem it an original file.**

(7) Upon transfer the probation officer of the transferring county must transmit, at a minimum, any court orders, probation or mandatory supervision reports, and case plans to the probation officer of the receiving county.

[1] **(8)** Upon transfer of the case, the probation officer of the transferring county must notify the supervised person of the transfer order. The supervised person must report to the probation officer of the receiving county no later than 30 days after transfer unless the transferring court orders the supervised person to report sooner. If the supervised person is in custody at the time of transfer, the supervised person must report to the probation officer of the receiving county no later than 30 days after being released from custody unless the transferring court orders the supervised person to report sooner. Any jail sentence imposed as a condition of probation or mandatory supervision prior to transfer must be served in the transferring county unless otherwise authorized by law.

(9) **Upon transfer of the case, only the receiving court may certify copies from the case file.**

(Subd (g) amended effective January 1, 2021; adopted effective July 1, 2010; previously amended effective November 1, 2012, and January 1, 2017.)

Rule 4.530(g). 2020 Deletes. [1] (7)

(h) Court-ordered debt

(1) In accordance with Penal Code section 1203.9(d) and (e):

(A) If the transferring court has ordered the defendant to pay fines, fees, forfeitures, penalties, assessments, or restitution, the transfer order must require that those and any other amounts ordered by the transferring court that are still unpaid at the time of transfer be paid by the defendant to the collection program for the transferring court for proper distribution and accounting once collected.

(B) The receiving court and receiving county probation department may impose additional local fees and costs as authorized.

(C) Upon approval of a transferring court, a receiving court may elect to collect all of the court-ordered payments from a defendant attributable to the case under which the defendant is being supervised.

(2) Policies and procedures for implementation of the collection, accounting, and disbursement of court-ordered debt under this rule must be consistent with Judicial Council fiscal procedures available at *www.courts.ca.gov.*

(Subd (h) adopted effective January 1, 2017.)

Rule 4.530 amended effective January 1, 2021; adopted effective July 1, 2010; previously amended effective November 1, 2012, February 20, 2014, and January 1, 2017.

Advisory Committee Comment

Subdivision (g)(5) requires the transferring court to transmit the entire original court file, except exhibits and any records of payments, to the court of the receiving county in all cases in which the supervisee is the sole defendant. Before transmitting the entire original court file, transferring courts should consider retaining copies of the court file in the event of an appeal or a writ. In cases involving more than one defendant, subdivision (g)(5) requires the transferring court to transmit certified copies of the entire original court file to ensure that transferring courts are able to properly adjudicate any pending or future codefendant proceedings. Only documents related to the transferring defendant must be transmitted to the receiving court.

Subdivision (g)(7) clarifies that any jail sentence imposed as a condition of probation or mandatory supervision before transfer must be served in the transferring county unless otherwise authorized by law. For example, Penal Code section 1208.5 authorizes the boards of supervisors of two or more counties with work furlough programs to enter into agreements to allow work-furlough-eligible persons sentenced to or imprisoned in one county jail to transfer to another county jail.

Subdivision (h) requires defendants still owing fines, fees, forfeitures, penalties, assessments, or restitution to pay the transferring court's collection program. In counties where the county probation department collects this court-ordered debt, the term "collection program" is intended to include the county probation department.

Chapter 2
Postrelease

Title 4, Criminal Rules—Division 6, Postconviction, Postrelease, and Writs— Chapter 2, Postrelease; adopted effective October 28, 2011.

Rule 4.540. Revocation of postrelease community supervision [Repealed]

Rule 4.540 repealed effective November 1, 2012; adopted effective October 28, 2011.

Rule 4.541. Minimum contents of supervising agency reports

(a) Application

This rule applies to supervising agency petitions for revocation of formal probation, parole, mandatory supervision under Penal Code section 1170(h)(5)(B), and postrelease community supervision under Penal Code section 3455.

(Subd (a) amended effective July 1, 2013; adopted effective October 28, 2011; previously amended effective November 1, 2012.)

(b) Definitions

As used in this rule:

(1) "Supervised person" means any person subject to formal probation, parole, mandatory supervision under Penal Code section 1170(h)(5)(B), or community supervision under Penal Code section 3451.

(2) "Formal probation" means the suspension of the imposition or execution of a sentence and the order of conditional and revocable release in the community under the supervision of a probation officer.

(3) "Court" includes any hearing officer appointed by a superior court and authorized to conduct revocation proceedings under Government Code section 71622.5.

(4) "Supervising agency" includes the county agency designated by the board of supervisors under Penal Code section 3451.

(Subd (b) amended effective July 1, 2013; adopted effective November 1, 2012.)

(c) Minimum contents

Except as provided in (d), a petition for revocation of supervision must include a written report that contains at least the following information:

(1) Information about the supervised person, including:

(A) Personal identifying information, including name and date of birth;

(B) Custody status and the date and circumstances of arrest;

(C) Any pending cases and case numbers;

(D) The history and background of the supervised person, including a summary of the supervised person's record of prior criminal conduct; and

(E) Any available information requested by the court regarding the supervised person's risk of recidivism, including any validated risk-needs assessments;

(2) All relevant terms and conditions of supervision and the circumstances of the alleged violations, including a summary of any statement made by the supervised person, and any victim information, including statements and type and amount of loss;

(3) A summary of any previous violations and sanctions; and

(4) Any recommended sanctions.

(Subd (c) amended and relettered effective November 1, 2012; adopted as subd (b) effective October 28, 2011.)

(d) Subsequent reports

If a written report was submitted as part of the original sentencing proceeding or with an earlier revocation petition, a subsequent report need only update the information required by (c). A subsequent report must include a copy of the original report if the original report is not contained in the court file.

(Subd (d) amended and relettered effective November 1, 2012; adopted as subd (c) effective October 28, 2011.)

(e) Parole and Postrelease Community Supervision Reports

In addition to the minimum contents described in (c), a report filed by the supervising agency in conjunction with a petition to revoke parole or postrelease community supervision must include the reasons for that agency's determination that intermediate sanctions without court intervention as authorized by Penal Code sections 3000.08(f) or 3454(b) are inappropriate responses to the alleged violations.

(Subd (e) amended effective July 1, 2013; adopted effective November 1, 2012.)
Rule 4.541 amended effective July 1, 2013; adopted effective October 28, 2011; previously amended effective November 1, 2012.

Advisory Committee Comment

Subdivision (c). This subdivision prescribes minimum contents for supervising agency reports. Courts may require additional contents in light of local customs and needs.

Subdivision (c)(1)(D). The history and background of the supervised person may include the supervised person's social history, including family, education, employment, income, military, medical, psychological, and substance abuse information.

Subdivision (c)(1)(E). Penal Code section 3451(a) requires postrelease community supervision to be consistent with evidence-based practices, including supervision policies, procedures, programs, and practices demonstrated by scientific research to reduce recidivism among supervised persons. "Evidence-based practices" refers to "supervision policies, procedures, programs, and practices demonstrated by scientific research to reduce recidivism among individuals under probation, parole, or postrelease supervision." (Pen. Code, § 3450(b)(9).)

Subdivision (e). Penal Code sections 3000.08(d) and 3454(b) authorize supervising agencies to impose appropriate responses to alleged violations of parole and postrelease community supervision without court intervention, including referral to a reentry court under Penal Code section 3015 or flash incarceration in a county jail. Penal Code sections 3000.08(f) and 3455(a) require the supervising agency to determine that the intermediate sanctions authorized by sections 3000.08(d) and 3454(b) are inappropriate responses to the alleged violation *before* filing a petition to revoke parole or postrelease community supervision.

Chapter 3
Habeas Corpus

Title 4, Criminal Rules—Division 6, Postconviction, Postrelease, and Writs—Chapter 3, Habeas Corpus; renumbered effective October 28, 2011; adopted as Chapter 2.

Article 1
General Provisions

Title 4, Criminal Rules—Division 6, Postconviction, Postrelease, and Writs—

Chapter 3, Habeas Corpus—Article 1, General Provisions; adopted effective April 25, 2019.

Rule 4.545.   Definitions

In this chapter, the following definitions apply:

(1) A "petition for writ of habeas corpus" is the petitioner's initial filing that commences a proceeding.

(2) An "order to show cause" is an order directing the respondent to file a return. The order to show cause is issued if the petitioner has made a prima facie showing that he or she is entitled to relief; it does not grant the relief requested. An order to show cause may also be referred to as "granting the writ."

(3) The "return" is the respondent's statement of reasons that the court should not grant the relief requested by the petitioner.

(4) The "denial" is the petitioner's pleading in response to the return. The denial may be also referred to as the "traverse."

(5) An "evidentiary hearing" is a hearing held by the trial court to resolve contested factual issues.

(6) An "order on writ of habeas corpus" is the court's order granting or denying the relief sought by the petitioner.

(7) The definitions in rule 8.601 also apply to this chapter.
Rule 4.545 adopted effective April 25, 2019.

Article 2
Noncapital Habeas Corpus Proceedings in the Superior Court

Title 4, Criminal Rules—Division 6, Postconviction, Postrelease, and Writs—Chapter 3, Habeas Corpus—Article 2, Noncapital Habeas Corpus Proceedings in the Superior Court; adopted effective April 25, 2019.

Rule 4.550.   Habeas corpus application

This article applies to habeas corpus proceedings in the superior court under Penal Code section 1473 et seq. or any other provision of law authorizing relief from unlawful confinement or unlawful conditions of confinement, except for death penalty–related habeas corpus proceedings, which are governed by rule 4.560 et seq.
Rule 4.550 amended effective April 25, 2019; adopted effective January 1, 2002; previously amended effective January 1, 2007.

Rule 4.551.   Habeas corpus proceedings

(a) Petition; form and court ruling

(1) Except as provided in (2), the petition must be on the *Petition for Writ of Habeas Corpus* (form HC-001).

(2) For good cause, a court may also accept for filing a petition that does not comply with (a)(1). A petition submitted by an attorney need not be on the Judicial Council form. However, a petition that is not on the Judicial Council form must comply with Penal Code section 1474 and must contain the pertinent information specified in the *Petition for Writ of Habeas Corpus* (form HC-001), including the information required regarding other petitions, motions, or applications filed in any court with respect to the conviction, commitment, or issue.

(3) (A) On filing, the clerk of the court must immediately deliver the petition to the presiding judge or his or her designee. The court must rule on a petition for writ of habeas corpus within 60 days after the petition is filed.

(B) If the court fails to rule on the petition within 60 days of its filing, the petitioner may file a notice and request for ruling.

(i) The petitioner's notice and request for ruling must include a declaration stating the date the petition was filed and the date of the notice and request for ruling, and indicating that the petitioner has not received a ruling on the petition. A copy of the original petition must be attached to the notice and request for ruling.

(ii) If the presiding judge or his or her designee determines that the notice is complete and the court has failed to rule, the presiding judge or his or her designee must assign the petition to a judge and calendar the matter for a decision without appearances within 30 days of the filing of the notice and request for ruling. If the judge assigned by the presiding judge rules on the petition before the date the petition is calendared for decision, the matter may be taken off calendar.

(4) For the purposes of (a)(3), the court rules on the petition by:

(A) Issuing an order to show cause under (c);

(B) Denying the petition for writ of habeas corpus; or

(C) Requesting an informal response to the petition for writ of habeas corpus under (b).

(5) The court must issue an order to show cause or deny the petition within 45 days after receipt of an informal response requested under (b).

(Subd (a) amended effective January 22, 2019; previously amended effective January 1, 2002, January 1, 2004, January 1, 2007, and January 1, 2009.)

(b) Informal response

(1) Before passing on the petition, the court may request an informal response from:

(A) The respondent or real party in interest; or

(B) The custodian of any record pertaining to the petitioner's case, directing the custodian to produce the record or a certified copy to be filed with the clerk of the court.

(2) A copy of the request must be sent to the petitioner. The informal response, if any, must be served on the petitioner by the party of whom the request is made. The informal response must be in writing and must be served and filed within 15 days. If any informal response is filed, the court must notify the petitioner that he or she may reply to the informal response within 15 days from the date of service of the response on the petitioner. If the informal response consists of records or copies of records, a copy of every record and document furnished to the court must be furnished to the petitioner.

(3) After receiving an informal response, the court may not deny the petition until the petitioner has filed a timely reply to the informal response or the 15-day period provided for a reply under (b)(2) has expired.

(Subd (b) amended effective January 1, 2007; adopted effective January 1, 2002.)

(c) Order to show cause

(1) The court must issue an order to show cause if the petitioner has made a prima facie showing that he or she is entitled to relief. In doing so, the court takes petitioner's factual allegations as true and makes a preliminary assessment regarding whether the petitioner would be entitled to relief if his or her factual allegations were proved. If so, the court must issue an order to show cause.

(2) On issuing an order to show cause, the court must appoint counsel for any unrepresented petitioner who desires but cannot afford counsel.

(3) An order to show cause is a determination that the petitioner has made a showing that he or she may be entitled to relief. It does not grant the relief sought in the petition.

(Subd (c) amended effective January 1, 2007; adopted effective January 1, 2002.)

(d) Return

If an order to show cause is issued as provided in (c), the respondent may, within 30 days thereafter, file a return. Any material allegation of the petition not controverted by the return is deemed admitted for purposes of the proceeding. The return must comply with Penal Code section 1480 and must be served on the petitioner.

(Subd (d) amended effective January 1, 2007; repealed and adopted effective January 1, 2002; previously amended effective January 1, 2004.)

(e) Denial

Within 30 days after service and filing of a return, the petitioner may file a denial. Any material allegation of the return not denied is deemed admitted for purposes of the proceeding. Any denial must comply with Penal Code section 1484 and must be served on the respondent.

(Subd (e) amended and relettered effective January 1, 2002; adopted as subd (b) effective January 1, 1982.)

(f) Evidentiary hearing; when required

Within 30 days after the filing of any denial or, if none is filed, after the expiration of the time for filing a denial, the court must either grant or deny the relief sought by the petition or order an evidentiary hearing. An evidentiary hearing is required if, after considering the verified petition, the return, any denial, any affidavits or declarations under penalty of perjury, and matters of which judicial notice may be taken, the court finds there is a reasonable likelihood that the petitioner may be entitled to relief and the petitioner's entitlement to relief depends on the resolution of an issue of fact. The petitioner must be produced at the evidentiary hearing unless the court, for good cause, directs otherwise.

(Subd (f) amended and relettered effective January 1, 2002; adopted as subd (c) effective January 1, 1982.)

(g) Reasons for denial of petition

Any order denying a petition for writ of habeas corpus must contain a brief statement of the reasons for the denial. An order only declaring the petition to be "denied" is insufficient.

(Subd (g) amended and relettered effective January 1, 2002; adopted as subd (e) effective January 1, 1982.)

(h) Extending or shortening time

On motion of any party or on the court's own motion, for good cause stated in the order, the court may shorten or extend the time for doing any act under this rule. A copy of the order must be mailed to each party.

(Subd (h) amended and relettered effective January 1, 2002; adopted as subd (f) effective January 1, 1982.)

Rule 4.551 amended effective January 22, 2019; adopted as rule 260 effective January 1, 1982; previously renumbered as rule 4.500 effective January 1, 2001; previously amended and renumbered effective January 1, 2002; previously amended effective January 1, 2004, January 1, 2007, and January 1, 2009.

Advisory Committee Comment

The court must appoint counsel on the issuance of an order to show cause. (*In re Clark* (1993) 5 Cal.4th 750, 780 and *People v. Shipman* (1965) 62 Cal.2d 226, 231-232.) The Court of Appeal has held that under Penal Code section 987.2, counties bear the expense of appointed counsel in a habeas corpus proceeding challenging the underlying conviction. (*Charlton v. Superior Court* (1979) 93 Cal.App.3d 858, 862.) Penal Code section 987.2 authorizes appointment of the public defender, or private counsel if there is no public defender available, for indigents in criminal proceedings.

Rule 4.552. Habeas corpus jurisdiction

(a) Proper court to hear petition

Except as stated in (b), the petition should be heard and resolved in the court in which it is filed.

(Subd (a) amended effective January 1, 2012; previously amended effective January 1, 2006, and January 1, 2007.)

(b) Transfer of petition

(1) The superior court in which the petition is filed must determine, based on the allegations of the petition, whether the matter should be heard by it or in the superior court of another county.

(2) If the superior court in which the petition is filed determines that the matter may be more properly heard by the superior court of another county, it may nonetheless retain jurisdiction in the matter or, without first determining whether a prima facie case for relief exists, order the matter transferred to the other county. Transfer may be ordered in the following circumstances:

(A) If the petition challenges the terms of a judgment, the matter may be transferred to the county in which judgment was rendered.

(B) If the petition challenges the conditions of an inmate's confinement, it may be transferred to the county in which the petitioner is confined. A change in the institution of confinement that effects a change in the conditions of confinement may constitute good cause to deny the petition.

(C) If the petition challenges the denial of parole or the petitioner's suitability for parole and is filed in a superior court other than the court that rendered the underlying judgment, the court in which the petition is filed should transfer the petition to the superior court in which the underlying judgment was rendered.

(3) The transferring court must specify in the order of transfer the reason for the transfer.

(4) If the receiving court determines that the reason for transfer is inapplicable, the receiving court must, within 30 days of receipt of the case, order the case returned to the transferring court. The transferring court must retain and resolve the matter as provided by these rules.

(Subd (b) amended effective January 1, 2012; previously amended effective January 1, 2006.)

(c) Single judge must decide petition

A petition for writ of habeas corpus filed in the superior court must be decided by a single judge; it must not be considered by the appellate division of the superior court.

(Subd (c) repealed and relettered effective January 1, 2012; adopted as subd (c) effective January 1, 2002; previously relettered as subd (d) effective January 1, 2006.)

Rule 4.552 amended effective January 1, 2012; adopted effective January 1, 2002; previously amended effective January 1, 2006, and January 1, 2007.

Advisory Committee Comment

Subdivision (b)(2)(C). This subdivision is based on the California Supreme Court decision in *In re Roberts* (2005) 36 Cal.4th 575, which provides that petitions for writ of habeas corpus challenging denial or suitability for parole should first be adjudicated in the trial court that rendered the underlying judgment.

Article 3
Death Penalty–Related Habeas Corpus Proceedings in the Superior Court

Title 4, Criminal Rules—Division 6, Postconviction, Postrelease, and Writs—

Chapter 3, Habeas Corpus—Article 3, Death Penalty–Related Habeas Corpus Proceedings in the Superior Court; adopted effective April 25, 2019.

Rule 4.560.   Application of article

This article governs procedures for death penalty–related habeas corpus proceedings in the superior courts.

Rule 4.560 adopted effective April 25, 2019.

Rule 4.561.   Superior court appointment of counsel in death penalty–related habeas corpus proceedings

(a) Purpose

This rule, in conjunction with rule 4.562, establishes a mechanism for superior courts to appoint qualified counsel to represent indigent persons in death penalty–related habeas corpus proceedings. This rule governs the appointment of counsel by superior courts only, including when the Supreme Court or a Court of Appeal has transferred a habeas corpus petition without having appointed counsel for the petitioner. It does not govern the appointment of counsel by the Supreme Court or a Court of Appeal.

(Subd (a) adopted effective April 25, 2019.)

(b) Prioritization of oldest judgments

In the interest of equity, both to the families of victims and to persons sentenced to death, California courts, whenever possible, should appoint death penalty–related habeas corpus counsel first for those persons subject to the oldest judgments of death.

(Subd (b) adopted effective April 25, 2019.)

(c) List of persons subject to a judgment of death

The Habeas Corpus Resource Center must maintain a list of persons subject to a judgment of death, organized by the date the judgment was entered by the sentencing court. The list must indicate whether death penalty–related habeas corpus counsel has been appointed for each person and, if so, the date of the appointment. The list must also indicate for each person whether a petition is pending in the Supreme Court.

(Subd (c) adopted effective April 25, 2019.)

(d) Notice of oldest judgments without counsel

(1) Within 30 days of the effective date of this rule, the Habeas Corpus Resource Center must identify the persons on the list required by (c) with the 25 oldest judgments of death for whom death penalty–related habeas corpus counsel have not been appointed.

(2) The Habeas Corpus Resource Center must notify the presiding judges of the superior courts in which these 25 judgments of death were entered that these are the oldest cases in which habeas corpus counsel have not been appointed. The Habeas Corpus Resource Center will send a copy of the notice to the administrative presiding justice of the appellate district in which the superior court is located.

(3) The presiding judge must identify the appropriate judge within the court to make an appointment and notify the judge that the case is among the oldest cases in which habeas corpus appointments are to be made.

(4) If qualified counsel is available for appointment to a case for which a petition is pending in the Supreme Court, the judge must provide written notice to the Supreme Court that counsel is available for appointment.

(5) On entry of an order appointing death penalty–related habeas corpus counsel, the appointing court must promptly send a copy of the appointment order to the Habeas Corpus Resource Center, which must update the list to reflect that counsel was appointed, and to the clerk/executive officer of the Supreme Court, the Attorney General, and the district attorney. The court must also send notice to the Habeas Corpus Resource Center, clerk/executive officer of the Supreme Court, Attorney General, and district attorney if, for any reason, the court determines that it does not need to make an appointment.

(6) When a copy of an appointment order, or information indicating that an appointment is for any reason not required, has been received by the Habeas Corpus Resource Center for 20 judgments, the center will identify the next 20 oldest judgments of death in cases in which death penalty–related habeas corpus counsel have not been appointed and send out a notice identifying these 20 judgments, and the procedures required by paragraphs (3) through (6) of this subdivision must be repeated.

(7) The presiding judge of a superior court may designate another judge within the court to carry out his or her duties in this subdivision.

(Subd (d) adopted effective April 25, 2019.)

(e) Appointment of counsel

(1) After the court receives a notice under (d)(2) and has made the findings required by Government Code section 68662, the appropriate judge must appoint a qualified attorney or attorneys to represent the person in death penalty–related habeas corpus proceedings.

(2) The superior court must appoint an attorney or attorneys from the statewide panel of counsel compiled under rule 4.562(d)(4); an entity that employs qualified attorneys, including the Habeas Corpus Resource Center, the local public defender's office, or alternate public defender's office; or if the court has adopted a local rule under 4.562(g), an attorney determined to be qualified under that court's local rules. The court must at this time also designate an assisting entity or counsel, unless the appointed counsel is employed by the Habeas Corpus Resource Center.

(3) When the court appoints counsel to represent a person in a death penalty–related habeas corpus proceeding under this subdivision, the court must complete and enter an *Order Appointing Counsel in Death Penalty–Related Habeas Corpus Proceeding* (form HC-101).

(Subd (e) adopted effective April 25, 2019.)

Rule 4.561 adopted effective April 25, 2019.

Rule 4.562.   Recruitment and determination of qualifications of attorneys for appointment in death penalty–related habeas corpus proceedings

(a) Purpose

This rule provides for a panel of attorneys from which superior courts may appoint counsel in death penalty–related habeas corpus proceedings.

(Subd (a) adopted effective April 25, 2019.)

(b) Regional habeas corpus panel committees

Each Court of Appeal must establish a death penalty–related habeas corpus panel committee as provided in this rule.

(Subd (b) adopted effective April 25, 2019.)

(c) Composition of regional habeas corpus panel committees

(1) The administrative presiding justice of the Court of Appeal appoints the members of each committee. Each committee must be composed of:

(A) One justice of the Court of Appeal to serve as the chair of the committee;

(B) A total of three judges from among those nominated by the presiding judges of the superior courts located within the appellate district; and

(C) A total of three attorneys from among those nominated by the entities in the six categories below. At least two of those appointed must have experience representing a petitioner in a death penalty–related habeas corpus proceeding.

(i) An attorney nominated by the Habeas Corpus Resource Center;

(ii) An attorney nominated by the California Appellate Project–San Francisco;

(iii) An attorney nominated by the appellate project with which the Court of Appeal contracts;

(iv) An attorney nominated by any of the federal public defenders' offices of the federal districts in which the participating courts are located;

(v) An attorney nominated by any of the public defenders' offices in a county where the participating courts are located; and

(vi) An attorney nominated by any entity not listed in this subparagraph, if the administrative presiding justice requests such a nomination.

(2) Each committee may also include advisory members, as authorized by the administrative presiding justice.

(3) The term of the chair and committee members is three years. Terms are staggered so that an approximately equal number of each committee's members changes annually. The administrative presiding justice has the discretion to remove or replace a chair or committee member for any reason.

(4) Except as otherwise provided in this rule, each committee is authorized to establish the procedures under which it is governed.

(Subd (c) adopted effective April 25, 2019.)

(d) Regional habeas corpus panel committee responsibilities

The committee has the following responsibilities:

(1) *Support superior court efforts to recruit applicants*

Each committee must assist the participating superior courts in their efforts to recruit attorneys to represent indigent petitioners in death penalty–related habeas corpus proceedings in the superior courts.

(2) *Accept applications*

Each committee must accept applications from attorneys who seek to be included on the panel of attorneys qualified for appointment in death penalty–related habeas corpus proceedings in the superior courts.

(A) The application must be on a *Declaration of Counsel re Minimum Qualifications for Appointment in Death Penalty–Related Habeas Corpus Proceedings* (form HC-100).

(B) Except as provided in (C), each committee must accept applications from attorneys whose principal place of business is within the appellate district and from only those attorneys.

(C) In addition to accepting applications from attorneys whose principal place of business is in its district, the First Appellate District committee must also accept applications from attorneys whose principal place of business is outside the state.

(3) *Review qualifications*

Each committee must review the applications it receives and determine whether the applicant meets the minimum qualifications stated in this division to represent persons in death penalty–related habeas corpus proceedings in the superior courts.

(4) *Provide names of qualified counsel for statewide panel*

(A) If a committee determines by a majority vote that an attorney is qualified to represent persons in death penalty–related habeas corpus proceedings in the superior court, it must include the name of the attorney on a statewide panel of qualified attorneys.

(B) Committees will provide to the Habeas Corpus Resource Center the names of attorneys who the committees determine meet the minimum qualifications. The Habeas Corpus Resource Center must consolidate the names into a single statewide panel, update the names on the panel at least quarterly, and make the most current panel available to superior courts on its website.

(C) Unless removed from the panel under (d)(6), an attorney included on the panel may remain on the panel for up to six years without submitting a renewed application.

(D) Inclusion on the statewide panel does not entitle an attorney to appointment by a superior court, nor does it compel an attorney to accept an appointment.

(5) *Match qualified attorneys to cases*

Each committee must assist a participating superior court in matching one or more qualified attorneys from the statewide panel to a person for whom counsel must be appointed under Government Code section 68662, if the court requests such assistance.

(6) *Remove attorneys from panel*

Suspension or disbarment of an attorney will result in removal of the attorney from the panel. Other disciplinary action, or a finding that counsel has provided ineffective assistance of counsel, may result in a reevaluation of the attorney's inclusion on the panel by the committee that initially determined the attorney to have met minimum qualifications.

(Subd (d) adopted effective April 25, 2019.)

(e) Consolidated habeas corpus panel committees

The administrative presiding justices of two or more Courts of Appeal may elect, following consultation with the presiding judges of the superior courts within their respective appellate districts, to operate a single committee to collectively fulfill the committee responsibilities for the superior courts in their appellate districts.

(Subd (e) adopted effective April 25, 2019.)

(f) Recruitment of qualified attorneys

The superior courts in which a judgment of death has been entered against an indigent person for whom habeas corpus counsel has not been appointed must develop and implement a plan to identify and recruit qualified counsel who may apply to be appointed.

(Subd (f) adopted effective April 25, 2019.)

(g) Local rule

A superior court may, by adopting a local rule, authorize appointment of qualified attorneys who are not members of the statewide panel. The local rule must establish procedures for submission and review of a *Declaration of Counsel re Minimum Qualifications for Appointment in Death Penalty–Related Habeas Corpus Proceedings* (form HC-100) and require attorneys to meet the minimum qualifications under rule 8.652(c).

(Subd (g) adopted effective April 25, 2019.)

Rule 4.562 adopted effective April 25, 2019.

Advisory Committee Comment

Subdivisions (d) and (f). In addition to the responsibilities identified in subdivisions (d) and (f), courts and regional committees are encouraged to support activities to expand the pool of attorneys that are qualified to represent petitioners in death penalty–related habeas corpus proceedings. Examples of such activities include providing mentoring and training programs and encouraging the use of supervised counsel.

Rule 4.571. Filing of petition in the superior court

(a) Petition

(1) A petition and supporting memorandum must comply with this rule and, except as otherwise provided in this rule, with rules 2.100–2.117 relating to the form of papers.

(2) A memorandum supporting a petition must comply with rule 3.1113(b), (c), (f), (h), (i), and (*l*).

(3) The petition and supporting memorandum must support any reference to a matter in the supporting documents or declarations, or other supporting materials, by a citation to its index number or letter and page and, if applicable, the paragraph or line number.

(Subd (a) adopted effective April 25, 2019.)

(b) Supporting documents

(1) The record prepared for the automatic appeal, including any exhibits admitted in evidence, refused, or lodged, and all briefs, rulings, and other documents filed in the automatic appeal are deemed part of the supporting documents for the petition.

(2) The petition must be accompanied by a copy of any petition, excluding exhibits, pertaining to the same judgment and petitioner that was previously filed in any state court or any federal court, along with any order in a proceeding on such a petition that disposes of any claim or portion of a claim.

(3) If the petition asserts a claim that was the subject of a hearing, the petition must be accompanied by a certified transcript of that hearing.

(4) If any supporting documents have previously been filed in the same superior court in which the petition is filed and the petition so states and identifies the documents by case number, filing date and title of the document, copies of these documents need not be included in the supporting documents.

(5) Rule 8.486(c)(1) governs the form of any supporting documents accompanying the petition.

(6) If any supporting documents accompanying the petition or any subsequently filed paper are sealed, rules 2.550 and 2.551 govern. Notwithstanding rule 8.45(a), if any supporting documents accompanying the petition or any subsequently filed papers are confidential records, rules 8.45(b), (c), and 8.47 govern, except that rules 2.550 and 2.551 govern the procedures for making a motion or application to seal such records.

(7) When other laws establish specific requirements for particular types of sealed or confidential records that differ from the requirements in this subdivision, those specific requirements supersede the requirements in this subdivision.

(Subd (b) adopted effective April 25, 2019.)

(c) Filing and service

(1) If the petition is filed in paper form, an original and one copy must be filed, along with an original and one copy of the supporting documents.

(2) A court that permits electronic filing must specify any requirements regarding electronically filed petitions as authorized under rules 2.250 et seq.

(3) Petitioner must serve one copy of the petition and supporting documents on the district attorney, the Attorney General, and on any assisting entity or counsel.

(Subd (c) adopted effective April 25, 2019.)

(d) Noncomplying filings

The clerk must file an attorney's petition not complying with this rule if it otherwise complies with the rules of court, but the court may notify the attorney that it may strike the petition or impose a lesser sanction if the petition is not brought into compliance within a stated reasonable time of not less than five court days.

(Subd (d) adopted effective April 25, 2019.)

(e) Ruling on the petition

(1) The court must rule on the petition within 60 days after the petition is filed with the court or transferred to the court from another superior court.

(2) For purposes of this subdivision, the court rules on a petition by:

(A) Requesting an informal response to the petition;

(B) Issuing an order to show cause; or

(C) Denying the petition.

(3) If the court requests an informal response, it must issue an order to show cause or deny the petition within 30 days after the filing of the reply, or if none is filed, after the expiration of the time for filing the reply under rule 4.573(a)(3).

(Subd (e) adopted effective April 25, 2019.)
Rule 4.571 adopted effective April 25, 2019.

Rule 4.572. Transfer of petitions

Unless the court finds good cause for it to consider the petition, a petition subject to this article that is filed in a superior court other than the court that imposed the sentence must be transferred to the court that imposed the sentence within 21 days of filing. The court in which the petition was filed must enter an order with the basis for its transfer or its finding of good cause for retaining the petition.

Rule 4.572 adopted effective April 25, 2019.

Rule 4.573. Proceedings after the petition is filed

(a) Informal response and reply

(1) If the court requests an informal written response, it must serve a copy of the request on the district attorney, the Attorney General, the petitioner and on any assisting entity or counsel.

(2) The response must be served and filed within 45 days of the filing of the request, or a later date if the court so orders. One copy of the informal response and any supporting documents must be served on the petitioner and on any assisting entity or counsel. If the response and supporting documents are served in paper form, two copies must be served on the petitioner.

(3) If a response is filed, the court must notify the petitioner that a reply may be served and filed within 30 days of the filing of the response, or a later date if the court so orders. The court may not deny the petition until that time has expired.

(4) If a reply is filed, the petitioner must serve one copy of the reply and any supporting documents on the district attorney, the Attorney General, and on any assisting entity or counsel.

(5) The formatting of the response, reply, and any supporting documents must comply with the applicable requirements for petitions in rule 4.571(a) and (b). The filing of the response, reply, and any supporting documents must comply with the requirements for petitions in rule 4.571(c)(1) and (2).

(6) On motion of any party or on the court's own motion, for good cause stated in the order, the court may extend the time for a party to perform any act under this subdivision. If a party requests extension of a deadline in this subdivision, the party must explain the additional work required to meet the deadline.

(Subd (a) adopted effective April 25, 2019.)

(b) Order to show cause

If the petitioner has made the required prima facie showing that petitioner is entitled to relief, the court must issue an order to show cause. An order to show cause does not grant the relief sought in the petition.

(Subd (b) adopted effective April 25, 2019.)
Rule 4.573 adopted effective April 25, 2019.

Rule 4.574. Proceedings following an order to show cause

(a) Return

(1) Any return must be served and filed within 45 days after the court issues the order to show cause, or a later date if the court so orders.

(2) The formatting of the return and any supporting documents must comply with the applicable requirements for petitions in rule 4.571(a) and (b). The filing of the return and any supporting documents must comply with the requirements for petitions in rule 4.571(c)(1) and (2).

(3) A copy of the return and any supporting documents must be served on the petitioner and on any assisting entity or counsel. If the return is served in paper form, two copies must be served on the petitioner.

(4) Any material allegation of the petition not controverted by the return is deemed admitted for purposes of the proceeding.

(Subd (a) adopted effective April 25, 2019.)

(b) Denial

(1) Unless the court orders otherwise, within 30 days after the return is filed, or a later date if the court so orders, the petitioner may serve and file a denial.

(2) The formatting of the denial and any supporting documents must comply with the applicable requirements for petitions in rule 4.571(a) and

(b). The filing of the denial and any supporting documents must comply with the requirements for petitions in rule 4.571(c)(1) and (2).

(3) A copy of the reply and any supporting documents must be served on the district attorney, the Attorney General, and on any assisting entity or counsel.

(4) Any material allegation of the return not controverted in the denial is deemed admitted for purposes of the proceeding.

(Subd (b) adopted effective April 25, 2019.)

(c) Ruling on the petition

Within 60 days after filing of the denial, or if none is filed, after the expiration of the deadline for filing the denial under (b)(1), the court must either grant or deny the relief sought by the petition or set an evidentiary hearing.

(Subd (c) adopted effective April 25, 2019.)

(d) Evidentiary hearing

(1) An evidentiary hearing is required if, after considering the verified petition, the return, any denial, any affidavits or declarations under penalty of perjury, exhibits, and matters of which judicial notice may be taken, the court finds there is a reasonable likelihood that the petitioner may be entitled to relief and the petitioner's entitlement to relief depends on the resolution of an issue of fact.

(2) The court must assign a court reporter who uses computer-aided transcription equipment to report all proceedings under this subdivision.

(A) All proceedings under this subdivision, whether in open court, in conference in the courtroom, or in chambers, must be conducted on the record with a court reporter present. The court reporter must prepare and certify a daily transcript of all proceedings.

(B) Any computer-readable transcript produced by court reporters under this subdivision must conform to the requirements of Code of Civil Procedure section 271.

(3) Rule 3.1306(c) governs judicial notice.

(Subd (d) adopted effective April 25, 2019.)

(e) Additional briefing

The court may order additional briefing during or following the evidentiary hearing.

(Subd (e) adopted effective April 25, 2019.)

(f) Submission of cause

For purposes of article VI, section 19, of the California Constitution, a death penalty–related habeas corpus proceeding is submitted for decision at the conclusion of the evidentiary hearing, if one is held. If there is supplemental briefing after the conclusion of the evidentiary hearing, the matter is submitted when all supplemental briefing is filed with the court.

(Subd (f) adopted effective April 25, 2019.)

(g) Extension of deadlines

On motion of any party or on the court's own motion, for good cause stated in the order, the court may extend the time for a party to perform any act under this rule. If a party requests extension of a deadline in this rule, the party must explain the additional work required to meet the deadline.

(Subd (g) adopted effective April 25, 2019.)
Rule 4.574 adopted effective April 25, 2019.

Rule 4.575. Decision on death penalty–related habeas corpus petition

On decision of the initial petition, the court must prepare and file a statement of decision specifying its order and explaining the factual and legal basis for its decision. The clerk of the court must serve a copy of the decision on the petitioner, the district attorney, the Attorney General, the clerk/executive officer of the Supreme Court, the clerk/executive officer of the Court of Appeal, and on any assisting entity or counsel.

Rule 4.575 adopted effective April 25, 2019.

Rule 4.576. Successive petitions

(a) Notice of intent to dismiss

Before dismissing a successive petition under Penal Code section 1509(d), a superior court must provide notice to the petitioner and an opportunity to respond.

(Subd (a) adopted effective April 25, 2019.)

(b) Certificate of appealability

The superior court must grant or deny a certificate of appealability concurrently with the issuance of its decision denying relief on a successive death penalty–related habeas corpus petition. Before issuing its decision, the superior court may order the parties to submit arguments on whether a certificate of appealability should be granted. If the superior court grants a certificate of appealability, the certificate must identify the substantial claim or claims for relief shown by the petitioner and the substantial claim that the requirements of Penal Code section 1509(d) have been met. The superior court clerk must send a copy of the certificate to the petitioner, the Attorney General, the district attorney, the clerk/ executive officer of the Court of Appeal and the district appellate project for the appellate district in which the superior court is located, the assisting counsel or entity, and the clerk/executive officer of the Supreme Court. The superior court clerk must send the certificate of appealability to the Court of Appeal when it sends the notice of appeal under rule 8.392(c).

(Subd (b) adopted effective April 25, 2019.)
Rule 4.576 adopted effective April 25, 2019.

Rule 4.577. Transfer of files

Counsel for the petitioner must deliver all files counsel maintained related to the proceeding to the attorney representing petitioner in any appeal taken from the proceeding.
Rule 4.577 adopted effective April 25, 2019.

Division 7
Miscellaneous

Rule 4.601. Judicial determination of factual innocence form
Rule 4.700. Firearm relinquishment procedures for criminal protective orders

Rule 4.601. Judicial determination of factual innocence form

(a) Form to be confidential

Any *Certificate of Identity Theft: Judicial Finding of Factual Innocence* (form CR-150) that is filed with the court is confidential. The clerk's office must maintain these forms in a manner that will protect and preserve their confidentiality.

(Subd (a) amended effective January 1, 2007.)

(b) Access to the form

Notwithstanding (a), the court, the identity theft victim, the prosecution, and law enforcement agencies may have access to the *Certificate of Identity Theft: Judicial Finding of Factual Innocence* (form CR-150). The court may allow access to any other person on a showing of good cause.

(Subd (b) amended effective January 1, 2007.)
Rule 4.601 amended effective January 1, 2007; adopted effective January 1, 2002.

Rule 4.700. Firearm relinquishment procedures for criminal protective orders

(a) Application of rule

This rule applies when a court issues a criminal protective order under Penal Code section 136.2 during a criminal case or as a condition of probation under Penal Code section 1203.097(a)(2) against a defendant charged with a crime of domestic violence as defined in Penal Code section 13700 and Family Code section 6211.

(Subd (a) amended effective January 22, 2019; adopted effective July 1, 2010.)

(b) Purpose

This rule is intended to:

(1) Assist courts issuing criminal protective orders to determine whether a defendant subject to such an order owns, possesses, or controls any firearms; and

(2) Assist courts that have issued criminal protective orders to determine whether a defendant has complied with the court's order to relinquish or sell the firearms under Code of Civil Procedure section 527.9.

(Subd (b) adopted effective July 1, 2010.)

(c) Setting review hearing

(1) At any hearing where the court issues a criminal protective order, the court must consider all credible information, including information provided on behalf of the defendant, to determine if there is good cause to believe that the defendant has a firearm within his or her immediate possession or control.

(2) If the court finds good cause to believe that the defendant has a firearm within his or her immediate possession or control, the court must set a review hearing to ascertain whether the defendant has complied with the requirement to relinquish the firearm as specified in Code of Civil Procedure section 527.9. Unless the defendant is in custody at the time, the review hearing should occur within two court days after issuance of the criminal protective order. If circumstances warrant, the court may extend the review hearing to occur within 5 court days after issuance of the criminal protective order. The court must give the defendant an opportunity to present information at the review hearing to refute the allegation that he or she owns any firearms. If the defendant is in custody at the time the criminal protective order is issued, the court should order the defendant to appear for a review hearing within two court days after the defendant's release from custody.

(3) If the proceeding is held under Penal Code section 136.2, the court may, under Penal Code section 977(a)(2), order the defendant to personally appear at the review hearing. If the proceeding is held under Penal Code section 1203.097, the court should order the defendant to personally appear.

(Subd (c) adopted effective July 1, 2010.)

(d) Review hearing

(1) If the court has issued a criminal protective order under Penal Code section 136.2, at the review hearing:

(A) If the court finds that the defendant has a firearm in or subject to his or her immediate possession or control, the court must consider whether bail, as set, or defendant's release on own recognizance is appropriate.

(B) If the defendant does not appear at the hearing and the court orders that bail be revoked, the court should issue a bench warrant.

(2) If the criminal protective order is issued as a condition of probation under Penal Code section 1203.097, and the court finds at the review hearing that the defendant has a firearm in or subject to his or her immediate possession or control, the court must proceed under Penal Code section 1203.097(a)(12).

(3) In any review hearing to determine whether a defendant has complied with the requirement to relinquish firearms as specified in Code of Civil Procedure section 527.9, the burden of proof is on the prosecution.

(Subd (d) adopted effective July 1, 2010.)
Rule 4.700 amended effective January 22, 2019; adopted effective July 1, 2010.

Advisory Committee Comment

When issuing a criminal protective order under Penal Code section 136.2 or 1203.097(a)(2), the court is required to order a defendant "to relinquish any firearm in that person's immediate possession or control, or subject to that person's immediate possession or control ...." (Code Civ. Proc., § 527.9(b).) Mandatory Judicial Council form CR-160, *Criminal Protective Order—Domestic Violence*, includes a mandatory order in bold type that the defendant "must surrender to local law enforcement or sell to a licensed gun dealer any firearm owned or subject to his or her immediate possession or control within 24 hours after service of this order and must file a receipt with the court showing compliance with this order within 48 hours of receiving this order."

Courts are encouraged to develop local procedures to calendar review hearings for defendants in custody beyond the two-court-day time frame to file proof of firearms relinquishment with the court under Code of Civil Procedure section 527.9.

TITLE 5
Family and Juvenile Rules

Title. Rule 5.1.
Division 1.   Family Rules. Rules 5.2–5.445.
Division 2.   Rules Applicable in Family and Juvenile Proceedings. Rules 5.451–5.495.
Division 3.   Juvenile Rules. Rules 5.500–5.906.

Rule 5.1.   Title
The rules in this title may be referred to as the Family and Juvenile Rules.
Rule 5.1 adopted effective January 1, 2007.

Division 1
Family Rules

Chapter 1
General Provisions

Article 1
General Provisions

Title 5, Family and Juvenile Rules—Division 1, Family Rules—Chapter 1, General Provisions—Article 1, General Provisions; adopted effective January 1, 2013.

Rule 5.2. Division title; definitions; application of rules and laws
Rule 5.4. Preemption; local rules and forms

Rule 5.2.   Division title; definitions; application of rules and laws

(a) Division title
The rules in this division may be referred to as the Family Rules.
(Subd (a) adopted effective January 1, 2013.)

(b) Definitions and use of terms
As used in this division, unless the context or subject matter otherwise requires, the following definitions apply:

(1) "Family Code" means that code enacted by chapter 162 of the Statutes of 1992 and any subsequent amendments to that code.

(2) "Action" is also known as a lawsuit, a case, or a demand brought in a court of law to defend or enforce a right, prevent or remedy a harm, or punish a crime. It includes all the proceedings in which a party requests orders that are available in the lawsuit.

(3) "Proceeding" is a court hearing in an action under the Family Code, including a hearing that relates to the dissolution or nullity of a marriage or domestic partnership, legal separation, custody and support of minor children, a parent and child relationship, adoptions, local child support agency actions under the Family Code, contempt proceedings relating to family law or local child support agency matters, and any action filed under the Domestic Violence Prevention Act, Uniform Parentage Act, Uniform Child Custody Jurisdiction and Enforcement Act, Indian Child Welfare Act, or Uniform Interstate Family Support Act.

(4) "Dissolution" is the legal term used for "divorce." "Divorce" commonly refers to a marriage that is legally ended.

(5) "Attorney" means a member of the State Bar of California. "Counsel" means an attorney.

(6) "Party" is a person appearing in an action. Parties include both self-represented persons and persons represented by an attorney of record. Any designation of a party encompasses the party's attorney of record, including "party," "petitioner," "plaintiff," "People of the State of California," "applicant," "defendant," "respondent," "other parent," "other parent/party," "protected person," and "restrained person."

(7) "Best interest of the child" is described in Family Code section 3011.

(8) "Parenting time," "visitation," and "visitation (parenting time)" refer to how parents share time with their children.

(9) "Property" includes assets and obligations.

(10) "Local rule" means every rule, regulation, order, policy, form, or standard of general application adopted by a court to govern practice and procedure in that court.

(11) "Reschedule the hearing" means the same as "continue the hearing" under the Family Code and refers to moving a hearing to another date and time.
(Subd (b) amended effective July 1, 2020; adopted effective January 1, 2013.)

(c) Application of rules
The rules in this division apply to every action and proceeding to which the Family Code applies and, unless these rules elsewhere explicitly make them applicable, do not apply to any other action or proceeding that is not found in the Family Code.
(Subd (c) adopted effective January 1, 2013.)

(d) General law applicable
Except as otherwise provided in these rules, all provisions of law applicable to civil actions generally apply to a proceeding under the Family Code if they would otherwise apply to such proceeding without reference to this rule. To the extent that these rules conflict with provisions in other statutes or rules, these rules prevail.
(Subd (d) adopted effective January 1, 2013.)

(e) Law applicable to other proceedings
In any action under the Family Code that is not considered a "proceeding" as defined in (b), all provisions of law applicable to civil actions generally apply. Such an action must be commenced by filing an appropriate petition, and the respondent must file an appropriate response within 30 days after service of the summons and a copy of the petition.
(Subd (e) adopted effective January 1, 2013.)

(f) Extensions of time
The time within which any act is permitted or required to be done by a party under these rules may be extended by the court upon such terms as may be just.
(Subd (f) adopted effective January 1, 2013.)

(g) Implied procedures
In the exercise of the court's jurisdiction under the Family Code, if the course of proceeding is not specifically indicated by statute or these rules, any suitable process or mode of proceeding may be adopted by the court that is consistent with the spirit of the Family Code and these rules.
(Subd (g) adopted effective January 1, 2013.)
Rule 5.2 amended effective July 1, 2020; adopted effective January 1, 2013.

Rule 5.4. Preemption; local rules and forms

Each local court may adopt local rules and forms regarding family law actions and proceedings that are not in conflict with or inconsistent with California law or the California Rules of Court. Effective January 1, 2013, local court rules and forms must comply with the Family Rules.

Rule 5.4 adopted effective January 1, 2013.

Advisory Committee Comment

The Family and Juvenile Law Advisory Committee agrees with the *Elkins Family Law Task Force: Final Report and Recommendations* (final report) regarding local rules of court (see final report at pages 31–32). The final report is available at *www.courts.ca.gov/elkins-finalreport.pdf.*

The advisory committee encourages local courts to continue piloting innovative family law programs and practices using local rules that are consistent with California law and the California Rules of Court.

Courts must not adopt local rules that create barriers for self-represented litigants or parties represented by counsel in getting their day in court. Further, courts should not adopt general rules for a courtroom as they pose substantial barriers to a party's access to justice.

Rule 5.5. Division title [Repealed]

Rule 5.5 repealed effective January 1, 2013; adopted effective January 1, 2007.

Article 2
Use of Forms

Title 5, Family and Juvenile Rules—Division 1, Family Rules—Chapter 1, General Provisions—Article 2, Use of Forms; adopted effective January 1, 2013.

Rule 5.7. Use of forms

(a) Status of family law and domestic violence forms

All forms adopted or approved by the Judicial Council for use in any proceeding under the Family Code, including any form in the FL, ADOPT, DV, and EJ series, are adopted as rules of court under the authority of Family Code section 211; article VI, section 6 of the California Constitution; and other applicable law.

(Subd (a) adopted effective January 1, 2013.)

(b) Forms in nonfamily law proceedings

The forms specified by this division may be used, at the option of the party, in any proceeding involving a financial obligation growing out of the relationship of parent and child or husband and wife or domestic partners, to the extent they are appropriate to that proceeding.

(Subd (b) adopted effective January 1, 2013.)

(c) Interstate forms

Notwithstanding any other provision of these rules, all Uniform Interstate Family Support Act forms approved by either the National Conference of Commissioners on Uniform State Laws or the U.S. Department of Health and Human Services are adopted for use in family law and other support actions in California.

(Subd (c) adopted effective January 1, 2013.)

Rule 5.7 adopted effective January 1, 2013.

Article 3
Appearance by Telephone

Title 5, Family and Juvenile Rules—Division 1, Family Rules—Chapter 1, General Provisions—Article 3, Appearance by Telephone; adopted effective January 1, 2013.

Rule 5.9. Appearance by telephone

(a) Application

This rule applies to all family law cases, except for actions for child support involving a local child support agency **and cases governed by the Indian Child Welfare Act**. Rule 5.324 governs telephone appearances in governmental child support cases. **Rule 5.482(g) governs telephone appearances in cases governed by the Indian Child Welfare Act.**

(Subd (a) amended effective January 1, 2021; adopted effective January 1, 2013.)

(b) Telephone appearance

The court may permit a party to appear by telephone at a hearing, conference, or proceeding if the court determines that a telephone appearance is appropriate.

(Subd (b) adopted effective January 1, 2013.)

(c) Need for personal appearance

(1) At its discretion, the court may require a party to appear in person at a hearing, conference, or proceeding if the court determines that a personal appearance would materially assist in the determination of the proceedings or in the effective management or resolution of the particular case.

(2) If, at any time during a hearing, conference, or proceeding conducted by telephone, the court determines that a personal appearance is necessary, the court may continue the matter and require a personal appearance.

(Subd (c) adopted effective January 1, 2013.)

(d) Local rules

Courts may develop local rules to specify procedures regarding appearances by telephone.

(Subd (d) adopted effective January 1, 2013.)

Rule 5.9 amended effective January 1, 2021; adopted effective January 1, 2013.

Rule 5.10. Definitions and use of terms [Repealed]

Rule 5.10 repealed effective January 1, 2013; adopted as rule 1201 effective January 1, 1970; previously amended effective January 1, 1994, January 1, 1999; previously amended and renumbered effective January 1, 2003; previously amended effective January 1, 2007, and January 1, 2008.

Article 4
Discovery

Title 5, Family and Juvenile Rules—Division 1, Family Rules—Chapter 1, General Provisions—Article 4, Discovery; adopted effective January 1, 2013.

Rule 5.12. Request for order regarding discovery

(a) Use of terms

In a family law proceeding, the term "request for order" has the same meaning as the terms "motion" or "notice of motion" when they are used in the Code of Civil Procedure.

(Subd (a) adopted effective July 1, 2016.

(b) Applicable law

A request for order regarding discovery in family court is subject to the provisions for discovery motions under Code of Civil Procedure sections 2016.010 through 2036.050 and Family Code sections 2100 through 2113 regarding disclosure of assets and liabilities.

(Subd (b) amended and relettered effective July 1, 2016; adopted as subd (a).)

(c) Applicable rules

Discovery proceedings brought in a case under the Family Code must comply with applicable civil rules for motions, including:

(1) The format of supplemental and further discovery (rule 3.1000);

(2) Oral deposition by telephone, videoconference, or other remote electronic means (rule 3.1010);

(3) Separate statement requirements (rule 3.1345);

(4) Service of motion papers on nonparty deponent (rule 3.1346); and

(5) Sanctions for failure to provide discovery (rule 3.1348).

(Subd (c) amended and relettered effective July 1, 2016; adopted as subd (b).)

Rule 5.12 amended effective July 1, 2016; adopted effective January 1, 2013.

Article 5
Sanctions

Title 5, Family and Juvenile Rules—Division 1, Family Rules—Chapter 1, General Provisions—Article 5, Sanctions; adopted effective January 1, 2013.

Rule 5.14. Sanctions for violations of rules of court in family law cases

(a) Application

This sanctions rule applies to any action or proceeding brought under the Family Code.

(Subd (a) adopted effective January 1, 2013.)

(b) Definition

For purposes of the rules in this division:

(1) "Sanctions" means a monetary fine or penalty ordered by the court.

(2) "Person" means a party, a party's attorney, a law firm, a witness, or any other individual or entity whose consent is necessary for the disposition of the case.

(Subd (b) adopted effective January 1, 2013.)

(c) Sanctions imposed on a person

In addition to any other sanctions permitted by law, the court may order a person, after written notice and an opportunity to be heard, to pay reasonable monetary sanctions to the court or to an aggrieved person, or both, for failure without good cause to comply with the applicable rules. The sanction must not put an unreasonable financial burden on the person ordered to pay.

(Subd (c) adopted effective January 1, 2013.)

(d) Notice and procedure

Sanctions must not be imposed under this rule except on a request for order by the person seeking sanctions or on the court's own motion after the court has provided notice and an opportunity to be heard.

(1) A party's request for sanctions must:

(A) State the applicable rule of court that has been violated;

(B) Describe the specific conduct that is alleged to have violated the rule; and

(C) Identify the party, attorney, law firm, witness, or other person against whom sanctions are sought.

(2) The court on its own motion may issue an order to show cause that must:

(A) State the applicable rule of court that has been violated;

(B) Describe the specific conduct that appears to have violated the rule; and

(C) Direct the attorney, law firm, party, witness, or other person to show cause why sanctions should not be imposed for violation of the rule.

(Subd (d) adopted effective January 1, 2013.)

(e) Award of expenses

In addition to the sanctions awardable under this rule, the court may order the person who has violated an applicable rule of court to pay to the party aggrieved by the violation that party's reasonable expenses, including reasonable attorney's fees and costs, incurred in connection with the motion or request for order for sanctions.

(Subd (e) adopted effective January 1, 2013.)

(f) Order

A court order awarding sanctions must be in writing and must recite in detail the conduct or circumstances justifying the order.

(Subd (f) adopted effective January 1, 2013.)
Rule 5.14 adopted effective January 1, 2013.

Rule 5.15.   Extensions of time [Repealed]

Rule 5.15 repealed effective January 1, 2013; adopted as rule 1203 effective January 1, 1970; previously renumbered effective January 1, 2003.

Chapter 2
Parties and Joinder of Parties

Title 5, Family and Juvenile Rules—Division 1, Family Rules—Chapter 2, Parties and Joinder of Parties; adopted effective January 1, 2013.

Art. 1.   Parties to Proceedings. Rules 5.16–5.18.
Art. 2.   Joinder of Parties. Rule 5.24.
Art. 3.   Employee Pension Benefit Plan. Rule 5.29.

Article 1
Parties to Proceedings

Title 5, Family and Juvenile Rules—Division 1, Family Rules—Chapter 2, Parties and Joinder of Parties—Article 1, Parties to Proceedings; adopted effective January 1, 2013.

Rule 5.16. Designation of parties
Rule 5.17. Other causes of action
Rule 5.18. Injunctive relief and reservation of jurisdiction

Rule 5.16.   Designation of parties

(a) Designation of parties

(1) In cases filed under the Family Code, the party starting the case is referred to as the "petitioner," and the other party is the "respondent."

(2) In local child support agency actions, the local child support agency starts the case and is the petitioner or plaintiff in the case. The parent sued by the child support agency is the "respondent" or "defendant," and the parent who is not the defendant is referred to as the "Other Parent." Every other proceeding must be prosecuted and defended in the names of the real parties in interest.

(Subd (a) adopted effective January 1, 2013.)

(b) Parties to proceeding

(1) The only persons permitted to be parties to a proceeding for dissolution, legal separation, or nullity of marriage are the spouses, except as provided in (3), a third party who is joined in the case under rule 5.24, or a local child support agency that intervenes in the case.

(2) The only persons permitted to be parties to a proceeding for dissolution, legal separation, or nullity of domestic partnership are the domestic partners, except as provided in (3), a third party who is joined in the case under rule 5.24, or a local child support agency that intervenes in the case.

(3) In a nullity proceeding, the case can be started by the spouses or domestic partners. The case may also be started by a parent or guardian, conservator, or other person specified in Family Code section 2211. For this type of case, the person starting the case is a party and the caption on all papers must be appropriately changed to reflect that fact.

(4) The only persons permitted to be parties to a proceeding under the Domestic Violence Prevention Act are those identified in Family Code section 6211.

(5) The only persons permitted to be parties to a family law proceeding to establish parentage are the presumed or putative parents of the minor child, the minor child, a third party who is joined in the case under rule 5.24, or a local child support agency that intervenes in the case.

(Subd (b) adopted effective January 1, 2013.)
Rule 5.16 adopted effective January 1, 2013.

Rule 5.17.   Other causes of action

A party in a family law proceeding may only ask that the court make orders against or involving the other party, or any other person, that are available to the party in these rules, Family Code sections 17400, 17402, and 17404, or other sections of the California Family Code.

Rule 5.17 adopted effective January 1, 2013.

Rule 5.18.   Injunctive relief and reservation of jurisdiction

(a) Injunctive relief

When a party in a family law case applies for a court order under rule 5.92, the court may grant injunctive or other relief against or for the following persons to protect the rights of either or both parties:

(1) A person who has or claims an interest in the case;

(2) A person who would be a necessary party to a complete disposition of the issues in the case, but is not permitted to be a party under rule 5.16; or

(3) A person who is acting as a trustee, agent, custodian, or similar fiduciary with respect to any property subject to disposition by the court in the proceeding, or other matter subject to the jurisdiction of the court in the proceeding.

(Subd (a) adopted effective January 1, 2013.)

(b) Reservation of jurisdiction

If the court is unable to resolve the issue in the proceeding under the Family Code, the court may reserve jurisdiction over the particular issue until such time as the rights of such person and the parties to the proceeding under the Family Code have been determined in a separate action or proceeding.

(Subd (b) adopted effective January 1, 2013.)
Rule 5.18 adopted effective January 1, 2013.

Rule 5.20.   Application of rules [Repealed]

Rule 5.20 repealed effective January 1, 2013; adopted as rule 1205 effective January 1, 1970; previously amended effective January 1, 1979, January 1, 1994, and January 1, 1999; previously amended and renumbered effective January 1, 2003; previously amended effective January 1, 2007.

Rule 5.21.   General law applicable [Repealed]

Rule 5.21 repealed effective January 1, 2013; adopted as rule 1206 effective January 1, 1970; previously amended effective January 1, 1994; previously amended and renumbered effective January 1, 2003.

Rule 5.22.   Other proceedings [Repealed]

Rule 5.22 repealed effective January 1, 2013; adopted as rule 1207 effective January 1, 1970; previously amended effective January 1, 1994; previously amended and renumbered effective January 1, 2003; previously amended effective January 1, 2007.

Article 2
Joinder of Parties

Title 5, Family and Juvenile Rules—Division 1, Family Rules—Chapter 2, Parties and Joinder of Parties—Article 2, Joinder of Parties; adopted effective January 1, 2013.

Rule 5.24.   Joinder of persons claiming interest

A person who claims or controls an interest in any matter subject to disposition in the proceeding may be joined as a party to the family law case only as provided in this chapter.

(a) Applicable rules

(1) All provisions of law relating to joinder of parties in civil actions generally apply to the joinder of a person as a party to a family law case, except as otherwise provided in this chapter.

(2) The law applicable to civil actions generally governs all pleadings, motions, and other matters pertaining to that portion of the proceeding as to which a claimant has been joined as a party to the proceeding in the same manner as if a separate action or proceeding not subject to these rules had been filed, except as otherwise provided in this chapter or by the court in which the proceeding is pending.

(b) "Claimant" defined

For purposes of this rule, a "claimant" is an individual or an entity joined or sought or seeking to be joined as a party to the family law proceeding.

(c) Persons who may seek joinder

(1) The petitioner or the respondent may apply to the court for an order joining a person as a party to the case who has or claims custody or physical control of any of the minor children subject to the action, or visitation rights with respect to such children, or who has in his or her possession or control or claims to own any property subject to the jurisdiction of the court in the proceeding.

(2) A person who has or claims custody or physical control of any of the minor children subject to the action, or visitation rights with respect to such children, may apply to the court for an order joining himself or herself as a party to the proceeding.

(3) A person served with an order temporarily restraining the use of property that is in his or her possession or control or that he or she claims to own, or affecting the custody of minor children subject to the action, or visitation rights with respect to such children, may apply to the court for an order joining himself or herself as a party to the proceeding.

(d) Form of joinder application

(1) All applications for joinder other than for an employee pension benefit plan must be made by serving and filing form a *Notice of Motion and Declaration for Joinder* (form FL-371). The hearing date must be less than 30 days from the date of filing the notice. The completed form must state with particularity the claimant's interest in the proceeding and the relief sought by the applicant, and it must be accompanied by an appropriate pleading setting forth the claim as if it were asserted in a separate action or proceeding.

(2) A blank copy of *Responsive Declaration to Motion for Joinder and Consent Order for Joinder* (form FL-373) must be served with the *Notice of Motion* and accompanying pleading.

(e) Court order on joinder

(1) *Mandatory joinder*

(A) The court must order that a person be joined as a party to the proceeding if the court discovers that person has physical custody or claims custody or visitation rights with respect to any minor child of the marriage, domestic partnership, or to any minor child of the relationship.

(B) Before ordering the joinder of a grandparent of a minor child in the proceeding under Family Code section 3104, the court must take the actions described in section 3104(a).

(2) *Permissive joinder*

The court may order that a person be joined as a party to the proceeding if the court finds that it would be appropriate to determine the particular issue in the proceeding and that the person to be joined as a party is either indispensable for the court to make an order about that issue or is necessary to the enforcement of any judgment rendered on that issue.

In deciding whether it is appropriate to determine the particular issue in the proceeding, the court must consider its effect upon the proceeding, including:

(A) Whether resolving that issue will unduly delay the disposition of the proceeding;

(B) Whether other parties would need to be joined to make an effective judgment between the parties;

(C) Whether resolving that issue will confuse other issues in the proceeding; and

(D) Whether the joinder of a party to determine the particular issue will complicate, delay, or otherwise interfere with the effective disposition of the proceeding.

(3) *Procedure upon joinder*

If the court orders that a person be joined as a party to the proceeding under this rule, the court must direct that a summons be issued on *Summons (Joinder)* (form FL-375) and that the claimant be served with a copy of *Notice of Motion and Declaration for Joinder* (form FL-371), the pleading attached thereto, the order of joinder, and the summons. The claimant has 30 days after service to file an appropriate response.

(Subd (e) amended effective January 1, 2017; adopted effective January 1, 2013.)

Rule 5.24 amended effective January 1, 2017; adopted effective January 1, 2013.

Rule 5.25. Status of family law and domestic violence forms [Repealed]

Rule 5.25 repealed effective January 1, 2013; adopted as rule 1278 effective January 1, 2001; previously amended and renumbered effective January 1, 2003.

Rule 5.26. Use of forms in nonfamily law proceedings [Repealed]

Rule 5.26 repealed effective January 1, 2013; adopted as rule 1275 effective July 1, 1985; previously amended and renumbered effective January 1, 2003.

Rule 5.27. Use of interstate forms [Repealed]

Rule 5.27 repealed effective January 1, 2013; adopted as rule 1276 effective July 1, 1988; previously amended effective January 1, 1998; previously renumbered effective January 1, 2003.

Rule 5.28. Domestic partnerships [Repealed]

Rule 5.28 repealed effective January 1, 2013; adopted effective January 1, 2005; previously amended effective January 1, 2007.

Article 3
Employee Pension Benefit Plan

Title 5, Family and Juvenile Rules—Division 1, Family Rules—Chapter 2, Parties and Joinder of Parties—Article 3, Employee Pension Benefit Plan; adopted effective January 1, 2013.

Rule 5.29. Joinder of employee pension benefit plan

(a) Request for joinder

Every request for joinder of employee pension benefit plan and order and every pleading on joinder must be submitted on *Request for Joinder of Employee Benefit Plan and Order* (form FL-372) and *Pleading on Joinder—Employee Benefit Plan* (form FL-370).

(Subd (a) adopted effective January 1, 2013.)

(b) Summons

Every summons issued on the joinder of employee pension benefit plan must be on *Summons (Joinder)* (form FL-375).

(Subd (b) adopted effective January 1, 2013.)

(c) Notice of Appearance

Every notice of appearance of employee pension benefit plan and responsive pleading filed under Family Code section 2063(b) must be given on *Notice of Appearance and Response of Employee Benefit Plan* (form FL-374).

(Subd (c) adopted effective January 1, 2013.)

Rule 5.29 adopted effective January 1, 2013.

Rule 5.30. Judicial education for family court judicial officers [Renumbered]

Rule 5.30 renumbered as rule 10.463 effective January 1, 2008.

Rule 5.35. Minimum standards for the Office of the Family Law Facilitator [Renumbered]

Rule 5.35 renumbered as rule 5.430 effective January 1, 2013.

Chapter 3
Filing Fees and Fee Waivers

Title 5, Family and Juvenile Rules—Division 1, Family Rules—Chapter 3, Filing Fees and Fee Waivers; adopted effective January 1, 2013.

Article 1
Filing Fees and Fee Waivers

Title 5, Family and Juvenile Rules—Division 1, Family Rules—Chapter 3, Filing Fees and Fee Waivers—Article 1, Filing Fees and Fee Waivers; adopted effective January 1, 2013.

Rule 5.40. Filing Fees
Rule 5.41. Waiver of fees and costs

Rule 5.40. Filing Fees

(a) Filing fees

Parties must pay filing fees to the clerk of the court at the time the parties file papers with the court.

(Subd (a) adopted effective January 1, 2013.)

(b) Authority

The amount of money required to pay filing fees in family court is established by the Uniform Civil Fees and Standard Fee Schedule Act of 2005 under Government Code section 70670 et seq. and is subject to change. The act covers fees the court may charge parties to file the first papers in a family law proceeding, motions, or other papers requiring a hearing. It also covers filing fees that courts may charge in proceedings relating to child custody or visitation (parenting time) to cover the costs of maintaining mediation services under Family Code section 3160 et seq.

(Subd (b) adopted effective January 1, 2013.)

(c) Other fees

(1) The court must not charge filing fees that are inconsistent with law or with the California Rules of Court and may not impose any tax, charge, or penalty upon a proceeding, or the filing of any pleading allowed by law, as provided by Government Code section 68070.

(2) In the absence of a statute or rule authorizing or prohibiting a fee by the superior court for a particular service or product, the court may charge a reasonable fee not to exceed the costs of providing the service or product, if the Judicial Council approves the fee, as provided by Government Code section 70631. Approved fees must be clearly posted and accessible to the public.

(Subd (c) adopted effective January 1, 2013.)

Rule 5.40 adopted effective January 1, 2013.

Rule 5.41.   Waiver of fees and costs

If unable to afford the costs to file an action in family court, a party may request that the court waive fees and costs. The procedure and forms needed to request an initial fee waiver in a family law action are the same as for all other civil actions, unless otherwise provided by a statute or the California Rules of Court.

(a) Forms

The forms required to request a fee waiver may be obtained from the clerk of the court, the public law library, or online at the California Courts website.

(b) Rules

Rules 3.50–3.56 of the California Rules of Court (title 3, division 2) govern fee waivers in family law cases. Parties may refer to the civil rules for information about:

(1) Applying for a fee waiver (rule 3.51);

(2) Forms for requesting a fee waiver (rule 3.51);

(3) How the court makes an order on a fee waiver application (rule 3.52);

(4) The time required for the court to grant a fee waiver (rule 3.53);

(5) The confidentiality of fee waiver applications and hearings (rule 3.54);

(6) Court fees and costs included in an initial fee waiver (rule 3.55); and

(7) Additional court fees and costs that may be included in the fee waiver (rule 3.56).

Rule 5.41 adopted effective January 1, 2013.

Article 2
Special Procedures

Title 5, Family and Juvenile Rules—Division 1, Family Rules—Chapter 3, Filing Fees and Fee Waivers—Article 2, Special Procedures; adopted effective January 1, 2013.

Rule 5.43. Fee waiver denials; voided actions; dismissal

Rule 5.45. Repayment of waived court fees and costs in family law support actions

Rule 5.46. Waiver of fees and costs—Supreme Court or Court of Appeal

Rule 5.43.   Fee waiver denials; voided actions; dismissal

(a) Voided paperwork

The clerk of the court must void the papers that were filed with a petitioner's or respondent's fee waiver application if 10 days pass after notice of the fee waiver denial and petitioner or respondent has not:

(1) Paid the fees owed;

(2) Submitted a new *Request to Waive Court Fees* (form FW-001) if the fee waiver was denied because the first form was incomplete; or

(3) Requested a hearing using *Request for Hearing About Court Fee Waiver Order (Superior Court)* (form FW-006).

(Subd (a) adopted effective January 1, 2013.)

(b) Effect of voided petition or complaint; dismissal or continuation of case

(1) *No response or notice of appearance filed*

If a petition or complaint is voided under (a) and a response to the petition or complaint has not been filed, or respondent has not appeared in the action, the court may dismiss the case without prejudice. If the court dismisses the case, the clerk of the court must notify the parties.

(2) *Response or notice of appearance filed; case continuation or dismissal*

If a petition or complaint is voided and a response has been filed with the court, or respondent has appeared in the action, the court must:

(A) Review the response, or documents constituting respondent's appearance, to determine whether or how the case will proceed based on the relief requested;

(B) Notify the parties of the court's determination; and

(C) Refund filing fees paid by the respondent if the court dismisses the case.

(Subd (b) adopted effective January 1, 2013.)

Rule 5.43 adopted effective January 1, 2013.

Rule 5.45.   Repayment of waived court fees and costs in family law support actions

(a) Determination of repayment required

When a judgment or support order is entered in a family law case, the court may order either party to pay all or part of the fees and costs that the court waived under Government Code section 68637. The court must consider and determine the repayment of waived fees as required by Government Code section 68637(d) and (e). The rule does not apply to actions initiated by a local child support agency.

(Subd (a) adopted effective January 1, 2013.)

(b) Required forms

(1) An order determining repayment of waived initial fees must be made on *Order to Pay Waived Court Fees and Costs (Superior Court)* (form FL-336). An order for payment of waived court fees must be accompanied by a blank *Application to Set Aside Order to Pay Waived Court Fees—Attachment* (form FL-337).

(2) An order granting or denying a request to set aside an order to pay waived court fees and costs must be made on *Order After Hearing on Motion to Set Aside Order to Pay Waived Court Fees (Superior Court)* (form FL-338).

(Subd (b) adopted effective January 1, 2013.)

Rule 5.45 adopted effective January 1, 2013.

Rule 5.46.   Waiver of fees and costs—Supreme Court or Court of Appeal

(a) Application

Rule 8.26 of the appellate rules specifies the procedure and forms for applying for an initial waiver of court fees and costs in the Supreme Court or Court of Appeal.

(Subd (a) adopted effective January 1, 2013.)

(b) Information

Parties may refer to rule 8.26 for information about:

(1) Applying for a fee waiver in appeals, writ proceedings, and petitions for review;

(2) Required forms requesting a fee waiver;

(3) The confidentiality of fee waiver applications and hearings;

(4) Time required for the court to grant a fee waiver; and

(5) Denial of a fee waiver application.

(Subd (b) adopted effective January 1, 2013.)

Rule 5.46 adopted effective January 1, 2013.

Chapter 4
Starting and Responding to a Family Law Case; Service of Papers

Title 5, Family and Juvenile Rules—Division 1, Family Rules—Chapter 4, Starting and Responding to a Family Law Case; Service of Papers; adopted effective January 1, 2013.

Article 1
Summonses, Notices, and Declarations

Title 5, Family and Juvenile Rules—Division 1, Family Rules—Chapter 4, Starting and Responding to a Family Law Case; Service of Papers—Article 1, Summonses, Notices, and Declarations; adopted effective January 1, 2013.

Rule 5.50. Papers issued by the court

Rule 5.52. Declaration Under Uniform Child Custody Jurisdiction and Enforcement Act (UCCJEA)

Rule 5.50.   Papers issued by the court

(a) Issuing the summons; form

If a summons is required to commence a family law case, the clerk of the court must issue the summons using the same procedure for issuing a summons in civil actions, generally.

(1) The clerk of the court must:

(A) Issue a *Summons (Family Law)* (form FL-110) for divorces, legal separations, or annulment cases involving married persons or domestic partnerships;

(B) Issue a *Summons (Uniform Parentage—Petition for Custody and Support)* (form FL-210) for parentage or custody and support cases;

(C) Issue a *Summons (UIFSA)* (form FL-510) when a party seeks to establish or enforce child support orders from other states; and

(D) Process a *Summons and Complaint or Supplemental Complaint Regarding Parental Obligations* (form FL-600) as specified in rule 5.325.

(2) The clerk of the court must not give the original summons to the petitioner, but must maintain it in the court file, except for support cases initiated by a local child support agency.

(Subd (a) adopted effective January 1, 2013.)

(b) Automatic temporary family law restraining order in summons; handling by clerk

Under Family Code section 233, in proceedings for dissolution, legal separation, or nullity of a marriage or domestic partnership and in parentage proceedings, the clerk of the court must issue a summons that includes automatic temporary (standard) restraining orders.

(1) The summons and standard restraining orders must be issued and filed in the same manner as a summons in a civil action and must be served and enforced in the manner prescribed for any other restraining order.

(2) If service is by publication, the publication need not include the standard restraining orders.

(Subd (b) amended effective January 1, 2016; adopted effective January 1, 2013.)

(c) Individual restraining order

(1) On application of a party and as provided in the Family Code, a court may issue any individual restraining order that appears to be reasonable or necessary, including those automatic temporary restraining orders in (b) included in the family law summons under Family Code section 233.

(2) Individual restraining orders supersede the standard family law restraining orders in the Family Law and Uniform Parentage Act summonses.

(Subd (c) amended effective January 1, 2016.)

Rule 5.50 amended effective January 1, 2016; adopted effective January 1, 2013.

Rule 5.52. Declaration Under Uniform Child Custody Jurisdiction and Enforcement Act (UCCJEA)

(a) Filing requirements; application

(1) Petitioner and respondent must each complete, serve, and file a *Declaration Under Uniform Child Custody Jurisdiction and Enforcement Act (UCCJEA)* (form FL-105/GC-120) if there are children of their relationship under the age of 18 years.

(2) The form is a required attachment to the petition and response in actions for divorce, to establish parentage, or actions for custody and support of minor children.

(Subd (a) adopted effective January 1, 2013.)

(b) Duty to update information

In any action or proceeding involving custody of a minor child, a party has a continuing duty to inform the court if he or she obtains further information about a custody proceeding in a California court or any other court concerning a child who is named in the petition, complaint, or response. To comply with this duty, a party must file an updated UCCJEA form with the court and have it served on the other party.

(Subd (b) adopted effective January 1, 2013.)

Rule 5.52 adopted effective January 1, 2013.

Article 2
Initial Pleadings

Title 5, Family and Juvenile Rules—Division 1, Family Rules—Chapter 4, Starting and Responding to a Family Law Case; Service of Papers—Article 2, Initial Pleadings; adopted effective January 1, 2013.

Rule 5.60. Petition or complaint; alternative relief
Rule 5.62. Appearance by respondent
Rule 5.63. Request for order to quash proceeding or responsive relief

Rule 5.60. Petition or complaint; alternative relief

(a) Format

A party starting a family law case must file an appropriate petition or complaint using a form approved by the Judicial Council. Where the Judicial Council has not approved a specific petition or complaint form, the party must submit the petition or complaint in an appropriate format under Trial Court Rules, rules 2.100 through 2.119.

(Subd (a) adopted effective January 1, 2013.)

(b) Request for alternative relief

The petitioner or respondent may request alternative relief when filing a family law action. The request for alternative relief must be indicated in the petition or response.

(Subd (b) adopted effective January 1, 2013.)

Rule 5.60 adopted effective January 1, 2013.

Rule 5.62. Appearance by respondent

(a) Use of terms

In a family law proceeding, the term "request for order" has the same meaning as the terms "motion" or "notice of motion" when they are used in the Code of Civil Procedure.

(Subd (a) adopted effective July 1, 2016.)

(b) Appearance

Except as provided in Code of Civil Procedure section 418.10 and Family Code sections 2012 and 3409, a respondent is deemed to have made a general appearance in a proceeding when he or she files:

(1) A response or answer;

(2) A request for order to strike, under section 435 of the Code of Civil Procedure;

(3) A request for order to transfer the proceeding under section 395 of the Code of Civil Procedure; or

(4) A written notice of his or her appearance.

(Subd (b) amended and relettered effective July 1, 2016; adopted as subd (a) effective January 1, 2013.)

(c) Notice required after appearance

After appearance, the respondent or his or her attorney is entitled to notice of all subsequent proceedings of which notice is required to be given by these rules or in civil actions generally.

(Subd (c) amended and relettered effective July 1, 2016; adopted as subd (b) effective January 1, 2013.)

(d) No notice required

Where a respondent has not appeared, notice of subsequent proceedings need not be given to the respondent except as provided in these rules.

(Subd (d) amended and relettered effective January 1, 2016; adopted as subd (c) effective January 1, 2013.)

Rule 5.62 amended effective July 1, 2016; adopted effective January 1, 2013.

Rule 5.63. Request for order to quash proceeding or responsive relief

(a) Use of terms

In a family law proceeding, the term "request for order" has the same meaning as the terms "motion" or "notice of motion" when they are used in the Code of Civil Procedure.

(Subd (a) adopted effective July 1, 2016.)

(b) Respondent's application

Within the time permitted to file a response, the respondent may move to quash the proceeding, in whole or in part, for any of the following reasons:

(1) Lack of legal capacity to sue;

(2) Prior judgment or another action pending between the same parties for the same cause;

(3) Failure to meet the residence requirement of Family Code section 2320; or

(4) Statute of limitations in Family Code section 2211.

(Subd (b) relettered effective July 1, 2016; adopted as subd (a) effective January 1, 2013.)

(c) Service of respondent's request for order to quash

The request for order to quash must be served in compliance with Code of Civil Procedure section 1005(b). If the respondent files a request for order to quash, no default may be entered, and the time to file a response will be extended until 15 days after service of the court's order denying the request for order to quash.

(Subd (c) amended and relettered effective July 1, 2016; adopted as subd (b) effective January 1, 2013.)

(d) Petitioner's application

Within 15 days after the filing of the response, the petitioner may move to quash, in whole or in part, any request for affirmative relief in the response for the grounds set forth in (a).

(Subd (d) relettered effective July 1, 2016; adopted as subd (c) effective January 1, 2013.)

(e) Waiver

The parties are deemed to have waived the grounds set forth in (b) if they do not file a request for order to quash within the time frame set forth.

(Subd (e) amended and relettered effective July 1, 2016; adopted as subd (d) effective January 1, 2013.)

(f) Relief

When a request for order to quash is granted, the court may grant leave to amend the petition or response and set a date for filing the amended pleadings. The court may also dismiss the action without leave to amend. The action may also be dismissed if the request for order has been sustained with leave to amend and the amendment is not made within the time permitted by the court.

(Subd (f) amended and relettered effective July 1, 2016; adopted as subd (e) effective January 1, 2013.)

Rule 5.63 amended effective July 1, 2016; adopted effective January 1, 2013.

Article 3
Service of Papers

Title 5, Family and Juvenile Rules—Division 1, Family Rules—Chapter 4, Starting and Responding to a Family Law Case; Service of Papers—Article 3, Service of Papers; adopted effective January 1, 2013.

Rule 5.66.   Proof of service
(a) Requirements to file proof of service

Parties must file with the court a completed form to prove that the other party received the petition or complaint or response to petition or complaint.

(Subd (a) amended and lettered effective January 1, 2017; adopted as unlettered subd.)

(b) Methods of proof of service

(1) The proof of service of summons may be on a form approved by the Judicial Council or a document or pleading containing the same information required in *Proof of Service of Summons* (form FL-115).

(2) The proof of service of response to petition or complaint may be on a form approved by the Judicial Council or a document or pleading containing the same information required in *Proof of Service by Mail* (form FL-335), *Proof of Personal Service* (form FL-330), or *Proof of Electronic Service* (form POS-050/EFS-050).

(Subd (b) amended and lettered effective January 1, 2017; adopted as unlettered subd.)

Rule 5.66 amended effective January 1, 2017; adopted effective January 1, 2013.

Article 4
Manner of Service

Title 5, Family and Juvenile Rules—Division 1, Family Rules—Chapter 4, Starting and Responding to a Family Law Case; Service of Papers—Article 4, Manner of Service; adopted effective January 1, 2013.

Rule 5.68. Manner of service of summons and petition; response; jurisdiction
Rule 5.72. Court order for service by publication or posting when respondent's address is unknown

Rule 5.68.   Manner of service of summons and petition; response; jurisdiction
(a) Service of summons and petition

The petitioner must arrange to serve the other party with a summons, petition, and other papers as required by one of the following methods:

(1) Personal service (Code Civ. Proc., § 415.10);

(2) Substituted service (Code Civ. Proc., § 415.20);

(3) Service by mail with a notice and acknowledgment of receipt (Code Civ. Proc., § 415.30);

(4) Service on person outside of the state (Code Civ. Proc., § 415.40);

(5) Service on a person residing outside of the United States, which must be done in compliance with service rules of the following:

(A) Hague Convention on the Service Abroad of Judicial and Extra-judicial Documents in Civil or Commercial Matters; or

(B) Inter-American Convention on Letters Rogatory and the Additional Protocol to the Inter-American Convention on Letters Rogatory.

(6) Service by posting or publication (Code Civ. Proc., §§ 415.50 and 413.30).

(Subd (a) amended effective January 1, 2014; adopted effective January 1, 2013.)

(b) Service of response to petition

A response to a family law petition may be served by the methods described in (a) but may also be served by mail without notice and acknowledgment of receipt.

(Subd (b) adopted effective January 1, 2013.)

(c) Continuing jurisdiction

The court has jurisdiction over the parties and control of all subsequent proceedings from the time of service of the summons and a copy of the petition. A general appearance of the respondent is equivalent to personal service within this state of the summons and a copy of the petition upon him or her.

(Subd (c) adopted effective January 1, 2013.)

Rule 5.68 amended effective January 1, 2014; adopted effective January 1, 2013.

Rule 5.70.   Nondisclosure of attorney assistance in preparation of court documents [Repealed]

Rule 5.70 repealed effective January 1, 2013; adopted as rule 5.170 effective July 1, 2003; previously renumbered effective January 1, 2004; previously amended effective January 1, 2007.

Rule 5.71.   Application to be relieved as counsel on completion of limited scope representation [Repealed]

Rule 5.71 repealed effective January 1, 2013; adopted as rule 5.171 effective July 1, 2003; previously renumbered effective January 1, 2004; previously amended effective January 1, 2007, and July 1, 2007.

Rule 5.72.   Court order for service by publication or posting when respondent's address is unknown

If the respondent cannot be found to be served a summons by any method described in Code of Civil Procedure sections 415.10 through 415.40, the petitioner may request an order for service of the summons by publication or posting under Code of Civil Procedure sections 415.50 and 413.30, respectively.

(a) Service of summons by publication or posting; forms

To request service of summons by publication or posting, the petitioner must complete and submit to the court *Application for Order for Publication or Posting* (form FL-980) and *Order for Publication or Posting* (form FL-982). Alternatively, petitioner may complete and submit to the court pleadings containing the same information as forms FL-980 and FL-982. The petitioner must list all the reasonable diligent efforts that have been made to find and serve the respondent.

(Subd (a) adopted effective January 1, 2013.)

(b) Service of summons by posting; additional requirements

Service of summons by posting may be ordered only if the court finds that the petitioner is eligible for a waiver of court fees and costs.

(1) To request service by posting, the petitioner must have obtained an order waiving court fees and costs. If the petitioner's financial situation has improved since obtaining the approved order on court fee waiver, the petitioner must file a *Notice to Court of Improved Financial Situation or Settlement* (form FW-010). If the court finds that the petitioner no longer qualifies for a fee waiver, the court may order service by publication of the documents.

(2) *Proof of Service by Posting* (form FL-985) (or a pleading containing the same information as form FL-985) must be completed by the person who posted the documents and then filed with the court once posting is completed.

(Subd (b) amended effective January 1, 2014; adopted effective January 1, 2013.)

Rule 5.72 amended effective January 1, 2014; adopted effective January 1, 2013.

Article 5
Pleadings and Amended Pleadings

Title 5, Family and Juvenile Rules—Division 1, Family Rules—Chapter 4, Starting and Responding to a Family Law Case; Service of Papers—Article 5, Pleadings and Amended Pleadings; adopted effective January 1, 2013.

Rule 5.74.   Pleadings and amended pleadings
(a) Definitions

(1) "Pleading" means a petition, complaint, application, objection, answer, response, notice, request for orders, statement of interest, report, or account filed in proceedings under the Family Code.

(2) "Amended pleading" means a pleading that completely restates and supersedes the pleading it amends for all purposes.

(3) "Amendment to a pleading" means a pleading that modifies another pleading and alleges facts or requests relief materially different from the facts alleged or the relief requested in the modified pleading. An amendment to a pleading does not restate or supersede the modified pleading but must be read together with that pleading.

(4) "Supplement to a pleading" and "supplement" mean a pleading that modifies another pleading but does not allege facts or request relief materially different from the facts alleged or the relief requested in the supplemented pleading. A supplement to a pleading may add information to or may correct omissions in the modified pleading.

(Subd (a) adopted effective January 1, 2013.)

(b) Forms of pleading

(1) The forms of pleading and the rules by which the sufficiency of pleadings is to be determined are solely those prescribed in these rules.

(2) Demurrers, motions for summary adjudication, and motions for summary judgment must not be used in family law actions.

(Subd (b) amended effective January 1, 2014; adopted effective January 1, 2013.)

(c) Amendment to pleadings

(1) Amendments to pleadings, amended pleadings, and supplemental pleadings may be served and filed in conformity with the provisions of law applicable to such matters in civil actions generally, but the petitioner is not required to file a reply if the respondent has filed a response.

(2) If both parties have filed initial pleadings (petition and response), there may be no default entered on an amended pleading of either party.

(Subd (c) adopted effective January 1, 2013.)

Rule 5.74 amended effective January 1, 2014; adopted effective January 1, 2013.

Article 6
Specific Proceedings

Title 5, Family and Juvenile Rules—Division 1, Family Rules—Chapter 4, Starting and Responding to a Family Law Case; Service of Papers—Article 6, Specific Proceedings; adopted effective January 1, 2013.

Rule 5.76. Domestic partnerships
Rule 5.77. Summary dissolution

Rule 5.76.   Domestic partnerships

To obtain a dissolution, a legal separation, or an annulment of a domestic partnership:

(1) Persons who qualify for a summary dissolution as described in the booklet *Summary Dissolution Information* (form FL-810) may act to dissolve their partnership through the California Secretary of State using forms found at *www.sos.ca.gov* or in the superior court following the procedures described in form FL-810.

(2) For persons who do not qualify for a summary dissolution proceeding, all forms and procedures used for the dissolution, legal separation, or annulment of a domestic partnership are the same as those used for the dissolution, legal separation, or annulment of a marriage.

Rule 5.76 amended effective January 1, 2015; adopted effective January 1, 2013.

Rule 5.77.   Summary dissolution

(a) Declaration of disclosure

To comply with the preliminary disclosure requirements of chapter 9 (beginning with section 2100) of part 1 of division 6 of the Family Code in proceedings for summary dissolution, each joint petitioner must complete and give each other copies of the following documents before signing a property settlement agreement or completing a divorce:

(1) An *Income and Expense Declaration* (form FL-150).

(2) Either of the following documents listing separate and community property assets and obligations:

(A) *Declaration of Disclosure* (form FL-140) and either a *Schedule of Assets and Debts* or a *Property Declaration* (form FL-160) with all attachments; or

(B) The completed worksheet pages indicated in *Summary Dissolution Information* (form FL-810).

(3) A written statement of all investment, business, or other income-producing opportunities that came up after the date of separation based on investments made or work done during the marriage or domestic partnership and before the date of separation.

(4) All tax returns filed by the spouse or domestic partner in the two year period before exchanging the worksheets or forms described in (2).

(Subd (a) amended effective July 1, 2013; adopted effective January 1, 2013.)

(b) Fee for filing

The joint petitioners must pay one fee for filing a *Joint Petition for Summary Dissolution of Marriage* (form FL-800) unless both parties are eligible for a fee waiver order. The fee is the same as that charged for filing a *Petition—Marriage* (form FL-100). No additional fee may be charged for the filing of any form prescribed for use in a summary dissolution proceeding.

(Subd (b) adopted effective January 1, 2013.)

Rule 5.77 amended effective July 1, 2013; adopted effective January 1, 2013.

Chapter 5
Family Centered Case Resolution Plans

Title 5, Family and Juvenile Rules—Division 1, Family Rules—Chapter 5, Family Centered Resolution Plans; adopted effective January 1, 2013.

Rule 5.83.   Family centered case resolution

(a) Purpose

This rule establishes processes and procedures for courts to manage cases from initial filing to final disposition in an effective and timely manner. It is intended to advance the goals of Family Code section 2450(a) and Standards of Judicial Administration, standard 5.30.

(Subd (a) adopted effective January 1, 2012.)

(b) Definitions

(1) "Family centered case resolution process" refers to the process employed by the court to ensure that family law cases move through the court process from filing to final disposition in a timely, fair, and effective manner.

(2) "Disposition" refers to final judgment, dismissal, change of venue, or consolidation of the case into a lead case. Courts may continue a case in, or return a case to, the family centered case resolution process after disposition.

(3) "Status conference" refers to court events scheduled with the parties and attorneys for the purpose of identifying the current status of the case and determining the next steps required to reach disposition.

(4) "Family centered case resolution conference" refers to a conference scheduled with parties, attorneys, and a judicial officer to develop and implement a family centered case resolution plan under Family Code section 2451.

(Subd (b) adopted effective January 1, 2012.)

(c) Family centered case resolution process

(1) Beginning January 1, 2012, courts must develop a family centered case resolution process which must be fully implemented by January 1, 2013. The family centered case resolution process must identify and assist all dissolution, legal separation, nullity, and parentage cases to progress through the court process toward disposition effectively in a timely manner. The court may identify other family law case types to include in the family centered case resolution process.

(2) For cases filed on or after January 1, 2013, the court must include as part of the family centered case resolution process a review of all dissolution, legal separation, nullity, and parentage cases within at least 180 days from the date of the initial filing and at a minimum, at least every 180 days thereafter until disposition in order to determine the most appropriate next steps to help ensure an effective, fair, and timely resolution. Unless the court determines that procedural milestones are being met, the review must include at least one of the following: (1) a status conference or (2) a family centered case resolution conference. Nothing in this section prohibits courts from setting more frequent review dates.

(3) If, after 18 months from the date the petition was filed, both parties have failed to participate in the case resolution process as determined by the court, the court's obligation for further review of the case is relieved until the case qualifies for dismissal under Code of Civil Procedure section 583.210 or 583.310, or until the parties reactivate participation in the case, and the case is not counted toward the goals for disposition set out in (c)(5).

(4) In deciding whether a case is progressing in an effective and timely manner, the court should consider procedural milestones including the following:

(A) A proof of service of summons and petition should be filed within 60 days of case initiation;

(B) If no response has been filed, and the parties have not agreed on an extension of time to respond, a request to enter default should be submitted within 60 days after the date the response was due;

(C) The petitioner's preliminary declaration of disclosure should be served within 60 days of the filing of the petition;

(D) When a default has been entered, a judgment should be submitted within 60 days of the entry of default;

(E) Whether a trial date has been requested or scheduled; and

(F) When the parties have notified the court that they are actively negotiating or mediating their case, a written agreement for judgment is submitted within six months of the date the petition was filed, or a request for trial date is submitted.

(5) For dissolution, legal separation, and nullity cases initially filed on or after January 1, 2014, the goals of any family centered case resolution process should be to finalize dispositions as follows:

(A) At least 20 percent are disposed within 6 months from the date the petition was filed;

(B) At least 75 percent are disposed within 12 months from the date the petition was filed; and

(C) At least 90 percent are disposed within 18 months from the date the petition was filed.

(6) The court may select various procedural milestones at which to assist cases in moving toward disposition in an effective and timely manner. Types of assistance that can be provided include the following:

(A) Notifying the parties and attorneys by mail, telephone, e-mail, or other electronic method of communication of the current status of the case and the next procedural steps required to reach disposition;

(B) Implementing a schedule of status conferences for cases to identify the status of the case and determine the next steps required to progress toward disposition;

(C) Providing assistance to the parties at the time scheduled for hearings on requests for orders to identify the status of the case and determine the next steps required to reach disposition;

(D) Providing financial and property settlement opportunities to the parties and their attorneys with judicial officers or qualified attorney settlement officers;

(E) Scheduling a family centered case resolution conference to develop and implement a family centered case resolution plan under Family Code section 2451.

(7) In deciding that a case requires a family centered case resolution conference, the court should consider, in addition to procedural milestones, factors including the following:

(A) Difficulty in locating and serving the respondent;

(B) Complexity of issues;

(C) Nature and extent of anticipated discovery;

(D) Number and locations of percipient and expert witnesses;

(E) Estimated length of trial;

(F) Statutory priority for issues such as custody and visitation of minor children;

(G) Extent of property and support issues in controversy;

(H) Existence of issues of domestic violence, child abuse, or substance abuse;

(I) Pendency of other actions or proceedings that may affect the case; and

(J) Any other factor that would affect the time for disposition.

(Subd (c) adopted effective January 1, 2012.)

(d) Family centered case resolution conferences

(1) The court may hold an initial family centered case resolution conference to develop a specific case resolution plan. The conference is not intended to be an evidentiary hearing.

(2) Family centered case resolution conferences must be heard by a judicial officer. On the court's initiative or at the request of the parties, to enhance access to the court, the conference may be held in person, by telephone, by videoconferencing, or by other appropriate means of communication.

(3) At the conference, counsel for each party and each self-represented litigant must be familiar with the case and must be prepared to discuss the party's positions on the issues.

(4) With the exception of mandatory child custody mediation and mandatory settlement conferences, before alternative dispute resolution (ADR) is included in a family centered case resolution plan under Family Code section 2451(a)(2), the court must inform the parties that their participation in any court recommended ADR services is voluntary and that ADR services can be part of a plan only if both parties voluntarily opt to use these services. Additionally, the court must:

(A) Inform the parties that ADR may not be appropriate in cases involving domestic violence and provide information about separate sessions; and

(B) Ensure that all court-connected providers of ADR services that are part of a family centered case resolution plan have been trained in assessing and handling cases that may involve domestic violence.

(5) Nothing in this rule prohibits an employee of the court from reviewing the file and notifying the parties of any deficiencies in their paperwork before the parties appear in front of a judicial officer at a family centered case resolution conference. This type of assistance can occur by telephone, in person, in writing, or by other means approved by the court, on or before each scheduled family centered case resolution conference. However, this type of procedural assistance is not intended to replace family centered case resolution plan management or to create a barrier to litigants' access to a judicial officer.

(Subd (d) amended effective January 1, 2016; adopted effective January 1, 2012.)

(e) Family centered case resolution plan order

(1) Family centered case resolution plans as ordered by the court must comply with Family Code sections 2450(b) and 2451.

(2) The family centered case resolution plan order should set a schedule for subsequent family centered case resolution conferences and otherwise provide for management of the case.

(Subd (e) adopted effective January 1, 2012.)

(f) Family centered case resolution order without appearance

If the court determines that appearances at a family centered case resolution conference are not necessary, the court may notify the parties and, if stipulated, issue a family centered case resolution order without an appearance at a conference.

(Subd (f) adopted effective January 1, 2012.)

(g) Family centered case resolution information

(1) Upon the filing of first papers in dissolution, legal separation, nullity, or parentage actions the court must provide the filing party with the following:

(A) Written information summarizing the process of a case through disposition;

(B) A list of local resources that offer procedural assistance, legal advice or information, settlement opportunities, and domestic violence services;

(C) Instructions for keeping the court informed of the person's current address and phone number, and e-mail address;

(D) Information for self-represented parties about the opportunity to meet with court self-help center staff or a family law facilitator; and

(E) Information for litigants on how to request a status conference, or a family centered case resolution conference earlier than or in addition to, any status conference or family centered case resolution conferences scheduled by the court.

(Subd (g) adopted effective January 1, 2012.)
Rule 5.83 amended effective January 1, 2016; adopted effective January 1, 2012.

Chapter 6
Request for Court Orders

Title 5, Family and Juvenile Rules—Division 1, Family Rules—Chapter 6, Request for Court Orders; adopted effective January 1, 2013.

Article 1
General Provisions

Title 5, Family and Juvenile Rules—Division 1, Family Rules—Chapter 6, Request for Court Orders—Article 1, General Provisions; adopted effective January 1, 2013.

Rule 5.90. Format of papers
Rule 5.91. Individual restraining order

Rule 5.90.   Format of papers

The rules regarding the format of a request for order are the same as the rules for format of motions in civil rules 3.1100 through 3.1116, except as otherwise provided in these Family Rules.
Rule 5.90 adopted effective January 1, 2013.

Rule 5.91.   Individual restraining order

On a party's request for order and as provided in the Family Code, a court may issue any individual restraining order that appears to be reasonable or necessary, including those automatic temporary restraining orders included in the family law summons. Individual orders supersede the standard family law restraining orders in the Family Law and Uniform Parentage Act summonses.
Rule 5.91 amended effective January 1, 2016; adopted effective January 1, 2013.

Article 2
Filing and Service

Title 5, Family and Juvenile Rules—Division 1, Family Rules—Chapter 6, Request for Court Orders—Article 2, Filing and Service; adopted effective January 1, 2013.

Rule 5.92. Request for court order; responsive declaration
Rule 5.94. Order shortening time; other filing requirements; failure to serve request for order

Rule 5.95. Request to reschedule hearing

Rule 5.96. Place and manner of filing

Rule 5.97. Time frames for transferring jurisdiction

Rule 5.92.   Request for court order; responsive declaration

(a) Application

(1) In a family law proceeding under the Family Code:

(A) The term "request for order" has the same meaning as the terms "motion" or "notice of motion" when they are used in the Code of Civil Procedure;

(B) A *Request for Order* (form FL-300) must be used to ask for court orders, unless another Judicial Council form has been adopted or approved for the specific request; and

(C) A *Responsive Declaration to Request for Order* (form FL-320) must be used to respond to the orders sought in form FL-300, unless another Judicial Council form has been adopted or approved for the specific purpose.

(2) In an action under the Domestic Violence Prevention Act, a *Request for Order* (form FL-300) must be used to request a modification or termination of all orders made after a hearing on *Restraining Order After Hearing* (form DV-130).

(3) In a local child support action under the Family Code, any party other than the local child support agency must use *Request for Order* (form FL-300) to ask for court orders.

(Subd (a) adopted effective July 1, 2016; previous subd (a) repealed effective July 1, 2016.)

(b) Request for order; required forms and filing procedure

(1) The *Request for Order* (form FL-300) must set forth facts sufficient to notify the other party of the moving party's contentions in support of the relief requested.

(2) When a party seeks orders for spousal or domestic partner support, attorney's fees and costs, or other orders relating to the parties' property or finances:

(A) The party must complete an *Income and Expense Declaration* (form FL-150) and file it with the *Request for Order* (form FL-300); and

(B) The *Income and Expense Declaration* (form FL-150) must be current, as described in rule 5.260 and include the documents specified in form FL-150 that demonstrate the party's income.

(3) When seeking child support orders:

(A) A party must complete an *Income and Expense Declaration* (form FL-150) and file it with the *Request for Order* (form FL-300);

(B) The *Income and Expense Declaration* (form FL-150) must be current, as described in rule 5.260 and include the documents specified in the form that demonstrate the party's income; and

(C) A party may complete a current *Financial Statement (Simplified)* (form FL-155) instead of a current *Income and Expense Declaration* (form FL-150) only if the party meets the requirements listed in form FL-155.

(4) The moving party may be required to complete, file and have additional forms or attachments served along with a *Request for Order* (form FL-300) when seeking court orders for child custody and visitation (parenting time), attorney's fees and costs, support, and other financial matters. For more information, see *Information Sheet for Order* (form FL-300-INFO).

(5) The moving party must file the documents with the court clerk to obtain a court date and then have a filed copy served on all parties in the case within the timelines required by law.

(6) No memorandum of points and authorities need to be filed with a *Request for Order* (form FL-300) unless required by the court on a case-by-case basis.

(Subd (b) adopted effective July 1, 2016; previous subd (b) repealed effective July 1, 2016.)

(c) Request for temporary emergency (ex parte) orders

If the moving party seeks temporary emergency orders pending the hearing, the moving party must:

(1) Comply with rules 5.151 through 5.169 of the California Rules of Court;

(2) Complete and include a proposed *Temporary Emergency (Ex Parte) Orders* (form FL-305) with the *Request for Order* (form FL-300); and

(3) Comply with specified local court procedures and/or local court rules about reserving the day for the temporary emergency hearing, submitting the paperwork to the court, and use of local forms.

(Subd (c) adopted effective July 1, 2016; previous subd (c) repealed effective July 1, 2016.)

(d) Request for order shortening time (for service or time until the hearing)

If the moving party seeks an order for a shorter time to serve documents or a shorter time until the hearing:

(1) The moving party must submit the request as a temporary emergency order on form FL-300 and comply with the requirements of rules 5.151 through 5.169 of the California Rules of Court; and

(2) The moving party's request must be supported by a declaration or a statement of facts showing good cause for the court to prescribe shorter times for the filing and service of the *Request for Order* (form FL-300) than the times specified in Code of Civil Procedure section 1005.

(3) The court may issue the order shortening time in the "Court Orders" section of the *Request for Order* (form FL-300).

(Subd (d) adopted effective July 1, 2016; previous subd (d) repealed effective July 1, 2016.)

(e) Issuance by court clerk

The court clerk's authority to issue a *Request for Order* (form FL-300) as a ministerial act is limited to those orders or notices:

(1) For the parties to attend orientation and confidential mediation or child custody recommending counseling; and

(2) That may be delegated by a judicial officer and do not require the use of judicial discretion.

(Subd (e) adopted effective July 1, 2016.)

(f) Request for order; service requirements

(1) The *Request for Order* (form FL-300) and appropriate documents or orders must be served in the manner specified for the service of a summons in Code of Civil Procedure sections 415.10 through 415.95, including personal service, if:

(A) The court granted temporary emergency orders pending the hearing;

(B) The responding party has not yet appeared in the case as described in rule 5.62; or

(C) The court ordered personal service on the other party.

(2) A *Request for Order* (form FL-300) must be served as specified in Family Code section 215 if filed after entry of a family law judgment or after a permanent order was made in any proceeding in which there was at issue the custody, visitation (parenting time), or support of a child.

(A) Requests to change a judgment or permanent order for custody, visitation (parenting time), or support of a child may be served by mail on the other party or parties only if the moving party can verify the other parties' current address.

(B) *Declaration Regarding Address Verification* (form FL-334) may be used as the address verification required by Family Code section 215. The completed form, or a declaration that includes the same information, must be filed with the proof of service of the *Request for Order*.

(3) All other requests for orders and appropriate documents may be served as specified in Code of Civil Procedure section 1010 et seq., including service by mail.

(4) The following blank forms must be served with a *Request for Order* (form FL-300):

(A) *Responsive Declaration to Request for Order* (form FL-320); and

(B) *Income and Expense Declaration* (form FL-150), when the requesting party is serving a completed FL-150 or FL-155.

(Subd (f) adopted effective July 1, 2016.)

(g) Responsive declaration to request for order; procedures

To respond to the issues raised in the *Request for Order* (form FL-300) and accompanying papers, the responding party must complete, file, and have a *Responsive Declaration to Request for Order* (form FL-320) served on all parties in the case.

(1) The *Responsive Declaration to Request for Order* (form FL-320) must set forth facts sufficient to notify the other party of the declarant's contentions in response to the request for order and in support of any relief requested.

(2) The responding party may request relief related to the orders requested in the moving papers. However, unrelated relief must be sought by scheduling a separate hearing using *Request for Order* (form FL-300) and following the filing and service requirements for a *Request for Order* described in this rule.

(3) A completed *Income and Expense Declaration* (form 150) must be filed with the *Responsive Declaration to Request for Order* (form FL-320)

following the same requirements specified above in rule 5.92(b)(2) and (b)(3).

(4) The responding party may be required to complete, file, and serve additional forms or attachments along with a *Responsive Declaration to Request for Order* (form FL-320) when responding to a *Request for Order* (form FL-300) about child custody and visitation (parenting time), attorney fees and costs, support, and other financial matters. For more information, read *Information Sheet: Responsive Declaration to Request for Order* (form FL-320-INFO).

(5) No memorandum of points and authorities need be filed with a *Responsive Declaration to Request for Order* (form FL-320) unless required by the court on a case-by-case basis.

(6) A *Responsive Declaration to Request for Order* (form FL-320) may be served on the parties by mail, unless otherwise required by court order.

(Subd (g) adopted effective July 1, 2016.)

Rule 5.92 amended effective July 1, 2016; adopted effective July 1, 2012.

Advisory Committee Comment

The Family and Juvenile Law Advisory Committee and the Elkins Implementation Task Force developed rule 5.92 and *Request for Order* (form FL-300) in response to *Elkins Family Law Task Force: Final Report and Recommendations (April 2010)* for one comprehensive form and related procedures to replace the *Order to Show Cause* (form FL-300) and *Notice of Motion* (form FL-301). (See page 35 of the final report online at *www.courts.ca.gov/elkins-finalreport.pdf.*)

Rule 5.93. Attorney's fees and costs [Renumbered]

Rule 5.93 renumbered as rule 5.427 effective January 1, 2013.

Rule 5.94. Order shortening time; other filing requirements; failure to serve request for order

(a) Order shortening time

The court, on its own motion or on application for an order shortening time supported by a declaration showing good cause, may prescribe shorter times for the filing and service of papers than the times specified in Code of Civil Procedure section 1005.

(Subd (a) adopted effective January 1, 2013.)

(b) Time for filing proof of service

Proof of service of the *Request for Order* (FL-300) and supporting papers should be filed five court days before the hearing date.

(Subd (b) adopted effective January 1, 2013.)

(c) Filing of late papers

No papers relating to a request for order or responsive declaration to the request may be rejected for filing on the ground that they were untimely submitted for filing. If the court, in its discretion, refuses to consider a late filed paper, the minutes or order must so indicate.

(Subd (c) amended and relettered effective July 1, 2016; adopted as subd (d) effective January 1, 2013.)

(d) Timely submission to court clerk

The papers requesting an order or responding to the request are deemed timely filed if they are submitted:

(1) Before the close of the court clerk's office to the public; and

(2) On or before the day the papers are due.

(Subd (d) amended and relettered effective July 1, 2016; adopted as subd (e) effective January 1, 2013.)

(e) Failure to serve request for order

The *Request for Order* (form FL-300) or other moving papers such as an order to show cause, along with any temporary emergency (ex parte) orders, will expire on the date and time of the scheduled hearing if the requesting party fails to:

(1) Have the other party [1] served before the hearing with the *Request for Order* (form FL-300) or other moving papers, such as an order to show cause; supporting documents; and any temporary emergency (ex parte) orders; or

(2) Obtain a court order to [2] **reschedule** the hearing, **as described in rule 5.95**.

(Subd (e) amended effective July 1, 2020; adopted as subd (c) effective January 1, 2013; previously amended and relettered as subd (e) effective July 1, 2016; previously amended effective September 1, 2017.)

Rule 5.94(e).   2020 Deletes. [1] timely [2] continue

(f) Procedures to request continued hearing date [Repealed]

(Subd (f) repealed effective July 1, 2020; adopted effective July 1, 2016; previously amended effective September 1, 2017.)

Rule 5.94 amended effective July 1, 2020; adopted effective January 1, 2013; previously amended effective July 1, 2016, and September 1, 2017.

Rule 5.95. Request to reschedule hearing

(a) Application

The rules in this chapter govern requests to reschedule a hearing in family law cases, unless otherwise provided by statute or rule. Unless specifically stated, these rules do not apply to ex parte applications for domestic violence restraining orders under the Domestic Violence Prevention Act.

(Subd (a) adopted effective July 1, 2020.)

(b) Reschedule a hearing because the other party was not served

If a *Request for Order* (form FL-300) (with or without temporary emergency [ex parte] orders), order to show cause, or other moving paper is not served on the other party as described in rule 5.92 or as ordered by the court and the requesting party still wishes to proceed with the hearing, the party must ask the court to reschedule the hearing date.

(1) To request that the court reschedule the hearing to serve papers on the other party, the party must take one of the following actions:

(A) *Before the date of the hearing*

(i) The party must complete and file with the court a written request and a proposed order. The following forms may be used for this purpose: *Request to Reschedule Hearing* (form FL-306) or *Request to Reschedule Hearing Involving Temporary Emergency (Ex Parte) Orders* (form FL-307), whichever form is appropriate for the case, and *Order on Request to Reschedule Hearing* (form FL-309); and

(ii) The party should submit the request to the court no later than five court days before the hearing set on the *Request for Order* (form FL-300), order to show cause, or other moving paper.

(B) *On the date of the hearing*

The party may appear and orally ask the court to reschedule the hearing. The party is not required to file a written request but must complete and submit a proposed *Order on Request to Reschedule Hearing* (form FL-309).

(2) The court may do any of the following:

(A) Grant or deny the request to reschedule the hearing.

(B) Delegate to the court clerk the authority to reschedule the hearing if:

(i) The request to reschedule the hearing is required to allow more time to serve the other party with notice of the hearing; and

(ii) The party asking to reschedule the hearing does not request a change to any temporary emergency (ex parte) orders issued with the *Request for Order* (form FL-300).

(3) If the court reschedules the hearing:

(A) The court, on a showing of good cause, may modify or terminate any temporary emergency (ex parte) orders initially granted with the *Request for Order* (form FL-300), order to show cause, or other moving papers.

(B) The requesting party must serve the *Order on Request to Reschedule Hearing* (form FL-309) on the other party in the case, along with the *Request for Order* (form FL-300) or other moving papers such as an order to show cause, any temporary emergency (ex parte) orders, and supporting documents.

(C) If the other party has not been served with the papers in (B) after the court granted the request to reschedule, the party must repeat the procedures in this rule, unless the court orders otherwise.

(Subd (b) adopted effective July 1, 2020.)

(c) Written agreements (stipulations) to reschedule a hearing

The court may reschedule the hearing date of a *Request for Order* (FL-300), order to show cause, or other moving paper based on a written agreement (stipulation) between the parties and/or their attorneys.

(1) The parties may complete *Agreement and Order to Reschedule Hearing* (form FL-308) for this purpose.

(2) The parties may agree to reschedule the hearing to a date that must be provided by the court clerk. Parties should follow the court's local rules and procedures for obtaining a new hearing date.

(3) Any temporary emergency orders will remain in effect until after the end of the new hearing date, unless modified by the court.

(4) The parties should submit the agreement to the court no later than five days before the hearing set on the *Request for Order* (form FL-300), order to show cause, or other moving paper.

(5) The court must approve and sign the agreement to make it a court order.

(6) The court may limit the number of times that parties can agree to reschedule a hearing.

(Subd (c) adopted effective July 1, 2020.)

(d) Reschedule a hearing after the other party was served with the request for order or other moving papers

The procedures in this section apply when a *Request for Order* (form FL-300), order to show cause, or other moving paper was served on the other party as described in rule 5.92 or as ordered by the court and either party seeks to reschedule the hearing date, and the parties are unable to reach an agreement about rescheduling the hearing.

(1) To reschedule a hearing, either party must submit a written request to reschedule before the hearing date as described below in (A) or appear in court on the date of the hearing and orally ask the court to reschedule, as described below in (B):

(A) *Before the date of the hearing*

(i) The party asking to reschedule the hearing must complete a written request and a proposed order. The following forms may be used for this purpose: *Request to Reschedule Hearing* (form FL-306) or *Request to Reschedule Hearing Involving Temporary Emergency (Ex Parte) Orders* (form FL-307), whichever form is appropriate for the case, and *Order on Request to Reschedule Hearing* (form FL-309).

(ii) The party must first notify and serve the other party. Notice and service to the other party of the documents in (i) must be completed as required by rules 5.151 through 5.169.

(iii) The party must file or submit to the court the forms in (i), along with a declaration describing how the other party was notified of the request to reschedule and served the documents. *Declaration Regarding Notice and Service of Request for Temporary Emergency (Ex Parte) Orders* (form FL-303), a local form, or a declaration that contains the same information as form FL-303 may be used for this purpose.

(iv) The party should submit the forms in (iii) to the court no later than five court days before the hearing date set on the *Request for Order* (form FL-300), order to show cause, or other moving paper.

(v) The party responding to a written request to reschedule may file and serve a responsive declaration to the request to reschedule before the court considers the written request. *Responsive Declaration to Request to Reschedule Hearing* (form FL-310) may be used for this purpose.

(B) *On the date of the hearing*

The party asking to reschedule the hearing may appear in court and orally request to reschedule the hearing. The party is not required to file a written request but must complete and submit a proposed *Order on Request to Reschedule Hearing* (form FL-309).

(2) The court may do any of the following:

(A) Grant the request to reschedule the hearing on a showing of good cause or as required by law.

(B) Deny the request to reschedule absent a showing of good cause.

(C) Modify or terminate any temporary emergency (ex parte) orders initially granted with the *Request for Order* (form FL-300), order to show cause, or other moving paper.

(Subd (d) adopted effective July 1, 2020.)

(e) Reschedule a hearing to attend mediation or child custody recommending counseling

(1) When parties need to reschedule a hearing relating to child custody and visitation (parenting time) because they have been unable to attend the family court services appointment, they should follow their local court rules and procedures for requesting and obtaining an order to reschedule the hearing.

(2) If the local court has no local rules and procedures for rescheduling hearings under (1), the parties may:

(A) Complete and file a written agreement (stipulation) for the court to sign as described in (c) of this rule; or

(B) Follow the procedures in (d) to ask for a court order to reschedule the hearing.

(Subd (e) adopted effective July 1, 2020.)
Rule 5.95 adopted effective July 1, 2020.

Rule 5.96.   Place and manner of filing

(a) Papers filed in clerk's office

All papers relating to a request for order proceeding must be filed in the clerk's office, unless otherwise provided by local rule or court order.

(Subd (a) adopted effective January 1, 2013.)

(b) General schedule

The clerk must post a general schedule showing the days and departments for hearing the matters indicated in the *Request for Order* (form FL-300).

(Subd (b) adopted effective January 1, 2013.)

(c) Duty to notify court of settlement

If the matter has been settled before the scheduled court hearing date, the moving party must immediately notify the court of the settlement.

(Subd (c) adopted effective January 1, 2013.)
Rule 5.96 adopted effective January 1, 2013.

Rule 5.97.   Time frames for transferring jurisdiction

(a) Application

This rule applies to family law actions or family law proceedings for which a transfer of jurisdiction has been ordered under part 2 of title 4 of the Code of Civil Procedure.

(Subd (a) adopted effective January 1, 2019.)

(b) Payment of fees; fee waivers

Responsibility for the payment of court costs and fees for the transfer of jurisdiction as provided in Government Code section 70618 is subject to the following provisions:

(1) If a transfer of jurisdiction is ordered in response to a motion made under title 4 of the Code of Civil Procedure by a party, the responsibility for costs and fees is subject to Code of Civil Procedure section 399(a). If the fees are not paid within the time specified in section 399(a), the court may, on a duly noticed motion by any party or on its own motion, dismiss the action without prejudice to the cause of action. Except as provided in (e), no other action on the cause may be commenced in another court before satisfaction of the court's order for fees and costs or a court-ordered waiver of such fees and costs.

(2) If a transfer of jurisdiction is ordered by the court on its own motion, the court must specify in its order which party is responsible for the Government Code section 70618 fees. If that party has not paid the fees within five days of service of notice of the transfer order, any other party interested in the action or proceeding may pay the costs and fees and the clerk must transmit the case file. If the fees are not paid within the time period set forth in Code of Civil Procedure section 399, the court may, on a duly noticed motion by any party or on its own motion, dismiss the action without prejudice to the cause or enter such other orders as the court deems appropriate. Except as provided in (e), no other action on the cause may be commenced in the original court or another court before satisfaction of the court's order for fees and costs or a court-ordered waiver of such fees and costs.

(3) If the party responsible for the fees has been granted a fee waiver by the sending court, the case file must be transmitted as if the fees and costs were paid and the fee waiver order must be transmitted with the case file in lieu of the fees and costs. If a partial fee waiver has been granted, the party responsible for the fees and costs must pay the required portion of the fees and costs before the case will be transmitted. In any case involving a fee waiver, the court receiving the case file has the authority under Government Code section 68636 to review the party's eligibility for a fee waiver based on additional information available to the court or pursuant to a hearing at final disposition of the case.

(4) At the hearing to transfer jurisdiction, the court must address any issues regarding fees. If a litigant indicates they cannot afford to pay the fees, a fee waiver request form should be provided by the clerk and the court should promptly rule on that request.

(Subd (b) adopted effective January 1, 2019.)

(c) Time frame for transfer of jurisdiction

After a court orders the transfer of jurisdiction over the action or proceeding, the clerk must transmit the case file to the clerk of the court to which the action or proceeding is transferred within five court days of the date of expiration of the 20-day time period to petition for a writ of mandate. If a writ is filed, the clerk must transmit the case file within five court days of the notice that the order is final. The clerk must send notice stating the date of the transmittal to all parties who have appeared in the action or proceeding and the court receiving the transfer.

(Subd (c) adopted effective January 1, 2019.)

(d) Time frame to assume jurisdiction over transferred matter

Within 20 court days of the date of the transmittal, the clerk of the court receiving the transferred action or proceeding must send notice to all parties who have appeared in the action or proceeding and the court that ordered the transfer stating the date of the filing of the case and the number assigned to the case in the court.

(Subd (d) adopted effective January 1, 2019.)

(e) Emergency orders while transfer is pending

Until the clerk of the receiving court sends notice of the date of filing, the transferring court retains jurisdiction over the matter to make orders designed to prevent immediate danger or irreparable harm to a party or the children involved in the matter, or immediate loss or damage to property subject to disposition in the matter. When an emergency order is requested, the transferring court must send notice to the receiving court that it is exercising its jurisdiction and must inform the receiving court of the action taken on the request. If the court makes a new order in the case, it must send a copy of the order to the receiving court if the case file has already been transmitted. The transferring court retains jurisdiction over the request until it takes action on it.

(Subd (e) adopted effective January 1, 2019.)

Rule 5.97 adopted effective January 1, 2019.

Article 3
Meet-and-Confer Conferences

Title 5, Family and Juvenile Rules—Division 1, Family Rules—Chapter 6, Request for Court Orders—Article 3, Meet-and-Confer Conferences; adopted effective January 1, 2013.

Rule 5.98.   Meet-and-confer requirements; document exchange

(a) Meet and confer

All parties and all attorneys are required to meet and confer in person, by telephone, or as ordered by the court, before the date of the hearing relating to a *Request for Order* (FL-300). During this time, parties must discuss and make a good faith attempt to settle all issues, even if a complete settlement is not possible and only conditional agreements are made. The requirement to meet and confer does not apply to cases involving domestic violence.

(Subd (a) adopted effective January 1, 2013.)

(b) Document exchange

Before or while conferring, parties must exchange all documentary evidence that is to be relied on for proof of any material fact at the hearing. At the hearing, the court may decline to consider documents that were not given to the other party before the hearing as required under this rule. The requirement to exchange documents does not relate to documents that are submitted primarily for rebuttal or impeachment purposes.

(Subd (b) adopted effective January 1, 2013.)

Rule 5.98 adopted effective January 1, 2013.

Rule 5.100.   Designation of parties [Repealed]

Rule 5.100 repealed effective January 1, 2013; adopted as rule 1210 effective January 1, 1970; previously amended effective January 1, 1999; previously amended and renumbered effective January 1, 2003.

Rule 5.102.   Parties to proceeding [Repealed]

Rule 5.102 repealed effective January 1, 2013; adopted as rule 1211 effective January 1, 1970; previously amended effective January 1, 1977, January 1, 1994, and January 1, 1999; previously amended and renumbered effective January 1, 2003; previously amended effective January 1, 2005.

Rule 5.104.   Other causes of action [Repealed]

Rule 5.104 repealed effective January 1, 2013; adopted as rule 1212 effective January 1, 1970; previously amended effective January 1, 1994, and January 1, 1999; previously amended and renumbered effective January 1, 2003.

Rule 5.106.   Injunctive relief and reservation of jurisdiction [Repealed]

Rule 5.106 repealed effective January 1, 2013; adopted as rule 1213 effective January 1, 1970; previously amended effective January 1, 1994; previously amended and renumbered effective January 1, 2003; previously amended effective January 1, 2007.

Rule 5.108.   Pleadings [Repealed]

Rule 5.108 repealed effective January 1, 2013; adopted as rule 1215 effective January 1, 1970; previously amended effective January 1, 1999; previously amended and renumbered effective January 1, 2003; previously amended effective January 1, 2007.

Rule 5.110.   Summons; restraining order [Repealed]

Rule 5.110 repealed effective January 1, 2013; adopted as rule 1216 effective January 1, 1970; previously amended effective July 1, 1990, January 1, 1994, January 1, 1999; previously amended and renumbered effective January 1, 2003; previously amended effective January 1, 2007.

Article 4
Evidence at Hearings

Title 5, Family and Juvenile Rules—Division 1, Family Rules—Chapter 6, Request for Court Orders—Article 4, Evidence at Hearings; adopted effective January 1, 2013.

Rule 5.111. Declarations supporting and responding to a request for court order

Rule 5.112.1. Declaration page limitation; exemptions

Rule 5.113. Live testimony

Rule 5.115. Judicial notice

Rule 5.111.   Declarations supporting and responding to a request for court order

Along with a *Request for Order* (form FL-300) or a *Responsive Declaration* (form FL-320), a party must file a supporting declaration with the court clerk and serve it on the other party. The declarations must comply with the following requirements:

(a) Length of declarations

A declaration included with a request for court order or a responsive declaration must not exceed 10 pages in length. A reply declaration must not exceed 5 pages in length, unless:

(1) The declaration is of an expert witness; or

(2) The court grants permission to extend the length of a declaration.

(b) Form, format, and content of declarations

(1) The form and format of each declaration submitted in a case filed under the Family Code must comply with the requirements set out in California Rules of Court, rule 2.100 et seq.

(2) A declaration must be based on personal knowledge and explain how the person has acquired that knowledge. The statements in the declaration must be admissible in evidence.

(c) Objections to declarations

(1) If a party thinks that a declaration does not meet the requirements of (b)(2) the party must file their objections in writing at least 2 court days before the time of the hearing, or any objection will be considered waived, and the declaration may be considered as evidence. Upon a finding of good cause, objections may be made in writing or orally at the time of the hearing.

(2) If the court does not specifically rule on the objection raised by a party, the objection is presumed overruled. If an appeal is filed, any presumed overrulings can be challenged.

Rule 5.111 adopted effective January 1, 2013.

Rule 5.112.   Continuing jurisdiction [Repealed]

Rule 5.112 repealed effective January 1, 2013; adopted as rule 1217 effective January 1, 1970; previously amended and renumbered effective January 1, 2003.

Rule 5.112.1.   Declaration page limitation; exemptions

The Judicial Council form portion of a declaration does not count toward the page limitation for declarations specified in rule 5.111. In addition, the following documents may be attached to a *Request for Order* (form FL-300) or *Responsive Declaration* (form FL-320) without being counted toward the page limitation for declarations:

(1) An *Income and Expense Declaration* (form FL-150) and its required attachments;

(2) A *Financial Statement (Simplified)* (form FL-155) and its required attachments;

(3) A *Property Declaration* (form FL-160) and required attachments;

(4) Exhibits attached to declarations; and

(5) A memorandum of points and authorities.

Rule 5.112.1 adopted effective January 1, 2013.

Rule 5.113.   Live testimony

(a) Purpose

Under Family Code section 217, at a hearing on any request for order brought under the Family Code, absent a stipulation of the parties or a finding of good cause under (b), the court must receive any live, competent, and admissible testimony that is relevant and within the scope of the hearing.

(Subd (a) adopted effective January 1, 2013.)

(b) Factors

In addition to the rules of evidence, a court must consider the following factors in making a finding of good cause to refuse to receive live testimony under Family Code section 217:

(1) Whether a substantive matter is at issue—such as child custody, visitation (parenting time), parentage, child support, spousal support, requests for restraining orders, or the characterization, division, or temporary use and control of the property or debt of the parties;

(2) Whether material facts are in controversy;

(3) Whether live testimony is necessary for the court to assess the credibility of the parties or other witnesses;

(4) The right of the parties to question anyone submitting reports or other information to the court;

(5) Whether a party offering testimony from a non-party has complied with Family Code section 217(c); and

(6) Any other factor that is just and equitable.

(Subd (b) adopted effective January 1, 2013.)

(c) Findings

If the court makes a finding of good cause to exclude live testimony, it must state its reasons on the record or in writing. The court is required to state only those factors on which the finding of good cause is based.

(Subd (c) adopted effective January 1, 2013.)

(d) Minor children

When receiving or excluding testimony from minor children, in addition to fulfilling the requirements of Evidence Code section 765, the court must follow the procedures in Family Code section 3042 and rule 5.250 of the California Rules of Court governing children's testimony.

(Subd (d) adopted effective January 1, 2013.)

(e) Witness lists

Witness lists required by Family Code section 217(c) must be served along with the request for order or responsive papers in the manner required for the service of those documents (*Witness List* (form FL-321) may be used for this purpose). If no witness list has been served, the court may require an offer of proof before allowing any nonparty witness to testify.

(Subd (e) adopted effective January 1, 2013.)

(f) Continuance

The court must consider whether or not a brief continuance is necessary to allow a litigant adequate opportunity to prepare for questioning any witness for the other parties. When a brief continuance is granted to allow time to prepare for questioning witnesses, the court should make appropriate temporary orders.

(Subd (f) adopted effective January 1, 2013.)

(g) Questioning by court

Whenever the court receives live testimony from a party or any witness it may elicit testimony by directing questions to the parties and other witnesses.

(Subd (g) adopted effective January 1, 2013.)
Rule 5.113 adopted effective January 1, 2013.

Rule 5.114.   Alternative relief [Repealed]

Rule 5.114 repealed effective January 1, 2013; adopted as rule 1221 effective January 1, 1970; previously amended and renumbered effective January 1, 2003.

Rule 5.115.   Judicial notice

A party requesting judicial notice of material under Evidence Code section 452 or 453 must provide the court and each party with a copy of the material. If the material is part of a file in the court in which the matter is being heard, the party must specify in writing the part of the court file sought to be judicially noticed and make arrangements with the clerk to have the file in the courtroom at the time of the hearing.

Rule 5.115 adopted effective January 1, 2013.

Rule 5.116.   Stipulation for judgment [Repealed]

Rule 5.116 repealed effective January 1, 2013; adopted as rule 1223 effective January 1, 1970; previously amended effective January 1, 1972; previously amended and renumbered effective January 1, 2003.

Rule 5.118.   Declarations supporting and responding to a request for court order [Repealed]

Rule 5.118 repealed effective January 1, 2013; adopted as rule 1225 effective January 1, 1970; previously amended effective January 1, 1972, July 1, 1977, January 1, 1980, and January 1, 1999; previously amended and renumbered effective January 1, 2003; previously amended effective January 1, 2004, January 1, 2007, July 1, 2011, and July 1, 2012.

Rule 5.119.   Live testimony [Repealed]

Rule 5.119 repealed effective January 1, 2013; adopted effective July 1, 2011.

Rule 5.120.   Appearance [Repealed]

Rule 5.120 repealed effective January 1, 2013; adopted as rule 1236 effective January 1, 1970; previously amended effective January 1, 1972, and January 1, 1999; previously amended and renumbered effective January 1, 2003; previously amended effective January 1, 2004, and January 1, 2006.

Rule 5.121.   Motion to quash proceeding or responsive relief [Repealed]

Rule 5.121 repealed effective January 1, 2013; adopted effective January 1, 2004; previously amended effective January 1, 2006.

Rule 5.122.   Default [Repealed]

Rule 5.122 repealed effective January 1, 2013; adopted as rule 1237 effective January 1, 1970; previously amended effective January 1, 1972, and January 1, 1980; previously amended and renumbered effective January 1, 2003; previously amended effective January 1, 2007.

Article 5
Reporting and Preparation of Order After Hearing

Title 5, Family and Juvenile Rules—Division 1, Family Rules—Chapter 6, Request for Court Orders—Article 5, Reporting and Preparation of Order After Hearing; adopted effective January 1, 2013.

Rule 5.123. Reporting of hearing proceedings
Rule 5.125. Preparation, service, and submission of order after hearing

Rule 5.123.   Reporting of hearing proceedings

A court that does not regularly provide for reporting of hearings on a request for order or motion must so state in its local rules. The rules must also provide a procedure by which a party may obtain a court reporter in order to provide the party with an official verbatim transcript.

Rule 5.123 adopted effective January 1, 2013.

Rule 5.124.   Request for default [Repealed]

Rule 5.124 repealed effective January 1, 2013; adopted as rule 1240 effective January 1, 1970; previously amended effective January 1, 1979, and January 1, 1980; previously amended and renumbered effective January 1, 2003.

Rule 5.125.   Preparation, service, and submission of order after hearing

The court may prepare the order after hearing and serve copies on the parties or their attorneys. Alternatively, the court may order one of the parties or attorneys to prepare the proposed order as provided in these rules. The court may also modify the timelines and procedures in this rule when appropriate to the case.

(a) In general

The term "party" or "parties" includes both self-represented persons and persons represented by an attorney of record. The procedures in this rule requiring a party to perform action related to the preparation, service, and submission of an order after hearing include the party's attorney of record.

(b) Submission of proposed order after hearing to the court

Within 10 calendar days of the court hearing, the party ordered to prepare the proposed order must:

(1) Serve the proposed order to the other party for approval; or

(2) If the other party did not appear at the hearing or the matter was uncontested, submit the proposed order directly to the court without the other party's approval. A copy must also be served to the other party or attorney.

(c) Other party approves or rejects proposed order after hearing

(1) Within 20 calendar days from the court hearing, the other party must review the proposed order to determine if it accurately reflects the orders made by the court and take one of the following actions:

(A) Approve the proposed order by signing and serving it on the party or attorney who drafted the proposed order; or

(B) State any objections to the proposed order and prepare an alternate proposed order. Any alternate proposed order prepared by the objecting party must list the findings and orders in the same sequence as the proposed order. After serving any objections and the alternate proposed order to the party or attorney, both parties must follow the procedure in (e).

(2) If the other party does not respond to the proposed order within 20 calendar days of the court hearing, the party ordered to prepare the proposed order must submit the proposed order to the court without approval within 25 calendar days of the hearing date. The correspondence to the court and to the other party must include:

(A) The date the proposed order was served on the other party;

(B) The other party's reasons for not approving the proposed order, if known;

(C) The date and results of any attempts to meet and confer, if relevant; and

(D) A request that the court sign the proposed order.

(d) Failure to prepare proposed order after hearing

(1) If the party ordered by the court to prepare the proposed order fails to serve the proposed order to the other party within 10 calendar days from the court hearing, the other party may prepare the proposed order and serve it to the party or attorney whom the court ordered to prepare the proposed order.

(2) Within 5 calendar days from service of the proposed order, the party who had been ordered to prepare the order must review the proposed order to determine if it accurately reflects the orders made by the court and take one of the following actions:

(A) Approve the proposed order by signing and serving it to the party or attorney who drafted the proposed order; or

(B) State any objections to the proposed order and prepare an alternate proposed order. Any alternate proposed order by the objecting party must list the findings and orders in the same sequence as the proposed order. After serving any objections and the alternate proposed order to the other party or attorney, both parties must follow the procedure in (e).

(3) If the party does not respond as described in (2), the party who prepared the proposed order must submit the proposed order to the court without approval within 5 calendar days. The cover letter to the court and to the other party or attorney must include:

(A) The facts relating to the preparation of the order, including the date the proposed order was due and the date the proposed order was served to the party whom the court ordered to draft the proposed order;

(B) The party's reasons for not preparing or approving the proposed order, if known;

(C) The date and results of any attempts to meet and confer, if relevant; and

(D) A request that the court sign the proposed order.

(e) Objections to proposed order after hearing

(1) If a party objects to the proposed order after hearing, both parties have 10 calendar days following service of the objections and the alternate proposed order after hearing to meet and confer by telephone or in person to attempt to resolve the disputed language.

(2) If the parties reach an agreement, the proposed findings and order after hearing must be submitted to the court within 10 calendar days following the meeting.

(3) If the parties fail to resolve their disagreement after meeting and conferring, each party will have 10 calendar days following the date of the meeting to submit to the court and serve on each other the following documents:

(A) A proposed *Findings and Order After Hearing* (FL-340) (and any form attachments);

(B) A copy of the minute order or official transcript of the court hearing; and

(C) A cover letter that explains the objections, describes the differences in the two proposed orders, references the relevant sections of the transcript or minute order, and includes the date and results of the meet-and-confer conferences.

(f) Unapproved order signed by the court; requirements

Before signing a proposed order submitted to the court without the other party's approval, the court must first compare the proposed order after hearing to the minute order; official transcript, if available; or other court record.

(g) Service of order after hearing signed by the court

After the proposed order is signed by the court, the court clerk must file the order. The party who prepared the order must serve an endorsed-filed copy to the other party.

Rule 5.125 adopted effective January 1, 2013.

Rule 5.126.   Alternate date of valuation [Repealed]

Rule 5.126 repealed effective January 1, 2013; adopted as rule 1242.5 effective July 1, 1995; previously amended and renumbered effective January 1, 2003; previously amended effective July 1, 2003.

Rule 5.128.   Financial declaration [Repealed]

Rule 5.128 repealed effective January 1, 2013; adopted as rule 1243 effective January 1, 1970; previously amended effective January 1, 1972, January 1, 1980, July 1, 1985, and January 1, 1999; previously amended and renumbered effective January 1, 2003.

Article 6
Special Immigrant Juvenile Findings

Title 5, Family and Juvenile Rules—Division 1, Family Rules—Chapter 6, Request for Court Orders—Article 6, Special Immigrant Juvenile Findings; adopted effective July 1, 2016.

Rule 5.130.   Summary dissolution [Repealed]

Rule 5.130 repealed effective January 1, 2013; adopted as rule 1271 effective January 1, 1979; previously amended effective January 1, 1993, and January 1, 1994; previously amended and renumbered effective January 1, 2003; previously amended effective January 1, 2007.

Another Rule 5.130 follows.

Rule 5.130.   Request for Special Immigrant Juvenile findings

(a) Application

This rule applies to a request by or on behalf of a minor child who is a party or the child of a party in a proceeding under the Family Code for the judicial findings needed as a basis for filing a federal petition for classification as a Special Immigrant Juvenile (SIJ). This rule also applies to an opposition to such a request, a hearing on such a request or opposition, and judicial findings in response to such a request.

(Subd (a) adopted effective July 1, 2016.)

(b) Request for findings

Unless otherwise required by law or this rule, the rules in this chapter governing a request for court orders in family law proceedings also apply to a request for SIJ findings in those proceedings.

(1) *Who may file*

Any person—including the child's parent, the child if authorized by statute, the child's guardian ad litem, or an attorney appointed to represent the child—authorized by the Family Code to file a petition, response, request for order, or responsive declaration to a request for order in a proceeding to determine custody of a child may file a request for SIJ findings with respect to that child.

(2) *Form of request*

A request for SIJ findings must be made using *Confidential Request for Special Immigrant Juvenile Findings—Family Law* (form FL-356). The completed form may be filed in any proceeding under the Family Code in which a party is requesting sole physical custody of the child who is the subject of the requested findings:

(A) At the same time as, or any time after, the petition or response;

(B) At the same time as, or any time after, a *Request for Order* (form FL-300) or a *Responsive Declaration to Request for Order* (form FL-320) requesting sole physical custody of the child; or

(C) In an initial action under the Domestic Violence Prevention Act, at the same time as, or any time after, a *Request for Domestic Violence Restraining Order (Domestic Violence Prevention)* (form DV-100) or *Response to Request for Domestic Violence Restraining Order (Domestic Violence Prevention)* (form DV-120) requesting sole physical custody of the child.

(3) *Separate filing*

A request on form FL-356 filed at the same time as any of the papers in (A), (B), or (C) must be filed separately from, and not as an attachment to, that paper.

(4) *Separate form for each child*

A separate form FL-356 must be filed for each child for whom SIJ findings are requested.

(Subd (b) adopted effective July 1, 2016.)

(c) Notice of hearing

Notice of a hearing on a request for SIJ findings must be served with a copy of the request and all supporting papers in the appropriate manner specified in rule 5.92(f)(1), (2) or (3), as applicable, on the following persons:

(1) All parties to the underlying family law case;

(2) All alleged, biological, and presumed parents of the child who is the subject of the request; and

(3) Any other person who has physical custody or is likely to claim a right to physical custody of the child who is the subject of the request.

(Subd (c) amended effective September 1, 2017; adopted effective July 1, 2016.)

(d) Response to request

Any person entitled under (c) to notice of a request for SIJ findings with respect to a child may file and serve a response to such a request using *Confidential Response to Request for Special Immigrant Juvenile Findings* (form FL-358).

(Subd (d) adopted effective July 1, 2016.)

(e) Hearing on request

To obtain a hearing on a request for SIJ findings, a person must file and serve a *Confidential Request for Special Immigrant Juvenile Findings—Family Law* (form FL-356) for each child who is the subject of such a request.

(1) A request for SIJ findings and a request for an order of sole physical custody of the same child may be heard and determined together.

(2) The court may consolidate into one hearing separate requests for SIJ findings for more than one sibling or half sibling named in the same family law case or in separate family law cases.

(3) If custody proceedings relating to siblings or half siblings are pending in multiple departments of a single court or in the courts of more than one California county, the departments or courts may communicate

about consolidation consistent with the procedures and limits in Family Code section 3410(b)–(e).

(Subd (e) adopted effective July 1, 2016.)

(f) Separate findings for each child

The court must make separate SIJ findings with respect to each child for whom a request is made, and the clerk must issue a separate *Special Immigrant Juvenile Findings* (form FL-357) for each child with respect to whom the court makes SIJ findings.

(Subd (f) adopted effective July 1, 2016.)

(g) Confidentiality (Code Civ. Proc., § 155(c))

The forms *Confidential Request for Special Immigrant Juvenile Findings—Family Law* (form FL-356), *Confidential Response to Request for Special Immigrant Juvenile Findings* (form FL-358), and *Special Immigrant Juvenile Findings* (form FL-357) must be kept in a confidential part of the case file or, alternatively, in a separate, confidential file. Any information regarding the child's immigration status contained in a record related to a request for SIJ findings kept in the public part of the file must be redacted to prevent its inspection by any person not authorized under Code of Civil Procedure section 155(c).

(Subd (g) adopted effective July 1, 2016.)

Rule 5.130 amended effective September 1, 2017; adopted effective July 1, 2016.

Rule 5.134. Notice of entry of judgment [Repealed]

Rule 5.134 repealed effective January 1, 2013; adopted as rule 1247 effective January 1, 1970; previously amended effective January 1, 1972, January 1, 1982, and January 1, 1999; previously amended and renumbered effective January 1, 2003; previously amended effective January 1, 2007.

Rule 5.136. Completion of notice of entry of judgment [Repealed]

Rule 5.136 repealed effective January 1, 2013; adopted as rule 1248 effective January 1, 1970; previously amended effective January 1, 1972, January 1, 1980, July 1, 1982, and January 1, 1999; previously amended and renumbered effective January 1, 2003; previously amended effective January 1, 2007.

Rule 5.140. Implied procedures [Repealed]

Rule 5.140 repealed effective January 1, 2013; adopted as rule 1249 effective January 1, 1970; previously amended effective January 1, 1994; previously amended and renumbered effective January 1, 2003.

Rule 5.146. Judgment checklists [Renumbered]

Rule 5.146 renumbered as rule 5.405 effective January 1, 2013; adopted effective July 1, 2012.

Rule 5.147. Review of judgments based on default and uncontested judgments submitted by declaration under Family Code section 2336 [Renumbered]

Rule 5.147 renumbered as rule 5.407 effective January 1, 2013; adopted effective July 1, 2012.

Rule 5.148. Default and uncontested hearings on judgments submitted on the basis of declarations under Family Code section 2336 [Renumbered]

Rule 5.148 renumbered as rule 5.409 effective January 1, 2013; adopted effective July 1, 2012.

Rule 5.150. Joinder of persons claiming interest [Repealed]

Rule 5.150 repealed effective January 1, 2013; adopted as rule 1250 effective November 23, 1970; previously amended effective January 1, 1978; previously renumbered effective January 1, 2003.

Chapter 7
Request for Emergency Orders (Ex Parte Orders)

Title 5, Family and Juvenile Rules—Division 1, Family Rules—Chapter 7, Request for Emergency Orders (Ex Parte Orders); adopted effective January 1, 2013.

Article 1
Request for Emergency Orders (Ex Parte Orders)

Title 5, Family and Juvenile Rules—Division 1, Family Rules—Chapter 7, Request for Emergency Orders (Ex Parte Orders)—Article 1, Request for Emergency Orders (Ex Parte Orders); adopted effective January 1, 2013.

Rule 5.151. Request for temporary emergency (ex parte) orders; application; required documents

(a) Application

The rules in this chapter govern applications for emergency orders (also known as ex parte applications) in family law cases, unless otherwise provided by statute or rule. These rules may be referred to as "the emergency orders rules." Unless specifically stated, these rules do not apply to ex parte applications for domestic violence restraining orders under the Domestic Violence Prevention Act.

(Subd (a) adopted effective January 1, 2013.)

(b) Purpose

The purpose of a request for emergency orders is to address matters that cannot be heard on the court's regular hearing calendar. In this type of proceeding, notice to the other party is shorter than in other proceedings. Notice to the other party can also be waived under exceptional and other circumstances as provided in these rules. The process is used to request that the court:

(1) Make orders to help prevent an immediate danger or irreparable harm to a party or to the children involved in the matter;

(2) Make orders to help prevent immediate loss or damage to property subject to disposition in the case; or

(3) Make orders about procedural matters, including the following:

(A) Setting a date for a hearing on the matter that is sooner than that of a regular hearing (granting an order shortening time for hearing);

(B) Shortening or extending the time required for the moving party to serve the other party with the notice of the hearing and supporting papers (grant an order shortening time for service); and

(C) [1] **Rescheduling** a hearing or trial.

(Subd (b) amended effective July 1, 2020; adopted effective January 1, 2013.)

Rule 5.151(b). 2020 Deletes. [1] Continuing

(c) Required documents

(1) *Request for order*

A request for emergency orders must be in writing and must include all of the following completed documents:

[1] **(A)** *Request for Order* (form FL-300) that identifies the relief requested.

[2] **(B)** When relevant to the relief requested, a current *Income and Expense Declaration* (form FL-150) or *Financial Statement (Simplified)* (form FL-155) and *Property Declaration* (form FL-160).

[3] **(C)** *Temporary Emergency (Ex Parte) Orders* (form FL-305) to serve as the proposed temporary order.

[4] **(D)** A written declaration regarding notice of application for emergency orders based on personal knowledge. *Declaration Regarding Notice and Service of Request for Temporary Emergency (Ex Parte) Orders* (form FL-303), a local court form, or a declaration that contains the same information as form FL-303 may be used for this purpose.

[5] **(E)** A memorandum of points and authorities only if required by the court.

(2) *Request to reschedule hearing*

A request to reschedule a hearing must comply with the requirements of rule 5.95.

(Subd (c) amended effective July 1, 2020; adopted effective January 1, 2013; previously amended effective July 1, 2016.)

Rule 5.151(c). 2020 Deletes. [1] (1) **[2]** (2) **[3]** (3) **[4]** (4) **[5]** (5)

(d) Contents of application and declaration

(1) *Identification of attorney or party*

An application for emergency orders must state the name, address, and telephone number of any attorney known to the applicant to be an attorney for any party or, if no such attorney is known, the name, address, and telephone number of the party, if known to the applicant.

(2) *Affirmative factual showing required in written declarations*

The declarations must contain facts within the personal knowledge of the declarant that demonstrate why the matter is appropriately handled as an emergency hearing, as opposed to being on the court's regular hearing calendar.

An applicant must make an affirmative factual showing of irreparable harm, immediate danger, or any other statutory basis for granting relief without notice or with shortened notice to the other party.

(3) *Disclosure of previous applications and orders*

An applicant should submit a declaration that fully discloses all previous applications made on the same issue and whether any orders were made on any of the applications, even if an application was previously made upon a different state of facts. Previous applications include an order to shorten time for service of notice or an order shortening time for hearing.

(4) *Disclosure of change in status quo*

The applicant has a duty to disclose that an emergency order will result in a change in the current situation or status quo. Absent such disclosure, attorney's fees and costs incurred to reinstate the status quo may be awarded.

(5) *Applications regarding child custody or visitation (parenting time)*

Applications for emergency orders granting or modifying child custody or visitation (parenting time) under Family Code section 3064 must:

(A) Provide a full, detailed description of the most recent incidents showing:

(i) Immediate harm to the child as defined in Family Code section 3064(b); or

(ii) Immediate risk that the child will be removed from the State of California.

(B) Specify the date of each incident described in (A);

(C) Advise the court of the existing custody and visitation (parenting time) arrangements and how they would be changed by the request for emergency orders;

(D) Include a copy of the current custody orders, if they are available. If no orders exist, explain where and with whom the child is currently living; and

(E) Include a completed *Declaration Under Uniform Child Custody Jurisdiction and Enforcement Act (UCCJEA)* (FL-105) if the form was not already filed by a party or if the information has changed since it was filed.

. (Subd (d) adopted effective January 1, 2013.)

(e) Contents of notice and declaration regarding notice of emergency hearing

(1) *Contents of notice*

When notice of a request for emergency orders is given, the person giving notice must:

(A) State with specificity the nature of the relief to be requested;

(B) State the date, time, and place for the presentation of the application;

(C) State the date, time, and place of the hearing, if applicable; and

(D) Attempt to determine whether the opposing party will appear to oppose the application (if the court requires a hearing) or whether he or she will submit responsive pleadings before the court rules on the request for emergency orders.

(2) *Declaration regarding notice*

An application for emergency orders must be accompanied by a completed declaration regarding notice that includes one of the following statements:

(A) The notice given, including the date, time, manner, and name of the party informed, the relief sought, any response, and whether opposition is expected and that, within the applicable time under rule 5.165, the applicant informed the opposing party where and when the application would be made;

(B) That the applicant in good faith attempted to inform the opposing party but was unable to do so, specifying the efforts made to inform opposing party; or

(C) That, for reasons specified, the applicant should not be required to inform the opposing party.

(Subd (e) adopted effective January 1, 2013.)

Rule 5.151 amended effective July 1, 2020; adopted effective January 1, 2013; previously amended effective July 1, 2016.

Rule 5.152.   "Claimant" defined [Repealed]

Rule 5.152 repealed effective January 1, 2013; adopted as rule 1251 effective November 23, 1970; previously amended effective January 1, 1972; previously renumbered effective January 1, 2003.

Rule 5.154.   Persons who may seek joinder [Repealed]

Rule 5.154 repealed effective January 1, 2013; adopted as rule 1252 effective November 23, 1970; previously amended and renumbered effective January 1, 2003; previously amended effective July 1, 1975, January 1, 2006, and January 1, 2007.

Rule 5.156.   Form of joinder application [Repealed]

Rule 5.156 repealed effective January 1, 2013; adopted as rule 1253 effective November 23, 1970; previously amended effective January 1, 1972, January 1, 1978, January 1, 1979, July 1, 1985, January 1, 1994, and January 1, 2001; previously amended and renumbered effective January 1, 2003; previously amended effective January 1, 2007.

Rule 5.158.   Determination on joinder [Repealed]

Rule 5.158 repealed effective January 1, 2013; adopted as rule 1254 effective November 23, 1970; previously amended effective July 1, 1997; previously

amended and renumbered effective January 1, 2003; previously amended effective July 1, 2003, and January 1, 2007.

Rule 5.160.   Pleading rules applicable [Repealed]

Rule 5.160 repealed effective January 1, 2013; adopted as rule 1255 effective November 23, 1970; previously amended and renumbered effective January 1, 2003.

Rule 5.162.   Joinder of employee pension benefit plan [Repealed]

Rule 5.162 repealed effective January 1, 2013; adopted as rule 1256 effective January 1, 1979; previously amended effective January 1, 1994; previously amended and renumbered effective January 1, 2003; previously amended effective January 1, 2007.

Article 2
Notice, Service, Appearance

Title 5, Family and Juvenile Rules—Division 1, Family Rules—Chapter 7, Request for Emergency Orders (Ex Parte Orders)—Article 2, Notice, Service, Appearance; adopted effective January 1, 2013.

Rule 5.165. Requirements for notice
Rule 5.167. Service of application; temporary restraining orders
Rule 5.169. Personal appearance at hearing for temporary emergency orders

Rule 5.165.   Requirements for notice

(a) Method of notice

Notice of appearance at a hearing to request emergency orders may be given **personally or** by telephone, [1] **voicemail, fax transmission, electronic means (if permitted), overnight mail, or other overnight carrier**.

(Subd (a) amended effective July 1, 2020; adopted effective January 1, 2013.)

Rule 5.165(a).   2020 Deletes. [1] in writing, or by voicemail message

(b) Notice to parties

A party seeking emergency orders under this chapter must give notice to all parties or their attorneys so that it is received no later than 10:00 a.m. on the court day before the matter is to be considered by the court. After providing notice, each party must be served with the documents requesting emergency orders as described in rule 5.167 or as required by local rule. This rule does not apply to a party seeking emergency orders under the Domestic Violence Prevention Act.

(1) *Explanation for shorter notice*

If a party provided notice of the request for emergency orders to all parties and their attorneys later than 10:00 a.m. the court day before the appearance, the party must request in a declaration regarding notice that the court approve the shortened notice. The party must provide facts in the declaration that show exceptional circumstances that justify the shorter notice.

(2) *Explanation for waiver of notice (no notice)*

A party may ask the court to waive notice to all parties and their attorneys of the request for emergency orders. To make the request, the party must file a written declaration signed under penalty of perjury that includes facts showing good cause not to give the notice. A judicial officer may approve a waiver of notice for good cause, which may include that:

(A) Giving notice would frustrate the purpose of the order;

(B) Giving notice would result in immediate and irreparable harm to the applicant or the children who may be affected by the order sought;

(C) Giving notice would result in immediate and irreparable damage to or loss of property subject to disposition in the case;

(D) The parties agreed in advance that notice will not be necessary with respect to the matter that is the subject of the request for emergency orders; and

(E) The party made reasonable and good faith efforts to give notice to the other party, and further efforts to give notice would probably be futile or unduly burdensome.

(Subd (b) adopted effective January 1, 2013.)

(c) Notice to the court

The court may adopt a local rule requiring that the party provide additional notice to the court that he or she will be requesting emergency orders the next court day. The local rule must include a method by which the party may give notice to the court by telephone.

(Subd (c) adopted effective January 1, 2013.)

Rule 5.165 amended effective July 1, 2020; adopted effective January 1, 2013.

Rule 5.167.   Service of application; temporary restraining orders

(a) Service of documents requesting emergency orders

A party seeking emergency orders and a party providing written opposition must serve the papers on the other party or on the other party's attorney at the first reasonable opportunity before the hearing. Absent exceptional circumstances, no hearing may be conducted unless such service has been made. The court may waive this requirement in extraordinary circumstances if good cause is shown that imminent harm is likely if documents are provided to the other party before the hearing. This rule does not apply in cases filed under the Domestic Violence Prevention Act.

(Subd (a) adopted effective January 1, 2013.)

(b) Service of temporary emergency orders

If the judicial officer signs the applicant's proposed emergency orders, the applicant must obtain and have the conformed copy of the orders personally served on all parties.

(Subd (b) adopted effective January 1, 2013.)
Rule 5.167 adopted effective January 1, 2013.

Rule 5.169.   Personal appearance at hearing for temporary emergency orders

Courts may require all parties to appear at a hearing before ruling on a request for emergency orders. Courts may also make emergency orders based on the documents submitted without requiring the parties to appear at a hearing.
Rule 5.169 adopted effective January 1, 2013.

Article 3
Procedural Matters Not Requiring Notice (Non-Emergency Orders)

Title 5, Family and Juvenile Rules—Division 1, Family Rules—Chapter 7, Request for Emergency Orders (Ex Parte Orders)—Article 3, Procedural Matters Not Requiring Notice (Non-Emergency Orders); adopted effective January 1, 2013.

Rule 5.170.   Matters not requiring notice to other parties

The courts may consider a party's request for order on the following issues without notice to the other parties or personal appearance at a hearing:

(1) Applications to restore a former name after judgment;

(2) Stipulations by the parties;

(3) An order or judgment after a default court hearing;

(4) An earnings assignment order based on an existing support order;

(5) An order for service of summons by publication or posting;

(6) An order or judgment that the other party or opposing counsel approved or agreed not to oppose; and

(7) Application for an order waiving filing fees.
Rule 5.170 adopted effective January 1, 2013.

Rule 5.175.   Bifurcation of issues [Repealed]

Rule 5.175 repealed effective January 1, 2013; adopted as rule 1269 effective July 1, 1989; previously amended effective January 1, 1994; previously amended and renumbered effective January 1, 2003; previously amended effective July 1, 2009.

Rule 5.180.   Interlocutory appeals [Renumbered]

Rule 5.180 renumbered as rule 5.392 effective January 1, 2013; adopted as rule 1269.5 effective July 1, 1989; previously amended effective January 1, 1994, and January 1, 2002; amended and renumbered effective January 1, 2003; previously amended effective January 1, 2007.

Chapter 8
Child Custody and Visitation (Parenting Time) Proceedings

Title 5, Family and Juvenile Rules—Division 1, Family Rules—Chapter 8, Child Custody and Visitation (Parenting Time) Proceedings; adopted effective January 1, 2013.

Art. 1.   Child Custody Mediation. Rules 5.210, 5.215.
Art. 2.   Child Custody Investigations and Evaluations. Rules 5.220–5.230.
Art. 3.   Ex parte Communication. Rule 5.235.
Art. 4.   Counsel Appointed to Represent a Child. Rules 5.240–5.242.
Art. 5.   Children's Participation in Family Court. Rule 5.250.

Article 1
Child Custody Mediation

Title 5, Family and Juvenile Rules—Division 1, Family Rules—Chapter 8, Child Custody and Visitation (Parenting Time) Proceedings—Article 1, Child Custody Mediation; adopted effective January 1, 2013.

Rule 5.210. Court-connected child custody mediation
Rule 5.215. Domestic violence protocol for Family Court Services

Rule 5.210.   Court-connected child custody mediation

(a) Authority

This rule of court is adopted under article VI, section 6 of the California Constitution and Family Code sections 211, 3160, and 3162(a).

(b) Purpose

This rule sets forth standards of practice and administration for court-connected child custody mediation services that are consistent with the requirements of Family Code section 3161.

(c) Definitions

(1) "Best interest of the child" is defined in Family Code section 3011.

(2) "Parenting plan" is a plan describing how parents or other appropriate parties will share and divide their decision making and caretaking responsibilities to protect the health, safety, welfare, and best interest of each child who is a subject of the proceedings.

(d) Responsibility for mediation services

(1) Each court must ensure that:

(A) Mediators are impartial, competent, and uphold the standards of practice contained in this rule of court.

(B) Mediation services and case management procedures implement state law and allow sufficient time for parties to receive orientation, participate fully in mediation, and develop a comprehensive parenting plan without unduly compromising each party's right to due process and a timely resolution of the issues.

(C) Mediation services demonstrate accountability by:

(i) Providing for acceptance of and response to complaints about a mediator's performance;

(ii) Participating in statewide data collection efforts; and

(iii) Disclosing the use of interns to provide mediation services.

(D) The mediation program uses a detailed intake process that screens for, and informs the mediator about, any restraining orders or safety-related issues affecting any party or child named in the proceedings to allow compliance with relevant law or court rules before mediation begins.

(E) Whenever possible, mediation is available from bilingual mediators or other interpreter services that meet the requirements of Evidence Code sections 754(f) and 755(a) and section 18 of the California Standards of Judicial Administration.

(F) Mediation services protect, in accordance with existing law, party confidentiality in:

(i) Storage and disposal of records and any personal information accumulated during the mediation process;

(ii) Interagency coordination or cooperation regarding a particular family or case; and

(iii) Management of child abuse reports and related documents.

(G) Mediation services provide a written description of limitations on the confidentiality of the process.

(H) Within one year of the adoption of this rule, the court adopts a local court rule regarding ex parte communications.

(2) Each court-connected mediator must:

(A) Maintain an overriding concern to integrate the child's best interest within the family context;

(B) Inform the parties and any counsel for a minor child if the mediator will make a recommendation to the court as provided under Family Code section 3184; and

(C) Use reasonable efforts and consider safety issues to:

(i) Facilitate the family's transition and reduce acrimony by helping the parties improve their communication skills, focus on the child's needs and areas of stability, identify the family's strengths, and locate counseling or other services;

(ii) Develop a comprehensive parenting agreement that addresses each child's current and future developmental needs; and

(iii) Control for potential power imbalances between the parties during mediation.

(Subd (d) amended effective January 1, 2007; previously amended effective January 1, 2002, and January 1, 2003.)

(e) Mediation process

All court-connected mediation processes must be conducted in accordance with state law and include:

(1) Review of the intake form and court file, if available, before the start of mediation;

(2) Oral or written orientation or parent education that facilitates the parties' informed and self-determined decision making about:

(A) The types of disputed issues generally discussed in mediation and the range of possible outcomes from the mediation process;

(B) The mediation process, including the mediator's role; the circumstances that may lead the mediator to make a particular recommendation to the court; limitations on the confidentiality of the process; and access to information communicated by the parties or included in the mediation file;

(C) How to make best use of information drawn from current research and professional experience to facilitate the mediation process, parties' communication, and co-parenting relationship; and

(D) How to address each child's current and future developmental needs;

(3) Interviews with children at the mediator's discretion and consistent with Family Code section 3180(a). The mediator may interview the child alone or together with other interested parties, including stepparents, siblings, new or step-siblings, or other family members significant to the child. If interviewing a child, the mediator must:

(A) Inform the child in an age-appropriate way of the mediator's obligation to disclose suspected child abuse and neglect and the local policies concerning disclosure of the child's statements to the court; and

(B) With parental consent, coordinate interview and information exchange among agency or private professionals to reduce the number of interviews a child might experience;

(4) Assistance to the parties, without undue influence or personal bias, in developing a parenting plan that protects the health, safety, welfare, and best interest of the child and that optimizes the child's relationship with each party by including, as appropriate, provisions for supervised visitation in high-risk cases; designations for legal and physical custody; a description of each party's authority to make decisions that affect the child; language that minimizes legal, mental health, or other jargon; and a detailed schedule of the time a child is to spend with each party, including vacations, holidays, and special occasions, and times when the child's contact with a party may be interrupted;

(5) Extension of time to allow the parties to gather additional information if the mediator determines that such information will help the discussion proceed in a fair and orderly manner or facilitate an agreement;

(6) Suspension or discontinuance of mediation if allegations of child abuse or neglect are made until a designated agency performs an investigation and reports a case determination to the mediator;

(7) Termination of mediation if the mediator believes that he or she is unable to achieve a balanced discussion between the parties;

(8) Conclusion of mediation with:

(A) A written parenting plan summarizing the parties' agreement or mediator's recommendation that is given to counsel or the parties before the recommendation is presented to the court; and

(B) A written or oral description of any subsequent case management or court procedures for resolving one or more outstanding custody or visitation issues, including instructions for obtaining temporary orders;

(9) Return to mediation to resolve future custody or visitation disputes.

(Subd (e) amended effective January 1, 2007; previously amended effective January 1, 2003.)

(f) Training, continuing education, and experience requirements for mediator, mediation supervisor, and family court services director

As specified in Family Code sections 1815 and 1816:

(1) All mediators, mediation supervisors, and family court service directors must:

(A) Complete a minimum of 40 hours of custody and visitation mediation training within the first six months of initial employment as a court-connected mediator;

(B) Annually complete 8 hours of related continuing education programs, conferences, and workshops. This requirement is in addition to the annual 4-hour domestic violence update training described in rule 5.215; and

(C) Participate in performance supervision and peer review.

(2) Each mediation supervisor and family court services director must complete at least 24 hours of additional training each calendar year. This requirement may be satisfied in part by the domestic violence training required by Family Code section 1816.

(Subd (f) amended effective January 1, 2005; previously amended effective January 1, 2003.)

(g) Education and training providers

Only education and training acquired from eligible providers meet the requirements of this rule. "Eligible providers" includes the Judicial Council and may include educational institutions, professional associations, professional continuing education groups, public or private for-profit or not-for-profit groups, and court-connected groups.

(1) Eligible providers must:

(A) Ensure that the training instructors or consultants delivering the education and training programs either meet the requirements of this rule or are experts in the subject matter;

(B) Monitor and evaluate the quality of courses, curricula, training, instructors, and consultants;

(C) Emphasize the importance of focusing child custody mediations on the health, safety, welfare, and best interest of the child;

(D) Develop a procedure to verify that participants complete the education and training program; and

(E) Distribute a certificate of completion to each person who has completed the training. The certificate must document the number of hours of training offered, the number of hours the person completed, the dates of the training, and the name of the training provider.

(2) Effective July 1, 2005, all education and training programs must be approved by Judicial Council staff in consultation with the Family and Juvenile Law Advisory Committee.

(Subd (g) amended effective January 1, 2016; adopted effective January 1, 2005.)

(h) Ethics

Mediation must be conducted in an atmosphere that encourages trust in the process and a perception of fairness. To that end, mediators must:

(1) Meet the practice and ethical standards of the Code of Ethics for the Court Employees of California and of related law;

(2) Maintain objectivity, provide and gather balanced information for both parties, and control for bias;

(3) Protect the confidentiality of the parties and the child in making any collateral contacts and not release information about the case to any individual except as authorized by the court or statute;

(4) Not offer any recommendations about a party unless that party has been evaluated directly or in consultation with another qualified neutral professional;

(5) Consider the health, safety, welfare, and best interest of the child in all phases of the process, including interviews with parents, extended family members, counsel for the child, and other interested parties or collateral contacts;

(6) Strive to maintain the confidential relationship between the child who is the subject of an evaluation and his or her treating psychotherapist;

(7) Operate within the limits of his or her training and experience and disclose any limitations or bias that would affect his or her ability to conduct the mediation;

(8) Not require children to state a custodial preference;

(9) Not disclose any recommendations to the parties, their attorneys, or the attorney for the child before having gathered the information necessary to support the conclusion;

(10) Disclose to the court, parties, attorneys for the parties, and attorney for the child conflicts of interest or dual relationships and not accept any appointment except by court order or the parties' stipulation;

(11) Be sensitive to the parties' socioeconomic status, gender, race, ethnicity, cultural values, religion, family structures, and developmental characteristics; and

(12) Disclose any actual or potential conflicts of interest. In the event of a conflict of interest, the mediator must suspend mediation and meet and confer in an effort to resolve the conflict of interest to the satisfaction of all parties or according to local court rules. The court may order mediation to continue with another mediator or offer the parties alternatives. The mediator cannot continue unless the parties agree in writing to continue mediation despite the disclosed conflict of interest.

(Subd (h) amended effective January 1, 2007; adopted as subd (g) effective July 1, 2001; previously amended effective January 1, 2003; previously relettered effective January 1, 2005.)

Rule 5.210 amended effective January 1, 2016; adopted as rule 1257.1 effective July 1, 2001; amended and renumbered as rule 5.210 effective January 1, 2003; previously amended effective January 1, 2003, January 1, 2005, and January 1, 2007.

Rule 5.215. Domestic violence protocol for Family Court Services

(a) Authority

This rule of court is adopted under Family Code sections 211, 1850(a), and 3170(b).

(Subd (a) amended effective January 1, 2007.)

(b) Purpose

This rule sets forth the protocol for Family Court Services' handling of domestic violence cases consistent with the requirement of Family Code section 3170(b).

(c) Definitions

(1) "Domestic violence" is used as defined in Family Code sections 6203 and 6211.

(2) "Protective order" is used as defined in Family Code section 6215, "Emergency protective order"; Family Code section 6218, "Protective order"; and Penal Code section 136.2 (orders by court). "Domestic violence restraining order" is synonymous with "protective order."

(3) "Mediation" refers to proceedings described in Family Code section 3161.

(4) "Evaluation" and "investigation" are synonymous terms.

(5) "Family Court Services" refers to court-connected child custody services and child custody mediation made available by superior courts under Family Code section 3160.

(6) "Family Court Services staff" refers to contract and employee mediators, evaluators, investigators, and counselors who provide services on behalf of Family Court Services.

(7) "Differential domestic violence assessment" is a process used to assess the nature of any domestic violence issues in the family so that Family Court Services may provide services in such a way as to protect any victim of domestic violence from intimidation, provide services for perpetrators, and correct for power imbalances created by past and prospective violence.

(Subd (c) amended effective January 1, 2003.)

(d) Family Court Services: Description and duties

(1) *Local protocols*

Family Court Services must handle domestic violence cases in accordance with pertinent state laws and all applicable rules of court and must develop local protocols in accordance with this rule.

(2) *Family Court Services duties relative to domestic violence cases*

Family Court Services is a court-connected service that must:

(A) Identify cases in Family Court Services that involve domestic violence, and code Family Court Services files to identify such cases;

(B) Make reasonable efforts to ensure the safety of victims, children, and other parties when they are participating in services provided by Family Court Services;

(C) Make appropriate referrals; and

(D) Conduct a differential domestic violence assessment in domestic violence cases and offer appropriate services as available, such as child custody evaluation, parent education, parent orientation, supervised visitation, child custody mediation, relevant education programs for children, and other services as determined by each superior court.

(3) *No negotiation of violence*

Family Court Services staff must not negotiate with the parties about using violence with each other, whether either party should or should not obtain or dismiss a restraining order, or whether either party should cooperate with criminal prosecution.

(4) *Domestic violence restraining orders*

Notwithstanding the above, to the extent permitted under Family Code section 3183(c), in appropriate cases, Family Court Services staff may recommend that restraining orders be issued, pending determination of the controversy, to protect the well-being of the child involved in the controversy.

(5) *Providing information*

Family Court Services staff must provide information to families accessing their services about the effects of domestic violence on adults and children. Family Court Services programs, including but not limited to orientation programs, must provide information and materials that describe Family Court Services policy and procedures with respect to domestic violence. Whenever possible, information delivered in video or audiovisual format should be closed-captioned.

(6) *Separate sessions*

In a Family Court Services case in which there has been a history of domestic violence between the parties or in which a protective order as defined in Family Code section 6218 is in effect, at the request of the party who is alleging domestic violence in a written declaration under penalty of perjury or who is protected by the order, the Family Court Services mediator, counselor, evaluator, or investigator must meet with the parties separately and at separate times. When appropriate, arrangements for separate sessions must protect the confidentiality of each party's times of arrival, departure, and meeting with Family Court Services. Family Court Services must provide information to the parties regarding their options for separate sessions under Family Code sections 3113 and 3181. If domestic violence is discovered after mediation or evaluation has begun, the Family Court Services staff member assigned to the case must confer with the parties separately regarding safety-related issues and the option of continuing in separate sessions at separate times. Family Court Services staff, including support staff, must not respond to a party's request for separate sessions as though it were evidence of his or her lack of cooperation with the Family Court Services process.

(7) *Referrals*

Family Court Services staff, where applicable, must refer family members to appropriate services. Such services may include but are not limited to programs for perpetrators, counseling and education for children, parent education, services for victims, and legal resources, such as family law facilitators.

(8) *Community resources*

Family Court Services should maintain a liaison with community-based services offering domestic violence prevention assistance and support so that referrals can be made based on an understanding of available services and service providers.

(Subd (d) amended effective January 1, 2016; previously amended effective January 1, 2003.)

(e) Intake

(1) *Court responsibility*

Each court must ensure that Family Court Services programs use a detailed intake process that screens for, and informs staff about, any restraining orders, dependency petitions under Welfare and Institutions Code section 300, and other safety-related issues affecting any party or child named in the proceedings.

(2) *Intake form*

Any intake form that an agency charged with providing family court services requires the parties to complete before the commencement of mediation or evaluation must state that, if a party alleging domestic violence in a written declaration under penalty of perjury or a party protected by a protective order so requests, the Family Court Services staff must meet with the parties separately and at separate times.

(3) *Review of intake form and case file*

All Family Court Services procedures must be conducted in accordance with state law and must include review of intake forms and court files, when available, by appropriate staff.

(f) Screening

(1) *Identification of domestic violence*

Screening for a history of domestic violence incidents must be done throughout the Family Court Services process. As early in the case as possible, Family Court Services staff should make every effort to identify cases in which incidents of domestic violence are present. The means by which Family Court Services elicits screening information may be determined by each program. Screening techniques may include but are not limited to questionnaires, telephone interviews, standardized screening devices, and face-to-face interviews.

(2) *Procedures for identification*

Procedures for identifying domestic violence may include, but are not limited to: (a) determination of an existing emergency protective order or domestic violence restraining order concerning the parties or minor; (b) review of court papers and declarations; (c) telephone interviews; (d) use of an intake form; (e) orientation; (f) information from attorneys, shelters, hospital reports, Child Protective Services, police reports, and criminal background checks; and (g) other collateral sources. Questions specific to incidents of domestic violence should request the following information: date of the parties' separation, frequency of domestic violence, most recent as well as past incidents of domestic violence, concerns about future domestic violence, identities of children and other individuals present at domestic violence incidents or otherwise exposed to the domestic violence, and severity of domestic violence.

(3) *Context for screening*

In domestic violence cases in which neither party has requested separate sessions at separate times, Family Court Services staff must confer with the parties separately and privately to determine whether joint or separate sessions are appropriate.

(g) Safety issues

(1) *Developing a safety plan*

When domestic violence is identified or alleged in a case, Family Court Services staff must consult with the party alleging domestic violence away from the presence of the party against whom such allegations are made and discuss the existence of or need for a safety plan. Safety planning may include but is not limited to discussion of safe housing, workplace safety, safety for other family members and children, access to financial resources, and information about local domestic violence agencies.

(2) *Safety procedures*

Each Family Court Services office should develop safety procedures for handling domestic violence cases.

(3) *Confidential addresses*

Where appropriate, Family Court Services staff must make reasonable efforts to keep residential addresses, work addresses, and contact information—including but not limited to telephone numbers and e-mail addresses—confidential in all cases and on all Family Court Services documents.

(Subd (g) amended effective January 1, 2007.)

(h) Support persons

(1) *Support person*

Family Court Services staff must advise the party protected by a protective order of the right to have a support person attend any mediation orientation or mediation sessions, including separate mediation sessions, under Family Code section 6303.

(2) *Excluding support person*

A Family Court Services staff person may exclude a domestic violence support person from a mediation session if the support person participates in the mediation session or acts as an advocate or the presence of a particular support person disrupts the process of mediation. The presence of the support person does not waive the confidentiality of the process, and the support person is bound by the confidentiality of the process.

(Subd (h) amended effective January 1, 2003.)

(i) Accessibility of services

To effectively address domestic violence cases, the court must make reasonable efforts to ensure the availability of safe and accessible services that include, but are not limited to:

(1) *Language accessibility*

Whenever possible, Family Court Services programs should be conducted in the languages of all participants, including those who are deaf. When the participants use only a language other than spoken English and the Family Court Services staff person does not speak their language, an interpreter—certified whenever possible—should be assigned to interpret at the session. A minor child of the parties must not be used as an interpreter. An adult family member may act as an interpreter only when appropriate interpreters are not available. When a family member is acting as an interpreter, Family Court Services staff should attempt to establish, away from the presence of the potential interpreter and the other party, whether the person alleging domestic violence is comfortable with having that family member interpret for the parties.

(2) *Facilities design*

To minimize contact between the parties and promote safety in domestic violence cases, courts must give consideration to the design of facilities. Such considerations must include but are not limited to the following: separate and secure waiting areas, separate conference rooms for parent education and mediation, signs providing directions to Family Court Services, and secure parking for users of Family Court Services.

(j) Training and education

(1) *Training, continuing education, and experience requirements for Family Court Services staff*

All Family Court Services staff must participate in programs of continuing instruction in issues related to domestic violence, including child abuse, as may be arranged for and provided to them, under Family Code section 1816(a).

(2) *Advanced domestic violence training*

Family Court Services staff must complete 16 hours of advanced domestic violence training within the first 12 months of employment and 4 hours of domestic violence update training each year thereafter. The content of the 16 hours of advanced domestic violence training and 4 hours of domestic violence update training must be the same as that required for court-appointed child custody investigators and evaluators as stated in rule 5.230. Those staff members employed by Family Court Services on January 1, 2002, who have not already fulfilled the require-

ments of rule 5.230 must participate in the 16-hour training within one year of the rule's effective date.

(3) *Support staff*

Family Court Services programs should, where possible, enable support staff, including but not limited to clerical staff, to participate in training on domestic violence and in handling domestic violence cases appropriately.

(Subd (j) amended effective January 1, 2003.)

Rule 5.215 amended effective January 1, 2016; adopted as rule 1257.2 effective January 1, 2002; previously amended and renumbered as rule 5.215 effective January 1, 2003; previously amended effective January 1, 2007.

Article 2
Child Custody Investigations and Evaluations

Title 5, Family and Juvenile Rules—Division 1, Family Rules—Chapter 8, Child Custody and Visitation (Parenting Time) Proceedings—Article 2, Child Custody Investigations and Evaluations; adopted effective January 1, 2013.

Rule 5.220. Court-ordered child custody evaluations
Rule 5.225. Appointment requirements for child custody evaluators
Rule 5.230. Domestic violence training standards for court-appointed child custody investigators and evaluators

Rule 5.220.   Court-ordered child custody evaluations

(a) Authority

This rule of court is adopted under Family Code sections 211 and 3117.
(Subd (a) amended effective January 1, 2007.)

(b) Purpose

Courts order child custody evaluations, investigations, and assessments to assist them in determining the health, safety, welfare, and best [1] **interests** of children with regard to disputed custody and visitation issues. This rule governs both court-connected and private child custody evaluators appointed under Family Code section 3111, **Family Code section 3118,** Evidence Code section 730, or **chapter 15 (commencing with section 2032.010) of title 4, part 4 of the** Code of Civil Procedure [2].

(Subd (b) amended effective January 1, 2021; previously amended effective January 1, 2003.)

Rule 5.220(b).   2020 Deletes. [1]&\ebf; interest [2] section 2032

(c) Definitions

For purposes of this rule:

(1) A "child custody evaluator" is a court-appointed investigator as defined in Family Code section 3110.

(2) The "best interest of the child" is as defined in Family Code section 3011.

(3) A "child custody evaluation" is an expert investigation and analysis of the health, safety, welfare, and best interest of children with regard to disputed custody and visitation issues.

(4) A "full evaluation, investigation, or assessment" is a comprehensive examination of the health, safety, welfare, and best interest of the child.

(5) A "partial evaluation, investigation, or assessment" is an examination of the health, safety, welfare, and best interest of the child that is limited by court order in either time or scope.

(6) "Evaluation," "investigation," and "assessment" are synonymous.
(Subd (c) amended effective January 1, 2003.)

(d) Responsibility for evaluation services

(1) Each court must:

(A) Adopt a local rule by January 1, 2000, to:

(i) Implement this rule of court;

(ii) Determine whether a peremptory challenge to a court-appointed evaluator is allowed and when the challenge must be exercised. The rules must specify whether a family court services staff member, other county employee, a mental health professional, or all of them may be challenged;

(iii) Allow evaluators to petition the court to withdraw from a case;

(iv) Provide for acceptance of and response to complaints about an evaluator's performance; and

(v) Address ex parte communications.

(B) Give the evaluator, before the evaluation begins, a copy of the court order that specifies:

(i) The appointment of the evaluator under Evidence Code section 730, Family Code section 3110, or Code of Civil Procedure 2032; and

(ii) The purpose and scope of the evaluation.

(C) Require child custody evaluators to adhere to the requirements of this rule.

(D) Determine and allocate between the parties any fees or costs of the evaluation.

(2) The child custody evaluator must:

(A) Consider the health, safety, welfare, and best interest of the child within the scope and purpose of the evaluation as defined by the court order;

(B) Strive to minimize the potential for psychological trauma to children during the evaluation process; and

(C) Include in the initial meeting with each child an age-appropriate explanation of the evaluation process, including limitations on the confidentiality of the process.

(Subd (d) amended effective January 1, 2007; previously amended effective January 1, 2003.)

(e) Scope of evaluations

All evaluations must include:

(1) A written explanation of the process that clearly describes the:

(A) Purpose of the evaluation;

(B) Procedures used and the time required to gather and assess information and, if psychological tests will be used, the role of the results in confirming or questioning other information or previous conclusions;

(C) Scope and distribution of the evaluation report;

(D) Limitations on the confidentiality of the process; and

(E) Cost and payment responsibility for the evaluation.

(2) Data collection and analysis that are consistent with the requirements of Family Code section 3118; that allow the evaluator to observe and consider each party in comparable ways and to substantiate (from multiple sources when possible) interpretations and conclusions regarding each child's developmental needs; the quality of attachment to each parent and that parent's social environment; and reactions to the separation, divorce, or parental conflict. This process may include:

(A) Reviewing pertinent documents related to custody, including local police records;

(B) Observing parent-child interaction (unless contraindicated to protect the best interest of the child);

(C) Interviewing parents conjointly, individually, or both conjointly and individually (unless contraindicated in cases involving domestic violence), to assess:

(i) Capacity for setting age-appropriate limits and for understanding and responding to the child's needs;

(ii) History of involvement in caring for the child;

(iii) Methods for working toward resolution of the child custody conflict;

(iv) History of child abuse, domestic violence, substance abuse, and psychiatric illness; and

(v) Psychological and social functioning;

(D) Conducting age-appropriate interviews and observation with the children, both parents, stepparents, step- and half-siblings conjointly, separately, or both conjointly and separately, unless contraindicated to protect the best interest of the child;

(E) Collecting relevant corroborating information or documents as permitted by law; and

(F) Consulting with other experts to develop information that is beyond the evaluator's scope of practice or area of expertise.

[1]

(Subd (e) amended effective January 1, 2021; previously amended effective January 1, 2003, July 1, 2003, and January 1, 2007.)

Rule 5.220(e). 2020 Deletes. [1] (3) A written or oral presentation of findings that is consistent with Family Code section 3111, Family Code section 3118, or Evidence Code section 730. In any presentation of findings, the evaluator must: (A) Summarize the data-gathering procedures, information sources, and time spent, and present all relevant information, including information that does not support the conclusions reached; (B) Describe any limitations in the evaluation that result from unobtainable information, failure of a party to cooperate, or the circumstances of particular interviews; (C) Only make a custody or visitation recommendation for a party who has been evaluated. This requirement does not preclude the evaluator from making an interim recommendation that is in the best interest of the child; and (D) Provide clear, detailed recommendations that are consistent with the health, safety, welfare, and best interest of the child if making any recommendations to the court regarding a parenting plan.

(f) Presentation of findings

All evaluations must include a written or oral presentation of findings that is consistent with Family Code section 3111, Family Code section 3118, or Evidence Code section 730. In any presentation of findings, the evaluator must do all of the following:

(1) Summarize the data-gathering procedures, information sources, and time spent, and present all relevant information, including information that does not support the conclusions reached;

(2) Describe any limitations in the evaluation that result from unobtainable information, failure of a party to cooperate, or the circumstances of particular interviews;

(3) Only make a custody or visitation recommendation for a party who has been evaluated. This requirement does not preclude the evaluator from making an interim recommendation that is in the best interests of the child; and

(4) Provide clear, detailed recommendations that are consistent with the health, safety, welfare, and best interests of the child if making any recommendations to the court regarding a parenting plan.

(Subd (f) adopted effective January 1, 2021.)

(g) Confidential written report; requirements

(1) *Family Code section 3111 evaluations.* An evaluator appointed under Family Code section 3111 must do all of the following:

(A) File and serve a report on the parties or their attorneys and any attorney appointed for the child under Family Code section 3150; and

(B) Attach a *Notice Regarding Confidentiality of Child Custody Evaluation Report* (form FL-328) as the first page of the child custody evaluation report when a court-ordered child custody evaluation report is filed with the clerk of the court and served on the parties or their attorneys, and any counsel appointed for the child, to inform them of the confidential nature of the report and the potential consequences for the unwarranted disclosure of the report.

(2) *Family Code section 3118 evaluations.* An evaluator appointed to conduct a child custody evaluation, investigation, or assessment based on (1) a serious allegation of child sexual abuse; or (2) an allegation of child abuse under Family Code section 3118 must do all of the following:

(A) Provide a full and complete analysis of the allegations raised in the proceeding and address the health, safety, welfare, and best interests of the child, as ordered by the court;

(B) Complete, file, and serve *Confidential Child Custody Evaluation Report* (form FL-329) on the parties or their attorneys and any attorney appointed for the child under Family Code section 3150; and

(C) Attach *Notice Regarding Confidentiality of Child Custody Evaluation Report* (form FL-328) as the first page of the child custody evaluation report in (B) to inform the parties or their attorneys of the confidential nature of the report and the potential consequences for the unwarranted disclosure of the report.

(Subd (g) adopted effective January 1, 2021.)

(h) Cooperation with professionals in another jurisdiction

When one party resides in another jurisdiction, the custody evaluator may rely on another qualified neutral professional for assistance in gathering information. In order to ensure a thorough and comparably reliable out-of-jurisdiction evaluation, the evaluator must:

(1) Make a written request that includes, as appropriate:

(A) A copy of all relevant court orders;

(B) An outline of issues to be explored;

(C) A list of the individuals who must or may be contacted;

(D) A description of the necessary structure and setting for interviews;

(E) A statement as to whether a home visit is required;

(F) A request for relevant documents such as police records, school reports, or other document review; and

(G) A request that a written report be returned only to the evaluator and that no copies of the report be distributed to parties or attorneys;

(2) Provide instructions that limit the out-of-jurisdiction report to factual matters and behavioral observations rather than recommendations regarding the overall custody plan; and

(3) Attach and discuss the report provided by the professional in another jurisdiction in the evaluator's final report.

(Subd (h) relettered effective January 1, 2021; adopted as subd (f); previously amended effective January 1, 2003.)

(i) Requirements for evaluator qualifications, training, continuing education, and experience

All child custody evaluators must meet the qualifications, training, and continuing education requirements specified in Family Code sections 1815, 1816, and 3111, and rules 5.225 and 5.230.

(Subd (i) repealed and relettered effective January 1, 2021; adopted as subd (g); previously amended effective July 1, 1999, January 1, 2003, and January 1, 2004.)

(j) Ethics

In performing an evaluation, the child custody evaluator must:

(1) Maintain objectivity, provide and gather balanced information for both parties, and control for bias;

(2) Protect the confidentiality of the parties and children in collateral contacts and not release information about the case to any individual except as authorized by the court or statute;

(3) Not offer any recommendations about a party unless that party has been evaluated directly or in consultation with another qualified neutral professional;

(4) Consider the health, safety, welfare, and best interest of the child in all phases of the process, including interviews with parents, extended family members, counsel for the child, and other interested parties or collateral contacts;

(5) Strive to maintain the confidential relationship between the child who is the subject of an evaluation and his or her treating psychotherapist;

(6) Operate within the limits of the evaluator's training and experience and disclose any limitations or bias that would affect the evaluator's ability to conduct the evaluation;

(7) Not pressure children to state a custodial preference;

(8) Inform the parties of the evaluator's reporting requirements, including, but not limited to, suspected child abuse and neglect and threats to harm one's self or another person;

(9) Not disclose any recommendations to the parties, their attorneys, or the attorney for the child before having gathered the information necessary to support the conclusion;

(10) Disclose to the court, parties, attorney for a party, and attorney for the child conflicts of interest or dual relationships; and not accept any appointment except by court order or the parties' stipulation; and

(11) Be sensitive to the socioeconomic status, gender, race, ethnicity, cultural values, religion, family structures, and developmental characteristics of the parties.

(Subd (j) relettered effective January 1, 2021; adopted as subd (h); previously amended effective January 1, 2003, and January 1, 2007.)

(k) Cost-effective procedures for cross-examination of evaluators

Each local court must develop procedures for expeditious and cost-effective cross-examination of evaluators, including, but not limited to, consideration of the following:

(1) Videoconferences;

(2) Telephone conferences;

(3) Audio or video examination; and

(4) Scheduling of appearances.

(Subd (k) relettered effective January 1, 2021; adopted as subd (i) effective January 1, 1999; previously amended effective January 1, 2003; previously relettered to subd (j) effective January 1, 2010.)

Rule 5.220 amended effective January 1, 2021; adopted as rule 1257.3 effective January 1, 1999; previously amended and renumbered effective January 1, 2003; previously amended effective July 1, 1999, July 1, 2003, January 1, 2004, January 1, 2007, and January 1, 2010.

Rule 5.225. Appointment requirements for child custody evaluators

(a) Purpose

This rule provides the licensing, education and training, and experience requirements for child custody evaluators who are appointed to conduct full or partial child custody evaluations under Family Code sections 3111 and 3118, Evidence Code section 730, or chapter 15 (commencing with section 2032.010) of title 4 of part 4 of the Code of Civil Procedure. This rule is adopted as mandated by Family Code section 3110.5.

(Subd (a) amended and relettered effective January 1, 2007; adopted as subd (b).)

(b) Definitions

For purposes of this rule:

(1) A "child custody evaluator" is a court-appointed investigator as defined in Family Code section 3110.

(2) A "child custody evaluation" is an investigation and analysis of the health, safety, welfare, and best interest of a child with regard to disputed custody and visitation issues conducted under Family Code sections 3111 and 3118, Evidence Code section 730, or Code of Civil Procedure section 2032.010 et seq.

(3) A "full evaluation, investigation, or assessment" is a child custody evaluation that is a comprehensive examination of the health, safety, welfare, and best interest of the child.

(4) A "partial evaluation, investigation, or assessment" is a child custody evaluation that is limited by the court in terms of its scope.

(5) The terms "evaluation," "investigation," and "assessment" are synonymous.

(6) "Best interest of the child" is described in Family Code section 3011.

(7) A "court-connected evaluator" is a superior court employee or a person under contract with a superior court who conducts child custody evaluations.

(Subd (b) amended and relettered effective January 1, 2007; adopted as subd (c).)

(c) Licensing requirements

A person appointed as a child custody evaluator meets the licensing criteria established by Family Code section 3110.5(c)(1)–(5) [1] if:

(1) The person is licensed as a:

(A) Physician and **either** is [2] **a board-certified** psychiatrist or has completed a residency in psychiatry;

(B) Psychologist;

(C) Marriage and family therapist; [3]

(D) Clinical social worker**; or**

(E) **Professional clinical counselor qualified to assess couples and families**.

(2) A person may be appointed as an evaluator even if he or she does not have a license as described in (c)(1) if:

(A) The court certifies that the person is a court-connected evaluator who meets all the qualifications specified in (j); or

(B) The court finds that all the following criteria have been met:

(i) There are no licensed or certified evaluators who are willing and available, within a reasonable period of time, to perform child custody evaluations;

(ii) The parties stipulate to the person; and

(iii) The court approves the person.

(Subd (c) amended effective January 1, 2020; adopted effective January 1, 2007; previously amended effective January 1, 2015.)

Rule 5.225(c). 2019 Deletes. [1] , **[2]** either a board certified **[3]** or

(d) Education and training requirements

Before appointment, a child custody evaluator must complete 40 hours of education and training, which must include all the following topics:

(1) The psychological and developmental needs of children, especially as those needs relate to decisions about child custody and visitation;

(2) Family dynamics, including, but not limited to, parent-child relationships, blended families, and extended family relationships;

(3) The effects of separation, divorce, domestic violence, child sexual abuse, child physical or emotional abuse or neglect, substance abuse, and interparental conflict on the psychological and developmental needs of children and adults;

(4) The assessment of child sexual abuse issues required by Family Code section 3118; local procedures for handling child sexual abuse cases; the effect that court procedures may have on the evaluation process when there are allegations of child sexual abuse; and the areas of training required by Family Code section 3110.5(b)(2)(A)–(F), as listed below:

(A) Children's patterns of hiding and disclosing sexual abuse in a family setting;

(B) The effects of sexual abuse on children;

(C) The nature and extent of sexual abuse;

(D) The social and family dynamics of child sexual abuse;

(E) Techniques for identifying and assisting families affected by child sexual abuse; and

(F) Legal rights, protections, and remedies available to victims of child sexual abuse;

(5) The significance of culture and religion in the lives of the parties;

(6) Safety issues that may arise during the evaluation process and their potential effects on all participants in the evaluation;

(7) When and how to interview or assess adults, infants, and children; gather information from collateral sources; collect and assess relevant data; and recognize the limits of data sources' reliability and validity;

(8) The importance of addressing issues such as general mental health, medication use, and learning or physical disabilities;

(9) The importance of staying current with relevant literature and research;

(10) How to apply comparable interview, assessment, and testing procedures that meet generally accepted clinical, forensic, scientific, diagnostic, or medical standards to all parties;

(11) When to consult with or involve additional experts or other appropriate persons;

(12) How to inform each adult party of the purpose, nature, and method of the evaluation;

(13) How to assess parenting capacity and construct effective parenting plans;

(14) Ethical requirements associated with the child custody evaluator's professional license and rule 5.220;

(15) The legal context within which child custody and visitation issues are decided and additional legal and ethical standards to consider when serving as a child custody evaluator;

(16) The importance of understanding relevant distinctions among the roles of evaluator, mediator, and therapist;

(17) How to write reports and recommendations, where appropriate;

(18) Mandatory reporting requirements and limitations on confidentiality;

(19) How to prepare for and give court testimony;

(20) How to maintain professional neutrality and objectivity when conducting child custody evaluations; and

(21) The importance of assessing the health, safety, welfare, and best interest of the child or children involved in the proceedings.

(Subd (d) repealed, amended, and relettered effective January 1, 2007; adopted as subd (e); previously amended effective January 1, 2005.)

(e) Additional training requirements

In addition to the requirements described in this rule, before appointment, child custody evaluators must comply with the basic and advanced domestic violence training requirements described in rule 5.230.

(Subd (e) adopted effective January 1, 2007.)

(f) Authorized education and training

The education and training described in (d) must be completed:

(1) After January 1, 2000;

(2) Through an eligible provider under this rule; and

(3) By either:

(A) Attending and participating in an approved course; or

(B) Serving as an instructor in an approved course. Each course taught may be counted only once. Instructors may claim and receive credit for only actual classroom time.

(Subd (f) adopted effective January 1, 2007.)

(g) Experience requirements

To satisfy the experience requirements of this rule, persons appointed as child custody evaluators must have participated in the completion of at least four partial or full court-appointed child custody evaluations within the preceding three years, as described below. Each of the four child custody evaluations must have resulted in a written or an oral report.

(1) The child custody evaluator participates in the completion of the child custody evaluations if the evaluator:

(A) Independently conducted and completed the child custody evaluation; or

(B) Materially assisted another child custody evaluator who meets all the following criteria:

(i) Licensing or certification requirements in (c);

(ii) Education and training requirements in (d);

(iii) Basic and advanced domestic violence training in (e);

(iv) Experience requirements in (g)(1)(A) or (g)(2); and

(v) Continuing education and training requirements in (h).

(2) The court may appoint an individual to conduct the child custody evaluation who does not meet the experience requirements described in (1), if the court finds that all the following criteria have been met:

(A) There are no evaluators who meet the experience requirements of this rule who are willing and available, within a reasonable period of time, to perform child custody evaluations;

(B) The parties stipulate to the person; and

(C) The court approves the person.

(3) Those who supervise court-connected evaluators meet the requirements of this rule by conducting or materially assisting in the completion of at least four partial or full court-connected child custody evaluations in the preceding three years.

(Subd (g) amended effective January 1, 2011; adopted as subd (f); previously amended and relettered effective January 1, 2007.)

(h) Appointment eligibility

After completing the licensing requirements in (c), the initial education and training requirements described in (d) and (e), and the experience requirements in (g), a person is eligible for appointment as a child custody evaluator.

(Subd (h) amended effective January 1, 2011; adopted as subd (g); previously amended and relettered effective January 1, 2005; previously amended effective January 1, 2007.)

(i) Continuing education and training requirements

(1) After a child custody evaluator completes the initial education and training requirements described in (d) and (e), the evaluator must complete these continuing education and training requirements to remain eligible for appointment:

(A) Domestic violence update training described in rule 5.230; and

(B) Eight hours of update training covering the subjects described in (d).

(2) The time frame for completing continuing education and training in (1) is as follows:

(A) A newly trained court-connected or private child custody evaluator who recently completed the education and training in (d) and (e) must:

(i) Complete the continuing education and training requirements of this rule within 18 months from the date he or she completed the initial education and training; and

(ii) Specify on form FL-325 or FL-326 the date by which he or she must complete the continuing education and training requirements of this rule.

(B) All other court-connected or private child custody evaluators must complete the continuing education and training requirements in (1) as follows:

(i) Court-connected child custody evaluators must complete the continuing education and training requirements within the 12-month period immediately preceding the date he or she signs the *Declaration of Court-Connected Child Custody Evaluator Regarding Qualifications* (form FL-325), which must be submitted as provided by (*l*) of this rule.

(ii) Private child custody evaluators must complete the continuing education and training requirements within the 12-month period immediately preceding his or her appointment to a case.

(3) Compliance with the continuing education and training requirements of this rule is determined at the time of appointment to a case.

(Subd (i) adopted effective January 1, 2011.)

(j) Court-connected evaluators

A court-connected evaluator who does not meet the education and training requirements in (d) may conduct child custody evaluations if, before appointment, he or she:

(1) Completed at least 20 of the 40 hours of education and training required by (d);

(2) Completes the remaining hours of education and training required by (d) within 12 months of conducting his or her first evaluation as a court-connected child custody evaluator;

(3) Complied with the basic and advanced domestic violence training requirements under Family Code sections 1816 and 3110.5 and rule 5.230;

(4) Complies with the experience requirements in (g); and

(5) Is supervised by a court-connected child custody evaluator who meets the requirements of this rule.

(Subd (j) relettered effective January 1, 2011; adopted as subd (h); previously relettered as subd (i) effective January 1, 2005; previously amended effective January 1, 2007.)

(k) Responsibility of the courts

Each court:

(1) Must develop local court rules that:

(A) Provide for acceptance of and response to complaints about an evaluator's performance; and

(B) Establish a process for informing the public about how to find qualified evaluators in that jurisdiction;

(2) Must use an *Order Appointing Child Custody Evaluator* (form FL-327) to appoint a private child custody evaluator or a court-connected evaluation service. Form FL-327 may be supplemented with local court forms;

(3) Must provide the Judicial Council with a copy of any local court forms used to implement this rule;

(4) As feasible and appropriate, may confer with education and training providers to develop and deliver curricula of comparable quality and relevance to child custody evaluations for both court-connected and private child custody evaluators; and

(5) Must use form *Declaration of Court-Connected Child Custody Evaluator Regarding Qualifications* (form FL-325) to certify that court-connected evaluators have met all the qualifications for court-connected evaluators under this rule for a given year. Form FL-325 may be supplemented with local court rules or forms.

(Subd (k) relettered effective January 1, 2011; adopted as subd (l); previously amended and relettered as subd (k) effective January 1, 2005, and as subd (j) effective January 1, 2007.)

(*l*) Child custody evaluator

A person appointed as a child custody evaluator must:

(1) Submit to the court a declaration indicating compliance with all applicable education, training, and experience requirements:

(A) Court-connected child custody evaluators must submit a *Declaration of Court-Connected Child Custody Evaluator Regarding Qualifications* (form FL-325) to the court executive officer or his or her designee. Court-connected child custody evaluators practicing as of January 1 of a given year must submit the form by January 30 of that year. Court-connected evaluators beginning practice after January 1 must submit the form before any work on the first child custody evaluation has begun and by January 30 of every year thereafter; and

(B) Private child custody evaluators must complete a *Declaration of Private Child Custody Evaluator Regarding Qualifications* (form FL-326) and file it with the clerk's office no later than 10 days after notification of each appointment and before any work on each child custody evaluation has begun;

(2) At the beginning of the child custody evaluation, inform each adult party of the purpose, nature, and method of the evaluation, and provide information about the evaluator's education, experience, and training;

(3) Use interview, assessment, and testing procedures that are consistent with generally accepted clinical, forensic, scientific, diagnostic, or medical standards;

(4) Have a license in good standing if licensed at the time of appointment, except as described in (c)(2) and Family Code section 3110.5(d);

(5) Be knowledgeable about relevant resources and service providers; and

(6) Before undertaking the evaluation or at the first practical moment, inform the court, counsel, and parties of possible or actual multiple roles or conflicts of interest.

(Subd (l) amended and relettered effective January 1, 2011; adopted as subd (m); previously amended and relettered as subd (l) effective January 1, 2005, and as subd (k) effective January 1, 2007.)

(m) Use of interns

Court-connected and court-appointed child custody evaluators may use interns to assist with the child custody evaluation, if:

(1) The evaluator:

(A) Before or at the time of appointment, fully discloses to the parties and attorneys the nature and extent of the intern's participation in the evaluation;

(B) Obtains the written agreement of the parties and attorneys as to the nature and extent of the intern's participation in the evaluation after disclosure;

(C) Ensures that the extent, kind, and quality of work performed by the intern being supervised is consistent with the intern's training and experience;

(D) Is physically present when the intern interacts with the parties, children, or other collateral persons in the evaluation; and

(E) Ensures compliance with all laws and regulations governing the professional practice of the supervising evaluator and the intern.

(2) The interns:

(A) Are enrolled in a master's or doctorate program or have obtained a graduate degree qualifying for licensure or certification as a clinical social worker, marriage and family therapist, psychiatrist, or psychologist;

(B) Are currently completing or have completed the coursework necessary to qualify for their degree in the subjects of child abuse assessment and spousal or partner abuse assessment; and

(C) Comply with the applicable laws related to the practice of their profession in California when interns are:

(i) Accruing supervised professional experience as defined in the California Code of Regulations; and

(ii) Providing professional services for a child custody evaluator that fall within the lawful scope of practice as a licensed professional.

(Subd (m) relettered effective January 1, 2011; adopted as subd (l) effective January 1, 2007.)

(n) Education and training providers

"Eligible providers" includes the Judicial Council and may include educational institutions, professional associations, professional continuing education groups, public or private for-profit or not-for-profit groups, and court-connected groups. Eligible providers must:

(1) Ensure that the training instructors or consultants delivering the training and education programs either meet the requirements of this rule or are experts in the subject matter;

(2) Monitor and evaluate the quality of courses, curricula, training, instructors, and consultants;

(3) Emphasize the importance of focusing child custody evaluations on the health, safety, welfare, and best interest of the child;

(4) Develop a procedure to verify that participants complete the education and training program;

(5) Distribute a certificate of completion to each person who has completed the training. The certificate must document the number of hours of training offered, the number of hours the person completed, the dates of the training, and the name of the training provider; and

(6) Meet the approval requirements described in (o).

(Subd (n) amended effective January 1, 2016; adopted as subd (n); previously amended and relettered as subd (m) effective January 1, 2005; previously amended effective January 1, 2007; previously amended and relettered as subd (n) effective January 1, 2011.)

(o) Program approval required

All education and training programs must be approved by Judicial Council staff in consultation with the Family and Juvenile Law Advisory Committee. Education and training courses that were taken between January 1, 2000, and July 1, 2003, may be applied toward the requirements of this rule if they addressed the subjects listed in (d) and either were certified or approved for continuing education credit by a professional provider group or were offered as part of a related postgraduate degree or licensing program.

(Subd (o) amended effective January 1, 2016; adopted as subd (o); previously amended and relettered as subd (n) effective January 1, 2005; previously amended effective January 1, 2007; relettered as subd (o) effective January 1, 2011.)
Rule 5.225 amended effective January 1, 2020; adopted as rule 1257.4 effective January 1, 2002; renumbered as rule 5.225 effective January 1, 2003; previously amended effective January 1, 2005, January 1, 2007, January 1, 2011, January 1, 2015, and January 1, 2016.

Rule 5.230. Domestic violence training standards for court-appointed child custody investigators and evaluators

(a) Authority

This rule of court is adopted under Family Code sections 211 and 3111(d) and (e).

(Subd (a) amended effective January 1, 2007.)

(b) Purpose

Consistent with Family Code sections 3020 and 3111, the purposes of this rule are to require domestic violence training for all court-appointed persons who evaluate or investigate child custody matters and to ensure that this training reflects current research and consensus about best practices for conducting child custody evaluations by prescribing standards that training in domestic violence must meet. Effective January 1, 1998, no person may be a court-appointed investigator under Family Code section 3111(d) or Evidence Code section 730 unless the person has completed domestic violence training described here and in Family Code section 1816.

(Subd (b) amended effective January 1, 2003.)

(c) Definitions

For purposes of this rule, "court-appointed investigator" is considered to be synonymous with "court-appointed evaluator" as defined in Family Code section 3110.

(d) Mandatory training

Persons appointed as child custody investigators under Family Code section 3110 or Evidence Code section 730, and persons who are professional staff or trainees in a child custody or visitation evaluation or investigation, must complete basic training in domestic violence issues as described in Family Code section 1816 and, in addition:

(1) *Advanced training*

Sixteen hours of advanced training must be completed within a 12-month period. The training must include the following:

(A) Twelve hours of instruction, as approved by Judicial Council staff, in:

(i) The appropriate structuring of the child custody evaluation process, including, but not limited to, maximizing safety for clients, evaluators, and court personnel; maintaining objectivity; providing and gathering balanced information from both parties and controlling for bias; providing for separate sessions at separate times (as specified in Family Code section 3113); and considering the impact of the evaluation report and recommendations with particular attention to the dynamics of domestic violence;

(ii) The relevant sections of local, state, and federal law or rules;

(iii) The range, availability, and applicability of domestic violence resources available to victims, including, but not limited to, battered women's shelters, specialized counseling, drug and alcohol counseling, legal advocacy, job training, parenting classes, battered immigrant victims, and welfare exceptions for domestic violence victims;

(iv) The range, availability, and applicability of domestic violence intervention available to perpetrators, including, but not limited to, arrest, incarceration, probation, applicable Penal Code sections (including Penal Code section 1203.097, which describes certified treatment programs for batterers), drug and alcohol counseling, legal advocacy, job training, and parenting classes; and

(v) The unique issues in family and psychological assessment in domestic violence cases, including the following concepts:

a. The effects of exposure to domestic violence and psychological trauma on children; the relationship between child physical abuse, child sexual abuse, and domestic violence; the differential family dynamics related to parent-child attachments in families with domestic violence; intergenerational transmission of familial violence; and manifestations of post-traumatic stress disorders in children;

b. The nature and extent of domestic violence, and the relationship of gender, class, race, culture, and sexual orientation to domestic violence;

c. Current legal, psychosocial, public policy, and mental health research related to the dynamics of family violence, the impact of victimization, the psychology of perpetration, and the dynamics of power and control in battering relationships;

d. The assessment of family history based on the type, severity, and frequency of violence;

e. The impact on parenting abilities of being a victim or perpetrator of domestic violence;

f. The uses and limitations of psychological testing and psychiatric diagnosis in assessing parenting abilities in domestic violence cases;

g. The influence of alcohol and drug use and abuse on the incidence of domestic violence;

h. Understanding the dynamics of high-conflict relationships and abuser/victim relationships;

i. The importance of, and procedures for, obtaining collateral information from probation departments, children's protective services, police incident reports, restraining order pleadings, medical records, schools, and other relevant sources;

j. Accepted methods for structuring safe and enforceable child custody and parenting plans that assure the health, safety, welfare, and best interest of the child, and safeguards for the parties; and

k. The importance of discouraging participants in child custody matters from blaming victims of domestic violence for the violence and from minimizing allegations of domestic violence, child abuse, or abuse against any family member.

(B) Four hours of community resource networking intended to acquaint the evaluator with domestic violence resources in the geographical communities where the families being evaluated may reside.

(2) *Annual update training*

Four hours of update training are required each year after the year in which the advanced training is completed. These four hours must consist of instruction focused on, but not limited to, an update of changes or modifications in local court practices, case law, and state and federal legislation related to domestic violence, and an update of current social science research and theory, particularly in regard to the impact on children of exposure to domestic violence.

(Subd (d) amended effective January 1, 2016; previously amended effective January 1, 2002, January 1, 2003, January 1, 2004, and January 1, 2005.)

(e) Education and training providers

Only education and training acquired from eligible providers meets the requirements of this rule. "Eligible providers" includes the Judicial Council and may include educational institutions, professional associations, professional continuing education groups, public or private for-profit or not-for-profit groups, and court-connected groups.

(1) Eligible providers must:

(A) Ensure that the training instructors or consultants delivering the education and training programs either meet the requirements of this rule or are experts in the subject matter;

(B) Monitor and evaluate the quality of courses, curricula, training, instructors, and consultants;

(C) Emphasize the importance of focusing child custody evaluations on the health, safety, welfare, and best interest of the child;

(D) Develop a procedure to verify that participants complete the education and training program; and

(E) Distribute a certificate of completion to each person who has completed the training. The certificate must document the number of hours of training offered, the number of hours the person completed, the dates of the training, and the name of the training provider.

(2) Effective July 1, 2005, all education and training programs must be approved by Judicial Council staff in consultation with the Family and Juvenile Law Advisory Committee.

(Subd (e) amended effective January 1, 2016; previously amended effective January 1, 2005.)

(f) Local court rules

Each local court may adopt rules regarding the procedures by which child custody evaluators who have completed the training in domestic violence as mandated by this rule will notify the local court. In the absence of such a local rule of court, child custody evaluators must attach copies of their certificates of completion of the initial 12 hours of advanced instruction and of the most recent annual 4-hour update training in domestic violence to each child custody evaluation report.

(Subd (f) relettered effective January 1, 2005; adopted as subd (g) effective January 1, 1999; amended effective January 1, 2003, and January 1, 2004.)

(g) Previous training accepted

Persons attending training programs offered after January 1, 1996, that meet all of the requirements set forth in subdivision (d)(1)(A) of this rule are deemed to have met the minimum standards set forth in subdivision (d)(1)(A) of this rule, but they must still meet the minimum standards listed in subdivisions (d)(1)(B) and (d)(2) of this rule.

(Subd (g) amended effective January 1, 2007; adopted as subd (h) effective January 1, 1999; relettered effective January 1, 2005.)

Rule 5.230 amended effective January 1, 2016; adopted as rule 1257.7 effective January 1, 1999; amended and renumbered as rule 5.230 effective January 1, 2003; previously amended effective January 1, 2004, January 1, 2005, and January 1, 2007.

Article 3
Ex Parte Communication

Title 5, Family and Juvenile Rules—Division 1, Family Rules—Chapter 8, Child Custody and Visitation (Parenting Time) Proceedings—Article 3, Ex Parte Communication; adopted effective January 1, 2013.

Rule 5.235. Ex parte communication in child custody proceedings

(a) Purpose

Generally, ex parte communication is prohibited in legal proceedings. In child custody proceedings, Family Code section 216 recognizes specific circumstances in which ex parte communication is permitted between court-connected or court-appointed child custody mediators or evaluators and the attorney for any party, the court-appointed counsel for a child, or the court. This rule of court establishes mandatory statewide standards of practice relating to when, and between whom, ex parte communication is permitted in child custody proceedings. This rule applies to all court-ordered child custody mediations or evaluations. As in Family Code section 216, this rule of court does not restrict communications between a court-connected or court-appointed child custody mediator or evaluator and a party in a child custody proceeding who is self-represented or represented by counsel.

(b) Definitions

For purposes of this rule,

(1) "Communication" includes any verbal statement made in person, by telephone, by voicemail, or by videoconferencing; any written statement, illustration, photograph, or other tangible item, contained in a letter, document, e-mail, or fax; or other equivalent means, either directly or through third parties.

(2) "Ex parte communication" is a direct or indirect communication on the substance of a pending case without the knowledge, presence, or consent of all parties involved in the matter.

(3) A "court-connected mediator or evaluator" is a superior court employee or a person under contract with a superior court who conducts child custody evaluations or mediations.

(4) A "court-appointed mediator or evaluator" is a professional in private practice appointed by the court to conduct a child custody evaluation or mediation.

(c) Ex parte communication prohibited

In any child custody proceeding under the Family Code, ex parte communication is prohibited between court-connected or court-appointed mediators or evaluators and the attorney for any party, a court-appointed counsel for a child, or the court, except as provided by this rule.

(d) Exception for parties' stipulation

The parties may enter into a stipulation either in open court or in writing to allow ex parte communication between a court-connected or court-appointed mediator or evaluator and:

(1) The attorney for any party; or

(2) The court.

(e) Ex parte communication permitted

In any proceeding under the Family Code, ex parte communication is permitted between a court-connected or court-appointed mediator or evaluator and (1) the attorney for any party, (2) the court-appointed counsel for a child, or (3) the court, only if:

(1) The communication is necessary to schedule an appointment;

(2) The communication is necessary to investigate or disclose an actual or potential conflict of interest or dual relationship as required under rule 5.210(h)(10) and (h)(12);

(3) The court-appointed counsel for a child is interviewing a mediator as provided by Family Code section 3151(c)(5);

(4) The court expressly authorizes ex parte communication between the mediator or evaluator and court-appointed counsel for a child in circumstances other than described in (3); or

(5) The mediator or evaluator is informing the court of the belief that a restraining order is necessary to prevent an imminent risk to the physical safety of the child or party.

(Subd (e) amended effective January 1, 2007.)

(f) Exception for mandated duties and responsibilities

This rule does not prohibit ex parte communication for the purpose of fulfilling the duties and responsibilities that:

(1) A mediator or evaluator may have as a mandated reporter of suspected child abuse;

(2) A mediator or evaluator may have to warn of threatened violent behavior against a reasonably identifiable victim or victims;

(3) A mediator or evaluator may have to address a case involving allegations of domestic violence under Family Code sections 3113, 3181, and 3192 and rule 5.215; and

(4) The court may have to investigate complaints.

(Subd (f) amended effective January 1, 2007.)

Rule 5.235 amended effective January 1, 2007; adopted effective July 1, 2006.

Article 4
Counsel Appointed to Represent a Child

Title 5, Family and Juvenile Rules—Division 1, Family Rules—Chapter 8, Child Custody and Visitation (Parenting Time) Proceedings—Article 4, Counsel Appointed to Represent a Child; adopted effective January 1, 2013.

Rule 5.240. Appointment of counsel to represent a child in family law proceedings

(a) Appointment considerations

In considering appointing counsel under Family Code section 3150, the court should take into account the following factors, including whether:

(1) The issues of child custody and visitation are highly contested or protracted;

(2) The child is subjected to stress as a result of the dispute that might be alleviated by the intervention of counsel representing the child;

(3) Counsel representing the child would be likely to provide the court with relevant information not otherwise readily available or likely to be presented;

(4) The dispute involves allegations of physical, emotional, or sexual abuse or neglect of the child.

(5) It appears that one or both parents are incapable of providing a stable, safe, and secure environment;

(6) Counsel is available for appointment who is knowledgeable about the issues being raised regarding the child in the proceeding;

(7) The best interest of the child appears to require independent representation; and

(8) If there are two or more children, any child would require separate counsel to avoid a conflict of interest.

(Subd (a) adopted effective January 1, 2008.)

(b) Request for appointment of counsel

The court may appoint counsel to represent the best interest of a child in a family law proceeding on the court's own motion or if requested to do so by:

(1) A party;

(2) The attorney for a party;

(3) The child, or any relative of the child;

(4) A mediator under Family Code section 3184;

(5) A professional person making a custody recommendation under Family Code sections 3111 and 3118, Evidence Code section 730, or Code of Civil Procedure section 2032.010 et seq.;

(6) A county counsel, district attorney, city attorney, or city prosecutor authorized to prosecute child abuse and neglect or child abduction cases under state law; or

(7) A court-appointed guardian ad litem or special advocate;

(8) Any other person who the court deems appropriate.

(Subd (b) adopted effective January 1, 2008.)

(c) Orders appointing counsel for a child

The court must issue written orders when appointing and terminating counsel for a child.

(1) The appointment orders must specify the:

(A) Appointed counsel's name, address, and telephone number;

(B) Name of the child for whom counsel is appointed; and

(C) Child's date of birth.

(2) The appointment orders may include the:

(A) Child's address, if appropriate;

(B) Issues to be addressed in the case;

(C) Tasks related to the case that would benefit from the services of counsel for the child;

(D) Responsibilities and rights of the child's counsel;

(E) Counsel's rate or amount of compensation;

(F) Allocation of fees payable by each party or the court;

(G) Source of funds and manner of reimbursement for counsel's fees and costs;

(H) Allocation of payment of counsel's fees to one party subject to reimbursement by the other party;

(I) Terms and amount of any progress or installment payments; and

(J) Ability of the court to reserve jurisdiction to retroactively modify the order on fees and payment.

(3) Courts may use *Order Appointing Counsel for a Child* (form FL-323) or may supplement form FL-323 with local forms developed under rule 10.613.

(Subd (c) amended effective January 1, 2013; adopted effective January 1, 2008.)

(d) Panel of counsel eligible for appointment

(1) Each court may create and maintain a list or panel of counsel meeting the minimum qualifications of this rule for appointment.

(2) If a list or panel of counsel is maintained, a court may appoint counsel not on the list or panel in special circumstances, taking into consideration factors including language, culture, and the special needs of a child in the following areas:

(A) Child abuse;

(B) Domestic violence;

(C) Drug abuse of a parent or the child;

(D) Mental health issues of a parent or the child;

(E) Particular medical issues of the child; and

(F) Educational issues.

(3) If the court maintains a panel of counsel eligible for appointment and the court appoints counsel who is not on the panel, the court must state the reason for not appointing a panel counsel in writing or on the record.

(4) Any lists maintained from which the court might appoint counsel should be reviewed at least annually to ensure that those on the list meet the education and training requirements. Courts should ask counsel annually to update their information and to notify the court if any changes would make them unable to be appointed.

(Subd (d) amended effective January 1, 2013; adopted effective January 1, 2008.)

(e) Complaint procedures

Rules of Court

By January 1, 2010, each court must develop local court rules in accordance with rule 10.613 that provide for acceptance and response to complaints about the performance of the court-appointed counsel for a child.

(Subd (e) adopted effective January 1, 2008.)

(f) Termination of appointment

On entering an appearance on behalf of a child, counsel must continue to represent that child until:

(1) The conclusion of the proceeding for which counsel was appointed;

(2) Relieved by the court;

(3) Substituted by the court with other counsel;

(4) Removed on the court's own motion or request of counsel or parties for good cause shown; or

(5) The child reaches the age of majority or is emancipated.

(Subd (f) adopted effective January 1, 2008.)

Rule 5.240 amended effective January 1, 2013; adopted effective January 1, 2008.

Rule 5.241. Compensation of counsel appointed to represent a child in a family law proceeding

(a) Determination of counsel's compensation

The court must determine the reasonable sum for compensation and expenses for counsel appointed to represent the child in a family law proceeding, and the ability of the parties to pay all or a portion of counsel's compensation and expenses.

(1) The court must set the compensation for the child's counsel:

(A) At the time of appointment;

(B) At the time the court determines the parties' ability to pay; or

(C) Within a reasonable time after appointment.

(2) No later than 30 days after counsel is relieved as attorney of record, the court may make a redetermination of counsel's compensation:

(A) On the court's own motion;

(B) At the request of a party or a party's counsel; or

(C) At the request of counsel for the child.

(Subd (a) adopted effective January 1, 2008.)

(b) Determination of ability to pay

The court must determine the respective financial ability of the parties to pay all or a portion of counsel's compensation.

(1) Before determining the parties' ability to pay:

(A) The court should consider factors such as the parties' income and assets reasonably available at the time of the determination, and eligibility for or existence of a fee waiver under Government Code section 68511.3; and

(B) The parties must have on file a current *Income and Expense Declaration* (form FL-150) or *Financial Statement (Simplified)* (form FL-155).

(2) The court should determine the parties' ability to pay:

(A) At the time counsel is appointed;

(B) Within 30 days after appointment; or

(C) At the next subsequent hearing.

(3) No later than 30 days after counsel is relieved as attorney of record, the court may redetermine the parties' ability to pay:

(A) On the court's own motion; or

(B) At the request of counsel or the parties.

(Subd (b) adopted effective January 1, 2008.)

(c) Payment to counsel

(1) If the court determines that the parties have the ability to pay all or a portion of the fees, the court must order that the parties pay in any manner the court determines to be reasonable and compatible with the parties' financial ability, including progress or installment payments.

(2) The court may use its own funds to pay counsel for a child and seek reimbursement from the parties.

(3) The court must inform the parties that the failure to pay fees to the appointed counsel or to the court may result in the attorney or the court initiating legal action against them to collect the money.

(Subd (c) adopted effective January 1, 2008.)

(d) Parties' inability to pay

If the court finds that the parties are unable to pay all or a portion of the cost of the child's counsel, the court must pay the portion the parties are unable to pay.

(Subd (d) adopted effective January 1, 2008.)

Rule 5.241 adopted effective January 1, 2008.

Rule 5.242. Qualifications, rights, and responsibilities of counsel appointed to represent a child in family law proceedings

(a) Purpose

This rule governs counsel appointed to represent the best interest of the child in a custody or visitation proceeding under Family Code section 3150.

(Subd (a) adopted effective January 1, 2008.)

(b) General appointment requirements

To be eligible for appointment as counsel for a child, counsel must:

(1) Be an active member in good standing of the State Bar of California;

(2) Have professional liability insurance or demonstrate to the court that he or she is adequately self-insured; and

(3) Meet the education, training, and experience requirements of this rule.

(Subd (b) adopted effective January 1, 2008.)

(c) Education and training requirements

Effective January 1, 2009, before being appointed as counsel for a child in a family law proceeding, counsel must have completed at least 12 hours of applicable education and training which must include all the following subjects:

(1) Statutes, rules of court, and case law relating to child custody and visitation litigation;

(2) Representation of a child in custody and visitation proceedings;

(3) Special issues in representing a child, including the following:

(A) Various stages of child development;

(B) Communicating with a child at various developmental stages and presenting the child's view;

(C) Recognizing, evaluating and understanding evidence of child abuse and neglect, family violence and substance abuse, cultural and ethnic diversity, and gender-specific issues;

(D) The effects of domestic violence and child abuse and neglect on children; and

(E) How to work effectively with multidisciplinary experts.

(Subd (c) adopted effective January 1, 2008.)

(d) Annual education and training requirements

Effective January 1, 2010, to remain eligible for appointment as counsel for a child, counsel must complete during each calendar year a minimum of eight hours of applicable education and training in the subjects listed in (c).

(Subd (d) adopted effective January 1, 2008.)

(e) Applicable education and training

(1) Education and training that addresses the subjects listed in (c) may be applied toward the requirements of this rule if completed through:

(A) A professional continuing education group;

(B) An educational institution;

(C) A professional association;

(D) A court-connected group; or

(E) A public or private for-profit or not-for-profit group.

(2) A maximum of two of the hours may be by self-study under the supervision of an education provider that provides evidence of completion.

(3) Counsel may complete education and training courses that satisfy the requirements of this rule offered by the education providers in (1) by means of video presentations or other delivery means at remote locations. Such courses are not self-study within the meaning of this rule.

(4) Counsel who serve as an instructor in an education and training course that satisfies the requirements of this rule may receive 1.5 hours of course participation credit for each hour of course instruction. All other counsel may claim credit for actual time he or she attended the education and training course.

(Subd (e) adopted effective January 1, 2008.)

(f) Experience requirements

(1) Persons appointed as counsel for a child in a family law proceeding must have represented a party or a child in at least six proceedings involving child custody within the preceding five years as follows:

(A) At least two of the six proceedings must have involved contested child custody and visitation issues in family law; and

(B) Child custody proceedings in dependency or guardianship cases can count for no more than three of the six required for appointment.

(2) Courts may develop local rules that impose additional experience requirements for persons appointed as counsel for a child in a family law proceeding.

(Subd (f) adopted effective January 1, 2008.)

(g) Alternative experience requirements

Counsel who does not meet the initial experience requirements in (f) may be appointed to represent a child in a family law proceeding if he or she meets one of the following alternative experience requirements. Counsel must:

(1) Be employed by a legal services organization, a governmental agency, or a private law firm that has been approved by the presiding or supervising judge of the local family court as qualified to represent a child in family law proceedings and be directly supervised by an attorney in an organization, an agency, or a private law firm who meets the initial experience requirements in (f);

(2) Be an attorney working in consultation with an attorney approved by the presiding or supervising judge of the local family court as qualified to represent a child in family law proceedings; or

(3) Demonstrate substantial equivalent experience as determined by local court rule or procedure.

(Subd (g) adopted effective January 1, 2008.)

(h) Compliance with appointment requirements

A person appointed as counsel for a child must:

(1) File a declaration with the court indicating compliance with the requirements of this rule no later than 10 days after being appointed and before beginning work on the case. Counsel may complete the *Declaration of Counsel for a Child Regarding Qualifications* (form FL-322) or other local court forms for this purpose; and

(2) Notify the court within five days of any disciplinary action taken by the State Bar of California, stating the basis of the complaint, result, and notice of any reproval, probation, or suspension.

(Subd (h) adopted effective January 1, 2008.)

(i) Rights of counsel for a child

Counsel has rights relating to the representation of a child's best interest under Family Code sections 3111, 3151, 3151.5, 3153, and Welfare and Institutions Code section 827, which include the right to:

(1) Reasonable access to the child;

(2) Seek affirmative relief on behalf of the child;

(3) Notice to any proceeding, and all phases of that proceeding, including a request for examination affecting the child;

(4) Take any action that is available to a party to the proceeding, including filing pleadings, making evidentiary objections, and presenting evidence;

(5) Be heard in the proceeding, which may include presenting motions and orders to show cause and participating in settlement conferences and trials, seeking writs, appeals, and arbitrations;

(6) Access the child's medical, dental, mental health, and other health-care records, and school and educational records;

(7) Inspect juvenile case files subject to the provisions of Welfare and Institutions Code section 827;

(8) Interview school personnel, caretakers, health-care providers, mental health professionals, and others who have assessed the child or provided care to the child; however, the release of this information to counsel does not constitute a waiver of the confidentiality of the reports, files, and any disclosed communications;

(9) Interview mediators, subject to the provisions of Family Code sections 3177 and 3182;

(10) Receive reasonable advance notice of and the right to refuse any physical or psychological examination or evaluation, for purposes of the proceeding, that has not been ordered by the court;

(11) Assert or waive any privilege on behalf of the child;

(12) Seek independent psychological or physical examination or evaluation of the child for purposes of the proceeding on approval by the court;

(13) Receive child custody evaluation reports;

(14) Not be called as a witness in the proceedings;

(15) Request the court to authorize release of relevant reports or files, concerning the child represented by the counsel, of the relevant local child protective services agency; and

(16) Receive reasonable compensation and expenses for representing the child, the amount of which will be determined by the court.

(Subd (i) adopted effective January 1, 2008.)

(j) Responsibilities of counsel for a child

Counsel is charged with the representation of the child's best interest. The role of the child's counsel is to gather evidence that bears on the best interest of the child and present that admissible evidence to the court in any manner appropriate for the counsel of a party. If the child so desires, the child's counsel must present the child's wishes to the court.

(1) Counsel's duties, unless under the circumstances it is inappropriate to exercise the duties, include those under Family Code section 3151:

(A) Interviewing the child;

(B) Reviewing the court files and all accessible relevant records available to both parties; and

(C) Making any further investigations that counsel considers necessary to ascertain the facts relevant to the custody or visitation hearings.

(2) Counsel must serve notices and pleadings on all parties consistent with the requirements for parties.

(3) Counsel may introduce and examine witnesses, present arguments to the court concerning the child's welfare, and participate further in the proceeding to the degree necessary to represent the child adequately.

(4) In any case in which counsel is representing a child who is called to testify in the proceeding, counsel must:

(A) Provide information to the child in an age-appropriate manner about the limitations on confidentiality and the possibility that information provided to the court may be on the record and provided to the parties in the case;

(B) Allow but not require the child to state a preference regarding custody or visitation and, in an age-appropriate manner, provide information about the process by which the court will make a decision;

(C) Provide procedures relevant to the child's participation and, if appropriate, provide an orientation to the courtroom where the child will be testifying; and

(D) Inform the parties and then the court about the client's desire to provide input.

(Subd (j) amended effective January 1, 2012; adopted effective January 1, 2008.)

(k) Other considerations

Counsel is not required to assume the responsibilities of a social worker, probation officer, child custody evaluator, or mediator and is not expected to provide nonlegal services to the child. Subject to the terms of the court's order of appointment, counsel for a child may take the following actions to implement his or her statutory duties in representing a child in a family law proceeding:

(1) Interview or observe the child as appropriate to the age and circumstances of the child. In doing so, counsel should consider all possible interview or observation environments and select a location most conducive to both conducting a meaningful interview of the child and investigating the issues relevant to the case at that time.

(2) In a manner and to the extent consistent with the child's age, level of maturity, and ability to understand, and consistent with the order of appointment for the case:

(A) Explain to the child at their first meeting counsel's role and the nature of the attorney-client relationship (including confidentiality issues); and

(B) Advise the child on a continuing basis of possible courses of action and of the risks and benefits of each course of action.

(3) Actively participate in the representation of the child at any hearings that affect custody and visitation of the child and attend and participate in any other hearings relevant to the child. In doing so, counsel may, as appropriate:

(A) Take positions relevant to the child on legal issues before the court;

(B) Seek and advocate for services for the child;

(C) Prepare for any hearings or trials;

(D) Work to settle contested issues and to define trial issues;

(E) Prepare witnesses, including the child if the child is to testify;

(F) Introduce and examine witnesses on behalf of the child;

(G) Cross-examine other witnesses;

(H) Make appropriate evidentiary objections;

(I) Review court files and other pertinent records;

(J) Prepare motions to advance the child's interest, including motions to quash subpoenas for the child and other protective orders;

(K) Present arguments to advance the child's interest;

(L) Prepare trial briefs and other documents if appropriate; and

(M) Request appointment of separate appellate counsel.

(4) Conduct thorough, continuing, and independent investigations and discovery to protect the child's interest, which may include:

(A) Obtaining necessary authorizations for the release of information.

(B) Reviewing the child's social services, mental health, drug and alcohol, medical, law enforcement, education, and other records relevant to the case;

(C) Reviewing the court files of the child and his or her siblings, case-related records of the social service agency, and case-related records of other service providers;

(D) Contacting attorneys for the parties and nonlawyer guardians ad litem, Court Appointed Special Advocates (CASAs), and other service professionals, to the extent permitted by local rule, for background information;

(E) Contacting and meeting with the child's parents, legal guardians, or caretakers, with permission of their attorneys;

(F) Interviewing witnesses and individuals involved with the child, including school personnel, child welfare caseworkers, foster parents and other caretakers, neighbors, relatives, coaches, clergy, mental health professionals, physicians, law enforcement officers, and other potential witnesses;

(G) Reviewing relevant photographs, video- or audio recordings, and other evidence;

(H) Documenting the results of these investigations;

(I) Monitoring compliance with court orders as appropriate, including the provision for and effectiveness of any court-ordered services;

(J) Promoting the timely progression of the case through the judicial system;

(K) Investigating the interests of the child beyond the scope of the proceeding and reporting to the court other interests of the child that may need to be protected by the institution of other administrative or judicial proceedings; however, counsel is not responsible for instituting those proceedings or representing the child in them unless expressly appointed by the court for that purpose; and

(L) After learning of other existing administrative or judicial proceedings involving the child, communicating and cooperating with others to the extent necessary and appropriate to protect the child's interest.

(5) Taking all other steps to represent the child adequately as appropriate to the case, including becoming knowledgeable in other areas affecting minors including:

(A) The Indian Child Welfare Act;

(B) Information about local experts who can provide evaluation, consultation, and testimony; and

(C) Delinquency, dependency, probate, family law, and other proceedings.

(Subd (k) amended effective January 1, 2016; adopted effective January 1, 2008.)

Rule 5.242 amended effective January 1, 2016; adopted effective January 1, 2008; previously amended effective January 1, 2012.

Article 5
Children's Participation in Family Court

Title 5, Family and Juvenile Rules—Division 1, Family Rules—Chapter 8, Child Custody and Visitation (Parenting Time) Proceedings—Article 5, Children's Participation in Family Court; adopted effective January 1, 2013.

Rule 5.250. Children's participation and testimony in family court proceedings

(a) Children's participation

This rule is intended to implement Family Code section 3042. Children's participation in family law matters must be considered on a case-by-case basis. No statutory mandate, rule, or practice requires children to participate in court or prohibits them from doing so. When a child wishes to participate, the court should find a balance between protecting the child, the statutory duty to consider the wishes of and input from the child, and the probative value of the child's input while ensuring all parties' due process rights to challenge evidence relied upon by the court in making custody decisions.

(Subd (a) adopted effective January 1, 2012.)

(b) Determining if the child wishes to address the court

(1) The following persons must inform the court if they have information indicating that a child in a custody or visitation (parenting time) matter wishes to address the court:

(A) A minor's counsel;

(B) An evaluator;

(C) An investigator; and

(D) A child custody recommending counselor who provides recommendations to the judge under Family Code section 3183.

(2) The following persons may inform the court if they have information indicating that a child wishes to address the court:

(A) A party; and

(B) A party's attorney.

(3) In the absence of information indicating a child wishes to address the court, the judicial officer may inquire whether the child wishes to do so.

(Subd (b) adopted effective January 1, 2012.)

(c) Guidelines for determining whether addressing the court is in the child's best interest

(1) When a child indicates that he or she wishes to address the court, the judicial officer must consider whether involving the child in the proceedings is in the child's best interest.

(2) If the child indicating an interest in addressing the court is 14 years old or older, the judicial officer must hear from that child unless the court makes a finding that addressing the court is not in the child's best interest and states the reasons on the record.

(3) In determining whether addressing the court is in a child's best interest, the judicial officer should consider the following:

(A) Whether the child is of sufficient age and capacity to reason to form an intelligent preference as to custody or visitation (parenting time);

(B) Whether the child is of sufficient age and capacity to understand the nature of testimony;

(C) Whether information has been presented indicating that the child may be at risk emotionally if he or she is permitted or denied the opportunity to address the court or that the child may benefit from addressing the court;

(D) Whether the subject areas about which the child is anticipated to address the court are relevant to the court's decisionmaking process; and

(E) Whether any other factors weigh in favor of or against having the child address the court, taking into consideration the child's desire to do so.

(Subd (c) adopted effective January 1, 2012.)

(d) Guidelines for receiving testimony and other input

(1) If the court precludes the calling of a child as a witness, alternatives for the court to obtain information or other input from the child may include, but are not limited to:

(A) The child's participation in child custody mediation under Family Code section 3180;

(B) Appointment of a child custody evaluator or investigator under Family Code section 3110 or Evidence Code section 730;

(C) Admissible evidence provided by the parents, parties, or witnesses in the proceeding;

(D) Information provided by a child custody recommending counselor authorized to provide recommendations under Family Code section 3183(a); and

(E) Information provided from a child interview center or professional so as to avoid unnecessary multiple interviews.

(2) If the court precludes the calling of a child as a witness and specifies one of the other alternatives, the court must require that the information or evidence obtained by alternative means and provided by a professional or nonparty:

(A) Be in writing and fully document the child's views on the matters on which the child wished to express an opinion;

(B) Describe the child's input in sufficient detail to assist the court in its adjudication process;

(C) Be provided to the court and to the parties by an individual who will be available for testimony and cross-examination; and

(D) Be filed in the confidential portion of the family law file.

(3) On deciding to take the testimony of a child, the judicial officer should balance the necessity of taking the child's testimony in the courtroom with parents and attorneys present with the need to create an environment in which the child can be open and honest. In each case in which a child's testimony will be taken, courts should consider:

(A) Where the testimony will be taken, including the possibility of closing the courtroom to the public or hearing from the child on the record in chambers;

(B) Who should be present when the testimony is taken, such as: both parents and their attorneys, only attorneys in the case in which both parents are represented, the child's attorney and parents, or only a court reporter with the judicial officer;

(C) How the child will be questioned, such as whether only the judicial officer will pose questions that the parties have submitted, whether attorneys or parties will be permitted to cross-examine the child, or whether a child advocate or expert in child development will ask the questions in the presence of the judicial officer and parties or a court reporter; and

(D) Whether a court reporter is available in all instances, but especially when testimony may be taken outside the presence of the parties and their attorneys and, if not, whether it will be possible to provide a listening device so that testimony taken in chambers may be heard simultaneously by the parents and their attorneys in the courtroom or to otherwise make a record of the testimony.

(4) In taking testimony from a child, the court must take special care to protect the child from harassment or embarrassment and to restrict the unnecessary repetition of questions. The court must also take special care to ensure that questions are stated in a form that is appropriate to the witness's age or cognitive level. If the child is not represented by an attorney, the court must inform the child in an age-appropriate manner about the limitations on confidentiality and that the information provided to the court will be on the record and provided to the parties in the case. In the process of listening to and inviting the child's input, the court must allow but not require the child to state a preference regarding custody or visitation and should, in an age-appropriate manner, provide information about the process by which the court will make a decision.

(5) In any case in which a child will be called to testify, the court may consider the appointment of minor's counsel for that child. The court may consider whether such appointment will cause unnecessary delay or otherwise interfere with the child's ability to participate in the process. In addition to adhering to the requirements for minor's counsel under Family Code section 3151 and rules 5.240, 5.241, and 5.242, minor's counsel must:

(A) Provide information to the child in an age-appropriate manner about the limitations on confidentiality and indicate to the child the possibility that information provided to the court will be on the record and provided to the parties in the case;

(B) Allow but not require the child to state a preference regarding custody or visitation (parenting time) and, in an age-appropriate manner, provide information about the process by which the court will make a decision;

(C) Provide procedures relevant to the child's participation and, if appropriate, provide an orientation to the courtroom where the child will be testifying; and

(D) Inform the parties and then the court about the client's desire to provide input.

(6) No testimony of a child may be received without such testimony being heard on the record or in the presence of the parties. This requirement may not be waived by stipulation.

(Subd (d) adopted effective January 1, 2012.)

(e) Responsibilities of court-connected or appointed professionals

A child custody evaluator, a child custody recommending counselor, an investigator, or a mediator appointed or assigned to meet with a child in a family court proceeding must:

(1) Provide information to the child in an age-appropriate manner about the limitations on confidentiality and the possibility that information provided to the professional may be shared with the court on the record and provided to the parties in the case;

(2) Allow but not require the child to state a preference regarding custody and visitation (parenting time), and, in an age-appropriate manner, provide information about the process by which the court will make a decision; and

(3) Provide to the parents of the child participating in the court process information about local court procedures relevant to the child's participation and information about how to best support the child in an age-appropriate manner during the court process.

(Subd (e) adopted effective January 1, 2012.)

(f) Methods of providing information to parents and supporting children

Courts should provide information to parties and parents and support for children when children want to participate or testify or are otherwise involved in family law proceedings. Such methods may include but are not limited to:

(1) Having court-connected professionals meet jointly or separately with the parents or parties to discuss alternatives to having a child provide direct testimony;

(2) Providing an orientation for a child about the court process and the role of the judicial officer in making decisions, how the courtroom or chambers will be set up, and what participating or testifying will entail;

(3) Providing information to parents or parties before and after a child participates or testifies so that they can consider the possible effect on their child of participating or not participating in a given case;

(4) Including information in child custody mediation orientation presentations and publications about a child's participation in family law proceedings;

(5) Providing a children's waiting room; and

(6) Providing an interpreter for the child, if needed.

(Subd (f) adopted effective January 1, 2012.)

(g) Education and training

Education and training content for court staff and judicial officers should include information on children's participation in family court processes, methods other than direct testimony for receiving input from children, and procedures for taking children's testimony.

(Subd (g) adopted effective January 1, 2012.)
Rule 5.250 adopted effective January 1, 2012.

Advisory Committee Comment

Rule 5.250 does not apply to probate guardianships except as and to the extent that the rule is incorporated or expressly made applicable by a rule of court in title 7 of the California Rules of Court.

Chapter 9
Child, Spousal, and Domestic Partner Support

Title 5, Family and Juvenile Rules—Division 1, Family Rules—Chapter 9, Child, Spousal, and Domestic Partner Support; adopted effective January 1, 2013.

Article 1
General Provisions

Title 5, Family and Juvenile Rules—Division 1, Family Rules—Chapter 9, Child, Spousal, and Domestic Partner Support—Article 1, General Provisions; adopted effective January 1, 2013.

Rule 5.260.   General provisions regarding support cases
(a) Financial declarations

Except as provided below, for all hearings involving child, spousal, or domestic partner support, both parties must complete, file, and serve a current *Income and Expense Declaration* (form FL-150) on all parties.

(1) A party requesting support orders must include a current, completed *Income and Expense Declaration* (form FL-150) with the *Request for Order* (form FL-300) that is filed with the court and served on all parties.

(2) A party responding to a request for support orders must include a current, completed *Income and Expense Declaration* (form FL-150) with the *Responsive Declaration to Request for Order* (form FL-320) that is filed with the court and served on all parties.

(3) "Current" means the form has been completed within the past three months providing no facts have changed. The form must be sufficiently completed to allow the court to make an order.

(4) In child support hearings, a party may complete a current *Financial Statement (Simplified)* (form FL-155) instead of a current *Income and Expense Declaration* (form FL-150) if he or she meets the requirements allowing submission of a *Financial Statement (Simplified)* (form FL-155).

(5) *Financial Statement (Simplified)* (form FL-155) is not appropriate for use in proceedings to determine or modify spousal or domestic partner support, to determine or modify family support, or to determine attorney's fees and costs.

(Subd (a) adopted effective January 1, 2013.)

(b) Deviations from guideline child support in orders and judgments

(1) If a party contends that the amount of support as calculated under the statewide uniform guideline formula is inappropriate, that party must file a declaration stating the amount of support alleged to be proper and the factual and legal bases justifying a deviation from guideline support under Family Code section 4057.

(2) In its discretion, for good cause shown, the court may deviate from the amount of guideline support resulting from the computer calculation. If the court finds good cause to deviate from the statewide uniform guideline formula for child support, the court must state its findings in

writing or on the record as required by Family Code sections 4056, 4057, and 4065.

(3) Stipulated agreements for child support that deviate from the statewide uniform guideline must include either a *Non-Guideline Child Support Findings Attachment* (form FL-342(A)) or language in the agreement or judgment conforming with Family Code sections 4056 and 4065.

(Subd (b) adopted effective January 1, 2013.)

(c) Request to change prior support orders

The supporting declaration submitted in a request to change a prior child, spousal, or domestic partner support order must include specific facts demonstrating a change of circumstances. No change of circumstances must be shown to change a previously agreed upon child support order that was below the child support guidelines.

(Subd (c) adopted effective January 1, 2013.)

(d) Notification to the local child support agency

The party requesting court orders must provide the local child support agency timely notice of any request to establish, change, or enforce any child, spousal, or domestic partner support order if the agency is providing support enforcement services or has intervened in the case as described in Family Code section 17400.

(Subd (d) adopted effective January 1, 2013.)

(e) Judgment for support

(1) If child support is an issue in a judgment:

(A) Each party should file a proposed support calculation with the proposed judgment that sets forth the party's assumptions with regard to gross income, tax filing status, time-share, add-on expenses, and any other factor relevant to the support calculation.

(B) The moving party should file the documents in (A) with the proposed judgment if the judgment is based on respondent's default or a stipulation of the parties.

(C) The court may use and must permit parties or their attorneys to use any software certified by the Judicial Council to present support calculations to the court.

(2) If spousal or domestic partner support is an issue in a judgment:

(A) Use of support calculation software is not appropriate when requesting a judgment or modification of a judgment for spousal or domestic partner support.

(B) Petitioner or the parties may use *Spousal or Partnership Support Declaration Attachment* (form FL-157) to address the issue of spousal or domestic partner support under Family Code section 4320 when relevant to the case.

(Subd (e) adopted effective January 1, 2013.)
Rule 5.260 adopted effective January 1, 2013.

Article 2
Certification of Statewide Uniform Guideline Support Calculators

Title 5, Family and Juvenile Rules—Division 1, Family Rules—Chapter 9, Child, Spousal, and Domestic Partner Support—Article 2, Certification of Statewide Uniform Guideline Support Calculators; amended effective January 1, 2013; adopted as Chapter 6.

Rule 5.275. Standards for computer software to assist in determining support

(a) Authority

This rule is adopted under Family Code section 3830.

(Subd (a) amended effective January 1, 2007; previously amended effective January 1, 2003.)

(b) Standards

The standards for computer software to assist in determining the appropriate amount of child or spousal support are:

(1) The software must accurately compute the net disposable income of each parent as follows:

(A) Permit entry of the "gross income" of each parent as defined by Family Code section 4058;

(B) Either accurately compute the state and federal income tax liability under Family Code section 4059(a) or permit the entry of a figure for this amount; this figure, in the default state of the program, must not include the tax consequences of any spousal support to be ordered;

(C) Ensure that any deduction for contributions to the Federal Insurance Contributions Act or as otherwise permitted by Family Code section 4059(b) does not exceed the allowable amount;

(D) Permit the entry of deductions authorized by Family Code sections 4059(c) through (f); and

(E) Permit the entry of deductions authorized by Family Code section 4059(g) (hardship) while ensuring that any deduction subject to the limitation in Family Code section 4071(b) does not exceed that limitation.

(2) Using examples provided by the Judicial Council, the software must calculate a child support amount, using its default settings, that is accurate to within 1 percent of the correct amount. In making this determination, the Judicial Council must calculate the correct amount of support for each example and must then calculate the amount for each example using the software program. Each person seeking certification of software must supply a copy of the software to the Judicial Council. If the software does not operate on a standard Windows 95 or later compatible or Macintosh computer, the person seeking certification of the software must make available to the Judicial Council any hardware required to use the software. The Judicial Council may delegate the responsibility for the calculation and determinations required by this rule.

(3) The software must contain, either on the screen or in written form, a glossary defining each term used on the computer screen or in printed hard copy produced by the software.

(4) The software must contain, either on the screen or in written form, instructions for the entry of each figure that is required for computation of child support using the default setting of the software. These instructions must include but not be limited to the following:

(A) The gross income of each party as provided for by Family Code section 4058;

(B) The deductions from gross income of each party as provided for by Family Code section 4059 and subdivision (b)(1) of this rule;

(C) The additional items of child support provided for in Family Code section 4062; and

(D) The following factors rebutting the presumptive guideline amount: Family Code section 4057(b)(2) (deferred sale of residence) and 4057(b)(3) (income of subsequent partner).

(5) In making an allocation of the additional items of child support under subdivision (b)(4)(C) of this rule, the software must, as its default setting, allocate the expenses one-half to each parent. The software must also provide, in an easily selected option, the alternative allocation of the expenses as provided for by Family Code section 4061(b).

(6) **The printout of the calculator results must display, on the first page of the results, the range of the low-income adjustment as permitted by Family Code section 4055(b)(7), if the low-income adjustment applies. If the software generates more than one report of the calculator results, the range of the low-income adjustment only must be displayed on the report that includes the user inputs.**

(7) The software or a license to use the software must be available to persons without restriction based on profession or occupation.

[1] (8) The sale or donation of software or a license to use the software to a court or a judicial officer must include a license, without additional charge, to the court or judicial officer to permit an additional copy of the software to be installed on a computer to be made available by the court or judicial officer to members of the public.

(Subd (b) amended effective January 1, 2020; previously amended effective January 1, 2003, and January 1, 2007.)

Rule 5.275(b). 2019 Deletes. [1] (7)

(c) Expiration of certification

Any certification provided by the Judicial Council under Family Code section 3830 and this rule must expire one year from the date of its issuance unless another expiration date is set forth in the certification. The Judicial Council may provide for earlier expiration of a certification if (1) the provisions involving the calculation of tax consequences change or (2) other provisions involving the calculation of support change.

(Subd (c) amended effective January 1, 2003.)

(d) Statement of certified public accountant

If the software computes the state and federal income tax liability as provided in subdivision (b)(1)(B) of this rule, the application for certification, whether for original certification or for renewal, must be accompanied by a statement from a certified public accountant that

(1) The accountant is familiar with the operation of the software;

(2) The accountant has carefully examined, in a variety of situations, the operation of the software in regard to the computation of tax liability;

(3) In the opinion of the accountant the software accurately calculates the estimated actual state and federal income tax liability consistent with Internal Revenue Service and Franchise Tax Board procedures;

(4) In the opinion of the accountant the software accurately calculates the deductions under the Federal Insurance Contributions Act (FICA),

including the amount for social security and for Medicare, and the deductions for California State Disability Insurance and properly annualizes these amounts; and

(5) States which calendar year the statement includes and must clearly indicate any limitations on the statement. The Judicial Council may request a new statement as often as it determines necessary to ensure accuracy of the tax computation.

(Subd (d) amended effective January 1, 2003.)

(e) Renewal of certification

At least three months prior to the expiration of a certification, a person may apply for renewal of the certification. The renewal must include a statement of any changes made to the software since the last application for certification. Upon request, the Judicial Council will keep the information concerning changes confidential.

(Subd (e) amended effective January 1, 2003.)

(f) Modifications to the software

The certification issued by the Judicial Council under Family Code section 3830 and this rule imposes a duty upon the person applying for the certification to promptly notify the Judicial Council of all changes made to the software during the period of certification. Upon request, the Judicial Council will keep the information concerning changes confidential. The Judicial Council may, after receipt of information concerning changes, require that the software be recertified under this rule.

(Subd (f) amended effective January 1, 2003.)

(g) Definitions

As used in this chapter:

(1) "Software" refers to any program or digital application used to calculate the appropriate amount of child or spousal support.

(2) "Default settings" refers to the status in which the software first starts when it is installed on a computer system. The software may permit the default settings to be changed by the user, either on a temporary or a permanent basis, if (1) the user is permitted to change the settings back to the default without reinstalling the software, (2) the computer screen prominently indicates whether the software is set to the default settings, and (3) any printout from the software prominently indicates whether the software is set to the default settings.

(3) "Contains" means, with reference to software, that the material is either displayed by the program code itself or is found in written documents supplied with the software.

(Subd (g) amended effective January 1, 2016; previously amended effective January 1, 2003.)

(h) Explanation of discrepancies

Before the Judicial Council denies a certificate because of failure to comply with the standards in paragraph (b)(1) or (b)(2) of this rule, the Judicial Council may request the person seeking certification to explain the differences in results.

(i) Application

[1] **A person seeking certification of software must apply in writing to the Judicial Council**.

(Subd (i) amended effective January 1, 2020; previously amended effective January 1, 2003.)

Rule 5.275(i). 2019 Deletes. [1] An application for certification must be on a form supplied by the Judicial Council and must be accompanied by an application fee of $250

(j) Acceptability in the courts

(1) In all actions for child or family support brought by or otherwise involving the local child support agency under title IV-D of the Social Security Act, the Department of Child Support Services' California Guideline Child Support Calculator software program must be used by:

(A) Parties and attorneys to present support calculations to the court; and

(B) The court to prepare support calculations.

(2) In all non-title IV-D proceedings, the court may use and must permit parties or attorneys to use any software certified by the Judicial Council under this rule.

(Subd (j) amended effective January 1, 2009; adopted as subd (k) effective January 1, 2000; previously relettered effective January 1, 2003.)

Rule 5.275 amended effective January 1, 2020; adopted as rule 1258 effective December 1, 1993; previously amended and renumbered as rule 5.275 effective January 1, 2003; previously amended effective January 1, 2000, January 1, 2007, January 1, 2009, and January 1, 2016.

Chapter 10
Government Child Support Cases (Title IV-D Support Cases)

Title 5, Family and Juvenile Rules—Division 1, Family Rules—Chapter 10, Government Child Support Cases (Title IV-D Support Cases); adopted effective January 1, 2013.

Rule 5.300. Purpose, authority, and definitions

(a) Purpose

The rules in this chapter are adopted to provide practice and procedure for support actions under title IV-D of the Social Security Act and under California statutory provisions concerning these actions.

(Subd (a) amended effective January 1, 2007.)

(b) Authority

These rules are adopted under Family Code sections 211, 3680(b), 4251(a), 4252(b), 10010, 17404, 17432, and 17400.

(Subd (b) amended effective January 1, 2007; previously amended effective January 1, 2003.)

(c) Definitions

As used in these rules, unless the context requires otherwise, "title IV-D support action" refers to an action for child or family support that is brought by or otherwise involves the local child support agency under title IV-D of the Social Security Act.

(Subd (c) amended effective January 1, 2007; previously amended effective January 1, 2003.)

Rule 5.300 amended effective January 1, 2007; adopted as rule 1280 effective January 1, 1977; previously amended and renumbered effective January 1, 2003.

Rule 5.305. Hearing of matters by a judge under Family Code sections 4251(a) and 4252(b)(7)

(a) Exceptional circumstances

The exceptional circumstances under which a judge may hear a title IV-D support action include:

(1) The failure of the judge to hear the action would result in significant prejudice or delay to a party including added cost or loss of work time;

(2) Transferring the matter to a commissioner would result in undue consumption of court time;

(3) Physical impossibility or difficulty due to the commissioner being geographically separate from the judge presently hearing the matter;

(4) The absence of the commissioner from the county due to illness, disability, death, or vacation; and

(5) The absence of the commissioner from the county due to service in another county and the difficulty of travel to the county in which the matter is pending.

(Subd (a) amended effective January 1, 2007; previously amended effective January 1, 2003.)

(b) Duty of judge hearing matter

A judge hearing a title IV-D support action under this rule and Family Code sections 4251(a) and 4252(b)(7) [1] **may make an order or may** make an interim order and refer the matter to the commissioner for further proceedings **when appropriate. As long as a local child support agency is a party to the action, any future proceedings must be heard by a commissioner, unless the commissioner is unavailable because of exceptional circumstances**.

(Subd (b) amended effective January 1, 2020; previously amended effective January 1, 2003, and January 1, 2007.)

Rule 5.305(b).   2019 Deletes. [1] must

(c) Discretion of the court

Notwithstanding (a) and (b) of this rule, a judge may, in the interests of justice, transfer a case to a commissioner for hearing.

(Subd (c) amended effective January 1, 2007.)

Rule 5.305 amended effective January 1, 2020; adopted as rule 1280.1 effective July 1, 1997; previously amended and renumbered effective January 1, 2003; previously amended effective January 1, 2007.

Rule 5.310.   Use of existing family law forms

When an existing family law form is required or appropriate for use in a title IV-D support action, the form may be used notwithstanding the absence of a notation for the other parent as a party under Family Code section 17404. The caption of the form must be modified by the person filing it by adding the words "Other parent:" and the name of the other parent to the form.

Rule 5.310 amended effective January 1, 2007; adopted as rule 1280.2 effective July 1, 1997; previously amended and renumbered effective January 1, 2003.

Rule 5.311.   Implementation of new and revised governmental forms by local child support agencies

(a) General extended implementation

A local child support agency providing services as required by Family Code section 17400 must implement any new or revised form approved or adopted by the Judicial Council for support actions under title IV-D of the Social Security Act, and under California statutory provisions concerning these actions, within six months of the effective date of the form. During that six-month period, the local child support agency may properly use and file the immediately prior version of the form.

(Subd (a) amended effective January 1, 2007.)

(b) Judgment regarding parental obligations

When the local child support agency files a proposed judgment or proposed supplemental judgment in any action using *Judgment Regarding Parental Obligations (Governmental)* (form FL-630), a final judgment or supplemental judgment may be filed on:

(1) The same version of the form that was used with the initial action or that was filed as an amended proposed judgment; or

(2) The most current version of the form, unless there have been amendments to the form that result in substantial changes from the filed version. If the most current version of the form has been substantially changed from the filed version, then the filed version must be used for the final judgment. A substantial change is one that would change the relief granted in a final judgment from that noticed in a proposed or amended proposed judgment.

(Subd (b) amended effective January 1, 2007.)

Rule 5.311 amended effective January 1, 2007; adopted effective January 1, 2004.

Rule 5.315.   Memorandum of points and authorities

Notwithstanding any other rule, including rule 313, a notice of motion in a title IV-D support action must not be required to contain points and authorities if the notice of motion uses a form adopted or approved by the Judicial Council. The absence of points and authorities under these circumstances may not be construed by the court as an admission that the motion is not meritorious and cause for its denial.

Rule 5.315 amended effective January 1, 2007; adopted as rule 1280.3 effective July 1, 1997; previously amended and renumbered effective January 1, 2003.

Rule 5.320.   Attorney of record in support actions under title IV-D of the Social Security Act

The attorney of record on behalf of a local child support agency appearing in any action under title IV-D of the Social Security Act is the director of the local child support agency, or if the director of that agency is not an attorney, the senior attorney of that agency or an attorney designated by the director for that purpose. Notwithstanding any other rule, including but not limited to rule 2.100–2.119, the name, address, and telephone number of the county child support agency and the name of the attorney of record are sufficient for any papers filed by the child support agency. The name of the deputy or assistant district attorney or attorney of the child support agency, who is not attorney of record, and the State Bar number of the attorney of record or any of his or her assistants are not required.

Rule 5.320 amended effective January 1, 2007; adopted as rule 1280.4 effective July 1, 1997; previously amended effective January 1, 2001; previously amended and renumbered effective January 1, 2003.

Rule 5.324.   Telephone appearance in title IV-D hearings and conferences

(a) Purpose

This rule is intended to improve the administration of the high volume of title IV-D child support hearings and conferences. Participation by both parents is needed for fair and accurate child support orders. The opportunity to appear by telephone fosters parental participation.

(b) Definition

"Telephone appearance," as used in this rule, includes any appearance by telephonic, audiovisual, videoconferencing, digital, or other electronic means.

(c) Permissibility of telephone appearances

Upon request, the court, in its discretion, may permit a telephone appearance in any hearing or conference related to an action for child support when the local child support agency is providing services under title IV-D of the Social Security Act.

(d) Exceptions

A telephone appearance is not permitted for any of the following except as permitted by Family Code section 5700.316:

(1) Contested trials, contempt hearings, orders of examination, and any matters in which the party or witness has been subpoenaed to appear in person; and

(2) Any hearing or conference for which the court, in its discretion on a case-by-case basis, decides that a personal appearance would materially assist in a determination of the proceeding or in resolution of the case.

(Subd (d) amended effective January 1, 2017; previously amended effective January 1, 2008.)

(e) Request for telephone appearance

(1) A party, an attorney, a witness, a parent who has not been joined to the action, or a representative of a local child support agency or government agency may request permission of the court to appear and testify by telephone. The local child support agency may request a telephone appearance on behalf of a party, a parent, or a witness when the local child support agency is appearing in the title IV-D support action, as defined by rule 5.300(c). The court may also, on its own motion, allow a telephone appearance.

(2) A party, an attorney, a witness, a parent who has not been joined to the action, or a representative of a local child support agency or government agency who wishes to appear by telephone at a hearing must file a request with the court clerk at least 12 court days before the hearing. A local child support agency that files the request for telephone appearance on behalf of a party, a parent, or a witness must file the request with the court clerk at least 12 court days before the hearing. This request must be served on the other parties, the local child support agency, and attorneys, if any. Service must be by personal delivery, fax, express mail, or other means reasonably calculated to ensure delivery by the close of the next court day.

(3) The mandatory *Request for Telephone Appearance (Governmental)* (form FL-679) must be filed to request a telephone appearance.

(Subd (e) amended effective January 1, 2008.)

(f) Opposition to telephone appearance

Any opposition to a request to appear by telephone must be made by declaration under penalty of perjury under the laws of the State of California. It must be filed with the court clerk and served at least eight court days before the court hearing. Service on the person or agency requesting the telephone appearance; all parties, including the other parent, a parent who has not been joined to the action, the local child support agency; and attorneys, if any, must be accomplished using one of the methods listed in (e)(2).

(Subd (f) amended effective January 1, 2007.)

(g) Shortening time

The court may shorten the time to file, submit, serve, respond, or comply with any of the procedures specified in this rule.

(h) Notice by court

At least five court days before the hearing, the court must notify the person or agency requesting the telephone appearance, the parties, and attorneys, if any, of its decision. The court may direct the court clerk, the court-approved vendor, the local child support agency, a party, or an attorney to provide the notification. This notice may be given in person or by telephone, fax, express mail, e-mail, or other means reasonably calculated to ensure notification no later than five court days before the hearing date.

(Subd (h) amended effective January 1, 2007.)

(i) Need for personal appearance

If, at any time during the hearing, the court determines that a personal appearance is necessary, the court may continue the matter and require a personal appearance.

(j) Vendors, procedure, audibility, reporting, and information

Rule 3.670(j)–(q) applies to telephone appearances under this rule.

(Subd (j) amended effective January 1, 2014; previously amended effective January 1, 2007, July 1, 2008, and July 1, 2011.)

(k) Technical equipment

Courts that lack the technical equipment to implement telephone appearances are exempt from the rule.

Rule 5.324 amended effective January 1, 2017; adopted effective July 1, 2005; previously amended effective January 1, 2007, January 1, 2008, July 1, 2008, July 1, 2011, and January 1, 2014.

Rule 5.325. Procedures for clerk's handling of combined summons and complaint

(a) Purpose

This rule provides guidance to court clerks in processing and filing the *Summons and Complaint or Supplemental Complaint Regarding Parental Obligations (Governmental)* (form FL-600) for actions under Family Code section 17400 or 17404.

(Subd (a) amended effective January 1, 2007; previously amended effective January 1, 2003.)

(b) Filing of complaint and issuance of summons

The clerk must accept the *Summons and Complaint or Supplemental Complaint Regarding Parental Obligations (Governmental)* (form FL-600) for filing under Code of Civil Procedure section 411.10. The clerk must issue the original summons in accordance with Code of Civil Procedure section 412.20 by filing the original form FL-600 and affixing the seal of the court. The original form FL-600 must be retained in the court's file.

(Subd (b) amended effective January 1, 2003.)

(c) Issuance of copies of combined summons and complaint

Upon issuance of the original summons, the clerk must conform copies of the filed form FL-600 to reflect that the complaint has been filed and the summons has been issued. A copy of form FL-600 so conformed must be served on the defendant in accordance with Code of Civil Procedure section 415.10 et seq.

(Subd (c) amended effective January 1, 2003.)

(d) Proof of service of summons

Proof of service of the *Summons and Complaint or Supplemental Complaint Regarding Parental Obligations (Governmental)* (form FL-600) must be on the form prescribed by rule 2.150 or any other proof of service form that meets the requirements of Code of Civil Procedure section 417.10.

(Subd (d) amended effective January 1, 2007; previously amended effective January 1, 2003.)

(e) Filing of proposed judgment and amended proposed judgment

The proposed judgment must be an attachment to the *Summons and Complaint or Supplemental Complaint Regarding Parental Obligations (Governmental)* (form FL-600) and must not be file-endorsed separately. An amended proposed judgment submitted for filing must be attached to the *Declaration for Amended Proposed Judgment* (form FL-616), as required by Family Code section 17430(c), and a proof of service by mail, if appropriate. Upon filing, the *Declaration for Amended Proposed Judgment* may be file-endorsed. The amended proposed judgment must not be file-endorsed.

(Subd (e) amended effective January 1, 2007; previously amended effective January 1, 2003.)

Rule 5.325 amended effective January 1, 2007; adopted as rule 1280.5 effective July 1, 1998; previously amended and renumbered effective January 1, 2003.

Rule 5.330. Procedures for child support case registry form

(a) Purpose

This rule provides guidance to court clerks in processing the *Child Support Case Registry Form* (form FL-191).

(Subd (a) amended effective January 1, 2007; previously amended effective January 1, 2003.)

(b) Application

This rule applies to any action or proceeding in which there is an order for child support or family support except for cases in which the local child support agency provides support enforcement services under Family Code section 17400. This rule does not apply to cases in which the local child support agency provides support enforcement services under Family Code section 17400.

(Subd (b) amended effective January 1, 2003.)

(c) Requirement that form be filed

The court must require that a *Child Support Case Registry Form* (form FL-191), completed by one of the parties, be filed each time an initial court order for child support or family support or a modification of a court order for child support or family support is filed with the court. A party attempting to file an initial judgment or order for child support or family support or a modification of an order for child or family support without a completed *Child Support Case Registry Form* (form FL-191) must be given a blank form to complete. The form must be accepted if legibly handwritten in ink or typed. No filing fees may be charged for filing the form.

(Subd (c) amended effective January 1, 2007; previously amended effective January 1, 2003.)

(d) Distribution of the form

Copies of the *Child Support Case Registry Form* (form FL-191) must be made available by the clerk's office and the family law facilitator's office to the parties without cost. A blank copy of the *Child Support Case Registry Form* (form FL-191) must be sent with the notice of entry of judgment to the party who did not submit the judgment or order.

(Subd (d) amended effective January 1, 2003.)

(e) Items on form that must be completed

A form must be considered complete if items 1b, 1c, 2, 5, and 6 are completed. Either item 3 or item 4 must also be completed as appropriate. If the form is submitted with the judgment or order for court approval, the clerk must complete item 1a once the judgment or order has been signed by the judicial officer and filed.

(Subd (e) amended effective January 1, 2003.)

(f) Clerk handling of form

The completed *Child Support Case Registry Form* (form FL-191) must not be stored in the court's file. It should be date and time stamped when received and stored in an area to which the public does not have access. At least once per month all forms received must be mailed to the California Department of Social Services.

(Subd (f) amended effective January 1, 2003.)

(g) Storage of confidential information

Provided that all information is kept confidential, the court may keep either a copy of the form or the information provided on the form in an electronic format.

Rule 5.330 amended effective January 1, 2007; adopted as rule 1280.6 effective July 1, 1999; previously amended and renumbered effective January 1, 2003.

Rule 5.335. Procedures for hearings on interstate income withholding orders

(a) Purpose

This rule provides a procedure for a hearing under Family Code section 4945 in response to an income withholding order.

(Subd (a) amended effective January 1, 2003.)

(b) Filing of request for hearing

A support obligor may contest the validity or enforcement of an income withholding order by filing a completed request for hearing. A copy of the income withholding order must be attached.

(c) Filing fee

The court must not require a filing fee to file the request for hearing under this rule.

(Subd (c) amended effective January 1, 2003.)

(d) Creation of court file

Upon receipt of the completed request for hearing and a copy of the income withholding order, the clerk must assign a case number and schedule a court date. The court date must be no earlier than 30 days from the date of filing and no later than 45 days from the date of filing.

(Subd (d) amended effective January 1, 2003.)

(e) Notice of hearing

The support obligor must provide the clerk with envelopes addressed to the obligor, the support enforcement agency that sent the income withholding order, and the obligor's employer. The support obligor must also provide an envelope addressed to the person or agency designated to receive the support payments if that person or agency is different than the paternity is [2] **canceled (set aside)**, the clerk must mail a copy of the order to the Department of Child Support Services in order that the voluntary declaration of **parentage or** paternity be purged from the records.

(Subd (e) amended effective January 1, 2020; previously amended effective January 1, 2003.)

Rule 5.350(e). 2019 Deletes. [1] *Set Aside* [2] set aside

(f) Use of court file in subsequent proceedings

Pleadings in any subsequent proceedings, including but not limited to proceedings under the Uniform Parentage Act, that involve the parties and child named in the voluntary declaration of **parentage or** paternity must be filed in the court file that was initiated by the filing of the *Request for Hearing and Application to* [1] *Cancel (Set Aside) Voluntary Declaration of Parentage or Paternity* (form FL-280).

(Subd (f) amended effective January 1, 2020; previously amended effective January 1, 2003.)

Rule 5.350(f). 2019 Deletes. [1] *Set Aside*

Rule 5.350 amended effective January 1, 2020; adopted as rule 1280.10 effective July 1, 2000; previously amended and renumbered effective January 1, 2003; previously amended effective January 1, 2006, and January 1, 2007.

Rule 5.355. Minimum standards of training for court clerk staff whose assignment includes title IV-D child support cases

Any court clerk whose assignment includes title IV-D child support cases must participate in a minimum of six hours of continuing education annually in federal and state laws concerning child support and related issues.

Rule 5.355 amended effective January 1, 2007; adopted as rule 1280.11 effective July 1, 2000; previously amended and renumbered effective January 1, 2003.

Rule 5.360. Appearance by local child support agency

When a local child support agency is providing services as required by Family Code section 17400, that agency may appear in any action or proceeding that it did not initiate by giving written notice to all parties, on *Notice Regarding Payment of Support* (form FL-632), that it is providing services in that action or proceeding under title IV-D of the Social Security Act. The agency must file the original of the notice in the action or proceeding with proof of service by mail on the parties. On service and filing of the notice, the court must not require the local child support agency to file any other notice or pleading before that agency appears in the action or proceeding.

Rule 5.360 amended effective January 1, 2007; adopted as rule 1280.12 effective January 1, 2001; previously amended and renumbered effective January 1, 2003.

Rule 5.365. Procedure for consolidation of child support orders

(a) When an order of consolidation of actions has been made under section 1048(a) of the Code of Civil Procedure in cases in which a local child support agency is appearing under section 17400 of the Family Code, or when a motion to consolidate or combine two or more child support orders has been made under section 17408 of the Family Code, the cases in which those orders were entered must be consolidated as follows:

(1) *Priority of consolidation*

The order consolidating cases that contain child support orders must designate the primary court file into which the support orders must be consolidated and must also designate the court files that are subordinate. Absent an order upon showing of good cause, the cases or child support orders must be consolidated into a single court file according to the following priority, including those cases or orders initiated or obtained by a local child support agency under division 17 of the Family Code that are consolidated under either section 1048(a) of the Code of Civil Procedure or section 17408 of the Family Code:

(A) If one of the cases or child support orders to be consolidated is in an action for nullity, dissolution, or legal separation brought under division 6 of the Family Code, all cases and orders so consolidated must be consolidated into that action, which must be the primary file.

(B) If none of the cases or child support orders to be consolidated is in an action for nullity, dissolution, or legal separation, but one of the child support orders to be consolidated has been issued in an action under the Uniform Parentage Act (Fam. Code, div. 12, pt. 3), all orders so consolidated must be consolidated into that action, which must be the primary file.

(C) If none of the cases or child support orders to be consolidated is in an action for nullity, dissolution, or legal separation or in an action under the Uniform Parentage Act, but one of the child support orders to be consolidated has been issued in an action commenced by a *Petition for Custody and Support of Minor Children* (form FL-260), all orders so consolidated must be consolidated into that action, which must be the primary file.

(D) If none of the cases or child support orders to be consolidated is in an action for nullity, dissolution, or legal separation or in an action under the Uniform Parentage Act, the case or cases with the higher number or numbers must be consolidated into the case with the lowest number, which must be the primary file. Child support orders in cases brought under the Domestic Violence Protection Act (Fam. Code, div. 10, pt. 4) or any similar law may be consolidated under this rule. However, a domestic violence case must not be designated as the primary file.

(2) *Notice of consolidation*

Upon issuance of the consolidation order, the local child support agency must prepare and file in each subordinate case a *Notice of Consolidation* (form FL-920), indicating that the support orders in those actions are consolidated into the primary file. The notice must state the date of the consolidation, the primary file number, and the case number of each of the cases so consolidated. If the local child support agency was not a participant in the proceeding in which the consolidation was ordered, the court must designate the party to prepare and file the notice.

(Subd (a) amended effective January 1, 2007; previously amended effective January 1, 2003.)

(b) Subsequent filings in consolidated cases

Notwithstanding any other rule, including but not limited to rule 367, upon consolidation of cases with child support orders, all filings in those cases, whether dealing with child support or not, must occur in the primary court action and must be filed under that case, caption, and number only. All further orders must be issued only in the primary action, and no further orders may be issued in a subordinate court file. All enforcement and modification of support orders in consolidated cases must occur in the primary court action regardless of in which action the order was originally issued.

(Subd (b) amended effective January 1, 2007; previously amended effective January 1, 2003.)

Rule 5.365 amended effective January 1, 2007; adopted as rule 1285.13 effective January 1, 2001; previously amended and renumbered effective January 1, 2003.

Rule 5.370.   Party designation in interstate and intrastate cases

When a support action that has been initiated in another county or another state is filed, transferred, or registered in a superior court of this state under the Uniform Interstate Family Support Act (Fam. Code, div. 9, pt. 5, ch. 6, commencing with § 4900), the intercounty support enforcement provisions of the Family Code (div. 9, pt. 5, ch. 8, art. 9, commencing with § 5600), or any similar law, the party designations in the caption of the action in the responding court must be as follows:

(1) *New actions initiated under the Uniform Interstate Family Support Act*

The party designation in the superior court of this state, responding to new actions initiated under the Uniform Interstate Family Support Act

(Fam. Code, div. 9, pt. 5, ch. 6, commencing with § 4900), must be the party designation that appears on the first page of *the Uniform Support Petition* (form FL-500/OMB 0970-0085) in the action.

(2) *Registered orders under the Uniform Interstate Family Support Act or state law*

The party designation in all support actions registered for enforcement or modification must be the one that appears in the original (earliest) order being registered.

Rule 5.370 amended effective January 1, 2007; adopted as rule 1285.14 effective January 1, 2001; previously amended and renumbered effective January 1, 2003.

Rule 5.372.   Transfer of title IV-D cases between tribal court and state court

(a) Purpose

This rule is intended to define the procedure for transfer of title IV-D child support cases between a California superior court and a tribal court.

(Subd (a) amended effective January 1, 2018; adopted effective January 1, 2014.)

(b) Definitions

(1) "Tribal court" means any tribal court of a federally recognized Indian tribe located in California that is receiving funding from the federal government to operate a child support program under title IV-D of the Social Security Act (42 U.S.C. § 654 et seq.).

(2) "Superior court" means a superior court of the state of California.

(3) "Title IV-D child support cases" include all cases where title IV-D services are being provided whether the case originates from the local child support agency's filing of a summons and complaint or later becomes a title IV-D cases when the local child support agency registers a child support order or intervenes in a child support action by filing a change of payee.

(Subd (b) adopted effective January 1, 2014.)

(c) Disclosure of related case

A party must disclose in superior court whether there is any related action in tribal court in the first pleading, in an attached affidavit, or under oath. A party's disclosure of a related action must include the names and addresses of the parties to the action, the name and address of the tribal court where the action is filed, the case number of the action, and the name of judge assigned to the action, if known.

(Subd (c) adopted effective January 1, 2014.)

(d) Notice of intent to transfer case

Before filing a motion for case transfer of a child support matter from a superior court to a tribal court, the party requesting the transfer, the state title IV-D agency, or the tribal IV-D agency must provide the parties with notice of their right to object to the case transfer and the procedures to make such an objection.

(Subd (d) adopted effective January 1, 2014.)

(e) Determination of concurrent jurisdiction by a superior court

(1) The superior court may, on its own motion or on the motion of any party and after notice to the parties of their right to object, transfer a child support and custody provision of an action in which the state is providing services under Family Code section 17400 to a tribal court, as defined in (a). This provision applies to both prejudgment and postjudgment cases.

(2) The motion for transfer to a tribal court must include the following information:

(A) Whether the child is a tribal member or eligible for tribal membership;

(B) Whether one or both of the child's parents are tribal members or eligible for tribal membership;

(C) Whether one or both of the child's parents live on tribal lands or in tribal housing, work for the tribe, or receive tribal benefits or services;

(D) Whether there are other children of the obligor subject to child support obligations;

(E) Any other factor supporting the child's or parents' connection to the tribe.

(3) When ruling on a motion to transfer, the superior court must first make a threshold determination that concurrent jurisdiction exists. Evidence to support this determination may include:

(A) Evidence contained within the motion for transfer;

(B) Evidence agreed to by stipulation of the parties; and

(C) Other evidence submitted by the parties or by the tribe.

The court may request that the tribal child support agency or the tribal court submit information concerning the tribe's jurisdiction.

(4) There is a presumption of concurrent jurisdiction if the child is a tribal member or eligible for tribal membership. If concurrent jurisdiction is found to exist, the transfer to tribal court will occur unless a party has objected within 20 days after service of notice of the right to object referenced in subdivision (e)(1) above. On the filing of a timely objection to the transfer, the superior court must conduct a hearing on the record considering all the relevant factors set forth in (f). The objecting party has the burden of proof to establish good cause not to transfer to tribal court.

(Subd (e) amended effective January 1, 2018; adopted effective January 1, 2014.)

(f) Evidentiary considerations

(1) In making a determination on the motion for case transfer, the superior court must consider:

(A) The identities of the parties;

(B) The convenience of the parties and witnesses;

(C) The remedy available in the superior court or tribal court; and

(D) Any other factors deemed necessary by the superior court.

(2) In making a determination on the motion for case transfer, the superior court may not consider the perceived adequacy of tribal justice systems.

(3) The superior court may, after notice to all parties, attempt to resolve any procedural issues by contacting the tribal court concerning a motion to transfer. The superior court must allow the parties to participate in, and must prepare a record of, any communication made with the tribal court judge.

(Subd (f) amended effective January 1, 2018; adopted effective January 1, 2014.)

(g) Order on request to transfer

If the superior court denies the request for transfer, the court must state on the record the basis for denying the request. If the superior court grants the request for transfer, it must issue a final order on the request to transfer including a determination of whether concurrent jurisdiction exists.

(Subd (g) amended effective January 1, 2018; adopted effective January 1, 2014.)

(h) Proceedings after order granting transfer

Once the superior court has granted the application to transfer and has received confirmation that the tribal court has accepted jurisdiction, the superior court clerk must deliver a copy of the entire file, including all pleadings and orders, to the clerk of the tribal court within 20 days of confirmation that the tribal court has accepted jurisdiction. With the exception of a filing by a tribal court as described by subdivision (i) of this rule, the superior court may not accept any further filings in the state court action in relation to the issues of child support and custody that were transferred to the tribal court.

(Subd (h) amended effective January 1, 2018; adopted effective January 1, 2014.)

(i) Transfer of proceedings from tribal court

(1) If a tribal court determines that it is not in the best interest of the child or the parties for the tribal court to retain jurisdiction of a child support case, the tribe may, upon noticed motion to all parties and the state child support agency, file a motion with the superior court to transfer the case to the jurisdiction of the superior court along with copies of the tribal court's order transferring jurisdiction and the entire file.

(2) The superior court must notify the tribal court upon receipt of the materials and the date scheduled for the hearing of the motion to transfer.

(3) If the superior court has concurrent jurisdiction, it must not reject the case.

(4) No filing fee may be charged for the transfer of a title IV-D child support case from a tribal court.

(Subd (i) adopted effective January 1, 2018.)

Rule 5.372 amended effective January 1, 2018; adopted effective January 1, 2014.

Advisory Committee Comment

This rule applies only to title IV-D child support cases. In the normal course, transfers from tribal court are initiated by the local child support agencies. Under Government Code sections 6103.9 and 70672, local child support agencies are exempt from payment of filing fees. The rule makes it clear that this exemption also applies when an eligible case is being transferred from a tribal court.

Rule 5.375. Procedure for a support obligor to file a motion regarding mistaken identity

(a) Purpose

This rule applies to a support obligor who claims that support enforcement actions have erroneously been taken against him or her by the local child support agency because of a mistake in the support obligor's identity. This rule sets forth the procedure for filing a motion in superior court to establish the mistaken identity under Family Code

section 17530 after the support obligor has filed a claim of mistaken identity with the local child support agency and the claim has been denied.

(Subd (a) amended effective January 1, 2003.)

(b) Procedure for filing motion in superior court

The support obligor's motion in superior court to establish mistaken identity must be filed on *Request for Order* (form FL-300) with appropriate attachments. The support obligor must also file as exhibits to the request for order a copy of the claim of mistaken identity that he or she filed with the local child support agency and a copy of the local child support agency's denial of the claim.

(Subd (b) amended effective January 1, 2013; previously amended effective January 1, 2003, and January 1, 2007.)

Rule 5.375 amended effective January 1, 2013; adopted as rule 1280.15 effective January 1, 2001; previously amended and renumbered effective January 1, 2003; previously amended effective January 1, 2007.

Chapter 11
Domestic Violence Cases

Title 5, Family and Juvenile Rules—Division 1, Family Rules—Chapter 11, Domestic Violence Cases; adopted effective January 1, 2013.

2012 Note: Chapter 11, effective January 1, 2013 was originally adopted as Chapter 8, effective July 1, 2012.

Article 1
Domestic Violence Prevention Act Cases

Title 5, Family and Juvenile Rules—Division 1, Family Rules—Chapter 11, Domestic Violence Cases—Article 1, Domestic Violence Prevention Act Cases; adopted effective January 1, 2013.

2012 Note: Article 1 of Chapter 11, effective January 1, 2013 was originally adopted as Article 1 of Chapter 8, effective July 1, 2012.

Rule 5.380. Agreement and judgment of parentage in Domestic Violence Prevention Act cases

(a) No requirement to open separate case; no filing fee

(1) If the court accepts the agreement of parentage and issues a judgment of parentage, the court may not require a party to open a separate parentage or other type of case in which to file the judgment. The court may open a separate type of case, but the court must not charge a fee for filing the judgment of parentage in the new case.

(2) When a judgment of parentage is filed in a Domestic Violence Prevention Act case in which a restraining order is currently in effect, no filing fee may be charged.

(Subd (a) adopted effective January 1, 2012.)

(b) Retention

The judgment must be retained by the court as a paternity record under Government Code section 68152.

(Subd (b) adopted effective January 1, 2012.)

(c) Notice of Entry of Judgment

When an *Agreement and Judgment of Parentage* (form DV-180) is filed, the court must serve a *Notice of Entry of Judgment* (form FL-190) on the parties.

(Subd (c) amended effective January 1, 2017; adopted effective January 1, 2012.)

Rule 5.380 amended effective January 1, 2017; adopted effective January 1, 2012.

Rule 5.381. Modification of child custody, visitation, and support orders in Domestic Violence Prevention Act cases

(a) Application of rule

This rule addresses court procedures for the modification of child custody, visitation, and support orders in accordance with Family Code section 6340(a).

(Subd (a) adopted effective January 1, 2012.)

(b) Filing fees

A filing fee may be charged on a request to modify a child custody, visitation, or support order only after a protective order, as defined in Family Code section 6218, is no longer in effect. The filing fee, if charged, is the same as the filing fee for a motion, application, or any other paper requiring a hearing after the first paper.

(Subd (b) adopted effective January 1, 2012.)

(c) Retention

The court must retain any child custody, visitation, or support order filed in a Domestic Violence Prevention Act as a Family Law order under Government Code section 68152(c)(5).

(Subd (c) adopted effective January 1, 2012.)

Rule 5.381 adopted effective January 1, 2012.

Rule 5.382.   Request to make minor's information confidential in domestic violence protective order proceedings

(a) Application of rule

This rule applies to requests and orders made under Family Code section 6301.5 to keep a minor's information confidential in a domestic violence protective order proceeding.

Wherever used in this rule, "legal guardian" means either parent if both parents have legal custody, or the parent or person having legal custody, or the guardian, of a minor.

(Subd (a) adopted effective January 1, 2019.)

(b) Information that may be made confidential

The information that may be made confidential includes:

(1) The minor's name;

(2) The minor's address;

(3) The circumstances surrounding the protective order with respect to the minor. These include the allegations in the *Request for Domestic Violence Retraining Order* (form DV-100) that involve conduct directed, in whole or in part, toward the minor; and

(4) Any other information that the minor or legal guardian believes should be confidential.

(Subd (b) adopted effective January 1, 2019.)

(c) Requests for confidentiality

(1) *Person making request*

A request for confidentiality may be made by a minor or legal guardian.

(2) *Number of minors*

A request for confidentiality by a legal guardian may be made for more than one minor. "Minor," as used in this rule, refers to all minors for whom a request for confidentiality is made.

(Subd (c) adopted effective January 1, 2019.)

(d) Procedures for making request

(1) *Timing of requests*

A request for confidentiality may be made at any time during the case.

(2) *Submission of request*

The person submitting a request must complete and file *Request to Keep Minor's Information Confidential* (form DV-160), a confidential form.

(3) *Ruling on request*

(A) *Ruling on request without notice*

The court must determine whether to grant a request for confidentiality without requiring that any notice of the request be given to the other party, or both parties if the minor is not a party in the proceeding. No adversarial hearing is to be held.

(B) *Request for confidentiality submitted at the same time as a request for restraining orders*

If a request for confidentiality is submitted at the same time as a request for restraining orders, the court must consider both requests consistent with Family Code section 6326, and must consider and rule on the request for confidentiality before the request for restraining order is filed.

Documents submitted with the restraining order request must not be filed until after the court has ruled on the request for confidentiality and must be consistent with (C) below.

(C) *Withdrawal of request*

If a request for confidentiality under (B) made by the person asking for the restraining order is denied and the requester seeks to withdraw the request for restraining orders, all of the following apply:

(i) The court must not file the request for restraining order and the accompanying proposed order forms and must return the documents to the requester personally, destroy the documents, or delete the documents from any electronic files;

(ii) The order denying confidentiality must be filed and maintained in a public file; and

(iii) The request for confidentiality must be filed and maintained in a confidential file.

(4) *Need for additional facts*

If the court finds that the request for confidentiality is insufficiently specific to meet the requirements under Family Code section 6301.5(b) for granting the request, the court may take testimony from the minor, or legal guardian, the person requesting a protective order, or other competent witness, in a closed hearing in order to determine if there are additional facts that would support granting the request.

(Subd (d) adopted effective January 1, 2019.)

(e) Orders on request for confidentiality

(1) *Rulings*

The court may grant the entire request, deny the entire request, or partially grant the request for confidentiality.

(2) *Order granting request for confidentiality*

(A) *Applicability*

An order made under Family Code section 6301.5 applies in this case and in any other civil case to all registers of actions, indexes, court calendars, pleadings, discovery documents, and other documents filed or served in the action, and at hearings, trial, and other court proceedings that are open to the public.

(B) *Minor's name*

If the court grants a request for confidentiality of the minor's name and:

(i) If the minor is a party to the action, the court must use the initials of the minor, or other initials at the discretion of the court. In addition, the court must use only initials to identify both parties to the action if using the other party's name would likely reveal the identity of the minor.

(ii) If the minor is not a party to the action, the court must not include any information that would likely reveal the identity of the minor, including whether the minor lives with the person making the request for confidentiality.

(C) *Circumstances surrounding protective order (statements related to minor)*

If the court grants a request for confidentiality, the order must specifically identify the information about the minor in *Request for Domestic Violence Restraining Order* (form DV-100) and any other applicable document that must be kept confidential. Information about the minor ordered confidential by the court must not be made available to the public.

(D) *Service and copies*

The other party, or both parties if the person making the request for confidentiality is not a party to the action, must be served with a copy of the [1] *Request to Keep Minor's Information Confidential* (form DV-160), *Order on Request to Keep Minor's Information Confidential* (form DV-165), and *Notice of Order Protecting Information of Minor* (form DV-170), redacted if required under (f)(4).

The protected person and the person requesting confidentiality (if not the protected person) must be provided up to three copies of redacted and unredacted copies of any request or order form.

(3) *Order denying request for confidentiality*

(A) The order denying confidentiality must be filed and maintained in a public file. The request for confidentiality must be filed and maintained in a confidential file.

(B) Notwithstanding denial of a request to keep the minor's address confidential, the address may be confidential under other statutory provisions

(C) Service

(i) If a request for confidentiality is denied and the request for restraining order has been withdrawn, and if no other action is pending before the court in the case, then the *Request to Keep Minor's Information Confidential* (form DV-160) and *Order on Request to Keep Minor's Information Confidential* (form DV-165) must not be served on the other party, or both parties if the person making the request for confidentiality is not a party to the action.

(ii) If a request for confidentiality is denied and the request for restraining order has not been withdrawn, or if an action between the same parties is pending before the court, then the *Request to Keep Minor's Information Confidential* (form DV-160) and *Order on Request to Keep Minor's Information Confidential* (form DV-165) must be served on the other party, or both parties if the person making the request for confidentiality is not a party to the action.

Rules of Court

(Subd (e) amended effective September 1, 2020; adopted effective January 1, 2019.)

Rule 5.382(e). 2020 Deletes. [1] *Request for Domestic Violence Restraining Order*

(f) Procedures to protect confidential information when order is granted

(1) If a request for confidentiality is granted in whole or in part, the court, in its discretion, and taking into consideration the factors stated in (g), must ensure that the order granting confidentiality is maintained in the most effective manner by:

(A) The judicial officer redacting all information to be kept confidential from all applicable documents;

(B) Ordering the requesting party or the requesting party's attorney to prepare a redacted copy of all applicable documents and submit all redacted copies to the court for review and filing; or

(C) Ordering any other procedure that facilitates the prompt and accurate preparation of a redacted copy of all applicable documents in compliance with the court's order granting confidentiality, provided the selected procedure is consistent with (g).

(2) The redacted copy or copies must be filed and maintained in a public file, and the unredacted copy or copies must be filed and maintained in a confidential file.

(3) Information that is made confidential from the public and the restrained person must be filed in a confidential file accessible only to the minor or minors who are subjects of the order of confidentiality, or legal guardian who requested confidentiality, law enforcement for enforcement purposes only, and the court.

(4) Any information that is made confidential from the restrained person must be redacted from the copy that will be served on the restrained person.

(Subd (f) adopted effective January 1, 2019.)

(g) Factors in selecting redaction procedures

In determining the procedures to follow under (f), the court must consider the following factors:

(1) Whether the requesting party is represented by an attorney;

(2) Whether the requesting party has immediate access to a self-help center or other legal assistance;

(3) Whether the requesting party is capable of preparing redacted materials without assistance;

(4) Whether the redactions to the applicable documents are simple or complex; and

(5) When applicable, whether the selected procedure will ensure that the orders on the request for restraining order and the request for confidentiality are entered in an expeditious and timely manner.

(Subd (g) adopted effective January 1, 2019.)

(h) Releasing minor's confidential information

(1) [1] *To respondent*

Information about a [2] minor must be shared with the respondent only as provided in Family Code section [3] **6301.5(d)(1)(B),** limited to information necessary to allow the respondent to respond to the request for the protective order [4] and to comply with the confidentiality order and the protective order.

(2) [5] *To law enforcement*

Information about a [6] minor must be shared with law enforcement [7] as provided in Family Code section [8] **6301.5(d)(1)(A) or by court order.**

(3) *To other persons*

If the court finds it is necessary to prevent abuse within the meaning of Family Code section 6220, or is in the best interest of the minor, the court may release confidential information on the request of any person or entity or on the court's own motion.

(A) *Request for release of confidential information*

(i) Any person or entity may request the release of confidential information by filing *Request for Release of Minor's Confidential Information* (form DV-176) and a proposed order, *Order on Request for Release of Minor's Confidential Information* (form DV-179), with the court.

(ii) Within 10 days after filing form DV-176 with the clerk, the clerk must serve, by first-class mail, the following documents on the minor or legal guardian who made the request to keep the minor's information confidential:

a. *Cover Sheet for Confidential Information* (form DV-175);

b. *Request for Release of Minor's Confidential Information* (form DV-176);

c. *Notice of Request for Release of Minor's Confidential Information* (form DV-177);

d. *Response to Request for Release of Minor's Confidential Information* (form DV-178) (blank copy);

e. *Order on Request for Release of Minor's Confidential Information* (form DV-179).

(B) *Opportunity to object*

(i) The person who made the request for confidentiality has the right to object by filing form DV-178 within 20 days from the date of the mailing of form DV-177, or verbally objecting at a hearing, if one is held.

(ii) The person filing a response must serve a copy of the response (form DV-178) on the person requesting release of confidential information. Service must occur before filing the response form with the court unless the response form contains confidential information. If the response form contains confidential information, service must be done as soon as possible after the response form has been redacted.

(iii) If the person who made the request for confidentiality objects to the release of information, the court may set the matter for a closed hearing.

(C) *Rulings*

The request may be granted or denied in whole or in part without a hearing. Alternatively, the court may set the matter for hearing on at least 10 days' notice to the person who made the request for release of confidential information and the person who made the request for confidential information. Any hearing must be confidential.

(i) *Order granting release of confidential information*

a. The order (form DV-179) granting the release of confidential information must be prepared in a manner consistent with the procedures outlined in (f).

b. A redacted copy of the order (form DV-179) must be filed in a public file and an unredacted copy of the order must be filed in a confidential file.

c. *Service*

If the court grants the request for release of information based on the pleadings, the court must mail a copy of form DV-179 to the person who filed form DV-176 and the person who made the request to keep the minor's information confidential. Parties may be served in court if present at the hearing.

(ii) *Order denying request to release minor's confidential information*

a. The court may deny a request to release confidential information based on the request alone.

b. The order (form DV-179) denying the release of confidential information must be filed in a public file and must not include any confidential information.

c. *Service*

If the court denies the request for release of information based on the pleadings, the court must mail a copy of form DV-179 to the person who filed form DV-176 and the person who made the request to keep the minor's information confidential. Parties may be served in court if present at the hearing.

(iii) If the court finds that the request to release confidential information is insufficiently specific to meet the requirements under Family Code section 6301.5(d)(3), the court may conduct a closed hearing to determine if there are additional facts that would support granting the request. The court may receive any relevant evidence, including testimony from the person requesting release of the minor's confidential information, the minor, the legal guardian, the person who requested the restraining order, or other competent witness.

(Subd (h) amended effective September 1, 2020; adopted effective January 1, 2019.)

Rule 5.382(h). 2020 Deletes. [1] *Sharing of information with the* [2] protected [3] 6301.5(d)(2) [4] , [5] *Sharing of information with* [6] protected [7] only [8] 6301.5(d)(1)

(i) Protecting information in subsequent filings and other civil cases

(1) *Filings made after an order granting confidentiality*

(A) A party seeking to file a document or form after an order for confidentiality has been made must submit the *Cover Sheet for Confiden-*

tial Information (form DV-175) attached to the front of the document to be filed.

(B) Upon receipt of form DV-175 with attached documents, the court must:

(i) Order a procedure for redaction consistent with the procedures stated in (f);

(ii) File the unredacted document in the confidential file pending receipt of the redacted document if the redacted document is not prepared on the same court day; and

(iii) File the redacted document in the public file after it has been reviewed and approved by the court for accuracy.

(2) *Other civil case*

(A) Information subject to an order of confidentiality issued under Family Code section 6301.5 must be kept confidential in **any family law case and** any other civil case **with the same parties.**

(B) The minor or person making the request for confidentiality and any person who has been served with a notice of confidentiality must submit a copy of the order of confidentiality (form DV-165) in **any family law case and** any other civil case [1] **with** the same parties.

(Subd (i) amended effective September 1, 2020; adopted effective January 1, 2019.)

Rule 5.382(i).   2020 Deletes. [1] involving

Rule 5.382 amended effective September 1, 2020; adopted effective January 1, 2019.

Advisory Committee Comment

Subdivisions (a), (b), (d), and (e). The process described in this rule need not be used if the request for confidentiality is merely to keep an address confidential and the minor has a mailing address which does not need to be kept private that can be listed on the forms, or if the minor's address can be made confidential under Family Code section 3429. In addition, the address need not be listed on the protective order for enforcement purposes under Family Code section 6225. The restraining order forms do not require the address of the nonpetitioning minor.

This rule and rule 2.551 provide a standard and procedures for courts to follow when a request is made to seal a record. The standard as reflected in Family Code section 6301.5 is based on *NBC Subsidiary (KNBC-TV), Inc. v. Superior Court* (1999) 20 Cal.4th 1178. The standard recognizes the First Amendment right of access to documents used at trial or as a basis of adjudication.

Article 2
Tribal Court Protective Orders

Title 5, Family and Juvenile Rules—Division 1, Family Rules—Chapter 11, Domestic Violence Cases—Article 2, Tribal Court Protective Orders; adopted effective January 1, 2013.

2012 Note: Article 2 of Chapter 11, effective January 1, 2013 was originally adopted as Article 2 of Chapter 8, effective July 1, 2012.

Rule 5.386.   Procedures for filing a tribal court protective order

(a) Request for written procedures for filing a tribal court protective order

At the request of any tribal court located within the county, a court must adopt a written procedure or local rule to permit the fax or electronic filing of any tribal court protective order that is entitled to be registered under Family Code section 6404.

(Subd (a) adopted effective July 1, 2012.)

(b) Process for registration of order

The written procedure or local rule developed in consultation with the local tribal court or courts must provide a process for:

(1) The tribal court or courts to contact a representative of the superior court to inform him or her that a request for registration of a tribal court protective order will be made;

(2) Confirmation of receipt of the request for registration of the order; and

(3) Return of copies of the registered order to the tribal court or the protected person.

(Subd (b) adopted effective July 1, 2012.)

(c) No filing fee required

In accordance with Family Code section 6404(b), no fee may be charged for the fax or electronic filing registration of a tribal court protective order.

(Subd (c) adopted effective July 1, 2012.)

(d) Facsimile coversheet

The *Fax Transmission Cover Sheet for Registration of Tribal Court Protective Order* (form DV-610) or similar cover sheet established by written procedure or local rule must be used when fax filing a tribal court

protective order. The cover sheet must be the first page transmitted, to be followed by any special handling instructions needed to ensure that the document will comply with local rules. Neither the cover sheet nor the special handling instructions are to be filed in the case. The court is not required to keep a copy of the cover sheet.

(Subd (d) adopted effective July 1, 2012.)
Rule 5.386 adopted effective July 1, 2012.

Chapter 12
Separate Trials (Bifurcation) and Interlocutory Appeals

Title 5, Family and Juvenile Rules—Division 1, Family Rules—Chapter 12, Separate Trials (Bifurcation) and Interlocutory Appeals; adopted effective January 1, 2013.

Art. 1.   Separate Trials. Rule 5.390.
Art. 2.   Interlocutory Appeals. Rule 5.392.

Article 1
Separate Trials

Title 5, Family and Juvenile Rules—Division 1, Family Rules—Chapter 12, Separate Trials (Bifurcation) and Interlocutory Appeals—Article 1, Separate Trials; adopted effective January 1, 2013.

Rule 5.390.   Bifurcation of issues

(a) Request for order to bifurcate

As part of the noticed *Request for Order* (FL-300) of a party, the stipulation of the parties, case management, or the court's own motion, the court may bifurcate one or more issues to be tried separately before other issues are tried. A party requesting a separate trial or responding to a request for a separate trial must complete *Application or Response to Application for Separate Trial* (form FL-315).

(Subd (a) adopted effective January 1, 2013.)

(b) When to bifurcate

The court may separately try one or more issues before trial of the other issues if resolution of the bifurcated issue is likely to simplify the determination of the other issues. Issues that may be appropriate to try separately in advance include:

(1) Validity of a postnuptial or premarital agreement;

(2) Date of separation;

(3) Date to use for valuation of assets;

(4) Whether property is separate or community;

(5) How to apportion increase in value of a business;

(6) Existence or value of business or professional goodwill;

(7) Termination of status of a marriage or domestic partnership;

(8) Child custody and visitation (parenting time);

(9) Child, spousal, or domestic partner support;

(10) Attorney's fees and costs;

(11) Division of property and debts;

(12) Reimbursement claims; or

(13) Other issues specific to a family law case.

(Subd (b) adopted effective January 1, 2013.)

(c) Alternate date of valuation

Requests for separate trial regarding alternate date of valuation under Family Code section 2552(b) must be accompanied by a declaration stating the following:

(1) The proposed alternate valuation date;

(2) Whether the proposed alternate valuation date applies to all or only a portion of the assets and, if the *Request for Order* (FL-300) is directed to only a portion of the assets, the declaration must separately identify each such asset; and

(3) The reasons supporting the alternate valuation date.

(Subd (c) adopted effective January 1, 2013.)

(d) Separate trial to terminate status of marriage or domestic partnership

(1) All pension plans that have not been divided by court order that require joinder must be joined as a party to the case before a petitioner or respondent may file a request for a separate trial to terminate marital status or the domestic partnership. Parties may refer to *Retirement Plan Joinder—Information Sheet* (form FL-318-INFO) to help determine whether their retirement benefit plans must be joined.

(2) The party not requesting termination of status may ask the court:

(A) To order that the judgment granting a dissolution include conditions that preserve his or her claims in retirement benefit plans, health insurance, and other assets; and

(B) For other orders made as conditions to terminating the parties' marital status or domestic partnership.

(3) The court must use *Bifurcation of Status of Marriage or Domestic Partnership—Attachment* (form FL-347) as an attachment to the order after hearing in these matters.

(4) In cases involving division of pension benefits acquired by the parties during the marriage or domestic partnership, the court must use *Pension Benefits—Attachment to Judgment* (form FL-348) to set out the orders upon severance of the status of marriage or domestic partnership. The form serves as a temporary qualified domestic relations order and must be attached to the status-only judgment and then served on the plan administrator. It can also be attached to a judgment to allow the parties time to prepare a qualified domestic relations order.

(Subd (d) adopted effective January 1, 2013.)

(e) Notice by clerk

Within 10 days after the order deciding the bifurcated issue and any statement of decision under rule 3.1591 have been filed, the clerk must serve copies to the parties and file a certificate of mailing or a certificate of electronic service.

(Subd (e) amended effective January 1, 2017; adopted effective January 1, 2013.)

Rule 5.390 amended effective January 1, 2017; adopted effective January 1, 2013.

Article 2
Interlocutory Appeals

Title 5, Family and Juvenile Rules—Division 1, Family Rules—Chapter 12, Separate Trials (Bifurcation) and Interlocutory Appeals—Article 2, Interlocutory Appeals; adopted effective January 1, 2013.

Rule 5.392. Interlocutory appeals

(a) Applicability

This rule does not apply to appeals from the court's termination of marital status as a separate issue, or to appeals from other orders that are separately appealable.

(Subd (a) amended effective January 1, 2003; previously amended effective January 1, 1994.)

(b) Certificate of probable cause for appeal

(1) The order deciding the bifurcated issue may include an order certifying that there is probable cause for immediate appellate review of the issue.

(2) If it was not in the order, within 10 days after the clerk serves the order deciding the bifurcated issue, a party may notice a motion asking the court to certify that there is probable cause for immediate appellate review of the order. The motion must be heard within 30 days after the order deciding the bifurcated issue is served.

(3) The clerk must promptly serve notice of the decision on the motion to the parties. If the motion is not determined within 40 days after serving the order on the bifurcated issue, it is deemed granted on the grounds stated in the motion.

(Subd (b) amended effective January 1, 2017; previously amended effective January 1, 2002, and January 1, 2003.)

(c) Content and effect of certificate

(1) A certificate of probable cause must state, in general terms, the reason immediate appellate review is desirable, such as a statement that final resolution of the issue:

(A) Is likely to lead to settlement of the entire case;

(B) Will simplify remaining issues;

(C) Will conserve the courts' resources; or

(D) Will benefit the well-being of a child of the marriage or the parties.

(2) If a certificate is granted, trial of the remaining issues may be stayed. If trial of the remaining issues is stayed, unless otherwise ordered by the trial court on noticed motion, further discovery must be stayed while the certification is pending. These stays terminate upon the expiration of time for filing a motion to appeal if none is filed, or upon the Court of Appeal denying all motions to appeal, or upon the Court of Appeal decision becoming final.

(Subd (c) amended effective January 1, 2003; previously amended effective January 1, 2002.)

(d) Motion to appeal

(1) If the certificate is granted, a party may, within 15 days after the court serves the notice of the order granting it, serve and file in the Court of Appeal a motion to appeal the decision on the bifurcated issue. On ex parte application served and filed within 15 days, the Court of Appeal or the trial court may extend the time for filing the motion to appeal by not more than an additional 20 days.

(2) The motion must contain:

(A) A brief statement of the facts necessary to an understanding of the issue;

(B) A statement of the issue; and

(C) A statement of why, in the context of the case, an immediate appeal is desirable.

(3) The motion must include or have attached:

(A) A copy of the decision of the trial court on the bifurcated issue;

(B) Any statement of decision;

(C) The certification of the appeal; and

(D) A sufficient partial record to enable the Court of Appeal to determine whether to grant the motion.

(4) A summary of evidence and oral proceedings, if relevant, supported by a declaration of counsel may be used when a transcript is not available.

(5) The motion must be accompanied by the filing fee for an appeal under rule 8.100(c) and Government Code sections 68926 and 68926.1.

(6) A copy of the motion must be served on the trial court.

(Subd (d) amended effective January 1, 2017; previously amended effective January 1, 2002, January 1, 2003, and January 1, 2007.)

(e) Proceedings to determine motion

(1) Within 10 days after service of the motion, an adverse party may serve and file an opposition to it.

(2) The motion to appeal and any opposition will be submitted without oral argument, unless otherwise ordered.

(3) The motion to appeal is deemed granted unless it is denied within 30 days from the date of filing the opposition or the last document requested by the court, whichever is later.

(4) Denial of a motion to appeal is final forthwith and is not subject to rehearing. A party aggrieved by the denial of the motion may petition for review by the Supreme Court.

(Subd (e) amended effective January 1, 2007; previously amended effective January 1, 2002, and January 1, 2003.)

(f) Proceedings if motion to appeal is granted

(1) If the motion to appeal is granted, the moving party is deemed an appellant, and the rules governing other civil appeals apply except as provided in this rule.

(2) The partial record filed with the motion will be considered the record for the appeal unless, within 10 days from the date notice of the grant of the motion is served, a party notifies the Court of Appeal of additional portions of the record that are needed for a full consideration of the appeal.

(3) If a party notifies the court of the need for an additional record, the additional material must be secured from the trial court by augmentation under rule 8.155, unless it appears to the Court of Appeal that some of the material is not needed.

(4) Briefs must be filed under a schedule set for the matter by the Court of Appeal.

(Subd (f) amended effective January 1, 2017; previously amended effective January 1, 2002, January 1, 2003, and January 1, 2007.)

(g) Review by writ or appeal

The trial court's denial of a certification motion under (b) does not preclude review of the decision on the bifurcated issue by extraordinary writ.

(Subd (g) amended effective January 1, 2003; previously amended effective January 1, 2002.)

(h) Review by appeal

None of the following precludes review of the decision on the bifurcated issue upon appeal of the final judgment:

(1) A party's failure to move for certification under (b) for immediate appeal;

(2) The trial court's denial of a certification motion under (b) for immediate appeal;

(3) A party's failure to move to appeal under (d); and

(4) The Court of Appeals denial of a motion to appeal under (d).

Rule 5.392 amended effective January 1, 2017; adopted as rule 1269.5 effective July 1, 1989; previously amended and renumbered as rule 5.180 effective January 1, 2003; previously renumbered as rule 5.392 effective January 1, 2013; previously amended effective January 1, 1994, January 1, 2002, and January 1, 2007.

Chapter 13
Trials and Long-Cause Hearings

Title 5, Family and Juvenile Rules—Division 1, Family Rules—Chapter 13, Trials and Long-Cause Hearings; adopted effective January 1, 2013.

Rule 5.393. Setting trials and long-cause hearings
Rule 5.394. Trial or hearing brief

Rule 5.393.   Setting trials and long-cause hearings

(a) Definitions

For purposes of this rule:

(1) A "trial day" is defined as a period no less than two and a half hours of a single court day.

(2) A "long-cause hearing" is defined as a hearing on a request for order that extends more than a single court day.

(3) A "trial brief" or "hearing brief" is a written summary or statement submitted by a party that explains to a judge the party's position on particular issues that will be part of the trial or hearing.

(Subd (a) adopted effective January 1, 2013.)

(b) Conference with judge before trial or long-cause hearing

The judge may schedule a conference with the parties and their attorneys before any trial or long-cause hearing.

(1) *Time estimates*

During the conference, each party must provide an estimate of the amount of time that will be needed to complete the trial or long-cause hearing. The estimate must take into account the time needed to examine witnesses and introduce evidence at the trial.

(2) *Trial or hearing brief*

The judge must determine at the conference whether to require each party to submit a trial or hearing brief. If trial briefs will be required, they must comply with the requirements of rule 5.394. Any additional requirements to the brief must be provided to the parties in writing before the end of the conference.

(Subd (b) adopted effective January 1, 2013.)

(c) Sequential days

Consistent with the goal of affording family law litigants continuous trials and long-cause hearings without interruption, when trials or long-cause hearings are set, they must be scheduled on as close to sequential days as the calendar of the trial judge permits.

(Subd (c) adopted effective January 1, 2013.)

(d) Intervals between trial or hearing days

When trials or long-cause hearings are not completed in the number of days originally scheduled, the court must schedule the remaining trial days as soon as possible on the earliest available days with the goal of minimizing intervals between days for trials or long-cause hearings.

(Subd (d) adopted effective January 1, 2013.)
Rule 5.393 adopted effective January 1, 2013.

Rule 5.394.   Trial or hearing brief

(a) Contents of brief

For cases in which the judge orders each party to complete a trial or hearing brief or other pleading, the contents of the brief must include at least:

(1) The statistical facts and any disputes about the statistical facts. Statistical facts that may apply to the case could include:

(A) Date of the marriage or domestic partnership;

(B) Date of separation;

(C) Length of marriage or domestic partnership in years and months; and

(D) Names and ages of the parties' minor children;

(2) A brief summary of the case;

(3) A statement of any issues that need to be resolved at trial;

(4) A brief statement summarizing the contents of any appraisal or expert report to be offered at trial;

(5) A list of the witnesses to be called at trial and a brief description of the anticipated testimony of each witness, as well as name, business address, and statement of qualifications of any expert witness;

(6) Any legal arguments on which a party intends to rely; and

(7) Any other matters determined by the judge to be necessary and provided to the parties in writing.

(Subd (a) adopted effective January 1, 2013.)

(b) Service of brief

The parties must serve the trial or hearing brief on all parties and file the brief with the court a minimum of 5 court days before the trial or long-cause hearing.

(Subd (b) adopted effective January 1, 2013.)
Rule 5.394 adopted effective January 1, 2013.

Chapter 14
Default Proceedings and Judgments

Title 5, Family and Juvenile Rules—Division 1, Family Rules—Chapter 14, Default Proceedings and Judgments; adopted effective January 1, 2013.

Rule 5.401. Default
Rule 5.402. Request for default; forms
Rule 5.405. Judgment checklists
Rule 5.407. Review of default and uncontested judgments submitted on the basis of declaration under Family Code section 2336
Rule 5.409. Default and uncontested judgment hearings on judgments submitted on the basis of declarations under Family Code section 2336
Rule 5.411. Stipulated judgments
Rule 5.413. Notice of entry of judgment
Rule 5.415. Completion of notice of entry of judgment

Rule 5.400.   Contact after adoption agreement [Renumbered]

Rule 5.400 renumbered as rule 5.451 effective January 1, 2013; adopted as rule 1180 effective July 1, 1998; previously amended effective July 1, 2001; previously amended and renumbered effective January 1, 2003; previously amended effective July 1, 2003, and January 1, 2007.

Rule 5.401.   Default

(a) Entry of default

Upon proper application of the petitioner, the clerk must enter a default if the respondent or defendant fails within the time permitted to:

(1) Make an appearance as stated in rule 5.62;

(2) File a notice of motion to quash service of summons under section 418.10 of the Code of Civil Procedure; or

(3) File a petition for writ of mandate under section 418.10 of the Code of Civil Procedure.

(Subd (a) adopted effective January 1, 2013.)

(b) Proof of facts

(1) The petitioner may apply to the court for the relief sought in the petition at the time default is entered. The court must require proof to be made of the facts stated in the petition and may enter its judgment based on that proof.

(2) The court may permit the use of a completed *Income and Expense Declaration* (form FL-150) or *Financial Statement (Simplified)* (form FL-155) and *Property Declaration* (form FL-160) for all or any part of the proof required or permitted to be offered on any issue to which they are relevant.

(Subd (b) adopted effective January 1, 2013.)

(c) Disposition of all matters required

A judgment based on a default must include disposition of all matters subject to the court's jurisdiction for which a party seeks adjudication or an explicit reservation of jurisdiction over any matter not proposed for disposition at that time.

(Subd (c) adopted effective January 1, 2013.)
Rule 5.401 adopted effective January 1, 2013.

Rule 5.402.   Request for default; forms

(a) Forms

No default may be entered in any proceeding unless a request has been completed on a *Request to Enter Default* (form FL-165) and filed by the petitioner. However, an *Income and Expense Declaration* (form FL-150) or *Financial Statement (Simplified)* (form FL-155) are not required if the petition contains no request for support, costs, or attorney's fees. A *Property Declaration* (form FL-160) is not required if the petition contains no request for property.

(Subd (a) adopted effective January 1, 2013.)

(b) Service address required

For the purpose of completing the declaration of mailing, unless service was by publication and the address of respondent is unknown, it is not sufficient to state that the address of the party to whom notice is given is unknown or unavailable.

(Subd (b) adopted effective January 1, 2013.)
Rule 5.402 adopted effective January 1, 2013.

Rule 5.405.   Judgment checklists

The *Judgment Checklist—Dissolution/Legal Separation* (form FL-182) lists the forms that courts may require to complete a judgment based on default or uncontested judgment in dissolution or legal separation cases based on a declaration under Family Code section 2336. The court may not require any additional forms or attachments.

Rule 5.405 renumbered effective January 1, 2013; adopted as rule 5.146 effective July 1, 2012.

Rule 5.407.   Review of default and uncontested judgments submitted on the basis of declaration under Family Code section 2336

Once a valid proof of service of summons has been filed with the court or respondent has made a general appearance in the case:

(a) Court review

The court must conduct a procedural review of all the documents submitted for judgment based on default or uncontested judgments submitted under Family Code section 2336 and notify the attorneys or self-represented litigants who submitted them of all identified defects.

(b) Notice of errors and omissions

Basic information for correction of the defects must be included in any notification to attorneys or self-represented litigants made under (a).

Rule 5.407 amended and renumbered effective January 1, 2013; adopted as rule 5.147 effective July 1, 2012.

Rule 5.409. Default and uncontested judgment hearings on judgments submitted on the basis of declarations under Family Code section 2336

The decision to hold a hearing in a case in which a judgment has been submitted on the basis of a declaration under Family Code section 2336 should be made on a case-by-case basis at the discretion of the court or request of a party. Courts must allow judgments in default and uncontested cases to be submitted by declaration pursuant to section 2336 and must not require that a hearing be conducted in all such cases.

Rule 5.409 renumbered effective January 1, 2013; adopted as rule 5.148 effective July 1, 2012.

Rule 5.410. Request for sibling contact information under Family Code section 9205 [Renumbered]

Rule 5.410 renumbered as rule 5.460 effective January 1, 2013; adopted effective January 1, 2008.

Rule 5.411. Stipulated judgments

(a) Format

A stipulated judgment (which must be attached to form FL-180 or form FL-250) may be submitted to the court for signature as an uncontested matter or at the time of the hearing on the merits and must contain the exact terms of any judgment proposed to be entered in the case. At the end, immediately above the space reserved for the judge's signature, the stipulated judgment must contain the following:

The foregoing is agreed to by:

_____   _____
(Petitioner)   (Respondent)

Approved as conforming to the agreement of the parties:

_____   _____
(Attorney for Petitioner)   (Attorney for Respondent)

(Subd (a) adopted effective January 1, 2013.)

(b) Disposition of all matters required

A stipulated judgment must include disposition of all matters subject to the court's jurisdiction for which a party seeks adjudication or an explicit reservation of jurisdiction over any matter not proposed for disposition at that time. A stipulated judgment constitutes a written agreement between the parties as to all matters covered by the stipulation.

(Subd (b) adopted effective January 1, 2013.)
Rule 5.411 adopted effective January 1, 2013.

Rule 5.413. Notice of entry of judgment

(a) Notice by clerk

Notwithstanding Code of Civil Procedure section 664.5, the clerk must give notice of entry of judgment, using *Notice of Entry of Judgment* (form FL-190), to the attorney for each party or to the party if self-represented, of the following:

(1) A judgment of legal separation;

(2) A judgment of dissolution;

(3) A judgment of nullity;

(4) A judgment establishing parental relationship (on form FL-190); or

(5) A judgment regarding custody or support.

(Subd (a) adopted effective January 1, 2013.)

(b) Notice to local child support agency form

This rule applies to local child support agency proceedings except that the notice of entry of judgment must be on *Notice of Entry of Judgment and Proof of Service by Mail* (form FL-635).

(Subd (b) adopted effective January 1, 2013.)
Rule 5.413 adopted effective January 1, 2013.

Rule 5.415. Completion of notice of entry of judgment

(a) Required attachments

Every person who submits a judgment for signature by the court must submit:

(1) Stamped envelopes addressed to the parties (if they do not have attorneys), or to the attorneys of record (if the parties are represented) that show the address of the court clerk as the return address; and

(2) An original and at least two additional copies of the *Notice of Entry of Judgment* (form FL-190).

(Subd (a) adopted effective January 1, 2013.)

(b) Fully completed

Form FL-190 must be fully completed except for the designation of the date entered, the date of mailing, and signatures. It must specify in the certificate of mailing the place where notices have been given to the other party.

(Subd (b) adopted effective January 1, 2013.)

(c) Address of respondent or defendant

If there has been no appearance by the other party, the address stated in the affidavit of mailing in part 3 of the *Request to Enter Default* (form FL-165) must be the party's last known address and must be used for mailing form FL-190 to that party. In support proceedings initiated by the local child support agency, an envelope addressed to the child support agency need not be submitted. If service was by publication and the address of respondent or defendant is unknown, those facts must be stated in place of the required address.

(Subd (c) adopted effective January 1, 2013.)

(d) Consequences of failure to comply

Failure to complete the form or to submit the envelopes is cause for refusal to sign the judgment until compliance with the requirements of this rule.

(Subd (d) adopted effective January 1, 2013.)

(e) Application to local child support agencies

This rule applies to local child support agency proceedings filed under the Family Code except that:

(1) The local child support agency must use form *Notice of Entry of Judgment and Proof of Service by Mail* (form FL-635);

(2) The local child support agency may specify in the certificate of mailing that the address where the *Notice of Entry of Judgment* (form FL-190) was mailed is on file with the local child support agency; and

(3) An envelope addressed to the local child support agency need not be submitted.

(Subd (e) adopted effective January 1, 2013.)
Rule 5.415 adopted effective January 1, 2013.

Chapter 15
Settlement Services

Title 5, Family and Juvenile Rules—Division 1, Family Rules—Chapter 15, Settlement Services; adopted effective January 1, 2013.

Rule 5.420. Domestic violence procedures for court-connected settlement service providers

(a) Purpose

This rule sets forth the protocol for court-connected settlement service providers handling cases involving domestic violence and not involving child custody or visitation (parenting time).

(Subd (a) adopted effective January 1, 2013.)

(b) Definitions

(1) "Domestic violence" is used as defined in Family Code sections 6203 and 6211.

(2) "Protective order" is synonymous with "domestic violence restraining order" as well as the following:

(A) "Emergency protective order" under Family Code section 6215;

(B) "Protective order" under Family Code section 6218;

(C) "Restraining order" under Welfare and Institutions Code section 213.5; and

(D) "Orders by court" under Penal Code section 136.2.

(3) "Settlement service(s)" refers to voluntary procedures in which the parties in a family law case agree to meet with a neutral third party professional for the purpose of identifying the issues involved in the case and attempting to reach a resolution of those issues by mutual agreement.

(Subd (b) adopted effective January 1, 2013.)

(c) Duties of settlement service providers

Courts providing settlement services must develop procedures for handling cases involving domestic violence. In developing these procedures, courts should consider:

(1) Reviewing court files or, if available, intake forms, to inform the person providing settlement services of any existing protective orders or history of domestic violence;

(2) Making reasonable efforts to ensure the safety of parties when they are participating in services;

(3) Avoiding negotiating with the parties about using violence with each other, whether either party should or should not obtain or dismiss a restraining order, or whether either party should cooperate with criminal prosecution;

(4) Providing information and materials that describe the settlement services and procedures with respect to domestic violence;

(5) Meeting first with the parties separately to determine whether joint meetings are appropriate in a case in which there has been a history of domestic violence between the parties or in which a protective order is in effect;

(6) Conferring with the parties separately regarding safety-related issues and the option of continuing in separate sessions at separate times if domestic violence is discovered after services have begun;

(7) Protecting the confidentiality of each party's times of arrival, departure, and meeting for separate sessions when appropriate; and

(8) Providing information to parties about support persons participating in joint or separate sessions.

(Subd (c) adopted effective January 1, 2013.)

(d) Training and education

All settlement service providers should participate in programs of continuing instruction in issues related to domestic violence, including child abuse.

(Subd (d) adopted effective January 1, 2013.)
Rule 5.420 adopted effective January 1, 2013.

Chapter 16
Limited Scope Representation; Attorney's Fees and Costs

Title 5, Family and Juvenile Rules—Division 1, Family Rules—Chapter 16, Limited Scope Representation; Attorney's Fees and Costs; adopted effective January 1, 2013.

Art. 1.   Limited Scope Representation. Rule 5.425.
Art. 2.   Attorney's Fees and Costs. Rule 5.427.

Article 1
Limited Scope Representation

Title 5, Family and Juvenile Rules—Division 1, Family Rules—Chapter 16, Limited Scope Representation; Attorney's Fees and Costs—Article 1, Limited Scope Representation; adopted effective January 1, 2013.

Rule 5.425.   Limited scope representation; application of rules

(a) Definition

"Limited scope representation" is a relationship between an attorney and a person seeking legal services in which they have agreed that the scope of the legal services will be limited to specific tasks that the attorney will perform for the person.

(Subd (a) adopted effective January 1, 2013.)

(b) Application

This rule applies to limited scope representation in family law cases. Rules 3.35 through 3.37 apply to limited scope representation in civil cases.

(Subd (b) adopted effective January 1, 2013.)

(c) Types of limited scope representation

These rules recognize two types of limited scope representation:

(1) *Noticed representation*

This type occurs when an attorney and a party notify the court and other parties of the limited scope representation. The procedures in (d) and (e) apply only to cases involving noticed limited scope representation.

(2) *Undisclosed representation*

In this type of limited scope representation, a party contracts with an attorney to draft or assist in drafting legal documents, but the attorney does not make an appearance in the case. The procedures in (f) apply to undisclosed representation.

(Subd (c) adopted effective January 1, 2013.)

(d) Noticed limited scope representation

(1) A party and an attorney must provide the required notice of their agreement for limited scope representation by serving other parties and filing with the court a *Notice of Limited Scope Representation* (form FL-950).

(2) After the notice in (1) is received and until a *Substitution of Attorney—Civil* (form MC-050), or a *Notice of Completion of Limited*

Scope Representation (form FL-955) with the "Final" box checked, or an order to be relieved as attorney is filed and served:

(A) The attorney must be served only with documents that relate to the issues identified in the *Notice of Limited Scope Representation* (form FL-950); and

(B) Documents that relate to all other issues outside the scope of the attorney's representation must be served directly on the party or the attorney representing the party on those issues.

(3) Electronic service of notices and documents described in this rule is permitted if the client previously agreed in writing to accept service of documents electronically from the attorney.

(4) Before being relieved as counsel, the limited scope attorney must file and serve the order after hearing or judgment following the hearing or trial at which he or she provided representation unless:

(A) Otherwise directed by the court; or

(B) The party agreed in the *Notice of Limited Scope Representation* (form FL-950) that completion of the order after hearing is not within the scope of the attorney's representation.

(Subd (d) amended effective September 1, 2017; adopted effective January 1, 2013.)

(e) Procedures to be relieved as counsel on completion of limited scope representation if client has not signed a substitution of attorney

An attorney who has completed the tasks specified in the *Notice of Limited Scope Representation* (form FL-950) may use the following procedures to request that he or she be relieved as attorney if the client has not signed a *Substitution of Attorney—Civil* (form MC-050):

(1) *Notice of completion of limited scope representation*

The limited scope attorney must serve the client with the following documents:

(A) A *Notice of Completion of Limited Scope Representation* (form FL-955) with the "Proposed" box marked and the deadline for the client to file the objection completed by the attorney;

(B) *Information for Client About Notice of Completion of Limited Scope Representation* (form FL-955-INFO); and

(C) A blank *Objection to Proposed Notice of Completion of Limited Scope Representation* (form FL-956).

(2) *No objection*

If the client does not file and serve an *Objection to Proposed Notice of Completion of Limited Scope Representation* (form FL-956) within 10 calendar days from the date that the *Notice of Completion of Limited Scope Representation* (form FL-955) was served, the limited scope attorney:

(A) Must serve the client and the other parties or, if represented, their attorneys, with a *Notice of Completion of Limited Scope Representation* (form FL-955) with the "Final" box marked;

(B) Must file the final *Notice of Completion of Limited Scope Representation* (form FL-955) with the court, and attach the proofs of service of both the "Proposed" and "Final" notices of completion;

(C) May not be charged a fee to file the final notice of completion, even if the attorney has not previously made an appearance in the case; and

(D) Is deemed to be relieved as attorney on the date that the final notice of completion is served on the client.

(3) *Objection*

If the client files the *Objection to Proposed Notice of Completion of Limited Scope Representation* (form FL-956) within 10 calendar days from the date that the proposed notice of completion was served, the following procedures apply:

(A) The clerk must set a hearing date on the *Objection to Proposed Notice of Completion of Limited Scope Representation* (form FL-956) to be conducted no later than 25 court days from the date the objection is filed.

(B) The court may charge a motion fee to file the objection and schedule the hearing.

(C) The objection—including the date, time, and location of the hearing—must be served on the limited scope attorney and all other parties in the case (or on their attorneys, if they are represented). Unless the court orders a different time for service, the objection must be served by the deadline specified in *Information for Client About Notice of Completion of Limited Scope Representation* (form FL-955-INFO).

(D) If the attorney wishes, he or she may file and serve a *Response to Objection to Proposed Notice of Completion of Limited Scope Representation* (form FL-957). Unless otherwise directed by the court, any response should be filed with the court and served on the client and other parties, or their attorneys, at least nine court days before the hearing.

(E) Unless otherwise directed by the court, the attorney must prepare the *Order on Completion of Limited Scope Representation* (form FL-958) and obtain the judge's signature.

(F) The attorney is responsible for filing and serving the order on the client and other parties after the hearing, unless the court directs otherwise.

(G) If the court finds that the attorney has completed the agreed-upon work, the representation is concluded on the date determined by the court in the *Order on Completion of Limited Scope Representation* (form FL-958).

(Subd (e) amended effective January 1, 2018; adopted effective January 1, 2013; previously amended and renumbered effective September 1, 2017.)

(f) Nondisclosure of attorney assistance in preparation of court documents

(1) *Nondisclosure*

In a family law proceeding, an attorney who contracts with a client to draft or assist in drafting legal documents, but does not make an appearance in the case, is not required to disclose within the text of the document that he or she was involved in preparing the documents.

(2) *Attorney's fees*

If a litigant seeks a court order for attorney's fees incurred as a result of document preparation, the litigant must disclose to the court information required for a proper determination of attorney's fees, including the name of the attorney who assisted in the preparation of the documents, the time involved or other basis for billing, the tasks performed, and the amount billed.

(3) *Applicability*

This rule does not apply to an attorney who has made a general appearance or has contracted with his or her client to make an appearance on any issue that is the subject of the pleadings.

(Subd (f) adopted effective January 1, 2013.)

Rule 5.425 amended effective January 1, 2018; adopted effective January 1, 2013; previously amended effective September 1, 2017.

Article 2
Attorney's Fees and Costs

Title 5, Family and Juvenile Rules—Division 1, Family Rules—Chapter 16, Limited Scope Representation; Attorney's Fees and Costs—Article 2, Attorney's Fees and Costs; adopted effective January 1, 2013.

Rule 5.427.   Attorney's fees and costs

(a) Application

This rule applies to attorney's fees and costs based on financial need, as described in Family Code sections 2030, 2032, 3121, 3557, and 7605.

(Subd (a) adopted effective January 1, 2012.)

(b) Request

(1) Except as provided in Family Code section 2031(b), to request attorney's fees and costs, a party must complete, file, and serve the following documents:

(A) *Request for Order* (form FL-300);

(B) *Request for Attorney's Fees and Costs Attachment* (form FL-319) or a comparable declaration that addresses the factors covered in form FL-319;

(C) A current *Income and Expense Declaration* (form FL-150);

(D) A personal declaration in support of the request for attorney's fees and costs, either using *Supporting Declaration for Attorney's Fees and Costs Attachment* (form FL-158) or a comparable declaration that addresses the factors covered in form FL-158; and

(E) Any other papers relevant to the relief requested.

(2) The party requesting attorney's fees and costs must provide the court with sufficient information about the attorney's hourly billing rate; the nature of the litigation; the attorney's experience in the particular type of work demanded; the fees and costs incurred or anticipated; and why the requested fees and costs are just, necessary, and reasonable.

(Subd (b) amended effective July 1, 2012; adopted effective January 1, 2012.)

(c) Response to request

To respond to the request for attorney's fees and costs, a party must complete, file, and serve the following documents:

(1) *Responsive Declaration to Request for Order* (form FL-320);

(2) A current *Income and Expense Declaration* (form FL-150);

(3) A personal declaration responding to the request for attorney's fees and costs, either using *Supporting Declaration for Attorney's Fees and*

Costs Attachment (form FL-158) or a comparable declaration that addresses the factors covered in form FL-158; and

(4) Any other papers relevant to the relief requested.

(Subd (c) amended effective July 1, 2012; adopted effective January 1, 2012.)

(d) Income and expense declaration

Both parties must complete, file, and serve a current *Income and Expense Declaration* (form FL-150). A *Financial Statement (Simplified)* (form FL-155) is not appropriate for use in proceedings to determine or modify attorney's fees and costs.

(1) "Current" is defined as being completed within the past three months, provided that no facts have changed. The form must be sufficiently completed to allow determination of the issues.

(2) When attorney's fees are requested by either party, the section on the *Income and Expense Declaration* (form FL-150) related to the amount in savings, credit union, certificates of deposit, and money market accounts must be fully completed, as well as the section related to the amount of attorney's fees incurred, currently owed, and the source of money used to pay such fees.

(Subd (d) adopted effective January 1, 2012.)

(e) Court findings and order

The court may make findings and orders regarding attorney's fees and costs by using *Attorney's Fees and Costs Order Attachment* (form FL-346). This form is an attachment to *Findings and Order After Hearing* (form FL-340), *Judgment* (form FL-180), and *Judgment (Uniform Parentage—Custody and Support)* (form FL-250).

(Subd (e) adopted effective January 1, 2012.)

Rule 5.427 renumbered effective January 1, 2013; adopted as rule 5.93 effective January 1, 2012; previously amended effective July 1, 2012.

Chapter 17
Family Law Facilitator

Title 5, Family and Juvenile Rules—Division 1, Family Rules—Chapter 17, Family Law Facilitator; adopted effective January 1, 2013.

Rule 5.430.   Minimum standards for the Office of the Family Law Facilitator

(a) Authority

These standards are adopted under Family Code section 10010.

(Subd (a) amended effective January 1, 2003.)

(b) Family law facilitator qualifications

The Office of the Family Law Facilitator must be headed by at least one attorney, who is an active member of the State Bar of California, known as the family law facilitator. Each family law facilitator must possess the following qualifications:

(1) A minimum of five years experience in the practice of law, which must include substantial family law practice including litigation and/or mediation;

(2) Knowledge of family law procedures;

(3) Knowledge of the child support establishment and enforcement process under Title IV-D of the federal Social Security Act (42 U.S.C. § 651 et seq.);

(4) Knowledge of child support law and the operation of the uniform state child support guideline; and

(5) Basic understanding of law and psychological issues related to domestic violence.

(Subd (b) amended effective January 1, 2003.)

(c) Substituted experience

Courts may substitute additional experience, skills, or background appropriate to their community for the qualifications listed above.

(d) Desirable experience

Additional desirable experience for a family law facilitator may include experience in working with low-income, semiliterate, self-represented, or non-English-speaking litigants.

(Subd (d) amended effective January 1, 2007.)

(e) Service provision

Services may be provided by other paid and volunteer members of the Office of the Family Law Facilitator under the supervision of the family law facilitator.

(f) Protocol required

Each court must develop a written protocol to provide services when a facilitator deems himself or herself disqualified or biased.

(g) Grievance procedure

Each court must develop a written protocol for a grievance procedure for processing and responding to any complaints against a family law facilitator.

(Subd (g) adopted effective January 1, 2003.)

(h) Training requirements

Each family law facilitator should attend at least one training per year for family law facilitators provided by the Judicial Council.

(Subd (h) relettered effective January 1, 2003; adopted as subd (g) effective January 1, 2000.)

Rule 5.430 renumbered effective January 1, 2013; adopted as rule 1208 effective January 1, 2000; previously amended and renumbered as rule 5.35 effective January 1, 2003; previously amended effective January 1, 2007.

Chapter 18
Court Coordination Rules

Title 5, Family and Juvenile Rules—Division 1, Family Rules—Chapter 18, Court Coordination Rules; adopted effective January 1, 2013.

Article 1
Related Cases

Title 5, Family and Juvenile Rules—Division 1, Family Rules—Chapter 18, Court Coordination Rules—Article 1, Related Cases; adopted effective January 1, 2013.

Rule 5.440. Related cases

Rule 5.445. Court communication protocol for domestic violence and child custody orders

Rule 5.440. Related cases

Where resources permit, courts should identify cases related to a pending family law case to avoid issuing conflicting orders and make effective use of court resources.

(a) Definition of "related case"

For purposes of this rule, a pending family law case is related to another pending case, or to a case that was dismissed with or without prejudice, or to a case that was disposed of by judgment, if the cases:

(1) Involve the same parties or the parties' minor children;

(2) Are based on issues governed by the Family Code or by the guardianship provisions of the Probate Code; or

(3) Are likely for other reasons to require substantial duplication of judicial resources if heard by different judges.

(Subd (a) adopted effective January 1, 2013.)

(b) Confidential information

Other than forms providing custody and visitation (parenting time) orders to be filed in the family court, where the identification of a related case includes a disclosure of information relating to a juvenile dependency or delinquency matter involving the children of the parties in the pending family law case, the clerk must file that information in the confidential portion of the court file.

(Subd (b) adopted effective January 1, 2013.)

(c) Coordination of title IV-D cases

To the extent possible, courts should coordinate title IV-D (government child support) cases with other related family law matters.

(Subd (c) adopted effective January 1, 2013.)

Rule 5.440 adopted effective January 1, 2013.

Rule 5.445. Court communication protocol for domestic violence and child custody orders

(a) Definitions

For purposes of this rule:

(1) "Criminal court protective order" means any court order issued under California Penal Code section 136.2 arising from a complaint, an information, or an indictment in which the victim or witness and the defendant have a relationship as defined in Family Code section 6211.

(2) "Court" means all departments and divisions of the superior court of a single county.

(3) "Cases involving child custody and visitation" include family, juvenile, probate, and guardianship proceedings.

(Subd (a) amended effective January 1, 2007.)

(b) Purpose

(1) This rule is intended to:

(A) Encourage courts to share information about the existence and terms of criminal court protective orders and other orders regarding child custody and visitation that involve the defendant and the victim or witness named in the criminal court protective orders.

(B) Encourage courts hearing cases involving child custody and visitation to take every action practicable to ensure that they are aware of the existence of any criminal court protective orders involving the parties to the action currently before them.

(C) Encourage criminal courts to take every action practicable to ensure that they are aware of the existence of any child custody or visitation court orders involving the defendant in the action currently before them.

(D) Permit appropriate visitation between a criminal defendant and his or her children under civil court orders, but at the same time provide for the safety of the victim or witness by ensuring that a criminal court protective order is not violated.

(E) Protect the rights of all parties and enhance the ability of law enforcement to enforce orders.

(F) Encourage courts to establish regional communication systems with courts in neighboring counties regarding the existence of and terms of criminal court protective orders.

(2) This rule is not intended to change the procedures, provided in Family Code section 6380, for the electronic entry of domestic violence restraining orders into the Domestic Violence Restraining Order System.

(Subd (b) amended effective January 1, 2007.)

(c) Local rule required

Every superior court must, by January 1, 2004, adopt local rules containing, at a minimum, the following elements:

(1) *Court communication*

A procedure for communication among courts issuing criminal court protective orders and courts issuing orders involving child custody and visitation, regarding the existence and terms of criminal protective orders and child custody and visitation orders, including:

(A) A procedure requiring courts issuing any orders involving child custody or visitation to make reasonable efforts to determine whether there exists a criminal court protective order that involves any party to the action; and

(B) A procedure requiring courts issuing criminal court protective orders to make reasonable efforts to determine whether there exist any child custody or visitation orders that involve any party to the action.

(2) *Modification*

A procedure by which the court that has issued a criminal court protective order may, after consultation with a court that has issued a subsequent child custody or visitation order, modify the criminal court protective order to allow or restrict contact between the person restrained by the order and his or her children.

(3) *Penal Code section 136.2*

The requirements of Penal Code section 136.2(f)(1) and (2).

(Subd (c) amended effective January 1, 2007; previously amended effective January 1, 2005.)

Rule 5.445 renumbered effective January 1, 2013; adopted as rule 5.500 effective January 1, 2003; previously amended effective January 1, 2005; previously amended and renumbered as rule 5.450 effective January 1, 2007.

Chapter 19
Minor Marriage or Domestic Partnership

Title 5, Family and Juvenile Rules—Division 1, Family Rules—Chapter 19, Minor Marriage or Domestic Partnership; adopted effective January 1, 2020.

Article 1
General Provisions

Title 5, Family and Juvenile Rules—Division 1, Family Rules—Chapter 19, Minor Marriage or Domestic Partnership—Article 1, General Provisions; adopted effective January 1, 2020.

Rule 5.448. Minor's request to marry or establish a domestic partnership

(a) Application

(1) This rule implements Family Code sections 297.1, 303, and 304, allowing a person under 18 years of age (a minor) to seek a court order for permission to marry or establish a domestic partnership.

(2) The responsibilities of Family Court Services under (c) apply equally to courts that adopt a confidential child custody mediation program, recommending child custody counseling, or a tiered/hybrid program.

(3) For the purpose of this rule, the terms "parent" and "parent with legal authority" are used interchangeably.

(Subd (a) adopted effective January 1, 2020.)

(b) Required initial filings

(1) The minor and the minor's proposed spouse or domestic partner must complete and file with the court clerk a *Request of Minor to Marry or Establish a Domestic Partnership* (form FL-910).

(2) Unless the minor has no parent or legal guardian capable of consenting, each minor must file, in addition to form FL-910, the written consent from a parent with legal authority to provide consent or a legal guardian. *Consent for Minor to Marry or Establish a Domestic Partnership* (form FL-912) may be used for this purpose.

(Subd (b) adopted effective January 1, 2020.)

(c) Responsibilities of Family Court Services

Unless the minor is 17 years of age and has achieved a high school diploma or a high school equivalency certificate, Family Court Services must:

(1) Interview the parties intending to marry or establish a domestic partnership.

(A) The parties must initially be interviewed separately; and

(B) The parties may subsequently be interviewed together.

(2) Interview at least one of the parents or the legal guardian of each party who is a minor, if the minor has a parent or legal guardian. If more than one parent or legal guardian is interviewed, the parents or guardians must be interviewed separately.

(3) Inform the parties that Family Court Services must:

(A) Prepare a written report, including recommendations for granting or denying the parties permission to marry or establish a domestic partnership;

(B) Provide the parties and the court with a copy of the report; and

(C) Submit a report of known or suspected child abuse or neglect to the county child protective services agency if Family Court Services knows or reasonably suspects that either party is a victim of child abuse or neglect.

(4) Prepare a written report, which must:

(A) Include an assessment of any potential force, threat, persuasion, fraud, coercion, or duress by either of the parties or their family members relating to the intended marriage or domestic partnership;

(B) Include recommendations for granting or denying the parties permission to marry or establish a domestic partnership; and

(C) Be submitted to the parties and the court.

(5) Protect party confidentiality in:

(A) Storage and disposal of records and any personal information gathered during the interviews; and

(B) Management of written reports containing recommendations for either granting or denying permission for a minor to marry or establish a domestic partnership.

(Subd (c) adopted effective January 1, 2020.)

(d) Responsibilities of judicial officer

In determining whether to issue a court order granting permission for the minor to marry or establish a domestic partnership:

(1) The judicial officer must:

(A) If Family Court Services is required to interview the parties, do the following before making a final determination:

(i) Separately and privately interview each of the parties; and

(ii) Consider whether there is any evidence of coercion or undue influence on the minor.

(B) Complete *Order and Notices to Minor on Request to Marry or Establish a Domestic Partnership* (form FL-915).

(2) The judicial officer may order that the parties:

(A) Appear at a hearing to consider whether it is in the best interest of the minor to marry or establish a domestic partnership.

(B) Participate in counseling concerning the social, economic, and personal responsibilities incident to the marriage or domestic partnership before the marriage or domestic partnership is established. The judicial officer:

(i) Must not require the parties to confer with counselors provided by religious organizations of any denomination;

(ii) Must consider, among other factors, the ability of the parties to pay for the counseling in determining whether to order the parties to participate in counseling;

(iii) May impose a reasonable fee to cover the cost of any counseling provided by the county or the court; and

(iv) May require the parties to file a certificate of completion of counseling before granting permission to marry or establish a domestic partnership.

(Subd (d) adopted effective January 1, 2020.)

(e) Waiting period

After obtaining a court order granting a minor permission to marry or establish a domestic partnership, the parties must wait 30 days from the date the court made the order before filing a marriage license or filing a declaration of domestic partnership. This waiting period is not required if the minor is:

(1) 17 years of age and has a high school diploma or a high school equivalency certificate; or

(2) 16 or 17 years of age and is pregnant or whose prospective spouse or domestic partner is pregnant.

(Subd (e) adopted effective January 1, 2020.)

Rule 5.448 adopted effective January 1, 2020.

Division 2
Rules Applicable in Family and Juvenile Proceedings

Chapter 1
Contact and Coordination

Chapter 1 adopted effective January 1, 2008.

Rule 5.450. Court communication protocol for domestic violence and child custody orders [Renumbered]

Rule 5.450 renumbered as rule 5.445 effective January 1, 2013; adopted as rule 5.500 effective January 1, 2003; previously amended effective January 1, 2005; previously amended and renumbered effective January 1, 2007.

2012 Note: Rule 5.445 appears under Division 1, Chapter 18.

Rule 5.451. Contact after adoption agreement

(a) Applicability of rule

This rule applies to any adoption of a child. The adoption petition must be filed under Family Code sections 8714 and 8714.5. If the child is a dependent of the juvenile court, the adoption petition may be filed in that juvenile court and the clerk must open a confidential adoption file for the child, and this file must be separate and apart from the dependency file, with an adoption case number different from the dependency case number. For the purposes of this rule, a "relative" is defined as follows:

(1) An adult related to the child or the child's sibling or half-sibling by blood or affinity, including a relative whose status is preceded by the word "step," "great," "great-great," or "grand"; or

(2) The spouse or domestic partner of any of the persons described in (1) even if the marriage or domestic partnership was terminated by dissolution or the death of the spouse related to the child.

(Subd (a) amended effective January 1, 2013; previously amended effective January 1, 2007.)

(b) Contact after adoption agreement

An adoptive parent or parents; a birth relative or relatives, including a birth parent or parents or any siblings of a child who is the subject of an adoption petition; or an Indian tribe that the child is a member of and the child may enter into a written agreement permitting postadoption contact between the child and birth relatives, including the birth parent or parents or any siblings, or an Indian tribe. No prospective adoptive parent or birth relative may be required by court order to enter into a contact-after-adoption agreement.

(Subd (b) amended effective January 1, 2018; previously amended effective July 1, 2001, January 1, 2003, July 1, 2003, and January 1, 2013.)

(c) Court approval; time of decree

If, at the time the adoption petition is granted, the court finds that the agreement is in the best interest of the child, the court may enter the decree of adoption and grant postadoption contact as reflected in the approved agreement.

(Subd (c) amended effective January 1, 2013; previously amended effective January 1, 2003.)

(d) Terms of agreement

The terms of the agreement are limited to the following, although they need not include all permitted terms:

(1) Provisions for visitation between the child and a birth parent or parents;

(2) Provisions for visitation between the child and other identified birth relatives, including siblings or half-siblings of the child;

(3) Provisions for contact between the child and a birth parent or parents;

(4) Provisions for contact between the child and other identified birth relatives, including siblings or half-siblings of the child;

(5) Provisions for contact between the adoptive parent or parents and a birth parent or parents;

(6) Provisions for contact between the adoptive parent or parents and other identified birth relatives, including siblings or half-siblings of the child;

(7) Provisions for the sharing of information about the child with a birth parent or parents;

(8) Provisions for the sharing of information about the child with other identified birth relatives, including siblings or half-siblings of the child; and

(9) The terms of any contact after adoption agreement entered into under a petition filed under Family Code section 8714 must be limited to the sharing of information about the child unless the child has an existing relationship with the birth relative.

(Subd (d) amended effective January 1, 2013; previously amended effective July 1, 2001, January 1, 2003, July 1, 2003, and January 1, 2007.)

(e) Child a party

The child who is the subject of the adoption petition is a party to the agreement whether or not specified as such.

(1) Written consent by a child 12 years of age or older to the terms of the agreement is required for enforcement of the agreement, unless the court finds by a preponderance of the evidence that the agreement is in the best interest of the child and waives the requirement of the child's written consent.

(2) If the child has been found by a juvenile court to be described by section 300 of the Welfare and Institutions Code, an attorney must be appointed to represent the child for purposes of participation in and consent to any contact after adoption agreement, regardless of the age of the child. If the child has been represented by an attorney in the dependency proceedings, that attorney must be appointed for the additional responsibilities of this rule. The attorney is required to represent the child only until the adoption is decreed and dependency terminated.

(Subd (e) amended effective January 1, 2013; previously amended effective July 1, 2001, January 1, 2003, and July 1, 2003.)

(f) Form and provisions of the agreement

The agreement must be prepared and submitted on *Contact After Adoption Agreement* (form ADOPT-310) with appropriate attachments.

(Subd (f) amended effective January 1, 2013; previously amended effective July 1, 2001, January 1, 2003, and January 1, 2007.)

(g) Report to the court

The department or agency participating as a party or joining in the petition for adoption must submit a report to the court. The report must include a criminal record check and descriptions of all social service referrals. If a contact after adoption agreement has been submitted, the report must include a summary of the agreement and a recommendation as to whether it is in the best interest of the child.

(Subd (g) amended effective January 1, 2013; previously amended effective July 1, 2001, January 1, 2003, and July 1, 2003.)

(h) Enforcement of the agreement

The court that grants the petition for adoption and approves the contact after adoption agreement must retain jurisdiction over the agreement.

(1) Any petition for enforcement of an agreement must be filed on *Request to: Enforce, Change, End Contact After Adoption Agreement* (form ADOPT-315). The form must not be accepted for filing unless completed in full, with documentary evidence attached of participation in, or attempts to participate in, mediation or other dispute resolution.

(2) The court may make its determination on the petition without testimony or an evidentiary hearing and may rely solely on documentary evidence or offers of proof. The court may order compliance with the agreement only if:

(A) There is sufficient evidence of good-faith attempts to resolve the issues through mediation or other dispute resolution; and

(B) The court finds enforcement is in the best interest of the child.

(3) The court must not order investigation or evaluation of the issues raised in the petition unless the court finds by clear and convincing evidence that:

(A) The best interest of the child may be protected or advanced only by such inquiry; and

(B) The inquiry will not disturb the stability of the child's home to the child's detriment.

(4) Monetary damages must not be ordered.

(Subd (h) amended effective January 1, 2013; previously amended effective July 1, 2001, January 1, 2003, July 1, 2003, and January 1, 2007.)

(i) Modification or termination of agreement

The agreement may be modified or terminated by the court. Any petition for modification or termination of an agreement must be filed on *Request to: Enforce, Change, End Contact After Adoption Agreement* (form ADOPT-315). The form must not be accepted for filing unless completed in full, with documentary evidence attached of participation in, or attempts to participate in, mediation or other appropriate dispute resolution.

(1) The agreement may be terminated or modified only if:

(A) All parties, including the child of 12 years or older, have signed the petition or have indicated on the *Answer to Request to: Enforce, Change, End Contact After Adoption Agreement* (form ADOPT-320) their consent or have executed a modified agreement filed with the petition; or

(B) The court finds all of the following:

(i) The termination or modification is necessary to serve the best interest of the child;

(ii) There has been a substantial change of circumstances since the original agreement was approved; and

(iii) The petitioner has participated in, or has attempted to participate in, mediation or appropriate dispute resolution.

(2) The court may make its determination without testimony or evidentiary hearing and may rely solely on documentary evidence or offers of proof.

(3) The court may order modification or termination without a hearing if all parties, including the child of 12 years or older, have signed the petition or have indicated on the *Answer to Request to: Enforce, Change, End Contact After Adoption Agreement* (form ADOPT-320) their consent or have executed a modified agreement filed with the petition.

(Subd (i) amended effective January 1, 2013; previously amended effective July 1, 2001, January 1, 2003, July 1, 2003, and January 1, 2007.)

(j) Costs and fees

The fee for filing a *Request to: Enforce, Change, End Contact After Adoption Agreement* (form ADOPT-315) must not exceed the fee assessed for the filing of an adoption petition. Costs and fees for mediation or other appropriate dispute resolution must be assumed by each party, with the exception of the child. All costs and fees of litigation, including any court-ordered investigation or evaluation, must be charged to the petitioner unless the court finds that a party other than the child has failed, without good cause, to comply with the approved agreement; all costs and fees must then be charged to that party.

(Subd (j) amended effective January 1, 2013; previously amended effective July 1, 2001, January 1, 2003, July 1, 2003, and January 1, 2007.)

(k) Adoption final

Once a decree of adoption has been entered, the court may not set aside the decree, rescind any relinquishment, modify or set aside any order terminating parental rights, or modify or set aside any other orders related to the granting of the adoption petition, due to the failure of any party to comply with the terms of a postadoption contact agreement or any subsequent modifications to it.

(Subd (k) amended effective January 1, 2013.)

Rule 5.451 amended effective January 1, 2018; adopted as rule 1180 effective July 1, 1998; previously amended and renumbered as rule 5.400 effective January 1, 2003; previously amended effective July 1, 2001, July 1, 2003; and January 1, 2007; previously renumbered effective January 1, 2013.

Rule 5.460. Request for sibling contact information

(a) Applicability of rule

This rule applies to all persons wishing to exchange contact information with their adopted siblings and all adopted persons wishing to have contact with their siblings, regardless of whether the adoption occurred in juvenile or family court.

(Subd (a) adopted effective January 1, 2008.)

(b) Definitions

As used in this rule:

(1) "Adoptee" means any person adopted under California law.

(2) "Department" means the California Department of Social Services (CDSS).

(3) "Licensed adoption agency" means an agency licensed by the department to provide adoption services and includes a licensed county

adoption agency and a licensed private adoption agency under Family Code sections 8521, 8530, and 8533.

(4) "Confidential intermediary" means either the department or a licensed adoption agency that provided adoption services for either sibling.

(5) "Alternate confidential intermediary" means a named entity or person designated by the court in place of a licensed adoption agency when the court finds that the agency would experience economic hardship by serving as confidential intermediary.

(6) "Sibling" means a biological sibling, half-sibling, or stepsibling of the adoptee.

(7) "Waiver" means *Waiver of Rights to Confidentiality for Siblings*, department form AD 904A (used for adoptees or siblings over the age of 18 years) or AD 904B (used for adoptees or siblings under the age of 18).

(8) "Consent" means the consent contained within the Department form AD 904B. It is the approval of the filing of a waiver by a person under the age of 18 years obtained from an adoptive parent, a legal parent, a legal guardian, or a dependency court when a child is currently a dependent of the court.

(9) "Petition" means Judicial Council form *Request for Appointment of Confidential Intermediary* (form ADOPT-330).

(10) "Order" means Judicial Council form *Order for Appointment of Confidential Intermediary* (form ADOPT-331).

(Subd (b) adopted effective January 1, 2008.)

(c) Waiver submitted by person under the age of 18 years

(1) *Adoptee or sibling waiver*

Each adoptee or sibling under the age of 18 years may submit a waiver to the department or the licensed adoption agency, provided that a consent is also completed.

(2) *Court consent*

If the sibling is currently under the jurisdiction of the juvenile court and his or her parent or legal guardian is unable or unavailable to sign the consent, the court may sign it.

(Subd (c) amended effective January 1, 2013; adopted effective January 1, 2008.)

(d) No waiver on file—sibling requesting contact

If, after contacting the department or licensed adoption agency, the sibling who is seeking contact learns that no waiver is on file for the other sibling, the sibling seeking contact should use the following procedure to ask the court that finalized the adoption of either sibling to designate a confidential intermediary to help locate the other sibling:

(1) *Sibling's request*

(A) A sibling requesting contact under Family Code section 9205 must file a petition and submit a blank order to the court that finalized the adoption of either sibling.

(B) If the sibling requesting contact is under the age of 18 years, the petition must be filed through the sibling's duly appointed guardian ad litem under Code of Civil Procedure section 373 or through the sibling's attorney.

(2) *Appointment of a confidential intermediary*

(A) The court must grant the petition unless the court finds that it would be detrimental to the adoptee or sibling with whom contact is sought. The court may consider any and all relevant information in making this determination, including, but not limited to, a review of the court file.

(B) The court will appoint the department or licensed adoption agency that provided adoption services for either sibling as the confidential intermediary.

(C) If the court finds that the licensed adoption agency that conducted the adoptee's adoption is unable to serve as the intermediary, owing to economic hardship, the court may then appoint any one of the following who agrees to serve as an alternate confidential intermediary:

(i) A CASA volunteer or CASA program staff member;

(ii) A court-connected mediator;

(iii) An adoption service provider as defined in Family Code section 8502(a);

(iv) An attorney; or

(v) Another California licensed adoption agency or the California Department of Social Services' Adoptions Support Bureau when no other individuals are available.

(D) When an alternate confidential intermediary is appointed, the licensed adoption agency must provide to the court all records related to the adoptee or sibling for inspection by the alternate confidential intermediary.

(3) *Role of the confidential intermediary*

(A) The confidential intermediary must:

(i) Have access to all records of the adoptee or the sibling, including the court adoption file and adoption agency or CDSS files of either sibling;

(ii) Make all reasonable efforts to locate the adoptee, the sibling, or the adoptive or birth parent;

(iii) Attempt to obtain the consent of the adoptee, the sibling, or the adoptive or birth parent; and

(iv) Notify any located adoptee, sibling, or adoptive or birth parent that consent is optional, not required by law, and does not affect the status of the adoption.

(B) The confidential intermediary must not make any further attempts to obtain consent if the individual denies the request for consent.

(C) The confidential intermediary must use information found in the records of the adoptee or the sibling for authorized purposes only and must not disclose any information obtained in this procedure unless specifically authorized.

(4) *Adopted sibling seeking contact with a sibling who is a dependent child*

An adoptee seeking contact with his or her sibling who is a dependent child must follow the procedure set forth under Welfare and Institutions Code section 388(b) to seek contact with the sibling.

(Subd (d) amended effective January 1, 2013; adopted effective January 1, 2008.)

Rule 5.460 amended and renumbered effective January 1, 2013; adopted as rule 5.410 effective January 1, 2008.

Rule 5.475. Custody and visitation orders following termination of a juvenile court proceeding or probate court guardianship proceeding

(a) Custody and visitation order from other courts or divisions

On termination of juvenile court jurisdiction under rule 5.700 or termination of a probate guardianship under rule 7.1008, the juvenile court or probate court will direct the transmission of its custody or visitation orders to any superior court in which a related family law custody proceeding or probate guardianship proceeding is pending for filing in that proceeding.

If no such proceeding is pending, the court terminating jurisdiction will direct the transmission of its order to the superior court of, in order of preference, the county in which the parent with sole physical custody resides; if none, the county where the child's primary residence is located; or, if neither exists, a county or location where any custodial parent resides.

(1) *Procedure for filing custody or visitation orders from juvenile or probate court*

(A) Except as directed in subparagraph (B), on receiving the custody or visitation order of a juvenile court or probate court, the clerk of the receiving court must file the order in any pending nullity, dissolution, legal separation, Uniform Parentage Act, Domestic Violence Prevention Act, or other family law custody proceeding, or in any probate guardianship proceeding that affects custody or visitation of the child.

(B) If the only pending proceeding related to the child in the receiving court is filed under Family Code section 17400 et seq., the clerk must proceed as follows.

(i) If the receiving court has issued a custody or visitation order in the pending proceeding, the clerk must file the received order in that proceeding.

(ii) If the receiving court has not issued a custody or visitation order in the pending proceeding, the clerk must not file the received order in that proceeding, but must instead proceed under subparagraph (C).

(C) If no dependency, family law, or guardianship proceeding affecting custody or visitation of the child is pending, the order must be used to open a new custody proceeding in the receiving court. The clerk must immediately open a family law file without charging a filing fee, assign a case number, and file the order in the new case file.

(2) *Endorsed filed copy—clerk's certificate of mailing*

Within 15 court days of receiving the order, the clerk must send an endorsed filed copy of the order showing the case number assigned by the receiving court by first-class mail to each of the child's parents and to the court that issued the order, with a completed clerk's certificate of mailing, for inclusion in the issuing court's file.

(Subd (a) amended effective January 1, 2016; previously amended effective January 1, 2007.)

(b) Modification of former guardian visitation orders—custodial parent

When a parent has custody of the child following termination of a probate guardianship, a former guardian's request for modification of the probate court visitation order, including an order denying visitation, must be brought in a proceeding under the Family Code.

(Subd (b) amended effective January 1, 2016; previously amended effective January 1, 2007.)

(c) Independent action for former guardian visitation

(1) If the court terminated a guardianship under the Probate Code and did not issue a visitation order, the former guardian may maintain an independent action for visitation if a dependency proceeding is not pending. The former guardian may bring the action without the necessity of a separate joinder action.

(2) If the child has at least one living parent and has no guardian, visitation must be determined in a proceeding under the Family Code. If the child does not have at least one living parent, visitation must be determined in a guardianship proceeding, which may be initiated for that purpose.

(3) *Declaration Under Uniform Child Custody Jurisdiction and Enforcement Act (UCCJEA)* (form FL-105/GC-120) must be filed with a petition or motion for visitation by a former guardian.

(Subd (c) amended effective January 1, 2007.)

Rule 5.475 amended effective January 1, 2016; adopted effective January 1, 2006; previously amended effective January 1, 2007.

Chapter 2
Indian Child Welfare Act

Chapter 2 adopted effective January 1, 2008.

Rule 5.480. Application
Rule 5.481. Inquiry and notice
Rule 5.482. Proceedings after notice
Rule 5.483. Dismissal and transfer of case
Rule 5.484. Emergency proceedings involving an Indian child
Rule 5.485. Placement of an Indian child
Rule 5.486. Termination of parental rights
Rule 5.487. Petition to invalidate orders
Rule 5.488. Adoption record keeping

Rule 5.480.   Application

This chapter addressing the Indian Child Welfare Act (25 [1] **U.S.C. §** 1901 et seq.) as codified in various sections of the [2] Family **Code**, Probate **Code**, and Welfare and Institutions [3] **Code**, applies to most proceedings involving Indian children that may result in an involuntary foster care placement; guardianship or conservatorship placement; custody placement under Family Code section 3041; declaration freeing a child from the custody and control of one or both parents; termination of parental rights; **preadoptive placement;** or adoptive placement. This chapter applies to:

(1) Proceedings under Welfare and Institutions Code section 300 et seq.;

(2) Proceedings under Welfare and Institutions Code sections 601 and 602 et seq., whenever the child is either in foster care or at risk of entering foster care. In these proceedings, inquiry is required in accordance with rule 5.481(a). The other requirements of this chapter contained in rules 5.481 through 5.487 apply only if:

(A) The court's jurisdiction is based on conduct that would not be criminal if the child were 18 years of age or over;

(B) The court has found that placement outside the home of the parent or legal guardian is based entirely on harmful conditions within the child's home. Without a specific finding, it is presumed that placement outside the home is based at least in part on the child's criminal conduct, and this chapter shall not apply; or

(C) The court is setting a hearing to terminate parental rights of the child's parents.

(3) Proceedings under Family Code section 3041;

(4) Proceedings under the Family Code resulting in adoption or termination of parental rights; and

(5) Proceedings listed in Probate Code section 1459.5 and rule 7.1015.

This chapter does not apply to voluntary foster care and guardianship placements where the child can be returned to the parent or Indian custodian on demand.

Rule 5.480 amended effective January 1, 2020; adopted effective January 1, 2008; previously amended effective January 1, 2013, and July 1, 2013.

Rule 5.480.   2019 Deletes. [1] United States Code section **[2]** California **[3]** Codes

Rule 5.481.   Inquiry and notice

(a) Inquiry

The court, court-connected investigator, and party seeking a foster-care placement, guardianship, conservatorship, custody placement under Family Code section 3041, declaration freeing a child from the custody or control of one or both parents, termination of parental rights, **preadoptive placement,** or adoption have an affirmative and continuing duty to inquire whether a child is or may be an Indian child in all proceedings identified in rule 5.480. The court, court-connected investigator, and party include the county welfare department, probation department, licensed adoption agency, adoption service provider, investigator, petitioner, appointed guardian or conservator of the person, and appointed fiduciary.

(1) The party seeking a foster-care placement, guardianship, conservatorship, custody placement under Family Code section 3041, declaration freeing a child from the custody or control of one or both parents, termination of parental rights, **preadoptive placement,** or adoption must ask the child, if the child is old enough, and the parents, Indian custodian, or legal guardians, **extended family members, others who have an interest in the child, and where applicable the party reporting child abuse or neglect,** whether the child is or may be an Indian child **and whether the residence or domicile of the child, the parents, or Indian custodian is on a reservation or in an Alaska Native village,** and must complete the *Indian Child Inquiry Attachment* (form ICWA-010(A)) and attach it to the petition unless the party is filing a subsequent petition [1] and there is no new information.

(2) At the first appearance by a parent, Indian custodian, or guardian, **and all other participants** in any dependency case; or in juvenile wardship proceedings in which the child is at risk of entering foster care or is in foster care; or at the initiation of any guardianship, conservatorship, proceeding for custody under Family Code section 3041, proceeding to terminate parental rights, proceeding to declare a child free of the custody and control of one or both parents, **preadoptive placement,** or adoption proceeding; **and at each hearing that may culminate in an order for foster care placement, termination of parental rights, preadoptive placement or adoptive placement, as described in Welfare and Institutions Code section 224.1(d)(1), or that may result in an order for guardianship, conservatorship, or custody under Family Code section 3041;** the court must:

(A) Ask each participant present whether the participant knows or has reason to know the child is an Indian child;

(B) Instruct the parties to inform the court if they subsequently receive information that provides reason to know the child is an Indian child; and

(C) Order the parent, Indian custodian, or guardian, if available, to complete *Parental Notification of Indian Status* (form ICWA-020).

(3) If the parent, Indian custodian, or guardian does not appear at the first hearing, or is unavailable at the initiation of a proceeding, the court must order the person or entity that has the inquiry duty under this rule to use reasonable diligence to find and inform the parent, Indian custodian, or guardian that the court has ordered the parent, Indian custodian, or guardian to complete *Parental Notification of Indian Status* (form ICWA-020).

(4) If the social worker, probation officer, licensed adoption agency, adoption service provider, investigator, or petitioner knows or has reason to know **or believe** that an Indian child is or may be involved, that person or entity must make further inquiry as soon as practicable by:

(A) Interviewing the parents, Indian custodian, and "extended family members" as defined in 25 United States Code [2] **section 1903**, to gather the information listed in Welfare and Institutions Code section [3] **224.3(a)(5),** Family Code section 180(b)(5), or Probate Code section 1460.2(b)(5) [4];

(B) Contacting the Bureau of Indian Affairs and the California Department of Social Services for assistance in identifying the names and contact information of the tribes in which the child may be a member or eligible for membership; and

(C) Contacting the tribes and any other person [5] **who** reasonably can be expected to have information regarding the child's membership status or eligibility. **These contacts must at a minimum include the contacts**

Rules of Court

and sharing of information listed in Welfare and Institutions Code section 224.2(e)(3).

(5) [6] **The petitioner must on an ongoing basis include in its filings a detailed description of all inquiries, and further inquiries it has undertaken, and all information received pertaining to the child's Indian status, as well as evidence of how and when this information was provided to the relevant tribes. Whenever new information is received, that information must be expeditiously provided to the tribes**.

(Subd (a) amended effective January 1, 2020; adopted effective January 1, 2008; previously amended effective January 1, 2013.)

Rule 5.481(a). 2019 Deletes. [1] , **[2]** sections 1901 and 1903(2) **[3]** 224.2(a)(5) **[4]** , which is required to complete the *Notice of Child Custody Proceeding for Indian Child* (form ICWA-030) **[5]** that **[6]** The circumstances that may provide reason to know the child is an Indian child include the following: (A) The child or a person having an interest in the child, including an Indian tribe, an Indian organization, an officer of the court, a public or private agency, or a member of the child's extended family, informs or otherwise provides information suggesting that the child is an Indian child to the court, the county welfare agency, the probation department, the licensed adoption agency or adoption service provider, the investigator, the petitioner, or any appointed guardian or conservator; (B) The residence or domicile of the child, the child's parents, or an Indian custodian is or was in a predominantly Indian community; or (C) The child or the child's family has received services or benefits from a tribe or services that are available to Indians from tribes or the federal government, such as the U.S. Department of Health and Human Services, Indian Health Service, or Tribal Temporary Assistance to Needy Families benefits

(b) Reason to know the child is an Indian child

(1) There is reason to know a child involved in a proceeding is an Indian child if:

(A) A person having an interest in the child, including the child, an officer of the court, a tribe, an Indian organization, a public or private agency, or a member of the child's extended family informs the court the child is an Indian child;

(B) The residence or domicile of the child, the child's parents, or Indian custodian is on a reservation or in an Alaska Native village;

(C) Any participant in the proceeding, officer of the court, Indian tribe, Indian organization, or agency informs the court that it has discovered information indicating that the child is an Indian child;

(D) The child who is the subject of the proceeding gives the court reason to know he or she is an Indian child;

(E) The court is informed that the child is or has been a ward of a tribal court; or

(F) The court is informed that either parent or the child possesses an identification card indicating membership or citizenship in an Indian tribe.

(2) When there is reason to know the child is an Indian child, but the court does not have sufficient evidence to determine that the child is or is not an Indian child, the court must confirm, by way of a report, declaration, or testimony included in the record that the agency or other party used due diligence to identify and work with all of the tribes of which there is reason to know the child may be a member, or eligible for membership, to verify whether the child is in fact a member or whether a biological parent is a member and the child is eligible for membership. Due diligence must include the further inquiry and tribal contacts discussed in (a)(4) above.

(3) Upon review of the evidence of due diligence, further inquiry, and tribal contacts, if the court concludes that the agency or other party has fulfilled its duty of due diligence, further inquiry, and tribal contacts, the court may:

(A) Find there is no reason to know the child is an Indian child and the Indian Child Welfare Act does not apply. Notwithstanding this determination, if the court or a party subsequently receives information that was not previously available relevant to the child's Indian status, the court must reconsider this finding; or

(B) Find it is known the child is an Indian child, and that the Indian Child Welfare Act applies, and order compliance with the requirements of the act, including notice in accordance with (c) below; or

(C) Find there is reason to know the child is an Indian child, order notice in accordance with (c) below, and treat the child as an Indian child unless and until the court determines on the record that the child is not an Indian child.

(4) A determination by an Indian tribe that a child is or is not a member of, or eligible for membership in, that tribe, or testimony attesting to that status by a person authorized by the tribe to provide that

determination, must be conclusive. Information that the child is not enrolled, or is not eligible for enrollment in, the tribe is not determinative of the child's membership status unless the tribe also confirms in writing that enrollment is a prerequisite for membership under tribal law or custom.

(Subd (b) adopted effective January 1, 2020.)

(c) Notice

(1) If it is known or there is reason to know [1] an Indian child is involved in a proceeding listed in rule 5.480, except for a wardship proceeding under Welfare and Institutions Code sections 601 and 602 et seq., the social worker, petitioner, or in probate guardianship and conservator proceedings, if the petitioner is unrepresented, the court, must send *Notice of Child Custody Proceeding for Indian Child* (form ICWA-030) to the parent or legal guardian and Indian custodian of an Indian child, and the Indian child's tribe, in the manner specified in Welfare and Institutions Code section [2] **224.3, Family** Code section 180, and Probate Code section 1460.2 **for all initial hearings that may result in the foster care placement, termination of parental rights, preadoptive placement, or adoptive placement, or an order of guardianship, conservatorship, or custody under Family Code section 3041. For all other hearings, and for continued hearings, notice must be provided to the child's parents, legal guardian or Indian custodian, and tribe in accordance with Welfare and Institutions Code sections 292, 293, and 295**.

(2) If it is known or there is reason to know that an Indian child is involved in a wardship proceeding under Welfare and Institutions Code sections 601 and 602 et seq., the probation officer must send *Notice of Child Custody Proceeding for Indian Child* (form ICWA-030) to the parent or legal guardian, Indian custodian, if any, and the child's tribe, in accordance with Welfare and Institutions Code section 727.4(a)(2) in any case described by rule 5.480(2)(A)–(C).

(3) The circumstances that may provide reason to know the child is an Indian child include the circumstances specified in [3] **(b)(1)**.

(4) Notice to an Indian child's tribe must be sent to the tribal chairperson unless the tribe has designated another agent for service.

(Subd (c) relettered and amended effective January 1, 2020; adopted as subd (b) effective January 1, 2008; previously amended effective January 1, 2013, and July 1, 2013.)

Rule 5.481(c). 2019 Deletes. [1] that **[2]** 224.2, Family Law **[3]** (a)(5)
Rule 5.481 amended effective January 1, 2020; adopted effective January 1, 2008; previously amended effective January 1, 2013, and July 1, 2013.

Advisory Committee Comment

Federal regulations (25 C.F.R. § 23.105) and state law (Welf. & Inst. Code, § 224.2(e)) contain detailed recommendations for contacting tribes to fulfill the obligations of inquiry, due diligence, information sharing, and notice under the Indian Child Welfare Act and state law.

Except for purposes of inquiry, the requirements of the Indian Child Welfare Act (ICWA) and related provisions of state law do not apply to most cases adjudicated under section 602 of the Welfare and Institutions Code for conduct that would be criminal if committed by an adult (see *In re W.B.* (2012) 55 Cal.4th 30). But in those cases where ICWA does not apply, following inquiry and receipt of information about Indian ancestry, the court is encouraged to communicate with and voluntarily provide informal or formal notice to the Indian child's tribe regarding resources and services to benefit the Indian child and his or her family. Such notice should particularly be encouraged wherever the Indian child's tribe has previously intervened or participated in other proceedings involving the child, such as earlier dependency or probate guardianship proceedings. The California Legislature has stated: "[i]t is in the interest of an Indian child that the child's membership in the child's Indian tribe and connection to the tribal community be encouraged and protected...." (See Welf. & Inst. Code, §§ 224(a)(2), 306.6.) Further, Welfare and Institutions Code section 727.1(a) mandates that in selecting a placement for a child under the supervision of a probation officer, the court "shall consider, in order of priority, placement with relatives, *tribal members*, and foster family...." (Emphasis added.) This mandate applies even if the case is not governed by ICWA.

As a matter of policy and best practice, culturally appropriate placements and services provide psychological benefit for the Indian child and family. By engaging the Indian child's tribe, tribal members, Indian Health Services, or other agencies and organizations providing services to Native Americans, additional resources and culturally appropriate services are often identified to assist in case planning. (See Welf. & Inst. Code, §§ 727.4(d)(5),(6) & 16501.1(c)(1) for information on services and case planning for children adjudicated under section 602.) Outreach to these entities is also an important part of family finding and engagement efforts for Indian children and of finding appropriate placements. By contacting the child's tribe, placement options and services—such as substance abuse treatment, counseling, and other services—may be available to Indian children and their families. A list of available services can be found on the California Courts website at Program, Tribal/State Programs, ICWA, Statewide Directory of Services for Native American Families, at *www.courts.ca.gov/5807.htm.*

Rule 5.482. Proceedings after notice

(a) Timing of Proceedings

(1) If it is known or there is reason to know [1] a child is an Indian child, [2] **a court hearing that may result in a foster care placement, termination of parental rights, preadoptive placement, or adoptive placement** must not proceed until at least 10 days after the parent, Indian custodian, the tribe, or the Bureau of Indian Affairs [3] **has** received notice, except as stated in sections (a)(2) and (3).

(2) The detention hearing in dependency cases and in delinquency cases in which the probation officer has assessed that the child is in foster care or it is probable the child will be entering foster care described by rule 5.480(2)(A)–(C) may proceed without delay, provided that:

(A) Notice of the detention hearing must be given as soon as possible after the filing of the petition initiating the proceeding; and

(B) Proof of notice must be filed with the court within 10 days after the filing of the petition.

(3) The parent, Indian custodian, or tribe must be granted a continuance, if requested, of up to 20 days to prepare for the proceeding, except for specified hearings in the following circumstances:

(A) The detention hearing in dependency cases and in delinquency cases described by rule 5.480(2)(A)–(C);

(B) The jurisdiction hearing in a delinquency case described by rule 5.480(2)(A)–(C) in which the court finds the continuance would not conform to speedy trial considerations under Welfare and Institutions Code section 657; and

(C) The disposition hearing in a delinquency case described by rule 5.480(2)(A)–(C) in which the court finds good cause to deny the continuance under Welfare and Institutions Code section 682. A good cause reason includes when probation is recommending the release of a detained child to his or her parent or to a less restrictive placement. The court must follow the placement preferences under rule [4] **5.485** when holding the disposition hearing.

(Subd (a) amended effective January 1, 2020; adopted effective January 1, 2008; previously amended effective January 1, 2013, and July 1, 2013.)

Rule 5.482(a). 2019 Deletes. [1] that [2] the [3] have [4] 5.484

(b) Proof of notice

Proof of notice **in accordance with this rule must be** filed with the court **in advance of the hearing, except for those excluded by (a)(2) and (3), and** must include *Notice of Child Custody Proceeding for Indian Child* (form ICWA-030), return receipts, and any responses received from the Bureau of Indian Affairs and tribes.

(Subd (b) amended effective January 1, 2020; adopted effective January 1, 2008; previously amended effective January 1, 2013.)

(c) Determination of applicability of the Indian Child Welfare Act

(1) If [1] **the court finds that proper and adequate inquiry, further inquiry, and due diligence were conducted under Welfare and Institutions Code section 224.2 and, if applicable, notice provided under Welfare and Institutions Code section 224.3, and the court determines there is no reason to know the child is an Indian child, the court may make a finding** that the Indian Child Welfare Act does not apply to the proceedings [2].

(2) **The determination of the court that the Indian Child Welfare Act does not apply in (c)(1) is subject to reversal based on sufficiency of the evidence. The court must reverse its determination if it subsequently receives information providing reason to believe that the** child is an Indian child [3] **and order the social worker or probation officer to conduct further inquiry under Welfare and Institutions Code section 224.3**.

(Subd (c) amended effective January 1, 2020; adopted as subd (d) effective January 1, 2008; previously amended effective January 1, 2013; previously repealed and relettered effective August 15, 2016.)

Rule 5.482(c). 2019 Deletes. [1] after notice has been provided as required by federal and state law and neither the tribe nor the Bureau of Indian Affairs has provided a determinative response within 60 days after receiving that notice, then the court may determine [2] , provided that the court must reverse its determination of the inapplicability of the act and must apply it prospectively if a tribe or the Bureau of Indian Affairs subsequently confirms that the child is an Indian child. (2) If at any time, based on the petition or other information, the court knows or has reason to know [3] , the court must proceed as if the child were an Indian child. (3) The court is not required to delay proceedings until a response to notice is received

(d) Intervention

The Indian child's tribe and Indian custodian [1] **are entitled to** intervene, orally or in writing, at any point in the proceedings [2]. **The tribe** may, but [3] **is** not required to, file with the court the *Notice of Designation of Tribal Representative* [4] *in a Court Proceeding Involving an Indian Child* (form ICWA-040) to give notice of [5] **its** intent to intervene.

(Subd (d) amended effective January 1, 2020; adopted as subd (e) effective January 1, 2008; previously amended effective January 1, 2013; previously relettered as subd (d) effective August 15, 2016.)

Rule 5.482(d). 2019 Deletes. [1] may [2] and [3] are [4] *and Notice of Intervention* [5] their

(e) Posthearing actions

Whenever an Indian child is removed from a guardian, conservator, other custodian, foster home, or institution for placement with a different guardian, conservator, custodian, foster home, institution, or preadoptive or adoptive home, the placement must comply with the placement preferences and standards specified in Welfare and Institutions Code section 361.31.

(Subd (e) relettered effective August 15, 2016; adopted as subd (f) effective January 1, 2008; previously amended effective January 1, 2013.)

(f) Consultation with tribe

Any person or court involved in the placement of an Indian child in a proceeding described by rule 5.480 must use the services of the Indian child's tribe, whenever available through the tribe, in seeking to secure placement within the order of placement preference specified in rule [1] **5.485**.

(Subd (f) amended effective January 1, 2020; adopted as subd (g) effective January 1, 2008; previously amended effective July 1, 2013; previously relettered as subd (f) effective August 15, 2016.)

Rule 5.482(f). 2019 Deletes. [1] 5.484

(g) Tribal appearance by telephone or other remote means

In any proceeding governed by the Indian Child Welfare Act involving an Indian child, the child's tribe may, on notification to the court, appear at any hearing, including the detention hearing, by telephone or other computerized remote means. The method of appearance may be determined by the court consistent with court capacity and contractual obligations, and taking into account the capacity of the tribe, as long as a method of effective remote appearance and participation sufficient to allow the tribe to fully exercise its rights is provided. No fee may be charged to the tribe for such telephonic or other remote appearance.

(Subd (g) adopted effective January 1, 2021.)

Rule 5.482 amended effective January 1, 2021; adopted effective January 1, 2008; previously amended effective January 1, 2013, July 1, 2013, August 15, 2016, and January 1, 2020.

Rule 5.483. Dismissal and transfer of case

(a) Dismissal when tribal court has exclusive jurisdiction

[1] **Subject to the terms of any agreement between the state and the tribe under 25 United States Code section 1919**:

(1) **If the court receives information at any stage of the proceeding suggesting that** the Indian child is [2] **already the** ward of the tribal court [3] **or** is domiciled or resides within a reservation of an Indian tribe that has exclusive jurisdiction over Indian child custody proceedings under **25 United States Code** section 1911 or 1918 [4]**, the court must expeditiously notify the tribe and the tribal court that it intends to dismiss the case upon receiving confirmation from the tribe or tribal court that the child is a ward of the tribal court or subject to the tribe's exclusive jurisdiction.**

(2) **When the court receives confirmation that the child is already a ward of a tribal court or is subject to the exclusive jurisdiction of an Indian tribe, the state court must dismiss the proceeding and ensure that the tribal court is sent all information regarding the proceeding, including, but not limited to, the pleadings and any state court record. If the local agency has not already transferred physical custody of the Indian child to the child's tribe, the state court must order that the local agency do so forthwith and hold in abeyance any dismissal order pending confirmation that the Indian child is in the physical custody of the tribe.**

(3) **This section does not preclude an emergency removal consistent with 25** United States Code **section 1922, 25 Code of Federal Regulations part 23.113, and Welfare and Institutions Code section 319 to protect the child from risk of imminent physical damage or harm and if more time is needed to facilitate the transfer of custody of the Indian child from the county welfare department to the tribe.**

(Subd (a) amended effective January 1, 2020; adopted effective January 1, 2008.)

Rule 5.483(a).   2019 Deletes. [1] The court must order transfer of a case to the tribal court of the child's tribe if **[2]** a **[3]** ; or (2) The Indian child **[4]** of title 25 of the

(b) Presumptive transfer of case to tribal court with concurrent state and tribal jurisdiction

Unless the court finds good cause under subdivision (d), the court must order transfer of a case to the tribal court of the child's tribe if the parent, the Indian custodian, or the child's tribe requests.

(Subd (b) adopted effective January 1, 2008.)

(c) Documentation of request to transfer a case to tribal court

(1) The parent, the Indian custodian, or the child's tribe may request transfer of the case, either orally or in writing or by filing *Notice of Petition and Petition to Transfer Case Involving an Indian Child to Tribal Jurisdiction* (form ICWA-050).

If the request is made orally, the court must document the request and make it part of the record.

(2) Upon receipt of a transfer petition, the state court must ensure that the tribal court is promptly notified in writing of the transfer petition. This notification may request a timely response regarding whether the tribal court wishes to decline the transfer.

(Subd (c) amended effective January 1, 2020; adopted effective January 1, 2008.)

(d) Cause to deny a request to transfer to tribal court with concurrent state and tribal jurisdiction

(1) [1] Either of the following circumstances constitutes mandatory good cause to deny a request to transfer:

(A) One or both of the child's parents objects to the transfer in open court or in an admissible writing for the record; **or**

(B) [2] The tribal court of the child's tribe declines the transfer.

(2) [3] In assessing whether good cause to deny the transfer exists, the court must not consider:

(A) Socioeconomic conditions and the perceived adequacy of tribal social services or judicial systems;

(B) Whether the child custody proceeding is at an advanced stage **[4] if the Indian child's parent, Indian custodian, or tribe did not receive notice of the child custody proceeding until an advanced stage. It must not, in and of itself, be considered an unreasonable delay for a party to wait until reunification efforts have failed and reunification services have been terminated before filing a petition to transfer;**

(C) Whether there have been prior proceedings involving the child for which no transfer petition was filed;

(D) Whether transfer could affect the placement of the child; or

(E) Whether the Indian child has cultural connections with the tribe or its reservation.

(3) If it appears that there is good cause to deny a transfer, the court must hold an evidentiary hearing on the transfer and make its findings on the record.

(Subd (d) amended effective January 1, 2020; adopted effective January 1, 2008; previously amended effective January 1, 2013.)

Rule 5.483(d).   2019 Deletes. [1] One or more **[2]** The child's tribe does not have a "tribal court" or any other administrative body as defined in section 1903 of the Indian Child Welfare Act: "a court with jurisdiction over child custody proceedings and which is either a Court of Indian Offenses, a court established and operated under the code or custom of an Indian tribe, or any other administrative body of a tribe which is vested with authority over child custody proceedings;" or (C) **[3]** One or more of the following circumstances may constitute discretionary good cause to deny a request to transfer: (A) The evidence necessary to decide the case cannot be presented in the tribal court without undue hardship to the parties or the witnesses, and the tribal court is unable to mitigate the hardship by making arrangements to receive and consider the evidence or testimony by use of remote communication, by hearing the evidence or testimony at a location convenient to the parties or witnesses, or by use of other means permitted in the tribal court's rules of evidence or discovery; (B) The proceeding was **[4]** when the request to transfer was received and the petitioner did not make the request within a reasonable time after receiving notice of the proceeding, provided the notice complied with statutory requirements. Waiting until reunification efforts have failed and reunification services have been terminated before filing a request to transfer may not, by itself, be considered an unreasonable delay; (C) The Indian child is over 12 years of age and objects to the transfer; or (D) The parents of a child over five years of age are not available and the child has had little or no contact with his or her tribe or members of the child's tribe

(e) Evidentiary burdens

(1) The burden of establishing good cause to deny a request to transfer is on the party opposing the transfer.

(2) If the court believes, or any party asserts, that good cause to deny the request exists, the reasons for that belief or assertion must be stated **orally on the record or** in writing, in advance of the hearing, and made available to all parties who are requesting the transfer, and the petitioner must have the opportunity to provide information or evidence in rebuttal of the belief or assertion.

(Subd (e) repealed, relettered and amended effective January 1, 2020; adopted as subd (f) effective January 1, 2008; previously amended effective January 1, 2013.)

(f) Order on request to transfer

(1) The court must issue its final order on the *Order on Petition to Transfer Case Involving an Indian Child to Tribal Jurisdiction* (form ICWA-060).

(2) When a matter is being transferred from the jurisdiction of a juvenile court, the order must include:

(A) All of the findings, orders, or modifications of orders that have been made in the case;

(B) The name and address of the tribe to which jurisdiction is being transferred;

(C) Directions for the agency to release the child case file to the tribe having jurisdiction under section 827.15 of the Welfare and Institutions Code;

(D) Directions that all papers contained in the child case file must be transferred to the tribal court; and

(E) Directions that a copy of the transfer order and the findings of fact must be maintained by the transferring court.

(Subd (f) relettered effective January 1, 2020; adopted as subd (g) effective January 1, 2008; previously amended effective January 1, 2016.)

(g) Advisement when transfer order granted

When the court grants a petition transferring a case to tribal court under Welfare and Institutions Code section 305.5, Family Code section 177(a), or Probate Code section 1459.5(b) and rule 5.483, the court must advise the parties orally and in writing that any appeal to the order for transfer to a tribal court must be made before the transfer to tribal jurisdiction is finalized and that failure to request and obtain a stay of the order for transfer will result in a loss of appellate jurisdiction.

(Subd (g) relettered effective January 1, 2020; adopted as subd (h) effective January 1, 2016.)

(h) Proceeding after transfer

When, under Welfare and Institutions Code section 305.5, Family Code section 177(a), or Probate Code section 1459.5(b), the court transfers any proceeding listed in rule 5.480, the court must proceed as follows:

(1) Dismiss the proceeding or terminate jurisdiction if the court has received proof that the tribal court has accepted the transfer of jurisdiction;

(2) Make an order transferring the physical custody of the child to a designated representative of the tribal court (not necessarily the same "designated representative" identified in the *Notice of Designation of Tribal Representative and Notice of Intervention in a Court Proceeding Involving an Indian Child* (form ICWA-040)); and

(3) Include in the *Order on Petition to Transfer Case Involving an Indian Child to Tribal Jurisdiction* (form ICWA-060) all contact information for the designated tribal court representative.

(Subd (h) relettered effective January 1, 2020; adopted as subd (h) effective January 1, 2008; previously relettered as subd (i) effective January 1, 2016.)
Rule 5.483 amended effective January 1, 2020; adopted effective January 1, 2008; previously amended effective January 1, 2013, and January 1, 2016.

Advisory Committee Comment

Once a transfer to tribal court is finalized as provided in rule 5.483(h), the appellate court lacks jurisdiction to order the case returned to state court (*In re M.M.* (2007) 154 Cal.App.4th 897).

As stated by the Court of Appeal in *In re M.M.*, the juvenile court has the discretion to stay the provisions of a judgment or order awarding, changing, or affecting custody of a minor child "pending review on appeal or for any other period or periods that it may deem appropriate" (Code Civ. Proc., § 917.7), and the party seeking review of the transfer order should first request a stay in the lower court. (See *Nuckolls v. Bank of California, Nat. Assn.* (1936) 7 Cal.2d 574, 577 [61 P.2d 927] ["Inasmuch as the [L]egislature has provided a method by which the trial court, in a proper case, may grant the stay, the appellate courts, assuming that they have the power, should not, except in some unusual emergency, exercise their power until the petitioner has first presented the matter to the trial court"].) If the juvenile court should deny the stay request, the aggrieved party may then petition this court for a writ of supersedeas pending appeal. (Cal. Rules of Court, rule 8.112).

Subdivision (g) and this advisory committee comment are added to help ensure that an objecting party does not inadvertently lose the right to appeal a transfer order.

Rule 5.484. Emergency proceedings involving an Indian child

(a) Standards for removal

Whenever it is known or there is reason to know the case involves an Indian child, the court may not order an emergency removal or placement of the child without a finding that the removal or placement is necessary to prevent imminent physical damage or harm to the child. The petition requesting emergency removal or continued emergency placement of the child or its accompanying documents must contain the following:

(1) A statement of the risk of imminent physical damage or harm to the child and any evidence that the emergency removal or placement continues to be necessary to prevent such imminent physical damage or harm to the child;

(2) The name, age, and last known address of the Indian child;

(3) The name and address of the child's parents and Indian custodian, if any;

(4) The steps taken to provide notice to the child's parents, Indian custodian, and tribe about the emergency proceeding;

(5) If the child's parents and Indian custodian are unknown, a detailed explanation of what efforts have been made to locate and contact them;

(6) The residence and the domicile of the Indian child;

(7) If either the residence or the domicile of the Indian child is believed to be on a reservation or in an Alaska Native village, the name of the tribe affiliated with that reservation or village;

(8) The tribal affiliation of the child and of the parents or Indian custodian;

(9) A specific and detailed account of the circumstances that led to the emergency removal of the child;

(10) If the child is believed to reside or be domiciled on a reservation where the tribe exercises exclusive jurisdiction over child custody matters, a statement of efforts that have been made and are being made to contact the tribe and transfer the child to the tribe's jurisdiction; and

(11) A statement of the efforts that have been taken to assist the parents or Indian custodian so the Indian child may safely be returned to their custody.

(Subd (a) adopted effective January 1, 2020.)

(b) Return of Indian child when emergency situation has ended

(1) Whenever it is known or there is reason to know the child is an Indian child and there has been an emergency removal of the child from parental custody, any party who asserts that there is new information indicating that the emergency situation has ended may request an ex parte hearing by filing a request on *Request for Ex Parte Hearing to Return Physical Custody of an Indian Child* (form ICWA-070) to determine whether the emergency situation has ended.

(2) If the request provides evidence of new information establishing that the emergency placement is no longer necessary, the court must promptly schedule a hearing. At the hearing the court must consider whether the child's removal and placement is still necessary to prevent imminent physical damage or harm to the child. If the court determines that the child's emergency removal or placement is no longer necessary to prevent imminent physical damage or harm to the child, the court must order the child returned to the physical custody of the parents or Indian custodian.

(3) In accordance with rules 3.10 and 3.20, this procedure is governed by the provisions of division 6, chapter 3 and division 11, chapter 4 of title 3 of the California Rules of Court.

(Subd (b) adopted effective January 1, 2020.)

(c) Time limitation on emergency proceedings

An emergency removal must not continue for more than 30 days unless the court makes the following determinations:

(1) Restoring the child to the parent or Indian custodian would subject the child to imminent physical damage or harm;

(2) The court has been unable to transfer the proceeding to the jurisdiction of the appropriate Indian tribe; and

(3) It has not been possible to have a hearing that complies with the substantive requirements of the Indian Child Welfare Act for a foster care placement proceeding.

(Subd (c) adopted effective January 1, 2020.)
Rule 5.484 adopted effective January 1, 2020.

Rule 5.485. Placement of an Indian child

(a) Evidentiary burdens

The court may only terminate parental rights to an Indian child or declare an Indian child free of the custody and control of one or both parents if at the hearing terminating parental rights or declaring the child free of the custody and control of one or both parents, the court:

(1) Finds by clear and convincing evidence that active efforts to provide remedial services and rehabilitative programs designed to prevent the breakup of the Indian family were made; and

(2) Makes a determination, supported by evidence beyond a reasonable doubt, including testimony of one or more "qualified expert witnesses" as defined in Welfare and Institutions Code section 224.6 and Family Code section 177(a), that the continued custody of the child by the parent is likely to result in serious emotional or physical damage to the child.

(Subd (a) adopted effective January 1, 2008.)

(b) Standards and preferences in placement of an Indian child

(1) **All placements of an Indian child must be in the least restrictive setting that most approximates a family situation and in which the child's special needs, if any, may be met.**

(2) Unless the court finds **by clear and convincing evidence that there is** good cause to [1] **deviate from them, whenever it is known or there is reason to know the child is an Indian child,** all placements [2] in any proceeding listed in [3] **rules** 5.480 **and 5.484** must follow the specified placement preferences in Family Code section 177(a), Probate Code section 1459(b), and Welfare and Institutions Code section 361.31.

[4] **(3) The court must analyze the availability of placements within the placement preferences in descending order without skipping.** The court may deviate from the preference order only for good cause, which may include the following considerations:

(A) The requests of the parent or Indian custodian **if they attest that they have reviewed the placement options, if any, that comply with the order of preference;**

(B) The requests of the Indian child, when of sufficient age **and capacity to understand the decision being made;**

(C) **The presence of a sibling attachment that can be maintained only through a particular placement;**

(D) The extraordinary physical, **mental,** or emotional needs of the Indian child [5]**, including specialized treatment services that may be unavailable in the community where families who meet the placement preferences live;** or

[6] **(E)** The unavailability of a suitable [7] **placement within the placement preferences** based on a documented diligent effort to identify [8] **placements** meeting the preference criteria. **The standard for determining whether a placement is unavailable must conform to the prevailing social and cultural standards of the Indian community in which the Indian child's parent or extended family resides or with which the Indian child's parent or extended family members maintain social and cultural ties.**

[9] **(4) The placement preferences must be analyzed and considered each time there is a change in the child's placement. A finding that there is good cause to deviate from the placement preferences does not affect the requirement that a diligent search be made for a subsequent placement within the placement preferences.**

(5) The burden of establishing good cause for the court to deviate from the preference order is on the party requesting that the preference order not be followed. **A placement may not depart from the preferences based on the socioeconomic status of any placement relative to another or solely on the basis of ordinary bonding or attachment that flowed from time spent in a nonpreferred placement that was made in violation of the Indian Child Welfare Act.**

[10] **(6)** The tribe, by resolution, may establish a different preference order, which must be followed if it provides for the least restrictive setting.

[11] **(7)** The preferences and wishes of the Indian child, when of sufficient age, and the parent must be considered, and weight given to a consenting parent's request for anonymity.

[12] **(8)** When no preferred placement is available, active efforts must be made and documented to place the child with a family committed to enabling the child to have visitation with "extended family members," as

defined in [13] **25 United States Code section 1903(2)**, and participation in the cultural and ceremonial events of the child's tribe.

(Subd (b) amended effective January 1, 2020; adopted effective January 1, 2008; previously amended effective January 1, 2013.)

Rule 5.485(b).   2019 Deletes. [1] the contrary [2] of Indian children [3] rule [4] (2) [5] as established by a qualified expert witness [6] (D) [7] families [8] families [9] (3) [10] (4) [11] (5) [12] (6) [13] rule 5.481(a)(4)(A)

(c) Active efforts

In addition to any other required findings to place an Indian child with someone other than a parent or Indian custodian, or to terminate parental rights, the court must find that active efforts have been made, in any proceeding listed in rule 5.480, to provide remedial services and rehabilitative programs designed to prevent the breakup of the Indian family, and must find that these efforts were unsuccessful. **These active efforts must include affirmative, active, thorough, and timely efforts intended primarily to maintain or reunite the child with his or her family, must be tailored to the facts and circumstances of the case, and must be consistent with the requirements of Welfare and Institutions Code section 224.1(f).**

(1) **The active efforts must be documented in detail in the record.**

(2) The court must consider whether active efforts were made in a manner consistent with the prevailing social and cultural conditions and way of life of the Indian child's tribe.

[1] **(3) Active** efforts to provide services must include pursuit of any steps necessary to secure tribal membership for a child if the child is eligible for membership in a given tribe, as well as attempts to use the available resources of extended family members, the tribe, tribal and other Indian social service agencies, and individual Indian caregivers.

(Subd (c) amended effective January 1, 2020; adopted effective January 1, 2008; previously amended effective January 1, 2013.)

Rule 5.485(c).   2019 Deletes. [1] (2)

Rule 5.485 renumbered and amended effective January 1, 2020; adopted as rule 5.484 effective January 1, 2008; previously amended effective January 1, 2013.

Rule 5.486.   Termination of parental rights

(a) Evidentiary burdens

The court may only terminate parental rights to an Indian child or declare an Indian child free of the custody and control of one or both parents if at the hearing terminating parental rights or declaring the child free of the custody and control of one or both parents, the court:

(1) Finds by clear and convincing evidence that active efforts to provide remedial services and rehabilitative programs designed to prevent the breakup of the Indian family were made; and

(2) Makes a determination, supported by evidence beyond a reasonable doubt, including testimony of one or more "qualified expert witnesses" as defined in Welfare and Institutions Code section 224.6 and Family Code section 177(a), that the continued custody of the child by the parent is likely to result in serious emotional or physical damage to the child.

(Subd (a) adopted effective January 1, 2008.)

(b) When parental rights may not be terminated

The court may not terminate parental rights to an Indian child or declare a child free from the custody and control of one or both parents if the court finds a compelling reason for determining that termination of parental rights would not be in the child's best interest. Such a reason may include:

(1) **The child is living with a relative who is unable or unwilling to adopt the child because of circumstances that do not include an unwillingness to accept legal or financial responsibility for the child, but who is willing and capable of providing the child with a stable and permanent environment through legal guardianship, and the removal of the child from the custody of his or her relative would be detrimental to the emotional well-being of the child. For purposes of an Indian child, "relative" must include an "extended family member," as defined in the Indian Child Welfare Act (25 U.S.C. § 1903(2));**

(2) Termination of parental rights would substantially interfere with the child's connection to his or her tribal community or the child's tribal membership rights; or

[1] **(3)** The child's tribe has identified **tribal customary adoption,** guardianship, long-term foster care with a fit and willing relative, or another planned permanent living arrangement for the child.

(Subd (b) amended effective January 1, 2020; adopted effective January 1, 2008.)

Rule 5.486(b).   2019 Deletes. [1] (2)

Rule 5.486 renumbered and amended effective January 1, 2020; adopted as rule 5.485 effective January 1, 2008; previously amended effective January 1, 2013.

Rule 5.487.   Petition to invalidate orders

(a) Who may petition

Any Indian child who is the subject of any action for foster-care placement, guardianship **or conservatorship** placement, **custody placement under Family Code section 3041, declaration freeing a child from the custody and control of one or both parents, preadoptive placement, adoptive placement,** or termination of parental rights; any parent or Indian custodian from whose custody such child was removed; and the Indian child's tribe may petition the court to invalidate the action on a showing that the action violated the Indian Child Welfare Act.

(Subd (a) amended effective January 1, 2020; adopted effective January 1, 2008.)

(b) Court of competent jurisdiction

If the Indian child is a dependent child or ward of the juvenile court or the subject of a pending petition, the juvenile court is a court of competent jurisdiction with the authority to hear the request to invalidate the foster placement or termination of parental rights.

(Subd (b) adopted effective January 1, 2008.)

(c) Request to return custody of the Indian child

If a final decree of adoption is vacated or set aside, or if the adoptive parents voluntarily consent to the termination of their parental rights, a biological parent or prior Indian custodian may request a return of custody of the Indian child.

(1) The court must reinstate jurisdiction.

(2) In a juvenile case, the juvenile court must hold a new disposition hearing in accordance with 25 United States Code section 1901 et seq. where the court may consider all placement options as stated in Welfare and Institutions Code sections 361.31(b), (c), (d), and (h).

(3) The court may consider placement with a biological parent or prior Indian custodian if the biological parent or prior Indian custodian can show that placement with him or her is not detrimental to the child and that the placement is in the best interests of the child.

(4) The hearing on the request to return custody of an Indian child must be conducted in accordance with statutory requirements and the relevant sections of this rule.

(Subd (c) adopted effective January 1, 2008.)

Rule 5.487 amended and renumbered effective January 1, 2020; adopted effective January 1, 2008; previously amended effective January 1, 2013.

Rule 5.488.   Adoption record keeping

(a) Copies of adoption decree and other information to the Secretary of the Interior

After granting a decree of adoption of an Indian child, the court must provide the Secretary of the Interior with a copy of the decree and the following information:

(1) The name and tribal affiliation of the Indian child;

(2) The names and addresses of the biological parents;

(3) The names and addresses of the adoptive parents; and

(4) The agency maintaining files and records regarding the adoptive placement.

(Subd (a) adopted effective January 1, 2008.)

(b) Affidavit of confidentiality to the Bureau of Indian Affairs

If a biological parent has executed an affidavit requesting that his or her identity remain confidential, the court must provide the affidavit to the Bureau of Indian Affairs, which must ensure the confidentiality of the information.

(Subd (b) adopted effective January 1, 2008.)

Rule 5.488 renumbered effective January 1, 2020; adopted effective January 1, 2008; previously amended effective January 1, 2013.

Advisory Committee Comment

This chapter was adopted, effective January 1, 2008, as the result of the passage of Senate Bill 678 (Ducheny; Stats. 2006, ch. 838), which codified the federal Indian Child Welfare Act into California's Family, Probate, and Welfare and Institutions Codes affecting all proceedings listed in rule 5.480. Rule 5.664, which applied the Indian Child Welfare Act but was limited in its effect to juvenile proceedings, was repealed effective January 1, 2008, and was replaced by this chapter.

As of January 1, 2008, only the Washoe Tribe of Nevada and California is authorized under the Indian Child Welfare Act to exercise exclusive jurisdiction as discussed in rule 5.483.

Chapter 3
Intercountry Adoptions

Title 5, Family and Juvenile Rules—Division 2, Rules Applicable in Family and

Juvenile Proceedings—Chapter 3, Intercountry Adoptions; amended effective January 1, 2021; adopted effective July 1, 2013.

Rule 5.490. Adoption of a child resident in the United States by a resident of a foreign country party to the Convention of 29 May 1993 on Protection of Children and Cooperation in Respect of Intercountry Adoption (Convention or Hague Adoption Convention)

Rule 5.491. Adoption of a child resident in the United States by a resident of a foreign country not party to the Hague Adoption Convention

Rule 5.492. Adoption by a United States resident of a child resident in a foreign country that is party to the Hague Adoption Convention

Rule 5.493. Requirement to request adoption under California law of a child born in a foreign country when the adoption is finalized in the foreign country (Fam. Code, §§ 8912, 8919)

Rule 5.490. Adoption of a child resident in the United States by a resident of a foreign country party to the Convention of 29 May 1993 on Protection of Children and Cooperation in Respect of Intercountry Adoption (Convention or Hague Adoption Convention)

(a) Purpose

The rules in this chapter are adopted to provide practice and procedure for intercountry adoptions conducted under the Hague Adoption Convention and applicable California law.

(Subd (a) adopted effective July 1, 2013.)

(b) Applicability of rule

This rule applies to any adoption of a child resident in the United States by an individual or individuals residing in a convention country, as defined in Family Code section 8900.5(f), if, in connection with the adoption, the child has moved or will move between the United States and the convention country.

(Subd (b) adopted effective July 1, 2013.)

(c) Adoption request and attachments

(1) The *Adoption Request* (form ADOPT-200) and *Verification of Compliance with Hague Adoption Convention Attachment* (ADOPT-216) must allege specific facts about the applicability of the Hague Adoption Convention and whether the petitioner is seeking a California adoption, will be petitioning for a Hague Adoption Certificate, or will be seeking a Hague Custody Declaration.

(2) The court must determine whether a child resident in the United States has been or will be moved to a convention country in connection with an adoption by an individual or individuals residing in a convention country.

(Subd (c) adopted effective July 1, 2013.)

(d) Evidence required to verify compliance with the Hague Adoption Convention

If the Hague Adoption Convention applies to the case, and the court is asked to issue findings and an order supporting a request for the U.S. Department of State to issue a Hague Adoption Certificate or a Hague Custody Declaration for the adoption placement, the court must receive sufficient evidence to conclude that the child is eligible for adoption and find that the placement is in the best interest of the child. The court must receive evidence of all of the following:

(1) The adoption agency or provider is accredited by the Council on Accreditation, is supervised by an accredited primary provider, or is acting as an exempted provider, as defined in Family Code section 8900.5(g), to provide intercountry adoption services for convention cases;

(2) A child background study has been completed and transmitted to a foreign authorized entity in accordance with the regulations governing convention adoptions with proof that the necessary consents have been obtained and the reason for its determination that the proposed placement is in the child's best interest, based on the home study and child background study and giving due consideration to the child's upbringing and his or her ethnic, religious, and cultural background;

(3) The child is eligible for adoption under California law;

(4) The adoption agency or provider has made reasonable efforts, as described under 22 Code of Federal Regulations section 96.54(a), to place the child in the United States, but was unable to do so, or an exception to this requirement applies to the case. Such reasonable efforts include: (1) disseminating information on the child and his or her availability for adoption through print, media, and Internet resources designed to communicate with potential prospective adoptive parents in the United States; (2) listing information about the child on a national or state adoption exchange or registry for at least 60 calendar days after the birth of the child; (3) responding to inquiries about adoption of the child; and (4) providing a copy of the child background study to potential U.S. prospective adoptive parent(s);

(5) The agency has determined that the placement is in the child's best interest;

(6) A home study on the petitioner(s) has been completed, which includes:

(A) Information on the petitioner(s), such as identity, eligibility and suitability to adopt, background, family and medical history, social environment, reasons for adoption, ability to undertake an intercountry adoption, an assessment of their ability to care for the child, and the characteristics of the child for whom they would be qualified to care;

(B) Confirmation that a competent authority has determined that the petitioner is eligible and suited to adopt and has ensured that the petitioner has been counseled as necessary; and

(C) The results of criminal background checks;

(7) The Hague Adoption Convention authority designated by the receiving country has declared that the child will be permitted to enter and reside permanently or on the same basis as the adopting parent(s) in the receiving country, and has consented to the adoption;

(8) All appropriate consents have been obtained in writing in accordance with the following standards:

(A) Counseling was provided to any biological or legal parent or legal guardian consenting to the adoption;

(B) All biological or legal parents or legal guardians were informed of the legal effect of adoption;

(C) Such consent was freely given without inducement by compensation;

(D) Such consent was not subsequently withdrawn; and

(E) Consents were taken only after the birth of the child.

(9) As appropriate in light of the child's age and maturity, the child has been counseled and informed of the effects of the adoption and the child's views have been considered. If the child's consent is required, the child has also been counseled and informed of the effects of granting consent and has freely given consent expressed or evidenced in writing in the required legal form without any inducement by compensation of any kind;

(10) The adoption agency or provider has committed to taking all steps to ensure the secure transfer of the child, including obtaining permission for the child to leave the United States;

(11) The adoption agency or provider has agreed to keep the receiving country's designated Hague Adoption Convention authority informed about the status of the case;

(12) The petitioner consents to adoption or has agreed to accept custody of the child for purposes of adoption;

(13) The adoption agency or provider demonstrates that any contact between the birth family and the adoptive family complies with applicable state law and federal regulations governing the timing of such communications; and

(14) The adoption agency or provider certifies that no one is deriving improper financial gain from the adoption and describes the financial arrangement with the prospective adoptive family.

(Subd (d) adopted effective July 1, 2013.)

(e) Court findings required to support the application for a Hague Adoption Certificate or Hague Custody Declaration

The court must make findings relating to the application for a Hague Adoption Certificate or Hague Custody Declaration from the Department of State. To meet the requirements for issuance of the certificate or declaration, the findings must include that:

(1) The adoption is in the child's best interest;

(2) The substantive regulatory requirements set forth in 22 Code of Federal Regulations sections 97.3(a)–(k) have been met; and

(3) The adoption services provider meets the requirements of 22 Code of Federal Regulations part 96.

(Subd (e) adopted effective July 1, 2013.)

(f) Court findings to verify that all Hague Adoption Convention requirements have been met

If the court is satisfied that all Hague Adoption Convention requirements have been met, the court must make findings of fact and order the following:

(1) The child is eligible for adoption;

(2) The grant of custody with respect to the proposed adoption is in the child's best interest; and

(3) The court grants custody of the child to the named family for purposes of adoption, as applicable.

(Subd (f) adopted effective July 1, 2013.)

(g) Petitioner's intent to finalize adoption

If the adoption is not finalized in California, a petition for a Hague Custody Declaration must state specific facts indicating that the petitioner intends to finalize the adoption in petitioner's country of residence or that petitioner will return to California after any required post-placement supervisory period to finalize the adoption in a superior court of California.

(Subd (g) adopted effective July 1, 2013.)
Rule 5.490 adopted effective July 1, 2013.

Advisory Committee Comment

The Hague Adoption Convention (HAC) is a treaty that entered into force with respect to the United States on April 1, 2008. The HAC strengthens protections for children, birth parents, and prospective adoptive parents and establishes internationally agreed-upon rules and procedures for adoptions between countries that have a treaty relationship under the HAC. It provides a framework for countries party to the Convention to work together to ensure that children are provided with permanent, loving homes; that adoptions take place in the best interest of a child; and that the abduction, sale, or traffic of children is prevented. This rule expands procedurally on Family Code sections 8900 through 8925, which address intercountry adoptions, by specifying the findings and evidence set forth in 22 Code of Federal Regulations section 97.3 that are required by a state court when the HAC applies to an adoption.

Rule 5.491. Adoption of a child resident in the United States by a resident of a foreign country not party to the Hague Adoption Convention

The adoption of a child resident in the United States by a resident of a foreign country not party to the Hague Adoption Convention must conform to the law governing California adoptions.

Rule 5.491 adopted effective July 1, 2013.

Rule 5.492. Adoption by a United States resident of a child resident in a foreign country that is party to the Hague Adoption Convention

A United States resident who plans to adopt, in California, a child resident in a foreign country that is party to the Hague Adoption Convention must provide to the California court the required proof, in the form of a Hague Custody Declaration, that all required Hague Adoption Convention findings have been made by the child's country of residence.

Rule 5.492 adopted effective July 1, 2013.

Rule 5.493. Requirement to request adoption under California law of a child born in a foreign country when the adoption is finalized in the foreign country (Fam. Code, §§ 8912, 8919)

(a) Responsibility to file request

(1) A resident of California who has finalized an intercountry adoption in a foreign country must:

(A) File a request to adopt the child in California within the earlier of 60 days from the adoptee's entry into the United States or the adoptee's 16th birthday; and

(B) Provide a copy of the adoption request to each adoption agency that provided the adoption services to the adoptive parent or parents.

(2) If the adopting parent fails to timely file a request to adopt the child under California law, the adoption agency that facilitated the adoption must:

(A) File the request within 90 days of the child's entry into the United States; and

(B) Provide a file-marked copy of the request to the adoptive parent and to any other adoption agency that provided services to the adoptive parent within five business days of filing.

(3) If an adoption agency files a request in accordance with (2), the adoptive parent or parents will be liable to the adoption agency for all costs and fees incurred as a result of good faith actions taken by the adoption agency to fulfill the requirement set forth in this rule.

(Subd (a) adopted effective January 1, 2021.)

(b) Contents of request

(1) A request to adopt under California law a child born in a foreign country whose adoption was finalized in a foreign country must include all of the following:

(A) A certified or otherwise official copy of the foreign decree, order, or certification of adoption that reflects finalization of the adoption in the foreign country;

(B) A certified or otherwise official copy of the child's foreign birth certificate;

(C) A certified translation of all documents described in this subdivision that are not written in English;

(D) Proof that the child was granted lawful entry into the United States as an immediate relative of the adoptive parent or parents;

(E) A report from at least one postplacement home visit by an intercountry adoption agency or a contractor of that agency licensed to provide intercountry adoption services in the state of California; and

(F) A copy of the home study report previously completed for the international finalized adoption by an adoption agency authorized to provide intercountry adoption services, in accordance with Family Code section 8900.

(2) If an adoption agency initiates a request in accordance with (a)(2), the filing must consist of the following:

(A) A signed cover sheet containing the name, date of birth, and date of entry to the United States of the child, the name and address of the adoptive parent or parents, and the name and contact information for the adoption agency;

(B) Blank copies of all forms required to initiate the request for adoption under California law; and

(C) Any document required in (b)(1) that is in the possession of the adoption agency.

(Subd (b) adopted effective January 1, 2021.)

(c) Clerk's notice of request and order

(1) When a request for adoption under California law of a child whose adoption was finalized in a foreign country is filed, the court clerk must immediately notify the California Department of Social Services in Sacramento in writing of the pendency of the proceeding and of any subsequent action taken.

(2) If a request for adoption under California law is initiated under (a)(2), the clerk of the court must file-stamp the request to allow the adoption agency to fulfill its obligations under (a)(2)(B).

(3) Within 10 business days of an order granting a request for adoption under California law, the clerk of the court must submit to the State Registrar the order granting the request.

(Subd (c) adopted effective January 1, 2021.)
Rule 5.493 adopted effective January 1, 2021.

Chapter 4
Protective Orders

Title 5, Family and Juvenile Rules—Division 2, Rules Applicable in Family and Juvenile Proceedings—Chapter 4, Protective Orders; adopted effective July 1, 2014.

Rule 5.495. Firearm relinquishment procedures

(a) Application of rule

This rule applies when a family or juvenile law domestic violence protective order as defined in Family Code section 6218 or Welfare and Institutions Code section 213.5 is issued or in effect.

(Subd (a) adopted effective July 1, 2014.)

(b) Purpose

This rule addresses situations in which information is presented to the court about firearms and provides the court with options for appropriately addressing the issue. This rule is intended to:

(1) Assist courts issuing domestic violence protective orders in determining whether a restrained person has a firearm in or subject to his or her immediate possession or control.

(2) Assist courts that have issued domestic violence protective orders in determining whether a restrained person has complied with the court's order to relinquish, store, or sell the firearm under Family Code section 6389(c).

(Subd (b) adopted effective July 1, 2014.)

(c) Firearm determination

When relevant information is presented to the court at any noticed hearing that a restrained person has a firearm, the court must consider that information to determine, by a preponderance of the evidence, whether the person subject to a protective order as defined in Family Code section 6218 or Welfare and Institutions Code section 213.5 has a firearm in or subject to his or her immediate possession or control in violation of Family Code section 6389.

(Subd (c) adopted effective July 1, 2014.)

(d) Determination procedures

(1) In making a determination under this rule, the court may consider whether the restrained person filed a firearm relinquishment, storage, or sales receipt or if an exemption from the firearm prohibition was granted under Family Code section 6389(h).

(2) The court may make the determination at any noticed hearing when a domestic violence protective order is issued, at a subsequent review hearing, or at any subsequent family or juvenile law hearing while the order remains in effect.

(3) If the court makes a determination that the restrained person has a firearm in violation of Family Code section 6389, the court must make a written record of the determination and provide a copy to any party who is present at the hearing and, upon request, to any party not present at the hearing.

(Subd (d) adopted effective July 1, 2014.)

(e) Subsequent review hearing

(1) When presented with information under (c), the court may set a review hearing to determine whether a violation of Family Code section 6389 has taken place.

(2) The review hearing must be held within 10 court days after the noticed hearing at which the information was presented. If the restrained person is not present when the court sets the review hearing, the protected person must provide notice of the review hearing to the restrained person at least 2 court days before the review hearing, in accordance with Code of Civil Procedure 414.10, by personal service or by mail to the restrained person's last known address.

(3) The court may for good cause extend the date of the review hearing for a reasonable period or remove it from the calendar.

(4) The court must order the restrained person to appear at the review hearing.

(5) The court may conduct the review hearing in the absence of the protected person.

(6) Nothing in this rule prohibits the court from permitting a party to appear by telephone under California Rules of Court, rule 5.9.

(Subd (e) adopted effective July 1, 2014.)

(f) Child custody and visitation

(1) If the court determines that the restrained person has a firearm in violation of Family Code section 6389, the court must consider that determination when deciding whether the restrained person has overcome the presumption in Family Code section 3044.

(2) An order for custody or visitation issued at any time during a family law matter must be made in a manner that ensures the health, safety, and welfare of the child and the safety of all family members, as specified in Family Code section 3020. The court must consider whether the best interest of the child, based on the circumstances of the case, requires that any visitation or custody arrangement be limited to situations in which a third person, specified by the court, is present, or that visitation or custody be suspended or denied, as specified in Family Code section 6323(d).

(3) An order for visitation issued at any time during a juvenile court matter must not jeopardize the safety of the child, as specified in Welfare and Institutions Code section 362.1.

(Subd (f) adopted effective July 1, 2014.)

(g) Other orders

(1) The court may consider a determination that the restrained person has a firearm in violation of Family Code section 6389 in issuing:

(A) An order to show cause for contempt under section 1209(a)(5) of the Code of Civil Procedure for failure to comply with the court's order to surrender or sell a firearm; or

(B) An order for money sanctions under section 177.5 of the Code of Civil Procedure.

(2) This rule should not be construed to limit the court's power to issue orders it is otherwise authorized or required to issue.

(Subd (g) adopted effective July 1, 2014.)

Rule 5.495 adopted effective July 1, 2014.

Advisory Committee Comment

When issuing a family or juvenile law domestic violence protective order as defined in Family Code section 6218 or Welfare and Institutions Code section 213.5, ex parte or after a noticed hearing, the court is required to order a restrained person "to relinquish any firearm in [that person's] immediate possession or control or subject to [that person's] immediate possession or control." (Fam. Code, § 6389(c)(1).) Several mandatory Judicial Council forms—*Temporary Restraining Order* (form DV-110), *Restraining Order After Hearing* (form DV-130), and *Notice of Hearing and Temporary Restraining Order—Juvenile* (form JV-250)—include

mandatory orders in bold type that the restrained person must sell to or store with a licensed gun dealer or turn in to a law enforcement agency any guns or other firearms within his or her immediate possession or control within 24 hours after service of the order and must file a receipt with the court showing compliance with the order within 48 hours of receiving the order. California law requires personal service of the request for and any temporary protective order at least five days before the hearing, unless the court issues an order shortening time for service. Therefore, by the date of the hearing, the restrained person should have relinquished, stored, or sold his or her firearms and submitted a receipt to the court.

Courts are encouraged to develop local procedures to calendar firearm relinquishment review hearings for restrained persons.

Section (f) of this rule restates existing law on the safety and welfare of children and family members and recognizes the safety issues associated with the presence of prohibited firearms.

Although this rule does not require the court to compel a restrained person to testify, the court may wish to advise a party of his or her privilege against self-incrimination under the Fifth Amendment to the United States Constitution. The court may also consider whether to grant use immunity under Family Code section 6389(d).

Division 3
Juvenile Rules

Chapter 1
Preliminary Provisions—Title and Definitions

Rule 5.500. Division title
Rule 5.501. Preliminary provisions
Rule 5.502. Definitions and use of terms
Rule 5.504. Judicial Council forms
Rule 5.505. Juvenile dependency court performance measures

Rule 5.500. Division title

The rules in this division may be referred to as the Juvenile Rules.
Rule 5.500 adopted effective January 1, 2007.

Rule 5.501. Preliminary provisions

(a) Application of rules (§§ 200–945)

The rules in this division solely apply to every action and proceeding to which the juvenile court law (Welf. & Inst. Code, div. 2, pt. 1, ch. 2, § 200 et seq.) applies, unless they are explicitly made applicable in any other action or proceeding. The rules in this division do not apply to an action or proceeding heard by a traffic hearing officer, nor to a rehearing or appeal from a denial of a rehearing following an order by a traffic hearing officer.

(Subd (a) amended effective January 1, 2007.)

(b) Authority for and purpose of rules (Cal. Const., art. VI, §§ 6, 265)

The Judicial Council adopted the rules in this division under its constitutional and statutory authority to adopt rules for court administration, practice, and procedure that are not inconsistent with statute. These rules implement the purposes of the juvenile court law by promoting uniformity in practice and procedure and by providing guidance to judicial officers, attorneys, social workers, probation officers, and others participating in the juvenile court.

(Subd (b) amended effective January 1, 2007.)

(c) Rules of construction

Unless the context otherwise requires, these preliminary provisions and the following rules of construction govern the construction of these rules:

(1) Insofar as these rules are substantially the same as existing statutory provisions relating to the same subject matter, these rules must be construed as restatements of those statutes; and

(2) Insofar as these rules may add to existing statutory provisions relating to the same subject matter, these rules must be construed so as to implement the purposes of the juvenile court law.

(Subd (c) amended effective January 1, 2007.)

(d) Severability clause

If a rule or a subdivision of a rule in this division is invalid, all valid parts that are severable from the invalid part remain in effect. If a rule or a subdivision of a rule in this division is invalid in one or more of its applications, the rule or subdivision remains in effect in all valid applications that are severable from the invalid applications.

Rule 5.501 amended and renumbered effective January 1, 2007; adopted as rule 1400 effective January 1, 1990.

Rule 5.502. Definitions and use of terms

Definitions (§§ 202(e), 303, 319, 361, 361.5(a)(3), 450, 628.1, 636, 726, 727.3(c)(2), 727.4(d), 4512(j), 4701.6(b), 11400(v), 11400(y), 16501(f)(16); 20 U.S.C. § 1415; 25 U.S.C. § 1903(2))

As used in these rules, unless the context or subject matter otherwise requires:

(1) "Affinity" means the connection existing between one spouse or domestic partner and the blood or adoptive relatives of the other spouse or domestic partner.

(2) "At risk of entering foster care" means that conditions within a child's family may require that the child be removed from the custody of a parent or guardian and placed in foster care unless or until those conditions are resolved.

(3) "CASA" means Court Appointed Special Advocate as defined in rule 5.655.

(4) "Child Abuse Prevention and Treatment Act (CAPTA) guardian ad litem for a child subject to a juvenile dependency petition" is defined in rule 5.662.

(5) "Child" means a person under the age of 18 years.

(6) "Clerk" means the clerk of the juvenile court.

(7) "Court" means the juvenile court and includes any judicial officer of the juvenile court.

(8) "Court-ordered services" or "court-ordered treatment program" means child welfare services or services provided by an appropriate agency ordered at a dispositional hearing at which the child is declared a dependent child or ward of the court, and any hearing thereafter, for the purpose of maintaining or reunifying a child with a parent or guardian.

(9) "Date the child entered foster care" means:

(A) In dependency, the date on which the court sustained the petition filed under section 300 or 60 days after the "initial removal" of the child as defined below, whichever is earlier; or

(B) In delinquency, the date 60 days after the date on which the child was initially removed from the home, unless one of the following exceptions applies:

(i) If the child is detained pending foster care placement and remains detained for more than 60 days, then the "date the child entered foster care" means the date the court declares the child a ward and orders the child placed in foster care under the supervision of the probation officer;

(ii) If, before the child is placed in foster care, the child is committed to a ranch, camp, school, or other institution pending placement, and remains in that facility for more than 60 days, then the "date the child entered foster care" is the date the child is physically placed in foster care; or

(iii) If, at the time the wardship petition was filed, the child was a dependent of the juvenile court and in out-of-home placement, then the "date the child entered foster care" is the date defined in (A).

(10) "De facto parent" means a person who has been found by the court to have assumed, on a day-to-day basis, the role of parent, fulfilling both the child's physical and psychological needs for care and affection, and who has assumed that role for a substantial period.

(11) "Detained" means any removal of the child from the person or persons legally entitled to the child's physical custody, or any release of the child on home supervision under section 628.1 or 636. A child released or placed on home supervision is not detained for the purposes of federal foster care funding.

(12) "Domestic partner" means one of two adults who have chosen to share one another's lives in an intimate and committed relationship of mutual caring as described in Family Code section 297.

(13) "Educational rights holder" means the adult identified or appointed by the court to make educational or developmental-services decisions for a child, nonminor, or nonminor dependent. If the court limits a parent's or guardian's decisionmaking rights and appoints an educational rights holder, the appointed rights holder acts as the child's or youth's parent, spokesperson, decision maker, and "authorized representative" as described in sections 4512(j) and 4701.6(b) in regard to all matters related to educational or developmental-services needs, including those described in sections 319, 361, 726, 4512, 4646–4648, and 4700–4731; Education Code sections 56028(b)(2), 56050, and 56055; Government Code sections 7579.5 and 7579.6; chapter 33 (commencing with section 1400) of title 20 of the United States Code; and part 300 (commencing with section 300.1) of title 34 of the Code of Federal Regulations, unless the court orders otherwise. An appointed educational rights holder is entitled to access to educational and developmental-services records and information to the extent permitted by law, including by sections 4514 and 5328, and to the same extent as a parent, as that term is used in title 20 United States Code section 1232g and defined in title 34 Code of Federal Regulations part 99.3.

(14) "Foster care" means residential care provided in any of the settings described in section 11402.

(15) "Foster parent" includes a relative with whom the child is placed.

(16) "General jurisdiction" means the jurisdiction the juvenile court maintains over a nonminor under section 303(b) at the time of the dismissal of dependency jurisdiction, delinquency jurisdiction, or transition jurisdiction for the purpose of considering a request to resume its dependency jurisdiction or to assume or resume its transition jurisdiction over the person as a nonminor dependent.

(17) "Guardian" means legal guardian of the child.

(18) "Hearing" means a noticed proceeding with findings and orders that are made on a case-by-case basis, heard by either of the following:

(A) A judicial officer, in a courtroom, in which the proceedings are recorded by a court reporter; or

(B) An administrative panel, provided that the hearing meets the conditions described in section 366.3(d) and (e) for dependents and section 727.4(d)(7)(B) for delinquents.

(19) "Indian child" means any unmarried person under 18 years of age who is either (a) a member of an Indian tribe or (b) eligible for membership in an Indian tribe and is the biological child of a member of an Indian tribe. In a court proceeding defined in section 224.1(d), the term also means a youth who satisfies the conditions in either (a) or (b), above, is 18 years of age but not yet 21 years of age, and remains under the jurisdiction of the juvenile court, unless that youth, directly or through his or her attorney, chooses not to be considered an Indian child for purposes of the proceeding.

(20) "Indian child's tribe" means (a) the Indian tribe of which the Indian child is a member or is eligible for membership, or (b), if an Indian child is a member of, or eligible for membership in, more than one tribe, the Indian tribe with which the Indian child has the more significant contacts, as determined under section 224.1(e).

(21) "Initial removal" means the date on which the child, who is the subject of a petition filed under section 300 or 600, was taken into custody by the social worker or a peace officer, or was deemed to have been taken into custody under section 309(b) or 628(c), if removal results in the filing of the petition before the court.

(22) "Member of the household," for purposes of section 300 proceedings, means any person continually or frequently found in the same household as the child.

(23) "Modification of parental rights" means a modification of parental rights through a tribal customary adoption under Welfare and Institutions Code section 366.24.

(24) "90-day Transition Plan" means the personalized plan developed at the direction of a child currently in a foster care placement during the 90-day period before the child's planned exit from foster care when she or he attains 18 years of age or, if applicable, developed at the direction of a nonminor during the 90-day period prior to his or her anticipated exit from foster care. A 90-day Transition Plan must also be developed for and at the direction of a former foster child who remains eligible for

Independent Living Program services during the 90-day period before he or she attains 18 years of age. The plan is as detailed as the child or nonminor chooses and includes information about a power of attorney for health care and specific options regarding housing, health insurance, education, local opportunities for mentors and continuing support services, workforce supports, and employment services. Inclusion of information in the plan relating to sexual health, services, and resources to ensure the child or nonminor is informed and prepared to make healthy decisions about his or her life is encouraged.

(25) "Nonminor" means a youth at least 18 years of age and not yet 21 years of age who remains subject to the court's dependency, delinquency, or general jurisdiction under section 303 but is not a "nonminor dependent."

(26) "Nonminor dependent" means a youth who is a dependent or ward of the court, or a nonminor under the transition jurisdiction of the court, is at least 18 years of age and not yet 21 years of age, and:

(A) Was under an order of foster care placement on [1] **the youth's** 18th birthday;

(B) Is currently in foster care under the placement and care authority of the county welfare department, the county probation department, or an Indian tribe that entered into an agreement under section 10553.1; and

(C) Is participating in a current Transitional Independent Living Case Plan as defined in this rule.

(27) "Notice" means a paper to be filed with the court accompanied by proof of service on each party required to be served in the manner prescribed by these rules. If a notice or other paper is required to be given to or served on a party, the notice or service must be given to or made on the party's attorney of record, if any.

(28) "Notify" means to inform, either orally or in writing.

(29) "Petitioner," in section 300 proceedings, means the county welfare department; "petitioner," in section 601 and 602 proceedings, means the probation officer or prosecuting attorney.

(30) "Preadoptive parent" means a licensed foster parent who has been approved to adopt a child by the California State Department of Social Services, when it is acting as an adoption agency, or by a licensed adoption agency, or, in the case of an Indian child for whom tribal customary adoption is the permanent plan, the individual designated by the child's identified Indian tribe as the prospective adoptive parent.

(31) "Probation officer," in section 300 proceedings, includes a social worker in the county agency responsible for the administration of child welfare.

(32) "Punishment" means the imposition of sanctions, as defined in section 202(e), on a child declared a ward of the court after a petition under section 602 is sustained. A court order to place a child in foster care must not be used as punishment.

(33) "Reasonable efforts" or "reasonable services" means those efforts made or services offered or provided by the county welfare agency or probation department to prevent or eliminate the need for removing the child, or to resolve the issues that led to the child's removal in order for the child to be returned home, or to finalize the permanent placement of the child.

(34) "Relative" means

(A) An adult who is related to the child by blood, adoption, or affinity within the fifth degree of kinship. This term includes:

(i) A parent, sibling, grandparent, aunt, uncle, nephew, niece, great-grandparent, great-aunt or -uncle (grandparents' sibling), first cousin, great-great-grandparent, great-great-aunt or -uncle (great-grandparents' sibling), first cousin once removed (parents' first cousin), and great-great-great-grandparent;

(ii) A stepparent or stepsibling; and

(iii) The spouse or domestic partner of any of the persons described in subparagraphs (A)(i) and (ii), even if the marriage or partnership was terminated by death or dissolution; or

(B) An extended family member as defined by the law or custom of an Indian child's tribe. (25 U.S.C. § 1903(2).)

(35) "Removal" means a court order that takes away the care, custody, and control of a dependent child or ward from the child's parent or guardian, and places the care, custody, and control of the child with the court, under the supervision of the agency responsible for the administration of child welfare or the county probation department.

(36) "Section" means a section of the Welfare and Institutions Code unless stated otherwise.

(37) "Sibling group" means two or more children related to each other by blood, adoption, or affinity through a common legal or biological parent.

(38) "Social study," in section 300, 601, or 602 proceedings, means any written report provided to the court and all parties and counsel by the social worker or probation officer in any matter involving the custody, status, or welfare of a child in a dependency or wardship proceeding.

(39) "Social worker," in section 300 proceedings, means an employee of the county child welfare agency and includes a probation officer performing the child welfare duties.

(40) "Subdivision" means a subdivision of the rule in which the term appears.

(41) "Transition dependent" means a ward of the court at least 17 years and five months of age but not yet 18 years of age who is subject to the court's transition jurisdiction under section 450.

(42) "Transition jurisdiction" means the juvenile court's jurisdiction over a child or nonminor described in Welfare and Institutions Code section 450.

(43) "Transitional independent living case plan" means a child's case plan submitted for the last review hearing held before he or she turns 18 years of age or a nonminor dependent's case plan, developed with the child or nonminor dependent and individuals identified as important to him or her, signed by the child or nonminor dependent and updated every six months, that describes the goals and objectives of how the child or nonminor will make progress in the transition to living independently and assume incremental responsibility for adult decision making; the collaborative efforts between the child or nonminor dependent and the social worker, probation officer, or Indian tribe and the supportive services as described in the Transitional Independent Living Plan (TILP) to ensure the child's or nonminor dependent's active and meaningful participation in one or more of the eligibility criteria described in subdivision (b) of section 11403; the child or nonminor dependent's appropriate supervised placement setting; the child or nonminor dependent's permanent plan for transition to living independently; and the steps the social worker, probation officer, or Indian tribe is taking to ensure the child or nonminor dependent achieves permanence, including maintaining or obtaining permanent connections to caring and committed adults, as set forth in paragraph (16) of subdivision (f) of section 16501.1.

(44) "Transitional Independent Living Plan" means the written unique, individualized service delivery plan for a child or nonminor mutually agreed upon by the child or nonminor and the social worker or probation officer that identifies the child's or nonminor's current level of functioning, emancipation goals, and the specific skills needed to prepare the child or nonminor to live independently upon leaving foster care.

(45) "Tribal customary adoption" means adoption by and through the tribal custom, traditions, or law of an Indian child's tribe as defined in Welfare and Institutions Code section 366.24 and to which a juvenile court may give full faith and credit under 366.26(e)(2). Termination of parental rights is not required to effect a tribal customary adoption.

(46) "Youth" means a person who is at least 14 years of age and not yet 21 years of age.

Rule 5.502 amended effective January 1, 2021; adopted as rule 1401 effective January 1, 1990; previously amended and renumbered as rule 5.502 effective January 1, 2007; previously amended effective July 1, 1992, July 1, 1997, January 1, 1998, January 1, 1999, January 1, 2001, July 1, 2002, January 1, 2003, January 1, 2008, July 1, 2010, January 1, 2011, January 1, 2012, July 1, 2012, January 1, 2014, and January 1, 2016.

Rule 5.502. 2020 Deletes. [1] his or her

Rule 5.504.   Judicial Council forms
(a) Explanation of Judicial Council legal forms
Rules 1.30–1.37 and 2.131–2.134 apply to Judicial Council legal forms, including forms applicable to the juvenile court.
(Subd (a) amended effective January 1, 2007; repealed and adopted effective January 1, 2001.)

(b) Electronically produced forms
The forms applicable to juvenile court may be produced entirely by computer, word-processor printer, or similar process, or may be produced by the California State Department of Social Services Child Welfare Systems Case Management System.
(Subd (b) amended effective July 1, 2006; adopted as subd (c) effective July 1, 1991; amended and relettered effective January 1, 2001; previously amended effective January 1, 1993, January 1, 1998, and January 1, 2006.)

(c) Implementation of new and revised mandatory forms

To help implement mandatory Judicial Council juvenile forms:

(1) New and revised mandatory forms produced by computer, word-processor printer, or similar process must be implemented within one year of the effective date of the form. During that one-year period the court may authorize the use of a legally accurate alternative form, including any existing local form or the immediate prior version of the Judicial Council form.

(2) A court may produce court orders in any form or format as long as:

(A) The document is substantively identical to the mandatory Judicial Council form it is modifying;

(B) Any electronically generated form is identical in both language and legally mandated elements, including all notices and advisements, to the mandatory Judicial Council form it is modifying;

(C) The order is an otherwise legally sufficient court order, as provided in rule 1.31(g), concerning orders not on Judicial Council mandatory forms; and

(D) The court sends written notice of its election to change the form or format of the mandatory form to the Family and Juvenile Law Advisory Committee and submits additional informational reports as requested by the committee.

(Subd (c) amended effective January 1, 2019; adopted effective January 1, 2006; previously amended effective January 1, 2007, January 1, 2012, and January 1, 2017.)

Rule 5.504 amended effective January 1, 2019; adopted as rule 1402 effective January 1, 1991; previously amended and renumbered effective January 1, 2007; previously amended effective July 1, 1991, January 1, 1992, July 1, 1992, January 1, 1993, January 1, 1994, January 1, 1998, January 1, 2001, January 1, 2006, July 1, 2006, January 1, 2012, and January 1, 2017.)

Rule 5.505. Juvenile dependency court performance measures

(a) Purpose

The juvenile dependency court performance measures and related procedures set forth in this rule are intended to:

(1) Protect abused and neglected children by assisting courts in promoting children's placement in safe and permanent homes, enhancing their well-being and that of their families, and ensuring that all participants receive timely and fair treatment;

(2) Assist trial courts in meeting the mandated timelines for dependency hearings, securing due process for all litigants, and, in collaboration with the child welfare agency, improving safety, permanency, and well-being outcomes for children and families under the jurisdiction of the juvenile dependency court; and

(3) Assist courts in making well-informed resource allocation decisions.

(Subd (a) adopted effective January 1, 2009.)

(b) Performance measures

Detailed definitions of the performance measures and descriptions of the methods for producing the performance measures in accordance with (c)(2) and (3) are contained in the Judicial Council–approved *Implementation Guide to Juvenile Dependency Court Performance Measures.*

The juvenile dependency court performance measures are:

(1) Hearing timeliness:

(A) Percentage of children for whom the initial hearing is completed within the statutory time frame following the filing of the initial petition;

(B) Percentage of children for whom the jurisdictional hearing is completed within the statutory time frame following the initial hearing;

(C) Percentage of children for whom the disposition hearing is completed within the statutory time frame following the finding of jurisdiction;

(D) Percentage of children for whom a 3-month or other interim review hearing is held;

(E) Percentage of children for whom the 6-month review hearing is completed within 6 months of the date the child entered foster care;

(F) Percentage of children for whom the 12-month permanency hearing is completed within 12 months of the date the child entered foster care;

(G) Percentage of children for whom the 18-month review hearing is completed within 18 months of the date of original protective custody;

(H) Percentage of children for whom the first section 366.26 hearing is completed within 120 days of the termination of reunification services;

(I) Percentage of children whose postpermanency hearing is completed within 6 months of the section 366.26 hearing or the last postpermanency hearing;

(J) Percentage of children in long-term foster care whose subsequent section 366.26 hearing is completed within 12 months of the previous section 366.26 hearing;

(K) Percentage of children whose adoption is finalized within 180 days after termination of parental rights;

(L) Median time from disposition or section 366.26 hearing to order establishing guardianship;

(M) Percentage of children for whom the first and subsequent postpermanency review hearings are completed within the statutory time frame;

(N) Percentage of hearings delayed by reasons for delay and hearing type;

(O) Median time from filing of original petition to implementation of a permanent plan by permanent plan type; and

(P) Median time from filing of original petition to termination of jurisdiction by reason for termination of jurisdiction.

(2) Court procedures and due process:

(A) Percentage of cases in which all hearings are heard by one judicial officer;

(B) Percentage of cases in which all parties and other statutorily entitled individuals are served with a copy of the original petition;

(C) Percentage of hearings in which notice is given to all statutorily entitled parties and individuals within the statutory time frame;

(D) Percentage of hearings in which child or parents are present if statutorily entitled to be present;

(E) Percentage of hearings in which a judicial inquiry is made when a child 10 years of age or older is not present at hearing;

(F) Percentage of hearings in which other statutorily entitled individuals who are involved in the case (e.g., CASA volunteers, caregivers, de facto parents, others) are present;

(G) Percentage of cases in which legal counsel for parents, children, and the child welfare agency are present at every hearing;

(H) Point at which children and parents are assigned legal counsel;

(I) Percentage of cases in which legal counsel for children or parents changes;

(J) Percentage of cases in which no reunification services are ordered and reasons;

(K) Percentage of cases for which youth have input into their case plans; and

(L) Cases in compliance with the requirements of the Indian Child Welfare Act (ICWA).

(3) Child safety in the child welfare system:

(A) Percentage of children who are not victims of another substantiated maltreatment allegation within 6 and 12 months after the maltreatment incident that led to the filing of the initial petition; and

(B) For all children served in foster care during the year, percentage of children who were not victims of substantiated maltreatment by a foster parent or facility staff member.

(4) Child permanency:

(A) Percentage of children reunified in less than 12 months;

(B) Percentage of children who were reunified but reentered foster care within 12 months;

(C) Percentage of children who were discharged from foster care to a finalized adoption within 24 months;

(D) Percentage of children in foster care who were freed for adoption;

(E) Percentage of children in long-term foster care who were discharged to a permanent home before their 18th birthdays;

(F) Of children discharged to emancipation or aging out of foster care, percentage who were in foster care 3 years or longer;

(G) Percentage of children with multiple foster-care placements;

(5) Child and family well-being:

(A) Percentage of children 14 years of age or older with current transitional independent living plans;

(B) Percentage of children for whom a section 391 termination of jurisdiction hearing was held;

(C) Percentage of section 391 termination of jurisdiction hearings that did not result in termination of jurisdiction and reasons jurisdiction did not terminate;

(D) Percentage of youth present at section 391 termination of jurisdiction hearing with judicial confirmation of receipt of all services and documents mandated by section 391(b)(1–5);

(E) Percentage of children placed with all siblings who are also under court jurisdiction, as appropriate;

(F) Percentage of children placed with at least one but not all siblings who are also under court jurisdiction, as appropriate;

(G) For children who have siblings under court jurisdiction but are not placed with all of them, percentage of cases in which sibling visitation is not ordered and reasons;

(H) Percentage of cases in which visitation is not ordered for parents and reasons;

(I) Number of visitation orders for adults other than parents and siblings, (e.g., grandparents, other relatives, extended family members, others) as appropriate;

(J) Number of cases in which the court has requested relative-finding efforts from the child welfare agency;

(K) Percentage of children placed with relatives;

(L) For children 10 years of age or older and in foster care for at least 6 months, percentage for whom the court has inquired whether the social worker has identified persons important to the child; and

(M) For children 10 years of age or older in foster care for at least 6 months, percentage for whom the court has made orders to enable the child to maintain relationships with persons important to that child.

(Subd (b) adopted effective January 1, 2009.)

(c) Data collection

(1) California's Court Case Management System (CCMS) family and juvenile law module must be capable of collecting the data described in the *Implementation Guide to Juvenile Dependency Court Performance Measures* in order to calculate the performance measures and to produce performance measure reports.

(2) Before implementation of the CCMS family and juvenile law module, each local court must collect and submit to the Judicial Council the subset of juvenile dependency data described in (b) and further delineated in the *Implementation Guide to Juvenile Dependency Court Performance Measures* that it is reasonably capable of collecting and submitting with its existing court case management system and resources.

(3) On implementation of the CCMS family and juvenile law module in a local court, and as the necessary data elements become electronically available, the local court must collect and submit to the Judicial Council the juvenile dependency data described in (b) and further delineated in the *Implementation Guide to Juvenile Dependency Court Performance Measures*. For the purposes of this subdivision, "implementation of the CCMS family and juvenile law module" in a local court means that the CCMS family and juvenile law module has been deployed in that court, is functioning, and has the ability to capture the required data elements and that local court staff has been trained to use the system.

(Subd (c) amended effective January 1, 2016; adopted effective January 1, 2009.)

(d) Use of data and development of measures before CCMS implementation

Before CCMS implementation, the Judicial Council must:

(1) Establish a program to assist the local courts in collecting, preparing, analyzing, and reporting the data required by this rule;

(2) Establish a procedure to assist the local courts in submitting the required data to the Judicial Council;

(3) Use the data submitted under (c)(2) to test and refine the detailed definitions of the performance measures and descriptions of the methods for producing the performance measures described in the *Implementation Guide to Juvenile Dependency Court Performance Measures*;

(4) Consult with local courts about the accuracy of the data submitted under (c)(2). After such consultation, use data to generate aggregate data reports on performance measures, consistent with section 16543, while not disclosing identifying information about children, parents, judicial officers, and other individuals in the dependency system; and

(5) Assist the courts in using the data to achieve improved outcomes for children and families in the dependency system, make systemic improvements, and improve resource allocation decisions.

(Subd (d) amended effective January 1, 2016; adopted effective January 1, 2009.)

(e) Use of data after CCMS implementation

On implementation of CCMS, the Judicial Council must:

(1) Use the data submitted under (c)(3) to conduct ongoing testing, refining, and updating of the information in the *Implementation Guide to Juvenile Dependency Court Performance Measures*;

(2) Use the data submitted under (c)(3) to generate aggregate data reports on performance measures, consistent with section 16543, while

not disclosing identifying information about children, parents, judicial officers, and other individuals in the dependency system;

(3) Upon the request of any local court, extract data from the system and prepare county-level reports to meet data reporting requirements; and

(4) Assist the courts in using the data to achieve improved outcomes for children and families in the dependency system, make systemic improvements, and improve resource allocation decisions.

(Subd (e) amended effective January 1, 2016; adopted effective January 1, 2009.)

Rule 5.505 amended effective January 1, 2016; adopted effective January 1, 2009.

Advisory Committee Comment

The juvenile dependency court performance measures and related procedures set forth in this rule fulfill the requirements of the Child Welfare Leadership and Accountability Act of 2006 (Welf. & Inst. Code, §§ 16540–16545).

Consistent with section 16545, the Child Welfare Council and the secretary of the California Health and Human Services Agency were consulted in adopting these performance measures. The appropriate court technology groups have also been consulted.

The *Implementation Guide to Juvenile Dependency Court Performance Measures* is a companion publication to this rule, approved by the Judicial Council.

It is anticipated that the Judicial Council will update the *Implementation Guide to Juvenile Dependency Court Performance Measures*, as appropriate, to stay current with Court Case Management System (CCMS) requirements, local court needs, and the most recent versions of the relevant state and federal child welfare measures. Proposed updates other than those that are purely technical will be circulated for public comment prior to publication.

Chapter 2
Commencement of Juvenile Court Proceedings

Rule 5.510. Proper court; determination of child's residence; exclusive jurisdiction

(a) Proper court (§§ 327, 651)

The proper court in which to commence proceedings to declare a child a dependent or ward of the court is the juvenile court in the county:

(1) In which the child resides;

(2) In which the child is found; or

(3) In which the acts take place or the circumstances exist that are alleged to bring the child within the provisions of section 300 or 601 or 602.

(Subd (a) amended effective January 1, 2007.)

(b) Determination of residence—general rule (§ 17.1)

Unless otherwise provided in the juvenile court law or in these rules, the residence of a child must be determined under section 17.1.

(c) Exclusive jurisdiction (§§ 304, 316.2, 726.4)

(1) Once a petition has been filed under section 300, the juvenile court has exclusive jurisdiction of the following:

(A) All issues regarding custody and visitation of the child, **including legal guardianship;** and

(B) All issues and actions regarding the parentage of the child under rule 5.635 and Family Code section 7630.

(2) Once a petition has been filed under section 601 or 602, the juvenile court has exclusive jurisdiction to hear an action filed under Family Code section 7630.

(Subd (c) amended effective January 1, 2021; adopted effective January 1, 1999; previously amended effective January 1, 2007, and January 1, 2015.)

Rule 5.510 amended effective January 1, 2021; adopted as rule 1403 effective January 1, 1991; previously amended effective January 1, 1999, and January 1, 2015; previously amended and renumbered effective January 1, 2007.

Rule 5.512. Joint assessment procedure

(a) Joint assessment requirement (§ 241.1)

Whenever a child appears to come within the description of section 300 and either section 601 or section 602, the responsible child welfare and probation departments must conduct a joint assessment to determine which status will serve the best interest of the child and the protection of society.

(1) The assessment must be completed as soon as possible after the child comes to the attention of either department.

(2) Whenever possible, the determination of status must be made before any petition concerning the child is filed.

(3) The assessment report need not be prepared before the petition is filed but must be provided to the court for the hearing as stated in (e).

(4) If a petition has been filed, on the request of the child, parent, guardian, or counsel, or on the court's own motion, the court may set a hearing for a determination under section 241.1 and order that the joint assessment report be made available as required in (f).

(Subd (a) amended effective January 1, 2007.)

(b) Proceedings in same county

If the petition alleging jurisdiction is filed in a county in which the child is already a dependent or ward, the child welfare and probation departments in that county must assess the child under a jointly developed written protocol and prepare a joint assessment report to be filed in that county.

(Subd (b) amended effective January 1, 2007.)

(c) Proceedings in different counties

If the petition alleging jurisdiction is filed in one county and the child is already a dependent or ward in another county, a joint assessment must be conducted by the responsible departments of each county. If the departments cannot agree on which will prepare the joint assessment report, then the department in the county where the petition is to be filed must prepare the joint assessment report.

(1) The joint assessment report must contain the recommendations and reasoning of both the child welfare and the probation departments.

(2) The report must be filed at least 5 calendar days before the hearing on the joint assessment in the county where the second petition alleging jurisdictional facts under sections 300, 601, or 602 has been filed.

(Subd (c) amended effective January 1, 2007.)

(d) Joint assessment report

The joint assessment report must contain the joint recommendation of the probation and child welfare departments if they agree on the status that will serve the best interest of the child and the protection of society, or the separate recommendation of each department if they do not agree. The report must also include:

(1) A description of the nature of the referral;

(2) The age of the child;

(3) The history of any physical, sexual, or emotional abuse of the child;

(4) The prior record of the child's parents for abuse of this or any other child;

(5) The prior record of the child for out-of-control or delinquent behavior;

(6) The parents' cooperation with the child's school;

(7) The child's functioning at school;

(8) The nature of the child's home environment;

(9) The history of involvement of any agencies or professionals with the child and his or her family;

(10) Any services or community agencies that are available to assist the child and his or her family;

(11) A statement by any counsel currently representing the child; and

(12) A statement by any CASA volunteer currently appointed for the child.

(Subd (d) amended effective January 1, 2007.)

(e) Hearing on joint assessment

If the child is detained, the hearing on the joint assessment report must occur as soon as possible after or concurrent with the detention hearing, but no later than 15 court days after the order of detention and before the jurisdictional hearing. If the child is not detained, the hearing on the joint assessment must occur before the jurisdictional hearing and within 30 days of the date of the petition. The juvenile court must conduct the hearing and determine which type of jurisdiction over the child best meets the child's unique circumstances.

(Subd (e) amended effective January 1, 2007.)

(f) Notice and participation

At least 5 calendar days before the hearing, notice of the hearing and copies of the joint assessment report must be provided to the child, the child's parent or guardian, all attorneys of record, any CASA volunteer,

and any other juvenile court having jurisdiction over the child. The notice must be directed to the judicial officer or department that will conduct the hearing.

(Subd (f) amended effective January 1, 2007.)

(g) Conduct of hearing

All parties and their attorneys must have an opportunity to be heard at the hearing. The court must make a determination regarding the appropriate status of the child and state its reasons on the record or in a written order.

(h) Notice of decision after hearing

Within 5 calendar days after the hearing, the clerk of the juvenile court must transmit the court's findings and orders to any other juvenile court with current jurisdiction over the child.

(i) Local protocols

On or before January 1, 2004, the probation and child welfare departments of each county must adopt a written protocol for the preparation of joint assessment reports, including procedures for resolution of disagreements between the probation and child welfare departments, and submit a copy to the Judicial Council.

Rule 5.512 amended and renumbered effective January 1, 2007; adopted as rule 1403.5 effective January 1, 2003.

Rule 5.514. Intake; guidelines

(a) Role of juvenile court

It is the duty of the presiding judge of the juvenile court to initiate meetings and cooperate with the probation department, welfare department, prosecuting attorney, law enforcement, and other persons and agencies performing an intake function. The goal of the intake meetings is to establish and maintain a fair and efficient intake program designed to promote swift and objective evaluation of the circumstances of any referral and to pursue an appropriate course of action.

(Subd (a) amended effective January 1, 2007.)

(b) Purpose of intake program

The intake program must be designed to:

(1) Provide for settlement at intake of:

(A) Matters over which the juvenile court has no jurisdiction;

(B) Matters in which there is insufficient evidence to support a petition; and

(C) Matters that are suitable for referral to a nonjudicial agency or program available in the community;

(2) Provide for a program of informal supervision of the child under sections 301 and 654; and

(3) **Establish a process for a judge to witness the consent of the parent or Indian custodian to a placement of an Indian child under section 16507.4(b) before a judge in accordance with section 16507.4(b)(3) that ensures the placement is consistent with the federal Indian Child Welfare Act and corresponding state law and all of the rights and protections of the Indian parent are respected, using** *Agreement of Parent or Indian Custodian to Temporary Custody of Indian Child* **(form ICWA-101). This process must ensure that the witnessing of the consent is scheduled within 72 hours of the request having been made. The original completed** *Agreement of Parent or Indian Custodian to Temporary Custody of Indian Child* **(form ICWA-101) must be retained by the court with a copy to the agency; and**

(4) Provide for the commencement of proceedings in the juvenile court only when necessary for the welfare of the child or protection of the public.

(Subd (b) amended effective January 1, 2021; previously amended effective January 1, 1995, and January 1, 2007.)

(c) Investigation at intake (§§ 309, 652.5)

The probation officer or the social worker must conduct an investigation and determine whether:

(1) The matter should be settled at intake by:

(A) Taking no action;

(B) Counseling the child and any others involved in the matter; or

(C) Referring the child, the child's family, and any others involved to other agencies and programs in the community for the purpose of receiving services to prevent or eliminate the need for removal;

(2) A program of informal supervision should be undertaken for not more than six months under section 301 or 654; or

(3) A petition should be filed under section 300 or 601, or the prosecuting attorney should be requested to file a petition under section 602.

(Subd (c) amended effective January 1, 2007; previously amended effective January 1, 1994, January 1, 1995, and January 1, 2001.)

(d) Mandatory referrals to the prosecuting attorney (§ 653.5)

Notwithstanding (c), the probation officer must refer to the prosecuting attorney, within 48 hours, all affidavits requesting that a petition be filed under section 602 if it appears to the probation officer that:

(1) The child, regardless of age:

(A) Is alleged to have committed an offense listed in section 707(b);

(B) Has been referred for the sale or possession for sale of a controlled substance under chapter 2 of division 10 of the Health and Safety Code;

(C) Has been referred for a violation of Health and Safety Code section 11350 or 11377 at a school, or for a violation of Penal Code sections 245.5, 626.9, or 626.10;

(D) Has been referred for a violation of Penal Code section 186.22;

(E) Has previously been placed on informal supervision under section 654; or

(F) Has been referred for an alleged offense in which restitution to the victim exceeds $1,000;

(2) The child was 16 years of age or older on the date of the alleged offense and the referral is for a felony offense; or

(3) The child was under 16 years of age on the date of the alleged offense and the referral is not the first referral for a felony offense.

Except for the offenses listed in (1)(C), the provisions of this subdivision do not apply to narcotics and drug offenses listed in Penal Code section 1000.

(Subd (d) amended effective January 1, 2007; previously amended effective January 1, 1994, and January 1, 1995.)

(e) Informal supervision (§§ 301, 654)

(1) If the child is placed on a program of informal supervision for not more than six months under section 301, the social worker may file a petition at any time during the six-month period. If the objectives of a service plan under section 301 have not been achieved within six months, the social worker may extend the period up to an additional six months, with the consent of the parent or guardian.

(2) If a child is placed on a program of informal supervision for not more than six months under section 654, the probation officer may file a petition under section 601, or request that the prosecuting attorney file a petition under section 602, at any time during the six-month period, or within 90 days thereafter. If a child on informal supervision under section 654 has not participated in the specific programs within 60 days, the probation officer must immediately file a petition under section 601, or request that the prosecuting attorney file one under section 602, unless the probation officer determines that the interests of the child and the community can be adequately protected by continuing under section 654.

(Subd (e) amended effective January 1, 2007; previously amended effective January 1, 1995.)

Rule 5.514 amended effective January 1, 2021; adopted as rule 1404 effective January 1, 1991; previously amended effective January 1, 1994, January 1, 1995, and January 1, 2001; previously amended and renumbered effective January 1, 2007.

Rule 5.516.   Factors to consider

(a) Settlement at intake (§ 653.5)

In determining whether a matter not described in rule 5.514(d) should be settled at intake, the social worker or probation officer must consider:

(1) Whether there is sufficient evidence of a condition or conduct to bring the child within the jurisdiction of the court;

(2) If the alleged condition or conduct is not considered serious, whether the child has previously presented significant problems in the home, school, or community;

(3) Whether the matter appears to have arisen from a temporary problem within the family that has been or can be resolved;

(4) Whether any agency or other resource in the community is available to offer services to the child and the child's family to prevent or eliminate the need to remove the child from the child's home;

(5) The attitudes of the child, the parent or guardian, and any affected persons;

(6) The age, maturity, and capabilities of the child;

(7) The dependency or delinquency history, if any, of the child;

(8) The recommendation, if any, of the referring party or agency; and

(9) Any other circumstances that indicate that settling the matter at intake would be consistent with the welfare of the child and the protection of the public.

(Subd (a) amended effective January 1, 2007; previously amended effective January 1, 2001.)

(b) Informal supervision

In determining whether to undertake a program of informal supervision of a child not described by rule 5.514(d), the social worker or probation officer must consider:

(1) If the condition or conduct is not considered serious, whether the child has had a problem in the home, school, or community that indicates that some supervision would be desirable;

(2) Whether the child and the parent or guardian seem able to resolve the matter with the assistance of the social worker or probation officer and without formal court action;

(3) Whether further observation or evaluation by the social worker or probation officer is needed before a decision can be reached;

(4) The attitudes of the child and the parent or guardian;

(5) The age, maturity, and capabilities of the child;

(6) The dependency or delinquency history, if any, of the child;

(7) The recommendation, if any, of the referring party or agency;

(8) The attitudes of affected persons; and

(9) Any other circumstances that indicate that a program of informal supervision would be consistent with the welfare of the child and the protection of the public.

(Subd (b) amended effective January 1, 2007.)

(c) Filing of petition

In determining whether to file a petition under section 300 or 601 or to request the prosecuting attorney to file a petition under section 602, the social worker or probation officer must consider:

(1) Whether any of the statutory criteria listed in rules 5.770 and 5.772 relating to the fitness of the child are present;

(2) Whether the alleged conduct would be a felony;

(3) Whether the alleged conduct involved physical harm or the threat of physical harm to person or property;

(4) If the alleged condition or conduct is not serious, whether the child has had serious problems in the home, school, or community that indicate that formal court action is desirable;

(5) If the alleged condition or conduct is not serious, whether the child is already a ward or dependent of the court;

(6) Whether the alleged condition or conduct involves a threat to the physical or emotional health of the child;

(7) Whether a chronic, serious family problem exists after other efforts to resolve the problem have been made;

(8) Whether the alleged condition or conduct is in dispute and, if proven, whether court-ordered disposition appears desirable;

(9) The attitudes of the child and the parent or guardian;

(10) The age, maturity, and capabilities of the child;

(11) Whether the child is on probation or parole;

(12) The recommendation, if any, of the referring party or agency;

(13) The attitudes of affected persons;

(14) Whether any other referrals or petitions are pending; and

(15) Any other circumstances that indicate that the filing of a petition is necessary to promote the welfare of the child or to protect the public.

(Subd (c) amended effective January 1, 2007.)

(d) Certification to juvenile court

Copies of the certification, the accusatory pleading, any police reports, and the order of a superior court, certifying that the accused person was under the age of 18 on the date of the alleged offense, must immediately be delivered to the clerk of the juvenile court.

(1) On receipt of the documents, the clerk must immediately notify the probation officer, who must immediately investigate the matter to determine whether to commence proceedings in juvenile court.

(2) If the child is under the age of 18 and is in custody, the child must immediately be transported to the juvenile detention facility.

(Subd (d) amended effective January 1, 2007.)

Rule 5.516 amended effective January 1, 2007; adopted as rule 1405 effective January 1, 1991; previously amended effective January 1, 2001.

Rule 5.518.   Court-connected child protection/dependency mediation

(a) Purpose (§ 350)

This rule establishes mandatory standards of practice and administration for court-connected dependency mediation services in accordance with section 350. This rule is intended to ensure fairness, accountability, and a high quality of service to children and families and to improve the safety, confidentiality, and consistency of dependency mediation programs statewide.

(Subd (a) amended effective January 1, 2007.)

(b) Definitions

(1) "Dependency mediation" is a confidential process conducted by specially trained, neutral third-party mediators who have no decision-making power. Dependency mediation provides a nonadversarial setting in which a mediator assists the parties in reaching a fully informed and mutually acceptable resolution that focuses on the child's safety and best interest and the safety of all family members. Dependency mediation is concerned with any and all issues related to child protection.

(2) "Safety and best interest of the child" refers to the child's physical, psychological, and emotional well-being. Determining the safety and best interest of the child includes consideration of all of the following:

(A) The preservation and strengthening of the family and family relationships whenever appropriate and possible;

(B) The manner in which the child may be protected from the risk of future abuse or neglect;

(C) The child's need for safety, stability, and permanency;

(D) The ongoing need of the child to cope with the issues that caused his or her involvement in the juvenile dependency system;

(E) The child's need for continuity of care and the effect that removal and subsequent placements have had, or may have, on the child; and

(F) The child's education, which includes the child's participation, progress, need for assistance, cognitive development and, if applicable, early childhood education and care, the need for special education and related services, and the extent to which the child has or has had limited English proficiency (LEP).

(3) "Safety of family members" refers to the physical, psychological, and emotional well-being of all family members, with consideration of the following:

(A) The role of domestic violence in creating a perceived or actual threat for the victim; and

(B) The ongoing need of family members to feel safe from physical, emotional, and psychological abuse.

(4) "Differential domestic violence assessment" is a process used to assess the nature of any domestic violence issues in the family so that the mediator may conduct the mediation in such a way as to protect any victim of domestic violence from intimidation and to correct for power imbalances created by past violence and the fear of prospective violence.

(5) "Protocols" refer to any local set of rules, policies, and procedures developed and implemented by juvenile dependency mediation programs. All protocols must be developed in accordance with pertinent state laws, California Rules of Court, and local court rules.

(Subd (b) amended effective January 1, 2008; previously amended effective January 1, 2007.)

(c) Responsibility for mediation services

(1) Each court that has a dependency mediation program must ensure that:

(A) Dependency mediators are impartial, are competent, and uphold the standards established by this rule;

(B) Dependency mediators maintain an appropriate focus on issues related to the child's safety and best interest and the safety of all family members;

(C) Dependency mediators provide a forum for all interested persons to develop a plan focused on the best interest of the child, emphasizing family preservation and strengthening and the child's need for permanency;

(D) Dependency mediation services and case management procedures are consistent with applicable state law without compromising each party's right to due process and a timely resolution of the issues;

(E) Dependency mediation services demonstrate accountability by:

(i) Providing for the processing of complaints about a mediator's performance; and

(ii) Participating in any statewide and national data-collection efforts;

(F) The dependency mediation program uses an intake process that screens for and informs the mediator about any restraining orders, domestic violence, or safety-related issues affecting the child or any other party named in the proceedings;

(G) Whenever possible, dependency mediation is conducted in the shared language of the participants. When the participants speak different languages, interpreters, court-certified when possible, should be assigned to translate at the mediation session; and

(H) Dependency mediation services preserve, in accordance with pertinent law, party confidentiality, whether written or oral, by the:

(i) Storage and disposal of records and any personal information accumulated by the mediation program; and

(ii) Management of any new child abuse reports and related documents.

(2) Each dependency mediator must:

(A) Attempt to assist the mediation participants in reaching a settlement of the issues consistent with preserving the safety and best interest of the child, first and foremost, and the safety of all family members and participants;

(B) Discourage participants from blaming the victim and from denying or minimizing allegations of child abuse or violence against any family member;

(C) Be conscious of the values of preserving and strengthening the family as well as the child's need for permanency;

(D) Not make any recommendations or reports of any kind to the court, except for the terms of any agreement reached by the parties;

(E) Treat all mediation participants in a manner that preserves their dignity and self-respect;

(F) Promote a safe and balanced environment for all participants to express and advocate for their positions and interests;

(G) Identify and disclose potential grounds on which a mediator's impartiality might reasonably be challenged through a procedure that allows for the selection of another mediator within a reasonable time. If a dependency mediation program has only one mediator and the parties are unable to resolve the conflict, the mediator must inform the court;

(H) Identify and immediately disclose to the participants any reasonable concern regarding the mediator's continuing capacity to be impartial, so they can decide whether the mediator should withdraw or continue;

(I) Promote the participants' understanding of the status of the case in relation to the ongoing court process, what the case plan requires of them, and the terms of any agreement reached during the mediation; and

(J) Conduct an appropriate review to evaluate the viability of any agreement reached, including the identification of any provision that depends on the action or behavior of any individual who did not participate in creating the agreement.

(Subd (c) amended effective January 1, 2007.)

(d) Mediation process

The dependency mediation process must be conducted in accordance with pertinent state laws, applicable rules of court, and local protocols. All local protocols must include the following:

(1) The process by which cases are sent to mediation, including:

(A) Who may request mediation;

(B) Who decides which cases are to be sent to mediation;

(C) Whether mediation is voluntary or mandatory;

(D) How mediation appointments are scheduled; and

(E) The consequences, if any, to a party who fails to participate in the mediation process.

(2) A policy on who participates in the mediation, according to the following guidelines:

(A) When at all possible, dependency mediation should include the direct and active participation of the parties, including but not limited to the child, the parents or legal guardian, a representative of the child protective agency, and, at some stage, their respective attorneys;

(B) The child has a right to participate in the dependency mediation process accompanied by his or her attorney. If the child makes an informed choice not to participate, then the child's attorney may participate. If the child is unable to make an informed choice, then the child's attorney may participate.

(C) Any attorney who has not participated in the mediation must have an opportunity to review and agree to any proposal before it is submitted to the court for approval.

(D) As appropriate, other family members and any guardian ad litem, CASA volunteer, or other involved person or professional may participate in the mediation.

(E) A mediation participant who has been a victim of violence allegedly perpetrated by another mediation participant has the right to be accompanied by a support person. Unless otherwise invited or ordered to participate under the protocols developed by the court, a support person may not actively participate in the mediation except to be present as a source of emotional support for the alleged victim.

(3) A method by which the mediator may review relevant case information before the mediation.

(4) A protocol for providing mediation in cases in which domestic violence or violence perpetrated by any other mediation participant has, or allegedly has, occurred. This protocol must include specialized procedures designed to protect victims of domestic violence from intimidation by perpetrators. The protocol must also appropriately address all family violence issues by encouraging the incorporation of appropriate safety and treatment interventions in any settlement. The protocol must require:

(A) A review of case-related information before commencing the mediation;

(B) The performance of a differential domestic violence assessment to determine the nature of the violence, for the purposes of:

(i) Assessing the ability of the victim to fully and safely participate and to reach a noncoerced settlement;

(ii) Clarifying the history and dynamics of the domestic violence issue in order to determine the most appropriate manner in which the mediation can proceed; and

(iii) Assisting the parties, attorneys, and other participants in formulating an agreement following a discussion of appropriate safeguards for the safety of the child and family members; and

(C) A mediation structure designed to meet the need of the victim of violence for safety and for full and noncoerced participation in the process, which structure must include:

(i) An option for the victim to attend the mediation session without the alleged perpetrator being present; and

(ii) Permission for the victim to have a support person present during the mediation process, whether he or she elects to be seen separately from or together with the alleged perpetrator.

(5) An oral or written orientation that facilitates participants' safe, productive, and informed participation and decision making by educating them about:

(A) The mediation process, the typical participants, the range of disputes that may be discussed, and the typical outcomes of mediation;

(B) The importance of keeping confidential all communications, negotiations, or settlement discussions by and between the participants in the course of mediation;

(C) The mediator's role and any limitations on the confidentiality of the process; and

(D) The right of a participant who has been a victim of violence allegedly perpetrated by another mediation participant to be accompanied by a support person and to have sessions with the mediators separate from the alleged perpetrator.

(6) Protocols related to the inclusion of children in the mediation, including a requirement that the mediator explain in an age-appropriate way the mediation process to a participating child. The following information must be explained to the child:

(A) How the child may participate in the mediation;

(B) What occurs during the mediation process;

(C) The role of the mediator;

(D) What the child may realistically expect from the mediation, and the limits on his or her ability to affect the outcome;

(E) Any limitations on the confidentiality of the process;

(F) The child's right to be accompanied, throughout the mediation, by his or her attorney and other support persons; and

(G) The child's right to leave the mediation session if his or her emotional or physical well-being is threatened.

(7) Policy and procedures for scheduling follow-up mediation sessions.

(8) A procedure for suspending or terminating the process if the mediator determines that mediation cannot be conducted in a safe or an appropriately balanced manner or if any party is unable to participate in an informed manner for any reason, including fear or intimidation.

(9) A procedure for ensuring that each participant clearly understands any agreement reached during the mediation, and a procedure for presenting the agreement to the court for its approval. This procedure must include the requirement that all parties and the attorneys who participate in the agreement review and approve it and indicate their agreement in writing before its submission to the court.

(Subd (d) amended effective January 1, 2007; previously amended effective January 1, 2005.)

(e) Education, experience, and training requirements for dependency mediators

Dependency mediators must meet the following minimum qualifications:

(1) Possession of one or more of the following:

(A) A master's or doctoral degree in psychology, social work, marriage and family therapy, conflict resolution, or another behavioral science substantially related to family relationships, family violence, child development, or conflict resolution from an accredited college or university; or

(B) A juris doctorate or bachelor of laws degree;

(2) At least two years of experience as an attorney, a referee, a judicial officer, a mediator, or a child welfare worker in juvenile dependency court, or at least three years of experience in mediation or counseling, preferably in a setting related to juvenile dependency or domestic relations; and

(3) Completion of at least 40 hours of initial dependency mediation training before or within 12 months of beginning practice as a dependency mediator. Currently practicing dependency mediators must complete the required 40 hours of initial training by January 1, 2006. The training must cover the following subject areas as they relate to the practice of dependency mediation:

(A) Multiparty, multi-issue, multiagency, and high-conflict cases, including:

(i) The roles and participation of parents, other family members, children, attorneys, guardians ad litem, children's caregivers, the child welfare agency staff, CASA volunteers, law enforcement, mediators, the court, and other involved professionals and interested participants in the mediation process;

(ii) The impact that the mediation process can have on a child's well-being, and when and how to involve the child in the process;

(iii) The methods to help parties collaboratively resolve disputes and jointly develop plans that consider the needs and best interest of the child;

(iv) The disclosure, recantation, and denial of child abuse and neglect;

(v) Adult mental health issues; and

(vi) The rights to educational and developmental services recognized or established by state and federal law and strategies for appropriately addressing the individual needs of persons with disabilities;

(B) Physical and sexual abuse, exploitation, emotional abuse, endangerment, and neglect of children, and the impacts on children, including safety and treatment issues related to child abuse, neglect, and family violence;

(C) Family violence, its relevance to child abuse and neglect, and its effects on children and adult victims, including safety and treatment issues related to child abuse, neglect, and family violence;

(D) Substance abuse and its impact on children;

(E) Child development and its relevance to child abuse, neglect, and child custody and visitation arrangements;

(F) Juvenile dependency and child welfare systems, including dependency law;

(G) Interfamilial relationships and the psychological needs of children, including, but not limited to:

(i) The effect of removal or nonremoval of children from their homes and family members; and

(ii) The effect of terminating parental rights;

(H) The effect of poverty on parenting and familial relationships;

(I) Awareness of differing cultural values, including cross-generational cultural issues and local demographics;

(J) An overview of the special needs of dependent children, including their educational, medical, psychosocial, and mental health needs; and

(K) Available community resources and services for dealing with domestic and family violence, substance abuse, and housing, educational, medical, and mental health needs for families in the juvenile dependency system.

(Subd (e) amended effective January 1, 2014; previously amended effective January 1, 2005, January 1, 2007, and January 1, 2008.)

(f) Substitution for education or experience

The court, on a case-by-case basis, may approve substitution of experience for the education, or education for the experience, required by (e)(1) and (e)(2).

(Subd (f) amended effective January 1, 2007.)

(g) Continuing education requirements for mediators

In addition to the 40 hours of training required by (e)(3), all dependency mediators, mediation supervisors, program coordinators and directors, volunteers, interns, and paraprofessionals must participate in at least 12 hours per year of continuing instruction designed to enhance dependency mediation practice, skills, and techniques, including at least 4 hours specifically related to the issue of family violence.

(Subd (g) amended effective January 1, 2007.)

(h) Volunteers, interns, or paraprofessionals

Dependency mediation programs may use volunteers, interns, or paraprofessionals as mediators, but only if they are supervised by a professional mediator who is qualified to act as a professional dependency mediator as described in (e). They must meet the training and continuing education requirements in (e)(3) and (g) unless they co-mediate with another professional who meets the requirements of this rule. They are exempt from meeting the education and experience requirements in (e)(1) and (e)(2).

(Subd (h) amended effective January 1, 2007.)

(i) Education and training providers

Only education and training acquired from eligible providers meet the requirements of this rule. "Eligible providers" includes the Judicial Council and may include educational institutions, professional associations, professional continuing education groups, public or private for-profit or not-for-profit groups, and court-connected groups.

(1) Eligible providers must:

(A) Ensure that the training instructors or consultants delivering the education and training programs either meet the requirements of this rule or are experts in the subject matter;

(B) Monitor and evaluate the quality of courses, curricula, training, instructors, and consultants;

(C) Emphasize the importance of focusing dependency mediations on the health, safety, welfare, and best interest of the child;

(D) Develop a procedure to verify that participants complete the education and training program; and

(E) Distribute a certificate of completion to each person who has completed the training. The certificate must document the number of hours of training offered, the number of hours the person completed, the dates of the training, and the name of the training provider.

(2) Effective July 1, 2005, all education and training programs must be approved by Judicial Council staff in consultation with the Family and Juvenile Law Advisory Committee.

(Subd (i) amended effective January 1, 2016; adopted effective January 1, 2005; previously amended effective January 1, 2007.)

(j) Ethics/standards of conduct

Mediators must:

(1) Meet the standards of the applicable code of ethics for court employees.

(2) Maintain objectivity, provide information to and gather information from all parties, and be aware of and control their own biases.

(3) Protect the confidentiality of all parties, including the child. Mediators must not release information or make any recommendations about the case to the court or to any individual except as required by statute (for example, the requirement to make mandatory child abuse reports or reports to authorities regarding threats of harm or violence). Any limitations to confidentiality must be clearly explained to all mediation participants before any substantive issues are discussed in the mediation session.

(4) Maintain the confidential relationship between any family member or the child and his or her treating counselor, including the confidentiality of any psychological evaluations.

(5) Decline to provide legal advice.

(6) Consider the health, safety, welfare, and best interest of the child and the safety of all parties and other participants in all phases of the process and encourage the formulation of settlements that preserve these values.

(7) Operate within the limits of their training and experience and disclose any limitations or bias that would affect their ability to conduct the mediation.

(8) Not require the child to state a preference for placement.

(9) Disclose to the court, to any participant, and to the participant's attorney any conflicts of interest or dual relationships, and not accept any referral except by court order or the parties' stipulation. In the event of a conflict of interest, the mediator must suspend mediation and meet and confer in an effort to resolve the conflict of interest either to the satisfaction of all parties or according to local court rules. The court may order mediation to continue with another mediator or offer the parties an alternative method of resolving the issues in dispute.

(10) Not knowingly assist the parties in reaching an agreement that would be unenforceable for a reason such as fraud, duress, illegality, overreaching, absence of bargaining ability, or unconscionability.

(11) Protect the integrity of the mediation process by terminating the mediation when a party or participant has no genuine interest in resolving the dispute and is abusing the process.

(12) Terminate any session in which an issue of coercion, inability to participate, lack of intention to resolve the issues at hand, or physical or emotional abuse during the mediation session is involved.

(Subd (j) amended effective January 1, 2007; adopted as subd (i) effective January 1, 2004; previously relettered effective January 1, 2005.)

Rule 5.518 amended effective January 1, 2016; adopted as rule 1405.5 effective January 1, 2004; previously amended and renumbered as rule 5.518 effective January 1, 2007; previously amended effective January 1, 2005, January 1, 2008, and January 1, 2014.

Rule 5.520. Filing the petition; application for petition

(a) Discretion to file (§§ 325, 650)

Except as provided in sections 331, 364, 604, 653.5, 654, and 655, the social worker or probation officer has the sole discretion to determine whether to file a petition under section 300 and 601. The prosecuting attorney has the sole discretion to file a petition under section 602.

(Subd (a) amended effective January 1, 2007.)

(b) Filing the petition (§§ 325, 650)

A proceeding in juvenile court to declare a child a dependent or a ward of the court is commenced by the filing of a petition.

(1) In proceedings under section 300, the social worker must file the petition;

(2) In proceedings under section 601, the probation officer must file the petition; and

(3) In proceedings under section 602, the prosecuting attorney must file the petition. The prosecuting attorney may refer the matter back to the probation officer for appropriate action.

(Subd (b) amended effective January 1, 2007.)

(c) Application for petition (§§ 329, 331, 653, 653.5, 655)

Any person may apply to the social worker or probation officer to commence proceedings. The application must be in the form of an affidavit alleging facts showing the child is described in sections 300, 601, or 602. The social worker or probation officer must proceed under sections 329, 653, or 653.5. The applicant may seek review of a decision not to file a petition by proceeding under section 331 or 655.

(Subd (c) amended effective January 1, 2007.)

Rule 5.520 amended and renumbered effective January 1, 2007; adopted as rule 1406 effective January 1, 1991.

Rule 5.522. Remote filing

(a) Applicability and definitions

(1) This rule applies to juvenile court proceedings in courts that permit fax or electronic filing by local rule.

(2) As used in this rule, "fax," "fax transmission," "fax machine," and "fax filing" are defined in rule 2.301. A fax machine also includes any electronic device capable of receiving a fax transmission, as defined in rule 2.301.

(3) As used in this rule, "electronic filing" is defined in rule 2.250. Rule 2.250 also defines other terms used in this rule related to electronic filing, such as "document," "electronic filer," and "electronic filing service provider."

(Subd (a) amended effective January 1, 2019; previously amended effective January 1, 2007, and January 1, 2015.)

(b) Electronic filing

A court may allow for the electronic filing of documents in juvenile proceedings in accordance with section 212.5.

(Subd (b) amended effective January 1, 2019; adopted effective January 1, 2015.)

(c) Fax filing

(1) *Juvenile court documents that may be filed by fax*

The following documents may be filed in juvenile court by the use of a fax machine: petitions filed under sections 300, 342, 387, 388, 601, 602, 777, and 778 [1]; **Tribal Information Form (form ICWA-100); and** other documents, may be filed by the use of a fax machine if permitted by local rule as specified in (a).

(2) *Persons and agencies that may file by fax*

Only the following persons and agencies may file documents by the use of a fax machine, as stated in (c)(1):

(A) Any named party to the proceeding;

(B) Any attorney of record in the proceeding;

(C) The county child welfare department;

(D) The probation department;

(E) The office of the district attorney;

(F) The office of the county counsel; [2]

(G) A Court Appointed Special Advocate (CASA) volunteer appointed in the case; **and**

(H) An Indian tribe.

(3) *Procedures for fax filing*

A person described in (c)(2) may file by fax directly to any juvenile court that has provided for fax filing by local rule. The local rule or other written instruction must provide the fax telephone number or numbers for filings and the business hours during which fax filings will be accepted.

(4) *Mandatory cover sheet*

A fax filing must be accompanied by *Fax Filing Cover Sheet* (form JV-520). The cover sheet must be the first page of the transferred document. The court is not required to retain or file a copy of the cover sheet.

(5) *Signatures*

Notwithstanding any provision of law to the contrary, a signature produced by fax transmission is an original signature.

(6) *Confidentiality requirements*

To secure the confidentiality of the documents subject to filing by fax, the following procedures are required:

(A) The clerk's office designated to receive such documents must have either a separate fax machine dedicated solely to the receipt of the documents described in (c)(1) or a fax machine that is set up with a protocol to preserve the confidentiality of the documents described in (c)(1); and

(B) Any document received for fax filing must be filed or submitted to the court immediately on receipt and must not be placed or stored where anyone not entitled to access may examine it.

(Subd (c) amended effective January 1, 2021; adopted and amended effective January 1, 2015; previously subd (b)–(g); previously amended effective January 1, 2007.)

Rule 5.522(c). 2020 Deletes. [1] . [2] and

Rule 5.522 amended effective January 1, 2021; adopted as rule 1406.5 effective January 1, 1999; previously amended and renumbered effective January 1, 2007; previously amended effective January 1, 2015, and January 1, 2019.

Rule 5.523.   Electronic service (§ 212.5)

(a) Electronic service—General provisions

(1) Electronic service is authorized only if the court and county agencies required to serve in juvenile court permit electronic service.

(2) Unless otherwise provided by law, a document in a juvenile court matter may be served electronically as prescribed by Code of Civil Procedure section 1010.6 and in accordance with Welfare and Institutions Code section 212.5.

(3) If the noticing entity knows or should know that a child or nonminor who has consented to electronic service is in custody at the time that a notice will issue, the entity must also provide service of the notice by first-class mail.

(Subd (a) adopted effective January 1, 2019.)

(b) Consent to electronic service by a child, age 10 to 15

Electronic service is permitted on a child who is 10 to 15 years of age only upon express consent of the child and the child's attorney by completing the appropriate Judicial Council form.

(Subd (b) adopted effective January 1, 2019.)

(c) Consent to electronic service by a child, age 16 or 17

Electronic service is permitted on a child who is 16 or 17 years of age only if the child, after consultation with his or her attorney, expressly consents by completing the appropriate Judicial Council form.

(Subd (c) adopted effective January 1, 2019.)

(d) Required consultation with attorney for child, age 16 or 17

In a consultation with a child who is 16 or 17 years old and who seeks to consent to electronic service in a juvenile matter, the child's attorney must discuss and encourage the child to consider the following:

(1) Whether the child has regular and reliable access to a means of electronic communication for purposes of communication regarding his or her case;

(2) The importance of maintaining confidentiality and what means of electronic communication the child intends to use to communicate about his or her case and whether it is private and secure; and

(3) Whether the child understands his or her rights with respect to the provision and withdrawal of consent to electronic service.

(Subd (d) adopted effective January 1, 2019.)

(e) Required notification to child, age 16 or 17

In addition to the required factors for consideration in consultation described in (d), the child's attorney must also notify the child who seeks to provide consent to electronic service of the following:

(1) Electronic service of medical or psychological documentation related to a child is prohibited, with the exception of the summary required under Welfare and Institutions Code section 16010 when included as part of a required report to the court.

(2) Electronic service on a party or other person is permitted only if the party or other person has expressly consented, as provided in Code of Civil Procedure section 1010.6.

(3) A party or other person may subsequently withdraw his or her consent to electronic service by completing the appropriate Judicial Council form.

(Subd (e) adopted effective January 1, 2019.)

Rule 5.523 adopted effective January 1, 2019.

Rule 5.524.   Form of petition; notice of hearing

(a) Form of petition—dependency (§§ 332, 333)

The petition to declare a child a dependent of the court must be verified and may be dismissed without prejudice if not verified. The petition must contain the information stated in section 332.

(Subd (a) amended effective January 1, 2007; previously amended effective January 1, 1995, and January 1, 2006.)

(b) Form of petition—delinquency (§§ 656, 656.1, 656.5, 661)

The petition to declare a child a ward of the court must be verified and may be dismissed without prejudice if not verified. The petition must contain the information stated in sections 656, 656.1, 656.5, 661, and, if applicable, the intent to aggregate other offenses under section 726.

(Subd (b) amended effective January 1, 2007; adopted effective January 1, 2006.)

(c) Use of forms

Dependency petitions must be filed on a Judicial Council form. The filing party must use *Juvenile Dependency Petition (Version One)* (form JV-100) with the *Additional Children Attachment (Juvenile Dependency Petition)* (form JV-101(A)) when appropriate, or *Juvenile Dependency Petition (Version Two)* (form JV-110) as prescribed by local rule or practice. Rules 1.31 and 1.35 govern the use of mandatory and optional forms, respectively.

(Subd (c) amended effective January 1, 2019; adopted as subd (b) effective January 1, 1991; previously amended and relettered effective January 1, 2006; previously amended effective January 1, 2007.)

(d) Amending the petition (§§ 348, 678)

Chapter 8 of title 6 of part 2 of the Code of Civil Procedure, beginning at section 469, applies to variances and amendments of petitions and proceedings in the juvenile court.

(Subd (d) amended and relettered effective January 1, 2006; adopted as subd (c) effective January 1, 1991.)

(e) Notice of hearing—dependency (§§ 290.1, 290.2, 297, 338)

(1) When the petition is filed, the probation officer or social worker must serve a notice of hearing under section 290.1, with a copy of the petition attached. On filing of the petition, the clerk must issue and serve notice as prescribed in section 290.2, along with a copy of the petition. CASA volunteers are entitled to the same notice as stated in sections 290.1 and 290.2. Notice under sections 290.1 and 290.2 may not be served electronically.

(2) If the county and the court choose to allow notice by electronic service of hearings under sections 291–295, the court must develop a process for obtaining consent from persons entitled to notice that complies with Welfare and Institutions Code section 212.5 and ensures that notice can be effectuated according to statutory timelines.

(Subd (e) amended effective January 1, 2019; adopted as subd (d) effective January 1, 1991; previously amended and relettered effective January 1, 2006; previously amended effective January 1, 2007, and July 1, 2016.)

(f) Notice of hearing—delinquency (§§ 630, 630.1, 658, 659, 660)

(1) Immediately after the filing of a petition to detain a child, the probation officer or the prosecuting attorney must issue and serve notice as prescribed in section 630.

(2) When a petition is filed, the clerk must issue and serve a notice of hearing in accordance with sections 658, 659, and 660 with a copy of the petition attached.

(3) After reasonable notification by counsel representing the child, or representing the child's parents or guardian, the clerk must notify such counsel of the hearings as prescribed in section 630.1.

(Subd (f) amended effective January 1, 2019; adopted effective January 1, 2006; previously amended effective January 1, 2007.)

(g) Waiver of service (§§ 290.2, 660)

A person may waive service of notice by a voluntary appearance noted in the minutes of the court, or by a written waiver of service filed with the clerk.

(Subd (g) amended and relettered effective January 1, 2006; adopted as subd (h) effective January 1, 1991.)

(h) Oral notice (§§ 290.1, 630)

Notice required by sections 290.1 and 630 may be given orally. The social worker or probation officer must file a declaration stating that oral notice was given and to whom.

(Subd (h) amended effective January 1, 2007; adopted as subd (j) effective January 1, 1991; previously amended and relettered effective January 1, 2006.) Rule 5.524 amended effective January 1, 2019; adopted as rule 1407 effective January 1, 1991; previously amended effective January 1, 1992, January 1, 1995, January 1, 2001, January 1, 2006, and July 1, 2016; previously amended and renumbered as rule 5.524 effective January 1, 2007.)

Rule 5.526. Citation to appear; warrants of arrest; subpoenas

(a) Citation to appear (§§ 338, 661)

In addition to the notice required under rule 5.524, the court may issue a citation directing a parent or guardian to appear at a hearing as specified in section 338 or 661.

(Subd (a) amended effective January 1, 2019; previously amended effective January 1, 2006, and January 1, 2007.)

(b) Warrant of arrest (§§ 339, 662)

The court may order a warrant of arrest to issue against the parent, guardian, or present custodian of the child as specified in section 339 or 662.

(Subd (b) amended effective January 1, 2019.)

(c) Protective custody or warrant of arrest for child (§§ 340, 663)

The court may order a protective custody warrant or a warrant of arrest for a child as specified in section 340 or 663.

(Subd (c) amended effective January 1, 2019.)

(d) Subpoenas (§§ 341, 664)

On the court's own motion or at the request of the petitioner, child, parent, guardian, or present caregiver, the clerk must issue subpoenas as specified in section 341 or 664.

(Subd (d) amended effective January 1, 2019; previously amended effective January 1, 2006.)

Rule 5.526 amended effective January 1, 2019; adopted as rule 1408 effective January 1, 1991; previously amended effective January 1, 2006; previously amended and renumbered effective January 1, 2007.

Chapter 3
General Conduct of Juvenile Court Proceedings

Rule 5.530. Persons present

(a) Separate session; restriction on persons present (§§ 345, 675)

All juvenile court proceedings must be heard at a special or separate session of the court, and no other matter may be heard at that session. No person on trial, awaiting trial, or accused of a crime, other than a parent, de facto parent, guardian, or relative of the child, may be present at the hearing, except while testifying as a witness.

(Subd (a) amended effective January 1, 2005.)

(b) Persons present (§§ 280, 290.1, 290.2, 332, 347, 349, 353, 656, 658, 677, 679, 681, 700; 25 U.S.C. §§ 1911, 1931–1934)

The following persons are entitled to be present:

(1) The child or nonminor dependent;

(2) All parents, de facto parents, Indian custodians, and guardians of the child or, if no parent or guardian resides within the state or their places of residence are not known, any adult relative residing within the county or, if none, the adult relative residing nearest the court;

(3) Counsel representing the child or the parent, de facto parent, guardian, adult relative, or Indian custodian or the tribe of an Indian child;

(4) The probation officer or social worker;

(5) The prosecuting attorney, as provided in (c) and (d);

(6) Any CASA volunteer;

(7) In a proceeding described by rule 5.480, a representative of the Indian child's tribe;

(8) The court clerk;

(9) The official court reporter, as provided in rule 5.532;

(10) At the court's discretion, a bailiff; and

(11) Any other persons entitled to notice of the hearing under sections 290.1 and 290.2.

(Subd (b) amended effective July 1, 2013; previously amended effective January 1, 1995, January 1, 1997, January 1, 2005, January 1, 2007, and January 1, 2012.)

(c) Presence of prosecuting attorney—section 601–602 proceedings (§ 681)

In proceedings brought under section 602, the prosecuting attorney must appear on behalf of the people of the State of California. In proceedings brought under section 601, the prosecuting attorney may appear to assist in ascertaining and presenting the evidence if:

(1) The child is represented by counsel; and

(2) The court consents to or requests the prosecuting attorney's presence, or the probation officer requests and the court consents to the prosecuting attorney's presence.

(Subd (c) amended effective January 1, 2007.)

(d) Presence of petitioner's attorney—section 300 proceedings (§ 317)

In proceedings brought under section 300, the county counsel or district attorney must appear and represent the petitioner if the parent or guardian is represented by counsel and the juvenile court requests the attorney's presence.

(Subd (d) amended effective January 1, 2007.)

(e) Others who may be admitted (§§ 346, 676, 676.5)

Except as provided below, the public must not be admitted to a juvenile court hearing. The court may admit those whom the court deems to have a direct and legitimate interest in the case or in the work of the court.

(1) If requested by a parent or guardian in a hearing under section 300, and consented to or requested by the child, the court may permit others to be present.

(2) In a hearing under section 602:

(A) If requested by the child and a parent or guardian who is present, the court may admit others.

(B) Up to two family members of a prosecuting witness may attend to support the witness, as authorized by Penal Code section 868.5.

(C) Except as provided in section 676(b), members of the public must be admitted to hearings concerning allegations of the offenses stated in section 676(a).

(D) A victim of an offense alleged to have been committed by the child who is the subject of the petition, and up to two support persons chosen by the victim, are entitled to attend any hearing regarding the offense.

(E) Any persons, including the child, may move to exclude a victim or a support person and must demonstrate a substantial probability that overriding interests will be prejudiced by the presence of the individual sought to be excluded. On such motion, the court must consider reasonable alternatives to the exclusion and must make findings as required under section 676.5.

(Subd (e) amended effective January 1, 2007; previously amended effective January 1, 2001.)

(f) Participation of incarcerated parent in dependency proceedings (§§ 290.1–294, 316.2, 349, 361.5(e); Pen. Code § 2625)

The incarcerated parent of a child on behalf of whom a petition under section 300 has been filed may appear and participate in dependency proceedings as provided in this subdivision.

(1) Notice must be sent to an incarcerated parent of a detention hearing under section 319 as required by sections 290.1 and 290.2; a jurisdictional hearing under section 355 or a dispositional hearing under section 358 or 361 as required by section 291; a review hearing under section 366.21, 366.22, or 366.25 as required by section 293; or a permanency planning hearing under section 366.26 as required by section 294.

(A) Notice to an incarcerated parent of a jurisdictional hearing, a dispositional hearing, or a section 366.26 permanency planning hearing at which termination of parental rights is at issue must inform the incarcerated parent of his or her right to be physically present at the hearing and explain how the parent may secure his or her presence or, if he or she waives the right to be physically present, appearance and participation.

(B) Notice to an incarcerated parent of a detention hearing, a review hearing, or any other hearing in a dependency proceeding must inform the incarcerated parent of his or her options for requesting physical or telephonic appearance at and participation in the hearing.

(C) The county welfare department must use the prisoner location system developed by the Department of Corrections and Rehabilitation to facilitate timely and effective notice of hearings to incarcerated parents.

(2) The court must order an incarcerated parent's temporary removal from the institution where he or she is confined and production before the court at the time appointed for any jurisdictional hearing held under section 355 or dispositional hearing held under section 358 or 361, and any permanency planning hearing held under section 366.26 in which termination of parental rights is at issue.

(3) For any other hearing in a dependency proceeding, including but not limited to a detention hearing or a review hearing, the court may order the temporary removal of the incarcerated parent from the institution where he or she is confined and the parent's production before the court at the time appointed for that hearing.

(4) No hearing described in (2) may be held without the physical presence of the incarcerated parent and the parent's attorney unless the court has received:

(A) A knowing waiver of the right to be physically present signed by the parent; or

(B) A declaration, signed by the person in charge of the institution in which the parent is incarcerated, or his or her designated representative, stating that the parent has, by express statement or action, indicated an intent not to be physically present at the hearing.

(5) When issuing an order under (2) or (3), the court must require that *Order for Prisoner's Appearance at Hearing Affecting Parental Rights* (form JV-450) and a copy of *Prisoner's Statement Regarding Appearance at Hearing Affecting Parental Rights* (form JV-451) be attached to the notice of hearing and served on the parent, the parent's attorney, the person in charge of the institution, and the sheriff's department of the county in which the order is issued by the person responsible for giving notice of the hearing at issue not less than 15 days before the date of the hearing.

(6) The court may, at the request of any party or on its own motion, permit an incarcerated parent, who has waived his or her right to be physically present at a hearing described in (2) or who has not been ordered to appear before the court, to appear and participate in a hearing by videoconference consistent with the requirements of rule 5.531. If video technology is not available, the court may permit the parent to appear by telephone consistent with the requirements of rule 5.531. The court must inform the parent that, if no technology complying with rule 5.531 is available, the court may proceed without his or her appearance and participation.

(7) The presiding judge of the juvenile court in each county should convene representatives of the county welfare department, the sheriff's department, parents' attorneys, and other appropriate entities to develop:

(A) Local procedures or protocols to ensure an incarcerated parent's notification of, transportation to, and physical presence at court hearings involving proceedings affecting his or her child as required or authorized by Penal Code section 2625 and this rule unless he or she has knowingly waived the right to be physically present; and

(B) Local procedures or protocols, consistent with (f)(6) and rule 5.531, to facilitate the appearance and participation by videoconference or telephone of an incarcerated parent who has knowingly waived the right to be physically present.

(Subd (f) adopted effective January 1, 2012.)

Rule 5.530 amended effective July 1, 2013; adopted as rule 1410 effective January 1, 1990; previously amended and renumbered effective January 1, 2007; previously amended effective January 1, 1995, January 1, 1997, January 1, 2001, January 1, 2005, and January 1, 2012.

Rule 5.531.   Appearance by telephone (§§ 224.2(k), 388; Pen. Code, § 2625)

(a) Application

The standards in (b) apply to any appearance or participation in court by telephone, videoconference, or other digital or electronic means authorized by law.

(Subd (a) adopted effective January 1, 2012.)

(b) Standards for local procedures or protocols

Local procedures or protocols must be developed to ensure the fairness and confidentiality of any proceeding in which a party is permitted by statute, rule of court, or judicial discretion to appear by telephone. These procedures or protocols must, at a minimum:

(1) **Allow an Indian child's tribe to appear by telephone or other computerized remote means at no charge in accordance with rule 5.482(g). The method of appearance may be determined by the court consistent with court capacity and contractual obligations, and taking account of the capacity of the tribe, as long as a method of effective remote appearance and participation sufficient to allow the tribe to fully exercise its rights is provided;**

(2) Ensure that the party appearing by telephone can participate in the hearing in real time, with no delay in aural or, if any, visual transmission or reception;

[1] (3) Ensure that the statements of participants are audible to all other participants and court staff and that the statements made by a participant are identified as being made by that participant;

[2] (4) Ensure that the proceedings remain confidential as required by law;

[3] (5) Establish a deadline of no more than three court days before the proceeding for notice to the court by the party or party's attorney (if any) of that party's intent to appear by telephone, and permit that notice to be conveyed by any method reasonably calculated to reach the court, including telephone, fax, or other electronic means;

[4] (6) Permit the party, on a showing of good cause, to appear by telephone even if he or she did not provide timely notice of intent to appear by telephone;

[5] (7) Permit a party to appear in person for a proceeding at the time and place for which the proceeding was noticed, even if that party had previously notified the court of an intent to appear by telephone;

[6] (8) Ensure that any hearing at which a party appears by telephone is recorded and reported to the same extent and in the same manner as if he or she had been physically present;

[7] (9) Ensure that the party appearing by telephone is able to communicate confidentially with his or her attorney (if any) during the proceeding and provide timely notice to all parties of the steps necessary to secure confidential communication; and

[8] (10) Provide for the development of the technological capacity to accommodate appearances by telephone that comply with the requirements of this rule.

(Subd (b) amended effective January 1, 2021; adopted effective January 1, 2012.)

Rule 5.531(b).   2020 Deletes. [1] (2) [2] (3) [3] (4) [4] (5) [5] (6) [6] (7) [7] (8) [8] (9)

(c) No independent right

Nothing in this rule confers on any person an independent right to appear by telephone, videoconference, or other electronic means in any proceeding.

(Subd (c) adopted effective January 1, 2012.)

Rule 5.531 amended effective January 1, 2021; adopted effective January 1, 2012.

Rule 5.532.   Court reporter; transcripts

(a) Hearing before judge (§§ 347, 677)

If the hearing is before a judge or a referee acting as a temporary judge by stipulation, an official court reporter or other authorized reporting procedure must record all proceedings.

(Subd (a) amended effective January 1, 2007.)

(b) Hearing before referee (§§ 347, 677)

If the hearing is before a referee not acting as a temporary judge, the judge may direct an official court reporter or other authorized reporting procedure to record all proceedings.

(c) Preparation of transcript (§§ 347, 677)

If directed by the judge or if requested by a party or the attorney for a party, the official court reporter or other authorized transcriber must prepare a transcript of the proceedings within such reasonable time after the hearing as the judge designates and must certify that the proceedings have been correctly reported and transcribed. If directed by the judge, the official court reporter or authorized transcriber must file the transcript with the clerk of the court.

(Subd (c) amended effective January 1, 2007.)

Rule 5.532 amended and renumbered effective January 1, 2007; adopted as rule 1411 effective January 1, 1990.

Rule 5.534.   General provisions—all proceedings

(a) De facto parents

On a sufficient showing, the court may recognize the child's present or previous custodian as a de facto parent and grant him or her standing to participate as a party in the dispositional hearing and any hearing thereafter at which the status of the dependent child is at issue. The de facto parent may:

(1) Be present at the hearing;

(2) Be represented by retained counsel or, at the discretion of the court, by appointed counsel; and

(3) Present evidence.

(Subd (a) relettered effective January 1, 2017; adopted as subd (e) effective January 1, 1991; previously amended effective January 1, 2007, and January 1, 2014.)

(b) Relatives

(1) On a sufficient showing, the court may permit a relative of the child or youth to:

(A) Be present at the hearing; and

(B) Address the court.

(2) A relative of the child has the right to submit information about the child to the court at any time. Written information about the child may be submitted to the court using *Relative Information* (form JV-285) or in a letter to the court.

(3) When a relative is located through the investigation required by rule 5.637, the social worker or probation officer must give that relative:

(A) The written notice required by section 309 or 628 and the "Important Information for Relatives" document as distributed in California Department of Social Services All County Letter No. 09-86;

(B) A copy of *Relative Information* (form JV-285), with the county and address of the court, the child's name and date of birth, and the case number already entered in the appropriate caption boxes by the social worker; and

(C) A copy of *Confidential Information* (form JV-287).

(4) When form JV-285 or a relative's letter is received by the court, the clerk must provide the social worker or probation officer, all self-represented parties, and all attorneys with a copy of the completed form or letter.

(5) When form JV-287 is received by the court, the clerk must place it in a confidential portion of the case file.

(Subd (b) relettered effective January 1, 2017; adopted as subd (f) effective January 1, 1991; previously amended effective January 1, 2007, January 1, 2011, and January 1, 2014.)

(c) Right to counsel (§§ 317, 633, 634, 700)

At each hearing, the court must advise any self-represented child, parent, or guardian of the right to be represented by counsel and, if applicable, of the right to have counsel appointed, subject to a claim by the court or the county for reimbursement as provided by law.

(Subd (c) relettered effective January 1, 2017; adopted as subd (g) effective January 1, 1991; previously amended effective July 1, 2002, January 1, 2007, and January 1, 2014.)

(d) Appointment of counsel (§§ 317, 353, 633, 634, 700)

(1) In cases petitioned under section 300:

(A) The court must appoint counsel for the child unless the court finds that the child would not benefit from the appointment and makes the findings required by rule 5.660(b); and

(B) The court must appoint counsel for any parent or guardian unable to afford counsel if the child is placed in out-of-home care or the recommendation of the petitioner is for out-of-home care, unless the court finds the parent or guardian has knowingly and intelligently waived the right to counsel.

(2) In cases petitioned under section 601 or 602:

(A) The court must appoint counsel for any child who appears without counsel, unless the child knowingly and intelligently waives the right to counsel. If the court determines that the parent or guardian can afford counsel but has not retained counsel for the child, the court must appoint counsel for the child and order the parent or guardian to reimburse the county;

(B) The court may appoint counsel for a parent or guardian who desires but cannot afford counsel; and

(C) If the parent has retained counsel for the child and a conflict arises, the court must take steps to ensure that the child's interests are protected.

(Subd (d) relettered effective January 1, 2017; adopted as subd (h) effective January 1, 1991; previously amended effective July 1, 2002, January 1, 2007, and January 1, 2014.)

(e) Tribal representatives (25 U.S.C. §§ 1911, 1931–1934)

The tribe of an Indian child is entitled to intervene as a party at any stage of a dependency proceeding concerning the Indian child.

(1) The tribe may appear by counsel or by a representative of the tribe designated by the tribe to intervene on its behalf. When the tribe appears as a party by a representative of the tribe, the name of the representative and a statement of authorization for that individual or agency to appear as the tribe must be submitted to the court in the form of a tribal resolution or other document evidencing an official act of the tribe.

(2) If the tribe of the Indian child does not intervene as a party, the court may permit an individual affiliated with the tribe or, if requested by the tribe, a representative of a program operated by another tribe or Indian organization to:

(A) Be present at the hearing;

(B) Address the court;

(C) Receive notice of hearings;

(D) Examine all court documents relating to the dependency case;

(E) Submit written reports and recommendations to the court; and

(F) Perform other duties and responsibilities as requested or approved by the court.

(Subd (e) relettered effective January 1, 2017; adopted as subd (i) effective January 1, 1997; previously amended effective July 1, 2002, and January 1, 2007.)

(f) Appointment of educational rights holder (§§ 319, 361, 366, 366.27, 726, 727.2; Gov. Code, §§ 7579.5–7579.6)

(1) If the court limits, even temporarily, the rights of a parent or guardian to make educational or developmental-services decisions for a child under rule 5.649, the court must immediately proceed under rule 5.650 to appoint a responsible adult as educational rights holder for the child.

(2) If a nonminor or nonminor dependent youth chooses not to make educational or developmental-services decisions for him- or herself or is deemed by the court to be incompetent, and the court also finds that the appointment of an educational rights holder would be in the best interests of the youth, then the court must immediately proceed under rule 5.650 to appoint or continue the appointment of a responsible adult as educational rights holder for the youth.

(Subd (f) relettered effective January 1, 2017; adopted as subd (j) effective January 1, 2008; previously amended effective January 1, 2014.)

(g) Advisement of hearing rights (§§ 301, 311, 341, 630, 702.5, 827)

(1) The court must advise the child, parent, and guardian in section 300 cases, and the child in section 601 or section 602 cases, of the following rights:

(A) The right to assert the privilege against self-incrimination;

(B) The right to confront and cross-examine the persons who prepared reports or documents submitted to the court by the petitioner and the witnesses called to testify at the hearing;

(C) The right to use the process of the court to bring in witnesses; and

(D) The right to present evidence to the court.

(2) The child, parent, guardian, and their attorneys have:

(A) The right to receive probation officer or social worker reports; and

(B) The right to inspect the documents used by the preparer of the report.

(3) Unless prohibited by court order, the child, parent, guardian, and their attorneys also have the right to receive all documents filed with the court.

(Subd (g) amended and relettered effective January 1, 2017; adopted as subd (i) effective January 1, 1991; previously relettered as subd (j) effective January 1, 1997, and as subd (k) effective January 1, 2008; previously amended effective July 1, 2002, and January 1, 2007.)

(h) Notice

At each hearing under section 300 et seq., the court must determine whether notice has been given as required by law and must make an appropriate finding noted in the minutes.

(Subd (h) relettered effective January 1, 2017; adopted as subd (j) effective January 1, 1991; previously relettered as subd (k) effective January 1, 1997, and as subd (l) effective January 1, 2008; previously amended effective July 1, 2002, and January 1, 2007.)

(i) Mailing address of parent or guardian (§ 316.1)

At the first appearance by a parent or guardian in proceedings under section 300 et seq., the court must order each parent or guardian to provide a mailing address.

(1) The court must advise that the mailing address provided will be used by the court, the clerk, and the social services agency for the purposes of notice of hearings and the mailing of all documents related to the proceedings.

(2) The court must advise that until and unless the parent or guardian, or the attorney of record for the parent or guardian, submits written notification of a change of mailing address, the address provided will be used, and notice requirements will be satisfied by appropriate service at that address.

(3) *Notification of Mailing Address* (form JV-140) is the preferred method of informing the court and the social services agency of the mailing address of the parent or guardian and change of mailing address.

(A) The form must be delivered to the parent or guardian, or both, with the petition.

(B) The form must be available in the courtroom, in the office of the clerk, and in the offices of the social services agency.

(C) The form must be printed and made available in both English and Spanish.

(Subd (i) amended effective January 1, 2019; adopted as subd (k) effective January 1, 1994; previously relettered as subd (l) effective January 1, 1997, as subd (m) effective January 1, 2008, and as subd (i) effective January 1, 2017; previously amended effective July 1, 2002, January 1, 2007, and July 1, 2016.)

(j) Electronic service address (§ 316.1)

At the first appearance by a party or person before the court, each party or person entitled to notice who consents to electronic service under section 212.5 must provide the court with an electronic service address by completing the appropriate Judicial Council form.

(1) The court must advise the party or person entitled to notice that the electronic service address will be used to serve notices and documents in the case, unless and until the party or person notifies the court of a new electronic service address in writing or unless the party or person withdraws consent to electronic service.

(2) A party or person entitled to notice may indicate his or her consent and provide his or her electronic service address or may withdraw his or her consent to electronic service or change his or her electronic service address by filing *Electronic Service: Consent, Withdrawal of Consent, Address Change (Juvenile)* (form EFS-005-JV/JV-141).

(3) If a person under 18 years old files form EFS-005-JV/JV-141, he or she must ask his or her attorney or another adult to serve the document on the other parties and persons required to be served in the case.

(4) The persons required to be served form EFS-005-JV/JV-141 are all legal parties to the action and their attorneys of record, including, but not limited to, the social services agency, the child, any parent, a legal guardian, a Court Appointed Special Advocate, and a guardian ad litem. In the case of an Indian child, the Indian custodian, if any, and the child's tribe must be served pursuant to section 224.2. The judge may order service to be made on additional parties or persons.

(Subd (j) adopted effective January 1, 2019.)

(k) Caregiver notice and right to be heard (§§ 290.1–297, 366.21)

For cases filed under section 300 et seq.:

(1) For any child who has been removed from the home, the court must ensure that notice of statutory review hearings, permanency hearings, and section 366.26 hearings has been provided to the current caregiver of the child, including foster parents, preadoptive parents, relative caregivers, and nonrelative extended family members. Notice of dispositional hearings also must be provided to these individuals when the dispositional hearing is serving as a permanency hearing under section 361.5(f).

(2) The current caregiver has the right to be heard in each proceeding listed in paragraph (1), including the right to submit information about the child to the court before the hearing. Written information about the child may be submitted to the court using the *Caregiver Information Form* (form JV-290) or in the form of a letter to the court.

(3) At least 10 calendar days before each hearing listed in paragraph (1), the social worker must provide to the current caregiver:

(A) A summary of his or her recommendations for disposition, and any recommendations for change in custody or status;

(B) *Caregiver Information Form* (form JV-290); and

(C) *Instruction Sheet for Caregiver Information Form* (form JV-290-INFO).

(4) If the caregiver chooses to provide written information to the court using form JV-290 or by letter, the caregiver must follow the procedures set forth below. The court may waive any element of this process for good cause.

(A) If filing in person, the caregiver must bring the original document and 8 copies to the court clerk's office for filing no later than five calendar days before the hearing.

(B) If filing by mail, the caregiver must mail the original document and 8 copies to the court clerk's office for filing no later than seven calendar days before the hearing.

(5) When form JV-290 or a caregiver letter is received by mail the court clerk must immediately file it.

(6) When form JV-290 or a caregiver letter is filed, the court clerk must provide the social worker, all unrepresented parties, and all attorneys with a copy of the completed form or letter immediately upon receipt. The clerk also must complete, file, and distribute *Proof of Service—Juvenile* (form JV-510). The clerk may use any technology designed to speed the distribution process, including drop boxes in the courthouse, e-mail, fax, or other electronic transmission, as defined in rule 2.250, to distribute the JV-290 form or letter and proof of service form.

(Subd (k) relettered effective January 1, 2019; adopted as subd (m) effective October 1, 2007; previously relettered as subd (n) effective January 1, 2008, and as subd (j) effective January 1, 2017; previously amended effective January 1, 2016.)

Rule 5.534 amended effective January 1, 2019; adopted as rule 1412 effective January 1, 1991; previously amended and renumbered as rule 5.534 effective January 1, 2007; previously amended effective January 1, 1994, July 1, 1995, January 1, 1997, January 1, 2000, July 1, 2002, January 1, 2005, October 1, 2007, January 1, 2008, January 1, 2010, January 1, 2011, January 1, 2014, January 1, 2016, July 1, 2016, and January 1, 2017.)

Advisory Committee Comment

Because the intent of subdivision (j) is to expand access to the courts for caregivers of children in out-of-home care, the rule should be liberally construed. To promote caregiver participation and input, judicial officers are encouraged to permit caregivers to orally address the court when caregivers would like to share information about the child. In addition, court clerks should allow filings by caregivers even if the caregiver has not strictly adhered to the requirements in the rule regarding number of copies and filing deadlines.

Rule 5.536. General provisions—proceedings held before referees

(a) Referees—appointment; powers (Cal. Const., art. VI, § 22)

One or more referees may be appointed under section 247 to perform subordinate judicial duties assigned by the presiding judge of the juvenile court.

(Subd (a) amended effective January 1, 2007.)

(b) Referee as temporary judge (Cal. Const., art. VI, § 21)

If the referee is an attorney admitted to practice in this state, the parties may stipulate under rule 2.816 that the referee is acting as a temporary judge with the same powers as a judge of the juvenile court. An official court reporter or other authorized reporting procedure must record all proceedings.

(Subd (b) amended effective January 1, 2007.)

Rule 5.536 amended and renumbered effective January 1, 2007; adopted as rule 1415 effective January 1, 1990.

Rule 5.538. Conduct of proceedings held before a referee not acting as a temporary judge

(a) General conduct (§§ 248, 347, 677)

Proceedings heard by a referee not acting as a temporary judge must be conducted in the same manner as proceedings heard by a judge, except:

(1) An official court reporter or other authorized reporting procedure must record the proceedings if directed by the court; and

(2) The referee must inform the child and parent or guardian of the right to seek review by a juvenile court judge.

(Subd (a) amended effective January 1, 2007.)

(b) Furnishing and serving findings and order; explanation of right to review (§§ 248, 248.5)

After each hearing before a referee, the referee must make findings and enter an order as provided elsewhere in these rules. In each case, the referee must furnish and serve the findings and order and provide an explanation of the right to review the order in accordance with sections 248 and 248.5.

(Subd (b) amended effective January 1, 2019; previously amended effective January 1, 2007, and January 1, 2016.)

Rule 5.538 amended effective January 1, 2019; adopted as rule 1416 effective January 1, 1990; previously amended and renumbered as rule 5.538 effective January 1, 2007; previously amended effective January 1, 2016.

Rule 5.540.   Orders of referees not acting as temporary judges

(a)   Effective date of order (§ 250)

Except as provided in (b) and subject to the right of review provided for in rule 5.542, all orders of a referee become effective immediately and continue in effect unless vacated or modified on rehearing by order of a juvenile court judge.

(Subd (a) amended effective January 1, 2007.)

(b)   Orders requiring express approval of judge (§§ 249, 251)

The following orders made by a referee do not become effective unless expressly approved by a juvenile court judge within two court days:

(1) Any order removing a child from the physical custody of the person legally entitled to custody; or

(2) Any order the presiding judge of the juvenile court requires to be expressly approved.

(Subd (b) amended effective January 1, 2007.)

(c)   Finality date of order

An order of a referee becomes final 10 calendar days after service of a copy of the order and findings under rule 5.538, if an application for rehearing has not been made within that time or if the judge of the juvenile court has not within the 10 days ordered a rehearing on the judge's own motion under rule 5.542.

(Subd (c) amended effective January 1, 2007.)

Rule 5.540 amended and renumbered effective January 1, 2007; adopted as rule 1417 effective January 1, 1990.

Rule 5.542.   Rehearing of proceedings before referees

(a)   Application for rehearing (§ 252)

An application for a rehearing of a proceeding before a referee not acting as a temporary judge may be made by the child, parent, or guardian at any time before the expiration of 10 calendar days after service of a copy of the order and findings. The application may be directed to all, or any specified part of, the order or findings and must contain a brief statement of the factual or legal reasons for requesting the rehearing.

(Subd (a) amended effective January 1, 2007.)

(b)   If no formal record (§ 252)

A rehearing must be granted if proceedings before the referee were not recorded by an official court reporter or other authorized reporting procedure.

(Subd (b) amended effective January 1, 2007.)

(c)   Hearing with court reporter (§ 252)

If the proceedings before the referee have been recorded by an official court reporter or other authorized reporting procedure, the judge of the juvenile court may, after reading the transcript of the proceedings, grant or deny the application for rehearing. If the application is not denied within 20 calendar days following the date of receipt of the application, or within 45 calendar days if the court for good cause extends the time, the application must be deemed granted.

(Subd (c) amended effective January 1, 2007.)

(d)   Rehearing on motion of judge (§ 253)

Notwithstanding (a), at any time within 20 court days after a hearing before a referee, the judge, on the judge's own motion, may order a rehearing.

(Subd (d) amended effective January 1, 2007.)

(e)   Hearing de novo (§ 254)

Rehearings of matters heard before a referee must be conducted de novo before a judge of the juvenile court. A rehearing of a detention hearing must be held within two court days after the rehearing is granted. A rehearing of other matters heard before a referee must be held within 10 court days after the rehearing is granted.

(Subd (e) amended effective January 1, 2007.)

(f)   Advisement of appeal rights—rule 5.590

If the judge of the juvenile court denies an application for rehearing directed in whole or in part to issues arising during a contested jurisdiction hearing, the judge must advise, either orally or in writing, the child and the parent or guardian of all of the following:

(1) The right of the child, parent, or guardian to appeal from the court's judgment;

(2) The necessary steps and time for taking an appeal;

(3) The right of an indigent appellant to have counsel appointed by the reviewing court; and

(4) The right of an indigent appellant to be provided a free copy of the transcript.

(Subd (f) amended effective January 1, 2007.)

Rule 5.542 amended and renumbered effective January 1, 2007; adopted as rule 1418 effective January 1, 1991.

Rule 5.544.   Prehearing motions (§ 700.1)

Unless otherwise ordered or specifically provided by law, prehearing motions and accompanying points and authorities must, absent a waiver, be served on the child and opposing counsel and filed with the court:

(1) At least 5 judicial days before the date the jurisdiction hearing is set to begin if the child is detained or the motion is one to suppress evidence obtained as a result of an unlawful search and seizure; or

(2) At least 10 judicial days before the date the jurisdiction hearing is set to begin if the child is not detained and the motion is other than one to suppress evidence obtained as a result of an unlawful search and seizure.

Prehearing motions must be specific, noting the grounds, and supported by points and authorities.

Rule 5.544 amended and renumbered effective January 1, 2007; adopted as rule 1419 effective January 1, 1991.

Rule 5.546.   Prehearing discovery

(a)   General purpose

This rule must be liberally construed in favor of informal disclosures, subject to the right of a party to show privilege or other good cause not to disclose specific material or information.

(Subd (a) amended effective January 1, 2007.)

(b)   Duty to disclose police reports

After filing the petition, petitioner must promptly deliver to or make accessible for inspection and copying by the child and the parent or guardian, or their counsel, copies of the police, arrest, and crime reports relating to the pending matter. Privileged information may be omitted if notice of the omission is given simultaneously.

(Subd (b) amended effective January 1, 2007.)

(c)   Affirmative duty to disclose

Petitioner must disclose any evidence or information within petitioner's possession or control favorable to the child, parent, or guardian.

(Subd (c) amended effective January 1, 2007.)

(d)   Material and information to be disclosed on request

Except as provided in (g) and (h), petitioner must, after timely request, disclose to the child and parent or guardian, or their counsel, the following material and information within the petitioner's possession or control:

(1) Probation reports prepared in connection with the pending matter relating to the child, parent, or guardian;

(2) Records of statements, admissions, or conversations by the child, parent, or guardian;

(3) Records of statements, admissions, or conversations by any alleged coparticipant;

(4) Names and addresses of witnesses interviewed by an investigating authority in connection with the pending matter;

(5) Records of statements or conversations of witnesses or other persons interviewed by an investigating authority in connection with the pending matter;

(6) Reports or statements of experts made regarding the pending matter, including results of physical or mental examinations and results of scientific tests, experiments, or comparisons;

(7) Photographs or physical evidence relating to the pending matter; and

(8) Records of prior felony convictions of the witnesses each party intends to call.

(Subd (d) amended effective January 1, 2007.)

(e)   Disclosure in section 300 proceedings

Except as provided in (g) and (h), the parent or guardian must, after timely request, disclose to petitioner relevant material and information within the parent's or guardian's possession or control. If counsel represents the parent or guardian, a disclosure request must be made through counsel.

(Subd (e) amended effective January 1, 2007.)

(f) Motion for prehearing discovery

If a party refuses to disclose information or permit inspection of materials, the requesting party or counsel may move the court for an order requiring timely disclosure of the information or materials. The motion must specifically and clearly designate the items sought, state the relevancy of the items, and state that a timely request has been made for the items and that the other party has refused to provide them. Each court may by local rule establish the manner and time within which a motion under this subdivision must be made.

(Subd (f) amended effective January 1, 2007.)

(g) Limits on duty to disclose—protective orders

On a showing of privilege or other good cause, the court may make orders restricting disclosures. All material and information to which a party is entitled must be disclosed in time to permit counsel to make beneficial use of them.

(h) Limits on duty to disclose—excision

When some parts of the materials are discoverable under (d) and (e) and other parts are not discoverable, the nondiscoverable material may be excised and need not be disclosed if the requesting party or counsel has been notified that the privileged material has been excised. Material ordered excised must be sealed and preserved in the records of the court for review on appeal.

(Subd (h) amended effective January 1, 2007.)

(i) Conditions of discovery

An order of the court granting discovery under this rule may specify the time, place, and manner of making the discovery and inspection and may prescribe terms and conditions. Discovery must be completed in a timely manner to avoid the delay or continuance of a scheduled hearing.

(Subd (i) amended effective January 1, 2007.)

(j) Failure to comply; sanctions

If at any time during the course of the proceedings the court learns that a person has failed to comply with this rule or with an order issued under this rule, the court may order the person to permit the discovery or inspection of materials not previously disclosed, grant a continuance, prohibit a party from introducing in evidence the material not disclosed, dismiss the proceedings, or enter any other order the court deems just under the circumstances.

(Subd (j) amended effective January 1, 2007.)

(k) Continuing duty to disclose

If subsequent to compliance with these rules or with court orders a party discovers additional material or information subject to disclosure, the party must promptly notify the child and parent or guardian, or their counsel, of the existence of the additional matter.

(Subd (k) amended effective January 1, 2007.)

Rule 5.546 amended and renumbered effective January 1, 2007; adopted as rule 1420 effective January 1, 1990.

Rule 5.548.   Granting immunity to witnesses

(a) Privilege against self-incrimination

If a person is called as a witness and it appears to the court that the testimony or other evidence being sought may tend to incriminate the witness, the court must advise the witness of the privilege against self-incrimination and of the possible consequences of testifying. The court must also inform the witness of the right to representation by counsel and, if indigent, of the right to have counsel appointed.

(Subd (a) amended effective January 1, 2007.)

(b) Authority of judge to grant immunity

If a witness refuses to answer a question or to produce evidence based on a claim of the privilege against self-incrimination, a judge may grant immunity to the witness under (c) or (d) and order the question answered or the evidence produced.

(Subd (b) amended effective January 1, 2007.)

(c) Request for immunity—section 602 proceedings

In proceedings under section 602, the prosecuting attorney may make a written or oral request on the record that the court order a witness to answer a question or produce evidence. The court must then proceed under Penal Code section 1324.

(1) After complying with an order to answer a question or produce evidence and if, but for those Penal Code sections or this rule, the witness would have been privileged to withhold the answer given or the evidence produced, no testimony or other information compelled under the order or information directly or indirectly derived from the testimony or other information may be used against the witness in any criminal case, including any juvenile court proceeding under section 602.

(2) The prosecuting attorney may request an order granting the witness use or transactional immunity.

(Subd (c) amended effective January 1, 2007; previously amended effective January 1, 1998.)

(d) Request for immunity—section 300 or 601 proceedings

In proceedings under section 300 or 601, the prosecuting attorney or petitioner may make a written or oral request on the record that the judge order a witness to answer a question or produce evidence. They may also make the request jointly.

(1) If the request is not made jointly, the other party must be given the opportunity to show why immunity is not to be granted and the judge may grant or deny the request as deemed appropriate.

(2) If jointly made, the judge must grant the request unless the judge finds that to do so would be clearly contrary to the public interest. The terms of a grant of immunity must be stated in the record.

(3) After complying with the order and if, but for this rule, the witness would have been privileged to withhold the answer given or the evidence produced, any answer given, evidence produced, or information derived there from must not be used against the witness in a juvenile court or criminal proceeding.

(Subd (d) amended effective January 1, 2007.)

(e) No immunity from perjury or contempt

Notwithstanding (c) or (d), a witness may be subject to proceedings under the juvenile court law or to criminal prosecution for perjury, false swearing, or contempt committed in answering or failing to answer or in producing or failing to produce evidence in accordance with the order.

(Subd (e) amended effective January 1, 2007.)

Rule 5.548 amended and renumbered effective January 1, 2007; adopted as rule 1421 effective January 1, 1990; previously amended effective January 1, 1998.

Rule 5.550.   Continuances

(a) Cases petitioned under section 300 (§§ 316.2, 352, 354)

(1) The court must not continue a hearing beyond the time set by statute unless the court determines the continuance is not contrary to the interest of the child. In considering the child's interest, the court must give substantial weight to a child's needs for stability and prompt resolution of custody status, and the damage of prolonged temporary placements.

(2) Continuances may be granted only on a showing of good cause, and only for the time shown to be necessary. Stipulation between counsel of parties, convenience of parties, and pending criminal or family law matters are not in and of themselves good cause.

(3) If a child has been removed from the custody of a parent or guardian, the court must not grant a continuance that would cause the disposition hearing under section 361 to be completed more than 60 days after the detention hearing unless the court finds exceptional circumstances. In no event may the disposition hearing be continued more than six months after the detention hearing.

(4) In order to obtain a continuance, written notice with supporting documents must be filed and served on all parties at least two court days before the date set for hearing, unless the court finds good cause for hearing an oral motion.

(5) The court must state in its order the facts requiring any continuance that is granted.

(Subd (a) amended effective July 1, 2016; previously amended effective January 1, 1999, July 1, 2002, and January 1, 2007.)

(b) Cases petitioned under section 601 or 602 (§ 682)

(1) A continuance may be granted only on a showing of good cause and only for the time shown to be necessary. Stipulation between counsel or parties and convenience of parties are not in and of themselves good cause.

(2) In order to obtain a continuance, written notice with supporting documents must be filed and served on all parties at least two court days before the date set for the hearing, unless the court finds good cause for failure to comply with these requirements.

(3) The court must state in its order the facts requiring any continuance that is granted.

(4) If the child is represented by counsel, failure of counsel or the child to object to an order continuing a hearing beyond the time limit is deemed a consent to the continuance.

(Subd (b) amended effective January 1, 2007; previously amended effective July 1, 2002.)

(c) Continuances of detention hearings (§§ 319, 322, 635, 636, 638)

(1) On the motion of the child, parent, or guardian, the court must continue the detention hearing for one court day or for a reasonable period to permit the moving party to prepare any relevant evidence on the issue of detention. Unless otherwise ordered by the court, the child must remain in custody pending the continued hearing.

(2) At the initial detention hearing, if the court continues the hearing under (c)(1) or for any other reason, or sets the matter for rehearing, the court must either find that the continuance of the child in the parent's or guardian's home is contrary to the child's welfare or order the child released to the custody of the parent or guardian. The court may enter this finding on a temporary basis, without prejudice to any party, and reevaluate the finding at the time of the continued detention hearing.

(3) When the court knows or has reason to know the child is an Indian child, the detention hearing may not be continued beyond 30 days unless the court makes the findings required by section 319(e)(2).

(Subd (c) amended effective January 1, 2020; adopted effective January 1, 1998; previously amended effective July 1, 2002, and January 1, 2007.)

(d) Continuances of a dispositional hearing when the court knows or has reason to know the child is an Indian child (§ 352(b))

(1) When the court knows or has reason to know that the case involves an Indian child, no continuance of a dispositional may be granted that would result in the hearing being held longer than 30 days after the hearing at which the minor was ordered removed or detained unless the court finds that there are exceptional circumstances requiring a continuance.

(2) The absence of an opinion from a qualified expert witness must not, in and of itself, support a finding that exceptional circumstances exist.

(Subd (d) adopted effective January 1, 2020.)

Rule 5.550 amended effective January 1, 2020; adopted effective January 1, 1991; previously amended effective January 1, 1998, January 1, 1999, July 1, 2002, and July 1, 2016; previously amended and renumbered as rule 5.550 effective January 1, 2007.

Rule 5.552.   Confidentiality of records (§§ 827, 827.12, 828)

(a) Definitions

For the purposes of this rule, "juvenile case file" includes:

(1) All documents filed in a juvenile court case;

(2) Reports to the court by probation officers, social workers of child welfare services programs, and CASA volunteers;

(3) Documents made available to probation officers, social workers of child welfare services programs, and CASA volunteers in preparation of reports to the court;

(4) Documents relating to a child concerning whom a petition has been filed in juvenile court that are maintained in the office files of probation officers, social workers of child welfare services programs, and CASA volunteers;

(5) Transcripts, records, or reports relating to matters prepared or released by the court, probation department, or child welfare services program; and

(6) Documents, video or audio tapes, photographs, and exhibits admitted into evidence at juvenile court hearings.

(Subd (a) amended effective January 1, 2007; previously amended effective January 1, 2001.)

(b) Petition

Juvenile case files may be obtained or inspected only in accordance with sections 827, 827.12, and 828. They may not be obtained or inspected by civil or criminal subpoena. With the exception of those persons permitted to inspect juvenile case files without court authorization under sections 827 and 828, and the specific requirements for accessing juvenile case files provided in section 827.12(a)(1), every person or agency seeking to inspect or obtain juvenile case files must petition the court for authorization using [1] *Petition for Access to Juvenile Case File* (form JV-570). A chief probation officer seeking juvenile court authorization to access and provide data from case files in the possession of the probation department under section 827.12(a)(2) must comply with the requirements [2] **in** (e) of this rule.

(1) The specific files sought must be identified based on knowledge, information, and belief that such files exist and are relevant to the purpose for which they are being sought.

(2) Petitioner must describe in detail the reasons the files are being sought and their relevancy to the proceeding or purpose for which petitioner wishes to inspect or obtain the files.

(Subd (b) amended effective September 1, 2020; adopted as subd (c); previously amended effective July 1, 1997, January 1, 2007, September 1, 2018, and January 1, 2019; previously repealed, amended and relettered effective January 1, 2018.)

Rule 5.552(b).   2020 Deletes. [1] *Request for Disclosure of Juvenile Case File* **[2]** of subdivision

(c) Notice of petition for access

(1) At least 10 days before the petition is submitted to the court, the petitioner must personally or by first-class mail serve [1] *Petition for Access to Juvenile Case File* (form JV-570), [2] *Notice of Petition for Access to Juvenile Case File* (form JV-571), and a blank copy of *Objection to Release of Juvenile Case File* (form JV-572) on the following:

(A) The county counsel, city attorney, or any other attorney representing the petitioning agency in a dependency action if the child's petition was filed under section 300;

(B) The district attorney if the child's petition was filed under section 601 or 602;

(C) The child if the child is 10 years of age or older;

(D) The attorney of record for the child who remains a ward or dependent of the court;

(E) The parents of the child if:

(i) The child is under 18 years of age; or

(ii) The child's petition was filed under section 300;

(F) The guardians of the child if:

(i) The child is under 18 years of age; or

(ii) The child's petition was filed under section 300;

(G) The probation department or child welfare agency, or both, if applicable;

(H) The Indian child's tribe; and

(I) The child's CASA volunteer.

(2) The petitioner must complete [3] *Proof of Service—Petition for Access to Juvenile Case File* (form JV-569) and file it with the court.

(3) If the petitioner **or the petitioner's counsel** does not know **or cannot reasonably determine** the identity or address of any of the parties in (c)(1) above, the clerk must:

(A) Serve personally or by first-class mail to the last known address a copy of [4] *Petition for Access to Juvenile Case File* (form JV-570), [5] *Notice of Petition for Access to Juvenile Case File* (form JV-571), and a blank copy of *Objection to Release of Juvenile Case File* (form JV-572); and

(B) Complete [6] *Proof of Service—Petition for Access to Juvenile Case File* (form JV-569) and file it with the court.

(4) For good cause, the court may, on the motion of the person seeking the order or on its own motion, shorten the time for service of the petition for [7] **access**.

(Subd (c) amended effective September 1, 2020; adopted as subd (d); previously amended effective January 1, 2007, and January 1, 2009; previously amended and relettered effective January 1, 2018.)

Rule 5.552(c).   2020 Deletes. [1] *Request for Disclosure of Juvenile Case File* **[2]** *Notice of Request for Disclosure of Juvenile Case File* **[3]** *Proof of Service—Request for Disclosure of Juvenile Case File* **[4]** *Request for Disclosure of Juvenile Case File* **[5]** *Notice of Request for Disclosure of Juvenile Case File* **[6]** *Proof of Service—Request for Disclosure* **[7]** disclosure

(d) Procedure

(1) The court must review the petition and, if petitioner does not show good cause, deny it summarily.

(2) If petitioner shows good cause, the court may set a hearing. The clerk must notice the hearing to the persons and entities listed in (c)(1) above.

(3) Whether or not the court holds a hearing, if the court determines that there may be information or documents in the records sought to which the petitioner may be entitled, the juvenile court judicial officer must conduct an in camera review of the juvenile case file and any objections and assume that all legal claims of privilege are asserted.

(4) In determining whether to authorize inspection or release of juvenile case files, in whole or in part, the court must balance the interests of the child and other parties to the juvenile court proceedings, the interests of the petitioner, and the interests of the public.

(5) If the court grants the petition, the court must find that the need for [1] **access** outweighs the policy considerations favoring confidentiality of juvenile case files. The confidentiality of juvenile case files is intended to protect the privacy rights of the child.

(6) The court may permit [2] **access to** juvenile case files only insofar as is necessary, and only if petitioner shows by a preponderance of the evidence that the records requested are necessary and have substantial relevance to the legitimate need of the petitioner.

(7) If, after [3] **in camera** review and review of any objections, the court determines that all or a portion of the juvenile case file may be [4] **accessed**, the court must make appropriate orders, specifying the information [5] **that may be accessed** and the procedure for providing access to it.

(8) The court may issue protective orders to accompany authorized disclosure, discovery, or access.

(Subd (d) amended effective September 1, 2020; adopted as subd (e); previously amended effective January 1, 2007, and January 1, 2009; previously amended and relettered effective January 1, 2018.)

Rule 5.552(d). 2020 Deletes. [1] discovery [2] disclosure of [3] in-camera [4] disclosed [5] to be disclosed

(e) Release of case file information for research (§ 872.12(a)(2))

The court may authorize a chief probation officer to access and provide data contained in juvenile delinquency case files and related juvenile records in the possession of the probation department for the purpose of data sharing or conducting or facilitating research on juvenile justice populations, practices, policies, or trends if the court finds the following:

(1) The research, evaluation, or study includes a sound method for the appropriate protection of the confidentiality of an individual whose juvenile delinquency case file is accessed for this purpose. In considering whether a method is sound, the court must have information on:

(A) The names and qualifications of any nonprobation personnel who will have access to personally identifying information as defined in Civil Code section 1798.79.8(b);

(B) Procedures to mask personally identifying information that is shared electronically; and

(C) Data security protocols to ensure that access to the information is limited to those people authorized by the court.

(2) No further release, dissemination, or publication of personally identifying information by the probation department or a program evaluator, researcher, or research organization that is retained by the probation department will take place for research or evaluation purposes.

(3) The disclosure requirements of section 10850 are met if any dependency information in a delinquency file may be disclosed.

(4) A date for destruction of records containing personally identifying information in the possession of nonprobation department personnel has been set to prevent inappropriate disclosure of the records.

If the information is being released for human subject research as defined in 45 Code of Federal Regulations part 46, the probation department must provide notice to the office of the public defender 30 days before the court authorizes the release of the information so that the office has an opportunity to file an objection to the release with the court. If such an objection is filed within the 30 day period the court must set a hearing on the objection within 30 days of the filing of the objection to consider the objection and make a determination on whether and how release of information should be accomplished. Upon receiving authorization, but prior to the release of information, the probation department must enter into a formal agreement with the entity or entities conducting the research that specifies what may and may not be done with the information disclosed.

(Subd (e) adopted effective September 1, 2018.)

(f) Reports of law enforcement agencies (§ 828)

Except as authorized under section 828, all others seeking to inspect or obtain information gathered and retained by a law enforcement agency regarding the taking of a child into custody must petition the juvenile court for authorization using *Petition to Obtain Report of Law Enforcement Agency* (form JV-575).

Subd (f) relettered effective September 1, 2018; adopted as subd (f) effective January 1, 1994; previously relettered as subd (g) effective January 1, 2001, and as subd (f) effective January 1, 2009; previously amended effective January 1, 2007; previously amended and relettered as subd (e) effective January 1, 2018.)

(g) Other applicable statutes

Under no circumstances must this rule or any section of it be interpreted to permit access to or release of records protected under any other federal or state law, including Penal Code section 11165 et seq., except as provided in those statutes, or to limit access to or release of records permitted under any other federal or state statute.

(Subd (g) relettered effective September 1, 2018; adopted as subd (f); previously amended and relettered as subd (h) effective July 1, 1995; previously relettered as subd (g) effective January 1, 1994, as subd (i) effective January 1, 2001, and as subd (h) effective January 1, 2009; previously amended effective January 1, 2007; previously amended and relettered as subd (f) effective January 1, 2018.)

Rule 5.552 amended effective September 1, 2020; adopted as rule 1423 effective July 1, 1992; previously amended effective January 1, 1994, July 1, 1995, July 1, 1997, January 1, 2001, January 1, 2004, January 1, 2009, January 1, 2018, September 1, 2018, and January 1, 2019; previously amended and renumbered effective January 1, 2007.

Rule 5.553. Juvenile case file of a deceased child

When the juvenile case file of a deceased child is sought, the court must proceed as follows:

(1) Under section 827(a)(2) if the request is made by a member of the public; or

(2) Under section 16502.5 if the request is made by a county board of supervisors.

Rule 5.553 adopted effective January 1, 2009.

Rule 5.555. Hearing to consider termination of juvenile court jurisdiction over a nonminor—dependents or wards of the juvenile court in a foster care placement and nonminor dependents (§§ 224.1(b), 303, 366.31, 391, 451, 452, 607.2, 607.3, 16501.1(g)(16))

(a) Applicability

(1) This rule applies to any hearing during which the termination of the juvenile court's jurisdiction over the following nonminors will be considered:

(A) A nonminor dependent as defined in section 11400(v);

(B) A ward or dependent of the juvenile court who is 18 years of age or older and subject to an order for a foster care placement; or

(C) A ward who was subject to an order for foster care placement at the time he or she attained 18 years of age, or a dependent of the juvenile court who is 18 years of age or older and is living in the home of the parent or former legal guardian.

(2) Nothing in the Welfare and Institutions Code or the California Rules of Court restricts the ability of the juvenile court to maintain dependency jurisdiction or delinquency jurisdiction over a person 18 years of age or older, who does not meet the eligibility requirements for status as a nonminor dependent and to proceed as to that person under the relevant sections of the Welfare and Institutions Code and California Rules of Court.

(Subd (a) amended effective January 1, 2014; adopted effective January 1, 2012; previously amended effective July 1, 2012.)

(b) Setting a hearing

(1) A court hearing must be placed on the appearance calendar and completed before juvenile court jurisdiction is terminated.

(2) The hearing under this rule may be held during any regularly scheduled review hearing or a hearing on a petition filed under section 388 or section 778.

(3) Notice of the hearing must be given as required by section 295.

(4) Notice of the hearing to the parent of a nonminor dependent as defined in section 11400(v) is not required, unless the parent is receiving court-ordered family reunification services or the nonminor is living in the home of the parent or former legal guardian.

(5) If juvenile court jurisdiction was resumed after having previously been terminated, a hearing under this rule must be held if the nonminor dependent wants juvenile court jurisdiction terminated again. The social worker or probation officer is not required to file the 90-day Transition Plan, and the court need not make the findings described in (d)(1)(L)(iii) or (d)(2)(E)(vi).

(6) The hearing must be continued for no more than five court days for the submission of additional information as ordered by the court if the court determines that the report, the Transitional Independent Living Plan, the Transitional Independent Living Case Plan, if required, or the 90-day Transition Plan submitted by the social worker or probation officer does not provide the information required by (c) and the court is unable to make the findings and orders required by (d).

(Subd (b) amended effective January 1, 2017; adopted effective January 1, 2012, previously amended effective July 1, 2012, and January 1, 2014.)

(c) Reports

(1) The report prepared by the social worker or probation officer for a hearing under this rule must, in addition to any other elements required by law, include:

(A) Whether remaining under juvenile court jurisdiction is in the nonminor's best interests and the facts supporting the conclusion reached;

(B) The specific criteria in section 11403(b) met by the nonminor that make him or her eligible to remain under juvenile court jurisdiction as a nonminor dependent as defined in section 11400(v);

(C) For a nonminor to whom the Indian Child Welfare Act applies, when and how the nonminor was provided with information about the right to continue to be considered an Indian child for the purposes of the ongoing application of the Indian Child Welfare Act to him or her as a nonminor;

(D) Whether the nonminor has applied for title XVI Supplemental Security Income benefits and, if so, the status of that application, and whether remaining under juvenile court jurisdiction until a final decision has been issued is in the nonminor's best interests;

(E) Whether the nonminor has applied for Special Immigrant Juvenile status or other immigration relief and, if so, the status of that application, and whether an active juvenile court case is required for that application;

(F) When and how the nonminor was provided with information about the potential benefits of remaining under juvenile court jurisdiction as a nonminor dependent, and the social worker's or probation officer's assessment of the nonminor's understanding of those benefits;

(G) When and how the nonminor was informed that if juvenile court jurisdiction is terminated, the court maintains general jurisdiction over him or her for the purpose of resuming jurisdiction and he or she has the right to file a request to return to foster care and have the juvenile court resume jurisdiction over him or her as a nonminor dependent until he or she has attained the age of 21 years;

(H) When and how the nonminor was informed that if juvenile court dependency jurisdiction or transition jurisdiction is continued over him or her, he or she has the right to have that jurisdiction terminated;

(I) If the social worker or probation officer has reason to believe that the nonminor will not appear at the hearing, documentation of the basis for that belief, including:

(i) Documentation of the nonminor's statement that he or she does not wish to appear in person or by telephone for the hearing; or

(ii) Documentation of reasonable efforts to find the nonminor when his or her location is unknown;

(J) Verification that the nonminor was provided with the information, documents, and services as required under section [1] **391(d)**; and

(K) When and how a nonminor who is under delinquency jurisdiction was provided with the notices and information required under section 607.5.

(2) The social worker or probation officer must file with the report a completed *Termination of Juvenile Court Jurisdiction—Nonminor* (form JV-365).

(3) The social worker or probation officer must also file with the report the nonminor's:

(A) Transitional Independent Living Case Plan when recommending continuation of juvenile court jurisdiction;

(B) Most recent Transitional Independent Living Plan; and

(C) Completed 90-day Transition Plan.

(4) The social worker's or probation officer's report and all documents required by (2)–(3) must be filed with the court at least 10 calendar days before the hearing, and the social worker or probation officer must provide copies of the report and other documents to the nonminor, the nonminor's parent, and all attorneys of record. If the nonminor is under juvenile court jurisdiction as a nonminor dependent, the social worker or probation officer is not required to provide copies of the report and other documents to the nonminor dependent's parent, unless the parent is receiving court-ordered family reunification services.

(Subd (c) amended effective January 1, 2021; adopted effective January 1, 2012; previously amended effective July 1, 2012, January 1, 2014, and January 1, 2017.)

Rule 5.555(c).   2020 Deletes. [1] 391(e)

(d) Findings and orders

The court must, in addition to any other determinations required by law, make the following findings and orders and include them in the written documentation of the hearing:

(1) *Findings*

(A) Whether the nonminor had the opportunity to confer with his or her attorney about the issues currently before the court;

(B) Whether remaining under juvenile court jurisdiction is in the nonminor's best interests and the facts in support of the finding made;

(C) Whether the nonminor meets one or more of the eligibility criteria in section 11403(b) to remain in foster care as a nonminor dependent under juvenile court jurisdiction and, if so, the specific criteria in section 11403(b) met by the nonminor;

(D) For a nonminor to whom the Indian Child Welfare Act applies, whether the nonminor was provided with information about the right to

continue to be considered an Indian child for the purposes of the ongoing application of the Indian Child Welfare Act to him or her;

(E) Whether the nonminor has an application pending for title XVI Supplemental Security Income benefits, and if so, whether it is in the nonminor's best interests to continue juvenile court jurisdiction until a final decision has been issued to ensure that the nonminor receives continued assistance with the application process;

(F) Whether the nonminor has an application pending for Special Immigrant Juvenile status or other immigration relief, and whether an active juvenile court case is required for that application;

(G) Whether the nonminor understands the potential benefits of remaining in foster care under juvenile court jurisdiction;

(H) Whether the nonminor has been informed that if juvenile court jurisdiction is continued, he or she may have the right to have juvenile court jurisdiction terminated and that the court will maintain general jurisdiction over him or her for the purpose of resuming dependency jurisdiction or assuming or resuming transition jurisdiction over him or her as a nonminor dependent;

(I) Whether the nonminor has been informed that if juvenile court jurisdiction is terminated, he or she has the right to file a request to return to foster care and have the juvenile court resume jurisdiction over him or her as a nonminor dependent until he or she has attained the age of 21 years;

(J) Whether the nonminor was provided with the information, documents, and services as required under section [1] **391(d)** and, if not, whether juvenile court jurisdiction should be continued to ensure that all information, documents, and services are provided;

(K) Whether a nonminor who is under delinquency jurisdiction was provided with the notices and information required under section 607.5; and

(L) Whether the nonminor's:

(i) Transitional Independent Living Case Plan, if required, includes a plan for a placement the nonminor believes is consistent with his or her need to gain independence, reflects the agreements made between the nonminor and social worker or probation officer to obtain independent living skills, and sets out the benchmarks that indicate how both will know when independence can be achieved;

(ii) Transitional Independent Living Plan identifies the nonminor's level of functioning, emancipation goals, and specific skills needed to prepare for independence and successful adulthood on leaving foster care; and

(iii) 90-day Transition Plan is a concrete individualized plan that specifically covers the following areas: housing, health insurance, education, local opportunities for mentors and continuing support services, workforce supports and employment services, and information that explains how and why to designate a power of attorney for health care.

(M) For a nonminor who does not appear in person or by telephone for the hearing, whether:

(i) The nonminor expressed a wish not to appear for the hearing; or

(ii) The nonminor's location remains unknown and, if so, whether reasonable efforts were made to find the nonminor.

(N) For a nonminor who has attained 21 years of age the court is only required to find that:

(i) Notice was given as required by law.

(ii) The nonminor was provided with the information, documents, and services required under section 391(e), and a completed *Termination of Juvenile Court Jurisdiction—Nonminor* (form JV-365) was filed with the court.

(iii) The 90-day Transition Plan is a concrete, individualized plan that specifically covers the following areas: housing, health insurance, education, local opportunities for mentoring and continuing support services, workforce supports and employment services, and information that explains how and why to designate a power of attorney for health care.

(iv) The nonminor has attained 21 years of age and is no longer subject to the jurisdiction of the court under section 303.

(2) *Orders*

(A) For a nonminor who meets one or more of the eligibility criteria in section 11403(b) to remain in placement under dependency jurisdiction as a nonminor dependent or under transition jurisdiction as a nonminor dependent, the court must order the continuation of juvenile court jurisdiction unless the court finds that:

(i) The nonminor does not wish to remain under juvenile court jurisdiction as a nonminor dependent;

(ii) The nonminor is not participating in a reasonable and appropriate Transitional Independent Living Case Plan; or

(iii) Reasonable efforts were made to locate the nonminor whose current location is unknown.

(B) When juvenile court jurisdiction is continued for the nonminor to remain in placement as a nonminor dependent:

(i) Order a permanent plan consistent with the nonminor's Transitional Independent Living Plan or Transitional Independent Living Case Plan;

(ii) Continue the nonminor's status as an Indian child for the purposes of the ongoing application of the Indian Child Welfare Act unless he or she has elected not to have his or her status as an Indian child continued; and

(iii) Set a status review hearing under rule 5.903 within six months of the date of his or her most recent status review hearing.

(C) For a nonminor who does not meet and does not intend to meet the eligibility requirements for nonminor dependent status but who is otherwise eligible to and will remain under juvenile court jurisdiction in a foster care placement, the court must set an appropriate statutory review hearing within six months of the date of the nonminor's most recent status review hearing.

(D) For a nonminor whose current location is unknown, the court may enter an order for termination of juvenile court jurisdiction only after finding that reasonable efforts were made to locate the nonminor;

(E) For a nonminor who does not meet one or more of the eligibility criteria of section 11403(b) and is not otherwise eligible to remain under juvenile court jurisdiction or, alternatively, who meets one or more of the eligibility criteria of section 11403(b) but either does not wish to remain under the jurisdiction of the juvenile court as a nonminor dependent or is not participating in a reasonable and appropriate Transitional Independent Living Case Plan, the court may order the termination of juvenile court jurisdiction only after entering the following findings:

(i) The nonminor was provided with the information, documents, and services as required under section [2] **391(d)**;

(ii) The nonminor was informed of the options available to him or her to assist with the transition from foster care to independence;

(iii) The nonminor was informed that if juvenile court jurisdiction is terminated, he or she has the right to file a request to return to foster care and have the juvenile court resume jurisdiction over him or her as a nonminor dependent until he or she has reached 21 years of age;

(iv) The nonminor was provided with a copy of *How to Return to Juvenile Court Jurisdiction and Foster Care* (form JV-464-INFO), *Request to Return to Juvenile Court Jurisdiction and Foster Care* (form JV-466), *Confidential Information—Request to Return to Juvenile Court Jurisdiction and Foster Care* (form JV-468), and an endorsed filed copy of the *Termination of Juvenile Court Jurisdiction—Nonminor* (form JV-365);

(v) The nonminor had an opportunity to confer with his or her attorney regarding the issues currently before the court;

(vi) The nonminor's 90-day Transition Plan includes specific options regarding housing, health insurance, education, local opportunities for mentors and continuing support services, workforce supports and employment services, and information that explains how and why to designate a power of attorney for health care.

(F) For a nonminor who has attained 21 years of age and is no longer subject to the jurisdiction of the juvenile court under section 303, the court must enter an order that juvenile court jurisdiction is dismissed and that the attorney for the nonminor dependent is relieved 60 days from the date of the order.

(Subd (d) amended effective January 1, 2021; adopted effective January 1, 2012; previously amended effective July 1, 2012, July 1, 2013, January 1, 2014, January 1, 2016, and January 1, 2017.)

Rule 5.555(d). 2020 Deletes. [1] 391(e) **[2]** 391(e)

Rule 5.555 amended effective January 1, 2021; adopted effective January 1, 2012; previously amended effective July 1, 2012, July 1, 2013, January 1, 2014, January 1, 2016, and January 1, 2017.

Chapter 4
Subsequent Petitions and Modifications

Rule 5.560. General provisions

Rule 5.565. Hearing on subsequent and supplemental petitions (§§ 342, 364, 386, 387)

Rule 5.570. Request to change court order (petition for modification)

Rule 5.575. Joinder of Agencies

Rule 5.580. Hearing on violation of probation (§ 777)

Rule 5.560.   General provisions

(a) General authority of the court (§ 385)

Subject to the procedural requirements prescribed by this chapter, an order made by the court may at any time be changed, modified, or set aside.

(Subd (a) amended effective January 1, 2001.)

(b) Subsequent petitions (§§ 297, 342, 360(b), 364)

All procedures and hearings required for an original petition are required for a subsequent petition. Petitioner must file a subsequent petition if:

(1) A child has previously been found to be a person described by section 300 and the petitioner alleges new facts or circumstances, other than those sustained in the original petition, sufficient to again describe the child as a person under section 300 based on these new facts or circumstances;

(2) At or after the disposition hearing the court has ordered that a parent or guardian retain custody of the dependent child and the petitioner receives information providing reasonable cause to believe the child is now, or once again, described by section 300(a), (d), or (e); or

(3) The family is unwilling or unable to cooperate with services previously ordered under section 301.

(Subd (b) amended effective July 1, 2007; previously amended effective January 1, 2001, January 1, 2006, and January 1, 2007.)

(c) Supplemental petition (§§ 297, 387)

A supplemental petition must be used if petitioner concludes that a previous disposition has not been effective in the protection of a child declared a dependent under section 300 and seeks a more restrictive level of physical custody. For purposes of this chapter, a more restrictive level of custody, in ascending order, is

(1) Placement in the home of the person entitled to legal custody;

(2) Placement in the home of a noncustodial parent;

(3) Placement in the home of a relative or friend;

(4) Placement in a foster home; or

(5) Commitment to a private institution.

(Subd (c) amended effective January 1, 2007; previously amended effective January 1, 2001, and January 1, 2006.)

(d) Petition for modification hearing (§§ 297, 388, 778)

A petition for modification hearing must be used if there is a change of circumstances or new evidence that may require the court to:

(1) Change, modify, or set aside an order previously made; or

(2) Terminate the jurisdiction of the court over the child.

(Subd (d) amended effective January 1, 2007; adopted as subd (e) effective January 1, 1991; previously amended and relettered effective January 1, 2001; previously amended effective January 1, 2006.)

(e) Filing of petition (§§ 297, 388, 778)

A petition for modification hearing may be filed by:

(1) The probation officer, the parent, the guardian, the child, the attorney for the child, or any other person having an interest in a child who is a ward if the requested modification is not for a more restrictive level of custody;

(2) The social worker, regarding a child who is a dependent, if the requested modification is not for a more restrictive level of custody; or

(3) The parent, the guardian, the child, the attorney for the child, or any other person having an interest in a child who is a dependent.

(Subd (e) amended effective January 1, 2007; adopted as subd (f) effective January 1, 1991; previously amended and relettered effective January 1, 2001; previously amended effective January 1, 2006.)

(f) Clerical errors

Clerical errors in judgments, orders, or other parts of the record may be corrected by the court at any time on the court's own motion or on motion of any party and may be entered nunc pro tunc.

(Subd (f) relettered effective January 1, 2001; adopted as subd (g) effective January 1, 1991.)

Rule 5.560 amended effective July 1, 2007; adopted as rule 1430 effective January 1, 1991; previously amended and renumbered effective January 1, 2007; previously amended effective January 1, 2001, and January 1, 2006.

Rule 5.565.   Hearing on subsequent and supplemental petitions (§§ 342, 364, 386, 387)

(a) Contents of subsequent and supplemental petitions (§§ 342, 364, 387)

A subsequent petition and a supplemental petition must be verified and, to the extent known to the petitioner, contain the information required in an original petition as described in rule 5.524. A supplemental petition must also contain a concise statement of facts sufficient to support the conclusion that the previous disposition has not been effective in the protection of the child or, in the case of a dependent child placed with a relative, that the placement is not appropriate in view of the criteria in section 361.3.

(Subd (a) amended effective January 1, 2007; repealed and adopted effective January 1, 1990; previously amended effective January 1, 1992, January 1, 1999, January 1, 2001, and January 1, 2006.)

(b) Setting the hearing (§§ 334, 342, 364, 386, 387)

When a subsequent or supplemental petition is filed, the clerk must immediately set it for hearing within 30 days of the filing date. The hearing must begin within the time limits prescribed for jurisdiction hearings on original petitions under rule 5.670.

(Subd (b) amended effective January 1, 2007; adopted as subd (c) effective January 1, 1990; previously amended and relettered effective January 1, 2001; previously amended effective January 1, 1992, July 1, 1995, and January 1, 2006.)

(c) Notice of hearing (§§ 292, 297)

(1) For petitions filed under section 342 or section 387, notice must be provided in accordance with section 297.

(2) For petitions filed under section 364, notice must be provided in accordance with section 292.

(Subd (c) amended effective January 1, 2019; adopted effective January 1, 2006.)

(d) Initial hearing (§ 387)

Chapter 12, article 1 of these rules applies to the case of a child who is the subject of a supplemental or subsequent petition.

(Subd (d) amended effective July 1, 2010; adopted as subd (d) effective January 1, 1990; previously amended and relettered as subd (c) effective January 1, 2001; previously amended and relettered effective January 1, 2006; previously amended effective January 1, 2007.)

(e) Requirement for bifurcated hearing

The hearing on a subsequent or supplemental petition must be conducted as follows:

(1) The procedures relating to jurisdiction hearings prescribed in chapter 12, article 2 apply to the determination of the allegations of a subsequent or supplemental petition. At the conclusion of the hearing on a subsequent petition the court must make a finding that the allegations of the petition are or are not true. At the conclusion of the hearing on a supplemental petition the court must make findings that:

(A) The factual allegations are or are not true; and

(B) The allegation that the previous disposition has not been effective is or is not true.

(2) The procedures relating to disposition hearings prescribed in chapter 12, article 3 apply to the determination of disposition on a subsequent or supplemental petition. If the court finds under a subsequent petition that the child is described by section 300(a), (d), or (e), the court must remove the child from the physical custody of the parent or guardian, if removal was not ordered under the previous disposition.

(Subd (e) amended effective July 1, 2010; adopted as subd (e) effective January 1, 1990; previously amended and relettered as subd (d) effective January 1, 2001; previously relettered effective January 1, 2006; previously amended effective January 1, 2007.)

(f) Supplemental petition (§ 387)—permanency planning

If a dependent child was returned to the custody of a parent or guardian at the 12-month review or the 18-month review or at an interim review between 12 and 18 months and a 387 petition is sustained and the child removed once again, the court must set a hearing under section 366.26 unless the court finds there is a substantial probability of return within the next 6 months or, if more than 12 months had expired at the time of the prior return, within whatever time remains before the expiration of the maximum 18-month period.

(Subd (f) amended effective January 1, 2007; adopted as subd (f) effective January 1, 1990; relettered as subd (e) effective January 1, 2001; previously amended and relettered effective January 1, 2006.)

Rule 5.565 amended effective January 1, 2019; adopted as rule 1431 effective January 1, 1990; previously amended effective January 1, 1992, July 1, 1995, January 1, 1999, July 1, 1999, January 1, 2001, January 1, 2006, and July 1, 2010; previously amended and renumbered effective January 1, 2007.

Rule 5.570. Request to change court order (petition for modification)

(a) Contents of petition (§§ 388, 778)

A petition for modification must be liberally construed in favor of its sufficiency. The petition must be verified and, to the extent known to the petitioner, must contain the following:

(1) The name of the court to which the petition is addressed;

(2) The title and action number of the original proceeding;

(3) The name and age of the child, nonminor, or nonminor dependent;

(4) The address of the child, nonminor, or nonminor dependent, unless confidential under (c);

(5) The name and address of the parent or guardian of the child or nonminor;

(6) The date and general nature of the order sought to be modified;

(7) A concise statement of any change of circumstance or new evidence that requires changing the order or, for requests under section 388(c)(1)(B), a concise statement of the relevant action or inaction of the parent or guardian;

(8) A concise statement of the proposed change of the order;

(9) A statement of the petitioner's relationship or interest in the child, nonminor, or nonminor dependent, if the petition is made by a person other than the child, nonminor, or nonminor dependent; and

(10) A statement whether or not all parties agree to the proposed change.

(Subd (a) amended effective January 1, 2014; previously amended effective July 1, 2002, January 1, 2007, January 1, 2009, and January 1, 2010.)

(b) 388 petition

A petition under Welfare and Institutions Code section 388 must be made on form *Request to Change Court Order* (form JV-180).

(Subd (b) adopted effective January 1, 2007.)

(c) Confidentiality

The addresses and telephone numbers of the person requesting to change the court order; the child, nonminor, or nonminor dependent; and the caregiver may be kept confidential by filing *Confidential Information (Request to Change Court Order)* (form JV-182) with form JV-180. Form JV-182 must be kept in the court file under seal, and only the court, the agency, and the attorney for the child, nonminor, or nonminor dependent may have access to this information.

(Subd (c) amended effective January 1, 2014; adopted effective January 1, 2007.)

(d) Denial of hearing

The court may deny the petition ex parte if:

(1) The petition filed under section 388(a) or section 778(a) fails to state a change of circumstance or new evidence that may require a change of order or termination of jurisdiction or fails to show that the requested modification would promote the best interest of the child, nonminor, or nonminor dependent.

(2) The petition filed under section 388(b) fails to demonstrate that the requested modification would promote the best interest of the dependent child;

(3) The petition filed under section 388(b) or 778(b) requests visits with a nondependent child and demonstrates that sibling visitation is contrary to the safety and well-being of any of the siblings;

(4) The petition filed under section 388(b) or 778(b) requests visits with a nondependent sibling who remains in the custody of a mutual parent who is not subject to the court's jurisdiction; or

(5) The petition filed under section 388(c) fails to state facts showing that the parent has failed to visit the child or that the parent has failed to participate regularly and make substantive progress in a court-ordered treatment plan or fails to show that the requested termination of services would promote the best interest of the child.

(Subd (d) amended effective January 1, 2016; adopted as subd (b); previously amended and relettered as subd (d) effective January 1, 2007; previously amended effective January 1, 2010, and January 1, 2014.)

(e) Grounds for grant of petition (§§ 388, 778)

(1) If the petition filed under section 388(a) or section 778(a) states a change of circumstance or new evidence and it appears that the best interest of the child, nonminor, or nonminor dependent may be promoted by the proposed change of order or termination of jurisdiction, the court may grant the petition after following the procedures in (f), (g), and (h), or (i).

(2) If the petition is filed under section 388(b) and it appears that the best interest of the child, nonminor, or nonminor dependent may be promoted by the proposed recognition of a sibling relationship or other requested orders, the court may grant the petition after following the procedures in (f), (g), and (h).

(3) If the petition is filed under section 388(b), the request is for visitation with a sibling who is not a dependent of the court and who is in the custody of a parent subject to the court's jurisdiction, and that sibling

visitation is not contrary to the safety and well-being of any of the siblings, the court may grant the request after following the procedures in (f), (g), and (h).

(4) If the petition is filed under section 778(b), the request is for visitation with a sibling who is not a dependent of the court and who is in the custody of a parent subject to the court's jurisdiction, and that sibling visitation is not contrary to the safety and well being of the ward or any of the siblings, the court may grant the request after following the procedures in (f), (g), and (i).

(5) For a petition filed under section 388(c)(1)(A), the court may terminate reunification services during the time periods described in section 388(c)(1) only if the court finds by a preponderance of evidence that reasonable services have been offered or provided, and, by clear and convincing evidence, that the change of circumstance or new evidence described in the petition satisfies a condition in section 361.5(b) or (e). **In the case of an Indian child, the court may terminate reunification services only if the court finds by clear and convincing evidence that active efforts have been made to provide remedial services and rehabilitative programs designed to prevent the breakup of the Indian family within the meaning of sections 224.1(f) and 361.7 and that these efforts have proved unsuccessful.** The court may grant the petition after following the procedures in (f), (g), and (h).

(6) For a petition filed under section 388(c)(1)(B), the court may terminate reunification services during the time periods described in section 388(c)(1) only if the court finds by a preponderance of evidence that reasonable services have been offered or provided, and, by clear and convincing evidence, that action or inaction by the parent or guardian creates a substantial likelihood that reunification will not occur. Such action or inaction includes, but is not limited to, failure to visit the child or failure to participate regularly and make substantive progress in a court-ordered treatment program. In determining whether the parent or guardian has failed to visit the child or to participate regularly or make progress in a court-ordered treatment plan, the court must consider factors including, but not limited to, the parent or guardian's incarceration, institutionalization, or participation in a residential substance abuse treatment program. **In the case of an Indian child, the court may terminate reunification services only if the court finds by clear and convincing evidence that active efforts have been made to provide remedial services and rehabilitative programs designed to prevent the breakup of the Indian family within the meaning of sections 224.1(f) and 361.7 and that these efforts have proved unsuccessful.** The court may grant the petition after following the procedures in (f), (g), and (h).

(7) If the petition filed under section 388(a) is filed before an order terminating parental rights and is seeking to modify an order that reunification services need not be provided under section 361.5(b)(4), (5), or (6) or to modify any orders related to custody or visitation of the child for whom reunification services were not ordered under section 361.5(b)(4), (5), or (6), the court may modify the orders only if the court finds by clear and convincing evidence that the proposed change is in the best interests of the child. The court may grant the petition after following the procedures in (f), (g), and (h).

(Subd (e) amended effective January 1, 2020; adopted as subd (c); previously amended and relettered as subd (e) effective January 1, 2007; previously amended effective January 1, 2010, January 1, 2014, and January 1, 2016.)

(f) Hearing on petition

If all parties stipulate to the requested modification, the court may order modification without a hearing. If there is no such stipulation and the petition has not been denied ex parte under section (d), the court must either:

(1) order that a hearing on the petition be held within 30 calendar days after the petition is filed; or

(2) order a hearing for the parties to argue whether an evidentiary hearing on the petition should be granted or denied. If the court then grants an evidentiary hearing on the petition, that hearing must be held within 30 calendar days after the petition is filed.

(Subd (f) amended effective January 1, 2016; adopted as subd (d); previously relettered as subd (f) effective January 1, 2007; previously amended effective July 1, 2002, and January 1, 2010.)

(g) Notice of petition and hearing (§§ 388, 778)

(1) If a petition is filed under section 388 or section 778 to terminate juvenile court jurisdiction over a nonminor, notice of the hearing must be given as required by section 295.

(2) For hearings on all other petitions filed under section 388 or section 778, notice of the hearing must be provided as required under section 297, or sections 776 and 779, except that notice to parents or former guardians of a nonminor must be provided only if the nonminor requests, in writing on the face of the petition, that such notice be provided, or if the parent or legal guardian is receiving court-ordered family reunification services.

(Subd (g) amended effective January 1, 2019; repealed and adopted as subd (e); previously amended effective January 1, 1992, July 1, 1995, July 1, 2000, July 1, 2002, and January 1, 2014; previously amended and relettered as subd (g) effective January 1, 2007.)

(h) Conduct of hearing (§ 388)

(1) The petitioner requesting the modification under section 388 has the burden of proof.

(A) If the request is for the removal of the child from the child's home, the petitioner must show by clear and convincing evidence that the grounds for removal in section 361(c) exist.

(B) If the request is for termination of court-ordered reunification services, the petitioner must show by clear and convincing evidence that one of the conditions in section 388(c)(1)(A) or (B) exists and must show by a preponderance of the evidence that reasonable services have been offered or provided. **In the case of an Indian child, the court may terminate reunification services only if the court finds by clear and convincing evidence that active efforts have been made to provide remedial services and rehabilitative programs designed to prevent the breakup of the Indian family within the meaning of sections 224.1(f) and 361.7 and that these efforts have proved unsuccessful.**

(C) If the request is to modify an order that reunification services were not ordered under section 361.5(b)(4), (5), or (6) or to modify any orders related to custody or visitation of the child for whom reunification services were not ordered under section 361.5(b)(4), (5), or (6), the petitioner must show by clear and convincing evidence that the proposed change is in the best interests of the child.

(D) All other requests require a preponderance of the evidence to show that the child's welfare requires such a modification.

(E) If the request is for visitation with a sibling who is not a dependent of the court, the court may grant the request unless the court determines that the sibling remains in the custody of a mutual parent who is not subject to the court's jurisdiction or that sibling visitation is contrary to the safety and well-being of any of the siblings.

(2) The hearing must be conducted as a dispositional hearing under rules 5.690 and 5.695 if:

(A) The request is for termination of court-ordered reunification services; or

(B) There is a due process right to confront and cross-examine witnesses.

Otherwise, proof may be by declaration and other documentary evidence, or by testimony, or both, at the discretion of the court.

(Subd (h) amended effective January 1, 2020; adopted as subd (f); previously amended and relettered as subd (h) effective January 1, 2007; previously amended effective July 1, 2000, July 1, 2002, January 1, 2003, January 1, 2010, January 1, 2014, and January 1, 2016.)

(i) Conduct of hearing (§ 778)

(1) The petitioner requesting the modification under section 778(a) has the burden of proving by a preponderance of the evidence that the ward's welfare requires the modification. Proof may be by declaration and other documentary evidence, or by testimony, or both, at the discretion of the court.

(2) If the request is for sibling visitation under section 778(b), the court may grant the request unless the court determines that the sibling remains in the custody of a mutual parent who is not subject to the court's jurisdiction or that sibling visitation is contrary to the safety and well-being of any of the siblings.

(Subd (i) amended effective January 1, 2016; adopted as subd (g); previously amended effective July 1, 2002; previously amended and relettered as subd (i) effective January 1, 2007.)

(j) Petitions for juvenile court to resume jurisdiction over nonminors (§§ 388(e), 388.1)

A petition filed by or on behalf of a nonminor requesting that the court resume jurisdiction over the nonminor as a nonminor dependent is not subject to this rule. Petitions filed under section 388(e) or section 388.1 are subject to rule 5.906.

(Subd (j) amended effective January 1, 2016; adopted effective January 1, 2014.)

Rule 5.570 amended effective January 1, 2020; adopted as rule 1432 effective January 1, 1991; previously amended and renumbered as rule 5.570 effective January 1, 2007; previously amended effective January 1, 1992, July 1, 1995, July 1, 2000, July 1, 2002, January 1, 2003, January 1, 2009, January 1, 2010, January 1, 2014, January 1, 2016, and January 1, 2019.

Rule 5.575. Joinder of Agencies

(a) Basis for joinder (§§ 362, 365, 727)

The court may, at any time after a petition has been filed, following notice and a hearing, join in the proceedings any agency (as defined in section 362) that the court determines has failed to meet a legal obligation to provide services to a child or a nonminor or nonminor dependent youth for whom a petition has been filed under section 300, 601, or 602. The court may not impose duties on an agency beyond those required by law.

(Subd (a) amended effective January 1, 2014; previously amended effective January 1, 2007.)

(b) Notice and Hearing

On application by a party, counsel, or CASA volunteer, or on the court's own motion, the court may set a hearing and require notice to the agency or provider subject to joinder.

(1) Notice of the hearing must be given to the agency on *Notice of Hearing on Joinder—Juvenile* (form JV-540). The notice must clearly describe the legal obligation at issue, the facts and circumstances alleged to constitute the agency's failure to meet that obligation, and any issues or questions the court expects the agency to address at the hearing.

(2) The hearing must be set to occur within 30 calendar days of the signing of the notice by the court. The hearing will proceed under the provisions of rule 5.570(h) or (i), as appropriate.

(3) The clerk must cause the notice to be served on the agency and all parties, attorneys of record, the CASA volunteer, any other person or entity entitled to notice under section 291 or 658, and, if the hearing might address educational or developmental-services issues, the educational rights holder by first-class mail within 5 court days of the signing of the notice.

(4) Nothing in this rule prohibits agencies from meeting before the hearing to coordinate the delivery of services. The court may request, using section 8 of form JV-540, that agency representatives meet before the hearing and that the agency or agencies submit a written response to the court at least 5 court days before the hearing.

(Subd (b) amended effective January 1, 2014; previously amended effective January 1, 2006, and January 1, 2007.)

Rule 5.575 amended effective January 1, 2014; adopted as rule 1434 effective January 1, 2002; previously amended effective January 1, 2006; amended and renumbered effective January 1, 2007.

Rule 5.580. Hearing on violation of probation (§ 777)

(a) Notice of hearing (§§ 656, 658, 660)

Notice of a hearing to be held under section 777 must be issued and served as provided in sections 658, 660, and 777 and prepared:

(1) By the probation officer if the child has been declared a ward under section 601; or

(2) By the probation officer or the district attorney if the child is a ward or is on probation under section 602, and the alleged violation of probation is not a crime.

(Subd (a) amended effective January 1, 2007; adopted effective January 1, 2001; previously amended effective January 1, 2006.)

(b) Motion to dismiss

If the probation officer files the notice of hearing, before jeopardy attaches the prosecuting attorney may move the court to dismiss the notice and request that the matter be referred to the probation officer for appropriate action under section 777(a)(3).

(Subd (b) adopted effective January 1, 2001.)

(c) Detention hearing

If the child has been brought into custody, the procedures described in rules 5.524 and 5.752 through 5.764 must be followed.

(Subd (c) amended effective January 1, 2007; adopted as subd (d) effective January 1, 2001; amended and relettered effective January 1, 2006.)

(d) Report of probation officer

Before every hearing the probation officer must prepare a report on those matters relevant to a determination of whether the child has violated a condition of probation. The report must be furnished to all parties at least 48 hours, excluding noncourt days, before the beginning of the hearing unless the child is represented by counsel and waives the right to service of the report.

(Subd (d) amended and relettered effective January 1, 2006; adopted as subd (b) effective January 1, 1990; amended and relettered as subd (e) effective January 1, 2001.)

(e) Evidence considered

The court must consider the report prepared by the probation officer and other relevant and material evidence offered by the parties to the proceeding.

(1) The court may admit and consider reliable hearsay evidence as defined by section 777(c).

(2) The probation officer or prosecuting attorney must prove the alleged violation by a preponderance of the evidence.

(Subd (e) amended and relettered effective January 1, 2006; adopted as subd (e) effective January 1, 1990; amended and relettered as subd (f) effective January 1, 2001.)

Rule 5.580 amended and renumbered effective January 1, 2007; adopted as rule 1433 effective January 1, 1990; previously amended effective January 1, 1992, January 1, 2001, and January 1, 2006.

Chapter 5
Appellate Review

Title 5, Family and Juvenile Rules—Division 3, Juvenile Rules—Chapter 5, Appellate Review; adopted effective January 1, 2007; amended effective July 1, 2010.

Rule 5.585. Rules governing appellate review
Rule 5.590. Advisement of right to review in section 300, 601, or 602 cases
Rule 5.595. Stay pending appeal

Rule 5.585. Review by appeal [Renumbered]

Rule 5.585 amended and renumbered to rule 5.590 effective July 1, 2010; adopted as rule 1435 effective January 1, 1990; previously amended effective January 1, 1992, January 1, 1993, January 1, 1994, January 1, 1995, and July 1, 1999; previously amended and renumbered effective January 1, 2007.

Another Rule 5.585 follows.

Rule 5.585. Rules governing appellate review

The rules in title 8, chapter 5 govern appellate review of judgments and orders in cases under Welfare and Institutions Code section 300, 601, or 602.

Rule 5.585 adopted effective July 1, 2010.

Advisory Committee Comment

Rules 8.450 and 8.452 describe how a party, including the petitioner, child, and parent or guardian, must proceed if seeking appellate court review of findings and orders of the juvenile court made at a hearing at which the court orders that a hearing under Welfare and Institutions Code section 366.26 be held.

Rule 5.590. Notification of appeal rights in juvenile cases [Repealed]

Rule 5.590 repealed effective July 1, 2010; adopted as rule 251 effective July 1, 1973; previously amended effective July 1, 1978; previously amended and renumbered effective January 1, 2007.

Another Rule 5.590 follows.

Rule 5.590. Advisement of right to review in section 300, 601, or 602 cases

(a) Advisement of right to appeal

If at a contested hearing on an issue of fact or law the court finds that the child is described by Welfare and Institutions Code section 300, 601, or 602 or sustains a supplemental or subsequent petition, the court after making its disposition order other than orders covered in (b) must advise, orally or in writing, the child, if of sufficient age, and [1] the parent or guardian of:

(1) The right of the child, parent, and guardian to appeal from the court order if there is a right to appeal;

(2) The necessary steps and time for taking an appeal;

(3) The right of an indigent appellant to have counsel appointed by the reviewing court; and

(4) The right of an indigent appellant to be provided with a free copy of the transcript.

If the parent or guardian is not present at the hearing, the advisement must be made by the clerk of the court by first-class mail to the last known address of the party or by electronic service in accordance with section 212.5.

(Subd (a) amended effective January 1, 2020; adopted as subd (d) effective January 1, 1990; previously amended effective January 1, 2007; previously amended and relettered as subd (a) effective July 1, 2010.)

Rule 5.590(a). 2019 Deletes. [1] , if present,

(b) Advisement of requirement for writ petition to preserve appellate rights when court orders hearing under section 366.26

When the court orders a hearing under section 366.26, the court must advise all parties and, if present, the child's parent, guardian, or adult relative, that if the party wishes to preserve any right to review on appeal of the order setting the hearing under section 366.26, the party is required to seek an extraordinary writ by filing a *Notice of Intent to File Writ Petition and Request for Record (California Rules of Court, Rule 8.450)* (form JV-820) or other notice of intent to file a writ petition and request for record and a *Petition for Extraordinary Writ (California Rules of Court, Rules 8.452, 8.456)* (form JV-825) or other petition for extraordinary writ.

(1) The advisement must be given orally to those present when the court orders the hearing under section 366.26.

(2) If a party is not present when the court orders a hearing under section 366.26, within 24 hours of the hearing, the advisement must be made by the clerk of the court by first-class mail to the last known address of the party or by electronic service in accordance with section 212.5. If the notice is for a hearing at which the social worker will recommend the termination of parental rights, the notice may be electronically served in accordance with section 212.5, but only in addition to service of the notice by first-class mail.

(3) The advisement must include the time for filing a notice of intent to file a writ petition.

(4) Copies of *Petition for Extraordinary Writ (California Rules of Court, Rules 8.452, 8.456)* (form JV-825) and *Notice of Intent to File Writ Petition and Request for Record (California Rules of Court, Rule 8.450)* (form JV-820) must be available in the courtroom and must accompany all mailed and electronically served notices informing the parties of their rights.

(Subd (b) amended effective January 1, 2019; adopted as subd (e) effective January 1, 1995; previously amended effective January 1, 2007; previously repealed, amended and relettered effective July 1, 2010.)

(c) Advisement requirements for appeal of order to transfer to tribal court

When the court grants a petition transferring a case to tribal court under Welfare and Institutions Code section 305.5, Family Code section 177(a), or Probate Code section 1459.5(b), and rule 5.483, the court must advise the parties orally and in writing, that an appeal of the order must be filed before the transfer to tribal jurisdiction is finalized, and that failure to request and obtain a stay of the order for transfer will result in a loss of appellate jurisdiction.

(Subd (c) adopted effective January 1, 2016.)

Rule 5.590 amended effective January 1, 2020; adopted as rule 1435 effective January 1, 1990; previously amended effective January 1, 1992, January 1, 1993, January 1, 1994, January 1, 1995, July 1, 1999, January 1, 2016, and January 1, 2019; previously amended and renumbered as rule 5.585 effective January 1, 2007; previously amended and renumbered as rule 5.590 effective July 1, 2010.

Advisory Committee Comment

Subdivision (a). The right to appeal in Welfare and Institutions Code section 601 or 602 (juvenile delinquency) cases is established by Welfare and Institutions Code section 800 and case law (see, for example, *In re Michael S.* (2007) 147 Cal.App.4th 1443, *In re Jeffrey M.* (2006) 141 Cal.App.4th 1017, and *In re Sean R.* (1989) 214 Cal.App.3d 662). The right to appeal in Welfare and Institutions Code section 300 (juvenile dependency) cases is established by Welfare and Institutions Code section 395 and case law (see, for example, *In re Aaron R.* (2005) 130 Cal.App.4th 697, and *In re Merrick V.* (2004) 122 Cal.App.4th 235).

Subdivision (b). Welfare and Institutions Code section 366.26(*l*) establishes important limitations on appeals of judgments, orders, or decrees setting a hearing under section 366.26, including requirements for the filing of a petition for an extraordinary writ and limitations on the issues that can be raised on appeal.

Rule 5.595.   Stay pending appeal

The court must not stay an order or judgment pending an appeal unless suitable provision is made for the maintenance, care, and custody of the child.

Rule 5.595 amended effective July 1, 2010; adopted as rule 1436 effective January 1, 1993; previously amended effective January 1, 1994, January 1, 1995, and January 1, 2006; previously amended and renumbered effective January 1, 2007.

Rule 5.600.   Writ petition after orders setting hearing under section 366.26; appeal [Repealed]

Rule 5.600 repealed effective July 1, 2010; adopted as rule 1436.5 effective January 1, 1995; previously amended effective July 1, 1995, January 1, 1996, July 1, 2006, and January 1, 2009; previously amended and renumbered effective January 1, 2007.

Chapter 6
Emancipation

Rule 5.605.   Emancipation of minors

(a) Petition

A petition for declaration of emancipation of a minor must be submitted on *Petition for Declaration of Emancipation of Minor, Order Prescribing Notice, Declaration of Emancipation, and Order Denying Petition* (form MC-300). Only the minor may petition the court for emancipation, and the petition may be filed in the county in which the minor can provide a verifiable residence address. The petitioner must complete and attach to the petition *Emancipation of Minor—Income and Expense Declaration* (form MC-306).

(Subd (a) amended effective January 1, 2007.)

(b) Dependents and wards of the juvenile court

Petitions to emancipate a child who is a dependent or ward of the juvenile court must be filed and heard in juvenile court.

(Subd (b) amended effective January 1, 2007; previously amended effective January 1, 1995.)

(c) Court

The petition to emancipate a minor other than a dependent or ward of the juvenile court must be filed and will be heard in juvenile court or other superior court department so designated by local rule or by order of the presiding judge.

(Subd (c) amended effective January 1, 2007.)

(d) Filing fee

Unless waived, the petitioner must pay the filing fee as specified. The ability or inability to pay the filing fee is not in and of itself evidence of the financial responsibility of the minor as required for emancipation.

(Subd (d) amended effective January 1, 2007.)

(e) Declaration of emancipation without hearing

If the court finds that all notice and consent requirements have been met or waived, and that emancipation is not contrary to the best interest of the petitioner, the court may grant the petition without a hearing. The presiding judge of the superior court must develop a protocol for the screening, evaluation, or investigation of petitions.

(Subd (e) amended effective January 1, 2007.)

(f) Time limits

The clerk of the court in which the petition is filed must immediately provide or direct the petitioner to provide the petition to the court. Within 30 days from the filing of the petition, the court must (1) grant the petition, (2) deny the petition, or (3) set a hearing on the petition to be conducted within 30 days thereafter. The clerk must immediately provide the petitioner with an endorsed-filed copy of the court's order.

(Subd (f) amended effective January 1, 2007.)

(g) Notice

If the court orders the matter set for hearing, the clerk must notify the district attorney of the time and date of the hearing, which must be within 30 days of the order prescribing notice and setting for hearing. The petitioner is responsible for notifying all other persons to whom the court requires notice.

(Subd (g) amended effective January 1, 2007.)

Rule 5.605 amended and renumbered effective January 1, 2007; adopted as rule 1437 effective July 1, 1994; previously amended effective January 1, 1995.

Chapter 7
Intercounty Transfers; Out-of-County Placements; Interstate Compact on the Placement of Children

Title 5, Family and Juvenile Rules—Division 3, Juvenile Rules—Chapter 7, Intercounty Transfers; Out-of-County Placements; Interstate Compact on the Placement of Children; amended effective January 1, 2020; previously amended effective January 1, 2019.

Rule 5.610. Transfer-out hearing
Rule 5.612. Transfer-in hearing
Rule 5.613. Transfer of nonminor dependents
Rule 5.614. Out-of-county placements
Rule 5.616. Interstate Compact on the Placement of Children

Rule 5.610.   Transfer-out hearing

(a) Determination of residence—special rule on intercounty transfers (§§ 375, 750)

(1) For purposes of rules 5.610, 5.612, and 5.614, the residence of the child is the residence of the person who has the legal right to physical custody of the child according to prior court order, including:

(A) A juvenile court order under section 361.2; and

(B) An order appointing a guardian of the person of the child.

(2) If there is no order determining custody, both parents are deemed to have physical custody.

(3) The juvenile court may make a finding of paternity under rule 5.635. If there is no finding of paternity, the mother is deemed to have physical custody.

(4) For the purposes of transfer of wardship, residence of a ward may be with the person with whom the child resides with approval of the court.

(Subd (a) amended effective January 1, 2019; previously amended effective January 1, 2004, and January 1, 2007.)

(b) Verification of residence

The residence of the person entitled to physical custody may be verified by declaration of a social worker or probation officer in the transferring or receiving county.

(Subd (b) amended effective January 1, 2017; previously amended effective January 1, 2004, and January 1, 2007.)

(c) Transfer to county of child's residence (§§ 375, 750)

(1) After making its jurisdictional finding, the court may order the case transferred to the juvenile court of the child's residence as specified in section 375 or section 750.

(2) If the court decides to transfer a delinquency case, the court must order the transfer before beginning the disposition hearing without adjudging the child to be a ward.

(3) If the court decides to transfer a dependency case, the court may order the transfer before or after the disposition hearing.

(Subd (c) amended effective January 1, 2019; previously amended effective January 1, 2004, and January 1, 2007.)

(d) Transfer on subsequent change in child's residence (§§ 375, 750)

If, after the child has been placed under a program of supervision, the residence is changed to another county, the court may, on an application for modification under rule 5.570, transfer the case to the juvenile court of the other county.

(Subd (d) amended effective January 1, 2007; previously amended effective January 1, 2004.)

(e) Conduct of hearing

(1) The request for transfer must be made on *Motion for Transfer Out* (form JV-548), which must include all required information.

(2) After the court determines the identity and residence of the child's custodian, the court must consider whether transfer of the case would be in the child's best interest. The court may not transfer the case unless it determines that the transfer will protect or further the child's best interest.

(Subd (e) amended effective January 1, 2017; repealed and adopted effective January 1, 1990; previously amended effective January 1, 1993, January 1, 2004, and January 1, 2007.)

(f) Date of transfer-in hearing

(1) If the transfer-out motion is granted, the sending court must set a date certain for the transfer-in hearing in the receiving court: within 5 court days of the transfer-out order if the child is in custody, and within 10 court days of the transfer-out order if the child is out of custody. The sending court must state on the record the date, time, and location of the hearing in the receiving court.

(2) The website for every court must include up-to-date contact information for the court clerks handling dependency and delinquency matters, as well as up-to-date information on when and where transfer-in hearings are held.

(Subd (f) adopted effective January 1, 2017.)

(g) Order of transfer (§§ 377, 752)

The order of transfer must be entered on *Juvenile Court Transfer-Out Orders* (form JV-550), which must include all required information and findings.

(Subd (g) amended and relettered effective January 1, 2017; repealed and adopted as subd (f) effective January 1, 1990; previously amended effective January 1, 1993, January 1, 2004, and January 1, 2007.)

(h) Modification of form JV-550

Juvenile Court Transfer Orders (form JV-550) may be modified as follows:

(1) Notwithstanding the mandatory use of form JV-550, the form may be modified for use by a formalized regional collaboration of courts to facilitate the efficient processing of transfer cases among those courts if the modification has been approved by the Judicial Council of California.

(2) The mandatory form must be used by a regional collaboration when transferring a case to a court outside the collaboration or when accepting a transfer from a court outside the collaboration.

(Subd (h) relettered effective January 1, 2017; adopted as subd (g) effective January 1, 2007; previously amended effective January 1, 2015.)

(i) Transport of child and transmittal of documents (§§ 377, 752)

(1) If the child is ordered transported in custody to the receiving county, the child must be delivered to the receiving county at least two business days before the transfer-in hearing, and the clerk of the court of the transferring county must prepare a certified copy of the complete case file so that it may be transported with the child to the court of the receiving county.

(2) If the child is not ordered transported in custody, the clerk of the transferring court must transmit to the clerk of the court of the receiving county within five court days a certified copy of the complete case file.

(3) The file may be transferred electronically, if possible. A certified copy of the complete case file is deemed an original.

(Subd (i) amended and relettered effective January 1, 2017; repealed and adopted as subd (g) effective, January 1, 1990; previously amended effective January 1, 1992, January 1, 1993, July 1, 1999, and January 1, 2004; previously amended and relettered as subd (h) effective January 1, 2007.)

(j) Appeal of transfer order (§§ 379, 754)

The order of transfer may be appealed by the transferring or receiving county and notice of appeal must be filed in the transferring county, under rule 8.400. Notwithstanding the filing of a notice of appeal, the receiving county must assume jurisdiction of the case on receipt and filing of the order of transfer.

(Subd (j) relettered effective January 1, 2017; repealed and adopted as subd (h) effective January 1, 1990; previously amended effective January 1, 1992, and January 1, 2004; previously amended and relettered as subd (i) effective January 1, 2007.)

Rule 5.610 amended effective January 1, 2019; adopted as rule 1425 effective January 1, 1990; previously amended and renumbered effective January 1, 2007; previously amended effective January 1, 1992, January 1, 1993, July 1, 1999, January 1, 2004, January 1, 2015, and January 1, 2017.

Advisory Committee Comment

Juvenile court judicial officers throughout the state have expressed concern that in determining whether or not to transfer a juvenile court case, the best interest of the subject child is being overlooked or at least outweighed by a desire to shift the financial burdens of case management and foster care. The advisory committee has clarified rule 5.610 in order to stress that in considering an intercounty transfer, as in all matters relating to children within its jurisdiction, the court has a mandate to act in the best interest of the subject children.

Juvenile Court Transfer-Out Orders (form JV-550) was adopted for mandatory use commencing January 1, 1992. Although the finding regarding the best interest of the child was noted on the original form, the language has been emphasized on the amended form.

Rule 5.612. Transfer-in hearing

(a) Procedure on transfer (§§ 378, 753)

On receipt and filing of a certified copy of a transfer order, the receiving court must accept jurisdiction of the case. The receiving court may not reject the case. The clerk of the receiving court must confirm the transfer-in hearing date scheduled by the sending court and ensure that date is on the receiving court's calendar. The receiving court must notify the transferring court on receipt and filing of the certified copies of the transfer order and complete case file.

(Subd (a) amended effective January 1, 2017; repealed and adopted effective January 1, 1990; previously amended effective January 1, 1992, July 1, 1999, January 1, 2004, and January 1, 2007.)

(b) Conduct of hearing

At the transfer-in hearing, the court must:

(1) Advise the child and the parent or guardian of the purpose and scope of the hearing;

(2) Provide for the appointment of counsel if appropriate; and

(3) If the child was transferred to the county in custody, determine whether the child must be further detained under rule 5.667.

(Subd (b) amended effective January 1, 2007; previously amended effective January 1, 2004.)

(c) Subsequent proceedings

The proceedings in the receiving court must commence at the same phase as when the case was transferred. The court may continue the hearing for an investigation and report to a date not to exceed 10 court days if the child is in custody or 15 court days if the child is not detained in custody.

(Subd (c) amended effective January 1, 2004; previously amended effective July 1, 1999.)

(d) Limitation on more restrictive custody (§§ 387, 777)

If a disposition order has already been made in the transferring county, a more restrictive level of physical custody may not be ordered in the receiving county, except after a hearing on a supplemental petition under rule 5.565.

(Subd (d) amended effective January 1, 2007; previously amended effective January 1, 2004.)

(e) Setting six-month review (§ 366)

When an order of transfer is received and filed relating to a child who has been declared a dependent, the court must set a date for a six-month review within six months of the disposition or the most recent review hearing.

(Subd (e) amended effective January 1, 2004.)

(f) Change of circumstances or additional facts (§§ 388, 778)

If the receiving court believes that a change of circumstances or additional facts indicate that the child does not reside in the receiving county, a transfer-out hearing must be held under rules 5.610 and 5.570. The court may direct the department of social services or the probation department to seek a modification of orders under section 388 or 778 and under rule 5.570.

(Subd (f) amended effective January 1, 2007; adopted effective January 1, 1992; previously amended effective July 1, 1999, and January 1, 2004.)

Rule 5.612 amended effective January 1, 2017; adopted as rule 1426 effective January 1, 1990; previously amended effective January 1, 1992, July 1, 1999, and January 1, 2004; previously amended and renumbered as rule 5.612 effective January 1, 2007.

Rule 5.613.   Transfer of nonminor dependents

(a) Purpose

This rule applies to requests to transfer the county of jurisdiction of a nonminor dependent as allowed by Welfare and Institutions Code section 375. This rule sets forth the procedures that a court is to follow when it seeks to order a transfer of a nonminor dependent and those to be followed by the court receiving the transfer. All other intercounty transfers of juveniles are subject to rules 5.610 and 5.612.

(Subd (a) adopted effective January 1, 2017.)

(b) Transfer-out hearing

(1) *Determination of residence—special rule on intercounty transfers (§§ 17.1, 375)*

(A) For purposes of this rule, the residence of a nonminor dependent who is placed in a planned permanent living arrangement may be either the county in which the court that has jurisdiction over the nonminor is located or the county in which the nonminor has resided continuously for at least one year as a nonminor dependent and the nonminor dependent has expressed his or her intent to remain.

(B) If a nonminor dependent's dependency jurisdiction has been resumed, or if transition jurisdiction has been assumed or resumed by the juvenile court that retained general jurisdiction over the nonminor under section 303, the county that the nonminor dependent is residing in may be deemed the county of residence of the nonminor dependent. The court may make this determination if the nonminor has established a continuous physical presence in the county for one year as a nonminor and has expressed his or her intent to remain in that county after the court grants the petition to resume jurisdiction. The period of continuous physical presence includes any period of continuous residence immediately before filing the petition.

(2) *Verification of residence*

The residence of a nonminor may be verified by declaration of a social worker or probation officer in the transferring or receiving county.

(3) *Transfer to county of nonminor's residence (§ 375)*

If the court is resuming dependency jurisdiction or assuming or resuming transition jurisdiction of a nonminor for whom the court has retained general jurisdiction under section 303(b) as a result of a petition filed under section 388(e), after granting the petition, the court may order the transfer of the case to the juvenile court of the county in which the nonminor is living if the nonminor establishes residency in that county as provided in (b)(1) and the court finds that the transfer is in the minor's best interest.

(4) *Transfer on change in nonminor's residence (§ 375)*

If a nonminor dependent under the dependency or transition jurisdiction of the court is placed in a planned permanent living arrangement in a county other than the county with jurisdiction over the nonminor, the court may, on an application for modification under rule 5.570, transfer the case to the juvenile court of the county in which the nonminor is living if the nonminor establishes residency in that county as provided in (b)(1).

(5) *Conduct of hearing*

(A) The request for transfer must be made on *Motion for Transfer Out* (form JV-548), which must include all required information.

(B) After the court determines whether a nonminor has established residency in another county as required in (b)(1), the court must consider whether transfer of the case would be in the nonminor's best interest. The court may not transfer the case unless it determines that the nonminor supports the transfer and that the transfer will protect or further the nonminor's best interest.

(C) If the transfer-out motion is granted, the sending court must set a date certain for the transfer-in hearing in the receiving court, which must be within 10 court days of the transfer-out order. The sending court must state on the record the date, time, and location of the hearing in the receiving court.

(6) *Order of transfer (§ 377)*

The order of transfer must be entered on *Juvenile Court Transfer-Out Orders—Nonminor Dependent* (form JV-552), which must include all required information and findings.

(7) *Modification of form JV-552*

Juvenile Court Transfer-Out Orders—Nonminor Dependent (form JV-552) may be modified as follows:

(A) Notwithstanding the mandatory use of form JV-552, the form may be modified for use by a formalized regional collaboration of courts to facilitate the efficient processing of transfer cases among those courts if the modification has been approved by the Judicial Council.

(B) The mandatory form must be used by a regional collaboration when transferring a case to a court outside the collaboration or when accepting a transfer from a court outside the collaboration.

(8) *Transmittal of documents (§ 377)*

The clerk of the transferring court must transmit to the clerk of the court of the receiving county no later than five court days from the date of the transfer-out order a certified copy of the entire nonminor file and, at a minimum, all documents associated with the last status review hearing held before the nonminor reached majority, including the court report and all findings and orders. The files may be transferred electronically, if possible. A certified copy of the complete case file is deemed an original.

(9) *Appeal of transfer order (§ 379)*

The order of transfer may be appealed by the transferring or receiving county, and notice of appeal must be filed in the transferring county, under rule 8.400. Notwithstanding the filing of a notice of appeal, the receiving county must assume jurisdiction of the case on receipt and filing of the order of transfer.

(Subd (b) adopted effective January 1, 2017.)

(c) Transfer-in hearing

(1) *Procedure on transfer (§ 378)*

On receipt and filing of a certified copy of a transfer order, the receiving court must accept jurisdiction of the case. The receiving court may not reject the case. The receiving court must notify the transferring court on receipt and filing of the certified copies of the transfer order and complete case file. The clerk of the receiving court must confirm the transfer-in hearing date scheduled by the sending court and ensure that date is on the receiving court's calendar.

(2) *Conduct of hearing*

At the transfer-in hearing, the court must:

(A) Advise the nonminor of the purpose and scope of the hearing; and

(B) Provide for the appointment of counsel, if appropriate.

(3) *Subsequent proceedings*

The proceedings in the receiving court must commence at the same phase as when the case was transferred. The court may continue the hearing for an investigation and a report to a date not to exceed 15 court days.

(4) *Setting six-month review (§ 366.31)*

When an order of transfer is received and filed relating to a nonminor dependent, the court must set a date for a six-month review within six months of the most recent review hearing or, if the sending court transferred the case immediately after assuming or resuming jurisdiction, within six months of the date a voluntary reentry agreement was signed.

(5) *Change of circumstances or additional facts (§§ 388, 778)*

If the receiving court believes that a change of circumstances or additional facts indicate that the nonminor does not reside in the receiving county, a transfer-out hearing must be held under this rule and rule 5.570. The court may direct the department of social services or the probation department to seek a modification of orders under section 388 or section 778 and under rule 5.570.

(Subd (c) adopted effective January 1, 2017.)

Rule 5.613 adopted effective January 1, 2017.

Rule 5.614.   Courtesy supervision (§§ 380, 755) [Repealed]

Rule 5.614 repealed effective January 1, 2019; adopted as rule 1427 effective January 1, 1990; previously amended and renumbered effective January 1, 2007.

Another Rule 5.614 follows.

Rule 5.614.   Out-of-county placements

(a) Procedure

Whenever a social worker intends to place a dependent child outside the child's county of residence, the procedures in section 361.2(h) must be followed.

(Subd (a) adopted effective January 1, 2019.)

(b) Required notices

Unless the requirements for emergency placement in section 361.4 are met **or the circumstances in section 361.2(h)(2)(A) exist**, before placing a child out of county, the agency must notify the following [1] of the proposed removal:

(1) The [2] **persons** listed in section 361.2(h);

(2) The Indian child's identified Indian tribe, if any;

(3) The Indian child's Indian custodian, if any; and

(4) The child's CASA program, if any.

(Subd (b) amended effective January 1, 2020; adopted effective January 1, 2019.)

Rule 5.614(b).   2019 Deletes. [1] participants **[2]** participants

(c) Form of notice

The social worker may provide the required written notice to the participants in (b) on *Notice of Intent to Place Child Out of County* (form JV-555). If form JV-555 is used, the social worker must also provide a blank copy of *Objection to Out-of-County Placement and Notice of Hearing* (form JV-556).

(Subd (c) adopted effective January 1, 2019.)

(d) Method of Service

The agency must serve notice of its intent to place the child out of county as follows:

(1) Notice must be served by either first-class mail, sent to the last known address of the person to be noticed; electronic service in accordance with Welfare and Institutions Code section 212.5; or personal service at least 14 days before the placement, unless the child's health or well-being is endangered by delaying the action or would be endangered if prior notice were given;

(2) Notice to the child's identified Indian tribe and Indian custodian must comply with the requirements of section [1] **224.3**; and

(3) *Proof of Notice* (form JV-326) must be filed with the court before any hearing on the proposed out-of-county placement.

(Subd (d) amended effective January 1, 2020; adopted effective January 1, 2019.)

Rule 5.614(d).   2019 Deletes. [1] 224.2

(e) Objection to proposed out-of-county placement

Each participant who receives notice under (b)(1)–(3) may object to the proposed removal of the child, and the court must set a hearing as required by section 361.2(h).

(1) An objection to the proposed [1] **out-of-county** placement may be made by using *Objection to Out-of-County Placement and Notice of Hearing* (form JV-556).

(2) An objection must be filed [2] **within the time frames in section 361.2(h).**

(Subd (e) amended effective January 1, 2020; adopted effective January 1, 2019.)

Rule 5.614(e).   2019 Deletes. [1] intercounty **[2]** no later than seven days after receipt of the notice

(f) Notice of hearing on proposed removal

If an objection is filed, the clerk must set a hearing, and notice of the hearing must be as follows:

(1) If the party objecting to the removal is not represented by counsel, the clerk must provide notice of the hearing to the agency and the participants listed in (b);

(2) If the party objecting to the removal is represented by counsel, that counsel must provide notice of the hearing to the agency and the participants listed in (b);

(3) Notice must be by either first-class mail, sent to the last known address of the person to be noticed; electronic service in accordance with Welfare and Institutions Code section 212.5; or personal service; [1]

(4) **Notice to the child's identified Indian tribe and Indian custodian must comply with the requirements of section 224.3; and**

(5) *Proof of Notice* (form JV-326) must be filed with the court before the hearing on the proposed removal.

(Subd (f) amended effective January 1, 2020; adopted effective January 1, 2019.)

Rule 5.614(f).   2019 Deletes. [1] and

(g) Burden of proof

At a hearing on an out-of-county placement, the agency intending to move the child must prove by a preponderance of the evidence that the standard in section 361.2(h) is met.

(Subd (g) adopted effective January 1, 2019.)

(h) Emergency placements

If the requirements for emergency placement in section 361.4 are met, the agency must provide notice as required in section 16010.6.

(Subd (h) adopted effective January 1, 2019.)

Rule 5.614 amended effective January 1, 2020; adopted effective January 1, 2019.

Rule 5.616.   Interstate Compact on the Placement of Children

(a) Applicability of rule (Fam. Code, § 7900 et seq.)

This rule implements the purposes and provisions of the Interstate Compact on the Placement of Children (ICPC, or the compact). California juvenile courts must apply this rule when placing children who are dependents or wards of the juvenile court and for whom placement is indicated in any other state, the District of Columbia, or the U.S. Virgin Islands.

(1) This rule applies to expedited placements as described in (h).

(2) This rule does not apply to placements made under the Interstate Compact for Juveniles (Welf. & Inst. Code, § 1400 et seq.).

(Subd (a) amended effective January 1, 2013; previously amended effective January 1, 2007.)

(b) Definitions (Fam. Code, § 7900 et seq.; ICPC Regulations)

(1) "Placement" is defined in article 2(d) of the compact. It includes placements with a relative, as defined in Regulation No. 3, paragraph 4, item 56; a legal guardian of the child; a placement recipient who is not related to the child; or a residential facility or group home as defined in Regulation No. 4.

(A) A court's directing or making an award of custody to a parent of the child or placing a child with his or her parent is not a placement requiring compliance with this rule.

(B) The following situations each constitute a placement, and the compact must be applied:

(i) An order causing a child to be sent or brought to a person, other than a parent, in a compact jurisdiction without a specific date of return to the sending jurisdiction;

(ii) An order causing a child to be sent or brought to a person, other than a parent, in a compact jurisdiction with a return date more than 30 days from the start of the visit or beyond the ending date of a school vacation period, under Regulation No. 9;

(iii) An out-of-state placement for the purpose of an anticipated adoption, whether independent, private, or public;

(iv) An out-of-state placement with a related or unrelated caregiver in a licensed or approved foster home;

(v) An out-of-state placement with relatives, except when a parent or relative sends or brings the child to the relative's home in the receiving state, as defined in article 8(a) of the ICPC; or

(vi) An out-of-state group home or residential placement of any child, including a child adjudicated delinquent.

(2) "Child," for the purposes of ICPC placement, includes nonminor dependents up to age 21. If a California nonminor dependent is to be placed out of state, the placing county may request supervision from the receiving state, but such services are discretionary. If the receiving state will not supervise the nonminor dependent, the sending county must make other supervision arrangements, which may include contracting with a private agency to provide the supervision.

(3) "Parent," as used in this rule, does not include de facto parents or legal guardians.

(4) ICPC Regulations Nos. 3, 4, 5, 9, 10, 11, and 12 contain additional definitions that apply to California ICPC cases, except where inconsistent with this rule or with California law.

(Subd (b) amended effective January 1, 2014; previously amended effective January 1, 2007, and January 1, 2013.)

(c) Compact requirements (Fam. Code, § 7901; ICPC Regulations)

Whenever the juvenile court makes a placement in another jurisdiction included in the compact or reviews a placement plan, the court must adhere to the provisions and regulations of the compact.

(1) Cases in which out-of-state placement is proposed in order to place a child for public adoption, in foster care, or with relatives, and where the criteria for expedited placement are not met, must meet all requirements of Regulation No. 2, except where inconsistent with California law.

(2) Expedited placement cases must meet the requirements in (h) and of Regulation No. 7, except where the requirements of Regulation No. 7 are inconsistent with California law.

(3) Cases in which out-of-state placement is proposed in order to place a child in a residential facility or group home must meet all the requirements of Regulation No. 4, except where inconsistent with California law.

(Subd (c) amended effective January 1, 2014; previously amended effective January 1, 2007, and January 1, 2013.)

(d) Notice of intention; authorization (Fam. Code, § 7901)

A sending jurisdiction must provide to the designated receiving jurisdiction written notice of intention to place the child, using Form ICPC-100A: Interstate Compact on the Placement of Children Request.

(1) The representative of the receiving jurisdiction may request and receive additional information as the representative deems necessary.

(2) The child must not be placed until the receiving jurisdiction has determined that the placement is not contrary to the interest of the child and has so notified the sending jurisdiction in writing.

(Subd (d) amended effective January 1, 2013; previously amended effective January 1, 2007.)

(e) Placement of delinquent children in institutional care (Fam. Code, §§ 7901, art. 6, and 7908; ICPC Reg. No. 4, § 2)

A child declared a ward of the court under Welfare and Institutions Code section 602 may be placed in an institution in another jurisdiction under the compact only when:

(1) Before the placement, the court has held a properly noticed hearing at which the child, parent, and guardian have had an opportunity to be heard;

(2) The court has found that equivalent facilities for the child are not available in the sending jurisdiction; and

(3) Institutional care in the other jurisdiction is in the best interest of the child and will not produce undue hardship for the child or his or her family.

(Subd (e) amended effective January 1, 2014; previously amended effective January 1, 2007, and January 1, 2013.)

(f) Relocation of Family Units (ICPC Reg. No. 1)

(1) The ICPC applies to family relocation cases when the child has been placed and continues to live with a family approved by California, the family relocates to another state with the child, and supervision by California is ongoing.

(2) The ICPC does not apply when the family with whom the child is placed relocates to another state and there will be no ongoing supervision by the sending state or the relocation will be temporary (90 days or less) and will not recur.

(3) Additional procedural requirements for cases involving relocation of family units are in ICPC Regulation No. 1.

(Subd (f) adopted effective January 1, 2013.)

(g) Placing a Child With an Out-of-State Parent (Fam. Code, §§ 7901, art. 5(b), and 7906; ICPC Reg. No. 2, § 3)

When a child will be placed with his or her parent in another state, compliance with the requirements of the ICPC is not required. However, the court has discretion to take the steps it deems necessary to ensure the child's safety and well-being in that placement. Those steps may include:

(1) Directing the child welfare agency to request an independent, non-ICPC home study or courtesy check;

(2) Directing the child welfare agency to enter into a contract with a public or private agency in the receiving state to obtain a home study or other needed information;

(3) Directing the child welfare agency to enter into an informal agreement with a public or private agency in the receiving state, or requesting a courtesy check from such an agency, to obtain needed information; or

(4) Any other steps that the court deems necessary to ensure the child's safety and well-being.

(Subd (g) adopted effective January 1, 2013.)

(h) Expedited placement (ICPC Reg. No. 7)

When seeking expedited approval of an out-of-state placement of a child with a relative or guardian, a California court may designate a proposed placement as an expedited placement by using procedures described in this section.

(1) Expedited placement under Regulation No. 7 does not apply to any situation in which a California child is being placed with his or her parent in another state.

(2) Before the court orders an expedited placement, the court must make express findings that the child is a dependent child removed from and no longer residing in the home of a parent and now being considered for placement in another state with a stepparent, grandparent, adult aunt or uncle, adult sibling, or legal guardian. In addition, the court must find that the child to be placed meets at least one of the following criteria:

(A) Unexpected dependency due to the sudden or recent incarceration, incapacitation, or death of a parent or guardian. *Incapacitation* means the parent or guardian is unable to care for the child due to the parent's medical, mental, or physical condition;

(B) The child is 4 years of age or younger;

(C) The child is part of a group of siblings who will be placed together, where one or more of the siblings is 4 years of age or younger;

(D) The child to be placed, or any of the child's siblings in a sibling group to be placed, has a substantial relationship with the proposed placement resource as defined in section 5(c) of Regulation No. 7; or

(E) The child is in an emergency placement.

(3) Before the court orders an expedited placement, the child welfare agency must provide to the court, at a minimum, the documents required by section 7(a) and (b) of Regulation No. 7:

(A) A signed statement of interest from the potential placement, or a written statement from the assigned case manager affirming that the potential placement resource confirms appropriateness for the ICPC expedited placement decision process. The statement must include all items listed in Regulation No. 7, section 7(a); and

(B) A statement from the assigned case manager or other child welfare agency representative stating that he or she knows of no reason why the child could not be placed with the proposed placement and that the agency has completed and is prepared to send all required paperwork.

(4) On findings of the court under (h)(2) and (3) that the child meets the criteria for an expedited placement and that the required statements have been provided to the court, the case must proceed as follows:

(A) The court must enter an order for expedited placement, stating on the record or in the written order the factual basis for that order. If the court is also requesting provisional approval of the proposed placement, the court must so order, and must state on the record or in the written order the factual basis for that request.

(B) The court's findings and orders must be noted in a written order using *Expedited Placement Under the Interstate Compact on the Placement of Children: Findings and Orders* (form JV-567), which must include the name, address, e-mail address, telephone number, and fax number of the clerk of court or designated court administrator.

(C) The order must be transmitted by the court to the sending agency of the court's jurisdiction within 2 business days of the hearing or consideration of the request.

(D) The sending child welfare agency must be ordered to transmit to the county ICPC Liaison in the sending jurisdiction within 3 business days of receipt of the order the following:

(i) A copy of the completed *Expedited Placement Under the Interstate Compact on the Placement of Children: Findings and Orders* (form JV-567); and

(ii) A completed Interstate Compact on the Placement of Children Request (form ICPC-100A), along with form ICPC-101, the statements required under section (h)(3), above, and all required supporting documentation.

(E) Within 2 business days after receipt of the paperwork, the county ICPC Liaison of the sending jurisdiction must transmit the documents described in (D) to the compact administrator of the receiving jurisdiction with a request for an expedited placement decision, as well as any request for provisional placement.

(5) The compact administrator of the receiving jurisdiction must determine immediately, and no later than 20 business days after receipt,

whether the placement is approved and must transmit the completed written report and form ICPC 100A, as required by Regulation 7, section 9, to the county ICPC Liaison in the sending jurisdiction.

(6) The transmission of any documentation, request for information, or decision may be by overnight mail, fax, e-mail, or other recognized, secure method of communication. The receiving state may also request original documents or certified copies if it considers them necessary for a legally sufficient record.

(7) When California is the sending state and there appears to be a lack of compliance with Regulation No. 7 requirements by state officials or the local child welfare agency in the receiving state regarding the expedited placement request, the California judicial officer may communicate directly with the judicial officer in the receiving state.

(A) This communication may be by telephone, e-mail, or any other recognized, secure communication method.

(B) The California judicial officer may do any one or more of the following:

(i) Contact the appropriate judicial officer in the receiving state to discuss the situation and possible solutions.

(ii) Provide, or direct someone else to provide, the judicial officer of the receiving state with copies of relevant documents and court orders.

(iii) Request assistance with obtaining compliance.

(iv) Use *Request for Assistance With Expedited Placement Under the Interstate Compact on the Placement of Children* (form JV-565) to communicate the request for assistance to the receiving state judicial officer. When this form is used, a copy should be provided to the county ICPC Liaison in the sending jurisdiction.

(8) All other requirements, exceptions, timelines, and instructions for expedited placement cases, along with procedures for provisional approval or denial of a placement and for removal of a child from the placement, are stated in Regulation No. 7.

(Subd (h) amended and relettered effective January 1, 2013; previously amended as subd (f) effective January 1, 2007.)

(i) Authority of sending court or agency to place child; timing (ICPC Reg. No. 2, § 8(d), and Reg. No. 4, § 8)

(1) When the receiving state has approved a placement resource, the sending court has the final authority to determine whether to use the approved placement resource. The sending court may delegate that decision to the sending state child welfare agency or probation department.

(2) For proposed placements of children for adoption, in foster care, or with relatives, the receiving state's approval expires six months from the date form ICPC-100A was signed by the receiving state.

(3) For proposed placements of children in residential facilities or group homes, the receiving state's approval expires 30 calendar days from the date form ICPC-100A was signed by the receiving state. The 30-day time frame can be extended by mutual agreement between the sending and receiving states.

(Subd (i) amended effective January 1, 2014; adopted effective January 1, 2013.)

(j) Ongoing jurisdiction

If a child is placed in another jurisdiction under the terms of the compact, the sending court must not terminate its jurisdiction until the child is adopted, reaches majority, or is emancipated, or the dependency is terminated with the concurrence of the receiving state authority.

(Subd (j) relettered effective January 1, 2013; previously amended as subd (g) effective January 1, 2007.)

Rule 5.616 amended effective January 1, 2014; adopted as rule 1428 effective January 1, 1999; previously amended and renumbered effective January 1, 2007; previously amended effective January 1, 2013.

Advisory Committee Comment

Urgency of ICPC Matters. Implementation of the ICPC has long frustrated judicial officers and other professionals. The overriding concern is that the process takes too long, and children cannot wait. In all ICPC actions, there should be a sense of urgency, and all professionals involved should take action as quickly as possible.

Subdivision (h)(7). Judicial officers requesting assistance under subdivision (h)(7) from the receiving state judge or judicial officer should be cognizant of ethical concerns raised by such ex parte communication. These concerns can be addressed in various ways, including but not limited to using form JV-565, obtaining a stipulation from all parties to permit judge-to-judge phone or e-mail contact, or conducting the discussion by phone with parties and a court reporter present.

Validity of California Placements in Receiving Jurisdictions. When a California child is placed with an out-of-state parent, and the placement is consistent with California law, the receiving jurisdiction may consider the placement invalid if it does not comply with the law of the receiving jurisdiction. In this situation, the receiving jurisdiction would have no obligation to provide services.

Regulations and Forms. The ICPC regulations and forms can be found on the website of the Association of Administrators of the Interstate Compact on the Placement of Children at *http://icpc.aphsa.org/*.

Chapter 8
Restraining Orders, Custody Orders, and Guardianships General Court Authority

Rule 5.620. Orders after filing under section 300
Rule 5.625. Orders after filing of petition under section 601 or 602
Rule 5.630. Restraining orders

Rule 5.620. Orders after filing under section 300

(a) Exclusive jurisdiction (§ 304)

Once a petition has been filed alleging that a child is described by section 300, and until the petition is dismissed or dependency is terminated, the juvenile court has exclusive jurisdiction to hear proceedings relating to the custody of the child and visitation with the child and establishing a **legal** guardianship for the child.

(Subd (a) amended effective January 1, 2021; previously amended effective January 1, 2016.)

(b) Restraining orders (§ 213.5)

After a petition has been filed under section 300, and until the petition is dismissed or dependency is terminated, the court may issue restraining orders as provided in rule 5.630. A temporary restraining order must be prepared on *Notice of Hearing and Temporary Restraining Order—Juvenile* (form JV-250). An order after hearing must be prepared on *Restraining Order—Juvenile* (form JV-255).

(Subd (b) amended effective January 1, 2014; previously amended effective January 1, 2007.)

(c) Custody and visitation (§ 361.2)

If the court sustains a petition, finds that the child is described by section 300, and removes physical custody from a parent or guardian, it may order the child placed in the custody of a previously noncustodial parent as described in rule 5.695(a)(7)(A) or (B).

(1) This order may be entered at the dispositional hearing, at any subsequent review hearing under rule 5.708(k), or on granting a request under section 388 for custody and visitation orders.

(2) If the court orders legal and physical custody to the previously noncustodial parent and terminates dependency jurisdiction under rule 5.695(a)(7)(A), the court must proceed under rule 5.700.

(3) If the court orders custody to the noncustodial parent subject to the continuing supervision of the court, the court may order services provided to either parent or to both parents under section 361.2(b)(3). If the court orders the provision of services, it must review its custody determination at each subsequent hearing held under section 366 and rule 5.708.

(Subd (c) amended effective January 1, 2016; previously amended effective January 1, 2007.)

(d) Appointment of a legal guardian (§§ 360, 366.26)

If the court finds that the child is described by section 300, it may appoint a legal guardian at the disposition hearing, as described in **section 360(a)** and rule [1] **5.695(a)**, or at the hearing under section 366.26, as described in **that section and** rule 5.735. The juvenile court maintains jurisdiction over the guardianship, and [2] **a petition** to terminate or modify [3] **that guardianship** must be heard in juvenile court under rule 5.740(c).

(Subd (d) amended effective January 1, 2021; previously amended effective January 1, 2007.)

Rule 5.620(d). 2020 Deletes. [1] 5.695(b) [2] petitions [3] such guardianships

(e) Termination or modification of previously established probate guardianships (§ 728)

At any time after the filing of a petition under section 300 and until the petition is dismissed or dependency is terminated, the court may terminate or modify a guardianship of the person previously established [1] **under the Probate Code.**

The social worker [2] **may recommend** to the court [3] **in a report accompanying an initial or supplemental petition** that an existing **probate** guardianship be modified or terminated [4]. **The probate guardian or the child's attorney may also file a motion to modify or terminate an existing probate guardianship.**

(1) The hearing on the **petition or** motion may be held simultaneously with any regularly scheduled hearing regarding the child. **The** notice requirements [5] **in section 294** apply.

(2) If the court terminates or modifies a previously established probate guardianship, the court must provide notice of the order to the probate court that made the original appointment. The clerk of the probate court must file the notice in the probate file and send a copy of the notice to all parties of record identified in that file.

(Subd (e) amended effective January 1, 2021; previously amended effective January 1, 2007.)

Rule 5.620(e). 2020 Deletes. [1] by the juvenile court or the probate court. If [2] recommends [3] , by filing *Juvenile Dependency Petition (Version One)* (form JV-100) and *Request to Change Court Order* (form JV-180), [4] , the court must order the appropriate county agency to file the recommended motion [5] under Probate Code section 1511

Rule 5.620 amended effective January 1, 2021; adopted as rule 1429.1 effective January 1, 2000; previously amended and renumbered as rule 5.620 effective January 1, 2007; previously amended effective January 1, 2014, and January 1, 2016.

Rule 5.625. Orders after filing of petition under section 601 or 602

(a) Restraining orders (§ 213.5)

After a petition has been filed under section 601 or 602, and until the petition is dismissed or wardship is terminated, the court may issue restraining orders as provided in rule 5.630. A temporary restraining order must be prepared on *Notice of Hearing and Temporary Restraining Order—Juvenile* (form JV-250). An order after hearing must be prepared on *Restraining Order—Juvenile* (form JV-255).

(Subd (a) amended effective January 1, 2014; previously amended effective January 1, 2003, and January 1, 2007.)

(b) Appointment of a legal guardian (§§ 727.3, 728)

At any time during wardship of a [1] **child** under 18 years **of age,** the court may appoint a **legal** guardian [2] **of the person for the child** in accordance with the requirements in **section 366.26 and** rule 5.815.

(1) On appointment of a legal guardian, the court may continue wardship and conditions of probation or may terminate wardship.

(2) The juvenile court retains jurisdiction over the guardianship. All proceedings to modify or terminate the guardianship must be held in juvenile court.

(Subd (b) amended effective January 1, 2021; adopted as subd (c) effective January 1, 2000; previously amended effective January 1, 2003; previously amended and relettered as subd (b) effective January 1, 2007.)

Rule 5.625(b). 2020 Deletes. [1] person [2] , or may terminate or modify a previously established guardianship,

(c) Termination or modification of previously established probate guardianships (§ 728)

At any time after the filing of a petition under section 601 or 602 and until the petition is dismissed or wardship is terminated, the court may terminate or modify a guardianship of the person previously established under the Probate Code. The probation officer may recommend to the court in a report accompanying an initial or supplemental petition that an existing probate guardianship be modified or terminated. The guardian or the child's attorney may also file a motion to modify or terminate the guardianship.

(1) The hearing on the petition or motion may be held simultaneously with any regularly scheduled hearing regarding the child. The notice requirements in section 294 apply.

(2) If the court terminates or modifies a previously established probate guardianship, the court must provide notice of the order to the probate court that made the original appointment. The clerk of the probate court must file the notice in the probate file and send a copy of the notice to all parties of record identified in that file.

(Subd (c) adopted effective January 1, 2021.)

Rule 5.625 amended effective January 1, 2021; adopted as rule 1429.3 effective January 1, 2000; previously amended effective January 1, 2003, and January 1, 2014; previously amended and renumbered effective January 1, 2007.

Rule 5.630. Restraining orders

(a) Court's authority

After a petition has been filed under section 300, 601, or 602, and until the petition is dismissed or dependency or wardship is terminated, or the ward is no longer on probation, the court may issue restraining orders as provided in section 213.5.

(Subd (a) amended effective January 1, 2012; adopted effective January 1, 2003.)

(b) Application for restraining orders

(1) Application for restraining orders may be made orally at any scheduled hearing regarding the child who is the subject of a petition under section 300, 601, or 602, or may be made by written application, or may be made on the court's own motion.

(2) The written application must be submitted on *Request for Restraining Order—Juvenile* (form JV-245).

(3) A person requesting a restraining order in writing must submit to the court with the request a completed *Confidential CLETS Information Form* (form CLETS-001) under rule 1.51.

(Subd (b) amended effective January 1, 2012; previously amended effective January 1, 2003, January 1, 2004, and January 1, 2007.)

(c) Definition of abuse

The definition of abuse in Family Code section 6203 applies to restraining orders issued under Welfare and Institutions Code section 213.5.

(Subd (c) repealed and adopted effective January 1, 2012.)

(d) Applications—procedure

The application may be submitted without notice, and the court may grant the petition and issue a temporary order.

(1) In determining whether or not to issue the temporary restraining order without notice, the court must consider all documents submitted with the application and may review the contents of the juvenile court file regarding the child.

(2) The temporary restraining order must be prepared on *Notice of Hearing and Temporary Restraining Order—Juvenile* (form JV-250) and must state on its face the date of expiration of the order.

(Subd (d) amended effective January 1, 2014; adopted as subd (c) effective January 1, 2000; previously amended and relettered as subd (f) effective January 1, 2003; previously amended effective January 1, 2007; previously repealed, amended and relettered effective January 1, 2012.)

(e) Continuance

(1) The court may grant a continuance under Welfare and Institutions Code section 213.5.

(2) Either *Request and Order to Continue Hearing (Temporary Restraining Order—Juvenile)* (form JV-251) or a new *Notice of Hearing and Temporary Restraining Order—Juvenile* (form JV-250) must be used for this purpose.

(Subd (e) amended effective July 1, 2016; adopted as subd (g) effective January 1, 2003; amended and relettered effective January 1, 2012; previously amended effective January 1, 2004, January 1, 2007, and January 1, 2014.)

(f) Hearing on application for restraining order

(1) Proof may be by the application and any attachments, additional declarations or documentary evidence, the contents of the juvenile court file, testimony, or any combination of these.

(2) The order after hearing must be prepared on *Restraining Order—Juvenile* (form JV-255) and must state on its face the date of expiration of the order.

(Subd (f) amended effective January 1, 2014; adopted as subd (d) effective January 1, 2000; previously amended and relettered as subd (h) effective January 1, 2003, and subd (f) effective January 1, 2012; previously amended effective January 1, 2007.)

(g) Service of restraining order

When service of *Notice of Hearing and Temporary Restraining Order—Juvenile* (form JV-250) or *Restraining Order—Juvenile* (form JV-255) is made, it must be served with a blank *Proof of Firearms Turned In, Sold, or Stored* (form DV-800/JV-252) and *How Do I Turn In, Sell, or Store My Firearms?* (form DV-800-INFO/JV-252-INFO). Failure to serve form JV-252 or JV-252-INFO does not make service of form JV-250 or form JV-255 invalid.

(Subd (g) amended effective July 1, 2014; adopted effective January 1, 2012; previously amended effective January 1, 2014.)

(h) Firearm relinquishment

The firearm relinquishment procedures in rule 5.495 apply to restraining orders issued under section 213.5.

(Subd (h) adopted effective July 1, 2014.)

(i) Expiration of restraining order

If the juvenile case is dismissed, the restraining order remains in effect until it expires or is terminated.

(Subd (i) relettered effective July 1, 2014; adopted as subd (h) effective January 1, 2012.)

(j) Criminal records search (§ 213.5 and Stats. 2001, ch. 572, § 7)

(1) Except as provided in (3), before any hearing on the issuance of a restraining order the court must ensure that a criminal records search is or has been conducted as described in Family Code section 6306(a). Before deciding whether to issue a restraining order, the court must consider the information obtained from the search.

(2) If the results of the search indicate that an outstanding warrant exists against the subject of the search, or that the subject of the search is currently on parole or probation, the court must proceed under section 213.5(k)(3).

(3) The requirements of (1) and (2) must be implemented in those courts identified by the Judicial Council as having resources currently available for these purposes. All other courts must implement the requirements to the extent that funds are appropriated for this purpose in the annual Budget Act.

(Subd (j) relettered effective July 1, 2014; adopted as subd (i) effective January 1, 2003; previously amended effective January 1, 2007, and January 1, 2012.)

(k) Modification of restraining order

(1) A restraining order may be modified on the court's own motion or in the manner provided for in Welfare and Institutions Code section 388 and rule 5.560.

(2) A termination or modification order must be made on *Change to Restraining Order After Hearing* (form JV-257). A new *Restraining Order—Juvenile* (form JV-255) may be prepared in addition to form JV-257.

(Subd (k) repealed and relettered effective July 1, 2014; adopted as subd (j) effective January 1, 2012; previously amended effective January 1, 2014.)
Rule 5.630 amended effective July 1, 2016; adopted as rule 1429.5 effective January 1, 2000; amended and renumbered effective January 1, 2007; previously amended effective January 1, 2003, January 1, 2004, January 1, 2012, January 1, 2014, and July 1, 2014.)

Chapter 9
Parentage

Rule 5.635. Parentage
Rule 5.637. Family Finding (§§ 309(e), 628(d))

Rule 5.635. Parentage

(a) Authority to declare; duty to inquire (§§ 316.2, 726.4)

The juvenile court has a duty to inquire about and to attempt to determine the parentage of each child who is the subject of a petition filed under section 300, 601, or 602. The court may establish and enter a judgment of parentage under the Uniform Parentage Act. (Fam. Code, § 7600 et seq.) Once a petition has been filed to declare a child a dependent or ward, and until the petition is dismissed or dependency or wardship is terminated, the juvenile court with jurisdiction over the action has exclusive jurisdiction to hear an action filed under Family Code section 7630.

(Subd (a) amended effective January 1, 2015; previously amended effective January 1, 2001, January 1, 2006, and January 1, 2007.)

(b) Parentage inquiry (§§ 316.2, 726.4)

At the initial hearing on a petition filed under section 300 or at the dispositional hearing on a petition filed under section 601 or 602, and at hearings thereafter until or unless parentage has been established, the court must inquire of the child's parents present at the hearing and of any other appropriate person present as to the identity and address of any and all presumed or alleged parents of the child. Questions, at the discretion of the court, may include the following and others that may provide information regarding parentage:

(1) Has there been a judgment of parentage?

(2) Was the mother married or did she have a registered domestic partner at or after the time of conception?

(3) Did the mother believe she was married or believe she had a registered domestic partner at or after the time of conception?

(4) Was the mother cohabiting with another adult at the time of conception?

(5) Has the mother received support payments or promises of support for the child or for herself during her pregnancy or after the birth of the child?

(6) Has a man formally or informally acknowledged [1] **parentage**, including the execution and filing of a voluntary declaration of **parentage or** paternity under Family Code section 7570 et seq., and agreed to have his name placed on the child's birth certificate?

(7) [2] **Has genetic testing** been administered, and, if so, what were the results?

(8) Has the child been raised jointly with another adult or in any other co-parenting arrangement?

(Subd (b) amended effective January 1, 2020; adopted effective January 1, 2001; previously amended effective January 1, 2006, January 1, 2007, and January 1, 2015.)

Rule 5.635(b). 2019 Deletes. [1] paternity [2] Have genetic tests

(c) Voluntary declaration

If a voluntary declaration as described in Family Code section 7570 et seq. has been executed and filed with the California Department of Child Support Services, the declaration establishes the [1] **parentage** of a child and has the same force and effect as a judgment of [2] **parentage** by a court. A [3] **person** is presumed to be the [4] **parent** of the child under Family Code section 7611 if the voluntary declaration has been properly executed and filed.

(Subd (c) amended effective January 1, 2020; adopted effective January 1, 2001; previously amended effective January 1, 2006, July 1, 2006, January 1, 2007, and January 1, 2015.)

Rule 5.635(c). 2019 Deletes. [1] paternity [2] paternity [3] man [4] father

(d) Issue raised; inquiry

If, at any proceeding regarding the child, the issue of parentage is addressed by the court:

(1) The court must ask the parent or the person alleging parentage, and others present, whether any parentage finding has been made, and, if so, what court made it, or whether a voluntary declaration has been executed and filed under the Family Code;

(2) The court must direct the court clerk to prepare and transmit *Parentage Inquiry—Juvenile* (form JV-500) to the local child support agency requesting an inquiry regarding whether parentage has been established through any superior court order or judgment or through the execution and filing of a voluntary declaration under the Family Code;

(3) The office of child support enforcement must prepare and return the completed *Parentage Inquiry—Juvenile* (form JV-500) within 25 judicial days, with certified copies of any such order or judgment or proof of the filing of any voluntary declaration attached; and

(4) The juvenile court must take judicial notice of the prior determination of parentage.

(Subd (d) amended effective January 1, 2015; adopted as subd (b) effective July 1, 1995; previously amended and relettered effective January 1, 2001; previously amended effective January 1, 2006, and January 1, 2007.)

(e) No prior determination

If the local child support agency states, or if the court determines through statements of the parties or other evidence, that there has been no prior determination of parentage of the child, the juvenile court must take appropriate steps to make such a determination.

(1) Any alleged father and his counsel must complete and submit *Statement Regarding Parentage (Juvenile)* (form JV-505). Form JV-505 must be made available in the courtroom.

(2) To determine parentage, the juvenile court may order the child and any alleged parents to submit to genetic tests and proceed under Family Code section 7550 et seq.

(3) The court may make its determination of parentage or nonparentage based on the testimony, declarations, or statements of the alleged parents. The court must advise any alleged parent that if parentage is determined, the parent will have responsibility for the financial support of the child, and, if the child receives welfare benefits, the parent may be subject to an action to obtain support payments.

(Subd (e) amended effective January 1, 2015; adopted as subd (c) effective July 1, 1995; previously amended and relettered effective January 1, 2001; previously amended effective January 1, 2006, and January 1, 2007.)

(f) Notice to office of child support enforcement

If the court establishes parentage of the child, the court must sign *Parentage—Finding and Judgment (Juvenile)* (form JV-501) and direct the clerk to transmit the signed form to the local child support agency.

(Subd (f) amended effective January 1, 2015; adopted as subd (d) effective July 1, 1995; previously amended and relettered effective January 1, 2001; previously amended effective January 1, 2006, and January 1, 2007.)

(g) Dependency and delinquency; notice to alleged parents

If, after inquiry by the court or through other information obtained by the county welfare department or probation department, one or more persons are identified as alleged parents of a child for whom a petition under section 300, 601, or 602 has been filed, the clerk must provide to each named alleged parent, at the last known address, by certified mail, return receipt requested, a copy of the petition, notice of the next scheduled hearing, and *Statement Regarding Parentage (Juvenile)* (form JV-505) unless:

(1) The petition has been dismissed;

(2) Dependency or wardship has been terminated;

(3) The alleged parent has previously filed a form JV-505 denying parentage and waiving further notice; or

(4) The alleged parent has relinquished custody of the child to the county welfare department.

(Subd (g) amended effective January 1, 2015; adopted as subd (e) effective July 1, 1995; previously amended and relettered effective January 1, 2001; previously amended effective January 1, 2006, and January 1, 2007.)

(h) Dependency and delinquency; alleged parents (§§ 316.2, 726.4)

If a person appears at a hearing in dependency matter or at a hearing under section 601 or 602 and requests a judgment of parentage on form JV-505, the court must determine:

(1) Whether that person is the biological parent of the child; and

(2) Whether that person is the presumed parent of the child, if that finding is requested.

(Subd (h) amended effective January 1, 2007; adopted as subd (f) effective January 1, 1999; previously amended and relettered effective January 1, 2001; previously amended effective January 1, 2006.)

Rule 5.635 amended effective January 1, 2020; adopted as rule 1413 effective July 1, 1995; previously amended effective January 1, 1999, January 1, 2001, January 1, 2006, July 1, 2006, January 1, 2007, and January 1, 2015.

Rule 5.637. Family Finding (§§ 309(e), 628(d))

(a) Within 30 days of a child's removal from the home of his or her parent or guardian, if the child is in or at risk of entering foster care, the social worker or probation officer must use due diligence in conducting an investigation to identify, locate, and notify all the child's adult relatives.

(Subd (a) adopted effective January 1, 2011.)

(b) The social worker or probation officer is not required to notify a relative whose personal history of family or domestic violence would make notification inappropriate.

(Subd (b) adopted effective January 1, 2011.)

Rule 5.637 adopted effective January 1, 2011.

Advisory Committee Comment

This rule restates the requirements of section 103 of the federal Fostering Connections to Success and Increasing Adoptions Act (Pub. L. No. 110-351, § 103 (Oct. 7, 2008) 122 Stat. 3949, 3956, codified at 42 U.S.C. § 671(a)(29)) as implemented by California Assembly Bill 938 (Com. on Judiciary; Stats. 2009, ch. 261, codified at Welf. & Inst. Code §§ 309(e) and 628(d)). These statutes enacted elements of the child welfare practice known as Family Finding and Engagement, which has been recommended to improve outcomes for children by the Judicial Council's California Blue Ribbon Commission on Children in Foster Care and the California Child Welfare Council. (*See* Cal. Blue Ribbon Com. on Children in Foster Care, *Fostering a New Future for California's Children*, pp. 30–31 (Admin. Off. of Cts., May 2009) (final report and action plan), *www.courts.ca.gov; Permanency Committee Recommendations to the Child Welfare Council*, pp. 1–4 (Sept. 10, 2009), *www.chhs.ca.gov.*)

Chapter 10
Medication, Mental Health, and Education

Rule 5.640. Psychotropic medications

(a) Definition (§§ 369.5(d), 739.5(d))

For the purposes of this rule, "psychotropic medication" means those medications prescribed to affect the central nervous system to treat psychiatric disorders or illnesses. They may include, but are not limited to, anxiolytic agents, antidepressants, mood stabilizers, antipsychotic medications, anti-Parkinson agents, hypnotics, medications for dementia, and psychostimulants.

(Subd (a) amended effective January 1, 2009; previously amended effective January 1, 2007.)

(b) Authorization to administer (§§ 369.5, 739.5)

(1) Once a child is declared a dependent child of the court and is removed from the custody of the parents [1], guardian, **or Indian custodian,** only a juvenile court judicial officer is authorized to make orders regarding the administration of psychotropic medication to the child, unless, under (e), the court orders that the parent or legal guardian is authorized to approve or deny the medication.

(2) Once a child is declared a ward of the court, removed from the custody of the parents [2], guardian, **or Indian custodian,** and placed into foster care, as defined in Welfare and Institutions Code section 727.4, only a juvenile court judicial officer is authorized to make orders regarding the administration of psychotropic medication to the child, unless, under (e), the court orders that the parent or legal guardian is authorized to approve or deny the medication.

(Subd (b) amended effective September 1, 2020; previously amended effective January 1, 2009, July 1, 2016, and January 1, 2018.)

Rule 5.640(b). 2020 Deletes. [1] or **[2]** or

(c) Procedure to obtain authorization

(1) To obtain authorization to administer psychotropic medication to a dependent child of the court who is removed from the custody of the parents [1], legal guardian, **or Indian custodian,** or to a ward of the court who is removed from the custody of the parents [2], legal guardian, **or Indian custodian** and placed into foster care, the following forms must be completed and filed with the court:

(A) *Application for Psychotropic Medication* (form JV-220);

(B) *Physician's Statement—Attachment* (form JV-220(A)), unless the request is to continue the same medication and maximum dosage by the same physician who completed the most recent JV-220(A); then the physician may complete *Physician's Request to Continue Medication—Attachment* (form JV-220(B)); and

(C) *Proof of Notice of Application* (form JV-221).

(2) The child, caregiver, parents [3], legal guardians, **or Indian custodian,** child's Indian tribe, and Court Appointed Special Advocate, if any, may provide input on the medications being prescribed.

(A) Input can be by *Child's Opinion About the Medicine* (form JV-218) or *Statement About Medicine Prescribed* (form JV-219); letter; talking to the judge at a court hearing; or through the social worker, probation officer, attorney of record, or Court Appointed Special Advocate.

(B) If form JV-218 or form JV-219 is filed, it must be filed within four court days after receipt of notice of the pending application for psychotropic medication. If a hearing is set on the application, form JV-218 and form JV-219 may be filed at any time before, or at, the hearing.

(C) Input from a Court Appointed Special Advocate can also be by a court report under local rule.

(3) *Input on Application for Psychotropic Medication* (form JV-222) may be filed by a parent [4], **guardian, or Indian custodian, their** attorney of record, a child's attorney of record, a child's Child Abuse Prevention and Treatment Act guardian ad litem appointed under rule 5.662 of the California Rules of Court, or the Indian child's tribe. If form JV-222 is filed, it must be filed within four court days of receipt of notice of the application.

(4) Additional information may be provided to the court through the use of local forms that are consistent with this rule.

(5) Local county practice and local rules of court determine the procedures for completing and filing the forms, except as otherwise provided in this rule.

(6) *Application for Psychotropic Medication* (form JV-220) may be completed by the prescribing physician, medical office staff, child welfare services staff, probation officer, or the child's caregiver. If the applicant is the social worker or probation officer, he or she must complete all items on form JV-220. If the applicant is the prescribing physician, medical office staff, or child's caregiver, he or she must complete and sign only page one of form JV-220.

(7) The physician prescribing the administration of psychotropic medication for the child must complete and sign *Physician's Statement—Attachment* (form JV-220(A)) or, if it is a request to continue the same medication by the same physician who completed the most recent JV-220(A), then the physician must complete and sign *Physician's Statement—Attachment* (form JV-220(A)) or *Physician's Request to Continue Medication—Attachment* (form JV-220(B)).

(8) The court must approve, deny, or set the matter for a hearing within seven court days of the receipt of the completed form JV-220 and form JV-220(A) or form JV-220(B).

Rules of Court

(9) The court must grant or deny the application using *Order on Application for Psychotropic Medication* (form JV-223).

(10) Notice of the application must be provided to the parents [5], legal guardians, **or Indian custodian,** their attorneys of record, the child's attorney of record, the child's Child Abuse Prevention and Treatment Act guardian ad litem, the child's current caregiver, the child's Court Appointed Special Advocate, if any, and where a child has been determined to be an Indian child, the Indian child's tribe (see also 25 U.S.C. § 1903(4)–(5); Welf. & Inst. Code, §§ 224.1(a) and (e) and 224.3).

(A) If the child is living in a group home or short-term residential therapeutic program, notice to the caregiver must be by notice to the facility administrator as defined in California Code of Regulations, title 22, section 84064, or to the administrator's designee.

(B) Local county practice and local rules of court determine the procedures for the provision of notice, except as otherwise provided in this rule and in section 212.5. Psychological or medical documentation related to a minor may not be served electronically. The person or persons responsible for providing notice as required by local court rules or local practice protocols are encouraged to use the most expeditious legally authorized manner of service possible to ensure timely notice.

(C) Notice must be provided as follows:

(i) Notice to the parents or legal guardians and their attorneys of record must include:

a. A statement that a physician is asking to treat the child's emotional or behavioral problems by beginning or continuing the administration of psychotropic medication to the child and the name of the psychotropic medication;

b. A statement that an *Application for Psychotropic Medication* (form JV-220) and a *Physician's Statement—Attachment* (form JV-220(A)) or *Physician's Request to Continue Medication—Attachment* (form JV-220(B)) are pending before the court;

c. A copy of *Guide to Psychotropic Medication Forms* (form JV-217-INFO);

d. A blank copy of *Statement About Medicine Prescribed* (form JV-219); and

e. A blank copy of *Input on Application for Psychotropic Medication* (form JV-222).

(ii) Notice to the child's current caregiver and Court Appointed Special Advocate, if one has been appointed, must include only:

a. A statement that a physician is asking to treat the child's emotional or behavioral problems by beginning or continuing the administration of psychotropic medication to the child and the name of the psychotropic medication;

b. A statement that an *Application for Psychotropic Medication* (form JV-220) and a *Physician's Statement—Attachment* (form JV-220(A)) or *Physician's Request to Continue Medication—Attachment* (form JV-220(B)) are pending before the court;

c. A copy of *Guide to Psychotropic Medication Forms* (form JV-217-INFO);

d. A blank copy of *Child's Opinion About the Medicine* (form JV-218); and

e. A blank copy of *Statement About Medicine Prescribed* (form JV-219).

(iii) Notice to the child's attorney of record and any Child Abuse Prevention and Treatment Act guardian ad litem for the child must include:

a. A completed copy of *Application for Psychotropic Medication* (form JV-220);

b. A completed copy of *Physician's Statement—Attachment* (form JV-220(A)) or *Physician's Request to Continue Medication—Attachment* (form JV-220(B));

c. A copy of *Guide to Psychotropic Medication Forms* (form JV-217-INFO) or information on how to obtain a copy of the form;

d. A blank copy of *Input on Application for Psychotropic Medication* (form JV-222) or information on how to obtain a copy of the form; [6]

e. A blank copy of *Child's Opinion About the Medicine* (form JV-218) or information on how to obtain a copy of the form**; and**

f. If the application could result in the authorization of three or more psychotropic medications for 90 days or longer, notice must also include a blank copy of *Position on Release of Information to Medical Board of California* (form JV-228), a copy of *Background on Release of Information to Medical Board of California* (form JV-228-INFO), a blank copy of *Withdrawal of Release of Information to Medical Board

of California (form JV-229), and the procedures in rule 5.642 must be followed.

(iv) Notice to the Indian child's tribe must include:

a. A statement that a physician is asking to treat the child's emotional or behavioral problems by beginning or continuing the administration of psychotropic medication to the child, and the name of the psychotropic medication;

b. A statement that an *Application for Psychotropic Medication* (form JV-220) and a *Physician's Statement—Attachment* (form JV-220(A)) or *Physician's Request to Continue Medication—Attachment* (form JV-220(B)) are pending before the court;

c. A copy of *Guide to Psychotropic Medication Forms* (form JV-217-INFO) or information on how to obtain a copy of the form;

d. A blank copy of *Input on Application for Psychotropic Medication* (form JV-222) or information on how to obtain a copy of the form; and

e. A blank copy of *Child's Opinion About the Medicine* (form JV-218) or information on how to obtain a copy of the form.

f. A blank copy of *Statement About Medicine Prescribed* (form JV-219) or information on how to obtain a copy of the form.

(v) Proof of notice of the application regarding psychotropic medication must be filed with the court using *Proof of Notice of Application* (form JV-221).

(11) If all the required information is not included in the request for authorization, the court must order the applicant to provide the missing information and set a hearing on the application.

(12) The court may grant the application without a hearing or may set the matter for hearing at the court's discretion. If the court sets the matter for a hearing, the clerk of the court must provide notice of the date, time, and location of the hearing to the parents [7], legal guardians, **or Indian custodian,** their attorneys of record, the dependent child if 12 years of age or older, a ward of the juvenile court of any age, the child's attorney of record, the child's current caregiver, the child's social worker or probation officer, the social worker's or probation officer's attorney of record, the child's Child Abuse Prevention and Treatment Act guardian ad litem, the child's Court Appointed Special Advocate, if any, and the Indian child's tribe at least two court days before the hearing. Notice must be provided to the child's probation officer and the district attorney, if the child is a ward of the juvenile court.

(Subd (c) amended effective September 1, 2020; previously amended effective January 1, 2007, January 1, 2008, January 1, 2009, January 1, 2014, July 1, 2016, January 1, 2018, and January 1, 2019.)

Rule 5.640(c). 2020 Deletes. [1] or [2] or [3] or [4] or guardian, his or her [5] or [6] and [7] or

(d) Conduct of hearing on application

At the hearing on the application, the procedures described in rule 5.570 and section 349 must be followed. The court may deny, grant, or modify the application for authorization. If the court grants or modifies the application for authorization, the court must set a date for review of the child's progress and condition. This review must occur at every status review hearing and may occur at any other time at the court's discretion.

(Subd (d) amended effective July 1, 2016; previously amended effective January 1, 2007.)

(e) Delegation of authority (§§ 369.5, 739.5)

If a child is removed from the custody of his or her parent [1], legal guardian, **or Indian custodian,** the court may order that the parent, **legal guardian, or Indian custodian** is authorized to approve or deny the administration of psychotropic medication. The order must be based on the findings in section 369.5 or section 739.5, which must be included in the order. The court may use *Order Delegating Judicial Authority Over Psychotropic Medication* (form JV-216) to document the findings and order.

(Subd (e) amended effective September 1, 2020; previously amended effective January 1, 2008, and January 1, 2018.)

Rule 5.640(e). 2020 Deletes. [1] or

(f) Continued treatment

If the court grants the request or modifies and then grants the request, the order for authorization is effective until terminated or modified by court order or until 180 days from the order, whichever is earlier.

(Subd (f) amended effective July 1, 2016.)

(g) Progress review

(1) After approving any application for authorization, regardless of whether the approval is made at a hearing, the court must set a progress review.

(2) A progress review must occur at every status review hearing and may occur at any other time at the court's discretion.

(3) If the progress review is held at the time of the status review hearing, notice must be provided as required under section 293 or 295, except that electronic service of psychological or medical documentation related to a child is not permitted. The notice must include a statement that the hearing will also be a progress review on previously ordered psychotropic medication, and must include a blank copy of *Child's Opinion About the Medicine* (form JV-218) and a blank copy of *Statement About Medicine Prescribed* (form JV-219).

(4) If the progress review is not held at the time of the status review hearing, notice must be provided as required under section 293 or 295, except that electronic service of psychological or medical documentation related to a child is not permitted. The notice must include a statement that the hearing will be a progress review on previously ordered psychotropic medication; and must include a blank copy of *Child's Opinion About the Medicine* (form JV-218) and a blank copy of *Statement About Medicine Prescribed* (form JV-219).

(5) Before each progress review, the social worker or probation officer must file a completed *County Report About Psychotropic Medication* (form JV-224) at least 10 calendar days before the hearing. If the progress review is set at the same time as a status review hearing, form JV-224 must be attached to and filed with the report.

(6) The child, caregiver, parents [1], legal guardians, **or Indian custodian,** and Court Appointed Special Advocate, if any, may provide input at the progress review as stated in (c)(2).

(7) At the progress review, the procedures described in section 349 must be followed.

(Subd (g) amended effective September 1, 2020; adopted effective July 1, 2016; previously amended effective January 1, 2018, and January 1, 2019.)

Rule 5.640(g). 2020 Deletes. [1] or

(h) Copy of order to caregiver

(1) Upon the approval or denial of the application, the county child welfare agency, probation department, or other person or entity who submitted the request must provide the child's caregiver with a copy of the court order approving or denying the request.

(2) The copy of the order must be provided in person or mailed within two court days of when the order is signed.

(3) If the court approves the request, the copy of the order must include the last two pages of form JV-220(A) or the last two pages of form JV-220(B) and all medication information sheets (medication monographs) that were attached to form JV-220(A) or form JV-220(B).

(4) If the child resides in a group home or short-term residential therapeutic program, a copy of the order, the last two pages of form JV-220(A) or the last two pages of form JV-220(B), and all medication information sheets (medication monographs) that were attached to form JV-220(A) or form JV-220(B) must be provided to the facility administrator, as defined in California Code of Regulations, title 22, section 84064, or to the administrator's designee.

(5) If the child changes placement, the social worker or probation officer must provide the new caregiver with a copy of the order, the last two pages of form JV-220(A) or the last two pages of form JV-220(B), and the medication information sheets (medication monographs) that were attached to form JV-220(A) or form JV-220(B).

(Subd (h) amended effective January 1, 2019; adopted effective July 1, 2016; previously amended effective January 1, 2018.)

(i) Emergency treatment

(1) Psychotropic medications may be administered without court authorization in an emergency situation. An emergency situation occurs when:

(A) A physician finds that the child requires psychotropic medication to treat a psychiatric disorder or illness; and

(B) The purpose of the medication is:

(i) To protect the life of the child or others, or

(ii) To prevent serious harm to the child or others, or

(iii) To treat current or imminent substantial suffering; and

(C) It is impractical to obtain authorization from the court before administering the psychotropic medication to the child.

(2) Court authorization must be sought as soon as practical but in no case more than two court days after the emergency administration of psychotropic medication.

(Subd (i) relettered effective July 1, 2016; adopted as subd (g); previously amended effective January 1, 2007, and January 1, 2008.)

(j) Section 601–602 wardships; local rules

A local rule of court may be adopted providing that authorization for the administration of such medication to a child declared a ward of the court under sections 601 or 602 and removed from the custody of the parent or guardian for placement in a facility that is not considered a foster-care placement may be similarly restricted to the juvenile court. If the local court adopts such a local rule, then the procedures under this rule apply; any reference to social worker also applies to probation officer.

(Subd (j) amended and relettered effective July 1, 2016; adopted as subd (i) effective January 1, 2001; previously relettered as subd (h) effective January 1, 2008; previously amended effective January 1, 2007, and January 1, 2009.)

(k) Public health nurses

Information may be provided to public health nurses as governed by Civil Code section 56.103.

(Subd (k) adopted effective July 1, 2016.)

Rule 5.640 amended effective September 1, 2020; adopted as rule 1432.5 effective January 1, 2001; previously amended and renumbered effective January 1, 2007; previously amended effective January 1, 2003, January 1, 2008, January 1, 2009, January 1, 2014, July 1, 2016, January 1, 2018, and January 1, 2019.

Rule 5.642. Authorization to release psychotropic medication prescription information to Medical Board of California

(a) Providing authorization forms

Whenever there is an *Application for Psychotropic Medication* (form JV-220) filed with the court under rule 5.640, the applicant must review the *Physician's Statement—Attachment* (form JV-220(A)) or *Physician's Request to Continue Medication—Attachment* (form JV-220(B)) to determine if the request would result in the child being prescribed three or more concurrent psychotropic medications for 90 days or more, as described in section 14028. If the request would result in the child being prescribed three or more psychotropic medications for 90 days or more, the applicant must provide blank copies of *Position on Release of Information to Medical Board of California* (form JV-228), *Background on Release of Information to Medical Board of California* (form JV-228-INFO), and *Withdrawal of Release of Information to Medical Board of California* (form JV-229) to the child and the child's attorney.

(Subd (a) adopted effective September 1, 2020.)

(b) Signing authorization form

(1) Form JV-228 may be signed by either the child, nonminor dependent, or the attorney, with the informed consent of the child if the child is found by the court to be of sufficient age and maturity to consent. Sufficient age and maturity to consent must be presumed, subject to rebuttal by clear and convincing evidence, if the child is 12 years of age or over. If the child does not want to sign form JV-228, the child's attorney may not sign it. The child's attorney may sign form JV-228 with the approval of a child 12 years of age or older, if the child is under 12 years of age, or if the court finds the child not to be of sufficient age and maturity to consent.

(2) The authorization is for the release of medical records only. It is not an authorization for the release of juvenile court case files as described in section 827.

(Subd (b) adopted effective September 1, 2020.)

(c) Filing and sending authorization form

(1) The child's attorney must review form JV-228 with the child and file it with the superior court.

(2) Within three court days of filing, the clerk of the superior court must send form JV-228 to the California Department of Social Services at the address indicated on the form.

(Subd (c) adopted effective September 1, 2020.)

(d) Withdrawal of authorization

At any time, the child, nonminor dependent, or attorney may withdraw the authorization to release information to the Medical Board of California.

(1) Withdrawal may be made by filing *Withdrawal of Release of Information to Medical Board of California* (form JV-229) or by written letter to the California Department of Social Services.

(2) The child, nonminor dependent, or attorney may sign (as specified in (b)) form JV-229.

(3) Within three court days of filing, the clerk of the superior court must send form JV-229 to the California Department of Social Services at the address indicated on the form.

(Subd (d) adopted effective September 1, 2020.)

(e) Notice of release of information to medical board

If the California Department of Social Services releases identifying information to the Medical Board of California, the California Department of Social Services must notify the child, nonminor dependent, or former dependent or ward, at the last known address. The California Department of Social Services must also notify the child's, nonminor dependent's, or former dependent's or ward's attorney, including in cases when jurisdiction has been terminated.

(Subd (e) adopted effective September 1, 2020.)
Rule 5.642 adopted effective September 1, 2020.

Rule 5.643.   Mental health or condition of child; court procedures

(a) Doubt concerning the mental health of a child (§§ 357, 705, 6550, 6551)

Whenever the court believes that the child who is the subject of a petition filed under section 300, 601, or 602 is mentally disabled or may be mentally ill, the court may stay the proceedings and order the child taken to a facility designated by the court and approved by the State Department of Mental Health as a facility for 72-hour treatment and evaluation. The professional in charge of the facility must submit a written evaluation of the child to the court.

(Subd (a) amended effective January 1, 2007.)

(b) Findings regarding a mental disorder (§ 6551)

Article 1 of chapter 2 of part 1 of division 5 (commencing with section 5150) applies.

(1) If the professional reports that the child is not in need of intensive treatment, the child must be returned to the juvenile court on or before the expiration of the 72-hour period, and the court must proceed with the case under section 300, 601, or 602.

(2) If the professional in charge of the facility finds that the child is in need of intensive treatment for a mental disorder, the child may be certified for not more than 14 days of involuntary intensive treatment according to the conditions of sections 5250(c) and 5260(b). The stay of the juvenile court proceedings must remain in effect during this time.

(A) During or at the end of the 14 days of involuntary intensive treatment, a certification may be sought for additional treatment under sections commencing with 5270.10 or for the initiation of proceedings to have a conservator appointed for the child under sections commencing with 5350. The juvenile court may retain jurisdiction over the child during proceedings under sections 5270.10 et seq. and 5350 et seq.

(B) For a child subject to a petition under section 602, if the child is found to be gravely disabled under sections 5300 et seq., a conservator is appointed under those sections, and the professional in charge of the child's treatment or of the treatment facility determines that proceedings under section 602 would be detrimental to the child, the juvenile court must suspend jurisdiction while the conservatorship remains in effect. The suspension of jurisdiction may end when the conservatorship is terminated, and the original 602 matter may be calendared for further proceedings.

(Subd (b) amended effective January 1, 2007.)

(c) Findings regarding developmental disability (§ 6551)

Article 1 of chapter 2 of part 1 of division 5 (commencing with section 5150) applies.

(1) If the professional finds that the child [1] **has a developmental disability** and recommends commitment to a state hospital, the court may direct the filing in the appropriate court of a petition for commitment of a child [2] **who has a developmental disability** to the State Department of Developmental Services for placement in a state hospital.

(2) If the professional finds that the child [3] **does not have a developmental disability**, the child must be returned to the juvenile court on or before the expiration of the 72-hour period, and the court must proceed with the case under section 300, 601, or 602.

(3) The jurisdiction of the juvenile court must be suspended while the child is subject to the jurisdiction of the appropriate court under a petition for commitment of a [4] person **who has a developmental disability**, or under remand for 90 days for intensive treatment or commitment ordered by that court.

(Subd (c) amended effective January 1, 2020; previously amended effective January 1, 2007, and January 1, 2009.)

Rule 5.643(c).   2019 Deletes. [1] is mentally retarded [2] as a mentally retarded person [3] is not mentally retarded [4] mentally retarded
Rule 5.643 amended and renumbered effective January 1, 2020; adopted as rule 1498 effective January 1, 1999; previously amended and renumbered as rule 5.645

effective January 1, 2007; previously amended effective January 1, 2009, and January 1, 2012.

Rule 5.645.   Mental health or condition of child; competency evaluations

(a) Doubt as to child's competency (§§ 601, 602, 709)

(1) If the court finds that there is substantial evidence regarding a child who is the subject of a petition filed under section 601 or 602 that raises a doubt as to the child's competency as defined in section 709, the court must suspend the proceedings and conduct a hearing regarding the child's competency.

(2) Unless the parties have stipulated to a finding of incompetency, the court must appoint an expert to evaluate the child and determine whether the child suffers from a mental illness, mental disorder, developmental disability, developmental immaturity, or other condition affecting competency and, if so, whether the child is incompetent as defined in section 709(a)(2).

(3) Following the hearing on competency, the court must proceed as directed in section 709.

(Subd (a) adopted effective January 1, 2020.)

(b) Expert qualifications

(1) To be appointed as an expert, an individual must be a:

(A) Licensed psychiatrist who has successfully completed four years of medical school and either four years of general psychiatry residency, including one year of internship and two years of child and adolescent fellowship training, or three years of general psychiatry residency, including one year of internship and one year of residency that focus on children and adolescents and one year of child and adolescent fellowship training; or

(B) Clinical, counseling, or school psychologist who has received a doctoral degree in psychology from an educational institution accredited by an organization recognized by the Council for Higher Education Accreditation and who is licensed as a psychologist.

(2) The expert, whether a licensed psychiatrist or psychologist, must:

(A) Possess demonstrable professional experience addressing child and adolescent developmental issues, including the emotional, behavioral, and cognitive impairments of children and adolescents;

(B) Have expertise in the cultural and social characteristics of children and adolescents;

(C) Possess a curriculum vitae reflecting training and experience in the forensic evaluation of children and adolescents;

(D) Be familiar with juvenile competency standards and accepted criteria used in evaluating juvenile competence;

(E) Be familiar with effective interventions, as well as treatment, training, and programs for the attainment of competency available to children and adolescents;

(F) Be proficient in the language preferred by the child, or if that is not feasible, employ the services of a certified interpreter and use assessment tools that are linguistically and culturally appropriate for the child; and

(G) Be familiar with juvenile competency remediation services available to the child.

(3) Nothing in this rule precludes involvement of clinicians with other professional qualifications from participation as consultants or witnesses or in other capacities relevant to the case.

(Subd (b) adopted effective January 1, 2020.)

(c) Interview of child

The expert must attempt to interview the child face-to-face. If an in-person interview is not possible because the child refuses an interview, the expert must try to observe and make direct contact with the child to attempt to gain clinical observations that may inform the expert's opinion regarding the child's competency.

(Subd (c) adopted effective January 1, 2020.)

(d) Review of records

(1) The expert must review all the records provided as required by section 709.

(2) The written protocol required under section 709(i) must include a description of the process for obtaining and providing the records to the expert to review, including who will obtain and provide the records to the expert.

(Subd (d) adopted effective January 1, 2020.)

(e) Consult with the child's counsel

(1) The expert must consult with the child's counsel as required by section 709. This consultation must include, but is not limited to, asking the child's counsel the following:

(A) If the child's counsel raised the question of competency, why the child's counsel doubts that the child is competent;

(B) What has the child's counsel observed regarding the child's behavior; and

(C) A description of how the child interacts with the child's counsel.

(2) No waiver of the attorney-client privilege will be deemed to have occurred from the child's counsel report of the child's statements to the expert, and all such statements are subject to the protections in (g)(2) of this rule.

(Subd (e) adopted effective January 1, 2020.)

(f) Developmental history

The expert must gather a developmental history of the child as required by section 709. This history must be documented in the report and must include the following:

(1) Whether there were complications or drug use during pregnancy that could have caused medical issues for the child;

(2) When the child achieved developmental milestones such as talking, walking, and reading;

(3) Psychosocial factors such as abuse, neglect, or drug exposure;

(4) Adverse childhood experiences, including early disruption in the parent-child relationship;

(5) Mental health services received during childhood and adolescence;

(6) School performance, including an Individualized Education Plan, testing, achievement scores, and retention;

(7) Acculturation issues;

(8) Biological and neurological factors such as neurological deficits and head trauma; and

(9) Medical history including significant diagnoses, hospitalizations, or head trauma.

(Subd (f) adopted effective January 1, 2020.)

(g) Written report

(1) Any court-appointed expert must examine the child and advise the court on the child's competency to stand trial. The expert's report must be submitted to the court, to the counsel for the child, to the probation department, and to the prosecution. The report must include the following:

(A) A statement identifying the court referring the case, the purpose of the evaluation, and the definition of competency in the state of California.

(B) A brief statement of the expert's training and previous experience as it relates to evaluating the competence of a child to stand trial.

(C) A statement of the procedure used by the expert, including:

(i) A list of all sources of information considered by the expert including those required by section 709(b)(3);

(ii) A list of all sources of information the expert tried or wanted to obtain but, for reasons described in the report, could not be obtained;

(iii) A detailed summary of the attempts made to meet the child face to-face and a detailed account of any accommodations made to make direct contact with the child; and

(iv) All diagnostic and psychological tests administered, if any.

(D) A summary of the developmental history of the child as required by this rule.

(E) A summary of the evaluation conducted by the expert on the child, including the current diagnosis or diagnoses that meet criteria under the most recent version of the *Diagnostic and Statistical Manual of Mental Disorders*, when applicable, and a summary of the child's mental or developmental status.

(F) A detailed analysis of the competence of the child to stand trial under section 709, including the child's ability or inability to understand the nature of the proceedings or assist counsel in the conduct of a defense in a rational manner as a result of a mental or developmental impairment.

(G) An analysis of whether and how the child's mental or developmental status is related to any deficits in abilities related to competency.

(H) If the child has significant deficits in abilities related to competency, an opinion with explanation as to whether treatment is needed to restore or attain competency, the nature of that treatment, its availability, and whether restoration is likely to be accomplished within the statutory time limit.

(I) A recommendation, as appropriate, for a placement or type of placement, services, and treatment that would be most appropriate for the child to attain or restore competence. The recommendation must be guided by the principle of section 709 that services must be provided in the least restrictive environment consistent with public safety.

(J) If the expert is of the opinion that a referral to a psychiatrist is appropriate, the expert must inform the court of this opinion and recommend that a psychiatrist examine the child.

(2) Statements made to the appointed expert during the child's competency evaluation and statements made by the child to mental health professionals during the remediation proceedings, and any fruits of these statements, must not be used in any other hearing against the child in either juvenile or adult court.

(Subd (g) adopted effective January 1, 2020.)
Rule 5.645 adopted effective January 1, 2020.

2019 Note: Subdivisions (a) and (b) were derived from former rule 5.645(d).

Rule 5.647.   Medi-Cal: Presumptive Transfer of Specialty Mental Health Services

(a) Applicability

This rule applies to the court's review under Welfare and Institutions Code section 14717.1 of the presumptive transfer of responsibility to arrange and provide for a child's or nonminor's specialty mental health services to the child's or nonminor's county of residence. The rule applies to presumptive transfer following any change of placement within California for a child or nonminor to a placement that is outside the county of original jurisdiction, including the initial placement. Nothing in this rule relieves the placing agency of the reporting requirements and duties under section 14717.1 when no hearing under this rule is held.

(Subd (a) adopted effective September 1, 2018.)

(b) Requesting a hearing to review the request for waiver of presumptive transfer (§ 14717.1)

(1) The following persons or agencies may make a request to the placing agency that presumptive transfer be waived and that the responsibility for providing specialty mental health services remain in the child's or nonminor's county of original jurisdiction:

(A) The foster child or nonminor;

(B) The person or agency that is responsible for making mental health care decisions on behalf of the foster child or nonminor;

(C) The child welfare services agency or the probation agency with responsibility for the care and placement of the child or nonminor; and

(D) Any other interested party who owes a legal duty to the child or nonminor involving the child's or nonminor's health or welfare, as defined by the department.

(2) The person or agency who requested the waiver, or any other party to the case who disagrees with the placing agency's determination on the request for the waiver of presumptive transfer, may request a judicial review of the placing agency's determination.

(3) A request for a hearing must be made by filing a *Request for Hearing on Waiver of Presumptive Transfer* (form JV-214). If a hearing is requested, form JV-214 must be provided to the placing agency within seven court days of the petitioner's being noticed of the placing agency's determination on the request for waiver of presumptive transfer.

(4) When a hearing is requested in (b)(3), the transfer of the responsibility for providing specialty mental health services cannot occur until the court makes a ruling as required in (c)(1).

(Subd (b) adopted effective September 1, 2018.)

(c) Setting of a hearing (§ 14717.1)

(1) The court on its own motion may direct the clerk to set a hearing no later than five court days after the request for a hearing was filed, or may deny the request for a hearing without ruling on the transfer of jurisdiction.

(2) If the court sets a hearing, the clerk must provide notice of the hearing date to:

(A) The parents—unless parental rights have been terminated—or guardians of the child;

(B) The petitioner;

(C) The social worker or probation officer;

(D) The mental health care decision maker for the child or nonminor, if one has been appointed under section 361(a)(1);

(E) The Indian child's tribe, if applicable, as defined in rule 5.502;

(F) The child—if 10 years of age or older—or nonminor; and

(G) All other persons entitled to notice under section 293 or section 727.4(a).

(3) If the court grants a hearing under (c)(1), responsibility for providing specialty mental health services cannot be transferred until the court makes a ruling as required in (e)(2) and section 14717.1(d)(4).

(Subd (c) adopted effective September 1, 2018.)

(d) Reports

When a hearing is granted under (c)(1), the social worker or probation officer must provide a report including discussion or documentation of the following:

(1) The placing agency's rationale for its decision on the request for a waiver of presumptive transfer, including:

(A) Any requests for waiver, and the exceptions claimed as the basis for those requests;

(B) The placing agency's determination of whether waiver of presumptive transfer is appropriate under section 14717.1(d)(5)(A)–(D);

(C) Any objections to the placing agency's determination in (B); and

(D) The ways that the child's or nonminor's best interests will be promoted by the placing agency's presumptive transfer determination.

(2) That the child or nonminor, his or her parents if applicable, the child and family team, and others who serve the child or nonminor as appropriate—such as the therapist, mental health care decision maker for the child or nonminor if one has been appointed under section 361(a)(1), and Court Appointed Special Advocate volunteer—were consulted regarding the waiver determination.

(3) That notice of the placing agency's determination of whether to waive presumptive transfer was provided to the individual who requested waiver of presumptive transfer, along with all parties to the case.

(4) Whether the mental health plan in the county of original jurisdiction demonstrates an existing contract with a specialty mental health care provider, or the ability to enter into a contract with a specialty mental health care provider within 30 days of the waiver decision, and the ability to deliver timely specialty mental health services directly to the foster child or nonminor.

(5) The child's or nonminor's current provision of specialty mental health services, and how those services will be affected by the placing agency's presumptive transfer determination.

(Subd (d) adopted effective September 1, 2018.)

(e) Conduct at the hearing

(1) The social worker or probation officer must provide the report in (d) to the court, all parties to the case, and the person or agency that requested the waiver no later than two court days after the hearing is set under (c)(1).

(2) At the hearing, the court may confirm or deny the transfer of jurisdiction or application of an exception based on the best interests of the child or nonminor. A waiver of presumptive transfer is contingent on the mental health plan in the county of original jurisdiction demonstrating an existing contract with a specialty mental health care provider, or the ability to enter into such a contract within 30 days of the waiver decision, and the ability to deliver timely specialty mental health services directly to the child or nonminor.

(3) The person or agency that requested the waiver of presumptive transfer bears the burden to show that an exception to presumptive transfer is in the best interests of the child or nonminor by a preponderance of the evidence.

(4) The hearing must conclude within five court days of the initial hearing date, unless a showing of good cause consistent with section 352 or section 682 supports a continuance of the hearing beyond five days.

(5) When considering whether it is in the child's or nonminor's best interests to confirm or deny the request for a waiver of presumptive transfer, the court may consider the following in addition to any other factors the court deems relevant:

(A) The child's or nonminor's access to specialty mental health services, the current provision of specialty mental health services to the child or nonminor, and whether any important service relationships will be affected by the transfer of jurisdiction or a waiver of presumptive transfer;

(B) If reunification services are being provided, the impact that the transfer of jurisdiction would have on reunification services;

(C) The anticipated length of stay in the child's or nonminor's new placement;

(D) The position of the child or nonminor, or of the child's or nonminor's attorney, on presumptive transfer; and

(E) The ability to maintain specialty mental health services in the county of original jurisdiction or to arrange for specialty mental health services in the county of residence after the child or nonminor changes placements.

(6) Findings and orders must be made on *Order after Hearing on Waiver of Presumptive Transfer* (form JV-215).

(Subd (e) adopted effective September 1, 2018.)

(f) Existing out-of-county placement

This rule applies to presumptive transfer for any child or nonminor who resided in a county other than the county of original jurisdiction after June 30, 2017, and who continues to reside outside his or her county of original jurisdiction after December 31, 2017, and has not had a presumptive transfer determination as required under Welfare and Institutions Code section 14717.1(c)(2). Unless amended by Judicial Council action effective after the effective date of this rule, this subdivision will be repealed effective January 1, 2020.

(Subd (f) adopted effective September 1, 2018.)
Rule 5.647 adopted effective September 1, 2018.

Advisory Committee Comment

The exceptions to the presumptive transfer of the responsibility to provide for and arrange for specialty mental health services to the county of the child's or nonminor's out-of-county residence are found in Welfare and Institutions Code section 14717.1(d)(5)(A–D). A court review hearing under this rule may not necessarily be common, but under section 14717.1(d)(7), for all cases, a request for waiver, the exceptions claimed as the basis for the request, a determination whether a waiver is appropriate under Welfare and Institutions Code section 14717.1, and any objections to the determination must be documented in the child's or nonminor's case plan under Welfare and Institutions Code section 16501.1. The Department of Health Care Services and California Department of Social Services are responsible for providing policy guidance and regulations to implement Assembly Bill 1299 (Ridley-Thomas; Stats. 2016, ch. 603). The policy guidance and regulations should be used during the administrative process related to presumptive transfer. This would include determining who is entitled to make a request for waiver under (b)(1)(D) of the rule and section 14717.1(d)(2), where "department" refers to the Department of Health Care Services. In the policy guidance and regulations, the Department of Health Care Services and California Department of Social Services will determine who owes a legal duty to the child or nonminor and thus may request a waiver of presumptive transfer. In addition, the policy guidance and regulations will address the timelines for the period to request a hearing. Presumptive transfer cannot occur until the court has made a ruling on the request for a hearing, and if a hearing is granted, makes a ruling as required in (c)(3). In accordance with the policy guidance issued by the Department of Health Care Services and California Department of Social Services, the delivery of existing specialty mental health services to the child or nonminor must however continue without interruption, and be provided or arranged for, and paid for by the Mental Health Plan in the county of original jurisdiction until the court makes a ruling on the request for a hearing or makes a ruling as required in (c)(3) if a hearing is granted.

Rule 5.649. Right to make educational or developmental-services decisions

The court must identify the educational rights holder for the child [1] at each hearing in a **juvenile** dependency or [2] **juvenile justice** proceeding. **At any hearing, where the court limits, restores, or modifies educational rights, or where there are updates to any contact or other information, in any juvenile proceeding, the findings and orders must be documented on form JV-535.** Unless [3] **the** rights **of the parent, guardian, or Indian custodian** have been limited by the court under this rule, the parent [4]**, guardian, or Indian custodian** holds the educational and developmental-services decisionmaking rights for [5] **the** child. In addition, a nonminor or nonminor dependent youth holds the rights to make educational and developmental-services decisions for [6] **the youth and should be identified on form JV-535,** unless rule 5.650(b) applies.

Rule 5.649 Introduction.   2020 Deletes. [1] on form JV-535 [2] delinquency [3] his or her [4] or [5] his or her [6] himself or herself

(a) Order (§§ 361, 366, 366.27, 366.3, 726, 727.2; 20 U.S.C. § 1415; 34 C.F.R. § 300.300)

At the dispositional hearing and each subsequent review or permanency hearing, the court must determine whether the rights of a parent [1]**,** guardian, **or Indian custodian** to make educational or developmental-services decisions for the child should be limited.

If necessary to protect a child who is adjudged a dependent or ward of the court under section 300, 601, or 602, the court may limit **the rights of** a [2] **parent, guardian, or Indian custodian** to make educational or developmental-services decisions for the child by making appropriate, specific orders on *Order Designating Educational Rights Holder* (form JV-535).

(Subd (a) amended effective September 1, 2020; adopted effective January 1, 2014.)

Rule 5.649(a).   2020 Deletes. [1] or [2] parent's or guardian's rights

(b) Temporary order (§ 319)

At the initial hearing on a petition filed under section 325 or at any time before a child is adjudged a dependent or the petition is dismissed, the court may, on making the findings required by section 319(g)(1), use form

JV-535 to temporarily limit **the rights of** a [1] **parent, guardian, or Indian custodian** to make educational or developmental-services decisions for the child. An order made under section 319(g) expires on dismissal of the petition, but in no circumstances later than the conclusion of the hearing held under section 361.

If the court does temporarily limit the [2] rights **of a parent, guardian, or Indian custodian** to make educational or developmental-services decisions, the court must, at the dispositional hearing, reconsider the need to limit those rights and must identify the authorized educational rights holder on form JV-535.

(Subd (b) amended effective September 1, 2020; adopted effective January 1, 2014.)

Rule 5.649(b).   2020 Deletes. [1] parent's or guardian's rights [2] parent's or guardian's

(c)   No delay of initial assessment

The child's initial assessment to determine any need for special education or developmental services need not be delayed to obtain parental or guardian consent or for the appointment of an educational rights holder if one or more of the following circumstances is met:

(1) The court has limited, even temporarily, the educational or developmental-services decisionmaking rights of the parent [1]**, guardian, or Indian custodian,** and consent for an initial assessment has been given by an individual appointed by the court to represent the child;

(2) The local educational agency or regional center, after reasonable efforts, cannot locate the parent [2]**, guardian, or Indian custodian**; or

(3) Parental rights have been terminated or the guardianship has been set aside.

(Subd (c) amended September 1, 2020; adopted effective January 1, 2014.)

Rule 5.649(c).   2020 Deletes. [1] or [2] or

(d)   Judicial determination

If the court determines that the child is in need of any assessments, evaluations, or services—including special education, mental health, developmental, and other related services—the court must direct an appropriate person to take the necessary steps to request those assessments, evaluations, or services.

(Subd (d) amended effective September 1, 2020; adopted effective January 1, 2014.)

(e)   Filing of order

Following the dispositional hearing and each statutory review hearing, the party that has requested a modification, limitation, or restoration of educational or developmental-services decisionmaking rights must complete form JV-535 and any required attachments to reflect the court's orders and submit the completed form within five court days for the court's review and signature. [1] **If there has been no request for modification, limitation, or restoration of educational or developmental-services decisionmaking rights, or there are no required updates to contact or other information, there is no need to file a new form JV-535. If a new form JV-535 is filed, the most recent** *Attachment to Order Designating Educational Rights Holder* **(form JV-535(A)) must be attached**. The court may **instead** direct the appropriate party to attach [2] **a new form JV-535(A)** to document the court's findings and orders.

(Subd (e) amended effective September 1, 2020; adopted effective January 1, 2014.)

Rule 5.649(e).   2020 Deletes. [1] If no request is made, the child's or youth's attorney must complete and file the form [2] *Attachment to Order Designating Educational Rights Holder* (form JV-535(A))

(f)   Service of process

After each hearing where a party has requested a modification, limitation, or restoration of educational or developmental-services decisionmaking rights, the court clerk must serve the most current forms JV-535 and JV-535(A) on each applicable party.

(Subd (f) adopted effective September 1, 2020.)

Rule 5.649 amended effective September 1, 2020; adopted effective January 1, 2014.

Rule 5.650.   Appointed educational rights holder

(a)   Order and appointment (§§ 319, 361, 366, 366.27, 366.3, 726, 727.2; Gov. Code, §§ 7579.5–7579.6; 20 U.S.C. § 1415; 34 C.F.R. § 300.519)

Whenever it limits, even temporarily, the rights of a parent or guardian to make educational or developmental-services decisions for a child, the court must use form JV-535 to appoint a responsible adult as educational rights holder or to document that one of the following circumstances exists:

(1) The child is a dependent child or ward of the court and has a court-ordered permanent plan of placement in a planned permanent living arrangement. The caregiver may, without a court order, exercise educational decisionmaking rights under Education Code section 56055 and developmental-services decisionmaking rights under section 361 or 726, and is not prohibited from exercising those rights by section 361, 726, or 4701.6(b), or by 34 Code of Federal Regulations section 300.519 or 303.422; or

(2) The court cannot identify a responsible adult to serve as the child's educational rights holder under section 319, 361, or 726 or under Education Code section 56055; and

(A) The child is a dependent child or ward of the court and is or may be eligible for special education and related services or already has a valid individualized education program, and the court:

(i) Refers the child to the local educational agency for the appointment of a surrogate parent under section 361 or 726, Government Code section 7579.5, and title 20 United States Code section 1415; and

(ii) Will, with the input of any interested person, make developmental-services decisions for the child; or

(B) The appointment of a surrogate parent is not warranted, and the court will, with the input of any interested person, make educational and developmental-services decisions for the child.

(C) If the court must temporarily make educational or developmental-services decisions for a child before disposition, it must order that every effort be made to identify a responsible adult to make future educational or developmental-services decisions for the child.

(Subd (a) amended and relettered effective January 1, 2014; adopted as subd (b) effective January 1, 2004; previously amended effective January 1, 2007, and January 1, 2008.)

(b)   Nonminor and nonminor dependent youth (§§ 361, 726, 366.3)

The court may, using form JV-535, appoint or continue the appointment of an educational rights holder to make educational or developmental-services decisions for a nonminor or nonminor dependent youth if:

(1) The youth has chosen not to make educational or developmental-services decisions for himself or herself or is deemed by the court to be incompetent; and

(2) With respect to developmental-services decisions, the court also finds that the appointment or continuance of a rights holder would be in the best interests of the youth.

(Subd (b) adopted effective January 1, 2014.)

(c)   Limits on appointment (§§ 319, 361, 726; Ed. Code, § 56055; Gov. Code, § 7579.5(i)–(j); 34 C.F.R. §§ 300.519, 303.422)

(1) The court must determine whether a responsible adult relative, nonrelative extended family member, or other adult known to the child is available and willing to serve as the educational rights holder and, if one of those adults is available and willing to serve, should consider appointing that person before appointing or temporarily appointing a responsible adult not known to the child.

(2) The court may not appoint any individual as the educational rights holder if that person is excluded under, or would have a conflict of interest as defined by, section 361(a) or 726(c), Education Code section 56055, Government Code section 7579.5(i)–(j), 20 United States Code section 1415(b)(2), or 34 Code of Federal Regulations section 300.519 or 303.422.

(Subd (c) amended effective January 1, 2014; adopted effective January 1, 2004; previously amended effective January 1, 2007, and January 1, 2008.)

(d)   Referral for appointment of surrogate parent (§§ 361, 726; Gov. Code, § 7579.5; 20 U.S.C. § 1415)

(1) If the court has limited a parent's or guardian's right to make educational decisions for a child and cannot identify a responsible adult to act as the educational rights holder, and the child is or may be eligible for special education and related services or already has an individualized education program, the court must use form JV-535 to refer the child to the responsible local educational agency for prompt appointment of a surrogate parent under Government Code section 7579.5.

(2) If the court refers a child to the local educational agency for appointment of a surrogate parent, the court must order that *Local Educational Agency Response to JV-535—Appointment of Surrogate Parent* (form JV-536) be attached to form JV-535 and served by first-class mail on the local educational agency no later than five court days from the date the order is signed.

(3) The court must direct the local educational agency that when the agency receives form JV-535 requesting prompt appointment of a surro-

gate parent, the agency must make reasonable efforts to identify and appoint a surrogate parent within 30 calendar days of service of the referral.

(A) Whenever the local educational agency appoints a surrogate parent for a dependent or ward under Government Code section 7579.5(a)(1), it must notify the court on form JV-536 within five court days of the appointment and, at the same time, must send copies of the notice to the child's attorney and to the social worker or probation officer identified on the form.

(B) If the local educational agency does not appoint a surrogate parent within 30 days of receipt of a judicial request, it must notify the court within the next five court days on form JV-536 of the following:

(i) Its inability to identify and appoint a surrogate parent; and

(ii) Its continuing reasonable efforts to identify and appoint a surrogate parent.

(4) Whenever a surrogate parent resigns or the local educational agency terminates the appointment of a surrogate parent, replaces a surrogate parent, or appoints another surrogate parent, it must notify the court, the child's attorney, and the social worker or probation officer on form JV-536 within five court days of the resignation, termination, replacement, or appointment. The child's attorney, the social worker, or the probation officer may request a hearing for appointment of a new educational rights holder by filing *Request for Hearing Regarding Child's Access to Services* (form JV-539) and must provide notice of the hearing as provided in (g)(2). The court may, on its own motion, direct the clerk to set a hearing.

(Subd (d) amended effective January 1, 2014; adopted as subd (b) effective July 1, 2002; previously amended and relettered effective January 1, 2004; previously amended effective January 1, 2007, and January 1, 2008.)

(e) Transfer of parent's or guardian's educational or developmental-services decisionmaking rights to educational rights holder

When the court appoints an educational rights holder after limiting a parent's or guardian's educational or developmental-services decisionmaking rights, those parental decisionmaking rights including the right to notice of educational or developmental-services meetings and activities, to participation in educational or developmental-services meetings and activities, and to decisionmaking authority regarding the child's education or developmental services, including the authority under sections 4512 and 4701.6, Education Code section 56028, 20 United States Code sections 1232g and 1401(23), and 34 Code of Federal Regulations section 300.30 are transferred to the educational rights holder unless the court specifies otherwise in its order.

(1) When returning a child to a parent or guardian, the court must consider the child's educational and developmental-services needs. The parent's or guardian's educational and developmental-services decisionmaking rights are reinstated when the court returns custody to the parent or guardian unless the court finds specifically that continued limitation of parental decisionmaking rights is necessary to protect the child.

(2) If the court appoints a guardian for the child under rule 5.735 or 5.815, all of the parent's or previous guardian's educational and developmental-services decisionmaking rights transfer to the newly appointed guardian unless the court determines that limitation of the new guardian's decisionmaking rights is necessary to protect the child.

(Subd (e) amended effective January 1, 2014; adopted effective January 1, 2004; previously amended effective January 1, 2007, and January 1, 2008.)

(f) Authority and responsibilities (§§ 317, 319, 360, 361, 635, 706.5, 726, 4514, 4646–4648, 4700–4731, 5328; Ed. Code, §§ 56055, 56340, 56345; Gov. Code, §§ 7579.5, 95014–95020; 34 C.F.R. § 300.519)

(1) The educational rights holder acts as and holds the rights of the parent or guardian with respect to all decisions regarding the child's education and developmental services, and is entitled:

(A) To access records and to authorize the disclosure of information to the same extent as a parent or guardian under the Family Educational Rights and Privacy Act (FERPA), 20 United States Code section 1232g;

(B) To be given notice of and participate in all meetings or proceedings relating to school discipline;

(C) To advocate for the interests of a child or youth with exceptional needs in matters relating to:

(i) The identification and assessment of those needs;

(ii) Instructional or service planning and program development—including the development of an individualized family service plan, an individualized educational program, an individual program plan, or the provision of other services and supports, as applicable;

(iii) Placement in the least restrictive program appropriate to the child's or youth's educational or developmental needs;

(iv) The review or revision of the individualized family service plan, the individualized education program, or the individual program plan; and

(v) The provision of a free, appropriate public education.

(D) To attend and participate in the child's or youth's individualized family service plan, individualized education program, individual program plan, and other educational or service planning meetings; to consult with persons involved in the provision of the child's or youth's education or developmental services; and to sign any written consent to educational or developmental services and plans; and

(E) Notwithstanding any other provision of law, to consent to the child's or youth's individualized family service plan, individualized education program, or individual program plan, including any related nonemergency medical services, mental health treatment services, and occupational or physical therapy services provided under sections 7570–7587 of the Government Code.

(2) The educational rights holder is responsible for investigating the child's or youth's educational and developmental-services needs, determining whether those needs are being met, and acting on behalf of the child or youth in all matters relating to the provision of educational or developmental services, as applicable, to ensure:

(A) The stability of the child's or youth's school placement. At any hearing following a change of educational placement, the educational rights holder must submit a statement to the court indicating whether the proposed change of placement is in the child's or youth's best interest and whether any efforts have been made to keep the pupil in the school of origin;

(B) Placement in the least restrictive educational program appropriate to the child's or youth's individual needs;

(C) The child's or youth's access to academic resources, services, and extracurricular and enrichment activities;

(D) The child's or youth's access to any educational and developmental services and supports needed to meet state standards for academic achievement and functional performance or, with respect to developmental services, to promote community integration, an independent, productive, and normal life, and a stable and healthy environment;

(E) The prompt and appropriate resolution of school disciplinary matters;

(F) The provision of any other elements of a free, appropriate public education; and

(G) The provision of any appropriate early intervention or developmental services required by law, including the California Early Intervention Services Act or the Lanterman Developmental Disabilities Services Act.

(3) The educational rights holder is also responsible for:

(A) Meeting with the child or youth at least once and as often as necessary to make educational or developmental-services decisions that are in the best interest of the child or youth;

(B) Being culturally sensitive to the child or youth;

(C) Complying with all federal and state confidentiality laws, including, but not limited to, sections 362.5, 827, 4514, and 5328, as well as Government Code section 7579.5(f);

(D) Participating in, and making decisions regarding, all matters affecting the child's or youth's educational or developmental-services needs—including, as applicable, the individualized family service planning process, the individualized education program planning process, the individual program planning process, the fair hearing process (including mediation and any other informal dispute resolution meetings), and as otherwise specified in the court order—in a manner consistent with the child's or youth's best interest; and

(E) Maintaining knowledge and skills that ensure adequate representation of the child's or youth's needs and interests with respect to education and developmental services.

(4) Before each statutory review hearing, the educational rights holder must do one or more of the following:

(A) Provide information and recommendations concerning the child's or youth's educational or developmental-services needs to the assigned social worker or probation officer;

(B) Make written recommendations to the court concerning the child's or youth's educational or developmental-services needs;

(C) Attend the review hearing and participate in any part of the hearing that concerns the child's or youth's education or developmental services.

(5) The educational rights holder may provide the contact information for the child's or youth's attorney to the local educational agency.

(Subd (f) amended effective January 1, 2014; adopted effective January 1, 2008.)

(g) Term of service; resignation (§§ 319, 361, 726; Gov. Code § 7579.5)

(1) An appointed educational rights holder must make educational or developmental-services decisions for the child or youth until:

(A) The dismissal of the petition or the conclusion of the dispositional hearing, if the rights holder is appointed under section 319(g);

(B) The rights of the parent or guardian to make educational or developmental-services decisions for the child are fully restored;

(C) The dependent or ward reaches 18 years of age, unless he or she chooses not to make his or her own educational or developmental-services decisions or is deemed incompetent by the court, in which case the court may, if it also finds that continuation would be in the best interests of the youth, continue the appointment until the youth reaches 21 years of age or the court's jurisdiction is terminated;

(D) The court appoints another responsible adult as educational rights holder for the child or youth under this rule;

(E) The court appoints a successor guardian or conservator; or

(F) The court designates an identified foster parent, relative caregiver, or nonrelative extended family member to make educational or developmental-services decisions because:

(i) Reunification services have been terminated and the child is placed in a planned permanent living arrangement with the identified caregiver under section 366.21(g)(5), 366.22, 366.26, 366.3(i), 727.3(b)(5), or 727.3(b)(6); and

(ii) The foster parent, relative caregiver, or nonrelative extended family member is not otherwise excluded from making education or developmental-services decisions by the court, by section 361 or 726, or by 34 Code of Federal Regulations section 300.519 or 303.422.

(2) If an appointed educational rights holder resigns his or her appointment, he or she must give notice to the court and to the child's attorney and may use *Educational Rights Holder Statement* (form JV-537) to provide this notice. Once notice is received, the child's or youth's attorney, or the social worker or probation officer may request a hearing for appointment of a new educational rights holder by filing form JV-539.

The attorney for the party requesting the hearing must provide notice of the hearing to:

(A) The parents or guardians, unless otherwise indicated on the most recent form JV-535, parental rights have been terminated, or the child has reached 18 years of age;

(B) Each attorney of record;

(C) The social worker or probation officer;

(D) The CASA volunteer; and

(E) All other persons or entities entitled to notice under section 293.

The hearing must be set within 14 days of receipt of the request for hearing. The court may, on its own motion, direct the clerk to set a hearing.

(Subd (g) amended effective January 1, 2014; adopted effective January 1, 2008.)

(h) Service of order

Whenever the order identifies or appoints a new or different educational rights holder or includes any other changes, the clerk will provide a copy of the completed and signed form JV-535, form JV-535(A) if attached, and any received form JV-536 or JV-537 to:

(1) The child, if 10 years or older, or youth;

(2) The attorney for the child or youth;

(3) The social worker or probation officer;

(4) The Indian child's tribe, if applicable, as defined in rule 5.502;

(5) The local foster youth educational liaison, as defined in Education Code section 48853.5;

(6) The county office of education foster youth services coordinator;

(7) The regional center service coordinator, if applicable; and

(8) The educational rights holder.

The completed and signed form must be provided no later than five court days from the date the order is signed. The clerk must also ensure that any immediately preceding educational rights holder, surrogate parent, or authorized representative, if any, is notified that the previous court order has been vacated and their appointment terminated.

The clerk will make copies of the form available to the parents or guardians, unless otherwise indicated on the form, parental rights have been terminated, or the child has reached 18 years of age and reunification services have been terminated; to the CASA volunteer; and, if requested, to all other persons or entities entitled to notice under section 293.

(Subd (h) amended effective January 1, 2014; adopted effective January 1, 2008.)

(i) Education and training of educational rights holder

If the educational rights holder, including a parent or guardian, asks for assistance in obtaining education and training in the laws incorporated in rule 5.651(a), the court must direct the clerk, social worker, or probation officer to inform the educational rights holder of all available resources, including resources available through the California Department of Education, the California Department of Developmental Services, the local educational agency, and the local regional center.

(Subd (i) amended effective January 1, 2015; adopted effective January 1, 2008; previously amended effective January 1, 2014.)

(j) Notice of and participation in hearings

(1) The educational rights holder must receive notice of all regularly scheduled juvenile court hearings and other judicial hearings that might affect the child's or youth's education and developmental services, including joint assessment hearings under rule 5.512 and joinder proceedings under rule 5.575.

(2) The educational rights holder may use form JV-537 to explain any educational or developmental-services needs to the court. The court must permit the educational rights holder to attend and participate in those portions of a court hearing, nonjudicial hearing, or mediation that concern education or developmental services.

(Subd (j) amended effective January 1, 2014; adopted effective January 1, 2008.) Rule 5.650 amended effective January 1, 2015; adopted as rule 1499 effective July 1, 2002; previously amended and renumbered effective January 1, 2007; previously amended effective January 1, 2004, January 1, 2008, and January 1, 2014.

Advisory Committee Comment

Under the Individuals With Disabilities Education Act (IDEA), the court may appoint a surrogate parent to speak and act on behalf of a pupil in all matters relating to the identification, evaluation, and educational placement of the child and to the provision of the child's free, appropriate public education. (20 U.S.C. § 1415(b)(2); 34 C.F.R. § 300.519.) Under Welfare and Institutions Code sections 361 and 726, the court must appoint a responsible adult as an educational representative or rights holder to make decisions regarding the child's educational or developmental-services needs when the parent's rights to make those decisions have been limited. A court-appointed educational rights holder is responsible for protecting the child's rights and interests with respect to educational or developmental services, including any special education and related services.

If the court limits the parent's decisionmaking rights and cannot identify a responsible adult to appoint as educational rights holder, and the appointment of a surrogate parent is not warranted, sections 361 and 726 authorize the court to make educational or developmental-services decisions for the child with the input of interested persons. If, however, the court cannot identify a responsible adult to appoint as educational rights holder and there is reason to believe that the child needs special education and related services, the court must refer the child to the local educational agency (LEA) for the appointment of a surrogate parent. Sections 361 and 726 do not authorize the court to make *educational* decisions for a child in these circumstances. The surrogate parent appointed by the LEA acts as a parent for the purpose of making decisions with respect to special education and related services and the provision of a free, appropriate public education on behalf of the child. (Gov. Code, § 7579.5(c); Ed. Code, § 56028; 34 C.F.R. § 300.30(b)(2); see 20 U.S.C. §§ 1401(9), 1414(d).) If, however, the LEA does not appoint a surrogate parent in a timely manner, the court has the authority to join the LEA in the dependency proceedings under section 362 and rule 5.575. In the period between the setting of the joinder hearing and the appointment of a surrogate parent by the LEA, the court may make educational decisions for the child under the general authority granted by section 362(a). The appointment of a surrogate parent notwithstanding, the court holds the authority under sections 361 and 726 to make *developmental-services* decisions if it cannot identify a responsible adult to do so.

Rule 5.651. Educational and developmental-services decisionmaking rights

(a) Applicability (§§ 213.5, 319(g), 358, 358.1, 361(a), 362(a), 364, 366.21, 366.22, 366.23, 366.26, 366.27(b), 366.3(e), 726, 727.2(e), 4500 et seq., 11404.1; Ed. Code, §§ 48645 et seq., 48850 et seq., 49069.5, 56028, 56055, and 56155 et seq.; Gov. Code, §§ 7573–7579.6; 20 U.S.C. § 1400 et seq.; 29 U.S.C. § 794; 42 U.S.C. § 12101 et seq.)

This rule incorporates all rights with respect to education or developmental services recognized or established by state or federal law and applies:

Rules of Court

(1) To any child, or any nonminor or nonminor dependent youth, for whom a petition has been filed under section 300, 601, or 602 until the petition is dismissed or the court has terminated dependency, delinquency, or transition jurisdiction over that person; and

(2) To every judicial hearing related to, or that might affect, the child's or youth's education or receipt of developmental services.

(Subd (a) amended effective January 1, 2014; adopted effective January 1, 2008.)

(b) Conduct of hearings

(1) To the extent the information is available, at the initial or detention hearing the court must consider:

(A) Who holds educational and developmental-services decisionmaking rights, and identify the rights holder or holders;

(B) Whether the child or youth is enrolled in, and is attending, the child's or youth's school of origin, as that term is defined in Education Code section 48853.5(f);

(C) If the child or youth is at risk of removal from or is no longer attending the school of origin, whether:

(i) In accordance with the child's or youth's best interest, the educational liaison, as described in Education Code section 48853.5(b), (d), and (e), in consultation with, and with the agreement of, the child or youth and the parent, guardian, or other person holding educational decisionmaking rights, recommends the waiver of the child's or youth's right to attend the school of origin;

(ii) Before making any recommendation to move a foster child or youth from his or her school of origin, the educational liaison provided the child or youth and the person holding the right to make educational decisions for the child or youth with a written explanation of the basis for the recommendation and how this recommendation serves the foster child's or youth's best interest as provided in Education Code section 48853.5(e)(7);

(iii) If the child or youth is no longer attending the school of origin, the local educational agency obtained a valid waiver of the child's or youth's right to continue in the school of origin under Education Code section 48853.5(e)(1) before moving the child or youth from that school; and

(iv) The child or youth was immediately enrolled in the new school as provided in Education Code section 48853.5(e)(8).

(D) In a dependency proceeding, whether the parent's or guardian's educational or developmental-services decisionmaking rights should be temporarily limited and an educational rights holder temporarily appointed using form JV-535; and

(E) Taking into account other statutory considerations regarding placement, whether the out-of-home placement:

(i) Is the environment best suited to meet the exceptional needs of a child or youth with disabilities and to serve the child's or youth's best interest if he or she has a disability; and

(ii) Promotes educational stability through proximity to the child's or youth's school of origin.

(2) At the dispositional hearing and at all subsequent hearings described in (a)(2), the court must:

(A) Consider and determine whether the child's or youth's educational, physical, mental health, and developmental needs, including any need for special education and related services, are being met;

(B) Identify the educational rights holder on form JV-535; and

(C) Direct the rights holder to take all appropriate steps to ensure that the child's or youth's educational and developmental needs are met.

The court's findings and orders must address the following:

(D) Whether the child's or youth's educational, physical, mental health, and developmental-services needs are being met;

(E) What services, assessments, or evaluations, including those for developmental services or for special education and related services, the child or youth may need;

(F) Who must take the necessary steps for the child or youth to receive any necessary assessments, evaluations, or services;

(G) If the child's or youth's educational placement changed during the period under review, whether:

(i) The child's or youth's educational records, including any evaluations of a child or youth with a disability, were transferred to the new educational placement within two business days of the request for the child's or youth's enrollment in the new educational placement; and

(ii) The child or youth is enrolled in and attending school.

(H) Whether the parent's or guardian's educational or developmental-services decisionmaking rights should be limited or, if previously limited, whether those rights should be restored.

(i) If the court finds that the parent's or guardian's educational or developmental-services decisionmaking rights should not be limited or should be restored, the court must explain to the parent or guardian his or her rights and responsibilities in regard to the child's education and developmental services as provided in rule 5.650(e), (f), and (j); or

(ii) If the court finds that the parent's or guardian's educational or developmental-services decisionmaking rights should be or remain limited, the court must designate the holder of those rights. The court must explain to the parent or guardian why the court is limiting his or her educational or developmental-services decisionmaking rights and must explain the rights and responsibilities of the educational rights holder as provided in rule 5.650(e), (f), and (j); and

(I) Whether, in the case of a nonminor or nonminor dependent youth who has chosen not to make educational or developmental-services decisions for himself or herself or has been deemed incompetent, it is in the best interests of the youth to appoint or to continue the appointment of an educational rights holder.

(Subd (b) amended effective January 1, 2014; adopted effective January 1, 2008.)

(c) Reports for hearings related to, or that may affect, education or developmental services

This subdivision applies at all hearings, including dispositional and joint assessment hearings. The court must ensure that, to the extent the information was available, the social worker or the probation officer provided the following information in the report for the hearing:

(1) The child's or youth's age, behavior, educational level, and developmental status and any discrepancies between that person's age and his or her level of achievement in education or level of cognitive, physical, and emotional development;

(2) The child's or youth's educational, physical, mental health, or developmental needs;

(3) Whether the child or youth is participating in developmentally appropriate extracurricular and social activities;

(4) Whether the child or youth is attending a comprehensive, regular, public or private school;

(5) Whether the child or youth may have physical, mental, or learning-related disabilities or other characteristics indicating a need for developmental services or special education and related services as provided by state of federal law;

(6) If the child is 0 to 3 years old, whether the child may be eligible for or is already receiving early intervention services or services under the California Early Intervention Services Act (Gov. Code, § 95000 et seq.) and, if the child is already receiving services, the specific nature of those services;

(7) If the child is between 3 and 5 years old and is or may be eligible for special education and related services, whether the child is receiving the early educational opportunities provided by Education Code section 56001 and, if so, the specific nature of those opportunities;

(8) Whether the child or youth is receiving special education and related services or any other services through a current individualized education program and, if so, the specific nature of those services;

(i) A copy of the current individualized education program should be attached to the report unless disclosure would create a risk of harm. In that case, the report should explain the risk.

(9) Whether the child or youth is receiving services under section 504 of the Rehabilitation Act of 1973 (29 U.S.C. § 701 et seq.) and, if so, the specific nature of those services;

(i) A copy of any current Section 504 plan should be attached to the report unless disclosure would create a risk of harm. In that case, the report should explain the risk.

(10) Whether the child or youth is or may be eligible for developmental services or is already receiving developmental services and, if that person is already receiving services, the specific nature of those services;

(i) A copy of any current individualized family service plan or individual program plan should be attached to the report unless disclosure would create a risk of harm. In that case, the report should explain the risk.

(11) Whether the parent's or guardian's educational or developmental-services decisionmaking rights have been or should be limited or restored;

(12) If the social worker or probation officer recommends that the court limit the parent's or guardian's rights to make educational or developmental-services decisions, the reasons those rights should be limited and the actions that the parent or guardian may take to restore those rights if they are limited;

(13) If the parent's or guardian's educational or developmental-services decisionmaking rights have been limited, the identity of the designated or appointed educational rights holder or surrogate parent;

(14) Recommendations and case plan goals to meet the child's or youth's identified educational, physical, mental health, and developmental-services needs, including all related information listed in section 16010(a) as required by section 16010(b);

(15) Whether any orders to direct an appropriate person to take the necessary steps for the child to receive assessments, evaluations, or services, including those for developmental services or for special education and related services, are requested; and

(16) In the case of a joint assessment, separate statements by the child welfare department and the probation department, each addressing whether the child or youth may have a disability and whether the child or youth needs developmental services or special education and related services or qualifies for any assessment or evaluation required by state or federal law.

(Subd (c) amended effective January 1, 2014; adopted effective January 1, 2008.)

(d) Continuance, stay, or suspension (§§ 357, 358, 702, 705)

If the court continues the dispositional hearing under rule 5.686 or 5.782 or stays the proceedings or suspends jurisdiction under rule 5.645, the child must continue to receive all services or accommodations required by state or federal law.

(Subd (d) amended effective January 1, 2014; adopted effective January 1, 2008.)

(e) Change of placement affecting the child's or youth's educational stability (§§ 16010, 16010.6; Ed. Code §§ 48850–48853.5)

This subdivision applies to all changes of placement, including the initial placement and any subsequent change of placement.

(1) At any hearing to which this rule applies that follows a decision to change the child's or youth's placement to a location that could lead to removal from the school of origin, the placement agency must demonstrate that, and the court must determine whether:

(A) The social worker or probation officer notified the court, the child's or youth's attorney, and the educational rights holder or surrogate parent, no more than one court day after making the placement decision, of the proposed placement decision.

(B) If the child or youth had a disability and an active individualized education program before removal, the social worker or probation officer, at least 10 days before the change of placement, notified in writing the local educational agency that provided a special education program for the child or youth before removal and the receiving special education local plan area, as described in Government Code section 7579.1, of the impending change of placement.

(2) After receipt of the notice in (1):

(A) The child's or youth's attorney must, as appropriate, discuss the proposed placement change and its effect on the child's or youth's right to attend the school of origin with the child or youth and the person who holds educational rights. The child's or youth's attorney may request a hearing by filing form JV-539. If requesting a hearing, the attorney must:

(i) File form JV-539 no later than two court days after receipt of the notice in (1); and

(ii) Provide notice of the hearing date, which will be no later than five court days after the form was filed, to the parents or guardians, unless otherwise indicated on form JV-535, parental rights have been terminated, or the youth has reached 18 years of age and reunification services have been terminated; the social worker or probation officer; the educational rights holder or surrogate parent; the foster youth educational liaison; Court Appointed Special Advocate (CASA) volunteer; and all other persons or entities entitled to notice under section 293.

(B) The person who holds educational rights may request a hearing by filing form JV-539 no later than two court days after receipt of the notice in (1). After receipt of the form, the clerk must notify the persons in (e)(2)(A)(ii) of the hearing date.

(C) The court on its own motion may direct the clerk to set a hearing.

(3) If removal from the school of origin is disputed, the child or youth must be allowed to remain in the school of origin pending this hearing and pending the resolution of any disagreement between the child or youth, the parent, guardian, or educational rights holder, and the local educational agency.

(4) If the court sets a hearing, the social worker or probation officer must provide a report no later than two court days after the hearing is set

that includes the information required by (b)(1)(C) as well as the following:

(A) Whether the foster child or youth has been allowed to continue his or her education in the school of origin to the extent required by Education Code section 48853.5(e)(1);

(B) Whether a dispute exists regarding the request of a foster child or youth to remain in the school of origin and whether the foster child or youth has been allowed to remain in the school of origin pending resolution of the dispute;

(C) Information addressing whether the information-sharing and other requirements in section 16501.1(c)(4) and Education Code section 49069.5 have been met;

(D) Information addressing how the proposed change serves the best interest of the child or youth;

(E) The responses of the child, if over 10 years old, or youth; the child's or youth's attorney; the parent, guardian, or other educational rights holder; the foster youth educational liaison; and the child's or youth's CASA volunteer to the proposed change of placement, specifying whether each person agrees or disagrees with the proposed change and, if any person disagrees, stating the reasons; and

(F) A statement from the social worker or probation officer confirming that the child or youth has not been segregated in a separate school, or in a separate program within a school, because the child or youth is placed in foster care.

(Subd (e) amended effective January 1, 2014; adopted effective January 1, 2008.)

(f) Court review of proposed change of placement affecting the right to attend the school of origin

(1) At a hearing set under (e)(2), the court must:

(A) Determine whether the placement agency and other relevant parties and advocates have fulfilled their obligations under section 16000(b), 16010(a), and 16501.1(f)(8);

(B) Determine whether the proposed school placement meets the requirements of this rule and Education Code sections 48853.5 and 49069.5, and whether the placement is in the best interest of the child or youth;

(C) Determine what actions are necessary to ensure the protection of the child's or youth's educational and developmental-services rights; and

(D) Make any findings and orders needed to enforce those rights, which may include an order to set a hearing under section 362 to join the necessary agencies regarding provision of services, including the provision of transportation services, so that the child or youth may remain in his or her school of origin.

(2) When considering whether it is in the child's or youth's best interest to remove him or her from the school of origin, the court must consider the following:

(A) Whether the parent, guardian, or other educational rights holder believes that removal from the school of origin is in the child's or youth's best interest;

(B) How the proposed change of placement will affect the stability of the child's or youth's school placement and the child's or youth's access to academic resources, services, and extracurricular and enrichment activities;

(C) Whether the proposed school placement would allow the child or youth to be placed in the least restrictive educational program; and

(D) Whether the child or youth has the educational and developmental services and supports, including those for special education and related services, necessary to meet state academic achievement standards.

(3) The court may make its findings and orders on *Findings and Orders Regarding Transfer From School of Origin* (form JV-538).

(Subd (f) amended effective January 1, 2014; adopted effective January 1, 2008.)
Rule 5.651 amended effective January 1, 2014; adopted effective January 1, 2008.

Advisory Committee Comment

A child or youth in, or at risk of entering, foster care has a statutory right to a meaningful opportunity to meet the state's academic achievement standards. To protect this right, the juvenile court, advocates, placing agencies, care providers, educators, and service providers must work together to maintain stable school placements and ensure that the child or youth is placed in the least restrictive educational programs and has access to the academic resources, services, and extracurricular and enrichment activities that are available to other pupils. This rule, sections 362 and 727, and rule 5.575 provide procedures for coordinating the provision of services to ensure that the child's or youth's educational and developmental-services needs are met.

Congress has found that improving the educational performance of children with disabilities is an essential prerequisite to ensuring their equality of opportunity, full participation in education, and economic self-sufficiency. Children and youth in foster care are disproportionately represented in the population of pupils with disabilities and face systemic challenges to attaining self-sufficiency. Children and youth in foster care have rights arising out of federal and state law, including the IDEA, the ADA, and section 504 of the Rehabilitation Act of 1973. To comply with federal requirements regarding the identification of children and youth with disabilities and the provision of services to those children and youth who qualify, the court, parent or guardian, placing agency, attorneys, CASA volunteer, local educational agencies, and educational rights holders must affirmatively address the child's or youth's educational and developmental-services needs. The court must continually inquire about the educational and developmental-services needs of the child or youth and the progress being made to enforce any rights the child or youth has under these laws.

Rule 5.652. Access to pupil records for truancy purposes

(a) Conditions of access (Ed. Code, § 49076)

Education Code section 49076 authorizes a school district to permit access to pupil records, including accurate copies, to any judicial officer or probation officer without consent of the pupil's parent or guardian and without a court order for the purposes of:

(1) Conducting a truancy mediation program for the pupil; or

(2) Presenting evidence in a truancy proceeding under section 681(b).

(Subd (a) amended effective January 1, 2007.)

(b) Written certification

The judicial officer or probation officer may request pupil records but must certify in writing that the requested information will be used only for purposes of truancy mediation or a truancy petition. A judicial officer or probation officer must complete and file *Certified Request for Pupil Records—Truancy* (form JV-530) and serve it with *Local Educational Agency Response to JV-530* (form JV-531), by first-class mail to the local educational agency.

(Subd (b) amended effective January 1, 2007.)

(c) Local educational agency response

Form JV-531 must be completed by the local educational agency and returned to the requesting judicial officer or probation officer within 15 calendar days of receipt of the request with copies of any responsive pupil records attached. After receipt the judicial officer or probation officer must file form JV-531 and the attached pupil records in the truancy proceedings.

(1) The school district must inform by telephone or other means, or provide written notification to, the child's parent or guardian within 24 hours of the release of the information.

(2) If a parent's or guardian's educational rights have been terminated, the school must notify the child's surrogate parent, relative, or other individual responsible for the child's education.

(Subd (c) amended effective January 1, 2007.)

Rule 5.652 amended and renumbered effective January 1, 2007; adopted as rule 1499.5 effective July 1, 2002.

Chapter 11
Advocates for Parties

Rule 5.655. Program requirements for Court Appointed Special Advocate programs

(a) General provisions

(1) A Court Appointed Special Advocate (CASA) program is a child advocacy program that recruits, screens, selects, trains, supervises, and supports lay volunteers for appointment by the court to help define the best interest of children and nonminors under the jurisdiction of the juvenile court, including the dependency and delinquency courts.

(2) To be authorized to serve children and nonminors in a county, the CASA program must be designated by the presiding judge of the juvenile court.

(3) A CASA program must comply with this rule to be eligible to receive Judicial Council funding.

(Subd (a) amended effective January 1, 2019; adopted effective January 1, 2005.)

(b) CASA program administration and management

(1) The court's designation of the CASA program must take the form of a memorandum of understanding (MOU) between the CASA program and the designating court.

(A) The MOU must state that the relationship between the CASA program and the designating court can be terminated for convenience by either the CASA program or the designating court.

(B) A CASA program may serve children and nonminors in more than one court if the program executes an MOU with each court.

(C) The CASA program and the designating court must be the only parties to the MOU.

(D) The MOU must indicate when and how the CASA program will have access to the juvenile case file and the nonminor dependent court file if applicable.

(2) A CASA program must function as a nonprofit organization or under the auspices of a public agency or nonprofit organization, and must adopt and adhere to a written plan for program governance and evaluation. The plan must include the following, as applicable:

(A) Articles of incorporation, a board of directors, and bylaws that specify a clear administrative relationship with the parent organization and clearly delineated delegations of authority and accountability.

(B) A clear statement of the purpose or mission of the CASA program that express goals and objectives to further that purpose. Where the CASA program is not an independent organization, but instead functions under the auspices of a public agency or a nonprofit organization, an active advisory council must be established. The role of the advisory council for CASA programs functioning under the auspices of a public agency or a nonprofit organization includes but is not limited to developing and approving policies for CASA, developing the CASA program's budget, promoting a collaborative relationship with the umbrella organization, monitoring and evaluating program operations, and developing and implementing fundraising activities to benefit the CASA program. The board of directors for the nonprofit organization or management of the public agency will function as the governing body for the CASA program, with guidance from the advisory council.

(C) A procedure for the recruitment, selection, hiring, and evaluation of an executive director for the CASA program.

(D) An administrative manual containing personnel policies, record-keeping practices, and data collection practices.

(E) Local juvenile court rules developed in consultation with the presiding judge of the juvenile court or a designee, as specified in section 100. One local rule must specify when CASA reports are to be submitted to the court, who is entitled to receive a copy of the report, and who will copy and distribute the report. This rule must also specify that the CASA court report must be distributed to the persons entitled to receive it at least two court days before the hearing for which the report was prepared.

(3) No CASA program may function under the auspices of a probation department or department of social services. CASA programs may receive funds from probation departments, local child welfare agencies, and the California Department of Social Services if:

(A) The CASA program and the contributing agency develop an MOU stating that the funds will be used only for general operating expenses as determined by the receiving CASA program, and the contributing agency will not oversee or monitor the funds;

(B) A procedure resolving any conflict between the CASA program and contributing agency is implemented so that conflict between the two agencies does not affect funding or the CASA program's ability to retain an independent evaluation separate from that of the contributing agency's; and

(C) Any MOU between a CASA program and the contributing agency is submitted to and approved by Judicial Council staff.

(4) If a CASA program serves more than one county, the CASA program is encouraged to seek representation on the board of directors and/or advisory council from each county it serves.

(Subd (b) repealed and adopted effective January 1, 2019.)

(c) Finance, facility, and risk management

(1) A CASA program must adopt a written plan for fiscal control. The fiscal plan must include an annual audit, conducted by a qualified professional, that is consistent with generally accepted accounting principles and the audit protocols in the program's Judicial Council contract.

(2) The fiscal plan must include a written budget with projections that guide the management of financial resources and a strategy for obtaining necessary funding for program operations.

(3) When the program has accounting oversight, it must adhere to written operational procedures in regard to accounting control.

(4) The CASA program's board of directors must set policies for and exercise control over fundraising activities carried out by its employees and volunteers.

(5) The CASA program must have the following insurance coverage for its staff and volunteers:

(A) General liability insurance with liability limits of not less than $1million ($1,000,000) for each person per occurrence/aggregate for bodily injury, and not less than $1million ($1,000,000) per occurrence/ aggregate for property damage;

(B) Nonowned automobile liability insurance and hired vehicle coverage with liability limits of not less than $1million ($1,000,000) combined single limit per occurrence and in the aggregate;

(C) Automobile liability insurance meeting the minimum state automobile liability insurance requirements, if the program owns a vehicle; and

(D) Workers' compensation insurance with a minimum limit of $500,000.

(6) The CASA program must require staff, volunteers, and members of the governing body, when applicable, to immediately notify the CASA program of any criminal charges against themselves.

(7) The nonprofit CASA program must plan for the disposition of property and confidential records in the event of its dissolution.

(Subd (c) adopted effective January 1, 2019.)

(d) Confidentiality

The presiding juvenile court judge and the CASA program director must adopt a written plan governing confidentiality of case information, case records, and personnel records. The plan must be included in the MOU or a local rule. The written plan must include the following provisions:

(1) All information concerning children and families, including nonminors, in the juvenile court process is confidential. Volunteers must not give case information to anyone other than the court, the parties and their attorneys, and CASA staff.

(2) CASA volunteers are required by law (Pen. Code, § 11166 et seq.) to report any reasonable suspicion that a child is a victim of child abuse or serious neglect as described by Penal Code section 273a.

(3) The child's original case file must be maintained in the CASA office by a custodian of records and must remain there. Copies of documents needed by a volunteer must be restricted to those actually needed to conduct necessary business outside of the office. No one may have access to the child's original case file except on the approval of the CASA program director or presiding judge of the juvenile court. Controls must be in place to ensure that records can be located at any time. The office must establish a written procedure for the maintenance of case files.

(4) If the nonminor provides consent for the CASA volunteer to obtain his or her nonminor dependent court file, the procedures stated in paragraph (3) related to maintenance of the case file must be followed.

(5) The volunteer's personnel file is confidential. No one may have access to the personnel file except the volunteer, the CASA program director or a designee, or the presiding judge of the juvenile court.

(Subd (d) adopted effective January 1, 2019.)

(e) Recruiting, screening, and selecting CASA volunteers

(1) A CASA volunteer is a person who has been recruited, screened, selected, and trained; is being supervised and supported by a local CASA program; and has been appointed by the juvenile court as a sworn officer of the court to help define the best interest of children or nonminors in juvenile court dependency and wardship proceedings.

(2) A CASA program must adopt and adhere to a written plan for the recruitment of potential CASA volunteers. The program staff, in its recruitment effort, must address the demographics of the jurisdiction by making all reasonable efforts to ensure that individuals representing all racial, ethnic, linguistic, and economic sectors of the community are recruited and made available for appointment as CASA volunteers.

(3) A CASA program must adopt and adhere to the following minimum written procedures for screening potential CASA volunteers under section 102(e):

(A) A written application that generates minimum identifying data; information regarding the applicant's education, training, and experience; minimum age requirements; and current and past employment.

(B) Notice to the applicant that a formal security check will be made, including inquiries through appropriate law enforcement agencies—including but not limited to the Department of Justice, Federal Bureau of Investigations, and Child Abuse Index—regarding any criminal record, driving record, or other record of conduct that would disqualify the applicant from service as a CASA volunteer. The security check must include fingerprinting. Refusal to consent to a formal security check is grounds for rejecting an applicant.

(C) A minimum of three completed references regarding the character, competence, and reliability of the applicant and his or her suitability for assuming the role of a CASA volunteer.

(4) If a CASA program allows its volunteers to transport children, the program must ensure that each volunteer transporting children:

(A) Possesses a valid and current driver's license;

(B) Possesses personal automobile insurance that meets the minimum state personal automobile insurance requirements;

(C) Obtains permission from the child's guardian or custodial agency; and

(D) Provides the CASA program with a Department of Motor Vehicles driving record report annually.

(5) A CASA program must adopt a written preliminary procedure for selecting CASA candidates to enter the CASA training program. The selection procedure must state that any applicant found to have been convicted of or to have current charges pending for a felony or misdemeanor involving a sex offense, child abuse, or child neglect must not be accepted as a CASA volunteer. This policy must be stated on the volunteer application form.

(6) An adult otherwise qualified to act as a CASA must not be discriminated against based on marital status, socioeconomic factors, race, national origin, ethnic group identification, religion, age, sex, sexual orientation, color, or disability or because of any other characteristic listed or defined in Government Code section 11135 or Welfare and Institutions Code section 103.

(Subd (e) amended and relettered effective January 1, 2019; adopted as subd (b) effective July 1, 1994; previously amended and relettered as subd (c) effective January 1, 2005; previously amended effective January 1, 1995, January 1, 2007, and January 1, 2010.)

(f) Initial training of CASA volunteers (§ 102(d))

A CASA program must adopt and adhere to a written plan for the initial training of CASA volunteers.

(1) The initial training curriculum must include at least 30 hours of formal instruction. This curriculum must include mandatory training topics as listed in section 102(d). The curriculum may also include additional appropriate topics, such as those stated in California Rules of Court, rule 5.664.

(2) The final selection process is contingent on the successful completion of the initial training program, as determined by the presiding judge of the juvenile court or designee.

(Subd (f) amended and relettered effective January 1, 2019; adopted as subd (c) effective July 1, 1994; previously amended and relettered as subd (d) effective January 1, 2005; previously amended effective January 1, 1995, and January 1, 2007.)

(g) Oath

At the completion of training, and before assignment to any child or nonminor's case, the CASA volunteer must take a court-administered oath describing the duties and responsibilities of the advocate under section 103(f). The CASA volunteer must also sign a written affirmation of that oath. The signed affirmation must be retained in the volunteer's file.

(Subd (g) amended and relettered effective January 1, 2019; adopted as subd (d) effective July 1, 1994; previously amended and relettered to subd (e) effective January 1, 2005; previously amended effective January 1, 2007.)

(h) Duties and responsibilities

CASA volunteers serve at the discretion of the court having jurisdiction over the proceeding in which the volunteer has been appointed. A CASA volunteer is an officer of the court and is bound by all court rules under section 103(e). A CASA program must develop and adopt a written description of duties and responsibilities, consistent with local court rules.

(Subd (h) amended and relettered effective January 1, 2019; adopted as subd (e) effective July 1, 1994; previously amended and relettered as subd (f) effective January 1, 2005; previously amended effective January 1, 1995, and January 1, 2007.)

(i) Prohibited activities

A CASA program must develop and adopt a written description of activities that are prohibited for CASA volunteers. The specified prohibited activities must include:

Rules of Court

(1) Taking a child or nonminor to the CASA volunteer's home;

(2) Giving legal advice or therapeutic counseling;

(3) Giving money or expensive gifts to the child, nonminor, or family of the child or nonminor;

(4) Being related to any parties involved in a case or being employed in a position and/or agency that might result in a conflict of interest; and

(5) Any other activities prohibited by the local juvenile court.

(Subd (i) amended and relettered effective January 1, 2019; adopted as subd (g) effective January 1, 2005.)

(j) The appointment of CASA volunteers

The CASA program director must develop, with the approval of the presiding juvenile court judge, a written procedure for the selection of cases and the appointment of CASA volunteers for children and nonminors in juvenile court proceedings.

(Subd (j) amended and relettered effective January 1, 2019; adopted as subd (f) effective July 1, 1994; previously amended effective January 1, 1995; previously amended and relettered as subd (h) effective January 1, 2005.)

(k) Oversight, support, and supervision of CASA volunteers

A CASA program must adopt and adhere to a written plan, approved by the presiding juvenile court judge, for the oversight, support, and supervision of CASA volunteers in the performance of their duties. The plan must:

(1) Include a grievance procedure that covers grievances by any person against a volunteer or CASA program staff and grievances by a volunteer against a CASA program or program staff. The grievance procedure must:

(A) Be incorporated into a document that contains a description of the roles and responsibilities of CASA volunteers. This document must be provided:

(i) When a copy of the court order that appointed the CASA volunteer is provided to any adult involved with the child's or nonminor's case, including but not limited to teachers, foster parents, therapists, and health-care workers;

(ii) To the nonminor upon appointment of the CASA; and

(iii) To any person, including a volunteer, who has a grievance against a volunteer or a CASA program employee.

(B) Include a provision that documentation of any grievance filed by or against a volunteer must be retained in the volunteer's personnel file.

(2) Include a provision for the ongoing training and continuing education of CASA volunteers. Ongoing training opportunities must be provided at least monthly under section 103(a). CASA volunteers must participate in a minimum of 12 hours of continuing education in each year of service.

(Subd (k) repealed, amended and relettered effective January 1, 2019; adopted as subd (g) effective July 1, 1994; previously amended and relettered as subd (i) effective January 1, 2005; previously amended effective January 1, 1995, and January 1, 2007.)

(l) Removal, resignation, and termination of a CASA volunteer

The CASA program must adopt a written plan for the removal, resignation, or involuntary termination of a CASA volunteer, including the following provisions:

(1) A volunteer may resign or be removed from an individual case at any time by the order of the juvenile court presiding judge or designee.

(2) A volunteer may be involuntarily terminated from the program by the program director.

(3) The volunteer has the right to appeal termination by the program director under the program's grievance procedure.

(Subd (l) repealed and relettered effective January 1, 2019; adopted as subd (h) effective July 1, 1994; previously amended and relettered as subd (j) effective January 1, 2005; previously amended effective January 1, 1995, and January 1, 2007.)

Rule 5.655 amended effective January 1, 2019; adopted as rule 1424 effective July 1, 1994; previously amended and renumbered as rule 5.655 effective January 1, 2007; previously amended effective January 1, 1995, January 1, 2000, January 1, 2001, January 1, 2005, January 1, 2010, and January 1, 2016.

Advisory Committee Comment

These 1995 guidelines implement the requirements of section 100, which establishes a grant program administered by the Judicial Council to establish or expand CASA programs to assist children involved in juvenile dependency proceedings, including guardianships, adoptions, and actions to terminate parental rights to custody and control.

CASA programs provide substantial benefits to children appearing in dependency proceedings and to the juvenile court having responsibility for these children. Child advocates improve the quality of judicial decision making by

providing information to the court concerning the child. Advocates help identify needed services for the children they are assisting and provide a consistent friend and support person for children throughout the long and complex dependency process.

The CASA concept was first implemented in Seattle in 1977. As of 1994, there were more than 30,000 volunteers working in more than 525 CASA programs in nearly every state. The programs recruit, screen, select, train, and supervise lay volunteers to become effective advocates in the juvenile court.

Currently, numerous jurisdictions in California use some variation of the CASA concept. These programs have developed over the past several years under the supervision of local juvenile courts under sections 356.5 and 358. Each program is unique and was designed to respond to the specific needs of the local jurisdiction and community it serves.

These guidelines provide a framework for ensuring the excellence of California CASA programs and volunteers. They are intended to be consistent with the guidelines established by the National CASA Association and to conform with the requirements of California law and procedure. The California CASA Association has assisted in developing these guidelines, which are meant to give the local bench, bar, child welfare professionals, children's advocates, and other interested citizens full rein to adapt the CASA concept to the special needs and circumstances of local communities.

Central to the intent of these guidelines is the effort to provide a vehicle for the presiding judge of the local juvenile court to exercise fully informed and effective oversight of the local CASA program and CASA volunteers. These guidelines are also intended to help CASA programs and juvenile courts develop local court rules. Nothing in these guidelines should limit or restrict the local juvenile court from developing and supporting multiple branches of a CASA program within the community to enable a county to offer comprehensive volunteer advocacy programs for children.

Rule 5.660. Attorneys for parties (§§ 317, 317.5, 317.6, 353, 366.26, 16010.6)

(a) Local rules

On or before January 1, 2002, the superior court of each county must amend its local rules regarding the representation of parties in dependency proceedings.

(1) The local rules must be amended after consultation by the court with representatives of the State Bar of California; local offices of the county counsel, district attorney, public defender, and other attorneys appointed to represent parties in these proceedings; county welfare departments; child advocates; current or recent foster youth; and others selected by the court in accordance with standard 5.40(c) of the Standards of Judicial Administration.

(2) The amended rules must address the following as needed:

(A) Representation of children in accordance with other sections of this rule;

(B) Timelines and procedures for settlements, mediation, discovery, protocols, and other issues related to contested matters;

(C) Procedures for the screening, training, and appointment of attorneys representing parties, with particular attention to the training requirements for attorneys representing children;

(D) Establishment of minimum standards of experience, training, and education of attorneys representing parties, including additional training and education in the areas of substance abuse and domestic violence as required;

(E) Establishment of procedures to determine appropriate caseloads for attorneys representing children;

(F) Procedures for reviewing and resolving complaints by parties regarding the performance of attorneys;

(G) Procedures for informing the court of interests of the dependent child requiring further investigation, intervention, or litigation; and

(H) Procedures for appointment of a Child Abuse Prevention and Treatment Act (CAPTA) guardian ad litem, who may be an attorney or a CASA volunteer, in cases in which a prosecution is initiated under the Penal Code arising from neglect or abuse of the child.

(3) Appropriate local forms may be used.

(Subd (a) amended effective January 1, 2007; previously amended effective July 1, 2001, and January 1, 2003.)

(b) Attorneys for children

The court must appoint counsel for a child who is the subject of a petition under section 300 and is unrepresented by counsel, unless the court finds that the child would not benefit from the appointment of counsel.

(1) In order to find that a child would not benefit from the appointment of counsel, the court must find all of the following:

(A) The child understands the nature of the proceedings;

(B) The child is able to communicate and advocate effectively with the court, other counsel, other parties, including social workers, and other professionals involved in the case; and

(C) Under the circumstances of the case, the child would not gain any benefit by being represented by counsel.

(2) If the court finds that the child would not benefit from representation by counsel, the court must make a finding on the record as to each of the criteria in (1) and state the reasons for each finding.

(3) If the court finds that the child would not benefit from representation by counsel, the court must appoint a CASA volunteer for the child, to serve as the CAPTA guardian ad litem, as required in section 326.5.

(Subd (b) amended effective January 1, 2007; adopted effective July 1, 2001; previously amended effective January 1, 2003.)

(c) Conflict of interest guidelines for attorneys representing siblings

(1) *Appointment*

(A) The court may appoint a single attorney to represent a group of siblings involved in the same dependency proceeding.

(B) An attorney must decline to represent one or more siblings in a dependency proceeding, and the court must appoint a separate attorney to represent the sibling or siblings, if, at the outset of the proceedings:

(i) An actual conflict of interest exists among those siblings; or

(ii) Circumstances specific to the case present a reasonable likelihood that an actual conflict of interest will arise among those siblings.

(C) The following circumstances, standing alone, do not necessarily demonstrate an actual conflict of interest or a reasonable likelihood that an actual conflict of interest will arise:

(i) The siblings are of different ages;

(ii) The siblings have different parents;

(iii) There is a purely theoretical or abstract conflict of interest among the siblings;

(iv) Some of the siblings appear more likely than others to be adoptable; or

(v) The siblings may have different permanent plans.

(2) *Withdrawal from appointment or continued representation*

(A) An attorney representing a group of siblings has an ongoing duty to evaluate the interests of each sibling and assess whether there is an actual conflict of interest.

(B) The following circumstances, standing alone, do not necessarily demonstrate an actual conflict of interest:

(i) The siblings are of different ages;

(ii) The siblings have different parents;

(iii) There is a purely theoretical or abstract conflict of interest among the siblings;

(iv) Some of the siblings are more likely to be adopted than others;

(v) The siblings have different permanent plans;

(vi) The siblings express conflicting desires or objectives, but the issues involved are not material to the case; or

(vii) The siblings give different or contradictory accounts of the events, but the issues involved are not material to the case.

(C) It is not necessary for an attorney to withdraw from representing some or all of the siblings if there is merely a reasonable likelihood that an actual conflict of interest will develop.

(D) If an attorney believes that an actual conflict of interest existed at appointment or developed during representation, the attorney must take any action necessary to ensure that the siblings' interests are not prejudiced, including:

(i) Notifying the juvenile court of the existence of an actual conflict of interest among some or all of the siblings; and

(ii) Requesting to withdraw from representation of some or all of the siblings.

(E) If the court determines that an actual conflict of interest exists, the court must relieve an attorney from representation of some or all of the siblings.

(F) After an actual conflict of interest arises, the attorney may continue to represent one or more siblings whose interests do not conflict only if:

(i) The attorney has successfully withdrawn from the representation of all siblings whose interests conflict with those of the sibling or siblings the attorney continues to represent;

(ii) The attorney has exchanged no confidential information with any sibling whose interest conflicts with those of the sibling or siblings the attorney continues to represent; and

(iii) Continued representation of one or more siblings would not otherwise prejudice the other sibling or siblings.

(Subd (c) amended effective January 1, 2007; adopted effective January 1, 2006.)

(d) Competent counsel

Every party in a dependency proceeding who is represented by an attorney is entitled to competent counsel.

(1) *Definition*

"Competent counsel" means an attorney who is a member in good standing of the State Bar of California, who has participated in training in the law of juvenile dependency, and who demonstrates adequate forensic skills, knowledge and comprehension of the statutory scheme, the purposes and goals of dependency proceedings, the specific statutes, rules of court, and cases relevant to such proceedings, and procedures for filing petitions for extraordinary writs.

(2) *Evidence of competency*

The court may require evidence of the competency of any attorney appointed to represent a party in a dependency proceeding.

(3) *Experience and education*

(A) Only those attorneys who have completed a minimum of eight hours of training or education in the area of juvenile dependency, or who have sufficient recent experience in dependency proceedings in which the attorney has demonstrated competency, may be appointed to represent parties. Attorney training must include:

(i) An overview of dependency law and related statutes and cases;

(ii) Information on child development, child abuse and neglect, substance abuse, domestic violence, family reunification and preservation, and reasonable efforts; and

(iii) For any attorney appointed to represent a child, instruction on cultural competency and sensitivity relating to, and best practices for, providing adequate care to lesbian, gay, bisexual, and transgender youth in out-of-home placement.

(B) Within every three years, attorneys must complete at least eight hours of continuing education related to dependency proceedings.

(4) *Standards of representation*

Attorneys or their agents are expected to meet regularly with clients, including clients who are children, regardless of the age of the child or the child's ability to communicate verbally, to contact social workers and other professionals associated with the client's case, to work with other counsel and the court to resolve disputed aspects of a case without contested hearing, and to adhere to the mandated timelines. The attorney for the child must have sufficient contact with the child to establish and maintain an adequate and professional attorney-client relationship. The attorney for the child is not required to assume the responsibilities of a social worker and is not expected to perform services for the child that are unrelated to the child's legal representation.

(5) *Attorney contact information*

The attorney for a child for whom a dependency petition has been filed must provide his or her contact information to the child's caregiver no later than 10 days after receipt of the name, address, and telephone number of the child's caregiver. If the child is 10 years of age or older, the attorney must also provide his or her contact information to the child for whom a dependency petition has been filed no later than 10 days after receipt of the caregiver's contact information. The attorney may give contact information to a child for whom a dependency petition has been filed who is under 10 years of age. At least once a year, if the list of educational liaisons is available online from the California Department of Education, the child's attorney must provide, in any manner permitted by section 317(e)(4), his or her contact information to the educational liaison of each local educational agency serving the attorney's clients in foster care in the county of jurisdiction.

(6) *Caseloads for children's attorneys*

The attorney for a child must have a caseload that allows the attorney to perform the duties required by section 317(e) and this rule, and to otherwise adequately counsel and represent the child. To enhance the quality of representation afforded to children, attorneys appointed under this rule must not maintain a maximum full-time caseload that is greater than that which allows them to meet the requirements stated in (3), (4), and (5).

(Subd (d) amended effective January 1, 2015; adopted as subd (b) effective January 1, 1996; amended and relettered as subd (c) effective July 1, 2001; previously relettered effective January 1, 2006; previously amended effective July 1, 1999, January 1, 2005, January 1, 2007, and January 1, 2014.)

(e) Client complaints

The court must establish a process for the review and resolution of complaints or questions by a party regarding the performance of an appointed attorney. Each party must be informed of the procedure for lodging the complaint. If it is determined that an appointed attorney has acted improperly or contrary to the rules or policies of the court, the court must take appropriate action.

(Subd (e) relettered effective January 1, 2006; adopted as subd (c) effective January 1, 1996; previously amended and relettered as subd (d) effective July 1, 2001.)

(f) CASA volunteer as CAPTA guardian ad litem (§ 326.5)

If the court makes the findings as outlined in (b) and does not appoint an attorney to represent the child, the court must appoint a CASA volunteer as the CAPTA guardian ad litem of the child.

(1) The required training of CASA volunteers is stated in rule 5.655.

(2) The caseload of a CASA volunteer acting as a CAPTA guardian ad litem must be limited to 10 cases. A case may include siblings, absent a conflict.

(3) CASA volunteers must not assume the responsibilities of attorneys for children.

(4) The appointment of an attorney to represent the child does not prevent the appointment of a CASA volunteer for that child, and courts are encouraged to appoint both an attorney and a CASA volunteer for the child in as many cases as possible.

(Subd (f) amended effective January 1, 2007; adopted as subd (e) effective July 1, 2001; previously amended effective January 1, 2003; previously relettered effective January 1, 2006.)

(g) Interests of the child

At any time following the filing of a petition under section 300 and until juvenile court jurisdiction is terminated, any interested person may advise the court of information regarding an interest or right of the child to be protected or pursued in other judicial or administrative forums.

(1) *Juvenile Dependency Petition (Version One)* (form JV-100) and *Request to Change Court Order* (form JV-180) may be used.

(2) If the attorney for the child, or a CASA volunteer acting as a CAPTA guardian ad litem, learns of any such interest or right, the attorney or CASA volunteer must notify the court immediately and seek instructions from the court as to any appropriate procedures to follow.

(3) If the court determines that further action on behalf of the child is required to protect or pursue any interests or rights, the court must appoint an attorney for the child, if the child is not already represented by counsel, and do one or all of the following:

(A) Refer the matter to the appropriate agency for further investigation and require a report to the court within a reasonable time;

(B) Authorize and direct the child's attorney to initiate and pursue appropriate action;

(C) Appoint a guardian ad litem for the child. The guardian may be the CASA volunteer already appointed as a CAPTA guardian ad litem or a person who will act only if required to initiate appropriate action; or

(D) Take any other action to protect or pursue the interests and rights of the child.

(Subd (g) amended effective January 1, 2007; adopted as subd (d) effective January 1, 1996; previously amended and relettered as subd (f) effective July 1, 2001; amended effective January 1, 2003; previously relettered effective January 1, 2006.)

Rule 5.660 amended effective January 1, 2015; adopted as rule 1438 effective January 1, 1996; previously amended and renumbered effective January 1, 2007; previously amended effectively July 1, 1999, July 1, 2001, January 1, 2003, January 1, 2005, January 1, 2006, and January 1, 2014.

Advisory Committee Comment

The court should initially appoint a single attorney to represent all siblings in a dependency matter unless there is an actual conflict of interest or a reasonable likelihood that an actual conflict of interest will arise. (*In re Celine R.* (2003) 31 Cal.4th 45, 58.) After the initial appointment, the court should relieve an attorney from representation of multiple siblings only if an actual conflict of interest arises. (*Ibid.*) Attorneys have a duty to use their best judgment in analyzing whether, under the particular facts of the case, it is necessary to decline appointment or request withdrawal from appointment due to a purported conflict of interest.

Nothing in this rule is intended to extend the permissible scope of any judicial inquiry into an attorney's reasons for declining to represent one or more siblings or requesting to withdraw from representation of one or more siblings, due to an actual or reasonably likely conflict of interest. (See State Bar Rules Prof. Conduct, rule 3-310(C).) While the court has the duty and authority to inquire as to the general nature of an asserted conflict of interest, it cannot require an attorney to disclose any privileged communication, even if such information forms the basis of

the alleged conflict. (*In re James S.* (1991) 227 Cal.App.3d 930, 934; *Aceves v. Superior Court* (1996) 51 Cal.App.4th 584, 592–593.)

Rule 5.661. Representation of the child on appeal

(a) Definition

For purposes of this rule, "guardian ad litem" means a person designated as the child's Child Abuse Prevention and Treatment Act (CAPTA) guardian ad litem as defined in rule 5.662.

(Subd (a) adopted effective July 1, 2007.)

(b) Child as appellant

A notice of appeal on behalf of the child must be filed by the child's trial counsel, guardian ad litem, or the child if the child is seeking appellate relief from the trial court's judgment or order.

(Subd (b) adopted effective July 1, 2007.)

(c) Recommendation from child's trial counsel or guardian ad litem

(1) In any juvenile dependency proceeding in which a party other than the child files a notice of appeal, if the child's trial counsel or guardian ad litem concludes that, for purposes of the appeal, the child's best interests cannot be protected without the appointment of separate counsel on appeal, the child's trial counsel or guardian ad litem must file a recommendation in the Court of Appeal requesting appointment of separate counsel.

(2) A child's trial counsel or guardian ad litem who recommends appointment of appellate counsel for a child who is not an appellant must follow the procedures outlined in (d)–(g).

(Subd (c) adopted effective July 1, 2007.)

(d) Time for trial counsel or guardian ad litem to file the recommendation with the Court of Appeal

A recommendation from the child's trial counsel or guardian ad litem may be filed at any time after a notice of appeal has been filed, but absent good cause, must be filed in the Court of Appeal no later than 20 calendar days after the filing of the last appellant's opening brief.

(Subd (d) adopted effective July 1, 2007.)

(e) Service of recommendation

The child's trial counsel or guardian ad litem must serve a copy of the recommendation filed in the Court of Appeal on the district appellate project and the trial court.

(Subd (e) amended effective January 1, 2015; adopted effective July 1, 2007.)

(f) Factors to be considered

The following are factors to be considered by a child's trial counsel or guardian ad litem in making a recommendation to the Court of Appeal:

(1) An actual or potential conflict exists between the interests of the child and the interests of any respondent;

(2) The child did not have an attorney serving as his or her guardian ad litem in the trial court;

(3) The child is of a sufficient age or development such that he or she is able to understand the nature of the proceedings and,

(A) The child expresses a desire to participate in the appeal, or

(B) The child's wishes differ from his or her trial counsel's position;

(4) The child took a legal position in the trial court adverse to that of one of his or her siblings, and an issue has been raised in an appellant's opening brief regarding the siblings' adverse positions;

(5) The appeal involves a legal issue regarding a determination of parentage, the child's inheritance rights, educational rights, privileges identified in division 8 of the Evidence Code, consent to treatment, or tribal membership;

(6) Postjudgment evidence completely undermines the legal underpinnings of the juvenile court's judgment under review, and all parties recognize this and express a willingness to stipulate to reversal of the juvenile court's judgment;

(7) The child's trial counsel or guardian ad litem, after reviewing the appellate briefs, believes that the legal arguments contained in the respondents' briefs do not adequately represent or protect the best interests of the child; and

(8) The existence of any other factors relevant to the child's best interests.

(Subd (f) adopted effective July 1, 2007.)

(g) Form of recommendation

The child's trial counsel, the guardian ad litem, or the child may use *Recommendation for Appointment of Appellate Attorney for Child* (form JV-810). Any recommendation for an appellate attorney for the child must state a factual basis for the recommendation, include the information provided on form JV-810, and be signed under penalty of perjury.

(Subd (g) adopted effective July 1, 2007.)

Rule 5.661 amended effective January 1, 2015; adopted effective July 1, 2007.

Advisory Committee Comment

Generally, separate counsel for a nonappealing child will not be appointed for the purpose of introducing postjudgment evidence. See California Code Civ. Proc., § 909; *In re Zeth S.* (2003) 31 Cal.4th 396; *In re Josiah Z.* (2005) 36 Cal.4th 664. For further discussion, see *In re Mary C.* (1995) 41 Cal.App.4th 71.

Rule 5.662. Child Abuse Prevention and Treatment Act (CAPTA) guardian ad litem for a child subject to a juvenile dependency petition

(a) Authority

This rule is adopted under section 326.5.

(Subd (a) amended effective January 1, 2007.)

(b) Applicability

The definition of the role and responsibilities of a CAPTA guardian ad litem in this rule applies exclusively to juvenile dependency proceedings and is distinct from the definitions of guardian ad litem in all other juvenile, civil, and criminal proceedings. No limitation period for bringing an action based on an injury to the child commences running solely by reason of the appointment of a CAPTA guardian ad litem under section 326.5 and this rule.

(Subd (b) amended effective January 1, 2007.)

(c) Appointment

A CAPTA guardian ad litem must be appointed for every child who is the subject of a juvenile dependency petition under section 300. An attorney appointed under rule 5.660 will serve as the child's CAPTA guardian ad litem under section 326.5. If the court finds that the child would not benefit from the appointment of counsel, the court must appoint a CASA volunteer to serve as the child's CAPTA guardian ad litem. The court must identify on the record the person appointed as the child's CAPTA guardian ad litem.

(Subd (c) amended effective January 1, 2007.)

(d) General duties and responsibilities

The general duties and responsibilities of a CAPTA guardian ad litem are:

(1) To obtain firsthand a clear understanding of the situation and needs of the child; and

(2) To make recommendations to the court concerning the best interest of the child as appropriate under (e) and (f).

(e) Attorney as guardian ad litem

The specific duties and responsibilities of the child's court-appointed attorney who is appointed to serve as the child's CAPTA guardian ad litem are stated in section 317(e) and rule 5.660.

(Subd (e) amended effective January 1, 2007.)

(f) CASA volunteer as CAPTA guardian ad litem

The specific duties and responsibilities of the child's CASA volunteer who is appointed to serve as the child's CAPTA guardian ad litem are stated in section 102(c) and rule 5.655.

(Subd (f) amended effective January 1, 2007.)

Rule 5.662 amended and renumbered effective January 1, 2007; adopted as rule 1448 effective January 1, 2003.

Rule 5.663. Responsibilities of children's counsel in delinquency proceedings (§§ 202, 265, 633, 634, 634.6, 679, 700)

(a) Purpose

This rule is designed to ensure public safety and the protection of the child's best interest at every stage of the delinquency proceedings by clarifying the role of the child's counsel in delinquency proceedings. This rule is not intended to affect any substantive duty imposed on counsel by existing civil standards or professional discipline standards.

(b) Responsibilities of counsel

A child's counsel is charged in general with defending the child against the allegations in all petitions filed in delinquency proceedings and with advocating, within the framework of the delinquency proceedings, that the child receive care, treatment, and guidance consistent with his or her best interest.

(c) Right to representation

A child is entitled to have the child's interests represented by counsel at every stage of the proceedings, including postdispositional hearings. Counsel must continue to represent the child unless relieved by the court on the substitution of other counsel or for cause.

(Subd (c) amended effective January 1, 2007.)

(d) Limits to responsibilities

A child's counsel is not required:

(1) To assume the responsibilities of a probation officer, social worker, parent, or guardian;

(2) To provide nonlegal services to the child; or

(3) To represent the child in any proceedings outside of the delinquency proceedings.

(Subd (d) amended effective January 1, 2007.)

Rule 5.663 amended and renumbered effective January 1, 2007; adopted as rule 1479 effective July 1, 2004.

Rule 5.664. Training requirements for children's counsel in delinquency proceedings (§ 634.3)

(a) Definition

"Competent counsel" means an attorney who is a member, in good standing, of the State Bar of California, who provides representation in accordance with Welfare and Institutions Code section 634.3(a)(1)–(3), and who has participated in training in the law and practice of juvenile delinquency as defined in this rule.

(Subd (a) adopted effective July 1, 2016.)

(b) Education and training requirements

(1) Only those attorneys who, during each of the most recent three calendar years, have dedicated at least 50 percent of their practice to juvenile delinquency and demonstrated competence or who have completed a minimum of 12 hours of training or education during the most recent 12-month period in the area of juvenile delinquency, may be appointed to represent youth.

(2) Attorney training must include:

(A) An overview of delinquency law and related statutes and cases;

(B) Trial skills, including drafting and filing pretrial motions, introducing evidence at trial, preserving the record for appeal, filing writs, notices of appeal, and posttrial motions;

(C) Advocacy at the detention phase;

(D) Advocacy at the dispositional phase;

(E) Child and adolescent development, including training on interviewing and working with adolescent clients;

(F) Competence and mental health issues, including capacity to commit a crime and the effects of trauma, child abuse, and family violence, as well as crossover issues presented by youth involved in the dependency system;

(G) Police interrogation methods, suggestibility of juveniles, and false confessions;

(H) Counsel's ethical duties, including racial, ethnic, and cultural understanding and addressing bias;

(I) Cultural competency and sensitivity relating to, and best practices for, providing adequate care to lesbian, gay, bisexual, and transgender youth;

(J) Understanding of the effects of and how to work with victims of human trafficking and commercial sexual exploitation of children and youth;

(K) Immigration consequences and the requirements of Special Immigrant Juvenile Status;

(L) General and special education, including information on school discipline;

(M) Extended foster care;

(N) Substance abuse;

(O) How to secure effective rehabilitative resources, including information on available community-based resources;

(P) Direct and collateral consequences of court involvement;

(Q) Transfer of jurisdiction to criminal court hearings and advocacy in adult court;

(R) Appellate advocacy; and

(S) Advocacy in the postdispositional phase.

(Subd (b) amended effective May 22, 2017; adopted effective July 1, 2016.)

(c) Continuing education requirements

(1) To remain eligible for appointment to represent delinquent youth, attorneys must engage in annual continuing education in the areas listed in (b)(2), as follows:

(A) Attorneys must complete at least 8 hours per calendar year of continuing education, for a total of 24 hours, during each MCLE compliance period.

(B) An attorney who is eligible to represent delinquent youth for only a portion of the corresponding MCLE compliance period must complete training hours in proportion to the amount of time the attorney was eligible. An attorney who is eligible to represent delinquent youth for only a portion of a calendar year must complete two hours of training for every three months of eligibility.

(C) The 12 hours of initial training may be applied toward the continuing training requirements for the first compliance period.

(2) Each individual attorney is responsible for complying with the training requirements in this rule; however, offices of the public defender and other agencies that work with delinquent youth are encouraged to provide MCLE training that meets the training requirements in (b)(2).

(3) Each individual attorney is encouraged to participate in policy meetings or workgroups convened by the juvenile court and to participate in local trainings designed to address county needs.

(Subd (c) adopted effective July 1, 2016.)

(d) Evidence of competency

The court may require evidence of the competency of any attorney appointed to represent a youth in a delinquency proceeding, including requesting documentation of trainings attended. The court may also require attorneys who represent youth in delinquency proceedings to complete *Declaration of Eligibility for Appointment to Represent Youth in Delinquency Court* (JV-700).

(Subd (d) adopted effective July 1, 2016.)

Rule 5.664 amended effective May 22, 2017; adopted effective July 1, 2016.

Chapter 12
Cases Petitioned Under
Section 300

Chapter 12 renumbered effective January 1, 2008; Adopted as Chapter 7 effective July, 1989; previously renumbered as Chapter 8 effective July 1, 1994, and as Chapter 9 effective January 1, 2000; previously renumbered and amended as Chapter 13 effective January 1, 2007.

Art. 1.   Initial Hearing. Rules 5.667–5.678.
Art. 2.   Jurisdiction. Rules 5.682, 5.684.
Art. 3.   Disposition. Rules 5.690–5.705.
Art. 4.   Reviews, Permanent Planning. Rules 5.706–5.740.

Article 1
Initial Hearing

Rule 5.667. Service and notice
Rule 5.668. Commencement of hearing—explanation of proceedings (§§ 316, 316.2)
Rule 5.670. Initial hearing; detention hearings; time limit on custody; setting jurisdiction hearing; visitation (§§ 309, 311, 313, 315, 362.1)
Rule 5.672. Continuances
Rule 5.674. Conduct of hearing; admission, no contest, submission
Rule 5.676. Requirements for detention
Rule 5.678. Findings in support of detention; factors to consider; reasonable efforts; active efforts; detention alternatives

Rule 5.667.   Service and notice

(a) In court order of notice (§ 296)

The court may order the child, or any parent or guardian or Indian custodian of the child who is present in court, to appear again before the court, social worker, probation officer, or county financial officer at a specified time and place as stated in the order.

(Subd (a) amended effective January 1, 2007; previously amended effective January 1, 2006.)

(b) Language of notice

If it appears that the parent or guardian does not read English, the social worker must provide notice in the language believed to be spoken by the parent or guardian.

(Subd (b) amended effective January 1, 2006.)

Rule 5.667 amended and renumbered effective January 1, 2007; repealed and adopted as rule 1440 effective January 1, 1998; previously amended effective January 1, 2006.

Rule 5.668.   Commencement of hearing—explanation of proceedings (§§ 316, 316.2)

(a) Commencement of hearing

At the beginning of the initial hearing on the petition, whether the child is detained or not detained, the court must give advisement as required by rule 5.534 and must inform each parent and guardian present, and the child, if present:

(1) Of the contents of the petition;

(2) Of the nature of, and possible consequences of, juvenile court proceedings;

(3) If the child has been taken into custody, of the reasons for the initial detention and the purpose and scope of the detention hearing; and

(4) If the petition is sustained and the child is declared a dependent of the court and removed from the custody of the parent or guardian, the court-ordered reunification services must be considered to have been offered or provided on the date the petition is sustained or 60 days after the child's initial removal, whichever is earlier. The time for services must not exceed 12 months for a child three years of age or older at the time of the initial removal and must not exceed 6 months for a child who was under three years of age or who is in a sibling group in which one sibling was under three years of age at the time of the initial removal if the parent or guardian fails to participate regularly and make substantive progress in any court-ordered treatment program.

(Subd (a) amended effective January 1, 2017; adopted effective January 1, 1999; previously amended effective January 1, 2001, and January 1, 2007.)

(b) Parentage inquiry

The court must also inquire of the child's mother and of any other appropriate person present as to the identity and address of any and all presumed or alleged parents of the child as set forth in section 316.2.

(Subd (b) amended effective January 1, 2017; adopted effective January 1, 1999; previously amended effective January 1, 2007, and January 1, 2015.)

(c) Indian Child Welfare Act inquiry (§ 224.2(c) & (g))

(1) At the first appearance in court of each party, the court must ask each participant present at the hearing whether:

(A) The participant knows or has reason to know the child is an Indian child;

(B) The residence or domicile of the child, the child's parents, or Indian custodian is on a reservation or in an Alaska Native village;

(C) The child is or has ever been a ward of a tribal court; and

(D) Either parent or the child possess an identification card indicating membership or citizenship in an Indian tribe.

(2) The court must also instruct all parties to inform the court if they subsequently receive information that provides reason to know the child is an Indian child, and order the parents, Indian custodian, or guardian, if available, to complete *Parental Notification of Indian Status* (form ICWA-020).

(3) If there is reason to believe that the case involves an Indian child, the court must require the agency to proceed in accordance with section 224.2(e).

(4) If it is known, or there is reason to know, the case involves an Indian child, the court must proceed in accordance with rules 5.481 et seq. and treat the child as an Indian child unless and until the court determines on the record after review of the report of due diligence described in section 224.2(g) that the child does not meet the definition of an Indian child.

(Subd (c) adopted effective January 1, 2020.)

(d) Health and education information (§ 16010)

The court must order each parent and guardian present either to complete *Your Child's Health and Education* (form JV-225) or to provide the information necessary for the social worker or probation officer, court staff, or representative of the local child welfare agency to complete the form. The social worker or probation officer assigned to the dependency matter must provide the child's attorney with a copy of the completed form. Before each periodic status review hearing, the social worker or probation officer must obtain and include in the reports prepared for the hearing all information necessary to maintain the accuracy of form JV-225.

(Subd (d) relettered effective January 1, 2020; adopted as subd (c) effective January 1, 2002; previously amended effective January 1, 2007, and January 1, 2008.)

Rule 5.668 amended effective January 1, 2020; repealed and adopted as rule 1441 effective January 1, 1998; previously amended and renumbered effective January 1, 2007; previously amended effective January 1, 1999, January 1, 2001, January 1, 2002, January 1, 2008, January 1, 2015, and January 1, 2017.

Rule 5.670.   Initial hearing; detention hearings; time limit on custody; setting jurisdiction hearing; visitation (§§ 309, 311, 313, 315, 362.1)

(a) Child not detained; filing petition, setting hearing

If the social worker does not take the child into custody but determines that a petition concerning the child should be filed, the social worker must file a petition with the clerk of the juvenile court as soon as possible. The clerk must set an initial hearing on the petition within 15 court days.

(Subd (a) amended effective January 1, 2007.)

(b) Detention hearing—warrant cases, transfers in, changes in placement

Notwithstanding section 309(b), and unless the child has been released sooner, a detention hearing must be held as soon as possible, but no later than 48 hours, excluding noncourt days, after the child arrives at a facility within the county if:

(1) The child was taken into custody in another county and transported in custody to the requesting county under a protective custody warrant issued by the juvenile court;

(2) The child was taken into custody in the county in which a protective custody warrant was issued by the juvenile court; or

(3) The matter was transferred from the juvenile court of another county under rule 5.610 and the child was ordered transported in custody.

At the hearing the court must determine whether the child is to continue to be detained in custody. If the hearing is not commenced within that time, the child must be immediately released from custody.

(Subd (b) amended and relettered effective January 1, 2017; adopted as subd (e) effective January 1, 1998; previously amended effective January 1, 2007.)

(c) Visitation

(1) The court must consider the issue of visitation between the child and other persons, determine if contact pending the jurisdiction hearing would be beneficial or detrimental to the child, and make appropriate orders.

(2) The court must consider the issue of visitation between the child and any sibling who was not placed with the child, and who was taken into custody with the child or is otherwise under the court's jurisdiction, and enter an order for sibling visitation pending the jurisdiction hearing, unless the court finds by clear and convincing evidence that sibling interaction between the child and the sibling is contrary to the safety or well-being of either child.

(Subd (c) relettered effective January 1, 2017; adopted as subd (g) effective January 1, 1998; previously amended effective January 1, 2007, and July 1, 2011.) Rule 5.670 amended effective January 1, 2017; repealed and adopted as rule 1442 effective January 1, 1998; previously amended and renumbered effective January 1, 2007; previously amended effective July 1, 2011.

Rule 5.672. Continuances

(a) Detention hearing; right to one-day continuance; custody pending continued hearing (§§ 319, 322)

On motion of the child, parent, or guardian, the court must continue the detention hearing for one court day. Unless otherwise ordered by the court, the child must remain detained pending completion of the detention hearing or a rehearing. The court must either find that continuance in the home of the parent or guardian is contrary to the child's welfare or order the child released to the custody of the parent or guardian. The court may enter this finding on a temporary basis, without prejudice to any party, and reevaluate the finding at the time of the continued detention hearing.

(Subd (a) amended effective January 1, 2007; previously amended effective July 1, 2002.)

(b) Initial hearing; child not detained

If the child is not detained, motions for continuances of the initial hearing must be made and ruled on under rule 5.550.

(Subd (b) amended effective January 1, 2007; previously amended effective July 1, 2002.)

Rule 5.672 amended and renumbered effective January 1, 2007; repealed and adopted as rule 1443 effective January 1, 1998; previously amended effective July 1, 2002.

Rule 5.674. Conduct of hearing; admission, no contest, submission

(a) Admission, no contest, submission

(1) At the initial hearing, whether or not the child is detained, the parent or guardian may admit the allegations of the petition, plead no contest, or submit the jurisdictional determination to the court based on the information provided to the court and waive further jurisdictional hearing.

(2) If the court accepts an admission, a plea of no contest, or a submission from each parent and guardian with standing to participate as a party, the court must then proceed according to rules 5.682 and 5.686.

(Subd (a) amended effective January 1, 2007; previously amended effective July 1, 2002.)

(b) Detention hearing; general conduct (§ 319; 42 U.S.C. § 600 et seq.)

(1) The court must read, consider, and reference any reports submitted by the social worker and any relevant evidence submitted by any party or counsel. All detention findings and orders must appear in the written orders of the court.

(2) The findings and orders that must be made on the record are:

(A) Continuance in the home is contrary to the child's welfare;

(B) Temporary placement and care are vested with the social services agency;

(C) Reasonable efforts, **or when it is known or there is reason to know the child is an Indian child, active efforts,** have been made to prevent removal; [1]

(D) The findings and orders required to be made on the record under section 319**; and**

(E) When it is known or there is reason to know the case involves an Indian child, that detention is necessary to prevent imminent physical damage or harm to the child, and there are no reasonable means by which the child can be protected if maintained in the physical custody of his or her parent or parents or Indian custodian.

(Subd (b) amended effective January 1, 2020; adopted effective July 1, 2002; previously amended effective January 1, 2007, and January 1, 2016.)

Rule 5.674(b).   2019 Deletes. [1] and

(c) Detention hearing; rights of child, parent, Indian custodian, or guardian (§§ 311, 319)

At the detention hearing, the child, the parent, **Indian custodian,** and the guardian have the right to assert the privilege against self-incrimination and the right to confront and cross-examine:

(1) The preparer of a police report, probation or social worker report, or other document submitted to the court; and

(2) Any person examined by the court under section 319. If the child, parent, **Indian custodian, Indian child's tribe,** or guardian asserts the right to cross-examine preparers of documents submitted for court consideration, the court may not consider any such report or document unless the preparer is made available for cross-examination.

(Subd (c) amended effective January 1, 2020; adopted as subd (c) effective January 1, 1998; previously amended and relettered as subd (d) effective July 1, 2002, amended and relettered as subd (c) effective January 1, 2017; previously amended effective January 1, 2007.)

(d) No parent, Indian custodian, or Indian child's tribe or guardian present and not noticed (§ 321)

If the court orders the child detained at the detention hearing and no parent, **Indian custodian, or Indian child's tribe** or guardian is present and no parent, **Indian custodian, or Indian child's tribe** or guardian has received actual notice of the detention hearing, a parent, **Indian custodian, or Indian child's tribe** or guardian may file an affidavit alleging the failure of notice and requesting a detention rehearing. The clerk must set the rehearing for a time within 24 hours of the filing of the affidavit, excluding noncourt days. At the rehearing the court must proceed under rules 5.670–5.678.

(Subd (d) amended effective January 1, 2020; adopted effective January 1, 2017.)

(e) Hearing for further evidence; prima facie case (§ 321)

If the court orders the child detained, and the child, a parent, **an Indian custodian, an Indian child's tribe,** a guardian, or counsel requests that evidence of the prima facie case be presented, the court must set a prima facie hearing for a time within 3 court days to consider evidence of the prima facie case or set the matter for jurisdiction hearing within 10 court days. If at the hearing the petitioner fails to establish the prima facie case, the child must be released from custody.

(Subd (e) amended effective January 1, 2020; adopted effective January 1, 2017.)

Rule 5.674 amended effective January 1, 2020; repealed and adopted as rule 1444 effective January 1, 1998; previously amended and renumbered as rule 5.674 effective January 1, 2007; previously amended effective July 1, 2002, January 1, 2016, and January 1, 2017.

Rule 5.676. Requirements for detention

(a) Requirements for detention (§ 319)

No child may be ordered detained by the court unless the court finds that:

(1) A prima facie showing has been made that the child is described by section 300;

(2) Continuance in the home of the parent, **Indian custodian,** or guardian is contrary to the child's welfare; and

(3) One or more of the grounds for detention in rule 5.678 is found.

(Subd (a) amended effective January 1, 2020; previously amended effective July 1, 2002, and January 1, 2007.)

(b) Additional requirements for detention of Indian child

If it is known, or there is reason to know the child is an Indian child, the child may not be ordered detained unless the court also finds that detention is necessary to prevent imminent physical damage or harm to the child. The court must state the facts supporting this finding on the record.

(Subd (b) adopted effective January 1, 2020.)

(c) Evidence required at detention hearing

In making the findings required to support an order of detention, the court may rely solely on written police reports, probation or social worker reports, or other documents.

The reports relied on must include:

(1) A statement of the reasons the child was removed from the parent's custody;

(2) A description of the services that have been provided, including those under section 306, and of any available services or safety plans that would prevent or eliminate the need for the child to remain in custody;

(3) If a parent is enrolled in a certified substance abuse treatment facility that allows a dependent child to reside with his or her parent, information and a recommendation regarding whether the child can be returned to the custody of that parent.

(4) Identification of the need, if any, for the child to remain in custody; and

(5) If continued detention is recommended, information about any parent or guardian of the child with whom the child was not residing at the time the child was taken into custody and about any relative or nonrelative extended family member as defined under section 362.7 with whom the child may be detained.

(Subd (c) relettered effective January 1, 2020; adopted as subd (b); previously amended effective July 1, 2002, January 1, 2007, and January 1, 2016.)

(d) Additional evidence required at detention hearing for Indian child

If it is known, or there is reason to know the child is an Indian child, the reports relied on must also include:

(1) A statement of the risk of imminent physical damage or harm to the Indian child and any evidence that the emergency removal or placement continues to be necessary to prevent the imminent physical damage or harm to the child;

(2) The steps taken to provide notice to the child's parents, Indian custodian, and tribe about the hearing under section 224.3;

(3) If the child's parents and Indian custodian are unknown, a detailed explanation of what efforts have been made to locate and contact them, including contact with the appropriate Bureau of Indian Affairs regional director;

(4) The residence and the domicile of the Indian child;

(5) If either the residence or the domicile of the Indian child is believed to be on a reservation or in an Alaska Native village, the name of the tribe affiliated with that reservation or village;

(6) The tribal affiliation of the child and of the parents or Indian custodian;

(7) A specific and detailed account of the circumstances that caused the Indian child to be taken into temporary custody;

(8) If the child is believed to reside or be domiciled on a reservation in which the tribe exercises exclusive jurisdiction over child custody matters, a statement of efforts that have been made and that are being made to contact the tribe and transfer the child to the tribe's jurisdiction; and

(9) A statement of the efforts that have been taken to assist the parents or Indian custodian so the Indian child may safely be returned to their custody.

(Subd (d) adopted effective January 1, 2020.)

Rule 5.676 amended effective January 1, 2020; repealed and adopted as rule 1445 effective January 1, 1998; previously amended effective July 1, 2002, and January 1, 2016; previously amended and renumbered as rule 5.676 effective January 1, 2007.

Rule 5.678. Findings in support of detention; factors to consider; reasonable efforts; active efforts; detention alternatives

(a) Findings in support of detention (§ 319; 42 U.S.C. § 672)

The court must order the child released from custody unless the court makes findings as specified in section [1] **319(c), and where it is known, or there is reason to know the child is an Indian child, the additional finding specified in section 319(d).**

(Subd (a) amended effective January 1, 2020; previously amended effective July 1, 2002, January 1, 2007, and January 1, 2019.)

Rule 5.678(a). 2019 Deletes. [1] 319(b)

(b) Factors to consider

In determining whether to release or detain the child under (a), the court must consider the factors in section [1] **319(f).**

(Subd (b) amended effective January 1, 2020; previously amended effective July 1, 2002, January 1, 2007, January 1, 2016, and January 1, 2019.)

Rule 5.678(b). 2019 Deletes. [1] 319(d)

(c) Findings of the court—reasonable or active efforts (§ 319; 42 U.S.C. § 672)

(1) Whether the child is released or detained at the hearing, the court must determine whether reasonable efforts have been made to prevent or eliminate the need for removal and must make one of the following findings:

(A) Reasonable efforts have been made; or

(B) Reasonable efforts have not been made.

(2) **Where it is known or there is reason to know the child is an Indian child, whether the child is released or detained at the hearing, the court must determine whether active efforts have been made to provide remedial services and rehabilitative programs designed to prevent the breakup of the Indian family and whether those efforts have been successful. Those active efforts must be documented in detail in the record, and the court must make one of the following findings:**

(A) **Active efforts have been made and were successful; or**

(B) **Active efforts have been made and were not successful; or**

(C) **Active efforts have not been made; and**

(D) **The court orders the department to initiate or continue services in accordance with section 358.**

(3) The court must also determine whether services are available that would prevent the need for further detention.

[1] **(4)** The court must not order the child detained unless the court, after inquiry regarding available services, finds that there are no reasonable services, **or where it is known or there is reason to know the child is an Indian child, active efforts to provide remedial services and rehabilitative programs designed to prevent the breakup of the Indian family** that would prevent or eliminate the need to detain the child or that would permit the child to return home.

[2] **(5)** If the court orders the child detained, the court must proceed under section [3] **319(g)–(h) and where it is known, or there is reason to know the child is an Indian child, subdivision (f) of this rule.**

(Subd (c) amended effective January 1, 2020; adopted as subd (d) effective January 1, 1998; previously amended and relettered effective July 1, 2002; previously amended effective January 1, 2007, and January 1, 2019.)

Rule 5.678(c). 2019 Deletes. [1] (3) [2] (4) [3] 319(d)–(e)

(d) Orders of the court (§ 319; 42 U.S.C. § 672)

If the court orders the child detained, the court must order that temporary care and custody of the child be vested with the county welfare department pending disposition or further order of the court and must make the other findings and orders specified in section [1] **319(g) and (h)(3).**

(Subd (d) amended effective January 1, 2020; adopted effective July 1, 2002; previously amended effective January 1, 2019.)

Rule 5.678(d). 2019 Deletes. [1] 319(e) and (f)(3)

(e) Detention alternatives (§ 319)

The court may order the child detained as specified in section [1] **319(h).**

(Subd (e) amended effective January 1, 2020; adopted effective January 1, 1999; previously amended effective July 1, 2002, January 1, 2007, and January 1, 2019.)

Rule 5.678(e). 2019 Deletes. [1] 319(f)

(f) Additional requirements regarding detention of Indian child (§ 319)

(1) If it is known, or there is reason to know the child is an Indian child, the child must be detained in a home that complies with the placement preferences in section 361.31 unless the court finds by clear and convincing evidence good cause exists not to follow the placement preferences in accordance with rule 5.485.

(2) If it is known, or there is reason to know the child is an Indian child, the detention hearing may not be continued beyond 30 days unless the court finds all of the following:

(A) Restoring the child to the parent, parents, or Indian custodian would subject the child to imminent physical damage or harm;

(B) The court is unable to transfer the proceeding to the jurisdiction of the appropriate Indian tribe; and

(C) It is not possible to initiate an Indian child custody proceeding as defined in section 224.1.

(Subd (f) adopted effective January 1, 2020.)

(g) Hearing for return of custody of Indian child after emergency removal when emergency has ended (§ 319.4)

If it is known or there is reason to know the child is an Indian child, a party may request a hearing under rule 5.484(b) for return of the child before disposition if the party asserts that there is new evidence that the emergency removal or placement is no longer necessary to prevent imminent physical damage or harm to the child.

(Subd (g) adopted effective January 1, 2020.)

Rule 5.678 amended effective January 1, 2020; repealed and adopted as rule 1446 effective January 1, 1998; previously amended and renumbered as rule 5.678 effective January 1, 2007; previously amended effective January 1, 1999, July 1, 2002, January 1, 2016, and January 1, 2019.

Rule 5.680.   Detention rehearings; prima facie hearings [Repealed]

Rule 5.680 repealed effective January 1, 2017; repealed and adopted as rule 1447 effective January 1, 1998; previously amended and renumbered effective January 1, 2007.

Article 2
Jurisdiction

Rule 5.682. Commencement of jurisdiction hearing—advisement of trial rights; admission, no contest, submission
Rule 5.684. Contested hearing on petition

Rule 5.682.   Commencement of jurisdiction hearing— advisement of trial rights; admission, no contest, submission

(a) Rights explained (§§ 341, 353, 361.1)

After giving the advisement required by rule 5.534, the court must advise the parent or guardian of the following rights:

(1) The right to a hearing by the court on the issues raised by the petition; and

(2) The right, if the child has been removed, to have the child returned to the parent or guardian within two working days after a finding by the court that the child does not come within the jurisdiction of the juvenile court under section 300, unless the parent or guardian and the child welfare agency agree that the child will be released on a later date.

(Subd (a) amended and relettered effective January 1, 2017; adopted as subd (b) effective January 1, 1991; previously amended effective January 1, 2005, and January 1, 2007.)

(b) Admission of allegations; prerequisites to acceptance

The court must then inquire whether the parent or guardian intends to admit or deny the allegations of the petition. If the parent or guardian neither admits nor denies the allegations, the court must state on the record that the parent or guardian does not admit the allegations. If the parent or guardian wishes to admit the allegations, the court must first find and state on the record that it is satisfied that the parent or guardian understands the nature of the allegations and the direct consequences of the admission, and understands and waives the rights in (a) and (e)(3).

(Subd (b) amended and relettered effective January 1, 2017; adopted as subd (c) effective January 1, 1991; previously amended effective January 1, 2007.)

(c) Parent or guardian must admit

An admission by the parent or guardian must be made personally by the parent or guardian.

(Subd (c) relettered effective January 1, 2017; adopted as subd (d) effective January 1, 1991; previously amended effective January 1, 2007.)

(d) Admission, no contest, submission

The parent or guardian may elect to admit the allegations of the petition or plead no contest and waive further jurisdictional hearing. The parent or guardian may elect to submit the jurisdictional determination to the court based on the information provided to the court and choose whether to waive further jurisdictional hearing. If the parent or guardian submits to the jurisdictional determination in writing, *Waiver of Rights— Juvenile Dependency* (form JV-190) must be completed by the parent or guardian and counsel and submitted to the court.

(Subd (d) amended and relettered effective January 1, 2017; adopted as subd (e) effective January 1, 1991; previously amended effective January 1, 2007.)

(e) Findings of court (§ 356)

After admission, plea of no contest, or submission, the court must make the following findings noted in the order of the court:

(1) Notice has been given as required by law;

(2) The birthdate and county of residence of the child;

(3) The parent or guardian has knowingly and intelligently waived the right to a trial on the issues by the court, the right to assert the privilege against self-incrimination, and the right to confront and to cross-examine adverse witnesses and to use the process of the court to compel the attendance of witnesses on the parent or guardian's behalf;

(4) The parent or guardian understands the nature of the conduct alleged in the petition and the possible consequences of an admission, plea of no contest, or submission;

(5) The admission, plea of no contest, or submission by the parent or guardian is freely and voluntarily made;

(6) There is a factual basis for the parent or guardian's admission;

(7) Those allegations of the petition as admitted are true as alleged; or

(8) Whether the allegations of the petition as submitted are true as alleged; and

(9) The child is described by one or more specific subdivisions of section 300.

(Subd (e) amended and relettered effective January 1, 2017; adopted as subd (f) effective January 1, 1991; previously amended effective January 1, 2007.)

(f) Disposition

After accepting an admission, plea of no contest, or submission, the court must proceed to a disposition hearing under rule 5.690 **or rule 5.697, if the youth will attain 18 years of age before the holding of the disposition hearing**.

(Subd (f) amended effective January 1, 2021; adopted as subd (g) effective January 1, 1991; previously amended effective January 1, 2007; previously amended and relettered as subd (f) effective January 1, 2017.)

Rule 5.682 amended effective January 1, 2021; adopted as rule 1449 effective January 1, 1991; previously amended effective January 1, 2005, and January 1, 2017; previously amended and renumbered as rule 5.682 effective January 1, 2007.

Rule 5.684.   Contested hearing on petition

(a) Contested jurisdiction hearing (§ 355)

If the parent or guardian denies the allegations of the petition, the court must hold a contested hearing and determine whether the allegations in the petition are true.

(Subd (a) amended effective January 1, 2007.)

(b) Admissibility of evidence—general (§§ 355, 355.1)

Except as provided in sections 355(c) and 355.1 and (c) and (d) of this rule, the admission and exclusion of evidence must be in accordance with the Evidence Code as it applies to civil cases.

(Subd (b) amended effective January 1, 2017; previously amended effective July 1, 1997, and January 1, 2007.)

(c) Reports

(1) A social study, with hearsay evidence contained in it, is admissible as provided in section 355.

(2) The social study must be provided to all parties and their counsel by the county welfare department within a reasonable time before the hearing.

(Subd (c) amended effective January 1, 2017; previously amended effective July 1, 1997, and January 1, 2007.)

(d) Inapplicable privileges (Evid. Code, §§ 972, 986)

The privilege not to testify or to be called as a witness against a spouse or domestic partner, and the confidential marital communication privilege, does not apply to dependency proceedings.

(Subd (d) relettered effective January 1, 2017; adopted as subd (e) effective January 1, 1991; previously amended effective July 1, 1997, and January 1, 2007.)

(e) Findings of court—allegations true (§ 356)

If the court determines by a preponderance of the evidence that the allegations of the petition are true, the court must make findings on each of the following, noted in the minutes:

(1) Notice has been given as required by law;

(2) The birthdate and county of residence of the child;

(3) The allegations of the petition are true; and

(4) The child is described by one or more subdivisions of section 300.

(Subd (e) amended and relettered effective January 1, 2017; adopted as subd (f) effective January 1, 1991; previously amended effective January 1, 2007.)

(f) Disposition and continuance pending disposition hearing (§§ 356, 358)

After making the findings in (e), the court must proceed to a disposition hearing under rule 5.690 **or rule 5.697, if the youth will attain 18 years of age before the holding of the disposition hearing**. The court may continue the disposition hearing as provided in section 358.

(Subd (f) amended effective January 1, 2021; adopted as subd (g) effective January 1, 1991; previously amended effective July 1, 1997, and January 1, 2007; previously amended and relettered as subd (f) effective January 1, 2017.)

Rules of Court

(g) Findings of court—allegations not proved (§§ 356, 361.1)

If the court determines that the allegations of the petition have not been proved by a preponderance of the evidence, the court must dismiss the petition and terminate any detention orders relating to the petition. The court must order that the child be returned to the physical custody of the parent or guardian immediately but, in any event, not more than two working days following the date of that finding, unless the parent or guardian and the agency with custody of the child agree to a later date for the child's release. The court must make the following findings, noted in the order of the court:

(1) Notice has been given as required by law;

(2) The birthdate and county of residence of the child; and

(3) The allegations of the petition are not proved.

(Subd (g) relettered effective January 1, 2017; adopted as subd (h) effective January 1, 1991; previously amended effective July 1, 1997, January 1, 2005, and January 1, 2007.)

Rule 5.684 amended effective January 1, 2021; adopted as rule 1450 effective January 1, 1991; previously amended effective July 1, 1997, January 1, 2005, and January 1, 2017; previously amended and renumbered as rule 5.684 effective January 1, 2007.

Rule 5.686. Continuance pending disposition hearing [Repealed]

Rule 5.686 repealed effective January 1, 2017; adopted as rule 1451 effective January 1, 1990; previously amended and renumbered as rule 5.684 effective January 1, 2007.

Rule 5.688. Failure to cooperate with services (§ 360(b)) [Repealed]

Rule 5.688 repealed effective January 1, 2017; adopted as rule 1452 effective January 1, 1990; previously amended effective July 1, 2000; previously amended and renumbered effective January 1, 2007.

Article 3
Disposition

Rule 5.690. General conduct of disposition hearing
Rule 5.695. Findings and orders of the court—disposition
Rule 5.697. Disposition Hearing for a Nonminor (Welf. & Inst. Code, §§ 224.1, 295, 303, 358, 358.1, 361, 366.31, 390, 391)
Rule 5.700. Termination of jurisdiction—custody and visitation orders (§§ 302, 304, 361.2, 362.4, 726.5)
Rule 5.705. Setting a hearing under section 366.26

Rule 5.690. General conduct of disposition hearing

(a) Social study (§§ 280, 309, 358, 358.1, 360, 361.5, 16002(b))

The petitioner must prepare a social study of the child. The social study must include a discussion of all matters relevant to disposition and a recommendation for disposition.

(1) The petitioner must comply with the following when preparing the social study:

(A) If petitioner recommends that the court appoint a legal guardian, petitioner must prepare an assessment under section 360(a), to be included in the social study report prepared for disposition or in a separate document.

(B) If petitioner recommends removal of the child from the home, the social study must include:

(i) A discussion of the reasonable efforts made to prevent or eliminate removal, **or if it is known or there is reason to know the child is an Indian child, the active efforts to provide remedial services and rehabilitative programs designed to prevent the breakup of the Indian family,** and a recommended plan for reuniting the child with the family, including a plan for visitation;

(ii) A plan for achieving legal permanence for the child if efforts to reunify fail; and

(iii) A statement that each parent has been advised of the option to participate in adoption planning and to voluntarily relinquish the child if an adoption agency is willing to accept the relinquishment, and the parent's response.

(C) The social study must include a discussion of the social worker's efforts to comply with **section 309(e) and** rule 5.637, including but not limited to:

(i) The number of relatives identified and the relationship of each to the child;

(ii) The number and relationship of those relatives described by item (i) who were located and notified;

(iii) The number and relationship of those relatives described by item (ii) who are interested in ongoing contact with the child; [1]

(iv) The number and relationship of those relatives described by item (ii) who are interested in providing placement for the child; **and**

(v) If it is known or there is reason to know the child is an Indian child, efforts to locate extended family members as defined in section 224.1, and evidence that all individuals contacted have been provided with information about the option of obtaining approval for placement through the tribe's license or approval procedure.

(D) If siblings are not placed together, the social study must include an explanation of why they have not been placed together in the same home, what efforts are being made to place the siblings together, or why making those efforts would be contrary to the safety and well-being of any of the siblings.

(E) If petitioner alleges that section 361.5(b) applies, the social study must state why reunification services should not be provided.

(F) All other relevant requirements of sections 358 and 358.1.

(2) The petitioner must submit the social study and copies of it to the clerk at least 48 hours before the disposition hearing is set to begin, and the clerk must make the copies available to the parties and attorneys. A continuance within statutory time limits must be granted on the request of a party who has not been furnished a copy of the social study in accordance with this rule.

(Subd (a) amended effective January 1, 2020; previously amended effective July 1, 1995, January 1, 2000, January 1, 2007, January 1, 2011, and January 1, 2017.)

Rule 5.690(a). 2019 Deletes. [1] and
(b) Evidence considered (§§ 358, 360)

The court must receive in evidence and consider the social study, a guardianship assessment, the report of any CASA volunteer, the case plan, and any relevant evidence offered by petitioner, the child, or the parent or guardian. The court may require production of other relevant evidence on its own motion. In the order of disposition, the court must state that the social study and the study or evaluation by the CASA volunteer, if any, have been read and considered by the court.

(Subd (b) amended effective January 1, 2007; previously amended effective July 1, 1995.)

(c) Case plan (§ 16501.1)

Whenever child welfare services are provided, the social worker must prepare a case plan.

(1) A written case plan must be completed and filed with the court by the date of disposition or within 60 calendar days of initial removal or of the in-person response required under section 16501(f) if the child has not been removed from his or her home, whichever occurs first.

(2) For a child of any age, the court must consider the case plan and must find as follows:

(A) The case plan meets the requirements of section 16501.1; or

(B) The case plan does not meet the requirements of section 16501.1, in which case the court must order the agency to comply with the requirements of section 16501.1; and

(C) The social worker solicited and integrated into the case plan the input of the child; the child's family; the child's identified Indian tribe, including consultation with the child's tribe on whether tribal customary adoption as defined in section 366.24 is an appropriate permanent plan for the child if reunification is unsuccessful; and other interested parties; or

(D) The social worker did not solicit and integrate into the case plan the input of the child, the child's family, the child's identified Indian tribe, and other interested parties, in which case the court must order that the social worker solicit and integrate into the case plan the input of the child, the child's family, the child's identified Indian tribe, and other interested parties, unless the court finds that each of these participants was unable, unavailable, or unwilling to participate.

(3) For a child 12 years of age or older and in a permanent placement, the court must consider the case plan and must also find as follows:

(A) The child was given the opportunity to review the case plan, sign it, and receive a copy; or

(B) The child was not given the opportunity to review the case plan, sign it, and receive a copy, in which case the court must order the agency to give the child the opportunity to review the case plan, sign it, and receive a copy.

(Subd (c) amended effective January 1, 2019; adopted effective January 1, 2007; previously amended effective January 1, 2009, July 1, 2010, and January 1, 2017.)

(d) Timing

Notwithstanding any other law, if a minor has been removed from the custody of the parents or Indian custodians or guardians, a continuance may not be granted that would result in the dispositional hearing, held under section 361, being completed more than 60 days, or 30 days in the case of an Indian child, after the hearing at which the minor was ordered removed or detained, unless the court finds that there are exceptional circumstances requiring a continuance. If the court knows or has reason to know that the child is an Indian child, the absence of the opinion of a qualified expert witness must not, in and of itself, support a finding that exceptional circumstances exist.

(Subd (d) adopted effective January 1, 2020.)

Rule 5.690 amended effective January 1, 2020; adopted as rule 1455 effective January 1, 1991; previously amended and renumbered effective January 1, 2007; previously amended effective July 1, 1995, January 1, 2000, January 1, 2009, July 1, 2010, January 1, 2011, January 1, 2017, and January 1, 2019.

Rule 5.695.   Findings and orders of the court—disposition

(a) Orders of the court (§§ 245.5, 358, 360, 361, 361.2, 390)

At the disposition hearing, the court may:

(1) Dismiss the petition with specific reasons stated in the minutes;

(2) Place the child under a program of supervision for a time period consistent with section 301 and order that services be provided;

(3) **If the requirements of section 360(a) are met,** appoint a legal guardian for the child without declaring dependency and order the clerk, **as soon as the guardian has signed the required affirmation,** to issue letters of guardianship, which are not subject to the confidential protections of juvenile court documents [1] in section 827;

(4) **If the requirements of section 360(a) are met,** declare dependency [2], appoint a legal guardian for the child [3], and order the clerk, **as soon as the guardian has signed the required affirmation,** to issue letters of guardianship, which are not subject to the confidential protections of juvenile court documents [4] in section 827;

(5) Declare dependency, permit the child to remain at home, and order that services be provided;

(6) Declare dependency, permit the child to remain at home, limit the control to be exercised by the parent or guardian, and order that services be provided; or

(7) Declare dependency, remove physical custody from the parent or guardian, and:

(A) After stating on the record or in writing the factual basis for the order, order custody to a noncustodial parent, terminate jurisdiction, and direct that *Custody Order—Juvenile—Final Judgment* (form JV-200) be prepared and filed under rule 5.700;

(B) After stating on the record or in writing the factual basis for the order, order custody to a noncustodial parent with services to one or both parents; or

(C) Make a placement order and consider granting specific visitation rights to the child's grandparents.

(Subd (a) amended effective January 1, 2021; previously amended effective July 1, 1995, January 1, 2007, January 1, 2015, and January 1, 2017.)

Rule 5.695(a). 2020 Deletes. [1] as described **[2]** and **[3]** if the requirements of section 360 are met **[4]** as described

(b) Limitations on parental control (§§ 245.5, 361, 362; Gov. Code, § 7579.5)

(1) If a child is declared a dependent, the court may clearly and specifically limit the control over the child by a parent or guardian.

(2) If the court orders that a parent or guardian retain physical custody of the child subject to court-ordered supervision, the parent or guardian must be ordered to participate in child welfare services or services provided by an appropriate agency designated by the court.

(3) The court must consider whether it is necessary to limit the rights of the parent or guardian to make educational or developmental-services decisions for the child or youth. If the court limits those rights, it must follow the procedures in rules 5.649–5.651.

(Subd (b) relettered effective January 1, 2017; adopted as subd (b) effective January 1, 1991; relettered as subd (c) effective July 1, 1995; previously amended effective July 1, 2002, January 1, 2004, January 1, 2007, January 1, 2008, and January 1, 2014.)

(c) Removal of custody—required findings (§ 361)

(1) The court may not order a dependent removed from the physical custody of a parent or guardian with whom the child resided at the time the petition was filed, unless the court makes one or more of the findings in section 361(c) by clear and convincing evidence.

(2) The court may not order a dependent removed from the physical custody of a parent with whom the child did not reside at the time the petition was initiated unless the juvenile court makes both of the findings in section 361(d) by clear and convincing evidence.

(Subd (c) amended effective January 1, 2019; adopted as subd (c) effective January 1, 1991; previously relettered as subd (d) effective July 1, 1995; previously amended effective July 1, 1997, July 1, 1999, July 1, 2002, and January 1, 2007; previously amended and relettered effective January 1, 2017.)

(d) Reasonable efforts finding

The court must consider whether reasonable efforts to prevent or eliminate the need for removal have been made and make one of the following findings:

(1) Reasonable efforts have been made to prevent removal; or

(2) Reasonable efforts have not been made to prevent removal.

(Subd (d) amended and relettered effective January 1, 2017; adopted as subd (d) effective January 1, 1991; relettered as subd (e) effective July 1, 1995; amended effective July 1, 2002, and January 1, 2006.)

(e) Family-finding determination (§ 309)

(1) If the child is removed, the court must consider and determine whether the social worker has exercised due diligence in conducting the required investigation to identify, locate, and notify the child's relatives. The court may consider the activities listed in (f) as examples of due diligence. The court must document its determination by making a finding on the record.

If the dispositional hearing is continued, the court may set a hearing to be held 30 days from the date of removal or as soon as possible thereafter to consider and determine whether the social worker has exercised due diligence in conducting the required investigation to identify, locate, and notify the child's relatives.

(2) If the court finds that the social worker has not exercised due diligence, the court may order the social worker to exercise due diligence in conducting an investigation to identify, locate, and notify the child's relatives—except for any individual the social worker identifies as inappropriate to notify under rule 5.637(b)—and may require a written or oral report to the court.

(Subd (e) amended and relettered effective January 1, 2017; adopted as subd (f) effective January 1, 2011; previously amended effective January 1, 2014, and January 1, 2015.)

(f) Due diligence (§ 309)

When making the determination required in (e), the court may consider, among other examples of due diligence, whether the social worker has done any of the following:

(1) Asked the child, in an age-appropriate manner and consistent with the child's best interest, about his or her relatives;

(2) Obtained information regarding the location of the child's relatives;

(3) Reviewed the child's case file for any information regarding relatives;

(4) Telephoned, e-mailed, or visited all identified relatives;

(5) Asked located relatives for the names and locations of other relatives;

(6) Used Internet search tools to locate relatives identified as supports; or

(7) Developed tools, including a genogram, family tree, family map, or other diagram of family relationships, to help the child or parents to identify relatives.

(Subd (f) amended and relettered effective January 1, 2017; adopted as subd (g) effective January 1, 2011; previously amended effective January 1, 2014, and January 1, 2015.)

(g) Provision of reunification services (§ 361.5)

(1) Unless the court makes a finding that reunification services need not be provided under subdivision (b) of section 361.5 if a child is removed from the custody of a parent or legal guardian, the court must order the county welfare department to provide reunification services to the child and the child's mother and statutorily presumed parent, or the child's legal guardian, to facilitate reunification of the family as required in section 361.5.

(2) On a finding and declaration of paternity by the juvenile court or proof of a prior declaration of paternity by any court of competent jurisdiction, the juvenile court may order services for the child and the biological father, if the court determines that such services will benefit the child.

(3) If a child is removed from the custody of a parent or guardian, and reunification services are ordered, the court must order visitation between

the child and the parent or guardian for whom services are ordered. Visits are to be as frequent as possible, consistent with the well-being of the child.

(4) Reunification services must not be provided when the parent has voluntarily relinquished the child and the relinquishment has been filed with the State Department of Social Services, or if the court has appointed a guardian under section 360.

(5) Except when the order is made under paragraph (1) of subdivision (b) of section 361.5, if the court orders no reunification services for every parent otherwise eligible for such services, the court must conduct a hearing under section 366.26 within 120 days and:

(A) Order that the social worker provide a copy of the child's birth certificate to the caregiver consistent with sections 16010.4(e)(5) and 16010.5(b)–(c); and

(B) Order that the social worker provide a child or youth 16 years of age or older with a certified copy of his or her birth certificate unless the court finds that provision of the birth certificate would be inappropriate.

(6) A judgment, order, or decree setting a hearing under section 366.26 is not an immediately appealable order. Review may be sought only by filing a *Notice of Intent to File Writ Petition and Request for Record (California Rules of Court, Rule 8.450)* (form JV-820) or other notice of intent to file a writ petition and request for record, and a *Petition for Extraordinary Writ (California Rules of Court, Rules 8.452, 8.456)* (form JV-825) or other petition for extraordinary writ. If a party wishes to preserve any right to review on appeal of the findings and orders made under this rule, the party must seek an extraordinary writ under rules 8.450 and 8.452.

(7) A judgment, order, or decree setting a hearing under section 366.26 may be reviewed on appeal following the order of the 366.26 hearing only if the following have occurred:

(A) An extraordinary writ was sought by the timely filing of a *Notice of Intent to File Writ Petition and Request for Record (California Rules of Court, Rule 8.450)* (form JV-820) or other notice of intent to file a writ petition and request for record and a *Petition for Extraordinary Writ (California Rules of Court, Rules 8.452, 8.456)* (form JV-825) or other petition for extraordinary writ; and

(B) The petition for extraordinary writ was summarily denied or otherwise not decided on the merits.

(8) Review on appeal of the order setting a hearing under section 366.26 is limited to issues raised in a previous petition for extraordinary writ that were supported by an adequate record.

(9) Failure to file a notice of intent to file a writ petition and request for record and a petition for extraordinary writ review within the period specified by rules 8.450 and 8.452 to substantively address the issues challenged, or to support the challenge by an adequate record, precludes subsequent review on appeal of the findings and orders made under this rule.

(10) When the court orders a hearing under section 366.26, the court must advise orally all parties present, and by first-class mail or by electronic service in accordance with section 212.5 for parties not present, that if the party wishes to preserve any right to review on appeal of the order setting the hearing under section 366.26, the party must seek an extraordinary writ by filing a *Notice of Intent to File Writ Petition and Request for Record (California Rules of Court, Rule 8.450)* (form JV-820) or other notice of intent to file a writ petition and request for record and a *Petition for Extraordinary Writ (California Rules of Court, Rules 8.452, 8.456)* (form JV-825) or other petition for extraordinary writ.

(A) Within 24 hours of the hearing, notice by first-class mail or by electronic service in accordance with section 212.5 must be provided by the clerk of the court to the last known address of any party who is not present when the court orders the hearing under section 366.26.

(B) Copies of *Petition for Extraordinary Writ (California Rules of Court, Rules 8.452, 8.456)* (form JV-825) and *Notice of Intent to File Writ Petition and Request for Record (California Rules of Court, Rule 8.450)* (form JV-820) must be available in the courtroom and must accompany all mailed notices informing the parties of their rights.

(C) If the notice is for a hearing at which the social worker will recommend the termination of parental rights, the notice may be electronically served in accordance with section 212.5, but only in addition to service of the notice by first-class mail.

(Subd (g) amended effective January 1, 2019; adopted as subd (e) effective January 1, 1991; previously relettered as subd (f) effective July 1, 1995, and as subd (h) effective January 1, 2011; previously amended effective January 1, 1993, *July 1, 1993, January 1, 1994, January 1, 1995, January 1, 1996, July 1, 1997, January 1, 1999, July 1, 1999, January 1, 2001, July 1, 2001, July 1, 2002, January 1, 2007, January 1, 2010, January 1, 2014, and January 1, 2015; previously amended and relettered effective January 1, 2017.)*

(h) Information regarding termination of parent-child relationship (§§ 361, 361.5)

If a child is removed from the physical custody of the parent or guardian under either section 361 or 361.5, the court must:

(1) State the facts on which the decision is based; and

(2) Notify the parents that their parental rights may be terminated if custody is not returned within 6 months of the dispositional hearing or within 12 months of the date the child entered foster care, whichever time limit is applicable.

(Subd (h) relettered effective January 1, 2017; adopted as subd (f) effective January 1, 1991; previously amended effective January 1, 2001, July 1, 2002, and January 1, 2015; previously relettered as subd (g) effective July 1, 1995, and as subd (i) effective January 1, 2011.)

(i) Setting a hearing under section 366.26

At the disposition hearing, the court may not set a hearing under section 366.26 to consider termination of the rights of only one parent unless that parent is the only surviving parent, or the rights of the other parent have been terminated by a California court of competent jurisdiction or by a court of competent jurisdiction of another state under the statutes of that state, or the other parent has relinquished custody of the child to the county welfare department.

(Subd (i) relettered effective January 1, 2017; adopted as subd (j) effective July 1, 1997; previously amended effective July 1, 2002; previously relettered as subd (l) effective January 1, 2011.)

Rule 5.695 amended effective January 1, 2021; adopted as rule 1456 effective January 1, 1991; previously amended and renumbered effective January 1, 2007; previously amended effective January 1, 1993, July 1, 1993, January 1, 1994, January 1, 1995, July 1, 1995, January 1, 1996, January 1, 1997, July 1, 1997, January 1, 1999, July 1, 1999, January 1, 2001, July 1, 2001, July 1, 2002, January 1, 2004, January 1, 2006, January 1, 2008, January 1, 2010, January 1, 2011, January 1, 2014, January 1, 2015, January 1, 2017, and January 1, 2019.

Rule 5.697. Disposition Hearing for a Nonminor (Welf. & Inst. Code, §§ 224.1, 295, 303, 358, 358.1, 361, 366.31, 390, 391)

(a) Purpose

This rule provides the procedures that must be followed when a disposition hearing for a nonminor is set under Welfare and Institutions Code section 358(d).

(Subd (a) adopted effective January 1, 2021.)

(b) Notice of hearing (§§ 291, 295)

(1) The social worker must serve written notice of the hearing in the manner provided in section 291 to all persons required to receive notice under section 295, including the nonminor's parent or guardian.

(2) The social worker must serve a copy of the *Nonminor's Informed Consent to Hold Disposition Hearing* (form JV-463) with the notice to the youth.

(Subd (b) adopted effective January 1, 2021.)

(c) Informed consent (§§ 317, 358)

(1) Unless the court has appointed a guardian ad litem for the nonminor or the nonminor is not locatable after reasonable and documented efforts have been made to locate the nonminor, the court must find that the nonminor:

(A) Understands the potential benefits of continued dependency;

(B) Has been informed of their right to seek termination of dependency jurisdiction under section 391 if the court establishes dependency;

(C) Has been informed of their right to have dependency reinstated under section 388(e) if the court establishes dependency; and

(D) Has had the opportunity to confer with their attorney regarding providing informed consent.

(2) The youth must give informed consent to the disposition hearing by completing and signing *Nonminor's Informed Consent to Hold Disposition Hearing* (form JV-463). The youth or their attorney must file the form with the court at or before the scheduled disposition hearing.

(3) If the nonminor is not competent to direct counsel and give informed consent in accordance with Code of Civil Procedure section 372 and Probate Code sections 810 thru 813, the court must appoint a guardian ad litem to determine whether to provide informed consent on the nonminor's behalf by completing and signing *Nonminor's Informed Consent to Hold Disposition Hearing* (form JV-463) and filing it with the court at or before the scheduled disposition hearing.

(Subd (c) adopted effective January 1, 2021.)

(d) Conduct of the hearing (§§ 295, 303, 358, 361)

(1) The hearing may be attended, as appropriate, by participants invited by the nonminor in addition to those entitled to notice under (b).

(2) The nonminor may appear by telephone as provided in rule 5.900(e).

(3) If the nonminor or the nonminor's guardian ad litem does not provide informed consent, the court must vacate the temporary orders made under section 319, and dependency or general jurisdiction must not be retained. Before dismissing jurisdiction, the court must make the following findings:

(A) Notice was given as required by law;

(B) The requirements of (c)(1) have been met unless a guardian ad litem has been appointed for the nonminor or the nonminor could not be located after reasonable and documented efforts have been made to locate the nonminor;

(C) If the reason the nonminor did not give informed consent is because the social worker could not locate the nonminor, the court must find that after reasonable and documented efforts the nonminor could not be located.

(4) If the nonminor or the nonminor's guardian ad litem does provide informed consent, the court must proceed to a disposition hearing consistent with this rule and section 358(d). The parent or guardian of the nonminor may participate as a party in the disposition hearing, receive the social study and other evidence submitted for the hearing, and present evidence. The parent's participation is limited to addressing the court's consideration of whether one of the conditions of section 361(c) existed immediately before the nonminor attained 18 years of age.

(Subd (d) adopted effective January 1, 2021.)

(e) Social study (§§ 358, 358.1)

The petitioner must prepare a social study of the nonminor if the court proceeds to a disposition hearing. The social study must include a discussion of all matters relevant to disposition and a recommendation for disposition.

(1) The petitioner's social study must include the following information:

(A) Whether one of the conditions of section 361(c) existed immediately before the youth attained 18 years of age.

(B) The reasonable efforts that were made to prevent or eliminate the need for removal.

(C) A plan for achieving legal permanence or successful adulthood, if reunification is not being considered.

(D) If reunification services are being considered:

(i) A plan for reuniting the nonminor with the family, including a plan of visitation, developed in collaboration with the nonminor, parent or guardian, and child and family team;

(ii) Whether the nonminor and parent or guardian were actively involved in the development of the case plan;

(iii) The extent of progress the parent or guardian has made toward alleviating or mitigating the causes necessitating placement in foster care;

(iv) Whether the nonminor and parent, parents, or guardian agree with the continuation of reunification services;

(v) Whether continued reunification services are in the best interest of the nonminor; and

(vi) Whether there is a substantial probability that the nonminor will be able to safely reside in the home of the parent or guardian by the next review hearing date.

(E) The social worker's efforts to comply with rule 5.637, including but not limited to:

(i) The number of relatives identified and the relationship of each to the nonminor;

(ii) The number and relationship of those relatives described by (i) who were located and notified;

(iii) The number and relationship of those relatives described by (ii) who are interested in ongoing contact with the nonminor;

(iv) The number and relationship of those relatives described by (ii) who are interested in providing placement for the nonminor; and

(v) If it is known or there is reason to know that the nonminor is an Indian child, efforts to locate extended family members as defined in section 224.1, and evidence that all individuals contacted have been provided with information about the option of obtaining approval for placement through the tribe's license or approval procedure.

(F) If siblings are not placed together, an explanation of why they have not been placed together in the same home, what efforts are being made to place the siblings together, or why making those efforts would be contrary to the safety and well-being of any of the siblings.

(G) How and when the Transitional Independent Living Case Plan was developed, including the nature and the extent of the nonminor's participation in its development and, for an Indian child who has elected to have the Indian Child Welfare Act apply to them, the extent of consultation with the tribal representative.

(H) The nonminor's plans to remain under juvenile court jurisdiction, including the criteria in section 11403(b) that the nonminor meets or plans to meet.

(I) The efforts made by the social worker to help the nonminor meet the criteria in section 11403(b).

(J) The efforts made by the social worker to comply with the nonminor's Transitional Independent Living Case Plan, including efforts to finalize the permanent plan and prepare the nonminor for successful adulthood.

(K) The continuing necessity for the nonminor's placement and the facts supporting the conclusion reached.

(L) The appropriateness of the nonminor's current foster care placement.

(M) Progress made by the nonminor toward meeting the Transitional Independent Living Case Plan goals and the need for any modifications to assist the nonminor in attaining the goals.

(N) Verification that the nonminor was provided with the information, documents, and services required under section 391.

(2) The petitioner must submit the social study and copies of it to the court clerk at least 48 hours before the disposition hearing is set to begin, and the clerk must make the copies available to the parties and attorneys. A continuance within statutory time limits must be granted on the request of a party who has not been furnished with a copy of the social study in accordance with this rule.

(Subd (e) adopted effective January 1, 2021.)

(f) Case plan and Transitional Independent Living Case Plan (§§ 11401, 16501.1)

(1) Whenever court-ordered services are provided, the social worker must prepare a case plan consistent with section 16501.1 and the requirements of rule 5.690(c).

(2) At least 48 hours before the hearing, the nonminor's Transitional Independent Living Case Plan must be submitted with the report that the social worker prepared for the hearing and must include:

(A) The individualized plan for the nonminor to satisfy one or more of the criteria in section 11403(b) and the nonminor's anticipated placement as specified in section 11402; and

(B) The nonminor's alternate plan for their transition to independence—including housing, education, employment, and a support system—in the event that the nonminor does not remain under juvenile court jurisdiction.

(Subd (f) adopted effective January 1, 2021.)

(g) Evidence considered (§§ 358, 360)

At a hearing held under this rule, the court must receive in evidence and consider the following:

(1) The social study described in (e), the report of any CASA volunteer, and any relevant evidence offered by the petitioner, nonminor, or parent or guardian. The court may require production of other relevant evidence on its own motion. In the order of disposition, the court must state that the social study and the study or evaluation by the CASA volunteer, if any, have been read and considered by the court.

(2) The case plan, if applicable, and the Transitional Independent Living Case Plan.

(Subd (g) adopted effective January 1, 2021.)

(h) Findings and orders (§§ 358, 358.1, 361, 390)

After the nonminor or the nonminor's guardian ad litem provides informed consent, the court must consider the safety of the nonminor, determine if notice was given as required by law, and determine if by clear and convincing evidence one of the conditions of section 361(c) existed immediately before the nonminor attained 18 years of age.

(1) If the court does not find by clear and convincing evidence that one of the conditions of section 361(c) existed immediately before the nonminor attained 18 years of age, the court must vacate the temporary orders made under section 319 and dismiss dependency jurisdiction.

(2) If the court finds by clear and convincing evidence that one of the conditions of section 361(c) existed immediately before the nonminor attained 18 years of age, the court must declare dependency and:

(A) Order the continuation of juvenile court jurisdiction and, consistent with (3), set a nonminor dependent review hearing under section 366.31 and rule 5.903 within 60 days or six months, or

(B) Set a hearing to consider termination of juvenile court jurisdiction over the nonminor dependent under rule 5.555 within 30 days, if the nonminor dependent chooses not to remain in foster care.

(3) If the court makes the finding in (2), the following findings and orders must be made and included in the written court documentation of the hearing, with the exception of those findings and orders stated in (C) that may be made at the nonminor disposition hearing or at a nonminor dependent status review hearing under section 366.31 and rule 5.903 to be held within 60 days:

(A) Findings

(i) Whether reasonable efforts have been made to prevent or eliminate the need for removal;

(ii) Whether the social worker has exercised due diligence in conducting the required investigation to identify, locate, and notify the nonminor dependent's relatives consistent with section 309(e); and

(iii) Whether a nonminor who is an Indian child chooses to have the Indian Child Welfare Act apply to them as a nonminor dependent.

(B) Orders

(i) Order that placement and care is vested with the placing agency.

(ii) Order the county agency to comply with rule 5.481, if there was no inquiry or determination of whether the nonminor dependent was an Indian child before the nonminor dependent attained 18 years of age and the nonminor dependent requests an Indian Child Welfare Act determination.

(iii) The court may order family reunification services under 361.6 for the nonminor and the parent or legal guardian. Court-ordered reunification services must not exceed the time frames as stated in section 361.5.

(C) The following findings and orders must be considered either at the nonminor disposition hearing held under this rule and section 358(d), or at a nonminor dependent status review hearing under rule 5.903 and section 366.31 held within 60 days of the nonminor disposition hearing:

(i) The findings contained in rule 5.903(e)(1)(A)–(P);

(ii) The orders contained in rule 5.903(e)(2)(A)(i) and (ii); and

(iii) For a nonminor dependent whose case plan is court-ordered family reunification services, a determination of the following:

a. The extent of the agency's compliance with the case plan in making reasonable efforts or, in the case of an Indian child, active efforts, as described in section 361.7, to create a safe home of the parent or guardian for the nonminor dependent to reside in or to complete whatever steps are necessary to finalize the permanent placement of the nonminor dependent; and

b. The extent of progress the parents or legal guardians have made toward alleviating or mitigating the causes necessitating placement in foster care.

(Subd (h) adopted effective January 1, 2021.)

Rule 5.697 adopted effective January 1, 2021.

Rule 5.700. Termination of jurisdiction—custody and visitation orders (§§ 302, 304, 361.2, 362.4, 726.5)

When the juvenile court terminates its jurisdiction over a dependent or ward of the court and places the child in the home of a parent, it may issue an order determining the rights to custody of and visitation with the child. The court may also issue protective orders as provided in section 213.5 or as described in Family Code section 6218.

(a) Effect of order

Any order issued under this rule continues in effect until modified or terminated by a later order of a superior court with jurisdiction to make determinations about the custody of the child. The order may be modified or terminated only if the superior court finds both that:

(1) There has been a significant change of circumstances since the juvenile court issued the order; and

(2) Modification or termination of the order is in the best interest of the child.

(Subd (a) adopted effective January 1, 2016.)

(b) Preparation and transmission of order

The order must be prepared on *Custody Order—Juvenile—Final Judgment* (form JV-200). The court must direct either the parent, parent's attorney, county counsel, or clerk to:

(1) Prepare the order for the court's signature; and

(2) Transmit the order within 10 calendar days after the order is signed to any superior court where a proceeding described in (c)(1) is pending or,

if no such proceeding exists, to the superior court of, in order of preference:

(A) The county in which the parent who has been given sole physical custody resides;

(B) The county in which the children's primary residence is located if no parent has been given sole physical custody; or

(C) A county or other location where any parent resides.

(Subd (b) amended and relettered effective January 1, 2016; adopted as part of subd (a).)

(c) Procedures for filing order—receiving court

On receiving a juvenile court custody order transmitted under (b)(2), the clerk of the receiving court must immediately file the juvenile court order as follows.

(1) Except as provided in paragraph (2), the juvenile court order must be filed in any pending nullity, dissolution, legal separation, guardianship, Uniform Parentage Act, Domestic Violence Prevention Act, or other family law custody proceeding and, when filed, becomes a part of that proceeding.

(2) If the only pending proceeding related to the child in the receiving court is filed under Family Code section 17400 et seq., the clerk must proceed as follows.

(A) If the receiving court has issued a custody or visitation order in the pending proceeding, the clerk must file the received order in that proceeding.

(B) If the receiving court has not issued a custody or visitation order in the pending proceeding, the clerk must not file the received order in that proceeding, but must instead proceed under paragraph (3).

(3) If no dependency, family law, or guardianship proceeding affecting custody or visitation of the child is pending, the order must be used to open a new custody proceeding in the receiving court. The clerk must immediately open a family law file without charging a filing fee, and assign a case number, and file the order in the new case file.

(Subd (c) amended and relettered effective January 1, 2016; adopted as part of subd (a).)

(d) Endorsed filed copy—clerk's certificate of service

Within 15 court days of receiving the order, the clerk of the receiving court must send an endorsed filed copy of the order showing the case number assigned by the receiving court by first-class mail or by electronic means in accordance with section 212.5 to the child's parents and the originating juvenile court, with a completed clerk's certificate of service, for inclusion in the child's file.

(Subd (d) amended effective January 1, 2019; adopted as part of subd (a); previously amended and relettered effective January 1, 2016.)

Rule 5.700 amended effective January 1, 2019; adopted as rule 1457 effective January 1, 1990; previously amended effective January 1, 1994, January 1, 2001, and January 1, 2016; previously amended and renumbered as rule 5.700 effective January 1, 2007.

Rule 5.705. Setting a hearing under section 366.26

At a disposition hearing, a review hearing, or at any other hearing regarding a dependent child, the court must not set a hearing under section 366.26 to consider termination of the rights of only one parent unless that parent is the only surviving parent, or the rights of the other parent have been terminated by a California court of competent jurisdiction or by a court of competent jurisdiction of another state under the statutes of that state, or the other parent has relinquished custody of the child to the county welfare department.

Rule 5.705 amended and renumbered effective January 1, 2007; adopted as rule 1459 effective July 1, 1990; previously amended effective January 1, 1994, and July 1, 1997.

Article 4
Reviews, Permanent Planning

Rule 5.735. Legal guardianship

Rule 5.740. Hearings after selection of a permanent plan (§§ 366.26, 366.3, 16501.1)

Rule 5.706.   Family maintenance review hearings (§ 364)

(a) Notice (§ 292)

The petitioner or the court clerk must give notice of review hearings on *Notice of Review Hearing* (form JV-280), in the manner provided in section 292, to all persons required to receive notice under section 292 and to any CASA volunteer that has been appointed on the case.

(Subd (a) relettered effective January 1, 2017; adopted as subd (b) effective January 1, 2010.)

(b) Release of Information to the Medical Board of California

If the child has signed *Position on Release of Information to Medical Board of California* (form JV-228), the social worker must provide the child with a blank copy of *Withdrawal of Release of Information to Medical Board of California* (form JV-229) before the hearing if it is the last hearing before the child turns 18 years of age or if the social worker is recommending termination of juvenile court jurisdiction.

(Subd (b) adopted effective September 1, 2020.)

(c) Court considerations and findings

(1) The court must consider the report prepared by the petitioner, the report of any CASA volunteer, and the case plan submitted for this hearing.

(2) In considering the case plan submitted for the hearing, the court must find as follows:

(A) The child was actively involved in the development of his or her own case plan as age and developmentally appropriate; or

(B) The child was not actively involved in the development of his or her own case plan. If the court makes such a finding, the court must order the agency to actively involve the child in the development of his or her own case plan, unless the court finds that the child is unable, unavailable, or unwilling to participate; and

(C) Each parent was actively involved in the development of the case plan; or

(D) Each parent was not actively involved in the development of the case plan. If the court makes such a finding, the court must order the agency to actively involve each parent in the development of the case plan, unless the court finds that each parent is unable, unavailable, or unwilling to participate.

(Subd (c) relettered effective September 1, 2020; adopted as subd (d) effective January 1, 2010; previously relettered as subd (b) effective January 1, 2017.)

(d) Conduct of hearing (§ 364)

If the court retains jurisdiction, the court must order continued services and set a review hearing within six months. The court must determine whether continued supervision is necessary under section 364(c).

(Subd (d) relettered effective September 1, 2020; adopted as subd (e) effective January 1, 2010; previously amended and relettered as subd (c) effective January 1, 2017.)

(e) Reasonable cause (§ 364)

In any case in which the court has ordered that a parent or legal guardian retain physical custody of a child subject to supervision by a social worker, and the social worker subsequently receives a report of acts or circumstances that indicate there is reasonable cause to believe that the child is a person described under section 300(a), (d), or (e), the social worker must file a subsequent petition under section 342 or a supplemental petition under section 387. If, as a result of the proceedings under the section 342 or 387 petition, the court finds that the child is a person described in section 300(a), (d), or (e), the court must remove the child from the care, custody, and control of the child's parent or legal guardian and must commit the child to the care, custody, and control of the social worker under section 361.

(Subd (e) relettered effective September 1, 2020; adopted as subd (f) effective January 1, 2010; previously relettered as subd (d) effective January 1, 2017.)

(f) Child's education (§§ 361, 366, 366.1)

The court must consider the child's education, including whether it is necessary to limit the right of the parent or legal guardian to make educational or developmental-services decisions for the child, following the requirements and procedures in rules 5.649, 5.650, and 5.651 and in section 361(a).

(Subd (f) relettered effective September 1, 2020; adopted as subd (g) effective January 1, 2010; previously amended and relettered as subd (e) effective January 1, 2017.)

Rule 5.706 amended effective September 1, 2020; adopted effective January 1, 2010; previously amended effective January 1, 2017.

Rule 5.707.   Review or dispositional hearing requirements for child approaching majority (§§ 224.1, 366(a)(1)(F), 366.3, 366.31, 16501.1(f)(16))

(a) Reports

At the last review hearing before the child attains 18 years of age held under section 366.21, 366.22, 366.25, or 366.3, or at the dispositional hearing held under section 360 if no review hearing will be set before the child attains 18 years of age, in addition to complying with all other statutory and rule requirements applicable to the report prepared by the social worker for the hearing, the report must include a description of:

(1) The child's plans to remain under juvenile court jurisdiction as a nonminor dependent including the criteria in section 11403(b) that he or she plans to meet;

(2) The efforts made by the social worker to help the child meet one or more of the criteria in section 11403(b);

(3) For an Indian child to whom the Indian Child Welfare Act applies, his or her plans to continue to be considered an Indian child for the purposes of the ongoing application of the Indian Child Welfare Act to him or her as a nonminor dependent;

(4) Whether the child has applied for and, if so, the status of any in-progress application pending for title XVI Supplemental Security Income benefits and, if such an application is pending, whether it will be in the child's best interest to continue juvenile court jurisdiction until a final decision is issued to ensure that the child receives continued assistance with the application process;

(5) Whether the child has an in-progress application pending for Special Immigrant Juvenile Status or other applicable application for legal residency and whether an active dependency case is required for that application;

(6) The efforts made by the social worker toward providing the child with the written information, documents, and services described in section 391, and to the extent that the child has not yet been provided with them, the barriers to providing the information, documents, or services and the steps that will be taken to overcome those barriers by the date the child attains 18 years of age;

(7) When and how the child was informed of his or her right to have juvenile court jurisdiction terminated when he or she attains 18 years of age;

(8) When and how the child was provided with information about the potential benefits of remaining under juvenile court jurisdiction as a nonminor dependent and the social worker's assessment of the child's understanding of those benefits; and

(9) When and how the child was informed that if juvenile court jurisdiction is terminated after he or she attains 18 years of age, he or she has the right to file a request to return to foster care and have the juvenile court resume jurisdiction over him or her as a nonminor dependent.

(Subd (a) amended effective January 1, 2016; adopted effective January 1, 2012; previously amended effective July 1, 2012.)

(b) Transitional Independent Living Case Plan

At the last review hearing before the child attains 18 years of age held under section 366.21, 366.22, 366.25, or 366.3, or at the dispositional hearing held under section 360 if no review hearing will be set before the child attains 18 years of age, the child's Transitional Independent Living Case Plan:

(1) Must be submitted with the social worker's report prepared for the hearing at least 10 calendar days before the hearing; and

(2) Must include:

(A) The individualized plan for the child to satisfy one or more of the criteria in section 11403(b) and the child's anticipated placement as specified in section 11402; and

(B) The child's alternate plan for his or her transition to independence, including housing, education, employment, and a support system in the event the child does not remain under juvenile court jurisdiction after attaining 18 years of age.

(Subd (b) amended effective January 1, 2016; adopted effective January 1, 2012.)

(c) Findings

(1) At the last review hearing before the child attains 18 years of age held under section 366.21, 366.22, 366.25, or 366.3, or at the dispositional hearing held under section 360 if no review hearing will be set before the child attains 18 years of age, in addition to complying with all other statutory and rule requirements applicable to the hearing, the court must

make the following findings in the written court documentation of the hearing:

(A) Whether the child's Transitional Independent Living Case Plan includes a plan for the child to satisfy one or more of the criteria in section 11403(b) and the specific criteria it is anticipated the child will satisfy;

(B) Whether there is included in the child's Transitional Independent Living Case Plan an alternative plan for the child's transition to independence, including housing, education, employment, and a support system in the event the child does not remain under juvenile court jurisdiction after attaining 18 years of age;

(C) For an Indian child to whom the Indian Child Welfare Act applies, whether he or she intends to continue to be considered an Indian child for the purposes of the ongoing application of the Indian Child Welfare Act to him or her as a nonminor dependent;

(D) Whether the child has an in-progress application pending for title XVI Supplemental Security Income benefits and, if such an application is pending, whether it is in the child's best interest to continue juvenile court jurisdiction until a final decision has been issued to ensure that the child receives continued assistance with the application process;

(E) Whether the child has an in-progress application pending for Special Immigrant Juvenile Status or other applicable application for legal residency and whether an active dependency case is required for that application;

(F) Whether all the information, documents, and services in sections 391(e) were provided to the child, and whether the barriers to providing any missing information, documents, or services can be overcome by the date the child attains 18 years of age;

(G) Whether the child has been informed of his or her right to have juvenile court jurisdiction terminated when he or she attains 18 years of age;

(H) Whether the child understands the potential benefits of remaining under juvenile court jurisdiction as a nonminor dependent; and

(I) Whether the child has been informed that if juvenile court jurisdiction is terminated after he or she attains 18 years of age, he or she has the right to file a request to return to foster care and have the juvenile court resume jurisdiction over him or her as a nonminor dependent.

(2) The hearing must be continued for no more than five court days for the submission of additional information as ordered by the court if the court finds that the report and Transitional Independent Living Case Plan submitted by the social worker do not provide the information required by (a) and (b) and the court is unable to make all the findings required by (c)(1).

(Subd (c) amended effective January 1, 2016; adopted effective January 1, 2012; previously amended effective July 1, 2012, and January 1, 2014.)

(d) Orders

(1) For a child who intends to remain under juvenile court jurisdiction as a nonminor dependent, as defined in section 11400(v), after attaining 18 years of age, the court must set a nonminor dependent status review hearing under rule 5.903 within six months from the date of the current hearing.

(2) For a child who does not intend to remain under juvenile court as a nonminor dependent, as defined in section 11400(v), after attaining 18 years of age, the court must:

(A) Set a hearing under rule 5.555 for a date within one month after the child's 18th birthday, for the child who requests that the juvenile court terminate its jurisdiction after he or she attains 18 years of age; or

(B) Set a hearing under section 366.21, 366.22, 366.25, or 366.3 no more than six months from the date of the current hearing, for a child who will remain under juvenile court jurisdiction in a foster care placement.

(Subd (d) amended effective July 1, 2012; adopted effective January 1, 2012.) Rule 5.707 amended effective January 1, 2016; adopted effective January 1, 2012; previously amended effective July 1, 2012, and January 1, 2014.

Rule 5.708. General review hearing requirements

(a) Notice of hearing (§ 293)

The petitioner or the clerk must serve written notice of review hearings on *Notice of Review Hearing* (form JV-280), in the manner provided in sections 224.2 or 293 as appropriate, to all persons or entities entitled to notice under sections 224.2 and 293 and to any CASA volunteer, educational rights holder, or surrogate parent appointed to the case.

(Subd (a) amended and relettered effective January 1, 2017; adopted as subd (b) effective January 1, 2010; previously amended effective January 1, 2014.)

(b) Reports (§§ 366.05, 366.1, 366.21, 366.22, 366.25, 16022)

Before the hearing, the social worker must investigate and file a report describing the services offered to the family, progress made, and, if relevant, the prognosis for return of the child to the parent or legal guardian.

(1) The report must include:

(A) Recommendations for court orders and the reasons for those recommendations;

(B) A description of the efforts made to achieve legal permanence for the child if reunification efforts fail;

(C) A factual discussion of each item listed in sections 366.1 and 366.21(c); and

(D) A factual discussion of the information required by section 16002(b).

(2) At least 10 calendar days before the hearing, the social worker must file the report and provide copies to the parent or legal guardian and his or her counsel, to counsel for the child, to any CASA volunteer, and, in the case of an Indian child, to the child's identified Indian tribe. The social worker must provide a summary of the recommendations to any foster parents, relative caregivers, or certified foster parents who have been approved for adoption.

(3) The court must read and consider, and state on the record that it has read and considered, the report of the social worker, the report of any CASA volunteer, the case plan submitted for the hearing, any report submitted by the child's caregiver under section 366.21(d), and any other evidence.

(Subd (b) relettered effective January 1, 2017; adopted as subd (c) effective January 1, 2010; previously amended effective July 1, 2010, and January 1, 2016.)

(c) Release of Information to the Medical Board of California

If the child has signed *Position on Release of Information to Medical Board of California* (form JV-228), the social worker must provide the child with a blank copy of *Withdrawal of Release of Information to Medical Board of California* (form JV-229) before the hearing if it is the last hearing before the child turns 18 years of age or if the social worker is recommending termination of juvenile court jurisdiction.

(Subd (c) adopted effective September 1, 2020.)

(d) Reasonable services (§§ 366, 366.21, 366.22, 366.25, 366.3)

(1) If the child is not returned to the custody of the parent or legal guardian, the court must consider whether reasonable services have been offered or provided. The court must find that reasonable services have been offered or provided or have not been offered or provided.

(2) If the child is not returned to the custody of the parent or legal guardian, the court must consider the safety of the child and make the findings listed in sections 366(a) and 16002.

(Subd (d) relettered effective September 1, 2020; adopted as subd (e) effective January 1, 2010; previously amended and relettered as subd (c) effective January 1, 2017.)

(e) Educational and developmental-services needs (§§ 361, 366, 366.1, 366.3)

The court must consider the educational and developmental-services needs of each child and nonminor or nonminor dependent, including whether it is necessary to limit the rights of the parent or legal guardian to make educational or developmental-services decisions for the child. If the court limits those rights or, in the case of a nonminor or nonminor dependent who has chosen not to make educational or developmental-services decisions for him- or herself or has been deemed incompetent, finds that appointment would be in the best interests of the nonminor or nonminor dependent, the court must appoint a responsible adult as the educational rights holder as defined in rule 5.502. Any limitation on the rights of a parent or guardian to make educational or developmental-services decisions for the child must be specified in the court order. The court must follow the procedures in rules 5.649–5.651.

(Subd (e) relettered effective September 1, 2020; adopted as subd (f) effective January 1, 2010; previously amended effective January 1, 2014, and January 1, 2016; previously relettered as subd (d) effective January 1, 2017.)

(f) Case plan (§§ 16001.9, 16501.1)

The court must consider the case plan submitted for the hearing and must find as follows:

(1) The case plan meets the requirements of section 16501.1; or

(2) The case plan does not meet the requirements of section 16501.1, in which case the court must order the agency to comply with the requirements of section 16501.1; and

(3) The child was actively involved, as age- and developmentally appropriate, in the development of the case plan and plan for permanent placement; or

(4) The child was not actively involved, as age- and developmentally appropriate, in the development of the case plan and plan for permanent placement, in which case the court must order the agency to actively involve the child in the development of the case plan and plan for permanent placement, unless the court finds the child is unable, unavailable, or unwilling to participate; and

(5) Each parent or legal guardian was actively involved in the development of the case plan and plan for permanent placement; or

(6) Each parent or legal guardian was not actively involved in the development of the case plan and plan for permanent placement, in which case the court must order the agency to actively involve that parent or legal guardian in the development of the case plan and plan for permanent placement, unless the court finds that the parent or legal guardian is unable, unavailable, or unwilling to participate; and

(7) In the case of an Indian child, the agency consulted with the Indian child's tribe, as defined in rule 5.502, and the tribe was actively involved in the development of the case plan and plan for permanent placement, including consideration of tribal customary adoption as an appropriate permanent plan for the child if reunification is unsuccessful; or

(8) The agency did not consult with the Indian child's tribe, as defined in rule 5.502, and the tribe was not actively involved in the development of the case plan and plan for permanent placement, including consideration of tribal customary adoption as an appropriate permanent plan for the child if reunification is unsuccessful, in which case the court must order the agency to do so, unless the court finds that the tribe is unable, unavailable, or unwilling to participate; and

(9) For a child 12 years of age or older in a permanent placement, the child was given the opportunity to review the case plan, sign it, and receive a copy; or

(10) The child was not given the opportunity to review the case plan, sign it, and receive a copy, in which case the court must order the agency to give the child the opportunity to review the case plan, sign it, and receive a copy.

(Subd (f) relettered effective September 1, 2020; adopted as subd (g) effective January 1, 2010; previously amended effective July 1, 2010, January 1, 2014, January 1, 2016, and January 1, 2019; amended and relettered as subd (e) effective January 1, 2016.)

(g) Sibling findings; additional findings (§§ 366, 16002)

(1) The court must determine whether the child has other siblings under the court's jurisdiction. If so, the court must make the additional determinations required by section 366(a)(1)(D); and

(2) The court must enter any additional findings as required by section 366 and section 16002.

(Subd (g) relettered effective September 1, 2020; adopted as subd (j) effective January 1, 2010; previously amended effective January 1, 2016; previously relettered as subd (f) effective January 1, 2017.)

(h) Placement with noncustodial parent (§ 361.2)

If at any review hearing the court places the child with a noncustodial parent, or if the court has previously made such a placement, the court may, after stating on the record or in writing the factual basis for the order:

(1) Continue supervision and reunification services;

(2) Order custody to the noncustodial parent, continue supervision, and order family maintenance services; or

(3) Order custody to the noncustodial parent, terminate jurisdiction, and direct that *Custody Order—Juvenile—Final Judgment* (form JV-200) be prepared and filed under rule 5.700.

(Subd (h) relettered effective September 1, 2020; adopted as subd (k) effective January 1, 2010; previously relettered as subd (g) effective January 1, 2017.)

(i) Setting a hearing under section 366.26 for one parent

The court may not set a hearing under section 366.26 to consider termination of the rights of only one parent unless:

(1) That parent is the only surviving parent;

(2) The rights of the other parent have been terminated by a California court of competent jurisdiction or by a court of competent jurisdiction of another state under the statutes of that state; or

(3) The other parent has relinquished custody of the child to the county welfare department.

(Subd (i) relettered effective September 1, 2020; adopted as subd (l) effective January 1, 2010; previously relettered as subd (h) effective January 1, 2017.)

(j) Requirements on setting a section 366.26 hearing (§§ 366.21, 366.22, 366.25)

The court must make the following orders and determinations when setting a hearing under section 366.26:

(1) The court must ensure that notice is provided as required by section 294.

(2) The court must follow all procedures in rule 5.590 regarding writ petition rights, advisements, and forms.

(Subd (j) relettered effective September 1, 2020; adopted as subd (n) effective January 1, 2010; previously amended effective July 1, 2010, January 1, 2014, January 1, 2015, January 1, 2016, and July 1, 2016; previously amended and relettered as subd (i) effective January 1, 2017.)

(k) Appeal of order setting section 366.26 hearing

An appeal of any order setting a hearing under section 366.26 is subject to the limitation stated in subdivision (*l*) of section 366.26 and must follow the procedures in rules 8.400–8.416.

(Subd (k) relettered effective September 1, 2020; adopted as subd (o) effective January 1, 2010; relettered as subd (j) effective January 1, 2017; previously amended effective January 1, 2019.)

Rule 5.708 amended effective September 1, 2020; adopted effective January 1, 2010; previously amended effective July 1, 2010, January 1, 2014, January 1, 2015, January 1, 2016, July 1, 2016, January 1, 2017, and January 1, 2019.

Rule 5.710.   Six-month review hearing

(a) Determinations and conduct of hearing (§§ 364, 366, 366.1, 366.21)

At the hearing, the court and all parties must comply with all relevant requirements and procedures in rule 5.708, General review hearing requirements. The court must make all appropriate findings and orders specified in rule 5.708 and proceed under section 366.21(e) and (g), and as follows:

(1) *Order return of the child or find that return would be detrimental*

If the child is returned, the court may order the termination of dependency jurisdiction or order continued dependency services and set a review hearing within 6 months.

(2) *Place with noncustodial parent*

If the court has previously placed or at this hearing places the child with a noncustodial parent, the court must follow the procedures in rule 5.708(g) and section 361.2.

(3) *Set a section 366.26 hearing*

If the court does not return custody of the child to the parent or legal guardian, the court may set a hearing under section 366.26 within 120 days, as provided in (b).

(4) *Continue the case for a 12-month permanency hearing*

If the child is not returned and the court does not set a section 366.26 hearing, the court must order that any reunification services previously ordered will continue to be offered to the parent or legal guardian, if appropriate. The court may modify those services as appropriate or order additional services reasonably believed to facilitate the return of the child to the parent or legal guardian. The court must set a date for the next hearing no later than 12 months from the date the child entered foster care as defined in section 361.49.

(Subd (a) amended effective January 1, 2018; repealed and adopted as subd (d) effective January 1, 1990; relettered as subd (e) effective January 1, 1992; previously amended effective January 1, 1999, July 1, 1999, January 1, 2001, July 1, 2002, January 1, 2004, January 1, 2005, and January 1, 2007; previously repealed, amended and relettered as subd (b) effective January 1, 2010 and as subd (a) effective January 1, 2017.)

(b) Setting a section 366.26 hearing (§§ 366.21, 366.215)

(1) The court may set a hearing under section 366.26 within 120 days if any of the conditions in section 366.21(e) are met; or the parent is deceased.

(2) At the hearing, the court and all parties must comply with all relevant requirements and procedures related to section 366.26 hearings in rule 5.708, General review hearing requirements. The court must make all appropriate findings and orders specified in rule 5.708.

(Subd (b) amended and relettered effective January 1, 2017; repealed and adopted as subd (e); previously amended and relettered as subd (f) effective January 1, 1992, and as subd (c) effective January 1, 2010; previously amended effective January 1, 1993, January 1, 1995, July 1, 1997, January 1, 1999, July 1, 1999, January 1, 2000, January 1, 2001, July 1, 2002, January 1, 2004, January 1, 2005, January 1, 2006, January 1, 2007, January 1, 2010, January 1, 2011, January 1, 2014, and January 1, 2015.)

Rule 5.710 amended effective January 1, 2018; adopted as rule 1460 effective January 1, 1990; previously amended and renumbered effective January 1, 2007; previously amended effective January 1, 1992, January 1, 1993, January 1, 1995, July 1, 1995, July 1, 1997, January 1, 1999, July 1, 1999, January 1, 2000, January 1, 2001, July 1, 2002, January 1, 2004, January 1, 2005, January 1, 2006, January 1, 2010, January 1, 2011, January 1, 2014, January 1, 2015, and January 1, 2017.

Rule 5.715.　Twelve-month permanency hearing

(a)　Requirement for 12-month review; setting of hearing (§§ 293, 366.21)

The case of any dependent child whom the court has removed from the custody of the parent or legal guardian must be set for a permanency hearing within 12 months of the date the child entered foster care, as defined in section 361.49, and no later than 18 months from the date of the initial removal.

(Subd (a) amended effective January 1, 2017; previously amended effective January 1, 2001, January 1, 2004, January 1, 2006, January 1, 2007, and January 1, 2010.)

(b)　Determinations and conduct of hearing (§§ 309(e), 361.5, 366, 366.1, 366.21)

At the hearing, the court and all parties must comply with all relevant requirements and procedures in rule 5.708, General review hearing requirements. The court must make all appropriate findings and orders specified in rule 5.708 and proceed under section 366.21(f) and (g), and as follows:

(1)　The requirements in rule 5.708(c) must be followed in entering a reasonable services finding.

(2)　If the court has previously placed or at this hearing places the child with a noncustodial parent, the court must follow the procedures in rule 5.708(g) and section 361.2.

(3)　The court may order that the name and address of the foster home remain confidential.

(4)　In the case of an Indian child, if the child is not returned to his or her parent or legal guardian, the court must determine whether:

(A)　The agency has consulted the child's tribe about tribal customary adoption;

(B)　The child's tribe concurs with tribal customary adoption; and

(C)　Tribal customary adoption is an appropriate permanent plan for the child.

(5)　If the child is not returned to his or her parent or legal guardian and the court terminates reunification services, the court must find as follows:

(A)　The agency has made diligent efforts to locate an appropriate relative; or

(B)　The agency has not made diligent efforts to locate an appropriate relative. If the court makes such a finding, the court or administrative review panel must order the agency to make diligent efforts to locate an appropriate relative; and

(C)　Each relative whose name has been submitted to the agency as a possible caregiver has been evaluated as an appropriate placement resource; or

(D)　Each relative whose name has been submitted to the agency as a possible caregiver has not been evaluated as an appropriate placement resource. If the court makes such a finding, the court must order the agency to evaluate as an appropriate placement resource, each relative whose name has been submitted to the agency as a possible caregiver.

(Subd (b) amended effective January 1, 2018; repealed and adopted as subd (c)(2) effective January 1, 1990; previously amended and relettered as subd (c) effective July 1, 1999, as subd (d) effective January 1, 2002, as subd (c) effective January 1, 2001, and as subd (b) effective January 1, 2010; previously amended effective January 1, 1992, January 1, 1993, January 1, 1995, July 1, 1995, July 1, 1997, January 1, 1999, January 1, 2004, January 1, 2005, January 1, 2007, July 1, 2010, January 1, 2014, and January 1, 2017.)

Rule 5.715 amended effective January 1, 2018; adopted as rule 1461 effective January 1, 1990; previously amended and renumbered effective January 1, 2007; previously amended effective January 1, 1992, January 1, 1993, January 1, 1994, January 1, 1995, July 1, 1995, July 1, 1997, January 1, 1999, July 1, 1999, January 1, 2000, January 1, 2001, January 1, 2004, January 1, 2005, January 1, 2006, January 1, 2010, July 1, 2010, January 1, 2014, and January 1, 2017.

Rule 5.720.　Eighteen-month permanency review hearing

(a)　Determinations and conduct of hearing (§§ 309(e), 361.5, 366.22)

At the hearing the court and all parties must comply with all relevant requirements and procedures in rule 5.708, General review hearing requirements. The court must make all appropriate findings and orders specified in rule 5.708, and proceed under section 366.22 and as follows:

(1)　If the court has previously placed or at this hearing places the child with a noncustodial parent, the court must follow the procedures in rule 5.708(g) and section 361.2.

(2)　The court may order that the name and address of the foster home remain confidential.

(3)　In the case of an Indian child, if the child is not returned to his or her parent or legal guardian, the court must determine whether:

(A)　The agency has consulted the child's tribe about tribal customary adoption;

(B)　The child's tribe concurs with tribal customary adoption; and

(C)　Tribal customary adoption is an appropriate permanent plan for the child.

(4)　If the child is not returned to his or her parent or legal guardian and the court terminates reunification services, the court must find as follows:

(A)　The agency has made diligent efforts to locate an appropriate relative; or

(B)　The agency has not made diligent efforts to locate an appropriate relative. If the court makes such a finding, the court must order the agency to make diligent efforts to locate an appropriate relative; and

(C)　Each relative whose name has been submitted to the agency as a possible caregiver has been evaluated as an appropriate placement resource; or

(D)　Each relative whose name has been submitted to the agency as a possible caregiver has not been evaluated as an appropriate placement resource. If the court makes such a finding, the court must order the agency to evaluate as an appropriate placement resource, each relative whose name has been submitted to the agency as a possible caregiver.

(Subd (a) amended and relettered effective January 1, 2017; repealed and adopted as subd (b) effective January 1, 1990; previously amended and relettered as subd (c) effective January 1, 2005, and as subd (b) effective January 1, 2010; previously amended effective July 1, 1991, January 1, 1992, January 1, 1993, January 1, 1995, July 1, 1995, January 1, 1999, July 1, 1999, January 1, 2006, July 1, 2006, January 1, 2007, July 1, 2007, July 1, 2010, January 1, 2014, and January 1, 2015.)

Rule 5.720 amended effective January 1, 2017; repealed and adopted as rule 1462 effective January 1, 1990; previously amended and renumbered effective January 1, 2007; previously amended effective July 1, 1991, January 1, 1992, January 1, 1993, January 1, 1994, January 1, 1995, July 1, 1995, July 1, 1997, January 1, 1999, July 1, 1999, January 1, 2001, January 1, 2005, January 1, 2006, July 1, 2006, July 1, 2007, January 1, 2010, July 1, 2010, January 1, 2014, and January 1, 2015.

Rule 5.722.　Twenty-four-month subsequent permanency review hearing

(a)　Determinations and conduct of hearing (§§ 309(e), 366, 366.1, 366.25)

At the hearing, the court and all parties must comply with all relevant requirements and procedures in rule 5.708, General review hearing requirements. The court must make all appropriate findings and orders specified in rule 5.708, and proceed under section 366.25 and as follows:

(1)　The requirements in rule 5.708(c) must be followed in entering a reasonable services finding.

(2)　If the court does not order the return of the child to the custody of the parent or legal guardian, the court must specify the factual basis for its finding of risk of detriment.

(3)　The court may order that the name and address of the foster home remain confidential. The court and all parties must comply with all relevant requirements, procedures, findings, and orders related to section 366.26 hearings in rule 5.708(h)–(j).

(4)　In the case of an Indian child, if the child is not returned to his or her parent or legal guardian, the court must determine whether:

(A)　The agency has consulted the child's tribe about tribal customary adoption;

(B)　The child's tribe concurs with tribal customary adoption; and

(C)　Tribal customary adoption is an appropriate permanent plan for the child.

(5)　If the child is not returned to his or her parent or legal guardian and the court terminates reunification services, the court must find as follows:

(A)　The agency has made diligent efforts to locate an appropriate relative; or

(B)　The agency has not made diligent efforts to locate an appropriate relative. If the court makes such a finding, the court must order the agency to make diligent efforts to locate an appropriate relative; and

(C)　Each relative whose name has been submitted to the agency as a possible caregiver has been evaluated as an appropriate placement resource; or

(D)　Each relative whose name has been submitted to the agency as a possible caregiver has not been evaluated as an appropriate placement resource. If the court makes such a finding, the court must order the agency to evaluate as an appropriate placement resource, each relative whose name has been submitted to the agency as a possible caregiver.

(Subd (a) amended and relettered effective January 1, 2017; adopted as subd (b) effective January 1, 2010; previously amended effective July 1, 2010.)

Rule 5.722 amended effective January 1, 2017; adopted effective January 1, 2010; previously amended effective July 1, 2010.

Rule 5.725. Selection of permanent plan (§§ 366.24, 366.26, 727.3, 727.31)

(a) Application of rule

This rule applies to children who have been declared dependents or wards of the juvenile court.

(1) The court may not terminate the rights of only one parent under section 366.26 unless that parent is the only surviving parent; or unless the rights of the other parent have been terminated by a California court of competent jurisdiction or by a court of competent jurisdiction of another state under the statutes of that state; or unless the other parent has relinquished custody of the child to the welfare department.

(2) **[1]** Sections **360,** 366.26 **[2], 727.3,** 727.31 **[3], and 728 provide the exclusive authority and procedures for the juvenile court to establish a** legal guardianship **for a dependent child or ward of the court**.

(3) For termination of the parental rights of an Indian child, the procedures in this rule and in rule 5.485 must be followed.

(Subd (a) amended effective January 1, 2021; previously amended effective January 1, 1994, July 1, 2002, January 1, 2007, January 1, 2009, and January 1, 2017.)

Rule 5.725(a). 2020 Deletes. [1] Only **[2]** and **[3]** apply for establishing

(b) Notice of hearing (§ 294)

In addition to the requirements stated in section 294, notice must be given to any CASA volunteer, Indian custodian, and de facto parent on *Notice of Hearing on Selection of a Permanent Plan* (form JV-300).

(Subd (b) amended effective January 1, 2017; previously amended effective January 1, 1992, July 1, 1992, July 1, 1995, July 1, 2002, January 1, 2005, January 1, 2006, and January 1, 2007.)

(c) Report

Before the hearing, petitioner must prepare an assessment under section 366.21(i). At least 10 calendar days before the hearing, the petitioner must file the assessment, provide copies to each parent or guardian and all counsel of record, and provide a summary of the recommendations to the present custodians of the child, to any CASA volunteer, and to the tribe of an Indian child.

(Subd (c) amended effective January 1, 2007; adopted effective January 1, 1992; previously amended effective July 1, 1995, and July 1, 2002.)

(d) Conduct of hearing

At the hearing, the court must state on the record that the court has read and considered the report of petitioner, the report of any CASA volunteer, the case plan submitted for this hearing, any report submitted by the child's caregiver under section 366.21(d), and any other evidence, and must proceed under section 366.26 and as follows:

(1) In the case of an Indian child, after the agency has consulted with the tribe, when the court has determined with the concurrence of the tribe that tribal customary adoption is the appropriate permanent plan for the child, order a tribal customary adoption in accordance with section 366.24.

(2) The party claiming that termination of parental rights would be detrimental to the child has the burden of proving the detriment.

(3) If the court finds that section 366.26(c)(1)(A) or section 366.26(c)(2)(A) applies, the court must appoint the present custodian or other appropriate person to become the child's legal guardian or must order the child to remain in foster care.

(A) If the court orders that the child remain in foster care, it may order that the name and address of the foster home remain confidential.

(B) If the court finds that removal of the child from the home of a foster parent or relative who is not willing to become a legal guardian for the child would be seriously detrimental to the emotional well-being of the child, then the child must not be removed. The foster parent or relative must be willing to provide, and capable of providing, a stable and permanent home for the child and must have substantial psychological ties with the child.

(4) The court must consider the case plan submitted for this hearing and must make the required findings and determinations in rule 5.708(e).

(Subd (d) amended effective January 1, 2017; repealed and adopted as subd (c) effective January 1, 1991; previously amended and relettered as subd (d) effective

January 1, 1992, and as subd (e) effective January 1, 2005; previously relettered as subd (d) effective January 1, 2010; previously amended effective July 1, 1994, January 1, 1999, July 1, 1999, July 1, 2002, January 1, 2006, January 1, 2007, January 1, 2009, July 1, 2010, and January 1, 2015.)*

(e) Procedures—adoption

(1) The court must follow the procedures in section 366.24 or 366.26, as appropriate.

(2) An order of the court terminating parental rights, ordering adoption under section 366.26 or, in the case of an Indian child, ordering tribal customary adoption under section 366.24, is conclusive and binding on the child, the parent, and all other persons who have been served under the provisions of section 294. **Once a final order of adoption has issued,** the order may not be set aside or modified by the court, except as provided in section **[1] 366.26(e)(3) and (i)(3)** and rules 5.538, 5.540, and 5.542 with regard to orders by a referee.

(Subd (e) amended effective January 1, 2020; adopted as subd (d) effective January 1, 1991; previously relettered as subd (e) effective January 1, 1992, as subd (f) effective January 1, 2005, and as subd (e) effective January 1, 2010; previously amended effective July 1, 1992, January 1, 1995, July 1, 2002, January 1, 2006, January 1, 2007, July 1, 2010, January 1, 2015, and January 1, 2017.)

Rule 5.725(e). 2019 Deletes. [1] 366.26(i)(3)

(f) Purpose of termination of parental rights

The purpose of termination of parental rights is to free the child for adoption. Therefore, the court must not terminate the rights of only one parent unless that parent is the only surviving parent, or the rights of the other parent have been terminated by a California court of competent jurisdiction or by a court of competent jurisdiction of another state under the statutes of that state, or the other parent has relinquished custody of the child to the county welfare department. The rights of all parents—whether natural, presumed, biological, alleged, or unknown—must be terminated in order to free the child for adoption.

(Subd (f) repealed and relettered effective January 1, 2021; adopted as subd (g) effective July 1, 1997; previously amended and relettered as subd (h) effective January 1, 2005; previously amended effective July 1, 2002, and January 1, 2015; previously relettered as subd (g) effective January 1, 2010.)

(g) Advisement of appeal rights

The court must advise all parties of their appeal rights as provided in rule 5.585 and section 366.26(*l*).

(Subd (g) relettered effective January 1, 2021; repealed and adopted as subd (f) effective January 1, 1991; previously relettered as subd (g) effective January 1, 1992; amended and relettered as subd (h) effective July 1, 1997; previously relettered as subd (i) effective January 1, 2005; previously relettered as subd (h) effective January 1, 2010; previously amended effective July 1, 2002, January 1, 2006, and January 1, 2007.)

Rule 5.725 amended effective January 1, 2021; repealed and adopted as rule 1463 effective January 1, 1991; previously amended and renumbered effective January 1, 2007; previously amended effective January 1, 1992, July 1, 1992, January 1, 1994, July 1, 1994, January 1, 1995, July 1, 1995, July 1, 1997, January 1, 1999, July 1, 1999, July 1, 2002, January 1, 2005, January 1, 2006, January 1, 2009, January 1, 2010, July 1, 2010, January 1, 2015, January 1, 2017, and January 1, 2020.

Rule 5.726. Prospective adoptive parent designation (§§ 366.26(n), 16010.6)

(a) Request procedure

A dependent child's caregiver may be designated as a prospective adoptive parent. The court may make the designation on its own motion or on a request by a caregiver, the child, a social worker, the child's identified Indian tribe, or the attorney for any of these parties.

(1) A request for designation as a prospective adoptive parent may be made at a hearing where parental rights are terminated or a plan of tribal customary adoption is ordered or thereafter, whether or not the child's removal from the home of the prospective adoptive parent is at issue.

(2) A request may be made orally.

(3) If a request for prospective adoptive parent designation is made in writing, it must be made on *Request for Prospective Adoptive Parent Designation* (form JV-321).

(4) The address and telephone number of the caregiver and the child may be kept confidential by filing *Confidential Information—Prospective Adoptive Parent* (form JV-322), with form JV-321. Form JV-322 must be kept in the court file under seal, and only the court, the child's attorney, the agency, and the child's CASA volunteer may have access to this information.

(Subd (a) amended effective July 1, 2010; previously amended effective January 1, 2007, and January 1, 2008.)

(b) Facilitation steps

Steps to facilitate the adoption process include those listed in section 366.26(n)(2) and, in the case of an Indian child when tribal customary adoption has been identified as the child's permanent plan, the child's identified Indian tribe has designated the caregiver as the prospective adoptive parent.

(Subd (b) amended effective January 1, 2017; previously amended effective January 1, 2007, and July 1, 2010.)

(c) Hearing on request for prospective adoptive parent designation

(1) The court must determine whether the caregiver meets the criteria in section 366.26(n)(1).

(2) If the court finds that the caregiver does not meet the criteria in section 366.26(n)(1), the court may deny the request without a hearing.

(3) If the court finds that the caregiver meets the criteria in section 366.26(n)(1), the court must set a hearing as set forth in (4) below.

(4) If it appears to the court that the request for designation as a prospective adoptive parent will be contested, or if the court wants to receive further evidence on the request, the court must set a hearing.

(A) If the request for designation is made at the same time a petition is filed to object to removal of the child from the caregiver's home, the court must set a hearing as follows:

(i) The hearing must be set as soon as possible and not later than five court days after the petition objecting to removal is filed with the court.

(ii) If the court for good cause cannot set the matter for hearing five court days after the petition objecting to removal is filed, the court must set the matter for hearing as soon as possible.

(iii) The matter may be set for hearing more than five court days after the petition objecting to removal is filed if this delay is necessary to allow participation by the child's identified Indian tribe or the child's Indian custodian.

(B) If the request for designation is made before the agency serves notice of a proposed removal or before an emergency removal has occurred, the court must set a hearing within 30 calendar days after the request for designation is made.

(5) If all parties stipulate to the designation of the caregiver as a prospective adoptive parent, the court may order the designation without a hearing.

(Subd (c) amended effective January 1, 2017; previously amended effective January 1, 2007.)

(d) Notice of designation hearing

After the court has ordered a hearing on a request for prospective-adoptive-parent designation, notice of the hearing must be as described below.

(1) The following participants must be noticed:

(A) The adoption agency;

(B) The current caregiver;

(C) The child's attorney;

(D) The child, if the child is 10 years of age or older;

(E) The child's identified Indian tribe if any;

(F) The child's Indian custodian if any; and

(G) The child's CASA program if any.

(2) If the request for designation is made at the same time as a request for hearing on a proposed or emergency removal, notice of the designation hearing must be provided with notice of the hearing on proposed removal, as stated in rule 5.727(f).

(3) If the request for designation is made before the agency serves notice of a proposed removal or before an emergency removal occurred, notice must be as follows:

(A) Service of the notice must be either by first-class mail or electronic service in accordance with section 212.5 sent at least 15 calendar days before the hearing date to the last known address of the person to be noticed, or by personal service on the person at least 10 calendar days before the hearing.

(B) *Prospective Adoptive Parent Designation Order* (form JV-327) must be used to provide notice of a hearing on the request for prospective adoptive parent designation.

(C) The clerk must provide notice of the hearing to the participants listed in (1) above, if the court, caregiver, or child requested the hearing.

(D) The child's attorney must provide notice of the hearing to the participants listed in (1) above, if the child's attorney requested the hearing.

(E) *Proof of Notice Under Section 366.26(n)* (form JV-326) must be filed with the court before the hearing on the request for prospective adoptive parent designation.

(Subd (d) amended effective January 1, 2019; previously amended effective January 1, 2007, January 1, 2008, and January 1, 2017.)

(e) Termination of designation

If the prospective adoptive parent no longer meets the criteria in section 366.26(n)(1), a request to vacate the order designating the caregiver as a prospective adoptive parent may be filed under section 388 and rule 5.570.

(Subd (e) amended effective January 1, 2017; previously amended effective January 1, 2007.)

(f) Confidentiality

If the telephone or address of the caregiver or the child is confidential, all forms must be kept in the court file under seal. Only the court, the child's attorney, the agency, and the child's CASA volunteer may have access to this information.

Rule 5.726 amended effective January 1, 2019; adopted as rule 1463.1 effective July 1, 2006; previously amended and renumbered effective January 1, 2007; previously amended effective January 1, 2008, July 1, 2010, and January 1, 2017.

Rule 5.727. Proposed removal (§ 366.26(n))

(a) Application of rule

This rule applies, after termination of parental rights or, in the case of tribal customary adoption, modification of parental rights, to the removal by the Department of Social Services (DSS) or a licensed adoption agency of a dependent child from a prospective adoptive parent or from a caregiver who may meet the criteria for designation as a prospective adoptive parent in section 366.26(n)(1). This rule does not apply if the caregiver requests the child's removal.

(Subd (a) amended effective January 1, 2017; previously amended effective January 1, 2007, and July 1, 2010.)

(b) Participants to be served with notice

Before removing a child from the home of a prospective adoptive parent as defined in section 366.26(n)(1) or from the home of a caregiver who may meet the criteria of a prospective adoptive parent in section 366.26(n)(1), and as soon as possible after a decision is made to remove the child, the agency must notify the following participants of the proposed removal:

(1) The court;

(2) The current caregiver, if that caregiver either is a designated prospective adoptive parent or, on the date of service of the notice, meets the criteria in section 366.26(n)(1);

(3) The child's attorney;

(4) The child, if the child is 10 years of age or older;

(5) The child's identified Indian tribe if any;

(6) The child's Indian custodian if any;

(7) The child's CASA program if any; and

(8) The child's sibling's attorney, if the change in placement of a dependent child will result in the separation of siblings currently placed together. Notice must be made in accordance with Code of Civil Procedure section 1010.6.

(Subd (b) amended effective January 1, 2019; previously amended effective January 1, 2007, and January 1, 2017.)

(c) Form of notice

DSS or the agency must provide notice on *Notice of Intent to Remove Child* (form JV-323). A blank copy of *Objection to Removal* (form JV-325) and *Request for Prospective Adoptive Parent Designation* (form JV-321) must also be provided to all participants listed in (b) except the court.

(Subd (c) amended effective January 1, 2017; previously amended effective January 1, 2007, and January 1, 2008.)

(d) Service of notice

DSS or the agency must serve notice of its intent to remove a child as follows:

(1) DSS or the agency must serve notice either by first-class mail or by electronic service in accordance with section 212.5, sent to the last known address of the person to be noticed, or by personal service.

(2) If service is by first-class mail, service is completed and time to respond is extended by five calendar days.

(3) If service is made through electronic means, service is completed and time to respond is extended in accordance with Code of Civil Procedure section 1010.6.

(4) Notice to the child's identified Indian tribe and Indian custodian must comply with the requirements of section 224.2.

(5) *Proof of Notice Under Section 366.26(n)* (form JV-326) must be filed with the court before the hearing on the proposed removal.

(Subd (d) amended effective January 1, 2019; previously amended effective January 1, 2007, January 1, 2008, January 1, 2011, and January 1, 2017.)

(e) Objection to proposed removal

Each participant who receives notice under (b) may object to the proposed removal of the child and may request a hearing.

(1) A request for hearing on the proposed removal must be made on *Objection to Removal* (form JV-325).

(2) A request for hearing on the proposed removal must be made within five court or seven calendar days from the date of notification, whichever is longer. If service of the notification is by mail, time to request a hearing is extended by five calendar days. If service of the notification is by electronic means, time to request a hearing is extended in accordance with Code of Civil Procedure section 1010.6.

(3) The court must set a hearing as follows:

(A) The hearing must be set as soon as possible and not later than five court days after the objection is filed with the court.

(B) If the court for good cause is unable to set the matter for hearing five court days after the petition is filed, the court must set the matter for hearing as soon as possible.

(C) The matter may be set for hearing more than five court days after the objection is filed if this delay is necessary to allow participation by the child's identified Indian tribe or the child's Indian custodian.

(Subd (e) amended effective January 1, 2019; previously amended effective January 1, 2007, January 1, 2008, and January 1, 2017.)

(f) Notice of hearing on proposed removal

After the court has ordered a hearing on a proposed removal, notice of the hearing must be as follows:

(1) The clerk must provide notice of the hearing to the agency and the participants listed in (b) above, if the court, caregiver, or child requested the hearing.

(2) The child's attorney must provide notice of the hearing to the agency and the participants listed in (b) above, if the child's attorney requested the hearing.

(3) Notice must be by personal service or by telephone. Notice by personal service must include a copy of the completed forms *Notice of Intent to Remove Child* (form JV-323) and *Objection to Removal* (form JV-325). Telephone notice must include the reasons for and against the removal, as indicated on forms JV-323 and JV-325.

(4) *Proof of Notice Under 366.26(n)* (form JV-326) must be filed with the court before the hearing on the proposed removal.

(Subd (f) amended effective January 1, 2019; previously amended effective January 1, 2007, January 1, 2008, and January 1, 2017.)

(g) Burden of proof

At a hearing on an intent to remove the child, the agency intending to remove the child must prove by a preponderance of the evidence that the proposed removal is in the best interest of the child.

(h) Confidentiality

If the telephone or address of the caregiver or the child is confidential, all forms must be kept in the court file under seal. Only the court, the child's attorney, the agency, and the child's CASA volunteer may have access to this information.

(i) Appeal

If the court order made after a hearing on an intent to remove a child is appealed, the appeal must be brought as petition for writ review under rules 8.454 and 8.456.

(Subd (i) amended effective January 1, 2017; previously amended effective January 1, 2007.)

Rule 5.727 amended effective January 1, 2019; adopted as rule 1463.3 effective July 1, 2006; previously amended and renumbered effective January 1, 2007; previously amended effective January 1, 2008, July 1, 2010, January 1, 2011, and January 1, 2017.

Rule 5.728.   Emergency removal (§ 366.26(n))

(a) Application of rule

This rule applies, after termination of parental rights or, in the case of tribal customary adoption, modification of parental rights, to the removal by the Department of Social Services (DSS) or a licensed adoption agency of a dependent child from the home of a prospective adoptive parent or a caregiver who may meet the criteria for designation as a prospective adoptive parent in section 366.26(n)(1) when the DSS or the licensed adoption agency has determined a removal must occur immediately due to a risk of physical or emotional harm. This rule does not apply if the child is removed at the request of the caregiver.

(Subd (a) amended effective January 1, 2017; previously amended effective January 1, 2007, and July 1, 2010.)

(b) Participants to be noticed

After removing a child from the home of a prospective adoptive parent, or from the home of a caregiver who may meet the criteria of a prospective adoptive parent in section 366.26(n)(1), because of risk of physical or emotional harm, the agency must notify the following participants of the emergency removal:

(1) The court;

(2) The caregiver, who is a prospective adoptive parent or who, on the date of service of the notice, may meet the criteria in section 366.26(n)(1);

(3) The child's attorney;

(4) The child if the child is 10 years of age or older;

(5) The child's identified Indian tribe if any;

(6) The child's Indian custodian if any;

(7) The child's CASA program if any; and

(8) The child's sibling's attorney, if the change in placement of a dependent child will result in the separation of siblings currently placed together. Notice must be made in accordance with section 1010.6 of the Code of Civil Procedure.

(Subd (b) amended effective January 1, 2019; previously amended effective January 1, 2007, and January 1, 2017.)

(c) Form and service of notice

Notice of Emergency Removal (form JV-324) must be used to provide notice of an emergency removal, as described below.

(1) The agency must provide notice of the emergency removal as soon as possible but no later than two court days after the removal.

(2) Notice must be either by telephone or by personal service of the form.

(3) Telephone notice must include the reasons for removal as indicated on the form, and notice of the right to object to the removal.

(4) Whenever possible, the agency, at the time of the removal, must give a blank copy of *Request for Prospective Adoptive Parent Designation* (form JV-321) and a blank copy of *Objection to Removal* (form JV-325) to the caregiver and, if the child is 10 years of age or older, to the child.

(5) Notice to the court must be served by filing *Notice of Emergency Removal* (form JV-324) and *Proof of Notice Under 366.26(n)* (form JV-326) with the court.

(6) *Proof of Notice Under Section 366.26(n)* (form JV-326) must be filed with the court before the hearing on the proposed removal.

(Subd (c) amended effective January 1, 2019; previously amended effective January 1, 2007, January 1, 2008, and January 1, 2017.)

(d) Objection to emergency removal

Each participant who receives notice under (b) may object to the removal of the child and may request a hearing.

(1) A request for hearing on the emergency removal must be made on *Objection to Removal* (form JV-325).

(2) The court must set a hearing as follows:

(A) The hearing must be set as soon as possible and not later than five court days after the petition objecting to removal is filed with the court.

(B) If the court for good cause cannot set the matter for hearing within five court days after the petition objecting to removal is filed, the court must set the matter for hearing as soon as possible.

(C) The matter may be set for hearing more than five court days after the petition objecting to removal is filed if this delay is necessary to allow participation by the child's identified Indian tribe or the child's Indian custodian.

(Subd (d) amended effective January 1, 2017; previously amended effective January 1, 2007, and January 1, 2008.)

(e) Notice of hearing on emergency removal

After the court has ordered a hearing on an emergency removal, notice of the hearing must be as follows:

(1) The clerk must provide notice of the hearing to the agency and the participants listed in (b) above, if the court, caregiver, or child requested the hearing.

(2) The child's attorney must provide notice of the hearing to the agency and the participants listed in (b) above, if the child's attorney requested the hearing.

(3) Notice must be by personal service or by telephone. Notice by personal service must include a copy of the completed *Notice of Emergency Removal* (form JV-324). Telephone notice must include the reasons for and against the removal, as indicated on forms JV-324 and JV-325.

(4) *Proof of Notice Under Section 366.26(n)* (form JV-326) must be filed with the court before the hearing on the emergency removal.

(Subd (e) amended effective January 1, 2019; previously amended effective January 1, 2007, January 1, 2008, and January 1, 2012.)

(f) Burden of proof

At a hearing on an emergency removal, the agency that removed the child must prove by a preponderance of the evidence that the removal is in the best interest of the child.

(g) Confidentiality

If the telephone or address of the caregiver or the child is confidential, all forms must be kept in the court file under seal. Only the court, the child's attorney, the agency, and the child's CASA volunteer and program may have access to this information.

Rule 5.728 amended effective January 1, 2019; adopted as rule 1463.5 effective July 1, 2006; previously amended and renumbered effective January 1, 2007; previously amended effective January 1, 2008, July 1, 2010, and January 1, 2017.

Rule 5.730.   Adoption (§§ 366.24, 366.26(e), Fam. Code, § 8600 et seq.)

(a) Procedures—adoption

(1) The petition for the adoption of a dependent child who has been freed for adoption may be filed in the juvenile court with jurisdiction over the dependency.

(2) All adoption petitions must be completed on *Adoption Request* (form ADOPT-200) and must be verified. In addition, the petitioner must complete *Adoption Agreement* (form ADOPT-210) and *Adoption Order* (form ADOPT-215).

(3) A petitioner seeking to adopt an Indian child must also complete *Adoption of Indian Child* (form ADOPT-220). If applicable, *Parent of Indian Child Agrees to End Parental Rights* (form ADOPT-225) may be filed.

(4) The clerk must open a confidential adoption file for each child and this file must be separate and apart from the dependency file, with an adoption case number different from the dependency case number.

(Subd (a) amended effective January 1, 2007; previously amended effective January 1, 1996, January 1, 1999, and January 1, 2004.)

(b) Notice

The clerk of the court must give notice of the adoption hearing to:

(1) Any attorney of record for the child;

(2) Any CASA volunteer;

(3) The child welfare agency;

(4) The tribe of an Indian child; and

(5) The California Department of Social Services. The notice to the California Department of Social Services must include a copy of the completed *Adoption Request* (form ADOPT-200) and a copy of any adoptive placement agreement or agency joinder filed in the case.

(Subd (b) amended effective January 1, 2007; previously amended effective January 1, 2004.)

(c) Hearing

If the petition for adoption is filed in the juvenile court, the proceeding for adoption must be heard in juvenile court once appellate rights have been exhausted. Each petitioner and the child must be present at the hearing. The hearing may be heard by a referee if the referee is acting as a temporary judge.

(Subd (c) amended effective January 1, 2007; previously amended effective January 1, 1999, and January 1, 2004.)

(d) Record

The record must reflect that the court has read and considered the assessment prepared for the hearing held under section 366.26 and as required by section 366.22(b), the report of any CASA volunteer, and any other reports or documents admitted into evidence.

(Subd (d) amended effective January 1, 2007; previously amended effective January 1, 2004.)

(e) Assessment

The preparer of the assessment may be called and examined by any party to the adoption proceeding.

(f) Consent

(1) At the hearing, each adoptive parent must execute *Adoption Agreement* (form ADOPT-210) in the presence of and with the acknowledgment of the court.

(2) If the child to be adopted is 12 years of age or older, he or she must also execute *Adoption Agreement* (form ADOPT-210), except in the case of a tribal customary adoption.

(Subd (f) amended effective July 1, 2010; previously amended effective January 1, 1999, January 1, 2004, and January 1, 2007.)

(g) Dismissal of jurisdiction

If the petition for adoption is granted, the juvenile court must dismiss the dependency, terminate jurisdiction over the child, and vacate any previously set review hearing dates. A completed *Termination of Dependency (Juvenile)* (form JV-364) must be filed in the child's juvenile dependency file.

(Subd (g) amended effective January 1, 2007; previously amended effective January 1, 1999, and January 1, 2004.)

Rule 5.730 amended effective January 1, 2017; adopted as rule 1464 effective July 1, 1995; previously amended effective January 1, 1996, January 1, 1999, January 1, 2004, and July 1, 2010; previously amended and renumbered effective January 1, 2007.

Advisory Committee Comment

Family Code section 8600.5 exempts tribal customary adoption from various provisions of the Family Code applicable to adoptions generally, including section 8602, which requires the consent of a child over the age of 12 to an adoption. However, under Welfare and Institutions Code section 366.24(c)(7), "[t]he child, birth parents, or Indian custodian and the tribal customary adoptive parents and their counsel, if applicable, may present evidence to the tribe regarding the tribal customary adoption and the child's best interest." Under Welfare and Institutions Code section 317(e), for all children over 4 years of age, the attorney for the child must determine the child's wishes and advise the court of the child's wishes. Welfare and Institutions Code section 361.31(e) provides that "[w]here appropriate, the placement preference of the Indian child, when of sufficient age, … shall be considered." This is consistent with Guideline F-3 of the *Guidelines for State Courts; Indian Child Custody Proceedings* issued by the Bureau of Indian Affairs on November 26, 1979, which recognizes that the request and wishes of a child of sufficient age are important in making an effective placement. The committee concludes, therefore, that while the consent of a child over the age of 12 is not required for a tribal customary adoption, the wishes of a child are still an important and appropriate factor for the court to consider and for children's counsel to ascertain and present to the court when determining whether tribal customary adoption is the appropriate permanent plan for an Indian child.

Rule 5.735.   Legal guardianship

(a) Proceedings in juvenile court (§§ 360, 366.26)

The proceedings for the appointment of a legal guardian for a dependent child must be **held** in the juvenile court. The [1] **recommendation** for appointment of a guardian must be included in the social study report prepared by the county welfare department or in the assessment prepared for the hearing under section 366.26. Neither a separate petition nor a separate hearing is required.

(Subd (a) amended effective January 1, 2021; previously amended effective July 1, 1997, July 1, 1999, January 1, 2006, and January 1, 2007.)

Rule 5.735(a).   2020 Deletes. [1] request

(b) Notice; hearing

Unless the court proceeds under section 360(a) at the dispositional hearing, notice [1] **of the** hearing **at which the court considers appointing a legal guardian** must be given under section 294, and the hearing must [2] **be conducted** under **the procedures in** section 366.26.

(Subd (b) amended effective January 1, 2021; previously amended effective July 1, 1999, and January 1, 2006.)

Rule 5.735(b).   2020 Deletes. [1] for the guardianship [2] proceed

(c) Findings and orders

(1) If the court finds that legal guardianship is the appropriate permanent plan, the court must appoint the guardian and order the clerk to issue letters of guardianship [1] (*Letters of Guardianship (Juvenile)* **(form JV-330)) as soon as the guardian has signed the required affirmation. These letters are not** subject to the confidentiality protections [2] in section 827.

(2) The court must issue orders regarding visitation of the child by a parent or former guardian, unless the court finds that visitation would be detrimental to the physical or emotional well-being of the child.

(3) The court may issue orders regarding visitation of the child by a relative.

(4) **Except as provided in (5),** on appointment of a **legal** guardian under section **360** or 366.26, the court may **retain dependency jurisdiction or** terminate dependency **jurisdiction and retain jurisdiction over the child as a ward of the guardianship under section 366.4**.

(5) **If the court appoints a relative or nonrelative extended family member as the child's legal guardian and the other requirements in section 366.3(a)(3) apply, the court must terminate dependency jurisdiction and retain jurisdiction over the child under section 366.4 unless the guardian objects or the court finds that exceptional circumstances require it to retain dependency jurisdiction.**

(Subd (c) amended effective January 1, 2021; adopted as subd (d) effective January 1, 1991; previously amended effective July 1, 1999, and January 1, 2006; previously amended and relettered as subd (c) effective January 1, 2017.)

Rule 5.735(c).   2020 Deletes. [1] , which will not be **[2]** described

(d) Notification of appeal rights

The court must advise all parties of their appeal rights as provided in rule 5.590.

(Subd (d) amended and relettered effective January 1, 2017; adopted as subd (e) effective January 1, 1991; previously amended effective January 1, 2006, and January 1, 2007.)

Rule 5.735 amended effective January 1, 2021; adopted as rule 1464 effective January 1, 1991; renumbered as rule 1465 effective July 1, 1995; previously amended effective July 1, 1999, January 1, 2006, and January 1, 2017; previously amended and renumbered effective January 1, 2007.

Rule 5.740.   Hearings after selection of a permanent plan (§§ 366.26, 366.3, 16501.1)

(a) Review hearings—adoption and guardianship

Following an order for termination of parental rights or, in the case of tribal customary adoption, modification of parental rights, or a plan for the establishment of a **legal** guardianship under section 366.26, the court must retain jurisdiction and conduct review hearings at least every 6 months to ensure the expeditious completion of the adoption or guardianship.

(1) At the review hearing, the court must consider the report of the petitioner required by section 366.3(g), the report of any CASA volunteer, the case plan submitted for this hearing, and any report submitted by the child's caregiver under section 366.21(d); inquire about the progress being made to provide a permanent home for the child; consider the safety of the child; and enter findings as required by section 366.3(e).

(2) The court or administrative review panel must consider the case plan and make the findings and determinations concerning the child in rule 5.708(e).

(3) When adoption is granted, the court must terminate its jurisdiction.

(4) **[1] After a** legal guardianship is **[2] established**, the court may continue dependency jurisdiction **[3] or** may terminate dependency jurisdiction and retain jurisdiction over the child as a ward of the guardianship **under section 366.4. If the court appoints a relative or nonrelative extended family member as the child's guardian and the other requirements in section 366.3(a)(3) apply, the court must terminate dependency jurisdiction and retain jurisdiction over the child under section 366.4 unless the guardian objects or the court finds that exceptional circumstances require it to retain dependency jurisdiction.**

(5) Notice of the hearing must be given as provided in section 295.

(6) If the child is not placed for adoption, the court or administrative review panel must find as follows:

(A) Whether the agency has made diligent efforts to locate an appropriate relative. If the court or administrative review panel finds the agency has not made diligent efforts to locate an appropriate relative, the court or administrative review panel must order the agency to do so.

(B) Whether each relative whose name has been submitted to the agency as a possible caregiver has been evaluated as an appropriate placement resource. If the court or administrative review panel finds the agency has not evaluated each relative whose name has been submitted as a possible caregiver, the court or administrative review panel must order the agency to do so.

(Subd (a) amended effective January 1, 2021; repealed and adopted effective January 1, 1991; previously amended effective January 1, 1992, January 1, 1993, July 1, 1999, January 1, 2005, January 1, 2006, January 1, 2007, July 1, 2010, January 1, 2015, and January 1, 2017.)

Rule 5.740(a).   2020 Deletes. [1] When **[2]** granted **[3]** if it is in the best interest of the child, or the court

(b) Review hearings—relative care or foster care

Following the establishment of a plan other than those provided for in (a), review hearings must be conducted at least every 6 months by the court or by a local administrative review panel.

(1) At the review hearing, the court or administrative review panel must consider the report of the petitioner, the report of any CASA volunteer, the case plan submitted for this hearing, and any report submitted by the child's caregiver under section 366.21(d); inquire about the progress being made to provide a permanent home for the child; consider the safety of the child; and enter findings as required by section 366.3(e).

(2) The court or administrative review panel must consider the case plan submitted for this hearing and make the findings and determinations concerning the child in rule 5.708(e).

(3) If the child is not placed for adoption, the court or administrative review panel must find as follows:

(A) Whether the agency has made diligent efforts to locate an appropriate relative. If the court or administrative review panel finds the agency has not made diligent efforts to locate an appropriate relative, the court or administrative review panel must order the agency to do so.

(B) Whether each relative whose name has been submitted to the agency as a possible caregiver has been evaluated as an appropriate placement resource. If the court or administrative review panel finds the agency has not evaluated each relative whose name has been submitted as a possible caregiver, the court or administrative review panel must order the agency to do so.

(4) No less frequently than once every 12 months, the court must conduct a review of the previously ordered permanent plan to consider whether the plan continues to be appropriate for the child. The review of the permanent plan may be combined with the 6-month review.

(5) If circumstances have changed since the permanent plan was ordered, the court may order a new permanent plan under section 366.26 at any subsequent hearing, or any party may seek a new permanent plan by a motion filed under section 388 and rule 5.570.

(6) Notice of the hearing must be given as provided in section 295.

(7) The court must continue the child in foster care unless the parents prove, by a preponderance of the evidence, that further efforts at reunification are the best alternative for the child. In those cases, the court may order reunification services for a period not to exceed 6 months.

(Subd (b) amended effective January 1, 2017; repealed and adopted effective January 1, 1991; previously amended effective January 1, 1992, January 1, 1994, January 1, 1998, January 1, 1999, July 1, 1999, January 1, 2005, January 1, 2006, and January 1, 2007.)

(c) Review hearings—youth 16 years of age and older

If the youth is 16 years of age or older, the procedures in section 391 must be followed.

(1) If it is the first review hearing after the youth turns 16 years of age, the social worker must provide the information, documents, and services required by section 391(a) and must use *First Review Hearing After Youth Turns 16 years of Age—Information, Documents, and Services* (form JV-361).

(2) If it is the last review hearing before the youth turns 18 years of age, the social worker must provide the information, documents, and services required by section 391(b)–(c) and must use *Review Hearing for Youth Approaching 18 Years of Age—Information, Documents, and Services* (form JV-362).

(3) If it is a review hearing after the youth turns 18 years of age, the social worker must provide the information, documents, and services required by section 391(c) and must use *Review Hearing for Youth 18 Years of Age or Older—Information, Documents, and Services* (form JV-363). If the court is terminating jurisdiction at this review hearing, the social worker must also provide the information, documents, and services required by section 391(h), must follow the procedures in rule 5.555, and must use *Termination of Juvenile Court Jurisdiction—Nonminor* (form JV-365).

(Subd (c) adopted effective January 1, 2021.)

(d) Hearing on petition to terminate guardianship or modify guardianship orders

A petition to terminate a guardianship established by the juvenile court, to appoint a successor guardian, or to modify or supplement orders concerning a guardianship must be filed in the juvenile court. The procedures described in rule 5.570 must be followed, and *Request to Change Court Order* (form JV-180) must be used.

(1) Proceedings on a petition to terminate a guardianship established under section 366.26 must be heard in the juvenile court. If dependency was terminated at the time of or subsequent to the appointment of the guardian, and dependency is later declared in another county, proceedings to terminate the guardianship may be held in the juvenile court with current dependency jurisdiction.

(2) Not less than 15 court days before the hearing date, the clerk must cause notice of the hearing to be given to the department of social services; the guardian; the child, if 10 years or older; parents whose parental rights have not been terminated; the court that established the

guardianship, if in another county; and counsel of record for those entitled to notice.

(3) At the hearing on the petition to terminate the guardianship, the court may do one of the following:

(A) Deny the petition to terminate guardianship;

(B) Deny the petition and request the county welfare department to provide services to the guardian and the ward for the purpose of maintaining the guardianship, consistent with section 301; or

(C) Grant the petition to terminate the guardianship.

(4) If the petition is granted and the court continues or resumes dependency, the court must order that a new plan be developed to provide stability and permanency to the child. Unless the court has already scheduled a hearing to review the child's status, the court must conduct a hearing within 60 days. Parents whose parental rights have not been terminated must be notified of the hearing on the new plan. The court may consider further efforts at reunification only if the parent proves, by a preponderance of the evidence, that the efforts would be the best alternative for the child.

(5) If the court terminates a guardianship established in another county, the clerk of the county of current dependency jurisdiction must transmit a certified copy of the order terminating guardianship within 15 days to the court that established the original guardianship.

(Subd (d) relettered effective January 1, 2021; adopted as subd (c); previously amended effective January 1, 1993, July 1, 1994, July 1, 1999, January 1, 2007, and January 1, 2017.)

Rule 5.740 amended effective January 1, 2021; adopted as rule 1465 effective January 1, 1991; previously renumbered as rule 1466 effective July 1, 1995; previously amended and renumbered effective January 1, 2007; previously amended effective January 1, 1992, January 1, 1993, January 1, 1994, July 1, 1994, January 1, 1998, January 1, 1999, July 1, 1999, July 1, 2002, January 1, 2005, January 1, 2006, July 1, 2010, January 1, 2012, January 1, 2015, and January 1, 2017.)

Chapter 13
Cases Petitioned Under Sections 601 and 602

Chapter 13 renumbered effective January 1, 2008; adopted as Chapter 11 effective July 1, 2002; previously amended and renumbered as Chapter 14, effective January 1, 2007.

Article 1
Initial Appearance

Rule 5.752.   Initial hearing; detention hearings; time limit on custody; setting jurisdiction hearing

(a) Child not detained; filing petition, setting hearing

If the child is not taken into custody and the authorized petitioner (district attorney or probation officer) determines that a petition or notice of probation violation concerning the child should be filed, the petition or notice must be filed with the clerk of the juvenile court as soon as possible. The clerk must set an initial hearing on the petition within 15 court days.

(Subd (a) amended effective January 1, 2007.)

(b) Time limit on custody; filing petition (§§ 604, 631, 631.1)

A child must be released from custody within 48 hours, excluding noncourt days, after first being taken into custody unless a petition or notice of probation violation has been filed either within that time or before the time the child was first taken into custody.

(Subd (b) amended effective January 1, 2007.)

(c) Time limit on custody—willful misrepresentation of age (§ 631.1)

If the child willfully misrepresents the child's age to be 18 years or older, and this misrepresentation causes an unavoidable delay in investigation that prevents the filing of a petition or of a criminal complaint within 48 hours, excluding noncourt days, after the child has been taken into custody, the child must be released unless a petition or complaint has been filed within 48 hours, excluding noncourt days, from the time the true age is determined.

(Subd (c) amended effective January 1, 2007.)

(d) Time limit on custody—certification of child detained in custody (§ 604)

A child must be released from custody within 48 hours, excluding noncourt days, after certification to juvenile court under rules 4.116 and 5.516(d) unless a petition has been filed.

(Subd (d) amended effective January 1, 2007.)

(e) Time limit for detention hearing—warrant or nonward charged with nonviolent misdemeanor (§ 632)

A detention hearing must be set and commenced as soon as possible, but no later than 48 hours, excluding noncourt days, after the child has been taken into custody, if:

(1) The child has been taken into custody on a warrant or by the authority of the probation officer; or

(2) The child is not on probation or parole and is alleged to have committed a misdemeanor not involving violence, the threat of violence, or the possession or use of a weapon.

(Subd (e) amended effective January 1, 2007.)

(f) Time limit for detention hearing—felony, violent misdemeanor, or ward (§ 632)

A detention hearing must be set and commenced as soon as possible, but no later than the expiration of the next court day after the petition or notice of probation violation has been filed, if:

(1) The child is alleged to have committed a felony;

(2) The child is alleged to have committed a misdemeanor involving violence, the threat of violence, or the possession or use of a weapon; or

(3) The child is a ward currently on probation or parole.

(Subd (f) amended effective January 1, 2007.)

(g) Time limit for hearing—arrival at detention facility (§ 632)

A detention hearing must be set and commenced as soon as possible, but no later than 48 hours, excluding noncourt days, after the child arrives at a detention facility within the county if:

(1) The child was taken into custody in another county and transported in custody to the requesting county;

(2) The child was ordered transported in custody when transferred by the juvenile court of another county under rule 5.610; or

(3) The child is a ward temporarily placed in a secure facility pending a change of placement.

(Subd (g) amended effective January 1, 2007.)

(h) Time limit for hearing—violation of home supervision (§§ 628.1, 636)

A child taken into custody for a violation of a written condition of home supervision, which the child has promised in writing to obey under section 628.1 or 636, must be brought before the court for a detention hearing as soon as possible, but no later than 48 hours, excluding noncourt days, after the child was taken into custody.

(Subd (h) amended effective January 1, 2007.)

(i) Time limits—remedy for not observing (§§ 632, 641)

If the detention hearing is not commenced within the time limits, the child must be released immediately, or, if the child is a ward under section 602 awaiting a change of placement, the child must be placed in a suitable, nonsecure facility.

(Subd (i) amended effective January 1, 2007.)

Rule 5.752 amended and renumbered effective January 1, 2007; repealed and adopted as rule 1471 effective January 1, 1998.

Rule 5.754.   Commencement of initial hearing—explanation, advisement, admission

(a) Explanation of proceedings (§ 633)

At the beginning of the initial hearing, whether the child is detained or not detained, the court must give the advisement required by rule 5.534 and must inform the child and each parent and each guardian present of the following:

(1) The contents of the petition;

(2) The nature and possible consequences of juvenile court proceedings; and

(3) If the child has been taken into custody, the reasons for the initial detention and the purpose and scope of the initial hearing.

(Subd (a) amended effective January 1, 2007.)

(b) Admission of allegations; no contest plea

If the child wishes to admit the allegations of the petition or enter a no contest plea at the initial hearing, the court may accept the admission or plea of no contest and must proceed according to rule 5.778.

(Subd (b) amended effective January 1, 2007.)

Rule 5.754 amended and renumbered effective January 1, 2007; repealed and adopted as rule 1472 effective January 1, 1998.

Rule 5.756.   Conduct of detention hearing

(a) Right to inspect (§ 827)

The child, the parent, the guardian, and counsel are permitted to inspect and receive copies of police reports, probation reports, and any other documents filed with the court or made available to the probation officer in preparing the probation recommendations.

(Subd (a) amended effective January 1, 2007.)

(b) Examination by court (§ 635)

Subject to the child's privilege against self-incrimination, the court may examine the child, the parent, the guardian, and any other person present who has knowledge or information relevant to the issue of detention and must consider any relevant evidence that the child, the parent, the guardian, or counsel presents.

(Subd (b) amended effective January 1, 2007.)

(c) Evidence required

The court may base its findings and orders solely on written police reports, probation reports, or other documents.

Rule 5.756 amended and renumbered effective January 1, 2007; repealed and adopted as rule 1473 effective January 1, 1998.

Rule 5.758.   Requirements for detention; prima facie case

(a) Requirements for detention (§§ 635, 636)

The court must release the child unless the court finds that:

(1) A prima facie showing has been made that the child is described by section 601 or 602;

(2) Continuance in the home is contrary to the child's welfare; and

(3) One or more of the grounds for detention stated in rule 5.760 exist. However, except as provided in sections 636.2 and 207, no child taken into custody solely on the basis of being a person described in section 601 may be detained in juvenile hall or any other secure facility.

(Subd (a) amended effective January 1, 2007; previously amended effective July 1, 2002.)

(b) Detention in adult facility

A child must not be detained in a jail or lockup used for the confinement of adults, except as provided in section 207.1.

(Subd (b) amended effective July 1, 2002.)

Rule 5.758 amended and renumbered effective January 1, 2007; repealed and adopted as rule 1474 effective January 1, 1998; previously amended effective July 1, 2002.

Rule 5.760.   Detention hearing; report; grounds; determinations; findings; orders; factors to consider for detention; restraining orders

(a) Conduct of detention hearing (§§ 635, 636)

The court must consider the written report of the probation officer and any other evidence and may examine the child, any parent or guardian, or any other person with relevant knowledge of the child.

(Subd (a) adopted effective January 1, 2007.)

(b) Written detention report (§§ 635, 636)

If the probation officer has reason to believe that the child is at risk of entering foster care placement, the probation officer must submit a written report to the court that includes the following:

(1) The reasons the child has been removed;

(2) Any prior referral for abuse or neglect of the child and any prior filing of a petition regarding the child under section 300;

(3) The need, if any, for continued detention;

(4) Available services to facilitate the return of the child;

(5) Whether there are any relatives able and willing to provide effective care and control over the child;

(6) Documentation that continuance in the home is contrary to the child's welfare; and

(7) Documentation that reasonable efforts were made to prevent or eliminate the need for removal of the child from the home and documentation of the nature and results of the services provided.

(Subd (b) amended and relettered effective January 1, 2007; adopted as subd (a) effective January 1, 2001; previously amended effective July 1, 2002.)

(c) Grounds for detention (§§ 625.3, 635, 636)

(1) The child must be released unless the court finds that continuance in the home of the parent or legal guardian is contrary to the child's welfare, and one or more of the following grounds for detention exist:

(A) The child has violated an order of the court;

(B) The child has escaped from a commitment of the court;

(C) The child is likely to flee the jurisdiction of the court;

(D) It is a matter of immediate and urgent necessity for the protection of the child; or

(E) It is reasonably necessary for the protection of the person or property of another.

(2) If the child is a dependent of the court under section 300, the court's decision to detain must not be based on the child's status as a dependent of the court or the child welfare services department's inability to provide a placement for the child.

(3) The court may order the child placed on home supervision under the conditions stated in sections 628.1 and 636, or detained in juvenile hall, or in a suitable place designated by the court.

(4) If the court orders the release of a child who is a dependent of the court under section 300, the court must order the child welfare services department either to ensure that the child's current caregiver takes physical custody of the child or to take physical custody of the child and place the child in a licensed or approved placement.

(Subd (c) amended effective January 1, 2016; adopted as subd (a); previously amended effective July 1, 2002; previously amended and relettered as subd (b) effective January 1, 2001, and as subd (c) effective January 1, 2007.)

(d) Required determinations before detention

Before detaining the child, the court must determine whether continuance in the home of the parent or legal guardian is contrary to the child's welfare and whether there are available services that would prevent the need for further detention. The court must make these determinations on a case-by-case basis and must state the evidence relied on in reaching its decision.

(1) If the court determines that the child can be returned to the home of the parent or legal guardian through the provision of services, the court must release the child to the parent or guardian and order that the probation department provide the required services.

(2) If the child cannot be returned to the home of the parent or legal guardian, the court must state the facts on which the detention is based.

(Subd (d) amended effective January 1, 2016; adopted as subd (c) effective July 1, 2002; previously amended and relettered as subd (d) effective January 1, 2007.)

(e) Required findings to support detention (§ 636)

If the court orders the child detained, the court must make the following findings on the record and in the written order. The court must reference the probation officer's report or other evidence relied on to make its determinations:

(1) Continuance in the home of the parent or guardian is contrary to the child's welfare;

(2) Temporary placement and care is the responsibility of the probation officer pending disposition or further order of the court; and

(3) Reasonable efforts have been made to prevent or eliminate the need for removal of the child, or reasonable efforts were not made.

(Subd (e) amended effective January 1, 2016; adopted as subd (b); previously relettered as subd (c) effective January 1, 2001; previously amended and relettered as subd (d) effective July 1, 2002, and as subd (e) effective January 1, 2007.)

(f) Required orders to support detention (§ 636)

If the court orders the child detained, the court must make the following additional orders:

(1) As soon as possible, the probation officer must provide services that will enable the child's parent or legal guardian to obtain such assistance as may be needed to effectively provide the care and control necessary for the child to return home; and

(2) The child's placement and care must be the responsibility of the probation department pending disposition or further order of the court.

(Subd (f) relettered effective January 1, 2007; adopted as subd (e) effective July 1, 2002.)

(g) Factors—violation of court order

Regarding ground for detention (c)(1), the court must consider:

(1) The specificity of the court order alleged to have been violated;

(2) The nature and circumstances of the alleged violation;

(3) The severity and gravity of the alleged violation;

(4) Whether the alleged violation endangered the child or others;

(5) The prior history of the child as it relates to any failure to obey orders or directives of the court or probation officer;

(6) Whether there are means to ensure the child's presence at any scheduled court hearing without detaining the child;

(7) The underlying conduct or offense that brought the child before the juvenile court; and

(8) The likelihood that if the petition is sustained, the child will be ordered removed from the custody of the parent or guardian at disposition.

(Subd (g) amended and relettered effective January 1, 2007; adopted as subd (c) effective January 1, 1998; previously relettered as subd (d) effective January 1, 2001; previously amended and relettered as subd (f) effective July 1, 2002.)

(h) Factors—escape from commitment

Regarding ground for detention (c)(2), the court must consider whether or not the child:

(1) Was committed to the California Department of Corrections and Rehabilitation, Division of Juvenile Justice; or a county juvenile home, ranch, camp, forestry camp, or juvenile hall; and

(2) Escaped from the facility or the lawful custody of any officer or person in which the child was placed during commitment.

(Subd (h) amended and relettered effective January 1, 2007; adopted as subd (d) effective January 1, 1998; previously relettered as subd (e) effective January 1, 2001; amended and relettered as subd (g) effective July 1, 2002; previously amended effective January 1, 2006.)

(i) Factors—likely to flee

Regarding ground for detention (c)(3), the court must consider whether or not:

(1) The child has previously fled the jurisdiction of the court or failed to appear in court as ordered;

(2) There are means to ensure the child's presence at any scheduled court hearing without detaining the child;

(3) The child promises to appear at any scheduled court hearing;

(4) The child has a prior history of failure to obey orders or directions of the court or the probation officer;

(5) The child is a resident of the county;

(6) The nature and circumstances of the alleged conduct or offense make it appear likely that the child would flee to avoid the jurisdiction of the court;

(7) The child's home situation is so unstable as to make it appear likely that the child would flee to avoid the jurisdiction of the court; and

(8) Absent a danger to the child, the child would be released on modest bail or own recognizance were the child appearing as an adult in adult court.

(Subd (i) amended and relettered effective January 1, 2007; adopted as subd (e) effective January 1, 1998; previously relettered as subd (f) effective January 1, 2001; previously amended and relettered as subd (h) effective July 1, 2002.)

(j) Factors—protection of child

Regarding ground for detention (c)(4), the court must consider whether or not:

(1) There are means to ensure the care and protection of the child until the next scheduled court appearance;

(2) The child is addicted to or is in imminent danger from the use of a controlled substance or alcohol; and

(3) There exist other compelling circumstances that make detention reasonably necessary.

(Subd (j) amended and relettered effective January 1, 2007; adopted as subd (f) effective January 1, 1998; previously relettered as subd (g) effective January 1, 2001; previously amended and relettered as subd (i) effective July 1, 2002.)

(k) Factors—protection of person or property of another

Regarding ground for detention (c)(5), the court must consider whether or not:

(1) The alleged offense involved physical harm to the person or property of another;

(2) The prior history of the child reveals that the child has caused physical harm to the person or property of another or has posed a substantial threat to the person or property of another; and

(3) There exist other compelling circumstances that make detention reasonably necessary.

(Subd (k) amended and relettered effective January 1, 2007; adopted as subd (g) effective January 1, 1998; previously relettered as subd (h) effective January 1, 2001; previously amended and relettered as subd (j) effective July 1, 2002.)

(l) Restraining orders

As a condition of release or home supervision, the court may issue restraining orders as stated in rule 5.630 or orders restraining the child from any or all of the following:

(1) Molesting, attacking, striking, sexually assaulting, or battering, or from any contact whatsoever with an alleged victim or victim's family;

(2) Presence near or in a particular area or building; or

(3) Associating with or contacting in writing, by phone, or in person any adult or child alleged to have been a companion in the alleged offense.

(Subd (l) amended effective January 1, 2016; adopted as subd (i) effective January 1, 1998; previously relettered as subd (j) effective January 1, 2001; previously amended and relettered as subd (k) effective July 1, 2002, and as subd (l) effective January 1, 2007.)

Rule 5.760 amended effective January 1, 2016; repealed and adopted as rule 1475 effective January 1, 1998; previously amended effective January 1, 2001, July 1, 2002, and January 1, 2006; previously amended and renumbered as rule 5.760 effective January 1, 2007.

Rule 5.762. Detention rehearings

(a) No parent or guardian present and not noticed

If the court orders the child detained at the detention hearing and no parent or guardian is present and no parent or guardian has received actual notice of the detention hearing, a parent or guardian may file an affidavit alleging the failure of notice and requesting a detention rehearing. The clerk must set the rehearing within 24 hours of the filing of the affidavit, excluding noncourt days. At the rehearing, the court must proceed under rules 5.752–5.760.

(Subd (a) amended effective January 1, 2007.)

(b) Parent or guardian noticed; parent or guardian not present (§ 637)

If the court determines that the parent or guardian has received adequate notice of the detention hearing, and the parent or guardian fails to appear at the hearing, a request from the parent or guardian for a detention rehearing must be denied, absent a finding that the failure was due to good cause.

(Subd (b) amended effective January 1, 2007.)

(c) Parent or guardian noticed; preparers available (§ 637)

If a parent or guardian received notice of the detention hearing, and the preparers of any reports or other documents relied on by the court in its order detaining the child are present at court or otherwise available for cross-examination, there is no right to a detention rehearing.

(Subd (c) amended effective January 1, 2007.)

Rule 5.762 amended and renumbered effective January 1, 2007; repealed and adopted as rule 1476 effective January 1, 1998.

Rule 5.764. Prima facie hearings

(a) Hearing for further evidence; prima facie case (§ 637)

If the court orders the child detained, and the child or the child's attorney requests that evidence of the prima facie case be presented, the court must set a prima facie hearing for a time within three court days to consider evidence of the prima facie case.

(b) Continuance (§ 637)

If the court determines that a prima facie hearing cannot be held within three court days because of the unavailability of a witness, a reasonable continuance not to exceed five court days may be granted. If at the hearing petitioner fails to establish the prima facie case, the child must be released from custody.

Rule 5.764 adopted effective January 1, 2007.

Article 2
Hearing on Transfer of Jurisdiction to Criminal Court

Title 5, Family and Juvenile Rules—Division 3, Juvenile Rules—Chapter 13, Cases Petitioned Under Sections 601 and 602—Article 2, Hearing on Transfer of Jurisdiction to Criminal Court; amended effective January 1, 2019.

Rule 5.766. General provisions
Rule 5.768. Report of probation officer
Rule 5.770. Conduct of transfer of jurisdiction hearing under section 707

Rule 5.766. General provisions

(a) Hearing on transfer of jurisdiction to criminal court (§ 707)

A child who is the subject of a petition under section 602 and who was 14 years or older at the time of the alleged felony offense may be considered for prosecution under the general law in a court of criminal jurisdiction. The district attorney or other appropriate prosecuting officer may make a motion to transfer the child from juvenile court to a court of criminal jurisdiction, in one of the following circumstances:

(1) The child was 14 years or older at the time of the alleged offense listed in section 707(b).

(2) The child was 16 years or older at the time of the alleged felony offense.

(Subd (a) amended effective May 22, 2017; previously amended effective January 1, 1996, and January 1, 2001.)

(b) Notice (§ 707)

Notice of the transfer hearing must be given at least five judicial days before the hearing. In no case may notice be given following the attachment of jeopardy.

(Subd (b) amended effective May 22, 2007; previously amended effective January 1, 2007.)

(c) Prima facie showing

On the child's motion, the court must determine whether a prima facie showing has been made that the offense alleged is an offense that makes the child subject to transfer as set forth in subdivision (a).

(Subd (c) adopted effective May 22, 2017.)

(d) Time of transfer hearing—rules 5.774, 5.776

The transfer of jurisdiction hearing must be held and the court must rule on the request to transfer jurisdiction before the jurisdiction hearing begins. Absent a continuance under rule 5.776 or the child's waiver of the statutory time period to commence the jurisdiction hearing, the jurisdiction hearing must begin within the time limits under rule 5.774.

(Subd (d) amended and relettered effective May 22, 2017; adopted as subd (c); previously amended effective January 1, 2007.)

Rule 5.766 amended effective May 22, 2017; adopted as rule 1486 effective January 1, 1991; previously amended and renumbered effective January 1, 2007.

Rule 5.768.   Report of probation officer

(a) Contents of report (§ 707)

The probation officer must prepare and submit to the court a report on the behavioral patterns and social history of the child being considered. The report must include information relevant to the determination of whether the child should be retained under the jurisdiction of the juvenile court or transferred to the jurisdiction of the criminal court, including information regarding all of the criteria in section 707(a)(2). The report must also include any written or oral statement offered by the victim pursuant to section 656.2.

(Subd (a) amended effective May 22, 2017; previously amended effective January 1, 2007.)

(b) Recommendation of probation officer (§§ 281, 707)

If the court, under section 281, orders the probation officer to include a recommendation, the probation officer must make a recommendation to the court as to whether the child should be retained under the jurisdiction of the juvenile court or transferred to the jurisdiction of the criminal court.

(Subd (b) amended effective May 22, 2017; previously amended effective January 1, 2007.)

(c) Copies furnished

The probation officer's report on the behavioral patterns and social history of the child must be furnished to the child, the parent or guardian, and all counsel at least two court days before commencement of the hearing on the motion. A continuance of at least 24 hours must be granted on the request of any party who has not been furnished the probation officer's report in accordance with this rule.

(Subd (c) amended effective May 22, 2017; previously amended effective January 1, 2007.)

Rule 5.768 amended effective May 22, 2017; adopted as rule 1481 effective January 1, 1991; previously amended and renumbered effective January 1, 2007.

Rule 5.770.   Conduct of transfer of jurisdiction hearing under section 707

(a) Burden of proof (§ 707)

In a transfer of jurisdiction hearing under section 707, the burden of proving that there should be a transfer of jurisdiction to criminal court jurisdiction is on the petitioner, by a preponderance of the evidence.

(Subd (a) amended effective May 22, 2017; previously amended effective January 1, 1996, January 1, 2001, and July 1, 2002.)

(b) Criteria to consider (§ 707)

Following receipt of the probation officer's report and any other relevant evidence, the court may order that the child be transferred to the jurisdiction of the criminal court if the court finds:

(1) The child was 16 years or older at the time of any alleged felony offense, or the child was 14 or 15 years at the time of an alleged felony offense listed in section 707(b); and

(2) The child should be transferred to the jurisdiction of the criminal court based on an evaluation of all of the criteria in section 707(a)(2) as provided in that section.

(Subd (b) amended effective May 22, 2017; adopted as subd (b) effective January 1, 1991; previously amended and relettered as subd (c) effective January 1, 1996;

previously amended and relettered effective January 1, 2001; previously amended effective January 1, 2007.)

(c) Basis for order of transfer

If the court orders a transfer of jurisdiction to the criminal court, the court must recite the basis for its decision in an order entered on the minutes.

(Subd (c) amended effective May 22, 2017; adopted as subd (c) effective January 1, 1991; previously amended and relettered as subd (d) effective January 1, 1996; amended and relettered effective January 1, 2001; previously amended effective July 1, 2002, and January 1, 2007.)

(d) Procedure following findings

(1) If the court finds the child should be retained within the jurisdiction of the juvenile court, the court must proceed to jurisdiction hearing under rule 5.774.

(2) If the court finds the child should be transferred to the jurisdiction of the criminal court, the court must make orders under section 707.1 relating to bail and to the appropriate facility for the custody of the child, or release on own recognizance pending prosecution. The court must set a date for the child to appear in criminal court and dismiss the petition without prejudice upon the date of that appearance.

(3) When the court rules on the request to transfer the child to the jurisdiction of the criminal court, the court must advise all parties present that appellate review of the order must be by petition for extraordinary writ. The advisement may be given orally or in writing when the court makes the ruling. The advisement must include the time for filing the petition for extraordinary writ as set forth in subdivision (g) of this rule.

(Subd (d) relettered and amended effective May 22, 2017; adopted as subd (d) effective January 1, 1991; previously relettered as subd (g) effective January 1, 1996, and as subd (f) effective January 1, 2001; previously amended effective July 1, 2002, and January 1, 2007.)

(e) Continuance to seek review

If the prosecuting attorney informs the court orally or in writing that a review of the court's decision not to transfer jurisdiction to the criminal court will be sought and requests a continuance of the jurisdiction hearing, the court must grant a continuance for not less than two judicial days to allow time within which to obtain a stay of further proceedings from the reviewing judge or appellate court.

(Subd (e) relettered and amended effective May 22, 2017; adopted as subd (e) effective January 1, 1991; previously relettered as subd (h) effective January 1, 1996, and as subd (g) effective January 1, 2001; previously amended effective July 1, 2002, and January 1, 2007.)

(f) Subsequent role of judicial officer

Unless the child objects, the judicial officer who has conducted a hearing on a motion to transfer jurisdiction may participate in any subsequent contested jurisdiction hearing relating to the same offense.

(Subd (f) relettered and amended effective May 22, 2017; adopted as subd (f) effective January 1, 1991; relettered as subd (i) effective January 1, 1996; previously amended and relettered as subd (h) effective January 1, 2001.)

(g) Review of determination on a motion to transfer jurisdiction to criminal court

An order granting or denying a motion to transfer jurisdiction of a child to the criminal court is not an appealable order. Appellate review of the order is by petition for extraordinary writ. Any petition for review of a judge's order to transfer jurisdiction of the child to the criminal court, or denying an application for rehearing of the referee's determination to transfer jurisdiction of the child to the criminal court, must be filed no later than 20 days after the child's first arraignment on an accusatory pleading based on the allegations that led to the transfer of jurisdiction order.

(Subd (g) relettered and amended effective May 22, 2017; adopted as subd (g) effective January 1, 1991; previously relettered as subd (j) effective January 1, 1996; amended and relettered effective 1, 2001; previously amended as subd (i) effective July 1, 2002.)

(h) Postponement of plea prior to transfer hearing

If a hearing for transfer of jurisdiction has been noticed under section 707, the court must postpone the taking of a plea to the petition until the conclusion of the transfer hearing, and no pleas that may have been entered already may be considered as evidence at the hearing.

(Subd (h) adopted effective May 22, 2017.)

Rule 5.770 amended effective May 22, 2017; adopted as rule 1482 effective January 1, 1991; previously amended effective January 1, 1996, January 1, 2001, and July 1, 2002; previously amended and renumbered effective January 1, 2007.

Advisory Committee Comment

Subdivision (b). This subdivision reflects changes to section 707 as a result of the passage of Senate Bill 382 (Lara; Stats. 2015, ch. 234) and Proposition 57, the

Public Safety and Rehabilitation Act of 2016. SB 382 was intended to clarify the factors for the juvenile court to consider when determining whether a case should be transferred to criminal court by emphasizing the unique developmental characteristics of children and their prior interactions with the juvenile justice system. Proposition 57 provided that its intent was to promote rehabilitation for juveniles and prevent them from reoffending, and to ensure that a judge makes the determination that a child should be tried in a criminal court. Consistent with this intent, the committee urges juvenile courts—when evaluating the statutory criteria to determine if transfer is appropriate—to look at the totality of the circumstances, taking into account the specific statutory language guiding the court in its consideration of the criteria.

Subdivision (c). While this rule and section 707 only require the juvenile court to recite the basis for its decision when the transfer motion is granted, the advisory committee believes that juvenile courts should, as a best practice, state the basis for their decisions on these motions in all cases so that the parties have an adequate record from which to seek subsequent review.

Rule 5.772.   Conduct of fitness hearings under sections 707(a)(2) and 707(c) [Repealed]

Rule 5.772 repealed effective May 22, 2017; adopted as rule 1483 effective January 1, 1991; previously amended effective January 1, 1996, and January 1, 2001; previously amended and renumbered effective January 1, 2007; previously amended effective January 1, 2009.

Article 3
Jurisdiction

Rule 5.774. Setting petition for hearing—detained and nondetained cases; waiver of hearing

Rule 5.776. Grounds for continuance of jurisdiction hearing

Rule 5.778. Commencement of hearing on section 601 or section 602 petition; right to counsel; advisement of trial rights; admission, no contest

Rule 5.780. Contested hearing on section 601 or section 602 petition

Rule 5.782. Continuance pending disposition hearing

Rule 5.774.   Setting petition for hearing—detained and nondetained cases; waiver of hearing

(a) Nondetention cases (§ 657)

If the child is not detained, the jurisdiction hearing on the petition must begin within 30 calendar days from the date the petition is filed.

(Subd (a) amended effective January 1, 2007.)

(b) Detention cases (§ 657)

If the child is detained, the jurisdiction hearing on the petition must begin within 15 judicial days from the date of the order of the court directing detention. If the child is released from detention before the jurisdiction hearing, the court may reset the jurisdiction hearing within the time limit in (a).

(Subd (b) amended effective January 1, 2007.)

(c) Tolling of time period

Any period of delay caused by the child's unavailability or failure to appear must not be included in computing the time limits of (a) and (b).

(Subd (c) amended effective January 1, 2007.)

(d) Dismissal

Absent a continuance under rule 5.776, when a jurisdiction hearing is not begun within the time limits of (a) and (b), the court must order the petition dismissed. This does not bar the filing of another petition based on the same allegations as in the original petition, but the child must not be detained.

(Subd (d) amended effective January 1, 2007.)

(e) Waiver of hearing (§ 657)

At the detention hearing, or at any time thereafter, a child may admit the allegations of the petition or plead no contest and waive further jurisdiction hearing. The court may accept the admission or no contest plea and proceed according to rules 5.778 and 5.782.

(Subd (e) amended effective January 1, 2007.)

Rule 5.774 amended and renumbered effective January 1, 2007; adopted as rule 1485 effective January 1, 1991.

Rule 5.776.   Grounds for continuance of jurisdiction hearing

(a) Request for continuance; consent (§ 682)

A continuance may be granted only on a showing of good cause and only for the time shown to be necessary. Stipulation between counsel or parties and convenience of parties are not in and of themselves good cause.

(1) In order to obtain a continuance, written notice with supporting documents must be filed and served on all parties at least two court days before the date set for the hearing, unless the court finds good cause for

failure to comply with these requirements. Absent a waiver of time, a child may not be detained beyond the statutory time limits.

(2) The court must state in its order the facts requiring any continuance that is granted.

(3) If the child is represented by counsel and no objection is made to an order setting or continuing the jurisdiction hearing beyond the time limits of rule 5.774, consent must be implied.

(Subd (a) amended effective January 1, 2007.)

(b) Grounds for continuance—mandatory (§ 700)

The court must continue the jurisdiction hearing for:

(1) A reasonable period to permit the child and the parent, guardian, or adult relative to prepare for the hearing; and

(2) No more than seven calendar days:

(A) For appointment of counsel;

(B) To enable counsel to become acquainted with the case; or

(C) To determine whether the parent, guardian, or adult relative can afford counsel.

(Subd (b) amended effective January 1, 2007.)

(c) Grounds for continuance—discretionary (§§ 700.5, 701)

The court may continue the jurisdiction hearing for no more than seven calendar days to enable the petitioner to subpoena witnesses if the child has made an extrajudicial admission and denies it, or has previously indicated to the court or petitioner an intention to admit the allegations of the petition, and at the time set for jurisdiction hearing denies the allegations.

(d) Grounds for continuance—section 654.2 (§§ 654.2, 654.3, 654.4)

In a case petitioned under section 602, the court may, with the consent of the child and the parent or guardian, continue the jurisdiction hearing for six months. If the court grants the continuance, the court must order the child and the parent or guardian to participate in a program of supervision under section 654, and must order the parent or guardian to participate with the child in a program of counseling or education under section 654.

(Subd (d) amended effective January 1, 2007.)

Rule 5.776 amended and renumbered effective January 1, 2007; adopted as rule 1486 effective January 1, 1991.

Rule 5.778.   Commencement of hearing on section 601 or section 602 petition; right to counsel; advisement of trial rights; admission, no contest

(a) Petition read and explained (§ 700)

At the beginning of the jurisdiction hearing, the petition must be read to those present. On request of the child, or the parent, guardian, or adult relative, the court must explain the meaning and contents of the petition, the nature of the hearing, the procedures of the hearing, and possible consequences.

(Subd (a) amended effective January 1, 2007.)

(b) Rights explained (§ 702.5)

After giving the advisement required by rule 5.534, the court must advise those present of each of the following rights of the child:

(1) The right to a hearing by the court on the issues raised by the petition;

(2) The right to assert the privilege against self-incrimination;

(3) The right to confront and to cross-examine any witness called to testify against the child; and

(4) The right to use the process of the court to compel the attendance of witnesses on the child's behalf.

(Subd (b) amended effective January 1, 2007.)

(c) Admission of allegations; prerequisites to acceptance

The court must then inquire whether the child intends to admit or deny the allegations of the petition. If the child neither admits nor denies the allegations, the court must state on the record that the child does not admit the allegations. If the child wishes to admit the allegations, the court must first find and state on the record that it is satisfied that the child understands the nature of the allegations and the direct consequences of the admission, and understands and waives the rights in (b).

(Subd (c) amended effective January 1, 2007.)

(d) Consent of counsel—child must admit

Counsel for the child must consent to the admission, which must be made by the child personally.

(Subd (d) amended effective January 1, 2007.)

(e) No contest

The child may enter a plea of no contest to the allegations, subject to the approval of the court.

(f) Findings of the court (§ 702)

On an admission or plea of no contest, the court must make the following findings noted in the minutes of the court:

(1) Notice has been given as required by law;

(2) The birthdate and county of residence of the child;

(3) The child has knowingly and intelligently waived the right to a hearing on the issues by the court, the right to confront and cross-examine adverse witnesses and to use the process of the court to compel the attendance of witnesses on the child's behalf, and the right to assert the privilege against self-incrimination;

(4) The child understands the nature of the conduct alleged in the petition and the possible consequences of an admission or plea of no contest;

(5) The admission or plea of no contest is freely and voluntarily made;

(6) There is a factual basis for the admission or plea of no contest;

(7) Those allegations of the petition as admitted are true as alleged;

(8) The child is described by section 601 or 602; and

(9) In a section 602 matter, the degree of the offense and whether it would be a misdemeanor or felony had the offense been committed by an adult. If any offense may be found to be either a felony or misdemeanor, the court must consider which description applies and expressly declare on the record that it has made such consideration and must state its determination as to whether the offense is a misdemeanor or a felony. These determinations may be deferred until the disposition hearing.

(Subd (f) amended effective January 1, 2007; previously amended effective January 1, 1998.)

(g) Disposition

After accepting an admission or plea of no contest, the court must proceed to disposition hearing under rules 5.782 and 5.785.

(Subd (g) amended effective January 1, 2007.)

Rule 5.778 amended and renumbered effective January 1, 2007; adopted as rule 1487 effective January 1, 1991; previously amended effective January 1, 1998.

Rule 5.780. Contested hearing on section 601 or section 602 petition

(a) Contested jurisdiction hearing (§ 701)

If the child denies the allegations of the petition, the court must hold a contested hearing to determine whether the allegations in the petition are true.

(Subd (a) amended effective January 1, 2007.)

(b) Admissibility of evidence—general (§ 701)

In a section 601 matter, the admission and exclusion of evidence must be in accordance with the Evidence Code as it applies in civil cases. In a section 602 matter, the admission and exclusion of evidence must be in accordance with the Evidence Code as it applies in criminal cases.

(Subd (b) amended effective January 1, 2007.)

(c) Probation reports

Except as otherwise provided by law, the court must not read or consider any portion of a probation report relating to the contested petition before or during a contested jurisdiction hearing.

(Subd (c) amended effective January 1, 2007.)

(d) Unrepresented children (§ 701)

If the child is not represented by counsel, objections that could have been made to the evidence must be deemed made.

(Subd (d) amended effective January 1, 2007.)

(e) Findings of court—allegations true (§ 702)

If the court determines by a preponderance of the evidence in a section 601 matter, or by proof beyond a reasonable doubt in a section 602 matter, that the allegations of the petition are true, the court must make findings on each of the following, noted in the order:

(1) Notice has been given as required by law;

(2) The birthdate and county of residence of the child;

(3) The allegations of the petition are true;

(4) The child is described by section 601 or 602; and

(5) In a section 602 matter, the degree of the offense and whether it would be a misdemeanor or a felony had the offense been committed by an adult. If any offense may be found to be either a felony or a misdemeanor, the court must consider which description applies and expressly declare on the record that it has made such consideration, and must state its determination as to whether the offense is a misdemeanor or a felony. These determinations may be deferred until the disposition hearing.

(Subd (e) amended effective January 1, 2007; previously amended effective January 1, 1998.)

(f) Disposition

After making the findings in (e), the court must then proceed to disposition hearing under rules 5.782 and 5.785.

(Subd (f) amended effective January 1, 2007.)

(g) Findings of court—allegations not proved (§ 702)

If the court determines that the allegations of the petition have not been proved by a preponderance of the evidence in a 601 matter, or beyond a reasonable doubt in a 602 matter, the court must make findings on each of the following, noted in the order:

(1) Notice has been given as required by law;

(2) The birthdate and county of residence of the child; and

(3) The allegations of the petition have not been proved.

The court must dismiss the petition and terminate detention orders related to this petition.

(Subd (g) amended effective January 1, 2007.)

Rule 5.780 amended and renumbered effective January 1, 2007; adopted as rule 1488 effective January 1, 1991; previously amended effective January 1, 1998.

Rule 5.782. Continuance pending disposition hearing

(a) Continuance pending disposition hearing (§ 702)

If the court finds that the child is described by section 601 or 602, it must proceed to a disposition hearing. The court may continue the disposition hearing up to 10 judicial days if the child is detained. If the child is not detained, the court may continue the disposition hearing up to 30 calendar days from the date of the filing of the petition and up to an additional 15 calendar days for good cause shown.

(Subd (a) amended effective January 1, 2007.)

(b) Detention pending hearing (§ 702)

The court may release or detain the child during the period of the continuance.

(c) Observation and diagnosis (§ 704)

If the child is eligible for commitment to the Youth Authority, the court may continue the disposition hearing up to 90 calendar days and order the child to be placed temporarily at a Youth Authority diagnostic and treatment center for observation and diagnosis. The court must order the Youth Authority to submit a diagnosis and recommendation within 90 days, and the probation officer or any other peace officer designated by the court must place the child in the diagnostic and treatment center and return the child to the court. After return from the diagnostic and treatment center, the child must be brought to court within 2 judicial days. A disposition hearing must be held within 10 judicial days thereafter.

(Subd (c) amended effective January 1, 2007.)

Rule 5.782 amended and renumbered effective January 1, 2007; adopted as rule 1489 effective January 1, 1991.

Article 4
Disposition

Rule 5.785. General conduct of hearing
Rule 5.790. Orders of the court
Rule 5.795. Required determinations
Rule 5.800. Deferred entry of judgment
Rule 5.805. California Department of Corrections and Rehabilitation, Division of Juvenile Justice, commitments

Rule 5.785. General conduct of hearing

(a) Social study (§§ 280, 702, 706.5)

The probation officer must prepare a social study of the child, which must contain all matters relevant to disposition, including any parole status information, and a recommendation for disposition.

(1) In any case in which the probation officer is recommending placement in foster care or in which the child is already in foster care placement or pending placement under an earlier order, the social study must include a case plan as described in (c).

(2) The probation officer must submit the social study and copies of it to the clerk at least 48 hours before the disposition hearing is set to begin, and the clerk must make the copies available to the parties and attorneys. A continuance of up to 48 hours must be granted on the request of a party who has not been furnished a copy of the social study in accordance with this rule.

(Subd (a) amended effective January 1, 2007; previously amended effective July 1, 2002.)

(b) Evidence considered (§ 706)

The court must receive in evidence and consider the social study and any relevant evidence offered by the petitioner, the child, or the parent or guardian. The court may require production of other relevant evidence on its own motion. In the order of disposition the court must state that the social study has been read and considered by the court.

(Subd (b) amended effective July 1, 2002.)

(c) Case plan

When a child is detained and is at risk of entering foster care placement, the probation officer must prepare a case plan.

(1) The plan must be completed and filed with the court by the date of disposition or within 60 calendar days of initial removal, whichever occurs first.

(2) The court must consider the case plan and must find as follows:

(A) The probation officer solicited and integrated into the case plan the input of the child, the child's family, in a case described by rule 5.480(2)(A)–(C) the child's identified Indian tribe, and other interested parties; or

(B) The probation officer did not solicit and integrate into the case plan the input of the child, the child's family, in a case described by rule 5.480(2)(A)–(C) the child's identified Indian tribe, and other interested parties. If the court finds that the probation officer did not solicit and integrate into the case plan the input of the child, the child's family, the child's identified Indian tribe, and other interested parties, the court must order that the probation officer solicit and integrate into the case plan the input of the child, the child's family, in a case described by rule 5.480(2)(A)–(C) the child's identified Indian tribe, and other interested parties, unless the court finds that each of these participants was unable, unavailable, or unwilling to participate.

(3) For a child 12 years of age or older and in a permanent placement, the court must consider the case plan and must find as follows:

(A) The child was given the opportunity to review the case plan, sign it, and receive a copy; or

(B) The child was not [1] **given** the opportunity to review the case plan, sign it, and receive a copy. If the court makes such a finding, the court must order the probation officer to give the child the opportunity to review the case plan, sign it, and receive a copy, unless the court finds that the child was unable, unavailable, or unwilling to participate.

(4) If the probation officer believes that the child will be able to return home through reasonable efforts by the child, the parents or guardian, and the probation officer, the case plan must include the elements described in section 636.1(b).

(5) If the probation officer believes that foster care placement is the most appropriate disposition for the child, the case plan must include all of the information required by section 706.6.

(Subd (c) amended effective January 1, 2021; adopted effective July 1, 2002; previously amended effective January 1, 2007, and July 1, 2013.)

Rule 5.785(c).   2020 Deletes. [1] give

Rule 5.785 amended effective January 1, 2021; adopted as rule 1492 effective January 1, 1991; previously amended effective July 1, 2002, and July 1, 2013; previously amended and renumbered effective January 1, 2007.

Rule 5.790.   Orders of the court

(a) Findings and orders of the court (§§ 654, 654.1, 654.2, 654.3, 654.4, 725, 725.5, 782)

At the disposition hearing:

(1) If the court has not previously considered whether any offense is a misdemeanor or felony, the court must do so at this time and state its finding on the record. If the offense may be found to be either a felony or a misdemeanor, the court must consider which description applies and must expressly declare on the record that it has made such consideration and must state its finding as to whether the offense is a misdemeanor or a felony.

(2) The court may then:

(A) Dismiss the petition in the interests of justice and the welfare of the child or, if the child does not need treatment or rehabilitation, with the specific reasons stated in the minutes;

(B) Place the child on probation for no more than six months, without declaring the child a ward; or

(C) Declare the child a ward of the court.

(Subd (a) amended effective January 1, 2007; previously amended effective January 1, 1998, and July 1, 2002.)

(b) Conditions of probation (§§ 725, 726, 727, 729.2, 729.9, 729.10)

If the child is placed on probation, with or without wardship, the court must set reasonable terms and conditions of probation. Unless the court finds and states its reasons on the record that any of the following conditions is inappropriate, the court must:

(1) Require the child to attend school;

(2) Require the parent to participate with the child in a counseling or education program; and

(3) Require the child to be at the child's residence between 10:00 p.m. and 6:00 a.m. unless accompanied by a parent or a guardian or an adult custodian.

(Subd (b) amended effective January 1, 2014; previously amended effective July 1, 2002, and January 1, 2007.)

(c) Custody and visitation (§ 726.5)

(1) At any time when a child is a ward of the juvenile court, the court may issue an order determining the custody of or visitation with the child. An order issued under this subdivision continues in effect until modified or terminated by a later order of the juvenile court.

(2) At the time wardship is terminated, the court may issue an order determining custody of or visitation with the child, as described in rule 5.700.

(Subd (c) amended effective January 1, 2016; adopted effective January 1, 2007.)

(d) Removal of custody—required findings (§ 726)

The court must not order a ward removed from the physical custody of a parent or guardian unless the court finds:

(1) The parent or guardian has failed or neglected to provide, or is incapable of providing, proper maintenance, training, and education for the child;

(2) The child has been on probation in the custody of the parent or guardian and during that time has failed to reform; or

(3) The welfare of the child requires that physical custody be removed from the parent or guardian.

(Subd (d) amended and relettered effective January 1, 2007; adopted as subd (c) effective January 1, 1991; previously amended effective July 1, 2002.)

(e) Removal of custody—orders regarding reunification services (§ 727.2)

(1) Whenever the court orders the care, custody, and control of the child to be under the supervision of the probation officer for placement, the court must order the probation department to ensure the provision of reunification services to facilitate the safe return of the child to his or her home or the permanent placement of the child and to address the needs of the child while in foster care.

(2) Reunification services need not be provided to the parent or guardian if the court finds, by clear and convincing evidence, that one or more of the exceptions listed in section 727.2(b) is true.

(Subd (e) amended and relettered effective January 1, 2007; adopted as subd (d) effective July 1, 2002; previously amended effective January 1, 2004.)

(f) Family-finding determination (§ 628(d))

(1) If the child is detained or at risk of entering foster care, the court must consider and determine whether the probation officer has exercised due diligence in conducting the required investigation to identify, locate, and notify the child's relatives. The court may consider the activities listed in (g) as examples of due diligence. The court must document its determination by making a finding on the record.

If the dispositional hearing is continued, the court may set a hearing to be held 30 days from the date of detention or as soon as possible thereafter to consider and determine whether the probation officer has exercised due diligence in conducting the required investigation to identify, locate, and notify the child's relatives.

(2) If the court finds that the probation officer has not exercised due diligence, the court may order the probation officer to exercise due diligence in conducting an investigation to identify, locate, and notify the child's relatives—except for any individual the probation officer identifies who is inappropriate to notify under rule 5.637(b)—and may require a written or oral report to the court.

(Subd (f) amended effective January 1, 2015; adopted effective January 1, 2014.)

(g) Due diligence

When making the determination required in (f), the court may consider, among other examples of due diligence, whether the probation officer has done any of the following:

(1) Asked the child, in an age-appropriate manner and consistent with the child's best interest, about his or her relatives;

(2) Obtained information regarding the location of the child's relatives;

(3) Reviewed the child's case file for any information regarding relatives;

(4) Telephoned, e-mailed, or visited all identified relatives;

(5) Asked located relatives for the names and locations of other relatives;

(6) Used Internet search tools to locate relatives identified as supports; or

(7) Developed tools, including a genogram, family tree, family map, or other diagram of family relationships, to help the child or parents to identify relatives.

(Subd (g) amended effective January 1, 2015; adopted effective January 1, 2014.)

(h) Wardship orders (§§ 726, 727, 727.1, 730, 731)

The court may make any reasonable order for the care, supervision, custody, conduct, maintenance, support, and medical treatment of a child adjudged a ward of the court.

(1) Subject to the provisions of section 727, the court may order the ward to be on probation without the supervision of the probation officer and may impose on the ward reasonable conditions of behavior.

(2) The court may order the care, custody, control, and conduct of the ward to be under the supervision of the probation officer in the home of a parent or guardian.

(3) If the court orders removal of custody under (d), it must authorize the probation officer to place the ward with a person or organization described in section 727. The decision regarding choice of placement must take into account the following factors:

(A) That the setting is safe;

(B) That the setting is the least restrictive or most family-like environment that is appropriate for the child and available;

(C) That the setting is in close proximity to the parent's home; and

(D) That the setting is the environment best suited to meet the child's special needs and best interest.

The selection must consider, in order of priority, placement with relatives, tribal members, and foster family, group care, and residential treatment under Family Code section 7950.

(4) If the child was declared a ward under section 602, the court may order treatment or commitment of the child under section 730 or 731.

(5) The court may limit the control exercised over the ward by a parent or guardian. Orders must clearly specify all limitations. In particular, the court must consider whether it is necessary to limit the rights of the parent or guardian to make educational or developmental-services decisions for the child. If the court limits those rights, it must follow the procedures in rules 5.649–5.651.

(Subd (h) amended and relettered effective January 1, 2014; adopted as subd (d) effective January 1, 1991; previously amended and relettered as subd (e) effective July 1, 2002, and as subd (f) effective January 1, 2007; previously amended effective January 1, 2004, and January 1, 2008.)

(i) California Department of Corrections and Rehabilitation, Division of Juvenile Justice

If, at the time of the disposition hearing, the child is a ward of the California Department of Corrections and Rehabilitation, Division of Juvenile Justice (DJJ) under a prior commitment, the court may either recommit or return the child to the DJJ. If the child is returned to the DJJ, the court may:

(1) Recommend that the ward's parole status be revoked;

(2) Recommend that the ward's parole status not be revoked; or

(3) Make no recommendation regarding revocation of parole.

(Subd (i) relettered effective January 1, 2014; adopted as subd (e) effective January 1, 1991; previously amended and relettered as subd (f) effective July 1, 2002, and as subd (g) effective January 1, 2007; previously amended effective January 1, 2006.)

(j) Fifteen-day reviews (§ 737)

If the child or nonminor is detained pending the implementation of a dispositional order, the court must review the case at least every 15 days as long as the child is detained. The review must meet all the requirements in section 737.

(Subd (j) amended effective January 1, 2016; adopted as subd (f) effective January 1, 1991; previously amended and relettered as subd (g) effective July 1, 2002, and as subd (h) effective January 1, 2007; previously relettered as subd (j) effective January 1, 2014.)

Rule 5.790 amended effective January 1, 2016; adopted as rule 1493 effective January 1, 1991; previously amended and renumbered as rule 5.790 effective January 1, 2007; previously amended effective January 1, 1998, July 1, 2002, January 1, 2004, January 1, 2006, January 1, 2008, January 1, 2014, and January 1, 2015.)

Rule 5.795. Required determinations

(a) Felony or misdemeanor (§ 702)

Unless determined previously, the court must find and note in the minutes the degree of the offense committed by the youth, and whether it would be a felony or a misdemeanor had it been committed by an adult. If any offense may be found to be either a felony or a misdemeanor, the court must consider which description applies and expressly declare on the record that it has made such consideration and must state its determination as to whether the offense is a misdemeanor or a felony.

(Subd (a) amended effective January 1, 2007; previously amended effective January 1, 2003.)

(b) Physical confinement (§ 726)

If the youth is declared a ward under section 602 and ordered removed from the physical custody of a parent or guardian, the court must specify and note in the minutes the maximum period of confinement under section 726.

(Subd (b) amended effective January 1, 2007; previously amended effective January 1, 2003.)

Rule 5.795 amended and renumbered effective January 1, 2007; adopted as rule 1494 effective January 1, 1991; previously amended effective January 1, 2001, and January 1, 2003.

Rule 5.800. Deferred entry of judgment

(a) Eligibility (§ 790)

A child who is the subject of a petition under section 602 alleging violation of at least one felony offense may be considered for a deferred entry of judgment if all of the following apply:

(1) The child is 14 years or older at the time of the hearing on the application for deferred entry of judgment;

(2) The offense alleged is not listed in section 707(b);

(3) The child has not been previously declared a ward of the court based on the commission of a felony offense;

(4) The child has not been previously committed to the California Department of Corrections and Rehabilitation, Division of Juvenile Justice;

(5) If the child is presently or was previously a ward of the court, probation has not been revoked before completion; and

(6) The child meets the eligibility standards stated in Penal Code section 1203.06.

(Subd (a) amended effective July 1, 2010; previously amended effective January 1, 2006.)

(b) Procedures for consideration (§ 790)

(1) Before filing a petition alleging a felony offense, or as soon as possible after filing, the prosecuting attorney must review the child's file to determine if the requirements of (a) are met. If the prosecuting attorney's review reveals that the requirements of (a) have been met, the prosecuting attorney must file *Determination of Eligibility—Deferred Entry of Judgment—Juvenile* (form JV-750) with the petition.

(2) If the court determines that the child is eligible and suitable for a deferred entry of judgment, and would derive benefit from education, treatment, and rehabilitation efforts, the court may grant deferred entry of judgment.

(Subd (b) amended effective July 1, 2010; previously amended effective January 1, 2007.)

(c) Citation (§ 792)

The court must issue *Citation and Written Notification for Deferred Entry of Judgment—Juvenile* (form JV-751) to the child's custodial parent, guardian, or foster parent. The form must be personally served on the custodial adult at least 24 hours before the time set for the appearance hearing.

(Subd (c) amended effective January 1, 2007.)

(d) Determination without a hearing; supplemental information (§ 791)

(1) The court may grant a deferred entry of judgment as stated in (2) or (3).

(2) If the child admits each allegation contained in the petition as charged and waives the right to a speedy disposition hearing, the court may summarily grant the deferred entry of judgment.

(3) When appropriate, the court may order the probation department to prepare a report with recommendations on the suitability of the child for deferred entry of judgment or set a hearing on the matter, with or without the order to the probation department for a report.

(A) The probation report must address the following:

(i) The child's age, maturity, educational background, family relationships, motivation, any treatment history, and any other relevant factors regarding the benefit the child would derive from education, treatment, and rehabilitation efforts; and

(ii) The programs best suited to assist the child and the child's family.

(B) The probation report must be submitted to the court, the child, the prosecuting attorney, and the child's attorney at least 48 hours, excluding noncourt days, before the hearing.

(Subd (d) amended effective July 1, 2010; previously amended effective January 1, 2007.)

(e) Written notification of ineligibility (§ 790)

If it is determined that the child is ineligible for deferred entry of judgment, the prosecuting attorney must complete and provide to the court, the child, and the child's attorney *Determination of Eligibility—Deferred Entry of Judgment—Juvenile* (form JV-750).

(Subd (e) amended effective January 1, 2007.)

(f) Conduct of hearing (§§ 791, 794)

At the hearing, the court must consider the declaration of the prosecuting attorney, any report and recommendations from the probation department, and any other relevant material provided by the child or other interested parties.

(1) If the child consents to the deferred entry of judgment, the child must enter an admission as stated in rule 5.778(c) and (d). A no-contest plea must not be accepted.

(2) The child must waive the right to a speedy disposition hearing.

(3) After acceptance of the child's admission, the court must set a date for review of the child's progress and a date by which the probation department must submit to the court, the child, the child's parent or guardian, the child's attorney, and the prosecuting attorney a report on the child's adherence to the conditions set by the court. Although the date set may be any time within the following 36 months, consideration of dismissal of the petition may not occur until at least 12 months have passed since the court granted the deferred entry of judgment.

(4) If the court grants the deferred entry of judgment, the court must order search-and-seizure probation conditions and may order probation conditions regarding the following:

(A) Education;

(B) Treatment;

(C) Testing for alcohol and other drugs, if appropriate;

(D) Curfew and school attendance requirements;

(E) Restitution; and

(F) Any other conditions consistent with the identified needs of the child and the factors that led to the conduct of the child.

(Subd (f) amended effective July 1, 2010; previously amended effective January 1, 2007.)

(g) Compliance with conditions; progress review

Twelve months after the court granted the deferred entry of judgment and on receipt of the progress report ordered at the hearing on the deferred entry of judgment, the court may:

(1) Find that the child has complied satisfactorily with the conditions imposed, dismiss the petition, seal the court records in compliance with section 793(c), and vacate the date set for review hearing; or

(2) Confirm the review hearing. At the hearing the court must:

(A) Find that the child has complied satisfactorily with the conditions imposed, dismiss the petition, and seal the court records in compliance with section 793(c); or

(B) Find that the child has not complied satisfactorily with the conditions imposed, lift the deferred entry of judgment, and set a disposition hearing.

(Subd (g) amended effective January 1, 2007.)

(h) Failure to comply with conditions (§ 793)

(1) Before the date of the progress hearing, if the child is found to have committed a misdemeanor offense or more than one misdemeanor offense on a single occasion, the court may schedule a hearing within 15 court days.

(A) At the hearing, the court must follow the procedure stated in rule 5.580(d) and (e) to determine if the deferred entry of judgment should be lifted, with a disposition hearing to be conducted thereafter.

(B) The disposition hearing must be conducted as stated in rules 5.785 through 5.795.

(C) The child's admission of the charges under a deferred entry of judgment must not constitute a finding that a petition has been sustained unless a judgment is entered under section 793(b).

(2) Before the date of the progress hearing, on the court's own motion, or if the court receives a declaration from the probation department or the prosecuting attorney alleging that the child has not complied with the conditions imposed or that the conditions are not benefiting the child, or if the child is found to have committed a felony offense or two or more misdemeanor offenses on separate occasions, the court must schedule a hearing within 10 court days.

(A) At the hearing, the court must follow the procedure stated in rule 5.580(d) and (e) to determine if the deferred entry of judgment should be lifted, with a disposition hearing to be conducted thereafter.

(B) The disposition hearing must be conducted as stated in rules 5.785 through 5.795.

(C) The child's admission of the charges under a deferred entry of judgment must not constitute a finding that a petition has been sustained unless a judgment is entered under section 793(b).

(3) If the child is found to have committed a felony offense or two or more misdemeanor offenses on separate occasions, the court must schedule a disposition hearing within 10 court days. The disposition hearing must be conducted as stated in rules 5.785 through 5.795.

(4) If the judgment previously deferred is imposed and a disposition hearing is scheduled under section 793(a), the juvenile court must report the complete criminal history of the child to the Department of Justice under section 602.5.

(Subd (h) amended effective January 1, 2007.)

Rule 5.800 amended effective July 1, 2010; adopted as rule 1495 effective January 1, 2001; previously amended effective January 1, 2006; previously amended and renumbered effective January 1, 2007.

Rule 5.805. California Department of Corrections and Rehabilitation, Division of Juvenile Justice, commitments

If the court orders the youth committed to the California Department of Corrections and Rehabilitation, Division of Juvenile Justice (DJJ):

(1) The court must complete *Commitment to the California Department of Corrections and Rehabilitation, Division of Juvenile Justice* (form JV-732).

(2) The court must specify whether the offense is one listed in section 707(b) or subdivision (c) of Penal Code section 290.008.

(3) The court must order the probation department to forward to the DJJ all required medical information, including previously executed medical releases.

(4) If the youth is taking a prescribed psychotropic medication, the DJJ may continue to administer the medication for up to 60 days, provided that a physician examines the youth on arrival at the facility, and the physician recommends that the medication continue.

(5) The court must provide to the DJJ information regarding the youth's educational needs, including the youth's current individualized education program if one exists. To facilitate this process, the court must ensure that the probation officer communicates with appropriate educational staff.

Rule 5.805 amended effective January 1, 2014; adopted as rule 1494.5 effective January 1, 2003; previously amended effective January 1, 2006; previously amended and renumbered effective January 1, 2007.

Article 5
Reviews and Sealing

Rule 5.810. Reviews, hearings, and permanency planning

(a) Six-month status review hearings (§§ 727.2, 11404.1)

For any ward removed from the custody of his or her parent or guardian under section 726 and placed in a home under section 727, the court must conduct a status review hearing no less frequently than once every six months from the date the ward entered foster care. The court may consider the hearing at which the initial order for placement is made as the first status review hearing.

(1) *Consideration of reports (§ 727.2(d))*

The court must review and consider the social study report and updated case plan submitted by the probation officer and the report submitted by any CASA volunteer, and any other reports filed with the court under section 727.2(d).

(2) *Return of child if not detrimental (§ 727.2(f))*

At any status review hearing before the first permanency hearing, the court must order the return of the ward to the parent or guardian unless it finds the probation department has established by a preponderance of evidence that return would create a substantial risk of detriment to the safety, protection, or physical or emotional well-being of the ward. The probation department has the burden of establishing that detriment. In making its determination, the court must review and consider all reports submitted to the court and must consider the efforts and progress demonstrated by the child and the family and the extent to which the child availed himself or herself of the services provided.

(3) *Findings and orders (§ 727.2(e))*

The court must consider the safety of the ward and make findings and orders that determine the following:

(A) The continuing necessity for and appropriateness of the placement;

(B) The extent of the probation department's compliance with the case plan in making reasonable efforts to safely return the child to the child's home and to complete whatever steps are necessary to finalize the permanent placement of the child;

(C) Whether it is necessary to limit the rights of the parent or guardian to make educational or developmental-services decisions for the child. If the court limits those rights or, if the ward is 18 years of age or older and has chosen not to make educational or developmental-services decisions for him- or herself or has been deemed incompetent, finds that it is in the best interests of the ward, the court must appoint a responsible adult as the educational rights holder as defined in rule 5.502. Any limitation on the rights of a parent or guardian to make educational or developmental-services decisions for a ward must be specified in the court order. The court must follow the procedures in rules 5.649–5.651;

(D) The extent of progress that has been made by the child and parent or guardian toward alleviating or mitigating the causes necessitating placement in foster care;

(E) The likely date by which the child may return to and be safely maintained in the home or placed for adoption, legal guardianship, or another permanent plan;

(F) In the case of a child who is 16 years of age or older, the services needed to assist the child in making the transition from foster care to independent living;

(G) Whether the child was actively involved, as age- and developmentally appropriate, in the development of his or her own case plan and plan for permanent placement. If the court finds that the child was not appropriately involved, the court must order the probation department to actively involve the child in the development of his or her own case plan and plan for permanent placement, unless the court finds that the child is unable, unavailable, or unwilling to participate;

(H) Whether each parent was actively involved in the development of the case plan and plan for permanent placement. If the court finds that any parent was not actively involved, the court must order the probation department to actively involve that parent in the development of the case plan and plan for permanent placement, unless the court finds that the parent is unable, unavailable, or unwilling to participate; and

(I) If sibling interaction has been suspended and will continue to be suspended, that sibling interaction is contrary to the safety or well-being of either child.

(4) *Basis for Findings and Orders (§ 727.2(e))*

The determinations required by (a)(3) must be made on a case-by-case basis, and the court must reference, in its written findings, the probation officer's report and any other evidence relied on in reaching its decision.

(Subd (a) amended effective January 1, 2016; previously amended effective January 1, 1998, January 1, 2001, January 1, 2003, January 1, 2004, January 1, 2007, and January 1, 2014.)

(b) Permanency planning hearings (§§ 727.2, 727.3, 11404.1)

A permanency planning hearing for any ward who has been removed from the custody of a parent or guardian and not returned at a previous review hearing must be held within 12 months of the date the ward entered foster care as defined in section 727.4(d)(4). However, when no reunification services are offered to the parents or guardians under section 727.2(b), the first permanency planning hearing must occur within 30 days of disposition.

(1) *Consideration of reports (§ 727.3)*

The court must review and consider the social study report and updated case plan submitted by the probation officer and the report submitted by any CASA volunteer, and any other reports filed with the court under section 727.3(a)(2).

(2) *Findings and orders (§§ 727.2(e), 727.3(a))*

At each permanency planning hearing, the court must consider the safety of the ward and make findings and orders regarding the following:

(A) The continuing necessity for and appropriateness of the placement;

(B) The extent of the probation department's compliance with the case plan in making reasonable efforts to safely return the child to the child's home and to complete whatever steps are necessary to finalize the permanent placement of the child;

(C) The extent of progress that has been made by the child and parent or guardian toward alleviating or mitigating the causes necessitating placement in foster care;

(D) The permanent plan for the child, as described in (3);

(E) Whether the child was actively involved, as age- and developmentally appropriate, in the development of his or her own case plan and plan for permanent placement. If the court finds that the child was not appropriately involved, the court must order the probation officer to actively involve the child in the development of his or her own case plan and plan for permanent placement, unless the court finds that the child is unable, unavailable, or unwilling to participate; and

(F) Whether each parent was actively involved in the development of the case plan and plan for permanent placement. If the court finds that any parent was not actively involved, the court must order the probation department to actively involve that parent in the development of the case plan and plan for permanent placement, unless the court finds that the parent is unable, unavailable, or unwilling to participate; and

(G) If sibling interaction has been suspended and will continue to be suspended, that sibling interaction is contrary to the safety or well-being of either child.

(3) *Selection of a permanent plan (§ 727.3(b))*

At the first permanency planning hearing, the court must select a permanent plan. At subsequent permanency planning hearings that must be held under section 727.2(g) and rule 5.810(c), the court must either make a finding that the current permanent plan is appropriate or select a different permanent plan, including returning the child home, if appropriate. The court must choose from one of the permanent plans listed in section 727.3(b).

(4) *Involvement of parents or guardians*

If the child has a continuing involvement with his or her parents or legal guardians, they must be involved in the planning for permanent placement. The permanent plan order must include an order regarding the nature and frequency of visitation with the parents or guardians.

(Subd (b) amended effective January 1, 2018; adopted effective January 1, 2001; previously amended effective January 1, 2003, January 1, 2007, January 1, 2014, and January 1, 2016.)

(c) Postpermanency status review hearings (§ 727.2)

A postpermanency status review hearing must be conducted for wards in placement no less frequently than once every six months.

(1) *Consideration of reports (§ 727.2(d))*

The court must review and consider the social study report and updated case plan submitted for this hearing by the probation officer and the report submitted by any CASA volunteer, and any other reports filed with the court under section 727.2(d).

(2) *Findings and orders (§ 727.2(g))*

At each postpermanency status review hearing, the court must consider the safety of the ward and make findings and orders regarding the following:

(A) Whether the current permanent plan continues to be appropriate. If not, the court must select a different permanent plan, including returning the child home, if appropriate. If the plan is another planned permanent living arrangement, the court must meet the requirements set forth in Welfare and Institutions Code section 727.3(a)(5);

(B) The continuing necessity for and appropriateness of the placement;

(C) The extent of the probation department's compliance with the case plan in making reasonable efforts to complete whatever steps are necessary to finalize the permanent plan for the child;

(D) Whether the child was actively involved, as age- and developmentally appropriate, in the development of his or her own case plan and plan for permanent placement. If the court finds that the child was not appropriately involved, the court must order the probation department to actively involve the child in the development of his or her own case plan and plan for permanent placement, unless the court finds that the child is unable, unavailable, or unwilling to participate; and

(E) If sibling interaction has been suspended and will continue to be suspended, sibling interaction is contrary to the safety or well-being of either child.

(3) Information, Documents, and Services (§ 391)

If the youth is 16 years of age or older, the procedures in section 391 must be followed.

(A) If it is the first review hearing after the youth turns 16 years of age, the probation officer must provide the information, documents, and services required by section 391(a) and must use *First Review Hearing After Youth Turns 16 Years of Age—Information, Documents, and Services* **(form JV-361).**

(B) If it is the last review hearing before the youth turns 18 years of age, the probation officer must provide the information, documents, and services required by section 391(b)–(c) and must use *Review Hearing for Youth Approaching 18 Years of Age—Information, Documents, and Services* **(form JV-362).**

(C) If it is a review hearing after the youth turns 18 years of age, the probation officer must provide the information, documents, and services required by section 391(c) and must use *Review Hearing for Youth 18 Years of Age or Older—Information, Documents, and Services* **(form JV-363). If the court is terminating jurisdiction at this review hearing, the probation officer must also provide the information, documents, and services required by section 391(h), must follow the procedures in rule 5.555, and must use** *Termination of Juvenile Court Jurisdiction—Nonminor* **(form JV-365).**

(Subd (c) amended effective January 1, 2021; adopted effective January 1, 2001; previously amended effective January 1, 2003, January 1, 2007, January 1, 2014, January 1, 2016, and January 1, 2018.)

(d) Notice of hearings; service; contents (§ 727.4)

No earlier than 30 nor later than 15 calendar days before each hearing date, the probation officer must serve written notice on all persons entitled to notice under section 727.4, as well as the current caregiver, any CASA volunteer or educational rights holder, and all counsel of record. A *Notice of Hearing—Juvenile Delinquency Proceeding* (form JV-625) must be used.

(Subd (d) amended effective January 1, 2014; adopted effective January 1, 2001; previously amended effective January 1, 2003, January 1, 2006, and January 1, 2007.)

(e) Report (§§ 706.5, 706.6, 727.2(c), 727.3(a)(1), 727.4(b), 16002)

Before each hearing described above, the probation officer must investigate and prepare a social study report that must include an updated case plan and all of the information required in sections 706.5, 706.6, 727.2, 727.3, and 16002.

(1) The report must contain recommendations for court findings and orders and must document the evidentiary basis for those recommendations.

(2) At least 10 calendar days before each hearing, the probation officer must file the report and provide copies of the report to the ward, the parent or guardian, all attorneys of record, and any CASA volunteer.

(Subd (e) amended effective January 1, 2016; adopted as subd (b) effective January 1, 1991; previously amended and relettered as subd (e) effective January 1, 2001; previously amended effective January 1, 1998, January 1, 2003, January 1, 2007, and January 1, 2014.)

(f) Release of Information to the Medical Board of California

If the child has signed *Position on Release of Information to Medical Board of California* (form JV-228), the probation officer must provide the child with a blank copy of *Withdrawal of Release of Information to Medical Board of California* (form JV-229) before the hearing if it is the last hearing before the child turns 18 years of age or if the social worker is recommending termination of juvenile court jurisdiction.

(Subd (f) adopted effective September 1, 2020.)

Rule 5.810 amended effective January 1, 2021; adopted as rule 1496 effective January 1, 1991; previously amended and renumbered as rule 5.810 effective January 1, 2007; previously amended effective January 1, 1998, January 1, 2001, January 1, 2003, January 1, 2004, January 1, 2006, January 1, 2014, January 1, 2016, January 1, 2018, and September 1, 2020.

Rule 5.811. Modification to transition jurisdiction for a ward older than 17 years and 5 months with a petition subject to dismissal (Welf. & Inst. Code, §§ 450, 451, 727.2(i)–(j), 778; Pen. Code, § 236.14)

(a) Purpose

This rule provides the procedures that must be followed to modify delinquency jurisdiction to transition jurisdiction for a young person who is older than 17 years, 5 months of age and:

(1) Is under a foster care placement order;

(2) Wants to remain in extended foster care under the transition jurisdiction of the juvenile court;

(3) Is not receiving reunification services;

(4) Does not have a hearing set for termination of parental rights or establishment of guardianship; and

(5) The underlying adjudication establishing wardship over the young person is subject to vacatur under Penal Code section 236.14.

(Subd (a) adopted effective January 1, 2019.)

(b) Setting and conduct of hearing

(1) The probation officer must request a hearing for the court to modify delinquency jurisdiction to transition jurisdiction and vacate the underlying adjudication.

(2) The hearing must be held before a judicial officer and recorded by a court reporter.

(3) The hearing must be continued for no more than five court days for the submission of additional evidence if the court finds that the report and, if required, the Transitional Independent Living Case Plan submitted by the probation officer do not provide the information required by (d), and the court is unable to make all the findings required by (e).

(Subd (b) adopted effective January 1, 2019.)

(c) Notice of hearing

(1) The probation officer must serve written notice of the hearing in the manner provided in section 295.

(2) Proof of service of notice must be filed by the probation officer at least five court days before the hearing.

(Subd (c) adopted effective January 1, 2019.)

(d) Reports

At least 10 calendar days before the hearing, the probation officer must submit a report to the court that includes information regarding:

(1) Whether the young person is subject to an order for foster care placement and is older than 17 years, 5 months of age and younger than 18 years of age;

(2) Whether the young person is a nonminor who was subject to an order for foster care placement on the day of the young person's 18th birthday and is within the age eligibility requirements for extended foster care;

(3) Whether the young person was removed from the physical custody of his or her parents, adjudged to be within the jurisdiction of the juvenile court under section 725, and ordered into foster care placement; or whether the young person was removed from the custody of his or her parents as a dependent of the court with an order for foster care placement in effect at the time the court adjudged him or her to be within the jurisdiction of the juvenile court under section 725 and was ordered into a foster care placement, including the date of the initial removal findings—"continuance in the home is contrary to the child's welfare" and "reasonable efforts were made to prevent removal"—as well as whether the young person continues to be removed from the parents or legal guardian from whom the young person was removed under the original petition;

(4) Whether each parent or legal guardian is currently able to provide the care, custody, supervision, and support the child requires in a safe and healthy environment;

(5) Whether the young person signed a mutual agreement with the probation department or social services agency for placement in a supervised setting as a transition dependent and, if so, a recommendation as to which agency should be responsible for placement and care of the transition dependent;

(6) Whether the young person plans to meet at least one of the conditions in section 11403(b) and what efforts the probation officer has made to help the young person meet any of these conditions;

(7) When and how the young person was informed of the benefits of remaining under juvenile court jurisdiction as a transition dependent and the probation officer's assessment of the young person's understanding of those benefits;

(8) When and how the young person was informed that he or she may decline to become a transition dependent and have the juvenile court terminate jurisdiction at a hearing under section 391 and rule 5.555; and

(9) When and how the young person was informed that if juvenile court jurisdiction is terminated, he or she can file a request to return to foster care and have the court resume jurisdiction over him or her as a nonminor.

(Subd (d) adopted effective January 1, 2019.)

(e) Findings

At the hearing, the court must make the following findings:

(1) Whether notice has been given as required by law;

(2) Whether the underlying adjudication is subject to vacatur under Penal Code section 236.14;

(3) Whether the young person has been informed that he or she may decline to become a transition dependent and have juvenile court jurisdiction terminated at a hearing set under rule 5.555;

(4) Whether the young person intends to sign a mutual agreement with the probation department or social services agency for placement in a supervised setting as a nonminor dependent;

(5) Whether the young person was informed that if juvenile court jurisdiction is terminated, the young person can file a request to return to foster care and may have the court resume jurisdiction over the young person as a nonminor dependent;

(6) Whether the benefits of remaining under juvenile court jurisdiction as a nonminor dependent were explained and whether the young person understands them;

(7) Whether the young person's Transitional Independent Living Case Plan includes a plan for the young person to satisfy at least one of the conditions in section 11403(b); and

(8) Whether the young person has had an opportunity to confer with his or her attorney.

In addition to the findings listed above, for children who are older than 17 years, 5 months of age but younger than 18 years of age, the court must make the following findings:

(A) Whether the young person's return to the home of his or her parent or legal guardian would create a substantial risk of detriment to the young person's safety, protection, or physical or emotional well-being—the facts supporting this finding must be stated on the record;

(B) Whether reunification services have been terminated; and

(C) Whether the young person's case has been set for a hearing to terminate parental rights or establish a guardianship.

(Subd (e) adopted effective January 1, 2019.)

(f) Orders

The court must enter the following orders:

(1) An order adjudging the young person a transition dependent as of the date of the hearing or pending his or her 18th birthday and granting status as a nonminor dependent under the general jurisdiction of the court. The order modifying the court's jurisdiction must contain all of the following provisions:

(A) A statement that "continuance in the home is contrary to the child or nonminor's welfare" and that "reasonable efforts have been made to prevent or eliminate the need for removal";

(B) A statement that the child continues to be removed from the parents or legal guardian from whom the child was removed under the original petition; and

(C) Identification of the agency that is responsible for placement and care of the child based on the modification of jurisdiction.

(2) An order vacating the underlying adjudication and dismissing the associated delinquency petition under Penal Code section 236.14.

(3) An order directing the Department of Justice and any law enforcement agency that has records of the arrest to seal those records and, three years from the date of the arrest or one year after the order to seal, whichever occurs later, destroy them.

(4) An order continuing the appointment of the attorney of record, or appointing a new attorney as the attorney of record for the nonminor dependent.

(5) An order setting a nonminor dependent status review hearing under section 366.31 and rule 5.903 within six months of the last hearing held under section 727.2 or 727.3.

(Subd (f) adopted effective January 1, 2019.)
Rule 5.811 adopted effective January 1, 2019.

Rule 5.812. Additional requirements for any hearing to terminate jurisdiction over child in foster care and for status review or dispositional hearing for child approaching majority (§§ 450, 451, 727.2(i)–(j), 778)

(a) Hearings subject to this rule

The following hearings are subject to this rule:

(1) The last review hearing under section 727.2 or 727.3 before the child turns 18 years of age and a dispositional hearing under section 702 for a child under an order of foster care placement who will attain 18 years of age before a subsequent review hearing will be held. If the hearing is the last review hearing under section 727.2 or 727.3, the hearing must be set at least 90 days before the child attains his or her 18th birthday and within six months of the previous hearing held under section 727.2 or 727.3.

(2) Any review hearing held under section 727.2 or 727.3 for a child less than 18 years of age during which a recommendation to terminate juvenile court jurisdiction will be considered;

(3) Any hearing to terminate juvenile court jurisdiction over a child less than 18 years of age who is subject to an order for foster care placement; and

(4) Any hearing to terminate juvenile court jurisdiction over a child less than 18 years of age who is not currently subject to an order for foster care placement but was previously removed from the custody of his or her parents or legal guardian as a dependent of the juvenile court and an order for a foster care placement as a dependent of the juvenile court was in effect at the time the juvenile court adjudged the child to be a ward of the juvenile court under section 725.

(Subd (a) amended effective January 1, 2016; adopted effective January 1, 2012; previously amended effective July 1, 2012.)

(b) Conduct of the hearing

(1) The hearing must be held before a judicial officer and recorded by a court reporter.

(2) The hearing must be continued for no more than five court days for the submission of additional information as ordered by the court if the court finds that the report and, if required, the Transitional Independent Living Case Plan and Transitional Independent Living Plan submitted by the probation officer do not provide the information required by (c) and the court is unable to make all the findings required by (d).

(Subd (b) amended effective July 1, 2012; adopted effective January 1, 2012.)

(c) Reports

(1) In addition to complying with all other statutory and rule requirements applicable to the report prepared by the probation officer for a hearing described in (a)(1)–(4), the report must state whether the child was provided with the notices and information required under section 607.5 and include a description of:

(A) The child's progress toward meeting the case plan goals that will enable him or her to be a law-abiding and productive member of his or her family and the community. This information is not required if dismissal of delinquency jurisdiction and vacatur of the underlying adjudication is based on Penal Code section 236.14.

(B) If reunification services have not been previously terminated, the progress of each parent or legal guardian toward participating in case plan service activities and meeting the case plan goals developed to resolve his or her issues that were identified and contributed to the child's removal from his or her custody.

(C) The current ability of each parent or legal guardian to provide the care, custody, supervision, and support the child requires in a safe and healthy environment.

(D) For a child previously determined to be a dual status child for whom juvenile court jurisdiction as a dependent was suspended under section 241.1(e)(5)(A), a joint assessment by the probation department and the child welfare services agency under section 366.5 regarding the detriment, if any, to the child of a return to the home of his or her parents or legal guardian and a recommendation on the resumption of dependency jurisdiction. The facts in support of the opinions expressed and the recommendations made must be included in the joint assessment section of the report. If the probation department and the child welfare services agency do not agree, the child welfare services agency must file a separate report with facts in support of its opinions and recommendations.

(E) For a child previously determined to be a dual status child for whom the probation department was designated the lead agency under section 241.1(e)(5)(B), the detriment, if any, to the child of a return to the home of his or her parents or legal guardian and the probation officer's recommendation regarding the modification of the court's jurisdiction over the child from that of a dual status child to that of a dependent under section 300 and the facts in support of the opinion expressed and the recommendation made.

(F) For a child other than a dual status child, including a child whose underlying adjudication is subject to vacatur under Penal Code section 236.14, the probation officer's recommendation regarding the modification of the juvenile court's jurisdiction over the child from that of a ward under section 601 or 602 to that of a dependent under section 300 or to that of a transition dependent under section 450 and the facts in support of his or her recommendation.

(2) For the review hearing held on behalf of a child approaching majority described in (a)(1) and any hearing described in (a)(2) or (a)(3) held on behalf of a child more than 17 years, 5 months old and less than 18 years of age, in addition to complying with all other report requirements set forth in (c)(1), the report prepared by the probation officer must include:

(A) The child's plans to remain under juvenile court jurisdiction as a nonminor dependent including the criteria in section 11403(b) that he or she plans to meet;

(B) The efforts made by the probation officer to help the child meet one or more of the criteria in section 11403(b);

(C) For an Indian child, his or her plans to continue to be considered an Indian child for the purposes of the ongoing application of the Indian Child Welfare Act to him or her as a nonminor dependent;

(D) Whether the child has applied for and, if so, the status of any in-progress application pending for title XVI Supplemental Security Income benefits and, if such an application is pending, whether it is in the child's best interest to continue juvenile court jurisdiction until a final decision has been issued to ensure that the child receives continued assistance with the application process;

(E) Whether the child has an in-progress application pending for Special Immigrant Juvenile Status or other applicable application for legal residency and whether an active juvenile court case is required for that application;

(F) The efforts made by the probation officer toward providing the child with the written information, documents, and services described in section 391 and, to the extent that the child has not yet been provided with them, the barriers to providing the information, documents or services and the steps that will be taken to overcome those barriers by the date the child attains 18 years of age;

(G) When and how the child was informed that upon reaching 18 years of age he or she may request the dismissal of juvenile court jurisdiction over him or her under section 778;

(H) When and how the child was provided with information regarding the potential benefits of remaining under juvenile court jurisdiction as a nonminor dependent and the probation officer's assessment of the child's understanding of those benefits;

(I) When and how the child was informed that if juvenile court jurisdiction is terminated after he or she attains 18 years of age, he or she has the right to file a request to return to foster care and have the juvenile court assume or resume transition jurisdiction over him or her as a nonminor dependent; and

(J) The child's Transitional Independent Living Case Plan and Transitional Independent Living Plan, which must include:

(i) The individualized plan for the child to satisfy one or more of the criteria in section 11403(b) and the child's anticipated placement as specified in section 11402; and

(ii) The child's alternate plan for his or her transition to independence, including housing, education, employment, and a support system in the event the child does not remain under juvenile court jurisdiction after attaining 18 years of age.

(Subd (c) amended effective January 1, 2019; adopted effective January 1, 2012; previously amended effective July 1, 2012.)

(d) Findings

(1) At the hearing described in (a)(1)–(4), in addition to complying with all other statutory and rule requirements applicable to the hearing, the court must make the following findings in the written documentation of the hearing:

(A) Whether the rehabilitative goals for this child have been met and juvenile court jurisdiction over the child as a ward is no longer required.

The facts supporting the finding must be stated on the record. This finding is not required where dismissal of delinquency jurisdiction is based on Penal Code section 236.14.

(B) For a dual status child for whom dependency jurisdiction was suspended under section 241.1(e)(5)(A), whether the return to the home of the parents or legal guardian would be detrimental to the minor. The facts supporting the finding must be stated on the record.

(C) For a child previously determined to be a dual status child for whom the probation department was designated the lead agency under section 241.1(e)(5)(B), whether the return to the home of the parents or legal guardian would be detrimental to the minor. The facts supporting the finding must be stated on the record.

(D) For a child other than a dual status child:

(i) Who was not subject to the court's dependency jurisdiction at the time he or she was adjudged a ward and is currently subject to an order for a foster care placement, including a child whose underlying adjudication is subject to vacatur under Penal Code section 236.14, whether the child appears to come within the description of section 300 and cannot be returned home safely. The facts supporting the finding must be stated on the record;

(ii) Who was subject to an order for a foster care placement as a dependent of the court at the time he or she was adjudged a ward, whether the child remains within the description of a dependent child under section 300 and whether the return to the home of the parents or legal guardian would create a substantial risk of detriment to the child's safety, protection, or physical or emotional well-being. The facts supporting the findings must be stated on the record;

(iii) Whether reunification services have been terminated;

(iv) Whether the matter has been set for a hearing to terminate parental rights or establish a guardianship; and

(v) Whether the minor intends to sign a mutual agreement for a placement in a supervised setting as a nonminor dependent.

(2) At the review hearing held on behalf of a child approaching majority described in (a)(1) and any hearing under (a)(2) or (a)(3) held on behalf of a child more than 17 years, 5 months old and less than 18 years of age, in addition to complying with all other statutory and rule requirements applicable to the hearing, the court must make the following findings in the written documentation of the hearing:

(A) Whether the child's Transitional Independent Living Case Plan, if required, or Transitional Independent Living Plan includes:

(i) A plan specific to the child for him or her to satisfy one or more of the criteria in section 11403(b) and the specific criteria in section 11403(b) it is anticipated the child will satisfy; and

(ii) The child's alternate plan for his or her transition to independence, including housing, education, employment, and a support system in the event the child does not remain under juvenile court jurisdiction after attaining 18 years of age.

(B) For an Indian child to whom the Indian Child Welfare Act applies, whether he or she intends to continue to be considered an Indian child for the purposes of the ongoing application of the Indian Child Welfare Act to him or her as a nonminor dependent;

(C) Whether the child has an in-progress application pending for title XVI Supplemental Security Income benefits and, if such an application is pending, whether it is in the child's best interest to continue juvenile court jurisdiction until a final decision has been issued to ensure that the child receives continued assistance with the application process;

(D) Whether the child has an in-progress application pending for Special Immigrant Juvenile Status or other applicable application for legal residency and whether an active juvenile court case is required for that application;

(E) Whether the child has been informed that he or she may decline to become a nonminor dependent;

(F) Whether the child has been informed that upon reaching 18 years of age he or she may request the dismissal of juvenile court jurisdiction over him or her under section 778;

(G) Whether the child understands the potential benefits of remaining under juvenile court jurisdiction as a nonminor dependent;

(H) Whether the child has been informed that if after reaching 18 years of age juvenile court jurisdiction is terminated, he or she has the right to file a request to return to foster care and have the juvenile court assume or resume transition jurisdiction over him or her as a nonminor dependent;

(I) Whether all the information, documents, and services in sections 391(e) were provided to the child, and whether the barriers to providing any missing information, documents, or services can be overcome by the date the child attains 18 years of age; and

(J) Whether the notices and information required under section 607.5 were provided to a child who is or was subject to an order for foster care placement.

(Subd (d) amended effective January 1, 2019; adopted effective January 1, 2012; previously amended effective July 1, 2012, and January 1, 2014.)

(e) Orders

(1) For a child previously determined to be a dual status child for whom dependency jurisdiction was suspended under section 241.1(e)(5)(A), dependency jurisdiction must be resumed if the court finds that the child's rehabilitative goals have been achieved and a return to the home of the parents or legal guardian would be detrimental to the child.

(2) For a child previously determined to be a dual status child for whom the probation department was designated the lead agency under section 241.1(e)(5)(B), the court must terminate dual status, dismiss delinquency jurisdiction, and continue dependency jurisdiction with the child welfare services department responsible for the child's placement if the court finds that the child's rehabilitative goals have been achieved and a return to the home of the parents or legal guardian would be detrimental to the child.

(3) For a child who comes within the description of section 450(a), other than a child described in (e)(1) or (e)(2), the court must enter an order modifying its jurisdiction over him or her from delinquency jurisdiction to transition jurisdiction and set a nonminor dependent status review hearing under rule 5.903 within six months of the last hearing held under section 727.2.

(4) For a child who was not subject to the court's dependency jurisdiction at the time he or she was adjudged a ward and is currently subject to an order for a foster care placement, including a child whose underlying adjudication is subject to vacatur under Penal Code section 236.14, the court must:

(A) Order the probation department or the child's attorney to submit an application under section 329 to the county child welfare services department to commence a proceeding to declare the child a dependent of the court by filing a petition under section 300 if the court finds:

(i) The child does not come within the description of section 450(a);

(ii) The rehabilitative goals for the child included in his or her case plan have been met and delinquency jurisdiction is no longer required, or the underlying adjudication is subject to vacatur under Penal Code section 236.14; and

(iii) The child appears to come within the description of section 300 and a return to the home of the parents or legal guardian may be detrimental to his or her safety, protection, or physical or emotional well-being.

(B) Set a hearing to review the county child welfare services department's decision within 20 court days of the date the order to file an application under section 329 was entered and at that hearing:

(i) Affirm the county child welfare services department's decision not to file a petition under section 300; or

(ii) Order the county child welfare services department to file a petition under section 300.

(C) If the court affirms the decision not to file a petition under section 300 or a petition filed under section 300 is not sustained, the court may:

(i) Return the child to the home of the parents or legal guardian and set a progress report hearing within the next six months;

(ii) Return the child to the home of the parents or legal guardian and terminate juvenile court jurisdiction over the child; or

(iii) Continue the child's foster care placement and set a hearing under section 727.2 no more than six months from the date of the most recent hearing held under 727.2.

(5) For a child who was subject to an order for foster care placement as a dependent of the court at the time he or she was adjudged a ward, the court must modify its delinquency jurisdiction over the child by vacating the order terminating jurisdiction over the child as a dependent of the court and resuming dependency jurisdiction over him or her if the court finds that:

(A) The child does not come within the description of section 450(a);

(B) The rehabilitative goals for the child included in his or her case plan have been met and delinquency jurisdiction may not be required; and

(C) The child remains within the description of a dependent child under section 300 and a return to the home of a parents or legal guardian would create a substantial risk of detriment to his or her safety, protection, or physical or emotional well-being.

(6) At a hearing described in (a)(1) for a child approaching majority or at any hearing described in (a)(2) or (a)(3) held on behalf of a child more than 17 years, 5 months old and less than 18 years old that did not result in modification of jurisdiction over the child from delinquency jurisdiction to dependency jurisdiction or transition jurisdiction, the court must:

(A) Return the child to the home of the parents or legal guardian and set a progress report hearing within the next six months; or

(B) Return the child to the home of the parents or legal guardian and terminate juvenile court jurisdiction over the child; or

(C) Continue the child's foster care placement and:

(i) For the child who intends to meet the eligibility requirements for status as a nonminor dependent after attaining 18 years of age, set a nonminor dependent status review hearing under rule 5.903 no more than six months from the most recent hearing held under section 727.2; or

(ii) For the child who does not intend to meet the eligibility requirements for nonminor dependent status after attaining 18 years of age:

a. Set a hearing to terminate delinquency jurisdiction under section 607.2(b)(4) and section 607.3 for a date within one month after the child's 18th birthday; or

b. Set a hearing under section 727.2 no more than six months from the date of the most recent hearing held under section 727.2 for the child who will remain under delinquency jurisdiction in a foster care placement.

(7) At any hearing under (a)(2) or (a)(3) held on behalf of a child 17 years, 5 months old or younger that did not result in modification of jurisdiction over the child from delinquency jurisdiction to dependency jurisdiction, the court must:

(A) Return the child to the home of the parents or legal guardian and set a progress report hearing within the next six months;

(B) Return the child to the home of the parents or legal guardian and terminate juvenile court jurisdiction over the child; or

(C) Continue the child's out-of-home placement and set a hearing under section 727.2 to occur within six months of the most recent hearing under section 727.2.

(8) At any hearing under (a)(4) on behalf of a child less than 18 years of age that did not result in modification of jurisdiction over the child from delinquency jurisdiction to dependency jurisdiction, the court must:

(A) Return the child to the home of the parents or legal guardian and set a progress report hearing within the next six months;

(B) Return the child to the home of the parents or legal guardian and terminate juvenile court jurisdiction over the child; or

(C) Continue the child's out-of-home placement and set a progress report hearing within the next six months.

(Subd (e) amended effective January 1, 2019; adopted effective January 1, 2012; previously amended effective July 1, 2012.)

(f) Modification of jurisdiction—conditions

(1) Whenever the court modifies its jurisdiction over a dependent or ward under section 241.1, 607.2, or 727.2, the court must ensure that all of the following conditions are met:

(A) The petition under which jurisdiction was taken at the time the dependent or ward was originally removed from his or her parents or legal guardian and placed in foster care is not dismissed until after the new petition is sustained; and

(B) The order modifying the court's jurisdiction contains all of the following provisions:

(i) A reference to the original removal findings, the date those findings were made, and a statement that the finding "continuation in the home is contrary to the child's welfare" and the finding "reasonable efforts were made to prevent removal" made at that hearing remain in effect;

(ii) A statement that the child continues to be removed from the parents or legal guardian from whom the child was removed under the original petition; and

(iii) Identification of the agency that is responsible for placement and care of the child based upon the modification of jurisdiction.

(2) Whenever the court modifies jurisdiction over a young person under section 450(a)(1)(B), the court must ensure that all of the following conditions are met:

(A) The order modifying the court's jurisdiction must be made before the underlying petition is vacated;

(B) The order modifying jurisdiction must contain the following provisions:

(i) Continuance in the home is contrary the child's welfare, and reasonable efforts were made to prevent removal;

(ii) The child continues to be removed from the parents or legal guardians;

(iii) Identification of the agency that is responsible for placement and care of the young person based on modification of jurisdiction;

(iv) A statement that the underlying adjudication is vacated and the arrest upon which it was based is expunged; and

(v) An order directing the Department of Justice and any law enforcement agency that has records of the arrest to seal those records and destroy them three years from the date of the arrest or one year after the order to seal, whichever occurs later.

(Subd (f) amended effective January 1, 2019; adopted effective January 1, 2012; previously amended effective July 1, 2012.)

Rule 5.812 amended effective January 1, 2019; adopted effective January 1, 2012; previously amended effective July 1, 2012, January 1, 2014, and January 1, 2016.

Rule 5.813. Modification to transition jurisdiction for a ward older than 18 years and younger than 21 years of age (§§ 450, 451)

(a) Purpose

This rule provides the procedures that must be followed when it appears to a probation officer that a ward who is at least 18 years of age and younger than 21 years of age has met his or her rehabilitative goals and wants to remain in extended foster care under the jurisdiction of the court.

(Subd (a) adopted effective January 1, 2014.)

(b) Setting and conduct of hearing

(1) The probation officer must request a hearing for the court to consider modifying delinquency jurisdiction to transition jurisdiction.

(2) The hearing must be held before a judicial officer and recorded by a court reporter.

(3) The hearing must be continued for no more than five court days for the submission of additional evidence as ordered by the court if the court finds that the report and, if required, the Transitional Independent Living Case Plan submitted by the probation officer do not provide the information required by (d) and the court is unable to make all the findings required by (e).

(Subd (b) adopted effective January 1, 2014.)

(c) Notice of hearing

(1) The probation officer must serve written notice of the hearing in the manner provided in section 295.

(2) Proof of service of notice must be filed by the probation officer at least five court days before the hearing.

(Subd (c) adopted effective January 1, 2014.)

(d) Reports

At least 10 calendar days before the hearing, the probation officer must submit a report to the court that includes information regarding:

(1) Whether the ward is a nonminor who was subject to an order for foster care placement on the day of the ward's 18th birthday and is within the age eligibility requirements for extended foster care;

(2) Whether the ward was removed from the physical custody of his or her parents, adjudged to be a ward of the juvenile court under section 725, and ordered into foster care placement as a ward; or whether the ward was removed from the custody of his or her parents as a dependent of the court with an order for foster care placement in effect at the time the court adjudged him or her to be a ward of the juvenile court under section 725 and was ordered into a foster care placement as a ward, including the date of the initial removal findings—"continuance in the home is contrary to the child's welfare" and "reasonable efforts were made to prevent removal"—as well as whether the ward continues to be removed from the parents or legal guardian from whom the child was removed under the original petition;

(3) Whether the ward's rehabilitative goals as stated in the case plan have been met and whether juvenile court jurisdiction over the ward is no longer required;

(4) Whether the probation officer recommends the modification of juvenile court jurisdiction over the ward from that of a ward under section 601 or 602 to that of a nonminor dependent under section 450 and the facts in support of that recommendation;

(5) Whether the ward signed a mutual agreement with the probation department or social services agency for placement in a supervised setting as a nonminor dependent and, if so, a recommendation as to which agency should be responsible for placement and care of the nonminor dependent;

(6) Whether the ward plans to meet at least one of the conditions in section 11403(b) and what efforts the probation officer has made to help the ward meet any of the conditions;

(7) When and how the ward was informed of the benefits of remaining under juvenile court jurisdiction as a nonminor dependent and the probation officer's assessment of the ward's understanding of those benefits;

(8) When and how the ward was informed that he or she may decline to become a nonminor dependent and have the juvenile court terminate jurisdiction at a hearing under section 391 and rule 5.555; and

(9) When and how the ward was informed that if juvenile court jurisdiction is terminated, he or she can file a request to return to foster care and have the court resume jurisdiction over him or her as a nonminor.

(Subd (d) adopted effective January 1, 2014.)

(e) Findings

At the hearing described in (a), the court must make the following findings:

(1) Whether notice has been given as required by law;

(2) Whether the nonminor comes within the description of section 450;

(3) Whether the ward has been informed that he or she may decline to become a nonminor dependent and have juvenile court jurisdiction terminated at a hearing set under rule 5.555;

(4) Whether the ward was informed that if juvenile court jurisdiction is terminated, the ward can file a request to return to foster care and may have the court resume jurisdiction over the ward as a nonminor;

(5) Whether the benefits of remaining under juvenile court jurisdiction as a nonminor dependent were explained and whether the ward understands them;

(6) Whether the ward has signed a mutual agreement with the probation department for placement in a supervised setting as a nonminor dependent;

(7) Whether the ward's Transitional Independent Living Case Plan includes a plan for the ward to satisfy at least one of the conditions in section 11403(b); and

(8) Whether the ward has had an opportunity to confer with his or her attorney.

(Subd (e) adopted effective January 1, 2014.)

(f) Orders

For a child who comes within the description of section 450(a), the court must enter the following orders:

(1) An order modifying the court's jurisdiction over the child from delinquency to transition jurisdiction and setting a nonminor dependent status review hearing under section 366.31 and rule 5.903 within six months of the last hearing held under section 727.2 or 366.31. The order modifying the court's jurisdiction must contain all of the following provisions:

(A) A reference to the initial removal findings, the date those findings were made, and a statement that the findings—"continuance in the home is contrary to the child's welfare" and "reasonable efforts were made to prevent removal"—made at that hearing remain in effect;

(B) A statement that the nonminor dependent continues to be removed from the parents or legal guardian from whom the nonminor dependent was removed under the original petition; and

(C) Identification of the agency that is responsible for placement and care of the nonminor dependent based on the modification of jurisdiction.

(2) An order continuing the appointment of the attorney of record or appointing a new attorney as the attorney of record for the nonminor dependent.

(Subd (f) adopted effective January 1, 2014.)

Rule 5.813 adopted effective January 1, 2014.

Rule 5.814. Modification to transition jurisdiction for a ward older than 17 years, 5 months of age and younger than 18 years of age (§§ 450, 451)

(a) Purpose

This rule provides the procedures that must be followed to modify delinquency jurisdiction to transition jurisdiction for a ward who is older than 17 years, 5 months of age, younger than 18 years of age, and:

(1) Has met his or her rehabilitative goals;

(2) Is under a foster care placement order;

(3) Wants to remain in extended foster care under the transition jurisdiction of the juvenile court;

(4) Is not receiving reunification services; and

(5) Does not have a hearing set for termination of parental rights or establishment of guardianship.

(Subd (a) adopted effective January 1, 2014.)

(b) Setting and conduct of hearing

(1) The probation officer must request a hearing for the court to consider modifying delinquency jurisdiction to transition jurisdiction.

(2) The hearing must be held before a judicial officer and recorded by a court reporter.

(3) The hearing must be continued for no more than five court days for the submission of additional evidence as ordered by the court if the court finds that the report and, if required, the Transitional Independent Living Case Plan submitted by the probation officer, do not provide the information required by (d) and the court is unable to make all the findings required by (e).

(Subd (b) adopted effective January 1, 2014.)

(c) Notice of hearing

(1) The probation officer must serve written notice of the hearing in the manner provided in section 295.

(2) Proof of service of notice must be filed by the probation officer at least five court days before the hearing.

(Subd (c) adopted effective January 1, 2014.)

(d) Reports

At least 10 calendar days before the hearing, the probation officer must submit a report to the court that includes information regarding:

(1) Whether the ward is subject to an order for foster care placement and is older than 17 years, 5 months of age and younger than 18 years of age;

(2) Whether the ward was removed from the physical custody of his or her parents, adjudged to be a ward of the juvenile court under section 725, and ordered into foster care placement as a ward; or whether the ward was removed from the custody of his or her parents as a dependent of the court with an order for foster care placement in effect at the time the court adjudged him or her to be a ward of the juvenile court under section 725 and was ordered into a foster care placement as a ward, including the date of the initial removal findings—"continuance in the home is contrary to the child's welfare" and "reasonable efforts were made to prevent removal"—as well as whether the ward continues to be removed from the parents or legal guardian from whom the child was removed under the original petition;

(3) Whether the ward's rehabilitative goals as stated in the case plan have been met and whether juvenile court jurisdiction over the ward is no longer required;

(4) Whether each parent or legal guardian is currently able to provide the care, custody, supervision, and support the child requires in a safe and healthy environment;

(5) Whether the probation officer recommends the modification of the juvenile court's jurisdiction over the ward from that of a ward under section 601 or 602 to that of a transition dependent under section 450;

(6) Whether the ward signed a mutual agreement with the probation department or social services agency for placement in a supervised setting as a transition dependent and, if so, a recommendation as to which agency should be responsible for placement and care of the transition dependent;

(7) Whether the ward plans to meet at least one of the conditions in section 11403(b) and what efforts the probation officer has made to help the ward meet any of these conditions;

(8) When and how the ward was informed of the benefits of remaining under juvenile court jurisdiction as a transition dependent and the probation officer's assessment of the ward's understanding of those benefits;

(9) When and how the ward was informed that he or she may decline to become a transition dependent and have the juvenile court terminate jurisdiction at a hearing under section 391 and rule 5.555; and

(10) When and how the ward was informed that if juvenile court jurisdiction is terminated, he or she can file a request to return to foster care and have the court resume jurisdiction over him or her as a nonminor.

(Subd (d) adopted effective January 1, 2014.)

(e) Findings

At the hearing, the court must make the following findings:

(1) Whether notice has been given as required by law;

(2) Whether the ward comes within the description of section 450;

(3) Whether the ward has been informed that he or she may decline to become a transition dependent and have juvenile court jurisdiction terminated at a hearing set under rule 5.555;

(4) Whether the ward's return to the home of his or her parent or legal guardian would create a substantial risk of detriment to the ward's safety, protection, or physical or emotional well-being. The facts supporting this finding must be stated on the record;

(5) Whether reunification services have been terminated;

(6) Whether the ward's case has been set for a hearing to terminate parental rights or establish a guardianship;

(7) Whether the ward intends to sign a mutual agreement with the probation department or social services agency for placement in a supervised setting as a nonminor dependent;

(8) Whether the ward was informed that if juvenile court jurisdiction is terminated, the ward can file a request to return to foster care and may have the court resume jurisdiction over the ward as a nonminor dependent;

(9) Whether the benefits of remaining under juvenile court jurisdiction as a nonminor dependent were explained and whether the ward understands them;

(10) Whether the ward's Transitional Independent Living Case Plan includes a plan for the ward to satisfy at least one of the conditions in section 11403(b); and

(11) Whether the ward has had an opportunity to confer with his or her attorney.

(Subd (e) adopted effective January 1, 2014.)

(f) Orders

For a child who comes within the description of section 450(a), the court must enter the following orders:

(1) An order modifying the court's jurisdiction over the child from delinquency to transition jurisdiction and adjudging the ward a transition dependent pending his or her 18th birthday and status as a nonminor dependent under the transition jurisdiction of the court. The order modifying the court's jurisdiction must contain all of the following provisions:

(A) A reference to the initial removal findings, the date those findings were made, and a statement that the findings—"continuance in the home is contrary to the child's welfare" and "reasonable efforts were made to prevent removal"—made at that hearing remain in effect;

(B) A statement that the child continues to be removed from the parents or legal guardian from whom the child was removed under the original petition; and

(C) Identification of the agency that is responsible for placement and care of the child based on the modification of jurisdiction.

(2) An order continuing the appointment of the attorney of record, or appointing a new attorney, as the attorney of record for the nonminor dependent.

(3) An order setting a nonminor dependent status review hearing under section 366.31 and rule 5.903 within six months of the last hearing held under section 727.2 or 727.3.

(Subd (f) adopted effective January 1, 2014.)
Rule 5.814 adopted effective January 1, 2014.

Rule 5.815. Legal guardianship—wards (§§ 366.26, 727.3, 728)

(a) Proceedings in juvenile court

Proceedings for the appointment of a legal guardian for a child who is a ward of the juvenile court [1] may be held in the juvenile court **under the procedures specified in section 366.26.**

(Subd (a) amended effective January 1, 2021; previously amended effective January 1, 2007.)

Rule 5.815(a). 2020 Deletes. [1] under section 725(b)

(b) Hearing to consider guardianship

On the recommendation of the probation officer supervising the child **in the social study and case plan required by sections 706.5(c)–(d) and 706.6(n),** the motion of the **child's** attorney [1] **under section 778,** or the court's [2] **determination under section 727.3** that a legal [3] **guardianship is the appropriate permanent plan** for the child, the court must set a hearing to consider the establishment of a legal guardianship and must order the probation officer to prepare an assessment that includes:

(1) [4] **All the elements required to be addressed in the assessment prepared under Welfare and Institutions Code section 727.31(b); and**

(2) A statement confirming that the proposed guardian has been provided with a copy of [5] *Becoming a Child's Guardian in Juvenile*

Court (form JV-350-INFO) or *La función de un tutor nombrado por la corte de menores* (form JV-350-INFO S).

(Subd (b) amended effective January 1, 2021; previously amended effective January 1, 2007.)

Rule 5.815(b).   2020 Deletes. [1] representing the child [2] own motion and order [3] guardian should be appointed [4] A review of the existing relationship between the child and the proposed guardian; (2) A summary of the child's medical, developmental, educational, mental, and emotional status; (3) A social history of the proposed guardian, including a screening for criminal records and any prior referrals for child abuse or neglect; (4) An assessment of the ability of the proposed guardian to meet the child's needs and the proposed guardian's understanding of the legal and financial rights and responsibilities of guardianship; and (5) [5] *Guardianship Pamphlet* (form JV-350) or *Guardianship Pamphlet (Spanish)* (form JV-350S)

(c) Probation officer's recommendation

The probation [1] **officer's recommendation for appointment of a legal guardian may be included in the social study report and case plan submitted under sections 706.5 and 706.6. Neither a separate petition nor a separate hearing is required.**

(Subd (c) amended effective January 1, 2021; previously amended effective January 1, 2007.)

Rule 5.815(c).   2020 Deletes. [1] officer or child's attorney may use *Juvenile Wardship Petition* (form JV-600) and *Petition to Modify Previous Orders—Change of Circumstances* (form JV-740) to request that a guardianship hearing be set

(d) Notice (§ 728(c))

The clerk must provide notice of the hearing to the child, the child's parents, and other individuals as required by section 294.

(Subd (d) amended effective July 1, 2016.)

(e) Conduct of hearing

The proceedings for appointment of a legal guardian must be conducted according to the procedural requirements of section 366.26, except for subdivision (j). The court must read and consider the assessment prepared by the probation officer and any other **relevant** evidence. The preparer of the assessment must be available for examination by the court or any party to the proceedings.

(Subd (e) amended effective January 1, 2021.)

(f) Findings and orders

If the court [1] **makes the necessary findings under section 366.26(c)(4)(A),** the court must appoint a legal guardian **for the child** and order the clerk to issue letters of guardianship *(Letters of Guardianship (Juvenile)* (form JV-330)) **as soon as the appointed guardian has signed them. These letters are not subject to the confidentiality protections in section 827**.

(1) The court may issue orders regarding visitation and contact between the child and a parent or other relative.

(2) After the appointment of a legal guardian, the court may continue juvenile court wardship and supervision or may terminate wardship.

(Subd (f) amended effective January 1, 2021; previously amended effective July 1, 2006, and January 1, 2007.)

Rule 5.815(f).   2020 Deletes. [1] finds that establishment of a legal guardianship is necessary or convenient and consistent with the rehabilitation and protection of the child and with public safety

(g) Modification or termination of juvenile court guardianship

A petition to **modify or** terminate a **legal** guardianship established by the juvenile court, **including a petition** to appoint a co-guardian or successor guardian, [1] **must be filed and heard in juvenile court.** The procedures described in rule 5.570 must be followed, and [2] *Request to Change Court Order* (form JV-180) must be used. The hearing on the [3] **petition** may be held [4] **concurrently** with any regularly scheduled hearing regarding the child.

(Subd (g) amended effective January 1, 2021; previously amended effective January 1, 2007.)

Rule 5.815(g).   2020 Deletes. [1] or to modify or supplement orders regarding the guardianship [2] *Juvenile Wardship Petition* (form JV-600) and *Petition to Modify Previous Orders—Change of Circumstances* (form JV-740) [3] motion [4] simultaneously

Rule 5.815 amended effective January 1, 2021; adopted as rule 1496.2 effective January 1, 2004; previously amended effective July 1, 2006, and July 1, 2016; previously amended and renumbered as rule 5.815 effective January 1, 2007.

Rule 5.820.   Termination of parental rights for child in foster care for 15 of the last 22 months

(a) Requirement (§§ 727.32(a), 16508.1)

Whenever a child has been declared a ward and has been in any foster care placement for 15 of the most recent 22 months, the probation department must follow the procedures described in section 727.31 to terminate the parental rights of the child's parents. The probation department is not required to follow these procedures if it has documented a compelling reason in the probation file, as defined in section 727.3(c), for determining that termination of parental rights would not be in the child's best interest, or if it has not provided the family with reasonable efforts necessary to achieve reunification.

(1) If the probation department sets a hearing under section 727.31, it must also make efforts to identify an approved family for adoption.

(2) If the probation department has determined that a compelling reason exists, it must document that reason in the case file. The documentation may be a separate document or may be included in another court document, such as the social study prepared for a permanency planning hearing.

(Subd (a) amended effective January 1, 2007.)

(b) Calculating time in foster care (§ 727.32(d))

The following guidelines must be used to determine if the child has been in foster care for 15 of the most recent 22 months:

(1) Determine the date the child entered foster care, as defined in rule 5.502(a)(9). In some cases, this will be the date the child entered foster care as a dependent.

(2) Calculate the total number of months since the date in (1) that the child has spent in foster care. Do not start over if a new petition is filed or for any other reason.

(3) If the child is in foster care for a portion of a month, calculate the total number of days in foster care during that month. Add one month to the total number of months for every 30 days the child is in foster care.

(4) Exclude time during which the child was detained in the home of a parent or guardian; the child was living at home on formal or informal probation, at home on a trial home visit, or at home with no probationary status; the child was a runaway or "absent without leave" (AWOL); or the child was out of home in a non–foster care setting, including juvenile hall; California Department of Corrections and Rehabilitation, Division of Juvenile Justice; a ranch; a camp; a school; or any other locked facility.

(5) Once the total number of months in foster care has been calculated, determine how many of those months occurred within the most recent 22 months. If that number is 15 or more, the requirement in (a) applies.

(6) If the requirement in (a) has been satisfied once, there is no need to take additional action or provide additional documentation after any subsequent 22-month period.

(Subd (b) amended effective January 1, 2007; previously amended effective January 1, 2006.)

Rule 5.820 amended and renumbered effective January 1, 2007; adopted as rule 1496.3 effective January 1, 2003; previously amended effective January 1, 2006.

Rule 5.825.   Freeing wards for adoption

(a) Applicable law (§§ 294, 366.26, 727.2, 727.3, 727.31)

Except as provided in section 727.31, the procedures for termination of parental rights to free children described in that section for adoption are stated in sections 294 and 366.26. Rules 5.725 and 5.730 are applicable to these proceedings.

(Subd (a) amended effective January 1, 2007; previously amended effective January 1, 2006.)

(b) Joint county protocol

In each county, the county probation department and the county child welfare department must jointly develop a protocol for freeing wards for adoption. The protocol should address questions such as:

(1) When and how will wards be referred to the licensed county adoption agency, or State Department of Social Services when it is acting as the adoption agency, for a determination of whether the ward is adoptable, as described by section 727.3(i)(2)?

(2) Once a finding has been made that the permanent plan for the ward must be adoption and the case is set for a section 727.31 hearing, how will the referral be made to the licensed county adoption agency, or to the State Department of Social Services when it is acting as the adoption agency, to prepare an adoption assessment, as required by section 727.3(j)?

(3) Will the probation department continue to have ongoing case management and supervision of the case, pending the termination of parental rights hearing?

(4) Will the probation department or the child welfare department prepare the notices and other legal documents required before a termination of parental rights hearing?

(5) In counties in which different judicial officers hear delinquency and dependency matters, what procedure will be used to ensure that the dependency judge will hear each 727.31 hearing?

(6) Will the probation department or the child welfare department prepare the petition for adoption and other forms needed after the 727.31 hearing to complete the adoption process?

(Subd (b) amended effective January 1, 2007.)

Rule 5.825 amended and renumbered effective January 1, 2007; adopted as rule 1496.5 effective January 1, 2001; previously amended effective January 1, 2006.

Rule 5.830.   Sealing records (§ 781)

(a) Sealing records—former wards

(1) A former ward of the court may apply to petition the court to order juvenile records sealed. Determinations under section 781 may be made by the court in any county in which wardship was terminated. A court may seal the records of another court when it determines that it is appropriate to do so, and must make a determination on sealing those records if the case has been transferred to its jurisdiction under rules 5.610 and 5.612.

(2) At the time jurisdiction is terminated or the case is dismissed, the court must provide or instruct the probation department to provide form JV-595-INFO, *How to Ask the Court to Seal Your Records,* and form JV-595, *Request to Seal Juvenile Records,* to the ward if the court does not seal the ward's records under section 786. If the court does seal the ward's records under section 786, the court must provide or instruct the probation department to provide form JV-596-INFO, *Sealing of Records for Satisfactory Completion of Probation,* and a copy of the sealing order as provided in rule 5.840.

(3) *Application—submission*

(A) The application for a petition to seal records must be submitted to the probation department in the county in which wardship was terminated.

(B) The application for a petition to seal juvenile records may be submitted on form JV-595, *Request to Seal Juvenile Records,* or on another form that includes all required information.

(4) *Investigation*

If the applicant is at least 18 years of age, or if it has been at least five years since the applicant's probation was last terminated or since the applicant was cited to appear before a probation officer or was taken before a probation officer under section 626 or before any officer of a law enforcement agency, the probation officer must do all of the following:

(A) Prepare the petition;

(B) Conduct an investigation under section 781 and compile a list of cases and contact addresses of every agency or person that the probation department knows has a record of the ward's case—including the date of each offense, case number(s), and date when the case was closed—to be attached to the sealing petition;

(C) Prepare a report to the court with a recommendation supporting or opposing the requested sealing; and

(D) Within 90 days from receipt of the application if only the records of the investigating county are to be reviewed, or within 180 days from receipt of the application if records of other counties are to be reviewed:

(i) File the petition;

(ii) Set the matter for a hearing, which may be nonappearance; and

(iii) Notify the prosecuting attorney of the hearing.

(5) The court must review the petition and the report of the probation officer, and the court must grant or deny the petition.

(6) If the petition is granted, the court must order the sealing of all records described in section 781 using form JV-590, *Order to Seal Juvenile Records—Welfare and Institutions Code Section 781,* or a similar form. The order must apply in the county of the court hearing the petition and in all other counties in which there are juvenile records concerning the petitioner. If the court determines that sealing the records of another court for a petition that has not been transferred is inappropriate, it must inform the petitioner that a petition to seal those records can be filed in the county where the other court is located.

(Subd (a) amended effective July 1, 2016; previously amended effective January 1, 2007.)

(b) Sealing—nonwards

(1) For all other persons described in section 781, application may be submitted to the probation department in any county in which there is a juvenile record concerning the petitioner, and the procedures of (a) must be followed.

(2) When jurisdiction is terminated or the case is closed, the probation department must provide the following forms to individuals described under section 781(h)(1)(A) and (B):

(A) If the individual's records have not been sealed under section 786, form JV-595-INFO, *How to Ask the Court to Seal Your Records,* and form JV-595, *Request to Seal Juvenile Records;* or

(B) If the individual's records have been sealed under section 786, form JV-596-INFO, *Sealing of Records for Satisfactory Completion of Probation,* and a copy of the sealing order.

(Subd (b) amended effective July 1, 2016; previously amended effective January 1, 2007.)

(c) Destruction of records

All records sealed must be destroyed according to section 781(d).

(Subd (c) amended effective January 1, 2007.)

(d) Distribution of order

The clerk of the issuing court must:

(1) Send a copy of the order to each agency and official listed in the order; and

(2) Send a certified copy of the order to the clerk in each county in which a record is ordered sealed.

(Subd (d) amended effective January 1, 2007.)

(e) Deadline for sealing

Each agency and official notified must immediately seal all records as ordered.

(Subd (e) amended effective January 1, 2007.)

Rule 5.830 amended effective July 1, 2016; adopted as rule 1499 effective January 1, 1991; previously renumbered as rule 1497 effective January 1, 1999; previously amended and renumbered as rule 5.830 effective January 1, 2007.

Advisory Committee Comment

This rule is intended to describe the legal process by which a person may apply to petition the juvenile court to order the sealing—that is, the prohibition of access and inspection—of the records related to specified cases in the custody of the juvenile court, the probation department, and other agencies and public officials. This rule establishes minimum legal standards but does not prescribe procedures for managing physical or electronic records or methods for preventing public inspection of the records at issue. These procedures remain subject to local discretion. Procedures may, but are not required to, include the actual sealing of physical records or files. Other permissible methods of sealing physical records pending their destruction under section 781(d) include, but are not limited to, storing sealed records separately from publicly accessible records, placing sealed records in a folder or sleeve of a color different from that in which publicly accessible records are kept, assigning a distinctive file number extension to sealed records, or designating them with a special stamp. Procedures for sealing electronic records must accomplish the same objectives as the procedures used to seal physical records, and appropriate access controls must be established to ensure that only authorized persons may access the sealed records.

Rule 5.840.   Dismissal of petition and sealing of records (§ 786)

(a) Applicability

This rule states the procedures to dismiss and seal the records of minors who are subject to section 786.

(Subd (a) adopted effective July 1, 2016.)

(b) Dismissal of petition

If the court finds that a minor subject to this rule has satisfactorily completed his or her informal or formal probation supervision, the court must order the petition dismissed. The court must not dismiss a petition if it was sustained based on the commission of an offense listed in subdivision (b) of section 707 when the minor was 14 or older unless the finding on that offense has been dismissed or was reduced to a misdemeanor or an offense not listed in subdivision (b) of section 707. The court may also dismiss prior petitions filed or sustained against the minor if they appear to the satisfaction of the court to meet the sealing and dismissal criteria in section 786. An unfulfilled order, condition, or restitution or an unpaid restitution fee must not be deemed to constitute unsatisfactory completion of probation supervision. The court may not extend the period of supervision or probation solely for the purpose of deferring or delaying eligibility for dismissal and sealing under section 786.

(Subd (b) amended effective September 1, 2018; adopted effective July 1, 2016.)

(c) Sealing of records

For any petition dismissed by the court under section 786, including any petition dismissed before adjudication, the court must also order sealed all records in the custody of the court, law enforcement agencies, the probation department, and the Department of Justice pertaining to those dismissed petition(s) using form JV-596, *Dismissal and Sealing of Records—Welfare and Institutions Code Section 786,* or a similar form. The court may also seal records pertaining to these cases in the custody of other public agencies upon a request by an individual who is eligible to have records sealed under section 786, if the court determines that sealing the additional record(s) will promote the successful reentry and rehabilitation of the individual. The prosecuting attorney, probation officer, and court must have access to these records as specifically provided in section 786. Access to the records for research purposes must be provided as required in section 787.

(Subd (c) amended effective September 1, 2018; adopted effective July 1, 2016.)

(d) Destruction of records

The court must specify in its order the date by which all sealed records must be destroyed. For court records this date may be no earlier than the date the subject of the order attains age 21 and no later than the end of the time frame set forth in section 781(d). For all other records, the date may be no earlier than the date the subject of the order attains age 18, and no later than the time frame set forth in section 781(d) unless that time frame expires prior to the date the subject attains 18 years of age.

(Subd (d) adopted effective July 1, 2016.)

(e) Distribution of order

The clerk of the issuing court must send a copy of the order to each agency and official listed in the order and provide a copy of the order to the individual whose records have been sealed and his or her attorney. The court shall also provide or instruct the probation department to provide the individual with form JV-596-INFO, *Sealing of Records for Satisfactory Completion of Probation.*

(Subd (e) adopted effective July 1, 2016.)

(f) Deadline for sealing

Each agency, individual, and official notified must immediately seal all records as ordered and advise the court that its sealing order has been completed using form JV-591, *Acknowledgment of Juvenile Record Sealed*, or another means.

(Subd (f) adopted effective July 1, 2016.)

Rule 5.840 amended effective September 1, 2018; adopted effective July 1, 2016.

Rule 5.850. Sealing of records by probation in diversion cases (§ 786.5)

(a) Applicability

This rule states the procedures to seal the records of persons who are subject to section 786.5.

(Subd (a) adopted effective September 1, 2018.)

(b) Sealing of records

Upon satisfactory completion of a program of diversion or supervision under a referral by the probation officer or the prosecutor instead of filing a petition to adjudge the person a ward of the juvenile court, including a program of informal supervision under section 654, the probation department must seal the arrest and other records in its custody relating to the arrest or referral and participation in the program. The probation department must also notify the public or private agency operating the diversion program to which the person has been referred to seal any records in its custody relating to the arrest or referral and participation in the program, and the operator of the program must do so promptly.

(Subd (b) adopted effective September 1, 2018.)

(c) Notice to participant

Within 60 days of the satisfactory completion of a program subject to this rule, the probation department must notify the person in writing that his or her records have been sealed. If the probation department determines that the program has not been completed satisfactorily, it must notify the person in writing of the reason or reasons for not sealing the record and provide the person with a copy of the *Petition to Review Denial of Sealing of Records After Diversion Program* (form JV-598) or similar local form to allow the person to seek court review of the probation department's determination within 60 days of making that determination.

(Subd (c) adopted effective September 1, 2018.)

(d) Review of unsatisfactory completion of program by the juvenile court

A person who receives notice from the probation department that he or she has not satisfactorily completed the program and that his or her records have not been sealed may seek review of that determination by the court by submitting a petition to the probation department on the *Petition to Review Denial of Sealing of Records After Diversion Program* (form JV-598) or similar local form, and the probation department must file that petition with the court for a hearing to review whether he or she has met the satisfactory completion requirement and is eligible for record sealing by the probation department. The petition must be provided to the probation department within 60 days of the date the notice from the probation department was sent, and must include a copy of that notice. The probation department must file the petition with the juvenile court in the county that issued the notice within 30 days of receiving it. The clerk

of the court must set the matter for hearing and notify the petitioner and the probation department of the date, time, and location of the hearing. The court must appoint counsel to represent the child before or at the hearing unless the court finds that the child has made an intelligent waiver of the right to counsel under section 634 or is already represented. If the court finds after the hearing that the petitioner is eligible to have the records sealed under section 786.5, it must order the probation department to promptly comply with the sealing and notice requirements of this rule.

(Subd (d) adopted effective September 1, 2018.)

Rule 5.850 adopted effective September 1, 2018.

Rule 5.860. Prosecuting attorney request to access sealed juvenile case files

(a) Applicability

This rule applies when a prosecuting attorney is seeking to access, inspect, utilize, or disclose a record that has been sealed by the court under sections 781, 786, or 793, or Penal Code section 851.7, and the attorney has reason to believe that access to the record is necessary to meet the attorney's statutory or constitutional obligation to disclose favorable or exculpatory evidence to a defendant in a criminal case.

(Subd (a) adopted effective January 1, 2021.)

(b) Contents of the request

Any request filed with the juvenile court under this rule must include the prosecuting attorney's rationale for believing that access to the information in the record may be necessary to meet the disclosure obligation and the date by which the records are needed. The date must allow for sufficient time to meet the notice and hearing requirements of this rule. Form JV-592, *Prosecutor Request for Access to Sealed Juvenile Case File*, may be used for this purpose.

(Subd (b) adopted effective January 1, 2021.)

(c) Notice and opportunity to respond

(1) *Notice requirements*

(A) The request must include a form for the court to notify the person whose records are to be accessed as well as that person's attorney of record, and a form for those individuals to respond in writing and to request an appearance before the juvenile court. Forms JV-593, *Notice of Prosecutor Request for Access to Sealed Juvenile Case File*, and JV-594, *Response to Prosecutor Request for Access to Sealed Juvenile Case File*, may be used for this purpose.

(B) The juvenile court must notify the person with the sealed record and that person's attorney of record using the documents prepared by the prosecuting attorney within two court days of the request being filed.

(2) *Requirements if a response is filed*

(A) If a written response is filed no more than 10 days after the date the notice was issued and no appearance has been requested, the clerk of the court must provide that response to the juvenile court for its consideration as it reviews the prosecuting attorney's request.

(B) If a response is filed no more than 10 days after the date the notice was issued and an appearance is requested, the clerk of the court must set a hearing and provide notice of the hearing to the person with the sealed record, the attorney of record for that person, and the prosecuting attorney who filed the request.

(Subd (c) adopted effective January 1, 2021.)

(d) Juvenile court review and order

The court must review the case file and records that have been referenced by the prosecuting attorney's request as well as any response provided as set forth in subdivision (c)(2). The court must approve the request, in whole or in part, if it determines that access to a specific sealed record or portion of a sealed record is necessary to enable the prosecuting attorney to comply with the disclosure obligation. If the court approves the request, the order must include appropriate limits on the access, inspection, utilization, and disclosure of the sealed record information in order to protect the confidentiality of the person whose sealed record is at issue. Such limits may include protective orders to accompany authorized disclosure, discovery, or access, including an order that the prosecuting attorney first submit the records to be disclosed to the court for its review and possible redaction to protect confidentiality. The court must make its initial order within 21 court days of when the request is filed, unless an appearance has been requested under subdivision (c)(2), in which case the court must act within five court days of the date set for the appearance.

(Subd (d) adopted effective January 1, 2021.)

Rule 5.860 adopted effective January 1, 2021.

Chapter 14
Nonminor Dependent

Title 5, Family and Juvenile Rules—Division 3, Juvenile Rules—Chapter 14, Nonminor Dependent; adopted effective January 1, 2012.

Rule 5.900. Nonminor dependent—preliminary provisions (§§ 224.1(b), 295, 303, 366, 366.3, 388, 391, 607(a))

Rule 5.903. Nonminor dependent status review hearing (§§ 224.1(b), 295, 366.1, 366.3, 366.31)

Rule 5.906. Request by nonminor for the juvenile court to resume jurisdiction (§§ 224.1(b), 303, 388(e), 388.1)

Rule 5.900.   Nonminor dependent—preliminary provisions (§§ 224.1(b), 295, 303, 366, 366.3, 388, 391, 607(a))

(a) Applicability

(1) The provisions of this chapter apply to nonminor dependents as defined in section 11400(v).

(2) Nothing in the Welfare and Institutions Code or in the California Rules of Court restricts the ability of the juvenile court to maintain dependency jurisdiction or delinquency jurisdiction over a person, 18 years of age and older, who does not meet the eligibility requirements for status as a nonminor dependent and to proceed as to that person under the relevant sections of the Welfare and Institutions Code and California Rules of Court.

(Subd (a) adopted effective January 1, 2012.)

(b) Purpose

(1) Maintaining juvenile court jurisdiction under sections 300 or 450 over a person as a nonminor dependent is the result of a consensual agreement between the person and child welfare services agency or the probation department for a voluntary placement in a supervised setting and includes the agreement between the social worker or probation officer and the person to work together to implement the mutually developed supervised placement agreement or reentry agreement.

(2) Maintaining juvenile court jurisdiction and supervision by the child welfare services agency or probation department under sections 300, 450, 601, or 602 over a person as a nonminor dependent is for the purpose of implementing the mutually developed Transitional Independent Living Case Plan and providing support, guidance, and foster care services to the person as a nonminor dependent so he or she is able to successfully achieve independence, including relationships with caring and committed adults who can serve as lifelong connections.

(Subd (b) amended effective January 1, 2014; adopted effective January 1, 2012.)

(c) Legal status

(1) Nothing in the Welfare and Institutions Code, including sections 340, 366.2, and 369.5, or in the California Rules of Court provides legal custody of a nonminor dependent to the child welfare services agency or the probation department or abrogates any right the nonminor dependent, as a person who has attained 18 years of age, may have as an adult under California law.

(2) A nonminor dependent retains all his or her legal decisionmaking authority as an adult. The decisionmaking authority of a nonminor dependent under delinquency jurisdiction may be limited by and subject to the care, supervision, custody, conduct, and maintenance orders in section 727.

(Subd (c) amended effective January 1, 2014; adopted effective January 1, 2012.)

(d) Conduct of hearings

(1) All hearings involving a person who is a nonminor dependent must be conducted in a manner that respects the person's legal status as an adult.

(2) Unless there is a contested issue of fact or law, the hearings must be informal and nonadversarial and all parties must work collaboratively with the nonminor dependent as he or she moves toward the achievement of his or her Transitional Independent Living Case Plan goals.

(3) The nonminor dependent may designate his or her attorney to appear on his or her behalf at a hearing under this chapter.

(Subd (d) adopted effective January 1, 2012.)

(e) Telephone appearance

(1) The person who is the subject of the hearing may appear, at his or her request, by telephone at a hearing to terminate juvenile court jurisdiction held under rule 5.555, a status review hearing under rule 5.903, or a hearing on a request to have juvenile court jurisdiction resumed held under rule 5.906. Rule 5.531 applies to telephone appearances under this paragraph.

(2) The court may require the nonminor dependent or the person requesting to return to juvenile court jurisdiction and foster care to appear personally on a showing of good cause and a showing that the personal appearance will not create an undue hardship for him or her.

(3) The telephone appearance must be permitted at no cost to the nonminor dependent or the person requesting to return juvenile court jurisdiction and foster care.

(Subd (e) adopted effective January 1, 2012.)

(f) Separate court file

The clerk of the superior court must open a separate court file for nonminor dependents under the dependency, delinquency, or transition jurisdiction of the court that ensures the confidentiality of the nonminor dependent and allows access only to those listed in section 362.5.

(Subd (f) adopted effective January 1, 2014.)

Rule 5.900 amended effective January 1, 2014; adopted effective January 1, 2012.

Advisory Committee Comment

A nonminor is entitled to be represented by an attorney of his or her choice rather than by a court-appointed attorney in proceedings under this chapter and under rule 5.555. (See Welf. & Inst. Code, § 349(b); *In re Akkiko M.* (1985) 163 Cal.App.3d 525.) Any fees for an attorney retained by the nonminor are the nonminor's responsibility.

Rule 5.903.   Nonminor dependent status review hearing (§§ 224.1(b), 295, 366.1, 366.3, 366.31)

(a) Purpose

The primary purpose of the nonminor dependent status review hearing is to focus on the goals and services described in the nonminor dependent's Transitional Independent Living Case Plan and the efforts and progress made toward achieving independence and establishing lifelong connections with caring and committed adults.

(Subd (a) adopted effective January 1, 2012.)

(b) Setting and conduct of a nonminor dependent status review hearing

(1) A status review hearing for a nonminor dependent conducted by the court or by a local administrative review panel must occur no less frequently than once every 6 months.

(2) The hearing must be placed on the appearance calendar, held before a judicial officer, and recorded by a court reporter under any of the following circumstances:

(A) The hearing is the first hearing following the nonminor dependent's 18th birthday;

(B) The hearing is the first hearing following the resumption of juvenile court jurisdiction over a person as a nonminor dependent under rule 5.906;

(C) The nonminor dependent or the nonminor dependent's attorney requests that the hearing be conducted by the court; or

(D) It has been 12 months since the hearing was conducted by the court.

(3) The hearing may be attended, as appropriate, by participants invited by the nonminor dependent in addition to those entitled to notice under (c). If delinquency jurisdiction is dismissed in favor of transition jurisdiction under Welfare and Institutions Code section 450, the prosecuting attorney is not permitted to appear at later review hearings for the nonminor dependent.

(4) The nonminor dependent may appear by telephone as provided in rule 5.900 at a hearing conducted by the court.

(5) The hearing must be continued for no more than five court days for the social worker, probation officer, or nonminor dependent to submit additional information as ordered by the court if the court determines that the report and Transitional Independent Living Case Plan submitted by the social worker or probation officer do not provide the information required by (d)(1) and the court is unable to make all the findings and orders required by (e).

(Subd (b) amended effective January 1, 2019; adopted effective January 1, 2012.)

(c) Notice of hearing (§ 295)

(1) The social worker or probation officer must serve written notice of the hearing in the manner provided in section 295, and to all persons required to receive notice under section 295, except notice to the parents of the nonminor dependent is not required.

(2) The written notice served on the nonminor dependent must include:

(A) A statement that he or she may appear for the hearing by telephone; and

(B) Instructions about the local court procedures for arranging to appear and appearing at the hearing by telephone.

(3) Proof of service of notice must be filed by the social worker or probation officer at least five court days before the hearing.

(Subd (c) adopted effective January 1, 2012.)

(d) Reports

(1) The social worker or probation officer must submit a report to the court that includes information regarding:

(A) The continuing necessity for the nonminor dependent's placement and the facts supporting the conclusion reached;

(B) The appropriateness of the nonminor dependent's current foster care placement;

(C) The nonminor dependent's plans to remain under juvenile court jurisdiction including the criteria in section 11403(b) that he or she meets;

(D) The efforts made by the social worker or probation officer to help the nonminor dependent meet the criteria in section 11403(b);

(E) Verification that the nonminor dependent was provided with the information, documents, and services as required under section 391(e);

(F) How and when the Transitional Independent Living Case Plan was developed, including the nature and the extent of the nonminor dependent's participation in its development, and for the nonminor dependent who has elected to have the Indian Child Welfare Act continue to apply, the extent of consultation with the tribal representative;

(G) The efforts made by the social worker or probation officer to comply with the nonminor dependent's Transitional Independent Living Case Plan, including efforts to finalize the permanent plan and prepare him or her for independence;

(H) Progress made toward meeting the Transitional Independent Living Case Plan goals and the need for any modifications to assist the nonminor dependent in attaining the goals;

(I) The efforts made by the social worker or probation officer to maintain relationships between the nonminor dependent and individuals who are important to him or her, including the efforts made to establish and maintain relationships with caring and committed adults who can serve as a lifelong connection;

(J) The efforts made by the social worker or probation officer to establish or maintain the nonminor dependent's relationship with his or her siblings who are under the juvenile court's jurisdiction as required in section 366(a)(1)(D);

(K) For a nonminor dependent whose case plan is continued court-ordered family reunification services, the information required in section 366.31(d); and

(L) For a nonminor who has returned to the home of the parent or former legal guardian, whether continued juvenile court jurisdiction is necessary and the facts in support of that conclusion.

(2) The social worker or probation officer must submit with his or her report the Transitional Independent Living Case Plan.

(3) The social worker or probation officer must file with the court the report prepared for the hearing and the Transitional Independent Living Case Plan at least 10 calendar days before the hearing, and provide copies of the report and other documents to the nonminor dependent, all attorneys of record, and for the nonminor dependent who has elected to have the Indian Child Welfare Act continue to apply, the tribal representative.

(Subd (d) amended effective January 1, 2014; adopted effective January 1, 2012.)

(e) Findings and orders

The court must consider the safety of the nonminor dependent, and the following judicial findings and orders must be made and included in the written court documentation of the hearing:

(1) *Findings*

(A) Whether notice was given as required by law;

(B) Whether the nonminor dependent's continuing placement is necessary;

(C) Whether the nonminor dependent's current placement is appropriate;

(D) Whether the Transitional Independent Living Case Plan includes a plan for the nonminor dependent to satisfy one or more of the criteria in section 11403(b);

(E) The specific criteria in section 11403(b) the nonminor dependent satisfied since the last hearing held under this rule;

(F) The specific criteria in section 11403(b) it is anticipated the nonminor dependent will satisfy during the next six months;

(G) Whether reasonable efforts were made and assistance provided by the social worker or probation officer to help the nonminor dependent establish and maintain compliance with section 11403(b);

(H) Whether the nonminor dependent was provided with the information, documents, and services as required under section 391(e);

(I) Whether the Transitional Independent Living Case Plan was developed jointly by the nonminor dependent and the social worker or probation officer, reflects the living situation and services that are consistent in the nonminor dependent's opinion with what he or she needs to gain independence, and sets out the benchmarks that indicate how both will know when independence can be achieved;

(J) For the nonminor dependent who has elected to have the Indian Child Welfare Act continue to apply, whether the representative from his or her tribe was consulted during the development of the Transitional Independent Living Case Plan;

(K) Whether reasonable efforts were made by the social worker or probation officer to comply with the Transitional Independent Living Case Plan, including efforts to finalize the nonminor dependent's permanent plan and prepare him or her for independence;

(L) Whether the Transitional Independent Living Case Plan includes appropriate and meaningful independent living skill services that will assist him or her with the transition from foster care to independent living;

(M) Whether the nonminor dependent signed and received a copy of his or her Transitional Independent Living Case Plan;

(N) The extent of progress made by the nonminor dependent toward meeting the Transitional Independent Living Case Plan goals and any modifications needed to assist in attaining the goals;

(O) Whether reasonable efforts were made by the social worker or probation officer to maintain relationships between the nonminor dependent and individuals who are important to him or her, including the efforts made to establish and maintain relationships with caring and committed adults who can serve as lifelong connections;

(P) Whether reasonable efforts were made by the social worker or probation officer to establish or maintain the nonminor dependent's relationship with his or her siblings who are under the juvenile court's jurisdiction as required in section 366(a)(1)(D);

(Q) For a nonminor dependent whose case plan is continued court-ordered family reunification services, the findings required in section 366.31(d); and

(R) For a nonminor who has returned to the home of the parent or former legal guardian, whether continued juvenile court jurisdiction is necessary.

(2) *Orders*

(A) Order the continuation of juvenile court jurisdiction and set a nonminor dependent review hearing under this rule within six months, and:

(i) Order a permanent plan consistent with the nonminor dependent's Transitional Independent Living Case Plan, and

(ii) Specify the likely date by which independence is anticipated to be achieved; and

(iii) For a nonminor dependent whose parents are receiving court-ordered family reunification services:

a. Order the continuation of reunification services;

b. Order the termination of reunification services; or

c. Order that the nonminor may reside in the home of the parent or former legal guardian and that juvenile court jurisdiction is terminated or that juvenile court jurisdiction is continued under section 303(a) and a status review hearing is set for within six months.

(B) Order the continuation of juvenile court jurisdiction and set a hearing to consider termination of juvenile court jurisdiction over a nonminor under rule 5.555 within 30 days; or

(C) Order termination of juvenile court jurisdiction pursuant to rule 5.555 if this nonminor dependent status review hearing was heard at the same time as a hearing under rule 5.555.

(Subd (e) amended effective January 1, 2014; adopted effective January 1, 2012.)

Rule 5.903 amended effective January 1, 2019; adopted effective January 1, 2012; previously amended effective January 1, 2014.

Rule 5.906.   Request by nonminor for the juvenile court to resume jurisdiction (§§ 224.1(b), 303, 388(e), 388.1)

(a) Purpose

This rule provides the procedures that must be followed when a nonminor wants to have juvenile court jurisdiction assumed or resumed over him or her as a nonminor dependent as defined in subdivisions (v) or (aa) of section 11400.

(Subd (a) amended effective January 1, 2016; adopted effective January 1, 2012; previously amended effective July 1, 2012, and January 1, 2014.)

(b) Contents of the request

(1) The request to have the juvenile court assume or resume jurisdiction must be made on the *Request to Return to Juvenile Court Jurisdiction and Foster Care* (form JV-466).

(2) The request must be liberally construed in favor of its sufficiency. It must be verified by the nonminor or if the nonminor is unable to provide verification due to a medical condition, the nonminor's representative, and to the extent known to the nonminor or the nonminor's representative, must include the following information:

(A) The nonminor's name and date of birth;

(B) The nonminor's address and contact information, unless the nonminor requests that this information be kept confidential from those persons entitled to access to the juvenile court file, including his or her parents, by filing *Confidential Information—Request to Return to Juvenile Court Jurisdiction and Foster Care* (form JV-468). Form JV-468 must be kept in the court file under seal, and only the court, the child welfare services agency, the probation department, or the Indian tribe with an agreement under section 10553.1 to provide child welfare services to Indian children (Indian tribal agency), the attorney for the child welfare services agency, the probation department, or the Indian tribe, and the nonminor's attorney may have access to this information;

(C) The name and action number or court file number of the nonminor's case and the name of the juvenile court that terminated its dependency jurisdiction, delinquency jurisdiction, or transition jurisdiction;

(D) The date the juvenile court entered the order terminating its dependency jurisdiction, delinquency jurisdiction, or transition jurisdiction;

(E) If the nonminor wants his or her parents or former legal guardians to receive notice of the filing of the request and the hearing, the name and residence addresses of the nonminor's parents or former guardians;

(F) The name and telephone number of the court-appointed attorney who represented the nonminor at the time the juvenile court terminated its dependency jurisdiction, delinquency jurisdiction, or transition jurisdiction if the nonminor wants that attorney to be appointed to represent him or her for the purposes of the hearing on the request;

(G) If the nonminor is an Indian child within the meaning of the Indian Child Welfare Act and chooses to have the Indian Child Welfare Act apply to him or her, the name of the tribe and the name, address, and telephone number of his or her tribal representative;

(H) If the nonminor had a Court Appointed Special Advocate (CASA) when he or she was a dependent or ward of the court and wants the CASA to receive notice of the filing of the request and the hearing, the CASA's name;

(I) The condition or conditions under section 11403(b) that the nonminor intends to satisfy; and

(J) Whether the nonminor requires assistance to maintain or secure an appropriate, supervised placement, or is in need of immediate placement and will agree to a supervised placement under a voluntary reentry agreement.

(3) The court may dismiss without prejudice a request filed under this rule that is not verified.

(Subd (b) amended effective January 1, 2016; adopted effective January 1, 2012; previously amended effective July 1, 2012.)

(c) Filing the request

(1) The form JV-466 must be completed and verified by the nonminor or the nonminor's representative if the nonminor is unable to provide verification due to a medical condition, and may be filed by the nonminor or the county child welfare services, probation department, or Indian tribe (placing agency) on behalf of the nonminor.

(2) For the convenience of the nonminor, the form JV-466 and, if the nonminor wishes to keep his or her contact information confidential, the *Confidential Information—Request to Return to Juvenile Court Jurisdiction and Foster Care* (form JV-468) may be:

(A) Filed with the juvenile court that maintained general jurisdiction or for cases petitioned under section 388.1, in the court that established the guardianship or had jurisdiction when the adoption was finalized; or

(B) Submitted to the juvenile court in the county in which the nonminor currently resides, after which:

(i) The court clerk must record the date and time received on the face of the originals submitted and provide a copy of the originals marked as received to the nonminor at no cost to him or her.

(ii) To ensure receipt of the original form JV-466 and, if submitted, the form JV-468 by the court of general jurisdiction within five court days as required in section 388(e), the court clerk must forward those originals to the clerk of the court of general jurisdiction within two court days of submission of the originals by the nonminor.

(iii) The court in the county in which the nonminor resides is responsible for all costs of processing, copying, and forwarding the form JV-466 and form JV-468 to the clerk of the court of general jurisdiction.

(iv) The court clerk in the county in which the nonminor resides must retain a copy of the documents submitted.

(v) The form JV-466 and, if submitted, the form JV-468 must be filed immediately upon receipt by the clerk of the juvenile court of general jurisdiction.

(C) For a nonminor living outside the state of California, the form JV-466 and, if the nonminor wishes to keep his or her contact information confidential, the form JV-468 must be filed with the juvenile court of general jurisdiction.

(3) If form JV-466 is filed by the nonminor, within two court days of its filing with the clerk of the court in the county of general jurisdiction, the clerk of that court must notify the placing agency that was supervising the nonminor when juvenile court jurisdiction was terminated that the nonminor has filed form JV-466 and provide the placing agency with the nonminor's contact information. The notification must be by telephone, fax, e-mail, or other method approved by the presiding juvenile court judge that will ensure prompt notification and inform the placing agency that a copy of form JV-466 will be served on the agency and that one is currently available in the office of the juvenile court clerk.

(4) If form JV-466 has not been filed at the time the nonminor completes the voluntary reentry agreement described in section 11400(z), the placing agency must file form JV-466 on the nonminor's behalf within 15 court days of the date the voluntary reentry agreement was signed, unless the nonminor files form JV-466 prior to the expiration of the 15 court days.

(5) No filing fees are required for the filing of form JV-466 and, if filed, form JV-468. An endorsed, filed copy of each form filed must be provided at no cost to the nonminor or the placing agency that filed the request on the nonminor's behalf.

(Subd (c) amended effective January 1, 2016; adopted effective January 1, 2012; previously amended effective July 1, 2012.)

(d) Determination of prima facie showing

(1) Within three court days of the filing of form JV-466 with the clerk of the juvenile court of general jurisdiction, a juvenile court judicial officer must review the form JV-466 and determine whether a prima facie showing has been made that the nonminor meets all of the criteria set forth below in (d)(1)(A)–(D) and enter an order as set forth in (d)(2) or (d)(3).

(A) The nonminor is eligible to seek assumption of dependency jurisdiction under the provisions of section 388.1(c), or the nonminor was previously under juvenile court jurisdiction subject to an order for foster care placement on the date he or she attained 18 years of age, including a nonminor whose adjudication was vacated under Penal Code section 236.14;

(B) The nonminor has not attained 21 years of age;

(C) The nonminor wants assistance to maintain or secure an appropriate, supervised placement or is in need of immediate placement and agrees to a supervised placement under a voluntary reentry agreement; and

(D) The nonminor intends to satisfy at least one of the eligibility criteria in section 11403(b).

(2) If the court determines that a prima facie showing has not been made, the court must enter a written order denying the request, listing the issues that resulted in the denial and informing the nonminor that a new form JV-466 may be filed when those issues are resolved.

(A) The court clerk must serve on the nonminor:

(i) A copy of the written order;

(ii) A blank copy of *Request to Return to Juvenile Court Jurisdiction and Foster Care* (form JV-466) and *Confidential Information—Request to Return to Juvenile Court Jurisdiction and Foster Care* (form JV-468);

(iii) A copy of *How to Ask to Return to Juvenile Court Jurisdiction and Foster Care* (form JV-464-INFO); and

(iv) The names and contact information for those attorneys approved by the court to represent children in juvenile court proceedings who have agreed to provide a consultation to any nonminor whose request was denied due to the failure to make a prima facie showing.

(B) The court clerk must serve on the placing agency a copy of the written order.

(C) Service must be by personal service, by first-class mail, or by electronic service in accordance with section 212.5 within two court days of the issuance of the order.

(D) A proof of service must be filed.

(3) If the judicial officer determines that a prima facie showing has been made, the judicial officer must issue a written order:

(A) Directing the court clerk to set the matter for a hearing; and

(B) Appointing an attorney to represent the nonminor solely for the hearing on the request.

(Subd (d) amended effective January 1, 2019; adopted effective January 1, 2012; previously amended effective July 1, 2012, January 1, 2014, and January 1, 2016.)

(e) Appointment of attorney

(1) If the nonminor included on the form JV-466 a request for the appointment of the court-appointed attorney who represented the nonminor during the period of time he or she was a ward or dependent or nonminor dependent, the judicial officer must appoint that attorney solely for the hearing on the request, if the attorney is available to accept such an appointment.

(2) If the nonminor did not request the appointment of his or her former court-appointed attorney, the judicial officer must appoint an attorney to represent the nonminor solely for the hearing on the request. The attorney must be selected from the panel or organization of attorneys approved by the court to represent children in juvenile court proceedings.

(3) In addition to complying with the requirements in (g)(1) for service of notice of the hearing, the juvenile court clerk must notify the attorney of his or her appointment as soon as possible, but no later than one court day from the date the order for his or her appointment was issued under (d)(3). This notification must be made by telephone, fax, e-mail, or other method approved by the presiding juvenile court judge that will ensure prompt notification. The notice must also include the nonminor's contact information and inform the attorney that a copy of the form JV-466 will be served on him or her and that one is currently available in the office of the juvenile court clerk.

(4) If the request is granted, the court must continue the attorney's appointment to represent the nonminor regarding matters related to his or her status as a nonminor dependent until the jurisdiction of the juvenile court is terminated, unless the court finds that the nonminor would not benefit from the appointment of an attorney.

(A) In order to find that a nonminor would not benefit from the appointment of an attorney, the court must find all of the following:

(i) The nonminor understands the nature of the proceedings;

(ii) The nonminor is able to communicate and advocate effectively with the court, other attorneys, and other parties, including social workers, probation officers, and other professionals involved in the case; and

(iii) Under the circumstances of the case, the nonminor would not gain any benefit from representation by an attorney.

(B) If the court finds that the nonminor would not benefit from representation by an attorney, the court must make a finding on the record as to each of the criteria in (e)(4)(A) and state the reasons for each finding.

(5) Representation of the nonminor by the court-appointed attorney for the hearing on the request to return to juvenile court jurisdiction and for matters related to his or her status as a nonminor dependent must be at no cost to the nonminor.

(6) If the nonminor chooses to be represented by an attorney other than a court-appointed attorney, the fees for an attorney retained by the nonminor are the nonminor's responsibility.

(Subd (e) amended effective July 1, 2012; adopted effective January 1, 2012.)

(f) Setting the hearing

(1) Within two court days of the issuance of the order directing the court clerk to do so, the court clerk must set a hearing on the juvenile court's calendar within 15 court days from the date the form JV-466 was filed with the court of general jurisdiction.

(2) The hearing must be placed on the appearance calendar, heard before a juvenile court judicial officer, and recorded by a court reporter.

(Subd (f) amended effective July 1, 2012; adopted effective January 1, 2012.)

(g) Notice of hearing

(1) The juvenile court clerk must serve notice as soon as possible, but no later than five court days before the date the hearing is set, as follows:

(A) The notice of the date, time, place, and purpose of the hearing and a copy of the form JV-466 must be served on the nonminor, the nonminor's attorney, the child welfare services agency, the probation department, or the Indian tribal agency that was supervising the nonminor when the juvenile court terminated its delinquency, dependency, or transition jurisdiction over the nonminor, and the attorney for the child welfare services agency, the probation department, or the Indian tribe. Notice must not be served on the prosecuting attorney if delinquency jurisdiction has been dismissed, and the nonminor's petition is for the court to assume or resume transition jurisdiction under Welfare and Institutions Code section 450.

(B) The notice of the date, time, place, and purpose of the hearing must be served on the nonminor's parents only if the nonminor included in the form JV-466 a request that notice be provided to his or her parents.

(C) The notice of the date, time, place, and purpose of the hearing must be served on the nonminor's tribal representative if the nonminor is an Indian child and indicated on the form JV-466 his or her choice to have the Indian Child Welfare Act apply to him or her as a nonminor dependent.

(D) The notice of the date, time, place, and purpose of the hearing must be served on the local CASA office if the nonminor had a CASA and included on the form JV-466 a request that notice be provided to his or her former CASA.

(2) The written notice served on the nonminor dependent must include:

(A) A statement that the nonminor may appear for the hearing by telephone; and

(B) Instructions regarding the local juvenile court procedures for arranging to appear and appearing at the hearing by telephone.

(3) Service of the notice must be by personal service, by first-class mail, or by electronic service in accordance with section 212.5.

(4) Proof of service of notice must be filed by the juvenile court clerk at least two court days prior to the hearing.

(Subd (g) amended effective January 1, 2019; adopted effective January 1, 2012; previously amended effective July 1, 2012.)

(h) Reports

(1) The social worker, probation officer, or Indian tribal agency case worker (tribal case worker) must submit a report to the court that includes:

(A) Confirmation that the nonminor was previously under juvenile court jurisdiction subject to an order for foster care placement when he or she attained 18 years of age and that he or she has not attained 21 years of age, or is eligible to petition the court to assume jurisdiction over the nonminor pursuant to section 388.1;

(B) The condition or conditions under section 11403(b) that the nonminor intends to satisfy;

(C) The social worker, probation officer, or tribal case worker's opinion as to whether continuing in a foster care placement is in the nonminor's best interests and recommendation about the assumption or resumption of juvenile court jurisdiction over the nonminor as a nonminor dependent;

(D) Whether the nonminor and the placing agency have entered into a reentry agreement for placement in a supervised setting under the placement and care responsibility of the placing agency;

(E) The type of placement recommended if the request to return to juvenile court jurisdiction and foster care is granted;

(F) If the type of placement recommended is a placement in a setting where minor dependents also reside, the results of the background check of the nonminor under section 16504.5.

(i) The background check under section 16504.5 is required only if a minor dependent resides in the placement under consideration for the nonminor.

(ii) A criminal conviction is not a bar to a return to foster care and the resumption of juvenile court jurisdiction over the nonminor as a nonminor dependent.

(2) At least two court days before the hearing, the social worker, probation officer, or tribal case worker must file the report and any supporting documentation with the court and provide a copy to the nonminor and to his or her attorney of record; and

(3) If the court determines that the report and other documentation submitted by the social worker, probation officer, or tribal case worker does not provide the information required by (h)(1) and the court is unable

to make the findings and orders required by (i), the hearing must be continued for no more than five court days for the social worker, probation officer, tribal case worker, or nonminor to submit additional information as ordered by the court.

(Subd (h) amended effective January 1, 2016; adopted effective January 1, 2012; previously amended effective July 1, 2012, and January 1, 2014.)

(i) Findings and orders

The court must read and consider, and state on the record that it has read and considered, the report; the supporting documentation submitted by the social worker, probation officer, or tribal caseworker; the evidence submitted by the nonminor; and any other evidence. The following judicial findings and orders must be made and included in the written court documentation of the hearing:

(1) *Findings*

(A) Whether notice was given as required by law;

(B) Whether the nonminor was previously under juvenile court jurisdiction subject to an order for foster care placement when he or she attained 18 years of age, or meets the requirements of subparagraph (5) of subdivision (c) of section 388.1;

(C) Whether the nonminor has attained 21 years of age;

(D) Whether the nonminor intends to satisfy a condition or conditions under section 11403(b);

(E) The condition or conditions under section 11403(b) that the nonminor intends to satisfy;

(F) Whether continuing or reentering and remaining in a foster care placement is in the nonminor's best interests;

(G) Whether the nonminor and the placing agency have entered into a reentry agreement for placement in a supervised setting under the placement and care responsibility of the placing agency; and

(H) Whether a nonminor who is an Indian child chooses to have the Indian Child Welfare Act apply to him or her as a nonminor dependent.

(2) *Orders*

(A) If the court finds that the nonminor has not attained 21 years of age, that the nonminor intends to satisfy at least one condition under section 11403(b), and that the nonminor and placing agency have entered into a reentry agreement, the court must:

(i) Grant the request and enter an order assuming or resuming juvenile court jurisdiction over the nonminor as a nonminor dependent and vesting responsibility for the nonminor's placement and care with the placing agency;

(ii) Order the social worker, probation officer, or tribal case worker to develop with the nonminor and file with the court within 60 days a new Transitional Independent Living Case Plan;

(iii) Order the social worker or probation officer to consult with the tribal representative regarding a new Transitional Independent Living Case Plan for the nonminor who chooses to have the Indian Child Welfare Act apply to him or her as a nonminor dependent and who is not under the supervision of a tribal case worker;

(iv) Set a nonminor dependent status review hearing under rule 5.903 within the next six months; and

(v) Make the findings and enter the appropriate orders under (e)(4) regarding appointment of an attorney for the nonminor.

(B) If the court finds that the nonminor has not attained 21 years of age, but the nonminor does not intend to satisfy at least one of the conditions under section 11403(b) and/or the nonminor and placing agency have not entered into a reentry agreement, the court must:

(i) Enter an order denying the request, listing the reasons for the denial, and informing the nonminor that a new form JV-466 may be filed when those circumstances change;

(ii) Enter an order terminating the appointment of the attorney appointed by the court to represent the nonminor, effective seven calendar days after the hearing; and

(iii) In addition to the service of a copy of the written order as required in (i)(3), the juvenile court clerk must cause to be served on the nonminor a blank copy of the *Request to Return to Juvenile Court Jurisdiction and Foster Care* (form JV-466) and *Confidential Information—Request to Return to Juvenile Court Jurisdiction and Foster Care* (form JV-468), and a copy of *How to Ask to Return to Juvenile Court Jurisdiction and Foster Care* (form JV-464-INFO).

(C) If the court finds that the nonminor is over 21 years of age, the court must:

(i) Enter an order denying the request to have juvenile court jurisdiction resumed; and

(ii) Enter an order terminating the appointment of the attorney appointed by the court to represent the nonminor, effective seven calendar days after the hearing.

(3) *Findings and order: service*

(A) The written findings and order must be served by the juvenile court clerk on all persons provided with notice of the hearing under (g)(1).

(B) Service must be by personal service, by first-class mail, or by electronic service in accordance with section 212.5 within three court days of the issuance of the order.

(C) A proof of service must be filed.

(Subd (i) amended effective January 1, 2019; adopted effective January 1, 2012; previously amended effective July 1, 2012, January 1, 2014, and January 1, 2016.) Rule 5.906 amended effective January 1, 2019; adopted effective January 1, 2012; previously amended effective July 1, 2012, January 1, 2014, and January 1, 2016.

Advisory Committee Comment

Assembly Bill 12 (Beall; Stats. 2010, ch. 559), known as the California Fostering Connections to Success Act, as amended by Assembly Bill 212 (Beall; Stats. 2011, ch. 459), implement the federal Fostering Connections to Success and Increasing Adoptions Act, Pub.L. No. 110-351, which provides funding resources to extend the support of the foster care system to children who are still in a foster care placement on their 18th birthday. Every effort was made in the development of the rules and forms to provide an efficient framework for the implementation of this important and complex legislation.

TITLE 6
[Reserved]

Rules of Court

TITLE 7
Probate Rules

Chapter 1
General Provisions

Rule 7.1. Probate Rules
Rule 7.2. Preliminary provisions
Rule 7.3. Definitions and use of terms
Rule 7.4. Waiver of rules in probate proceedings
Rule 7.5. Waivers of court fees in decedents' estates, conservatorships, and guardianships
Rule 7.10. Ex parte communications in proceedings under the probate code and certain other proceedings

Rule 7.1. Probate Rules

The rules in this title may be referred to as the Probate Rules.
Rule 7.1 adopted effective January 1, 2007.

Rule 7.2. Preliminary provisions

(a) Application of rules

The rules in this title apply to every action and proceeding to which the Probate Code applies and, unless they are elsewhere explicitly made applicable, do not apply to any other action or proceeding.
(Subd (a) amended effective January 1, 2007.)

(b) Purpose of rules

The rules in this title are designed to implement the purposes of the probate law by promoting uniformity in practice and procedure.
(Subd (b) amended effective January 1, 2007.)

(c) Rules of construction

Unless the context otherwise requires, these preliminary provisions and the following rules of construction govern the construction of the rules in this title:

(1) To the extent that the rules in this title are substantially the same as existing statutory provisions relating to the same subject matter, they must be construed as a restatement and a continuation of those statutes; and

(2) To the extent that the rules in this title may add to existing statutory provisions relating to the same subject matter, they must be construed so as to implement the purposes of the probate law.
(Subd (c) amended effective January 1, 2007; previously amended effective January 1, 2003.)

(d) Jurisdiction

The rules in this title are not intended to expand, limit, or restrict the jurisdiction of the court in proceedings under the Probate Code.

(Subd (d) adopted effective January 1, 2003.)
Rule 7.2 amended and renumbered effective January 1, 2007; adopted as rule 7.1 effective January 1, 2000; previously amended effective January 1, 2003.

Rule 7.3. Definitions and use of terms

As used in the rules in this title, unless the context or subject matter otherwise requires:

(1) The definitions in division 1, part 2 of the Probate Code apply.

(2) "Pleading" means a contest, answer, petition, application, objection, response, statement of interest, report, or account filed in proceedings under the Probate Code.

(3) "Amended pleading" means a pleading that completely restates and supersedes the pleading it amends for all purposes.

(4) "Amendment to a pleading" means a pleading that modifies another pleading and alleges facts or requests relief materially different from the facts alleged or the relief requested in the modified pleading. An amendment to a pleading does not restate or supersede the modified pleading but must be read together with that pleading.

(5) "Supplement to a pleading" and "supplement" mean a pleading that modifies another pleading but does not allege facts or request relief materially different from the facts alleged or the relief requested in the supplemented pleading. A supplement to a pleading may add information to or may correct omissions in the modified pleading.
Rule 7.3 amended and renumbered effective January 1, 2007; adopted as rule 7.2 effective January 1, 2000; previously amended effective January 1, 2002, and January 1, 2003.

Rule 7.4. Waiver of rules in probate proceedings

The court for good cause may waive the application of the rules in this title in an individual case.
Rule 7.4 renumbered effective January 1, 2007; adopted as rule 7.3 effective January 1, 2000; previously amended effective January 1, 2003.

Rule 7.5. Waivers of court fees in decedents' estates, conservatorships, and guardianships

(a) Scope of rule

This rule governs initial fee waivers, as defined in rule 3.50(b), that are requested by petitioners for the appointment of fiduciaries, or by fiduciaries after their appointment, in decedents' estates, conservatorships, and guardianships under the Probate Code. The rule also governs initial fee waivers in other civil actions or proceedings in which conservators or guardians are parties representing the interests of their conservatees or wards.
(Subd (a) adopted effective September 1, 2015.)

(b) Court fee waiver requested by a petitioner for the appointment of a conservator or guardian of the person, estate, or person and estate of a conservatee or ward

A petitioner for the appointment of a conservator or guardian of the person, estate, or person and estate of a conservatee or ward must base an application for an initial fee waiver on the personal financial condition of the proposed conservatee or ward.
(Subd (b) adopted effective September 1, 2015.)

(c) Court fee waiver requested by a petitioner for the appointment of a personal representative of a decedent's estate

A petitioner for the appointment of a personal representative of a decedent's estate must base an application for an initial fee waiver on the petitioner's personal financial condition.
(Subd (c) adopted effective September 1, 2015.)

(d) Effect of appointment of a personal representative of a decedent's estate on a court fee waiver

The appointment of a personal representative of a decedent's estate may be a change of financial condition for fee waiver purposes under Government Code section 68636 in accordance with the following:

(1) If the successful petitioner is an appointed personal representative:

(A) The petitioner's continued eligibility for an initial fee waiver must be based on the combined financial condition of the petitioner and the decedent's estate.

(B) Upon marshaling or collecting assets of the decedent's estate following the petitioner's appointment and qualification as personal representative, the petitioner must notify the court of a change in financial condition under Government Code section 68636(a) that may affect his or her ability to pay all or a portion of the waived court fees and costs.

(C) The court may make a preliminary determination under Government Code section 68636(b) that the petitioner's appointment as fiduciary is a change of financial condition that makes the petitioner no longer eligible for an initial fee waiver based, in whole or in part, on the estimates of estate value and income contained in the petitioner's *Petition for Probate*. In that event, the court must give notice and conduct the hearing required by section 68636(b).

(2) If the successful petitioner is not an appointed personal representative:

(A) An initial fee waiver for that petitioner continues in effect according to its terms for subsequent fees incurred by that petitioner in the proceeding solely in his or her individual capacity.

(B) The appointed personal representative may apply for an initial fee waiver. The application must be based on the combined financial condition of the personal representative and the decedent's estate.

(Subd (d) adopted effective September 1, 2015.)

(e) Financial condition of the conservatee or ward

(1) The financial condition of the conservatee or ward for purposes of this rule includes:

(A) The financial condition—to the extent of the information known or reasonably available to the conservator or guardian, or the petitioner for the conservator's or guardian's appointment, upon reasonable inquiry—of any person who has a duty to support the conservatee or ward, including a spouse, registered domestic partner, or parent. A divorced spouse's or divorced registered domestic partner's duty to support a conservatee and a parent's duty to support a ward under this subparagraph is limited to the amount of support ordered by a court. Consideration of a support order as an element of the conservatee's or ward's financial condition under this rule is subject to the provisions of Government Code sections 68637(d) and (e), concerning the likelihood that the obligated person will pay all or any portion of the support ordered by the court;

(B) A conservatee's interest in community property that is outside the conservatorship estate and under the management or control of the conservatee's spouse or registered domestic partner; and

(C) The right to receive support, income, or other distributions from a trust or under a contract.

(2) Following the appointment of a conservator or guardian and the grant of an initial fee waiver based on the financial condition of the conservatee or ward, the conservator or guardian is the "person who received the initial fee waiver" for purposes of Government Code section 68636(a), whether or not he or she was the successful applicant for the initial waiver. The conservator or guardian must report to the court any changes in the financial condition of the conservatee or ward that affects his or her ability to pay all or a portion of the court fees and costs that were initially waived, including any changes in the financial condition of the persons or property mentioned in subparagraphs (1)(A) and (1)(B) of this subdivision of which the conservator or guardian becomes aware after reasonable investigation.

(Subd (e) adopted effective September 1, 2015.)

(f) Additional discretionary factors in the financial condition or circumstances of a decedent's, conservatee's, or ward's estate

(1) The financial condition of the decedent's, conservatee's, or ward's estate for purposes of this rule may, in the court's discretion, include consideration of:

(A) The estate's liquidity;

(B) Whether estate property or income is necessary for the support of a person entitled to a family allowance from the estate of a decedent, the conservatee or a person entitled to support from the conservatee, or the ward; or

(C) Whether property in a decedent's estate is specifically devised.

(2) If property of the estate is eliminated from consideration for initial court fee waiver purposes because of one or more of the factors listed in (1), the court may determine that the estate can pay a portion of court fees, can pay court fees over time, or can pay court fees at a later time, under an equitable arrangement within the meaning of Government Code sections 68632(c) and 68634(e)(5). An equitable arrangement under this paragraph may include establishment of a lien for initially waived court fees against property distributable from a decedent's estate or payable to the conservatee or ward or other successor in interest at the termination of a conservatorship or guardianship.

(Subd (f) adopted effective September 1, 2015.)

(g) Payment of previously waived court fees by a decedent's estate

If the financial condition of a decedent's estate is a change of financial condition of a fee waiver applicant under this rule that results in withdrawal of a previously granted initial waiver of fees in favor of a petitioner for the appointment of a personal representative, the estate must pay to the court, as an allowable expense of administration, the fees and costs previously waived.

(Subd (g) adopted effective September 1, 2015.)

(h) Termination or modification of previously granted initial fee waivers

(1) *Conservatorships and guardianships of the estate or person and estate*

Upon establishment of a conservatorship or guardianship of the estate or person and estate, the court may collect all or a portion of court fees previously waived from the estate of the conservatee or ward if the court finds that the estate has the ability to pay the fees, or a portion thereof, immediately, over a period of time, or under some other equitable agreement, without using moneys that normally would pay for the common necessaries of life for the conservatee or ward and his or her family. The court must comply with the notice and hearing requirements of the second paragraph of Government Code section 68634(e)(5) to make the findings authorized in this paragraph.

(2) *Conservatorships and guardianships of the person*

In a conservatorship or guardianship of the person, if the court seeks to reconsider or modify a court fee waiver previously granted based on collection, application, or consideration of support, assets, or income described in (e), it must proceed as provided in Government Code section 68636 and comply with the notice and hearing requirements of the second paragraph of Government Code section 68634(e)(5), including notice to the conservator or guardian, any support obligor, and any person in possession of the assets or income. The conservator or guardian must appear at the hearing on behalf of the conservatee or ward, and the court may also appoint counsel for the conservatee or ward under Probate Code section 1470.

(Subd (h) adopted effective September 1, 2015.)

(i) Civil actions in which a conservator or guardian is a party representing the interests of a conservatee or ward

In a civil action in which a conservator or guardian is a party representing the interests of a conservatee or ward against another party or parties, for purposes of Government Code sections 68631.5, 68636, and 68637:

(1) The conservator or guardian is the person with a duty to notify the court of a change of financial condition under section 68636(a) and the person the court may require to appear at a court hearing under sections 68636(b) and (c);

(2) The conservatee or ward and the persons identified in subparagraphs (1)(A) and (B) of subdivision (e) of this rule is the person or persons whose change of financial condition or circumstances of which the court is to be notified under section 68636(a); and

(3) The conservatee or ward is the person or party whose initial fees and costs were initially waived under sections 68636(c) and 68637.

(Subd (i) adopted effective September 1, 2015.)

(j) Advances of court fees and costs by legal counsel

(1) Government Code section 68633(g)—concerning agreements between applicants for initial court fee waivers and their legal counsel for counsel to advance court fees and costs and court hearings to determine the effect of the presence or absence of such agreements on the applications—applies to proceedings described in this rule.

(2) Conservators, guardians, and petitioners for their appointment applying for initial fee waivers under this rule represented by legal counsel, and their counsel, must complete the *Request to Waive Court Fees (Ward or Conservatee)* (form FW-001-GC), including items 2a and 2b, and, if a request to waive additional court fees is made, the *Request to Waive Additional Court Fees (Superior Court) (Ward or Conservatee)* (form FW-002-GC), including items 2a and 2b. The reference to "legal-aid type services" in these forms refers to legal services provided to an applicant by counsel for or affiliated with a qualified legal services project defined in Business and Professions Code section 6213.

(Subd (j) adopted effective September 1, 2015.)

(k) Expiration of initial court fee waivers in decedents' estates, conservatorships, and guardianships

"Final disposition of the case" in decedent's estate, conservatorship, and guardianship proceedings for purposes of determining the expiration of fee waivers under Government Code section 68639 occurs on the later of the following events:

(1) Termination of the proceedings by order of court or under operation of law in conservatorships and guardianships of the person; or

(2) Discharge of personal representatives of decedents' estates and discharge of conservators or guardians of estates.

(Subd (k) adopted effective September 1, 2015.)
Rule 7.5 adopted effective September 1, 2015.

Rule 7.10.   Ex parte communications in proceedings under the probate code and certain other proceedings

(a) Definitions

As used in this rule, the following terms have the meanings stated below:

(1) "Fiduciary" has the meaning specified in Probate Code section 39, and includes LPS conservators.

(2) "Person" has the meaning specified in Probate Code section 56.

(3) "Pleading" has the meaning specified in rule 7.3, but also includes petitions and objections or other opposition filed in LPS conservatorships. The term does not include creditors' claims and requests for special notice.

(4) A "party" is a fiduciary appointed in a proceeding under the Probate Code or an LPS conservatorship proceeding, and any other person who has filed a pleading in the proceeding concerning a matter then pending in the court.

(5) A "ward" is a minor subject to a guardianship under Division 4 of the Probate Code, including a proposed ward concerning whom a petition for appointment of a guardian has been filed.

(6) "Ex parte communication" is a communication between any party, attorney, or person in a proceeding under the Probate Code or an LPS conservatorship proceeding and the court outside the presence of all parties and attorneys, including written communications sent to the court without copies having been provided to other interested persons.

(7) "LPS Act" is the Lanterman-Petris-Short Act, part 1 of division 5 of the Welfare and Institutions Code, commencing with section 5000.

(8) "LPS Conservatorship" is a conservatorship proceeding under chapter 3 of the LPS Act, commencing with section 5350 of the Welfare and Institutions Code, for persons gravely disabled as the result of a mental disorder or impairment by chronic alcoholism.

(9) A "conservatee" is a person subject to a conservatorship under division 4 of the Probate Code or chapter 3 of the LPS Act, including a proposed conservatee concerning whom a petition for appointment of a conservator has been filed.

(10) A "matter then pending in the court" in proceedings under the Probate Code or in an LPS conservatorship proceeding refers to a request for relief or opposition in pleadings filed in the proceeding that has not yet been resolved by a decision of the court or an agreement of the parties.

(11) Concerning a proceeding under the Probate Code or an LPS conservatorship proceeding, the term "open proceeding" refers to a proceeding that has been commenced and has not been concluded by the final discharge of all fiduciaries or otherwise terminated as provided by law, whether or not there is a matter then pending in the court in the proceeding at any point in time.

(Subd (a) adopted effective January 1, 2008.)

(b) Ex parte communications by parties and attorneys prohibited

(1) Except under a stipulation of all parties to the contrary, no ex parte communications may be made by a party or an attorney for a party and the court concerning a matter then pending in the court in proceedings under the Probate Code or in an LPS conservatorship proceeding.

(2) Except as provided in (c)(1), the court must treat an ex parte communication to the court described in (1) in the same way that an ex parte communication from a party or attorney for a party must be treated in other civil actions or proceedings or in criminal actions.

(Subd (b) adopted effective January 1, 2008.)

(c) Ex parte communications received and considered

(1) Notwithstanding (b)(2), a judicial officer or court staff may receive an ex parte communication concerning an open proceeding under the Probate Code or an open LPS conservatorship proceeding for the limited purpose of ascertaining whether it is a communication described in (b) or a communication described in (c)(2).

(2) Subject to the requirements of (c)(3), a judicial officer may consider an ex parte communication from a person about a fiduciary's performance of his or her duties and responsibilities or regarding a

conservatee or ward in an open proceeding under the Probate Code or an open LPS conservatorship proceeding. The court may decline to take further action on the communication, with or without replying to the person or returning any written communication received from the person. The court may also take appropriate action, consistent with due process and California law, including one or any combination of the following:

(A) Review the court file and take any action that is supported by the record, including ordering a status report or accounting if it appears that a status report or accounting should have been filed by a fiduciary but is delinquent.

(B) Refer the communication to a court investigator for further action, and receive, consider, and respond to any report from the investigator concerning it;

(C) If the communication discloses possible criminal activity, refer the matter to the appropriate law enforcement agency or prosecutor's office;

(D) If the communication discloses conduct that might subject a person or organization to disciplinary action on a license, refer the matter to the appropriate licensing agency;

(E) If the communication discloses possible elder or dependent adult abuse, or child abuse, refer the matter to appropriate state or local governmental agencies, including adult protective or child protective service departments; and

(F) Set a hearing regarding the communication, compel the fiduciary's attendance, and require a response from the fiduciary concerning the issues raised by the communication.

(3) The court must fully disclose communications described in (c)(2) and any response made by the court to the fiduciary and all other parties to any matter then pending in the court, and their attorneys, unless the court finds good cause to dispense with the disclosure if necessary to protect a conservatee or ward from harm. If the court dispenses with disclosure to any party or attorney, it must make written findings in support of its determination of good cause, and preserve the communication received and any response made by the court. The court may place its findings and the preserved communication under seal or otherwise secure their confidentiality.

(Subd (c) adopted effective January 1, 2008.)
Rule 7.10 adopted effective January 1, 2008.

Chapter 2
Notices, Publication, and Service

Rule 7.50.   Description of pleading in notice of hearing

The notice of hearing on a pleading filed in a proceeding under the Probate Code must state the complete title of the pleading to which the notice relates.

Rule 7.50 adopted effective January 1, 2003.

Rule 7.51.   Service of notice of hearing

(a) Direct notice required

(1) Except as otherwise permitted in the Probate Code, a notice sent by mail under Probate Code section 1220 must be mailed individually and directly to the person entitled to notice.

(2) A notice mailed to a person in care of another person is insufficient unless the person entitled to notice is an adult and has directed the party giving notice in writing to send the notice in care of the second person.

(3) Notices mailed to more than one person in the same household must be sent separately to each person.

(b) Notice to attorney

If a notice is required or permitted to be given to a person who is represented by an attorney of record in the proceeding, the notice must be sent as required in Probate Code section 1214.

(c) Notice to guardian or conservator

(1) When a guardian or conservator has been appointed for a person entitled to notice, the notice must be sent to the guardian or conservator.

(2) A copy of the notice must also be sent to the ward or conservatee unless:

(A) The court dispenses with such notice; or

(B) Under Probate Code section 1210 in a decedent's estate proceeding, the notice is personally served on a California-resident guardian or conservator of the estate of the ward or conservatee.

(Subd (c) amended effective January 1, 2004.)

(d) Notice to minor

Except as permitted in Probate Code section 1460.1 for guardianships, conservatorships, and certain protective proceedings under division 4 of the Probate Code, notice to a minor must be sent directly to the minor. A separate copy of the notice must be sent to the person or persons having legal custody of the minor, with whom the minor resides.

(e) Notice required in a decedent's estate when a beneficiary has died

(1) *Notice when a beneficiary dies after the decedent*

Notice must be sent to the personal representative of a beneficiary who died after the decedent and survived for a period required by the decedent's will. If no personal representative has been appointed for the postdeceased beneficiary, notice must be sent to his or her beneficiaries or other persons entitled to succeed to his or her interest in the decedent's estate.

(2) *Notice when a beneficiary of the decedent's will dies before the decedent*

When a beneficiary under the will of the decedent died before the decedent or fails to survive the decedent for a period required by the decedent's will, notice must be sent to the persons named in the decedent's will as substitute beneficiaries of the gift to the predeceased beneficiary. If the decedent's will does not make a substitute disposition of that gift, notice must be sent as follows:

(A) If the predeceased beneficiary is a "transferee" under Probate Code section 21110(c), to the issue of the predeceased beneficiary determined under Probate Code section 240 and to the residuary beneficiaries of the decedent or to the decedent's heirs if decedent's will does not provide for distribution of the residue of the estate.

(B) If the predeceased beneficiary is not a "transferee" under Probate Code section 21110(c), to the residuary beneficiaries of the decedent or to the decedent's heirs if decedent's will does not provide for distribution of the residue of the estate.

Rule 7.51 amended effective January 1, 2004; adopted effective January 1, 2003.

Rule 7.52. Service of notice when recipient's address unknown

(a) Declaration of diligent search

Petitioner must file a declaration describing efforts made to locate a person entitled to notice in a proceeding under the Probate Code, but whose address is unknown, before the court will prescribe an alternate form of notice or dispense with notice under (c). The declaration must state the name of the person whose address is unknown, the last known address of the person, the approximate date when the person was last known to reside there, the efforts made to locate the person, and any facts that explain why the person's address cannot be obtained. The declaration must include a description of the attempts to learn of the person's business and residence addresses by:

(1) Inquiry of the relatives, friends, acquaintances, and employers of the person entitled to notice and of the person who is the subject of the proceeding;

(2) Review of appropriate city telephone directories and directory assistance; and

(3) Search of the real and personal property indexes in the recorder's and assessor's offices for the county where the person was last known or believed to reside.

(b) Mailed notice to county seat

Mailing notice to a person at a county seat is not a manner of giving notice reasonably calculated to give actual notice.

(c) The court may prescribe or dispense with notice

If a person entitled to notice cannot be located after diligent search, the court may prescribe the manner of giving notice to that person or may dispense with notice to that person.

Rule 7.52 adopted effective January 1, 2003.

Rule 7.53. Notice of hearing of amended or supplemented pleadings

(a) Amended pleading and amendment to a pleading

An amended pleading or an amendment to a pleading requires the same notice of hearing (including publication) as the pleading it amends.

(b) Supplement to a pleading

A supplement to a pleading does not require additional notice of hearing, but a copy of a supplement to a pleading must be served if service of a copy of the pleading was required, unless waived by the court.

Rule 7.53 adopted effective January 1, 2003.

Rule 7.54. Publication of Notice of Petition to Administer Estate

Publication and service of a *Notice of Petition to Administer Estate* (form DE-121) under Probate Code sections 8110–8125 is sufficient notice of any instrument offered for probate that is filed with, and specifically referred to in, the petition for which notice is given. Any other instrument must be presented in an amended petition, and a new notice must be published and served.

Rule 7.54 amended effective January 1, 2007; adopted effective January 1, 2003.

Rule 7.55. Ex parte application for order

(a) Special notice allegation

An ex parte application for an order must allege whether special notice has been requested.

(Subd (a) amended effective January 1, 2007.)

(b) Allegation if special notice requested

If special notice has been requested, the application must identify each person who has requested special notice and must allege that special notice has been given to or waived by each person who has requested it.

(Subd (b) amended effective January 1, 2007.)

(c) Proof of service or waiver of special notice

Proofs of service of special notice or written waivers of special notice must be filed with the application.

(Subd (c) amended effective January 1, 2007.)

Rule 7.55 amended effective January 1, 2007; adopted effective January 1, 2003.

Chapter 3
Pleadings

Rule 7.101. Use of Judicial Council forms
Rule 7.102. Titles of pleadings and orders
Rule 7.103. Signature and verification of pleadings
Rule 7.104. Execution and verification of amended pleadings, amendments to pleadings, and supplements to pleadings; use of Judicial Council forms

Rule 7.101. Use of Judicial Council forms

(a) Use of mandatory forms

If a petition, an order, or another document to be submitted to the court is one for which the Judicial Council has adopted a mandatory form, that form must be used. Except as provided in this rule, if the Judicial Council has adopted a mandatory form in more than one alternative version, one of the alternative versions must be used. If that form is inadequate in a particular situation, an addendum may be attached to it.

(Subd (a) amended and lettered effective January 1, 2007; adopted as untitled subd effective January 1, 2001.)

(b) Alternative mandatory forms

The following forms have been adopted by the Judicial Council as alternative mandatory forms for use in probate proceedings or other proceedings governed by provisions of the Probate Code:

(1) *Petition for Appointment of Guardian of Minor* (form GC-210) and *Petition for Appointment of Guardian of the Person* (form GC-210(P);

(2) *Petition for Appointment of Temporary Guardian* (form GC-110) and *Petition for Appointment of Temporary Guardian of the Person* (form GC-110(P));

(3) *Petition* [1] **for Approval of Compromise of Claim or** *Action or Disposition of Proceeds of Judgment for Minor or Person With a Disability* (form MC-350) and [2] **Petition for Expedited Approval of Compromise of Claim or** *Action or Disposition of Proceeds of Judgment for Minor or Person With a Disability* (form MC-350EX).

(Subd (b) amended effective January 1, 2021; adopted effective January 1, 2007; previously amended effective January 1, 2010, and January 1, 2014.)

Rule 7.101(b). 2020 Deletes. [1] *to Approve Compromise of Disputed Claim or Pending* [2] *Expedited Petition to Approve Compromise of Disputed Claim or Pending*

(c) Use of guardianship petitions

Notwithstanding any other provision of this rule, a party petitioning for appointment of a temporary guardian of the person of a minor may file either form GC-110 or form GC-110(P). A party petitioning for appointment of a general guardian of the person of a minor may file either form GC-210 or form GC-210(P). A party petitioning for appointment of a temporary guardian of the estate or the person and estate of a minor must file form GC-110. A party petitioning for appointment of a general guardian of the estate or the person and estate of a minor must file form GC-210.

(Subd (c) adopted effective January 1, 2007.)

Rule 7.101 amended effective January 1, 2021; adopted effective January 1, 2001; previously amended effective January 1, 2002, January 1, 2007, January 1, 2010, and January 1, 2014.

Rule 7.101.5. Electronic generation of mandatory Judicial Council form orders [Repealed]

Rule 7.101.5 repealed effective January 1, 2012; adopted effective January 1, 2007.

Rule 7.102. Titles of pleadings and orders

The title of each pleading and of each proposed order must clearly and completely identify the nature of the relief sought or granted.

Rule 7.102 amended effective January 1, 2003; adopted effective January 1, 2001; previously amended effective January 1, 2002.

Rule 7.103. Signature and verification of pleadings

(a) Signature of parties

A pleading must be in writing and must be signed by all persons joining in it.

(b) Verification by parties

All pleadings filed in proceedings under the Probate Code must be verified. If two or more persons join in a pleading, it may be verified by any of them.

(c) Signature and verification by attorney

If a person is absent from the county where his or her attorney's office is located, or for some other cause is unable to sign or verify a pleading, the attorney may sign or verify it, unless the person is, or is seeking to become, a fiduciary appointed in the proceeding.

Rule 7.103 adopted effective January 1, 2003.

Rule 7.104. Execution and verification of amended pleadings, amendments to pleadings, and supplements to pleadings; use of Judicial Council forms

(a) Amended pleading and amendment to a pleading

(1) All persons required to sign a pleading must sign an amended pleading. One of the persons required to verify a pleading must verify an amended pleading.

(2) All persons required to sign a pleading must sign an amendment to that pleading. One of the persons required to verify a pleading must verify an amendment to that pleading.

(3) A Judicial Council form must be used for an amended pleading, with the word "Amended" added to its caption, if the form was used for the pleading that is amended. A Judicial Council form must not be used for an amendment to a pleading.

(b) Supplement to a pleading

(1) A supplement to a pleading must be signed and verified by one of the persons who were required to sign and verify the pleading that is supplemented. However, the court may, in the exercise of its discretion, accept for filing and consider a supplement to a pleading signed under penalty of perjury by an attorney for the party offering it, where the information contained in the supplement is particularly within the knowledge of the attorney.

(2) A Judicial Council form must not be used for a supplement to a pleading.

Rule 7.104 adopted effective January 1, 2003.

Chapter 4
Appointment of Executors and Administrators

Rule 7.150. Acknowledgment of receipt of statement of duties and liabilities of personal representative

Before the court issues letters, each personal representative of a decedent's estate (other than a company authorized to conduct a trust business in California) must execute and file an acknowledgment of receipt of *Duties and Liabilities of Personal Representative* (form DE-147).

Rule 7.150 amended effective January 1, 2007; adopted effective January 1, 2000; previously amended effective January 1, 2002.

Rule 7.151. Reimbursement of graduated filing fee by successful subsequent petitioner [Repealed]

Rule 7.151 repealed effective January 1, 2020; adopted effective January 1, 2004; previously amended effective January 1, 2007, and March 1, 2008.

Chapter 5
Bonding of Personal Representatives, Guardians, Conservators, and Trustees

Rule 7.201. Waiver of bond in will

Rule 7.201. Waiver of bond in will

(a) Statement of waiver in petition

If the will waives bond, the Petition for Probate must so state.

(Subd (a) amended effective January 1, 2007; previously amended effective January 1, 2001, and January 1, 2002.)

(b) Court's discretion to require bond

The court may require bond if the proposed personal representative resides outside California or for other good cause, even if the will waives bond.

(Subd (b) amended effective January 1, 2001.)

Rule 7.201 amended effective January 1, 2007; adopted effective January 1, 2000; previously amended effective January 1, 2001, and January 1, 2002.

Rule 7.202. Two or more personal representatives

If a will admitted to probate names two or more persons to serve as executors but not all serve and the will does not expressly waive bond if fewer than all of the named persons serve, the court must require each executor to give a bond unless the court waives this requirement under Probate Code section 8481(a)(2).

Rule 7.202 amended effective January 1, 2002; adopted effective January 1, 2000.

Rule 7.203. Separate bonds for individuals

Because a corporate fiduciary (whether personal representative, guardian, conservator, or trustee) cannot assume responsibility for the acts of an individual cofiduciary, an individual cofiduciary who is required to give a bond must provide a separate bond, except to the extent that the court orders the assets to be held solely by the corporate cofiduciary.

Rule 7.203 amended effective January 1, 2002; adopted effective January 1, 2000.

Rule 7.204. Duty to apply for order increasing bond

(a) Ex parte application for order

Immediately upon the occurrence of facts making it necessary or appropriate to increase the amount of the bond, the personal representative, or the guardian or conservator of the estate, must make an ex parte application for an order increasing the bond.

(Subd (a) amended effective January 1, 2003; previously amended effective January 1, 2002.)

(b) Attorney's duty

If the personal representative, or the guardian or conservator of the estate, has not already made application under (a), the attorney for the personal representative, or the attorney for the guardian or conservator of the estate, must make the ex parte application immediately upon becoming aware of the need to increase bond.

(Subd (b) amended effective January 1, 2003; previously amended effective January 1, 2002.)

(c) Amount

(1) The application by a personal representative under (a) or by the attorney for a personal representative under (b) must show the value of the estate's personal property and the probable annual gross income of the estate.

(2) The application by a guardian or conservator of the estate under (a) or by the attorney for a guardian or conservator of the estate under (b) must show the value of the estate's personal property, the probable annual gross income of all of the property of the estate, and the sum of the probable annual gross payments of the public benefits of the ward or conservatee identified in Probate Code section 2320(c)(3).

(3) If the personal representative has full Independent Administration of Estates Act (IAEA) authority or the guardian or conservator of the estate has authority to sell estate real property without court confirmation, the application must also show the amount of the equity in estate real property.

(Subd (c) amended effective January 1, 2003; previously amended effective January 1, 2002.)

Rule 7.204 amended effective January 1, 2002; adopted effective January 1, 2000.

Rule 7.205. Independent power to sell real property

If the personal representative requests or has been granted an independent power to sell or hypothecate real estate or to lease it for a term of more than one year, the personal representative must state in the request to fix the amount of the bond the value of the real property less encumbrances.

Rule 7.205 amended effective January 1, 2002; adopted effective January 1, 2000.

Rule 7.206.   Bond upon sale of real property

If a bond or additional bond is required in an order confirming sale of real estate, the court must not file the order until the additional bond is filed.

Rule 7.206 amended effective January 1, 2002; adopted effective January 1, 2000.

Rule 7.207.   Bonds of conservators and guardians

(a) Bond includes reasonable amount for recovery on the bond

Except as otherwise provided by statute, every conservator or guardian of the estate must furnish a bond that includes an amount determined under (b) as a reasonable amount for the cost of recovery to collect on the bond under Probate Code section 2320(c)(4).

(Subd (a) amended effective January 1, 2010; adopted effective January 1, 2008.)

(b) Amount of bond for the cost of recovery on the bond

The reasonable amount of bond for the cost of recovery to collect on the bond, including attorney's fees and costs, under Probate Code section 2320(c)(4) is:

(1) Ten percent (10%) of the value up to and including $500,000 of the following:

(A) The value of personal property of the estate;

(B) The value, less encumbrances, of real property of the estate that the guardian or conservator has the independent power to sell without approval or confirmation of the court under Probate Code sections 2590 and 2591(d);

(C) The probable annual income from all assets of the estate; and

(D) The probable annual gross payments described in Probate Code section 2320(c)(3); and

(2) Twelve percent (12%) of the value above $500,000 up to and including $1,000,000 of the property, income, and payments described in (1); and

(3) Two percent (2%) of the value above $1,000,000 of the property, income, and payments described in (1).

(Subd (b) repealed, amended and relettered effective January 1, 2010; adopted as subd (c) effective January 1, 2008.)

Rule 7.207 amended effective January 1, 2010; adopted effective January 1, 2008.

Chapter 6
Independent Administration of Estates

Rule 7.250.   Report of actions taken under the Independent Administration of Estates Act

(a) Report required

In any accounting, report, petition for preliminary distribution, or petition for final distribution, the petitioner must list and describe all actions taken without prior court approval under the Independent Administration of Estates Act (IAEA) if notice of the proposed action was required. The description of the action must include the following:

(1) The nature of the action;

(2) When the action was taken;

(3) A statement of when and to whom notice was given;

(4) Whether notice was waived, and if so, by whom; and

(5) Whether any objections were received.

(Subd (a) amended effective January 1, 2002.)

(b) Actions reported in previous reports

An action taken under the IAEA that was (1) properly listed and described in a prior accounting, report, or petition for distribution, and (2) approved by the court, need not be listed and described in a subsequent account, report, or petition for distribution.

(Subd (b) amended effective January 1, 2007.)

Rule 7.250 amended effective January 1, 2007; adopted effective January 1, 2000; previously amended effective January 1, 2002.

Chapter 7
Spousal or Domestic Partner Property Petitions

Rule 7.301.   Spousal or domestic partner property petition filed with petition for probate

A petition for spousal or domestic partner property determination or confirmation must be filed separately from a petition for probate of will or for letters of administration, even if both petitions are filed at the same time. The two petitions must be filed under the same case number.

Rule 7.301 amended effective January 1, 2007; adopted effective January 1, 2000; previously amended effective January 1, 2002.

Chapter 8
Petitions for Instructions
[Reserved]

Chapter 9
Creditors' Claims

Rule 7.401. Personal representative's action on the claim
Rule 7.402. Court's action on the claim
Rule 7.403. Listing all claims in the final report

Rule 7.401.   Personal representative's action on the claim

For each creditor's claim filed with the court, the personal representative (whether or not acting under the Independent Administration of Estates Act (IAEA)) must:

(1) Allow or reject in whole or in part the claim in writing;

(2) Serve a copy of the allowance or rejection on the creditor and the creditor's attorney; and

(3) File a copy of the allowance or rejection with proof of service with the court.

Rule 7.401 amended effective January 1, 2002; adopted effective January 1, 2000.

Rule 7.402.   Court's action on the claim

Except as to claims of the personal representative or the attorney, if the personal representative has authority to act under the Independent Administration of Estates Act (IAEA), the court must not act on the personal representative's allowance or rejection of a creditor's claim unless good cause is shown.

Rule 7.402 amended effective January 1, 2002; adopted effective January 1, 2000.

Rule 7.403.   Listing all claims in the final report

For each claim presented, the personal representative must state in the final report or petition for final distribution:

(1) The claimant's name;

(2) The date of filing of the claim;

(3) The nature of the claim;

(4) The amount claimed;

(5) The disposition of the claim; and

(6) If the claim was rejected, the date of service of the rejection and whether or not a lawsuit was filed.

Rule 7.403 amended effective January 1, 2002; adopted effective January 1, 2000.

Chapter 10
Sales of Real and Personal Property

Rule 7.451. Refusal to show property to prospective buyers
Rule 7.452. Petitioner or attorney required at hearing
Rule 7.453. Petition for exclusive listing
Rule 7.454. Ex parte application for order authorizing sale of securities or other personal property

Rule 7.451.   Refusal to show property to prospective buyers

Upon a showing that the fiduciary has denied any bona fide prospective buyer or his or her broker a reasonable opportunity to inspect the property, the court must not confirm the sale but must continue the sale to allow inspection unless good cause is shown for the court to confirm the sale.

Rule 7.451 amended effective January 1, 2002; adopted effective January 1, 2000.

Rule 7.452.   Petitioner or attorney required at hearing

The court must not proceed with the hearing on a petition to confirm a sale of property unless the petitioner's attorney or petitioner, if unrepresented, is present.

Rule 7.452 amended effective January 1, 2002; adopted effective January 1, 2000.

Rule 7.453.   Petition for exclusive listing

A petition for approval of an exclusive listing under Probate Code section 10150(c) must state the following:

(1) A description of the property to be sold;

(2) The name of the broker to be employed;

(3) A summary of the terms of the exclusive listing agreement or include a copy of the listing agreement; and

(4) A detailed statement of the facts supporting the "necessity and the advantage" to the estate of having the exclusive listing.

Rule 7.453 amended effective January 1, 2002; adopted effective January 1, 2000.

Rule 7.454.   Ex parte application for order authorizing sale of securities or other personal property

An ex parte application for authority to sell or to surrender tangible or

intangible personal property must state whether or not the property is specifically devised. If it is specifically devised, the written consent of the specific devisee to the sale or surrender must be filed.
Rule 7.454 adopted effective January 1, 2003.

Chapter 11
Inventory and Appraisal

Rule 7.501. Inventory and Appraisal to show sufficiency of bond

(a) Statement required

Every Inventory and Appraisal must contain one of the following statements:

(1) "Bond is waived";

(2) "Bond has been filed in the amount of $ *(specify amount)* and is insufficient"; or

(3) "Bond has been filed in the amount of $ *(specify amount)* and is sufficient."

(Subd (a) amended effective January 1, 2007; previously amended effective January 1, 2002.)

(b) Insufficient bond

If the bond is insufficient, the fiduciary (the personal representative, or the guardian or conservator of the estate), or the attorney for the fiduciary, must immediately make ex parte application as provided in rule 7.204 for an order increasing the amount of the bond.

(Subd (b) amended effective January 1, 2003; previously amended effective January 1, 2002.)

(c) Statement signed by attorney

The statement required by (a) must be signed by the attorney of record for each fiduciary who has an attorney of record and by each fiduciary who does not.

(Subd (c) amended effective January 1, 2003; previously amended effective January 1, 2002.)

Rule 7.501 amended effective January 1, 2007; adopted effective January 1, 2000; previously amended effective January 1, 2002, and January 1, 2003.

Chapter 12
Accounts and Reports of Executors, Administrators, Conservators, and Guardians

Chapter 12 amended effective January 1, 2008.

Rule 7.550. Effect of waiver of account
Rule 7.575. Accounts of conservators and guardians

Rule 7.550. Effect of waiver of account

(a) Waiver of account

Except as provided in (b), if an accounting is waived under Probate Code section 10954, the details of receipts and disbursements need not be listed in the report required under section 10954(c)(1).

(Subd (a) amended effective January 1, 2007; adopted as part of unlettered subdivision effective January 1, 2003; previously amended effective January 1, 2004.)

(b) Information required in report on waiver of account

The report required when an account has been waived must list the information required by law, including information as to:

(1) Creditors' claims;

(2) Sales, purchases, or exchanges of assets;

(3) Changes in the form of assets;

(4) Assets on hand;

(5) Whether the estate is solvent;

(6) Detailed schedules of receipts and gains or losses on sale (where an amount other than the amount of the Inventory and Appraisal is used as a basis for calculating fees or commissions);

(7) Costs of administration (if reimbursement of these costs is requested);

(8) The amount of any fees or commissions paid or to be paid;

(9) The calculation of such fees or commissions as described in rule 7.705 [1].

(Subd (b) amended effective January 1, 2020; adopted as part of unlettered subdivision effective January 1, 2003; previously amended effective January 1, 2004, and January 1, 2007.)

Rule 7.550(b).   2019 Deletes. [1] ; and (10) For decedent's estate proceedings commenced on or after August 18, 2003, the information required by rule 7.552(a) and (b)

Rule 7.550 amended effective January 1, 2020; adopted effective January 1, 2003; previously amended effective January 1, 2004, and January 1, 2007.

Rule 7.551. Final accounts or reports in estates with nonresident beneficiaries [Repealed]

Rule 7.551 repealed effective January 1, 2015; adopted effective January 1, 2004.

Rule 7.552. Graduated filing fee adjustments for estates commenced on or after August 18, 2003, and before January 1, 2008 [Repealed]

Rule 7.552 repealed effective January 1, 2015; adopted effective January 1, 2004; previously amended effective January 1, 2007, and March 1, 2008.

Rule 7.553. Graduated filing fee statements for decedents' estates commenced on or after January 1, 2008 [Repealed]

Rule 7.553 repealed effective January 1, 2015; adopted effective March 1, 2008.

Rule 7.575. Accountings of conservators and guardians

[1] **Unless waived by the court** under Probate Code section [2] **2628, a conservator or guardian of the estate must file accountings in the frequency, manner, and circumstances specified in Probate Code section 2620. The court may order accountings to be filed more frequently than required by the statute. An** accounting must [3] be filed [4] **as a standard accounting unless this rule authorizes filing a simplified accounting.**

(a) Information required in all accountings

[5] **Notwithstanding any other provision of this rule or the Judicial Council accounting forms, each accounting filed with the court must include:**

(1) **All information required by Probate Code section 1061 in the** *Summary of Account—Standard and Simplified Accounts* **(form GC-400(SUM)/GC-405(SUM));**

(2) **All information required by Probate Code sections 1062–1063 in the supporting schedules; and**

(3) **All information required by Probate Code section 1064 in the petition for approval of the accounting or the report accompanying the petition.**

(Subd (a) amended effective January 1, 2020; adopted effective January 1, 2008.)

Rule 7.575(a).   2019 Deletes. [1] This rule defines standard and simplified accountings filed by conservators and guardians [2] 2620(a), provides when each type of [3] or may [4] , and prescribes the use of Judicial Council accounting forms in both types of accountings [5] A standard accounting lists receipts and disbursements in subject-matter categories, with each receipt and disbursement category subtotaled. A simplified accounting lists receipts and disbursements chronologically, by receipt or payment date, without subject-matter categories

(b) Supporting documents

Each accounting filed with the court must include the supporting documents, including all original statements, specified in section 2620(c) of the Probate Code.

(1) If a conservator or guardian receives a statement from the issuing institution in electronic form but not in paper form, the court has discretion to accept a computer-generated printout of that statement as an original in satisfaction of the requirements in section 2620(c) if:

(A) The fiduciary submitting the printout verifies under penalty of perjury that the statement was received in electronic form and printed without alteration; and

(B) The printout is an "original," as defined in Evidence Code section 255.

(2) This rule does not authorize a fiduciary to submit, or a court to accept, a copy of a statement in support of an accounting filed under section 2620.

(Subd (b) adopted effective January 1, 2020.)

(c) Standard accounting

[1] **A "standard accounting" reports receipts and disbursements in subject-matter categories, with each category subtotaled on a separate form. A conservator, guardian, or trustee must file each accounting** as a standard accounting [2] **unless** a simplified accounting [3] **is authorized in (d)(1).**

(Subd (c) relettered and amended effective January 1, 2020; adopted as subd (b) effective January 1, 2008.)

Rule 7.575(c).   2019 Deletes. [1] A conservator or guardian may file any accounting required or authorized by Probate Code section 2620 [2] under this rule and must file a standard accounting if: (1) The estate contains income real property; (2) The estate contains a whole or partial interest in a trade or business; (3) The appraised value of the estate is $500,000 or more, exclusive of the conservatee's or ward's personal residence; (4) Except as provided in (c), Schedule A (receipts) or Schedule C (disbursements) prepared in [3] format exceeds five pages in length; or (5) The court directs that a standard accounting be filed

(d) Simplified accounting

A "simplified accounting" reports individual receipts and disbursements chronologically, by receipt or payment date, without separating them into subject matter categories.

(1) A conservator [1]**,** guardian**, or trustee** may file a simplified accounting [2] **only if all the following requirements are met:**

(A) The estate or trust contains no income-generating real property;

(B) The estate or trust contains neither a whole nor a partial interest in a trade or business;

(C) The appraised value of the estate or trust, excluding the value of the conservatee's or ward's personal residence, is less than $500,000; and

(D) The court has not directed the fiduciary to file a standard accounting.

(2) If the requirements in (1) are met, but either *Schedule A, Receipts—Simplified Account* **(form GC-405(A)) or** *Schedule C, Disbursements—Simplified Account* **(form GC-405(C)) would be longer than five pages, the fiduciary must use the standard receipt forms— forms GC-400(A)(1)–(6)—or the standard disbursement forms— forms GC-400(C)(1)–(11)—as applicable, but may otherwise file a simplified accounting.**

(Subd (d) relettered and amended effective January 1, 2020; adopted as subd (c) effective January 1, 2008.)

Rule 7.575(d). 2019 Deletes. [1] or [2] in all cases not listed in (b). If required by this rule to file a standard accounting only because a receipts or disbursements schedule is longer than five pages under (b)(4), a conservator or guardian may file a simplified accounting, except for that schedule, which must be prepared in a standard accounting format.

(e) Judicial Council forms

[1] The Judicial Council has approved two overlapping sets of forms for accountings in conservatorships and guardianships.

(1) Forms intended for use in standard accountings are numbered GC-400.

(2) Forms intended for use in simplified accountings are numbered GC-405.

(3) Forms intended for use in both accounting formats bear both numbers.

(4) Each form number is followed by a suffix—for example, GC-405(A)—to specify that form's intended use. The suffix indicates either the letter or the subject matter of the form's schedule.

(5) The *Summary of Account—Standard and Simplified Accounts* **(form GC-400(SUM)/GC-405(SUM)) must be used in all accountings.**

(6) Except for the *Summary of Account,* **all standard accounting forms are optional. A fiduciary who files a standard accounting and elects not to use the Judicial Council forms must:**

(A) Report receipts and disbursements in the subject-matter categories specified on the Judicial Council standard accounting forms for receipts and disbursements schedules;

(B) Provide the same information about any asset, property, transaction, receipt, disbursement, or other matter that is required on the applicable Judicial Council standard accounting form; and

(C) Provide the information in the same general format as that of the applicable Judicial Council standard accounting form, except that instructional material and material contained or requested in the form's header and footer may be omitted.

(7) *Schedule A, Receipts—Simplified Account* **(form GC-405(A)) and** *Schedule C, Disbursements—Simplified Account* **(form GC-405(C)) must be used in all simplified accountings unless (d)(2) requires use of the standard forms for Schedule A or Schedule C.**

(8) A fiduciary filing a simplified accounting must use the appropriate form in the GC-405 series whenever the accounting covers an asset, a transaction, or an event to which that form applies.

(Subd (e) relettered and amended effective January 1, 2020; adopted as subd (d) effective January 1, 2008.)

Rule 7.575(e). 2019 Deletes. [1] Judicial Council forms designated as GC-400 are standard accounting forms. Forms designated as GC-405 are simplified accounting forms. Forms designated as GC-400/GC-405 are forms for both standard and simplified accountings. Each form is also designated by a suffix following its accounting designator that identifies the form's intended use, based either on the form's schedule letter as shown in the *Summary of Account* (form GC-400(SUM)/GC-405(SUM)) or the form's subject matter

(f) Order waiving an accounting

The court may make an order waiving an otherwise required accounting if all the conditions in Probate Code section 2628(a) are met. If the conservatee or ward owns a personal residence, the request for an order waiving the accounting must include, in addition to the information needed to verify that all the conditions in section 2628(a) are met, the following information and documents regarding the personal residence:

(1) The street address of the residence;

(2) A true copy of the most recent residential property tax bill;

(3) A true copy of the declarations page from the homeowner's insurance policy covering the residence;

(4) A true copy of the most recent statement for any mortgage or loan secured by the residence; and

(5) A true copy of the most recent fee or dues statement for any homeowners' association or similar association.

(Subd (f) repealed and adopted effective January 1, 2020.)
Rule 7.575 amended effective January 1, 2020; adopted effective January 1, 2008.

Chapter 13
Taxes
[Reserved]
Chapter 14
Preliminary and Final Distributions

Rule 7.650. Decree of distribution establishing testamentary trusts
Rule 7.651. Description of property in petition for distribution
Rule 7.652. Allegations in petition for distribution concerning character of property

Rule 7.650. Decree of distribution establishing testamentary trusts

(a) Determining the trust

Upon distribution, the court must:

(1) Determine whether or not a valid trust has been created by the will;

(2) Determine the terms of the trust; and

(3) Order distribution of the trust property to the trustee.

(Subd (a) amended effective January 1, 2002.)

(b) Terms of the trust

The order for distribution must incorporate the terms of the trust so as to give effect to the conditions existing at the time distribution is ordered. The pertinent provisions must be stated in the present tense and in the third person instead of quoting the will verbatim.

(Subd (b) amended effective January 1, 2002.)
Rule 7.650 amended effective January 1, 2002; adopted effective January 1, 2000.

Rule 7.651. Description of property in petition for distribution

(a) Property description

A petition for distribution must list and describe in detail the property to be distributed, in the body of the petition or in an attachment that is incorporated in the petition by reference. If an account is filed with the petition, the description must be included in a schedule in the account.

(b) Specific description requirements

The description under (a) must:

(1) Include the amount of cash on hand;

(2) Indicate whether promissory notes are secured or unsecured, and describe in detail the security interest of any secured notes;

(3) Include the complete legal description, street address (if any), and assessor's parcel number (if any) of real property; and

(4) Include the complete description of each individual security held in "street name" in security brokers' accounts.

Rule 7.651 adopted effective January 1, 2004.

Rule 7.652. Allegations in petition for distribution concerning character of property

(a) Required allegations

If the character of property to be distributed may affect the distribution, a petition for distribution must allege:

(1) The character of the property to be distributed, whether separate, community, or quasi-community; and

(2) That the community or quasi-community property to be distributed is either the decedent's one-half interest only, or the entire interest of the decedent and the decedent's spouse.

(b) Compliance with Probate Code section 13502

If any property is to be distributed outright to the surviving spouse, a written election by the surviving spouse that complies with Probate Code section 13502 must have been filed, and the petition must show the filing date of the election.

Rule 7.652 adopted effective January 1, 2004.

Chapter 15
Compensation of Personal Representatives and Attorneys

Rule 7.700. Compensation paid in advance
Rule 7.701. Allowance on account of statutory compensation
Rule 7.702. Petition for extraordinary compensation
Rule 7.703. Extraordinary compensation
Rule 7.704. Apportionment of statutory compensation
Rule 7.705. Calculation of statutory compensation
Rule 7.706. Compensation when personal representative is an attorney
Rule 7.707. Application of compensation provisions

Rule 7.700.   Compensation paid in advance

(a) No compensation in advance of court order

The personal representative must neither pay nor receive, and the attorney for the personal representative must not receive, statutory commissions or fees or fees for extraordinary services in advance of an order of the court authorizing their payment.

(b) Surcharge for payment or receipt of advance compensation

In addition to removing the personal representative and imposing any other sanctions authorized by law against the personal representative or the attorney for the personal representative, the court may surcharge the personal representative for payment or receipt of statutory commissions or fees or fees for extraordinary services in advance of an order of the court authorizing their payment. The surcharge may include interest at the legal rate from the date of payment.

Rule 7.700 adopted effective January 1, 2003.

Rule 7.701.   Allowance on account of statutory compensation

The court may authorize an allowance of statutory fees or commissions on account before approval of the final account and the decree of final distribution. Any allowance made before settlement of the final account must be low enough to avoid the possibility of overpayment. The allowance:

(1) Must be based on the estimated amount of statutory compensation payable on the estate determined as of the date of the petition for allowance;

(2) Must be in proportion to the work actually performed; and

(3) Must be based upon a detailed description of the ordinary services performed and remaining to be performed.

Rule 7.701 adopted effective January 1, 2003.

Rule 7.702.   Petition for extraordinary compensation

A petition for extraordinary compensation must include, or be accompanied by, a statement of the facts upon which the petition is based. The statement of facts must:

(1) Show the nature and difficulty of the tasks performed;

(2) Show the results achieved;

(3) Show the benefit of the services to the estate;

(4) Specify the amount requested for each category of service performed;

(5) State the hourly rate of each person who performed services and the hours spent by each of them;

(6) Describe the services rendered in sufficient detail to demonstrate the productivity of the time spent; and

(7) State the estimated amount of statutory compensation to be paid by the estate, if the petition is not part of a final account or report.

Rule 7.702 adopted effective January 1, 2003.

Rule 7.703.   Extraordinary compensation

(a) Discretion of the court

An award of extraordinary compensation to the personal representative or to the attorney for the personal representative is within the discretion of the court. The court may consider the amount of statutory compensation when determining compensation for extraordinary services.

(b) Examples of extraordinary services by personal representative

The following is a nonexclusive list of activities for which extraordinary compensation may be awarded to the personal representative:

(1) Selling, leasing, exchanging, financing, or foreclosing real or personal property;

(2) Carrying on decedent's business if necessary to preserve the estate or under court order;

(3) Preparing tax returns; and

(4) Handling audits or litigation connected with tax liabilities of the decedent or of the estate.

(c) Examples of extraordinary services by attorney

The following is a nonexclusive list of activities for which extraordinary compensation may be awarded to the attorney for the personal representative:

(1) Legal services in connection with the sale of property held in the estate;

(2) Services to secure a loan to pay estate debts;

(3) Litigation undertaken to benefit the estate or to protect its interests;

(4) Defense of the personal representative's account;

(5) Defense of a will contested after its admission to probate;

(6) Successful defense of a will contested before its admission to probate;

(7) Successful defense of a personal representative in a removal proceeding;

(8) Extraordinary efforts to locate estate assets;

(9) Litigation in support of attorney's request for extraordinary compensation, where prior compensation awards are not adequate compensation under all the circumstances;

(10) Coordination of ancillary administration; and

(11) Accounting for a deceased, incapacitated, or absconded personal representative under Probate Code section 10953.

(d) Contingency fee agreement for extraordinary legal services

An attorney may agree to perform extraordinary services for a personal representative on a contingent-fee basis on the following conditions:

(1) The agreement must be in writing and must comply with section 6147 of the Business and Professions Code;

(2) The court must approve the agreement in the manner provided in Probate Code section 10811(c), based on findings that the compensation under the agreement is just and reasonable, that the agreement is to the advantage of the estate, and that the agreement is in the best interest of the persons interested in the estate; and

(3) In the absence of an emergency or other unusual circumstances, the personal representative must obtain the court's approval of the contingency fee agreement before services are performed under it.

(Subd (d) amended effective January 1, 2007.)

(e) Use of paralegals in the performance of extraordinary services

Extraordinary legal services may include the services of a paralegal as defined in Business and Professions Code section 6450(a) only if the request for extraordinary legal fees for the paralegal's services:

(1) Describes the qualifications of the paralegal (including education, certification, continuing education, and experience). The description must state that the paralegal:

(A) Acted under the direction and supervision of an attorney;

(B) Satisfies one or more of the minimum qualifications specified in Business and Professions Code section 6450(c); and

(C) Has completed mandatory continuing education required by Business and Professions Code section 6450(d) for the last two-year certification period ending before the year during which any part of the paralegal's services were performed.

(2) States the hours spent by the paralegal and the hourly rate requested for the paralegal's services;

(3) Describes the services performed by the paralegal;

(4) States why it was appropriate to use the paralegal's services in the particular case; and

(5) Demonstrates that the total amount requested for the extraordinary services of the attorney and the paralegal does not exceed the amount appropriate if the attorney had performed the services without the paralegal's assistance.

(Subd (e) amended effective July 1, 2010.)

Rule 7.703 amended effective July 1, 2010; adopted effective January 1, 2003; previously amended effective January 1, 2007.

Rule 7.704.   Apportionment of statutory compensation

(a) One statutory commission and fee

There is one statutory commission for ordinary services by the personal representative of the estate and one statutory attorney fee for ordinary legal services to the personal representative, regardless of the number of personal representatives or attorneys performing the services. The court may apportion statutory commissions and fees among multiple, successive, and concurrent personal representatives or attorneys. The apportionment must be based on the agreement of the multiple personal representatives or attorneys or, if there is no agreement, according to the services actually rendered by each of them.

(b) Notice of hearing

If there has been a change of personal representative or a substitution of attorneys for the personal representative, notice of hearing of any interim or final petition seeking or waiving an award of statutory compensation must be given to all prior personal representatives or attorneys unless:

(1) A waiver of notice executed by all prior personal representatives or attorneys is on file or is filed with the petition;

(2) A written, signed agreement on the allocation of statutory commissions or fees between the present personal representative or attorney and all prior personal representatives or attorneys is on file or is included in or filed with the petition; or

(3) The court's file and the petition demonstrate that the commissions or fees of the prior personal representatives or attorneys have been previously provided for and allowed by the court.

Rule 7.704 adopted effective January 1, 2003.

Rule 7.705. Calculation of statutory compensation

(a) Account filed

A petition for statutory commissions or attorney fees must state the amount of statutory compensation payable and set forth the estate accounted for and the calculation of statutory compensation. The calculation must be stated in the petition in substantially the following form:

COMMISSION OR FEE BASE

Inventory and Appraisal	$____
Receipts, Excluding Principal	$____
Gains on Sales	$____
Losses on Sales	$(____)
TOTAL COMMISSION OR FEE BASE	$____

COMMISSION OR FEE COMPUTATION

4% on first $100,000	($__)[1]	$__[2]
3% on next $100,000	($__)	$__
2% on next $800,000	($__)	$__
1% on next $9,000,000	($__)	$__
½ of 1% on next $15,000,000	($__)	$__
Amount requested from the court for estates above $25,000,000	($__)	$__
TOTAL COMMISSION OR FEE		$__[3]

1. Enter in this column the amount of the estate accounted for in each category. The sum of the entries in this column would equal the total commission or fee base.
2. Enter in this column the product of the amount of the estate accounted for in each category multiplied by the percentage for that category.
3. Enter here the sum of the products entered in this column.

(b) Account waived

When an account has been waived, the report must contain the information required by rule 7.550. If the report is accompanied by a request for statutory commissions or fees, the basis for their computation must be included in the petition substantially in the form provided in (a). Notwithstanding the waiver of account, if the petition and report requests statutory commissions or fees based on any amount other than the amount of the Inventory and Appraisal, detailed schedules of receipts and gains and losses on sales must be included.

Rule 7.705 adopted effective January 1, 2003.

Rule 7.706. Compensation when personal representative is an attorney

(a) Personal representative's compensation only

Notwithstanding the provisions of the decedent's will, a personal representative who is an attorney may receive the personal representative's compensation but may not receive compensation for legal services as the attorney for the personal representative unless the court approves the right to compensation for legal services in advance and finds the arrangement is to the advantage, benefit, and best interest of the decedent's estate.

(b) Agreement not to participate in compensation

A law firm of which the personal representative is a partner or shareholder may request compensation for legal services in addition to the personal representative's compensation if a written agreement not to participate in each other's compensation, signed by the personal representative and by authorized representatives of the law firm, has been filed in the estate proceeding.

Rule 7.706 adopted effective January 1, 2003.

Rule 7.707. Application of compensation provisions

For proceedings commenced after June 30, 1991, the law in effect on the date of the court's order awarding statutory compensation determines the amount of such compensation.

Rule 7.707 adopted effective January 1, 2003.

Chapter 16
Compensation in All Matters Other Than Decedents' Estates

Rule 7.750. Application of rules to guardianships and conservatorships

The rules in this chapter apply to guardianships and conservatorships under division 4 of the Probate Code (Prob. Code, § 1400 et seq.) and to conservatorships under the Lanterman-Petris-Short Act (Welf. & Inst. Code, §§ 5350–5371). They do not apply to guardianships under chapter 2 of division 2 of the Welfare and Institutions Code (Welf. & Inst. Code, § 200 et seq.). Under Probate Code section 2646, the rules in this chapter applicable to guardianships and conservatorships apply only to compensation payable from the estate of the ward or conservatee or from money or property recovered or collected for the estate of the ward or conservatee.

Rule 7.750 adopted effective January 1, 2003.

Rule 7.751. Petitions for orders allowing compensation for guardians or conservators and their attorneys

(a) Petition for allowance of compensation for services performed before appointment of guardian or conservator

A petition for allowance of compensation to a guardian or conservator or to the attorney for a guardian or conservator may include a request for compensation for services rendered before an order appointing a guardian or conservator. The petition must show facts demonstrating the necessity for preappointment services.

(Subd (a) amended effective January 1, 2007.)

(b) Required showing in petition for allowance of compensation

All petitions for orders fixing and allowing compensation must comply with the requirements of rule 7.702 concerning petitions for extraordinary compensation in decedents' estates, to the extent applicable to guardianships and conservatorships, except that the best interest of the ward or conservatee is to be considered instead of the interest of beneficiaries of the estate.

Rule 7.751 amended effective January 1, 2007; adopted effective January 1, 2003.

Rule 7.752. Court may order accounting before allowing compensation

Notwithstanding the time period after which a petition may be filed for an allowance of compensation to a guardian, conservator, or an attorney for a guardian or conservator, the court may order the guardian or conservator to file an accounting before or at the time a petition for an allowance of compensation is filed or heard.

Rule 7.752 adopted effective January 1, 2003.

Rule 7.753. Contingency fee agreements in guardianships and conservatorships

A guardian or conservator of the estate may contract with an attorney for a contingency fee for the attorney's services on behalf of the ward or conservatee, or the estate, in connection with a matter that is of a type

customarily the subject of a contingency fee agreement, if the court has authorized the guardian or conservator to do so, or if the agreement has been approved by the court under Probate Code section 2644. The agreement must also satisfy the requirements of rule 7.703(d)(1).
Rule 7.753 adopted effective January 1, 2003.

Rule 7.754.   Use of paralegals in the performance of legal services for the guardian or conservator

An attorney for a guardian or conservator may use the services of a paralegal acting under the direction and supervision of the attorney. A request for an allowance of compensation for the services of a paralegal must satisfy the requirements of rule 7.703(e).
Rule 7.754 adopted effective January 1, 2003.

Rule 7.755.   Advance payments and periodic payments to guardians, conservators, and to their attorneys on account for future services

(a) No advance payments

A guardian or conservator must neither pay nor receive, and the attorney for a guardian or conservator must not receive, any payment from the estate of the ward or conservatee for services rendered in advance of an order of the court authorizing the payment. If an advance payment is made or received, the court may surcharge the guardian or conservator in the manner provided in rule 7.700(b), in addition to removing the guardian or conservator or imposing any other sanction authorized by law on the guardian or conservator or on the attorney.

(b) Periodic payments to attorneys on account

A guardian or conservator may request the court to authorize periodic payment of attorney fees on account of future services under Probate Code section 2643 on a showing of an ongoing need for legal services.
Rule 7.755 adopted effective January 1, 2003.

Rule 7.756.   Compensation of trustees [Renumbered]

Rule 7.756 renumbered as rule 7.776 effective January 1, 2008.

Another Rule 7.756 follows.

Rule 7.756.   Compensation of conservators and guardians

(a) Standards for determining just and reasonable compensation

The court may consider the following nonexclusive factors in determining just and reasonable compensation for a conservator from the estate of the conservatee or a guardian from the estate of the ward:

(1) The size and nature of the conservatee's or ward's estate;

(2) The benefit to the conservatee or ward, or his or her estate, of the conservator's or guardian's services;

(3) The necessity for the services performed;

(4) The conservatee's or ward's anticipated future needs and income;

(5) The time spent by the conservator or guardian in the performance of services;

(6) Whether the services performed were routine or required more than ordinary skill or judgment;

(7) Any unusual skill, expertise, or experience brought to the performance of services;

(8) The conservator's or guardian's estimate of the value of the services performed; and

(9) The compensation customarily allowed by the court in the community where the court is located for the management of conservatorships or guardianships of similar size and complexity.
(Subd (a) adopted effective January 1, 2008.)

(b) No single factor determinative

No single factor listed in (a) should be the exclusive basis for the court's determination of just and reasonable compensation.
(Subd (b) adopted effective January 1, 2008.)

(c) No inflexible maximum or minimum compensation or maximum approved hourly rate

This rule is not authority for a court to set an inflexible maximum or minimum compensation or a maximum approved hourly rate for compensation.
(Subd (c) adopted effective January 1, 2008.)
Rule 7.756 adopted effective January 1, 2008.

Rule 7.776.   Compensation of trustees

In determining or approving compensation of a trustee, the court may consider, among other factors, the following:

(1) The gross income of the trust estate;

(2) The success or failure of the trustee's administration;

(3) Any unusual skill, expertise, or experience brought to the trustee's work;

(4) The fidelity or disloyalty shown by the trustee;

(5) The amount of risk and responsibility assumed by the trustee;

(6) The time spent in the performance of the trustee's duties;

(7) The custom in the community where the court is located regarding compensation authorized by settlors, compensation allowed by the court, or charges of corporate trustees for trusts of similar size and complexity; and

(8) Whether the work performed was routine, or required more than ordinary skill or judgment.
Rule 7.776 renumbered effective January 1, 2008; adopted as rule 7.756 effective January 1, 2003; previously amended effective January 1, 2007.

Chapter 17
Contested Hearings and Trials

Rule 7.801. Objections and responses
Rule 7.802. Electronic filing and service in contested probate proceedings

Rule 7.801.   Objections and responses

If the court continues a matter to allow a written objection or response to be made, and the responding or objecting party fails to serve and file a timely objection or response, the court may deem the objections or responses waived.
Rule 7.801 adopted effective January 1, 2000.

Rule 7.802.   Electronic filing and service in contested probate proceedings

The provisions of Code of Civil Procedure section 1010.6 and rules 2.250–2.261 of the California Rules of Court concerning filing and service by electronic means apply to contested proceedings under the Probate Code and the Probate Rules to the same extent as they apply to other contested civil proceedings in each superior court in this state.
Rule 7.802 adopted effective January 1, 2016.

Chapter 18
Discovery
[Reserved]
Chapter 19
Trusts

Rule 7.901. Trustee's accounts
Rule 7.902. Beneficiaries to be listed in petitions and accounts
Rule 7.903. Trusts funded by court order

Rule 7.901.   Trustee's accounts

(a) Period covered

A trustee's account must state the period covered by the account.
(Subd (a) amended effective January 1, 2002.)

(b) First account

The first account in a testamentary trust must reconcile the initial assets on hand with the decree of distribution of the estate.
(Subd (b) amended effective January 1, 2002.)

(c) Principal and income

All trustee's accounts in a trust that distributes income to a beneficiary must allocate receipts and disbursements between (1) principal receipts and disbursements, and (2) income receipts and disbursements.
(Subd (c) amended effective January 1, 2002.)
Rule 7.901 amended effective January 1, 2002; adopted effective January 1, 2001.

Rule 7.902.   Beneficiaries to be listed in petitions and accounts

A petition and account involving a trust must state the names and last known addresses of all vested or contingent beneficiaries, including all persons in being who may or will receive income or corpus of the trust, provided, however, that (1) during the time that the trust is revocable and the person holding the power to revoke the trust is competent, the names and last known addresses of beneficiaries who do not hold the power to revoke do not need to be stated, and (2) the petition or account does not need to state the name and last known address of any beneficiary who need not be given notice under Probate Code section 15804.
Rule 7.902 amended effective January 1, 2007; adopted effective January 1, 2002.

Rule 7.903.   Trusts funded by court order

(a) Definitions

(1) "Trust funded by court order" under this rule means and refers to a trust that will receive funds under Probate Code section 2580 et seq. (substituted judgment); section 3100 et seq. (proceedings for particular transactions involving disabled spouses or registered domestic partners); or section 3600 et seq. (settlement of claims or actions or disposition of judgments involving minors or persons with disabilities).

(2) "Continuing jurisdiction of the court" under (b) means and refers to the court's continuing subject matter jurisdiction over trust proceedings under division 9 of the Probate Code (Prob. Code, § 15000 et seq.).

(3) "Court supervision under the Probate Code" under (b) means and refers to the court's authority to require prior court approval or subsequent confirmation of the actions of the trustee as for the actions of a guardian or conservator of the estate under division 4 of the Probate Code (Prob. Code, § 1400 et seq.).

(b) Continuing jurisdiction and court supervision

The order creating or approving the funding of a trust funded by court order must provide that the trust is subject to the continuing jurisdiction of the court and may provide that the trust is to be subject to court supervision under the Probate Code.

(c) Required provisions in trust instruments

Except as provided in (d), unless the court otherwise orders for good cause shown, trust instruments for trusts funded by court order must:

(1) Not contain "no-contest" provisions;

(2) Prohibit modification or revocation without court approval;

(3) Clearly identify the trustee and any other person with authority to direct the trustee to make disbursements;

(4) Prohibit investments by the trustee other than those permitted under Probate Code section 2574;

(5) Require persons identified in (3) to post bond in the amount required under Probate Code section 2320 et seq.;

(6) Require the trustee to file accounts and reports for court approval in the manner and frequency required by Probate Code sections 1060 et seq. and 2620 et seq.;

(7) Require court approval of changes in trustees and a court order appointing any successor trustee; and

(8) Require compensation of the trustee, the members of any advisory committee, or the attorney for the trustee, to be in just and reasonable amounts that must be fixed and allowed by the court. The instrument may provide for periodic payments of compensation on account, subject to the requirements of Probate Code section 2643 and rule 7.755.

(Subd (c) amended effective January 1, 2007; previously amended effective July 1, 2005.)

(d) Trust instruments for smaller trusts

Unless the court otherwise orders for good cause shown, the requirements of (c)(5)–(8) of this rule do not apply to trust instruments for trusts that will have total assets of $20,000 or less after receipt of the property ordered by the court.

Rule 7.903 amended effective January 1, 2007; adopted effective January 1, 2005; previously amended effective July 1, 2005.

Advisory Committee Comment

Subdivision (a) of this rule defines a court-funded trust as a product of three court proceedings. Two of these—a petition for substituted judgment in a probate conservatorship (Prob. Code, § 2580) and a proceeding for a particular transaction in the property of an impaired spouse or domestic partner without a conservator (Prob. Code, § 3100; Fam. Code, § 297.5)—are regularly heard in the probate department of the court. The third proceeding, an application for an order approving the settlement of a minor's claim or a pending action involving a minor or person with a disability or approving the disposition of the proceeds of a judgment in favor of a minor or person with a disability (Prob. Code, § 3600), may be heard in either a probate or a civil department.

The Judicial Council has adopted standard 7.10 of the Standards of Judicial Administration to address proceedings under Probate Code section 3600 that involve court-funded trusts and are heard in civil departments. The standard makes two recommendations concerning the expertise of judicial officers who hear these proceedings on trust issues. The recommendations are to develop practices and procedures that (1) provide for determination of the trust issues in these matters by the probate department of the court or by a judicial officer who regularly hears probate proceedings or (2) ensure that judicial officers who hear these matters have experience or receive training in substantive and technical issues involving trusts, including special needs trusts.

Chapter 20
Claims of Minors and Persons With Disabilities

Rule 7.950. Petition for approval of compromise of claim or action or disposition of proceeds of judgment for minor or person with a disability

Rule 7.950. Petition for approval of compromise of claim or action or disposition of proceeds of judgment for minor or person with a disability

A petition for court approval of a compromise of, or a covenant not to sue or enforce judgment on, a minor's disputed claim; a compromise or settlement of a pending action or proceeding to which a minor or person with a disability is a party; or **the** disposition of the proceeds of a judgment for a minor or person with a disability under [1] Probate Code [2] **sections 3500 and 3600–3613** or Code of Civil Procedure section 372 must be verified by the petitioner and must contain a full disclosure of all information that has any bearing [3] **on** the reasonableness of the compromise, covenant, settlement, or disposition. Except as provided in rule 7.950.5, the petition must be [4] **submitted on a completed *Petition for Approval of Compromise of Claim or* Action or Disposition of Proceeds of Judgment for Minor or Person With a Disability** (form MC-350).

Rule 7.950 amended effective January 1, 2021; adopted effective January 1, 2002; previously amended effective January 1, 2007, and January 1, 2010.

Rule 7.950. 2020 Deletes. [1] chapter 4 of part 8 of division 4 of the [2] (commencing with section 3600) [3] upon [4] prepared on a fully completed *Petition to Approve Compromise of Disputed Claim or Pending*

Rule 7.950.5. Petition for expedited approval of compromise of claim or action or disposition of proceeds of judgment for minor or person with a disability

(a) Authorized use of petition for expedited approval

[1] **If all the circumstances specified in paragraphs (1) through (9) of this rule exist**, a petitioner for court approval of a compromise of, or a covenant not to sue or enforce judgment on, a minor's disputed claim; a compromise or settlement of a pending action or proceeding to which a minor or person with a disability is a party; or **the** disposition of the proceeds of a judgment for a minor or person with a disability under [2] Probate Code [3] **sections 3500 and 3600–3613** or Code of Civil Procedure section 372 may [4] satisfy the [5] **disclosure requirements of rule 7.950 by submitting the petition on a completed *Petition for Expedited Approval of Compromise of Claim or* Action or Disposition of Proceeds of Judgment for Minor or Person With a Disability** (form MC-350EX) [6]**.**

(1) The petitioner is represented by an attorney authorized to practice in the courts of this state;

(2) The claim is not for damages for the wrongful death of a person;

(3) No portion of the net proceeds of the compromise, settlement, or judgment in favor of the minor or disabled claimant is to be placed in a trust;

(4) There are no unresolved disputes concerning liens to be satisfied from the proceeds of the compromise, settlement, or judgment;

(5) The petitioner's attorney did not become involved in the matter at the direct or indirect request of a person against whom the claim is asserted or an insurance carrier for that person;

(6) The petitioner's attorney is neither employed by nor associated with a defendant or insurance carrier in connection with the petition;

(7) If an action has been filed on the claim:

(A) All defendants that have appeared in the action are participating in the compromise; or

(B) The court has finally determined that the settling parties entered into the settlement in good faith;

(8) The judgment for the minor or [7] claimant **with a disability** (exclusive of interest and costs) or the total amount payable to the minor or [8] claimant **with a disability** and all other parties under the proposed compromise or settlement is $50,000 or less or, if greater:

(A) The total amount payable to the minor or [9] claimant **with a disability** represents payment of the individual-person policy limits of all liability insurance policies covering all proposed contributing parties; and

(B) All proposed contributing parties would be substantially unable to discharge an adverse judgment on the [10] claim from assets other than the proceeds of their liability insurance policies; and

(9) The court does not otherwise order [11].

(Subd (a) amended effective January 1, 2021; adopted effective January 1, 2010.)

Rule 7.950.5(a). 2020 Deletes. [1] Notwithstanding the provisions of rule 7.950 [2] chapter 4 of part 8 of division 4 of the [3] (commencing with section 3600) [4] , in the following circumstances, [5] information requirements of that rule by fully completing the *Expedited Petition to Approve Compromise of Disputed Claim or Pending* [6] : [7] disabled [8] disabled [9] disabled [10] minor's or disabled person's [11] ;

(b) Determination of petition

[1] A petition **for expedited approval** must be determined by the court not more than 35 days after it is filed, unless a hearing is requested, required, or scheduled under (c)**,** or the time for determination is extended for good cause by order of the court.

(Subd (b) amended effective January 1, 2021; adopted effective January 1, 2010.)

Rule 7.950.5(b). 2020 Deletes. [1] An expedited

(c) Hearing on petition

(1) The [1] petition **for expedited approval** must be determined by the court without a hearing unless**:**

(A) A hearing is requested by the petitioner at the time the [2] petition is filed [3]**;**

(B) An objection or other opposition to the petition is filed by an interested party [4]**;** or

(C) A hearing is scheduled by the court under (2) or (3).

(2) The court may**,** on its own motion**,** elect to schedule and conduct a hearing on [5] a petition **for expedited approval**. The court must make its election to schedule the hearing and must give notice of its election and the date, time, and place of the hearing to the petitioner and all other interested parties not more than 25 days after the date the [6] petition is filed.

(3) If the court decides not to grant [7] a petition **for expedited approval** in full as requested, it must schedule a hearing and give notice of its intended ruling and the date, time, and place of the hearing to the petitioner and all other interested parties within the time provided in (2).

(Subd (c) amended effective January 1, 2021; adopted effective January 1, 2010.)

Rule 7.950.5(c). 2020 Deletes. [1] expedited [2] expedited [3] , [4] , [5] an expedited [6] expedited [7] an expedited

Rule 7.950.5 amended effective January 1, 2021; adopted effective January 1, 2010.

Rule 7.951.   Disclosure of attorney's interest in petition for approval of compromise of claim

If the petitioner has been represented or assisted by an attorney in preparing the petition [1] **for approval of the** compromise **of** the claim or in any other respect with regard to the claim, the petition must disclose the following information:

(1) The name, state bar number, law firm, if any, and business address of the attorney;

(2) Whether the attorney became involved with the petition, directly or indirectly, at the instance of any party against whom the claim is asserted or of any party's insurance carrier;

(3) Whether the attorney represents or is employed by any other party or any insurance carrier involved in the matter;

(4) Whether the attorney has received any attorney's fees or other compensation for services provided in connection with the claim giving rise to the petition or with the preparation of the petition, and, if so, the amounts and the identity of the person who paid the fees or other compensation;

(5) If the attorney has not received any attorney's fees or other compensation for services provided in connection with the claim giving rise to the petition or with the preparation of the petition, whether the attorney expects to receive any fees or other compensation for these services, and, if so, the amounts and the identity of the person who is expected to pay the fees or other compensation; and

(6) The terms of any agreement between the petitioner and the attorney.

Rule 7.951 amended effective January 1, 2021; adopted effective January 1, 2002.

Rule 7.951. 2020 Deletes. [1] to

Rule 7.952.   Attendance at hearing on petition for approval of compromise of claim

(a) Attendance of petitioner and claimant

The person [1] **petitioning for approval of the compromise of** the claim on behalf of the minor or person with a disability and the minor or person with a disability must attend the hearing on the [2] **petition** unless the court for good cause dispenses with their personal appearance.

(Subd (a) amended effective January 1, 2021; previously amended effective January 1, 2007.)

Rule 7.952(a). 2020 Deletes. [1] compromising [2] compromise of the claim

(b) Attendance of physician and other witnesses

[1] The court may require the presence and testimony of witnesses, including the attending or examining physician, **at the hearing**.

(Subd (b) amended effective January 1, 2021.)

Rule 7.952(b). 2020 Deletes. [1] At the hearing,

Rule 7.952 amended effective January 1, 2021; adopted effective January 1, 2002; previously amended effective January 1, 2007.

Rule 7.953.   Order for the deposit of funds of a minor or a person with a disability

(a) Acknowledgment of receipt by financial institution

In any case in which the court orders that funds to be received by a minor or a person with a disability must be deposited in a financial institution and not disbursed without further order of the court, the order must include a provision that a certified or filed endorsed copy of the order must be delivered to a manager at the financial institution where the funds are to be deposited, and that a receipt from the financial institution must be promptly filed with the court, acknowledging receipt of both the funds deposited and the order for deposit of funds.

(Subd (a) amended effective January 1, 2007.)

(b) Order permitting the withdrawal of funds by a former minor

If, in the order approving the compromise of a minor's claim, there is a finding that the minor will attain the age of majority on a definite date, the order for deposit may require that the depository permit the withdrawal of funds by the former minor after that date, without further order of the court.

Rule 7.953 amended effective January 1, 2007; adopted effective January 1, 2002.

Rule 7.954.   Petition for the withdrawal of funds deposited for a minor or a person with a disability

(a) Verified petition required

A petition for the withdrawal of funds deposited for a minor or a person with a disability must be verified and must include the identity of the depository, a showing of the amounts previously withdrawn, a statement of the balance on deposit at the time of the filing of the petition, and a justification for the withdrawal.

(Subd (a) amended effective January 1, 2007.)

(b) Ex parte or noticed hearing

A petition for the withdrawal of funds may be considered ex parte or set for a hearing at the discretion of the court.

Rule 7.954 amended effective January 1, 2007; adopted effective January 1, 2002.

Rule 7.955.   Attorney's fees for services to minor or person with a disability

(a) Reasonable attorney's fees

(1) In all cases under Code of Civil Procedure section 372 or Probate Code sections 3600–3601, unless the court has approved the fee agreement in advance, the court must use a reasonable fee standard when approving and allowing the amount of attorney's fees payable from money or property paid or to be paid for the benefit of a minor or a person with a disability.

(2) The court must give consideration to the terms of any representation agreement made between the attorney and the representative of the minor or person with a disability and must evaluate the agreement based on the facts and circumstances existing at the time the agreement was made, except where the attorney and the representative of the minor or person with a disability contemplated that the attorney's fee would be affected by later events.

(Subd (a) amended and lettered effective January 1, 2010; adopted as unlettered subd effective January 1, 2003.)

(b) Factors the court may consider in determining a reasonable attorney's fee

In determining a reasonable attorney's fee, the court may consider the following nonexclusive factors:

(1) The fact that a minor or person with a disability is involved and the circumstances of that minor or person with a disability.

(2) The amount of the fee in proportion to the value of the services performed.

(3) The novelty and difficulty of the questions involved and the skill required to perform the legal services properly.

(4) The amount involved and the results obtained.

(5) The time limitations or constraints imposed by the representative of the minor or person with a disability or by the circumstances.

(6) The nature and length of the professional relationship between the attorney and the representative of the minor or person with a disability.

(7) The experience, reputation, and ability of the attorney or attorneys performing the legal services.

(8) The time and labor required.

(9) The informed consent of the representative of the minor or person with a disability to the fee.

(10) The relative sophistication of the attorney and the representative of the minor or person with a disability.

(11) The likelihood, if apparent to the representative of the minor or person with a disability when the representation agreement was made, that the attorney's acceptance of the particular employment would preclude other employment.

(12) Whether the fee is fixed, hourly, or contingent.

(13) If the fee is contingent:

(A) The risk of loss borne by the attorney;

(B) The amount of costs advanced by the attorney; and

(C) The delay in payment of fees and reimbursement of costs paid by the attorney.

(14) Statutory requirements for representation agreements applicable to particular cases or claims.

(Subd (b) adopted effective January 1, 2010.)

(c) Attorney's declaration

A petition requesting court approval and allowance of an attorney's fee under (a) must include a declaration from the attorney that addresses the factors listed in (b) that are applicable to the matter before the court.

(Subd (c) adopted effective January 1, 2010.)

(d) Preemption

The Judicial Council has preempted all local rules relating to the determination of reasonable attorney's fees to be awarded from the proceeds of a compromise, settlement, or judgment under Probate Code sections 3600–3601. No trial court, or any division or branch of a trial court, may enact or enforce any local rule concerning this field, except a rule pertaining to the assignment or scheduling of a hearing on a petition or application for court approval or allowance of attorney's fees under sections 3600–3601. All local rules concerning this field are null and void unless otherwise permitted by a statute or a rule in the California Rules of Court.

(Subd (d) adopted effective January 1, 2010.)

Rule 7.955 amended effective January 1, 2021; adopted effective January 1, 2003; previously amended effective January 1, 2007, and January 1, 2010.

Advisory Committee Comment

This rule requires the court to approve and allow attorney's fees in an amount that is reasonable under all the facts and circumstances, under Probate Code section 3601. The rule is declaratory of existing law concerning attorney's fees under a contingency fee agreement when the fees must be approved by the court. The facts and circumstances that the court may consider are discussed in a large body of decisional law under section 3601 and under other statutes that require the court to determine reasonable attorney's fees. The factors listed in rule 7.955(b) are modeled in part after those provided in rule 1.5 of the Rules of Professional Conduct of the State Bar of California concerning an unconscionable attorney's fee, but the advisory committee does not intend to suggest or imply that an attorney's fee must be found to be unconscionable under rule 1.5 to be determined to be unreasonable under this rule.

The rule permits, but does not require, the court to allow attorney's fees in an amount specified in a contingency fee agreement. The amount of attorney's fees allowed by the court must meet the reasonableness standard of section 3601 no matter how they are determined.

Chapter 21
Guardianships

Rule 7.1001. Guardian screening form

(a) Screening form to be submitted with petition

Each proposed probate guardian, except a public guardian, or a bank or other entity entitled to conduct the business of a trust company, must submit to the court with the petition for appointment of guardian a completed *Confidential Guardian Screening Form* (form GC-212).

(Subd (a) amended effective January 1, 2002.)

(b) Use of form

The information on the *Confidential Guardian Screening Form* is used by the court and by persons or agencies designated by the court to assist the court in determining whether a proposed guardian should be appointed.

(Subd (b) amended effective January 1, 2002.)

(c) Form to be confidential

The *Confidential Guardian Screening Form* and the information contained on the form are confidential. The clerk must maintain these forms in a manner that will protect and preserve their confidentiality.

(Subd (c) amended effective January 1, 2007; previously amended effective January 1, 2002.)

Rule 7.1001 amended effective January 1, 2007; adopted effective January 1, 2001; previously amended effective January 1, 2002.

Rule 7.1002. Acknowledgment of receipt of *Duties of Guardian*

Before the court issues letters, each guardian must execute and file an acknowledgment of receipt of the *Duties of Guardian* (form GC-248).

Rule 7.1002 amended effective July 1, 2016; adopted effective January 1, 2001; previously amended effective January 1, 2002, and January 1, 2007.

Rule 7.1002.5. Guardianship of ward 18 to 20 years of age

(a) Authority

The court may extend an existing guardianship of the person past a ward's 18th birthday or appoint a new guardian of the person for a ward who is at least 18 but not yet 21 years of age if the ward is the petitioner or has given consent as provided in section 1510.1 of the Probate Code and this rule.

(Subd (a) adopted effective July 1, 2016.)

(b) Consent to appointment of guardian of the person

The court may appoint a new guardian of the person under this rule only if the ward has given consent, both to the appointment and to the guardian's performance of the duties of a guardian, by signing the petition.

(Subd (b) adopted effective July 1, 2016.)

(c) Consent to extension of guardianship of the person

The court may extend a guardianship of the person under this rule only if the ward has given consent, both to the extension and to the guardian's continued performance of the duties of a guardian, by signing the *Petition to Extend Guardianship of the Person* (form GC-210(PE)).

(Subd (c) adopted effective July 1, 2016.)

(d) Dispute

In the event of a dispute over the guardian's intended action, the guardian may not act against the ward's desires without the ward's express consent unless failure to act as intended would breach the guardian's fiduciary duties to the ward.

(Subd (d) adopted effective July 1, 2016.)

(e) Modification of consent

(1) A ward may withdraw his or her consent to the establishment or extension of a guardianship under this rule by filing a petition to terminate the guardianship under rule 7.1004(b)(2)(B).

(2) In addition to any other petition authorized by section 2359(a), the ward may file a petition at any time during a guardianship established or extended under this rule to withdraw or modify his or her consent to the guardian's performance of a specific duty or duties.

(Subd (e) adopted effective July 1, 2016.)
Rule 7.1002.5 adopted effective July 1, 2016.

Rule 7.1003. Confidential guardianship status report form

(a) Due date of status report

Each guardian required by the court to complete, sign, and file the status report authorized by Probate Code section 1513.2 must file the completed and signed report no later than one month after the anniversary of the date of the order appointing him or her as guardian. Co-guardians may sign and file their reports jointly.

(b) Court clerk's duties

The clerk of each court that requires guardians to file the status report authorized by Probate Code section 1513.2 must:

(1) Determine the annual due date for the completed report from each appointed guardian required to file the report;

(2) Fill in the due date for the completed report, in the space provided in the form for that purpose, on each blank copy of the form that must be mailed to appointed guardians under (3); and

(3) Mail by first class mail to each appointed guardian no later than one month prior to the date the status report is due under (a) a blank copy of *Confidential Guardianship Status Report* (form GC-251) for each child under guardianship under the same case number.

(Subd (b) amended effective January 1, 2007.)
Rule 7.1003 amended effective January 1, 2007; adopted effective January 1, 2004.

Rule 7.1004. Termination of guardianship

(a) Operation of law or court order

A guardianship of the person or estate of a minor may terminate by operation of law or may be terminated by court order where the court determines that it would be in the ward's best interest to terminate the guardianship.

(b) Guardian of the person

(1) Under Probate Code section 1600 a guardianship of the person terminates by operation of law, and the guardian of the person need not file a petition for its termination, when the ward attains majority except as provided in (2), dies, is adopted, or is emancipated.

(2) If the court has appointed a guardian of the person for a ward 18 years of age or older or extended a guardianship of the person past the ward's 18th birthday, the guardianship terminates:

(A) By operation of law when the ward attains 21 years of age, marries, or dies; or

(B) By order of the court when the ward files a petition under Probate Code section 1601.

(Subd (b) amended effective July 1, 2016.)

(c) Duty of guardian of estate on termination

A guardian of the estate whose administration is terminated by operation of law or court order must file and obtain the court's approval of a final account or report of the administration.

Rule 7.1004 amended effective July 1, 2016; adopted effective January 1, 2004.

Rule 7.1005. Service of copy of final account or report after resignation or removal of guardian

A resigned or removed guardian of the estate must serve a copy of the guardian's final account or report and the petition for its settlement, with the notice of hearing that must be served on the successor guardian of the estate under Probate Code section 1460(b)(1), unless the court dispenses with such service.

Rule 7.1005 adopted effective January 1, 2004.

Rule 7.1006. Service of copy of final account on termination of guardianship

(a) Minor living

In addition to service of notices of hearing required under Probate Code section 1460(b), on termination of the guardianship the guardian of the estate must serve a copy of the guardian's final account and petition for its settlement on the minor, unless the court dispenses with such service.

(b) Personal representative of deceased minor

If the minor is deceased, in addition to service of notices of hearing required under Probate Code section 1460(b), on termination of the guardianship the guardian of the estate must serve a notice of hearing and a copy of the guardian's final account and petition for its settlement on the personal representative of the deceased minor's estate, unless the court dispenses with such service.

(c) Successors in interest to deceased minor

If the minor is deceased and no personal representative of the minor's estate has been appointed or qualified or if the personal representative of the minor's estate is also the guardian, on termination of the guardianship, in addition to the notices of hearing required under Probate Code section 1460(b), the guardian of the estate must serve a notice of hearing and a copy of the guardian's final account and petition for its settlement on the persons entitled to succeed to the deceased minor's estate, unless the court dispenses with such service.

Rule 7.1006 adopted effective January 1, 2004.

Rule 7.1007. Settlement of accounts and release by former minor

(a) Release of guardian of estate by ward after majority

A ward who has attained majority may settle accounts with his or her guardian of the estate and may give a valid release to the guardian if the court determines, at the time of the hearing on the final account, or on the final report and petition for termination on waiver of account, that the release has been obtained fairly and without undue influence. The release is not effective to discharge the guardian until one year after the ward has attained majority.

(b) Appearance of ward

The court may require the personal appearance of the ward at the hearing on the final account or report of the guardian of the estate after termination of the guardianship.

Rule 7.1007 adopted effective January 1, 2004.

Rule 7.1008. Visitation by former guardian after termination of guardianship

(a) Visitation order at time of termination of guardianship

Subject to the provisions of Welfare and Institutions Code section 304, a guardian may request the court to order visitation with the child under guardianship at the time of termination of the guardianship either in the guardian's petition for termination or in the guardian's objections or other pleading filed in response to the petition of another party for termination. The court may then order visitation if it is in the best interest of the child.

(b) Request for visitation after termination of guardianship

If no order was entered under (a) concerning visitation between the former guardian and the former ward at termination of the guardianship and no dependency proceedings for the child are pending, the former guardian may request the court to order visitation with the former ward after termination of the guardianship as provided in Family Code section 3105, Probate Code section 1602, rule 5.475, and this rule, as follows:

(1) If either parent of the former ward is living, in an independent action for visitation under the Family Code; or

(2) If neither parent of the former ward is living, in a guardianship proceeding under the Probate Code, including a proceeding commenced for that purpose.

(c) Declaration under UCCJEA

A guardian or former guardian requesting visitation under this rule must file a *Declaration Under Uniform Child Custody Jurisdiction and Enforcement Act (UCCJEA)* (form FL-105/GC-120) with his or her request for visitation.

(Subd (c) amended effective January 1, 2007.)

(d) Transmission of visitation order

Following the termination of the guardianship the clerk of the superior court issuing the visitation order concerning the guardian or former guardian and the ward or former ward must promptly transmit an endorsed filed copy of the order to the superior court of the county where a custody proceeding under the Family Code is pending or, if none, to the superior court of the county in which the custodial parent resides. An order transmitted to the court in the county where the custodial parent resides may be sent to the receiving court's Court Operations Manager, Family Division, or similar senior manager or clerk responsible for the operations of the family law departments of the court. If the receiving court has more than one location, the order may be sent to the main or central district of the court.

Rule 7.1008 amended effective January 1, 2007; adopted effective January 1, 2006.

Rule 7.1009.   Standards of conduct for the guardian of the estate

Except as otherwise required by statute, in the exercise of ordinary care and diligence in managing and controlling the estates of the ward, the guardian of the estate is to be guided by the following principles:

(a) Avoidance of actual and apparent conflicts of interest with the ward

The guardian must avoid actual conflicts of interest and, consistent with his or her fiduciary duty to the ward, the appearance of conflicts of interest. The guardian must avoid any personal, business, or professional interest or relationship that is or reasonably could be perceived as being self-serving or adverse to the best interest of the ward. In particular:

(1) Except as appropriate for guardians who are not professional fiduciaries with full disclosure to the court, the guardian should not personally provide medical or legal services to the ward;

(2) The guardian must be independent from all service providers, except when (a) no other guardian or service providers are reasonably available, (b) the exception is in the best interest of the ward, (c) the circumstances are fully disclosed to the court, and (d) prior court approval has been obtained;

(3) The guardian must neither solicit nor accept incentives from service providers; and

(4) The guardian must not engage his or her family members to provide services to the ward for a profit or fee when other alternatives are reasonably available. Where family members do provide such services, their relationship to the guardian must be fully disclosed to the court, the terms of engagement must be in the best interest of the ward compared to the terms available from independent service providers, the services must be competently performed, and the guardian must be able to exercise appropriate control and supervision.

A guardian's employees, including family members, are not service providers and are not providing services to the ward for a profit or fee within the meaning of this rule if their compensation is paid by the guardian and their services are either included in the guardian's petition for allowance of the guardian's compensation or are not paid from the ward's estate.

(Subd (a) adopted effective January 1, 2008.)

(b) Guardianship estate management

In addition to complying with applicable standards of estate management specified in rule 7.1059(b), the guardian of the estate must:

(1) Manage the estate primarily for the ward's long-term benefit if the ward has a parent available who can provide sufficient support;

(2) If it would be in the best interest of the ward and the estate, consider requesting court authority to support the ward from the estate if the ward does not have a parent available who can provide sufficient support.

(Subd (b) adopted effective January 1, 2008.)
Rule 7.1009 adopted effective January 1, 2008.

Advisory Committee Comment

The Probate and Mental Health Advisory Committee consulted with several organizations in the development of rule 7.1009, including the National Guardianship Association, a nationwide voluntary association of professional and family fiduciaries, guardians, and allied professionals. In developing this rule, the Probate and Mental Health Advisory Committee considered the National Guardianship Association's Standards of Practice. Some of these standards have been incorporated into the rule.

Rule 7.1010.   Qualifications and continuing education requirements for private professional guardians [Repealed]

Rule 7.1010 repealed effective July 1, 2008; amended effective January 1, 2007; adopted effective January 1, 2006; previously amended effective July 1, 2006.

Rule 7.1011.   Taking possession of an asset of the ward at an institution or opening or changing ownership of an account or safe-deposit box in a financial institution

(a) Definitions

As used in this rule, the following terms have the meanings stated below:

(1) An "institution" is an insurance company, insurance broker, insurance agent, investment company, investment bank, securities broker-dealer, investment advisor, financial planner, financial advisor, or any other person who takes, holds, or controls an asset subject to a guardianship that is not a "financial institution" within the meaning of this rule;

(2) A "financial institution" is a bank, trust (except as provided in (d)), savings and loan association, savings bank, industrial bank, or credit union; and

(3) "Taking possession" or "taking control" of an asset held or controlled by an institution includes changing title to the asset, withdrawing all or any portion of the asset, or transferring all or any portion of the asset from the institution.

(Subd (a) adopted effective January 1, 2009.)

(b) Responsibilities of the guardian when taking possession or control of an asset of the ward at an institution

When taking possession or control of an asset held by an institution in the name of the ward, the temporary or general guardian of the estate must provide the following to the institution:

(1) A certified copy of the guardian's *Letters of Temporary Guardianship or Conservatorship* (form GC-150) or *Letters of Guardianship* (form GC-250) containing the Notice to Institutions and Financial Institutions on the second page; and

(2) A blank copy of a *Notice of Taking Possession or Control of an Asset of Minor or Conservatee* (form GC-050).

(Subd (b) adopted effective January 1, 2009.)

(c) Responsibilities of the guardian when opening or changing the name on an account or a safe-deposit box in a financial institution

When opening or changing the name on an account or a safe-deposit box in a financial institution, the temporary or general guardian of the estate must provide the following to the financial institution:

(1) A certified copy of the guardian's *Letters of Temporary Guardianship or Conservatorship* (form GC-150) or *Letters of Guardianship* (form GC-250) containing the Notice to Institutions and Financial Institutions on the second page; and

(2) A blank copy of a *Notice of Opening or Changing a Guardianship or Conservatorship Account or Safe-Deposit Box* (form GC-051).

(Subd (c) adopted effective January 1, 2009.)

(d) Application of this rule to trust arrangements

This rule applies to Totten trust accounts but does not apply to any other trust arrangement described in Probate Code section 82(b).

(Subd (d) adopted effective January 1, 2009.)
Rule 7.1011 adopted effective January 1, 2009.

Rule 7.1012.   The good cause exception to notice of the hearing on a petition for appointment of a temporary guardian

(a) Purpose

The purpose of this rule is to establish uniform standards for the good cause exception to the notice of the hearing required on a petition for appointment of a temporary guardian under Probate Code section 2250(e).

(Subd (a) amended effective January 1, 2009; adopted effective January 1, 2008.)

(b) Good cause for exceptions to notice limited

Good cause for an exception to the notice required by section 2250(e) must be based on a showing that the exception is necessary to protect the proposed ward or his or her estate from immediate and substantial harm.

(Subd (b) amended effective January 1, 2009; adopted effective January 1, 2008.)

(c) Court may waive or change the time or manner of giving notice

An exception to the notice requirement of section 2250(e) may include one or any combination of the following:

(1) Waiving notice to one, more than one, or all persons entitled to notice;

(2) Requiring a different period of notice; and

(3) Changing the required manner of giving notice, including requiring notice by telephone, fax, e-mail, or a combination of these methods, instead of notice by personal delivery to the proposed ward's parents or to a person with a visitation order.

(Subd (c) amended effective January 1, 2009; adopted effective January 1, 2008.)

(d) Good cause exceptions to notice

Good cause for an exception to the notice requirement of section 2250(e) may include a showing of:

(1) Harm caused by the passage of time. The showing must demonstrate the immediate and substantial harm to the ward or the ward's estate that could occur during the notice period.

(2) Harm that one or more persons entitled to notice might do to the proposed ward, including abduction; or harm to the proposed ward's estate if notice to those persons is given. Such a showing would not

support an exception to the requirement to give notice to any other person entitled to notice unless it also demonstrates that notice cannot reasonably be given to the other person without also giving notice to the persons who might cause harm.

(3) The death or incapacity of the proposed ward's custodial parent and the petitioner's status as the custodial parent's nominee.

(4) Medical emergency. The emergency must be immediate and substantial and treatment (1) must be reasonably unavailable unless a temporary guardian is appointed and (2) cannot be deferred for the notice period because of the proposed ward's pain or extreme discomfort or a significant risk of harm.

(5) Financial emergency. The emergency must be immediate and substantial and other means shown likely to be ineffective to prevent loss or further loss to the proposed ward's estate or loss of support for the proposed ward during the notice period.

(Subd (d) amended effective January 1, 2009; adopted effective January 1, 2008.)

(e) Contents of request for good cause exception to notice

(1) When the temporary guardianship petition is prepared on the *Petition for Appointment of Temporary Guardian* (form GC-110), a request for a good cause exception to the notice requirement of section 2250(e) must be in writing, separate from the petition for appointment of a temporary guardian, and must include:

(A) An application containing the case caption and stating the relief requested;

(B) An affirmative factual showing in support of the application in a declaration under penalty of perjury containing competent testimony based on personal knowledge;

(C) A declaration under penalty of perjury based on personal knowledge containing the information required for an ex parte application under rule 3.1204(b); and

(D) A proposed order.

(2) When the temporary guardianship petition is prepared on the *Petition for Appointment of Temporary Guardian of the Person* (form GC-110(P)), a request for a good cause exception to the notice requirement of section 2250(e) may be included in the petition.

(Subd (e) amended effective January 1, 2009; adopted effective January 1, 2008.)

Rule 7.1012 amended effective January 1, 2009; adopted effective January 1, 2008.

Rule 7.1013. Change of ward's residence

(a) Pre-move notice of change of personal residence required

Unless an emergency requires a shorter period of notice, the guardian of the person must mail copies of a notice of an intended change of the ward's personal residence to the persons listed below at least 15 days before the date of the proposed change, and file the original notice with proof of mailing with the court. Copies of the notice must be mailed to:

(1) The ward if he or she is 12 years of age or older;

(2) The attorney of record for the ward;

(3) The ward's parents;

(4) Any person who had legal custody of the ward when the first petition for appointment of a guardian was filed in the proceeding;

(5) A guardian of the ward's estate; and

(6) Any person who was nominated as guardian of the ward under Probate Code sections 1500 or 1501 but was not appointed guardian in the proceeding.

(Subd (a) adopted effective January 1, 2008.)

(b) Ward's personal residence

The "ward's personal residence" under (a) is the ward's residence when the first petition for appointment of a guardian was filed in the proceeding.

(Subd (b) adopted effective January 1, 2008.)

(c) Post-move notice of a change of residence required

The guardian of the person of a minor must file a notice of a change of the ward's residence with the court within 30 days of the date of any change. Unless waived by the court for good cause to prevent harm to the ward, the guardian, the guardian's attorney, or an employee of the guardian's attorney must also mail a copy of the notice to the persons listed below and file a proof of mailing with the original notice. Unless waived, copies of the notice must be mailed to:

(1) The ward's attorney of record;

(2) The ward's parents;

(3) Any person who had legal custody of the ward when the first petition for appointment of a guardian was filed in the proceeding;

(4) A guardian of the ward's estate; and

(5) Any person who was nominated as guardian of the ward under Probate Code sections 1500 or 1501 but was not appointed guardian in the proceeding.

(Subd (c) adopted effective January 1, 2008.)

(d) Ward's residence

The "ward's residence" under (c) is the ward's residence at any time after appointment of a guardian.

(Subd (d) adopted effective January 1, 2008.)

(e) Use of Judicial Council forms GC-079 and GC-080

(1) The *Pre-Move Notice of Proposed Change of Personal Residence of Conservatee or Ward* (form GC-079) must be used for the pre-move notice required under (a) and Probate Code section 2352(e)(3). The guardian, the guardian's attorney, or an employee of the attorney may complete the mailing and sign the proof of mailing on page 2 of the form. If the notice is mailed less than 15 days before the date of the move because an emergency requires a shorter period of notice, the basis for the emergency must be stated in the notice.

(2) The *Post-Move Notice of Change of Residence of Conservatee or Ward* (form GC-080) must be used for the post-move notice required under (c) and Probate Code section 2352(e)(1) and (2). The guardian, the guardian's attorney, or an employee of the attorney may complete the mailing and sign the proof of mailing on page 2 of the form.

(Subd (e) adopted effective January 1, 2008.)

(f) Prior court approval required to establish ward's residence outside California

Notwithstanding any other provision of this rule, prior court approval is required before a ward's residence may be established outside the state of California.

(Subd (f) adopted effective January 1, 2008.)

(g) Wards 18 to 20 years of age

For a ward who is at least 18 but not yet 21 years of age, a copy of any notice under this rule must be mailed only to the ward and the ward's attorney of record.

(Subd (g) adopted effective July 1, 2016.)

Rule 7.1013 amended effective July 1, 2016; adopted effective January 1, 2008.

Rule 7.1014. Communications between courts in different California counties concerning guardianship venue

(a) Purpose of rule

This rule addresses the communications between courts concerning guardianship venue required by Probate Code section 2204(b). These communications are between the superior court in one California county where a guardianship proceeding has been filed (referred to in this rule as the guardianship court) and one or more superior courts in one or more other California counties where custody or visitation proceedings under the Family Code involving the ward or proposed ward were previously filed (referred to in this rule as the family court or courts, or the other court or courts).

(Subd (a) adopted effective January 1, 2013.)

(b) Substantive communications between judicial officers

Before making a venue decision on a petition for appointment of a general guardian in a guardianship proceeding described in (a), or a decision on a petition to transfer under Probate Code section 2212 filed in the proceeding before the appointment of a guardian or temporary guardian, the judicial officer responsible for the proceeding in the guardianship court must communicate with the judicial officer or officers responsible for the custody proceeding or proceedings in the family court or courts concerning which county provides the venue for the guardianship proceeding that is in the best interests of the ward or the proposed ward.

(1) If the currently responsible judicial officer in the family court or courts cannot be identified, communication must be made with the managing or supervising judicial officer of the family departments of the other court or courts, if any, or his or her designee, or with the presiding judge of the other court or courts or his or her designee.

(2) If courts in more than two counties are involved, simultaneous communications among judicial officers of all of the courts are recommended, if reasonably practicable. If communications occur between some but not all involved courts, the record of these communications must be made available to those judicial officers of the courts who were not included at or before the time the judicial officer of the guardianship court communicates with them.

(3) A record must be made of all communications between judicial officers under this subdivision.

(4) The parties to the guardianship proceeding, including a petitioner for transfer; all persons entitled to notice of the hearing on the petition for appointment of a guardian; and any additional persons ordered by the guardianship court must promptly be informed of the communications and given access to the record of the communications.

(5) The provisions of Family Code section 3410(b) apply to communications between judicial officers under this subdivision, except that the term "jurisdiction" in that section corresponds to "venue" in this context, and the term "parties" in that section identifies the persons listed in (4).

(Subd (b) adopted effective January 1, 2013.)

(c) Preliminary communications

To assist the judicial officer in making the communication required in (b), the guardianship court may have preliminary communications with each family court to collect information about the proceeding in that court or for other routine matters, including calendar management, and scheduling.

(1) The guardianship court should attempt to collect, and each family court is encouraged to provide, as much of the following information about the proceeding in the family court as is reasonable under the circumstances:

(A) The case number or numbers and the nature of each family court proceeding;

(B) The names of the parties to each family court proceeding, including contact information for self-represented parties; their relationship or other connection to the ward or proposed ward in the guardianship proceeding, and the names and contact information of counsel for any parties represented by counsel;

(C) The current status (active or inactive) of each family court proceeding, whether any future hearings are set in each proceeding, and if so, their dates and times, locations, and nature;

(D) The contents and dates filed of orders in the each family court proceeding that decide or resolve custody or visitation issues concerning the ward or proposed ward in the guardianship proceeding;

(E) Whether any orders of each family court are final, were appealed from, or were the subject of extraordinary writ proceedings, and the current status of any such appeal or proceeding;

(F) The court branch and department where each family court proceeding was assigned and where the proceeding is currently assigned or pending;

(G) The identity of the judicial officer currently assigned to or otherwise responsible for each family court proceeding; and

(H) Other information about each family court proceeding requested by the judicial officer of the guardianship court.

(2) In the discretion of the judicial officer of the guardianship court, preliminary communications under this rule may be between judicial officers of the courts involved or between staff of the guardianship court and judicial officers or court staff of each other court.

(3) Family Code section 3410(c) applies to preliminary communications under this rule.

(Subd (c) adopted effective January 1, 2013.)

(d) Applicability of this rule to petitions to transfer filed after the appointment of a guardian or temporary guardian

Subdivisions (b) and (c) of this rule may, in the discretion of the guardianship court, apply to petitions for transfer described in Probate Code section 2204(b)(2).

(Subd (d) adopted effective January 1, 2013.)

(e) "Record" under this rule

"Record" under this rule has the meaning provided in Family Code section 3410(e).

(Subd (e) adopted effective January 1, 2013.)

Rule 7.1014 adopted effective January 1, 2013.

Rule 7.1015. Indian Child Welfare Act in guardianship and certain conservatorship proceedings

(a) Definitions

As used in this rule, unless the context or subject matter otherwise requires:

(1) "Act" means the Indian Child Welfare Act (25 United States Code sections 1901–1963).

(2) "Petitioner" means and refers to a petitioner for the appointment of a guardian of the person of a child or a petitioner for the appointment of a conservator of the person of a formerly married minor child.

(Subd (a) adopted effective January 1, 2008.)

(b) Applicability of this rule and rules 5.480 through 5.487

(1) This rule applies to the following proceedings under division 4 of the Probate Code when the proposed ward or conservatee is an Indian child, within the meaning of the act:

(A) A guardianship of the person or the person and estate in which the proposed guardian of the person is not the proposed ward's natural parent or Indian custodian within the meaning of the act;

(B) A conservatorship of the person or the person and estate of a formerly married minor in which the proposed conservator is not a natural parent or Indian custodian of the minor and is seeking physical custody of the proposed conservatee.

(2) Unless the context otherwise requires, rules 5.480 through 5.487 apply to the proceedings listed in (1).

(3) When applied to the proceedings listed in (1), references in rules 5.480 through 5.487 to social workers, probation officers, county probation departments, or county social welfare departments are references to the petitioner or petitioners for the appointment of a guardian or conservator of the person of an Indian child and to an Indian child's appointed temporary or general guardian or conservator of the person.

(4) If the court appoints a temporary or general guardian or conservator of the person of the child involved in a proceeding listed in (1), the duties and responsibilities of a petitioner under this rule are transferred to and become the duties and responsibilities of the appointed guardian or conservator. The petitioner must cooperate with and provide any information the petitioner has concerning the child to the appointed guardian or conservator.

(Subd (b) adopted effective January 1, 2008.)

(c) Notice

If, at any time after the filing of a petition for appointment of a guardian or conservator for a minor child, the court or petitioner knows or has reason to know, within the meaning of Probate Code sections 1449 and 1459.5 and Welfare and Institutions Code section 224.3(b), that an Indian child is involved, the petitioner and the court must notify the child's parents or legal guardian and Indian custodian, and the Indian child's tribe, of the pending proceeding and the right of the tribe to intervene, as follows:

(1) Notice to the Indian child's parents, Indian custodian, and Indian tribe of the commencement of a guardianship or conservatorship must be given by serving copies of the completed *Notice of Child Custody Proceeding for Indian Child* (form ICWA-030), the petition for appointment of a guardian or conservator, and all attachments, by certified or registered mail, fully prepaid with return receipt requested.

(2) The petitioner and his or her attorney, if any, must complete the *Notice* and the petitioner must date and sign the declaration. If there is more than one petitioner, the statements about the child's ancestors and background provided in the *Notice of Child Custody Proceeding for Indian Child* (form ICWA-030) must be based on all information known to each petitioner, and all petitioners must sign the declaration.

(3) When the petitioner is represented by an attorney in the proceeding, the attorney must serve copies of the *Notice of Child Custody Proceeding for Indian Child* (form ICWA-030) in the manner described in (1) and sign the declaration of mailing on the *Notice*.

(4) When the guardianship or conservatorship petitioner or petitioners are not represented by an attorney in the proceeding, the clerk of the court must serve the *Notice* in the manner described in (1) and sign the certificate of mailing on the *Notice*.

(5) The original of all *Notices of Child Custody Proceeding for Indian Child* (form ICWA-030) served under the act, and all return receipts and responses received, must be filed with the court before the hearing.

(6) Notice to an Indian child's tribe must be sent to the tribal chairperson unless the tribe has designated another agent for service.

(7) Notice must be served on all tribes of which the child may be a member or eligible for membership. If there are more tribes or bands to be served than can be listed on the last page of the *Notice*, the additional tribes or bands may be listed on an *Attachment to Notice of Child Custody Proceeding for Indian Child* (form ICWA-030(A)).

(8) Notice under the act must be served whenever there is any reason to know that the child is or may be an Indian child and for every hearing after the first hearing unless and until it is determined that the act does not apply to the proceeding.

(9) If, after a reasonable time following the service of notice under the act—but in no event less than 60 days—no determinative response to the

Notice of Child Custody Proceeding for Indian Child (form ICWA-030) is received, the court may determine that the act does not apply to the proceeding unless further evidence of its applicability is later received.

(10) If an Indian child's tribe intervenes in the proceeding, service of the *Notice of Child Custody Proceeding for Indian Child* (form ICWA-030) is no longer required and subsequent notices to the tribe may be sent to all parties in the form and in the manner required under the Probate Code and these rules. All other provisions of the act, this rule, and rules 5.480 through 5.487 continue to apply.

(11) Notice under the act must be served in addition to all notices otherwise required for the particular proceeding under the provisions of the Probate Code.

(Subd (c) adopted effective January 1, 2008.)

(d) Duty of inquiry

(1) The court, a court investigator or county officer appointed to conduct an investigation under Probate Code section 1513 or 1826, a petitioner, and an appointed temporary or general guardian or conservator of the person of a minor child each have an affirmative and continuing duty to inquire whether the child involved in the matters identified in (b)(1) is or may be an Indian child.

(2) Before filing his or her petition, the petitioner must ask the child involved in the proceeding, if the child is old enough, and the parents, any other legal guardian, and any Indian custodian, whether the child is or may be an Indian child, and must complete items 1c and 8 of the *Guardianship Petition—Child Information Attachment* (form GC-210(CA)) and attach it to his or her petition.

(3) At the first personal appearance by a parent or previously appointed legal guardian at a hearing in a guardianship or conservatorship, the court must if requested by petitioner, or may on its own motion, order the parent or legal guardian to complete a *Parental Notification of Indian Status* (form ICWA-020) and deliver the completed form to the petitioner.

(4) If the parent, Indian custodian, or guardian does not personally appear at a hearing in a proceeding identified in (b)(1), the court may order the petitioner to use reasonable diligence to find and ask the parent, Indian custodian, or legal guardian to complete and deliver to petitioner a *Parental Notification of Indian Status* (form ICWA-020).

(5) If the court or county investigator, petitioner, appointed guardian or conservator, or the attorney for a petitioner or appointed guardian or conservator, knows or has reason to know that an Indian child is involved in the proceeding, he or she must make further inquiry as soon as practicable by:

(A) Interviewing the parents, Indian custodian, and "extended family members" as defined in 25 United States Code section 1903(2), to gather the information listed in Probate Code section 1460.2(b)(5) that is required to complete the *Notice of Child Custody Proceeding for Indian Child* (form ICWA-030);

(B) Contacting the U.S. Department of the Interior, Bureau of Indian Affairs and the California Department of Social Services for assistance in identifying the names and contact information of the tribes of which the child may be a member or eligible for membership; and

(C) Contacting the tribes and any other person who reasonably can be expected to have information regarding the child's tribal membership status or eligibility for membership.

(6) If the court knows or has reason to know that an Indian child is involved in the proceeding, the court may direct any of the persons named in (5) to conduct the inquiry described in that paragraph.

(7) The circumstances that may provide reason to know the child is an Indian child include the following:

(A) The child or person having an interest in the child, including an Indian tribe, an Indian organization, an officer of the court, a public or private agency, or a member of the child's extended family, informs or otherwise provides information suggesting that the child is an Indian child to the court or to any person listed in (5);

(B) The residence or domicile of the child, the child's parents, or an Indian custodian is in a predominantly Indian community; or

(C) The child or the child's family has received services or benefits from a tribe or services that are available to Indians from tribes or the federal government, such as the U.S. Department of Health and Human Services, Indian Health Service, or Tribal Temporary Assistance to Needy Families benefits.

(Subd (d) amended effective July 1, 2012; adopted effective January 1, 2008.)
Rule 7.1015 amended effective July 1, 2012; adopted effective January 1, 2008.

Rule 7.1016.   Participation and testimony of wards in guardianship proceedings

(a) Definitions

As used in this rule, the following terms have the meanings specified:

(1) "Ward" includes "proposed ward."

(2) A "proceeding" is a matter before the court for decision in a probate guardianship of the person that concerns appointment or removal of a guardian, visitation, determination of the ward's place of residence, or termination of the guardianship by court order.

(3) "Party," as used in this rule to refer to the ward, means a ward who has filed a petition or opposition to a petition concerning a proceeding or other matter subject to this rule.

(Subd (a) adopted effective January 1, 2013.)

(b) Purpose and scope of rule

(1) This rule applies Family Code section 3042 to the participation and testimony of the ward in a proceeding in a probate guardianship of the person. The testimony of other minors in a guardianship case is governed by Evidence Code sections 765(b) and 767(b).

(2) The court in its discretion may apply this rule, in whole or in part, to the participation and testimony of a ward in a guardianship of the estate or in a matter before the court in a guardianship of the person that is not a proceeding within the meaning of this rule. The phrase "or other matter subject to this rule" following the term "proceeding" is a reference to the matters described in this paragraph.

(3) No statutory mandate, rule, or practice requires a ward who is not a party to the proceeding or other matter subject to this rule to participate in court or prohibits him or her from doing so. When a ward desires to participate but is not a party to the proceeding or other matter subject to this rule, the court must balance the protection of the ward, the statutory duty to consider the wishes of and input from the ward, and the probative value of the ward's input while ensuring all parties' due process rights to challenge evidence relied on by the court in making decisions affecting the ward in matters covered by the rule.

(4) This rule rather than rule 5.250, on children's participation and testimony in family court proceedings, applies in probate guardianship proceedings.

(Subd (b) adopted effective January 1, 2013.)

(c) Determining whether the nonparty ward wishes to address the court

(1) The following persons must inform the court if they have information indicating that a ward who is not a party wishes to address the court in a proceeding or other matter subject to this rule:

(A) The ward's counsel;

(B) A court or county guardianship investigator;

(C) A child custody recommending counselor who provides recommendations to the judicial officer under Family Code section 3183;

(D) An expert appointed by the court under Evidence Code section 730 to assist the court in the matter; or

(E) The ward's guardian ad litem.

(2) The following persons may inform the court if they have information indicating that a ward who is not a party wishes to address the court in a proceeding or other matter subject to this rule:

(A) A party in the guardianship case; and

(B) An attorney for a party in the guardianship case.

(3) In the absence of information indicating that a ward who is not a party wishes to address the court in a proceeding or other matter subject to this rule, the judicial officer may inquire whether the ward wishes to do so.

(Subd (c) adopted effective January 1, 2013.)

(d) Guidelines for determining whether addressing the court is in the nonparty ward's best interest

(1) When a ward who is not a party indicates that he or she wishes to address the court, the judicial officer must consider whether involving the ward in the proceeding or other matter subject to this rule is in the ward's best interest.

(2) If the ward is 12 years old or older, the judicial officer must hear from the ward unless the court makes a finding that addressing the court is not in the ward's best interest and states the reasons on the record.

(3) In determining whether addressing the court is in the ward's best interest, the judicial officer should consider the following:

(A) Whether the ward is of sufficient age and capacity to form an intelligent preference as to the matter to be decided;

(B) Whether the ward is of sufficient age and capacity to understand the nature of testimony;

(C) Whether information has been presented indicating that the ward may be at risk emotionally if he or she is permitted or denied the opportunity to address the court or that the ward may benefit from addressing the court;

(D) Whether the subject areas about which the ward is anticipated to address the court are relevant to the decision the court must make;

(E) Whether the appointment of counsel under Probate Code section 1470 or a guardian ad litem for the ward would be helpful to the determination or would be necessary to protect the ward's interests; and

(F) Whether any other factors weigh in favor of or against having the ward address the court, taking into consideration the ward's desire to do so.

(Subd (d) adopted effective January 1, 2013.)

(e) Guidelines for receiving testimony and other input from the nonparty ward

(1) No testimony of a ward may be received without such testimony being heard on the record or in the presence of the parties. This requirement may not be waived.

(2) On deciding to take the testimony of a ward who is not a party in a proceeding or other matter subject to this rule, the judicial officer should balance the necessity of taking the ward's testimony in the courtroom with parents, the guardian or proposed guardian, other parties, and attorneys present with the need to create an environment in which the ward can be open and honest. In each case in which a ward's testimony will be taken, the judicial officer should consider:

(A) Where the testimony will be taken;

(B) Who should be present when the testimony is taken;

(C) How the ward will be questioned; and

(D) Whether a court reporter is available in all instances, but especially when the ward's testimony may be taken outside the presence of the parties and their attorneys. If the court reporter will not be available, whether there are other means to collect, preserve, transcribe, and make the ward's testimony available to parties and their attorneys.

(3) In taking testimony from a ward who is not a party to the proceeding or other matter subject to this rule, the court must take the special care required by Evidence Code section 765(b). If the ward is not represented by an attorney, the court must inform the ward in an age-appropriate manner about the limitations on confidentiality of testimony and that the information provided to the court will be on the record and provided to the parties in the case.

(4) In the process of listening to and inviting the ward's input, the court must allow but not require the ward to state a preference regarding the matter to be decided in the proceeding or other matter subject to this rule and should provide information in an age-appropriate manner about the process by which the court will make a decision.

(5) In any case in which a ward who is not a party to the proceeding or other matter subject to this rule will be called to testify, the court must consider the appointment of counsel for the ward under Probate Code section 1470 and may consider the appointment of a guardian ad litem for the ward. In addition to satisfying the requirements for minor's counsel under rule 7.1101, minor's counsel must:

(A) Provide information to the ward in an age-appropriate manner about the limitations on the confidentiality of testimony and indicate to the ward the possibility that information provided to the court will be on the record and provided to the parties in the case;

(B) Allow but not require the ward to state a preference regarding the issues to be decided in the proceeding or other matter subject to this rule, and provide information in an age-appropriate manner about the process by which the court will make a decision;

(C) If appropriate, provide the ward with an orientation to the courtroom or other place where the ward will testify; and

(D) Inform the parties and the court about the ward's desire to provide input.

(6) If the court precludes the calling of a ward who is not a party as a witness in a proceeding or other matter subject to this rule, alternatives for the court to obtain information or other input from the ward may include:

(A) A court or county guardianship investigator participating in the case under Probate Code section 1513 or 1513.2;

(B) Appointment of a child custody evaluator or investigator under Evidence Code section 730;

(C) Appointment of counsel or a guardian ad litem for the ward;

(D) Admissible evidence provided by the ward's parents, parties, or witnesses in the proceeding or other matter subject to this rule;

(E) Information provided by a child custody recommending counselor authorized under Family Code section 3183 to make a recommendation to the court; and

(F) Information provided from a child interview center or professional to avoid unnecessary multiple interviews.

(7) If the court precludes the calling of a ward who is not a party as a witness in a proceeding or other matter subject to this rule and specifies one of the other alternatives, the court must require that the information or evidence obtained by alternative means and provided by a professional (other than counsel for the ward or counsel for any party) or a nonparty:

(A) Be in writing and fully document the ward's views on the matters on which he or she wished to express an opinion;

(B) Describe the ward's input in sufficient detail to assist the court in making its decision;

(C) Be provided to the court and to the parties by a person who will be available for testimony and cross-examination; and

(D) Be filed in the confidential portion of the case file.

(Subd (e) adopted effective January 1, 2013.)

(f) Responsibilities of court-connected or appointed professionals—all wards

A child custody evaluator, an expert witness appointed under Evidence Code section 730, an investigator, a child custody recommending counselor or other custody mediator appointed or assigned to meet with a ward must:

(1) Provide information to the ward in an age-appropriate manner about the limitations on confidentiality of testimony and the possibility that information provided to the professional may be shared with the court on the record and provided to the parties in the case;

(2) Allow but not require the ward to state a preference regarding the issues to be decided in the proceeding or other matter subject to this rule, and provide information in an age-appropriate manner about the process by which the court will make a decision; and

(3) Provide to the other parties in the case information about how best to support the interest of the ward during the court process.

(Subd (f) adopted effective January 1, 2013.)

(g) Methods of providing information to parties and supporting nonparty wards

Courts should provide information to the parties and the ward who is not a party to the proceeding or other matter subject to this rule when the ward wants to participate or testify. Methods of providing information may include:

(1) Having court or county guardianship investigators and experts appointed under Evidence Code section 730 meet jointly or separately with the parties and their attorneys to discuss alternatives to having the ward provide direct testimony;

(2) Providing an orientation for the ward about the court process and the role of the judicial officer in making decisions, how the courtroom or chambers will be set up, and what participating or testifying will entail;

(3) Providing information to parties before the ward participates or testifies so that they can consider the possible effect on the ward of participating or not participating in the proceeding or other matter subject to this rule;

(4) Appointing counsel under Probate Code section 1470 or a guardian ad litem for the ward to assist in the provision of information to the ward concerning his or her decision to participate in the proceeding or testify;

(5) Including information in guardianship orientation presentations and publications about the options available to a ward who is not a party to the proceeding or other matter subject to this rule to participate or testify or not to do so, and the consequences of a ward's decision whether to become a party to the proceeding or other matter subject to this rule; and

(6) Providing an interpreter for the ward.

(Subd (g) adopted effective January 1, 2013.)

(h) If the ward is a party to the proceeding

(1) A ward who is a party to the proceeding or other matter subject to this rule is subject to the law of discovery applied to parties in civil actions and may be called as a witness by any other party unless the court makes a finding that providing information in response to discovery requests or testifying as a witness is not in the ward's best interest and states the reasons on the record.

(2) The court must consider appointing counsel under Probate Code section 1470 or a guardian ad litem for a ward who is a party to the proceeding or other matter subject to this rule if the ward is not represented by counsel.

(3) In determining whether providing information in response to discovery requests or testifying as a witness is in the ward's best interest, the judicial officer should consider the following:

(A) Whether information has been presented indicating that the ward may be at risk emotionally if he or she is permitted or denied the opportunity to provide information in response to discovery requests or by testimony;

(B) Whether the subject areas about which the ward is anticipated to provide information in response to discovery requests or by testimony are relevant to the decision the court must make; and

(C) Whether any other factors weigh in favor of or against having the ward provide information in response to discovery requests or by testimony.

(4) In taking testimony from a ward who is a party to the proceeding or other matter subject to this rule, the court must take the special care required by Evidence Code section 765(b). If the ward is not represented by an attorney, the court must inform the ward in an age-appropriate manner about the limitations on confidentiality of testimony and that the information provided to the court will be on the record and provided to the parties in the case.

(Subd (h) adopted effective January 1, 2013.)

(i) Education and training of judicial officers and court staff

Education and training content for court staff and judicial officers should include information on wards' participation in proceedings or other matters subject to this rule, methods other than direct testimony for receiving input from a ward, procedures for taking a ward's testimony, and differences in the application of this rule to wards who are and are not parties to the proceeding or other matters subject to this rule.

(Subd (i) adopted effective January 1, 2013.)

Rule 7.1016 adopted effective January 1, 2013.

Rule 7.1020.　Special Immigrant Juvenile findings in guardianship proceedings

(a) Application

This rule applies to a request by or on behalf of a minor who is a ward or a proposed ward in a probate guardianship proceeding for judicial findings needed as a basis for filing a petition for classification as a Special Immigrant Juvenile (SIJ) under federal immigration law. The term "request under this rule" as used in this rule refers exclusively to such a request. This rule also applies to any opposition to a request under this rule, any hearing on such a request and opposition, and any findings of the court in response to such a request.

(Subd (a) adopted effective January 1, 2016.)

(b) Request for findings

(1) *Who may file request*

Any person or entity authorized under Probate Code section 1510 or 1510.1 to petition for the appointment of a guardian of the person of a minor, including the ward or proposed ward if 12 years of age or older, may file a request for findings regarding the minor under this rule.

(A) If there is more than one ward or proposed ward in the proceeding, a minor eligible to file a request for findings under this rule may do so only for himself or herself.

(B) The court may appoint an attorney under Probate Code section 1470 or a guardian ad litem under Probate Code sections 1003 and 1003.5 to file and present a request for findings under this rule for a minor or to represent the interests of a minor in a proceeding to decide a request filed on the minor's behalf by another.

(2) *Form of request*

(A) A request for findings under this rule must be made by verified petition. A separate request must be filed for each minor seeking SIJ findings.

(B) A request for findings under this rule by or on behalf of a minor filed concurrently with a petition for the appointment of a guardian of the person or for extension of a guardianship of the person past the 18th birthday of the minor must be prepared and filed as a separate petition, not as an attachment to the petition for appointment.

(Subd (b) amended effective July 1, 2016; adopted effective January 1, 2016.)

(c) Notice of hearing

Notice of a hearing of a request for findings under this rule, and a copy of the request, must be sent to the minor's parents and the persons listed in section 1460(b) of the Probate Code, in the manner and within the time provided in that section, subject to the provisions of subdivision (e) of that section and sections 1202 and 1460.1 of that code.

(Subd (c) adopted effective January 1, 2016.)

(d) Opposition to request

Any of the persons who must be given notice of hearing of a request for findings under this rule may file an objection or other opposition to the request.

(Subd (d) adopted effective January 1, 2016.)

(e) Hearing on request

(1) If filed concurrently, a request for findings under this rule by or on behalf of a minor and a petition for appointment of a guardian of the person or extension of a guardianship of the person past the 18th birthday of that minor may be heard and determined together.

(2) Hearings on separate requests for findings under this rule by or on behalf of more than one ward or proposed ward in the same guardianship proceeding may be consolidated on the motion of any party or on the court's own motion.

(3) Hearings on requests for findings under this rule by or on behalf of minors who are siblings or half-siblings and are wards or proposed wards in separate guardianship proceedings may be consolidated on the motion of any party in either proceeding or on the motion of the court in either proceeding. If multiple departments of a single court or courts in more than one county are involved, they may communicate with each other on consolidation issues in the manner provided for inter-court communications on venue issues in guardianship and family law matters under section 2204 of the Probate Code and rule 7.1014.

(4) Hearings on contested requests for findings under this rule must be conducted in the same manner as hearings on other contested petitions under the Probate Code.

(5) Probate Code section 1022 applies to uncontested requests for findings under this rule.

(Subd (e) amended effective July 1, 2016; adopted effective January 1, 2016.)

(f) Separate findings in multi-ward cases under this rule

The court must issue separate findings for each minor in a guardianship proceeding in which more than one minor is the subject of a request under this rule.

(Subd (f) adopted effective January 1, 2016.)

Rule 7.1020 amended effective July 1, 2016; adopted effective January 1, 2016.

Chapter 22
Conservatorships

Rule 7.1050.　Conservator forms

(a) Forms to be submitted with petition

Each petitioner, unless the petitioner is a bank or other entity entitled to conduct the business of a trust company, must submit to the court with the petition for appointment of conservator a completed *Confidential Supplemental Information* statement (form GC-312). In addition, each proposed conservator, except a bank or other entity entitled to conduct the business of a trust company, or a public guardian, must submit a completed *Confidential Conservator Screening Form* (form GC-314).

(Subd (a) amended effective January 1, 2007; previously amended effective January 1, 2002.)

(b) Use of form

The information on the *Confidential Conservator Screening Form* is used by the court and by persons or agencies designated by the court to assist the court in determining whether a proposed conservator should be appointed.

(Subd (b) amended effective January 1, 2002.)

(c) Forms to be confidential

The *Confidential Conservator Screening Form*, the *Confidential Supplemental Information* statement, and the information contained on these forms are confidential. The clerk must maintain these forms in a manner that will protect and preserve their confidentiality.

(Subd (c) amended effective January 1, 2007; previously amended effective January 1, 2002.)

Rule 7.1050 amended effective January 1, 2007; adopted effective January 1, 2001; previously amended effective January 1, 2002.

Rule 7.1051. Acknowledgment of receipt of Duties of Conservator

Before the court issues letters, each conservator must execute and file an acknowledgment of receipt of the *Duties of Conservator and Acknowledgment of Receipt of Handbook* (form GC-348).

Rule 7.1051 amended effective January 1, 2002; adopted effective January 1, 2001.

Rule 7.1052. Termination of conservatorship

(a) Operation of law or court order

A conservatorship of the person or estate may terminate by operation of law or may be terminated by court order if the court determines that it is no longer required.

(b) Conservator of the person

Under Probate Code section 1860(a), a conservatorship of the person terminates by operation of law when the conservatee dies, and the conservator of the person need not file a petition for its termination.

(c) Duty of conservator of estate on termination

A conservator of the estate whose administration is terminated by operation of law or by court order must file and obtain the court's approval of a final account of the administration.

Rule 7.1052 adopted effective January 1, 2004.

Rule 7.1053. Service of final account of removed or resigned conservator

A resigned or removed conservator of the estate must serve a copy of the conservator's final account and the petition for its settlement with the notice of hearing that must be served on the successor conservator of the estate under Probate Code section 1460(b)(1), unless the court dispenses with such service.

Rule 7.1053 adopted effective January 1, 2004.

Rule 7.1054. Service of final account after termination of conservatorship

After termination of the conservatorship, the conservator of the estate must serve copies of the conservator's final account and the petition for its settlement with the notices of hearing that must be served on the former conservatee and on the spouse or domestic partner of the former conservatee under Probate Code sections 1460(b)(2) and (3), unless the court dispenses with such service.

Rule 7.1054 adopted effective January 1, 2004.

Rule 7.1059. Standards of conduct for the conservator of the estate

Except as otherwise required by statute, in the exercise of ordinary care and diligence in managing and controlling the estate of the conservatee, the conservator of the estate is to be guided by the following principles:

(a) Avoidance of actual and apparent conflicts of interest with the conservatee

The conservator must avoid actual conflicts of interest and, consistent with his or her fiduciary duty to the conservatee, the appearance of conflicts of interest. The conservator must avoid any personal, business, or professional interest or relationship that is or reasonably could be perceived as being self-serving or adverse to the best interest of the conservatee. In particular:

(1) Except as appropriate for conservators who are not professional fiduciaries with full disclosure to the court, the conservator should not personally provide housing, medical, or legal services to the conservatee;

(2) The conservator must be independent from all service providers, except when (a) no other conservator or service providers are reasonably available, (b) the exception is in the best interest of the conservatee, (c) the circumstances are fully disclosed to the court, and (d) prior court approval has been obtained;

(3) The conservator must neither solicit nor accept incentives from service providers; and

(4) The conservator must not engage his or her family members to provide services to the conservatee for a profit or fee when other alternatives are reasonably available. Where family members do provide such services, their relationship to the conservator must be fully disclosed to the court, the terms of engagement must be in the best interest of the conservatee compared to the terms available from independent service providers, the services must be competently performed, and the conservator must be able to exercise appropriate control and supervision.

A conservator's employees, including family members, are not service providers and are not providing services to the conservatee for a profit or fee within the meaning of this rule if their compensation is paid by the conservator and their services are either included in the conservator's petition for allowance of the conservator's compensation or are not paid from the conservatee's estate.

(Subd (a) adopted effective January 1, 2008.)

(b) Conservatorship estate management

The conservator of the estate must:

(1) Provide competent management of the conservatee's property, with the care of a prudent person dealing with someone else's property;

(2) Refrain from unreasonably risky investments;

(3) Refrain from making loans or gifts of estate property, except as authorized by the court after full disclosure;

(4) Manage the estate for the benefit of the conservatee;

(5) Subject to the duty of full disclosure to the court and persons entitled under law to receive it, closely guard against unnecessary or inappropriate disclosure of the conservatee's financial information;

(6) Keep the money and property of the estate separate from the conservator's or any other person's money or property, except as may be permitted under statutes authorizing public guardians or public conservators and certain regulated private fiduciaries to maintain common trust funds or similar common investments;

(7) Hold title reflecting the conservatorship in individual securities, mutual funds, securities broker accounts, and accounts with financial institutions;

(8) Keep accurate records of all transactions. Professional fiduciaries must maintain prudent accounting systems and procedures designed to protect against embezzlement and other cash-asset mismanagement;

(9) Undertake as soon as possible after appointment and qualification to locate and safeguard the conservatee's estate planning documents, including wills, living trusts, powers of attorney for health care and finances, life insurance policies, and pension records;

(10) Undertake as soon as possible after appointment and qualification to secure the real and personal property of the estate, insuring it at appropriate levels, and protecting it against damage, destruction, or loss;

(11) Make reasonable efforts to preserve property identified in the conservatee's estate planning documents;

(12) Communicate as necessary and appropriate with the conservator of the person of the conservatee, if any, and with the trustee of any trust of which the conservatee is a beneficiary;

(13) Pursue claims against others on behalf of the conservatee or the estate to do so. Consider requesting prior court authority to pursue or compromise large or complex claims, particularly those that might require litigation and the assistance of counsel and those that might result in an award of attorneys' fees for the other party against the estate if unsuccessful, and request such approval before entering into a contingent fee agreement with counsel;

(14) Defend against actions or claims against the estate when it would be in the best interest of the conservatee or the estate to do so. Consider requesting court approval or instructions concerning the defense or compromise of litigation against the estate;

(15) Collect all public and insurance benefits for which the conservatee is eligible;

(16) Evaluate the conservatee's ability to manage cash or other assets and take appropriate action, including obtaining prior court approval when necessary or appropriate, to enable the conservatee to do so to the level of his or her ability;

(17) When disposing of the conservatee's tangible personal property, inform the conservatee's family members in advance and give them an opportunity to acquire the property, with approval or confirmation of the court; and

(18) In deciding whether it is in the best interest of the conservatee to dispose of property of the estate, consider the following factors, among others, as appropriate in the circumstances:

(A) The likely benefit or improvement of the conservatee's life that disposing of the property would bring;

(B) The likelihood that the conservatee would need or benefit from the property in the future;

(C) Subject to the factors specified in Probate Code section 2113, the previously expressed or current desires of the conservatee concerning the property;

(D) The provisions of the conservatee's estate plan concerning the property;

(E) The tax consequences of the disposition transaction;

(F) The impact of the disposition transaction on the conservatee's entitlement to public benefits;

(G) The condition of the entire estate;

(H) Alternatives to disposition of the property;

(I) The likelihood that the property will deteriorate or be subject to waste if retained in the estate; and

(J) The benefit versus the cost or liability of maintaining the property in the estate.

(Subd (b) adopted effective January 1, 2008.)
Rule 7.1059 adopted effective January 1, 2008.

Advisory Committee Comment

The Probate and Mental Health Advisory Committee consulted with several organizations in the development of rule 7.1059, including the National Guardianship Association, a nationwide voluntary association of professional and family fiduciaries, guardians, and allied professionals. In developing this rule, the Probate and Mental Health Advisory Committee considered the National Guardianship Association's Standards of Practice. Some of these standards have been incorporated into the rules.

Rule 7.1060. Qualifications and continuing education requirements for private professional conservators [Repealed]

Rule 7.1060 repealed effective July 1, 2008; amended effective January 1, 2007; adopted effective January 1, 2006.

Another Rule 7.1060 follows.

Rule 7.1060. Investigations and reports by court investigators

(a) *Order Appointing Court Investigator* (form GC-330)

Order Appointing Court Investigator (form GC-330) is an optional form within the meaning of rule 1.35 of these rules, except as follows:

(1) A court may, by local rule, require that form GC-330 be used for orders appointing court investigators and directing them to conduct all or any of the investigations described in the form and to prepare, file, and serve copies of reports concerning those investigations. The local rule may also prescribe the form's preparation, service, and delivery to the court for execution and filing.

(2) A court may, by local rule, require that a general order, a court-prepared order, or a local form order instead of form GC-330 be used to appoint and direct the actions of court investigators concerning all or any of the investigations and reports described in form GC-330.

(Subd (a) adopted effective January 1, 2011.)

(b) *Order Appointing Court Investigator (Review and Successor Conservator Investigations)* (form GC-331)

Order Appointing Court Investigator (Review and Successor Conservator Investigations) (form GC-331) is an optional form within the meaning of rule 1.35 of these rules, except as follows:

(1) A court may, by local rule, require that form GC-331 be used for orders appointing court investigators and directing them to conduct all or any of the review investigations under Probate Code sections 1850 and 1851 or investigations concerning the appointment of successor conservators under Probate Code sections 2684 and 2686 described in the form and to prepare, file, and serve copies of reports concerning those investigations. Form GC-331 is to be prepared by the court only.

(2) A court may, by local rule, require that a general order, a court-prepared order, or a local form order instead of form GC-331 be used to appoint and direct the actions of court investigators concerning all or any of the investigations and reports described in form GC-331.

(Subd (b) adopted effective January 1, 2011.)

(c) *Order Setting Biennial Review Investigation and Directing Status Report Before Review* (form GC-332)

Order Setting Biennial Review Investigation and Directing Status Report Before Review (form GC-332) is an optional form within the meaning of rule 1.35 of these rules, except as follows:

(1) A court may, by local rule, require that form GC-332 be used for orders setting biennial review investigations and directing status reports

under Probate Code section 1850(a)(2). Form GC-332 is to be prepared by the court only.

(2) A court may, by local rule, require that a general order, a court-prepared order, or a local form order instead of form GC-332 be used concerning the matters described in form GC-332.

(Subd (c) adopted effective January 1, 2011.)
Rule 7.1060 adopted effective January 1, 2011.

Rule 7.1061. Taking possession of an asset of the conservatee at an institution or opening or changing ownership of an account or safe-deposit box in a financial institution

(a) Definitions

As used in this rule, the following terms have the meanings stated below:

(1) An "institution" is an insurance company, insurance broker, insurance agent, investment company, investment bank, securities broker-dealer, investment advisor, financial planner, financial advisor, or any other person who takes, holds, or controls an asset subject to a guardianship that is not a "financial institution" within the meaning of this rule;

(2) A "financial institution" is a bank, trust (except as provided in (d)), savings and loan association, savings bank, industrial bank, or credit union; and

(3) "Taking possession" or "taking control" of an asset held or controlled by an institution includes changing title to the asset, withdrawing all or any portion of the asset, or transferring all or any portion of the asset from the institution.

(Subd (a) adopted effective January 1, 2009.)

(b) Responsibilities of the conservator when taking possession or control of an asset of the conservatee at an institution

When taking possession or control of an asset held by an institution in the name of the conservatee, the temporary, general, or limited conservator of the estate must provide the following to the institution:

(1) A certified copy of the conservator's *Letters of Temporary Guardianship or Conservatorship* (form GC-150) or *Letters of Conservatorship* (form GC-350) containing the Notice to Institutions and Financial Institutions on the second page; and

(2) A blank copy of a *Notice of Taking Possession or Control of an Asset of Minor or Conservatee* (form GC-050).

(Subd (b) adopted effective January 1, 2009.)

(c) Responsibilities of the conservator when opening or changing the name on an account or a safe-deposit box at a financial institution

When opening or changing the name on an account or a safe-deposit box in a financial institution, the temporary, general, or limited conservator of the estate must provide the following to the financial institution:

(1) A certified copy of the guardian's *Letters of Temporary Guardianship or Conservatorship* (form GC-150) or *Letters of Conservatorship* (form GC-350) containing the Notice to Institutions and Financial Institutions on the second page; and

(2) A blank copy of a *Notice of Opening or Changing a Guardianship or Conservatorship Account or Safe-Deposit Box* (form GC-051).

(Subd (c) adopted effective January 1, 2009.)

(d) Application of this rule to Totten trust accounts

This rule applies to Totten trust accounts but does not apply to any other trust arrangement described in Probate Code section 82(b).

(Subd (d) adopted effective January 1, 2009.)
Rule 7.1061 adopted effective January 1, 2009.

Rule 7.1062. The good cause exception to notice of the hearing on a petition for appointment of a temporary conservator

(a) Purpose

The purpose of this rule is to establish uniform standards for the good cause exception to the notice of the hearing required on a petition for appointment of a temporary conservator under Probate Code section 2250(e).

(Subd (a) amended effective January 1, 2009; adopted effective January 1, 2008.)

(b) Good cause for exceptions to notice limited

Good cause for an exception to the notice required by section 2250(e) must be based on a showing that the exception is necessary to protect the proposed conservatee or his or her estate from immediate and substantial harm.

(Subd (b) amended effective January 1, 2009; adopted effective January 1, 2008.)

(c) Court may change the time or manner of giving notice

An exception to the notice requirement of section 2250(e) may include one or any combination of the following:

(1) Waiving notice to one, more than one, or all persons entitled to notice;

(2) Requiring a different period of notice; and

(3) Changing the required manner of giving notice, including requiring notice by telephone, fax, e-mail, or personal delivery, or a combination of these methods, instead of or in addition to notice by mail to the proposed conservatee's spouse or registered domestic partner and relatives.

(Subd (c) amended effective July 1, 2008; adopted effective January 1, 2008.)

(d) Good cause exceptions to notice

Good cause for an exception to the notice requirement of section 2250(e) may include a showing of:

(1) Harm caused by the passage of time. The showing must demonstrate the immediate and substantial harm to the conservatee or the conservatee's estate that could occur during the notice period.

(2) Harm that one or more persons entitled to notice might do to the proposed conservatee or the proposed conservatee's estate if notice is given. Such a showing would not support an exception to the requirement to give notice to any other person entitled to notice unless it also demonstrates that notice cannot reasonably be given to the other person without also giving notice to the persons who might cause harm.

(3) Medical emergency. The emergency must be immediate and substantial and treatment (1) must be reasonably unavailable unless a temporary conservator is appointed and (2) cannot be deferred for the notice period because of the proposed conservatee's pain or extreme discomfort or a significant risk of harm.

(4) Financial emergency. The emergency must be immediate and substantial and other means shown likely to be ineffective to prevent loss or further loss to the proposed conservatee's estate during the notice period.

(Subd (d) amended effective January 1, 2009; adopted effective January 1, 2008.)

(e) Contents of request for good cause exception to notice

A request for a good cause exception to the notice requirement of section 2250(e) must be in writing, separate from the petition for appointment of a temporary conservator, and must include:

(1) An application containing the case caption and stating the relief requested;

(2) An affirmative factual showing in support of the application in a declaration under penalty of perjury containing competent testimony based on personal knowledge;

(3) A declaration under penalty of perjury based on personal knowledge containing the information required for an ex parte application under rule 3.1204(b); and

(4) A proposed order.

(Subd (e) amended effective January 1, 2009; adopted effective January 1, 2008.)

Rule 7.1062 amended effective January 1, 2009; adopted effective January 1, 2008; previously amended effective July 1, 2008.

Rule 7.1063. Change of conservatee's residence

(a) Pre-move notice of change of personal residence required

Unless an emergency requires a shorter period of notice, the conservator of the person must mail copies of a notice of an intended change of the conservatee's personal residence to the persons listed below at least 15 days before the date of the proposed change, and file the original notice with proof of mailing with the court. Copies of the notice must be mailed to:

(1) The conservatee;

(2) The conservatee's attorney of record;

(3) The conservatee's spouse or registered domestic partner; and

(4) The conservatee's relatives named in the *Petition for Appointment of Probate Conservator* (form GC-310), including the conservatee's "deemed relatives" under Probate Code section 1821(b)(1)–(4) if the conservatee has no spouse or registered domestic partner and no second-degree relatives.

(Subd (a) adopted effective January 1, 2008.)

(b) Conservatee's personal residence

(1) The "conservatee's personal residence" under (a) is the residence the conservatee understands or believes, or reasonably appears to understand or believe, to be his or her permanent residence on the date the first petition for appointment of a conservator was filed in the proceeding, whether or not the conservatee is living in that residence on that date. A residential care facility, including a board and care, intermediate care, skilled nursing, or secured perimeter facility, may be the conservatee's personal residence under this rule.

(2) If the conservatee cannot form or communicate an understanding or belief concerning his or her permanent residence on the date the first petition for appointment of a conservator was filed in the proceeding, his or her personal residence under this rule is the residence he or she last previously understood or believed, or appeared to understand or believe, to be his or her permanent residence.

(3) For purposes of this rule, the following changes of residence are or are not changes of the conservatee's personal residence, as indicated:

(A) A move from the conservatee's personal residence under this rule to a residential care facility or other residence is a change of the conservatee's personal residence under (a).

(B) A move from a residential care facility or other residence to another residence that is not the conservatee's personal residence under this rule is a change of the conservatee's personal residence under (a).

(C) A move from a residential care facility or other residence to the conservatee's personal residence under this rule is not a change of the conservatee's personal residence under (a).

(Subd (b) adopted effective January 1, 2008.)

(c) Post-move notice of a change of residence required

The conservator of the person must file a notice of a change of the conservatee's residence with the court within 30 days of the date of the change. Unless waived by the court for good cause to prevent harm to the conservatee, the conservator must mail a copy of the notice to the persons named below and file a proof of mailing with the original notice filed with the court. Unless waived, the notice must be mailed to:

(1) The conservatee's attorney of record;

(2) The conservatee's spouse or registered domestic partner; and

(3) The conservatee's relatives named in the *Petition for Appointment of Probate Conservator* (form GC-310), including the conservatee's "deemed relatives" under Probate Code section 1821(b)(1)–(4) if the conservatee has no spouse or registered domestic partner and no second-degree relatives.

(Subd (c) adopted effective January 1, 2008.)

(d) Conservatee's residence

The "conservatee's residence" under (c) is the conservatee's residence at any time after appointment of a conservator.

(Subd (d) adopted effective January 1, 2008.)

(e) Use of Judicial Council forms GC-079 and GC-080

(1) The *Pre-Move Notice of Proposed Change of Personal Residence of Conservatee or Ward* (form GC-079) must be used for the pre-move notice required under (a) and Probate Code section 2352(e)(3). The conservator, the conservator's attorney, or an employee of the attorney may complete the mailing and sign the Proof of Mailing on page 2 of the form. If the notice is mailed less than 15 days before the date of the move because an emergency requires a shorter period of notice, the basis for the emergency must be stated in the notice.

(2) The *Post-Move Notice of Change of Residence of Conservatee or Ward* (form GC-080) must be used for the post-move notice required under (c) and Probate Code section 2352(e)(1) and (2). The conservator, the conservator's attorney, or an employee of the attorney may complete the mailing and sign the Proof of Mailing on page 2 of the form.

(Subd (e) adopted effective January 1, 2008.)

(f) Prior court approval required to establish conservatee's residence outside California

Notwithstanding any other provision of this rule, prior court approval is required before a conservatee's residence may be established outside the state of California.

(Subd (f) adopted effective January 1, 2008.)

Rule 7.1063 adopted effective January 1, 2008.

Chapter 23
Appointed Counsel

Chapter 23 amended effective January 1, 2020; adopted effective January 1, 2008.

Rule 7.1101. Scope, definitions, and general qualifications

Rule 7.1102. Qualifications and annual education required for counsel ap-

pointed to represent a ward or proposed ward (Prob. Code, §§ 1456, 1470(a))

Rule 7.1103. Qualifications and annual education required for counsel appointed to represent a conservatee, proposed conservatee, or person alleged to lack legal capacity (Prob. Code, §§ 1456, 1470(a), 1471)

Rule 7.1104. Local administration

Rule 7.1105. Certification of attorney qualifications

Rule 7.1101.   Qualifications and continuing education required of counsel appointed by the court in guardianships and conservatorships [Repealed]

Rule 7.1101 repealed effective January 1, 2020; adopted effective January 1, 2008; previously amended effective January 1, 2009, January 1, 2011, and January 1, 2016.

Another Rule 7.1101 follows.

Rule 7.1101.   Scope, definitions, and general qualifications

(a) Scope (Prob. Code, §§ 1456, 1470–1471)

The rules in this chapter establish minimum qualifications, annual education requirements, and certification requirements that an attorney must meet as conditions of court appointment as counsel under Probate Code section 1470 or 1471 in a proceeding under division 4 of that code.

(1) The rules in this chapter apply to an appointed attorney regardless of whether the attorney is a sole practitioner or works for a private law firm, a legal services organization, or a public defender's office.

(2) The rules in this chapter do not apply to:

(A) Retained counsel;

(B) Counsel appointed under the authority of any law other than Probate Code section 1470 or 1471.

(Subd (a) adopted effective January 1, 2020.)

(b) Definitions

For purposes of this chapter, the following terms are used as defined below:

(1) "Appointed counsel" or "appointed attorney" means an attorney appointed by the court under Probate Code section 1470 or 1471 who assumes direct personal responsibility for representing a ward or proposed ward, a conservatee or proposed conservatee, or a person alleged to lack legal capacity in a proceeding under division 4 of the Probate Code.

(2) "Probate guardianship" means any proceeding related to a general or temporary guardianship under division 4 of the Probate Code.

(3) "Probate conservatorship" means any proceeding related to a conservatorship or limited conservatorship, general or temporary, under division 4 of the Probate Code.

(4) "LPS Act" refers to the Lanterman-Petris-Short Act (Welf. & Inst. Code, §§ 5000–5556), which provides for involuntary mental health treatment and conservatorship for persons who are gravely disabled as the result of a mental health disorder.

(5) A "contested matter" is a matter that requires a noticed hearing and in which an objection is filed in writing or made orally in open court by any person entitled to appear at the hearing and support or oppose the petition.

(6) "Trial" means the determination of one or more disputed issues of fact by means of an evidentiary hearing.

(Subd (b) adopted effective January 1, 2020.)

(c) General qualifications

To qualify for any appointment under Probate Code section 1470 or 1471, an attorney must:

(1) Be an active member in good standing of the State Bar of California or a registered legal aid attorney qualified to practice law in California under rule 9.45;

(2) Have had no professional discipline imposed in the 12 months immediately preceding the date of submitting any initial or annual certification of compliance; and

(3) Have demonstrated to the court that the attorney or the attorney's firm or employer:

(A) Is covered by professional liability insurance with coverage limits no less than $100,000 per claim and $300,000 per year; or

(B) Is covered for professional liability at an equivalent level through a self-insurance program;

(4) Have met the applicable qualifications and annual education requirements in this chapter and have a current certification on file with the appointing court; and

(5) Have satisfied any additional requirements established by local rule.

(Subd (c) adopted effective January 1, 2020.)

(d) Local rules

The rules in this chapter establish minimum qualifications and requirements. Nothing in this chapter prohibits a court from establishing, by local rule adopted under rule 10.613, additional or more rigorous qualifications or requirements.

(Subd (d) adopted effective January 1, 2020.)

(e) Retroactivity

The amendments to this chapter adopted effective January 1, 2020, are not retroactive. They do not require an attorney who submitted an initial certification of qualifications under this chapter as it read on or before December 31, 2019, to submit a new initial certification.

(Subd (e) adopted effective January 1, 2020.)

Rule 7.1101 adopted effective January 1, 2020.

Rule 7.1102.   Qualifications and annual education required for counsel appointed to represent a ward or proposed ward (Prob. Code, §§ 1456, 1470(a))

Except as provided in rule 7.1104(b), an attorney appointed for a ward or proposed ward must have met the qualifications in either (a) or (b) and, in every calendar year after first availability for appointment, must meet the annual education requirements in (c).

(a) Experience-based qualifications

An attorney is qualified for appointment if the attorney has met the experience requirements described in either (1) or (2).

(1) Within the five years immediately before first availability for appointment, the attorney has personally represented a petitioner, an objector, a respondent, a minor child, or a nonminor dependent in at least three of any combination of the following proceedings, at least one of which must have been a contested matter or trial:

(A) A probate guardianship proceeding;

(B) A juvenile court child welfare proceeding; or

(C) A family law child custody proceeding.

(2) At the time of first availability for appointment, the attorney meets the experience requirements:

(A) In rule 5.660(d) and any applicable local rules for appointment to represent a minor child or nonminor dependent in a juvenile court child welfare proceeding; or

(B) In rule 5.242(f) for appointment to represent a minor child in a family law child custody proceeding.

(Subd (a) adopted effective January 1, 2020.)

(b) Alternative qualifications

An attorney who does not yet meet the experience-based qualifications in (a) may, until the attorney has gained the necessary experience, qualify for appointment if the attorney meets the requirements in (1) or (2).

(1) At the time of appointment, the attorney works for an attorney, a private law firm, or a legal services organization approved by the court for appointment under Probate Code section 1470 to represent wards or proposed wards, and the attorney is supervised by or working in close professional consultation with a qualified attorney who has satisfied the experience requirements in (a); or

(2) In the 12 months immediately before first availability for appointment, the attorney has completed at least three hours of professional education approved by the State Bar of California for Minimum Continuing Legal Education (MCLE) credit in the subjects listed in (d) and, at the time of appointment, the attorney is working in close professional consultation with a qualified attorney who has satisfied the experience requirements in (a).

(Subd (b) adopted effective January 1, 2020.)

(c) Annual education

Each calendar year after first availability for appointment, an attorney appointed by the court to represent a ward or proposed ward must complete at least three hours of professional education approved by the State Bar for MCLE credit in the subjects listed in (d).

(Subd (c) adopted effective January 1, 2020.)

(d) Subject matter and delivery of education

Education in the following subjects—delivered in person or by any State Bar–approved method of distance learning—may be used to satisfy this rule's education requirements:

(1) State and federal statutes—including the federal Indian Child Welfare Act of 1978 (25 U.S.C. §§ 1901–1963)—rules of court, and case law governing probate guardianship proceedings and the legal rights of parents and children;

(2) Child development, including techniques for communicating with a child client; and

(3) Risk factors for child abuse and neglect and family violence.

(Subd (d) adopted effective January 1, 2020.)

Rule 7.1102 adopted effective January 1, 2020.

Rule 7.1103. Qualifications and annual education required for counsel appointed to represent a conservatee, proposed conservatee, or person alleged to lack legal capacity (Prob. Code, §§ 1456, 1470(a), 1471)

Except as provided in rule 7.1104(b), an attorney appointed to represent the interests of a conservatee, proposed conservatee, or person alleged to lack legal capacity must have met the qualifications in (a) or (b) and, in every calendar year after first availability for appointment, must meet the annual education requirements in (c).

(a) Experience-based qualifications

An attorney is qualified for appointment if, within the five years immediately preceding first availability for appointment, the attorney has personally represented a petitioner, an objector, a conservatee or proposed conservatee, or a person alleged to lack legal capacity or be gravely disabled in at least three separate proceedings under either division 4 of the Probate Code or the LPS Act, including at least one contested matter or trial.

(Subd (a) adopted effective January 1, 2020.)

(b) Alternative qualifications

An attorney who does not yet meet the experience-based qualifications in (a) may, until the attorney has gained the necessary experience, qualify for appointment if the attorney meets the requirements in (1) or (2).

(1) At the time of appointment, the attorney works for an attorney, a private law firm, a public defender's office, or a legal services organization (including the organization designated by the Governor as the state protection and advocacy agency, as defined in section 4900(i) of the Welfare and Institutions Code) approved by the court for appointment to represent conservatees, proposed conservatees, and persons alleged to lack legal capacity, and the attorney is supervised by or working in close professional consultation with a qualified attorney who has satisfied the experience requirements in (a); or

(2) In the 12 months immediately before first availability for appointment, the attorney has completed at least three hours of professional education approved by the State Bar of California for Minimum Continuing Legal Education (MCLE) credit in the subjects listed in (d), and, at the time of appointment, the attorney is working in close professional consultation with a qualified attorney who has satisfied the experience requirements in (a).

(Subd (b) adopted effective January 1, 2020.)

(c) Annual education

Each calendar year after first availability for appointment, an attorney appointed by the court to represent a conservatee, proposed conservatee, or person alleged to lack legal capacity must complete at least three hours of professional education approved by the State Bar for MCLE credit in the subjects listed in (d).

(Subd (c) adopted effective January 1, 2020.)

(d) Subject matter and delivery of education

Education in the following subjects—delivered in person or by any State Bar–approved method of distance learning—may be used to satisfy this rule's education requirements:

(1) State and federal statutes—including the federal Americans with Disabilities Act (42 U.S.C. §§ 12101–12213)—rules of court, and case law governing probate conservatorship proceedings, capacity determinations, and the legal rights of conservatees, persons alleged to lack legal capacity, and persons with disabilities;

(2) The attorney-client relationship and lawyer's ethical duties to a client under the California Rules of Professional Conduct and other applicable law; and

(3) Special considerations for representing an older adult or a person with a disability, including:

(A) Communicating with an older client or a client with a disability;

(B) Vulnerability of older adults and persons with disabilities to undue influence, physical and financial abuse, and neglect;

(C) Effects of aging, major neurocognitive disorders (including dementia), and intellectual and developmental disabilities on a person's ability to perform the activities of daily living; and

(D) Less-restrictive alternatives to conservatorship, including supported decisionmaking.

(Subd (d) adopted effective January 1, 2020.)

Rule 7.1103 adopted effective January 1, 2020.

Rule 7.1104. Local administration

(a) Procedures

(1) A local court may create and maintain lists or panels of certified attorneys or approve the public defender's office and one or more legal services organizations to provide qualified attorneys for appointment under Probate Code sections 1470 and 1471 to represent specific categories of persons in proceedings under division 4 of that code.

(2) A court may establish, by local rule adopted under rule 10.613, procedural requirements, including submission of an application, as conditions for approval for appointment or placement on a list or panel.

(Subd (a) adopted effective January 1, 2020.)

(b) Exception to qualifications

A court may appoint an attorney who is not qualified under rule 7.1102 or 7.1103 on an express finding, on the record or in writing, of circumstances that make such an appointment necessary. These circumstances may include, but are not limited to, when:

(1) No qualified attorney is available for appointment; or

(2) The needs or interests of the person to be represented cannot be served without the appointment of an attorney who has other specific knowledge, skills, or experience.

(Subd (b) adopted effective January 1, 2020.)

Rule 7.1104 adopted effective January 1, 2020.

Rule 7.1105. Certification of attorney qualifications

(a) Initial certification

Before first availability for appointment under Probate Code section 1470 or 1471, an attorney must certify to the court that the attorney:

(1) Meets the licensing, disciplinary status, and insurance requirements in rule 7.1101(c)(1)–(3); and

(2) Meets the qualifications in rule 7.1102 for appointment to represent wards or the qualifications in rule 7.1103 for appointment to represent conservatees, or both, depending on the appointments the attorney wishes to be available for.

(Subd (a) adopted effective January 1, 2020.)

(b) Annual certification

To remain eligible for appointment under Probate Code section 1470 or 1471, an attorney who has submitted an initial certification must certify to the court, no later than March 31 of each following year, that:

(1) The attorney meets the licensing, disciplinary status, and insurance requirements in rule 7.1101(c)(1)–(3); and

(2) The attorney has completed the applicable annual education—in rule 7.1102, 7.1103, or both—required for the previous calendar year.

(Subd (b) adopted effective January 1, 2020.)

(c) Notification of disciplinary action

An appointed attorney must notify the court in writing within five court days of any disciplinary action taken against the attorney by the State Bar of California. The notification must describe the charges, disposition, and terms of any reproof, probation, or suspension.

(Subd (c) adopted effective January 1, 2020.)

(d) Documentation

A court to which an attorney has submitted a certification under this rule may require the attorney to submit documentation or other information in support of any statement in the certification.

(Subd (d) adopted effective January 1, 2020.)

(e) Confidentiality

The certifications required by this rule and any supporting documentation or information submitted to the court must be maintained confidentially by the court. They must not be filed or lodged in a case file.

(Subd (e) adopted effective January 1, 2020.)

Rule 7.1105 adopted effective January 1, 2020.

TITLE 8
Appellate Rules

Division 1
Rules Relating to the Supreme Court and Courts of Appeal

Chapter 1
General Provisions

Article 1
In General

Rule 8.1.   Title

The rules in this title may be referred to as the Appellate Rules. All references in this title to "these rules" are to the Appellate Rules.
Rule 8.1 adopted effective January 1, 2007.

Rule 8.4.   Application of division

The rules in this division apply to:

(1) Appeals from the superior courts, except appeals to the appellate divisions of the superior courts;

(2) Original proceedings, motions, applications, and petitions in the Courts of Appeal and the Supreme Court; and

(3) Proceedings for transferring cases within the appellate jurisdiction of the superior court to the Court of Appeal for review, unless rules 8.1000–8.1018 provide otherwise.
Rule 8.4 amended and renumbered effective January 1, 2007; repealed and adopted as rule 53 effective January 1, 2005.

Rule 8.7.   Construction

The rules of construction stated in rule 1.5 apply to these rules. In addition, in these rules the headings of divisions, chapters, articles, rules, and subdivisions are substantive.

Rule 8.7 adopted effective January 1, 2007.

Rule 8.10.   Definitions and use of terms

Unless the context or subject matter requires otherwise, the definitions and use of terms in rule 1.6 apply to these rules. In addition, the following apply:

(1) "Appellant" means the appealing party.

(2) "Respondent" means the adverse party.

(3) "Party" includes any attorney of record for that party.

(4) "Judgment" includes any judgment or order that may be appealed.

(5) "Superior court" means the court from which an appeal is taken.

(6) "Reviewing court" means the Supreme Court or the Court of Appeal to which an appeal is taken, in which an original proceeding is begun, or to which an appeal or original proceeding is transferred.

(7) The word "briefs" includes petitions for rehearing, petitions for review, and answers thereto. It does not include petitions for extraordinary relief in original proceedings.

(8) "Attach" or "attachment" may refer to either physical attachment or electronic attachment, as appropriate.

(9) "Copy" or "copies" may refer to electronic copies, as appropriate.

(10) "Cover" includes the cover page of a document filed electronically.

(11) "Written" and "writing" include electronically created written materials, whether or not those materials are printed on paper.
Rule 8.10 amended effective January 1, 2016; repealed and adopted as rule 40 effective January 1, 2005; previously amended and renumbered as rule 8.10 effective January 1, 2007.

Rule 8.11.   Scope of rules

These rules apply to documents filed and served electronically as well as in paper form, unless otherwise provided.
Rule 8.11 adopted effective January 1, 2016.

Rule 8.13.   Amendments to rules

Only the Judicial Council may amend these rules, except the rules in division 5, which may be amended only by the Supreme Court. An amendment by the Judicial Council must be published in the advance pamphlets of the Official Reports and takes effect on the date ordered by the Judicial Council.
Rule 8.13 amended and renumbered effective January 1, 2007; repealed and adopted as rule 54 effective January 1, 2005.

Rule 8.16.   Amendments to statutes

In these rules, a reference to a statute includes any subsequent amendment to the statute.
Rule 8.16 adopted effective January 1, 2007.

Rule 8.18.   Documents violating rules not to be filed

Except as these rules provide otherwise, the reviewing court clerk must not file any record or other document that does not conform to these rules.
Rule 8.18 amended effective January 1, 2009; repealed and adopted as rule 46 effective January 1, 2005; previously amended and renumbered effective January 1, 2007.

Advisory Committee Comment

The exception in this rule acknowledges that there are different rules that apply to certain non-conforming documents. For example, this rule does not apply to nonconforming or late briefs, which are addressed by rules 8.204(e) and 8.220(a), respectively, or to nonconforming supporting documents accompanying a writ petition under chapter 7, which are addressed by rule 8.486(c)(2).

Rule 8.20.   California Rules of Court prevail

A Court of Appeal must accept for filing a record, brief, or other document that complies with the California Rules of Court despite any local rule imposing other requirements.

Rule 8.20 amended and renumbered effective January 1, 2007; repealed and adopted as rule 80 effective January 1, 2005.

Rule 8.23. Sanctions to compel compliance

The failure of a court reporter or clerk to perform any duty imposed by statute or these rules that delays the filing of the appellate record is an unlawful interference with the reviewing court's proceedings. It may be treated as an interference in addition to or instead of any other sanction that may be imposed by law for the same breach of duty. This rule does not limit the reviewing court's power to define and remedy any other interference with its proceedings.

Rule 8.23 renumbered effective January 1, 2007; repealed and adopted as rule 46.5 effective January 1, 2005.

Article 2
Service, Filing, Filing Fees, Form, and Privacy

Title 8, Appellate Rules—Division 1, Rules Relating to the Supreme Court and Courts of Appeal—Chapter 1, General Provisions—Article 2, Service, Filing Fees, Form, and Privacy; amended effective January 1, 2017; previously amended effective October 28, 2011.

Rule 8.25. Service, filing, and filing fees
Rule 8.26. Waiver of fees and costs
Rule 8.29. Service on nonparty public officer or agency
Rule 8.32. Address and other contact information of record; notice of change
Rule 8.36. Substituting parties; substituting or withdrawing attorneys
Rule 8.40. Cover requirements for documents filed in paper form
Rule 8.41. Protection of privacy in documents and records
Rule 8.42. Requirements for signatures of multiple parties on filed documents
Rule 8.44. Number of copies of filed documents

Rule 8.25.   Service, filing, and filing fees

(a) Service

(1) Before filing any document, a party must serve [1] one copy of the document on the attorney for each party separately represented, on each unrepresented party, and on any other person or entity when required by statute or rule.

(2) The party must attach to the document presented for filing a proof of service showing service on each person or entity required to be served under (1), **or, if using an electronic filing service provider's automatic electronic document service, the party may have the electronic filing service provider generate a proof of service**. The proof must name each party represented by each attorney served.

(Subd (a) amended effective January 1, 2021; previously amended effective January 1, 2007.)

Rule 8.25(a). 2020 Deletes. [1] , by any method permitted by the Code of Civil Procedure,

(b) Filing

(1) A document is deemed filed on the date the clerk receives it.

(2) Unless otherwise provided by these rules or other law, a filing is not timely unless the clerk receives the document before the time to file it expires.

(3) A brief, an application to file an amicus curiae brief, an answer to an amicus curiae brief, a petition for rehearing, an answer to a petition for rehearing, a petition for transfer of an appellate division case to the Court of Appeal, an answer to such a petition for transfer, a petition for review, an answer to a petition for review, or a reply to an answer to a petition for review is timely if the time to file it has not expired on the date of:

(A) Its mailing by priority or express mail as shown on the postmark or the postal receipt; or

(B) Its delivery to a common carrier promising overnight delivery as shown on the carrier's receipt.

(4) The provisions of (3) do not apply to original proceedings.

(5) If the clerk receives a document by mail from an inmate or a patient in a custodial institution after the period for filing the document has expired but the envelope shows that the document was mailed or delivered to custodial officials for mailing within the period for filing the document, the document is deemed timely. The clerk must retain in the case file the envelope in which the document was received.

(Subd (b) amended effective July 1, 2012; previously amended effective January 1, 2007, January 1, 2009, July 1, 2010, and January 1, 2011.)

(c) Filing fees

(1) Unless otherwise provided by law, any document for which a filing fee is required under Government Code sections 68926 or 68927 must be accompanied at the time of filing by the required fee or an application for a waiver of court fees under rule 8.26.

(2) Documents for which a filing fee may be required under Government Code sections 68926 or 68927 include:

(A) A notice of appeal in a civil case. For purposes of this rule, "notice of appeal" includes a notice of cross-appeal;

(B) A petition for a writ within the original civil jurisdiction of the Supreme Court or Court of Appeal;

(C) A petition for review in a civil case in the Supreme Court;

(D) The following where the document is the first document filed in the Court of Appeal or Supreme Court by a party other than the appellant or petitioner in a civil case. For purposes of this rule, a "party other than the appellant" does not include a respondent who files a notice of cross-appeal.

(i) An application or an opposition or other response to an application;

(ii) A motion or an opposition or other response to a motion;

(iii) A respondent's brief;

(iv) A preliminary opposition to a petition for a writ, excluding a preliminary opposition requested by the court unless the court has notified the parties that it is considering issuing a peremptory writ in the first instance;

(v) A return (by demurrer, verified answer, or both) after the court issues an alternative writ or order to show cause;

(vi) Any answer to a petition for review in the Supreme Court; and

(vii) Any brief filed in the Supreme Court after the Court grants review.

(3) If a document other than the notice of appeal or a petition for a writ is not accompanied by the filing fee or an application for a waiver of court fees under rule 8.26, the clerk must file the document and must promptly notify the filing party in writing that the court may strike the document unless, within the stated time of not less than 5 court days after the notice is sent, the filing party either:

(A) Pays the filing fee; or

(B) Files an application for a waiver under rule 8.26 if the party has not previously filed such an application.

(4) If the party fails to take the action specified in a notice given under (3), the reviewing court may strike the document, but may vacate the striking of the document for good cause.

(Subd (c) amended effective January 1, 2018; adopted effective October 28, 2011.)

Rule 8.25 amended effective January 1, 2021; adopted as rule 40.1 effective January 1, 2005; previously amended and renumbered effective January 1, 2007; previously amended effective January 1, 2009, July 1, 2010, January 1, 2011, October 28, 2011, July 1, 2012, and January 1, 2018.

Advisory Committee Comment

Subdivision (a). Code of Civil Procedure sections 1010.6–1013a describe generally permissible methods of service. *Information Sheet for Proof of Service (Court of Appeal)* (form APP-009-INFO) provides additional information about how to serve documents and how to provide proof of service. In the Supreme Court and the Courts of Appeal, registration with the court's electronic filing service provider is deemed to show agreement to accept service electronically at the email address provided, unless a party affirmatively opts out of electronic service under rule 8.78(a)(2)(B). This procedure differs from the procedure for electronic service in the superior courts, including their appellate divisions. See rules 2.250–2.261.

Subdivision (b). In general, to be filed on time, a document must be received by the clerk before the time for filing that document expires. There are, however, some limited exceptions to this general rule. For example, (5) provides that if the clerk receives a document by mail from a custodial institution after the deadline for filing the document has expired but the envelope shows that the document was mailed or delivered to custodial officials for mailing before the deadline expired, the document is deemed timely. This provision applies to notices of appeal as well as to other documents mailed from a custodial institution and reflects the "prison-delivery" exception articulated by the California Supreme Court in *In re Jordan* (1992) 4 Cal.4th 116 and *Silverbrand v. County of Los Angeles* (2009) 46 Cal.4th 106.

Note that if a deadline runs from the date of filing, it runs from the date that the document is actually received and deemed filed under (b)(1); neither (b)(3) nor (b)(5) changes that date. Nor do these provisions extend the date of finality of an appellate opinion or any other deadline that is based on finality, such as the deadline for the court to modify its opinion or order rehearing. Subdivision (b)(5) is also not intended to limit a criminal defendant's appeal rights under the case law of constructive filing. (See, e.g., *In re Benoit* (1973) 10 Cal.3d 72.)

Subdivision (b)(3). This rule includes applications to file amicus curiae briefs because, under rules 8.200(c)(4) and 8.520(f)(5), a proposed amicus curiae brief must accompany the application to file the brief.

Subdivision (c). Government Code section 68926 establishes fees in civil cases for filing a notice of appeal, filing a petition for a writ within the original jurisdiction of the Supreme Court or a Court of Appeal, and for a party other than appellant or petitioner filing its first document in such an appeal or writ proceeding in the Supreme Court or a Court of Appeal. Government Code section 68927 establishes fees for filing a petition for review in a civil case in the Supreme Court and for a party other than the petitioner filing its first document in a civil case in the Supreme Court. These statutes provide that fees may not be charged in appeals from, petitions for writs involving, or petitions for review from decisions in juvenile cases or proceedings to declare a minor free from parental custody or control, or proceedings under the Lanterman-Petris-Short Act (Part 1 (commencing with Section 5000) of Division 5 of the Welfare and Institutions Code).

Subdivision (c)(2)(A) and (D). Under rule 8.100(f), "notice of appeal" includes a notice of a cross-appeal and a respondent who files a notice of cross-appeal in a civil appeal is considered an appellant and is required to pay the fee for filing a notice of appeal under Government Code section 68926.

A person who files an application to file an amicus brief is not a "party" and therefore is not subject to the fees applicable to a party other than the appellant or petitioner.

Subdivision (c)(3). Rule 8.100 establishes the procedures applicable when an appellant in a civil appeal fails to pay the fee for filing a notice of appeal or the deposit for the clerk's transcript that must also be paid at that time.

Rule 8.26.   Waiver of fees and costs

(a) Application form

An application for initial waiver of court fees and costs in the Supreme Court or Court of Appeal must be made on *Request to Waive Court Fees* (form FW-001) or, if the application is made for the benefit of a (proposed) ward or conservatee, on *Request to Waive Court Fees (Ward or Conservatee)* (form FW-001-GC). The clerk must provide *Request to Waive Court Fees* (form FW-001) or *Request to Waive Court Fees (Ward or Conservatee)* (form FW-001-GC) and the *Information Sheet on Waiver of Fees and Costs (Supreme Court, Court of Appeal, or Appellate Division)* (form APP-015/FW-015-INFO) without charge to any person who requests any fee waiver application or states that he or she is unable to pay any court fee or cost.

(Subd (a) amended effective September 1, 2015; adopted effective July 1, 2009.)

(b) Filing the application

(1) *Appeals*

(A) The appellant should submit any application for initial waiver of court fees and costs for an appeal with the notice of appeal in the superior court that issued the judgment or order being appealed. For purposes of this rule, a respondent who files a notice of cross-appeal is an "appellant."

(B) A party other than the appellant should submit any application for initial waiver of the court fees and costs for an appeal at the time the fees are to be paid to the court.

(2) *Writ proceedings*

(A) The petitioner should submit the application for waiver of the court fees and costs for a writ proceeding with the writ petition.

(B) A party other than the petitioner should submit any application for initial waiver of the court fees and costs at the time the fees for filing its first document in the writ proceeding are to be paid to the reviewing court.

(3) *Petitions for review*

(A) The petitioner should submit the application for waiver of the court fees and costs for a petition for review in the Supreme Court with the petition.

(B) A party other than the petitioner should submit any application for initial waiver of the court fees and costs at the time the fees for filing its first document in the proceeding are to be paid to the Supreme Court.

(Subd (b) amended effective October 28, 2011; adopted effective July 1, 2009.)

(c) Procedure for determining application

The application must be considered and determined as required by Government Code section 68634.5. An order from the Supreme Court or Court of Appeal determining the application for initial fee waiver or setting a hearing on the application in the Supreme Court or Court of Appeal may be made on *Order on Court Fee Waiver (Court of Appeal or Supreme Court)* (form APP-016/FW-016) or, if the application is made for the benefit of a (proposed) ward or conservatee, on *Order on Court Fee Waiver (Court of Appeal or Supreme Court) (Ward or Conservatee)* (form APP-016-GC/FW-016-GC).

(Subd (c) amended effective September 1, 2015; adopted effective July 1, 2009.)

(d) Application granted unless acted on by the court

The application for initial fee waiver is deemed granted unless the court gives notice of action on the application within five court days after the application is filed.

(Subd (d) adopted effective July 1, 2009.)

(e) Court fees and costs waived

Court fees and costs that must be waived on granting an application for initial waiver of court fees and costs in the Supreme Court or Court of Appeal include:

(1) The fee for filing the notice of appeal and the fee required for a party other than the appellant filing its first document under Government Code section 68926;

(2) The fee for filing an original proceeding and the fee required for a party other than the petitioner filing its first document under Government Code section 68926;

(3) The fee for filing a petition for review and the fee required for a party other than the petitioner filing its first document under Government Code section 68927; and

(4) Any court fee for telephonic oral argument.

(Subd (e) amended effective October 28, 2011; adopted effective July 1, 2009.)

(f) Denial of the application

If an application is denied, the applicant must pay the court fees and costs or submit the new application or additional information requested by the court within 10 days after the clerk gives notice of the denial.

(Subd (f) adopted effective July 1, 2009.)

(g) Confidential records

(1) No person may have access to an application for an initial fee waiver submitted to the court except the court and authorized court personnel, any persons authorized by the applicant, and any persons authorized by order of the court. No person may reveal any information contained in the application except as authorized by law or order of the court. An order granting access to an application or financial information may include limitations on who may access the information and on the use of the information after it has been released.

(2) Any person seeking access to an application or financial information provided to the court by an applicant must make the request by motion, supported by a declaration showing good cause as to why the confidential information should be released.

(Subd (g) adopted effective July 1, 2009.)

Rule 8.26 amended effective September 1, 2015; adopted effective July 1, 2009; previously amended effective October 28, 2011.

Advisory Committee Comment

Subdivision (a). The waiver of court fees and costs is called an "initial" waiver because, under Government Code section 68630 and following, any such waiver may later be modified, terminated, or retroactively withdrawn if the court determines that the applicant was not or is no longer eligible for a waiver. The court may, at a later time, order that the previously waived fees be paid.

Subdivision (b)(1). If an applicant is requesting waiver of both Court of Appeal fees, such as the fee for filing the notice of appeal, and superior court fees, such as the fee for preparing, certifying, copying, and transmitting the clerk's transcript, the clerk of the superior court may ask the applicant to provide two signed copies of *Request to Waive Court Fees* (form FW-001).

Subdivision (e). The parties in an appeal may also ask the superior court to waive the deposit required under Government Code section 68926.1 and the fees under rule 8.122 for preparing, certifying, copying, and transmitting the clerk's transcript to the reviewing court and to the requesting party.

Rule 8.29.   Service on nonparty public officer or agency

(a) Proof of service

When a statute or this rule requires a party to serve any document on a nonparty public officer or agency, the party must file proof of such service with the document unless a statute permits service after the document is filed, in which case the proof of service must be filed immediately after the document is served on the public officer or agency.

(Subd (a) relettered effective January 1, 2007; adopted as subd (b) effective January 1, 2004.)

(b) Identification on cover

When a statute or this rule requires a party to serve any document on a nonparty public officer or agency, the cover of the document must contain a statement that identifies the statute or rule requiring service of the document on the public officer or agency in substantially the following form: "Service on [insert name of the officer or agency] required by [insert citation to the statute or rule]."

(Subd (b) relettered effective January 1, 2007; adopted as subd (c) effective January 1, 2004.)

(c) Service on the Attorney General

In addition to any statutory requirements for service of briefs on public officers or agencies, a party must serve its brief or petition on the Attorney General if the brief or petition:

(1) Questions the constitutionality of a state statute; or

(2) Is filed on behalf of the State of California, a county, or an officer whom the Attorney General may lawfully represent in:

(A) A criminal case;

(B) A case in which the state or a state officer in his or her official capacity is a party; or

(C) A case in which a county is a party, unless the county's interest conflicts with that of the state or a state officer in his or her official capacity.

(Subd (c) adopted effective January 1, 2007.)

Rule 8.29 amended and renumbered effective January 1, 2007; adopted as rule 44.5 effective January 1, 2004; previously amended effective July 1, 2004.

Advisory Committee Comment

Rule 8.29 refers to statutes that require a party to serve documents on a nonparty public officer or agency. For a list of examples of such statutory requirements, please see the *Civil Case Information Statement* (form APP-004).

Rule 8.32. Address and other contact information of record; notice of change

(a) Address and other contact information of record

In any case pending before the court, the court will use the mailing address, telephone number, fax number, and e-mail address that an attorney or unrepresented party provides on the first document filed in that case as the mailing address, telephone number, fax number, and e-mail address of record unless the attorney or unrepresented party files a notice under (b).

(Subd (a) amended effective January 1, 2013; adopted effective January 1, 2007.)

(b) Notice of change

(1) An attorney or unrepresented party whose mailing address, telephone number, fax number, or e-mail address changes while a case is pending must promptly serve and file a written notice of the change in the reviewing court in which the case is pending.

(2) The notice must specify the title and number of the case or cases to which it applies. If an attorney gives the notice, the notice must include the attorney's California State Bar number.

(Subd (b) amended effective January 1, 2013; adopted as subd (a) effective January 1, 2005; previously amended and relettered effective January 1, 2007; previously amended effective July 1, 2008.)

(c) Multiple addresses or other contact information

If an attorney or an unrepresented party has more than one mailing address, telephone number, fax number, or e-mail address, only one mailing address, telephone number, fax number, or e-mail address for that attorney or unrepresented party may be used in a given case.

(Subd (c) repealed, amended and relettered effective January 1, 2013; adopted as subd (c) effective January 1, 2005; previously amended and relettered as subd (d) effective January 1, 2007; previously amended effective January 1, 2008, and July 1, 2008.)

Rule 8.32 amended effective January 1, 2013; repealed and adopted as rule 40.5 effective January 1, 2005; previously amended and renumbered effective January 1, 2007; previously amended effective January 1, 2008, and July 1, 2008.

Rule 8.36. Substituting parties; substituting or withdrawing attorneys

(a) Substituting parties

Substitution of parties in an appeal or original proceeding must be made by serving and filing a motion in the reviewing court. The clerk of that court must notify the superior court of any ruling on the motion.

(b) Substituting attorneys

A party may substitute attorneys by serving and filing in the reviewing court a substitution signed by the party represented and the new attorney. In all appeals and in original proceedings related to a superior court proceeding, the party must also serve the superior court.

(c) Withdrawing attorney

(1) An attorney may request withdrawal by filing a motion to withdraw. Unless the court orders otherwise, the motion need be served only on the party represented and the attorneys directly affected.

(2) The proof of service need not include the address of the party represented. But if the court grants the motion, the withdrawing attorney must promptly provide the court and the opposing party with the party's current or last known address and telephone number.

(3) In all appeals and in original proceedings related to a superior court proceeding, the reviewing court clerk must notify the superior court of any ruling on the motion.

(4) If the motion is filed in any proceeding pending in the Supreme Court after grant of review, the clerk/executive officer of the Supreme Court must also notify the Court of Appeal of any ruling on the motion.

(Subd (c) amended effective January 1, 2018.)

Rule 8.36 amended effective January 1, 2018; repealed and adopted as rule 48 effective January 1, 2005; previously renumbered effective January 1, 2007.

Rule 8.40. Cover requirements for documents filed in paper form

(a) Cover color

(1) As far as practicable, the covers of briefs and petitions filed in paper form must be in the following colors:

Appellant's opening brief or appendix	green
Respondent's brief or appendix	yellow
Appellant's reply brief or appendix	tan
Joint appendix	white
Amicus curiae brief	gray
Answer to amicus curiae brief	blue
Petition for rehearing	orange
Answer to petition for rehearing	blue
Petition for original writ	red
Answer (or opposition) to petition for original writ	red
Reply to answer (or opposition) to petition for original writ	red
Petition for transfer of appellate division case to Court of Appeal	white
Answer to petition for transfer of appellate division case to Court of Appeal	blue
Petition for review	white
Answer to petition for review	blue
Reply to answer to petition for review	white
Opening brief on the merits	white
Answer brief on the merits	blue
Reply brief on the merits	white

(2) In appeals under rule 8.216, the cover of a combined respondent's brief and appellant's opening brief filed in paper form must be yellow, and the cover of a combined reply brief and respondent's brief filed in paper form must be tan.

(3) A **paper** brief or petition not conforming to (1) or (2) must be accepted for filing, but in case of repeated violations by an attorney or party, the court may proceed as provided in rule 8.204(e)(2).

(Subd (a) repealed, amended and relettered effective January 1, 2020; adopted as subd (c) effective January 1, 2005; previously amended and relettered effective January 1, 2007; previously amended effective January 1, 2011, and January 1, 2016.)

(b) Cover information

(1) Except as provided in (2), the cover—or first page if there is no cover—of every document filed in a reviewing court must include the name, mailing address, telephone number, fax number (if available), e-mail address (if available), and California State Bar number of each attorney filing or joining in the document, or of the party if he or she is unrepresented. The inclusion of a fax number or e-mail address on any document does not constitute consent to service by fax or e-mail unless otherwise provided by law.

(2) If more than one attorney from a law firm, corporation, or public law office is representing one party and is joining in the document, the name and State Bar number of each attorney joining in the document must be provided on the cover. The law firm, corporation, or public law office representing each party must designate one attorney to receive notices and other communication in the case from the court by placing an asterisk before that attorney's name on the cover and must provide the contact information specified under (1) for that attorney. Contact information for the other attorneys from the same law firm, corporation, or public law office is not required but may be provided.

(Subd (b) relettered effective January 1, 2020; adopted as subd (d) effective January 1, 2005; previously amended and relettered effective January 1, 2007; previously amended effective January 1, 2013.)

Rule 8.40 amended effective January 1, 2020; repealed and adopted as rule 44 effective January 1, 2005; previously amended and renumbered as rule 8.40 effective January 1, 2007; previously amended effective January 1, 2006, January 1, 2011, January 1, 2013, and January 1, 2016.

Rule 8.41. Protection of privacy in documents and records

The provisions on protection of privacy in rule 1.201 apply to documents and records under these rules.

Rule 8.41 adopted effective January 1, 2017.

Rule 8.42. Requirements for signatures of multiple parties on filed documents

When a document to be filed in paper form, such as a stipulation, requires the signatures of multiple parties, the original signature of at least one party must appear on the document filed in the reviewing court; the other signatures may be in the form of copies of the signed signature page of the document. Electronically filed documents must comply with the relevant provisions of rule 8.77.

Rule 8.42 amended effective January 1, 2016; adopted effective January 1, 2014.

Rule 8.44.   Number of copies of filed documents

(a) Documents filed in the Supreme Court

Except as these rules provide otherwise, the number of copies of every brief, petition, motion, application, or other document that must be filed in the Supreme Court and that is filed in paper form is as follows:

(1) An original of a petition for review, an answer, a reply, a brief on the merits, an amicus curiae brief, an answer to an amicus curiae brief, a petition for rehearing, or an answer to a petition for rehearing and either

(A) 13 paper copies; or

(B) 8 paper copies and one electronic copy;

(2) Unless the court orders otherwise, an original of a petition for a writ within the court's original jurisdiction, an opposition or other response to the petition, or a reply; and either:

(A) 10 paper copies; or

(B) 8 paper copies and one electronic copy;

(3) Unless the court orders otherwise, an original and 2 copies of any supporting document accompanying a petition for writ of habeas corpus, an opposition or other response to the petition, or a reply;

(4) An original and 8 copies of a petition for review to exhaust state remedies under rule 8.508, an answer, or a reply, or an amicus curiae letter under rule 8.500(g);

(5) An original and 8 copies of a motion or an opposition or other response to a motion; and

(6) An original and 1 copy of an application, including an application to extend time, or any other document.

(Subd (a) amended effective January 1, 2016; previously amended effective January 1, 2014.)

(b) Documents filed in a Court of Appeal

Except as these rules provide otherwise, the number of copies of every brief, petition, motion, application, or other document that must be filed in a Court of Appeal and that is filed in paper form is as follows:

(1) An original and 4 paper copies of a brief, an amicus curiae brief, or an answer to an amicus curiae brief. In civil appeals, for briefs other than petitions for rehearing or answers thereto, 1 electronic copy or, in case of undue hardship, proof of delivery of 4 paper copies to the Supreme Court, as provided in rule 8.212(c) is also required;

(2) An original of a petition for writ of habeas corpus filed under rule 8.380 by a person who is not represented by an attorney and 1 set of any supporting documents;

(3) An original and 4 copies of any other petition, an answer, an opposition or other response to a petition, or a reply;

(4) Unless the court orders otherwise, an original and 1 copy of a motion or an opposition or other response to a motion;

(5) Unless the court provides otherwise by local rule or order, 1 set of any separately bound supporting documents accompanying a document filed under (3) or (4);

(6) An original and 1 copy of an application, other than an application to extend time, or any other document; and

(7) An original and 1 copy of an application to extend time. In addition, 1 copy for each separately represented and unrepresented party must be provided to the court.

(Subd (b) amended effective January 1, 2016; previously amended effective January 1, 2011, January 1, 2013, and January 1, 2014.)

(c) Electronic copies of paper documents

[1] **Even when filing a paper document is permissible**, a court may provide by local rule for the submission of an electronic copy of [2] **the paper document** either in addition to the copies of a document required to be filed under (a) or (b) or as a substitute for one or more of these copies. The local rule must [3] provide for an exception if it would cause undue hardship for a party to submit an electronic copy.

(Subd (c) amended effective January 1, 2020; adopted effective January 1, 2014; previously amended effective January 1, 2016.)

Rule 8.44(c). 2019 Deletes. [1] A court that permits electronic filing will specify any requirements regarding electronically filed documents in the electronic filing requirements published under rule 8.74. In addition **[2]** a document that is not electronically filed **[3]** specify the format of the electronic copy and

Rule 8.44 amended effective January 1, 2020; adopted effective January 1, 2007; previously amended effective January 1, 2007, January 1, 2011, January 1, 2013, January 1, 2014, and January 1, 2016.

Advisory Committee Comment

The initial sentence of this rule acknowledges that there are exceptions to this rule's requirements concerning the number of copies. See, for example, rule 8.150, which specifies the number of copies of the record that must be filed.

Information about electronic submission of copies of documents can be found on the web page for the Supreme Court at: *www.courts.ca.gov/appellatebriefs* or for the Court of Appeal District in which the brief is being filed at: *www.courts.ca.gov/courtsofappeal*.

Note that submitting an electronic copy of a document under this rule or under a local rule adopted pursuant to subdivision (c) does not constitute filing a document electronically under rules 8.70–8.79 and thus does not substitute for the filing of the original document with the court in paper format.

Article 3
Sealed and Confidential Records

Division 1, Rules Relating to the Supreme Court and Courts of Appeal—Chapter 1, General Provisions—Article 3, Sealed and Confidential Records; adopted effective January 1, 2014.

Rule 8.45.   General provisions

(a) Application

The rules in this article establish general requirements regarding sealed and confidential records in appeals and original proceedings in the Supreme Court and Courts of Appeal. Where other laws establish specific requirements for particular types of sealed or confidential records that differ from the requirements in this article, those specific requirements supersede the requirements in this article.

(Subd (a) adopted effective January 1, 2014.)

(b) Definitions

As used in this article:

(1) "Record" means all or part of a document, paper, exhibit, transcript, or other thing filed or lodged with the court by electronic means or otherwise.

(2) A "lodged" record is a record temporarily deposited with the court but not filed.

(3) A "sealed" record is a record that is closed to inspection by the public or a party by order of a court under rules 2.550–2.551 or rule 8.46.

(4) A "conditionally sealed" record is a record that is filed or lodged subject to a pending application or motion to file it under seal.

(5) A "confidential" record is a record that, in court proceedings, is required by statute, rule of court, or other authority except a court order under rules 2.550–2.551 or rule 8.46 to be closed to inspection by the public or a party.

(6) A "redacted version" is a version of a filing from which all portions that disclose material contained in a sealed, conditionally sealed, or confidential record have been removed.

(7) An "unredacted version" is a version of a filing or a portion of a filing that discloses material contained in a sealed, conditionally sealed, or confidential record.

(Subd (b) amended effective January 1, 2016; adopted effective January 1, 2014.)

(c) Format of sealed and confidential records

(1) Unless otherwise provided by law or court order, sealed or confidential records that are part of the record on appeal or the supporting documents or other records accompanying a motion, petition for a writ of habeas corpus, other writ petition, or other filing in the reviewing court must be kept separate from the rest of a clerk's or reporter's transcript, appendix, supporting documents, or other records sent to the reviewing court and in a secure manner that preserves their confidentiality.

(A) If the records are in paper format, they must be placed in a sealed envelope or other appropriate sealed container. This requirement does not apply to a juvenile case file but does apply to any record contained within a juvenile case file that is sealed or confidential under authority other than Welfare and Institutions Code section 827 et seq.

(B) Sealed records, and if applicable the envelope or other container, must be marked as "Sealed by Order of the Court on *(Date)*."

(C) Confidential records, and if applicable the envelope or other container, must be marked as "Confidential *(Basis)*—May Not Be Examined Without Court Order." The basis must be a citation to or other brief description of the statute, rule of court, case, or other authority that establishes that the record must be closed to inspection in the court proceeding.

(D) The superior court clerk or party transmitting sealed or confidential records to the reviewing court must prepare a sealed or confidential index of these materials. If the records include a transcript of any in-camera proceeding, the index must list the date and the names of all parties present at the hearing and their counsel. This index must be transmitted and kept with the sealed or confidential records.

(2) Except as provided in (3) or by court order, the alphabetical and chronological indexes to a clerk's or reporter's transcript, appendix, supporting documents, or other records sent to the reviewing court that are available to the public must list each sealed or confidential record by title, not disclosing the substance of the record, and must identify it as "Sealed" or "Confidential"—May Not Be Examined Without Court Order."

(3) Records relating to a request for funds under Penal Code section 987.9 or other proceedings the occurrence of which is not to be disclosed under the court order or applicable law must not be bound together with, or electronically transmitted as a single document with, other sealed or confidential records and must not be listed in the index required under (1)(D) or the alphabetical or chronological indexes to a clerk's or reporter's transcript, appendix, supporting documents to a petition, or other records sent to the reviewing court.

(Subd (c) amended effective January 1, 2016; adopted effective January 1, 2014.)

(d) Transmission of and access to sealed and confidential records

(1) A sealed or confidential record must be transmitted in a secure manner that preserves the confidentiality of the record.

(2) Unless otherwise provided by (3)–(5) or other law or court order, a sealed or confidential record that is part of the record on appeal or the supporting documents or other records accompanying a motion, petition for a writ of habeas corpus, other writ petition, or other filing in the reviewing court must be transmitted only to the reviewing court and the party or parties who had access to the record in the trial court or other proceedings under review and may be examined only by the reviewing court and that party or parties. If a party's attorney but not the party had access to the record in the trial court or other proceedings under review, only the party's attorney may examine the record.

(3) Except as provided in (4), if the record is a reporter's transcript or any document related to any in-camera hearing from which a party was excluded in the trial court, the record must be transmitted to and examined by only the reviewing court and the party or parties who participated in the in-camera hearing.

(4) A reporter's transcript or any document related to an in-camera hearing concerning a confidential informant under Evidence Code sections 1041–1042 must be transmitted only to the reviewing court.

(5) A probation report must be transmitted only to the reviewing court and to appellate counsel for the People and the defendant who was the subject of the report.

(Subd (d) amended effective January 1, 2019; adopted effective January 1, 2014.)

Rule 8.45 amended effective January 1, 2019; adopted effective January 1, 2014; previously amended effective January 1, 2016.

Advisory Committee Comment

Subdivision (a). Many laws address sealed and confidential records. These laws differ from each other in a variety of respects, including what information is closed to inspection, from whom it is closed, under what circumstances it is closed, and what procedures apply to closing or opening it to inspection. It is very important to determine if any such law applies with respect to a particular record because where other laws establish specific requirements that differ from the requirements in this article, those specific requirements supersede the requirements in this article.

Subdivision (b)(5). Examples of confidential records are records in juvenile proceedings (Welf. & Inst. Code, § 827 and California Rules of Court, rule 8.401), records of the family conciliation court (Fam. Code, § 1818(b)), fee waiver applications (Gov. Code, § 68633(f)), and court-ordered diagnostic reports (Penal Code, § 1203.03). This term also encompasses records closed to inspection by a court order other than an order under rules 2.550–2.551 or 8.46, such as situations in which case law, statute, or rule has established a category of records that must be closed to inspection and a court has found that a particular record falls within that category and has ordered that it be closed to inspection. Examples include discovery material subject to a protective order under Code of Civil Procedure sections 2030.090, 2032.060, or 2033.080 and records closed to inspection by court order under *People v. Marsden* (1970) 2 Cal.3d 118 or *Pitchess v. Superior Court* (1974) 11 Cal.3d 531. For more examples of confidential records, please see appendix 1 of the *Trial Court Records Manual* at *www.courts.ca.gov/documents/trial-court-records-manual.pdf.*

Subdivisions (c) and (d). The requirements in this rule for format and transmission of and access to sealed and confidential records apply only unless otherwise provided by law. Special requirements that govern transmission of and/or access to particular types of records may supersede the requirements in this rule. For example, rules 8.619(g) and 8.622(e) require copies of reporters' transcripts in capital cases to be sent to the Habeas Corpus Resource Center and the California Appellate Project in San Francisco, and under rules 8.336(g)(2) and 8.409(e)(2), in non-capital felony appeals, if the defendant—or in juvenile appeals, if the appellant or the respondent—is not represented by appellate counsel when the clerk's and reporter's transcripts are certified as correct, the clerk must send that counsel's copy of the transcripts to the district appellate project.

Subdivision (c)(1)(C). For example, for juvenile records, this mark could state "Confidential—Welf. & Inst. Code, § 827" or "Confidential—Juvenile Case File"; for a fee waiver application, this mark could state "Confidential—Gov. Code, § 68633(f)" or "Confidential—Fee Waiver Application"; and for a transcript of an in-camera hearing under *People v. Marsden* (1970) 2 Cal.3d 118, this mark could say "Confidential—*Marsden* Hearing."

Subdivision (c)(2). Subdivision (c)(2) requires that, with certain exceptions, the alphabetical and chronological indexes to the clerk's and reporter's transcripts, appendixes, and supporting documents must list any sealed and confidential records but identify them as sealed or confidential. The purpose of this provision is to assist the parties in making—and the court in adjudicating—motions to unseal sealed records or to provide confidential records to a party. To protect sealed and confidential records from disclosure until the court issues an order, however, each index must identify sealed and confidential records without disclosing their substance.

Subdivision (c)(3). Under certain circumstances, the Attorney General has a statutory right to request copies of documents filed under Penal Code section 987.9(d). To facilitate compliance with such requests, this subdivision requires that such documents not be bound with other confidential documents.

Subdivision (d). See rule 8.47(b) for special requirements concerning access to certain confidential records.

Subdivision (d)(2) and (3). Because the term "party" includes any attorney of record for that party, under rule 8.10(3), when a party who had access to a record in the trial court or other proceedings under review or who participated in an in-camera hearing—such as a *Marsden* hearing in a criminal or juvenile proceeding—is represented by appellate counsel, the confidential record or transcript must be transmitted to that party's appellate counsel. Under rules 8.336(g)(2) and 8.409(e)(2), in non-capital felony appeals, if the defendant—or in juvenile appeals, if the appellant or the respondent—is not represented by appellate counsel when the clerk's and reporter's transcripts are certified as correct, the clerk must send the copy of the transcripts that would go to appellate counsel, including confidential records such as transcripts of *Marsden* hearings, to the district appellate project.

Subdivision (d)(5). This rule limits to whom a copy of a probation report is transmitted based on the provisions of Penal Code section 1203.05, which limit who may inspect or copy probation reports.

Rule 8.46.   Sealed records

(a) Application

This rule applies to sealed records and records proposed to be sealed on appeal and in original proceedings, but does not apply to confidential records.

(Subd (a) amended effective January 1, 2014; previously amended effective January 1, 2006, and January 1, 2007.)

(b) Record sealed by the trial court

If a record sealed by order of the trial court is part of the record on appeal or the supporting documents or other records accompanying a motion, petition for a writ of habeas corpus, other writ petition, or other filing in the reviewing court:

(1) The sealed record must remain sealed unless the reviewing court orders otherwise under (e). Rule 8.45 governs the form and transmission of and access to sealed records.

(2) The record on appeal or supporting documents filed in the reviewing court must also include:

(A) The motion or application to seal filed in the trial court;

(B) All documents filed in the trial court supporting or opposing the motion or application; and

(C) The trial court order sealing the record.

(Subd (b) repealed, amended and relettered effective January 1, 2014; adopted as subd (c); previously amended effective January 1, 2004, and January 1, 2007.)

(c) Record not sealed by the trial court

A record filed or lodged publicly in the trial court and not ordered sealed by that court must not be filed under seal in the reviewing court.

(Subd (c) relettered effective January 1, 2014; adopted as subd (d).)

(d) Record not filed in the trial court; motion or application to file under seal

(1) A record not filed in the trial court may be filed under seal in the reviewing court only by order of the reviewing court; it must not be filed under seal solely by stipulation or agreement of the parties.

(2) To obtain an order under (1), a party must serve and file a motion or application in the reviewing court, accompanied by a declaration containing facts sufficient to justify the sealing. At the same time, the party must lodge the record under (3), unless good cause is shown not to lodge it.

(3) To lodge a record, the party must transmit the record to the court in a secure manner that preserves the confidentiality of the record to be lodged. The record must be transmitted [1] **separately** from the rest of a clerk's or reporter's transcript, appendix, supporting documents, or other records sent to the reviewing court with a cover sheet that complies with rule [2] **8.40(b) if the record is in paper form or rule 8.74(a)(9) if the record is in electronic form,** and **that** labels the contents as "CONDITIONALLY UNDER SEAL." If the record is in paper [3] **form**, it must be placed in a sealed envelope or other appropriate sealed container.

(4) If necessary to prevent disclosure of material contained in a conditionally sealed record, any motion or application, any opposition, and any supporting documents must be filed in a redacted version and lodged in a complete unredacted version conditionally under seal. The cover of the redacted version must identify it as "Public—Redacts material from conditionally sealed record." In juvenile cases, the cover of the redacted version must identify it as "Redacted version—Redacts material from conditionally sealed record." The cover of the unredacted version must identify it as "May Not Be Examined Without Court Order—Contains material from conditionally sealed record." Unless the court orders otherwise, any party that had access to the record in the trial court or other proceedings under review must be served with a complete, unredacted version of all papers as well as a redacted version.

(5) On receiving a lodged record, the clerk must note the date of receipt on the cover sheet and retain but not file the record. The record must remain conditionally under seal pending determination of the motion or application.

(6) The court may order a record filed under seal only if it makes the findings required by rule 2.550(d)–(e).

(7) If the court denies the motion or application to seal the record, the lodging party may notify the court that the lodged record is to be filed unsealed. This notification must be received within 10 days of the order denying the motion or application to seal, unless otherwise ordered by the court. On receipt of this notification, the clerk must unseal and file the record. If the lodging party does not notify the court within 10 days of the order, the clerk must (1) return the lodged record to the lodging party if it is in paper form, or (2) permanently delete the lodged record if it is in electronic form.

(8) An order sealing the record must direct the sealing of only those documents and pages or, if reasonably practical, portions of those documents and pages, that contain the material that needs to be placed under seal. All other portions of each document or page must be included in the public file.

(9) Unless the sealing order provides otherwise, it prohibits the parties from disclosing the contents of any materials that have been sealed in anything that is subsequently publicly filed.

(Subd (d) amended effective January 1, 2020; adopted as subd (e); previously amended effective July 1, 2002, January 1, 2004, January 1, 2007, January 1, 2016, and January 1, 2019; previously amended and relettered as subd (d) effective January 1, 2014.)

Rule 8.46(d).   2019 Deletes. [1] separate **[2]** 8.40(c) **[3]** format

(e) Challenge to an order denying a motion or application to seal a record

Notwithstanding the provisions in (d)(1)–(2), when an appeal or original proceeding challenges an order denying a motion or application to seal a record, the appellant or petitioner must lodge the subject record labeled as conditionally under seal in the reviewing court as provided in (d)(3)–(5), and the reviewing court must maintain the record conditionally under seal during the pendency of the appeal or original proceeding. Once the reviewing court's decision on the appeal or original proceeding becomes final, the clerk must (1) return the lodged record to the lodging party if it is in paper form, or (2) permanently delete the lodged record if it is in electronic form.

(Subd (e) adopted effective January 1, 2019.)

(f) Unsealing a record in the reviewing court

(1) A sealed record must not be unsealed except on order of the reviewing court.

(2) Any person or entity may serve and file a motion, application, or petition in the reviewing court to unseal a record.

(3) If the reviewing court proposes to order a record unsealed on its own motion, the court must send notice to the parties stating the reason for unsealing the record. Unless otherwise ordered by the court, any party may serve and file an opposition within 10 days after the notice is sent, and any other party may serve and file a response within 5 days after an opposition is filed.

(4) If necessary to prevent disclosure of material contained in a sealed record, the motion, application, or petition under (2) and any opposition, response, and supporting documents under (2) or (3) must be filed in both a redacted version and a complete unredacted version. The cover of the redacted version must identify it as "Public—Redacts material from sealed record." In juvenile cases, the cover of the redacted version must identify it as "Redacted version—Redacts material from sealed record." The cover of the unredacted version must identify it as "May Not Be Examined Without Court Order—Contains material from sealed record." Unless the court orders otherwise, any party that had access to the sealed record in the trial court or other proceedings under review must be served with a complete, unredacted version of all papers as well as a redacted version. If a party's attorney but not the party had access to the record in the trial court or other proceedings under review, only the party's attorney may be served with the complete, unredacted version.

(5) In determining whether to unseal a record, the court must consider the matters addressed in rule 2.550(c)–(e).

(6) The order unsealing a record must state whether the record is unsealed entirely or in part. If the order unseals only part of the record or unseals the record only as to certain persons, the order must specify the particular records that are unsealed, the particular persons who may have access to the record, or both.

(7) If, in addition to the record that is the subject of the sealing order, a court has previously ordered the sealing order itself, the register of actions, or any other court records relating to the case to be sealed, the unsealing order must state whether these additional records are unsealed.

(Subd (f) amended and relettered effective January 1, 2019; adopted as subd (f); previously amended effective January 1, 2004, January 1, 2007, and January 1, 2016; previously amended and relettered as subd (e) effective January 1, 2014.)

(g) Disclosure of nonpublic material in public filings prohibited

(1) Nothing filed publicly in the reviewing court—including any application, brief, petition, or memorandum—may disclose material contained in a record that is sealed, lodged conditionally under seal, or otherwise subject to a pending motion to file under seal.

(2) If it is necessary to disclose material contained in a sealed record in a filing in the reviewing court, two versions must be filed:

(A) A public redacted version. The cover of this version must identify it as "Public—Redacts material from sealed record." In juvenile cases, the cover of the redacted version must identify it as "Redacted Version—Redacts material from sealed record."

(B) An unredacted version. If this version is in paper format, it must be placed in a sealed envelope or other appropriate sealed container. The cover of this version, and if applicable the envelope or other container, must identify it as "May Not Be Examined Without Court Order—Contains material from sealed record." Sealed material disclosed in this version must be identified as such in the filing and accompanied by a citation to the court order sealing that material.

(C) Unless the court orders otherwise, any party who had access to the sealed record in the trial court or other proceedings under review must be served with both the unredacted version of all papers as well as the redacted version. Other parties must be served with only the public redacted version. If a party's attorney but not the party had access to the record in the trial court or other proceedings under review, only the party's attorney may be served with the unredacted version.

(3) If it is necessary to disclose material contained in a conditionally sealed record in a filing in the reviewing court:

(A) A public redacted version must be filed. The cover of this version must identify it as "Public—Redacts material from conditionally sealed record." In juvenile cases, the cover of the redacted version must identify it as "Redacted version—Redacts material from conditionally sealed record."

(B) An unredacted version must be lodged. The filing must be transmitted in a secure manner that preserves the confidentiality of the filing being lodged. If this version is in paper format, it must be placed in a sealed envelope or other appropriate sealed container. The cover of this version, and if applicable the envelope or other container, must identify it as "May Not Be Examined Without Court Order—Contains material from conditionally sealed record." Conditionally sealed material disclosed in this version must be identified as such in the filing.

(C) Unless the court orders otherwise, any party who had access to the conditionally sealed record in the trial court or other proceedings under review must be served with both the unredacted version of all papers as well as the redacted version. Other parties must be served with only the public redacted version.

(D) If the court denies the motion or application to seal the record, the party who filed the motion or application may notify the court that the unredacted version lodged under (B) is to be filed unsealed. This notification must be received within 10 days of the order denying the motion or application to seal, unless otherwise ordered by the court. On receipt of this notification, the clerk must unseal and file the lodged unredacted version. If the party who filed the motion or application does not notify the court within 10 days of the order, the clerk must (1) return the lodged unredacted version to the lodging party if it is in paper form, or (2) permanently delete the lodged unredacted version if it is in electronic form.

(Subd (g) amended and relettered effective January 1, 2019; adopted as subd (g); previously amended effective January 1, 2007; previously amended and relettered as subd (f) effective January 1, 2014.)

Rule 8.46 amended effective January 1, 2020; repealed and adopted as rule 12.5 effective January 1, 2002; previously amended and renumbered as rule 8.160 effective January 1, 2007; previously renumbered as rule 8.46 effective January 1, 2010; previously amended effective July 1, 2002, January 1, 2004, January 1, 2006, January 1, 2014, January 1, 2016, and January 1, 2019.

Advisory Committee Comment

This rule and rules 2.550–2.551 for the trial courts provide a standard and procedures for courts to use when a request is made to seal a record. The standard is based on *NBC Subsidiary (KNBC-TV), Inc. v. Superior Court* (1999) 20 Cal.4th 1178. The sealed records rules apply to civil and criminal cases. They recognize the First Amendment right of access to documents used at trial or as a basis of adjudication. Except as otherwise expressly provided in this rule, motions in a reviewing court relating to the sealing or unsealing of a record must follow rule 8.54.

Subdivision (e). This subdivision is not intended to expand the availability of existing appellate review for any person aggrieved by a court's denial of a motion or application to seal a record.

Rule 8.47.   Confidential records

(a) Application

This rule applies to confidential records but does not apply to records sealed by court order under rules 2.550–2.551 or rule 8.46 or to conditionally sealed records under rule 8.46. Unless otherwise provided by this rule or other law, rule 8.45 governs the form and transmission of and access to confidential records.

(Subd (a) adopted effective January 1, 2014.)

(b) Records of *Marsden* hearings and other in-camera proceedings

(1) This subdivision applies to reporter's transcripts of and documents filed or lodged by a defendant in connection with:

(A) An in-camera hearing conducted by the superior court under *People v. Marsden* (1970) 2 Cal.3d 118; or

(B) Another in-camera hearing at which the defendant was present but from which the People were excluded in order to prevent disclosure of information about defense strategy or other information to which the prosecution was not allowed access at the time of the hearing.

(2) Except as provided in (3), if the defendant raises a *Marsden* issue or an issue related to another in-camera hearing covered by this rule in a brief, petition, or other filing in the reviewing court, the following procedures apply:

(A) The brief, including any portion that discloses matters contained in the transcript of the in-camera hearing, and other documents filed or lodged in connection with the hearing, must be filed publicly. The requirement to publicly file this brief does not apply in juvenile cases; rule 8.401 governs the format of and access to such briefs in juvenile cases.

(B) The People may serve and file an application requesting a copy of the reporter's transcript of, and documents filed or lodged by a defendant in connection with, the in-camera hearing.

(C) Within 10 days after the application is filed, the defendant may serve and file opposition to this application on the basis that the transcript or documents contain confidential material not relevant to the issues raised by the defendant in the reviewing court. Any such opposition must identify the page and line numbers of the transcript or documents containing this irrelevant material.

(D) If the defendant does not timely serve and file opposition to the application, the reviewing court clerk must send to the People a copy of the reporter's transcript of, and documents filed or lodged by a defendant in connection with, the in-camera hearing.

(3) A defendant may serve and file a motion or application in the reviewing court requesting permission to file under seal a brief, petition, or other filing that raises a *Marsden* issue or an issue related to another in-camera hearing covered by this subdivision, and requesting an order maintaining the confidentiality of the relevant material from the reporter's transcript of, or documents filed or lodged in connection with, the in-camera hearing.

(A) Except as otherwise provided in this rule, rule 8.46(d) governs a motion or application under this subdivision.

(B) The declaration accompanying the motion or application must contain facts sufficient to justify an order maintaining the confidentiality of the relevant material from the reporter's transcript of, or documents filed or lodged in connection with, the in-camera hearing and sealing of the brief, petition, or other filing.

(C) At the time the motion or application is filed, the defendant must:

(i) File a public redacted version of the brief, petition, or other filing that he or she is requesting be filed under seal. The cover of this version must identify it as "Public—Redacts material from conditionally sealed record." The requirement to publicly file the redacted version does not apply in juvenile cases; rule 8.401 generally governs access to filings in juvenile cases. In juvenile cases, the cover of the redacted version must identify it as "Redacted version—Redacts material from conditionally sealed record."

(ii) Lodge an unredacted version of the brief, petition, or other filing that he or she is requesting be filed under seal. The filing must be transmitted in a secure manner that preserves the confidentiality of the filing being lodged. If this version is in paper format, it must be placed in a sealed envelope or other appropriate sealed container. The cover of the unredacted version of the document, and if applicable the envelope or other container, must identify it as "May Not Be Examined Without Court Order—Contains material from conditionally sealed record." Conditionally sealed material disclosed in this version must be identified as such in the filing.

(D) If the court denies the motion or application to file the brief, petition, or other filing under seal, the defendant may notify the court that the unredacted brief, petition, or other filing lodged under (C)(ii) is to be filed unsealed. This notification must be received within 10 days of the order denying the motion or application to file the brief, petition, or other filing under seal, unless otherwise ordered by the court. On receipt of this notification, the clerk must unseal and file the lodged unredacted brief, petition, or other filing. If the defendant does not notify the court within 10 days of the order, the clerk must (1) return the lodged unredacted brief, petition, or other filing to the defendant if it is in paper form, or (2) permanently delete the lodged unredacted brief, petition, or other filing if it is in electronic form.

(Subd (b) amended effective January 1, 2019; adopted effective January 1, 2014; previously amended effective January 1, 2016.)

(c) Other confidential records

Except as otherwise provided by law or order of the reviewing court:

(1) Nothing filed publicly in the reviewing court—including any application, brief, petition, or memorandum—may disclose material contained in a confidential record, including a record that, by law, a party may choose to be kept confidential in reviewing court proceedings and that the party has chosen to keep confidential.

(2) To maintain the confidentiality of material contained in a confidential record, if it is necessary to disclose such material in a filing in the reviewing court, a party may serve and file a motion or application in the reviewing court requesting permission for the filing to be under seal.

(A) Except as otherwise provided in this rule, rule 8.46(d) governs a motion or application under this subdivision.

(B) The declaration accompanying the motion or application must contain facts sufficient to establish that the record is required by law to be closed to inspection in the reviewing court and to justify sealing of the brief, petition, or other filing.

(C) At the time the motion or application is filed, the party must:

(i) File a redacted version of the brief, petition, or other filing that he or she is requesting be filed under seal. The cover of this version must identify it as "Public—Redacts material from conditionally sealed record." In juvenile cases, the cover of this version must identify it as "Redacted version—Redacts material from conditionally sealed record."

(ii) Lodge an unredacted version of the brief, petition, or other filing that he or she is requesting be filed under seal. The filing must be transmitted in a secure manner that preserves the confidentiality of the filing being lodged. If this version is in paper format, it must be placed in a sealed envelope or other appropriate sealed container. The cover of the unredacted version of the document, and if applicable the envelope or other container, must identify it as "May Not Be Examined Without Court Order—Contains material from conditionally sealed record." Material from a confidential record disclosed in this version must be identified and accompanied by a citation to the statute, rule of court, case, or other authority establishing that the record is required by law to be closed to inspection in the reviewing court.

(D) If the court denies the motion or application to file the brief, petition, or other filing under seal, the party who filed the motion or application may notify the court that the unredacted brief, petition, or other filing lodged under (C)(ii) is to be filed unsealed. This notification must be received within 10 days of the order denying the motion or application to file the brief, petition, or other filing under seal, unless otherwise ordered by the court. On receipt of this notification, the clerk must unseal and file the lodged unredacted brief, petition, or other filing. If the party who filed the motion or application does not notify the court within 10 days of the order, the clerk must (1) return the lodged unredacted brief, petition, or other filing to the lodging party if it is in paper form, or (2) permanently delete the lodged unredacted brief, petition, or other filing if it is in electronic form.

(Subd (c) amended effective January 1, 2019; adopted effective January 1, 2014; previously amended effective January 1, 2016.)

Rule 8.47 amended effective January 1, 2019; adopted effective January 1, 2014; previously amended effective January 1, 2016.

Advisory Committee Comment

Subdivisions (a) and (c). Note that there are many laws that address the confidentiality of various records. These laws differ from each other in a variety of respects, including what information is closed to inspection, from whom it is closed, under what circumstances it is closed, and what procedures apply to closing or opening it to inspection. It is very important to determine if any such law applies with respect to a particular record because this rule applies only to confidential records as defined in rule 8.45, and the procedures in this rule apply only "unless otherwise provided by law." Thus, where other laws establish specific requirements that differ from the requirements in this rule, those specific requirements supersede the requirements in this rule. For example, although Penal Code section 1203.05 limits who may inspect or copy probation reports, much of the material contained in such reports—such as the factual summary of the offense(s); the evaluations, analyses, calculations, and recommendations of the probation officer; and other nonpersonal information—is not considered confidential under that statute and is routinely discussed in openly filed appellate briefs (see *People v. Connor* (2004) 115 Cal.App.4th 669, 695–696). In addition, this rule does not alter any existing authority for a court to open a confidential record to inspection by the public or another party to a proceeding.

Subdivision (c)(1). The reference in this provision to records that a party may choose to be kept confidential in reviewing court proceedings is intended to encompass situations in which a record may be subject to a privilege that a party may choose to maintain or choose to waive.

Subdivision (c)(2). Note that when a record has been sealed by court order, rule 8.46(g)(2) requires a party to file redacted (public) and unredacted (sealed) versions of any filing that discloses material from the sealed record; it does not require the party to make a motion or application for permission to do so. By contrast, this rule requires court permission before redacted (public) and unredacted (sealed) filings may be made to prevent disclosure of material from confidential records.

Article 4
Applications and Motions; Extending and Shortening Time

Division 1, Rules Relating to the Supreme Court and Courts of Appeal—Chapter 1, General Provisions—Article 4, Applications and Motions; Extending and Shortening Time; renumbered effective January 1, 2014; adopted as Article 3.

Rule 8.50.   Applications
(a) Service and filing

Except as these rules provide otherwise, parties must serve and file all applications in the reviewing court, including applications to extend the time to file records, briefs, or other documents, and applications to shorten time. For good cause, the Chief Justice or presiding justice may excuse advance service.

(Subd (a) amended effective January 1, 2007.)

(b) Contents

The application must state facts showing good cause—or making an exceptional showing of good cause, when required by these rules—for granting the application and must identify any previous application filed by any party.

(Subd (b) amended effective January 1, 2007.)

(c) Disposition

Unless the court determines otherwise, the Chief Justice or presiding justice may rule on the application.

(Subd (c) relettered effective January 1, 2016; adopted as subd (d).)

Rule 8.50 amended effective January 1, 2016; repealed and adopted as rule 43 effective January 1, 2005; previously amended and renumbered as 8.50 effective January 1, 2007.

Advisory Committee Comment

Rule 8.50 addresses applications generally. Rules 8.60, 8.63, and 8.68 address applications to extend or shorten time.

Subdivision (a). A party other than the appellant or petitioner who files an application or opposition to an application may be required to pay a filing fee under Government Code sections 68926 or 68927 if the application or opposition is the first document filed in the appeal or writ proceeding in the reviewing court by that party. See rule 8.25(c).

Subdivision (b). An exceptional showing of good cause is required in applications in certain juvenile proceedings under rules 8.416, 8.450, 8.452, and 8.454.

Rule 8.54.   Motions
(a) Motion and opposition

(1) Except as these rules provide otherwise, a party wanting to make a motion in a reviewing court must serve and file a written motion stating the grounds and the relief requested and identifying any documents on which the motion is based.

(2) A motion must be accompanied by a memorandum and, if it is based on matters outside the record, by declarations or other supporting evidence.

(3) Any opposition must be served and filed within 15 days after the motion is filed.

(Subd (a) amended effective January 1, 2007.)

(b) Disposition

(1) The court may rule on a motion at any time after an opposition or other response is filed or the time to oppose has expired.

(2) On a party's request or its own motion, the court may place a motion on calendar for a hearing. The clerk must promptly send each party a notice of the date and time of the hearing.

(c) Failure to oppose motion

A failure to oppose a motion may be deemed a consent to the granting of the motion.

Rule 8.54 amended and renumbered effective January 1, 2007; repealed and adopted as rule 41 effective January 1, 2005.

Advisory Committee Comment

Subdivision (a). A party other than the appellant or petitioner who files a motion or opposition to a motion may be required to pay a filing fee under Government Code sections 68926 or 68927 if the motion or opposition is the first document filed in the appeal or writ proceeding in the reviewing court by that party. See rule 8.25(c).

Subdivision (c). Subdivision (c) provides that a "failure to oppose a motion" may be deemed a consent to the granting of the motion. The provision is not intended to indicate a position on the question whether there is an implied right to a hearing to oppose a motion to dismiss an appeal.

Rule 8.57.   Motions before the record is filed
(a) Motion to dismiss appeal

A motion to dismiss an appeal before the record is filed in the reviewing court must be accompanied by a certificate of the superior court clerk, a declaration, or both, stating:

(1) The nature of the action and the relief sought by the complaint and any cross-complaint or complaint in intervention;

(2) The names, addresses, and telephone numbers of all attorneys of record—stating whom each represents—and unrepresented parties;

(3) A description of the judgment or order appealed from, its entry date, and the service date of any written notice of its entry;

(4) The factual basis of any extension of the time to appeal under rule 8.108;

(5) The filing dates of all notices of appeal and the courts in which they were filed;

(6) The filing date of any document necessary to procure the record on appeal; and

(7) The status of the record preparation process, including any order extending time to prepare the record.

(Subd (a) amended effective January 1, 2007.)

(b) Other motions

Any other motion filed before the record is filed in the reviewing court must be accompanied by a declaration or other evidence necessary to advise the court of the facts relevant to the relief requested.

Rule 8.57 amended and renumbered effective January 1, 2007; repealed and adopted as rule 42 effective January 1, 2005.

Rule 8.60.   Extending time

(a) Computing time

The Code of Civil Procedure governs computing and extending the time to do any act required or permitted under these rules.

(b) Extending time

Except as these rules provide otherwise, for good cause—or on an exceptional showing of good cause, when required by these rules—the Chief Justice or presiding justice may extend the time to do any act required or permitted under these rules.

(Subd (b) amended effective January 1, 2007.)

(c) Application for extension

(1) An application to extend time must include a declaration stating facts, not mere conclusions, and must be served on all parties. For good cause, the Chief Justice or presiding justice may excuse advance service.

(2) The application must state:

(A) The due date of the document to be filed;

(B) The length of the extension requested;

(C) Whether any earlier extensions have been granted and, if so, their lengths and whether granted by stipulation or by the court; and

(D) Good cause—or an exceptional showing of good cause, when required by these rules—for granting the extension, consistent with the factors in rule 8.63(b).

(Subd (c) amended and relettered effective January 1, 2007; adopted as subd (d) effective January 1, 2005.)

(d) Relief from default

For good cause, a reviewing court may relieve a party from default for any failure to comply with these rules except the failure to file a timely notice of appeal or a timely statement of reasonable grounds in support of a certificate of probable cause.

(Subd (d) relettered effective January 1, 2007; adopted as subd (e) effective January 1, 2005.)

(e) No extension by superior court

Except as these rules provide otherwise, a superior court may not extend the time to do any act to prepare the appellate record.

(Subd (e) relettered effective January 1, 2007; adopted as subd (f) effective January 1, 2005.)

(f) Notice to party

(1) In a civil case, counsel must deliver to his or her client or clients a copy of any stipulation or application to extend time that counsel files. Counsel must attach evidence of such delivery to the stipulation or application, or certify in the stipulation or application that the copy has been delivered.

(2) In a class action, the copy required under (1) need be delivered to only one represented party.

(3) The evidence or certification of delivery under (1) need not include the address of the party notified.

(Subd (f) amended and relettered effective January 1, 2007; adopted as subd (g) effective January 1, 2005.)

Rule 8.60 amended and renumbered effective January 1, 2007; repealed and adopted as rule 45 effective January 1, 2005.

Advisory Committee Comment

Subdivisions (b) and (c). An exceptional showing of good cause is required in applications in certain juvenile proceedings under rules 8.416, 8.450, 8.452, and 8.454.

Rule 8.63.   Policies and factors governing extensions of time

(a) Policies

(1) The time limits prescribed by these rules should generally be met to ensure expeditious conduct of appellate business and public confidence in the efficient administration of appellate justice.

(2) The effective assistance of counsel to which a party is entitled includes adequate time for counsel to prepare briefs or other documents that fully advance the party's interests. Adequate time also allows the preparation of accurate, clear, concise, and complete submissions that assist the courts.

(3) For a variety of legitimate reasons, counsel may not always be able to prepare briefs or other documents within the time specified in the rules of court. To balance the competing policies stated in (1) and (2), applications to extend time in the reviewing courts must demonstrate good cause—or an exceptional showing of good cause, when required by these rules—under (b). If good cause is shown, the court must extend the time.

(Subd (a) amended effective January 1, 2007.)

(b) Factors considered

In determining good cause—or an exceptional showing of good cause, when required by these rules—the court must consider the following factors when applicable:

(1) The degree of prejudice, if any, to any party from a grant or denial of the extension. A party claiming prejudice must support the claim in detail.

(2) In a civil case, the positions of the client and any opponent with regard to the extension.

(3) The length of the record, including the number of relevant trial exhibits. A party relying on this factor must specify the length of the record. In a civil case, a record containing one volume of clerk's transcript or appendix and two volumes of reporter's transcript is considered an average-length record.

(4) The number and complexity of the issues raised. A party relying on this factor must specify the issues.

(5) Whether there are settlement negotiations and, if so, how far they have progressed and when they might be completed.

(6) Whether the case is entitled to priority.

(7) Whether counsel responsible for preparing the document is new to the case.

(8) Whether other counsel or the client needs additional time to review the document.

(9) Whether counsel responsible for preparing the document has other time-limited commitments that prevent timely filing of the document. Mere conclusory statements that more time is needed because of other pressing business will not suffice. Good cause requires a specific showing of other obligations of counsel that:

(A) Have deadlines that as a practical matter preclude filing the document by the due date without impairing its quality; or

(B) Arise from cases entitled to priority.

(10) Illness of counsel, a personal emergency, or a planned vacation that counsel did not reasonably expect to conflict with the due date and cannot reasonably rearrange.

(11) Any other factor that constitutes good cause in the context of the case.

(Subd (b) amended effective January 1, 2007.)

Rule 8.63 amended and renumbered effective January 1, 2007; repealed and adopted as rule 45.5 effective January 1, 2005.

Advisory Committee Comment

An exceptional showing of good cause is required in applications in certain juvenile proceedings under rules 8.416, 8.450, 8.452, and 8.454.

Rule 8.66.   Tolling or extending time because of public emergency

(a) Emergency tolling or extensions of time

If made necessary by the occurrence or danger of an earthquake, fire, **public health crisis,** or other public emergency, or by the destruction of or danger to a building housing a reviewing court, the Chair of the Judicial Council, notwithstanding any other rule in this title, may:

(1) **Toll for up to 30 days or** extend by no more than [1] **30 days any time periods specified by** these rules; or

(2) Authorize specified courts to **toll for up to 30 days or** extend by no more than 30 [2] **days any time periods specified by** these rules.

(Subd (a) amended effective April 4, 2020; previously amended effective January 1, 2007.)

Rule 8.66(a).   2020 Deletes. [1] 14 additional days the time to do any act required or permitted under **[2]** additional days the time to do any act required or permitted under

(b) Applicability of order

(1) An order under [1] **(a)(1)** must specify **the length of the tolling or extension and** whether [2] **the order** applies throughout the state, only to specified courts, or only to courts or attorneys in specified geographic areas, or applies in some other manner.

(2) An order [3] under (a)(2) must specify the length of the authorized **tolling or** extension.

(Subd (b) amended effective April 4, 2020.)

Rule 8.66(b).   2020 Deletes. [1] (a) **[2]** it **[3]** of the Chair of the Judicial Council

(c) Renewed orders

If made necessary by the nature or extent of the public emergency, **with or without a request,** the Chair of the Judicial Council may [1] renew an order issued under [2] **this rule prior to its expiration. An order may be renewed for additional periods not to exceed 30 days per renewal**.

(Subd (c) amended effective April 4, 2020; previously amended effective January 1, 2007.)

Rule 8.66(c).   2020 Deletes. [1] extend or **[2]** (a) for an additional period of: (1) No more than 14 days for an order under (a)(1); or (2) No more than 30 days for an order under (a)(2)

Rule 8.66 amended effective April 4, 2020; previously amended and renumbered effective January 1, 2007; repealed and adopted as rule 45.1 effective January 1, 2005.

Advisory Committee Comment

The Chief Justice of California is the Chair of the Judicial Council (see rule 10.2).

Any tolling ordered under this rule is excluded from the time period specified by the rules. (See *Woods v. Young* (1991) 53 Cal.3d 315, 326, fn. 3 ["Tolling may be analogized to a clock that is stopped and then restarted. Whatever period of time that remained when the clock is stopped is available when the clock is restarted, that is, when the tolling period has ended."].)

The tolling and extension of time authorized under this rule include and apply to all rules of court that govern finality in both the Supreme Court and the Courts of Appeal.

Rule 8.68.   Shortening time

For good cause and except as these rules provide otherwise, the Chief Justice or presiding justice may shorten the time to do any act required or permitted under these rules.

Rule 8.68 adopted effective January 1, 2007.

Article 5
E-filing

Division 1, Rules Relating to the Supreme Court and Courts of Appeal—Chapter 1, General Provisions—Article 5, E-filing; renumbered effective January 1, 2014; adopted as Article 4; previously amended effective January 1, 2012.

Rule 8.70. Application, construction, and definitions
Rule 8.71. Electronic filing
Rule 8.72. Responsibilities of court and electronic filer
Rule 8.73. Contracts with electronic filing service providers
Rule 8.74. Format of electronic documents
Rule 8.75. Requirements for signatures on documents
Rule 8.76. Payment of filing fees
Rule 8.77. Actions by court on receipt of electronically submitted document; date and time of filing
Rule 8.78. Electronic service
Rule 8.79. Court order requiring electronic service

Rule 8.70.   Application, construction, and definitions

(a) Application

Notwithstanding any other rules to the contrary, the rules in this article govern filing and service by electronic means in the Supreme Court and the Courts of Appeal.

(Subd (a) amended and relettered effective January 1, 2017; adopted as subd (b) effective July 1, 2010; previously amended effective January 1, 2012.)

(b) Construction

The rules in this article must be construed to authorize and permit filing and service by electronic means to the extent feasible.

(Subd (b) relettered effective January 1, 2017; adopted as subd (c) effective July 1, 2010.)

(c) Definitions

As used in this article, unless the context otherwise requires:

(1) "The court" means the Supreme Court or a Court of Appeal.

(2) A "document" is:

(A) Any filing submitted to the reviewing court, including a brief, a petition, an appendix, or a motion;

(B) Any document transmitted by a trial court to the reviewing court, including a notice or a clerk's or reporter's transcript;

(C) Any writing prepared by the reviewing court, including an opinion, an order, or a notice.

(D) A document may be in paper or electronic form.

(3) "Electronic service" is service of a document on a party or other person by either electronic transmission or electronic notification. Electronic service may be performed directly by a party, by an agent of a party including the party's attorney, through an electronic filing service provider, or by a court.

(4) "Electronic transmission" means the transmission of a document by electronic means to the electronic service address at or through which a party or other person has authorized electronic service.

(5) "Electronic notification" means the notification of a party or other person that a document is served by sending an electronic message to the electronic service address at or through which the party or other person has authorized electronic service, specifying the exact name of the document served and providing a hyperlink at which the served document can be viewed and downloaded.

(6) "Electronic service address" of a party means the electronic address at or through which the party has authorized electronic service.

(7) An "electronic filer" is a party filing a document in electronic form directly with the court, by an agent, or through an electronic filing service provider.

(8) "Electronic filing" is the electronic transmission to a court of a document in electronic form.

(9) An "electronic filing service provider" is a person or entity that receives an electronic filing from a party for retransmission to the court or for electronic service on other parties, or both. In submission of filings, the electronic filing service provider does so on behalf of the electronic filer and not as an agent of the court.

(Subd (c) amended and relettered effective January 1, 2017; adopted as subd (d) effective January 1, 2011; previously amended effective January 1, 2012.)
Rule 8.70 amended effective January 1, 2017; adopted effective July 1, 2010; previously amended effective January 1, 2011, and January 1, 2012.

Advisory Committee Comment

The definition of "electronic service" has been amended to provide that a party may effectuate service not only by the electronic transmission of a document, but also by providing electronic notification of where a document served electronically may be located and downloaded. This amendment is intended to modify the rules on electronic service to expressly authorize electronic notification as a legally effective alternative means of service to electronic transmission. This rules amendment is consistent with the amendment of Code of Civil Procedure section 1010.6, effective January 1, 2011, to authorize service by electronic notification. (See Stats. 2010, ch. 156 (Sen. Bill 1274).) The amendments change the law on electronic service as understood by the appellate court in *Insyst, Ltd. v. Applied Materials, Inc.* (2009) 170 Cal.App.4th 1129, which interpreted the rules as authorizing electronic transmission as the only effective means of electronic service.

Rule 8.71.   Definitions [Repealed]

Rule 8.71 repealed effective January 1, 2011; adopted effective July 1, 2010.

Rule 8.71.   Electronic service [Renumbered]

Rule 8.71 amended and renumbered as rule 8.78 effective January 1, 2017; adopted as rule 8.80 effective July 1, 2010; previously amended and renumbered as rule 8.71 effective January 1, 2011; previously amended effective January 1, 2016.

Another Rule 8.71 follows.

Rule 8.71.   Electronic filing

(a) Mandatory electronic filing

Except as otherwise provided by these rules, the [1] ***Supreme Court Rules Regarding Electronic Filing***, or court order, all parties are required to file all documents electronically in the reviewing court.

(Subd (a) amended effective January 1, 2020; adopted effective January 1, 2017.)

Rule 8.71(a).   2019 Deletes. [1] local rules of the reviewing court

(b) Self-represented parties

(1) Self-represented parties are exempt from the requirement to file documents electronically.

(2) A self-represented party may agree to file documents electronically. By electronically filing any document with the court, a self-represented party agrees to file documents electronically.

(3) In cases involving both represented and self-represented parties, represented parties are required to file documents electronically; however, in these cases, each self-represented party may file documents in paper form.

(Subd (b) adopted effective January 1, 2017.)

(c) Trial courts

Trial courts are exempt from the requirement to file documents electronically, but are permitted to file documents electronically.

(Subd (c) adopted effective January 1, 2017.)

(d) Excuse for undue hardship or significant prejudice

A party must be excused from the requirement to file documents electronically if the party shows undue hardship or significant prejudice. A court must have a process for parties, including represented parties, to apply for relief and a procedure for parties excused from filing documents electronically to file them in paper form.

(Subd (d) adopted effective January 1, 2017.)

(e) Applications for fee waivers

The court may permit electronic filing of an application for waiver of court fees and costs in any proceeding in which the court accepts electronic filings.

(Subd (e) adopted effective January 1, 2017.)

(f) Effect of document filed electronically

(1) A document that the court, a party, or a trial court files electronically under the rules in this article has the same legal effect as a document in paper form.

(2) Filing a document electronically does not alter any filing deadline.

(Subd (f) adopted effective January 1, 2017.)

(g) Paper documents

When it is not feasible for a party to convert a document to electronic form by scanning, imaging, or another means, the court may allow that party to file the document in paper form.

(Subd (g) adopted effective January 1, 2017.)

Rule 8.71 amended effective January 1, 2020; adopted effective January 1, 2017.

Rule 8.72. Documents that may be filed electronically [Repealed]

Rule 8.72 repealed effective January 1, 2017; adopted effective July 1, 2010.

Another Rule 8.72 follows.

Rule 8.72. Responsibilities of court and electronic filer

(a) Responsibilities of court

(1) The court will publish, in both electronic **form** and print [1] **form,** the court's electronic filing requirements.

[2] **(2)** If the court is aware of a problem that impedes or precludes electronic filing, it must promptly take reasonable steps to provide notice of the problem.

(Subd (a) amended effective January 1, 2020; adopted effective July 1, 2010; previously amended effective January 1, 2017.)

Rule 8.72(a). 2019 Deletes. [1] formats **[2] (b) Problems with electronic filing**

(b) Responsibilities of electronic filer

Each electronic filer must:

(1) Take all reasonable steps to ensure that the filing does not contain computer code, including viruses, that might be harmful to the court's electronic filing system and to other users of that system;

(2) Furnish one or more electronic service addresses, in the manner specified by the court, at which the electronic filer agrees to accept **receipt and filing confirmations under rule 8.77 and, if applicable, at which the electronic filer agrees to receive electronic** service; and

(3) Immediately provide the court and all parties with any change to the electronic filer's electronic service address.

(Subd (b) amended effective January 1, 2021; adopted effective January 1, 2020.)

Rule 8.72 amended effective January 1, 2021; adopted as rule 8.74 effective July 1, 2010; previously amended and renumbered effective January 1, 2017; previously amended effective January 1, 2020.

Advisory Committee Comment

Subdivision (b)(1). One example of a reasonable step an electronic filer may take is to use a commercial virus scanning program. Compliance with this subdivision requires more than an absence of intent to harm the court's electronic filing system or other users' systems.

Rule 8.73. Court order requiring electronic service or filing [Renumbered]

Rule 8.73 amended and renumbered as rule 8.79 effective January 1, 2017; adopted as rule 8.73 effective July 1, 2010; previously amended effective January 1, 2011.

Another Rule 8.73 follows.

Rule 8.73. Contracts with electronic filing service providers

(a) Right to contract

(1) The court may contract with one or more electronic filing service providers to furnish and maintain an electronic filing system for the court.

(2) If the court contracts with an electronic filing service provider, the court may require electronic filers to transmit the documents to the provider.

(3) If the court contracts with an electronic service provider or the court has an in-house system, the provider or system must accept filing from other electronic filing service providers to the extent the provider or system is compatible with them.

(Subd (a) amended effective January 1, 2011; adopted effective July 1, 2010.)

(b) Provisions of contract

The court's contract with an electronic filing service provider may allow the provider to charge electronic filers a reasonable fee in addition to the court's filing fee. Whenever possible, the contract should require that the electronic filing service provider agree to waive a fee that normally would be charged to a party when the court orders that the fee be waived for that party. The contract may also allow the electronic filing service provider to make other reasonable requirements for use of the electronic filing system.

(Subd (b) amended effective January 1, 2017; adopted effective July 1, 2010.)

(c) Transmission of filing to court

An electronic filing service provider must promptly transmit any electronic filing and any applicable filing fee to the court.

(Subd (c) amended effective January 1, 2011; adopted effective July 1, 2010.)

(d) Confirmation of receipt and filing of document

(1) An electronic filing service provider must promptly send to an electronic filer its confirmation of the receipt of any document that the filer has transmitted to the provider for filing with the court.

(2) The electronic filing service provider must send its confirmation to the filer's electronic service address and must indicate the date and time of receipt, in accordance with rule 8.77.

(3) After reviewing the documents, the court must arrange to promptly transmit confirmation of filing or notice of rejection to the electronic filer in accordance with rule 8.77.

(Subd (d) amended effective January 1, 2017; adopted effective July 1, 2010; previously amended effective January 1, 2011.)

(e) Ownership of information

All contracts between the court and electronic filing service providers must acknowledge that the court is the owner of the contents of the filing system and has the exclusive right to control the system's use.

(Subd (e) adopted effective July 1, 2010.)

Rule 8.73 amended and renumbered effective January 1, 2017; adopted as rule 8.75 effective July 1, 2010; previously amended effective January 1, 2011.

Rule 8.74. Responsibilities of court [Renumbered]

Rule 8.74 amended and renumbered as rule 8.72 effective January 1, 2017; adopted as rule 8.74 effective July 1, 2010.

Another Rule 8.74 follows.

Rule 8.74. Format of electronic documents

(a) Formatting requirements applicable to all electronic documents

[1] **(1)** *Text-searchable portable document format:* **Electronic documents must be in text-searchable portable document format (PDF) while maintaining the original document formatting. In the limited circumstances in which a document cannot practicably be converted to a text-searchable PDF, the document may be scanned or converted to non-text-searchable PDF. An** electronic filer [2] **is not required to use a specific vendor, technology, or software for creation of a searchable-format document, unless** the electronic filer agrees to [3] **such use.** The software for creating and reading **electronic** documents must be in the public domain or generally available at a reasonable cost. [4] The printing of [5] **an electronic document** must not result in the loss of document text, [6] **formatting,** or appearance. [7] **The electronic filer is responsible for ensuring that any document filed is complete and readable.**

(2) *Pagination:* **The electronic page counter for the electronic document must match the page number for each page of the document.** The page numbering of a document filed electronically must begin with the first page or cover page as page 1 and [8] **thereafter be paginated consecutively using only arabic** numerals (e.g., 1, 2, 3). The page number **for the cover page** may be suppressed and need not appear on the cover page. [9] **When** a document is filed [10] **in both paper form and electronic form, the pagination in both versions must comply with this paragraph.**

(3) *Bookmarking:* **An electronic bookmark is a descriptive text link that appears in the bookmarks panel of an electronic document. Each electronic document must include an electronic bookmark to each heading, subheading, and the first page of any component of the document, including any table of contents, table of authorities, petition, verification, memorandum, declaration, certificate of word count, certificate of interested entities or persons, proof of service, exhibit, or attachment. Each electronic bookmark must briefly describe the item to which it is linked. For example, an electronic bookmark to a heading must provide the text of the heading, and an electronic bookmark to an exhibit or attachment must include the letter or number of the exhibit or attachment and a brief description of the exhibit or attachment. An electronic appendix must have bookmarks to the indexes and to the first page of each separate exhibit or attachment. Exhibits or attachments within an exhibit or attachment must be bookmarked. All bookmarks must be set to retain the reader's selected zoom setting.**

(4) *Protection of sensitive information:* **Electronic filers must comply with rules 1.201, 8.45, 8.46, 8.47, and 8.401 regarding the protection of sensitive information, except for those requirements exclusively applicable to paper form.**

(5) *Size and multiple files:* **An electronic filing may not be larger than 25 megabytes. This rule does not change the limitations on word count or number of pages otherwise established by the California Rules of Court for documents filed in the court. Although certain provisions** in the California Rules of Court [11] **require volumes of no more than 300 pages (see, e.g., rules 8.124(d)(1), 8.144(b)(6), 8.144(g)), an electronic filing may exceed 300 pages so long as its individual components comply with the 300-page volume requirement and the electronic filing does not exceed 25 megabytes. If a document exceeds the 25-megabyte file-size limitation, the electronic filer must submit the document in more than one file, with each file 25 megabytes or less. The first file must include a master chronological and alphabetical index stating the contents for all files. Each file must have a cover page stating (a) the file number for that file and the total number of files for that document, (b) the volumes contained in that file, and (c) the page numbers contained in that file. (For example: File 2 of 4, Volumes 3–4, pp. 301–499.) In addition, each file must be paginated consecutively across all files in the document, including the cover pages for each file. (For example, if the first file ends on page 300, the cover of the second file must be page 301.) If a multiple-file document is submitted to the court in both electronic form and paper form, the cover pages for each file must be included in the paper documents.**

(6) *Manual Filing:*

(A) When an electronic filer seeks to file an electronic document consisting of more than 10 files, or when the document cannot or should not be electronically filed in multiple files, or when electronically filing the document would cause undue hardship, the document must not be electronically filed but must be manually filed with the court on an electronic medium such as a flash drive, DVD, or compact disc (CD). When an electronic filer files with the court one or more documents on an electronic medium, the electronic filer must electronically file, on the same day, a "manual filing notification" notifying the court and the parties that one or more documents have been filed on electronic media, explaining the reason for the manual filing. The electronic media must be served on the parties in accordance with the requirements for service of paper documents. To the extent practicable, each document or file on electronic media must comply with the format requirements of this rule.

(B) Electronic media files such as audio or video must be manually filed. Audio files must be filed in .wav or mp3 format. Video files must be filed in .avi or mp4 format.

(C) If manually filed, photographs must be filed in .jpg, .png, .tif, or .pdf format.

(D) If an original electronic media file is converted to a required format for manual filing, the electronic filer must retain the original.

(7) *Page size:* **All documents must have a page size of 8-1/2 by 11 inches.**

(8) *Color:* **An electronic document with a color component may be electronically filed or manually filed on electronic media, depending on its file size. An electronic document must not have a color cover.**

(9) *Cover or first-page information:*

(A) Except as provided in (B), the cover—or first page, if there is no cover—of every electronic document filed in a reviewing court must include the name, mailing address, telephone number, fax number (if available), email address (if available), and California State Bar number of each attorney filing or joining in the document, or of the party if he or she is unrepresented. The inclusion of a fax number or email address on any electronic document does not constitute consent to service by fax or email unless otherwise provided by law.

(B) If more than one attorney from a law firm, corporation, or public law office is representing one party and is joining in the document, the name and State Bar number of each attorney joining in the electronic document must be provided on the cover. The law firm, corporation, or public law office representing each party must designate one attorney to receive notices and other communication in the case from the court by placing an asterisk before that attorney's name on the cover and must provide the contact information specified under (A) for that attorney. Contact information for the other attorneys from the same law firm, corporation, or public law office is not required but may be provided.

(Subd (a) amended effective January 1, 2020; adopted effective July 1, 2010; previously amended effective January 1, 2011.)

Rule 8.74(a). 2019 Deletes. [1] Each [2] must: (1) Comply with any court requirements designed to ensure the integrity of electronic filing and to protect sensitive personal information; (2) Furnish information that the court requires for case processing; (3) Take all reasonable steps to ensure that the filing does not contain computer code, including viruses, that might be harmful to the court's electronic filing system and to other users of that system; (4) Furnish one or more electronic service addresses, in the manner specified by the court, at which [3] accept service; and (5) Immediately provide the court and all parties with any change to the electronic filer's electronic service address. **(b) Format of documents to be filed electronically** (1) A document that is filed electronically with the court must be in a format specified by the court unless it cannot be created in that format. (2) The format adopted by a court must meet the following minimum requirements: (A) The format must be text-searchable while maintaining original document formatting. (B) [4] (C) [5] documents [6] format [7] (3) [8] use only Arabic [9] (4) If [10] electronically under the rules in this article and cannot be formatted to be consistent with a formatting rule elsewhere [11] , the rules in this article prevail

(b) Additional formatting requirements applicable to documents prepared for electronic filing in the first instance in a reviewing court

(1) *Font:* The font style must be a proportionally spaced serif face. Century Schoolbook is preferred. A sans-serif face may be used for headings, subheadings, and captions. Font size must be 13-points, including in footnotes. Case names must be italicized or underscored. For emphasis, italics or boldface may be used or the text may be underscored. Do not use all capitals (i.e., ALL CAPS) for emphasis.

(2) *Spacing:* Lines of text must be 1.5 spaced. Footnotes, headings, subheadings, and quotations may be single-spaced. The lines of text must be unnumbered.

(3) *Margins:* The margins must be set at 1-1/2 inches on the left and right and 1 inch on the top and bottom. Quotations may be block-indented.

(4) *Alignment:* Paragraphs must be left-aligned, not justified.

(5) *Hyperlinks:* Hyperlinks to legal authorities and appendixes or exhibits are encouraged but not required. However, if an electronic filer elects to include hyperlinks in a document, the hyperlink must be active as of the date of filing, and if the hyperlink is to a legal authority, it should be formatted to standard citation format as provided in the California Rules of Court.

(Subd (b) adopted effective January 1, 2020.)

(c) Additional formatting requirements for certain electronic documents

(1) *Brief:* In addition to compliance with this rule, an electronic brief must also comply with the contents and length requirements stated in rule 8.204(a) and (c). The brief need not be signed. The cover must state:

(A) The title of the brief;

(B) The title, trial court number, and Court of Appeal number of the case;

(C) The names of the trial court and each participating trial judge; and

(D) The name of the party that each attorney on the brief represents.

(2) *Request for judicial notice or request, application, or motion supported by documents:* When seeking judicial notice of matter not already in the appellate record, or when a request, application, or motion is supported by matter not already in the appellate record, the electronic filer must attach a copy of the matter to the request, application, or motion, or an explanation of why it is not practicable to do so. The request, application, or motion and its attachments must comply with this rule.

(3) *Appendix:* The format of an appendix must comply with this rule and rule 8.144 pertaining to clerks' transcripts.

(4) *Agreed statement and settled statement:* The format for an agreed statement or a settled statement must comply with this rule and rule 8.144.

(5) *Reporter's transcript and clerk's transcript:* The format for an electronic reporter's transcript must comply with Code of Civil Procedure section 271 and rule 8.144. The format for an electronic clerk's transcript must comply with this rule and rule 8.144.

(6) *Exhibits:* Electronic exhibits must be submitted in files no larger than 25 megabytes, rather than as individual documents.

(7) *Sealed and confidential records:* Under rule 8.45(c)(1), electronic records that are sealed or confidential must be filed separately from publicly filed records. If one or more pages are omitted from a record and filed separately as a sealed or confidential record, an omission page or pages must be inserted in the publicly filed record at the location of the omitted page or pages. The omission page or pages must identify the type of page or pages omitted. Each omission page must be paginated consecutively with the rest of the publicly filed record. Each single omission page or the first omission page in a range of omission pages must be bookmarked and must be listed in any indexes included in the publicly filed record. The PDF counter for each omission page must match the page number of the page omitted from the publicly filed record. Separately-filed sealed or confidential records must comply with this rule and rules 8.45, 8.46, and 8.47.

(Subd (c) adopted effective January 1, 2020.)

(d) Other formatting rules

This rule prevails over other formatting rules.

(Subd (d) adopted effective January 1, 2020.)

Rule 8.74 amended effective January 1, 2020; adopted as rule 8.76 effective July 1, 2010; previously amended effective January 1, 2011; previously amended and renumbered effective January 1, 2017.

Advisory Committee Comment

Subdivision (a)(1). If an electronic filer must file a document that the electronic filer possesses only in paper form, use of a scanned image is a permitted means of conversion to PDF, but optical character recognition must be used, if possible. If a document cannot practicably be converted to a text-searchable PDF (e.g., if the document is entirely or substantially handwritten, a photograph, or a graphic such as a chart or diagram that is not primarily text based), the document may be converted to a non-text-searchable PDF file.

Subdivision (a)(3). An electronic bookmark's brief description of the item to which it is linked should enable the reader to easily identify the item. For example, if a declaration is attached to a document, the bookmark to the declaration might say "Robert Smith Declaration," and if a complaint is attached to a declaration as an exhibit, the bookmark to the complaint might say "Exhibit A, First Amended Complaint filed 8/12/17."

Subdivision (b). Subdivision (b) governs documents prepared for electronic filing in the first instance in a reviewing court and does not apply to previously created documents (such as exhibits), whose formatting cannot or should not be altered.

Subdivision (c)(7). In identifying the type of pages omitted, the omission page might say, for example, "probation report" or "*Marsden* hearing transcript."

Rule 8.75. Contracts with electronic filing service providers [Renumbered]

Rule 8.75 amended and renumbered as rule 8.73 effective January 1, 2017; adopted as rule 8.75 effective July 1, 2010; previously amended effective January 1, 2011.

Another Rule 8.75 follows.

Rule 8.75. Requirements for signatures on documents

(a) Documents signed under penalty of perjury

If a document to be filed electronically must be signed under penalty of perjury, the following procedure applies:

(1) The document is deemed signed by the declarant if, before filing, the declarant has signed a printed form of the document.

(2) By electronically filing the document, the electronic filer certifies that (1) has been complied with and that the original signed document is available for inspection and copying at the request of the court or any other party.

(3) At any time after the document is filed, any other party may serve a demand for production of the original signed document. The demand must be served on all other parties but need not be filed with the court.

(4) Within five days of service of the demand under (3), the party on whom the demand is made must make the original signed document available for inspection and copying by all other parties.

(5) At any time after the document is filed, the court may order the filing party to produce the original signed document in court for inspection and copying by the court. The order must specify the date, time, and place for the production and must be served on all parties.

(Subd (a) amended effective January 1, 2014; adopted effective July 1, 2010.)

(b) Documents not signed under penalty of perjury

If a document does not require a signature under penalty of perjury, the document is deemed signed by the party if the document is filed electronically.

(Subd (b) adopted effective July 1, 2010.)

(c) Documents requiring signatures of multiple parties

When a document to be filed electronically, such as a stipulation, requires the signatures of multiple parties, the following procedure applies:

(1) The party filing the document must obtain the signatures of all parties either in the form of an original signature on a printed form of the document or in the form of a copy of the signed signature page of the document. By electronically filing the document, the electronic filer indicates that all parties have signed the document and that the filer has the signatures of all parties in a form permitted by this rule in his or her possession.

(2) The party filing the document must maintain the original signed document and any copies of signed signature pages and must make them available for inspection and copying as provided in (a)(2). The court and any other party may demand production of the original signed document and any copies of signed signature pages in the manner provided in (a)(3)–(5).

(Subd (c) amended effective January 1, 2014; adopted effective July 1, 2010.)

(d) Digital signature

A party is not required to use a digital signature on an electronically filed document.

(Subd (d) adopted effective July 1, 2010.)

(e) Judicial signatures

If a document requires a signature by a court or a judicial officer, the document may be electronically signed in any manner permitted by law.

(Subd (e) adopted effective July 1, 2010.)

Rule 8.75 renumbered effective January 1, 2017; adopted as rule 8.77 effective July 1, 2010; previously amended effective January 1, 2014.

Rule 8.76. Responsibilities of electronic filer [Renumbered]

Rule 8.76 amended and renumbered to rule 8.74 effective January 1, 2017; adopted as rule 8.76 effective July 1, 2010; previously amended effective January 1, 2011.

Another Rule 8.76 follows.

Rule 8.76. Payment of filing fees

(a) Use of credit cards and other methods

The court may permit the use of credit cards, debit cards, electronic fund transfers, or debit accounts for the payment of filing fees associated with electronic filing, as provided in Government Code section 6159 and other applicable law. The court may also authorize other methods of payment.

(Subd (a) adopted effective July 1, 2010.)

(b) Fee waivers

Eligible persons may seek a waiver of court fees and costs, as provided in Government Code section 68634.5 and rule 8.26.

(Subd (b) adopted effective July 1, 2010.)

Rule 8.76 renumbered effective January 1, 2017; adopted as rule 8.78 effective July 1, 2010.

Advisory Committee Comment

Subdivision (b). A fee charged by an electronic filing service provider under rule 8.73(b) is not a court fee that can be waived under Government Code section 68634.5 and rule 8.26.

Rule 8.77. Requirements for signatures on documents [Renumbered]

Rule 8.77 amended and renumbered to rule 8.75 effective January 1, 2017; adopted as rule 8.77 effective July 1, 2010; previously amended effective January 1, 2014.

Another Rule 8.77 follows.

Rule 8.77. Actions by court on receipt of electronically submitted document; date and time of filing

(a) Confirmation of receipt and filing of document

(1) *Confirmation of receipt*

When the court receives an electronically submitted document, the court must arrange to promptly send the electronic filer confirmation of the court's receipt of the document, indicating the date and time of receipt [1] **by the court.**

(2) *Filing*

If the electronically submitted document received by the court complies with filing requirements, the document is [2] **deemed filed on** the date and time **it was received by the court as stated in** the confirmation of receipt [3]**.**

(3) *Confirmation of filing*

[4] **When the court files an electronically submitted document**, the court must arrange to promptly send the electronic filer confirmation that the document has been filed. The filing confirmation must indicate the date and time of filing **as specified in the confirmation of receipt,** and [5] must also specify:

(A) Any transaction number associated with the filing; and

(B) The titles of the documents as filed by the court.

[6] **(4)** *Transmission of confirmations*

The court must arrange to send receipt and filing confirmation to the electronic filer at the electronic service address that the filer furnished to the court under rule [7] **8.72(b)(2).** The court or the electronic filing service provider must maintain a record of all receipt and filing confirmations.

[8] **(5)** *Filer responsible for verification*

In the absence of confirmation of receipt and filing, there is no presumption that the court received and filed the document. The electronic filer is responsible for verifying that the court received and filed any document that the electronic filer submitted to the court electronically.

(Subd (a) amended effective January 1, 2021; adopted effective July 1, 2010; previously amended effective January 1, 2011, January 1, 2017, and January 1, 2020.)

Rule 8.77(a). 2020 Deletes. [1] . A [2] considered received at [3] is created. (2) [4] If the document received by the court under (1) complies with filing requirements [5] is proof that the document was filed on the date and at the time specified. The filing confirmation [6] (3) [7] 8.74(a)(4) [8] (4)

(b) Notice of rejection of document for filing

If the clerk does not file a document because it does not comply with applicable filing requirements, the court must arrange to promptly send notice of the rejection of the document for filing to the electronic filer. The notice must state the reasons that the document was rejected for filing.

(Subd (b) amended effective January 1, 2017; adopted effective July 1, 2010.)

(c) Document received after close of business

A document that is received electronically by the court after 11:59 p.m. is deemed to have been received on the next court day.

(Subd (c) amended effective January 1, 2011; adopted effective July 1, 2010.)

(d) Delayed delivery

If a filer fails to meet a filing deadline imposed by court order, rule, or statute because of a failure at any point in the electronic transmission and receipt of a document, the filer may file the document on paper or electronically as soon thereafter as practicable and accompany the filing with a motion to accept the document as timely filed. For good cause shown, the court may enter an order permitting the document to be filed nunc pro tunc to the date the filer originally sought to transmit the document electronically.

(Subd (d) amended effective January 1, 2017; adopted effective July 1, 2010.)

(e) Endorsement

(1) The court's endorsement of a document electronically filed must contain the following: "Electronically filed by [Name of Court], on _____ (date)," followed by the name of the court clerk.

(2) The endorsement required under (1) has the same force and effect as a manually affixed endorsement stamp with the signature and initials of the court clerk.

(3) A record on appeal, brief, or petition in an appeal or original proceeding that is filed and endorsed electronically may be printed and served on the appellant or respondent in the same manner as if it had been filed in paper form.

(Subd (e) amended effective January 1, 2012; adopted effective July 1, 2010.)
Rule 8.77 amended effective January 1, 2021; adopted as rule 8.79 effective July 1, 2010; previously amended effective January 1, 2011, January 1, 2012, and January 1, 2020; previously amended and renumbered effective January 1, 2017.

Rule 8.78. Payment of filing fees [Renumbered]

Rule 8.78 renumbered to rule 8.76 effective January 1, 2017; adopted as rule 8.78 effective July 1, 2010.

Another Rule 8.78 follows.

Rule 8.78. Electronic service

(a) Authorization for electronic service; exceptions

(1) A document may be electronically served under these rules:

(A) If electronic service is provided for by law or court order; or

(B) If the recipient agrees to [1] **accept-electronic** services as provided by these rules and the document is otherwise authorized to be served by mail, express mail, overnight delivery, or fax transmission.

(2) A party indicates that the party agrees to accept electronic service by:

(A) Serving a notice on all parties that the party accepts electronic service and filing the notice with the court. The notice must include the electronic service address at which the party agrees to accept service; or

(B) [2] **Registering with the court's** electronic filing [3] **service provider and providing the party's electronic service address. Registration with the court's electronic filing service provider is** deemed to show that the party agrees to accept service at the electronic service address that the party has [4] **provided,** unless the party serves a notice on all parties and files the notice with the court that the party does not accept electronic service and chooses instead to be served paper copies at an address specified in the notice.

(3) A document may be electronically served on a nonparty if the nonparty consents to electronic service or electronic service is otherwise provided for by law or court order. All provisions of this rule that apply or relate to a party also apply to any nonparty who has agreed to or is otherwise required by law or court order to accept electronic service or to electronically serve documents.

(Subd (a) amended effective January 1, 2021; adopted effective July 1, 2010; previously amended effective January 1, 2011, January 1, 2016, January 1, 2017, and January 1, 2020.)

Rule 8.78(a). 2020 Deletes. [1] accept electronic [2] Electronically filing any document with the court. The act of [3] shall be [4] furnished to the court under rule 8.72(b)(2)

(b) Maintenance of electronic service lists

When the court orders or permits electronic service in a case, it must maintain and make available electronically to the parties an electronic service list that contains the parties' current electronic service addresses as provided by the parties that have been ordered to or have consented to electronic service in the case.

(Subd (b) amended effective January 1, 2017; adopted effective July 1, 2010; previously amended effective January 1, 2011.)

(c) Service by the parties

Notwithstanding (b), parties are responsible for electronic service on all other parties in the case. A party may serve documents electronically directly, by an agent, or through a designated electronic filing service provider.

(Subd (c) amended effective January 1, 2016; adopted effective July 1, 2010, and January 1, 2011.)

(d) Change of electronic service address

(1) A party whose electronic service address changes while the appeal or original proceeding is pending must promptly file a notice of change of address electronically with the court and must serve this notice electronically on all other parties.

(2) A party's election to contract with an electronic filing service provider to electronically file and serve documents or to receive electronic service of documents on the party's behalf does not relieve the party of its duties under (1).

(Subd (d) amended effective January 1, 2017; adopted effective July 1, 2010; previously amended effective January 1, 2011.)

(e) Reliability and integrity of documents served by electronic notification

A party that serves a document by means of electronic notification must:

(1) Ensure that the documents served can be viewed and downloaded using the hyperlink provided;

(2) Preserve the document served without any change, alteration, or modification from the time the document is posted until the time the hyperlink is terminated; and

(3) Maintain the hyperlink until the case is final.

(Subd (e) repealed and adopted effective January 1, 2011.)

(f) Proof of service

(1) Proof of electronic service may be by any of the methods provided in Code of Civil Procedure section 1013a, with the following exceptions:

(A) The proof of electronic service does not need to state that the person making the service is not a party to the case.

(B) The proof of electronic service must state:

(i) The electronic service address of the person making the service, in addition to that person's residence or business address;

(ii) The date of the electronic service, instead of the date and place of deposit in the mail;

(iii) The name and electronic service address of the person served, in place of that person's name and address as shown on the envelope; and

(iv) That the document was served electronically, in place of the statement that the envelope was sealed and deposited in the mail with postage fully prepaid.

(2) Proof of electronic service may be in electronic form and may be filed electronically with the court.

(3) The party filing the proof of electronic service must maintain the printed form of the document bearing the declarant's original signature and must make the document available for inspection and copying on the request of the court or any party to the action or proceeding in which it is filed, in the manner provided in rule 8.75.

(Subd (f) amended effective January 1, 2017; adopted effective July 1, 2010; previously amended effective January 1, 2011.)

(g) Electronic delivery by court and electronic service on court

(1) The court may [1] **deliver** any notice, order, opinion, or other document issued by the court [2] by electronic [3] **means**.

(2) A document may be electronically served on a court if the court consents to electronic service or electronic service is otherwise provided for by law or court order. A court indicates that it agrees to accept electronic service by:

(A) Serving a notice on all parties that the court accepts electronic service. The notice must include the electronic service address at which the court agrees to accept service; or

(B) Adopting a local rule stating that the court accepts electronic service. The rule must indicate where to obtain the electronic service address at which the court agrees to accept service.

(Subd (g) amended effective January 1, 2021; adopted effective July 1, 2010; previously amended effective January 1, 2016.)

Rule 8.78(g). 2020 Deletes. [1] electronically serve [2] in the same manner that parties may serve documents [3] service

Rule 8.78 amended effective January 1, 2021; adopted as rule 8.80 effective July 1, 2010; previously amended and renumbered as rule 8.71 effective January 1, 2011, and amended and renumbered as rule 8.78 effective January 1, 2017; previously amended effective January 1, 2016, and January 1, 2020.

Advisory Committee Comment

In the Supreme Court and the Courts of Appeal, registration with the court's electronic filing service provider is deemed to show agreement to accept service electronically at the email address provided, unless a party affirmatively opts out of electronic service under rule 8.78(a)(2)(B). This procedure differs from the procedure for electronic service in the superior courts, including their appellate divisions. See rules 2.250–2.261.

Rule 8.79. Actions by court on receipt of electronic filing [Renumbered]

Rule 8.79 amended and renumbered as rule 8.77 effective January 1, 2017; adopted as rule 8.79 effective July 1, 2010; previously amended effective January 1, 2011, and January 1, 2012.

Another Rule 8.79 follows.

Rule 8.79. Court order requiring electronic service

(a) Court order

(1) The court may, on the motion of any party or on its own motion, provided that the order would not cause undue hardship or significant prejudice to any party, order some or all parties to do either or both of the following:

(A) Serve all documents electronically, except when personal service is required by statute or rule; or

(B) Accept electronic service of documents.

(2) The court will not:

(A) Order a self-represented party to electronically serve or accept electronic service of documents; or

(B) Order a trial court to electronically serve documents.

(3) If the reviewing court proposes to make an order under (1) on its own motion, the court must mail notice to the parties. Any party may serve and file an opposition within 10 days after the notice is mailed or as the court specifies.

(Subd (a) amended effective January 1, 2017; adopted effective July 1, 2010; previously amended effective January 1, 2011.)

(b) Serving in paper form

When it is not feasible for a party to convert a document to electronic form by scanning, imaging, or another means, the court may allow that party to serve the document in paper form.

(Subd (b) amended and relettered effective January 1, 2017; adopted as subd (c) effective July 1, 2010.)

Rule 8.79 amended and renumbered effective January 1, 2017; adopted as rule 8.73 effective July 1, 2010; previously amended effective January 1, 2011.

Rule 8.80. Electronic service [Renumbered]

Rule 8.80 renumbered as rule 8.71 effective January 1, 2011.

Another Rule 8.80 follows in Article 6.

Article 6
Public Access to Electronic Appellate Court Records

Title 8, Appellate Rules—Division 1, Rules Relating to the Supreme Court and Courts of Appeal—Chapter 1, General Provisions—Article 6, Public Access to Electronic Appellate Court Records; adopted effective January 1, 2016.

Rule 8.80. Statement of purpose

(a) Intent

The rules in this article are intended to provide the public with reasonable access to appellate court records that are maintained in electronic form, while protecting privacy interests.

(Subd (a) adopted effective January 1, 2016.)

(b) Benefits of electronic access

Improved technologies provide courts with many alternatives to the historical paper-based record receipt and retention process, including the creation and use of court records maintained in electronic form. Providing public access to appellate court records that are maintained in electronic form may save the courts and the public time, money, and effort and encourage courts to be more efficient in their operations. Improved access to appellate court records may also foster in the public a more comprehensive understanding of the appellate court system.

(Subd (b) adopted effective January 1, 2016.)

(c) No creation of rights

The rules in this article are not intended to give the public a right of access to any record that they are not otherwise entitled to access. The rules do not create any right of access to sealed or confidential records.

(Subd (c) adopted effective January 1, 2016.)

Rule 8.80 adopted effective January 1, 2016.

Advisory Committee Comment

The rules in this article acknowledge the benefits that electronic court records provide but attempt to limit the potential for unjustified intrusions into the privacy of individuals involved in litigation that can occur as a result of remote access to electronic court records. The proposed rules take into account the limited resources currently available in the appellate courts. It is contemplated that the rules may be modified to provide greater electronic access as the courts' technical capabilities improve and with the knowledge gained from the experience of the courts in providing electronic access under these rules.

Subdivision (c). Rules 8.45–8.47 govern sealed and confidential records in the appellate courts.

Rule 8.81. Application and scope

(a) Application

The rules in this article apply only to records of the Supreme Court and Courts of Appeal.

(Subd (a) adopted effective January 1, 2016.)

(b) Access by parties and attorneys

The rules in this article apply only to access to court records by the public. They do not limit access to court records by a party to an action or proceeding, by the attorney of a party, or by other persons or entities that are entitled to access by statute or rule.

(Subd (b) adopted effective January 1, 2016.)

Rule 8.81 adopted effective January 1, 2016.

Rule 8.82. Definitions

As used in this article, the following definitions apply:

(1) "Court record" is any document, paper, exhibit, transcript, or other thing filed in an action or proceeding; any order, judgment, or opinion of the court; and any court minutes, index, register of actions, or docket. The term does not include the personal notes or preliminary memoranda of justices, judges, or other judicial branch personnel.

(2) "Electronic record" is a court record that requires the use of an electronic device to access. The term includes both a record that has been filed electronically and an electronic copy or version of a record that was filed in paper form.

(3) "The public" means an individual, a group, or an entity, including print or electronic media, or the representative of an individual, a group, or an entity.

(4) "Electronic access" means computer access to court records available to the public through both public terminals at the courthouse and remotely, unless otherwise specified in the rules in this article.

(5) Providing electronic access to electronic records "to the extent it is feasible to do so" means that electronic access must be provided to the extent the court determines it has the resources and technical capacity to do so.

(6) "Bulk distribution" means distribution of multiple electronic records that is not done on a case-by-case basis.

Rule 8.82 adopted effective January 1, 2016.

Rule 8.83. Public access

(a) General right of access

All electronic records must be made reasonably available to the public in some form, whether in electronic or in paper form, except sealed or confidential records.

(Subd (a) adopted effective January 1, 2016.)

(b) Electronic access required to extent feasible

(1) Electronic access, both remote and at the courthouse, will be provided to the following court records, except sealed or confidential records, to the extent it is feasible to do so:

(A) Dockets or registers of actions;

(B) Calendars;

(C) Opinions; and

(D) The following Supreme Court records:

i. Results from the most recent Supreme Court weekly conference;

ii. Party briefs in cases argued in the Supreme Court for at least the preceding three years;

iii. Supreme Court minutes from at least the preceding three years.

(2) If a court maintains records in civil cases in addition to those listed in (1) in electronic form, electronic access to these records, except those listed in (c), must be provided both remotely and at the courthouse, to the extent it is feasible to do so.

(Subd (b) adopted effective January 1, 2016.)

(c) Courthouse electronic access only

If a court maintains the following records in electronic form, electronic access to these records must be provided at the courthouse, to the extent it is feasible to do so, but remote electronic access may not be provided to these records:

(1) Any reporter's transcript for which the reporter is entitled to receive a fee; and

(2) Records other than those listed in (b)(1) in the following proceedings:

(A) Proceedings under the Family Code, including proceedings for dissolution, legal separation, and nullity of marriage; child and spousal support proceedings; child custody proceedings; and domestic violence prevention proceedings;

(B) Juvenile court proceedings;

(C) Guardianship or conservatorship proceedings;

(D) Mental health proceedings;

(E) Criminal proceedings;

(F) Civil harassment proceedings under Code of Civil Procedure section 527.6;

(G) Workplace violence prevention proceedings under Code of Civil Procedure section 527.8;

(H) Private postsecondary school violence prevention proceedings under Code of Civil Procedure section 527.85;

(I) Elder or dependent adult abuse prevention proceedings under Welfare and Institutions Code section 15657.03; and

(J) Proceedings to compromise the claims of a minor or a person with a disability.

(Subd (c) adopted effective January 1, 2016.)

(d) Remote electronic access allowed in extraordinary cases

Notwithstanding (c)(2), the presiding justice of the court, or a justice assigned by the presiding justice, may exercise discretion, subject to (d)(1), to permit remote electronic access by the public to all or a portion of the public court records in an individual case if (1) the number of requests for access to documents in the case is extraordinarily high and (2) responding to those requests would significantly burden the operations of the court. An individualized determination must be made in each case in which such remote electronic access is provided.

(1) In exercising discretion under (d), the justice should consider the relevant factors, such as:

(A) The privacy interests of parties, victims, witnesses, and court personnel, and the ability of the court to redact sensitive personal information;

(B) The benefits to and burdens on the parties in allowing remote electronic access; and

(C) The burdens on the court in responding to an extraordinarily high number of requests for access to documents.

(2) The following information must be redacted from records to which the court allows remote access under (d): driver's license numbers; dates of birth; social security numbers; Criminal Identification and Information and National Crime Information numbers; addresses, e-mail addresses, and phone numbers of parties, victims, witnesses, and court personnel; medical or psychiatric information; financial information; account numbers; and other personal identifying information. The court may order any party who files a document containing such information to provide the court with both an original unredacted version of the document for filing in the court file and a redacted version of the document for remote electronic access. No juror names or other juror identifying information may be provided by remote electronic access. Subdivision (d)(2) does not apply to any document in the original court file; it applies only to documents that are made available by remote electronic access.

(3) Five days' notice must be provided to the parties and the public before the court makes a determination to provide remote electronic access under this rule. Notice to the public may be accomplished by posting notice on the court's website. Any person may file comments with the court for consideration, but no hearing is required.

(4) The court's order permitting remote electronic access must specify which court records will be available by remote electronic access and what categories of information are to be redacted. The court is not required to make findings of fact. The court's order must be posted on the court's website and a copy sent to the Judicial Council.

(Subd (d) adopted effective January 1, 2016.)

(e) Access only on a case-by-case basis

With the exception of the records covered by (b)(1), electronic access to an electronic record may be granted only when the record is identified by the number of the case, the caption of the case, the name of a party, the name of the attorney, or the date of oral argument, and only on a case-by-case basis.

(Subd (e) adopted effective January 1, 2016.)

(f) Bulk distribution

Bulk distribution may be provided only of the records covered by (b)(1).

(Subd (f) adopted effective January 1, 2016.)

(g) Records that become inaccessible

If an electronic record to which electronic access has been provided is made inaccessible to the public by court order or by operation of law, the court is not required to take action with respect to any copy of the record that was made by a member of the public before the record became inaccessible.

(Subd (g) adopted effective January 1, 2016.)

Rule 8.83 adopted effective January 1, 2016.

Advisory Committee Comment

The rule allows a level of access by the public to all electronic records that is at least equivalent to the access that is available for paper records and, for some types of records, is much greater. At the same time, it seeks to protect legitimate privacy concerns.

Subdivision (b). Courts should encourage availability of electronic access to court records at public off-site locations.

Subdivision (c). This subdivision excludes certain records (those other than the register, calendar, opinions, and certain Supreme Court records) in specified types of cases (notably criminal, juvenile, and family court matters) from remote electronic access. The committees recognized that while these case records are public records and should remain available at the courthouse, either in paper or electronic form, they often contain sensitive personal information. The court should not publish that information over the Internet. However, the committees also recognized that the use of the Internet may be appropriate in certain individual cases of extraordinary public interest where information regarding a case will be widely disseminated through the media. In such cases, posting of selected nonconfidential court records, redacted where necessary to protect the privacy of the participants, may provide more timely and accurate information regarding the court proceedings, and may relieve substantial burdens on court staff in responding to individual requests for documents and information. Thus, under subdivision (d), if the presiding justice makes individualized determinations in a specific case, certain records in individual cases may be made available over the Internet.

Subdivision (d). Courts must send a copy of the order permitting remote electronic access in extraordinary cases to: Legal Services, Judicial Council of California, 455 Golden Gate Avenue, San Francisco, CA 94102-3688.

Subdivisions (e) and (f). These subdivisions limit electronic access to records (other than the register, calendars, opinions, and certain Supreme Court records) to a case-by-case basis and prohibit bulk distribution of those records. These limitations are based on the qualitative difference between obtaining information from a specific case file and obtaining bulk information that may be manipulated to compile personal information culled from any document, paper, or exhibit filed in a lawsuit. This type of aggregate information may be exploited for commercial or other purposes unrelated to the operations of the courts, at the expense of privacy rights of individuals.

Rule 8.84. Limitations and conditions

(a) Means of access

Electronic access to records required under this article must be provided by means of a network or software that is based on industry standards or is in the public domain.

(Subd (a) adopted effective January 1, 2016.)

(b) Official record

Unless electronically certified by the court, a court record available by electronic access is not the official record of the court.

(Subd (b) adopted effective January 1, 2016.)

(c) Conditions of use by persons accessing records

Electronic access to court records may be conditioned on:

(1) The user's consent to access the records only as instructed; and

(2) The user's consent to monitoring of access to its records.

The court must give notice of these conditions, in any manner it deems appropriate. Access may be denied to a member of the public for failure to comply with either of these conditions of use.

(Subd (c) adopted effective January 1, 2016.)

(d) Notices to persons accessing records

The court must give notice of the following information to members of the public accessing its records electronically, in any manner it deems appropriate:

(1) The identity of the court staff member to be contacted about the requirements for accessing the court's records electronically.

(2) That copyright and other proprietary rights may apply to information in a case file, absent an express grant of additional rights by the holder of the copyright or other proprietary right. This notice must advise the public that:

(A) Use of such information in a case file is permissible only to the extent permitted by law or court order; and

(B) Any use inconsistent with proprietary rights is prohibited.

(3) Whether electronic records are the official records of the court. The notice must describe the procedure and any fee required for obtaining a certified copy of an official record of the court.

(4) That any person who willfully destroys or alters any court record maintained in electronic form is subject to the penalties imposed by Government Code section 6201.

(Subd (d) adopted effective January 1, 2016.)

(e) Access policy

A privacy policy must be posted on the California Courts public-access website to inform members of the public accessing its electronic records of the information collected regarding access transactions and the uses that may be made of the collected information.

(Subd (e) adopted effective January 1, 2016.)
Rule 8.84 adopted effective January 1, 2016.

Rule 8.85. Fees for copies of electronic records

The court may impose fees for the costs of providing copies of its electronic records, under Government Code section 68928.

Rule 8.85 adopted effective January 1, 2016.

Article 7
Privacy

Title 8, Appellate Rules—Division 1, Rules Relating to the Supreme Court and Courts of Appeal—Chapter 1, General Provisions—Article 7, Privacy; adopted effective January 1, 2017.

Rule 8.90. Privacy in opinions

(a) Application

(1) This rule provides guidance on the use of names in appellate court opinions.

(2) Reference to juveniles in juvenile court proceedings is governed by rule 8.401(a).

(3) Where other laws establish specific privacy-protection requirements that differ from the provisions in this rule, those specific requirements supersede the provisions in this rule.

(Subd (a) adopted effective January 1, 2017.)

(b) Persons protected

To protect personal privacy interests, in all opinions, the reviewing court should consider referring to the following people by first name and last initial or, if the first name is unusual or other circumstances would defeat the objective of anonymity, by initials only:

(1) Children in all proceedings under the Family Code and protected persons in domestic violence-prevention proceedings;

(2) Wards in guardianship proceedings and conservatees in conservatorship proceedings;

(3) Patients in mental health proceedings;

(4) Victims in criminal proceedings;

(5) Protected persons in civil harassment proceedings under Code of Civil Procedure section 527.6;

(6) Protected persons in workplace violence-prevention proceedings under Code of Civil Procedure section 527.8;

(7) Protected persons in private postsecondary school violence-prevention proceedings under Code of Civil Procedure section 527.85;

(8) Protected persons in elder or dependent adult abuse-prevention proceedings under Welfare and Institutions Code section 15657.03;

(9) Minors or persons with disabilities in proceedings to compromise the claims of a minor or a person with a disability;

(10) Persons in other circumstances in which personal privacy interests support not using the person's name; and

(11) Persons in other circumstances in which use of that person's full name would defeat the objective of anonymity for a person identified in (1)–(10).

(Subd (b) adopted effective January 1, 2017.)
Rule 8.90 adopted effective January 1, 2017.

Advisory Committee Comment

Subdivision (b)(1)–(9) lists people in proceedings under rule 8.83 for which remote electronic access to records—except dockets or registers of actions, calendars, opinions, and certain Supreme Court records—may not be provided. If the court maintains these records in electronic form, electronic access must be provided at the courthouse only, to the extent it is feasible to do so. (Cal. Rules of Court, rule 8.83(c).) Subdivision (b)(1)–(9) recognize the privacy considerations of certain persons subject to the proceedings listed in rule 8.83(c). Subdivision (b)(10) recognizes people in circumstances other than the listed proceedings, such as witnesses, in which the court should consider referring to a person by first name and last initial, or, if the first name is unusual or other circumstances would defeat the objective of protecting personal privacy interests, by initials. Subdivision (b)(11) recognizes people in circumstances other than the listed proceedings, such as relatives, in which the court should consider referring to a person by first name and last initial or by initials if the use of that person's full name would identify another person whose personal privacy interests support remaining anonymous.

Chapter 2
Civil Appeals

Article 1
Taking the Appeal

Rule 8.100.   Filing the appeal

(a) Notice of appeal

(1) To appeal from a superior court judgment or an appealable order of a superior court, other than in a limited civil case, an appellant must serve and file a notice of appeal in that superior court. The appellant or the appellant's attorney must sign the notice.

(2) The notice of appeal must be liberally construed. The notice is sufficient if it identifies the particular judgment or order being appealed. The notice need not specify the court to which the appeal is taken; the appeal will be treated as taken to the Court of Appeal for the district in which the superior court is located.

(3) Failure to serve the notice of appeal neither prevents its filing nor affects its validity, but the appellant may be required to remedy the failure.

(b) Fee and deposit

(1) Unless otherwise provided by law, the notice of appeal must be accompanied by the $775 filing fee under Government Code sections 68926 and 68926.1(b), an application for a waiver of court fees and costs on appeal under rule 8.26, or an order granting such an application. The fee may be paid by check or money order payable to "Clerk/Executive Officer, Court of Appeal"; if the fee is paid in cash, the clerk must give a receipt. The fee may also be paid by any method permitted by the court pursuant to rules 2.258 and 8.78.

(2) The appellant must also deposit $100 with the superior court clerk as required under Government Code section 68926.1, unless otherwise provided by law or the superior court waives the deposit.

(3) The clerk must file the notice of appeal even if the appellant does not present the filing fee, the deposit, or an application for, or order granting, a waiver of fees and costs.

(Subd (b) amended effective January 1, 2018; previously amended effective August 17, 2003, January 1, 2007, July 1, 2009, July 27, 2012, and January 1, 2016.)

(c) Failure to pay filing fee

(1) The reviewing court clerk must promptly notify the appellant in writing if:

(A) The reviewing court receives a notice of appeal without the filing fee required by (b)(1), a certificate of cash payment under (e)(5), or an application for, or order granting, a fee waiver under rule 8.26;

(B) A check for the filing fee is dishonored; or

(C) An application for a waiver under rule 8.26 is denied.

(2) A clerk's notice under (1)(A) or (B) must state that the court may dismiss the appeal unless, within 15 days after the notice is sent, the appellant either:

(A) Pays the fee; or

(B) Files an application for a waiver under rule 8.26 if the appellant has not previously filed such an application.

(3) If the appellant fails to take the action specified in a notice given under (2), the reviewing court may dismiss the appeal, but may vacate the dismissal for good cause.

(Subd (c) amended effective July 1, 2009; previously amended effective January 1, 2007, and January 1, 2008.)

(d) Failure to pay deposit

(1) If the appellant fails to pay the deposit to the superior court required under (b)(2), the superior court clerk must promptly notify the appellant in writing that the reviewing court may dismiss the appeal unless, within 15 days after the notice is sent, the appellant either:

(A) Makes the deposit; or

(B) Files an application in the superior court for a waiver of fees and costs if the appellant has not previously filed such an application or an order granting such an application.

(2) If the appellant fails to take the action specified in a notice given under (1), the superior court clerk must notify the reviewing court of the default.

(3) If the superior court clerk notifies the reviewing court of a default under (2), the reviewing court may dismiss the appeal, but may vacate the dismissal for good cause.

(Subd (d) amended effective July 1, 2009; adopted effective January 1, 2008.)

(e) Superior court clerk's duties

(1) The superior court clerk must promptly send a notification of the filing of the notice of appeal to the attorney of record for each party, to any unrepresented party, and to the reviewing court clerk.

(2) The notification must show the date it was sent and must state the number and title of the case and the date the notice of appeal was filed. If the information is available, the notification must include:

(A) The name, address, telephone number, e-mail address, and California State Bar number of each attorney of record in the case;

(B) The name of the party each attorney represented in the superior court; and

(C) The name, address, telephone number and e-mail address of any unrepresented party.

(3) A copy of the notice of appeal is sufficient notification under (1) if the required information is on the copy or is added by the superior court clerk.

(4) The sending of a notification under (1) is a sufficient performance of the clerk's duty despite the death of the party or the discharge, disqualification, suspension, disbarment, or death of the attorney.

(5) With the notification of the appeal, the superior court clerk must send the reviewing court the filing fee or an application for, or order granting, a waiver of that fee. If the fee was paid in cash, the clerk must send the reviewing court a certificate of payment and thereafter a check for the amount of the fee.

(6) Failure to comply with any provision of this subdivision does not affect the validity of the notice of appeal.

(Subd (e) amended effective January 1, 2016; adopted as subd (d) effective January 1, 2002; previously amended effective January 1, 2007; relettered effective January 1, 2008.)

(f) Notice of cross-appeal

As used in this rule, "notice of appeal" includes a notice of cross-appeal and "appellant" includes a respondent filing a notice of cross-appeal.

(Subd (f) relettered effective January 1, 2008; adopted as subd (e) effective January 1, 2002.)

(g) Civil case information statement

(1) Within 15 days after the superior court clerk sends the notification of the filing of the notice of appeal required by (e)(1), the appellant must serve and file in the reviewing court a completed *Civil Case Information Statement* (form APP-004), attaching a copy of the judgment or appealed order that shows the date it was entered.

(2) If the appellant fails to timely file a case information statement under (1), the reviewing court clerk must notify the appellant in writing that the appellant must file the statement within 15 days after the clerk's notice is sent and that if the appellant fails to comply, the court may either impose monetary sanctions or dismiss the appeal. If the appellant fails to file the statement as specified in the notice, the court may impose the sanctions specified in the notice.

(Subd (g) amended effective January 1, 2016; adopted as subd (f) effective January 1, 2003; previously amended and relettered as subd (g) effective January 1, 2008; previously amended effective January 1, 2007, and January 1, 2014.)
Rule 8.100 amended effective January 1, 2018; repealed and adopted as rule 1 effective January 1, 2002; previously amended and renumbered as rule 8.100 effective January 1, 2007; previously amended effective January 1, 2003, August 17, 2003, January 1, 2008, July 1, 2009, July 27, 2012, January 1, 2014, and January 1, 2016.

Advisory Committee Comment

Subdivision (a). In subdivision (a)(1), the reference to "judgment" is intended to include part of a judgment. Subdivision (a)(1) includes an explicit reference to "appealable order" to ensure that litigants do not overlook the applicability of this rule to such orders.

Subdivision (c)(2). This subdivision addresses the content of a clerk's notice that a check for the filing fee has been dishonored or that the reviewing court has received a notice of appeal without the filing fee, a certificate of cash payment, or an application for, or order granting, a fee waiver. Rule 8.26(f) addresses what an appellant must do when a fee waiver application is denied.

Subdivision (e). Under subdivision (e)(2), a notification of the filing of a notice of appeal must show the date that the clerk sent the document. This provision is intended to establish the date when the 20-day extension of the time to file a cross-appeal under rule 8.108(e) begins to run.

Subdivision (e)(1) requires the clerk to send a notification of the filing of notice of appeal to the appellant's attorney or to the appellant if unrepresented. Knowledge of the date of that notification allows the appellant's attorney or the appellant to track the running of the 20-day extension of time to file a cross-appeal under rule 8.108(e).

Rule 8.104.   Time to appeal

(a) Normal time

(1) Unless a statute or rules 8.108, 8.702, or 8.712 provide otherwise, a notice of appeal must be filed on or before the earliest of:

(A) 60 days after the superior court clerk serves on the party filing the notice of appeal a document entitled "Notice of Entry" of judgment or a filed-endorsed copy of the judgment, showing the date either was served;

(B) 60 days after the party filing the notice of appeal serves or is served by a party with a document entitled "Notice of Entry" of judgment or a filed-endorsed copy of the judgment, accompanied by proof of service; or

(C) 180 days after entry of judgment.

(2) Service under (1)(A) and (B) may be by any method permitted by the Code of Civil Procedure, including electronic service when permitted under Code of Civil Procedure section 1010.6 and rules 2.250–2.261.

(3) If the parties stipulated in the trial court under Code of Civil Procedure section 1019.5 to waive notice of the court order being appealed, the time to appeal under (1)(C) applies unless the court or a party serves notice of entry of judgment or a filed-endorsed copy of the judgment to start the time period under (1)(A) or (B).

(Subd (a) amended effective July 1, 2017; previously amended effective January 1, 2007, January 1, 2010, July 1, 2012, July 1, 2014, and January 1, 2016.)

(b) No extension of time; late notice of appeal

Except as provided in rule 8.66, no court may extend the time to file a notice of appeal. If a notice of appeal is filed late, the reviewing court must dismiss the appeal.

(Subd (b) amended effective January 1, 2007; adopted effective January 1, 2005.)

(c) What constitutes entry

For purposes of this rule:

(1) The entry date of a judgment is the date the judgment is filed under Code of Civil Procedure section 668.5, or the date it is entered in the judgment book.

(2) The entry date of an appealable order that is entered in the minutes is the date it is entered in the permanent minutes. But if the minute order directs that a written order be prepared, the entry date is the date the signed order is filed; a written order prepared under rule 3.1312 or similar local rule is not such an order prepared by direction of a minute order.

(3) The entry date of an appealable order that is not entered in the minutes is the date the signed order is filed.

(4) The entry date of a decree of distribution in a probate proceeding is the date it is entered at length in the judgment book or other permanent court record.

(5) An order signed electronically has the same effect as an order signed on paper.

(Subd (c) amended effective January 1, 2017; adopted as subd (c) effective January 1, 2002; relettered as subd (d) effective January 1, 2005; previously amended effective January 1, 2007; previously repealed and relettered as subd (c) effective January 1, 2011.)

(d) Premature notice of appeal

(1) A notice of appeal filed after judgment is rendered but before it is entered is valid and is treated as filed immediately after entry of judgment.

(2) The reviewing court may treat a notice of appeal filed after the superior court has announced its intended ruling, but before it has rendered judgment, as filed immediately after entry of judgment.

(Subd (d) relettered effective January 1, 2011; adopted as subd (d) effective January 1, 2002; previously relettered as subd (e) effective January 1, 2005.)

(e) Appealable order

As used in (a) and (d), "judgment" includes an appealable order if the appeal is from an appealable order.

(Subd (e) amended effective July 1, 2011; adopted as subd (f); previously amended effective January 1, 2005; previously relettered effective January 1, 2011.)

Rule 8.104 amended effective July 1, 2017; repealed and adopted as rule 2 effective January 1, 2002; previously amended and renumbered as rule 8.104 effective January 1, 2007; previously amended effective January 1, 2005, January 1, 2010, January 1, 2011, July 1, 2011, July 1, 2012, July 1, 2014, January 1, 2016, and January 1, 2017.

Advisory Committee Comment

Subdivision (a). This subdivision establishes the standard time for filing a notice of appeal and identifies rules that establish very limited exceptions to this standard time period for cases involving certain postjudgment motions and cross-appeals (rule 8.108), certain expedited appeals under the California Environmental Quality Act (rule 8.702), and appeals under Code of Civil Procedure section 1294.4 of an order dismissing or denying a petition to compel arbitration (rule 8.712).

Under subdivision (a)(1)(A), a notice of entry of judgment (or a copy of the judgment) must show the date on which the clerk served the document. The proof of service establishes the date that the 60-day period under subdivision (a)(1)(A) begins to run.

Subdivision (a)(1)(B) requires that a notice of entry of judgment (or a copy of the judgment) served by or on a party be accompanied by proof of service. The proof of service establishes the date that the 60-day period under subdivision (a)(1)(B)

begins to run. Although the general rule on service (rule 8.25(a)) requires proof of service for all documents served by parties, the requirement is reiterated here because of the serious consequence of a failure to file a timely notice of appeal (see subd. (e)).

Subdivision (b). See rule 8.25(b)(5) for provisions concerning the timeliness of documents mailed by inmates and patients from custodial institutions. Subdivision (b) is declarative of the case law, which holds that the reviewing court lacks jurisdiction to excuse a late-filed notice of appeal. (*Hollister Convalescent Hosp., Inc. v. Rico* (1975) 15 Cal.3d 660, 666–674; *Estate of Hanley* (1943) 23 Cal.2d 120, 122–124.)

In criminal cases, the time for filing a notice of appeal is governed by rule 8.308 and by the case law of "constructive filing." (See, e.g., *In re Benoit* (1973) 10 Cal.3d 72.)

Rule 8.108. Extending the time to appeal

(a) Extension of time

This rule operates only to extend the time to appeal otherwise prescribed in rule 8.104(a); it does not shorten the time to appeal. If the normal time to appeal stated in rule 8.104(a) is longer than the time provided in this rule, the time to appeal stated in rule 8.104(a) governs.

(Subd (a) adopted effective January 1, 2008.)

(b) Motion for new trial

If any party serves and files a valid notice of intention to move for a new trial, the following extensions of time apply:

(1) If the motion for a new trial is denied, the time to appeal from the judgment is extended for all parties until the earliest of:

(A) 30 days after the superior court clerk or a party serves an order denying the motion or a notice of entry of that order;

(B) 30 days after denial of the motion by operation of law; or

(C) 180 days after entry of judgment.

(2) If the trial court makes a finding of excessive or inadequate damages and grants the motion for a new trial subject to the condition that the motion is denied if a party consents to the additur or remittitur of damages, the time to appeal is extended as follows:

(A) If a party serves an acceptance of the additur or remittitur within the time for accepting the additur or remittitur, the time to appeal from the judgment is extended for all parties until 30 days after the date the party serves the acceptance.

(B) If a party serves a rejection of the additur or remittitur within the time for accepting the additur or remittitur or if the time for accepting the additur or remittitur expires, the time to appeal from the new trial order is extended for all parties until the earliest of 30 days after the date the party serves the rejection or 30 days after the date on which the time for accepting the additur or remittitur expired.

(Subd (b) amended effective July 1, 2012; adopted as subd (a) effective January 1, 2002; previously amended and relettered effective January 1, 2008; previously amended effective January 1, 2011.)

(c) Motion to vacate judgment

If, within the time prescribed by rule 8.104 to appeal from the judgment, any party serves and files a valid notice of intention to move—or a valid motion—to vacate the judgment, the time to appeal from the judgment is extended for all parties until the earliest of:

(1) 30 days after the superior court clerk or a party serves an order denying the motion or a notice of entry of that order;

(2) 90 days after the first notice of intention to move—or motion—is filed; or

(3) 180 days after entry of judgment.

(Subd (c) amended effective January 1, 2011; adopted as subd (b) effective January 1, 2002; previously amended effective January 1, 2007; previously relettered effective January 1, 2008.)

(d) Motion for judgment notwithstanding the verdict

(1) If any party serves and files a valid motion for judgment notwithstanding the verdict and the motion is denied, the time to appeal from the judgment is extended for all parties until the earliest of:

(A) 30 days after the superior court clerk or a party serves an order denying the motion or a notice of entry of that order;

(B) 30 days after denial of the motion by operation of law; or

(C) 180 days after entry of judgment.

(2) Unless extended by (g)(2), the time to appeal from an order denying a motion for judgment notwithstanding the verdict is governed by rule 8.104.

(Subd (d) amended effective January 1, 2015; adopted as subd (c) effective January 1, 2002; previously relettered as subd (d) effective January 1, 2008; previously amended effective January 1, 2007, and January 1, 2011.)

(e) Motion to reconsider appealable order

If any party serves and files a valid motion to reconsider an appealable order under Code of Civil Procedure section 1008, subdivision (a), the time to appeal from that order is extended for all parties until the earliest of:

(1) 30 days after the superior court clerk or a party serves an order denying the motion or a notice of entry of that order;

(2) 90 days after the first motion to reconsider is filed; or

(3) 180 days after entry of the appealable order.

(Subd (e) amended effective January 1, 2011; adopted as subd (d) effective January 1, 2002; previously relettered effective January 1, 2008.)

(f) Public entity actions under Government Code section 962, 984, or 985

If a public entity defendant serves and files a valid request for a mandatory settlement conference on methods of satisfying a judgment under Government Code section 962, an election to pay a judgment in periodic payments under Government Code section 984 and rule 3.1804, or a motion for a posttrial hearing on reducing a judgment under Government Code section 985, the time to appeal from the judgment is extended for all parties until the earliest of:

(1) 90 days after the superior court clerk serves the party filing the notice of appeal with a document entitled "Notice of Entry" of judgment, or a filed-endorsed copy of the judgment, showing the date either was served;

(2) 90 days after the party filing the notice of appeal serves or is served by a party with a document entitled "Notice of Entry" of judgment or a filed-endorsed copy of the judgment, accompanied by proof of service; or

(3) 180 days after entry of judgment.

(Subd (f) amended effective January 1, 2016; adopted effective January 1, 2011.)

(g) Cross-appeal

(1) If an appellant timely appeals from a judgment or appealable order, the time for any other party to appeal from the same judgment or order is extended until 20 days after the superior court clerk serves notification of the first appeal.

(2) If an appellant timely appeals from an order granting a motion for new trial, an order granting—within 150 days after entry of judgment—a motion to vacate the judgment, or a judgment notwithstanding the verdict, the time for any other party to appeal from the original judgment or from an order denying a motion for judgment notwithstanding the verdict is extended until 20 days after the clerk serves notification of the first appeal.

(Subd (g) amended and relettered effective January 1, 2011; adopted as subd (e) effective January 1, 2002; previously relettered as subd (f) effective January 1, 2008.)

(h) Service; proof of service

Service under this rule may be by any method permitted by the Code of Civil Procedure, including electronic service when permitted under Code of Civil Procedure section 1010.6 and rules 2.250–2.261. An order or notice that is served must be accompanied by proof of service.

(Subd (h) amended and relettered effective January 1, 2011; adopted as subd (f) effective January 1, 2002; previously relettered as subd (g) effective January 1, 2008.)

Rule 8.108 amended effective January 1, 2016; repealed and adopted as rule 3 effective January 1, 2002; previously amended and renumbered as rule 8.108 effective January 1, 2007; previously amended effective January 1, 2008, January 1, 2011, July 1, 2012, and January 1, 2015.

Advisory Committee Comment

Subdivisions (b)–(f) operate only when a party serves and files a "valid" motion, election, request, or notice of intent to move for the relief in question. As used in these provisions, the word "valid" means only that the motion, election, request, or notice complies with all procedural requirements; it does not mean that the motion, election, request, or notice must also be substantively meritorious. For example, under the rule a timely new trial motion on the ground of excessive damages (Code Civ. Proc., § 657) extends the time to appeal from the judgment even if the trial court ultimately determines the damages were not excessive. Similarly, a timely motion to reconsider (*id.*, § 1008) extends the time to appeal from an appealable order for which reconsideration was sought even if the trial court ultimately determines the motion was not "based upon new or different facts, circumstances, or law," as subdivision (a) of section 1008 requires.

Subdivision (b). Subdivision (b)(1) provides that the denial of a motion for new trial triggers a 30-day extension of the time to appeal from the judgment beginning on the date that the superior court clerk or a party serves either the order of denial or a notice of entry of that order. This provision is intended to eliminate a trap for litigants and to make the rule consistent with the primary rule on the time to appeal from the judgment (rule 8.104(a)).

Subdivision (c). The Code of Civil Procedure provides two distinct statutory motions to vacate a judgment: (1) a motion to vacate a judgment and enter "another and different judgment" because of judicial error (*id.*, § 663), which requires a notice of intention to move to vacate (*id.*, § 663a); and (2) a motion to vacate a judgment because of mistake, inadvertence, surprise, or neglect, which requires a motion to vacate but not a notice of intention to so move (*id.*, § 473, subd. (b)). The courts also recognize certain nonstatutory motions to vacate a judgment, e.g., when the judgment is void on the face of the record or was obtained by extrinsic fraud. (See 8 Witkin, Cal. Procedure (4th ed. 1997) Attack on Judgment in Trial Court, §§ 222–236, pp. 726–750.) Subdivision (c) is intended to apply to all such motions.

In subdivision (c) the phrase "within the time prescribed by rule 8.104 to appeal from the judgment" is intended to incorporate in full the provisions of rule 8.104(a).

Under subdivision (c)(1), the 30-day extension of the time to appeal from the judgment begins when the superior court clerk or a party serves the order denying the motion or notice of entry of that order. This provision is discussed further under subdivision (b) of this comment.

Subdivision (d). Subdivision (d)(1) provides an extension of time after an order denying a motion for judgment notwithstanding the verdict regardless of whether the moving party also moved unsuccessfully for a new trial.

Subdivision (d) further specifies the times to appeal when, as often occurs, a motion for judgment notwithstanding the verdict is joined with a motion for new trial and both motions are denied. Under subdivision (b), the appellant has 30 days after notice of the denial of the new trial motion to appeal from the judgment. Subdivision (d) allows the appellant the longer time provided by rule 8.104 to appeal from the order denying the motion for judgment notwithstanding the verdict, subject to that time being further extended in the circumstances covered by subdivision (g)(2).

Under subdivision (d)(1)(A), the 30-day extension of the time to appeal from the judgment begins when the superior court clerk or a party serves the order denying the motion or notice of entry of that order. This provision is discussed further under subdivision (b) of this comment.

Subdivision (e). The scope of subdivision (e) is specific. It applies to any "appealable order," whether made before or after judgment (see Code Civ. Proc., § 904.1, subd. (a)(2)–(12)), but it extends only the time to appeal "from that order." The subdivision thus takes no position on whether a judgment is subject to a motion to reconsider (see, e.g., *Ramon v. Aerospace Corp.* (1996) 50 Cal.App.4th 1233, 1236–1238 [postjudgment motion to reconsider order granting summary judgment did not extend time to appeal from judgment because trial court had no power to rule on such motion after entry of judgment]), or whether an order denying a motion to reconsider is itself appealable (compare *Santee v. Santa Clara County Office of Education* (1990) 220 Cal.App.3d 702, 710–711 [order appealable if motion based on new facts] with *Rojes v. Riverside General Hospital* (1988) 203 Cal.App.3d 1151, 1160–1161 [order not appealable under any circumstances]). Both these issues are legislative matters.

Subdivision (e) applies only when a "party" makes a valid motion to "reconsider" an appealable order under subdivision (a) of Code of Civil Procedure section 1008; it therefore does not apply when a court reconsiders an order on its own motion (*id.*, subd. (d)) or when a party makes "a subsequent application for the same order" (*id.*, subd. (c)). The statute provides no time limits within which either of the latter events must occur.

Under subdivision (e)(1), the 30-day extension of the time to appeal from the order begins when the superior court clerk or a party serves the order denying the motion or notice of entry of that order. The purpose of this provision is discussed further under subdivision (b) of this comment.

Among its alternative periods of extension of the time to appeal, subdivision (e) provides in paragraph (2) for a 90-day period beginning on the filing of the motion to reconsider or, if there is more than one such motion, the filing of the first such motion. The provision is consistent with subdivision (c)(2), governing motions to vacate judgment; as in the case of those motions, there is no time limit for a ruling on a motion to reconsider.

Subdivision (g). Consistent with case law, subdivision (g)(1) extends the time to appeal after another party appeals only if the later appeal is taken "from the same order or judgment as the first appeal." (*Commercial & Farmers Nat. Bank v. Edwards* (1979) 91 Cal.App.3d 699, 704.)

The former rule (former rule 3(c), second sentence) provided an extension of time for filing a protective cross-appeal from the judgment when the trial court granted a motion for new trial or a motion to vacate the judgment, but did not provide the same extension when the trial court granted a motion for judgment notwithstanding the verdict. One case declined to infer that the omission was unintentional, but suggested that the Judicial Council might consider amending the rule to fill the gap. (*Lippert v. AVCO Community Developers, Inc.* (1976) 60 Cal.App.3d 775, 778 & fn. 3.) Rule 8.108(e)(2) fills the gap thus identified.

Subdivision (h). Under subdivision (h), an order or notice that is served under this rule must be accompanied by proof of service. The date of the proof of service establishes the date when an extension of the time to appeal begins to run after service of such an order or notice.

Rule 8.112. Petition for writ of supersedeas

(a) Petition

(1) A party seeking a stay of the enforcement of a judgment or order pending appeal may serve and file a petition for writ of supersedeas in the reviewing court.

(2) The petition must bear the same title as the appeal and, if known, the appeal's docket number.

(3) The petition must explain the necessity for the writ and include a memorandum.

(4) If the record has not been filed in the reviewing court:

(A) The petition must include a statement of the case sufficient to show that the petitioner will raise substantial issues on appeal, including a fair summary of the material facts and the issues that are likely to be raised on appeal.

(B) The petitioner must file the following documents with the petition:

(i) The judgment or order, showing its date of entry;

(ii) The notice of appeal, showing its date of filing;

(iii) A reporter's transcript of any oral statement by the court supporting its rulings related to the issues that are likely to be raised on appeal, or, if a transcript is unavailable, a declaration fairly summarizing any such statements;

(iv) Any application for a stay filed in the trial court, any opposition to that application, and a reporter's transcript of the oral proceedings concerning the stay or, if a transcript is unavailable, a declaration fairly summarizing the proceedings, including the parties' arguments and any statement by the court supporting its ruling; and

(v) Any other document from the trial court proceeding that is necessary for proper consideration of the petition.

(C) The documents listed in (B) must comply with the following requirements:

(i) If filed in paper form, they must be bound together at the end of the petition or in separate volumes not exceeding 300 pages each. The pages must be consecutively numbered;

(ii) If filed in paper form, they must be index-tabbed by number or letter, and

(iii) They must begin with a table of contents listing each document by its title and its index number or letter.

(5) The petition must be verified.

(Subd (a) amended effective January 1, 2016; previously amended effective January 1, 2007, January 1, 2008, January 1, 2010, and July 1, 2013.)

(b) Opposition

(1) Unless otherwise ordered, any opposition must be served and filed within 15 days after the petition is filed.

(2) An opposition must state any material facts not included in the petition and include a memorandum.

(3) The court may not issue a writ of supersedeas until the respondent has had the opportunity to file an opposition.

(Subd (b) amended effective January 1, 2007.)

(c) Temporary stay

(1) The petition may include a request for a temporary stay under rule 8.116 pending the ruling on the petition.

(2) A separately filed request for a temporary stay must be served on the respondent. For good cause, the Chief Justice or presiding justice may excuse advance service.

(Subd (c) amended effective January 1, 2007.)

(d) Issuing the writ

(1) The court may issue the writ on any conditions it deems just.

(2) The court must hold a hearing before it may issue a writ staying an order that awards or changes the custody of a minor.

(3) The court must notify the superior court, under rule 8.489, of any writ or temporary stay that it issues.

(Subd (d) amended effective January 1, 2009; previously amended effective January 1, 2007, and January 1, 2008.)

Rule 8.112 amended effective January 1, 2016; repealed and adopted as rule 49 effective January 1, 2005; previously amended and renumbered as rule 8.112 effective January 1, 2007; previously amended effective January 1, 2008, January 1, 2009, January 1, 2010, and July 1, 2013.

Advisory Committee Comment

Subdivision (a). If the preparation of a reporter's transcript has not yet been completed at that time a petition for a writ of supersedeas is filed, that transcript is "unavailable" within the meaning of (a)(4)(B).

Rule 8.116. Request for writ of supersedeas or temporary stay

(a) Information on cover

If a petition for original writ, petition for review, or any other document requests a writ of supersedeas or temporary stay from a reviewing court, the cover of the document must:

(1) Prominently display the notice "STAY REQUESTED"; and

(2) Identify the nature and date of the proceeding or act sought to be stayed.

(Subd (a) amended effective January 1, 2007.)

(b) Additional information

The following information must appear either on the cover or at the beginning of the text:

(1) The trial court and department involved; and

(2) The name and telephone number of the trial judge whose order the request seeks to stay.

(Subd (b) amended effective January 1, 2007.)

(c) Sanction

If the document does not comply with (a) and (b), the reviewing court may decline to consider the request for writ of supersedeas or temporary stay.

Rule 8.116 amended and renumbered effective January 1, 2007; repealed and adopted as rule 49.5 effective January 1, 2005.

Article 2
Record on Appeal

Rule 8.120. Clerk's transcript [Renumbered]

Rule 8.120 renumbered as Rule 8.122 effective January 1, 2008.

Another Rule 8.120 follows.

Rule 8.120. Record on appeal

Except as otherwise provided in this chapter, the record on an appeal in a civil case must contain the records specified in (a) and (b), which constitute the normal record on appeal.

(a) Record of written documents

(1) A record of the written documents from the superior court proceedings in the form of one of the following:

(A) A clerk's transcript under rule 8.122;

(B) An appendix under rule 8.124;

(C) The original superior court file under rule 8.128, if a local rule of the reviewing court permits this form of the record;

(D) An agreed statement under rule 8.134(a)(2); or

(E) A settled statement under rule 8.137.

(2) If an appellant intends to raise any issue that requires consideration of the record of an administrative proceeding that was admitted in evidence, refused, or lodged in the superior court, the record on appeal must include that administrative record, transmitted under rule 8.123.

(Subd (a) adopted effective January 1, 2008.)

(b) Record of the oral proceedings

If an appellant intends to raise any issue that requires consideration of the oral proceedings in the superior court, the record on appeal must include a record of these oral proceedings in the form of one of the following:

(1) A reporter's transcript under rule 8.130;

(2) An agreed statement under rule 8.134; or

(3) A settled statement under rule 8.137.

(Subd (b) adopted effective January 1, 2008.)

Rule 8.120 adopted effective January 1, 2008.

Advisory Committee Comment

Rules 8.45–8.47 address the appropriate handling of sealed and confidential records that are included in the record on appeal. Examples of confidential records include records of the family conciliation court (Fam. Code, § 1818 (b)) and fee waiver applications (Gov. Code, § 68633(f)).

Rule 8.121. Notice designating the record on appeal

(a) Time to file

Within 10 days after filing the notice of appeal, an appellant must serve and file a notice in the superior court designating the record on appeal. The appellant may combine its notice designating the record with its notice of appeal.

(Subd (a) adopted effective January 1, 2008.)

(b) Contents

(1) The notice must:

(A) Specify the date the notice of appeal was filed.

(B) Specify which form of the record of the written documents from the superior court proceedings listed in rule 8.120(a)(1) the appellant elects to use. If the appellant elects to use a clerk's transcript, the notice must also designate the documents to be included in the clerk's transcript as required under rule 8.122(b)(1).

(C) Specify whether the appellant elects to proceed with or without a record of the oral proceedings in the trial court. If the appellant elects to proceed with a record of the oral proceedings in the trial court, the notice must specify which form of the record listed in rule 8.120(b) the appellant elects to use. If the appellant elects to use a reporter's transcript, the notice must designate the proceedings to be included in the transcript as required under rule 8.130.

(2) If an appellant intends to raise any issue that requires consideration of the record of an administrative proceeding that was admitted in evidence, refused, or lodged in the superior court, the notice must also request that this administrative record be transmitted to the reviewing court under rule 8.123.

(Subd (b) adopted effective January 1, 2008.)

(c) Copy to the reviewing court

The clerk must promptly send the reviewing court a copy of any notice filed under this rule.

(Subd (c) adopted effective January 1, 2008.)

Rule 8.121 adopted effective January 1, 2008.

Advisory Committee Comment

The Judicial Council has adopted an optional form—*Appellant's Notice Designating Record on Appeal* (form APP-003)—that can be used to provide the notice required by this rule.

This rule makes the filing of a notice designating the record an "act required to procure the record" within the meaning of rule 8.140(a). Under that rule, a failure to file such a notice triggers the clerk's duty to issue a 15-day notice of default and thereby allows the appellant to cure the default in superior court.

Rule 8.122.   Clerk's transcript

(a) Designation

(1) A notice designating documents to be included in a clerk's transcript must identify each designated document by its title and filing date or, if the filing date is not available, the date it was signed. The notice may specify portions of designated documents that are not to be included in the transcript. For minute orders or instructions, it is sufficient to collectively designate all minute orders or all minute orders entered between specified dates, or all written jury instructions given, refused, or withdrawn.

(2) Within 10 days after the appellant serves its notice designating a clerk's transcript, the respondent may serve and file a notice in superior court designating any additional documents the respondent wants included in the transcript.

(3) Except as provided in (b)(4), all exhibits admitted in evidence, refused, or lodged are deemed part of the record, but a party wanting a copy of an exhibit included in the transcript must specify that exhibit by number or letter in its notice of designation. If the superior court has returned a designated exhibit to a party, the party in possession of the exhibit must deliver it to the superior court clerk within 10 days after the notice designating the exhibit is served.

(Subd (a) amended effective January 1, 2010; previously amended effective January 1, 2005, January 1, 2007, and January 1, 2008.)

(b) Contents of transcript

(1) The transcript must contain:

(A) The notice of appeal;

(B) Any judgment appealed from and any notice of its entry;

(C) Any order appealed from and any notice of its entry;

(D) Any notice of intention to move for a new trial or motion to vacate the judgment, for judgment notwithstanding the verdict, or for reconsideration of an appealed order, and any order on such motion and any notice of its entry;

(E) Any notices or stipulations to prepare clerk's or reporter's transcripts or to proceed by agreed or settled statement; and

(F) The register of actions, if any.

(2) Each document listed in (1)(A), (B), (C), and (D) must show the date necessary to determine the timeliness of the appeal under rule 8.104 or 8.108.

(3) Except as provided in (4), if designated by any party, the transcript must also contain:

(A) Any other document filed or lodged in the case in superior court;

(B) Any exhibit admitted in evidence, refused, or lodged; and

(C) Any jury instruction that any party submitted in writing and the cover page required by rule 2.1055(b)(2) indicating the party requesting it, and any written jury instructions given by the court.

(4) Unless the reviewing court orders or the parties stipulate otherwise:

(A) The clerk must not copy or transmit to the reviewing court the original of a deposition except those portions of a deposition presented or offered into evidence under rule 2.1040.

(B) The clerk must not include in the transcript the record of an administrative proceeding that was admitted in evidence, refused, or lodged in the trial court. Any such administrative record must be transmitted to the reviewing court as specified in rule 8.123.

(Subd (b) amended effective July 1, 2011; previously amended effective January 1, 2007, January 1, 2008, and January 1, 2011.)

(c) Deposit for cost of transcript

(1) Within 30 days after the respondent files a designation under (a)(2) or the time for filing it expires, whichever first occurs, the superior court clerk must send:

(A) To the appellant, notice of the estimated cost to prepare an original and one copy of the clerk's transcript; and

(B) To each party other than the appellant, notice of the estimated cost to prepare a copy of the clerk's transcript for that party's use.

(2) A notice under (1) must show the date it was sent.

(3) Unless otherwise provided by law, within 10 days after the clerk sends a notice under (1), the appellant and any party wanting to purchase a copy of the clerk's transcript must either deposit the estimated cost specified in the notice under (1) with the clerk or submit an application for, or an order granting, a waiver of the cost.

(4) If the appellant does not submit a required deposit or an application for, or an order granting, a waiver of the cost within the required period, the clerk must promptly issue a notice of default under rule 8.140.

(Subd (c) amended effective January 1, 2014; previously amended effective January 1, 2007, January 1, 2008, and July 1, 2009.)

(d) Preparation of transcript

(1) Within the time specified in (2), the clerk must:

(A) Prepare and certify the original transcript;

(B) Prepare one copy of the transcript for the appellant; and

(C) Prepare additional copies for parties that have requested a copy of the clerk's transcript and have made deposits as provided in (c)(3) or received an order waiving the cost.

(2) Except as provided in (3), the clerk must complete preparation of the transcripts required under (1) within 30 days after either:

(A) The appellant deposits either the estimated cost of the clerk's transcript or a preexisting order granting a waiver of that cost; or

(B) The court grants an application submitted under (c)(3) to waive that cost.

(3) If the appellant elects under rule 8.121 to proceed with a reporter's transcript, the clerk need not complete preparation of the transcripts required under (1) until 30 days after the appellant deposits the estimated cost of the reporter's transcript or one of the substitutes under rule 8.130(b).

(4) If the appeal is abandoned or dismissed before the clerk has completed preparation of the transcript, the clerk must refund any portion of the deposit under (c) exceeding the preparation cost actually incurred.

(Subd (d) amended effective January 1, 2014; previously amended effective January 1, 2003, and January 1, 2007.)

Rule 8.122 amended effective January 1, 2014; repealed and adopted as rule 5 effective January 1, 2002; previously amended effective January 1, 2003, January 1, 2005; previously amended and renumbered as rule 8.120 effective January 1, 2007, and as rule 8.122 effective January 1, 2008; previously amended effective July 1, 2009, January 1, 2010, January 1, 2011, and July 1, 2011.

Advisory Committee Comment

Subdivision (a). Subdivision (a)(1) allows a party designating documents for inclusion in the clerk's transcript to specify *portions* of such documents that are not to be included, e.g., because they are duplicates of other designated documents or are not necessary for proper consideration of the issues raised in the appeal. The notice of designation should identify any portion to be omitted by means of a descriptive reference, e.g., by specific page or exhibit numbers. This provision is intended to simplify and therefore expedite the preparation of the clerk's transcript, to reduce its cost to the parties, and to relieve the courts of the burden of reviewing a record containing redundant, irrelevant, or immaterial documents.

Subdivision (b). The supporting and opposing memoranda and attachments to any motion to vacate the judgment, for judgment notwithstanding the verdict, or for reconsideration of an appealed order are not required to be included in the clerk's transcript under subdivision (b)(1)(D) but may be included by designation of a party under (b)(3) or on motion of a party or the reviewing court under rule 8.155.

Subdivision (b)(1)(F) requires the clerk's transcript to include the register of actions, if any. This provision is intended to assist the reviewing court in determining the accuracy of the clerk's transcript.

Subdivision (c). Under subdivision (c)(2), a clerk who sends a notice under subdivision (c)(1) must include a certificate stating the date on which the clerk sent it. This provision is intended to establish the date when the 10-day period for depositing the cost of the clerk's transcript under this rule begins to run.

The Superior Court will make the determination on any application to waive the fees for preparing, certifying, copying, and transmitting the clerk's transcript.

Subdivision (d). The different timelines for preparing a clerk's transcript under subdivision (d)(2)(A) and (B) recognize that an appellant may apply for and receive a waiver of fees at different points during the appellate process. Some appellants may have applied for and obtained an order waiving fees before receiving the estimate of the cost of the clerk's transcript and thus may be able to provide that order to the court in lieu of making a deposit for the clerk's transcript. Other appellants may not apply for a waiver until after they receive the estimate of the cost for the clerk's transcript, in which case the time for preparing the transcript runs from the granting of that waiver.

In cases in which a reporter's transcript has been designated, subdivision (d)(3) gives the clerk the option of waiting until the deposit for the reporter's transcript has been made before beginning preparation of the clerk's transcript.

Rule 8.123. Record of administrative proceedings

(a) Application

This rule applies if the record of an administrative proceeding was admitted in evidence, refused, or lodged in the superior court.

(Subd (a) adopted effective January 1, 2008.)

(b) Designation

(1) An appellant's notice designating the record on appeal under rule 8.121 that requests a record of an administrative proceeding be transmitted to the reviewing court must identify the administrative record by the title and date or dates of the administrative proceedings.

(2) If an appellant does not request that an administrative record admitted in evidence, refused, or lodged in the superior court be transmitted to the reviewing court, the respondent, within 10 days after the appellant serves its notice designating the record on appeal, may serve and file in the superior court a notice requesting that this administrative record be transmitted to the reviewing court.

(Subd (b) adopted effective January 1, 2008.)

(c) Transmittal to the reviewing court

Except as provided in (d), if any administrative record is designated by a party, the superior court clerk must transmit the original administrative record, or electronic administrative record, with any clerk's or reporter's transcript sent to the reviewing court under rule 8.150. If the appellant has elected under rule 8.121 to use neither a clerk's transcript nor a reporter's transcript, the superior court clerk must transmit any administrative record designated by a party to the reviewing court no later than 45 days after the respondent files a designation under (b)(2) or the time for filing it expires, whichever first occurs.

(Subd (c) amended effective January 1, 2016; adopted as subd (d) effective January 1, 2008; previously amended and relettered as subd (c) effective January 1, 2013.)

(d) Administrative records returned to parties

(1) If the superior court has returned a designated administrative record to a party, the party in possession of the administrative record must make that record available to the other parties in the case for copying within 15 days after the notice designating the record on appeal is served and lodge the record with the clerk of the reviewing court at the time the last respondent's brief is due.

(2) A party seeking an administrative record that was returned to another party must first ask the possessing party to provide a copy or lend it for copying. The possessing party should reasonably cooperate with such requests.

(3) If the request under (2) is unsuccessful, the requesting party may serve and file in the reviewing court a notice identifying the administrative record and requesting that the possessing party deliver the administrative record to the requesting party or, if the possessing party prefers, to the reviewing court. The possessing party must comply with the request within 10 days after the notice was served.

(4) If the possessing party sends the administrative record to the requesting party, that party must copy and return it to the possessing party within 10 days after receiving it.

(5) If the possessing party sends the administrative record to the reviewing court, that party must:

(A) Include with the administrative record a copy of the notice served by the requesting party; and

(B) Immediately notify the requesting party that it has sent the administrative record to the reviewing court.

(Subd (d) amended and relettered effective January 1, 2013; adopted as subd (c) effective January 1, 2008.)

(e) Return by reviewing court

On request, the reviewing court may return an administrative record to the superior court or, if the record was lodged by a party under (d), to the lodging party. When the remittitur issues, the reviewing court must return any administrative record to the superior court or, if the record was lodged by a party under (d), to the lodging party.

(Subd (e) amended effective January 1, 2013; adopted effective January 1, 2008.)

Rule 8.123 amended effective January 1, 2016; adopted effective January 1, 2008; previously amended effective January 1, 2013.

Rule 8.124. Appendixes

(a) Notice of election

(1) Unless the superior court orders otherwise on a motion served and filed within 10 days after the notice of election is served, this rule governs if:

(A) The appellant elects to use an appendix under this rule in the notice designating the record on appeal under rule 8.121; or

(B) The respondent serves and files a notice in the superior court electing to use an appendix under this rule within 10 days after the notice of appeal is filed and no waiver of the fee for a clerk's transcript is granted to the appellant.

(2) When a party files a notice electing to use an appendix under this rule, the superior court clerk must promptly send a copy of the register of actions, if any, to the attorney of record for each party and to any unrepresented party.

(3) The parties may prepare separate appendixes or they may stipulate to a joint appendix.

(Subd (a) amended effective January 1, 2016; previously amended effective January 1, 2005, January 1, 2007, January 1, 2008, and January 1, 2010.)

(b) Contents of appendix

(1) A joint appendix or an appellant's appendix must contain:

(A) All items required by rule 8.122(b)(1), showing the dates required by rule 8.122(b)(2);

(B) Any item listed in rule 8.122(b)(3) that is necessary for proper consideration of the issues, including, for an appellant's appendix, any item that the appellant should reasonably assume the respondent will rely on;

(C) The notice of election; and

(D) For a joint appendix, the stipulation designating its contents.

(2) An appendix may incorporate by reference all or part of the record on appeal in another case pending in the reviewing court or in a prior appeal in the same case.

(A) The other appeal must be identified by its case name and number. If only part of a record is being incorporated by reference, that part must be identified by citation to the volume and page numbers of the record where it appears and either the title of the document or documents or the date of the oral proceedings to be incorporated. The parts of any record incorporated by reference must be identified both in the body of the appendix and in a separate section at the end of the index.

(B) If the appendix incorporates by reference any such record, the cover of the appendix must prominently display the notice "Record in case number: _____ incorporated by reference," identifying the number of the case from which the record is incorporated.

(C) On request of the reviewing court or any party, the designating party must provide a copy of the materials incorporated by reference to the court or another party or lend them for copying as provided in (c).

(3) An appendix must not:

(A) Contain documents or portions of documents filed in superior court that are unnecessary for proper consideration of the issues.

(B) Contain transcripts of oral proceedings that may be designated under rule 8.130.

(C) Contain the record of an administrative proceeding that was admitted in evidence, refused, or lodged in the trial court. Any such administrative record must be transmitted to the reviewing court as specified in rule 8.123.

(D) Incorporate any document by reference except as provided in (2).

(4) All exhibits admitted in evidence, refused, or lodged are deemed part of the record, whether or not the appendix contains copies of them.

(5) A respondent's appendix may contain any document that could have been included in the appellant's appendix or a joint appendix.

(6) An appellant's reply appendix may contain any document that could have been included in the respondent's appendix.

(Subd (b) amended effective January 1, 2010; previously amended effective January 1, 2007, and January 1, 2008.)

(c) Document or exhibit held by other party

If a party preparing an appendix wants it to contain a copy of a document or an exhibit in the possession of another party:

(1) The party must first ask the party possessing the document or exhibit to provide a copy or lend it for copying. All parties should reasonably cooperate with such requests.

(2) If the attempt under (1) is unsuccessful, the party may serve and file in the reviewing court a notice identifying the document or specifying the exhibit's trial court designation and requesting the party possessing the document or exhibit to deliver it to the requesting party or, if the possessing party prefers, to the reviewing court. The possessing party must comply with the request within 10 days after the notice was served.

(3) If the party possessing the document or exhibit sends it to the requesting party non-electronically, that party must copy and return it to the possessing party within 10 days after receiving it.

(4) If the party possessing the document or exhibit sends it to the reviewing court, that party must:

(A) Accompany the document or exhibit with a copy of the notice served by the requesting party; and

(B) Immediately notify the requesting party that it has sent the document or exhibit to the reviewing court.

(5) On request, the reviewing court may return a document or an exhibit to the party that sent it non-electronically. When the remittitur issues, the reviewing court must return all documents or exhibits to the party that sent them, if they were sent non-electronically.

(Subd (c) amended effective January 1, 2016; adopted effective January 1, 2005; previously amended effective January 1, 2007, and January 1, 2010.)

(d) Form of appendix

(1) An appendix must comply with the requirements of rule 8.144 for a clerk's transcript.

(2) In addition to the information required on the cover of a brief by rule 8.204(b)(10), the cover of an appendix must prominently display the title "Joint Appendix" or "Appellant's Appendix" or "Respondent's Appendix" or "Appellant's Reply Appendix."

(3) An appendix must not be bound or transmitted electronically as one document with a brief.

(Subd (d) amended effective January 1, 2018; adopted as subd (c) effective January 1, 2002; relettered as subd (d) effective January 1, 2005; previously amended effective January 1, 2007, January 1, 2016, and January 1, 2017.)

(e) Service and filing

(1) A party preparing an appendix must:

(A) Serve the appendix on each party, unless otherwise agreed by the parties or ordered by the reviewing court; and

(B) File the appendix in the reviewing court.

(2) A joint appendix or an appellant's appendix must be served and filed with the appellant's opening brief.

(3) A respondent's appendix, if any, must be served and filed with the respondent's brief.

(4) An appellant's reply appendix, if any, must be served and filed with the appellant's reply brief.

(Subd (e) amended effective January 1, 2007; adopted as subd (d) effective January 1, 2002; relettered as subd (d) effective January 1, 2005.)

(f) Cost of appendix

(1) Each party must pay for its own appendix.

(2) The cost of a joint appendix must be paid:

(A) By the appellant;

(B) If there is more than one appellant, by the appellants equally; or

(C) As the parties may agree.

(Subd (f) amended effective January 1, 2007; adopted as subd (e) effective January 1, 2002; relettered effective January 1, 2005.)

(g) Inaccurate or noncomplying appendix

Filing an appendix constitutes a representation that the appendix consists of accurate copies of documents in the superior court file. The reviewing court may impose monetary or other sanctions for filing an appendix that contains inaccurate copies or otherwise violates this rule.

(Subd (g) adopted as subd (f) effective January 1, 2002; relettered effective January 1, 2005.)

Rule 8.124 amended effective January 1, 2018; repealed and adopted as rule 5.1 effective January 1, 2002; previously amended and renumbered as rule 8.124 effective January 1, 2007; previously amended effective January 1, 2005, January 1, 2008, January 1, 2010, January 1, 2016, and January 1, 2017.

Advisory Committee Comment

Subdivision (a). Under this provision either party may elect to have the appeal proceed by way of an appendix. If the appellant's fees for a clerk's transcript are not waived and the respondent timely elects to use an appendix, that election will govern unless the superior court orders otherwise. This election procedure differs from all other appellate rules governing designation of a record on appeal. In those rules, the appellant's designation, or the stipulation of the parties, determines the type of record on appeal. Before making this election, respondents should check whether the appellant has been granted a fee waiver that is still in effect. If the trial court has granted appellant a fee waiver for the clerk's transcript, or grants such a waiver after the notice of appeal is filed, respondent cannot elect to proceed by way of an appendix.

Subdivision (a)(2) is intended to assist appellate counsel in preparing an appendix by providing them with the list of pleadings and other filings found in the register of actions or "docket sheet" in those counties that maintain such registers. (See Gov. Code, § 69845.) The provision is derived from rule 10-1 of the United States Circuit Rules (9th Cir.).

Subdivision (b). Under subdivision (b)(1)(A), a joint appendix or an appellant's appendix must contain any register of actions that the clerk sent to the parties under subdivision (a)(2). This provision is intended to assist the reviewing court in determining the accuracy of the appendix. The provision is derived from rule 30-1.3(a)(ii) of the United States Circuit Rules (9th Cir.).

In support of or opposition to pleadings or motions, the parties may have filed a number of lengthy documents in the proceedings in superior court, including, for example, declarations, memorandums, trial briefs, documentary exhibits (e.g., insurance policies, contracts, deeds), and photocopies of judicial opinions or other publications. Subdivision (b)(3)(A) prohibits the inclusion of such documents in an appendix when they are not necessary for proper consideration of the issues raised in the appeal. Even if a document is otherwise includable in an appendix, the rule prohibits the inclusion of any substantial *portion* of the document that is not necessary for proper consideration of the issues raised in the appeal. The prohibition is intended to simplify and therefore expedite the preparation of the appendix, to reduce its cost to the parties, and to relieve the courts of the burden of reviewing a record containing redundant, irrelevant, or immaterial documents. The provision is adapted from rule 30-1.4 of the United States Circuit Rules (9th Cir.).

Subdivision (b)(3)(B) prohibits the inclusion in an appendix of transcripts of oral proceedings that may be made part of a reporter's transcript. (Compare rule 8.130(e)(3) [the reporter must not copy into the reporter's transcript any document includable in the clerk's transcript under rule 8.122].) The prohibition is intended to prevent a party filing an appendix from evading the requirements and safeguards imposed by rule 8.130 on the process of designating and preparing a reporter's transcript, or the requirements imposed by rule 8.144(e) on the use of daily or other transcripts instead of a reporter's transcript (i.e., renumbered pages, required indexes). In addition, if an appellant were to include in its appendix a transcript of less than all the proceedings, the respondent would not learn of any need to designate additional proceedings (under rule 8.130(a)(3)) until the appellant had served its appendix with its brief, when it would be too late to designate them. Note also that a party may file a certified transcript of designated proceedings instead of a deposit for the reporter's fee (rule 8.130(b)(3)).

Subdivision (d). In current practice, served copies of filed documents often bear no clerk's date stamp and are not conformed by the parties serving them. Consistently with this practice, subdivision (d) does not require such documents to be conformed. The provision thereby relieves the parties of the burden of obtaining conformed copies at the cost of considerable time and expense and expedites the preparation of the appendix and the processing of the appeal. It is to be noted, however, that under subdivision (b)(1)(A) each document necessary to determine the timeliness of the appeal must show the date required under rule 8.104 or 8.108. Note also that subdivision (g) of rule 8.124 provides that a party filing an appendix represents under penalty of sanctions that its copies of documents are accurate.

Subdivision (e). Subdivision (e)(2) requires a joint appendix to be filed with the appellant's opening brief. The provision is intended to improve the briefing process by enabling the appellant's opening brief to include citations to the record. To provide for the case in which a respondent concludes in light of the appellant's opening brief that the joint appendix should have included additional documents, subdivision (b)(5) permits such a respondent to present in an appendix filed with its respondent's brief (see subd. (e)(3)) any document that could have been included in the joint appendix.

Under subdivision (e)(2)–(4) an appendix is required to be filed "with" the associated brief. This provision is intended to clarify that an extension of a briefing period ipso facto extends the filing period of an appendix associated with the brief.

Subdivision (g). Under subdivision (g), sanctions do not depend on the degree of culpability of the filing party—i.e., on whether the party's conduct was willful or negligent—but on the nature of the inaccuracies and the importance of the documents they affect.

Rule 8.128. Superior court file instead of clerk's transcript

(a) Stipulation; time to file

(1) If a local rule of the reviewing court permits, the parties may stipulate to use the original superior court file instead of a clerk's transcript under rule 8.122. This rule and any supplemental provisions of the local rule then govern unless the superior court orders otherwise after notice to the parties.

(2) Parties intending to proceed under this rule must file their stipulation in superior court with the appellant's notice designating the record on appeal under rule 8.121. The parties must serve the reviewing court with a copy of the stipulation.

(Subd (a) amended effective January 1, 2008; previously amended effective January 1, 2007.)

(b) Cost estimate; preparation of file; transmittal

(1) Within 10 days after a stipulation under (a) is filed, the superior court clerk must send the appellant an estimate of the cost to prepare the file, including the cost of sending the index under (3). The appellant must deposit the cost or file an application for, or an order granting, a waiver of the cost within 10 days after the clerk sends the estimate.

(2) Within 10 days after the appellant deposits the cost or the court files an order waiving that cost, the superior court clerk must put the superior court file in chronological order, number the pages, and attach a chronological index and a list of all attorneys of record, the parties they represent, and any unrepresented parties.

(3) The clerk must send copies of the index to all attorneys of record and any unrepresented parties for their use in paginating their copies of the file to conform to the index.

(4) The clerk must send the prepared file to the reviewing court with the reporter's transcript. If the appellant elected to proceed without a reporter's transcript, the clerk must immediately send the prepared file to the reviewing court.

(Subd (b) amended effective January 1, 2016; previously amended effective July 1, 2009.)

Rule 8.128 amended effective January 1, 2016; repealed and adopted as rule 5.2 effective January 1, 2002; previously amended and renumbered as rule 8.128 effective January 1, 2007; previously amended effective January 1, 2008, and July 1, 2009.

Advisory Committee Comment

Subdivision (b). The Superior Court will make the determination on any application to waive the fees for preparing and transmitting the trial court file.

Rule 8.130. Reporter's transcript

(a) Notice

(1) A notice under rule 8.121 designating a reporter's transcript must specify the date of each proceeding to be included in the transcript and may specify portions of designated proceedings that are not to be included. The notice must identify any proceeding for which a certified transcript has previously been prepared by checking the appropriate box on *Appellant's Notice Designating Record on Appeal (Unlimited Civil)* (form APP-003) or, if that form is not used, placing an asterisk before that proceeding in the notice.

(2) If the appellant designates less than all the testimony, the notice must state the points to be raised on appeal; the appeal is then limited to those points unless, on motion, the reviewing court permits otherwise.

(3) If the appellant serves and files a notice designating a reporter's transcript, the respondent may, within 10 days after such service, serve and file a notice in superior court designating any additional proceedings the respondent wants included in the transcript. The notice must identify any proceeding for which a certified transcript has previously been prepared by checking the appropriate box on *Respondent's Notice Designating Record on Appeal (Unlimited Civil Case)* (form APP-010) or, if that form is not used, placing an asterisk before that proceeding in the notice.

(4) If the appellant elects to proceed without a reporter's transcript, the respondent cannot require that a reporter's transcript be prepared. But the

reviewing court, on its own or the respondent's motion, may order the record augmented under rule 8.155 to prevent a miscarriage of justice. Unless the court orders otherwise, the appellant is responsible for the cost of any reporter's transcript the court may order under this subdivision.

(5) Except when a party submits a certified transcript that contains all the designated proceedings under (b)(3)(C) with the notice of designation, the notice of designation must be served on each known reporter of the designated proceedings.

(Subd (a) amended effective January 1, 2014; previously amended effective January 1, 2005, January 1, 2007, and January 1, 2008.)

(b) Deposit or substitute for cost of transcript

(1) With its notice of designation, a party must deposit with the superior court clerk the approximate cost of transcribing the proceedings it designates and a fee of $50 for the superior court to hold this deposit in trust. The deposit must be either:

(A) The amount specified in the reporter's written estimate; or

(B) An amount calculated as follows:

(i) For proceedings that have not previously been transcribed: $325 per fraction of the day's proceedings that did not exceed three hours, or $650 per day or fraction that exceeded three hours.

(ii) For proceedings that have previously been transcribed: $80 per fraction of the day's proceedings that did not exceed three hours, or $160 per day or fraction that exceeded three hours.

(2) If the reporter believes the deposit is inadequate, within 15 days after the clerk sends the notice under (d)(1) the reporter may file with the clerk and send to the designating party an estimate of the transcript's total cost at the statutory rate, showing the additional deposit required. The party must deposit the additional sum within 10 days after the reporter sends the estimate.

(3) Instead of a deposit under (1), the party may substitute:

(A) The reporter's written waiver of a deposit. A reporter may waive the deposit for a part of the designated proceedings, but such a waiver replaces the deposit for only that part.

(B) A copy of a Transcript Reimbursement Fund application filed under (c)(1).

(C) A certified transcript of all of the proceedings designated by the party. The transcript must comply with the format requirements of rule 8.144.

(Subd (b) amended effective January 1, 2016; previously amended effective January 1, 2007, January 1, 2010, and January 1, 2014.)

(c) Transcript Reimbursement Fund application

(1) With its notice of designation, a party may serve and file a copy of its application to the Court Reporters Board for payment or reimbursement from the Transcript Reimbursement Fund under Business and Professions Code section 8030.2 et seq.

(2) Within 90 days after the appellant serves and files a copy of its application to the Court Reporters Board, the appellant must either file with the superior court a copy of the Court Reporters Board's provisional approval of the application or take one of the following actions:

(A) Deposit the amount required under (b) or the reporter's written waiver of this deposit;

(B) File an agreed statement or a stipulation that the parties are attempting to agree on a statement under rule 8.134;

(C) File a motion to use a settled statement instead of a reporter's transcript under rule 8.137;

(D) Notify the superior court clerk that it elects to proceed without a record of the oral proceedings; or

(E) Serve and file an abandonment under rule 8.244.

(3) Within 90 days after the respondent serves and files a copy of its application to the Court Reporters Board, the respondent must either file with the superior court a copy of the Court Reporters Board's provisional approval of the application or take one of the following actions:

(A) Deposit the amount required under (b) or the reporter's written waiver of this deposit; or

(B) Notify the superior court clerk that it no longer wants the additional proceedings it designated for inclusion in the reporter's transcript.

(4) If the appellant fails to timely take one of the actions specified in (2) or the respondent fails to timely make the deposit or send the notice under (3), the superior court clerk must promptly issue a notice of default under rule 8.140.

(5) If the Court Reporters Board provisionally approves the application, the reporter's time to prepare the transcript under (f)(1) begins when

the reporter receives notice of the provisional approval from the clerk under (d)(2).

(Subd (c) amended effective January 1, 2014; previously amended effective January 1, 2007.)

(d) Superior court clerk's duties

(1) The clerk must file a party's notice of designation even if the party does not present the required deposit under (b)(1) or a substitute under (b)(3) with its notice of designation.

(2) The clerk must promptly send the reporter notice of the designation and of the deposit or substitute and notice to prepare the transcript, showing the date the notice was sent to the reporter, when the court receives:

(A) The required deposit under (b)(1);

(B) A reporter's written waiver of a deposit under (b)(3); or

(C) A copy of the Court Reporters Board's provisional approval of the party's application for payment from the Transcript Reimbursement Fund under (c).

(3) If the appellant does not present the deposit under (b)(1) or a substitute under (b)(3) with its notice of designation or does not present an additional deposit required under (b)(2):

(A) The clerk must promptly notify the appellant in writing that, within 15 days after the notice is sent, the appellant must take one of the following actions or the court may dismiss the appeal:

(i) Deposit the amount required or a substitute permitted under (b);

(ii) File an agreed statement or a stipulation that the parties are attempting to agree on a statement under rule 8.134;

(iii) File a motion to use a settled statement instead of a reporter's transcript under rule 8.137;

(iv) Notify the superior court clerk that it elects to proceed without a record of the oral proceedings; or

(v) Serve and file an abandonment under rule 8.244.

(B) If the appellant elects to use a reporter's transcript and fails to take one of the actions specified in the notice under (A), rule 8.140(b) and (c) apply.

(4) If the respondent does not present the deposit under (b)(1) or a substitute under (b)(3) with its notice of designation or does not present an additional deposit required under (b)(2), the clerk must file the notice of designation and promptly issue a notice of default under rule 8.140.

(5) The clerk must promptly notify the reporter if a check for a deposit is dishonored or an appeal is abandoned or is dismissed before the reporter has filed the transcript.

(Subd (d) amended effective January 1, 2016; previously amended effective January 1, 2007, January 1, 2008, and January 1, 2014.)

(e) Contents of transcript

(1) Except when a party deposits a certified transcript of all the designated proceedings under (b)(3)(C), the reporter must transcribe all designated proceedings that have not previously been transcribed and include in the transcript a copy of all designated proceedings that have previously been transcribed. The reporter must note in the transcript where any proceedings were omitted and the nature of those proceedings. The reporter must also note where any exhibit was marked for identification and where it was admitted or refused, identifying such exhibits by number or letter.

(2) If a party designates a portion of a witness's testimony to be transcribed, the reporter must transcribe the witness's entire testimony unless the parties stipulate otherwise.

(3) The reporter must not copy any document includable in the clerk's transcript under rule 8.122.

(Subd (e) amended effective January 1, 2014; previously amended effective January 1, 2007, and January 1, 2008.)

(f) Filing the transcript; copies; payment

(1) Within 30 days after notice is sent under (d)(2), the reporter must prepare and certify an original of the transcript and file it in superior court. The reporter must also file one copy of the original transcript, or more than one copy if multiple appellants equally share the cost of preparing the record (see rule 8.147(a)(2)). Only the reviewing court can extend the time to prepare the reporter's transcript (see rule 8.60).

(2) When the transcript is completed, the reporter must notify all parties to the appeal that the transcript is complete, bill each designating party at the statutory rate, and send a copy of the bill to the superior court clerk. The clerk must pay the reporter from that party's deposited funds and refund any excess deposit or notify the party of any additional funds needed. In a multiple reporter case, the clerk must pay each reporter who

certifies under penalty of perjury that his or her transcript portion is completed.

(3) If the appeal is abandoned or is dismissed before the reporter has filed the transcript, the reporter must inform the superior court clerk of the cost of the portion of the transcript that the reporter has completed. The clerk must pay that amount to the reporter from the appellant's deposited funds and refund any excess deposit.

(Subd (f) amended effective January 1, 2018; previously amended effective January 1, 2007, July 1, 2008, January 1, 2014, January 1, 2016, and January 1, 2017.)

(g) Disputes over transcript costs

Notwithstanding any dispute that may arise over the estimated or billed costs of a reporter's transcript, a designating party must timely comply with the requirements under this rule regarding deposits for transcripts. If a designating party believes that a reporter's estimate or bill is excessive, the designating party may file a complaint with the Court Reporters Board.

(Subd (g) adopted effective January 1, 2014.)

(h) Agreed or settled statement when proceedings cannot be transcribed

(1) If any portion of the designated proceedings cannot be transcribed, the superior court clerk must so notify the designating party in writing; the notice must show the date it was sent. The party may then substitute an agreed or settled statement for that portion of the designated proceedings by complying with either (A) or (B):

(A) Within 10 days after the notice is sent, the party may file in superior court, under rule 8.134, an agreed statement or a stipulation that the parties are attempting to agree on a statement. If the party files a stipulation, within 30 days thereafter the party must file the agreed statement, move to use a settled statement under rule 8.137, or proceed without such a statement; or

(B) Within 10 days after the notice is sent, the party may move in superior court to use a settled statement. If the court grants the motion, the statement must be served, filed, and settled as rule 8.137 provides, but the order granting the motion must fix the times for doing so.

(2) If the agreed or settled statement contains all the oral proceedings, it will substitute for the reporter's transcript; if it contains a portion of the proceedings, it will be incorporated into that transcript.

(3) This remedy supplements any other available remedies.

(Subd (h) amended effective January 1, 2016; adopted as subd (g); previously amended effective January 1, 2007; previously relettered as subd (h) effective January 1, 2014.)

Rule 8.130 amended effective January 1, 2018; repealed and adopted as rule 4 effective January 1, 2002; previously amended and renumbered as rule 8.130 effective January 1, 2007; previously amended effective January 1, 2005, January 1, 2008, July 1, 2008, January 1, 2010, January 1, 2014, January 1, 2016, and January 1, 2017.

Advisory Committee Comment

Subdivision (a). Subdivision (a)(1) requires that every notice designating a reporter's transcript identify which proceedings are to be included, and that it do so by specifying the date or dates on which those proceedings took place. Those proceedings for which a certified transcript has previously been prepared must be identified in the party's designation. If the appellant does not want a portion of the proceedings on a given date to be included, the notice should identify that portion by means of a descriptive reference (e.g., "August 3, 2004, but not the proceedings on defendant's motion to tax costs").

As used in subdivision (a)(1), the phrase "proceedings" includes all instructions that the court gives, whether or not submitted in writing, and any instructions that counsel orally propose but the court refuses; all such instructions are included in the reporter's transcript if designated under this rule. All instructions that counsel submit in writing, whether or not given to the jury, are lodged with the superior court clerk and are included in the clerk's transcript if designated under rule 8.122.

Under subdivision (a), portions of depositions read in open court but not reported, or not read but lodged with the superior court clerk, are included in the clerk's transcript if designated under rule 8.122.

Subdivision (b). Where a certified transcript has been previously prepared, subdivision (b) makes clear that the certified transcript may be filed in lieu of a deposit for the transcript only where the certified transcript contains all of the proceedings identified in the notice of designation and the transcript complies with the format requirements of rule 8.144. Otherwise, where a certified transcript has been previously prepared for only some of the designated proceedings, subdivision (b)(1) authorizes a reduced fee to be deposited for those proceedings. This reduced deposit amount was established in recognition of the holding in *Hendrix v. Superior Court of San Bernardino County* (2011) 191 Cal.App.4th 889 that the statutory rate for an original transcript only applies to the first transcription of the reporter's notes. The amount of the deposit is based on the rate established by Government

Code section 69950(b) for a first copy of a reporter's transcript purchased by any court, party, or other person who does not simultaneously purchase the original.

To eliminate any ambiguity, subdivision (b)(3) recognizes, first, that a party may substitute a court reporter's written waiver of a deposit for part of the designated proceedings and, second, that in such event the waiver replaces the deposit for only that part.

Subdivision (b) and subdivision (f) refer to the "statutory rate" for reporter's transcripts. The fees for reporter's transcripts are established by Government Code sections 69950 and 69554.

Subdivision (c). Under subdivision (c), an application to the Court Reporters Board for payment or reimbursement of the cost of the reporter's transcript from the Transcript Reimbursement Fund (Bus. & Prof. Code, §8030.8) is a permissible substitute for the required deposit of the reporter's fee (subd. (b)(3)) and thereby prevents issuance of a notice of default (subd. (d)(5)).

Business and Professions Code sections 8030.6 and 8030.8 use the term "reimbursement" to mean not only a true reimbursement, i.e., repaying a party who has previously paid the reporter out of the party's own funds (see *id.*, §8030.8, subd. (d)), but also a direct payment to a reporter who has not been previously paid by the party (see *id.*, §8030.6, subds. (b) and (d)). Subdivision (f) recognizes this special dual meaning by consistently using the compound phrase "payment or reimbursement."

Subdivision (d). Under subdivision (d)(2), the clerk's notice to the reporter must show the date on which the clerk sent the notice. This provision is intended to establish the date when the period for preparing the reporter's transcript under subdivision (f)(1) begins to run.

Subdivision (e). Subdivision (e)(1) clarifies that: (1) when a certified transcript containing all of the proceedings identified in the notice of designation is submitted in lieu of a deposit, the court reporter will not prepare a reporter's transcript; and (2) that the court reporter will only transcribe those proceedings that have not previously been transcribed and will include a copy of those proceedings that have previously been transcribed in the reporter's transcript. Under rule 8.144, the full transcript, including the previously transcribed material, must meet the format requirements for a reporter's transcript.

Subdivision (e)(3) is not intended to relieve the reporter of the duty to report all oral proceedings, including the reading of instructions or other documents.

Subdivision (f). Subdivision (f)(1) requires the reporter to prepare and file additional copies of the record "if multiple appellants equally share the cost of preparing the record ...." The reason for the requirement is explained in the comment to rule 8.147(a)(2).

Rule 8.134.   Agreed statement

(a) Contents of statement

(1) The record on appeal may consist wholly or partly of an agreed statement. The statement must explain the nature of the action, the basis of the reviewing court's jurisdiction, and how the superior court decided the points to be raised on appeal. The statement should recite only those facts needed to decide the appeal and must be signed by the parties.

(2) If the agreed statement replaces a clerk's transcript, the statement must be accompanied by copies of all items required by rule 8.122(b)(1), showing the dates required by rule 8.122(b)(2).

(3) The statement may be accompanied by copies of any document includable in the clerk's transcript under rule 8.122(b)(3) and (4).

(Subd (a) amended effective January 1, 2008; previously amended effective January 1, 2007.)

(b) Time to file; extension of time

(1) An appellant intending to proceed under this rule must file either an agreed statement or a stipulation that the parties are attempting to agree on a statement in superior court with its notice designating the record on appeal under rule 8.121.

(2) If the appellant files the stipulation and the parties can agree on the statement, the appellant must file the statement within 40 days after filing the notice of appeal.

(3) If the appellant files the stipulation and the parties cannot agree on the statement, the appellant must file a new notice designating the record on appeal under rule 8.121 within 50 days after filing the notice of appeal.

(Subd (b) amended effective January 1, 2008; previously amended effective January 1, 2007.)

Rule 8.134 amended effective January 1, 2008; repealed and adopted as rule 6 effective January 1, 2002; previously amended and renumbered effective January 1, 2007.

Advisory Committee Comment

Subdivision (b). Subdivision (b)(1) requires the appellant to file, with the appellant's notice designating the record under rule 8.121, either an agreed statement or a stipulation that the parties are attempting to agree on a statement. The provision is intended to prevent issuance of a notice of default while the parties are preparing an agreed statement.

Rule 8.137.   Settled statement

(a) Description

A settled statement is a summary of the superior court proceedings approved by the superior court. An appellant may either elect under (b)(1) or move under (b)(2) to use a settled statement as the record of the oral proceedings in the superior court, instead of a reporter's transcript.

(Subd (a) adopted effective January 1, 2018.)

(b) When a settled statement may be used

(1) An appellant may elect in his or her notice designating the record on appeal under rule 8.121 to use a settled statement as the record of the oral proceedings in the superior court without filing a motion under (2) if:

(A) The designated oral proceedings in the superior court were not reported by a court reporter; or

(B) The appellant has an order waiving his or her court fees and costs.

(2) An appellant intending to proceed under this rule for reasons other than those listed in (1) must serve and file in superior court with its notice designating the record on appeal under rule 8.121 a motion to use a settled statement instead of a reporter's transcript.

(A) The motion must be supported by a showing that:

(i) A substantial cost saving will result and the statement can be settled without significantly burdening opposing parties or the court;

(ii) The designated oral proceedings cannot be transcribed; or

(iii) Although the appellant does not have a fee waiver, he or she is unable to pay for a reporter's transcript and funds are not available from the Transcript Reimbursement Fund (see rule 8.130(c)).

(B) If the court denies the motion, the appellant must file a new notice designating the record on appeal under rule 8.121 within 10 days after the superior court clerk sends, or a party serves, the order of denial.

(3) An appellant's notice under (1) or motion under (2) must:

(A) Specify the date of each oral proceeding to be included in the settled statement;

(B) Identify whether each proceeding designated under (A) was reported by a court reporter and, if so, for each such proceeding:

(i) Provide the name of the court reporter, if known; and

(ii) Identify whether a certified transcript has previously been prepared by checking the appropriate box on *Appellant's Notice Designating Record on Appeal (Unlimited Civil Case)* (form APP-003) or, if that form is not used, placing an asterisk before that proceeding in the notice.

(4) If the designated oral proceedings in the superior court were reported by a court reporter:

(A) Within 10 days after the appellant serves either a notice under (1) or a motion under (2), the respondent may serve and file a notice indicating that he or she is electing to provide a reporter's transcript in lieu of proceeding with a settled statement. The respondent must also either:

(i) Deposit a certified transcript of all of the proceedings designated by the appellant under (3) and any additional proceedings designated by the respondent under rule 8.130(b)(3)(C); or

(ii) Serve and file a notice that the respondent is requesting preparation, at the respondent's expense, of a reporter's transcript of all proceedings designated by the appellant under (3) and any additional proceedings designated by the respondent. This notice must be accompanied by either the required deposit for the reporter's transcript under rule 8.130(b)(1) or the reporter's written waiver of the deposit in lieu of all or a portion of the deposit under rule 8.130(b)(3)(A).

(B) If the respondent timely deposits the certified transcript as required under (i), the appellant's motion to use a settled statement will be dismissed. If the respondent timely files the notice and makes the deposit or files the waiver as provided under (ii), the appellant's motion to use a settled statement will be dismissed and the clerk must promptly send the reporter notice of the designation and of the deposit, waiver, or both—and notice to prepare the transcript—as provided under rule 8.130(d).

(Subd (b) relettered and amended effective January 1, 2018; previously amended effective January 1, 2007, January 1, 2008, and January 1, 2016.)

(c) Time to file proposed statement

(1) If the respondent does not file a notice under (b)(4)(A) electing to provide a reporter's transcript in lieu of proceeding with a settled statement, the appellant must serve and file a proposed statement in superior court within 30 days after filing its notice under (b)(1) or within 30 days after the superior court clerk sends, or a party serves, an order granting a motion under (b)(2).

(2) Appellants who are not represented by an attorney are encouraged to file their proposed statement on *Proposed Statement on Appeal (Unlimited Civil Case)* (form APP-014). The court may order an appellant to use form APP-014.

(Subd (c) relettered and amended effective January 1, 2018; adopted as subd (b); previously amended effective January 1, 2007, January 1, 2008, and January 1, 2016.)

(d) Contents of proposed statement

The proposed statement must:

(1) Contain a statement of the points the appellant is raising on appeal. If the condensed narrative under (2) covers only a portion of the oral proceedings, the appeal is then limited to the points identified in the statement unless the reviewing court determines that the record permits the full consideration of another point or, on motion, the reviewing court permits otherwise.

(2) Contain a condensed narrative of the oral proceedings that the appellant specified under (b)(3).

(A) The condensed narrative must include a concise factual summary of the evidence and the testimony of each witness relevant to the points that the appellant states under (1) are being raised on appeal. Subject to the court's approval in settling the statement, the appellant may present some or all of the evidence by question and answer. Any evidence or portion of a proceeding not included will be presumed to support the judgment or order appealed from.

(B) If one of the points that the appellant states will be raised on appeal is a challenge to the giving, refusal, or modification of a jury instruction, the condensed narrative must include any instructions submitted orally and not in writing and must identify the party that requested the instruction and any modification.

(3) Have attached to it a copy of the judgment or order being appealed.

(Subd (d) adopted effective January 1, 2018.)

(e) Respondent's response to proposed statement

Within 20 days after the appellant serves the proposed statement, the respondent may serve and file either:

(1) Proposed amendments to the proposed statement; or

(2) A notice indicating that he or she is electing to provide a reporter's transcript in lieu of proceeding with a settled statement. The respondent must also either:

(A) Deposit a certified transcript of all the proceedings specified by the appellant under (b)(3) of this rule and any additional proceedings designated by the respondent under rule 8.130(b)(3)(C); or

(B) Serve and file a notice that the respondent is requesting preparation, at the respondent's expense, of a reporter's transcript of all proceedings specified by the appellant under (b)(3) of this rule and any additional proceedings designated by the respondent. This notice must be accompanied by either the required deposit for the reporter's transcript under rule 8.130(b)(1) or the reporter's written waiver of the deposit in lieu of all or a portion of the deposit under rule 8.130(b)(3)(A).

(Subd (e) adopted effective January 1, 2018.)

(f) Review of appellant's proposed statement

(1) No later than 10 days after the respondent files proposed amendments or the time to do so expires, whichever is earlier, a party may request a hearing to review and correct the proposed statement. No hearing will be held unless ordered by the trial court judge, and the judge will not ordinarily order a hearing unless there is a factual dispute about a material aspect of the trial court proceedings.

(2) The trial court judge may order that a transcript be prepared as the record of the oral proceedings instead of correcting a proposed statement on appeal if the trial court proceedings were reported by a court reporter, the trial court judge determines that doing so would save court time and resources, and the court has a local rule permitting such an order. The court will pay for any transcript ordered under this subdivision.

(3) Except as provided in (2), if no hearing is ordered, no later than 10 days after the time for requesting a hearing expires, the trial court judge must review the proposed statement and any proposed amendments filed by the respondent and take one of the following actions:

(A) If the proposed statement does not contain material required under (d), the trial court judge may order the appellant to prepare a new proposed statement. The order must identify the additional material that must be included in the statement to comply with (d) and the date by which the new proposed statement must be served and filed. If the appellant does not serve and file a new proposed statement as directed, the appellant will be deemed to be in default, and rule 8.140 will apply.

(B) If the trial court judge does not issue an order under (A), the judge must either:

(i) Make any corrections or modifications to the statement necessary to ensure that it is an accurate summary of the evidence and the testimony of each witness relevant to the points that the appellant states under (d)(1) are being raised on appeal; or

(ii) Identify the necessary corrections and modifications, and order the appellant to prepare a statement incorporating these corrections and modifications.

(4) If a hearing is ordered, the court must promptly set the hearing date and provide the parties with at least 5 days' written notice of the hearing date. No later than 10 days after the hearing, the trial court judge must either:

(A) Make any corrections or modifications to the statement necessary to ensure that it is an accurate summary of the evidence and the testimony of each witness relevant to the points that the appellant states under (d)(1) are being raised on appeal; or

(B) Identify the necessary corrections and modifications and order the appellant to prepare a statement incorporating these corrections and modifications.

(5) The trial court judge must not eliminate the appellant's specification of grounds of appeal from the proposed statement.

(Subd (f) relettered and amended effective January 1, 2018; adopted as subd (c).)

(g) Review of the corrected statement

(1) If the trial court judge makes any corrections or modifications to the proposed statement under (f), the clerk must serve copies of the corrected or modified statement on the parties. If under (f) the trial court judge orders the appellant to prepare a statement incorporating corrections and modifications, the appellant must serve and file the corrected or modified statement within the time ordered by the court. If the appellant does not serve and file a corrected or modified statement as directed, the appellant will be deemed to be in default and rule 8.140 will apply.

(2) Within 10 days after the corrected or modified statement is served on the parties, any party may serve and file proposed modifications or objections to the statement.

(3) Within 10 days after the time for filing proposed modifications or objections under (2) has expired, the trial court judge must review the corrected or modified statement and any proposed modifications or objections to the statement filed by the parties. The procedures in (2) or in (f)(3) apply if the trial court judge determines that further corrections or modifications are necessary to ensure that the statement is an accurate summary of the evidence and the testimony of each witness relevant to the points that the appellant states under (d)(1) are being raised on appeal.

(Subd (g) adopted effective January 1, 2018.)

(h) Certification of the statement on appeal

(1) If the trial court judge does not order the preparation of a transcript under (f)(2) in lieu of correcting the proposed statement or order any corrections or modifications to the proposed statement under (f)(3), (f)(4), or (g)(3), the judge must promptly certify the statement.

(2) The parties may serve and file a stipulation that the statement as originally served under (c) or as corrected or modified under (f)(3), (f)(4), or (g)(3) is correct. Such a stipulation is equivalent to the judge's certification of the statement.

(3) Upon certification of the statement under (1) or receipt of a stipulation under (2), the certified statement must immediately be transmitted to the clerk for filing of the record under rule 8.150.

(Subd (h) adopted effective January 1, 2018.)

Rule 8.137 amended effective January 1, 2018; repealed and adopted as rule 7 effective January 1, 2002; previously amended and renumbered as rule 8.137 effective January 1, 2007; previously amended January 1, 2008, and January 1, 2016.

Advisory Committee Comment

Subdivision (b). This rule requires the appellant to file only one copy of the settled statement, i.e., for the use of the reviewing court. Because all parties participate in preparing the settled statement, it may be assumed that each will retain a copy for its own use.

Rule 8.140. Failure to procure the record

(a) Notice of default

Except as otherwise provided by these rules, if a party fails to timely do an act required to procure the record, the superior court clerk must promptly notify the party in writing that it must do the act specified in the notice within 15 days after the notice is sent, and that if it fails to comply, the reviewing court may impose one of the following sanctions:

(1) If the defaulting party is the appellant, the court may dismiss the appeal; or

(2) If the defaulting party is the respondent, the court may proceed with the appeal on the record designated by the appellant.

(Subd (a) amended effective January 1, 2016; previously amended effective January 1, 2007, January 1, 2008, and January 1, 2014.)

(b) Sanctions

If a party fails to take the action specified in a notice given under (a), the superior court clerk must promptly notify the reviewing court of the default, and the reviewing court may impose one of the following sanctions:

(1) If the defaulting party is the appellant, the reviewing court may dismiss the appeal. If the appeal is dismissed, the reviewing court must promptly notify the superior court. The reviewing court may vacate the dismissal for good cause.

(2) If the defaulting party is the respondent, the reviewing court may order the appeal to proceed on the record designated by the appellant, but the respondent may obtain relief from default under rule 8.60(d).

(Subd (b) amended effective January 1, 2014; previously amended effective January 1, 2007, and January 1, 2008.)

(c) Motion for sanctions

If the superior court clerk fails to give a notice required by (a), a party may serve and file a motion for sanctions under (b) in the reviewing court, but the motion must be denied if the defaulting party cures the default within 15 days after the motion is served.

Rule 8.140 amended effective January 1, 2016; adopted as rule 8 effective January 1, 2002; previously amended and renumbered as rule 8.140 effective January 1, 2007; previously amended effective January 1, 2008, and January 1, 2014.

Advisory Committee Comment

Subdivision (a). In subdivision (a), the reference to a failure to "timely" do a required act is intended to include any valid extension of that time.

Rule 8.144.   Form of the record

(a) The provisions of this rule must be applied in a manner consistent with Code of Civil Procedure section 271.

(Subd (a) adopted effective January 1, 2018.)

(b) Format

(1) *Application to electronic and paper clerks' and reporters' transcripts*

The requirements for clerks' and reporters' transcripts in this subdivision apply to clerks' and reporters' transcripts delivered in electronic form and in paper form.

(2) *General*

In the clerk's and reporter's transcripts:

(A) All documents filed must have a page size of 8½ by 11 inches;

(B) The text must be reproduced as legibly as printed matter;

(C) The contents must be arranged chronologically;

(D) The pages must be consecutively numbered, except as provided in (f), beginning with volume one's cover as page 1 and continuing throughout the transcript, including the indexes, certificates, and cover pages for subsequent volumes, and using only Arabic numerals (i.e., 1, 2, 3); and

(E) The margin must be at least 1¼ inches from the left edge.

(3) *Line numbering*

In the reporter's transcript the lines on each page must be consecutively numbered, and must be double-spaced or one-and-a-half-spaced; double-spaced means three lines to a vertical inch.

(4) *Sealed and confidential records*

The clerk's and reporter's transcripts must comply with rules 8.45–8.47 relating to sealed and confidential records.

(5) *Indexes*

Except as provided in rule 8.45:

(A) The clerk's transcript must contain, at the beginning of the first volume, alphabetical and chronological indexes listing each document and the volume, where applicable, and page where it first appears;

(B) The reporter's transcript must contain:

(i) Alphabetical and chronological indexes listing the volume, where applicable, and page where each witness's direct, cross, and any other examination begins; and

(ii) An index listing the volume, where applicable, and page where any exhibit is marked for identification and where it is admitted or refused. The index must identify each exhibit by number or letter and a brief description of the exhibit.

(C) Each index prepared under this paragraph must begin on a separate page.

(6) *Volumes*

Clerks' and reporters' transcripts must be produced in volumes of no more than 300 pages.

(7) *Cover*

(A) The cover of each volume of the clerk's and reporter's transcripts must state the title and trial court number of the case, the names of the trial court and each participating trial judge, the names and addresses of appellate counsel for each party, the volume number, the total number of volumes in the transcript, and the inclusive page numbers of that volume.

(B) In reporters' transcripts, in addition to the information required by (A), the cover of each volume must state the dates of the proceedings reported in that volume.

(Subd (b) amended effective January 1, 2018; previously amended effective January 1, 2007, January 1, 2014, January 1, 2016, and January 1, 2017.)

(c) Additional requirements for record in paper form

In addition to complying with (b), if the clerk's or reporter's transcript is filed in paper form:

(1) The paper must be white or unbleached and of at least 20-pound weight;

(2) In the clerk's transcript only one side of the paper may be used; in the reporter's transcript both sides may be used, but the margins must then be 1¼ inches on each edge; and

(3) Clerks' and reporters' transcripts must be bound on the left margin.

(Subd (c) adopted effective January 1, 2018.)

(d) Additional requirements for reporter's transcript delivered in electronic form

(1) *General*

In addition to complying with (b), a reporter's transcript delivered in electronic format must:

(A) Be generated electronically; it must not be created from a scanned document unless ordered by the court.

(B) Be in full text-searchable PDF (portable document format) or other searchable format approved by the court.

(C) Ensure that the electronic page counter in the PDF file viewer matches the transcript page numbering.

(D) Include an electronic bookmark to each heading and subheading; all sessions or hearings (date lines); all witness examinations where each witness's direct, cross, and any other examination begins; all indexes; and all exhibits where any exhibit is marked for identification and where it is admitted or refused. All bookmarks, when clicked, must retain the user's currently selected zoom settings.

(E) Be digitally and electronically signed by the court reporter, unless the court reporter lacks the technical ability to provide a digital signature, in which case only an electronic signature is required.

(F) Permit users to copy and paste, keeping the original formatting, but with headers, footers, line numbers, and page numbers excluded.

(G) Permit courts to electronically add filed/received stamps.

(2) *Multivolume or multireporter transcripts*

In addition to the requirements in (1), for multivolume or multireporter transcripts delivered in electronic format, each individual reporter must provide a digitally and electronically signed certificate with his or her respective portion of the transcript. If the court reporter lacks the technical ability to provide a digital signature, then only an electronic signature is required.

(3) *Additional functionality or enhancements*

Nothing in this rule prohibits courts from accepting additional functionality or enhancements in reporters' transcripts delivered in electronic form.

(Subd (d) adopted effective January 1, 2018.)

(e) Daily transcripts

Daily or other certified transcripts may be used for all or part of the reporter's transcript, but the pages must be renumbered consecutively and the required indexes and covers must be added.

(Subd (e) relettered effective January 1, 2018; adopted as subd (d).)

(f) Pagination in multiple reporter cases

(1) In a multiple reporter case, each reporter must estimate the number of pages in each segment reported and inform the designated primary reporter of the estimate. The primary reporter must then assign beginning and ending page numbers for each segment.

(2) If a segment exceeds the assigned number of pages, the reporter must number the additional pages with the ending page number, a hyphen, and a new number, starting with 1 and continuing consecutively.

(3) If a segment has fewer than the assigned number of pages, on the last page of the segment, before the certificate page, the reporter must state in parentheses "(next volume and page number is _____)," and

on the certificate page, the reporter must add a hyphen to the last page number used, followed by the segment's assigned ending page number.

(Subd (f) amended and relettered effective January 1, 2018; adopted as subd (e).)

(g) Agreed or settled statements

Agreed or settled statements must conform with this rule insofar as practicable.

(Subd (g) relettered effective January 1, 2018; adopted as subd (f).)

Rule 8.144 amended effective January 1, 2018; repealed and adopted as rule 9 effective January 1, 2002; previously amended and renumbered as rule 8.144 effective January 1, 2007; previously amended effective January 1, 2008, January 1, 2014, January 1, 2016, and January 1, 2017.

Advisory Committee Comment

Subdivision (b). Paragraph (1) of subdivision (b) clarifies that the format requirements for reporters' transcripts, including the requirements for indexes, volumes, and covers, that previously applied to transcripts delivered in paper form now apply to transcripts delivered in both paper and electronic form.

Paragraphs (4) and (5) of subdivision (b) refer to special requirements concerning sealed and confidential records established by rules 8.45–8.47. Rule 8.45(c)(2) and (3) establishes special requirements regarding references to sealed and confidential records in the alphabetical and chronological indexes to clerks' and reporters' transcripts.

Rule 8.147. Record in multiple or later appeals in same case

(a) Multiple appeals

(1) If more than one appeal is taken from the same judgment or a related order, only one record need be prepared, which must be filed within the time allowed for filing the record in the latest appeal.

(2) If there is more than one separately represented appellant, they must equally share the cost of preparing the record, unless otherwise agreed by the appellants or ordered by the superior court. Appellants equally sharing the cost are each entitled to a copy of the record.

(b) Later appeal

In an appeal in which the parties are using either a clerk's transcript under rule 8.122 or a reporter's transcript under rule 8.130:

(1) A party wanting to incorporate by reference all or parts of a record in a prior appeal in the same case must specify those parts in its designation of the record.

(A) The prior appeal must be identified by its case name and number. If only part of a record is being incorporated by reference, that part must be identified by citation to the volume, where applicable, and page numbers of the record where it appears and either the title of the document or documents or the date of the oral proceedings to be incorporated. The parts of any record incorporated by reference must be identified in a separate section at the end of the designation of the record.

(B) If the transcript incorporates by reference any such record, the cover of the transcript must prominently display the notice "Record in case number: _____ incorporated by reference," identifying the number of the case from which the record is incorporated.

(C) On request of the reviewing court or any party, the designating party must provide a copy of the materials incorporated by reference to the reviewing court or another party or lend them as provided in rule 8.153.

(2) A party wanting any parts of a clerk's transcript or other record of the written documents from a prior appeal in the same case to be copied into the clerk's transcript in a later appeal must specify those parts in its designation of the record as provided in (1). The estimated cost of copying these materials must be included in the clerk's estimate of the cost of preparing the transcript under rule 8.122(c)(1). On request of the trial court clerk, the designating party must provide a copy of or lend the materials to be copied to the clerk. The parts of any record from a prior appeal that are copied into a clerk's transcript under this rule must be placed in a separate section at the end of the transcript and identified in a separate section at the end of the indexes.

(Subd (b) amended effective January 1, 2016; previously amended effective January 1, 2007, January 1, 2008, and January 1, 2010.)

Rule 8.147 amended effective January 1, 2016; repealed and adopted as rule 10 effective January 1, 2002; previously amended and renumbered as rule 8.147 effective January 1, 2007; previously amended effective January 1, 2008, and January 1, 2010.

Advisory Committee Comment

Subdivision (a). Subdivision (a)(1) provides broadly for a single record whenever there are multiple appeals "from the same judgment or a related order." Multiple appeals from the *same judgment* include all cases in which opposing parties, or multiple parties on the same side of the case, appeal from the judgment. Multiple appeals from a judgment *and a related order* include all cases in which one party appeals from the judgment and another party appeals from any appealable order arising from or related to the judgment, i.e., not only orders contemplated by rule 8.108 (e.g., denying a motion for judgment notwithstanding the verdict) but also, for example, posttrial orders granting or denying attorney fees. The purpose is to encourage, when practicable, the preparation of a single record for all appeals taken in the same case. In specifying that "only one *record* need be prepared," of course, the rule does not depart from the basic requirement that an *original* and at least one *copy* of the record be prepared.

The second sentence of subdivision (a)(2) applies when multiple appellants equally share the cost of preparing the record and that cost includes the cost of a copy for each appellant. An appellant wanting the reporter to prepare an additional copy of the record—i.e., additional to the copy required by rule 8.130(f)(1)—must make a timely deposit adequate to cover the cost of that copy.

Rule 8.149. When the record is complete

(a) Record of written documents

If the appellant elected to proceed without a record of the oral proceedings in the trial court and the parties are not proceeding by appendix under rule 8.124, the record is complete:

(1) If a clerk's transcript will be used, when the clerk's transcript is certified under rule 8.122(d);

(2) If the original superior court file will be used instead of the clerk's transcript, when that original file is ready for transmission as provided under rule 8.128(b);

(3) If an agreed statement will be used instead of the clerk's transcript, when the appellant files the agreed statement under rule 8.134(b);

(4) If a settled statement will be used instead of the clerk's transcript, when the statement has been certified by the trial court under rule 8.137(c); or

(5) If any party requested that a record of an administrative proceeding held by the superior court be transmitted to the reviewing court, when that record of that administrative proceeding is ready for transmittal to the reviewing court and any clerk's transcript or other record of the documents from the trial court is complete as provided in (1)–(4).

(Subd (a) adopted effective January 1, 2014.)

(b) Record of the oral proceedings

(1) If the parties are not proceeding by appendix under rule 8.124 and the appellant elected to proceed with a record of the oral proceedings in the trial court, the record is complete when the clerk's transcript or other record of the documents from the trial court is complete as provided in (a) and:

(A) If the appellant elected to use a reporter's transcript, when the certified reporter's transcript is delivered to the court under rule 8.130;

(B) If an agreed statement will be used instead of the reporter's transcript, when the appellant files the agreed statement under rule 8.134(b); or

(C) If a settled statement will be used instead of the reporter's transcript, when the statement has been certified by the trial court under rule 8.137(c).

(2) If the parties are proceeding by appendix under rule 8.124 and the appellant elected to proceed with a record of the oral proceedings in the trial court, the record is complete when the record of the oral proceedings is complete—as provided in (1)(A), (B), or (C)—and the record of any administrative proceeding held by the superior court that a party requested be transmitted to the reviewing court is ready for transmittal to the reviewing court.

(Subd (b) adopted effective January 1, 2014.)

Rule 8.149 adopted effective January 1, 2014.

Rule 8.150. Filing the record

(a) Superior court clerk's duties

When the record is complete, the superior court clerk must promptly send the original to the reviewing court and the copy to the appellant.

(Subd (a) amended effective January 1, 2007.)

(b) Reviewing court clerk's duties

On receiving the record, the reviewing court clerk must promptly file the original and send notice of the filing date to the parties.

(Subd (b) amended effective January 1, 2016; adopted as part of subd (a) effective January 1, 2002; previously amended and lettered as subd (b) effective January 1, 2007.)

Rule 8.150 amended effective January 1, 2016; repealed and adopted as rule 11 effective January 1, 2002; previously amended and renumbered as rule 8.150 effective January 1, 2007.

Subdivision (a). Under rule 8.71(c), the superior court clerk may send the record to the reviewing court in electronic form.

Rule 8.153.   Lending the record

(a) Request

Within 20 days after the record is filed in the reviewing court, a party that has not purchased its own copy of the record may request another party, in writing, to lend it that party's copy of the record. The other party must then lend its copy of the record when it serves its brief.

(b) Time to return

The borrowing party must return the copy of the record when it serves its brief or the time to file its brief has expired.

(c) Cost

The borrowing party must bear the cost of sending the copy of the record to and from the borrowing party.

Rule 8.153 adopted effective January 1, 2007.

Rule 8.155.   Augmenting and correcting the record

(a) Augmentation

(1) At any time, on motion of a party or its own motion, the reviewing court may order the record augmented to include:

(A) Any document filed or lodged in the case in superior court; or

(B) A certified transcript—or agreed or settled statement—of oral proceedings not designated under rule 8.130. Unless the court orders otherwise, the appellant is responsible for the cost of any additional transcript the court may order under this subdivision.

(2) A party must attach to its motion a copy, if available, of any document or transcript that it wants added to the record. The pages of the attachments must be consecutively numbered, beginning with the number one. If the reviewing court grants the motion it may augment the record with the copy.

(3) If the party cannot attach a copy of the matter to be added, the party must identify it as required under rules 8.122 and 8.130.

(Subd (a) amended effective January 1, 2008; previously amended effective January 1, 2007.)

(b) Omissions

(1) If a clerk or reporter omits a required or designated portion of the record, a party may serve and file a notice in superior court specifying the omitted portion and requesting that it be prepared, certified, and sent to the reviewing court. The party must serve a copy of the notice on the reviewing court.

(2) The clerk or reporter must comply with a notice under (1) within 10 days after it is filed. If the clerk or reporter fails to comply, the party may serve and file a motion to augment under (a), attaching a copy of the notice.

(c) Corrections

(1) On motion of a party, on stipulation, or on its own motion, the reviewing court may order the correction or certification of any part of the record.

(2) The reviewing court may order the superior court to settle disputes about omissions or errors in the record.

(d) Notice

The reviewing court clerk must send all parties notice of the receipt and filing of any matter under this rule.

Rule 8.155 amended effective January 1, 2008; repealed and adopted as rule 12 effective January 1, 2002; previously amended and renumbered effective January 1, 2007.

Subdivision (a). Subdivision (a)(1) makes it clear that a party may apply for—and the reviewing court may order—augmentation of the record at any time. Whether the motion is made within a reasonable time and is not for the purpose of delay, however, are among the factors the reviewing court may consider in ruling on such a motion.

Rule 8.160.   Sealed records [Renumbered]

Rule 8.160 renumbered to rule 8.46 effective January 1, 2010; repealed and adopted as rule 12.5 effective January 1, 2002; previously amended and renumbered as rule 8.160 effective January 1, 2007; previously amended effective July 1, 2002, January 1, 2004, and January 1, 2006.

Rule 8.163.   Presumption from the record

The reviewing court will presume that the record in an appeal includes all matters material to deciding the issues raised. If the appeal proceeds without a reporter's transcript, this presumption applies only if the claimed error appears on the face of the record.

Rule 8.163 amended and renumbered effective January 1, 2007; repealed and adopted as rule 52 effective January 1, 2005.

The intent of rule 8.163 is explained in the case law. (See, e.g., *Dumas v. Stark* (1961) 56 Cal.2d 673, 674.)

Article 3
Briefs in the Court of Appeal

Rule 8.200. Briefs by parties and amici curiae
Rule 8.204. Contents and format of briefs
Rule 8.208. Certificate of Interested Entities or Persons
Rule 8.212. Service and filing of briefs
Rule 8.216. Appeals in which a party is both appellant and respondent
Rule 8.220. Failure to file a brief
Rule 8.224. Transmitting exhibits

Rule 8.200.   Briefs by parties and amici curiae

(a) Parties' briefs

(1) Each appellant must serve and file an appellant's opening brief.

(2) Each respondent must serve and file a respondent's brief.

(3) Each appellant may serve and file a reply brief.

(4) No other brief may be filed except with the permission of the presiding justice, unless it qualifies under (b) or (c)(7).

(5) Instead of filing a brief, or as part of its brief, a party may join in or adopt by reference all or part of a brief in the same or a related appeal.

(Subd (a) amended effective January 1, 2017; previously amended effective January 1, 2003.)

(b) Supplemental briefs after remand or transfer from Supreme Court

(1) Within 15 days after finality of a Supreme Court decision remanding or order transferring a cause to a Court of Appeal for further proceedings, any party may serve and file a supplemental opening brief in the Court of Appeal. Within 15 days after such a brief is filed, any opposing party may serve and file a supplemental responding brief.

(2) Supplemental briefs must be limited to matters arising after the previous Court of Appeal decision in the cause, unless the presiding justice permits briefing on other matters.

(3) Supplemental briefs may not be filed if the previous decision of the Court of Appeal was a denial of a petition for a writ within its original jurisdiction without issuance of an alternative writ or order to show cause.

(Subd (b) adopted effective January 1, 2003.)

(c) Amicus curiae briefs

(1) Within 14 days after the last appellant's reply brief is filed or could have been filed under rule 8.212, whichever is earlier, any person or entity may serve and file an application for permission of the presiding justice to file an amicus curiae brief. For good cause, the presiding justice may allow later filing.

(2) The application must state the applicant's interest and explain how the proposed amicus curiae brief will assist the court in deciding the matter.

(3) The application must also identify:

(A) Any party or any counsel for a party in the pending appeal who:

(i) Authored the proposed amicus brief in whole or in part; or

(ii) Made a monetary contribution intended to fund the preparation or submission of the brief; and

(B) Every person or entity who made a monetary contribution intended to fund the preparation or submission of the brief, other than the amicus curiae, its members, or its counsel in the pending appeal.

(4) The proposed brief must be served and must accompany the application, and may be combined with it.

(5) The covers of the application and proposed brief must identify the party the applicant supports, if any.

(6) If the court grants the application, any party may file an answer within the time the court specifies. The answer must be served on all parties and the amicus curiae.

(7) The Attorney General may file an amicus curiae brief without the presiding justice's permission, unless the brief is submitted on behalf of another state officer or agency. The Attorney General must serve and file the brief within 14 days after the last appellant's reply brief is filed or could have been filed under rule 8.212, whichever is earlier, and must provide the information required by (2) and comply with (5). Any party may serve and file an answer within 14 days after the brief is filed.

(Subd (c) amended effective January 1, 2009; adopted as subd (b) effective January 1, 2002; previously relettered effective January 1, 2003; previously amended effective January 1, 2007, and January 1, 2008.)

Rule 8.200 amended effective January 1, 2017; repealed and adopted as rule 13 effective January 1, 2002; previously amended and renumbered effective January 1, 2007; previously amended effective January 1, 2003, January 1, 2008, and January 1, 2009.

Advisory Committee Comment

Subdivision (a)(2). A respondent, other than a respondent who has filed a notice of cross-appeal, who files a respondent's brief may be required to pay a filing fee under Government Code sections 68926 if the respondent's brief is the first document filed in the appellate proceeding in the Court of Appeal by that party. See rule 8.25(c).

Subdivision (b). After the Supreme Court remands or transfers a cause to the Court of Appeal for further proceedings (i.e., under rules 8.528(c)–(e) or 10.1000(a)(1)(B)), the parties are permitted to file supplemental briefs. The first 15-day briefing period begins on the day of *finality* (under rule 8.532) of the Supreme Court decision remanding or order transferring the cause to the Court of Appeal. The rule specifies that "any party" may file a supplemental opening brief, and if such a brief is filed, "any opposing party" may file a supplemental responding brief. In this context the phrase "any party" is intended to mean any *or all* parties. Such a decision or order of transfer to the Court of Appeal thus triggers, first, a 15-day period in which any or all parties may file supplemental opening briefs and, second—if any party files such a brief—an additional 15-day period in which any opposing party may file a supplemental responding brief.

Subdivision (c)(1). The time within which a reply brief "could have been filed under rule 8.212" includes any authorized extension of the deadline specified in rule 8.212.

Rule 8.204.   Contents and format of briefs

(a) Contents

(1) Each brief must:

(A) Begin with a table of contents and a table of authorities separately listing cases, constitutions, statutes, court rules, and other authorities cited;

(B) State each point under a separate heading or subheading summarizing the point, and support each point by argument and, if possible, by citation of authority; and

(C) Support any reference to a matter in the record by a citation to the volume and page number of the record where the matter appears. If any part of the record is submitted in an electronic format, citations to that part must identify, with the same specificity required for the printed record, the place in the record where the matter appears.

(2) An appellant's opening brief must:

(A) State the nature of the action, the relief sought in the trial court, and the judgment or order appealed from;

(B) State that the judgment appealed from is final, or explain why the order appealed from is appealable; and

(C) Provide a summary of the significant facts limited to matters in the record.

(Subd (a) amended effective January 1, 2006.)

(b) Format of briefs filed in paper form

(1) A brief may be reproduced by any process that produces a clear, black image of letter quality. All documents filed must have a page size of 8½ by 11 inches. If filed in paper form, the paper must be white or unbleached and of at least 20-pound weight.

(2) Any conventional font may be used. The font may be either proportionally spaced or monospaced.

(3) The font style must be roman; but for emphasis, italics or boldface may be used or the text may be underscored. Case names must be italicized or underscored. Headings may be in uppercase letters.

(4) Except as provided in (11), the font size, including footnotes, must not be smaller than 13-point, and both sides of the paper may be used.

(5) The lines of text must be unnumbered and at least one-and-a-half-spaced. Headings and footnotes may be single-spaced. Quotations may be block-indented and single-spaced. Single-spaced means six lines to a vertical inch.

(6) The margins must be at least 1½ inches on the left and right and 1 inch on the top and bottom.

(7) The pages must be consecutively numbered. The page numbering must begin with the cover page as page 1 and use only Arabic numerals (e.g., 1, 2, 3). The page number may be suppressed and need not appear on the cover page.

(8) If filed in paper form, the brief must be filed unbound unless otherwise provided by local rule or court order.

(9) The brief need not be signed.

(10) If filed in paper form, the cover must be in the color prescribed by rule [1] **8.40(a)**. In addition to providing the cover information required by rule [2] **8.40(b)**, the cover must state:

(A) The title of the brief;

(B) The title, trial court number, and Court of Appeal number of the case;

(C) The names of the trial court and each participating trial judge; **and**

(D) The name of the party that each attorney on the brief represents.

(11) If the brief is produced on a typewriter:

(A) A typewritten original and carbon copies may be filed only with the presiding justice's permission, which will ordinarily be given only to unrepresented parties proceeding in forma pauperis. All other typewritten briefs must be filed as photocopies.

(B) Both sides of the paper may be used if a photocopy is filed; only one side may be used if a typewritten original and carbon copies are filed.

(C) The type size, including footnotes, must not be smaller than standard pica, 10 characters per inch. Unrepresented incarcerated litigants may use elite type, 12 characters per inch, if they lack access to a typewriter with larger characters.

(Subd (b) amended effective January 1, 2020; previously amended effective January 1, 2004, July 1, 2004, January 1, 2006, January 1, 2007, January 1, 2013, January 1, 2014, January 1, 2016, and January 1, 2017.)

Rule 8.204(b).   2019 Deletes. [1] 8.40(b) [2] 8.40(c)

(c) Length

(1) **Except as provided in (5),** a brief produced on a computer must not exceed 14,000 words, including footnotes. Such a brief must include a certificate by appellate counsel or an unrepresented party stating the number of words in the brief. The person certifying may rely on the word count of the computer program used to prepare the brief.

(2) **Except as provided in (5),** a brief produced on a typewriter must not exceed 50 pages.

(3) The tables required under (a)(1), the cover information required under (b)(10), the Certificate of Interested Entities or Persons required under rule 8.208, a certificate under (1), any signature block, and any attachment under (d) are excluded from the limits stated in (1) or (2).

(4) A combined brief in an appeal governed by rule 8.216 must not exceed double the limits stated in (1) or (2).

(5) **A petition for rehearing or an answer to a petition for rehearing produced on a computer must not exceed 7,000 words, including footnotes. A petition or answer produced on a typewriter must not exceed 25 pages.**

(6) On application, the presiding justice may permit a longer brief for good cause.

(Subd (c) amended effective January 1, 2020; previously amended effective January 1, 2007, and January 1, 2011.)

(d) Attachments to briefs

A party filing a brief may attach copies of exhibits or other materials in the appellate record or copies of relevant local, state, or federal regulations or rules, out-of-state statutes, or other similar citable materials that are not readily accessible. These attachments must not exceed a combined total of 10 pages, but on application the presiding justice may permit additional pages of attachments for good cause. A copy of an opinion required to be attached to the brief under rule 8.1115(c) does not count toward this 10-page limit.

(Subd (d) amended effective January 1, 2007.)

(e) Noncomplying briefs

If a brief does not comply with this rule:

(1) The reviewing court clerk may decline to file it, but must mark it "received but not filed" and return it to the party; or

(2) If the brief is filed, the reviewing court may, on its own or a party's motion, with or without notice:

(A) Order the brief returned for corrections and refiling within a specified time;

(B) Strike the brief with leave to file a new brief within a specified time; or

(C) Disregard the noncompliance.

(Subd (e) amended effective January 1, 2006.)

Rule 8.204 amended effective January 1, 2020; repealed and adopted as rule 14 effective January 1, 2002; previously amended and renumbered as rule 8.204 effective January 1, 2007; previously amended effective January 1, 2004, July 1, 2004, January 1, 2006, January 1, 2011, January 1, 2013, January 1, 2014, January 1, 2016, and January 1, 2017.

Advisory Committee Comment

Subdivision (b). The first sentence of subdivision (b)(1) confirms that any method of reproduction is acceptable provided it results in a clear black image of letter quality. The provision is derived from subdivision (a)(1) of rule 32 of the Federal Rules of Appellate Procedure (28 U.S.C.) (FRAP 32).

Paragraphs (2), (3), and (4) of subdivision (b) state requirements of *font, font style,* and *font size* (see also subd. (b)(11)(C)).

Subdivision (b)(2) allows the use of any conventional font—e.g., Times New Roman, Courier, Arial, Helvetica, etc.—and permits the font to be either proportionally spaced or monospaced.

Subdivision (b)(3) requires the font style to be roman, but permits the use of italics, boldface, or underscoring for emphasis; it also requires case names to be italicized or underscored. These provisions are derived from FRAP 32(a)(6).

Subdivision (b)(5) allows headings to be single-spaced; it is derived from FRAP 32(a)(4). The provision also permits quotations of any length to be block-indented and single-spaced at the discretion of the brief writer.

See also rule 1.200 concerning the format of citations. Brief writers are encouraged to follow the citation form of the *California Style Manual* (4th ed., 2000).

Subdivision (c). Subdivision (c) governs the maximum permissible length of a brief. It is derived from the federal procedure of measuring the length of a brief produced on a computer by the number of words in the brief. (FRAP 32(a)(7).) Subdivision (c)(1), like FRAP 32(a)(7)(B)(i), imposes a limit of 14,000 words if the brief is produced on a computer. Subdivision (c)(1) implements this provision by requiring the writer of a brief produced on a computer to include a certificate stating the number of words in the brief, but allows the writer to rely on the word count of the computer program used to prepare the brief. This requirement, too, is adapted from the federal rule. (FRAP 32(a)(7)(C).) For purposes of this rule, a "brief produced on a computer" includes a commercially printed brief.

Subdivision (c)(3) specifies certain items that are not counted toward the maximum brief length. Signature blocks, as referenced in this provision, include not only the signatures, but also the printed names, titles, and affiliations of any attorneys filing or joining in the brief, which may accompany the signature.

Subdivision (c)(5) clarifies that a party seeking permission to exceed the page or word limits stated in subdivision (c)(1) and (2) must proceed by application under rule 8.50 rather than by motion under rule 8.54, and must show good cause.

Subdivision (d). Subdivision (d) permits a party filing a brief to attach copies of exhibits or other materials, provided they are part of the record on appeal and do not exceed a total of 10 pages. If the brief writer attaches, under rule 8.1115(c), a copy of an unpublished opinion or an opinion available only in computerized form, that opinion does not count toward the 10-page limit stated in rule 8.204(d).

Subdivision (e). Subdivision (e) states the consequences of submitting briefs that do not comply with this rule: (e)(1) recognizes the power of the reviewing court clerk to decline to file such a brief, and (e)(2) recognizes steps the reviewing court may take to obtain a brief that does comply with the rule. Subdivision (e)(2) does not purport to limit the inherent power of the reviewing court to fashion other sanctions for such noncompliance.

Rule 8.208. Certificate of Interested Entities or Persons

(a) Purpose and intent

The California Code of Judicial Ethics states the circumstances under which an appellate justice must disqualify himself or herself from a proceeding. The purpose of this rule is to provide justices of the Courts of Appeal with additional information to help them determine whether to disqualify themselves from a proceeding.

(b) Application

This rule applies in appeals in civil cases other than family, juvenile, guardianship, and conservatorship cases.

(Subd (b) adopted effective January 1, 2008.)

(c) Definitions

For purposes of this rule:

(1) "Certificate" means a Certificate of Interested Entities or Persons signed by appellate counsel or an unrepresented party.

(2) "Entity" means a corporation, a partnership, a firm, or any other association, but does not include a governmental entity or its agencies or a natural person.

(Subd (c) relettered effective January 1, 2008; adopted as subd (b) effective July 1, 2006.)

(d) Serving and filing a certificate

(1) Except as otherwise provided in this rule, if a party files a motion, an application, or an opposition to such motion or application in the Court of Appeal before filing its principal brief, the party must serve and file its certificate at the time it files the first such motion, application, or opposition and must include a copy of this certificate in the party's principal brief. If no motion, application, or opposition to such motion or application is filed before the parties file their principal briefs, each party must include its certificate in its principal brief. The certificate must appear after the cover and before the tables.

(2) If the identity of any party or any entity or person subject to disclosure under this rule has not been publicly disclosed in the proceedings and a party wants to keep that identity confidential, the party may serve and file an application for permission to file its certificate under seal separately from its principal brief, motion, application, or opposition. If the application is granted, the party must file the certificate under seal and without service within 10 days of the court's order granting the application.

(3) If a party fails to file a certificate as required under (1), the clerk must notify the party in writing that the party must file the certificate within 15 days after the clerk's notice is sent and that if the party fails to comply, the court may impose one of the following sanctions:

(A) If the party is the appellant, the court may strike the document or dismiss the appeal; or

(B) If the party is the respondent, the court may strike the document or decide the appeal on the record, the opening brief, and any oral argument by the appellant.

(4) If the party fails to file the certificate as specified in the notice under (2), the court may impose the sanctions specified in the notice.

(Subd (d) amended effective January 1, 2016; adopted as subd (c) effective July 1, 2006; previously amended and relettered effective January 1, 2008; previously amended effective January 1, 2009.)

(e) Contents of certificate

(1) If an entity is a party, that party's certificate must list any other entity or person that the party knows has an ownership interest of 10 percent or more in the party.

(2) If a party knows of any person or entity, other than the parties themselves, that has a financial or other interest in the outcome of the proceeding that the party reasonably believes the justices should consider in determining whether to disqualify themselves under canon 3E of the Code of Judicial Ethics, the party's certificate must list that entity or person and identify the nature of the interest of the person or entity. For purposes of this subdivision:

(A) A mutual or common investment fund's ownership of securities or bonds issued by an entity does not constitute a financial interest in that entity.

(B) An interest in the outcome of the proceeding does not arise solely because the entity or person is in the same industry, field of business, or regulatory category as a party and the case might establish a precedent that would affect that industry, field of business, or regulatory category.

(C) A party's insurer does not have a financial interest in the outcome of the proceeding solely on the basis of its status as insurer for that party.

(3) If the party knows of no entity or person that must be listed under (1) or (2), the party must so state in the certificate.

(Subd (e) amended effective January 1, 2009; adopted as subd (d) effective July 1, 2006; previously amended effective January 1, 2007; previously relettered effective January 1, 2008.)

(f) Supplemental information

A party that learns of changed or additional information that must be disclosed under (e) must promptly serve and file a supplemental certificate in the reviewing court.

(Subd (f) amended and relettered effective January 1, 2008; adopted as subd (e) effective July 1, 2006.)

Rule 8.208 amended effective January 1, 2016; adopted as rule 14.5 effective July 1, 2006; previously amended and renumbered as rule 8.208 effective January 1, 2007; previously amended effective January 1, 2008, and January 1, 2009.

Advisory Committee Comment

The Judicial Council has adopted an optional form, *Certificate of Interested Entities or Persons* (form APP-008), that can be used to file the certificate required by this rule.

Subdivision (e). This subdivision requires a party to list on its certificate entities or persons that the party *knows* have specified interests. This subdivision does not impose a duty on a party to gather information not already known by that party.

Rule 8.212. Service and filing of briefs

(a) Time to file

(1) An appellant must serve and file its opening brief within:

(A) 40 days after the record—or the reporter's transcript, after a rule 8.124 election—is filed in the reviewing court; or

(B) 70 days after the filing of a rule 8.124 election, if the appeal proceeds without a reporter's transcript.

(2) A respondent must serve and file its brief within 30 days after the appellant files its opening brief.

(3) An appellant must serve and file its reply brief, if any, within 20 days after the respondent files its brief.

(Subd (a) amended effective January 1, 2010; previously amended effective January 1, 2007.)

(b) Extensions of time

(1) Except as otherwise provided by statute or when the time to file the brief has previously been extended under (3) or rule 8.220(d), the parties may extend each period under (a) by up to 60 days by filing one or more stipulations in the reviewing court before the brief is due. Stipulations must be signed by and served on all parties.

(2) A stipulation under (1) is effective on filing. The reviewing court may not shorten a stipulated extension.

(3) Before the brief is due, a party may apply to the presiding justice for an extension of each period under (a), or under rule 8.200(c)(6) or (7), on a showing that there is good cause and that:

(A) The applicant was unable to obtain—or it would have been futile to seek—the extension by stipulation; or

(B) The parties have stipulated to the maximum extension permitted under (1) and the applicant seeks a further extension.

(4) A party need not apply for an extension or relief from default if it can file its brief within the time prescribed by rule 8.220(a). The clerk must file a brief submitted within that time if it otherwise complies with these rules.

(Subd (b) amended effective January 1, 2015; previously amended effective January 1, 2003, July 1, 2005, January 1, 2007, January 1, 2010, January 1, 2011, January 1, 2013, and January 1, 2014.)

(c) Service

(1) One copy of each brief must be served on the superior court clerk for delivery to the trial judge.

(2) If a brief is not filed electronically under rules 8.70–8.79, one electronic copy of each brief must be submitted to the Court of Appeal. For purposes of this requirement, the term "brief" does not include a petition for rehearing or an answer thereto.

(A) The copy must be a single computer file in text-searchable Portable Document Format (PDF), and it must exactly duplicate the appearance of the paper copy, including the order and pagination of all of the brief's components. By electronically submitting the copy, the filer certifies that the copy complies with these requirements and that all reasonable steps have been taken to ensure that the copy does not contain computer code, including viruses, that might be harmful to the court's system for receipt of electronic copies or to other users of that system.

(B) If the brief discloses material contained in a sealed or conditionally sealed record, the party serving the brief must comply with rule 8.46(f) and include as the first page in the PDF document a cover sheet that contains the information required by rule 8.204(b)(10).

(C) If it would cause undue hardship for the party filing the brief to submit an electronic copy of the brief to the Court of Appeal, the party may instead serve four paper copies of the brief on the Supreme Court. If the brief discloses material contained in a sealed or conditionally sealed record, the party serving the brief must comply with rule 8.46(f) and attach a cover sheet that contains the information required by rule 8.204(b)(10). The clerk/executive officer of the Court of Appeal must promptly notify the Supreme Court of any court order unsealing the brief. In the absence of such notice, the clerk/executive officer of the Supreme Court must keep all copies of the unredacted brief under seal.

(3) One copy of each brief must be served on a public officer or agency when required by rule 8.29.

(Subd (c) amended effective January 1, 2018; previously amended effective January 1, 2004, January 1, 2005, January 1, 2007, January 1, 2008, January 1, 2013, January 1, 2014, and January 1, 2015.)

Rule 8.212 amended effective January 1, 2018; repealed and adopted as rule 15 effective January 1, 2002; previously amended and renumbered effective January 1, 2007; previously amended effective January 1, 2003, January 1, 2004, January 1, 2005, July 1, 2005, January 1, 2008, January 1, 2010, January 1, 2011, January 1, 2013, January 1, 2014, and January 1, 2015.)

Advisory Committee Comment

Subdivision (a). Note that the sequence and timing of briefing in appeals in which a party is both appellant and respondent (cross-appeals) are governed by rule 8.216. Typically, a cross-appellant's combined respondent's brief and opening brief must be filed within the time specified in (a)(2) for the respondent's brief.

Subdivision (b). Extensions of briefing time are limited by statute in some cases. For example, under Public Resources Code section 21167.6(h) in cases under section 21167, extensions are limited to one 30-day extension for the opening brief and one 30-day extension for "preparation of responding brief."

Under rule 8.42, the original signature of only one party is required on the stipulation filed with the court; the signatures of the other parties may be in the form of copies of the signed signature page of the document. Signatures on electronically filed documents are subject to the requirements of rule 8.77.

Subdivision (b)(2) clarifies that a party seeking an extension of time from the presiding justice must proceed by application under rule 8.50 rather than by motion under rule 8.54.

Subdivision (c). In subdivision (c)(2) the word "brief" means only (1) an appellant's opening brief, (2) a respondent's brief, (3) an appellant's reply brief, (4) an amicus curiae brief, or (5) an answer thereto. It follows that no other documents or papers filed in the Court of Appeal, whatever their nature, should be served on the Supreme Court. Further, only briefs filed in the Court of Appeal "in a civil appeal" must be served on the Supreme Court. It follows that no briefs filed in the Court of Appeal in criminal appeals or in original proceedings should be served on the Supreme Court.

Information about electronic submission of copies of briefs to the Court of Appeal can be found on the web page for the Court of Appeal district in which the brief is being filed on the California Courts website at *www.courts.ca.gov/courtsofappeal*.

Examples of "undue hardship" under (2)(C) include but are not limited to when a party does not have access to a computer or the software necessary to prepare an electronic copy of a brief or does not have e-mail access to electronically submit a brief to the Court of Appeal.

Rule 8.216. Appeals in which a party is both appellant and respondent

(a) Briefing sequence and time to file briefs

In an appeal in which any party is both an appellant and a respondent:

(1) The parties must jointly—or separately if unable to agree—submit a proposed briefing sequence to the reviewing court within 20 days after the second notice of appeal is filed.

(2) After receiving the proposal, the reviewing court must order a briefing sequence and prescribe briefing periods consistent with rule 8.212(a).

(3) Extensions of time are governed by rule 8.212(b).

(Subd (a) amended effective January 1, 2007.)

(b) Contents of briefs

(1) A party that is both an appellant and a respondent must combine its respondent's brief with its appellant's opening brief or its reply brief, if any, whichever is appropriate under the briefing sequence that the reviewing court orders.

(2) A combined brief must address the points raised in each appeal separately but may include a single summary of the significant facts.

(3) A party must confine a reply brief, or the reply portion of a combined brief, to points raised in its appeal.

(Subd (b) amended effective January 1, 2009; previously amended effective January 1, 2007.)

Rule 8.216 amended effective January 1, 2009; repealed and adopted as rule 16 effective January 1, 2002; previously amended and renumbered effective January 1, 2007.

Advisory Committee Comment

Rule 8.216 applies, first, to all cases in which opposing parties both appeal from the judgment. In addition, it applies to all cases in which one party appeals from the judgment and another party appeals from any appealable order arising from or related to the judgment, i.e., not only orders contemplated by rule 8.108 (denying a motion for judgment notwithstanding the verdict) but also, for example, posttrial orders granting or denying attorney fees. The purpose of the rule is to provide, in all such appeals, a single unified procedure for resolving uncertainties as to the order in which the parties must file their briefs.

As used in this rule, "appellant" includes cross-appellant and "respondent" includes cross-respondent. (Compare rule 8.100(e).)

Subdivision (a). Subdivision (a) implements the above-stated purpose by providing a procedure for determining both the briefing *sequence*—i.e., the order in which the parties must file their briefs—and the briefing *periods*—i.e., the periods of time (e.g., 30 days or 70 days, etc.) within which the briefs must be filed. Subdivision (a)(1) places the burden on the parties in the first instance to propose a briefing sequence, jointly if possible but separately if not. The purpose of this requirement is to assist the reviewing court by giving it the benefit of the parties' views on what is the most efficient briefing sequence in the circumstances of the case. Subdivision (a)(2) then prescribes the role of the reviewing court: after considering the parties' proposal, the court will decide on the briefing sequence, prescribe the briefing periods, and notify the parties of both. The reviewing court, of course, may thereafter modify its order just as it may do in a single-appeal case. Extensions of time are governed by rule 8.212(b).

Subdivision (b). The purpose of subdivision (b)(3) is to ensure that in its reply brief a party addresses only issues germane to its own appeal. For example, a cross-appellant may not use its *cross-appellant's* reply brief to answer points raised in the *appellant's* reply brief.

Rule 8.220. Failure to file a brief

(a) Notice to file

If a party fails to timely file an appellant's opening brief or a respondent's brief, the reviewing court clerk must promptly notify the party in writing that the brief must be filed within 15 days after the notice is sent and that if the party fails to comply, the court may impose one of the following sanctions:

(1) If the brief is an appellant's opening brief, the court may dismiss the appeal;

(2) If the brief is a respondent's brief, the court may decide the appeal on the record, the opening brief, and any oral argument by the appellant.

(Subd (a) amended effective January 1, 2016; previously amended effective January 1, 2007, and January 1, 2008.)

(b) Combined brief

A party that is both an appellant and a respondent under rule 8.216 may file its combined respondent's brief and appellant's reply brief within the period specified in the notice under (a).

(Subd (b) amended effective January 1, 2007.)

(c) Sanction

If a party fails to file the brief as specified in a notice under (a), the court may impose the sanction specified in the notice.

(Subd (c) amended effective January 1, 2008.)

(d) Extension of time

Within the period specified in the notice under (a), a party may apply to the presiding justice for an extension of that period for good cause. If the extension is granted and the brief is not filed within the extended period, the court may impose the sanction under (c) without further notice.

Rule 8.220 amended effective January 1, 2016; repealed and adopted as rule 17 effective January 1, 2002; previously amended and renumbered as rule 8.220 effective January 1, 2007; previously amended effective January 1, 2008.

Advisory Committee Comment

Subdivision (a). Subdivision (a) applies to all appellant's opening briefs and respondent's briefs, but does not apply to reply briefs.

A brief is "timely" under subdivision (a) if it is filed within the normal rule time prescribed for that brief or any extension of that time.

A party that fails to timely file a required brief need not make a formal motion to permit a late filing (e.g., under rule 8.60(d)); it is sufficient to file the brief within the 15-day grace period specified in the notice under subdivision (a).

Subdivision (d). Subdivision (d) clarifies that a party seeking an extension of time from the presiding justice must proceed by application under rule 8.50 rather than by motion under rule 8.54. In conformity with current practice, the subdivision also clarifies that if a brief is not filed within an extension granted by the court, the court may impose sanctions without further notice.

Rule 8.224. Transmitting exhibits

(a) Notice of designation

(1) Within 10 days after the last respondent's brief is filed or could be filed under rule 8.220, a party wanting the reviewing court to consider any original exhibits that were admitted in evidence, refused, or lodged but that were not copied in the clerk's transcript under rule 8.122 or the appendix under rule 8.124 must serve and file a notice in superior court designating such exhibits.

(2) Within 10 days after a notice under (1) is served, any other party wanting the reviewing court to consider additional exhibits must serve and file a notice in superior court designating such exhibits.

(3) A party filing a notice under (1) or (2) must serve a copy on the reviewing court.

(Subd (a) amended effective January 1, 2008; previously amended effective January 1, 2007.)

(b) Transmittal

Unless the reviewing court orders otherwise, within 20 days after the first notice under (a) is filed:

(1) The superior court clerk must put any designated exhibits in clerk's possession into numerical or alphabetical order and send them to the reviewing court. The superior court clerk must also send a list of the exhibits sent. If the exhibits are not transmitted electronically, the superior court clerk must send two copies of the list. If the reviewing court clerk finds the list correct, the clerk must sign and return a copy to the superior court clerk.

(2) Any party in possession of designated exhibits returned by the superior court must put them into numerical or alphabetical order and send them to the reviewing court. The party must also send a list of the exhibits sent. If the exhibits are not transmitted electronically, the party must send two copies of the list. If the reviewing court clerk finds the list correct, the clerk must sign and return a copy to the party.

(Subd (b) amended effective January 1, 2016.)

(c) Application for later transmittal

After the periods specified in (a) have expired, a party may apply to the reviewing court for permission to send an exhibit to that court.

(d) Request and return by reviewing court

At any time the reviewing court may direct the superior court or a party to send it an exhibit. On request, the reviewing court may return an exhibit to the superior court or to the party that sent it. When the remittitur issues, the reviewing court must return all exhibits not transmitted electronically to the superior court or to the party that sent them.

(Subd (d) amended effective January 1, 2016.)

Rule 8.224 amended effective January 1, 2016; repealed and adopted as rule 18 effective January 1, 2002; previously amended and renumbered as rule 8.224 effective January 1, 2007; previously amended effective January 1, 2008.

Advisory Committee Comment

Subdivision (b). Subdivision (b)(2) provides a procedure by which parties send designated exhibits directly to the reviewing court in cases in which the superior court has returned the exhibits to the parties under Code of Civil Procedure section 1952 or other provision. (See also rule 8.122(a)(3).)

Subdivision (c). Subdivision (c) addresses the case in which a party's need to designate a certain exhibit does not arise until after the period specified in subdivision (a) has expired—for example, when the appellant makes a point in its reply brief that the respondent reasonably believes justifies the reviewing court's consideration of an exhibit it had not previously designated. In that event, the subdivision authorizes the party to apply to the reviewing court for permission to send the exhibit on a showing of good cause.

Article 4
Hearing and Decision in the Court of Appeal

Rule 8.240. Calendar preference

A party seeking calendar preference must promptly serve and file a motion for preference in the reviewing court. As used in this rule, "calendar preference" means an expedited appeal schedule, which may include expedited briefing and preference in setting the date of oral argument.

Rule 8.240 amended and renumbered effective January 1, 2007; repealed and adopted as rule 19 effective January 1, 2003.

Advisory Committee Comment

Rule 8.240 requires a party claiming preference to file a motion for preference in the reviewing court. The motion requirement relieves the reviewing court of the burden of searching the record to determine if preference should be ordered. The requirement is not intended to bar the court from ordering preference without a motion when the ground is apparent on the face of the appeal, e.g., in appeals from judgments of dependency (Welf. & Inst. Code, §395).

The rule is broad in scope: it includes motions for preference on the grounds (1) that a statute provides for preference in the reviewing court (e.g., Code Civ. Proc., §§44 [probate proceedings, contested elections, libel by public official], 45 [judgment freeing minor from parental custody]); (2) that the reviewing court should exercise its discretion to grant preference when a statute provides for trial preference (e.g., *id.*, §§35 [certain election matters], 36 [party over 70 and in poor health; party with terminal illness; minor in wrongful death action]; see *Warren v. Schecter* (1997) 57 Cal.App.4th 1189, 1198–1199); and (3) that the reviewing court should exercise its discretion to grant preference on a nonstatutory ground (e.g., economic hardship).

Because valid grounds for preference could arise after the filing of the reply brief, e.g., a diagnosis of terminal illness, the rule requires the motion to be filed "promptly," i.e., as soon as the ground for preference arises.

Rule 8.244. Settlement, abandonment, voluntary dismissal, and compromise

(a) Notice of settlement

(1) If a civil case settles after a notice of appeal has been filed either as a whole or as to any party, the appellant who has settled must immediately serve and file a notice of settlement in the Court of Appeal. If the parties have designated a clerk's or a reporter's transcript and the

record has not been filed in the Court of Appeal, the appellant must also immediately serve a copy of the notice on the superior court clerk.

(2) If the case settles after the appellant receives a notice setting oral argument or a prehearing conference, the appellant must also immediately notify the Court of Appeal of the settlement by telephone or other expeditious method.

(3) Within 45 days after filing a notice of settlement—unless the court has ordered a longer time period on a showing of good cause—the appellant who filed the notice of settlement must file either an abandonment under (b), if the record has not yet been filed in the Court of Appeal, or a request to dismiss under (c), if the record has already been filed in the Court of Appeal.

(4) If the appellant does not file an abandonment, a request to dismiss, or a letter stating good cause why the appeal should not be dismissed within the time period specified under (3), the court may dismiss the appeal as to that appellant and order each side to bear its own costs on appeal.

(5) This subdivision does not apply to settlements requiring findings to be made by the Court of Appeal under Code of Civil Procedure section 128(a)(8).

(Subd (a) amended effective January 1, 2007; previously amended effective January 1, 2006.)

(b) Abandonment

(1) Before the record is filed in the Court of Appeal, the appellant may serve and file in superior court an abandonment of the appeal or a stipulation to abandon the appeal. The filing effects a dismissal of the appeal and restores the superior court's jurisdiction.

(2) The superior court clerk must promptly notify the Court of Appeal and the parties of the abandonment or stipulation.

(c) Request to dismiss

(1) After the record is filed in the Court of Appeal, the appellant may serve and file in that court a request or a stipulation to dismiss the appeal.

(2) On receipt of a request or stipulation to dismiss, the court may dismiss the appeal and direct immediate issuance of the remittitur.

(d) Approval of compromise

If a guardian or conservator seeks approval of a proposed compromise of a pending appeal, the Court of Appeal may, before ruling on the compromise, direct the trial court to determine whether the compromise is in the minor's or the conservatee's best interests and to report its findings.

Rule 8.244 amended and renumbered effective January 1, 2007; repealed and adopted as rule 20 effective January 1, 2003; previously amended effective January 1, 2006.

Rule 8.248.   Prehearing conference

(a) Statement and conference

After the notice of appeal is filed in a civil case, the presiding justice may:

(1) Order one or more parties to serve and file a concise statement describing the nature of the case and the issues presented; and

(2) Order all necessary persons to attend a conference to consider case management issues, settlement, and other relevant matters.

(Subd (a) amended effective January 1, 2016; previously amended effective January 1, 2007.)

(b) Agreement

An agreement reached in a conference must be signed by the parties and filed. Unless the Court of Appeal orders otherwise, the agreement governs the appeal.

(c) Proceedings after conference

(1) Unless allowed by a filed agreement, no matter recited in a statement under (a)(1) or discussed in a conference under (a)(2) may be considered in any subsequent proceeding in the appeal other than in another conference.

(2) If settlement is addressed at the conference, other than an inquiry solely about the parties' interest in settlement, neither the presiding officer nor any court personnel present at the conference may participate in or influence the determination of the appeal.

(Subd (c) amended effective January 1, 2016.)

(d) Time to file brief

The time to file a party's brief under rule 8.212(a) is tolled from the date the Court of Appeal sends notice of the conference until the date it sends notice that the conference is concluded.

(Subd (d) amended effective January 1, 2016; previously amended effective January 1, 2007.)

Rule 8.248 amended effective January 1, 2016; repealed and adopted as rule 21 effective January 1, 2003; previously amended and renumbered as rule 8.248 effective January 1, 2007.

Advisory Committee Comment

Subdivision (a). Subdivision (a)(1) requires each party to *serve* any statement it files. (Cf. rule 3.1380(c) [pretrial settlement conference statement must be served on each party].) The service requirement is not intended to prohibit the presiding justice from ordering the parties to submit additional, confidential material in appropriate cases.

Subdivision (d). If a prehearing conference is ordered before the due date of the appellant's opening brief, the time to file the brief is not *extended* but *tolled*, in order to avoid unwarranted lengthening of the briefing process. For example, if the conference is ordered 15 days after the start of the normal 30-day briefing period, the rule simply *suspends* the running of that period; when the period resumes, the party will not receive an automatic extension of a full 30 days but rather the remaining 15 days of the original briefing period, unless the period is otherwise extended.

Under subdivision (d) the tolling period continues "until the date [the Court of Appeal] sends notice that the conference is *concluded*" (italics added). This provision is intended to accommodate the possibility that the conference may not conclude on the date it begins.

Whether or not the conference concludes on the date it begins, subdivision (d) requires the clerk/executive officer of the Court of Appeal to send the parties a notice that the conference is concluded. This provision is intended to facilitate the calculation of the new briefing due dates.

Rule 8.252.   Judicial notice; findings and evidence on appeal

(a) Judicial notice

(1) To obtain judicial notice by a reviewing court under Evidence Code section 459, a party must serve and file a separate motion with a proposed order.

(2) The motion must state:

(A) Why the matter to be noticed is relevant to the appeal;

(B) Whether the matter to be noticed was presented to the trial court and, if so, whether judicial notice was taken by that court;

(C) If judicial notice of the matter was not taken by the trial court, why the matter is subject to judicial notice under Evidence Code section 451, 452, or 453; and

(D) Whether the matter to be noticed relates to proceedings occurring after the order or judgment that is the subject of the appeal.

(3) If the matter to be noticed is not in the record, the party must [1] **attach to the motion a copy of the matter to be noticed or an explanation of** why it is not practicable to do so. The [2] **motion with attachments must comply with rule 8.74 if filed in electronic form**.

(Subd (a) amended effective January 1, 2020; previously amended effective January 1, 2009, January 1, 2013, and January 1, 2015.)

Rule 8.252(a). 2019 Deletes. [1] serve and file a copy with the motion or explain **[2]** pages of the copy of the matter or matters to be judicially noticed must be consecutively numbered, beginning with the number 1

(b) Findings on appeal

A party may move that the reviewing court make findings under Code of Civil Procedure section 909. The motion must include proposed findings.

(c) Evidence on appeal

(1) A party may move that the reviewing court take evidence.

(2) An order granting the motion must:

(A) State the issues on which evidence will be taken;

(B) Specify whether the court, a justice, or a special master or referee will take the evidence; and

(C) Give notice of the time and place for taking the evidence.

(3) For documentary evidence, a party may offer [1] an electronic **copy, or if filed in paper form, the original, a certified copy, or a photocopy**. The court may admit the document in evidence without a hearing.

(Subd (c) amended effective January 1, 2020; previously amended effective January 1, 2007, and January 1, 2016.)

Rule 8.252(c). 2019 Deletes. [1] the original, a certified copy, a photocopy, or, in a case in which electronic filing is permitted,

Rule 8.252 amended effective January 1, 2020; repealed and adopted as rule 22 effective January 1, 2003; previously amended and renumbered as rule 8.252 effective January 1, 2007; previously amended effective January 1, 2009, January 1, 2013, January 1, 2015, and January 1, 2016.

Advisory Committee Comment

Subdivisions (b) and (c). Although appellate courts are authorized to take evidence and make findings of fact on appeal by Code of Civil Procedure section

909 and this rule, this authority should be exercised sparingly. (See *In re Zeth S.* (2003) 31 Cal.4th 396.)

Rule 8.254. New Authorities

(a) Letter to court

If a party learns of significant new authority, including new legislation, that was not available in time to be included in the last brief that the party filed or could have filed, the party may inform the Court of Appeal of this authority by letter.

(Subd (a) adopted effective July 1, 2012.)

(b) Form and content

The letter may provide only a citation to the new authority and identify, by citation to a page or pages in a brief on file, the issue on appeal to which the new authority is relevant. No argument or other discussion of the authority is permitted in the letter.

(Subd (b) adopted effective July 1, 2012.)

(c) Service and filing

The letter must be served and filed before the court files its opinion and as soon as possible after the party learns of the new authority. If the letter is served and filed after oral argument is heard, it may address only new authority that was not available in time to be addressed at oral argument.

(Subd (c) adopted effective July 1, 2012.)
Rule 8.254 adopted effective July 1, 2012.

Advisory Committee Comment

This rule does not preclude a party from asking the presiding justice for permission to file supplemental briefing under rule 8.200(a)(4). A letter filed under this rule does not change the date of submission under rule 8.256.

Rule 8.256. Oral argument and submission of the cause

(a) Frequency and location of argument

(1) Each Court of Appeal and division must hold a session at least once each quarter.

(2) A Court of Appeal may hold sessions at places in its district other than the court's permanent location.

(3) Subject to approval by the Chair of the Judicial Council, a Court of Appeal may hold a session in another district to hear a cause transferred to it from that district.

(b) Notice of argument

The clerk/executive officer of the Court of Appeal must send a notice of the time and place of oral argument to all parties at least 20 days before the argument date. The presiding justice may shorten the notice period for good cause; in that event, the clerk/executive officer must immediately notify the parties by telephone or other expeditious method.

(Subd (b) amended effective January 1, 2018.)

(c) Conduct of argument

Unless the court provides otherwise by local rule or order:

(1) The appellant, petitioner, or moving party has the right to open and close. If there are two or more such parties, the court must set the sequence of argument.

(2) Each side is allowed 30 minutes for argument. If multiple parties are represented by separate counsel, or if an amicus curiae—on written request—is granted permission to argue, the court may apportion or expand the time.

(3) Only one counsel may argue for each separately represented party.

(d) When the cause is submitted

(1) A cause is submitted when the court has heard oral argument or approved its waiver and the time has expired to file all briefs and papers, including any supplemental brief permitted by the court.

(2) If the Supreme Court transfers a cause to the Court of Appeal and supplemental briefs may be filed under rule 8.200(b), the cause is submitted when the last such brief is or could be timely filed. The Court of Appeal may order the cause submitted at an earlier time if the parties so stipulate.

(Subd (d) amended effective January 1, 2007.)

(e) Vacating submission

(1) Except as provided in (2), the court may vacate submission only by an order stating its reasons and setting a timetable for resubmission.

(2) If a cause is submitted under (d)(2), an order setting oral argument vacates submission and the cause is resubmitted when the court has heard oral argument or approved its waiver.

(Subd (e) amended effective January 1, 2007.)
Rule 8.256 amended effective January 1, 2018; repealed and adopted as rule 23 effective January 1, 2003; previously amended and renumbered effective January 1, 2007.

Rule 8.260. Opinions [Reserved]
Rule 8.260 adopted effective January 1, 2007.

Rule 8.264. Filing, finality, and modification of decision

(a) Filing the decision

(1) The clerk/executive officer of the Court of Appeal must promptly file all opinions and orders of the court and promptly send copies showing the filing date to the parties and, when relevant, to the lower court or tribunal.

(2) A decision by opinion must identify the participating justices, including the author of the majority opinion and of any concurring or dissenting opinion, or the justices participating in a "by the court" opinion.

(Subd (a) amended effective January 1, 2018.)

(b) Finality of decision

(1) Except as otherwise provided in this rule, a Court of Appeal decision in a civil appeal, including an order dismissing an appeal involuntarily, is final in that court 30 days after filing.

(2) The following Court of Appeal decisions are final in that court on filing:

(A) The denial of a petition for writ of supersedeas; and

(B) The dismissal of an appeal on request or stipulation.

(3) If a Court of Appeal certifies its opinion for publication or partial publication after filing its decision and before its decision becomes final in that court, the finality period runs from the filing date of the order for publication.

(Subd (b) amended effective January 1, 2009; previously amended effective January 1, 2007.)

(c) Modification of decision

(1) A reviewing court may modify a decision until the decision is final in that court. If the office of the clerk/executive officer is closed on the date of finality, the court may modify the decision on the next day the office is open.

(2) An order modifying an opinion must state whether it changes the appellate judgment. A modification that does not change the appellate judgment does not extend the finality date of the decision. If a modification changes the appellate judgment, the finality period runs from the filing date of the modification order.

(Subd (c) amended effective January 1, 2018.)

(d) Consent to increase or decrease in amount of judgment

If a Court of Appeal decision conditions the affirmance of a money judgment on a party's consent to an increase or decrease in the amount, the judgment is reversed unless, before the decision is final under (b), the party serves and files a copy of a consent in the Court of Appeal. If a consent is filed, the finality period runs from the filing date of the consent. The clerk/executive officer must send one filed-endorsed copy of the consent to the superior court with the remittitur.

(Subd (d) amended effective January 1, 2018; previously amended effective January 1, 2016.)
Rule 8.264 amended effective January 1, 2018; repealed and adopted as rule 24 effective January 1, 2003; previously amended and renumbered as rule 8.264 effective January 1, 2007; previously amended effective January 1, 2009, and January 1, 2016.

Advisory Committee Comment

Subdivision (b). As used in subdivision (b)(1), "decision" includes all interlocutory orders of the Court of Appeal. (See Advisory Committee Comment to rule 8.500(a) and (e).) This provision addresses the finality of decisions in civil appeals and, through a cross-reference in rule 8.470, in juvenile appeals. See rule 8.366 for provisions addressing the finality of decisions in proceedings under chapter 3, relating to criminal appeals; rule 8.387 for provisions addressing finality of decisions under chapter 4, relating to habeas corpus proceedings; and rule 8.490 for provisions addressing the finality of decisions in proceedings under chapter 7, relating to writs of mandate, certiorari, and prohibition.

Subdivision (b)(3) provides that a postfiling decision of the Court of Appeal to publish its opinion in whole under rule 8.1105(c) or in part under rule 8.1100(a) restarts the 30-day finality period. This provision is based on rule 40-2 of the United States Circuit Rules (9th Cir.). It is intended to allow parties sufficient time to petition the Court of Appeal for rehearing and/or the Supreme Court for review—and to allow potential amici curiae sufficient time to express their views—when the Court of Appeal changes the publication status of an opinion. The rule thus recognizes that the publication status of an opinion may affect a party's decision whether to file a petition for rehearing and/or a petition for review.

Rule 8.268. Rehearing
(a) Power to order rehearing

(1) On petition of a party or on its own motion, a reviewing court may order rehearing of any decision that is not final in that court on filing.

(2) An order for rehearing must be filed before the decision is final. If the clerk's office is closed on the date of finality, the court may file the order on the next day the clerk's office is open.

(b) Petition and answer

(1) A party may serve and file a petition for rehearing within 15 days after:

(A) The filing of the decision;

(B) A publication order restarting the finality period under rule 8.264(b)(3), if the party has not already filed a petition for rehearing;

(C) A modification order changing the appellate judgment under rule 8.264(c)(2); or

(D) The filing of a consent under rule 8.264(d).

(2) A party must not file an answer to a petition for rehearing unless the court requests an answer. The clerk must promptly send to the parties copies of any order requesting an answer and immediately notify the parties by telephone or another expeditious method. Any answer must be served and filed within 8 days after the order is filed unless the court orders otherwise. A petition for rehearing normally will not be granted unless the court has requested an answer.

(3) The petition and answer must comply with the relevant provisions of rule 8.204, **including the length provisions in subdivision (c)(5)**.

(4) Before the decision is final and for good cause, the presiding justice may relieve a party from a failure to file a timely petition or answer.

(Subd (b) amended effective January 1, 2020; previously amended effective January 1, 2004, January 1, 2007, and January 1, 2009.)

(c) No extension of time

The time for granting or denying a petition for rehearing in the Court of Appeal may not be extended. If the court does not rule on the petition before the decision is final, the petition is deemed denied.

(d) Effect of granting rehearing

An order granting a rehearing vacates the decision and any opinion filed in the case and sets the cause at large in the Court of Appeal.

Rule 8.268 amended effective January 1, 2020; repealed and adopted as rule 25 effective January 1, 2003; previously amended effective January 1, 2004, and January 1, 2009; previously amended and renumbered effective January 1, 2007.

Rule 8.272.   Remittitur

(a) Issuance of remittitur

A Court of Appeal must issue a remittitur after a decision in an appeal.

(Subd (a) amended effective January 1, 2008; previously amended effective January 1, 2007.)

(b) Clerk's duties

(1) If a Court of Appeal decision is not reviewed by the Supreme Court:

(A) The clerk/executive officer of the Court of Appeal must issue a remittitur immediately after the Supreme Court denies review, or the period for granting review expires, or the court dismisses review under rule 8.528(b); and

(B) The clerk/executive officer must send the lower court or tribunal the Court of Appeal remittitur and a filed-endorsed copy of the opinion or order.

(2) After Supreme Court review of a Court of Appeal decision:

(A) On receiving the Supreme Court remittitur, the clerk/executive officer of the Court of Appeal must issue a remittitur immediately if there will be no further proceedings in the Court of Appeal; and

(B) The clerk must send the lower court or tribunal the Court of Appeal remittitur, a copy of the Supreme Court remittitur, and a filed-endorsed copy of the Supreme Court opinion or order.

(Subd (b) amended effective January 1, 2018; previously amended effective January 1, 2007, and January 1, 2016.)

(c) Immediate issuance, stay, and recall

(1) A Court of Appeal may direct immediate issuance of a remittitur only on the parties' stipulation or on dismissal of the appeal under rule 8.244(c)(2).

(2) On a party's or its own motion or on stipulation, and for good cause, the court may stay a remittitur's issuance for a reasonable period or order its recall.

(3) An order recalling a remittitur issued after a decision by opinion does not supersede the opinion or affect its publication status.

(Subd (c) amended effective January 1, 2007.)

(d) Notice

(1) The remittitur is deemed issued when the clerk/executive officer enters it in the record. The clerk/executive officer must immediately send the parties notice of issuance of the remittitur, showing the date of entry.

(2) If, without requiring further proceedings in the trial court, the decision changes the length of a state prison sentence, applicable credits, or the maximum permissible confinement to the Department of Corrections and Rehabilitation, Division of Juvenile Justice, the clerk/executive officer must send a copy of the remittitur and opinion or order to either the Department of Corrections and Rehabilitation or the Division of Juvenile Justice.

(Subd (d) amended effective January 1, 2018; previously amended effective January 1, 2007.)

Rule 8.272 amended effective January 1, 2018; repealed and adopted as rule 26 effective January 1, 2003; previously amended effective January 1, 2007, January 1, 2008, and January 1, 2016.

Advisory Committee Comment

See rule 8.386 for provisions addressing remittitur in habeas corpus proceedings and rule 8.490 for provisions addressing remittitur in other writ proceedings.

Rule 8.276.   Sanctions

(a) Grounds for sanctions

On motion of a party or its own motion, a Court of Appeal may impose sanctions, including the award or denial of costs under rule 8.278, on a party or an attorney for:

(1) Taking a frivolous appeal or appealing solely to cause delay;

(2) Including in the record any matter not reasonably material to the appeal's determination;

(3) Filing a frivolous motion; or

(4) Committing any other unreasonable violation of these rules.

(Subd (a) amended and relettered effective January 1, 2008; adopted as subd (e) effective January 1, 2003; previously amended effective January 1, 2007.)

(b) Motions for sanctions

(1) A party's motion under (a) must include a declaration supporting the amount of any monetary sanction sought and must be served and filed before any order dismissing the appeal but no later than 10 days after the appellant's reply brief is due.

(2) If a party files a motion for sanctions with a motion to dismiss the appeal and the motion to dismiss is not granted, the party may file a new motion for sanctions within 10 days after the appellant's reply brief is due.

(Subd (b) amended and lettered effective January 1, 2008; adopted as part of subd (e) effective January 1, 2003; previously amended effective January 1, 2007.)

(c) Notice

The court must give notice in writing if it is considering imposing sanctions.

(Subd (c) amended and lettered effective January 1, 2008; adopted as part of subd (e) effective January 1, 2003; previously amended effective January 1, 2007.)

(d) Opposition

Within 10 days after the court sends such notice, a party or attorney may serve and file an opposition, but failure to do so will not be deemed consent. An opposition may not be filed unless the court sends such notice.

(Subd (d) amended and lettered effective January 1, 2008; adopted as part of subd (e) effective January 1, 2003; previously amended effective January 1, 2007.)

(e) Oral argument

Unless otherwise ordered, oral argument on the issue of sanctions must be combined with oral argument on the merits of the appeal.

(Subd (e) amended and lettered effective January 1, 2008; adopted as part of subd (e) effective January 1, 2003; previously amended effective January 1, 2007.)

Rule 8.276 amended effective January 1, 2008; repealed and adopted as rule 27 effective January 1, 2003; previously amended and renumbered effective January 1, 2007.

Rule 8.278.   Costs on appeal

(a) Award of costs

(1) Except as provided in this rule, the party prevailing in the Court of Appeal in a civil case other than a juvenile case is entitled to costs on appeal.

(2) The prevailing party is the respondent if the Court of Appeal affirms the judgment without modification or dismisses the appeal. The prevailing party is the appellant if the court reverses the judgment in its entirety.

(3) If the Court of Appeal reverses the judgment in part or modifies it, or if there is more than one notice of appeal, the opinion must specify the award or denial of costs.

(4) In probate cases, the prevailing party must be awarded costs unless the Court of Appeal orders otherwise, but the superior court must decide who will pay the award.

(5) In the interests of justice, the Court of Appeal may also award or deny costs as it deems proper.

(Subd (a) adopted effective January 1, 2008.)

(b) Judgment for costs

(1) The clerk/executive officer of the Court of Appeal must enter on the record, and insert in the remittitur, a judgment awarding costs to the prevailing party under (a)(2) or as directed by the court under (a)(3), (a)(4), or (a)(5).

(2) If the clerk/executive officer fails to enter judgment for costs, the court may recall the remittitur for correction on its own motion, or on a party's motion made not later than 30 days after the remittitur issues.

(Subd (b) amended effective January 1, 2018; adopted effective January 1, 2008.)

(c) Procedure for claiming or opposing costs

(1) Within 40 days after issuance of the remittitur, a party claiming costs awarded by a reviewing court must serve and file in the superior court a verified memorandum of costs under rule 3.1700.

(2) A party may serve and file a motion in the superior court to strike or tax costs claimed under (1) in the manner required by rule 3.1700.

(3) An award of costs is enforceable as a money judgment.

(Subd (c) amended effective January 1, 2016; adopted effective January 1, 2008.)

(d) Recoverable costs

(1) A party may recover only the following costs, if reasonable:

(A) Filing fees;

(B) The amount the party paid for any portion of the record, whether an original or a copy or both. The cost to copy parts of a prior record under rule 8.147(b)(2) is not recoverable unless the Court of Appeal ordered the copying;

(C) The cost to produce additional evidence on appeal;

(D) The costs to notarize, serve, mail, and file the record, briefs, and other papers;

(E) The cost to print and reproduce any brief, including any petition for rehearing or review, answer, or reply;

(F) The cost to procure a surety bond, including the premium, the cost to obtain a letter of credit as collateral, and the fees and net interest expenses incurred to borrow funds to provide security for the bond or to obtain a letter of credit, unless the trial court determines the bond was unnecessary; and

(G) The fees and net interest expenses incurred to borrow funds to deposit with the superior court in lieu of a bond or undertaking, unless the trial court determines the deposit was unnecessary.

(2) Unless the court orders otherwise, an award of costs neither includes attorney's fees on appeal nor precludes a party from seeking them under rule 3.1702.

(Subd (d) amended effective January 1, 2013; adopted effective January 1, 2008.)

Rule 8.278 amended effective January 1, 2018; adopted effective January 1, 2008; previously amended effective January 1, 2009, January 1, 2013, and January 1, 2016.

Advisory Committee Comment

This rule is not intended to expand the categories of appeals subject to the award of costs. See rule 8.493 for provisions addressing costs in writ proceedings.

Subdivision (c). Subdivision (c)(2) provides the procedure for a party to move in the trial court to strike or tax costs that another party has claimed under subdivision (c)(1). It is not intended that the trial court's authority to strike or tax unreasonable costs be limited by any failure of the moving party to move for sanctions in the Court of Appeal under rule 8.276; a party may seek to strike or tax costs on the ground that an opponent included unnecessary materials in the record even if the party did not move the Court of Appeal to sanction the opponent under that rule.

Subdivision (d). Subdivision (d)(1)(B) is intended to refer not only to a normal record prepared by the clerk and the reporter under rules 8.122 and 8.130 but also, for example, to an appendix prepared by a party under rule 8.124 and to a superior court file to which the parties stipulate under rule 8.128.

Subdivision (d)(1)(D), allowing recovery of the "costs to notarize, serve, mail, and file the record, briefs, and other papers," is intended to include fees charged by electronic filing service providers for electronic filing and service of documents.

"Net interest expenses" in subdivisions (d)(1)(F) and (G) means the interest expenses incurred to borrow the funds that are deposited minus any interest earned by the borrower on those funds while they are on deposit.

Chapter 3
Criminal Appeals

Article 1
Taking the Appeal

Rule 8.300.   Appointment of appellate counsel by the Court of Appeal

(a) Procedures

(1) Each Court of Appeal must adopt procedures for appointing appellate counsel for indigents not represented by the State Public Defender in all cases in which indigents are entitled to appointed counsel.

(2) The procedures must require each attorney seeking appointment to complete a questionnaire showing the attorney's California State Bar number, date of admission, qualifications, and experience.

(b) List of qualified attorneys

(1) The Court of Appeal must evaluate the attorney's qualifications for appointment and, if the attorney is qualified, place the attorney's name on a list to receive appointments in appropriate cases.

(2) Each court's appointments must be based on criteria approved by the Judicial Council or its designated oversight committee.

(Subd (b) amended effective January 1, 2007.)

(c) Demands of the case

In matching counsel with the demands of the case, the Court of Appeal should consider:

(1) The length of the sentence;

(2) The complexity or novelty of the issues;

(3) The length of the trial and of the reporter's transcript; and

(4) Any questions concerning the competence of trial counsel.

(Subd (c) amended effective January 1, 2007.)

(d) Evaluation

The court must review and evaluate the performance of each appointed counsel to determine whether counsel's name should remain on the list at the same level, be placed on a different level, or be deleted from the list.

(e) Contracts to perform administrative functions

(1) The court may contract with an administrator having substantial experience in handling appellate court appointments to perform any of the duties prescribed by this rule.

(2) The court must provide the administrator with the information needed to fulfill the administrator's duties.

Rule 8.300 amended and renumbered effective January 1, 2007; repealed and adopted as rule 76.5 effective January 1, 2005.

Advisory Committee Comment

Subdivision (b). The "designated oversight committee" referred to in subdivision (b)(2) is currently the Appellate Indigent Defense Oversight Advisory Committee. The criteria approved by this committee can be found on the judicial branch's public website at *www.courts.ca.gov/4206.htm.*

Rule 8.304.   Filing the appeal; certificate of probable cause

(a) Notice of appeal

(1) To appeal from a judgment or an appealable order of the superior court in a felony case—other than a judgment imposing a sentence of death—the defendant or the People must file a notice of appeal in that superior court. To appeal after a plea of guilty or nolo contendere or after an admission of probation violation, the defendant must also comply with (b).

(2) As used in (1), "felony case" means any criminal action in which a felony is charged, regardless of the outcome. A felony is "charged" when an information or indictment accusing the defendant of a felony is filed or a complaint accusing the defendant of a felony is certified to the superior court under Penal Code section 859a. A felony case includes an action in which the defendant is charged with:

(A) A felony and a misdemeanor or infraction, but is convicted of only the misdemeanor or infraction;

(B) A felony, but is convicted of only a lesser offense; or

(C) An offense filed as a felony but punishable as either a felony or a misdemeanor, and the offense is thereafter deemed a misdemeanor under Penal Code section 17(b).

(3) If the defendant appeals, the defendant or the defendant's attorney must sign the notice of appeal. If the People appeal, the attorney for the People must sign the notice.

(4) The notice of appeal must be liberally construed. Except as provided in (b), the notice is sufficient if it identifies the particular judgment or order being appealed. The notice need not specify the court to which the appeal is taken; the appeal will be treated as taken to the Court of Appeal for the district in which the superior court is located.

(Subd (a) amended effective January 1, 2007.)

(b) Appeal after plea of guilty or nolo contendere or after admission of probation violation

(1) Except as provided in (4), to appeal from a superior court judgment after a plea of guilty or nolo contendere or after an admission of probation violation, the defendant must file in that superior court—with the notice of appeal required by (a)—the statement required by Penal Code section 1237.5 for issuance of a certificate of probable cause.

(2) Within 20 days after the defendant files a statement under (1), the superior court must sign and file either a certificate of probable cause or an order denying the certificate.

(3) If the defendant does not file the statement required by (1) or if the superior court denies a certificate of probable cause, the superior court clerk must mark the notice of appeal "Inoperative," notify the defendant, and send a copy of the marked notice of appeal to the district appellate project.

(4) The defendant need not comply with (1) if the notice of appeal states that the appeal is based on:

(A) The denial of a motion to suppress evidence under Penal Code section 1538.5; or

(B) Grounds that arose after entry of the plea and do not affect the plea's validity.

(5) If the defendant's notice of appeal contains a statement under (4), the reviewing court will not consider any issue affecting the validity of the plea unless the defendant also complies with (1).

(Subd (b) amended effective July 1, 2007; previously amended effective January 1, 2007.)

(c) Notification of the appeal

(1) When a notice of appeal is filed, the superior court clerk must promptly send a notification of the filing to the attorney of record for each party, to any unrepresented defendant, to the reviewing court clerk, to each court reporter, and to any primary reporter or reporting supervisor. If the defendant also files a statement under (b)(1), the clerk must not send the notification unless the superior court files a certificate under (b)(2).

(2) The notification must show the date it was sent, the number and title of the case, and the dates the notice of appeal and any certificate under (b)(2) were filed. If the information is available, the notification must also include:

(A) The name, address, telephone number, e-mail address, and California State Bar number of each attorney of record in the case;

(B) The name of the party each attorney represented in the superior court; and

(C) The name, address, telephone number and e-mail address of any unrepresented defendant.

(3) The notification to the reviewing court clerk must also include a copy of the notice of appeal, any certificate filed under (b), and the sequential list of reporters made under rule 2.950.

(4) A copy of the notice of appeal is sufficient notification under (1) if the required information is on the copy or is added by the superior court clerk.

(5) The sending of a notification under (1) is a sufficient performance of the clerk's duty despite the discharge, disqualification, suspension, disbarment, or death of the attorney.

(6) Failure to comply with any provision of this subdivision does not affect the validity of the notice of appeal.

(Subd (c) amended effective January 1, 2016; previously amended effective January 1, 2007.)

Rule 8.304 amended effective January 1, 2016; repealed and adopted as rule 30 effective January 1, 2004; previously amended and renumbered as rule 8.304 effective January 1, 2007; previously amended effective July 1, 2007.

Advisory Committee Comment

Subdivision (a). Penal Code section 1235(b) provides that an appeal from a judgment or appealable order in a "felony case" is taken to the Court of Appeal, and

Penal Code section 691(f) defines "felony case" to mean "a criminal action in which a felony is charged...." Rule 8.304(a)(2) makes it clear that a "felony case" is an action in which a felony is charged *regardless of the outcome of the action.* Thus the question whether to file a notice of appeal under this rule or under the rules governing appeals to the appellate division of the superior court (rule 8.800 et seq.) is answered simply by examining the accusatory pleading: if that document charged the defendant with at least one count of felony (as defined in Penal Code, section 17(a)), the Court of Appeal has appellate jurisdiction and the appeal must be taken under this rule *even if the prosecution did not result in a punishment of imprisonment in a state prison.*

It is settled case law that an appeal is taken to the Court of Appeal not only when the defendant is charged with and convicted of a felony, but also when the defendant is charged with both a felony and a misdemeanor (Pen. Code, § 691(f)) but is convicted of only the misdemeanor (e.g., *People v. Brown* (1970) 10 Cal.App.3d 169); when the defendant is charged with a felony but is convicted of only a lesser offense (Pen. Code, § 1159; e.g., *People v. Spreckels* (1954) 125 Cal.App.2d 507); and when the defendant is charged with an offense filed as a felony but punishable as either a felony or a misdemeanor, and the offense is thereafter deemed a misdemeanor under Penal Code section 17(b) (e.g., *People v. Douglas* (1999) 20 Cal.4th 85; *People v. Clark* (1971) 17 Cal.App.3d 890).

Trial court unification did not change this rule: after as before unification, "Appeals in felony cases lie to the [C]ourt of [A]ppeal, regardless of whether the appeal is from the superior court, the municipal court, or the action of a magistrate. *Cf.* Cal. Const. art. VI, § 11(a) [except in death penalty cases, Courts of Appeal have appellate jurisdiction when superior courts have original jurisdiction 'in causes of a type within the appellate jurisdiction of the [C]ourts of [A]ppeal on June 30, 1995....'.]" ("Recommendation on Trial Court Unification" (July 1998) 28 *Cal. Law Revision Com. Rep.* 455–56.)

Subdivision (b). Under (b)(1), the defendant is required to file both a notice of appeal and the statement required by Penal Code section 1237.5(a) for issuance of a certificate of probable cause. Requiring a notice of appeal in all cases simplifies the rule, permits compliance with the signature requirement of rule 8.304(a)(3), ensures that the defendant's intent to appeal will not be misunderstood, and makes the provision consistent with the rule in civil appeals and with current practice as exemplified in the Judicial Council form governing criminal appeals.

Because of the drastic consequences of failure to file the statement required for issuance of a certificate of probable cause in an appeal after a plea of guilty or nolo contendere or after an admission of probation violation, (b)(5) alerts appellants to a relevant rule of case law, i.e., that although such an appeal may be maintained without a certificate of probable cause if the notice of appeal states the appeal is based on the denial of a motion to suppress evidence or on grounds arising after entry of the plea and not affecting its validity (rule 8.304(b)(4)), no *issue* challenging the validity of the plea is cognizable on that appeal without a certificate of probable cause. (*People v. Mendez* (1999) 19 Cal.4th 1084, 1104.)

Rule 8.308.   Time to appeal

(a) Normal time

Except as provided in (b) or as otherwise provided by law, a notice of appeal and any statement required by Penal Code section 1237.5 must be filed within 60 days after the rendition of the judgment or the making of the order being appealed. Except as provided in rule 8.66, no court may extend the time to file a notice of appeal.

(Subd (a) amended effective July 1, 2007; previously amended effective January 1, 2005, and January 1, 2007.)

(b) Cross-appeal

If the defendant or the People timely appeals from a judgment or appealable order, the time for any other party to appeal from the same judgment or order is either the time specified in (a) or 30 days after the superior court clerk sends notification of the first appeal, whichever is later.

(Subd (b) amended effective January 1, 2016; adopted effective January 1, 2007; previously amended effective January 1, 2008.)

(c) Premature notice of appeal

A notice of appeal filed before the judgment is rendered or the order is made is premature, but the reviewing court may treat the notice as filed immediately after the rendition of judgment or the making of the order.

(Subd (c) relettered effective January 1, 2007; adopted as subd (b) effective January 1, 2004.)

(d) Late notice of appeal

The superior court clerk must mark a late notice of appeal "Received [date] but not filed," notify the party that the notice was not filed because it was late, and send a copy of the marked notice of appeal to the district appellate project.

(Subd (d) relettered effective January 1, 2007; adopted as subd (c) effective January 1, 2004.)

Rule 8.308 amended effective January 1, 2016; adopted as rule 30.1 effective January 1, 2004; previously amended and renumbered as rule 8.308 effective January 1, 2007; previously amended effective January 1, 2005, July 1, 2007, January 1, 2008, and July 1, 2010.

Advisory Committee Comment

Subdivision (c). The subdivision requires the clerk to send a copy of a late notice of appeal, marked with the date it was received but not filed, to the appellate project for the district; that entity is charged with the duty, among others, of dealing with indigent criminal appeals that suffer from procedural defect, but it can do so efficiently only if it is promptly notified of such cases.

Subdivision (d). See rule 8.25(b)(5) for provisions concerning the timeliness of documents mailed by inmates or patients from custodial institutions.

Rule 8.312. Stay of execution and release on appeal

(a) Application

Pending appeal, the defendant may apply to the reviewing court:

(1) For a stay of execution after a judgment of conviction or an order granting probation; or

(2) For bail, to reduce bail, or for release on other conditions.

(Subd (a) amended effective January 1, 2007.)

(b) Showing

The application must include a showing that the defendant sought relief in the superior court and that the court unjustifiably denied the application.

(c) Service

The application must be served on the district attorney and on the Attorney General.

(d) Interim relief

Pending its ruling on the application, the reviewing court may grant the relief requested. The reviewing court must notify the superior court under rule 8.489 of any stay that it grants.

(Subd (d) amended effective January 1, 2009; previously amended effective January 1, 2007.)

Rule 8.312 amended effective January 1, 2009; adopted as rule 30.2 effective January 1, 2004; previously amended and renumbered effective January 1, 2007.

Advisory Committee Comment

Subdivision (a). The remedy of an application for bail under (a)(2) is separate from but consistent with the statutory remedy of a petition for habeas corpus under Penal Code section 1490. (*In re Brumback* (1956) 46 Cal.2d 810, 815, fn. 3.)

An order of the Court of Appeal denying bail or reduction of bail, or for release on other conditions, is final on filing. (See rule 8.366(b)(2)(A).)

Subdivision (d). The first sentence of (d) recognizes the case law holding that a reviewing court may grant bail or reduce bail, or release the defendant on other conditions, pending its ruling on an application for that relief. (See, e.g., *In re Fishman* (1952) 109 Cal.App.2d 632, 633; *In re Keddy* (1951) 105 Cal.App.2d 215, 217.) The second sentence of the subdivision requires the reviewing court to notify the superior court under rule 8.489 when it grants either (1) a stay to preserve the status quo pending its ruling on a stay application or (2) the stay requested by that application.

Rule 8.316. Abandoning the appeal

(a) How to abandon

An appellant may abandon the appeal at any time by filing an abandonment of the appeal signed by the appellant or the appellant's attorney of record.

(b) Where to file; effect of filing

(1) If the record has not been filed in the reviewing court, the appellant must file the abandonment in the superior court. The filing effects a dismissal of the appeal and restores the superior court's jurisdiction.

(2) If the record has been filed in the reviewing court, the appellant must file the abandonment in that court. The reviewing court may dismiss the appeal and direct immediate issuance of the remittitur.

(c) Clerk's duties

(1) The clerk of the court in which the appellant files the abandonment must immediately notify the adverse party of the filing or of the order of dismissal. If the defendant abandons the appeal, the clerk must notify both the district attorney and the Attorney General.

(2) If the appellant files the abandonment in the superior court, the clerk must immediately notify the reviewing court.

(3) The clerk must immediately notify the reporter if the appeal is abandoned before the reporter has filed the transcript.

Rule 8.316 renumbered effective January 1, 2007; adopted as rule 30.3 effective January 1, 2004.

Article 2
Record on Appeal

Rule 8.320. Normal record; exhibits

(a) Contents

If the defendant appeals from a judgment of conviction, or if the People appeal from an order granting a new trial, the record must contain a clerk's transcript and a reporter's transcript, which together constitute the normal record.

(b) Clerk's transcript

The clerk's transcript must contain:

(1) The accusatory pleading and any amendment;

(2) Any demurrer or other plea;

(3) All court minutes;

(4) All jury instructions that any party submitted in writing and the cover page required by rule 2.1055(b)(2) indicating the party requesting each instruction, and any written jury instructions given by the court;

(5) Any written communication between the court and the jury or any individual juror;

(6) Any verdict;

(7) Any written opinion of the court;

(8) The judgment or order appealed from and any abstract of judgment or commitment;

(9) Any motion for new trial, with supporting and opposing memoranda and attachments;

(10) The notice of appeal and any certificate of probable cause filed under rule 8.304(b);

(11) Any transcript of a sound or sound-and-video recording furnished to the jury or tendered to the court under rule 2.1040;

(12) Any application for additional record and any order on the application;

(13) And, if the appellant is the defendant:

(A) Any written defense motion denied in whole or in part, with supporting and opposing memoranda and attachments;

(B) If related to a motion under (A), any search warrant and return and the reporter's transcript of any preliminary examination or grand jury hearing;

(C) Any document admitted in evidence to prove a prior juvenile adjudication, criminal conviction, or prison term;

(D) The probation officer's report; and

(E) Any court-ordered diagnostic or psychological report required under Penal Code section 1203.03(b) or 1369.

(Subd (b) amended effective January 1, 2014; previously amended effective January 1, 2005, January 1, 2007, January 1, 2008, and January 1, 2010.)

(c) Reporter's transcript

The reporter's transcript must contain:

(1) The oral proceedings on the entry of any plea other than a not guilty plea;

(2) The oral proceedings on any motion in limine;

(3) The oral proceedings at trial, but excluding the voir dire examination of jurors and any opening statement;

(4) All instructions given orally;

(5) Any oral communication between the court and the jury or any individual juror;

(6) Any oral opinion of the court;

(7) The oral proceedings on any motion for new trial;

(8) The oral proceedings at sentencing, granting or denying of probation, or other dispositional hearing;

(9) And, if the appellant is the defendant:

(A) The oral proceedings on any defense motion denied in whole or in part except motions for disqualification of a judge and motions under Penal Code section 995;

(B) The closing arguments; and

(C) Any comment on the evidence by the court to the jury.

(Subd (c) amended effective January 1, 2007.)

(d) Limited normal record in certain appeals

If the People appeal from a judgment on a demurrer to the accusatory pleading, or if the defendant or the People appeal from an appealable order other than a ruling on a motion for new trial, the normal record is composed of:

(1) *Clerk's transcript*

A clerk's transcript containing:

(A) The accusatory pleading and any amendment;

(B) Any demurrer or other plea;

(C) Any written motion or notice of motion granted or denied by the order appealed from, with supporting and opposing memoranda and attachments;

(D) The judgment or order appealed from and any abstract of judgment or commitment;

(E) Any court minutes relating to the judgment or order appealed from and:

(i) If there was a trial in the case, any court minutes of proceedings at the time the original verdict is rendered and any subsequent proceedings; or

(ii) If the original judgment of conviction is based on a guilty plea or nolo contendere plea, any court minutes of the proceedings at the time of entry of such plea and any subsequent proceedings;

(F) The notice of appeal; and

(G) If the appellant is the defendant, all probation officer reports and any court-ordered diagnostic report required under Penal Code section 1203.03(b).

(2) *Reporter's transcript*

(A) A reporter's transcript of any oral proceedings incident to the judgment or order being appealed; and

(B) If the appeal is from an order after judgment, a reporter's transcript of:

(i) The original sentencing proceeding; and

(ii) If the original judgment of conviction is based on a guilty plea or nolo contendere plea, the proceedings at the time of entry of such plea.

(Subd (d) amended effective January 1, 2013; previously amended effective January 1, 2007.)

(e) Exhibits

Exhibits admitted in evidence, refused, or lodged are deemed part of the record, but may be transmitted to the reviewing court only as provided in rule 8.224.

(Subd (e) amended effective January 1, 2007.)

(f) Stipulation for partial transcript

If counsel for the defendant and the People stipulate in writing before the record is certified that any part of the record is not required for proper determination of the appeal, that part must not be prepared or sent to the reviewing court.

Rule 8.320 amended effective January 1, 2014; repealed and adopted as rule 31 effective January 1, 2004; previously amended and renumbered effective January 1, 2007; previously amended effective January 1, 2005, January 1, 2008, January 1, 2010, and January 1, 2013.

Advisory Committee Comment

Rules 8.45–8.46 address the appropriate handling of sealed and confidential records that must be included in the record on appeal. Examples of confidential records include Penal Code section 1203.03 diagnostic reports, records closed to inspection by court order under *People v. Marsden* (1970) 2 Cal.3d 118 or *Pitchess v. Superior Court* (1974) 11 Cal.3d 531, in-camera proceedings on a confidential informant, and defense expert funding requests (Pen. Code, § 987.9; *Keenan v. Superior Court* (1982) 31 Cal.3d 424, 430).

Subdivision (d)(1)(E). This rule identifies the minutes that must be included in the record. The trial court clerk may include additional minutes beyond those identified in this rule if that would be more cost-effective.

Rule 8.483 governs the normal record and exhibits in civil commitment appeals.

Rule 8.324. Application in superior court for addition to normal record

(a) Appeal by the People

The People, as appellant, may apply to the superior court for inclusion in the record of any item that would be part of the normal record in a defendant's appeal.

(b) Application by either party

Either the People or the defendant may apply to the superior court for inclusion in the record of any of the following items:

(1) In the clerk's transcript: any written defense motion granted in whole or in part or any written motion by the People, with supporting and opposing memoranda and attachments;

(2) In the reporter's transcript:

(A) The voir dire examination of jurors;

(B) Any opening statement; and

(C) The oral proceedings on motions other than those listed in rule 8.320(c).

(Subd (b) amended effective January 1, 2007.)

(c) Application

(1) An application for additional record must describe the material to be included and explain how it may be useful in the appeal.

(2) The application must be filed in the superior court with the notice of appeal or as soon thereafter as possible, and will be treated as denied if it is filed after the record is sent to the reviewing court.

(3) The clerk must immediately present the application to the trial judge.

(d) Order

(1) Within five days after the application is filed, the judge must order that the record include as much of the additional material as the judge finds proper to fully present the points raised by the applicant. Denial of the application does not preclude a motion in the reviewing court for augmentation under rule 8.155.

(2) If the judge does not rule on the application within the time prescribed by (1), the requested material—other than exhibits—must be included in the clerk's transcript or the reporter's transcript without a court order.

(3) The clerk must immediately notify the reporter if additions to the reporter's transcript are required under (1) or (2).

(Subd (d) amended effective January 1, 2007.)

Rule 8.324 amended and renumbered effective January 1, 2007; adopted as rule 31.1 effective January 1, 2004.

Rule 8.328. Confidential records [Repealed]

Rule 8.328 repealed effective January 1, 2014; adopted as rule 31.2 effective January 1, 2004; previously amended effective January 1, 2005, and January 1, 2011; previously amended and renumbered effective January 1, 2007.

Rule 8.332. Juror-identifying information

(a) Application

A clerk's transcript, a reporter's transcript, or any other document in the record that contains juror-identifying information must comply with this rule.

(Subd (a) amended effective January 1, 2007.)

(b) Juror names, addresses, and telephone numbers

(1) The name of each trial juror or alternate sworn to hear the case must be replaced with an identifying number wherever it appears in any document. The superior court clerk must prepare and keep under seal in the case file a table correlating the jurors' names with their identifying numbers. The clerk and the reporter must use the table in preparing all transcripts or other documents.

(2) The addresses and telephone numbers of trial jurors and alternates sworn to hear the case must be deleted from all documents.

(c) Potential jurors

Information identifying potential jurors called but not sworn as trial jurors or alternates must not be sealed unless otherwise ordered under Code of Civil Procedure section 237(a)(1).

Rule 8.332 amended and renumbered effective January 1, 2007; adopted as rule 31.3 effective January 1, 2004.

Advisory Committee Comment

Rule 8.332 implements Code of Civil Procedure section 237.

Rule 8.336. Preparing, certifying, and sending the record

(a) Immediate preparation when appeal is likely

(1) The reporter and the clerk must begin preparing the record immediately after a verdict or finding of guilt of a felony is announced following a trial on the merits, unless the judge determines that an appeal is unlikely under (2).

(2) In determining the likelihood of an appeal, the judge must consider the facts of the case and the fact that an appeal is likely if the defendant has been convicted of a crime for which probation is prohibited or is prohibited except in unusual cases, or if the trial involved a contested question of law important to the outcome.

(3) A determination under (2) is an administrative decision intended to further the efficient operation of the court and not intended to affect any substantive or procedural right of the defendant or the People. The determination cannot be cited to prove or disprove any legal or factual issue in the case and is not reviewable by appeal or writ.

(b) Appeal after plea of guilty or nolo contendere or after admission of probation violation

In an appeal under rule 8.304(b)(1), the time to prepare, certify, and file the record begins when the court files a certificate of probable cause under rule 8.304(b)(2).

(Subd (b) amended effective January 1, 2007.)

(c) Clerk's transcript

(1) Except as provided in (a) or (b), the clerk must begin preparing the clerk's transcript immediately after the notice of appeal is filed.

(2) Within 20 days after the notice of appeal is filed, the clerk must complete preparation of an original and two copies of the clerk's transcript, one for defendant's counsel and one for the Attorney General or the district attorney, whichever is the counsel for the People on appeal.

(3) On request, the clerk must prepare an extra copy for the district attorney or the Attorney General, whichever is not counsel for the People on appeal.

(4) If there is more than one appealing defendant, the clerk must prepare an extra copy for each additional appealing defendant represented by separate counsel.

(5) The clerk must certify as correct the original and all copies of the clerk's transcript.

(Subd (c) amended effective January 1, 2007.)

(d) Reporter's transcript

(1) Except as provided in (a) or (b), the reporter must begin preparing the reporter's transcript immediately on being notified by the clerk under rule 8.304(c)(1) that the notice of appeal has been filed.

(2) The reporter must prepare an original and the same number of copies of the reporter's transcript as (c) requires of the clerk's transcript, and must certify each as correct.

(3) The reporter must deliver the original and all copies to the superior court clerk as soon as they are certified, but no later than 20 days after the notice of appeal is filed.

(4) Any portion of the transcript transcribed during trial must not be retyped unless necessary to correct errors, but must be repaginated and combined with any portion of the transcript not previously transcribed. Any additional copies needed must not be retyped but, if the transcript is in paper form, must be prepared by photocopying or an equivalent process.

(5) In a multireporter case, the clerk must accept any completed portion of the transcript from the primary reporter one week after the time prescribed by (3) even if other portions are uncompleted. The clerk must promptly pay each reporter who certifies that all portions of the transcript assigned to that reporter are completed.

(Subd (d) amended effective January 1, 2018; previously amended effective January 1, 2007, January 1, 2014, January 1, 2016, and January 1, 2017.)

(e) Extension of time

(1) The superior court may not extend the time for preparing the record.

(2) The reviewing court may order one or more extensions of time for preparing the record, including a reporter's transcript, not exceeding a total of 60 days, on receipt of:

(A) A declaration showing good cause; and

(B) In the case of a reporter's transcript, certification by the superior court presiding judge, or a court administrator designated by the presiding judge, that an extension is reasonable and necessary in light of the workload of all reporters in the court.

(Subd (e) amended effective January 1, 2014; previously amended effective January 1, 2007.)

(f) Form of record

The clerk's and reporter's transcripts must comply with rules 8.45–8.47, relating to sealed and confidential records, and rule 8.144.

(Subd (f) adopted effective January 1, 2014.)

(g) Sending the transcripts

(1) When the clerk and reporter's transcripts are certified as correct, the clerk must promptly send:

(A) The original transcripts to the reviewing court, noting the sending date on each original;

(B) One copy of each transcript to appellate counsel for each defendant represented by separate counsel and to the Attorney General or the district attorney, whichever is counsel for the People on appeal; and

(C) One copy of each transcript to the district attorney or Attorney General if requested under (c)(3).

(2) If the defendant is not represented by appellate counsel when the transcripts are certified as correct, the clerk must send that defendant's counsel's copy of the transcripts to the district appellate project.

(Subd (g) repealed and relettered effective January 1, 2014; previously amended as subd (f) effective January 1, 2007.)

(h) Supervision of preparation of record

Each clerk/executive officer of the Court of Appeal, under the supervision of the administrative presiding justice or the presiding justice, must take all appropriate steps to ensure that superior court clerks and reporters promptly perform their duties under this rule. This provision does not affect the superior courts' responsibility for the prompt preparation of appellate records.

(Subd (h) amended effective January 1, 2018.)

Rule 8.336 amended effective January 1, 2018; repealed and adopted as rule 32 effective January 1, 2004; previously amended and renumbered as rule 8.336 effective January 1, 2007; previously amended effective January 1, 2010, January 1, 2014, January 1, 2016, January 1, 2017, and January 1, 2018.

Advisory Committee Comment

Subdivision (a). Subdivision (a) implements Code of Civil Procedure section 269(b).

Subdivision (f). Examples of confidential records include Penal Code section 1203.03 diagnostic reports, records closed to inspection by court order under *People v. Marsden* (1970) 2 Cal.3d 118 or *Pitchess v. Superior Court* (1974) 11 Cal.3d 531, in-camera proceedings on a confidential informant, and defense expert funding requests (Pen. Code, § 987.9; *Keenan v. Superior Court* (1982) 31 Cal.3d 424, 430).

Subdivision (g). Under rule 8.71(c), the superior court clerk may send the record to the reviewing court in electronic form.

Rule 8.340. Augmenting or correcting the record in the Court of Appeal

(a) Subsequent trial court orders

(1) If, after the record is certified, the trial court amends or recalls the judgment or makes any other order in the case, including an order affecting the sentence or probation, the clerk must promptly certify and send a copy of the amended abstract of judgment or other order—as an augmentation of the record—to:

(A) The reviewing court, the probation officer, the defendant,

(B) The defendant's appellate counsel for each defendant represented by separate counsel, and the Attorney General or the district attorney, whichever is counsel for the People on appeal; and

(C) The district attorney or Attorney General, whichever is not counsel for the People on appeal, if he or she requested a copy of the clerk's transcript under 8.336(c)(3).

(2) If there is any additional document or transcript related to the amended judgment or new order that any rule or order requires be included in the record, the clerk must send this document or transcript with the amended abstract of judgment or other order. The clerk must promptly copy and certify any such document, and the reporter must promptly prepare and certify any such transcript.

(Subd (a) amended effective January 1, 2007.)

(b) Omissions

(1) If, after the record is certified, the superior court clerk or the reporter learns that the record omits a document or transcript that any rule or order requires to be included, the clerk must promptly copy and certify the document or the reporter must promptly prepare and certify the transcript. Without the need for a court order, the clerk must promptly send the document or transcript—as an augmentation of the record—to all those who are listed under (a)(1).

(Subd (b) amended effective January 1, 2007.)

(c) Augmentation or correction by the reviewing court

At any time, on motion of a party or on its own motion, the reviewing court may order the record augmented or corrected as provided in rule 8.155. The clerk must send any document or transcript added to the record to all those who are listed under (a)(1).

(Subd (c) amended and relettered effective January 1, 2007; adopted as subd (d) effective January 1, 2004.)

(d) Defendant not yet represented

If the defendant is not represented by appellate counsel when the record is augmented or corrected, the clerk must send that defendant's counsel's copy of the augmentations or corrections to the district appellate project.

(Subd (d) adopted effective January 1, 2007.)

Rule 8.340 amended and renumbered effective January 1, 2007; adopted as rule 32.1 effective January 1, 2004.

Advisory Committee Comment

Subdivision (b). The words "or order" in the first sentence of (b) are intended to refer to any court order to include additional material in the record, e.g., an order of the superior court under rule 8.324(d)(1).

Rule 8.344. Agreed statement

If the parties present the appeal on an agreed statement, they must comply with the relevant provisions of rule 8.134, but the appellant must file an original and, if the statement is filed in paper form, three copies of the statement in superior court within 25 days after filing the notice of appeal.

Rule 8.344 amended effective January 1, 2016; adopted as rule 32.2 effective January 1, 2004; amended and renumbered as rule 8.344 effective January 1, 2007.

Rule 8.346. Settled statement

(a) Application

As soon as a party learns that any portion of the oral proceedings cannot be transcribed, the party may serve and file in superior court an application for permission to prepare a settled statement. The application must explain why the oral proceedings cannot be transcribed.

(b) Order and proposed statement

The judge must rule on the application within five days after it is filed. If the judge grants the application, the parties must comply with the relevant provisions of rule 8.137, but the applicant must deliver a proposed statement to the judge for settlement within 30 days after it is ordered, unless the reviewing court extends the time.

(Subd (b) amended effective January 1, 2007.)

(c) Serving and filing the settled statement

The applicant must prepare, serve, and file in superior court an original and, if the statement is filed in paper form, three copies of the settled statement.

(Subd (c) amended effective January 1, 2016.)

Rule 8.346 amended effective January 1, 2016; adopted as rule 32.3 effective January 1, 2004; amended and renumbered as rule 8.346 effective January 1, 2007.

Article 3
Briefs, Hearing, and Decision

Rule 8.360. Briefs by parties and amici curiae
Rule 8.361. Certificate of interested entities or persons
Rule 8.366. Hearing and decision in the Court of Appeal
Rule 8.368. Hearing and decision in the Supreme Court

Rule 8.360. Briefs by parties and amici curiae

(a) Contents and form

Except as provided in this rule, briefs in criminal appeals must comply as nearly as possible with rules 8.200 and 8.204.

(Subd (a) amended effective January 1, 2007.)

(b) Length

(1) A brief produced on a computer must not exceed 25,500 words, including footnotes. Such a brief must include a certificate by appellate counsel or an unrepresented defendant stating the number of words in the brief; the person certifying may rely on the word count of the computer program used to prepare the brief.

(2) A typewritten brief must not exceed 75 pages.

(3) The tables required under rule 8.204(a)(1), the cover information required under rule 8.204(b)(10), any Certificate of Interested Entities or Persons required under rule 8.361, a certificate under (1), any signature block, and any attachment permitted under rule 8.204(d) are excluded from the limits stated in (1) or (2).

(4) A combined brief in an appeal governed by (e) must not exceed double the limit stated in (1) or (2).

(5) On application, the presiding justice may permit a longer brief for good cause.

(Subd (b) amended effective January 1, 2011; previously amended effective January 1, 2007.)

(c) Time to file

(1) The appellant's opening brief must be served and filed within 40 days after the record is filed in the reviewing court.

(2) The respondent's brief must be served and filed within 30 days after the appellant's opening brief is filed.

(3) The appellant must serve and file a reply brief, if any, within 20 days after the respondent files its brief.

(4) The time to serve and file a brief may not be extended by stipulation, but only by order of the presiding justice under rule 8.60.

(5) If a party fails to timely file an appellant's opening brief or a respondent's brief, the reviewing court clerk must promptly notify the party in writing that the brief must be filed within 30 days after the notice is sent, and that failure to comply may result in one of the following sanctions:

(A) If the brief is an appellant's opening brief:

(i) If the appellant is the People, the court will dismiss the appeal;

(ii) If the appellant is the defendant and is represented by appointed counsel on appeal, the court will relieve that appointed counsel and appoint new counsel;

(iii) If the appellant is the defendant and is not represented by appointed counsel, the court will dismiss the appeal; or

(B) If the brief is a respondent's brief, the court will decide the appeal on the record, the opening brief, and any oral argument by the appellant.

(6) If a party fails to comply with a notice under (5), the court may impose the sanction specified in the notice.

(Subd (c) amended effective January 1, 2016; previously amended effective January 1, 2007.)

(d) Service

(1) Defendant's appellate counsel must serve each brief for the defendant on the People and the district attorney, and must send a copy of each to the defendant personally unless the defendant requests otherwise.

(2) The proof of service under (1) must state that a copy of the defendant's brief was sent to the defendant, or counsel must file a signed statement that the defendant requested in writing that no copy be sent.

(3) The People must serve two copies of their briefs on the appellate counsel for each defendant who is a party to the appeal and one copy on the district appellate project. If the district attorney is representing the People, one copy of the district attorney's brief must be served on the Attorney General.

(4) A copy of each brief must be served on the superior court clerk for delivery to the trial judge.

(Subd (d) amended effective January 1, 2013.)

(e) When a defendant and the People appeal

When both a defendant and the People appeal, the defendant must file the first opening brief unless the reviewing court orders otherwise, and rule 8.216(b) governs the contents of the briefs.

(Subd (e) amended effective January 1, 2007.)

(f) Amicus curiae briefs

Amicus curiae briefs may be filed as provided in rule 8.200(c).

(Subd (f) amended effective January 1, 2007.)

Rule 8.360 amended effective January 1, 2016; repealed and adopted as rule 33 effective January 1, 2004; previously amended and renumbered as rule 8.360 effective January 1, 2007; previously amended effective January 1, 2011, and January 1, 2013.

Advisory Committee Comment

Subdivision (b). Subdivision (b)(1) states the maximum permissible length of a brief produced on a computer in terms of word count rather than page count. This provision tracks a provision in rule 8.204(c) governing Court of Appeal briefs and is explained in the comment to that provision. The word count assumes a brief using one-and-one-half spaced lines of text, as permitted by rule 8.204(b)(5). Subdivision (b)(3) specifies certain items that are not counted toward the maximum brief length. Signature blocks as referenced in this provision, include not only the signatures, but also the printed names, titles, and affiliations of any attorneys filing or joining in the brief, which may accompany the signature.

The maximum permissible length of briefs in death penalty appeals is prescribed in rule 8.630.

Rule 8.361. Certificate of interested entities or persons

In criminal cases in which an entity is a defendant, that defendant must comply with the requirements of rule 8.208 concerning serving and filing a certificate of interested entities or persons.

Rule 8.361 adopted effective January 1, 2009.

Advisory Committee Comment

Under rule 8.208(c), for purposes of certificates of interested entities or persons, an "entity" means a corporation, a partnership, a firm, or any other association but does not include a governmental entity or its agencies or a natural person.

Rule 8.366. Hearing and decision in the Court of Appeal

(a) General application of rules 8.252–8.272

Except as provided in this rule, rules 8.252–8.272 govern the hearing and decision in the Court of Appeal of an appeal in a criminal case.

(Subd (a) amended and lettered effective January 1, 2009; adopted as unlettered subd effective January 1, 2004.)

(b) Finality

(1) Except as otherwise provided in this rule, a Court of Appeal decision in a proceeding under this chapter, including an order dismissing an appeal involuntarily, is final in that court 30 days after filing.

(2) The following Court of Appeal decisions are final in that court on filing:

(A) The denial of an application for bail or to reduce bail pending appeal; and

(B) The dismissal of an appeal on request or stipulation.

(3) If a Court of Appeal certifies its opinion for publication or partial publication after filing its decision and before its decision becomes final

in that court, the finality period runs from the filing date of the order for publication.

(4) If an order modifying an opinion changes the appellate judgment, the finality period runs from the filing date of the modification order.

(Subd (b) adopted effective January 1, 2009.)

(c) Sanctions

Except for (a)(1), rule 8.276 applies in criminal appeals.

(Subd (c) amended and lettered effective January 1, 2009; adopted as unlettered subd effective January 1, 2004.)

Rule 8.366 amended effective January 1, 2009; adopted as rule 33.1 effective January 1, 2004; previously amended and renumbered effective January 1, 2007; previously amended effective January 1, 2008.

Advisory Committee Comment

Subdivision (b). As used in subdivision (b)(1), "decision" includes all interlocutory orders of the Court of Appeal. (See Advisory Committee Comment to rule 8.500(a) and (e).) This provision addresses the finality of decisions in criminal appeals. See rule 8.264(b) for provisions addressing the finality of decisions in proceedings under chapter 2, relating to civil appeals, and rule 8.490 for provisions addressing the finality of proceedings under chapter 7, relating to writs of mandate, certiorari, and prohibition.

Rule 8.368. Hearing and decision in the Supreme Court

Rules 8.500 through 8.552 govern the hearing and decision in the Supreme Court of an appeal in a criminal case.

Rule 8.368 amended and renumbered effective January 1, 2007; adopted as rule 33.2 effective January 1, 2004.

Chapter 4
Habeas Corpus Appeals and Writs

Art. 1. Habeas Corpus Proceedings Not Related to Judgment of Death. Rules 8.380–8.388.

Art. 2. Appeals From Superior Court Decisions in Death Penalty–Related Habeas Corpus Proceedings. Rules 8.390–8.398.

Article 1
Habeas Corpus Proceedings Not Related to Judgment of Death

Title 8, Appellate Rules—Division 1, Rules Relating to the Supreme Court and Courts of Appeal—Chapter 4, Habeas Corpus Appeals and Writs—Article 1, Habeas Corpus Proceedings Not Related to Judgment of Death adopted effective April 25, 2019.

Rule 8.380. Petition for writ of habeas corpus filed by petitioner not represented by an attorney

Rule 8.384. Petition for writ of habeas corpus filed by an attorney for a party

Rule 8.385. Proceedings after the petition is filed

Rule 8.386. Proceedings if the return is ordered to be filed in the reviewing court

Rule 8.387. Decision in habeas corpus proceedings

Rule 8.388. Appeal from order granting relief by writ of habeas corpus

Rule 8.380. Petition for writ of habeas corpus filed by petitioner not represented by an attorney

(a) Required Judicial Council form

A person who is not represented by an attorney and who petitions a reviewing court for writ of habeas corpus seeking release from, or modification of the conditions of, custody of a person confined in a state or local penal institution, hospital, narcotics treatment facility, or other institution must file the petition on *Petition for Writ of Habeas Corpus* (form [1] **HC-001**). For good cause the court may permit the filing of a petition that is not on that form, but the petition must be verified.

(Subd (a) amended effective January 1, 2020; previously amended effective January 1, 2006, January 1, 2007, January 1, 2009, and January 1, 2018.)

Rule 8.380(a). 2019 Deletes. [1] MC-275

(b) Form and content

A petition filed under (a) need not comply with the provisions of rules 8.40, 8.204, or 8.486 that prescribe the form and content of a petition and require the petition to be accompanied by a memorandum. If any supporting documents accompanying the petition are sealed or confidential records, rules 8.45–8.47 govern these documents.

(Subd (b) amended effective January 1, 2014; adopted as part of subd (a) effective January 1, 2005; previously repealed, amended and lettered effective January 1, 2009.)

(c) Number of copies

In the Court of Appeal, the petitioner must file the original of the petition under (a) and one set of any supporting documents. In the Supreme Court, the petitioner must file an original and, if the petition is

filed in paper form, 10 copies of the petition and an original and, if the document is filed in paper form, 2 copies of any supporting document accompanying the petition unless the court orders otherwise.

(Subd (c) amended effective January 1, 2016; adopted as part of subd (a) effective January 1, 2005; previously repealed, amended, and lettered as subd (c) effective January 1, 2009.)

Rule 8.380 amended effective January 1, 2020; repealed and adopted as rule 60 effective January 1, 2005; previously amended and renumbered as rule 8.380 effective January 1, 2007; previously amended effective January 1, 2006, January 1, 2009, January 1, 2014, January 1, 2016, and January 1, 2018.

Advisory Committee Comment

Subdivision (b). Examples of confidential records include Penal Code section 1203.03 diagnostic reports, records closed to inspection by court order under *People v. Marsden* (1970) 2 Cal.3d 118 or *Pitchess v. Superior Court* (1974) 11 Cal.3d 531, in-camera proceedings on a confidential informant, and defense expert funding requests (Pen. Code, § 987.9; *Keenan v. Superior Court* (1982) 31 Cal.3d 424, 430).

Rule 8.384. Petition for writ of habeas corpus filed by an attorney for a party

(a) Form and content of petition and memorandum

(1) A petition for habeas corpus filed by an attorney need not be filed on *Petition for Writ of Habeas Corpus* (form [1] **HC-001**), but must contain the information requested in that form and must be verified. All petitions filed by attorneys, whether or not on form [2] **HC-001**, must be either typewritten or produced on a computer, and must comply with this rule and rule 8.40(b)–(c) relating to document covers and rule 8.204(a)(1)(A) relating to tables of contents and authorities. A petition that is not on form [3] **HC-001** must also comply with the remainder of rule 8.204(a)–(b).

(2) Any memorandum accompanying the petition must comply with rule 8.204(a)–(b). Except in habeas corpus proceedings related to sentences of death, any memorandum must also comply with the length limits in rule 8.204(c).

(3) The petition and any memorandum must support any reference to a matter in the supporting documents by a citation to its index number or letter and page.

(Subd (a) amended effective January 1, 2020; adopted as part of subd (b) effective January 1, 2006; previously repealed, amended, and lettered as subd (a) effective January 1, 2009; previously amended effective January 1, 2016, and January 1, 2018.)

Rule 8.384(a). 2019 Deletes. [1] MC-275 [2] MC-275 [3] MC-275

(b) Supporting documents

(1) The petition must be accompanied by a copy of any petition—excluding exhibits—pertaining to the same judgment and petitioner that was previously filed in any state court or any federal court. If such documents have previously been filed in the same Court of Appeal where the petition is filed or in the Supreme Court and the petition so states and identifies the documents by case name and number, copies of these documents need not be included in the supporting documents.

(2) If the petition asserts a claim that was the subject of an evidentiary hearing, the petition must be accompanied by a certified transcript of that hearing.

(3) Rule 8.486(c)(1) and (2) govern the form of any supporting documents accompanying the petition.

(4) If any supporting documents accompanying the petition are sealed or confidential records, rules 8.45–8.47 govern these documents.

(Subd (b) amended effective January 1, 2014; previously amended effective January 1, 2007, and January 1, 2009.)

(c) Number of copies

If the petition is filed in the Supreme Court, the attorney must file the number of copies of the petition and supporting documents required by rule 8.44(a). If the petition is filed in the Court of Appeal, the attorney must file the number of copies of the petition and supporting documents required by rule 8.44(b).

(Subd (c) amended and lettered effective January 1, 2009; adopted as part of subd (b) effective January 1, 2006.)

(d) Noncomplying petitions

The clerk must file an attorney's petition not complying with (a)–(c) if it otherwise complies with the rules of court, but the court may notify the attorney that it may strike the petition or impose a lesser sanction if the petition is not brought into compliance within a stated reasonable time of not less than five days.

(Subd (d) amended and lettered effective January 1, 2009; adopted as part of subd (b) effective January 1, 2006.)

Rule 8.384 amended effective January 1, 2020; adopted as rule 60.5 effective January 1, 2006; previously amended and renumbered as rule 8.384 effective January 1, 2007; previously amended effective January 1, 2009, January 1, 2014, January 1, 2016, and January 1, 2018.

Advisory Committee Comment

Subdivision (b)(4). Examples of confidential records include Penal Code section 1203.03 diagnostic reports, records closed to inspection by court order under *People v. Marsden* (1970) 2 Cal.3d 118 or *Pitchess v. Superior Court* (1974) 11 Cal.3d 531, in-camera proceedings on a confidential informant, and defense expert funding requests (Pen. Code, § 987.9; *Keenan v. Superior Court* (1982) 31 Cal.3d 424, 430).

Rule 8.385.   Proceedings after the petition is filed

(a) Production of record

Before ruling on the petition, the court may order the custodian of any relevant record to produce the record or a certified copy to be filed with the court. Sealed and confidential records are governed by rules 8.45–8.47.

(Subd (a) amended effective January 1, 2014; adopted effective January 1, 2009.)

(b) Informal response

(1) Before ruling on the petition, the court may request an informal written response from the respondent, the real party in interest, or an interested person. The court must send a copy of any request to the petitioner.

(2) The response must be served and filed within 15 days or as the court specifies. If the petitioner is not represented by counsel in the habeas corpus proceeding, one copy of the informal response and any supporting documents must be served on the petitioner. If the petitioner is represented by counsel in the habeas corpus proceeding, the response must be served on the petitioner's counsel. If the response is served in paper form, two copies must be served on the petitioner's counsel. If the petitioner is represented by court-appointed counsel other than the State Public Defender's Office or Habeas Corpus Resource Center, one copy must also be served on the applicable appellate project.

(3) If a response is filed, the court must notify the petitioner that a reply may be served and filed within 15 days or as the court specifies. The court may not deny the petition until that time has expired.

(Subd (b) amended effective January 1, 2016; adopted effective January 1, 2009; previously amended effective January 1, 2014.)

(c) Petition filed in an inappropriate court

(1) A Court of Appeal may deny without prejudice a petition for writ of habeas corpus that is based primarily on facts occurring outside the court's appellate district, including petitions that question:

(A) The validity of judgments or orders of trial courts located outside the district; or

(B) The conditions of confinement or the conduct of correctional officials outside the district.

(2) A Court of Appeal should deny without prejudice a petition for writ of habeas corpus that challenges the denial of parole or the petitioner's suitability for parole if the issue was not first adjudicated by the trial court that rendered the underlying judgment.

(3) If the court denies a petition solely under (1), the order must state the basis of the denial and must identify the appropriate court in which to file the petition.

(Subd (c) amended effective January 1, 2012; adopted effective January 1, 2009.)

(d) Order to show cause

If the petitioner has made the required prima facie showing that he or she is entitled to relief, the court must issue an order to show cause. An order to show cause does not grant the relief sought in the petition.

(Subd (d) adopted effective January 1, 2009.)

(e) Return to the superior court

The reviewing court may order the respondent to file a return in the superior court. The order vests jurisdiction over the cause in the superior court, which must proceed under rule 4.551.

(Subd (e) adopted effective January 1, 2009.)

(f) Return to the reviewing court

If the return is ordered to be filed in the Supreme Court or the Court of Appeal, rule 8.386 applies and the court in which the return is ordered filed must appoint counsel for any unrepresented petitioner who desires but cannot afford counsel.

(Subd (f) adopted effective January 1, 2009.)

Rule 8.385 amended effective January 1, 2016; adopted effective January 1, 2009; previously amended effective January 1, 2012, and January 1, 2014.

Advisory Committee Comment

Subdivision (a). Examples of confidential records include Penal Code section 1203.03 diagnostic reports, records closed to inspection by court order under *People v. Marsden* (1970) 2 Cal.3d 118 or *Pitchess v. Superior Court* (1974) 11 Cal.3d 531, in-camera proceedings on a confidential informant, and defense expert funding requests (Pen. Code, § 987.9; *Keenan v. Superior Court* (1982) 31 Cal.3d 424, 430).

Subdivision (c). Except for subdivision (c)(2), rule 8.385(c) restates former section 6.5 of the Standards of Judicial Administration. Subdivision (c)(2) is based on the California Supreme Court decision in *In re Roberts* (2005) 36 Cal.4th 575, which provides that petitions for writ of habeas corpus challenging denial or suitability for parole should first be adjudicated in the trial court that rendered the underlying judgment. The committee notes, however, that courts of appeal have original jurisdiction in writ proceedings and may, under appropriate circumstances, adjudicate a petition that challenges the denial or suitability of parole even if the petition was not first adjudicated by the trial court that rendered the underlying judgment. (*In re Kler* (2010) 188 Cal.App.4th 1399.) A court of appeal may, for example, adjudicate a petition that follows the court's prior reversal of a denial of parole by the Board of Parole Hearings where the issues presented by the petition directly flow from the court of appeal's prior decision and the limited hearing conducted. (*Id.* at 1404–05.)

Subdivision (d). Case law establishes the specificity of the factual allegations and support for these allegations required in a petition for a writ of habeas corpus (see, e.g., *People v. Duvall* (1995) 9 Cal.4th 464, 474–475, and *Ex parte Swain* (1949) 34 Cal.2d 300, 303–304). A court evaluating whether a petition meeting these requirements makes a prima facie showing asks whether, assuming the petition's factual allegations are true, the petitioner would be entitled to relief (*People v. Duvall*, supra).

Issuing an order to show cause is just one of the actions a court might take on a petition for a writ of habeas corpus. Examples of other actions that a court might take include denying the petition summarily, requesting an informal response from the respondent under (b), or denying the petition without prejudice under (c) because it is filed in an inappropriate court.

Rule 8.386.   Remittitur in habeas corpus proceedings [Renumbered]

Rule 8.386 amended and renumbered to rule 8.387 effective January 1, 2009; adopted effective January 1, 2008.

Another Rule 8.386 follows.

Rule 8.386.   Proceedings if the return is ordered to be filed in the reviewing court

(a) Application

This rule applies if the Supreme Court orders the return to be filed in the Supreme Court or the Court of Appeal or if the Court of Appeal orders the return to be filed in the Court of Appeal.

(Subd (a) adopted effective January 1, 2009.)

(b) Serving and filing return

(1) Unless the court orders otherwise, any return must be served and filed within 30 days after the court issues the order to show cause.

(2) If the return is filed in the Supreme Court, the respondent must file the number of copies of the return and any supporting documents required by rule 8.44(a). If the return is filed in the Court of Appeal, the respondent must file the number of copies of the return and any supporting documents required by rule 8.44(b).

(3) The return and any supporting documents must be served on the petitioner's counsel. If the return is served in paper form, two copies must be served on the petitioner's counsel. If the petitioner is represented for the habeas corpus proceeding by court-appointed counsel other than the State Public Defender's Office or Habeas Corpus Resource Center, one copy must be served on the applicable appellate project.

(Subd (b) amended effective January 1, 2016; adopted effective January 1, 2009; previously amended effective January 1, 2014.)

(c) Form and content of return

(1) The return must be either typewritten or produced on a computer and must comply with Penal Code section 1480 and rules 8.40(b)–(c) and 8.204(a)–(b). Except in habeas corpus proceedings related to sentences of death, any memorandum accompanying a return must also comply with the length limits in rule 8.204(c).

(2) Rule 8.486(c)(1) and (2) govern the form of any supporting documents accompanying the return. The return must support any reference to a matter in the supporting documents by a citation to its index number or letter and page.

(3) Any material allegation of the petition not controverted by the return is deemed admitted for purposes of the proceeding.

(Subd (c) amended effective January 1, 2016; adopted effective January 1, 2009; previously amended effective January 1, 2014.)

(d) Traverse

(1) Unless the court orders otherwise, within 30 days after the respondent files a return, the petitioner may serve and file a traverse.

(2) Any traverse must be either typewritten or produced on a computer and must comply with Penal Code section 1484 and rules 8.40(b)–(c) and 8.204(a)–(b). Except in habeas corpus proceedings related to sentences of death, any memorandum accompanying a traverse must also comply with the length limits in rule 8.204(c).

(3) Rule 8.486(c)(1) and (2) govern the form of any supporting documents accompanying the traverse.

(4) Any material allegation of the return not denied in the traverse is deemed admitted for purposes of the proceeding.

(5) If the return is filed in the Supreme Court, the attorney must file the number of copies of the traverse required by rule 8.44(a). If the return is filed in the Court of Appeal, the attorney must file the number of copies of the traverse required by rule 8.44(b).

(Subd (d) amended effective January 1, 2014; adopted effective January 1, 2009.)

(e) Judicial notice

Rule 8.252(a) governs judicial notice in the reviewing court.

(Subd (e) adopted effective January 1, 2009.)

(f) Evidentiary hearing ordered by the reviewing court

(1) An evidentiary hearing is required if, after considering the verified petition, the return, any traverse, any affidavits or declarations under penalty of perjury, and matters of which judicial notice may be taken, the court finds there is a reasonable likelihood that the petitioner may be entitled to relief and the petitioner's entitlement to relief depends on the resolution of an issue of fact.

(2) The court may appoint a referee to conduct the hearing and make recommended findings of fact.

(Subd (f) adopted effective January 1, 2009.)

(g) Oral argument and submission of the cause

Unless the court orders otherwise:

(1) Rule 8.256 governs oral argument and submission of the cause in the Court of Appeal.

(2) Rule 8.524 governs oral argument and submission of the cause in the Supreme Court.

(Subd (g) adopted effective January 1, 2009.)

Rule 8.386 amended effective January 1, 2016; adopted effective January 1, 2009; previously amended effective January 1, 2014.

Rule 8.387. Decision in habeas corpus proceedings

(a) Filing the decision

(1) Rule 8.264(a) governs the filing of the decision in the Court of Appeal.

(2) Rule 8.532(a) governs the filing of the decision in the Supreme Court.

(Subd (a) adopted effective January 1, 2009.)

(b) Finality of decision in the Court of Appeal

(1) *General finality period*

Except as otherwise provided in this rule, a Court of Appeal decision in a habeas corpus proceeding is final in that court 30 days after filing.

(2) *Denial of a petition for writ of habeas corpus without issuance of an order to show cause*

(A) Except as provided in (B), a Court of Appeal decision denying a petition for writ of habeas corpus without issuance of an order to show cause is final in the Court of Appeal upon filing.

(B) A Court of Appeal decision denying a petition for writ of habeas corpus without issuing an order to show cause is final in that court on the same day that its decision in a related appeal is final if the two decisions are filed on the same day. If the Court of Appeal orders rehearing of the decision in the appeal, its decision denying the petition for writ of habeas corpus is final when its decision on rehearing is final.

(3) *Decision in a habeas corpus proceeding after issuance of an order to show cause*

(A) If necessary to prevent mootness or frustration of the relief granted or to otherwise promote the interests of justice, a Court of Appeal may order early finality in that court of a decision in a habeas corpus proceeding after issuing an order to show cause. The decision may provide for finality in that court on filing or within a stated period of less than 30 days.

(B) If a Court of Appeal certifies its opinion for publication or partial publication after filing its decision and before its decision becomes final

in that court, the finality period runs from the filing date of the order for publication.

(Subd (b) adopted effective January 1, 2009.)

(c) Finality of decision in the Supreme Court

Rule 8.532(b) governs finality of a decision in the Supreme Court.

(Subd (c) adopted effective January 1, 2009.)

(d) Modification of decision

(1) A reviewing court may modify a decision until the decision is final in that court. If the clerk's office is closed on the date of finality, the court may modify the decision on the next day the clerk's office is open.

(2) An order modifying an opinion must state whether it changes the appellate judgment. A modification that does not change the appellate judgment does not extend the finality date of the decision. If a modification changes the appellate judgment, the finality period runs from the filing date of the modification order.

(Subd (d) adopted effective January 1, 2009.)

(e) Rehearing

(1) Rule 8.268 governs rehearing in the Court of Appeal.

(2) Rule 8.536 governs rehearing in the Supreme Court.

(Subd (e) adopted effective January 1, 2009.)

(f) Remittitur

(1) A Court of Appeal must issue a remittitur in a habeas corpus proceeding under this chapter except when the court denies the petition without issuing an order to show cause or orders the return filed in the superior court.

(2) A Court of Appeal must also issue a remittitur if the Supreme Court issues a remittitur to the Court of Appeal.

(3) Rule 8.272(b)–(d) governs issuance of a remittitur by a Court of Appeal in habeas corpus proceedings, including the clerk's duties; immediate issuance, stay, and recall of remittitur; and notice of issuance.

(Subd (f) amended effective January 1, 2014; adopted as unlettered subd effective January 1, 2008; previously amended and lettered effective January 1, 2009.)

Rule 8.387 amended effective January 1, 2014; adopted as rule 8.386 effective January 1, 2008; previously amended and renumbered effective January 1, 2009.

Advisory Committee Comment

A party may seek review of a Court of Appeal decision in a habeas corpus proceeding by way of a petition for review in the Supreme Court under rule 8.500.

Subdivision (f). Under this rule, a remittitur serves as notice that the habeas corpus proceedings have concluded.

Rule 8.388. Appeal from order granting relief by writ of habeas corpus

(a) Application

Except as otherwise provided in this rule, rules 8.304–8.368 and 8.508 govern appeals under Penal Code section 1506 or 1507 from orders granting all or part of the relief sought in a petition for writ of habeas corpus. This rule does not apply to appeals under Penal Code section 1509.1 from superior court decisions in death penalty–related habeas corpus proceedings.

(Subd (a) amended effective April 25, 2019; previously amended effective January 1, 2007.)

(b) Contents of record

In an appeal under this rule, the record must contain:

(1) The petition, the return, and the traverse;

(2) The order to show cause;

(3) All court minutes;

(4) All documents and exhibits submitted to the court;

(5) The reporter's transcript of any oral proceedings;

(6) Any written opinion of the court;

(7) The order appealed from; and

(8) The notice of appeal.

(Subd (b) amended effective January 1, 2007.)

Rule 8.388 amended effective April 25, 2019; repealed and adopted as rule 39.2 effective January 1, 2005; previously amended and renumbered as rule 8.388 effective January 1, 2007.

Article 2
Appeals From Superior Court Decisions in Death Penalty–Related Habeas Corpus Proceedings

Title 8, Appellate Rules—Division 1, Rules Relating to the Supreme Court and Courts of Appeal—Chapter 4, Habeas Corpus Appeals and Writs—Article 2, Appeals From Superior Court Decisions in Death Penalty–Related Habeas Corpus Proceedings adopted effective April 25, 2019.

Rule 8.390. Application

Rule 8.390.   Application

(a) Application

The rules in this article apply only to appeals under Penal Code section 1509.1 from superior court decisions in death penalty–related habeas corpus proceedings.

(Subd (a) adopted effective April 25, 2019.)

(b) General application of rules for criminal appeals

Except as otherwise provided in this article, rules 8.300, 8.316, 8.332, 8.340–8.346, and 8.366–8.368 govern appeals subject to the rules in this article.

(Subd (b) adopted effective April 25, 2019.)

Rule 8.390 adopted effective April 25, 2019.

Rule 8.391.   Qualifications and appointment of counsel by the Court of Appeal

(a) Qualifications

To be appointed by the Court of Appeal to represent an indigent petitioner not represented by the State Public Defender in an appeal under this article, an attorney must:

(1) Meet the minimum qualifications established by rule 8.652 for attorneys to be appointed to represent a person in a death penalty–related habeas corpus proceeding, including being willing to cooperate with an assisting counsel or entity that the court may designate;

(2) Be familiar with appellate practices and procedures in the California courts, including those related to death penalty appeals; and

(3) Not have represented the petitioner in the habeas corpus proceedings that are the subject of the appeal unless the petitioner and counsel expressly request, in writing, continued representation.

(Subd (a) adopted effective April 25, 2019.)

(b) Designation of assisting entity or counsel

Either before or at the time it appoints counsel, the court must designate an assisting entity or counsel.

(Subd (b) adopted effective April 25, 2019.)

Rule 8.391 adopted effective April 25, 2019.

Rule 8.392.   Filing the appeal; certificate of appealability

(a) Notice of appeal

(1) To appeal from a superior court decision in a death penalty–related habeas corpus proceeding, the petitioner or the People must serve and file a notice of appeal in that superior court. To appeal a decision denying relief on a successive habeas corpus petition, the petitioner must also comply with (b).

(2) If the petitioner appeals, petitioner's counsel, or, in the absence of counsel, the petitioner, is responsible for signing the notice of appeal. If the People appeal, the attorney for the People must sign the notice.

(Subd (a) adopted effective April 25, 2019.)

(b) Appeal of decision denying relief on a successive habeas corpus petition

(1) The petitioner may appeal the decision of the superior court denying relief on a successive death penalty–related habeas corpus petition only if the superior court or the Court of Appeal grants a certificate of appealability under Penal Code section 1509.1(c).

(2) The petitioner must identify in the notice of appeal that the appeal is from a superior court decision denying relief on a successive petition and indicate whether the superior court granted or denied a certificate of appealability.

(3) If the superior court denied a certificate of appealability, the petitioner must attach to the notice of appeal a request to the Court of Appeal for a certificate of appealability. The request must identify the petitioner's claim or claims for relief and explain how the requirements of Penal Code section 1509(d) have been met.

(4) On receiving the request for a certificate of appealability, the Court of Appeal clerk must promptly file the request and send notice of the filing date to the parties.

(5) The People need not file an answer to a request for a certificate of appealability unless the court requests an answer. The clerk must promptly send to the parties and the assisting entity or counsel copies of any order requesting an answer and immediately notify the parties by telephone or another expeditious method. Any answer must be served on the parties and the assisting entity or counsel and filed within five days after the order is filed unless the court orders otherwise.

(6) The Court of Appeal must grant or deny the request for a certificate of appealability within 10 days of the filing of the request in that court. If the Court of Appeal grants a certificate of appealability, the certificate must identify the substantial claim or claims for relief shown by the petitioner. The clerk must send a copy of the certificate or its order denying the request for a certificate to:

(A) The attorney for the petitioner or, if unrepresented, to the petitioner;

(B) The district appellate project and, if designated, any assisting entity or counsel other than the district appellate project;

(C) The Attorney General;

(D) The district attorney;

(E) The superior court clerk; and

(F) The clerk/executive officer of the Supreme Court.

(7) If both the superior court and the Court of Appeal deny a certificate of appealability, the clerk/executive officer of the Court of Appeal must mark the notice of appeal "Inoperative," notify the petitioner, and send a copy of the marked notice of appeal to the superior court clerk, the clerk/executive officer of the Supreme Court, the district appellate project, and, if designated, any assisting entity or counsel other than the district appellate project.

(Subd (b) adopted effective April 25, 2019.)

(c) Notification of the appeal

(1) Except as provided in (2), when a notice of appeal is filed, the superior court clerk must promptly—and no later than five days after the notice of appeal is filed—send a notification of the filing to:

(A) The attorney for the petitioner or, if unrepresented, to the petitioner;

(B) The district appellate project and, if designated, any assisting entity or counsel other than the district appellate project;

(C) The Attorney General;

(D) The district attorney;

(E) The clerk/executive officer of the Court of Appeal;

(F) The clerk/executive officer of the Supreme Court;

(G) Each court reporter; and

(H) Any primary reporter or reporting supervisor.

(2) If the petitioner is appealing from a superior court decision denying relief on a successive petition and the superior court did not issue a certificate of appealability, the clerk must not send the notification of the filing of a notice of appeal to the court reporter or reporters unless the clerk receives a copy of a certificate of appealability issued by the Court of Appeal under (b)(6). The clerk must send the notification no later than five days after the superior court receives the copy of the certificate of appealability.

(3) The notification must show the date it was sent, the number and title of the case, and the dates the notice of appeal was filed and any certificate of appealability was issued. If the information is available, the notification must also include:

(A) The name, address, telephone number, e-mail address, and California State Bar number of each attorney of record in the case; and

(B) The name of the party each attorney represented in the superior court.

(4) The notification to the clerk/executive officer of the Court of Appeal must also include a copy of the notice of appeal, any certificate of appealability or denial of a certificate of appealability issued by the superior court, and the sequential list of reporters made under rule 2.950.

(5) A copy of the notice of appeal is sufficient notification under (1) if the required information is on the copy or is added by the superior court clerk.

(6) The sending of a notification under (1) is a sufficient performance of the clerk's duty despite the discharge, disqualification, suspension, disbarment, or death of the attorney.

(7) Failure to comply with any provision of this subdivision does not affect the validity of the notice of appeal.

(Subd (c) adopted effective April 25, 2019.)

Rule 8.392 adopted effective April 25, 2019.

Advisory Committee Comment

Subdivision (b). This subdivision addresses issuance of a certificate of appealability by the Court of Appeal. Rule 4.576(b) addresses issuance of a certificate of appealability by the superior court.

Rule 8.393.   Time to appeal

A notice of appeal under this article must be filed within 30 days after the rendition of the judgment or the making of the order being appealed.
Rule 8.393 adopted effective April 25, 2019.

Rule 8.394.   Stay of execution on appeal

(a) Application

Pending appeal under this article, the petitioner may apply to the reviewing court for a stay of execution of the death penalty. The application must be served on the People.

(Subd (a) adopted effective April 25, 2019.)

(b) Interim relief

Pending its ruling on the application, the reviewing court may grant the relief requested. The reviewing court must notify the superior court under rule 8.489 of any stay that it grants. Notification must also be sent to the clerk/executive officer of the Supreme Court.

(Subd (b) adopted effective April 25, 2019.)
Rule 8.394 adopted effective April 25, 2019.

Rule 8.395.   Record on appeal

(a) Contents

In an appeal under this article, the record must contain:

(1) A clerk's transcript containing:

(A) The petition;

(B) Any informal response to the petition and any reply to the informal response;

(C) Any order to show cause;

(D) Any reply, return, answer, denial, or traverse;

(E) All supporting documents under rule 4.571, including the record prepared for the automatic appeal and all briefs, rulings, and other documents filed in the automatic appeal;

(F) Any other documents and exhibits submitted to the court, including any transcript of a sound or sound-and-video recording tendered to the court under rule 2.1040 and any visual aids submitted to the court;

(G) Any written communication between the court and the parties, including printouts of any e-mail messages and their attachments;

(H) All court minutes;

(I) Any statement of decision required by Penal Code section 1509(f) and any other written decision of the court;

(J) The order appealed from;

(K) The notice of appeal; and

(L) Any certificate of appealability issued by the superior court or the Court of Appeal.

(2) A reporter's transcript of any oral proceedings.

(Subd (a) adopted effective April 25, 2019.)

(b) Stipulation for partial transcript

If counsel for the petitioner and the People stipulate in writing before the record is certified that any part of the record is not required for proper determination of the appeal, that part need not be prepared or sent to the reviewing court.

(Subd (b) adopted effective April 25, 2019.)

(c) Preparation of record

(1) The reporter and the clerk must begin preparing the record immediately after the superior court issues the decision on an initial petition under Penal Code section 1509.

(2) If either party appeals from a superior court decision on a successive petition under Penal Code section 1509.1(c):

(A) The clerk must begin preparing the clerk's transcript immediately after the filing of the notice of appeal or, if one is required, the superior court's issuance of a certificate of appealability or the clerk's receipt of a copy of a certificate of appealability issued by the Court of Appeal under rule 8.391(b)(5), whichever is later. If a certificate of appealability is required to appeal the decision of the superior court, the clerk must not begin preparing the clerk's transcript until a certificate of appealability has issued.

(B) The reporter must begin preparing the reporter's transcript immediately on being notified by the clerk under rule 8.392(c) that the notice of appeal has been filed.

(Subd (c) adopted effective April 25, 2019.)

(d) Clerk's transcript

(1) Within 30 days after the clerk is required to begin preparing the transcript, the clerk must complete preparation of an original and four copies of the clerk's transcript.

(2) On request, the clerk must prepare an extra copy for the district attorney or the Attorney General, whichever is not counsel for the People on appeal.

(3) The clerk must certify as correct the original and all copies of the clerk's transcript.

(Subd (d) adopted effective April 25, 2019.)

(e) Reporter's transcript

(1) The reporter must prepare an original and the same number of copies of the reporter's transcript as (d) requires of the clerk's transcript, and must certify each as correct.

(2) As soon as the transcripts are certified, but no later than 30 days after the reporter is required to begin preparing the transcript, the reporter must deliver the original and all copies to the superior court clerk.

(3) Any portion of the transcript transcribed during superior court habeas corpus proceedings must not be retyped unless necessary to correct errors, but must be repaginated and combined with any portion of the transcript not previously transcribed. Any additional copies needed must not be retyped but, if the transcript is in paper form, must be prepared by photocopying or an equivalent process.

(4) In a multireporter case, the clerk must accept any completed portion of the transcript from the primary reporter one week after the time prescribed by (2) even if other portions are uncompleted. The clerk must promptly pay each reporter who certifies that all portions of the transcript assigned to that reporter are completed.

(Subd (e) adopted effective April 25, 2019.)

(f) Extension of time

(1) Except as provided in this rule, rules 8.60 and 8.63 govern requests for extension of time to prepare the record.

(2) On request of the clerk or a reporter showing good cause, the superior court may extend the time prescribed in (d) or (e) for preparing the clerk's or reporter's transcript for no more than 30 days. If the superior court orders an extension, the order must specify the reason justifying the extension. The clerk must promptly send a copy of the order to the reviewing court.

(3) For any further extension, the clerk or reporter must file a request in the reviewing court showing good cause.

(4) A request under (2) or (3) must be supported by:

(A) A declaration showing good cause. The court may presume good cause if the clerk's and reporter's transcripts combined will likely exceed 10,000 pages, not including the supporting documents submitted with the petition, any informal response, reply to the informal response, return, answer, or traverse; and

(B) In the case of a reporter's transcript, certification by the superior court presiding judge or a court administrator designated by the presiding judge that an extension is reasonable and necessary in light of the workload of all reporters in the court.

(Subd (f) adopted effective April 25, 2019.)

(g) Form of record

(1) The reporter's transcript must be in electronic form. The clerk is encouraged to send the clerk's transcript in electronic form if the court is able to do so.

(2) The clerk's and reporter's transcripts must comply with rules 8.45–8.47, relating to sealed and confidential records, and rule 8.144.

(Subd (g) adopted effective April 25, 2019.)

(h) Sending the transcripts

(1) When the clerk's and reporter's transcripts are certified as correct, the clerk must promptly send:

(A) The original transcripts to the reviewing court, noting the sending date on each original; and

(B) One copy of each transcript to:

(i) Appellate counsel for the petitioner;

(ii) The assisting entity or counsel, if designated, or the district appellate project;

(iii) The Attorney General or the district attorney, whichever is counsel for the People on appeal;

(iv) The district attorney or Attorney General if requested under (d)(2); and

(v) The Governor.

(2) If the petitioner is not represented by appellate counsel when the transcripts are certified as correct, the clerk must send that copy of the transcripts to the assisting entity or counsel, if designated, or the district appellate project.

(Subd (h) adopted effective April 25, 2019.)

(i) Supervision of preparation of record

The clerk/executive officer of the Court of Appeal, under the supervision of the administrative presiding justice or the presiding justice, must take all appropriate steps to ensure that superior court clerks and reporters promptly perform their duties under this rule. This provision does not affect the responsibility of the superior courts for the prompt preparation of appellate records.

(Subd (i) adopted effective April 25, 2019.)

(j) Augmenting or correcting the record in the Court of Appeal

Rule 8.340 governs augmenting or correcting the record in the Court of Appeal, except that copies of augmented or corrected records must be sent to those listed in (h).

(Subd (j) adopted effective April 25, 2019.)

(k) Judicial notice

Rule 8.252(a) governs judicial notice in the reviewing court.

(Subd (k) adopted effective April 25, 2019.)

Rule 8.395 adopted effective April 25, 2019.

Rule 8.396.   Briefs by parties and amici curiae

(a) Contents and form

(1) Except as provided in this rule, briefs in appeals governed by the rules in this article must comply as nearly as possible with rules 8.200 and 8.204.

(2) If, as permitted by Penal Code section 1509.1(b), the petitioner wishes to raise a claim in the appeal of ineffective assistance of trial counsel that was not raised in the superior court habeas corpus proceedings, that claim must be raised in the first brief filed by the petitioner. A brief containing such a claim must comply with the additional requirements in rule 8.397.

(3) If the petitioner is appealing from a decision of the superior court denying relief on a successive death penalty–related habeas corpus petition, the petitioner may only raise claims in the briefs that were identified in the certificate of appealability that was issued and any additional claims added by the Court of Appeal as provided in Penal Code section 1509.1(c).

(Subd (a) adopted effective April 25, 2019.)

(b) Length

(1) A brief produced on a computer must not exceed the following limits, including footnotes, except that if the presiding justice permits the appellant to file an opening brief that exceeds the limit set in (1)(A) or (3)(A), the respondent's brief may not exceed the same length:

(A) Appellant's opening brief: 102,000 words.

(B) Respondent's brief: 102,000 words.

(C) Reply brief: 47,600 words.

(2) A brief under (1) must include a certificate by appellate counsel stating the number of words in the brief; counsel may rely on the word count of the computer program used to prepare the brief.

(3) A typewritten brief must not exceed the following limits, except that if the presiding justice permits the appellant to file an opening brief that exceeds the limit set in (1)(A) or (3)(A), the respondent's brief may not exceed the same length:

(A) Appellant's opening brief: 300 pages.

(B) Respondent's brief: 300 pages.

(C) Reply brief: 140 pages.

(4) The tables required under rule 8.204(a)(1), the cover information required under rule 8.204(b)(10), a certificate under (2), any signature block, and any attachment permitted under rule 8.204(d) are excluded from the limits stated in (1) and (3).

(5) A combined brief in an appeal governed by (e) must not exceed double the limit stated in (1) or (3).

(6) On application, the presiding justice may permit a longer brief for good cause.

(Subd (b) adopted effective April 25, 2019.)

(c) Time to file

(1) The appellant's opening brief must be served and filed within 210 days after either the record is filed or appellate counsel is appointed, whichever is later.

(2) The respondent's brief must be served and filed within 120 days after the appellant's opening brief is filed.

(3) The appellant must serve and file a reply brief, if any, within 60 days after the filing of respondent's brief.

(4) If the clerk's and reporter's transcripts combined exceed 10,000 pages, the time limits stated in (1) and (2) are extended by 15 days for each 1,000 pages of combined transcript over 10,000 pages, up to 20,000 pages. The time limits in (1) and (2) may be extended further by order of the presiding justice under rule 8.60.

(5) The time to serve and file a brief may not be extended by stipulation, but only by order of the presiding justice under rule 8.60.

(6) If a party fails to timely file an appellant's opening brief or a respondent's brief, the clerk/executive officer of the Court of Appeal must promptly notify the party in writing that the brief must be filed within 30 days after the notice is sent, and that failure to comply may result in sanctions specified in the notice.

(Subd (c) adopted effective April 25, 2019.)

(d) Service

(1) The petitioner's appellate counsel must serve each brief for the petitioner on the assisting entity or counsel, the Attorney General, and the district attorney, and must deliver a copy of each to the petitioner unless the petitioner requests otherwise.

(2) The proof of service must state that a copy of the petitioner's brief was delivered to the petitioner or will be delivered in person to the petitioner within 30 days after the filing of the brief, or counsel must file a signed statement that the petitioner requested in writing that no copy be delivered.

(3) The People must serve each of their briefs on the appellate counsel for the petitioner, the assisting entity or counsel, and either the district attorney or the Attorney General, whichever is not representing the People on appeal.

(4) A copy of each brief must be served on the superior court clerk for delivery to the superior court judge who issued the order being appealed.

(Subd (d) adopted effective April 25, 2019.)

(e) When the petitioner and the People appeal

When both the petitioner and the People appeal, the petitioner must file the first opening brief unless the reviewing court orders otherwise, and rule 8.216(b) governs the contents of the briefs.

(Subd (e) adopted effective April 25, 2019.)

(f) Amicus curiae briefs

Amicus curiae briefs may be filed as provided in rule 8.200(c), except that an application for permission of the presiding justice to file an amicus curiae brief must be filed within 14 days after the last appellant's reply brief is filed or could have been filed under (c), whichever is earlier.

(Subd (f) adopted effective April 25, 2019.)

Rule 8.396 adopted effective April 25, 2019.

Advisory Committee Comment

Subdivision (a)(3). This subdivision is intended to implement the sentence in Penal Code section 1509.1(c) providing that "[t]he jurisdiction of the court of appeal is limited to the claims identified in the certificate [of appealability] and any additional claims added by the court of appeal within 60 days of the notice of appeal."

Subdivision (b)(4). This subdivision specifies certain items that are not counted toward the maximum brief length. Signature blocks referred to in this provision include not only the signatures, but also the printed names, titles, and affiliations of any attorneys filing or joining in the brief, which may accompany the signature.

Rule 8.397.   Claim of ineffective assistance of trial counsel not raised in the superior court

(a) Application

This rule governs claims under Penal Code section 1509.1(b) of ineffective assistance of trial counsel not raised in the superior court habeas corpus proceeding giving rise to an appeal under this article.

(Subd (a) adopted effective April 25, 2019.)

(b) Discussion of claim in briefs

(1) A claim subject to this rule must be raised in the first brief filed by the petitioner.

(2) All discussion of claims subject to this rule must be addressed in a separate part of the brief under a heading identifying this part as addressing claims of ineffective assistance of trial counsel that were not raised in a superior court habeas corpus proceeding.

(3) Discussion of each claim within this part of the brief must be under a separate subheading identifying the claim. Petitioner's brief must include a summary of the claim under the subheading, and each claim must be supported by argument and, if possible, by citation of authority.

(4) This part of the brief may include references to matters:

(A) In the record on appeal prepared under rule 8.395. Any reference to a matter in the record must be supported by a citation to the volume and page number of the record where the matter appears.

(B) Of which the court has taken judicial notice.

(C) In a proffer required under (c). Any reference to a matter in a proffer must be supported by a citation to its index number or letter and page.

(Subd (b) adopted effective April 25, 2019.)

(c) Proffer

(1) A brief raising a claim under Penal Code section 1509.1(b) of ineffective assistance of trial counsel not raised in a superior court habeas corpus proceeding must be accompanied by a proffer of any reasonably available documentary evidence supporting the claim that is not in either the record on appeal prepared under rule 8.395 or matters of which the court has taken judicial notice. A brief responding to such a claim must be accompanied by a proffer of any reasonably available documentary evidence the People are relying on that is not in the petitioner's proffer, the record on appeal prepared under rule 8.395, or matters of which the court has taken judicial notice.

(A) If a brief raises a claim that was the subject of an evidentiary hearing, the proffer must include a certified transcript of that hearing.

(B) Evidence may be in the form of affidavits or declarations under penalty of perjury.

(2) The proffer must comply with the following formatting requirements:

(A) The pages must be consecutively numbered.

(B) It must begin with a table of contents listing each document by its title and its index number or letter. If a document has attachments, the table of contents must give the title of each attachment and a brief description of its contents.

(C) If submitted in paper form:

(i) It must be bound together at the end of the brief or in separate volumes not exceeding 300 pages each.

(ii) It must be index-tabbed by number or letter.

(3) The clerk must file any proffer not complying with (2), but the court may notify the filer that it may strike the proffer and the portions of the brief referring to the proffer if the documents are not brought into compliance within a stated reasonable time of not less than five court days.

(4) If any documents in the proffer are sealed or confidential records, rules 8.45–8.47 govern these documents.

(Subd (c) adopted effective April 25, 2019.)

(d) Evidentiary hearing

An evidentiary hearing is required if, after considering the briefs, the proffer, and matters of which judicial notice may be taken, the court finds there is a reasonable likelihood that the petitioner may be entitled to relief and the petitioner's entitlement to relief depends on the resolution of an issue of fact. The reviewing court may take one of the following actions:

(1) Order a limited remand to the superior court to consider the claim under Penal Code section 1509.1(b). The order for limited remand vests jurisdiction over the claim in the superior court, which must proceed under rule 4.574(d)(2)–(3) and (e)–(g) and rule 4.575 for death penalty–related habeas corpus proceedings in the superior court. The clerk/executive officer of the Court of Appeal must send a copy of any such order to the clerk/executive officer of the Supreme Court.

(2) Appoint a referee to conduct the hearing and make recommended findings of fact.

(3) Conduct the hearing itself or designate a justice of the court to conduct the hearing.

(Subd (d) adopted effective April 25, 2019.)

(e) Procedures following limited remand

(1) If the reviewing court orders a limited remand to the superior court to consider a claim under Penal Code section 1509.1(b), it may stay the proceedings on the remainder of the appeal pending the decision of the superior court on remand. The clerk/executive officer of the Court of Appeal must send a copy of any such stay to the clerk/executive officer of the Supreme Court.

(2) If any party wishes to appeal from the superior court decision on remand, the party must file a notice of appeal as provided in rule 8.392.

(3) If an appeal is filed from the superior court decision on remand, the reviewing court may consolidate this appeal with any pending appeal under Penal Code section 1509.1 from the superior court's decisions in the same habeas corpus proceeding. A copy of any consolidation order must be promptly sent to the superior court clerk. The superior court clerk must then augment the record on appeal to include all items listed in rule 8.395(a) from the remanded proceedings.

(Subd (e) adopted effective April 25, 2019.)

Rule 8.397 adopted effective April 25, 2019.

Advisory Committee Comment

Penal Code section 1509.1(b) states when a claim of ineffective assistance of trial counsel not raised in the superior court habeas corpus proceeding may be raised in an appeal under this article.

Rule 8.398.   Finality

(a) General rule

Except as otherwise provided in this rule, rule 8.366(b) governs the finality of a Court of Appeal decision in a proceeding under this article.

(Subd (a) adopted effective April 25, 2019.)

(b) Denial of certificate of appealability

The Court of Appeal's denial of an application for a certificate of appealability in a proceeding under this article is final in that court on filing.

(Subd (b) adopted effective April 25, 2019.)

Rule 8.398 adopted effective April 25, 2019.

Chapter 5
Juvenile Appeals and Writs

Article 1
General Provisions

Title 8, Appellate Rules—Division 1, Rules Relating to the Supreme Court and Courts of Appeal—Chapter 5, Juvenile Appeals and Writs—Article 1, General Provisions; adopted effective July 1, 2010.

Rule 8.400.   Application

The rules in this chapter govern:

(1) Appeals from judgments or appealable orders in:

(A) Cases under Welfare and Institutions Code sections 300, 601, and 602; and

(B) Actions to free a child from parental custody and control under Family Code section 7800 et seq. and Probate Code section 1516.5;

(2) Appeals of orders requiring or dispensing with an alleged father's consent for the adoption of a child under Family Code section 7662 et seq.; and

(3) Writ petitions under Welfare and Institutions Code sections 366.26 and 366.28.

Rule 8.400 amended effective January 1, 2017; adopted as rule 37 effective January 1, 2005; previously amended effective January 1, 2006, January 1, 2008, and July 1, 2010; previously amended and renumbered effective January 1, 2007.

Rule 8.401.   Confidentiality

(a) References to juveniles or relatives in documents

To protect the anonymity of juveniles involved in juvenile court proceedings:

(1) In all documents filed by the parties in proceedings under this chapter, a juvenile must be referred to by first name and last initial; but if the first name is unusual or other circumstances would defeat the objective of anonymity, the initials of the juvenile may be used.

(2) In opinions that are not certified for publication and in court orders, a juvenile may be referred to either by first name and last initial or by his or her initials. In opinions that are certified for publication in proceedings under this chapter, a juvenile must be referred to by first name and last initial; but if the first name is unusual or other circumstances would defeat the objective of anonymity, the initials of the juvenile may be used.

(3) In all documents filed by the parties and in all court orders and opinions in proceedings under this chapter, if use of the full name of a juvenile's relative would defeat the objective of anonymity for the juvenile, the relative must be referred to by first name and last initial; but if the first name is unusual or other circumstances would defeat the objective of anonymity for the juvenile, the initials of the relative may be used.

(Subd (a) adopted effective January 1, 2012.)

(b) Access to filed documents and records

For the purposes of this rule, "filed document" means a brief, petition, motion, application, or other thing filed by the parties in the reviewing court in a proceeding under this chapter; "record on

appeal" means the documents referenced in rule 8.407; "record on a writ petition" means the documents referenced in rules 8.450 and 8.454; and "records in the juvenile case file" means all or part of a document, paper, exhibit, transcript, opinion, order, or other thing filed or lodged in the juvenile court.

(1) Except as provided in [1] **(2)–(4), a filed document**, the record on appeal [2], **or the record on a writ petition** may be inspected only by the reviewing court [3], appellate project personnel, the parties [4], **attorneys for the parties, or** other persons the **reviewing** court may designate.

(2) **Access to records in the juvenile case file, including any such records made part of the record on appeal or the record on a writ petition, is governed by Welfare and Institutions Code section 827. A person who is not described in section 827(a)(1)(A)–(P) may not access records in the juvenile case file, including any such records made part of the record on appeal or the record on a writ petition, unless that person petitioned the juvenile court under section 827(a)(1)(Q) and was granted access by order of the juvenile court.**

(3) A filed [5] **document that protects** anonymity as required by (a) may be inspected by any person or entity that is considering filing an amicus curiae brief.

[6] **(4)** Access to [7] **a filed document or items in the record on appeal or the record on a writ petition** that are sealed or confidential under authority other than Welfare and Institutions Code section 827 is governed by rules 8.45–8.47 and the applicable statute, rule, sealing order, or other authority.

(Subd (b) amended effective September 1, 2020; adopted as subd (a) effective July 1, 2010; previously amended and relettered effective January 1, 2012; previously amended effective January 1, 2014.)

Rule 8.401(b).   2020 Deletes. [1] (2)–(3) [2] and documents filed by the parties in proceedings under this chapter [3] and [4] or their attorneys, and [5] documents that protect [6] (3) [7] records

(c) Access to oral argument

The court may limit or prohibit public admittance to oral argument.

(Subd (c) relettered effective January 1, 2012; adopted as subd (b) effective July 1, 2010.)

Rule 8.401 amended effective September 1, 2020; adopted effective July 1, 2010; previously amended effective January 1, 2012, and January 1, 2014.

Advisory Committee Comment

Subdivision (b)(2). Welfare and Institutions Code section 827(a)(1)(Q) authorizes a petition by which a person may request access to records in the juvenile case file. The petition process is stated in rule 5.552. The Judicial Council has adopted a mandatory form—*Petition for Access to Juvenile Case File* (form JV-570)—that must be filed in the juvenile court to make the request. This form is available at any courthouse or county law library or online at *www.courts.ca.gov/forms.*

Article 2
Appeals

Title 8, Appellate Rules—Division 1, Rules Relating to the Supreme Court and Courts of Appeal—Chapter 5, Juvenile Appeals and Writs—Article 2, Appeals; renumbered effective July 1, 2010; adopted as article 1 effective January 1, 2007.

Rule 8.403.   Right to appointment of appellate counsel and prerequisites for appeal

(a) Welfare and Institutions Code section 601 or 602 proceedings

In appeals of proceedings under Welfare and Institutions Code section 601 or 602, the child is entitled to court-appointed counsel.

(Subd (a) amended effective January 1, 2013; adopted effective July 1, 2010.)

(b) Welfare and Institutions Code section 300 proceedings

(1) Any judgment, order, or decree setting a hearing under Welfare and Institutions Code section 366.26 may be reviewed on appeal following the order at the Welfare and Institutions Code section 366.26 hearing only if:

(A) The procedures in rules 8.450 and 8.452 regarding writ petitions in these cases have been followed; and

(B) The petition for an extraordinary writ was summarily denied or otherwise not decided on the merits.

(2) The reviewing court may appoint counsel to represent an indigent child, parent, or guardian.

(3) Rule 5.661 governs the responsibilities of trial counsel in Welfare and Institutions Code section 300 proceedings with regard to appellate representation of the child.

(Subd (b) adopted effective July 1, 2010.)

Rule 8.403 amended effective January 1, 2013; adopted effective July 1, 2010.

Advisory Committee Comment

The right to appeal in Welfare and Institutions Code section 601 or 602 (juvenile delinquency) cases is established by Welfare and Institutions Code section 800 and case law (see, for example, *In re Michael S.* (2007) 147 Cal.App.4th 1443, *In re Jeffrey M.* (2006) 141 Cal.App.4th 1017 and *In re Sean R.* (1989) 214 Cal.App.3d 662). The right to appeal in Welfare and Institutions Code section 300 (juvenile dependency) cases is established by Welfare and Institutions Code section 395 and case law (see, for example, *In re Aaron R.* (2005) 130 Cal.App.4th 697, and *In re Merrick V.* (2004) 122 Cal.App.4th 235).

Subdivision (b)(1). Welfare and Institutions Code section 366.26(*l*) establishes important limitations on appeals of judgments, orders, or decrees setting a hearing under section 366.26, including requirements for the filing of a petition for an extraordinary writ and limitations on the issues that can be raised on appeal.

Rule 8.404.   Record on appeal [Renumbered]

Rule 8.404 amended and renumbered to rule 8.407 effective July 1, 2010; adopted as rule 37.1 effective January 1, 2005; previously amended and renumbered effective January 1, 2007.

Another Rule 8.404 follows.

Rule 8.404.   Stay pending appeal

The court must not stay an order or judgment pending an appeal unless suitable provision is made for the maintenance, care, and custody of the child.

Rule 8.404 adopted effective July 1, 2010.

Rule 8.405.   Filing the appeal

(a) Notice of appeal

(1) To appeal from a judgment or appealable order under these rules, the appellant must file a notice of appeal in the superior court. Any notice of appeal on behalf of the child in a Welfare and Institutions Code section 300 proceeding must be authorized by the child or the child's CAPTA guardian ad litem.

(2) The appellant or the appellant's attorney must sign the notice of appeal.

(3) The notice of appeal must be liberally construed, and is sufficient if it identifies the particular judgment or order being appealed. The notice need not specify the court to which the appeal is taken; the appeal will be treated as taken to the Court of Appeal for the district in which the superior court is located.

(Subd (a) adopted effective July 1, 2010.)

(b) Superior court clerk's duties

(1) When a notice of appeal is filed, the superior court clerk must immediately:

(A) Send a notification of the filing to:

(i) Each party other than the appellant, including the child if the child is 10 years of age or older;

(ii) The attorney of record for each party;

(iii) Any person currently awarded by the juvenile court the status of the child's de facto parent;

(iv) Any Court Appointed Special Advocate (CASA) volunteer;

(v) If the court knows or has reason to know that an Indian child is involved, the Indian custodian, if any, and tribe of the child or the Bureau of Indian Affairs, as required under Welfare and Institutions Code section 224.2; and

(vi) The reviewing court clerk; and

(B) Notify the reporter [1], **in a manner providing immediate notice,** to prepare a reporter's transcript and deliver it to the clerk within 20 days after the notice of appeal is filed.

(2) The notification must show the name of the appellant, the date it was sent, the number and title of the case, and the date the notice of appeal was filed. If the information is available, the notification must also include:

(A) The name, address, telephone number, e-mail address, and California State Bar number of each attorney of record in the case;

Rules of Court

(B) The name of the party that each attorney represented in the superior court; and

(C) The name, address, telephone number and e-mail address of any unrepresented party.

(3) The notification to the reviewing court clerk must also include a copy of the notice of appeal and any sequential list of reporters made under rule 2.950.

(4) A copy of the notice of appeal is sufficient notification if the required information is on the copy or is added by the superior court clerk.

(5) The sending of a notification is a sufficient performance of the clerk's duty despite the discharge, disqualification, suspension, disbarment, or death of the attorney.

(6) Failure to comply with any provision of this subdivision does not affect the validity of the notice of appeal.

(Subd (b) amended effective January 1, 2021; adopted effective July 1, 2010; previously amended effective January 1, 2016.)

Rule 8.405(b). 2020 Deletes. [1] by telephone and in writing
Rule 8.405 amended effective January 1, 2021; adopted effective July 1, 2010; previously amended effective January 1, 2016.

Advisory Committee Comment

Subdivision (a). *Notice of Appeal—Juvenile (California Rules of Court, Rule 8.400) (form JV-800) may be used to file the notice of appeal required under this rule. This form is available at any courthouse or county law library or online at www.courts.ca.gov/forms.*

Rule 8.406. Record in multiple appeals in the same case [Renumbered]
Rule 8.406 renumbered to rule 8.408 effective July 1, 2010; adopted effective January 1, 2007.

Another Rule 8.406 follows.

Rule 8.406. Time to appeal
(a) Normal time
(1) Except as provided in (2) and (3), a notice of appeal must be filed within 60 days after the rendition of the judgment or the making of the order being appealed.

(2) In matters heard by a referee not acting as a temporary judge, a notice of appeal must be filed within 60 days after the referee's order becomes final under rule 5.540(c).

(3) When an application for rehearing of an order of a referee not acting as a temporary judge is denied under rule 5.542, a notice of appeal from the referee's order must be filed within 60 days after that order is served under rule 5.538(b)(3) or 30 days after entry of the order denying rehearing, whichever is later.

(Subd (a) adopted effective July 1, 2010.)

(b) Cross-appeal
If an appellant timely appeals from a judgment or appealable order, the time for any other party to appeal from the same judgment or order is either the time specified in (a) or 20 days after the superior court clerk sends notification of the first appeal, whichever is later.

(Subd (b) amended effective January 1, 2016; adopted effective July 1, 2010.)

(c) No extension of time; late notice of appeal
Except as provided in rule 8.66, no court may extend the time to file a notice of appeal. The superior court clerk must mark a late notice of appeal "Received [date] but not filed," notify the party that the notice was not filed because it was late, and send a copy of the marked notice of appeal to the district appellate project.

(Subd (c) repealed and relettered effective July 1, 2010; adopted as subd (d) effective July 1, 2010.)

(d) Premature notice of appeal
A notice of appeal is premature if filed before the judgment is rendered or the order is made, but the reviewing court may treat the notice as filed immediately after the rendition of judgment or the making of the order.

(Subd (d) relettered effective July 1, 2010; adopted as subd (e) effective July 1, 2010.)
Rule 8.406 amended effective January 1, 2016; adopted effective July 1, 2010; previously amended effective July 1, 2010.

Advisory Committee Comment

Subdivision (c). See rule 8.25(b)(5) for provisions concerning the timeliness of documents mailed by inmates or patients from custodial institutions.

Rule 8.407. Record on appeal
(a) Normal record: clerk's transcript
The clerk's transcript must contain:
(1) The petition;

(2) Any notice of hearing;

(3) All court minutes;

(4) Any report or other document submitted to the court;

(5) The jurisdictional and dispositional findings and orders;

(6) The judgment or order appealed from;

(7) Any application for rehearing;

(8) The notice of appeal and any order pursuant to the notice;

(9) Any transcript of a sound or sound-and-video recording tendered to the court under rule 2.1040;

(10) Any application for additional record and any order on the application;

(11) Any opinion or dispositive order of a reviewing court in the same case; and

(12) Any written motion or notice of motion by any party, with supporting and opposing memoranda and attachments, and any written opinion of the court.

(Subd (a) amended effective January 1, 2017; previously amended effective January 1, 2007, and July 1, 2010.)

(b) Normal record: reporter's transcript
The reporter's transcript must contain any oral opinion of the court and:
(1) In appeals from disposition orders, the oral proceedings at hearings on:

(A) Jurisdiction;

(B) Disposition;

(C) Any motion by the appellant that was denied in whole or in part; and

(D) In cases under Welfare and Institutions Code section 300 et seq., hearings:

(i) On detention; and

(ii) At which a parent of the child made his or her initial appearance.

(2) In appeals from an order terminating parental rights under Welfare and Institutions Code section 300 et seq., the oral proceedings at all section 366.26 hearings.

(3) In all other appeals, the oral proceedings at any hearing that resulted in the order or judgment being appealed.

(Subd (b) amended effective January 1, 2017; previously amended effective January 1, 2007.)

(c) Application in superior court for addition to normal record
(1) Any party or Indian tribe that has intervened in the proceedings may apply to the superior court for inclusion of any oral proceedings in the reporter's transcript.

(2) An application for additional record must describe the material to be included and explain how it may be useful in the appeal.

(3) The application must be filed in the superior court with the notice of appeal or as soon thereafter as possible, and will be treated as denied if it is filed after the record is sent to the reviewing court.

(4) The clerk must immediately present the application to the trial judge.

(5) Within five days after the application if filed, the judge must order that the record include as much of the additional material as the judge finds proper to fully present the points raised by the applicant. Denial of the application does not preclude a motion in the reviewing court for augmentation under rule 8.155.

(6) If the judge does not rule on the application within the time prescribed by (5), the requested material–other than exhibits–must be included in the clerk's transcript or the reporter's transcript without a court order.

(7) The clerk must immediately notify the reporter if additions to the reporter's transcript are required under (5) or (6).

(Subd (c) amended effective July 1, 2010; previously amended effective January 1, 2007.)

(d) Agreed or settled statement
To proceed by agreed or settled statement, the parties must comply with rule 8.344 or 8.346, as applicable.

(Subd (d) amended effective January 1, 2007.)

(e) Transmitting exhibits
Exhibits that were admitted in evidence, refused, or lodged may be transmitted to the reviewing court as provided in rule 8.224.

(Subd (e) repealed and relettered effective January 1, 2014; previously amended as subd (f) effective January 1, 2007.)
Rule 8.407 amended effective January 1, 2017; adopted as rule 37.1 effective January 1, 2005; previously amended and renumbered as rule 8.404 effective January 1, 2007, and July 1, 2010; previously amended effective January 1, 2014.

Advisory Committee Comment

Rules 8.45–8.47 address the appropriate handling of sealed or confidential records that must be included in the record on appeal. Examples of confidential records include records of proceedings closed to inspection by court order under *People v. Marsden* (1970) 2 Cal.3d 118 and in-camera proceedings on a confidential informant.

Subdivision (a)(4). Examples of the documents that must be included in the clerk's transcript under this provision include all documents filed with the court relating to the Indian Child Welfare Act, including but not limited to all inquiries regarding a child under the Indian Child Welfare Act (*Indian Child Inquiry Attachment* [form ICWA-010(A)]), any *Parental Notification of Indian Status* (form ICWA-020), any *Notice of Child Custody Proceeding for Indian Child* (form ICWA-030) sent, any signed return receipts for the mailing of form ICWA-030, and any responses received to form ICWA-030.

Subdivision (b). Subdivision (b)(1) provides that only the reporter's transcript of a hearing that resulted in the order being appealed must be included in the normal record. This provision is intended to achieve consistent record requirements in all appeals of cases under Welfare and Institutions Code section 300, 601, or 602 and to reduce the delays and expense caused by transcribing proceedings not necessary to the appeal.

Subdivision (b)(1)(A) recognizes that findings made in a jurisdictional hearing are not separately appealable and can be challenged only in an appeal from the ensuing disposition order. The rule therefore specifically provides that a reporter's transcript of jurisdictional proceedings must be included in the normal record on appeal from a disposition order.

Subdivision (b)(1)(C) specifies that the oral proceedings on any motion by the appellant that was denied in whole or in part must be included in the normal record on appeal from a disposition order. Rulings on such motions usually have some impact on either the jurisdictional findings or the subsequent disposition order. Routine inclusion of these proceedings in the record will promote expeditious resolution of appeals of cases under Welfare and Institutions Code section 300, 601, or 602.

Rule 8.408. Preparing, sending, augmenting, and correcting the record [Renumbered]

Rule 8.408 amended and renumbered to rule 8.409 effective July 1, 2010; adopted as rule 37.2 effective January 1, 2005; previously amended and renumbered effective January 1, 2007.

Another Rule 8.408 follows.

Rule 8.408. Record in multiple appeals in the same case

If more than one appeal is taken from the same judgment or related order, only one appellate record need be prepared, which must be filed within the time allowed for filing the record in the latest appeal.

Rule 8.408 renumbered effective July 1, 2010; adopted as rule 8.406 effective January 1, 2007.

Rule 8.409. Preparing and sending the record

(a) Application

This rule applies to appeals in juvenile cases except cases governed by rule 8.416.

(Subd (a) amended effective January 1, 2015; previously amended effective January 1, 2007, and July 1, 2010.)

(b) Form of record

The clerk's and reporter's transcripts must comply with rules 8.45–8.47, relating to sealed and confidential records, and with rule 8.144.

(Subd (b) amended effective January 1, 2015; adopted effective January 1, 2014.)

(c) Preparing and certifying the transcripts

Within 20 days after the notice of appeal is filed:

(1) The clerk must prepare and certify as correct an original of the clerk's transcript and one copy each for the appellant, the respondent, the child's Indian tribe if the tribe has intervened, and the child if the child is represented by counsel on appeal or if a recommendation has been made to the Court of Appeal for appointment of counsel for the child under rule 8.403(b)(2) and that recommendation is either pending with or has been approved by the Court of Appeal but counsel has not yet been appointed; and

(2) The reporter must prepare, certify as correct, and deliver to the clerk an original of the reporter's transcript and the same number of copies as (1) requires of the clerk's transcript.

(Subd (c) amended effective January 1, 2018; adopted as subd (b); previously amended as subd (b) effective January 1, 2007; previously amended and relettered as subd (c) effective January 1, 2014; previously amended effective January 1, 2015, and January 1, 2017.)

(d) Extension of time

(1) The superior court may not extend the time to prepare the record.

(2) The reviewing court may order one or more extensions of time for preparing the record, including a reporter's transcript, not exceeding a total of 60 days, on receipt of:

(A) A declaration showing good cause; and

(B) In the case of a reporter's transcript, certification by the superior court presiding judge, or a court administrator designated by the presiding judge, that an extension is reasonable and necessary in light of the workload of all reporters in the court.

(Subd (d) amended and relettered effective January 1, 2014; previously amended as subd (c) effective January 1, 2007.)

(e) Sending the record

(1) When the transcripts are certified as correct, the court clerk must immediately send:

(A) The original transcripts to the reviewing court, noting the sending date on each original; and

(B) One copy of each transcript to the appellate counsel for the following, if they have appellate counsel:

(i) The appellant;

(ii) The respondent;

(iii) The child's Indian tribe if the tribe has intervened; and

(iv) The child.

(2) If appellate counsel has not yet been retained or appointed for the appellant or the respondent, or if a recommendation has been made to the Court of Appeal for appointment of counsel for the child under rule 8.403(b)(2) and that recommendation is either pending with or has been approved by the Court of Appeal but counsel has not yet been appointed, when the transcripts are certified as correct, the clerk must send that counsel's copy of the transcripts to the district appellate project. If a tribe that has intervened is not represented by counsel when the transcripts are certified as correct, the clerk must send that counsel's copy of the transcripts to the tribe.

(3) The clerk must not send a copy of the transcripts to the Attorney General or the district attorney unless that office represents a party.

(Subd (e) amended effective January 1, 2015; adopted as subd (d); previously amended effective January 1, 2007, and January 1, 2013; previously relettered as subd (e) effective January 1, 2014.)

Rule 8.409 amended effective January 1, 2018; adopted as rule 37.2 effective January 1, 2005; previously amended and renumbered as rule 8.408 effective January 1, 2007, and as rule 8.409 effective July 1, 2010; previously amended effective January 1, 2013, January 1, 2014, January 1, 2015, and January 1, 2017.

Advisory Committee Comment

Subdivision (a). Subdivision (a) calls litigants' attention to the fact that a different rule (rule 8.416) governs the record in appeals from judgments or orders terminating parental rights and in dependency appeals in certain counties.

Subdivision (b). Examples of confidential records include records closed to inspection by court order under *People v. Marsden* (1970) 2 Cal.3d 118 and in-camera proceedings on a confidential informant.

Subdivision (e). Under rule 8.71(c), the superior court clerk may send the record to the reviewing court in electronic form. Subsection (1)(B) clarifies that when a child's Indian tribe has intervened in the proceedings, the tribe is a party who must receive a copy of the appellate record. The statutes that require notices to be sent to a tribe by registered or certified mail return receipt requested and generally be addressed to the tribal chairperson (25 U.S.C. § 1912(a), 25 C.F.R. § 23.11, and Welf. & Inst. Code, § 224.2) do not apply to the sending of the appellate record.

Rule 8.410. Augmenting and correcting the record in the reviewing court

(a) Omissions

If, after the record is certified, the superior court clerk or the reporter learns that the record omits a document or transcript that any rule or order requires to be included, without the need for a motion or court order, the clerk must promptly copy and certify the document or the reporter must promptly prepare and certify the transcript and the clerk must promptly send the document or transcript—as an augmentation of the record—to all those who are listed under 8.409(e).

(Subd (a) amended effective January 1, 2015; adopted effective July 1, 2010.)

(b) Augmentation or correction by the reviewing court

(1) On motion of a party or on its own motion, the reviewing court may order the record augmented or corrected as provided in rule 8.155(a) and (c).

(2) If, after the record is certified, the trial court amends or recalls the judgment or makes any other order in the case, the trial court clerk must notify each entity and person to whom the record is sent under rule 8.409(e).

(Subd (b) amended effective January 1, 2015; adopted effective July 1, 2010.)

Rule 8.410 amended effective January 1, 2015; adopted effective July 1, 2010.

Rule 8.411. Abandoning the appeal

(a) How to abandon

An appellant may abandon the appeal at any time by filing an abandonment of the appeal. The abandonment must be authorized by the appellant and signed by either the appellant or the appellant's attorney of record. In a Welfare and Institutions Code section 300 proceeding in which the child is the appellant, the abandonment must be authorized by the child or, if the child is not capable of giving authorization, by the child's CAPTA guardian ad litem.

(Subd (a) adopted effective July 1, 2010.)

(b) Where to file; effect of filing

(1) If the record has not been filed in the reviewing court, the appellant must file the abandonment in the superior court. The filing effects a dismissal of the appeal and restores the superior court's jurisdiction.

(2) If the record has been filed in the reviewing court, the appellant must file the abandonment in that court. The reviewing court may dismiss the appeal and direct immediate issuance of the remittitur.

(Subd (b) adopted effective July 1, 2010.)

(c) Clerk's duties

(1) If the abandonment is filed in the superior court, the clerk must immediately send a notification of the abandonment to:

(A) Every other party;

(B) The reviewing court; and

(C) The reporter if the appeal is abandoned before the reporter has filed the transcript.

(2) If the abandonment is filed in the reviewing court and the reviewing court orders the appeal dismissed, the clerk must immediately send a notification of the order of dismissal to every party.

(Subd (c) amended effective January 1, 2016; adopted effective July 1, 2010.)
Rule 8.411 amended January 1, 2016; adopted effective July 1, 2010.

Advisory Committee Comment

The Supreme Court has held that appellate counsel for an appealing minor has the power to move to dismiss a dependency appeal based on counsel's assessment of the child's best interests, but that the motion to dismiss requires the authorization of the child or, if the child is incapable of giving authorization, the authorization of the child's CAPTA guardian ad litem (*In re Josiah Z.* (2005) 36 Cal.4th 664).

Rule 8.412. Briefs by parties and amici curiae

(a) Contents, form, and length

(1) Rule 8.200 governs the briefs that may be filed by parties and amici curiae.

(2) Except as provided in (3), rule 8.204 governs the form and contents of briefs. Rule 8.216 also applies in appeals in which a party is both appellant and respondent.

(3) Rule 8.360(b) governs the length of briefs.

(Subd (a) amended effective July 1, 2010; previously amended effective January 1, 2007.)

(b) Time to file

(1) Except in appeals governed by rule 8.416, the appellant must serve and file the appellant's opening brief within 40 days after the record is filed in the reviewing court.

(2) The respondent must serve and file the respondent's brief within 30 days after the appellant's opening brief is filed.

(3) The appellant must serve and file any reply brief within 20 days after the respondent's brief is filed.

(4) In dependency cases in which the child is not an appellant but has appellate counsel, the child must serve and file any brief within 10 days after the respondent's brief is filed.

(5) Rule 8.220 applies if a party fails to timely file an appellant's opening brief or a respondent's brief, but the period specified in the notice required by that rule must be 30 days.

(Subd (b) amended effective July 1, 2010; previously amended effective January 1, 2007.)

(c) Extensions of time

The superior court may not order any extensions of time to file briefs. Except in appeals governed by rule 8.416, the reviewing court may order extensions of time for good cause.

(Subd (c) amended effective July 1, 2010; previously amended effective January 1, 2007.)

(d) Failure to file a brief

(1) Except in appeals governed by rule 8.416, if a party fails to timely file an appellant's opening brief or a respondent's brief, the reviewing court clerk must promptly notify the party's counsel or the party, if not represented, in writing that the brief must be filed within 30 days after the notice is sent and that failure to comply may result in one of the following sanctions:

(A) If the brief is an appellant's opening brief:

(i) If the appellant is the county, the court will dismiss the appeal;

(ii) If the appellant is other than the county and is represented by appointed counsel on appeal, the court will relieve that appointed counsel and appoint new counsel;

(iii) If the appellant is other than the county and is not represented by appointed counsel, the court will dismiss the appeal.

(B) If the brief is a respondent's brief, the court will decide the appeal on the record, the opening brief, and any oral argument by the appellant.

(2) If a party fails to comply with a notice under (1), the court may impose the sanction specified in the notice.

(3) Within the period specified in the notice under (1), a party may apply to the presiding justice for an extension of that period for good cause. If an extension is granted beyond the 30-day period and the brief is not filed within the extended period, the court may impose the sanction under (2) without further notice.

(Subd (d) amended effective January 1, 2016; adopted effective January 1, 2007; previously amended effective July 1, 2010.)

(e) Additional service requirements

(1) A copy of each brief must be served on the superior court clerk for delivery to the superior court judge.

(2) A copy of each brief must be served on the child's trial counsel, or, if the child is not represented by trial counsel, on the child's guardian ad litem appointed under rule 5.662.

(3) If the Court of Appeal has appointed counsel for any party:

(A) The county child welfare department and the People must serve two copies of their briefs on that counsel; and

(B) Each party must serve a copy of its brief on the district appellate project.

(4) In delinquency cases the parties must serve copies of their briefs on the Attorney General and the district attorney. In all other cases the parties must not serve copies of their briefs on the Attorney General or the district attorney unless that office represents a party.

(5) The parties must not serve copies of their briefs on the Supreme Court under rule 8.44(b)(1).

(Subd (e) amended effective July 1, 2007; adopted as subd (d) effective January 1, 2005; previously amended and relettered effective January 1, 2007.)
Rule 8.412 amended effective January 1, 2016; adopted as rule 37.3 effective January 1, 2005; previously amended and renumbered as rule 8.412 effective January 1, 2007; previously amended effective July 1, 2007, and July 1, 2010.

Advisory Committee Comment

Subdivision (b). Subdivision (b)(1) calls litigants' attention to the fact that a different rule (rule 8.416(e)) governs the time to file an appellant's opening brief in appeals from judgments or orders terminating parental rights and in dependency appeals in certain counties.

Subdivision (c). Subdivision (c) calls litigants' attention to the fact that a different rule (rule 8.416(f)) governs the showing required for extensions of time to file briefs in appeals from judgments or orders terminating parental rights and in dependency appeals in certain counties.

Rule 8.416. Appeals from all terminations of parental rights; dependency appeals in Orange, Imperial, and San Diego Counties and in other counties by local rule

(a) Application

(1) This rule governs:

(A) Appeals from judgments or appealable orders of all superior courts terminating parental rights under Welfare and Institutions Code section 366.26 or freeing a child from parental custody and control under Family Code section 7800 et seq.; and

(B) Appeals from judgments or appealable orders in all juvenile dependency cases of:

(i) The Superior Courts of Orange, Imperial, and San Diego Counties; and

(ii) Other superior courts when the superior court and the District Court of Appeal with jurisdiction to hear appeals from that superior court have agreed and have adopted local rules providing that this rule will govern appeals from that superior court.

(2) In all respects not provided for in this rule, rules 8.403–8.412 apply.

(Subd (a) amended effective July 1, 2010; previously amended effective January 1, 2007.)

(b) Form of record

(1) The clerk's and reporter's transcripts must comply with rules 8.45–8.47, relating to sealed and confidential records, and, except as provided in (2) and (3), with rule 8.144.

(2) In appeals under (a)(1)(A), the cover of the record must prominently display the title "Appeal From [Judgment or Order] Terminating Parental Rights Under [Welfare and Institutions Code Section 366.26 or Family Code Section 7800 et seq.]," whichever is appropriate.

(3) In appeals under (a)(1)(B), the cover of the record must prominently display the title "Appeal From [Judgment or Order] Under [Welfare and Institutions Code Section 300 et seq. or Family Code Section 7800 et seq.]," whichever is appropriate.

(Subd (b) amended effective January 1, 2015; previously amended effective July 1, 2010.)

(c) Preparing, certifying, and sending the record

(1) Within 20 days after the notice of appeal is filed:

(A) The clerk must prepare and certify as correct an original of the clerk's transcript and one copy each for the appellant, the respondent, the district appellate project, the child's Indian tribe if the tribe has intervened, and the child if the child is represented by counsel on appeal or if a recommendation has been made to the Court of Appeal for appointment of counsel for the child under rule 8.403(b)(2) and that recommendation is either pending with or has been approved by the Court of Appeal but counsel has not yet been appointed; and

(B) The reporter must prepare, certify as correct, and deliver to the clerk an original of the reporter's transcript and the same number of copies as (A) requires of the clerk's transcript.

(2) When the clerk's and reporter's transcripts are certified as correct, the clerk must immediately send:

(A) The original transcripts to the reviewing court by the most expeditious method, noting the sending date on each original; and

(B) One copy of each transcript to the district appellate project and to the appellate counsel for the following, if they have appellate counsel, by any method as fast as United States Postal Service express mail:

(i) The appellant;

(ii) The respondent;

(iii) The child's Indian tribe if the tribe has intervened; and

(iv) The child.

(3) If appellate counsel has not yet been retained or appointed for the appellant or the respondent or if a recommendation has been made to the Court of Appeal for appointment of counsel for the child under rule 8.403(b)(2) and that recommendation is either pending with or has been approved by the Court of Appeal but counsel has not yet been appointed, when the transcripts are certified as correct, the clerk must send that counsel's copies of the transcripts to the district appellate project. If a tribe that has intervened is not represented by counsel when the transcripts are certified as correct, the clerk must send that counsel's copy of the transcripts to the tribe.

(Subd (c) amended effective January 1, 2018; previously amended effective January 1, 2007, July 1, 2010, January 1, 2015, and January 1, 2017.)

(d) Augmenting or correcting the record

(1) Except as provided in (2) and (3), rule 8.410 governs any augmentation or correction of the record.

(2) An appellant must serve and file any motion for augmentation or correction within 15 days after receiving the record. A respondent must serve and file any such motion within 15 days after the appellant's opening brief is filed.

(3) The clerk and the reporter must prepare any supplemental transcripts within 20 days, giving them the highest priority.

(4) The clerk must certify and send any supplemental transcripts as required by (c).

(Subd (d) amended effective July 1, 2010; previously amended effective January 1, 2007.)

(e) Time to file briefs

(1) To permit determination of the appeal within 250 days after the notice of appeal is filed, the appellant must serve and file the appellant's opening brief within 30 days after the record is filed in the reviewing court.

(2) Rule 8.412(b) governs the time for filing other briefs.

(Subd (e) amended effective July 1, 2010.)

(f) Extensions of time

The superior court may not order any extensions of time to prepare the record or to file briefs; the reviewing court may order extensions of time, but must require an exceptional showing of good cause.

(g) Failure to file a brief

Rule 8.412(d) applies if a party fails to timely file an appellant's opening brief or a respondent's brief, but the period specified in the notice required by that rule must be 15 days.

(Subd (g) amended effective July 1, 2010; adopted effective January 1, 2007.)

(h) Oral argument and submission of the cause

(1) Unless the reviewing court orders otherwise, counsel must serve and file any request for oral argument no later than 15 days after the appellant's reply brief is filed or due to be filed. Failure to file a timely request will be deemed a waiver.

(2) The court must hear oral argument within 60 days after the appellant's last reply brief is filed or due to be filed, unless the court extends the time for good cause or counsel waive argument.

(3) If counsel waive argument, the cause is deemed submitted no later than 60 days after the appellant's reply brief is filed or due to be filed.

(Subd (h) relettered effective January 1, 2007; adopted as subd (g) effective January 1, 2005.)

Rule 8.416 amended effective January 1, 2018; adopted as rule 37.4 effective January 1, 2005; previously amended and renumbered effective January 1, 2007; previously amended effective July 1, 2010, January 1, 2015, and January 1, 2017.

Advisory Committee Comment

Subdivision (c). Under rule 8.71(c), the superior court clerk may send the record to the reviewing court in electronic form.

Subdivision (g). Effective January 1, 2007, revised rule 8.416 incorporates a new subdivision (g) to address a failure to timely file a brief in all termination of parental rights cases and in dependency appeals in Orange, Imperial, and San Diego Counties. Under the new subdivision, appellants would not have the full 30-day grace period given in rule 8.412(d) in which to file a late brief, but instead would have the standard 15-day grace period that is given in civil cases. The intent of this revision is to balance the need to determine the appeal within 250 days with the need to protect appellants' rights in this most serious of appeals.

Subdivision (h). Subdivision (h)(1) recognizes certain reviewing courts' practice of requiring counsel to file any request for oral argument within a time period other than 15 days after the appellant's reply brief is filed or due to be filed. The reviewing court is still expected to determine the appeal "within 250 days after the notice of appeal is filed." (Subdivision (e).)

Article 3
Writs

Title 8, Appellate Rules—Division 1, Rules Relating to the Supreme Court and Courts of Appeal—Chapter 5, Juvenile Appeals and Writs—Article 3, Writs; renumbered effective July 1, 2010; adopted as article 2 effective January 1, 2007.

Rule 8.450. Notice of intent to file writ petition to review order setting hearing under Welfare and Institutions Code section 366.26

Rule 8.452. Writ petition to review order setting hearing under Welfare and Institutions Code section 366.26

Rule 8.454. Notice of intent to file writ petition under Welfare and Institutions Code section 366.28 to review order designating specific placement of a dependent child after termination of parental rights

Rule 8.456. Writ petition under Welfare and Institutions Code section 366.28 to review order designating or denying specific placement of a dependent child after termination of parental rights

Rule 8.450. Notice of intent to file writ petition to review order setting hearing under Welfare and Institutions Code section 366.26

(a) Application

Rules 8.450–8.452 and 8.490 govern writ petitions to review orders setting a hearing under Welfare and Institutions Code section 366.26.

(Subd (a) amended effective July 1, 2010; previously amended effective January 1, 2006, July 1, 2006, January 1, 2007, and January 1, 2009.)

(b) Purpose

Rules 8.450–8.452 are intended to encourage and assist the reviewing courts to determine on their merits all writ petitions filed under these rules within the 120-day period for holding a hearing under Welfare and Institutions Code section 366.26.

(Subd (b) amended effective January 1, 2007.)

(c) Who may file

The petitioner's trial counsel, or, in the absence of trial counsel, the party, is responsible for filing any notice of intent and writ petition under rules 8.450–8.452. Trial counsel is encouraged to seek assistance from or consult with attorneys experienced in writ procedure.

(Subd (c) amended effective January 1, 2008; previously amended effective January 1, 2007.)

(d) Extensions of time

The superior court may not extend any time period prescribed by rules 8.450–8.452. The reviewing court may extend any time period but must require an exceptional showing of good cause.

(Subd (d) amended effective January 1, 2013; previously amended effective January 1, 2007, and July 1, 2010.)

(e) Notice of intent

(1) A party seeking writ review under rules 8.450–8.452 must file in the superior court a notice of intent to file a writ petition and a request for the record.

(2) The notice must include all known dates of the hearing that resulted in the order under review.

(3) The notice must be authorized by the party intending to file the petition and must be signed by that party or by the attorney of record for that party.

(4) The date of the order setting the hearing is the date on which the court states the order on the record orally, or issues an order in writing, whichever occurs first. The notice of intent must be filed according to the following timeline requirements:

(A) If the party was present at the hearing when the court ordered a hearing under Welfare and Institutions Code section 366.26, the notice of intent must be filed within 7 days after the date of the order setting the hearing.

(B) If the party was notified of the order setting the hearing only by mail, the notice of intent must be filed within 12 days after the date the clerk mailed the notification.

(C) If the party was notified of the order setting the hearing by mail, and the notice was mailed to an address outside California but within the United States, the notice of intent must be filed within 17 days after the date the clerk mailed the notification.

(D) If the party was notified of the order setting the hearing by mail, and the notice was mailed to an address outside the United States, the notice of intent must be filed within 27 days after the date the clerk mailed the notification.

(E) If the order was made by a referee not acting as a temporary judge, the party has an additional 10 days to file the notice of intent as provided in rule 5.540(c).

(Subd (e) amended effective July 1, 2010; previously amended effective January 1, 2007, and July 1, 2010.)

(f) Premature or late notice of intent to file writ petition

(1) A notice of intent to file a writ petition under Welfare and Institutions Code section 366.26 is premature if filed before an order setting a hearing under Welfare and Institutions Code section 366.26 has been made.

(2) If a notice of intent is premature or late, the superior court clerk must promptly:

(A) Mark the notice of intent "Received [date] but not filed;"

(B) Return the marked notice of intent to the party with a notice stating that:

(i) The notice of intent was not filed either because it is premature, as no order setting a hearing under Welfare and Institutions Code section 366.26 has been made, or because it was late; and

(ii) The party should contact his or her attorney as soon as possible to discuss this notice, because the time available to take appropriate steps to protect the party's interests may be short; and

(C) Send a copy of the marked notice of intent and clerk's notice to the party's counsel of record, if applicable.

(Subd (f) adopted effective January 1, 2013.)

(g) Sending the notice of intent

(1) When the notice of intent is filed, the superior court clerk must immediately send a copy of the notice to:

(A) The attorney of record for each party;

(B) Each party, including the child if the child is 10 years of age or older;

(C) Any known sibling of the child who is the subject of the hearing if that sibling either is the subject of a dependency proceeding or has been adjudged to be a dependent child of the juvenile court as follows:

(i) If the sibling is under 10 years of age, on the sibling's attorney; or

(ii) If the sibling is 10 years of age or over, on the sibling and the sibling's attorney.

(D) The mother, the father, and any presumed and alleged parents;

(E) The child's legal guardian, if any;

(F) Any person currently awarded by the juvenile court the status of the child's de facto parent;

(G) The probation officer or social worker;

(H) Any Court Appointed Special Advocate (CASA) volunteer;

(I) The grandparents of the child, if their address is known and if the parents' whereabouts are unknown; and

(J) If the court knows or has reason to know that an Indian child is involved, the Indian custodian, if any, and tribe of the child or the Bureau of Indian Affairs, as required under Welfare and Institutions Code section 224.2.

(2) The clerk must promptly send by first-class mail, e-mail, or fax a copy of the notice of intent and a list of those to whom the notice of intent was sent to:

(A) The reviewing court; and

(B) The petitioner if the clerk sent the notice of intent to the Indian custodian, tribe of the child, or the Bureau of Indian Affairs.

(3) If the party was notified of the order setting the hearing only by mail, the clerk must include the date that the notification was mailed.

(Subd (g) amended effective January 1, 2017; previously amended effective January 1, 2006, July 1, 2006, January 1, 2007, and July 1, 2010; previously amended and relettered effective January 1, 2013.)

(h) Preparing the record

When the notice of intent is filed, the superior court clerk must:

(1) Immediately notify each court reporter [1]**, in a manner providing immediate notice,** to prepare a reporter's transcript of the oral proceedings at each session of the hearing that resulted in the order under review and deliver the transcript to the clerk within 12 calendar days after the notice of intent is filed; and

(2) Within 20 days after the notice of intent is filed, prepare a clerk's transcript that includes the notice of intent, proof of service, and all items listed in rule 8.407(a).

(Subd (h) amended effective January 1, 2021; adopted as subd (g); previously amended effective January 1, 2006, January 1, 2007, January 1, 2008, and July 1, 2010; previously amended and relettered as subd (h) effective January 1, 2013.)

Rule 8.450(h). 2020 Deletes. [1] by telephone and in writing

(i) Sending the record

When the transcripts are certified as correct, the superior court clerk must immediately send:

(1) The original transcripts to the reviewing court by the most expeditious method, noting the sending date on each original, and

(2) One copy of each transcript to each counsel of record and any unrepresented party by any means as fast as United States Postal Service express mail.

(Subd (i) relettered effective January 1, 2013; previously amended as subd (h) effective January 1, 2007.)

(j) Reviewing court clerk's duties

(1) The reviewing court clerk must immediately lodge the notice of intent. When the notice is lodged, the reviewing court has jurisdiction of the writ proceedings.

(2) When the record is filed in the reviewing court, that court's clerk must immediately notify the parties, stating the date on which the 10-day period for filing the writ petition under rule 8.452(c)(1) will expire.

(Subd (j) relettered effective January 1, 2013; previously amended as subd (i) effective January 1, 2007.)

Rule 8.450 amended effective January 1, 2021; adopted as rule 38 effective January 1, 2005; previously amended and renumbered effective January 1, 2007; previously amended effective January 1, 2006, July 1, 2006, January 1, 2008, January 1, 2009, July 1, 2010, January 1, 2013, and January 1, 2017.

Advisory Committee Comment

Subdivision (d). The case law generally recognizes that the reviewing courts may grant extensions of time under these rules for exceptional good cause. (See, e.g., *Jonathan M. v. Superior Court* (1995) 39 Cal.App.4th 1826, and *In re Cathina W.* (1998) 68 Cal.App.4th 716 [recognizing that a late notice of intent may be filed on a showing of exceptional circumstances not under the petitioner's control].) It may constitute exceptional good cause for an extension of the time to file a notice of intent if a premature notice of intent is returned to a party shortly before the issuance of an order setting a hearing under Welfare and Institutions Code section 366.26.

Subdivision (e)(4). See rule 8.25(b)(5) for provisions concerning the timeliness of documents mailed by inmates or patients from custodial institutions.

Subdivision (f)(1). A party who prematurely attempts to file a notice of intent to file a writ petition under Welfare and Institutions Code section 366.26 is not precluded from later filing such a notice after the issuance of an order setting a hearing under Welfare and Institutions Code section 366.26.

Subdivision (i). Under rule 8.71(c), the superior court clerk may send the record to the reviewing court in electronic form.

Rule 8.452. Writ petition to review order setting hearing under Welfare and Institutions Code section 366.26

(a) Petition

(1) The petition must be liberally construed and must include:

(A) The identities of the parties;

(B) The date on which the superior court made the order setting the hearing;

(C) The date on which the hearing is scheduled to be held;

(D) A summary of the grounds of the petition; and

(E) The relief requested.

(2) The petition must be verified.

(3) The petition must be accompanied by a memorandum.

(Subd (a) amended effective January 1, 2018; previously amended effective January 1, 2007, and July 1, 2010.)

(b) Contents of the memorandum

(1) The memorandum must provide a summary of the significant facts, limited to matters in the record.

(2) The memorandum must state each point under a separate heading or subheading summarizing the point and support each point by argument and citation of authority.

(3) The memorandum must support any reference to a matter in the record by a citation to the record. The memorandum should explain the significance of any cited portion of the record and note any disputed aspects of the record.

(Subd (b) amended effective January 1, 2007.)

(c) Serving and filing the petition and response

(1) The petition must be served and filed within 10 days after the record is filed in the reviewing court. The petitioner must serve a copy of the petition on:

(A) Each attorney of record;

(B) Any unrepresented party, including the child if the child is 10 years of age or older;

(C) Any known sibling of the child who is the subject of the hearing if that sibling either is the subject of a dependency proceeding or has been adjudged to be a dependent child of the juvenile court as follows:

(i) If the sibling is under 10 years of age, on the sibling's attorney;

(ii) If the sibling is 10 years of age or over, on the sibling and the sibling's attorney.

(D) The child's Court Appointed Special Advocate (CASA) volunteer;

(E) Any person currently awarded by the juvenile court the status of the child's de facto parent; and

(F) If the court sent the notice of intent to file the writ petition to an Indian custodian, tribe, or Bureau of Indian Affairs, then to that Indian custodian, tribe of the child, or the Bureau of Indian Affairs as required under Welfare and Institutions Code section 224.2.

(2) Any response must be served on each of the people and entities listed above and filed:

(A) Within 10 days—or, if the petition was served by mail, within 15 days—after the petition is filed; or

(B) Within 10 days after a respondent receives a request from the reviewing court for a response, unless the court specifies a shorter time.

(Subd (c) amended effective July 1, 2010; previously amended effective January 1, 2007.)

(d) Order to show cause or alternative writ

If the court intends to determine the petition on the merits, it must issue an order to show cause or alternative writ.

(Subd (d) repealed and relettered effective July 1, 2010; adopted as subd (d) effective January 1, 2006; previously relettered as subd (e) effective January 1, 2006.)

(e) Augmenting or correcting the record in the reviewing court

(1) Except as provided in (2) and (3), rule 8.410 governs any augmentation or correction of the record.

(2) The petitioner must serve and file any request for augmentation or correction within 5 days—or, if the record exceeds 300 pages, within 7 days; or, if the record exceeds 600 pages, within 10 days—after receiving the record. A respondent must serve and file any such request within 5 days after the petition is filed or an order to show cause has issued, whichever is later.

(3) A party must attach to its motion a copy, if available, of any document or transcript that the party wants added to the record. The pages of the attachment must be consecutively numbered, beginning with the number one. If the reviewing court grants the motion, it may augment the record with the copy.

(4) If the party cannot attach a copy of the matter to be added, the party must identify it as required under rules 8.122 and 8.130.

(5) An order augmenting or correcting the record may grant no more than 15 days for compliance. The clerk and the reporter must give the order the highest priority.

(6) The clerk must certify and send any supplemental transcripts as required by rule 8.450(h). If the augmentation or correction is ordered, the time to file any petition or response is extended by the number of additional days granted to augment or correct the record.

(Subd (e) amended and relettered effective July 1, 2010; adopted as subd (e) effective January 1, 2005; previously relettered as subd (f) effective January 1, 2006; previously amended effective January 1, 2007.)

(f) Stay

The reviewing court may stay the hearing set under Welfare and Institutions Code section 366.26, but must require an exceptional showing of good cause.

(Subd (f) relettered effective July 1, 2010; adopted as subd (f) effective January 1, 2005; previously relettered as subd (g) effective January 1, 2006.)

(g) Oral argument

(1) The reviewing court must hear oral argument within 30 days after the response is filed or due to be filed, unless the court extends the time for good cause or counsel waive argument.

(2) If argument is waived, the cause is deemed submitted not later than 30 days after the response is filed or due to be filed.

(Subd (g) relettered effective July 1, 2010; adopted as subd (g) effective January 1, 2005; previously relettered as subd (h) effective January 1, 2006.)

(h) Decision

(1) Absent exceptional circumstances, the reviewing court must decide the petition on the merits by written opinion.

(2) The reviewing court clerk must promptly notify the parties of any decision and must promptly send a certified copy of any writ or order to the court named as respondent.

(3) If the writ or order stays or prohibits proceedings set to occur within 7 days or requires action within 7 days—or in any other urgent situation—the reviewing court clerk must make a reasonable effort to notify the clerk of the respondent court by telephone or e-mail. The clerk of the respondent court must then notify the judge or officer most directly concerned.

(4) The reviewing court clerk need not give telephonic or e-mail notice of the summary denial of a writ, unless a stay previously issued will be dissolved.

(Subd (h) amended effective January 1, 2017; adopted as subd (h) effective January 1, 2005; previously relettered as subd (i) effective January 1, 2006, and subd (h) effective July 1, 2010; previously amended effective January 1, 2007.)

(i) Filing, modification, finality of decision, and remittitur

Rule 8.490 governs the filing, modification, finality of decisions, and remittitur in writ proceedings under this rule.

(Subd (i) adopted effective July 1, 2010.)

Rule 8.452 amended effective January 1, 2018; adopted as rule 38.1 effective January 1, 2005; previously amended and renumbered effective January 1, 2007; previously amended effective January 1, 2006, July 1, 2010, and January 1, 2017.)

Advisory Committee Comment

Subdivision (d). Subdivision (d) tracks the second sentence of former rule 39.1B(*l*). (But see *Maribel M. v. Superior Court* (1998) 61 Cal.App.4th 1469, 1471–1476.)

Subdivision (h). Subdivision (h)(1) tracks former rule 39.1B(o). (But see *Maribel M. v. Superior Court* (1998) 61 Cal.App.4th 1469, 1471–1476.)

Rule 8.454. Notice of intent to file writ petition under Welfare and Institutions Code section 366.28 to review order designating specific placement of a dependent child after termination of parental rights

(a) Application

Rules 8.454–8.456 and 8.490 govern writ petitions to review placement orders following termination of parental rights entered on or after January 1, 2005. "Posttermination placement order" as used in this rule and rule 8.456 refers to orders following termination of parental rights.

(Subd (a) amended effective July 1, 2010; previously amended effective January 1, 2007, and January 1, 2009.)

(b) Purpose

The purpose of this rule is to facilitate and implement Welfare and Institutions Code section 366.28. Delays caused by appeals from court orders designating the specific placement of a dependent child after parental rights have been terminated may cause a substantial detriment to the child.

(c) Who may file

The petitioner's trial counsel, or, in the absence of trial counsel, the party, is responsible for filing any notice of intent and writ petition under rules 8.454–8.456. Trial counsel is encouraged to seek assistance from, or consult with, attorneys experienced in writ procedure.

(Subd (c) amended effective January 1, 2008; previously amended effective January 1, 2007.)

(d) Extensions of time

The superior court may not extend any time period prescribed by rules 8.454–8.456. The reviewing court may extend any time period, but must require an exceptional showing of good cause.

(Subd (d) amended effective January 1, 2007.)

(e) Notice of intent

(1) A party seeking writ review under rules 8.454–8.456 must file in the superior court a notice of intent to file a writ petition and a request for the record.

(2) The notice must include all known dates of the hearing that resulted in the order under review.

(3) The notice must be authorized by the party intending to file the petition and signed by the party or by the attorney of record for that party.

(4) The notice must be served and filed within 7 days after the date of the posttermination placement order or, if the order was made by a referee not acting as a temporary judge, within 7 days after the referee's order becomes final under rule 5.540(c). The date of the posttermination placement order is the date on which the court states the order on the record orally or in writing, whichever first occurs.

(5) If the party was notified of the posttermination placement order only by mail, the notice of intent must be filed within 12 days after the date that the clerk mailed the notification.

(Subd (e) amended effective July 1, 2010; previously amended effective January 1, 2007.)

(f) Premature or late notice of intent to file writ petition

(1) A notice of intent to file a writ petition under Welfare and Institutions Code section 366.28 is premature if filed before a date for a posttermination placement order has been made. The reviewing court may treat the notice as filed immediately after the posttermination order has been made.

(2) The superior court clerk must mark a late notice of intent to file a writ petition under section 366.28 "Received [date] but not filed," notify the party that the notice was not filed because it was late, and send a copy of the marked notice to the party's counsel of record, if applicable.

(Subd (f) amended effective July 1, 2013; adopted effective January 1, 2006; previously amended effective January 1, 2007.)

(g) Sending the notice of intent

(1) When the notice of intent is filed, the superior court clerk must immediately send a copy of the notice to:

(A) The attorney of record for each party;

(B) Each party, including the child if the child is 10 years of age or older;

(C) Any known sibling of the child who is the subject of the hearing if that sibling either is the subject of a dependency proceeding or has been adjudged to be a dependent child of the juvenile court as follows:

(i) If the sibling is under 10 years of age, on the sibling's attorney;

(ii) If the sibling is 10 years of age or over, on the sibling and the sibling's attorney;

(D) Any prospective adoptive parent;

(E) The child's legal guardian if any;

(F) Any person currently awarded by the juvenile court the status of the child's de facto parent;

(G) The probation officer or social worker;

(H) The child's Court Appointed Special Advocate (CASA) volunteer, if any; and

(I) If the court knows or has reason to know that an Indian child is involved, the Indian custodian, if any, and tribe of the child or the Bureau of Indian Affairs as required under Welfare and Institutions Code section 224.2.

(2) The clerk must promptly send by first-class mail, e-mail, or fax a copy of the notice of intent and a list of those to whom the notice of intent was sent to:

(A) The reviewing court; and

(B) The petitioner if the clerk sent a copy of the notice of intent to the Indian custodian, tribe of the child, or the Bureau of Indian Affairs.

(3) If the party was notified of the posttermination placement order only by mail, the clerk must include the date that the notification was mailed.

(Subd (g) amended effective January 1, 2017; adopted as subd (f) effective January 1, 2005; relettered effective January 1, 2006; previously amended effective January 1, 2007, and July 1, 2010.)

(h) Preparing the record

When the notice of intent is filed, the superior court clerk must:

(1) Immediately notify each court reporter [1], **in a manner providing immediate notice,** to prepare a reporter's transcript of the oral proceedings at each session of the hearing that resulted in the order under review and to deliver the transcript to the clerk within 12 calendar days after the notice of intent is filed; and

(2) Within 20 days after the notice of intent is filed, prepare a clerk's transcript that includes the notice of intent, proof of service, and all items listed in rule 8.407(a).

(Subd (h) amended effective January 1, 2021; adopted as subd (g) effective January 1, 2005; previously amended and relettered effective January 1, 2006; previously amended effective July 1, 2006, January 1, 2007, January 1, 2008, July 1, 2010, and July 1, 2013.)

Rule 8.454(h).   2020 Deletes. [1] by telephone and in writing

(i) Sending the record

When the transcripts are certified as correct, the superior court clerk must immediately send:

(1) The original transcripts to the reviewing court by the most expeditious method, noting the sending date on each original; and

(2) One copy of each transcript to each counsel of record and any unrepresented party and unrepresented custodian of the dependent child by any means as fast as United States Postal Service express mail.

(Subd (i) amended effective January 1, 2007; adopted as subd (h) effective January 1, 2005; relettered effective January 1, 2006.)

(j) Reviewing court clerk's duties

(1) The reviewing court clerk must promptly lodge the notice of intent. When the notice is lodged, the reviewing court has jurisdiction over the writ proceedings.

(2) When the record is filed in the reviewing court, that court's clerk must immediately notify the parties, stating the date on which the 10-day period for filing the writ petition under rule 8.456(c)(1) will expire.

(Subd (j) amended effective January 1, 2007; adopted as subd (i) effective January 1, 2005; relettered effective January 1, 2006.)

Rule 8.454 amended effective January 1, 2021; adopted as rule 38.2 effective January 1, 2005; previously amended and renumbered effective January 1, 2007; previously amended effective January 1, 2006, July 1, 2006, January 1, 2008, January 1, 2009, July 1, 2010, July 1, 2013, and January 1, 2017.

Advisory Committee Comment

Subdivision (f)(2). See rule 8.25(b)(5) for provisions concerning the timeliness of documents mailed by inmates or patients from custodial institutions.

Subdivision (i). Under rule 8.71(c), the superior court clerk may send the record to the reviewing court in electronic form.

Rule 8.456.   Writ petition under Welfare and Institutions Code section 366.28 to review order designating or denying specific placement of a dependent child after termination of parental rights

(a) Petition

(1) The petition must be liberally construed and must include:

(A) The identities of the parties;

(B) The date on which the superior court made the posttermination placement order;

(C) A summary of the grounds of the petition; and

(D) The relief requested.

(2) The petition must be verified.

(3) The petition must be accompanied by a memorandum.

(Subd (a) amended effective January 1, 2018; previously amended effective January 1, 2007, and July 1, 2010.)

(b) Contents of memorandum

(1) The memorandum must provide a summary of the significant facts, limited to matters in the record.

(2) The memorandum must state each point under a separate heading or subheading summarizing the point and support each point by argument and citation of authority.

(3) The memorandum must support any reference to a matter in the record by a citation to the record. The memorandum should explain the

significance of any cited portion of the record and note any disputed aspects of the record.

(Subd (b) amended effective January 1, 2007.)

(c) Serving and filing the petition and response

(1) The petition must be served and filed within 10 days after the record is filed in the reviewing court. The petitioner must serve the petition on:

(A) Each attorney of record;

(B) Any unrepresented party, including the child if the child is 10 years of age or older;

(C) Any known sibling of the child who is the subject of the hearing if that sibling either is the subject of a dependency proceeding or has been adjudged to be a dependent child of the juvenile court as follows:

(i) If the sibling is under 10 years of age, on the sibling's attorney;

(ii) If the sibling is 10 years of age or over, on the sibling and the sibling's attorney;

(D) Any prospective adoptive parent;

(E) The child's Court Appointed Special Advocate (CASA) volunteer;

(F) Any person currently awarded by the juvenile court the status of the child's de facto parent; and

(G) If the court sent the notice of intent to file the writ petition to an Indian custodian, tribe, or Bureau of Indian Affairs, then to that Indian custodian, tribe, or the Bureau of Indian Affairs as required under Welfare and Institutions Code section 224.2.

(2) Any response must be served on each of the people and entities listed in (1) and filed:

(A) Within 10 days—or, if the petition was served by mail, within 15 days—after the petition is filed; or

(B) Within 10 days after a respondent receives a request from the reviewing court for a response, unless the court specifies a shorter time.

(Subd (c) amended effective July 1, 2010; previously amended effective January 1, 2006, and January 1, 2007.)

(d) Order to show cause or alternative writ

If the court intends to determine the petition on the merits, it must issue an order to show cause or alternative writ.

(Subd (d) repealed and relettered effective July 1, 2010; adopted as subd (d) effective January 1, 2005; previously relettered as subd (e) effective January 1, 2006.)

(e) Augmenting or correcting the record in the reviewing court

(1) Except as provided in (2) and (3), rule 8.410 governs augmentation or correction of the record.

(2) The petitioner must serve and file any request for augmentation or correction within 5 days—or, if the record exceeds 300 pages, within 7 days; or, if the record exceeds 600 pages, within 10 days—after receiving the record. A respondent must serve and file any such request within 5 days after the petition is filed or an order to show cause has issued, whichever is later.

(3) A party must attach to its motion a copy, if available, of any document or transcript that it wants added to the record. The pages of the attachment must be consecutively numbered, beginning with the number one. If the reviewing court grants the motion, it may augment the record with the copy.

(4) If the party cannot attach a copy of the matter to be added, the party must identify it as required under rules 8.122 and 8.130.

(5) An order augmenting or correcting the record may grant no more than 15 days for compliance. The clerk and the reporter must give the order the highest priority.

(6) The clerk must certify and send any supplemental transcripts as required by rule 8.454(i). If the augmentation or correction is ordered, the time to file any petition or response is extended by the number of additional days granted to augment or correct the record.

(Subd (e) amended and relettered effective July 1, 2010; adopted as subd (e) effective January 1, 2005; previously relettered as subd (f) effective January 1, 2006; previously amended effective January 1, 2007.)

(f) Stay

A request by petitioner for a stay of the posttermination placement order will not be granted unless the writ petition shows that implementation of the superior court's placement order pending the reviewing court's decision is likely to cause detriment to the child if the order is ultimately reversed.

(Subd (f) relettered effective July 1, 2010; adopted as subd (f) effective January 1, 2005; previously relettered as subd (g) effective January 1, 2006; previously amended effective February 24, 2006.)

(g) Oral argument

(1) The reviewing court must hear oral argument within 30 days after the response is filed or due to be filed, unless the court extends the time for good cause or counsel waive argument.

(2) If argument is waived, the cause is deemed submitted not later than 30 days after the response is filed or due to be filed.

(Subd (g) relettered effective July 1, 2010; adopted as subd (g) effective January 1, 2005; previously relettered as subd (h) effective January 1, 2006; previously amended effective January 1, 2007.)

(h) Decision

(1) Absent exceptional circumstances, the reviewing court must review the petition and decide it on the merits by written opinion.

(2) The reviewing court clerk must promptly notify the parties of any decision and must promptly send a certified copy of any writ or order to the court named as respondent.

(3) If the writ or order stays or requires action within 7 days—or in any other urgent situation—the reviewing court clerk must make a reasonable effort to notify the clerk of the respondent court by telephone or e-mail. The clerk of the respondent court must then notify the judge or officer most directly concerned.

(4) The reviewing court clerk need not give telephonic or e-mail notice of the summary denial of a writ, unless a stay previously issued and will be dissolved.

(5) Rule 8.490 governs the filing, modification, finality of decisions, and remittitur in writ proceedings under this rule.

(Subd (h) amended effective January 1, 2017; adopted as subd (h) effective January 1, 2005; previously relettered as subd (i) effective January 1, 2006; previously amended and relettered as subd (h) effective July 1, 2010.)

(i) Right to appeal other orders

This section does not affect the right of a parent, a legal guardian, or the child to appeal any order that is otherwise appealable and that is issued at a hearing held under Welfare and Institutions Code section 366.26.

(Subd (i) relettered effective July 1, 2010; adopted as subd (i) effective January 1, 2005; previously relettered as subd (j) effective January 1, 2006; previously amended effective January 1, 2007.)

Rule 8.456 amended effective January 1, 2018; adopted as rule 38.3 effective January 1, 2005; previously amended and renumbered effective January 1, 2007; previously amended effective January 1, 2006, February 24, 2006, July 1, 2010, and January 1, 2017.

Article 4
Hearing and Decision

Division 1, Rules Relating to the Supreme Court and Courts of Appeal—Chapter 5, Juvenile Appeals and Writs—Article 4, Hearing and Decision, renumbered effective January 1, 2011.

Rule 8.470. Hearing and decision in the Court of Appeal
Rule 8.472. Hearing and decision in the Supreme Court
Rule 8.474. Procedures and data

Rule 8.470.   Hearing and decision in the Court of Appeal

Except as provided in rules 8.400–8.456, rules 8.252–8.272 govern hearing and decision in the Court of Appeal in juvenile cases.

Rule 8.470 amended and renumbered effective January 1, 2007; adopted as rule 38.4 effective January 1, 2005; previously amended effective July 1, 2005.

Rule 8.472.   Hearing and decision in the Supreme Court

Rules 8.500–8.552 govern hearing and decision in the Supreme Court in juvenile cases.

Rule 8.472 amended and renumbered effective January 1, 2007; adopted as rule 38.5 effective January 1, 2005; previously amended effective July 1, 2005.

Rule 8.474.   Procedures and data

(a) Procedures

The judges and clerks of the superior courts and the reviewing courts must adopt procedures to identify the records and expedite the processing of all appeals and writs in juvenile cases.

(b) Data

The clerks of the superior courts and the reviewing courts must provide the data required to assist the Judicial Council in evaluating the effectiveness of the rules governing appeals and writs in juvenile cases.

(Subd (b) amended effective January 1, 2016.)

Rule 8.474 amended effective January 1, 2016; adopted as rule 38.6 effective January 1, 2005; previously renumbered as rule 8.474 effective January 1, 2007.

Chapter 6
Conservatorship and Civil Commitment Appeals

Title 8, Appellate Rules—Division 1, Rules Relating to the Supreme Court and Courts of Appeal—Chapter 6, Conservatorship and Civil Commitment Appeals amended effective January 1, 2020.

Rule 8.480. Appeal from order establishing conservatorship

Rule 8.482. Appeal from judgment authorizing conservator to consent to sterilization of conservatee

Rule 8.483. Appeal from order of civil commitment

Rule 8.480.   Appeal from order establishing conservatorship

(a) Application

Except as otherwise provided in this rule, rules 8.304–8.368 and 8.508 govern appeals from orders establishing conservatorships under Welfare and Institutions Code section 5350 et seq.

(Subd (a) amended effective January 1, 2007.)

(b) Clerk's transcript

The clerk's transcript must contain:

(1) The petition;

(2) Any demurrer or other plea;

(3) Any written motion with supporting and opposing memoranda and attachments;

(4) Any filed medical or social worker reports;

(5) All court minutes;

(6) All instructions submitted in writing, each noting the party requesting it;

(7) Any verdict;

(8) Any written opinion of the court;

(9) The judgment or order appealed from;

(10) The notice of appeal; and

(11) Any application for additional record and any order on the application.

(Subd (b) amended effective January 1, 2007.)

(c) Reporter's transcript

The reporter's transcript must contain all oral proceedings, excluding the voir dire examination of jurors and any opening statement.

(d) Sending the record

The clerk must not send a copy of the record to the Attorney General or the district attorney unless that office represents a party.

(e) Briefs

The parties must not serve copies of their briefs:

(1) On the Attorney General or the district attorney, unless that office represents a party; or

(2) On the Supreme Court under rule 8.44(b)(1).

(Subd (e) amended effective January 1, 2007.)

Rule 8.480 amended and renumbered effective January 1, 2007; repealed and adopted as rule 39 effective January 1, 2005.

Advisory Committee Comment

Subdivision (a). Under rule 8.71(c), the superior court clerk may send the record to the reviewing court in electronic form.

Rule 8.482.   Appeal from judgment authorizing conservator to consent to sterilization of conservatee

(a) Application

Except as otherwise provided in this rule, rules 8.304–8.368 and 8.508 govern appeals from judgments authorizing a conservator to consent to the sterilization of a developmentally disabled adult conservatee.

(Subd (a) amended effective January 1, 2007.)

(b) When appeal is taken automatically

An appeal from a judgment authorizing a conservator to consent to the sterilization of a developmentally disabled adult conservatee is taken automatically, without any action by the conservatee, when the judgment is rendered.

(c) Superior court clerk's duties

After entering the judgment, the clerk must immediately:

(1) Begin preparing a clerk's transcript and notify the reporter to prepare a reporter's transcript; and

(2) Send certified copies of the judgment to the Court of Appeal and the Attorney General.

(Subd (c) amended effective January 1, 2016; previously amended effective January 1, 2007.)

(d) Clerk's transcript

The clerk's transcript must contain:

(1) The petition and notice of hearing;

(2) All court minutes;

(3) Any application, motion, or notice of motion, with supporting and opposing memoranda and attachments;

(4) Any report or other document submitted to the court;

(5) Any transcript of a proceeding pertaining to the case;

(6) The statement of decision; and

(7) The judgment or order appealed from.

(Subd (d) amended effective January 1, 2007.)

(e) Reporter's transcript

The reporter's transcript must contain all oral proceedings, including:

(1) All proceedings at the hearing on the petition, with opening statements and closing arguments;

(2) All proceedings on motions;

(3) Any comments on the evidence by the court; and

(4) Any oral opinion or oral statement of decision.

(Subd (e) amended effective January 1, 2007.)

(f) Preparing and sending transcripts

(1) The clerk and the reporter must prepare and send an original and two copies of each of the transcripts as provided in rule 8.336.

(2) Probate Code section 1963 governs the cost of preparing the record on appeal.

(Subd (f) amended effective January 1, 2007.)

(g) Confidential material

(1) Written reports of physicians, psychologists, and clinical social workers, and any other matter marked confidential by the court, may be inspected only by court personnel, the parties and their counsel, the district appellate project, and other persons designated by the court.

(2) Material under (1) must be sent to the reviewing court in a secure manner that preserves its confidentiality. If the material is in paper format, it must be sent to the reviewing court in a sealed envelope marked "CONFIDENTIAL—MAY NOT BE EXAMINED WITHOUT COURT ORDER."

(Subd (g) amended effective January 1, 2016.)

(h) Trial counsel's continuing representation

To expedite preparation and certification of the record, the conservatee's trial counsel must continue to represent the conservatee until appellate counsel is retained or appointed.

(i) Appointment of appellate counsel

If appellate counsel has not been retained for the conservatee, the reviewing court must appoint such counsel.

Rule 8.482 amended effective January 1, 2016; repealed and adopted as rule 39.1 effective January 1, 2005; previously amended and renumbered as rule 8.482 effective January 1, 2007.

Advisory Committee Comment

Subdivision (a). Under rule 8.71(c), the superior court clerk may send the record to the reviewing court in electronic form.

Rule 8.483.   Appeal from order of civil commitment

(a) Application and contents

(1) *Application*

Except as otherwise provided in this rule, rules 8.300–8.368 and 8.508 govern appeals from civil commitment orders under Penal Code sections 1026 et seq. (not guilty by reason of insanity), 1370 et seq. (incompetent to stand trial), 1600 et seq. (outpatient placement and revocation), and 2962 et seq. (mentally disordered offenders); Welfare and Institutions Code sections 1800 et seq. (extended detention of dangerous persons), 6500 et seq. (developmentally disabled persons), and 6600 et seq. (sexually violent predators); and former Welfare and Institutions Code section 6300 et seq. (mentally disordered sex offenders).

(2) *Contents*

In an appeal from a civil commitment order, the record must contain a clerk's transcript and a reporter's transcript, which together constitute the normal record.

(Subd (a) adopted effective January 1, 2020.)

(b) Clerk's transcript

The clerk's transcript must contain:

(1) The petition and any supporting documents filed along with the petition;

(2) Any demurrer or other plea, admission, or denial;

(3) All court minutes;

(4) All jury instructions that any party submitted in writing and the cover page required by rule 2.1055(b)(2) indicating the party requesting each instruction, and any written jury instructions given by the court;

(5) Any written communication between the court and the jury or any individual juror;

(6) Any verdict;

(7) Any written opinion of the court;

(8) The commitment order and any judgment or other order appealed from;

(9) Any motion for new trial, with supporting and opposing memoranda and attachments;

(10) The notice of appeal;

(11) Any transcript of a sound or sound-and-video recording furnished to the jury or tendered to the court under rule 2.1040;

(12) Any application for additional record and any order on the application;

(13) Any diagnostic or psychological reports submitted to the court, including at the trial or probable cause hearing;

(14) Any written waiver of the right to a jury trial or the right to be present; and

(15) If the appellant is the person subject to the civil commitment order:

(A) Any written defense motion denied in whole or in part, with supporting and opposing memoranda and attachments; and

(B) Any document admitted in evidence to prove a juvenile adjudication, criminal conviction, or prison term.

(Subd (b) adopted effective January 1, 2020.)

(c) Reporter's transcript

The reporter's transcript must contain:

(1) The oral proceedings on the entry of any admission or submission to the commitment petition;

(2) The oral proceedings on any motion in limine;

(3) The oral proceedings at trial, excluding the voir dire examination of jurors and any opening statement;

(4) All instructions given orally;

(5) Any oral communication between the court and the jury or any individual juror;

(6) Any oral opinion of the court;

(7) The oral proceedings on any motion for new trial;

(8) The oral proceedings of the commitment hearing or other dispositional hearing, including any probable cause hearing;

(9) Any oral waiver of the right to a jury trial or the right to be present; and

(10) If the appellant is the person subject to the civil commitment order:

(A) The oral proceedings on any defense motion denied in whole or in part except motions for disqualification of a judge;

(B) The closing arguments; and

(C) Any comment on the evidence by the court to the jury.

(Subd (c) adopted effective January 1, 2020.)

(d) Exhibits

Exhibits admitted in evidence, refused, or lodged are deemed part of the record, but may be transmitted to the reviewing court only as provided in rule 8.224.

(Subd (d) adopted effective January 1, 2020.)

(e) Stipulation for partial transcript

If counsel for the person subject to the civil commitment order and the People stipulate in writing before the record is certified that any part of the record is not required for proper determination of the appeal, that part must not be prepared or sent to the reviewing court.

(Subd (e) adopted effective January 1, 2020.)

Rule 8.483 adopted effective January 1, 2020.

Advisory Committee Comment

The record on appeal of orders establishing conservatorships under Welfare and Institutions Code section 5350 et seq., including Murphy conservatorships for persons who are gravely disabled as defined in Welfare and Institutions Code section 5008(h)(1)(B), is governed by rule 8.480.

Chapter 7
Writs of Mandate, Certiorari, and Prohibition in the Supreme Court and Court of Appeal

Title 8, Appellate Rules—Division 1, Rules Relating to the Supreme Court and Courts of Appeal—Chapter 7, Writs of Mandate, Certiorari, and Prohibition in the Supreme Court and Court of Appeal adopted effective January 1, 2009.

Rule 8.485.   Application

(a) Writ proceedings governed

Except as provided in (b), the rules in this chapter govern petitions to the Supreme Court and Court of Appeal for writs of mandate, certiorari, or prohibition, or other writs within the original jurisdiction of these courts. In all respects not provided for in these rules, rule 8.204 governs the form and content of documents in the proceedings governed by this chapter.

(Subd (a) adopted effective January 1, 2009.)

(b) Writ proceedings not governed

These rules do not apply to proceedings for writs of mandate, certiorari, or prohibition in the appellate division of the superior court under rules 8.930–8.936, writs of supersedeas under rule 8.116, writs of habeas corpus except as provided in rule 8.384, writs to review orders setting a hearing under Welfare and Institutions Code section 366.26, writs under Welfare and Institutions Code section 366.28 to review orders designating or denying a specific placement of a dependent child after termination of parental rights, and writs under rules 8.450–8.456 except as provided in rules 8.452 and 8.456, or writs under rules 8.495–8.498.

(Subd (b) amended effective January 1, 2014; adopted effective January 1, 2009; previously amended effective July 1, 2012.)

Rule 8.485 amended effective January 1, 2014; adopted effective January 1, 2009; previously amended effective July 1, 2012.

Rule 8.486.   Petitions

(a) Contents of petition

(1) If the petition could have been filed first in a lower court, it must explain why the reviewing court should issue the writ as an original matter.

(2) If the petition names as respondent a judge, court, board, or other officer acting in a public capacity, it must disclose the name of any real party in interest.

(3) If the petition seeks review of trial court proceedings that are also the subject of a pending appeal, the notice "Related Appeal Pending" must appear on the cover of the petition and the first paragraph of the petition must state:

(A) The appeal's title, trial court docket number, and any reviewing court docket number; and

(B) If the petition is filed under Penal Code section 1238.5, the date the notice of appeal was filed.

(4) The petition must be verified.

(5) The petition must be accompanied by a memorandum, which need not repeat facts alleged in the petition.

(6) Rule 8.204(c) governs the length of the petition and memorandum, but, in addition to the exclusions provided in that rule, the verification and any supporting documents are excluded from the limits stated in rule 8.204(c)(1) and (2).

(7) If the petition requests a temporary stay, it must comply with the following or the reviewing court may decline to consider the request for a temporary stay:

(A) The petition must explain the urgency.

(B) The cover of the petition must prominently display the notice "STAY REQUESTED" and identify the nature and date of the proceeding or act sought to be stayed.

(C) The trial court and department involved and the name and telephone number of the trial judge whose order the request seeks to stay must appear either on the cover or at the beginning of the text.

(Subd (a) amended effective January 1, 2011; adopted as subd (b) effective January 1, 2005; previously amended effective January 1, 2006, and January 1, 2007; previously repealed, amended and relettered effective January 1, 2009.)

(b) Contents of supporting documents

(1) A petition that seeks review of a trial court ruling must be accompanied by an adequate record, including copies of:

(A) The ruling from which the petition seeks relief;

(B) All documents and exhibits submitted to the trial court supporting and opposing the petitioner's position;

(C) Any other documents or portions of documents submitted to the trial court that are necessary for a complete understanding of the case and the ruling under review; and

(D) A reporter's transcript of the oral proceedings that resulted in the ruling under review.

(2) In exigent circumstances, the petition may be filed without the documents required by (1)(A)–(C) but must include a declaration that

explains the urgency and the circumstances making the documents unavailable and fairly summarizes their substance.

(3) If a transcript under (1)(D) is unavailable, the record must include a declaration:

(A) Explaining why the transcript is unavailable and fairly summarizing the proceedings, including the parties' arguments and any statement by the court supporting its ruling. This declaration may omit a full summary of the proceedings if part of the relief sought is an order to prepare a transcript for use by an indigent criminal defendant in support of the petition and if the declaration demonstrates the need for and entitlement to the transcript; or

(B) Stating that the transcript has been ordered, the date it was ordered, and the date it is expected to be filed, which must be a date before any action requested of the reviewing court other than issuance of a temporary stay supported by other parts of the record.

(4) If the petition does not include the required record or explanations or does not present facts sufficient to excuse the failure to submit them, the court may summarily deny a stay request, the petition, or both.

(Subd (b) amended effective January 1, 2014; adopted as subd (c) effective January 1, 2005; previously amended effective January 1, 2006, July 1, 2006, January 1, 2007, and July 1, 2009; previously amended and relettered effective January 1, 2009.)

(c) Form of supporting documents

(1) Documents submitted under (b) must comply with the following requirements:

(A) If submitted in paper form, they must be bound together at the end of the petition or in separate volumes not exceeding 300 pages each. The pages must be consecutively numbered.

(B) If submitted in paper form, they must be index-tabbed by number or letter.

(C) They must begin with a table of contents listing each document by its title and its index number or letter. If a document has attachments, the table of contents must give the title of each attachment and a brief description of its contents.

(2) The clerk must file any supporting documents not complying with (1), but the court may notify the petitioner that it may strike or summarily deny the petition if the documents are not brought into compliance within a stated reasonable time of not less than 5 days.

(3) Rule 8.44(a) governs the number of copies of supporting documents to be filed in the Supreme Court. Rule 8.44(b) governs the number of supporting documents to be filed in the Court of Appeal.

(Subd (c) amended effective January 1, 2016; adopted as subd (d) effective January 1, 2005; previously amended effective January 1, 2006, and January 1, 2007; previously amended and relettered as subd (c) effective January 1, 2009.)

(d) Sealed and confidential records

Rules 8.45–8.47 govern sealed and confidential records in proceedings under this chapter.

(Subd (d) amended effective January 1, 2014; adopted as subd (e) effective January 1, 2005; previously amended effective January 1, 2007, and January 1, 2011; previously relettered effective January 1, 2009.)

(e) Service

(1) If the respondent is the superior court or a judge of that court, the petition and one set of supporting documents must be served on any named real party in interest, but only the petition must be served on the respondent.

(2) If the respondent is not the superior court or a judge of that court, both the petition and one set of supporting documents must be served on the respondent and on any named real party in interest.

(3) In addition to complying with the requirements of rule 8.25, the proof of service must give the telephone number of each attorney served.

(4) The petition must be served on a public officer or agency when required by statute or rule 8.29.

(5) The clerk must file the petition even if its proof of service is defective, but if the petitioner fails to file a corrected proof of service within 5 days after the clerk gives notice of the defect the court may strike the petition or impose a lesser sanction.

(6) The court may allow the petition to be filed without proof of service.

(Subd (e) relettered effective January 1, 2009; adopted as subd (f) effective January 1, 2005; previously amended effective January 1, 2007.)

Rule 8.486 amended effective January 1, 2016; repealed and adopted as rule 56 effective January 1, 2005; previously amended and renumbered as rule 8.490 effective January 1, 2007, and as rule 8.486 effective January 1, 2009; previously
amended effective July 1, 2005, January 1, 2006, July 1, 2006, January 1, 2008, July 1, 2009, January 1, 2011, and January 1, 2014.

Advisory Committee Comment

Subdivision (a). Because of the importance of the point, rule 8.486(a)(6) explicitly states that the provisions of rule 8.204(c)—and hence the word-count limits imposed by that rule—apply to a petition for original writ.

Subdivision (d). Examples of confidential records include records of the family conciliation court (Fam. Code, § 1818 (b)) and fee waiver applications (Gov. Code, § 68633(f)).

Subdivision (e). Rule 8.25, which generally governs service and filing in reviewing courts, also applies to the original proceedings covered by this rule.

Rule 8.487. Opposition and amicus curiae briefs

(a) Preliminary opposition

(1) Within 10 days after the petition is filed, the respondent or any real party in interest, separately or jointly, may serve and file a preliminary opposition.

(2) A preliminary opposition must contain a memorandum and a statement of any material fact not included in the petition.

(3) Within 10 days after a preliminary opposition is filed, the petitioner may serve and file a reply.

(4) Without requesting preliminary opposition or waiting for a reply, the court may grant or deny a request for temporary stay, deny the petition, issue an alternative writ or order to show cause, or notify the parties that it is considering issuing a peremptory writ in the first instance.

(Subd (a) adopted effective January 1, 2009.)

(b) Return or opposition; reply

(1) If the court issues an alternative writ or order to show cause, the respondent or any real party in interest, separately or jointly, may serve and file a return by demurrer, verified answer, or both. If the court notifies the parties that it is considering issuing a peremptory writ in the first instance, the respondent or any real party in interest may serve and file an opposition.

(2) Unless the court orders otherwise, the return or opposition must be served and filed within 30 days after the court issues the alternative writ or order to show cause or notifies the parties that it is considering issuing a peremptory writ in the first instance.

(3) Unless the court orders otherwise, the petitioner may serve and file a reply within 15 days after the return or opposition is filed.

(4) If the return is by demurrer alone and the demurrer is not sustained, the court may issue the peremptory writ without granting leave to answer.

(Subd (b) adopted effective January 1, 2009.)

(c) Supporting documents

Any supporting documents accompanying a preliminary opposition, return or opposition, or reply must comply with rule 8.486(c)–(d).

(Subd (c) adopted effective January 1, 2014.)

(d) Attorney General's amicus curiae brief

(1) If the court issues an alternative writ or order to show cause, the Attorney General may file an amicus curiae brief without the permission of the Chief Justice or presiding justice, unless the brief is submitted on behalf of another state officer or agency.

(2) The Attorney General must serve and file the brief within 14 days after the return is filed or, if no return is filed, within 14 days after the date it was due. For good cause, the Chief Justice or presiding justice may allow later filing.

(3) The brief must provide the information required by rule 8.200(c)(2) and comply with rule 8.200(c)(5).

(4) Any party may serve and file an answer within 14 days after the brief is filed.

(Subd (d) amended effective January 1, 2017; adopted as subd (c) effective January 1, 2009; previously relettered as subd (d) effective January 1, 2014.)

(e) Other amicus curiae briefs

(1) This subdivision governs amicus curiae briefs when the court issues an alternative writ or order to show cause.

(2) Any person or entity may serve and file an application for permission of the Chief Justice or presiding justice to file an amicus curiae brief.

(3) The application must be filed no later than 14 days after the return is filed or, if no return is filed, within 14 days after the date it was due. For good cause, the Chief Justice or presiding justice may allow later filing.

(4) The proposed brief must be served on all parties. It must accompany the application and may be combined with it.

(5) The proposed brief must provide the information required by rule 8.200(c)(2) and (3) and comply with rule 8.200(c)(5).

(6) If the court grants the application, any party may file either an answer to the individual amicus curiae brief or a consolidated answer to multiple amicus curiae briefs filed in the case. If the court does not specify a due date, the answer must be filed within 14 days after either the court rules on the last timely filed application to file an amicus curiae brief or the time for filing applications to file an amicus curiae brief expires, whichever is later. The answer must be served on all parties and the amicus curiae.

(Subd (e) adopted effective January 1, 2017.)

Rule 8.487 amended effective January 1, 2017; adopted effective January 1, 2009; previously amended effective January 1, 2014.

Advisory Committee Comment

A party other than the petitioner who files a preliminary opposition under (a) or a return or opposition under (b) may be required to pay a filing fee under Government Code section 68926 if the preliminary opposition, return, or opposition is the first document filed in the writ proceeding in the reviewing court by that party. See rule 8.25(c).

Subdivision (a). Consistent with practice, rule 8.487 draws a distinction between a "preliminary opposition," which the respondent or a real party in interest may file before the court takes any action on the petition ((a)(1)), and a more formal "opposition," which the respondent or a real party in interest may file if the court notifies the parties that it is considering issuing a peremptory writ in the first instance ((b)(1)).

Subdivision (a)(1) allows the respondent or any real party in interest to serve and file a preliminary opposition within 10 days after the petition is filed. The reviewing court retains the power to act in any case without obtaining preliminary opposition ((a)(4)).

Subdivision (a)(3) allows a petitioner to serve and file a reply within 10 days after a preliminary opposition is filed. To permit prompt action in urgent cases, however, the provision recognizes that the reviewing court may act on the petition without waiting for a reply.

Subdivision (a)(4) recognizes that the reviewing court may "grant or deny a request for temporary stay" without requesting preliminary opposition or waiting for a reply.

The several references in rule 8.487 to the power of the court to issue a peremptory writ in the first instance after notifying the parties that it is considering doing so ((a)–(b)) implement the rule of *Palma v. U.S. Industrial Fasteners, Inc.* (1984) 36 Cal.3d 171.

Subdivision (b). Subdivision (b)(2) requires that the return or opposition be served and filed within 30 days after the court issues the alternative writ or order to show cause or notifies the parties that it is considering issuing a peremptory writ in the first instance. To permit prompt action in urgent cases, however, the provision recognizes that the reviewing court may order otherwise.

Subdivision (b)(3) formalizes the common practice of permitting petitioners to file replies to returns and specifies that such a reply must be served and filed within 15 days after the return is filed. To permit prompt action in urgent cases, however, the provision recognizes that the reviewing court may order otherwise.

Subdivision (c). Examples of confidential records include records of the family conciliation court (Fam. Code, § 1818 (b)) and fee waiver applications (Gov. Code, § 68633(f)).

Subdivisions (d) and (e). These provisions do not alter the court's authority to request or permit the filing of amicus briefs or amicus letters in writ proceedings in circumstances not covered by these subdivisions, such as before the court has determined whether to issue an alternative writ or order to show cause or when it notifies the parties that it is considering issuing a peremptory writ in the first instance.

Rule 8.488.   Certificate of Interested Entities or Persons

(a) Application

This rule applies in writ proceedings in criminal cases in which an entity is the defendant and in civil cases other than family, juvenile, guardianship, and conservatorship cases.

(Subd (a) adopted effective January 1, 2009.)

(b) Compliance with rule 8.208

Each party in a civil case and any entity that is a defendant in a criminal case must comply with the requirements of rule 8.208 concerning serving and filing a certificate of interested entities or persons.

(Subd (b) adopted effective January 1, 2009.)

(c) Placement of certificates

(1) The petitioner's certificate must be included in the petition.

(2) The certificates of the respondent and real party in interest must be included in their preliminary opposition or, if no such opposition is filed, in their return, if any.

(3) The certificate must appear after the cover and before the tables.

(4) If the identity of any party has not been publicly disclosed in the proceedings, the party may file an application for permission to file its certificate under seal separately from the petition, preliminary opposition, or return.

(Subd (c) adopted effective January 1, 2009.)

(d) Failure to file a certificate

(1) If a party fails to file a certificate as required under (b) and (c), the clerk must notify the party in writing that the party must file the certificate within 10 days after the clerk's notice is sent and that if the party fails to comply, the court may impose one of the following sanctions:

(A) If the party is the petitioner, the court may strike the petition; or

(B) If the party is the respondent or the real party in interest, the court may strike that party's document.

(2) If the party fails to file the certificate as specified in the notice under (1), the court may impose the sanctions specified in the notice.

(Subd (d) amended effective January 1, 2016; adopted effective January 1, 2009.)

Rule 8.488 amended effective January 1, 2016; adopted effective January 1, 2009.

Advisory Committee Comment

The Judicial Council has adopted an optional form, *Certificate of Interested Entities or Persons* (form APP-008), that can be used to file the certificate required by this provision.

Subdivision (a). Under rule 8.208(c), for purposes of certificates of interested entities or persons, an "entity" means a corporation, a partnership, a firm, or any other association, but does not include a governmental entity or its agencies or a natural person.

Rule 8.489.   Notice to trial court

(a) Notice if writ issues

If a writ or order issues directed to any judge, court, board, or other officer, the reviewing court clerk must promptly send a certified copy of the writ or order to the person or entity to whom it is addressed.

(Subd (a) adopted effective January 1, 2009.)

(b) Notice by telephone

(1) If the writ or order stays or prohibits proceedings set to occur within 7 days or requires action within 7 days—or in any other urgent situation—the reviewing court clerk must make a reasonable effort to notify the clerk of the respondent court by telephone or e-mail. The clerk of the respondent court must then notify the judge or officer most directly concerned.

(2) The clerk need not give telephonic or e-mail notice of the summary denial of a writ, whether or not a stay previously issued.

(Subd (b) amended effective January 1, 2017; adopted effective January 1, 2009.)

Rule 8.489 amended effective January 1, 2017; adopted effective January 1, 2009.

Rule 8.490.   Petitions for writ of mandate, certiorari, or prohibition [Renumbered]

Rule 8.490 renumbered to rule 8.486 effective January 1, 2009; repealed and adopted as rule 56 effective January 1, 2005; previously amended effective July 1, 2005, January 1, 2006, July 1, 2006 and January 1, 2008; previously amended and renumbered effective January 1, 2007.

Another Rule 8.490 follows.

Rule 8.490.   Filing, finality, and modification of decisions; rehearing; remittitur

(a) Filing and modification of decisions

Rule 8.264(a) and (c) govern the filing and modification of decisions in writ proceedings.

(Subd (a) adopted effective January 1, 2009.)

(b) Finality of decision

(1) Except as otherwise ordered by the court, the following decisions regarding petitions for writs within the court's original jurisdiction are final in the issuing court when filed:

(A) An order denying or dismissing such a petition without issuance of an alternative writ, order to show cause, or writ of review; and

(B) An order denying or dismissing such a petition as moot after issuance of an alternative writ, order to show cause, or writ of review.

(2) All other decisions in a writ proceeding are final 30 days after the decision is filed, except as follows:

(A) If necessary to prevent mootness or frustration of the relief granted or to otherwise promote the interests of justice, the court may order early finality in that court of a decision granting a petition for a writ within its original jurisdiction or denying such a petition after issuing an alternative writ, order to show cause, or writ of review. The decision may provide for finality in that court on filing or within a stated period of less than 30 days.

(B) If a Court of Appeal certifies its opinion for publication or partial publication after filing its decision and before the decision becomes final

Rules of Court

in that court, the 30 days or other finality period ordered under (A) runs from the filing date of the order for publication.

(C) If an order modifying a decision changes the appellate judgment, the 30 days or other finality period ordered under (A) runs from the filing date of the modification order.

(Subd (b) amended effective January 1, 2014; adopted effective January 1, 2009.)

(c) Rehearing

(1) Rule 8.268 governs rehearing in the Courts of Appeal.

(2) Rule 8.536 governs rehearing in the Supreme Court.

(Subd (c) adopted effective January 1, 2014.)

(d) Remittitur

A Court of Appeal must issue a remittitur in a writ proceeding under this chapter except when the court issues one of the orders listed in (b)(1). Rule 8.272(b)–(d) governs issuance of a remittitur by a Court of Appeal in writ proceedings under this chapter.

(Subd (d) amended and relettered effective January 1, 2014; adopted as subd (c) effective January 1, 2009.)

Rule 8.490 amended effective January 1, 2014; adopted effective January 1, 2009.

Advisory Committee Comment

Subdivision (b). This provision addresses the finality of decisions in proceedings relating to writs of mandate, certiorari, and prohibition. See rule 8.264(b) for provisions addressing the finality of decisions in proceedings under chapter 2, relating to civil appeals, and rule 8.366 for provisions addressing the finality of decisions in proceedings under chapter 3, relating to criminal appeals.

Subdivision (b)(1). Examples of situations in which the court may issue an order dismissing a writ petition include when the petitioner fails to comply with an order of the court, when the court recalls the alternative writ, order to show cause, or writ of review as improvidently granted, or when the petition becomes moot.

Subdivision (d). Under this rule, a remittitur serves as notice that the writ proceedings have concluded.

Rule 8.491. Responsive pleading under Code of Civil Procedure section 418.10

If the Court of Appeal denies a petition for writ of mandate brought under Code of Civil Procedure section 418.10(c) and the Supreme Court denies review of the Court of Appeal's decision, the time to file a responsive pleading in the trial court is extended until 10 days after the Supreme Court files its order denying review.

Rule 8.491 adopted effective January 1, 2009.

Rule 8.492. Sanctions

(a) Grounds for sanctions

On motion of a party or its own motion, a Court of Appeal may impose sanctions, including the award or denial of costs under rule 8.493, on a party or an attorney for:

(1) Filing a frivolous petition or filing a petition solely to cause delay; or

(2) Committing any other unreasonable violation of these rules.

(Subd (a) adopted effective January 1, 2009.)

(b) Notice

The court must give notice in writing if it is considering imposing sanctions.

(Subd (b) adopted effective January 1, 2009.)

(c) Opposition

Within 10 days after the court sends such notice, a party or attorney may serve and file an opposition, but failure to do so will not be deemed consent. An opposition may not be filed unless the court sends such notice.

(Subd (c) adopted effective January 1, 2009.)

(d) Oral argument

Unless otherwise ordered, oral argument on the issue of sanctions must be combined with any oral argument on the merits of the petition.

(Subd (d) adopted effective January 1, 2009.)

Rule 8.492 adopted effective January 1, 2009.

Rule 8.493. Costs

(a) Award of costs

(1) Except in a criminal or juvenile or other proceeding in which a party is entitled to court-appointed counsel:

(A) Unless otherwise ordered by the court under (B), the prevailing party in an original proceeding is entitled to costs if the court resolves the proceeding by written opinion after issuing an alternative writ, an order to show cause, or a peremptory writ in the first instance.

(B) In the interests of justice, the court may also award or deny costs as it deems proper in the proceedings listed in (A) and in other circumstances.

(2) The opinion or order resolving the proceeding must specify the award or denial of costs.

(Subd (a) adopted effective January 1, 2009.)

(b) Procedures for recovering costs

Rule 8.278(b)–(d) governs the procedure for recovering costs under this rule.

(Subd (b) adopted effective January 1, 2009.)

Rule 8.493 adopted effective January 1, 2009.

Rule 8.494. Review of Workers' Compensation Appeals Board cases [Renumbered]

Rule 8.494 renumbered to rule 8.495 effective January 1, 2009; repealed and adopted as rule 57 effective January 1, 2005; previously amended effective July 1, 2006; previously amended and renumbered effective January 1, 2007.

Chapter 8
[Reserved]

Title 8, Appellate Rules—Division 1, Rules Relating to the Supreme Court and Courts of Appeal—Chapter 8, [Reserved] amended effective April 25, 2019; adopted as chapter 7 effective January 1, 2007; amended and renumbered effective January 1, 2009; previously amended effective July 1, 2012.

Rule 8.495. Review of Workers' Compensation Appeals Board cases [Renumbered]

Rule 8.495 renumbered as rule 8.720 effective April 25, 2019; repealed and adopted as rule 57 effective January 1, 2005; previously amended effective July 1, 2006, January 1, 2016, and January 1, 2018; previously amended and renumbered as rule 8.494 effective January 1, 2007; previously renumbered as rule 8.495 effective January 1, 2009.

Rule 8.496. Review of Public Utilities Commission cases [Renumbered]

Rule 8.496 renumbered as rule 8.724 effective April 25, 2019; repealed and adopted as rule 58 effective January 1, 2005; previously amended effective July 1, 2006, and January 1, 2016; previously amended and renumbered as rule 8.496 effective January 1, 2007.

Rule 8.497. Review of California Environmental Quality Act cases under Public Resources Code sections 21178–21189.3 [Repealed]

Rule 8.497 repealed effective July 1, 2014; adopted effective July 1, 2012.

Rule 8.498. Review of Agricultural Labor Relations Board and Public Employment Relations Board cases [Renumbered]

Rule 8.498 renumbered as rule 8.728 effective April 25, 2019; repealed and adopted as rule 59 effective January 1, 2005; previously amended effective July 1, 2006, and January 1, 2016; previously amended and renumbered as rule 8.498 effective January 1, 2007.

Rule 8.499. Filing, modification, and finality of decision; remittitur [Renumbered]

Rule 8.499 renumbered as rule 8.730 effective April 25, 2019; adopted effective January 1, 2008; previously amended effective January 1, 2011, and July 1, 2012.

Chapter 9
Proceedings in the Supreme Court

Title 8, Appellate Rules—Division 1, Rules Relating to the Supreme Court and Courts of Appeal—Chapter 9, Proceedings in the Supreme Court renumbered effective January 1, 2009; adopted as chapter 8 effective January 1, 2007.

Rule 8.500. Petition for review

(a) Right to file a petition, answer, or reply

(1) A party may file a petition in the Supreme Court for review of any decision of the Court of Appeal, including any interlocutory order, except

the denial of a transfer of a case within the appellate jurisdiction of the superior court.

(2) A party may file an answer responding to the issues raised in the petition. In the answer, the party may ask the court to address additional issues if it grants review.

(3) The petitioner may file a reply to the answer.

(Subd (a) amended effective January 1, 2004.)

(b) Grounds for review

The Supreme Court may order review of a Court of Appeal decision:

(1) When necessary to secure uniformity of decision or to settle an important question of law;

(2) When the Court of Appeal lacked jurisdiction;

(3) When the Court of Appeal decision lacked the concurrence of sufficient qualified justices; or

(4) For the purpose of transferring the matter to the Court of Appeal for such proceedings as the Supreme Court may order.

(Subd (b) amended effective January 1, 2007.)

(c) Limits of review

(1) As a policy matter, on petition for review the Supreme Court normally will not consider an issue that the petitioner failed to timely raise in the Court of Appeal.

(2) A party may petition for review without petitioning for rehearing in the Court of Appeal, but as a policy matter the Supreme Court normally will accept the Court of Appeal opinion's statement of the issues and facts unless the party has called the Court of Appeal's attention to any alleged omission or misstatement of an issue or fact in a petition for rehearing.

(d) Petitions in nonconsolidated proceedings

If the Court of Appeal decides an appeal and denies a related petition for writ of habeas corpus without issuing an order to show cause and without formally consolidating the two proceedings, a party seeking review of both decisions must file a separate petition for review in each proceeding.

(e) Time to serve and file

(1) A petition for review must be served and filed within 10 days after the Court of Appeal decision is final in that court. For purposes of this rule, the date of finality is not extended if it falls on a day on which the office of the clerk/executive officer is closed.

(2) The time to file a petition for review may not be extended, but the Chief Justice may relieve a party from a failure to file a timely petition for review if the time for the court to order review on its own motion has not expired.

(3) If a petition for review is presented for filing before the Court of Appeal decision is final in that court, the clerk/executive officer of the Supreme Court must accept it and file it on the day after finality.

(4) Any answer to the petition must be served and filed within 20 days after the petition is filed.

(5) Any reply to the answer must be served and filed within 10 days after the answer is filed.

(Subd (e) amended effective January 1, 2018; previously amended effective January 1, 2007, and January 1, 2009.)

(f) Additional requirements

(1) The petition must also be served on the superior court clerk and, **if filed in paper format,** the clerk/executive officer of the Court of Appeal. **Electronic filing of a petition constitutes service of the petition on the clerk/executive officer of the Court of Appeal.**

(2) A copy of each brief must be served on a public officer or agency when required by statute or by rule 8.29.

(3) The clerk/executive officer of the Supreme Court must file the petition even if its proof of service is defective, but if the petitioner fails to file a corrected proof of service within 5 days after the clerk gives notice of the defect the court may strike the petition or impose a lesser sanction.

(Subd (f) amended effective January 1, 2020; previously amended effective January 1, 2004, January 1, 2007, and January 1, 2018.)

(g) Amicus curiae letters

(1) Any person or entity wanting to support or oppose a petition for review or for an original writ must serve on all parties and send to the Supreme Court an amicus curiae letter rather than a brief.

(2) The letter must describe the interest of the amicus curiae. Any matter attached to the letter or incorporated by reference must comply with rule 8.504(e).

(3) Receipt of the letter does not constitute leave to file an amicus curiae brief on the merits under rule 8.520(f).

(Subd (g) amended effective January 1, 2007; previously amended effective July 1, 2004.)

Rule 8.500 amended effective January 1, 2020; repealed and adopted as rule 28 effective January 1, 2003; previously amended effective January 1, 2004, July 1, 2004, January 1, 2009, and January 1, 2018; previously amended and renumbered effective January 1, 2007.

Advisory Committee Comment

Subdivision (a). A party other than the petitioner who files an answer may be required to pay a filing fee under Government Code section 68927 if the answer is the first document filed in the proceeding in the Supreme Court by that party. See rule 8.25(c).

Subdivision (a)(1) makes it clear that any interlocutory order of the Court of Appeal—such as an order denying an application to appoint counsel, to augment the record, or to allow oral argument—is a "decision" that may be challenged by petition for review.

Subdivision (e). Subdivision (e)(1) provides that a petition for review must be served and filed within 10 days after the Court of Appeal decision is *final in that court*. Finality in the Court of Appeal is generally governed by rules 8.264(b) (civil appeals), 8.366(b) (criminal appeals), 8.387(b) (habeas corpus proceedings), and 8.490(b) (proceedings for writs of mandate, certiorari, and prohibition). These rules declare the general rule that a Court of Appeal decision is final in that court 30 days after filing. They then carve out specific exceptions—decisions that they declare to be final immediately on filing (see rules 8.264(b)(2), 8.366(b)(2), and 8.490(b)(1)). The plain implication is that all other Court of Appeal orders—specifically, interlocutory orders that may be the subject of a petition for review—are *not* final on filing. This implication is confirmed by current practice, in which parties may be allowed to apply for—and the Courts of Appeal may grant—reconsideration of such interlocutory orders; reconsideration, of course, would be impermissible if the orders were in fact final on filing.

Contrary to paragraph (2) of subdivision (e), paragraphs (4) and (5) do not prohibit extending the time to file an answer or reply; because the subdivision thus expressly forbids an extension of time only with respect to the petition for review, by clear negative implication it permits an application to extend the time to file an answer or reply under rule 8.50.

See rule 8.25(b)(5) for provisions concerning the timeliness of documents mailed by inmates or patients from custodial institutions.

Subdivision (f). The general requirements relating to service of documents in the appellate courts are established by rule 8.25. Subdivision (f)(1) requires that the petition (but not an answer or reply) be served on the clerk/executive officer of the Court of Appeal. To assist litigants, (f)(1) also states explicitly what is impliedly required by rule 8.212(c), i.e., that the petition must also be served on the superior court clerk (for delivery to the trial judge).

Rule 8.504. Form and contents of petition, answer, and reply

(a) In general

Except as provided in this rule, a petition for review, answer, and reply must comply with the relevant provisions of rule 8.204.

(Subd (a) amended effective January 1, 2007.)

(b) Contents of a petition

(1) The body of the petition must begin with a concise, nonargumentative statement of the issues presented for review, framing them in terms of the facts of the case but without unnecessary detail.

(2) The petition must explain how the case presents a ground for review under rule 8.500(b).

(3) If a petition for rehearing could have been filed in the Court of Appeal, the petition for review must state whether it was filed and, if so, how the court ruled.

(4) If the petition seeks review of a Court of Appeal opinion, a copy of the opinion showing its filing date and a copy of any order modifying the opinion or directing its publication must be bound at the back of the original petition and each copy filed in the Supreme Court or, if the petition is not filed in paper form, attached.

(5) If the petition seeks review of a Court of Appeal order, a copy of the order showing the date it was entered must be bound at the back of the original petition and each copy filed in the Supreme Court or, if the petition is not filed in paper form, attached.

(6) The title of the case and designation of the parties on the cover of the petition must be identical to the title and designation in the Court of Appeal opinion or order that is the subject of the petition.

(7) Rule 8.508 governs the form and content of a petition for review filed by the defendant in a criminal case for the sole purpose of exhausting state remedies before seeking federal habeas corpus review.

(Subd (b) amended effective January 1, 2016; previously amended effective January 1, 2004, January 1, 2007, and January 1, 2009.)

(c) Contents of an answer

An answer that raises additional issues for review must contain a concise, nonargumentative statement of those issues, framing them in terms of the facts of the case but without unnecessary detail.

(d) Length

(1) If produced on a computer, a petition or answer must not exceed 8,400 words, including footnotes, and a reply must not exceed 4,200 words, including footnotes. Each petition, answer, or reply must include a certificate by appellate counsel or an unrepresented party stating the number of words in the document. The person certifying may rely on the word count of the computer program used to prepare the document.

(2) If typewritten, a petition or answer must not exceed 30 pages and a reply must not exceed 15 pages.

(3) The tables, the cover information required under rule 8.204(b)(10), the Court of Appeal opinion, a certificate under (1), any signature block, and any attachment under (e)(1) are excluded from the limits stated in (1) and (2).

(4) On application and for good cause, the Chief Justice may permit a longer petition, answer, reply, or attachment.

(Subd (d) amended effective January 1, 2011; adopted as subd (e) effective January 1, 2003; previously relettered effective January 1, 2004; previously amended effective January 1, 2007.)

(e) Attachments and incorporation by reference

(1) No attachments are permitted except:

(A) An opinion or order required to be attached under (b)(4) or (5);

(B) Exhibits or orders of a trial court or Court of Appeal that the party considers unusually significant;

(C) Copies of relevant local, state, or federal regulations or rules, out-of-state statutes, or other similar citable materials that are not readily accessible; and

(D) An opinion required to be attached under rule 8.1115(c).

(2) The attachments under (1)(B)–(C) must not exceed a combined total of 10 pages.

(3) No incorporation by reference is permitted except a reference to a petition, an answer, or a reply filed by another party in the same case or filed in a case that raises the same or similar issues and in which a petition for review is pending or has been granted.

(Subd (e) amended effective January 1, 2009; adopted as subd (f) effective January 1, 2003; previously relettered effective January 1, 2004; previously amended effective January 1, 2007.)

Rule 8.504 amended effective January 1, 2016; adopted as rule 28.1 effective January 1, 2003; previously amended and renumbered as rule 8.504 effective January 1, 2007; previously amended effective January 1, 2004, January 1, 2009, and January 1, 2011.

Advisory Committee Comment

Subdivision (d). Subdivision (d) states in terms of word counts rather than page counts the maximum permissible lengths of a petition for review, answer, or reply produced on a computer. This provision tracks a provision in rule 8.204(c) governing Court of Appeal briefs and is explained in the advisory committee comment to that provision. Subdivision (d)(3) specifies certain items that are not counted toward the maximum length of a petition, answer, or reply. Signature blocks, as referenced in this provision include not only the signatures, but also the printed names, titles, and affiliations of any attorneys filing or joining in the petition, answer, or reply, which may accompany the signature.

Rule 8.508. Petition for review to exhaust state remedies

(a) Purpose

After decision by the Court of Appeal in a criminal case, a defendant may file an abbreviated petition for review in the Supreme Court for the sole purpose of exhausting state remedies before presenting a claim for federal habeas corpus relief.

(b) Form and contents

(1) The words "Petition for Review to Exhaust State Remedies" must appear prominently on the cover of the petition.

(2) Except as provided in (3), the petition must comply with rule 8.504.

(3) The petition need not comply with rule 8.504(b)(1)–(2) but must include:

(A) A statement that the case presents no grounds for review under rule 8.500(b) and the petition is filed solely to exhaust state remedies for federal habeas corpus purposes;

(B) A brief statement of the underlying proceedings, including the nature of the conviction and the punishment imposed; and

(C) A brief statement of the factual and legal bases of the claim.

(Subd (b) amended effective January 1, 2007.)

(c) Service

The petition must be served on the clerk/executive officer of the Court of Appeal but need not be served on the superior court clerk.

(Subd (c) amended effective January 1, 2018.)

Rule 8.508 amended effective January 1, 2018; adopted as rule 33.3 effective January 1, 2004; previously amended and renumbered effective January 1, 2007.

Advisory Committee Comment

Subdivision (b). Although a petition under this rule must state that "the case presents no grounds for review under rule 8.500(b)" (see (b)(3)(A)), this does not mean the Supreme Court cannot order review if it determines the case warrants review. The list of grounds for granting review in rule 8.500(b) is not intended to be exclusive, and from time to time the Supreme Court has exercised its discretion to order review in a case that does not present one of the listed grounds. (Compare U.S. Supreme Court Rule 10 [the listed grounds for granting certiorari, "although neither controlling nor fully measuring the Court's discretion, indicate the character of the reasons the Court considers"].)

Subdivision (b)(3)(C) requires the petition to include a statement of the factual and legal bases of the claim. This showing is required by federal law: "for purposes of exhausting state remedies, a claim for relief [in state court] … must include reference to a specific federal constitutional guarantee, as well as a statement of the facts that entitle the petitioner to relief." (*Gray v. Netherland* (1996) 518 U.S. 152, 162–163, citing *Picard v. Connor* (1971) 404 U.S. 270.) The federal courts will decide whether a petition filed in compliance with this rule satisfies federal exhaustion requirements, and practitioners should consult federal law to determine whether the petition's statement of the factual and legal bases for the claim is sufficient for that purpose.

Rule 8.512. Ordering review

(a) Transmittal of record

On receiving a copy of a petition for review or on request of the Supreme Court, whichever is earlier, the clerk/executive officer of the Court of Appeal must promptly send the record to the Supreme Court. If the petition is denied, the clerk/executive officer of the Supreme Court must promptly return the record to the Court of Appeal if the record was transmitted in paper form.

(Subd (a) amended effective January 1, 2018; previously amended effective January 1, 2016.)

(b) Determination of petition

(1) The court may order review within 60 days after the last petition for review is filed. Before the 60-day period or any extension expires, the court may order one or more extensions to a date not later than 90 days after the last petition is filed.

(2) If the court does not rule on the petition within the time allowed by (1), the petition is deemed denied.

(Subd (b) amended effective January 1, 2004.)

(c) Review on the court's own motion

(1) If no petition for review is filed, the Supreme Court may, on its own motion, order review of a Court of Appeal decision within 30 days after the decision is final in that court. Before the 30-day period or any extension expires, the Supreme Court may order one or more extensions to a date not later than 90 days after the decision is final in the Court of Appeal. If any such period ends on a day on which the office of the clerk/executive officer is closed, the court may order review on its own motion on the next day the office is open.

(2) If a petition for review is filed, the Supreme Court may deny the petition but order review on its own motion within the periods prescribed in (b)(1).

(Subd (c) amended effective January 1, 2018; adopted as subd (d) effective January 1, 2003; previously amended and relettered effective January 1, 2004.)

(d) Order; grant and hold

(1) An order granting review must be signed by at least four justices; an order denying review may be signed by the Chief Justice alone.

(2) On or after granting review, the court may order action in the matter deferred until the court disposes of another matter or pending further order of the court.

(Subd (d) adopted effective January 1, 2004.)

Rule 8.512 amended effective January 1, 2018; adopted as rule 28.2 effective January 1, 2003; previously amended effective January 1, 2004, and January 1, 2016; previously renumbered as rule 8.512 effective January 1, 2007.

Advisory Committee Comment

Subdivision (b). The Supreme Court deems the 60-day period within which it may grant review to begin on the filing date of the last petition for review that either (1) is timely in the sense that it is filed within the rule time for such petitions (i.e., 10 days after finality of the Court of Appeal decision) or (2) is treated as timely—although presented for filing after expiration of the rule time—in the sense that it is filed with permission of the Chief Justice on a showing of good cause for relief from default. In each circumstance it is the filing of the petition that triggers the 60-day period.

Rule 8.516.   Issues on review

(a) Issues to be briefed and argued

(1) On or after ordering review, the Supreme Court may specify the issues to be briefed and argued. Unless the court orders otherwise, the parties must limit their briefs and arguments to those issues and any issues fairly included in them.

(2) Notwithstanding an order specifying issues under (1), the court may, on reasonable notice, order oral argument on fewer or additional issues or on the entire cause.

(b) Issues to be decided

(1) The Supreme Court may decide any issues that are raised or fairly included in the petition or answer.

(2) The court may decide an issue that is neither raised nor fairly included in the petition or answer if the case presents the issue and the court has given the parties reasonable notice and opportunity to brief and argue it.

(3) The court need not decide every issue the parties raise or the court specifies.

Rule 8.516 renumbered effective January 1, 2007; repealed and adopted as rule 29 effective January 1, 2003.

Rule 8.520.   Briefs by parties and amici curiae; judicial notice

(a) Parties' briefs; time to file

(1) Within 30 days after the Supreme Court files the order of review, the petitioner must serve and file in that court either an opening brief on the merits or the brief it filed in the Court of Appeal.

(2) Within 30 days after the petitioner files its brief or the time to do so expires, the opposing party must serve and file either an answer brief on the merits or the brief it filed in the Court of Appeal.

(3) The petitioner may file a reply brief on the merits or the reply brief it filed in the Court of Appeal. A reply brief must be served and filed within 20 days after the opposing party files its brief.

(4) A party filing a brief it filed in Court of Appeal must attach to the cover a notice of its intent to rely on the brief in the Supreme Court.

(5) The time to serve and file a brief may not be extended by stipulation but only by order of the Chief Justice under rule 8.60.

(6) The court may designate which party is deemed the petitioner or otherwise direct the sequence in which the parties must file their briefs.

(Subd (a) amended effective January 1, 2007.)

(b) Form and content

(1) Briefs filed under this rule must comply with the relevant provisions of rule 8.204.

(2) The body of the petitioner's brief on the merits must begin by quoting either:

(A) Any order specifying the issues to be briefed; or, if none,

(B) The statement of issues in the petition for review and, if any, in the answer.

(3) Unless the court orders otherwise, briefs on the merits must be limited to the issues stated in (2) and any issues fairly included in them.

(Subd (b) amended effective January 1, 2007.)

(c) Length

(1) If produced on a computer, an opening or answering brief on the merits must not exceed 14,000 words, including footnotes, and a reply brief on the merits must not exceed 8,400 words, including footnotes. Each brief must include a certificate by appellate counsel or an unrepresented party stating the number of words in the brief. The person certifying may rely on the word count of the computer program used to prepare the brief.

(2) If typewritten, an opening or answering brief on the merits must not exceed 50 pages and a reply brief on the merits must not exceed 30 pages.

(3) The tables required under rule 8.204(a)(1), the cover information required under rule 8.204(b)(10), a certificate under (1), any signature block, any attachment under (h), and any quotation of issues required by (b)(2) are excluded from the limits stated in (1) and (2).

(4) On application and for good cause, the Chief Justice may permit a longer brief.

(Subd (c) amended effective January 1, 2011; previously amended effective January 1, 2007, and January 1, 2009.)

(d) Supplemental briefs

(1) A party may file a supplemental brief limited to new authorities, new legislation, or other matters that were not available in time to be included in the party's brief on the merits.

(2) A supplemental brief must not exceed 2,800 words, including footnotes, if produced on a computer or 10 pages if typewritten, and must be served and filed no later than 10 days before oral argument.

(Subd (d) amended effective January 1, 2007.)

(e) Briefs on the court's request

The court may request additional briefs on any or all issues, whether or not the parties have filed briefs on the merits.

(f) Amicus curiae briefs

(1) After the court orders review, any person or entity may serve and file an application for permission of the Chief Justice to file an amicus curiae brief.

(2) The application must be filed no later than 30 days after all briefs that the parties may file under this rule—other than supplemental briefs—have been filed or were required to be filed. For good cause, the Chief Justice may allow later filing.

(3) The application must state the applicant's interest and explain how the proposed amicus curiae brief will assist the court in deciding the matter.

(4) The application must also identify:

(A) Any party or any counsel for a party in the pending appeal who:

(i) Authored the proposed amicus brief in whole or in part; or

(ii) Made a monetary contribution intended to fund the preparation or submission of the brief; and

(B) Every person or entity who made a monetary contribution intended to fund the preparation or submission of the brief, other than the amicus curiae, its members, or its counsel in the pending appeal.

(5) The proposed brief must be served. It must accompany the application and may be combined with it.

(6) The covers of the application and proposed brief must identify the party the applicant supports, if any.

(7) If the court grants the application, any party may file either an answer to the individual amicus curiae brief or a consolidated answer to multiple amicus curiae briefs filed in the case. The answer must be filed within 30 days after either the court rules on the last timely filed application to file an amicus curiae brief or the time for filing applications to file an amicus curiae brief expires, whichever is later. The answer must be served on all parties and the amicus curiae.

(8) The Attorney General may file an amicus curiae brief without the Chief Justice's permission unless the brief is submitted on behalf of another state officer or agency. The Attorney General must serve and file the brief within the time specified in (2) and must provide the information required by (3) and comply with (6). Any answer must comply with (7).

(Subd (f) amended effective January 1, 2011; previously amended effective January 1, 2008, and January 1, 2009.)

(g) Judicial notice

To obtain judicial notice by the Supreme Court under Evidence Code section 459, a party must comply with rule 8.252(a).

(Subd (g) amended effective January 1, 2007.)

(h) Attachments

A party filing a brief may attach copies of relevant local, state, or federal regulations or rules, out-of-state statutes, or other similar citable materials that are not readily accessible. These attachments must not exceed a combined total of 10 pages. A copy of an opinion required to be attached to the brief under rule 8.1115(c) does not count toward this 10-page limit.

(Subd (h) adopted effective January 1, 2007.)

Rule 8.520 amended effective January 1, 2011; adopted as rule 29.1 effective January 1, 2003; previously amended and renumbered effective January 1, 2007; previously amended effective January 1, 2008, and January 1, 2009.

Advisory Committee Comment

Subdivision (a). A party other than the petitioner who files a brief may be required to pay a filing fee under Government Code section 68927 if the brief is the first document filed in the proceeding in the Supreme Court by that party. See rule 8.25(c).

Subdivisions (c) and (d). Subdivisions (c) and (d) state in terms of word count rather than page count the maximum permissible lengths of Supreme Court briefs produced on a computer. This provision tracks an identical provision in rule 8.204(c) governing Court of Appeal briefs and is explained in the advisory committee comment to that provision. Subdivision (c)(3) specifies certain items that are not counted toward the maximum brief length. The signature block referenced in this provision includes not only the signatures, but also the printed names, titles, and affiliations of any attorneys filing or joining in the brief, which may accompany the signature.

Rule 8.524.   Oral argument and submission of the cause

(a) Application

This rule governs oral argument in the Supreme Court unless the court provides otherwise in its Internal Operating Practices and Procedures or by order.

(b) Place of argument

The Supreme Court holds regular sessions in San Francisco, Los Angeles, and Sacramento on a schedule fixed by the court, and may hold special sessions elsewhere.

(c) Notice of argument

The Supreme Court clerk must send notice of the time and place of oral argument to all parties at least 20 days before the argument date. The Chief Justice may shorten the notice period for good cause; in that event, the clerk must immediately notify the parties by telephone or other expeditious method.

(d) Sequence of argument

The petitioner for Supreme Court relief has the right to open and close. If there are two or more petitioners—or none—the court must set the sequence of argument.

(e) Time for argument

Each side is allowed 30 minutes for argument.

(f) Number of counsel

(1) Only one counsel on each side may argue—regardless of the number of parties on the side—unless the court orders otherwise on request.

(2) Requests to divide oral argument among multiple counsel must be filed within 10 days after the date of the order setting the case for argument.

(3) Multiple counsel must not divide their argument into segments of less than 10 minutes per person, except that one counsel for the opening side—or more, if authorized by the Chief Justice on request—may reserve any portion of that counsel's time for rebuttal.

(g) Argument by amicus curiae

An amicus curiae is not entitled to argument time but may ask a party for permission to use a portion or all of the party's time, subject to the 10-minute minimum prescribed in (f)(3). If permission is granted, counsel must file a request under (f)(2).

(h) Submission of the cause

(1) A cause is submitted when the court has heard oral argument or approved its waiver and the time has expired to file all briefs and papers, including any supplemental brief permitted by the court.

(2) The court may vacate submission only by an order stating the court's reasons and setting a timetable for resubmission.

Rule 8.524 renumbered effective January 1, 2007; repealed and adopted as rule 29.2 effective January 1, 2003.

Advisory Committee Comment

Subdivision (d). In subdivision (d), "The petitioner for Supreme Court relief" can be a petitioner for review, a petitioner for transfer (rule 8.552), a petitioner in an original proceeding in the Supreme Court, or a party designated as petitioner in a proceeding on request of a court of another jurisdiction (rule 8.548(b)(1)).

The number of petitioners is "none" when the court grants review on its own motion or transfers a cause to itself on its own motion.

Subdivision (e). The time allowed for argument in death penalty appeals is prescribed in rule 8.638.

Subdivision (f). The number of counsel allowed to argue on each side in death penalty appeals is prescribed in rule 8.638.

Rule 8.528.   Disposition

(a) Normal disposition

After review, the Supreme Court normally will affirm, reverse, or modify the judgment of the Court of Appeal, but may order another disposition.

(b) Dismissal of review

(1) The Supreme Court may dismiss review. The clerk/executive officer of the Supreme Court must promptly send an order dismissing review to all parties and the Court of Appeal.

(2) When the Court of Appeal receives an order dismissing review, the decision of that court is final and its clerk/executive officer must promptly issue a remittitur or take other appropriate action.

(3) An order dismissing review does not affect the publication status of the Court of Appeal opinion unless the Supreme Court orders otherwise.

(Subd (b) amended effective January 1, 2018; previously amended effective January 1, 2017.)

(c) Remand for decision on remaining issues

If it decides fewer than all the issues presented by the case, the Supreme Court may remand the cause to a Court of Appeal for decision on any remaining issues.

(d) Transfer without decision

After ordering review, the Supreme Court may transfer the cause to a Court of Appeal without decision but with instructions to conduct such proceedings as the Supreme Court orders.

(e) Retransfer without decision

After transferring to itself, before decision, a cause pending in the Court of Appeal, the Supreme Court may retransfer the cause to a Court of Appeal without decision.

(f) Court of Appeal briefs after remand or transfer

Any supplemental briefing in the Court of Appeal after remand or transfer from the Supreme Court is governed by rule 8.200(b).

(Subd (f) amended effective January 1, 2007.)

Rule 8.528 amended effective January 1, 2018; repealed and adopted as rule 29.3 effective January 1, 2003; previously amended and renumbered effective January 1, 2007; previously amended effective January 1, 2017.

Advisory Committee Comment

Subdivision (a). Subdivision (a) serves two purposes. First, it declares that the Supreme Court's normal disposition of a cause after completing its review is to affirm, reverse, or modify *the judgment of the Court of Appeal*. Second, the subdivision recognizes that, when necessary, the Supreme Court may order "another disposition" appropriate to the circumstances. Subdivisions (b)–(e) provide examples of such "other dispositions," but the list is not intended to be exclusive.

As used in subdivision (a), "the judgment of the Court of Appeal" includes a decision of that court denying a petition for original writ without issuing an alternative writ or order to show cause. The Supreme Court's method of disposition after reviewing such a decision, however, has evolved. In earlier cases the Supreme Court itself denied or granted the requested writ, in effect treating the matter as if it were an original proceeding in the Supreme Court. (E.g., *City of San Jose v. Superior Court* (1993) 5 Cal.4th 47, 58 ["The alternative writ of mandate is discharged and the petition for a peremptory writ of mandate is denied."].) By contrast, current Supreme Court practice is to affirm or reverse the judgment of the Court of Appeal summarily denying the writ petition. (E.g., *People v. Superior Court (Laff)* (2001) 25 Cal.4th 703, 742–743 ["The judgment of the Court of Appeal is reversed with directions to vacate its order denying the petition, and to issue a writ of mandate…."]; *State Comp. Ins. Fund v. Superior Court* (2001) 24 Cal.4th 930, 944 ["The judgment of the Court of Appeal summarily denying the petition for writ of mandate is affirmed and the order to show cause … is discharged."].) As the cited cases illustrate, if the Supreme Court affirms such a judgment it will normally discharge any alternative writ or order to show cause it issued when granting review; if the court reverses the judgment it will normally include a direction to the Court of Appeal, e.g., to issue the requested writ or to reconsider the petition.

Subdivision (b). An earlier version of this rule purported to limit Supreme Court *dismissals of review* to cases in which the court had "improvidently" granted review. In practice, however, the court may dismiss review for a variety of other reasons. For example, after the court decides a "lead" case, its current practice is to dismiss review in any pending companion case (i.e., a "grant and hold" matter under rule 8.512(c)) that appears correctly decided in light of the lead case and presents no additional issue requiring resolution by the Supreme Court or the Court of Appeal. The Supreme Court may also dismiss review when a supervening event renders the case moot for any reason, e.g., when the parties reach a settlement, when a party seeking personal relief dies, or when the court orders review to construe a statute that is then repealed before the court can act. Reflecting this practice, the Supreme Court now dismisses review—even in the rare case in which the grant of review was arguably "improvident"—by an order that says simply that "review is dismissed."

An order of review ipso facto transfers jurisdiction of the cause to the Supreme Court. By the same token, an order dismissing review ipso facto retransfers jurisdiction to the Court of Appeal. The Court of Appeal has no discretion to exercise after the Supreme Court dismisses review: the clerk/executive officer of the Supreme Court must promptly send the dismissal order to the Court of Appeal; when the clerk/executive officer of the Court of Appeal files that order, the Court of Appeal decision immediately becomes final.

If the decision of the Court of Appeal made final by (b)(2) requires issuance of a remittitur under rule 8.272(a), the clerk/executive officer must issue the remittitur; if the decision does not require issuance of a remittitur—e.g., if the decision is an interlocutory order (see rule 8.500(a)(1))—the clerk/executive officer must take whatever action is appropriate in the circumstances.

Subdivision (d). Subdivision (d) is intended to apply primarily to two types of cases: (1) those in which the court granted review "for the purpose of transferring the matter to the Court of Appeal for such proceedings as the Supreme Court may order" (rule 8.500(b)(4)) and (2) those in which the court, after deciding a "lead case," determines that a companion "grant and hold" case (rule 8.512(c)) should be reconsidered by the Court of Appeal in light of the lead case or presents an additional issue or issues that require resolution by the Court of Appeal.

Subdivision (e). Subdivision (e) is intended to apply to cases in which the Supreme Court, after *transferring* to itself before decision a cause pending in the Court of Appeal, *retransfers* the matter to that court without decision and with or without instructions.

Rule 8.532.   Filing, finality, and modification of decision

(a) Filing the decision

The clerk/executive officer of the Supreme Court must promptly file all opinions and orders issued by the court and promptly send copies showing the filing date to the parties and, when relevant, to the lower court or tribunal.

(Subd (a) amended effective January 1, 2018.)

(b) Finality of decision

(1) Except as provided in (2), a Supreme Court decision is final 30 days after filing unless:

(A) The court orders a shorter period; or

(B) Before the 30-day period or any extension expires the court orders one or more extensions, not to exceed a total of 60 additional days.

(2) The following Supreme Court decisions are final on filing:

(A) The denial of a petition for review of a Court of Appeal decision;

(B) A disposition ordered under rule 8.528(b), (d), or (e);

(C) The denial of a petition for a writ within the court's original jurisdiction without issuance of an alternative writ or order to show cause; and

(D) The denial of a petition for writ of supersedeas.

(Subd (b) amended effective January 1, 2007.)

(c) Modification of decision

The Supreme Court may modify a decision as provided in rule 8.264(c).

(Subd (c) amended effective January 1, 2007.)

Rule 8.532 amended effective January 1, 2018; repealed and adopted as rule 29.4 effective January 1, 2003; previously amended and renumbered effective January 1, 2007.

Advisory Committee Comment

Subdivision (b). Subdivision (b)(2)(A) recognizes the general rule that the denial of a petition for review of a Court of Appeal decision is final on filing. Subdivision (b)(2)(B)–(D) recognizes several additional types of Supreme Court decisions that are final on filing. Thus (b)(2)(B) recognizes that a dismissal, a transfer, and a retransfer under (b), (d), and (e), respectively, of rule 8.528 are decisions final on filing. A remand under rule 8.528(c) is not a decision final on filing because it is not a separately filed order; rather, as part of its appellate judgment at the end of its opinion in such cases the Supreme Court simply orders the cause remanded to the Court of Appeal for disposition of the remaining issues in the appeal.

Subdivision (b)(2)(C) recognizes that an order denying a petition for a writ within the court's original jurisdiction without issuance of an alternative writ or order to show cause is final on filing. The provision reflects the settled Supreme Court practice, since at least 1989, of declining to file petitions for rehearing in such matters. (See, e.g., *In re Hayes* (S004421) Minutes, Cal. Supreme Ct., July 28, 1989 ["The motion to vacate this court's order of May 18, 1989 [denying a petition for habeas corpus without opinion] is denied. Because the California Rules of Court do not authorize the filing of a petition for rehearing of such an order, the alternate request to consider the matter as a petition for rehearing is denied."].)

Subdivision (b)(2)(D) recognizes that an order denying a petition for writ of supersedeas is final on filing.

Rule 8.536.   Rehearing

(a) Power to order rehearing

The Supreme Court may order rehearing as provided in rule 8.268(a).

(Subd (a) amended effective January 1, 2007.)

(b) Petition and answer

A petition for rehearing and any answer must comply with rule 8.268(b)(1) and (3). Any answer to the petition must be served and filed within eight days after the petition is filed. Before the Supreme Court decision is final and for good cause, the Chief Justice may relieve a party from a failure to file a timely petition or answer.

(Subd (b) amended effective January 1, 2007; previously amended effective January 1, 2004.)

(c) Extension of time

The time for granting or denying a petition for rehearing in the Supreme Court may be extended under rule 8.532(b)(1)(B). If the court does not rule on the petition before the decision is final, the petition is deemed denied.

(Subd (c) amended effective January 1, 2007.)

(d) Determination of petition

An order granting a rehearing must be signed by at least four justices; an order denying rehearing may be signed by the Chief Justice alone.

(e) Effect of granting rehearing

An order granting a rehearing vacates the decision and any opinion filed in the case and sets the cause at large in the Supreme Court.

Rule 8.536 amended and renumbered effective January 1, 2007; repealed and adopted as rule 29.5 effective January 1, 2003; previously amended effective January 1, 2004.

Rule 8.540.   Remittitur

(a) Proceedings requiring issuance of remittitur

The Supreme Court must issue a remittitur after a decision in:

(1) A review of a Court of Appeal decision; or

(2) An appeal from a judgment of death or in a cause transferred to the court under rule 8.552.

(Subd (a) amended effective January 1, 2007.)

(b) Clerk's duties

(1) The clerk must issue a remittitur when a decision of the court is final. The remittitur is deemed issued when the clerk enters it in the record.

(2) After review of a Court of Appeal decision, the clerk/executive officer of the Supreme Court must address the remittitur to the Court of Appeal and send that court a copy of the remittitur and a filed-endorsed copy of the Supreme Court opinion or order. The clerk must send two copies of any document sent in paper form.

(3) After a decision in an appeal from a judgment of death or in a cause transferred to the court under rule 8.552, the clerk must send the remittitur and a filed-endorsed copy of the Supreme Court opinion or order to the lower court or tribunal.

(4) The clerk must comply with the requirements of rule 8.272(d).

(Subd (b) amended effective January 1, 2018; previously amended effective January 1, 2007, and January 1, 2016.)

(c) Immediate issuance, stay, and recall

(1) The Supreme Court may direct immediate issuance of a remittitur on the parties' stipulation or for good cause.

(2) On a party's or its own motion and for good cause, the court may stay a remittitur's issuance for a reasonable period or order its recall.

(3) An order recalling a remittitur issued after a decision by opinion does not supersede the opinion or affect its publication status.

Rule 8.540 amended effective January 1, 2018; repealed and adopted as rule 29.6 effective January 1, 2003; previously amended and renumbered as rule 8.540 effective January 1, 2007; previously amended effective January 1, 2016.

Rule 8.544.   Costs and sanctions

In a civil case, the Supreme Court may direct the Court of Appeal to award costs, if any; or may order the parties to bear their own costs; or may make any other award of costs the Supreme Court deems proper. The Supreme Court may impose sanctions on a party or an attorney under rule 8.276 for committing any unreasonable violation of these rules.

Rule 8.544 amended effective July 1, 2008; adopted as rule 29.7 effective January 1, 2003; previously amended and renumbered effective January 1, 2007.

Advisory Committee Comment

If the Supreme Court makes an award of costs, the party claiming such costs must proceed under rule 8.278(c).

Rule 8.548.   Decision on request of a court of another jurisdiction

(a) Request for decision

On request of the United States Supreme Court, a United States Court of Appeals, or the court of last resort of any state, territory, or commonwealth, the Supreme Court may decide a question of California law if:

(1) The decision could determine the outcome of a matter pending in the requesting court; and

(2) There is no controlling precedent.

(Subd (a) amended effective January 1, 2007.)

(b) Form and contents of request

The request must take the form of an order of the requesting court containing:

(1) The title and number of the case, the names and addresses of counsel and any unrepresented party, and a designation of the party to be deemed the petitioner if the request is granted;

(2) The question to be decided, with a statement that the requesting court will accept the decision;

(3) A statement of the relevant facts prepared by the requesting court or by the parties and approved by the court; and

(4) An explanation of how the request satisfies the requirements of (a).

(Subd (b) amended effective January 1, 2007.)

(c) Supporting materials

Copies of all relevant briefs must accompany the request. At any time, the Supreme Court may ask the requesting court to furnish additional record materials, including transcripts and exhibits.

(d) Serving and filing the request

The requesting court clerk must file an original, and if the request is filed in paper form, 10 copies, of the request in the Supreme Court with a certificate of service on the parties.

(Subd (d) amended effective January 1, 2016.)

(e) Letters in support or opposition

(1) Within 20 days after the request is filed, any party or other person or entity wanting to support or oppose the request must send a letter to the Supreme Court, with service on the parties and on the requesting court.

(2) Within 10 days after service of a letter under (1), any party may send a reply letter to the Supreme Court, with service on the other parties and the requesting court.

(3) A letter or reply asking the court to restate the question under (f)(5) must propose new wording.

(f) Proceedings in the Supreme Court

(1) In exercising its discretion to grant or deny the request, the Supreme Court may consider whether resolution of the question is necessary to secure uniformity of decision or to settle an important question of law, and any other factor the court deems appropriate.

(2) An order granting the request must be signed by at least four justices; an order denying the request may be signed by the Chief Justice alone.

(3) If the court grants the request, the rules on review and decision in the Supreme Court govern further proceedings in that court.

(4) If, after granting the request, the court determines that a decision on the question may require an interpretation of the California Constitution or a decision on the validity or meaning of a California law affecting the public interest, the court must direct the clerk to send to the Attorney General—unless the Attorney General represents a party to the litigation—a copy of the request and the order granting it.

(5) At any time, the Supreme Court may restate the question or ask the requesting court to clarify the question.

(6) After filing the opinion, the clerk must promptly send filed-endorsed copies to the requesting court and the parties and must notify that court and the parties when the decision is final.

(7) Supreme Court decisions pursuant to this rule are published in the Official Reports and have the same precedential effect as the court's other decisions.

(Subd (f) amended effective January 1, 2016; previously amended effective January 1, 2007.)

Rule 8.548 amended effective January 1, 2016; adopted as rule 29.8 effective January 1, 2003; previously amended and renumbered as rule 8.548 effective January 1, 2007.

Rule 8.552. Transfer for decision

(a) Time of transfer

On a party's petition or its own motion, the Supreme Court may transfer to itself, for decision, a cause pending in a Court of Appeal.

(b) When a cause is pending

For purposes of this rule, a cause within the appellate jurisdiction of the superior court is not pending in the Court of Appeal until that court orders it transferred under rule 8.1002. Any cause pending in the Court of Appeal remains pending until the decision of the Court of Appeal is final in that court.

(Subd (b) amended effective January 1, 2009; previously amended effective January 1, 2007.)

(c) Grounds

The Supreme Court will not order transfer under this rule unless the cause presents an issue of great public importance that the Supreme Court must promptly resolve.

(d) Petition and answer

A party seeking transfer under this rule must promptly serve and file in the Supreme Court a petition explaining how the cause satisfies the requirements of (c). Within 20 days after the petition is filed, any party may serve and file an answer. The petition and any answer must conform to the relevant provisions of rule 8.504.

(Subd (d) amended effective January 1, 2007.)

(e) Order

Transfer under this rule requires a Supreme Court order signed by at least four justices; an order denying transfer may be signed by the Chief Justice alone.

Rule 8.552 amended effective January 1, 2009; repealed and adopted as rule 29.9 effective January 1, 2003; previously amended and renumbered effective January 1, 2007.

Advisory Committee Comment

Rule 8.552 applies only to causes that the Supreme Court transfers to itself for the purpose of reaching a decision on the merits. The rule implements a portion of article VI, section 12(a) of the Constitution. As used in article VI, section 12(a) and the rule, the term "cause" is broadly construed to include " 'all cases, matters, and proceedings of every description' " adjudicated by the Courts of Appeal and the Supreme Court. *(In re Rose* (2000) 22 Cal.4th 430, 540, quoting *In re Wells* (1917) 174 Cal. 467, 471.)

Subdivision (b). For provisions addressing the finality of Court of Appeal decisions, see rules 8.264(b) (civil appeals), 8.366(b) (criminal appeals), 8.490 (proceedings for writs of mandate, certiorari, and prohibition), and 8.1018(a) (transfer of appellate division cases).

Division 2
Rules Relating to Death Penalty Appeals and Habeas Corpus Proceedings

Title 8, Appellate Rules—Division 2, Rules Relating to Death Penalty Appeals and Habeas Corpus Proceedings adopted effective April 25, 2019.

Chap. 1. General Provisions. Rule 8.601.

Chap. 2. Automatic Appeals From Judgments of Death. Rules 8.603–8.642.

Chap. 3. Death Penalty–Related Habeas Corpus Proceedings. Rule 8.652.

Chapter 1
General Provisions

Title 8, Appellate Rules—Division 2, Rules Relating to Death Penalty Appeals and Habeas Corpus Proceedings—Chapter 1, General Provisions adopted effective April 25, 2019.

Rule 8.600. In general [Renumbered]

Rule 8.600 renumbered as rule 8.603 effective April 25, 2019; repealed and adopted as rule 34 effective January 1, 2004; previously amended and renumbered effective January 1, 2007; previously amended effective January 1, 2018.

Rule 8.601. Definitions

For purposes of this division:

(1) "Appointed counsel" or "appointed attorney" means an attorney appointed to represent a person in a death penalty appeal, death penalty–related habeas corpus proceedings, or an appeal of a decision in death penalty–related habeas corpus proceedings. Appointed counsel may be either lead counsel or associate counsel.

(2) "Lead counsel" means an appointed attorney or an attorney in the Office of the State Public Defender, the Habeas Corpus Resource Center, the California Appellate Project–San Francisco, or a Court of Appeal district appellate project who is responsible for the overall conduct of the case and for supervising the work of associate and supervised counsel. If two or more attorneys are appointed to represent a person jointly in a death penalty appeal, in death penalty–related habeas corpus proceedings, or in both classes of proceedings together, one such attorney will be designated as lead counsel.

(3) "Associate counsel" means an appointed attorney who does not have the primary responsibility for the case but nevertheless has casewide responsibility. Associate counsel must meet the same minimum qualifications as lead counsel.

(4) "Supervised counsel" means an attorney who works under the immediate supervision and direction of lead or associate counsel but is not appointed by the court. Supervised counsel must be an active member of the State Bar of California.

(5) "Assisting counsel or entity" means an attorney or entity designated by the appointing court to provide appointed counsel with consultation and resource assistance. An assisting counsel must be an experienced capital appellate counsel or habeas corpus practitioner, as appropriate. An assisting counsel in an automatic appeal must, at a minimum,

meet the qualifications for appointed appellate counsel, including the case experience requirements in rule 8.605(c)(2). An assisting counsel in a habeas corpus proceeding must, at a minimum, meet the qualifications for appointed habeas corpus counsel, including the case experience requirements in rule 8.652(c)(2)(A). Entities that may be designated include the Office of the State Public Defender, the Habeas Corpus Resource Center, the California Appellate Project–San Francisco, and a Court of Appeal district appellate project.

(6) "Trial counsel" means both the defendant's trial counsel and the prosecuting attorney.

(7) "Panel" means a panel of attorneys from which superior courts may appoint counsel in death penalty–related habeas corpus proceedings.

(8) "Committee" means a death penalty–related habeas corpus panel committee that accepts and reviews attorney applications to determine whether applicants are qualified for inclusion on a panel.

Rule 8.601 adopted effective April 25, 2019.

Advisory Committee Comment

Number (3). The definition of "associate counsel" in (3) is intended to make it clear that, although appointed lead counsel has overall and supervisory responsibility in a capital case, appointed associate counsel also has casewide responsibility.

Chapter 2
Automatic Appeals From Judgments of Death

Title 8, Appellate Rules—Division 2, Rules Relating to Death Penalty Appeals and Habeas Corpus Proceedings—Chapter 2, Automatic Appeals From Judgments of Death; amended and renumbered effective April 25, 2019; adopted as chapter 9 effective January 1, 2007; previously amended and renumbered as chapter 10 effective January 1, 2009.

Art. 1.   General Provisions. Rules 8.603, 8.605.
Art. 2.   Record on Appeal. Rules 8.608–8.622.
Art. 3.   Briefs, Hearing, and Decision. Rules 8.630–8.642.

Article 1
General Provisions

Rule 8.603. In general
Rule 8.605. Qualifications of counsel in death penalty appeals

Rule 8.603.   In general

(a) Automatic appeal to Supreme Court

If a judgment imposes a sentence of death, an appeal by the defendant is automatically taken to the Supreme Court.

(b) Copies of judgment

When a judgment of death is rendered, the superior court clerk must immediately send certified copies of the commitment to the Supreme Court, the Attorney General, the Governor, the Habeas Corpus Resource Center, and the California Appellate Project–San Francisco.

(Subd (b) amended effective April 25, 2019.)

Rule 8.603 amended and renumbered effective April 25, 2019; repealed and adopted as rule 34 effective January 1, 2004; previously amended and renumbered as rule 8.600 effective January 1, 2007; previously amended effective January 1, 2018.

Rule 8.605.   Qualifications of counsel in death penalty appeals

(a) Purpose

This rule defines the minimum qualifications for attorneys appointed by the Supreme Court in death penalty appeals. These minimum qualifications are designed to promote competent representation and to avoid unnecessary delay and expense by assisting the court in appointing qualified counsel. Nothing in this rule is intended to be used as a standard by which to measure whether the defendant received effective assistance of counsel. An attorney is not entitled to appointment simply because the attorney meets these minimum qualifications.

(Subd (a) amended effective April 25, 2019.)

(b) General qualifications

The Supreme Court may appoint an attorney only if it has determined, after reviewing the attorney's experience, writing samples, references, and evaluations under (c) and (d), that the attorney has demonstrated the commitment, knowledge, and skills necessary to competently represent the defendant. An appointed attorney must be willing to cooperate with an assisting counsel or entity that the court may designate.

(Subd (b) amended effective April 25, 2019.)

(c) Qualifications for appointed appellate counsel

Except as provided in (d), an attorney appointed as lead or associate counsel in a death penalty appeal must satisfy the following minimum qualifications and experience:

(1) *California legal experience*

Active practice of law in California for at least four years.

(2) *Criminal appellate experience*

Either:

(A) Service as counsel of record for either party in seven completed felony appeals, including as counsel of record for a defendant in at least four felony appeals, one of which was a murder case; or

(B) Service as:

(i) Counsel of record for either party in five completed felony appeals, including as counsel of record for a defendant in at least three of these appeals; and

(ii) Supervised counsel for a defendant in two death penalty appeals in which the opening brief has been filed. Service as supervised counsel in a death penalty appeal will apply toward this qualification only if lead or associate counsel in that appeal attests that the supervised attorney performed substantial work on the case and recommends the attorney for appointment.

(3) *Knowledge*

Familiarity with Supreme Court practices and procedures, including those related to death penalty appeals.

(4) *Training*

(A) Within three years before appointment, completion of at least nine hours of Supreme Court–approved appellate criminal defense training, continuing education, or course of study, at least six hours of which involve death penalty appeals. Counsel who serves as an instructor in a course that satisfies the requirements of this rule may receive course participation credit for instruction, on request to and approval by the Supreme Court, in an amount to be determined by the Supreme Court.

(B) If the Supreme Court has previously appointed counsel to represent a person in a death penalty appeal or a related habeas corpus proceeding, and counsel has provided active representation within three years before the request for a new appointment, the court, after reviewing counsel's previous work, may find that such representation constitutes compliance with some or all of this requirement.

(5) *Skills*

Proficiency in issue identification, research, analysis, writing, and advocacy, taking into consideration all of the following:

(A) Two writing samples—ordinarily appellate briefs—written by the attorney and presenting an analysis of complex legal issues;

(B) If the attorney has previously been appointed in a death penalty appeal or death penalty–related habeas corpus proceeding, the evaluation of the assisting counsel or entity in that proceeding;

(C) Recommendations from two attorneys familiar with the attorney's qualifications and performance; and

(D) If the attorney is on a panel of attorneys eligible for appointments to represent indigents in the Court of Appeal, the evaluation of the administrator responsible for those appointments.

(Subd (c) repealed, amended and relettered effective April 25, 2019; adopted as subd (d) effective January 1, 2005; previously amended effective January 1, 2007.)

(d) Alternative qualifications

The Supreme Court may appoint an attorney who does not meet the California law practice requirement of (c)(1) or the criminal appellate experience requirements of (c)(2) if the attorney has the qualifications described in (c)(3)–(5) and:

(1) The court finds that the attorney has extensive experience in another jurisdiction or a different type of practice (such as civil trials or appeals, academic work, or work for a court or prosecutor) for at least four years, providing the attorney with experience in complex cases substantially equivalent to that of an attorney qualified under (c).

(2) Ongoing consultation is available to the attorney from an assisting counsel or entity designated by the court.

(3) Within two years before appointment, the attorney has completed at least 18 hours of Supreme Court–approved appellate criminal defense or habeas corpus defense training, continuing education, or course of study, at least nine hours of which involve death penalty appellate or habeas corpus proceedings. The Supreme Court will determine in each case whether the training, education, or course of study completed by a particular attorney satisfies the requirements of this subdivision in light of the attorney's individual background and experience. If the Supreme Court has previously appointed counsel to represent a person in a death penalty appeal or a related habeas corpus proceeding, and counsel has provided active representation within three years before the request for a new appointment, the court, after reviewing counsel's previous work, may

Rules of Court

find that such representation constitutes compliance with some or all of this requirement.

(Subd (d) repealed, amended and relettered effective April 25, 2019; adopted as subd (f) effective January 1, 2005.)

(e) Use of supervised counsel

An attorney who does not meet the qualifications described in (c) or (d) may assist lead or associate counsel, but must work under the immediate supervision and direction of lead or associate counsel.

(Subd (e) repealed, amended and relettered effective April 25, 2019; adopted as subd (h) effective January 1, 2005.)

(f) Appellate and habeas corpus appointment

(1) An attorney appointed to represent a person in both a death penalty appeal and death penalty–related habeas corpus proceedings must meet the minimum qualifications of both (c) or (d) and rule 8.652.

(2) Notwithstanding (1), two attorneys together may be eligible for appointment to represent a person jointly in both a death penalty appeal and death penalty–related habeas corpus proceedings if the Supreme Court finds that one attorney satisfies the minimum qualifications set forth in (c) or (d), and the other attorney satisfies the minimum qualifications set forth in rule 8.652.

(Subd (f) repealed, amended and relettered effective April 25, 2019; adopted as subd (i) effective January 1, 2005.)

(g) Designated entities as appointed counsel

(1) Notwithstanding any other provision of this rule, both the State Public Defender and the California Appellate Project–San Francisco are qualified to serve as appointed counsel in death penalty appeals

(2) When serving as appointed counsel in a death penalty appeal, the State Public Defender or the California Appellate Project–San Francisco must not assign any attorney as lead counsel unless it finds the attorney qualified under (c)(1)–(5) or the Supreme Court finds the attorney qualified under (d).

(Subd (g) repealed, amended and relettered effective April 25, 2019; adopted as subd (j) effective January 1, 2005.)

Rule 8.605 amended effective April 25, 2019; repealed and adopted as rule 76.6 effective January 1, 2005; previously amended and renumbered effective January 1, 2007.

Article 2
Record on Appeal

Rule 8.608. General provisions
Rule 8.610. Contents and form of the record
Rule 8.611. Juror-identifying information
Rule 8.613. Preparing and certifying the record of preliminary proceedings
Rule 8.616. Preparing the trial record
Rule 8.619. Certifying the trial record for completeness
Rule 8.622. Certifying the trial record for accuracy

Rule 8.608.   General provisions

(a) Supervising preparation of record

The clerk/executive officer of the Supreme Court, under the supervision of the Chief Justice, must take all appropriate steps to ensure that superior court clerks and reporters promptly perform their duties under the rules in this article. This provision does not affect the superior courts' responsibility for the prompt preparation of appellate records in capital cases.

(Subd (a) adopted effective April 25, 2019.)

(b) Extensions of time

When a rule in this article authorizes a trial court to grant an extension of a specified time period, the court must consider the relevant policies and factors stated in rule 8.63.

(Subd (b) adopted effective April 25, 2019.)

(c) Delivery date

The delivery date of a transcript sent by mail is the mailing date plus five days.

(Subd (c) adopted effective April 25, 2019.)
Rule 8.608 adopted effective April 25, 2019.

Rule 8.610.   Contents and form of the record

(a) Contents of the record

(1) The record must include a clerk's transcript containing:

(A) The accusatory pleading and any amendment;

(B) Any demurrer or other plea;

(C) All court minutes;

(D) All instructions submitted in writing, the cover page required by rule 2.1055(b)(2) indicating the party requesting each instruction, and any written jury instructions given by the court;

(E) Any written communication, including printouts of any e-mail or text messages and their attachments, between the court and the parties, the jury or any individual juror or prospective juror;

(F) Any verdict;

(G) Any written opinion of the court;

(H) The judgment or order appealed from and any abstract of judgment or commitment;

(I) Any motion for new trial, with supporting and opposing memoranda and attachments;

(J) Any transcript of a sound or sound-and-video recording furnished to the jury or tendered to the court under rule 2.1040, including witness statements;

(K) Any application for additional record and any order on the application;

(L) Any written defense motion or any written motion by the People, with supporting and opposing memoranda and attachments;

(M) If related to a motion under (L), any search warrant and return and the reporter's transcript of any preliminary examination or grand jury hearing;

(N) Any document admitted in evidence to prove a prior juvenile adjudication, criminal conviction, or prison term;

(O) The probation officer's report;

(P) Any court-ordered diagnostic or psychological report required under Penal Code section 1369;

(Q) Any copies of visual aids provided to the clerk under rule 4.230(f). If a visual aid is oversized, a photograph of that visual aid must be included in place of the original. For digital or electronic presentations, printouts showing the full text of each slide or image must be included;

(R) Each juror questionnaire, whether or not the juror was selected;

(S) The table correlating the jurors' names with their identifying numbers required by rule 8.611;

(T) The register of actions;

(U) All documents filed under Penal Code section 987.2 or 987.9; and

(V) Any other document filed or lodged in the case.

(2) The record must include a reporter's transcript containing:

(A) The oral proceedings on the entry of any plea other than a not guilty plea;

(B) The oral proceedings on any motion in limine;

(C) The voir dire examination of jurors;

(D) Any opening statement;

(E) The oral proceedings at trial;

(F) All instructions given orally;

(G) Any oral communication between the court and the jury or any individual juror;

(H) Any oral opinion of the court;

(I) The oral proceedings on any motion for new trial;

(J) The oral proceedings at sentencing, granting or denying of probation, or other dispositional hearing;

(K) The oral proceedings on any motion under Penal Code section 1538.5 denied in whole or in part;

(L) The closing arguments;

(M) Any comment on the evidence by the court to the jury;

(N) The oral proceedings on motions in addition to those listed above; and

(O) Any other oral proceedings in the case, including any proceedings that did not result in a verdict or sentence of death because the court ordered a mistrial or a new trial.

(3) All exhibits admitted in evidence, refused, or lodged are deemed part of the record, but, except as provided in rule 8.622, may be transmitted to the reviewing court only as provided in rule 8.634.

(4) The superior court or the Supreme Court may order that the record include additional material.

(Subd (a) amended effective April 25, 2019; previously amended effective January 1, 2007.)

(b) Sealed and confidential records

Rules 8.45–8.47 govern sealed and confidential records in appeals under this chapter.

(Subd (b) amended effective April 25, 2019; previously amended effective January 1, 2007, and January 1, 2014.)

(c) Juror-identifying information

Any document in the record containing juror-identifying information must be edited in compliance with rule 8.611. Unedited copies of all such documents and a copy of the table required by the rule, under seal and bound together if filed in paper form, must be included in the record sent to the Supreme Court.

(Subd (c) amended effective April 25, 2019; previously amended effective January 1, 2007, and January 1, 2016.)

(d) Form of record

The clerk's transcript and the reporter's transcript must comply with rules 8.45 8.47, relating to sealed and confidential records, and rule 8.144.

(Subd (d) amended effective January 1, 2014; previously amended effective January 1, 2005, and January 1, 2007.)

Rule 8.610 amended effective April 25, 2019; adopted as rule 34.1 effective January 1, 2004; previously amended and renumbered as rule 8.610 effective January 1, 2007; previously amended effective January 1, 2005, January 1, 2014, and January 1, 2016.

Advisory Committee Comment

Subdivision (a). Subdivision (a) implements Penal Code section 190.7(a).

Subdivision (b). The clerk's and reporter's transcripts may contain records that are sealed or confidential. Rules 8.45–8.47 address the handling of such records, including requirements for the format, labeling, and transmission of and access to such records. Examples of confidential records include Penal Code section 1203.03 diagnostic reports, records closed to inspection by court order under *People v. Marsden* (1970) 2 Cal.3d 118 or *Pitchess v. Superior Court* (1974) 11 Cal.3d 531, in-camera proceedings on a confidential informant, and defense investigation and expert funding requests (Pen. Code, §§ 987.2 and 987.9; *Puett v. Superior Court* (1979) 96 Cal.App.3d 936, 940, fn. 2; *Keenan v. Superior Court* (1982) 31 Cal.3d 424, 430).

Rule 8.611. Juror-identifying information

(a) Application

A clerk's transcript, a reporter's transcript, or any other document in the record that contains juror-identifying information must comply with this rule.

(Subd (a) adopted effective April 25, 2019.)

(b) Juror names, addresses, and telephone numbers

(1) The name of each trial juror or alternate sworn to hear the case must be replaced with an identifying number wherever it appears in any document. The superior court clerk must prepare and keep under seal in the case file a table correlating the jurors' names with their identifying numbers. The clerk and the reporter must use the table in preparing all transcripts or other documents.

(2) The addresses and telephone numbers of trial jurors and alternates sworn to hear the case must be deleted from all documents.

(Subd (b) adopted effective April 25, 2019.)

(c) Potential jurors

Information identifying potential jurors called but not sworn as trial jurors or alternates must not be sealed unless otherwise ordered under Code of Civil Procedure section 237(a)(1).

(Subd (c) adopted effective April 25, 2019.)

Rule 8.611 adopted effective April 25, 2019.

Advisory Committee Comment

Rule 8.611 implements Code of Civil Procedure section 237.

Rule 8.613. Preparing and certifying the record of preliminary proceedings

(a) Definitions

For purposes of this rule:

(1) The "preliminary proceedings" are all proceedings held before and including the filing of the information or indictment, whether in open court or otherwise, and include the preliminary examination or grand jury proceeding;

(2) The "record of the preliminary proceedings" is the court file and the reporter's transcript of the preliminary proceedings;

(3) The "responsible judge" is the judge assigned to try the case or, if none is assigned, the presiding superior court judge or designee of the presiding judge; and

(4) The "designated judge" is the judge designated by the presiding judge to supervise preparation of the record of preliminary proceedings.

(Subd (a) amended effective January 1, 2007.)

(b) Notice of intent to seek death penalty

In any case in which the death penalty may be imposed:

(1) If the prosecution notifies the responsible judge that it intends to seek the death penalty, the judge must notify the presiding judge and the clerk. The clerk must promptly enter the information in the court file.

(2) If the prosecution does not give notice under (1)—and does not give notice to the contrary—the clerk must notify the responsible judge 60 days before the first date set for trial that the prosecution is presumed to seek the death penalty. The judge must notify the presiding judge, and the clerk must promptly enter the information in the court file.

(c) Assignment of judge designated to supervise preparation of record of preliminary proceedings

(1) Within five days after receiving notice under (b), the presiding judge must designate a judge to supervise preparation of the record of the preliminary proceedings.

(2) If there was a preliminary examination, the designated judge must be the judge who conducted it.

(d) Notice to prepare transcript and lists

Within five days after receiving notice under (b)(1) or notifying the judge under (b)(2), the clerk must do the following:

(1) Notify each reporter who reported a preliminary proceeding to prepare a transcript of the proceeding. If there is more than one reporter, the designated judge may assign a reporter or another designee to perform the functions of the primary reporter.

(2) Notify trial counsel to submit the lists of appearances, exhibits, and motions required by rule 4.119.

(Subd (d) amended effective April 25, 2019.)

(e) Reporter's duties

(1) The reporter must prepare an original and five copies of the reporter's transcript in electronic form and two additional copies in electronic form for each codefendant against whom the death penalty is sought. The transcript must include the preliminary examination or grand jury proceeding unless a transcript of that examination or proceeding has already been filed in superior court for inclusion in the clerk's transcript.

(2) The reporter must certify the original and all copies of the reporter's transcript as correct.

(3) Within 20 days after receiving the notice to prepare the reporter's transcript, the reporter must deliver the original and all copies of the transcript to the clerk.

(Subd (e) amended effective April 25, 2019.)

(f) Review by counsel

(1) Within five days after the reporter delivers the transcript, the clerk must deliver the original transcript and the lists of appearances, exhibits, and motions required by rule 4.119 to the designated judge and one copy of the transcript and each list required by rule 4.119 that is not required to be sealed to each trial counsel. If a different attorney represented the defendant or the People in the preliminary proceedings, both attorneys must perform the tasks required by (2).

(2) Each trial counsel must promptly:

(A) Review the reporter's transcript and the lists of appearances, exhibits, and motions to identify any errors or omissions in the transcript;

(B) Review the docket sheets and minute orders to determine whether all preliminary proceedings have been transcribed; and

(C) Review the court file to determine whether it is complete.

(3) Within 21 days after the clerk delivers the transcript and lists under (1), trial counsel must confer regarding any errors or omissions in the reporter's transcript or court file identified by trial counsel during the review required under (2) and determine whether any other proceedings or discussions should have been transcribed.

(Subd (f) amended effective April 25, 2019; previously amended effective January 1, 2007.)

(g) Declaration and request for corrections or additions

(1) Within 30 days after the clerk delivers the reporter's transcript and lists, each trial counsel must serve and file:

(A) A declaration stating that counsel or another person under counsel's supervision has performed the tasks required by (f), including conferring with opposing counsel; and

(B) Either:

(i) A request for corrections or additions to the reporter's transcript or court file. Immaterial typographical errors that cannot conceivably cause confusion are not required to be brought to the court's attention; or

(ii) A statement that counsel does not request any corrections or additions.

(C) The requirements of (B) may be satisfied by a joint statement or request filed by counsel for all parties.

(2) If a different attorney represented the defendant in the preliminary proceedings, that attorney must also file the declaration required by (1).

(3) A request for additions to the reporter's transcript must state the nature and date of the proceedings and, if known, the identity of the reporter who reported them.

(4) If any counsel fails to timely file a declaration under (1), the designated judge must not certify the record and must set the matter for hearing, require a showing of good cause why counsel has not complied, and fix a date for compliance.

(Subd (g) amended effective April 25, 2019; previously amended effective January 1, 2007.)

(h) Corrections or additions to the record of preliminary proceedings

If any counsel files a request for corrections or additions:

(1) Within 15 days after the last request is filed, the designated judge must hold a hearing and order any necessary corrections or additions.

(2) If any portion of the proceedings cannot be transcribed, the judge may order preparation of a settled statement under rule 8.346.

(3) Within 20 days after the hearing under (1), the original reporter's transcript and court file must be corrected or augmented to reflect all corrections or additions ordered. The clerk must promptly send copies of the corrected or additional pages to trial counsel.

(4) The judge may order any further proceedings to correct or complete the record of the preliminary proceedings.

(5) When the judge is satisfied that all corrections and additions ordered have been made and copies of all corrected or additional pages have been sent to the parties, the judge must certify the record of the preliminary proceedings as complete and accurate.

(6) The record of the preliminary proceedings must be certified as complete and accurate within 120 days after the presiding judge orders preparation of the record.

(Subd (h) amended effective January 1, 2007.)

(i) Transcript delivered in electronic form

(1) When the record of the preliminary proceedings is certified as complete and accurate, the clerk must promptly notify the reporter to prepare five copies of the transcript in electronic form and two additional copies in electronic form for each codefendant against whom the death penalty is sought.

(2) Each transcript delivered in electronic form must comply with the applicable requirements of rule 8.144 and any additional requirements prescribed by the Supreme Court, and must be further labeled to show the date it was made.

(3) A copy of a sealed or confidential transcript delivered in electronic form must be separated from any other transcripts and labeled as required by rule 8.45.

(4) The reporter is to be compensated for copies delivered in electronic form as provided in Government Code section 69954(b).

(5) Within 20 days after the clerk notifies the reporter under (1), the reporter must deliver the copies in electronic form to the clerk.

(Subd (i) amended effective April 25, 2019; previously amended effective January 1, 2007, January 1, 2017, and January 1, 2018.)

(j) Delivery to the superior court

Within five days after the reporter delivers the copies in electronic form, the clerk must deliver to the responsible judge, for inclusion in the record:

(1) The certified original reporter's transcript of the preliminary proceedings and the copies that have not been distributed to counsel; and

(2) The complete court file of the preliminary proceedings or a certified copy of that file.

(Subd (j) amended effective April 25, 2019; previously amended effective January 1, 2007, and January 1, 2018.)

(k) Extension of time

(1) Except as provided in (2), the designated judge may extend for good cause any of the periods specified in this rule.

(2) The period specified in (h)(6) may be extended only as follows:

(A) The designated judge may request an extension of the period by presenting a declaration to the responsible judge explaining why the time limit cannot be met; and

(B) The responsible judge may order an extension not exceeding 90 additional days; in an exceptional case the judge may order an extension exceeding 90 days, but must state on the record the specific reason for the greater extension.

(Subd (k) amended effective January 1, 2007.)

(*l*) Notice that the death penalty is no longer sought

After the clerk has notified the court reporter to prepare the pretrial record, if the death penalty is no longer sought, the clerk must promptly notify the reporter that this rule does not apply.

(Subd (l) amended effective April 25, 2019; previously amended effective January 1, 2007.)

Rule 8.613 amended effective April 25, 2019; adopted as rule 34.2 effective January 1, 2004; previously amended and renumbered as rule 8.613 effective January 1, 2007; previously amended effective January 1, 2017, and January 1, 2018.

Advisory Committee Comment

Rule 8.613 implements Penal Code section 190.9(a). Rules 8.613–8.622 govern the process of preparing and certifying the record in any appeal from a judgment of death; specifically, rule 8.613 provides for the record of the preliminary proceedings in such an appeal.

Subdivision (f). As used in subdivision (f)—as in all rules in this chapter—trial counsel "means both the defendant's trial counsel and the prosecuting attorney." (Rule 8.600(e)(2).)

Subdivision (i). Subdivision (i)(4) restates a provision of former rule 35(b), second paragraph, as it was in effect on December 31, 2003.

Rule 8.616.　Preparing the trial record

(a) Clerk's duties

(1) The clerk must promptly—and no later than five days after the judgment of death is rendered:

(A) Notify the reporter to prepare the reporter's transcript; and

(B) Notify trial counsel to submit the lists of appearances, exhibits, and motions required by rule 4.230.

(2) The clerk must prepare an original and eight copies of the clerk's transcript and two additional copies for each codefendant sentenced to death. The clerk is encouraged to send the clerk's transcript in electronic form if the court is able to do so.

(3) The clerk must certify the original and all copies of the clerk's transcript as correct.

(Subd (a) amended effective April 25, 2019.)

(b) Reporter's duties

(1) The reporter must prepare an original and five copies of the reporter's transcript in electronic form and two additional copies in electronic form for each codefendant sentenced to death.

(2) Any portion of the transcript transcribed during trial must not be retyped unless necessary to correct errors, but must be repaginated and combined with any portion of the transcript not previously transcribed. Any additional copies needed must not be retyped but, if the transcript is in paper form, must be prepared by photocopying or an equivalent process.

(3) The reporter must certify the original and all copies of the reporter's transcript as correct and deliver them to the clerk.

(Subd (b) amended effective April 25, 2019; previously amended effective January 1, 2016.)

(c) Sending the record to trial counsel

Within 30 days after the judgment of death is rendered, the clerk must deliver one copy of the clerk's and reporter's transcripts and one copy of each list of appearances, exhibits, and motions required by rule 4.230 that is not required to be sealed to each trial counsel. The clerk must retain the original transcripts and any remaining copies. If counsel does not receive the transcripts within that period, counsel must promptly notify the superior court.

(Subd (c) amended effective April 25, 2019.)

(d) Extension of time

(1) On request of the clerk or a reporter and for good cause, the superior court may extend the period prescribed in (c) for no more than 30 days. For any further extension the clerk or reporter must file a request in the Supreme Court, showing good cause.

(2) A request under (1) must be supported by a declaration explaining why the extension is necessary. The court may presume good cause if the clerk's and reporter's transcripts combined will likely exceed 10,000 pages.

(3) If the superior court orders an extension under (1), the order must specify the reason justifying the extension. The clerk must promptly send a copy of the order to the Supreme Court.

Rule 8.616 amended effective April 25, 2019; repealed and adopted as rule 35 effective January 1, 2004; previously renumbered as rule 8.606 effective January 1, 2007; previously amended effective January 1, 2016.

Advisory Committee Comment

Rule 8.616 implements Penal Code section 190.8(b).

Rule 8.619.　Certifying the trial record for completeness

(a) Review by counsel after trial

(1) When the clerk delivers the clerk's and reporter's transcripts and the lists of appearances, exhibits, motions, and jury instructions required by rule 4.230 to trial counsel, each counsel must promptly:

(A) Review the docket sheets, minute orders, and the lists of appearances, exhibits, motions, and jury instructions to determine whether the reporter's transcript is complete; and

(B) Review the court file to determine whether the clerk's transcript is complete.

(2) Within 21 days after the clerk delivers the transcripts and lists under (1), trial counsel must confer regarding any errors or omissions in the reporter's transcript or clerk's transcript identified by trial counsel during the review required under (1).

(Subd (a) repealed, amended and relettered effective April 25, 2019; adopted as subd (b); previously amended effective January 1, 2007.)

(b) Declaration and request for additions or corrections

(1) Within 30 days after the clerk delivers the transcripts, each trial counsel must serve and file:

(A) A declaration stating that counsel or another person under counsel's supervision has performed the tasks required by (a), including conferring with opposing counsel; and

(B) Either:

(i) A request to include additional materials in the record or to correct errors that have come to counsel's attention. Immaterial typographical errors that cannot conceivably cause confusion are not required to be brought to the court's attention; or

(ii) A statement that counsel does not request any additions or corrections.

(2) The requirements of (1)(B) may be satisfied by a joint statement or request filed by counsel for all parties.

(3) If the clerk's and reporter's transcripts combined exceed 10,000 pages, the time limits stated in (a)(2) and (b)(1) are extended by three days for each 1,000 pages of combined transcript over 10,000 pages.

(4) A request for additions to the reporter's transcript must state the nature and date of the proceedings and, if known, the identity of the reporter who reported them.

(5) If any counsel fails to timely file a declaration under (1), the judge must not certify the record and must set the matter for hearing, require a showing of good cause why counsel has not complied, and fix a date for compliance.

(Subd (b) amended and relettered effective April 25, 2019; adopted as subd (c); previously amended effective January 1, 2007.)

(c) Completion of the record

If any counsel files a request for additions or corrections:

(1) The clerk must promptly deliver the original transcripts to the judge who presided at the trial.

(2) Within 15 days after the last request is filed, the judge must hold a hearing and order any necessary additions or corrections. The order must require that any additions or corrections be made within 10 days of its date.

(3) The clerk must promptly—and in any event within five days—notify the reporter of an order under (2). If any portion of the proceedings cannot be transcribed, the judge may order preparation of a settled statement under rule 8.346.

(4) The original transcripts must be augmented or corrected to reflect all additions or corrections ordered. The clerk must promptly send copies of the additional or corrected pages to trial counsel.

(5) Within five days after the augmented or corrected transcripts are filed, the judge must set another hearing to determine whether the record has been completed or corrected as ordered. The judge may order further proceedings to complete or correct the record.

(6) When the judge is satisfied that all additions or corrections ordered have been made and copies of all additional or corrected pages have been sent to trial counsel, the judge must certify the record as complete and redeliver the original transcripts to the clerk.

(7) The judge must certify the record as complete within 30 days after the last request to include additional materials or make corrections is filed or, if no such request is filed, after the last statement that counsel does not request any additions or corrections is filed.

(Subd (c) amended and relettered effective April 25, 2019; adopted as subd (d); previously amended effective January 1, 2007.)

(d) Transcript delivered in electronic form

(1) When the record is certified as complete, the clerk must promptly notify the reporter to prepare five copies of the transcript in electronic form and two additional copies in electronic form for each codefendant sentenced to death.

(2) Each copy delivered in electronic form must comply with the applicable requirements of rule 8.144 and any additional requirements prescribed by the Supreme Court, and must be further labeled to show the date it was made.

(3) A copy of a sealed or confidential transcript delivered in electronic form must be separated from any other transcripts and labeled as required by rule 8.45.

(4) The reporter is to be compensated for copies delivered in electronic form as provided in Government Code section 69954(b).

(5) Within 10 days after the clerk notifies the reporter under (1), the reporter must deliver the copies in electronic form to the clerk.

(Subd (d) amended and relettered effective April 25, 2019; adopted as subd (e); previously amended effective January 1, 2017, and January 1, 2018.)

(e) Extension of time

(1) The court may extend for good cause any of the periods specified in this rule.

(2) An application to extend the period to review the record under (a) or the period to file a declaration under (b) must be served and filed within the relevant period.

(3) If the court orders an extension of time, the order must specify the justification for the extension. The clerk must promptly send a copy of the order to the Supreme Court.

(Subd (e) amended and relettered effective April 25, 2019; adopted as subd (f).)

(f) Sending the certified record

(1) When the record is certified as complete, the clerk must promptly send one copy of the clerk's transcript and one copy of the reporter's transcript:

(A) To each defendant's appellate counsel and each defendant's habeas corpus counsel. If either counsel has not been retained or appointed, the clerk must keep that counsel's copies until counsel is retained or appointed.

(B) To the Attorney General, the Habeas Corpus Resource Center, and the California Appellate Project in San Francisco.

(2) The reporter's transcript must be in electronic form. The clerk is encouraged to send the clerk's transcript in electronic form if the court is able to do so.

(Subd (f) amended and relettered effective April 25, 2019; adopted as subd (g); previously amended effective January 1, 2018.)

(g) Notice of delivery

When the clerk sends the record to the defendant's appellate counsel, the clerk must serve a notice of delivery on the clerk/executive officer of the Supreme Court.

(Subd (g) amended and relettered effective April 25, 2019; adopted as subd (h); previously amended effective January 1, 2018.)

Rule 8.619 amended effective April 25, 2019; adopted as rule 35.1 effective January 1, 2004; previously amended and renumbered as rule 8.619 effective January 1, 2007; previously amended effective January 1, 2017, and January 1, 2018.

Advisory Committee Comment

Rule 8.619 implements Penal Code section 190.8(c)–(e).

Subdivision (d)(4) restates a provision of former rule 35(b), second paragraph, as it was in effect on December 31, 2003.

Rule 8.622. Certifying the trial record for accuracy

(a) Request for corrections or additions

(1) Within 90 days after the clerk delivers the record to defendant's appellate counsel:

(A) Any party may serve and file a request for corrections or additions to the record. Immaterial typographical errors that cannot conceivably cause confusion are not required to be brought to the court's attention. Items that a party may request to be added to the clerk's transcript include a copy of any exhibit admitted in evidence, refused, or lodged that is a document in paper or electronic format. The requesting party must state the reason that the exhibit needs to be included in the clerk's transcript. Parties may file a joint request for corrections or additions.

(B) Appellate counsel must review all sealed records that they are entitled to access under rule 8.45 and file an application to unseal any such records that counsel determines no longer meet the criteria for sealing specified in rule 2.550(d). Notwithstanding rule 8.46(e), this application must be filed in the trial court and these records may be unsealed on order of the trial court.

(2) A request for additions to the reporter's transcript must state the nature and date of the proceedings and, if known, the identity of the

reporter who reported them. A request for an exhibit to be included in the clerk's transcript must specify that exhibit by number or letter.

(3) Unless otherwise ordered by the court, within 10 days after a party serves and files a request for corrections or additions to the record, defendant's appellate counsel and the trial counsel from the prosecutor's office must confer regarding the request and any application to unseal records served on the prosecutor's office.

(4) If the clerk's and reporter's transcripts combined exceed 10,000 pages, the time limits stated in (1), (3), and (b)(4) are extended by 15 days for each 1,000 pages of combined transcript over 10,000 pages.

(Subd (a) amended effective April 25, 2019.)

(b) Correction of the record

(1) If any counsel files a request for corrections or additions, the procedures and time limits of rule 8.619(c)(1)–(5) must be followed.

(2) If any application to unseal a record is filed, the judge must grant or deny the application before certifying the record as accurate.

(3) When the judge is satisfied that all corrections or additions ordered have been made, the judge must certify the record as accurate and redeliver the record to the clerk.

(4) The judge must certify the record as accurate within 30 days after the last request to include additional materials or make corrections is filed.

(Subd (b) amended effective April 25, 2019; previously amended effective January 1, 2007.)

(c) Copies of the record

(1) When the record is certified as accurate, the clerk must promptly notify the reporter to prepare six copies of the reporter's transcript in electronic form and two additional copies in electronic form for each codefendant sentenced to death.

(2) In preparing the copies, the procedures and time limits of rule 8.619(d)(2)–(5) must be followed.

(Subd (c) amended effective April 25, 2019; previously amended effective January 1, 2007, and January 1, 2018.)

(d) Extension of time

(1) The court may extend for good cause any of the periods specified in this rule.

(2) An application to extend the period to request corrections or additions under (a) must be served and filed within that period.

(3) If the court orders an extension of time, the order must specify the justification for the extension. The clerk must promptly send a copy of the order to the Supreme Court.

(4) If the court orders an extension of time, the court may conduct a status conference or require the counsel who requested the extension to file a status report on counsel's progress in reviewing the record.

(Subd (d) amended effective April 25, 2019.)

(e) Sending the certified record

When the record is certified as accurate, the clerk must promptly send:

(1) To the Supreme Court: the corrected original record, including the judge's certificate of accuracy. The reporter's transcript must be in electronic form. The clerk is encouraged to send the clerk's transcript in electronic form if the court is able to do so.

(2) To each defendant's appellate counsel, each defendant's habeas corpus counsel, the Attorney General, the Habeas Corpus Resource Center, and the California Appellate Project in San Francisco: a copy of the order certifying the record and a copy of the reporter's transcript in electronic form.

(3) To the Governor: the copies of the transcripts required by Penal Code section 1218, with copies of any corrected or augmented pages inserted.

(Subd (e) amended effective April 25, 2019; previously amended effective January 1, 2018.)
Rule 8.622 amended effective April 25, 2019; adopted as rule 35.2 effective January 1, 2004; previously amended and renumbered as rule 8.622 effective January 1, 2007; previously amended effective January 1, 2018.

Advisory Committee Comment

Rule 8.622 implements Penal Code section 190.8(g).

Rule 8.625. Certifying the record in pre-1997 trials [Repealed]

Rule 8.625 repealed effective April 25, 2019; adopted as rule 35.3 effective January 1, 2004; previously amended and renumbered as rule 8.625 effective January 1, 2007; previously amended effective January 1, 2017, and January 1, 2018.

Article 3
Briefs, Hearing, and Decision

Rule 8.630. Briefs by parties and amicus curiae

Rule 8.630. Briefs by parties and amicus curiae

(a) Contents and form

Except as provided in this rule, briefs in appeals from judgments of death must comply as nearly as possible with rules 8.200 and 8.204.

(Subd (a) amended effective January 1, 2007.)

(b) Length

(1) A brief produced on a computer must not exceed the following limits, including footnotes:

(A) Appellant's opening brief: 102,000 words.

(B) Respondent's brief: 102,000 words. If the Chief Justice permits the appellant to file an opening brief that exceeds the limit set in (1)(A) or (3)(A), respondent's brief may not exceed the length of appellant's opening brief approved by the Chief Justice.

(C) Reply brief: 47,600 words.

(D) Petition for rehearing and answer: 23,800 words each.

(2) A brief under (1) must include a certificate by appellate counsel stating the number of words in the brief; counsel may rely on the word count of the computer program used to prepare the brief.

(3) A typewritten brief must not exceed the following limits:

(A) Appellant's opening brief: 300 pages.

(B) Respondent's brief: 300 pages. If the Chief Justice permits the appellant to file an opening brief that exceeds the limit set in (1)(A) or (3)(A), respondent's brief may not exceed the length of appellant's opening brief approved by the Chief Justice.

(C) Reply brief: 140 pages.

(D) Petition for rehearing and answer: 70 pages each.

(4) The tables required under rule 8.204(a)(1), the cover information required under rule 8.204(b)(10), a certificate under (2), any signature block, and any attachment permitted under rule 8.204(d) are excluded from the limits stated in (1) and (3).

(5) On application, the Chief Justice may permit a longer brief for good cause. An application in any case in which the certified record is filed in the California Supreme Court on or after January 1, 2008, must comply with rule 8.631.

(Subd (b) amended effective January 1, 2011; previously amended effective January 1, 2007, and January 1, 2008.)

(c) Time to file

(1) Except as provided in (2), the times to file briefs in an appeal from a judgment of death are as follows:

(A) The appellant's opening brief must be served and filed within 210 days after the record is certified as complete or the superior court clerk delivers the completed record to the defendant's appellate counsel, whichever is later. The clerk/executive officer of the Supreme Court must promptly notify the defendant's appellate counsel and the Attorney General of the due date for the appellant's opening brief.

(B) The respondent's brief must be served and filed within 120 days after the appellant's opening brief is filed. The clerk/executive officer of the Supreme Court must promptly notify the defendant's appellate counsel and the Attorney General of the due date for the respondent's brief.

(C) If the clerk's and reporter's transcripts combined exceed 10,000 pages, the time limits stated in (A) and (B) are extended by 15 days for each 1,000 pages of combined transcript over 10,000 pages.

(D) The appellant must serve and file a reply brief, if any, within 60 days after the respondent files its brief.

(2) In any appeal from a judgment of death imposed after a trial that began before January 1, 1997, the time to file briefs is governed by rule 8.360(c).

(3) The Chief Justice may extend the time to serve and file a brief for good cause.

(Subd (c) amended effective January 1, 2018; previously amended effective January 1, 2007.)

(d) Supplemental briefs

Supplemental briefs may be filed as provided in rule 8.520(d).

(Subd (d) amended effective January 1, 2007.)

(e) Amicus curiae briefs

Amicus curiae briefs may be filed as provided in rule 8.520(f).

(Subd (e) amended effective January 1, 2007.)

(f) Briefs on the court's request

The court may request additional briefs on any or all issues.

(g) Service

(1) The Supreme Court Policy on Service of Process by Counsel for Defendant governs service of the defendant's briefs.

(2) The Attorney General must serve two paper copies or one electronic copy of the respondent's brief on each defendant's appellate counsel and, for each defendant sentenced to death, one copy on the California Appellate Project in San Francisco.

(3) A copy of each brief must be served on the superior court clerk for delivery to the trial judge.

(Subd (g) amended effective January 1, 2016.)

(h) Judicial notice

To obtain judicial notice by the Supreme Court under Evidence Code section 459, a party must comply with rule 8.252(a).

(Subd (h) amended effective January 1, 2007.)

Rule 8.630 amended effective January 1, 2018; repealed and adopted as rule 36 effective January 1, 2004; previously amended and renumbered as rule 8.630 effective January 1, 2007; previously amended effective January 1, 2008, January 1, 2011, and January 1, 2016.

Advisory Committee Comment

Subdivision (b). Subdivision (b)(1) states the maximum permissible lengths of briefs produced on a computer in terms of word count rather than page count. This provision tracks a provision in rule 8.204(c) governing Court of Appeal briefs and is explained in the comment to that provision. Each word count assumes a brief using one-and-one-half spaced lines of text, as permitted by rule 8.204(b)(5).

Subdivision (b)(4) specifies certain items that are not counted toward the maximum brief length. Signature blocks, as referenced in this provision includes not only the signatures, but also the printed names, titles, and affiliations of any attorneys filing or joining in the brief, which may accompany the signature.

Subdivision (g). Subdivision (g)(1) is a cross-reference to Policy 4 of the Supreme Court Policies Regarding Cases Arising From Judgments of Death.

Rule 8.631. Applications to file overlength briefs in appeals from a judgment of death

(a) Cases in which this rule applies

This rule applies in appeals from a judgment of death in which the certified record is filed in the California Supreme Court on or after January 1, 2008.

(Subd (a) adopted effective January 1, 2008.)

(b) Policies

(1) The brief limits set by rule 8.630 are substantially higher than for other appellate briefs in recognition of the number, significance, and complexity of the issues generally presented in appeals from judgments of death and are designed to be sufficient to allow counsel to prepare adequate briefs in the majority of such appeals.

(2) In a small proportion of such appeals, counsel may not be able to prepare adequate briefs within the limits set by rule 8.630. In those cases, necessary additional briefing will be permitted.

(3) A party may not file a brief that exceeds the limit set by rule 8.630 unless the court finds that good cause has been shown in an application filed within the time limits set in (d).

(Subd (b) adopted effective January 1, 2008.)

(c) Factors considered

The court will consider the following factors in determining whether good cause exists to grant an application to file a brief that exceeds the limit set by rule 8.630:

(1) The unusual length of the record. A party relying on this factor must specify the length of each of the following components of the record:

(A) The reporter's transcript;

(B) The clerk's transcript; and

(C) The portion of the clerk's transcript that is made up of juror questionnaires.

(2) The number of codefendants in the case and whether they were tried separately from the appellant;

(3) The number of homicide victims in the case and whether the homicides occurred in more than one incident;

(4) The number of other crimes in the case and whether they occurred in more than one incident;

(5) The number of rulings by the trial court on unusual, factually intensive, or legally complex motions that the party may assert are erroneous and prejudicial. A party relying on this factor must briefly describe the nature of these motions;

(6) The number of rulings on objections by the trial court that the party may assert are erroneous and prejudicial;

(7) The number and nature of unusual, factually intensive, or legally complex hearings held in the trial court that the party may assert raise issues on appeal; and

(8) Any other factor that is likely to contribute to an unusually high number of issues or unusually complex issues on appeal. A party relying on this factor must briefly specify those issues.

(Subd (c) adopted effective January 1, 2008.)

(d) Time to file and contents of application

(1) An application to file a brief that exceeds the limits set by rule 8.630 must be served and filed as follows:

(A) For an appellant's opening brief or respondent's brief:

(i) If counsel has not filed an application requesting an extension of time to file the brief, no later than 45 days before the brief is due.

(ii) If counsel has filed an application requesting an extension of time to file the brief, within the time specified by the court in its order regarding the extension of time.

(B) For an appellant's reply brief:

(i) If counsel has not filed an application requesting an extension of time to file the brief, no later than 30 days before the brief is due.

(ii) If counsel has filed an application requesting an extension of time to file the brief, within the time specified by the court in its order regarding the extension of time.

(2) After the time specified in (1), an application to file a brief that exceeds the applicable limit may be filed only under the following circumstances:

(A) New authority substantially affects the issues presented in the case and cannot be adequately addressed without exceeding the applicable limit. Such an application must be filed within 30 days of finality of the new authority; or

(B) Replacement counsel has been appointed to represent the appellant and has determined that it is necessary to file a brief that exceeds the applicable limit. Such an application must be filed within the time specified by the court in its order setting the deadline for replacement counsel to file the appellant's brief.

(3) The application must:

(A) State the number of additional words or typewritten pages requested.

(B) State good cause for granting the additional words or pages requested, consistent with the factors in (c). The number of additional words or pages requested must be commensurate with the good cause shown. The application must explain why the factors identified demonstrate good cause in the particular case. The application must not state mere conclusions or make legal arguments regarding the merits of the issues on appeal.

(C) Not exceed 5,100 words if produced on a computer or 15 pages if typewritten.

(Subd (d) adopted effective January 1, 2008.)

Rule 8.631 adopted effective January 1, 2008.

Advisory Committee Comment

Subdivision (a). In all cases in which a judgment of death was imposed after a trial that began after January 1, 1997, the record filed with the Supreme Court will be the record that has been certified for accuracy under rule 8.622. In cases in which a judgment of death was imposed after a trial that began before January 1, 1997, the record filed with the Supreme Court will be the certified record under rule 8.625.

Subdivision (c)(1)(A). As in guideline 8 of the Supreme Court's Guidelines for Fixed Fee Appointments, juror questionnaires generally will not be taken into account in considering whether the length of the record is unusual unless these questionnaires are relevant to an issue on appeal. A record of 10,000 pages or less, excluding juror questionnaires, is not considered a record of unusual length; 70 percent of the records in capital appeals filed between 2001 and 2004 were 10,000 pages or less, excluding juror questionnaires.

Subdivision (c)(1)(E). Examples of unusual, factually intensive, or legally complex motions include motions to change venue, admit scientific evidence, or determine competency.

Subdivisions (c)(1)(E)–(I). Because an application must be filed before briefing is completed, the issues identified in the application will be those that the party anticipates *may* be raised on appeal. If the party does not ultimately raise all of these issues on appeal, the party is expected to have reduced the length of the brief accordingly.

Subdivision (c)(1)(I). Examples of unusual, factually intensive, or legally complex hearings include jury composition proceedings and hearings to determine the defendant's competency or sanity, whether the defendant is mentally retarded, and whether the defendant may represent himself or herself.

Subdivision (d)(1)(A)(ii). To allow the deadline for an application to file an overlength brief to be appropriately tied to the deadline for filing that brief, if counsel requests an extension of time to file a brief, the court will specify in its order regarding the request to extend the time to file the brief, when any application to file an overlength brief is due. Although the order will specify the deadline by which an application must be filed, counsel are encouraged to file such applications sooner, if possible.

Subdivision (d)(3). These requirements apply to applications filed under either (d)(1) or (d)(2).

Rule 8.634. Transmitting exhibits; augmenting the record in the Supreme Court

(a) Application

Except as provided in (b), rule 8.224 governs the transmission of exhibits to the Supreme Court.

(Subd (a) amended effective January 1, 2007; previously amended effective January 1, 2004.)

(b) Time to file notice of designation

No party may file a notice designating exhibits under rule 8.224(a) until the clerk/executive officer of the Supreme Court notifies the parties of the time and place of oral argument.

(Subd (b) amended effective January 1, 2018; previously amended effective January 1, 2007.)

(c) Augmenting the record in the Supreme Court

At any time, on motion of a party or on its own motion, the Supreme Court may order the record augmented or corrected as provided in rule 8.155.

(Subd (c) amended effective January 1, 2007; adopted effective January 1, 2004.)

Rule 8.634 amended effective January 1, 2018; adopted as rule 36.1 effective January 1, 2003; previously amended effective January 1, 2004; previously amended and renumbered effective January 1, 2007.

Rule 8.638. Oral argument and submission of the cause

(a) Application

Except as provided in (b), rule 8.524 governs oral argument and submission of the cause in the Supreme Court unless the court provides otherwise in its Internal Operating Practices and Procedures or by order.

(Subd (a) amended effective January 1, 2007; previously amended effective January 1, 2004.)

(b) Procedure

(1) The appellant has the right to open and close.

(2) Each side is allowed 45 minutes for argument.

(3) Two counsel may argue on each side if, within 10 days after the date of the order setting the case for argument, they notify the court that the case requires it.

(Subd (b) amended effective January 1, 2004.)

Rule 8.638 amended and renumbered effective January 1, 2007; adopted as rule 36.2 effective January 1, 2003; previously amended effective January 1, 2004.

Rule 8.642. Filing, finality, and modification of decision; rehearing; remittitur

Rules 8.532 through 8.540 govern the filing, finality, and modification of decision, rehearing, and issuance of remittitur by the Supreme Court in an appeal from a judgment of death.

Rule 8.642 amended and renumbered effective January 1, 2007; adopted as rule 36.3 effective January 1, 2004.

Chapter 3
Death Penalty–Related Habeas Corpus Proceedings

Title 8, Appellate Rules—Division 2, Rules Relating to Death Penalty Appeals and Habeas Corpus Proceedings—Chapter 3, Death Penalty–Related Habeas Corpus Proceedings adopted effective April 25, 2019.

Rule 8.652. Qualifications of counsel in death penalty–related habeas corpus proceedings

Rule 8.652. Qualifications of counsel in death penalty–related habeas corpus proceedings

(a) Purpose

This rule defines the minimum qualifications for attorneys to be appointed by a court to represent a person in a habeas corpus proceeding related to a sentence of death. These minimum qualifications are designed to promote competent representation in habeas corpus proceedings related to sentences of death and to avoid unnecessary delay and expense by assisting the courts in appointing qualified counsel. Nothing in this rule is intended to be used as a standard by which to measure whether a person received effective assistance of counsel. An attorney is not entitled to appointment simply because the attorney meets these minimum qualifications.

(Subd (a) adopted effective April 25, 2019.)

(b) General qualifications

An attorney may be included on a panel, appointed by the Supreme Court, or appointed by a court under a local rule as provided in rule 4.562, only if it is determined, after reviewing the attorney's experience, training, writing samples, references, and evaluations, that the attorney meets the minimum qualifications in this rule and has demonstrated the commitment, knowledge, and skills necessary to competently represent a person in a habeas corpus proceeding related to a sentence of death. An appointed attorney must be willing to cooperate with an assisting counsel or entity that the appointing court designates.

(Subd (b) adopted effective April 25, 2019.)

(c) Qualifications for appointed habeas corpus counsel

An attorney included on a panel, appointed by the Supreme Court, or appointed by a court under a local rule as provided in rule 4.562, must satisfy the following minimum qualifications:

(1) *California legal experience*

Active practice of law in California for at least five years.

(2) *Case experience*

The case experience identified in (A), (B), or (C).

(A) Service as counsel of record for a petitioner in a death penalty–related habeas corpus proceeding in which the petition has been filed in the California Supreme Court, a Court of Appeal, or a superior court.

(B) Service as:

(i) Supervised counsel in two death penalty–related habeas corpus proceedings in which the petition has been filed. Service as supervised counsel in a death penalty–related habeas corpus proceeding will apply toward this qualification only if lead or associate counsel in that proceeding attests that the attorney performed substantial work on the case and recommends the attorney for appointment; and

(ii) Counsel of record for either party in a combination of at least five completed appeals, habeas corpus proceedings, or jury trials in felony cases, including as counsel of record for a petitioner in at least two habeas corpus proceedings, each involving a serious felony in which the petition has been filed. Service as counsel of record in an appeal where counsel did not file a brief, or in a habeas corpus proceeding where counsel did not file a petition, informal response, or a return, does not satisfy any part of this combined case experience. The combined case experience must be sufficient to demonstrate proficiency in investigation, issue identification, and writing.

(C) Service as counsel of record for either party in a combination of at least eight completed appeals, habeas corpus proceedings, or jury trials in felony cases, including as counsel of record for a petitioner in at least two habeas corpus proceedings, each involving a serious felony in which the petition has been filed. Service as counsel of record in an appeal where counsel did not file a brief, or in a habeas corpus proceeding where counsel did not file a petition, informal response, or a return, does not satisfy any part of this combined case experience. The combined case experience must be sufficient to demonstrate proficiency in investigation, issue identification, and writing.

(3) *Knowledge*

Familiarity with the practices and procedures of the California courts and the federal courts in death penalty–related habeas corpus proceedings.

(4) *Training*

(A) Within three years before being included on a panel, appointed by the Supreme Court, or appointed by a court under a local rule as provided in rule 4.562, completion of at least 15 hours of appellate criminal defense or habeas corpus defense training approved for Minimum Continuing Legal Education credit by the State Bar of California, at least 10 hours of which address death penalty–related habeas corpus proceedings.

(B) Counsel who serves as an instructor in a course that satisfies the requirements of this rule may receive course participation credit for instruction, on request to and approval by the committee, the Supreme Court, or a court appointing counsel under a local rule as provided in rule 4.562, in an amount to be determined by the approving entity.

(C) If the attorney has previously represented a petitioner in a death penalty–related habeas corpus proceeding, the committee, the Supreme Court, or the court appointing counsel under a local rule as provided in rule 4.562, after reviewing counsel's previous work, may find that such representation constitutes compliance with some or all of this requirement.

(5) *Skills*

Demonstrated proficiency in issue identification, research, analysis, writing, investigation, and advocacy. To enable an assessment of the attorney's skills:

(A) The attorney must submit:

(i) Three writing samples written by the attorney and presenting analyses of complex legal issues. If the attorney has previously served as lead counsel of record for a petitioner in a death penalty–related habeas corpus proceeding, these writing samples must include one or more habeas corpus petitions filed by the attorney in that capacity. If the attorney has previously served as associate or supervised counsel for a petitioner in a death penalty–related habeas corpus proceeding, these writing samples must include the portion of the habeas corpus petition prepared by the attorney in that capacity. If the attorney has not served as lead counsel of record for a petitioner in a death penalty–related habeas corpus proceeding, these writing samples must include two or more habeas corpus petitions filed by the attorney as counsel of record for a petitioner in a habeas corpus proceeding involving a serious felony; and

(ii) Recommendations from two attorneys familiar with the attorney's qualifications and performance.

(B) The committee, the Supreme Court, or the court appointing counsel under a local rule as provided in rule 4.562, must obtain and review:

(i) If the attorney has previously been appointed in a death penalty appeal or death penalty–related habeas corpus proceeding, the evaluation of the assisting counsel or entity in those proceedings; and

(ii) If the attorney is on a panel of attorneys eligible for appointments to represent indigent appellants in the Court of Appeal, the evaluation of the administrator responsible for those appointments.

(Subd (c) adopted effective April 25, 2019.)

(d) Alternative experience

An attorney who does not meet the experience requirements of (c)(1) and (2) may be included on a panel or appointed by the Supreme Court if the attorney meets the qualifications described in (c)(3) and (5), excluding the writing samples described in (c)(5)(A)(i), and:

(1) The committee or the Supreme Court finds that the attorney has:

(A) Extensive experience as an attorney at the Habeas Corpus Resource Center or the California Appellate Project–San Francisco, or in another jurisdiction or a different type of practice (such as civil trials or appeals, academic work, or work for a court or as a prosecutor), for at least five years, providing the attorney with experience in complex cases substantially equivalent to that of an attorney qualified under (c)(1) and (2); and

(B) Demonstrated proficiency in issue identification, research, analysis, writing, investigation, and advocacy. To enable an assessment of the attorney's skills, the attorney must submit three writing samples written by the attorney and presenting analyses of complex legal issues, including habeas corpus petitions filed by the attorney, if any.

(2) Ongoing consultation is available to the attorney from an assisting counsel or entity designated by the court.

(3) Within two years before being included on a panel or appointed by the Supreme Court, the attorney has completed at least 18 hours of appellate criminal defense or habeas corpus defense training approved for Minimum Continuing Legal Education credit by the State Bar of California, at least 10 hours of which involve death penalty–related habeas corpus proceedings. The committee or the Supreme Court will determine whether the training completed by an attorney satisfies the requirements of this subdivision in light of the attorney's individual background and experience.

(Subd (d) adopted effective April 25, 2019.)

(e) Attorneys without trial experience

If an evidentiary hearing is ordered in a death penalty–related habeas corpus proceeding and an attorney appointed under (c) or (d) to represent a person in that proceeding lacks experience in conducting trials or evidentiary hearings, the attorney must associate with an attorney who has such experience.

(Subd (e) adopted effective April 25, 2019.)

(f) Use of supervised counsel

An attorney who does not meet the qualifications described in (c) or (d) may assist lead or associate counsel, but must work under the immediate supervision and direction of lead or associate counsel.

(Subd (f) adopted effective April 25, 2019.)

(g) Appellate and habeas corpus appointment

(1) An attorney appointed to represent a person in both a death penalty appeal and death penalty–related habeas corpus proceedings must meet the minimum qualifications of both (c) or (d) and rule 8.605.

(2) Notwithstanding (1), two attorneys together may be eligible for appointment to represent a person jointly in both a death penalty appeal and death penalty–related habeas corpus proceedings if it is determined that one attorney satisfies the minimum qualifications stated in (c) or (d) and the other attorney satisfies the minimum qualifications stated in rule 8.605.

(Subd (g) adopted effective April 25, 2019.)

(h) Entities as appointed counsel

(1) Notwithstanding any other provision of this rule, the Habeas Corpus Resource Center and the California Appellate Project–San Francisco are qualified to serve as appointed counsel in death penalty–related habeas corpus proceedings.

(2) When serving as appointed counsel in a death penalty–related habeas corpus proceeding, the Habeas Corpus Resource Center or the California Appellate Project–San Francisco must not assign any attorney as lead counsel unless it finds the attorney is qualified under (c) or (d).

(Subd (h) adopted effective April 25, 2019.)

(i) Attorney appointed by federal court

Notwithstanding any other provision of this rule, a court may appoint an attorney who is under appointment by a federal court in a death penalty–related habeas corpus proceeding for the purpose of exhausting state remedies in the California courts if the court finds that the attorney has the commitment, proficiency, and knowledge necessary to represent the person competently in state proceedings. Counsel under appointment by a federal court is not required to also be appointed by a state court in order to appear in a state court proceeding.

(Subd (i) adopted effective April 25, 2019.)
Rule 8.652 adopted effective April 25, 2019.

Division 3
Rules Relating to Miscellaneous Appeals and Writ Proceedings

Title 8, Appellate Rules—Division 3, Rules Relating to Miscellaneous Appeals and Writ Proceedings adopted effective April 25, 2019.

Chapter 1
Review of California Environmental Quality Act Cases Under Public Resources Code Sections 21168.6.6, 21178–21189.3, and 21189.50–21189.57

Title 8, Appellate Rules—Division 3, Rules Relating to Miscellaneous Appeals and Writ Proceedings—Chapter 1, Review of California Environmental Quality Act Cases Under Public Resources Code Sections 21168.6.6, 21178–21189.3, and 21189.50–21189.57 renumbered from chapter 11 effective April 25, 2019; adopted effective July 1, 2014; previously amended effective January 1, 2017.

Rule 8.700.   Definitions and application

(a) Definitions

As used in this chapter:

(1) An "environmental leadership development project" or "leadership project" means a project certified by the Governor under Public Resources Code sections 21182–21184.

(2) The "Sacramento entertainment and sports center project" or "Sacramento arena project" means the entertainment and sports center project as defined by Public Resources Code section 21168.6.6, for which

the proponent provided notice of election to proceed under that statute as described in section 21168.6.6(j)(1).

(3) A "capitol building annex project" means a capitol building annex project as defined by Public Resources Code section 21189.50.

(Subd (a) amended effective January 1, 2017; adopted effective July 1, 2014.)

(b) Proceedings governed

The rules in this chapter govern appeals and writ proceedings in the Court of Appeal to review a superior court judgment or order in an action or proceeding brought to attack, review, set aside, void, or annul the certification of the environmental impact report or the granting of any project approvals for an environmental leadership development project, the Sacramento arena project, or a capitol building annex project.

(Subd (b) amended effective January 1, 2017; adopted effective July 1, 2014.)
Rule 8.700 amended effective January 1, 2017; adopted effective July 1, 2014.

Rule 8.701.   Filing and service

(a) Service

Except when the court orders otherwise under (b) or as otherwise provided by law, all documents that the rules in this chapter require be served on the parties must be served by personal delivery, electronic service, express mail, or other means consistent with Code of Civil Procedure sections 1010, 1011, 1012, and 1013 and reasonably calculated to ensure delivery of the document to the parties not later than the close of the business day after the document is filed or lodged with the court.

(Subd (a) adopted effective July 1, 2014.)

(b) Electronic filing and service

(1) In accordance with rule 8.71, all parties except self-represented parties are required to file all documents electronically except as otherwise provided by these rules, the local rules of the reviewing court, or court order. Notwithstanding rule 8.71(b), a court may order a self-represented party to file documents electronically.

(2) All documents must be served electronically on parties who have consented to electronic service or who are otherwise required by law or court order to accept electronic service. All parties represented by counsel are deemed to have consented to electronic service. All self-represented parties may so consent.

(Subd (b) amended effective January 1, 2017; adopted effective July 1, 2014.)

(c) Exemption from extension of time

The extension of time provided in Code of Civil Procedure section 1010.6 for service completed by electronic means does not apply to any service in actions governed by these rules.

(Subd (c) adopted effective July 1, 2014.)
Rule 8.701 amended effective January 1, 2017; adopted effective July 1, 2014.

Rule 8.702.   Appeals

(a) Application of general rules for civil appeals

Except as otherwise provided by the rules in this chapter, rules 8.100–8.278, relating to civil appeals, apply to appeals under this chapter.
(Subd (a) adopted effective July 1, 2014.)

(b) Notice of appeal

(1) *Time to appeal*

The notice of appeal must be served and filed on or before the earlier of:

(A) Five court days after the superior court clerk serves on the party filing the notice of appeal a document entitled "Notice of Entry" of judgment or a filed-endorsed copy of the judgment, showing the date either was served; or

(B) Five court days after the party filing the notice of appeal serves or is served by a party with a document entitled "Notice of Entry" of judgment or a filed-endorsed copy of the judgment, accompanied by proof of service.

(2) *Contents of notice of appeal*

The notice of appeal must:

(A) State that the superior court judgment or order being appealed is governed by the rules in this chapter;

(B) Indicate whether the judgment or order pertains to the Sacramento arena project, a leadership project, or a capitol building annex project; and

(C) If the judgment or order being appealed pertains to a leadership project, provide notice that the person or entity that applied for certification of the project as a leadership project must make the payments required by rule 8.705.

(Subd (b) amended effective January 1, 2017; adopted effective July 1, 2014; previously amended effective January 1, 2016.)

(c) Extending the time to appeal

(1) *Motion for new trial*

If any party serves and files a valid notice of intention to move for a new trial or, under rule 3.2237, a valid motion for a new trial and that motion is denied, the time to appeal from the judgment is extended for all parties until the earlier of:

(A) Five court days after the superior court clerk or a party serves an order denying the motion or a notice of entry of that order; or

(B) Five court days after denial of the motion by operation of law.

(2) *Motion to vacate judgment*

If, within the time prescribed by subdivision (b) to appeal from the judgment, any party serves and files a valid notice of intention to move—or a valid motion—to vacate the judgment and that motion is denied, the time to appeal from the judgment is extended for all parties until five court days after the superior court clerk or a party serves an order denying the motion or a notice of entry of that order.

(3) *Motion to reconsider appealable order*

If any party serves and files a valid motion to reconsider an appealable order under Code of Civil Procedure section 1008, subdivision (a), the time to appeal from that order is extended for all parties until five court days after the superior court clerk or a party serves an order denying the motion or a notice of entry of that order.

(4) *Cross-appeal*

If an appellant timely appeals from a judgment or appealable order, the time for any other party to appeal from the same judgment or order is extended until five court days after the superior court clerk serves notification of the first appeal.

(Subd (c) adopted effective July 1, 2014.)

(d) Record on appeal

(1) *Record of written documents*

The record of the written documents from the superior court proceedings other than the administrative record must be in the form of a joint appendix or separate appellant's and respondent's appendixes under rule 8.124.

(2) *Record of the oral proceedings*

(A) The appellant must serve and file with its notice of appeal a notice designating the record under rule 8.121 specifying whether the appellant elects to proceed with or without a record of the oral proceedings in the trial court. If the appellant elects to proceed with a record of the oral proceedings in the trial court, the notice must designate a reporter's transcript.

(B) Any party that submits a copy of a Transcript Reimbursement Fund application in lieu of a deposit under rule 8.130(b)(3) must serve all other parties with notice of this submission when the party serves its notice of designation of the record. Within five days after service of this notice, any other party may submit to the trial court the required deposit for the reporter's transcript under rule 8.130(b)(1), the reporter's written waiver of the deposit under rule 8.130(b)(3)(A), or a certified transcript of all of the proceedings designated by the party under rule 8.130(b)(3)(C).

(C) Within 10 days after the superior court notifies the court reporter to prepare the transcript under rule 8.130(d)(2), the reporter must prepare and certify an original of the transcript and file the original and required number of copies in superior court.

(D) If the appellant does not present its notice of designation as required under (A) or if any designating party does not submit the required deposit for the reporter's transcript under rule 8.130(b)(1) or a permissible substitute under rule 8.130(b)(3) with its notice of designation or otherwise fails to timely do another act required to procure the record, the superior court clerk must serve the defaulting party with a notice indicating that the party must do the required act within two court days of service of the clerk's notice or the reviewing court may impose one of the following sanctions:

(i) If the defaulting party is the appellant, the court may dismiss the appeal; or

(ii) If the defaulting party is the respondent, the court may proceed with the appeal on the record designated by the appellant.

(Subd (d) adopted effective July 1, 2014.)

(e) Superior court clerk duties

Within five court days following the filing of a notice of appeal under this rule, the superior court clerk must:

(1) Serve the following on each party:

(A) Notification of the filing of the notice of appeal; and

(B) A copy of the register of actions, if any.

(2) Transmit the following to the reviewing court clerk:

(A) A copy of the notice of appeal;

(B) A copy of the appellant's notice designating the record; and

(C) An electronic copy of the administrative record.

(Subd (e) adopted effective July 1, 2014.)

(f) Briefing

(1) *Electronic filing*

Unless otherwise ordered by the reviewing court, all briefs must be electronically filed.

(2) *Time to serve and file briefs*

Unless otherwise ordered by the reviewing court:

(A) An appellant must serve and file its opening brief within 25 days after the notice of appeal is served and filed.

(B) A respondent must serve and file its brief within 25 days after the appellant files its opening brief.

(C) An appellant must serve and file its reply brief, if any, within 15 days after the respondent files its brief.

(3) *Contents and form of briefs*

(A) The briefs must comply as nearly as possible with rule 8.204.

(B) If a designated reporter's transcript has not been filed at least 5 days before the date by which a brief must be filed, an initial version of the brief may be served and filed in which references to a matter in the reporter's transcript are not supported by a citation to the volume and page number of the reporter's transcript where the matter appears. Within 10 days after the reporter's transcript is filed, a revised version of the brief must be served and filed in which all references to a matter in the reporter's transcript must be supported by a citation to the volume and page number of the reporter's transcript where the matter appears.

(C) Unless otherwise ordered by the court, within 5 days after filing its brief, each party must submit an electronic version of the brief that contains hyperlinks to material cited in the brief, including electronically searchable copies of the record on appeal, cited decisions, and the parties' other briefs. Such briefs must comply with any local requirements of the reviewing court relating to e-briefs.

(4) *Extensions of time to file briefs*

If the parties stipulate to extend the time to file a brief under rule 8.212(b), they are deemed to have agreed that the time for resolving the action may be extended beyond 270 days by the number of days by which the parties stipulated to extend the time for filing the brief and, to that extent, to have waived any objection to noncompliance with the deadlines for completing review stated in Public Resources Code sections 21168.6.6(c)–(d), 21185, and 21189.51 for the duration of the stipulated extension.

(5) *Failure to file brief*

If a party fails to timely file an appellant's opening brief or a respondent's brief, the reviewing court clerk must serve the party with a notice indicating that if the required brief is not filed within two court days of service of the clerk's notice, the court may impose one of the following sanctions:

(A) If the brief is an appellant's opening brief, the court may dismiss the appeal;

(B) If the brief is a respondent's brief, the court may decide the appeal on the record, the opening brief, and any oral argument by the appellant; or

(C) Any other sanction that the court finds appropriate.

(Subd (f) amended effective January 1, 2017; adopted effective July 1, 2014.)

(g) Oral argument

Unless otherwise ordered by the reviewing court, oral argument will be held within 45 days after the last reply brief is filed. The reviewing court clerk must send a notice of the time and place of oral argument to all parties at least 15 days before the argument date. The presiding justice may shorten the notice period for good cause; in that event, the clerk must immediately notify the parties by telephone or other expeditious method.

(Subd (g) adopted effective July 1, 2014.)

Rule 8.702 amended effective January 1, 2017; adopted effective July 1, 2014; previously amended effective January 1, 2016.

Advisory Committee Comment

Subdivision (b). It is very important to note that the time period to file a notice of appeal under this rule is the same time period for filing most postjudgment motions in a case regarding the Sacramento arena project, and in a case regarding a leadership project or capitol building annex project, the deadline for filing a notice of appeal may be earlier than the deadline for filing a motion for a new trial, a motion for reconsideration, or a motion to vacate the judgment.

Rule 8.703. Writ proceedings

(a) Application of general rules for writ proceedings

Except as otherwise provided by the rules in this chapter, rules 8.485–8.493—relating to writs of mandate, certiorari, and prohibition in the Supreme Court and Court of Appeal—apply to writ proceedings under this chapter.

(Subd (a) adopted effective July 1, 2014.)

(b) Petition

(1) *Time for filing petition*

A petition for a writ challenging a superior court judgment or order governed by the rules in this chapter must be served and filed on or before the earliest of:

(A) Thirty days after the superior court clerk serves on the party filing the petition a document entitled "Notice of Entry" of judgment or order, or a filed-endorsed copy of the judgment or order, showing the date either was served; or

(B) Thirty days after the party filing the petition serves or is served by a party with a document entitled "Notice of Entry" of judgment or order, or a filed-endorsed copy of the judgment or order, accompanied by proof of service.

(2) *Contents of petition*

In addition to any other applicable requirements, the petition must:

(A) State that the superior court judgment or order being challenged is governed by the rules in this chapter;

(B) Indicate whether the judgment or order pertains to the Sacramento arena project, a leadership project, or a capitol building annex project; and

(C) If the judgment or order pertains to a leadership project, provide notice that the person or entity that applied for certification of the project as a leadership project must make the payments required by 8.705.

(Subd (b) amended effective January 1, 2017; adopted effective July 1, 2014; previously amended effective January 1, 2016.)

Rule 8.703 amended effective January 1, 2017; adopted effective July 1, 2014; previously amended effective January 1, 2016.

Rule 8.705. Court of Appeal costs in leadership projects

In fulfillment of the provision in Public Resources Code section 21183 regarding payment of the Court of Appeal's costs with respect to cases concerning leadership projects:

(1) Within 10 days after service of the notice of appeal or petition in a case concerning a leadership project, the person who applied for certification of the project as a leadership project must pay a fee of $100,000 to the Court of Appeal.

(2) If the Court of Appeal incurs any of the following costs, the person who applied for certification of the project as a leadership project must also pay, within 10 days of being ordered by the court, the following costs or estimated costs:

(A) The costs of any special master appointed by the Court of Appeal in the case; and

(B) The costs of any contract personnel retained by the Court of Appeal to work on the case.

(3) If the party fails to timely pay the fee or costs specified in this rule, the court may impose sanctions that the court finds appropriate after notifying the party and providing the party with an opportunity to pay the required fee or costs.

Rule 8.705 adopted effective July 1, 2014.

Chapter 2
Appeals Under Code of Civil Procedure Section 1294.4 From an Order Dismissing or Denying a Petition to Compel Arbitration

Title 8, Appellate Rules—Division 3, Rules Relating to Miscellaneous Appeals and Writ Proceedings—Chapter 2, Appeals Under Code of Civil Procedure Section 1294.4 From an Order Dismissing or Denying a Petition to Compel Arbitration renumbered from chapter 12 effective April 25, 2019; adopted effective July 1, 2017.

Rule 8.710. Application
Rule 8.711. Filing and service
Rule 8.712. Notice of appeal
Rule 8.713. Record on appeal
Rule 8.714. Superior court clerk duties
Rule 8.715. Briefing
Rule 8.716. Oral argument
Rule 8.717. Extensions of time

Rule 8.710. Application

(a) Application of the rules in this chapter

The rules in this chapter govern appeals under Code of Civil Procedure section 1294.4 from a superior court order dismissing or denying a petition to compel arbitration.

(Subd (a) adopted effective July 1, 2017.)

(b) Application of general rules for civil appeals

Except as otherwise provided by the rules in this chapter, rules 8.100–8.278, relating to civil appeals, apply to appeals under this chapter.

(Subd (b) adopted effective July 1, 2017.)

Rule 8.710 adopted effective July 1, 2017.

Rule 8.711.   Filing and service

(a) Method of service

Except as otherwise provided by law:

(1) All documents must be served electronically on parties who have consented to electronic service or who are otherwise required by law or court order to accept electronic service. All parties represented by counsel are deemed to have consented to electronic service. All self-represented parties may so consent.

(2) All documents that the rules in this chapter require be served on the parties that are not served electronically must be served by personal delivery, express mail, or other means consistent with Code of Civil Procedure sections 1010, 1011, 1012, and 1013, and reasonably calculated to ensure delivery of the document to the parties not later than the close of the business day after the document is filed or lodged with the court.

(Subd (a) adopted effective July 1, 2017.)

(b) Electronic filing

In accordance with rule 8.71, all parties except self-represented parties are required to file all documents electronically except as otherwise provided by these rules, the local rules of the reviewing court, or court order. Notwithstanding rule 8.71(b), in appeals governed by this chapter, a court may order a self-represented party to file documents electronically.

(Subd (b) adopted effective July 1, 2017.)

(c) Exemption from extension of time

The extension of time provided in Code of Civil Procedure section 1010.6 for service completed by electronic means does not apply to any service in actions governed by these rules.

(Subd (c) adopted effective July 1, 2017.)

Rule 8.711 adopted effective July 1, 2017.

Rule 8.712.   Notice of appeal

(a) Contents of notice of appeal

(1) The notice of appeal must state that the superior court order being appealed is governed by the rules in this chapter.

(2) Copies of the order being appealed and the order granting preference under Code of Civil Procedure section 36 must be attached to the notice of appeal.

(Subd (a) adopted effective July 1, 2017.)

(b) Time to appeal

The notice of appeal must be served and filed on or before the earlier of:

(1) Twenty days after the superior court clerk serves on the party filing the notice of appeal a document entitled "Notice of Entry" of the order dismissing or denying a petition to compel arbitration or a filed-endorsed copy of the order, showing the date either was served; or

(2) Twenty days after the party filing the notice of appeal serves or is served by a party with a document entitled "Notice of Entry" of the order dismissing or denying a petition to compel arbitration or a filed-endorsed copy of the order, accompanied by proof of service.

(Subd (b) adopted effective July 1, 2017.)

(c) Extending the time to appeal

(1) *Motion to reconsider appealable order*

If any party serves and files a valid motion under subdivision (a) of Code of Civil Procedure section 1008 to reconsider the order dismissing or denying a petition to compel arbitration, the time to appeal from that order is extended for all parties until five court days after the superior court clerk or a party serves an order denying the motion or a notice of entry of that order.

(2) *Cross-appeal*

If an appellant timely appeals from the order dismissing or denying a petition to compel arbitration, the time for any other party to appeal from the same order is extended until five court days after the superior court clerk serves notification of the first appeal.

(Subd (c) adopted effective July 1, 2017.)

Rule 8.712 adopted effective July 1, 2017.

Rule 8.713.   Record on appeal

(a) Record of written documents

The record of the written documents from the superior court proceedings must be in the form of a joint appendix or separate appellant's and respondent's appendixes under rule 8.124.

(Subd (a) adopted effective July 1, 2017.)

(b) Record of the oral proceedings

(1) The appellant must serve and file with its notice of appeal a notice designating the record under rule 8.121 specifying whether the appellant elects to proceed with or without a record of the oral proceedings in the trial court. If the appellant elects to proceed with a record of the oral proceedings in the trial court, the notice must designate a reporter's transcript.

(2) Within 10 days after the superior court notifies the court reporter to prepare the transcript under rule 8.130(d)(2), the reporter must prepare and certify an original of the transcript and file the original and required number of copies in superior court.

(3) If the appellant does not present its notice of designation as required under (1) or if any designating party does not submit the required deposit for the reporter's transcript under rule 8.130(b)(1) or a permissible substitute under rule 8.130(b)(3) with its notice of designation or otherwise fails to timely do another act required to procure the record, the superior court clerk must serve the defaulting party with a notice indicating that the party must do the required act within two court days of service of the clerk's notice or the reviewing court may impose one of the following sanctions:

(A) If the defaulting party is the appellant, the court may dismiss the appeal; or

(B) If the defaulting party is the respondent, the court may proceed with the appeal on the record designated by the appellant.

(4) Within 10 days after the record is filed in the reviewing court, a party that has not purchased its own copy of the record may request the appellant, in writing, to lend it the appellant's copy of the record at the time that the appellant serves its final opening brief under rule 8.715(b)(2). The borrowing party must return the copy of the record when it serves its brief or the time to file its brief has expired. The cost of sending the copy of the record to and from the borrowing party shall be treated as a cost on appeal under rule 8.891(d)(1)(B).

(Subd (b) adopted effective July 1, 2017.)

Rule 8.713 adopted effective July 1, 2017.

Rule 8.714.   Superior court clerk duties

Within five court days following the filing of a notice of appeal under this rule, the superior court clerk must:

(1) Serve the following on each party:

(A) Notification of the filing of the notice of appeal; and

(B) A copy of the register of actions, if any.

(2) Transmit the following to the reviewing court clerk:

(A) A copy of the notice of appeal, with the copies of the order being appealed and the order granting preference under Code of Civil Procedure section 36 attached; and

(B) A copy of the appellant's notice designating the record.

Rule 8.714 adopted effective July 1, 2017.

Rule 8.715.   Briefing

(a) Time to serve and file briefs

Unless otherwise ordered by the reviewing court:

(1) An appellant must serve and file its opening brief within 10 days after the notice of appeal is served and filed;

(2) A respondent must serve and file its brief within 25 days after the appellant files its opening brief; and

(3) An appellant must serve and file its reply brief, if any, within 15 days after the respondent files its brief.

(Subd (a) adopted effective July 1, 2017.)

(b) Contents and form of briefs

(1) The briefs must comply as nearly as possible with rule 8.204.

(2) If a designated reporter's transcript has not been filed at least 5 days before the date by which a brief must be filed, an initial version of the brief may be served and filed in which references to a matter in the reporter's transcript are not supported by a citation to the volume and page number of the reporter's transcript where the matter appears. Within 10 days after the reporter's transcript is filed, a revised version of the brief must be served and filed in which all references to a matter in the reporter's transcript must be supported by a citation to the volume and

page number of the reporter's transcript where the matter appears. No other changes to the initial version of the brief are permitted.

(Subd (b) adopted effective July 1, 2017.)

(c) Stipulated extensions of time to file briefs

If the parties stipulate to extend the time to file a brief under rule 8.212(b), they are deemed to have agreed that such an extension will promote the interests of justice, that the time for resolving the action may be extended beyond 100 days by the number of days by which the parties stipulated to extend the time for filing the brief, and that to that extent, they have waived any objection to noncompliance with the deadlines for completing review stated in Code of Civil Procedure section 1294.4 for the duration of the stipulated extension.

(Subd (c) adopted effective July 1, 2017.)

(d) Failure to file brief

If a party fails to timely file an appellant's opening brief or a respondent's brief, the reviewing court clerk must serve the party with a notice indicating that if the required brief is not filed within two court days of service of the clerk's notice, the court may impose one of the following sanctions:

(1) If the brief is an appellant's opening brief, the court may dismiss the appeal;

(2) If the brief is a respondent's brief, the court may decide the appeal on the record, the opening brief, and any oral argument by the appellant; or

(3) Any other sanction that the court finds appropriate.

(Subd (d) adopted effective July 1, 2017.)

Rule 8.715 adopted effective July 1, 2017.

Rule 8.716.   Oral argument

The reviewing court clerk must send a notice of the time and place of oral argument to all parties at least 10 days before the argument date. The presiding justice may shorten the notice period for good cause; in that event, the clerk must immediately notify the parties by telephone or other expeditious method.

Rule 8.716 adopted effective July 1, 2017.

Rule 8.717.   Extensions of time

The Court of Appeal may grant an extension of the time in appeals governed by this chapter only if good cause is shown and the extension will promote the interests of justice.

Rule 8.717 adopted effective July 1, 2017.

Chapter 3
Miscellaneous Writs

Title 8, Appellate Rules—Division 3, Rules Relating to Miscellaneous Appeals and Writ Proceedings—Chapter 3, Miscellaneous Writs amended and renumbered as chapter 3 effective April 25, 2019; adopted as chapter 7 effective January 1, 2007; amended and renumbered as chapter 8 effective January 1, 2009; previously amended effective July 1, 2012.

Rule 8.720.   Review of Workers' Compensation Appeals Board cases

(a) Petition

(1) A petition to review an order, award, or decision of the Workers' Compensation Appeals Board must include:

(A) The order, award, or decision to be reviewed; and

(B) The workers' compensation judge's minutes of hearing and summary of evidence, findings and opinion on decision, and report and recommendation on the petition for reconsideration.

(2) If the petition claims that the board's ruling is not supported by substantial evidence, it must fairly state and attach copies of all the relevant material evidence.

(3) The petition must be verified.

(4) The petition must be accompanied by proof of service of a copy of the petition on the Secretary of the Workers' Compensation Appeals Board in San Francisco, or two copies if the petition is served in paper form, and one copy on each party who appeared in the action and whose interest is adverse to the petitioner. Service on the board's local district office is not required.

(Subd (a) amended effective January 1, 2018; previously amended effective January 1, 2007, and January 1, 2016.)

(b) Answer and reply

(1) Within 25 days after the petition is filed, the board or any real party in interest may serve and file an answer and any relevant exhibits not included in the petition.

(2) Within 15 days after an answer is filed, the petitioner may serve and file a reply.

(c) Certificate of Interested Entities or Persons

(1) Each party other than the board must comply with the requirements of rule 8.208 concerning serving and filing a Certificate of Interested Entities or Persons.

(2) The petitioner's certificate must be included in the petition and the real party in interest's certificate must be included in the answer. The certificate must appear after the cover and before the tables.

(3) If a party fails to file a certificate as required under (1) and (2), the clerk must notify the party in writing that the party must file the certificate within 10 days after the clerk's notice is sent and that failure to comply will result in one of the following sanctions:

(A) If the party is the petitioner, the court will strike the petition; or

(B) If the party is the real party in interest, the court will strike the document.

(4) If the party fails to comply with the notice under (3), the court may impose the sanctions specified in the notice.

(Subd (c) amended effective January 1, 2016; adopted effective July 1, 2006; previously amended effective January 1, 2007.)

Rule 8.720 renumbered effective April 25, 2019; repealed and adopted as rule 57 effective January 1, 2005; previously amended effective July 1, 2006, January 1, 2016, and January 1, 2018; previously amended and renumbered as rule 8.494 effective January 1, 2007; previously renumbered as rule 8.495 effective January 1, 2009.

Advisory Committee Comment

Subdivision (a). Subdivision (a)(3) specifies that the petition must be served on the Secretary of the Workers' Compensation Appeals Board in San Francisco. Neither the petition nor a courtesy copy should be served on the local district office of the board.

Subdivision (b). To clarify that a respondent may rely on exhibits filed with the petition without duplicating them in the answer, (b)(1) specifies that exhibits filed with an answer must be limited to exhibits "not included in the petition."

Rule 8.724.   Review of Public Utilities Commission cases

(a) Petition

(1) A petition to review an order or decision of the Public Utilities Commission must be verified and must be served on the executive director and general counsel of the commission and any real parties in interest.

(2) A real party in interest is one who was a party of record to the proceeding and took a position adverse to the petitioner.

(b) Answer and reply

(1) Within 35 days after the petition is filed, the commission or any real party in interest may serve and file an answer.

(2) Within 25 days after an answer is filed, the petitioner may serve and file a reply.

(c) Certificate of Interested Entities or Persons

(1) Each party other than the commission must comply with the requirements of rule 8.208 concerning serving and filing a Certificate of Interested Entities or Persons.

(2) The petitioner's certificate must be included in the petition and the real party in interest's certificate must be included in the answer. The certificate must appear after the cover and before the tables.

(3) If a party fails to file a certificate as required under (1) and (2), the clerk must notify the party in writing that the party must file the certificate within 10 days after the clerk's notice is sent and that failure to comply will result in one of the following sanctions:

(A) If the party is the petitioner, the court will strike the petition; or

(B) If the party is the real party in interest, the court will strike the document.

(4) If the party fails to comply with the notice under (3), the court may impose the sanctions specified in the notice.

(Subd (c) amended effective January 1, 2016; adopted effective July 1, 2006; previously amended effective January 1, 2007.)

Rule 8.724 renumbered effective April 25, 2019; repealed and adopted as rule 58 effective January 1, 2005; previously amended effective July 1, 2006, and January 1, 2016; previously amended and renumbered as rule 8.496 effective January 1, 2007.

Advisory Committee Comment

Subdivision (b). A party other than the petitioner who files an answer may be required to pay a filing fee under Government Code section 68926 if the answer is the first document filed in the writ proceeding in the reviewing court by that party. See rule 8.25(c).

Rule 8.728. Review of Agricultural Labor Relations Board and Public Employment Relations Board cases

(a) Petition

(1) A petition to review an order or decision of the Agricultural Labor Relations Board or the Public Employment Relations Board must be filed in the Court of Appeal and served on the executive secretary of the Agricultural Labor Relations Board or the general counsel of the Public Employment Relations Board in Sacramento and on any real parties in interest.

(2) A real party in interest is a party of record to the proceeding.

(3) The petition must be verified.

(b) Record

Within the time permitted by statute, the board must file the certified record of the proceedings and simultaneously file and serve on all parties an index to that record.

(c) Briefs

(1) The petitioner must serve and file its brief within 35 days after the index is filed.

(2) Within 35 days after the petitioner's brief is filed, the board must—and any real party in interest may—serve and file a respondent's brief.

(3) Within 25 days after the respondent's brief is filed, the petitioner may serve and file a reply brief.

(d) Certificate of Interested Entities or Persons

(1) Each party other than the board must comply with the requirements of rule 8.208 concerning serving and filing a Certificate of Interested Entities or Persons.

(2) The petitioner's certificate must be included in the petition and the real party in interest's certificate must be included in the answer. The certificate must appear after the cover and before the tables.

(3) If a party fails to file a certificate as required under (1) and (2), the clerk must notify the party in writing that the party must file the certificate within 10 days after the clerk's notice is sent and that failure to comply will result in one of the following sanctions:

(A) If the party is the petitioner, the court will strike the petition; or

(B) If the party is the real party in interest, the court will strike the document.

(4) If the party fails to comply with the notice under (3), the court may impose the sanctions specified in the notice.

(Subd (d) amended effective January 1, 2016; adopted effective July 1, 2006; previously amended effective January 1, 2007.)

Rule 8.728 renumbered effective April 25, 2019; repealed and adopted as rule 59 effective January 1, 2005; previously amended effective July 1, 2006, and January 1, 2016; previously amended and renumbered as rule 8.498 effective January 1, 2007.

Advisory Committee Comment

A party other than the petitioner who files an answer or brief may be required to pay a filing fee under Government Code section 68926 if the answer or brief is the first document filed in the writ proceeding in the reviewing court by that party. See rule 8.25(c).

Rule 8.730. Filing, modification, and finality of decision; remittitur

(a) Filing of decisions

Rule 8.264(a) governs the filing of decisions in writ proceedings under this chapter in the Court of Appeal and rule 8.532(a) governs the filing of decisions in the Supreme Court.

(Subd (a) adopted effective January 1, 2011.)

(b) Modification of decisions

Rule 8.264(c) governs the modification of decisions in writ proceedings under this chapter.

(Subd (b) adopted effective January 1, 2011.)

(c) Finality of decision

(1) A court's denial of a petition for a writ under rule 8.495, 8.496, or 8.498 without issuance of a writ of review is final in that court when filed.

(2) Except as otherwise provided in this rule, a decision in a writ proceeding under this chapter is final in that court 30 days after the decision is filed.

(3) If necessary to prevent mootness or frustration of the relief granted or to otherwise promote the interests of justice, the court may order early finality in that court of a decision granting a petition for a writ under this chapter or, except as provided in (1), a decision denying such a petition. The decision may provide for finality in that court on filing or within a stated period of less than 30 days.

(4) If a Court of Appeal certifies its opinion for publication or partial publication after filing its decision and before its decision becomes final in that court, the finality period runs from the filing date of the order for publication.

(5) If an order modifying an opinion changes the appellate judgment, the finality period runs from the filing date of the modification order.

(Subd (c) amended effective July 1, 2012; adopted effective January 1, 2011.)

(d) Remittitur

A Court of Appeal must issue a remittitur in a writ proceeding under this chapter except when the court denies the petition under rule 8.495, 8.496, or 8.498 without issuing a writ of review. Rule 8.272(b)–(d) governs issuance of a remittitur in writ proceedings under this chapter.

(Subd (d) amended effective July 1, 2012; adopted as unlettered subd effective January 1, 2008; previously lettered and amended effective January 1, 2011.)

Rule 8.730 renumbered effective April 25, 2019; adopted as rule 8.499 effective January 1, 2008; previously amended effective January 1, 2011, and July 1, 2012.

Division 4
Rules Relating to the Superior Court Appellate Division

Title 8, Appellate Rules—Division 4, Rules Relating to the Superior Court Appellate Division renumbered from Division 2 effective April 25, 2019; adopted as Division 2 effective January 1, 2009.

Advisory Committee Comment

Division 4. The rules relating to the superior court appellate division begin with Chapter 1, which contains general rules applicable to appeals in all three types of cases within the jurisdiction of the appellate division—limited civil, misdemeanor, and infraction. Because the procedures relating to taking appeals and preparing the record in limited civil, misdemeanor, and infraction appeals differ, there are separate chapters addressing these topics: Chapter 2 addresses taking appeals and record preparation in limited civil cases, and Chapter 3 addresses taking appeals and record preparation in misdemeanor cases. Because the procedures for briefing and rendering decisions are generally the same in limited civil and misdemeanor appeals, Chapter 4 addresses these procedures in appeals of both types of cases. To make the distinct procedures for appeals in infraction proceedings easier to find and understand, these procedures are located in a separate chapter—Chapter 5. Chapter 6 addresses writ proceedings in the appellate division.

Chap. 1. General Rules Applicable to Appellate Division Proceedings. Rules 8.800–8.819.

Chap. 2. Appeals and Records in Limited Civil Cases. Rules 8.820–8.845.

Chap. 3. Appeals and Records in Misdemeanor Cases. Rules 8.850–8.874.

Chap. 4. Briefs, Hearing, and Decision in Limited Civil and Misdemeanor Appeals. Rules 8.880–8.891.

Chap. 5. Appeals in Infraction Cases. Rules 8.900–8.929.

Chap. 6. Writ Proceedings. Rules 8.930–8.936.

Chapter 1
General Rules Applicable to Appellate Division Proceedings

Chapter 1 adopted effective January 1, 2009.

Rule 8.800. Application of division and scope of rules
Rule 8.802. Construction
Rule 8.803. Definitions
Rule 8.804. Requirements for signatures on documents
Rule 8.805. Amendments to rules and statutes
Rule 8.806. Applications
Rule 8.808. Motions
Rule 8.809. Judicial notice
Rule 8.810. Extending time
Rule 8.811. Policies and factors governing extensions of time
Rule 8.812. Relief from default
Rule 8.813. Shortening time
Rule 8.814. Substituting parties; substituting or withdrawing attorneys
Rule 8.815. Form of filed documents
Rule 8.816. Address and other contact information of record; notice of change
Rule 8.817. Service and filing
Rule 8.818. Waiver of fees and costs
Rule 8.819. Sealed records

Rule 8.800. Application of division and scope of rules

(a) Application

The rules in this division apply to:

(1) Appeals in the appellate division of the superior court; and

(2) Writ proceedings, motions, applications, and petitions in the appellate division of the superior court.

(Subd (a) amended and lettered effective January 1, 2016; adopted as unlettered subdivision.)

(b) Scope of rules

The rules in this division apply to documents filed and served electronically as well as in paper form, unless otherwise provided.

(Subd (b) adopted effective January 1, 2016.)

Rule 8.800 amended effective January 1, 2016; adopted effective January 1, 2009.

Rule 8.802. Construction

(a) Construction

The rules in this division must be construed to ensure that the proceedings they govern will be justly and speedily determined.

(Subd (a) adopted effective January 1, 2009.)

(b) Terminology

As used in this division:

(1) "Must" is mandatory;

(2) "May" is permissive;

(3) "May not" means is not permitted to;

(4) "Will" expresses a future contingency or predicts action by a court or person in the ordinary course of events, but does not signify a mandatory duty; and

(5) "Should" expresses a preference or a nonbinding recommendation.

(Subd (b) adopted effective January 1, 2009.)

(c) Construction of additional terms

In the rules:

(1) Each tense (past, present, or future) includes the others;

(2) Each gender (masculine, feminine, or neuter) includes the others;

(3) Each number (singular or plural) includes the other; and

(4) The headings of divisions, chapters, articles, rules, and subdivisions are substantive.

(Subd (c) adopted effective January 1, 2009.)

Rule 8.802 adopted effective January 1, 2009.

Rule 8.803. Definitions

As used in this division, unless the context or subject matter otherwise requires:

(1) "Action" includes special proceeding.

(2) "Case" includes action or proceeding.

(3) "Civil case" means a case prosecuted by one party against another for the declaration, enforcement, or protection of a right or the redress or prevention of a wrong. Civil cases include all cases except criminal cases.

(4) "Unlimited civil cases" and "limited civil cases" are defined in Code of Civil Procedure section 85 et seq.

(5) "Criminal case" means a proceeding by which a party charged with a public offense is accused and brought to trial and punishment.

(6) "Rule" means a rule of the California Rules of Court.

(7) "Local rule" means every rule, regulation, order, policy, form, or standard of general application adopted by a court to govern practice and procedure in that court or by a judge of the court to govern practice or procedure in that judge's courtroom.

(8) "Presiding judge" includes the acting presiding judge or the judge designated by the presiding judge.

(9) "Judge" includes, as applicable, a judge of the superior court, a commissioner, or a temporary judge.

(10) "Person" includes a corporation or other legal entity as well as a natural person.

(11) "Appellant" means the appealing party.

(12) "Respondent" means the adverse party.

(13) "Party" is a person appearing in an action. Parties include both self-represented persons and persons represented by an attorney of record. "Party," "applicant," "petitioner," or any other designation of a party includes the party's attorney of record.

(14) "Attorney" means a member of the State Bar of California.

(15) "Counsel" means an attorney.

(16) "Prosecuting attorney" means the city attorney, county counsel, or district attorney prosecuting an infraction or misdemeanor case.

(17) "Complaint" includes a citation.

(18) "Service" means service in the manner prescribed by a statute or rule.

(19) "Declaration" includes "affidavit."

(20) "Trial court" means the superior court from which an appeal is taken.

(21) "Reviewing court" means the appellate division of the superior court.

(22) "Judgment" includes any judgment or order that may be appealed.

(23) "Attach" or "attachment" may refer to either physical attachment or electronic attachment, as appropriate.

(24) "Copy" or "copies" may refer to electronic copies, as appropriate.

(25) "Cover" includes the cover page of a document filed electronically.

(26) "Written" and "writing" include electronically created written materials, whether or not those materials are printed on paper.

Rule 8.803 amended and renumbered effective January 1, 2016; adopted as rule 8.804 effective January 1, 2009; previously amended effective January 1, 2014.

Advisory Committee Comment

Item (18). See rule 1.21 for general requirements relating to service, including proof of service.

Rule 8.804. Definitions [Renumbered]

Rule 8.804 renumbered as rule 8.803 effective January 1, 2016.

Another Rule 8.804 follows.

Rule 8.804. Requirements for signatures on documents

Except as otherwise provided, or required by order of the court, signatures on electronically filed documents must comply with the requirements of rule 8.77.

Rule 8.804 adopted effective January 1, 2016.

Rule 8.805. Amendments to rules and statutes

(a) Amendments to rules

Only the Judicial Council may amend these rules, except the rules in division 5, which may be amended only by the Supreme Court. An amendment by the Judicial Council must be published in the advance pamphlets of the Official Reports and takes effect on the date ordered by the Judicial Council.

(Subd (a) adopted effective January 1, 2009.)

(b) Amendments to statutes

In these rules, a reference to a statute includes any subsequent amendment to the statute.

(Subd (b) adopted effective January 1, 2009.)

Rule 8.805 adopted effective January 1, 2009.

Rule 8.806. Applications

(a) Service and filing

Except as these rules provide otherwise, parties must serve and file all applications, including applications to extend time to file records, briefs, or other documents and applications to shorten time. Applications to extend the time to prepare the record on appeal may be filed in either the trial court or the appellate division. All other applications must be filed in the appellate division. For good cause, the presiding judge of the court where the application was filed, or his or her designee, may excuse advance service.

(Subd (a) adopted effective January 1, 2009.)

(b) Contents

The application must:

(1) State facts showing good cause to grant the application; and

(2) Identify any previous applications relating to the same subject filed by any party in the same appeal or writ proceeding.

(Subd (b) adopted effective January 1, 2009.)

(c) Envelopes

If any party or parties in the case are served in paper form, an application must be accompanied by addressed, postage-prepaid envelopes for the clerk's use in mailing copies of the order on the application to those parties.

(Subd (c) amended effective January 1, 2016; adopted effective January 1, 2009.)

(d) Disposition

Unless the court determines otherwise, the presiding judge of the court in which the application was filed, or his or her designee, may rule on the application.

(Subd (d) adopted effective January 1, 2009.)

Rule 8.806 amended effective January 1, 2016; adopted effective January 1, 2009.

Advisory Committee Comment

Subdivision (a). See rule 1.21 for the meaning of "serve and file," including the requirements for proof of service.

Subdivisions (a) and (d). These provisions permit the presiding judge to designate another judge, such as the trial judge, to handle applications.

Rule 8.808.   Motions

(a) Motion and opposition

(1) Except as these rules provide otherwise, to make a motion in the appellate division a party must serve and file a written motion, stating the grounds and the relief requested and identifying any documents on which it is based.

(2) A motion must be accompanied by a memorandum and, if it is based on matters outside the record, by declarations or other supporting evidence.

(3) Any opposition to the motion must be served and filed within 15 days after the motion is filed.

(Subd (a) adopted effective January 1, 2009.)

(b) Disposition

(1) The court may rule on a motion at any time after an opposition or other response is filed or the time to oppose has expired.

(2) On a party's request or its own motion, the appellate division may place a motion on calendar for a hearing. The clerk must promptly send each party a notice of the date and time of the hearing.

(Subd (b) adopted effective January 1, 2009.)

Rule 8.808 adopted effective January 1, 2009.

Advisory Committee Comment

Subdivision (a)(1). See rule 1.21 for the meaning of "serve and file," including the requirements for proof of service.

Subdivision (b). Although a party may request a hearing on a motion, a hearing will be held only if the court determines that one is needed.

Rule 8.809.   Judicial notice

(a) Motion required

(1) To obtain judicial notice by a reviewing court under Evidence Code section 459, a party must serve and file a separate motion with a proposed order.

(2) The motion must state:

(A) Why the matter to be noticed is relevant to the appeal;

(B) Whether the matter to be noticed was presented to the trial court and, if so, whether judicial notice was taken by that court;

(C) If judicial notice of the matter was not taken by the trial court, why the matter is subject to judicial notice under Evidence Code section 451, 452, or 453; and

(D) Whether the matter to be noticed relates to proceedings occurring after the order or judgment that is the subject of the appeal.

(Subd (a) amended effective January 1, 2013; adopted effective January 1, 2011.)

(b) Copy of matter to be judicially noticed

If the matter to be noticed is not in the record, the party must serve and file a copy with the motion or explain why it is not practicable to do so. The pages of the copy of the matter or matters to be judicially noticed must be consecutively numbered, beginning with the number 1.

(Subd (b) amended effective January 1, 2015; adopted effective January 1, 2011.)

Rule 8.809 amended effective January 1, 2015; adopted effective January 1, 2011; previously amended effective January 1, 2013.

Rule 8.810.   Extending time

(a) Computing time

The Code of Civil Procedure governs computing and extending the time to do any act required or permitted under these rules.

(Subd (a) adopted effective January 1, 2009.)

(b) Extension by trial court

(1) For good cause and except as these rules provide otherwise, the presiding judge of the trial court, or his or her designee, may extend the time to do any act to prepare the record on appeal.

(2) The trial court may not extend:

(A) The time to do an act if that time—including any valid extension—has expired; or

(B) The time for a court reporter to prepare a transcript.

(3) Notwithstanding anything in these rules to the contrary, the trial court may grant an initial extension to any party to do any act to prepare the record on appeal on an ex parte basis.

(Subd (b) amended effective March 1, 2014; adopted effective January 1, 2009.)

(c) Extension by appellate division

For good cause and except as these rules provide otherwise, the presiding judge of the appellate division, or his or her designee, may extend the time to do any act required or permitted under these rules, except the time to file a notice of appeal.

(Subd (c) adopted effective January 1, 2009.)

(d) Application for extension

(1) An application to extend time, including an application requesting an extension of time to prepare a transcript from either a court reporter or a person preparing a transcript of an official electronic recording, must be served on all parties. For good cause, the presiding judge of the appellate division, or his or her designee, may excuse advance service.

(2) The application must include a declaration stating facts, not mere conclusions, that establish good cause for granting the extension. For applications filed by counsel or self-represented litigants, the facts provided to establish good cause must be consistent with the policies and factors stated in rule 8.811.

(3) The application must state:

(A) The due date of the document to be filed;

(B) The length of the extension requested; and

(C) Whether any earlier extensions have been granted and, if so, their lengths.

(Subd (d) amended effective March 1, 2014; adopted effective January 1, 2009.)

(e) Notice to party

(1) In a civil case, counsel must deliver to his or her client or clients a copy of any stipulation or application to extend time that counsel files. Counsel must attach evidence of such delivery to the stipulation or application or certify in the stipulation or application that the copy has been delivered.

(2) The evidence or certification of delivery under (1) need not include the address of the party notified.

(Subd (e) adopted effective January 1, 2009.)

Rule 8.810 amended effective March 1, 2014; adopted effective January 1, 2009.

Advisory Committee Comment

Subdivision (b)(1). This provision permits the presiding judge to designate another judge, such as the trial judge, to handle applications to extend time.

Rule 8.811.   Policies and factors governing extensions of time

(a) Policies

(1) The time limits prescribed by these rules should generally be met to ensure expeditious conduct of appellate business and public confidence in the efficient administration of appellate justice.

(2) The effective assistance of counsel to which a party is entitled includes adequate time for counsel to prepare briefs or other documents that fully advance the party's interests. Adequate time also allows the preparation of accurate, clear, concise, and complete submissions that assist the courts.

(3) For a variety of legitimate reasons, counsel or self-represented litigants may not always be able to prepare briefs or other documents within the time specified in the rules of court. To balance the competing policies stated in (1) and (2), applications to extend time in the appellate division must demonstrate good cause under (b). If good cause is shown, the court must extend the time.

(Subd (a) adopted effective January 1, 2009.)

(b) Factors considered

In determining good cause, the court must consider the following factors when applicable:

(1) The degree of prejudice, if any, to any party from a grant or denial of the extension. A party claiming prejudice must support the claim in detail.

(2) In a civil case, the positions of the client and any opponent with regard to the extension.

(3) The length of the record, including the number of relevant trial exhibits. A party relying on this factor must specify the length of the record.

(4) The number and complexity of the issues raised. A party relying on this factor must specify the issues.

(5) Whether there are settlement negotiations and, if so, how far they have progressed and when they might be completed.

(6) Whether the case is entitled to priority.

(7) Whether counsel responsible for preparing the document is new to the case.

(8) Whether other counsel or the client needs additional time to review the document.

(9) Whether counsel or a self-represented party responsible for preparing the document has other time-limited commitments that prevent timely filing of the document. Mere conclusory statements that more time is needed because of other pressing business will not suffice. Good cause requires a specific showing of other obligations of counsel or a self-represented party that:

(A) Have deadlines that as a practical matter preclude filing the document by the due date without impairing its quality; or

(B) Arise from cases entitled to priority.

(10) Illness of counsel or a self-represented party, a personal emergency, or a planned vacation that counsel or a self-represented party did not reasonably expect to conflict with the due date and cannot reasonably rearrange.

(11) Any other factor that constitutes good cause in the context of the case.

(Subd (b) adopted effective January 1, 2009.)
Rule 8.811 adopted effective January 1, 2009.

Rule 8.812. Relief from default

For good cause, the presiding judge of the appellate division, or his or her designee, may relieve a party from a default for any failure to comply with these rules, except the failure to file a timely notice of appeal.
Rule 8.812 adopted effective January 1, 2009.

Rule 8.813. Shortening time

For good cause and except as these rules provide otherwise, the presiding judge of the appellate division, or his or her designee, may shorten the time to do any act required or permitted under these rules.
Rule 8.813 adopted effective January 1, 2009.

Rule 8.814. Substituting parties; substituting or withdrawing attorneys

(a) Substituting parties

Substitution of parties in an appeal or original proceeding must be made by serving and filing a motion in the appellate division. The clerk of the appellate division must notify the trial court of any ruling on the motion.
(Subd (a) adopted effective January 1, 2009.)

(b) Substituting attorneys

A party may substitute attorneys by serving and filing in the appellate division a stipulation signed by the party represented and the new attorney.
(Subd (b) adopted effective January 1, 2009.)

(c) Withdrawing attorney

(1) An attorney may request withdrawal by filing a motion to withdraw. Unless the court orders otherwise, the motion need be served only on the party represented and the attorneys directly affected.

(2) The proof of service need not include the address of the party represented. But if the court grants the motion, the withdrawing attorney must promptly provide the court and the opposing party with the party's current or last known address, e-mail address, and telephone number.

(3) In all appeals and in original proceedings related to a trial court proceeding, the appellate division clerk must notify the trial court of any ruling on the motion.
(Subd (c) amended effective January 1, 2016; adopted effective January 1, 2009.)
Rule 8.814 amended effective January 1, 2016; adopted effective January 1, 2009.

Rule 8.815. Form of filed documents

Except as these rules provide otherwise, documents filed in the appellate division may be either produced on a computer or typewritten and must comply with the relevant provisions of rule 8.883(c).
Rule 8.815 adopted effective January 1, 2020.

Rule 8.816. Address and other contact information of record; notice of change

(a) Address and other contact information of record

(1) Except as provided in (2), the cover—or first page if there is no cover—of every document filed in the appellate division must include the name, mailing address, telephone number, fax number (if available), e-mail address (if available), and California State Bar number of each attorney filing or joining in the document, or of the party if he or she is unrepresented. The inclusion of a fax number or e-mail address on any document does not constitute consent to service by fax or e-mail unless otherwise provided by law.

(2) If more than one attorney from a law firm, corporation, or public law office is representing one party and is joining in the document, the name and State Bar number of each attorney joining in the document must be provided on the cover. The law firm, corporation, or public law office representing each party must designate one attorney to receive notices and other communication in the case from the court by placing an asterisk before that attorney's name on the cover and must provide the contact information specified under (1) for that attorney. Contact information for the other attorneys from the same law firm, corporation, or public law office is not required but may be provided.

(3) In any case pending before the appellate division, the appellate division will use the mailing address, telephone number, fax number, and e-mail address that an attorney or unrepresented party provides on the first document filed in that case as the mailing address, telephone number, fax number, and e-mail address of record unless the attorney or unrepresented party files a notice under (b).
(Subd (a) amended effective January 1, 2013; adopted effective January 1, 2009.)

(b) Notice of change

(1) An attorney or unrepresented party whose mailing address, telephone number, fax number, or e-mail address changes while a case is pending must promptly serve and file a written notice of the change in the appellate division in which the case is pending.

(2) The notice must specify the title and number of the case or cases to which it applies. If an attorney gives the notice, the notice must include the attorney's California State Bar number.
(Subd (b) amended effective January 1, 2013; adopted effective January 1, 2009.)

(c) Multiple addresses or other contact information

If an attorney or unrepresented party has more than one mailing address, telephone number, fax number, or e-mail address, only one mailing address, telephone number, fax number, and e-mail address may be used in a given case.
(Subd (c) repealed, relettered and amended effective January 1, 2013; adopted as subd (d) effective January 1, 2009.)
Rule 8.816 amended effective January 1, 2013; adopted effective January 1, 2009.

Rule 8.817. Service and filing

(a) Service

(1) Before filing any document, a party must serve, by any method permitted by the Code of Civil Procedure, one copy of the document on the attorney for each party separately represented, on each unrepresented party, and on any other person or entity when required by statute or rule.

(2) The party must attach to the document presented for filing a proof of service showing service on each person or entity required to be served under (1). The proof must name each party represented by each attorney served.
(Subd (a) adopted effective January 1, 2009.)

(b) Filing

(1) A document is deemed filed on the date the clerk receives it.

(2) Unless otherwise provided by these rules or other law, a filing is not timely unless the clerk receives the document before the time to file it expires.

(3) A brief, a petition for rehearing, or an answer to a petition for rehearing is timely if the time to file it has not expired on the date of:

(A) Its mailing by priority or express mail as shown on the postmark or the postal receipt; or

(B) Its delivery to a common carrier promising overnight delivery as shown on the carrier's receipt.

(4) The provisions of (3) do not apply to original proceedings.

(5) If the clerk receives a document by mail from an inmate or a patient in a custodial institution after the period for filing the document has expired but the envelope shows that the document was mailed or delivered to custodial officials for mailing within the period for filing the document, the document is deemed timely. The clerk must retain in the case file the envelope in which the document was received.
(Subd (b) amended effective July 1, 2010; adopted effective January 1, 2009.)
Rule 8.817 amended effective July 1, 2010; adopted effective January 1, 2009.

Advisory Committee Comment

Subdivision (a). Subdivision (a)(1) requires service "by any method permitted by the Code of Civil Procedure." The reference is to the several permissible methods of service provided in Code of Civil Procedure sections 1010–1020. *What Is Proof of Service?* (form APP-109-INFO) provides additional information about how to serve documents and how to provide proof of service.

Subdivision (b). In general, to be filed on time, a document must be received by the clerk before the time for filing that document expires. There are, however, some limited exceptions to this general rule. For example, (5) provides that if the superior court clerk receives a document by mail from a custodial institution after the deadline for filing the document has expired but the envelope shows that the document was mailed or delivered to custodial officials for mailing before the deadline expired, the document is deemed timely. This provision reflects the "prison-delivery" exception articulated by the California Supreme Court in *In re Jordan* (1992) 4 Cal.4th 116 and *Silverbrand v. County of Los Angeles* (2009) 46 Cal.4th 106.

Note that if a deadline runs from the date of filing, it runs from the date that the document is actually received and deemed filed under (b)(1); neither (b)(3) nor (b)(5) changes that date. Nor do these provisions extend the date of finality of an appellate opinion or any other deadline that is based on finality, such as the deadline for the court to modify its opinion or order rehearing. Subdivision (b)(5) is also not intended to limit a criminal defendant's appeal rights under the case law of constructive filing. (See, e.g., *In re Benoit* (1973) 10 Cal.3d 72.)

Rule 8.818.   Waiver of fees and costs

(a) Applications for waiver of fees and costs

(1) *Appeals*

(A) If the trial court previously issued an order granting a party's request to waive court fees and costs in a case, and that fee waiver is still in effect, all of the court fees for an appeal to the appellate division in that case that are listed in (d) are waived by that order, and the party is not required to file a new application for waiver of court fees and costs for an appeal to the appellate division in that case.

(B) If the trial court did not previously issue an order granting a party's request to waive court fees and costs in a case or an order that was previously issued is no longer in effect, an application for initial waiver of court fees and costs for an appeal must be made on *Request to Waive Court Fees* (form FW-001). The appellant should file the application with the notice of appeal in the trial court that issued the judgment or order being appealed. The respondent should file any application at the time the fees are to be paid to the court.

(2) *Writ Proceedings*

To request the waiver of fees and costs in a writ proceeding, the petitioner must complete *Request to Waive Court Fees* (form FW-001). The petitioner should file the application with the writ petition.

(3) *Forms*

The clerk must provide *Request to Waive Court Fees* (form FW-001) and *Information Sheet on Waiver of Fees and Costs (Supreme Court, Court of Appeal, Appellate Division)* (form APP-015/FW-015-INFO) without charge to any person who requests any fee waiver application or states that he or she is unable to pay any court fee or cost.

(Subd (a) adopted effective July 1, 2009.)

(b) Procedure for determining application

The application must be considered and determined as required by Government Code section 68634.5. An order determining the application for initial fee waiver or setting a hearing on the application may be made on *Order on Court Fee Waiver (Superior Court)* (form FW-003).

(Subd (b) adopted effective July 1, 2009.)

(c) Application granted unless acted on by the court

The application for initial fee waiver is deemed granted unless the court gives notice of action on the application within five court days after the application is filed.

(Subd (c) adopted effective July 1, 2009.)

(d) Court fees and costs waived

Court fees and costs that must be waived upon granting an application for initial waiver of court fees and costs are listed in rule 3.55. The court may waive other necessary court fees and costs itemized in the application upon granting the application, either at the outset or upon later application.

(Subd (d) amended effective July 1, 2015; adopted effective July 1, 2009.)

(e) Denial of the application

If an application is denied, the applicant must pay the court fees and costs or submit the new application or additional information requested by the court within 10 days after the clerk gives notice of the denial.

(Subd (e) adopted effective July 1, 2009.)

(f) Confidential Records

(1) No person may have access to an application for an initial fee waiver submitted to the court except the court and authorized court personnel, any person authorized by the applicant, and any persons authorized by order of the court. No person may reveal any information contained in the application except as authorized by law or order of the court. An order granting access to an application or financial information may include limitations on who may access the information and on the use of the information after it has been released.

(2) Any person seeking access to an application or financial information provided to the court by an applicant must make the request by motion, supported by a declaration showing good cause as to why the confidential information should be released.

(Subd (f) adopted effective July 1, 2009.)

Rule 8.818 amended effective July 1, 2015; adopted effective July 1, 2009.

Advisory Committee Comment

Subdivision (a)(1)(B). The waiver of court fees and costs is called an "initial" waiver because, under Government Code section 68630 and following, any such waiver may later be modified, ended, or retroactively withdrawn if the court determines that the applicant was not or is no longer eligible for a waiver. The court may, at a later time, order that the previously waived fees be paid.

Rule 8.819.   Sealed records

Rule 8.46 governs records sealed by court order under rules 2.550–2.551 and records proposed to be sealed in the appellate division.

Rule 8.819 adopted effective January 1, 2010.

Chapter 2
Appeals and Records in Limited Civil Cases

Chapter 2 adopted effective January 1, 2009.

Article 1
Taking Civil Appeals

Article 1 adopted effective January 1, 2009.

Rule 8.820.   Application of chapter

The rules in this chapter apply to appeals in limited civil cases, except small claims cases.

Rule 8.820 adopted effective January 1, 2009.

Advisory Committee Comment

Chapters 1 and 4 of this division also apply in appeals in limited civil cases.

Rule 8.821.   Notice of appeal

(a) Notice of appeal

(1) To appeal from a judgment or appealable order in a limited civil case, except a small claims case, an appellant must serve and file a notice of appeal in the superior court that issued the judgment or order being appealed. The appellant or the appellant's attorney must sign the notice.

(2) The notice of appeal must be liberally construed and is sufficient if it identifies the particular limited civil case judgment or order being appealed.

(3) Failure to serve the notice of appeal neither prevents its filing nor affects its validity, but the appellant may be required to remedy the failure.

(Subd (a) adopted effective January 1, 2009.)

(b) Filing fee

(1) Unless otherwise provided by law, the notice of appeal must be accompanied by the filing fee required under Government Code sections 70621 and 70602.5, an application for a waiver of court fees and costs on appeal under rule 8.818, or an order granting an application for a waiver of court fees and costs. The filing fee is nonrefundable.

(2) The clerk must file the notice of appeal even if the appellant does not present the filing fee or an application for, or order granting, a waiver of court fees and costs.

(Subd (b) amended effective January 1, 2013; adopted effective January 1, 2009; previously amended effective July 1, 2009.)

(c) Failure to pay filing fee

(1) The clerk must promptly notify the appellant in writing if:

(A) The court receives a notice of appeal without the filing fee required by (b) or an application for, or order granting, a waiver of court fees and costs;

(B) A check for the filing fee is dishonored; or

(C) An application for a waiver under rule 8.818 is denied.

(2) A clerk's notice under (1)(A) or (B) must state that the court may dismiss the appeal unless, within 15 days after the notice is sent, the appellant either:

(A) Pays the fee; or

(B) Files an application for a waiver under rule 8.818 if the appellant has not previously filed such an application or an order granting such an application.

(3) If the appellant fails to take the action specified in the notice given under (2), the appellate division may dismiss the appeal, but may vacate the dismissal for good cause.

(Subd (c) amended effective July 1, 2009; adopted effective January 1, 2009.)

(d) Notification of the appeal

(1) When the notice of appeal is filed, the trial court clerk must promptly send a notification of the filing of the notice of appeal to the attorney of record for each party and to any unrepresented party. The clerk must also send or deliver this notification to the appellate division clerk.

(2) The notification must show the date it was sent and must state the number and title of the case and the date the notice of appeal was filed.

(3) A copy of the notice of appeal is sufficient notification under (1) if the required information is on the copy or is added by the trial court clerk.

(4) The sending of a notification under (1) is a sufficient performance of the clerk's duty despite the death of the party or the discharge, disqualification, suspension, disbarment, or death of the attorney.

(5) Failure to comply with any provision of this subdivision does not affect the validity of the notice of appeal.

(Subd (d) amended effective January 1, 2016; adopted effective January 1, 2009.)

(e) Notice of cross-appeal

As used in this rule, "notice of appeal" includes a notice of cross-appeal and "appellant" includes a respondent filing a notice of cross-appeal.

(Subd (e) adopted effective January 1, 2009.)

Rule 8.821 amended effective January 1, 2016; adopted effective January 1, 2009; previously amended effective July 1, 2009, and January 1, 2013.

Advisory Committee Comment

Subdivision (a). *Notice of Appeal/Cross-Appeal (Limited Civil Case)* (form APP-102) may be used to file the notice of appeal required under this rule. This form is available at any courthouse or county law library or online at *www.courts.ca.gov/forms.htm.*

Subdivision (b). For information about the amount of the filing fee, see the current Statewide Civil Fee Schedule linked at *www.courts.ca.gov/7646.htm* (note that the "Appeal and Writ Related Fees" section appears near the end of the schedule and that there are different fees for limited civil cases depending on the amount demanded in the case.)

Subdivision (c)(2). This subdivision addresses the content of a clerk's notice that a check for the filing fee has been dishonored or that the reviewing court has received a notice of appeal without the filing fee, a certificate of cash payment, or an application for, or order granting, a fee waiver. Rule 8.818(e) addresses what an appellant must do when a fee waiver application is denied.

Rule 8.822. Time to appeal

(a) Normal time

(1) Unless a statute or rule 8.823 provides otherwise, a notice of appeal must be filed on or before the earliest of:

(A) 30 days after the trial court clerk serves the party filing the notice of appeal a document entitled "Notice of Entry" of judgment or a filed-endorsed copy of the judgment, showing the date it was served;

(B) 30 days after the party filing the notice of appeal serves or is served by a party with a document entitled "Notice of Entry" of judgment or a filed-endorsed copy of the judgment, accompanied by proof of service; or

(C) 90 days after the entry of judgment.

(2) Service under (1)(A) and (B) may be by any method permitted by the Code of Civil Procedure, including electronic service when permitted under Code of Civil Procedure section 1010.6 and rules 2.250–2.261.

(3) If the parties stipulated in the trial court under Code of Civil Procedure section 1019.5 to waive notice of the court order being appealed, the time to appeal under (1)(C) applies unless the court or a party serves notice of entry of judgment or a filed-endorsed copy of the judgment to start the time period under (1)(A) or (B).

(Subd (a) amended effective January 1, 2016; adopted effective January 1, 2009; previously amended effective January 1, 2011, July 1, 2012, and March 1, 2014.)

(b) What constitutes entry

For purposes of this rule:

(1) The entry date of a judgment is the date the judgment is filed under Code of Civil Procedure section 668.5 or the date it is entered in the judgment book.

(2) The date of entry of an appealable order that is entered in the minutes is the date it is entered in the permanent minutes. But if the minute order directs that a written order be prepared, the entry date is the date the signed order is filed; a written order prepared under rule 3.1312 or similar local rule is not such an order prepared by direction of a minute order.

(3) The entry date of an order that is not entered in the minutes is the date the signed order is filed.

(Subd (b) adopted effective January 1, 2009.)

(c) Premature notice of appeal

(1) A notice of appeal filed after judgment is rendered but before it is entered is valid and is treated as filed immediately after entry of judgment.

(2) The appellate division may treat a notice of appeal filed after the trial court has announced its intended ruling, but before it has rendered judgment, as filed immediately after entry of judgment.

(Subd (c) adopted effective January 1, 2009.)

(d) Late notice of appeal

If a notice of appeal is filed late, the appellate division must dismiss the appeal.

(Subd (d) adopted effective January 1, 2009.)

Rule 8.822 amended effective January 1, 2016; adopted effective January 1, 2009; previously amended effective January 1, 2011, July 1, 2012, and March 1, 2014.

Advisory Committee Comment

Under rule 8.804(23), the term "judgment" includes any order that may be appealed.

Subdivision (d). See rule 8.817(b)(5) for provisions concerning the timeliness of documents mailed by inmates or patients from custodial institutions.

Rule 8.823. Extending the time to appeal

(a) Extension of time

This rule operates only to increase the time to appeal otherwise prescribed in rule 8.822(a); it does not shorten the time to appeal. If the normal time to appeal stated in rule 8.822(a) would be longer than the time provided in this rule, the time to appeal stated in rule 8.822(a) governs.

(Subd (a) adopted effective January 1, 2009.)

(b) Motion for a new trial

If any party serves and files a valid notice of intention to move for a new trial, the following extensions of time apply:

(1) If the motion is denied, the time to appeal from the judgment is extended for all parties until the earliest of:

(A) 15 days after the trial court clerk or a party serves an order denying the motion or a notice of entry of that order;

(B) 15 days after denial of the motion by operation of law; or

(C) 90 days after entry of judgment; or

(2) If the trial court makes a finding of excessive or inadequate damages and grants the motion for a new trial subject to the condition that the motion is denied if a party consents to the additur or remittitur of damages:

(A) If a party serves an acceptance of the additur or remittitur within the time for accepting the additur or remittitur, the time to appeal from the judgment is extended for all parties until 15 days after the date the party serves the acceptance.

(B) If a party serves a rejection of the additur or remittitur within the time for accepting the additur or remittitur or if the time for accepting the additur or remittitur expires, the time to appeal from the new trial order is extended for all parties until the earliest of 30 days after the date the party serves the rejection or 30 days after the date on which the time for accepting the additur or remittitur expired.

(Subd (b) amended effective March 1, 2014; adopted effective January 1, 2009; previously amended effective July 1, 2012.)

(c) Motion to vacate judgment

If, within the time prescribed by rule 8.822 to appeal from the judgment, any party serves and files a valid notice of intention to move to vacate the judgment or a valid motion to vacate the judgment, the time to appeal from the judgment is extended for all parties until the earliest of:

(1) 15 days after the trial court clerk or a party serves an order denying the motion or a notice of entry of that order;

(2) 45 days after the first notice of intention to move or motion is filed; or

(3) 90 days after entry of judgment.

(Subd (c) amended effective March 1, 2014; adopted effective January 1, 2009.)

(d) Motion for judgment notwithstanding the verdict

(1) If any party serves and files a valid motion for judgment notwithstanding the verdict and the motion is denied, the time to appeal from the judgment is extended for all parties until the earliest of:

(A) 15 days after the trial court clerk or a party serves an order denying the motion or a notice of entry of that order;

(B) 15 days after denial of the motion by operation of law; or

(C) 90 days after entry of judgment.

(2) Unless extended by (e)(2), the time to appeal from an order denying a motion for judgment notwithstanding the verdict is governed by rule 8.822.

(Subd (d) amended effective March 1, 2014; adopted effective January 1, 2009.)

(e) Motion to reconsider appealable order

If any party serves and files a valid motion to reconsider an appealable order under Code of Civil Procedure section 1008(a), the time to appeal from that order is extended for all parties until the earliest of:

(1) 15 days after the superior court clerk or a party serves an order denying the motion or a notice of entry of that order;

(2) 45 days after the first motion to reconsider is filed; or

(3) 90 days after entry of the appealable order.

(Subd (e) amended effective March 1, 2014; adopted effective January 1, 2009.)

(f) Public entity actions under Government Code section 962, 984, or 985

If a public entity defendant serves and files a valid request for a mandatory settlement conference on methods of satisfying a judgment under Government Code section 962, an election to pay a judgment in periodic payments under Government Code section 984 and rule 3.1804, or a motion for a posttrial hearing on reducing a judgment under Government Code section 985, the time to appeal from the judgment is extended for all parties until the earliest of:

(1) 60 days after the superior court clerk serves the party filing the notice of appeal with a document entitled "Notice of Entry" of judgment or a filed-endorsed copy of the judgment, showing the date either was served;

(2) 60 days after the party filing the notice of appeal serves or is served by a party with a document entitled "Notice of Entry" of judgment or a filed-endorsed copy of the judgment, accompanied by proof of service; or

(3) 90 days after entry of judgment.

(Subd (f) amended effective January 1, 2016; adopted effective January 1, 2011.)

(g) Cross-appeal

(1) If an appellant timely appeals from a judgment or appealable order, the time for any other party to appeal from the same judgment or order is extended until 10 days after the trial court clerk serves notification of the first appeal.

(2) If an appellant timely appeals from an order granting a motion for a new trial, an order granting—within 75 days after entry of judgment—a motion to vacate the judgment, or a judgment notwithstanding the verdict, the time for any other party to appeal from the original judgment or from an order denying a motion for judgment notwithstanding the verdict is extended until 10 days after the clerk serves notification of the first appeal.

(Subd (g) amended effective March 1, 2014; adopted as subd (f) effective January 1, 2009; previously relettered as subd (g) effective January 1, 2011.)

(h) Proof of service

Service under this rule may be by any method permitted by the Code of Civil Procedure, including electronic service when permitted under Code of Civil Procedure section 1010.6 and rules 2.250–2.261. An order or notice that is served must be accompanied by proof of service.

(Subd (h) amended effective March 1, 2014; adopted as subd (g) effective January 1, 2009; previously amended and relettered as subd (h) effective January 1, 2011.)

Rule 8.823 amended effective January 1, 2016; adopted effective January 1, 2009; previously amended effective January 1, 2011, July 1, 2012, and March 1, 2014.

Rule 8.824. Writ of supersedeas

(a) Petition

(1) A party seeking a stay of the enforcement of a judgment or order pending appeal may serve and file a petition for writ of supersedeas in the appellate division.

(2) The petition must bear the same title as the appeal.

(3) The petition must explain the necessity for the writ and include a memorandum.

(4) If the record has not been filed in the reviewing court:

(A) The petition must include a statement of the case sufficient to show that the petitioner will raise substantial issues on appeal, including a fair summary of the material facts and the issues that are likely to be raised on appeal.

(B) The petitioner must file the following documents with the petition:

(i) The judgment or order, showing its date of entry;

(ii) The notice of appeal, showing its date of filing;

(iii) A reporter's transcript of any oral statement by the court supporting its rulings related to the issues that are likely to be raised on appeal, or, if a transcript is unavailable, a declaration fairly summarizing any such statements;

(iv) Any application for a stay filed in the trial court, any opposition to that application, and a reporter's transcript of the oral proceedings concerning the stay or, if a transcript is unavailable, a declaration fairly summarizing the proceedings, including the parties' arguments and any statement by the court supporting its ruling; and

(v) Any other document from the trial court proceeding that is necessary for proper consideration of the petition.

(C) The documents listed in (B) must comply with the following requirements:

(i) If filed in paper form, they must be bound together at the end of the petition or in separate volumes not exceeding 300 pages each. The pages must be consecutively numbered;

(ii) If filed in paper form, they must be index-tabbed by number or letter; and

(iii) They must begin with a table of contents listing each document by its title and its index number or letter.

(5) The petition must be verified.

(Subd (a) amended effective January 1, 2016; adopted effective January 1, 2009; previously amended effective January 1, 2010.)

(b) Opposition

(1) Unless otherwise ordered, any opposition must be served and filed within 15 days after the petition is filed.

(2) An opposition must state any material facts not included in the petition and include a memorandum.

(3) The court may not issue a writ of supersedeas until the respondent has had the opportunity to file an opposition.

(Subd (b) adopted effective January 1, 2009.)

(c) Temporary stay

(1) The petition may include a request for a temporary stay pending the ruling on the petition.

(2) A separately filed request for a temporary stay must be served on the respondent. For good cause, the presiding judge may excuse advance service.

(Subd (c) adopted effective January 1, 2009.)

(d) Issuing the writ

(1) The court may issue the writ on any conditions it deems just.

(2) The court must notify the trial court, under rule 8.904, of any writ or stay that it issues.

(Subd (d) adopted effective January 1, 2009.)

Rule 8.824 amended effective January 1, 2016; adopted effective January 1, 2009; previously amended effective January 1, 2010.

Advisory Committee Comment

Subdivision (a). If the preparation of a reporter's transcript has not yet been completed at that time a petition for a writ of supersedeas is filed, that transcript is "unavailable" within the meaning of (a)(4)(B).

Rule 8.825. Abandonment, voluntary dismissal, and compromise

(a) Notice of settlement

(1) If a civil case settles after a notice of appeal has been filed, either as a whole or as to any party, the appellant who has settled must immediately serve and file a notice of settlement in the appellate division. If the parties have designated a clerk's or a reporter's transcript and the record has not been filed in the appellate division, the appellant must also immediately serve a copy of the notice on the trial court clerk.

(2) If the case settles after the appellant receives a notice setting oral argument, the appellant must also immediately notify the appellate division of the settlement by telephone or other expeditious method.

(3) Within 45 days after filing a notice of settlement—unless the court has ordered a longer time period on a showing of good cause—the appellant who filed the notice of settlement must file an abandonment under (b).

(4) If the appellant does not file an abandonment or a letter stating good cause why the appeal should not be dismissed within the time period

specified under (3), the court may dismiss the appeal as to that appellant and order each side to bear its own costs on appeal.

(5) Subdivision (a) does not apply to settlements requiring findings to be made by the Court of Appeal under Code of Civil Procedure section 128(a)(8).

(Subd (a) adopted effective January 1, 2009.)

(b) Abandonment

(1) The appellant may serve and file an abandonment of the appeal or a stipulation to abandon the appeal in the appellate division.

(2) If the record has not been filed in the appellate division, the filing of an abandonment effects a dismissal of the appeal and restores the trial court's jurisdiction. If the record has been filed in the appellate division, the appellate division may dismiss the appeal and direct immediate issuance of the remittitur.

(3) The clerk must promptly notify the adverse party of an abandonment. If the record has not been filed in the appellate division, the clerk must also immediately notify the trial court.

(4) If the appeal is abandoned before the clerk has completed preparation of the transcript, the clerk must refund any portion of a deposit exceeding the preparation cost actually incurred.

(5) If the appeal is abandoned before the reporter has filed the transcript, the reporter must inform the trial court clerk of the cost of the portion of the transcript that the reporter has completed. The clerk must pay that amount to the reporter from the appellant's deposited funds and refund any excess deposit.

(Subd (b) adopted effective January 1, 2009.)

(c) Approval of compromise

If a guardian or conservator seeks approval of a proposed compromise of a pending appeal, the appellate division may, before ruling on the compromise, direct the trial court to determine whether the compromise is in the minor's or the conservatee's best interest and to report its findings.

(Subd (c) adopted effective January 1, 2009.)

Rule 8.825 adopted effective January 1, 2009.

Advisory Committee Comment

Abandonment of Appeal (Limited Civil Case) (form APP-107) may be used to file an abandonment under this rule. This form is available at any courthouse or county law library or online at *www.courts.ca.gov/forms.*

Article 2
Record in Civil Appeals

Article 2 adopted effective January 1, 2009.

Rule 8.830. Record on appeal
Rule 8.831. Notice designating the record on appeal
Rule 8.832. Clerk's transcript
Rule 8.833. Trial court file instead of clerk's transcript
Rule 8.834. Reporter's transcript
Rule 8.835. Record when trial proceedings were officially electronically recorded
Rule 8.836. Agreed statement
Rule 8.837. Statement on appeal
Rule 8.838. Form of the record
Rule 8.839. Record in multiple appeals
Rule 8.840. Completion and filing of the record
Rule 8.841. Augmenting and correcting the record in the appellate division
Rule 8.842. Failure to procure the record
Rule 8.843. Transmitting exhibits
Rule 8.845. Appendixes

Rule 8.830. Record on appeal

(a) Normal record

Except as otherwise provided in this chapter, the record on an appeal to the appellate division in a civil case must contain the following, which constitute the normal record on appeal:

(1) A record of the written documents from the trial court proceedings in the form of one of the following:

(A) A clerk's transcript under rule 8.832;

(B) **An appendix under rule 8.845;**

(C) If the court has a local rule for the appellate division electing to use this form of the record, the original trial court file under rule 8.833; or

[1] **(D)** An agreed statement under rule 8.836.

(2) If an appellant wants to raise any issue that requires consideration of the oral proceedings in the trial court, the record on appeal must include a record of these oral proceedings in the form of one of the following:

(A) A reporter's transcript under rule 8.834 or a transcript prepared from an official electronic recording under rule 8.835;

(B) If the court has a local rule for the appellate division permitting this form of the record, an official electronic recording of the proceedings under rule 8.835;

(C) An agreed statement under rule 8.836; or

(D) A statement on appeal under rule 8.837.

(Subd (a) amended effective January 1, 2021; adopted effective January 1, 2009.)

Rule 8.830(a). 2020 Deletes. [1] (C)

(b) Presumption from the record

The appellate division will presume that the record in an appeal includes all matters material to deciding the issues raised. If the appeal proceeds without a reporter's transcript, this presumption applies only if the claimed error appears on the face of the record.

(Subd (b) adopted effective January 1, 2009.)

Rule 8.830 amended effective January 1, 2021; adopted effective January 1, 2009.

Advisory Committee Comment

Subdivision (a). The options of using the original trial court file instead of a clerk's transcript under (1)(C) or an electronic recording itself, rather than a transcript, under (2)(B) are available only if the court has local rules for the appellate division authorizing these options.

Rule 8.831. Notice designating the record on appeal

(a) Time to file

Within 10 days after filing the notice of appeal, an appellant must serve and file a notice in the trial court designating the record on appeal. The appellant may combine its notice designating the record with its notice of appeal.

(Subd (a) adopted effective January 1, 2009.)

(b) Contents

The notice must specify:

(1) The date the notice of appeal was filed;

(2) Which form of the record of the written documents from the trial court proceedings listed in rule 8.830(a)(1) the appellant elects to use. If the appellant elects to use a clerk's transcript, the notice must also:

(A) Provide the filing date of each document that is required to be included in the clerk's transcript under 8.832(a)(1) or, if the filing date is not available, the date it was signed; and

(B) Designate, as provided under 8.832(b), any documents in addition to those required under 8.832(a)(1) that the appellant wants included in the clerk's transcript;

(3) Whether the appellant elects to proceed with or without a record of the oral proceedings in the trial court;

(4) If the appellant elects to proceed with a record of the oral proceedings in the trial court, the notice must specify which form of the record listed in rule 8.830(a)(2) the appellant elects to use;

(5) If the appellant elects to use a reporter's transcript, the notice must designate the proceedings to be included in the transcript as required under rule 8.834;

(6) If the appellant elects to use an official electronic recording, the appellant must attach a copy of the stipulation required under rule 8.835(c); and

(7) If the appellant elects to use an agreed statement, the appellant must attach to the notice either the agreed statement or stipulation as required under rule 8.836(c)(1).

(Subd (b) adopted effective January 1, 2009.)

Rule 8.831 adopted effective January 1, 2009.

Advisory Committee Comment

Appellant's Notice Designating Record on Appeal (Limited Civil Case) (form APP-103) may be used to file the designation required under this rule. This form is available at any courthouse or county law library or online at *www.courts.ca.gov/forms.* To assist parties in making appropriate choices, courts are encouraged to include information about whether the proceedings were recorded by a court reporter or officially electronically recorded in any information that the court provides to parties concerning their appellate rights.

If the appellant designates a clerk's transcript or reporter's transcript under this rule, the respondent will have an opportunity to designate additional documents to be included in the clerk's transcript under rule 8.832(b)(2) or additional proceedings to be included in the reporter's transcript under rule 8.834(a)(3).

Rule 8.832. Clerk's transcript

(a) Contents of clerk's transcript

(1) The clerk's transcript must contain:

(A) The notice of appeal;

(B) Any judgment appealed from and any notice of its entry;

(C) Any order appealed from and any notice of its entry;

(D) Any notice of intention to move for a new trial or motion to vacate the judgment, for judgment notwithstanding the verdict, or for reconsideration of an appealed order, and any order on such motion and any notice of its entry;

(E) The notice designating the record on appeal; and

(F) The register of actions, if any.

(2) Each document listed in (1)(A), (B), (C), and (D) must show the date necessary to determine the timeliness of the appeal under rule 8.822 or 8.823.

(3) If designated by any party, the clerk's transcript must also contain:

(A) Any other document filed or lodged in the case in the trial court;

(B) Any exhibit admitted in evidence, refused, or lodged; and

(C) Any jury instructions that any party submitted in writing, the cover page required by rule 2.1055(b)(2), and any written jury instructions given by the court.

(Subd (a) amended effective January 1, 2011; adopted effective January 1, 2009.)

(b) Notice of designation

(1) Within 10 days after the appellant serves a notice under rule 8.831 indicating that the appellant elects to use a clerk's transcript, the respondent may serve and file a notice in the trial court designating any additional documents the respondent wants included in the clerk's transcript.

(2) A notice designating documents to be included in a clerk's transcript must identify each designated document by its title and filing date or, if the filing date is not available, the date it was signed. A notice designating documents in addition to those listed in (a)(1) may specify portions of designated documents that are not to be included in the clerk's transcript. For minute orders or jury instructions, it is sufficient to collectively designate all minute orders or all minute orders entered between specified dates, or all written instructions given, refused, or withdrawn.

(3) All exhibits admitted in evidence, refused, or lodged are deemed part of the record, but a party wanting an exhibit included in the transcript must specify that exhibit by number or letter in its designation. If the trial court has returned a designated exhibit to a party, the party in possession of the exhibit must deliver it to the trial court clerk within 10 days after the notice designating the exhibit is served.

(Subd (b) amended effective January 1, 2010; adopted effective January 1, 2009.)

(c) Deposit for cost of clerk's transcript

(1) Within 30 days after the respondent files a designation under (b)(1) or the time to file it expires, whichever first occurs, the trial court clerk must send:

(A) To the appellant, notice of the estimated cost to prepare an original and one copy of the clerk's transcript; and

(B) To each party other than the appellant, notice of the estimated cost to prepare a copy of the clerk's transcript for that party's use.

(2) A notice under (1) must show the date it was sent.

(3) Unless otherwise provided by law, within 10 days after the clerk sends a notice under (1), the appellant and any party wanting to purchase a copy of the clerk's transcript must either deposit the estimated cost specified in the notice under (1) with the clerk or submit an application for a waiver of the cost under rule 8.818 or an order granting a waiver of this cost.

(4) If the appellant does not submit a required deposit or an application for, or an order granting a waiver of the cost within the required period, the clerk must promptly issue a notice of default under rule 8.842.

(Subd (c) amended effective January 1, 2014; adopted effective January 1, 2009; previously amended effective July 1, 2009.)

(d) Preparing the clerk's transcript

(1) The clerk must:

(A) Prepare and certify the original transcript;

(B) Prepare one copy of the transcript for the appellant; and

(C) Prepare any additional copies for parties that have requested a copy of the clerk's transcript and have made deposits as provided in (c)(3) or received an order waiving the cost.

(2) Except as provided in (3), the clerk must complete preparation of the transcripts required under (1) within 30 days after either:

(A) The appellant deposits either the estimated cost of the clerk's transcript or a preexisting order granting a waiver of that cost; or

(B) The court grants an application submitted under (c)(3) to waive that cost.

(3) If the appellant elects under rule 8.831 to proceed with a reporter's transcript, the clerk need not complete preparation of the transcripts required under (1) until 30 days after the appellant deposits the estimated cost of the reporter's transcript or one of the substitutes under rule 8.834(b).

(4) If the appeal is abandoned or dismissed before the clerk has completed preparation of the transcript, the clerk must refund any portion of the deposit under (c)(3) exceeding the preparation cost actually incurred.

(Subd (d) amended effective January 1, 2014; adopted effective January 1, 2009.)

Rule 8.832 amended effective January 1, 2014; adopted effective January 1, 2009; previously amended effective July 1, 2009, January 1, 2010, and January 1, 2011.

Advisory Committee Comment

Subdivision (a). The supporting and opposing memoranda and attachments to any motion to vacate the judgment, for judgment notwithstanding the verdict, or for reconsideration of an appealed order are not required to be included in the clerk's transcript under subdivision (a)(1)(D) but may be included by designation of a party under (a)(3) or on motion of a party or the reviewing court under rule 8.841.

Subdivision (d). The different timelines for preparing a clerk's transcript under subdivision (d)(2)(A) and (B) recognize that an appellant may apply for and receive a waiver of fees at different points during the appellate process. Some appellants may have applied for and obtained an order waiving fees before receiving the estimate of the cost of the clerk's transcript and thus may be able to provide that order to the court in lieu of making a deposit for the clerk's transcript. Other appellants may not apply for a waiver until after they receive the estimate of the cost for the clerk's transcript, in which case the time for preparing the transcript runs from the granting of that waiver.

In cases in which a reporter's transcript has been designated, subdivision (d)(3) gives the clerk the option of waiting until the deposit for the reporter's transcript has been made before beginning preparation of the clerk's transcript.

Rule 8.833. Trial court file instead of clerk's transcript

(a) Application

If the court has a local rule for the appellate division electing to use this form of the record, the original trial court file may be used instead of a clerk's transcript. This rule and any supplemental provisions of the local rule then govern unless the trial court orders otherwise after notice to the parties.

(Subd (a) adopted effective January 1, 2009.)

(b) Cost estimate; preparation of file; transmittal

(1) Within 10 days after the appellant serves a notice under rule 8.831 indicating that the appellant elects to use a clerk's transcript, the trial court clerk may send the appellant a notice indicating that the appellate division for that court has elected by local court rule to use the original trial court file instead of a clerk's transcript and providing the appellant with an estimate of the cost to prepare the file, including the cost of sending the index under (4).

(2) Within 10 days after the clerk sends the estimate under (1), the appellant must deposit the estimated cost with the clerk, unless otherwise provided by law or the party submits an application for a waiver of the cost under rule 8.818 or an order granting a waiver of this cost.

(3) Within 10 days after the appellant deposits the cost or the court files an order waiving that cost, the trial court clerk must put the trial court file in chronological order, number the pages, and attach a chronological index and a list of all attorneys of record, the parties they represent, and any unrepresented parties.

(4) The clerk must send copies of the index to all attorneys of record and any unrepresented parties for their use in paginating their copies of the file to conform to the index.

(5) If the appellant elected to proceed with a reporter's transcript, the clerk must send the prepared file to the appellate division with the reporter's transcript. If the appellant elected to proceed without a reporter's transcript, the clerk must immediately send the prepared file to the appellate division.

(Subd (b) amended effective January 1, 2016; adopted effective January 1, 2009; previously amended effective July 1, 2009.)

Rule 8.833 amended effective January 1, 2016; adopted effective January 1, 2009; previously amended effective July 1, 2009.

Rule 8.834. Reporter's transcript

(a) Notice

(1) A notice designating a reporter's transcript under rule 8.831 must specify the date of each proceeding to be included in the transcript and may specify portions of the designated proceedings that are not to be included. The notice must identify any proceeding for which a certified

transcript has previously been prepared by checking the appropriate box on *Appellant's Notice Designating Record on Appeal (Limited Civil Case)* (form APP-103) or, if that form is not used, placing an asterisk before that proceeding.

(2) If the appellant designates less than all the testimony, the notice must state the points to be raised on the appeal; the appeal is then limited to those points unless, on motion, the appellate division permits otherwise.

(3) If the appellant serves and files a notice under rule 8.831 designating a reporter's transcript, the respondent may, within 10 days after such service, serve and file a notice in the trial court designating any additional proceedings the respondent wants included in the reporter's transcript. The notice must identify any proceeding for which a certified transcript has previously been prepared by checking the appropriate box on *Respondent's Notice Designating Record on Appeal (Limited Civil Case)* (form APP-110) or, if that form is not used, placing an asterisk before that proceeding.

(4) Except when a party deposits a certified transcript of all the designated proceedings under (b)(2)(D) with the notice of designation, the clerk must promptly send a copy of each notice to the reporter. The copy must show the date it was sent.

(Subd (a) amended effective January 1, 2016; adopted effective January 1, 2009; previously amended effective January 1, 2014.)

(b) Deposit or substitute for cost of transcript

(1) Within 10 days after the clerk sends a notice under (a)(4), the reporter must file the estimate with the clerk—or notify the clerk in writing of the date that he or she notified the appellant directly—of the estimated cost of preparing the reporter's transcript at the statutory rate.

(2) Within 10 days after the clerk notifies the appellant of the estimated cost of preparing the reporter's transcript or within 10 days after the reporter notifies the appellant directly—the appellant must do one of the following:

(A) Deposit with the clerk an amount equal to the estimated cost and a fee of $50 for the superior court to hold this deposit in trust;

(B) File with the clerk a written waiver of the deposit signed by the reporter;

(C) File a copy of a Transcript Reimbursement Fund application filed under (3);

(D) File a certified transcript of all of the designated proceedings. The transcript must comply with the format requirements of rule 8.144; or

(E) Notify the clerk that:

(i) He or she now elects to use a statement on appeal instead of a reporter's transcript. The appellant must prepare, serve, and file a proposed statement on appeal within 20 days after serving and filing the notice and must otherwise comply with the requirements for statements on appeal under rule 8.837;

(ii) He or she now elects to proceed without a record of the oral proceedings in the trial court; or

(iii) He or she is abandoning the appeal by filing an abandonment in the reviewing court under rule 8.825.

(3) With its notice of designation, a party may serve and file a copy of its application to the Court Reporters Board for payment or reimbursement from the Transcript Reimbursement Fund under Business and Professions Code section 8030.2 et seq.

(A) Within 90 days after the appellant serves and files a copy of its application to the Court Reporters Board, the appellant must either file with the court a copy of the Court Reporters Board's provisional approval of the application or take one of the following actions:

(i) Deposit the amount required under (2) or the reporter's written waiver of this deposit;

(ii) Notify the superior court that he or she now elects to use a statement on appeal instead of a reporter's transcript. The appellant must prepare, serve, and file a proposed statement on appeal within 20 days after serving and filing the notice and must otherwise comply with the requirements for statements on appeal under rule 8.837;

(iii) Notify the superior court that that he or she elects to proceed without a record of the oral proceedings; or

(iv) Notify the superior court that he or she is abandoning the appeal by filing an abandonment in the reviewing court under rule 8.825.

(B) Within 90 days after the respondent serves and files a copy of its application to the Court Reporters Board, the respondent must either file with the court a copy of the Court Reporters Board's provisional approval of the application or take one of the following actions:

(i) Deposit the amount required under (2) or the reporter's written waiver of this deposit; or

(ii) Notify the superior court that the respondent no longer wants the additional proceedings it designated for inclusion in the reporter's transcript.

(C) If the appellant fails to timely take one of the actions specified in (A) or the respondent fails to timely make the deposit or send the notice under (B), the clerk must promptly issue a notice of default under rule 8.842.

(D) If the Court Reporters Board provisionally approves the application, the reporter's time to prepare the transcript under (d)(1) begins when the clerk sends notice of the provisional approval under (4).

(4) The clerk must promptly notify the reporter to prepare the transcript when the court receives:

(A) The required deposit under (2)(A);

(B) A waiver of the deposit signed by the reporter under (2)(B); or

(C) A copy of the Court Reporters Board's provisional approval of the party's application for payment from the Transcript Reimbursement Fund under (3).

(Subd (b) amended effective January 1, 2016; adopted effective January 1, 2009; previously amended effective January 1, 2014.)

(c) Contents of reporter's transcript

(1) Except when a party deposits a certified transcript of all the designated proceedings under (b)(2)(D), the reporter must transcribe all designated proceedings that have not previously been transcribed and provide a copy of all designated proceedings that have previously been transcribed. The reporter must note in the transcript where any proceedings were omitted and the nature of those proceedings. The reporter must also note where any exhibit was marked for identification and where it was admitted or refused, identifying such exhibits by number or letter.

(2) The reporter must not transcribe the voir dire examination of jurors, any opening statement, or the proceedings on a motion for new trial, unless they are designated.

(3) If a party designates a portion of a witness's testimony to be transcribed, the reporter must transcribe the witness's entire testimony unless the parties stipulate otherwise.

(4) The reporter must not copy any document includable in the clerk's transcript under rule 8.832.

(Subd (c) amended effective January 1, 2014; adopted effective January 1, 2009.)

(d) Filing the reporter's transcript; copies; payment

(1) Within 20 days after the clerk notifies the reporter to prepare the transcript under (b)(2), the reporter must prepare and certify an original of the reporter's transcript and file it in the trial court. The reporter must also file one copy of the original transcript or more than one copy if multiple appellants equally share the cost of preparing the record. Only the presiding judge of the appellate division, or his or her designee, may extend the time to prepare the reporter's transcript (see rule 8.810).

(2) When the transcript is completed, the reporter must notify all parties to the appeal that the transcript is complete, bill each designating party at the statutory rate, and send a copy of the bill to the clerk. The clerk must pay the reporter from that party's deposited funds and refund any excess deposit or notify the party of any additional funds needed. In a multiple reporter case, the clerk must pay each reporter who certifies under penalty of perjury that his or her transcript portion is completed.

(3) If the appeal is abandoned or is dismissed before the reporter has filed the transcript, the reporter must inform the clerk of the cost of the portion of the transcript that the reporter has completed. The clerk must pay that amount to the reporter from the appellant's deposited funds and refund any excess deposit.

(Subd (d) amended effective January 1, 2018; adopted effective January 1, 2009; previously amended effective January 1, 2014, March 1, 2014, and January 1, 2017.)

(e) Disputes over transcript costs

Notwithstanding any dispute that may arise over the estimated or billed costs of a reporter's transcript, a designating party must timely comply with the requirements under this rule regarding deposits for transcripts. If a designating party believes that a reporter's estimate or bill is excessive, the designating party may file a complaint with the Court Reporters Board.

(Subd (e) adopted effective January 1, 2014.)

(f) Notice when proceedings cannot be transcribed

(1) If any portion of the designated proceedings were not reported or cannot be transcribed, the trial court clerk must so notify the designating party in writing; the notice must:

(A) Indicate whether the identified proceedings were officially electronically recorded under Government Code section 69957; and

(B) Show the date it was sent.

(2) Within 10 days after the notice under (1) is sent, the designating party must file a new election notifying the court whether the party elects to proceed with or without a record of the identified oral proceedings. If the party elects to proceed with a record of these oral proceedings, the notice must specify which form of the record listed in rule 8.830(a)(2) the party elects to use.

(A) The party may not elect to use a reporter's transcript.

(B) The party may not elect to use an official electronic recording or a transcript prepared from an official electronic recording under rule 8.835 unless the clerk's notice under (1) indicates that proceedings were officially electronically recorded under Government Code section 69957.

(C) The party must comply with the requirements applicable to the form of the record elected.

(3) This remedy supplements any other available remedies.

(Subd (f) amended effective January 1, 2016; adopted as subd (e) effective January 1, 2009; previously relettered as subd (f) effective January 1, 2014; previously amended effective March 1, 2014.)

Rule 8.834 amended effective January 1, 2018; adopted effective January 1, 2009; previously amended effective January 1, 2014, March 1, 2014, January 1, 2016, January 1, 2017.

Rule 8.835. Record when trial proceedings were officially electronically recorded

(a) Application

This rule applies only if:

(1) The trial court proceedings were officially recorded electronically under Government Code section 69957; and

(2) The electronic recording was prepared in compliance with applicable rules regarding electronic recording of court proceedings.

(Subd (a) adopted effective January 1, 2009.)

(b) Transcripts from official electronic recording

Written transcripts of official electronic recordings may be prepared under rule 2.952. A transcript prepared and certified as provided in that rule is prima facie a true and complete record of the oral proceedings it purports to cover and satisfies any requirement in these rules or in any statute for a reporter's transcript of oral proceedings.

(Subd (b) adopted effective January 1, 2009.)

(c) Use of official recording as record of oral proceedings

If the court has a local rule for the appellate division permitting this, on stipulation of the parties or on order of the trial court under rule 8.837(d)(6), the original of an official electronic recording of the trial court proceedings, or a copy made by the court, may be transmitted as the record of these oral proceedings without being transcribed. Such an official electronic recording satisfies any requirement in these rules or in any statute for a reporter's transcript of these proceedings.

(Subd (c) amended effective July 1, 2010; adopted effective January 1, 2009.)

(d) Notice when proceedings were not officially electronically recorded or cannot be transcribed

(1) If the appellant elects under rule 8.831 to use a transcript prepared from an official electronic recording or the recording itself, the trial court clerk must notify the appellant in writing if any portion of the designated proceedings was not officially electronically recorded or cannot be transcribed. The notice must:

(A) Indicate whether the identified proceedings were reported by a court reporter; and

(B) Show the date it was sent.

(2) Within 10 days after the notice under (1) is sent, the appellant must file a new election notifying the court whether the appellant elects to proceed with or without a record of the oral proceedings that were not recorded or cannot be transcribed. If the appellant elects to proceed with a record of these oral proceedings, the notice must specify which form of the record listed in rule 8.830(a)(2) the appellant elects to use.

(A) The appellant may not elect to use an official electronic recording or a transcript prepared from an official electronic recording.

(B) The appellant may not elect to use a reporter's transcript unless the clerk's notice under (1) indicates that proceedings were reported by a court reporter.

(C) The appellant must comply with the requirements applicable to the form of the record elected.

(Subd (d) amended effective January 1, 2016; adopted effective January 1, 2009; previously amended effective March 1, 2014.)

Rule 8.835 amended effective January 1, 2016; adopted effective January 1, 2009; previously amended effective July 1, 2010, and March 1, 2014.

Rule 8.836. Agreed statement

(a) What is an agreed statement

An agreed statement is a summary of the trial court proceedings that is agreed to by the parties. If the parties have prepared an agreed statement or stipulated to prepare one, the appellant can elect under rule 8.831 to use an agreed statement as the record of the documents filed in the trial court, replacing the clerk's transcript, and as the record of the oral proceedings in the trial court, replacing the reporter's transcript.

(Subd (a) adopted effective January 1, 2009.)

(b) Contents of an agreed statement

(1) The agreed statement must explain the nature of the action, the basis of the appellate division's jurisdiction, and the rulings of the trial court relating to the points to be raised on appeal. The statement should recite only those facts that a party considers relevant to decide the appeal and must be signed by the parties.

(2) If the agreed statement replaces a clerk's transcript, the statement must be accompanied by copies of all items required by rule 8.832(a)(1), showing the dates required by rule 8.832(a)(2).

(3) The statement may be accompanied by copies of any document includable in the clerk's transcript under rule 8.832(a)(3).

(Subd (b) adopted effective January 1, 2009.)

(c) Time to file; extension of time

(1) If an appellant indicates on its notice designating the record under rule 8.831 that it elects to use an agreed statement under this rule, the appellant must file with the notice designating the record either the agreed statement or a stipulation that the parties are attempting to agree on a statement.

(2) If the appellant files a stipulation under (1), within 30 days after filing the notice of designation under rule 8.831, the appellant must either:

(A) File the statement if the parties were able to agree on the statement; or

(B) File both a notice stating that the parties were not able to agree on the statement and a new notice designating the record under rule 8.831. In the new notice designating the record, the appellant may not elect to use an agreed statement.

(Subd (c) adopted effective January 1, 2009.)

Rule 8.836 adopted effective January 1, 2009.

Rule 8.837. Statement on appeal

(a) Description

A statement on appeal is a summary of the trial court proceedings that is approved by the trial court. An appellant can elect under rule 8.831 to use a statement on appeal as the record of the oral proceedings in the trial court, replacing the reporter's transcript.

(Subd (a) adopted effective January 1, 2009.)

(b) Preparing the proposed statement

(1) If the appellant elects in its notice designating the record under rule 8.831 to use a statement on appeal, the appellant must serve and file a proposed statement within 20 days after filing the notice under rule 8.831. If the appellant does not serve and file a proposed statement within this time, rule 8.842 applies.

(2) Appellants who are not represented by an attorney must file their proposed statement on *Statement on Appeal (Limited Civil Case)* (form APP-104). For good cause, the court may permit the filing of a statement that is not on form APP-104.

(Subd (b) amended effective March 1, 2014; adopted effective January 1, 2009.)

(c) Contents of the proposed statement

The proposed statement must contain:

(1) A statement of the points the appellant is raising on appeal. If the condensed narrative under (3) covers only a portion of the oral proceedings, then the appeal is limited to the points identified in the statement unless the appellate division determines that the record permits the full consideration of another point or, on motion, the appellate division permits otherwise.

(A) The statement must specify the intended grounds of appeal by clearly stating each point to be raised but need not identify each particular ruling or matter to be challenged.

(B) If one of the grounds of appeal is insufficiency of the evidence, the statement must specify how it is insufficient.

(2) A summary of the trial court's rulings and judgment.

(3) A condensed narrative of the oral proceedings that the appellant believes necessary for the appeal.

(A) The condensed narrative must include a concise factual summary of the evidence and the testimony of each witness that is relevant to the points which the appellant states under (1) are being raised on appeal. Any evidence or portion of a proceeding not included will be presumed to support the judgment or order appealed from.

(B) If one of the points which the appellant states under (1) is being raised on appeal is a challenge to the giving, refusal, or modification of a jury instruction, the condensed narrative must include any instructions submitted orally and not in writing and must identify the party that requested the instruction and any modification.

(Subd (c) amended effective March 1, 2014; adopted effective January 1, 2009.)

(d) Review of the appellant's proposed statement

(1) Within 10 days after the appellant files the proposed statement, the respondent may serve and file proposed amendments to that statement.

(2) No later than 10 days after the respondent files proposed amendments or the time to do so expires, a party may request a hearing to review and correct the proposed statement. No hearing will be held unless ordered by the trial court judge, and the judge will not ordinarily order a hearing unless there is a factual dispute about a material aspect of the trial court proceedings.

(3) Except as provided in (6), if no hearing is ordered, no later than 10 days after the time for requesting a hearing expires, the trial court judge must review the proposed statement and any proposed amendments filed by the respondent and take one of the following actions:

(A) If the proposed statement does not contain material required under (c), the trial judge may order the appellant to prepare a new proposed statement. The order must identify the additional material that must be included in the statement to comply with (c) and the date by which the new proposed statement must be served and filed. If the appellant does not serve and file a new proposed statement as directed, rule 8.842 applies.

(B) If the trial judge does not issue an order under (A), the trial judge must either:

(i) Make any corrections or modifications to the statement necessary to ensure that it is an accurate summary of the evidence and the testimony of each witness that is relevant to the points which the appellant states under (c)(1) are being raised on appeal; or

(ii) Identify the necessary corrections and modifications and order the appellant to prepare a statement incorporating these corrections and modifications.

(4) If a hearing is ordered, the court must promptly set the hearing date and provide the parties with at least 5 days' written notice of the hearing date. No later than 10 days after the hearing, the trial court judge must either:

(A) Make any corrections or modifications to the statement necessary to ensure that it is an accurate summary of the evidence and the testimony of each witness that is relevant to the points which the appellant states under (c)(1) are being raised on appeal; or

(B) Identify the necessary corrections and modifications and order the appellant to prepare a statement incorporating these corrections and modifications.

(5) The trial court judge must not eliminate the appellant's specification of grounds of appeal from the proposed statement.

(6) If the trial court proceedings were reported by a court reporter or officially electronically recorded under Government Code section 69957 and the trial court judge determines that it would save court time and resources, instead of correcting a proposed statement on appeal:

(A) If the court has a local rule for the appellate division permitting the use of an official electronic recording as the record of the oral proceedings, the trial court judge may order that the original of an official electronic recording of the trial court proceedings, or a copy made by the court, be transmitted as the record of these oral proceedings without being transcribed. The court will pay for any copy of the official electronic recording ordered under this subdivision; or

(B) If the court has a local rule permitting this, the trial court judge may order that a transcript be prepared as the record of the oral proceedings. The court will pay for any transcript ordered under this subdivision.

(Subd (d) amended effective March 1, 2014; adopted effective January 1, 2009.)

(e) Review of the corrected statement

(1) If the trial court judge makes any corrections or modifications to the proposed statement under (d), the clerk must serve copies of the corrected or modified statement on the parties. If under (d) the trial court judge orders the appellant to prepare a statement incorporating corrections

and modifications, the appellant must serve and file the corrected or modified statement within the time ordered by the court. If the appellant does not serve and file a corrected or modified statement as directed, rule 8.842 applies.

(2) Within 10 days after the corrected or modified statement is served on the parties, any party may serve and file proposed modifications or objections to the statement.

(3) Within 10 days after the time for filing proposed modifications or objections under (2) has expired, the judge must review the corrected or modified statement and any proposed modifications or objections to the statement filed by the parties. The procedures in (d)(3) or (4) apply if the judge determines that further corrections or modifications are necessary to ensure that the statement is an accurate summary of the evidence and the testimony of each witness relevant to the points which the appellant states under (c)(1) are being raised on appeal.

(Subd (e) amended effective March 1, 2014; adopted effective January 1, 2009.)

(f) Certification of the statement on appeal

If the trial court judge does not make or order any corrections or modifications to the proposed statement under (d)(3), (d)(4), or (e)(3) and does not order either the use of an official electronic recording or the preparation of a transcript in lieu of correcting the proposed statement under (d)(6), the judge must promptly certify the statement.

(Subd (f) amended effective March 1, 2014; adopted effective January 1, 2009.)
Rule 8.837 amended effective March 1, 2014; adopted effective January 1, 2009.

Advisory Committee Comment

Subdivision (b)(2). *Proposed Statement on Appeal (Limited Civil Case)* (form APP-104) is available at any courthouse or county law library or online at *www.courts.ca.gov/forms*.

Subdivision (d). Under rule 8.804, the term "judge" includes a commissioner or a temporary judge.

Subdivisions (d)(3)(B), (d)(4), and (f). The judge need not ensure that the statement as modified or corrected is complete, but only that it is an accurate summary of the evidence and testimony relevant to the issues identified by the appellant.

Rule 8.838. Form of the record

(a) Paper and format

Except as otherwise provided in this rule, clerk's and reporter's transcripts must comply with the requirements of rule 8.144(b)(1)–(4), (c), and (d).

(Subd (a) amended effective January 1, 2018; adopted effective January 1, 2009.)

(b) Indexes

At the beginning of the first volume of each:

(1) The clerk's transcript must contain alphabetical and chronological indexes listing each document and the volume, where applicable, and page where it first appears;

(2) The reporter's transcript must contain alphabetical and chronological indexes listing the volume, where applicable, and page where each witness's direct, cross, and any other examination, begins; and

(3) The reporter's transcript must contain an index listing the volume, where applicable, and page where any exhibit is marked for identification and where it is admitted or refused.

(Subd (b) amended effective January 1, 2016; adopted effective January 1, 2009.)

(c) Binding and cover

(1) If filed in paper form, clerk's and reporter's transcripts must be bound on the left margin in volumes of no more than 300 sheets, except that transcripts may be bound at the top if required by a local rule of the appellate division.

(2) Each volume's cover must state the title and trial court number of the case, the names of the trial court and each participating trial judge, the names and addresses of appellate counsel for each party, the volume number, and the inclusive page numbers of that volume.

(3) In addition to the information required by (2), the cover of each volume of the reporter's transcript must state the dates of the proceedings reported in that volume.

(Subd (c) amended effective January 1, 2016; adopted effective January 1, 2009; previously amended effective January 1, 2014.)
Rule 8.838 amended effective January 1, 2018; adopted effective January 1, 2009; previously amended effective January 1, 2014, and January 1, 2016.

Rule 8.839. Record in multiple appeals

(a) Single record

If more than one appeal is taken from the same judgment or a related order, only one record need be prepared, which must be filed within the time allowed for filing the record in the latest appeal.

(Subd (a) adopted effective January 1, 2009.)

(b) Cost

If there is more than one separately represented appellant, they must equally share the cost of preparing the record, unless otherwise agreed by the appellants or ordered by the trial court. Appellants equally sharing the cost are each entitled to a copy of the record.

(Subd (b) adopted effective January 1, 2009.)
Rule 8.839 adopted effective January 1, 2009.

Rule 8.840.   Completion and filing of the record

(a) When the record is complete

(1) If the appellant elected under rule 8.831 or 8.834(b) to proceed without a record of the oral proceedings in the trial court **and the parties are not proceeding by appendix under rule 8.845**, the record is complete:

(A) If a clerk's transcript will be used, when the clerk's transcript is certified under rule 8.832(d);

(B) If the original trial court file will be used instead of the clerk's transcript, when that original file is ready for transmission as provided under rule 8.833(b); or

(C) If an agreed statement will be used instead of the clerk's transcript, when the appellant files the agreed statement under rule 8.836(b).

(2) If **the parties are not proceeding by appendix under rule 8.845 and** the appellant elected under rule 8.831 to proceed with a record of the oral proceedings in the trial court, the record is complete when the clerk's transcript or other record of the documents from the trial court is complete as provided in (1) and:

(A) If the appellant elected to use a reporter's transcript, when the certified reporter's transcript is delivered to the court under rule 8.834(d);

(B) If the appellant elected to use a transcript prepared from an official electronic recording, when the transcript has been prepared under rule 8.835;

(C) If the parties stipulated to the use of an official electronic recording of the proceedings, when the electronic recording has been prepared under rule 8.835; or

(D) If the appellant elected to use a statement on appeal, when the statement on appeal has been certified by the trial court or a transcript or an official electronic recording has been prepared under rule 8.837(d)(6).

(3) If the parties are proceeding by appendix under rule 8.845 and the appellant elected under rule 8.831 to proceed with a record of the oral proceedings in the trial court, the record is complete when the record of the oral proceedings is complete as provided in (2)(A), (B), (C), or (D).

(Subd (a) amended effective January 1, 2021; adopted effective January 1, 2014.)

(b) Filing the record

When the record is complete, the trial court clerk must promptly send the original to the appellate division and send to the appellant and respondent copies of any certified statement on appeal and any copies of transcripts or official electronic recordings that they have purchased. The appellate division clerk must promptly file the original and send notice of the filing date to the parties.

(Subd (b) amended effective January 1, 2016; adopted as unlettered subd effective January 1, 2009; previously amended and lettered as subd (b) effective January 1, 2014.)
Rule 8.840 amended effective January 1, 2021; adopted effective January 1, 2009; previously amended effective January 1, 2014, and January 1, 2016.

Rule 8.841.   Augmenting and correcting the record in the appellate division

(a) Augmentation

(1) At any time, on motion of a party or its own motion, the appellate division may order the record augmented to include:

(A) Any document filed or lodged in the case in the trial court; or

(B) A certified transcript—or agreed statement or a statement on appeal—of oral proceedings not designated under rule 8.831.

(2) A party must attach to its motion a copy, if available, of any document or transcript that it wants added to the record. The pages of the attachments must be consecutively numbered, beginning with the number 1. If the appellate division grants the motion, it may augment the record with the copy.

(3) If the party cannot attach a copy of the matter to be added, the party must identify it as required under rules 8.831.

(b) Correction

(1) On agreement of the parties, motion of a party, or on its own motion, the appellate division may order the correction or certification of any part of the record.

(2) The appellate division may order the trial court to settle disputes about omissions or errors in the record or to make corrections pursuant to stipulation filed by the parties in that court.

(Subd (b) adopted effective January 1, 2009.)

(c) Omissions

(1) If a clerk or reporter omits a required or designated portion of the record, a party may serve and file a notice in the trial court specifying the omitted portion and requesting that it be prepared, certified, and sent to the appellate division. The party must serve a copy of the notice on the appellate division.

(2) The clerk or reporter must comply with a notice under (1) within 10 days after it is filed. If the clerk or reporter fails to comply, the party may serve and file a motion to augment under (a), attaching a copy of the notice.

(Subd (c) adopted effective January 1, 2009.)

(d) Notice

The appellate division clerk must send all parties notice of the receipt and filing of any matter under this rule.

(Subd (d) adopted effective January 1, 2009.)
Rule 8.841 adopted effective January 1, 2009.

Rule 8.842.   Failure to procure the record

(a) Notice of default

Except as otherwise provided by these rules, if a party fails to do any act required to procure the record, the trial court clerk must promptly notify that party in writing that it must do the act specified in the notice within 15 days after the notice is sent and that, if it fails to comply, the reviewing court may impose the following sanctions:

(1) If the defaulting party is the appellant, the court may dismiss the appeal; or

(2) If the defaulting party is the respondent, the court may proceed with the appeal on the record designated by the appellant.

(Subd (a) amended effective January 1, 2016; adopted effective January 1, 2009; previously amended effective January 1, 2014.)

(b) Sanctions

If the party fails to take the action specified in a notice given under (a), the trial court clerk must promptly notify the appellate division of the default, and the appellate division may impose one of the following sanctions:

(1) If the defaulting party is the appellant, the reviewing court may dismiss the appeal. If the appeal is dismissed, the reviewing court must promptly notify the superior court. The reviewing court may vacate the dismissal for good cause.

(2) If the defaulting party is the respondent, the reviewing court may order the appeal to proceed on the record designated by the appellant, but the respondent may obtain relief from default under rule 8.812.

(Subd (b) amended effective January 1, 2014; adopted effective January 1, 2009; previously amended effective January 1, 2011.)
Rule 8.842 amended effective January 1, 2016; adopted effective January 1, 2009; previously amended effective January 1, 2011, and January 1, 2014.

Rule 8.843.   Transmitting exhibits

(a) Notice of designation

(1) If a party wants the appellate division to consider any original exhibits that were admitted in evidence, refused, or lodged but that were not copied in the clerk's transcript under rule 8.832 **or the appendix under rule 8.845** or included in the original file under rule 8.833, within 10 days after the last respondent's brief is filed or could be filed under rule 8.882 the party must serve and file a notice in the trial court designating such exhibits.

(2) Within 10 days after a notice under (1) is served, any other party wanting the appellate division to consider additional exhibits must serve and file a notice in the trial court designating such exhibits.

(3) A party filing a notice under (1) or (2) must serve a copy on the appellate division.

(Subd (a) amended effective January 1, 2021; adopted effective January 1, 2009.)

(b) Application for later transmittal

After the periods specified in (a) have expired, a party may apply to the appellate division for permission to send an exhibit to that court.

(Subd (b) adopted effective January 1, 2009.)

(c) Request by appellate division

At any time the appellate division may direct the trial court or a party to send it an exhibit.

(Subd (c) adopted effective January 1, 2009.)

(d) Transmittal

Unless the appellate division orders otherwise, within 20 days after notice under (a) is filed or after the appellate division directs that an exhibit be sent:

(1) The trial court clerk must put any designated exhibits in the clerk's possession into numerical or alphabetical order and send them to the appellate division. The trial court clerk must also send a list of the exhibits sent. If the exhibits are not transmitted electronically, the trial court clerk must send two copies of the list. If the appellate division clerk finds the list correct, the clerk must sign and return a copy to the trial court clerk.

(2) Any party in possession of designated exhibits returned by the trial court must put them into numerical or alphabetical order and send them to the appellate division. The party must also send a list of the exhibits sent. If the exhibits are not transmitted electronically, the party must send two copies of the list. If the appellate division clerk finds the list correct, the clerk must sign and return a copy to the party.

(Subd (d) amended effective January 1, 2016; adopted effective January 1, 2009.)

(e) Return by appellate division

On request, the appellate division may return an exhibit to the trial court or to the party that sent it. When the remittitur issues, the appellate division must return all exhibits not transmitted electronically to the trial court or to the party that sent them.

(Subd (e) amended effective January 1, 2016; adopted effective January 1, 2009.)

Rule 8.843 amended effective January 1, 2021; adopted effective January 1, 2009; previously amended effective January 1, 2016.

Rule 8.845. Appendixes

(a) Notice of election

(1) Unless the superior court orders otherwise on a motion served and filed within 10 days after the notice of election is served, this rule governs if:

(A) The appellant elects to use an appendix under this rule in the notice designating the record on appeal under rule 8.831; or

(B) The respondent serves and files a notice in the superior court electing to use an appendix under this rule within 10 days after the notice of appeal is filed, and no waiver of the fee for a clerk's transcript is granted to the appellant.

(2) When a party files a notice electing to use an appendix under this rule, the superior court clerk must promptly send a copy of the register of actions, if any, to the attorney of record for each party and to any unrepresented party.

(3) The parties may prepare separate appendixes or they may stipulate to a joint appendix.

(Subd (a) adopted effective January 1, 2021.)

(b) Contents of appendix

(1) A joint appendix or an appellant's appendix must contain:

(A) All items required by rule 8.832(a)(1), showing the dates required by rule 8.832(a)(2);

(B) Any item listed in rule 8.832(a)(3) that is necessary for proper consideration of the issues, including, for an appellant's appendix, any item that the appellant should reasonably assume the respondent will rely on;

(C) The notice of election; and

(D) For a joint appendix, the stipulation designating its contents.

(2) An appendix may incorporate by reference all or part of the record on appeal in another case pending in the reviewing court or in a prior appeal in the same case.

(A) The other appeal must be identified by its case name and number. If only part of a record is being incorporated by reference, that part must be identified by citation to the volume and page numbers of the record where it appears and either the title of the document or documents or the date of the oral proceedings to be incorporated. The parts of any record incorporated by reference must be identified both in the body of the appendix and in a separate section at the end of the index.

(B) If the appendix incorporates by reference any such record, the cover of the appendix must prominently display the notice "Record in case number: _____ incorporated by reference," identifying the number of the case from which the record is incorporated.

(C) On request of the reviewing court or any party, the designating party must provide a copy of the materials incorporated by reference to the court or another party or lend them for copying as provided in (c).

(3) An appendix must not:

(A) Contain documents or portions of documents filed in superior court that are unnecessary for proper consideration of the issues.

(B) Contain transcripts of oral proceedings that may be designated under rule 8.834.

(C) Incorporate any document by reference except as provided in (2).

(4) All exhibits admitted in evidence, refused, or lodged are deemed part of the record, whether or not the appendix contains copies of them.

(5) A respondent's appendix may contain any document that could have been included in the appellant's appendix or a joint appendix.

(6) An appellant's reply appendix may contain any document that could have been included in the respondent's appendix.

(Subd (b) adopted effective January 1, 2021.)

(c) Document or exhibit held by other party

If a party preparing an appendix wants it to contain a copy of a document or an exhibit in the possession of another party:

(1) The party must first ask the party possessing the document or exhibit to provide a copy or lend it for copying. All parties should reasonably cooperate with such requests.

(2) If the request under (1) is unsuccessful, the party may serve and file in the reviewing court a notice identifying the document or specifying the exhibit's trial court designation and requesting the party possessing the document or exhibit to deliver it to the requesting party or, if the possessing party prefers, to the reviewing court. The possessing party must comply with the request within 10 days after the notice was served.

(3) If the party possessing the document or exhibit sends it to the requesting party nonelectronically, that party must copy and return it to the possessing party within 10 days after receiving it.

(4) If the party possessing the document or exhibit sends it to the reviewing court, that party must:

(A) Accompany the document or exhibit with a copy of the notice served by the requesting party; and

(B) Immediately notify the requesting party that it has sent the document or exhibit to the reviewing court.

(5) On request, the reviewing court may return a document or an exhibit to the party that sent it nonelectronically. When the remittitur issues, the reviewing court must return all documents or exhibits to the party that sent them, if they were sent nonelectronically.

(Subd (c) adopted effective January 1, 2021.)

(d) Form of appendix

(1) An appendix must comply with the requirements of rule 8.838 for a clerk's transcript.

(2) In addition to the information required on the cover of a brief by rule 8.883(c)(8), the cover of an appendix must prominently display the title "Joint Appendix" or "Appellant's Appendix" or "Respondent's Appendix" or "Appellant's Reply Appendix."

(3) An appendix must not be bound with or transmitted electronically with a brief as one document.

(Subd (d) adopted effective January 1, 2021.)

(e) Service and filing

(1) A party preparing an appendix must:

(A) Serve the appendix on each party, unless otherwise agreed by the parties or ordered by the reviewing court; and

(B) File the appendix in the reviewing court.

(2) A joint appendix or an appellant's appendix must be served and filed with the appellant's opening brief.

(3) A respondent's appendix, if any, must be served and filed with the respondent's brief.

(4) An appellant's reply appendix, if any, must be served and filed with the appellant's reply brief.

(Subd (e) adopted effective January 1, 2021.)

(f) Cost of appendix

(1) Each party must pay for its own appendix.

(2) The cost of a joint appendix must be paid:

(A) By the appellant;

(B) If there is more than one appellant, by the appellants equally; or

(C) As the parties may agree.

(Subd (f) adopted effective January 1, 2021.)

(g) Inaccurate or noncomplying appendix

Filing an appendix constitutes a representation that the appendix consists of accurate copies of documents in the superior court file. The reviewing court may impose monetary or other sanctions for filing an appendix that contains inaccurate copies or otherwise violates this rule.

(Subd (g) adopted effective January 1, 2021.)

Rule 8.845 adopted effective January 1, 2021.

Advisory Committee Comment

Subdivision (a). Under this provision, either party may elect to have the appeal proceed by way of an appendix. If the appellant's fees for a clerk's transcript are not waived and the respondent timely elects to use an appendix, that election will govern unless the superior court orders otherwise. This election procedure differs from all other appellate rules governing designation of a record on appeal. In those rules, the appellant's designation, or the stipulation of the parties, determines the type of record on appeal. Before making this election, respondents should check whether the appellant has been granted a fee waiver that is still in effect. If the trial court has granted the appellant a fee waiver for the clerk's transcript, or grants such a waiver after the notice of appeal is filed, the respondent cannot elect to proceed by way of an appendix.

Subdivision (a)(2) is intended to assist appellate counsel in preparing an appendix by providing counsel with the list of pleadings and other filings found in the register of actions or "docket sheet" in those counties that maintain such registers. (See Gov. Code, § 69845.) The provision is derived from rule 10-1 of the United States Circuit Rules (9th Cir.).

Subdivision (b). Under subdivision (b)(1)(A), a joint appendix or an appellant's appendix must contain any register of actions that the clerk sent to the parties under subdivision (a)(2). This provision is intended to assist the reviewing court in determining the accuracy of the appendix. The provision is derived from rule 30-1.3(a)(ii) of the United States Circuit Rules (9th Cir.).

In support of or opposition to pleadings or motions, the parties may have filed a number of lengthy documents in the proceedings in superior court, including, for example, declarations, memorandums, trial briefs, documentary exhibits (e.g., insurance policies, contracts, deeds), and photocopies of judicial opinions or other publications. Subdivision (b)(3)(A) prohibits the inclusion of such documents in an appendix when they are not necessary for proper consideration of the issues raised in the appeal. Even if a document is otherwise includable in an appendix, the rule prohibits the inclusion of any substantial *portion* of the document that is not necessary for proper consideration of the issues raised in the appeal. The prohibition is intended to simplify and therefore expedite the preparation of the appendix, to reduce its cost to the parties, and to relieve the courts of the burden of reviewing a record containing redundant, irrelevant, or immaterial documents. The provision is adapted from rule 30-1.4 of the United States Circuit Rules (9th Cir.).

Subdivision (b)(3)(B) prohibits the inclusion in an appendix of transcripts of oral proceedings that may be made part of a reporter's transcript. (Compare rule 8.834(c)(4) [the reporter must not copy into the reporter's transcript any document includable in the clerk's transcript under rule 8.832].) The prohibition is intended to prevent a party filing an appendix from evading the requirements and safeguards imposed by rule 8.834 on the process of designating and preparing a reporter's transcript. In addition, if an appellant were to include in its appendix a transcript of less than all the proceedings, the respondent would not learn of any need to designate additional proceedings (under rule 8.834(a)(3)) until the appellant had served its appendix with its brief, when it would be too late to designate them. Note also that a party may file a certified transcript of designated proceedings instead of a deposit for the reporter's fee (Cal. Rules of Court, rule 8.834(b)(2)(D)).

Subdivision (d). In current practice, served copies of filed documents often bear no clerk's date stamp and are not conformed by the parties serving them. Consistent with this practice, subdivision (d) does not require such documents to be conformed. The provision thereby relieves the parties of the burden of obtaining conformed copies at the cost of considerable time and expense, and expedites the preparation of the appendix and the processing of the appeal. It is to be noted, however, that under subdivision (b)(1)(A) each document necessary to determine the timeliness of the appeal must show the date required under rule 8.822 or 8.823. Note also that subdivision (g) of rule 8.845 provides that a party filing an appendix represents under penalty of sanctions that its copies of documents are accurate.

Subdivision (e). Subdivision (e)(2) requires a joint appendix to be filed with the appellant's opening brief. The provision is intended to improve the briefing process by enabling the appellant's opening brief to include citations to the record. To provide for the case in which a respondent concludes in light of the appellant's opening brief that the joint appendix should have included additional documents, subdivision (b)(5) permits such a respondent to present in an appendix filed with its respondent's brief (see subd. (e)(3)) any document that could have been included in the joint appendix.

Under subdivision (e)(2)–(4), an appendix is required to be filed "with" the associated brief. This provision is intended to clarify that an extension of a briefing period ipso facto extends the filing period of an appendix associated with the brief.

Subdivision (g). Under subdivision (g), sanctions do not depend on the degree of culpability of the filing party—i.e., on whether the party's conduct was willful or negligent—but on the nature of the inaccuracies and the importance of the documents they affect.

Chapter 3
Appeals and Records in Misdemeanor Cases

Chapter 3 adopted effective January 1, 2009.

Article 1
Taking Appeals in Misdemeanor Cases

Article 1 adopted effective January 1, 2009.

Rule 8.850.   Application of chapter

The rules in this chapter apply only to appeals in misdemeanor cases. In postconviction appeals, misdemeanor cases are cases in which the defendant was convicted of a misdemeanor and was not charged with any felony. In preconviction appeals, misdemeanor cases are cases in which the defendant was charged with a misdemeanor but was not charged with any felony. A felony is "charged" when an information or indictment accusing the defendant of a felony is filed or a complaint accusing the defendant of a felony is certified to the superior court under Penal Code section 859a.

Rule 8.850 adopted effective January 1, 2009.

Advisory Committee Comment

Chapters 1 and 4 of this division also apply in appeals from misdemeanor cases. The rules that apply in appeals in felony cases are located in chapter 3 of division 1 of this title.

Penal Code section 1466 provides that an appeal in a "misdemeanor or infraction case" is to the appellate division of the superior court, and Penal Code section 1235(b), in turn, provides that an appeal in a "felony case" is to the Court of Appeal. Penal Code section 691(g) defines "misdemeanor or infraction case" to mean "a criminal action in which a misdemeanor or infraction is charged *and does not include a criminal action in which a felony is charged* in conjunction with a misdemeanor or infraction" (emphasis added), and section 691(f) defines "felony case" to mean "a criminal action in which a felony is charged *and includes a criminal action in which a misdemeanor or infraction is charged in conjunction with a felony*" (emphasis added).

As rule 8.304 from the rules on felony appeals provides, the following types of cases are felony cases, not misdemeanor cases: (1) an action in which the defendant is charged with a felony and a misdemeanor, but is convicted of only the misdemeanor; (2) an action in which the defendant is charged with felony, but is convicted of only a lesser offense; or (3) an action in which the defendant is charged with an offense filed as a felony but punishable as either a felony or a misdemeanor, and the offense is thereafter deemed a misdemeanor under Penal Code section 17(b). Rule 8.304 makes it clear that a "felony case" is an action in which a felony is charged *regardless of the outcome of the action.* Thus the question of which rules apply—these rules governing appeals in misdemeanor cases or the rules governing appeals in felony cases—is answered simply by examining the accusatory pleading: if that document charged the defendant with at least one count of felony (as defined in Penal Code, section 17(a)), the Court of Appeal has appellate jurisdiction and the appeal must be taken under the rules on felony appeals *even if the prosecution did not result in a punishment of imprisonment in a state prison.*

It is settled case law that an appeal is taken to the Court of Appeal not only when the defendant is charged with and convicted of a felony, but also when the defendant is charged with both a felony and a misdemeanor (Pen. Code, § 691(f)) but is convicted of only the misdemeanor (e.g., *People v. Brown* (1970) 10 Cal.App.3d 169); when the defendant is charged with a felony but is convicted of only a lesser offense (Pen. Code, § 1159; e.g., *People v. Spreckels* (1954) 125 Cal.App.2d 507); and when the defendant is charged with an offense filed as a felony but punishable as either a felony or a misdemeanor, and the offense is thereafter deemed a misdemeanor under Penal Code section 17(b) (e.g., *People v. Douglas* (1999) 20 Cal.4th 85; *People v. Clark* (1971) 17 Cal.App.3d 890).

Trial court unification did not change this rule: after as before unification, "Appeals in felony cases lie to the [C]ourt of [A]ppeal, regardless of whether the appeal is from the superior court, the municipal court, or the action of a magistrate. *Cf.* Cal. Const. art. VI, § 11(a) [except in death penalty cases, Courts of Appeal have appellate jurisdiction when superior courts have original jurisdiction 'in causes of a type within the appellate jurisdiction of the [C]ourts of [A]ppeal on June

30, 1995....']." ("Recommendation on Trial Court Unification" (July 1998) 28 *Cal. Law Revision Com. Rep.* 455–56.)

Rule 8.851.   Appointment of appellate counsel

(a) Standards for appointment

(1) On application, the appellate division must appoint appellate counsel for a defendant [1] **who was represented by appointed counsel in the trial court or establishes indigency and** who:

(A) Was convicted of a misdemeanor and is subject to incarceration or a fine of more than $500 (including penalty and other assessments), or who is likely to suffer significant adverse collateral consequences as a result of the conviction; [2] **or**

(B) Is charged with a misdemeanor and the appeal is a critical stage of the criminal process.

(2) On application, the appellate division may appoint counsel for any other indigent defendant **charged with or** convicted of a misdemeanor.

(3) **For applications under (1)(A),** a defendant is subject to incarceration or a fine if the incarceration or fine is in a sentence, is a condition of probation, or may be ordered if the defendant violates probation.

(Subd (a) amended effective September 1, 2020; adopted effective January 1, 2009.)

Rule 8.851(a).   2020 Deletes. [1] convicted of a misdemeanor [2] and (B) Was represented by appointed counsel in the trial court or establishes indigency

(b) Application; duties of trial counsel and clerk

(1) If defense trial counsel has reason to believe that the client is indigent and will file an appeal **or is a party in an appeal described in (a)(1)(B),** counsel must prepare and file in the trial court an application to the appellate division for appointment of counsel.

(2) If the defendant was represented by appointed counsel in the trial court, the application must include trial counsel's declaration to that effect. If the defendant was not represented by appointed counsel in the trial court, the application must include a declaration of indigency in the form required by the Judicial Council.

(3) Within 15 court days after an application is filed in the trial court, the clerk must send it to the appellate division. A defendant may, however, apply directly to the appellate division for appointment of counsel at any time after [1] the notice of appeal **is filed**.

(4) The appellate division must grant or deny a defendant's application for appointment of counsel within 30 days after the application is filed.

(Subd (b) amended effective September 1, 2020; adopted effective January 1, 2009; previously amended effective March 1, 2014.)

Rule 8.851(b).   2020 Deletes. [1] filing

(c) Defendant found able to pay in trial court

(1) If a defendant was represented by appointed counsel in the trial court and was found able to pay all or part of the cost of counsel in proceedings under Penal Code section 987.8 or 987.81, the findings in those proceedings must be included in the record or, if the findings were made after the record is sent to the appellate division, must be sent as an augmentation of the record.

(2) In cases under (1), the appellate division may determine the defendant's ability to pay all or part of the cost of counsel on appeal, and if it finds the defendant able, may order the defendant to pay all or part of that cost.

(Subd (c) adopted effective January 1, 2009.)

Rule 8.851 amended effective September 1, 2020; adopted effective January 1, 2009; previously amended effective March 1, 2014.

Advisory Committee Comment

Request for Court-Appointed Lawyer in Misdemeanor Appeal (form CR-133) may be used to request that appellate counsel be appointed in a misdemeanor case. If the defendant was not represented by the public defender or other appointed counsel in the trial court, the defendant must use *Defendant's Financial Statement on Eligibility for Appointment of Counsel and Reimbursement and Record on Appeal at Public Expense* (form CR-105) to show indigency. These forms are available at any courthouse or county law library or online at *www.courts.ca.gov/forms*.

Subdivision (a)(1)(B). In *Gardner v. Appellate Division of Superior Court* (2019) 6 Cal.5th 998, the California Supreme Court addressed what constitutes a critical stage of the criminal process. The court provided the analysis for determining whether a defendant has a right to counsel in confrontational proceedings other than trial, and held that the pretrial prosecution appeal of an order granting the defendant's motion to suppress evidence was a critical stage of the process at which the defendant, who was represented by appointed counsel in the trial court, had a right to appointed counsel as a matter of state constitutional law.

Rule 8.852.   Notice of appeal

(a) Notice of appeal

(1) To appeal from a judgment or an appealable order of the trial court in a misdemeanor case, the defendant or the People must file a notice of appeal in the trial court. The notice must specify the judgment or order—or part of it—being appealed.

(2) If the defendant appeals, the defendant or the defendant's attorney must sign the notice of appeal. If the People appeal, the attorney for the People must sign the notice.

(3) The notice of appeal must be liberally construed in favor of its sufficiency.

(Subd (a) adopted effective January 1, 2009.)

(b) Notification of the appeal

(1) When a notice of appeal is filed, the trial court clerk must promptly send a notification of the filing to the attorney of record for each party and to any unrepresented defendant. The clerk must also send or deliver this notification to the appellate division clerk.

(2) The notification must show the date it was sent or delivered, the number and title of the case, the date the notice of appeal was filed, and whether the defendant was represented by appointed counsel.

(3) The notification to the appellate division clerk must also include a copy of the notice of appeal.

(4) A copy of the notice of appeal is sufficient notification under (1) if the required information is on the copy or is added by the trial court clerk.

(5) The sending of a notification under (1) is a sufficient performance of the clerk's duty despite the discharge, disqualification, suspension, disbarment, or death of the attorney.

(6) Failure to comply with any provision of this subdivision does not affect the validity of the notice of appeal.

(Subd (b) amended effective January 1, 2016; adopted effective January 1, 2009.)

Rule 8.852 amended effective January 1, 2016; adopted effective January 1, 2009.

Advisory Committee Comment

Notice of Appeal (Misdemeanor) (form CR-132) may be used to file the notice of appeal required under this rule. This form is available at any courthouse or county law library or online at *www.courts.ca.gov/forms*.

Subdivision (a). The only orders that a defendant can appeal in a misdemeanor case are (1) orders granting or denying a motion to suppress evidence (Penal Code section 1538.5(j)); and (2) orders made after the final judgment that affects the substantial rights of the defendant (Penal Code section 1466).

Rule 8.853.   Time to appeal

(a) Normal time

A notice of appeal must be filed within 30 days after the rendition of the judgment or the making of the order being appealed. If the defendant is committed before final judgment for insanity or narcotics addiction, the notice of appeal must be filed within 30 days after the commitment.

(Subd (a) adopted effective January 1, 2009.)

(b) Cross-appeal

If the defendant or the People timely appeal from a judgment or appealable order, the time for any other party to appeal from the same judgment or order is either the time specified in (a) or 15 days after the trial court clerk sends notification of the first appeal, whichever is later.

(Subd (b) amended effective January 1, 2016; adopted effective January 1, 2009.)

(c) Premature notice of appeal

A notice of appeal filed before the judgment is rendered or the order is made is premature, but the appellate division may treat the notice as filed immediately after the rendition of the judgment or the making of the order.

(Subd (c) adopted effective January 1, 2009.)

(d) Late notice of appeal

The trial court clerk must mark a late notice of appeal "Received [date] but not filed" and notify the party that the notice was not filed because it was late.

(Subd (d) adopted effective January 1, 2009.)

Rule 8.853 amended effective January 1, 2016; adopted effective January 1, 2009; previously amended effective July 1, 2010.

Advisory Committee Comment

Subdivision (d). See rule 8.817(b)(5) for provisions concerning the timeliness of documents mailed by inmates or patients from custodial institutions.

Rule 8.854.   Stay of execution and release on appeal

(a) Application

Pending appeal, the defendant may apply to the appellate division:

(1) For a stay of execution after a judgment of conviction or an order granting probation; or

(2) For bail for release from custody, to reduce bail for release from custody, or for release on other conditions.

(Subd (a) adopted effective January 1, 2009.)

(b) Showing

The application must include a showing that the defendant sought relief in the trial court and that the court unjustifiably denied the application.

(Subd (b) adopted effective January 1, 2009.)

(c) Service

The application must be served on the prosecuting attorney.

(Subd (c) adopted effective January 1, 2009.)

(d) Interim relief

Pending its ruling on the application, the appellate division may grant the relief requested. The appellate division must notify the trial court of any stay that it grants.

(Subd (d) adopted effective January 1, 2009.)
Rule 8.854 adopted effective January 1, 2009.

Advisory Committee Comment

Subdivision (c). As defined in rule 8.804, the "prosecuting attorney" may be the city attorney, county counsel, district attorney, or state Attorney General, depending on what government agency filed the criminal charges.

Rule 8.855.   Abandoning the appeal

(a) How to abandon

An appellant may abandon the appeal at any time by filing an abandonment of the appeal signed by the appellant or the appellant's attorney of record.

(Subd (a) adopted effective January 1, 2009.)

(b) Where to file; effect of filing

(1) The appellant must file the abandonment in the appellate division.

(2) If the record has not been filed in the appellate division, the filing of an abandonment effects a dismissal of the appeal and restores the trial court's jurisdiction.

(3) If the record has been filed in the appellate division, the appellate division may dismiss the appeal and direct immediate issuance of the remittitur.

(Subd (b) adopted effective January 1, 2009.)

(c) Clerk's duties

(1) The appellate division clerk must immediately notify the adverse party of the filing or of the order of dismissal.

(2) If the record has not been filed in the appellate division, the clerk must immediately notify the trial court.

(3) If a reporter's transcript has been requested, the clerk must immediately notify the reporter if the appeal is abandoned before the reporter has filed the transcript.

(Subd (c) adopted effective January 1, 2009.)
Rule 8.855 adopted effective January 1, 2009.

Advisory Committee Comment

Abandonment of Appeal (Misdemeanor) (form CR-137) may be used to file an abandonment under this rule. This form is available at any courthouse or county law library or online at *www.courtinfo.ca.gov/forms.*

Article 2
Record in Misdemeanor Appeals

Article 2 adopted effective January 1, 2009.

Rule 8.860.   Normal record on appeal

(a) Contents

Except as otherwise provided in this chapter, the record on an appeal to a superior court appellate division in a misdemeanor criminal case must contain the following, which constitute the normal record on appeal:

(1) A record of the written documents from the trial court proceedings in the form of one of the following:

(A) A clerk's transcript under rule 8.861 or 8.867; or

(B) If the court has a local rule for the appellate division electing to use this form of the record, the original trial court file under rule 8.863.

(2) If an appellant wants to raise any issue that requires consideration of the oral proceedings in the trial court, the record on appeal must include a record of the oral proceedings in the form of one of the following:

(A) A reporter's transcript under rules 8.865–8.867 or a transcript prepared from an official electronic recording under rule 8.868;

(B) If the court has a local rule for the appellate division permitting this form of the record, an official electronic recording of the proceedings under rule 8.868; or

(C) A statement on appeal under rule 8.869.

(Subd (a) adopted effective January 1, 2009.)

(b) Stipulation for limited record

If, before the record is certified, the appellant and the respondent stipulate in writing that any part of the record is not required for proper determination of the appeal and file that stipulation in the trial court, that part of the record must not be prepared or sent to the appellate division.

(Subd (b) amended effective July 1, 2009; adopted effective January 1, 2009.)
Rule 8.860 amended effective July 1, 2009; adopted effective January 1, 2009.

Rule 8.861.   Contents of clerk's transcript

Except in appeals covered by rule 8.867 or when the parties have filed a stipulation under rule 8.860(b) that any of these items is not required for proper determination of the appeal, the clerk's transcript must contain:

(1) The complaint, including any notice to appear, and any amendment;

(2) Any demurrer or other plea;

(3) All court minutes;

(4) Any jury instructions that any party submitted in writing, the cover page required by rule 2.1055(b)(2), and any written jury instructions given by the court;

(5) Any written communication between the court and the jury or any individual juror;

(6) Any verdict;

(7) Any written findings or opinion of the court;

(8) The judgment or order appealed from;

(9) Any motion or notice of motion for new trial, in arrest of judgment, or to dismiss the action, with supporting and opposing memoranda and attachments;

(10) Any transcript of a sound or sound-and-video recording furnished to the jury or tendered to the court under rule 2.1040; and

(11) The notice of appeal; and

(12) If the appellant is the defendant:

(A) Any written defense motion denied in whole or in part, with supporting and opposing memoranda and attachments;

(B) If related to a motion under (A), any search warrant and return;

(C) Any document admitted in evidence to prove a prior juvenile adjudication, criminal conviction, or prison term. If a record was closed to public inspection in the trial court because it is required to be kept confidential by law, it must remain closed to public inspection in the appellate division unless that court orders otherwise;

(D) The probation officer's report; and

(E) Any court-ordered psychological report required under Penal Code section 1369.

Rule 8.861 amended effective January 1, 2010; adopted effective January 1, 2009.

Advisory Committee Comment

Rule 8.862(c) addresses the appropriate handling of probation officers' reports that must be included in the clerk's transcript under (12)(D).

Rule 8.862.   Preparation of clerk's transcript

(a) When preparation begins

Unless the original court file will be used in place of a clerk's transcript under rule 8.863, the clerk must begin preparing the clerk's transcript immediately after the notice of appeal is filed.

(Subd (a) adopted effective January 1, 2009.)

(b) Format of transcript

The clerk's transcript must comply with rule 8.144.

(Subd (b) adopted effective January 1, 2009.)

(c) Probation officer's reports

A probation officer's report included in the clerk's transcript under rule 8.861(12)(D) must appear in only the copies of the appellate record that are sent to the reviewing court, to appellate counsel for the People, and to appellate counsel for the defendant who was the subject of the report or to the defendant if he or she is self-represented. If the report is in paper form, it must be placed in a sealed envelope. The reviewing court's copy of the report, and if applicable, the envelope, must be marked "CONFIDENTIAL—MAY NOT BE EXAMINED WITHOUT COURT ORDER—PROBATION OFFICER REPORT."

(Subd (c) amended effective January 1, 2016; adopted effective January 1, 2010.)

(d) When preparation must be completed

Within 20 days after the notice of appeal is filed, the clerk must complete preparation of an original clerk's transcript for the appellate division, one copy for the appellant, and one copy for the respondent. If there is more than one appellant, the clerk must prepare an extra copy for each additional appellant who is represented by separate counsel or self-represented.

(Subd (d) relettered effective January 1, 2010; adopted as subd (c) effective January 1, 2009; previously amended effective July 1, 2009.)

(e) Certification

The clerk must certify as correct the original and all copies of the clerk's transcript.

(Subd (e) relettered effective January 1, 2010; adopted as subd (d) effective January 1, 2009.)

Rule 8.862 amended effective January 1, 2016; adopted effective January 1, 2009; previously amended effective July 1, 2009, and January 1, 2010.

Advisory Committee Comment

Rule 8.872 addresses when the clerk's transcript is sent to the appellate division in misdemeanor appeals.

Rule 8.863.   Trial court file instead of clerk's transcript

(a) Application

If the court has a local rule for the appellate division electing to use this form of the record, the original trial court file may be used instead of a clerk's transcript. This rule and any supplemental provisions of the local rule then govern unless the trial court orders otherwise after notice to the parties.

(Subd (a) adopted effective January 1, 2009.)

(b) When original file must be prepared

Within 20 days after the filing of the notice of appeal, the trial court clerk must put the trial court file in chronological order, number the pages, and attach a chronological index and a list of all attorneys of record, the parties they represent, and any unrepresented parties.

(Subd (b) adopted effective January 1, 2009.)

(c) Copies

The clerk must send a copy of the index to the appellant and the respondent for use in paginating their copies of the file to conform to the index. If there is more than one appellant, the clerk must prepare an extra copy of the index for each additional appellant who is represented by separate counsel or self-represented.

(Subd (c) amended effective July 1, 2009; adopted effective January 1, 2009.)

Rule 8.863 amended effective July 1, 2009; adopted effective January 1, 2009.

Advisory Committee Comment

Rule 8.872 addresses when the original file is sent to the appellate division in misdemeanor appeals.

Rule 8.864.   Record of oral proceedings

(a) Appellant's election

The appellant must notify the trial court whether he or she elects to proceed with or without a record of the oral proceedings in the trial court. If the appellant elects to proceed with a record of the oral proceedings in the trial court, the notice must specify which form of the record of the oral proceedings in the trial court the appellant elects to use:

(1) A reporter's transcript under rules 8.865–8.867 or a transcript prepared from an official electronic recording of the proceedings under rule 8.868(b). If the appellant elects to use a reporter's transcript, the clerk must promptly send a copy of appellant's notice making this election and the notice of appeal to each court reporter;

(2) An official electronic recording of the proceedings under rule 8.868(c). If the appellant elects to use the official electronic recording itself, rather than a transcript prepared from that recording, the appellant must attach a copy of the stipulation required under rule 8.868(c); or

(3) A statement on appeal under rule 8.869.

(Subd (a) amended effective January 1, 2016; adopted effective January 1, 2009.)

(b) Time for filing election

The notice of election required under (a) must be filed no later than the following:

(1) If no application for appointment of counsel is filed, 20 days after the notice of appeal is filed; or

(2) If an application for appointment of counsel is filed before the period under (A) expires, either 10 days after the court appoints counsel to represent the defendant on appeal or denies the application for appointment of counsel or 20 days after the notice of appeal is filed, whichever is later.

(Subd (b) adopted effective January 1, 2009.)

(c) Failure to file election

If the appellant does not file an election within the time specified in (b), rule 8.874 applies.

(Subd (c) amended effective March 1, 2014; adopted effective January 1, 2010.)

Rule 8.864 amended effective January 1, 2016; adopted effective January 1, 2009; previously amended effective January 1, 2010, and March 1, 2014.

Advisory Committee Comment

Notice Regarding Record of Oral Proceedings (Misdemeanor) (form CR-134) may be used to file the election required under this rule. This form is available at any courthouse or county law library or online at *www.courtinfo.ca.gov/forms*. To assist parties in making an appropriate election, courts are encouraged to include information about whether the proceedings were recorded by a court reporter or officially electronically recorded in any information that the court provides to parties concerning their appellate rights.

Rule 8.865.   Contents of reporter's transcript

(a) Normal contents

Except in appeals covered by rule 8.867, when the parties have filed a stipulation under rule 8.860(b), or when, under a procedure established by a local rule adopted pursuant to (b), the trial court has ordered that any of these items is not required for proper determination of the appeal, the reporter's transcript must contain:

(1) The oral proceedings on the entry of any plea other than a not guilty plea;

(2) The oral proceedings on any motion in limine;

(3) The oral proceedings at trial, but excluding the voir dire examination of jurors and any opening statement;

(4) Any jury instructions given orally;

(5) Any oral communication between the court and the jury or any individual juror;

(6) Any oral opinion of the court;

(7) The oral proceedings on any motion for new trial;

(8) The oral proceedings at sentencing, granting or denying probation, or other dispositional hearing;

(9) If the appellant is the defendant, the reporter's transcript must also contain:

(A) The oral proceedings on any defense motion denied in whole or in part except motions for disqualification of a judge;

(B) Any closing arguments; and

(C) Any comment on the evidence by the court to the jury.

(Subd (a) lettered and amended effective March 1, 2014; adopted effective January 1, 2009.)

(b) Local procedure for determining contents

A court may adopt a local rule that establishes procedures for determining whether any of the items listed in (a) is not required for proper determination of the appeal or whether a form of the record other than a reporter's transcript constitutes a record of sufficient completeness for proper determination of the appeal.

(Subd (b) adopted effective March 1, 2014.)

Rule 8.865 amended effective March 1, 2014; adopted effective January 1, 2009.

Advisory Committee Comment

Subdivision (b). Both the United States Supreme Court and the California Supreme Court have held that, where the State has established a right to appeal, an indigent defendant convicted of a criminal offense has a constitutional right to a "'record of sufficient completeness' to permit proper consideration of [his] claims." (*Mayer v. Chicago* (1971) 404 U.S. 189, 193–194; *March v. Municipal Court* (1972) 7 Cal.3d 422, 427–428.) The California Supreme Court has also held that an indigent appellant is denied his or her right under the Fourteenth Amendment to the competent assistance of counsel on appeal if counsel fails to obtain an appellate record adequate for consideration of appellant's claims of errors (*People v. Barton* (1978) 21 Cal.3d 513, 518–520).

The *Mayer* and *March* decisions make clear, however, that the constitutionally required "record of sufficient completeness" does not necessarily mean a complete verbatim transcript; other forms of the record, such as a statement on appeal, or a partial transcript may be sufficient. The record that is necessary depends on the grounds for the appeal in the particular case. Under these decisions, where the grounds of appeal make out a colorable need for a complete transcript, the burden is on the State to show that only a portion of the transcript or an alternative form of the record will suffice for an effective appeal on those grounds. The burden of overcoming the need for a verbatim reporter's transcript appears to be met where a verbatim recording of the proceedings is provided. (*Mayer, supra,* 404 U.S. at p. 195; cf. *Eyrich v. Mun. Court* (1985) 165 Cal.App.3d 1138, 1140 ["Although use of a court reporter is one way of obtaining a verbatim record, it may also be acquired through an electronic recording when no court reporter is available"].)

Some courts have adopted local rules that establish procedures for determining whether only a portion of a verbatim transcript or an alternative form of the record will be sufficient for an effective appeal, including (1) requiring the appellant to specify the points the appellant is raising on appeal; (2) requiring the appellant and respondent to meet and confer about the content and form of the record; and (3) holding a hearing on the content and form of the record. Local procedures can be tailored to reflect the methods available in a particular court for making a record of the trial court proceedings that is sufficient for an effective appeal.

Rule 8.866. Preparation of reporter's transcript

(a) When preparation begins

(1) Unless the court has adopted a local rule under rule 8.865(b) that provides otherwise, the reporter must immediately begin preparing the reporter's transcript if the notice sent to the reporter by the clerk under rule 8.864(a)(1) indicates either:

(A) That the defendant was represented by appointed counsel at trial; or

(B) That the appellant is the People.

(2) If the notice sent to the reporter by the clerk under rule 8.864(a)(1) indicates that the appellant is the defendant and that the defendant was not represented by appointed counsel at trial:

(A) Within 10 days after the date the clerk sent the notice under rule 8.864(a)(1), the reporter must file with the clerk the estimated cost of preparing the reporter's transcript.

(B) The clerk must promptly notify the appellant and his or her counsel of the estimated cost of preparing the reporter's transcript. The notification must show the date it was sent.

(C) Within 10 days after the date the clerk sent the notice under (B), the appellant must do one of the following:

(i) Deposit with the clerk an amount equal to the estimated cost of preparing the transcript;

(ii) File a waiver of the deposit signed by the reporter;

(iii) File a declaration of indigency supported by evidence in the form required by the Judicial Council;

(iv) File a certified transcript of all of the proceedings required to be included in the reporter's transcript under rule 8.865. The transcript must comply with the format requirements of rule 8.144;

(v) Notify the clerk by filing a new election that he or she will be using a statement on appeal instead of a reporter's transcript. The appellant must prepare, serve, and file a proposed statement on appeal within 20 days after serving and filing the notice and must otherwise comply with the requirements for statements on appeal under rule 8.869; or

(vi) Notify the clerk by filing a new election that he or she now elects to proceed without a record of the oral proceedings in the trial court; or

(vii) Notify the clerk that he or she is abandoning the appeal by filing an abandonment in the reviewing court under rule 8.855.

(D) If the trial court determines that the appellant is not indigent, within 10 days after the date the clerk sends notice of this determination to the appellant, the appellant must do one of the following:

(i) Deposit with the clerk an amount equal to the estimated cost of preparing the transcript;

(ii) File with the clerk a waiver of the deposit signed by the reporter;

(iii) File a certified transcript of all of the proceedings required to be included in the reporter's transcript under rule 8.865. The transcript must comply with the format requirements of rule 8.144;

(iv) Notify the clerk by filing a new election that he or she will be using a statement on appeal instead of a reporter's transcript. The appellant must prepare, serve, and file a proposed statement on appeal within 20 days after serving and filing the notice and must otherwise comply with the requirements for statements on appeal under rule 8.869; or

(v) Notify the clerk by filing a new election that he or she now elects to proceed without a record of the oral proceedings in the trial court; or

(vi) Notify the clerk that he or she is abandoning the appeal by filing an abandonment in the reviewing court under rule 8.855.

(E) The clerk must promptly notify the reporter to begin preparing the transcript when:

(i) The clerk receives the required deposit under (C)(i) or (D)(i);

(ii) The clerk receives a waiver of the deposit signed by the reporter under (C)(ii) or (D)(ii); or

(iii) The trial court determines that the appellant is indigent and orders that the appellant receive the transcript without cost.

(Subd (a) amended effective January 1, 2016; adopted effective January 1, 2009; previously amended effective March 1, 2014.)

(b) Format of transcript

The reporter's transcript must comply with rule 8.144.

(Subd (b) adopted effective January 1, 2009.)

(c) Copies and certification

The reporter must prepare an original and the same number of copies of the reporter's transcript as rule 8.862 requires of the clerk's transcript and must certify each as correct.

(Subd (c) adopted effective January 1, 2009.)

(d) When preparation must be completed

(1) The reporter must deliver the original and all copies to the trial court clerk as soon as they are certified but no later than 20 days after the reporter is required to begin preparing the transcript under (a). Only the presiding judge of the appellate division or his or her designee may extend the time to prepare the reporter's transcript (see rule 8.810).

(2) If the appellant deposited with the clerk an amount equal to the estimated cost of preparing the transcript and the appeal is abandoned or dismissed before the reporter has filed the transcript, the reporter must inform the clerk of the cost of the portion of the transcript that the reporter has completed. The clerk must pay that amount to the reporter from the appellant's deposited funds and refund any excess deposit to the appellant.

(Subd (d) amended effective March 5, 2018; adopted effective January 1, 2009; previously amended effective March 1, 2014, January 1, 2017, and January 1, 2018.)

(e) Multi-reporter cases

In a multi-reporter case, the clerk must accept any completed portion of the transcript from the primary reporter one week after the time prescribed by (d) even if other portions are uncompleted. The clerk must promptly pay each reporter who certifies that all portions of the transcript assigned to that reporter are completed.

(Subd (e) adopted effective January 1, 2009.)

(f) Notice when proceedings were not reported or cannot be transcribed

(1) If any portion of the oral proceedings to be included in the reporter's transcript was not reported or cannot be transcribed, the trial court clerk must so notify the parties in writing. The notice must:

(A) Indicate whether the identified proceedings were officially electronically recorded under Government Code section 69957; and

(B) Show the date it was sent.

(2) Within 15 days after this notice is sent by the clerk, the appellant must serve and file a notice with the court stating whether the appellant elects to proceed with or without a record of the identified proceedings. When the party elects to proceed with a record of these oral proceedings:

(A) If the clerk's notice under (1) indicates that the proceedings were officially electronically recorded under Government Code section 69957, the appellant's notice must specify which form of the record listed in rule 8.864(a) other than a reporter's transcript the appellant elects to use. The appellant must comply with the requirements applicable to the form of the record elected.

(B) If the clerk's notice under (1) indicates that the proceedings were not officially electronically recorded under Government Code section 69957, the appellant must prepare, serve, and file a proposed statement on appeal within 20 days after serving and filing the notice.

(Subd (f) amended effective January 1, 2016; adopted effective March 1, 2014.)
Rule 8.866 amended effective March 5, 2018; adopted effective January 1, 2009; previously amended effective March 1, 2014, January 1, 2016, January 1, 2017, and January 1, 2018.

Advisory Committee Comment

Subdivision (a). If the appellant was not represented by the public defender or other appointed counsel in the trial court, the appellant must use *Defendant's Financial Statement on Eligibility for Appointment of Counsel and Reimbursement and Record on Appeal at Public Expense* (form CR-105) to show indigency. This form is available at any courthouse or county law library or online at *www.courts.ca.gov/forms.*

Subdivisions (a)(2)(C)(iv) and (a)(2)(D)(iii). Sometimes a party in a trial court proceeding will purchase reporter's transcripts of all or part of the proceedings before any appeal is filed. In recognition of the fact that such transcripts may already have been purchased, this rule allows an appellant, in lieu of depositing funds for a reporter's transcript, to deposit with the trial court a certified transcript of the proceedings necessary for the appeal. Subdivisions (a)(2)(C)(iv) and (a)(2)(D)(iii) make clear that the certified transcript may be filed in lieu of a deposit for a reporter's transcript only where the certified transcript contains all of the proceedings required under rule 8.865 and the transcript complies with the format requirements of rule 8.144.

Rule 8.867. Limited normal record in certain appeals

(a) Application and additions

This rule establishes a limited normal record for certain appeals. This rule does not alter the parties' right to request that exhibits be transmitted to the reviewing court under rule 8.870 nor preclude either an application in the superior court under (e) for additions to the limited normal record or a motion in the reviewing court for augmentation under rule 8.841.

(Subd (a) adopted effective March 1, 2014.)

(b) Pretrial appeals of rulings on motions under Penal Code section 1538.5

If before trial either the defendant or the People appeal a ruling on a motion under Penal Code section 1538.5 for the return of property or the suppression of evidence, the normal record is composed of:

(1) *Record of the documents filed in the trial court*

A clerk's transcript or original trial court file containing:

(A) The complaint, including any notice to appear, and any amendment;

(B) The motion under Penal Code section 1538.5, with supporting and opposing memoranda, and attachments;

(C) The order on the motion under Penal Code section 1538.5;

(D) Any court minutes relating to the order; and

(E) The notice of appeal.

(2) *Record of the oral proceedings in the trial court*

If an appellant wants to raise any issue that requires consideration of the oral proceedings in the trial court, a reporter's transcript, a transcript prepared under rule 8.868, an official electronic recording under rule 8.868, or a statement on appeal under rule 8.869 summarizing any oral proceedings incident to the order on the motion under Penal Code section 1538.5.

(Subd (b) adopted effective March 1, 2014.)

(c) Appeals from judgments on demurrers or certain appealable orders

If the People appeal from a judgment on a demurrer to the complaint, including any notice to appear, or if the defendant or the People appeal from an appealable order other than a ruling on a motion for new trial or a ruling covered by (a), the normal record is composed of:

(1) *Record of the documents filed in the trial court*

A clerk's transcript or original trial court file containing:

(A) The complaint, including any notice to appear, and any amendment;

(B) Any demurrer or other plea;

(C) Any motion or notice of motion granted or denied by the order appealed from, with supporting and opposing memoranda and attachments;

(D) The judgment or order appealed from and any abstract of judgment or commitment;

(E) Any court minutes relating to the judgment or order appealed from and

(i) If there was a trial in the case, any court minutes of proceedings at the time the original verdict is rendered and any subsequent proceedings; or

(ii) If the original judgment of conviction is based on a guilty plea or nolo contendere plea, any court minutes of the proceedings at the time of entry of such plea and any subsequent proceedings;

(F) The notice of appeal; and

(G) If the appellant is the defendant, all probation officer reports.

(2) *Record of the oral proceedings in the trial court*

If an appellant wants to raise any issue which requires consideration of the oral proceedings in the trial court:

(A) A reporter's transcript, a transcript prepared under rule 8.868, an official electronic recording under rule 8.868, or a statement on appeal under rule 8.869 summarizing any oral proceedings incident to the judgment or order being appealed.

(B) If the appeal is from an order after judgment, a reporter's transcript, a transcript prepared under rule 8.868, an official electronic recording under rule 8.868, or a statement on appeal under rule 8.869 summarizing any oral proceedings from:

(i) The original sentencing proceeding; and

(ii) If the original judgment of conviction is based on a guilty plea or nolo contendere plea, the proceedings at the time of entry of such plea.

(Subd (c) amended and lettered effective March 1, 2014; adopted effective January 1, 2009; previously amended effective January 1, 2013.)

(d) Appeals of the conditions of probation

If a defendant's appeal of the judgment contests only the conditions of probation, the normal record is composed of:

(1) *Record of the documents filed in the trial court*

A clerk's transcript or original trial court file containing:

(A) The complaint, including any notice to appear, and any amendment;

(B) The judgment or order appealed from and any abstract of judgment or commitment;

(C) Any court minutes relating to the judgment or order appealed from and:

(i) If there was a trial in the case, any court minutes of proceedings at the time the original verdict is rendered and any subsequent proceedings; or

(ii) If the original judgment of conviction is based on a guilty plea or nolo contendere plea, any court minutes of the proceedings at the time of entry of such plea and any subsequent proceedings;

(D) The notice of appeal; and

(E) All probation officer reports.

(2) *Record of the oral proceedings in the trial court*

If an appellant wants to raise any issue that requires consideration of the oral proceedings in the trial court, a reporter's transcript, a transcript prepared under rule 8.868, an official electronic recording under rule 8.868, or a statement on appeal under rule 8.869 summarizing any oral proceedings from:

(A) The sentencing proceeding; and

(B) If the judgment of conviction is based on a guilty plea or nolo contendere plea, the proceedings at the time of entry of such plea.

(Subd (d) adopted effective March 1, 2014.)

(e) Additions to the record

Either the People or the defendant may apply to the superior court for inclusion in the record under (b), (c), or (d) of any item that would ordinarily be included in the clerk's transcript under rule 8.861 or a reporter's transcript under rule 8.865.

(1) An application for additional record must describe the material to be included and explain how it may be useful in the appeal.

(2) The application must be filed in the superior court with the notice of appeal or as soon thereafter as possible, and will be treated as denied if it is filed after the record is sent to the reviewing court.

(3) The clerk must immediately present the application to the trial judge.

(4) Within five days after the application is filed, the judge must order that the record include as much of the additional material as the judge finds proper to fully present the points raised by the applicant. Denial of the application does not preclude a motion in the reviewing court for augmentation under rule 8.841.

(5) If the judge does not rule on the application within the time prescribed by (4), the requested material—other than exhibits—must be included in the clerk's transcript or the reporter's transcript without a court order.

(6) The clerk must immediately notify the reporter if additions to the reporter's transcript are required under (4) or (5).

(Subd (e) adopted effective March 1, 2014.)

Rule 8.867 amended effective March 1, 2014; adopted effective January 1, 2009; previously amended effective January 1, 2013.

Advisory Committee Comment

Subdivisions (b)(1)(D), (c)(1)(E), and (d)(1)(C). These provisions identify the minutes that must be included in the record. The trial court clerk may include additional minutes beyond those identified in these subdivisions if that would be more cost-effective.

Subdivisions (c)(1)(G) and (d)(1)(E). Rule 8.862(c) addresses the appropriate handling of probation officers' reports that must be included in the clerk's transcript.

Rule 8.868. Record when trial proceedings were officially electronically recorded

(a) Application

This rule applies only if:

(1) The trial court proceedings were officially recorded electronically under Government Code section 69957; and

(2) The electronic recording was prepared in compliance with applicable rules regarding electronic recording of court proceedings.

(Subd (a) adopted effective January 1, 2009.)

(b) Transcripts from official electronic recording

Written transcripts of an official electronic recording may be prepared under rule 2.952. A transcript prepared and certified as provided in that rule is prima facie a true and complete record of the oral proceedings it purports to cover, and satisfies any requirement in these rules or in any statute for a reporter's transcript of oral proceedings.

(Subd (b) adopted effective January 1, 2009.)

(c) Use of official recording as record of oral proceedings

If the court has a local rule for the appellate division permitting this, on stipulation of the parties or on order of the trial court under rule 8.869(d)(6), the original of an official electronic recording of the trial court proceedings, or a copy made by the court, may be transmitted as the record of these oral proceedings without being transcribed. Such an electronic recording satisfies any requirement in these rules or in any statute for a reporter's transcript of these proceedings.

(Subd (c) amended effective July 1, 2010; adopted effective January 1, 2009.)

(d) Contents

Except in appeals when either the parties have filed a stipulation under rule 8.860(b) or the trial court has ordered that any of these items is not required for proper determination of the appeal, rules 8.865 and 8.867 govern the contents of a transcript of an official electronic recording.

(Subd (d) adopted effective March 1, 2014.)

(e) When preparation begins

(1) If the appellant files an election under rule 8.864 to use a transcript of an official electronic recording or a copy of the official electronic recording as the record of the oral proceedings, unless the trial court has a local rule providing otherwise, preparation of a transcript or a copy of the recording must begin immediately if either:

(A) The defendant was represented by appointed counsel at trial; or

(B) The appellant is the People.

(2) If the appellant is the defendant and the defendant was not represented by appointed counsel at trial:

(A) Within 10 days after the date the defendant files the election under rule 8.864(a)(1), the clerk must notify the appellant and his or her counsel of the estimated cost of preparing the transcript or the copy of the recording. The notification must show the date it was sent.

(B) Within 10 days after the date the clerk sent the notice under (A), the appellant must do one of the following:

(i) Deposit with the clerk an amount equal to the estimated cost of preparing the transcript or the copy of the recording;

(ii) File a declaration of indigency supported by evidence in the form required by the Judicial Council;

(iii) Notify the clerk by filing a new election that he or she will be using a statement on appeal instead of a transcript or copy of the recording. The appellant must prepare, serve, and file a proposed statement on appeal within 20 days after serving and filing the notice and must otherwise comply with the requirements for statements on appeal under rule 8.869;

(iv) Notify the clerk by filing a new election that he or she now elects to proceed without a record of the oral proceedings in the trial court; or

(v) Notify the clerk that he or she is abandoning the appeal by filing an abandonment in the reviewing court under rule 8.855.

(C) If the trial court determines that the appellant is not indigent, within 10 days after the date the clerk sends notice of this determination to the appellant, the appellant must do one of the following:

(i) Deposit with the clerk an amount equal to the estimated cost of preparing the transcript or the copy of the recording;

(ii) Notify the clerk by filing a new election that he or she will be using a statement on appeal instead of a reporter's transcript. The appellant must prepare, serve, and file a proposed statement on appeal within 20 days after serving and filing the notice and must otherwise comply with the requirements for statements on appeal under rule 8.869;

(iii) Notify the clerk by filing a new election that he or she now elects to proceed without a record of the oral proceedings in the trial court; or

(iv) Notify the clerk that he or she is abandoning the appeal by filing an abandonment in the reviewing court under rule 8.855.

(D) Preparation of the transcript or the copy of the recording must begin when:

(i) The clerk receives the required deposit under (B)(i) or (C)(i); or

(ii) The trial court determines that the defendant is indigent and orders that the defendant receive the transcript or the copy of the recording without cost.

(Subd (e) amended effective January 1, 2016; adopted as subd (d) effective January 1, 2009; previously amended and relettered as subd (e) effective March 1, 2014.)

(f) Notice when proceedings were not officially electronically recorded or cannot be transcribed

(1) If any portion of the oral proceedings to be included in the transcript was not officially electronically recorded under Government Code section 69957 or cannot be transcribed, the trial court clerk must so notify the parties in writing. The notice must:

(A) Indicate whether the identified proceedings were reported by a court reporter; and

(B) Show the date it was sent.

(2) Within 15 days after this notice is sent by the clerk, the appellant must serve and file a notice with the court stating whether the appellant elects to proceed with or without a record of the identified oral proceedings. When the party elects to proceed with a record of these oral proceedings:

(A) If the clerk's notice under (1) indicates that the proceedings were reported by a court reporter, the appellant's notice must specify which form of the record listed in rule 8.864(a) other than an official electronic recording or a transcript prepared from an official electronic recording the appellant elects to use. The appellant must comply with the requirements applicable to the form of the record elected.

(B) If the clerk's notice under (1) indicates that the proceedings were not reported by a court reporter, the appellant must prepare, serve, and file a proposed statement on appeal within 20 days after serving and filing the notice.

(Subd (f) amended effective January 1, 2016; adopted effective March 1, 2014.)
Rule 8.868 amended effective January 1, 2016; adopted effective January 1, 2009; previously amended effective July 1, 2010, and March 1, 2014.

Advisory Committee Comment

Subdivision (d). If the appellant was not represented by the public defender or other appointed counsel in the trial court, the appellant must use *Defendant's Financial Statement on Eligibility for Appointment of Counsel and Reimbursement and Record on Appeal at Public Expense* (form CR-105) to show indigency. This form is available at any courthouse or county law library or online at *www.courtinfo.ca.gov/forms.*

Rule 8.869. Statement on appeal

(a) Description

A statement on appeal is a summary of the trial court proceedings that is approved by the trial court. An appellant can elect under rule 8.864 to use a statement on appeal as the record of the oral proceedings in the trial court, replacing the reporter's transcript.

(Subd (a) adopted effective January 1, 2009.)

(b) Preparing the proposed statement

(1) If the appellant elects under rule 8.864 to use a statement on appeal, the appellant must prepare, serve, and file a proposed statement within 20 days after filing the record preparation election.

(2) Appellants who are not represented by an attorney must file their proposed statement on *Proposed Statement on Appeal (Misdemeanor)* (form CR-135). For good cause, the court may permit the filing of a statement that is not on form CR-135.

(3) If the appellant does not serve and file a proposed statement within the time specified in (1), rule 8.874 applies.

(Subd (b) amended effective March 1, 2014; adopted effective January 1, 2009.)

(c) Contents of the proposed statement on appeal

A proposed statement prepared by the appellant must contain:

(1) A statement of the points the appellant is raising on appeal. The appeal is then limited to those points unless the appellate division determines that the record permits the full consideration of another point.

(A) The statement must specify the intended grounds of appeal by clearly stating each point to be raised but need not identify each particular ruling or matter to be challenged.

(B) If one of the grounds of appeal is insufficiency of the evidence, the statement must specify how it is insufficient.

(2) A summary of the trial court's rulings and the sentence imposed on the defendant.

(3) A condensed narrative of the oral proceedings that the appellant believes necessary for the appeal.

(A) The condensed narrative must include a concise factual summary of the evidence and the testimony of each witness that is relevant to the points which the appellant states under (1) are being raised on appeal. Any evidence or portion of a proceeding not included will be presumed to support the judgment or order appealed from.

(B) If one of the points which the appellant states under (1) is being raised on appeal is a challenge to the giving, refusal, or modification of a jury instruction, the condensed narrative must include any instructions submitted orally and not in writing and must identify the party that requested the instruction and any modification.

(Subd (c) amended effective March 1, 2014; adopted effective January 1, 2009; previously amended effective July 1, 2009.)

(d) Review of the appellant's proposed statement

(1) Within 10 days after the appellant files the proposed statement, the respondent may serve and file proposed amendments to that statement.

(2) No later than 10 days after either the respondent files proposed amendments or the time to do so expires, a party may request a hearing to review and correct the proposed statement. No hearing will be held unless ordered by the trial court judge, and the judge will not ordinarily order a hearing unless there is a factual dispute about a material aspect of the trial court proceedings.

(3) Except as provided in (6), if no hearing is ordered, no later than 10 days after the time for requesting a hearing expires, the trial court judge must review the proposed statement and any proposed amendments filed by the respondent and take one of the following actions:

(A) If the proposed statement does not contain material required under (c), the trial court judge may order the appellant to prepare a new proposed statement. The order must identify the additional material that must be included in the statement to comply with (c) and the date by which the new proposed statement must be served and filed. If the appellant does not serve and file a new proposed statement as directed, rule 8.874 applies.

(B) If the trial court judge does not issue an order under (A), the trial court judge must either:

(i) Make any corrections or modifications to the statement necessary to ensure that it is an accurate summary of the evidence and the testimony of each witness that is relevant to the points which the appellant states under (c)(1) are being raised on appeal; or

(ii) Identify the necessary corrections and modifications and order the appellant to prepare a statement incorporating these corrections and modifications.

(4) If a hearing is ordered, the court must promptly set the hearing date and provide the parties with at least 5 days' written notice of the hearing date. No later than 10 days after the hearing, the trial court judge must either:

(A) Make any corrections or modifications to the statement necessary to ensure that it is an accurate summary of the evidence and the testimony of each witness that is relevant to the points which the appellant states under (c)(1) are being raised on appeal; or

(B) Identify the necessary corrections and modifications and order the appellant to prepare a statement incorporating these corrections and modifications.

(5) The trial court judge must not eliminate the appellant's specification of grounds of appeal from the proposed statement.

(6) If the trial court proceedings were reported by a court reporter or officially recorded electronically under Government Code section 69957 and the trial court judge determines that it would save court time and resources, instead of correcting a proposed statement on appeal:

(A) If the court has a local rule for the appellate division permitting the use of an official electronic recording as the record of the oral proceedings, the trial court judge may order that the original of an official electronic recording of the trial court proceedings, or a copy made by the court, be transmitted as the record of these oral proceedings without being transcribed. The court will pay for any copy of the official electronic recording ordered under this subdivision; or

(B) If the court has a local rule permitting this, the trial court judge may order that a transcript be prepared as the record of the oral proceedings. The court will pay for any transcript ordered under this subdivision.

(Subd (d) amended effective March 1, 2014; adopted effective January 1, 2009.)

(e) Review of the corrected or modified statement

(1) If the trial court judge makes any corrections or modifications to the proposed statement under (d), the clerk must serve copies of the corrected or modified statement on the parties. If under (d) the trial court judge orders the appellant to prepare a statement incorporating corrections and modifications, the appellant must serve and file the corrected or modified statement within the time ordered by the court. If the appellant does not serve and file a corrected or modified statement as directed, rule 8.874 applies.

(2) Within 10 days after the corrected or modified statement is served on the parties, any party may serve and file proposed modifications or objections to the statement.

(3) Within 10 days after the time for filing proposed modifications or objections under (2) has expired, the judge must review the corrected or modified statement and any proposed modifications or objections to the statement filed by the parties. The procedures in (d)(3) or (4) apply if the judge determines that further corrections or modifications are necessary to ensure that the statement is an accurate summary of the evidence and the testimony of each witness relevant to the points which the appellant states under (c)(1) are being raised on appeal.

(Subd (e) amended effective March 1, 2014; adopted effective January 1, 2009.)

(f) Certification of the statement on appeal

If the trial court judge does not make or order any corrections or modifications to the proposed statement under (d)(3), (d)(4), or (e)(3) and does not order either the use of an official electronic recording or preparation of a transcript in lieu of correcting the proposed statement under (d)(6), the judge must promptly certify the statement.

(Subd (f) amended effective March 1, 2014; adopted effective January 1, 2009.)

(g) Extensions of time

For good cause, the trial court may grant an extension of not more than 15 days to do any act required or permitted under this rule.

(Subd (g) adopted effective January 1, 2009.)

Rule 8.869 amended effective March 1, 2014; adopted effective January 1, 2009; previously amended effective July 1, 2009.

Advisory Committee Comment

Rules 8.806, 8.810, and 8.812 address applications for extensions of time and relief from default.

Subdivision (b)(2). *Proposed Statement on Appeal (Misdemeanor)* (form CR-135) is available at any courthouse or county law library or online at *www.courts.ca.gov/forms*.

Subdivision (d). Under rule 8.804, the term "judge" includes a commissioner or a temporary judge.

Subdivisions (d)(3)(B), (d)(4), and (f). The judge need not ensure that the statement as modified or corrected is complete, but only that it is an accurate summary of the evidence and testimony relevant to the issues identified by the appellant.

Rule 8.870.   Exhibits

(a) Exhibits deemed part of record

Exhibits admitted in evidence, refused, or lodged are deemed part of the record, but may be transmitted to the appellate division only as provided in this rule.

(Subd (a) adopted effective January 1, 2009.)

(b) Notice of designation

(1) Within 10 days after the last respondent's brief is filed or could be filed under rule 8.882, if the appellant wants the appellate division to consider any original exhibits that were admitted in evidence, refused, or lodged, the appellant must serve and file a notice in the trial court designating such exhibits.

(2) Within 10 days after a notice under (1) is served, any other party wanting the appellate division to consider additional exhibits must serve and file a notice in trial court designating such exhibits.

(3) A party filing a notice under (1) or (2) must serve a copy on the appellate division.

(Subd (b) adopted effective January 1, 2009.)

(c) Request by appellate division

At any time, the appellate division may direct the trial court or a party to send it an exhibit.

(Subd (c) adopted effective January 1, 2009.)

(d) Transmittal

Unless the appellate division orders otherwise, within 20 days after the first notice under (b) is filed or after the appellate division directs that an exhibit be sent:

Rules of Court

(1) The trial court clerk must put any designated exhibits in the clerk's possession into numerical or alphabetical order and send them to the appellate division. The trial court clerk must also send a list of the exhibits sent. If the exhibits are not transmitted electronically, the trial court clerk must send two copies of the list. If the appellate division clerk finds the list correct, the clerk must sign and return a copy to the trial court clerk.

(2) Any party in possession of designated exhibits returned by the trial court must put them into numerical or alphabetical order and send them to the appellate division. The party must also send a list of the exhibits sent. If the exhibits are not transmitted electronically, the party must send two copies of the list. If the appellate division clerk finds the list correct, the clerk must sign and return a copy to the party.

(Subd (d) amended effective January 1, 2016; adopted effective January 1, 2009.)

(e) Return by appellate division

On request, the appellate division may return an exhibit to the trial court or to the party that sent it. When the remittitur issues, the appellate division must return all exhibits not transmitted electronically to the trial court or to the party that sent them.

(Subd (e) amended effective January 1, 2016; adopted effective January 1, 2009.)

Rule 8.870 amended effective January 1, 2016; adopted effective January 1, 2009.

Rule 8.871. Juror-identifying information

(a) Applicability

In a criminal case, a clerk's transcript, a reporter's transcript, or any other document in the record that contains juror-identifying information must comply with this rule.

(Subd (a) adopted effective January 1, 2009.)

(b) Juror names, addresses, and telephone numbers

(1) The name of each trial juror or alternate sworn to hear the case must be replaced with an identifying number wherever it appears in any document. The trial court clerk must prepare and keep under seal in the case file a table correlating the jurors' names with their identifying numbers. The clerk and the reporter must use the table in preparing all transcripts or other documents.

(2) The addresses and telephone numbers of trial jurors and alternates sworn to hear the case must be deleted from all documents.

(Subd (b) adopted effective January 1, 2009.)

(c) Potential jurors

Information identifying potential jurors called but not sworn as trial jurors or alternates must not be sealed unless otherwise ordered under Code of Civil Procedure section 237(a)(1).

(Subd (c) adopted effective January 1, 2009.)

Rule 8.871 adopted effective January 1, 2009.

Advisory Committee Comment

This rule implements Code of Civil Procedure section 237.

Rule 8.872. Sending and filing the record in the appellate division

(a) When the record is complete

(1) If the appellant elected under rule 8.864 to proceed without a record of the oral proceedings in the trial court, the record is complete when the clerk's transcript is certified as correct or, if the original trial court file will be used instead of the clerk's transcript, when that original file is ready for transmission as provided under rule 8.863(b).

(2) If the appellant elected under rule 8.864 to proceed with a record of the oral proceedings in the trial court, the record is complete when the clerk's transcript is certified as correct or the original file is ready for transmission as provided in (1) and:

(A) If the appellant elected to use a reporter's transcript, the certified reporter's transcript is delivered to the court under rule 8.866;

(B) If the appellant elected to use a transcript prepared from an official electronic recording, the transcript has been prepared under rule 8.868;

(C) If the parties stipulated to the use of an official electronic recording of the proceedings, the electronic recording has been prepared under rule 8.868; or

(D) If the appellant elected to use a statement on appeal, the statement on appeal has been certified by the trial court or a transcript or an official electronic recording has been prepared under rule 8.869(d)(6).

(Subd (a) adopted effective January 1, 2009.)

(b) Sending the record

When the record is complete, the clerk must promptly send:

(1) The original record to the appellate division;

(2) One copy of the clerk's transcript or index to the original court file and one copy of any record of the oral proceedings to each appellant who is represented by separate counsel or is self-represented; and

(3) One copy of the clerk's transcript or index to the original court file and one copy of any record of the oral proceedings to the respondent.

(Subd (b) adopted effective January 1, 2009.)

(c) Filing the record

On receipt, the appellate division clerk must promptly file the original record and send notice of the filing date to the parties.

(Subd (c) amended effective January 1, 2016; adopted effective January 1, 2009.)

Rule 8.872 amended effective January 1, 2016; adopted effective January 1, 2009.

Rule 8.873. Augmenting or correcting the record in the appellate division

(a) Subsequent trial court orders

If, after the record is certified, the trial court amends or recalls the judgment or makes any other order in the case, including an order affecting the sentence or probation, the clerk must promptly certify and send a copy of the amended abstract of judgment or other order as an augmentation of the record to all those who received the record under rule 8.872(b). If there is any additional document or transcript related to the amended judgment or new order that any rule or order requires be included in the record, the clerk must send these documents or transcripts with the amended abstract of judgment or other order. The clerk must promptly copy and certify any such document and the reporter must promptly prepare and certify any such transcript.

(Subd (a) adopted effective January 1, 2009.)

(b) Omissions

If, after the record is certified, the trial court clerk or the reporter learns that the record omits a document or transcript that any rule or order requires to be included, the clerk must promptly copy and certify the document or the reporter must promptly prepare and certify the transcript. Without the need for a court order, the clerk must promptly send the document or transcript as an augmentation of the record to all those who received the record under rule 8.872(b).

(Subd (b) adopted effective January 1, 2009.)

(c) Augmentation or correction by the appellate division

At any time, on motion of a party or on its own motion, the appellate division may order the record augmented or corrected as provided in rule 8.841.

(Subd (c) adopted effective January 1, 2009.)

Rule 8.873 adopted effective January 1, 2009.

Rule 8.874. Failure to procure the record

(a) Notice of default

If a party fails to do any act required to procure the record, the trial court clerk must promptly notify that party in writing that it must do the act specified in the notice within 15 days after the notice is sent and that, if it fails to comply, the appellate division may impose the following sanctions:

(1) When the defaulting party is the appellant:

(A) If the appellant is the defendant and is represented by appointed counsel on appeal, the appellate division may relieve that appointed counsel and appoint new counsel; or

(B) If the appellant is the People or the appellant is the defendant and is not represented by appointed counsel, the appellate division may dismiss the appeal.

(2) When the defaulting party is the respondent:

(A) If the respondent is the defendant and is represented by appointed counsel on appeal, the appellate division may relieve that appointed counsel and appoint new counsel; or

(B) If the respondent is the People or the respondent is the defendant and is not represented by appointed counsel, the appellate division may proceed with the appeal on the record designated by the appellant.

(Subd (a) amended effective January 1, 2016; adopted effective March 1, 2014.)

(b) Sanctions

If the party fails to take the action specified in a notice given under (a), the trial court clerk must promptly notify the appellate division of the default and the appellate division may impose the sanction specified in the notice. If the appellate division dismisses the appeal, it may vacate the dismissal for good cause. If the appellate division orders the appeal to proceed on the record designated by the appellant, the respondent may obtain relief from default under rule 8.812.

(Subd (b) adopted effective March 1, 2014.)

Rule 8.874 amended effective January 1, 2016; adopted effective March 1, 2014.

Chapter 4
Briefs, Hearing, and Decision in Limited Civil and Misdemeanor Appeals

Chapter 4 adopted effective January 1, 2009.

Rule 8.880.   Application

Except as otherwise provided, the rules in this chapter apply to both civil and misdemeanor appeals in the appellate division.
Rule 8.880 adopted effective January 1, 2009.

Rule 8.881.   Notice of briefing schedule

When the record is filed, the clerk of the appellate division must promptly send a notice to each appellate counsel or unrepresented party giving the dates the briefs are due.
Rule 8.881 amended effective January 1, 2016; adopted effective January 1, 2009.

Rule 8.882.   Briefs by parties and amici curiae

(a) Briefs by parties

(1) The appellant must serve and file an appellant's opening brief within:

(A) 30 days after the record—**or the reporter's transcript, after a rule 8.845 election in a civil case**—is filed in the appellate division**; or**

(B) 60 days after the filing of a rule 8.845 election in a civil case, if the appeal proceeds without a reporter's transcript.

(2) Any respondent's brief must be served and filed within 30 days after the appellant files its opening brief.

(3) Any appellant's reply brief must be served and filed within 20 days after the respondent files its brief.

(4) No other brief may be filed except with the permission of the presiding judge.

(5) Instead of filing a brief, or as part of its brief, a party may join in a brief or adopt by reference all or part of a brief in the same or a related appeal.

(Subd (a) amended effective January 1, 2021; adopted effective January 1, 2009.)

(b) Extensions of time

(1) Except as otherwise provided by statute, in a civil case, the parties may extend each period under (a) by up to 30 days by filing one or more stipulations in the appellate division before the brief is due. Stipulations must be signed by and served on all parties. If the stipulation is filed in paper form, the original signature of at least one party must appear on the stipulation filed in the appellate division; the signatures of the other parties may be in the form of fax copies of the signed signature page of the stipulation. If the stipulation is electronically filed, the signatures must comply with the requirements of rule 8.77.

(2) A stipulation under (1) is effective on filing. The appellate division may not shorten such a stipulated extension.

(3) Before the brief is due, a party may apply to the presiding judge of the appellate division for an extension of the time period for filing a brief under (a). The application must show that there is good cause to grant an extension under rule 8.811(b). In civil appeals, the application must also show that:

(A) The applicant was unable to obtain—or it would have been futile to seek—the extension by stipulation; or

(B) The parties have stipulated to the maximum extension permitted under (1) and the applicant seeks a further extension.

(4) A party need not apply for an extension or relief from default if it can file its brief within the time prescribed by (c). The clerk must file a brief submitted within that time if it otherwise complies with these rules.

(Subd (b) amended effective January 1, 2016; adopted effective January 1, 2009; previously amended effective January 1, 2010, and January 1, 2013.)

(c) Failure to file a brief

(1) If a party in a civil appeal fails to timely file an appellant's opening brief or a respondent's brief, the appellate division clerk must promptly notify the party in writing that the brief must be filed within 15 days after the notice is sent and that if the party fails to comply, the court may impose one of the following sanctions:

(A) If the brief is an appellant's opening brief, the court may dismiss the appeal; or

(B) If the brief is a respondent's brief, the court may decide the appeal on the record, the appellant's opening brief, and any oral argument by the appellant.

(2) If the appellant in a misdemeanor appeal fails to timely file an opening brief, the appellate division clerk must promptly notify the appellant in writing that the brief must be filed within 30 days after the notice is sent and that if the appellant fails to comply, the court may impose one of the following sanctions:

(A) If the appellant is the defendant and is represented by appointed counsel on appeal, the court may relieve that appointed counsel and appoint new counsel; or

(B) In all other cases, the court may dismiss the appeal.

(3) If the respondent in a misdemeanor appeal fails to timely file a brief, the appellate division clerk must promptly notify the respondent in writing that the brief must be filed within 30 days after the notice is sent and that if the respondent fails to comply, the court may impose one of the following sanctions:

(A) If the respondent is the defendant and is represented by appointed counsel on appeal, the court may relieve that appointed counsel and appoint new counsel; or

(B) In all other cases, the court may decide the appeal on the record, the appellant's opening brief, and any oral argument by the appellant.

(4) If a party fails to comply with a notice under (1), (2), or (3), the court may impose the sanction specified in the notice.

(Subd (c) amended effective January 1, 2016; adopted as subd (b) effective January 1, 2009; previously relettered as subd (c) effective January 1, 2009; previously amended effective March 1, 2014.)

(d) Amicus curiae briefs

(1) Within 14 days after the appellant's reply brief is filed or was required to be filed, whichever is earlier, any person or entity may serve and file an application for permission of the presiding judge to file an amicus curiae brief. For good cause, the presiding judge may allow later filing.

(2) The application must state the applicant's interest and explain how the proposed amicus curiae brief will assist the court in deciding the matter.

(3) The application must also identify:

(A) Any party or any counsel for a party in the pending appeal who:

(i) Authored the proposed amicus brief in whole or in part; or

(ii) Made a monetary contribution intended to fund the preparation or submission of the brief; and

(B) Every person or entity who made a monetary contribution intended to fund the preparation or submission of the brief, other than the amicus curiae, its members, or its counsel in the pending appeal.

(4) The proposed brief must be served and must accompany the application and may be combined with it.

(5) The Attorney General may file an amicus curiae brief without the presiding judge's permission, unless the brief is submitted on behalf of another state officer or agency; but the presiding judge may prescribe reasonable conditions for filing and answering the brief.

(Subd (d) amended and relettered effective January 1, 2009; adopted as subd (c) effective January 1, 2009.)

(e) Service and filing

(1) Copies of each brief must be served as required by rule 8.817.

(2) Unless the court provides otherwise by local rule or order in the specific case, only the original brief, with proof of service, must be filed in the appellate division.

(3) A copy of each brief must be served on the trial court clerk for delivery to the judge who tried the case.

(4) A copy of each brief must be served on a public officer or agency when required by rule 8.817.

(5) In misdemeanor appeals:

(A) Defendant's appellate counsel must serve each brief for the defendant on the People and must send a copy of each brief to the defendant personally unless the defendant requests otherwise;

Rules of Court

(B) The proof of service under (A) must state that a copy of the defendant's brief was sent to the defendant, or counsel must file a signed statement that the defendant requested in writing that no copy be sent; and

(C) The People must serve two copies of their briefs on the appellate counsel for each defendant who is a party to the appeal.

(Subd (e) amended effective January 1, 2018; adopted as subd (d) effective January 1, 2009; previously amended and relettered as subd (e) effective January 1, 2009.)

Rule 8.882 amended effective January 1, 2021; adopted effective January 1, 2009; previously amended effective January 1, 2009, January 1, 2010, January 1, 2013, March 1, 2014, January 1, 2016, and January 1, 2018.

Advisory Committee Comment

Subdivision (a). Note that the sequence and timing of briefing in appeals in which a party is both appellant and respondent (cross-appeals) are governed by rule 8.884. Typically, a cross-appellant's combined respondent's brief and opening brief must be filed within the time specified in (a)(2) for the respondent's brief.

Subdivision (b). Extensions of briefing time are limited by statute in some cases. For example, under Public Resources Code section 21167.6(h) in cases under section 21167 extensions are limited to one 30-day extension for the opening brief and one 30-day extension for "preparation of responding brief."

Rule 8.883.   Contents and form of briefs

(a) Contents

(1) Each brief must:

(A) State each point under a separate heading or subheading summarizing the point and support each point by argument and, if possible, by citation of authority; and

(B) Support any reference to a matter in the record by a citation to the volume and page number of the record where the matter appears.

(2) An appellant's opening brief must:

(A) State the nature of the action, the relief sought in the trial court, and the judgment or order appealed from;

(B) State that the judgment appealed from is final or explain why the order appealed from is appealable; and

(C) Provide a summary of the significant facts limited to matters in the record.

(Subd (a) adopted effective January 1, 2009.)

(b) Length

(1) A brief produced on a computer must not exceed 6,800 words, including footnotes. Such a brief must include a certificate by appellate counsel or an unrepresented party stating the number of words in the brief. The person certifying may rely on the word count of the computer program used to prepare the brief.

(2) A brief produced on a typewriter must not exceed 20 pages.

(3) The information listed on the cover, any table of contents or table of authorities, the certificate under (1), and any signature block are excluded from the limits stated in (1) or (2).

(4) On application, the presiding judge may permit a longer brief for good cause. A lengthy record or numerous or complex issues on appeal will ordinarily constitute good cause. If the court grants an application to file a longer brief, it may order that the brief include a table of contents and a table of authorities.

(Subd (b) amended effective January 1, 2013; adopted effective January 1, 2009; previously amended effective January 1, 2011.)

(c) Form

(1) A brief may be reproduced by any process that produces a clear, black image of letter quality. All documents filed must have a page size of 8½ by 11 inches. If filed in paper form, the paper must be white or unbleached and of at least 20-pound weight. Both sides of the paper may be used if the brief is not bound at the top.

(2) Any conventional font may be used. The font may be either proportionally spaced or monospaced.

(3) The font style must be roman; but for emphasis, italics or boldface may be used or the text may be underscored. Case names must be italicized or underscored. Headings may be in uppercase letters.

(4) Except as provided in (11), the font size, including footnotes, must not be smaller than 13-point.

(5) The lines of text must be at least one-and-a-half-spaced. Headings and footnotes may be single-spaced. Quotations may be block-indented and single-spaced. Single-spaced means six lines to a vertical inch.

(6) The margins must be at least 1½ inches on the left and right and 1 inch on the top and bottom.

(7) The pages must be consecutively numbered.

(8) The cover—or first page if there is no cover—must include the information required by rule 8.816(a)(1).

(9) If filed in paper form, the brief must be bound on the left margin, except that briefs may be bound at the top if required by a local rule of the appellate division. If the brief is stapled, the bound edge and staples must be covered with tape.

(10) The brief need not be signed.

(11) If the brief is produced on a typewriter:

(A) A typewritten original and carbon copies may be filed only with the presiding judge's permission, which will ordinarily be given only to unrepresented parties proceeding in forma pauperis. All other typewritten briefs must be filed as photocopies.

(B) Both sides of the paper may be used if a photocopy is filed; only one side may be used if a typewritten original and carbon copies are filed.

(C) The type size, including footnotes, must not be smaller than standard pica, 10 characters per inch. Unrepresented incarcerated litigants may use elite type, 12 characters per inch, if they lack access to a typewriter with larger characters.

(Subd (c) amended effective January 1, 2016; adopted effective January 1, 2009; previously amended effective January 1, 2011, January 1, 2013, and January 1, 2014.)

(d) Noncomplying briefs

If a brief does not comply with this rule:

(1) The reviewing court clerk may decline to file it, but must mark it "received but not filed" and return it to the party; or

(2) If the brief is filed, the presiding judge may with or without notice:

(A) Order the brief returned for corrections and refiling within a specified time;

(B) Strike the brief with leave to file a new brief within a specified time; or

(C) Disregard the noncompliance.

(Subd (d) adopted effective January 1, 2009.)

Rule 8.883 amended effective January 1, 2016; adopted effective January 1, 2009; previously amended effective January 1, 2011, January 1, 2013, and January 1, 2014.

Advisory Committee Comment

Subdivision (b). Subdivision (b)(1) states the maximum permissible lengths of briefs produced on a computer in terms of word count rather than page count. This provision tracks a provision in rule 8.204(c) governing Court of Appeal briefs and is explained in the comment to that provision. Subdivision (b)(3) specifies certain items that are not counted toward the maximum brief length. Signature blocks, as referenced in this provision, include not only the signatures, but also the printed names, titles, and affiliations of any attorneys filing or joining in the brief, which may accompany the signature.

Rule 8.884.   Appeals in which a party is both appellant and respondent

(a) Briefing sequence and time to file briefs

In an appeal in which any party is both an appellant and a respondent:

(1) The parties must jointly—or separately if unable to agree—submit a proposed briefing sequence to the appellate division within 20 days after the second notice of appeal is filed.

(2) After receiving the proposal, the appellate division must order a briefing sequence and prescribe briefing periods consistent with rule 8.882(a).

(Subd (a) adopted effective January 1, 2009.)

(b) Contents of briefs

(1) A party that is both an appellant and a respondent must combine its respondent's brief with its appellant's opening brief or its reply brief, if any, whichever is appropriate under the briefing sequence that the appellate division orders under (a).

(2) A party must confine a reply brief to points raised in its own appeal.

(3) A combined brief must address the points raised in each appeal separately but may include a single summary of the significant facts.

(Subd (b) amended effective January 1, 2009; adopted effective January 1, 2009.)

Rule 8.884 amended effective January 1, 2009; adopted effective January 1, 2009.

Rule 8.885.   Oral argument

(a) Calendaring and sessions

(1) Unless otherwise ordered, **and except as provided in (2),** all appeals in which the last reply brief was filed or the time for filing this brief expired 45 or more days before the date of a regular appellate division session must be placed on the calendar for that session by the

appellate division clerk. By order of the presiding judge or the division, any appeal may be placed on the calendar for oral argument at any session.

(2) Oral argument will not be set in appeals under *People v. Wende* (1979) 25 Cal.3d 436 where no arguable issue is raised.

(Subd (a) amended effective January 1, 2020; adopted effective January 1, 2009.)

(b) Oral argument by videoconference

(1) Oral argument may be conducted by videoconference if:

(A) It is ordered by the presiding judge of the appellate division or the presiding judge's designee on application of any party or on the court's own motion. An application from a party requesting that oral argument be conducted by videoconference must be filed within 10 days after the court sends notice of oral argument under (c)(1); or

(B) A local rule authorizes oral argument to be conducted by videoconference consistent with these rules.

(2) If oral argument is conducted by videoconference:

(A) Each judge of the appellate division panel assigned to the case must participate in the entire oral argument either in person at the superior court that issued the judgment or order that is being appealed or by videoconference from another court.

(B) Unless otherwise allowed by local rule or ordered by the presiding judge of the appellate division or the presiding judge's designee, all the parties must appear at oral argument in person at the superior court that issued the judgment or order that is being appealed.

(C) The oral argument must be open to the public at the superior court that issued the judgment or order that is being appealed. If provided by local rule or ordered by the presiding judge of the appellate division or the presiding judge's designee, oral argument may also be open to the public at any of the locations from which a judge of the appellate division is participating in oral argument.

(D) The appellate division must ensure that:

(i) During oral argument, the participants in oral argument are visible and their statements are audible to all other participants, court staff, and any members of the public attending the oral argument;

(ii) Participants are identified when they speak; and

(iii) Only persons who are authorized to participate in the proceedings speak.

(E) A party must not be charged any fee to participate in oral argument by videoconference if the party participates from the superior court that issued the judgment or order that is being appealed or from a location from which a judge of the appellate division panel is participating in oral argument.

(Subd (b) adopted effective January 1, 2010.)

(c) Notice of argument

(1) **Except for appeals covered by (a)(2),** as soon as all parties' briefs are filed or the time for filing these briefs has expired, the appellate division clerk must send a notice of the time and place of oral argument to all parties. The notice must be sent at least 20 days before the date for oral argument. The presiding judge may shorten the notice period for good cause; in that event, the clerk must immediately notify the parties by telephone or other expeditious method.

(2) If oral argument will be conducted by videoconference under (b), the clerk must specify, either in the notice required under (1) or in a supplemental notice sent to all parties at least 5 days before the date for oral argument, the location from which each judge of the appellate division panel assigned to the case will participate in oral argument.

(Subd (c) amended effective January 1, 2020; adopted as subd (b) effective January 1, 2009; previously amended and relettered as subd (c) effective January 1, 2010.)

(d) Waiver of argument

(1) Parties may waive oral argument **in advance by filing a notice of waiver of oral argument within 7 days after the notice of oral argument is sent.**

(2) The court may vacate oral argument if all parties waive oral argument.

(3) If the court vacates oral argument, the court must notify the parties that no oral argument will be held.

(4) If all parties do not waive oral argument, or if the court rejects a waiver request, the matter will remain on the oral argument calendar. Any party who previously filed a notice of waiver may participate in the oral argument.

(Subd (d) amended effective January 1, 2020; adopted as subd (c) effective January 1, 2009; previously relettered as subd (d) effective January 1, 2010.)

(e) Conduct of argument

Unless the court provides otherwise:

(1) The appellant, petitioner, or moving party has the right to open and close. If there are two or more such parties, the court must set the sequence of argument.

(2) Each side is allowed 10 minutes for argument. The appellant may reserve part of this time for reply argument. If multiple parties are represented by separate counsel, or if an amicus curiae—on written request—is granted permission to argue, the court may apportion or expand the time.

(3) Only one counsel may argue for each separately represented party.

(Subd (e) amended and relettered effective January 1, 2010; adopted as subd (d) effective January 1, 2009.)

Rule 8.885 amended effective January 1, 2020; adopted effective January 1, 2009; previously amended effective January 1, 2010.

Advisory Committee Comment

Subdivision (a). Under rule 10.1108, the appellate division must hold a session at least once each quarter, unless no matters are set for oral argument that quarter, but may choose to hold sessions more frequently.

Rule 8.886. Submission of the cause

(a) When the cause is submitted

(1) Except as provided in (2), a cause is submitted when the court has heard oral argument or approved its waiver and the time has expired to file all briefs and papers, including any supplemental brief permitted by the court. The appellate division may order the cause submitted at an earlier time if the parties so stipulate.

(2) For appeals that raise no arguable issues under *People v. Wende* (1979) 25 Cal.3d 436, the cause is submitted when the time has expired to file all briefs and papers, including any supplemental brief permitted by the court.

(Subd (a) amended effective January 1, 2020; adopted effective January 1, 2009.)

(b) Vacating submission

The court may vacate submission only by an order stating its reasons and setting a timetable for resubmission.

(Subd (b) adopted effective January 1, 2009.)

Rule 8.886 amended effective January 1, 2020; adopted effective January 1, 2009.

Rule 8.887. Decisions

(a) Written opinions

Appellate division judges are not required to prepare a written opinion in any case but may do so when they deem it advisable or in the public interest. A decision by opinion must identify the participating judges, including the author of the majority opinion and of any concurring or dissenting opinion, or the judges participating in a "by the court" opinion.

(Subd (a) adopted effective January 1, 2009.)

(b) Filing the decision

The appellate division clerk must promptly file all opinions and orders of the court and on the same day send copies (by e-mail where permissible under rule 2.251) showing the filing date to the parties and, when relevant, to the trial court.

(Subd (b) amended effective January 1, 2019; adopted effective January 1, 2009.)

(c) Opinions certified for publication

(1) Opinions certified for publication must comply to the extent practicable with the *California Style Manual.*

(2) When the opinion is certified for publication, the clerk must immediately send:

(A) Two paper copies and one electronic copy to the Reporter of Decisions in a format approved by the Reporter.

(B) One copy to the Court of Appeal for the district. The copy must bear the notation "This opinion has been certified for publication in the Official Reports. It is being sent to assist the Court of Appeal in deciding whether to order the case transferred to the court on the court's own motion under rules 8.1000–8.1018." The clerk/executive officer of the Court of Appeal must promptly file that copy or make a docket entry showing its receipt.

(Subd (c) amended effective January 1, 2018; adopted effective January 1, 2009; previously amended effective January 1, 2011, and March 1, 2014.)

Rule 8.887 amended effective January 1, 2019; adopted effective January 1, 2009; previously amended effective January 1, 2011, March 1, 2014, and January 1, 2018.

Rule 8.888.   Finality and modification of decision

(a) Finality of decision

(1) Except as otherwise provided in this rule, an appellate division decision, including an order dismissing an appeal involuntarily, is final 30 days after the decision is sent by the court clerk to the parties.

(2) If the appellate division certifies a written opinion for publication or partial publication after its decision is filed and before its decision becomes final in that court, the finality period runs from the date the order for publication is sent by the court clerk to the parties.

(3) The following appellate division decisions are final in that court when filed:

(A) The denial of a petition for writ of supersedeas;

(B) The denial of an application for bail or to reduce bail pending appeal; and

(C) The dismissal of an appeal on request or stipulation.

(Subd (a) amended effective January 1, 2019; adopted effective January 1, 2009.)

(b) Modification of judgment

(1) The appellate division may modify its decision until the decision is final in that court. If the clerk's office is closed on the date of finality, the court may modify the decision on the next day the clerk's office is open.

(2) An order modifying a decision must state whether it changes the appellate judgment. A modification that does not change the appellate judgment does not extend the finality date of the decision. If a modification changes the appellate judgment, the finality period runs from the date the modification order is sent by the court clerk to the parties.

(Subd (b) amended effective January 1, 2019; adopted effective January 1, 2009.)

(c) Consent to increase or decrease in amount of judgment

If an appellate division decision conditions the affirmance of a money judgment on a party's consent to an increase or decrease in the amount, the judgment is reversed unless, before the decision is final under (a), the party serves and files a copy of a consent in the appellate division. If a consent is filed, the finality period runs from the filing date of the consent. The clerk must send one filed-endorsed copy of the consent to the trial court with the remittitur.

(Subd (c) amended effective January 1, 2016; adopted effective January 1, 2009.)

Rule 8.888 amended effective January 1, 2019; adopted effective January 1, 2009; previously amended effective January 1, 2016.

Rule 8.889.   Rehearing

(a) Power to order rehearing

(1) On petition of a party or on its own motion, the appellate division may order rehearing of any decision that is not final in that court on filing.

(2) An order for rehearing must be filed before the decision is final. If the clerk's office is closed on the date of finality, the court may file the order on the next day the clerk's office is open.

(Subd (a) adopted effective January 1, 2009.)

(b) Petition and answer

(1) A party may serve and file a petition for rehearing within 15 days after the following, whichever is later:

(A) The decision is sent by the court clerk to the parties;

(B) A publication order restarting the finality period under rule 8.888(a)(2), if the party has not already filed a petition for rehearing, is sent by the court clerk to the parties;

(C) A modification order changing the appellate judgment under rule 8.888(b) is sent by the court clerk to the parties; or

(D) A consent is filed under rule 8.888(c).

(2) A party must not file an answer to a petition for rehearing unless the court requests an answer. The clerk must promptly send to the parties copies of any order requesting an answer and immediately notify the parties by telephone or another expeditious method. Any answer must be served and filed within 8 days after the order is filed unless the court orders otherwise. A petition for rehearing normally will not be granted unless the court has requested an answer.

(3) The petition and answer must comply with the relevant provisions of rule 8.883.

(4) Before the decision is final and for good cause, the presiding judge may relieve a party from a failure to file a timely petition or answer.

(Subd (b) amended effective January 1, 2019; adopted effective January 1, 2009.)

(c) No extensions of time

The time for granting or denying a petition for rehearing in the appellate division may not be extended. If the court does not rule on the petition before the decision is final, the petition is deemed denied.

(Subd (c) adopted effective January 1, 2009.)

(d) Effect of granting rehearing

An order granting a rehearing vacates the decision and any opinion filed in the case. If the appellate division orders rehearing, it may place the case on calendar for further argument or submit it for decision.

(Subd (d) adopted effective January 1, 2009.)

Rule 8.889 amended effective January 1, 2019; adopted effective January 1, 2009.

Rule 8.890.   Remittitur

(a) Proceedings requiring issuance of remittitur

An appellate division must issue a remittitur after a decision in an appeal.

(Subd (a) adopted effective January 1, 2009.)

(b) Clerk's duties

(1) If an appellate division case is not transferred to the Court of Appeal under rule 8.1000 et seq., the appellate division clerk must:

(A) Issue a remittitur immediately after the Court of Appeal denies transfer or the period for granting transfer under rule 8.1008(a) expires if there will be no further proceedings in the appellate division;

(B) Send the remittitur to the trial court with a filed-endorsed copy of the opinion or order; and

(C) Return to the trial court with the remittitur all original records, exhibits, and documents sent nonelectronically to the appellate division in connection with the appeal, except any certification for transfer under rule 8.1005, the transcripts or statement on appeal, briefs, and the notice of appeal.

(2) If an appellate division case is transferred to a Court of Appeal under rule 8.1000 et seq., on receiving the Court of Appeal remittitur, the appellate division clerk must issue a remittitur and return documents to the trial court as provided in rule 8.1018.

(Subd (b) amended effective January 1, 2016; adopted effective January 1, 2009; previously amended effective January 1, 2011.)

(c) Immediate issuance, stay, and recall

(1) The appellate division may direct immediate issuance of a remittitur only on the parties' stipulation or on dismissal of the appeal on the request or stipulation of the parties under rule 8.825(b)(2).

(2) On a party's or its own motion or on stipulation, and for good cause, the court may stay a remittitur's issuance for a reasonable period or order its recall.

(3) An order recalling a remittitur issued after a decision by opinion does not supersede the opinion or affect its publication status.

(Subd (c) amended effective March 1, 2014; adopted effective January 1, 2009.)

(d) Notice

The remittitur is deemed issued when the clerk enters it in the record. The clerk must immediately send the parties notice of issuance of the remittitur, showing the date of entry.

(Subd (d) adopted effective January 1, 2009.)

Rule 8.890 amended effective January 1, 2016; adopted effective January 1, 2009; previously amended effective January 1, 2011, and March 1, 2014.

Rule 8.891.   Costs and sanctions in civil appeals

(a) Right to costs

(1) Except as provided in this rule, the prevailing party in a civil appeal is entitled to costs on appeal.

(2) The prevailing party is the respondent if the appellate division affirms the judgment without modification or dismisses the appeal. The prevailing party is the appellant if the appellate division reverses the judgment in its entirety.

(3) If the appellate division reverses the judgment in part or modifies it, or if there is more than one notice of appeal, the appellate division must specify the award or denial of costs in its decision.

(4) In the interests of justice, the appellate division may also award or deny costs as it deems proper.

(Subd (a) adopted effective January 1, 2009.)

(b) Judgment for costs

(1) The appellate division clerk must enter on the record and insert in the remittitur judgment awarding costs to the prevailing party under (a).

(2) If the clerk fails to enter judgment for costs, the appellate division may recall the remittitur for correction on its own motion or on a party's motion made not later than 30 days after the remittitur issues.

(Subd (b) adopted effective January 1, 2009.)

(c) Procedure for claiming or opposing costs

(1) Within 30 days after the clerk sends notice of issuance of the remittitur, a party claiming costs awarded by the appellate division must serve and file in the trial court a verified memorandum of costs under rule 3.1700(a)(1).

(2) A party may serve and file a motion in the trial court to strike or tax costs claimed under (1) in the manner required by rule 3.1700.

(3) An award of costs is enforceable as a money judgment.

(Subd (c) amended effective January 1, 2011; adopted effective January 1, 2009.)

(d) Recoverable costs

(1) A party may recover only the costs of the following, if reasonable:

(A) Filing fees;

(B) The amount the party paid for any portion of the record, whether an original or a copy or both, subject to reduction by the appellate division under subdivision (e);

(C) The cost to produce additional evidence on appeal;

(D) The costs to notarize, serve, mail, and file the record, briefs, and other papers;

(E) The cost to print and reproduce any brief, including any petition for rehearing or review, answer, or reply;

(F) The cost to procure a surety bond, including the premium, the cost to obtain a letter of credit as collateral, and the fees and net interest expenses incurred to borrow funds to provide security for the bond or to obtain a letter of credit, unless the trial court determines the bond was unnecessary; and

(G) The fees and net interest expenses incurred to borrow funds to deposit with the superior court in lieu of a bond or undertaking, unless the trial court determines the deposit was unnecessary.

(2) Unless the court orders otherwise, an award of costs neither includes attorney's fees on appeal nor precludes a party from seeking them under rule 3.1702.

(Subd (d) amended effective January 1, 2013; adopted effective January 1, 2009.)

(e) Sanctions

(1) On motion of a party or its own motion, the appellate division may impose sanctions, including the award or denial of costs, on a party or an attorney for:

(A) Taking a frivolous appeal or appealing solely to cause delay; or

(B) Committing any unreasonable violation of these rules.

(2) A party's motion under (1) must include a declaration supporting the amount of any monetary sanction sought and must be served and filed before any order dismissing the appeal but no later than 10 days after the appellant's reply brief is due. If a party files a motion for sanctions with a motion to dismiss the appeal and the motion to dismiss is not granted, the party may file a new motion for sanctions within 10 days after the appellant's reply brief is due.

(3) The court must give notice in writing if it is considering imposing sanctions. Within 10 days after the court sends such notice, a party or attorney may serve and file an opposition, but failure to do so will not be deemed consent. An opposition may not be filed unless the court sends such notice.

(4) Unless otherwise ordered, oral argument on the issue of sanctions must be combined with oral argument on the merits of the appeal.

(Subd (e) adopted effective January 1, 2009.)

Rule 8.891 amended effective January 1, 2013; adopted effective January 1, 2009; previously amended effective January 1, 2011.

Advisory Committee Comment

Subdivision (d). "Net interest expenses" in subdivisions (d)(1)(F) and (G) means the interest expenses incurred to borrow the funds that are deposited minus any interest earned by the borrower on those funds while they are on deposit.

Subdivision (d)(1)(D), allowing recovery of the "costs to notarize, serve, mail, and file the record, briefs, and other papers," is intended to include fees charged by electronic filing service providers for electronic filing and service of documents.

Chapter 5
Appeals in Infraction Cases

Chapter 5 adopted effective January 1, 2009.

Art. 1.   Taking Appeals in Infraction Cases. Rules 8.900–8.904.
Art. 2.   Record in Infraction Appeals. Rules 8.910–8.924.
Art. 3.   Briefs, Hearing, and Decision in Infraction Appeals. Rules 8.925–8.929.

Article 1
Taking Appeals in Infraction Cases

Article 1 adopted effective January 1, 2009.

Rule 8.900.   Application [Renumbered]

Rule 8.900 renumbered to rule 8.950 effective January 1, 2009; adopted as rule 151 effective July 1, 1964; previously amended effective January 1, 1977, and January 1, 2005; previously amended and renumbered effective January 1, 2007.

Another Rule 8.900 follows.

Rule 8.900.   Application of chapter

The rules in this chapter apply only to appeals in infraction cases. An infraction case is a case in which the defendant was convicted only of an infraction and was not charged with any felony. A felony is "charged" when an information or indictment accusing the defendant of a felony is filed or a complaint accusing the defendant of a felony is certified to the superior court under Penal Code section 859a.

Rule 8.900 adopted effective January 1, 2009.

Advisory Committee Comment

Chapter 1 of this division also applies in appeals from infraction cases. Chapters 3 and 4 of this division apply to appeals in misdemeanor cases. The rules that apply in appeals in felony cases are located in chapter 3 of division 1 of this title.

Penal Code section 1466 provides that an appeal in a "misdemeanor or infraction case" is to the appellate division of the superior court, and Penal Code section 1235(b), in turn, provides that an appeal in a "felony case" is to the Court of Appeal. Penal Code section 691(g) defines "misdemeanor or infraction case" to mean "a criminal action in which a misdemeanor or infraction is charged *and does not include a criminal action in which a felony is charged* in conjunction with a misdemeanor or infraction" (emphasis added), and section 691(f) defines "felony case" to mean "a criminal action in which a felony is charged *and includes a criminal action in which a misdemeanor or infraction is charged in conjunction with a felony*" (emphasis added).

As rule 8.304 from the rules on felony appeals makes clear, a "felony case" is an action in which a felony is charged *regardless of the outcome of the action.* Thus the question of which rules apply—these appellate division rules or the rules governing appeals in felony cases—is answered simply by examining the accusatory pleading: if that document charged the defendant with at least one count of felony (as defined in Penal Code, section 17(a)), the Court of Appeal has appellate jurisdiction and the appeal must be taken under the rules on felony appeals *even if the prosecution did not result in a punishment of imprisonment in a state prison.*

It is settled case law that an appeal is taken to the Court of Appeal not only when the defendant is charged with and convicted of a felony, but also when the defendant is charged with both a felony and a misdemeanor (Pen. Code, § 691(f)) but is convicted of only the misdemeanor (e.g., *People v. Brown* (1970) 10 Cal.App.3d 169); when the defendant is charged with a felony but is convicted of only a lesser offense (Pen. Code, § 1159; e.g., *People v. Spreckels* (1954) 125 Cal.App.2d 507); and when the defendant is charged with an offense filed as a felony but punishable as either a felony or a misdemeanor, and the offense is thereafter deemed a misdemeanor under Penal Code section 17(b) (e.g., *People v. Douglas* (1999) 20 Cal.4th 85; *People v. Clark* (1971) 17 Cal.App.3d 890).

Trial court unification did not change this rule: after as before unification, "Appeals in felony cases lie to the [C]ourt of [A]ppeal, regardless of whether the appeal is from the superior court, the municipal court, or the action of a magistrate. *Cf.* Cal. Const. art. VI, § 11(a) [except in death penalty cases, Courts of Appeal have appellate jurisdiction when superior courts have original jurisdiction 'in causes of a type within the appellate jurisdiction of the [C]ourts of [A]ppeal on June 30, 1995....']." ("Recommendation on Trial Court Unification" (July 1998) 28 *Cal. Law Revision Com. Rep.* 455–56.)

Rule 8.901.   Notice of appeal

(a) Notice of appeal

(1) To appeal from a judgment or an appealable order in an infraction case, the defendant or the People must file a notice of appeal in the trial court that issued the judgment or order being appealed. The notice must specify the judgment or order—or part of it—being appealed.

(2) If the defendant appeals, the defendant or the defendant's attorney must sign the notice of appeal. If the People appeal, the attorney for the People must sign the notice.

(3) The notice of appeal must be liberally construed in favor of its sufficiency.

(Subd (a) adopted effective January 1, 2009.)

(b) Notification of the appeal

(1) When a notice of appeal is filed, the trial court clerk must promptly send a notification of the filing to the attorney of record for each party and to any unrepresented defendant. The clerk must also send or deliver this notification to the appellate division clerk.

(2) The notification must show the date it was sent or delivered, the number and title of the case, and the date the notice of appeal was filed.

(3) The notification to the appellate division clerk must also include a copy of the notice of appeal.

(4) A copy of the notice of appeal is sufficient notification under (1) if the required information is on the copy or is added by the trial court clerk.

(5) The sending of a notification under (1) is a sufficient performance of the clerk's duty despite the discharge, disqualification, suspension, disbarment, or death of the attorney.

(6) Failure to comply with any provision of this subdivision does not affect the validity of the notice of appeal.

(Subd (b) amended effective January 1, 2016; adopted effective January 1, 2009.)

Rule 8.901 amended effective January 1, 2016; adopted effective January 1, 2009.

Advisory Committee Comment

Notice of Appeal and Record on Appeal (Infraction) (form CR-142) may be used to file the notice of appeal required under this rule. This form is available at any courthouse or county law library or online at *www.courts.ca.gov/forms.*

Rule 8.902.   Definitions [Renumbered]

Rule 8.902 renumbered to rule 8.952 effective January 1, 2009; adopted as rule 158 effective July 1, 1964; previously amended and renumbered as rule 156 effective July 1, 1991; previously amended effective January 1, 2005; previously amended and renumbered effective January 1, 2007.

Another Rule 8.902 follows.

Rule 8.902.   Time to appeal

(a) Normal time

A notice of appeal must be filed within 30 days after the rendition of the judgment or the making of the order being appealed. If the defendant is committed before final judgment for insanity or narcotics addiction, the notice of appeal must be filed within 30 days after the commitment.

(Subd (a) adopted effective January 1, 2009.)

(b) Cross-appeal

If the defendant or the People timely appeals from a judgment or appealable order, the time for any other party to appeal from the same judgment or order is either the time specified in (a) or 30 days after the trial court clerk sends notification of the first appeal, whichever is later.

(Subd (b) amended effective January 1, 2016; adopted effective January 1, 2009.)

(c) Premature notice of appeal

A notice of appeal filed before the judgment is rendered or the order is made is premature, but the appellate division may treat the notice as filed immediately after the rendition of the judgment or the making of the order.

(Subd (c) adopted effective January 1, 2009.)

(d) Late notice of appeal

The trial court clerk must mark a late notice of appeal "Received [date] but not filed" and notify the party that the notice was not filed because it was late.

(Subd (d) adopted effective January 1, 2009.)

Rule 8.902 amended effective January 1, 2016; adopted effective January 1, 2009; previously amended effective July 1, 2010.

Advisory Committee Comment

Subdivision (d). See rule 8.817(b)(5) for provisions concerning the timeliness of documents mailed by inmates or patients from custodial institutions.

Rule 8.903.   Stay of execution on appeal

(a) Application

Pending appeal, the defendant may apply to the appellate division for a stay of execution after a judgment of conviction.

(Subd (a) adopted effective January 1, 2009.)

(b) Showing

The application must include a showing that the defendant sought relief in the trial court and that the court unjustifiably denied the application.

(Subd (b) adopted effective January 1, 2009.)

(c) Service

The application must be served on the prosecuting attorney.

(Subd (c) adopted effective January 1, 2009.)

(d) Interim relief

Pending its ruling on the application, the appellate division may grant the relief requested. The appellate division must notify the trial court of any stay that it grants.

(Subd (d) adopted effective January 1, 2009.)

Rule 8.903 adopted effective January 1, 2009.

Advisory Committee Comment

Subdivision (c). Under rule 8.804, the prosecuting attorney means the city attorney, county counsel, or district attorney prosecuting the infraction.

Rule 8.904.   Filing the appeal [Renumbered]

Rule 8.904 renumbered to rule 8.954 effective January 1, 2009; adopted as rule 152 effective July 1, 1964; previously amended effective July 1, 1973, January 1, 1977, January 1, 1979, January 1, 1984, July 1, 1991, and January 1, 2005; previously amended and renumbered effective January 1, 2007.

Another Rule 8.904 follows.

Rule 8.904.   Abandoning the appeal

(a) How to abandon

An appellant may abandon the appeal at any time by filing an abandonment of the appeal signed by the appellant or the appellant's attorney of record.

(Subd (a) adopted effective January 1, 2009.)

(b) Where to file; effect of filing

(1) The appellant must file the abandonment in the appellate division.

(2) If the record has not been filed in the appellate division, the filing of an abandonment effects a dismissal of the appeal and restores the trial court's jurisdiction.

(3) If the record has been filed in the appellate division, the appellate division may dismiss the appeal and direct immediate issuance of the remittitur.

(Subd (b) adopted effective January 1, 2009.)

(c) Clerk's duties

(1) The appellate division clerk must immediately notify the adverse party of the filing or of the order of dismissal.

(2) If the record has not been filed in the appellate division, the clerk must immediately notify the trial court.

(3) If a reporter's transcript has been requested, the clerk must immediately notify the reporter if the appeal is abandoned before the reporter has filed the transcript.

(Subd (c) adopted effective January 1, 2009.)

Rule 8.904 adopted effective January 1, 2009.

Advisory Committee Comment

Abandonment of Appeal (Infraction) (form CR-145) may be used to file an abandonment under this rule. This form is available at any courthouse or county law library or online at *www.courts.ca.gov/forms.*

Rule 8.907.   Record on appeal [Renumbered]

Rule 8.907 renumbered to rule 8.957 effective January 1, 2009; adopted as rule 153 effective July 1, 1964; previously amended effective July 1, 1972, July 1, 1973, January 1, 1977, and January 1, 2005; previously amended and renumbered effective January 1, 2007.

Article 2
Record in Infraction Appeals

Article 2 adopted effective January 1, 2009.

Rule 8.910.   Continuances [Renumbered]

Rule 8.910 renumbered to rule 8.960 effective January 1, 2009; adopted as rule 154 effective July 1, 1964; previously amended effective January 1, 1977, July 1, 1991, and January 1, 2005; previously renumbered effective January 1, 2007.

Another Rule 8.910 follows.

Rule 8.910.   Normal record on appeal

(a) Contents

Except as otherwise provided in this chapter, the record on an appeal to a superior court appellate division in an infraction criminal case must contain the following, which constitute the normal record on appeal:

(1) A record of the written documents from the trial court proceedings in the form of one of the following:

(A) A clerk's transcript under rule 8.912 or 8.920; or

(B) If the court has a local rule for the appellate division electing to use this form of the record, the original trial court file under rule 8.914.

(2) If an appellant wants to raise any issue that requires consideration of the oral proceedings in the trial court, the record on appeal must include a record of the oral proceedings in the form of one of the following:

(A) A statement on appeal under rule 8.916;

(B) If the court has a local rule for the appellate division permitting this form of the record, an official electronic recording of the proceedings under rule 8.917; or

(C) A reporter's transcript under rules 8.918–8.920 or a transcript prepared from an official electronic recording under rule 8.917.

(Subd (a) adopted effective January 1, 2009.)

(b) Stipulation for limited record

If before the record is certified, the appellant and the respondent stipulate in writing that any part of the record is not required for proper determination of the appeal and file the stipulation in the trial court, that part of the record must not be prepared or sent to the appellate division.

(Subd (b) amended effective January 1, 2010; adopted effective January 1, 2009.)

Rule 8.910 amended effective January 1, 2010; adopted effective January 1, 2009.

Rule 8.911.   Prosecuting attorney's notice regarding the record

If the prosecuting attorney does not want to receive a copy of the record on appeal, within 10 days after the notification of the appeal under rule 8.901(b) is sent to the prosecuting attorney, the prosecuting attorney must serve and file a notice indicating that he or she does not want to receive the record.

Rule 8.911 amended effective January 1, 2016; adopted effective January 1, 2009.

Rule 8.912.   Contents of clerk's transcript

Except in appeals covered by rule 8.920 or when the parties have filed a stipulation under rule 8.910(b) that any of these items is not required for proper determination of the appeal, the clerk's transcript must contain:

(1) The complaint, including any notice to appear, and any amendment;

(2) Any demurrer or other plea;

(3) All court minutes;

(4) Any written findings or opinion of the court;

(5) The judgment or order appealed from;

(6) Any motion or notice of motion for new trial, in arrest of judgment, or to dismiss the action, with supporting and opposing memoranda and attachments;

(7) Any transcript of a sound or sound-and-video recording tendered to the court under rule 2.1040;

(8) The notice of appeal; and

(9) If the appellant is the defendant:

(A) Any written defense motion denied in whole or in part, with supporting and opposing memoranda and attachments; and

(B) If related to a motion under (A), any search warrant and return.

Rule 8.912 adopted effective January 1, 2009.

Rule 8.913.   Abandonment, dismissal, and judgment for failure to bring to trial [Renumbered]

Rule 8.913 renumbered to rule 8.963 effective January 1, 2009; adopted as rule 157 effective July 1, 1964; amended and renumbered as rule 155 effective July 1, 1991; previously amended effective January 1, 1972, July 1, 1972, and January 1, 2005; previously amended and renumbered effective January 1, 2007.

Another Rule 8.913 follows.

Rule 8.913.   Preparation of clerk's transcript

(a) When preparation begins

Unless the original court file will be used in place of a clerk's transcript under rule 8.914, the clerk must begin preparing the clerk's transcript immediately after the notice of appeal is filed.

(Subd (a) adopted effective January 1, 2009.)

(b) Format of transcript

The clerk's transcript must comply with rule 8.144.

(Subd (b) adopted effective January 1, 2009.)

(c) When preparation must be completed

Within 20 days after the notice of appeal is filed, the clerk must complete preparation of an original clerk's transcript for the appellate division and one copy for the appellant. If there is more than one

appellant, the clerk must prepare an extra copy for each additional appellant who is represented by separate counsel or self-represented. If the defendant is the appellant, a copy must also be prepared for the prosecuting attorney unless the prosecuting attorney has notified the court under rule 8.911 that he or she does not want to receive the record. If the People are the appellant, a copy must also be prepared for the respondent.

(Subd (c) adopted effective January 1, 2009.)

(d) Certification

The clerk must certify as correct the original and all copies of the clerk's transcript.

(Subd (d) adopted effective January 1, 2009.)

Rule 8.913 adopted effective January 1, 2009.

Advisory Committee Comment

Rule 8.922 addresses when the clerk's transcript is sent to the appellate division in infraction appeals.

Rule 8.914.   Trial court file instead of clerk's transcript

(a) Application

If the court has a local rule for the appellate division electing to use this form of the record, the original trial court file may be used instead of a clerk's transcript. This rule and any supplemental provisions of the local rule then govern unless the trial court orders otherwise after notice to the parties.

(Subd (a) adopted effective January 1, 2009.)

(b) When original file must be prepared

Within 20 days after the filing of the notice of appeal, the trial court clerk must put the trial court file in chronological order, number the pages, and attach a chronological index and a list of all attorneys of record, the parties they represent, and any unrepresented parties.

(Subd (b) adopted effective January 1, 2009.)

(c) Copies

The clerk must send a copy of the index to the appellant for use in paginating his or her copy of the file to conform to the index. If there is more than one appellant, the clerk must prepare an extra copy of the index for each additional appellant who is represented by separate counsel or self-represented. If the defendant is the appellant, a copy must also be prepared for the prosecuting attorney unless the prosecuting attorney has notified the court under rule 8.911 that he or she does not want to receive the record. If the People are the appellant, a copy must also be prepared for the respondent.

(Subd (c) adopted effective January 1, 2009.)

Rule 8.914 adopted effective January 1, 2009.

Advisory Committee Comment

Rule 8.922 addresses when the original file is sent to the appellate division in infraction appeals.

Rule 8.915.   Record of oral proceedings

(a) Appellant's election

The appellant must notify the trial court whether he or she elects to proceed with or without a record of the oral proceedings in the trial court. If the appellant elects to proceed with a record of the oral proceedings in the trial court, the notice must specify which form of the record of the oral proceedings in the trial court the appellant elects to use:

(1) A statement on appeal under rule 8.916;

(2) If the court has a local rule for the appellate division permitting this, an official electronic recording of the proceedings under rule 8.917(c). The appellant must attach to the notice a copy of the stipulation required under rule 8.917(c); or

(3) A reporter's transcript under rules 8.918–8.920 or a transcript prepared from an official electronic recording of the proceedings under rule 8.917(b). If the appellant elects to use a reporter's transcript, the clerk must promptly send a copy of appellant's notice making this election and the notice of appeal to each court reporter.

(Subd (a) amended effective January 1, 2016; adopted effective January 1, 2009.)

(b) Time for filing election

The notice of election required under (a) must be filed with the notice of appeal.

(Subd (b) adopted effective January 1, 2009.)

(c) Failure to file election

If the appellant does not file an election within the time specified in (b), rule 8.924 applies.

(Subd (c) amended effective March 1, 2014; adopted effective January 1, 2010.)

Rules of Court

Rule 8.915 amended effective January 1, 2016; adopted effective January 1, 2009; previously amended effective January 1, 2010, and March 1, 2014.

Advisory Committee Comment

Notice of Appeal and Record of Oral Proceedings (Infraction) (form CR-142) may be used to file the election required under this rule. This form is available at any courthouse or county law library or online at *www.courtinfo.ca.gov/forms*. To assist appellants in making an appropriate election, courts are encouraged to include information about whether the proceedings were recorded by a court reporter or officially electronically recorded in any information that the court provides to parties concerning their appellate rights.

Rule 8.916. Examination of witnesses [Renumbered]
Rule 8.916 renumbered to rule 8.966 effective January 1, 2009; adopted as rule 157 effective July 1, 1999; previously amended and renumbered effective January 1, 2007.

Another Rule 8.916 follows.

Rule 8.916. Statement on appeal

(a) Description
A statement on appeal is a summary of the trial court proceedings that is approved by the trial court.

(Subd (a) adopted effective January 1, 2009.)

(b) Preparing the proposed statement
(1) If the appellant elects under rule 8.915 to use a statement on appeal, the appellant must prepare and file a proposed statement within 20 days after filing the record preparation election. If the defendant is the appellant and the prosecuting attorney appeared in the case, the defendant must serve a copy of the proposed statement on the prosecuting attorney. If the People are the appellant, the prosecuting attorney must serve a copy of the proposed statement on the respondent.

(2) Appellants who are not represented by an attorney must file their proposed statements on *Proposed Statement on Appeal (Infraction)* (form CR-143). For good cause, the court may permit the filing of a statement that is not on form CR-143.

(3) If the appellant does not serve and file a proposed statement within the time specified in (1), rule 8.924 applies.

(Subd (b) amended effective March 1, 2014; adopted effective January 1, 2009.)

(c) Contents of the proposed statement on appeal
A proposed statement prepared by the appellant must contain:

(1) A statement of the points the appellant is raising on appeal. The appeal is then limited to those points unless the appellate division determines that the record permits the full consideration of another point.

(A) The statement must specify the intended grounds of appeal by clearly stating each point to be raised but need not identify each particular ruling or matter to be challenged.

(B) If one of the grounds of appeal is insufficiency of the evidence, the statement must specify how it is insufficient.

(2) A summary of the trial court's rulings and the sentence imposed on the defendant.

(3) A condensed narrative of the oral proceedings that the appellant believes necessary for the appeal. The condensed narrative must include a concise factual summary of the evidence and the testimony of each witness that is relevant to the points which the appellant states under (1) are being raised on appeal. Any evidence or portion of a proceeding not included will be presumed to support the judgment or order appealed from.

(Subd (c) amended effective March 1, 2014; adopted effective January 1, 2009; previously amended effective July 1, 2009.)

(d) Review of the appellant's proposed statement
(1) Within 10 days after the appellant files the proposed statement, the respondent may serve and file proposed amendments to that statement.

(2) No later than 10 days after the respondent files proposed amendments or the time to do so expires, a party may request a hearing to review and correct the proposed statement. No hearing will be held unless ordered by the trial court judge, and the judge will not ordinarily order a hearing unless there is a factual dispute about a material aspect of the trial court proceedings.

(3) Except as provided in (6), if no hearing is ordered, no later than 10 days after the time for requesting a hearing expires, the trial court judge must review the proposed statement and any proposed amendments filed by the respondent and take one of the following actions:

(A) If the proposed statement does not contain material required under (c), the trial court judge may order the appellant to prepare a new proposed statement. The order must identify the additional material that must be included in the statement to comply with (c) and the date by which the new proposed statement must be served and filed. If the appellant does not serve and file a new proposed statement as directed, rule 8.924 applies.

(B) If the trial court judge does not issue an order under (A), the trial court judge must either:

(i) Make any corrections or modifications to the statement necessary to ensure that it is an accurate summary of the evidence and the testimony of each witness that is relevant to the points which the appellant states under (c)(1) are being raised on appeal; or

(ii) Identify the necessary corrections and modifications and order the appellant to prepare a statement incorporating these corrections and modifications.

(4) If a hearing is ordered, the court must promptly set the hearing date and provide the parties with at least 5 days' written notice of the hearing date. No later than 10 days after the hearing, the trial court judge must either:

(A) Make any corrections or modifications to the statement necessary to ensure that it is an accurate summary of the evidence and the testimony of each witness that is relevant to the points which the appellant states under (c)(1) are being raised on appeal; or

(B) Identify the necessary corrections and modifications and order the appellant to prepare a statement incorporating these corrections and modifications.

(5) The trial court judge must not eliminate the appellant's specification of grounds of appeal from the proposed statement.

(6) If the trial court proceedings were reported by a court reporter or officially electronically recorded electronically under Government Code section 69957 and the trial court judge determines that it would save court time and resources, instead of correcting a proposed statement on appeal:

(A) If the court has a local rule for the appellate division permitting the use of an official electronic recording as the record of the oral proceedings, the trial court judge may order that the original of an official electronic recording of the trial court proceedings, or a copy made by the court, be transmitted as the record of these oral proceedings without being transcribed. The court will pay for any copy of the official electronic recording ordered under this subdivision; or

(B) If the court has a local rule permitting this, the trial court judge may order that a transcript be prepared as the record of the oral proceedings. The court will pay for any transcript ordered under this subdivision.

(Subd (d) amended effective March 1, 2014; adopted effective January 1, 2009.)

(e) Review of the corrected or modified statement
(1) If the trial court judge makes any corrections or modifications to the proposed statement under (d), the clerk must serve copies of the corrected or modified statement on the parties. If under (d) the trial court judge orders the appellant to prepare a statement incorporating corrections and modifications, the appellant must serve and file the corrected or modified statement within the time ordered by the court. If the prosecuting attorney did not appear at the trial, no copy of the statement is to be sent to or served on the prosecuting attorney. If the appellant does not serve and file a corrected or modified statement as directed, rule 8.924 applies.

(2) Within 10 days after the statement is served on the parties, any party may serve and file proposed modifications or objections to the statement.

(3) Within 10 days after the time for filing proposed modifications or objections under (2) has expired, the judge must review the corrected or modified statement and any proposed modifications or objections to the statement filed by the parties. The procedures in (d)(3) or (d)(4) apply if the judge determines that further corrections or modifications are necessary to ensure that the statement is an accurate summary of the evidence and the testimony of each witness relevant to the points which the appellant states under (c)(1) are being raised on appeal.

(Subd (e) amended effective March 1, 2014; adopted effective January 1, 2009.)

(f) Certification of the statement on appeal
If the trial court judge does not make or order any corrections or modifications to the proposed statement under (d)(3), (d)(4), or (e)(3) and does not direct the preparation of a transcript in lieu of correcting the proposed statement under (d)(6), the judge must promptly certify the statement.

(Subd (f) amended effective March 1, 2014; adopted effective January 1, 2009.)

(g) Extensions of time
For good cause, the trial court may grant an extension of not more than 15 days to do any act required or permitted under this rule.

(Subd (g) adopted effective January 1, 2009.)
Rule 8.916 amended effective March 1, 2014; adopted effective January 1, 2009;
previously effective July 1, 2009.

Advisory Committee Comment

Rules 8.806, 8.810, and 8.812 address applications for extensions of time and
relief from default.

Subdivision (b)(2). *Proposed Statement on Appeal (Infraction)* (form CR-143)
is available at any courthouse or county law library or online at *www.courts.ca.gov/
forms.*

Subdivision (d). Under rule 8.804, the term "judge" includes a commissioner or
a temporary judge.

Subdivisions (d)(3)(B), (d)(4), and (f). The judge need not ensure that the
statement as modified or corrected is complete, but only that it is an accurate
summary of the evidence and testimony relevant to the issues identified by the
appellant.

Rule 8.917.   Record when trial proceedings were officially electronically recorded

(a) Application

This rule applies only if:

(1) The trial court proceedings were officially recorded electronically
under Government Code section 69957; and

(2) The electronic recording was prepared in compliance with applicable rules regarding electronic recording of court proceedings.

(Subd (a) adopted effective January 1, 2009.)

(b) Transcripts from official electronic recording

Written transcripts of official electronic recordings may be prepared
under rule 2.952. A transcript prepared and certified as provided in that
rule is prima facie a true and complete record of the oral proceedings it
purports to cover, and satisfies any requirement in these rules or in any
statute for a reporter's transcript of oral proceedings.

(Subd (b) adopted effective January 1, 2009.)

(c) Use of official recording as record of oral proceedings

If the court has a local rule for the appellate division permitting this, on
stipulation of the parties or on order of the trial court under rule
8.916(d)(6), the original of an official electronic recording of the trial
court proceedings, or a copy made by the court, may be transmitted as the
record of these oral proceedings without being transcribed. This official
electronic recording satisfies any requirement in these rules or in any
statute for a reporter's transcript of these proceedings.

(Subd (c) amended effective July 1, 2010; adopted effective January 1, 2009.)

(d) Contents

Except in appeals when either the parties have filed a stipulation under
rule 8.910(b) or the trial court has ordered that any of these items is not
required for proper determination of the appeal, rules 8.918 and 8.920
govern the contents of a transcript of an official electronic recording.

(Subd (d) adopted effective March 1, 2014.)

(e) When preparation begins

(1) If the appellant is the People, preparation of a transcript or a copy
of the recording must begin immediately after the appellant files an
election under rule 8.915(a) to use a transcript of an official electronic
recording or a copy of the official electronic recording as the record of the
oral proceedings.

(2) If the appellant is the defendant:

(A) Within 10 days after the date the appellant files the election under
rule 8.915(a), the clerk must notify the appellant and his or her counsel of
the estimated cost of preparing the transcript or the copy of the recording.
The notification must show the date it was sent.

(B) Within 10 days after the date the clerk sent the notice under (A),
the appellant must do one of the following:

(i) Deposit with the clerk an amount equal to the estimated cost of
preparing the transcript or the copy of the recording;

(ii) File a declaration of indigency supported by evidence in the form
required by the Judicial Council; or

(iii) Notify the clerk by filing a new election that he or she will be
using a statement on appeal instead of a transcript or copy of the
recording. The appellant must prepare, serve, and file a proposed
statement on appeal within 20 days after serving and filing the notice and
must otherwise comply with the requirements for statements on appeal
under rule 8.869;

(iv) Notify the clerk by filing a new election that he or she now elects
to proceed without a record of the oral proceedings in the trial court; or

(v) Notify the clerk that he or she is abandoning the appeal by filing
an abandonment in the reviewing court under rule 8.904.

(C) If the trial court determines that the appellant is not indigent,
within 10 days after the date the clerk sends notice of this determination
to the appellant, the appellant must do one of the following:

(i) Deposit with the clerk an amount equal to the estimated cost of
preparing the transcript or the copy of the recording;

(ii) Notify the clerk by filing a new election that he or she will be using
a statement on appeal instead of a reporter's transcript. The appellant must
prepare, serve, and file a proposed statement on appeal within 20 days
after serving and filing the notice and must otherwise comply with the
requirements for statements on appeal under rule 8.869;

(iii) Notify the clerk by filing a new election that he or she now elects
to proceed without a record of the oral proceedings in the trial court; or

(iv) Notify the clerk that he or she is abandoning the appeal by filing
an abandonment in the reviewing court under rule 8.904.

(D) Preparation of the transcript or the copy of the recording must
begin when:

(i) The clerk receives the required deposit under (B)(i) or (C)(i); or

(ii) The trial court determines that the defendant is indigent and orders
that the defendant receive the transcript or the copy of the recording
without cost.

*(Subd (e) amended effective January 1, 2016; adopted as subd (d) effective
January 1, 2009; previously amended and relettered as subd (e) effective March 1,
2014.)*

(f) Notice when proceedings were not officially electronically recorded or cannot be transcribed

(1) If any portion of the oral proceedings to be included in the
transcript were not officially electronically recorded under Government
Code section 69957 or cannot be transcribed, the trial court clerk must so
notify the parties in writing. The notice must:

(A) Indicate whether the identified proceedings were reported by a
court reporter; and

(B) Show the date it was sent.

(2) Within 15 days after this notice is sent by the clerk, the appellant
must serve and file a notice with the court stating whether the appellant
elects to proceed with or without a record of the identified proceedings.
When the party elects to proceed with a record of these oral proceedings:

(A) If the clerk's notice under (1) indicates that the proceedings were
reported by a court reporter, the appellant's notice must specify which
form of the record listed in rule 8.915(a) other than an official electronic
recording or a transcript prepared from an official electronic recording the
appellant elects to use. The appellant must comply with the requirements
applicable to the form of the record elected.

(B) If the clerk's notice under (1) indicates that the proceedings were
not reported by a court reporter, the appellant must prepare, serve, and file
a proposed statement on appeal within 20 days after serving and filing the
notice.

(Subd (f) amended effective January 1, 2016; adopted effective March 1, 2014.)
*Rule 8.917 amended effective January 1, 2016; adopted effective January 1, 2009;
previously amended effective July 1, 2010, and March 1, 2014.*

Advisory Committee Comment

Subdivision (d). The appellant must use *Defendant's Financial Statement on
Eligibility for Appointment of Counsel and Reimbursement and Record on Appeal
at Public Expense* (form CR-105) to show indigency. This form is available at any
courthouse or county law library or online at *www.courtinfo.ca.gov/forms.*

Rule 8.918.   Contents of reporter's transcript

(a) Normal contents

Except in appeals covered by rule 8.920, when the parties have filed a
stipulation under rule 8.910(b), or when, under a procedure established by
a local rule adopted pursuant to (b), the trial court has ordered that any of
these items is not required for proper determination of the appeal, the
reporter's transcript must contain:

(1) The oral proceedings on the entry of any plea other than a not
guilty plea;

(2) The oral proceedings on any motion in limine;

(3) The oral proceedings at trial, but excluding any opening statement;

(4) Any oral opinion of the court;

(5) The oral proceedings on any motion for new trial;

(6) The oral proceedings at sentencing or other dispositional hearing;

(7) If the appellant is the defendant, the reporter's transcript must also
contain:

(A) The oral proceedings on any defense motion denied in whole or in
part except motions for disqualification of a judge; and

(B) The closing arguments.

(Subd (a) amended and lettered effective March 1, 2014; adopted effective January 1, 2009.)

(b) Local procedure for determining contents

A trial court may adopt a local rule that establishes procedures for determining whether any of the items listed in (a) is not required for proper determination of the appeal or whether a form of the record other than a reporter's transcript constitutes a record of sufficient completeness for proper determination of the appeal.

(Subd (b) adopted effective March 1, 2014.)

Rule 8.918 amended effective March 1, 2014; adopted effective January 1, 2009.

Advisory Committee Comment

Subdivision (b). Both the United States Supreme Court and the California Supreme Court have held that, where the State has established a right to appeal, an indigent defendant convicted of a criminal offense has a constitutional right to a "'record of sufficient completeness' to permit proper consideration of [his] claims." (*Mayer v. Chicago* (1971) 404 U.S. 189, 193–194; *March v. Municipal Court* (1972) 7 Cal.3d 422, 427–428.) The California Supreme Court has also held that an indigent appellant is denied his or her right under the Fourteenth Amendment to the competent assistance of counsel on appeal if counsel fails to obtain an appellate record adequate for consideration of appellant's claims of errors (*People v. Barton* (1978) 21 Cal.3d 513, 518–520).

The *Mayer* and *March* decisions make clear, however, that the constitutionally required "record of sufficient completeness" does not necessarily mean a complete verbatim transcript; other forms of the record, such as a statement on appeal or a partial transcript, may be sufficient. The record that is necessary depends on the grounds for the appeal in the particular case. Under these cases, where the grounds of appeal make out a colorable need for a complete transcript, the burden is on the State to show that only a portion of the transcript or an alternative form of the record will suffice for an effective appeal on those grounds. The burden of overcoming the need for a verbatim reporter's transcript appears to be met where a verbatim recording of the proceedings is provided. (*Mayer, supra,* 404 U.S. at p. 195; cf. *Eyrich v. Mun. Court* (1985) 165 Cal.App.3d 1138, 1140 ["Although use of a court reporter is one way of obtaining a verbatim record, it may also be acquired through an electronic recording when no court reporter is available"].)

Some courts have adopted local rules that establish procedures for determining whether only a portion of a verbatim transcript or an alternative form of the record will be sufficient for an effective appeal, including: (1) requiring the appellant to specify the points the appellant is raising on appeal; (2) requiring the appellant and respondent to meet and confer about the content and form of the record; and (3) holding a hearing on the content and form of the record. Local procedures can be tailored to reflect the methods available in a particular court for making a record of the trial court proceedings that is sufficient for an effective appeal.

Rule 8.919. Preparation of reporter's transcript

(a) When preparation begins

(1) Unless the court has adopted a local rule under rule 8.920(b) that provides otherwise, the reporter must immediately begin preparing the reporter's transcript if the notice sent to the reporter by the clerk under rule 8.915(a)(3) indicates that the appellant is the People.

(2) If the notice sent to the reporter by the clerk under rule 8.915(a)(3) indicates that the appellant is the defendant:

(A) Within 10 days after the date the clerk sent the notice under rule 8.915(a)(3), the reporter must file with the clerk the estimated cost of preparing the reporter's transcript; and

(B) The clerk must promptly notify the appellant and his or her counsel of the estimated cost of preparing the reporter's transcript. The notification must show the date it was sent.

(C) Within 10 days after the date the clerk sent the notice under (B), the appellant must do one of the following:

(i) Deposit with the clerk an amount equal to the estimated cost of preparing the transcript;

(ii) File a waiver of the deposit signed by the reporter;

(iii) File a declaration of indigency supported by evidence in the form required by the Judicial Council;

(iv) File a certified transcript of all of the proceedings required to be included in the reporter's transcript under rule 8.918. The transcript must comply with the format requirements of rule 8.144;

(v) Notify the clerk by filing a new election that he or she will be using a statement on appeal instead of a reporter's transcript. The appellant must prepare, serve, and file a proposed statement on appeal within 20 days after serving and filing the notice and must otherwise comply with the requirements for statements on appeal under rule 8.916;

(vi) Notify the clerk by filing a new election that he or she now elects to proceed without a record of the oral proceedings in the trial court; or

(vii) Notify the clerk that he or she is abandoning the appeal by filing an abandonment in the reviewing court under rule 8.904.

(D) If the trial court determines that the appellant is not indigent, within 10 days after the date the clerk sends notice of this determination to the appellant, the appellant must do one of the following:

(i) Deposit with the clerk an amount equal to the estimated cost of preparing the transcript;

(ii) File with the clerk a waiver of the deposit signed by the reporter;

(iii) File a certified transcript of all of the proceedings required to be included in the reporter's transcript under rule 8.918. The transcript must comply with the format requirements of rule 8.144;

(iv) Notify the clerk by filing a new election that he or she will be using a statement on appeal instead of a reporter's transcript. The appellant must prepare, serve, and file a proposed statement on appeal within 20 days after serving and filing the notice and must otherwise comply with the requirements for statements on appeal under rule 8.916;

(v) Notify the clerk by filing a new election that he or she now elects to proceed without a record of the oral proceedings in the trial court; or

(vi) Notify the clerk that he or she is abandoning the appeal by filing an abandonment in the reviewing court under rule 8.904.

(E) The clerk must promptly notify the reporter to begin preparing the transcript when:

(i) The clerk receives the required deposit under (C)(i) or (D)(i); or

(ii) The clerk receives a waiver of the deposit signed by the reporter under (C)(ii) or (D)(ii); or

(iii) The trial court determines that the defendant is indigent and orders that the defendant receive the transcript without cost.

(Subd (a) amended effective January 1, 2016; adopted effective January 1, 2009; previously amended effective March 1, 2014.)

(b) Format of transcript

The reporter's transcript must comply with rule 8.144.

(Subd (b) adopted effective January 1, 2009.)

(c) Copies and certification

The reporter must prepare an original and the same number of copies of the reporter's transcript as rule 8.913(c) requires of the clerk's transcript and must certify each as correct.

(Subd (c) adopted effective January 1, 2009.)

(d) When preparation must be completed

The reporter must deliver the original and all copies to the trial court clerk as soon as they are certified but no later than 20 days after the reporter is required to begin preparing the transcript under (a). Only the presiding judge of the appellate division or his or her designee may extend the time to prepare the reporter's transcript (see rule 8.810).

(Subd (d) amended effective January 1, 2018; adopted effective January 1, 2009; previously amended effective March 1, 2014, January 1, 2017, and January 1, 2018.)

(e) Multi-reporter cases

In a multi-reporter case, the clerk must accept any completed portion of the transcript from the primary reporter one week after the time prescribed by (d) even if other portions are uncompleted. The clerk must promptly pay each reporter who certifies that all portions of the transcript assigned to that reporter are completed.

(Subd (e) adopted effective January 1, 2009.)

(f) Notice when proceedings cannot be transcribed

(1) If any portion of the oral proceedings to be included in the reporter's transcript was not reported or cannot be transcribed, the trial court clerk must so notify the parties in writing. The notice must:

(A) Indicate whether the identified proceedings were officially electronically recorded under Government Code section 69957; and

(B) Show the date it was sent.

(2) Within 15 days after this notice is sent by the clerk, the appellant must serve and file a notice with the court stating whether the appellant elects to proceed with or without a record of the identified proceedings. When the party elects to proceed with a record of these oral proceedings:

(A) If the clerk's notice under (1) indicates that the proceedings were officially electronically recorded under Government Code section 69957, the appellant's notice must specify which form of the record listed in rule 8.915(a) other than a reporter's transcript the appellant elects to use. The appellant must comply with the requirements applicable to the form of the record elected.

(B) If the clerk's notice under (1) indicates that the proceedings were not officially electronically recorded under Government Code section 69957, the appellant must prepare, serve, and file a proposed statement on appeal within 20 days after serving and filing the notice.

(Subd (f) amended effective January 1, 2016; adopted effective March 1, 2014.)

Rule 8.919 amended effective January 1, 2018; adopted effective January 1, 2009; previously amended effective March 1, 2014, January 1, 2016, January 1, 2017, and January 1, 2018.

Advisory Committee Comment

Subdivision (a). The appellant must use *Defendant's Financial Statement on Eligibility for Appointment of Counsel and Reimbursement and Record on Appeal at Public Expense* (form CR-105) to show indigency. This form is available at any courthouse or county law library or online at *www.courts.ca.gov/forms.*

Subdivisions (a)(2)(C)(iv) and (a)(2)(D)(iii). Sometimes a party in a trial court proceeding will purchase a reporter's transcripts of all or part of the proceedings before any appeal is filed. In recognition of the fact that such transcripts may already have been purchased, this rule allows an appellant, in lieu of depositing funds for a reporter's transcript, to deposit with the trial court a certified transcript of the proceedings necessary for the appeal. Subdivisions (a)(2)(C)(iv) and (a)(2)(D)(iii) make clear that the certified transcript may be filed in lieu of a deposit for a reporter's transcript only where the certified transcript contains all of the proceedings required under rule 8.865 and the transcript complies with the format requirements of rule 8.144.

Rule 8.920.   Limited normal record in certain appeals

If the People appeal from a judgment on a demurrer to the complaint, including any notice to appear, or if the defendant or the People appeal from an appealable order other than a ruling on a motion for new trial, the normal record is composed of:

(1) *Record of the documents filed in the trial court*

A clerk's transcript or original trial court file containing:

(A) The complaint, including any notice to appear, and any amendment;

(B) Any demurrer or other plea;

(C) Any motion or notice of motion granted or denied by the order appealed from, with supporting and opposing memoranda and attachments;

(D) The judgment or order appealed from and any abstract of judgment;

(E) Any court minutes relating to the judgment or order appealed from and

(i) If there was a trial in the case, any court minutes of proceedings at the time the original judgment is rendered and any subsequent proceedings; or

(ii) If the original judgment of conviction is based on a guilty plea or nolo contendere plea, any court minutes of the proceedings at the time of entry of such plea and any subsequent proceedings; and

(F) The notice of appeal.

(2) *Record of the oral proceedings in the trial court*

If an appellant wants to raise any issue that requires consideration of the oral proceedings in the trial court:

(A) A reporter's transcript, a transcript prepared under rule 8.917, an official electronic recording under rule 8.917, or a statement on appeal under rule 8.916 summarizing any oral proceedings incident to the judgment or order being appealed.

(B) If the appeal is from an order after judgment, a reporter's transcript, a transcript prepared under rule 8.917, an official electronic recording under rule 8.917, or a statement on appeal under rule 8.916 summarizing any oral proceedings from:

(i) The original sentencing proceeding; and

(ii) If the original judgment of conviction is based on a guilty plea or nolo contendere plea, the proceedings at the time of entry of such plea.

Rule 8.920 amended effective January 1, 2013; adopted effective January 1, 2009.

Advisory Committee Comment

Subdivision (1)(E). This rule identifies the minutes that must be included in the record. The trial court clerk may include additional minutes beyond those identified in this rule if that would be more cost-effective.

Rule 8.921.   Exhibits

(a) Exhibits deemed part of record

Exhibits admitted in evidence, refused, or lodged are deemed part of the record but may be transmitted to the appellate division only as provided in this rule.

(Subd (a) adopted effective January 1, 2009.)

(b) Notice of designation

(1) Within 10 days after the last respondent's brief is filed or could be filed under rule 8.927, if the appellant wants the appellate division to consider any original exhibits that were admitted in evidence, refused, or lodged, the appellant must serve and file a notice in the trial court designating such exhibits.

(2) Within 10 days after a notice under (1) is served, any other party wanting the appellate division to consider additional exhibits must serve and file a notice in trial court designating such exhibits.

(3) A party filing a notice under (1) or (2) must serve a copy on the appellate division.

(Subd (b) adopted effective January 1, 2009.)

(c) Request by appellate division

At any time the appellate division may direct the trial court or a party to send it an exhibit.

(Subd (c) adopted effective January 1, 2009.)

(d) Transmittal

Unless the appellate division orders otherwise, within 20 days after notice under (b) is filed or after the appellate division directs that an exhibit be sent:

(1) The trial court clerk must put any designated exhibits in the clerk's possession into numerical or alphabetical order and send them to the appellate division. The trial court clerk must also send a list of the exhibits sent. If the exhibits are not transmitted electronically, the trial court clerk must send two copies of the list. If the appellate division clerk finds the list correct, the clerk must sign and return a copy to the trial court clerk.

(2) Any party in possession of designated exhibits returned by the trial court must put them into numerical or alphabetical order and send them to the appellate division. The party must also send a list of the exhibits sent. If the exhibits are not transmitted electronically, the party must send two copies of the list. If the appellate division clerk finds the list correct, the clerk must sign and return a copy to the party.

(Subd (d) amended effective January 1, 2016; adopted effective January 1, 2009.)

(e) Return by appellate division

On request, the appellate division may return an exhibit to the trial court or to the party that sent it. When the remittitur issues, the appellate division must return all exhibits not transmitted electronically to the trial court or to the party that sent them.

(Subd (e) amended effective January 1, 2016; adopted effective January 1, 2009.)

Rule 8.921 amended effective January 1, 2016; adopted effective January 1, 2009.

Rule 8.922.   Sending and filing the record in the appellate division

(a) When the record is complete

(1) If the appellant elected under rule 8.915 to proceed without a record of the oral proceedings in the trial court, the record is complete when the clerk's transcript is certified as correct or, if the original trial court file will be used instead of the clerk's transcript, when that original file is ready for transmission as provided under rule 8.914(b).

(2) If the appellant elected under rule 8.915 to proceed with a record of the oral proceedings in the trial court, the record is complete when the clerk's transcript is certified as correct or the original file is ready for transmission as provided in (1) and:

(A) If the appellant elected to use a reporter's transcript, the certified reporter's transcript is delivered to the court under rule 8.919;

(B) If the appellant elected to use a transcript prepared from an official electronic recording, the transcript has been prepared under rule 8.917;

(C) If the parties stipulated to the use of an official electronic recording of the proceedings, the electronic recording has been prepared under rule 8.917; or

(D) If the appellant elected to use a statement on appeal, the statement on appeal has been certified by the trial court or a transcript or copy of an official electronic recording has been prepared under rule 8.916(d)(6).

(Subd (a) adopted effective January 1, 2009.)

(b) Sending the record

When the record is complete, the clerk must promptly send:

(1) The original record to the appellate division;

(2) One copy of the clerk's transcript or index to the original court file and one copy of any record of the oral proceedings to each appellant who is represented by separate counsel or is self-represented;

(3) If the defendant is the appellant, one copy of the clerk's transcript or index to the original court file and one copy of any record of the oral proceedings to the prosecuting attorney unless the prosecuting attorney has notified the court under rule 8.911 that he or she does not want to receive the record; and

(4) If the People are the appellant, a copy of the clerk's transcript or index to the original court file and one copy of any record of the oral proceedings to the respondent.

(Subd (b) adopted effective January 1, 2009.)

(c) Filing the record

On receipt, the appellate division clerk must promptly file the original record and send notice of the filing date to the parties.

(Subd (c) amended effective January 1, 2016; adopted effective January 1, 2009.)

Rule 8.922 amended effective January 1, 2016; adopted effective January 1, 2009.

Rule 8.923. Augmenting or correcting the record in the appellate division

(a) Subsequent trial court orders

If, after the record is certified, the trial court amends or recalls the judgment or makes any other order in the case, including an order affecting the sentence or probation, the clerk must promptly certify and send a copy of the amended abstract of judgment or other order as an augmentation of the record to all those who received the record under rule 8.872(b). If there is any additional document or transcript related to the amended judgment or new order that any rule or order requires be included in the record, the clerk must send these documents or transcripts with the amended abstract of judgment or other order. The clerk must promptly copy and certify any such document and the reporter must promptly prepare and certify any such transcript.

(Subd (a) adopted effective January 1, 2009.)

(b) Omissions

If, after the record is certified, the trial court clerk or the reporter learns that the record omits a document or transcript that any rule or order requires to be included, the clerk must promptly copy and certify the document or the reporter must promptly prepare and certify the transcript. Without the need for a court order, the clerk must promptly send the document or transcript as an augmentation of the record to all those who received the record under rule 8.922(b).

(Subd (b) adopted effective January 1, 2009.)

(c) Augmentation or correction by the appellate division

At any time, on motion of a party or on its own motion, the appellate division may order the record augmented or corrected as provided in rule 8.841.

(Subd (c) adopted effective January 1, 2009.)

Rule 8.923 adopted effective January 1, 2009.

Rule 8.924. Failure to procure the record

(a) Notice of default

If a party fails to do any act required to procure the record, the trial court clerk must promptly notify that party in writing that it must do the act specified in the notice within 15 days after the notice is sent and that, if it fails to comply, the reviewing court may impose the following sanctions:

(1) If the defaulting party is the appellant, the court may dismiss the appeal or, if the default relates only to procurement of the record of the oral proceedings, may proceed on the clerk's transcript or other record of the written documents from the trial court proceedings; or

(2) If the defaulting party is the respondent, the court may proceed with the appeal on the record designated by the appellant.

(Subd (a) amended effective January 1, 2016; adopted effective March 1, 2014.)

(b) Sanctions

If the party fails to take the action specified in a notice given under (a), the trial court clerk must promptly notify the appellate division of the default and the appellate division may impose the sanction specified in the notice. If the appellate division dismisses the appeal, it may vacate the dismissal for good cause. If the appellate division orders the appeal to proceed on the record designated by the appellant, the respondent may obtain relief from default under rule 8.812.

(Subd (b) adopted effective March 1, 2014.)

Rule 8.924 amended effective January 1, 2016; adopted effective March 1, 2014.

Article 3
Briefs, Hearing, and Decision in Infraction Appeals

Article 3 adopted effective January 1, 2009.

Rule 8.925. General application of chapter 4

Except as provided in this article, rules 8.880–8.890 govern briefs, hearing, and decision in the appellate division in infraction cases.

Rule 8.925 adopted effective January 1, 2009.

Rule 8.926. Notice of briefing schedule

When the record is filed, the clerk of the appellate division must promptly send, to each appellate counsel or unrepresented party, a notice giving the dates the briefs are due.

Rule 8.926 amended effective January 1, 2016; adopted effective January 1, 2009.

Rule 8.927. Briefs

(a) Time to file briefs

(1) The appellant must serve and file an appellant's opening brief within 30 days after the record is filed in the appellate division.

(2) Any respondent's brief must be served and filed within 30 days after the appellant files its opening brief.

(3) Any appellant's reply brief must be served and filed within 20 days after the respondent files its brief.

(4) No other brief may be filed except with the permission of the presiding judge.

(5) Instead of filing a brief, or as part of its brief, a party may join in a brief or adopt by reference all or part of a brief in the same or a related appeal.

(Subd (a) adopted effective January 1, 2009.)

(b) Failure to file a brief

(1) If the appellant fails to timely file an opening brief, the appellate division clerk must promptly notify the appellant in writing that the brief must be filed within 20 days after the notice is sent and that if the appellant fails to comply, the court may dismiss the appeal.

(2) If the respondent fails to timely file a brief, the appellate division clerk must promptly notify the respondent in writing that the brief must be filed within 20 days after the notice is sent and that if the respondent fails to comply, the court will decide the appeal on the record, the appellant's opening brief, and any oral argument by the appellant.

(3) If a party fails to comply with a notice under (1) or (2), the court may impose the sanction specified in the notice.

(Subd (b) amended effective January 1, 2016; adopted effective January 1, 2009; previously amended effective March 1, 2014.)

(c) Service and filing

(1) Copies of each brief must be served as required by rule 8.25.

(2) Unless the appellate division provides otherwise by local rule or order in the specific case, only the original brief, with proof of service, must be filed in the appellate division.

(3) A copy of each brief must be served on the trial court clerk for delivery to the judge who tried the case.

(4) A copy of each brief must be served on a public officer or agency when required by rule 8.29.

(Subd (c) adopted effective January 1, 2009.)

Rule 8.927 amended effective January 1, 2016; adopted effective January 1, 2009; previously amended effective March 1, 2014.

Rule 8.928. Contents and form of briefs

(a) Contents

(1) Each brief must:

(A) State each point under a separate heading or subheading summarizing the point and support each point by argument and, if possible, by citation of authority; and

(B) Support any reference to a matter in the record by a citation to the volume and page number of the record where the matter appears.

(2) An appellant's opening brief must:

(A) State the nature of the action, the relief sought in the trial court, and the judgment or order appealed from;

(B) State that the judgment appealed from is final or explain why the order appealed from is appealable; and

(C) Provide a summary of the significant facts limited to matters in the record.

(Subd (a) adopted effective January 1, 2009.)

(b) Length

(1) A brief produced on a computer must not exceed 5,100 words, including footnotes. Such a brief must include a certificate by appellate counsel or an unrepresented party stating the number of words in the brief. The person certifying may rely on the word count of the computer program used to prepare the brief.

(2) A brief produced on a typewriter must not exceed 15 pages.

(3) The information listed on the cover, any table of contents or table of authorities, the certificate under (1), and any signature block are excluded from the limits stated in (1) or (2).

(4) On application, the presiding judge may permit a longer brief for good cause. A lengthy record or numerous or complex issues on appeal will ordinarily constitute good cause.

(Subd (b) amended effective January 1, 2013; adopted effective January 1, 2009; previously amended effective January 1, 2011.)

(c) Form

(1) A brief may be reproduced by any process that produces a clear, black image of letter quality. All documents filed must have a page size of 8½ by 11 inches. If filed in paper form, the paper must be white or unbleached and of at least 20-pound weight. Both sides of the paper may be used if the brief is not bound at the top.

(2) Any conventional font may be used. The font may be either proportionally spaced or monospaced.

(3) The font style must be roman; but for emphasis, italics or boldface may be used or the text may be underscored. Case names must be italicized or underscored. Headings may be in uppercase letters.

(4) Except as provided in (11), the font size, including footnotes, must not be smaller than 13-point.

(5) The lines of text must be unnumbered and at least one-and-a-half-spaced. Headings and footnotes may be single-spaced. Quotations may be block-indented and single-spaced. Single-spaced means six lines to a vertical inch.

(6) The margins must be at least 1½ inches on the left and right and 1 inch on the top and bottom.

(7) The pages must be consecutively numbered.

(8) The cover—or first page if there is no cover—must include the information required by rule 8.816(a)(1).

(9) If filed in paper form, the brief must be bound on the left margin, except that briefs may be bound at the top if required by a local rule of the appellate division. If the brief is stapled, the bound edge and staples must be covered with tape.

(10) The brief need not be signed.

(11) If the brief is produced on a typewriter:

(A) A typewritten original and carbon copies may be filed only with the presiding justice's permission, which will ordinarily be given only to unrepresented parties proceeding in forma pauperis. All other typewritten briefs must be filed as photocopies.

(B) Both sides of the paper may be used if a photocopy is filed; only one side may be used if a typewritten original and carbon copies are filed.

(C) The type size, including footnotes, must not be smaller than standard pica, 10 characters per inch. Unrepresented incarcerated litigants may use elite type, 12 characters per inch, if they lack access to a typewriter with larger characters.

(Subd (c) amended effective January 1, 2016; adopted effective January 1, 2009; previously amended effective January 1, 2013, and March 1, 2014.)

(d) Noncomplying briefs

If a brief does not comply with this rule:

(1) The reviewing court clerk may decline to file it, but must mark it "received but not filed" and return it to the party; or

(2) If the brief is filed, the presiding judge may with or without notice:

(A) Order the brief returned for corrections and refiling within a specified time;

(B) Strike the brief with leave to file a new brief within a specified time; or

(C) Disregard the noncompliance.

(Subd (d) adopted effective January 1, 2009.)

Rule 8.928 amended effective January 1, 2016; adopted effective January 1, 2009; previously amended effective January 1, 2011, January 1, 2013, and March 1, 2014.

Advisory Committee Comment

Subdivision (b). Subdivision (b)(1) states the maximum permissible lengths of briefs produced on a computer in terms of word count rather than page count. This provision tracks a provision in rule 8.204(c) governing Court of Appeal briefs and is explained in the comment to that provision. Subdivision (b)(3) specifies certain items that are not counted toward the maximum brief length. Signature blocks, as referenced in this provision include not only the signatures, but also the printed names, titles, and affiliations of any attorneys filing or joining in the brief, which may accompany the signature.

Rule 8.929. Oral argument

(a) Calendaring and sessions

Unless otherwise ordered, all appeals in which the last reply brief was filed or the time for filing this brief expired 45 or more days before the date of a regular appellate division session must be placed on the calendar for that session by the appellate division clerk. By order of the presiding judge or the appellate division, any appeal may be placed on the calendar for oral argument at any session.

(Subd (a) adopted effective January 1, 2009.)

(b) Oral argument by videoconference

(1) Oral argument may be conducted by videoconference if:

(A) It is ordered by the presiding judge of the appellate division or the presiding judge's designee on application of any party or on the court's own motion. An application from a party requesting that oral argument be conducted by videoconference must be filed within 10 days after the court sends notice of oral argument under (c)(1); or

(B) A local rule authorizes oral argument to be conducted by videoconference consistent with these rules.

(2) If oral argument is conducted by videoconference:

(A) Each judge of the appellate division panel assigned to the case must participate in the entire oral argument either in person at the superior court that issued the judgment or order that is being appealed or by videoconference from another court.

(B) Unless otherwise allowed by local rule or ordered by the presiding judge of the appellate division or the presiding judge's designee, all of the parties must appear at oral argument in person at the superior court that issued the judgment or order that is being appealed.

(C) The oral argument must be open to the public at the superior court that issued the judgment or order that is being appealed. If provided by local rule or ordered by the presiding judge of the appellate division or the presiding judge's designee, oral argument may also be open to the public at any of the locations from which a judge of the appellate division is participating in oral argument.

(D) The appellate division must ensure that:

(i) During oral argument, the participants in oral argument are visible and their statements are audible to all other participants, court staff, and any members of the public attending the oral argument;

(ii) Participants are identified when they speak; and

(iii) Only persons who are authorized to participate in the proceedings speak.

(E) A party must not be charged any fee to participate in oral argument by videoconference if the party participates from the superior court that issued the judgment or order that is being appealed or from a location from which a judge of the appellate division panel is participating in oral argument.

(Subd (b) adopted effective January 1, 2010.)

(c) Notice of argument

(1) As soon as all parties' briefs are filed or the time for filing these briefs has expired, the appellate division clerk must send a notice of the time and place of oral argument to all parties. The notice must be sent at least 20 days before the date for oral argument. The presiding judge may shorten the notice period for good cause; in that event, the clerk must immediately notify the parties by telephone or other expeditious method.

(2) If oral argument will be conducted by videoconference under (b), the clerk must specify, either in the notice required under (1) or in a supplemental notice sent to all parties at least 5 days before the date for oral argument, the location from which each judge of the appellate division panel assigned to the case will participate in oral argument.

(Subd (c) amended and relettered effective January 1, 2010; adopted as subd (b) effective January 1, 2009.)

(d) Waiver of argument

Parties may waive oral argument.

(Subd (d) relettered effective January 1, 2010; adopted as subd (c) effective January 1, 2009.)

(e) Conduct of argument

Unless the court provides otherwise:

(1) The appellant, petitioner, or moving party has the right to open and close. If there are two or more such parties, the court must set the sequence of argument.

(2) Each side is allowed 5 minutes for argument. The appellant may reserve part of this time for reply argument. If multiple parties are represented by separate counsel, or if an amicus curiae—on written request—is granted permission to argue, the court may apportion or expand the time.

(3) Only one counsel may argue for each separately represented party.

(Subd (e) amended and relettered effective January 1, 2010; adopted as subd (d) effective January 1, 2009.)

Rule 8.929 amended effective January 1, 2010; adopted effective January 1, 2009.

Advisory Committee Comment

Subdivision (a). Under rule 10.1108, the appellate division must hold a session at least once each quarter, unless no matters are set for oral argument that quarter, but may choose to hold sessions more frequently.

Chapter 6
Writ Proceedings

Chapter 6 adopted effective January 1, 2009.

Rule 8.930. Application
Rule 8.931. Petitions filed by persons not represented by an attorney
Rule 8.932. Petitions filed by an attorney for a party
Rule 8.933. Opposition
Rule 8.934. Notice to trial court
Rule 8.935. Filing, finality, and modification of decisions; rehearing; remittitur
Rule 8.936. Costs

Rule 8.930. Application

(a) Writ proceedings governed

Except as provided in (b), the rules in this chapter govern proceedings in the appellate division for writs of mandate, certiorari, or prohibition, or other writs within the original jurisdiction of the appellate division, including writs relating to a postjudgment enforcement order of the small claims division. In all respects not provided for in this chapter, rule 8.883, regarding the form and content of briefs, applies.

(Subd (a) amended effective January 1, 2016; adopted effective January 1, 2009.)

(b) Writ proceedings not governed

The rules in this chapter do not apply to:

(1) Petitions for writs of supersedeas under rule 8.824;

(2) Petitions for writs relating to acts of the small claims division other than a postjudgment enforcement order; or

(3) Petitions for writs not within the original jurisdiction of the appellate division.

(Subd (b) amended effective January 1, 2016; adopted effective January 1, 2009.)

Rule 8.930 amended effective January 1, 2016; adopted effective January 1, 2009.

Advisory Committee Comment

Information on Writ Proceedings in Misdemeanor, Infraction, and Limited Civil Cases (form APP-150-INFO) provides additional information about proceedings for writs in the appellate division of the superior court. This form is available at any courthouse or county law library or online at *www.courts.ca.gov/forms.*

Subdivision (b)(1). The superior courts, not the appellate divisions, have original jurisdiction in habeas corpus proceedings (see Cal. Const., art. VI, § 10). Habeas corpus proceedings in the superior courts are governed by rules 4.550 et seq.

Subdivision (b)(2). A petition that seeks a writ relating to an act of the small claims division other than a postjudgment enforcement order is heard by a single judge of the appellate division (see Code Civ. Proc. § 116.798(a)) and is governed by rules 8.970 et seq.

Rule 8.931. Petitions filed by persons not represented by an attorney

(a) Petitions

A person who is not represented by an attorney and who petitions the appellate division for a writ under this chapter must file the petition on *Petition for Writ (Misdemeanor, Infraction, or Limited Civil Case)* (form APP-151). For good cause the court may permit an unrepresented party to file a petition that is not on form APP-151, but the petition must be verified.

(Subd (a) amended effective January 1, 2018; adopted effective January 1, 2009.)

(b) Contents of supporting documents

(1) The petition must be accompanied by an adequate record, including copies of:

(A) The ruling from which the petition seeks relief;

(B) All documents and exhibits submitted to the trial court supporting and opposing the petitioner's position;

(C) Any other documents or portions of documents submitted to the trial court that are necessary for a complete understanding of the case and the ruling under review; and

(D) A reporter's transcript, a transcript of an electronic recording or, if the court has a local rule permitting this, an electronic recording of the oral proceedings that resulted in the ruling under review.

(2) In extraordinary circumstances, the petition may be filed without the documents required by (1)(A)–(C) but must include a declaration that

explains the urgency and the circumstances making the documents unavailable and fairly summarizes their substance.

(3) If a transcript or electronic recording under (1)(D) is unavailable, the record must include a declaration:

(A) Explaining why the transcript or electronic recording is unavailable and fairly summarizing the proceedings, including the parties' arguments and any statement by the court supporting its ruling. This declaration may omit a full summary of the proceedings if part of the relief sought is an order to prepare a transcript for use by an indigent criminal defendant in support of the petition and if the declaration demonstrates the need for and entitlement to the transcript; or

(B) Stating that the transcript or electronic recording has been ordered, the date it was ordered, and the date it is expected to be filed, which must be a date before any action requested of the appellate division other than issuance of a temporary stay supported by other parts of the record.

(4) If the petition does not include the required record or explanations or does not present facts sufficient to excuse the failure to submit them, the court may summarily deny a stay request, the petition, or both.

(Subd (b) amended effective January 1, 2014; adopted effective January 1, 2009; previously amended effective January 1, 2009.)

(c) Form of supporting documents

(1) Documents submitted under (b) must comply with the following requirements:

(A) If submitted in paper form, they must be bound together at the end of the petition or in separate volumes not exceeding 300 pages each. The pages must be consecutively numbered.

(B) If submitted in paper form, they must be index-tabbed by number or letter.

(C) They must begin with a table of contents listing each document by its title and its index number or letter. If a document has attachments, the table of contents must give the title of each attachment and a brief description of its contents.

(2) The clerk must file any supporting documents not complying with (1), but the court may notify the petitioner that it may strike or summarily deny the petition if the documents are not brought into compliance within a stated reasonable time of not less than five days.

(3) Unless the court provides otherwise by local rule or order, only one set of the supporting documents needs to be filed in support of a petition, an answer, an opposition, or a reply.

(Subd (c) amended effective January 1, 2016; adopted effective January 1, 2009; previously amended effective January 1, 2011.)

(d) Service

(1) The petition and one set of supporting documents must be served on any named real party in interest, but only the petition must be served on the respondent.

(2) The proof of service must give the telephone number of each attorney or unrepresented party served.

(3) The petition must be served on a public officer or agency when required by statute or rule 8.29.

(4) The clerk must file the petition even if its proof of service is defective, but if the petitioner fails to file a corrected proof of service within five days after the clerk gives notice of the defect the court may strike the petition or impose a lesser sanction.

(5) The court may allow the petition to be filed without proof of service.

(Subd (d) adopted effective January 1, 2009.)

Rule 8.931 amended effective January 1, 2018; adopted effective January 1, 2009; previously amended effective January 1, 2009, January 1, 2011, January 1, 2014, and January 1, 2016.

Advisory Committee Comment

Subdivision (a). *Petition for Writ (Misdemeanor, Infraction, or Limited Civil Case)* (form APP-151) is available at any courthouse or county law library or online at *www.courts.ca.gov/forms.*

Subdivision (b). Rule 2.952 addresses the use of electronic recordings and transcripts of such recordings as the official record of proceedings.

Subdivision (d). Rule 8.25, which generally governs service and filing in appellate divisions, also applies to the original proceedings covered by this rule.

Rule 8.932. Petitions filed by an attorney for a party

(a) General application of rule 8.931

Except as provided in this rule, rule 8.931 applies to any petition for an extraordinary writ filed by an attorney.

(Subd (a) adopted effective January 1, 2009.)

(b) Form and content of petition

(1) A petition for an extraordinary writ filed by an attorney may, but is not required to be, filed on *Petition for Writ (Misdemeanor, Infraction, or Limited Civil Case)* (form APP-151).

(2) The petition must disclose the name of any real party in interest.

(3) If the petition seeks review of trial court proceedings that are also the subject of a pending appeal, the notice "Related Appeal Pending" must appear on the cover of the petition, and the first paragraph of the petition must state the appeal's title and any appellate division docket number.

(4) The petition must be verified.

(5) The petition must be accompanied by a memorandum, which need not repeat facts alleged in the petition.

(6) Rule 8.883(b) governs the length of the petition and memorandum, but the verification and any supporting documents are excluded from the limits stated in rule 8.883(b)(1) and (2).

(7) If the petition requests a temporary stay, it must explain the urgency.

(Subd (b) adopted effective January 1, 2009.)

Rule 8.932 adopted effective January 1, 2009.

Rule 8.933. Opposition

(a) Preliminary opposition

(1) Within 10 days after the petition is filed, the respondent or any real party in interest, separately or jointly, may serve and file a preliminary opposition.

(2) An opposition must contain a memorandum and a statement of any material fact not included in the petition.

(3) Within 10 days after an opposition is filed, the petitioner may serve and file a reply.

(4) Without requesting opposition or waiting for a reply, the court may grant or deny a request for temporary stay, deny the petition, issue an alternative writ or order to show cause, or notify the parties that it is considering issuing a peremptory writ in the first instance.

(Subd (a) adopted effective January 1, 2009.)

(b) Return or opposition; reply

(1) If the court issues an alternative writ or order to show cause, the respondent or any real party in interest, separately or jointly, may serve and file a return by demurrer, verified answer, or both. If the court notifies the parties that it is considering issuing a peremptory writ in the first instance, the respondent or any real party in interest may serve and file an opposition.

(2) Unless the court orders otherwise, the return or opposition must be served and filed within 30 days after the court issues the alternative writ or order to show cause or notifies the parties that it is considering issuing a peremptory writ in the first instance.

(3) Unless the court orders otherwise, the petitioner may serve and file a reply within 15 days after the return or opposition is filed.

(4) If the return is by demurrer alone and the demurrer is not sustained, the court may issue the peremptory writ without granting leave to answer.

(Subd (b) adopted effective January 1, 2009.)

(c) Form of preliminary opposition, return, or opposition

Any preliminary opposition, return, or opposition must comply with rule 8.931(c). If it is filed by an attorney, it must also comply with rule 8.932(b)(3)–(7).

(Subd (c) adopted effective January 1, 2014.)

Rule 8.933 amended effective January 1, 2014; adopted effective January 1, 2009.

Rule 8.934. Notice to trial court

(a) Notice if writ issues

If a writ or order issues directed to any judge, court, or other officer, the appellate division clerk must promptly send a certified copy of the writ or order to the person or entity to whom it is directed.

(Subd (a) adopted effective January 1, 2009.)

(b) Notice by telephone

(1) If the writ or order stays or prohibits proceedings set to occur within seven days or requires action within seven days—or in any other urgent situation—the appellate division clerk must make a reasonable effort to notify the clerk of the respondent court by telephone. The clerk of the respondent court must then notify the judge or officer most directly concerned.

(2) The clerk need not give notice by telephone of the summary denial of a writ, whether or not a stay previously issued.

(Subd (b) adopted effective January 1, 2009.)

Rule 8.934 adopted effective January 1, 2009.

Rule 8.935. Filing, finality, and modification of decisions; rehearing; remittitur

(a) Filing of decision

(1) The appellate division clerk must promptly file all opinions and orders of the court and on the same day send copies (by e-mail where permissible under rule 2.251) showing the filing date to the parties and, when relevant, to the trial court.

(2) A decision must identify the participating judges, including the author of any majority opinion and of any concurring or dissenting opinion, or the judges participating in a "by the court" decision.

(Subd (a) amended effective January 1, 2019; adopted effective January 1, 2014.)

(b) Finality of decision

(1) Except as otherwise ordered by the court, the following appellate division decisions regarding petitions for writs within the court's original jurisdiction are final in the issuing court when filed:

(A) An order denying or dismissing such a petition without issuance of an alternative writ, order to show cause, or writ of review; and

(B) An order denying or dismissing such a petition as moot after issuance of an alternative writ, order to show cause, or writ of review.

(2) Except as otherwise provided in (3), all other appellate division decisions in a writ proceeding are final 30 days after the decision is sent by the court clerk to the parties.

(3) If necessary to prevent mootness or frustration of the relief granted or to otherwise promote the interests of justice, an appellate division may order early finality in that court of a decision granting a petition for a writ within its original jurisdiction or denying such a petition after issuing an alternative writ, order to show cause, or writ of review. The decision may provide for finality in that court on filing or within a stated period of less than 30 days.

(Subd (b) amended effective January 1, 2019; adopted as subd (a) effective January 1, 2009; previously amended and relettered effective January 1, 2014.)

(c) Modification of decisions

Rule 8.888(b) governs the modification of appellate division decisions in writ proceedings.

(Subd (c) adopted effective January 1, 2014.)

(d) Rehearing

Rule 8.889 governs rehearing in writ proceedings in the appellate division.

(Subd (d) adopted effective January 1, 2014.)

(e) Remittitur

Except as provided in rule 8.1018 for cases transferred to the Court of Appeal, the appellate division must issue a remittitur after the court issues a decision in a writ proceeding except when the court issues one of the orders listed in (b)(1). Rule 8.890(b)–(d) govern issuance of a remittitur in these proceedings, including the clerk's duties, immediate issuance, stay, and recall of remittitur, and notice of issuance.

(Subd (e) amended and relettered effective January 1, 2014; adopted as subd (b) effective January 1, 2009.)

Rule 8.935 amended effective January 1, 2019; adopted effective January 1, 2009; previously amended effective January 1, 2014.

Advisory Committee Comment

Subdivision (b). This provision addresses the finality of decisions in proceedings relating to writs of mandate, certiorari, and prohibition. See rule 8.888(a) for provisions addressing the finality of decisions in appeals.

Subdivision (b)(1). Examples of situations in which the appellate division may issue an order dismissing a writ petition include when the petitioner fails to comply with an order of the court, when the court recalls the alternative writ, order to show cause, or writ of review as improvidently granted, or when the petition becomes moot.

Subdivision (d). Under this rule, a remittitur serves as notice that the writ proceedings have concluded.

Rule 8.936. Costs

(a) Entitlement to costs

Except in a criminal proceeding or other proceeding in which a party is entitled to court-appointed counsel, the prevailing party in an original proceeding is entitled to costs if the court resolves the proceeding after issuing an alternative writ, an order to show cause, or a peremptory writ in the first instance.

(Subd (a) adopted effective January 1, 2009.)

(b) Award of costs

(1) In the interests of justice, the court may award or deny costs as it deems proper.

(2) The opinion or order resolving the proceeding must specify the award or denial of costs.

(3) Rule 8.891(b)–(d) governs the procedure for recovering costs under this rule.

(Subd (b) adopted effective January 1, 2009.)
Rule 8.936 adopted effective January 1, 2009.

Division 5
Rules Relating to Appeals and Writs in Small Claims Cases

Title 8, Appellate Rules—Division 5, Rules Relating to Appeals and Writs in Small Claims renumbered from Division 3 effective April 25, 2019; amended effective January 1, 2016.

Chapter 1
Trial of Small Claims Cases on Appeal

Title 8, Appellate Rules—Division 3, Rules Relating to Appeals and Writs in Small Claims—Chapter 1, Trial of Small Claims Cases on Appeal; adopted effective January 1, 2016.

Rule 8.950.   Application

The rules in this chapter supplement article 7 of the Small Claims Act, Code of Civil Procedure sections 116.710 et seq., providing for new trials of small claims cases on appeal, and must be read in conjunction with those statutes.

Rule 8.950 amended effective January 1, 2016; adopted as rule 151 effective July 1, 1964; previously amended effective January 1, 1977, and January 1, 2005; previously amended and renumbered as rule 8.900 effective January 1, 2007; previously renumbered as rule 8.950 effective January 1, 2009.

Rule 8.952.   Definitions

The definitions in rule 1.6 apply to these rules unless the context or subject matter requires otherwise. In addition, the following definitions apply to these rules:

(1) "Small claims court" means the trial court from which the appeal is taken.

(2) "Appeal" means a new trial before a different judge on all claims, whether or not appealed.

(3) "Appellant" means the party appealing; "respondent" means the adverse party. "Plaintiff" and "defendant" refer to the parties as they were designated in the small claims court.

Rule 8.952 renumbered effective January 1, 2009; adopted as rule 158 effective July 1, 1964; previously amended and renumbered as rule 156 effective July 1, 1991; previously amended effective January 1, 2005; previously amended and renumbered as rule 8.902 effective January 1, 2007.

Rule 8.954.   Filing the appeal

(a) Notice of appeal

To appeal from a judgment in a small claims case, an appellant must file a notice of appeal in the small claims court. The appellant or the appellant's attorney must sign the notice. The notice is sufficient if it states in substance that the appellant appeals from a specified judgment or, in the case of a defaulting defendant, from the denial of a motion to vacate the judgment. A notice of appeal must be liberally construed.

(Subd (a) amended effective January 1, 2007; previously amended effective July 1, 1973, January 1, 1977, January 1, 1979, January 1, 1984, July 1, 1991, and January 1, 2005.)

(b) Notification by clerk

(1) The clerk of the small claims court must promptly mail a notification of the filing of the notice of appeal to each other party at the party's last known address.

(2) The notification must state the number and title of the case and the date the notice of appeal was filed. If a party dies before the clerk mails the notification, the mailing is a sufficient performance of the clerk's duty.

(3) A failure of the clerk to give notice of the judgment or notification of the filing of the notice of appeal does not extend the time for filing the notice of appeal or affect the validity of the appeal.

(Subd (b) amended effective January 1, 2007; previously amended and relettered effective January 1, 1977; previously amended effective July 1, 1991, and January 1, 2005.)

(c) Premature notice of appeal

A notice of appeal filed after judgment is rendered but before it is entered is valid and is treated as filed immediately after entry. A notice of appeal filed after the judge has announced an intended ruling but before judgment is rendered may, in the discretion of the reviewing court be treated as filed immediately after entry of the judgment.

(Subd (c) amended effective January 1, 2007; adopted as subd (d) effective July 1, 1964; relettered effective January 1, 1977; previously amended effective July 1, 1991, and January 1, 2005.)

Rule 8.954 renumbered effective January 1, 2009; adopted as rule 152 effective July 1, 1964; previously amended effective July 1, 1973, January 1, 1977, January 1, 1979, January 1, 1984, July 1, 1991, and January 1, 2005; previously amended and renumbered as rule 8.904 effective January 1, 2007.

Rule 8.957.   Record on appeal

Within five days after the filing of the notice of appeal and the payment of any fees required by law, the clerk of the small claims court must transmit the file and all related papers, including the notice of appeal, to the clerk of the court assigned to hear the appeal.

Rule 8.957 renumbered effective January 1, 2009; adopted as rule 153 effective July 1, 1964; previously amended effective July 1, 1972, July 1, 1973, January 1, 1977, and January 1, 2005; previously amended and renumbered as rule 8.907 effective January 1, 2007.

Rule 8.960.   Continuances

For good cause, the court assigned to hear the appeal may continue the trial. A request for a continuance may be presented by one party or by stipulation. The court may grant a continuance not to exceed 30 days, but in a case of extreme hardship the court may grant a continuance exceeding 30 days.

Rule 8.960 renumbered effective January 1, 2009; adopted as rule 154 effective July 1, 1964; previously amended effective January 1, 1977, July 1, 1991, and January 1, 2005; previously renumbered as rule 8.910 effective January 1, 2007.

Rule 8.963.   Abandonment, dismissal, and judgment for failure to bring to trial

(a) Before the record is filed

Before the record has been transmitted to the court assigned to hear the appeal, the appellant may file in the small claims court an abandonment of the appeal or a stipulation to abandon the appeal. Either filing operates to dismiss the appeal and return the case to the small claims court.

(Subd (a) amended effective January 1, 2007; previously amended effective July 1, 1972, January 1, 1977, and January 1, 2005.)

(b) After the record is filed

After the record has been transmitted to the court assigned to hear the appeal, the court may dismiss the appeal on the appellant's written request or the parties' stipulation filed in that court.

(Subd (b) amended effective January 1, 2007; previously amended effective January 1, 2005.)

(c) Dismissal or judgment by the court

(1) The court must dismiss the appeal if the case is not brought to trial within one year after the date of filing the appeal. If a new trial is ordered, the court must dismiss the appeal if the case is not brought to trial within one year after the entry date of the new trial order.

(2) Notwithstanding (1), the court must not order dismissal or enter judgment if there was in effect a written stipulation extending the time for trial or on a showing that the appellant exercised reasonable diligence to bring the case to trial.

(3) Notwithstanding (1) and (2), the court must dismiss the appeal if the case is not brought to trial within three years after either the notice of appeal is filed or the most recent new trial order is entered in the court assigned to hear the appeal.

(Subd (c) amended effective January 1, 2007; previously amended effective January 1, 1977, July 1, 1991, and January 1, 2005.)

(d) Notification by clerk

If an appellant files an abandonment, the clerk of the court in which it is filed must immediately notify the adverse party of the filing. The clerk of the court assigned to hear the appeal must immediately notify the parties of any order of dismissal or any judgment for defendant made by the court under (c).

(Subd (d) amended effective January 1, 2007; previously amended effective January 1, 2005.)

(e) Return of papers

If an appeal is dismissed, the clerk of the court assigned to hear the appeal must promptly transmit to the small claims court a copy of the dismissal order and all original papers and exhibits sent to the court assigned to hear the appeal. The small claims court must then proceed with the case as if no appeal had been taken.

(Subd (e) amended effective January 1, 2007; previously amended effective January 1, 2005.)

(f) Approval of compromise

If a guardian or conservator seeks approval of a proposed compromise of a pending appeal in which a new trial has been ordered, the court assigned to hear the appeal may, before ruling on the compromise, hear and determine whether the proposed compromise is for the best interest of the ward or conservatee.

(Subd (f) amended effective January 1, 2007; previously amended effective January 1, 2005.)

Rule 8.963 renumbered effective January 1, 2009; adopted as rule 157 effective July 1, 1964; amended and renumbered as rule 155 effective July 1, 1991; previously amended effective January 1, 1972, July 1, 1972, and January 1, 2005; previously amended and renumbered as rule 8.913 effective January 1, 2007.

Rule 8.966. Examination of witnesses

The court may allow parties or attorneys representing parties to the appeal to conduct direct and cross-examination, subject to the court's discretion to control the manner, mode, and duration of examination in keeping with informality and the circumstances.

Rule 8.966 renumbered effective January 1, 2009; adopted as rule 157 effective July 1, 1999; previously amended and renumbered as rule 8.916 effective January 1, 2007.

Chapter 2
Writ Petitions

Title 8, Appellate Rules—Division 3, Rules Relating to Appeals and Writs in Small Claims Cases—Chapter 2, Writ Petitions; adopted effective January 1, 2016.

Rule 8.970. Application

(a) Writ proceedings governed

Except as provided in (b), the rules in this chapter govern proceedings under Code of Civil Procedure section 116.798(a) for writs of mandate, certiorari, or prohibition, relating to an act of the small claims division, other than a postjudgment enforcement order. In all respects not provided for in this chapter, rule 8.883, regarding the form and content of briefs, applies.

(Subd (a) adopted effective January 1, 2016.)

(b) Writ proceedings not governed

The rules in this chapter do not apply to:

(1) Proceedings under Code of Civil Procedure section 116.798(c) for writs relating to a postjudgment enforcement order of the small claims division, which are governed by rules 8.930–8.936.

(2) Proceedings under Code of Civil Procedure section 116.798(b) for writs relating to an act of a superior court in a small claims appeal, which are governed by rules 8.485–8.493.

(Subd (b) adopted effective January 1, 2016.)

Rule 8.970 adopted effective January 1, 2016.

Advisory Committee Comment

Code of Civil Procedure section 116.798 provides where writs in small claims actions may be heard.

The Judicial Council form *Information on Writ Proceedings in Small Claims Actions* (form SC-300-INFO) provides additional information about proceedings for writs in small claims actions in the appellate division of the superior court. This form is available at any courthouse or county law library or online at *www.courts.ca.gov/forms.*

Rule 8.971. Definitions

The definitions in rule 1.6 apply to these rules unless the context or subject matter requires otherwise. In addition, the following definitions apply to these rules:

(1) "Writ" means an order telling the small claims court to do something that the law says it must do, or not do something the law says it must not do. The various types of writs covered by this chapter are described in statutes beginning at section 1067 of the Code of Civil Procedure.

(2) "Petition" means a request for a writ.

(3) "Petitioner" means the person asking for the writ.

(4) "Respondent" and "small claims court" mean the court against which the writ is sought.

(5) "Real party in interest" means any other party in the small claims court case who would be affected by a ruling regarding the request for a writ.

Rule 8.971 adopted effective January 1, 2016.

Rule 8.972. Petitions filed by persons not represented by an attorney

(a) Petitions

(1) A person who is not represented by an attorney and who requests a writ under this chapter must file the petition on a *Petition for Writ (Small Claims)* (form SC-300). For good cause the court may permit an unrepresented party to file a petition that is not on that form, but the petition must be verified.

(2) If the petition raises any issue that would require the appellate division judge considering it to understand what was said in the small claims court, it must include a statement that fairly summarizes the proceedings, including the parties' arguments and any statement by the small claims court supporting its ruling.

(3) The clerk must file the petition even if it is not verified but if the party asking for the writ fails to file a verification within five days after the clerk gives notice of the defect, the court may strike the petition.

(Subd (a) amended effective January 1, 2018; adopted effective January 1, 2016.)

(b) Contents of supporting documents

(1) The petition must be accompanied by copies of the following:

(A) The small claims court ruling from which the petition seeks relief;

(B) All documents and exhibits submitted to the small claims court supporting and opposing the petitioner's position; and

(C) Any other documents or portions of documents submitted to the small claims court that are necessary for a complete understanding of the case and the ruling under review.

(2) If the petition does not include the required documents or does not present facts sufficient to excuse the failure to submit them, the appellate division judge may summarily deny a stay request, the petition, or both.

(Subd (b) adopted effective January 1, 2016.)

(c) Form of supporting documents

(1) Documents submitted under (b) must comply with the following requirements:

(A) They must be attached to the petition. The pages must be consecutively numbered.

(B) They must each be given a number or letter.

(2) The clerk must file any supporting documents not complying with (1), but the court may notify the petitioner that it may strike or summarily deny the petition if the documents are not brought into compliance within a stated reasonable time of not less than five days.

(Subd (c) adopted effective January 1, 2016.)

(d) Service

(1) The petition and all its attachments, and a copy of *Information on Writ Proceedings in Small Claims Cases* (form SC-300-INFO) must be served personally or by mail on all the parties in the case, and the petition must be served on the small claims court.

(2) The petitioner must file a proof of service at the same time the petition is filed.

(3) The clerk must file the petition even if its proof of service is defective but if the party asking for the writ fails to file a corrected proof of service within five days after the clerk gives notice of the defect, the court may strike the petition or allow additional time to file a corrected proof of service.

(4) The court may allow the petition to be filed without proof of service.

(Subd (d) adopted effective January 1, 2016.)

Rule 8.972 amended effective January 1, 2018; adopted effective January 1, 2016.

Advisory Committee Comment

Subdivision (a). *Petition for Writ (Small Claims)* (form SC-300) and *Information on Writ Proceedings in Small Claims Actions* (form SC-300-INFO) are available at any courthouse or county law library or online at *www.courts.ca.gov/forms.*

Rule 8.973. Petitions filed by an attorney for a party

(a) General application of rule 8.972

Except as provided in this rule, rule 8.972 applies to any petition for an extraordinary writ filed by an attorney under this chapter.

(Subd (a) adopted effective January 1, 2016.)

(b) Form and content of petition

(1) A petition for an extraordinary writ filed by an attorney may, but is not required to be, filed on *Petition for Writ (Small Claims)* (form SC-300). It must contain all the information requested in that form.

(2) The petition must disclose the name of any real party in interest.

(3) If the petition seeks review of small claims court proceedings that are also the subject of a pending appeal, the notice "Related Appeal Pending" must appear on the cover of the petition, and the first paragraph of the petition must state the appeal's title and any appellate division docket number.

(4) The petition must be verified.

(5) The petition must be accompanied by a memorandum, which need not repeat facts alleged in the petition.

(6) Rule 8.883(b) governs the length of the petition and memorandum, but the verification and any supporting documents are excluded from the limits stated in rule 8.883(b)(1) and (2).

(7) If the petition requests a temporary stay, it must explain the urgency.

(Subd (b) adopted effective January 1, 2016.)
Rule 8.973 adopted effective January 1, 2016.

Rule 8.974.   Opposition

(a) Preliminary opposition

(1) The respondent and real party in interest are not required to file any opposition to the petition unless asked to do so by the appellate division judge.

(2) Within 10 days after the petition is filed, the respondent or any real party in interest may serve and file a preliminary opposition.

(3) A preliminary opposition should contain any legal arguments the party wants to make as to why the appellate division judge should not issue a writ and a statement of any material facts not included in the petition.

(4) Without requesting opposition, the appellate division judge may grant or deny a request for temporary stay, deny the petition, issue an alternative writ or order to show cause, or notify the parties that the judge is considering issuing a peremptory writ in the first instance.

(Subd (a) adopted effective January 1, 2016.)

(b) Return or opposition; reply

(1) If the appellate division judge issues an alternative writ or order to show cause, the respondent or any real party in interest, individually or jointly, may serve and file a return (which is a response to the petition) by demurrer, verified answer, or both. If the appellate division judge notifies the parties that he or she is considering issuing a peremptory writ in the first instance, the respondent or any real party in interest may serve and file an opposition.

(2) Unless the appellate division judge orders otherwise, the return or opposition must be served and filed within 30 days after the appellate division judge issues the alternative writ or order to show cause or notifies the parties that it is considering issuing a peremptory writ in the first instance.

(3) Unless the appellate division judge orders otherwise, the petitioner may serve and file a reply within 15 days after the return or opposition is filed.

(4) If the return is by demurrer alone and the demurrer is not sustained, the appellate division judge may issue the peremptory writ without granting leave to answer.

(Subd (b) adopted effective January 1, 2016.)

(c) Form of preliminary opposition, return, or opposition

Any preliminary opposition, return, or opposition must comply with rule 8.931(c). If it is filed by an attorney, it must also comply with rule 8.932(b)(3)–(7).

(Subd (c) adopted effective January 1, 2016.)
Rule 8.974 adopted effective January 1, 2016.

Rule 8.975.   Notice to small claims court

(a) Notice if writ issues

If a writ or order issues directed to any judge, court, or other officer, the appellate division clerk must promptly send a certified copy of the writ or order to the person or entity to whom it is directed.

(Subd (a) adopted effective January 1, 2016.)

(b) Notice by telephone

(1) If the writ or order stays or prohibits proceedings set to occur within seven days or requires action within seven days—or in any other urgent situation—the appellate division clerk must make a reasonable effort to notify the clerk of the respondent small claims court by telephone. The clerk of the respondent small claims court must then notify the judge or officer most directly concerned.

(2) The appellate division clerk need not give notice by telephone of the summary denial of a writ, whether or not a stay was previously issued.

(Subd (b) adopted effective January 1, 2016.)
Rule 8.975 adopted effective January 1, 2016.

Rule 8.976.   Filing, finality, and modification of decisions; remittitur

(a) Filing of decision

The appellate division clerk must promptly file all opinions and orders in proceedings under this chapter and on the same day send copies (by e-mail where permissible under rule 2.251) showing the filing date to the parties and, when relevant, to the small claims court.

(Subd (a) amended effective January 1, 2019; adopted effective January 1, 2016.)

(b) Finality of decision

(1) Except as otherwise ordered by the appellate division judge, the following decisions regarding petitions for writs under this chapter are final in the issuing court when filed:

(A) An order denying or dismissing such a petition without issuance of an alternative writ, order to show cause, or writ of review; and

(B) An order denying or dismissing such a petition as moot after issuance of an alternative writ, order to show cause, or writ of review.

(2) Except as otherwise provided in (3), all other decisions in a writ proceeding under this chapter are final 30 days after the decision is sent by the court clerk to the parties.

(3) If necessary to prevent mootness or frustration of the relief granted or to otherwise promote the interests of justice, a judge in the appellate division may order early finality of a decision granting a petition for a writ under this chapter or denying such a petition after issuing an alternative writ, order to show cause, or writ of review. The decision may provide for finality on filing or within a stated period of less than 30 days.

(Subd (b) amended effective January 1, 2019; adopted effective January 1, 2016.)

(c) Modification of decisions

Rule 8.888(b) governs the modification of decisions in writ proceedings under this chapter.

(Subd (c) adopted effective January 1, 2016.)

(d) Remittitur

The appellate division must issue a remittitur after the judge issues a decision in a writ proceeding under this chapter except when the judge issues one of the orders listed in (b)(1). The remittitur is deemed issued when the clerk enters it in the record. The clerk must immediately send the parties notice of issuance of the remittitur, showing the date of entry.

(Subd (d) adopted effective January 1, 2016.)
Rule 8.976 amended effective January 1, 2019; adopted effective January 1, 2016.

Advisory Committee Comment

Subdivision (b)(1). Examples of situations in which the appellate division judge may issue an order dismissing a writ petition include when the petitioner fails to comply with an order, when the judge recalls the alternative writ, order to show cause, or writ of review as improvidently granted, or when the petition becomes moot.

Rule 8.977.   Costs

(a) Entitlement to costs

The prevailing party in an original proceeding is entitled to costs if the appellate division judge resolves the proceeding after issuing an alternative writ, an order to show cause, or a peremptory writ in the first instance.

(Subd (a) adopted effective January 1, 2016.)

(b) Award of costs

(1) In the interests of justice, the appellate division judge may award or deny costs as the court deems proper.

(2) The opinion or order resolving the proceeding must specify the award or denial of costs.

(3) Rule 8.891(b)–(d) governs the procedure for recovering costs under this rule.

(Subd (b) adopted effective January 1, 2016.)
Rule 8.977 adopted effective January 1, 2016.

Division 6
Transfer of Appellate Division Cases to the Court of Appeal

Title 8, Appellate Rules—Division 6, Transfer of Appellate Division Cases to the Court of Appeal renumbered from Division 4 effective April 25, 2019.

Rule 8.1000. Application
Rule 8.1002. Transfer authority
Rule 8.1005. Certification for transfer by the appellate division
Rule 8.1006. Petition for transfer
Rule 8.1007. Transmitting record to Court of Appeal
Rule 8.1008. Order for transfer
Rule 8.1012. Briefs and argument
Rule 8.1014. Proceedings in the appellate division after certification or transfer
Rule 8.1016. Disposition of transferred case
Rule 8.1018. Finality and remittitur

Rule 8.1000.   Application

Rules 8.1000–8.1018 govern the transfer of cases within the appellate jurisdiction of the superior court—other than appeals in small claims cases—to the Court of Appeal. Unless the context requires otherwise, the term "case" as used in these rules means cases within that jurisdiction.
Rule 8.1000 amended effective January 1, 2011; repealed and adopted as rule 61 effective January 1, 2003; previously amended and renumbered effective January 1, 2007.

Advisory Committee Comment

The rules in this division implement the authority of the Court of Appeal under Code of Civil Procedure section 911 and Penal Code section 1471 to order any case on appeal to a superior court in its district transferred to the Court of Appeal if it determines that transfer is necessary to secure uniformity of decision or to settle important questions of law.

Rule 8.1002.   Transfer authority

A Court of Appeal may order a case transferred to it for hearing and decision if it determines that transfer is necessary to secure uniformity of decision or to settle an important question of law. Transfer may be ordered on:

(1) Certification of the case for transfer by the superior court appellate division under rule 8.1005;

(2) Petition for transfer under rule 8.1006; or

(3) The Court of Appeal's own motion.

Rule 8.1002 amended effective January 1, 2011; repealed and adopted as rule 62 effective January 1, 2003; previously amended and renumbered effective January 1, 2007.

Rule 8.1005.   Certification for transfer by the appellate division

(a) Authority to certify

(1) The appellate division may certify a case for transfer to the Court of Appeal on its own motion or on a party's application if it determines that transfer is necessary to secure uniformity of decision or to settle an important question of law.

(2) Except as provided in (3), a case may be certified for transfer by a majority of the appellate division judges to whom the case has been assigned or who decided the appeal or, if the case has not yet been assigned, by any two appellate division judges.

(3) If an appeal from a conviction of a traffic infraction is assigned to a single appellate division judge under Code of Civil Procedure section 77, the case may be certified for transfer by that judge.

(4) If an assigned or deciding judge is unable to act on the certification for transfer, a judge designated or assigned to the appellate division by the chair of the Judicial Council may act in that judge's place.

(Subd (a) amended effective January 1, 2011; previously amended effective January 1, 2007.)

(b) Application for certification

(1) A party may serve and file an application asking the appellate division to certify a case for transfer at any time after the record on appeal is filed in the appellate division but no later than 15 days after:

(A) The decision is sent by the court clerk to the parties;

(B) A publication order restarting the finality period under rule 8.888(a)(2) is sent by the court clerk to the parties;

(C) A modification order changing the appellate judgment under rule 8.888(b) is sent by the court clerk to the parties; or

(D) A consent is filed under rule 8.888(c).

(2) The party may include the application in a petition for rehearing.

(3) The application must explain why transfer is necessary to secure uniformity of decision or to settle an important question of law.

(4) Within five days after the application is filed, any other party may serve and file an answer.

(5) No hearing will be held on the application. Failure to certify the case within the time specified in (c) is deemed a denial of the application.

(Subd (b) amended effective January 1, 2019; previously amended effective January 1, 2011.)

(c) Time to certify

The appellate division may certify a case for transfer at any time after the record on appeal is filed in the appellate division and before the appellate division decision is final in that court.

(Subd (c) repealed, amended and relettered effective January 1, 2011; adopted as subd (d).)

(d) Contents of order certifying case for transfer

An order certifying a case for transfer must:

(1) Clearly state that the appellate division is certifying the case for transfer to the Court of Appeal;

(2) Briefly describe why transfer is necessary to secure uniformity of decision or to settle an important question of law; and

(3) State whether there was a decision on appeal and, if so, its date and disposition.

(Subd (d) amended and relettered effective January 1, 2011; adopted as subd (e); previously amended effective January 1, 2007.)

(e) Superior court clerk's duties

(1) If the appellate division orders a case certified for transfer, the clerk must promptly send a copy of the certification order to the clerk/executive officer of the Court of Appeal, the parties, and, in a criminal case, the Attorney General.

(2) If the appellate division denies a certification application by order, the clerk must promptly send a copy of the order to the parties.

(Subd (e) amended effective January 1, 2018; adopted as subd (f); previously amended and relettered effective January 1, 2011.)
Rule 8.1005 amended effective January 1, 2019; repealed and adopted as rule 63 effective January 1, 2003; previously amended and renumbered effective January 1, 2007; previously amended effective January 1, 2010, January 1, 2011, and January 1, 2018.

Rule 8.1006.   Petition for transfer

(a) Right to file petition

A party may file a petition in the Court of Appeal asking for an appellate division case to be transferred to that court only if an application for certification for transfer was first filed in the appellate division and denied.

(Subd (a) adopted effective January 1, 2011.)

(b) Time to file petition

(1) The petition must be served and filed in the Court of Appeal after the appellate division issues its decision in the case but no later than 15 days after the decision is final in that court. A copy of the petition must also be served on the appellate division.

(2) The time to file a petition for transfer may not be extended, but the presiding justice may relieve a party from a failure to file a timely petition for transfer if the time for the Court of Appeal to order transfer on its own motion has not expired.

(Subd (b) adopted effective January 1, 2011.)

(c) Form and contents of petition

(1) Except as provided in this rule, a petition must comply with the form and contents requirements of rule 8.204(a)(1), (b), and (d).

(2) The body of the petition must begin with a concise, nonargumentative statement of the issues presented for review, framing them in terms of the facts of the case but without unnecessary detail.

(3) The petition must explain why transfer is necessary to secure uniformity of decision or to settle an important question of law.

(4) The petition must not exceed 5,600 words, including footnotes, if produced on a computer, and 20 pages if typewritten. A petition produced on a computer must include a certificate by counsel or an unrepresented party stating the number of words in the document. The person certifying may rely on the word count of the computer program used to prepare the document. A certificate stating the number of words, the tables required by rule 8.204(a)(1), the cover information required under rule 8.204(b)(10), any signature block, and any attachment permitted under rule 8.204(d) are excluded from these length limits.

(Subd (c) adopted effective January 1, 2011.)

(d) Answer to petition

(1) Any answer must be served and filed within 10 days after the petition is filed unless the court orders otherwise.

(2) Except as provided in this rule, any answer must comply with the form and contents requirements of rule 8.204(a)(1), (b), and (d).

(3) An answer must comply with the length requirements of (c)(4).

(Subd (d) adopted effective January 1, 2011.)

Rule 8.1006 adopted effective January 1, 2011.

Advisory Committee Comment

See rule 8.40 for requirements regarding the covers of documents filed in the appellate courts and rule 8.44(b) for the number of copies of documents that must be provided to the Court of Appeal.

Rule 8.1007.   Transmitting record to Court of Appeal

(a) Clerks' duties

(1) To assist the Court of Appeal in determining whether to order transfer, the superior court clerk must send the record specified in (b) to the Court of Appeal within five days after:

(A) The appellate division certifies a case for transfer under rule 8.1005;

(B) The superior court clerk sends a copy of an appellate division opinion certified for publication to the Court of Appeal under rule 8.887;

(C) The superior court clerk receives a copy of a petition for transfer under rule 8.1006; or

(D) The superior court receives a request for the record from the Court of Appeal.

(2) The clerk/executive officer of the Court of Appeal must promptly notify the parties when the clerk files the record.

(Subd (a) amended effective January 1, 2018; adopted as subd (b); previously amended effective January 1, 2007, and July 1, 2009; previously amended and relettered effective January 1, 2011.)

(b) Contents

The record sent to the Court of Appeal under (a) must contain:

(1) The original record on appeal prepared under rules 8.830–8.843, 8.860–8.873, or 8.910–8.923;

(2) Any briefs filed in the appellate division;

(3) The decision of the appellate division; and

(4) Any application for certification for transfer, any answer to that application, and the appellate division's order on the application.

(Subd (b) amended and relettered effective January 1, 2011; adopted as subd (a); previously amended effective January 1, 2007, and July 1, 2009.)

Rule 8.1007 amended effective January 1, 2018; repealed and adopted as rule 65 effective January 1, 2003; previously amended and renumbered as rule 8.1010 effective January 1, 2007, and as rule 8.1007 effective January 1, 2011; previously amended effective July 1, 2009.

Advisory Committee Comment

Under rule 8.71(c), the superior court clerk may send the record to the reviewing court in electronic form.

Rule 8.1008.   Order for transfer

(a) Time to transfer

(1) The Court of Appeal may order transfer

(A) After the appellate division certifies the case for transfer or on petition for transfer, within 20 days after the record sent under rule 8.1007 is filed in the Court of Appeal; or

(B) On its own motion, within 30 days after the appellate division decision is final in that court.

(2) Within either period specified in (1), the Court of Appeal may order an extension not exceeding 20 days.

(3) If the Court of Appeal does not timely order transfer, transfer is deemed denied.

(Subd (a) repealed, amended and relettered effective January 1, 2011; adopted as subd (c); previously amended effective January 1, 2007.)

(b) Court of Appeal clerk's duties

(1) When a transfer order is filed, the clerk must promptly send a copy of the order to the superior court clerk, the parties, and, in a criminal case, the Attorney General.

(2) With the copy of the transfer order sent to the parties and the Attorney General, the clerk must send notice of the time to serve and file any briefs ordered under rule 8.1012 and, if specified by the Court of Appeal, the issues to be briefed and argued.

(3) If the court denies transfer after the appellate division certifies a case for transfer or after a party files a petition for transfer, the clerk must promptly send notice of the denial to the parties, the appellate division, and, in a criminal case, the Attorney General.

(4) Failure to send any order or notice under this subdivision does not affect the jurisdiction of the Court of Appeal.

(Subd (b) repealed, amended and relettered effective January 1, 2011; adopted as subd (f); previously amended effective January 1, 2007.)

Rule 8.1008 amended effective January 1, 2011; repealed and adopted as rule 64 effective January 1, 2003; previously amended and renumbered effective January 1, 2007; previously amended effective July 1, 2003, and January 1, 2008.

Rule 8.1010.   Record on transfer [Renumbered]

Rule 8.1010 renumbered as rule 8.1007 effective January 1, 2011.

Rule 8.1012.   Briefs and argument

(a) When briefs permitted

(1) After the Court of Appeal orders transfer, the parties may file briefs in the Court of Appeal only if ordered by the court. The court may order briefs either on a party's application or the court's own motion. The court must prescribe the briefing sequence in any briefing order.

(2) Instead of filing a brief, or as part of its brief, a party may join in or adopt by reference all or part of a brief filed in the Court of Appeal in the same or a related case.

(Subd (a) amended effective January 1, 2011.)

(b) Time to file briefs

Unless otherwise provided in the court's order under (a):

(1) The opening brief must be served and filed within 20 days after entry of the briefing order.

(2) The responding brief must be served and filed within 20 days after the opening brief is filed.

(3) Any reply brief must be served and filed within 10 days after the responding brief is filed.

(Subd (b) amended effective January 1, 2011.)

(c) Additional service requirements

(1) Any brief of a defendant in a criminal case must be served on the prosecuting attorney and the Attorney General.

(2) Every brief must be served on the appellate division from which the case was transferred.

(Subd (c) amended effective January 1, 2011.)

(d) Form and contents of briefs

(1) Except as provided in this rule, briefs must comply with the form and contents requirements of rule 8.204(a)(1), (b), and (d).

(2) No brief may exceed 5,600 words if produced on a computer or 20 pages if typewritten. The person certifying may rely on the word count of the computer program used to prepare the document. A certificate stating the number of words, the tables required by rule 8.204(a)(1), the cover information required under rule 8.204(b)(10), any signature block, and any attachment permitted under rule 8.204(d) are excluded from these length limits.

(Subd (d) amended effective January 1, 2011; previously amended effective January 1, 2007.)

(e) Limitation of issues

(1) On or after ordering transfer, the Court of Appeal may specify the issues to be briefed and argued. Unless the court orders otherwise, the parties must limit their briefs and arguments to those issues and any issues fairly included in those issues.

(2) Notwithstanding an order specifying issues under (1), the court may, on reasonable notice, order oral argument on fewer or additional issues or on the entire case.

(Subd (e) adopted effective January 1, 2011.)

Rule 8.1012 amended effective January 1, 2011; repealed and adopted as rule 66 effective January 1, 2003; previously amended and renumbered effective January 1, 2007.

Rule 8.1014.   Proceedings in the appellate division after certification or transfer

When the appellate division certifies a case for transfer or the Court of Appeal orders transfer, further action by the appellate division is limited to preparing and sending the record under rule 8.1007 until termination of the proceedings in the Court of Appeal.

Rule 8.1014 amended effective January 1, 2011; repealed and adopted as rule 67 effective January 1, 2003; previously renumbered effective January 1, 2007.

Rule 8.1016.   Disposition of transferred case

(a) Decision on limited issues

The Court of Appeal may decide fewer than all the issues raised and may retransfer the case to the appellate division for decision on any remaining issues.

(b) Retransfer without decision

The Court of Appeal may vacate a transfer order without decision and retransfer the case to the appellate division with or without directions to conduct further proceedings.

(Subd (b) amended effective January 1, 2011; previously amended effective January 1, 2007.)

Rule 8.1016 amended effective January 1, 2011; repealed and adopted as rule 68 effective January 1, 2003; previously amended and renumbered effective January 1, 2007.

Rule 8.1018.　Finality and remittitur

(a)　When transfer is denied

If the Court of Appeal denies transfer of a case from the appellate division of the superior court after the appellate division certifies the case for transfer or after a party files a petition for transfer, the denial is final immediately. On receiving notice under rule 8.1008(b) that the Court of Appeal has denied transfer or if the period for ordering transfer under rule 8.1008(a) expires, the appellate division clerk must promptly issue a remittitur if there will be no further proceedings in that court.

(Subd (a) amended effective January 1, 2011; adopted effective January 1, 2009.)

(b)　When transfer order is vacated

If the appellate division issued a decision before transfer and the Court of Appeal vacates its transfer order under rule 8.1016(b) and retransfers the case without directing further proceedings, the appellate division's decision is final when the appellate division receives the order vacating transfer. The appellate division clerk must promptly issue a remittitur.

(Subd (b) adopted effective January 1, 2011.)

(c)　When the Court of Appeal issues a decision

If the Court of Appeal issues a decision on a case it has ordered transferred from the appellate division of the superior court, filing, finality, and modification of that decision are governed by rule 8.264 and remittitur is governed by rule 8.272, except that the clerk/executive officer must address the remittitur to the appellate division and send that court a copy of the remittitur and a filed-endorsed copy of the Court of Appeal opinion or order. If the remittitur and opinion are sent in paper format, two copies must be sent. On receipt of the Court of Appeal remittitur, the appellate division clerk must promptly issue a remittitur if there will be no further proceedings in that court.

(Subd (c) amended effective January 1, 2018; adopted as subd (a); previously relettered as subd (b) effective January 1, 2009; previously repealed, amended and relettered as subd (c) effective January 1, 2011; previously amended effective January 1, 2016.)

(d)　Documents to be returned

When the Court of Appeal denies or vacates transfer or issues a remittitur under (c), the clerk/executive officer must return to the appellate division any part of the record sent nonelectronically to the Court of Appeal under rule 8.1007 and any exhibits that were sent nonelectronically.

(Subd (d) amended effective January 1, 2018; adopted as subd (c) effective January 1, 2003; previously relettered subd (d) effective January 1, 2009; previously amended effective January 1, 2011, and January 1, 2016.)

Rule 8.1018 amended effective January 1, 2018; repealed and adopted as rule 69 effective January 1, 2003; previously renumbered as rule 8.1018 effective January 1, 2007; previously amended effective January 1, 2009, January 1, 2011, and January 1, 2016.

Advisory Committee Comment

Subdivision (a). The finality of Court of Appeal decisions in appeals is generally addressed in rules 8.264 (civil appeals) and 8.366 (criminal appeals).

Division 7
Publication of Appellate Opinions

Title 8, Appellate Rules—Division 7, Publication of Appellate Opinions renumbered from Division 5 effective April 25, 2019.

Rule 8.1100. Authority
Rule 8.1105. Publication of appellate opinions
Rule 8.1110. Partial publication
Rule 8.1115. Citation of opinions
Rule 8.1120. Requesting publication of unpublished opinions
Rule 8.1125. Requesting depublication of published opinions

Rule 8.1100.　Authority

The rules governing the publication of appellate opinions are adopted by the Supreme Court under section 14 of article VI of the California Constitution and published in the California Rules of Court at the direction of the Judicial Council.

Rule 8.1100 adopted effective January 1, 2007.

Rule 8.1105.　Publication of appellate opinions

(a)　Supreme Court

All opinions of the Supreme Court are published in the Official Reports.

(b)　Courts of Appeal and appellate divisions

Except as provided in (e), an opinion of a Court of Appeal or a superior court appellate division is published in the Official Reports if a majority of the rendering court certifies the opinion for publication before the decision is final in that court.

(Subd (b) amended effective July 23, 2008; adopted effective April 1, 2007.)

(c)　Standards for certification

An opinion of a Court of Appeal or a superior court appellate division — whether it affirms or reverses a trial court order or judgment — should be certified for publication in the Official Reports if the opinion:

(1)　Establishes a new rule of law;

(2)　Applies an existing rule of law to a set of facts significantly different from those stated in published opinions;

(3)　Modifies, explains, or criticizes with reasons given, an existing rule of law;

(4)　Advances a new interpretation, clarification, criticism, or construction of a provision of a constitution, statute, ordinance, or court rule;

(5)　Addresses or creates an apparent conflict in the law;

(6)　Involves a legal issue of continuing public interest;

(7)　Makes a significant contribution to legal literature by reviewing either the development of a common law rule or the legislative or judicial history of a provision of a constitution, statute, or other written law;

(8)　Invokes a previously overlooked rule of law, or reaffirms a principle of law not applied in a recently reported decision; or

(9)　Is accompanied by a separate opinion concurring or dissenting on a legal issue, and publication of the majority and separate opinions would make a significant contribution to the development of the law.

(Subd (c) amended effective April 1, 2007; previously amended effective January 1, 2007.)

(d)　Factors not to be considered

Factors such as the workload of the court, or the potential embarrassment of a litigant, lawyer, judge, or other person should not affect the determination of whether to publish an opinion.

(Subd (d) adopted effective April 1, 2007.)

(e)　Changes in publication status

(1)　Unless otherwise ordered under (2):

(A)　An opinion is no longer considered published if the rendering court grants rehearing.

(B)　Grant of review by the Supreme Court of a decision by the Court of Appeal does not affect the appellate court's certification of the opinion for full or partial publication under rule 8.1105(b) or rule 8.1110, but any such Court of Appeal opinion, whether officially published in hard copy or electronically, must be accompanied by a prominent notation advising that review by the Supreme Court has been granted.

(2)　The Supreme Court may order that an opinion certified for publication is not to be published or that an opinion not certified is to be published. The Supreme Court may also order depublication of part of an opinion at any time after granting review.

(Subd (e) amended effective July 1, 2016; adopted as subd (d) effective January 1, 2005; previously relettered as subd (e) effective April 1, 2007.)

(f)　Editing

(1)　Computer versions of all opinions of the Supreme Court and Courts of Appeal must be provided to the Reporter of Decisions on the day of filing. Opinions of superior court appellate divisions certified for publication must be provided as prescribed in rule 8.887.

(2)　The Reporter of Decisions must edit opinions for publication as directed by the Supreme Court. The Reporter of Decisions must submit edited opinions to the courts for examination, correction, and approval before finalization for the Official Reports.

(Subd (f) amended effective July 1, 2009; adopted as subd (e) effective January 1, 2005; previously amended effective January 1, 2007; previously relettered effective April 1, 2007.)

Rule 8.1105 amended effective July 1, 2016; repealed and adopted as rule 976 effective January 1, 2005; previously amended and renumbered effective January 1, 2007; previously amended effective April 1, 2007, July 23, 2008, and July 1, 2009.

Comment

Subdivision (e)(2). This subdivision allows the Supreme Court to order depublication of an opinion that is under review by that court.

Rule 8.1110.   Partial publication

(a) Order for partial publication

A majority of the rendering court may certify for publication any part of an opinion meeting a standard for publication under rule 8.1105.

(Subd (a) amended effective January 1, 2007.)

(b) Opinion contents

The published part of the opinion must specify the part or parts not certified for publication. All material, factual and legal, including the disposition, that aids in the application or interpretation of the published part must be published.

(c) Construction

For purposes of rules 8.1105, 8.1115, and 8.1120, the published part of the opinion is treated as a published opinion and the unpublished part as an unpublished opinion.

(Subd (c) amended effective January 1, 2007.)

Rule 8.1110 amended and renumbered effective January 1, 2007; repealed and adopted as rule 976.1 effective January 1, 2005.

Rule 8.1115.   Citation of opinions

(a) Unpublished opinion

Except as provided in (b), an opinion of a California Court of Appeal or superior court appellate division that is not certified for publication or ordered published must not be cited or relied on by a court or a party in any other action.

(b) Exceptions

An unpublished opinion may be cited or relied on:

(1) When the opinion is relevant under the doctrines of law of the case, res judicata, or collateral estoppel; or

(2) When the opinion is relevant to a criminal or disciplinary action because it states reasons for a decision affecting the same defendant or respondent in another such action.

(Subd (b) amended effective January 1, 2007.)

(c) Citation procedure

On request of the court or a party, a copy of an opinion citable under (b) must be promptly furnished to the court or the requesting party.

(Subd (c) amended effective July 1, 2016.)

(d) When a published opinion may be cited

A published California opinion may be cited or relied on as soon as it is certified for publication or ordered published.

(e) When review of published opinion has been granted

(1) *While review is pending*

Pending review and filing of the Supreme Court's opinion, unless otherwise ordered by the Supreme Court under (3), a published opinion of a Court of Appeal in the matter has no binding or precedential effect, and may be cited for potentially persuasive value only. Any citation to the Court of Appeal opinion must also note the grant of review and any subsequent action by the Supreme Court.

(2) *After decision on review*

After decision on review by the Supreme Court, unless otherwise ordered by the Supreme Court under (3), a published opinion of a Court of Appeal in the matter, and any published opinion of a Court of Appeal in a matter in which the Supreme Court has ordered review and deferred action pending the decision, is citable and has binding or precedential effect, except to the extent it is inconsistent with the decision of the Supreme Court or is disapproved by that court.

(3) *Supreme Court order*

At any time after granting review or after decision on review, the Supreme Court may order that all or part of an opinion covered by (1) or (2) is not citable or has a binding or precedential effect different from that specified in (1) or (2).

(Subd (e) adopted effective July 1, 2016.)

Rule 8.1115 amended effective July 1, 2016; repealed and adopted as rule 977 effective January 1, 2005; previously amended and renumbered as rule 8.115 effective January 1, 2007.

Comment

Subdivision (e)(1). In two respects, this subdivision alters the effect of published Court of Appeal decisions after review is granted by the Supreme Court and while a decision on review is pending.

Under *Auto Equity Sales, Inc. v. Superior Court* (1962) 57 Cal.2d 450, published "[d]ecisions of every division of the District Courts of Appeal are binding upon all the … superior courts of this state …." (*Id.*, at p. 455.) The nature of this binding effect changes when there are conflicting published Court of Appeal opinions: in that circumstance, the superior court is still bound, but it "can and must make a choice between the conflicting decisions." (*Id.*, at p. 456.) Because the practice and

rule in effect before July 1, 2016, automatically depublished the decision under review, superior courts were not allowed to choose to be bound by the appellate court decision that was under review. Under new subdivision (e)(1) of this rule, if the Supreme Court grants review of a published Court of Appeal decision, that decision now remains published and citable while review is pending and yet — similar to the result under the former rule — it will not have binding or precedential effect on the superior courts, but will instead have a lesser status of "potentially persuasive value only." Accordingly, pursuant to the new rule (as before), when a decision that is pending review conflicts with another published Court of Appeal decision that is not under review, only that other published decision will continue to have binding or precedential effect on the superior court.

Subdivision (e)(1) also slightly alters practice with respect to the Court of Appeal pending-decision after grant of review. It has long been the rule that no published Court of Appeal decision has *binding* effect on any other Court of Appeal (e.g., *In re Marriage of Hayden* (1981) 124 Cal.App.3d 72, 77, fn. 1; *Froyd v. Cook* (E.D.Cal. 1988) 681 F.Supp. 669, 672, fn. 9, and cases cited) or on the Supreme Court. Under prior practice and the former rule, because a grant of review automatically depublished the decision under review, the Court of Appeal was not allowed to cite or quote that review-granted decision concerning any substantive point. Under the new subdivision, a published Court of Appeal decision as to which review has been granted remains published and is citable, while review is pending, for any potentially persuasive value.

Subdivision (e)(2). The fact that a Supreme Court decision does not discuss an issue addressed in the prior Court of Appeal decision does not constitute an expression of the Supreme Court's opinion concerning the correctness of the result of the decision on that issue or of any law stated in the Court of Appeal decision with respect to any such issue.

Subdivision (e)(3). This subdivision specifically provides that the Supreme Court can order that an opinion under review by that court, or after decision on review by that court, have an effect other than the effect otherwise specified under this rule. For example, the court could order that, while review is pending, specified parts of the published Court of Appeal opinion have binding or precedential effect, rather than only potentially persuasive value. For purposes of subdivision (e)(2) and (3), a "decision on review" includes any order by the Supreme Court dismissing review. (See rules 8.528(b) [addressing an "order dismissing review"] & 8.532(b)(2)(B) [listing, among "decisions final on filing," an order filed under rule 8.528(b)].) Accordingly, upon dismissal of review, any published Court of Appeal opinion regains binding or precedential effect under rule 8.1115(e)(2) unless the court orders otherwise under that rule's subdivision (e)(3).

Rule 8.1120.   Requesting publication of unpublished opinions

(a) Request

(1) Any person may request that an unpublished opinion be ordered published.

(2) The request must be made by a letter to the court that rendered the opinion, concisely stating the person's interest and the reason why the opinion meets a standard for publication.

(3) The request must be delivered to the rendering court within 20 days after the opinion is filed.

(4) The request must be served on all parties.

(b) Action by rendering court

(1) If the rendering court does not or cannot grant the request before the decision is final in that court, it must forward the request to the Supreme Court with a copy of its opinion, its recommendation for disposition, and a brief statement of its reasons. The rendering court must forward these materials within 15 days after the decision is final in that court.

(2) The rendering court must also send a copy of its recommendation and reasons to all parties and any person who requested publication.

(c) Action by Supreme Court

The Supreme Court may order the opinion published or deny the request. The court must send notice of its action to the rendering court, all parties, and any person who requested publication.

(d) Effect of Supreme Court order to publish

A Supreme Court order to publish is not an expression of the court's opinion of the correctness of the result of the decision or of any law stated in the opinion.

Rule 8.1120 renumbered effective January 1, 2007; repealed and adopted as rule 978 effective January 1, 2005.

Advisory Committee Comment

Subdivision (a). This rule previously required generally that a publication request be made "promptly," but in practice the term proved so vague that requests were often made after the Court of Appeal had lost jurisdiction. To assist persons intending to request publication and to give the Court of Appeal adequate time to act, this rule was revised to specify that the request must be made within 20 days after the opinion is filed. The change is substantive.

Subdivision (b). This rule previously did not specify the time within which the Court of Appeal was required to forward to the Supreme Court a publication request that it had not or could not have granted. In practice, however, it was not uncommon for the court to forward such a request after the Supreme Court had denied a petition for review in the same case or, if there was no such petition, had lost jurisdiction to grant review on its own motion. To assist the Supreme Court in timely processing publication requests, therefore, this rule was revised to require the Court of Appeal to forward the request within 15 days after the decision is final in that court. The change is substantive.

Rule 8.1125. Requesting depublication of published opinions

(a) Request

(1) Any person may request the Supreme Court to order that an opinion certified for publication not be published.

(2) The request must not be made as part of a petition for review, but by a separate letter to the Supreme Court not exceeding 10 pages.

(3) The request must concisely state the person's interest and the reason why the opinion should not be published.

(4) The request must be delivered to the Supreme Court within 30 days after the decision is final in the Court of Appeal.

(5) The request must be served on the rendering court and all parties.

(b) Response

(1) Within 10 days after the Supreme Court receives a request under (a), the rendering court or any person may submit a response supporting or opposing the request. A response submitted by anyone other than the rendering court must state the person's interest.

(2) A response must not exceed 10 pages and must be served on the rendering court, all parties, and any person who requested depublication.

(c) Action by Supreme Court

(1) The Supreme Court may order the opinion depublished or deny the request. It must send notice of its action to the rendering court, all parties, and any person who requested depublication.

(2) The Supreme Court may order an opinion depublished on its own motion, notifying the rendering court of its action.

(d) Effect of Supreme Court order to depublish

A Supreme Court order to depublish is not an expression of the court's opinion of the correctness of the result of the decision or of any law stated in the opinion.

Rule 8.1125 renumbered effective January 1, 2007; repealed and adopted as rule 979 effective January 1, 2005.

Advisory Committee Comment

Subdivision (a). This subdivision previously required depublication requests to be made "by letter to the Supreme Court," but in practice many were incorporated in petitions for review. To clarify and emphasize the requirement, the subdivision was revised specifically to state that the request "must not be made as part of a petition for review, but by a separate letter to the Supreme Court not exceeding 10 pages." The change is not substantive.

TITLE 9
Rules on Law Practice, Attorneys, and Judges

Division 1. General Provisions. Rule 9.0.
Division 2. Attorney Admission and Disciplinary Proceedings and Review of State Bar Proceedings. Rules 9.1–9.31.
Division 3. Legal Specialists. Rule 9.35.
Division 4. Appearances and Practice by Individuals Who Are Not Licensees of the State Bar of California. Rules 9.40–9.48.
Division 5. Censure, Removal, Retirement, or Private or Public Admonishment of Judges. Rules 9.60, 9.61.
Division 6. Judicial Ethics Opinions. Rule 9.80.
Division 7. State Bar Trustees. Rule 9.90.

Division 1
General Provisions

Rule 9.0. Title and source
(a) Title
The rules in this title may be referred to as the Rules on Law Practice, Attorneys, and Judges.
(b) Source
The rules in this title were adopted by the Supreme Court under its inherent authority over the admission and discipline of attorneys and under subdivisions (d) and (f) of section 18 of article VI of the Constitution of the State of California.
Rule 9.0 amended and renumbered effective January 1, 2018; adopted as rules 9.1 and 9.2 effective January 1, 2007.

Division 2
Attorney Admission and Disciplinary Proceedings and Review of State Bar Proceedings

Chap. 1. General Provisions. Rules 9.1, 9.2.
Chap. 2. Attorney Admissions. Rules 9.3–9.9.5.
Chap. 3. Attorney Disciplinary Proceedings. Rules 9.10–9.23.
Chap. 4. Legal Education. Rules 9.30, 9.31.

Chapter 1
General Provisions

Rule 9.1. Definitions
Rule 9.2. Interim Special Regulatory Assessment for Attorney Discipline

Rule 9.1. Title [Renumbered]
Rule 9.1 renumbered as rule 9.0(a) effective January 1, 2018.

Another Rule 9.1 follows.

Rule 9.1. Definitions
As used in this division, unless the context otherwise requires:
(1) "Licensee" means a person licensed by the State Bar to practice law in this state.
(2) "State Bar Court" means the Hearing Department or the Review Department established under Business and Professions Code sections 6079.1 and 6086.65.
(3) "Review Department" means the Review Department of the State Bar Court established under Business and Professions Code section 6086.65.
(4) "General Counsel" means the general counsel of the State Bar of California.
(5) "Chief Trial Counsel" means the chief trial counsel of the State Bar of California appointed under Business and Professions Code section 6079.5.
Rule 9.1 amended effective January 1, 2019; adopted as rule 950 effective December 1, 1990; previously amended and renumbered as rule 9.5 effective January 1, 2007; previously renumbered as rule 9.1 effective January 1, 2018.

Rule 9.2. Source [Renumbered]
Rule 9.2 renumbered as rule 9.0(b) effective January 1, 2018.

Another Rule 9.2 follows.

Rule 9.2. Interim Special Regulatory Assessment for Attorney Discipline
(a) This rule is adopted by the Supreme Court solely as an emergency interim measure to protect the public, the courts, and the legal profession from the harm that may be caused by the absence of an adequately functioning attorney disciplinary system. The Supreme Court contemplates that the rule may be modified or repealed once legislation designed to fund an adequate attorney disciplinary system is enacted and becomes effective.

(b)(1) Each active licensee shall pay a mandatory regulatory assessment of two hundred ninety-seven dollars ($297) to the State Bar of California. This assessment is calculated as the sum of the following amounts:
(A) Two hundred eighty-three dollars ($283) to support the following departments and activities:
Office of Chief Trial Counsel
Office of Probation
State Bar Court
Mandatory Fee Arbitration program
Office of Professional Competence
Office of General Counsel
Office of Licensee Records and Compliance
Licensee Billing
Office of Communications (support of discipline only)
California Young Lawyers Association (discipline-related only).
(B) Nine dollars ($9) to fund implementation of the workforce plan recommendations from the National Center for State Courts.
(C) Five dollars ($5) to make up for revenue the State Bar will forgo because of assessment scaling and assessment waivers, as provided for under this rule.
(2) The $297 assessment specifically excludes any funding for the State Bar's legislative lobbying, elimination of bias, and bar relations programs.
(3) Payment of this assessment is due by March 1, 2017. Late payment or nonpayment of the assessment shall subject a licensee to the same penalties and/or sanctions applicable to mandatory fees authorized by statute.
(4) The provisions regarding fee scaling, fee waivers, and penalty waivers contained in Business and Professions Code section 6141.1 and rules 2.15 and 2.16 of the Rules of the State Bar of California shall apply to requests for relief from payment of the assessment or any penalty under this rule. Applications for relief from payment shall be made to the State Bar, which may grant or deny waivers in conformance with its existing rules and regulations. The State Bar shall keep a record of all fee scaling and fee waivers approved and the amount of fees affected.
(Subd (b) amended effective January 1, 2019.)
(c) A special master appointed by the Supreme Court shall establish the Special Master's Attorney Discipline Fund, into which all money collected pursuant to this rule shall be deposited. The special master shall oversee the disbursement and allocation of funds from the Special Master's Attorney Discipline Fund for the limited purpose of maintaining, operating, and supporting an attorney disciplinary system, including payment of the reasonable costs and expenses of the special master as ordered by the Supreme Court. The special master shall exercise authority pursuant to the charge of the Supreme Court and shall submit quarterly reports and recommendations to the Supreme Court regarding the supervision and use of these funds. The State Bar shall respond in timely and accurate fashion to the special master's requests for information and reports.
Should any funds collected pursuant to this rule not be used for the limited purpose set forth in the rule, the Supreme Court may order the refund of an appropriate amount to licensees or take any other action that it deems appropriate.
(Subd (c) amended effective January 1, 2019.)

Rule 9.2 amended effective January 1, 2019; adopted as rule 9.9 effective November 16, 2016; previously renumbered effective January 1, 2018.

Chapter 2
Attorney Admissions

Title 9, Rules on Law Practice, Attorneys, and Judges—Division 2, Attorney Admission and Disciplinary Proceedings and Review of State Bar Proceedings—Chapter 2, Attorney Admissions; adopted effective January 1, 2018.

Rule 9.3. Inherent power of Supreme Court
Rule 9.4. Nomination and appointment of Members to Committee of Bar Examiners
Rule 9.5. Supreme Court approval of admissions rules
Rule 9.6. Supreme Court approval of bar examination
Rule 9.7. Oath required when admitted to practice law
Rule 9.8. Roll of attorneys admitted to practice
Rule 9.9. Online reporting by attorneys
Rule 9.9.5. Attorney Fingerprinting

Rule 9.3. Inherent power of Supreme Court
(a) Inherent power over admissions
The Supreme Court has the inherent power to admit persons to practice law in California. The State Bar serves as the administrative arm of the Supreme Court for admissions matters and in that capacity acts under the authority and at the direction of the Supreme Court. The Committee of Bar Examiners, acting under authority delegated to it by the State Bar Board of Trustees, is authorized to administer the requirements for admission to practice law, to examine all applicants for admission, and to certify to the Supreme Court for admission those applicants who fulfill the admission requirements.

(Subd (a) amended effective January 1, 2019; adopted effective January 1, 2018.)

(b) Inherent jurisdiction over practice of law
Nothing in this chapter may be construed as affecting the power of the Supreme Court to exercise its inherent jurisdiction over the practice of law in this state.

(Subd (b) adopted effective January 1, 2018.)
Rule 9.3 amended effective January 1, 2019; adopted effective January 1, 2018.

Rule 9.4. Oath required when admitted to practice law [Renumbered]
Rule 9.4 renumbered as rule 9.7 effective January 1, 2018.

Another Rule 9.4 follows.

Rule 9.4. Nomination and appointment of members to the Committee of Bar Examiners
(a) Appointments
The Supreme Court is responsible for appointing ten examiners to the Committee of Bar Examiners, each for a four-year term. At least one of the ten examiners must be a judicial officer in this state, and the balance must be licensees of the State Bar. At least one of the attorney examiners shall have been admitted to practice law in California within three years from the date of his or her appointment. The court may reappoint an attorney or judicial officer examiner to serve no more than three additional full terms, and may fill any vacancy in the term of any appointed attorney or judicial officer examiner.

(Subd (a) amended effective January 1, 2019; adopted effective January 1, 2018.)

(b) Nominations
The Supreme Court must make its appointments from a list of candidates nominated by the Board of Trustees of the State Bar pursuant to a procedure approved by the court.

(Subd (b) adopted effective January 1, 2018.)
Rule 9.4 amended effective January 1, 2019; adopted effective January 1, 2018.

Rule 9.5. Definitions [Renumbered]
Rule 9.5 renumbered as rule 9.1 effective January 1, 2018.

Another Rule 9.5 follows.

Rule 9.5. Supreme Court approval of admissions rules
All State Bar rules adopted by the State Bar Committee of Bar Examiners pertaining to the admission to practice law must be approved by the Board of Trustees and then submitted to the Supreme Court for its review and approval.
Rule 9.5 amended effective January 1, 2019; adopted effective January 1, 2018.

Rule 9.6. Roll of attorneys admitted to practice [Renumbered]
Rule 9.6 renumbered as rule 9.8 effective January 1, 2018.

Another Rule 9.6 follows.

Rule 9.6. Supreme Court approval of bar examination
(a) Bar examination
The Committee of Bar Examiners, pursuant to the authority delegated to it by the Board of Trustees, is responsible for determining the bar examination's format, scope, topics, content, questions, and grading process, subject to review and approval by the Supreme Court. The Supreme Court must set the passing score of the examination.

(Subd (a) amended effective January 1, 2019; adopted effective January 1, 2018.)

(b) Analysis of validity
The State Bar must conduct an analysis of the validity of the bar examination at least once every seven years, or whenever directed by the Supreme Court. The State Bar must prepare and submit a report summarizing its findings and recommendations, if any, to the Supreme Court. Any recommendations proposing significant changes to the bar examination, and any recommended change to the passing score, must be submitted to the Supreme Court for its review and approval.

(Subd (b) amended effective January 1, 2019; adopted effective January 1, 2018.)

(c) Report on examination
The State Bar must provide the Supreme Court a report on each administration of the bar examination in a timely manner.

(Subd (c) adopted effective January 1, 2018.)
Rule 9.6 amended effective January 1, 2019; adopted effective January 1, 2018.

Rule 9.7. Online reporting by attorneys [Renumbered]
Rule 9.7 renumbered as rule 9.9 effective January 1, 2018.

Another Rule 9.7 follows.

Rule 9.7. Oath required when admitted to practice law
In addition to the language required by Business and Professions Code section 6067, the oath to be taken by every person on admission to practice law is to conclude with the following: "As an officer of the court, I will strive to conduct myself at all times with dignity, courtesy and integrity."

Rule 9.7 renumbered effective January 1, 2018; adopted as rule 9.4 effective May 27, 2014.

Rule 9.8. Roll of attorneys admitted to practice
(a) State Bar to maintain the roll of attorneys
The State Bar must maintain, as part of the official records of the State Bar, a roll of attorneys, which is a list of all persons admitted to practice in this state. Such records must include the information specified in Business and Professions Code section 6002.1 and 6064 and other information as directed by the Supreme Court.

(Subd (a) amended effective January 1, 2019; adopted as unlettered subdivision effective May 1, 1996; previously amended effective January 1, 2007; previously lettered effective June 1, 2007.)

(b) Annual State Bar recommendation for one-time expungement of suspension for nonpayment of license fees
The State Bar is authorized to transmit to the Supreme Court on an annual basis the names of those licensees who meet all of the following criteria, along with a recommendation that their public record of suspension for nonpayment of license fees be expunged:

(1) The licensee has not on any previous occasion obtained an expungement under the terms of this rule or rule 9.31;

(2) The suspension was for 90 days or less;

(3) The suspension ended at least seven years before the date of the submission of the licensee's name to the Supreme Court;

(4) The licensee has no other record of suspension or involuntary inactive enrollment for discipline or otherwise.

(Subd (b) amended effective January 1, 2019; adopted effective June 1, 2007; previously amended effective August 1, 2017.)

(c) Records to be maintained by State Bar
Upon order of the Supreme Court of expungement of a licensee's record under (b) of this rule, the State Bar will remove or delete the record of such suspension from the licensee's public record. Notwithstanding any other provision of this rule, the State Bar must maintain such internal records as are necessary to apply the terms of (b) of this rule and to report to the Commission on Judicial Nominees Evaluation or appropriate governmental entities involved in judicial elections the licensee's eligibility for a judgeship under the California Constitution, article VI, section 15.

(Subd (c) amended effective January 1, 2019; adopted effective June 1, 2007.)

(d) Duty of disclosure by licensee

Expungement of a licensee's suspension under (b) of this rule will not relieve the licensee of his or her duty to disclose the suspension for purpose of determining the licensee's eligibility for a judgeship under the California Constitution, article VI, section 15. For all other purposes the suspension expunged under (b) of this rule is deemed not to have occurred and the licensee may answer accordingly any question relating to his or her record.

(Subd (d) amended effective January 1, 2019; adopted effective June 1, 2007.)

(e) Authorization for the Board of Trustees of the State Bar to adopt rules and regulations

The Board of Trustees of the State Bar is authorized to adopt such rules and regulations as it deems necessary and appropriate in order to comply with this rule.

(Subd (e) amended effective August 1, 2017; adopted effective June 1, 2007.)

(f) Inherent power of Supreme Court

Nothing in this rule may be construed as affecting the power of the Supreme Court to exercise its inherent power to direct the State Bar to expunge its records.

(Subd (f) adopted effective June 1, 2007.)

Rule 9.8 amended effective January 1, 2019; adopted as rule 950.5 by the Supreme Court effective May 1, 1996; previously amended and renumbered as rule 9.6 effective January 1, 2007; previously amended effective June 1, 2007, and August 1, 2017; previously renumbered effective January 1, 2018.

Rule 9.9. Interim Special Regulatory Assessment for Attorney Discipline [Renumbered]

Rule 9.9 renumbered as rule 9.2 effective January 1, 2018.

Another Rule 9.9 follows.

Rule 9.9. Online reporting by attorneys

(a) Required information

To maintain the roll of attorneys required by rule 9.8 and to facilitate communications by the State Bar with its licensees, each licensee must use an online account on a secure system provided by the State Bar to report a current:

(1) Office address and telephone number, or if none, an alternative address; and

(2) An e-mail address not to be disclosed on the State Bar's website or otherwise to the public without the licensee's consent.

(Subd (a) amended effective January 1, 2019; adopted effective February 1, 2010.)

(b) Optional information

A licensee may also use an online attorney records account to:

(1) Provide an e-mail address for disclosure to the public on the State Bar Web site; and

(2) Provide additional information as authorized by statute, rule or Supreme Court directive, or as requested by the State Bar.

(Subd (b) amended effective January 1, 2019; adopted effective February 1, 2010.)

(c) Exclusions

Unless otherwise permitted by law or the Supreme Court, the State Bar may not use e-mail as substitute means of providing a notice required to initiate a State Bar disciplinary or regulatory proceeding or to otherwise change a licensee's status involuntarily.

(Subd (c) amended effective January 1, 2019; adopted effective February 1, 2010.)

(d) Exemption

A licensee who does not have online access or an e-mail address may claim an exemption from the reporting requirements of this rule. The exemption must be requested in the manner prescribed by the State Bar.

(Subd (d) amended effective January 1, 2019; adopted effective February 1, 2010.)

Rule 9.9 amended effective January 1, 2019; adopted as rule 9.7 effective February 1, 2010; previously renumbered effective January 1, 2018.

Rule 9.9.5. Attorney Fingerprinting

(a) Subsequent arrest notification

(1) The State Bar must enter into a contract with the California Department of Justice for subsequent arrest notification services for attorneys whose license is on active status with the State Bar ("active licensed attorneys") and attorneys permitted to practice in the State of California pursuant to rules 9.44, 9.45, and 9.46 of the California Rules of Court ("special admissions attorneys").

(2) The State Bar must consider those active licensed attorneys and special admissions attorneys for whom it is already receiving subsequent arrest notification services as having satisfied the fingerprinting require-

ment of this rule and thereby exempt. The State Bar must adopt a procedure for notification of all attorneys as to whether they have been deemed to have already satisfied the requirement.

(Subd (a) adopted effective June 1, 2018.)

(b) Active licensed attorneys

Each active licensed attorney, with the exception of those attorneys specifically exempt under (a)(2) of this rule, must, pursuant to the procedure identified by the State Bar, be fingerprinted for the purpose of obtaining criminal offender record information regarding state and federal level convictions and arrests from the Department of Justice and the Federal Bureau of Investigation. These fingerprints will be retained by the Department of Justice for the limited purpose of subsequent arrest notification.

(Subd (b) adopted effective June 1, 2018.)

(c) Inactive licensed attorneys

An attorney whose license is on inactive status with the State Bar ("inactive licensed attorneys"), with the exception of those attorneys specifically exempt under (a)(2) of this rule, must, pursuant to the procedure identified by the State Bar, be fingerprinted prior to being placed on active status for the purposes described in (b) of this rule.

(Subd (c) adopted effective June 1, 2018.)

(d) Active licensed attorneys in foreign countries

Active licensed attorneys who are residing outside the United States and required to submit fingerprints under this rule should have their fingerprints taken by a licensed fingerprinting service agency and submit the hard copy fingerprint card to the State Bar. If fingerprinting services are not provided in the jurisdiction where the attorney is physically located, or the attorney is able to provide evidence that he/she is unable to access or afford such services, the attorney must notify the State Bar pursuant to the procedure identified by the State Bar. The attorney will be exempt from providing fingerprints until he or she returns to the United States for a period of not less than 60 days.

(Subd (d) adopted effective June 1, 2018.)

(e) Special admissions attorneys

Attorneys permitted to practice in the State of California pursuant to rules 9.44, 9.45, and 9.46 of the California Rules of Court, with the exception of those attorneys specifically exempt under (a)(2) of this rule, must, pursuant to the procedure identified by the State Bar, be fingerprinted for the purpose of obtaining criminal offender record information regarding state and federal level convictions and arrests from the Department of Justice and the Federal Bureau of Investigation. These fingerprints will be retained by the Department of Justice for the limited purpose of subsequent arrest notification.

(Subd (e) adopted effective June 1, 2018.)

(f) Implementation schedule and penalty for noncompliance

(1) The State Bar must develop a schedule for implementation that requires all attorneys subject to fingerprinting under (b) of this rule to be fingerprinted by December 1, 2019. The State Bar must develop a schedule for implementation that requires all special admissions attorneys subject to fingerprinting under (e) of this rule to be fingerprinted by the renewal of their application to practice law in the State of California.

(2) The State Bar has ongoing authority to require submission of fingerprints after December 1, 2019 for attorneys for whom it is not receiving subsequent arrest notification services and for attorneys transferring to active status. Failure to be fingerprinted if required by this rule may result in involuntary inactive enrollment pursuant to Business and Professions Code section 6054(d).

(3) The State Bar has ongoing authority to require submission of fingerprints after December 1, 2019, for special admissions attorneys for whom it is not receiving subsequent arrest notification services. Failure to be fingerprinted if required may result in a State Bar determination that the attorney cease providing legal services in California.

(Subd (f) adopted effective June 1, 2018.)

(g) Information obtained by fingerprint submission; disclosure limitations

Any information obtained by the State Bar as a result of fingerprint submission under this rule must be kept confidential and used solely for State Bar licensing and regulatory purposes.

(Subd (g) adopted effective June 1, 2018.)

(h) Fingerprint submission and processing costs

(1) Except as described in (h)(2), all costs incurred for the processing of fingerprints for the State Bar, including print furnishing and encoding,

as required by Business and Professions Code section 6054, must be borne by the licensed attorney or special admissions attorney.

(2) The State Bar must develop procedures for granting waivers of the processing costs of running Department of Justice and Federal Bureau of Investigation background checks for licensed attorneys with demonstrable financial hardship.

(Subd (h) adopted effective June 1, 2018.)

(i) Attorneys who are physically unable to be fingerprinted

(1) If the Department of Justice makes a determination pursuant to Penal Code section 11105.7 that any attorney required to be fingerprinted under this rule is presently unable to provide legible fingerprints, the attorney will be deemed to have complied with the fingerprinting requirements of this rule.

(2) Attorneys required to be fingerprinted under this rule may also submit notification to the State Bar that they are unable to submit fingerprints due to disability, illness, accident, or other circumstances beyond their control. The State Bar must evaluate the notification and may require additional evidence. If the State Bar determines that the attorney is unable to submit fingerprints based on the information provided, the attorney will be deemed to have complied with the fingerprinting requirements of this rule.

(3) A determination of deemed compliance under (i)(1) and (i)(2) will apply only to those attorneys who are unable to supply legible fingerprints due to disability, illness, accident, or other circumstances beyond their control and will not apply to attorneys who are unable to provide fingerprints because of actions they have taken to avoid submitting their fingerprints.

(Subd (i) adopted effective June 1, 2018.)
Rule 9.9.5 adopted effective June 1, 2018.

Chapter 3
Attorney Disciplinary Proceedings

Title 9, Rules on Law Practice, Attorneys, and Judges—Division 2, Attorney Admission and Disciplinary Proceedings and Review of State Bar Proceedings— Chapter 3, Attorney Disciplinary Proceedings; renumbered from Chapter 2 effective January 1, 2018.

Rule 9.10. Authority of the State Bar Court

(a) Conviction proceedings

The State Bar Court exercises statutory powers under Business and Professions Code sections 6101 and 6102 with respect to the discipline of attorneys convicted of crimes. (See Bus. & Prof. Code §6087.) For purposes of this rule, a judgment of conviction is deemed final when the availability of appeal has been exhausted and the time for filing a petition for certiorari in the United States Supreme Court on direct review of the judgment of conviction has elapsed and no petition has been filed, or if filed the petition has been denied or the judgment of conviction has been affirmed. The State Bar Court must impose or recommend discipline in conviction matters as in other disciplinary proceedings. The power conferred upon the State Bar Court by this rule includes the power to place attorneys on interim suspension under subdivisions (a) and (b) of section 6102, and the power to vacate, delay the effective date of, and temporarily stay the effect of such orders.

(Subd (a) amended effective January 1, 2007.)

(b) Professional responsibility examination

The State Bar Court may:

(1) Extend the time within which a licensee of the State Bar must take and pass a professional responsibility examination;

(2) Suspend a licensee for failing to take and pass such examination; and

(3) Vacate licensee's suspension for failing to take and pass such examination.

(Subd (b) amended effective January 1, 2019; previously amended effective January 1, 2007.)

(c) Probation

The State Bar Court for good cause, may:

(1) Approve stipulations between the licensee and the Chief Trial Counsel for modification of the terms of a licensee's probation; and

(2) Make corrections and minor modifications to the terms of a licensee's disciplinary probation.

The order of the State Bar Court must be filed promptly with the Clerk of the Supreme Court.

(Subd (c) amended effective January 1, 2019; previously amended effective January 1, 2007.)

(d) Rule 9.20 compliance

The State Bar Court for good cause, may extend the time within which a licensee must comply with the provisions of rule 9.20 of the California Rules of Court.

(Subd (d) amended effective January 1, 2019; previously amended effective January 1, 2007.)

(e) Commencement of suspension

The State Bar Court for good cause, may delay temporarily the effective date of, or temporarily stay the effect of, an order for a licensee's disciplinary suspension from practice.

(Subd (e) amended effective January 1, 2019; previously amended effective January 1, 2007.)

(f) Readmission and reinstatement

Applications for readmission or reinstatement must, in the first instance, be filed and heard by the State Bar Court, except that no applicant who has been disbarred by the Supreme Court on two previous occasions may apply for readmission or reinstatement. Applicants for readmission or reinstatement must:

(1) Pass a professional responsibility examination;

(2) Establish their rehabilitation and present moral qualifications for readmission; and

(3) Establish present ability and learning in the general law. Applicants who resigned without charges pending more than five years before filing an application for reinstatement or readmission must establish present ability and learning in the general law by providing proof, at the time of filing the application, that they have taken and passed the Attorneys' Examination administered by the Committee of Bar Examiners pursuant to the authority delegated to it by the Board of Trustees within five years prior to the filing of the application for readmission or reinstatement. Applicants who resigned with charges pending or who were disbarred must establish present ability and learning in the general law by providing proof, at the time of filing the application for readmission or reinstatement, that they have taken and passed the Attorneys' Examination by State Bar within three years prior to the filing of the application for readmission or reinstatement.

(Subd (f) amended effective January 1, 2019; previously amended effective January 1, 2007, and January 1, 2010.)

(g) Inherent power of Supreme Court

Nothing in these rules may be construed as affecting the power of the Supreme Court to exercise its inherent jurisdiction over the lawyer discipline and admissions system.

(Subd (g) amended effective January 1, 2007.)

Rule 9.10 amended effective January 1, 2019; adopted as rule 951 effective December 1, 1990; previously amended by the Supreme Court effective April 1, 1996, and January 1, 2007; previously amended and renumbered effective January 1, 2010.

Rule 9.11. State Bar Court judges

(a) Applicant Evaluation and Nomination Committee

(1) In order to ensure that individuals appointed by the Supreme Court or by the executive or legislative branches have been evaluated objectively, the Supreme Court has established an independent Applicant Evaluation and Nomination Committee to solicit, receive, screen, and evaluate all applications for appointment or reappointment to any position of judge of the State Bar Court (hearing judge, presiding judge, and review department judge). The role of the committee is to determine whether appointees possess not only the statutorily enumerated qualifica-

tions, but also any qualifications that may be required by the Supreme Court to assist in the exercise of its ultimate authority over the discipline and admission of attorneys (see *Obrien v. Jones* (2000) 23 Cal.4th 40; *In re Attorney Discipline System* (1998) 19 Cal.4th 582; Cal. Const., art. VI, sec. 9).

(2) The committee serves at the pleasure of the Supreme Court. It shall consist of seven members appointed by the court of whom four must be licensees of the State Bar in good standing, two must be retired or active judicial officers, and one must be a public member who has never been a licensee of the State Bar or admitted to practice before any court in the United States. Two members of the committee must be present members of the Board of Trustees of the State Bar (neither of whom may be from the Board's Discipline Committee).

(3) The committee must adopt, and implement upon approval by the Supreme Court, procedures for:

(A) Timely notice to potential applicants of vacancies;

(B) Receipt of applications for appointments to those positions from both incumbents and other qualified persons;

(C) Solicitation and receipt of public comment;

(D) Evaluation and rating of applicants; and

(E) Transmittal of the materials specified in (b) of this rule to the Supreme Court and, as applicable, other appointing authorities.

The procedures adopted by the committee must include provisions to ensure confidentiality comparable to those followed by the Judicial Nominees Evaluation Commission established under Government Code section 12011.5.

(4) The Board of Trustees of the State Bar, in consultation with the Supreme Court if necessary, must provide facilities and support staff needed by the committee to carry out its obligations under this rule.

(Subd (a) amended effective January 1, 2019; previously amended effective February 15, 1995, July 1, 2000, January 1, 2007, and January 1, 2009.)

(b) Evaluations

(1) The committee must evaluate the qualifications of and rate all applicants for positions appointed by the Supreme Court and must submit to the Supreme Court the nominations of at least three qualified candidates for each vacancy. Candidates shall be rated as "not recommended," "recommended," and "highly recommended." A rating of "not recommended" relates only to the position under consideration and does not indicate any lack of ability or expertise of the applicant generally. The committee must report in confidence to the Supreme Court its evaluation, rating and recommendation for applicants for appointment and the reasons therefore, including a succinct summary of their qualifications, at a time to be designated by the Supreme Court. The report must include written comments received by the committee, which must be transmitted to the Supreme Court together with the nominations.

(2) The committee must evaluate the qualifications of and rate all applicants for positions appointed by the Governor, the Senate Committee on Rules, or the Speaker of the Assembly, and must submit in confidence to the Supreme Court and, as applicable, to other appointing authorities, all applications for such positions together with the committee's evaluation, rating and recommendation for these applicants, including any written comments received by the committee, at a time to be designated by the Supreme Court.

(3) In determining the qualifications of an applicant for appointment or reappointment the committee must consider, among other appropriate factors, the following: industry, legal and judicial experience (including prior service as a judge of the State Bar Court), judicial temperament, honesty, objectivity, community respect, integrity, and ability. The committee must consider legal work experience broadly, including, but not limited to, litigation and non-litigation experience, legal work for a business or nonprofit entity, experience as a law professor or other academic position, legal work in any of the three branches of government, and legal work in dispute resolution.

The committee shall consider whether an applicant has demonstrated the ability to write cogently and to analyze legal provisions and principles. Among the issues the committee may also consider are (1) the applicant's demonstrated capacity to work independently and to set and meet performance goals, (2) the applicant's knowledge and experience relevant to issues that give rise to the majority of State Bar Court proceedings, including professional ethics and fiduciary obligations, (3) knowledge of practice and demeanor in the courtroom, and (4) whether the applicant has been in practice for 10 or more years. The committee shall accord weight to all experience that has provided the applicant with legal experience and

exposure during which the individual has demonstrated the underlying skills necessary to serve as an effective State Bar Court judge. The committee shall apply the same criteria to candidates seeking appointment from all of the appointing authorities. Any evaluation or rating of an applicant and any recommendation for appointment or reappointment by the committee must be made in conformity with Business and Professions Code section 6079.1(b) and in light of the factors specified in Government Code section 12011.5(d), and those specified in this paragraph.

(4) Upon transmittal of its report to the Supreme Court, the committee must notify any incumbent who has applied for reappointment by the Supreme Court if he or she is or is not among the applicants recommended for appointment to the new term by the committee. The applicable appointing authority must notify as soon as possible an incumbent who has applied for reappointment but is not selected.

(Subd (b) amended effective January 1, 2019; adopted effective February 15, 1995; previously amended effective July 1, 2000, January 1, 2007, and January 1, 2009.)

(c) Appointments

Only applicants who are rated as recommended or highly recommended by the committee or by the Supreme Court may be appointed. At the request of the Governor, the Senate Committee on Rules, or the Speaker of the Assembly, the Supreme Court will reconsider a finding by the committee that a particular applicant is not recommended. The Supreme Court may make such orders as to the appointment of applicants as it deems appropriate, including extending the term of incumbent judges pending such order or providing for staggered terms.

(Subd (c) amended effective January 1, 2009; adopted effective February 15, 1995; previously amended effective July 1, 2000 and January 1, 2007.)

(d) Discipline for misconduct or disability

A judge of the State Bar Court is subject to discipline or retirement on the same grounds as a judge of a court of this state. Complaints concerning the conduct of a judge of the State Bar Court must be addressed to the Executive Director–Chief Counsel of the Commission on Judicial Performance, who is the Supreme Court's investigator for the purpose of evaluating those complaints, conducting any necessary further investigation, and determining whether formal proceedings should be instituted. If there is reasonable cause to institute formal proceedings, the investigator must notify the Supreme Court of that fact and must serve as or appoint the examiner and make other appointments and arrangements necessary for the hearing. The Supreme Court will then appoint one or more active or retired judges of superior courts or Courts of Appeal as its special master or masters to hear the complaint and the results of the investigation, and to report to the Supreme Court on the resulting findings, conclusions, and recommendations as to discipline. The procedures of the Commission on Judicial Performance must be followed by the investigator and special masters, to the extent feasible. The procedures in the Supreme Court after a discipline recommendation is filed will, to the extent feasible, be the same as the procedures followed when a determination of the Commission on Judicial Performance is filed.

(Subd (d) amended effective January 1, 2007; adopted as subd (b) effective December 1, 1990; relettered effective February 15, 1995; previously amended effective July 1, 2000.)

Rule 9.11 amended effective January 1, 2019; adopted as rule 961 effective December 1, 1990; previously amended February 15, 1995, July 1, 2000, and January 1, 2009; previously amended and renumbered effective January 1, 2007.

Rule 9.12.   Standard of review for State Bar Court Review Department

In reviewing the decisions, orders, or rulings of a hearing judge under rule 301 of the Rules of Procedure of the State Bar of California or such other rule as may be adopted governing the review of any decisions, orders, or rulings by a hearing judge that fully disposes of an entire proceeding, the Review Department of the State Bar Court must independently review the record and may adopt findings, conclusions, and a decision or recommendation different from those of the hearing judge.

Rule 9.12 amended and renumbered effective January 1, 2007; adopted as rule 951.5 by the Supreme Court effective February 23, 2000.

Rule 9.13.   Review of State Bar Court decisions

(a) Review of recommendation of disbarment or suspension

A petition to the Supreme Court by a licensee to review a decision of the State Bar Court recommending his or her disbarment or suspension from practice must be served and filed within 60 days after a certified copy of the decision complained of is filed with the Clerk of the Supreme Court. The State Bar may serve and file an answer to the petition within

15 days after filing of the petition. Within 5 days after filing of the answer, the petitioner may serve and file a reply. If review is ordered by the Supreme Court, the State Bar must serve and file a supplemental brief within 45 days after the order is filed. Within 15 days after filing of the supplemental brief, the petitioner may serve and file a reply brief.

(Subd (a) amended effective January 1, 2019; previously relettered and amended effective October 1, 1973; previously amended effective July 1, 1968, December 1, 1990, and January 1, 2007.)

(b) Review of recommendation to set aside stay of suspension or modify probation

A petition to the Supreme Court by a licensee to review a recommendation of the State Bar Court that a stay of an order of suspension be set aside or that the duration or conditions of probation be modified on account of a violation of probation must be served and filed within 15 days after a certified copy of the recommendation complained of is filed with the Clerk of the Supreme Court. Within 15 days after filing of the petition, the State Bar may serve and file an answer. Within 5 days after filing of the answer, the petitioner may serve and file a reply.

(Subd (b) amended effective January 1, 2019; adopted effective October 1, 1973; previously amended effective December 1, 1990, and January 1, 2007.)

(c) Review of interim decisions

A petition to the Supreme Court by a licensee to review a decision of the State Bar Court regarding interim suspension, the exercise of powers delegated by rule 9.10(b)–(e), or another interlocutory matter must be served and filed within 15 days after written notice of the adverse decision of the State Bar Court is mailed by the State Bar to the petitioner and to his or her counsel of record, if any, at their respective addresses under section 6002.1. Within 15 days after filing of the petition, the State Bar may serve and file an answer. Within 5 days after filing of the answer, the petitioner may serve and file a reply.

(Subd (c) amended effective January 1, 2019; adopted effective December 1, 1990; previously amended effective January 1, 2007.)

(d) Review of other decisions

A petition to the Supreme Court to review any other decision of the State Bar Court or action of the Board of Trustees of the State Bar, or of any board or committee appointed by it and authorized to make a determination under the provisions of the State Bar Act, or of the chief executive officer of the State Bar or the designee of the chief executive officer authorized to make a determination under article 10 of the State Bar Act or these rules of court, must be served and filed within 60 days after written notice of the action complained of is mailed to the petitioner and to his or her counsel of record, if any, at their respective addresses under Business and Professions Code section 6002.1. Within 15 days after filing of the petition, the State Bar may serve and file an answer and brief. Within 5 days after filing of the answer and brief, the petitioner may serve and file a reply. If review is ordered by the Supreme Court, the State Bar, within 45 days after filing of the order, may serve and file a supplemental brief. Within 15 days after filing of the supplemental brief, the petitioner may serve and file a reply brief.

(Subd (d) amended effective January 1, 2019; previously amended effective July 1, 1968, May 1, 1986, April 2, 1987, and January 1, 2007; previously relettered and amended effective October 1, 1973, and December 1, 1990.)

(e) Contents of petition

(1) A petition to the Supreme Court filed under (a) or (b) of this rule must be verified, must specify the grounds relied upon, must show that review within the State Bar Court has been exhausted, must address why review is appropriate under one or more of the grounds specified in rule 9.16, and must have attached a copy of the State Bar Court decision from which relief is sought.

(2) When review is sought under (c) or (d) of this rule, the petition must also be accompanied by a record adequate to permit review of the ruling, including:

(A) Legible copies of all documents and exhibits submitted to State Bar Court or the State Bar supporting and opposing petitioner's position;

(B) Legible copies of all other documents submitted to the State Bar Court or the State Bar that are necessary for a complete understanding of the case and the ruling; and

(C) A transcript of the proceedings in the State Bar Court leading to the decision or, if a transcript is unavailable, a declaration by counsel explaining why a transcript is unavailable and fairly summarizing the proceedings, including arguments by counsel and the basis of the State Bar Court's decision, if stated; or a declaration by counsel stating that the transcript has been ordered, the date it was ordered, and the date it is

expected to be filed, which must be a date before any action is requested from the Supreme Court other than issuance of a stay supported by other parts of the record.

(3) A petitioner who requests an immediate stay must explain in the petition the reasons for the urgency and set forth all relevant time constraints.

(4) If a petitioner does not submit the required record, the court may summarily deny the stay request, the petition, or both.

(Subd (e) amended effective January 1, 2019; previously repealed and adopted by the Supreme Court effective December 1, 1990, and February 1, 1991; previously repealed and adopted effective March 15, 1991; previously amended effective January 1, 2007.)

(f) Service

All petitions, briefs, reply briefs, and other pleadings filed by a petitioner under this rule must be accompanied by proof of service of three copies on the General Counsel of the State Bar at the San Francisco office of the State Bar, and of one copy on the Clerk of the State Bar Court at the Los Angeles office of the State Bar Court. The State Bar must serve the licensee at his or her address under Business and Professions Code section 6002.1, and his or her counsel of record, if any.

(Subd (f) amended effective January 1, 2019; adopted by the Supreme Court effective December 1, 1990; previously amended by the Supreme Court effective February 1, 1991; previously amended effective March 15, 1991, and January 1, 2007.)

Rule 9.13 amended effective January 1, 2019; adopted as rule 59 by the Supreme Court effective April 20, 1943, and by the Judicial Council effective July 1, 1943; previously amended and renumbered as rule 952 effective October 1, 1973, and as rule 9.13 effective January 1, 2007; previously amended effective July 1, 1976, May 1, 1986, April 2, 1987, December 1, 1990, February 1, 1991, and March 15, 1991.

Rule 9.14.   Petitions for review by the Chief Trial Counsel

(a) Time for filing

The Chief Trial Counsel may petition for review of recommendations and decisions of the State Bar Court as follows:

(1) From recommendations that a licensee be suspended, within 60 days of the date the recommendation is filed with the Supreme Court.

(2) From recommendations that the duration or conditions of probation be modified, or a reinstatement application be granted, within 15 days of the date the recommendation is filed with the Supreme Court.

(3) From decisions not to place an eligible licensee on interim suspension, or vacating interim suspension, or a denial of a petition brought under Business and Professions Code section 6007(c), within 15 days of notice under the rules adopted by the State Bar.

(4) From decisions dismissing disciplinary proceedings or recommending approval, within 60 days of notice under the rules adopted by the State Bar.

(Subd (a) amended effective January 1, 2019; adopted effective March 15, 1991; previously adopted by the Supreme Court effective December 10, 1990; previously amended effective January 1, 2007.)

(b) Procedures

Proceedings under this rule with regard to briefing, service of process, and applicable time periods therefor must correspond to proceedings brought under rule 9.13, except that the rights and duties of the licensee and the State Bar under that rule are reversed.

(Subd (b) amended effective January 1, 2019; adopted as part of subd (d) effective March 15, 1991; previously adopted by the Supreme Court effective December 10, 1991; previously amended and relettered effective January 1, 2007.)
Rule 9.14 amended effective January 1, 2019; adopted as rule 952.5 effective March 15, 1991; previously amended and renumbered effective January 1, 2007.

Rule 9.15.   Petitions for review by State Bar; grounds for review; confidentiality

(a) Petition for review by the State Bar

The State Bar may petition for review of the decision of the Review Department of the State Bar Court in moral character proceedings. All petitions under this rule must be served and filed with the Clerk of the Supreme Court within 60 days after the State Bar Court decision is filed and served on the General Counsel of the State Bar at the San Francisco office of the State Bar. The applicant may file and serve an answer within 15 days after filing of the petition. Within 5 days after filing of the answer the State Bar may serve and file a reply. If review is ordered by the Supreme Court, within 45 days after filing and service of the order, the applicant may serve and file a supplemental brief. Within 15 days after filing of the supplemental brief, the petitioner may serve and file a reply brief.

(Subd (a) amended effective January 1, 2019; previously amended effective January 1, 2007.)

(b) Contents of petition

A petition to the Supreme Court filed under this rule must show that review within the State Bar Court has been exhausted, must address why review is appropriate under one or more of the grounds specified in rule 9.16, and must have attached a copy of the State Bar Court decision for which review is sought.

(Subd (b) amended effective January 1, 2007.)

(c) Service

All petitions, briefs, reply briefs, and other pleadings filed by the State Bar must include a proof of service by mail to the applicant's last address provided to the State Bar or the applicant's attorney of record, if any. Filings by the applicant must include a proof of service of three copies on the General Counsel of the State Bar at the San Francisco office of the State Bar and one copy on the Clerk of the State Bar Court at the Los Angeles office of the State Bar Court.

(Subd (c) amended effective January 1, 2019; previously amended effective April 20, 1998, and January 1, 2007.)

(d) Confidentiality

All filings under this rule are confidential unless: (1) the applicant waives confidentiality in writing; or (2) the Supreme Court grants review. Once the Supreme Court grants review, filings under this rule are open to the public; however, if good cause exists, the Supreme Court may order portions of the record or the identity of witnesses or other third parties to the proceedings to remain confidential.

(Subd (d) amended effective January 1, 2007; adopted effective April 20, 1998.) Rule 9.15 amended effective January 1, 2019; adopted as rule 952.6 by the Supreme Court effective July 1, 1993, and by the Judicial Council May 6, 1998; previously amended by the Supreme Court effective April 20, 1998; previously amended and renumbered effective January 1, 2007.

Rule 9.16.   Grounds for review of State Bar Court decisions in the Supreme Court

(a) Grounds

The Supreme Court will order review of a decision of the State Bar Court recommending disbarment or suspension from practice when it appears:

(1) Necessary to settle important questions of law;

(2) The State Bar Court has acted without or in excess of jurisdiction;

(3) Petitioner did not receive a fair hearing;

(4) The decision is not supported by the weight of the evidence; or

(5) The recommended discipline is not appropriate in light of the record as a whole.

(Subd (a) amended effective January 1, 2007; adopted by the Supreme Court effective February 1, 1991.)

(b) Denial of review

Denial of review of a decision of the State Bar Court is a final judicial determination on the merits and the recommendation of the State Bar Court will be filed as an order of the Supreme Court.

(Subd (b) amended effective January 1, 2007; adopted by the Supreme Court effective February 1, 1991.) Rule 9.16 amended and renumbered effective January 1, 2007; adopted as rule 954 effective February 1, 1991.

Rule 9.17.   Remand with instructions

The Supreme Court may at any time remand a matter filed under this chapter to the State Bar Court or the State Bar with instructions to take such further actions or conduct such further proceedings as the Supreme Court deems necessary.

Rule 9.17 amended effective January 1, 2019; adopted as rule 953.5 effective February 1, 1991; previously amended and renumbered effective January 1, 2007.

Rule 9.18.   Effective date of disciplinary orders and decisions

(a) Effective date of Supreme Court orders

Unless otherwise ordered, all orders of the Supreme Court imposing discipline or opinions deciding causes involving the State Bar become final 30 days after filing. The Supreme Court may grant a rehearing at any time before the decision or order becomes final. Petitions for rehearing must be served and filed within 15 days after the date the decision or order was filed. Unless otherwise ordered, when petitions for review under rules 9.13(c) and 9.14(a)(3) are acted upon summarily, the orders of the Supreme Court are final forthwith and do not have law-of-the-case effect in subsequent proceedings in the Supreme Court.

(Subd (a) amended effective January 1, 2019; adopted effective March 15, 1991; previously adopted by the Supreme Court effective December 1, 1990; previously amended effective January 1, 2007.)

(b) Effect of State Bar Court orders when no review sought

Unless otherwise ordered, if no petition for review is filed within the time allowed by rule 9.13 (a), (b), and (d), or rule 9.14 (a)(1) and (2), as to a recommendation of the State Bar Court for the disbarment, suspension, or reinstatement of a licensee, the vacation of a stay, or modification of the duration or conditions of a probation, the recommendation of the State Bar Court will be filed as an order of the Supreme Court following the expiration of the time for filing a timely petition. The Clerk of the Supreme Court will mail notice of this effect to the licensee and his or her attorney of record, if any, at their respective addresses under Business and Professions Code section 6002.1 and to the State Bar.

(Subd (b) amended effective January 1, 2019; adopted effective March 15, 1991; previously adopted by the Supreme Court effective December 1, 1990; previously amended effective January 1, 2007.)

(c) Effect of State Bar Court orders in moral character proceedings when no review sought

Unless otherwise ordered, if no petition for review is filed within the time allowed by rule 9.15(a), as to a recommendation of the State Bar Court in moral character proceedings, the recommendation of the State Bar Court will be filed as an order of the Supreme Court following the expiration of the time for filing a timely petition. The Clerk of the Supreme Court will mail notice of this effect to the applicant's last address provided to the State Bar or to the applicant's attorney of record, if any, and to the State Bar.

(Subd (c) amended effective January 1, 2007.) Rule 9.18 amended effective January 1, 2019; adopted as rule 953 effective March 15, 1991; previously amended effective February 1, 1996; previously amended and renumbered effective January 1, 2007.

Rule 9.19.   Conditions attached to reprovals

(a) Attachment of conditions to reprovals

The State Bar may attach conditions, effective for a reasonable time, to a public or private reproval administered upon a licensee of the State Bar. Conditions so attached must be based on a finding by the State Bar that protection of the public and the interests of the licensee will be served thereby. The State Bar when administering the reproval must give notice to the licensee that failure to comply with the conditions may be punishable.

(Subd (a) amended effective January 1, 2019; previously amended effective January 1, 2007.)

(b) Sanctions for failure to comply

A licensee's failure to comply with conditions attached to a public or private reproval may be cause for a separate proceeding for willful breach of 8.1.1 of the Rules of Professional Conduct.

(Subd (b) amended effective January 1, 2019; previously amended effective January 1, 2007.) Rule 9.19 amended effective January 1, 2019; adopted as rule 956 effective November 18, 1983; previously amended and renumbered effective January 1, 2007.

Rule 9.20.   Duties of disbarred, resigned, or suspended attorneys

(a) Disbarment, suspension, and resignation orders

The Supreme Court may include in an order disbarring or suspending a licensee of the State Bar, or accepting his or her resignation, a direction that the licensee must, within such time limits as the Supreme Court may prescribe:

(1) Notify all clients being represented in pending matters and any co-counsel of his or her disbarment, suspension, or resignation and his or her consequent disqualification to act as an attorney after the effective date of the disbarment, suspension, or resignation, and, in the absence of co-counsel, also notify the clients to seek legal advice elsewhere, calling attention to any urgency in seeking the substitution of another attorney or attorneys;

(2) Deliver to all clients being represented in pending matters any papers or other property to which the clients are entitled, or notify the clients and any co-counsel of a suitable time and place where the papers and other property may be obtained, calling attention to any urgency for obtaining the papers or other property;

(3) Refund any part of fees paid that have not been earned; and

(4) Notify opposing counsel in pending litigation or, in the absence of counsel, the adverse parties of the disbarment, suspension, or resignation

and consequent disqualification to act as an attorney after the effective date of the disbarment, suspension, or resignation, and file a copy of the notice with the court, agency, or tribunal before which the litigation is pending for inclusion in the respective file or files.

(Subd (a) amended effective January 1, 2019; previously amended effective December 1, 1990, and January 1, 2007.)

(b) Notices to clients, co-counsel, opposing counsel, and adverse parties

All notices required by an order of the Supreme Court or the State Bar Court under this rule must be given by registered or certified mail, return receipt requested, and must contain an address where communications may be directed to the disbarred, suspended, or resigned licensee.

(Subd (b) amended effective January 1, 2019; previously amended effective December 1, 1990, and January 1, 2007.)

(c) Filing proof of compliance

Within such time as the order may prescribe after the effective date of the licensee's disbarment, suspension, or resignation, the licensee must file with the Clerk of the State Bar Court an affidavit showing that he or she has fully complied with those provisions of the order entered under this rule. The affidavit must also specify an address where communications may be directed to the disbarred, suspended, or resigned licensee.

(Subd (c) amended effective January 1, 2019; previously amended effective December 1, 1990, and January 1, 2007.)

(d) Sanctions for failure to comply

A disbarred or resigned licensee's willful failure to comply with the provisions of this rule is a ground for denying his or her application for reinstatement or readmission. A suspended licensee's willful failure to comply with the provisions of this rule is a cause for disbarment or suspension and for revocation of any pending probation. Additionally, such failure may be punished as a contempt or a crime.

(Subd (d) amended effective January 1, 2019; previously relettered and amended effective December 1, 1990; previously amended effective January 1, 2007.)
Rule 9.20 amended effective January 1, 2019; adopted as rule 955 effective April 4, 1973; previously amended effective December 1, 1990; previously amended and renumbered effective January 1, 2007.

Rule 9.21. Resignations of licensees of the State Bar with disciplinary charges pending

(a) General provisions

A licensee of the State Bar against whom disciplinary charges are pending may tender a written resignation from the State Bar and relinquishment of the right to practice law. The written resignation must be signed and dated by the licensee at the time it is tendered and must be tendered to the Office of the Clerk, State Bar Court, [1] **845 S. Figueroa Street**, Los Angeles, California [2] **90017**. The resignation must be substantially in the form specified in (b) of this rule. In submitting a resignation under this rule, a licensee of the State Bar agrees to be transferred to inactive status in the State Bar effective on the filing of the resignation by the State Bar. Within 30 days after filing of the resignation, the licensee must perform the acts specified in rule 9.20(a)(1)–(4) and (b) and within 40 days after filing of the resignation, the licensee must file with the Office of the Clerk, State Bar Court, at the above address, the proof of compliance specified in rule 9.20(c). No resignation is effective unless and until it is accepted by the Supreme Court after consideration and recommendation by the State Bar Court.

(Subd (a) amended effective January 1, 2021; previously amended effective January 1, 2007, January 1, 2010, and January 1, 2019.)

Rule 9.21(a).   2020 Deletes. [1] 1149 South Hill Street [2] 90015

(b) Form of resignation

The licensee's written resignation must be in substantially the following form:

"I, [*name of licensee,*] against whom charges are pending, hereby resign from the State Bar of California and relinquish all right to practice law in the State of California. I agree that, in the event that this resignation is accepted and I later file a petition for reinstatement, the State Bar will consider in connection therewith all disciplinary matters and proceedings against me at the time this resignation is accepted, in addition to other appropriate matters, I also agree that the Supreme Court may decline to accept my resignation unless I reach agreement with the Chief Trial Counsel on a written stipulation as to facts and conclusions of law regarding the disciplinary matters and proceedings that were pending against me at the time of my resignation. I further agree that, on the filing of this resignation by the Office of the Clerk, State Bar Court, I will be transferred to inactive status with the State Bar. On such transfer, I

acknowledge that I will be ineligible to practice law or to advertise or hold myself out as practicing or as entitled to practice law. I further acknowledge that in the event the Supreme Court does not accept my resignation, I will remain an inactive licensee of the State Bar, pending any further order of the Supreme Court or the State Bar Court. I further agree that, within 30 days of the filing of the resignation by the Office of the Clerk, State Bar Court, I will perform the acts specified in rule 9.20(a)–(b) of the California Rules of Court, and within 40 days of the date of filing of this resignation by the Office of the Clerk, State Bar Court, I will notify that office as specified in rule 9.20(c) of the California Rules of Court."

(Subd (b) amended effective January 1, 2019; previously amended effective January 1, 2007, January 1, 2010, and January 1, 2014.)

(c) Consideration of resignation by State Bar Court and Supreme Court

When the Office of the Clerk of the State Bar Court receives a licensee's resignation tendered in conformity with this rule, it must promptly file the resignation. The State Bar Court must thereafter consider the licensee's resignation and the stipulated facts and conclusions of law, if any, agreed upon between the licensee and the Chief Trial Counsel, and must recommend to the Supreme Court whether the resignation should be accepted. The State Bars Court's recommendation must be made in light of the grounds set forth in (d) of this rule and, if the State Bar Court recommends acceptance of the resignation notwithstanding the existence of one or more of the grounds set forth in subsection (d), the State Bar Court's recommendation must include an explanation of the reasons for the recommendation that the resignation be accepted. The Office of the Clerk of the State Bar Court must transmit to the Clerk of the Supreme Court, three certified copies of the State Bar Court's recommendation together with the licensee's resignation, when, by the terms of the State Bar Court's recommendation, the resignation should be transmitted to the Supreme Court.

(Subd (c) amended effective January 1, 2019; previously amended effective January 1, 2007, and January 1, 2010.)

(d) Grounds for rejection of resignation by the Supreme Court

The Supreme Court will make such orders concerning the licensee's resignation as it deems appropriate. The Supreme Court may decline to accept the resignation based on a report by the State Bar Court that:

(1) Preservation of necessary testimony is not complete;

(2) After transfer to inactive status, the licensee has practiced law or has advertised or held himself or herself out as entitled to practice law;

(3) The licensee has failed to perform the acts specified by rule 9.20(a)–(b);

(4) The licensee has failed to provide proof of compliance as specified in rule 9.20(c);

(5) The Supreme Court has filed an order of disbarment as to the licensee;

(6) The State Bar Court has filed a decision or opinion recommending the licensee's disbarment;

(7) The licensee has previously resigned or has been disbarred and reinstated to the practice of law;

(8) The licensee and the Chief Trial Counsel have not reached agreement on a written stipulation as to facts and conclusions of law regarding the disciplinary matters and proceedings that were pending against the licensee at the time the resignation was tendered; or

(9) Acceptance of the resignation of the licensee will reasonably be inconsistent with the need to protect the public, the courts, or the legal profession.

(Subd (d) amended effective January 1, 2019; adopted as part of subd (c) effective December 14, 1984; previously amended and relettered effective January 1, 2007; previously amended effective January 1, 2010.)

(e) Rejection of resignation by the Supreme Court

A licensee whose resignation with charges pending is not accepted by the Supreme Court will remain an inactive licensee of the State Bar. The licensee may move the Review Department of the State Bar Court to be restored to active status, at which time the Office of the Chief Trial Counsel may demonstrate any basis for the licensee's continued ineligibility to practice law. The Review Department will expedite a motion to be restored to active status. Any return to active status will be conditioned on the licensee's payment of any due, penalty payments, and restitution owed by the licensee.

(Subd (e) amended effective January 1, 2019; adopted effective January 1, 2014.)
Rule 9.21 amended effective January 1, 2021; adopted as rule 960 by the Supreme Court effective December 14, 1984; previously amended and renumbered effective

January 1, 2007; previously amended effective January 1, 2010, January 1, 2014, and January 1, 2019.

Rule 9.22. Suspension of licensees of the State Bar for failure to comply with judgment or order for child or family support

(a) Annual State Bar recommendation for suspension of delinquent licensees

Under Family Code section 17520, the State Bar is authorized to transmit to the Supreme Court on an annual basis the names of those licensees listed by the State Department of Social Services as delinquent in their payments of court-ordered child or family support with a recommendation for their suspension from the practice of law.

(Subd (a) amended effective January 1, 2019; previously amended effective January 1, 2007.)

(b) Condition for reinstatement of suspended licensees

A licensee suspended under this rule may be reinstated only after receipt by the Supreme Court of notification from the State Bar that the licensee's name has been removed from the State Department of Social Services list.

(Subd (b) amended effective January 1, 2019; adopted as part of subd (a) effective January 31, 1993; previously amended and lettered effective January 1, 2007.)

(c) Additional recommendation for suspension by the State Bar

Under Family Code section 17520(*l*), the State Bar is further authorized to promptly transmit to the Supreme Court with a recommendation for their suspension from the practice of law the names of those licensees previously listed by the State Department of Social Services as delinquent in their payments of court-ordered child or family support, who obtained releases under Family Code section 17520(h), and who have subsequently been identified by the Department of Social Services as again being delinquent.

(Subd (c) amended effective January 1, 2019; adopted as part of subd (a) effective January 31, 1993; previously amended and lettered effective January 1, 2007.)

(d) Authorization for the Board of Trustees of the State Bar to adopt rules and regulations

The Board of Trustees of the State Bar is authorized to adopt such rules and regulations as it deems necessary and appropriate in order to comply with this rule. The rules and regulations of the State Bar must contain procedures governing the notification, suspension, and reinstatement of licensees of the State Bar in a manner not inconsistent with Family Code section 17520.

(Subd (d) amended effective January 1, 2019; adopted as subd (b) effective January 31, 1993; previously amended and relettered effective January 1, 2007.) Rule 9.22 amended effective January 1, 2019; adopted as rule 962 effective January 31, 1993; previously amended by the Supreme Court effective April 1, 1996; previously amended and renumbered effective January 1, 2007.

Rule 9.23. Enforcement as money judgment disciplinary orders directing the payment of costs and disciplinary orders requiring reimbursement of the Client Security Fund

(a) Authority to obtain money judgment

Under Business and Professions Code section 6086.10(a) the State Bar is authorized to enforce as a money judgment any disciplinary order assessing costs. Under Business and Professions Code section 6140.5(d) the State Bar is authorized to enforce as a money judgment any disciplinary order requiring reimbursement of the State Bar Client Security Fund.

(Subd (a) adopted by the Supreme Court effective April 1, 2007.)

(b) Duty of clerk of the superior court

The State Bar may file a certified copy of a final disciplinary order assessing costs or requiring reimbursement to the Client Security Fund, along with a certified copy of the certificate of costs and any record of Client Security Fund payments and costs, with the clerk of the superior court of any county. The clerk must immediately enter judgment in conformity with the order.

(Subd (b) amended effective January 1, 2019; adopted by the Supreme Court effective April 1, 2007.)

(c) Compromise of judgment

Motions for the compromise of any judgment entered under this rule must, in the first instance, be filed and heard by the State Bar Court.

(Subd (c) adopted by the Supreme Court effective April 1, 2007.)

(d) Power of the Supreme Court

Nothing in this rule may be construed as affecting the power of the Supreme Court to alter the amounts owed.

(Subd (d) adopted by the Supreme Court effective April 1, 2007.) Rule 9.23 amended effective January 1, 2019; adopted by the Supreme Court effective April 1, 2007.

Chapter 4
Legal Education

Title 9, Rules on Law Practice, Attorneys, and Judges—Division 2, Attorney Admission and Disciplinary Proceedings and Review of State Bar Proceedings—Chapter 4, Legal Education; renumbered from Chapter 3 effective January 1, 2018.

Rule 9.30. Law school study in schools other than those accredited by the examining committee
Rule 9.31. Minimum continuing legal education

Rule 9.30. Law school study in schools other than those accredited by the examining committee

(a) Receipt of credit

A person who seeks to be certified to the Supreme Court for admission in and licensed to practice law under section 6060(e)(2) of the Business and Professions Code may receive credit for:

(1) Study in a law school in the United States other than one accredited by the examining committee established by the Board of Trustees of the State Bar under Business and Professions Code section 6046 only if the law school satisfies the requirements of (b) or (c) of this rule; or

(2) Instruction in law from a correspondence school only if the correspondence school requires 864 hours of preparation and study per year for four years and satisfies the requirements of (d) of this rule; or

(3) Study in a law school outside the United States other than one accredited by the examining committee established by the Board of Trustees of the State Bar under Business and Professions Code section 6046 only if the examining committee is satisfied that the academic program of such law school is substantially equivalent to that of a law school qualified under (b) of this rule.

(Subd (a) amended effective January 1, 2019; previously amended effective April 2, 1984, and January 1, 2007.)

(b) Requirements for unaccredited law schools in state

A law school in this state that is not accredited by the examining committee must:

(1) Be authorized to confer professional degrees by the laws of this state;

(2) Maintain a regular course of instruction in law, with a specified curriculum and regularly scheduled class sessions;

(3) Require classroom attendance of its students for a minimum of 270 hours a year for at least four years, and further require regular attendance of each student at not less than 80 percent of the regularly scheduled class hours in each course in which such student was enrolled and maintain attendance records adequate to determine each student's compliance with these requirements;

(4) Maintain, in a fixed location, physical facilities capable of accommodating the classes scheduled for that location;

(5) Have an adequate faculty of instructors in law. The faculty will prima facie be deemed adequate if at least 80 percent of the instruction in each academic period is by persons who possess one or more of the following qualifications:

(A) Admission to the general practice of the law in any jurisdiction in the United States;

(B) Judge of a United States court or a court of record in any jurisdiction in the United States; or

(C) Graduation from a law school accredited by the examining committee.

(6) Own and maintain a library consisting of not less than the following sets of books, all of which must be current and complete:

(A) The published reports of the decisions of California courts, with advance sheets and citator;

(B) A digest or encyclopedia of California law;

(C) An annotated set of the California codes; and

(D) A current, standard text or treatise for each course or subject in the curriculum of the school for which such a text or treatise is available.

(7) Establish and maintain standards for academic achievement, advancement in good standing and graduation, and provide for periodic testing of all students to determine the quality of their performance in relation to such standards; and

(8) Register with the examining committee, and maintain such records (available for inspection by the examining committee) and file with the examining committee such reports, notices, and certifications as may be required by the rules of the examining committee.

(Subd (b) amended effective January 1, 2007; previously amended effective April 2, 1984.)

(c) Requirements for unaccredited law schools outside the state

A law school in the United States that is outside the state of California and is not accredited by the examining committee must:

(1) Be authorized to confer professional degrees by the law of the state in which it is located;

(2) Comply with (b)(2), (3), (4), (5), (7), and (8) of this rule; and

(3) Own and maintain a library that is comparable in content to that specified in (b)(6) of this rule.

(Subd (c) amended effective January 1, 2007; previously amended effective April 2, 1984.)

(d) Registration and reports

A correspondence law school must register with the examining committee and file such reports, notices, and certifications as may be required by the rules of the examining committee concerning any person whose mailing address is in the state of California or whose application to, contract with, or correspondence with or from the law school indicates that the instruction by correspondence is for the purpose or with the intent of qualifying that person for admission to practice law in California.

(Subd (d) amended effective January 1, 2007.)

(e) Inspections

The examining committee may make such inspection of law schools not accredited by the committee or correspondence schools as may be necessary or proper to give effect to the provisions of Business and Professions Code section 6060, this rule, and the rules of the examining committee.

(Subd (e) amended effective January 1, 2007.)

(f) Application

This rule does not apply to any person who, on the effective date of the rule, had commenced the study of law in a manner authorized by Business and Professions Code section 6060(e) and registered as a law student before January 1, 1976 (as provided in Business and Professions Code section 6060(d) and otherwise satisfies the requirements of Business and Professions Code section 6060(e), provided that after January 1, 1976, credit will be given such person for any study in an unaccredited law school or by correspondence only if the school complies with the requirements of (b)(8) or (d) of this rule, whichever is applicable, and permits inspection under (e) of this rule.

(Subd (f) amended effective January 1, 2007.)

Rule 9.30 amended effective January 1, 2019; adopted as rule 957 by the Supreme Court effective October 8, 1975; previously amended effective April 2, 1984; previously amended and renumbered effective January 1, 2007.

Rule 9.31. Minimum continuing legal education

(a) Statutory authorization

This rule is adopted under Business and Professions Code section 6070.

(Subd (a) amended effective January 1, 2007.)

(b) State Bar minimum continuing legal education program

The State Bar must establish and administer a minimum continuing legal education program under rules adopted by the Board of Trustees of the State Bar. These rules may provide for carryforward of excess credit hours, staggering of the education requirement for implementation purposes, and retroactive credit for legal education.

(Subd (b) amended effective August 1, 2017; previously amended effective September 27, 2000, and January 1, 2007.)

(c) Minimum continuing legal education requirements

Each active licensee of the State Bar (1) not exempt under Business and Professions Code section 6070, (2) not a full-time employee of the United States Government, its departments, agencies, and public corporations, acting within the scope of his or her employment, and (3) not otherwise exempt under rules adopted by the Board of Trustees of the State Bar, must, within 36-month periods designated by the State Bar, complete at least 25 hours of legal education approved by the State Bar or offered by a State Bar-approved provider. Four of those hours must address legal ethics. Licensees may be required to complete legal education in other specified areas within the 25-hour requirement under rules adopted by the State Bar. Each active licensee must report his or her compliance to the State Bar under rules adopted by the Board of Trustees of the State Bar.

(Subd (c) amended effective January 1, 2019; previously amended effective September 27, 2000, January 1, 2007, and August 1, 2017.)

(d) Failure to comply with program

A licensee of the State Bar who fails to satisfy the requirements of the State Bar's minimum continuing legal education program must be enrolled as an inactive licensee of the State Bar under rules adopted by the Board of Trustees of the State Bar.

(Subd (d) amended effective January 1, 2019; previously amended effective January 1, 2007, and August 1, 2017.)

(e) Fees and penalties

The State Bar has the authority to set and collect appropriate fees and penalties.

(Subd (e) amended effective January 1, 2007.)

(f) One-time expungement of a record of inactive enrollment for failure to comply with program

The State Bar is authorized to expunge a public record of a period of inactive enrollment for failure to comply with the minimum continuing legal education program for those licensees who meet all of the following criteria:

(1) The licensee has not on any previous occasion obtained an expungement under the terms of this rule or rule 9.6;

(2) The period of inactive enrollment was for 90 days or less;

(3) The period of inactive enrollment ended at least seven years before the date of expungement;

(4) The licensee has no other record of suspension or involuntary inactive enrollment for discipline or otherwise.

(Subd (f) amended effective January 1, 2019; adopted effective August 1, 2017.)

(g) Records to be maintained by State Bar

Under (f) of this rule, the State Bar will remove or delete the record of such period of inactive enrollment from the licensee's record. Notwithstanding any other provision of this rule, the State Bar must maintain such internal records as are necessary to apply the terms of (f) of this rule and to report to the Commission on Judicial Nominees Evaluation or appropriate governmental entities involved in judicial elections the licensee's eligibility for a judgeship under the California Constitution, article VI, section 15.

(Subd (g) amended effective January 1, 2019; adopted effective August 1, 2017.)

(h) Duty of disclosure by licensee

Expungement of the record of a licensee's period of inactive enrollment under (f) of this rule will not relieve the licensee of his or her duty to disclose the period of inactive enrollment for purpose of determining the licensee's eligibility for a judgeship under the California Constitution, article VI, section 15. For all other purposes, the record of inactive enrollment expunged under (f) of this rule is deemed not to have occurred and the licensee may answer accordingly any question relating to his or her record.

(Subd (h) amended effective January 1, 2019; adopted effective August 1, 2017.)
Rule 9.31 amended effective January 1, 2019; adopted as rule 958 effective December 6, 1990; previously amended effective December 25, 1992; previously amended by the Supreme Court effective September 27, 2000; previously amended and renumbered as rule 9.31 effective January 1, 2007; previously amended effective August 1, 2017.

Division 3
Legal Specialists

Rule 9.35. Certified legal specialists

(a) Definition

A "certified specialist" is a California attorney who holds a current certificate as a specialist issued by the State Bar of California Board of Legal Specialization or any other entity approved by the State Bar to designate specialists.

(b) State Bar Legal Specialization Program

The State Bar must establish and administer a program for certifying legal specialists and may establish a program for certifying entities that certify legal specialists under rules adopted by the Board of Trustees of the State Bar.

(Subd (b) amended effective January 1, 2019; previously amended effective January 1, 2007.)

(c) Authority to practice law

No attorney may be required to obtain certification as a certified specialist as a prerequisite to practicing law in this state. Any attorney, alone or in association with any other attorney, has the right to practice in any field of law in this state and to act as counsel in every type of case, even though he or she is not certified as a specialist.

(Subd (c) amended effective January 1, 2007.)

(d) Failure to comply with program

A certified specialist who fails to comply with the requirements of the Legal Specialization Program of the State Bar will have her or his certification suspended or revoked under rules adopted by the Board of Trustees of the State Bar.

(Subd (d) amended effective January 1, 2019; previously amended effective January 1, 2007.)

(e) Fee and penalty

The State Bar has the authority to set and collect appropriate fees and penalties for this program.

(Subd (e) amended effective January 1, 2007.)

(f) Inherent power of Supreme Court

Nothing in these rules may be construed as affecting the power of the Supreme Court to exercise its inherent jurisdiction over the practice of law in California.

(Subd (f) amended effective January 1, 2007.)

Rule 9.35 amended effective January 1, 2019; adopted as rule 983.5 effective January 1, 1996; previously amended and renumbered effective January 1, 2007.

Division 4
Appearances and Practice by Individuals Who Are Not Licensees of the State Bar of California

Rule 9.40. Counsel *pro hac vice*
Rule 9.41. Appearances by military counsel
Rule 9.41.1. Registered military spouse attorney
Rule 9.42. Certified law students
Rule 9.43. Out-of-state attorney arbitration counsel
Rule 9.44. Registered foreign legal consultant
Rule 9.45. Registered legal aid attorneys
Rule 9.46. Registered in-house counsel
Rule 9.47. Attorneys practicing law temporarily in California as part of litigation
Rule 9.48. Nonlitigating attorneys temporarily in California to provide legal services

Rule 9.40.   Counsel *pro hac vice*

(a) Eligibility

A person who is not a licensee of the State Bar of California but who is an attorney in good standing of and eligible to practice before the bar of any United States court or the highest court in any state, territory, or insular possession of the United States, and who has been retained to appear in a particular cause pending in a court of this state, may in the discretion of such court be permitted upon written application to appear as counsel *pro hac vice*, provided that an active licensee of the State Bar of California is associated as attorney of record. No person is eligible to appear as counsel *pro hac vice* under this rule if the person is:

(1) A resident of the State of California;

(2) Regularly employed in the State of California; or

(3) Regularly engaged in substantial business, professional, or other activities in the State of California.

(Subd (a) amended effective January 1, 2019; previously amended effective January 1, 2007.)

(b) Repeated appearances as a cause for denial

Absent special circumstances, repeated appearances by any person under this rule is a cause for denial of an application.

(Subd (b) lettered effective January 1, 2007; adopted as part of subd (a) effective September 13, 1972.)

(c) Application

(1) *Application in superior court*

A person desiring to appear as counsel *pro hac vice* in a superior court must file with the court a verified application together with proof of service by mail in accordance with Code of Civil Procedure section 1013a of a copy of the application and of the notice of hearing of the application on all parties who have appeared in the cause and on the State Bar of California at its San Francisco office. The notice of hearing must be given at the time prescribed in Code of Civil Procedure section 1005 unless the court has prescribed a shorter period.

(2) *Application in Supreme Court or Court of Appeal*

An application to appear as counsel *pro hac vice* in the Supreme Court or a Court of Appeal must be made as provided in rule 8.54, with proof of service on all parties who have appeared in the cause and on the State Bar of California at its San Francisco office.

(Subd (c) amended and relettered effective January 1, 2007; adopted as part of subd (b) effective September 13, 1972; subd (b) previously amended effective October 3, 1973, September 3, 1986, January 17, 1991, and March 15, 1991.)

(d) Contents of application

The application must state:

(1) The applicant's residence and office address;

(2) The courts to which the applicant has been admitted to practice and the dates of admission;

(3) That the applicant is a licensee in good standing in those courts;

(4) That the applicant is not currently suspended or disbarred in any court;

(5) The title of each court and cause in which the applicant has filed an application to appear as counsel *pro hac vice* in this state in the preceding two years, the date of each application, and whether or not it was granted; and

(6) The name, address, and telephone number of the active licensee of the State Bar of California who is attorney of record.

(Subd (d) amended effective January 1, 2019; adopted as part of subd (b) effective September 13, 1972; subd (b) previously amended effective October 3, 1973, September 3, 1986, January 17, 1991, and March 15, 1991; previously amended and lettered effective January 1, 2007.)

(e) Fee for application

An applicant for permission to appear as counsel *pro hac vice* under this rule must pay a reasonable fee not exceeding $50 to the State Bar of California with the copy of the application and the notice of hearing that is served on the State Bar. The Board of Trustees of the State Bar of California will fix the amount of the fee:

(1) To defray the expenses of administering the provisions of this rule that are applicable to the State Bar and the incidental consequences resulting from such provisions; and

(2) Partially to defray the expenses of administering the Board's other responsibilities to enforce the provisions of the State Bar Act relating to the competent delivery of legal services and the incidental consequences resulting therefrom.

(Subd (e) amended effective January 1, 2019; adopted as subd (c) effective September 3, 1986; previously amended and relettered effective January 1, 2007.)

(f) Counsel *pro hac vice* subject to jurisdiction of courts and State Bar

A person permitted to appear as counsel *pro hac vice* under this rule is subject to the jurisdiction of the courts of this state with respect to the law of this state governing the conduct of attorneys to the same extent as a licensee of the State Bar of California. The counsel *pro hac vice* must familiarize himself or herself and comply with the standards of professional conduct required of licensees of the State Bar of California and will be subject to the disciplinary jurisdiction of the State Bar with respect to any of his or her acts occurring in the course of such appearance. Article 5 of chapter 4, division 3 of the Business and Professions Code and the Rules of Procedure of the State Bar govern in any investigation or proceeding conducted by the State Bar under this rule.

(Subd (f) amended effective January 1, 2019; previously relettered as subd (d) effective September 3, 1986; previously amended and relettered effective January 1, 2007.)

(g) Representation in cases governed by the Indian Child Welfare Act (25 U.S.C. §1903 et seq.)

(1) The requirement in (a) that the applicant associate with an active licensee of the State Bar of California does not apply to an applicant seeking to appear in a California court to represent an Indian tribe in a child custody proceeding governed by the Indian Child Welfare Act; and

(2) An applicant seeking to appear in a California court to represent an Indian tribe in a child custody proceeding governed by the Indian Child Welfare Act constitutes a special circumstance for the purposes of the restriction in (b) that an application may be denied because of repeated appearances.

(Subd (g) adopted effective January 1, 2019.)

(h) Supreme Court and Court of Appeal not precluded from permitting argument in a particular case

This rule does not preclude the Supreme Court or a Court of Appeal from permitting argument in a particular case from a person who is not a licensee of the State Bar, but who is licensed to practice in another jurisdiction and who possesses special expertise in the particular field affected by the proceeding.

(Subd (h) amended and relettered effective January 1, 2019; previously relettered as subd (e) effective September 3, 1986; previously amended and relettered as subd (g) effective January 1, 2007.)

Rule 9.40 amended effective January 1, 2019; adopted as rule 983 by the Supreme Court effective September 13, 1972; previously amended and renumbered effective January 1, 2007; previously amended effective October 3, 1973, September 3, 1986, January 17, 1991, and March 15, 1991.

Rule 9.41. Appearances by military counsel
(a) Permission to appear

A judge advocate (as that term is defined at 10 U.S.C. §801(13)) who is not a licensee of the State Bar of California but who is an attorney in good standing of and eligible to practice before the bar of any United States court or of the highest court in any state, territory, or insular possession of the United States may, in the discretion of a court of this state, be permitted to appear in that court to represent a person in the military service in a particular cause pending before that court, under the Servicemembers Civil Relief Act, 50 United States Code Appendix section 501 et seq., if:

(1) The judge advocate has been made available by the cognizant Judge Advocate General (as that term is defined at 10 United States Code section 801(1)) or a duly designated representative; and

(2) The court finds that retaining civilian counsel likely would cause substantial hardship for the person in military service or that person's family; and

(3) The court appoints a judge advocate as attorney to represent the person in military service under the Servicemembers Civil Relief Act.

Under no circumstances is the determination of availability of a judge advocate to be made by any court within this state, or reviewed by any court of this state. In determining the likelihood of substantial hardship as a result of the retention of civilian counsel, the court may take judicial notice of the prevailing pay scales for persons in the military service.

(Subd (a) amended effective January 1, 2019; previously amended effective January 1, 2007.)

(b) Notice to parties

The clerk of the court considering appointment of a judge advocate under this rule must provide written notice of that fact to all parties who have appeared in the cause. A copy of the notice, together with proof of service by mail in accordance with Code of Civil Procedure section 1013a, must be filed by the clerk of the court. Any party who has appeared in the matter may file a written objection to the appointment within 10 days of the date on which notice was given unless the court has prescribed a shorter period. If the court determines to hold a hearing in relation to the appointment, notice of the hearing must be given at least 10 days before the date designated for the hearing unless the court has prescribed a shorter period.

(Subd (b) amended effective January 1, 2007.)

(c) Appearing judge advocate subject to court and State Bar jurisdiction

A judge advocate permitted to appear under this rule is subject to the jurisdiction of the courts of this state with respect to the law of this state governing the conduct of attorneys to the same extent as a licensee of the State Bar of California. The judge advocate must become familiar with and comply with the standards of professional conduct required of licensees of the State Bar of California and is subject to the disciplinary jurisdiction of the State Bar of California. Division 3, chapter 4, article 5 of the Business and Professions Code and the Rules of Procedure of the State Bar of California govern any investigation or proceeding conducted by the State Bar under this rule.

(Subd (c) amended effective January 1, 2019; previously amended effective January 1, 2007.)

(d) Appearing judge advocate subject to rights and obligations of State Bar licensees concerning professional privileges

A judge advocate permitted to appear under this rule is subject to the rights and obligations with respect to attorney-client privilege, work-product privilege, and other professional privileges to the same extent as a licensee of the State Bar of California.

(Subd (d) amended effective January 1, 2019; previously amended effective January 1, 2007.)

Rule 9.41 amended effective January 1, 2019; adopted as rule 983.1 by the Supreme Court effective February 19, 1992; adopted by the Judicial Council effective February 21, 1992; previously amended and renumbered effective January 1, 2007.

Rule 9.41.1. Registered military spouse attorney
(a) Definitions

(1) "Military Spouse Attorney" means an active licensee in good standing of the bar of a United States state, jurisdiction, possession, territory, or dependency and who is married to, in a civil union with, or a registered domestic partner of, a Service Member.

(2) "Service Member" means an active duty member of the United States Uniformed Services who has been ordered stationed within California.

(3) "Active licensee in good standing of the bar of a United States state, jurisdiction, possession, territory, or dependency" means an attorney who:

(A) Is a licensee in good standing of the entity governing the practice of law in each jurisdiction in which the attorney is licensed to practice law, who has not been disbarred, has not resigned with charges pending, or is not suspended from practicing law for disciplinary misconduct in any other jurisdiction; and

(B) Remains an active licensee in good standing of the entity governing the practice of law in at least one United States state, jurisdiction, possession, territory, or dependency other than California while practicing law as a registered military spouse attorney in California.

(Subd (a) adopted effective March 1, 2019.)

(b) Scope of Practice

Subject to all applicable rules, regulations, and statutes, an attorney practicing law under this rule is permitted to practice law in California, under supervision, in all forms of legal practice that are permissible for a licensed attorney of the State Bar of California, including pro bono legal services.

(Subd (b) adopted effective March 1, 2019.)

(c) Requirements

For an attorney to qualify to practice law under this rule, the attorney must:

(1) Be an active licensee in good standing of the bar of a United States state, jurisdiction, possession, territory, or dependency;

(2) Be married to, be in a civil union with, or be a registered domestic partner of, a Service Member, except that the attorney may continue to practice as a registered military spouse attorney for one year after the termination of the marriage, civil union, or domestic partnership as provided in (i)(1)(G);

(3) Reside in California;

(4) Meet all of the requirements for admission to the State Bar of California, except that the attorney:

(A) Need not take the California bar examination or the Multistate Professional Responsibility Examination; and

(B) May practice law while awaiting the result of his or her Application for Determination of Moral Character from the State Bar of California.

(5) Comply with the rules adopted by the Board of Trustees relating to the State Bar Registered Military Spouse Attorney Program;

(6) Practice law under the supervision of an attorney who is an active licensee in good standing of the State Bar of California who has been admitted to the practice of law for two years or more;

(7) Abide by all of the laws and rules that govern licensees of the State Bar of California, including the Minimum Continuing Legal Education ("MCLE") requirements;

(8) Satisfy in his or her first year of practice under this rule all of the MCLE requirements, including ethics education, that licensees of the State Bar of California must complete every three years and, thereafter, satisfy the MCLE requirements for the registered military spouse attorney's compliance group as set forth in State Bar Rules 2.70 and 2.71. If the registered military spouse attorney's compliance group is required to report in less than thirty-six months, the MCLE requirements will be reduced proportionally ; and

(9) Not have taken and failed the California bar examination within five years immediately preceding initial application to register under this rule.

(Subd (c) adopted effective March 1, 2019.)

(d) Application

The attorney must comply with the following registration requirements:

(1) Register as an attorney applicant, file an Application for Determination of Moral Character with the Committee of Bar Examiners, and comply with Rules of Court, rule 9.9.5, governing attorney fingerprinting;

(2) Submit to the State Bar of California a declaration signed by the attorney agreeing that he or she will be subject to the disciplinary authority of the Supreme Court of California and the State Bar of California and attesting that he or she will not practice law in California other than under supervision of a California attorney during the time he or she practices law as a military spouse attorney in California; and

(3) Submit to the State Bar of California a declaration signed by a qualifying supervising attorney. The declaration must attest:

(A) that the applicant will be supervised as specified in this rule; and

(B) that the supervising attorney assumes professional responsibility for any work performed by the registered military spouse attorney under this rule.

(Subd (d) adopted effective March 1, 2019.)

(e) Application and Registration Fees

The State Bar of California may set appropriate application fees and initial and annual registration fees to be paid by registered military spouse attorney.

(Subd (e) adopted effective March 1, 2019.)

(f) State Bar Registered Military Spouse Attorney Program

The State Bar may establish and administer a program for registering registered military spouse attorneys under rules adopted by the Board of Trustees of the State Bar.

(Subd (f) adopted effective March 1, 2019.)

(g) Supervision

To meet the requirements of this rule, an attorney supervising a registered military spouse attorney:

(1) Must have practiced law as a full-time occupation for at least four years in any United States jurisdiction;

(2) Must have actively practiced law in California for at least two years immediately preceding the time of supervision and be a licensee in good standing of the State Bar of California;

(3) Must assume professional responsibility for any work that the registered military spouse attorney performs under the supervising attorney's supervision;

(4) Must assist, counsel, and provide direct supervision of the registered military spouse attorney in the activities authorized by this rule, approve in writing any appearance in court, deposition, arbitration or any proceeding by the registered military spouse attorney, and review such activities with the supervised military spouse attorney, to the extent required for the protection of the client or customer;

(5) Must read, approve, and personally sign any pleadings, briefs, or other similar documents prepared by the registered military spouse attorney before their filing, and must read and approve any documents prepared by the registered military spouse attorney before their submission to any other party;

(6) Must agree to assume control of the work of the registered military spouse attorney in the event the registration of the military spouse attorney is terminated, in accordance with applicable laws; and

(7) May, in his or her absence, designate another attorney meeting the requirements of (g)(1) through (g)(6) to provide the supervision required under this rule.

(Subd (g) adopted effective March 1, 2019.)

(h) Duration of Practice

A registered military spouse attorney must renew his or her registration annually and may practice for no more than a total of five years under this rule.

(Subd (h) adopted effective March 1, 2019.)

(i) Termination of Military Spouse Attorney Registration

(1) Registration as a registered military spouse attorney is terminated

(A) upon receipt of a determination by the Committee of Bar Examiners that the registered military spouse attorney is not of good moral character;

(B) for failure to annually register as a registered military spouse attorney and submit any related fee set by the State Bar;

(C) for failure to comply with the Minimum Continuing Legal Education requirements and to pay any related fee set by the State Bar;

(D) if the registered military spouse attorney no longer meets the requirements under (a)(3) of this section;

(E) upon the imposition of any discipline by the State Bar of California or any other professional or occupational licensing authority, including administrative or stayed suspension;

(F) for failure to otherwise comply with these rules or with the laws or standards of professional conduct applicable to a licensee of the State Bar of California;

(G) if the Service Member is no longer an active member of the United States Uniformed Services or is transferred to another state, jurisdiction, territory outside of California, except that if the Service Member has been assigned to an unaccompanied or remote assignment with no dependents authorized, the military spouse attorney may continue to practice pursuant to the provisions of this rule until the Service Member is assigned to a location with dependents authorized; or

(H) one year after the date of termination of the registered military spouse attorney's marriage, civil union, or registered domestic partnership.

(2) The supervising attorney of registered military spouse attorney suspended by these rules will assume the work of the registered military spouse attorney in accordance with applicable laws.

(Subd (i) adopted effective March 1, 2019.)

(j) Inherent Power of Supreme Court

Nothing in this rule may be construed as affecting the power of the Supreme Court of California to exercise its inherent jurisdiction over the practice of law in California.

(Subd (j) adopted effective March 1, 2019.)

(k) Effect of Rule on Multijurisdictional Practice

Nothing in this rule limits the scope of activities permissible under existing law by attorneys who are not licensees of the State Bar of California.

(Subd (k) adopted effective March 1, 2019.)

Rule 9.41.1 adopted by the Supreme Court effective March 1, 2019.

Rule 9.42. Certified law students

(a) Definitions

(1) A "certified law student" is a law student who has a currently effective certificate of registration as a certified law student from the State Bar.

(2) A "supervising attorney" is a licensee of the State Bar who agrees to supervise a certified law student under rules established by the State Bar and whose name appears on the application for certification.

(Subd (a) amended effective January 1, 2019; previously amended effective January 1, 2007.)

(b) State Bar certified law student program

The State Bar must establish and administer a program for registering law students under rules adopted by the Board of Trustees of the State Bar.

(Subd (b) amended effective January 1, 2019; previously amended effective January 1, 2007.)

(c) Eligibility for certification

To be eligible to become a certified law student, an applicant must:

(1) Have successfully completed one full year of studies (minimum of 270 hours) at a law school accredited by the American Bar Association or the State Bar of California, or both, or have passed the first year law students' examination;

(2) Have been accepted into, and be enrolled in, the second, third, or fourth year of law school in good academic standing or have graduated from law school, subject to the time period limitations specified in the rules adopted by the Board of Trustees of the State Bar; and

(3) Have either successfully completed or be currently enrolled in and attending academic courses in evidence and civil procedure.

(Subd (c) amended effective January 1, 2019.)

(d) Permitted activities

Subject to all applicable rules, regulations, and statutes, a certified law student may:

(1) Negotiate for and on behalf of the client subject to final approval thereof by the supervising attorney or give legal advice to the client, provided that the certified law student:

(A) Obtains the approval of the supervising attorney to engage in the activities;

(B) Obtains the approval of the supervising attorney regarding the legal advice to be given or plan of negotiation to be undertaken by the certified law student; and

(C) Performs the activities under the general supervision of the supervising attorney;

(2) Appear on behalf of the client in depositions, provided that the certified law student:

(A) Obtains the approval of the supervising attorney to engage in the activity;

(B) Performs the activity under the direct and immediate supervision and in the personal presence of the supervising attorney (or, exclusively in the case of government agencies, any deputy, assistant, or other staff attorney authorized and designated by the supervising attorney); and

(C) Obtains a signed consent form from the client on whose behalf the certified law student acts (or, exclusively in the case of government agencies, from the chief counsel or prosecuting attorney) approving the performance of such acts by such certified law student or generally by any certified law student;

(3) Appear on behalf of the client in any public trial, hearing, arbitration, or proceeding, or before any arbitrator, court, public agency, referee, magistrate, commissioner, or hearing officer, to the extent approved by such arbitrator, court, public agency, referee, magistrate, commissioner, or hearing officer, provided that the certified law student:

(A) Obtains the approval of the supervising attorney to engage in the activity;

(B) Performs the activity under the direct and immediate supervision and in the personal presence of the supervising attorney (or, exclusively in the case of government agencies, any deputy, assistant, or other staff attorney authorized and designated by the supervising attorney);

(C) Obtains a signed consent form from the client on whose behalf the certified law student acts (or, exclusively in the case of government agencies, from the chief counsel or prosecuting attorney) approving the performance of such acts by such certified law student or generally by any certified law student; and

(D) As a condition to such appearance, either presents a copy of the consent form to the arbitrator, court, public agency, referee, magistrate, commissioner, or hearing officer, or files a copy of the consent form in the court case file; and

(4) Appear on behalf of a government agency in the prosecution of criminal actions classified as infractions or other such minor criminal offenses with a maximum penalty or a fine equal to the maximum fine for infractions in California, including any public trial:

(A) Subject to approval by the court, commissioner, referee, hearing officer, or magistrate presiding at such public trial; and

(B) Without the personal appearance of the supervising attorney or any deputy, assistant, or other staff attorney authorized and designated by the supervising attorney, but only if the supervising attorney or the designated attorney has approved in writing the performance of such acts by the certified law student and is immediately available to attend the proceeding.

(Subd (d) amended effective January 1, 2007.)

(e) Failure to comply with program

A certified law student who fails to comply with the requirements of the State Bar certified law student program must have his or her certification withdrawn under rules adopted by the Board of Trustees of the State Bar.

(Subd (e) amended effective January 1, 2019; previously amended effective January 1, 2007.)

(f) Fee and penalty

The State Bar has the authority to set and collect appropriate fees and penalties for this program.

(Subd (f) amended effective January 1, 2007.)

(g) Inherent power of Supreme Court

Nothing in these rules may be construed as affecting the power of the Supreme Court to exercise its inherent jurisdiction over the practice of law in California.

(Subd (g) amended effective January 1, 2007.)

Rule 9.42 amended effective January 1, 2019; adopted as rule 983.2 by the Supreme Court effective December 29, 1993; previously amended and renumbered effective January 1, 2007.

Rule 9.43.   Out-of-state attorney arbitration counsel

(a) Definition

An "out-of-state attorney arbitration counsel" is an attorney who is:

(1) Not a licensee of the State Bar of California but who is an attorney in good standing of and eligible to practice before the bar of any United States court or the highest court in any state, territory, or insular possession of the United States, and who has been retained to appear in the course of, or in connection with, an arbitration proceeding in this state;

(2) Has served a certificate in accordance with the requirements of Code of Civil Procedure section 1282.4 on the arbitrator, the arbitrators, or the arbitral forum, the State Bar of California, and all other parties and counsel in the arbitration whose addresses are known to the attorney; and

(3) Whose appearance has been approved by the arbitrator, the arbitrators, or the arbitral forum.

(Subd (a) amended effective January 1, 2019; previously amended effective January 1, 2007.)

(b) State Bar out-of-state attorney arbitration counsel program

The State Bar of California must establish and administer a program to implement the State Bar of California's responsibilities under Code of Civil Procedure section 1282.4. The State Bar of California's program may be operative only as long as the applicable provisions of Code of Civil Procedure section 1282.4 remain in effect.

(Subd (b) amended effective January 1, 2007.)

(c) Eligibility to appear as an out-of-state attorney arbitration counsel

To be eligible to appear as an out-of-state attorney arbitration counsel, an attorney must comply with all of the applicable provisions of Code of Civil Procedure section 1282.4 and the requirements of this rule and the related rules and regulations adopted by the State Bar of California.

(Subd (c) amended effective January 1, 2007.)

(d) Discipline

An out-of-state attorney arbitration counsel who files a certificate containing false information or who otherwise fails to comply with the standards of professional conduct required of licensees of the State Bar of California is subject to the disciplinary jurisdiction of the State Bar with respect to any of his or her acts occurring in the course of the arbitration.

(Subd (d) amended effective January 1, 2019; previously amended effective January 1, 2007.)

(e) Disqualification

Failure to timely file and serve a certificate or, absent special circumstances, appearances in multiple separate arbitration matters are grounds for disqualification from serving in the arbitration in which the certificate was filed.

(Subd (e) amended effective January 1, 2007.)

(f) Fee

Out-of-state attorney arbitration counsel must pay a reasonable fee not exceeding $50 to the State Bar of California with the copy of the certificate that is served on the State Bar.

(Subd (f) amended effective January 1, 2007.)

(g) Inherent power of Supreme Court

Nothing in these rules may be construed as affecting the power of the Supreme Court to exercise its inherent jurisdiction over the practice of law in California.

(Subd (g) amended effective January 1, 2007.)

Rule 9.43 amended effective January 1, 2019; adopted as rule 983.4 by the Supreme Court effective July 1, 1999; previously amended and renumbered effective January 1, 2007.

Rule 9.44.   Registered foreign legal consultant

(a) Definition

A "registered foreign legal consultant" is a person who:

(1) Is admitted to practice and is in good standing as an attorney or counselor-at-law or the equivalent in a foreign country; and

(2) Has a currently effective certificate of registration as a registered foreign legal consultant from the State Bar.

(Subd (a) amended effective January 1, 2007.)

(b) State Bar registered foreign legal consultant program

The State Bar must establish and administer a program for registering foreign attorneys or counselors-at-law or the equivalent under rules adopted by the Board of Trustees of the State Bar.

(Subd (b) amended effective January 1, 2019; previously amended effective January 1, 2007.)

(c) Eligibility for certification

To be eligible to become a registered foreign legal consultant, an applicant must:

(1) Present satisfactory proof that the applicant has been admitted to practice and has been in good standing as an attorney or counselor-at-law or the equivalent in a foreign country for at least four of the six years immediately preceding the application and, while so admitted, has actually practiced the law of that country;

(2) Present satisfactory proof that the applicant possesses the good moral character requisite for a person to be licensed as a licensee of the State Bar of California and proof of compliance with California Rules of Court, rule 9.9.5, governing attorney fingerprinting;

(3) Agree to comply with the provisions of the rules adopted by the Board of Trustees of the State Bar relating to security for claims against a foreign legal consultant by his or her clients;

(4) Agree to comply with the provisions of the rules adopted by the Board of Trustees of the State Bar relating to maintaining an address of record for State Bar purposes;

(5) Agree to notify the State Bar of any change in his or her status in any jurisdiction where he or she is admitted to practice or of any discipline with respect to such admission;

(6) Agree to be subject to the jurisdiction of the courts of this state with respect to the laws of the State of California governing the conduct of attorneys, to the same extent as a licensee of the State Bar of California;

(7) Agree to become familiar with and comply with the standards of professional conduct required of licensees of the State Bar of California;

(8) Agree to be subject to the disciplinary jurisdiction of the State Bar of California;

(9) Agree to be subject to the rights and obligations with respect to attorney client privilege, work-product privilege, and other professional privileges, to the same extent as attorneys admitted to practice law in California; and

(10) Agree to comply with the laws of the State of California, the rules and regulations of the State Bar of California, and these rules.

(Subd (c) amended effective January 1, 2019; previously amended effective January 1, 2007.)

(d) Authority to practice law

Subject to all applicable rules, regulations, and statutes, a registered foreign legal consultant may render legal services in California, except that he or she may not:

(1) Appear for a person other than himself or herself as attorney in any court, or before any magistrate or other judicial officer, in this state or prepare pleadings or any other papers or issue subpoenas in any action or proceeding brought in any court or before any judicial officer;

(2) Prepare any deed, mortgage, assignment, discharge, lease, or any other instrument affecting title to real estate located in the United States;

(3) Prepare any will or trust instrument affecting the disposition on death of any property located in the United States and owned by a resident or any instrument relating to the administration of a decedent's estate in the United States;

(4) Prepare any instrument in respect of the marital relations, rights, or duties of a resident of the United States, or the custody or care of the children of a resident; or

(5) Otherwise render professional legal advice on the law of the State of California, any other state of the United States, the District of Columbia, the United States, or of any jurisdiction other than the jurisdiction named in satisfying the requirements of (c) of this rule, whether rendered incident to preparation of legal instruments or otherwise.

(Subd (d) amended effective January 1, 2007.)

(e) Failure to comply with program

A registered foreign legal consultant who fails to comply with the requirements of the State Bar Registered Foreign Legal Consultant Program will have her or his certification suspended or revoked under rules adopted by the Board of Trustees of the State Bar.

(Subd (e) amended effective January 1, 2019; previously amended effective January 1, 2007.)

(f) Fee and penalty

The State Bar has the authority to set and collect appropriate fees and penalties for this program.

(Subd (f) amended effective January 1, 2007.)

(g) Inherent power of Supreme Court

Nothing in these rules may be construed as affecting the power of the Supreme Court to exercise its inherent jurisdiction over the practice of law in California.

(Subd (g) amended effective January 1, 2007.)

Rule 9.44 amended effective January 1, 2019; adopted as rule 988 effective December 1, 1993; previously amended and renumbered effective January 1, 2007.

Rule 9.45.   Registered legal aid attorneys

(a) Definitions

The following definitions apply in this rule:

(1) "Eligible legal aid organization" means any of the following:

(A) A nonprofit entity in good standing in California and in the state in which it is incorporated, if other than California, that provides legal aid in civil matters, including family law and immigration law, to indigent and disenfranchised persons, especially underserved client groups, such as the elderly, persons with disabilities, people of color, juveniles, and limited English proficient persons; or

(B) A nonprofit law school approved by the American Bar Association located in California or accredited by the State Bar of California that provides legal aid as described above in subdivision (A).

(C) Entities that receive IOLTA funds pursuant to Business and Professions Code, section 6210, et seq., are deemed to be eligible legal aid organizations.

(2) "Active licensee in good standing of the bar of a United States state, jurisdiction, possession, territory, or dependency" means an attorney who:

(A) Is a licensee in good standing of the entity governing the practice of law in each jurisdiction in which the attorney is licensed to practice law, who has not been disbarred, has not resigned with charges pending, or is not suspended from practicing law for disciplinary misconduct in any other jurisdiction; and

(B) Remains an active licensee in good standing of the entity governing the practice of law in at least one United States state, jurisdiction, possession, territory, or dependency other than California while practicing law as a registered legal aid attorney in California.

(Subd (a) amended effective March 1, 2019; adopted as subd (j) effective November 15, 2004; previously relettered effective January 1, 2007; previously amended effective January 1, 2019.)

(b) Scope of practice

Subject to all applicable rules, regulations, and statutes, an attorney practicing law under this rule may practice law in California only while working, with or without pay, at an eligible legal aid organization, as defined in this rule, and, at that institution and only on behalf of its clients or customers, may engage, under supervision, in all forms of legal practice that are permissible for a licensee of the State Bar of California.

(Subd (b) amended effective March 1, 2019; adopted as subd (a) effective November 15, 2004; previously amended and relettered effective January 1, 2007; previously amended effective January 1, 2019.)

(c) Requirements

For an attorney to qualify to practice law under this rule, the attorney must:

(1) Be an active licensee in good standing of the bar of a United States state, jurisdiction, possession, territory, or dependency;

(2) Meet all of the requirements for admission to the State Bar of California, except that the attorney:

(A) Need not take the California bar examination or the Multistate Professional Responsibility Examination; and

(B) May practice law while awaiting the result of his or her Application for Determination of Moral Character;

(3) Comply with the rules adopted by the Board of Trustees relating to the State Bar Registered Legal Aid Attorney Program;

(4) Practice law under the supervision of an attorney who is employed by the eligible legal aid organization and who is a licensee in good standing of the State Bar of California;

(5) Abide by all of the laws and rules that govern licensees of the State Bar of California, including the Minimum Continuing Legal Education (MCLE) requirements;

(6) Satisfy in his or her first year of practice under this rule all of the MCLE requirements, including ethics education, that licensees of the State Bar of California must complete every three years and, thereafter, satisfy the MCLE requirements for the registered legal aid attorney's compliance group as set forth in State Bar Rules 2.70 and 2.71. If the registered legal aid attorney's compliance group is required to report in less than thirty-six months, the MCLE requirements will be reduced proportionally; and

(7) Not have taken and failed the California bar examination within five years immediately preceding initial application to register under this rule.

(Subd (c) amended and renumbered effective March 1, 2019; adopted as subd (b) effective November 15, 2004; previously relettered effective January 1, 2007; previously amended effective January 1, 2019.)

(d) Application

The attorney must comply with the following registration requirements:

(1) Register as a legal aid attorney; submit a separate application for each eligible legal aid organization; file an Application for Determination of Moral Character with the State Bar of California; and comply with Rules of Court, rule 9.9.5, governing attorney fingerprinting;

(2) Submit to the State Bar of California a declaration signed by the attorney agreeing that he or she will be subject to the disciplinary authority of the Supreme Court of California and the State Bar of California and attesting that he or she will not practice law in California other than under supervision of an attorney at an eligible legal aid

organization during the time he or she practices law as a registered legal aid attorney in California; and

(3) Submit to the State Bar of California a declaration signed by a qualifying supervisor from each eligible legal aid organization in California. The declaration must attest:

(A) that the applicant will work, with or without pay, as an attorney for the organization;

(B) that the applicant will be supervised as specified in this rule;

(C) that the eligible legal aid organization and the supervising attorney assume professional responsibility for any work performed by the applicant under this rule;

(D) that the organization will notify the State Bar of California within 30 days of the cessation of the applicant's employment with that employer in California; and

(E) that the person signing the declaration believes, to the best of his or her knowledge after reasonable inquiry, that the applicant qualifies for registration under this rule and is an individual of good moral character.

(Subd (d) amended effective March 1, 2019; adopted as subd (c) effective November 15, 2004; previously relettered effective January 1, 2007.)

(e) Duration of practice

A registered legal aid attorney must renew his or her registration annually and may practice for no more than a total of five years under this rule.

(Subd (e) amended effective March 1, 2019; adopted as subd (d) effective November 15, 2004; previously relettered effective January 1, 2007.)

(f) Application and registration fees

The State Bar of California may set appropriate application fees and initial and annual registration fees to be paid by registered legal aid attorneys.

(Subd (f) amended effective March 1, 2019; adopted as subd (e) effective November 15, 2004; previously amended and relettered effective January 1, 2007.)

(g) State Bar Registered Legal Aid Attorney Program

The State Bar may establish and administer a program for registering California legal aid attorneys under rules adopted by the Board of Trustees of the State Bar.

(Subd (g) amended effective March 1, 2019; adopted as subd (f) effective November 15, 2004; previously relettered effective January 1, 2007; previously amended effective January 1, 2019.)

(h) Supervision

To meet the requirements of this rule, an attorney supervising a registered legal aid attorney:

(1) Must have practiced law as a full-time occupation for at least four years in any United States jurisdiction;

(2) Must have actively practiced law in California for at least two years immediately preceding the time of supervision and be a licensee in good standing of the State Bar of California;

(3) Must assume professional responsibility for any work that the registered legal aid attorney performs under the supervising attorney's supervision;

(4) Must assist, counsel, and provide direct supervision of the registered legal aid attorney in the activities authorized by this rule, approve in writing any appearance in court, deposition, arbitration or any proceeding by the registered legal aid attorney, and review such activities with the supervised registered legal aid attorney, to the extent required for the protection of the client or customer;

(5) Must read, approve, and personally sign any pleadings, briefs, or other similar documents prepared by the registered legal aid attorney before their filing, and must read and approve any documents prepared by the registered legal aid attorney before their submission; and

(6) May, in his or her absence, designate another attorney meeting the requirements of (1) through (5) to provide the supervision required under this rule.

(Subd (h) amended and renumbered effective March 1, 2019; adopted as subd (g) effective November 15, 2004; previously relettered effective January 1, 2007; previously amended effective January 1, 2019.)

(i) Inherent power of Supreme Court

Nothing in this rule may be construed as affecting the power of the Supreme Court of California to exercise its inherent jurisdiction over the practice of law in California.

(Subd (i) amended and relettered effective January 1, 2007; adopted as subd (h) effective November 15, 2004.)

(j) Effect of rule on multijurisdictional practice

Nothing in this rule limits the scope of activities permissible under existing law by attorneys who are not licensees of the State Bar of California.

(Subd (j) amended effective January 1, 2019; previously relettered effective January 1, 2007; adopted as subd (i) effective November 15, 2004.)

Rule 9.45 amended effective March 1, 2019; adopted as rule 964 by the Supreme Court effective November 15, 2004; previously amended and renumbered effective January 1, 2007; previously amended effective January 1, 2019.

Rule 9.46. Registered in-house counsel

(a) Definitions

The following definitions apply to terms used in this rule:

(1) "Qualifying institution" means a corporation, a partnership, an association, or other legal entity, including its subsidiaries and organizational affiliates, which has an office located in California. Neither a governmental entity nor an entity that provides legal services to others can be a qualifying institution for purposes of this rule. A qualifying institution must:

(A) Employ at least 5 full time employees; or

(B) Employ in California an attorney who is an active licensee in good standing of the State Bar of California.

(2) "Active licensee in good standing of the bar of a United States state, jurisdiction, possession, territory, or dependency" means an attorney who:

(A) Is a licensee in good standing of the entity governing the practice of law in each jurisdiction in which the attorney is licensed to practice law, who has not been disbarred, has not resigned with charges pending, or is not suspended from practicing law for disciplinary misconduct in any other jurisdiction; and

(B) Remains an active licensee in good standing of the entity governing the practice of law in at least one United States state, jurisdiction, possession, territory, or dependency, other than California, while practicing law as registered in-house counsel in California.

(Subd (a) amended effective March 1, 2019; adopted as subd (j) effective November 15, 2004; previously relettered effective January 1, 2007; previously amended effective January 1, 2019.)

(b) Scope of practice

Subject to all applicable rules, regulations, and statutes, an attorney practicing law under this rule is:

(1) Permitted to provide legal services in California to the qualifying institution that employs him or her;

(2) Permitted to provide *pro bono* legal services under supervision of a California attorney for either eligible legal aid organizations as defined by Rules of Court, rule 9.45(a)(1), or the qualifying institution that employs him or her;

(3) Not permitted to make court appearances in California state courts or to engage in any other activities for which *pro hac vice* admission is required if they are performed in California by an attorney who is not a licensee of the State Bar of California; and

(4) Not permitted to provide personal or individual representation to any customers, shareholders, owners, partners, officers, employees, servants, or agents of the qualifying institution, except as described in subdivision (b)(2).

(Subd (b) amended effective March 1, 2019; adopted as subd (a) effective November 15, 2004; previously amended and relettered effective January 1, 2007; previously amended effective January 1, 2019.)

(c) Requirements

For an attorney to qualify to practice law under this rule, the attorney must:

(1) Be an active licensee in good standing of the bar of a United States state, jurisdiction, possession, territory, or dependency;

(2) Meet all of the requirements for admission to the State Bar of California, except that the attorney:

(A) Need not take the California bar examination or the Multistate Professional Responsibility Examination; and

(B) May practice law while awaiting the result of his or her Application for Determination of Moral Character;

(3) Comply with the rules adopted by the Board of Trustees relating to the State Bar Registered In-House Counsel Program;

(4) Practice law exclusively for a single qualifying institution, except that, while practicing under this rule, the attorney may provide *pro bono* services through eligible legal aid organizations;

(5) Abide by all of the laws and rules that govern licensees of the State Bar of California, including the Minimum Continuing Legal Education (MCLE) requirements;

(6) Satisfy in his or her first year of practice under this rule all of the MCLE requirements, including ethics education, that licensees of the

State Bar of California must complete every three years and, thereafter, satisfy the MCLE requirements for the registered in-house counsel's compliance group as set forth in State Bar Rules 2.70 and 2.71. If the registered in-house counsel's compliance group is required to report in less than thirty-six months, the MCLE requirement will be reduced proportionally; and

(7) Reside in California.

(Subd (c) amended effective March 1, 2019; adopted as subd (b) effective November 15, 2004; previously relettered effective January 1, 2007; previously amended effective January 1, 2019.)

(d) Application

The attorney must comply with the following registration requirements:

(1) Register as an in-house counsel; submit an application for the qualifying institution; file an Application for Determination of Moral Character with the State Bar of California; and comply with Rules of Court, rule 9.9.5, governing attorney fingerprinting;

(2) Submit a supplemental form identifying the eligible legal aid organizations as defined by Rules of Court, rule 9.45(a)(1) and the supervising attorney, through which an in-house counsel intends to provide *pro bono* services, if applicable;

(3) Submit to the State Bar of California a declaration signed by the attorney agreeing that he or she will be subject to the disciplinary authority of the Supreme Court of California and the State Bar of California and attesting that he or she will not practice law in California other than on behalf of the qualifying institution during the time he or she is registered in-house counsel in California, except if supervised, a registered in-house counsel may provide *pro bono* services through an eligible legal aid organization; and

(4) Submit to the State Bar of California a declaration signed by an officer, a director, or a general counsel of the applicant's employer, on behalf of the applicant's employer. The declaration must attest:

(A) that the applicant is employed as an attorney for the employer;

(B) that the nature of the employment conforms to the requirements of this rule;

(C) that the employer will notify the State Bar of California within 30 days of the cessation of the applicant's employment in California; and

(D) that the person signing the declaration believes, to the best of his or her knowledge after reasonable inquiry, that the applicant qualifies for registration under this rule and is an individual of good moral character.

(Subd (d) amended effective March 1, 2019; adopted as subd (c) effective November 15, 2004; previously relettered effective January 1, 2007.)

(e) Duration of practice

A registered in-house counsel must renew his or her registration annually. There is no limitation on the number of years in-house counsel may register under this rule. Registered in-house counsel may practice law under this rule only for as long as he or she remains employed by the same qualifying institution that provided the declaration in support of his or her application. If an attorney practicing law as registered in-house counsel leaves the employment of his or her employer or changes employers, he or she must notify the State Bar of California within 30 days. If an attorney wishes to practice law under this rule for a new employer, he or she must first register as in-house counsel for that employer.

(Subd (e) amended and relettered effective January 1, 2007; adopted as subd (d) effective November 15, 2004.)

(f) Application and registration fees

The State Bar of California may set appropriate application fees and initial and annual registration fees to be paid by registered in-house counsel.

(Subd (f) relettered effective March 1, 2019; adopted as subd (f) effective November 15, 2004; previously amended and relettered as subd (g) effective January 1, 2007.)

(g) State Bar Registered In-House Counsel Program

The State Bar must establish and administer a program for registering California in-house counsel under rules adopted by the Board of Trustees.

(Subd (g) relettered effective March 1, 2019; adopted as subd (g) effective November 15, 2004; previously amended and relettered as subd (h) effective January 1, 2007; previously amended effective January 1, 2019.)

(h) Inherent power of Supreme Court

Nothing in this rule may be construed as affecting the power of the Supreme Court of California to exercise its inherent jurisdiction over the practice of law in California.

(Subd (h) relettered effective March 1, 2019; adopted as subd (h) effective November 15, 2004; previously amended and relettered as subd (i) effective January 1, 2007.)

(i) Effect of rule on multijurisdictional practice

Nothing in this rule limits the scope of activities permissible under existing law by attorneys who are not licensees of the State Bar of California.

(Subd (i) relettered effective March 1, 2019; adopted as subd (i) effective November 15, 2004; previously relettered as subd (j) effective January 1, 2007; previously amended effective January 1, 2019.)

Rule 9.46 amended effective March 1, 2019; adopted as rule 965 by the Supreme Court effective November 15, 2004; previously amended and renumbered effective January 1, 2007; previously amended effective January 1, 2019.

Rule 9.47. Attorneys practicing law temporarily in California as part of litigation

(a) Definitions

The following definitions apply to the terms used in this rule:

(1) "A formal legal proceeding" means litigation, arbitration, mediation, or a legal action before an administrative decision-maker.

(2) "Authorized to appear" means the attorney is permitted to appear in the proceeding by the rules of the jurisdiction in which the formal legal proceeding is taking place or will be taking place.

(3) "Active attorney in good standing of the bar of a United States state, jurisdiction, possession, territory, or dependency" means an attorney who meets all of the following criteria:

(A) Is a licensee in good standing of the entity governing the practice of law in each jurisdiction in which the attorney is licensed to practice law;

(B) Remains an active licensee in good standing of the entity governing the practice of law in at least one United States state, jurisdiction, possession, territory, or dependency while practicing law under this rule; and

(C) Has not been disbarred, has not resigned with charges pending, or is not suspended from practicing law in any other jurisdiction.

(Subd (a) amended effective January 1, 2019; adopted as subd (g) effective November 15, 2004; previously relettered effective January 1, 2007.)

(b) Requirements

For an attorney to practice law under this rule, the attorney must:

(1) Maintain an office in a United States jurisdiction other than California and in which the attorney is licensed to practice law;

(2) Already be retained by a client in the matter for which the attorney is providing legal services in California, except that the attorney may provide legal advice to a potential client, at the potential client's request, to assist the client in deciding whether to retain the attorney;

(3) Indicate on any Web site or other advertisement that is accessible in California either that the attorney is not a licensee of the State Bar of California or that the attorney is admitted to practice law only in the states listed; and

(4) Be an active attorney in good standing of the bar of a United States state, jurisdiction, possession, territory, or dependency.

(Subd (b) amended effective January 1, 2019; adopted as subd (a) effective November 15, 2004; previously relettered effective January 1, 2007.)

(c) Permissible activities

An attorney meeting the requirements of this rule, who complies with all applicable rules, regulations, and statutes, is not engaging in the unauthorized practice of law in California if the attorney's services are part of:

(1) A formal legal proceeding that is pending in another jurisdiction and in which the attorney is authorized to appear;

(2) A formal legal proceeding that is anticipated but is not yet pending in California and in which the attorney reasonably expects to be authorized to appear;

(3) A formal legal proceeding that is anticipated but is not yet pending in another jurisdiction and in which the attorney reasonably expects to be authorized to appear; or

(4) A formal legal proceeding that is anticipated or pending and in which the attorney's supervisor is authorized to appear or reasonably expects to be authorized to appear.

The attorney whose anticipated authorization to appear in a formal legal proceeding serves as the basis for practice under this rule must seek that authorization promptly after it becomes possible to do so. Failure to seek that authorization promptly, or denial of that authorization, ends eligibility to practice under this rule.

(Subd (c) relettered effective January 1, 2007; adopted as subd (b) effective November 15, 2004.)

(d) Restrictions

To qualify to practice law in California under this rule, an attorney must not:

(1) Hold out to the public or otherwise represent that he or she is admitted to practice law in California;

(2) Establish or maintain a resident office or other systematic or continuous presence in California for the practice of law;

(3) Be a resident of California;

(4) Be regularly employed in California;

(5) Regularly engage in substantial business or professional activities in California; or

(6) Have been disbarred, have resigned with charges pending, or be suspended from practicing law in any other jurisdiction.

(Subd (d) relettered effective January 1, 2007; adopted as subd (c) effective November 15, 2004.)

(e) Conditions

By practicing law in California under this rule, an attorney agrees that he or she is providing legal services in California subject to:

(1) The jurisdiction of the State Bar of California;

(2) The jurisdiction of the courts of this state to the same extent as is a licensee of the State Bar of California; and

(3) The laws of the State of California relating to the practice of law, the State Bar Rules of Professional Conduct, the rules and regulations of the State Bar of California, and these rules.

(Subd (e) amended effective January 1, 2019; adopted as subd (d) effective November 15, 2004; previously relettered effective January 1, 2007.)

(f) Inherent power of Supreme Court

Nothing in this rule may be construed as affecting the power of the Supreme Court of California to exercise its inherent jurisdiction over the practice of law in California.

(Subd (f) amended and relettered effective January 1, 2007; adopted as subd (e) effective November 15, 2004.)

(g) Effect of rule on multijurisdictional practice

Nothing in this rule limits the scope of activities permissible under existing law by attorneys who are not licensees of the State Bar of California.

(Subd (g) amended effective January 1, 2019; adopted as subd (f) effective November 15, 2004; previously relettered effective January 1, 2007.)

Rule 9.47 amended effective January 1, 2019; adopted as rule 966 by the Supreme Court effective November 15, 2004; previously amended and renumbered effective January 1, 2007.

Rule 9.48. Nonlitigating attorneys temporarily in California to provide legal services

(a) Definitions

The following definitions apply to terms used in this rule:

(1) "A transaction or other nonlitigation matter" includes any legal matter other than litigation, arbitration, mediation, or a legal action before an administrative decision-maker.

(2) "Active attorney in good standing of the bar of a United States state, jurisdiction, possession, territory, or dependency" means an attorney who meets all of the following criteria:

(A) Is a licensee in good standing of the entity governing the practice of law in each jurisdiction in which the attorney is licensed to practice law;

(B) Remains an active attorney in good standing of the entity governing the practice of law in at least one United States state, jurisdiction, possession, territory, or dependency other than California while practicing law under this rule; and

(C) Has not been disbarred, has not resigned with charges pending, or is not suspended from practicing law in any other jurisdiction.

(Subd (a) amended effective January 1, 2019; adopted as subd (h) effective November 15, 2004; previously relettered effective January 1, 2007.)

(b) Requirements

For an attorney to practice law under this rule, the attorney must:

(1) Maintain an office in a United States jurisdiction other than California and in which the attorney is licensed to practice law;

(2) Already be retained by a client in the matter for which the attorney is providing legal services in California, except that the attorney may provide legal advice to a potential client, at the potential client's request, to assist the client in deciding whether to retain the attorney;

(3) Indicate on any Web site or other advertisement that is accessible in California either that the attorney is not a licensee of the State Bar of California or that the attorney is admitted to practice law only in the states listed; and

(4) Be an active attorney in good standing of the bar of a United States state, jurisdiction, possession, territory, or dependency.

(Subd (b) amended effective January 1, 2019; adopted as subd (a) effective November 15, 2004; previously relettered effective January 1, 2007.)

(c) Permissible activities

An attorney who meets the requirements of this rule and who complies with all applicable rules, regulations, and statutes is not engaging in the unauthorized practice of law in California if the attorney:

(1) Provides legal assistance or legal advice in California to a client concerning a transaction or other nonlitigation matter, a material aspect of which is taking place in a jurisdiction other than California and in which the attorney is licensed to provide legal services;

(2) Provides legal assistance or legal advice in California on an issue of federal law or of the law of a jurisdiction other than California to attorneys licensed to practice law in California; or

(3) Is an employee of a client and provides legal assistance or legal advice in California to the client or to the client's subsidiaries or organizational affiliates.

(Subd (c) relettered effective January 1, 2007; adopted as subd (b) effective November 15, 2004.)

(d) Restrictions

To qualify to practice law in California under this rule, an attorney must not:

(1) Hold out to the public or otherwise represent that he or she is admitted to practice law in California;

(2) Establish or maintain a resident office or other systematic or continuous presence in California for the practice of law;

(3) Be a resident of California;

(4) Be regularly employed in California;

(5) Regularly engage in substantial business or professional activities in California; or

(6) Have been disbarred, have resigned with charges pending, or be suspended from practicing law in any other jurisdiction.

(Subd (d) amended and relettered effective January 1, 2007; adopted as subd (c) effective November 15, 2004.)

(e) Conditions

By practicing law in California under this rule, an attorney agrees that he or she is providing legal services in California subject to:

(1) The jurisdiction of the State Bar of California;

(2) The jurisdiction of the courts of this state to the same extent as is a licensee of the State Bar of California; and

(3) The laws of the State of California relating to the practice of law, the State Bar Rules of Professional Conduct, the rules and regulations of the State Bar of California, and these rules.

(Subd (e) amended effective January 1, 2019; adopted as subd (d) effective November 15, 2004; previously amended and relettered effective January 1, 2007.)

(f) Scope of practice

An attorney is permitted by this rule to provide legal assistance or legal services concerning only a transaction or other nonlitigation matter.

(Subd (f) relettered effective January 1, 2007; adopted as subd (e) effective November 15, 2004.)

(g) Inherent power of Supreme Court

Nothing in this rule may be construed as affecting the power of the Supreme Court of California to exercise its inherent jurisdiction over the practice of law in California.

(Subd (g) amended and relettered effective January 1, 2007; adopted as subd (f) effective November 15, 2004.)

(h) Effect of rule on multijurisdictional practice

Nothing in this rule limits the scope of activities permissible under existing law by attorneys who are not licensees of the State Bar of California.

(Subd (h) amended effective January 1, 2019; adopted as subd (g) effective November 15, 2004; previously relettered effective January 1, 2007.)

Rule 9.48 amended effective January 1, 2019; adopted as rule 967 by the Supreme Court effective November 15, 2004; previously amended and renumbered effective January 1, 2007.

Division 5
Censure, Removal, Retirement, or Private or Public Admonishment of Judges

Rule 9.60. Review of determinations by the Commission on Judicial Performance

Rule 9.61. Proceedings involving private or public admonishment, censure, removal, retirement, or disqualification of a judge of the Supreme Court

Rule 9.60. Review of determinations by the Commission on Judicial Performance

(a) Time for petition for review to Supreme Court

A petition to the Supreme Court by a judge or former judge to review a determination by the Commission on Judicial Performance to retire, remove, censure, admonish, or disqualify the judge or former judge must be served and filed within 60 days after:

(1) The Commission, under its rules, notifies the judge or former judge that its determination has been filed or entered in its records; or

(2) The determination becomes final as to the Commission under its rules, whichever event is later.

(Subd (a) amended effective January 1, 2007.)

(b) Time for answer to petition for review and reply

Within 45 days after service of the petition, the Commission may serve and file an answer. Within 20 days after service of the answer, the judge or former judge may serve and file a reply. Each petition, answer, or reply submitted for filing must be accompanied by proof of service, including service on the Commission of three copies of any petition or reply filed by a judge or former judge. Extensions of time to file the petition, answer, or reply are disfavored and will be granted only upon a specific and affirmative showing of good cause. Good cause does not include ordinary press of business.

(Subd (b) lettered effective January 1, 2007; adopted as part of subd (a) effective December 1, 1996.)

(c) Contents and form

The petition, answer, and reply must address both the appropriateness of review and the merits of the Commission's determination, and they will serve as briefs on the merits in the event review is granted. Except as provided in these rules, the form of the petition, answer, and reply must, insofar as practicable, conform to rule 8.504 except that the lengths of the petition, answer, and reply must conform to the limits specified in rule 8.204(c). Each copy of the petition must contain:

(1) A copy of the Commission's determination;

(2) A copy of the notice of filing or entry of the determination in the records of the Commission;

(3) A copy of any findings of fact and conclusions of law; and

(4) A cover that bears the conspicuous notation "PETITION FOR REVIEW OF DETERMINATION BY COMMISSION ON JUDICIAL PERFORMANCE (RULE 9.60)" or words of like effect.

(Subd (c) amended and relettered effective January 1, 2007; adopted as subd (b) effective December 1, 1996.)

(d) Transmission of the record

Promptly upon the service and filing of the petition, the Commission must transmit to the Clerk of the Supreme Court the original record, including a transcript of the testimony, briefs, and all original papers and exhibits on file in the proceeding.

(Subd (d) amended and relettered effective January 1, 2007; adopted as subd (c) effective December 1, 1996.)

(e) Applicable rules on review

In the event review is granted, the rules adopted by the Judicial Council governing appeals from the superior court in civil cases, other than rule 8.272 relating to costs, apply to proceedings in the Supreme Court for review of a determination of the Commission except where express provision is made to the contrary or where such application would otherwise be clearly impracticable or inappropriate.

(Subd (e) amended and relettered effective January 1, 2007; adopted as subd (d) effective December 1, 1996.)

Rule 9.60 amended and renumbered effective January 1, 2007; adopted as rule 935 effective December 1, 1996.

Rule 9.61. Proceedings involving private or public admonishment, censure, removal, retirement, or disqualification of a judge of the Supreme Court

(a) Selection of appellate tribunal

Immediately on the filing of a petition to review a determination by the Commission on Judicial Performance to retire, remove, censure, admonish, or disqualify a justice of the Supreme Court, the Clerk of the Supreme Court must select, by lot, seven Court of Appeal justices who must elect one of their number presiding justice and perform the duties of the tribunal created under article VI, section 18(f) of the Constitution. This selection must be made upon notice to the Commission, the justice, and the counsel of record in a proceeding open to the public. No court of appeal justice who has served as a master or a member of the Commission in the particular proceeding or is otherwise disqualified may serve on the tribunal.

(Subd (a) amended effective January 1, 2007; previously amended effective December 1, 1996.)

(b) Clerk of Supreme Court as clerk of tribunal

The Clerk of the Supreme Court serves as the clerk of the tribunal.

(Subd (b) amended effective January 1, 2007.)

Rule 9.61 amended effective January 1, 2019; adopted as rule 921 effective November 13, 1976; previously amended and renumbered as rule 936 effective December 1, 1996, and as rule 9.61 effective January 1, 2007.

2019 Note: The amendment effective January 1, 2019, only amended the rule heading.

Division 6
Judicial Ethics Opinions

Rule 9.80. Committee on Judicial Ethics Opinions

(a) Purpose

The Supreme Court has established the Committee on Judicial Ethics Opinions to provide judicial ethics advisory opinions and advice to judicial officers and candidates for judicial office.

(Subd (a) adopted effective July 1, 2009.)

(b) Committee determinations

In providing its opinions and advice, the committee acts independently of the Supreme Court, the Commission on Judicial Performance, and all other entities. The committee must rely on the California Code of Judicial Ethics, the decisions of the Supreme Court and of the Commission on Judicial Performance, and may rely on other relevant sources in its opinions and advice.

(Subd (b) amended effective January 1, 2019; adopted effective July 1, 2009.)

(c) Membership

The committee consists of twelve members appointed by the Supreme Court, including at least one justice from a Court of Appeal and one member who is a subordinate judicial officer employed full-time by a superior court. The remaining members must be justices of a Court of Appeal or judges of a superior court, active or retired. No more than a total of two retired justices or judges may serve on the committee at one time, except that if an active justice or judge retires during his or her term, he or she will be permitted to complete his or her term. A retired justice or judge may only serve so long as he or she is not an active licensee of the State Bar of California and is not engaged in privately compensated dispute resolution activities.

(Subd (c) amended effective January 1, 2019; adopted effective July 1, 2009.)

(d) Terms

(1) Except as provided in (2), all full terms are for four years. Appointments to fill a vacancy will be for the balance of the term vacated. A member may be reappointed by the Supreme Court or may continue to serve until a successor is appointed. Members may serve no more than three terms, except that members who are appointed to fill a vacancy for the balance of a term are eligible to serve three full terms in addition to the remainder of the term for which they were appointed.

(2) To create staggered terms among the members of the committee, the Supreme Court appointed initial members of the committee as follows:

(A) Three members each to serve an initial term of five years. The Court may reappoint these members to two full terms.

(B) Three members each to serve an initial term of four years. The Court may reappoint these members to two full terms.

(C) Three members each to serve an initial term of three years. The Court may reappoint these members to two full terms.

(D) Three members each to serve an initial term of two years. The Court may reappoint these members to two full terms.

(3) Committee members may not simultaneously serve as members of the Commission on Judicial Performance or the California Judges Association's Judicial Ethics Committee. If a member of the committee accepts appointment to serve on one of these entities, that member will be deemed to have resigned from the committee and the Supreme Court will appoint a replacement.

(Subd (d) amended effective January 1, 2016; adopted effective July 1, 2009.)

(e) Powers and duties

The committee is authorized to provide ethics advice to judicial officers and candidates for judicial office, including formal written opinions, informal written opinions, and oral advice. Specifically, the committee is authorized to:

(1) Issue formal written opinions, informal written opinions, and oral advice on proper judicial conduct under the California Code of Judicial Ethics, the California Constitution, statutes, and any other authority deemed appropriate by the committee.

(2) Make recommendations to the Supreme Court for amending the Code of Judicial Ethics or these rules;

(3) Make recommendations regarding appropriate subjects for judicial education programs; and

(4) Make other recommendations to the Supreme Court as deemed appropriate by the committee or as requested by the Court.

(Subd (e) adopted effective July 1, 2009.)

(f) Referrals to California Judges Association's Judicial Ethics Committee

The committee may adopt a revocable policy of referring requests for oral advice, with conditions and exceptions as approved by the committee, to the California Judges Association's Judicial Ethics Committee.

(Subd (f) adopted effective July 1, 2009.)

(g) Chair and vice-chair

The Supreme Court will appoint a chair, and vice-chair from the members of the committee to serve a term of four years each. The chair and the vice-chair may be reappointed by the Supreme Court or may continue to serve until a successor is appointed. The chair and vice-chair may serve no more than three terms each. The chair may call meetings as needed, and to otherwise coordinate the work of the committee.

(Subd (g) amended effective January 1, 2019; adopted effective July 1, 2009; previously amended effective January 1, 2016.)

(h) Confidentiality

Communications to and from the committee are confidential except as described here. Encouraging judicial officers and candidates for judicial office to seek ethics opinions and advice from the committee will promote ethical conduct and the fair administration of justice. Establishing the confidentiality of committee proceedings and communications to and from the committee is critical to encourage judicial officers and candidates for judicial office to seek ethics opinions and advice from the committee. The necessity for preserving the confidentiality of these proceedings and communications to and from the committee outweighs the necessity for disclosure in the interest of justice. Therefore, to promote ethical conduct by judicial officers and candidates for judicial office and to encourage them to seek ethics opinions and advice from the committee, the following confidentiality requirements, and exceptions, apply to proceedings and other matters under this rule:

(1) Notwithstanding any other provision of law, and with the exception of formal written opinions, summaries of informal written opinions and oral advice, and public comments where confidentiality has been waived, all opinions, inquiries, replies, circulated drafts, records, documents, writings, files, communications with staff, and proceedings of the committee are confidential. All communications, written or verbal, from or to the person or entity requesting an opinion or advice are deemed to be official information within the meaning of the Evidence Code. In addition, all communications and documents regarding opinions or advice of the California Judges Association forwarded by the California Judges Association to the committee are deemed to be confidential information.

(2) Members of the committee or its staff may not disclose outside the committee or its staff any confidential information, including identifying information, obtained by the committee or its staff concerning an individual whose inquiry or conduct was the subject of any communication with the committee or its staff.

(3) A judicial officer or candidate for judicial office may waive confidentiality; any such waiver must be in writing. If the judicial officer or candidate making the request for an opinion or advice waives confidentiality or asserts reliance on an opinion or advice in judicial or attorney discipline proceedings, such opinion or advice no longer is confidential under these rules. Notwithstanding any waiver, committee deliberations and records are confidential.

(Subd (h) amended effective January 1, 2019; adopted effective July 1, 2009.)

(i) Opinion requests

(1) The committee may issue formal written opinions, informal written opinions, or oral advice on any subject it deems appropriate. Any person or entity may suggest to the committee, in writing, topics to be addressed in a formal written opinion.

(2) Only judicial officers and candidates for judicial office may request informal written opinions and oral advice.

(3) A judicial officer or candidate for judicial office requesting a written opinion, formal or informal, must submit the request in writing, including by electronic mail. The request must be in a form approved by the committee and must describe the facts and discuss the issues presented in the request. The identity, organizational affiliation, and geographic location of persons requesting opinions are confidential.

(4) A judicial officer or candidate for judicial office requesting oral advice may communicate in person, in writing, including by electronic mail, or by telephone to committee staff or any member of the committee.

(5) A judicial officer or candidate for judicial office requesting an opinion or advice must disclose to the committee whether the issue that is the subject of the inquiry is also the subject of pending litigation involving the inquiring judicial officer or candidate or a pending Commission on Judicial Performance or State Bar disciplinary proceeding involving the inquiring judicial officer or candidate.

(Subd (i) amended effective January 1, 2019; adopted effective July 1, 2009.)

(j) Consideration of requests

(1) The committee will determine whether a written request for an opinion should be resolved with a formal written opinion, an informal written opinion, oral advice, or any combination thereof. The committee may decline to issue an opinion or advice.

(2) Eight members must vote affirmatively to adopt a formal written opinion. After the committee authorizes a formal written opinion and before it becomes final, it will be posted in draft form on the committee web site and made available for public comment for at least 45 days, unless the committee in its discretion decides such an opinion should be issued in final form in less time or with no prior notice. Public comments may be posted on the web site following the public comment period for at least 90 days. After the public comment period has expired, eight members must vote affirmatively to publish the opinion in its original form, or modify or withdraw the formal written opinion.

(3) Informal written opinions and oral advice must be decided by vote of the committee members. The committee must adopt procedures concerning the number of votes required to issue an informal written opinion or oral advice.

(4) The committee must adopt procedures concerning the handling and determination of requests for opinions or advice.

(5) The committee will inform the inquiring judicial officer or candidate for judicial office that he or she must disclose all relevant information and that any opinion or advice issued by the committee is based on the premise that the inquiring judicial officer or candidate has disclosed all relevant information.

(6) The committee may confer in person, in writing, including by electronic mail, by telephone, or by videoconference as often as needed to conduct committee business and resolve pending requests.

(Subd (j) amended effective January 1, 2019; adopted effective July 1, 2009.)

(k) Opinion distribution

(1) The committee will, upon final approval of a formal written opinion, ensure distribution of the opinion, including to the person or entity who requested the opinion, all California judicial officers, and other interested persons.

(2) The committee's informal written opinions and written confirmation of oral advice will, upon approval by the committee, be provided to the inquiring judicial officer or candidate for judicial office.

(3) The committee will post all formal written opinions on the committee's website. The committee may post summaries of its informal written opinions and of oral advice on the committee's website.

(4) The committee must maintain records of committee determinations and opinions at the committee's office.

(Subd (k) amended effective January 1, 2019; adopted effective July 1, 2009.)

(*l*) Withdrawn, modified, and superseding opinions

The committee may withdraw, modify, or supersede an opinion at any time.

(Subd (l) adopted effective July 1, 2009.)

(m) Internal operating rules

The committee must adopt procedures, subject to approval by the Supreme Court, to implement this rule.

(Subd (m) amended effective January 1, 2019; adopted effective July 1, 2009.)

(n) Website, e-mail address, and toll-free telephone number

The committee must maintain a website, e-mail address, and toll-free telephone number.

Rules of Court

(Subd (n) amended effective January 1, 2019; adopted effective July 1, 2009.)
Rule 9.80 amended effective January 1, 2019; adopted effective July 1, 2009; previously amended effective January 1, 2016.

Division 7
State Bar Trustees

Rule 9.90. Nominations and appointments of State Bar trustees

(a) State Bar Trustees Nominating Committee

(1) The Supreme Court appoints five attorneys to the State Bar Board of Trustees, each for a four-year term. The court may reappoint an attorney for one additional term. The court may also fill any vacancy in the term of, and make any reappointment of, any appointed attorney member. Each appointee must be an active licensee of the State Bar and have his or her principal office in California.

(2) In order to ensure that individuals appointed by the Supreme Court to the State Bar Board of Trustees have been evaluated objectively, the court has established an independent "State Bar Trustees Nominating Committee" to receive applications and screen and evaluate prospective appointees. The role of the committee is to determine whether applicants possess not only the statutorily enumerated qualifications, but also any other qualifications that may be required to carry out the duties of the Board of Trustees.

(3) The committee serves at the pleasure of the court. The committee will consist of seven members appointed by the court of whom five must be active licensees of the State Bar in good standing, and two must be active or retired judicial officers. A committee chair and vice-chair are designated by the court. The court will seek to create a broadly representative body to assist it in its considerations.

Except as provided below, all full terms are for three years. Members may not serve more than two consecutive full terms. Members will continue to serve until a successor is appointed. Appointments to fill a vacancy will be for the balance of the term vacated. Members who are appointed to fill a vacancy for the balance of a term are eligible to serve two full terms in addition to the remainder of the term for which they were appointed.

To create staggered terms among the members of the committee, the Supreme Court will appoint initial members of the committee as follows:

(A) Four members each to serve a term of three years. The court may reappoint these members to one full term.

(B) Three members each to serve a term of two years. The court may reappoint these members to one full term.

(4) The committee must adopt, and implement upon approval by the Supreme Court, procedures for:

(A) Receipt of applications and initial screening of applicants for appointments to fill the vacant positions, including adoption of a comprehensive application form;

(B) Receipt of evaluations concerning selected applicants;

(C) Evaluation and rating of applicants; and

(D) Transmittal of the materials specified in (b) of this rule to the Supreme Court.

The procedures adopted by the committee must include provisions to ensure the confidentiality of its evaluations.

(5) In recommending candidates, in order to provide for the appointment of trustees who bring to the board a variety of experiences, the committee should consider:

(A) Legal services attorneys, solo practitioners, attorneys with small firms, and attorneys with governmental entities;

(B) Historically underrepresented groups, such as those underrepresented because of race, ethnicity, gender, and sexual orientation;

(C) Legal academics;

(D) Geographic distribution;

(E) Years of practice;

(F) Attorneys who are in their first five years of practice;

(G) Participation in voluntary local or state bar activities;

(H) Participation in activities to benefit the public; and

(I) Other factors demonstrating a background that will help inform the work of the board.

(6) The State Bar must provide the support the committee requires to discharge its obligations under this rule.

(Subd (a) amended effective January 1, 2019; adopted effective January 23, 2013.)

(b) Evaluations

(1) The committee must evaluate the qualifications of and rate all applicants and must submit to the court the nominations of at least three qualified candidates for each vacancy. Candidates are to be rated as "not recommended," "recommended," and "highly recommended." A rating of "not recommended" relates only to the position under consideration and does not indicate any lack of ability or expertise of the applicant generally. The committee must report in confidence to the Supreme Court its evaluation, rating, and recommendation for applicants for appointment and the reasons therefore, including a succinct summary of their qualifications, at a time to be designated by the Supreme Court. The report must include written comments regarding the nominees received by the committee, which must be transmitted to the Supreme Court together with the nominations.

(2) In determining the qualifications of an applicant for appointment or reappointment the committee should, in addition to the factors cited in (a)(5), consider the following: focus on the public interest, public service, commitment to the administration of justice, objectivity, community respect, integrity, ability to work collaboratively, and balanced temperament.

(Subd (b) amended effective January 1, 2019; adopted effective January 23, 2013.)

Rule 9.90 amended effective January 1, 2019; adopted effective January 23, 2013.

TITLE 10
Judicial Administration Rules

Division 1
Judicial Council

Chapter 1
The Judicial Council and Internal Committees

Rule 10.1.   Authority, duties, and goals of the Judicial Council

(a) The Judicial Council

(1) The Judicial Council of California is a state entity established by the California Constitution and chaired by the Chief Justice of California. The Judicial Council sets the direction for improving the quality of justice and advancing the consistent, independent, impartial, and accessible administration of justice by the judicial branch for the benefit of the public.

(2) The council establishes policies and sets priorities for the judicial branch of government. The council may seek advice and recommendations from committees, task forces, and the public.

(3) The Judicial Council Governance Policies are located in Appendix D of these rules of court. The policies describe the council's:

(A) Purposes;

(B) Responsibilities;

(C) Policymaking role;

(D) Members and officers and their roles;

(E) Internal organization;

(F) Relationship with its advisory groups;

(G) Relationship with the Administrative Director and the Judicial Council staff that he or she directs; and

(H) Internal policies and procedures.

(Subd (a) amended effective July 29, 2014; previously amended effective January 1, 2007, and August 14, 2009.)

(b) Constitutional authority and duties

Article VI, section 6 of the California Constitution requires the council to improve the administration of justice by doing the following:

(1) Surveying judicial business;

(2) Making recommendations to the courts;

(3) Making annual recommendations to the Governor and the Legislature;

(4) Adopting rules for court administration and rules of practice and procedure that are not inconsistent with statute; and

(5) Performing other functions prescribed by statute.

(Subd (b) amended effective August 14, 2009.)

(c) Judicial branch goals

The Judicial Council develops judicial branch goals in its strategic and operational plans. At six-year intervals, the council develops and approves a long-range strategic plan. At three-year intervals, the council develops and approves an operational plan for the implementation of the strategic plan. Each plan is developed in consultation with branch stakeholders and justice system partners.

(Subd (c) amended effective August 14, 2009; previously amended effective January 1, 2007.)

(d) Judicial Council staff

The Judicial Council staff supports the council in performing its functions. The Administrative Director is the Secretary of the Judicial Council.

(Subd (d) amended effective July 29, 2014; adopted as subd (e) effective January 1, 1999; previously amended effective January 1, 2007; previously repealed and relettered as subd (d) effective August 14, 2009.)

Rule 10.1 amended effective July 29, 2014; adopted as rule 6.1 effective January 1, 1999; previously amended and renumbered effective January 1, 2007; previously amended effective August 14, 2009.

Rule 10.2.   Judicial Council membership and terms

(a) Constitutional provision on membership and terms

(1) Under article VI, section 6 of the California Constitution, the Judicial Council consists of the Chief Justice and one other justice of the Supreme Court, 3 justices of Courts of Appeal, 10 judges of superior courts, 2 nonvoting court administrators, and such other nonvoting members as determined by the voting membership of the council, each appointed by the Chief Justice to three-year terms; 4 members of the State Bar appointed by its governing body to three-year terms; and 1 member of each house of the Legislature appointed as provided by the house.

(2) Council membership terminates if a member ceases to hold the position that qualified the member for appointment. A vacancy is filled by the appointing power for the remainder of the term.

(Subd (a) amended effective August 14, 2009; previously amended effective January 1, 2007.)

(b) Council officers and duties

(1) *Chair and vice-chair*

(A) The Chief Justice of California is the Chair of the Judicial Council and performs those functions prescribed by the Constitution and the laws of the State of California. The Chair is a voting member of the council. A reference to the Chair of the Judicial Council in the statutes or rules of this state means the Chief Justice of California.

(B) The Chief Justice appoints a vice-chair from among the judicial members of the council. When the chair is absent, unable to serve, or so directs, the vice-chair performs all of the duties of the chair.

(C) The Chief Justice appoints a Judicial Council member to serve as chair of the council in the event that both the Chief Justice and the council vice-chair are absent or unable to serve. The Chief Justice determines individuals to serve as chair from among the internal committee chairs and vice-chairs.

(2) *Chairs and vice-chairs of the internal committees*

The Judicial Council has five internal committees composed of Judicial Council members, as specified in rule 10.10. The Chief Justice appoints for a one-year term the chair and vice-chair of each of the council's internal committees. Chairs call meetings, as necessary, and provide reports to the council on the activities of the internal committees.

(3) *Officers*

The Judicial Council has eight officers: the chair, vice-chair, secretary, and the chairs of the council's five internal committees.

(4) *Administrative Director*

The Administrative Director is the secretary to the Judicial Council and performs administrative and policymaking functions as provided by the Constitution and the laws of the State of California and as delegated by the Judicial Council and the Chief Justice. The secretary is not a voting member of the council.

(Subd (b) amended effective January 1, 2016; previously amended effective August 14, 2009.)

(c) Role of members

(1) Council members are a governing body for California's judicial branch of government. In accepting appointment, they commit themselves to act in the best interest of the public and the judicial system for the purposes of maintaining and enhancing public access to the justice system, as well as preserving and enhancing impartial judicial decisionmaking and an independent judicial branch of government.

(2) Council members do not represent any particular constituency notwithstanding any of their other affiliations or roles.

(3) Council members communicate as representatives of the Judicial Council with the public, the courts, judicial officers, Judicial Council advisory bodies, other government entities, and justice system partners. They communicate about the council's processes, purposes, responsibilities, and issues and reasons for policy decisions, including those policy decisions where there is disagreement.

(Subd (c) amended effective August 14, 2009.)

(d) Terms

Council members are appointed to terms beginning September 15 and ending September 14. Terms for judge members are staggered. To the extent feasible, the State Bar and the Legislature should create staggered terms for their appointees.

(e) Restrictions on advisory committee membership

Unless otherwise provided by these rules or the Chief Justice waives this provision, neither council members nor nonvoting advisory council members may concurrently serve on a council advisory committee. This provision does not apply to members of the following advisory committees:

(1) Administrative Presiding Justices;

(2) Trial Court Presiding Judges; and

(3) Court Executives.

(Subd (e) amended effective January 1, 2015; previously amended effective January 1, 2007, and August 14, 2009.)

Rule 10.2 amended effective January 1, 2016; adopted as rule 6.2 effective January 1, 1999; previously amended and renumbered as rule 10.2 effective January 1, 2007; previously amended effective August 14, 2009, and January 1, 2015.

Rule 10.3.   Nonvoting members

(a) Appointment

The Chief Justice appoints nonvoting advisory council members as specified in article VI, section 6 of the California Constitution or as approved by the Judicial Council.

(b) Voting

A nonvoting council member may make or second motions at a council meeting but may not vote. A nonvoting member may vote on an internal committee matter as specified in rule 10.10(e).

(Subd (b) amended effective September 1, 2017; previously amended January 1, 2007.)

Rule 10.3 amended effective September 1, 2017; adopted as rule 6.3 effective January 1, 1999; previously amended and renumbered effective January 1, 2007.

Rule 10.4.   Nominations and appointments to the Judicial Council

(a) Nomination procedures

The Executive and Planning Committee assists the Chief Justice in selecting council members by submitting a list of nominees for each position. The committee uses the following procedures:

(1) The committee publicizes vacancies and solicits nominations. Nominations for advisory member positions are solicited from the Court Executives Advisory Committee, the Appellate Court Clerks Association, the California Court Commissioners Association, and other related bodies. The selected nominees should represent diverse backgrounds, experiences, and geographic locations.

(2) The committee submits a list of at least three nominees to the Chief Justice for each vacant position, except for the Supreme Court associate justice position. The committee gives added consideration to persons who have served on advisory committees or task forces.

(3) If the Chief Justice is a member of the Executive and Planning Committee, the Chief Justice does not participate in discussions relating to nominations.

(Subd (a) amended effective January 1, 2007.)

(b) Appointing order

The Chief Justice makes appointments to the council by order.

Rule 10.4 amended and renumbered effective January 1, 2007; adopted as rule 6.4 effective January 1, 1999.

Rule 10.5.   Notice and agenda of council meetings

(a) Generally

The Judicial Council meets at the call of the Chief Justice no fewer than four times a year.

(Subd (a) amended effective January 1, 2004.)

(b) Meeting schedule

The Judicial Council must publish a regular annual schedule that states the planned date and location of each meeting. Additional meetings may be scheduled as necessary.

(Subd (b) amended effective January 1, 2016; previously amended effective January 1, 2004, and January 1, 2007.)

(c) Notice of business meetings

"Business meetings" are council meetings at which a majority of voting members are present to discuss and decide matters within the council's jurisdiction. The Judicial Council must give public notice of the date, location, and agenda of each business meeting at least seven days before the meeting. The notice must state whether the meeting is open or closed. If the meeting is partly closed, the notice must indicate which agenda items are closed. A meeting may be conducted without notice in case of an emergency requiring prompt action.

(Subd (c) amended effective January 1, 2016; previously amended effective January 1, 2004.)

(d) Budget meetings

A "budget meeting" is that portion of any business meeting at which trial court budgets are to be discussed. The Judicial Council must provide notice of a budget meeting in the same manner as any other business meeting. Budget meetings normally are scheduled as follows:

(1) A budget priority meeting, normally in February of each year, at which the Judicial Council adopts budget priorities for the trial courts for the budget year that begins July 1 of the next calendar year.

(2) A meeting at which the proposed budget is approved, normally in August of each year, at which the Judicial Council takes action on the following:

(A) Staff recommendations on trial court budget change requests for the next fiscal year;

(B) A total baseline budget for each trial court for the next fiscal year; and

(C) Any proposed changes in funding for a trial court.

(3) A budget allocation meeting, normally at the first council meeting after the state's budget is enacted, at which the Judicial Council approves the final budget allocations for each trial court, including approved budget adjustments.

(4) Other meetings following substantive changes to the trial court portion of the proposed State Budget made by the Governor in the proposed Governor's budget or by a committee or house of the Legislature, at which the Judicial Council will take appropriate action, if any.

(Subd (d) amended effective January 1, 2016; adopted effective January 1, 2004.)

(e) Form of notice

The notice and agenda for council meetings must be posted on the California Courts website (*www.courts.ca.gov*). In addition, the notice and agenda for budget meetings must be provided to designated employee representatives who have submitted a written request to the Judicial Council (attention Judicial Council Support).

(Subd (e) amended effective January 1, 2016; adopted as subd (d) effective January 1, 1999; previously amended and relettered as subd (e) effective January 1, 2004; previously amended effective January 1, 2007.)

(f) Contents of agenda

The agenda must contain a brief description of each item to be considered at the council meeting. All items are classified as discussion items, consent items, or informational items.

(1) *Consent items deemed approved*

All consent items are deemed approved without further action at the adjournment of each council meeting.

(2) *Moving consent items to discussion agenda*

A consent item must be moved to the discussion agenda if a council member so requests by giving 48 hours' advance notice to the Executive and Planning Committee, or if the Chief Justice moves the item to the discussion agenda.

(Subd (f) amended and relettered effective January 1, 2004; adopted as subd (e) effective January 1, 1999.)

(g) Meeting materials

(1) *General materials*

General meeting materials must be distributed to council members at least three business days before the date of the meeting, except in extraordinary circumstances. The Administrative Director may make copies of materials available to the media or attendees in advance of a business meeting and may specify that the materials are provided on agreement by the recipient that they will be kept confidential until the council has discussed or acted on specified items. The council may charge a fee to cover the costs of replicating and mailing these materials to members of the public.

(2) *Budget materials*

(A) *When available*

Materials involving trial court budgets must be made available at least five business days before the meeting if they have been distributed by that time to the members of the council. All other materials involving trial court budgets must be made available at the same time as the information is distributed to the council.

(B) *Distribution*

Materials must be made available by posting on the California Courts website and by distribution to designated employee representatives who have submitted a written request to the Judicial Council of California (attention Judicial Council Support).

(C) *Contents at the budget approval meeting*

Materials involving trial court budget proposals presented at the budget approval meeting must include proposed statewide requests for funding, existing trial court baseline budgets, adjustments proposed for any trial court baseline budget, and any court-specific budget change requests.

(Subd (g) amended effective January 1, 2016; adopted as subd (f) effective January 1, 1999; previously amended and relettered effective January 1, 2004; previously amended effective January 1, 2007.)

(h) Circulating orders

Between business meetings, the council may act by circulating order on urgent matters if the Chief Justice or the Administrative Director approves. Prior public notice of a proposed circulating order is not required. Each circulating order adopted by the council must be included on the agenda for the next business meeting as an information item.

(Subd (h) amended and relettered effective January 1, 2004; adopted as subd (g) effective January 1, 1999.)

Rule 10.5 amended effective January 1, 2016; adopted as rule 6.5 effective January 1, 1999; previously amended effective January 1, 2004; previously amended and renumbered as rule 10.5 effective January 1, 2007.

Rule 10.6.   Judicial Council meetings

(a) Open meeting policy

Business meetings are open to the public unless they are closed under (b). Other meetings, such as orientation, planning, and educational meetings, may be made open to the public at the discretion of the Chief Justice. The Chief Justice may seek a recommendation from the Executive and Planning Committee on whether all or part of any meeting should be open or closed. Any discussion or decision of the full council at a business meeting regarding a trial court budget allocation must take place in an open meeting of the council, except for an executive session as provided in (b).

(Subd (a) amended effective January 1, 2007; previously amended effective January 1, 2004.)

(b) Closed sessions

The Chief Justice may close all or part of a business meeting because of the nature of the meeting or of matters to be discussed. The following matters will ordinarily be discussed in closed session:

(1) A personnel matter or a discussion of the character, competence, or physical or mental health of an individual;

(2) Claims or litigation in which the Judicial Council has an interest;

(3) Contract, labor, or legislative negotiations;

(4) The purchase, sale, or lease of real property;

(5) Security plans or procedures;

(6) Allegations of criminal or professional misconduct; and

(7) Discussions protected by the attorney-client privilege.

(c) Conduct at meeting

Members of the public who attend open meetings must remain orderly. The Chief Justice may order the removal of any disorderly persons.

(Subd (c) amended effective January 1, 2004.)

(d) Requests to speak—general

The Executive and Planning Committee, in its discretion, may allow a member of the public to speak at a business meeting. Unless the Chief Justice waives this requirement, any member of the public who wishes to speak at a business meeting must submit a request of no more than two pages to the chair of the Executive and Planning Committee by delivering it to the Judicial Council (attention Judicial Council Support) at least four business days before the meeting.

(1) *Contents of the request*

The request must include the following:

(A) A description of the agenda item to be addressed;

(B) A specific recitation of the proposed statement with an explanation of its relevance to the agenda item and the reasons it would be of benefit to the council in its deliberations;

(C) The name, residence, and occupation of the person asking to speak and, if applicable, the name, address, and purpose of the agency or organization that the speaker represents;

(D) If available, telephone and fax numbers and e-mail address of the person asking to speak and, if applicable and available, the telephone, fax numbers, and e-mail address of the agency or organization that the speaker represents;

(E) The words "Request to Speak at Judicial Council Meeting" displayed prominently in letters at least one-quarter-inch high on the envelope containing the request; and

(F) A copy of any written materials the speaker proposes to distribute at the meeting.

(2) *Notice of decision*

The Executive and Planning Committee must respond to the request at least two business days before the meeting. The committee may grant the request in part or whole, request additional information, circulate any written materials, or take other action it deems appropriate.

(Subd (d) amended effective January 1, 2016; previously amended effective January 1, 2004, and January 1, 2007.)

(e) Presentation of information on trial court budget matters

(1) *Presentation of written information*

Any designated employee representative has a right to provide written information on trial court budget allocations to the council.

(2) *Oral presentation*

Any designated employee representative who wishes to make an oral presentation to the Judicial Council must make a written request to the Judicial Council of California (attention Judicial Council Support) no later than 24 hours before the meeting unless the issue has arisen within the last five business days before the meeting, in which case the written request may be made on the day of the meeting.

(3) *Limit on number and time*

The Chief Justice or his or her designee may limit the number and time of speakers in order to avoid cumulative discussion.

(Subd (e) amended effective January 1, 2016; adopted effective January 1, 2004; previously amended effective January 1, 2007.)

(f) Video recording, photographing, and broadcasting at meeting

The Chief Justice may permit video recording, photographing, or broadcasting of a meeting. Any such video recording, photographing, or broadcasting is subject to regulations that ensure the meeting's security and dignity. A request to record, photograph, or broadcast a council meeting must be received by the Chief Justice at least two business days before the meeting.

(Subd (f) relettered effective January 1, 2004; adopted as subd (e) effective January 1, 1999.)

(g) Minutes as official records

The Secretary of the Judicial Council must prepare written minutes of each council meeting for approval at the next council meeting. When approved by the council, the minutes constitute the official record of the meeting.

(Subd (g) amended and relettered effective January 1, 2004; adopted as subd (f) effective January 1, 1999.)

Rule 10.6 amended effective January 1, 2016; adopted as rule 6.6 effective January 1, 1999; previously amended effective January 1, 2004; previously amended and renumbered as rule 10.6 effective January 1, 2007.

Rule 10.10.   Judicial Council internal committees

(a) Judicial Council internal committees

The internal committees are:

(1) Executive and Planning Committee;

(2) [1] **Legislation** Committee;

(3) Rules [2] Committee;

(4) Litigation Management Committee;

(5) Technology Committee; and

(6) Judicial Branch Budget Committee.

(Subd (a) amended effective April 16, 2020; adopted effective August 14, 2009, previously amended effective February 20, 2014, and January 1, 2019.)

Rule 10.10(a). 2020 Deletes. [1] Policy Coordination and Liaison [2] and Projects

(b) Purpose of the internal committees

The internal committees of the Judicial Council assist the full membership of the council in its responsibilities by providing recommendations in their assigned areas, including rules for court administration, practice, and procedure, and by performing duties delegated by the council. Internal committees generally work at the same policy level as the council, focusing on the establishment of policies that emphasize long-term strategic leadership and that align with judicial branch goals.

(Subd (b) repealed and adopted effective August 14, 2009.)

(c) Membership and appointment

The Chief Justice appoints each council member and advisory council member to one or more internal committees for a one-year term.

(Subd (c) relettered effective August 14, 2009; adopted as subd (a) effective January 1, 1999; previously amended effective January 1, 2007.)

(d) Meetings

Each internal committee meets as often as necessary to perform its responsibilities. The Administrative Director, as secretary of the Judicial Council, may attend and participate in the meetings of each internal committee.

(Subd (d) amended effective January 1, 2016; adopted as subd (c) effective January 1, 1999; previously amended and relettered as subd (d) effective August 14, 2009.)

(e) Voting

An advisory council member may vote on any internal committee matter unless the committee is taking final action on behalf of the council.

(Subd (e) relettered effective August 14, 2009; adopted as subd (d) effective January 1, 1999.)

(f) Council review

The council may overrule or modify an action taken by an internal committee.

(Subd (f) relettered effective August 14, 2009; adopted as subd (e) effective January 1, 1999.)

(g) Reporting to the council

As often as necessary, each internal committee must report to the council on the committee's activities.

(Subd (g) relettered effective August 14, 2009; adopted as subd (f) effective January 1, 1999; previously amended effective January 1, 2007.)

(h) Oversight of advisory committees and other bodies

When an internal committee has been assigned by the Chief Justice with the responsibility for oversight over one or more advisory committees or other bodies, the internal committee ensures that the activities of each advisory body overseen by it are consistent with the council's goals and policies. To achieve these outcomes, the internal committee:

(1) Communicates the council's annual charge to each advisory body;

(2) Reviews the proposed annual agenda of each to determine whether the agenda is consistent with the advisory body's charge and with the priorities established by the council; and

(3) After review, approves the final annual agenda for each advisory body.

(Subd (h) adopted effective January 1, 2019.)

Rule 10.10 amended effective April 16, 2020; adopted as rule 6.10 effective January 1, 1999; previously amended and renumbered as rule 10.10 effective January 1, 2007; previously amended effective August 14, 2009, February 20, 2014, January 1, 2016, and January 1, 2019.

Rule 10.11. Executive and Planning Committee

(a) Actions on behalf of the Judicial Council

The Executive and Planning Committee may take action on behalf of the council between council meetings, except for:

(1) Adopting rules of court, standards of judicial administration, and forms;

(2) Making appointments that by statute must be made by the council; and

(3) Taking actions that are delegated to other council internal committees.

(Subd (a) adopted effective August 14, 2009.)

2009 Note: Subdivision (a) was derived from former subdivision (d).

(b) Planning

The committee oversees the council's strategic planning process.

(Subd (b) adopted effective August 14, 2009.)

2009 Note: Subdivision (b) was derived from former subdivision (e).

(c) Court facilities

The committee oversees the council's policies and procedures regarding court facilities, including development of policies, procedures, and guidelines for facilities; site selection; and capital appropriations.

(Subd (c) adopted effective August 14, 2009.)

(d) Agendas for council meetings

The committee establishes agendas for council meetings by determining:

(1) Whether items submitted for the council's agenda require the council's action and are presented in a form that provides the council with the information it needs to make well-informed decisions; and

(2) Whether each item should be on the consent, discussion, or information agenda; how much time should be allotted for discussion; what presenters should be invited to speak; and, when appropriate, which specific issues should be discussed.

(Subd (d) repealed and relettered effective January 1, 2019; adopted as subd (e) effective August 14, 2009.)

(e) Topics for making policy and receiving updates

The committee develops a schedule of topics that the council intends to consider for making policy and receives updates from the Administrative Director or Judicial Council staff.

(Subd (e) relettered effective January 1, 2019; adopted as subd (f) effective August 14, 2009; previously amended effective January 1, 2016.)

(f) Governance

The committee makes recommendations to the council regarding governance and oversees the council's review of its governance policies and principles.

(Subd (f) relettered effective January 1, 2019; adopted as subd (g) effective August 14, 2009.)

(g) Nominations

The committee recommends candidates to the Chief Justice for appointment to the Judicial Council and its advisory bodies.

(Subd (g) relettered effective January 1, 2019; adopted as subd (h) effective August 14, 2009.)

(h) Communications

The committee promotes effective policies for communications between the Judicial Council and the judicial branch.

(Subd (h) relettered effective January 1, 2019; adopted as subd (j) effective August 14, 2009.)

Rule 10.11 amended effective January 1, 2019; adopted as rule 6.11 effective January 1, 1999; previously amended and renumbered as rule 10.11 effective January 1, 2007; previously amended effective January 1, 2002, September 1, 2003, January 1, 2005, August 14, 2009, and January 1, 2016.

Rule 10.12. Legislation Committee

(a) Legislative activities

The [1] **Legislation** Committee performs the following functions:

(1) Taking a position on behalf of the council on pending legislative bills, after evaluating input from the council advisory bodies and Judicial Council staff, and any other input received from the courts, provided that the position is consistent with the council's established policies and precedents;

(2) Making recommendations to the council on all proposals for council-sponsored legislation and on an annual legislative agenda after evaluating input from council advisory bodies and Judicial Council staff, and any other input received from the courts; and

(3) Representing the council's position before the Legislature and other bodies or agencies and acting as liaison with other governmental entities, the bar, the media, the judiciary, and the public regarding council-sponsored legislation, pending legislative bills, and the council's legislative positions and agendas.

(Subd (a) amended effective April 16, 2020; adopted as subd (b); previously amended effective September 1, 2003, and January 1, 2016; previously amended and relettered as subd (a) effective August 14, 2009.)

Rule 10.12(a). 2020 Deletes. [1] Policy Coordination and Liaison

(b) Building consensus

The committee builds consensus on issues of importance to the judicial branch consistent with the council's strategic plan with entities and individuals outside of the branch.

(Subd (b) adopted effective August 14, 2009.)

(c) Coordination

The committee develops an annual plan for communication and interaction with other branches and levels of government, components of the justice system, the bar, the media, and the public.

(Subd (c) amended effective August 14, 2009; previously amended effective September 1, 2003.)

(d) Advisory committees

The committee may direct any advisory committee to provide it with analysis or recommendations on any pending or proposed legislation, and reviews all recommendations from advisory committees regarding pending or proposed legislation.

(Subd (d) amended effective January 1, 2007; adopted effective September 1, 2003.)

Rule 10.12 amended effective April 16, 2020; adopted as rule 6.12 effective January 1, 1999; previously amended and renumbered as rule 10.12 effective January 1, 2007; previously amended effective September 1, 2003, August 14, 2009, and January 1, 2016.

Rule 10.13. Rules Committee

(a) Rules, standards, and forms

The Rules [1] Committee establishes and maintains a rule-making process that is understandable and accessible to justice system partners and the public. The committee:

(1) Identifies the need for new rules, standards, and forms;

(2) Establishes and publishes procedures for the proposal, adoption, and approval of rules of court, forms, and standards of judicial administration that ensure that relevant input from the public is solicited and considered;

(3) Reviews proposed rules, standards, and forms and circulates those proposals for public comment in accordance with its procedures and guidelines.

(4) Provides guidelines for the style and format of rules, forms, and standards and ensures that proposals are consistent with the guidelines;

(5) Ensures that proposals for new or amended rules, standards, and forms do not conflict with statutes or other rules; and

(6) Determines whether proposals for new or amended rules, standards, or forms have complied with its procedures.

(Subd (a) amended effective April 16, 2020; adopted effective August 14, 2009.)

Rule 10.13(a). 2020 Deletes. [1] and Projects

(b) Jury instructions

The committee establishes and maintains a process for obtaining public comment on the jury instructions and assists the council in making informed decisions about jury instructions.

(Subd (b) adopted effective August 14, 2009.)

2009 Note: Subdivision (b) was derived from former subdivision (d).

(c) Recommendations

The Rules [1] Committee assists the council in making informed decisions about rules of court, forms, standards of judicial administration, and jury instructions. The committee:

(1) Recommends whether the council should approve, modify, or reject each proposal;

(2) Recommends to the Executive and Planning Committee whether a proposal should be on the council's consent or discussion agenda and how much time should be allocated for discussion; and

(3) When appropriate, identifies issues for discussion.

If the Rules [2] Committee recommends against approval, it states the reasons for its recommendation.

(Subd (c) amended effective April 16, 2020; adopted effective August 14, 2009.)

Rule 10.13(c). 2020 Deletes. [1] and Projects **[2]** and Projects

2009 Note: Subdivision (c) was derived from former subdivision (b).

(d) Circulating orders

The committee initiates circulating orders to allow the council to adopt rules, standards, and forms between council meetings, if necessary.

(Subd (d) adopted effective August 14, 2009.)

(e) Responsibility of the Administrative Director

The Administrative Director is responsible for ensuring that items submitted to the committee for circulation for comment and the council's agenda comply with the committee's procedures and its guidelines on format and style.

(Subd (e) repealed and relettered effective January 1, 2019; adopted as subd (f) effective August 14, 2009; previously amended January 1, 2016.)

Rule 10.13 amended effective April 16, 2020; adopted as rule 6.13 effective January 1, 1999; previously amended and renumbered as rule 10.13 effective January 1, 2007; previously amended effective September 1, 2003, August 14, 2009, January 1, 2016, and January 1, 2019.

Rule 10.14. Litigation Management Committee

(a) Litigation oversight

The Litigation Management Committee oversees litigation and claims against trial court judges, appellate court justices, the Judicial Council, its staff, the trial and appellate courts, and the employees of those bodies in which the likely monetary exposure is $100,000 or more or that raise issues of significance to the judicial branch by:

(1) Reviewing and approving any proposed settlement, stipulated judgment, or offer of judgment; and

(2) Consulting with the Administrative Director or Chief Counsel, on request, regarding important strategy issues.

(Subd (a) amended effective January 1, 2016; previously amended effective January 1, 2003, January 1, 2007, December 9, 2008, and August 14, 2009.)

(b) Recommendations

The committee makes recommendations to the Judicial Council for policies governing the management of litigation involving the courts.

(Subd (b) amended effective August 14, 2009.)

(c) Strategic decisions

The committee resolves written objections described in rule 10.202(d) presented by Legal Services.

(Subd (c) amended effective January 1, 2016; adopted effective January 1, 2003; previously amended effective January 1, 2007, and August 14, 2009.)

Rule 10.14 amended effective January 1, 2016; adopted as rule 6.14 effective January 1, 2001; previously amended and renumbered as rule 10.14 effective January 1, 2007; previously amended effective January 1, 2003, December 9, 2008, and August 14, 2009.

Rule 10.15. Interim Court Facilities Panel [Repealed]

Rule 10.15 repealed by its own provision effective June 30, 2007; adopted as rule 6.15 effective June 23, 2004; previously amended and renumbered effective January 1, 2007.

Another Rule 10.15 follows.

Rule 10.15. Judicial Branch Budget Committee

(a) Purpose

The Judicial Branch Budget Committee assists the council to exercise its responsibilities under rule 10.101 with respect to the branch budget.

(Subd (a) adopted effective January 1, 2019.)

(b) Budget responsibilities

In assisting the council on the branch budget, the committee:

(1) Ensures that proposed judicial branch budgets, allocation schedules, and related budgetary issues are brought to the Judicial Council in a timely manner and in a format that permits the council to establish funding priorities in the context of the council's annual program objectives, statewide policies, and long-range strategic and operational plans;

(2) Reviews and makes recommendations annually to the council on submitted budget change proposals for the judicial branch, coordinates these budget change proposals, and ensures that they are submitted to the council in a timely manner;

(3) Reviews and makes recommendations on the use of statewide emergency funding for the judicial branch;

(4) Reviews and makes recommendations on the funding of grants on programs assigned to the committee; and

(5) Acts on other assignments referred to it by the council.

(Subd (b) adopted effective January 1, 2019.)

Rule 10.15 adopted effective January 1, 2019.

Rule 10.16. Technology Committee

(a) Technology policies

The Technology Committee oversees the council's policies concerning information technology. The committee assists the council by providing technology recommendations focusing on the establishment of policies that emphasize long-term strategic leadership and that align with judicial branch goals. The committee is responsible for determining that council policies are complied with on specific projects approved and funded by the council and that those projects proceed on schedule and within scope and budget.

(Subd (a) amended effective September 1, 2015; adopted effective February 20, 2014.)

(b) Coordination

The committee coordinates the activities of the Administrative Director, council internal committees and advisory committees, the courts, justice partners, and stakeholders on matters relating to court information technology. The committee also, in collaboration or consultation with the

[1] Legislation Committee, coordinates with other branches of government on information technology issues.

(Subd (b) amended effective April 16, 2020; previously amended effective September 1, 2015, and January 1, 2016.)

Rule 10.16(b). 2020 Deletes. [1] Policy Coordination and Liaison

(c) Reports

The committee seeks reports and recommendations from the Administrative Director, the courts, and stakeholders on information technology issues. It ensures that information technology reports to the council are clear, are comprehensive, and provide relevant options so that the council can make effective final information technology policy decisions.

(Subd (c) adopted effective February 20, 2014.)

(d) Strategic and tactical technology plans

(1) *Strategic technology plan*

The strategic technology plan describes the technology goals for the branch. With input from advisory committees and individual courts, the committee is responsible for developing and recommending a strategic technology plan for the branch and the courts.

(2) *Tactical technology plan*

The tactical technology plan outlines the technology initiatives and projects that provide a road map for achieving the goals in the strategic technology plan. The committee provides oversight approval and prioritization of the tactical technology plan, which is developed and recommended by advisory committees with input from the courts.

(Subd (d) adopted effective September 1, 2015.)

(e) Technology needs, standards, and systems

The committee will, in partnership with the courts, develop timelines and recommendations to the council for:

(1) Establishing an approach and vision for implementing information technology that serves the courts, litigants, attorneys, justice partners, and the public, while considering available resources and information technology needs;

(2) Improving judicial branch information technology governance to best serve the implementation of technological solutions;

(3) Reviewing and recommending information technology standards; and

(4) Encouraging the courts to leverage their collective economic purchasing power in acquiring technological systems.

(Subd (e) amended and relettered effective September 1, 2015; adopted as subd (d) effective February 20, 2014.)

(f) Sponsorship of branchwide technology initiatives

The committee may act as executive sponsor of branchwide technology initiatives under the workstream model in rule 10.53(c).

(Subd (f) adopted effective September 1, 2015.)

(g) Funding of branchwide technology initiatives and projects

The committee reviews, prioritizes, and recommends requests for the funding of branchwide technology initiatives and projects with input from advisory committees. Factors to be considered by the committee include overall return on investment, business risk, alignment with the technology goals approved by the council in the strategic technology plan, and the availability of sufficient funding from an identifiable funding source.

(Subd (g) adopted effective September 1, 2015.)

(h) Collaboration and consultation with the committee

Other committees and advisory bodies should collaborate or consult with the committee (1) before making decisions or recommendations on technology policies, standards, and projects, and (2) before recommending funding priorities or making recommendations to approve funding requests for branchwide technology initiatives and projects.

(Subd (h) adopted effective September 1, 2015.)

(i) Oversight of advisory committees and other bodies

In addition to performing its oversight responsibilities under rule 10.10(h), the Technology Committee oversees the branchwide technology initiatives sponsored by each advisory body for which it is responsible.

(Subd (i) amended effective January 1, 2019; adopted as subd (e) effective February 20, 2014; previously amended and relettered effective September 1, 2015.)

Rule 10.16 amended effective April 16, 2020; adopted effective February 20, 2014; previously amended effective September 1, 2015, January 1, 2016, and January 1, 2019.

Rule 10.20. Proposals for new or amended rules, standards, or forms; rule-making process in general

(a) Council meetings to consider proposals

The Judicial Council meets twice a year, generally in April and October, to consider proposals for the adoption, amendment, or repeal of California Rules of Court, California Standards of Judicial Administration, and Judicial Council forms.

(b) Proposals

The council will consider proposals that are submitted to it by an internal committee, an advisory committee, a task force, or Judicial Council staff, in accordance with rule 10.22 and any policies and procedures established by the Rules [1] Committee.

(Subd (b) amended effective April 16, 2020; repealed and adopted effective January 1, 2002; previously amended effective January 1, 2007, and January 1, 2016.)

Rule 10.20(b). 2020 Deletes. [1] and Projects

(c) Statewide uniformity

The council will establish uniform statewide practices and procedures where appropriate to achieve equal access to justice throughout California.

(Subd (c) relettered effective January 1, 2002; adopted as subd (g) effective January 1, 1999.)

Rule 10.20 amended effective April 16, 2020; adopted as rule 6.20 effective January 1, 1999; previously amended effective January 1, 2002, and January 1, 2016; previously amended and renumbered as rule 10.20 effective January 1, 2007.

Rule 10.21. Proposals from members of the public for changes to rules, standards, or forms

(a) Application

This rule applies to proposals for changes to rules, standards, or forms by a member of the public (any person or organization other than a Judicial Council internal committee, advisory committee, or task force, or Judicial Council staff).

(Subd (a) amended effective January 1, 2016.)

(b) Submission and content of proposals

Proposals must be submitted in writing to: Judicial Council of California, Attention: Chief Counsel. Proposals should include:

(1) The text of the proposed rule, standard, form, or amendment;

(2) A description of the problem to be addressed;

(3) The proposed solution and alternative solutions;

(4) Any likely implementation problems;

(5) Any need for urgent consideration;

(6) Known proponents and opponents;

(7) Any known fiscal impact; and

(8) If known, any previous action by the council or an advisory committee on the proposal.

(Subd (b) amended effective January 1, 2016.)

(c) Advisory committee's review of proposal

The Chief Counsel must refer each proposal from a member of the public to an appropriate advisory committee for consideration and recommendation, or, if no appropriate advisory committee exists, to the Rules [1] Committee. A Judicial Council staff member may independently review the proposal and present an analysis and a recommendation to the committee. The committee may take one of the following actions:

(1) Accept the proposal, either as submitted or modified, and proceed under rule 10.22;

(2) Request further information or analysis; or

(3) Reject the proposal.

(Subd (c) amended effective April 16, 2020; previously amended effective January 1, 2007, and January 1, 2016.)

Rule 10.21(c). 2020 Deletes. [1] and Projects

Rule 10.21 amended effective April 16, 2020; adopted as rule 6.21 effective January 1, 2002; previously amended and renumbered as rule 10.21 effective January 1, 2007; previously amended effective January 1, 2016.

Rule 10.22. Rule-making procedures

(a) Who may make proposals

A Judicial Council internal committee, advisory committee, task force, or Judicial Council staff may recommend that the council adopt, amend, or repeal a rule or standard or adopt, approve, revise, or revoke a form.

(Subd (a) amended effective January 1, 2016; previously amended effective January 1, 2007.)

(b) Legal and advisory committee review

The internal committee, advisory committee, task force, or Judicial Council staff (the proponent) must first submit its proposal to Legal Services for legal and drafting review. If the proponent is not an advisory committee, and an appropriate advisory committee exists, the proponent must also submit the proposal to that advisory committee for review.

(Subd (b) amended effective January 1, 2016; previously amended effective January 1, 2007.)

(c) Recommendation to Rules Committee

After the proposal has been reviewed by Legal Services and any appropriate advisory committee, the proponent must submit the proposal to the Rules [1] Committee with a recommendation that it be (1) circulated for public comment or (2) submitted to the council for approval without public comment.

(Subd (c) amended effective April 16, 2020; previously amended effective January 1, 2016.)

Rule 10.22(c).   2020 Deletes. [1] and Projects

(d) Review by Rules Committee

The Rules [1] Committee must review the recommendation and may take one of the following actions:

(1) Circulate the proposal for public comment;

(2) If the proposal presents a nonsubstantive technical change or correction or a minor substantive change that is unlikely to create controversy, recommend that the council adopt it without circulating it for comment;

(3) Postpone circulation for comment and either request further information or analysis by the proponent or refer the matter to another council internal or advisory committee, the full council, or the Chief Justice; or

(4) Reject the proposal if it is contrary to statute, conflicts with other rules or standards, or is contrary to established council policy.

(Subd (d) amended April 16, 2020; previously amended effective January 1, 2007.)

Rule 10.22(d).   2020 Deletes. [1] and Projects

(e) Review of comments

After a proposal is circulated, the proponent must review the comments and decide whether to reject the proposal or to recommend that the council adopt it, with or without modifications.

(f) Submission to council

If, after reviewing the comments, the proponent recommends that the council adopt the proposal, the matter will be placed on the council's agenda. The Rules [1] Committee must review the recommendation and submit its own recommendation to the council. The council may adopt, modify, or reject the proposal.

(Subd (f) amended effective April 16, 2020.)

Rule 10.22(f).   2020 Deletes. [1] and Projects

(g) Compelling circumstances

The procedures established in this rule must be followed unless the Rules [1] Committee finds that compelling circumstances necessitate a different procedure. The committee's finding and a summary of the procedure used must be presented to the council with any recommendation to the council made under this subdivision.

(Subd (g) amended effective April 16, 2020.)

Rule 10.22(g).   2020 Deletes. [1] and Projects

Rule 10.22 amended effective April 16, 2020; adopted as rule 6.22 effective January 1, 2002; previously amended and renumbered as rule 10.22 effective January 1, 2007; previously amended effective January 16, 2016.

Chapter 2
Judicial Council Advisory Committees and Task Forces

Rule 10.30.   Judicial Council advisory bodies

(a) Types of bodies

Judicial Council advisory bodies are typically advisory committees and task forces.

(Subd (a) adopted effective August 14, 2009.)

(b) Functions

The advisory bodies:

(1) Use the individual and collective experience, opinions, and wisdom of their members to provide policy recommendations and advice to the council on topics the Chief Justice or the council specifies;

(2) Work at the same policy level as the council, developing recommendations that focus on strategic goals and long-term impacts that align with judicial branch goals;

(3) Generally do not implement policy. The council may, however, assign policy-implementation and programmatic responsibilities to an advisory body and may request it make recommendations to the Administrative Director on implementation of council policy or programs;

(4) Do not speak or act for the council except when formally given such authority for specific and time-limited purposes; and

(5) Are responsible, through Judicial Council staff, for gathering stakeholder perspectives on policy recommendations they plan to present to the council.

(Subd (b) amended effective January 1, 2016; adopted effective August 14, 2009.)

2009 Note: Subdivision (b) was derived from former subdivision (b).

(c) Subcommittees

With the approval of the internal committee with oversight responsibility for the advisory body, an advisory body may form subcommittees, composed entirely of members, to carry out the body's duties, subject to available resources.

(Subd (c) amended effective February 20, 2014; adopted effective August 14, 2009.)

2009 Note: Subdivision (c) was derived from former subdivision (e).

(d) Oversight

The Chief Justice assigns oversight of each council advisory body to an internal committee. The council gives a general charge to each advisory body specifying the body's subject matter jurisdiction. The council and its internal committees provide direction to the advisory bodies.

(Subd (d) adopted effective August 14, 2009.)

(e) Preference for using existing advisory committees

Unless substantial reasons dictate otherwise, new projects requiring committee involvement must be assigned to existing advisory committees.

(Subd (e) adopted effective August 14, 2009.)

2009 Note: Subdivision (e) was derived from former subdivision (f).

(f) Role of the Administrative Director

The Administrative Director sits as an ex officio member of each advisory body.

(Subd (f) amended effective January 1, 2016; adopted effective August 14, 2009.)

(g) Creation

In addition to the advisory committees established by the rules in this division, the Chief Justice may create additional advisory bodies by order.

(Subd (g) adopted effective August 14, 2009.)

2009 Note: Subdivision (g) was derived from former subdivision (a).

Rule 10.30 amended effective January 1, 2016; adopted as rule 6.30 effective January 1, 1999; previously amended and renumbered as rule 10.30 effective January 1, 2007; previously amended effective September 1, 2003, August 14, 2009, and February 20, 2014.

Rule 10.31.   Advisory committee membership and terms

(a) Membership

The categories of membership of each advisory committee are specified in the rules in this chapter. Each advisory committee consists of between 12 and 18 members, unless a different number is specified by the

Chief Justice or required by these rules. Advisory committee members do not represent a specific constituency but must act in the best interests of the public and the entire court system.

(Subd (a) amended effective September 1, 2003.)

(b) Terms

The Chief Justice appoints advisory committee members to three-year terms unless another term is specified in these rules or in the order appointing a member. Terms are staggered so that an approximately equal number of each committee's members changes annually. Members may apply for reappointment but there is no presumption of reappointment. All appointments and reappointments are at the sole discretion of the Chief Justice.

(Subd (b) amended effective February 1, 2018; previously amended effective November 1, 2004, and January 1, 2007.)

(c) Chair and vice-chair

The Chief Justice appoints an advisory committee member to be a committee chair or vice-chair for a one-year term except for the chair and vice-chair of the Court Executives Advisory Committee, who may be appointed to two-year terms. Except for the Court Executives Advisory Committee, when a member's term as the chair of an advisory committee ends, that member's term on the committee also ends, unless the Chief Justice orders otherwise.

(Subd (c) amended effective February 1, 2018; previously amended effective September 1, 2000, January 1, 2004, and January 1, 2007.)

(d) Advisory members

On the request of the advisory committee, the Chief Justice may designate an advisory member to assist an advisory committee or a subcommittee. Advisory members are appointed for three-year terms unless another term is specified in the order appointing the advisory member. Advisory members may participate in discussions and make or second motions but cannot vote.

(Subd (d) amended effective February 1, 2018; previously amended effective January 1, 2007.)

(e) Termination of membership

Committee membership terminates if a member leaves the position that qualified the member for the advisory committee unless (g) applies or the Chief Justice determines that the individual may complete the current term.

(Subd (e) amended effective February 1, 2018.)

(f) Vacancies

Vacancies are filled as they occur according to the nomination procedures described in rule 10.32.

(Subd (f) amended effective January 1, 2007.)

(g) Retired judges

A judge's retirement does not cause a vacancy on the committee if the judge is eligible for assignment. A retired judge who is eligible for assignment may hold a committee position based on his or her last judicial position.

Rule 10.31 amended effective February 1, 2018; adopted as rule 6.31 effective January 1, 1999; previously amended and renumbered as rule 10.31 effective January 1, 2007; previously amended effective September 1, 2000, September 1, 2003, January 1, 2004, and November 1, 2004.

Rule 10.32.   Nominations and appointments to advisory committees

(a) Nomination procedures

The Executive and Planning Committee assists the Chief Justice in selecting advisory committee members by submitting a list of nominees for each position. Unless otherwise specified in the rule applicable to a particular advisory committee, the nomination procedures are as follows:

(1) The Executive and Planning Committee must publicize vacancies and solicit nominations. If any group is designated to submit nominations for a position, the Executive and Planning Committee will request that the group submit at least three nominations for each advisory committee vacancy.

(2) The Executive and Planning Committee must submit at least three nominees for each advisory committee vacancy to the Chief Justice. The nominees should represent diverse backgrounds and experiences as well as geographic locations throughout California.

(Subd (a) amended effective September 1, 2003.)

(b) Court executive or administrator members

A court executive or administrator member may be a county clerk, a court administrator, or an executive officer if the member also serves as the clerk of the court.

(c) Judicial administrator member

A judicial administrator member may be any person experienced in court administration and is not required to be currently employed by a court.

(d) Judicial officer

A judicial officer member may be a judge of the superior court or a court commissioner or referee.

(Subd (d) amended effective September 1, 2003.)

(e) Appointing order

The Chief Justice appoints advisory committee members by order.

(Subd (e) amended effective September 1, 2003.)

Rule 10.32 amended and renumbered effective January 1, 2007; adopted as rule 6.32 effective January 1, 1999; previously amended effective September 1, 2003.

Rule 10.33.   Advisory committee meetings

Each advisory committee may meet as often as its chair deems necessary, within available resources. Meetings may be in person or by teleconference.

Rule 10.33 renumbered effective January 1, 2007; adopted as rule 6.33 effective January 1, 1999; previously amended effective September 1, 2003.

Rule 10.34.   Duties and responsibilities of advisory committees

(a) Role

Advisory committees are standing committees created by rule of court or the Chief Justice to make recommendations and offer policy alternatives to the Judicial Council for improving the administration of justice within their designated areas of focus by doing the following:

(1) Identifying issues and concerns affecting court administration and recommending solutions to the council;

(2) Proposing necessary changes to rules, standards, forms, and jury instructions;

(3) Reviewing pending legislation and making recommendations to the [1] **Legislation** Committee on whether to support or oppose it;

(4) Recommending new legislation to the council;

(5) Recommending to the council pilot projects and other programs to evaluate new procedures or practices;

(6) Acting on assignments referred by the council or an internal committee; and

(7) Making other appropriate recommendations to the council.

(Subd (a) amended effective April 16, 2020; adopted effective August 14, 2009.)

Rule 10.34(a).   2020 Deletes. [1] Policy Coordination and Liaison

2009 Note: Subdivision (a) was derived from former subdivision (a).

(b) Annual charges

(1) Advisory committees are assigned annual charges by the council or an internal committee specifying what should be achieved in a given year. The council or an internal committee may amend an advisory committee's annual charge at any time.

(2) Advisory committees have limited discretion to pursue matters in addition to those specified in each committee's annual charge, as long as the matters are consistent with a committee's general charge, within the limits of resources available to the committee, and within any other limits specified by the council, the designated internal committee, or the Administrative Director.

(Subd (b) amended effective January 1, 2016; adopted effective August 14, 2009.)

(c) Responsibilities of the chair

Advisory committee chairs are responsible, with the assistance of staff, to:

(1) Develop a realistic annual agenda for the advisory committee, consistent with the committee's annual charge by the Judicial Council or Judicial Council internal committee;

(2) Present the advisory committee's recommendations to the Judicial Council;

(3) Discuss with the Administrative Director or the Administrative Director's designee appropriate staffing and other resources for projects within the advisory committee's agenda; and

(4) Submit recommendations with respect to advisory committee membership.

(Subd (c) adopted effective August 14, 2009.)

(d) Role of the Administrative Director

(1) The Administrative Director determines whether projects undertaken by council advisory bodies in addition to those specified in the council's or internal committee's annual charge to the advisory body are

consistent with the body's general charge, its approved annual agenda, and the Judicial Council's strategic plan. The Administrative Director also determines whether any additional matters are within the body's authorized budget and available resources.

(2) The Administrative Director is not bound by the recommendations of an advisory committee and may make alternative recommendations to the Judicial Council or recommend that an advisory committee's annual charge be amended.

(Subd (d) amended effective January 1, 2016; adopted effective August 14, 2009.)

(e) Role of staff

(1) Advisory committees are assisted by Judicial Council staff. The duties of staff members include drafting committee annual agendas, managing the committee's budget and resources, coordinating committee activities, providing legal and policy analysis to the committee, organizing and drafting reports, selecting and supervising consultants, providing technical assistance, and assisting committee chairs in presenting the committee's recommendations to the Judicial Council. Staff may provide independent legal or policy analysis of issues that is different from the committee's position, if authorized to do so by the Administrative Director.

(2) Staff report to the Administrative Director. The decisions or instructions of an advisory body or its chair are not binding on the staff except in instances when the council or the Administrative Director has specifically authorized such exercise of authority.

(Subd (e) amended effective January 1, 2016; adopted effective August 14, 2009.)

(f) Review of annual agendas

(1) Each committee must submit a proposed annual agenda that is reviewed by the internal committee with oversight responsibility, as designated by the Chief Justice. This subdivision does not apply to the Administrative Presiding Justices Advisory Committee.

(2) The internal committee that is responsible for oversight of the advisory committee reviews the proposed annual agenda and provides the advisory committee with an annual charge to ensure that its activities are consistent with the council's goals and priorities. The annual charge may:

(A) Approve or disapprove the annual agenda in whole or in part;

(B) Direct the committee to pursue specific projects on the annual agenda;

(C) Add or delete specific projects; and

(D) Reassign priorities.

(3) To pursue matters in addition to those specified in its annual charge, an advisory committee must have the approval of the internal committee with oversight responsibility for the advisory committee. The matters must be consistent with the advisory committee's general charge, as set forth in the rules of court, its approved annual agenda, and the council's long-range strategic plan. The additional matters must also be within the committee's authorized budget and available resources, as specified by the council or the Administrative Director.

(Subd (f) amended effective January 1, 2016; adopted effective August 14, 2009; previously amended effective February 20, 2014.)

2009 Note: Subdivision (f) was derived from former subdivision (d).

Rule 10.34 amended effective April 16, 2020; adopted as rule 6.34 effective January 1, 1999; previously amended and renumbered as rule 10.34 effective January 1, 2007; previously amended effective January 1, 2002, September 1, 2003, August 14, 2009, February 20, 2014, and January 16, 2016.

Rule 10.40.   Appellate Advisory Committee

(a) Area of focus

The committee makes recommendations to the council for improving the administration of justice in appellate proceedings.

(Subd (a) amended effective January 1, 2007; previously amended effective January 1, 2002.)

(b) Additional duty

In addition to the duties described in rule 10.34 the committee makes proposals on training for justices and appellate support staff to the Governing Committee of the Center for Judicial Education and Research.

(Subd (b) amended effective January 1, 2007; previously amended effective January 1, 2002.)

(c) Membership

The committee must include at least one member from each of the following categories:

(1) Supreme Court justice;

(2) Court of Appeal justice;

(3) Trial court judicial officer with experience in the appellate division;

(4) Supreme Court clerk/executive officer;

(5) Appellate court clerk/executive officer;

(6) Trial court judicial administrator;

(7) Civil appellate lawyer;

(8) Criminal defense appellate lawyer;

(9) State Public Defender;

(10) Appellate lawyer of the Attorney General's Office; and

(11) Appellate lawyer of the Court of Appeal or Supreme Court.

(Subd (c) amended effective January 1, 2018; previously amended effective January 1, 2002, January 1, 2007, and July 1, 2014.)

Rule 10.40 amended effective January 1, 2018; adopted as rule 6.40 effective January 1, 1999; previously amended effective January 1, 2002, and July 1, 2014; previously amended and renumbered effective January 1, 2007.

Rule 10.41.   Civil and Small Claims Advisory Committee

(a) Area of focus

The committee makes recommendations to the council for improving the administration of justice in civil and small claims proceedings.

(Subd (a) amended effective January 1, 2007.)

(b) Membership

The committee must include at least one member from each of the following categories:

(1) Appellate court justice;

(2) Trial court judicial officer;

(3) Judicial administrator;

(4) Lawyer whose primary area of practice is civil law;

(5) Legal secretary;

(6) Person knowledgeable about small claims law and procedure; and

(7) Person knowledgeable about court-connected alternative dispute resolution programs for civil and small claims cases.

(Subd (b) amended effective January 1, 2011; previously amended effective January 1, 2007.)

Rule 10.41 amended effective January 1, 2011; adopted as rule 6.41 effective January 1, 1999; previously amended and renumbered effective January 1, 2007.

Rule 10.42.   Criminal Law Advisory Committee

(a) Area of focus

The committee makes recommendations to the council for improving the administration of justice in criminal proceedings.

(Subd (a) amended effective January 1, 2007.)

(b) Membership

The committee must include at least one member from each of the following categories:

(1) Appellate court justice;

(2) Trial court judicial officer;

(3) Judicial administrator;

(4) Prosecutor;

(5) Criminal defense lawyer;

(6) Probation officer; and

(7) Mental health professional with experience in criminal law issues.

(Subd (b) amended effective February 1, 2018; previously amended effective January 1, 2007, and January 1, 2011.)

Rule 10.42 amended effective February 1, 2018; adopted as rule 6.42 effective January 1, 1999; previously amended and renumbered as rule 10.42 effective January 1, 2007; previously amended effective January 1, 2011.

Rule 10.43.   Family and Juvenile Law Advisory Committee

(a) Area of focus

The committee makes recommendations to the council for improving the administration of justice in all cases involving marriage, family, or children.

(Subd (a) amended effective January 1, 2007.)

(b) Membership

The committee must include at least one member from each of the following categories:

(1) Appellate court justice;

(2) Trial court judicial officer;

(3) Judicial administrator;

(4) Child custody mediator;

(5) Lawyer whose primary practice area is family law;

(6) Lawyer from a public or private defender's office whose primary practice area is juvenile law;

(7) Chief probation officer;

(8) Child welfare director;

(9) Court Appointed Special Advocate (CASA) director;

(10) County counsel assigned to juvenile dependency cases;

(11) Domestic violence prevention advocate;

(12) District attorney assigned to juvenile delinquency cases;

(13) Lawyer from the California Department of Child Support Services or a local child support agency;

(14) Public-interest children's rights lawyer; and

(15) Mental health professional with experience with family and children's issues.

(Subd (b) amended effective February 1, 2018; previously amended effective July 1, 2005, and January 1, 2007.)

Rule 10.43 amended effective February 1, 2018; adopted as rule 6.43 effective January 1, 1999; previously amended and renumbered as rule 10.43 effective January 1, 2007; previously amended effective July 1, 2005.

Rule 10.44. Probate and Mental Health Advisory Committee

(a) Area of focus

The committee makes recommendations to the council for improving the administration of justice in proceedings involving:

(1) Decedents' estates, trusts, conservatorships, guardianships, and other probate matters; and

(2) Mental health and developmental disabilities issues.

(Subd (a) amended effective January 1, 2007.)

(b) Additional duty

The committee must coordinate activities and work with the Family and Juvenile Law Advisory Committee in areas of common concern and interest.

(Subd (b) amended effective January 1, 2007.)

(c) Membership

The committee must include at least one member from each of the following categories:

(1) Judicial officer with experience in probate;

(2) Lawyer whose primary practice involves decedents' estates, trusts, guardianships, conservatorships, or elder abuse law;

(3) Lawyer or examiner who works for the court on probate or mental health matters;

(4) Lawyer working for a public interest organization or a court self-help center whose practice focuses on guardianships or conservatorships;

(5) Investigator who works for the court to investigate probate guardianships or conservatorships;

(6) Person knowledgeable in mental health or developmental disability law;

(7) Person knowledgeable in private management of probate matters in a fiduciary capacity; and

(8) County counsel, public guardian, or other similar public officer familiar with guardianship and conservatorship issues.

(Subd (c) amended effective February 1, 2018; previously amended effective January 1, 2007, and January 1, 2008.)

Rule 10.44 amended effective February 1, 2018; adopted as rule 6.44 effective July 1, 2000; previously amended and renumbered as rule 10.44 effective January 1, 2007; previously amended effective January 1, 2008.

Rule 10.45. Trial Court Budget Working Group [Renumbered]

Rule 10.45 renumbered as rule 10.107 effective August 14, 2009.

Rule 10.46. Trial Court Presiding Judges Advisory Committee

(a) Area of focus

The committee contributes to the statewide administration of justice by monitoring areas of significance to the justice system and making recommendations to the Judicial Council on policy issues affecting the trial courts.

(Subd (a) amended effective January 1, 2007; previously amended effective September 1, 2000, and April 18, 2003.)

(b) Additional duties

In addition to the duties specified in rule 10.34, the committee may:

(1) Recommend methods and policies within its area of focus to improve trial court presiding judges' access to and participation in council decision making, increase communication between the council and the trial courts, and provide for training programs for judicial and court support staff;

(2) Respond and provide input to the Judicial Council, appropriate advisory committees, or Judicial Council staff on pending policy proposals and offer new recommendations on policy initiatives in the areas of legislation, rules, forms, standards, studies, and recommendations concerning court administration; and

(3) Provide for liaison between the trial courts and the Judicial Council, its advisory committees, task forces, and working groups, and Judicial Council staff.

(Subd (b) amended effective January 1, 2016; previously amended effective September 1, 2000, April 18, 2003, and January 1, 2007.)

(c) Membership

The committee consists of the presiding judge of each superior court.

(Subd (c) amended effective January 1, 2007; previously amended effective September 1, 2000, and April 18, 2003.)

(d) Executive Committee

The advisory committee may establish an Executive Committee that, in addition to other powers provided by the advisory committee, may act on behalf of the full advisory committee between its meetings.

(Subd (d) amended effective April 18, 2003; adopted effective September 1, 2000.)

(e) Subcommittee membership

The committee has standing subcommittees on rules and legislation. The chair may create other subcommittees as he or she deems appropriate. The chair must strive for representation of courts of all sizes on subcommittees.

(Subd (e) repealed and adopted effective April 18, 2003.)

(f) Chair

The advisory committee must annually submit to the Chief Justice one nomination for the chair of the advisory committee. Any member of the advisory committee whose term as presiding judge would extend at least through the term of the advisory committee chair is eligible for nomination. The nomination must be made by a majority vote of the full advisory committee. In the event that no candidate receives a majority vote on the first ballot, subsequent ballots of the top two candidates will occur until a candidate receives a majority vote. The chair of the advisory committee serves as chair of any Executive Committee established under (d) and as an advisory member of the Judicial Council.

(Subd (f) amended effective July 1, 2013; adopted as subd (d) effective January 1, 1999; previously amended and relettered effective September 1, 2000; previously amended effective April 18, 2003, and January 1, 2007.)

Rule 10.46 amended effective January 1, 2016; adopted as rule 6.46 effective January 1, 1999; previously amended and renumbered as rule 10.46 effective January 1, 2007; previously amended effective September 1, 2000, April 18, 2003, and July 1, 2013.

Advisory Committee Comment

Subdivision (f): An advisory committee member may submit his or her own name, the name of another member of the advisory committee, or the name of an incoming member of the advisory committee to be considered for nomination. An incoming member of the advisory committee may be nominated by a current member of the advisory committee, but he or she may not participate in the voting process. Only current members of the advisory committee may vote. The successful candidate must receive 30 or more votes.

Rule 10.48. Court Executives Advisory Committee

(a) Area of focus

The committee makes recommendations to the council on policy issues affecting the trial courts.

(Subd (a) amended effective January 1, 2004.)

(b) Additional duties

In addition to the duties specified in rule 10.34, the committee must:

(1) Recommend methods and policies to improve trial court administrators' access to and participation in council decision making;

(2) Review and comment on legislation, rules, forms, standards, studies, and recommendations concerning court administration proposed to the council;

(3) Review and make proposals concerning the Judicial Branch Statistical Information System or other large-scope data collection efforts;

(4) Suggest methods and policies to increase communication between the council and the trial courts; and

(5) Meet periodically with the Judicial Council's executive team to enhance branch communications.

(Subd (b) amended effective January 1, 2016; previously amended effective January 1, 2004, January 1, 2007, and February 20, 2014.)

(c) Membership

The committee consists of the court executive officer of each superior court.

(Subd (c) repealed, relettered and amended effective February 20, 2014; adopted as subd (d) effective January 1, 1999; previously amended effective January 1, 2004, and January 1, 2007.)

(d) Executive Committee

The advisory committee may establish an Executive Committee that, in addition to other powers provided by the advisory committee, acts on behalf of the full advisory committee. To assist it in formulating proposals and making recommendations to the council, the Executive Committee may seek the advice of the advisory committee. The Executive Committee consists of the following members:

(1) The nine court executive officers or interim/acting court executive officers from the nine trial courts that have 48 or more judges;

(2) Four court executive officers from trial courts that have 16 to 47 judges;

(3) Two court executive officers from trial courts that have 6 to 15 judges;

(4) Two court executive officers from trial courts that have 2 to 5 judges; and

(5) One court executive officer from the trial courts as an at-large member appointed by the committee chair to a one-year term.

(Subd (d) adopted effective February 20, 2014.)

(e) Nominations

(1) The advisory committee must submit nominations for each vacancy on the Executive Committee. The Executive Committee will recommend three nominees for each Executive Committee vacancy from the nominations received and submit its recommendations to the Executive and Planning Committee of the Judicial Council. The list of nominees must enable the Chief Justice to appoint an Executive Committee that reflects a variety of experience, expertise, and locales (e.g., urban, suburban, and rural). Membership on the Executive Committee does not preclude appointment to any other advisory committee or task force.

(2) The Executive Committee must review and recommend to the Executive and Planning Committee of the Judicial Council the following:

(A) Members of the Executive Committee;

(B) Nonvoting court administrator members of the Judicial Council; and

(C) Members of other advisory committees who are court executives or judicial administrators.

(Subd (e) amended effective February 20, 2014; previously amended effective January 1, 2004, and January 1, 2007.)

(f) Chair and vice-chair

The Chief Justice may appoint the chair and vice-chair of the advisory committee for up to a two-year term from the current or incoming membership of the Executive Committee. The chair and vice-chair of the advisory committee serve as the chair and vice-chair of the Executive Committee established by subdivision (d).

(Subd (f) amended effective February 20, 2014; previously amended effective January 1, 2004, January 1, 2007, and January 1, 2008.)

(g) Meetings

The Executive Committee will meet approximately every two months, which includes the statewide meetings with the advisory committee. The advisory committee will meet during at least two statewide meetings per year.

(Subd (g) adopted effective February 20, 2014.)

Rule 10.48 amended effective January 1, 2016; adopted as rule 6.48 effective January 1, 1999; previously amended and renumbered as rule 10.48 effective January 1, 2007; previously amended effective January 1, 2004, January 1, 2008, and February 20, 2014.

Rule 10.49.　Conference of Court Executives [Repealed]

Rule 10.49 repealed effective February 20, 2014; adopted as rule 6.49 effective January 1, 1999; previously amended effective January 1, 2004; previously amended and renumbered effective January 1, 2007.

Rule 10.50.　Center for Judicial Education and Research Advisory Committee

(a) Establishment and purpose

In 1973, the Judicial Council of California and the California Judges Association created the Center for Judicial Education and Research (CJER). The oversight body then known as the Governing Committee of CJER was made an advisory committee to the council in 1993 through the adoption of former rule 1029. In 2001, the rule that specifies the duties of that advisory committee was made consistent with the rules pertaining to other Judicial Council advisory committees.

(Subd (a) amended effective January 1, 2019; adopted effective December 18, 2001; previously amended effective January 1, 2007, and January 1, 2016.)

(b) Area of focus

The committee makes recommendations to the council for improving the administration of justice through comprehensive and quality education and training for judicial officers and other judicial branch personnel.

(Subd (b) relettered and amended effective December 18, 2001; adopted as subd (a).)

(c) Additional duties

In addition to the duties described in rule 10.34, the committee must:

(1) Recommend rules, standards, policies, and procedures for judicial branch education;

(2) Recommend a strategic long-range plan for judicial branch education;

(3) Evaluate the effectiveness of judicial branch education, the quality of participation, the efficiency of delivery, and the impact on service to the public;

(4) Review and comment on proposals from other advisory committees and task forces that include education and training of judicial officers or court staff in order to ensure coordination, consistency, and collaboration in educational services;

(5) Establish educational priorities for implementation of curricula, programs, publications, and delivery systems;

(6) Identify the need for and appoint education committees to implement the priorities, long-range plan, and programs and products of judicial branch education; create and adopt procedures for their operation; and review and approve their projects and products;

(7) Identify and foster collaborative opportunities with courts to promote and ensure the availability of training at the local court level;

(8) Identify, analyze, and implement systems to enhance the delivery of education and training statewide; and

(9) Identify and foster collaborative opportunities with internal and external partners to maximize the resources dedicated to education and training.

(Subd (c) amended effective January 1, 2007; adopted as subd (b) effective January 1, 1999; previously relettered and amended effective December 18, 2001.)

(d) Membership

The committee consists of at least the following members:

(1) Eleven sitting judicial officers, including at least one appellate court justice and one immediate past presiding judge;

(2) Three judicial administrators, including a supervisor or manager from a trial or appellate court;

(3) The Administrative Director as an advisory member;

(4) The president of the California Judges Association or his or her designee as an advisory member; and

(5) Other advisory members as the Chief Justice may appoint.

(Subd (d) amended effective January 1, 2015; adopted as subd (c); previously relettered and amended effective December 18, 2001.)

(e) Nominations

Nominations for vacant positions on the CJER Advisory Committee will be solicited under the procedures described in rule 10.32. The president of the California Judges Association may submit nominations to the Executive and Planning Committee.

(Subd (e) amended effective January 1, 2019; previously amended effective December 18, 2001, and January 1, 2007.)

(f) Chair and vice-chair

The Chief Justice appoints the chair and vice-chair. The committee may make recommendations to the Chief Justice for these two positions.

(Subd (f) amended effective December 18, 2001.)

Rule 10.50 amended effective January 1, 2019; adopted as rule 6.50 effective January 1, 1999; previously amended and renumbered as rule 10.50 effective January 1, 2007; previously amended effective December 18, 2001, January 1, 2015, and January 1, 2016.

Rule 10.51.　Court Interpreters Advisory Panel

(a) Area of focus

To assist the council in performing its duties under Government Code sections 68560 through 68566 and to promote access to spoken-language interpreters and interpreters for deaf and hearing-impaired persons, the advisory panel is charged with making recommendations to the council on:

(1) Interpreter use and need for interpreters in court proceedings; and

(2) Certification, registration, renewal of certification and registration, testing, recruiting, training, continuing education, and professional conduct of interpreters.

(Subd (a) amended effective October 1, 2004.)

(b) Additional duty

The advisory panel is charged with reviewing and making recommendations to the council on the findings of the study of language and interpreter use and need for interpreters in court proceedings that is conducted by the Judicial Council every five years under Government Code section 68563.

(Subd (b) amended effective January 1, 2016; previously amended effective October 1, 2004.)

(c) Membership

The advisory panel consists of 11 members. A majority of the members must be court interpreters. The advisory panel must include the specified numbers of members from the following categories:

(1) Four certified or registered court interpreters working as employees in trial courts, one from each of the four regions established by Government Code section 71807. For purposes of the appointment of members under this rule, the Superior Court of California, County of Ventura, is considered part of Region 1 as specified in section 71807, and the Superior Court of California, County of Solano, is considered part of Region 2 as specified in section 71807;

(2) Two interpreters certified or registered in a language other than Spanish, each working either in a trial court as an independent contractor or in an educational institution;

(3) One appellate court justice;

(4) Two trial court judges; and

(5) Two court administrators, including at least one trial court executive officer.

(Subd (c) amended effective October 1, 2004; previously amended effective July 1, 1999.)

(d) Advisors

The Chief Justice may also appoint nonmember advisors to assist the advisory panel.

(Subd (d) adopted effective October 1, 2004.)

Rule 10.51 amended effective January 1, 2016; adopted as rule 6.51 effective January 1, 1999; previously amended effective July 1, 1999, and October 1, 2004; previously renumbered as rule 10.51 effective January 1, 2007.

Rule 10.52. Administrative Presiding Justices Advisory Committee

(a) Area of focus

The committee makes recommendations to the council on policy issues affecting the administration and operation of the Courts of Appeal.

(Subd (a) amended effective January 1, 2007.)

(b) Additional duties

In addition to the duties described in rule 10.34, the committee must:

(1) Establish administrative policies that promote the quality of justice by advancing the efficient functioning of the appellate courts;

(2) Advise the council of the appellate courts' resource requirements and solicit the council's support in meeting budget, administrative, and staffing requirements;

(3) Make proposals on training for justices and appellate support staff to the Governing Committee of the Center for Judicial Education and Research; and

(4) Comment on and make recommendations to the council about appellate court operations, including:

(A) Initiatives to be pursued by the council or its staff; and

(B) The council's goals and strategies.

(Subd (b) amended effective January 1, 2016; previously amended effective January 1, 2007.)

(c) Membership

The committee consists of:

(1) The Chief Justice as chair; and

(2) The administrative presiding justices of the Courts of Appeal designated under rule 10.1004.

(Subd (c) amended effective January 1, 2007.)

(d) Funding

Each year, the committee must recommend budget change proposals to be submitted to the Chief Justice for legislative funding to operate the appellate courts. These proposals must be consistent with the budget management guidelines of the Judicial Council's Finance office.

(Subd (d) amended effective January 1, 2016; previously amended effective January 1, 2007.)

(e) Allocations

The committee allocates resources among the appellate courts and approves budget management guidelines based on the actual allocation made by the Chief Justice.

(Subd (e) amended effective January 1, 2007.)

(f) Administrative Director

The Administrative Director must meet regularly with the committee and must notify and, when appropriate, consult with the committee about appellate court personnel matters.

(Subd (f) amended effective January 1, 2016; previously amended effective January 1, 2007.)

Rule 10.52 amended effective January 1, 2016; adopted as rule 6.52 effective January 1, 1999; previously amended and renumbered as rule 10.52 effective January 1, 2007.

Rule 10.53. Information Technology Advisory Committee

(a) Areas of focus

The committee makes recommendations to the council for improving the administration of justice through the use of technology and for fostering cooperative endeavors to resolve common technological issues with other stakeholders in the justice system. The committee promotes, coordinates, and acts as executive sponsor for projects and initiatives that apply technology to the work of the courts.

(Subd (a) amended effective September 1, 2015; previously amended effective January 1, 2007.)

(b) Additional duties

In addition to the duties described in rule 10.34, the committee must:

(1) Oversee branchwide technology initiatives funded in whole or in part by the state;

(2) Recommend rules, standards, and legislation to ensure compatibility in information and communication technologies in the judicial branch;

(3) Provide input to the Judicial Council Technology Committee on the technology and business requirements of court technology projects and initiatives in funding requests;

(4) Review and recommend legislation, rules, or policies to balance the interests of privacy, access, and security in relation to court technology;

(5) Make proposals for technology education and training in the judicial branch;

(6) Assist courts in acquiring and developing useful technologies;

(7) Establish mechanisms to collect, preserve, and share best practices across the state;

(8) Maintain a long-range plan. Develop and recommend a tactical technology plan, described in rule 10.16, with input from the individual appellate and trial courts; and

(9) Develop and recommend the committee's annual agenda, identifying individual technology initiatives scheduled for the next year.

(Subd (b) amended effective September 1, 2015; previously amended effective January 1, 2007.)

(c) Sponsorship of branchwide technology initiatives

(1) *Oversight of branchwide technology initiatives*

The committee is responsible for overseeing branchwide technology initiatives that are approved as part of the committee's annual agenda. The committee may oversee these initiatives through a workstream model, a subcommittee model, or a hybrid of the two. Under the workstream model, committee members sponsor discrete technology initiatives executed by ad hoc teams of technology experts and experienced project and program managers from throughout the branch. Under the subcommittee model, committee members serve on subcommittees that carry out technology projects and develop and recommend policies and rules.

(2) *Technology workstreams*

Each technology workstream has a specific charge and duration that align with the objective and scope of the technology initiative assigned to the workstream. The individual tasks necessary to complete the initiative may be carried out by dividing the workstream into separate tracks. Technology workstreams are not advisory bodies for purposes of rule 10.75.

(3) Executive *sponsorship* of technology workstreams

The committee chair designates a member or two members of the committee to act as executive sponsors of each technology initiative monitored through the workstream model. The executive sponsor assumes overall executive responsibility for project deliverables and periodically provides high-level project status updates to the advisory committee and council. The executive sponsor is responsible for facilitating work plans for the initiative.

(4) Responsibilities and composition of technology workstream teams

A workstream team serves as staff on the initiative and is responsible for structuring, tracking, and managing the progress of individual tasks and milestones necessary to complete the initiative. The executive sponsor recommends, and the chair appoints, a workstream team of technology experts and experienced project and program managers from throughout the branch.

(Subd (c) adopted effective September 1, 2015.)

(d) Membership

The committee must include at least one member from each of the following categories:

(1) Appellate justice;

(2) Trial court judicial officer;

(3) Trial court judicial administrator;

(4) Appellate court judicial administrator;

(5) Trial court information technology officer;

(6) Member of the Senate;

(7) Member of the Assembly;

(8) Representative of the executive branch; and

(9) Lawyer.

(Subd (d) amended and relettered effective September 1, 2015; adopted as subd (c); previously amended effective January 1, 2007.)

(e) Member selection

The two legislative members are appointed by the respective houses. The executive member is appointed by the Governor. The lawyer member is appointed by the State Bar. In making all other appointments to the committee, factors to be considered include a candidate's technology expertise and experience, as well as an ability to act as lead executive sponsor for technology initiatives.

(Subd (e) amended and relettered effective September 1, 2015; adopted as subd (d).)

(f) Chair

The Chief Justice appoints a judicial officer to serve as chair.

(Subd (f) amended and relettered effective September 1, 2015; adopted as subd (e).)

Rule 10.53 amended effective September 1, 2015; adopted as rule 6.53 effective January 1, 1999; previously amended and renumbered effective January 1, 2007.

Rule 10.54. Traffic Advisory Committee

(a) Area of focus

The committee makes recommendations to the council for improving the administration of justice in the area of traffic procedure, practice, and case management and in other areas as stated in the fish and game, boating, forestry, public utilities, parks and recreation, and business licensing bail schedules.

(Subd (a) amended effective January 1, 2007.)

(b) Membership

The committee must include at least one member from each of the following categories:

(1) Trial court judicial officer;

(2) Judicial administrator;

(3) Juvenile hearing officer;

(4) Representative from the California Highway Patrol;

(5) Representative from the Department of Motor Vehicles;

(6) Representative from the Office of Traffic Safety; and

(7) Criminal defense lawyer.

(Subd (b) amended effective January 1, 2010; previously amended effective January 1, 2007.)

Rule 10.54 amended effective January 1, 2010; adopted as rule 6.54 effective January 1, 1999; previously amended and renumbered effective January 1, 2007.

Rule 10.55. Advisory Committee on Providing Access and Fairness

(a) Area of focus

The committee makes recommendations for improving access to the judicial system, fairness in the state courts, diversity in the judicial branch, and court services for self-represented parties.

(Subd (a) amended effective February 20, 2014; previously amended effective January 1, 2007.)

(b) Additional duties

In addition to the duties described in rule 10.34, the committee must recommend to the Governing Committee of the Center for Judicial Education and Research, proposals for the education and training of judicial officers and court staff.

(Subd (b) amended effective February 20, 2014; previously amended effective January 1, 2007.)

(c) Membership

The committee must include at least one member from each of the following categories:

(1) Appellate justice;

(2) Trial court judicial officer;

(3) Lawyer with expertise or interest in disability issues;

(4) Lawyer with expertise or interest in additional access, fairness, and diversity issues addressed by the committee;

(5) Lawyer from a trial court self-help center;

(6) Legal services lawyer;

(7) Court executive officer or trial court manager who has experience with self-represented litigants;

(8) County law librarian or other related professional;

(9) Judicial administrator; and

(10) Public member.

(Subd (c) amended effective February 20, 2014; previously amended effective January 1, 2007.)

(d) Cochairs

The Chief Justice appoints two advisory committee members to serve as cochairs. Each cochair is responsible for leading the advisory committee's work in the following areas:

(1) Physical, programmatic, and language access; fairness in the courts; and diversity in the judicial branch; and

(2) Issues confronted by self-represented litigants and those of limited or moderate income, including economic, education, and language challenges.

(Subd (d) adopted effective February 20, 2014.)

Rule 10.55 amended effective February 20, 2014; adopted as rule 6.55 effective January 1, 1999; previously amended and renumbered effective January 1, 2007.

Advisory Committee Comment

The advisory committee's area of focus includes assisting courts to improve access and fairness by recommending methods and tools to identify and address physical, programmatic, and language access; fairness in the courts; and diversity in the judicial branch, as well as addressing issues that affect the ability of litigants to access the courts including economic, education, and language challenges. An additional responsibility of the advisory committee to recommend to the council updated guidelines and procedures for court self-help centers, as needed, is stated in rule 10.960.

Rule 10.56. Collaborative Justice Courts Advisory Committee

(a) Area of focus

The committee makes recommendations to the Judicial Council on criteria for identifying and evaluating collaborative justice courts and for improving the processing of cases in these courts, which include drug courts, domestic violence courts, youth courts, and other collaborative justice courts. Those recommendations include "best practices" guidelines and methods for collecting data to evaluate the long-term effectiveness of collaborative justice courts.

(Subd (a) amended effective January 1, 2007.)

(b) Additional duties

In addition to the duties described in rule 10.34, the committee must:

(1) Assess and measure the success and effectiveness of local collaborative justice courts;

(2) Identify and disseminate to trial courts locally generated best practices;

(3) Recommend minimum judicial education standards and educational activities to support those standards to the Governing Committee of the Center for Judicial Education and Research;

(4) Advise the council of potential funding sources;

(5) Make recommendations regarding grant funding programs that are administered by Judicial Council staff for drug courts and other treatment courts; and

(6) Recommend appropriate outreach activities needed to support collaborative justice courts.

(Subd (b) amended effective January 1, 2016; previously amended effective January 1, 2007.)

(c) Membership

The committee must include the following:

(1) At least five judicial officers. Nominations for these appointments must be made in accordance with rule 10.32. The list of nominees should enable the Chair of the Judicial Council to appoint a committee that reflects a variety of court experience (e.g., criminal, juvenile, family, general civil), expertise, and court sizes and types (e.g., urban, suburban, and rural; and small, medium, and large).

(2) At least one member from each of the following categories:

(A) Judicial administrator;

(B) District attorney;

(C) Criminal defense attorney;

(D) Law enforcement (police/sheriff);

(E) Treatment provider or rehabilitation provider;

(F) Probation officer;

(G) Court-treatment coordinator;

(H) Treatment court graduate; and

(I) Public member.

(Subd (c) amended effective January 1, 2007.)

Rule 10.56 amended effective January 1, 2016; adopted as rule 6.56 effective January 1, 2000; previously amended effective January 1, 2002; previously amended and renumbered as rule 10.56 effective January 1, 2007.

Rule 10.57.   Judicial Service Advisory Committee [Repealed]

Rule 10.57 repealed effective October 25, 2013; adopted as rule 6.57 effective January 1, 2003; previously amended and renumbered effective January 1, 2007.

Rule 10.58.   Advisory Committee on Civil Jury Instructions

(a) Area of focus

The committee regularly reviews case law and statutes affecting jury instructions and makes recommendations to the Judicial Council for updating, amending, and adding topics to the council's civil jury instructions.

(Subd (a) amended effective January 1, 2007.)

(b) Membership

The committee must include at least one member from each of the following categories, and a majority of the members must be judges:

(1) Appellate court justice;

(2) Trial court judge;

(3) Lawyer whose primary area of practice is civil law; and

(4) Law professor whose primary area of expertise is civil law.

Rule 10.58 amended and renumbered effective January 1, 2007; adopted as rule 6.58 effective September 1, 2003.

Rule 10.59.   Advisory Committee on Criminal Jury Instructions

(a) Area of focus

The committee regularly reviews case law and statutes affecting jury instructions and makes recommendations to the Judicial Council for updating, amending, and adding topics to the council's criminal jury instructions.

(b) Membership

The committee must include at least one member from each of the following categories, and a majority of the members must be judges:

(1) Appellate court justice;

(2) Trial court judge;

(3) Lawyer whose primary area of practice is criminal defense;

(4) Deputy district attorney or other attorney who represents the People of the State of California in criminal matters; and

(5) Law professor whose primary area of expertise is criminal law.

Rule 10.59 renumbered effective January 1, 2007; adopted as rule 6.59 effective July 1, 2005.

Rule 10.60.   Tribal Court–State Court Forum

(a) Area of focus

The forum makes recommendations to the council for improving the administration of justice in all proceedings in which the authority to exercise jurisdiction by the state judicial branch and the tribal justice systems overlaps.

(Subd (a) adopted effective October 25, 2013.)

(b) Additional duties

In addition to the duties described in rule 10.34, the forum must:

(1) Identify issues of mutual importance to tribal and state justice systems, including those concerning the working relationship between tribal and state courts in California;

(2) Make recommendations relating to the recognition and enforcement of court orders that cross jurisdictional lines, the determination of jurisdiction for cases that might appear in either court system, and the sharing of services between jurisdictions;

(3) Identify, develop, and share with tribal and state courts local rules of court, protocols, standing orders, and other agreements that promote tribal court–state court coordination and cooperation, the use of concurrent jurisdiction, and the transfer of cases between jurisdictions;

(4) Recommend appropriate activities needed to support local tribal court–state court collaborations; and

(5) Make proposals to the Governing Committee of the Center for Judicial Education and Research on educational publications and programming for judges and judicial support staff.

(Subd (b) adopted effective October 25, 2013.)

(c) Membership

The forum must include the following members:

(1) Tribal court judges or justices selected by tribes in California, as described in (d), but no more than one tribal court judge or justice from each tribe;

(2) At least three trial court judges from counties in which a tribal court is located;

(3) At least one appellate justice of the California Courts of Appeal;

(4) At least one member from each of the following committees: the Access and Fairness Advisory Committee, Civil and Small Claims Advisory Committee, Criminal Law Advisory Committee, Family and Juvenile Law Advisory Committee, Governing Committee of the Center for Judicial Education and Research, Probate and Mental Health Advisory Committee, and Traffic Advisory Committee; and

(5) At least one, but no more than three, California executive branch officials responsible for tribal-related work.

The composition of the forum must have an equal or a close-to-equal number of judges or justices from tribal courts and state courts.

(Subd (c) amended effective February 1, 2018; adopted effective October 25, 2013.)

(d) Member Selection

(1) The Chief Justice appoints all forum members, except tribal court judges and tribal court justices, who are appointed as described in (2).

(2) For each tribe in California with a tribal court, the tribal leadership will appoint the tribal court judge or justice member to the forum consistent with the following selection and appointment process.

(A) The forum cochairs will notify the tribal leadership of a vacancy for a tribal court judge or justice and request that they submit names of tribal court judges or justices to serve on the forum.

(B) A vacancy for a tribal court judge or justice will be filled as it occurs either on the expiration of a member's term or when the member has left the position that qualified the member for the forum.

(C) If there are more names of tribal court judges and justices submitted by the tribal leadership than vacancies, then the forum cochairs will confer and decide which tribal court judges or justices should be appointed. Their decision will be based on the diverse background and experience, as well as the geographic location, of the current membership.

(Subd (d) adopted effective October 25, 2013.)

(e) Cochairs

The Chief Justice appoints a state appellate justice or trial court judge and a tribal court appellate justice or judge to serve as cochairs, consistent with rule 10.31(c).

(Subd (e) adopted effective October 25, 2013.)

Rule 10.60 amended effective February 1, 2018; adopted effective October 25, 2013.

Judicial Council Comment

Tribes are recognized as distinct, independent political nations (see *Worcester v. Georgia* (1832) 31 U.S. 515, 559, and *Santa Clara Pueblo v. Martinez* (1978) 436 U.S. 49, 55, citing *Worcester*), which retain inherent authority to establish their own form of government, including tribal justice systems. (25 U.S.C.A. §3601(4).) Tribal justice systems are an essential part of tribal governments and serve to ensure the public health and safety and the political integrity of tribal governments. (25 U.S.C.A. §3601(5).) Traditional tribal justice practices are essential to the maintenance of the culture and identity of tribes. (25 U.S.C.A. §3601(7).)

The constitutional recognition of tribes as sovereigns in a government-to-government relationship with all other sovereigns is a well-established principle of federal Indian law. (See *Cohen's Handbook of Federal Indian Law* (2005) p.207.) In recognition of this sovereignty, the council's oversight of the forum, through an internal committee under rule 10.30(d), is limited to oversight of the forum's work and activities and does not include oversight of any tribe or tribal court.

Rule 10.61.   Court Security Advisory Committee

(a) Area of Focus

The committee makes recommendations to the council for improving court security, including personal security and emergency response planning.

(Subd (a) adopted effective October 25, 2013.)

(b) Membership

The committee must include at least one member from each of the following categories:

(1) Appellate court justice;

(2) Appellate court administrator;

(3) Trial court judge;

(4) Trial court judicial administrator;

(5) Member of the Court Facilities Advisory Committee; and

(6) Member of the Trial Court Facility Modification Advisory Committee.

At least one member of the committee should be from a trial court that uses a marshal for court security services.

(Subd (b) adopted effective October 25, 2013.)

Rule 10.61 adopted effective October 25, 2013.

Rule 10.62. Court Facilities Advisory Committee

(a) Area of focus

The committee makes recommendations to the council concerning the judicial branch capital program for the trial and appellate courts.

(Subd (a) adopted effective February 20, 2014.)

(b) Membership

The committee must include at least one member from each of the following categories:

(1) Appellate court justice;

(2) Appellate court clerk/executive officer;

(3) Superior court judge;

(4) Court executive officer;

(5) Lawyer;

(6) Local government official or administrator; and

(7) Public member with expertise in real estate acquisition, construction, architecture, cost estimating, or facilities management and operations.

The committee also includes the chair and vice-chair of the Trial Court Facility Modification Advisory Committee, as non-voting members.

(Subd (b) amended effective January 1, 2018; adopted effective February 20, 2014.)

Rule 10.62 amended effective January 1, 2018; adopted effective February 20, 2014.

Rule 10.63. Advisory Committee on Audits and Financial Accountability for the Judicial Branch

(a) Purpose of the rule

One of the most important functions of government is to ensure that public funds are properly spent and accounted for. This committee is charged with advising and assisting the council in performing its responsibilities to ensure that the fiscal affairs of the judicial branch are managed efficiently, effectively, and transparently, and in performing its specific responsibilities relating to audits and contracting, as required by law and good public policy.

(Subd (a) adopted effective July 28, 2017.)

(b) Area of focus

The committee makes recommendations to the council on audits and practices that will promote financial accountability and efficiency in the judicial branch.

(Subd (b) amended and relettered effective July 28, 2017; adopted as subd (a) effective February 20, 2014.)

(c) Additional duties

In addition to the duties specified in rule 10.34, the committee must:

(1) Review and approve a yearly audit plan for the judicial branch that will ensure the adequacy and effectiveness of the judicial branch's accounting, financial reporting, compliance, and internal control system; review all audit reports of the judicial branch; recommend council action on audit reports that identify substantial issues; approve all other audit reports and have them posted publicly; and, where appropriate, make recommendations to the council on individual or systemic issues identified in audit reports;

(2) Advise and assist the council in performing its responsibilities and exercising its authority under Government Code sections 77009 and 77206 and under part 2.5 of the Public Contract Code (commencing with section 19201; the California Judicial Branch Contract Law);

(3) Review and recommend to the council proposed updates and revisions to the *Judicial Branch Contracting Manual*; and

(4) Make recommendations concerning any proposed changes to the annual compensation plan for Judicial Council staff.

(Subd (c) amended and relettered effective July 28, 2017; adopted as subd (b) effective February 20, 2014.)

(d) Membership

The committee may include members with experience in public or judicial branch finance and must include at least one member from each of the following categories:

(1) Justices of the Courts of Appeal;

(2) Judges of the superior courts;

(3) Clerk/executive officers of the Courts of Appeal; and

(4) Court executive officers of the superior courts.

The committee membership must also include at least one nonvoting advisory member who has significant governmental auditing experience.

The California Judges Association will recommend three nominees for a superior court judge position and submit its recommendations to the Executive and Planning Committee of the Judicial Council.

(Subd (d) amended and relettered effective July 28, 2017; adopted as subd (c) effective February 20, 2014.)

Rule 10.63 amended effective July 28, 2017; adopted effective February 20, 2014.

Advisory Committee Comment

The purpose of the Advisory Committee on Audits and Financial Accountability for the Judicial Branch is to advise and assist the council in performing its constitutional and statutory responsibilities relating to the fiscal affairs of the judicial branch. To improve the administration of the courts, article VI, section 6 of the California Constitution requires the council to survey judicial business and make recommendations. To ensure that the fiscal affairs of the courts are managed efficiently, effectively, and responsibly, Government Code section 77206 authorizes the council to regulate the fiscal management of the courts and provides for audits of the courts and Judicial Council staff by the council, its representatives, and other entities. Government Code section 77009(h) provides that the "Judicial Council or its representatives may perform audits, reviews, and investigations of superior court operations and records wherever they may be located." The Public Contract Code provides that the council shall publish a *Judicial Branch Contracting Manual* (Pub. Contract Code, §19206). It also provides that the California State Auditor, subject to appropriations, shall biennially identify and audit five or more judicial branch entities to assess the implementation of the California Judicial Branch Contract Law (JBCL) (Pub. Contract Code, §19210(a), (b)) and shall biennially conduct audits of Judicial Council staff to assess the implementation of, and compliance with, the JBCL (Pub. Contract Code, §19210(c)).

Rule 10.64. Trial Court Budget Advisory Committee

(a) Area of focus

The Trial Court Budget Advisory Committee makes recommendations to the council on the preparation, development, and implementation of the budget for the trial courts and provides input to the council on policy issues affecting trial court funding.

(Subd (a) adopted effective February 20, 2014.)

(b) Additional duties

In addition to the duties specified in rule 10.34, the committee may make recommendations to the council on:

(1) Trial court budget priorities to guide the development of the budget for the upcoming fiscal year;

(2) The allocation of trial court funding, including any changes to existing methodologies for allocating trial court budget augmentations and reductions; and

(3) Budget policies and procedures, as appropriate.

(Subd (b) adopted effective February 20, 2014.)

(c) Membership

(1) The advisory committee consists of an equal number of trial court presiding judges and court executive officers reflecting diverse aspects of state trial courts, including urban, suburban, and rural locales; the size and adequacy of budgets; and the number of authorized judgeships. For purposes of this rule, "presiding judge" means a current presiding judge or a judge who has served as a presiding judge within six years of the year of the appointment as a committee member. An existing presiding judge or past presiding judge member is eligible to be reappointed.

(2) No more than two members may be from the same court.

(3) The chairs of the Trial Court Presiding Judges Advisory Committee and the Court Executives Advisory Committee serve as ex officio voting members.

(4) Notwithstanding rule 10.31(e), a presiding judge is qualified to complete his or her term on the advisory committee even if his or her term as presiding judge of a trial court ends.

(5) The Judicial Council's chief administrative officer, and director of Budget Services serve as nonvoting members.

(Subd (c) amended effective January 1, 2019; adopted effective February 20, 2014; previously amended effective October 28, 2014.)

Rule 10.64 amended effective January 1, 2019; adopted effective February 20, 2014; previously amended effective October 28, 2014.

Rule 10.65. Trial Court Facility Modification Advisory Committee

(a) Area of focus

The committee makes recommendations to the council on facilities modifications, maintenance, and operations; environmental services; and utility management.

(Subd (a) adopted effective January 1, 2015.)

(b) Additional duties

In addition to the duties specified in rule 10.34, the committee:

(1) Makes recommendations to the council on policy issues, business practices, and budget monitoring and control for all facility-related matters in existing branch facilities.

(2) Makes recommendations to the council on funding and takes additional action in accordance with council policy, both for facility modifications and for operations and maintenance.

(3) Collaborates with the Court Facilities Advisory Committee in the development of the capital program, including providing input to design standards, prioritization of capital projects, and methods to reduce construction cost without impacting long-term operations and maintenance cost.

(4) Provides quarterly and annual reports on the facilities modification program in accordance with the council policy.

(Subd (b) adopted effective January 1, 2015.)

(c) Membership

The committee consists of members from the following categories:

(1) Trial court judges; and

(2) Court executive officers.

The committee includes the chair and vice-chair of the Court Facilities Advisory Committee, as nonvoting members.

(Subd (c) adopted effective January 1, 2015.)

Rule 10.65 adopted effective January 1, 2015.

Advisory Committee Comment

The Judicial Council policy referred to in the rule is contained in the *Trial Court Facility Modifications Policy* adopted by the council.

Rule 10.66.   Workload Assessment Advisory Committee

(a) Area of focus

The committee makes recommendations to the council on judicial administration standards and measures that provide for the equitable allocation of resources across courts to promote the fair and efficient administration of justice.

(Subd (a) adopted effective January 1, 2015.)

(b) Additional duties

In addition to the duties specified in rule 10.34, the committee must recommend:

(1) Improvements to performance measures and implementation plans and any modifications to the Judicial Workload Assessment and the Resource Assessment Study Model;

(2) Processes, study design, and methodologies that should be used to measure and report on court administration; and

(3) Studies and analyses to update and amend case weights through time studies, focus groups, or other methods.

(Subd (b) adopted effective January 1, 2015.)

(c) Membership

(1) The advisory committee consists of an equal number of superior court judicial officers and court executive officers reflecting diverse aspects of state trial courts, including urban, suburban, and rural locales; size and adequacy of resources; number of authorized judgeships; and for judicial officers, diversity of case type experience.

(2) A judicial officer and court executive officer may be from the same court.

(Subd (c) adopted effective January 1, 2015.)

Rule 10.66 adopted effective January 1, 2015.

Rule 10.67.   Judicial Branch Workers' Compensation Program Advisory Committee

(a) Area of focus

The committee makes recommendations to the council for improving the statewide administration of the Judicial Branch Workers' Compensation Program and on allocations to and from the Judicial Branch Workers' Compensation Fund established under Government Code section 68114.10.

(Subd (a) adopted effective January 1, 2015.)

(b) Additional duties

In addition to the duties specified in rule 10.34, the committee must review:

(1) The progress of the Judicial Branch Workers' Compensation Program;

(2) The annual actuarial report; and

(3) The annual allocation, including any changes to existing methodologies for allocating workers' compensation costs.

(Subd (b) adopted effective January 1, 2015.)

(c) Membership

The advisory committee consists of persons from trial courts and state judicial branch entities knowledgeable about workers' compensation matters, including court executive officers, appellate court clerks/executive officers, and human resources professionals.

(Subd (c) amended effective January 1, 2018; adopted effective January 1, 2015.)

Rule 10.67 amended effective January 1, 2018; adopted effective January 1, 2015; previously amended effective July 1, 2016.

Advisory Committee Comment

The Judicial Branch Workers' Compensation Program is administered by the Judicial Council staff under rule 10.350.

Rule 10.70.   Task forces, working groups, and other advisory bodies

(a) Established by Chief Justice or Judicial Council

The Chief Justice or the council may establish task forces and other advisory bodies to work on specific projects that cannot be addressed by the council's standing advisory committees. These task forces and other advisory bodies may be required to report to one of the internal committees, as designated in their charges.

(Subd (a) lettered and amended effective July 1, 2015; adopted as unlettered subd effective January 1, 1999.)

(b) Established by Administrative Director

The Administrative Director may establish working groups to work on specific projects identified by the Administrative Director that address areas and topics within the Administrative Director's purview.

(Subd (b) adopted effective July 1, 2015.)

Rule 10.70 amended effective July 1, 2015; adopted as rule 6.70 effective January 1, 1999; previously renumbered effective January 1, 2007; previously amended effective September 1, 2003, and August 14, 2009.

Rule 10.71.   Court Facilities Transitional Task Force [Repealed]

Rule 10.71 repealed by its own provision effective June 30, 2007; adopted as rule 6.60 effective June 23, 2004; previously amended and renumbered effective January 1, 2007.

Chapter 3
Judicial Council Advisory Body Meetings

Title 10, Judicial Administration Rules—Division 1, Judicial Council—Chapter 3, Judicial Council Advisory Body Meetings; adopted effective July 1, 2014.

Rule 10.75.   Meetings of advisory bodies

(a) Intent

The Judicial Council intends by this rule to supplement and expand on existing rules and procedures providing public access to the council and its advisory bodies. Existing rules and procedures provide for circulation of advisory body proposals regarding rules, forms, standards, and jury instructions for public comment, posting of written reports for the council on the California Courts website (*www.courts.ca.gov*), public attendance and comment during council meetings, real time audio casts of council meetings, and public posting of council meeting minutes. This rule expands public access to advisory body meetings.

(Subd (a) adopted effective July 1, 2014.)

(b) Advisory bodies and chairs

(1) "Advisory bodies," as used in this rule, means any multimember body created by the Judicial Council to review issues and report to the council. For purposes of this rule, subcommittees that are composed of less than a majority of the members of the advisory body are not advisory bodies. However, standing subcommittees that are charged with addressing a topic as a continuing matter are advisory bodies for purposes of this rule irrespective of their composition.

(2) "Chair," as used in this rule, includes a chair's designee.

(Subd (b) adopted effective July 1, 2014.)

(c) Open meetings

(1) *Meetings*

Advisory body meetings to review issues that the advisory body will report to the Judicial Council are open to the public, except as otherwise provided in this rule. A meeting open to the public includes a budget meeting, which is a meeting or portion of a meeting to discuss a proposed recommendation of the advisory body that the Judicial Council approve an allocation or direct an expenditure of public funds. A majority of advisory body members must not decide a matter included on a posted agenda for an upcoming meeting in advance of the meeting.

(2) *Exempt bodies*

The meetings of the following advisory bodies and their subcommittees are exempt from the requirements of this rule:

(A) Advisory Committee on Civil Jury Instructions;

(B) Advisory Committee on Criminal Jury Instructions; and

(C) Litigation Management Committee.

(3) *Rule committees*

With the exception of any budget meetings, the meetings of the rule committees listed in this subdivision and of their subcommittees are closed unless the chair concludes that a particular agenda item may be addressed in open session. Any budget meeting must be open to the public.

(A) Appellate Advisory Committee;

(B) Civil and Small Claims Advisory Committee;

(C) Criminal Law Advisory Committee;

(D) Family and Juvenile Law Advisory Committee;

(E) Probate and Mental Health Advisory Committee; and

(F) Traffic Advisory Committee.

(Subd (c) adopted effective July 1, 2014.)

(d) Closed sessions

The chair of an advisory body or an advisory body subcommittee may close a meeting, or portion of a meeting, to discuss any of the following:

(1) The appointment, qualifications, performance, or health of an individual, or other information that, if discussed in public, would constitute an unwarranted invasion of personal privacy;

(2) Claims, administrative claims, agency investigations, or pending or reasonably anticipated litigation naming, or reasonably anticipated to name, a judicial branch entity or a member, officer, or employee of such an entity;

(3) Negotiations concerning a contract, a labor issue, or legislation;

(4) The price and terms of payment for the purchase, sale, exchange, or lease of real property for a judicial branch facility before the property has been acquired or the relevant contracts have been executed;

(5) Security plans or procedures or other matters that if discussed in public would compromise the safety of the public or of judicial branch officers or personnel or the security of judicial branch facilities or equipment, including electronic data;

(6) Non-final audit reports or proposed responses to such reports;

(7) Trade secrets or privileged or confidential commercial and financial information;

(8) Development, modification, or approval of any licensing or other professional examination or examination procedure;

(9) Evaluation of individual grant applications; or

(10) Topics that judicial officers may not discuss in public without risking a violation of the California Code of Judicial Ethics, necessitating recusal, or encouraging disqualification motions or peremptory challenges against them, including proposed legislation, rules, forms, standards of judicial administration, or jury instructions.

(Subd (d) adopted effective July 1, 2014.)

(e) Notice of meetings

(1) *Regular meetings*

Public notice must be given of the date and agenda of each meeting that is subject to this rule, whether open or closed, at least five business days before the meeting.

(2) *Urgent circumstances*

A meeting that is subject to this rule may be conducted on 24-hours notice in case of urgent circumstances requiring prompt action. The minutes of such meetings must briefly state the facts creating the urgent circumstances requiring prompt action and the action taken.

(Subd (e) adopted effective July 1, 2014.)

(f) Form of notice

(1) The notice and agenda for a meeting subject to this rule, whether open or closed, must be posted on the California Courts website.

(2) The notice for meetings subject to this rule must state whether the meeting is open or closed. If a meeting is closed or partially closed, the notice must identify the closed agenda items and the specific subdivision of this rule authorizing the closure.

(3) For meetings that are open in part or in full, the notice must provide:

(A) The telephone number or other electronic means that a member of the public may use to attend the meeting;

(B) The time of the meeting, whether the public may attend in person, and, if so, the meeting location; and

(C) The e-mail address or other electronic means that the public may use to submit written comments regarding agenda items or requests to make an audio recording of a meeting.

(Subd (f) adopted effective July 1, 2014.)

(g) Contents of agenda

The agenda for a meeting subject to this rule, whether open or closed, must contain a brief description of each item to be considered during the meeting. If a meeting is closed or partially closed, the agenda must identify the specific subdivision of this rule authorizing the closure.

(Subd (g) adopted effective July 1, 2014.)

(h) Meeting materials

Materials for an open meeting must be posted on the California Courts website at least three business days before the date of the meeting, except in extraordinary circumstances.

(Subd (h) adopted effective July 1, 2014.)

(i) Public attendance

The public may attend open sessions of advisory body meetings by telephone or other available electronic means. If the members of an advisory body gather in person at a single location for a meeting, the public may attend in person at that location if the chair concludes security measures permit.

(Subd (i) adopted effective July 1, 2014.)

(j) Conduct at meeting

Members of the public who attend open meetings in person must remain orderly. The chair may order the removal of any disorderly person.

(Subd (j) adopted effective July 1, 2014.)

(k) Public comment

(1) *Written comment*

The public may submit written comments for any agenda item of a regularly noticed open meeting up to one complete business day before the meeting.

(2) *In-person comment*

If security measures permit public attendance at an open in-person advisory body meeting, the meeting must include an opportunity for public comment on each agenda item before the advisory body considers the item. Requests to comment on an agenda item must be submitted before the meeting begins, indicating the speaker's name, the name of the organization that the speaker represents, if any, and the agenda item that the public comment will address. The advisory body chair may grant a request to comment on an agenda item that is received after a meeting has begun.

(3) *Reasonable limits and timing*

The advisory body chair has discretion to establish reasonable limits on the length of time for each speaker and the total amount of time permitted for public comment. The chair may also decide whether public comments will be heard at the beginning of the meeting or in advance of the agenda items.

(Subd (k) adopted effective July 1, 2014.)

(l) Making an audio recording of a meeting

An advisory body chair may permit a member of the public to make an audio recording of an open meeting, or the open portion of a meeting, if a written request is submitted at least two business days before the meeting.

(Subd (l) adopted effective July 1, 2014.)

(m) Minutes as official records

Minutes of each meeting subject to this rule, whether open or closed, must be prepared for approval at a future meeting. When approved by the advisory body, the minutes constitute the official record of the meeting. Approved minutes for the open portion of a meeting must be posted on the California Courts website.

(Subd (m) adopted effective July 1, 2014.)

(n) Adjourned meetings

An advisory body chair may adjourn a meeting to reconvene at a specified time without issuing a new notice under (e)(1), provided that, if open agenda items remain for discussion, notice of the adjourned meeting is posted on the California Courts website 24 hours before the meeting reconvenes. The notice must identify any remaining open agenda items to be discussed, the time that the meeting will reconvene, the telephone number that the public may use to attend the meeting, and if the public may attend the reconvened meeting in person, the location. The advisory body may not consider new agenda items when the meeting reconvenes except as permitted under (e)(2).

(Subd (n) adopted effective July 1, 2014.)

(o) Action by e-mail between meetings

An advisory body may take action by e-mail between meetings in circumstances specified in this subdivision.

(1) *Circumstances*

An advisory body chair may distribute a proposal by e-mail to all advisory body members for action between meetings if:

(A) The advisory body discussed and considered the proposal at a previous meeting but concluded additional information was needed; or

(B) The chair concludes that prompt action is needed.

(2) *Notice*

If an e-mail proposal concerns a matter that otherwise must be discussed in an open meeting, the advisory body must provide public notice and allow one complete business day for public comment concerning the proposal before acting on the proposal. The notice must be posted on the California Courts website and must provide an e-mail address to which the public may submit written comments. The advisory body may forego public comment if the chair concludes that prompt action is required.

(3) *Communications*

If an e-mail proposal concerns a matter that otherwise must be discussed in an open meeting, after distribution of the proposal and until the advisory body has acted, advisory body members must restrict their communications with each other about the proposal to e-mail. This restriction only applies to proposals distributed under this subdivision.

(4) *Official record*

Written minutes describing the action taken on an e-mail proposal that otherwise must be discussed in an open meeting must be prepared for approval at a future meeting. The minutes must attach any public comments received. When approved by the advisory body, the minutes constitute the official record of the proposal. Approved minutes for such a proposal must be posted to the California Courts website. The e-mails exchanged concerning a proposal that otherwise would have been considered in a closed meeting will constitute the official record of the proposal.

(Subd (o) adopted effective July 1, 2014.)

(p) Review requirement

The Judicial Council will review the impact of this rule within one year of the rule's adoption and periodically thereafter to determine whether amendments are needed. In conducting its review, the council will consider, among other factors, the public interest in access to meetings of the council's advisory bodies, the obligation of the judiciary to comply with judicial ethics standards, and the public interest in the ability of advisory bodies to effectively assist the Judicial Council by offering policy recommendations and alternatives for improving the administration of justice.

(Subd (p) adopted effective July 1, 2014.)
Rule 10.75 adopted effective July 1, 2014.

Advisory Committee Comment

Subdivisions (a) and (c)(1). This rule expands public access to Judicial Council advisory bodies. The council recognizes the important public interest in access to those meetings and to information regarding administration and governance of the judicial branch. Meetings of the Judicial Council are open, and notice and materials for those meetings are provided to the public, under rules 10.5 and 10.6. Rules in Division 1 of Title 10 describe the council's advisory bodies and require that proposals for rules, standards, forms, and jury instructions be circulated for public comment. (See Cal. Rules of Court, rules 10.10–10.22, 10.30–10.70.) Reports to the council presenting proposals and recommendations are publicly posted on the California Courts website (*www.courts.ca.gov*). Internal committee chairs report at each council meeting regarding the activities of the internal committees in the period since the last council meeting, and internal committee meeting minutes also are posted on the California Courts website. This rule expands on those existing rules and procedures to increase public access by opening the meetings of advisory bodies to review issues that the advisory body will report to the council. The rule does not apply to meetings that do not involve review of issues to be reported to the council, such as meetings providing education and training of members, discussion of best practices, or sharing of information of general interest unrelated to advice or reports to the council. Those non-advisory matters are outside the scope of this rule.

Subdivision (b)(1). The definition provided in (b)(1) is intended exclusively for this rule and includes internal committees, advisory committees, task forces, and other similar multimember bodies that the council creates to review issues and

report to it. (Cf. Cal. Rules of Court, rule 10.30(a) ["Judicial Council advisory bodies are typically advisory committees and task forces"].)

Subdivisions (c)(2), (c)(3), and (d)(10). The Code of Judicial Ethics governs the conduct of judges and is binding upon them. It establishes high standards of conduct that judges must personally observe, maintain, and enforce at all times to promote and protect public confidence in the integrity and impartiality of the judiciary. (See Code Judicial Ethics, Preamble, canon 1, canon 2A.) Among other things, compliance with these high ethical standards means avoiding conduct that could suggest a judge does not have an open mind in considering issues that may come before the judge. (*Id.*, canon 2A.) Judges also are prohibited from making public comments about a pending or impending proceeding (*id.*, canon 3B(9)), signifying that they may not publicly discuss case law that has not reached final disposition through the appellate process, or pending or anticipated litigation, conduct that would be required to participate in the work covered by the referenced subdivisions. Ethical standards also direct that they hear and decide all matters assigned to them, avoiding extrajudicial duties that would lead to their frequent disqualification. (*Id.*, canons 3B(1), 4A(4).)

The work of the three advisory bodies listed in subdivision (c)(2) exclusively involves discussion of topics that are uniquely difficult or impossible for judges to address while honoring the detailed ethical standards governing the judiciary. For example, as required by rule, the Litigation Management Committee discusses pending or anticipated claims and litigation against judicial officers, courts, and court employees. Jury instruction committees also may discuss decisions or rulings issued in cases that have not reached final resolution through the appellate process. Thus, opening the meetings of these three committees would result in precluding judges, who are specially learned in the law, from meaningful participation on those committees. Subdivision (c)(2) is added to avoid this result.

The work of the six rule committees listed in subdivision (c)(3) almost always will trigger similar issues. Those bodies focus primarily on developing, and providing input concerning, proposed legislation, rules, forms, and standards of judicial administration. That work necessarily entails a complex interchange of views, consideration of multiple perspectives, and the vetting of opposing legal arguments, which judges cannot undertake in public without risk that their comments will be misunderstood or used as a basis for disqualification or challenge. Service on the referenced committees, and public participation in discussing the referenced topics, may make it difficult for a judge to hear and decide all matters assigned to the judge and conceivably could lead to frequent disqualification of the judge, exposing the judge to risk of an ethical violation. This may create significant practical issues for courts related to judicial workloads, while also deterring individuals specially learned in the law from serving on advisory bodies, in turn depriving the public of the benefits of their training and experience in crafting procedures for the effective and efficient administration of justice. Subdivisions (c)(3) and (d)(10) are intended to prevent such deleterious results by clarifying that meetings of the six rule committees whose work almost entirely focuses on these topics ordinarily will be closed and that meetings of other bodies performing similar functions also will be closed as the chairs deem appropriate, with the exception that any budget meetings must be open.

Subdivision (d)(7). Definitions of the terms "trade secret," "privileged information," and "confidential commercial and financial information," are provided in rule 10.500(f)(10).

Subdivision (k)(1). Due to budget constraints, members' schedules, and the geographic diversity of most committees' membership, advisory body meetings typically are held via teleconference or other method not requiring the members' in person attendance. Because judicial officer and attorney members may have limited time for meetings (e.g., only a lunch hour), the volume of advisory body business to be accomplished in those periods may be considerable, and the costs of coordinating teleconferences that would accommodate spoken comments from the public would be significant in the aggregate, the rule only provides for public comment in writing. To ensure sufficient time for advisory body staff to gather and distribute written comments to members, and for members to review comments before the meeting, the rule requires that comments be submitted one complete business day before the meeting.

Chapter 4
Judicial Council staff

Title 10, Judicial Administration Rules—Division 1, Judicial Council—Chapter 4, Judicial Council staff; amended effective July 29, 2014; renumbered effective July 1, 2014.

Rule 10.80. Administrative Director of the Courts (Administrative Director)
Rule 10.81. Judicial Council staff

Rule 10.80. Administrative Director of the Courts (Administrative Director)

(a) Functions

The Administrative Director, appointed by the Judicial Council under article VI, section 6 of the Constitution, performs those functions prescribed by the Constitution and laws of the state, or delegated to the director by the Judicial Council or the Chief Justice.

(Subd (a) amended effective July 29, 2014; adopted as unlettered subd effective January 1, 1999; previously lettered subd (a) and amended effective August 14, 2009.)

(b) Accountability

The Administrative Director is accountable to the council and the Chief Justice for the performance of the Judicial Council staff. The Administrative Director's charge is to accomplish the council's goals and priorities.

(Subd (b) amended effective July 29, 2014; adopted effective August 14, 2009.)

(c) Interpretation of policies

The Administrative Director may use any reasonable interpretation of Judicial Council policies to achieve the council's goals, consistent with the limitations from the council and the Chief Justice.

(Subd (c) adopted effective August 14, 2009.)

(d) Responsibilities

In carrying out these duties, the Administrative Director is responsible for allocating the financial and other resources relating to the Judicial Council staff (including, for example, funding the operation of advisory bodies and other activities) to achieve the branch goals and policies adopted by the Judicial Council of California.

(Subd (d) amended effective July 29, 2014; adopted effective August 14, 2009.)

(e) Reports

The Administrative Director reports to the Judicial Council at least once annually on the progress made toward achieving the council's goals. When the council sets the direction on projects or programs that require more than one year to complete, the Administrative Director will report back to the council at regular intervals on their status and significant developments.

(Subd (e) adopted effective August 14, 2009.)

Rule 10.80 amended effective July 29, 2014; adopted as rule 6.80 effective January 1, 1999; previously amended and renumbered effective January 1, 2007; previously amended effective August 14, 2009.

Rule 10.81.   Judicial Council staff

(a) Establishment

The Administrative Director, under the supervision of the Chief Justice, employs, organizes, and directs a staff that assists the council and its chair in carrying out their duties under the Constitution and laws of the state.

(Subd (a) amended effective July 29, 2014; previously amended effective January 1, 2007, and August 14, 2009.)

(b) References to "Administrative Office of the Courts"

The Judicial Council in the past referred to its staff as the "Administrative Office of the Courts". The following applies where the term "Administrative Office of the Courts" is used:

(1) Rules of Court

Throughout these rules of court and in all Judicial Council forms, all references to "Administrative Office of the Courts" or "AOC" are deemed to refer to the Judicial Council, the Administrative Director, or the Judicial Council staff, as appropriate.

(2) Other Judicial Council materials and actions

All references to "Administrative Office of the Courts" or "AOC" in any policy, procedure, manual, guideline, publication, or other material issued by the Judicial Council or its staff are deemed to refer to the Judicial Council, the Administrative Director, or the Judicial Council staff, as appropriate. Judicial Council staff will continue to be responsible for any active delegations or directives the Judicial Council made to the Administrative Office of the Court.

(3) Statutes

The Judicial Council, its staff, or the Administrative Director, as appropriate, will continue to perform all functions, duties, responsibilities, and other obligations imposed by statute or regulation on the Administrative Office of the Courts.

(4) Agreements and proceedings

The Judicial Council will continue to perform all duties, responsibilities, functions, or other obligations, and bear all liabilities, and exercise all rights, powers, authorities, benefits, and other privileges attributed to the "Administrative Office of the Courts" or "AOC" arising from contracts, memorandums of understanding, or other legal agreements, documents, proceedings, or transactions. The Judicial Council may be substituted for the "Administrative Office of the Courts" or "AOC" wherever necessary, with no prejudice to the substantive rights of any party.

(Subd (b) amended effective July 29, 2014; previously amended effective January 1, 2007.)

Rule 10.81 amended effective July 29, 2014; adopted as rule 6.81 effective January 1, 1999; previously amended and renumbered effective January 1, 2007; previously amended effective August 14, 2009.

Advisory Committee Comment

The Judicial Council in 1961 adopted a resolution that named its staff the "Administrative Office of the California Courts." In 1970, the council adopted a rule of court that renamed its staff the "Administrative Office of the Courts."

In recent years, the council became aware of recurring confusion about the relationship between the Administrative Office of the Courts and the Judicial Council. There was a common misperception that the Administrative Office of the Courts was a separate entity from the council having independent policymaking authority, when in fact, the members of the Judicial Council set policy, and staff, by whatever name, support the work of the council under the members' direction and oversight. The confusion about the role of the Administrative Office of the Courts impeded the council's ability to advance the interests of the judicial branch.

To allow the council to better achieve its mission, it decided in 2014 to retire the name "Administrative Office of the Courts." This adjustment underscored the unity of identity of the Judicial Council and its staff, and clarified that there has always been only a single entity. The retirement conformed the Judicial Council's practice with that of other state government entities, which do not assign a separate name to their staffs.

The 2014 amendments to this rule are intended to implement the retirement of the name "Administrative Office of the Courts" and clarify that in retiring the name no substantive legal change has occurred. The Judicial Council and its staff will continue to discharge any legal obligations and duties they may have, regardless of the discontinuance of the use of the name "Administrative Office of the Courts."

Division 2
Administration of the Judicial Branch

Chapter 1
Budget and Fiscal Management

Rule 10.101.   Role of the Judicial Council

(a) Purpose

This rule specifies the responsibilities of the Judicial Council, the Chief Justice, the Administrative Director, and council staff with respect to the judicial branch budget.

(Subd (a) amended effective July 1, 2015; previously amended effective January 1, 2005, January 1, 2007, and August 14, 2009.)

(b) Duties of the Judicial Council

The Judicial Council must:

(1) Establish responsible fiscal priorities that best enable the judicial branch to achieve its goals and the Judicial Council to achieve its mission;

(2) Develop policies and procedures for the creation and implementation of a yearly budget for the judicial branch;

(3) Develop the budget of the judicial branch based on the priorities established and the needs of the courts;

(4) Communicate and advocate the budget of the judicial branch to the Governor and the Legislature;

(5) Allocate funds in a manner that ensures equal access to justice for all citizens of the state, ensures the ability of the courts to carry out their functions effectively, promotes implementation of statewide policies as established by statute and the Judicial Council, and promotes implementation of efficiencies and cost-saving measures;

(6) Resolve appeals on budget and allocation issues; and

(7) Ensure that the budget of the judicial branch remains within the limits of the appropriation set by the Legislature.

(Subd (b) amended effective July 1, 2015; previously amended effective January 1, 2007, and August 14, 2009.)

(c) Authority of the Chief Justice and Administrative Director

(1) The Chief Justice and the Administrative Director may take the following actions, on behalf of the Judicial Council, with regard to any of the Judicial Council's recommended budgets for the Supreme Court, the

Courts of Appeal, the trial courts, the Judicial Council, the Habeas Corpus Resource Center, and council staff:

(A) Make technical changes to the proposed budget; and

(B) Make changes during their negotiations with the legislative and executive branches consistent with the goals and priorities adopted by the Judicial Council.

(2) The Chief Justice, on behalf of the Judicial Council, may allocate funding appropriated in the annual State Budget to the Supreme Court, the Courts of Appeal, the Judicial Council, the Habeas Corpus Resource Center, and council staff.

(3) After the end of each fiscal year, the Administrative Director must report to the Judicial Council on the actual expenditures from the budgets for the Supreme Court, the Courts of Appeal, the trial courts, the Judicial Council, the Habeas Corpus Resource Center, and council staff.

(Subd (c) amended effective July 1, 2015; adopted effective January 1, 2005; previously amended effective August 14, 2009.)

(d) Duties of the Administrative Director

The Administrative Director implements the directives of the Judicial Council and must:

(1) Present the judicial branch budget in negotiations with the Governor and the Legislature; and

(2) Allocate to the trial courts, on behalf of the Judicial Council, a portion of the prior fiscal year baseline allocation for the trial courts following approval of the State Budget and before the allocation of state trial court funding by the Judicial Council. The portion of the prior fiscal year baseline allocation that may be so allocated is limited to the amount estimated to be necessary for the operation of the courts pending action by the Judicial Council, and may not exceed 25 percent of the prior fiscal year baseline allocation for each trial court.

(Subd (d) amended effective July 1, 2015; adopted as subd (c) effective July 1, 1998; previously relettered effective January 1, 2005; previously amended effective January 1, 2001, January 1, 2007, and August 14, 2009.)

(e) Duties of the director of Finance

The director of Finance for the Judicial Council, under the direction of the Administrative Director, administers the budget policies and procedures developed and approved by the Judicial Council. The director of Finance must:

(1) Develop and administer a budget preparation process for the judicial branch, and ensure the submission of a final budget recommendation for the judicial branch to the Department of Finance by November 1 of each year;

(2) Develop, in consultation with the State Controller's Office and the Department of Finance, a manual of procedures for the budget request process, revenues, expenditures, allocations, and payments;

(3) Monitor all revenues and expenditures for the judicial branch;

(4) Develop recommendations for fiscal priorities and the allocation and reallocation of funds; and

(5) Assist all courts and the Administrative Director in preparing and managing budgets.

(Subd (e) amended effective July 1, 2015; adopted as subd (d) effective July 1, 1998; previously relettered effective January 1, 2005; previously amended effective January 1, 2007, and August 14, 2009.)

Rule 10.101 amended effective July 1, 2015; adopted as rule 2301 effective July 1, 1998; renumbered as rule 6.101 effective January 1, 1999; previously amended and renumbered effective January 1, 2007; previously amended effective January 1, 2001, January 1, 2005, and August 14, 2009.

Advisory Committee Comment

Subdivision (c)(1)(A). Examples of technical changes to the budget include calculation of fiscal need, translation of an approved concept to final fiscal need, and simple non-policy-related baseline adjustments such as health and retirement benefits, Pro Rata, and the Statewide Cost Allocation Plan.

Rule 10.102.   Acceptance of gifts

(a) Administrative Director's authority to accept gifts

The Administrative Director may accept on behalf of any entity listed in (b) any gift of real or personal property if the gift and any terms and conditions are found to be in the best interest of the state. Any applicable standards used by the Director of Finance under Government Code section 11005.1 may be considered in accepting gifts.

(Subd (a) amended effective January 1, 2016; adopted as unlettered subd; previously amended and lettered as subd (a) effective January 1, 2004; previously amended effective January 1, 2007.)

(b) Delegation of authority

The Administrative Director may delegate the authority to accept gifts to the following, under any guidelines established by the Administrative Director:

(1) The executive officer of a superior court, for gifts to the superior court;

(2) The clerk/executive officer of a Court of Appeal, for gifts to that Court of Appeal;

(3) The clerk/executive officer of the Supreme Court, for gifts to the Supreme Court; and

(4) The Judicial Council's director of Finance, for gifts to the Judicial Council.

(Subd (b) amended effective January 1, 2018; previously adopted effective January 1, 2004; previously amended effective January 1, 2007, and January 1, 2016.)

Rule 10.102 amended effective January 1, 2018; adopted as rule 989.7 effective September 13, 1991; previously amended and renumbered as rule 6.102 effective January 1, 2004, and as rule 10.102 effective January 1, 2007; previously amended effective January 1, 2016.

Rule 10.103.   Limitation on intrabranch contracting

(a) Definitions

For purposes of this rule, "judicial branch entity" includes a trial court, a Court of Appeal, the Supreme Court, and the Judicial Council.

(Subd (a) amended effective January 1, 2016.)

(b) Application

This rule is not applicable to:

(1) Part-time commissioners, with respect to services as a commissioner;

(2) Part-time court interpreters who are not subject to the cross-assignment system under Government Code section 71810, with respect to interpreter services provided to a court; and

(3) Court reporters, with respect to reporter services provided to a court.

(Subd (b) amended effective January 1, 2007.)

(c) Intrabranch limitations

An employee of a judicial branch entity must not:

(1) Engage in any employment, enterprise, or other activity from which he or she receives compensation or in which he or she has a financial interest and that is sponsored or funded by any judicial branch entity through or by a contract for goods or services for which compensation is paid, unless the activity is required as a condition of his or her regular judicial branch employment; or

(2) Contract with any judicial branch entity, on his or her own behalf, to provide goods or services for which compensation is paid.

(Subd (c) amended effective January 1, 2007.)

(d) Multiple employment

This rule does not prohibit any person from being employed by more than one judicial branch entity.

Rule 10.103 amended effective January 1, 2016; adopted as rule 6.103 effective January 1, 2004; previously amended and renumbered as rule 10.103 effective January 1, 2007.

Rule 10.104.   Limitation on contracting with former employees

(a) Trial and appellate court contracts with former employees

A trial or appellate court may not enter into a contract for goods or services for which compensation is paid with a person previously employed by that court or by the Judicial Council:

(1) For a period of 12 months following the date of the former employee's retirement, dismissal, or separation from service, if he or she was employed in a policymaking position in the same general subject area as the proposed contract within the 12-month period before his or her retirement, dismissal, or separation; or

(2) For a period of 24 months following the date of the former employee's retirement, dismissal, or separation from service, if he or she engaged in any of the negotiations, transactions, planning, arrangements, or any part of the decision-making process relevant to the contract while employed in any capacity by the court or the Judicial Council.

(Subd (a) amended effective January 1, 2016.)

(b) Judicial Council contracts with former employees

The Judicial Council may not enter into a contract for goods or services for which compensation is paid with a person previously employed by it:

(1) For a period of 12 months following the date of the former employee's retirement, dismissal, or separation from service, if he or she was employed in a policymaking position at the Judicial Council in the same general subject area as the proposed contract within the 12-month period before his or her retirement, dismissal, or separation; or

(2) For a period of 24 months following the date of the former employee's retirement, dismissal, or separation from service, if he or she engaged in any of the negotiations, transactions, planning, arrangements, or any part of the decision-making process relevant to the contract while employed in any capacity by the Judicial Council.

(Subd (b) amended effective January 1, 2016; previously amended effective January 1, 2007.)

(c) Policymaking position

"Policymaking position" includes:

(1) In a trial court, the court's executive officer and any other position designated by the court as a policymaking position;

(2) In an appellate court, the clerk/executive officer and any other position designated by the court as a policymaking position; and

(3) In the Judicial Council, the Administrative Director, Chief of Staff, Chief Operating Officer, Chief Administrative Officer, any director, and any other position designated by the Administrative Director as a policymaking position.

(Subd (c) amended effective January 1, 2018; previously amended effective January 1, 2016.)

(d) Scope

This rule does not prohibit any court or the Judicial Council from (1) employing any person or (2) contracting with any former judge or justice.

(Subd (d) amended effective January 1, 2016.)

Rule 10.104 amended effective January 1, 2018; adopted as rule 6.104 effective January 1, 2004; previously amended and renumbered as rule 10.104 effective January 1, 2007; previously amended effective January 1, 2016.

Rule 10.105.   Allocation of new fee, fine, and forfeiture revenue

(a) Allocation

The Judicial Council must annually allocate 80 percent of the amount of fee, fine, and forfeiture revenue deposited in the Trial Court Improvement Fund under Government Code section 77205(a) that exceeds the amount of fee, fine, and forfeiture revenue deposited in the Trial Court Improvement Fund in fiscal year 2002–2003 to one or more of the following:

(1) To the trial courts in the counties from which the increased amount is attributable;

(2) To other trial courts to support trial court operations; or

(3) For retention in the Trial Court Improvement Fund.

(Subd (a) amended effective January 1, 2007.)

(b) Methodology

The Judicial Council staff must recommend a methodology for the allocation and must recommend an allocation based on this methodology. On approval of a methodology by the Judicial Council, Judicial Council staff must issue a Finance Memo stating the methodology adopted by the Judicial Council.

(Subd (b) amended effective January 1, 2016; previously amended effective January 1, 2007.)

Rule 10.105 amended effective January 1, 2016; adopted as rule 6.105 effective December 10, 2004; previously amended and renumbered as rule 10.105 effective January 1, 2007.

Rule 10.106.   Judicial branch travel expense reimbursement policy

(a) Adoption

The Judicial Council must adopt a fiscally responsible judicial branch travel expense reimbursement policy, under Government Code section 68506.5, that provides appropriate accountability for the use of public resources. Before adopting the initial policy, the Judicial Council must receive comments from the courts, court employee organizations, and other interested groups.

(Subd (a) adopted effective July 1, 2008.)

(b) Applicability

The judicial branch travel expense reimbursement policy applies to official state business travel by:

(1) Judicial officers and judicial officers sitting by assignment;

(2) Officers, employees, retired annuitants, and members of the Supreme Court, the Courts of Appeal, superior courts, the Judicial Council and its staff, the Habeas Corpus Resource Center, and the Commission on Judicial Performance; and

(3) Members of task forces, working groups, commissions, or similar bodies appointed by the Chief Justice, the Judicial Council, or the Administrative Director.

(Subd (b) amended effective January 1, 2016; adopted effective July 1, 2008.)

(c) Amendments

The Judicial Council delegates to the Administrative Director, under article VI, section 6(c) of the California Constitution and other applicable law, the authority to make technical changes and clarifications to the judicial branch travel expense reimbursement policy. The changes and clarifications must be fiscally responsible, provide for appropriate accountability, and be in general compliance with the policy initially adopted by the Judicial Council.

(Subd (c) amended effective January 1, 2016; adopted effective July 1, 2008.)
Rule 10.106 amended effective January 1, 2016; adopted effective July 1, 2008.

Rule 10.107.   Trial Court Budget Working Group [Repealed]

Rule 10.107 repealed effective January 1, 2015; repealed and adopted as rule 6.45 effective January 1, 2005; previously renumbered as rule 10.45 effective January 1, 2007, and as rule 10.107 effective August 14, 2009.

Chapter 2
Court Security

Rule 10.170.   Working Group on Court Security [Repealed]

Rule 10.170 repealed effective October 25, 2013; adopted as rule 6.170 effective October 15, 2003; previously amended and renumbered effective January 1, 2007.

Rule 10.171.   Working Group on Court Security Fiscal Guidelines [Repealed]

Rule 10.171 repealed effective October 25, 2013; adopted as rule 6.170 effective January 1, 2003; adopted as rule 6.171 effective October 15, 2003; previously amended and renumbered effective January 1, 2007.

Rule 10.172.   Court security plans

(a) Responsibility

The presiding judge and the sheriff or marshal are responsible for developing an annual or multiyear comprehensive, countywide court security plan.

(Subd (a) adopted effective January 1, 2009.)

(b) Scope of security plan

(1) Each court security plan must, at a minimum, address the following general security subject areas:

(A) Composition and role of court security committees;

(B) Composition and role of executive team;

(C) Incident command system;

(D) Self-assessments and audits of court security;

(E) Mail handling security;

(F) Identification cards and access control;

(G) Courthouse landscaping security plan;

(H) Parking plan security;

(I) Interior and exterior lighting plan security;

(J) Intrusion and panic alarm systems;

(K) Fire detection and equipment;

(L) Emergency and auxiliary power;

(M) Use of private security contractors;

(N) Use of court attendants and employees;

(O) Administrative/clerk's office security;

(P) Jury personnel and jury room security;

(Q) Security for public demonstrations;

(R) Vital records storage security;

(S) Evacuation planning;

(T) Security for after-hours operations;

(U) Custodial services;

(V) Computer and data security;

(W) Workplace violence prevention; and

(X) Public access to court proceedings.

(2) Each court security plan must, at a minimum, address the following law enforcement subject areas:

(A) Security personnel and staffing;

(B) Perimeter and entry screening;

(C) Prisoner and inmate transport;

(D) Holding cells;

(E) Interior and public waiting area security;

(F) Courtroom security;

(G) Jury trial procedures;

(H) High-profile and high-risk trial security;

(I) Judicial protection;

(J) Incident reporting and recording;

(K) Security personnel training;

(L) Courthouse security communication;

(M) Hostage, escape, lockdown, and active shooter procedures;

(N) Firearms policies and procedures; and

(O) Restraint of defendants.

(3) Each court security plan should address additional security issues as needed.

(Subd (b) adopted effective January 1, 2009.)

(c) Court security assessment and assessment report

At least once every two years, the presiding judge and the sheriff or marshal are responsible for conducting an assessment of security with respect to all court operations. The assessment must include a comprehensive review of the court's physical security profile and security protocols and procedures. The assessment should identify security weaknesses, resource deficiencies, compliance with the court security plan, and any need for changes to the court security plan. The assessment must be summarized in a written assessment report.

(Subd (c) adopted effective January 1, 2009.)

(d) Submission of court security plan to the Judicial Council

On or before November 1, 2009, each superior court must submit a court security plan to the Judicial Council. On or before February 1, 2011, and each succeeding February 1, each superior court must give notice to the Judicial Council whether it has made any changes to the court security plan and, if so, identify each change made and provide copies of the current court security plan and current assessment report. In preparing any submission, a court may request technical assistance from Judicial Council staff.

(Subd (d) amended effective January 1, 2016; adopted effective January 1, 2009.)

(e) Plan review process

Judicial Council staff will evaluate for completeness submissions identified in (d). Annually, the submissions and evaluations will be provided to the Court Security Advisory Committee. Any submissions determined by the advisory committee to be incomplete or deficient must be returned to the submitting court for correction and completion.

(Subd (e) amended effective January 1, 2016; adopted effective January 1, 2009.)

(f) Delegation

The presiding judge may delegate any of the specific duties listed in this rule to another judge or, if the duty does not require the exercise of judicial authority, to the court executive officer or other court employee. The presiding judge remains responsible for all duties listed in this rule even if he or she has delegated particular tasks to someone else.

(Subd (f) adopted effective January 1, 2009.)

Rule 10.172 amended effective January 1, 2016; adopted effective January 1, 2009.

Advisory Committee Comment

This rule is adopted to comply with the mandate in Government Code section 69925, which requires the Judicial Council to provide for the areas to be addressed in a court security plan and to establish a process for the review of such plans.

Rule 10.173. Court security committees

(a) Establishment

Each superior court must establish a standing court security committee.

(Subd (a) adopted effective January 1, 2009.)

(b) Role of the court security committee

The court security committee and any subcommittees advise the presiding judge and sheriff or marshal on the preparation of court security plans and on the formulation and implementation of all other policies and procedures related to security for court operations and security for facilities where the court conducts its operations. The presiding judge and sheriff or marshal may delegate to a court security committee or subcommittee the responsibility for conducting the court security assessment and preparing the assessment report.

(Subd (b) adopted effective January 1, 2009.)

(c) Members

(1) The court security committee must be chaired by the presiding judge or a judge designated by the presiding judge.

(2) In addition to the chair, each court security committee must include at least one representative designated by the sheriff or marshal and either the court executive officer or other court administrator as designated by the presiding judge.

(3) The chair may appoint additional members as appropriate. Additional members may include representatives from other government agencies, including:

(A) The facilities management office of the government entity, or entities, that hold title to or are responsible for the facilities where the court conducts its operations;

(B) Local fire protection agencies;

(C) Agencies that occupy portions of a court facility; and

(D) Agencies other than the sheriff that manage local corrections or state prison facilities.

(Subd (c) adopted effective January 1, 2009.)

(d) Facility contact person

In those courts having more than one court facility, the chair of the court security committee must designate for each facility a single contact person to coordinate activities in the event of an emergency and to collaborate with the court security committee, at its request.

(Subd (d) adopted effective January 1, 2009.)

(e) Subcommittees

The chair of the court security committee may form subcommittees if appropriate, including a subcommittee for each court facility. The chair must determine the composition of each subcommittee based on the individual court's circumstances.

(Subd (e) adopted effective January 1, 2009.)

Rule 10.173 adopted effective January 1, 2009.

Rule 10.174. Petition Regarding Disputes Related to Court Security Memoranda of Understanding

(a) Application

This rule applies to petitions filed under Government Code section 69926(e).

(Subd (a) adopted effective November 1, 2012.)

(b) Request for assignment of Court of Appeal justice

(1) If a sheriff, county, or superior court is unable to resolve a dispute related to the memorandum of understanding required by Government Code section 69926(b), the sheriff, county, or superior court may file a petition for a writ of mandamus or writ of prohibition.

(2) On the first page, below the case number, the petition must include the following language in the statement of the character of the proceeding (see rule 2.111(6)): "Petition filed under Government Code section 69926(e): Assignment of Court of Appeal justice requested."

(3) On receipt of a petition, the superior court clerk must submit a request to the Chief Justice asking that he or she assign a Court of Appeal justice from an appellate district other than the one in which the county, the superior court, and the sheriff are located to hear and decide the petition.

(Subd (b) adopted effective November 1, 2012.)

(c) Superior court hearing

A petition filed under this rule must be heard and decided on an expedited basis and must be given priority over other matters to the extent permitted by law and the rules of court.

(Subd (c) adopted effective November 1, 2012.)

(d) Appeal

(1) Any notice of appeal of a decision under (c) must be filed in the same superior court in which the petition was initially filed and must include on the first page the following language, below the case number, in the statement of the character of the proceeding (see rule 2.111(6)): "Notice of Appeal Relating to Petition filed under Government Code section 69926(e): Transfer Requested."

(2) On receipt of the notice of appeal, the Court of Appeal must request that the Supreme Court transfer the appeal to an appellate district other than the one in which the county, the superior court, and the sheriff are located.

(Subd (d) adopted effective November 1, 2012.)

Rule 10.174 adopted effective November 1, 2012.

Chapter 3
Court Facilities

Rule 10.180. Court facilities standards

(a) Development of standards

Judicial Council staff is responsible for developing and maintaining standards for the alteration, remodeling, renovation, and expansion of existing court facilities and for the construction of new court facilities.

(Subd (a) amended effective January 1, 2016; previously amended effective April 21, 2006.)

(b) Adoption by the Judicial Council

The standards developed by Judicial Council staff must be submitted to the Judicial Council for review and adoption as the standards to be used for court facilities in the state. Nonsubstantive changes to the standards may be made by the Judicial Council staff; substantive changes must be submitted to the Judicial Council for review and adoption.

(Subd (b) amended effective January 1, 2016; previously amended effective April 21, 2006.)

(c) Use of standards

The Judicial Council and its staff, affected courts, and advisory groups on court facilities issues created under these rules must use the standards adopted under (b) in reviewing or recommending proposed alteration, remodeling, renovation, or expansion of an existing court facility or new construction. Courts and advisory groups must report deviations from the standards to Judicial Council staff through a process established for that purpose.

(Subd (c) amended effective January 1, 2016; previously amended effective June 23, 2004, and April 21, 2006.)

Rule 10.180 amended effective January 1, 2016; adopted as rule 6.150 effective July 1, 2002; previously amended effective June 23, 2004, and April 21, 2006; previously renumbered as rule 10.180 effective January 1, 2007.

Rule 10.181. Court facilities policies, procedures, and standards

(a) Responsibilities of Judicial Council staff

Judicial Council staff, after consultation with the Court Facilities Transitional Task Force, must prepare and present to the Judicial Council recommendations for policies, procedures, and standards concerning the operation, maintenance, alteration, remodeling, renovation, expansion, acquisition, space programming, design, and construction of appellate and trial court facilities under Government Code sections 69204(c) and 70391(e).

(Subd (a) amended effective January 1, 2016; adopted as part of unlettered subd; previously amended and lettered as subd (a) effective January 1, 2007.)

(b) Consultations with the affected court and with local governmental and community interests

The policies, procedures, and standards must ensure that decisions are made in consultation with the affected court, when appropriate, and that decisions concerning acquisition, design, and construction of court facilities are made in consultation with local governmental and community interests, when appropriate.

(Subd (b) lettered and amended effective January 1, 2007; adopted as part of unlettered subd.)

Rule 10.181 amended effective January 1, 2016; adopted as rule 6.180 effective June 23, 2004; previously amended effective April 21, 2006; previously amended and renumbered as rule 10.181 effective January 1, 2007.

Rule 10.182. Operation and maintenance of court facilities

(a) Intent

The intent of this rule is to allocate responsibility and decision making for the operation and maintenance of court facilities among the courts and Judicial Council staff.

(Subd (a) amended effective January 1, 2016.)

(b) Responsibilities of Judicial Council staff

(1) In addition to those matters expressly authorized by statute, Judicial Council staff are responsible for:

(A) Taking action on the operation of court facilities, including the day-to-day operation of a building and maintenance of a facility. Judicial Council staff must, in cooperation with the court, perform its responsibilities concerning operation of the court facility to effectively and efficiently support the day-to-day operation of the court system and services of the court. These actions include maintaining proper heating, ventilation, and air conditioning levels; providing functional electrical, fire safety, vertical transportation, mechanical, and plumbing systems through preventive maintenance and responsive repairs; and maintaining structural, nonstructural, security, and telecommunications infrastructures.

(B) Preparing and submitting budget allocation proposals to the Judicial Council, as part of the yearly judicial branch budget development cycle, specifying the amounts to be spent for the operation of court facilities as provided in (A).

(C) Developing policies, procedures, and guidelines concerning court facilities for submission to the Judicial Council.

(2) Judicial Council staff must consult with affected courts concerning the annual operations and maintenance needs assessment, development of annual priorities, and fiscal planning for the operational and maintenance needs of court facilities.

(3) Judicial Council staff may, when appropriate, delegate its responsibilities for ongoing operation and management to the court for some or all of the existing court facilities used by that court. Any delegation of responsibility must ensure that:

(A) The management of court facilities is consistent with the statewide goals and policies of the judicial branch;

(B) Access to all court facilities in California is promoted;

(C) Facilities decisions are made with consideration of operational costs and enhance economical, efficient, and effective court operations; and

(D) Courts have adequate and sufficient facilities and appropriate resources to undertake these delegated tasks.

(4) Judicial Council staff must, whenever feasible, seek review and recommendations from the Court Facilities Transitional Task Force before recommending action on appellate and trial court facilities issues to the Judicial Council.

(Subd (b) amended effective January 1, 2016; previously amended effective January 1, 2007.)

(c) Responsibilities of the courts

(1) The affected courts must consult with Judicial Council staff concerning the annual operations and maintenance needs assessment, development of annual priorities, and fiscal planning for the operational and maintenance needs of court facilities, including contingency planning for unforeseen facility maintenance needs.

(2) Each court to which responsibility is delegated under (b)(3) must report to Judicial Council staff quarterly or more often, as provided in the delegation. The report must include the activities and expenditures related to the delegation that are specified for reporting in the delegation. Each court must also account to Judicial Council staff for all expenditures related to the delegation. Judicial Council staff may conduct an internal audit of any receipts and expenditures.

(Subd (c) amended effective January 1, 2016; previously amended effective January 1, 2007.)

Rule 10.182 amended effective January 1, 2016; adopted as rule 6.181 effective June 23, 2004; previously amended and renumbered as rule 10.182 effective January 1, 2007.

Rule 10.183. Decision making on transfer of responsibility for trial court facilities

(a) Intent

The intent of this rule is to allocate among the Judicial Council, the trial courts, and Judicial Council staff, responsibility and decision making for the transfer of responsibility for trial court facilities from the counties to the Judicial Council.

(Subd (a) amended effective January 1, 2016.)

(b) Definitions

As used in this rule, the following terms have the same meaning as provided by Government Code section 70301:

(1) "Court facilities";

(2) "Maintenance";

(3) "Responsibility for facilities"; and

(4) "Shared use."

(Subd (b) amended effective January 1, 2007.)

(c) Responsibilities of the Judicial Council and the Executive and Planning Committee

The Judicial Council must determine the following issues concerning transfer of responsibility of court facilities, except in the case of a need for urgent action between meetings of the council, in which case the Executive and Planning Committee is authorized to act under rule 10.11(d).

(1) Rejection of transfer of responsibility for a building under Government Code section 70326; and

(2) A decision to dispose of a surplus court facility under Government Code section 70391(c).

(Subd (c) amended effective January 1, 2007.)

(d) Responsibilities of Judicial Council staff

Judicial Council staff are responsible for the following matters related to transfer of responsibility for court facilities, in addition to matters expressly authorized by statute:

(1) Keeping the courts informed and involved, as appropriate, in the negotiations with the counties for transfer of responsibility for court facilities;

(2) Except as provided in (c)(1), approving an agreement transferring responsibility for a court facility to the state;

(3) Administering a shared-use court facility, including:

(A) Making a decision to displace a minority county tenant under Government Code section 70344(b);

(B) Seeking a change in the amount of court space under Government Code section 70342; and

(C) Responding to a county seeking a change in the amount of county space under Government Code section 70342; and

(4) Auditing the collection of fees by trial courts under Government Code section 70391(d)(1) and the money in local courthouse construction funds under Government Code section 70391(d)(2).

(Subd (d) amended effective January 1, 2016; previously amended effective January 1, 2007.)

(e) Appeal of county facilities payment amount

The Administrative Director must obtain the approval of the Executive and Planning Committee before pursuing correction of a county facilities payment amount under Government Code section 70367. This provision does not preclude the Administrative Director from submitting a declaration as required by Government Code section 70367(a). The Administrative Director must report to the Executive and Planning Committee any decision not to appeal a county facilities payment amount.

(Subd (e) amended effective January 1, 2016.)

Rule 10.183 amended effective January 1, 2016; adopted as rule 6.182 effective June 23, 2004; previously amended and renumbered as rule 10.183 effective January 1, 2007.

Rule 10.184. Acquisition, space programming, construction, and design of court facilities

(a) Intent

The intent of this rule is to allocate responsibility and decision making for acquisition, space programming, construction, and design of court facilities among the courts, the Judicial Council, and its staff.

(Subd (a) amended effective January 1, 2016.)

(b) Responsibilities of Judicial Council staff

(1) In addition to those matters expressly provided by statute, Judicial Council staff are responsible for the acquisition, space programming, construction, and design of a court facility, consistent with the facilities policies and procedures adopted by the Judicial Council and the California Rules of Court.

(2) Judicial Council staff must prepare and submit to the Judicial Council separate annual capital outlay proposals for the appellate courts and the trial courts, as part of the yearly judicial branch budget development cycle, specifying the amounts to be spent for these purposes. The capital outlay proposal for the trial courts must specify the money that is proposed to be spent from the State Court Facilities Construction Fund and from other sources. The annual capital outlay proposals must be consistent with the Five-Year Capital Infrastructure Plan or must recommend appropriate changes in the Five-Year Capital Infrastructure Plan. Judicial Council staff must, whenever feasible, seek review and recommendations from the Court Facilities Transitional Task Force before recommending action to the Judicial Council on these issues.

(3) Judicial Council staff must consult with the affected courts concerning the annual capital needs of the courts.

(Subd (b) amended effective January 1, 2016; previously amended effective January 1, 2007.)

(c) Responsibilities of the courts

(1) Affected courts must consult with Judicial Council staff concerning the courts' annual capital needs.

(2) An affected court must work with the advisory group that is established for any court construction or major renovation project.

(Subd (c) amended effective January 1, 2016.)

(d) Advisory group for construction projects

Judicial Council staff, in consultation with the leadership of the affected court, must establish and work with an advisory group for each court construction or major renovation project. The advisory group consists of court judicial officers, other court personnel, and others affected by the court facility. The advisory group must work with Judicial Council staff on issues involved in the construction or renovation, from the selection of a space programmer and architect through occupancy of the facility.

(Subd (d) amended effective January 1, 2016.)

Rule 10.184 amended effective January 1, 2016; adopted as rule 6.183 effective June 23, 2004; previously amended and renumbered as rule 10.184 effective January 1, 2007.

Chapter 4
Management of Claims and Litigation

Rule 10.201. Claim and litigation procedure
Rule 10.202. Claims and litigation management
Rule 10.203. Contractual indemnification

Rule 10.201. Claim and litigation procedure

(a) Definitions

As used in this chapter:

(1) "Judicial branch entity" is as defined in Government Code section 900.3;

(2) "Judge" means a judge or justice of a judicial branch entity;

(3) "Legal Services" means the Judicial Council's Legal Services office; and

(4) "Litigation Management Committee" means the Litigation Management Committee of the Judicial Council.

(Subd (a) amended effective January 1, 2016; previously amended effective January 1, 2007.)

(b) Procedure for action on claims

To carry out the Judicial Council's responsibility under Government Code section 912.7 to act on a claim, claim amendment, or application for leave to present a late claim against a judicial branch entity or a judge, Legal Services, under the direction of the Administrative Director, must:

(1) On receipt of a claim, claim amendment, or application for leave to present a late claim forwarded by a judicial branch entity, promptly consult with a representative of that entity about the merits of the claim, claim amendment, or application for leave to present a late claim;

(2) Grant or deny an application for leave to present a late claim under Government Code section 911.6(b);

(3) If determined by Legal Services to be appropriate, refer a claim or claim amendment for further investigation to a claims adjuster or other investigator under contract with the Judicial Council;

(4) Reject a claim if it is not a proper charge against the judicial branch entity or judge;

(5) Allow a claim in the amount justly due as determined by Legal Services if it is a proper charge against the judicial branch entity and the amount is less than $100,000; and

(6) Make recommendations to the Litigation Management Committee regarding proposed settlements of claims requiring payments of $100,000 or more.

(Subd (b) amended effective January 1, 2016; previously amended effective January 1, 2007, and December 9, 2008.)

(c) Allowance and payment of claims

The following may allow and authorize payment of any claim arising out of the activities of a judicial branch entity or judge:

(1) Legal Services, under the direction of the Administrative Director, if the payment is less than $100,000; or

(2) The Litigation Management Committee, for any claim.

(Subd (c) amended effective January 1, 2016; previously amended effective December 9, 2008.)

(d) Settlement of lawsuits and payment of judgments

The following may settle lawsuits, after consultation with the affected entity and any judge or employee being defended by the Judicial Council, and authorize payment of judgments arising out of the activities of a judicial branch entity or judge:

(1) Legal Services, under the direction of the Administrative Director, if the payment is less than $100,000 and the lawsuit does not raise issues of significance to the judicial branch; or

(2) The Litigation Management Committee, for any settlement or judgment.

(Subd (d) amended effective January 1, 2016; previously amended effective December 9, 2008.)

Rule 10.201 amended effective January 1, 2016; adopted as rule 6.201 effective January 1, 2003; previously amended and renumbered as rule 10.201 effective January 1, 2007; previously amended effective December 9, 2008.

Rule 10.202. Claims and litigation management

(a) Intent

The intent of this rule is to:

(1) Ensure that the trial and appellate courts are provided with timely, quality legal assistance; and

(2) Promote the cost-effective, prompt, and fair resolution of actions, proceedings, and claims that affect the trial and appellate courts and involve justices of the Courts of Appeal or the Supreme Court, trial court judges, subordinate judicial officers, court executive officers or administrators, or employees of the trial and appellate courts.

(Subd (a) amended effective January 1, 2007; previously amended effective January 1, 2003.)

(b) Duties of Legal Services

To carry out the duty of the Judicial Council to provide for the representation, defense, and indemnification of justices of the Courts of Appeal or the Supreme Court, judges, subordinate judicial officers, court executive officers and administrators, and trial and appellate court employees under part 1 (commencing with section 810) to part 7 (commencing with section 995), inclusive, of the Government Code, Legal Services, under the direction of the Administrative Director and the Chief Counsel, must:

(1) Develop, manage, and administer a litigation management program for investigating and resolving all claims and lawsuits affecting the trial and appellate courts;

(2) Provide legal assistance to the trial or appellate court, and to any justice, judge, subordinate judicial officer, court executive officer or administrator, and trial or appellate court employee who is named as a defendant or responsible party, subject to the defense and indemnification provisions of part 1 (commencing with section 810) to part 7 (commencing with section 995), inclusive, of the Government Code, on receipt of notice of a claim or lawsuit affecting the trial or appellate court or of a dispute that is likely to result in a claim or lawsuit;

(3) Select and direct any counsel retained to represent any trial or appellate court, justice, judge, subordinate judicial officer, court executive officer or administrator, and trial or appellate court employee being provided legal representation under (2), after consultation with the trial or appellate court and any such individual defendant;

(4) Make settlement decisions in all claims and lawsuits other than those identified in (5), after consultation with the affected trial or appellate court, and any justice, judge, subordinate judicial officer, court executive officer or administrator, and trial or appellate court employee being provided legal representation under (2);

(5) Make recommendations to the Litigation Management Committee regarding proposed settlements of claims or lawsuits requiring payments of $100,000 or more or raising issues of significance to the judicial branch;

(6) Develop and implement risk avoidance programs for the trial and appellate courts;

(7) Provide an annual report to the Litigation Management Committee concerning the litigation management program; and

(8) Provide an annual report to each trial and appellate court concerning claims and lawsuits filed against that trial or appellate court.

(Subd (b) amended effective January 1, 2016; previously amended effective July 1, 2002, January 1, 2003, January 1, 2007, and December 9, 2008.)

(c) Duties of trial and appellate courts

The trial and appellate courts must:

(1) Notify Legal Services promptly on receipt of notice of a dispute that is likely to result in a claim or lawsuit, or of a claim or lawsuit filed, against the court, a justice, a judge or subordinate judicial officer, a court executive officer or administrator, or a court employee, and forward the claim and lawsuit to Legal Services for handling; and

(2) Consult with Legal Services regarding strategic and settlement decisions in claims and lawsuits.

(Subd (c) amended effective January 1, 2016; previously amended effective July 1, 2002, January 1, 2003, and January 1, 2007.)

(d) Disagreements about major strategic decisions

Following consultation with Legal Services, a presiding judge or administrative presiding justice may object to a proposed decision of Legal Services about major strategic decisions, such as retention of counsel and proposed settlements, by presenting to Legal Services a written statement of the objection. Legal Services must present the written objection to the Litigation Management Committee, which will resolve the objection.

(Subd (d) amended effective January 1, 2016; adopted effective January 1, 2003; previously amended effective January 1, 2007.)

Rule 10.202 amended effective January 1, 2016; adopted as rule 6.800 effective January 1, 2001; previously renumbered as rule 6.202 effective January 1, 2003; previously amended and renumbered as rule 10.202 effective January 1, 2007; previously amended effective July 1, 2002, and December 9, 2008.

Rule 10.203.   Contractual indemnification

(a) Intent

The intent of this rule is to facilitate the use of contractual indemnities that allocate legal risk and liability to parties that contract with a superior court or Court of Appeal, the Supreme Court, or the Judicial Council (a "judicial branch entity" as defined in Gov. Code, § 900.3).

(Subd (a) amended effective January 1, 2016.)

(b) Defense and indemnification provisions

Notwithstanding rule 10.14, 10.201, or 10.202, a judicial branch entity may enter into a contract that requires the contractor or the contractor's insurer to indemnify, defend, and hold harmless the entity and its officers, agents, and employees against claims, demands, liability, damages, attorney fees, costs, expenses, or losses arising from the performance of the contract. Upon receipt of notice of a claim or lawsuit that may be subject to contractual indemnities, the judicial branch entity must notify Legal Services, which will manage the claim or lawsuit to obtain the benefits of the contractual indemnities to the extent consistent with the interests of the public and the judicial branch.

(Subd (b) amended effective January 1, 2016; previously amended effective January 1, 2007.)

Rule 10.203 amended effective January 1, 2016; adopted as rule 6.203 effective October 15, 2003; previously amended and renumbered as rule 10.203 effective January 1, 2007.

Chapter 5
Ethics Training
[Repealed]

Title 10, Judicial Administration Rules—Division 2, Administration of the Judicial Branch—Chapter 5, Ethics Training; repealed effective January 1, 2013; adopted as Chapter 6.

Rule 10.301.   Ethics training for Judicial Council members and judicial branch employees [Renumbered]

Rule 10.301 renumbered to rule 10.455 effective January 1, 2013; adopted as rule 6.301 effective January 1, 2004; previously amended and renumbered effective January 1, 2007.

Another Chapter 5 follows.

Chapter 5
Management of Human Resources

Title 10, Judicial Administration Rules—Division 2, Administration of the Judicial Branch—Chapter 5, Management of Human Resources; renumbered effective January 1, 2013; adopted as Chapter 6.

Rule 10.350. Workers' compensation program
Rule 10.351. Judicial branch policies on workplace conduct

Rule 10.350.   Workers' compensation program

(a) Intent

The intent of this rule is to:

(1) Establish procedures for the Judicial Council's workers' compensation program for the trial courts; and

(2) Ensure that the trial courts' workers' compensation coverage complies with applicable law and is cost-efficient.

(Subd (a) amended effective January 1, 2016; previously amended effective January 1, 2007.)

(b) Duties of Judicial Council staff

To carry out the duty of the Judicial Council to establish a workers' compensation program for the trial courts, the council's Human Resources office must:

(1) Maintain a contract with a vendor to provide courts, on a voluntary basis, with a cost-efficient workers' compensation coverage program;

(2) Monitor the performance of the vendor with which it contracts to provide such services;

(3) Timely notify the trial courts concerning the terms of the workers' compensation coverage program;

(4) Timely inform the trial courts about the legal requirements with which a workers' compensation program must comply;

(5) Make personnel available by telephone to consult with trial courts regarding the cost and benefits of the plan being offered by the Judicial Council; and

(6) Review and approve or disapprove any other workers' compensation programs identified by a trial court for consideration as a vendor to provide workers' compensation benefits to its employees.

(Subd (b) amended effective January 1, 2016; previously amended effective January 1, 2007.)

(c) Duties of the trial courts

(1) Each trial court that elects to participate in the program made available through the Judicial Council must:

(A) Timely notify the Human Resources office of its decision to participate in the workers' compensation program being offered through the Judicial Council;

(B) Timely complete and return necessary paperwork to the Human Resources office; and

(C) Timely pay all costs associated with the program.

(2) Each trial court that elects not to participate in the workers' compensation program available through the Judicial Council must:

(A) Independently identify a workers' compensation benefits provider that fulfills all legal responsibilities to offer such benefits in California in a cost-efficient manner;

(B) Timely submit to the Human Resources office for its approval the information necessary to evaluate the workers' compensation program identified by the trial court to provide benefits for its employees; and

(C) Maintain a contract with a workers' compensation benefits provider that fulfills all legal responsibilities to offer such benefits in California in a cost-efficient manner.

(Subd (c) amended effective January 1, 2016; previously amended effective January 1, 2007.)

Rule 10.350 amended effective January 1, 2016; adopted as rule 6.302 effective January 1, 2005; previously amended and renumbered as rule 10.350 effective January 1, 2007.

Rule 10.351. Judicial branch policies on workplace conduct

The judicial branch is committed to providing a workplace free of harassment, discrimination, retaliation, and inappropriate workplace conduct based on a protected classification. Consistent with this commitment, each court must take reasonable steps to prevent and address such conduct, including adopting policies prohibiting harassment, discrimination, retaliation, and inappropriate workplace conduct based on a protected classification and establishing for such conduct complaint reporting and response procedures that satisfy the minimum requirements stated in this rule.

(a) Prohibition policies

Each court must ensure that its policies prohibiting harassment, discrimination, retaliation, and inappropriate workplace conduct based on a protected classification conform with the minimum requirements stated in this rule. These policies must contain:

(1) A prohibition against harassment, discrimination, retaliation, and inappropriate workplace conduct based on a protected classification by judicial officers, managers, supervisors, employees, other personnel, and other individuals with whom employees come into contact;

(2) A list of all protected classifications under applicable state and federal laws, including all protected classifications listed in Government Code section 12940(a);

(3) Definitions and a nonexhaustive list of examples of harassment, discrimination, retaliation, and inappropriate workplace conduct based on a protected classification;

(4) A clear prohibition of retaliation against anyone making a complaint or participating in an investigation of harassment, discrimination, retaliation, or inappropriate workplace conduct based on a protected classification; and

(5) Comprehensive complaint reporting, intake, investigatory, and follow-up processes.

(Subd (a) adopted effective January 17, 2020.)

(b) Complaint reporting process

Each court must adopt a process for employees to report complaints of harassment, discrimination, retaliation, and inappropriate workplace conduct based on a protected classification. These reporting processes must:

(1) Establish effective open-door policies and procedures for reporting complaints;

(2) Offer multiple avenues for raising complaints, either orally or in writing, and not require that the employee bring concerns to an immediate supervisor;

(3) Clearly identify individuals to whom complaints may be made regarding the conduct of administrative presiding justices, appellate court clerk/executive officers, presiding judges, court executive officers, judicial officers, and court management;

(4) Identify the Commission on Judicial Performance, California Department of Fair Employment and Housing, and U.S. Equal Employment Opportunity Commission as additional avenues for employees to lodge complaints, and provide contact information for those entities; and

(5) Instruct supervisors, managers, and directors with knowledge of harassment, discrimination, retaliation, or inappropriate workplace conduct based on a protected classification to report this information to the administrative presiding justice or an appellate court clerk/executive officer, a presiding judge, a court executive officer, human resources, or another appropriate judicial officer who is not involved with the conduct or named in the complaint.

(Subd (b) adopted effective January 17, 2020.)

(c) Court responsibility on receipt of complaint or knowledge of potential misconduct

Each court must develop processes to intake, investigate, and respond to complaints or known instances of harassment, discrimination, retaliation, or inappropriate workplace conduct based on a protected classification. These processes must provide for:

(1) Appropriate reassurances to complainants that their confidentiality in making a complaint will be preserved to the extent possible, including an explanation that disclosure of information will be limited to the extent consistent with conducting a fair, effective, and thorough investigation;

(2) Fair, timely, and thorough investigations of complaints that provide all parties with appropriate consideration and an opportunity to be heard. These investigations should be conducted by impartial, qualified investigators;

(3) Communication with complainants throughout the investigation process, including initial acknowledgment of complaints, follow-up communication as appropriate, and communication at the end of the process;

(4) Consideration of appropriate options for remedial action and resolution based on the evidence collected in the investigation; and

(5) Timely case closures.

(Subd (c) adopted effective January 17, 2020.)

(d) Implementation

All courts must implement the requirements of this rule by [1] December 31, 2020, or as soon thereafter as possible, subject to any applicable obligations to meet and confer or consult with recognized employee organizations.

(Subd (d) amended effective April 16, 2020.)

Rule 10.351(d). 2020 Deletes. [1] June 30

Rule 10.351 amended effective April 16, 2020; adopted effective January 17, 2020.

Chapter 6
Court Technology, Information, and Automation

Title 10, Judicial Administration Rules—Division 2, Administration of the Judicial Branch—Chapter 6, Court Technology, Information, and Automation; renumbered effective January 1, 2013; adopted as Chapter 7.

Rule 10.400. Judicial Branch Statistical Information System (JBSIS)

(a) Purpose of rule

Consistent with article VI, section 6 of the California Constitution and Government Code section 68505, the Judicial Branch Statistical Information System (JBSIS) is established by the Judicial Council to provide accurate, consistent, and timely information for the judicial branch, the Legislature, and other state agencies that require information from the courts to fulfill their mandates.

(Subd (a) amended effective January 1, 2007.)

(b) Reporting required

Each trial court must collect and report to the Judicial Council information according to its capability and level of automation as prescribed by the *JBSIS Manual* adopted by the Judicial Council.

(Subd (b) amended effective January 1, 2007.)

(c) Automated JBSIS collection and reporting

By July 1, 1998, each trial court must develop a plan for meeting reporting requirements prescribed by the *JBSIS Manual*. By January 1, 2001, subject to adequate funding being made available, each trial court must develop, upgrade, replace, or procure automated case management systems needed to meet or exceed JBSIS data collection and reporting requirements prescribed by the *JBSIS Manual.*

(Subd (c) amended effective January 1, 2007; previously amended effective January 1, 2000.)

Rule 10.400 amended and renumbered effective January 1, 2007; adopted as rule 996 effective January 1, 1998; previously amended effective January 1, 2000.

Chapter 7
Minimum Education Requirements, Expectations, and Recommendations

Title 10, Judicial Administration Rules—Division 2, Administration of the Judicial Branch—Chapter 7, Minimum Education Requirements, Expectations, and Recommendations; renumbered effective January 1, 2013; adopted as Chapter 8.

Rule 10.451. Judicial branch education
Rule 10.452. Minimum education requirements, expectations, and recommendations
Rule 10.455. Ethics orientation for Judicial Council members and for judicial branch employees required to file a statement of economic interests
Rule 10.461. Minimum education requirements for Supreme Court and Court of Appeal justices
Rule 10.462. Minimum education requirements and expectations for trial court judges and subordinate judicial officers
Rule 10.463. Education requirements for family court judges and subordinate judicial officers
Rule 10.464. Education requirements and expectations for judges and subordinate judicial officers on domestic violence issues
Rule 10.468. Content-based and hours-based education for superior court judges and subordinate judicial officers regularly assigned to hear probate proceedings
Rule 10.469. Judicial education recommendations for justices, judges, and subordinate judicial officers, and additional requirements
Rule 10.471. Minimum education requirements for Supreme Court and Court of Appeal clerks/executive officers
Rule 10.472. Minimum education requirements for Supreme Court and Court of Appeal managing attorneys, supervisors, and other personnel
Rule 10.473. Minimum education requirements for trial court executive officers
Rule 10.474. Trial court managers, supervisors, and other personnel
Rule 10.478. Content-based and hours-based education for court investigators, probate attorneys, and probate examiners
Rule 10.479. Education recommendations for appellate and trial court personnel
Rule 10.481. Approved providers; approved course criteria
Rule 10.491. Minimum education requirements for Judicial Council employees

Rule 10.451.   Judicial branch education

(a) Purpose

Judicial branch education for all justices, judges, subordinate judicial officers, and court personnel is essential to enhance the fair, effective, and efficient administration of justice. Participation in education activities is part of the official duties of judicial officers and court personnel. Judicial branch education is acknowledged as a vital component in achieving the goals of the Judicial Council's Long-Range Strategic Plan, which include access, fairness, and diversity; branch independence and accountability; modernization of management and administration; and quality of justice and service to the public. The responsibility for planning, conducting, and overseeing judicial branch education properly resides in the judicial branch.

(Subd (a) adopted effective January 1, 2007.)

(b) Education objectives

Justices, judges, subordinate judicial officers, court personnel, education committees, and others who plan and deliver education will endeavor to achieve the following objectives:

(1) To provide justices, judges, subordinate judicial officers, and court personnel with the knowledge, skills, and abilities required to perform their responsibilities competently, fairly, and efficiently;

(2) To ensure that education, including opportunities for orientation, continuing education, and professional development, is available to all justices, judges, subordinate judicial officers, and court personnel;

(3) To assist justices, judges, subordinate judicial officers, and court personnel in preserving the integrity and impartiality of the judicial system through their efforts to ensure that all members of the public have equal access to the courts and equal ability to participate in court proceedings and are treated in a fair and just manner;

(4) To promote the adherence of justices, judges, subordinate judicial officers, and court personnel to the highest ideals of personal and official

conduct, as set forth in the California Code of Judicial Ethics and the Code of Ethics for the Court Employees of California;

(5) To improve the administration of justice, reduce court delay, and promote fair and efficient management of court proceedings;

(6) To promote standardized court practices and procedures; and

(7) To implement the recommendations adopted by the Judicial Council in the California Standards of Judicial Administration.

(Subd (b) adopted effective January 1, 2007.)
Rule 10.451 adopted effective January 1, 2007.

Rule 10.452.   Minimum education requirements, expectations, and recommendations

(a) Purpose

Justices, judges, and subordinate judicial officers are entrusted by the public with the impartial and knowledgeable handling of proceedings that affect the freedom, livelihood, and happiness of the people involved. Court personnel assist justices, judges, and subordinate judicial officers in carrying out their responsibilities and must provide accurate and timely services to the public. Each justice, judge, and subordinate judicial officer and each court staff member is responsible for maintaining and improving his or her professional competence. To assist them in enhancing their professional competence, the judicial branch will develop and maintain a comprehensive and high-quality education program, including minimum education requirements, expectations, and recommendations, to provide educational opportunities for all justices, judges, subordinate judicial officers, and court personnel.

(Subd (a) amended effective January 1, 2008; adopted effective January 1, 2007.)

(b) Goals

The minimum education requirements, expectations, and recommendations set forth in rules 10.461–10.479 are intended to achieve two complementary goals:

(1) To ensure that both individuals who are new to the bench or the court and those who are experienced on the bench or court but are beginning a new assignment or role obtain education on the tasks, skills, abilities, and knowledge necessary to be successful in the new roles; and

(2) To establish broad parameters, based on time, for continuing education for individuals who are experienced both on the bench or court and in their assignments or roles, while preserving the ability of the individual, working with the individual who oversees his or her work, to determine the appropriate content and provider.

(Subd (b) amended effective January 1, 2008; adopted effective January 1, 2007.)

(c) Relationship of minimum education requirements and expectations to education recommendations

The education requirements and expectations set forth in rules 10.461–10.462 and 10.471–10.474 are minimums. Justices, judges, and subordinate judicial officers should participate in more judicial education than is required and expected, related to each individual's responsibilities and particular judicial assignment or assignments and in accordance with the judicial education recommendations set forth in rule 10.469. Additional education requirements related to specific responsibilities are set forth in rule 10.463 (for those hearing family law matters), rule 10.464 (for those hearing domestic violence issues), and rule 10.468 (for those hearing probate proceedings).

(Subd (c) amended effective January 1, 2012; adopted effective January 1, 2007; previously amended effective January 1, 2008.)

(d) Responsibilities of Chief Justice and administrative presiding justices

The Chief Justice and each administrative presiding justice:

(1) Must grant sufficient leave to Supreme Court and Court of Appeal justices, the clerk/executive officer, and the managing attorney to enable them to complete the minimum education requirements stated in rules 10.461, 10.471, and 10.472, respectively;

(2) To the extent compatible with the efficient administration of justice, must grant to all justices, the clerk/executive officer, and the managing attorney sufficient leave to participate in education programs consistent with the education recommendations stated in rules 10.469 and 10.479. After a justice has completed any new justice education required under rule 10.461 or after a justice has completed the first year on the bench, the Chief Justice or the administrative presiding justice should grant each justice at least eight court days per calendar year to participate in continuing education relating to the justice's responsibilities;

(3) In addition to the educational leave required under (d)(1)–(2), should grant leave to a justice, clerk/executive officer, or managing attorney to serve on education committees and as a faculty member at education programs when the individual's services have been requested for these purposes by Judicial Council staff, the California Judges Association, or the court. If a court's calendar would not be adversely affected, the court should grant additional leave for a justice, the clerk/executive officer, or the managing attorney to serve on an educational committee or as a faculty member for judicial branch education;

(4) Should establish an education plan for his or her court to facilitate the involvement of justices, the clerk/executive officer, and the managing attorney as both participants and faculty in judicial education activities;

(5) Must ensure that justices, the clerk/executive officer, and the managing attorney are reimbursed by their court in accordance with the travel policies issued by the Judicial Council for travel expenses incurred in attending in-state education programs as a participant, except to the extent that: (i) certain expenses are covered by the Judicial Council; or (ii) the education provider or sponsor of the program pays the expenses. Provisions for these expenses must be part of every court's budget. The Chief Justice or the administrative presiding justice may approve reimbursement of travel expenses incurred by justices, the clerk/executive officer, and the managing attorney in attending out-of-state education programs as a participant; and

(6) Must retain the records and cumulative histories of participation provided by justices. These records and cumulative histories are subject to periodic audit by Judicial Council staff. The Chief Justice and the administrative presiding justice must report the data from the records and cumulative histories on an aggregate basis to the Judicial Council, on a form provided by the Judicial Council, within six months after the end of each three-year period.

(Subd (d) amended effective January 1, 2018; adopted effective January 1, 2007; previously amended effective January 1, 2008, and January 1, 2016.)

(e) Responsibilities of presiding judges

Each presiding judge:

(1) Must grant sufficient leave to all judges and subordinate judicial officers and to the court executive officer to enable them to complete the minimum education requirements and expectations stated in rules 10.462 and 10.473, respectively;

(2) To the extent compatible with the efficient administration of justice, must grant to all judges and subordinate judicial officers and to the court executive officer sufficient leave to participate in education programs consistent with the education recommendations stated in rules 10.469 and 10.479. After a judge or subordinate judicial officer has completed the new judge education required under rule 10.462, the presiding judge should grant each judge and subordinate judicial officer at least eight court days per calendar year to participate in continuing education relating to the judge or subordinate judicial officer's responsibilities or current or future court assignment;

(3) In addition to the educational leave required or authorized under rule 10.603 or (e)(1)–(2), should grant leave to a judge or subordinate judicial officer or the executive officer to serve on education committees and as a faculty member at education programs when the judicial officer's or executive officer's services have been requested for these purposes by Judicial Council staff, the California Judges Association, or the court. If a court's calendar would not be adversely affected, the presiding judge should grant additional leave for a judge or subordinate judicial officer or executive officer to serve on an educational committee or as a faculty member for judicial branch education;

(4) Should establish an education plan for his or her court to facilitate the involvement of judges, subordinate judicial officers, and the executive officer as both participants and faculty in education activities and should consult with each judge, each subordinate judicial officer, and the executive officer regarding their education needs and requirements related to their current and future assignments;

(5) Should use his or her assignment powers to enable all judges and subordinate judicial officers, particularly those assigned to specific calendar courts, to participate in educational activities;

(6) Must ensure that judges, subordinate judicial officers, and the court executive officer are reimbursed by their court in accordance with the Trial Court Financial Policies and Procedures Manual for travel expenses incurred in attending in-state education programs as a participant, except to the extent that: (i) certain expenses are covered by the Judicial Council; or (ii) the education provider or sponsor of the program pays the expenses.

Provisions for these expenses must be part of every court's budget. The presiding judge may approve reimbursement of travel expenses incurred by judges, subordinate judicial officers, and the court executive officer in attending out-of-state education programs as a participant; and

(7) Must retain the records and cumulative histories of participation provided by judges. These records and cumulative histories are subject to periodic audit by Judicial Council staff. The presiding judge must report the data from the records and cumulative histories on an aggregate basis to the Judicial Council, on a form provided by the Judicial Council, within six months after the end of each three-year period.

(Subd (e) amended effective January 1, 2016; adopted effective January 1, 2007; previously amended effective January 1, 2008.)

(f) Responsibilities of Supreme Court and Court of Appeal justices, clerks/executive officers, managing attorneys, and supervisors

Each court's justices, clerk/executive officer, managing attorney, and supervisors:

(1) Must grant sufficient leave to all court personnel to enable them to complete the minimum education requirements stated in rule 10.472;

(2) To the extent compatible with the efficient administration of justice, must grant to all court personnel sufficient leave to participate in education programs consistent with the education recommendations stated in rule 10.479;

(3) Should allow and encourage court personnel, in addition to participating as students in educational activities, to serve on court personnel education committees and as faculty at court personnel education programs when an employee's services have been requested for these purposes by Judicial Council staff or the court; and

(4) Should establish an education plan for their court to facilitate the involvement of court personnel as both participants and faculty in educational activities, and should consult with each court staff member regarding his or her education needs and requirements and professional development.

(5) Must ensure that supervisors and other court personnel are reimbursed by their court in accordance with the travel policies issued by the Judicial Council for travel expenses incurred in attending in-state education programs as a participant, except to the extent that: (i) certain expenses are covered by the Judicial Council; or (ii) the education provider or sponsor of the program pays the expenses. Provisions for these expenses must be part of every court's budget. The clerk/executive officer or the managing attorney may approve reimbursement of travel expenses incurred by supervisors and other court personnel in attending out-of-state education programs as a participant.

(Subd (f) amended effective January 1, 2018; adopted effective January 1, 2008; previously amended effective January 1, 2016.)

(g) Responsibilities of trial court executive officers, managers, and supervisors

Each trial court's executive officer, managers, and supervisors:

(1) Must grant sufficient leave to all court personnel to enable them to complete the minimum education requirements stated in rule 10.474;

(2) To the extent compatible with the efficient administration of justice, must grant to all court personnel sufficient leave to participate in education programs consistent with the education recommendations stated in rule 10.479;

(3) Should allow and encourage court personnel, in addition to participating as students in education activities, to serve on court personnel education committees and as faculty at court personnel education programs when an employee's services have been requested for these purposes by Judicial Council staff or the court;

(4) Should establish an education plan for their court to facilitate the involvement of court personnel as both participants and faculty in educational activities, and should consult with each court staff member regarding his or her education needs and requirements and professional development; and

(5) Must ensure that managers, supervisors, and other court personnel are reimbursed by their court in accordance with the Trial Court Financial Policies and Procedures Manual for travel expenses incurred in attending in-state education programs as a participant, except to the extent that: (i) certain expenses are covered by the Judicial Council; or (ii) the education provider or sponsor of the program pays the expenses. Provisions for these expenses must be part of every court's budget. The court executive officer may approve reimbursement of travel expenses incurred by managers, supervisors, and other court personnel in attending out-of-state education programs as a participant.

(Subd (g) amended effective January 1, 2016; adopted as subd (f) effective January 1, 2007; previously amended and relettered as subd (g) effective January 1, 2008.)

Rule 10.452 amended effective January 1, 2018; adopted effective January 1, 2007; previously amended effective January 1, 2008, January 1, 2012, and January 1, 2016.

Rule 10.455. Ethics orientation for Judicial Council members and for judicial branch employees required to file a statement of economic interests

(a) Authority

This rule is adopted under Government Code section 11146 et seq. and article VI, section 6 of the California Constitution.

(Subd (a) amended effective January 1, 2007.)

(b) Definitions

For purposes of this rule, "judicial branch employee" includes an employee of a trial or appellate court or the Judicial Council, but does not include court commissioners or referees.

(Subd (b) amended effective January 1, 2016.)

(c) Judicial Council members and judicial branch employees

(1) Judicial Council staff must provide an ethics orientation course for Judicial Council members and for judicial branch employees who are required to file a statement of economic interests.

(2) Judicial Council members must take the orientation course within six months of appointment. If a member is appointed to a subsequent term, he or she must take the course within six months of the reappointment.

(3) Judicial branch employees who are required to file a statement of economic interests must take the orientation course as follows:

(A) For employees who have taken the orientation course before the effective date of this rule, at least once during each consecutive two calendar years after the date of the last attendance.

(B) For new employees, within six months of becoming an employee and at least once during each consecutive two calendar years thereafter.

(C) For all other employees, within six months of the effective date of this rule and at least once during each consecutive two calendar years thereafter.

(Subd (c) amended effective January 1, 2016.)

Rule 10.455 amended effective January 1, 2016; adopted as rule 6.301 effective January 1, 2004; previously amended and renumbered as rule 10.301 effective January 1, 2007, and as rule 10.455 effective January 1, 2013.

2012 Note: In addition to renumbering the rule, the amendment, effective January 1, 2013, consisted of revising the heading.

Rule 10.461. Minimum education requirements for Supreme Court and Court of Appeal justices

(a) Applicability

All California Court of Appeal justices must complete the minimum judicial education requirements for new justices under (b), and all Supreme Court and Court of Appeal justices must complete minimum continuing education requirements as outlined under (c). All justices should participate in more judicial education than is required, related to each individual's responsibilities and in accordance with the judicial education recommendations set forth in rule 10.469.

(Subd (a) adopted effective January 1, 2008.)

(b) Content-based requirement

Each new Court of Appeal justice, within two years of confirmation of appointment, must attend a new appellate justice orientation program sponsored by a national provider of appellate orientation programs or by the Judicial Council's Center for Judicial Education and Research.

(Subd (b) amended effective January 1, 2016; adopted as unlettered subd effective January 1, 2007; previously amended and lettered as subd (b) effective January 1, 2008; previously amended effective January 1, 2012.)

(c) Hours-based continuing education

(1) Each justice must complete 30 hours of continuing judicial education every three years, beginning on the dates outlined:

(A) A new Supreme Court justice enters the three-year continuing education period on January 1 of the year following confirmation of appointment, and a new Court of Appeal justice enters the three-year continuing education period on January 1 of the year following completion of the required new justice education; continuing education requirements are prorated based on the number of years remaining in the three-year period.

(B) For all other justices, the first continuing education period begins January 1, 2008.

(C) The first continuing education period for Supreme Court and Court of Appeal justices is for two years from January 1, 2008, through December 31, 2009, rather than three years. The continuing education requirements and limitations in (c) are consequently prorated for this two-year period. The first three-year period then begins January 1, 2010.

(2) The following education applies toward the required 30 hours of continuing judicial education:

(A) Any education offered by an approved provider (see rule 10.481(a)) and any other education, including education taken to satisfy a statutory or other education requirement, approved by the Chief Justice or the administrative presiding justice as meeting the criteria listed in rule 10.481(b).

(B) Each hour of participation in traditional (live, face-to-face) education; distance education such as broadcasts, videoconferences, and online coursework; self-directed study; and faculty service counts toward the continuing education requirement on an hour-for-hour basis. Each justice must complete at least half of his or her continuing education hours requirement as a participant in traditional (live, face-to-face) education. The justice may complete the balance of his or her education hours requirement through any other means with no limitation on any particular type of education.

(C) A justice who serves as faculty by teaching legal or judicial education to a legal or judicial audience may apply education hours as faculty service. Credit for faculty service counts toward the continuing education requirement in the same manner as all other types of education—on an hour-for-hour basis.

(Subd (c) amended effective January 1, 2013; adopted effective January 1, 2008; previously amended effective January 1, 2012.)

(d) Extension of time

(1) For good cause, the Chief Justice or the administrative presiding justice may grant a one-year extension of time to complete the continuing education requirement in (c).

(2) If the Chief Justice or the administrative presiding justice grants a request for an extension of time, the justice, in consultation with the Chief Justice or the administrative presiding justice, should also pursue interim means of obtaining relevant educational content.

(3) An extension of time to complete the hours-based continuing education requirement does not affect what is required in the next three-year period.

(Subd (d) adopted effective January 1, 2008.)

(e) Records and summaries of participation for justices

Each justice is responsible for:

(1) Tracking his or her own participation in education and keeping a record of participation for three years after each course or activity that is applied toward the requirements, on a form provided by the Chief Justice for the Supreme Court or by the administrative presiding justice for each appellate district of the Court of Appeal. The form must include the information regarding a justice's participation in education that is needed by the Chief Justice or the administrative presiding justice to complete the aggregate form required by rule 10.452(d)(6);

(2) At the end of each year, giving the Chief Justice or the administrative presiding justice a copy of his or her record of participation in education for that year, on the form provided by the Chief Justice or the administrative presiding justice; and

(3) At the end of each three-year period, giving the Chief Justice or the administrative presiding justice a copy of his or her record of participation in education for that year and a cumulative history of participation for that three-year period, on the form provided by the Chief Justice or the administrative presiding justice.

(Subd (e) amended effective August 15, 2008; adopted effective January 1, 2008.)

Rule 10.461 amended effective January 1, 2016; adopted effective January 1, 2007; previously amended effective January 1, 2008, August 15, 2008, January 1, 2012, and January 1, 2013.

Advisory Committee Comment

The requirements formerly contained in subdivision (e)(2) of rule 970, which has been repealed, are carried forward without change in rule 10.461(b).

Judicial Council staff have developed both a manual format and an automated format of the individual justice's recording and reporting form referenced in rule 10.461(e) that gathers all the information needed by the Chief Justice or the administrative presiding justice to complete the aggregate report to the Judicial Council required under rule 10.452(d)(6). The Chief Justice or the administrative presiding justice may determine which form should be used in his or her court and may provide the manual or automated format of the council-developed form (available from the council's Center for Judicial Education and Research) or may provide another appropriate form that has been developed by his or her court or by another court that gathers all the information needed by the Chief Justice or the administrative presiding justice to complete the aggregate report to the Judicial Council.

Rule 10.462. Minimum education requirements and expectations for trial court judges and subordinate judicial officers

(a) Applicability

All California trial court judges must complete the minimum judicial education requirements for new judges under (c)(1) and are expected to participate in continuing education as outlined under (d). All subordinate judicial officers must complete the minimum education requirements for new subordinate judicial officers under (c)(1) and for continuing education as outlined under (d). All trial court judges and subordinate judicial officers who hear family law matters must complete additional education requirements set forth in rule 10.463. All trial court judges and subordinate judicial officers who hear certain types of matters must participate in education on domestic violence issues as provided in rule 10.464. All trial court judges and subordinate judicial officers regularly assigned to hear probate proceedings must complete additional education requirements set forth in rule 10.468. All trial court judges and subordinate judicial officers should participate in more judicial education than is required and expected, related to each individual's responsibilities and particular judicial assignment or assignments and in accordance with the judicial education recommendations set forth in rule 10.469.

(Subd (a) amended effective January 1, 2012; adopted effective January 1, 2007; previously amended effective January 1, 2008.)

(b) Definitions

Unless the context or subject matter otherwise requires, "subordinate judicial officers" as used in this rule means subordinate judicial officers as defined in rule 10.701.

(Subd (b) adopted effective January 1, 2007.)

(c) Content-based requirements

(1) Each new trial court judge and subordinate judicial officer must complete the "new judge education" provided by the Judicial Council's Center for Judicial Education and Research (CJER) as follows:

(A) The New Judge Orientation Program within six months of taking the oath as a judge or subordinate judicial officer. For purposes of the New Judge Orientation Program, a judge or subordinate judicial officer is considered "new" only once, and any judge or subordinate judicial officer who has completed the New Judge Orientation Program, as required under this rule or under former rule 970, is not required to complete the program again. A judge or subordinate judicial officer who was appointed, elected, or hired before rule 970 was adopted on January 1, 1996, is not required to complete the program.

(B) An orientation course in his or her primary assignment (civil, criminal, family, juvenile delinquency or dependency, probate, or traffic) within one year of taking the oath as a judge or subordinate judicial officer; and

(C) The B. E. Witkin Judicial College of California within two years of taking the oath as a judge or subordinate judicial officer, unless the new judge completed the Judicial College as a new subordinate judicial officer, in which case the presiding judge may determine whether the new judge must complete it again.

(2) Each judge beginning a supervising judge role is expected to complete the following education, unless he or she is returning to a similar supervising judge role after less than two years in another assignment or is beginning a supervising judge role less than two years after serving in the presiding judge role and completing the Presiding Judges Orientation and Court Management Program.

(A) For a judge who has administrative responsibility, CJER's Supervising Judges Overview course within one year of beginning the supervising judge role, preferably before beginning the role;

(B) For a judge who has calendar management responsibility, a calendar management overview course, provided either by the local court or by CJER, within one year of beginning the supervising judge role, preferably before beginning the role;

(C) For a judge who has both administrative and calendar management responsibility, both overview courses within one year of beginning the role.

(3) Each judge beginning a presiding judge role is expected to complete CJER's Presiding Judges Orientation and Court Management Program within one year of beginning the presiding judge role, preferably before beginning the role unless he or she is returning to a presiding judge role after two years or less in another role or assignment.

(4) Each judge is expected to and each subordinate judicial officer must, if beginning a new primary assignment (unless he or she is returning to an assignment after less than two years in another assignment), complete a course on the new primary assignment, provided by CJER, the California Judges Association (CJA), or the local court, within six months of beginning the new assignment. CJER is responsible for identifying content for these courses and will share the identified content with CJA and the local courts.

(Subd (c) amended effective January 1, 2016; adopted effective January 1, 2007; previously amended effective January 1, 2008, July 1, 2008, and January 1, 2012.)

(d) Hours-based continuing education

(1) Each judge is expected to and each subordinate judicial officer must complete 30 hours of continuing judicial education every three years, beginning on the dates outlined:

(A) A new judge or new subordinate judicial officer enters the three-year continuing education period on January 1 of the year following the period provided for completion of the required new judge education; continuing education expectations for judges and requirements for subordinate judicial officers are prorated based on the number of years remaining in the three-year period.

(B) For all other judges and subordinate judicial officers, the first three-year period begins on January 1, 2007.

(2) The following education applies toward the expected or required 30 hours of continuing judicial education:

(A) The content-based courses under (c)(2), (3), and (4) for a new supervising judge, a new presiding judge, and a judge beginning a new primary assignment (the "new judge education" required under (c)(1) does not apply); and

(B) Any other education offered by an approved provider (see rule 10.481(a)) and any other education, including education taken to satisfy a statutory or other education requirement, approved by the presiding judge as meeting the criteria listed in rule 10.481(b).

(3) Each hour of participation in traditional (live, face-to-face) education; distance education such as broadcasts, videoconferences, and online coursework; self-directed study; and faculty service counts toward the continuing education expectation or requirement on an hour-for-hour basis. Each judge and subordinate judicial officer must complete at least half of his or her continuing education hours expectation or requirement as a participant in traditional (live, face-to-face) education. The judge or subordinate judicial officer may complete the balance of his or her judicial education hours expectation or requirement through any other means with no limitation on any particular type of education.

(4) A judge or subordinate judicial officer who serves as faculty by teaching legal or judicial education for a legal or judicial audience may apply education hours as faculty service. Credit for faculty service counts toward the continuing education expectation or requirement in the same manner as all other types of education—on an hour-for-hour basis.

(5) The presiding judge may require subordinate judicial officers to participate in specific courses or participate in education in a specific subject matter area as part of their continuing education.

(Subd (d) amended effective January 1, 2013; previously amended effective January 1, 2008, and January 1, 2012.)

(e) Extension of time

(1) For good cause, a presiding judge may grant an extension of time to complete the education expectations or requirements in (c)(2)–(4) and the continuing education expectation or requirement in (d) as follows:

(A) A time extension to complete the content-based expectations or requirements in (c)(2)–(4) is limited to the original time period provided for completion—that is, one year, one year, or six months, respectively.

(B) A time extension to complete the hours-based continuing education expectation or requirement in (d) is limited to one year.

(2) If the presiding judge grants a request for an extension of time, the judge or subordinate judicial officer, in consultation with the presiding judge, should also pursue interim means of obtaining relevant educational content.

(3) An extension of time to complete the hours-based continuing education expectation or requirement does not affect what is expected or required in the next three-year period.

(Subd (e) adopted effective January 1, 2007.)

(f) Records and cumulative histories of participation for judges

Each judge is responsible for:

(1) Tracking his or her own participation in education and keeping a record of participation for three years after each course or activity that is applied toward the requirements and expectations, on a form provided by the presiding judge. The form must include the information regarding a judge's participation in education that is needed by the presiding judge to complete the aggregate form required by rule 10.452(e)(7);

(2) At the end of each year, giving the presiding judge a copy of his or her record of participation in education for that year, on the form provided by the presiding judge; and

(3) At the end of each three-year period, giving the presiding judge a copy of his or her record of participation in education for that year and a cumulative history of participation for that three-year period, on the form provided by the presiding judge.

(Subd (f) amended effective August 15, 2008; adopted effective January 1, 2007; previously amended effective January 1, 2008.)

(g) Records of participation for subordinate judicial officers

(1) Each court is responsible for tracking participation in education and for tracking completion of minimum education requirements for its subordinate judicial officers.

(2) Each subordinate judicial officer must keep records of his or her own participation for three years after each course or activity that is applied toward the requirements.

(Subd (g) adopted effective January 1, 2007.)

Rule 10.462 amended effective January 1, 2016; adopted effective January 1, 2007; previously amended effective January 1, 2008, July 1, 2008, August 15, 2008, January 1, 2012, and January 1, 2013.

Advisory Committee Comment

The minimum judicial education requirements in rule 10.462 do not apply to retired judges seeking to sit on regular court assignment in the Assigned Judges Program. Retired judges who seek to serve in the Assigned Judges Program must comply with the Chief Justice's Standards and Guidelines for Judges Who Serve on Assignment, which includes education requirements.

Judicial Council staff have developed both a manual format and an automated format of the individual judge's recording and reporting form referenced in rule 10.462(f) that gathers all the information needed by the presiding judge to complete the aggregate report to the Judicial Council required under rule 10.452(e)(7). The presiding judge may determine which form should be used in his or her court and may provide the manual or automated format of the council-developed form (available from the Judicial Council's Center for Judicial Education and Research) or may provide another appropriate form that has been developed by his or her court or by another court that gathers all the information needed by the presiding judge to complete the aggregate report to the Judicial Council.

Rule 10.463. Trial court executive officers [Renumbered]

Rule 10.463 renumbered as rule 10.473 effective January 1, 2008.

Another Rule 10.463 follows.

Rule 10.463. Education requirements for family court judges and subordinate judicial officers

Each judge or subordinate judicial officer whose primary assignment is to hear family law matters or who is the sole judge hearing family law matters must complete the following education:

(a) Basic family law education

Within six months of beginning a family law assignment, or within one year of beginning a family law assignment in courts with five or fewer judges, the judge or subordinate judicial officer must complete a basic educational program on California family law and procedure designed primarily for judicial officers. A judge or subordinate judicial officer who has completed the basic educational program need not complete the basic educational program again. All other judicial officers who hear family law matters, including retired judges who sit on court assignment, must complete appropriate family law educational programs.

(Subd (a) amended effective January 1, 2008; adopted as (1) effective January 1, 1992; previously amended and lettered effective January 1, 2003.)

(b) Continuing family law education

The judge or subordinate judicial officer must complete a periodic update on new developments in California family law and procedure.

(Subd (b) amended effective January 1, 2008; adopted as (2) effective January 1, 1992; previously amended and lettered effective January 1, 2003.)

(c) Other family law education

To the extent that judicial time and resources are available, the judge or subordinate judicial officer must complete additional educational programs on other aspects of family law including interdisciplinary subjects relating to the family.

(Subd (c) amended effective January 1, 2008; adopted as (3) effective January 1, 1992; previously amended and lettered effective January 1, 2003.)

Rule 10.463 amended and renumbered effective January 1, 2008; adopted as rule 1200 effective January 1, 1992; previously amended and renumbered as rule 5.30 effective January 1, 2003.

Rule 10.464. Trial court managers, supervisors, and personnel [Renumbered]

Rule 10.464 renumbered as rule 10.474 effective January 1, 2008.

Another Rule 10.464 follows.

Rule 10.464. Education requirements and expectations for judges and subordinate judicial officers on domestic violence issues

(a) Judges and subordinate judicial officers hearing specified matters

Each judge or subordinate judicial officer who hears criminal, family, juvenile delinquency, juvenile dependency, or probate matters must participate in appropriate education on domestic violence issues as part of his or her requirements and expectations under rule 10.462. Each judge or subordinate judicial officer whose primary assignment is in one of these areas also must participate in a periodic update on domestic violence as part of these requirements and expectations.

(Subd (a) adopted effective January 1, 2010.)

(b) Specified courses to include education on domestic violence issues

The education provider must include education on domestic violence issues at the Judicial College under rule 10.462(c)(1)(C) and in courses for primary assignments in criminal, family, juvenile delinquency, juvenile dependency, or probate under rule 10.462(c)(1)(B) or (c)(4).

(Subd (b) adopted effective January 1, 2010.)

Rule 10.464 adopted effective January 1, 2010.

Advisory Committee Comment

In determining what constitutes "appropriate" education, each judge or subordinate judicial officer should determine the number of hours of education on domestic violence that is adequate for his or her assignment, taking into account the size of the court, the nature of his or her assignment, the mix of assignments, and other factors.

Rule 10.468. Content-based and hours-based education for superior court judges and subordinate judicial officers regularly assigned to hear probate proceedings

(a) Definitions

As used in this rule, the following terms have the meanings stated below:

(1) "Judge" means a judge of the superior court.

(2) "Subordinate judicial officer" has the meaning specified in rule 10.701(a).

(3) "Judicial officer" means a judge or a subordinate judicial officer.

(4) "Probate proceedings" are decedents' estates, guardianships and conservatorships under division 4 of the Probate Code, trust proceedings under division 9 of the Probate Code, and other matters governed by provisions of that code and the rules in title 7 of the California Rules of Court.

(5) A judicial officer "regularly assigned to hear probate proceedings" is a judicial officer who is:

(A) Assigned to a dedicated probate department where probate proceedings are customarily heard on a full-time basis;

(B) Responsible for hearing most of the probate proceedings filed in a court that does not have a dedicated probate department; or

(C) Responsible for hearing probate proceedings on a regular basis in a department in a branch or other location remote from the main or central courthouse, whether or not he or she also hears other kinds of matters in that department and whether or not there is a dedicated probate department in the main or central courthouse; or

(D) Designated by the presiding judge of a court with four or fewer authorized judges.

(6) "CJER" is the Judicial Council's Center for Judicial Education and Research.

(7) "CJA" is the California Judges Association.

(Subd (a) amended effective January 1, 2016; adopted effective January 1, 2008.)

(b) Content-based requirements

(1) Each judicial officer beginning a regular assignment to hear probate proceedings after the effective date of this rule—unless he or she

is returning to this assignment after less than two years in another assignment—must complete, as soon as possible but not to exceed six months from the assignment's commencement date, 6 hours of education on probate guardianships and conservatorships, including court-supervised fiduciary accounting.

(2) The education required in (1) is in addition to the New Judge Orientation program for new judicial officers and the B. E. Witkin Judicial College required under rule 10.462(c)(1)(A) and (C) and may be applied toward satisfaction of the 30 hours of continuing education expected of judges and required of subordinate judicial officers under rule 10.462(d).

(3) The education required in (1) must be provided by CJER, CJA, or the judicial officer's court. CJER is responsible for identifying content for this education and will share the identified content with CJA and the courts.

(4) The education required in (1) may be by traditional (face to face) or distance-learning means, such as broadcasts, videoconferences, or online coursework, but may not be by self-study.

(Subd (b) adopted effective January 1, 2008.)

(c) Hours-based continuing education

(1) In a court with five or more authorized judges, each judicial officer regularly assigned to hear probate proceedings must complete 18 hours of continuing education every three years, with a minimum of six hours required in the first year, on probate guardianships and conservatorships, including court-supervised fiduciary accounting. The three-year period begins on January 1 of the year following the judicial officer's completion of the education required in (b)(1) or, if he or she is exempt from that education, on January 1 of the year the assignment commenced after the effective date of this rule.

(2) In a court with four or fewer authorized judges, each judicial officer regularly assigned to hear probate proceedings must complete nine hours of continuing education every three years, with a minimum of three hours per year, on probate guardianships and conservatorships, including court-supervised fiduciary accounting. The three-year period begins on January 1 of the year following the judicial officer's completion of the education required in (b)(1) or, if he or she is exempt from that education, on January 1 of the year the assignment commenced after the effective date of this rule.

(3) The first continuing education period for judicial officers who were regularly assigned to hear probate proceedings before the effective date of this rule and who continue in the assignment after that date is two years, from January 1, 2008, through December 31, 2009, rather than three years. The continuing education requirements in (1) are prorated for the first continuing education period under this paragraph. The first full three-year period of continuing education for judicial officers under this paragraph begins on January 1, 2010.

(4) The number of hours of education required in (1) or (2) may be reduced proportionately for judicial officers whose regular assignment to hear probate proceedings is for a period of less than three years.

(5) The education required in (1) or (2) may be applied toward satisfaction of the 30 hours of continuing education expected of judges or required of subordinate judicial officers under rule 10.462(d).

(6) A judicial officer may fulfill the education requirement in (1) or (2) through council-sponsored education, an approved provider (see rule 10.481(a)), or education approved by the judicial officer's presiding judge as meeting the education criteria specified in rule 10.481(b).

(7) The education required in (1) or (2) may be by traditional (live, face-to-face) or distance learning, such as broadcasts, videoconferences, or online coursework, but may not be by self-study.

(Subd (c) amended effective January 1, 2016; adopted effective January 1, 2008; previously amended effective January 1, 2012.)

(d) Extension of time

The provisions of rule 10.462(e) concerning extensions of time apply to the content-based and hours-based education required under (b) and (c) of this rule.

(Subd (d) adopted effective January 1, 2008.)

(e) Record keeping and reporting

(1) The provisions of rule 10.462(f) and (g) concerning, respectively, tracking participation, record keeping, and summarizing participation by judges and tracking participation by subordinate judicial officers, apply to the education required under this rule.

(2) Presiding judges' records of judicial officer participation in the education required by this rule are subject to audit by Judicial Council staff under rule 10.462. Judicial Council staff may require courts to report participation by judicial officers in the education required by this rule to ensure compliance with Probate Code section 1456.

(Subd (e) amended effective January 1, 2016; adopted effective January 1, 2008.)
Rule 10.468 amended effective January 1, 2016; adopted effective January 1, 2008; previously amended effective January 1, 2012.

Rule 10.469.   Judicial education recommendations for justices, judges, and subordinate judicial officers, and additional requirements

(a) Judicial education recommendations generally

Each justice, judge and subordinate judicial officer, as part of his or her continuing judicial education, should regularly participate in educational activities related to his or her responsibilities and particular judicial assignment or assignments. Minimum education requirements and expectations related to judicial responsibilities and assignments are set forth in rules 10.461–10.462. Additional education requirements related to specific responsibilities are set forth in rule 10.463 (for those hearing family law matters), rule 10.464 (for those hearing domestic violence issues), and rule 10.468 (for those hearing probate proceedings). The following recommendations illustrate for some specific responsibilities and assignments how justices, judges, and subordinate judicial officers should participate in more judicial education than is required and expected.

(Subd (a) amended effective January 1, 2012; adopted effective January 1, 2008.)

(b) Jury trial assignment

Each judge or subordinate judicial officer assigned to jury trials should regularly use the Judicial Council CJER educational materials or other appropriate materials and should regularly complete CJER or other appropriate educational programs devoted to the conduct of jury voir dire and the treatment of jurors.

(Subd (b) amended effective January 1, 2016; adopted effective January 1, 2008; previously amended effective January 1, 2012.)

(c) Hearing of juvenile dependency matters

Each judge or subordinate judicial officer who hears juvenile dependency matters, including retired judges who sit on court assignment, should regularly use appropriate educational materials and should annually complete appropriate education programs on juvenile dependency law and procedure, consistent with the requirements in Welfare and Institutions Code section 304.7.

(Subd (c) adopted effective January 1, 2008.)

(d) Capital case assignment

Each judge assigned to hear a capital case should complete before the commencement of the trial a comprehensive education program on California law and procedure relevant to capital cases provided by CJER. A judge with a subsequent assignment to a capital case should complete a periodic update course within two years before the commencement of the trial. The periodic update may be provided through actual classroom instruction or through video, audio, or other media as determined by CJER.

(Subd (d) adopted effective January 1, 2008.)

(e) Education on fairness and access, unconscious bias, and prevention of harassment, discrimination, retaliation, and inappropriate workplace conduct

(1) In order to achieve the objective of assisting judicial officers in preserving the integrity and impartiality of the judicial system through the prevention of bias, each justice, judge, and subordinate judicial officer should regularly participate in education on fairness and access. The education should include the following subjects: race and ethnicity, gender, sexual orientation, **and** persons with disabilities [1].

(2) Each justice, judge, and subordinate judicial officer must participate in education on unconscious bias, as well as the prevention of harassment, discrimination, retaliation, and inappropriate workplace conduct. This education must be taken at least once every three-year continuing education period as determined by rules 10.461(c)(1) and 10.462(d).

(Subd (e) amended effective January 1, 2021; adopted effective January 1, 2008.)

Rule 10.469(e).   2020 Deletes. [1] , and sexual harassment
Rule 10.469 amended effective January 1, 2021; adopted effective January 1, 2008; previously amended effective January 1, 2012, and January 1, 2016.

Rule 10.471.   Approved providers; approved course criteria [Renumbered]

Rule 10.471 renumbered as rule 10.481 effective January 1, 2008.

Another Rule 10.471 follows.

Rule 10.471. Minimum education requirements for Supreme Court and Court of Appeal clerks/executive officers

(a) Applicability

All clerks/executive officers of the California Supreme Court and Courts of Appeal must complete these minimum education requirements. All clerks/executive officers should participate in more education than is required, related to each individual's responsibilities and in accordance with the education recommendations set forth in rule 10.479.

(Subd (a) amended effective January 1, 2018; adopted effective January 1, 2008.)

(b) Hours-based requirement

(1) Each clerk/executive officer must complete 30 hours of continuing education every three years beginning on the following date:

(A) For a new clerk/executive officer, the first three-year period begins on January 1 of the year following his or her hire.

(B) For all other clerks/executive officers, the first three-year period begins on January 1, 2008.

(2) The following education applies toward the required 30 hours of continuing education:

(A) Any education offered by an approved provider (see rule 10.481(a)) and any other education, including education taken to satisfy a statutory or other education requirement, approved by the Chief Justice or the administrative presiding justice as meeting the criteria listed in rule 10.481(b).

(B) Each hour of participation in traditional (live, face-to-face) education; distance education such as broadcasts, videoconferences, and online coursework; faculty service; and self-directed study counts toward the requirement on an hour-for-hour basis. Each clerk/executive officer must complete at least half of his or her continuing education hours requirement as a participant in traditional (live, face-to-face) education. The clerk/executive officer may complete the balance of his or her education hours requirement through any other means with no limitation on any particular type of education.

(C) A clerk/executive officer who serves as faculty by teaching legal or judicial education to a legal or judicial audience may apply education hours as faculty service. Credit for faculty service counts toward the continuing education requirement in the same manner as all other types of education—on an hour-for-hour basis.

(Subd (b) amended effective January 1, 2018; adopted effective January 1, 2008; previously amended effective January 1, 2012, and January 1, 2014.)

(c) Extension of time

(1) For good cause, the Chief Justice or the administrative presiding justice may grant a one-year extension of time to complete the education requirements in (b).

(2) If the Chief Justice or the administrative presiding justice grants a request for an extension of time, the clerk/executive officer, in consultation with the Chief Justice or the administrative presiding justice, must also pursue interim means of obtaining relevant educational content.

(3) An extension of time to complete the hours-based requirement does not affect the timing of the clerk/executive officer's next three-year period.

(Subd (c) amended effective January 1, 2018; adopted effective January 1, 2008.)

(d) Record of participation; statement of completion

Each clerk/executive officer is responsible for:

(1) Tracking his or her own participation in education and keeping a record of participation for three years after each course or activity that is applied toward the requirements;

(2) At the end of each year, giving the Chief Justice or the administrative presiding justice a copy of his or her record of participation in education for that year; and

(3) At the end of each three-year period, giving the Chief Justice or the administrative presiding justice a signed statement of completion for that three-year period.

(Subd (d) amended effective January 1, 2018; adopted effective January 1, 2008.)

Rule 10.471 amended effective January 1, 2018; adopted effective January 1, 2008; previously amended effective January 1, 2012, and January 1, 2014.

Rule 10.472. Minimum education requirements for Supreme Court and Court of Appeal managing attorneys, supervisors, and other personnel

(a) Applicability

All California Supreme Court and Court of Appeal managing attorneys, supervisors, and other personnel must complete these minimum education requirements. All managing attorneys, supervisors, and other personnel should participate in more education than is required related to each individual's responsibilities and in accordance with the education recommendations set forth in rule 10.479.

(Subd (a) adopted effective January 1, 2008.)

(b) Content-based requirements

(1) Each new managing attorney or supervisor must complete orientation courses within six months of becoming a managing attorney or supervisor, unless the individual's supervisor determines that the new managing attorney or supervisor has already completed these orientation courses or courses covering equivalent content. The courses must include orientation about:

(A) The judicial branch of California;

(B) The local court; and

(C) Basic management and supervision.

(2) Each new court employee who is not a managing attorney or supervisor must complete orientation courses within six months of becoming a court employee, unless the employee's supervisor determines that the new court employee has already completed these orientation courses or courses covering equivalent content. The courses must include orientation about:

(A) The judicial branch of California;

(B) The local court;

(C) Basic employee issues, such as sexual harassment and safety; and

(D) The employee's specific job.

(3) The clerk/executive officer, the managing attorney, or the employee's supervisor may determine the appropriate content, delivery mechanism, and length of orientation based on the needs and role of each individual employee.

(Subd (b) amended effective January 1, 2018; adopted effective January 1, 2008.)

(c) Hours-based requirements

(1) Each managing attorney, supervisor, or appellate judicial attorney must complete 12 hours of continuing education every two years.

(2) Each court employee who is not a managing attorney, supervisor, or appellate judicial attorney must complete 8 hours of continuing education every two years, with the exception of employees who do not provide court administrative or operational services. Those employees are not subject to the continuing education hours-based requirement but must complete any education or training required by law and any other education required by the clerk/executive officer.

(3) The first two-year period for all managing attorneys, supervisors, and other personnel begins on January 1, 2008. The orientation education required for new managing attorneys, supervisors, and other personnel under (b) does not apply toward the required hours of continuing education because it must be completed before they enter the two-year period. Each new managing attorney, supervisor, or employee enters the two-year continuing education period on the first day of the quarter following his or her completion of the orientation education required under (b); the quarters begin on January 1, April 1, July 1, and October 1. Each managing attorney, supervisor, or employee who enters the two-year continuing education period after it has begun must complete a prorated number of continuing education hours for that two-year period, based on the number of quarters remaining in it.

(4) Any education offered by an approved provider (see rule 10.481(a)) and any other education, including education taken to satisfy a statutory, rules-based, or other education requirement, that is approved by the clerk/executive officer, the managing attorney, or the employee's supervisor as meeting the criteria listed in rule 10.481(b) applies toward the orientation education required under (b) and the continuing education required under (c)(1) and (2).

(5) Each hour of participation in traditional (live, face-to-face) education; distance education such as broadcasts, videoconferences, online coursework; and faculty service counts toward the requirement on an hour-for-hour basis. Each managing attorney, supervisor, and other employee must complete at least half of his or her continuing education hours requirement as a participant in traditional (live, face-to-face) education. The managing attorney, supervisor, or other employee may complete the balance of his or her education hours requirement through any other means with no limitation on any particular type of education.

Self-directed study is encouraged for professional development but does not apply toward the required hours.

(6) A managing attorney, supervisor, or other employee who serves as faculty by teaching legal or judicial education for a legal or judicial audience may apply education hours for the faculty service. Credit for faculty service counts toward the continuing education requirement in the same manner as all other types of education—on an hour-for-hour basis.

(7) The clerk/executive officer, the managing attorney, or the employee's supervisor may require supervisors and other court personnel to participate in specific courses or to participate in education in a specific subject matter area as part of their continuing education.

(Subd (c) amended effective January 1, 2018; adopted effective January 1, 2008; previously amended effective January 1, 2012.)

(d) Extension of time

(1) For good cause, a justice (for that justice's chambers staff), the managing attorney, the clerk/executive officer, or a supervisor, if delegated by the clerk/executive officer, or the employee's supervisor may grant a six-month extension of time to complete the education requirements in this rule.

(2) If the justice, managing attorney, clerk/executive officer, or supervisor grants a request for an extension of time, the managing attorney, supervisor, or employee who made the request, in consultation with the justice, managing attorney, clerk/executive officer, or supervisor, must also pursue interim means of obtaining relevant educational content.

(3) An extension of time to complete the hours-based requirement does not affect the timing of the next two-year period.

(Subd (d) amended effective January 1, 2018; adopted effective January 1, 2008.)

(e) Records of participation

(1) Each court is responsible for tracking participation in education and for tracking completion of minimum education requirements for its managing attorneys, supervisors, and other personnel.

(2) Each managing attorney, supervisor, and employee must keep records of his or her own participation for two years after each course or activity that is applied toward the requirements.

(Subd (e) adopted effective January 1, 2008.)

Rule 10.472 amended effective January 1, 2018; adopted effective January 1, 2008; previously amended effective January 1, 2012.

Rule 10.473. Minimum education requirements for trial court executive officers

(a) Applicability

All California trial court executive officers must complete these minimum education requirements. All executive officers should participate in more education than is required, related to each individual's responsibilities and in accordance with the education recommendations set forth in rule 10.479.

(Subd (a) amended effective January 1, 2008; adopted effective January 1, 2007.)

(b) Content-based requirement

(1) Each new executive officer must complete the Presiding Judges Orientation and Court Management Program provided by the Judicial Council's Center for Judiciary Education and Research (CJER) within one year of becoming an executive officer and should participate in additional education during the first year.

(2) Each executive officer should participate in CJER's Presiding Judges Orientation and Court Management Program each time a new presiding judge from his or her court participates in the course and each time the executive officer becomes the executive officer in a different court.

(Subd (b) amended effective July 1, 2015; adopted effective January 1, 2007.)

(c) Hours-based requirement

(1) Each executive officer must complete 30 hours of continuing education, including at least three hours of ethics education, every three years.

(2) For a new executive officer, the first three-year period begins on January 1 of the year following completion of the required education for new executive officers.

(3) The following education applies toward the required 30 hours of continuing education:

(A) Any education offered by an approved provider (see rule 10.481(a)) and any other education, including education taken to satisfy a statutory or other education requirement, approved by the presiding judge as meeting the criteria listed in rule 10.481(b).

(B) Each hour of participation in traditional (live, face-to-face) education; distance education such as broadcasts, videoconferences, and online coursework; self-directed study; and faculty service counts toward the requirement on an hour-for-hour basis. The presiding judge has discretion to determine the number of hours, if any, of traditional (live, face-to-face) education required to meet the continuing education requirement.

(C) An executive officer who serves as faculty by teaching legal or judicial education to a legal or judicial audience may apply education hours as faculty service. Credit for faculty service counts toward the continuing education requirement in the same manner as all other types of education—on an hour-for-hour basis.

(Subd (c) amended effective July 1, 2015; previously amended effective January 1, 2008, January 1, 2011, January 1, 2012, and January 1, 2013.)

(d) Extension of time

(1) For good cause, a presiding judge may grant a one-year extension of time to complete the education requirements in (b) and (c).

(2) If the presiding judge grants a request for an extension of time, the executive officer, in consultation with the presiding judge, must also pursue interim means of obtaining relevant educational content.

(3) An extension of time to complete the hours-based requirement does not affect the timing of the executive officer's next three-year period.

(Subd (d) adopted effective January 1, 2007.)

(e) Record of participation; statement of completion

Each executive officer is responsible for:

(1) Tracking his or her own participation in education and keeping a record of participation for three years after each course or activity that is applied toward the requirements;

(2) At the end of each year, giving the presiding judge a copy of his or her record of participation in education for that year; and

(3) At the end of each three-year period, giving the presiding judge a signed statement of completion for that three-year period.

(Subd (e) amended effective January 1, 2008; adopted effective January 1, 2007.)

Rule 10.473 amended effective July 1, 2015; adopted as rule 10.463 effective January 1, 2007; previously amended and renumbered effective January 1, 2008; previously amended effective January 1, 2011, January 1, 2012, and January 1, 2013.

Rule 10.474. Trial court managers, supervisors, and other personnel

(a) Applicability

All California trial court managers, supervisors, and other personnel must complete these minimum education requirements. All managers, supervisors, and other personnel should participate in more education than is required, related to each individual's responsibilities and in accordance with the education recommendations set forth in rule 10.479.

(Subd (a) amended effective January 1, 2008; adopted effective January 1, 2007.)

(b) Content-based requirements

(1) Each new manager or supervisor must complete orientation courses within six months of becoming a manager or supervisor, unless the court's executive officer determines that the new manager or supervisor has already completed these orientation courses or courses covering equivalent content. The courses must include orientation about:

(A) The judicial branch of California;

(B) The local court; and

(C) Basic management and supervision.

(2) Each new court employee who is not a manager or supervisor must complete orientation courses within six months of becoming a court employee, unless the employee's supervisor determines that the new court employee has already completed these orientation courses or courses covering equivalent content. The courses must include orientation about:

(A) The judicial branch of California;

(B) The local court;

(C) Basic employee issues, such as sexual harassment and safety; and

(D) The employee's specific job.

(3) The court executive officer may determine the appropriate content, delivery mechanism, and length of orientation based on the needs and role of each individual employee.

(Subd (b) amended effective January 1, 2008; adopted effective January 1, 2007.)

(c) Hours-based requirements

(1) Each court manager or supervisor must complete 12 hours of continuing education every two years.

(2) Each court employee who is not a manager or supervisor must complete 8 hours of continuing education every two years, with the exception of employees who do not provide court administrative or operational services. Those employees are not subject to the continuing education hours-based requirement but must complete any education or training required by law and any other education required by the court executive officer.

(3) The orientation education required for new managers, supervisors, and other personnel under (b) does not apply toward the required hours of continuing education because it must be completed before they enter the two-year period. Each new manager, supervisor, or employee enters the two-year continuing education period on the first day of the quarter following his or her completion of the orientation education required under (b); the quarters begin on January 1, April 1, July 1, and October 1. Each manager, supervisor, or employee who enters the two-year continuing education period after it has begun must complete a prorated number of continuing education hours for that two-year period, based on the number of quarters remaining in it.

(4) Any education offered by an approved provider (see rule 10.481(a)) and any other education, including education taken to satisfy a statutory, rules-based, or other education requirement, that is approved by the executive officer or the employee's supervisor as meeting the criteria listed in rule 10.481(b) applies toward the orientation education required under (b) and the continuing education required under (c)(1) and (2).

(5) Each hour of participation in traditional (live, face-to-face) education; distance education such as broadcasts, videoconferences, and online coursework; and faculty service counts toward the requirement on an hour-for-hour basis. The court executive officer has discretion to determine the number of hours, if any, of traditional (live, face-to-face) education required to meet the continuing education requirement. Self-directed study is encouraged for professional development but does not apply toward the required hours.

(6) A manager, supervisor, or employee who serves as faculty by teaching legal or judicial education to a legal or judicial audience may apply education hours as faculty service. Credit for faculty service counts toward the continuing education requirement in the same manner as all other types of education—on an hour-for-hour basis.

(7) The court executive officer may require managers, supervisors and other court personnel to participate in specific courses or to participate in education in a specific subject matter area as part of their continuing education.

(Subd (c) amended effective January 1, 2015; previously amended effective January 1, 2008, January 1, 2012, and January 1, 2013.)

(d) Extension of time

(1) For good cause, the executive officer may grant a one-year extension of time to complete the education requirements in this rule. If an extension is granted, the subsequent two-year compliance period begins immediately after the extended compliance period ends, unless otherwise determined by the executive officer.

(2) If the executive officer grants a request for an extension of time, the manager, supervisor, or employee who made the request, in consultation with the executive officer, must also pursue interim means of obtaining relevant educational content.

(Subd (d) amended effective January 1, 2015; adopted effective January 1, 2007.)

(e) Records of participation

(1) Each court is responsible for tracking participation in education and for tracking completion of minimum education requirements for its managers, supervisors, and other personnel.

(2) Each manager, supervisor, and employee must keep records of his or her own participation for two years after each course or activity that is applied toward the requirements.

(Subd (e) adopted effective January 1, 2007.)

Rule 10.474 amended effective January 1, 2015; adopted as rule 10.464 effective January 1, 2007; previously amended and renumbered effective January 1, 2008; previously amended effective January 1, 2012, and January 1, 2013.

Advisory Committee Comment

The time frame for completion of compliance courses based on statutory or regulatory mandates is unaffected by the one-year extension in (d)(1).

Rule 10.478. Content-based and hours-based education for court investigators, probate attorneys, and probate examiners

(a) Definitions

As used in this rule, the following terms have the meanings specified below, unless the context or subject matter otherwise require:

(1) A "court investigator" is a person described in Probate Code section 1454(a) employed by or under contract with a court to provide the investigative services for the court required or authorized by law in guardianships, conservatorships, and other protective proceedings under division 4 of the Probate Code;

(2) A "probate attorney" is an active member of the State Bar of California who is employed by a court to perform the functions of a probate examiner and also to provide legal analysis, recommendations, advice, and other services to the court pertaining to probate proceedings;

(3) A "probate examiner" is a person employed by a court to review filings in probate proceedings in order to assist the court and the parties to get the filed matters properly ready for consideration by the court in accordance with the requirements of the Probate Code, the rules in title 7 of the California Rules of Court, and the court's local rules;

(4) "Probate proceedings" are decedents' estates, guardianships and conservatorships under division 4 of the Probate Code, trust proceedings under division 9 of the Probate Code, and other matters governed by provisions of that code and the rules in title 7 of the California Rules of Court;

(5) "CJER" is the Judicial Council's Center for Judicial Education and Research.

(Subd (a) amended effective January 1, 2016; adopted effective January 1, 2008.)

(b) Content-based requirements for court investigators

(1) Each court investigator must complete 18 hours of education within one year of his or her start date after the effective date of this rule. The education must include the following general topics:

(A) Court process and legal proceedings;

(B) Child abuse and neglect and the effect of domestic violence on children (guardianship investigators); elder and dependent adult abuse, including undue influence and other forms of financial abuse (conservatorship investigators);

(C) Medical issues;

(D) Access to and use of criminal-record information, confidentiality, ethics, conflicts of interest;

(E) Accessing and evaluating community resources for children and mentally impaired elderly or developmentally disabled adults; and

(F) Interviewing children and persons with mental function or communication deficits.

(2) A court investigator may fulfill the education requirement in (1) through council-sponsored education, an approved provider (see rule 10.481(a)), or education approved by the court executive officer or the court investigator's supervisor as meeting the education criteria specified in rule 10.481(b).

(3) The education required in (1) may be applied to the specific-job portion of the orientation course required for all new court employees under rule 10.474(b)(2)(D) and the continuing education required for all nonmanagerial or non-supervisory court employees under rule 10.474(c)(2).

(4) The education required in (1) may be by traditional (face-to-face) or distance-learning means, such as broadcasts, videoconferences, or online coursework, but may not be by self-study.

(Subd (b) amended effective January 1, 2016; adopted effective January 1, 2008; previously amended effective January 1, 2012.)

(c) Content-based education for probate attorneys

(1) Each probate attorney must complete 18 hours of education within six months of his or her start date after January 1, 2008, in probate-related topics, including guardianships, conservatorships, and court-supervised fiduciary accounting.

(2) A probate attorney may fulfill the education requirement in (1) through council-sponsored education, an approved provider (see rule 10.481(a)), or education approved by the court executive officer or the probate attorney's supervisor as meeting the education criteria specified in rule 10.481(b).

(3) The education required in (1) may be applied to the specific-job portion of the orientation course required for all new court employees under rule 10.474(b)(2)(D) and the continuing education required for all nonmanagerial or non-supervisory court employees under rule 10.474(c)(2).

(4) The education required in (1) may be by traditional (face-to-face) or distance-learning means, such as broadcasts, videoconferences, or online coursework, but may not be by self-study.

(d) Content-based education for probate examiners

(1) Each probate examiner must complete 30 hours of education within one year of his or her start date after January 1, 2008, in probate-related topics, of which 18 hours must be in guardianships and conservatorships, including court-appointed fiduciary accounting.

(2) A probate examiner may fulfill the education requirement in (1) through council-sponsored education, an approved provider (see rule 10.481(a)), or education approved by the court executive officer or the probate examiner's supervisor as meeting the education criteria specified in rule 10.481(b).

(3) The education required in (1) may be applied to the specific-job portion of the orientation course required for all new court employees under rule 10.474(b)(2)(D) and the continuing education required for all nonmanagerial or non-supervisory court employees under rule 10.474(c)(2).

(4) The education required in (1) may be by traditional (face-to-face) or distance-learning means, such as broadcasts, videoconferences, or online coursework, but may not be by self-study.

(Subd (d) amended effective January 1, 2016; adopted effective January 1, 2008; previously amended effective January 1, 2012.)

(e) Hours-based education for court investigators

(1) Each court investigator must complete 12 hours of continuing education on some or all of the general topics listed in (b)(1) each calendar year. For court investigators employed by or performing services under contract with the court before the effective date of this rule, the first calendar year the education is required begins on January 1, 2008. For court investigators who begin their employment or performance of services under contract with the court after the effective date of this rule, the first year this education is required begins on January 1 of the year immediately following completion of the education required in (b).

(2) A court investigator may fulfill the education requirement in (1) through council-sponsored education, an approved provider (see rule 10.481(a)), or education approved by the court executive officer or the court investigator's supervisor as meeting the education criteria specified in rule 10.481(b).

(3) The education required in (1) may be applied to the continuing education required for all nonmanagerial or nonsupervisory court employees under rule 10.474(c)(2).

(4) The education required in (1) may be by traditional (face-to-face) or distance-learning means, such as broadcasts, videoconferences, or online coursework, but may not be by self-study.

(Subd (e) amended effective January 1, 2016; adopted effective January 1, 2008; previously amended effective January 1, 2012.)

(f) Hours-based education for probate attorneys

(1) Each probate attorney must complete 12 hours of continuing education each calendar year in probate-related subjects, of which six hours per year must be in guardianships and conservatorships, including court-supervised fiduciary accounting. For probate attorneys employed by or performing services under contract with the court before the effective date of this rule, the first calendar year the education is required begins on January 1, 2008. For probate attorneys who begin their employment with the court after the effective date of this rule, the first year this education is required begins on January 1 of the year immediately following completion of the education required in (c).

(2) A probate attorney may fulfill the education requirement in (1) through council-sponsored education, an approved provider (see rule 10.481(a)), or education approved by the court executive officer or the probate attorney's supervisor as meeting the education criteria specified in rule 10.481(b).

(3) The education required in (1) may be applied to the continuing education required for all nonmanagerial or nonsupervisory court employees under rule 10.474(c)(2).

(4) The education required in (1) may be by traditional (face-to-face) or distance-learning means, such as broadcasts, videoconferences, or online coursework, but may not be by self-study.

(Subd (f) amended effective January 1, 2016; adopted effective January 1, 2008; previously amended effective January 1, 2012.)

(g) Hours-based education for probate examiners

(1) Each probate examiner must complete 12 hours of continuing education each calendar year in probate-related subjects, of which six hours per year must be in guardianships and conservatorships, including court-appointed fiduciary accounting. For probate examiners employed by

the court before the effective date of this rule, the first calendar year the education is required begins on January 1, 2008. For probate examiners who begin their employment with the court after the effective date of this rule, the first year this education is required begins on January 1 of the year immediately following completion of the education required in (d).

(2) A probate examiner may fulfill the education requirement in (1) through council-sponsored education, an approved provider (see rule 10.481(a)), or education approved by the court executive officer or the probate examiner's supervisor as meeting the education criteria specified in rule 10.481(b).

(3) The education required in (1) may be applied to the continuing education required for all nonmanagerial or nonsupervisory court employees under rule 10.474(c)(2).

(4) The education required in (1) may be by traditional (face-to-face) or distance-learning means, such as broadcasts, videoconferences, or online coursework, but may not be by self-study.

(Subd (g) amended effective January 1, 2016; adopted effective January 1, 2008; previously amended effective January 1, 2012.)

(h) Extension of time

The provisions of rule 10.474(d) concerning extensions of time apply to the content-based and hours-based education required under this rule.

(Subd (h) adopted effective January 1, 2008.)

(i) Record keeping and reporting

(1) The provisions of rule 10.474(e) concerning the responsibilities of courts and participating court employees to keep records and track the completion of educational requirements apply to the education required under this rule.

(2) Judicial Council staff may require courts to report participation by court investigators, probate attorneys, and probate examiners in the education required by this rule as necessary to ensure compliance with Probate Code section 1456.

(Subd (i) amended effective January 1, 2016; adopted effective January 1, 2008.)
Rule 10.478 amended effective January 1, 2016; adopted effective January 1, 2008; previously amended effective January 1, 2012.

Rule 10.479.   Education recommendations for appellate and trial court personnel

(a) Education recommendations generally

Each appellate and trial court executive or administrative officer, manager, supervisor, and other employee, as part of his or her continuing education, should regularly participate in educational activities related to his or her responsibilities. Minimum education requirements for court personnel are set forth in rules 10.471–10.474. The following recommendations illustrate for some specific responsibilities how executive and administrative officers, managers, supervisors, and other personnel should participate in more education than is required.

(Subd (a) adopted effective January 1, 2008.)

(b) Education on treatment of jurors

The presiding judge of each trial court should ensure that all court executives and all court employees who interact with jurors are properly trained in the appropriate treatment of jurors. Court executives and jury staff employees should regularly use CJER educational materials or other appropriate materials and should regularly participate in CJER programs or other appropriate programs devoted to the treatment of jurors.

(Subd (b) adopted effective January 1, 2008.)

(c) Fairness and access education

In order to achieve the objective of assisting court employees in preserving the integrity and impartiality of the judicial system through the prevention of bias, all court personnel should regularly participate in education on fairness and access. The education should include instruction on race and ethnicity, gender, sexual orientation, persons with disabilities, and sexual harassment.

(Subd (c) adopted effective January 1, 2008.)

(d) Education on quality service to court users

Employees should regularly participate in education covering appropriate skills and conduct for working with court customers offered locally or by the Judicial Council through CJER.

(Subd (d) adopted effective January 1, 2008.)
Rule 10.479 adopted effective January 1, 2008.

Rule 10.481.   Approved providers; approved course criteria

(a) Approved providers

The Judicial Council's Center for Judicial Education and Research (CJER) is responsible for maintaining a current list of approved providers. The list of approved providers must include the Judicial Council, the

California Judges Association, and all California state courts and should include other reputable national and state organizations that regularly offer education directed to justices, judges, and court personnel. The director of CJER may add or remove organizations from the list of approved providers as appropriate according to these criteria. Any education program offered by any of the approved providers that is relevant to the work of the courts or enhances the individual participant's ability to perform his or her job may be applied toward the education requirements and expectations stated in rules 10.461–10.479, except for the requirements stated in rules 10.461(b), 10.462(c), and 10.473(b), for which specific providers are required.

(Subd (a) amended effective January 1, 2016; adopted effective January 1, 2007; previously amended effective January 1, 2008, and January 1, 2012.)

(b) Approved education criteria

Education is not limited to the approved providers referred to in (a). Any education from another provider that is approved by the Chief Justice, the administrative presiding justice, or the presiding judge as meeting the criteria listed below may be applied toward the continuing education expectations and requirements for justices, judges, and subordinate judicial officers or requirements for clerks/executive officers or court executive officers. Similarly, any education from another provider that is approved by the clerk/executive officer, the court executive officer, or the employee's supervisor as meeting the criteria listed below may be applied toward the orientation or continuing education requirements for managers, supervisors, and other employees or the content-based or continuing education requirements for probate court investigators, probate attorneys, and probate examiners in rule 10.478.

(1) The education must meet the following three criteria:

(A) The subject matter is relevant to the work of the courts or the judicial branch;

(B) The education is at least one hour in length; and

(C) Anticipated learning outcomes (how new knowledge, skills, or abilities will be applied, demonstrated, or used) are identified prior to the education work.

(2) The education must also meet at least two of the following five criteria:

(A) The learning environment is educationally sound (e.g., distractions are limited and the physical location is conducive to learning the subject matter);

(B) The participant receives or has access to all the reference tools and other materials and resources (such as handouts) that are required for learning and applying the content (such as job aids or scripts);

(C) The participant has an opportunity to practice using or applying the new information or skill (through direct experience, role-play, or case studies/hypothetical situations) as part of the learning experience;

(D) The participant has the opportunity to interact with knowledgeable faculty or other experts in the topical area to pose questions or clarify understanding;

(E) An assessment tool or activity (such as the development of an action plan to apply the newly gained knowledge or skill) enables the participant to determine whether the skills, abilities, or knowledge gained through the education can be used in the future in his or her work.

(Subd (b) amended effective January 1, 2018; adopted effective January 1, 2007; previously amended effective January 1, 2008, and January 1, 2012.)

Rule 10.481 amended effective January 1, 2018; adopted as rule 10.471 effective January 1, 2007; previously amended and renumbered as rule 10.481 effective January 1, 2008; previously amended effective January 1, 2008, January 1, 2012, and January 1, 2016.

Advisory Committee Comment

Subdivision (b). The director of CJER is available to assist those authorized to approve a request to apply education offered by a non-approved provider in determining whether the education meets the listed criteria.

Rule 10.491. Minimum education requirements for Judicial Council employees

(a) Applicability

Orientation and ongoing professional development for Judicial Council staff enables them to effectively provide service, leadership and expertise to the courts and to enhance trust and confidence in the judicial branch. All Judicial Council employees must complete minimum education requirements. These education requirements are included as a part of the employee performance evaluation process.

(Subd (a) amended effective January 1, 2017; adopted effective January 1, 2008; previously amended effective January 1, 2016.)

(b) Education requirements for new employees and new managers and supervisors

(1) Each new employee with supervisory or management responsibilities must complete the New Manager/Supervisor Orientation within six months of being hired or appointed or as soon as possible after being hired or appointed.

(2) Each new employee, including those with supervisory or management responsibilities, must complete the New Employee Orientation within six months of being hired or as soon as possible after being hired.

(3) Completion of the orientation courses counts toward the education hours requirement in (c).

(Subd (b) amended effective January 1, 2017; adopted effective January 1, 2008; previously amended effective January 1, 2016.)

(c) Continuing education requirements

(1) Each employee must complete 20 hours of continuing education every two years, beginning on January 1, 2017.

(2) For new employees beginning employment after July 1 of any year, the education hours may be prorated for that year at the discretion of the employee's supervisor.

(3) The Administrative Director may require employees to complete specific compliance courses or specific courses for management. This compliance education applies toward the continuing education requirement in (c)(1) on an hour-for-hour basis.

(4) Education offered by an approved provider described in rule 10.481(a), as well as education that is approved by the employee's supervisor as meeting the criteria listed in rule 10.481(b), applies toward the employee's continuing education requirement.

(5) Continuing education may be live (face-to-face) or distance education, such as webinars, videoconferencing, online courses, and broadcasts.

(6) Participation in education, whether as a learner or as faculty, counts toward an employee's continuing education requirement under this rule on an hour-for-hour basis.

(Subd (c) amended effective January 1, 2017; previously amended effective January 1, 2012, July 1, 2013, and January 1, 2016.)

Rule 10.491 amended effective January 1, 2017; adopted effective January 1, 2008; previously amended effective July 1, 2008, January 1, 2012, July 1, 2013, and January 1, 2016.

Division 3
Judicial Administration Rules
Applicable to All Courts

Rule 10.500. Public access to judicial administrative records

(a) Intent

(1) The Judicial Council intends by this rule to implement Government Code section 68106.2(g), added by Senate Bill X4 13 (Stats. 2009–10, 4th Ex. Sess. ch. 22), which requires adoption of rules of court that provide public access to nondeliberative and nonadjudicative court records, budget and management information.

(2) This rule clarifies and expands the public's right of access to judicial administrative records and must be broadly construed to further the public's right of access.

(Subd (a) adopted effective January 1, 2010.)

(b) Application

(1) This rule applies to public access to judicial administrative records, including records of budget and management information relating to the administration of the courts.

(2) This rule does not apply to, modify or otherwise affect existing law regarding public access to adjudicative records.

(3) This rule does not restrict the rights to disclosure of information otherwise granted by law to a recognized employee organization.

(4) This rule does not affect the rights of litigants, including parties to administrative proceedings, under the laws of discovery of this state, nor does it limit or impair any rights of discovery in a criminal case.

(5) This rule does not apply to electronic mail and text messages sent or received before the effective date of this rule.

(Subd (b) adopted effective January 1, 2010.)

(c) Definitions

As used in this rule:

(1) "Adjudicative record" means any writing prepared for or filed or used in a court proceeding, the judicial deliberation process, or the assignment or reassignment of cases and of justices, judges (including temporary and assigned judges), and subordinate judicial officers, or of counsel appointed or employed by the court.

(2) "Judicial administrative record" means any writing containing information relating to the conduct of the people's business that is prepared, owned, used, or retained by a judicial branch entity regardless of the writing's physical form or characteristics, except an adjudicative record. The term "judicial administrative record" does not include records of a personal nature that are not used in or do not relate to the people's business, such as personal notes, memoranda, electronic mail, calendar entries, and records of Internet use.

(3) "Judicial branch entity" means the Supreme Court, each Court of Appeal, each superior court, and the Judicial Council.

(4) "Judicial branch personnel" means justices, judges (including temporary and assigned judges), subordinate judicial officers, members of the Judicial Council and its advisory bodies, and directors, officers, employees, volunteers, and agents of a judicial branch entity.

(5) "Person" means any natural person, corporation, partnership, limited liability company, firm, or association.

(6) "Writing" means any handwriting, typewriting, printing, photographing, photocopying, electronic mail, fax, and every other means of recording on any tangible thing any form of communication or representation, including letters, words, pictures, sounds, symbols, or combinations, regardless of the manner in which the record has been stored.

(Subd (c) amended effective January 1, 2016; adopted effective January 1, 2010.)

(d) Construction of rule

(1) Unless otherwise indicated, the terms used in this rule have the same meaning as under the Legislative Open Records Act (Gov. Code, § 9070 et seq.) and the California Public Records Act (Gov. Code, § 6250 et seq.) and must be interpreted consistently with the interpretation applied to the terms under those acts.

(2) This rule does not require the disclosure of a record if the record is exempt from disclosure under this rule or is the type of record that would not be subject to disclosure under the Legislative Open Records Act or the California Public Records Act.

(Subd (d) adopted effective January 1, 2010.)

(e) Public access

(1) *Access*

(A) A judicial branch entity must allow inspection and copying of judicial administrative records unless the records are exempt from disclosure under this rule or by law.

(B) Nothing in this rule requires a judicial branch entity to create any record or to compile or assemble data in response to a request for judicial administrative records if the judicial branch entity does not compile or assemble the data in the requested form for its own use or for provision to other agencies. For purposes of this rule, selecting data from extractable fields in a single database using software already owned or licensed by the judicial branch entity does not constitute creating a record or compiling or assembling data.

(C) If a judicial administrative record contains information that is exempt from disclosure and the exempt portions are reasonably segregable, a judicial branch entity must allow inspection and copying of the record after deletion of the portions that are exempt from disclosure. A judicial branch entity is not required to allow inspection or copying of the portion of a writing that is a judicial administrative record unless that portion is reasonably segregable from the portion that constitutes an adjudicative record.

(D) If requested, a superior court must provide a copy of the certified judicial administrative record if the judicial administrative record requested has previously been certified by the superior court.

(2) *Examples*

Judicial administrative records subject to inspection and copying unless exempt from disclosure under subdivision (f) include, but are not limited to, the following:

(A) Budget information submitted to the Judicial Council after enactment of the annual Budget Act;

(B) Any other budget and expenditure document pertaining to the administrative operation of the courts, including quarterly financial statements and statements of revenue, expenditure, and reserves;

(C) Actual and budgeted employee salary and benefit information;

(D) Copies of executed contracts with outside vendors and payment information and policies concerning goods and services provided by outside vendors without an executed contract;

(E) Final audit reports; and

(F) Employment contracts between judicial branch entities and their employees.

(3) *Procedure for requesting records*

A judicial branch entity must make available on its public Web site or otherwise publicize the procedure to be followed to request a copy of or to inspect a judicial administrative record. At a minimum, the procedure must include the address to which requests are to be addressed, to whom requests are to be directed, and the office hours of the judicial branch entity.

(4) *Costs of duplication, search, and review*

(A) A judicial branch entity, on request, must provide a copy of a judicial administrative record not exempt from disclosure if the record is of a nature permitting copying, subject to payment of the fee specified in this rule or other applicable statutory fee. A judicial branch entity may require advance payment of any fee.

(B) A judicial branch entity may impose on all requests a fee reasonably calculated to cover the judicial branch entity's direct costs of duplication of a record or of production of a record in an electronic format under subdivision (i). The fee includes:

(i) A charge per page, per copy, or otherwise, as established and published by the Judicial Council, or as established by the judicial branch entity following a notice and comment procedure specified by the Judicial Council, representing the direct costs of equipment, supplies, and staff time required to duplicate or produce the requested record; and

(ii) Any other direct costs of duplication or production, including, but not limited to, the costs incurred by a judicial branch entity in retrieving the record from a remote storage facility or archive and the costs of mailing responsive records.

(C) In the case of requests for records for commercial use, a judicial branch entity may impose, in addition to the fee in (B), a fee reasonably calculated to cover the actual costs of staff search and review time, based on an hourly rate for salary and benefits of each employee involved.

(D) For purposes of this rule:

(i) "Commercial use" means a request for a use or purpose that furthers the commercial, trade, or profit interests of the requester or the person on whose behalf the request is being made. A request from a representative of the news media that supports its news-dissemination function is not a request for a commercial use.

(ii) "Representative of the news media" means a person who regularly gathers, prepares, collects, photographs, records, writes, edits, reports, or publishes news or information that concerns local, national, or international events or other matters of public interest for dissemination to the public for a substantial portion of the person's livelihood or for substantial financial gain.

(iii) "Search and review time" means actual time spent identifying and locating judicial administrative records, including material within documents, responsive to a request; determining whether any portions are exempt from disclosure; and performing all tasks necessary to prepare the records for disclosure, including redacting portions exempt from disclosure. "Search and review time" does not include time spent resolving general legal or policy issues regarding the applicability of particular exemptions.

(E) By January 1, 2012, the Judicial Council will review and evaluate the numbers of requests received, the time necessary to respond, and the fees imposed by judicial branch entities for access to records and information. The Judicial Council's review will consider the impact of this rule on both the public's access to records and information and on judicial branch entities' ability to carry out and fund core judicial operations.

(5) *Inspection*

A judicial branch entity must make judicial administrative records in its possession and not exempt from disclosure open to inspection at all times during the office hours of the judicial branch entity provided that the record is of a nature permitting inspection.

(6) *Time for determination of disclosable records*

A judicial branch entity, on a request that reasonably describes an identifiable record or records, must determine, within 10 calendar days from receipt of the request, whether the request, in whole or in part, seeks disclosable judicial administrative records in its possession and must promptly notify the requesting party of the determination and the reasons for the determination.

(7) *Response*

If a judicial branch entity determines that a request seeks disclosable judicial administrative records, the judicial branch entity must make the disclosable judicial administrative records available promptly. The judicial branch entity must include with the notice of the determination the estimated date and time when the records will be made available. If the judicial branch entity determines that the request, in whole or in part, seeks nondisclosable judicial administrative records, it must convey its determination in writing, include a contact name and telephone number to which inquiries may be directed, and state the express provision of this rule justifying the withholding of the records not disclosed.

(8) *Extension of time for determination of disclosable records*

In unusual circumstances, to the extent reasonably necessary to the proper processing of the particular request, a judicial branch entity may extend the time limit prescribed for its determination under (e)(6) by no more than 14 calendar days by written notice to the requesting party, stating the reasons for the extension and the date on which the judicial branch entity expects to make a determination. As used in this section, "unusual circumstances" means the following:

(A) The need to search for and collect the requested records from multiple locations or facilities that are separate from the office processing the request;

(B) The need to search for, collect, and appropriately examine a voluminous amount of records that are included in a single request; or

(C) The need for consultation, which must be conducted with all practicable speed, with another judicial branch entity or other governmental agency having substantial subject matter interest in the determination of the request, or with two or more components of the judicial branch entity having substantial subject matter interest in the determination of the request.

(9) *Reasonable efforts*

(A) On receipt of a request to inspect or obtain a copy of a judicial administrative record, a judicial branch entity, in order to assist the requester in making a focused and effective request that reasonably describes an identifiable judicial administrative record, must do all of the following to the extent reasonable under the circumstances:

(i) Assist the requester in identifying records and information responsive to the request or to the purpose of the request, if stated;

(ii) Describe the information technology and physical location in which the records exist; and

(iii) Provide suggestions for overcoming any practical basis for denying inspection or copying of the records or information sought.

(B) The requirements of (A) will be deemed to have been satisfied if the judicial branch entity is unable to identify the requested information after making a reasonable effort to elicit additional clarifying information from the requester that helps identify the record or records.

(C) The requirements of (A) do not apply to a request for judicial administrative records if the judicial branch entity makes the requested records available or determines that the requested records are exempt from disclosure under this rule.

(10) *No obstruction or delay*

Nothing in this rule may be construed to permit a judicial branch entity to delay or obstruct the inspection or copying of judicial administrative records that are not exempt from disclosure.

(11) *Greater access permitted*

Except as otherwise prohibited by law, a judicial branch entity may adopt requirements for itself that allow for faster, more efficient, or greater access to judicial administrative records than prescribed by the requirements of this rule.

(12) *Control of records*

A judicial branch entity must not sell, exchange, furnish, or otherwise provide a judicial administrative record subject to disclosure under this rule to a private entity in a manner that prevents a judicial branch entity from providing the record directly under this rule. A judicial branch entity must not allow a private entity to control the disclosure of information that is otherwise subject to disclosure under this rule.

(Subd (e) amended effective January 1, 2016; adopted effective January 1, 2010.)

(f) Exemptions

Nothing in this rule requires the disclosure of judicial administrative records that are any of the following:

(1) Preliminary writings, including drafts, notes, working papers, and inter-judicial branch entity or intra-judicial branch entity memoranda, that are not retained by the judicial branch entity in the ordinary course of business, if the public interest in withholding those records clearly outweighs the public interest in disclosure;

(2) Records pertaining to pending or anticipated claims or litigation to which a judicial branch entity is a party or judicial branch personnel are parties, until the pending litigation or claim has been finally adjudicated or otherwise resolved;

(3) Personnel, medical, or similar files, or other personal information whose disclosure would constitute an unwarranted invasion of personal privacy, including, but not limited to, records revealing home addresses, home telephone numbers, cellular telephone numbers, private electronic mail addresses, and social security numbers of judicial branch personnel and work electronic mail addresses and work telephone numbers of justices, judges (including temporary and assigned judges), subordinate judicial officers, and their staff attorneys;

(4) Test questions, scoring keys, and other examination data used to develop, administer, and score examinations for employment, certification, or qualification;

(5) Records whose disclosure is exempted or prohibited under state or federal law, including provisions of the California Evidence Code relating to privilege, or by court order in any court proceeding;

(6) Records whose disclosure would compromise the security of a judicial branch entity or the safety of judicial branch personnel, including but not limited to, court security plans, and security surveys, investigations, procedures, and assessments;

(7) Records related to evaluations of, complaints regarding, or investigations of justices, judges (including temporary and assigned judges), subordinate judicial officers, and applicants or candidates for judicial office. This exemption does not apply to any settlement agreement entered into on or after January 1, 2010 for which public funds were spent in payment of the settlement, including any settlement agreement arising from claims or complaints of sexual harassment or sexual discrimination. The names of judicial officers may not be redacted from any settlement agreement that is produced under this rule; however, the names of complainants or witnesses, and other information that would identify complainants or witnesses, may be redacted;

(8) The contents of real estate appraisals or engineering or feasibility estimates and evaluations made for or by the judicial branch entity related to the acquisition of property or to prospective public supply and construction contracts, until all of the property has been acquired or the relevant contracts have been executed. This provision does not affect the law of eminent domain;

(9) Records related to activities governed by Government Code sections 71600 et seq. and 71800 et seq. that reveal deliberative processes, impressions, evaluations, opinions, recommendations, meeting minutes, research, work products, theories, or strategy or that provide instruction, advice, or training to employees who are not represented by employee organizations under those sections. Nothing in this subdivision limits the disclosure duties of a judicial branch entity with respect to any other records relating to the activities governed by the employee relations acts referred to in this subdivision;

(10) Records that contain trade secrets or privileged or confidential commercial and financial information submitted in response to a judicial branch entity's solicitation for goods or services or in the course of a judicial branch entity's contractual relationship with a commercial entity. For purposes of this rule:

(A) "Trade secret" means information, including a formula, pattern, compilation, program, device, method, technique, or process, that:

(i) Derives independent economic value, actual or potential, from not being generally known to the public or to other persons who can obtain economic value from its disclosure or use; and

(ii) Is the subject of efforts that are reasonable under the circumstances to maintain its secrecy;

(B) "Privileged information" means material that falls within recognized constitutional, statutory, or common law privileges;

(C) "Confidential commercial and financial information" means information whose disclosure would:

(i) Impair the judicial branch entity's ability to obtain necessary information in the future; or

(ii) Cause substantial harm to the competitive position of the person from whom the information was obtained.

(11) Records whose disclosure would disclose the judicial branch entity's or judicial branch personnel's decision-making process, provided that, on the facts of the specific request for records, the public interest served by nondisclosure clearly outweighs the public interest served by disclosure of the record; or

(12) If, on the facts of the specific request for records, the public interest served by nondisclosure of the record clearly outweighs the public interest served by disclosure of the record.

(Subd (f) amended effective June 1, 2018; adopted effective January 1, 2010.)

(g) Computer software; copyrighted materials

(1) Computer software developed by a judicial branch entity or used by a judicial branch entity for the storage or manipulation of data is not a judicial administrative record under this rule. For purposes of this rule "computer software" includes computer mapping systems, computer graphic systems, and computer programs, including the source, object, and other code in a computer program.

(2) This rule does not limit a judicial branch entity's ability to sell, lease, or license computer software for commercial or noncommercial use.

(3) This rule does not create an implied warranty on the part of any judicial branch entity for errors, omissions, or other defects in any computer software.

(4) This rule does not limit any copyright protection. A judicial branch entity is not required to duplicate records under this rule in violation of any copyright.

(5) Nothing in this subdivision is intended to affect the judicial administrative record status of information merely because the information is stored in a computer. Judicial administrative records stored in a computer will be disclosed as required in this rule.

(Subd (g) adopted effective January 1, 2010.)

(h) Waiver of exemptions

(1) Disclosure of a judicial administrative record that is exempt from disclosure under this rule or provision of law by a judicial branch entity or judicial branch personnel acting within the scope of their office or employment constitutes a waiver of the exemptions applicable to that particular record.

(2) This subdivision does not apply to disclosures:

(A) Made through discovery proceedings;

(B) Made through other legal proceedings or as otherwise required by law;

(C) Made to another judicial branch entity or judicial branch personnel for the purposes of judicial branch administration;

(D) Within the scope of a statute that limits disclosure of specified writings to certain purposes; or

(E) Made to any governmental agency or to another judicial branch entity or judicial branch personnel if the material will be treated confidentially.

(Subd (h) adopted effective January 1, 2010.)

(i) Availability in electronic format

(1) A judicial branch entity that has information that constitutes an identifiable judicial administrative record not exempt from disclosure under this rule and that is in an electronic format must, on request, produce that information in the electronic format requested, provided that:

(A) No law prohibits disclosure;

(B) The record already exists in the requested electronic format, or the judicial branch entity has previously produced the judicial administrative record in the requested format for its own use or for provision to other agencies;

(C) The requested electronic format is customary or standard for records of a similar type and is commercially available to private entity requesters; and

(D) The disclosure does not jeopardize or compromise the security or integrity of the original record or the computer software on which the original record is maintained.

(2) In addition to other fees imposed under this rule, the requester will bear the direct cost of producing a record if:

(A) In order to comply with (1), the judicial branch entity would be required to produce a record and the record is one that is produced only at otherwise regularly scheduled intervals or;

(B) Producing the requested record would require data compilation or extraction or any associated programming that the judicial branch entity is not required to perform under this rule but has agreed to perform in response to the request.

(3) Nothing in this subdivision shall be construed to require a judicial branch entity to reconstruct a record in an electronic format if the judicial branch entity no longer has the record available in an electronic format.

(Subd (i) adopted effective January 1, 2010.)

(j) Public access disputes

(1) Unless the petitioner elects to proceed under (2) below, disputes and appeals of decisions with respect to disputes with the Judicial Council or a superior court regarding access to budget and management information required to be maintained under rule 10.501 are subject to the process described in rule 10.803.

(2) Any person may institute proceedings for injunctive or declarative relief or writ of mandate in any court of competent jurisdiction to enforce his or her right to inspect or to receive a copy of any judicial administrative record under this rule.

(3) Whenever it is made to appear by verified petition that a judicial administrative record is being improperly withheld from disclosure, the court with jurisdiction will order the judicial branch entity to disclose the records or show cause why it should not do so. The court will decide the case after examining the record (in camera if appropriate), papers filed by the parties, and any oral argument and additional evidence as the court may allow.

(4) If the court finds that the judicial branch entity's decision to refuse disclosure is not justified under this rule, the court will order the judicial branch entity to make the record public. If the court finds that the judicial branch entity's decision was justified, the court will issue an order supporting the decision.

(5) An order of the court, either directing disclosure or supporting the decision of the judicial branch entity refusing disclosure, is not a final judgment or order within the meaning of Code of Civil Procedure section 904.1 from which an appeal may be taken, but will be immediately reviewable by petition to the appellate court for the issuance of an extraordinary writ. Upon entry of an order under this subdivision, a party must, in order to obtain review of the order, file a petition within 20 days after service of a written notice of entry of the order or within such further time not exceeding an additional 20 days as the court may for good cause allow. If the notice is served by mail, the period within which to file the petition will be extended by 5 days. A stay of an order or judgment will not be granted unless the petitioning party demonstrates it will otherwise sustain irreparable damage and probable success on the merits. Any person who fails to obey the order of the court will be cited to show cause why that is not in contempt of court.

(6) The court will award court costs and reasonable attorney fees to the plaintiff should the plaintiff prevail in litigation filed under this subdivision. The costs and fees will be paid by the judicial branch entity and will not become a personal liability of any individual. If the court finds that the plaintiff's case is clearly frivolous, it will award court costs and reasonable attorney fees to the judicial branch entity.

(Subd (j) amended effective January 1, 2016; adopted effective January 1, 2010.)
Rule 10.500 amended effective June 1, 2018; adopted effective January 1, 2010; previously amended effective January 1, 2016.

Advisory Committee Comment

Subdivision (a). By establishing a public access rule applicable to all judicial administrative records, the proposed rule would expand public access to these records. The Judicial Council recognizes the important public interest in access to records and information relating to the administration of the judicial branch. The Judicial Council also recognizes the importance of the privacy rights of individuals working in or doing business with judicial branch entities and the public's interest in an effective and independent judicial branch of state government. The report on this rule includes the Judicial Council's findings on the impact of this rule on these interests, and how these interests are protected by the rule.

Subdivisions (b)(1) and (b)(2). This rule does not apply to adjudicative records, and is not intended to modify existing law regarding public access to adjudicative records. California case law has established that, in general, subject to specific statutory exceptions, case records that accurately and officially reflect the work of the court are public records open to inspection. (*Estate of Hearst* (1977) 67 Cal.App.3d 777, 782–83.) However, documents prepared in the course of adjudicative work and not regarded as official case records, such as preliminary drafts, personal notes, and rough records of proceedings, are not subject to public access because the perceived harm to the judicial process by requiring this material to be available to the public is greater than the benefit the public might derive from its disclosure. (*Copley Press, Inc. v. Superior Court* (1992) 6 Cal.App.4th 106.)

Subdivision (c)(2). The application of this rule is intended to reflect existing case law under the California Public Records Act that exempts from the definition of "public record" certain types of personal records and information. The concept was first discussed in the California Assembly and establishes that if personal correspondence and information are "unrelated to the conduct of the people's business" they are therefore not public records. (*San Gabriel Tribune v. Superior Court* (1983) 143 Cal.App.3d 762, 774, citing Assembly Committee on Statewide Information Policy California Public Records Act of 1968, section B, page 9, Appendix to Assembly Journal (1970 Reg. Sess.).) Case law has further established that only records necessary or convenient to the discharge of official duty, or kept as necessary or convenient to the discharge of official duty, are public records for the purposes of the California Public Records Act and its predecessors. (*Braun v. City of Taft* (1984) 154 Cal.App.3d 332; *City Council of Santa Monica v. Superior Court* (1962) 204 Cal.App.2d 68.)

Subdivision (e)(4). The fees charged by a judicial branch entity under this rule are intended to allow the entity to recover an amount not to exceed the reasonable costs of responding to a request for records or information. In accordance with existing practice within the judicial branch and the other branches of government, the Judicial Council intends agencies and entities of the executive and legislative branches of the California state government to receive records or information requested from judicial branch entities for the agency's or entity's use free of charge. This subdivision is intended to provide, however, that requesters of records or information for the purpose of furthering the requester's commercial interests will be charged for costs incurred by the judicial branch entity in responding to the request, and that such costs will not be a charge against the budget of the judicial branch of the state General Fund.

Subdivision (f)(3). In addition to the types of records and information exempt from disclosure under the corresponding provision of the California Public Records Act, Government Code section 6254(c), this provision includes a further nonexclusive list of specific information that is exempt under this rule. The rule does not attempt to list each category of information that is specific to judicial branch entities and that may also be exempt under this rule. For example, although they are not specifically listed, this provision exempts from disclosure records maintained by any court or court-appointed counsel administrator for the purpose of evaluating attorneys seeking or being considered for appointment to cases.

Subdivision (f)(7). The 2018 amendments to (f)(7) clarify that settlement agreements are not exempt from disclosure. All judicial branch entities, including the Judicial Council, must disclose settlement agreements under a rule 10.500 request, given the public nature of these records. (See *Register Div. of Freedom Newspapers, Inc. v. County of Orange* (1984) 158 Cal.App.3d 893, 909.) By clarifying the public nature of settlement agreements and judicial branch entities' obligation to disclose them, the amended rule also clarifies that a judicial branch entity's disclosure of these agreements, whether maintained by the entity or its attorneys, would not implicate any ethical or legal obligations under Business and Professions Code section 6068(e)(1) or rule 3-100(A) of the State Bar Rules of Professional Conduct. The duty of a judicial branch entity to disclose public records of settlements is not constrained by which persons, division, or office within the entity maintains the records.

The 2018 amendments to rule 10.500 do not apply to records maintained by the Commission on Judicial Performance, an independent state entity established under article VI, section 18 of the California Constitution. Rule 10.500 is not applicable to the Commission on Judicial Performance which has separate rules that apply to its work and records.

Subdivision (f)(10). The definition of "trade secret" restates the definition in Civil Code section 3426.1.

Subdivision (f)(11). This subdivision is intended to reflect California law on the subject of the "deliberative process" exemption under the California Public Records Act, which is currently stated in the Supreme Court's decision in *Times Mirror Co. v. Superior Court* (1991) 53 Cal.3d 29 1325 and the later Court of Appeal decisions *California First Amendment Coalition v. Superior Court* (1998) 67 Cal.App.4th 159 and *Wilson v. Superior Court* (1996) 51 Cal.App.4th 1136.

Subdivision (j)(1). Under current rule 10.803 a petitioner may file a writ in a superior court regarding a dispute with a superior court or the Judicial Council with respect to disclosure of records and information required to be maintained under current rule 10.802. The writ petition must be heard on an expedited basis and includes a right to an appeal. The statutory authority for the hearing process set forth in current rule 10.803, Government Code section 71675(b), does not extend this procedure to other disputes with respect to public access. The rule provides that petitioners with a dispute with any other judicial branch entity, or with respect to records that are not required to be maintained under rule 10.802, may follow the procedure set forth in (j)(2) through (j)(6), which is equivalent to the dispute resolution procedure of the California Public Records Act. A petitioner eligible for the dispute resolution process set out in current rule 10.803 may also elect to proceed with his or her dispute under the procedure set forth in (j)(2) through (j)(6).

Rule 10.501.   Judicial education [Repealed]

Rule 10.501 repealed effective January 1, 2007; adopted as rule 970 effective January 1, 1996. The repealed rule related to judicial education.

Another Rule 10.501 follows.

Rule 10.501.   Maintenance of budget and management information

(a) Maintenance of information by the superior court

Each superior court must maintain for a period of three years from the close of the fiscal year to which the following relate:

(1) Official documents of the superior court pertaining to the approved superior court budget allocation adopted by the Judicial Council and actual final year-end superior court revenue and expenditure reports as required in budget procedures issued by Judicial Council staff to be maintained or reported to the council, including budget allocation, revenue, and expenditure reports;

(2) Records or other factual management information on matters that are within the scope of representation as defined in Government Code section 71634 unless distribution is otherwise precluded by law; and

(3) Records or other factual management information on other matters referred to in Government Code section 71634 unless distribution is otherwise precluded by law.

(Subd (a) amended effective January 1, 2016; adopted effective January 1, 2010.)

(b) Maintenance of information by Judicial Council staff

Judicial Council staff must maintain for a period of three years from the close of the fiscal year to which the following relate:

(1) Official approved budget allocations for each superior court;

(2) Actual final year-end superior court revenue and expenditure reports required by budget procedures issued by Judicial Council staff to be maintained or reported to the council that are received from the courts, including budget revenues and expenditures for each superior court;

(3) Budget priorities as adopted by the council; and

(4) Documents concerning superior court budgets considered or adopted by the council at council business meetings on court budgets.

(Subd (b) amended effective January 1, 2016; adopted effective January 1, 2010.)

Rule 10.501 amended effective January 1, 2016; adopted effective January 1, 2010.

Rule 10.502.   Judicial sabbatical program

(a) Objective

Sabbatical leave is a privilege available to jurists by statute. The objective of sabbatical leave is to facilitate study that will benefit the administration of justice and enhance judges' performance of their duties.

(Subd (a) amended effective July 23, 2018.)

(b) Eligibility

Any judge is eligible to apply for an unpaid sabbatical under Government Code section 68554.

(Subd (b) amended effective July 23, 2018.)

(c) Application

(1) A judge may apply for a sabbatical by submitting a sabbatical proposal to the Administrative Director with a copy to the presiding judge or justice.

(2) The sabbatical proposal must include:

(A) The beginning and ending dates of the proposed sabbatical;

(B) A description of the sabbatical project, including an explanation of how the sabbatical will benefit the administration of justice and the judge's performance of his or her duties; and

(C) A statement from the presiding judge or justice of the affected court, indicating approval or disapproval of the sabbatical request and the reasons for such approval or disapproval, forwarded to the Executive and Planning Committee with a copy to the judge.

(Subd (c) amended effective July 23, 2018; previously amended effective January 1, 2007, and January 1, 2016.)

(d) Review of applications

The Executive and Planning Committee will make recommendations to the Judicial Council regarding sabbatical requests, with support from the council's human resources staff.

(Subd (d) amended effective July 23, 2018; previously amended effective January 1, 2007, and January 1, 2016.)

(e) Evaluation

(1) The Administrative Director must forward all sabbatical requests that comply with (c) to the Executive and Planning Committee.

(2) The Executive and Planning Committee must recommend granting or denying the sabbatical request after it considers the following factors:

(A) Whether the sabbatical will benefit the administration of justice in California and the judge's performance of his or her duties; and

(B) Whether the sabbatical leave will be detrimental to the affected court.

(Subd (e) amend effective July 23, 2018; previously amended effective January 1, 2016.)

(f) Length

A unpaid judicial sabbatical taken under Government Code section 68554 may not exceed one year.

(Subd (f) amended effective July 23, 2018.)

(g) Ethics and compensation

A judge on unpaid sabbatical leave is subject to the California Code of Judicial Ethics and may receive compensation and reimbursement for expenses for activities performed during that sabbatical leave as provided in canon 4H of the Code of Judicial Ethics.

(Subd (g) amended effective July 23, 2018.)

(h) Retirement and benefits

A judge on unpaid sabbatical leave under Government Code section 68554 receives no compensation, and the period of absence does not count as service toward retirement. The leave does not affect the term of office.

(Subd (h) amended and relettered effective July 23, 2018; adopted as subd (i) effective January 1, 2007.)

(i) Judge's report

On completion of a sabbatical leave, the judge must report in writing to the Judicial Council on how the leave benefited the administration of justice in California and on its effect on his or her official duties as a judicial officer.

(Subd (i) amended and relettered effective July 23, 2018; adopted as subd (h) effective January 1, 2007.)

Rule 10.502 amended effective July 23, 2018; adopted as rule 6.151 effective January 1, 2003; previously amended and renumbered as rule 10.502 effective January 1, 2007; previously amended effective January 1, 2016.

Rule 10.503. Use of recycled paper by all courts [Repealed]

Rule 10.503 repealed effective January 1, 2014; adopted as rule 989.1 effective January 1, 1994; previously amended and renumbered effective January 1, 2007.

Rule 10.504. Smoking prohibited in all courts

(a) Definition

"Court facilities" means courthouses and all areas of multipurpose buildings used for court operations.

(b) Smoking prohibited

Smoking is prohibited in all court facilities.

(Subd (b) amended effective January 1, 2007.)

(c) Signs

Conspicuous no-smoking signs must be placed in all court facilities.

(Subd (c) amended effective January 1, 2007.)

Rule 10.504 amended and renumbered effective January 1, 2007; adopted as rule 989.5 effective July 1, 1991.

Rule 10.505. Judicial robes

(a) Color and length

The judicial robe required by Government Code section 68110 must be black, must extend in front and back from the collar and shoulders to below the knees, and must have sleeves to the wrists.

(Subd (a) amended and lettered effective January 1, 2007; adopted as subd (e) effective September 24, 1959; relettered as subd (d) effective July 1, 1963; amended as an unlettered subd effective January 1, 2003.)

(b) Style

The judicial robe must conform to the style customarily worn in courts in the United States.

(Subd (b) amended and lettered effective January 1, 2007; adopted as subd (e) effective September 24, 1959; relettered as subd (d) effective July 1, 1963; amended as an unlettered subd effective January 1, 2003.)

Rule 10.505 amended and renumbered effective January 1, 2007; adopted as rule 249 effective January 1, 1949; previously amended effective September 24, 1959, and July 1, 1963; amended and renumbered as rule 299 effective January 1, 2003.

Division 4
Trial Court Administration

Chapter 1
General Rules on Trial Court Management

Rule 10.601. Superior court management

(a) Purpose

The rules in this division establish a system of trial court management that:

(1) Promotes equal access to the courts;

(2) Establishes decentralized management of trial court resources; and

(3) Enables the trial courts to operate in an efficient, effective, and accountable manner in serving the people of California.

(Subd (a) amended effective January 1, 2007.)

(b) Goals

The rules in this division are intended to ensure the authority and responsibility of the superior courts to do the following, consistent with statutes, rules of court, and standards of judicial administration:

(1) Manage their day-to-day operations with sufficient flexibility to meet the needs of those served by the courts;

(2) Establish the means of selecting presiding judges, assistant presiding judges, executive officers or court administrators, clerks of court, and jury commissioners;

(3) Manage their personnel systems, including the adoption of personnel policies;

(4) Manage their budget and fiscal operations, including allocating funding and moving funding between functions or line items;

(5) Provide input to the Judicial Council, the Trial Court Budget Advisory Committee, and Judicial Council on the trial court budget process; and

(6) Develop and implement processes and procedures to improve court operations and responsiveness to the public.

(Subd (b) amended effective January 1, 2016; previously amended effective January 1, 2002, and January 1, 2007.)

(c) Decentralized management

"Decentralized management" as used in the rules in this division refers to the administration of the trial courts on a countywide basis, unless an alternative structure has been approved by the Judicial Council, consistent with applicable statutes, rules, and standards of judicial administration.

(Subd (c) amended effective January 1, 2007.)

Rule 10.601 amended effective January 1, 2016; adopted as rule 2501 effective July 1, 1998; renumbered as rule 6.601 effective January 1, 1999; previously amended effective January 1, 2002; previously amended and renumbered as rule 10.601 effective January 1, 2007.

Rule 10.602. Selection and term of presiding judge

(a) Selection

(1) *Courts with three or more judges*

Each court that has three or more judges must select a presiding judge. Selection of the presiding judge may be by secret ballot. The court should establish an internal local rule or policy for the selection of the presiding judge and assistant presiding judge, if any.

(2) *Two-judge courts*

In a court having two judges, the selection of the presiding judge must conform to Government Code section 69508.5. If selection cannot be agreed on and neither judge has at least four years of experience, the senior judge must hold the office of presiding judge until both judges have at least four years of experience.

(Subd (a) amended effective January 1, 2007; previously amended effective January 1, 2005.)

(b) Requisite experience and waiver

A presiding judge must have at least four years of experience as a judge, unless this requirement is waived by a majority vote of the judges of the court. Nomination and selection of a presiding judge should take into consideration the judge's:

(1) Management and administrative ability;

(2) Interest in serving in the position;

(3) Experience and familiarity with a variety of trial court assignments;

(4) Ability to motivate and educate other judicial officers and court personnel;

(5) Ability to evaluate the strengths of the court's bench officers and make assignments based on those strengths as well as the best interests of the public and the court; and

(6) Other appropriate factors.

(Subd (b) amended effective January 1, 2007; previously amended effective January 1, 2005.)

(c) Term

A presiding judge in a court with two judges must be elected for a term of not less than one year. A presiding judge in a court with three or more judges must be elected for an initial term of not less than two years. The presiding judge may be elected for additional terms. The court may change the duration of the initial or additional term by local rule or policy so long as the initial term is not less than the duration specified in this rule. A presiding judge may be removed by a majority vote of the judges of the court.

(Subd (c) amended effective January 1, 2007; previously amended effective January 1, 2005.)

(d) Assistant presiding judge and acting presiding judge

(1) The court may elect an assistant presiding judge.

(2) If the court's internal local rule or policy does not provide for the designation of an acting presiding judge to serve if the presiding judge is absent or unable to act, the presiding judge must designate one.

(3) The court should provide the assistant presiding judge with training to foster an orderly succession to the office of presiding judge.

(Subd (d) amended effective January 1, 2007; previously amended effective January 1, 2005.)

(e) Caseload adjustment

To the extent possible, the judicial caseload should be adjusted to provide the presiding judge with sufficient time and resources to devote to the management and administrative duties of the office.

Rule 10.602 amended and renumbered effective January 1, 2007; adopted as rule 6.602 effective January 1, 2001; previously amended effective January 1, 2005.

Advisory Committee Comment

The internal local rule described in this rule relates only to the internal management of the court, and as such is exempt from the requirements in rule 10.613. (See rule 10.613(j).)

Rule 10.603. Authority and duties of presiding judge

(a) General responsibilities

The presiding judge is responsible, with the assistance of the court executive officer, for leading the court, establishing policies, and allocating resources in a manner that promotes access to justice for all members of the public, provides a forum for the fair and expeditious resolution of disputes, maximizes the use of judicial and other resources, increases efficiency in court operations, and enhances service to the public. The presiding judge is responsible for:

(1) Ensuring the effective management and administration of the court, consistent with any rules, policies, strategic plan, or budget adopted by the Judicial Council or the court;

(2) Ensuring that the duties of all judges specified under rule 10.608 are timely and orderly performed; and

(3) Ensuring that the court has adopted written policies and procedures allowing the presiding judge to perform efficiently the administrative duties of that office.

(Subd (a) amended effective January 1, 2007.)

(b) Authority

(1) The presiding judge is authorized to:

(A) Assign judges to departments and designate supervising judges for divisions, districts, or branch courts;

(B) Apportion the business of the court, including assigning and reassigning cases to departments;

(C) Call meetings of the judges;

(D) Appoint standing and special committees of judges;

(E) Act as the spokesperson for the court;

(F) Authorize and direct expenditures from the court's Trial Court Operations Fund; and

(G) Perform all acts necessary to accomplish the duties specified by the rules of court.

(2) No local rule or policy may limit the authority of the presiding judge as granted in the rules of court.

(Subd (b) amended effective January 1, 2007.)

(c) Duties

(1) *Assignments*

The presiding judge has ultimate authority to make judicial assignments. The presiding judge must:

(A) Designate a judge to preside in each department, including a master calendar judge when appropriate, and designate a presiding judge of the juvenile division and a supervising judge for each division, district, or branch court. In making judicial assignments, the presiding judge must take into account the following:

(i) The needs of the public and the court, as they relate to the efficient and effective management of the court's calendar;

(ii) The knowledge and abilities demanded by the assignment;

(iii) The judge's judicial and nonjudicial experience, including specialized training or education;

(iv) The judge's interests;

(v) The need for continuity in the assignment;

(vi) The desirability of exposing the judge to a particular type of assignment; and

(vii) Other appropriate factors. Judicial assignments must not be based solely or primarily on seniority;

(B) Assign to a master calendar judge any of the duties that may more appropriately be performed by that department;

(C) Supervise the court's calendar, apportion the business of the court among the several departments of the court as equally as possible, and publish for general distribution copies of a current calendar specifying the judicial assignments of the judges and the times and places assigned for hearings;

(D) Reassign cases between departments as convenience or necessity requires; and

(E) Designate a judge to act if by law or the rules of court a matter is required to be presented to or heard by a particular judge and that judge is absent, deceased, or unable to act.

(2) *Judicial schedules*

(A) The presiding judge must adopt a process for scheduling judges' vacations and absences from court for attendance at schools, conferences, workshops, and community outreach activities, and must prepare a plan for these vacations and absences from court.

(B) The plan should take into account the principles contained in standards 10.11–10.13 (on judicial education) and standard 10.5 (on community activities) of the Standards of Judicial Administration.

(C) The presiding judge must review requests from judges for time absent from court and may approve any request that is consistent with the plan and with the orderly operation of the court.

(D) The presiding judge must allow each judge to take two days of personal leave per year. Personal leave may be taken at any time that is approved by the presiding judge.

(E) The presiding judge must allow the following number of days of vacation for each judge annually:

(i) 24 days for judges with less than 7 years of service as a California judge;

(ii) 27 days for judges with at least 7 but less than 14 years of service as a California judge; and

(iii) 30 days for judges with 14 or more years of service as a California judge.

(F) The presiding judge may authorize a judge to take more time off than is specified in (c)(2)(E) as justified by extraordinary circumstances, if the circumstances are documented and the authorization is in writing.

(G) The presiding judge, in his or her discretion, may allow a judge to take additional vacation days equal to the number of vacation days that the judge did not use in the previous year, up to a maximum of 30 such days. A court may, by local rule, establish a lower maximum number of such days. This paragraph applies only to vacation days accrued after January 1, 2001. It does not affect any unused vacation days that a judge may have accrued before January 1, 2001, which are governed by local court policy, nor does it create any right to compensation for unused vacation days.

(H) The court must, by local rule, define a day of vacation. Absence from court to attend an authorized education program, conference, or workshop for judges, or to participate in Judicial Council or other authorized committees or community outreach activities, is not vacation time if attendance is in accordance with the plan and has the prior approval of the presiding judge. Absence from court due to illness is not vacation time. This rule does not limit the time a judge may be absent from court when unable to work because of illness.

(I) To ensure compliance with the plan, the presiding judge must establish a system to monitor judges' absences from court and maintain records of those absences.

(3) *Submitted cases*

The presiding judge must supervise and monitor the number of causes under submission before the judges of the court and ensure that no cause under submission remains undecided and pending for longer than 90 days. As an aid in accomplishing this goal, the presiding judge must:

(A) Require each judge to report to the presiding judge all causes under submission for more than 30 days and, with respect to each cause, designate whether it has been under submission for 30 through 60 days, 61 through 90 days, or over 90 days;

(B) Compile a list of all causes under submission before judges of the court, designated as the submitted list, which must include the name of each judge, a list of causes under submission before that judge, and the length of time each cause has been under submission;

(C) Circulate monthly a complete copy of the submitted list to each judge of the court;

(D) Contact and alert each judge who has a cause under submission for over 30 days and discuss ways to ensure that the cause is timely decided;

(E) Consider providing assistance to a judge who has a cause under submission for over 60 days; and

(F) Consider requesting the services of Judicial Council staff to review the court's calendar management procedures and make recommendations whenever either of the following condition exists in the court for the most recent three months:

(i) More than 90 civil active cases are pending for each judicial position; or

(ii) More than 10 percent of the cases on the civil active list have been pending for one year or more.

(4) *Oversight of judicial officers*

The presiding judge must:

(A) *Judges*

Notify the Commission on Judicial Performance of:

(i) A judge's substantial failure to perform judicial duties, including any habitual neglect of duty, persistent refusal to carry out assignments as assigned by the presiding judge, or persistent refusal to carry out the directives of the presiding judge as authorized by the rules of court; or

(ii) Any absences caused by disability totaling more than 90 court days in a 12-month period, excluding absences authorized under (c)(2);

(B) *Notice*

Give the judge a copy of the notice to the commission under (A) if appropriate. If a copy is not given to the judge, the presiding judge must inform the commission of the reasons why so notifying the judge was deemed inappropriate;

(C) *Commissioners*

(i) Prepare and submit to the judges for consideration and adoption procedures for receiving, inquiring into, and resolving complaints lodged against subordinate judicial officers, consistent with rule 10.703; and

(ii) Notify the Commission on Judicial Performance if a subordinate judicial officer is disciplined or resigns, consistent with rule 10.703(j).

(D) *Temporary judges*

Be responsible for the recruitment, training, supervision, approval, and performance of temporary judges as provided in rules 2.810–2.819 and rules 10.740–10.746; and

(E) *Assigned judges*

For each assigned retired judge:

(i) Complete a confidential evaluation form;

(ii) Submit the form annually to the Administrative Director;

(iii) Direct complaints against the assigned judge to the Chief Justice, by forwarding them to the attention of the Administrative Director, and provide requested information in writing to the Administrative Director in a timely manner; and

(iv) Assist the Administrative Director in the process of investigating, evaluating, and making recommendations to the Chief Justice regarding complaints against retired judges who serve on assignment.

(5) *Personnel*

(A) The presiding judge must provide general direction to and supervision of the court executive officer, or, if the court has no executive officer, perform the duties of the court executive regarding personnel as specified in rule 10.610(c)(1).

(B) The presiding judge must approve, in writing, the total compensation package (salary and all benefits) offered to the court executive officer at the time of the executive officer's appointment and any subsequent changes to the executive officer's total compensation package.

(6) *Budget and fiscal management*

The presiding judge must:

(A) Establish a process for consulting with the judges of the court on budget requests, expenditure plans, and other budget or fiscal matters that the presiding judge deems appropriate;

(B) Establish responsible budget priorities and submit budget requests that will best enable the court to achieve its goals;

(C) Establish a documented process for setting and approving any changes to the court executive officer's total compensation package in a fiscally responsible manner consistent with the court's established budget; and

(D) Approve procurements, contracts, expenditures, and the allocation of funds in a manner that promotes the implementation of state and local budget priorities and that ensures equal access to justice and the ability of the court to carry out its functions effectively. In a court with an executive officer, the presiding judge may delegate these duties to the court executive officer, but the presiding judge must ensure that the court executive officer performs such delegated duties consistent with the court's established budget.

(7) *Meetings and committees*

The presiding judge must establish a process for consulting with the judges of the court and may call meetings of the judges as needed. The presiding judge may appoint standing and special committees of judges as needed to assist in the proper performance of the duties and functions of the court.

(8) *Liaison*

The presiding judge must:

(A) Provide for liaison between the court and the Judicial Council, Judicial Council staff, and other governmental and civic agencies;

(B) Meet with or designate a judge or judges to meet with any committee of the bench, bar, news media, or community to review problems and to promote understanding of the administration of justice, when appropriate; and

(C) Support and encourage the judges to actively engage in community outreach to increase public understanding of and involvement with the justice system and to obtain appropriate community input regarding the administration of justice, consistent with the California Code of Judicial Ethics and standard 10.5 of the Standards of Judicial Administration.

(9) *Planning*

The presiding judge must:

(A) Prepare, with the assistance of appropriate court committees and appropriate input from the community, a long-range strategic plan that is consistent with the plan and policies of the Judicial Council, for adoption in accordance with procedures established by local rules or policies; and

(B) Ensure that the court regularly and actively examines access issues, including any physical, language, or economic barriers that impede the fair administration of justice.

(10) *Appellate records*

The presiding judge is responsible for ensuring the timely preparation of records on appeal.

(A) The presiding judge ordinarily should delegate the following duties to the executive officer:

(i) Maintaining records of outstanding transcripts to be completed by each court reporter;

(ii) Reassigning court reporters as necessary to facilitate prompt completion of transcripts; and

(iii) Reviewing court reporters' requests for extensions of time to complete transcripts in appeals of criminal cases.

(B) After reasonable notice and hearing, the presiding judge must declare any reporter of the court who is delinquent in completing a transcript on appeal not competent to act as a reporter in court, under Government Code section 69944.

(11) *Local rules*

The presiding judge must prepare, with the assistance of appropriate court committees, proposed local rules to expedite and facilitate court business in accordance with Government Code section 68071 and rules 2.100, 3.20, and 10.613.

(Subd (c) amended effective January 1, 2016; previously amended effective January 1, 2001, January 1, 2002, January 1, 2006, July 1, 2006, January 1, 2007, and July 1, 2010.)

(d) Delegation

The presiding judge may delegate any of the specific duties listed in this rule to another judge. Except for the duties listed in (c)(5)(B) and (c)(6)(C), the presiding judge may delegate to the court executive officer any of the duties listed in this rule that do not require the exercise of judicial authority. The presiding judge remains responsible for all duties listed in this rule even if he or she has delegated particular tasks to someone else.

(Subd (d) amended effective July 1, 2010; previously amended effective January 1, 2007.)

Rule 10.603 amended effective January 1, 2016; adopted as rule 6.603 effective January 1, 2001; previously amended and renumbered effective January 1, 2007; previously amended effective January 1, 2002, January 1, 2006, July 1, 2006, and July 1, 2010.

Rule 10.605. Executive committee

In accordance with the internal policies of the court, an executive committee may be established by the court to advise the presiding judge or to establish policies and procedures for the internal management of the court. An executive committee may be appointed by the presiding judge to advise the presiding judge.

Rule 10.605 renumbered effective January 1, 2007; adopted rule 6.605 effective January 1, 2001.

Rule 10.608. Duties of all judges

Each judge must:

(1) Hear all assigned matters unless:

(A) He or she is disqualified; or

(B) He or she has stated in writing the reasons for refusing to hear a cause assigned for trial, and the presiding judge, supervising judge, or master calendar judge has concurred;

(2) Immediately notify the master calendar judge or the presiding judge on the completion or continuation of a trial or any other matter assigned for hearing;

(3) Request approval of the presiding judge for any intended absence of one-half day or more, within a reasonable time before the intended absence;

(4) Follow the court's personnel plan in dealing with employees; and

(5) Follow directives of the presiding judge in matters of court management and administration, as authorized by the rules of court and the local rules and internal policies of the court.

Rule 10.608 amended and renumbered effective January 1, 2007; adopted as rule 6.608 effective January 1, 2001; previously amended effective January 1, 2006.

Rule 10.609. Notification to State Bar of attorney misconduct

(a) Notification by judge

When notification to the State Bar is required under Business and Professions Code section 6086.7, the judge issuing the order that triggers the notification requirement under section 6086.7 is responsible for notifying the State Bar. The judge may direct court staff to notify the State Bar.

(Subd (a) adopted effective January 1, 2014.)

(b) Contents of notice

The notice must include the State Bar member's full name and State Bar number, if known, and a copy of the order that triggered the notification requirement.

(Subd (b) adopted effective January 1, 2014.)

(c) Notification to attorney

If notification to the State Bar is made under this rule, the person who notified the State Bar must also inform the attorney who is the subject of the notification that the matter has been referred to the State Bar.

(Subd (c) adopted effective January 1, 2014.)

Rule 10.609 adopted effective January 1, 2014.

Advisory Committee Comment

Business and Professions Code section 6086.7 requires a court to notify the State Bar of any of the following: (1) a final order of contempt imposed on an attorney that may involve grounds warranting discipline under the State Bar Act; (2) a modification or reversal of a judgment in a judicial proceeding based in whole or in part on the misconduct, incompetent representation, or willful misrepresentation of an attorney; (3) the imposition of any judicial sanctions on an attorney of $1,000 or more, except sanctions for failure to make discovery; or (4) the imposition of any civil penalty on an attorney under Family Code section 8620. If the notification pertains to a final order of contempt, Business and Professions Code section 6086.7(a)(1) requires the court to transmit to the State Bar a copy of the relevant minutes, final order, and transcript, if one exists. This rule is intended to clarify who has the responsibility of notifying the State Bar under section 6086.7 and the required contents of the notice.

In addition to the requirements stated in Business and Professions Code section 6086.7, judges are subject to canon 3D(2) of the California Code of Judicial Ethics, which states: "Whenever a judge has personal knowledge, or concludes in a judicial decision, that a lawyer has committed misconduct or has violated any provision of the Rules of Professional Conduct, the judge shall take appropriate corrective action, which may include reporting the violation to the appropriate authority." The Advisory Committee Commentary states: "Appropriate corrective action could include direct communication with the judge or lawyer who has committed the violation, other direct action, such as a confidential referral to a judicial or lawyer assistance program, or a report of the violation to the presiding judge, appropriate authority, or other agency or body. Judges should note that in addition to the action required by Canon 3D(2), California law imposes mandatory additional reporting requirements on judges regarding lawyer misconduct. See Business and Professions Code section 6086.7."

Rule 10.610. Duties of court executive officer

(a) Selection

A court may employ an executive officer selected in accordance with procedures adopted by the court.

(b) General responsibilities

Acting under the direction of the presiding judge, the court executive officer is responsible for overseeing the management and administration of the nonjudicial operations of the court and allocating resources in a manner that promotes access to justice for all members of the public, provides a forum for the fair and expeditious resolution of disputes, maximizes the use of judicial and other resources, increases efficiency in court operations, and enhances service to the public.

(Subd (b) amended effective January 1, 2007.)

(c) Duties

Under the direction of the presiding judge and consistent with the law and rules of court, the court executive officer must perform the following duties, where they are not inconsistent with the authorized duties of the clerk of the court:

(1) *Personnel*

Provide general direction to and supervision of the employees of the court, and draft for court approval and administer a personnel plan for court employees that complies with rule 10.670. The court executive officer has the authority, consistent with the personnel plan, to hire, discipline, and terminate nonjudicial employees of the court.

(2) *Budget*

Make recommendations to the presiding judge on budget priorities; prepare and implement court budgets, including accounting, payroll, and financial controls; and employ sound budget and fiscal management practices and procedures to ensure that annual expenditures are within the court's budget.

(3) *Contracts*

Negotiate contracts on behalf of the court, in accordance with established contracting procedures and all applicable laws.

(4) *Calendar management*

Supervise and employ efficient calendar and case flow management systems, including analyzing and evaluating pending caseloads and recommending effective calendar management techniques.

(5) *Technology*

Analyze, evaluate, and implement technological and automated systems to assist the court.

(6) *Jury management*

Manage the jury system in the most efficient and effective way.

(7) *Facilities*

Plan physical space needs, and purchase and manage equipment and supplies.

(8) *Records*

Create and manage uniform record-keeping systems, collecting data on pending and completed judicial business and the internal operation of the court, as required by the court and the Judicial Council.

(9) *Recommendations*

Identify problems, recommending procedural and administrative changes to the court.

(10) *Public relations*

Provide a clearinghouse for news releases and other publications for the media and public.

(11) *Liaison*

Act as liaison to other governmental agencies.

(12) *Committees*

Provide staff for judicial committees.

(13) *Other*

Perform other duties as the presiding judge directs.

(Subd (c) amended effective January 1, 2007.)

Rule 10.610 amended and renumbered effective January 1, 2007; adopted as rule 6.610 effective January 1, 2001.

Rule 10.611.   Nondiscrimination in court appointments

Each court should select attorneys, arbitrators, mediators, referees, masters, receivers, and other persons appointed by the court on the basis of merit. No court may discriminate in such selection on the basis of gender, race, ethnicity, disability, sexual orientation, or age.

Rule 10.611 amended and renumbered effective January 1, 2007; adopted as rule 989.2 effective January 1, 1999.

Rule 10.612.   Use of gender-neutral language

Each court must use gender-neutral language in all new local rules, forms, and documents and must review and revise those now in use to ensure that they are written in gender-neutral language.

Rule 10.612 adopted effective January 1, 2007.

Rule 10.613.   Local court rules—adopting, filing, distributing, and maintaining

(a) Definitions

As used in this rule:

(1) "Court" means a trial court; and

(2) "Local rule" means every rule, regulation, order, policy, form, or standard of general application adopted by a court to govern practice or procedure in that court or by a judge of the court to govern practice or procedure in that judge's courtroom.

(Subd (a) amended and relettered effective July 1, 1999; adopted as subd (b) and repealed effective July 1, 1991.)

(b) Local inspection and copying of rules

Each court must make its local rules available for inspection and copying in every location of the court that generally accepts filing of papers. The court may impose a reasonable charge for copying the rules and may impose a reasonable page limit on copying. The rules must be accompanied by a notice indicating where a full set of the rules may be purchased or otherwise obtained.

(Subd (b) amended effective January 1, 2003; adopted as subd (c) effective July 1, 1991; previously relettered effective July 1, 1999.)

(c) Publication of rules

(1) Each court executive officer must be the official publisher of the court's local rules unless the court, by a majority vote of the judges, appoints another public agency or a private company.

(2) The official publisher must have the local rules reproduced and make copies available for distribution to attorneys and litigants.

(3) The court must adopt rules in sufficient time to permit reproduction of the rules by the official publisher before the effective date of the changes.

(4) The official publisher may charge a reasonable fee.

(5) Within 30 days of selecting an official publisher or changing an official publisher, each court must notify the Judicial Council of the name, address, and telephone number of the official publisher. Within 30 days of

a change in the cost of the rules, each court must notify the Judicial Council of the charge for the local rules. This information will be published annually by the Judicial Council.

(Subd (c) amended effective January 1, 2003; adopted as subd (d) effective July 1, 1991; amended and relettered effective July 1, 1999.)

(d) Filing rules with the Judicial Council

(1) Forty-five days before the effective date of January 1 or July 1, each court must file with the Judicial Council an electronic copy of rules and amendments to rules adopted by the court in a format authorized by the Judicial Council.

(2) The filing must be accompanied by a certificate from the presiding judge or court executive officer stating that:

(A) The court has complied with the applicable provisions of this rule;

(B) The court does or does not post local rules on the court's Web site; and

(C) The court does or does not provide assistance to members of the public in accessing the Internet or the court has delegated to and obtained the written consent of the county law librarian to provide public assistance under (e).

(3) Rules that do not comply with this rule will not be accepted for filing by the Judicial Council.

(Subd (d) amended effective January 1, 2009; adopted as subd (e) effective July 1, 1991; amended and relettered effective July 1, 1999; previously amended effective January 1, 2003, and January 1, 2007.)

(e) Deposit and maintenance of rules statewide for public inspection

(1) The Judicial Council must publish a list of courts that have filed rules and amendments to rules with the Judicial Council. The Judicial Council must deposit a paper copy of each rule and amendment in the office of the executive officer of each superior court that does not provide assistance to members of the public in accessing the Internet or has not obtained agreement from the county law librarian to provide assistance under this subdivision.

(2) The executive officer must make a complete current set of local rules and amendments available for public examination either in paper copy or through the Internet with public assistance. In a county maintaining an organized county law library, if the executive officer is satisfied that the rules and amendments will be maintained as required by this paragraph, the executive officer, with the approval of the superior court and the written consent of the county law librarian, may delegate the authority to the county law librarian to either receive and maintain paper copies of the rules and amendments, or make the rules and amendments available through the Internet with assistance to members of the public.

(3) On or before January 1 of each year, the executive officer of each court must notify the Judicial Council of the street address and room number of the place where the rules are maintained under this subdivision.

(Subd (e) amended effective January 1, 2007; adopted as subd (f) effective July 1, 1991; amended and relettered effective July 1, 1999; previously amended effective January 1, 2003.)

(f) Format of rules

(1) *Paper and electronic copies*

Paper copies may be typewritten or printed or produced by other process of duplication at the option of the court. Electronic rules must be prepared in a format authorized by the Judicial Council. All copies must be clear and legible.

(2) *Format of paper copies*

Paper copies must conform, as far as is practicable, to the requirements of chapter 1 of division 2 of title 2, except that both sides of the paper may be used, lines need not be numbered and may be single spaced, and the pages must not be permanently bound across the top but may be bound at the left side. ("Permanently bound" does not include binding with staples.) The left margin on the front and the right margin on the reverse must be at least one inch. The name of the court must be at the top of each page. The effective date of each rule and amended rule must be stated in parentheses following the text of the rule.

(3) *New pages and filing instructions*

New pages must be issued for added, repealed, or amended rules, with a list of currently effective rules and the date of adoption or of the latest amendment to each rule. Filing instructions must accompany each set of replacement pages.

(4) *Table of contents*

The rules must have a table of contents. The rules must list all local forms and indicate whether their use is mandatory or optional. If the total length of the court rules exceeds five pages, the rules must have an alphabetical subject matter index at the end of the rules. All courts must use any subject matter index the Judicial Council may have specified.

(Subd (f) amended effective January 1, 2007; adopted as subd (g) effective July 1, 1991; amended and relettered effective July 1, 1999; previously amended effective January 1, 2003.)

(g) Comment period for proposed rules

(1) *Timing*

Except for rules specifying the time of hearing and similar calendaring matters, the court must distribute each proposed rule for comment at least 45 days before it is adopted.

(2) *Organizations*

A proposed rule must be distributed for comment to the following organizations in each county located within a 100-mile radius of the county seat of the county in which the court is located:

(A) Civil rules to the county bar association in each county, the nearest office of the State Attorney General, and the county counsel in each county;

(B) Criminal rules to the county bar association in each county, the nearest office of the State Attorney General, the district attorney in each county, and the public defender in each county; and

(C) On request, any bar organization, newspaper, or other interested party.

(3) *Methods*

A court may distribute a proposed rule for comment by either of the following methods:

(A) Distributing a copy of the proposal to every organization listed in (g)(2); or

(B) Posting the proposal on the court's Web site and distributing to every organization listed in (g)(2) a notice that the proposed rule has been posted for comment and that a hard copy of the proposal is available on request.

(Subd (g) amended effective January 1, 2007; adopted as subd (h) effective July 1, 1991; relettered effective July 1, 1999; previously amended effective January 1, 2003.)

(h) Periodic review

Each court must periodically review its local rules and repeal rules that have become outdated, unnecessary, or inconsistent with statewide rules or statutes.

(Subd (h) amended effective January 1, 2007; adopted as subd (g) effective July 1, 1991; relettered effective July 1, 1999; previously amended effective January 1, 2003.)

(i) Alternative effective date

A court may adopt a rule to take effect on a date other than as provided by Government Code section 68071 if:

(1) The presiding judge submits to the Judicial Council the proposed rule and a statement of reasons constituting good cause for making the rule effective on the stated date;

(2) The Chair of the Judicial Council authorizes the rule to take effect on the date proposed; and

(3) The rule is made available for inspection as provided in (b) on or before the effective date.

(Subd (i) amended effective January 1, 2007; adopted as subd (j) effective January 1, 1993; relettered effective July 1, 1999; previously amended effective July 1, 2001.)

(j) Limitation

Except for (i), this rule does not apply to local rules that relate only to the internal management of the court.

(Subd (j) amended effective January 1, 2007; adopted effective July 1, 1999; previously amended effective July 1, 2001.)

Rule 10.613 amended effective January 1, 2009; adopted as rule 981 effective July 1, 1991; previously amended effective January 1, 1993, July 1, 1999, July 1, 2001, and January 1, 2003; previously amended and renumbered effective January 1, 2007.

Rule 10.614. Local court forms

Local forms must comply with the following:

(1) Each form must be on paper measuring no more than 8½ by 11 inches and no less than 8½ by 5 inches.

(2) The court must make copies of its forms available in the clerk's office. A court may, as an alternative, make its forms available in a booklet from which photocopies of the forms may be made. The court may charge for either copies of forms or the booklet of forms.

(3) The court must assign to each form a unique designator consisting of numbers or letters, or both. The designator must be positioned on the form in the same manner as the designator on a Judicial Council form.

(4) The effective date of each form must be placed on the form in the same manner as the effective date on a Judicial Council form, and each form must state whether it is a "Mandatory Form" or an "Optional Form" in the lower left corner of the first page.

(5) Each court must make available a current list of forms adopted or approved by that court. The list must include, for each form, its name, number, effective date, and whether the form is mandatory or optional. There must be two versions of the list, one organized by form number and one organized by form name. The court must modify its lists whenever it adopts, approves, revises, or repeals any form.

(6) Each form must be designed so that no typing is required on it within 1 inch of the top or within ½ inch of the bottom.

(7) All forms presented for filing must be firmly bound at the top and must contain two prepunched, normal-sized holes centered 2½ inches apart and ⅝ inch from the top of the form.

(8) If a form is longer than one page, the form may be filed on sheets printed on only one side even if the original form has two printed sides to a sheet. If a form is filed on a sheet printed on two sides, the reverse side must be rotated 180 degrees (printed head to foot).

Rule 10.614 amended effective January 1, 2014; adopted as rule 201.3 effective January 1, 2003; previously amended and renumbered effective January 1, 2007.

Rule 10.620. Public access to administrative decisions of trial courts

(a) Interpretation

The provisions of this rule concern public access to administrative decisions by trial courts as provided in this rule. This rule does not modify existing law regarding public access to the judicial deliberative process and does not apply to the adjudicative functions of the trial courts or the assignment of judges.

(b) Budget priorities

The Administrative Director may request, on 30 court days' notice, recommendations from the trial courts concerning judicial branch budget priorities. The notice must state that if a trial court is to make recommendations, the trial court must also give notice, as provided in (g), that interested members of the public may send input to the Judicial Council.

(Subd (b) amended effective January 1, 2016; previously amended effective January 1, 2005, and January 1, 2007.)

(c) Budget requests

Before making recommendations, if any, to the Judicial Council on items to be included in the judicial branch budget that is submitted annually to the Governor and the Legislature, a trial court must seek input from the public, as provided in (e), on what should be included in the recommendations.

(Subd (c) amended effective January 1, 2007.)

(d) Other decisions requiring public input

Each trial court must seek input from the public, as provided in (e), before making the following decisions:

(1) A request for permission from Judicial Council staff to reallocate budget funds from one program component to another in an amount greater than $400,000 or 10 percent of the total trial court budget, whichever is greater.

(2) The execution of a contract without competitive bidding in an amount greater than $400,000 or 10 percent of the total trial court budget, whichever is greater. This subdivision does not apply to a contract entered into between a court and a county that is provided for by statute.

(3) The cessation of any of the following services at a court location:

(A) The Family Law Facilitator; or

(B) The Family Law Information Center.

(Subd (d) amended effective January 1, 2016; previously amended effective January 1, 2007.)

(e) Manner of seeking public input

When a trial court is required to seek public input under this rule, it must provide public notice of the request at least 15 court days before the date on which the decision is to be made or the action is to be taken. Notice must be given as provided in (g). Any interested person or entity who wishes to comment must send the comment to the court in writing or electronically unless the court requires that all public comment be sent either by e-mail or through a response system on the court's Web site. For good cause, in the event an urgent action is required, a trial court may take immediate action if it (1) gives notice of the action as provided in (f), (2) states the reasons for urgency, and (3) gives any public input received to the person or entity making the decision.

(Subd (e) amended effective January 1, 2007.)

(f) Information about other trial court administrative matters

A trial court must provide notice, not later than 15 court days after the event, of the following:

(1) Receipt of the annual allocation of the trial court budget from the Judicial Council after enactment of the Budget Act.

(2) The awarding of a grant to the trial court that exceeds the greater of $400,000 or 10 percent of the total trial court budget.

(3) The solicitation of proposals or the execution of a contract that exceeds the greater of $400,000 or 10 percent of the trial court budget.

(4) A significant permanent increase in the number of hours that a court location is open during any day for either court sessions or filing of papers. As used in this paragraph, a significant increase does not include an emergency or one-time need to increase hours.

(5) The action taken on any item for which input from the public was required under (d). The notice must show the person or persons who made the decision and a summary of the written and e-mail input received.

(Subd (f) amended effective January 1, 2016; previously amended effective January 1, 2007.)

(g) Notice

When notice is required to be given by this rule, it must be given in the following ways:

(1) Posted on the trial court's Web site, if any.

(2) Sent to any of the following persons or entities—subject to the requirements of (h)—who have requested in writing or by electronic mail to the court executive officer to receive such notice:

(A) A newspaper, radio station, and television station in the county;

(B) The president of a local or specialty bar association in the county;

(C) Representatives of a trial court employees organization;

(D) The district attorney, public defender, and county counsel;

(E) The county administrative officer; and

(F) If the court is sending notice electronically using the provisions of (h), any other person or entity that submits an electronic mail address to which the notice will be sent.

(3) Posted at all locations of the court that accept papers for filing.

(Subd (g) amended effective January 1, 2007.)

(h) Electronic notice

A trial court may require a person or entity that is otherwise entitled to receive notice under (g)(2) to submit an electronic mail address to which the notice will be sent.

(Subd (h) amended effective January 1, 2007.)

(i) Materials

When a trial court is required to seek public input under (b), (c), or (d), it must also provide for public viewing at one or more locations in the county of any written factual materials that have been specifically gathered or prepared for the review at the time of making the decision of the person or entity making the decision. This subdivision does not require the disclosure of materials that are otherwise exempt from disclosure or would be exempt from disclosure under the state Public Records Act (beginning with Government Code section 6250). The materials must be mailed or otherwise be made available not less than five court days before the decision is to be made except if the request is made within the five court days before the decision is to be made, the materials must be mailed or otherwise be made available the next court day after the request is made. A court must either (1) provide copies to a person or entity that requests copies of these materials in writing or by electronic mail to the executive officer of the court or other person designated by the executive office in the notice, if the requesting person or entity pays all mailing and copying costs as determined by any mailing and copy cost recovery policies established by the trial court, or (2) make all materials available electronically either on its Web site or by e-mail. This subdivision does not require the trial court to prepare reports. A person seeking documents may request the court to hold the material for pickup by that person instead of mailing.

(Subd (i) amended effective January 1, 2007.)

(j) Other requirements

This rule does not affect any other obligations of the trial court including any obligation to meet and confer with designated employee representatives. This rule does not change the procedures a court must otherwise follow in entering into a contract or change the types of matters for which a court may contract.

(Subd (j) amended effective January 1, 2007.)

(k) Enforcement

This rule may be enforced under Code of Civil Procedure section 1085.

Rule 10.620 amended effective January 1, 2016; adopted as rule 6.620 effective January 1, 2004; previously amended effective January 1, 2005; previously amended and renumbered as rule 10.620 effective January 1, 2007.

Advisory Committee Comment

The procedures required under this rule do not apply where statutes specify another procedure for giving public notice and allowing public input. (See, e.g., Gov. Code, § 68106 [notice of reduced court services]; *id.*, § 68511.7 [notice of proposed court budget plan].)

Rule 10.625. Certain demographic data relating to regular grand jurors

(a) Definitions

The following definitions apply under this rule:

(1) "Regular grand jury" means a body of citizens of a county selected by the court to investigate matters of civil concern in the county, whether or not that body has jurisdiction to return indictments.

(2) "Race or ethnicity" reflects the concept of race used by the United States Census Bureau and reflects self-identification by people according to the race or races with which they most closely identify. These categories are sociopolitical constructs and should not be interpreted as being scientific or anthropological in nature. The categories include both racial and national-origin groups.

(3) "Prospective regular grand juror" means those citizens who (a) respond in person to the jury summonses or questionnaires from the court for the purposes of grand jury service and are eligible to serve as regular grand jurors, or (b) either submit applications, are recruited, or are nominated by judicial officers and are eligible to serve as regular grand jurors.

(4) "Eligible to serve" means that the prospective regular grand juror meets each of the criteria set forth in Penal Code section 893(a) and is not disqualified by any factor set forth in section 893(b).

(Subd (a) adopted effective January 1, 2007.)

(b) Jury commissioner duties and responsibilities

(1) The jury commissioner or designee must create a method to capture the following data from prospective regular grand jurors:

(A) Age range, specifically:

(i) 18–25

(ii) 26–34

(iii) 35–44

(iv) 45–54

(v) 55–64

(vi) 65–74

(vii) 75 and over

(B) Gender; and

(C) Race or ethnicity from the following categories (candidates may select more than one category):

(i) American Indian or Alaska Native

(ii) Asian

(iii) Black or African American

(iv) Hispanic/Latino

(v) Native Hawaiian or other Pacific Islander

(vi) White

(vii) Other race or ethnicity (please state: _____)

(viii) Decline to answer

(2) Develop and maintain a database containing the following information regarding prospective regular grand jurors, the candidates who are ultimately selected by the court to serve as grand jurors, and any carry-over grand jurors: name, age range, occupation, gender, race or ethnicity, and the year(s) served on the regular grand jury. The database should indicate how the juror initially became a candidate (by random draw, application, or nomination).

(Subd (b) adopted effective January 1, 2007.)

(c) Annual summary

(1) The court must develop and maintain an annual summary of the information in the database maintained under (b)(2). The summary must not include the names of the candidates and must be made available to the public.

(Subd (c) adopted effective January 1, 2007.)

Rule 10.625 adopted effective January 1, 2007.

Advisory Committee Comment

This rule is intended to facilitate the courts' continued efforts to achieve the goals stated in standard 10.50 [formerly section 17] of the Standards of Judicial Administration, which encourages courts to employ various methods of soliciting prospective candidates to serve on regular grand juries that reflect a representative cross-section of the community they serve. Those methods include obtaining recommendations for grand jurors who encompass a cross-section of the county's population base, solicited from a broad representation of community-based organizations, civic leaders, and superior court judges, referees, and commissioners subdivision (b)(2)); having the court consider carry-over grand jury selections under Penal Code section 901(b) to ensure broad-based representation (Subd (c)); and encouraging judges who nominate persons for grand jury service under Penal Code section 903.4 to select candidates from the list returned by the jury commissioner or otherwise employing a nomination procedure to ensure broad-based representation from the community.

This rule is also intended to assist the courts in establishing a formal mechanism whereby they can monitor the extent to which they achieve the goal of seating representative regular grand juries through a process comparable to that stated in Penal Code section 904.6(e), which requires that persons selected for the "criminal grand jury shall be selected at random from a source or sources reasonably representative of a cross section of the population which is eligible for jury service in the county."

Rule 10.630.   Reciprocal assignment orders

A "reciprocal assignment order" is an order issued by the Chief Justice that permits judges in courts of different counties to serve in each other's courts.

Rule 10.630 amended effective July 1, 2015; adopted as rule 813 effective July 1, 1990; previously amended and renumbered effective January 1, 2007.

Chapter 2
Trial Court Management of Human Resources

Art. 1.   Trial Court Employee Labor Relations. Rules 10.650–10.660.
Art. 2.   Other Human Resources Rules. Rule 10.670.

Article 1
Trial Court Employee Labor Relations

Rule 10.650. Court Employee Labor Relations Rules
Rule 10.651. Purpose
Rule 10.652. Definitions
Rule 10.653. Right and obligation to meet and confer
Rule 10.654. Scope of representation
Rule 10.655. Governing court employee labor relations
Rule 10.656. Transition provisions
Rule 10.657. Construction
Rule 10.658. Interpretation
Rule 10.659. Other provisions
Rule 10.660. Enforcement of agreements—petitions (Gov. Code, §§ 71639.5, 71825.2)

Rule 10.650.   Court Employee Labor Relations Rules

Rules 10.651–10.659 in this chapter are referred to as the Court Employee Labor Relations Rules.
Rule 10.650 adopted effective January 1, 2007.

Rule 10.651.   Purpose

The purpose of the Court Employee Labor Relations Rules is to extend to trial court employees the right, and to require trial courts, to meet and confer in good faith over matters that the court, as opposed to the county, has authority to determine that are within the scope of representation, consistent with the procedures stated in this division.

The adoption of the Court Employee Labor Relations Rules is not intended to require changes in existing representation units, memoranda of agreements, statutes, or court rules relating to trial court employees, except as they would otherwise normally occur as provided for in this division.
Rule 10.651 amended and renumbered effective January 1, 2007; adopted as rule 2201 effective January 1, 1998, the effective date of Stats. 1997, ch. 850.

Rule 10.652.   Definitions

As used in the Court Employee Labor Relations Rules:
(1) "Court" means a superior court.
(2) "Court employee" means any employee of a court, except those employees whose job classification confers safety retirement status.
(3) "Meet and confer in good faith" means that a court or such representatives as it may designate, and representatives of recognized employee organizations, have the mutual obligation personally to meet and confer promptly on request by either party and to continue for a reasonable period of time in order to exchange freely information, opinions, and proposals, and to endeavor to reach agreement on matters within the scope of representation. The process should include adequate time for the resolution of impasses where specific procedures for such

resolution are contained in this division or a local rule, regulation, or ordinance, or when such procedures are used by mutual consent.
(4) "Recognized employee organization" means an employee organization that has been formally acknowledged by the county to represent court employees under the provisions of Government Code sections 3500–3510 or by the court under its rules or policies.
Rule 10.652 amended and renumbered effective January 1, 2007; adopted as rule 2202 effective January 1, 1998, the effective date of Stats. 1997, ch. 850.

Rule 10.653.   Right and obligation to meet and confer
(a) Recognized employee organization
A recognized employee organization has the right to represent its court employee members in their employment relations with a court as to matters covered by the Court Employee Labor Relations Rules. Nothing in these rules prohibits any court employee from appearing in his or her own behalf regarding employment relations with a court.
(Subd (a) amended effective January 1, 2007.)
(b) Representatives of a court
Representatives of a court must meet and confer in good faith regarding matters within the scope of representation, as defined in the Court Employee Labor Relations Rules, with representatives of a recognized employee organization, and must consider fully such presentations as are made by the recognized employee organization on behalf of its members before arriving at a determination of policy or course of action. In meeting this obligation a court must also comply with the procedures and provisions stated in Government Code sections 3504.5, 3505.1, 3505.2, and 3505.3 applicable to a public agency.
(Subd (b) amended effective January 1, 2007.)
(c) Joint negotiations and designations
In fulfilling the provisions of (b), the court and the county must consult with each other, may negotiate jointly, and each may designate the other in writing as its agent on any matters within the scope of representation.
(Subd (c) amended effective January 1, 2007.)
(d) Intimidation
A court or a recognized employee organization must not interfere with, intimidate, restrain, coerce, or discriminate against court employees because of their exercise of any rights they may have under the Court Employee Labor Relations Rules or Government Code sections 3500–3510.
(Subd (d) amended effective January 1, 2007.)
Rule 10.653 amended and renumbered effective January 1, 2007; adopted as rule 2203 effective January 1, 1998, the effective date of Stats. 1997, ch. 850.

Rule 10.654.   Scope of representation
(a) Matters included in the scope of representation
For purposes of the Court Employee Labor Relations Rules, the scope of representation includes all matters within the court's authority to determine relating to employment conditions and employer-employee relations, including, but not limited to, wages, hours, and terms and other conditions of employment, except, however, that the scope of representation does not include consideration of the merits, necessity, or organization of any service or activity provided by law or executive order.
(Subd (a) amended effective January 1, 2007.)
(b) Matters outside the scope of representation
In view of the unique and special responsibilities of the courts in the administration of justice, decisions regarding the following matters are not included within the scope of representation:
(1) The merits and administration of the court system;
(2) Coordination, consolidation, and merger of trial courts and support staff;
(3) Automation, including but not limited to fax filing, electronic recording, and implementation of information systems;
(4) Design, construction, and location of court facilities;
(5) Delivery of court services; and
(6) Hours of operation of the courts and court system.
(Subd (b) amended effective January 1, 2007.)
(c) Impact
Impact from such matters as in (b) must be included within the scope of representation as those matters affect wages, hours, terms, and conditions of employment of court employees, to the extent such matters are within the court's authority to determine.
(Subd (c) amended effective January 1, 2007.)
(d) Assignments and transfers
The superior court continues to have the right to determine assignments and transfers of court employees, provided that the process,

procedures, and criteria for assignments and transfers are included within the scope of representation.

(Subd (d) amended effective January 1, 2007.)

Rule 10.654 amended and renumbered effective January 1, 2007; adopted as rule 2204 effective January 1, 1998, the effective date of Stats. 1997, ch. 850.

Rule 10.655. Governing court employee labor relations

(a) County rules and procedures

As they relate to court employees in their relations with the court, matters described in Government Code section 3507(a) through (d) are governed by any rules and administrative procedures and provisions adopted by the county under section 3507 that may apply to county employees generally, with the right of review by the appropriate Court of Appeal.

(Subd (a) amended effective January 1, 2007.)

(b) Court rules and policies

A court may adopt reasonable rules and policies after consultation in good faith with representatives of a recognized employee organization or organizations for the administration of employer-employee relations under this rule as to matters described in Government Code section 3507(e)–(i). The court and county jointly will establish procedures to determine the appropriateness of any bargaining unit of court employees. The court must consult with the county about any rules and policies that the court may adopt under this section. If the court does not adopt rules by January 1, 1998, the court is bound by existing county rules until the court adopts rules.

(Subd (b) amended effective January 1, 2007.)

Rule 10.655 amended and renumbered effective January 1, 2007; adopted as rule 2205 effective January 1, 1998, the effective date of Stats. 1997, ch. 850.

Rule 10.656. Transition provisions

(a) Court employee organization

On the effective date of the Court Employee Labor Relations Rules, the court must recognize the employee organization that represented its court employees at the time of adoption. The court and the recognized employee organization are bound by the terms of any memorandum of understanding or agreement to which the court is a party that is in effect as of the date of adoption of the Court Employee Labor Relations Rules for its duration, or until it expires or, before then, is replaced by a subsequent memorandum of understanding.

(Subd (a) amended effective January 1, 2007.)

(b) Court personnel rules and policies

A court's local rules governing court employees and a court's personnel rules, policies, and practices in effect at the time of the adoption of the Court Employee Labor Relations Rules, to the extent they are not contrary to or inconsistent with the obligations and duties provided for in these rules, continue in effect until changed by the court. Before changing any rule, policy, or practice that affects any matter within the scope of representation as stated in these rules, the court must meet and confer in good faith with the recognized employee organization as provided for in these rules.

(Subd (b) amended effective January 1, 2007.)

(c) County employee representation units

Nothing contained in these rules is intended to preclude court employees from continuing to be included in representation units that contain county employees.

(Subd (c) amended effective January 1, 2007.)

Rule 10.656 amended and renumbered effective January 1, 2007; adopted as rule 2206 effective January 1, 1998, the effective date of Stats. 1997, ch. 850.

Rule 10.657. Construction

The enactment of the Court Employee Labor Relations Rules is not to be construed as making the provisions of Labor Code section 923 applicable to court employees.

Rule 10.657 amended and renumbered effective January 1, 2007; adopted as rule 2207 effective January 1, 1998, the effective date of Stats. 1997, ch. 850.

Rule 10.658. Interpretation

Where the language of the Court Employee Labor Relations Rules is the same or substantially the same as that contained in Government Code sections 3500 to 3510, it must be interpreted and applied in accordance with judicial interpretations of the same language.

Rule 10.658 amended and renumbered effective January 1, 2007; adopted as rule 2208 effective January 1, 1998, the effective date of Stats. 1997, ch. 850.

Rule 10.659. Other provisions

(a) Mediation

If, after a reasonable period of time, representatives of the court and the recognized employee organization fail to reach agreement, the court and the recognized employee organization or recognized employee organizations together may agree on the appointment of a mediator mutually agreeable to the parties. Costs of mediation are to be divided one-half to the court and one-half to the recognized employee organization or recognized employee organizations.

(Subd (a) amended effective January 1, 2007.)

(b) Submission for dispute resolution

In the absence of local procedures and provisions for resolving disputes on the appropriateness of a unit of representation, on the request of any of the parties, the dispute must be submitted to the Division of Conciliation of the Department of Industrial Relations for mediation or for recommendation for resolving the dispute.

(Subd (b) amended effective January 1, 2007.)

(c) Dues deduction

Nothing in the Court Employee Labor Relations Rules affects the right of a court employee to authorize a dues deduction from his or her salary or wages under Government Code sections 1157.1, 1157.2, 1157.3, 1157.4, 1157.5, or 1157.7.

(Subd (c) amended effective January 1, 2007.)

(d) Applicability of Government Code section 3502.5

The procedures and provisions stated in Government Code section 3502.5 are applicable to court employees.

(Subd (d) amended effective January 1, 2007.)

Rule 10.659 amended and renumbered effective January 1, 2007; adopted as rule 2209 effective January 1, 1998, the effective date of Stats. 1997, ch. 850.

Rule 10.660. Enforcement of agreements—petitions (Gov. Code, §§ 71639.5, 71825.2)

(a) Application

This rule applies to petitions filed under Government Code sections 71639.5 and 71825.2.

(Subd (a) amended effective October 24, 2008; previously amended effective December 10, 2004, and January 1, 2007.)

(b) Assignment of Court of Appeal justice to hear the petition

(1) The petition must state the following on the first page, below the case number, in the statement of the character of the proceeding (see rule 2.111(6)): "Petition filed under Government Code sections 71639.5 and 71825.2—Assignment of Court of Appeal justice required."

(2) When the petition is filed, the clerk of the court must immediately request of the Judicial Council's Assigned Judges Program the assignment of a hearing judge from the panel established under (e).

(3) The judge assigned to hear the petition in the superior court must be a justice from a Court of Appeal for a district other than the district for that superior court.

(Subd (b) amended effective January 1, 2016; previously amended effective December 10, 2004, and January 1, 2007.)

(c) Superior court hearing

(1) The superior court must hear and decide the petition on an expedited basis and must give the petition priority over other matters to the extent permitted by law and the rules of court.

(2) The petition must be heard by a judge assigned by the Chief Justice from the panel of hearing judges established under (e).

(Subd (c) amended effective January 1, 2007.)

(d) Appeal

An appeal of the superior court decision must be heard and decided on an expedited basis in the Court of Appeal for the district in which the petition was heard and must be given priority over other matters to the extent permitted by law and the rules of court. The notice of appeal must state the following on the first page, below the case number, in the statement of the character of the proceeding (see rule 2.111(6)): "Notice of Appeal on Petition filed under Government Code sections 71639.5 and 71825.2—Expedited Processing Requested."

(Subd (d) amended effective January 1, 2007; previously amended effective December 10, 2004.)

(e) Panel of hearing judges

The panel of judges who may hear the petitions in the superior court must consist of Court of Appeal justices selected by the Chief Justice as follows:

(1) The panel must include at least one justice from each district of the Court of Appeal.

(2) Each justice assigned to hear a petition under (c)(2) must have received training on hearing the petitions as specified by the Chief Justice.

Rule 10.660 amended effective January 1, 2016; adopted as rule 2211 effective January 1, 2001; previously amended and renumbered as rule 10.660 effective January 1, 2007; previously amended effective December 10, 2004, and October 24, 2008.

Article 2
Other Human Resources Rules

Rule 10.670. Trial court personnel plans
(a) Purpose
This rule establishes the authority and responsibility of the superior courts, on a countywide basis, to create and implement a system of personnel management designed to achieve lawful, uniform, and fair employment practices and procedures.

(Subd (a) amended effective January 1, 2007.)

(b) Countywide personnel plans
The superior court of each county must establish a single personnel plan on a countywide basis, consistent with applicable statutes, rules, and standards of judicial administration.

(Subd (b) amended effective January 1, 2007.)

(c) Provisions of a personnel plan
The personnel plan must ensure that treatment of employees complies with current law. The personnel plan should address the following issues:

(1) A salary-setting procedure;

(2) Regular review of job classifications and titles;

(3) An equal employment opportunity policy applying to all employees in accordance with applicable state and federal law;

(4) Recruitment, selection, and promotion policies;

(5) A sexual harassment prevention policy;

(6) A reasonable accommodation policy;

(7) Grievance or complaint procedures covering, but not limited to, sexual harassment, discrimination, and denial of reasonable accommodation;

(8) An employee benefits plan that includes health benefits, retirement benefits, workers' compensation benefits, disability leave, and paid and unpaid leave in compliance with state and federal law;

(9) Timekeeping and payroll policies and procedures that comply with applicable state and federal law;

(10) A records management policy, including confidentiality and retention of personnel records;

(11) Job-related training and continuing education programs for all personnel concerning at least the following:

(A) Sexual harassment awareness;

(B) Discrimination and bias; and

(C) Safety;

(12) A policy statement on professional behavior requiring that all employees conduct themselves in a professional manner at all times and refrain from offensive conduct or comments that reflect bias or harassment;

(13) A policy regarding conflicts of interest and incompatible activities;

(14) Procedures for discipline and discharge; and

(15) A labor policy consistent with rules 10.653–10.659.

(Subd (c) amended effective January 1, 2007.)

(d) Optional provisions
A personnel plan may contain additional provisions, including the following:

(1) Criteria and schedules for performance evaluations for all levels of employees;

(2) Job-related training and continuing education programs for all personnel as appropriate, with provisions for both paid and unpaid educational leave concerning:

(A) Career development, including basic and managerial skills; and

(B) Equal employment opportunity concepts and recruitment methods.

(3) An employee benefit plan that may include:

(A) Flex-time, part-time, job-sharing, and other alternative work schedules;

(B) Cafeteria options to use pretax dollars for dependent care and medical care and for sick leave for the care of dependents;

(C) An employee assistance program; and

(D) A deferred compensation plan.

(Subd (d) amended effective January 1, 2007.)

(e) Submission of personnel plans

The superior court of each county must submit to the Judicial Council a personnel plan in compliance with these provisions by March 1, 1999. The superior court of each county must submit to the Judicial Council any changes to this plan by March 1 of every following year. If requested by a superior court, Judicial Council staff must review the court's personnel plan and provide the court with technical assistance in preparing the plan.

(Subd (e) amended effective January 1, 2016; previously amended effective January 1, 2007.)

Rule 10.670 amended effective January 1, 2016; adopted as rule 2520 effective July 1, 1998; previously renumbered as rule 6.650 effective January 1, 1999; previously amended and renumbered as rule 10.670 effective January 1, 2007.

Chapter 3
Subordinate Judicial Officers

Rule 10.700. Role of subordinate judicial officers
Rule 10.701. Qualifications and education of subordinate judicial officers
Rule 10.702. Subordinate judicial officers: practice of law
Rule 10.703. Subordinate judicial officers: complaints and notice requirements

Rule 10.700. Role of subordinate judicial officers
(a) Application
This rule applies to all subordinate judicial officers except those acting as child support commissioners under Family Code section 4251.

(b) Role of subordinate judicial officers
The primary role of subordinate judicial officers is to perform subordinate judicial duties. However, a presiding judge may assign a subordinate judicial officer to sit as a temporary judge where lawful, if the presiding judge determines that, because of a shortage of judges, it is necessary for the effective administration of justice.

Rule 10.700 renumbered effective January 1, 2007; adopted as rule 6.609 effective July 1, 2002.

Rule 10.701. Qualifications and education of subordinate judicial officers
(a) Definition
For purposes of this rule, "subordinate judicial officer" means a person appointed by a court to perform subordinate judicial duties as authorized by article VI, section 22 of the California Constitution, including a commissioner, a referee, and a hearing officer.

(Subd (a) amended effective January 1, 2007.)

(b) Qualifications
Except as provided in (d), a person is ineligible to be a subordinate judicial officer unless the person is a member of the State Bar and:

(1) Has been admitted to practice law in California for at least 10 years or, on a finding of good cause by the presiding judge, for at least 5 years; or

(2) Is serving as a subordinate judicial officer in a trial court as of January 1, 2003.

(Subd (b) amended effective January 1, 2007.)

(c) Education
A subordinate judicial officer must comply with the education requirements of any position to which he or she is assigned, even if it is not his or her principal assignment. Such requirements include the following, as applicable: rules 5.30, 5.340, and 10.462 of the California Rules of Court, and Welfare and Institutions Code section 304.7.

(Subd (c) amended effective January 1, 2017; previously amended effective January 1, 2007.)

(d) Juvenile referees and hearing officers
A person appointed as a juvenile referee or as a hearing officer under Welfare and Institutions Code sections 255 or 5256.1 must meet the qualification requirements established by those sections. Such a person is ineligible to exercise the powers and perform the duties of another type of subordinate judicial officer unless he or she meets the qualifications established in (b).

(Subd (d) amended effective July 1, 2008; previously amended effective January 1, 2007.)

Rule 10.701 amended effective January 1, 2017; adopted as rule 6.660 effective January 1, 2003; previously amended and renumbered effective January 1, 2007; previously amended effective July 1, 2008.

Rule 10.702. Subordinate judicial officers: practice of law
A subordinate judicial officer may practice law only to the extent permitted by the Code of Judicial Ethics.

Rule 10.702 renumbered effective January 1, 2007; adopted as rule 6.665 effective January 1, 2003.

Rule 10.703. Subordinate judicial officers: complaints and notice requirements

(a) Intent

The procedures in this rule for processing complaints against subordinate judicial officers do not:

(1) Create a contract of employment;

(2) Change the existing employee-employer relationship between the subordinate judicial officer and the court;

(3) Change the status of a subordinate judicial officer from an employee terminable at will to an employee terminable only for cause; or

(4) Restrict the discretion of the presiding judge in taking appropriate corrective action.

(Subd (a) amended effective January 1, 2016; previously amended effective January 1, 2007.)

(b) Definitions

Unless the context requires otherwise, the following definitions apply to this rule:

(1) "Subordinate judicial officer" means an attorney employed by a court to serve as a commissioner, referee, or hearing officer, whether the attorney is acting as a commissioner, referee, hearing officer, or temporary judge. The term does not include any other attorney acting as a temporary judge.

(2) "Presiding judge" includes the person or group the presiding judge designates to perform any duty required by this rule to be performed by a presiding judge.

(3) "Commission" means the Commission on Judicial Performance. The commission exercises discretionary jurisdiction over the discipline of subordinate judicial officers under article VI, section 18.1 of the California Constitution.

(4) "Written reprimand" means written disciplinary action that is warranted either because of the seriousness of the misconduct or because previous corrective action has been ineffective.

(Subd (b) amended effective January 1, 2016.)

(c) Application

(1) A court that employs a subordinate judicial officer must use the procedures in this rule for processing complaints against the subordinate judicial officer if the complaint alleges conduct that if alleged against a judge would be within the jurisdiction of the commission under article VI, section 18 of the California Constitution.

(2) If a complaint against a subordinate judicial officer as described in (f) does not allege conduct that would be within the jurisdiction of the commission, the local procedures adopted under rule 10.603(c)(4)(C) apply. The local process may include any procedures from this rule for the court's adjudication of the complaint other than the provisions for referring the matter to the commission under (g) or giving notice of commission review under (k)(2)(B).

(3) A court may adopt additional policies and procedures for the adjudication of complaints against subordinate judicial officers not inconsistent with this rule.

(Subd (c) amended effective January 1, 2016; previously amended effective July 1, 2002, and January 1, 2007.)

(d) Promptness required

The presiding judge must ensure that the court processes each complaint promptly. To the extent reasonably possible, the court must complete action on each complaint within 90 days after the complaint is submitted.

(Subd (d) amended effective January 1, 2007.)

(e) Confidentiality

(1) All proceedings by a presiding judge under this rule must be conducted in a manner that is as confidential as is reasonably possible consistent with the need to conduct a thorough and complete investigation and the need for proper administration of the court.

(2) This rule does not prohibit access by the commission to any information relevant to the investigation of a complaint against a subordinate judicial officer.

(Subd (e) amended effective January 1, 2007.)

(f) Written complaints to presiding judge

(1) A complaint about the conduct of a subordinate judicial officer must be in writing and must be submitted to the presiding judge.

(2) Persons who are unable to file a written complaint because of a disability may present an oral complaint, which the presiding judge must commit to writing.

(3) The presiding judge has discretion to investigate complaints that are anonymous.

(4) The presiding judge must give written notice of receipt of the complaint to the complainant, if known.

(Subd (f) amended effective January 1, 2016; previously amended effective January 1, 2007.)

(g) Initial review of the complaint

(1) The presiding judge must review each complaint and determine if the complaint:

(A) May be closed after initial review;

(B) Requires investigation by the presiding judge; or

(C) Should be referred to the commission or to the presiding judge of another court for investigation or for investigation and adjudication.

(2) A presiding judge may request that the commission investigate and adjudicate the complaint if a local conflict of interest or disqualification prevents the court from acting on the complaint.

(3) In exceptional circumstances, a presiding judge may request the commission or the presiding judge of another court to investigate a complaint on behalf of the court and provide the results of the investigation to the court for adjudication.

(4) The court must maintain a file on every complaint received, containing the following:

(A) The complaint;

(B) The response of the subordinate judicial officer, if any;

(C) All evidence and reports produced by the investigation of the complaint, if any; and

(D) The final action taken on the complaint.

(Subd (g) amended effective January 1, 2016; previously amended effective January 1, 2007.)

(h) Closing a complaint after initial review

(1) After an initial review, the presiding judge may close without further action any complaint that:

(A) Relates to the permissible exercise of judicial or administrative discretion by the subordinate judicial officer; or

(B) Does not allege conduct that if alleged against a judge would be within the jurisdiction of the commission under article VI, section 18 of the California Constitution.

(2) If the presiding judge decides to close the complaint under (h)(1), the presiding judge must notify the complainant in writing of the decision to close the complaint. The notice must include the information required under (k).

(3) The presiding judge may, in his or her discretion, advise the subordinate judicial officer in writing of the decision to close the complaint.

(Subd (h) amended effective January 1, 2016; previously amended effective January 1, 2007.)

(i) Complaints requiring investigation

(1) If after an initial review of the complaint the presiding judge finds a basis for further inquiry, the presiding judge must conduct an investigation appropriate to the nature of the complaint.

(2) The investigation may include interviews of witnesses and a review of court records.

(3) The presiding judge may give the subordinate judicial officer a copy of the complaint or a summary of its allegations and allow him or her an opportunity to respond to the allegations during the investigation. The presiding judge must give the subordinate judicial officer a copy of the complaint or a summary of its allegations and allow the subordinate judicial officer an opportunity to respond to the allegations before the presiding judge decides to take any disciplinary action against the subordinate judicial officer.

(4) After completing the investigation, the presiding judge must, in his or her discretion:

(A) Close action on the complaint if the presiding judge finds the complaint lacks merit; or

(B) Impose discipline; or

(C) Take other appropriate corrective action, which may include, but is not limited to, oral counseling, oral reprimand, or warning of the subordinate judicial officer.

(5) If the presiding judge closes action on the complaint under (i)(4)(A) and the presiding judge is aware that the subordinate judicial officer knows of the complaint, the presiding judge must give the subordinate judicial officer written notice of the final action taken on the complaint.

(6) If the presiding judge decides to impose discipline or take other appropriate corrective action under (i)(4)(B) or (C), within 10 days after the completion of the investigation or as soon thereafter as is reasonably possible, the presiding judge must give the subordinate judicial officer the following in writing:

(A) Notice of the intended final action on the complaint; and

(B) The facts and other information forming the basis for the proposed action and the source of the facts and information.

(7) The notice of the intended final action on the complaint in (i)(6)(A) must include the following advice:

(A) The subordinate judicial officer may request an opportunity to respond to the intended final action within 10 days after service of the notice; and

(B) If the subordinate judicial officer does not request an opportunity to respond within 10 days after service of the notice, the proposed action will become final.

(8) If the subordinate judicial officer requests an opportunity to respond, the presiding judge must allow the subordinate judicial officer an opportunity to respond to the notice of the intended final action, either orally or in writing as specified by the presiding judge, in accordance with local rules.

(9) Within 10 days after the subordinate judicial officer has responded, the presiding judge must give the subordinate judicial officer written notice of the final action taken on the complaint.

(10) If the subordinate judicial officer does not request an opportunity to respond, the presiding judge must promptly give written notice of the final action to the complainant. The notice must include the information required under (k).

(Subd (i) amended effective January 1, 2016; previously amended effective January 1, 2006, and January 1, 2007.)

(j) Notice to the Commission on Judicial Performance

(1) If a court disciplines a subordinate judicial officer by written reprimand, suspension, or termination for conduct that, if alleged against a judge, would be within the jurisdiction of the commission under article VI, section 18 of the California Constitution, the presiding judge must promptly forward to the commission a copy of the portions of the court file that reasonably reflect the basis of the action taken by the court, including the complaint or allegations of misconduct and the subordinate judicial officer's response. This provision is applicable even when the disciplinary action does not result from a written complaint.

(2) If a subordinate judicial officer resigns (A) while an investigation under (i) is pending concerning conduct that, if alleged against a judge, would be within the jurisdiction of the commission under article VI, section 18 of the California Constitution, or (B) under circumstances that would lead a reasonable person to conclude that the resignation was due, at least in part, to a complaint or allegation of misconduct that, if alleged against a judge, would be within the jurisdiction of the commission under article VI, section 18 of the California Constitution, the presiding judge must, within 15 days of the resignation or as soon thereafter as is reasonably possible, forward to the commission the entire court file on any pending complaint about or allegation of misconduct committed by the subordinate judicial officer.

(3) On request by the commission, the presiding judge must forward to the commission any requested information regarding a complaint about or allegation of misconduct committed by a subordinate judicial officer.

(Subd (j) repealed, relettered and amended effective January 1, 2016; adopted as subd (k); previously amended effective January 1, 2007, and July 1, 2010.)

(k) Notice of final court action

(1) When the court has completed its action on a complaint, the presiding judge must promptly notify the complainant, if known, of the final court action.

(2) The notice to the complainant of the final court action must:

(A) Provide a general description of the action taken by the court consistent with any law limiting the disclosure of confidential employee information; and

(B) Include the following statement:

If you are dissatisfied with the court's action on your complaint, you have the right to request the Commission on Judicial Performance to review this matter under its discretionary jurisdiction to oversee the discipline of subordinate judicial officers. No further action will be taken on your complaint unless the commission receives your written request within 30 days after the date this notice was mailed. The commission's address is:

Commission on Judicial Performance
455 Golden Gate Avenue, Suite 14400
San Francisco, California 94102-3660

(Subd (k) relettered and amended effective January 1, 2016; adopted as subd (l); previously amended effective April 29, 1999, and January 1, 2007.)

Rule 10.703 amended effective January 1, 2016; adopted as rule 6.655 effective November 20, 1998; previously amended and renumbered effective January 1, 2007; previously amended effective April 29, 1999, July 1, 2002, January 1, 2006, and July 1, 2010.

Chapter 4
Referees
[Reserved]
Chapter 5
Temporary Judges

Rule 10.740.   Responsibilities of the trial courts for temporary judge programs

Each trial court that uses temporary judges must develop, institute, and operate—by itself or in collaboration with another court or courts—a program to recruit, select, train, and evaluate attorneys qualified to serve as temporary judges.

Rule 10.740 amended and renumbered effective January 1, 2007; adopted as rule 6.740 effective July 1, 2006.

Rule 10.741.   Duties and authority of the presiding judge

(a) General duties

The presiding judge is responsible for the recruitment, selection, training, appointment, supervision, assignment, performance, and evaluation of court-appointed temporary judges. In carrying out these responsibilities, the presiding judge is assisted by the Temporary Judge Administrator as provided in rule 10.743.

(Subd (a) amended effective January 1, 2007.)

(b) Publicizing the opportunity to serve as a temporary judge

(1) Except for those courts that have nine or fewer authorized judge positions or use only research attorneys as temporary judges, each trial court that uses court-appointed temporary judges must publicize the opportunity to serve as a temporary judge whenever the court seeks to add attorneys to its pool of temporary judges or within a reasonable time before conducting its mandatory training for temporary judges but, in any case, no less than once every three years.

(2) Courts must publicize this opportunity in a manner that maximizes the potential for a diverse applicant pool, which includes publicizing the opportunity to legal communities and organizations, including all local bar associations, in their geographical area. This publicity should encourage and must provide an equal opportunity for all eligible individuals to seek positions as court-appointed temporary judges and not exclude individuals based on their gender, race, ethnicity, disability, religion, sexual orientation, age, or other protected class.

(Subd (b) adopted effective July 1, 2012.)

(c) Nondiscrimination in application and selection procedure

Each trial court that uses court-appointed temporary judges must conduct an application and selection procedure for temporary judges that ensures the most qualified applicants for appointment are selected and must not reject applicants who otherwise meet the requirements for appointment based on their gender, race, ethnicity, disability, religion, sexual orientation, age, or other protected class. Among the qualifications to be considered in the selection procedure are the applicant's exposure to and experience with diverse populations and issues related to those populations.

(Subd (c) adopted effective July 1, 2012.)

(d) Authority to remove or discontinue

The presiding judge has the discretion to remove a court-appointed temporary judge or to discontinue using an attorney as a court-appointed temporary judge at any time.

(Subd (d) relettered effective July 1, 2012; adopted as subd (b) effective July 1, 2006.)

Rule 10.741 amended effective July 1, 2012; adopted as rule 6.741 effective July 1, 2006; previously amended and renumbered effective January 1, 2007.

Advisory Committee Comment

Subdivision (b). This subdivision is intended to offer all attorneys who satisfy the requirements for appointment under rule 2.812 the opportunity to serve as temporary judges and to expand the size and diversity of the pool of eligible candidates. Pursuant to the rule, courts that do not use temporary judges, that have nine or fewer authorized and funded judge positions, or that only use their research attorneys as temporary judges are exempt from the requirement to publicize the opportunity to serve as a temporary judge. Courts that use temporary judges may publicize the opportunity in a manner they determine to be most effective, given their individual circumstances. In attempting to broaden the diversity of the temporary judge applicant pool, courts also have the flexibility to widen the geographical areas in which they publicize the opportunity. Thus, courts are not limited to publicizing their temporary judge program through the local or state bar associations. However, they must include *all* local bar associations when they do so. Further, the method of publication is purposefully left to the court's discretion. No-cost methods exist, such as email, use of the court's public website, and oral announcements at local bar association or legal organization events. Publicizing this opportunity no less than once every three years should increase the potential for greater diversity among the temporary judges who serve the courts.

Subdivision (c). This subdivision emphasizes that the selection and appointment process must be devoid of discrimination. These provisions are intended to discourage favoritism in the appointment process and permit the courts to consider, as an additional qualification, an attorney's exposure to and experience with the diverse populations and issues unique to that population in the county where they are seeking appointment. "Exposure to and experience with diverse populations" includes work, social interaction, educational experiences, or community involvement with individuals or groups from diverse communities that may appear in court.

Rule 10.742. Use of attorneys as court-appointed temporary judges

(a) Responsibility of the presiding judge

The presiding judge of the trial court is responsible for determining whether that court needs to use attorneys as temporary judges and, if so, the specific purposes for which attorneys are to be appointed as temporary judges.

(b) Conditions for the use of court-appointed temporary judges

The presiding judge may appoint an attorney as a court-appointed temporary judge only if all the following circumstances apply:

(1) The appointment of an attorney to serve as a temporary judge is necessary to fill a judicial need in that court;

(2) The attorney serving as a temporary judge has been approved by the court where the attorney will serve under rule 2.810 et seq.;

(3) The appointment of the attorney as a temporary judge does not result in any conflict of interest; and

(4) There is no appearance of impropriety resulting from the appointment of the attorney to serve as a temporary judge.

(Subd (b) amended effective January 1, 2007.)

Rule 10.742 amended effective January 1, 2017; adopted as rule 6.742 effective July 1, 2006; previously amended and renumbered as rule 10.742 effective January 1, 2007; previously amended effective January 1, 2016.

Advisory Committee Comment

Subdivisions (a)–(b). These subdivisions provide that the presiding judge in each court is responsible for determining whether court-appointed temporary judges need to be used in that court, and these subdivisions furnish the criteria for determining when their use is proper. Under (b)(1), the use and appointment of court-appointed temporary judges must be based on judicial needs. Under (b)(3), an attorney serving as a temporary judge would have a conflict of interest if the disqualifying factors in the Code of Judicial Ethics exist. Under (b)(4), the test for the appearance of impropriety is whether a person aware of the facts might entertain a doubt that the judge would be able to act with integrity, impartiality, and competence. In addition to the disqualifying factors listed in the Code of Judicial Ethics, an appearance of impropriety would be generated if any of the limitations in family law, unlawful detainer, and other cases identified in the Code of Judicial Ethics are present.

Rule 10.743. Administrator of temporary judges program

(a) Administrator

The presiding judge who appoints attorneys as temporary judges must designate a clerk, executive officer, or other court employee knowledgeable about temporary judges to serve as the Temporary Judge Administrator in that court.

(b) Duties of administrator

Under the supervision of the presiding judge, the Temporary Judge Administrator is responsible for the management of the temporary judges program in the court. The administrator's duties include:

(1) Receiving and processing applications from attorneys to serve as temporary judges with the court;

(2) Verifying the information on the applications;

(3) Assisting the presiding judge in the recruitment and selection of attorneys to serve as temporary judges, as provided in rule 10.741;

(4) Administering the court's program for the education and training of temporary judges;

(5) Maintaining records of attendance and completion of required courses by all attorneys serving as temporary judges in the court;

(6) Determining that attorneys have satisfied all the conditions required to be appointed as a temporary judge in that court, including continuing education requirements;

(7) Maintaining a list of attorneys currently appointed and qualified to serve as temporary judges in the court;

(8) Managing support services for temporary judges, such as providing mentoring programs and reference materials;

(9) Receiving and processing complaints and other information concerning the performance of attorneys serving as temporary judges;

(10) Assisting the presiding judge in identifying judicial needs that require the use of temporary judges and in addressing these needs; and

(11) Maintaining records, gathering statistics, and preparing and transmitting quarterly reports on the court's use of temporary judges as required under rule 10.742(c).

(Subd (b) amended effective July 1, 2012; previously amended effective January 1, 2007.)

Rule 10.743 amended effective July 1, 2012; adopted as rule 6.743 effective July 1, 2006; previously amended and renumbered effective January 1, 2007.

Advisory Committee Comment

The goal of this rule is to ensure the effective and efficient administration of the courts' use of temporary judges. The rule should be applied flexibly. In courts with large temporary judge programs, the court may want to designate a full-time administrator, and some of the administrator's duties may be delegated to other individuals. On the other hand, in courts that use only a few temporary judges, the Temporary Judge Administrator position may consume only part of the administrator's time and be combined with other duties. Also, courts that use only a small number of temporary judges may work with other courts, or may cooperate on a regional basis, to perform the functions and duties prescribed under this rule.

Rule 10.744. Application procedures to serve as a court-appointed temporary judge

(a) Application

Every attorney who applies for appointment as a temporary judge in a trial court must complete an application to serve as a temporary judge.

(b) Information required

The attorney must provide all applicable information requested on the application. This information must include:

(1) The attorney's name and contact information as required by the court;

(2) The attorney's State Bar number;

(3) The date of the attorney's admission to the State Bar of California and the dates of his or her admissions to practice in any other state;

(4) Length of membership in the State Bar of California and of practice in any other state;

(5) Whether the attorney is in good standing with the State Bar of California and in good standing as an attorney in any other state where the attorney has been admitted to practice;

(6) Whether the attorney has ever been disciplined, or is the subject of a pending disciplinary proceeding, by the State Bar of California or by any other state bar association or court of record; and, if so, an explanation of the circumstances;

(7) The areas of specialization for which the attorney has been certified in California or in any other state;

(8) The attorney's major area or areas of practice;

(9) Whether the attorney holds himself or herself out publicly as representing exclusively one side in any of the areas of litigation in which the attorney practices;

(10) Whether the attorney represents one side in more than 90 percent of all cases in any areas of litigation in which the attorney specializes or concentrates his or her practice;

(11) The location or locations in which the attorney principally practices;

(12) How often the attorney appears in the court where he or she is applying to serve as a temporary judge;

(13) A list of the attorney's previous service as a temporary judge in the court where the attorney is applying and in any other court;

(14) Whether the attorney has ever been removed as a temporary judge by any court;

(15) The types of cases on which the attorney is willing to serve as a temporary judge;

(16) Whether the attorney has ever been convicted of a felony or misdemeanor, or is a defendant in any pending felony or misdemeanor proceeding, and, if so, a statement about the conviction or pending proceeding;

(17) Whether the attorney has been a party in any legal proceeding and, if so, a brief description of the proceedings;

(18) Information concerning any circumstances or conditions that would adversely affect or limit the attorney's ability to serve as a temporary judge;

(19) Any facts concerning the attorney's background that may reflect positively or negatively on the attorney or that should be disclosed to the court; and

(20) Such additional information as the court may require.

(c) Continuing duty to disclose

An attorney appointed by a court to serve as a temporary judge has a continuing duty to disclose to the court any material changes in facts or circumstances that affect his or her ability to serve as a temporary judge. The attorney must disclose the changes to the court before the next time the attorney is assigned to serve as a temporary judge.

(d) Review of application

The presiding judge, assisted by the Temporary Judge Administrator, must review all applications and determine whether each applicant is qualified, has satisfied the requirements of rule 2.812, and should be appointed as a temporary judge. The presiding judge may delegate this task to another judge or a committee of judges, assisted by the Temporary Judge Administrator. In appointing attorneys as temporary judges, the presiding judge may go beyond the minimum qualifications and standards required under the California Rules of Court. The decision whether to appoint, use, retrain, remove, or discontinue using any particular attorney as a temporary judge is at the sole discretion of the presiding judge.

(Subd (d) amended effective January 1, 2007.)

Rule 10.744 amended and renumbered effective January 1, 2007; adopted as rule 6.744 effective July 1, 2006.

Rule 10.745.   Performance

(a) Review required

The court must review on a regular basis the performance of temporary judges appointed by that court.

(b) Monitoring performance

In monitoring and reviewing the performance of court-appointed temporary judges, the court may use direct observation, audiotaping of hearings, reports by court staff, comments from mentor judges, and such other means as may be helpful.

Rule 10.745 renumbered effective January 1, 2007; adopted as rule 6.745 effective July 1, 2006.

Rule 10.746.   Complaints

Each court must have procedures for receiving, investigating, and resolving complaints against court-appointed temporary judges.

Rule 10.746 renumbered effective January 1, 2007; adopted as rule 6.746 effective July 1, 2006.

Chapter 6
Court Interpreters

Rule 10.761. Regional Court Interpreter Employment Relations Committees
Rule 10.762. Cross-assignments for court interpreter employees

Rule 10.761.   Regional Court Interpreter Employment Relations Committees

(a) Creation

Government Code sections 71807–71809 establish four Regional Court Interpreter Employment Relations Committees. Each committee has the authority, for spoken language court interpreters within its region as defined under Government Code section 71807(a), to:

(1) Set the terms and conditions of employment for court interpreters, subject to meet and confer in good faith, as authorized by Government Code section 71808;

(2) Adopt reasonable rules and regulations for the administration of employer-employee relations with recognized employee organizations, as authorized by Government Code section 71823(a); and

(3) Act as the representative of the superior courts within the region in bargaining with a recognized employee organization as authorized by Government Code section 71809.

(b) Membership

(1) Each Regional Court Interpreter Employment Committee consists of one representative from each superior court that has at least one interpreter employed as a court interpreter as defined by Government Code section 71806 and not excluded by section 71828(d).

(2) The following regions are established by Government Code section 71807:

(A) Region 1: Los Angeles, Santa Barbara, and San Luis Obispo Counties.

(B) Region 2: Counties of the First and Sixth Appellate Districts, except Solano County.

(C) Region 3: Counties of the Third and Fifth Appellate Districts.

(D) Region 4: Counties of the Fourth Appellate District.

(3) The court executive officer of each superior court may appoint the court's representative, under rule 10.610, which authorizes the court executive officer, acting under the direction of the presiding judge, to oversee the management and administration of the nonjudicial operations of the court.

(4) Each Regional Court Interpreter Employment Relations Committee may appoint a chief negotiator to bargain with recognized employee organizations. The chief negotiator may be Judicial Council staff.

(5) Any superior court that is not entitled to appoint a representative under this rule, including the superior courts of Ventura and Solano Counties, may appoint an advisory member to the committee for its region.

(Subd (b) amended effective January 1, 2016; previously amended effective January 1, 2006, and January 1, 2007.)

(c) Rules of procedure

Each Regional Court Interpreter Employment Relations Committee may adopt its own rules of procedure, including the procedure for selecting its chair, advisory members, and chief negotiator.

(d) Voting

(1) Each representative of a superior court has a number of votes equal to the number of court interpreter employees in that trial court as defined by Government Code section 71806 and not excluded by section 71828(d).

(2) On July 1, 2004, and annually thereafter each Regional Court Interpreter Employment Relations Committee must recalculate the number of votes of each representative of a superior court to equal the number of court interpreter employees in that court.

(Subd (d) amended effective January 1, 2006.)

(e) Judicial Council staff

Judicial Council staff will assist each Regional Court Interpreter Employment Relations Committee in performing its functions.

(Subd (e) amended effective January 1, 2016.)

Rule 10.761 amended effective January 1, 2016; adopted as rule 6.661 effective March 1, 2003; previously amended effective January 1, 2006; previously amended and renumbered as rule 10.761 effective January 1, 2007.

Rule 10.762.   Cross-assignments for court interpreter employees

(a) Purpose

This rule implements a process for cross-assignment of a court interpreter employed by a superior court under Government Code section 71810(b).

(Subd (a) amended effective January 1, 2007.)

(b) Definitions

As used in this rule:

(1) "Home court" means the superior court in which the court interpreter is an employee. An employee's home court includes all locations of a superior court within a county.

(2) "Away court" means the superior court to which the court interpreter is temporarily cross-assigned.

(3) "Cross-assignment" means any assignment to perform spoken language interpretation for a superior court other than the interpreter's home court.

(4) "Regional court interpreter coordinator" means a Judicial Council employee whose duty it is to locate, assign, and schedule available court

interpreter employees for courts within and across regions, which are described under Government Code section 71807(a).

(5) "Local court interpreter coordinator" means an employee of a superior court whose duty it is to locate, assign, and schedule available court interpreter employees for his or her court.

(Subd (b) amended effective January 1, 2016; previously amended effective January 1, 2007.)

(c) Procedure for cross-assignments

(1) Under Government Code section 71804.5(b) a court interpreter employed by a superior court is not permitted to be an employee of more than one superior court. A court interpreter employed by a superior court may not contract with another court, but may accept appointments to provide services to more than one court through cross-assignments.

(2) A superior court may attempt to fill an interpreting assignment with the employee of another court before hiring an independent contract court interpreter.

(3) If a superior court wants to fill an interpreting assignment with the employee of another court, the court must notify the regional court interpreter coordinator to locate an employee of a court within or across regions.

(4) Each local court interpreter coordinator must provide the schedule of each court interpreter employee available for cross-assignment to the regional court interpreter coordinator.

(5) A superior court may adopt additional internal procedures for cross-assigning a court interpreter employee that are not inconsistent with Government Code section 71810 and this rule.

(6) A Regional Court Interpreter Employment Relations Committee may approve alternative procedures for cross-assigning a court interpreter employee that permit the interpreter to directly arrange cross-assignments with an "away" court, provided that the procedures require notice to the regional coordinator.

(Subd (c) amended effective January 1, 2007.)

(d) Payment for cross-assignments

The home court must issue payment to the court interpreter for all cross-assignments, including per diem compensation and mileage reimbursement. Judicial Council staff will administer funding to the home court for payments associated with cross-assignments.

(Subd (d) amended effective January 1, 2016; previously amended effective January 1, 2007.)

(e) Duties of a court interpreter on cross-assignment

A court interpreter who accepts a cross-assignment is responsible for following the personnel rules of the home court while performing services for the away court.

(f) Superior courts of Ventura and Solano Counties

The superior courts of Ventura and Solano Counties may participate in the procedure for cross-assignments as follows:

(1) The Superior Court of Ventura County may accept or provide interpreters on cross-assignment under the procedures established in Region 1, as defined by Government Code section 71807.

(2) The Superior Court of Solano County may accept or provide interpreters on cross-assignment under the procedures established in Region 2, as defined by Government Code section 71807.

(Subd (f) amended effective January 1, 2007.)

Rule 10.762 amended effective January 1, 2016; adopted as rule 6.662 effective March 1, 2003; previously amended and renumbered as rule 10.672 effective January 1, 2007.

Chapter 7
Qualifications of Court Investigators, Probate Attorneys, and Probate Examiners

Chapter 7 adopted effective January 1, 2008.

Rule 10.776. Definitions
Rule 10.777. Qualifications of court investigators, probate attorneys, and probate examiners

Rule 10.776. Definitions

As used in the rules in this chapter, the following terms have the meanings stated below:

(1) A "court investigator" is a person described in Probate Code section 1454(a) employed by or under contract with a court to provide the investigative services for the court required or authorized by law in guardianships, conservatorships, and other protective proceedings under division 4 of the Probate Code;

(2) A "probate examiner" is a person employed by a court to review filings in probate proceedings in order to assist the court and the parties to get the filed matters ready for consideration by the court in accordance with the requirements of the Probate Code, title 7 of the California Rules of Court, and the court's local rules;

(3) A "probate attorney" is an active member of the State Bar of California who is employed by a court to perform the functions of a probate examiner and also to provide legal analysis, recommendations, advice, and other services to the court pertaining to probate proceedings;

(4) "Probate proceedings" are decedents' estates, guardianships and conservatorships under division 4 of the Probate Code, trust proceedings under division 9 of the Probate Code, and other matters governed by provisions of that code and the rules in title 7 of the California Rules of Court;

(5) An "accredited educational institution" is a college or university, including a community or junior college, accredited by a regional accrediting organization recognized by the Council for Higher Education Accreditation.

Rule 10.776 amended effective January 1, 2016; adopted effective January 1, 2008.

Rule 10.777.   Qualifications of court investigators, probate attorneys, and probate examiners

(a) Qualifications of court investigators

Except as otherwise provided in this rule, a person who begins employment with a court or enters into a contract to perform services with a court as a court investigator on or after January 1, 2008, must:

(1) Have a bachelor of arts or bachelor of science degree in a science, a social science, a behavioral science, liberal arts, or nursing from an accredited educational institution; and

(2) Have a minimum of two years' employment experience performing casework or investigations in a legal, financial, law enforcement, or social services setting.

(Subd (a) adopted effective January 1, 2008.)

(b) Qualifications of probate attorneys

Except as otherwise provided in this rule, a person who begins employment with a court as a probate attorney on or after January 1, 2008, must:

(1) Be an active member of the State Bar of California for:

(A) A minimum of five years; or

(B) A minimum of two years, plus a minimum of five years' current or former active membership in the equivalent organization of another state or eligibility to practice in the highest court of another state or in a court of the United States; and

(2) Have a minimum of two years' total experience, before or after admission as an active member of the State Bar of California, in one or more of the following positions:

(A) Court-employed staff attorney;

(B) Intern, court probate department (minimum six-month period);

(C) Court-employed probate examiner or court-employed or court-contracted court investigator;

(D) Attorney in a probate-related public or private legal practice;

(E) Deputy public guardian or conservator;

(F) Child protective services or adult protective services worker or juvenile probation officer; or

(G) Private professional fiduciary appointed by a court or employee of a private professional fiduciary or bank or trust company appointed by a court, with significant fiduciary responsibilities, including responsibility for court accountings.

(Subd (b) adopted effective January 1, 2008.)

(c) Qualifications of probate examiners

Except as otherwise provided in this rule, a person who begins employment with a court as a probate examiner on or after January 1, 2008, must have:

(1) A bachelor of arts or bachelor of science degree from an accredited educational institution and a minimum of two years' employment experience with one or more of the following employers:

(A) A court;

(B) A public or private law office; or

(C) A public administrator, public guardian, public conservator, or private professional fiduciary; or

(2) A paralegal certificate or an Associate of Arts degree from an accredited educational institution and a minimum of a total of four years' employment experience with one or more of the employers listed in (1); or

(3) A juris doctor degree from an educational institution approved by the American Bar Association or accredited by the Committee of Bar Examiners of the State Bar of California and a minimum of six months' employment experience with an employer listed in (1).

(Subd (c) adopted effective January 1, 2008.)

(d) Additional court-imposed qualifications and requirements

The qualifications in (a), (b), and (c) are minimums. A court may establish higher qualification standards for any position covered by this rule and may require applicants to comply with its customary hiring or personal-service contracting practices, including written applications, personal references, personal interviews, or entrance examinations.

(Subd (d) adopted effective January 1, 2008.)

(e) Exemption for smaller courts

The qualifications required under this rule may be waived by a court with eight or fewer authorized judges if it cannot find suitable qualified candidates for the positions covered by this rule or for other grounds of hardship. A court electing to waive a qualification under this subdivision must make express written findings showing the circumstances supporting the waiver and disclosing all alternatives considered, including those not selected.

(Subd (e) adopted effective January 1, 2008.)

(f) Record keeping and reporting

The Judicial Council may require courts to report on the qualifications of the court investigators, probate attorneys, or probate examiners hired or under contract under this rule, and on waivers made under (e), as necessary to ensure compliance with Probate Code section 1456.

(Subd (f) amended effective January 1, 2016; adopted effective January 1, 2008.)
Rule 10.777 amended effective January 1, 2016; adopted effective January 1, 2008.

Chapter 8
Alternative Dispute Resolution Programs

Chapter 8 renumbered effective January 1, 2008; adopted as Chapter 7 effective January 1, 2007.

Rule 10.780. Administration of alternative dispute resolution (ADR) programs
Rule 10.781. Court-related ADR neutrals
Rule 10.782. ADR program information
Rule 10.783. ADR program administration

Rule 10.780.   Administration of alternative dispute resolution (ADR) programs

The rules in this chapter concern alternative dispute resolution (ADR) programs administered by the trial courts. General provisions concerning ADR are located in title 3, division 8.

Rule 10.780 amended effective January 1, 2008; adopted effective January 1, 2007.

Rule 10.781.   Court-related ADR neutrals

(a) Qualifications of mediators for general civil cases

Each superior court that makes a list of mediators available to litigants in general civil cases or that recommends, selects, appoints, or compensates mediators to mediate any general civil case pending in the court must establish minimum qualifications for the mediators eligible to be included on the court's list or to be recommended, selected, appointed, or compensated by the court. A court that approves the parties' agreement to use a mediator who is selected by the parties and who is not on the court's list of mediators or that memorializes the parties' agreement in a court order has not thereby recommended, selected, or appointed that mediator within the meaning of this rule. In establishing these qualifications, courts are encouraged to consider the Model Qualification Standards for Mediators in Court-Connected Mediation Programs for General Civil Cases issued by the Judicial Council staff.

(Subd (a) amended effective January 1, 2016; adopted effective January 1, 2011.)

(b) Lists of neutrals

If a court makes available to litigants a list of ADR neutrals, the list must contain, at a minimum, the following information concerning each neutral listed:

(1) The types of ADR services available from the neutral;

(2) The neutral's résumé, including his or her general education and ADR training and experience; and

(3) The fees charged by the neutral for each type of service.

(Subd (b) amended and relettered effective January 1, 2011; adopted as subd (a); amended effective January 1, 2007.)

(c) Requirements to be on lists

In order to be included on a court list of ADR neutrals, an ADR neutral must sign a statement or certificate agreeing to:

(1) Comply with all applicable ethics requirements and rules of court; and

(2) Serve as an ADR neutral on a pro bono or modest-means basis in at least one case per year, not to exceed eight hours, if requested by the court. The court must establish the eligibility requirements for litigants to receive, and the application process for them to request, ADR services on a pro bono or modest-means basis.

(Subd (c) relettered effective January 1, 2011; adopted as subd (b); previously amended effective January 1, 2007.)

(d) Privilege to serve as a court-program neutral

Inclusion on a court list of ADR neutrals and eligibility to be recommended, appointed, or compensated by the court to serve as a neutral are privileges that are revocable and confer no vested right on the neutral.

(Subd (d) relettered effective January 1, 2011; adopted as subd (c) effective July 1, 2009.)
Rule 10.781 amended effective January 1, 2016; adopted as rule 1580.1 effective January 1, 2001; previously amended and renumbered as rule 10.781 effective January 1, 2007; previously amended effective July 1, 2009, and January 1, 2011.

Advisory Committee Comment

Subdivision (c). A court has absolute discretion to determine who may be included on a court list of ADR neutrals or is eligible to be recommended, selected, appointed, or compensated by the court to serve as a neutral (except as otherwise expressly provided by statute or rule of court).

Rule 10.782.   ADR program information

(a) Report to Judicial Council

Each court must report information on its ADR programs to the Judicial Council, as requested by Judicial Council staff.

(Subd (a) amended effective January 1, 2016; previously amended effective January 1, 2007.)

(b) Parties and ADR neutrals to supply information

Subject to applicable limitations, including the confidentiality requirements in Evidence Code section 1115 et seq., courts must require parties and ADR neutrals, as appropriate, to supply pertinent information for the reports required under (a).

(Subd (b) amended effective January 1, 2007.)
Rule 10.782 amended effective January 1, 2016; adopted as rule 1580.2 effective January 1, 2001; previously amended and renumbered as rule 10.782 effective January 1, 2007.

Rule 10.783.   ADR program administration

(a) ADR program administrator

The presiding judge in each trial court must designate the clerk or executive officer, or another court employee who is knowledgeable about ADR processes, to serve as ADR program administrator. The duties of the ADR program administrator must include:

(1) Developing informational material concerning the court's ADR programs;

(2) Educating attorneys and litigants about the court's ADR programs;

(3) Supervising the development and maintenance of any panels of ADR neutrals maintained by the court; and

(4) Gathering statistical and other evaluative information concerning the court's ADR programs.

(Subd (a) amended effective January 1, 2007; previously amended effective January 1, 2004.)

(b) ADR committee

(1) *Membership in courts with 18 or more authorized judges*

In each superior court that has 18 or more authorized judges, there must be an ADR committee. The members of the ADR committee must include, insofar as is practicable:

(A) The presiding judge or a judge designated by the presiding judge;

(B) One or more other judges designated by the presiding judge;

(C) The ADR program administrator;

(D) Two or more active members of the State Bar chosen by the presiding judge as representatives of those attorneys who regularly represent parties in general civil cases before the court, including an equal number of attorneys who represent plaintiffs and who represent defendants in these cases;

(E) One or more members of the court's panel of arbitrators chosen by the presiding judge; and

(F) If the court makes available to litigants a list of any ADR neutrals other than arbitrators, one or more neutrals chosen by the presiding judge from that list.

(2) *Additional members*

The ADR committee may include additional members selected by the presiding judge.

(3) *ADR committee in other courts*

Any other court may by rule establish an ADR committee as provided in (b)(1). Otherwise, the presiding judge or a judge designated by the presiding judge must perform the functions and have the powers of an ADR committee as provided in these rules.

(4) *Term of membership*

ADR committee membership is for a two-year term. The members of the ADR committee may be reappointed and may be removed by the presiding judge.

(5) *Responsibilities of ADR committee*

The ADR committee is responsible for overseeing the court's alternative dispute resolution programs for general civil cases, including those responsibilities relating to the court's judicial arbitration program specified in rule 3.813(b).

(Subd (b) amended effective January 1, 2007; previously adopted effective January 1, 2004.)

Rule 10.783 amended and renumbered effective January 1, 2007; adopted as rule 1580.3 effective January 1, 2001; previously amended effective January 1, 2004.

Chapter 9
Trial Court Budget and Fiscal Management

Chapter 9 renumbered effective January 1, 2008; adopted as Chapter 3 effective July 1, 1998; previously renumbered as Chapter 8 effective January 1, 2007.

Rule 10.800. Superior court budgeting
Rule 10.801. Superior court budget procedures
Rule 10.803. Information access disputes—writ petitions (Gov. Code, § 71675)
Rule 10.804. Superior court financial policies and procedures
Rule 10.805. Notice of change in court-county relationship
Rule 10.810. Court operations
Rule 10.811. Reimbursement of costs associated with homicide trials
Rule 10.815. Fees to be set by the court
Rule 10.820. Acceptance of credit cards by the superior courts
Rule 10.821. Acceptance of checks and other negotiable paper
Rule 10.830. Disposal of surplus court personal property

Rule 10.800. Superior court budgeting

(a) Purpose

This rule provides for local authority and accountability for development of budget requests and management of court operations within the authorized funding level. Superior courts must manage their budgets in a manner that is responsive to local needs, ensures equal access to justice, is consistent with Judicial Council policy and legislative direction, and does not exceed the total allocated budget.

(Subd (a) amended effective January 1, 2007; previously amended effective January 1, 2002.)

(b) Development of budget requests

Each superior court must prepare and submit to the Judicial Council a budget according to the schedule and procedures established by the council.

(Subd (b) amended effective January 1, 2016; previously amended effective January 1, 2002, and January 1, 2007.)

(c) Allocation of funding

(1) The funding allocation to each superior court is based on the amounts incorporated for that court in budget change proposals that have been funded through the Budget Act, except as otherwise ordered by the Judicial Council. The superior court of each county may distribute and periodically redistribute its annual allocation between programs, locations, and line items as needed, within the parameters of the *Trial Court Financial Policies and Procedures Manual* and consistent with council policy direction, to promote accessible justice and the effective, efficient, and accountable operation of the courts. The Judicial Council may make additional allocations as it deems appropriate.

(2) Each superior court is accountable for achieving the expected outcomes of the programs funded for that year. If a court is unable to do so, it must report the reasons to the Judicial Council.

(Subd (c) amended effective January 1, 2007; previously amended effective January 1, 2002.)

Rule 10.800 amended effective January 1, 2016; adopted as rule 2530 effective July 1, 1998; renumbered as rule 6.700 effective January 1, 1999; previously amended effective January 1, 2002; previously amended and renumbered as rule 10.800 effective January 1, 2007.

Rule 10.801. Superior court budget procedures

(a) Adoption of budget procedures by Judicial Council staff

Judicial Council staff must adopt superior court budget procedures to be included in the *Trial Court Financial Policies and Procedures Manual*, the annual Baseline Budget Development Package, and the annual *Budget Change Request Package*. These procedures include the following:

(1) Procedures permitting the superior courts to comment on the proposed budget procedures;

(2) Procedures for budget development, submission, and appeal;

(3) Procedures for budget implementation, including expenditure and revenue reporting;

(4) Reasonable time frames to comply with requirements or changes in the budget procedures;

(5) Procedures to ensure the reporting to the Judicial Council of relevant information on the implementation of programs funded;

(6) Procedures for providing timely management information to the Judicial Council on the baseline budget, revenues, and expenditures.

(7) An annual budget development and implementation calendar;

(8) Procedures for a superior court to follow if it projects that its budget will be exhausted before the end of the fiscal year, preventing the court from meeting its financial obligations or continuing operations; and

(9) Procedures governing the transfer of funds between individual programs and operations of expenditure.

(Subd (a) amended effective January 1, 2016; previously amended effective January 1, 2002, and January 1, 2007.)

(b) Technical assistance

Judicial Council staff, on request, provide technical assistance and ongoing training in budget development and implementation to the superior courts.

(Subd (b) amended effective January 1, 2016; previously amended effective January 1, 2002, and January 1, 2007.)

Rule 10.801 amended effective January 1, 2016; adopted as rule 2531 effective July 1, 1998; renumbered as rule 6.701 effective January 1, 1999; previously amended effective January 1, 2002; previously amended and renumbered as rule 10.801 effective January 1, 2007.

Rule 10.802. Maintenance of and public access to budget and management information [Repealed]

Rule 10.802 repealed effective January 1, 2010; adopted as rule 6.702 effective January 1, 2001; previously amended effective July 1, 2001, July 1, 2002, and January 1, 2004; previously amended and renumbered effective January 1, 2007.

Rule 10.803. Information access disputes—writ petitions (Gov. Code, § 71675)

(a) Availability

This rule applies to petitions filed under rule 10.500(j)(1) and Government Code section 71675(b).

(Subd (a) amended effective January 1, 2010; previously amended effective January 1, 2007.)

(b) Assignment of Court of Appeal justice to hear the petition

(1) The petition must state the following on the first page, below the case number, in the statement of the character of the proceeding (see rule 2.111(6)):

"Writ petition filed under rule 10.500(j)(1) and Government Code section 71675—Assignment of Court of Appeal justice required."

(2) When the petition is filed, the clerk of the court must immediately request of the Chief Justice the assignment of a hearing judge from the panel established under (e).

(3) If an assignment is made, the judge assigned to hear the petition in the superior court must be a justice from a Court of Appeal for a district other than the district for that superior court.

(Subd (b) amended effective January 1, 2010; previously amended effective January 1, 2007.)

(c) Superior court hearing

(1) The superior court must hear and decide the petition on an expedited basis and must give the petition priority over other matters to the extent permitted by law and the rules of court.

(2) The petition must be heard by a judge assigned by the Chief Justice from the panel of hearing judges established under (e).

(Subd (c) amended effective January 1, 2007.)

(d) Appeal

An appeal of the superior court decision must be heard and decided on an expedited basis in the Court of Appeal for the district in which the petition was heard and must be given priority over other matters to the extent permitted by law and rules of court. The notice of appeal must state the following on the first page, below the case number, in the statement of the character of the proceeding (see rule 2.111(6)):

"Notice of Appeal on Writ Petition filed under rule 10.500(j)(1) and Government Code section 71675—Expedited Processing Requested."

(Subd (d) amended effective January 1, 2010; previously amended effective January 1, 2007.)

(e) Panel of hearing judges

The panel of judges who may hear the petitions in the superior court must consist of Court of Appeal justices selected by the Chief Justice as follows:

(1) The panel must include at least one justice from each district of the Court of Appeal.

(2) Each justice assigned to hear a petition under (c)(2) must have received training on hearing the petitions as specified by the Chief Justice.

Rule 10.803 amended effective January 1, 2010; adopted as rule 6.710 effective October 15, 2004; previously amended and renumbered effective January 1, 2007.

Rule 10.804. Superior court financial policies and procedures

(a) Adoption

As part of its responsibility for regulating the budget and fiscal management of the trial courts, the Judicial Council adopts the *Trial Court Financial Policies and Procedures Manual*. The manual contains regulations establishing budget procedures, recordkeeping, accounting standards, and other financial guidelines for superior courts. The manual sets out a system of fundamental internal controls that will enable the trial courts to monitor their use of public funds, provide consistent and comparable financial statements, and demonstrate accountability.

(Subd (a) amended effective August 26, 2016; previously amended effective January 1, 2007, and July 1, 2015.)

(b) Amendments

(1) Before making any substantive amendments to the *Trial Court Financial Policies and Procedures Manual*, the Judicial Council must make the amendments available to the superior courts, the California Department of Finance, and the State Controller's Office for 30 days for comment.

(2) The Judicial Council delegates to the Administrative Director, under article VI, section 6 of the California Constitution and other applicable law, the authority to make technical changes and clarifications to the manual, provided the changes and clarifications are consistent with council policies.

(Subd (b) amended effective August 26, 2016; previously amended effective January 1, 2007, and July 1, 2015.)

(c) Date of adherence

Superior courts must adhere to the requirements contained in the *Trial Court Financial Policies and Procedures Manual*, except as otherwise provided in the manual. Superior courts must not be required to adhere to any substantive amendment to the manual sooner than 60 days after the amendment is adopted.

(Subd (c) amended effective August 26, 2016; previously amended January 1, 2007.)

Rule 10.804 amended effective August 26, 2016; adopted as rule 6.707 effective January 1, 2001; previously amended and renumbered effective January 1, 2007; previously amended effective July 1, 2015.

Advisory Committee Comment

Subdivision (a). Procurement and contracting policies and procedures for judicial branch entities, including superior courts, are addressed separately in the *Judicial Branch Contracting Manual*, which the Judicial Council adopted under Public Contract Code section 19206.

Subdivision (b)(2). Technical changes and clarifications include clarifying language that (1) does not change any substantive requirement imposed on courts; and (2) corrects typographical errors or citations, or makes reimbursement rate adjustments and other changes that result from changes in federal, state, or local rules, regulations or applicable law.

Rule 10.805. Notice of change in court-county relationship

If, under Government Code section 77212, the county gives notice to the superior court that the county will no longer provide a specific county service or the court gives notice to the county that the court will no longer use a specific county service, the court must, within 10 days of receiving or giving such notice, provide a copy of this notice to the Judicial Council's Finance office.

Rule 10.805 amended effective January 1, 2016; adopted as rule 6.705 effective January 1, 2000; previously amended and renumbered as rule 10.805 effective January 1, 2007.

Rule 10.810. Court operations

(a) Definition

Except as provided in subdivision (b) and subject to the requirements of subdivisions (c) and (d), "court operations" as defined in Government Code section 77003 includes the following costs:

(1) *(judicial salaries and benefits)* salaries, benefits, and public agency retirement contributions for superior and municipal court judges and for subordinate judicial officers;

(2) *(nonjudicial salaries and benefits)* salaries, benefits, and public agency retirement contributions for superior and municipal court staff whether permanent, temporary, full- or part-time, contract or per diem, including but not limited to all municipal court staff positions specifically prescribed by statute and county clerk positions directly supporting the superior courts;

(3) salaries and benefits for those sheriff, marshal, and constable employees as the court deems necessary for court operations in superior and municipal courts and the supervisors of those sheriff, marshal, and constable employees who directly supervise the court security function;

(4) court-appointed counsel in juvenile dependency proceedings, and counsel appointed by the court to represent a minor as specified in Government Code section 77003;

(5) *(services and supplies)* operating expenses in support of judicial officers and court operations;

(6) *(collective bargaining)* collective bargaining with respect to court employees; and

(7) *(indirect costs)* a share of county general services as defined in subdivision (d), Function 11, and used by the superior and municipal courts.

(Subd (a) amended effective July 1, 1995; previously amended effective January 1, 1989, July 1, 1990, and July 1, 1991.)

(b) Exclusions

Excluded from the definition of "court operations" are the following:

(1) law library operations conducted by a trust pursuant to statute;

(2) courthouse construction and site acquisition, including space rental (for other than court records storage), alterations/remodeling, or relocating court facilities;

(3) district attorney services;

(4) probation services;

(5) indigent criminal and juvenile delinquency defense;

(6) civil and criminal grand jury expenses and operations (except for selection);

(7) pretrial release services;

(8) equipment and supplies for use by official reporters of the courts to prepare transcripts as specified by statute; and

(9) county costs as provided in subdivision (d) as unallowable.

(Subd (b) amended effective July 1, 1995; adopted effective July 1, 1988 as subd (c); previously amended effective January 1, 1989, and July 1, 1990.)

(c) Budget appropriations

Costs for court operations specified in subdivision (a) shall be appropriated in county budgets for superior and municipal courts, including contract services with county agencies or private providers except for the following:

(1) salaries, benefits, services, and supplies for sheriff, marshal, and constable employees as the court deems necessary for court operations in superior and municipal courts;

(2) salaries, benefits, services, and supplies for county clerk activities directly supporting the superior court; and

(3) costs for court-appointed counsel specified in Government Code section 77003.

Except as provided in this subdivision, costs not appropriated in the budgets of the courts are unallowable.

(Subd (c) amended effective July 1, 1995; adopted as subd (d) effective July 1, 1990.)

(d) Functional budget categories

Trial court budgets and financial reports shall identify all allowable court operations in the following eleven (11) functional budget categories. Costs for salary, wages, and benefits of court employees are to be shown in the appropriate functions provided the individual staff member works at least 25 percent time in that function. Individual staff members whose time spent in a function is less than 25 percent are reported in Function 10, All Other Court Operations. The functions and their respective costs are as follows:

Function 1. Judicial Officers
Costs reported in this function are
    Salaries and state benefits of
        Judges
        Full- or part-time court commissioners
        Full- or part-time court referees
    Assigned judges' in-county travel expenses

Costs not reported in this function include
    County benefits of judicial officers (Function 10)
    Juvenile traffic hearing officers (Function 10)
    Mental health hearing officers (Function 10)
    Pro tem hearing officers (Function 10)
    Commissioner and referee positions specifically excluded by statute from state trial court funding (unallowable)
    Related data processing (Function 9)
    Any other related services, supplies, and equipment (Function 10)

Function 2. Jury Services
Costs reported in this function are
    Juror expenses of per diem fees and mileage
    Meals and lodging for sequestered jurors
    Salaries, wages, and benefits of jury commissioner and jury services staff (including selection of grand jury)
    Contractual jury services
    Jury-related office expenses (other than information technology)
    Jury-related communications, including "on call" services

Costs not reported in this function include
    Juror parking (unallowable)
    Civil and criminal grand jury costs (unallowable)
    Jury-related information systems (Function 9)

Function 3. Verbatim Reporting
Costs reported in this function are
    Salaries, wages, and benefits of court reporters who are court employees
    Salaries, wages, and benefits of electronic monitors and support staff
    Salaries, wages, and benefits of verbatim reporting coordinators and clerical support staff
    Contractual court reporters and monitors
    Transcripts for use by appellate or trial courts, or as otherwise required by law
    Related office expenses and equipment (purchased, leased, or rented) used to record court proceedings, except as specified in Government Code
    § 68073, e.g.,
        notepaper, pens, and pencils
        ER equipment and supplies

Costs not reported in this function include
    Office expenses and equipment for use by reporters to prepare transcripts (unallowable)
    Expenses specified in Government Code § 69073 (unallowable)
    Space use charges for court reporters (unallowable)

Function 4. Court Interpreters
Costs reported in this function are
    Salaries, wages, and benefits of courtroom interpreters and interpreter coordinators
    Per diem and contractual courtroom interpreters, including contractual transportation and travel allowances

Costs not reported in this function include
    Related data processing (Function 9)
    Any other related services, supplies, and equipment (Function 10)

Function 5. Collections Enhancement
Collections performed in the enforcement of court orders for fees, fines, forfeitures, restitutions, penalties, and assessments (beginning with the
establishment of the accounts receivable record)

Costs reported in this function are
    Salaries, wages, and benefits of collection employees of the court, e.g.,
        financial hearing officers
        evaluation officers
        collection staff
    Contract collections costs
    County charges for collection services provided to the court by county agencies
    Related services, supplies, and equipment (except data processing, Function 9)

Costs not reported in this function include
    Staff whose principal involvement is in collecting "forthwith" payments, e.g.,
        counter clerks (Function 10)
        cashiers (Function 10)

Function 6. Dispute Resolution Programs

Costs reported in this function are

Arbitrators' fees in mandatory judicial arbitration programs

Salaries, wages, and benefits of court staff providing child custody and visitation mediation and related investigation services, e.g.,

Director of Family Court Services

mediators

conciliators

investigators

clerical support staff

Contract mediators providing child custody and visitation mediation services

Salaries, wages, benefits, fees, and contract costs for other arbitration and mediation programs (programs not mandated by statute), e.g.,

arbitration administrators

clerical support staff

arbitrators' fees and expenses

Costs not reported in this function include

Related data processing (Function 9)

Any other related services, supplies, and equipment (Function 10)

Function 7. Court-Appointed Counsel (Noncriminal)

Costs reported in this function are

Expenses for court-appointed counsel as specified in Government Code § 77003

Function 8. Court Security

Court security services as deemed necessary by the court. Includes only the duties of

(a) courtroom bailiff,

(b) perimeter security (i.e., outside the courtroom but inside the court facility), and

(c) at least .25 FTE dedicated supervisors of these activities.

Costs reported in this function are

Salary, wages, and benefits (including overtime) of sheriff, marshal, and constable employees who perform the court's security, i.e.,

bailiffs

weapons-screening personnel

Salary, wages, and benefits (including overtime) of court staff performing court security, e.g.,

court attendants

Contractual security services

Salary, wages, and benefits of supervisors of sheriff, marshal, and constable employees whose duties are greater than .25 FTE dedicated to this function

Sheriff, marshal, and constable employee training

Purchase of security equipment

Maintenance of security equipment

Costs not reported in this function include

Other sheriff, marshal, or constable employees (unallowable)

Court attendant training (Function 10)

Overhead costs attributable to the operation of the sheriff and marshal offices (unallowable)

Costs associated with the transportation and housing of detainees from the jail to the courthouse (unallowable)

Service of process in civil cases (unallowable)

Services and supplies, including data processing, not specified above as allowable

Supervisors of bailiffs and perimeter security personnel of the sheriff, marshal, or constable office who supervise these duties less than .25 FTE time (unallowable)

Function 9. Information Technology

Costs reported in this function are

Salaries, wages, and benefits of court employees who plan, implement, and maintain court data processing and information technologies, e.g.,

programmers

analysts

Contract and consulting services associated with court information/data processing needs and systems

County Information Systems/Data Processing Department charges made to court for court systems, e.g.,

jury-related systems

court and case management, including courts' share of a criminal justice information system

accounts receivable/collections systems

Related services, supplies, and equipment, e.g.,

software purchases and leases

maintenance of automation equipment

training associated with data processing systems' development

Costs not reported in this function include

Information technology services not provided directly to the courts (i.e., services used by other budget units)

Data processing for county general services, e.g., payroll, accounts payable (Function 11)

Function 10. All Other Court Operations

Costs reported in this function are

Salaries, wages, and benefits (including any pay differentials and overtime) of court staff

(a) not reported in Functions 2–9, or

(b) whose time cannot be allocated to Functions 2-9 in increments of at least 25 percent time (.25 FTE);

Judicial benefits, county-paid

Allowable costs not reported in Functions 2-9.

(Nonjudicial staff) Cost items may include, for example,

> juvenile traffic hearing officer
> mental health hearing officer
> court-appointed hearing officer (pro tem)
> executive officer
> court administrator
> clerk of the court
> administrative assistant
> personnel staff
> legal research personnel; staff attorney; planning and research staff
> secretary
> courtroom clerk
> clerical support staff
> calendar clerk
> deputy clerk
> accountant
> cashier
> counter clerk
> microfilming staff
> management analyst
> probate conservatorship and guardianship investigators
> probate examiner
> training staff employed by the court

Personnel costs not reported in this function:

> Any of the above not employed by the court

(Services and supplies) Cost items may include, for example,

> office supplies
> printing
> postage
> communications
> publications and legal notices, by the court
> miscellaneous departmental expenses
> books, publications, training fees, and materials for court personnel (judicial and nonjudicial)
> travel and transportation (judicial and nonjudicial)
> professional dues
> memberships and subscriptions
> statutory multidistrict judges' association expenses
> research, planning, and program coordination expenses
> small claims advisor program costs
> court-appointed expert witness fees (for the court's needs)
> court-ordered forensic evaluations and other professional services (for the court's own use)
> pro tem judges' expenses
> micrographics expenses
> public information services
> vehicle use, including automobile insurance
> equipment (leased, rented, or purchased) and furnishings, including interior painting, replacement/maintenance of flooring, and furniture repair
> maintenance of office equipment
> janitorial services
> legal services for allowable court operations (County Counsel and contractual)
> fidelity and faithful performance insurance (bonding and personal liability insurance on judges and court employees)
> insurance on cash money and securities (hold-up and burglary)
> general liability/comprehensive insurance for other than faulty maintenance or design of facility (e.g., "slip and fall," other injury, theft and damage of court equipment, slander, discrimination)
> risk management services related to allowable insurance
> space rental for court records
> county records retention/destruction services
> county messenger/mail service
> court audits mandated under Government Code § 71383

Service and supply costs not reported in this function include

> Civic association dues (unallowable)
> Facility damages insurance (unallowable)
> County central service department charges not appropriated in the court budget (unallowable)

Function 11. County General Services ("Indirect Costs")

General county services are defined as all eligible accounting, payroll, budgeting, personnel, purchasing, and county administrator costs rendered in support of court operations. Costs for included services are allowable to the extent the service is provided to the court. The following costs, regardless of how characterized by the county or by which county department they are performed, are reported in this function only and are subject to the statutory maximum for indirect costs as specified in Government Code § 77003. To the extent costs are allowable under this rule, a county's approved Cost Plan may be used to determine the specific cost although the cost categories, or functions, may differ.

Cost items within the meaning of rule 10.810(a)(7) and the county departments often performing the service may include, for example,

> County Administrator
>> budget development and administration
>> interdepartmental budget unit administration and operations
>> personnel (labor) relations and administration

Auditor-Controller
   payroll
   financial audits
   warrant processing
   fixed asset accounting
   departmental accounting for courts, e.g., fines, fees, forfeitures, restitutions, penalties, and assessments; accounting for the Trial Court Special
   Revenue Fund
   accounts payable
   grant accounting
   management reporting
   banking
Personnel
   recruitment and examination of applicants
   maintenance and certification of eligible lists
   position classification
   salary surveys
   leave accounting
   employment physicals
   handling of appeals
Treasurer/Tax Collector
   warrant processing
   bank reconciliation
   retirement system administration
   receiving, safeguarding, investing, and disbursing court funds
Purchasing Agent
   process departmental requisitions
   issue and analyze bids
   make contracts and agreements for the purchase or rental of personal property
   store surplus property and facilitate public auctions
Unallowable costs
   Unallowable court-related costs are those
      (a) in support of county operations,
      (b) expressly prohibited by statute,
      (c) facility-related, or
      (d) exceptions of the nature referenced in Functions 1-11.
Unallowable cost items, including any related data processing costs, are not reported in Functions 1-11 and may include, for example,
Communications
   central communication control and maintenance for county emergency and general government radio equipment
Central Collections
   processing accounts receivable for county departments (not courts)
County Administrator
   legislative analysis and activities
   preparation and operation of general directives and operating procedures
   responses to questions from the Board, outside agencies, and the public executive functions: Board of Supervisors
   county advisory councils
Treasurer/Tax Collector
   property tax determination, collection, etc.
General Services
   rental and utilities support
   coordinate county's emergency services
Property Management
   negotiations for the acquisition, sale, or lease of property, except for space rented for storage of court records
   making appraisals
   negotiating utility relocations
   assisting County Counsel in condemnation actions
   preparing deeds, leases, licenses, easements
   collecting rents
   building lease management services (except for storage of court records)
Facility-related
   construction services
   right-of-way and easement services
   purchase of land and buildings
   construction
   depreciation of buildings/use allowance
   space rental/building rent (except for storage of court records)
   building maintenance and repairs (except interior painting and to replace/repair flooring)
   purchase, installation, and maintenance of H/V/A/C equipment
   maintenance and repair of utilities
   utility use charges (e.g., heat, light, water)
   elevator purchase and maintenance
   alterations/remodeling
   landscaping and grounds maintenance services
   exterior lighting and security
   insurance on building damages (e.g., fire, earthquake, flood, boiler and machinery)
   grounds' liability insurance
   parking lot or facility maintenance
   juror parking

(Subd (d) amended effective January 1, 2007; previously amended and relettered effective July 1, 1995.)

Rule 10.810 amended and renumbered effective January 1, 2007; adopted as rule 810 effective July 1, 1988; previously amended effective July 1, 1989, July 1, 1990, July 1, 1991, and July 1, 1995.

Advisory Committee Comment

Rule 10.810 is identical to former rule 810, except for the rule number. All references in statutes or rules to rule 810 apply to this rule.

Rule 10.811. Reimbursement of costs associated with homicide trials

(a) Intent

This rule permits courts that meet certain criteria to request reimbursement of extraordinary costs of homicide trials.

(Subd (a) amended effective January 1, 2007.)

(b) Criteria

A court that requests reimbursement of extraordinary costs of a homicide trial must meet all the following criteria:

(1) Be located in a county with a population of 300,000 or less;

(2) Have incurred extraordinary costs of a homicide trial; and

(3) Demonstrate an actual need for reimbursement.

(c) Submission

A request for reimbursement must be submitted by the court's presiding judge or executive officer to Judicial Council staff. All requests for reimbursement must comply with guidelines approved by the Judicial Council and include a completed *Request for Reimbursement of Extraordinary Homicide Trial Costs* form.

(Subd (c) amended effective January 1, 2016.)

Rule 10.811 amended effective January 1, 2016; adopted as rule 6.711 effective January 1, 2005; previously amended and renumbered as rule 10.811 effective January 1, 2007.

Rule 10.815. Fees to be set by the court

(a) Authority

Under Government Code section 70631, a superior court may charge a reasonable fee for a service or product not to exceed the costs of providing the service or product, if the Judicial Council approves the fee.

(b) Approved fees

The Judicial Council authorizes courts to charge a reasonable fee not to exceed costs for the following products and services unless courts are prohibited by law from charging a fee for, or providing, the product or service:

(1) Forms;

(2) Packages of forms;

(3) Information materials;

(4) Publications, including books, pamphlets, and local rules;

(5) Compact discs;

(6) DVDs;

(7) Audiotapes;

(8) Videotapes;

(9) Microfiches;

(10) Envelopes;

(11) Postage;

(12) Shipping;

(13) Off-site retrieval of documents;

(14) Direct fax filing under rule 2.304 (fee per page);

(15) Returning filed-stamped copies of documents by fax to persons who request that a faxed copy be sent to them;

(16) Training programs for attorneys who serve as court-appointed temporary judges, including the materials and food provided to the participants; and

(17) Other training programs or events, including materials and food provided to the participants.

(Subd (b) amended effective January 1, 2007; previously amended effective July 1, 2006.)

(c) Guidelines for determining costs

The fee charged for any product or service listed in (b) may not exceed the court's cost in providing the product or service. In determining the costs of a product or service, the court must:

(1) Identify the specific product or service; and

(2) Prepare an analysis of the direct and indirect costs on which the fee is based.

(d) Reasonableness

In deciding what specific fee or fees, if any, to charge for a product or service under (b), the court must determine that the fee charged is reasonable considering relevant factors such as the benefits to the court and the public from providing the product or service and the effects of charging the fee on public access to the court.

(e) Reporting requirement

Each court that charges a fee under this rule must provide Judicial Council staff with a description of the fee, how the amount of the fee was determined, and how the fee is applied.

(Subd (e) amended effective January 1, 2016.)

(f) Public notice

The court must notify the public of any fee that it charges under this rule by providing information concerning the fee in a conspicuous place such as the court's fee schedule.

(g) Procedure for adoption of fee

If a court proposes to change any fee authorized under (b) that it is already charging or to charge any new fee authorized under (b), the court must follow the procedures for adopting or amending a local rule under rule 10.613 of the California Rules of Court.

(Subd (g) amended effective January 1, 2007; previously amended effective July 1, 2006.)

Rule 10.815 amended effective January 1, 2016; adopted as rule 6.712 effective January 1, 2006; previously amended effective July 1, 2006; amended and renumbered as rule 10.815 effective January 1, 2007.

Rule 10.820. Acceptance of credit cards by the superior courts

(a) Delegation of authority to Administrative Director

The Administrative Director is authorized, under rule 10.80, to approve on behalf of the Judicial Council requests from the superior courts to accept credit cards for the payment of court fees or to impose a charge for the use of credit cards. The authority is given to the Judicial Council by Government Code section 6159.

(Subd (a) amended effective January 1, 2016; previously amended effective January 1, 2007.)

(b) Standards for use of credit cards

The Administrative Director is authorized to approve requests under (a) for acceptance of credit cards if all of the following are true:

(1) The court (A) imposes a fee for the use of the credit card, or (B) demonstrates that the cost of acceptance of credit cards is not greater than the cost of acceptance of other means of payment of fees, or (C) demonstrates that it can absorb the cost of the acceptance of the credit card;

(2) The court has obtained a credit card acceptance contract that is competitive with other possible contracts the court could obtain; and

(3) The court provides alternative means for a person to pay court fees.

(Subd (b) amended effective January 1, 2016; previously amended effective January 1, 2007.)

(c) Standards for charge for the use of credit cards

The Administrative Director is authorized to approve requests under (a) for the imposition of a charge for the use of credit cards if both of the following are true:

(1) The proposed fee is not greater than the cost for acceptance of a credit card; and

(2) The proposed fee would not result in an undue hardship on people wishing to use credit cards for payment of fees.

(Subd (c) amended effective January 1, 2016; previously amended effective January 1, 2007.)

(d) Referral to Judicial Council

The Administrative Director may refer any request under (a) to the Judicial Council for its action.

(Subd (d) amended effective January 1, 2016; previously amended effective January 1, 2007.)

(e) Existing approvals ratified

The approval of any board of supervisors for any superior court to accept credit cards or charge a fee for the use of credit cards that was effective as of December 31, 1999, is ratified by the council as of January 1, 2000.

(Subd (e) amended effective January 1, 2009; previously amended effective January 1, 2007.)

Rule 10.820 amended effective January 1, 2016; adopted as rule 6.703 effective January 1, 2000; previously amended and renumbered as rule 10.820 effective January 1, 2007; previously amended effective January 1, 2009.

Rule 10.821. Acceptance of checks and other negotiable paper

(a) Conditions for acceptance

A personal check, bank cashier's check, money order, or traveler's check tendered in payment of any fee, fine, or bail deposit under Government Code section 71386 or Vehicle Code section 40510 or 40521 must be accepted by the court:

(1) If the personal check is drawn on a banking institution located in California by a person furnishing satisfactory proof of residence in California, is payable to the court without a second party endorsement, and is in an amount not exceeding the amount of the payment and is not postdated or staledated, unless the person drawing the check is known to have previously tendered worthless checks; or

(2) If the bank cashier's check or money order is drawn on a banking institution located in the United States and is in an amount not exceeding the amount of the payment; or

(3) If the person presenting the traveler's check shows satisfactory identification.

(Subd (a) amended effective January 1, 2007.)

(b) Requiring satisfactory proof of good credit

Except for checks tendered under the conditions specified in Vehicle Code section 40521(a), a court may require that a person drawing a personal check furnish satisfactory proof of good credit by showing a valid recognized credit card or by any other reasonable means.

(Subd (b) amended effective January 1, 2007.)

(c) Written policy for acceptance or rejection

A court may accept or reject any check or money order not meeting the requirements of this rule, under a written policy adopted by the court under Government Code section 71386(a).

(Subd (c) amended effective January 1, 2007.)

Rule 10.821 amended and renumbered effective January 1, 2007; adopted as rule 805 effective July 1, 1981.

Rule 10.830.   Disposal of surplus court personal property

(a) Disposal of surplus property

Except as provided in (b), a superior court may:

(1) Sell, at fair market value, any personal property of the court that is no longer needed for court use;

(2) Trade or exchange any surplus personal property of the court, according to such terms and conditions as are agreed on, for personal property of another court, the state, a county, a city, a federal agency, a community redevelopment agency, a housing authority, a community development commission, a surplus property authority, a school district, or any irrigation, flood control, county board of education, or other special district, if the property to be acquired by the court is needed for court use;

(3) Donate, sell at less than fair market value, or otherwise transfer to another court, the state, a county, a city, a federal agency, a community redevelopment agency, a housing authority, a community development commission, a surplus property authority, a school district, or any irrigation, flood control, county board of education, or other special district, according to such terms and conditions as are agreed on, any personal property of the court that is no longer needed for court use; and

(4) Dispose of any personal property of the court that is no longer needed for court use, and that has negligible or no economic value, in any manner the court deems appropriate.

(Subd (a) amended effective January 1, 2007.)

(b) Exception for disposal of technology equipment acquired on or after July 1, 2000

A superior court that wishes to dispose of surplus technology equipment to which the court acquired title on or after July 1, 2000 must provide a written description of such technology equipment to the Administrative Director. If, within 60 days of receipt of the description, the Administrative Director determines that another court of record of the State of California is in need of the surplus technology equipment, the court holding title to the equipment must donate it to the court determined to be in need. If the Administrative Director determines that no other court needs the equipment or makes no determination within 60 days of receiving the written description of it, the court holding title to the equipment may dispose of it as provided in (a), (c), and (d). The Administrative Director must provide to the courts a definition of the term "technology equipment" as used in this rule and must provide 30 days' notice of any amendment to the definition.

(Subd (b) amended effective January 1, 2016; previously amended effective January 1, 2007.)

(c) Notice of disposal

Unless the property to be transferred under this rule is valued at $500 or less or the entity to which the property is to be transferred is another

court of record of the State of California, the transferring superior court must, at least one week before the transfer, place a notice of its intended action:

(1) In three public places; or

(2) On the court's Web site; or

(3) In a newspaper of general circulation published in the county.

(Subd (c) amended effective January 1, 2007.)

(d) Proceeds of disposal

Any proceeds of a sale or other transfer under this rule must be deposited in the superior court's operations fund.

(Subd (d) amended effective January 1, 2007.)

Rule 10.830 amended effective January 1, 2016; adopted as rule 6.709 effective January 1, 2001; previously amended and renumbered as rule 10.830 effective January 1, 2007.

Chapter 10
Trial Court Records Management

Chapter 10 renumbered effective January 1, 2008; adopted as Chapter 4 effective January 1, 2001; previously amended and renumbered as Chapter 9 effective January 1, 2007.

Rule 10.850.   Trial court records

Unless otherwise provided, "court records" as used in this chapter consist of the records as defined in Government Code section 68151(a).
Rule 10.850 adopted effective January 1, 2011.

Rule 10.851.   Court indexes—automated maintenance

(a) Authorized media

The clerk of each trial court may create, maintain, update, and make accessible the indexes required by law by photographic, microphotographic, photocopy, mechanical, magnetic, or electronic means. The clerk must make provision for preserving the information on a medium that will ensure its permanence and protect it from loss or damage arising from electronic failure or mechanical defect.

(Subd (a) amended effective January 1, 2007; adopted as unlettered subd; previously amended and relettered effective January 1, 2001.)

(b) Alphabetic index

A single alphabetic index may be maintained so long as the plaintiff-defendant distinction is retained.

(Subd (b) adopted effective January 1, 2001.)

(c) Public access

The indexes maintained under automated procedures must be accessible for public examination and use.

(Subd (c) amended effective January 1, 2007; adopted as part of unlettered subd; previously lettered and amended effective January 1, 2001.)

Rule 10.851 amended and renumbered effective January 1, 2007; adopted as rule 1010 effective January 1, 1975; renumbered as rule 999 effective January 1, 2003; amended and renumbered as rule 6.751 effective January 1, 2001.

Rule 10.854.   Standards and guidelines for trial court records

(a) The standards and guidelines

Judicial Council staff, in collaboration with trial court presiding judges and court executives, must prepare, maintain, and distribute a manual providing standards and guidelines for the creation, maintenance, and retention of trial court records (the *Trial Court Records Manual*), consistent with the Government Code and the rules of court and policies adopted by the Judicial Council. The manual should assist the courts and the public to have complete, accurate, efficient, and accessible court records. Before the manual is issued, it must be made available for comment from the trial courts.

(Subd (a) amended effective January 1, 2016; adopted effective January 1, 2011.)

(b) Contents of the *Trial Court Records Manual*

The *Trial Court Records Manual* must provide standards and guidelines for the creation, maintenance, and retention of trial court records. These standards and guidelines must ensure that all court records subject to permanent retention are retained and made available to the public in perpetuity as legally required.

(Subd (b) adopted effective January 1, 2011.)

(c) Updating the manual

Judicial Council staff, in collaboration with trial court presiding judges and court executives, must periodically update the *Trial Court Records Manual* to reflect changes in technology that affect the creation, maintenance, and retention of court records. Except for technical changes, corrections, or minor substantive changes not likely to create controversy, proposed changes in the manual must be made available for comment from the courts before the manual is updated or changed. Courts must be notified of any changes in the standards or guidelines, including all those relating to the permanent retention of records.

(Subd (c) amended effective January 1, 2016; adopted effective January 1, 2011.)

(d) Adherence to standards and guidelines

Trial courts must adhere to the requirements contained in the *Trial Court Records Manual*, except as otherwise provided in the manual.

(Subd (d) adopted effective January 1, 2011.)

Rule 10.854 amended effective January 1, 2016; adopted effective January 1, 2011.

Rule 10.855. Superior court records sampling program

(a) Purpose

This rule establishes a program to preserve in perpetuity for study by historians and other researchers all superior court records filed before 1911 and a sample of superior court records filed after December 31, 1910, to document the progress and development of the judicial system, and to preserve evidence of significant events and social trends. This rule is not intended to restrict a court from preserving more records than the minimum required.

(Subd (a) amended effective January 1, 2007.)

(b) Scope

"Records" of the superior court, as used in this rule, does not include records of limited civil, small claims, misdemeanor, or infraction cases.

(Subd (b) adopted effective January 1, 2001.)

(c) Comprehensive and significant records

Each superior court must preserve forever comprehensive and significant court records as follows:

(1) All records filed before 1911;

(2) If practicable, all records filed after 1910 and before 1950;

(3) All case indexes; and

(4) All noncapital cases in which the California Supreme Court has issued a written opinion.

(Subd (c) amended effective July 1, 2016; adopted as subd (b) effective July 1, 1992; previously amended and relettered effective January 1, 2001; previously amended effective January 1, 2007.)

(d) Sample records

If a superior court destroys court records without preserving them in a medium described in (g), the court must preserve forever a sample of court records as provided by this rule of all cases, including sealed, expunged, and other confidential records to the extent permitted by law.

(Subd (d) amended effective July 1, 2016; adopted as subd (c) effective July 1, 1992; relettered effective January 1, 2001; previously amended effective January 1, 2007.)

(e) Court record defined

The "court record" under this rule consists of the following:

(1) All papers and documents in the case folder; but if no case folder is created by the court, all papers and documents that would have been in the case folder if one had been created; and

(2) The case folder, unless all information on the case folder is in papers and documents preserved in a medium described in (g); and

(3) If available, corresponding depositions, daily transcripts, and tapes of electronically recorded proceedings.

(Subd (e) amended effective July 1, 2016; adopted as subd (d) effective July 1, 1992; previously amended and relettered effective January 1, 2001; previously amended effective January 1, 2007.)

(f) Sampling technique

Three courts assigned in rotation by the Judicial Council must preserve the following:

(1) A random sample of 25 percent of their court records for a calendar year, with the exception of the Superior Court of Los Angeles County, which must preserve a random sample of 10 percent of its court records for a calendar year.

(2) All judgment books, minute books, and registers of action if maintained separately from the case files, for the calendar year.

(Subd (f) amended effective July 1, 2016; adopted as subd (e) effective July 1, 1992; repealed, amended, and relettered effective January 1, 2001; previously amended effective January 1, 2007.)

(g) Preservation medium

(1) Comprehensive and significant court records under (c) filed before 1911 must be preserved in their original paper form unless the paper is not available.

(2) Comprehensive and significant court records under (c) filed after 1910 and sample records under (d) must be retained permanently in accord with the requirements of the *Trial Court Records Manual*.

(Subd (g) amended and relettered effective July 1, 2016; adopted as subd (h); previously amended effective January 1, 2001, January 1, 2007, and January 1, 2011.)

(h) Access

The court must ensure the following:

(1) The comprehensive, significant, and sample court records are made reasonably available to all members of the public.

(2) Sealed and confidential records are made available to the public only as provided by law.

(3) If the records are preserved in a medium other than paper, equipment is provided to permit public viewing of the records.

(4) Reasonable provision is made for duplicating the records at cost.

(Subd (h) amended and relettered effective July 1, 2016; adopted as subd (j); previously amended effective January 1, 2007.)

(i) Storage

(1) Until statewide or regional archival facilities are established, each court is responsible for maintaining its comprehensive, significant, and sample court records in a secure and safe environment consistent with the archival significance of the records. The court may deposit the court records in a suitable California archival facility such as a university, college, library, historical society, museum, archive, or research institution whether publicly supported or privately endowed. The court must ensure that the records are kept and preserved according to commonly recognized archival principles and practices of preservation.

(2) If a local archival facility is maintaining the court records, the court may continue to use that facility's services if it meets the storage and access requirements under (h) and (i)(1). If the court solicits archival facilities interested in maintaining the comprehensive, significant, and sample court records, the court must follow the procedures specified under rule 10.856, except that the comprehensive, significant, and sample court records must not be destroyed. Courts may enter into agreements for long-term deposit of records subject to the storage and access provisions of this rule.

(Subd (i) amended and relettered effective July 1, 2016; adopted as subd (k); previously amended effective January 1, 1994, January 1, 2001, and January 1, 2007.)

(j) Application

The sampling program provided in this rule, as amended effective July 1, 2016, applies retroactively to all superior courts.

(Subd (j) repealed and relettered effective January 1, 2018; adopted effective July 1, 2016.)

Rule 10.855 amended effective January 1, 2018; adopted as rule 243.5 effective July 1, 1992; previously amended and renumbered as rule 6.755 effective January 1, 2001, and as rule 10.855 January 1, 2007; previously amended effective January 1, 1994, January 1, 1995, January 1, 2011, July 1, 2013, and July 1, 2016.

Advisory Committee Comment

Subdivision (c)(4). Capital cases are excluded under subdivision (c)(4) because these cases have an automatic right of appeal to the California Supreme Court, and trial court records are retained permanently under Government Code section 68152(c)(1) if the defendant is sentenced to death. Each year, the Judicial Council will make available to the superior courts a list of all noncapital cases in which the California Supreme Court has issued a written opinion.

Subdivision (j). Because the destruction of court records is discretionary, all courts may elect to apply the rule retroactively and destroy court records that are not required to be preserved under subdivisions (c), (d), and (f), but they are not required to do so.

Superior courts that destroyed court records under the prior sampling rule may have preserved only 10 percent of their records (formerly known as the "systematic sample") for the year that they are now assigned to preserve the sample defined in subdivision (f). Except for the Superior Court of Los Angeles County, these courts would not be able to meet the requirement in subdivision (f)(1). So long as these courts continue preserving the 10-percent sample for their assigned year, they will be deemed to have satisfied subdivision (f)(1).

Rule 10.856. Notice of superior court records destruction

(a) Scope

"Records" of the superior court, as used in this rule, do not include records of limited civil, small claims, misdemeanor, or infraction cases.

(Subd (a) adopted effective January 1, 2007.)

(b) Notice

The superior court must give 30 days' written notice of its intent to destroy court records open to public inspection to entities maintained on a master list by the Judicial Council and to any other entities that have informed the court directly that they wish to be notified.

(Subd (b) amended and relettered effective January 1, 2007; adopted as subd (a); previously amended effective January 1, 2001, and July 1, 2001.)

(c) Transfer to requesting entity

Records scheduled for destruction must be permanently transferred to the entity requesting possession of the records on written order of the presiding judge unless the request is denied for good cause shown. The cost of transferring the records must be paid by the requesting party.

(Subd (c) amended and relettered effective January 1, 2007; adopted as subd (b); previously amended effective January 1, 2001.)

(d) Request by two or more entities

If two or more entities request the same records, the presiding judge must order the transfer of those records to the entity that shows the greatest capability of caring for and preserving the records according to commonly recognized archival principles and practices of preservation and access, and that provides the greatest likelihood of making them available for historical or research purposes.

(Subd (d) amended and relettered effective January 1, 2007; adopted as subd (c); previously amended effective January 1, 2001.)

(e) Public access

No entity may receive the records unless the entity agrees to make the records reasonably available to all members of the public. Provision must be made for duplicating the records at cost.

(Subd (e) amended and relettered effective January 1, 2007; adopted as subd (d); previously amended effective January 1, 2001.)

(f) Destruction

If after 30 days no request for transfer of records scheduled for destruction has been received by the court, the clerk may destroy the records not designated for the historical and research program under rule 10.855, under a written order of the presiding judge of the court and in accordance with provisions of the Government Code.

(Subd (f) amended and relettered effective January 1, 2007; adopted as subd (e); previously amended effective January 1, 2001.)

(g) Extension of time

The time for retention of any of the court records specified in the notice may be extended by order of the court on its own motion, or on application of any interested member of the public for good cause shown and on such terms as are just. No fee may be charged for making the application.

(Subd (g) amended and relettered effective January 1, 2007; adopted as subd (f); previously amended effective January 1, 2001.)

(h) Forms

The court must use the following forms to implement the requirements of this rule:

(1) *Notice of Intent to Destroy Superior Court Records; Offer to Transfer Possession* (form REC-001(N)), with a form on the reverse titled *Request for Transfer or Extension of Time for Retention of Superior Court Records* (form REC-001(R)), for optional use by the recipient of the notice; and

(2) *Notice of Hearing on Request for Transfer or Extension of Time for Retention of Superior Court Records; Court Order; Release and Receipt of Superior Court Records* (form REC-002(N)).

(Subd (h) amended effective July 1, 2010; adopted as subd (g); previously amended effective January 1, 2001; previously amended and relettered effective January 1, 2007.)

Rule 10.856 amended effective July 1, 2010; adopted as rule 243.6 effective January 1, 1994; previously amended effective July 1, 2001; previously amended and renumbered as rule 6.756 effective January 1, 2001, and as rule 10.856 effective January 1, 2007.

Chapter 11
Trial Court Automation

Chapter 11 renumbered effective January 1, 2008; adopted as Chapter 5 effective January 1, 2001; previously amended and renumbered as Chapter 10 effective January 1, 2007.

Rule 10.870.   Trial court automation standards

Each superior court that acquires, develops, enhances, or maintains automated accounting or case management systems through funding provided under Government Code section 68090.8 must comply with the standards approved by the Judicial Council. The approved standards are stated in *Judicial Council Trial Court Automation Standards.*

Rule 10.870 amended effective January 1, 2016; adopted as rule 1011 effective March 1, 1992; renumbered as rule 999.1 effective July 1, 1993; previously amended and renumbered as rule 10.870 effective January 1, 2007.

Chapter 12
Trial Court Management of Civil Cases

Chapter 12 renumbered effective January 1, 2008; adopted as Chapter 11 effective January 1, 2007.

Rule 10.900.   Case management and calendaring system

Each superior court must adopt a case management and calendaring system for general civil cases that will advance the goals stated in standard 2.1 of the California Standards of Judicial Administration.

Rule 10.900 amended and renumbered effective January 1, 2007; adopted as rule 204.1 effective July 1, 2002.

Rule 10.901.   Internal management procedures

Each court must:

(1) Maintain a calendar and caseflow management system that will ensure that a sufficient number of cases are set for trial, based on the court's experience, so that all departments will be occupied with judicial business;

(2) Adopt for judges and court personnel an internal operations manual of policies and procedures necessary for the efficient operation and management of the court;

(3) Maintain and periodically review for accuracy written local court procedures, policies, and operating practices not contained in local rules for quick, accurate, and complete reference; and

(4) Ensure that calendaring functions are performed as directed by the court and that personnel rendering direct and immediate service to the court are within its administrative control to the maximum extent consistent with the existing organizational structures.

Rule 10.901 amended and renumbered effective January 1, 2007; adopted as rule 208 effective January 1, 1985; previously amended and renumbered as rule 204.2 effective July 1, 2002.

Rule 10.910.   Assigned cases to be tried or dismissed—notification to presiding judge

(a) Assignment of cases for trial

In a court employing the master calendar, each case transferred to a trial department must be tried, ordered off the calendar, or dismissed unless, for good cause arising after the commencement of the trial, the judge of the trial department continues the case for further hearing or, with the consent of the judge supervising the master calendar, reassigns the case to the judge supervising the master calendar for further disposition.

(Subd (a) amended effective January 1, 2007; adopted as untitled subd effective January 1, 1985; previously amended and lettered effective July 1, 2002.)

(b) Notification to presiding judge

A judge who has finished or continued the trial of a case or any special matter must immediately notify the judge supervising the master calendar. The judge to whose department a cause is assigned for trial or for hearing must accept the assignment unless disqualified or, for other good cause stated to the judge supervising the master calendar, the judge supervising the master calendar determines that in the interest of justice the cause should not be tried or heard before the judge. When the judge has refused a cause and is not disqualified, the judge must state the reasons in writing unless the judge supervising the master calendar has concurred.

(Subd (b) amended and lettered effective July 1, 2002; adopted as untitled subd effective January 1, 1985.)

Rule 10.910 amended and renumbered effective January 1, 2007; adopted as rule 226 effective January 1, 1985; previously amended effective July 1, 2002.

Chapter 13
Trial Court Management of Criminal Cases

Chapter 13 renumbered effective January 1, 2008; adopted as Chapter 12 effective January 1, 2007.

Rule 10.950.   Role of presiding judge, supervising judge, criminal division, and master calendar department in courts having more than three judges

The presiding judge of a court having more than three judges may designate one or more departments primarily to hear criminal cases. Two or more departments so designated must be the criminal division. The presiding judge may designate supervising judges for the criminal division, but retains final authority over all criminal and civil case assignments.

Rule 10.950 amended and renumbered effective January 1, 2007; adopted as rule 227.1 effective January 1, 1985.

Rule 10.951.   Duties of supervising judge of the criminal division

(a) Duties

In addition to any other duties assigned by the presiding judge or imposed by these rules, a supervising judge of the criminal division must assign criminal matters requiring a hearing or cases requiring trial to a trial department.

(Subd (a) amended effective January 1, 2007.)

(b) Arraignments, pretrial motions, and readiness conferences

The presiding judge, supervising judge, or other designated judge must conduct arraignments, hear and determine any pretrial motions, preside over readiness conferences, and, where not inconsistent with law, assist in the disposition of cases without trial.

(Subd (b) amended effective January 1, 2008; previously amended effective January 1, 2007.)

(c) Mental health case protocols

The presiding judge, supervising judge, or other designated judge, in conjunction with the justice partners designated in rule 10.952, is encouraged to develop local protocols for cases involving offenders with mental illness or co-occurring disorders to ensure early identification of and appropriate treatment for offenders with mental illness or co-occurring disorders with the goals of reducing recidivism, responding to public safety concerns, and providing better outcomes for those offenders while using resources responsibly and reducing costs.

(Subd (c) adopted effective January 1, 2014.)

(d) Additional judges

To the extent that the business of the court requires, the presiding judge may designate additional judges under the direction of the supervising judge to perform the duties specified in this rule.

(Subd (d) relettered effective January 1, 2014; adopted as subd (c).)

(e) Courts without supervising judge

In a court having no supervising judge, the presiding judge performs the duties of a supervising judge.

(Subd (e) relettered effective January 1, 2014; previously amended as subd (d) effective January 1, 2007.)

Rule 10.951 amended effective January 1, 2014; adopted as rule 227.2 effective January 1, 1985; previously amended and renumbered effective January 1, 2007; previously amended effective January 1, 2008.

Rule 10.952.   Meetings concerning the criminal court system

The supervising judge or, if none, the presiding judge must designate judges of the court to attend regular meetings to be held with the district attorney; public defender; representatives of the local bar, probation department, parole office, sheriff department, police departments, and Forensic Conditional Release Program (CONREP); county mental health director or his or her designee; county alcohol and drug programs director or his or her designee; court personnel; and other interested persons to identify and eliminate problems in the criminal court system and to discuss other problems of mutual concern.

Rule 10.952 amended effective January 1, 2015; adopted as rule 227.8 effective January 1, 1985; previously amended and renumbered effective January 1, 2007; previously amended effective January 1, 2014.

Rule 10.953.   Procedures for disposition of cases before the preliminary hearing

(a) Disposition before preliminary hearing

Superior courts having more than three judges must, in cooperation with the district attorney and defense bar, adopt procedures to facilitate dispositions before the preliminary hearing and at all other stages of the proceedings. The procedures may include:

(1) Early, voluntary, informal discovery, consistent with part 2, title 6, chapter 10 of the Penal Code (commencing with section 1054); and

(2) The use of superior court judges as magistrates to conduct readiness conferences before the preliminary hearing and to assist, where not inconsistent with law, in the early disposition of cases.

(Subd (a) amended effective January 1, 2007; previously amended effective June 6, 1990, and January 1, 1991.)

(b) Case to be disposed of under rule 4.114

Pleas of guilty or no contest resulting from proceedings under (a) must be disposed of as provided in rule 4.114.

(Subd (b) amended effective January 1, 2007; previously amended effective July 1, 2001.)

Rule 10.953 amended and renumbered effective January 1, 2007; adopted as rule 227.10 effective January 1, 1985; previously amended effective June 6, 1990, January 1, 1991, and July 1, 2001.

Chapter 14
Management of Self-Help Centers

Chapter 14 adopted effective July 1, 2008.

Rule 10.960.   Court self-help centers

(a) Scope and application

This rule applies to all court-based self-help centers whether the services provided by the center are managed by the court or by an entity other than the court.

(Subd (a) adopted effective January 1, 2008.)

(b) Purpose and core court function

Providing access to justice for self-represented litigants is a priority for California courts. The services provided by court self-help centers facilitate the timely and cost-effective processing of cases involving self-represented litigants and improve the delivery of justice to the public. Court programs, policies, and procedures designed to assist self-represented litigants and effectively manage cases involving self-represented litigants at all stages must be incorporated and budgeted as core court functions.

(Subd (b) adopted effective January 1, 2008.)

(c) Staffing

Court self-help centers provide assistance to self-represented litigants. A court self-help center must include an attorney and other qualified staff who provide information and education to self-represented litigants about the justice process, and who work within the court to provide for the effective management of cases involving self-represented litigants.

(Subd (c) adopted effective January 1, 2008.)

(d) Neutrality and availability

The information and education provided by court self-help centers must be neutral and unbiased, and services must be available to all sides of a case.

(Subd (d) adopted effective January 1, 2008.)

(e) Guidelines and procedures

The Advisory Committee on Providing Access and Fairness must recommend to the council updates to the *Guidelines for the Operation of Self-Help Centers in California Trial Courts* as needed. It should, in collaboration with judges, court executives, attorneys, and other parties with demonstrated interest in services to self-represented litigants, develop and disseminate guidelines, procedures and best practices for the operation of court self-help centers. The guidelines and procedures must address the following topics:

(1) Location and hours of operation;

(2) Scope of services;

(3) Attorney qualifications;

(4) Other staffing qualifications and supervision requirements;

(5) Language access;

(6) Contracts with entities other than the court that provide self-help services;

(7) Use of technology;

(8) Ethics;

(9) Efficiency of operation; and

(10) Security.

(Subd (e) amended effective January 1, 2015; adopted effective January 1, 2008; previously amended effective February 20, 2014.)

(f) Budget and funding

A court must include in its annual budget funding necessary for operation of its self-help center. In analyzing and making recommendations on the allocation of funding for a court self-help center, Judicial Council staff will consider the degree to which individual courts have been successful in meeting the guidelines and procedures for the operation of the self-help center.

(Subd (f) amended effective January 1, 2016; adopted effective January 1, 2008.)
Rule 10.960 amended effective January 1, 2016; adopted effective January 1, 2008; previously amended effective February 20, 2014, and January 1, 2015.

Division 5
Appellate Court Administration

Chap. 1.   Rules Relating to the Supreme Court and Courts of Appeal. Rules 10.1000–10.1030.
Chap. 2.   Rules Relating to the Superior Court Appellate Division. Rules 10.1100–10.1108.

Chapter 1
Rules Relating to the Supreme Court and Courts of Appeal

Rule 10.1000.   Transfer of causes

(a) Transfer by Supreme Court

(1) The Supreme Court may transfer a cause:

(A) To itself from a Court of Appeal;

(B) From itself to a Court of Appeal;

(C) Between Courts of Appeal; or

(D) Between divisions of a Court of Appeal.

(2) The clerk of the transferee court must promptly send each party a copy of the transfer order with the new case number, if any.

(Subd (a) amended effective January 1, 2007.)

(b) Transfer by a Court of Appeal administrative presiding justice

(1) A Court of Appeal administrative presiding justice may transfer causes between divisions of that court as follows:

(A) If multiple appeals or writ petitions arise from the same trial court action or proceeding, the presiding justice may transfer the later appeals or petitions to the division assigned the first appeal or petition.

(B) If, because of recusals, a division does not have three justices qualified to decide a cause, the presiding justice may transfer it to a division randomly selected by the clerk.

(2) The clerk must promptly notify the parties of the division to which the cause was transferred.

Rule 10.1000 amended and renumbered effective January 1, 2007; adopted as rule 47.1 effective January 1, 2003.

Advisory Committee Comment

Subdivision (a). Subdivision (a)(1) implements article VI, section 12(a) of the Constitution. As used in article VI, section 12(a) and in the rule, the term "cause" is broadly construed to include " 'all cases, matters, and proceedings of every description' " adjudicated by the Courts of Appeal and the Supreme Court. *(In re Rose* (2000) 22 Cal.4th 430, 540, quoting *In re Wells* (1917) 174 Cal. 467, 471.)

Rule 10.1004.   Court of Appeal administrative presiding justice

(a) Designation

(1) In a Court of Appeal with more than one division, the Chief Justice may designate a presiding justice to act as administrative presiding justice. The administrative presiding justice serves at the pleasure of the Chief Justice for the period specified in the designation order.

(2) The administrative presiding justice must designate another member of the court to serve as acting administrative presiding justice in the administrative presiding justice's absence. If the administrative presiding justice does not make that designation, the Chief Justice must do so.

(3) In a Court of Appeal with only one division, the presiding justice acts as the administrative presiding justice.

(Subd (a) amended effective January 1, 2007.)

(b) Responsibilities

The administrative presiding justice is responsible for leading the court, establishing policies, promoting access to justice for all members of the public, providing a forum for the fair and expeditious resolution of disputes, and maximizing the use of judicial and other resources.

(c) Duties

The administrative presiding justice must perform any duties delegated by a majority of the justices in the district with the Chief Justice's concurrence. In addition, the administrative presiding justice has responsibility for the following matters:

(1) *Personnel*

The administrative presiding justice has general direction and supervision of the clerk/executive officer and all court employees except those assigned to a particular justice or division;

(2) *Unassigned matters*

The administrative presiding justice has the authority of a presiding justice with respect to any matter that has not been assigned to a particular division;

(3) *Judicial Council*

The administrative presiding justice cooperates with the Chief Justice and any officer authorized to act for the Chief Justice in connection with the making of reports and the assignment of judges or retired judges under article VI, section 6 of the California Constitution;

(4) *Transfer of cases*

The administrative presiding justice cooperates with the Chief Justice in expediting judicial business and equalizing the work of judges by recommending, when appropriate, the transfer of cases by the Supreme Court under article VI, section 12 of the California Constitution;

(5) *Administration*

The administrative presiding justice supervises the administration of the court's day-to-day operations, including personnel matters, but must secure the approval of a majority of the justices in the district before implementing any change in court policies;

(6) *Budget*

The administrative presiding justice has sole authority in the district over the budget as allocated by the Chair of the Judicial Council, including budget transfers, execution of purchase orders, obligation of funds, and approval of payments; and

(7) *Facilities*

The administrative presiding justice, except as provided in (d), has sole authority in the district over the operation, maintenance, renovation, expansion, and assignment of all facilities used and occupied by the district.

(Subd (c) amended effective January 1, 2018; previously amended effective January 1, 2007.)

(d) Geographically separate divisions

Under the general oversight of the administrative presiding justice, the presiding justice of a geographically separate division:

(1) Generally directs and supervises all of the division's court employees not assigned to a particular justice;

(2) Has authority to act on behalf of the division regarding day-to-day operations;

(3) Administers the division budget for day-to-day operations, including expenses for maintenance of facilities and equipment; and

(4) Operates, maintains, and assigns space in all facilities used and occupied by the division.

(Subd (d) amended effective January 1, 2007.)

Rule 10.1004 amended effective January 1, 2018; repealed and adopted as rule 75 effective January 1, 2005; previously amended and renumbered effective January 1, 2007.

Rule 10.1008.   Courts of Appeal with more than one division

Appeals and original proceedings filed in a Court of Appeal with more than one division, or transferred to such a court without designation of a division, may be assigned to divisions in a way that will equalize the distribution of business among them. The clerk/executive officer of the Court of Appeal must keep records showing the divisions in which cases and proceedings are pending.

Rule 10.1008 amended effective January 1, 2018; repealed and adopted as rule 47 effective January 1, 2005; previously amended and renumbered effective January 1, 2007.

Rule 10.1012.   Supervising progress of appeals

(a) Duty to ensure prompt filing

The administrative presiding justices of Courts of Appeal with more than one division in the same city and the presiding justices of all other Courts of Appeal are generally responsible for ensuring that all appellate records and briefs are promptly filed. Staff must be provided for that purpose, to the extent that funds are appropriated and available.

(Subd (a) amended effective January 1, 2007.)

(b) Authority

Notwithstanding any other rule, the administrative presiding justices and presiding justices referred to in (a) may:

(1) Grant or deny applications to extend the time to file records, briefs, and other documents, except that a presiding justice may extend the time to file briefs in conjunction with an order to augment the record;

(2) Order the dismissal of an appeal or any other authorized sanction for noncompliance with these rules, if no application to extend time or for relief from default has been filed before the order is entered; and

(3) Grant relief from default or from a sanction other than dismissal imposed for the default.

(Subd (b) amended effective January 1, 2007.)

Rule 10.1012 amended and renumbered effective January 1, 2007; repealed and adopted as rule 77 effective January 1, 2005.

Rule 10.1016.   Notice of failure to perform judicial duties

(a) Notice

(1) The Chief Justice or presiding justice must notify the Commission on Judicial Performance of a reviewing court justice's:

(A) Substantial failure to perform judicial duties, including any habitual neglect of duty; or

(B) Disability-caused absences totaling more than 90 court days in a 12-month period, excluding absences for authorized vacations and for attending schools, conferences, and judicial workshops.

(2) If the affected justice is a presiding justice, the administrative presiding justice must give the notice.

(Subd (a) amended effective January 1, 2007.)

(b) Copy to justice

The Chief Justice, administrative presiding justice, or presiding justice must give the affected justice a copy of any notice under (a).

Rule 10.1016 amended and renumbered effective January 1, 2007; repealed and adopted as rule 78 effective January 1, 2005.

Rule 10.1017.   Notification to State Bar of attorney misconduct

(a) Notification by justice

When notification to the State Bar is required under Business and Professions Code section 6086.7, the senior justice issuing the order or the justice authoring the opinion that triggers the notification requirement under section 6086.7 is responsible for notifying the State Bar. The justice may direct the Clerk to notify the State Bar.

(Subd (a) adopted effective January 1, 2014.)

(b) Contents of notice

The notice must include the State Bar member's full name and State Bar number, if known, and a copy of the order or opinion that triggered the notification requirement.

(Subd (b) adopted effective January 1, 2014.)

(c) Notification to attorney

If notification to the State Bar is made under this rule, the person who notified the State Bar must also inform the attorney who is the subject of the notification that the matter has been referred to the State Bar.

(Subd (c) adopted effective January 1, 2014.)

Rule 10.1017 adopted effective January 1, 2014.

Advisory Committee Comment

Business and Professions Code section 6086.7 requires a court to notify the State Bar of any of the following: (1) a final order of contempt imposed on an attorney that may involve grounds warranting discipline under the State Bar Act; (2) a modification or reversal of a judgment in a judicial proceeding based in whole or in part on the misconduct, incompetent representation, or willful misrepresentation of an attorney; (3) the imposition of any judicial sanctions on an attorney of $1,000 or more, except sanctions for failure to make discovery; or (4) the imposition of any civil penalty on an attorney under Family Code section 8620. If the notification pertains to a final order of contempt, Business and Professions Code section 6086.7(a)(1) requires the court to transmit to the State Bar a copy of the relevant minutes, final order, and transcript, if one exists. This rule is intended to clarify which justice has the responsibility of notifying the State Bar under section 6086.7 and the required contents of the notice. In addition to the requirements stated in Business and Professions Code section 6086.7, judges are subject to canon 3D(2) of the California Code of Judicial Ethics, which states: "Whenever a judge has personal knowledge, or concludes in a judicial decision, that a lawyer has committed misconduct or has violated any provision of the Rules of Professional Conduct, the judge shall take appropriate corrective action, which may include reporting the violation to the appropriate authority." The Advisory Committee

Commentary states: "Appropriate corrective action could include direct communication with the judge or lawyer who has committed the violation, other direct action, such as a confidential referral to a judicial or lawyer assistance program, or a report of the violation to the presiding judge, appropriate authority, or other agency or body. Judges should note that in addition to the action required by Canon 3D(2), California law imposes mandatory additional reporting requirements on judges regarding lawyer misconduct. See Business and Professions Code section 6068.7."

Rule 10.1020.   Reviewing court clerk/executive officer

(a) Selection

A reviewing court may employ a clerk/executive officer selected in accordance with procedures adopted by the court.

(Subd (a) amended effective January 1, 2018.)

(b) Responsibilities

Acting under the general direction and supervision of the administrative presiding justice, the clerk/executive officer is responsible for planning, organizing, coordinating, and directing, with full authority and accountability, the management of the office of the clerk/executive officer and all nonjudicial support activities in a manner that promotes access to justice for all members of the public, provides a forum for the fair and expeditious resolution of disputes, and maximizes the use of judicial and other resources.

(Subd (b) amended effective January 1, 2018.)

(c) Duties

Under the direction of the administrative presiding justice, the clerk/executive officer has the following duties:

(1) *Personnel*

The clerk/executive officer directs and supervises all court employees assigned to the clerk/executive officer by the administrative presiding justice and ensures that the court receives a full range of human resources support;

(2) *Budget*

The clerk/executive officer develops, administers, and monitors the court budget and develops practices and procedures to ensure that annual expenditures are within the budget;

(3) *Contracts*

The clerk/executive officer negotiates contracts on the court's behalf in accord with established contracting procedures and applicable laws;

(4) *Calendar management*

The clerk/executive officer employs and supervises efficient calendar and caseflow management, including analyzing and evaluating pending caseloads and recommending effective calendar management techniques;

(5) *Technology*

The clerk/executive officer coordinates technological and automated systems activities to assist the court;

(6) *Facilities*

The clerk/executive officer coordinates facilities, space planning, court security, and business services support, including the purchase and management of equipment and supplies;

(7) *Records*

The clerk/executive officer creates and manages uniform record-keeping systems, collecting data on pending and completed judicial business and the court's internal operation as the court and Judicial Council require;

(8) *Recommendations*

The clerk/executive officer identifies problems and recommends policy, procedural, and administrative changes to the court;

(9) *Public relations*

The clerk/executive officer represents the court to internal and external customers—including the other branches of government—on issues pertaining to the court;

(10) *Liaison*

The clerk/executive officer acts as liaison with other governmental agencies;

(11) *Committees*

The clerk/executive officer provides staff for judicial committees;

(12) *Administration*

The clerk/executive officer develops and implements administrative and operational programs and policies for the court and the office of the clerk/executive officer; and

(13) *Other*

The clerk/executive officer performs other duties as the administrative presiding justice directs.

(Subd (c) amended effective January 1, 2018; previously amended effective January 1, 2007.)

(d) Geographically separate divisions

Under the general oversight of the clerk/executive officer, an assistant clerk/executive officer of a geographically separate division has responsibility for the nonjudicial support activities of that division.

(Subd (d) amended effective January 1, 2018.)

Rule 10.1020 amended effective January 1, 2018; repealed and adopted as rule 76.1 effective January 1, 2005; previously amended and renumbered effective January 1, 2007.

Rule 10.1024.   Court of Appeal minutes

(a) Purpose

Court of Appeal minutes should record the court's significant public acts and permit the public to follow the major events in the history of cases coming before the court.

(b) Required contents of minutes

The minutes must include:

(1) The filing date of each opinion, showing whether it was ordered published;

(2) Orders granting or denying rehearings or modifying opinions;

(3) Orders affecting an opinion's publication status, if issued after the opinion was filed;

(4) Summaries of all courtroom proceedings, showing at a minimum:

(A) The cases called for argument;

(B) The justices hearing argument;

(C) The name of the attorney arguing for each party; and

(D) Whether the case was submitted at the close of argument or the court requested further briefing;

(5) The date of submission, if other than the date of argument;

(6) Orders vacating submission, including the reason for vacating and the resubmission date;

(7) Orders dismissing appeals for lack of jurisdiction;

(8) Orders consolidating cases;

(9) Orders affecting a judgment or its finality date; and

(10) Orders changing or correcting any of the above.

(Subd (b) amended effective January 1, 2007.)

(c) Optional contents of minutes

At the court's discretion, the minutes may include such other matter as:

(1) Assignments of justices by the Chief Justice;

(2) Reports of the Commission on Judicial Appointments confirming justices; and

(3) Memorials.

(Subd (c) amended effective January 1, 2007.)

Rule 10.1024 amended and renumbered effective January 1, 2007; adopted as rule 71 effective January 1, 2005.

Rule 10.1028.   Preservation and destruction of Court of Appeal records

(a) Form or forms in which records may be preserved

(1) Court of Appeal records may be created, maintained, and preserved in any form or forms of communication or representation, including paper or optical, electronic, magnetic, micrographic, or photographic media or other technology, if the form or forms of representation or communication satisfy the standards or guidelines for the creation, maintenance, reproduction, and preservation of court records established under rule 10.854.

(2) If records are preserved in a medium other than paper, the following provisions of Government Code section 68150 apply: subdivisions (c)–(*l*), excluding subdivision (i)(1).

(Subd (a) amended effective January 1, 2013.)

(b) Methods for signing, subscribing, or verifying documents

Any notice, order, ruling, decision, opinion, memorandum, certificate of service, or similar document issued by an appellate court or by a judicial officer of an appellate court may be signed, subscribed, or verified using a computer or other technology in accordance with procedures, standards, and guidelines established by the Judicial Council. Notwithstanding any other provision of law, all notices, orders, rulings, decisions, opinions, memoranda, certificates of service, or similar documents that are signed, subscribed, or verified by computer or other technological means under this subdivision shall have the same validity, and the same legal force and effect, as paper documents signed, subscribed, or verified by an appellate court or a judicial officer of the court.

(Subd (b) adopted effective January 1, 2013.)

(c) Permanent records

The clerk/executive officer of the Court of Appeal must permanently keep the court's minutes and a register of appeals and original proceedings.

(Subd (c) amended effective January 1, 2018; relettered from subd (b) effective January 1, 2013.)

(d) Time to keep other records

(1) Except as provided in (2), the clerk/executive officer may destroy all other records in a case 10 years after the decision becomes final, as ordered by the administrative presiding justice or, in a court with only one division, by the presiding justice.

(2) In a criminal case in which the court affirms a judgment of conviction, the clerk/executive officer must keep the original reporter's transcript or a true and correct electronic copy of the transcript for 20 years after the decision becomes final.

(Subd (d) amended effective January 1, 2018; relettered from subd (c) effective January 1, 2013; previously amended effective January 1, 2017.)

Rule 10.1028 amended effective January 1, 2018; adopted as rule 70 effective January 1, 2005; previously renumbered effective January 1, 2007; previously amended effective January 1, 2013, and January 1, 2017.

Advisory Committee Comment

Subdivision (d). Subdivision (d) permits the Court of Appeal to keep an electronic copy of the reporter's transcript in lieu of keeping the original. Although subdivision (a) allows the Court of Appeal to maintain its records in any format that satisfies the otherwise applicable standards for maintenance of court records, including electronic formats, the original of a reporter's transcript is required to be on paper under Code of Civil Procedure section 271(a). Subdivision (d) therefore specifies that an electronic copy may be kept, to clarify that the paper original need not be kept by the court.

Rule 10.1030.   Local rules of Courts of Appeal

(a) Publication

(1) A Court of Appeal must submit any local rule it adopts to the Reporter of Decisions for publication in the advance pamphlets of the Official Reports.

(2) As used in this rule, "publication" means printing in the manner in which amendments to the California Rules of Court are printed.

(Subd (a) relettered effective January 1, 2007.)

(b) Effective date

A local rule cannot take effect sooner than 45 days after the publication date of the advance pamphlet in which it is printed.

(Subd (b) relettered effective January 1, 2007.)

Rule 10.1030 amended and renumbered effective January 1, 2007; repealed and adopted as rule 80 effective January 1, 2005.

Chapter 2
Rules Relating to the Superior Court Appellate Division

Chapter 2 adopted effective January 1, 2009.

Rule 10.1100. Assignments to the appellate division
Rule 10.1104. Presiding judge
Rule 10.1108. Sessions

Rule 10.1100.   Assignments to the appellate division

(a) Goal

In making assignments to the appellate division, the Chief Justice will consider the goal of promoting the independence and the quality of the appellate division.

(Subd (a) adopted effective January 1, 2009.)

(b) Factors considered

Factors considered in making the assignments may include:

(1) Length of service as a judge;

(2) Reputation in the judicial community;

(3) Degree of separateness of the appellate division work from the judge's regular assignments; and

(4) Any recommendation of the presiding judge.

(Subd (b) adopted effective January 1, 2009.)

(c) Who may be assigned

Judges assigned may include judges from another county, judges retired from the superior court or a court of higher jurisdiction, or a panel of judges from different superior courts who sit in turn in each of those superior courts.

(Subd (c) adopted effective January 1, 2009.)

(d) Terms of service

In specifying terms of service to the appellate division, the Chief Justice will consider the needs of the court.

(Subd (d) adopted effective January 1, 2009.)
Rule 10.1100 adopted effective January 1, 2009.

Advisory Committee Comment

The Chief Justice is responsible for assigning judges to the appellate division as provided in article VI, section 4 of the California Constitution and by statute.

Rule 10.1104.   Presiding judge
(a) Designation of acting presiding judge
(1) The presiding judge of the appellate division must designate another member of the appellate division to serve as acting presiding judge in the absence of the presiding judge. If the presiding judge does not make that designation, the appellate division judge among those present who has the greatest seniority in the appellate division must act as presiding judge. When the judges are of equal seniority in the appellate division, the judge who is also senior in service in the superior court must act as presiding judge.

(2) As used in these rules, "presiding judge" includes acting presiding judge.

(Subd (a) adopted effective January 1, 2009.)

(b) Responsibilities
The presiding judge of the appellate division may convene the appellate division at any time and must supervise the business of the division.

(Subd (b) adopted effective January 1, 2009.)
Rule 10.1104 adopted effective January 1, 2009.

Advisory Committee Comment

Under Code of Civil Procedure section 77(a), the Chief Justice is responsible for designating one of the judges of each appellate division as the presiding judge.

Rule 10.1108.   Sessions
The appellate division of each superior court must hold a session at least once each quarter unless there are no matters set for oral argument that quarter. The time and place of any session is determined by the presiding judge of the appellate division.

Rule 10.1108 adopted effective January 1, 2009.

Standards of Judicial Administration

Title 1
Standards for All Courts
[Reserved]

Title 2
Standards for Proceedings in the Trial Courts

Standard 2.1. Case management and delay reduction—statement of general principles
Standard 2.2. Trial court case disposition time goals
Standard 2.10. Procedures for determining the need for an interpreter and a preappearance interview
Standard 2.11. Interpreted proceedings—instructing participants on procedure
Standard 2.20. Trial management standards
Standard 2.25. Uninterrupted jury selection
Standard 2.30. Judicial comment on verdict or mistrial

Standard 2.1.   Case management and delay reduction—statement of general principles

(a) Elimination of all unnecessary delays

Trial courts should be guided by the general principle that from the commencement of litigation to its resolution, whether by trial or settlement, any elapsed time other than reasonably required for pleadings, discovery, preparation, and court events is unacceptable and should be eliminated.

(Subd (a) amended and lettered effective January 1, 2004; adopted as part of unlettered subdivision effective July 1, 1987.)

(b) Court responsible for the pace of litigation

To enable the just and efficient resolution of cases, the court, not the lawyers or litigants, should control the pace of litigation. A strong judicial commitment is essential to reducing delay and, once achieved, maintaining a current docket.

(Subd (b) amended and lettered effective January 1, 2004; adopted as part of unlettered subdivision effective July 1, 1987.)

(c) Presiding judge's role

The presiding judge of each court should take an active role in advancing the goals of delay reduction and in formulating and implementing local rules and procedures to accomplish the following:

(1) The expeditious and timely resolution of cases, after full and careful consideration consistent with the ends of justice;

(2) The identification and elimination of local rules, forms, practices, and procedures that are obstacles to delay reduction, are inconsistent with statewide case management rules, or prevent the court from effectively managing its cases;

(3) The formulation and implementation of a system of tracking cases from filing to disposition; and

(4) The training of judges and nonjudicial administrative personnel in delay reduction rules and procedures adopted in the local jurisdiction.

(Subd (c) amended and lettered effective January 1, 2004; adopted as part of unlettered subdivision effective July 1, 1987.)

Standard 2.1 amended and renumbered effective January 1, 2007; adopted as sec. 2 effective July 1, 1987; previously amended effective January 1, 1994, and January 1, 2004.

Standard 2.2.   Trial court case disposition time goals
(a) Trial Court Delay Reduction Act

The recommended goals for case disposition time in the trial courts in this standard are adopted under Government Code sections 68603 and 68620.

(Subd (a) amended effective January 1, 2007; adopted effective July 1, 1987; relettered effective January 1, 1989; previously amended effective January 1, 2004.)

(b) Statement of purpose

The recommended time goals are intended to guide the trial courts in applying the policies and principles of standard 2.1. They are administrative, justice-oriented guidelines to be used in the management of the courts. They are intended to improve the administration of justice by encouraging prompt disposition of all matters coming before the courts. The goals apply to all cases filed and are not meant to create deadlines for individual cases. Through its case management practices, a court may achieve or exceed the goals stated in this standard for the overall disposition of cases. The goals should be applied in a fair, practical, and flexible manner. They are not to be used as the basis for sanctions against any court or judge.

(Subd (b) amended effective January 1, 2007; adopted effective July 1, 1987, as (1); relettered effective January 1, 1989; previously amended effective January 1, 2004.)

(c) Definition

The definition of "general civil case" in rule 1.6 applies to this section. It includes both unlimited and limited civil cases.

(Subd (c) amended effective January 1, 2007; adopted effective January 1, 2004.)

(d) Civil cases—processing time goals

The goal of each trial court should be to process general civil cases so that all cases are disposed of within two years of filing.

(Subd (d) amended and relettered effective January 1, 2004; adopted effective July 1, 1987, as (2); previously amended effective July 1, 1988; amended and relettered as subd (c) effective January 1, 1989.)

(e) Civil cases—rate of disposition

Each trial court should dispose of at least as many civil cases as are filed each year and, if necessary to meet the case-processing goal in (d), dispose of more cases than are filed. As the court disposes of inactive cases, it should identify active cases that may require judicial attention.

(Subd (e) amended effective January 1, 2007; adopted effective July 1, 1987, as (3); previously amended effective July 1, 1988; previously amended and relettered as subd (d) effective January 1, 1989, and as subd (e) effective January 1, 2004.)

(f) General civil cases—case disposition time goals

The goal of each trial court should be to manage general civil cases, except those exempt under (g), so that they meet the following case disposition time goals:

(1) *Unlimited civil cases:*

The goal of each trial court should be to manage unlimited civil cases from filing so that:

(A) 75 percent are disposed of within 12 months;

(B) 85 percent are disposed of within 18 months; and

(C) 100 percent are disposed of within 24 months.

(2) *Limited civil cases:*

The goal of each trial court should be to manage limited civil cases from filing so that:

(A) 90 percent are disposed of within 12 months;

(B) 98 percent are disposed of within 18 months; and

(C) 100 percent are disposed of within 24 months.

(3) *Individualized case management*

The goals in (1) and (2) are guidelines for the court's disposition of all unlimited and limited civil cases filed in that court. In managing individual civil cases, the court must consider each case on its merits. To enable the fair and efficient resolution of civil cases, each case should be set for trial as soon as appropriate for that individual case consistent with rule 3.729.

(Subd (f) amended effective January 1, 2007; adopted as subd (g) effective July 1, 1987; relettered as subd (h) effective January 1, 1989; amended effective July 1, 1991; previously amended and relettered as subd (f) effective January 1, 2004.)

(g) Exceptional civil cases

A general civil case that meets the criteria in rules 3.715 and 3.400 and that involves exceptional circumstances or will require continuing review is exempt from the time goals in (d) and (f). Every exceptional case should be monitored to ensure its timely disposition consistent with the exceptional circumstances, with the goal of disposing of the case within three years.

(Subd (g) amended effective January 1, 2007; adopted effective January 1, 2004.)

(h) Small claims cases

The goals for small claims cases are:

(1) 90 percent disposed of within 75 days after filing; and

(2) 100 percent disposed of within 95 days after filing.

(Subd (h) adopted effective January 1, 2004.)

(i) Unlawful detainer cases

The goals for unlawful detainer cases are:

(1) 90 percent disposed of within 30 days after filing; and

(2) 100 percent disposed of within 45 days after filing.

(Subd (i) adopted effective January 1, 2004.)

(j) Felony cases—processing time goals

Except for capital cases, all felony cases disposed of should have a total elapsed processing time of no more than one year from the defendant's first arraignment to disposition.

(Subd (j) amended effective January 1, 2007; adopted effective January 1, 2004.)

(k) Misdemeanor cases

The goals for misdemeanor cases are:

(1) 90 percent disposed of within 30 days after the defendant's first arraignment on the complaint;

(2) 98 percent disposed of within 90 days after the defendant's first arraignment on the complaint; and

(3) 100 percent disposed of within 120 days after the defendant's first arraignment on the complaint.

(Subd (k) adopted effective January 1, 2004.)

(l) Felony preliminary examinations

The goal for felony cases at the time of the preliminary examination (excluding murder cases in which the prosecution seeks the death penalty) should be disposition by dismissal, by interim disposition by certified plea of guilty, or by finding of probable cause, so that:

(1) 90 percent of cases are disposed of within 30 days after the defendant's first arraignment on the complaint;

(2) 98 percent of cases are disposed of within 45 days after the defendant's first arraignment on the complaint; and

(3) 100 percent of cases are disposed of within 90 days after the defendant's first arraignment on the complaint.

(Subd (l) adopted effective January 1, 2004.)

(m) Exceptional criminal cases

An exceptional criminal case is not exempt from the time goal in (j), but case progress should be separately reported under the Judicial Branch Statistical Information System (JBSIS) regulations.

(Subd (m) amended effective January 1, 2007; adopted effective January 1, 2004.)

(n) Cases removed from court's control excluded from computation of time

If a case is removed from the court's control, the period of time until the case is restored to court control should be excluded from the case disposition time goals. The matters that remove a case from the court's control for the purposes of this section include:

(1) Civil cases:

(A) The filing of a notice of conditional settlement under rule 3.1385;

(B) An automatic stay resulting from the filing of an action in a federal bankruptcy court;

(C) The removal of the case to federal court;

(D) An order of a federal court or higher state court staying the case;

(E) An order staying the case based on proceedings in a court of equal standing in another jurisdiction;

(F) The pendency of contractual arbitration under Code of Civil Procedure section 1281.4;

(G) The pendency of attorney fee arbitration under Business and Professions Code section 6201;

(H) A stay by the reporting court for active military duty or incarceration; and

(I) For 180 days, the exemption for uninsured motorist cases under rule 3.712(b).

(2) Felony or misdemeanor cases:

(A) Issuance of warrant;

(B) Imposition of a civil assessment under Penal Code section 1214.1;

(C) Pendency of completion of diversion under Penal Code section 1000 et seq.;

(D) Evaluation of mental competence under Penal Code section 1368;

(E) Evaluation as a narcotics addict under Welfare and Institutions Code sections 3050 and 3051;

(F) 90-day diagnostic and treatment program under Penal Code section 1203.3;

(G) 90-day evaluation period for a juvenile under Welfare and Institutions Code section 707.2;

(H) Stay by a higher court or by a federal court for proceedings in another jurisdiction;

(I) Stay by the reporting court for active military duty or incarceration; and

(J) Time granted by the court to secure counsel if the defendant is not represented at the first appearance.

(Subd (n) amended effective January 1, 2007; adopted effective January 1, 2004.)

(o) Problems

A court that finds its ability to comply with these goals impeded by a rule of court or statute should notify the Judicial Council.

(Subd (o) amended effective January 1, 2007; adopted effective January 1, 2004.)

Standard 2.2 amended and renumbered effective January 1, 2007; adopted as sec. 2.1 effective July 1, 1987; previously amended effective January 1, 1988, July 1, 1988, January 1, 1989, January 1, 1990, July 1, 1991, and January 1, 2004.

Standard 2.10. Procedures for determining the need for an interpreter and a preappearance interview

(a) When an interpreter is needed

An interpreter is needed if, after an examination of a party or witness, the court concludes that:

(1) The party cannot understand and speak English well enough to participate fully in the proceedings and to assist counsel; or

(2) The witness cannot speak English so as to be understood directly by counsel, court, and jury.

(Subd (a) amended effective January 1, 2007.)

(b) When an examination is required

The court should examine a party or witness on the record to determine whether an interpreter is needed if:

(1) A party or counsel requests such an examination; or

(2) It appears to the court that the party or witness may not understand and speak English well enough to participate fully in the proceedings.

(Subd (b) amended effective January 1, 2007.)

(c) Examination of party or witness

To determine if an interpreter is needed, the court should normally include questions on the following:

(1) Identification (for example: name, address, birthdate, age, place of birth);

(2) Active vocabulary in vernacular English (for example: "How did you come to the court today?" "What kind of work do you do?" "Where did you go to school?" "What was the highest grade you completed?" "Describe what you see in the courtroom." "What have you eaten today?"). Questions should be phrased to avoid "yes" or "no" replies;

(3) The court proceedings (for example: the nature of the charge or the type of case before the court, the purpose of the proceedings and function of the court, the rights of a party or criminal defendant, and the responsibilities of a witness).

(Subd (c) amended effective January 1, 2007.)

(d) Record of examination

After the examination, the court should state its conclusion on the record. The file in the case should be clearly marked and data entered electronically when appropriate by court personnel to ensure that an interpreter will be present when needed in any subsequent proceeding.

(Subd (d) amended effective January 1, 2007.)

(e) Good cause for preappearance interview

For good cause, the court should authorize a preappearance interview between the interpreter and the party or witness. Good cause exists if the interpreter needs clarification on any interpreting issues, including: colloquialisms, culturalisms, dialects, idioms, linguistic capabilities and traits, regionalisms, register, slang, speech patterns, or technical terms.

(Subd (e) amended effective January 1, 2007.)

Standard 2.10 amended and renumbered effective January 1, 2007; repealed and adopted as sec. 18 effective January 1, 1999.

Standard 2.11. Interpreted proceedings—instructing participants on procedure

(a) Instructions to interpreters

The court or the court's designee should give the following instructions to interpreters, either orally or in writing:

(1) Do not discuss the pending proceedings with a party or witness.

(2) Do not disclose communications between counsel and client.

(3) Do not give legal advice to a party or witness. Refer legal questions to the attorney or to the court.

(4) Inform the court if you are unable to interpret a word, expression, special terminology, or dialect, or have doubts about your linguistic expertise or ability to perform adequately in a particular case.

(5) Interpret all words, including slang, vulgarisms, and epithets, to convey the intended meaning.

(6) Use the first person when interpreting statements made in the first person. (For example, a statement or question should not be introduced with the words, "He says ….")

(7) Direct all inquiries or problems to the court and not to the witness or counsel. If necessary, you may request permission to approach the bench with counsel to discuss a problem.

(8) Position yourself near the witness or party without blocking the view of the judge, jury, or counsel.

(9) Inform the court if you become fatigued during the proceedings.

(10) When interpreting for a party at the counsel table, speak loudly enough to be heard by the party or counsel but not so loudly as to interfere with the proceedings.

(11) Interpret everything, including objections.

(12) If the court finds good cause under rule 2.893(e), hold a preappearance interview with the party or witness to become familiar with speech patterns and linguistic traits and to determine what technical or special terms may be used. Counsel may be present at the preappearance interview.

(13) During the preappearance interview with a non-English-speaking witness, give the witness the following instructions on the procedure to be followed when the witness is testifying:

(A) The witness must speak in a loud, clear voice so that the entire court and not just the interpreter can hear.

(B) The witness must direct all responses to the person asking the question, not to the interpreter.

(C) The witness must direct all questions to counsel or to the court and not to the interpreter. The witness may not seek advice from or engage in any discussion with the interpreter.

(14) During the preappearance interview with a non-English-speaking party, give the following instructions on the procedure to be used when the non-English-speaking party is not testifying:

(A) The interpreter will interpret all statements made in open court.

(B) The party must direct any questions to counsel. The interpreter will interpret all questions to counsel and the responses. The party may not seek advice from or engage in discussion with the interpreter.

(Subd (a) amended effective January 1, 2007.)

(b) Instructions to counsel

The court or the court's designee should give the following instructions to counsel, either orally or in writing:

(1) When examining a non-English-speaking witness, direct all questions to the witness and not to the interpreter. (For example, do not say to the interpreter, "Ask him if ….")

(2) If there is a disagreement with the interpretation, direct any objection to the court and not to the interpreter. Ask permission to approach the bench to discuss the problem.

(3) If you have a question regarding the qualifications of the interpreter, you may request permission to conduct a supplemental examination on the interpreter's qualifications.

Standard 2.11 amended and renumbered effective January 1, 2007; repealed and adopted as sec. 18.1 effective January 1, 1999.

Standard 2.20. Trial management standards

(a) General principles

The trial judge has the responsibility to manage the trial proceedings. The judge should take appropriate action to ensure that all parties are prepared to proceed, the trial commences as scheduled, all parties have a fair opportunity to present evidence, and the trial proceeds to conclusion without unnecessary interruption. When the trial involves a jury, the trial judge should manage proceedings with particular emphasis on the needs of the jury.

(Subd (a) amended effective January 1, 2007.)

(b) Techniques of trial management

The trial judge should employ the following trial management techniques:

(1) Participate with trial counsel in a trial management conference before trial.

(2) After consultation with counsel, set reasonable time limits.

(3) Arrange the court's docket to start trial as scheduled and inform parties of the number of hours set each day for the trial.

(4) Ensure that once trial has begun, momentum is maintained.

(5) Be receptive to using technology in managing the trial and the presentation of evidence.

(6) Attempt to maintain continuity in days of trial and hours of trial.

(7) Schedule arguments on legal issues at the beginning or end of the day so as not to interrupt the presentation of evidence.

(8) Permit sidebar conferences only when necessary, and keep them as short as possible.

(9) In longer trials, consider scheduling trial days to permit jurors time for personal business.

(Subd (b) amended effective January 1, 2007.)

Standard 2.20 amended and renumbered effective January 1, 2007; adopted as sec. 8.9 effective July 1, 1997.

Standard 2.25. Uninterrupted jury selection

When practical, the trial judge, with the cooperation of the other judges of the court, should schedule court business to allow for jury selection uninterrupted by other court business.

Standard 2.25 amended and renumbered effective January 1, 2007; adopted as sec. 8.6 effective July 1, 1990.

Standard 2.30. Judicial comment on verdict or mistrial

At the conclusion of a trial, or on declaring a mistrial for failure of a jury to reach a verdict, it is appropriate for the trial judge to thank jurors for their public service, but the judge's comments should not include praise or criticism of the verdict or the failure to reach a verdict.

Standard 2.30 amended and renumbered effective January 1, 2007; adopted as sec. 14 effective January 1, 1976.

Title 3
Standards for Civil Cases

Standard 3.1. Appearance by telephone

(a) Recommended criteria for telephone equipment

Each court should have adequate telephone equipment for use in hearings at which counsel may appear by telephone. This equipment should:

(1) Permit each person participating in the hearing, whether in person or by telephone, to hear all other persons;

(2) Handle at least three incoming calls at one time and place those calls into a conference call in a simple and quick manner;

(3) Have a silent (visible) ringer;

(4) Be simple to learn and use;

(5) Be reasonable in cost; and

(6) Have full-duplex, simultaneous bidirectional speaker capability.

(Subd (a) amended effective January 1, 2007.)

(b) Optional features for telephone equipment

It is desirable if the telephone equipment can:

(1) Dial previously stored telephone numbers;

(2) Record conversations;

(3) Be moved easily from location to location; and

(4) Automatically queue incoming calls.

(Subd (b) amended effective January 1, 2007.)

(c) Award of attorney's fees

A court should consider, in awarding attorney's fees under any applicable provision of law, whether an attorney is claiming fees for appearing in person in a proceeding in which that attorney could have appeared by telephone.

(Subd (c) repealed and relettered effective January 1, 2008; adopted as subd (d) effective January 1, 1989; previously amended effective January 1, 2007.)

(d) Local procedures for telephone appearance

Each court should adopt a local rule or uniform local written policy specifying the following:

(1) Whether the court or the attorney initiates the telephone call for a telephone appearance;

(2) Whether the court sets a specified time for a telephone appearance or a time range; and

(3) How the parties are notified, in advance of the hearing, of the time or time range of the telephone appearance. In those courts using a tentative ruling recording system, that notice should be part of the tentative ruling recording.

(Subd (d) relettered effective January 1, 2008; adopted as subd (e) effective January 1, 1989; previously amended effective January 1, 2007.)

Standard 3.1 amended effective January 1, 2008; repealed and adopted as sec. 21 effective January 1, 1989; previously amended effective July 1, 1992, and January 1, 2007.

Standard 3.10. Complex civil litigation

(a) Judicial management

In complex litigation, judicial management should begin early and be applied continuously and actively, based on knowledge of the circumstances of each case.

(b) All-purpose assignment

Complex litigation should be assigned to one judge for all purposes. If such an assignment is not possible, a single judge should be assigned to hear law and motion matters and discovery matters.

(Subd (b) amended effective January 1, 2007; adopted as subd (d) effective July 1, 1982; previously relettered effective January 1, 2000.)

(c) Selection of judges for complex litigation assignments

In selecting judges for complex litigation assignments, the presiding judge should consider the needs of the court and the judge's ability, interest, training, experience (including experience with complex civil cases), and willingness to participate in educational programs related to the management of complex cases. Commissioners should not be employed in any phase of complex litigation, except under the judge's direct supervision to assist in the management of the case.

(Subd (c) amended and relettered effective January 1, 2000; adopted as subd (e) effective July 1, 1982.)

(d) Establishing time limits

Time limits should be regularly used to expedite major phases of complex litigation. Time limits should be established early, tailored to the circumstances of each case, firmly and fairly maintained, and accompanied by other methods of sound judicial management.

(Subd (d) relettered effective January 1, 2000; adopted as subd (f) effective July 1, 1982.)

(e) Preparation for trial

Litigants in complex litigation cases should be required to minimize evidentiary disputes and to organize efficiently their exhibits and other evidence before trial.

(Subd (e) amended and relettered effective January 1, 2007; adopted as subd (i) effective July 1, 1982; previously relettered as subd (g) effective January 1, 2000.)

(f) Dilatory tactics

Judges involved in complex litigation should be sensitive to dilatory or abusive litigation tactics and should be prepared to invoke disciplinary procedures for violations.

(Subd (f) relettered effective January 1, 2007; adopted as subd (j) effective July 1, 1982; previously relettered as subd (h) effective January 1, 2000.)

(g) Educational programs

Judges should be encouraged to attend educational programs on the management of complex litigation.

(Subd (g) relettered effective January 1, 2007; adopted as subd (k) effective July 1, 1982; previously amended and relettered as subd (i) effective January 1, 2000.)

(h) Staff assignment

Judges assigned to handle complex cases should be given research attorney and administrative staff assistance when possible.

(Subd (h) amended and relettered effective January 1, 2007; adopted as subd (j) effective January 1, 2000.)

Standard 3.10 amended and renumbered effective January 1, 2007; adopted as sec. 19 effective July 1, 1982; previously amended effective January 1, 1995, and January 1, 2000.

Standard 3.25. Examination of prospective jurors in civil cases

(a) In general

(1) *Methods and scope of examination*

The examination of prospective jurors in a civil case may be oral, by written questionnaire, or by both methods, and should include all questions necessary to ensure the selection of a fair and impartial jury. The *Juror Questionnaire for Civil Cases* (form MC-001) may be used. During any supplemental examination conducted by counsel for the parties, the trial judge should permit liberal and probing examination calculated to discover possible bias or prejudice with regard to the circumstances of the particular case.

(2) *Examination by counsel*

When counsel requests to be allowed to conduct a supplemental voir dire examination, the trial judge should permit counsel to conduct such examination without requiring prior submission of the questions to the judge unless a particular counsel has demonstrated unwillingness to avoid the type of examination proscribed in (f). In exercising his or her sound discretion as to the form and subject matter of voir dire questions, the trial judge should consider, among other criteria: (1) any unique or complex elements, legal or factual, in the case, and (2) the individual responses or conduct of jurors that may evince attitudes inconsistent with suitability to serve as a fair and impartial juror in the particular case. Questions regarding personal relationships of jurors should be relevant to the subject matter of the case.

(Subd (a) amended effective January 1, 2007; adopted effective January 1, 1972; previously amended effective January 1, 1974, July 1, 1993, and January 1, 2004.)

(b) Pre-voir dire conference

Before the examination the trial judge should, outside the prospective jurors' hearing and with a court reporter present, confer with counsel, at which time specific questions or areas of inquiry may be proposed that the judge in his or her discretion may inquire of the jurors. Thereafter, the judge should advise counsel of the questions or areas to be inquired into during the examination and voir dire procedure. The judge should also obtain from counsel the names of the witnesses whom counsel then plan to call at trial and a brief outline of the nature of the case, including any alleged injuries or damages and, in an eminent domain action, the respective contentions of the parties concerning the value of the property taken and any alleged severance damages and special benefits.

(Subd (b) amended effective January 1, 2007; adopted effective January 1, 1972; previously amended effective January 1, 1974.)

(c) Examination of jurors

Except as otherwise provided in (d), the trial judge's examination of prospective jurors should include the following areas of inquiry and any other matters affecting their qualifications to serve as jurors in the case:

(1) *To the entire jury panel after it has been sworn and seated:*

I am now going to question the prospective jurors who are seated in the jury box concerning their qualifications to serve as jurors in this case. All members of this jury panel, however, should pay close attention to my questions, making note of the answers you would give if these questions were put to you personally. If and when any other member of this panel is called to the jury box, the member will be asked to give his or her answers to these questions.

(2) In the trial of this case the parties are entitled to have a fair, unbiased, and unprejudiced jury. If there is any reason why any of you might be biased or prejudiced in any way, you must disclose such reason when you are asked to do so. It is your duty to make this disclosure.

(3) *In lengthy trials:*

This trial will likely take _____ days to complete, but it may take longer. Will any of you find it difficult or impossible to participate for this period of time?

(4) The nature of this case is as follows: *(Describe briefly, including any alleged injuries or damages and, in an eminent domain action, the name of the condemning agency, a description of the property being acquired, and the particular public project or purpose of the condemnation.)*

(5) The parties to this case and their respective attorneys are: *(Specify.)* Have you heard of or been acquainted with any of these parties or their attorneys?

(6) During the trial of this case, the following witnesses may be called to testify on behalf of the parties. These witnesses are: *(Do not identify the party on whose behalf the witnesses might be called.)* Have any of you heard of or been otherwise acquainted with any of the witnesses just

named? The parties are not required and might not wish to call all of these witnesses, and they may later find it necessary to call other witnesses.

(7) Have any of you heard of, or have you any knowledge of, the facts or events in this case? Are any of you familiar with the places or property mentioned in this case?

(8) Do any of you believe that a case of this nature should not be brought into court for determination by a jury?

(9) Do any of you have any belief or feeling toward any of the parties, attorneys, or witnesses that might be regarded as a bias or prejudice for or against any of them? Do you have any interest, financial or otherwise, in the outcome of this case?

(10) Have any of you served as a juror or witness involving any of these parties, attorneys, or witnesses?

(11) Have any of you served as a juror in any other case? (If so, was it a civil or criminal case?) You must understand that there is a basic difference between a civil case and a criminal case. In a criminal case a defendant must be found guilty beyond a reasonable doubt; in a civil case such as this, you need only find that the evidence you accept as the basis of your decision is more convincing, and thus has the greater probability of truth, than the contrary evidence.

In the following questions I will be using the terms "family," "close friend," and "anyone with whom you have a significant personal relationship." The term "anyone with whom you have a significant personal relationship" means a domestic partner, life partner, former spouse, or anyone with whom you have an influential or intimate relationship that you would characterize as important.

(12) *If a corporation or "company" is a party:*

(A) Have you or, to your knowledge, has any member of your family, a close friend, or anyone with whom you have a significant personal relationship ever had any connection with, or any dealings with, the _____ corporation (or company)?

(B) Are any of you or them related to any officer, director, or employee of this corporation (or company) to your knowledge?

(C) Do you or they own any stock or other interest in this corporation (or company) to your knowledge?

(D) Have you or they ever done business as a corporation (or company)?

(E) The fact that a corporation (or company) is a party in this case must not affect your deliberations or your verdict. You may not discriminate between corporations (or companies) and natural individuals. Both are persons in the eyes of the law and both are entitled to have a fair and impartial trial based on the same legal standards. Do any of you have any belief or feeling for or against corporations (or companies) that might prevent you from being a completely fair and impartial juror in this case?

(13) Have you or, to your knowledge, has any member of your family, a close friend, or anyone with whom you have a significant personal relationship ever sued anyone, or presented a claim against anyone in connection with a matter similar to this case? (If so, did the matter terminate satisfactorily so far as you were concerned?)

(14) Has anyone ever sued you, or presented a claim against you or, to your knowledge, against any member of your family, a close friend, or anyone with whom you have a significant personal relationship, in connection with a matter similar to this case? (If so, did the matter terminate satisfactorily so far as you were concerned?)

(15) Are you or, to your knowledge, is any member of your family, a close friend, or anyone with whom you have a significant personal relationship presently involved in a lawsuit of any kind?

(16) *When appropriate:*

It may appear that one or more of the parties, witnesses, or attorneys come from a particular national, racial, or religious group (or may have a lifestyle different than your own). Would this in any way affect your judgment or the weight and credibility you would give to their testimony or to their contentions?

(17) Have you or, to your knowledge, has any member of your family, a close friend, or anyone with whom you have a significant personal relationship had any special training in: *(Describe briefly the fields of expertise involved in the case, such as law, medicine, nursing, or any other branch of the healing arts.)*

(18) *In personal injury or wrongful death cases:*

(A) You may be called on in this case to award damages for personal injury, pain, and suffering. Do any of you have any religious or other belief that pain and suffering are not real or any belief that would prevent you from awarding damages for pain and suffering if liability for them is established?

(B) Are there any of you who would not employ a medical doctor?

(C) Have you or, to your knowledge, has any member of your family, a close friend, or anyone with whom you have a significant personal relationship ever engaged in investigating or otherwise acting on claims for damages?

(D) Have you or they, to your knowledge, ever been in an accident with the result that a claim for personal injuries or for substantial property damage was made by someone involved in that accident, whether or not a lawsuit was filed?

(E) Have you or they, to your knowledge, ever been involved in an accident in which someone died or received serious personal injuries, whether or not a lawsuit was filed?

(F) Are there any of you who do not drive an automobile? (If so, have you ever driven an automobile, and if you have, give your reason for not presently driving.) Does your spouse or anyone with whom you have a significant personal relationship drive an automobile? (If that person does not drive but did so in the past, why did that person stop driving?)

(G) Plaintiff (or cross-complainant) _____ is claiming injuries. *(Describe briefly the general nature of the alleged injuries.)* Do you or, to your knowledge, does any member of your family, a close friend, or anyone with whom you have a significant personal relationship suffer from similar injuries? Have you or they, to your knowledge, suffered from similar injuries in the past? (If so, would that fact affect your point of view in this case to the extent that you might not be able to render a completely fair and impartial verdict?)

(19) It is important that I have your assurance that you will, without reservation, follow my instructions and rulings on the law and will apply that law to this case. To put it somewhat differently, whether you approve or disapprove of the court's rulings or instructions, it is your solemn duty to accept as correct these statements of the law. You may not substitute your own idea of what you think the law ought to be. Will all of you follow the law as given to you by me in this case?

(20) Each of you should now state your:

(A) Name;
(B) Children's ages and the number of children, if any;
(C) Occupation;
(D) Occupational history; and
(E) Present employer;

And for your spouse or anyone with whom you have a significant personal relationship, their:

(F) Names;
(G) Occupations;
(H) Occupational histories; and
(I) Present employers.

Please begin with juror number one.

(21) Do you know of any other reason, or has anything occurred during this question period, that might make you doubtful you would be a completely fair and impartial juror in this case? If there is, it is your duty to disclose the reason at this time.

(Subd (c) amended effective January 1, 2007; adopted effective January 1, 1972; previously amended effective January 1, 1974, and January 1, 2004.)

(d) Examination of jurors in eminent domain cases

In eminent domain cases, the trial judge's examination of prospective jurors should include, in the areas of inquiry in (c)(1) through (c)(12), the following matters, and any other matters affecting their qualifications to serve as jurors in the case:

(1) Have you or, to your knowledge, has any member of your family, a close friend, or anyone with whom you have a significant personal relationship ever had any connection with, or dealings with, the plaintiff agency? Are you or any of them related to any officer or employee of the plaintiff agency?

(2) Have you or, to your knowledge, has any member of your family, a close friend, or anyone with whom you have a significant personal relationship ever been involved in an eminent domain proceeding such as this or are you or they likely to become involved in such a proceeding in the future?

(3) To your knowledge, do you have relatives, close friends, or anyone with whom you have a significant personal relationship who has been or will be affected by the proposed project or a similar public project? (If so, who and how affected?)

(4) Have you or, to your knowledge, has any member of your family, a close friend, or anyone with whom you have a significant personal relationship ever sold property to a public agency having the power of eminent domain?

(5) Are you or, to your knowledge, is any member of your family, a close friend, or anyone with whom you have a significant personal relationship presently involved in a lawsuit of any kind? (If so, does the lawsuit involve a public agency?)

(6) Have you or, to your knowledge, has any member of your family, a close friend, or anyone with whom you have a significant personal relationship ever been involved in a lawsuit involving a public agency?

(7) *When appropriate:*

It may appear that one or more of the parties, witnesses, or attorneys come from a particular national, racial, or religious group (or may have a lifestyle different from your own). Would this in any way affect your judgment or the weight and credibility you would give to their testimony or contentions?

(8) Have you or, to your knowledge, has any member of your family, a close friend, or anyone with whom you have a significant personal relationship had any special training in: *(Describe briefly the fields of expertise involved in the case, such as law, real estate, real estate appraising, engineering, surveying, geology, etc.)*

(9) Have you, has your spouse, or, to your knowledge, has any member of your family, a close friend, or anyone with whom you have a significant personal relationship ever been engaged in any phase of the real estate business including:

(A) Acting as a real estate agent, broker, or salesperson;

(B) Acting as a real estate appraiser;

(C) Dealing in trust deeds;

(D) Buying or selling real property as a business;

(E) Owning or managing income property; or

(F) Engaging in the construction business?

(10) Have you or, to your knowledge, has any member of your family, a close friend, or anyone with whom you have a significant personal relationship ever studied or engaged in: (State type of business, if any, conducted on subject property.)

(11) Have you or, to your knowledge, has any member of your family, a close friend, or anyone with whom you have a significant personal relationship ever been engaged in any work involving the acquisition of private property for public purposes? Or involving the zoning or planning of property?

(12) Under the law of this state, all private property is held subject to the necessary right of eminent domain, which is the right of the state or its authorized agencies to take private property for public use whenever the public interest so requires. The right of eminent domain is exercised through proceedings commonly called a condemnation action. This is a condemnation action.

(13) The Constitution of this state requires that a property owner be paid just compensation for the taking (or damaging) of his or her property for public use. It will be the duty of the jury ultimately selected in this case to determine the just compensation to be paid.

(14) *If no claim of severance damages:*

In order to find the amount of just compensation in this case, the jury will be called on to determine the fair market value of the real property being acquired.

(15) *If severance damages are claimed:*

In order to find the amount of just compensation in this case, the jury will be called on to determine the following:

(A) The fair market value of the real property being acquired.

(B) Severance damages, if any, to the defendant's remaining real property; that is, the depreciation in market value by reason of the severance of the part taken, or by the construction of the improvements in the manner proposed by the plaintiff, or both.

(C) *When applicable:* Special benefits, if any, to the defendant's remaining real property. *(The trial judge on request may advise the jury on the concept of special benefits.)*

(16) Just compensation is measured in terms of fair market value as of *(date)*, the date of value in this case.

(17) I will give you more specific instructions on the issues and determinations to be made in this case at the conclusion of all the evidence. However, I will now advise you of the definition of fair market value: *(See CACI 3501.)*

(18) *Private ownership of property:*

(A) Do you have any objection to the concept of private ownership of property?

(B) Do you have any objection to the right of the owner of private property to develop or use that property in whatever lawful way its owner sees fit?

(19) Do you have any objection to the plaintiff acquiring private property for a public use as long as just compensation is paid for the property?

(20) Do you have any objection to the defendant(s) seeking just compensation in these proceedings in the form of the fair market value of the subject property (and the damages that the defendant(s) contend will be caused to the remaining property)?

(21) Do you have any objection to the particular public project involved in this proceeding, previously referred to as the *(name of project)*?

(22) Are you or, to your knowledge, is any member of your family, a close friend, or anyone with whom you have a significant personal relationship a member of any organization that is opposed to such public projects?

(23) Do you have any objection to the concept that just compensation is measured by fair market value as I have defined that term for you earlier?

(24) Do you have any feeling that, because the plaintiff needs the property for public purposes, it should pay anything other than its fair market value?

(25) In these cases, the evidence of value is introduced for the most part by what the courts sometimes refer to as expert testimony. This expert testimony frequently is introduced through appraisers or real estate brokers. Do you have any prejudice against real estate brokers or appraisers, or that type of testimony?

(26) In a condemnation case the property owner produces all of his or her evidence of value first, then the government calls its witnesses. Having this in mind, will you keep your mind open throughout all the case and not determine the matter in your mind until all of the evidence is in?

(27) It is important that I have your assurance that you will, without reservation, follow my instructions and rulings on the law and will apply that law to this case. To put it somewhat differently, whether you approve or disapprove of the court's rulings or instructions, it is your solemn duty to accept as correct these statements of the law. You may not substitute your own idea of what you think the law ought to be. Will all of you follow the law as given to you by me in this case?

(28) Each of you should now state your:

(A) Name;

(B) Children's ages and number of children, if any;

(C) Occupation;

(D) Occupational history; and

(E) Present employer;

And for your spouse or anyone with whom you have a significant personal relationship, their:

(F) Names;

(G) Occupations;

(H) Occupational histories; and

(I) Present employers.

Please begin with juror number one.

(29) Each of you should now state whether you, your spouse, or anyone with whom you have a significant personal relationship owns or has an interest in any real property and, if so, whether its value or use is affected by the public project involved in this case.

We will again start with juror number one.

(30) Do you know of any other reason, or has anything occurred during this question period, that might make you doubtful you would be a completely fair and impartial juror in this case? If there is, it is your duty to disclose the reason at this time.

(Subd (d) amended effective January 1, 2007; adopted effective January 1, 1974; previously amended effective January 1, 1989, and January 1, 2004.)

(e) Subsequent conference and examination

On completion of the initial examination and on request of counsel for any party that the trial judge put additional questions to the jurors, the judge should, outside the jurors' hearing and with a court reporter present, confer with counsel, at which time additional questions or areas of inquiry may be proposed that the judge may inquire of the jurors.

(Subd (e) amended effective January 1, 2007; adopted effective January 1, 1972; previously amended effective January 1, 1974.)

(f) Improper questions

When any counsel examines the prospective jurors, the trial judge should not permit counsel to attempt to precondition the prospective jurors to a particular result or allow counsel to comment on the personal lives and families of the parties or their attorneys. Nor should the trial judge allow counsel to question the jurors concerning the pleadings, the applicable law, the meaning of particular words and phrases, or the comfort of the jurors, except in unusual circumstances, where, in the trial judge's sound discretion, such questions become necessary to insure the selection of a fair and impartial jury.

(Subd (f) amended effective January 1, 2007; adopted effective January 1, 1972; previously amended effective January 1, 1974.)

Standard 3.25 amended and renumbered effective January 1, 2007; adopted as sec. 8 effective January 1, 1972; previously amended effective January 1, 1974, January 1, 1989, July 1, 1993, and January 1, 2004.

Title 4
Standards for Criminal Cases

Standard 4.10. Guidelines for diversion drug court programs
Standard 4.15. Vacatur relief under Penal Code section 236.14
Standard 4.30. Examination of prospective jurors in criminal cases
Standard 4.35. Court use of risk/needs assessments at sentencing
Standard 4.40. Traffic infraction procedures
Standard 4.42. Traffic infraction trial scheduling

Standard 4.10.   Guidelines for diversion drug court programs

(a) Minimum components

The components specified in this standard should be included as minimum requirements in any pre-plea diversion drug court program developed under Penal Code section 1000.5.

(Subd (a) amended effective January 1, 2007.)

(b) Early entry

Eligible participants should be identified early and enter into a supervision and treatment program promptly.

(1) A declaration of eligibility should be filed by the district attorney no later than the date of the defendant's first appearance in court.

(2) Participants designated as eligible by the district attorney should be ordered by the assigned drug court judge to report for assessment and treatment supervision within five days of the first court appearance.

(c) Treatment services

Participants should be given access to a continuum of treatment and rehabilitative services.

(1) The county drug program administrator should specify and certify appropriate drug treatment programs under Penal Code section 1211.

(2) The certified treatment programs should provide a minimum of two levels of treatment services to match participants to programs according to their needs for treatment, recognizing that some divertees may be at the stage of experimenting with illicit drugs while others may be further along in the addiction's progression.

(3) Each treatment level should be divided into phases in order to provide periodic reviews of treatment progress. Each phase may vary in length. It should be recognized that a participant is expected to progress in treatment but may relapse. Most participants, however, should be able to successfully complete the treatment program within 12 months.

(4) Each pre-plea diversion drug court program should have an assessment component to ensure that participants are initially screened and then periodically assessed by treatment personnel to ensure that appropriate treatment services are provided and to monitor the participants' progress through the phases.

(5) Treatment services should include educational and group outpatient treatment. Individual counseling, however, should be made available in special circumstances if an assessment based on acceptable professional standards indicates that individual counseling is the only appropriate form of treatment. Referrals should be made for educational and vocational counseling if it is determined to be appropriate by the judge.

(Subd (c) amended effective January 1, 2007.)

(d) Monitoring

Abstinence from and use of drugs should be monitored by frequent drug testing.

(1) Alcohol and other drug (AOD) testing is essential and should be mandatory in each pre-plea diversion drug court program to monitor participant compliance.

(2) Testing may be administered randomly or at scheduled intervals, but should occur no less frequently than one time per week during the first 90 days of treatment.

(3) The probation officer and court should be immediately notified when a participant has tested positive, has failed to submit to AOD testing, or has submitted an adulterated sample. In such cases, an interim hearing should be calendared and required as outlined in (e)(4).

(4) Participants should not be considered to have successfully completed the treatment program unless they have consistently had negative test results for a period of four months.

(Subd (d) amended effective January 1, 2007.)

(e) Judicial supervision

There should be early and frequent judicial supervision of each diversion drug court participant.

(1) Each participant should appear in court before a specifically assigned diversion drug court judge within 30 days after the first court appearance. At this time the participant should provide proof of registration, proof of completion of assessment, proof of entry into a specific treatment program, and initial drug test results.

(2) The second drug court appearance should be held no later than 30 days after the first drug court appearance. The third drug court appearance should be held no later than 60 days after the second drug court appearance.

(3) A final drug court appearance should be required no sooner than 12 months from entry into treatment unless continued treatment is found to be appropriate and necessary.

(4) Interim drug court appearances should be required within one week of the following: positive drug test results, failure to test, adulterated test, or failure to appear or participate in treatment.

(5) At each drug court appearance, the judge should receive a report of the participant's progress in treatment and drug test results and should review, monitor, and impose rewards and sanctions based on the participant's progress or lack of progress.

(f) Sanctions and incentives

The drug court responds directly to each participant's compliance or noncompliance with graduated sanctions or incentives.

(1) A clear regimen of incentives and sanctions should be established and implemented at each court hearing.

(2) The suggested range of incentives should be as follows:

(A) Encouragement;

(B) Advancement to next treatment phase;

(C) Reduction in diversion program fees (other than state-mandated fees);

(D) Completion of treatment and required court appearances and shortening of the term of diversion; and

(E) Other incentives the court may deem necessary or appropriate.

(3) The suggested range of sanctions should be as follows:

(A) Demotion to earlier treatment phase;

(B) Increased frequency of testing, supervision, or treatment requirements;

(C) Graduated length of incarceration for violating diversion order to abstain from use of illegal drugs and for nonparticipation in treatment; and

(D) Reinstatement of criminal proceedings.

(4) A participant should be terminated from the pre-plea diversion drug court, and criminal proceedings reinstated, if the drug court judge, after a hearing, makes a final and specific finding and determination at any time during the period of diversion that the participant has:

(A) Not performed satisfactorily in treatment;

(B) Failed to benefit from education, treatment, or rehabilitation;

(C) Been convicted of a misdemeanor that reflects the participant's propensity for violence; or

(D) Engaged in criminal conduct rendering him or her unsuitable for continued treatment.

(Subd (f) amended effective January 1, 2007.)

(g) National standards

In addition to meeting the minimum guidelines provided in this standard, courts are encouraged to look to the nationally accepted guidelines, *Defining Drug Courts: The Key Components,* developed by the National Association of Drug Court Professionals in cooperation with the Department of Justice, for further and detailed guidance in developing an effective diversion drug court program.

(Subd (g) amended effective January 1, 2007.)

Standard 4.10 amended and renumbered effective January 1, 2007; adopted as sec. 36 effective January 1, 1998.

Standard 4.15.   Vacatur relief under Penal Code section 236.14

(a) Request to consolidate hearings for arrests and convictions that occurred in the same county

(1) The court should allow the filing of a single petition requesting vacatur relief under Penal Code section 236.14(a) for multiple arrests and convictions that occurred in the same county.

(2) The court should favor consolidating hearings for multiple arrests and convictions that occurred in the same county.

(3) The court may require the following documentation before granting a request to consolidate hearings:

(A) An agreement between the petitioner and all of the involved state or local prosecutorial agencies, as defined in Penal Code section 236.14(c), to consolidate the hearings;

(B) Documentation that states whether any of the involved state or local prosecutorial agencies, as defined in Penal Code section 236.14(c), intend to file an opposition to the petition; and

(C) Proof of service of the request to consolidate hearings on all of the involved state or local prosecutorial agencies, as defined in Penal Code section 236.14(c).

(4) The court should consider the following nonexclusive list of factors when deciding whether to consolidate hearings:

(A) The common questions of fact or law, if any;

(B) The convenience of parties, witnesses, and counsel;

(C) The efficient utilization of judicial facilities and staff resources;

(D) The calendar of the court; and

(E) The disadvantages of duplicative and inconsistent orders.

(Subd (a) adopted effective January 1, 2020.)

(b) Confidentiality

(1) The court should designate the petition and related filings and court records as confidential.

(2) At the hearing or any other proceeding accessible to the public, the court should consider implementing procedures consistent with Penal Code section 236.14(q), such as ordering the identity of the petitioner to be either "Jane Doe" or "John Doe."

(Subd (b) adopted effective January 1, 2020.)

(c) Initial court review and orders

(1) After 45 days from the filing of the petition, the court should conduct an initial review of the case. Concurrent with granting or denying a request to consolidate hearings, the court should:

(A) Grant relief without a hearing when the prosecuting agency files no opposition within 45 days from the date of service and the court finds that the petitioner meets the requirements for relief;

(B) Set a hearing date if an opposition is filed or a hearing is otherwise warranted; or

(C) Deny the petition without prejudice if the petitioner fails to provide the information required by Penal Code section 236.14(b).

(Subd (c) adopted effective January 1, 2020.)

(d) Notification

(1) The court should timely notify the petitioner and prosecuting agency of its decisions under subdivision (c)(1).

(2) The court should timely notify the relevant probation department of any decision to terminate probation.

(Subd (d) adopted effective January 1, 2020.)

(e) Additional relief

When granting the petition for vacatur relief under Penal Code section 236.14(a), the court should consider ordering the following additional relief, including, but not limited to:

(1) Sealing or destruction of probation or other postconviction supervision agency records related to the conviction;

(2) Expungement of DNA profiles and destruction of DNA samples, if they qualify under Penal Code section 299;

(3) Recall or return of court fines and fees, if paid;

(4) Sealing of the court file, if warranted under the factors in rule 2.550(d); and

(5) Additional relief that will carry out the purposes of Penal Code section 236.14.

(Subd (e) adopted effective January 1, 2020.)
Standard 4.15 adopted effective January 1, 2020.

Standard 4.30.   Examination of prospective jurors in criminal cases

(a) In general

(1) This standard applies in all criminal cases.

(2) The examination of prospective jurors in a criminal case should include all questions necessary to insure the selection of a fair and impartial jury.

(3) The court may consider conducting sequestered voir dire on issues that are sensitive to prospective jurors, on questions concerning media reports of the case, and on any other issue that the court deems advisable.

(Subd (a) amended effective January 1, 2007; previously amended effective January 1, 1988, January 1, 1990, June 6, 1990, and January 1, 2006.)

(b) Examination of jurors

The trial judge's examination of prospective jurors in criminal cases should include the areas of inquiry listed below and any other matters affecting their qualifications to serve as jurors in the case. The trial judge may want to use the *Juror Questionnaire for Criminal Cases* (form MC-002) to assist in the examination of prospective jurors. Form MC-002 is an optional form and is not intended to constitute the complete examination of prospective jurors. Form MC-002 is a tool for trial judges to use to make the initial examination of prospective jurors more efficient. If the court chooses to use form MC-002, its use and any supplemental questions submitted by counsel must be discussed at the pre-voir dire conference required by rule 4.200. Excusing jurors based on questionnaire answers alone is generally not advisable.

(1) *Address to entire jury panel:*

Do any of you have any vision, hearing, or medical difficulties that may affect your jury service? *(Response.)*

(2) *In particular, for lengthy trials. Address to entire jury panel:*

This trial will likely take _____ days to complete, but it may take longer. *(State the days and times during the day when the trial will be in session.)*

Will any of you find it difficult or impossible to participate for this period of time? *(After the entire panel has been screened for time hardships, direct the excused jurors to return to the jury assembly room for possible reassignment to other courtrooms for voir dire.)*

(3) *At this point the court may wish to submit any juror questionnaire that has been developed to assist in voir dire. The court should remind panel members that their answers on the questionnaire are given under penalty of perjury. In addition, if a questionnaire is used, the court and counsel may wish to question individual prospective jurors further based on their responses to particular questions, and a procedure for doing so should be established at the pre-voir dire conference. Therefore, it may not be necessary to ask all of the prospective jurors questions 5 through 25 that follow, although the text may assist the court with following up with individual jurors about answers given on the questionnaire.*

To the entire jury panel:

I am now going to question the prospective jurors who are seated in the jury box concerning their qualifications to serve as jurors in this case. All the remaining members of this jury panel, however, should pay close attention to my questions, making note of the answers you would give if these questions were put to you personally. If and when any other member of this panel is called to the jury box, he or she will be asked to answer these questions.

(4) *To the prospective jurors seated in the jury box:*

In the trial of this case each side is entitled to have a fair, unbiased, and unprejudiced jury. If there is any fact or any reason why any of you might be biased or prejudiced in any way, you must disclose such reasons when you are asked to do so. It is your duty to make this disclosure.

(5) *To the prospective jurors seated in the jury box:*

Do any of you know anyone else on this jury panel? *(Response.)*

(6) Ladies and gentlemen of the jury: This is a criminal case entitled The People of the State of California v. _____. The (defendant is)(defendants are) seated _____.

(A) (Mr.)(Ms.)(defendant), please stand and face the prospective jurors in the jury box and in the audience seats. *(Defendant complies.)* Is there any member of the jury panel who is acquainted with the defendant or who may have heard (his)(her) name before today? If your answer is yes, please raise your hand.

(B) The defendant, _____, is represented by (his)(her) attorney, _____, who is seated _____ (Mr.)(Ms.)(defense attorney), would you please stand? Is there any member of the jury panel who knows or who has seen (Mr.)(Ms.) _____ before today?

(C) *(If there is more than one defendant, repeat (a) and (b) for each codefendant.)*

(7) The People are represented by _____, Deputy District Attorney, who is seated _____. (Mr.)(Ms.)(district attorney), would you please stand? Is there any member of the jury panel who knows or who has seen (Mr.)(Ms.) _____ before today?

(8) The defendant is charged by an (information)(indictment) filed by the district attorney with having committed the crime of _____, in violation of section _____ of the _____ Code, it being alleged that on or about _____ in the County of _____, the defendant did *(describe the offense)*. To (this charge)(these charges) the defendant has pleaded not guilty, and the jury will have to decide whether the defendant's guilt has been proved beyond a reasonable doubt. Having heard the charge(s) that (has)(have) been filed against the defendant, is there any member of the jury panel who feels that he or she cannot give this defendant a fair trial because of the nature of the charge(s) against (him)(her)?

(9) Have any of you heard of, or have you any prior knowledge of, the facts or events in this case?

(10) Do any of you have any ethical, religious, political, or other beliefs that would prevent you from serving as a juror in this case?

(11) During the trial of this case, the following persons may be called as witnesses to testify on behalf of the parties or their names may be mentioned in evidence: _____ *(Do not identify the side on whose behalf the witness might be called.)* Have any of you heard of or otherwise been acquainted with any of the witnesses just named? You should note that the parties are not required and might not wish to call all of these witnesses, and they may later find it necessary to call other witnesses.

(12) Do any of you have any financial or personal interest in the outcome of this case?

(13) How many of you have served previously as jurors in a criminal case?

To each person whose hand is raised:

(A) (Mr.)(Ms.)_____(or Juror ID number), you indicated you have been a juror in a criminal case. What were the charges in that case? *(Response.)*

(B) Do you feel you can put aside whatever you heard in that case and decide this case on the evidence to be presented and the law as I will state it to you? *(Response.)*

(14) May I see the hands of those jurors who have served on civil cases, but who have never served on a criminal case? *(Response.)* You must understand that there are substantial differences in the rules applicable to the trial of criminal cases from those applicable to the trial of civil cases. This is particularly true respecting the burden of proof that is placed on the People. In a civil case we say that the plaintiff must prove (his) (her) case by a preponderance of the evidence. In a criminal case, the defendant is presumed to be innocent, and before (he)(she) may be found guilty, the People must prove (his)(her) guilt beyond a reasonable doubt. If the jury has a reasonable doubt, the defendant must be acquitted. Will each of you be able to set aside the instructions that you received in your previous cases and try this case on the instructions given by me in this case?

(15) The fact that the defendant is in court for trial, or that charges have been made against (him)(her), is no evidence whatever of (his)(her) guilt. The jurors are to consider only evidence properly received in the courtroom in determining whether the defendant's guilt has been proved beyond a reasonable doubt. The defendant has entered a plea of "not guilty," which is a complete denial, making it necessary for the People, acting through the district attorney, to prove beyond a reasonable doubt the case against the defendant. If the evidence does not convince you of the truth of the charges beyond a reasonable doubt, the defendant is entitled to a verdict of not guilty.

In the following questions I will be using the terms "relative," "close friend," and "anyone with whom you have a significant personal relationship." The term "anyone with whom you have a significant personal relationship" means a domestic partner, life partner, former spouse, or anyone with whom you have an influential or intimate relationship that you would characterize as important.

(16) Have you or, to your knowledge, has any relative, close friend, or anyone with whom you have a significant personal relationship, ever been the victim of any crime? *(Response.)*

(17) Have you or, to your knowledge, has any relative, close friend, or anyone with whom you have a significant personal relationship, ever had any contact with law enforcement, including being: (a) stopped by the police? (b) accused of misconduct, whether or not it was a crime? (c) investigated as a suspect in a criminal case? (d) charged with a crime? or (e) a criminal defendant? *(Response.)*

(18) Have you or, to your knowledge, has any relative, close friend, or anyone with whom you have a significant personal relationship, had any law enforcement training or experience or been a member of or been employed by any law enforcement agency? By law enforcement agency, I include any police department, sheriff's office, highway patrol, district attorney's office, city attorney's office, attorney general's office, United States attorney's office, FBI, and others. *(If so, elicit the details of the experience or connection.)*

(19) Would you be able to listen to the testimony of a police or other peace officer and measure it the same way you would that of any other witness?

(20) *When appropriate:*

It may appear that one or more of the parties, attorneys, or witnesses come from a particular national, racial, or religious group (or may have a lifestyle different from your own). Would this in any way affect your judgment or the weight and credibility you would give to their testimony?

(21) It is important that I have your assurance that you will follow my instructions and rulings on the law and will apply that law to this case. To put it somewhat differently, whether you approve or disapprove of the court's rulings or instructions, it is your solemn duty to accept as correct these statements of the law. You must accept and follow my instructions even if you disagree with the law. You may not substitute your own idea of what you think the law ought to be. Will all of you follow the law as given to you by me in this case?

(22) Each of you should now state your:

(A) (Name)(or juror ID number);

(B) Children's ages and the number of children, if any;

(C) Occupation;

(D) Occupational history; and

(E) Present employer;

And for your spouse or anyone with whom you have a significant personal relationship, their:

(F) Occupations;

(G) Occupational histories; and

(H) Present employers;

And for your adult children, their:

(I) Occupations;

(J) Occupational histories; and

(K) Present employers.

Please begin with juror number one.

(23) Do you know of any other reason, or has anything occurred during this question period, that might make you doubtful you would be a completely fair and impartial juror in this case or why you should not be on this jury? If there is, it is your duty to disclose the reason at this time.

(24) *After the court conducts the initial examination, Code of Civil Procedure section 223 allows counsel to ask supplemental questions for the purposes of uncovering possible bias or prejudice relevant to challenges for cause. The court may, in the exercise of its discretion, limit the oral and direct questioning of prospective jurors by counsel. The court may specify the maximum amount of time that counsel for each party may question an individual juror, or may specify an aggregate amount of time for each party, which can then be allocated among the prospective jurors by counsel.*

(25) *After the conclusion of counsel questioning, the court asks each side to exercise any challenges for cause.*

(26) *After ruling on challenges for cause, if any, the court calls on each side, alternately, to exercise any preemptory challenges.*

(27) *If a new prospective juror is seated, the court should ask him or her:*

(A) Have you heard my questions to the other prospective jurors?

(B) Have any of the questions I have asked raised any doubt in your mind as to whether you could be a fair and impartial juror in this case?

(C) Can you think of any other reason why you might not be able to try this case fairly and impartially to both the prosecution and defendant, or why you should not be on this jury?

(D) Give us the personal information requested concerning your occupation, that of your spouse or anyone with whom you have a significant personal relationship, that of your adult children, and your prior jury experience.

(Thereupon, as to each new juror seated, the court must permit counsel to ask supplemental questions, and proceed with challenges as above.)

(Subd (b) amended effective January 1, 2007; adopted as subd (c) effective July 1, 1974; amended and relettered effective June 6, 1990; previously amended effective January 1, 1997, January 1, 2004, and January 1, 2006.)

(c) Improper questions

When any counsel examines the prospective jurors, the trial judge should not permit counsel to attempt to precondition the prospective jurors to a particular result or allow counsel to comment on the personal lives and families of the parties or their attorneys.

(Subd (c) amended effective January 1, 2006; adopted as subd (e) effective July 1, 1974; previously amended and relettered as subd (d) effective June 6, 1990; relettered as subd (c) effective January 1, 1997.)
Standard 4.30 amended and renumbered effective January 1, 2007; adopted as sec. 8.5 July 1, 1974; previously amended effective January 1, 1988, January 1, 1990, June 6, 1990, January 1, 1997, January 1, 2004, and January 1, 2006.

Standard 4.35.   Court use of risk/needs assessments at sentencing

(a) Application and purpose

(1) This standard applies only to the use of the results of risk/needs assessments at sentencing.

(2) The use of the results of risk/needs assessments at sentencing is intended to:

(A) Prevent biases in sentencing;

(B) Reduce the risk of recidivism by focusing services and resources on medium- and high-risk offenders, who are most likely to reoffend;

(C) Reduce a defendant's risk of future recidivism by targeting that defendant's needs with appropriate intervention services through community supervision programs demonstrated to reduce recidivism; and

(D) Advance the legislative directive to improve public safety outcomes by routing offenders into community-based supervision informed by evidence-based practices.

(Subd (a) adopted effective January 1, 2018.)

(b) Definitions

(1) "Risk" refers to the likelihood that a person will reoffend without regard, unless otherwise specified, to the nature of the original offense or the nature of the reoffense.

(2) "Risk factors" refers to the "static" and "dynamic" factors that contribute to the risk score.

(3) "Static risk factors" refers to those risk factors that cannot be changed through treatment or intervention, such as age or prior criminal history.

(4) "Dynamic risk factors," also known as "needs," are factors that can be changed through treatment or intervention.

(5) "Results of a risk/needs assessment" refers to both a risk score and an assessment of a person's needs.

(6) A "risk score" refers to a descriptive evaluation of a person's risk level as a result of conducting an actuarial assessment with a validated risk/needs assessment instrument and may include such terms as "high," "medium," or "low" risk.

(7) "Amenability" or "suitability" refers to the likelihood that the person can be safely and effectively supervised in the community and benefit from supervision services that are informed by evidence-based practices that have been demonstrated to reduce recidivism.

(8) A "validated risk/needs assessment instrument" refers to a risk/needs assessment instrument demonstrated by scientific research to be accurate and reliable in assessing the risks and needs of the specific population on which it was validated.

(9) "Supervision" includes all forms of supervision referenced in Penal Code section 1203.2(a).

(Subd (b) adopted effective January 1, 2018.)

(c) Validation

The risk/needs assessment instrument should be validated.

(Subd (c) adopted effective January 1, 2018.)

(d) Proper uses of the results of a risk/needs assessment at sentencing

(1) The results of a risk/needs assessment should be considered only in context with all other information considered by the court at the time of sentencing, including the probation report, statements in mitigation and aggravation, evidence presented at a sentencing proceeding conducted under section 1204, and comments by counsel and any victim.

(2) The results of a risk/needs assessment should be one of many factors that may be considered and weighed at a sentencing hearing. Information generated by the risk/needs assessment should be used along with all other information presented in connection with the sentencing

hearing to inform and facilitate the decision of the court. Risk/needs assessment information should not be used as a substitute for the sound independent judgment of the court.

(3) Although they may not be determinative, the results of a risk/needs assessment may be considered by the court as a relevant factor in assessing:

(A) Whether a defendant who is presumptively ineligible for probation has overcome the statutory limitation on probation;

(B) Whether an offender can be supervised safely and effectively in the community; and

(C) The appropriate terms and conditions of supervision and responses to violations of supervision.

(4) If a court uses the results of a risk/needs assessment, it should consider any limitations of the instrument that have been raised in the probation report or by counsel, including:

(A) That the instrument's risk scores are based on group data, such that the instrument is able to identify only groups of high-risk offenders, for example, not a particular high-risk individual;

(B) Whether the instrument's proprietary nature has been invoked to prevent the disclosure of information relating to how it weighs static and dynamic risk factors and how it determines risk scores;

(C) Whether any scientific research has raised questions that the instrument unfairly classifies offenders by gender, race, or ethnicity; and

(D) Whether the instrument has been validated on a relevant population.

(Subd (d) adopted effective January 1, 2018.)

(e) Improper uses of the results of a risk/needs assessment at sentencing

(1) The results of a risk/needs assessment should not be used to determine:

(A) Whether to incarcerate a defendant; or

(B) The severity of the sentence.

(2) The results of a risk/needs assessment should not be considered by the court for defendants statutorily ineligible for supervision.

(Subd (e) adopted effective January 1, 2018.)

(f) Amenability to or suitability for supervision

(1) A court should not interpret a "high" or "medium" risk score as necessarily indicating that a defendant is not amenable to or suitable for community-based supervision. Community-based supervision may be most effective for defendants with "high" and "medium" risk scores. A "low" risk score often, but not necessarily, indicates that a defendant is amenable to or suitable for community-based supervision.Risk scores must be interpreted in the context of all relevant sentencing information received by the court.

(2) Ordinarily a defendant's level of supervision should correspond to his or her level of risk of recidivism. In most cases, a court should order that a low-risk defendant receive less supervision and a high-risk defendant more.

(3) A court should order services that address the defendant's needs.

(Subd (f) adopted effective January 1, 2018.)

(g) Education regarding the nature, purpose, and limits of risk/needs assessment information is critical to the proper use of such information. Education should include all justice system partners.

(Subd (g) adopted effective January 1, 2018.)
Standard 4.35 adopted effective January 1, 2018.

Advisory Committee Comment

Subdivision (d)(1)–(2). Although the results of risk/needs assessments provide important information for use by the court at sentencing, they are not designed as a substitute for the exercise of judicial discretion and judgment. The information should not be used as the sole basis of the court's decision, but should be considered in the context of all of the information received in a sentencing proceeding. If justified by the circumstances of the case, it is appropriate for the court to impose a disposition not supported by the results of a risk/needs assessment. (See *State v. Loomis* (2016) 371 Wis.2d 235, 266 ["Just as corrections staff should disregard risk scores that are inconsistent with other factors, we expect that … courts will exercise discretion when assessing a … risk score with respect to each individual defendant"].)

Subdivision (d)(4). Court and justice partners should understand any limitations of the particular instrument used to generate the results of a risk/needs assessment. (See *State v. Loomis, supra,* 371 Wis.2d at p. 264 [requiring presentence investigation reports to state the limitations of the instrument used, including the proprietary nature of that instrument, any absence of a cross-validation study for relevant populations, and any questions raised in studies about whether the instrument disproportionately classifies minority offenders as having a higher risk of recidivism].) The Wisconsin court also required that all presentence investigation reports caution that risk/needs assessment tools must be constantly monitored and renormed for accuracy because of changing populations and subpopulations. (*Ibid.*) California courts should similarly consider any such limitations in the accuracy of the particular instrument employed in the case under review. (See *ibid.* ["Providing information to sentencing courts on the limitations and cautions attendant with the use of … risk assessments will enable courts to better assess the accuracy of the assessment and the appropriate weight to be given to the risk score"].)

Subdivision (d)(4)(D). Validating a risk/needs assessment instrument will increase its accuracy and reliability. Validation on a relevant population or subpopulation is recommended to account for differences in local policies, implementation practices, and offender populations. Ongoing monitoring and renorming of the instrument may be necessary to reflect changes in a population or subpopulation. Revalidation of the instrument is also necessary if any of its dynamic or static risk factors are modified.

Subdivision (e). When the court is considering whether to place a person on supervision at an original sentencing proceeding or after a violation of supervision, the results of a risk/needs assessment may assist the court in assessing the person's amenability to supervision and services in the community. But when the person is ineligible for supervision, or the court has otherwise decided not to grant or reinstate probation, the results of a risk/needs assessment should not be used in determining the period of incarceration to be imposed. (See *State v. Loomis, supra,* 371 Wis.2d at p. 256 [holding that risk/needs assessments should not be used to determine the severity of a sentence or whether a defendant is incarcerated]; *Malenchik v. State* (Ind. 2010) 928 N.E.2d 564, 573 ["It is clear that [risk/needs assessment instruments are neither intended] nor recommended to substitute for the judicial function of determining the length of sentence appropriate for each offender"].)

Subdivision (f). Risk/needs assessment instruments generally produce a numerical or descriptive "risk score" such as "high," "moderate," or "low" risk. It is critical that courts and justice partners understand the meaning and limitations of such designations. First, because risk assessments are based on group data, they are able to identify groups of high-risk offenders, not a particular high-risk individual. Second, in some assessment instruments, "risk" refers only to a generalized risk of committing a new offense, not to the seriousness of the subsequent offense (e.g., violent, sex, drug, or theft). Nor does "high risk" necessarily mean "highly dangerous." A high-risk drug offender, for example, may present a high risk that he or she will use drugs again, but does not necessarily present a high risk to commit a violent felony. Third, scientific research indicates that medium- and high-risk offenders may most benefit from evidence-based supervision and programs that address critical risk factors. Courts and probation departments should also consider how presentence investigation reports present risk assessment information. A report that merely refers to the defendant as "high risk" may incorrectly imply that the defendant presents a great danger to public safety and must therefore be incarcerated. Conversely, "low risk" does not necessarily mean "no risk."

Subdivision (g). An instrument's accuracy and reliability depend on its proper administration. Training and continuing education should be required for anyone who administers the instrument. Judges with sentencing assignments should receive appropriate training on the purpose, use, and limits of risk/needs assessments. (See Guiding Principle 4, Stakeholder Training, in Pamela M. Casey et al., *Using Offender Risk and Needs Assessment Information at Sentencing: Guidance for Courts from a National Working Group* (National Center for State Courts, 2011) pp. 21–22.)

Standard 4.40.   Traffic infraction procedures

To insure the prompt and efficient disposition of traffic infraction cases, each court should:

(1) Authorize the clerk, within limits set by the court, to grant defendants extensions of time for the posting of bail and payment of fines.

(2) Authorize the clerk or other court official to accept offers of proof of correction or compliance in accordance with the bail schedule without the necessity of a court appearance.

Standard 4.40 amended and renumbered effective January 1, 2007; adopted as sec. 10.5 effective July 1, 1977.

Standard 4.41.   Courtesy notice—traffic procedures [Repealed]

Standard 4.41 repealed effective January 1, 2017; adopted as sec. 10.6 effective January 1, 1987; previously amended and renumbered effective January 1, 2007.

Standard 4.42.   Traffic infraction trial scheduling

(a) Review of procedures

Courts should adopt and periodically review procedures governing the scheduling of traffic infraction trials that minimize appearance time and costs for defendants, witnesses, and law enforcement officers.

(Subd (a) amended and lettered effective January 1, 2007; adopted as part of unlettered subdivision effective January 1, 1987.)

(b) Meetings

Courts should hold periodic meetings with representatives from local law enforcement agencies, the prosecution and defense bars, and other interested groups as appropriate in an effort to achieve this goal.

(Subd (b) amended and lettered effective January 1, 2007; adopted as part of unlettered subdivision effective January 1, 1987.)

Standard 4.42 amended and renumbered effective January 1, 2007; adopted as sec. 10.7 effective January 1, 1987.

Title 5
Standards for Cases Involving Children and Families

Standard 5.20. Uniform standards of practice for providers of supervised visitation

Standard 5.30. Family court matters

Standard 5.40. Juvenile court matters

Standard 5.45. Resource guidelines for child abuse and neglect cases

Standard 5.10.   Guidelines for determining payment for costs of appointed counsel for children in family court [Repealed]

Standard 5.10 repealed effective January 1, 2008; adopted as sec. 20.6 effective January 1, 1992; previously amended effective January 1, 2005, and July 1, 2005; previously amended and renumbered effective January 1, 2007.

Standard 5.11.   Guidelines for appointment of counsel for minors when time with or responsibility for the minor is disputed [Repealed]

Standard 5.11 repealed effective January 1, 2008; adopted as sec. 20.5 effective January 1, 1990; previously amended and renumbered effective January 1, 2007.

Standard 5.20.   Uniform standards of practice for providers of supervised visitation

(a) Scope of service

This standard defines the standards of practice, including duties and obligations, for providers of supervised visitation under Family Code sections 3200 and 3200.5. Unless specified otherwise, the standards of practice are designed to apply to all providers of supervised visitation, whether the provider is a friend, relative, paid independent contractor, employee, intern, or volunteer operating independently or through a supervised visitation center or agency. The goal of these standards of practice is to assure the safety and welfare of the child, adults, and providers of supervised visitation. Once safety is assured, the best interest of the child is the paramount consideration at all stages and particularly in deciding the manner in which supervision is provided. Each court is encouraged to adopt local court rules necessary to implement these standards of practice.

(Subd (a) amended effective January 1, 2015; previously amended effective January 1, 2007.)

(b) Definitions

For purposes of this standard, the following definitions apply:

(1) A "nonprofessional provider," as defined in Family Code section 3200.5, is any person who is not paid for providing supervised visitation services.

(2) A "professional provider," as defined in Family Code section 3200.5, is any person who is paid for providing supervised visitation services, or an independent contractor, employee, intern, or volunteer operating independently or through a supervised visitation center or agency.

(3) A "provider," as defined in Family Code section 3200 [1], **includes** any individual [2] **who functions as a visitation monitor, as well as** supervised visitation [3] **centers.**

(4) "Supervised visitation" is contact between a noncustodial party and one or more children in the presence of a neutral third person.

(5) A "TrustLine provider," is a professional supervised visitation provider who is registered on TrustLine, a database that is administered by the California Department of Social Services.

(Subd (b) amended effective January 1, 2021; previously amended effective January 1, 2007, and January 1, 2015.)

Standard 5.20(b).   2020 Deletes. [1] defines the term "provider" as including [2] or [3] center that monitors visitation. Supervised visitation

(c) Type of provider

Who provides the supervision and the manner in which supervision is provided depends on different factors, including local resources, the financial situation of the parties, and the degree of risk in each case. While the court makes the final decision as to the manner in which supervision is provided and any terms or conditions, the court may consider recommendations by the attorney for the child, the parties and their attorneys, Family Court Services staff, evaluators, and therapists. As specified in Family Code section 3200.5, in any case in which the court has determined that there is domestic violence or child abuse or neglect, as defined in section 11165.6 of the Penal Code, and the court determines supervision is necessary, the court must consider whether to use a professional or nonprofessional provider based on the child's best interest.

(Subd (c) amended effective January 1, 2015; previously amended effective January 1, 2007.)

(d) Qualifications of nonprofessional providers

(1) [1] Unless otherwise ordered by the court or stipulated by the parties, the nonprofessional provider must:

(A) Have no record of a conviction for child molestation, child abuse, or other crimes against a person;

(B) Have proof of automobile insurance if transporting the child;

(C) Have no current or past court order in which the provider is the person being supervised; and

(D) Agree to adhere to and enforce the court order regarding supervised visitation.

(2) Unless otherwise ordered by the court or stipulated by the parties, the nonprofessional provider should:

(A) Be 21 years of age or older;

(B) Have no record of conviction for driving under the influence (DUI) within the last 5 years;

(C) Not have been on probation or parole for the last 10 years;

(D) Have no civil, criminal, or juvenile restraining orders within the last 10 years; and

(E) Not be financially dependent on the person being supervised.

(3) Sign a local court form or *Declaration of Supervised Visitation Provider (Nonprofessional)* (form FL-324(NP)) stating that all requirements to be a nonprofessional provider have been met.

(Subd (d) amended effective January 1, 2021; adopted as part of subd (c); previously relettered and amended effective January 1, 2015.)

Standard 5.20(d). 2020 Deletes. [1] A "nonprofessional provider" is any person who is not paid for providing supervised visitation services.

(e) Qualifications of professional providers

[1] The professional provider must:

(1) Be 21 years of age or older;

(2) Have no record of conviction for driving under the influence (DUI) within the last 5 years;

(3) Not have been on probation or parole for the last 10 years;

(4) Have no record of a conviction for child molestation, child abuse, or other crimes against a person;

(5) Have proof of automobile insurance if transporting the child;

(6) Have no civil, criminal, or juvenile restraining orders within the last 10 years;

(7) Have no current or past court order in which the provider is the person being supervised;

(8) Be able to speak the language of the party being supervised and of the child, or the provider must provide a neutral interpreter over the age of 18 who is able to do so;

(9) Agree to adhere to and enforce the court order regarding supervised visitation;

(10) Complete a Live Scan criminal background check, at the expense of the provider or the supervised visitation center or agency, before providing visitation services;

(11) Be registered as a TrustLine provider under chapter 3.35 (commencing with section 1596.60) of division 2 of the Health and Safety Code. Notwithstanding any other law, a person is ineligible to be a professional provider if the California Department of Social Services either:

(A) Denies that person's TrustLine registration under Health and Safety Code sections 1596.605 or 1596.607; or

(B) Revokes that person's TrustLine registration under Health and Safety Code section 1596.608;

(12) Meet the training requirements [2] **listed** in (f); [3]

(13) Sign a [4] *Declaration of Supervised Visitation Provider* [5] *(Professional)* (form FL-324(P)) stating that all requirements to be a professional provider have been met**; and**

(14) Sign a separate, updated form FL-324(P) each time the professional provider submits a report to the court.

(Subd (e) amended effective January 1, 2021; adopted as part of subd (c); previously relettered as subd (e) and amended effective January 1, 2015.)

Standard 5.20(e). 2020 Deletes. [1] A "professional provider" is any person paid for providing supervised visitation services, or an independent contractor, employee, intern, or volunteer operating independently or through a supervised visitation center or agency. **[2]** stated **[3]** and (11) **[4]** declaration or **[5]** (form FL-324)

(f) Training for professional providers

(1) [1] **Before providing services**, professional providers must [2] **complete** 24 hours of training [3], **including at least 12 hours of classroom instruction in** the following subjects:

(A) The role of a professional provider;

(B) Child abuse reporting laws;

(C) Record-keeping procedures;

(D) Screening, monitoring, and termination of visitation;

(E) Developmental needs of children;

(F) Legal responsibilities and obligations of a provider;

(G) Cultural sensitivity;

(H) Conflicts of interest, **including the acceptance of gifts**;

(I) Confidentiality;

(J) Issues relating to substance abuse, child abuse, sexual abuse, and domestic violence; and

(K) Basic knowledge of family and juvenile law.

(2) Of the 24 hours of training required in (1), the training must include at least:

(A) Three hours on the screening, monitoring, and termination of visitation;

(B) Three hours on the developmental needs of children;

(C) Three hours on issues relating to substance abuse, child abuse, sexual abuse, and domestic violence; and

(D) One hour on basic knowledge of family law.

(3) On or after January 1, 2021, to complete the required training in child abuse reporting laws under (1)(B), a professional provider must complete an online training required for mandated reporters that is provided by the California Department of Social Services. This mandatory online training is not intended to increase the total of 24 hours of training required in (1).

(Subd (f) amended effective January 1, 2021; adopted as subd (d) effective January 1, 2007; previously amended and relettered as subd (f) effective January 1, 2015.)

Standard 5.20(f). 2020 Deletes. [1] Each court is encouraged to make available to all providers informational materials about the role of a provider, the terms and conditions of supervised visitation, and the legal responsibilities and obligations of a provider under this standard. (2) In addition **[2]** receive **[3]** that includes

(g) Safety and security procedures

All providers must make every reasonable effort to assure the safety and welfare of the child and adults during the visitation. Professional providers should establish a written protocol, with the assistance of the local law enforcement agency, that describes the emergency assistance and responses that can be expected from the local law enforcement agency. In addition, the professional provider should:

(1) Establish and state in writing minimum security procedures and inform the parties of these procedures before the commencement of supervised visitation;

(2) Conduct comprehensive intake and screening to understand the nature and degree of risk for each case. The procedures for intake should include separate interviews with the parties before the first visit. During the interview, the provider should obtain identifying information and explain the reasons for temporary suspension or termination of a visit under this standard. If the child is of sufficient age and capacity, the provider should include the child in part of the intake or orientation process. Any discussion should be presented to the child in a manner appropriate to the child's developmental stage;

(3) Obtain during the intake process:

(A) Copies of any protective order;

(B) Current court orders;

(C) Any Judicial Council form relating to supervised visitation orders;

(D) A report of any written records of allegations of domestic violence or abuse; and

(E) An account of the child's health needs if the child has a chronic health condition; and

(4) Establish written procedures that must be followed in the event a child is abducted during supervised visitation.

(Subd (g) amended and relettered effective January 1, 2015; adopted as subd (d) effective January 1, 1998; previously amended and relettered as subd (e) effective January 1, 2007.)

(h) Ratio of children to provider

The ratio of children to a professional provider must be contingent on:

(1) The degree of risk factors present in each case;

(2) The nature of supervision required in each case;

(3) The number and ages of the children to be supervised during a visit;

(4) The number of people, as provided in the court order, visiting the child during the visit;

(5) The duration and location of the visit; and

(6) The experience of the provider.

(Subd (h) amended and relettered effective January 1, 2015; adopted as subd (e) effective January 1, 1998; previously amended and relettered as subd (f) effective January 1, 2007.)

(i) Conflict of interest

All providers should maintain neutrality by refusing to discuss the merits of the case or agree with or support one party over another. Any discussion between a provider and the parties should be for the purposes of arranging visitation and providing for the safety of the children. In order to avoid a conflict of interest, the professional provider should not:

(1) Be financially dependent on the person being supervised;

(2) Be an employee of the person being supervised;

(3) Be an employee of or affiliated with any superior court in the county in which the supervision is ordered unless specified in the employment contract; or

(4) Be in an intimate relationship with the person being supervised.

(Subd (i) amended and relettered effective January 1, 2015; adopted as subd (f) effective January 1, 1998; previously amended and relettered as subd (g) effective January 1, 2007.)

(j) Maintenance and disclosure of records for professional providers

(1) Professional providers must keep a record for each case, including the following:

(A) A written record of each contact and visit;

(B) Who attended the visit;

(C) Any failure to comply with the terms and conditions of the visitation; and

(D) Any incidence of abuse as required by law.

(2) Case recordings should be limited to facts, observations, and direct statements made by the parties, not personal conclusions, suggestions, or opinions of the provider. All contacts by the provider in person, in writing, or by telephone with either party, the children, the court, attorneys, mental health professionals, and referring agencies should be documented in the case file. All entries should be dated and signed by the person recording the entry.

(3) If ordered by the court or requested by either party or the attorney for either party or the attorney for the child, a report about the supervised visit must be produced. These reports should include facts, observations, and direct statements and not opinions or recommendations regarding future visitation. The original report must be sent to the court if so ordered, or to the requesting party or attorney, and copies should be sent to all parties, their attorneys, and the attorney for the child.

(4) Any identifying information about the parties and the child, including addresses, telephone numbers, places of employment, and schools, is confidential, should not be disclosed, and should be deleted from documents before releasing them to any court, attorney, attorney for the child, party, mediator, evaluator, mental health professional, social worker, or referring agency, except as required in reporting suspected child abuse.

(Subd (j) amended and relettered effective January 1, 2015; adopted as subd (g) effective January 1, 1998; previously amended and relettered as subd (h) effective January 1, 2007.)

(k) Confidentiality

Communications between parties and providers of supervised visitation are not protected by any privilege of confidentiality. Professional providers should, whenever possible, maintain confidentiality regarding the case except when:

(1) Ordered by the court;

(2) Subpoenaed to produce records or testify in court;

(3) Requested to provide information about the case by a mediator or evaluator in conjunction with a court-ordered mediation, investigation, or evaluation;

(4) Required to provide information about the case by Child Protective Services; or

(5) Requested to provide information about the case by law enforcement.

(Subd (k) amended and relettered effective January 1, 2015; adopted as subd (h) effective January 1, 1998; previously amended and relettered as subd (i) effective January 1, 2007.)

(l) Delineation of terms and conditions

The provider bears the sole responsibility for enforcement of all the terms and conditions of any supervised visitation. Unless otherwise ordered by the court, the provider should implement the following terms and conditions:

(1) Monitor conditions to assure the safety and welfare of the child;

(2) Enforce the frequency and duration of the visits as ordered by the court;

(3) Avoid any attempt to take sides with either party;

(4) Ensure that all contact between the child and the noncustodial party is within the provider's hearing and sight at all times, and that discussions are audible to the provider;

(5) Speak in a language spoken by the child and the noncustodial party;

(6) Allow no derogatory comments about the other parent, his or her family, caretaker, child, or child's siblings;

(7) Allow no discussion of the court case or possible future outcomes;

(8) Allow neither the provider nor the child to be used to gather information about the other party or caretaker or to transmit documents, information, or personal possessions;

(9) Allow no spanking, hitting, or threatening the child;

(10) Allow no visits to occur while the visiting party appears to be under the influence of alcohol or illegal drugs;

(11) Allow no emotional, verbal, physical, or sexual abuse;

(12) Allow no contact between the custodial and noncustodial parents unless ordered by the court; and

(13) Ensure that the parties follow any additional rules set forth by the provider or the court.

(Subd (l) amended and relettered effective January 1, 2015; adopted as subd (i) effective January 1, 1998; previously amended and relettered as subd (j) effective January 1, 2007.)

(m) Safety considerations for sexual abuse cases

In cases where there are allegations of sexual abuse, in addition to the requirements of (l), the provider should comply with the following terms and conditions, unless otherwise ordered by the court:

(1) Allow no exchanges of gifts, money, or cards;

(2) Allow no photographing, audiotaping, or videotaping of the child;

(3) Allow no physical contact with the child such as lap sitting, hair combing, stroking, hand holding, hugging, wrestling, tickling, horseplaying, changing diapers, or accompanying the child to the bathroom;

(4) Allow no whispering, passing notes, hand signals, or body signals; and

(5) Allow no supervised visitation in the location where the alleged sexual abuse occurred.

(Subd (m) amended and relettered effective January 1, 2015; adopted as subd (j) effective January 1, 1998; previously amended and relettered as subd (k) effective January 1, 2007.)

(n) Legal responsibilities and obligations of a provider

All nonprofessional providers of supervised visitation should, and all professional providers must:

(1) Advise the parties before commencement of supervised visitation that no confidential privilege exists;

(2) Report suspected child abuse to the appropriate agency, as provided by law, and inform the parties of the provider's obligation to make such reports; and

(3) Suspend or terminate visitation under (p).

(Subd (n) amended and relettered effective January 1, 2015; adopted as subd (k) effective January 1, 1998; previously amended and relettered as subd (l) effective January 1, 2007.)

(o) Additional legal responsibilities of professional providers

In addition to the legal responsibilities and obligations required in (n), professional providers must:

(1) Prepare a written contract to be signed by the parties before commencement of the supervised visitation. The contract should inform each party of the terms and conditions of supervised visitation; and

(2) Review custody and visitation orders relevant to the supervised visitation.

(Subd (o) amended and relettered effective January 1, 2015; adopted as subd (l) effective January 1, 1998; previously amended and relettered as subd (m) effective January 1, 2007.)

(p) Temporary suspension or termination of supervised visitation

(1) All providers must make every reasonable effort to provide a safe visit for the child and the noncustodial party.

(2) However, if a provider determines that the rules of the visit have been violated, the child has become acutely distressed, or the safety of the child or the provider is at risk, the visit may be temporarily interrupted, rescheduled at a later date, or terminated.

(3) All interruptions or terminations of visits must be recorded in the case file.

(4) All providers must advise both parties of the reasons for interruption of a visit or termination.

(Subd (p) amended and relettered effective January 1, 2015; adopted as subd (m) effective January 1, 1998; previously amended and relettered as subd (n) effective January 1, 2007.)

(q) Additional requirements for professional providers

Professional providers must state the reasons for temporary suspension or termination of supervised visitation in writing and provide the written statement to both parties, their attorneys, the attorney for the child, and the court.

(Subd (q) amended and relettered effective January 1, 2015; adopted as subd (n) effective January 1, 1998; previously amended and relettered to subd (o) effective January 1, 2007.)

(r) Informational materials; procedures

(1) Each court is encouraged to make available to all providers informational materials about the role of a provider, the terms and conditions of supervised visitation, and the legal responsibilities and obligations of a provider under this standard.

(2) By January 1, 2022, each court must develop and adopt local rules that establish procedures for processing and maintaining:

(A) *Declaration of Supervised Visitation Provider (Professional)* (form FL-324(P)), along with the professional provider's original report required in (j)(3) of this standard; and

(B) The nonprofessional supervised visitation provider's declaration regarding qualifications, whether the provider uses the court's local form or *Declaration of Supervised Visitation Provider (Nonprofessional)* (form FL-324(NP)).

(Subd (r) adopted effective January 1, 2021.)

Standard 5.20 amended effective January 1, 2021; adopted as sec. 26.2 effective January 1, 1998; previously amended and renumbered effective January 1, 2007; previous amended effective January 1, 2015.

Standard 5.30. Family court matters

(a) Judicial assignments to family court

In a court with a separate family court, the presiding judge of the superior court should assign judges to the family court to serve for a minimum of three years. In selecting judges for family court assignments, the presiding judge should consider, in addition to rule 10.603(c)(1)(A) of the California Rules of Court, the judge's prior experience in family law litigation and mediation, as well as whether the judge prefers to serve in a family law department.

(Subd (a) adopted effective January 1, 2007.)

(b) Case assignment to same department

To the extent possible, family law actions related to the same family should be assigned to the same judicial officer for all purposes, so that all decisions that are made in a case through final judgment are issued by the same judicial officer.

(Subd (b) adopted effective January 1, 2007.)

(c) Importance of family court

The supervising judge in the family court, in consultation with the presiding judge of the superior court, should:

(1) Motivate and educate other judges regarding the significance of family court; and

(2) Work to ensure that sufficient judicial officers, court staff, family law facilitators, child custody mediators and evaluators, interpreters, financial resources, and adequate facilities are assigned to the family court to allow adequate time to hear and decide the matters before it.

(Subd (c) adopted effective January 1, 2007.)

(d) Compensation for court-appointed attorneys

The supervising judge of the family court should ensure that court-appointed attorneys in the family court are compensated at a level equivalent to attorneys appointed by the court in comparable types of cases.

(Subd (d) adopted effective January 1, 2007.)

(e) Training and education

Family court law is a specialized area of the law that requires dedication and study. The supervising judge of the family court has a responsibility to maintain high-quality services in family court. The quality of services provided by judicial officers and court staff depends, in significant part, on appropriate training and education, from the beginning of the family court assignment and on a continuing basis thereafter.

(1) Family court judicial officers, family law facilitators, child custody mediators and evaluators, interpreters, other court staff, and court-appointed attorneys should have sufficient training to perform their jobs competently.

(2) The supervising judge of the family court should promote access to printed, electronic, Internet, and other family law resources.

(Subd (e) adopted effective January 1, 2007.)

(f) Unique role of a family court

Under the direction of the presiding judge of the superior court, the family court, to the extent that it does not interfere with the adjudication process or violate any ethical constraints, is encouraged to:

(1) Provide active leadership within the community in determining the needs of, and obtaining and developing resources and services for children and families who participate in the family law court system;

(2) Investigate and determine the availability of specific prevention, intervention, and treatment services in the community for families who come before the family courts;

(3) Take an active role in helping the court develop rules and procedures that will result in the ordering of appropriate treatment and services for children and families;

(4) Exercise a leadership role in the development and maintenance of services for self-represented and financially disadvantaged litigants;

(5) Take an active part in the formation of a community-wide network to promote and coordinate private- and public-sector efforts to focus attention and resources on the needs of family law litigants;

(6) Educate the community and its institutions, including the media, concerning the role of the family court in meeting the complex needs of families;

(7) Encourage the development of community services and resources to assist families and children in the family court system, including self-help information; supervised visitation; substance abuse and drug prevention, intervention, and treatment; services for families with domestic violence issues; counseling; parenting education; vocational training; mediation; alternative dispute resolution options; and other resources to support families;

(8) Manage cases more efficiently and effectively to avoid conflicting orders;

(9) Take an active role in promoting completion of cases in a timely manner;

(10) Appoint counsel for children in appropriate family law custody cases; and

(11) Ensure that the best interest of children is served throughout the family court process.

(Subd (f) adopted effective January 1, 2007.)

(g) Appointment of attorneys and other persons

A court should follow the guidelines of standard 10.21 of the California Standards of Judicial Administration when appointing attorneys, arbitrators, mediators, referees, masters, receivers, and other persons.

(Subd (g) adopted effective January 1, 2007.)

Standard 5.30 adopted effective January 1, 2007.

Advisory Committee Comment

Standard 5.30. Family court matters include proceedings under the Family Code for dissolution of marriage, nullity of marriage, legal separation, custody and support of minor children; or actions under the Domestic Violence Prevention Act, the Uniform Parentage Act, the Uniform Child Custody Jurisdiction and Enforcement Act, Domestic Partner Registration Act, and the Uniform Interstate Family Support Act; local child support agency actions under the Family Code; and contempt proceedings relating to family law or local child support agency actions.

Subdivision (a). This subdivision implements the legislative mandate of Family Code section 2330.3(b) requiring the Judicial Council to adopt a standard of judicial administration prescribing a minimum length of a judge's family law assignment. Standard 5.30 sets a standard in family court that is similar to the juvenile court standards stated in standard 5.40, Juvenile Court Matters.

Family law is complex and constantly evolving. The laws concerning child custody, support, domestic violence, and property division are always changing. Not only does the family law judge have to understand family law and procedure but also issues that involve bankruptcy, estate planning, insurance, state and federal tax law, business, immigration, and criminal law, which can frequently arise in the context of a family law case. Because of the complexity and long-range impact of the judicial determinations, the presiding judge should strive to place experienced judges in family law assignments.

Considering the constantly evolving changes in the law, as well as the unique nature of the proceedings in family court, the family court judge should be willing to commit to a minimum tenure of three years. Not only does this tenure afford the judge the opportunity to become well acquainted with the complexity of the family court process, but it also provides continuity to a system that demands it.

Subdivision (b). This subdivision implements the legislative mandate of Family Code section 2330.3(a), which requires that dissolution actions, to the greatest extent possible, be assigned to the same superior court department for all purposes, so that all decisions in a case are made by the same judicial officer. This subdivision expands the Legislature's requirement by including other related family court matters, such as those filed under the Uniform Parentage Act, Domestic Violence Prevention Act, in recognition that the same families may enter the family court through a variety of actions.

The committee recognizes that having the same judicial officer hear all actions involving the same family may not be practical in all cases for reasons that include funding limitations, assignment rotations, illness, vacations, and retirements. In some courts, one judge does not hear all aspects of a family's legal problems because of multiple courthouse locations or specifically designated funding of certain issues (e.g., Title IV-D child support issues). However, the committee agrees with the legislative intent in enacting section 2330.3(a), which was to expedite and simplify the dissolution process, reduce the litigation expenses and costs, and encourage greater judicial supervision of cases involving dissolution of marriage. Family law actions often involve a succession of hearings to resolve the various issues that arise. A single judge's involvement over this period of time allows the judge to be more familiar with the particular actions and issues, which creates judicial efficiencies that expedite their handling. One judge hearing all actions involving a family also helps avoid conflicting orders, alleviates the need to hold multiple hearings on the same issue, improves the court process, promotes consistency, and enhances fairness in family proceedings.

Subdivision (c). The family court is an integral part of the justice system. Decisions made by family law judges can have significant and lasting impacts on the lives of the parties and their children. The work of the family court has a significant impact on the health of families and ultimately on the strength of the community. The parties deserve to have adequate time to present their cases, and the judges should have the resources they need to enable them to make informed decisions. It is only through the constant exertion of pressure to maintain resources and the continuous education of court-related personnel and administrators that the historic trend to give less priority and provide fewer resources to the family court can be changed.

Subdivision (d). Fees paid to court-appointed attorneys who represent children in family court are sometimes less than the fees paid attorneys doing other comparable legal work thereby demeaning the work of the family court and leading many to believe that such work is less important. It may also discourage attorneys from accepting these appointments. Compensation for legal work in the family court should reflect the importance of the work.

Subdivision (e)(2). A significant barrier to having well-trained attorneys and educated self-represented litigants is a lack of current educational materials relating to family court practice. Law libraries, law offices, and court systems traditionally have not devoted adequate resources to purchase such educational materials. With advances in technology, resources can be accessed, shared, developed, or made available through electronic/computer-based, online, and multimedia means, audiotape and videotape, DVD, CD, Web-based audiocasts and videocasts, and other media to supplement print materials.

Subdivision (f). In addition to the traditional role of fairly and efficiently resolving disputes before the court, a family court judge occupies a unique position within California's judiciary. California law empowers the family court judge not only to order relief related to the needs of families under its jurisdiction but also to enforce and review the compliance with such orders. This oversight function includes the obligation to understand and work with those public and private agencies that provide services for families. As such, the family court assignment requires a dramatic shift in emphasis from judging in the traditional sense. Active and public judicial support and encouragement of programs serving children and families in family court poses no conflict with traditional concepts of judicial ethics and is an important function of the family court judge. These efforts enhance the overall administration of justice for families.

Standard 5.40. Juvenile court matters

(a) Assignments to juvenile court

The presiding judge of the superior court should assign judges to the juvenile court to serve for a minimum of three years. Priority should be given to judges who have expressed an interest in the assignment.

(Subd (a) adopted effective July 1, 1989.)

(b) Importance of juvenile court

The presiding judge of the juvenile court, in consultation with the presiding judge of the superior court, should:

(1) Motivate and educate other judges regarding the significance of juvenile court.

(2) Work to ensure that sufficient judges and staff, facilities, and financial resources are assigned to the juvenile court to allow adequate time to hear and decide the matters before it.

(Subd (b) amended effective January 1, 2007; adopted effective July 1, 1989.)

(c) Standards of representation and compensation

The presiding judge of the juvenile court should:

(1) Encourage attorneys who practice in juvenile court, including all court-appointed and contract attorneys, to continue their practice in juvenile court for substantial periods of time. A substantial period of time is at least two years and preferably from three to five years.

(2) Confer with the county public defender, county district attorney, county counsel, and other public law office leaders and encourage them to raise the status of attorneys working in the juvenile courts as follows: hire attorneys who are interested in serving in the juvenile court for a substantial part of their careers; permit and encourage attorneys, based on interest and ability, to remain in juvenile court assignments for significant periods of time; and work to ensure that attorneys who have chosen to serve in the juvenile court have the same promotional and salary opportunities as attorneys practicing in other assignments within a law office.

(3) Establish minimum standards of practice to which all court-appointed and public office attorneys will be expected to conform. These standards should delineate the responsibilities of attorneys relative to investigation and evaluation of the case, preparation for and conduct of hearings, and advocacy for their respective clients.

(4) In conjunction with other leaders in the legal community, ensure that attorneys appointed in the juvenile court are compensated in a manner equivalent to attorneys appointed by the court in other types of cases.

(Subd (c) amended effective January 1, 2007; adopted effective July 1, 1992.)

(d) Training and orientation

The presiding judge of the juvenile court should:

(1) Establish relevant prerequisites for court-appointed attorneys and advocates in the juvenile court.

(2) Develop orientation and in-service training programs for judicial officers, attorneys, volunteers, law enforcement personnel, court personnel, and child advocates to ensure that all are adequately trained concerning all issues relating to special education rights and responsibilities, including the right of each child with exceptional needs to receive a free, appropriate public education and the right of each child with educational disabilities to receive accommodations.

(3) Promote the establishment of a library or other resource center in which information about juvenile court practice (including books, periodicals, videotapes, and other training materials) can be collected and made available to all participants in the juvenile system.

(4) Ensure that attorneys who appear in juvenile court have sufficient training to perform their jobs competently, as follows: require that all court-appointed attorneys meet minimum training and continuing legal education standards as a condition of their appointment to juvenile court matters; and encourage the leaders of public law offices that have responsibilities in juvenile court to require their attorneys who appear in juvenile court to have at least the same training and continuing legal education required of court-appointed attorneys.

(Subd (d) amended effective January 1, 2001; adopted effective July 1, 1989; previously amended and relettered effective July 1, 1992.)

(e) Unique role of a juvenile court judge

Judges of the juvenile court, in consultation with the presiding judge of the juvenile court and the presiding judge of the superior court, to the extent that it does not interfere with the adjudication process, are encouraged to:

(1) Provide active leadership within the community in determining the needs of and obtaining and developing resources and services for at-risk children and families. At-risk children include delinquents, dependents, and status offenders.

(2) Investigate and determine the availability of specific prevention, intervention, and treatment services in the community for at-risk children and their families.

(3) Exercise their authority by statute or rule to review, order, and enforce the delivery of specific services and treatment for at-risk children and their families.

(4) Exercise a leadership role in the development and maintenance of permanent programs of interagency cooperation and coordination among the court and the various public agencies that serve at-risk children and their families.

(5) Take an active part in the formation of a communitywide network to promote and unify private and public sector efforts to focus attention and resources for at-risk children and their families.

(6) Maintain close liaison with school authorities and encourage coordination of policies and programs.

(7) Educate the community and its institutions through every available means, including the media, concerning the role of the juvenile court in meeting the complex needs of at-risk children and their families.

(8) Evaluate the criteria established by child protection agencies for initial removal and reunification decisions and communicate the court's expectations of what constitutes "reasonable efforts" to prevent removal or hasten return of the child.

(9) Encourage the development of community services and resources to assist homeless, truant, runaway, and incorrigible children.

(10) Be familiar with all detention facilities, placements, and institutions used by the court.

(11) Act in all instances consistent with the public safety and welfare.

(Subd (e) amended effective January 1, 2007; adopted effective July 1, 1989; previously relettered effective July 1, 1992.)

(f) Appointment of attorneys and other persons

For the appointment of attorneys, arbitrators, mediators, referees, masters, receivers, and other persons, each court should follow rule 10.611 and the guidelines of standard 10.21.

(Subd (f) amended effective January 1, 2007; adopted effective January 1, 1999.)

(g) Educational rights of children in the juvenile court

The juvenile court should be guided by certain general principles:

(1) A significant number of children in the juvenile court process have exceptional needs that, if properly identified and assessed, would qualify such children to receive special education and related services under federal and state education law (a free, appropriate public education) (see Ed. Code, § 56000 et seq. and 20 U.S.C. § 1400 et seq.);

(2) Many children in the juvenile court process have disabilities that, if properly identified and assessed, would qualify such children to receive educational accommodations (see § 504 of the Rehabilitation Act of 1973 [29 U.S.C. § 794; 34 C.F.R. § 104.1 et seq.]);

(3) Unidentified and unremediated exceptional needs and unaccommodated disabilities have been found to correlate strongly with juvenile delinquency, substance abuse, mental health issues, teenage pregnancy, school failure and dropout, and adult unemployment and crime; and

(4) The cost of incarcerating children is substantially greater than the cost of providing special education and related services to exceptional needs children and providing educational accommodations to children with disabilities.

(Subd (g) adopted effective January 1, 2001.)

(h) Role of the juvenile court

The juvenile court should:

(1) Take responsibility, with the other juvenile court participants at every stage of the child's case, to ensure that the child's educational needs are met, regardless of whether the child is in the custody of a parent or is suitably placed in the custody of the child welfare agency or probation department and regardless of where the child is placed in school. Each child under the jurisdiction of the juvenile court with exceptional needs has the right to receive a free, appropriate public education, specially designed, at no cost to the parents, to meet the child's unique special education needs. (See Ed. Code, § 56031 and 20 U.S.C. § 1401(8).) Each child with disabilities under the jurisdiction of the juvenile court has the right to receive accommodations. (See § 504 of the Rehabilitation Act of 1973 [29 U.S.C. § 794; 34 C.F.R. § 104.1 et seq. (1980)].) The court should also ensure that each parent or guardian receives information and assistance concerning his or her child's educational entitlements as provided by law.

(2) Provide oversight of the social service and probation agencies to ensure that a child's educational rights are investigated, reported, and monitored. The court should work within the statutory framework to accommodate the sharing of information between agencies. A child who comes before the court and is suspected of having exceptional needs or other educational disabilities should be referred in writing for an assessment to the child's school principal or to the school district's special education office. (See Ed. Code, §§ 56320–56329.) The child's parent, teacher, or other service provider may make the required written referral for assessment. (See Ed. Code, § 56029.)

(3) Require that court reports, case plans, assessments, and permanency plans considered by the court address a child's educational entitlements and how those entitlements are being satisfied, and contain information to assist the court in deciding whether the right of the parent or guardian to make educational decisions for the child should be limited by the court under Welfare and Institutions Code section 361(a) or 726(b). Information concerning whether the school district has met its obligation to provide educational services to the child, including special educational services if the child has exceptional needs under Education Code section 56000 et seq., and to provide accommodations if the child has disabilities as defined in section 504 of the Rehabilitation Act of 1973 (29 U.S.C. § 794; 34 C.F.R. § 104.1 et seq. (1980)) should also be included, along with a recommendation for disposition.

(4) Facilitate coordination of services by joining the local educational agency as a party when it appears that an educational agency has failed to fulfill its legal obligations to provide special education and related services or accommodations to a child in the juvenile court who has been identified as having exceptional needs or educational disabilities. (See Welf. & Inst. Code, §§ 362(a), 727(a).)

(5) Make appropriate orders limiting the educational rights of a parent or guardian who cannot be located or identified, or who is unwilling or unable to be an active participant in ensuring that the child's educational needs are met, and appoint a responsible adult as educational representative for such a child or, if a representative cannot be identified and the child may be eligible for special education and related services or already has an individualized education program, use form JV-535 to refer the child to the local educational agency for special education and related services and prompt appointment of a surrogate parent. (Welf. & Inst. Code, §§ 361, 726; Ed. Code, § 56156.)

(6) Ensure that special education, related services, and accommodations to which the child is entitled are provided whenever the child's school placement changes. (See Ed. Code, § 56325.)

(Subd (h) amended effective January 1, 2007; adopted effective January 1, 2001; previously amended effective January 1, 2004.)

Standard 5.40 amended and renumbered effective January 1, 2007; adopted as sec. 24 effective January 1, 1989; previously amended effective July 1, 1992, January 1, 1999; January 1, 2001, and January 1, 2004.

Advisory Committee Comment

Subdivision (a). Considering the constantly evolving changes in the law, as well as the unique nature of the proceedings in juvenile court, the juvenile court judge should be willing to commit to a tenure of three years. Not only does this tenure afford the judge the opportunity to become well acquainted with the total juvenile justice complex, but it also provides continuity to a system that demands it.

Dependency cases under Welfare and Institutions Code section 300 for the most part last 18 months. The juvenile court judge has a responsibility to oversee these cases, and a single judge's involvement over this period of time is important to help ensure positive results. The ultimate goal should be to perfect a system that serves the needs of both recipients and providers. This can only be done over time and with constant application of effective energy.

Subdivision (b)(2). The juvenile court is an integral part of the justice system. It is only through the constant exertion of pressure to maintain resources and the continuous education of court-related personnel and administrators that the historic trend to minimize the juvenile court can be contained.

Subdivision (c)(4). The quality of justice in the juvenile court is in large part dependent on the quality of the attorneys who appear on behalf of the different parties before the court. The presiding judge of the juvenile court plays a significant role in ensuring that a sufficient number of attorneys of high quality are available to the parties appearing in juvenile court.

Juvenile court practice requires attorneys who have both a special interest in and a substantive understanding of the work of the court. Obtaining and retaining qualified attorneys for the juvenile court requires effective recruiting, training, and employment considerations.

The importance of juvenile court work must be stressed to ensure that juvenile court assignments have the same status and career enhancement opportunities as other assignments for public law office attorneys.

The presiding judge of the juvenile court should urge leaders of public law offices serving the juvenile court to assign experienced, interested, and capable attorneys to that court, and to establish hiring and promotional policies that will encourage the development of a division of the office dedicated to working in the juvenile court.

National commentators are in accord with these propositions: "Court-appointed and public attorneys representing children in abuse and neglect cases, as well as judges, should be specially trained or experienced. Juvenile and family courts should not be the 'training ground' for inexperienced attorneys or judges." (Metropolitan Court Judges Committee, National Council of Juvenile and Family

Court Judges, *Deprived Children: A Judicial Response—73 Recommendations* (1986) p. 14.)

Fees paid to attorneys appearing in juvenile court are sometimes less than the fees paid attorneys doing other legal work. Such a payment scheme demeans the work of the juvenile court, leading many to believe that such work is less important. It may discourage attorneys from selecting juvenile court practice as a career option. The incarceration of a child in a detention facility or a child's permanent loss of his or her family through a termination of parental rights proceeding is at least as important as any other work in the legal system. Compensation for the legal work in the juvenile court should reflect the importance of this work.

Subdivision (d)(4). Juvenile court law is a specialized area of the law that requires dedication and study. The juvenile court judge has a responsibility to maintain high quality in the practice of law in the juvenile court. The quality of representation in the juvenile court depends in good part on the education of the lawyers who appear there. In order to make certain that all parties receive adequate representation, it is important that attorneys have adequate training before they begin practice in juvenile court and on a continuing basis thereafter. The presiding judge of the juvenile court should mandate such training for all court-appointed attorneys and urge leaders of public law offices to provide at least comparable training for attorneys assigned to juvenile court.

A minimum of six hours of continuing legal education is suggested; more hours are recommended. Education methods can include lectures and tapes that meet the legal education requirements.

In addition to basic legal training in juvenile dependency and delinquency law, evidentiary issues, and effective trial practice techniques, training should also include important related issues, including child development, alternative resources for families, effects and treatment of substance abuse, domestic violence, abuse, neglect, modification and enforcement of all court orders, dependency, delinquency, guardianships, conservatorships, interviewing children, and emancipation. Education may also include observational experience such as site visits to institutions and operations critical to the juvenile court.

A significant barrier to the establishment and maintenance of well-trained attorneys is a lack of educational materials relating to juvenile court practice. Law libraries, law offices, and court systems traditionally do not devote adequate resources to the purchase of such educational materials.

Effective January 1, 1993, guidelines and training material will be available from Judicial Council staff.

Subdivision (e)(11). A superior court judge assigned to the juvenile court occupies a unique position within California's judiciary. In addition to the traditional role of fairly and efficiently resolving disputes before the court, the juvenile court judge is statutorily required to discharge other duties. California law empowers the juvenile court judge not only to order services for children under its jurisdiction, but also to enforce and review the delivery of those services. This oversight function includes the obligation to understand and work with the public and private agencies, including school systems, that provide services and treatment programs for children and families. As such, the juvenile court assignment requires a dramatic shift in emphasis from judging in the traditional sense.

The legislative directive to juvenile court judges to "improve system performance in a vigorous and ongoing manner" (Welf. & Inst. Code, § 202) poses no conflict with traditional concepts of judicial ethics. Active and public judicial support and encouragement of programs serving children and families at risk are important functions of the juvenile court judge that enhance the overall administration of justice.

The standards in (e) are derived from statutory requirements in the following sections of the Welfare and Institutions Code as well as the supplementary material promulgated by the National Council of Juvenile and Family Court Judges and others: (1) Welfare and Institutions Code, sections 202, 209, 300, 317, 318, 319, 362, 600, 601, 654, 702, 727; (2) California Code of Judicial Conduct, canon 4; (3) Metropolitan Court Judges Committee, National Council of Juvenile and Family Court Judges, *Deprived Children: A Judicial Response—73 Recommendations* (1986), Recommendations 1–7, 14, 35, 40; and (4) National Council of Juvenile and Family Court Judges, Child Welfare League of America, Youth Law Center, and the National Center for Youth Law, *Making Reasonable Efforts: Steps for Keeping Families Together* pp. 43–59.

Standard 5.45.   Resource guidelines for child abuse and neglect cases

(a) Guidelines

To improve the fair and efficient administration of child abuse and neglect cases in the California juvenile dependency system, judges and judicial officers assigned to the juvenile court, in consultation with the presiding judge of the juvenile court and the presiding judge of the superior or consolidated court, are encouraged to follow the resource guidelines of the National Council of Juvenile and Family Court Judges, titled "Resource Guidelines: Improving Court Practice in Child Abuse & Neglect Cases." The guidelines are meant to be goals to help courts achieve, among other objectives, the following:

(1) Adherence to statutory timelines;

(2) Effective calendar management;

(3) Effective representation by counsel;

(4) Child-friendly court facilities;

(5) Timely and thorough reports and services to ensure informed judicial decisions, including reasonable efforts findings; and

(6) Minimum time allocations for specified hearings.

(Subd (a) amended effective January 1, 2007.)

(b) Distribution of guidelines

Judicial Council staff will distribute a copy of the resource guidelines to each juvenile court and will provide individual copies to judicial officers and court administrators on written request.

(Subd (b) amended effective January 1, 2016; previously amended effective January 1, 2007.)

Standard 5.45 amended effective January 1, 2016; adopted as sec. 24.5 effective July 1, 1997; previously amended and renumbered as standard 5.45 effective January 1, 2007.

Advisory Committee Comment

Child abuse and neglect cases impose a special obligation on juvenile court judges to oversee case progress. Case oversight includes monitoring the agency's fulfillment of its responsibilities and parental cooperation with the case plan. Court involvement in child welfare cases occurs simultaneously with agency efforts to assist the family. Federal and state legal mandates assign to the juvenile court a series of interrelated and complex decisions that shape the course of state intervention and determine the future of the child and family.

Unlike almost all other types of cases in the court system, child abuse and neglect cases deal with an ongoing and changing situation. In a child welfare case, the court must focus on agency casework and parental behavior over an extended period of time. In making a decision, the court must take into account the agency's plan to help the family and anticipated changes in parental behavior. At the same time, the court must consider the evolving circumstances and needs of each child.

The purpose of these resource guidelines is to specify the essential elements of properly conducted court hearings. The guidelines describe the requirements of juvenile courts in fulfilling their oversight role under federal and state laws, and they specify the necessary elements of a fair, thorough, and speedy court process in child abuse and neglect cases. The guidelines cover all stages of the court process, from the initial removal hearing to the end of juvenile court involvement. These guidelines assume that the court will remain involved until after the child has been safely returned home, has been placed in another permanent home, or has reached adulthood.

Currently, juvenile courts in California operate under the same juvenile court law and rules, and yet the rules are implemented with considerable variation throughout the state. In part, this is due to the lack of resource guidelines. The adoption of the proposed resource guidelines will help encourage more consistent juvenile court procedures in the state.

The guidelines are meant to be goals and, as such, some of them may appear out of reach because of fiscal constraints or lack of judicial and staff resources. The Judicial Council Family and Juvenile Law Advisory Committee and Judicial Council staff are committed to providing technical assistance to each juvenile court to aid in implementing these goals.

Title 6
[Reserved]
Title 7
Standards for Probate Proceedings

Standard 7.10.   Settlements or judgments in certain civil cases involving minors or persons with disabilities

In matters assigned to or pending in civil departments of the court where court approval of trusts that will receive proceeds of settlements or judgments is required under Probate Code section 3600, each court should develop practices and procedures that:

(1) Provide for determination of the trust issues by the probate department of the court or, in a court that does not have a probate department, a judicial officer who regularly hears proceedings under the Probate Code; or

(2) Ensure that judicial officers who hear these matters are experienced or have received training in substantive and technical issues involving trusts (including special needs trusts).

Standard 7.10 amended and renumbered effective January 1, 2007; adopted as sec. 40 effective January 1, 2005.

Title 8
Standards for the Appellate Courts

Standard 8.1.   Memorandum opinions

The Courts of Appeal should dispose of causes that raise no substantial issues of law or fact by memorandum or other abbreviated form of opinion. Such causes could include:

(1) An appeal that is determined by a controlling statute which is not challenged for unconstitutionality and does not present any substantial question of interpretation or application;

(2) An appeal that is determined by a controlling decision which does not require a reexamination or restatement of its principles or rules; or

(3) An appeal raising factual issues that are determined by the substantial evidence rule.

Standard 8.1 amended and renumbered effective January 1, 2007; adopted as sec. 6 effective July 1, 1970.

Title 9
Standards on Law Practice, Attorneys, and Judges
[Reserved]
Title 10
Standards for Judicial Administration

Standard 10.5.   The role of the judiciary in the community

(a) Community outreach an official judicial function

Judicial participation in community outreach activities should be considered an official judicial function to promote public understanding of and confidence in the administration of justice. This function should be performed in a manner consistent with the California Code of Judicial Ethics.

(Subd (a) lettered effective January 1, 2007; adopted as part of unlettered subdivision effective April 1, 1999.)

(b) Encouraged outreach activities

The judiciary is encouraged to:

(1) Provide active leadership within the community in identifying and resolving issues of access to justice within the court system;

(2) Develop local education programs for the public designed to increase public understanding of the court system;

(3) Create local mechanisms for obtaining information from the public about how the court system may be more responsive to the public's needs;

(4) Serve as guest speakers, during or after normal court hours, to address local civic, educational, business, and charitable groups that have an interest in understanding the court system but do not espouse a particular political agenda with which it would be inappropriate for a judicial officer to be associated; and

(5) Take an active part in the life of the community where the participation of the judiciary will serve to increase public understanding and promote public confidence in the integrity of the court system.

(Subd (b) amended effective January 1, 2007.)

Standard 10.5 amended and renumbered effective January 1, 2007; adopted as sec. 39 effective April 1, 1999.

Standard 10.10.   Judicial branch education [Repealed]

Standard 10.10 repealed effective January 1, 2008; adopted as sec. 25 effective January 1, 1999; previously amended and renumbered effective January 1, 2007.

Standard 10.11.   General judicial education standards [Repealed]

Standard 10.11 repealed effective January 1, 2008; adopted as sec. 25 effective

January 1, 1990; previously amended and renumbered as Sec. 25.1 effective January 1, 1999; previously amended and renumbered effective January 1, 2007.

Standard 10.12.   Judicial education for judicial officers in particular judicial assignments [Repealed]

Standard 10.12 repealed effective January 1, 2008; adopted as sec. 25.2 effective January 1, 1999; previously amended and renumbered effective January 1, 2007.

Standard 10.13.   Judicial education curricula provided in particular judicial assignments [Repealed]

Standard 10.13 repealed effective January 1, 2008; repealed and adopted as sec. 25.3 effective January 1, 1999; previously amended and renumbered effective January 1, 2007.

Standard 10.14.   Judicial education for judges hearing capital cases [Repealed]

Standard 10.14 repealed effective January 1, 2008; adopted as sec. 25.4 effective January 1, 2004; previously amended and renumbered effective January 1, 2007.

Standard 10.15.   General court employee education standards [Repealed]

Standard 10.15 repealed effective January 1, 2008; adopted as sec. 25.6 effective January 1, 1999; previously amended and renumbered effective January 1, 2007.

Standard 10.16.   Model code of ethics for court employees

Each trial and appellate court should adopt a code of ethical behavior for its support staff, and in doing so should consider rule 10.670(c)(12) of the California Rules of Court, and the model Code of Ethics for the Court Employees of California approved by the Judicial Council on May 17, 1994, and any subsequent revisions. The approved model code is published by the Judicial Council.

Standard 10.16 amended effective January 1, 2016; adopted as sec. 35 effective July 1, 1994; previously amended and renumbered as standard 10.16 effective January 1, 2007; previously amended effective July 1, 2008.

Standard 10.17.   Trial court performance standards

(a) Purpose

These standards are intended to be used by trial courts, in cooperation with the Judicial Council, for purposes of internal evaluation, self-assessment, and self-improvement. They are not intended as a basis for cross-court comparisons, nor are they intended as a basis for evaluating the performance of individual judges.

(Subd (a) lettered effective January 1, 2007; adopted as part of unlettered subdivision effective January 25, 1995.)

(b) Standards

The standards for trial court performance are as follows:

(1) *Access to justice*

(A) The court conducts its proceedings and other public business openly.

(B) Court facilities are safe, accessible, and convenient to use.

(C) All who appear before the court are given the opportunity to participate effectively without undue hardship or inconvenience.

(D) Judges and other trial court personnel are courteous and responsive to the public and accord respect to all with whom they come into contact.

(E) The costs of access to the trial court's proceedings and records—whether measured in terms of money, time, or the procedures that must be followed—are reasonable, fair, and affordable.

(2) *Expedition and timeliness*

(A) The trial court establishes and complies with recognized guidelines for timely case processing while, at the same time, keeping current with its incoming caseload.

(B) The trial court disburses funds promptly, provides reports and information according to required schedules, and responds to requests for information and other services on an established schedule that assures their effective use.

(C) The trial court promptly implements changes in law and procedure.

(3) *Equality, fairness, and integrity*

(A) Trial court procedures faithfully adhere to relevant laws, procedural rules, and established policies.

(B) Jury lists are representative of the jurisdiction from which they are drawn.

(C) Trial courts give individual attention to cases, deciding them without undue disparity among like cases and on legally relevant factors.

(D) Decisions of the trial court unambiguously address the issues presented to it and make clear how compliance can be achieved.

(E) The trial court takes appropriate responsibility for the enforcement of its orders.

(F) Records of all relevant court decisions and actions are accurate and properly preserved.

(4) *Independence and accountability*

(A) A trial court maintains its institutional integrity and observes the principle of comity in its governmental relations.

(B) The trial court responsibly seeks, uses, and accounts for its public resources.

(C) The trial court uses fair employment practices.

(D) The trial court informs the community of its programs.

(E) The trial court anticipates new conditions or emergent events and adjusts its operations as necessary.

(5) *Public trust and confidence*

(A) The trial court and the justice it delivers are perceived by the public as accessible.

(B) The public has trust and confidence that the basic trial court functions are conducted expeditiously and fairly and that its decisions have integrity.

(C) The trial court is perceived to be independent, not unduly influenced by other components of government, and accountable.

(Subd (b) lettered effective January 1, 2007; adopted as part of unlettered subdivision effective January 25, 1995.)

Standard 10.17 amended and renumbered effective January 1, 2007; adopted as sec. 30 effective January 25, 1995.

Standard 10.20. Court's duty to prohibit bias

(a) General

To preserve the integrity and impartiality of the judicial system, each judge should:

(1) *Ensure fairness*

Ensure that courtroom proceedings are conducted in a manner that is fair and impartial to all of the participants.

(2) *Refrain from and prohibit biased conduct*

In all courtroom proceedings, refrain from engaging in conduct and prohibit others from engaging in conduct that exhibits bias, including but not limited to bias based on disability, gender, race, religion, ethnicity, and sexual orientation, whether that bias is directed toward counsel, court personnel, witnesses, parties, jurors, or any other participants.

(3) *Ensure unbiased decisions*

Ensure that all orders, rulings, and decisions are based on the sound exercise of judicial discretion and the balancing of competing rights and interests and are not influenced by stereotypes or biases.

(Subd (a) amended effective January 1, 2007; previously amended effective January 1, 1994, and January 1, 1998.)

(b) Creation of local committees on bias

Each court should establish a local committee with local bar associations to assist in maintaining a courtroom environment free of bias or the appearance of bias. Courts within one or more counties may choose to form a single committee. The local committee should:

(1) Be composed of representative members of the court community, including but not limited to judges, lawyers, court administrators, and representatives and individuals from minority, women's, and gay and lesbian bar associations and from organizations that represent persons with disabilities;

(2) Sponsor or support educational programs designed to eliminate bias within the court and legal communities, including but not limited to bias based on disability, gender, race, religion, ethnicity, and sexual orientation; and

(3) Develop and maintain an informal procedure for receiving complaints relating to bias in the courtroom, including but not limited to bias based on disability, gender, race, religion, ethnicity, and sexual orientation.

(Subd (b) amended effective January 1, 2007; adopted effective January 1, 1994; previously amended effective January 1, 1998.)

(c) Minimum components of a complaint procedure

An informal complaint procedure developed and maintained by a local committee on bias should:

(1) Contain a provision specifying that the intent of the procedure is to educate with the purpose of ameliorating the problem rather than disciplining the person who is the subject of the complaint;

(2) Accommodate local needs and allow for local flexibility;

(3) Apply to all participants in courtroom proceedings;

(4) Apply only to complaints as to which the identity of the complainant is known;

(5) To the extent possible and unless disclosure is required by law, protect the confidentiality of the complainant, the person who is the subject of the complaint, and other interested persons;

(6) Relate to incidents of behavior or conduct occurring in courtroom proceedings;

(7) Apply to incidents of bias whether they relate to race, sex, religion, national origin, disability, age, sexual orientation, or socioeconomic status;

(8) Contain a provision that exempts activities constituting legitimate advocacy when matters of race, sex, religion, national origin, disability, age, sexual orientation, or socioeconomic status are relevant to issues in the courtroom proceeding;

(9) Focus on incidents that do not warrant discipline but that should be corrected;

(10) With respect to those incidents that if substantiated would warrant discipline, advise the complaining party of the appropriate disciplinary authority;

(11) Contain a provision specifying that nothing in the procedure in any way limits the ability of any person to submit a complaint of misconduct to the appropriate disciplinary body; and

(12) To the extent possible and unless disclosure is required by law, prohibit retention of written records of complaints received but permit collection of data on types of complaints or underlying anecdotes that might be useful in educational programs.

(Subd (c) amended effective January 1, 2007; adopted effective January 1, 1994.)

(d) Application of local rules

The existence of the local committee, its purpose, and the features of the informal complaint procedure should be memorialized in the applicable local rules of court.

(Subd (d) amended effective January 1, 2007; adopted effective January 1, 1994.)

Standard 10.20 amended and renumbered effective January 1, 2007; adopted as sec. 1 effective January 1, 1987; previously amended effective January 1, 1994, and January 1, 1998.

Standard 10.21. Appointment of attorneys, arbitrators, mediators, referees, masters, receivers, and other persons

(a) Nondiscrimination in appointment lists

In establishing and maintaining lists of qualified attorneys, arbitrators, mediators, referees, masters, receivers, and other persons who are eligible for appointment, courts should ensure equal access for all applicants regardless of gender, race, ethnicity, disability, sexual orientation, or age.

(b) Nondiscrimination in recruitment

Each trial court should conduct a recruitment procedure for the appointment of attorneys, arbitrators, mediators, referees, masters, receivers, and other persons appointed by the court (the "appointment programs") by publicizing the existence of the appointment programs at least once annually through state and local bar associations, including specialty bar associations. This publicity should encourage and provide an opportunity for all eligible individuals, regardless of gender, race, ethnicity, disability, sexual orientation, or age, to seek positions on the rosters of the appointment programs. Each trial court also should use other methods of publicizing the appointment programs that maximize the opportunity for a diverse applicant pool.

(c) Nondiscrimination in application and selection procedure

Each trial court should conduct an application and selection procedure for the appointment programs that ensures that the most qualified applicants for an appointment are selected, regardless of gender, race, ethnicity, disability, sexual orientation, or age.

(Subd (c) amended effective January 1, 2007.)

Standard 10.21 amended and renumbered effective January 1, 2007; adopted as sec. 1.5 effective January 1, 1999.

Standard 10.24. Children's waiting room

Each court should endeavor to provide a children's waiting room located in the courthouse for the use of minors under the age of 16 who are present on court premises as participants or who accompany persons who are participants in court proceedings. The waiting room should be supervised and open during normal court hours. If a court does not have sufficient space in the courthouse for a children's waiting room, the court should create the necessary space when court facilities are reorganized or remodeled or when new facilities are constructed.

Standard 10.24 renumbered effective January 1, 2007; adopted as sec. 1.3 effective January 1, 1987.

Standard 10.25. Reasonable accommodation for court personnel

At least to the extent required by state and federal law, each court should evaluate existing facilities, programs, and services available to employees to ensure that no barriers exist to prevent otherwise-qualified employees with known disabilities from performing their jobs or participating fully in court programs or activities.

Standard 10.25 renumbered effective January 1, 2007; adopted as sec. 1.4 effective January 1, 1998.

Standard 10.31. Master jury list

The jury commissioner should use the National Change of Address System or other comparable means to update jury source lists and create as accurate a master jury list as reasonably practical.

Standard 10.31 amended and renumbered effective January 1, 2007; adopted as sec. 4.6 effective July 1, 1997.

Standard 10.40. Court security [Repealed]

Standard 10.40 repealed effective January 1, 2009; adopted as sec. 7 effective July 1, 1971; previously amended and renumbered effective January 1, 2007.

Standard 10.41. Court sessions at or near state penal institutions

(a) Provision of adequate protection

Facilities used regularly for judicial proceedings should not be located on the grounds of or immediately adjacent to a state penal institution unless the location, design, and setting of the court facility provide adequate protection against the possible adverse influence that the prison facilities and activities might have on the fairness of judicial proceedings.

(Subd (a) amended effective January 1, 2007.)

(b) Factors to be considered

In determining whether adequate protection is provided, the following factors should be considered:

(1) The physical and visual remoteness of the court facility from the facilities and activities of the prison;

(2) The location and appearance of the court facility with respect to the adjacent public areas through which jurors and witnesses would normally travel in going to and from the court;

(3) The accessibility of the facility to the press and the general public; and

(4) Any other factors that might affect the fairness of the judicial proceedings.

(Subd (b) lettered effective January 1, 2007; adopted as part of subd (a) effective July 1, 1975.)

(c) Compelling reasons of safety or court convenience

Unless the location, design, and setting of the facility for conducting court sessions meet the criteria in (a) and (b):

(1) Court sessions should not be conducted in or immediately adjacent to a state penal institution except for compelling reasons of safety or convenience of the court; and

(2) Court sessions should not be conducted at such a location when the trial is by jury or when the testimony of witnesses who are neither inmates nor employees of the institution will be required.

(Subd (c) amended and relettered effective January 1, 2007; adopted as subd (b) effective July 1, 1975.)

Standard 10.41 amended and renumbered effective January 1, 2007; adopted as sec. 7.5 effective July 1, 1975.

Standard 10.50. Selection of regular grand jury

(a) Definition

"Regular grand jury" means a body of citizens of a county selected by the court to investigate matters of civil concern in the county, whether or not that body has jurisdiction to return indictments.

(b) Regular grand jury list

The list of qualified candidates prepared by the jury commissioner to be considered for nomination to the regular grand jury should be obtained by one or more of the following methods:

(1) Names of members of the public obtained at random in the same manner as the list of trial jurors. However, the names obtained for nomination to the regular grand jury should be kept separate and distinct from the trial jury list, consistent with Penal Code section 899.

(2) Recommendations for grand jurors that encompass a cross-section of the county's population base, solicited from a broad representation of community-based organizations, civic leaders, and superior court judges, referees, and commissioners.

(3) Applications from interested citizens solicited through the media or a mass mailing.

(Subd (b) amended effective January 1, 2007.)

(c) Carryover grand jurors

The court is encouraged to consider carryover grand jury selections under Penal Code section 901(b) to ensure broad-based representation.

(d) Nomination of grand jurors

Judges who nominate persons for grand jury selection under Penal Code section 903.4 are encouraged to select candidates from the list returned by the jury commissioner or to otherwise employ a nomination procedure that will ensure broad-based representation from the community.

(Subd (d) amended effective January 1, 2007.)

(e) Disfavored nominations

Judges should not nominate to the grand jury a spouse or immediate family member (within the first degree of consanguinity) of any superior court judge, commissioner, or referee; elected official; or department head of any city, county, or governmental entity subject to grand jury scrutiny.

(Subd (e) amended effective January 1, 2007.)

Standard 10.50 amended and renumbered effective January 1, 2007; adopted as sec. 17 effective July 1, 1992.

Standard 10.51. Juror complaints

Each court should establish a reasonable mechanism for receiving and responding to juror complaints.

Standard 10.51 renumbered effective January 1, 2007; adopted as sec. 4.5 effective July 1, 1997.

Standard 10.55. Local program on waste reduction and recycling

Each court should adopt a program for waste reduction and recycling or participate in a county program.

Standard 10.55 amended and renumbered effective January 1, 2007; adopted as sec. 17.5 effective January 1, 1991.

Standard 10.70. Implementation and coordination of mediation and other alternative dispute resolution (ADR) programs

(a) Implementation of mediation programs for civil cases

Superior courts should implement mediation programs for civil cases as part of their core operations.

(Subd (a) adopted effective January 1, 2006.)

(b) Promotion of ADR programs

Superior courts should promote the development, implementation, maintenance, and expansion of successful mediation and other alternative dispute resolution (ADR) programs, through activities that include:

(1) Establishing appropriate criteria for determining which cases should be referred to ADR, and what ADR processes are appropriate for those cases. These criteria should include whether the parties are likely to benefit from the use of the ADR process;

(2) Developing, refining, and using lists of qualified ADR neutrals;

(3) Adopting appropriate criteria for referring cases to qualified ADR neutrals;

(4) Developing ADR information and providing educational programs for parties who are not represented by counsel; and

(5) Providing ADR education for judicial officers.

(Subd (b) amended effective January 1, 2007; adopted as unlettered subdivision effective July 1, 1992; lettered and amended effective January 1, 2006.)

(c) Coordination of ADR programs

Superior courts should coordinate ADR promotional activities and explore joint funding and administration of ADR programs with each other and with professional and community-based organizations.

(Subd (c) adopted effective January 1, 2006.)

Standard 10.70 amended and renumbered effective January 1, 2007; adopted as sec. 32 effective July 1, 1992; previously amended effective January 1, 2006.

Standard 10.71. Alternative dispute resolution (ADR) committees

Courts that are not required and that do not elect to have an ADR administrative committee as provided in rule 10.783 of the California Rules of Court should form committees of judges, attorneys, alternative dispute resolution (ADR) neutrals, and county ADR administrators, if any, to oversee the court's ADR programs and panels of neutrals for general civil cases.

Standard 10.71 amended and renumbered effective January 1, 2007; adopted as sec. 32.1 effective January 1, 2006.

Standard 10.72.   ADR committees and criteria for referring cases to dispute resolution neutrals

(a) Training, experience, and skills

Courts should evaluate the ADR training, experience, and skills of potential ADR neutrals.

(Subd (a) amended effective January 1, 2006.)

(b) Additional considerations for continuing referrals

After a court has sufficient experience with an ADR neutral, the court should also consider indicators of client satisfaction, settlement rate, continuing ADR education, and adherence to applicable standards of conduct in determining whether to continue referrals to that neutral.

(Subd (b) amended effective January 1, 2006.)

Standard 10.72 amended and renumbered effective January 1, 2007; adopted as sec. 33 effective July 1, 1992; previously amended effective January 1, 2006.

Advisory Committee Comment

Although settlement rate is an important indicator of a neutral's effectiveness, it should be borne in mind that some disputes will not resolve, despite the best efforts of a skilled neutral. Neutrals should not feel pressure to achieve a high settlement rate through resolutions that may not be in the interest of one or more parties. Accordingly, settlement rate should be used with caution as a criterion for court referral of disputes to neutrals.

Standard 10.80.   Court records management standards

Each court should develop records management practices consistent with the standards approved by the Judicial Council. The approved standards are specified in Judicial Council Court Records Management Standards, published by the Judicial Council.

Implementation of these standards, which cover creation, use, maintenance, and destruction of records, should lead to more efficient court administration, better protection and preservation of records, and improved public access to records.

Standard 10.80 amended effective January 1, 2016; adopted as sec. 34 effective January 1, 1993; previously amended and renumbered as standard 10.80 effective January 1, 2007.

Ethics Standards for Neutral Arbitrators in Contractual Arbitration

The Ethics Standards for Neutral Arbitrators in Contractual Arbitration *were adopted by the Judicial Council effective July, 2002, and further substantially amended and reorganized effective January 1, 2003.*

Standard 1.   Purpose, intent, and construction.

(a) These standards are adopted under the authority of Code of Civil Procedure section 1281.85 and establish the minimum standards of conduct for neutral arbitrators who are subject to these standards. They are intended to guide the conduct of arbitrators, to inform and protect participants in arbitration, and to promote public confidence in the arbitration process.

(b) For arbitration to be effective there must be broad public confidence in the integrity and fairness of the process. Arbitrators are responsible to the parties, the other participants, and the public for conducting themselves in accordance with these standards so as to merit that confidence.

(c) These standards are to be construed and applied to further the purpose and intent expressed in subdivisions (a) and (b) and in conformance with all applicable law.

(d) These standards are not intended to affect any existing civil cause of action or create any new civil cause of action.

Comment to Standard 1

Code of Civil Procedure section 1281.85 provides that, beginning July 1, 2002, a person serving as a neutral arbitrator pursuant to an arbitration agreement shall comply with the ethics standards for arbitrators adopted by the Judicial Council pursuant to that section.

While the grounds for vacating an arbitration award are established by statute, not these standards, an arbitrator's violation of these standards may, under some circumstances, fall within one of those statutory grounds. (See Code Civ. Proc., §1286.2.) A failure to disclose within the time required for disclosure a ground for disqualification of which the arbitrator was then aware is a ground for vacatur of the arbitrator's award. (See Code Civ. Proc., §1286.2(a)(6)(A).) Violations of other obligations under these standards may also constitute grounds for vacating an arbitration award under section 1286.2(a)(3) if "the rights of the party were substantially prejudiced" by the violation.

While vacatur may be an available remedy for violation of these standards, these standards are not intended to affect any civil cause of action that may currently exist nor to create any new civil cause of action. These standards are also not intended to establish a ceiling on what is considered good practice in arbitration or to discourage efforts to educate arbitrators about best practices.

Standard 2.   Definitions.

As used in these standards:

(a) **Arbitrator and neutral arbitrator**

(1) "Arbitrator" and "neutral arbitrator" mean any arbitrator who is subject to these standards and who is to serve impartially, whether selected or appointed:

(A) Jointly by the parties or by the arbitrators selected by the parties;

(B) By the court, when the parties or the arbitrators selected by the parties fail to select an arbitrator who was to be selected jointly by them; or

(C) By a dispute resolution provider organization, under an agreement of the parties.

(2) Where the context includes events or acts occurring before an appointment is final, "arbitrator" and "neutral arbitrator" include a person who has been served with notice of a proposed nomination or appointment. For purposes of these standards, "proposed nomination" does not include nomination of persons by a court under Code of Civil Procedure section 1281.6 to be considered for possible selection as an arbitrator by the parties or appointment as an arbitrator by the court.

(Subd (a) amended effective July 1, 2014.)

(b) "Applicable law" means constitutional provisions, statutes, decisional law, California Rules of Court, and other statewide rules or regulations that apply to arbitrators who are subject to these standards.

(c) "Conclusion of the arbitration" means the following:

(1) When the arbitrator is disqualified or withdraws or the case is settled or dismissed before the arbitrator makes an award, the date on which the arbitrator's appointment is terminated;

(2) When the arbitrator makes an award and no party makes a timely application to the arbitrator to correct the award, the final date for making an application to the arbitrator for correction; or

(3) When a party makes a timely application to the arbitrator to correct the award, the date on which the arbitrator serves a corrected award or a denial on each party, or the date on which denial occurs by operation of law.

(d) "Consumer arbitration" means an arbitration conducted under a predispute arbitration provision contained in a contract that meets the criteria listed in paragraphs (1) through (3) below. "Consumer arbitration" excludes arbitration proceedings conducted under or arising out of public or private sector labor-relations laws, regulations, charter provisions, ordinances, statutes, or agreements.

(1) The contract is with a consumer party, as defined in these standards;

(2) The contract was drafted by or on behalf of the nonconsumer party; and

(3) The consumer party was required to accept the arbitration provision in the contract.

(e) "Consumer party" is a party to an arbitration agreement who, in the context of that arbitration agreement, is any of the following:

(1) An individual who seeks or acquires, including by lease, any goods or services primarily for personal, family, or household purposes including, but not limited to, financial services, insurance, and other goods and services as defined in section 1761 of the Civil Code;

(2) An individual who is an enrollee, a subscriber, or insured in a health-care service plan within the meaning of section 1345 of the Health and Safety Code or health-care insurance plan within the meaning of section 106 of the Insurance Code;

(3) An individual with a medical malpractice claim that is subject to the arbitration agreement; or

(4) An employee or an applicant for employment in a dispute arising out of or relating to the employee's employment or the applicant's prospective employment that is subject to the arbitration agreement.

(f) "Dispute resolution neutral" means a temporary judge appointed under article VI, section 21 of the California Constitution, a referee appointed under Code of Civil Procedure section 638 or 639, an arbitrator, a neutral evaluator, a special master, a mediator, a settlement officer, or a settlement facilitator.

(g) "Dispute resolution provider organization" and "provider organization" mean any nongovernmental entity that, or individual who, coordinates, administers, or provides the services of two or more dispute resolution neutrals.

(h) "Domestic partner" means a domestic partner as defined in Family Code section 297.

(i) "Financial interest" means a financial interest within the meaning of Code of Civil Procedure section 170.5.

(j) "Gift" means a gift as defined in Code of Civil Procedure section 170.9(*l*).

(k) "Honoraria" means honoraria as defined in Code of Civil Procedure section 170.9(h) and (i).

(*l*) "Lawyer in the arbitration" means the lawyer hired to represent a party in the arbitration.

(m)   "Lawyer for a party" means the lawyer hired to represent a party in the arbitration and any lawyer or law firm currently associated in the practice of law with the lawyer hired to represent a party in the arbitration.

(n)   "Member of the arbitrator's immediate family" means the arbitrator's spouse or domestic partner and any minor child living in the arbitrator's household.

(o)   "Member of the arbitrator's extended family" means the parents, grandparents, great-grandparents, children, grandchildren, great-grandchildren, siblings, uncles, aunts, nephews, and nieces of the arbitrator or the arbitrator's spouse or domestic partner or the spouse or domestic partner of such person.

(Subd (o) amended effective July 1, 2014.)

(p)   **Party**

(1)   "Party" means a party to the arbitration agreement:

(A)   Who seeks to arbitrate a controversy pursuant to the agreement;

(B)   Against whom such arbitration is sought; or

(C)   Who is made a party to such arbitration by order of a court or the arbitrator upon such party's application, upon the application of any other party to the arbitration, or upon the arbitrator's own determination.

(2)   "Party" includes the representative of a party, unless the context requires a different meaning.

(q)   "Party-arbitrator" means an arbitrator selected unilaterally by a party.

(r)   "Private practice of law" means private practice of law as defined in Code of Civil Procedure section 170.5.

(s)   "Significant personal relationship" includes a close personal friendship.

Standard 2 amended effective July 1, 2014.

Comment to Standard 2

Subdivision (a). The definition of "arbitrator" and "neutral arbitrator" in this standard is intended to include all arbitrators who are to serve in a neutral and impartial manner and to exclude unilaterally selected arbitrators.

Subdivisions (l) and (m). Arbitrators should take special care to note that there are two different terms used in these standards to refer to lawyers who represent parties in the arbitration. In particular, arbitrators should note that the term "lawyer for a party" includes any lawyer or law firm currently associated in the practice of law with the lawyer hired to represent a party in the arbitration.

Subdivision (p)(2). While this provision generally permits an arbitrator to provide required information or notices to a party's attorney as that party's representative, a party's attorney should not be treated as a "party" for purposes of identifying matters that an arbitrator must disclose under standards 7 or 8, as those standards contain separate, specific requirements concerning the disclosure of relationships with a party's attorney.

Other terms that may be pertinent to these standards are defined in Code of Civil Procedure section 1280.

Standard 3.   Application and effective date.

(a)   Except as otherwise provided in this standard and standard 8, these standards apply to all persons who are appointed to serve as neutral arbitrators on or after July 1, 2002, in any arbitration under an arbitration agreement, if:

(1)   The arbitration agreement is subject to the provisions of title 9 of part III of the Code of Civil Procedure (commencing with section 1280); or

(2)   The arbitration hearing is to be conducted in California.

(b)   These standards do not apply to:

(1)   Party arbitrators, as defined in these standards; or

(2)   Any arbitrator serving in:

(A)   An international arbitration proceeding subject to the provisions of title 9.3 of part III of the Code of Civil Procedure;

(B)   A judicial arbitration proceeding subject to the provisions of chapter 2.5 of title 3 of part III of the Code of Civil Procedure;

(C)   An attorney-client fee arbitration proceeding subject to the provisions of article 13 of chapter 4 of division 3 of the Business and Professions Code;

(D)   An automobile warranty dispute resolution process certified under California Code of Regulations title 16, division 33.1 or an informal dispute settlement procedure under Code of Federal Regulations title 16, chapter 1, part 703;

(E)   An arbitration of a workers' compensation dispute under Labor Code sections 5270 through 5277;

(F)   An arbitration conducted by the Workers' Compensation Appeals Board under Labor Code section 5308;

(G)   An arbitration of a complaint filed against a contractor with the Contractors State License Board under Business and Professions Code sections 7085 through 7085.7;

(H)   An arbitration conducted under or arising out of public or private sector labor-relations laws, regulations, charter provisions, ordinances, statutes, or agreements; or

(I)   An arbitration proceeding governed by rules adopted by a securities self-regulatory organization and approved by the United States Securities and Exchange Commission under federal law.

(Subd (b) amended effective July 1, 2014.)

(c)   The following persons are not subject to the standards or to specific amendments to the standards in certain arbitrations:

(1)   Persons who are serving in arbitrations in which they were appointed to serve as arbitrators before July 1, 2002, are not subject to these standards in those arbitrations.

(2)   Persons who are serving in arbitrations in which they were appointed to serve as arbitrators before January 1, 2003, are not subject to standard 8 in those arbitrations.

(3)   Persons who are serving in arbitrations in which they were appointed to serve as arbitrators before July 1, 2014, are not subject to the amendments to standards 2, 7, 8, 12, 16, and 17 that took effect July 1, 2014 in those arbitrations.

(Subd (c) amended effective July 1, 2014.)
Standard 3 amended effective July 1, 2014.

Comment to Standard 3

With the exception of standard 8 and the amendments to standards 2, 7, 8, 12, 16, and 17 that took effect July 1, 2014, these standards apply to all neutral arbitrators appointed on or after July 1, 2002, who meet the criteria of subdivision (a). Arbitration provider organizations, although not themselves subject to these standards, should be aware of them when performing administrative functions that involve arbitrators who are subject to these standards. A provider organization's policies and actions should facilitate, not impede, compliance with the standards by arbitrators who are affiliated with the provider organization.

Subdivision (b)(2)(I) is intended to implement the decisions of the California Supreme Court in *Jevne v. Superior Court* ((2005) 35 Cal.4th 935) and of the United States Court of Appeals for the Ninth Circuit in *Credit Suisse First Boston Corp. v. Grunwald* ((9th Cir. 2005) 400 F.3d 1119).

Standard 4.   Duration of duty.

(a)   Except as otherwise provided in these standards, an arbitrator must comply with these ethics standards from acceptance of appointment until the conclusion of the arbitration.

(b)   If, after the conclusion of the arbitration, a case is referred back to the arbitrator for reconsideration or rehearing, the arbitrator must comply with these ethics standards from the date the case is referred back to the arbitrator until the arbitration is again concluded.

Standard 5.   General duty.

An arbitrator must act in a manner that upholds the integrity and fairness of the arbitration process. He or she must maintain impartiality toward all participants in the arbitration at all times.

Comment to Standard 5

This standard establishes the overarching ethical duty of arbitrators. The remaining standards should be construed as establishing specific requirements that implement this overarching duty in particular situations.

Maintaining impartiality toward all participants during all stages of the arbitration is central to upholding the integrity and fairness of the arbitration. An arbitrator must perform his or her duties impartially, without bias or prejudice, and must not, in performing these duties, by words or conduct manifest partiality, bias, or prejudice, including but not limited to partiality, bias, or prejudice based upon race, sex, religion, national origin, disability, age, sexual orientation, socioeconomic status, or the fact that a party might select the arbitrator to serve as an arbitrator in additional cases. After accepting appointment, an arbitrator should avoid entering into any relationship or acquiring any interest that might reasonably create the appearance of partiality, bias, or prejudice. An arbitrator does not become partial, biased, or prejudiced simply by having acquired knowledge of the parties, the issues or arguments, or the applicable law.

Standard 6.   Duty to refuse appointment.

Notwithstanding any contrary request, consent, or waiver by the parties, a proposed arbitrator must decline appointment if he or she is not able to be impartial.

Standard 7.   Disclosure.

(a)   **Intent**

This standard is intended to identify the matters that must be disclosed by a person nominated or appointed as an arbitrator. To the extent that this standard addresses matters that are also addressed by statute, it is intended to include those statutory disclosure requirements, not to eliminate, reduce, or otherwise limit them.

(b) **General provisions**

For purposes of this standard:

(1) *Collective bargaining cases excluded*

The terms "cases" and "any arbitration" do not include collective bargaining cases or arbitrations conducted under or arising out of collective bargaining agreements between employers and employees or between their respective representatives.

(2) *Offers of employment or professional relationship*

(A) Except as provided in (B), if an arbitrator has disclosed to the parties in an arbitration that he or she will entertain offers of employment or of professional relationships from a party or lawyer for a party while the arbitration is pending as required by subdivision (b) of standard 12, the arbitrator is not also required under this standard to disclose to the parties in that arbitration any such offer from a party or lawyer for a party that he or she subsequently receives or accepts while that arbitration is pending.

(B) In a consumer arbitration, if an arbitrator has disclosed to the parties that he or she will entertain offers of employment or of professional relationships from a party or lawyer for a party while the arbitration is pending as required by subdivision (b) of standard 12 and has informed the parties in the pending arbitration about any such offer and the acceptance of any such offer as required by subdivision (d) of standard 12, the arbitrator is not also required under this standard to disclose that offer or the acceptance of that offer to the parties in that arbitration.

(3) *Names of parties in cases*

When making disclosures about other pending or prior cases, in order to preserve confidentiality, it is sufficient to give the name of any party who is not a party to the pending arbitration as "claimant" or "respondent" if the party is an individual and not a business or corporate entity.

(Subd (b) amended effective July 1, 2014.)

(c) **Time and manner of disclosure**

(1) *Initial disclosure*

Within 10 calendar days of service of notice of the proposed nomination or appointment, a proposed arbitrator must disclose to all parties in writing all matters listed in subdivisions (d) and (e) of this standard of which the arbitrator is then aware.

(2) *Supplemental disclosure*

If an arbitrator subsequently becomes aware of a matter that must be disclosed under either subdivision (d) or (e) of this standard, the arbitrator must disclose that matter to the parties in writing within 10 calendar days after the arbitrator becomes aware of the matter.

(Subd (c) amended effective July 1, 2014.)

(d) **Required disclosures**

A proposed arbitrator or arbitrator must disclose all matters that could cause a person aware of the facts to reasonably entertain a doubt that the arbitrator would be able to be impartial, including, but not limited to, all of the following:

(1) *Family relationships with party*

The arbitrator or a member of the arbitrator's immediate or extended family is:

(A) A party;

(B) The spouse or domestic partner of a party; or

(C) An officer, director, or trustee of a party.

(2) *Family relationships with lawyer in the arbitration*

(A) Current relationships

The arbitrator, or the spouse, former spouse, domestic partner, child, sibling, or parent of the arbitrator or the arbitrator's spouse or domestic partner is:

(i) A lawyer in the arbitration;

(ii) The spouse or domestic partner of a lawyer in the arbitration; or

(iii) Currently associated in the private practice of law with a lawyer in the arbitration.

(B) Past relationships

The arbitrator or the arbitrator's spouse or domestic partner was associated in the private practice of law with a lawyer in the arbitration within the preceding two years.

(3) *Significant personal relationship with party or lawyer for a party*

The arbitrator or a member of the arbitrator's immediate family has or has had a significant personal relationship with any party or lawyer for a party.

(4) *Service as arbitrator for a party or lawyer for party*

(A) The arbitrator is serving or, within the preceding five years, has served:

(i) As a neutral arbitrator in another prior or pending noncollective bargaining case involving a party to the current arbitration or a lawyer for a party.

(ii) As a party-appointed arbitrator in another prior or pending noncollective bargaining case for either a party to the current arbitration or a lawyer for a party.

(iii) As a neutral arbitrator in another prior or pending noncollective bargaining case in which he or she was selected by a person serving as a party-appointed arbitrator in the current arbitration.

(B) Case information

If the arbitrator is serving or has served in any of the capacities listed under (A), he or she must disclose:

(i) The names of the parties in each prior or pending case and, where applicable, the name of the attorney representing the party in the current arbitration who is involved in the pending case, who was involved in the prior case, or whose current associate is involved in the pending case or was involved in the prior case.

(ii) The results of each prior case arbitrated to conclusion, including the date of the arbitration award, identification of the prevailing party, the amount of monetary damages awarded, if any, and the names of the parties' attorneys.

(C) Summary of case information

If the total number of the cases disclosed under (A) is greater than five, the arbitrator must provide a summary of these cases that states:

(i) The number of pending cases in which the arbitrator is currently serving in each capacity;

(ii) The number of prior cases in which the arbitrator previously served in each capacity;

(iii) The number of prior cases arbitrated to conclusion; and

(iv) The number of such prior cases in which the party to the current arbitration, the party represented by the lawyer for a party in the current arbitration or the party represented by the party-arbitrator in the current arbitration was the prevailing party.

(5) *Compensated service as other dispute resolution neutral*

The arbitrator is serving or has served as a dispute resolution neutral other than an arbitrator in another pending or prior noncollective bargaining case involving a party or lawyer for a party and the arbitrator received or expects to receive any form of compensation for serving in this capacity.

(A) Time frame

For purposes of this paragraph (5), "prior case" means any case in which the arbitrator concluded his or her service as a dispute resolution neutral within two years before the date of the arbitrator's proposed nomination or appointment.

(B) Case information

If the arbitrator is serving or has served in any of the capacities listed under this paragraph (5), he or she must disclose:

(i) The names of the parties in each prior or pending case and, where applicable, the name of the attorney in the current arbitration who is involved in the pending case, who was involved in the prior case, or whose current associate is involved in the pending case or was involved in the prior case;

(ii) The dispute resolution neutral capacity (mediator, referee, etc.) in which the arbitrator is serving or served in the case; and

(iii) In each such case in which the arbitrator rendered a decision as a temporary judge or referee, the date of the decision, the prevailing party, the amount of monetary damages awarded, if any, and the names of the parties' attorneys.

(C) Summary of case information

If the total number of cases disclosed under this paragraph (5) is greater than five, the arbitrator must also provide a summary of the cases that states:

(i) The number of pending cases in which the arbitrator is currently serving in each capacity;

(ii) The number of prior cases in which the arbitrator previously served in each capacity;

(iii) The number of prior cases in which the arbitrator rendered a decision as a temporary judge or referee; and

(iv) The number of such prior cases in which the party to the current arbitration or the party represented by the lawyer for a party in the current arbitration was the prevailing party.

(6) *Current arrangements for prospective neutral service*

Whether the arbitrator has any current arrangement with a party concerning prospective employment or other compensated service as a dispute resolution neutral or is participating in or, within the last two years, has participated in discussions regarding such prospective employment or service with a party.

(7) *Attorney-client relationship*

Any attorney-client relationship the arbitrator has or has had with a party or lawyer for a party. Attorney-client relationships include the following:

(A) An officer, a director, or a trustee of a party is or, within the preceding two years, was a client of the arbitrator in the arbitrator's private practice of law or a client of a lawyer with whom the arbitrator is or was associated in the private practice of law;

(B) In any other proceeding involving the same issues, the arbitrator gave advice to a party or a lawyer in the arbitration concerning any matter involved in the arbitration; and

(C) The arbitrator served as a lawyer for or as an officer of a public agency which is a party and personally advised or in any way represented the public agency concerning the factual or legal issues in the arbitration.

(8) *Employee, expert witness, or consultant relationships*

The arbitrator or a member of the arbitrator's immediate family is or, within the preceding two years, was an employee of or an expert witness or a consultant for a party or for a lawyer in the arbitration.

(9) *Other professional relationships*

Any other professional relationship not already disclosed under paragraphs (2)–(8) that the arbitrator or a member of the arbitrator's immediate family has or has had with a party or lawyer for a party.

(10) *Financial interests in party*

The arbitrator or a member of the arbitrator's immediate family has a financial interest in a party.

(11) *Financial interests in subject of arbitration*

The arbitrator or a member of the arbitrator's immediate family has a financial interest in the subject matter of the arbitration.

(12) *Affected interest*

The arbitrator or a member of the arbitrator's immediate family has an interest that could be substantially affected by the outcome of the arbitration.

(13) *Knowledge of disputed facts*

The arbitrator or a member of the arbitrator's immediate or extended family has personal knowledge of disputed evidentiary facts relevant to the arbitration. A person who is likely to be a material witness in the proceeding is deemed to have personal knowledge of disputed evidentiary facts concerning the proceeding.

(14) *Membership in organizations practicing discrimination*

The arbitrator is a member of any organization that practices invidious discrimination on the basis of race, sex, religion, national origin, or sexual orientation. Membership in a religious organization, an official military organization of the United States, or a nonprofit youth organization need not be disclosed unless it would interfere with the arbitrator's proper conduct of the proceeding or would cause a person aware of the fact to reasonably entertain a doubt concerning the arbitrator's ability to act impartially.

(15) Any other matter that:

(A) Might cause a person aware of the facts to reasonably entertain a doubt that the arbitrator would be able to be impartial;

(B) Leads the proposed arbitrator to believe there is a substantial doubt as to his or her capacity to be impartial, including, but not limited to, bias or prejudice toward a party, lawyer, or law firm in the arbitration; or

(C) Otherwise leads the arbitrator to believe that his or her disqualification will further the interests of justice.

(Subd (d) amended effective July 1, 2014.)

(e) Other required disclosures

In addition to the matters that must be disclosed under subdivision (d), a proposed arbitrator or arbitrator must also disclose:

(1) *Professional discipline*

(A) If the arbitrator has been disbarred or had his or her license to practice a profession or occupation revoked by a professional or occupational disciplinary agency or licensing board, whether in California or elsewhere. The disclosure must specify the date of the revocation, what professional or occupational disciplinary agency or licensing board revoked the license, and the reasons given by that professional or occupational disciplinary agency or licensing board for the revocation.

(B) If the arbitrator has resigned his or her membership in the State Bar or another professional or occupational licensing agency or board, whether in California or elsewhere, while public or private disciplinary charges were pending. The disclosure must specify the date of the resignation, what professional or occupational disciplinary agency or licensing board had charges pending against the arbitrator at the time of the resignation, and what those charges were.

(C) If within the preceding 10 years public discipline other than that covered under (A) has been imposed on the arbitrator by a professional or occupational disciplinary agency or licensing board, whether in California or elsewhere. "Public discipline" under this provision means any disciplinary action imposed on the arbitrator that the professional or occupational disciplinary agency or licensing board identifies in its publicly available records or in response to a request for information about the arbitrator from a member of the public. The disclosure must specify the date the discipline was imposed, what professional or occupational disciplinary agency or licensing board imposed the discipline, and the reasons given by that professional or occupational disciplinary agency or licensing board for the discipline.

(2) *Inability to conduct or timely complete proceedings*

(A) If the arbitrator is not able to properly perceive the evidence or properly conduct the proceedings because of a permanent or temporary physical impairment; and

(B) Any constraints on his or her availability known to the arbitrator that will interfere with his or her ability to commence or complete the arbitration in a timely manner.

(Subd (e) amended effective July 1, 2014.)

(f) Continuing duty

An arbitrator's duty to disclose the matters described in subdivisions (d) and (e) of this standard is a continuing duty, applying from service of the notice of the arbitrator's proposed nomination or appointment until the conclusion of the arbitration proceeding.

Standard 7 amended effective July 1, 2014.

Comment to Standard 7

This standard requires proposed arbitrators to disclose to all parties, in writing within 10 days of service of notice of their proposed nomination or appointment, all matters they are aware of at that time that could cause a person aware of the facts to reasonably entertain a doubt that the proposed arbitrator would be able to be impartial as well as those matters listed under subdivision (e). This standard also requires that if arbitrators subsequently become aware of any additional such matters, they must make supplemental disclosures of these matters within 10 days of becoming aware of them. This latter requirement is intended to address both matters existing at the time of nomination or appointment of which the arbitrator subsequently becomes aware and new matters that arise based on developments during the arbitration, such as the hiring of new counsel by a party.

Timely disclosure to the parties is the primary means of ensuring the impartiality of an arbitrator. It provides the parties with the necessary information to make an informed selection of an arbitrator by disqualifying or ratifying the arbitrator following disclosure. See also standard 12, concerning disclosure and disqualification requirements relating to concurrent and subsequent employment or professional relationships between an arbitrator and a party or attorney in the arbitration. A party may disqualify an arbitrator for failure to comply with statutory disclosure obligations (see Code Civ. Proc., § 1281.91(a)). Failure to disclose, within the time required for disclosure, a ground for disqualification of which the arbitrator was then aware is a ground for *vacatur* of the arbitrator's award (see Code Civ. Proc., § 1286.2(a)(6)(A)).

The arbitrator's overarching duty under subdivision (d) of this standard, which mirrors the duty set forth in Code of Civil Procedure section 1281.9, is to inform parties about matters that could cause a person aware of the facts to reasonably entertain a doubt that the arbitrator would be able to be impartial. While the remaining subparagraphs of subdivision (d) require the disclosure of specific interests, relationships, or affiliations, these are only examples of common matters that could cause a person aware of the facts to reasonably entertain a doubt that the arbitrator would be able to be impartial. The fact that none of the interests, relationships, or affiliations specifically listed in the subparagraphs of (d) are present in a particular case does not necessarily mean that there is no matter that could reasonably raise a question about the arbitrator's ability to be impartial and that therefore must be disclosed. Similarly, the fact that a particular interest, relationship, or affiliation present in a case is not specifically enumerated in one of the examples given in these subparagraphs does not mean that it must be disclosed. An arbitrator must make determinations concerning disclosure on a case-by-case basis, applying the general criteria for disclosure under subdivision (d): is the matter something that could cause a person aware of the facts to reasonably entertain a doubt that the arbitrator would be able to be impartial?

Code of Civil Procedure section 1281.85 specifically requires that the ethics standards adopted by the Judicial Council address the disclosure of interests, relationships, or affiliations that may constitute conflicts of interest, including prior service as an arbitrator or other dispute resolution neutral entity. Section 1281.85 further provides that the standards "shall be consistent with the standards established for arbitrators in the judicial arbitration program and may expand but may not limit the disclosure and disqualification requirements established by this chapter [chapter 2 of title 9 of part III, Code of Civil Procedure, sections 1281–1281.95]."

Code of Civil Procedure section 1281.9 already establishes detailed requirements concerning disclosures by arbitrators, including a specific requirement that arbitrators disclose the existence of any ground specified in Code of Civil Procedure section 170.1 for disqualification of a judge. This standard does not eliminate or otherwise limit those requirements; in large part, it simply consolidates and integrates those existing statutory disclosure requirements by topic area. This standard does, however, expand upon or clarify the existing statutory disclosure requirements in the following ways:

- Requiring arbitrators to make supplemental disclosures to the parties regarding any matter about which they become aware after the time for making an initial disclosure has expired, within 10 calendar days after the arbitrator becomes aware of the matter (subdivision (c)).
- Expanding required disclosures about the relationships or affiliations of an arbitrator's family members to include those of an arbitrator's domestic partner (subdivisions (d)(1) and (2); see also definitions of immediate and extended family in standard 2).
- Requiring arbitrators, in addition to making statutorily required disclosures regarding prior service as an arbitrator for a party or attorney for a party, to disclose both prior service as a neutral arbitrator selected by a party arbitrator in the current arbitration and prior compensated service as any other type of dispute resolution neutral for a party or attorney in the arbitration (e.g., temporary judge, mediator, or referee) (subdivisions (d)(4)(A)(iii) and (5)).
- If a disclosure includes information about five or more cases, requiring arbitrators to provide a summary of that information (subdivisions (d)(4)(C) and (5)(C).
- Requiring the arbitrator to disclose if he or she or a member of his or her immediate family is or, within the preceding two years, was an employee, expert witness, or consultant for a party or a lawyer in the arbitration (subdivision (d)(8)).
- Requiring the arbitrator to disclose if he or she or a member of his or her immediate family has an interest that could be substantially affected by the outcome of the arbitration (subdivision (d)(12)).
- Requiring arbitrators to disclose membership in organizations that practice invidious discrimination on the basis of race, sex, religion, national origin, or sexual orientation (subdivision (d)(14)).
- Requiring the arbitrator to disclose if he or she was disbarred or had his or her license to practice a profession or occupation revoked by a professional or occupational disciplinary agency or licensing board, resigned membership in the State Bar or another licensing agency or board while disciplinary charges were pending, or had any other public discipline imposed on him or her by a professional or occupational disciplinary agency or licensing board within the preceding 10 years (subdivision (e)(1)). The standard identifies the information that must be included in such a disclosure; however, arbitrators may want to provide additional information to assist parties in determining whether to disqualify an arbitrator based on such a disclosure.
- Requiring the arbitrator to disclose any constraints on his or her availability known to the arbitrator that will interfere with his or her ability to commence or complete the arbitration in a timely manner (subdivision (e)(2)).
- Clarifying that the duty to make disclosures is a continuing obligation, requiring disclosure of matters that were not known at the time of nomination or appointment but that become known afterward (subdivision (f)).

It is good practice for an arbitrator to ask each participant to make an effort to disclose any matters that may affect the arbitrator's ability to be impartial.

Standard 8. Additional disclosures in consumer arbitrations administered by a provider organization.

(a) General provisions

(1) *Reliance on information provided by provider organization*

Except as to the information in (c)(1), an arbitrator may rely on information supplied by the administering provider organization in making the disclosures required by this standard only if the provider organization represents that the information the arbitrator is relying on is current through the end of the immediately preceding calendar quarter or more recent. If the information that must be disclosed is available on the Internet, the arbitrator may comply with the obligation to disclose this information by providing in the disclosure statement required under standard 7(c)(1) the Internet address of the specific web page at which the information is located and notifying the party that the arbitrator will supply hard copies of this information upon request.

(2) *Reliance on representation that not a consumer arbitration*

An arbitrator is not required to make the disclosures required by this standard if he or she reasonably believes that the arbitration is not a

consumer arbitration based on reasonable reliance on a consumer party's representation that the arbitration is not a consumer arbitration.

(Subd (a) amended effective July 1, 2014.)

(b) Additional disclosures required

In addition to the disclosures required under standard 7, in a consumer arbitration as defined in standard 2 in which a dispute resolution provider organization is coordinating, administering, or providing the arbitration services, a proposed arbitrator who is nominated or appointed as an arbitrator on or after January 1, 2003 must disclose the following within the time and in the same manner as the disclosures required under standard 7(c)(1):

(1) *Relationships between the provider organization and party or lawyer in arbitration*

Any significant past, present, or currently expected financial or professional relationship or affiliation between the administering dispute resolution provider organization and a party or lawyer in the arbitration. Information that must be disclosed under this standard includes:

(A) The provider organization has a financial interest in a party.

(B) A party, a lawyer in the arbitration, or a law firm with which a lawyer in the arbitration is currently associated is a member of or has a financial interest in the provider organization.

(C) Within the preceding two years the provider organization has received a gift, bequest, or favor from a party, a lawyer in the arbitration, or a law firm with which a lawyer in the arbitration is currently associated.

(D) The provider organization has entered into, or the arbitrator currently expects that the provider organization will enter into, an agreement or relationship with any party or lawyer in the arbitration or a law firm with which a lawyer in the arbitration is currently associated under which the provider organization will administer, coordinate, or provide dispute resolution services in other noncollective bargaining matters or will provide other consulting services for that party, lawyer, or law firm.

(E) The provider organization is coordinating, administering, or providing dispute resolution services or has coordinated, administered, or provided such services in another pending or prior noncollective bargaining case in which a party or lawyer in the arbitration was a party or a lawyer. For purposes of this paragraph, "prior case" means a case in which the dispute resolution neutral affiliated with the provider organization concluded his or her service within the two years before the date of the arbitrator's proposed nomination or appointment, but does not include any case in which the dispute resolution neutral concluded his or her service before July 1, 2002.

(2) *Case information*

If the provider organization is acting or has acted in any of the capacities described in paragraph (1)(E), the arbitrator must disclose:

(A) The names of the parties in each prior or pending case and, where applicable, the name of the attorney in the current arbitration who is involved in the pending case or who was involved in the prior case;

(B) The type of dispute resolution services (arbitration, mediation, reference, etc.) coordinated, administered, or provided by the provider organization in the case; and

(C) In each prior case in which a dispute resolution neutral affiliated with the provider organization rendered a decision as an arbitrator, a temporary judge appointed under article VI, §4 of the California Constitution, or a referee appointed under Code of Civil Procedure sections 638 or 639, the date of the decision, the prevailing party, the amount of monetary damages awarded, if any, and the names of the parties' attorneys.

(3) *Summary of case information*

If the total number of cases disclosed under paragraph (1)(E) is greater than five, the arbitrator must also provide a summary of these cases that states:

(A) The number of pending cases in which the provider organization is currently providing each type of dispute resolution services;

(B) The number of prior cases in which the provider organization previously provided each type of dispute resolution services;

(C) The number of such prior cases in which a neutral affiliated with the provider organization rendered a decision as an arbitrator, a temporary judge, or a referee; and

(D) The number of prior cases in which the party to the current arbitration or the party represented by the lawyer in the current arbitration was the prevailing party.

(Subd (b) amended effective July 1, 2014.)

(c) Relationship between provider organization and arbitrator

If a relationship or affiliation is disclosed under subdivision (b), the arbitrator must also provide information about the following:

(1) Any financial relationship or affiliation the arbitrator has with the provider organization other than receiving referrals of cases, including whether the arbitrator has a financial interest in the provider organization or is an employee of the provider organization;

(2) The provider organization's process and criteria for recruiting, screening, and training the panel of arbitrators from which the arbitrator in this case is to be selected;

(3) The provider organization's process for identifying, recommending, and selecting potential arbitrators for specific cases; and

(4) Any role the provider organization plays in ruling on requests for disqualification of the arbitrator.

(Subd (c) amended effective July 1, 2014.)

(d) Effective date

The provisions of this standard take effect on January 1, 2003. Persons who are serving in arbitrations in which they were appointed to serve as arbitrators before January 1, 2003, are not subject to this standard in those pending arbitrations.

Standard 8 amended effective July 1, 2014.

Comment to Standard 8

This standard only applies in consumer arbitrations in which a dispute resolution provider organization is administering the arbitration. Like standard 7, this standard expands upon the existing statutory disclosure requirements. Code of Civil Procedure section 1281.95 requires arbitrators in certain construction defect arbitrations to make disclosures concerning relationships between their employers or arbitration services and the parties in the arbitration. This standard requires arbitrators in all consumer arbitrations to disclose any financial or professional relationship between the administering provider organization and any party, attorney, or law firm in the arbitration and, if any such relationship exists, then the arbitrator must also disclose his or her relationship with the dispute resolution provider organization. This standard requires an arbitrator to disclose if the provider organization has a financial interest in a party or lawyer in the arbitration or if a party or lawyer in the arbitration has a financial interest in the provider organization even though provider organizations are prohibited under Code of Civil Procedure section 1281.92 from administering any consumer arbitration where any such relationship exists.

Subdivision (b). Currently expected relationships or affiliations that must be disclosed include all relationships or affiliations that the arbitrator, at the time the disclosure is made, expects will be formed. For example, if the arbitrator knows that the administering provider organization has agreed in concept to enter into a business relationship with a party, but they have not yet signed a written agreement formalizing that relationship, this would be a "currently expected" relationship that the arbitrator would be required to disclose.

Standard 9. Arbitrators' duty to inform themselves about matters to be disclosed.

(a) General duty to inform him or herself

A person who is nominated or appointed as an arbitrator must make a reasonable effort to inform himself or herself of matters that must be disclosed under standards 7 and 8.

(b) Obligation regarding extended family

An arbitrator can fulfill the obligation under this standard to inform himself or herself of relationships or other matters involving his or her extended family and former spouse that are required to be disclosed under standard 7 by:

(1) Seeking information about these relationships and matters from the members of his or her immediate family and any members of his or her extended family living in his or her household; and

(2) Declaring in writing that he or she has made the inquiry in (1).

(c) Obligation regarding relationships with associates of lawyer in the arbitration

An arbitrator can fulfill the obligation under this standard to inform himself or herself of relationships with any lawyer associated in the practice of law with the lawyer in the arbitration that are required to be disclosed under standard 7 by:

(1) Informing the lawyer in the arbitration, in writing, of all such relationships within the arbitrator's knowledge and asking the lawyer if the lawyer is aware of any other such relationships; and

(2) Declaring in writing that he or she has made the inquiry in (1) and attaching to this declaration copies of his or her inquiry and any response from the lawyer in the arbitration.

(d) Obligation regarding service as a neutral other than an arbitrator before July 1, 2002

An arbitrator can fulfill the obligation under this standard to inform himself or herself of his or her service as a dispute resolution neutral other than as an arbitrator in cases that commenced prior to July 1, 2002 by:

(1) Asking any dispute resolution provider organization that administered those prior services for this information; and

(2) Declaring in writing that he or she has made the inquiry in (1) and attaching to this declaration copies of his or her inquiry and any response from the provider organization.

(e) Obligation regarding relationships with provider organization

An arbitrator can fulfill his or her obligation under this standard to inform himself or herself of the information that is required to be disclosed under standard 8 by:

(1) Asking the dispute resolution provider organization for this information; and

(2) Declaring in writing that he or she has made the inquiry in (1) and attaching to this declaration copies of his or her inquiry and any response from the provider organization.

Comment to Standard 9

This standard expands arbitrators existing duty of reasonable inquiry that applies with respect to financial interests under Code of Civil Procedure section 170.1(a)(3), to require arbitrators to make a reasonable effort to inform themselves about all matters that must be disclosed. This standard also clarifies what constitutes a reasonable effort by an arbitrator to inform himself or herself about specified matters, including relationships or other matters concerning his or her extended family and relationships with attorneys associated in the practice of law with the attorney in the arbitration (such as associates encompassed within the term "lawyer for a party").

Standard 10. Disqualification.

(a) An arbitrator is disqualified if:

(1) The arbitrator fails to comply with his or her obligation to make disclosures and a party serves a notice of disqualification in the manner and within the time specified in Code of Civil Procedure section 1281.91;

(2) The arbitrator complies with his or her obligation to make disclosures within 10 calendar days of service of notice of the proposed nomination or appointment and, based on that disclosure, a party serves a notice of disqualification in the manner and within the time specified in Code of Civil Procedure section 1281.91;

(3) The arbitrator makes a required disclosure more than 10 calendar days after service of notice of the proposed nomination or appointment and, based on that disclosure, a party serves a notice of disqualification in the manner and within the time specified in Code of Civil Procedure section 1281.91; or

(4) A party becomes aware that an arbitrator has made a material omission or material misrepresentation in his or her disclosure and, within 15 days after becoming aware of the omission or misrepresentation and within the time specified in Code of Civil Procedure section 1281.91(c), the party serves a notice of disqualification that clearly describes the material omission or material misrepresentation and how and when the party became aware of this omission or misrepresentation; or

(5) If any ground specified in Code of Civil Procedure section 170.1 exists and the party makes a demand that the arbitrator disqualify himself or herself in the manner and within the time specified in Code of Civil Procedure section 1281.91(d).

(b) For purposes of this standard, "obligation to make disclosure" means an arbitrator's obligation to make disclosures under standards 7 or 8 or Code of Civil Procedure section 1281.9.

(c) Notwithstanding any contrary request, consent, or waiver by the parties, an arbitrator must disqualify himself or herself if he or she concludes at any time during the arbitration that he or she is not able to conduct the arbitration impartially.

Comment to Standard 10

Code of Civil Procedure section 1281.91 already establishes requirements concerning disqualification of arbitrators. This standard does not eliminate or otherwise limit those requirements or change existing authority or procedures for challenging an arbitrator's failure to disqualify himself or herself. The provisions of subdivisions (a)(1), (2), and (5) restate existing disqualification procedures under section 1281.91; (b) and (d) when an arbitrator makes, or fails to make, initial disclosures or where a section 170.1 ground exists. The provisions of subdivisions (a)(3) and (4) clarify the requirements relating to disqualification based on disclosure made by the arbitrator after appointment or based on the discovery by the party of a material omission or misrepresentation in the arbitrator's disclosure.

Standard 11. Duty to refuse gift, bequest, or favor.

(a) An arbitrator must not, under any circumstances, accept a gift, bequest, favor, or honoraria from a party or any other person or entity whose interests are reasonably likely to come before the arbitrator in the arbitration.

(b) From service of notice of appointment or appointment until two years after the conclusion of the arbitration, an arbitrator must not, under any circumstances, accept a gift, bequest, favor, or honoraria from a party or any other person or entity whose interests have come before the arbitrator in the arbitration.

(c) An arbitrator must discourage members of his or her family residing in his or her household from accepting a gift, bequest, favor, or honoraria that the arbitrator would be prohibited from accepting under subdivisions (a) or (b).

(d) This standard does not prohibit an arbitrator from demanding or receiving a fee for services or expenses.

Comment to Standard 11

Gifts and favors do not include any rebate or discount made available in the regular course of business to members of the public.

Standard 12. Duties and limitations regarding future professional relationships or employment.

(a) Offers as lawyer, expert witness, or consultant

From the time of appointment until the conclusion of the arbitration, an arbitrator must not entertain or accept any offers of employment or new professional relationships as a lawyer, an expert witness, or a consultant from a party or a lawyer for a party in the pending arbitration.

(b) Offers for employment or professional relationships other than as a lawyer, expert witness, or consultant

(1) In addition to the disclosures required by standards 7 and 8, within ten calendar days of service of notice of the proposed nomination or appointment, a proposed arbitrator must disclose to all parties in writing if, while that arbitration is pending, he or she will entertain offers of employment or new professional relationships in any capacity other than as a lawyer, expert witness, or consultant from a party or a lawyer for a party, including offers to serve as a dispute resolution neutral in another case.

(2) If the arbitrator discloses that he or she will entertain such offers of employment or new professional relationships while the arbitration is pending:

(A) In consumer arbitrations, the disclosure must also state that the arbitrator will inform the parties as required under (d) if he or she subsequently receives an offer while that arbitration is pending.

(B) In all other arbitrations, the disclosure must also state that the arbitrator will not inform the parties if he or she subsequently receives an offer while that arbitration is pending.

(3) A party may disqualify the arbitrator based on this disclosure by serving a notice of disqualification in the manner and within the time specified in Code of Civil Procedure section 1281.91(b).

(Subd (b) amended effective July 1, 2014.)

(c) Acceptance of offers under (b) prohibited unless intent disclosed

If an arbitrator fails to make the disclosure required by subdivision (b) of this standard, from the time of appointment until the conclusion of the arbitration the arbitrator must not entertain or accept any such offers of employment or new professional relationships, including offers to serve as a dispute resolution neutral.

(Subd (c) amended effective July 1, 2014.)

(d) Required notice of offers under (b)

If, in the disclosure made under subdivision (b), the arbitrator states that he or she will entertain offers of employment or new professional relationships covered by (b), the arbitrator may entertain such offers. However, in consumer arbitrations, from the time of appointment until the conclusion of the arbitration, the arbitrator must inform all parties to the current arbitration of any such offer and whether it was accepted as provided in this subdivision.

(1) The arbitrator in a consumer arbitration must notify the parties in writing of any such offer within five days of receiving the offer and, if the arbitrator accepts the offer, must notify the parties in writing within five days of that acceptance. The arbitrator's notice must identify the party or attorney who made the offer and provide a general description of the employment or new professional relationship that was offered including,

if the offer is to serve as a dispute resolution neutral, whether the offer is to serve in a single case or multiple cases.

(2) If the arbitrator fails to inform the parties of an offer or an acceptance as required under (1), that constitutes a failure to comply with the arbitrator's obligation to make a disclosure required under these ethics standards.

(3) If an arbitrator has informed the parties in a pending arbitration about an offer as required under (1):

(A) Receiving or accepting that offer does not, by itself, constitute corruption in or misconduct by the arbitrator;

(B) The arbitrator is not also required to disclose that offer or its acceptance under standard 7; and

(C) The arbitrator is not subject to disqualification under standard 10(a)(2), (3), or (5) solely on the basis of that offer or the arbitrator's acceptance of that offer.

(4) An arbitrator is not required to inform the parties in a pending arbitration about an offer under this subdivision if:

(A) He or she reasonably believes that the pending arbitration is not a consumer arbitration based on reasonable reliance on a consumer party's representation that the arbitration is not a consumer arbitration;

(B) The offer is to serve as an arbitrator in an arbitration conducted under or arising out of public or private sector labor-relations laws, regulations, charter provisions, ordinances, statutes, or agreements; or

(C) The offer is for uncompensated service as a dispute resolution neutral.

(Subd (d) adopted effective July 1, 2014.)

(e) Relationships and use of confidential information related to the arbitrated case

An arbitrator must not at any time:

(1) Without the informed written consent of all parties, enter into any professional relationship or accept any professional employment as a lawyer, an expert witness, or a consultant relating to the case arbitrated; or

(2) Without the informed written consent of the party, enter into any professional relationship or accept employment in another matter in which information that he or she has received in confidence from a party by reason of serving as an arbitrator in a case is material.

(Subd (e) relettered effective July 1, 2014; adopted as subd (d).)
Standard 12 amended effective July 1, 2014.

Comment to Standard 12

Subdivision (d)(1). A party may disqualify an arbitrator for failure to make required disclosures, including disclosures required by these ethics standards (see Code Civ. Proc., § 1281.91(a) and standard 10(a)). Failure to disclose, within the time required for disclosure, a ground for disqualification of which the arbitrator was then aware is also a ground for *vacatur* of the arbitrator's award (see Code Civ. Proc., § 1286.2(a)(6)(A)).

Subdivision (d)(4)(B). The arbitrations identified under this provision are only those in which, under Code of Civil Procedure section 1281.85(b) and standard 3(b)(2)(H), the ethics standards do not apply to the arbitrator.

Standard 13. Conduct of proceeding.

(a) An arbitrator must conduct the arbitration fairly, promptly, and diligently and in accordance with the applicable law relating to the conduct of arbitration proceedings.

(b) In making the decision, an arbitrator must not be swayed by partisan interests, public clamor, or fear of criticism.

Comment to Standard 13

Subdivision (a). The arbitrator's duty to dispose of matters promptly and diligently must not take precedence over the arbitrator's duty to dispose of matters fairly.

Conducting the arbitration in a procedurally fair manner includes conducting a balanced process in which each party is given an opportunity to participate. When one but not all parties are unrepresented, an arbitrator must ensure that the party appearing without counsel has an adequate opportunity to be heard and involved. Conducting the arbitration promptly and diligently requires expeditious management of all stages of the proceeding and concluding the case as promptly as the circumstances reasonably permit. During an arbitration, an arbitrator may discuss the issues, arguments, and evidence with the parties or their counsel, make interim rulings, and otherwise to control or direct the arbitration. This standard is not intended to restrict these activities.

The arbitrator's duty to uphold the integrity and fairness of the arbitration process includes an obligation to make reasonable efforts to prevent delaying tactics, harassment of any participant, or other abuse of the arbitration process. It is recognized, however, that the arbitrator's reasonable efforts may not successfully control all conduct of the participants.

For the general law relating to the conduct of arbitration proceedings, see chapter 3 of title 9 of part III of the Code of Civil Procedure, sections 1282–1284.2, relating to the conduct of arbitration proceedings. See also Code of Civil Procedure section 1286.2 concerning an arbitrator's unreasonable refusal to grant a continuance as grounds for *vacatur* of the award.

Standard 14.   Ex parte communications.

(a) An arbitrator must not initiate, permit, or consider any ex parte communications or consider other communications made to the arbitrator outside the presence of all of the parties concerning a pending or impending arbitration, except as permitted by this standard, by agreement of the parties, or by applicable law.

(b) An arbitrator may communicate with a party in the absence of other parties about administrative matters, such as setting the time and place of hearings or making other arrangements for the conduct of the proceedings, as long as the arbitrator reasonably believes that the communication will not result in a procedural or tactical advantage for any party. When such a discussion occurs, the arbitrator must promptly inform the other parties of the communication and must give the other parties an opportunity to respond before making any final determination concerning the matter discussed.

(c) An arbitrator may obtain the advice of a disinterested expert on the subject matter of the arbitration if the arbitrator notifies the parties of the person consulted and the substance of the advice and affords the parties a reasonable opportunity to respond.

Comment to Standard 14

See also Code of Civil Procedure sections 1282.2(e) regarding the arbitrator's authority to hear a matter when a party fails to appear and 1282.2(g) regarding the procedures that must be followed if an arbitrator intends to base an award on information not obtained at the hearing.

Standard 15.   Confidentiality.

(a) An arbitrator must not use or disclose information that he or she received in confidence by reason of serving as an arbitrator in a case to gain personal advantage. This duty applies from acceptance of appointment and continues after the conclusion of the arbitration.

(b) An arbitrator must not inform anyone of the award in advance of the time that the award is given to all parties. This standard does not prohibit an arbitrator from providing all parties with a tentative or draft decision for review or from providing an award to an assistant or to the provider organization that is coordinating, administering, or providing the arbitration services in the case for purposes of copying and distributing the award to all parties.

Standard 16.   Compensation.

(a) An arbitrator must not charge any fee for services or expenses that is in any way contingent on the result or outcome of the arbitration.

(b) Before accepting appointment, an arbitrator, a dispute resolution provider organization, or another person or entity acting on the arbitrator's behalf must inform all parties in writing of the terms and conditions of the arbitrator's compensation. This information must include any basis to be used in determining fees; any special fees for cancellation, research and preparation time, or other purposes; any requirements regarding advance deposit of fees; and any practice concerning situations in which a party fails to timely pay the arbitrator's fees, including whether the arbitrator will or may stop the arbitration proceedings.

(Subd (b) amended effective July 1, 2014.)
Standard 16 amended effective July 1, 2014.

Comment to Standard 16

This standard is not intended to affect any authority a court may have to make orders with respect to the enforcement of arbitration agreements or arbitrator fees. It is also not intended to require any arbitrator or arbitration provider organization to establish a particular requirement or practice concerning fees or deposits, but only to inform the parties if such a requirement or practice has been established.

Standard 17.   Marketing.

(a) An arbitrator must be truthful and accurate in marketing his or her services. An arbitrator may advertise a general willingness to serve as an arbitrator and convey biographical information and commercial terms of employment but must not make any representation that directly or indirectly implies favoritism or a specific outcome. An arbitrator must ensure that his or her personal marketing activities and any activities carried out on his or her behalf, including any activities of a provider organization with which the arbitrator is affiliated, comply with this requirement.

(Subd (a) amended effective July 1, 2014.)

(b) An arbitrator must not solicit business from a participant in the arbitration while the arbitration is pending.

(c) An arbitrator must not solicit appointment as an arbitrator in a specific case or specific cases.

(Subd (c) adopted effective July 1, 2014.)

(d) As used in this standard, "solicit" means to communicate in person, by telephone, or through real-time electronic contact to any prospective participant in the arbitration concerning the availability for professional employment of the arbitrator in which a significant motive is pecuniary gain. The term solicit does not include: (1) responding to a request from all parties in a case to submit a proposal to provide arbitration services in that case; or (2) responding to inquiries concerning the arbitrator's availability, qualifications, experience, or fee arrangements.

(Subd (d) adopted effective July 1, 2014.)
Standard 17 amended effective July 1, 2014.

Comment to Standard 17

Subdivision (b) and (c). Arbitrators should keep in mind that, in addition to these restrictions on solicitation, several other standards contain related disclosure requirements. For example, under standard 7(d)(4)–(6), arbitrators must disclose information about their past, current, and prospective service as an arbitrator or other dispute resolution for a party or attorney in the arbitration. Under standard 8(b)(1)(C) and (D), in consumer arbitrations administered by a provider organization, arbitrators must disclose if the provider organization has coordinated, administered, or provided dispute resolution services, is coordinating, administering, or providing such services, or has an agreement to coordinate, administer, or provide such services for a party or attorney in the arbitration. And under standard 12 arbitrators must disclose if, while an arbitration is pending, they will entertain offers from a party or attorney in the arbitration to serve as a dispute resolution neutral in another case.

These provisions are not intended to prohibit an arbitrator from accepting another arbitration from a party or attorney in the arbitration while the first matter is pending, as long as the arbitrator complies with the provisions of standard 12 and there was no express solicitation of this business by the arbitrator.

Appendix A
Judicial Council Legal Forms List

Under Government Code section 68511, the Judicial Council may "prescribe" certain forms. Use of prescribed forms is mandatory. Under rule 1.31, each mandatory Judicial Council legal form is identified as mandatory by an asterisk (*) on the list of Judicial Council legal forms published in this appendix. Mandatory forms bear the word "adopted" in the lower left corner of the first page.

Optional forms bear the word "approved" in the lower left corner of the

first page. Use of an approved (optional) form is not mandatory, but the form must be accepted by all courts in appropriate cases (rule 1.35(a)).

A local court may not reject any Judicial Council form, optional or mandatory, for any of the reasons listed in rule 1.42.

The forms are available on the California Courts Web site in both a fillable and a PDF format at *www.courts.ca.gov/forms*.

JUDICIAL COUNCIL FORMS

Form No.	Year	Title	[Rev. Jan. 1, 2021]

ADOPTION

ADOPT-050-INFO	1/1/2021	How to Adopt a Child in California
ADOPT-200*	1/1/2021	Adoption Request
ADOPT-205	1/1/2016	Declaration Confirming Parentage in Stepparent Adoption
ADOPT-206	1/1/2021	Declaration Confirming Parentage in Stepparent Adoption: Gestational Surrogacy
ADOPT-210*	1/1/2021	Adoption Agreement
ADOPT-210* S	1/1/2016	Adoption Agreement (Spanish)
ADOPT-215*	1/1/2021	Adoption Order
ADOPT-215* S	1/1/2016	Adoption Order (Spanish)
ADOPT-216*	7/1/2013	Verification of Compliance with Hague Adoption Convention Attachment
ADOPT-216* S	7/1/2013	Verification of Compliance with Hague Adoption Convention Attachment (Spanish)
ADOPT-220*	7/1/2010	Adoption of Indian Child
ADOPT-225*	1/1/2005	Parent Of Indian Child Agrees To End Parental Rights
ADOPT-226*	1/1/2008	*[Revoked]* Notice of Adoption Proceedings for a Possible Indian Child
ADOPT-230*	1/1/2007	Adoption Expenses
ADOPT-310*	1/1/2018	Contact After Adoption Agreement
ADOPT-315*	1/1/2018	Request to: Enforce, Change, End Contact After Adoption Agreement
ADOPT-320*	1/1/2018	Answer to Request to: Enforce, Change, End Contact After Adoption Agreement
ADOPT-325*	1/1/2018	Judge's Order to: Enforce, Change, End Contact After Adoption Agreement
ADOPT-330*	1/1/2008	Request for Appointment of Confidential Intermediary
ADOPT-331*	1/1/2008	Order for Appointment of Confidential Intermediary

ALTERNATIVE DISPUTE RESOLUTION

ADR-100*	7/1/2012	Statement of Agreement or Nonagreement
ADR-101*	3/1/1994	ADR Information Form
ADR-102	1/1/2012	Request for Trial De Novo After Judicial Arbitration
ADR-103	7/1/2010	Petition to Confirm, Correct, or Vacate Attorney-Client Fee Arbitration Award
ADR-104	1/1/2004	Rejection of Award and Request for Trial After Attorney-Client Fee Arbitration
ADR-105	1/1/2009	Information Regarding Rights After Attorney-Client Fee Arbitration
ADR-106	1/1/2004	Petition to Confirm, Correct, or Vacate Contractual Arbitration Award
ADR-107	7/1/2009	Attendance Sheet for Court-Program Mediation of Civil Case
ADR-109	1/1/2007	Stipulation or Motion For Order Appointing Referee
ADR-110	7/1/2011	Order Appointing Referee
ADR-111	1/1/2006	Report of Referee
ADR-200	1/1/2020	Mediation Disclosure Notification and Acknowledgement

APPELLATE

APP-001	7/1/2015	*[Revoked]* Information on Appeal Procedures for Unlimited Civil Cases *[renumbered to APP-001-INFO]*
APP-001-INFO	1/1/2019	Information on Appeal Procedures for Unlimited Civil Cases *[renumbered from APP-001]*
APP-002	1/1/2017	Notice of Appeal/Cross-Appeal (Unlimited Civil Case)
APP-003	1/1/2019	Appellant's Notice Designating Record on Appeal (Unlimited Civil Case)
APP-004*	1/1/2021	Civil Case Information Statement
APP-005	1/1/2017	Abandonment Of Appeal (Unlimited Civil Case)
APP-006	1/1/2017	Application for Extension of Time to File Brief (Civil Case)
APP-007	1/1/2017	Request for Dismissal of Appeal (Civil Case)
APP-008	1/1/2017	Certificate of Interested Entities or Persons
APP-009	1/1/2017	Proof of Service (Court of Appeal)
APP-009E	1/1/2017	Proof of Electronic Service
APP-009-INFO	1/1/2021	Information Sheet For Proof of Service (Court of Appeal)
APP-010	1/1/2019	Respondent's Notice Designating Record on Appeal (Unlimited Civil Case)
APP-011	1/1/2017	Respondent's Notice Electing to Use an Appendix (Unlimited Civil Case)
APP-012	1/1/2017	Stipulation for Extension of Time to File Brief (Civil Case)
APP-013*	1/1/2020	Memorandum of Costs on Appeal
APP-014	1/1/2018	*[Revoked]* Proposed Statement on Appeal (Unlimited Civil Case)
APP-014	1/1/2021	Appellant's Proposed Settled Statement (Unlimited Civil Case)
APP-014A	1/1/2019	Other Party and Nonparty Witness Testimony and other Evidence Attachment (Unlimited Civil Case)
APP-014-INFO	1/1/2019	Information Sheet for Proposed Settled Statement
APP-015-INFO*	3/24/2020	Information Sheet on Waiver of Appellate Court Fees — Supreme Court, Court of Appeal, Appellate Division *[same as FW-015-INFO*]*
APP-016	7/1/2010	Order on Court Fee Waiver (Court of Appeal or Supreme Court) *[same as FW-016]*
APP-016 S	7/1/2010	Order on Court Fee Waiver (Court of Appeal or Supreme Court) (Spanish) *[same as FW-016 S]*

---

* Adopted for mandatory use by all courts.

APP-016-GC	1/1/2021	Order on Court Fee Waiver (Court of Appeal or Supreme Court) (Ward or Conservatee) *[same as FW-016-GC]*
APP-016-GC S	9/1/2015	Order on Court Fee Waiver (Ward or Conservatee) (Spanish) *[same as FW-016-GC S]*
APP-020	1/1/2019	Response to Appellant's Proposed Settled Statement (Unlimited Civil Case)
APP-022	1/1/2019	Order on Appellant's Proposed Settled Statement (Unlimited Civil Case)
APP-025	1/1/2019	Appellant Motion to Use a Settled Statement (Unlimited Civil Case)
APP-031A	1/1/2015	Attached Declaration (Court of Appeal)
APP-060	1/1/2020	Notice of Appeal—Civil Commitment/Mental Health Proceedings
APP-101-INFO	1/1/2021	Information on Appeal Procedures for Limited Civil Cases
APP-102	1/1/2019	Notice of Appeal/Cross-Appeal (Limited Civil Case)
APP-103	1/1/2021	Appellant's Notice Designating Record on Appeal (Limited Civil Case)
APP-104	1/1/2021	Proposed Statement on Appeal (Limited Civil Case)
APP-105	3/1/2014	Order Concerning Appellant's Proposed Statement on Appeal (Limited Civil Case)
APP-106	1/1/2017	Application for Extension of Time to File Brief (Limited Civil Case)
APP-107	1/1/2017	Abandonment of Appeal (Limited Civil Case)
APP-108	1/1/2020	Notice of Waiver of Oral Argument (Limited Civil Case)
APP-109	1/1/2017	Proof of Service (Appellate Division)
APP-109E	1/1/2017	Proof of Electronic Service (Appellate Division)
APP-109-INFO	1/1/2021	What Is Proof of Service?
APP-110	1/1/2019	Respondent's Notice Designating Record on Appeal (Limited Civil Case)
APP-111	1/1/2021	Respondent's Notice Electing to Use an Appendix (Limited Civil Case)
APP-150-INFO	1/1/2021	Information on Writ Proceedings in Misdemeanor, Infraction, and Limited Civil Cases
APP-151	1/1/2017	Petition for Writ (Misdemeanor, Infraction, or Limited Civil Case)

ATTACHMENT

AT-105	7/1/2010	Application for Right to Attach Order, Temporary Protective Order, Etc.
AT-115	7/1/2010	Notice of Application and Hearing for Right to Attach Order and Writ of Attachment
AT-120	7/1/2010	Right to Attach Order After Hearing and Order for Issuance of Writ of Attachment
AT-125	7/1/2010	Ex Parte Right to Attach Order and Order for Issuance of Writ of Attachment (Resident)
AT-130	7/1/2010	Ex Parte Right to Attach Order and Order for Issuance of Writ of Attachment (Nonresident)
AT-135*	1/1/2003	Writ of Attachment
AT-138*	1/1/2017	Application and Order for Appearance and Examination *[same as EJ-125*]*
AT-140	7/1/2011	Temporary Protective Order
AT-145	7/1/1983	Application and Notice of Hearing for Order to Terminate, Modify, or Vacate Temporary Protective Order
AT-150	7/1/1983	Order to Terminate, Modify, or Vacate Temporary Protective Order
AT-155	7/1/1983	Notice of Opposition to Right to Attach Order and Claim of Exemption
AT-160*	1/1/2006	Undertaking by Personal Sureties *[same as CD-140*]*
AT-165	1/1/2003	Notice of Attachment
AT-167	7/1/2013	Memorandum of Garnishee (Attachment—Enforcement of Judgment) *[same as EJ-152]*
AT-170	7/1/1983	Application to Set Aside Right to Attach Order and Release Attached Property, Etc.
AT-175	7/1/1983	Order to Set Aside Attachment, to Substitute Undertaking, Etc.
AT-180	1/1/1985	Notice of Lien *[same as EJ-185]*

BIRTH, MARRIAGE, DEATH

BMD-001*	9/1/2018	Petition to Establish Fact, Time, and Place of Birth *[renumbered from MC-361]*
BMD-001A*	9/1/2018	Declaration in Support of Petition to Establish Fact, Time, and Place of Birth *[renumbered from MC-361A]*
BMD-002*	9/1/2018	Petition to Establish Fact, Date, and Place of Marriage *[renumbered from MC-362]*
BMD-002A*	9/1/2018	Declaration in Support of Petition to Establish Fact, Date, and Place of Marriage *[renumbered from MC-362A]*
BMD-003*	9/1/2018	Petition to Establish Fact, Time, and Place of Death *[renumbered from MC-360]*
BMD-003A*	9/1/2018	Declaration in Support of Petition to Establish Fact, Time, and Place of Death *[renumbered from MC-360A]*

CASE MANAGEMENT

CM-010*	7/1/2007	Civil Case Cover Sheet
CM-011*	9/1/2018	Confidential Cover Sheet False Claims Action *[renumbered from MC-060]*
CM-015	7/1/2007	Notice of Related Case
CM-020	1/1/2008	Ex Parte Application for Extension of Time to Serve Pleading and Orders
CM-110*	7/1/2011	Case Management Statement
CM-180*	1/1/2007	Notice of Stay of Proceedings
CM-181*	1/1/2007	Notice of Termination or Modification of Stay
CM-200*	1/1/2007	Notice of Settlement of Entire Case

---

* Adopted for mandatory use by all courts.

CIVIL

CIV-010*	1/1/2008	Application and Order for Appointment of Guardian Ad Litem—Civil
CIV-020	1/1/2016	Notice of Intent to Appear by Telephone
CIV-025	1/1/2007	Application and Order for Reissuance of Order to Show Cause and Temporary Restraining Order
CIV-050*	1/1/2007	Statement of Damages (Personal Injury or Wrongful Death)
CIV-090	1/1/2008	Offer to Compromise and Acceptance Under Code of Civil Procedure Section 998
CIV-100*	1/1/2020	Request for Entry of Default (Application to Enter Default)
CIV-105*	1/1/2020	Request for Entry of Default (Fair Debt Buying Practices Act)
CIV-110*	1/1/2013	Request for Dismissal
CIV-120*	1/1/2012	Notice of Entry of Dismissal and Proof of Service
CIV-130	1/1/2010	Notice of Entry of Judgment or Order
CIV-140	1/1/2019	Declaration of Demurring Party Regarding Meet and Confer
CIV-141	1/1/2019	Declaration of Demurring Party in Support of Automatic Extension
CIV-150*	9/1/2018	Notice of Limited Scope Representation *[renumbered from MC-950]*
CIV-151	9/1/2018	Application to Be Relieved as Attorney on Completion of Limited Scope Representation *[renumbered from MC-955]*
CIV-152	9/1/2018	Objection to Application to Be Relieved as Attorney on Completion of Limited Scope Representation *[renumbered from MC-956]*
CIV-153	9/1/2018	Order on Application to Be Relieved as Attorney on Completion of Limited Scope Representation *[renumbered from MC-958]*
CIV-160	9/1/2018	Petition for Order Striking and Releasing Lien, Etc. (Government Employee) *[renumbered from MC-100]*
CIV-161	9/1/2018	Order to Show Cause (Government Employee) *[renumbered from MC-101]*
CIV-165*	9/1/2019	Order on Unlawful Use of Personal Identifying Information
CIV-170*	9/1/2018	Petition and Declaration Regarding Unresolved Claims and Deposit of Undistributed Surplus Proceeds of Trustee's Sale *[renumbered from MC-095]*
GDC-001*	1/1/2019	Gender Discrimination Notice

CIVIL HARASSMENT

CH-100*	1/1/2018	Request for Civil Harassment Restraining Orders
CH-100* C	1/1/2018	Request for Civil Harassment Restraining Orders (Chinese)
CH-100* K	1/1/2018	Request for Civil Harassment Restraining Orders (Korean)
CH-100* S	1/1/2018	Request for Civil Harassment Restraining Orders (Spanish)
CH-100* V	1/1/2018	Request for Civil Harassment Restraining Orders (Vietnamese)
CH-100-INFO	7/1/2014	Can a Civil Harassment Restraining Order Help Me? (Civil Harassment Prevention) *[Renumbered from CH-150]*
CH-101*	7/1/2007	*[Revoked]* Request and Order for Free Service of Restraining Order (Sexual Assault or Stalking) *[same as DV-290*]*
CH-101* C	7/1/2007	*[Revoked]* Request and Order for Free Service of Restraining Order (Sexual Assault or Stalking) (Chinese) *[same as DV-290* C]*
CH-101* K	7/1/2007	*[Revoked]* Request and Order for Free Service of Restraining Order (Sexual Assault or Stalking) (Korean) *[same as DV-290* K]*
CH-101* S	7/1/2007	*[Revoked]* Request and Order for Free Service of Restraining Order (Sexual Assault or Stalking) (Spanish) *[same as DV-290* S]*
CH-101* V	7/1/2007	*[Revoked]* Request and Order for Free Service of Restraining Order (Sexual Assault or Stalking) (Vietnamese) *[same as DV-290* V]*
CH-102*	1/1/2012	*[Revoked]* Confidential CLETS Information (Domestic Violence, Civil Harassment, Elder Abuse, Juvenile Law) *[same as DV-260*, EA-102* and JV-248*]*
CH-109*	9/1/2020	Notice of Court Hearing
CH-109* C	1/1/2019	Notice of Court Hearing (Chinese)
CH-109* K	1/1/2019	Notice of Court Hearing (Korean)
CH-109* S	1/1/2019	Notice of Court Hearing (Spanish)
CH-109* V	1/1/2019	Notice of Court Hearing (Vietnamese)
CH-110*	3/15/2019	Temporary Restraining Order (CLETS—TCH) *[Renumbered from CH-120*]*
CH-110* C	1/1/2017	Temporary Restraining Order (CLETS-TCH) (Chinese)
CH-110* K	1/1/2017	Temporary Restraining Order (CLETS-TCH) (Korean)
CH-110* S	1/1/2017	Temporary Restraining Order (CLETS-TCH) (Spanish)
CH-110* V	1/1/2017	Temporary Restraining Order (CLETS-TCH) (Vietnamese)
CH-115*	1/1/2020	Request to Continue Court Hearing *[Renumbered from CH-125*]*
CH-115-INFO	1/1/2020	How to Ask for a New Hearing Date
CH-116*	1/1/2020	Order on Request to Continue Hearing (CLETS—TCH)
CH-120*	1/1/2018	Response to Request for Civil Harassment Restraining Orders *[Renumbered from CH-110*]*
CH-120* C	1/1/2018	Response to Request for Civil Harassment Restraining Orders (Chinese)
CH-120* K	1/1/2018	Response to Request for Civil Harassment Restraining Orders (Korean)
CH-120* S	1/1/2018	Response to Request for Civil Harassment Restraining Orders (Spanish)
CH-120* V	1/1/2018	Response to Request for Civil Harassment Restraining Orders (Vietnamese)

---

* Adopted for mandatory use by all courts.

CH-120-INFO	7/1/2014	How Can I Respond to a Request for Civil Harassment Restraining Orders? (Civil Harassment Prevention) *[Renumbered from CH-151]*
CH-125*	1/1/2005	Reissue Temporary Restraining Order (Civil Harassment) *[Renumbered to CH-115*]*
CH-130*	3/15/2019	Civil Harassment Restraining Order After Hearing (CLETS—CHO) *[Renumbered from CH-140*]*
CH-130* C	1/1/2018	Civil Harassment Restraining Order After Hearing (CLETS-CHO) (Chinese)
CH-130* K	1/1/2018	Civil Harassment Restraining Order After Hearing (CLETS-CHO) (Korean)
CH-130* S	1/1/2018	Civil Harassment Restraining Order After Hearing (CLETS-CHO) (Spanish)
CH-130* V	1/1/2018	Civil Harassment Restraining Order After Hearing (CLETS-CHO) (Vietnamese)
CH-131	1/1/2005	Proof of Service by Mail (Civil Harassment) *[Renumbered to CH-250]*
CH-135	1/1/2005	What Is Proof of Service? (Civil Harassment) *[Renumbered to CH-200-INFO]*
CH-140*	7/1/2007	Restraining Order After Hearing to Stop Harassment (CLETS) (Civil Harassment) *[Renumbered to CH-130*]*
CH-145	1/1/2005	Proof of Firearms Turned in or Sold (Civil Harassment) *[Renumbered to CH-800]*
CH-150	7/1/2007	Can a Civil Harassment Restraining Order Help Me? (Civil Harassment) *[Renumbered to CH-100-INFO]*
CH-151	1/1/2005	How Can I Answer a Request for Orders to Stop Harassment? (Civil Harassment) *[Renumbered to CH-120-INFO]*
CH-160*	9/1/2020	Request to Keep Minor's Information Confidential
CH-160-INFO	9/1/2020	Privacy Protection for a Minor (Person Under 18 Years Old)
CH-165*	1/1/2021	Order on Request to Keep Minor's Information Confidential
CH-170*	9/1/2020	Notice of Order Protecting Information of Minor
CH-175*	9/1/2020	Cover Sheet for Confidential Information
CH-176*	9/1/2020	Request for Release of Minor's Confidential Information
CH-177*	1/1/2021	Notice of Request for Release of Minor's Confidential Information
CH-178*	9/1/2020	Response to Request for Release of Minor's Confidential Information
CH-179*	9/1/2020	Order on Request for Release of Minor's Confidential Information
CH-200	7/1/2014	Proof of Personal Service *[Renumbered from CH-130]*
CH-200-INFO	1/1/2012	What Is "Proof of Personal Service"? *[Renumbered from CH-135]*
CH-200-INFO C	1/1/2012	What Is "Proof of Personal Service"? (Chinese)
CH-200-INFO K	1/1/2012	What Is "Proof of Personal Service"? (Korean)
CH-200-INFO S	1/1/2012	What Is "Proof of Personal Service"? (Spanish)
CH-200-INFO V	1/1/2012	What Is "Proof of Personal Service"? (Vietnamese)
CH-250	1/1/2012	Proof of Service of Response by Mail *[Renumbered from CH-131]*
CH-250 C	1/1/2012	Proof of Service of Response by Mail (Chinese)
CH-250 K	1/1/2012	Proof of Service of Response by Mail (Korean)
CH-250 S	1/1/2012	Proof of Service of Response by Mail (Spanish)
CH-250 V	1/1/2012	Proof of Service of Response by Mail (Vietnamese)
CH-260	1/1/2012	Proof of Service of Order After Hearing by Mail
CH-260 C	1/1/2012	Proof of Service of Order After Hearing by Mail (Chinese)
CH-260 K	1/1/2012	Proof of Service of Order After Hearing by Mail (Korean)
CH-260 S	1/1/2012	Proof of Service of Order After Hearing by Mail (Spanish)
CH-260 V	1/1/2012	Proof of Service of Order After Hearing by Mail (Vietnamese)
CH-600*	1/1/2018	Request to Modify/Terminate Civil Harassment Restraining Order
CH-610*	1/1/2018	Notice of Hearing on Request to Modify/Terminate Civil Harassment Restraining Order
CH-620*	1/1/2018	Response to Request to Modify/Terminate Civil Harassment Restraining Order
CH-630*	1/1/2018	Order on Request to Modify/Terminate Civil Harassment Restraining Order
CH-700*	1/1/2016	Request to Renew Restraining Order
CH-700* C	1/1/2012	Request to Renew Restraining Order (Chinese)
CH-700* K	1/1/2012	Request to Renew Restraining Order (Korean)
CH-700* S	1/1/2012	Request to Renew Restraining Order (Spanish)
CH-700* V	1/1/2012	Request to Renew Restraining Order (Vietnamese)
CH-710*	1/1/2016	Notice of Hearing to Renew Restraining Order
CH-710* C	1/1/2012	Notice of Hearing to Renew Restraining Order (Chinese)
CH-710* K	1/1/2012	Notice of Hearing to Renew Restraining Order (Korean)
CH-710* S	1/1/2012	Notice of Hearing to Renew Restraining Order (Spanish)
CH-710* V	1/1/2012	Notice of Hearing to Renew Restraining Order (Vietnamese)
CH-720*	1/1/2016	Response to Request to Renew Restraining Order
CH-730*	1/1/2012	Order Renewing Civil Harassment Restraining Order (CLETS)
CH-730* C	1/1/2012	Order Renewing Civil Harassment Restraining Order (CLETS) (Chinese)
CH-730* K	1/1/2012	Order Renewing Civil Harassment Restraining Order (CLETS) (Korean)
CH-730* S	1/1/2012	Order Renewing Civil Harassment Restraining Order (CLETS) (Spanish)
CH-730* V	1/1/2012	Order Renewing Civil Harassment Restraining Order (CLETS) (Vietnamese)
CH-800	7/1/2014	Proof of Firearms Turned In, Sold, or Stored *[Renumbered from CH-145]*
CH-800-INFO	7/1/2014	How Do I Turn In, Sell, or Store My Firearms?

CLAIM AND DELIVERY

CD-100*	1/1/2006	Application for Writ of Possession
CD-110*	1/1/2006	Notice of Application for Writ of Possession and Hearing
CD-120*	1/1/2006	Order for Writ of Possession

---

* Adopted for mandatory use by all courts.

CD-130*	1/1/2006	Writ of Possession
CD-140*	1/1/2006	Undertaking By Personal Sureties [same as AT-160*]
CD-160*	1/1/2006	Application and Notice of Application and Hearing for Order to Quash Ex Parte Writ of Possession
CD-170*	1/1/2006	Order for Release and Redelivery of Property
CD-180*	1/1/2006	Declaration for Ex Parte Writ of Possession
CD-190*	1/1/2006	Application for Temporary Restraining Order
CD-200*	1/1/2006	Temporary Restraining Order

CLETS

| CLETS-001* | 1/1/2012 | Confidential CLETS Information |

COURT RECORDS

REC-001(N)*[1]	1/1/2007	Notice of Intent to Destroy Superior Court Records; Offer to Transfer Possession (*formerly 982.8(1)(N)*)
REC-001(R)*	1/1/2007	Request for Transfer or Extension of Time for Retention of Superior Court Records (*formerly 982.8(1)(R)*)
REC-002(N)*[2]	1/1/2007	Notice of Hearing on Request for Transfer or Extension of Time for Retention of Superior Court Records; Court Record; Release and Receipt of Records (*formerly 982.8(2)(N)*)
REC-002(R)*	1/1/2007	Release and Receipt of Superior Court Records (*formerly 982.8(2)(R)*)
REC-003*	1/1/2007	Report to the Judicial Council: Superior Court Records Destroyed, Preserved, and Transferred (*formerly 982.8A*)
REC-033*	1/1/2018	*[Revoked]* Report to the Judicial Council: Superior Court Records Destroyed, Preserved, and Transferred

CRIMINAL

CR-100*	1/24/2012	Fingerprint Form
CR-101	1/1/2021	Plea Form, With Explanations and Waiver of Rights—Felony
CR-102	1/1/2020	Domestic Violence Plea Form With Waiver Of Rights—Misdemeanor
CR-105	9/1/2018	Defendant's Financial Statement on Eligibility for Appointment of Counsel and Reimbursement and Record on Appeal at Public Expense [renumbered from MC-210]
CR-106	1/1/2020	Proof of Service—Criminal Record Clearing
CR-106-INFO	1/1/2020	Information on How to File a Proof of Service in Criminal Record Clearing Requests
CR-110	3/5/2018	Order for Victim Restitution [same as JV-790]
CR-111	7/1/2015	Abstract of Judgment—Restitution [same as JV-791]
CR-112	9/1/2018	Instructions: Order for Victim Restitution [same as JV-792]
CR-113	1/1/2014	Instructions: Abstract of Judgment—Restitution [same as JV-793]
CR-115*	1/1/2020	Defendant's Statement of Assets
CR-117	1/1/2004	Instructions: Defendant's Statement of Assets
CR-118	1/1/2005	Information Regarding Income Deduction Order (Pen. Code, §1202.42)
CR-119	1/1/2005	Order for Income Deduction (Pen. Code, §1202.42)
CR-120	1/1/2017	Notice of Appeal—Felony (Defendant)
CR-125*	7/1/2007	Order to Attend Court or Provide Documents: Subpoena/Subpoena Duces Tecum [same as JV-525*]
CR-126	1/1/2017	Application for Extension of Time to File Brief (Criminal Case)
CR-130	1/1/2009	*[Revoked]* Notice of Appeal—Misdemeanor (Defendant)
CR-131-INFO	9/1/2020	Information on Appeal Procedures for Misdemeanors
CR-132	1/1/2020	Notice of Appeal (Misdemeanor)
CR-133	9/1/2020	Request for Court-Appointed Lawyer in Misdemeanor Appeal
CR-134	1/1/2020	Notice Regarding Record on Appeal (Misdemeanor)
CR-135	1/1/2021	Proposed Statement on Appeal (Misdemeanor)
CR-136	3/1/2014	Order Concerning Appellant's Proposed Statement on Appeal (Misdemeanor)
CR-137	1/1/2017	Abandonment of Appeal (Misdemeanor)
CR-138	1/1/2020	Notice of Waiver of Oral Argument (Misdemeanor)
CR-141-INFO	1/1/2020	Information on Appeal Procedures for Infractions
CR-142	1/1/2020	Notice of Appeal and Record on Appeal
CR-143	1/1/2021	Proposed Statement on Appeal (Infraction)
CR-144	3/1/2014	Order Concerning Appellant's Proposed Statement on Appeal (Infraction)
CR-145	1/1/2017	Abandonment of Appeal (Infraction)
CR-150*	1/1/2021	Certificate of Identity Theft: Judicial Finding of Factual Innocence
CR-151	1/1/2005	Petition for Certificate of Identity Theft (Pen. Code, §530.6)
CR-160*	1/22/2019	Criminal Protective Order—Domestic Violence (CLETS—CPO)
CR-160* S	1/22/2019	Criminal Protective Order—Domestic Violence (CLETS—CPO) (Spanish)
CR-161*	1/1/2017	Criminal Protective Order—Other Than Domestic Violence (CLETS—CPO)
CR-162*	1/1/2021	Order to Surrender Firearms in Domestic Violence Case (CLETS—CPO) (Penal Code, § 136.2(a)(1)(G)(ii))

---

[1] Form REC-001(R) to be printed on reverse side of form REC-001(N).

[2] Form REC-002(R) to be printed on reverse side of form REC-002(N).

* Adopted for mandatory use by all courts.

CR-165*	7/1/2016	Notice of Termination of Protective Order in Criminal Proceeding (CLETS—CANCEL)
CR-168	1/1/2007	Batterer Intervention Program Progress Report
CR-170	1/1/2020	Notification of Decision Whether to Challenge Recommendation (Pen. Code, § 2972.1)
CR-173	9/1/2018	Order for Commitment (Sexually Violent Predator) *[renumbered from MC-280]*
CR-174	9/1/2018	Order for Extended Commitment (Sexually Violent Predator) *[renumbered from MC-281]*
CR-175	9/1/2018	*[Renumbered]* Notice and Request for Ruling (Criminal) *[renumbered to HC-004]*
CR-180	1/1/2019	Petition for Dismissal
CR-181	1/1/2019	Order for Dismissal
CR-183	1/1/2016	Petition for Dismissal (Military Personnel) *[same as MIL-183]*
CR-184	1/22/2019	Order for Dismissal (Military Personnel) *[same as MIL-184]*
CR-185	1/1/2009	Petition for Expungement of DNA Profiles and Samples (Pen. Code, §299) *[same as JV-796]*
CR-186	1/1/2009	Order for Expungement of DNA Profiles and Samples (Pen. Code, §299) *[same as JV-798]*
CR-187	7/1/2017	*[Revoked]* Petition/Application Adult Crimes
CR-187	1/1/2020	Motion to Vacate Conviction or Sentence *[renumbered from MC-245]*
CR-188	7/1/2017	*[Renumbered]* Order After Petition/Application Adult Crimes *[Renumbered to CR-403]*
CR-188	1/1/2020	Order on Motion to Vacate Conviction or Sentence *[renumbered from MC-246]*
CR-190*	1/1/2004	Order Appointing Counsel in Capital Case
CR-191*	1/22/2019	Declaration of Counsel for Appointment in Capital Case
CR-200	1/1/2021	Form Interrogatories—Crime Victim Restitution
CR-210	1/1/2018	Prohibited Persons Relinquishment Form Findings (Pen. Code, § 29810(c))
CR-220	1/22/2019	Proof of Enrollment or Completion Alcohol or Drug Program *[renumbered from MC-400]*
CR-221	1/1/2021	Order to Install Ignition Interlock Device *[renumbered from ID-100]*
CR-222	1/1/2021	Ignition Interlock Installation Verification *[renumbered from ID-110]*
CR-223	1/1/2021	Ignition Interlock Calibration Verification *[renumbered from ID-120]*
CR-224	1/1/2021	Ignition Interlock Noncompliance Report *[renumbered from ID-130]*
CR-225	1/1/2021	Ignition Interlock Removal and Modification to Probation Order *[renumbered from ID-140]*
CR-226	1/1/2021	Notice to Employers of Ignition Interlock Restriction *[renumbered from ID-150]*
CR-250*	11/1/2012	Notice and Motion for Transfer
CR-251*	1/1/2021	Order for Transfer
CR-252*	11/1/2012	Receiving Court Comment Form
CR-290*	7/1/2012	Felony Abstract of Judgment—Determinate
CR-290(A)*	7/1/2012	Felony Abstract of Judgment Attachment Page
CR-290.1*	7/1/2012	Felony Abstract of Judgment—Determinate Single, Concurrent, or Full-Term Consecutive Count Form
CR-292*	1/1/2012	Abstract of Judgment—Prison Commitment—Indeterminate
CR-300	1/1/2021	Petition for Revocation (Pen. Code, §§ 1170(h)(5)(B), 1203.2, 3000.08, and 3455)
CR-301	7/1/2013	Warrant Request and Order
CR-302	7/1/2013	Request and Order to Recall Warrant
CR-320	4/1/2018	Can't Afford to Pay Fine: Traffic and Other Infractions *[same as TR-320]*
CR-321	4/1/2018	Can't Afford to Pay Fine: Traffic and Other Infractions (Court Order) *[same as TR-321]*
CR-400	7/1/2017	Petition/Application (Health and Safety Code, § 11361.8) Adult Crime(s)
CR-401	7/1/2017	Proof of Service for Petition/Application (Health and Safety Code, § 11361.8) Adult Crime(s)
CR-402	7/1/2017	Prosecuting Agency Response to Petition/Application (Health and Safety Code, § 11361.8) Adult Crime(s)
CR-403	7/1/2017	Order After Petition/Application (Health and Safety Code, § 11361.8) Adult Crime(s) *[Renumbered from CR-188]*
CR-404	1/1/2019	Petition/Application for Resentencing and Dismissal
CR-405	1/1/2019	Order After Petition/Application for Resentencing and Dismissal
CR-409	1/1/2019	Petition to Seal Arrest and Related Records
CR-409-INFO	1/1/2019	Information on How to File a Petition to Seal Arrest and Related Records Under Penal Code Section 851.91
CR-410	1/1/2019	Order to Seal arrest and Related Records (Pen. Code, sections 851.91, 851.92)
CR-412	1/1/2020	Petition for Resentencing Based on Health Conditions Due to Military Service Listed in Penal Code Section 1170.91(b) *[same as MIL-412]*
CR-600*	4/25/2019	Capital Case Attorney Pretrial Checklist
CR-601*	4/25/2019	Capital Case Attorney List of Appearances
CR-602*	4/25/2019	Capital Case Attorney List of Exhibits
CR-603*	4/25/2019	Capital Case Attorney List of Motions
CR-604*	4/25/2019	Capital Case Attorney List of Jury Instructions
CR-605*	4/25/2019	Capital Case Attorney Trial Checklist

DISABILITY ACCESS LITIGATION

DAL-001*	7/1/2016	Important Advisory Information for Building Owners and Tenants
DAL-001* C	10/23/2009	Important Advisory Information for Building Owners and Tenants (Chinese)
DAL-001* K	10/23/2009	Important Advisory Information for Building Owners and Tenants (Korean)
DAL-001* S	10/23/2009	Important Advisory Information for Building Owners and Tenants (Spanish)
DAL-001* V	10/23/2009	Important Advisory Information for Building Owners and Tenants (Vietnamese)
DAL-002	7/1/2016	Answer—Disability Access
DAL-005*	7/1/2016	Defendant's Application for Stay of Proceedings and Early Evaluation Conference, Joint Inspection

---

* Adopted for mandatory use by all courts.

Rules of Court

DAL-006*	7/1/2013	Confidential Cover Sheet and Declaration Re Documents for Stay and Early Evaluation Conference
DAL-010*	7/1/2016	Notice of Stay of Proceedings and Early Evaluation Conference, Joint Inspection
DAL-012	1/1/2016	Proof of Service—Disability Access Litigation
DAL-015*	1/1/2015	Application for Mandatory Evaluation Conference Under Civil Code Section 55.545
DAL-020*	7/1/2013	Notice of Mandatory Evaluation Conference

DISCOVERY

DISC-001	1/1/2008	Form Interrogatories—General
DISC-002	1/1/2009	Form Interrogatories—Employment Law
DISC-003	1/1/2014	Form Interrogatories—Unlawful Detainer *[same as UD-106]*
DISC-004	1/1/2007	Form Interrogatories—Limited Civil Cases (Economic Litigation)
DISC-005	7/1/2013	Form Interrogatories—Construction Litigation
DISC-010*	1/1/2007	Case Questionnaire—For Limited Civil Cases (Under $25,000)
DISC-015*	1/1/2007	Request For Statement Of Witnesses And Evidence—For Limited Civil Cases (Under $25,000)
DISC-020	1/1/2008	Request for Admission
DISC-030	1/1/2008	Commission to Take Deposition Outside California

DOMESTIC VIOLENCE PREVENTION

DV-100*	7/1/2016	Request for Domestic Violence Restraining Order
DV-100* C	7/1/2014	Request for Domestic Violence Restraining Order (Chinese)
DV-100* K	7/1/2016	Request for Domestic Violence Restraining Order (Korean)
DV-100* S	7/1/2016	Request for Domestic Violence Restraining Order (Spanish)
DV-100* V	7/1/2016	Request for Domestic Violence Restraining Order (Vietnamese)
DV-101	1/1/2017	Description of Abuse
DV-101 C	1/1/2017	Description of Abuse (Chinese)
DV-101 K	1/1/2017	Description of Abuse (Korean)
DV-101 S	1/1/2017	Description of Abuse (Spanish)
DV-101 V	1/1/2017	Description of Abuse (Vietnamese)
DV-105*	1/1/2012	Request for Child Custody and Visitation Orders
DV-105* C	1/1/2012	Request for Child Custody and Visitation Orders (Chinese)
DV-105* K	1/1/2012	Request for Child Custody and Visitation Orders (Korean)
DV-105* S	1/1/2012	Request for Child Custody and Visitation Orders (Spanish)
DV-105* V	1/1/2012	Request for Child Custody and Visitation Orders (Vietnamese)
DV-108*	1/1/2012	Request for Order: No Travel with Children
DV-108* C	1/1/2012	Request for Order: No Travel with Children (Chinese)
DV-108* K	1/1/2012	Request for Order: No Travel with Children (Korean)
DV-108* S	1/1/2012	Request for Order: No Travel with Children (Spanish)
DV-108* V	1/1/2012	Request for Order: No Travel with Children (Vietnamese)
DV-109*	9/1/2020	Notice of Court Hearing
DV-109* C	1/1/2012	Notice of Court Hearing (Chinese)
DV-109* K	1/1/2012	Notice of Court Hearing (Korean)
DV-109* S	1/1/2012	Notice of Court Hearing (Spanish)
DV-109* V	1/1/2012	Notice of Court Hearing (Vietnamese)
DV-110*	7/1/2016	Temporary Restraining Order (CLETS—TRO)
DV-110* C	7/1/2014	Temporary Restraining Order (CLETS—TRO) (Chinese)
DV-110* K	7/1/2016	Temporary Restraining Order (CLETS—TRO) (Korean)
DV-110* S	7/1/2016	Temporary Restraining Order (CLETS—TRO) (Spanish)
DV-110* V	7/1/2016	Temporary Restraining Order (CLETS—TRO) (Vietnamese)
DV-112	1/1/2012	Waiver of Hearing on Denied Request for Temporary Restraining Order
DV-112 C	1/1/2012	Waiver of Hearing on Denied Request for Temporary Restraining Order (Chinese)
DV-112 K	1/1/2012	Waiver of Hearing on Denied Request for Temporary Restraining Order (Korean)
DV-112 S	1/1/2012	Waiver of Hearing on Denied Request for Temporary Restraining Order (Spanish)
DV-112 V	1/1/2012	Waiver of Hearing on Denied Request for Temporary Restraining Order (Vietnamese)
DV-115*	1/1/2020	Request to Continue Hearing (Temporary Restraining Order) *[Renumbered from DV-125*]*
DV-115* C	1/1/2012	Request to Continue Court Hearing and Reissue Temporary Restraining Order (Chinese)
DV-115* K	7/1/2016	Request to Continue Hearing (Korean)
DV-115* S	7/1/2016	Request to Continue Hearing (Spanish)
DV-115* V	7/1/2016	Request to Continue Hearing (Vietnamese)
DV-115-INFO	1/1/2020	How to Ask for a New Hearing Date
DV-115-INFO C	1/1/2013	How to Ask for a New Hearing Date (Chinese)
DV-115-INFO K	7/1/2016	How to Ask for a New Hearing Date (Korean)
DV-115-INFO S	7/1/2016	How to Ask for a New Hearing Date (Spanish)
DV-115-INFO V	7/1/2016	How to Ask for a New Hearing Date (Vietnamese)
DV-116*	1/1/2020	Order on Request to Continue Hearing (Temporary Restraining Order) (CLETS—TRO)
DV-116* K	7/1/2016	Order on Request to Continue Hearing (CLETS—TRO) (Korean)
DV-116* S	7/1/2016	Order on Request to Continue Hearing (CLETS—TRO) (Spanish)
DV-116* V	7/1/2016	Order on Request to Continue Hearing (CLETS—TRO) (Vietnamese)
DV-117*	1/1/2020	Order Granting Alternative Service

---

* Adopted for mandatory use by all courts.

DV-120*	7/1/2016	Response to Request for Domestic Violence Restraining Order
DV-120* K	7/1/2016	Response to Request for Domestic Violence Restraining Order (Korean)
DV-120* S	7/1/2016	Response to Request for Domestic Violence Restraining Order (Spanish)
DV-120* V	7/1/2016	Response to Request for Domestic Violence Restraining Order (Vietnamese)
DV-120-INFO	7/1/2016	How Can I Respond to a Request for Domestic Violence Restraining Order? *[Renumbered from DV-540-INFO]*
DV-120-INFO K	7/1/2016	How Can I Respond to a Request for Domestic Violence Restraining Order? (Korean)
DV-120-INFO S	7/1/2016	How Can I Respond to a Request for Domestic Violence Restraining Order? (Spanish)
DV-120-INFO V	7/1/2016	How Can I Respond to a Request for Domestic Violence Restraining Order? (Vietnamese)
DV-125*	1/1/2010	Reissue Notice of Court Hearing and Temporary Restraining Order (Domestic Violence Prevention) *[Renumbered to DV-115*]*
DV-126-INFO	1/1/2012	*[Revoked]* How to Reissue a Temporary Restraining Order (Domestic Violence Prevention)
DV-130*	7/1/2016	Restraining Order After Hearing (CLETS—OAH) (Order of Protection)
DV-130* K	7/1/2016	Restraining Order After Hearing (CLETS—OAH) (Order of Protection) (Korean)
DV-130* S	7/1/2016	Restraining Order After Hearing (CLETS—OAH) (Order of Protection) (Spanish)
DV-130* V	7/1/2016	Restraining Order After Hearing (CLETS—OAH) (Order of Protection) (Vietnamese)
DV-140*	1/1/2012	Child Custody and Visitation Order
DV-140* C	1/1/2012	Child Custody and Visitation Order (Chinese)
DV-140* K	1/1/2012	Child Custody and Visitation Order (Korean)
DV-140* S	1/1/2012	Child Custody and Visitation Order (Spanish)
DV-140* V	1/1/2012	Child Custody and Visitation Order (Vietnamese)
DV-145*	1/1/2012	Order: No Travel With Children
DV-145* C	1/1/2012	Order: No Travel With Children (Chinese)
DV-145* K	1/1/2012	Order: No Travel With Children (Korean)
DV-145* S	1/1/2012	Order: No Travel With Children (Spanish)
DV-145* V	1/1/2012	Order: No Travel With Children (Vietnamese)
DV-150*	1/1/2016	Supervised Visitation and Exchange Order
DV-160*	9/1/2020	Request to Keep Minor's Information Confidential
DV-160 C	1/1/2019	Request to Keep Minor's Information Confidential (Domestic Violence Prevention) (Chinese)
DV-160 K	1/1/2019	Request to Keep Minor's Information Confidential (Domestic Violence Prevention) (Korean)
DV-160 S	1/1/2019	Request to Keep Minor's Information Confidential (Domestic Violence Prevention) (Spanish)
DV-160 V	1/1/2019	Request to Keep Minor's Information Confidential (Domestic Violence Prevention) (Vietnamese)
DV-160-INFO	1/1/2021	Privacy Protection for a Minor (Person Under 18 Years Old)
DV-165*	1/1/2021	Order on Request to Keep Minor's Information Confidential
DV-165* C	1/1/2019	Order on Request to Keep Minor's Information Confidential (Domestic Violence Prevention) (Chinese)
DV-165* K	1/1/2019	Order on Request to Keep Minor's Information Confidential (Domestic Violence Prevention) (Korean)
DV-165* S	1/1/2019	Order on Request to Keep Minor's Information Confidential (Domestic Violence Prevention) (Spanish)
DV-165* V	1/1/2019	Order on Request to Keep Minor's Information Confidential (Domestic Violence Prevention) (Vietnamese)
DV-170*	9/1/2020	Notice of Order Protecting Information of Minor
DV-170* C	1/1/2019	Other Orders (Domestic Violence Prevention) (Chinese)
DV-170* K	1/1/2019	Other Orders (Domestic Violence Prevention) (Korean)
DV-170* S	1/1/2019	Other Orders (Domestic Violence Prevention) (Spanish)
DV-170* V	1/1/2019	Other Orders (Domestic Violence Prevention) (Vietnamese)
DV-175*	9/1/2020	Cover Sheet for Confidential Information
DV-175* C	1/1/2019	Cover Sheet for Confidential Information (Domestic Violence Prevention) (Chinese)
DV-175* K	1/1/2019	Cover Sheet for Confidential Information (Domestic Violence Prevention) (Korean)
DV-175* S	1/1/2019	Cover Sheet for Confidential Information (Domestic Violence Prevention) (Spanish)
DV-175* V	1/1/2019	Cover Sheet for Confidential Information (Domestic Violence Prevention) (Vietnamese)
DV-176*	9/1/2020	Request for Release of Minor's Confidential Information
DV-177*	1/1/2021	Notice of Request for Release of Minor's Confidential Information
DV-178*	9/1/2020	Response to Request for Release of Minor's Confidential Information
DV-179*	9/1/2020	Order on Request for Release of Minor's Confidential Information
DV-180*	7/1/2014	Agreement and Judgment of Parentage
DV-180* C	7/1/2014	Agreement and Judgment of Parentage (Chinese)
DV-180* K	7/1/2014	Agreement and Judgment of Parentage (Korean)
DV-180* S	7/1/2014	Agreement and Judgment of Parentage (Spanish)
DV-180* V	7/1/2014	Agreement and Judgment of Parentage (Vietnamese)
DV-200	7/1/2016	Proof of Personal Service (CLETS)
DV-200 K	7/1/2016	Proof of Personal Service (CLETS) (Domestic Violence Prevention) (Korean)
DV-200 S	7/1/2016	Proof of Personal Service (CLETS) (Domestic Violence Prevention) (Spanish)
DV-200 V	7/1/2016	Proof of Personal Service (CLETS) (Domestic Violence Prevention) (Vietnamese)
DV-200-INFO	1/1/2020	What Is "Proof of Personal Service"? *[Renumbered from DV-210-INFO]*
DV-200-INFO K	7/1/2016	What Is "Proof of Personal Service"? (Korean)
DV-200-INFO S	7/1/2016	What Is "Proof of Personal Service"? (Spanish)
DV-200-INFO V	7/1/2016	What Is "Proof of Personal Service"? (Vietnamese)
DV-205-INFO	1/1/2020	What if the Person I Want Protection From is Avoiding (Evading) Service?

---

* Adopted for mandatory use by all courts.

DV-210*	1/1/2020	Summons (Domestic Violence Restraining Order)
DV-210-INFO	1/1/2010	What is "Proof of Service"? (Domestic Violence Prevention) *[Renumbered to DV-200-INFO]*
DV-250	1/1/2020	Proof of Service by Mail (CLETS)
DV-250 C	1/1/2012	Proof of Service by Mail (CLETS) (Chinese)
DV-250 K	1/1/2012	Proof of Service by Mail (CLETS) (Korean)
DV-250 S	1/1/2012	Proof of Service by Mail (CLETS) (Spanish)
DV-250 V	1/1/2012	Proof of Service by Mail (CLETS) (Vietnamese)
DV-260*	1/1/2012	*[Revoked]* Confidential CLETS Information (Domestic Violence, Civil Harassment, Elder Abuse, Juvenile Law) *[same as CH-102*, EA-102* and JV-248*]*
DV-290*	7/1/2007	*[Revoked]* Request and Order for Free Service of Restraining Order (Sexual Assault or Stalking) *[same as CH-101*]*
DV-290* C	7/1/2007	*[Revoked]* Request and Order for Free Service of Restraining Order (Sexual Assault or Stalking) (Chinese) *[same as CH-101* C]*
DV-290* K	7/1/2007	*[Revoked]* Request and Order for Free Service of Restraining Order (Sexual Assault or Stalking) (Korean) *[same as CH-101* K]*
DV-290* S	7/1/2007	*[Revoked]* Request and Order for Free Service of Restraining Order (Sexual Assault or Stalking) (Spanish) *[same as CH-101* S]*
DV-290* V	7/1/2007	*[Revoked]* Request and Order for Free Service of Restraining Order (Sexual Assault or Stalking) (Vietnamese) *[same as CH-101* V]*
DV-400*	7/1/2016	Findings and Order to Terminate Restraining Order After Hearing (CLETS—CANCEL)
DV-400* S	7/1/2016	Findings and Order to Terminate Restraining Order After Hearing (CLETS—CANCEL) (Spanish)
DV-400-INFO	7/1/2016	How Do I Ask to Change or End a Domestic Violence Restraining Order After Hearing?
DV-400-INFO C	7/1/2016	How Do I Ask to Change or End a Domestic Violence Restraining Order After Hearing? (Chinese)
DV-400-INFO K	7/1/2016	How Do I Ask to Change or End a Domestic Violence Restraining Order After Hearing? (Korean)
DV-400-INFO S	7/1/2016	How Do I Ask to Change or End a Domestic Violence Restraining Order After Hearing? (Spanish)
DV-400-INFO V	7/1/2016	How Do I Ask to Change or End a Domestic Violence Restraining Order After Hearing? (Vietnamese)
DV-500-INFO	1/1/2012	Can a Domestic Violence Restraining Order Help Me?
DV-500-INFO C	1/1/2012	Can a Domestic Violence Restraining Order Help Me? (Chinese)
DV-500-INFO K	1/1/2012	Can a Domestic Violence Restraining Order Help Me? (Korean)
DV-500-INFO S	1/1/2012	Can a Domestic Violence Restraining Order Help Me? (Spanish)
DV-500-INFO V	1/1/2012	Can a Domestic Violence Restraining Order Help Me? (Vietnamese)
DV-505-INFO	7/1/2016	How Do I Ask for a Temporary Restraining Order? *[Renumbered from DV-510-INFO]*
DV-505-INFO K	7/1/2016	How Do I Ask for a Temporary Restraining Order? (Korean)
DV-505-INFO S	7/1/2016	How Do I Ask for a Temporary Restraining Order? (Spanish)
DV-505-INFO V	7/1/2016	How Do I Ask for a Temporary Restraining Order? (Vietnamese)
DV-510-INFO	1/1/2010	I Filled Out the Forms—What Now? *[Renumbered to DV-505-INFO]*
DV-520-INFO	1/1/2016	Get Ready for the Court Hearing
DV-520-INFO C	1/1/2012	Get Ready for the Court Hearing (Chinese)
DV-520-INFO K	1/1/2012	Get Ready for the Court Hearing (Korean)
DV-520-INFO S	1/1/2012	Get Ready for the Court Hearing (Spanish)
DV-520-INFO V	1/1/2012	Get Ready for the Court Hearing (Vietnamese)
DV-530-INFO	1/1/2012	How to Enforce Your Restraining Order
DV-530-INFO C	1/1/2012	How to Enforce Your Restraining Order (Chinese)
DV-530-INFO K	1/1/2012	How to Enforce Your Restraining Order (Korean)
DV-530-INFO S	1/1/2012	How to Enforce Your Restraining Order (Spanish)
DV-530-INFO V	1/1/2012	How to Enforce Your Restraining Order (Vietnamese)
DV-540-INFO	1/1/2010	Information for the Restrained Person (Domestic Violence Prevention) *[Renumbered to DV-120-INFO]*
DV-550-INFO	1/1/2012	*[Revoked]* Get Ready for Your Hearing (For Restrained Person) (Domestic Violence Prevention)
DV-560	1/1/2012	*[Revoked]* How Can I Make the Order Permanent? (Domestic Violence Prevention)
DV-570	1/1/2003	Which Financial Form—FL-155 or FL-150?
DV-570 C	1/1/2003	Which Financial Form—FL-155 or FL-150? (Chinese)
DV-570 K	1/1/2003	Which Financial Form—FL-155 or FL-150? (Korean)
DV-570 S	1/1/2003	Which Financial Form—FL-155 or FL-150? (Spanish)
DV-570 V	1/1/2003	Which Financial Form—FL-155 or FL-150? (Vietnamese)
DV-600*	7/1/2015	Order to Register Out-of-State or Tribal Court Protective/Restraining Order (CLETS—OOS)
DV-600* C	7/1/2015	Order to Register Out-of-State or Tribal Court Protective/Restraining Order (CLETS—OOS) (Chinese)
DV-600* K	7/1/2015	Order to Register Out-of-State or Tribal Court Protective/Restraining Order (CLETS—OOS) (Korean)
DV-600* S	7/1/2015	Order to Register Out-of-State or Tribal Court Protective/Restraining Order (CLETS—OOS) (Spanish)
DV-600* V	7/1/2015	Order to Register Out-of-State or Tribal Court Protective/Restraining Order (CLETS—OOS) (Vietnamese)
DV-610	7/1/2012	Fax Transmission Cover Sheet for Registration of Tribal Court Protective Order
DV-630*	1/22/2019	Order to Register Canadian Domestic Violence Protective/Restraining Order (Domestic Violence Prevention)
DV-630* C	1/22/2019	Order to Register Canadian Domestic Violence Protective/Restraining Order (Domestic Violence Prevention) (Chinese)

_____

* Adopted for mandatory use by all courts.

DV-630* K	1/22/2019	Order to Register Canadian Domestic Violence Protective/Restraining Order (Domestic Violence Prevention) (Korean)
DV-630* S	1/22/2019	Order to Register Canadian Domestic Violence Protective/Restraining Order (Domestic Violence Prevention) (Spanish)
DV-630* V	1/22/2019	Order to Register Canadian Domestic Violence Protective/Restraining Order (Domestic Violence Prevention) (Vietnamese)
DV-700*	1/1/2012	Request to Renew Restraining Order
DV-700* C	1/1/2012	Request to Renew Restraining Order (Chinese)
DV-700* K	1/1/2012	Request to Renew Restraining Order (Korean)
DV-700* S	1/1/2012	Request to Renew Restraining Order (Spanish)
DV-700* V	1/1/2012	Request to Renew Restraining Order (Vietnamese)
DV-700-INFO	1/1/2012	How Do I Ask the Court to Renew My Restraining Order? [Renumbered from DV-720-INFO]
DV-700-INFO C	1/1/2012	How Do I Ask the Court to Renew My Restraining Order? (Chinese)
DV-700-INFO K	1/1/2012	How Do I Ask the Court to Renew My Restraining Order? (Korean)
DV-700-INFO S	1/1/2012	How Do I Ask the Court to Renew My Restraining Order? (Spanish)
DV-700-INFO V	1/1/2012	How Do I Ask the Court to Renew My Restraining Order? (Vietnamese)
DV-710*	7/1/2014	Notice of Hearing to Renew Restraining Order (CLETS)
DV-710* C	7/1/2014	Notice of Hearing to Renew Restraining Order (CLETS) (Chinese)
DV-710* K	7/1/2014	Notice of Hearing to Renew Restraining Order (CLETS) (Korean)
DV-710* S	7/1/2014	Notice of Hearing to Renew Restraining Order (CLETS) (Spanish)
DV-710* V	7/1/2014	Notice of Hearing to Renew Restraining Order (CLETS) (Vietnamese)
DV-720*	1/1/2012	Response to Request to Renew Restraining Order
DV-720* C	1/1/2012	Response to Request to Renew Restraining Order (Chinese)
DV-720* K	1/1/2012	Response to Request to Renew Restraining Order (Korean)
DV-720* S	1/1/2012	Response to Request to Renew Restraining Order (Spanish)
DV-720* V	1/1/2012	Response to Request to Renew Restraining Order (Vietnamese)
DV-720-INFO	7/1/2006	How Do I Ask the Court to Renew my Restraining Order? [Renumbered to DV-700-INFO]
DV-730*	1/1/2012	Order to Renew Domestic Violence Restraining Order (CLETS)
DV-730* C	1/1/2012	Order to Renew Domestic Violence Restraining Order (CLETS) (Chinese)
DV-730* K	1/1/2012	Order to Renew Domestic Violence Restraining Order (CLETS) (Korean)
DV-730* S	1/1/2012	Order to Renew Domestic Violence Restraining Order (CLETS) (Spanish)
DV-730* V	1/1/2012	Order to Renew Domestic Violence Restraining Order (CLETS) (Vietnamese)
DV-800	1/1/2019	Proof of Firearms Turned In, Sold, or Stored [same as JV-252]
DV-800-INFO	7/1/2014	How Do I Turn In, Sell, or Store My Firearms? [Renumbered from DV-810; same as JV-252-INFO]
DV-800-INFO C	7/1/2014	How Do I Turn In, Sell, or Store My Firearms? (Chinese) [same as JV-252-INFO C]
DV-800-INFO K	7/1/2014	How Do I Turn In, Sell, or Store My Firearms? (Korean) [same as JV-252-INFO K]
DV-800-INFO S	7/1/2014	How Do I Turn In, Sell, or Store My Firearms? (Spanish) [same as JV-252-INFO S]
DV-800-INFO V	7/1/2014	How Do I Turn In, Sell, or Store My Firearms? (Vietnamese) [same as JV-252-INFO V]
DV-805*	7/1/2016	Proof of Enrollment for Batterer Intervention Program
DV-805* C	7/1/2016	Proof of Enrollment for Batterer Intervention Program (Chinese)
DV-805* K	7/1/2016	Proof of Enrollment for Batterer Intervention Program (Korean)
DV-805* S	7/1/2016	Proof of Enrollment for Batterer Intervention Program (Spanish)
DV-805* V	7/1/2016	Proof of Enrollment for Batterer Intervention Program (Vietnamese)
DV-810	1/1/2003	What Do I Do With My Gun or Firearm? [Renumbered to DV-800-INFO and JV-252-INFO]
DV-815	7/1/2016	Batterer Intervention Program Progress Report
DV-815 C	7/1/2016	Batterer Intervention Program Progress Report (Chinese)
DV-815 K	7/1/2016	Batterer Intervention Program Progress Report (Korean)
DV-815 S	7/1/2016	Batterer Intervention Program Progress Report (Spanish)
DV-815 V	7/1/2016	Batterer Intervention Program Progress Report (Vietnamese)
DV-900*	7/1/2016	Order Transferring Wireless Phone Account
DV-900* C	7/1/2016	Order Transferring Wireless Phone Account (Chinese)
DV-900* K	7/1/2016	Order Transferring Wireless Phone Account (Korean)
DV-900* S	7/1/2016	Order Transferring Wireless Phone Account (Spanish)
DV-900* V	7/1/2016	Order Transferring Wireless Phone Account (Vietnamese)
DV-901*	7/1/2016	Attachment to Order Transferring Wireless Phone Account
DV-901* C	7/1/2016	Attachment to Order Transferring Wireless Phone Account (Chinese)
DV-901* K	7/1/2016	Attachment to Order Transferring Wireless Phone Account (Korean)
DV-901* S	7/1/2016	Attachment to Order Transferring Wireless Phone Account (Spanish)
DV-901* V	7/1/2016	Attachment to Order Transferring Wireless Phone Account (Vietnamese)

ELDER OR DEPENDENT ADULT ABUSE

EA-100*	1/1/2021	Request for Elder or Dependent Adult Abuse Restraining Orders
EA-100* C	1/1/2018	Request for Elder or Dependent Adult Abuse Restraining Orders (Chinese)
EA-100* K	1/1/2018	Request for Elder or Dependent Adult Abuse Restraining Orders (Korean)
EA-100* S	1/1/2018	Request for Elder or Dependent Adult Abuse Restraining Orders (Spanish)
EA-100* V	1/1/2018	Request for Elder or Dependent Adult Abuse Restraining Orders (Vietnamese)
EA-100-INFO	1/1/2012	Can a Restraining Order to Prevent Elder or Dependent Adult Abuse Help Me? [Renumbered from EA-150-INFO]

---

* Adopted for mandatory use by all courts.

EA-102*	1/1/2012	*[Revoked]* Confidential CLETS Information *[same as CH-102*, DV-260* and JV-248*]*
EA-109*	1/1/2012	Notice of Court Hearing (Elder or Dependent Adult Abuse Prevention)
EA-110*	1/1/2017	Temporary Restraining Order (CLETS—TEA or TEF) *[Renumbered from EA-120*]*
EA-110* C	1/1/2017	Temporary Restraining Order (CLETS—TEA or TEF) (Chinese)
EA-110* K	1/1/2017	Temporary Restraining Order (CLETS—TEA or TEF) (Korean)
EA-110* S	1/1/2017	Temporary Restraining Order (CLETS—TEA or TEF) (Spanish)
EA-110* V	1/1/2017	Temporary Restraining Order (CLETS—TEA or TEF) (Vietnamese)
EA-115*	1/1/2020	Request to Continue Court Hearing (Temporary Restraining Order) *[Renumbered from EA-125*]*
EA-115-INFO	1/1/2020	How to Ask for a New Hearing Date
EA-116*	1/1/2020	Order on Request to Continue Hearing (Temporary Restraining Order) (CLETS—TEA or TEF)
EA-120*	1/1/2021	Response to Request for Elder or Dependent Adult Abuse Restraining Orders *[Renumbered from EA-110*]*
EA-120* C	1/1/2018	Response to Request for Elder or Dependent Adult Abuse Restraining Orders (Chinese)
EA-120* K	1/1/2018	Response to Request for Elder or Dependent Adult Abuse Restraining Orders (Korean)
EA-120* S	1/1/2018	Response to Request for Elder or Dependent Adult Abuse Restraining Orders (Spanish)
EA-120* V	1/1/2018	Response to Request for Elder or Dependent Adult Abuse Restraining Orders (Vietnamese)
EA-120-INFO	7/1/2014	How Can I Respond to a Request for Elder or Dependent Adult Abuse Restraining Orders? *[Renumbered from EA-151-INFO]*
EA-125*	1/1/2007	Request and Order for Reissuance of Temporary Restraining Order (CLETS—TEA or TEF) *[Renumbered to EA-115*]*
EA-130*	1/1/2021	Elder or Dependent Adult Abuse Restraining Order After Hearing (CLETS—EAR or EAF)
EA-130* C	1/1/2018	Elder or Dependent Adult Abuse Restraining Order After Hearing (CLETS—EAR or EAF) (Chinese)
EA-130* K	1/1/2018	Elder or Dependent Adult Abuse Restraining Order After Hearing (CLETS—EAR or EAF) (Korean)
EA-130* S	1/1/2018	Elder or Dependent Adult Abuse Restraining Order After Hearing (CLETS—EAR or EAF) (Spanish)
EA-130* V	1/1/2018	Elder or Dependent Adult Abuse Restraining Order After Hearing (CLETS—EAR or EAF) (Vietnamese)
EA-140	1/1/2007	Proof of Personal Service—CLETS *[Renumbered to EA-200]*
EA-141	1/1/2007	Proof of Service by Mail—CLETS *[Renumbered to EA-250]*
EA-142-INFO	7/1/2008	What Is "Proof of Service"? *[Renumbered to EA-200-INFO]*
EA-145	1/1/2007	Proof of Firearms Turned In or Sold *[Renumbered to EA-800]*
EA-150	7/1/2008	*[Revoked]* Instructions on Petition for a Protective Order to Prevent Elder of Dependent Adult Abuse
EA-150-INFO	7/1/2008	Can a Restraining Order To Prevent Elder or Dependent Adult Abuse Help Me? *[Renumbered to EA-100-INFO; formerly EA-150]*
EA-151-INFO	1/1/2007	How Can I Respond to a Request for Orders to Stop Elder or Dependent Adult Abuse? *[Renumbered to EA-120-INFO]*
EA-200	7/1/2014	Proof of Personal Service *[Renumbered from EA-140]*
EA-200-INFO	1/1/2012	What Is "Proof of Personal Service"? *[Renumbered from EA-142-INFO]*
EA-250	1/1/2012	Proof of Service of Response by Mail *[Renumbered from EA-141]*
EA-260	1/1/2012	Proof of Service of Order After Hearing by Mail
EA-600*	1/1/2018	Request to Modify/Terminate Elder or Dependent Adult Abuse Restraining Order
EA-610*	1/1/2018	Notice of Hearing on Request to Modify/Terminate Elder or Dependent Adult Abuse Restraining Order
EA-620*	1/1/2018	Response to Request to Modify/Terminate Elder or Dependent Adult Abuse Restraining Order
EA-630*	1/1/2018	Order on Request to Modify/Terminate Elder or Dependent Adult Abuse Restraining Order
EA-700*	1/1/2012	Request to Renew Restraining Order
EA-710*	1/1/2012	Notice of Hearing to Renew Restraining Order
EA-720*	1/1/2012	Response to Request to Renew Restraining Order
EA-730*	1/1/2012	Order Renewing Elder or Dependent Adult Abuse Restraining Order (CLETS)
EA-800	7/1/2014	Proof of Firearms Turned In, Sold, or Stored *[Renumbered from EA-145]*
EA-800-INFO	7/1/2014	How Do I Turn In, Sell, or Store My Firearms?

ELECTRONIC FILING AND SERVICE

EFS-005	7/1/2016	Consent to Electronic Service and Notice of Electronic Service Address *[Renumbered to EFS-005-CV]*
EFS-005-CV	7/1/2016	Consent to Electronic Service and Notice of Electronic Service Address *[Renumbered from EFS-005]*
EFS-005-JV*	1/1/2019	Electronic Service: Consent, Withdrawal of Consent, Address Change (Juvenile) *[same as JV-141*]*
EFS-006	1/1/2019	Withdrawal of Consent to Electronic Service
EFS-007	7/1/2013	Request for Exemption from Mandatory Electronic Filing and Service
EFS-008	7/1/2013	Order of Exemption from Mandatory Electronic Filing and Service
EFS-010	1/1/2011	Notice of Change of Electronic Service Address
EFS-020*	2/1/2017	Proposed Order (Cover Sheet)
EFS-050	2/1/2017	Proof of Electronic Service *[same as POS-050]*
EFS-050(D)	1/1/2010	Attachment to Proof of Electronic Service (Documents Served) *[same as POS-050(D)]*
EFS-050(P)	2/1/2017	Attachment to Proof of Electronic Service (Persons Served) *[same as POS-050(P)]*

---

* Adopted for mandatory use by all courts.

EMANCIPATION OF MINORS

EM-100*	9/1/2018	Petition for Declaration of Emancipation of Minor, Order Prescribing Notice, Declaration of Emancipation, and Order Denying Petition *[renumbered from MC-300*]*
EM-100-INFO	9/1/2018	Emancipation Pamphlet *[renumbered from MC-301*]*
EM-100-INFO C	9/1/2018	Emancipation Pamphlet (Chinese) *[renumbered from MC-301 C]*
EM-100-INFO K	9/1/2018	Emancipation Pamphlet (Korean) *[renumbered from MC-301 K]*
EM-100-INFO S	9/1/2018	Emancipation Pamphlet (Spanish) *[renumbered from MC-301 S]*
EM-100-INFO V	9/1/2018	Emancipation Pamphlet (Vietnamese) *[renumbered from MC-301 V]*
EM-109*	9/1/2018	Notice of Hearing—Emancipation of Minor *[renumbered from MC-305]*
EM-115*	9/1/2018	Emancipation of Minor Income and Expense Declaration *[renumbered from MC-306]*
EM-130*	9/1/2018	Declaration of Emancipation of Minor After Hearing *[renumbered from MC-310*]*
EM-140	9/1/2018	Emancipated Minor's Application to California Department of Motor Vehicles *[renumbered from MC-315]*

EMERGENCY PROTECTIVE ORDER

EPO-001*	1/1/2014	Emergency Protective Order (CLETS—EPO) (Domestic Violence, Child Abuse, Elder or Dependent Adult Abuse, or Stalking)
EPO-001* C	1/1/2014	Emergency Protective Order (CLETS—EPO) (Domestic Violence, Child Abuse, Elder or Dependent Adult Abuse, or Stalking (Workplace Violence, Civil Harassment)) (Chinese)
EPO-001* K	1/1/2014	Emergency Protective Order (CLETS—EPO) (Domestic Violence, Child Abuse, Elder or Dependent Adult Abuse, or Stalking (Workplace Violence, Civil Harassment)) (Korean)
EPO-001* S	1/1/2014	Emergency Protective Order (CLETS—EPO) (Domestic Violence, Child Abuse, Elder or Dependent Adult Abuse, or Stalking (Workplace Violence, Civil Harassment)) (Spanish)
EPO-001* V	1/1/2014	Emergency Protective Order (CLETS—EPO) (Domestic Violence, Child Abuse, Elder or Dependent Adult Abuse, or Stalking (Workplace Violence, Civil Harassment)) (Vietnamese)
EPO-002*	9/1/2020	Gun Violence Emergency Protective Order (CLETS—EGV)
EPO-002* C	1/1/2017	Gun Violence Emergency Protective Order (CLETS—EGV) (Chinese)
EPO-002* K	1/1/2017	Gun Violence Emergency Protective Order (CLETS—EGV) (Korean)
EPO-002* V	1/1/2017	Gun Violence Emergency Protective Order (CLETS—EGV) (Vietnamese)

ENFORCEMENT OF JUDGMENT

EJ-001*	7/1/2014	Abstract of Judgment—Civil and Small Claims
EJ-100	7/1/2014	Acknowledgment of Satisfaction of Judgment
EJ-105	7/1/1983	Application for Entry of Judgment on Sister-State Judgment
EJ-110	7/1/1983	Notice of Entry of Judgment on Sister-State Judgment
EJ-115*	7/1/2015	Notice of Application for Recognition and Entry of Tribal Court Money Judgment
EJ-125*	1/1/2017	Application and Order for Appearance and Examination *[same as AT-138*]*
EJ-130	9/1/2020	Writ of Execution
EJ-150	9/1/2020	Notice of Levy
EJ-152	7/1/2013	Memorandum of Garnishee *[same as AT-167]*
EJ-155*	9/1/2020	Exemptions From the Enforcement of Judgments
EJ-156	9/1/2020	Current Dollar Amounts of Exemptions From Enforcement of Judgments (Code of Civil Procedure sections 703.140(b) and 704.010 et seq.)
EJ-157	1/1/2021	Ex Parte Application for Order on Deposit Account Exemption
EJ-157-INFO	9/1/2020	Instructions for Ex Parte Application for Order on Deposit Account Exemption
EJ-158	1/1/2021	Declaration Regarding Notice and Service for Ex Parte Application for Order on Deposit Account Exemption
EJ-159	1/1/2021	Order on Application for Designation of Deposit Account Exemption
EJ-160	1/1/2009	Claim of Exemption
EJ-165*	1/1/2007	Financial Statement *[same as WG-007*]*
EJ-170	7/1/1983	Notice of Opposition to Claim of Exemption
EJ-175	1/1/2007	Notice of Hearing on Claim of Exemption *[same as WG-010]*
EJ-180	1/1/1985	Notice of Hearing on Right to Homestead Exemption
EJ-182	1/1/1985	Notice of Rehearing on Right to Homestead Exemption
EJ-185	1/1/1985	Notice of Lien *[same as AT-180]*
EJ-190	7/1/2014	Application for and Renewal of Judgment
EJ-195*	1/1/2007	Notice of Renewal of Judgment

EXPEDITED JURY TRIAL

EJT-001-INFO*	7/1/2016	Expedited Jury Trial Information Sheet *[Renumbered from EJT-010-INFO*]*
EJT-003*	7/1/2016	Request to Opt Out of Mandatory Expedited Jury Trial Procedures
EJT-004*	7/1/2016	Objection to Request to Opt Out of Mandatory Expedited Jury Trial Procedures
EJT-005	7/1/2016	Order on Request to Opt Out of Mandatory Expedited Jury Trial Procedures
EJT-010-INFO*	7/1/2016	Expedited Jury Trial Information Sheet *[Renumbered to EJT-001-INFO*]*
EJT-018	7/1/2016	Agreement of Parties (Mandatory Expedited Jury Trial Procedures)

---

* Adopted for mandatory use by all courts.

EJT-020	7/1/2016	[Proposed] Consent Order for Voluntary Expedited Jury Trial
EJT-020A	7/1/2016	Attachment to [Proposed] Consent Order for Expedited Jury Trial *[Renumbered to EJT-022A]*
EJT-022A	7/1/2016	Attachment to [Proposed] Consent Order or Agreement of Parties *[Renumbered from EJT-020A]*

FAMILY LAW
Dissolution, Legal Separation and Annulment

FL-100*	1/1/2020	Petition—Marriage/Domestic Partnership
FL-100* A	7/1/2016	Petition—Marriage/Domestic Partnership (Arabic)
FL-100* C	7/1/2016	Petition—Marriage/Domestic Partnership (Chinese)
FL-100* S	7/1/2016	Petition—Marriage/Domestic Partnership (Spanish)
FL-103*	1/1/2015	*[Revoked]* Petition—Domestic Partnership/Marriage (Family Law)
FL-105*	1/1/2009	Declaration Under Uniform Child Custody Jurisdiction and Enforcement Act (UCCJEA) *[same as GC-120*]*
FL-105* S	1/1/2009	Declaration Under Uniform Child Custody Jurisdiction and Enforcement Act (UCCJEA) (Spanish) *[same as GC-120* S]*
FL-105(A)*	1/1/2009	Attachment to Declaration Under Uniform Child Custody Jurisdiction and Enforcement Act (UCCJEA) *[same as GC-120(A)*]*
FL-107-INFO	1/1/2015	Legal Steps for a Divorce or Legal Separation
FL-107-INFO C	1/1/2015	Legal Steps for a Divorce or Legal Separation (Chinese)
FL-107-INFO K	1/1/2015	Legal Steps for a Divorce or Legal Separation (Korean)
FL-107-INFO S	1/1/2015	Legal Steps for a Divorce or Legal Separation (Spanish)
FL-107-INFO V	1/1/2015	Legal Steps for a Divorce or Legal Separation (Vietnamese)
FL-110*	1/1/2015	Summons (Family Law)
FL-110* A	1/1/2015	Summons (Family Law) (Arabic)
FL-110* C	1/1/2015	Summons (Family Law) (Chinese)
FL-115	1/1/2021	Proof of Service of Summons
FL-117	1/1/2021	Notice and Acknowledgment of Receipt
FL-120*	1/1/2020	Response—Marriage/Domestic Partnership
FL-120* A	7/1/2016	Response—Marriage/Domestic Partnership (Arabic)
FL-120* C	7/1/2016	Response—Marriage/Domestic Partnership (Chinese)
FL-120* S	7/1/2016	Response—Marriage/Domestic Partnership (Spanish)
FL-123*	1/1/2015	*[Revoked]* Response—Domestic Partnership/Marriage (Family Law)
FL-130	1/1/2021	Appearance, Stipulations, and Waivers
FL-130 S	1/1/2011	Appearance, Stipulations, and Waivers (Spanish)
FL-130(A)	1/1/2011	Declaration and Conditional Waiver of Rights Under the Servicemembers Civil Relief Act of 2003
FL-140*	7/1/2013	Declaration of Disclosure
FL-140* S	7/1/2013	Declaration of Disclosure (Spanish)
FL-141*	7/1/2013	Declaration Regarding Service of Declaration of Disclosure and Income and Expense Declaration
FL-142	1/1/2005	Schedule of Assets and Debts
FL-142 S	1/1/2005	Schedule of Assets and Debts (Spanish)
FL-144	1/1/2007	Stipulation and Waiver of Final Declaration of Disclosure
FL-145	1/1/2006	Form Interrogatories—Family Law
FL-150*	1/1/2019	Income and Expense Declaration
FL-150* S	1/1/2019	Income and Expense Declaration (Spanish)
FL-155	1/1/2004	Financial Statement (Simplified)
FL-155 S	1/1/2004	Financial Statement (Simplified) (Spanish)
FL-157	1/1/2021	Spousal or Domestic Partner Support Declaration Attachment
FL-157 S	1/1/2012	Spousal or Partnership Support Declaration Attachment (Spanish)
FL-158	1/1/2012	Supporting Declaration for Attorney's Fees and Costs Attachment
FL-160*	7/1/2016	Property Declaration
FL-160* S	7/1/2016	Property Declaration (Spanish)
FL-161*	7/1/2013	Continuation of Property Declaration
FL-165*	1/1/2005	Request to Enter Default
FL-170*	1/17/2020	Declaration for Default or Uncontested Dissolution or Legal Separation
FL-172	1/1/2012	Case Information—Family Law
FL-174	1/1/2012	Family Centered Case Resolution Order
FL-180*	7/1/2012	Judgment
FL-180* S	7/1/2012	Judgment (Spanish)
FL-182	7/1/2012	Judgment Checklist—Dissolution/Legal Separation
FL-190*	1/1/2005	Notice of Entry of Judgment
FL-191*	7/1/2005	Child Support Case Registry Form
FL-191 S	7/1/2005	Child Support Case Registry Form — Spanish
FL-192	1/1/2021	Notice of Rights and Responsibilities Health-Care Costs and Reimbursement Procedures
FL-192 S	1/1/2015	Notice of Rights and Responsibilities (Health-Care Costs and Reimbursement Procedures) (Spanish)
FL-195	1/1/2018	Income Withholding for Support (IWO)
FL-196	1/1/2018	Income Withholding for Support—Instructions

---

* Adopted for mandatory use by all courts.

FAMILY LAW
Parentage Actions

FL-200	1/1/2020	Petition to Determine Parental Relationship (Uniform Parentage)
FL-200 S	1/1/2003	Petition to Establish Parental Relationship (Spanish)
FL-210*	1/1/2015	Summons
FL-210* C	1/1/2015	Summons (Chinese)
FL-220	1/1/2020	Response to Petition to Determine Parental Relationship (Uniform Parentage)
FL-220 S	1/1/2006	Response to Petition to Establish Parental Relationship (Spanish)
FL-230*	1/1/2020	Declaration for Default or Uncontested Judgment (Uniform Parentage, Custody and Support)
FL-235	1/1/2020	Advisement and Waiver of Rights Re: Determination of Parental Relationship
FL-235 S	1/1/2003	Advisement and Waiver of Rights Re: Establishment of Parental Relationship (Spanish)
FL-240*	1/1/2021	Stipulation for Entry of Judgment Re: Determination of Parental Relationship
FL-240* S	1/1/2015	Stipulation for Entry of Judgment Re: Establishment of Parental Relationship (Spanish)
FL-250*	1/1/2020	Judgment (Uniform Parentage—Custody and Support)
FL-250* S	1/1/2004	Judgment (Spanish)
FL-260*	1/1/2020	Petition for Custody and Support of Minor Children
FL-260 S	1/1/2004	Petition for Custody and Support of Minor Children (Spanish)
FL-270*	1/1/2020	Response to Petition for Custody and Support of Minor Children
FL-270 S	1/1/2004	Response to Petition for Custody and Support of Minor Children (Spanish)
FL-272*	1/1/2020	Notice of Motion to Cancel (Set Aside) Judgment of Parentage
FL-272* S	1/1/2006	Notice of Motion to Set Aside Judgment of Paternity (Spanish)
FL-273*	1/1/2020	Declaration in Support of Motion to Cancel (Set Aside) Judgment of Parentage
FL-273* S	1/1/2006	Declaration in Support of Motion to Set Aside Judgment of Paternity (Spanish)
FL-274	1/1/2020	Information Sheet for Completing Notice of Motion to Cancel (Set Aside) Judgment of Parentage
FL-274 S	1/1/2006	Information Sheet for Completing Notice of Motion to Set Aside Judgment of Paternity (Spanish)
FL-276*	1/1/2020	Response to Notice of Motion to Cancel (Set Aside) Judgment of Parentage
FL-276* S	1/1/2006	Response to Notice of Motion to Set Aside Judgment of Paternity (Spanish)
FL-278*	1/1/2020	Order After Hearing on Motion to Cancel (Set Aside) Judgment of Parentage
FL-278* S	1/1/2006	Order After Hearing on Motion to Set Aside Judgment of Paternity (Spanish)
FL-280*	1/1/2020	Request for Hearing and Application to Cancel (Set Aside) Voluntary Declaration of Parentage or Paternity
FL-280* S	1/1/2006	Request for Hearing and Application to Set Aside Voluntary Declaration of Paternity (Spanish)
FL-281	1/1/2020	Information Sheet for Completing Request for Hearing and Application to Cancel (Set Aside) Voluntary Declaration of Parentage or Paternity
FL-281 S	1/1/2006	Information Sheet for Completing Request for Hearing and Application to Set Aside Voluntary Declaration of Paternity (Spanish)
FL-285*	1/1/2020	Responsive Declaration to Application to Cancel (Set Aside) Voluntary Declaration of Parentage or Paternity
FL-285* S	1/1/2006	Responsive Declaration to Application to Set Aside Voluntary Declaration of Paternity (Spanish)
FL-290*	1/1/2020	Order After Hearing on Motion to Cancel (Set Aside) Voluntary Declaration of Parentage or Paternity
FL-290* S	1/1/2006	Order After Hearing on Motion to Set Aside Voluntary Declaration of Paternity (Spanish)

FAMILY LAW
Motions and Attachments

FL-300*	7/1/2016	Request for Order
FL-300* S	7/1/2016	Request for Order (Spanish)
FL-300-INFO	1/1/2020	Information Sheet for Request for Order
FL-300-INFO S	7/1/2016	Information Sheet for Request for Order (Spanish)
FL-301*	7/1/2012	*[Revoked]* Notice of Motion
FL-303	7/1/2020	Declaration Regarding Notice and Service of Request for Temporary Emergency (Ex Parte) Orders
FL-303 S	9/1/2017	Declaration Regarding Notice and Service of Request for Temporary Emergency (Ex Parte) Orders (Spanish)
FL-304-INFO	7/1/2020	How to Reschedule a Hearing in Family Court
FL-305*	7/1/2016	Temporary Emergency (Ex Parte) Orders
FL-305* S	7/1/2016	Temporary Emergency (Ex Parte) Orders (Spanish)
FL-306*	1/1/2014	*[Revoked]* Request and Order to Continue Hearing and Extend Temporary Emergency (Ex Parte) Orders
FL-306	7/1/2020	Request to Reschedule Hearing (Family Law—Governmental—Uniform Parentage—Custody and Support)
FL-306* S	9/1/2017	Request to Continue Hearing (Spanish)
FL-307*	9/1/2017	*[Revoked]* Order on Request to Continue Hearing
FL-307	7/1/2020	Request to Reschedule Hearing Involving Temporary Emergency (Ex Parte) Orders (Family Law—Governmental—Uniform Parentage—Custody and Support)
FL-307* S	9/1/2017	Order on Request to Continue Hearing (Spanish)
FL-308	7/1/2020	Agreement and Order to Reschedule Hearing (Family Law—Governmental—Uniform Parentage—Custody and Support)

* Adopted for mandatory use by all courts.

FL-309*	7/1/2020	Order on Request to Reschedule Hearing (Family Law—Governmental—Uniform Parentage—Custody and Support)
FL-310*	7/1/2012	*[Revoked]* Application for Order and Supporting Declaration
FL-310	7/1/2020	Responsive Declaration to Request to Reschedule Hearing (Family Law—Governmental—Uniform Parentage—Custody and Support)
FL-311	7/1/2016	Child Custody and Visitation (Parenting Time) Application Attachment
FL-311 S	7/1/2016	Child Custody and Visitation (Parenting Time) Application Attachment (Spanish)
FL-312*	7/1/2016	Request for Child Abduction Prevention Orders
FL-312* S	7/1/2016	Request for Child Abduction Prevention Orders (Spanish)
FL-313-INFO	1/1/2012	Child Custody Information Sheet—Recommending Counseling
FL-313-INFO C	1/1/2012	Child Custody Information Sheet—Recommending Counseling (Chinese)
FL-313-INFO K	1/1/2012	Child Custody Information Sheet—Recommending Counseling (Korean)
FL-313-INFO S	1/1/2012	Child Custody Information Sheet—Recommending Counseling (Spanish)
FL-313-INFO T	1/1/2012	Child Custody Information Sheet—Recommending Counseling (Tagalog)
FL-313-INFO V	1/1/2012	Child Custody Information Sheet—Recommending Counseling (Vietnamese)
FL-314-INFO	1/1/2012	Child Custody Information Sheet—Child Custody Mediation
FL-314-INFO C	1/1/2012	Child Custody Information Sheet—Child Custody Mediation (Chinese)
FL-314-INFO K	1/1/2012	Child Custody Information Sheet—Child Custody Mediation (Korean)
FL-314-INFO S	1/1/2012	Child Custody Information Sheet—Child Custody Mediation (Spanish)
FL-314-INFO V	1/1/2012	Child Custody Information Sheet—Child Custody Mediation (Vietnamese)
FL-315*	1/1/2018	Request or Response to Request for Separate Trial
FL-316	7/1/2012	Request for Orders Regarding Noncompliance With Disclosure Requirements
FL-318-INFO	1/1/2009	Retirement Plan Joinder—Information Sheet (Family Law)
FL-319	1/1/2012	Request for Attorney's Fees and Costs Attachment (Family Law)
FL-320*	7/1/2016	Responsive Declaration to Request for Order
FL-320* S	7/1/2016	Responsive Declaration to Request for Order (Spanish)
FL-320-INFO	7/1/2016	Information Sheet: Responsive Declaration to Request for Order
FL-320-INFO S	7/1/2016	Information Sheet: Responsive Declaration to Request for Order (Spanish)
FL-321	7/1/2012	Witness List
FL-321-INFO	7/1/2017	Attorney for Child in a Family Law Case—Information Sheet *[Renumbered to FL-323-INFO]*
FL-322	1/1/2008	Declaration of Counsel for a Child Regarding Qualifications
FL-322 S	1/1/2008	Declaration of Counsel for a Child Regarding Qualifications (Spanish)
FL-323	1/1/2012	Order Appointing Counsel for a Child
FL-323 C	1/1/2012	Order Appointing Counsel for a Child (Chinese)
FL-323 K	1/1/2012	Order Appointing Counsel for a Child (Korean)
FL-323 S	1/1/2012	Order Appointing Counsel for a Child (Spanish)
FL-323 V	1/1/2012	Order Appointing Counsel for a Child (Vietnamese)
FL-323-INFO	7/1/2017	Attorney for Child in a Family Law Case—Information Sheet *[Renumbered from FL-321-INFO]*
FL-323-INFO C	1/1/2012	Attorney for Child in a Family Law Case—Information Sheet (Chinese)
FL-323-INFO K	1/1/2012	Attorney for Child in a Family Law Case—Information Sheet (Korean)
FL-323-INFO S	1/1/2012	Attorney for Child in a Family Law Case—Information Sheet (Spanish)
FL-323-INFO V	1/1/2012	Attorney for Child in a Family Law Case—Information Sheet (Vietnamese)
FL-324	1/1/2014	Declaration of Supervised Visitation Provider *[renumbered to FL-324(P)*]*
FL-324 S	1/1/2014	Declaration of Supervised Visitation Provider (Spanish)
FL-324(NP)	1/1/2021	Declaration of Supervised Visitation Provider (Nonprofessional)
FL-324(P)*	1/1/2021	Declaration of Supervised Visitation Provider (Professional) *[renumbered from FL-324]*
FL-325*	1/1/2020	Declaration of Court-Connected Child Custody Evaluator Regarding Qualifications
FL-326*	1/1/2020	Declaration of Private Child Custody Evaluator Regarding Qualifications
FL-327*	1/1/2021	Order Appointing Child Custody Evaluator
FL-327(A)*	1/1/2021	Additional Orders Regarding Child Custody Evaluations Under Family Code Section 3118
FL-328*	1/1/2010	Notice Regarding Confidentiality of Child Custody Evaluation Report
FL-329*	1/1/2021	Confidential Child Custody Evaluation Report
FL-329-INFO	1/1/2010	Child Custody Evaluation Information Sheet
FL-329-INFO S	1/1/2010	Child Custody Evaluation Information Sheet (Spanish)
FL-330	1/1/2012	Proof of Personal Service
FL-330-INFO	1/1/2012	Information Sheet for Proof of Personal Service
FL-334	1/1/2012	Declaration Regarding Address Verification—Postjudgment Request to Modify a Child Custody, Visitation, or Child Support Order
FL-335	1/1/2012	Proof of Service by Mail
FL-335-INFO	1/1/2012	Information Sheet for Proof of Service by Mail
FL-336*	7/1/2016	Order to Pay Waived Court Fees and Costs (Superior Court)
FL-337*	7/1/2016	Application to Set Aside Order to Pay Waived Court Fees—Attachment
FL-338*	7/1/2009	Order After Hearing on Motion to Set Aside Order to Pay Waived Court Fees
FL-340*	1/1/2012	Findings and Order After Hearing
FL-341	7/1/2016	Child Custody and Visitation (Parenting Time) Order Attachment
FL-341 S	7/1/2006	Child Custody and Visitation (Parenting Time) Order Attachment (Spanish)
FL-341(A)*	1/1/2015	Supervised Visitation Order
FL-341(A)* S	1/1/2015	Supervised Visitation Order (Spanish)
FL-341(B)*	7/1/2016	Child Abduction Prevention Order Attachment
FL-341(B)* S	7/1/2016	Child Abduction Prevention Order Attachment (Spanish)

---

* Adopted for mandatory use by all courts.

FL-341(C)	7/1/2016	Children's Holiday Schedule Attachment
FL-341(C) S	7/1/2016	Children's Holiday Schedule Attachment (Spanish)
FL-341(D)	7/1/2016	Additional Provisions—Physical Custody Attachment
FL-341(D) S	7/1/2016	Additional Provisions—Physical Custody Attachment (Spanish)
FL-341(E)	7/1/2016	Joint Legal Custody Attachment
FL-341(E) S	7/1/2016	Joint Legal Custody Attachment (Spanish)
FL-342*	1/1/2020	Child Support Information and Order Attachment
FL-342* S	1/1/2017	Child Support Information and Order Attachment (Spanish)
FL-342(A)*	1/1/2008	Non-Guideline Child Support Findings Attachment
FL-343	1/1/2021	Spousal, Domestic Partner, or Family Support Order Attachment
FL-344*	1/1/2007	Property Order Attachment To Findings And Order After Hearing
FL-344* S	1/1/2007	Property Order Attachment To Findings And Order After Hearing (Spanish)
FL-345	1/1/2021	Property Order Attachment To Judgment
FL-345 S	1/1/2007	Property Order Attachment To Judgment (Spanish)
FL-346	1/1/2012	Attorney's Fees and Costs Order Attachment
FL-347*	1/1/2018	Bifurcation of Status of Marriage or Domestic Partnership—Attachment
FL-348	1/1/2009	Pension Benefits—Attachment to Judgment *(Attach to form FL-180)*
FL-348 S	1/1/2009	Pension Benefits—Attachment to Judgment *(Attach to form FL-180)* (Spanish)
FL-349	1/1/2021	Spousal or Domestic Partner Support Factors Under Family Code Section 4320—Attachment
FL-350	1/1/2020	Stipulation to Establish or Modify Child Support and Order
FL-350* S	1/1/2017	Stipulation to Establish or Modify Child Support and Order (Spanish)
FL-355	1/1/2004	Stipulation and Order for Custody and/or Visitation of Children
FL-355 S	1/1/2004	Stipulation and Order for Custody and/or Visitation of Children (Spanish)
FL-356*	1/1/2021	Confidential Request for Special Immigrant Juvenile Findings—Family Law
FL-356* S	7/1/2016	Confidential Request for Special Immigrant Juvenile Findings—Family Law (Spanish)
FL-357*	7/1/2016	Special Immigrant Juvenile Findings *[same as JV-357*, GC-224*]*
FL-357* S	7/1/2016	Special Immigrant Juvenile Findings (Spanish) *[same as JV-357* S, GC-224* S]*
FL-358*	7/1/2016	Confidential Response to Request for Special Immigrant Juvenile Findings
FL-358* S	7/1/2016	Confidential Response to Request for Special Immigrant Juvenile Findings (Spanish)
FL-360*	1/1/2007	Request For Hearing And Application To Set Aside Support Order Under Family Code Section 3691
FL-365*	1/1/2003	Responsive Declaration to Application to Set Aside Support Order
FL-367*	1/1/2003	Order After Hearing on Motion to Set Aside Support Order
FL-370*	1/1/2003	Pleading on Joinder—Employees Benefit Plan
FL-371*	1/1/2003	Notice of Motion and Declaration for Joinder
FL-372*	1/1/2003	Request for Joinder of Employee Benefit Plan Order
FL-373*	1/1/2003	Responsive Declaration to Motion for Joinder and Consent Order of Joinder
FL-374*	1/1/2003	Notice of Appearance and Response of Employee Benefit Plan
FL-375*	1/1/2003	Summons (Joinder)
FL-380*	1/1/2003	Application for Expedited Child Support Order
FL-381*	1/1/2003	Response to Application for Expedited Child Support Order and Notice of Hearing
FL-382*	1/1/2003	Expedited Child Support Order
FL-390*	1/1/2003	Notice of Motion and Motion for Simplified Modification of Order for Child, Spousal, or Family Support
FL-391	7/1/2008	Information Sheet—Simplified Way to Change Child, Spousal, or Family Support
FL-392*	1/1/2003	Responsive Declaration to Motion for Simplified Modification of Order for Child, Spousal, or Family Support
FL-393	7/1/2008	Information Sheet—How to Oppose a Request to Change Child, Spousal, or Family Support
FL-395*	1/1/2003	Ex Parte Application for Restoration of Former Name After Entry of Judgment and Order (Family Law)
FL-396*	1/1/2003	Request for Production of an Income and Expense Declaration After Judgment
FL-397*	1/1/2003	Request for Income and Benefit Information From Employer
FL-398*	12/2/2005	Notice of Activation of Military Service and Deployment and Request to Modify a Support Order

FAMILY LAW
Enforcement

FL-400*	1/1/2003	Order for Child Support Security Deposit and Evidence of Deposit
FL-401*	1/1/2003	Application for Disbursement and Order for Disbursement From Child Support Security Deposit
FL-410*	1/1/2015	Order to Show Cause and Affidavit for Contempt
FL-411*	1/1/2003	Affidavit of Facts Constituting Contempt (Financial and Injunctive Orders)
FL-412*	1/1/2003	Affidavit of Facts Constituting Contempt
FL-415	7/1/2003	Findings and Order Regarding Contempt
FL-420*	1/1/2003	Declaration of Payment History
FL-421	7/1/2003	Payment History Attachment
FL-430*	1/1/2014	Ex Parte Application to Issue, Modify, or Terminate an Earnings Assignment Order
FL-435*	1/1/2005	Earnings Assignment Order for Spousal or Partner Support
FL-440	1/1/2003	Statement for Registration of California Support Order
FL-445*	1/1/2021	Request for Hearing Regarding Registration of California Support Order
FL-450*	7/1/2008	Request for Hearing Regarding Earnings Assignment

---

* Adopted for mandatory use by all courts.

FL-455*	1/1/2003	Stay of Service of Earnings Assignment and Order
FL-460	1/1/2003	Qualified Domestic Relations Order for Support
FL-461	1/1/2003	Attachment to Qualified Domestic Relations Order for Support
FL-470*	1/1/2007	Application and Order For Health Insurance Coverage
FL-475*	1/1/2003	Employer's Health Insurance Return
FL-478*	1/1/2007	Request and Notice of Hearing Regarding Health Insurance Assignment
FL-478-INFO	1/1/2007	Information Sheet and Instructions for Request and Notice of Hearing Regarding Health Insurance Assignment
FL-480*	1/1/2015	Abstract of Support Judgment
FL-485*	7/1/2013	Notice of Delinquency
FL-490*	1/1/2020	Application to Determine Arrears
FL-490* S	1/1/2017	Application to Determine Arrears (Spanish)

FAMILY LAW
Interstate Actions

FL-500	1/1/2008	*[Revoked]* Uniform Support Petition
FL-505	1/1/2008	*[Revoked]* Child Support Enforcement Transmittal #1—Initial Request
FL-510*	7/1/2017	Summons (UIFSA)
FL-511*	1/1/2017	*[Revoked]* Ex Parte Application for Order for Nondisclosure of Address and Order (UIFSA)
FL-515*	1/1/2017	*[Revoked]* Order to Show Cause (UIFSA)
FL-520*	1/1/2017	Response to Uniform Support Petition (UIFSA)
FL-525	1/1/2008	*[Revoked]* Affidavit in Support of Establishing Paternity
FL-526	1/1/2008	*[Revoked]* General Testimony
FL-530*	1/1/2020	Judgment Regarding Parental Obligations (UIFSA)
FL-530* S	1/1/2017	Judgment Regarding Parental Obligations (UIFSA) (Spanish)
FL-556	1/1/2008	*[Revoked]* Registration Statement
FL-557	1/1/2008	*[Revoked]* Child Support Enforcement Transmittal #2—Subsequent Actions
FL-558	1/1/2008	*[Revoked]* Locate Data Sheet
FL-559	1/1/2008	*[Revoked]* Child Support Enforcement Transmittal #3—Request for Assistance/Discovery
FL-560*	1/1/2017	Ex Parte Application for Transfer and Order (UIFSA)
FL-570	1/1/2020	Notice of Registration of Out-of-State Support Order
FL-571	1/1/2008	*[Revoked]* Notice of Determination of Controlling Order
FL-575*	1/1/2021	Request for Hearing Regarding Registration of Out-of-State Support Order
FL-580	1/1/2006	Registration of Out-of-State Custody Order
FL-585	1/1/2003	Request for Hearing Regarding Registration of Out-of-State Custody Decree
FL-590A*	7/1/2017	UIFSA Child Support Order Jurisdictional Attachment
FL-592*	7/1/2017	Notice of Registration of an International Hague Convention Support Order
FL-594*	1/1/2017	Request for Hearing Regarding Registration of an International Hague Convention Support Order

FAMILY LAW
Governmental Child Support

FL-600*	1/1/2020	Summons and Complaint or Supplemental Complaint Regarding Parental Obligations (Governmental)
FL-605*	1/1/2007	Notice and Acknowledgment of Receipt
FL-610*	1/1/2020	Answer to Complaint or Supplemental Complaint Regarding Parental Obligations (Governmental)
FL-611	1/1/2003	Information Sheet for Service of Process
FL-615*	1/1/2020	Stipulation for Judgment or Supplemental Judgment Regarding Parental Obligations and Judgment
FL-615* S	1/1/2017	Stipulation for Judgment or Supplemental Judgment Regarding Parental Obligations and Judgment (Spanish)
FL-616*	1/1/2003	Declaration for Amended Proposed Judgment
FL-618*	1/1/2010	Request for Dismissal
FL-618* S	1/1/2010	Request for Dismissal (Spanish)
FL-620*	1/1/2005	Request to Enter Default Judgment
FL-625*	1/1/2020	Stipulation and Order
FL-625* S	1/1/2017	Stipulation and Order (Spanish)
FL-626	1/1/2009	Stipulation and Order Waiving Unassigned Arrears
FL-626 C	1/1/2009	Stipulation and Order Waiving Unassigned Arrears (Chinese)
FL-626 K	1/1/2009	Stipulation and Order Waiving Unassigned Arrears (Korean)
FL-626 S	1/1/2009	Stipulation and Order Waiving Unassigned Arrears (Spanish)
FL-626 T	1/1/2009	Stipulation and Order Waiving Unassigned Arrears (Tagalog)
FL-626 V	1/1/2009	Stipulation and Order Waiving Unassigned Arrears (Vietnamese)
FL-627*	1/1/2003	Order for Genetic (Parentage) Testing
FL-630*	1/1/2020	Judgment Regarding Parental Obligations
FL-630* S	1/1/2017	Judgment Regarding Parental Obligations (Spanish)
FL-632*	7/1/2015	Notice Regarding Payment of Support
FL-634*	1/1/2011	Notice of Change of Responsibility for Managing Child Support Case
FL-634* S	1/1/2011	Notice of Change of Responsibility for Managing Child Support Case (Spanish)
FL-635*	7/1/2004	Notice of Entry of Judgment and Proof of Service by Mail

---

* Adopted for mandatory use by all courts.

FL-640*	1/1/2012	Notice and Motion to Cancel (Set Aside) Support Order Based on Presumed Income
FL-640* S	1/1/2012	Notice and Motion to Cancel (Set Aside) Support Order Based on Presumed Income (Spanish)
FL-640-INFO	1/1/2012	Information Sheet for Notice and Motion to Cancel (Set Aside) Support Order Based on Presumed Income
FL-640-INFO S	1/1/2012	Information Sheet for Notice and Motion to Cancel (Set Aside) Support Order Based on Presumed Income (Spanish)
FL-643	1/1/2007	Declaration Of Obligor's Income During Judgment Period—Presumed Income Set-Aside Request
FL-645*	1/1/2003	Notice to Local Child Support Agency of Intent to Take Independent Action to Enforce Support Order
FL-646*	1/1/2003	Response of Local Child Support Agency to Notice of Intent to Take Independent Action to Enforce Support Order
FL-650*	1/1/2003	Statement for Registration of California Support Order
FL-651*	1/1/2004	Notice of Registration of California Support Order
FL-660*	1/1/2003	Ex Parte Motion by Local Child Support Agency and Declaration for Joinder of Other Parent
FL-661	1/1/2012	Notice of Motion and Declaration for Joinder of Other Parent in Governmental Action
FL-661-INFO	1/1/2012	Information Sheet for Notice of Motion and Declaration for Joinder of Other Parent in Governmental Action
FL-662*	1/1/2012	Responsive Declaration to Motion for Joinder of Other Parent—Consent Order of Joinder
FL-662-INFO	1/1/2012	Information Sheet for Responsive Declaration to Motion for Joinder of Other Parent—Consent Order of Joinder
FL-663*	1/1/2009	Stipulation and Order for Joinder of Other Parent
FL-663 C*	1/1/2009	Stipulation and Order for Joinder of Other Parent (Chinese)
FL-663 K*	1/1/2009	Stipulation and Order for Joinder of Other Parent (Korean)
FL-663 S*	1/1/2009	Stipulation and Order for Joinder of Other Parent (Spanish)
FL-663 T*	1/1/2009	Stipulation and Order for Joinder of Other Parent (Tagalog)
FL-663 V*	1/1/2009	Stipulation and Order for Joinder of Other Parent (Vietnamese)
FL-665*	1/1/2020	Findings and Recommendation of Commissioner
FL-665* S	1/1/2017	Findings and Recommendation of Commissioner (Spanish)
FL-666*	1/1/2003	Notice of Objection
FL-667*	1/1/2003	Review of Commissioner's Findings of Fact and Recommendation
FL-670*	1/1/2003	Notice of Motion for Judicial Review of License Denial
FL-675*	1/1/2003	Order After Judicial Review of License Denial
FL-676*	1/1/2020	Request for Determination of Support Arrears
FL-676 S*	1/1/2017	Request for Determination of Support Arrears or Adjustment of Child Support Arrears Due to Incarceration or Involuntary Institutionalization (Spanish)
FL-676-INFO	1/1/2020	Information Sheet: Request for Determination of Support Arrears
FL-677*	1/1/2012	Notice of Opposition and Notice of Motion on Claim of Exemption
FL-678*	1/1/2003	Order Determining Claim of Exemption or Third-Party Claim
FL-679*	1/1/2012	Request for Telephone Appearance
FL-679* S	1/1/2012	Request for Telephone Appearance (Spanish)
FL-679-INFO*	1/1/2008	Information Sheet—Request for Telephone Appearance
FL-679-INFO S	1/1/2008	Information Sheet—Request for Telephone Appearance (Spanish)
FL-680*	1/1/2012	Notice of Motion
FL-681	7/1/2005	Clerk Calendar Cover Sheet (For Court Clerk Use Only)
FL-683*	7/1/2005	Order to Show Cause
FL-684*	1/1/2010	Request for Order and Supporting Declaration
FL-685*	1/1/2012	Response to Governmental Notice of Motion or Order to Show Cause
FL-686*	1/1/2020	Proof of Service by Mail
FL-687*	1/1/2020	Order After Hearing
FL-687* S	1/1/2017	Order After Hearing (Spanish)
FL-688*	1/1/2020	Short Form Order After Hearing
FL-688* S	1/1/2017	Short Form Order After Hearing (Spanish)
FL-692*	1/1/2020	Minutes and Order or Judgment
FL-692* S	1/1/2017	Minutes and Order or Judgment (Spanish)
FL-693	1/1/2003	Guideline Findings Attachment
FL-694	1/1/2020	Advisement and Waiver of Rights for Stipulation
FL-694 C	1/1/2003	Advisement and Waiver of Rights for Stipulation (Chinese)
FL-694 K	1/1/2003	Advisement and Waiver of Rights for Stipulation (Korean)
FL-694 S	1/1/2003	Advisement and Waiver of Rights for Stipulation (Spanish)
FL-694 T	1/1/2003	Advisement and Waiver of Rights for Stipulation (Tagalog)
FL-694 V	1/1/2003	Advisement and Waiver of Rights for Stipulation (Vietnamese)
FL-697*	1/1/2003	Declaration for Default or Uncontested Judgment

FAMILY LAW
Summary Dissolutions

FL-800*	9/1/2019	Joint Petition for Summary Dissolution
FL-810*	9/1/2019	Summary Dissolution Information
FL-810* S	7/1/2017	Summary Dissolution Information (Spanish)
FL-820*	1/1/2012	Request for Judgment, Judgment of Dissolution of Marriage, and Notice of Entry of Judgment

---

* Adopted for mandatory use by all courts.

| FL-825* | 1/1/2012 | Judgment of Dissolution and Notice of Entry of Judgment |
| FL-830* | 7/1/2015 | Notice of Revocation of Joint Petition for Summary Dissolution |

FAMILY LAW
Miscellaneous

FL-910*	1/1/2020	Request of Minor to Marry or Establish a Domestic Partnership
FL-912	1/1/2020	Consent for Minor to Marry or Establish a Domestic Partnerhip
FL-915*	1/1/2020	Order and Notices to Minor on Request to Marry or Establish a Domestic Partnership
FL-920	1/1/2003	Notice of Consolidation
FL-935	1/1/2008	Application and Order for Appointment of Guardian Ad Litem of Minor—Family Law
FL-940	1/1/2003	Office of the Family Law Facilitator Disclosure
FL-940 C	1/1/2003	Office of the Family Law Facilitator Disclosure (Chinese)
FL-940 K	1/1/2003	Office of the Family Law Facilitator Disclosure (Korean)
FL-940 S	1/1/2003	Office of the Family Law Facilitator Disclosure (Spanish)
FL-940 V	1/1/2003	Office of the Family Law Facilitator Disclosure (Vietnamese)
FL-945	1/1/2003	Family Law Information Center Disclosure
FL-950*	9/1/2017	Notice of Limited Scope Representation
FL-955*	9/1/2017	Notice of Completion of Limited Scope Representation
FL-955-INFO	9/1/2017	Information for Client About Notice of Completion of Limited Scope Representation
FL-955-INFO S	9/1/2017	Information for Client About Notice of Completion of Limited Scope Representation (Spanish)
FL-956*	9/1/2017	Objection to Proposed Notice of Completion of Limited Scope Representation
FL-957*	9/1/2017	Response to Objection to Proposed Notice of Completion of Limited Scope Representation
FL-958*	1/1/2018	Order on Completion of Limited Scope Representation
FL-960*	1/1/2003	Notice of Withdrawal of Attorney of Record
FL-970*	1/1/2003	Request and Declaration for Final Judgment of Dissolution of Marriage
FL-980	1/1/2013	Application for Order for Publication or Posting
FL-982	1/1/2013	Order for Publication or Posting
FL-985	1/1/2013	Proof of Service by Posting

FEE WAIVER

FW-001*	3/24/2020	Request to Waive Court Fees
FW-001* S	3/1/2017	Request to Waive Court Fees (Spanish)
FW-001-GC*	3/24/2020	Request to Waive Court Fees (Ward or Conservatee)
FW-001-GC* S	9/1/2015	Request to Waive Court Fees (Ward or Conservatee) (Spanish)
FW-001-INFO	1/1/2021	Information Sheet on Waiver of Superior Court Fees and Costs
FW-001-INFO* S	9/1/2015	Information Sheet on Waiver of Superior Court Fees and Costs (California Rules of Court, rule 3.51) (Spanish)
FW-002*	7/1/2015	Request to Waive Additional Court Fees (Superior Court)
FW-002* S	7/1/2009	Request to Waive Additional Court Fees (Superior Court) (Spanish)
FW-002-GC*	9/1/2015	Request to Waive Additional Court Fees (Superior Court) (Ward or Conservatee)
FW-002-GC* S	9/1/2015	Request to Waive Additional Court Fees (Superior Court) (Ward or Conservatee) (Spanish)
FW-003*	9/1/2019	Order on Court Fee Waiver (Superior Court)
FW-003* S	7/1/2015	Order on Court Fee Waiver (Superior Court) (Spanish)
FW-003-GC*	9/1/2019	Order on Court Fee Waiver (Superior Court) (Ward or Conservatee)
FW-003-GC* S	9/1/2015	Order on Court Fee Waiver (Superior Court) (Ward or Conservatee) (Spanish)
FW-004*	7/1/2009	*[Revoked]* Order on Application for Waiver of Additional Court Fees and Costs (*formerly 982(a)(18.1)*)
FW-005*	9/1/2019	Notice: Waiver of Court Fees (Superior Court)
FW-005* S	7/1/2009	Notice: Waiver of Court Fees (Spanish)
FW-005-GC*	9/1/2019	Notice: Waiver of Court Fees (Superior Court) (Ward or Conservatee)
FW-005-GC* S	9/1/2015	Notice: Waiver of Court Fees (Superior Court) (Ward or Conservatee) (Spanish)
FW-006*	7/1/2009	Request for Hearing About Court Fee Waiver Order (Superior Court)
FW-006* S	7/1/2009	Request for Hearing About Court Fee Waiver Order (Superior Court) (Spanish)
FW-006-GC*	9/1/2015	Request for Hearing About Court Fee Waiver Order (Superior Court) (Ward or Conservatee)
FW-006-GC* S	9/1/2015	Request for Hearing About Court Fee Waiver Order (Superior Court) (Ward or Conservatee) (Spanish)
FW-007*	1/1/2010	Notice on Hearing About Court Fees
FW-007* S	1/1/2010	Notice on Hearing About Court Fees (Spanish)
FW-007-GC*	9/1/2015	Notice on Hearing About Court Fees (Ward or Conservatee)
FW-007-GC* S	9/1/2015	Notice on Hearing About Court Fees (Ward or Conservatee) (Spanish)
FW-008*	9/1/2019	Order on Court Fee Waiver After Hearing (Superior Court)
FW-008* S	1/1/2010	Order on Court Fee Waiver After Hearing (Superior Court) (Spanish)
FW-008-GC*	9/1/2019	Order on Court Fee Waiver After Hearing (Superior Court) (Ward or Conservatee)
FW-008-GC* S	9/1/2015	Order on Court Fee Waiver After Hearing (Superior Court) (Ward or Conservatee) (Spanish)
FW-010*	7/1/2009	Notice to Court of Improved Financial Situation or Settlement
FW-010* S	7/1/2009	Notice to Court of Improved Financial Situation or Settlement (Spanish)
FW-010-GC*	9/1/2015	Notice to Court of Improved Financial Situation or Settlement (Ward or Conservatee)
FW-010-GC* S	9/1/2015	Notice to Court of Improved Financial Situation or Settlement (Ward or Conservatee) (Spanish)

---

* Adopted for mandatory use by all courts.

FW-011*	7/1/2009	Notice to Appear for Reconsideration of Fee Waiver
FW-011* S	7/1/2009	Notice to Appear for Reconsideration of Fee Waiver (Spanish)
FW-011-GC*	9/1/2015	Notice to Appear for Reconsideration of Fee Waiver (Ward or Conservatee)
FW-011-GC* S	9/1/2015	Notice to Appear for Reconsideration of Fee Waiver (Ward or Conservatee) (Spanish)
FW-012*	9/1/2019	Order on Court Fee Waiver After Reconsideration Hearing (Superior Court)
FW-012* S	7/1/2009	Order on Court Fee Waiver After Reconsideration Hearing (Superior Court) (Spanish)
FW-012-GC*	9/1/2019	Order on Court Fee Waiver After Reconsideration Hearing (Superior Court) (Ward or Conservatee)
FW-012-GC* S	9/1/2015	Order on Court Fee Waiver After Reconsideration Hearing (Superior Court) (Ward or Conservatee) (Spanish)
FW-015-INFO*	3/24/2020	Information Sheet on Waiver of Appellate Court Fees — Supreme Court, Court of Appeal, Appellate Division [same as APP-015-INFO*]
FW-015-INFO* S	9/1/2015	Information Sheet on Waiver of Appellate Court Fees (Supreme Court, Court of Appeal, Appellate Division) (Spanish)
FW-016	7/1/2010	Order on Court Fee Waiver (Court of Appeal or Supreme Court) [same as APP-016]
FW-016 S	7/1/2010	Order on Court Fee Waiver (Court of Appeal or Supreme Court) (Spanish) [same as APP-016 S]
FW-016-GC	1/1/2021	Order on Court Fee Waiver (Court of Appeal or Supreme Court) (Ward or Conservatee) [same as APP-016-GC]
FW-016-GC S	9/1/2015	Order on Court Fee Waiver (Ward or Conservatee) (Spanish) [same as APP-016-GC S]
FW-020	1/1/2021	Request for Court Reporter by Party With Fee Waiver

GUN VIOLENCE PREVENTION

GV-009	9/1/2020	Notice of Court Hearing
GV-020*	9/1/2020	Response to Gun Violence Emergency Protective Order
GV-020-INFO	9/1/2020	How Can I Respond to a Gun Violence Emergency Protective Order?
GV-025	9/1/2019	Proof of Service by Mail
GV-030*	9/1/2020	Gun Violence Restraining Order After Hearing on EPO-002 (CLETS—HGV)
GV-100*	9/1/2020	Petition for Gun Violence Restraining Order
GV-100* C	1/1/2018	Petition for Gun Violence Restraining Order (Chinese)
GV-100* K	1/1/2018	Petition for Gun Violence Restraining Order (Korean)
GV-100* S	1/1/2018	Petition for Gun Violence Restraining Order (Spanish)
GV-100* V	1/1/2018	Petition for Gun Violence Restraining Order (Vietnamese)
GV-100-INFO	9/1/2020	Can a Gun Violence Restraining Order Help Me?
GV-100-INFO C	1/1/2016	Can a Gun Violence Restraining Order Help Me? (Chinese)
GV-100-INFO K	1/1/2016	Can a Gun Violence Restraining Order Help Me? (Korean)
GV-100-INFO S	1/1/2016	Can a Gun Violence Restraining Order Help Me? (Spanish)
GV-100-INFO V	1/1/2016	Can a Gun Violence Restraining Order Help Me? (Vietnamese)
GV-109*	9/1/2020	Notice of Court Hearing
GV-109* C	1/1/2016	Notice of Court Hearing (Chinese)
GV-109* K	1/1/2016	Notice of Court Hearing (Korean)
GV-109* V	1/1/2016	Notice of Court Hearing (Vietnamese)
GV-110*	9/1/2020	Temporary Gun Violence Restraining Order (CLETS—TGV)
GV-110* C	1/1/2016	Temporary Gun Violence Restraining Order (CLETS—TGV) (Chinese)
GV-110* K	1/1/2016	Temporary Gun Violence Restraining Order (CLETS—TGV) (Korean)
GV-110* S	1/1/2016	Temporary Gun Violence Restraining Order (CLETS—TGV) (Spanish)
GV-110* V	1/1/2016	Temporary Gun Violence Restraining Order (CLETS—TGV) (Vietnamese)
GV-115*	1/1/2020	Request to Continue Court Hearing for Gun Violence Restraining Order (EPO-002 or Temporary Restraining Order)
GV-115* C	1/1/2016	Request to Continue Court Hearing for Gun Violence Restraining Order (Chinese)
GV-115* K	1/1/2016	Request to Continue Court Hearing for Gun Violence Restraining Order (Korean)
GV-115* V	1/1/2016	Request to Continue Court Hearing for Gun Violence Restraining Order (Vietnamese)
GV-116*	1/1/2020	Order on Request to Continue Hearing (EPO-002 or Temporary Restraining Order) (CLETS—EGV or CLETS—TGV)
GV-116* C	1/1/2017	Order for Continuance and Notice of New Hearing Date (Chinese)
GV-116* K	1/1/2017	Order for Continuance and Notice of New Hearing Date (Korean)
GV-116* V	1/1/2017	Order for Continuance and Notice of New Hearing Date (Vietnamese)
GV-120*	9/1/2020	Response to Petition for Gun Violence Restraining Order
GV-120* C	1/1/2018	Response to Petition for Gun Violence Restraining Order (Chinese)
GV-120* K	1/1/2018	Response to Petition for Gun Violence Restraining Order (Korean)
GV-120* S	1/1/2018	Response to Petition for Gun Violence Restraining Order (Spanish)
GV-120* V	1/1/2018	Response to Petition for Gun Violence Restraining Order (Vietnamese)
GV-120-INFO	9/1/2020	How Can I Respond to a Petition for a Gun Violence Restraining Order?
GV-120-INFO C	1/1/2016	How Can I Respond to a Petition for a Gun Violence Restraining Order? (Chinese)
GV-120-INFO K	1/1/2016	How Can I Respond to a Petition for a Gun Violence Restraining Order? (Korean)
GV-120-INFO V	1/1/2016	How Can I Respond to a Petition for a Gun Violence Restraining Order? (Vietnamese)
GV-125*	9/1/2020	Consent to Gun Violence Restraining Order and Surrender of Firearms
GV-130*	9/1/2020	Gun Violence Restraining Order After Hearing or Consent to Gun Violence Restraining Order (CLETS—OGV)
GV-130* C	1/1/2016	Gun Violence Restraining Order After Hearing (CLETS—OGV) (Chinese)
GV-130* K	1/1/2016	Gun Violence Restraining Order After Hearing (CLETS—OGV) (Korean)

---

* Adopted for mandatory use by all courts.

GV-130* V	1/1/2016	Gun Violence Restraining Order After Hearing (CLETS—OGV) (Vietnamese)
GV-200	9/1/2019	Proof of Personal Service
GV-200 C	1/1/2016	Proof of Personal Service (Chinese)
GV-200 K	1/1/2016	Proof of Personal Service (Korean)
GV-200 S	1/1/2016	Proof of Personal Service (Spanish)
GV-200 V	1/1/2016	Proof of Personal Service (Vietnamese)
GV-200-INFO	1/1/2019	What Is "Proof of Personal Service"?
GV-200-INFO C	1/1/2016	What Is "Proof of Personal Service"? (Chinese)
GV-200-INFO K	1/1/2016	What Is "Proof of Personal Service"? (Korean)
GV-200-INFO S	1/1/2016	What Is "Proof of Personal Service"? (Spanish)
GV-200-INFO V	1/1/2016	What Is "Proof of Personal Service"? (Vietnamese)
GV-250	1/1/2019	Proof of Service by Mail
GV-250 C	1/1/2016	Proof of Service by Mail (Chinese)
GV-250 K	1/1/2016	Proof of Service by Mail (Korean)
GV-250 S	1/1/2016	Proof of Service by Mail (Spanish)
GV-250 V	1/1/2016	Proof of Service by Mail (Vietnamese)
GV-600*	9/1/2020	Request to Terminate Gun Violence Restraining Order
GV-600* C	1/1/2016	Request to Terminate Gun Violence Restraining Order (Chinese)
GV-600* K	1/1/2016	Request to Terminate Gun Violence Restraining Order (Korean)
GV-600* S	1/1/2016	Request to Terminate Gun Violence Restraining Order (Spanish)
GV-600* V	1/1/2016	Request to Terminate Gun Violence Restraining Order (Vietnamese)
GV-610*	9/1/2020	Notice of Hearing on Request to Terminate Gun Violence Restraining Order
GV-610* C	1/1/2016	Notice of Hearing on Request to Terminate Gun Violence Restraining Order (Chinese)
GV-610* K	1/1/2016	Notice of Hearing on Request to Terminate Gun Violence Restraining Order (Korean)
GV-610* S	1/1/2016	Notice of Hearing on Request to Terminate Gun Violence Restraining Order (Spanish)
GV-610* V	1/1/2016	Notice of Hearing on Request to Terminate Gun Violence Restraining Order (Vietnamese)
GV-620*	9/1/2020	Response to Request to Terminate Gun Violence Restraining Order
GV-620* C	1/1/2016	Response to Request to Terminate Gun Violence Restraining Order (Chinese)
GV-620* K	1/1/2016	Response to Request to Terminate Gun Violence Restraining Order (Korean)
GV-620* S	1/1/2016	Response to Request to Terminate Gun Violence Restraining Order (Spanish)
GV-620* V	1/1/2016	Response to Request to Terminate Gun Violence Restraining Order (Vietnamese)
GV-630*	9/1/2020	Order on Request to Terminate Gun Violence Restraining Order
GV-630* C	1/1/2016	Order on Request to Terminate Gun Violence Restraining Order (Chinese)
GV-630* K	1/1/2016	Order on Request to Terminate Gun Violence Restraining Order (Korean
GV-630* S	1/1/2016	Order on Request to Terminate Gun Violence Restraining Order (Spanish)
GV-630* V	1/1/2016	Order on Request to Terminate Gun Violence Restraining Order (Vietnamese)
GV-700*	9/1/2020	Request to Renew Gun Violence Restraining Order
GV-700* C	1/1/2016	Request to Renew Gun Violence Restraining Order (Chinese)
GV-700* K	1/1/2016	Request to Renew Gun Violence Restraining Order (Korean)
GV-700* S	1/1/2016	Request to Renew Gun Violence Restraining Order (Spanish)
GV-700* V	1/1/2016	Request to Renew Gun Violence Restraining Order (Vietnamese)
GV-710*	9/1/2020	Notice of Hearing on Request to Renew Gun Violence Restraining Order
GV-710* C	1/1/2016	Notice of Hearing on Request to Renew Gun Violence Restraining Order (Chinese)
GV-710* K	1/1/2016	Notice of Hearing on Request to Renew Gun Violence Restraining Order (Korean)
GV-710* S	1/1/2016	Notice of Hearing on Request to Renew Gun Violence Restraining Order (Spanish)
GV-710* V	1/1/2016	Notice of Hearing on Request to Renew Gun Violence Restraining Order (Vietnamese)
GV-720*	1/1/2019	Response to Request to Renew Gun Violence Restraining Order
GV-720* C	1/1/2016	Response to Request to Renew Gun Violence Restraining Order (Chinese)
GV-720* K	1/1/2016	Response to Request to Renew Gun Violence Restraining Order (Korean)
GV-720* S	1/1/2016	Response to Request to Renew Gun Violence Restraining Order (Spanish)
GV-720* V	1/1/2016	Response to Request to Renew Gun Violence Restraining Order (Vietnamese)
GV-730*	1/1/2019	Order on Request to Renew Gun Violence Restraining Order
GV-730* C	1/1/2016	Order on Request to Renew Gun Violence Restraining Order (Chinese)
GV-730* K	1/1/2016	Order on Request to Renew Gun Violence Restraining Order (Korean)
GV-730* S	1/1/2016	Order on Request to Renew Gun Violence Restraining Order (Spanish)
GV-730* V	1/1/2016	Order on Request to Renew Gun Violence Restraining Order (Vietnamese)
GV-800	9/1/2019	Proof of Firearms, Ammunition, and Magazines Turned In, Sold, or Stored
GV-800 C	1/1/2016	Proof of Firearms Turned in, Sold, or Stored (Chinese)
GV-800 K	1/1/2016	Proof of Firearms Turned in, Sold, or Stored (Korean)
GV-800 S	1/1/2016	Proof of Firearms Turned in, Sold, or Stored (Spanish)
GV-800 V	1/1/2016	Proof of Firearms Turned in, Sold, or Stored (Vietnamese)
GV-800-INFO	9/1/2019	How Do I Turn In, Sell, or Store My Firearms, Ammunition, and Magazines?
GV-800-INFO C	1/1/2016	How Do I Turn In, Sell, or Store My Firearms? (Chinese)
GV-800-INFO K	1/1/2016	How Do I Turn In, Sell, or Store My Firearms? (Korean)
GV-800-INFO S	1/1/2016	How Do I Turn In, Sell, or Store My Firearms? (Spanish)
GV-800-INFO V	1/1/2016	How Do I Turn In, Sell, or Store My Firearms? (Vietnamese)

HABEAS CORPUS

HC-001	1/1/2019	Petition for Writ of Habeas Corpus *[renumbered from MC-275]*

---

* Adopted for mandatory use by all courts.

HC-002	9/1/2018	Petition for Writ of Habeas Corpus—LPS Act (Mental Health) *[renumbered from MC-265]*
HC-003	9/1/2018	Petition for Writ of Habeas Corpus—Penal Commitment (Mental Health) *[renumbered from MC-270]*
HC-004	9/1/2018	Notice and Request for Ruling *[renumbered from CR-175]*
HC-100*	4/25/2019	Declaration of Counsel Re Minimum Qualifications for Appointment in Dealth Penalty–Related Habeas Corpus Proceedings
HC-101*	4/25/2019	Order Appointing Counsel in Death Penalty–Related Habeas Corpus Proceeding
HC-200*	4/25/2019	Petitioner's Notice of Appeal—Dealth Penalty–Related Habeas Corpus Decision

IGNITION INTERLOCK DEVICE

ID-100	7/1/2008	Order to Install Ignition Interlock Device *[renumbered to CR-221]*
ID-110	7/1/2005	Ignition Interlock Installation Verification *[renumbered to CR-222]*
ID-120	7/1/2005	Ignition Interlock Calibration Verification and Tamper Report *[renumbered to CR-223]*
ID-130	1/1/2000	Ignition Interlock Noncompliance Report *[renumbered to CR-224]*
ID-140	7/1/2008	Ignition Interlock Removal and Modification to Probation Order *[renumbered to CR-225]*
ID-150	7/1/2005	Notice to Employers of Ignition Interlock Restriction *[renumbered to CR-226]*

INDIAN CHILD WELFARE ACT

ICWA-005-INFO	1/1/2020	Information Sheet on Indian Child Inquiry Attachments and Notice of Child Custody Proceeding for Indian Child
ICWA-010(A)*	1/1/2020	Indian Child Inquiry Attachment
ICWA-010(A)* S	1/1/2008	Indian Child Inquiry Attachment (Spanish)
ICWA-020*	3/25/2020	Parental Notification of Indian Status
ICWA-020* S	1/1/2008	Parental Notification of Indian Status (Spanish)
ICWA-030*	1/1/2021	Notice of Child Custody Proceeding for Indian Child
ICWA-030* S	1/1/2008	Notice of Child Custody Proceeding for Indian Child (Spanish)
ICWA-030(A)	1/1/2008	Attachment to Notice of Child Custody Proceeding for Indian Child
ICWA-030(A) S	1/1/2008	Attachment to Notice of Child Custody Proceeding for Indian Child (Spanish)
ICWA-040	1/1/2020	Notice of Designation of Tribal Representative in a Court Proceeding Involving an Indian Child
ICWA-050	1/1/2008	Notice of Petition and Petition to Transfer Case Involving an Indian Child to Tribal Jurisdiction
ICWA-060*	1/1/2020	Order on Petition to Transfer Case Involving an Indian Child to Tribal Jurisdiction
ICWA-070*	1/1/2020	Request for Ex Parte Hearing to Return Physical Custody of an Indian Child
ICWA-080*	1/1/2020	Order on Request for Ex Parte Hearing to Return Physical Custody of an Indian Child
ICWA-090*	1/1/2021	Order After Hearing on Ex Parte Request to Return Physical Custody of an Indian Child
ICWA-100	1/1/2021	Tribal Information Form
ICWA-100-INFO	1/1/2021	Instructions Sheet for Tribal Information Form
ICWA-101*	1/1/2021	Agreement of Parent or Indian Custodian to Temporary Custody of Indian Child

INTERPRETER

INT-001*	1/1/2009	Semiannual Report to the Judicial Council on the Use of Noncertified or Nonregistered Interpreters
INT-002(A)*	1/1/2009	Semiannual Report to the Judicial Council on the Use of Nonregistered Interpreters *(Attachment to INT-001)*
INT-100-INFO*	1/1/2018	*[Revoked]* Procedures and Guidelines to Appoint a Noncertified or Nonregistered Interpreter in Criminal and Juvenile Delinquency Proceedings
INT-100-INFO*	1/1/2018	Procedures to Appoint a Noncertified or Nonregistered Spoken Language Interpreter as Either Provisionally Qualified or Temporary
INT-110*	1/1/2018	Qualifications of a Noncertified or Nonregistered Spoken Language Interpreter
INT-120*	1/1/2009	Certification of Unavailability of Certified or Registered Interpreter
INT-140	1/1/2018	Temporary Use of a Noncertified or Nonregistered Spoken Language Interpreter
INT-200	7/1/2008	Foreign Language Interpreter's Duties—Civil and Small Claims (For Noncertified and Nonregistered Interpreters)
INT-300	7/1/2016	Request for Interpreter (Civil)
INT-300 C	1/1/2018	Request for Interpreter (Civil) (Chinese)
INT-300 CT	1/1/2018	Request for Interpreter (Civil) (Chinese Traditional)
INT-300 F	1/1/2018	Request for Interpreter (Civil) (Farsi)
INT-300 K	1/1/2018	Request for Interpreter (Civil) (Korean)
INT-300 P	1/1/2018	Request for Interpreter (Civil) (Punjabi)
INT-300 R	1/1/2018	Request for Interpreter (Civil) (Russian)
INT-300 S	1/1/2018	Request for Interpreter (Civil) (Spanish)
INT-300 TG	1/1/2018	Request for Interpreter (Civil) (Tagalog)
INT-300 V	1/1/2018	Request for Interpreter (Civil) (Vietnamese)

JUDGMENT

| JUD-100 | 1/1/2002 | Judgment |

---

* Adopted for mandatory use by all courts.

JURY SELECTION

JURY-001	9/1/2018	Juror Questionnaire for Civil Cases/Code of Civil Procedure section 205(c)-(d) *[renumbered from MC-001]*
JURY-002	9/1/2018	Juror Questionnaire for Criminal Cases/Code of Civil Procedure section 205(c)-(d) *[renumbered from MC-002]*
JURY-003	9/1/2018	Juror Questionnaire for Expedited Jury Trials *[renumbered from MC-003]*
JURY-010	9/1/2018	Juror's Motion to Set Aside Sanctions and Order *[renumbered from MC-070]*

JUVENILE LAW

JV-050	1/1/2015	*[Revoked]* Information for Parents (Juvenile Dependency)
JV-050-INFO	1/1/2015	What happens if your child is taken from your home?
JV-050-INFO C	1/1/2015	What happens if your child is taken from your home? (Chinese)
JV-050-INFO CM	1/1/2015	What happens if your child is taken from your home? (Cambodian)
JV-050-INFO H	1/1/2015	What happens if your child is taken from your home? (Hmong)
JV-050-INFO K	1/1/2015	What happens if your child is taken from your home? (Korean)
JV-050-INFO R	1/1/2015	What happens if your child is taken from your home? (Russian)
JV-050-INFO S	1/1/2015	What happens if your child is taken from your home? (Spanish)
JV-050-INFO V	1/1/2015	What happens if your child is taken from your home? (Vietnamese)
JV-055	1/1/2015	*[Revoked]* Juvenile Court—The Dependency Court: How It Works
JV-060	9/1/2017	Juvenile Court—Information for Parents *[renumbered to JV-060-INFO]*
JV-060 S	9/1/2017	Juvenile Court—Information for Parents (Spanish)
JV-060-INFO	1/1/2019	Juvenile Justice Court: Information for Parents *[renumbered from JV-060]*
JV-060-INFO C	1/1/2019	Juvenile Justice Court: Information for Parents (Chinese)
JV-060-INFO K	1/1/2019	Juvenile Justice Court: Information for Parents (Korean)
JV-060-INFO S	1/1/2019	Juvenile Justice Court: Information for Parents (Spanish)
JV-060-INFO V	1/1/2019	Juvenile Justice Court: Information for Parents (Vietnamese)
JV-100*	1/1/2020	Juvenile Dependency Petition (Version One)
JV-100* S	7/1/2016	Juvenile Dependency Petition (Version One) (Spanish)
JV-101(A)*	1/1/2021	Additional Children Attachment—Juvenile Dependency Petition
JV-101(A)* S	7/1/2016	Additional Children Attachment—Juvenile Dependency Petition (Spanish)
JV-110*	1/1/2021	Juvenile Dependency Petition (Version Two)
JV-110* S	1/1/2008	Juvenile Dependency Petition (Version Two) (Spanish)
JV-120	1/1/2007	Serious Physical Harm (§ 300(a))
JV-120 S	1/1/2007	Serious Physical Harm (§ 300(a)) (Spanish)
JV-121	7/1/2016	Failure to Protect (§ 300(b))
JV-121 S	7/1/2016	Failure to Protect (§ 300(b)) (Spanish)
JV-122	1/1/2007	Serious Emotional Damage (§ 300(c))
JV-122 S	1/1/2007	Serious Emotional Damage (§ 300(c)) (Spanish)
JV-123*	1/1/2007	Sexual Abuse (§ 300(d))
JV-123* S	1/1/2007	Sexual Abuse (§ 300(d)) (Spanish)
JV-124	1/1/2007	Severe Physical Abuse (§ 300(e))
JV-124 S	1/1/2007	Severe Physical Abuse (§ 300(e)) (Spanish)
JV-125	1/1/2007	Caused Another Child's Death Through Abuse or Neglect (§ 300(f))
JV-125 S	1/1/2007	Caused Another Child's Death Through Abuse or Neglect (§ 300(f)) (Spanish)
JV-126	1/1/2007	No Provision for Support (§ 300(g))
JV-126 S	1/1/2007	No Provision for Support (§ 300(g)) (Spanish)
JV-127	1/1/2007	Freed for Adoption (§ 300(h))
JV-127 S	1/1/2007	Freed for Adoption (§ 300(h)) (Spanish)
JV-128	1/1/2007	Cruelty (§ 300(i))
JV-128 S	1/1/2007	Cruelty (§ 300(i)) (Spanish)
JV-129	1/1/2007	Abuse of Sibling (§ 300(i))
JV-129 S	1/1/2007	Abuse of Sibling (§ 300(i)) (Spanish)
JV-130*	1/1/2008	*[Revoked]* Parental Notification of Indian Status (Juvenile Court)
JV-130-INFO	1/1/2013	Paying for Lawyers in Dependency Court—Information for Parents and Guardians
JV-130-INFO S	1/1/2013	Paying for Lawyers in Dependency Court—Information for Parents and Guardians (Spanish)
JV-131	1/1/2013	Order to Appear for Financial Evaluation
JV-132	3/24/2020	Financial Declaration—Juvenile Dependency
JV-133	1/1/2013	Recommendation Regarding Ability to Repay Cost of Legal Services
JV-134	1/1/2013	Response to Recommendation Regarding Ability to Repay Cost of Legal Services
JV-135	1/1/2013	Order for Repayment of Cost of Legal Services
JV-136	1/1/2013	Juvenile Dependency—Cost of Appointed Counsel: Repayment Recommendation/Response/Order
JV-140*	1/1/2007	Notification of Mailing Address
JV-140* S	1/1/2007	Notification of Mailing Address (Spanish)
JV-141*	1/1/2019	Electronic Service: Consent, Withdrawal of Consent, Address Change (Juvenile) *[same as EFS-005-JV*]*
JV-150*	1/1/2007	Supplemental Petition for More Restrictive Placement (Attachment) (Welfare and Institutions Code, § 387)

---

* Adopted for mandatory use by all courts.

JV-150* S	1/1/2007	Supplemental Petition for More Restrictive Placement (Attachment) (Welfare and Institutions Code, § 387) (Spanish)
JV-180*	1/1/2020	Request to Change Court Order
JV-180 S*	1/1/2014	Request to Change Court Order (Spanish)
JV-182*	1/1/2007	Confidential Information (Request to Change Court Order)
JV-183*	1/1/2016	Court Order on Form JV-180, *Request to Change Court Order*
JV-184*	1/1/2009	Order After Hearing on Form JV-180, *Request to Change Court Order*
JV-185	1/1/2016	Child's Information Sheet—Request to Change Court Order
JV-190*	1/1/2007	Waiver of Rights—Juvenile Dependency
JV-190* S	1/1/2007	Waiver of Rights—Juvenile Dependency (Spanish)
JV-195*	7/1/1998	Waiver of Reunification Services
JV-195 S	7/1/1998	Waiver of Reunification Services (Spanish)
JV-200*	1/1/2016	Custody Order—Juvenile—Final Judgment
JV-200* S	1/1/2016	Custody Order—Juvenile—Final Judgment (Spanish)
JV-205*	1/1/2016	Visitation (Parenting Time) Order—Juvenile
JV-205* S	1/1/2016	Visitation (Parenting Time) Order—Juvenile (Spanish)
JV-206	1/1/2016	Reasons for No or Supervised Visitation—Juvenile
JV-206 S	1/1/2016	Reasons for No or Supervised Visitation—Juvenile (Spanish)
JV-210	7/1/2010	Application to Commence Proceedings by Affidavit and Decision by Social Worker (Welf. & Inst. Code, §329)
JV-212	9/1/2018	Application to Review Decision by Social Worker Not to Commence Proceedings (Welf. & Inst. Code, §331) *[renumbered from JV-215]*
JV-212 S	9/1/2018	Application to Review Decision by Social Worker Not to Commence Proceedings (Welf. & Inst. Code, §331) (Spanish)
JV-214*	9/1/2018	Request for Hearing on Waiver of Presumptive Transfer
JV-214(A)*	9/1/2018	Notice of and Order on Request for Hearing on Waiver of Presumptive Transfer
JV-214-INFO	9/1/2018	Instructions for Requesting a Hearing to Review Waiver of Presumptive Transfer of Specialty Mental Health Services
JV-214-INFO S	9/1/2018	Instructions for Requesting a Hearing to Review Waiver of Presumptive Transfer of Specialty Mental Health Services (Spanish)
JV-215*	9/1/2018	Order After Hearing on Waiver of Presumptive Transfer
JV-216	9/1/2018	Order Delegating Judicial Authority Over Psychotropic Medication
JV-217-INFO	1/1/2019	Guide to Psychotropic Medication Forms
JV-218	7/1/2016	Child's Opinion About the Medicine
JV-218 S	7/1/2016	Child's Opinion About the Medicine (Spanish)
JV-219	1/1/2018	Statement About Medicine Prescribed
JV-219 S	1/1/2018	Statement About Medicine Prescribed (Spanish)
JV-219-INFO	7/1/2016	Information About Psychotropic Medication Forms *[Renumbered to JV-217-INFO]*
JV-220*	1/1/2018	Application For Psychotropic Medication
JV-220(A)*	1/1/2018	Physician's Statement—Attachment
JV-220(A)* S	7/1/2016	Physician's Statement—Attachment (Spanish)
JV-220(B)*	1/1/2018	Physician's Request to Continue Medication—Attachment
JV-221*	1/1/2021	Proof of Notice of Application
JV-221* S	7/1/2016	Proof of Notice of Application (Spanish)
JV-222	1/1/2018	Input on Application for Psychotropic Medication
JV-222* S	1/1/2018	Input on Application for Psychotropic Medication (Spanish)
JV-223*	9/1/2020	Order on Application for Psychotropic Medication
JV-223* S	7/1/2016	Order on Application for Psychotropic Medication (Spanish)
JV-224*	1/1/2016	*[Revoked]* Order Regarding Eligibility for Special Immigrant Juvenile Status
JV-224*	9/1/2020	County Report on Psychotropic Medication
JV-225*	1/1/2014	Your Child's Health and Education
JV-225* S	1/1/2014	Your Child's Health and Education (Spanish)
JV-226	7/1/2013	Authorization to Release Health and Mental Health Information (Dependency)
JV-227	1/1/2014	Consent to Release Education Information (Dependency)
JV-228	9/1/2020	Position on Release of Information to Medical Board of California
JV-228-INFO	9/1/2020	Background on Release of Information to Medical Board of California
JV-229*	9/1/2020	Withdrawal of Release of Information to Medical Board of California
JV-245*	1/1/2017	Request for Restraining Order—Juvenile
JV-245* C	1/1/2017	Request for Restraining Order—Juvenile (Chinese)
JV-245* K	1/1/2017	Request for Restraining Order—Juvenile (Korean)
JV-245* S	1/1/2017	Request for Restraining Order—Juvenile (Spanish)
JV-245* V	1/1/2017	Request for Restraining Order—Juvenile (Vietnamese)
JV-247*	7/1/2014	Answer to Request for Restraining Order—Juvenile
JV-247* S	7/1/2014	Answer to Request for Restraining Order—Juvenile (Spanish)
JV-248*	1/1/2012	*[Revoked]* Confidential CLETS Information (Domestic Violence, Civil Harassment, Elder Abuse, Juvenile Law) *[same as CH-102*, DV-260* and EA-102*]*
JV-250*	9/1/2019	Notice of Hearing and Temporary Restraining Order—Juvenile
JV-250* C	1/1/2017	Notice of Hearing and Temporary Restraining Order—Juvenile (Chinese)
JV-250* K	1/1/2017	Notice of Hearing and Temporary Restraining Order—Juvenile (Korean)
JV-250* S	1/1/2017	Notice of Hearing and Temporary Restraining Order—Juvenile (Spanish)

* Adopted for mandatory use by all courts.

JV-250* V	1/1/2017	Notice of Hearing and Temporary Restraining Order—Juvenile (Vietnamese)
JV-251	7/1/2016	Request and Order to Continue Hearing (CLETS—JUV)
JV-251 S	7/1/2016	Request and Order to Continue Hearing (CLETS—JUV) (Spanish)
JV-252	1/1/2019	Proof of Firearms Turned In, Sold, or Stored *[same as DV-800]*
JV-252-INFO	7/1/2014	How Do I Turn In, Sell, or Store My Firearms? (Domestic Violence Prevention/Juvenile) *[Renumbered from DV-810; same as DV-800-INFO]*
JV-252-INFO C	7/1/2014	How Do I Turn In, Sell, or Store My Firearms? (Domestic Violence Prevention/Juvenile) (Chinese) *[same as DV-800-INFO C]*
JV-252-INFO K	7/1/2014	How Do I Turn In, Sell, or Store My Firearms? (Domestic Violence Prevention/Juvenile) (Korean) *[same as DV-800-INFO K]*
JV-252-INFO S	7/1/2014	How Do I Turn In, Sell, or Store My Firearms? (Domestic Violence Prevention/Juvenile) (Spanish) *[same as DV-800-INFO S]*
JV-252-INFO V	7/1/2014	How Do I Turn In, Sell, or Store My Firearms? (Domestic Violence Prevention/Juvenile) (Vietnamese) *[same as DV-800-INFO V]*
JV-255*	9/1/2019	Restraining Order—Juvenile (CLETS—JUV)
JV-255* C	1/1/2017	Restraining Order—Juvenile (CLETS—JUV) (Chinese)
JV-255* K	1/1/2017	Restraining Order—Juvenile (CLETS—JUV) (Korean)
JV-255* S	1/1/2017	Restraining Order—Juvenile (CLETS—JUV) (Spanish)
JV-255* V	1/1/2017	Restraining Order—Juvenile (CLETS—JUV) (Vietnamese)
JV-257*	1/1/2014	Change to Restraining Order After Hearing—Juvenile (CLETS—JUV) *[Renumbered from JV-255*]*
JV-257* C	1/1/2014	Change to Restraining Order After Hearing—Juvenile (CLETS—JUV) (Chinese)
JV-257* K	1/1/2014	Change to Restraining Order After Hearing—Juvenile (CLETS—JUV) (Korean)
JV-257* S	1/1/2014	Change to Restraining Order After Hearing—Juvenile (CLETS—JUV) (Spanish)
JV-257* V	1/1/2014	Change to Restraining Order After Hearing—Juvenile (CLETS—JUV) (Vietnamese)
JV-280*	1/1/2007	Notice of Review Hearing
JV-280* S	1/1/2007	Notice of Review Hearing (Spanish)
JV-281	1/1/2014	Notice of Hearing—Nonminor
JV-282	1/1/2019	Proof of service—Nonminor
JV-285	9/1/2020	Relative Information
JV-285 S	1/1/2011	Relative Information (Spanish)
JV-287	9/1/2020	Confidential Information
JV-287 S	1/1/2011	Confidential Information (Spanish)
JV-290	9/1/2020	Caregiver Information Form
JV-290 C	10/1/2007	Caregiver Information Form (Chinese)
JV-290 K	10/1/2007	Caregiver Information Form (Korean)
JV-290 S	10/1/2007	Caregiver Information Form (Spanish)
JV-290 V	10/1/2007	Caregiver Information Form (Vietnamese)
JV-290-INFO	10/1/2007	Instruction Sheet for Caregiver Information Form
JV-290-INFO C	10/1/2007	Instruction Sheet for Caregiver Information Form (Chinese)
JV-290-INFO K	10/1/2007	Instruction Sheet for Caregiver Information Form (Korean)
JV-290-INFO S	10/1/2007	Instruction Sheet for Caregiver Information Form (Spanish)
JV-290-INFO V	10/1/2007	Instruction Sheet for Caregiver Information Form (Vietnamese)
JV-291-INFO	9/1/2020	Information on Requesting Access to Records for Persons With a Limited Right to Appeal
JV-295*	9/1/2020	De Facto Parent Request
JV-295* S	1/1/2007	De Facto Parent Request (Spanish)
JV-296*	1/1/2007	De Facto Parent Statement
JV-296* S	1/1/2007	De Facto Parent Statement (Spanish)
JV-297*	9/1/2019	De Facto Parent Order
JV-297* S	1/1/2007	De Facto Parent Order (Spanish)
JV-298*	1/1/2007	Order Ending De Facto Parent Status
JV-298* S	1/1/2007	Order Ending De Facto Parent Status (Spanish)
JV-299	9/1/2019	De Facto Parent Pamphlet
JV-299 C	1/1/2007	De Facto Parent Pamphlet (Chinese)
JV-299 K	1/1/2007	De Facto Parent Pamphlet (Korean)
JV-299 S	1/1/2007	De Facto Parent Pamphlet (Spanish)
JV-299 V	1/1/2007	De Facto Parent Pamphlet (Vietnamese)
JV-300*	7/1/2010	Notice of Hearing on Selection of a Permanent Plan
JV-300* S	7/1/2010	Notice of Hearing on Selection of a Permanent Plan (Spanish)
JV-305*	1/1/2007	Citation for Publication Under Welfare and Institutions Code Section 294
JV-305* S	1/1/2007	Citation for Publication Under Welfare and Institutions Code Section 294 (Spanish)
JV-310*	1/1/2019	Proof of Service Under Section 366.26 of the Welfare and Institutions Code
JV-310* S	1/1/2007	Proof of Service Under Section 366.26 of the Welfare and Institutions Code (Spanish)
JV-320*	1/1/2021	Orders Under Welfare and Institutions Code Sections 366.24, 366.26, 727.3, 727.31
JV-321*	9/1/2020	Request for Prospective Adoptive Parent Designation
JV-322*	1/1/2007	Confidential Information—Prospective Adoptive Parent
JV-323*	1/1/2008	Notice of Intent to Remove Child
JV-324*	1/1/2008	Notice of Emergency Removal
JV-325*	1/1/2008	*[Revoked]* Proof of Notice of Hearing
JV-325*	9/1/2020	Objection to Removal
JV-325-INFO	1/1/2008	*[Revoked]* Instructions for Notice of Prospective Adoptive Parent Hearing

* Adopted for mandatory use by all courts.

JV-326*	1/1/2019	Proof of Notice Under Section 366.26(n)
JV-326-INFO	1/1/2019	Instructions for Notice of Hearings Under Section 366.26(n)
JV-327*	7/1/2010	Prospective Adoptive Parent Designation Order
JV-328*	1/1/2008	Prospective Adoptive Parent Order After Hearing
JV-330*	9/1/2019	Letters of Guardianship (Juvenile)
JV-330* S	7/1/2006	Letters of Guardianship (Juvenile) (Spanish) *(formerly JV-325)*
JV-350*	9/1/2019	*[Renumbered]* Guardianship Pamphlet *[Renumbered to JV-350-INFO*]*
JV-350 C	1/1/2001	Guardianship Pamphlet (Chinese)
JV-350 K	1/1/2001	Guardianship Pamphlet (Korean)
JV-350 S	1/1/2001	Guardianship Pamphlet (Spanish)
JV-350 V	1/1/2001	Guardianship Pamphlet (Vietnamese)
JV-350-INFO*	9/1/2019	Becoming a Child's Guardian in Juvenile Court *[Renumbered from JV-350*]*
JV-356*	1/1/2016	Request for Special Immigrant Juvenile Findings
JV-357*	7/1/2016	Special Immigrant Juvenile Findings *[same as FL-357*, GC-224*]*
JV-357* S	7/1/2016	Special Immigrant Juvenile Findings (Spanish) *[same as FL-357* S, GC-224* S]*
JV-361*	1/1/2021	First Review Hearing After Youth Turns 16 Years of Age—Information, Documents, and Services
JV-362*	1/1/2021	Review Hearing for Youth Approaching 18 Years of Age—Information, Documents, and Services
JV-363*	1/1/2021	Review Hearing for Youth 18 Years of Age or Older—Information, Documents, and Services
JV-364*	1/1/2020	Termination of Dependency for Adoption
JV-364* S	1/1/2007	Termination of Dependency (Spanish)
JV-365*	1/1/2021	Termination of Juvenile Court Jurisdiction—Nonminor
JV-365* S	1/1/2017	Termination of Juvenile Court Jurisdiction—Nonminor (Spanish)
JV-367*	1/1/2021	Findings and Orders After Hearing to Consider Termination of Juvenile Court Jurisdiction Over a Nonminor
JV-400	1/1/2007	Visitation Attachment: Parent, Legal Guardian, Indian Custodian, Other Important Person
JV-401	1/1/2015	Visitation Attachment: Sibling
JV-402	1/1/2007	Visitation Attachment: Grandparent
JV-403	1/1/2016	Sibling Attachment: Contact and Placement
JV-405	1/1/2020	Continuance—Dependency Detention Hearing
JV-406	7/1/2011	Continuance—Dependency General
JV-410	1/1/2021	Findings and Orders After Detention Hearing (Welf. & Inst. Code, § 319)
JV-412	1/1/2020	Findings and Orders After Jurisdictional Hearing (Welf. & Inst. Code, § 356)
JV-415	1/1/2020	Findings and Orders After Dispositional Hearing (Welf. & Inst. Code, § 361 et seq.)
JV-416	7/1/2011	Dispositional Attachment: Dismissal of Petition With Or Without Informal Supervision (Welf. & Inst. Code, § 360(b))
JV-417	7/1/2011	Dispositional Attachment: In-Home Placement With Formal Supervision (Welf. & Inst. Code, § 361)
JV-418	1/1/2021	Dispositional Attachment: Appointment of Guardian (Welf. & Inst. Code, § 360(a))
JV-419	1/1/2007	Guardianship—Consent and Waiver of Rights
JV-419A	1/1/2007	Guardianship—Child's Consent and Waiver of Rights
JV-420	7/1/2011	Dispositional Attachment: Removal From Custodial Parent—Placement With Previously Noncustodial Parent (Welf. & Inst. Code, §§ 361, 361.2)
JV-421	1/1/2020	Dispositional Attachment: Removal From Custodial Parent—Placement With Nonparent (Welf. & Inst. Code, §§ 361, 361.2)
JV-425	7/1/2011	Findings and Orders After In-Home Status Review Hearing (Welf. & Inst. Code, § 364)
JV-426	7/1/2011	Findings and Orders After In-Home Status Review Hearing—Child Placed With Previously Noncustodial Parent (Welf. & Inst. Code, §§ 364, 366.21)
JV-430	1/1/2020	Findings and Orders After Six-Month Status Review Hearing (Welf. & Inst. Code, § 366.21(e))
JV-431	7/1/2011	Six-Month Prepermanency Attachment: Child Reunified (Welf. & Inst. Code, § 366.21(e))
JV-432	1/1/2020	Six-Month Permanency Attachment: Reunification Services Continued (Welf. & Inst. Code, § 366.21(e))
JV-433	1/1/2020	Six-Month Permanency Attachment: Reunification Services Terminated (Welf. & Inst. Code, § 366.21(e))
JV-435	1/1/2020	Findings and Orders After 12-Month Permanency Hearing (Welf. & Inst. Code, § 366.21(f))
JV-436	7/1/2011	Twelve-Month Permanency Attachment: Child Reunified (Welf. & Inst. Code, § 366.21(f))
JV-437	1/1/2020	Twelve-Month Permanency Attachment: Reunification Services Continued (Welf. & Inst. Code, § 366.21(f))
JV-438	1/1/2020	Twelve-Month Permanency Attachment: Reunification Services Terminated (Welf. & Inst. Code, § 366.21(f))
JV-440	1/1/2020	Findings and Orders After 18-Month Permanency Hearing (Welf. & Inst. Code, § 366.22)
JV-441	7/1/2011	Eighteen-Month Permanency Attachment: Child Reunified (Welf. & Inst. Code, § 366.22)
JV-442	1/1/2020	Eighteen-Month Permanency Attachment: Reunification Services Terminated (Welf. & Inst. Code, § 366.22)
JV-443	1/1/2020	Eighteen-Month Permanency Attachment: Reunification Services Continued (Welf. & Inst. Code, § 366.22)
JV-445	1/1/2018	Findings and Orders After Postpermanency Hearing—Parental Rights Terminated; Permanent Plan of Adoption (Welf. & Inst. Code, § 366.3(f))
JV-446	1/1/2018	Findings and Orders After Postpermanency Hearing—Permanent Plan Other Than Adoption (Welf. & Inst. Code, § 366.3)

---

* Adopted for mandatory use by all courts.

JV-448	1/1/2006	Order Granting Authority to Consent to Medical, Surgical, and Dental Care (Welf. & Inst. Code, § 366.27)
JV-450*	1/1/2012	Order for Prisoner's Appearance at Hearing Affecting Parental Rights
JV-451*	1/1/2012	Prisoner's Statement Regarding Appearance at Hearing Affecting Parental Rights
JV-455	1/1/2020	Findings and Orders After 24-Month Permanency Hearing (Welf. & Inst. Code, § 366.25)
JV-456	7/1/2011	Twenty-Four-Month Permanency Attachment: Child Reunified (Welf. & Inst. Code, § 366.25)
JV-457	1/1/2021	Twenty-Four-Month Prepermanency Attachment: Reunification Services Terminated (Welf. & Inst. Code, § 366.25)
JV-460	1/1/2021	Attachment: Additional Findings and Orders For Child Approaching Majority—Dependency
JV-461*	1/1/2021	Findings and Orders After Nonminor Disposition Hearing
JV-461(A)*	1/1/2021	Dispositional Attachment: Nonminor Dependent
JV-462	1/1/2021	Findings and Orders After Nonminor Dependent Status Review Hearing
JV-463*	1/1/2021	Nonminor's Informed Consent to Hold Disposition Hearing
JV-464-INFO*	1/1/2019	How to Ask to Return to Juvenile Court Jurisdiction and Foster Care
JV-464-INFO* C	1/1/2019	How to Ask to Return to Juvenile Court Jurisdiction and Foster Care (Chinese)
JV-464-INFO* K	1/1/2019	How to Ask to Return to Juvenile Court Jurisdiction and Foster Care (Korean)
JV-464-INFO* S	1/1/2019	How to Ask to Return to Juvenile Court Jurisdiction and Foster Care (Spanish)
JV-464-INFO* V	1/1/2019	How to Ask to Return to Juvenile Court Jurisdiction and Foster Care (Vietnamese)
JV-466*	1/1/2019	Request to Return to Juvenile Court Jurisdiction and Foster Care
JV-468*	7/1/2012	Confidential Information—Request to Return to Juvenile Court Jurisdiction and Foster Care
JV-470	1/1/2019	Findings and Orders Regarding Prima Facie Showing on Nonminor's Request to Reenter Foster Care
JV-472	1/1/2019	Findings and Orders After Hearing to Consider Nonminor's Request to Reenter Foster Care
JV-474	1/1/2019	Nonminor Dependent—Consent to Copy and Inspect Nonminor Dependent Court File
JV-475	10/25/2013	Agreement of Adoption of Nonminor or Dependent
JV-477	10/25/2013	Consent of Spouse or Registered Domestic Partner to Adoption of Nonminor Dependent
JV-479	10/25/2013	Order of Adoption of Nonminor Dependent
JV-500*	1/1/2007	Parentage Inquiry
JV-500* S	1/1/2007	Parentage Inquiry (Spanish)
JV-501*	1/1/2007	Parentage—Findings and Judgment
JV-501* S	1/1/2007	Parentage—Findings and Judgment (Spanish)
JV-505*	1/1/2008	Statement Regarding Parentage
JV-505* S	1/1/2008	Statement Regarding Parentage (Spanish)
JV-510*	1/1/2019	Proof of Service—Juvenile
JV-510(A)	1/1/2019	Attachment to Proof of Service—Juvenile (Additional Persons Served)
JV-520*	1/1/2007	Fax Filing Cover Sheet
JV-520* S	1/1/2007	Fax Filing Cover Sheet (Spanish)
JV-525*	7/1/2007	Order to Attend Court or Provide Documents: Subpoena/Subpoena Duces Tecum [same as CR-125*]
JV-530*	7/1/2002	Certified Request for Pupil Records—Truancy
JV-530 S	7/1/2002	Certified Request for Pupil Records—Truancy (Spanish)
JV-531*	7/1/2002	Local Educational Agency Response to JV-530
JV-531 S	7/1/2002	Local Educational Agency Response to JV-530 (Spanish)
JV-535*	1/1/2021	Order Designating Educational Rights Holder
JV-535* S	1/1/2014	Order Designating Educational Rights Holder (Spanish)
JV-535(A)*	9/1/2020	Attachment to Order Designating Educational Rights Holder
JV-535(A) S	1/1/2014	Attachment to Order Designating Educational Rights Holder (Spanish)
JV-535-INFO	9/1/2020	Information on Educational Rights Holders
JV-536*	1/1/2014	Local Educational Agency Response to JV-535—Appointment of Surrogate Parent
JV-536* S	1/1/2014	Local Educational Agency Response to JV-535—Appointment of Surrogate Parent (Spanish)
JV-537	1/1/2014	Educational Rights Holder Statement
JV-537 S	1/1/2014	Educational Rights Holder Statement (Spanish)
JV-538	1/1/2014	Findings and Orders Regarding Transfer from School of Origin
JV-539	1/1/2014	Request for Hearing Regarding Child's Access to Services
JV-539 S	1/1/2014	Request for Hearing Regarding Child's Education (Spanish)
JV-540*	1/1/2014	Notice of Hearing on Joinder—Juvenile
JV-540 S	1/1/2014	Notice of Hearing on Joinder—Juvenile (Spanish)
JV-548*	1/1/2017	Motion for Transfer Out
JV-550*	1/1/2017	Juvenile Court Transfer-Out Orders
JV-550* S	1/1/2007	Juvenile Court Transfer Orders — Spanish
JV-552*	1/1/2017	Juvenile Court Transfer-Out Orders—Nonminor Dependent
JV-552* S	1/1/2017	Juvenile Court Transfer-Out Orders—Nonminor Dependent (Spanish)
JV-555	1/1/2020	Notice of Intent to Place Child Out of County
JV-556	1/1/2019	Objection to Out-of-County Placement and Notice of Hearing
JV-565	1/1/2013	Request for Assistance With Expedited Placement Under the Interstate Compact on the Placement of Children
JV-567*	1/1/2013	Expedited Placement Under the Interstate Compact on the Placement of Children: Findings and Orders
JV-569*	9/1/2020	Proof of Service—Petition for Access to Juvenile Case File
JV-570*	9/1/2020	Petition for Access to Juvenile Case File

* Adopted for mandatory use by all courts.

JV-570 S*	1/1/2009	Request for Disclosure of Juvenile Case File (Spanish)
JV-571*	9/1/2020	Notice of Petition for Access to Juvenile Case File
JV-572*	9/1/2020	Objection to Release of Juvenile Case File
JV-573*	1/1/2021	Order on Petition for Access to Juvenile Case File
JV-574*	1/1/2021	Order After Judicial Review on Petition for Access to Juvenile Case File
JV-575*	1/1/2007	Petition to Obtain Report of Law Enforcement Agency
JV-575* S	1/1/2007	Petition to Obtain Report of Law Enforcement Agency (Spanish)
JV-580*	1/1/2006	Notice to Child and Parent/Guardian RE: Release of Juvenile Police Records and Objection
JV-580 S	1/1/2006	Notice to Child and Parent/Guardian RE: Release of Juvenile Police Records and Objection (Spanish)
JV-590	9/1/2018	Order to Seal Juvenile Records—Welfare and Institutions Code Section 781
JV-590* S	9/1/2018	Order to Seal Juvenile Records—Welfare and Institutions Code Section 781 (Spanish)
JV-591	7/1/2016	Acknowledgment of Juvenile Record Sealed
JV-592	1/1/2021	Prosecutor Request for Access to Sealed Juvenile Case File
JV-593	1/1/2021	Notice of Prosecutor Request for Access to Sealed Juvenile Case File
JV-594	1/1/2021	Response to Prosecutor Request for Access to Sealed Juvenile Case File
JV-595	1/1/2021	Request to Seal Juvenile Records
JV-595-INFO*	1/1/2021	How to Ask the Court to Seal Your Records
JV-595-INFO* S	9/1/2017	How to Ask the Court to Seal Your Records (Spanish)
JV-596	9/1/2018	Dismissal and Sealing of Records—Welfare and Institutions Code Section 786
JV-596-INFO*	1/1/2020	Sealing of Records for Satisfactory Completion of Probation
JV-596-INFO* S	9/1/2017	Sealing of Records for Satisfactory Completion of Probation (Spanish)
JV-597	9/1/2018	Probation Department Notice on Sealing of Records After Diversion Program (Welf. & Inst. Code § 786.5)
JV-598	9/1/2018	Petition to Review Denial of Sealing of Records After Diversion Program
JV-599	1/1/2021	Order on Prosecutor Request for Access to Sealed File
JV-600	1/1/2020	Juvenile Wardship Petition
JV-600 S	9/1/2018	Juvenile Wardship Petition (Spanish)
JV-610	1/1/2007	Child Habitually Disobedient (§ 601(a))
JV-610 S	1/1/2007	Child Habitually Disobedient (§ 601(a)) (Spanish)
JV-611	1/1/2007	Child Habitually Truant (§ 601(b))
JV-611 S	1/1/2007	Child Habitually Truant (§ 601(b)) (Spanish)
JV-615	1/1/2012	Deferred Entry of Judgment Notice of Noncompliance
JV-615 S	1/1/2012	Deferred Entry of Judgment Notice of Noncompliance (Spanish)
JV-618	1/1/2020	Waiver of Rights—Juvenile Justice
JV-618 S	1/1/2014	Waiver of Rights—Juvenile Delinquency (Spanish)
JV-620*	1/1/2007	Violation of Law By Child
JV-620* S	1/1/2007	Violation of Law By Child (Spanish)
JV-622	1/1/2006	Informal Probation Agreement
JV-624	1/1/2012	Terms and Conditions
JV-625	9/1/2018	Notice of Hearing—Juvenile Delinquency Proceeding
JV-625 S	1/1/2012	Notice of Hearing—Juvenile Delinquency Proceeding (Spanish)
JV-635*	5/22/2017	Promise to Appear—Juvenile Delinquency (Juvenile 14 Years or Older)
JV-635* S	5/22/2017	Promise to Appear—Juvenile Delinquency (Juvenile 14 years or Older) (Spanish)
JV-640	1/1/2012	Delinquency Court Proceeding Findings and Orders
JV-642	5/22/2017	Initial Appearance Hearing—Juvenile Delinquency
JV-644	1/1/2012	Jurisdiction Hearing—Juvenile Delinquency
JV-665	1/1/2016	Disposition—Juvenile Delinquency
JV-667	1/1/2016	Custodial and Out-of-Home Placement Disposition Attachment
JV-672	1/1/2018	Findings and Orders After Six-Month Prepermanency Hearing—Delinquency
JV-674	1/1/2018	Findings and Orders After Permanency Hearing—Delinquency
JV-678	1/1/2018	Findings and Orders After Postpermanency Hearing—Delinquency
JV-680	1/1/2021	Findings and Orders for Child Approaching Majority—Delinquency
JV-681	7/1/2012	Attachment: Hearing for Dismissal—Additional Findings and Orders—Foster Care Placement—Delinquency
JV-682	3/15/2019	Findings and Orders After Hearing to Modify Delinquency Jurisdiction to Transition Jurisdiction for Child Younger Than 18 Years of Age [Renumbered to JV-688]
JV-683	3/15/2019	Findings and Orders After Hearing to Modify Delinquency Jurisdiction to Transition Jurisdiction for Ward Older Than 18 Years of Age
JV-688	1/1/2014	Continuance—Juvenile Delinquency [Renumbered from JV-682]
JV-690	1/1/2019	School Notification of Court Adjudication (Welfare & Institutions Code Section 827(b) and Education Code Section 48267)
JV-692	1/1/2012	Notification to Sheriff of Juvenile Delinquency Felony Adjudication (Welfare & Institutions Code Section 827.2)
JV-700	7/1/2016	Declaration of Eligibility for Appointment to Represent Youth in Delinquency Court
JV-710	1/1/2021	Order to Transfer Juvenile to Criminal Court Jurisdiction (Welfare and Institutions Code, § 707)
JV-710 S	5/22/2017	Order to Transfer Juvenile to Criminal Court Jurisdiction (Welfare and Institutions Code, § 707) (Spanish)
JV-720	1/1/2008	*[Revoked]* Supplemental Petition for More Restrictive Placement (Attachment) (Welfare & Institutions Code, § 777(a))

---

* Adopted for mandatory use by all courts.

JV-720 S	1/1/2008	*[Revoked]* Supplemental Petition for More Restrictive Placement (Attachment) Welfare and Institutions Code, §777(a) (Spanish)
JV-730	1/1/2008	*[Revoked]* Supplemental Petition for Commitment for 30 Days or Less (Attachment) (Welfare & Institutions Code, § 777(b))
JV-730 S	1/1/2008	*[Revoked]* Supplemental Petition for Commitment for 30 Days or Less (Attachment) Welfare and Institutions Code, § 777(b) (Spanish)
JV-732*	9/1/2017	Commitment to the California Department of Corrections and Rehabilitation, Division of Juvenile Facilities
JV-732 S	9/1/2017	Commitment to the California Department of Corrections and Rehabilitation, Division of Juvenile Facilities (Spanish)
JV-735	5/22/2017	Juvenile Notice of Violation of Probation
JV-735 S	5/22/2017	Juvenile Notice of Violation of Probation (Spanish)
JV-740	1/1/2012	Petition to Modify, Change, or Set Aside Previous Orders—Change of Circumstances
JV-740 S	1/1/2012	Petition to Modify, Change, or Set Aside Previous Orders—Change of Circumstances (Spanish)
JV-742	1/1/2019	Request to Vacate Disposition and Dismiss Penal Code Section 647f Adjudication
JV-743	1/1/2019	Order after Request to Vacate Disposition and Dismiss Penal Code Section 647f Adjudication
JV-744	7/1/2017	Request to Reduce Juvenile Marijuana Offense (Health and Safety Code, § 11361.8(m))
JV-744A	7/1/2017	Attachment to Request to Reduce Juvenile Marijuana Offense (Health and Safety Code, § 11361.8(m))
JV-745	7/1/2017	*[Revoked]* Juvenile Order After Request to Reduce Marijuana Offense
JV-745	7/1/2017	Prosecuting Agency Response to Request to Reduce Juvenile Marijuana Offense (Health and Safety Code, § 11361.8(m))
JV-746	7/1/2017	Order After Request to Reduce Juvenile Marijuana Offense (Health and Safety Code, § 11361.8(m))
JV-748	1/1/2019	Request to Expunge Arrest or Vacate Adjudication (Human Trafficking Victim) (Penal Code, § 236.14)
JV-749	1/1/2019	Order after Request to Expunge Arrest or Vacate Adjudication (Human Trafficking Victim) (Penal Code, § 236.14)
JV-750*	9/1/2018	Determination of Eligibility—Deferred Entry of Judgment—Juvenile
JV-750* S	9/1/2018	Determination of Eligibility—Deferred Entry of Judgment—Juvenile (Spanish)
JV-751*	7/1/2010	Citation and Written Notification for Deferred Entry of Judgment—Juvenile
JV-755	1/1/2012	Deferred Entry of Judgment—Dismissal and Sealing of Juvenile Records
JV-755 S	1/1/2012	Deferred Entry of Judgment—Dismissal and Sealing of Juvenile Records (Spanish)
JV-760	1/1/2012	Deferred Entry of Judgment Order
JV-790	3/5/2018	Order for Victim Restitution *[same as CR-110]*
JV-791	7/1/2015	Abstract of Judgment—Restitution *[same as CR-111]*
JV-792	9/1/2018	Instructions: Order for Victim Restitution *[same as CR-112]*
JV-792 S	9/1/2018	Instructions: Order for Restitution and Abstract of Judgment (Spanish)
JV-793	1/1/2014	Instructions: Abstract of Judgment—Restitution *[same as CR-113]*
JV-794	9/1/2017	Petition to Terminate Wardship and Order
JV-796	1/1/2009	Petition for Expungement of DNA Profiles and Samples (Pen. Code, §299) *[same as CR-185]*
JV-798	1/1/2009	Order for Expungement of DNA Profiles and Samples (Pen. Code, §299) *[same as CR-186]*
JV-800	9/1/2020	Notice of Appeal—Juvenile
JV-805-INFO	1/1/2020	Information Regarding Appeal Rights
JV-810	1/1/2021	Recommendation for Appointment of Appellate Attorney for Child
JV-816	1/1/2017	Application for Extension of Time to File Brief (Juvenile Delinquency Case)
JV-817	1/1/2017	Application for Extension of Time to File Brief (Juvenile Dependency Case)
JV-820	9/1/2020	Notice of Intent to File Writ Petition and Request for Record to Review Order Setting a Hearing Under Welfare and Institutions Code Section 366.26 (California Rules of Court, Rule 8.450)
JV-822	9/1/2020	Notice of Intent to File Writ Petition and Request for Record to Review Order Designating or Denying Specific Placement of a Dependent Child After Termination of Parental Rights (California Rules of Court, Rule 8.454)
JV-825	1/1/2017	Petition for Extraordinary Writ
JV-826	1/1/2007	Denial of Petition (California Rules of Court, Rules 8.452, 8.456)
JV-826 S	1/1/2007	Denial of Petition (California Rules of Court, Rules 8.452, 8.456) (Spanish)
JV-828	7/1/2010	Notice of Action (California Rules of Court, Rule 8.452)

LANGUAGE ACCESS

LA-350	9/1/2019	Notice of Available Language Assistance—Service Provider
LA-400	9/1/2019	Service Not Available in My Language: Request to Change Court Order
LA-450	9/1/2019	Service Not Available in My Language: Order

MENACING DOG

MD-100	9/1/2018	Petition to Determine If Dog Is Potentially Dangerous or Vicious *[renumbered from MC-600]*
MD-109	9/1/2018	Notice of Hearing *[renumbered from MC-601]*
MD-130	9/1/2018	Order After Hearing *[renumbered from MC-602]*
MD-140	9/1/2018	Notice of Appeal *[renumbered from MC-603]*

---

* Adopted for mandatory use by all courts.

MILITARY SERVICE

MIL-010*	1/1/2012	Notice of Petition and Petition for Relief From Financial Obligation During Military Service
MIL-015*	1/1/2012	Declaration In Support of Petition for Relief From Financial Obligations During Military Service
MIL-020	1/1/2012	Order on Petition for Relief From Financial Obligations During Military Service
MIL-100	1/1/2021	Notification of Military Veteran/Reserve/Active Status
MIL-183	1/1/2016	Petition for Dismissal (Military Personnel) *[same as CR-183]*
MIL-184	1/22/2019	Order for Dismissal (Military Personnel) *[same as CR-184]*
MIL-412	1/1/2020	Petition for Resentencing Based on Health Conditions Due to Military Service Listed in Penal Code Section 1170.91(b) *[same as CR-412]*

MISCELLANEOUS

MC-001	9/1/2018	*[Renumbered]* Juror Questionnaire for Civil Cases *[renumbered to JURY-001]*
MC-002	9/1/2018	*[Renumbered]* Juror Questionnaire for Criminal Cases/Capital Case Supplement *[renumbered to JURY-002]*
MC-003	9/1/2018	*[Renumbered]* Juror Questionnaire for Expedited Jury Trials *[renumbered to JURY-003]*
MC-005*	1/1/2007	Facsimile Transmission Cover Sheet (Fax Filing)
MC-010	9/1/2017	Memorandum of Costs (Summary)
MC-011	9/1/2017	Memorandum of Costs (Worksheet)
MC-012*	9/1/2018	Memorandum of Costs After Judgment, Acknowledgment of Credit, and Declaration of Accrued Interest
MC-013-INFO	1/1/2018	Information Sheet for Calculating Interest and Amount Owed on a Judgment
MC-020	1/1/1987	Additional Page [to be attached to any form]
MC-025	7/1/2009	Attachment to Judicial Council Form
MC-025 S	7/1/2009	Attachment to Judicial Council Form (Spanish)
MC-030	1/1/2006	Declaration
MC-031	7/1/2005	Attached Declaration
MC-040	1/1/2013	Notice of Change of Address or Other Contact Information
MC-050*	1/1/2009	Substitution of Attorney—Civil (Without Court Order)
MC-051*	1/1/2007	Notice of Motion and Motion to Be Relieved as Counsel—Civil
MC-052*	1/1/2007	Declaration in Support of Attorney's Motion to Be Relieved as Counsel—Civil
MC-053*	1/1/2007	Order Granting Attorney's Motion to Be Relieved as Counsel—Civil
MC-060*	9/1/2018	*[Renumbered]* Confidential Cover Sheet False Claims Action *[renumbered to CM-011*]*
MC-070	9/1/2018	*[Renumbered]* Juror's Motion to Set Aside Sanctions and Order *[renumbered to JURY-010]*
MC-095*	9/1/2018	*[Renumbered]* Petition and Declaration Regarding Unresolved Claims and Deposit of Undistributed Surplus Proceeds of Trustee's Sale *[renumbered to CIV-170*]*
MC-100	9/1/2018	*[Renumbered]* Petition for Order Striking and Releasing Lien, etc. (Government Employee) *[renumbered to CIV-160]*
MC-101	9/1/2018	*[Renumbered]* Order to Show Cause (Government Employee) *[renumbered to CIV-161]*
MC-120*	1/1/2017	Confidential Reference List of Identifiers
MC-125*	1/1/2019	Confidential Information From Under Civil Code Section 1708.85
MC-200	1/1/2018	Claim Opposing Forfeiture (Health & Saf. Code, § 11488.5)
MC-201	1/1/2009	Claim Opposing Forfeiture of Vehicle (Vehicle Code, § 14607.6)
MC-202	2/1/1995	Petition for Forfeiture of Vehicle and Notice of Hearing
MC-210	9/1/2018	*[Renumbered]* Defendant's Financial Statement on Eligibility for Appointment of Counsel and Reimbursement and Record on Appeal at Public Expense *[renumbered to CR-105]*
MC-245	1/1/2018	*[Renumbered]* Motion to Vacate Conviction or Sentence (Pen. Code, §§ 1016.5, 1473.7) *[renumbered to CR-187]*
MC-246	1/1/2018	*[Renumbered]* Order on Motion to Vacate Conviction or Sentence (Pen. Code, §§ 1016.5, 1473.7) *[renumbered to CR-188]*
MC-265	9/1/2018	*[Renumbered]* Petition for Writ of Habeas Corpus—LPS Act (Mental Health) *[renumbered to HC-002]*
MC-270	9/1/2018	*[Renumbered]* Petition for Writ of Habeas Corpus—Penal Commitment (Mental Health) *[renumbered to HC-003]*
MC-275	9/1/2018	*[Renumbered]* Petition for Writ of Habeas Corpus *[renumbered to HC-001]*
MC-280	9/1/2018	*[Renumbered]* Order for Commitment (Sexually Violent Predator) *[renumbered to CR-173]*
MC-281	9/1/2018	*[Renumbered]* Order for Extended Commitment (Sexually Violent Predator) *[renumbered to CR-174]*
MC-300*	9/1/2018	*[Renumbered]* Petition for Declaration of Emancipation of Minor, Order Prescribing Notice, Declaration of Emancipation, and Order Denying Petition *[renumbered to EM-100*]*
MC-301*	9/1/2018	*[Renumbered]* Emancipation Pamphlet *[renumbered to EM-100-INFO]*
MC-301 C	9/1/2018	*[Renumbered]* Emancipation Pamphlet (Chinese) *[renumbered to EM-100-INFO C]*
MC-301 K	9/1/2018	*[Renumbered]* Emancipation Pamphlet (Korean) *[renumbered to EM-100-INFO K]*
MC-301 S	9/1/2018	*[Renumbered]* Emancipation Pamphlet (Spanish) *[renumbered to EM-100-INFO S]*
MC-301 V	9/1/2018	*[Renumbered]* Emancipation Pamphlet (Vietnamese) *[renumbered to EM-100-INFO V]*
MC-305*	9/1/2018	*[Renumbered]* Notice of Hearing—Emancipation of Minor *[renumbered to EM-109*]*
MC-306*	9/1/2018	*[Renumbered]* Emancipation of Minor Income and Expense Declaration *[renumbered to EM-115*]*
MC-310*	9/1/2018	*[Renumbered]* Declaration of Emancipation of Minor After Hearing *[renumbered to EM-130*]*

---

* Adopted for mandatory use by all courts.

MC-315	9/1/2018	*[Renumbered]* Emancipated Minor's Application to California Department of Motor Vehicles *[renumbered to EM-140]*
MC-350*	1/1/2021	Petition for Approval of Compromise of Claim or Action or Disposition of Proceeds of Judgment for Minor or Person With A Disability
MC-350(A-12b(5))	1/1/2021	Additional Medical Service Providers Attachment to Petition for Approval of Compromise of Claim or Action or Disposition of Proceeds of Judgment *[renumbered from MC-350(A-13b(5))]*
MC-350(A-13b(5))	1/1/2010	Medical Service Provider Attachment to Petition to Approve Compromise of Claim or Action or Disposition of Proceeds of Judgment *[renumbered to MC-350(A-12b(5))]*
MC-350EX*	1/1/2021	Petition for Expedited Approval of Compromise of Claim or Action or Disposition of Proceeds of Judgment for Minor or Person With a Disability
MC-351*	1/1/2021	Order Approving Compromise of Claim or Action or Disposition of Proceeds of Judgment for Minor or Person With a Disability
MC-355*	1/1/2021	Order to Deposit Funds in Blocked Account
MC-356*	1/1/2021	Acknowledgment of Receipt of Order and Funds for Deposit in Blocked Account
MC-357*	1/1/2021	Petition to Withdraw Funds From Blocked Account
MC-358*	1/1/2021	Order Authorizing Withdrawal of Funds From Blocked Account
MC-360*	9/1/2018	*[Renumbered]* Petition to Establish Fact, Time, and Place of Death (Miscellaneous) *[renumbered to BMD-003*]*
MC-360A*	9/1/2018	*[Renumbered]* Declaration in Support of Petition to Establish Fact, Time, and Place of Death (Miscellaneous) *[renumbered to BMD-003A*]*
MC-361*	9/1/2018	*[Renumbered]* Petition to Establish Fact, Time, and Place of Birth (Miscellaneous) *[renumbered to BMD-001*]*
MC-361A*	9/1/2018	*[Renumbered]* Declaration in Support of Petition to Establish Fact, Time, and Place of Birth (Miscellaneous) *[renumbered to BMD-001A*]*
MC-362*	9/1/2018	*[Renumbered]* Petition to Establish Fact, Date, and Place of Marriage (Miscellaneous) *[renumbered to BMD-002*]*
MC-362A*	9/1/2018	*[Renumbered]* Declaration in Support of Petition to Establish Fact, Date, and Place of Marriage (Miscellaneous) *[renumbered to BMD-002A*]*
MC-400	9/1/2018	*[Renumbered]* Proof of Enrollment or Completion (Alcohol or Drug Program) *[renumbered to CR-220]*
MC-410	1/1/2021	Disability Accommodation Request
MC-410-INFO	1/1/2021	How to Request a Disability Accommodation for Court
MC-500*	1/1/2007	Media Request to Photograph, Record, or Broadcast
MC-510*	1/1/2007	Order on Media Request to Permit Coverage
MC-600	9/1/2018	*[Renumbered]* Petition to Determine if Dog is Potentially Dangerous or Vicious (Menacing Dog) *[renumbered to MD-100]*
MC-601	9/1/2018	*[Renumbered]* Notice of Hearing (Menacing Dog) *[renumbered to MD-109]*
MC-602	9/1/2018	*[Renumbered]* Order After Hearing (Menacing Dog) *[renumbered to MD-130]*
MC-603	9/1/2018	*[Renumbered]* Notice of Appeal (Menacing Dog) *[renumbered to MD-140]*
MC-700*	9/1/2018	*[Renumbered]* Prefiling Order—Vexatious Litigant *[renumbered to VL-100*]*
MC-701	9/1/2018	*[Renumbered]* Request to File New Litigation by Vexatious Litigant *[renumbered to VL-110]*
MC-702	9/1/2018	*[Renumbered]* Order to File New Litigation by Vexatious Litigant *[renumbered to VL-115]*
MC-703	9/1/2018	*[Renumbered]* Application for Order to Vacate Prefiling Order and Remove Plaintiff/Petitioner From Judicial Council Vexatious Litigant List *[renumbered to VL-120]*
MC-704	9/1/2018	*[Renumbered]* Order on Application to Vacate Prefiling Order and Remove Plaintiff/Petitioner From Judicial Council Vexatious Litigant List *[renumbered to VL-125]*
MC-800	1/1/2002	Court Clerks Office: Signage
MC-950*	9/1/2018	*[Renumbered]* Notice of Limited Scope Representation *[renumbered to CIV-150*]*
MC-955	9/1/2018	*[Renumbered]* Application to Be Relieved as Attorney on Completion of Limited Scope Representation *[renumbered to CIV-151]*
MC-956	9/1/2018	*[Renumbered]* Objection to Application to Be Relieved as Attorney on Completion of Limited Scope Representation *[renumbered to CIV-152]*
MC-958	9/1/2018	*[Renumbered]* Order on Application to Be Relieved as Attorney on Completion of Limited Scope Representation *[renumbered to CIV-153]*
MC-1000	1/1/2019	Request for Review of Denial of Request to Remove Name From Gang Database

NAME CHANGE

NC-100*	9/1/2018	Petition for Change of Name
NC-100-INFO	1/1/2019	Instructions for Filing a Petition for Change of Name
NC-110*	9/1/2018	Attachment to Petition for Change of Name
NC-110G*	1/1/2001	Supplemental Attachment to Petition for Change of Name (Declaration of Guardian)
NC-120*	7/1/2007	Order to Show Cause for Change of Name (Change of Name)
NC-121*	1/1/2019	Proof of Service of Order to Show Cause
NC-125*	1/1/2019	Order to Show Cause for Change of Name to Conform to Gender Identity *[same as NC-225*]*
NC-130*	9/1/2018	Decree Changing Name
NC-130G*	9/1/2018	Decree Changing Name of Minor (By Guardian)
NC-150	9/1/2018	Notice of Hearing on Petition
NC-200*	9/1/2018	Petition for Change of Name, Recognition of Change of Gender, and Issuance of New Birth Certificate

* Adopted for mandatory use by all courts.

NC-210	9/1/2018	*[Revoked]* Declaration of Physician—Attachment to Petition (Change of Name and Gender/Change of Gender) *[same as NC-310]*
NC-220*	9/1/2018	*[Revoked]* Order to Show Cause for Change of Name
NC-225*	1/1/2019	Order to Show Cause for Change of Name to Conform to Gender Identity *[same as NC-125*]*
NC-230*	9/1/2018	Decree Changing Name and Order Recognizing Change of Gender and for Issuance of New Birth Certificate
NC-300	9/1/2018	Petition for Recognition of Change of Gender and for Issuance of New Birth Certificate
NC-310	9/1/2018	*[Revoked]* Declaration of Physician—Attachment to Petition (Change of Name and Gender/Change of Gender) *[same as NC-210]*
NC-320	9/1/2018	*[Revoked]* Setting of Hearing on Petition for Change of Gender and Issuance of New Birth Certificate
NC-330	9/1/2018	Order Recognizing Change of Gender and for Issuance of New Birth Certificate
NC-400*	1/1/2019	Confidential Cover Sheet—Name Change Proceeding Under Address Confidentiality Program (Safe at Home)
NC-400-INFO	1/1/2019	Information Sheet for Name Change Proceedings Under Address Confidentiality Program (Safe at Home)
NC-410*	1/1/2010	Application to File Documents Under Seal in Name Change Proceeding Under Address Confidentiality Program (Safe at Home)
NC-420*	1/1/2019	Declaration in Support of Application to File Documents Under Seal in Name Change Proceeding Under Address Confidentiality Program (Safe at Home)
NC-425	1/1/2010	Order on Application to File Documents Under Seal in Name Change Proceeding Under Address Confidentiality Program (Safe at Home)
NC-500*	1/1/2019	Petition for Recognition of Minor's Change of Gender and Issuance of New Birth Certificate and Change of Name
NC-500-INFO	9/1/2019	Instructions for Filing Petition for Recognition of Minor's Change of Gender and Issuance of New Birth Certificate and Change of Name
NC-510G*	1/1/2019	Declaration of Guardian or Dependency Attorney (Supplemental Attachment to Form NC-500)
NC-520*	9/1/2019	Order to Show Cause for Recognition of Minor's Change of Gender and Issuance of New Birth Certificate and Change of Name
NC-530G*	1/1/2019	Order Recognizing Minor's Change of Gender and for Issuance of New Birth Certificate (By Guardian or Dependency Attorney)

PLEADINGS
Contract

PLD-C-001	1/1/2007	Complaint—Contract *(formerly 982.1(20))*
PLD-C-001(1)	1/1/2007	Cause of Action—Breach of Contract *(formerly 982.1(21))*
PLD-C-001(2)	1/1/2009	Cause of Action—Common Counts *(formerly 982.1(22))*
PLD-C-001(3)	1/1/2007	Cause of Action—Fraud *(formerly 982.1(23))*
PLD-C-010	1/1/2007	Answer—Contract *(formerly 982.1(35))*

PLEADINGS
General

| PLD-050* | 1/1/2009 | General Denial *(formerly 982(a)(13))* |

PLEADINGS
Personal Injury, Property Damage, Wrongful Death

PLD-PI-001	1/1/2007	Complaint—Personal Injury, Property Damage, Wrongful Death *(formerly 982.1(1))*
PLD-PI-001(1)	1/1/2007	Cause of Action—Motor Vehicle *(formerly 982.1(2))*
PLD-PI-001(2)	1/1/2007	Cause of Action—General Negligence *(formerly 982.1(3))*
PLD-PI-001(3)	1/1/2007	Cause of Action—Intentional Tort *(formerly 982.1(4))*
PLD-PI-001(4)	1/1/2007	Cause of Action—Premises Liability *(formerly 982.1(5))*
PLD-PI-001(5)	1/1/2007	Cause of Action—Products Liability *(formerly 982.1(6))*
PLD-PI-001(6)	1/1/2007	Exemplary Damages Attachment *(formerly 982.1(13))*
PLD-PI-002	1/1/2007	Cross-Complaint—Personal Injury, Property Damage, Wrongful Death *(formerly 982.1(14))*
PLD-PI-003	1/1/2007	Answer—Personal Injury, Property Damage, Wrongful Death *(formerly 982.1(15))*

PLEADINGS
Unlawful Detainer (Landlord/Tenant)

CP10	7/1/2017	Claim of Right to Possession and Notice of Hearing
CP10.5	6/15/2015	Prejudgment Claim of Right to Possession
UD-100	9/1/2020	Complaint—Unlawful Detainer
UD-101*	10/5/2020	Plaintiff's Mandatory Cover Sheet and Supplemental Allegations—Unlawful Detainer
UD-104	10/5/2020	Cover Sheet for Declaration of Covid-19—Related Financial Distress
UD-104(A)	10/5/2020	Attachment—Declaration of Covid-19—Related Financial Distress
UD-105	10/5/2020	Answer—Unlawful Detainer
UD-106	1/1/2014	Form Interrogatories—Unlawful Detainer *[same as DISC-003]*

---

* Adopted for mandatory use by all courts.

UD-110	1/1/2003	Judgment—Unlawful Detainer
UD-110 S	1/1/2003	Judgment—Unlawful Detainer Attachment
UD-115	1/1/2003	Stipulation for Entry of Judgment (Unlawful Detainer)
UD-116	7/1/2003	Declaration for Default Judgment by Court (Unlawful Detainer—Civ. Proc., §585(d))
UD-150*	1/1/2005	Request/Counter-Request To Set Case For Trial—Unlawful Detainer

PROBATE
Decedents Estates

DE-111*	7/1/2017	Petition for Probate
DE-111(A-3d)*	7/1/2017	Waiver of Bond by Heir or Beneficiary [Renumbered to DE-111(A-3e); same as DE-142*]
DE-111(A-3e)*	7/1/2017	Waiver of Bond by Heir or Beneficiary [Renumbered from DE-111(A-3d); same as DE-142*]
DE-115*	1/1/2020	Notice of Hearing on Petition to Determine Claim to Property [same as GC-015*]
DE-120*	1/1/2020	Notice of Hearing—Decedent's Estate or Trust
DE-120(MA)	7/1/2005	Attachment to Notice of Hearing Proof of Service by Mail [same as GC-020(MA)]
DE-120(P)	7/1/2005	Proof of Personal Service of Notice of Hearing—Decedent's Estate or Trust
DE-120(PA)	7/1/2005	Attachment to Notice of Hearing Proof of Personal Service [same as GC-020(PA)]
DE-121*	1/1/2013	Notice of Petition to Administer Estate
DE-121(MA)	1/1/2006	Attachment to Notice of Petition to Administer Estate—Proof of Service by Mail
DE-122*	1/1/2006	Citation—Probate [same as GC-322*]
DE-125*	1/1/1998	Summons (Probate)
DE-131*	1/1/1998	Proof of Subscribing Witness
DE-135*	1/1/1998	Proof of Holographic Instrument
DE-140*	1/1/1998	Order for Probate
DE-142*	7/1/2017	Waiver of Bond by Heir or Beneficiary [same as DE-111(A-3e)*]
DE-147*	1/1/2002	Duties and Liabilities of Personal Representative
DE-147* S	1/1/2001	Confidential Supplement to Duties and Liabilities of Personal Representative
DE-150*	1/1/1998	Letters
DE-154*	1/1/1998	Request for Special Notice [same as GC-035*]
DE-157*	1/1/2013	Notice of Administration to Creditors
DE-160*	1/1/2007	Inventory and Appraisal [same as GC-040*]
DE-161*	1/1/1998	Inventory and Appraisal Attachment [same as GC-041*]
DE-165*	1/1/1998	Notice of Proposed Action (Objection—Consent)
DE-166*	1/1/1998	Waiver of Notice of Proposed Action
DE-172*	1/1/1998	Creditor's Claim
DE-174*	1/1/2009	Allowance or Rejection of Creditor's Claim
DE-200*	1/1/1998	Order Prescribing Notice [same as GC-022*]
DE-221*	1/1/2014	Spousal or Domestic Partner Property Petition
DE-226*	1/1/2015	Spousal or Domestic Partner Property Order
DE-260*	1/1/2006	Report of Sale and Petition for Order Confirming Sale of Real Property [same as GC-060*]
DE-265*	1/1/2015	Order Confirming Sale of Real Property [same as GC-065*]
DE-270*	1/1/1998	Ex Parte Petition for Authority to Sell Securities and Order [same as GC-070*]
DE-275*	1/1/1998	Ex Parte Petition for Approval of Sale of Personal Property and Order [same as GC-075*]
DE-295*	1/1/2006	Ex Parte Petition for Final Discharge and Order [same as GC-395*]
DE-305*	1/1/2020	Affidavit re Real Property of Small Value ($55,425 or Less)
DE-310*	1/1/2020	Petition to Determine Succession to Real Property (Estates of $166,250 or less)
DE-315*	1/1/2020	Order Determining Succession to Real Property (Estates of $166,250 or Less)
DE-350*	1/1/2008	Petition for Appointment of Guardian Ad Litem—Probate [same as GC-100*]
DE-351*	1/1/2004	Order Appointing Guardian Ad Litem—Probate [same as GC-101*]

PROBATE
Guardianships and Conservatorships

GC-005	1/1/2019	Application for Appointment of Counsel
GC-006	1/1/2019	Order Appointing Legal Counsel
GC-010	1/1/2020	Certification of Attorney Qualifications
GC-011*	1/1/2020	[Revoked] Annual Certification of Court-Appointed Attorney
GC-015*	1/1/2020	Notice of Hearing on Petition to Determine Claim to Property [same as DE-115*]
GC-020*	7/1/2005	Notice of Hearing—Guardianship or Conservatorship
GC-020(C)*	7/1/2005	Clerk's Certificate of Posting Notice of Hearing—Guardianship or Conservatorship
GC-020(MA)	7/1/2005	Attachment to Notice of Hearing Proof of Service by Mail [same as DE-120(MA)]
GC-020(P)	7/1/2005	Proof of Personal Service of Notice of Hearing—Guardianship or Conservatorship
GC-020(PA)	7/1/2005	Attachment to Notice of Hearing Proof of Personal Service [same as DE-120(PA)]
GC-021*	1/1/1998	Order Dispensing with Notice
GC-022*	1/1/1998	Order Prescribing Notice [same as DE-200*]
GC-035*	1/1/1998	Request for Special Notice [same as DE-154*]
GC-040*	1/1/2007	Inventory and Appraisal [same as DE-160*]
GC-041*	1/1/1998	Inventory and Appraisal Attachment [same as DE-161*]
GC-042*	1/1/2008	Notice of Filing of Inventory and Appraisal and How to Object to the Inventory or the Appraised Value of Property

---

* Adopted for mandatory use by all courts.

GC-042(MA)	1/1/2008	Attachment to Notice of Filing of Inventory and Appraisal and How to Object to the Inventory or the Appraised Value of Property
GC-045	1/1/2008	Objections to Inventory and Appraisal of Conservator or Guardian
GC-050*	1/1/2009	Notice of Taking Possession or Control of an Asset of Minor or Conservatee
GC-051*	7/1/2005	Notice of Opening or Changing a Guardianship or Conservatorship Account or Safe Deposit Box
GC-060*	1/1/2006	Report of Sale and Petition for Order Confirming Sale of Real Property [same as DE-260*]
GC-065*	1/1/2015	Order Confirming Sale of Real Property [same as DE-265*]
GC-070*	1/1/1998	Ex Parte Petition for Authority to Sell Securities and Order [same as DE-270*]
GC-075*	1/1/1998	Ex Parte Petition for Approval of Sale of Personal Property and Order [same as DE-275*]
GC-079*	1/1/2008	Pre-Move Notice of Proposed Change of Personal Residence of Conservatee or Ward
GC-079(MA)	1/1/2008	Attachment to Pre-Move Notice of Proposed Change of Personal Residence of Conservatee or Ward
GC-080*	1/1/2008	Change of Residence Notice
GC-080(MA)	1/1/2008	Attachment to Post-Move Notice of Change of Residence of Conservatee or Ward
GC-085*	1/1/2000	Petition to Fix Residence Outside the State of California
GC-090*	1/1/2000	Order Fixing Residence Outside the State of California
GC-100*	1/1/2008	Petition for Appointment of Guardian Ad Litem—Probate [same as DE-350*]
GC-101*	1/1/2004	Order Appointing Guardian Ad Litem — Probate [same as DE-351*]
GC-110*	7/1/2008	Petition for Appointment of Temporary Guardian
GC-110(P)*	1/1/2009	Petition for Appointment of Temporary Guardian of the Person
GC-111*	7/1/2008	Petition for Appointment of Temporary Conservator
GC-112	1/1/2009	Ex Parte Application for Good Cause Exception to Notice of Hearing on Petition for Appointment of Temporary Conservator
GC-112(A-1)	1/1/2009	Declaration in Support of Ex Parte Application for Good Cause Exception to Notice of Hearing on Petition for Appointment of Temporary Conservator
GC-112(A-2)	1/1/2009	Declaration Continuation Page
GC-115	1/1/2009	Order on Ex Parte Application for Good Cause Exception to Notice of Hearing on Petition for Appointment of Temporary Conservator
GC-120*	1/1/2009	Declaration Under Uniform Child Custody Jurisdiction and Enforcement Act (UCCJEA) [same as FL-105*]
GC-120* S	1/1/2009	Declaration Under Uniform Child Custody Jurisdiction and Enforcement Act (UCCJEA) (Spanish) [same as FL-105* S]
GC-120(A)*	1/1/2009	Attachment to Declaration Under Uniform Child Custody Jurisdiction and Enforcement Act (UCCJEA) [same as FL-105(A)*]
GC-140*	1/1/2009	Order Appointing Temporary Guardian
GC-141*	1/1/2009	Order Appointing Temporary Conservator
GC-150*	1/1/2015	Letters of Temporary Guardianship or Conservatorship
GC-205*	1/1/2001	Guardianship Pamphlet
GC-205 C	1/1/2001	Guardianship Pamphlet (Chinese)
GC-205 K	1/1/2001	Guardianship Pamphlet (Korean)
GC-205 S	1/1/2001	Guardianship Pamphlet (Spanish)
GC-205 V	1/1/2001	Guardianship Pamphlet (Vietnamese)
GC-210*	7/1/2016	Petition for Appointment of Guardian of Minor
GC-210(A-PF)*	7/1/2009	Professional Fiduciary Attachment to Petition for Appointment of Guardian or Conservator [same as GC-310(A-PF)*]
GC-210(CA)*	7/1/2012	Guardianship Petition—Child Information Attachment (Probate—Guardianships and Conservatorships)
GC-210(P)*	7/1/2016	Petition for Appointment of Guardian of the Person
GC-210(PE)*	7/1/2016	Petition to Extend Guardianship of the Person
GC-211*	1/1/2004	Consent of Proposed Guardian, Nomination of Guardian, and Consent to Appointment of Guardian and Waiver of Notice
GC-212*	7/1/2009	Confidential Guardian Screening Form
GC-220*	1/1/2016	Petition for Special Immigrant Juvenile Findings
GC-220* S	1/1/2016	Petition for Special Immigrant Juvenile Findings (Spanish)
GC-224*	1/1/2016	[Revoked] Order Regarding Eligibility for Special Immigrant Juvenile Status—Probate Guardianship (Probate—Guardianships and Conservatorships)
GC-224*	7/1/2016	Special Immigrant Juvenile Findings [same as FL-357*, JV-357*]
GC-224* S	7/1/2016	Special Immigrant Juvenile Findings (Spanish) [same as FL-357* S, JV-357* S]
GC-240*	7/1/2016	Order Appointing Guardian or Extending Guardianship of the Person
GC-248*	1/1/2001	Duties of Guardian (Probate)
GC-248* S	1/1/2001	Duties of Guardian (Probate) (Spanish)
GC-250*	7/1/2016	Letters of Guardianship
GC-251*	7/1/2003	Confidential Guardianship Status Report
GC-255*	1/1/2006	Petition for Termination of Guardianship
GC-260*	1/1/2006	Order Terminating Guardianship
GC-310*	1/1/2019	Petition for Appointment of Probate Conservator
GC-310(A-PF)*	7/1/2009	Professional Fiduciary Attachment to Petition for Appointment of Guardian or Conservator [same as GC-210(A-PF)*]
GC-312*	1/1/2001	Confidential Supplemental Information
GC-313*	1/1/2019	Attachment Requesting Special Orders Regarding a Major Neurocognitive Disorder

* Adopted for mandatory use by all courts.

GC-314*	7/1/2009	Confidential Conservator Screening Form
GC-320*	7/1/2016	Citation for Conservatorship
GC-322*	1/1/2006	Citation—Probate [same as DE-122*]
GC-330	7/1/2016	Order Appointing Court Investigator
GC-331	7/1/2016	Order Appointing Court Investigator (Review and Successor Conservator Investigations)
GC-332	1/1/2011	Order Setting Biennial Review Investigation and Directing Status Report Before Review
GC-333*	1/1/2019	Ex Parte Application for Order Authorizing Completion of Capacity Declaration—HIPAA
GC-334*	1/1/2019	Ex Parte Order Re Completion of Capacity Declaration—HIPAA
GC-335*	1/1/2019	Capacity Declaration—Conservatorship
GC-335A*	1/1/2019	Major Neurocognitive Disoder Attachment to Capacity Declaration—Conservatorship
GC-336*	1/1/2009	Ex Parte Order Authorizing Disclosure of (Proposed) Conservatee's Health Information to Court Investigator—HIPAA
GC-340*	1/15/2016	Order Appointing Probate Conservator
GC-341*	1/1/2008	Notice of Conservatee's Rights
GC-341* S	1/1/2008	Notice of Conservatee's Rights (Spanish)
GC-341(MA)	1/1/2008	Attachment to Notice of Conservatee's Rights
GC-348*	1/1/2011	Duties of Conservator and Acknowledgment of Receipt of *Handbook for Conservators*
GC-348* S	1/1/2011	Duties of Conservator and Acknowledgment of Receipt of *Handbook for Conservators* (Spanish)
GC-350*	7/1/2015	Letters of Conservatorship
GC-355*	7/1/2011	Determination of Conservatee's Appropriate Level of Care
GC-360*	1/1/2016	Conservatorship Registration Cover Sheet and Attestation of Conservatee's Non-Residence in California
GC-361*	1/1/2016	Notice of Intent to Register Conservatorship
GC-362*	1/1/2016	Conservatorship Registrant's Acknowledgment of Receipt of Handbook for Conservators
GC-363	1/1/2020	Petition for Transfer Orders (California Conservatorship Jurisdiction Act)
GC-364	1/1/2019	Provisional Order for Transfer (California Conservatorship Jurisdiction Act)
GC-365	1/1/2019	Final Order Confirming Transfer (California Conservatorship Jurisdiction Act)
GC-366	1/1/2020	Petition for Orders Accepting Transfer (California Conservatorship Jurisdiction Act)
GC-367	1/1/2019	Provisional Order Accepting Transfer (California Conservatorship Jurisdiction Act)
GC-368	1/1/2019	Final Order Accepting Transfer (California Conservatorship Jurisdiction Act)
GC-380*	1/1/2019	Petition for Exclusive Authority to Give Consent for Medical Treatment
GC-385*	1/1/2019	Order Authorizing Conservator to Give Consent for Medical Treatment
GC-395*	1/1/2006	Ex Parte Petition for Final Discharge and Order [same as DE-295*]
GC-399*	1/1/2017	Notice of the Conservatee's Death
GC-400(A)(1)	1/1/2008	Schedule A, Receipts, Dividends—Standard Account
GC-400(A)(2)	1/1/2008	Schedule A, Receipts, Interest—Standard Account
GC-400(A)(3)	1/1/2008	Schedule A, Receipts, Pensions, Annuities, and Other Regular Periodic Payments—Standard Account
GC-400(A)(4)	1/1/2008	Schedule A, Receipts, Rent—Standard Account
GC-400(A)(5)	1/1/2008	Schedule A, Receipts, Social Security, Veterans' Benefits, Other Public Benefits—Standard Account
GC-400(A)(6)	1/1/2008	Schedule A, Receipts, Other Receipts—Standard Account
GC-400(A)(C)	1/1/2008	Schedule A and C, Receipts and Disbursements Worksheet—Standard Account
GC-400(AP)	1/1/2008	Additional Property Received During Period of Account—Standard and Simplified Accounts [same as GC-405(AP)]
GC-400(B)	1/1/2015	Schedule B, Gains on Sales—Standard and Simplified Accounts [same as GC-405(B)]
GC-400(C)(1)	1/1/2008	Schedule C, Disbursements, Conservatee's Caregiver Expenses—Standard Account
GC-400(C)(2)	1/1/2008	Schedule C, Disbursements, Conservatee's Residential or Long-Term Care Facility Living Expenses—Standard Account
GC-400(C)(3)	1/1/2008	Schedule C, Disbursements, Ward's Education Expenses—Standard Account
GC-400(C)(4)	1/1/2008	Schedule C, Disbursements, Fiduciary and Attorney Fees—Standard Account
GC-400(C)(5)	1/1/2008	Schedule C, Disbursements, General Administration Expenses—Standard Account
GC-400(C)(6)	1/1/2008	Schedule C, Disbursements, Investment Expenses—Standard Account
GC-400(C)(7)	1/1/2008	Schedule C, Disbursements, Living Expenses—Standard Account
GC-400(C)(8)	1/1/2008	Schedule C, Disbursements, Medical Expenses—Standard Account
GC-400(C)(9)	1/1/2008	Schedule C, Disbursements, Property Sale Expenses—Standard Account
GC-400(C)(10)	1/1/2008	Schedule C, Disbursements, Rental Property Expenses—Standard Account
GC-400(C)(11)	1/1/2008	Schedule C, Disbursements, Other Expenses—Standard Account
GC-400(D)	1/1/2015	Schedule D, Losses on Sales—Standard and Simplified Accounts [same as GC-405(D)]
GC-400(DIST)	1/1/2008	Distributions to Conservatee or Ward—Standard and Simplified Accounts [same as GC-405(DIST)]
GC-400(E)(1)	1/1/2008	Cash Assets on Hand at End of Account Period—Standard and Simplified Accounts [same as GC-405(E)(1)]
GC-400(E)(2)	1/1/2008	Non-Cash Assets on Hand at End of Account Period—Standard and Simplified Accounts [same as GC-405(E)(2)]
GC-400(F)	1/1/2008	Schedule F, Changes in Form of Assets—Standard and Simplified Accounts [same as GC-405(F)]
GC-400(G)	1/1/2008	Schedule G, Liabilities at End of Account Period—Standard and Simplified Accounts [same as GC-405(G)]
GC-400(NI)	1/1/2008	Net Income From a Trade or Business—Standard Account
GC-400(NL)	1/1/2008	Net Loss From a Trade or Business—Standard Account
GC-400(OCH)	1/1/2008	Other Charges—Standard and Simplified Accounts [same as GC-405(OCH)]
GC-400(OCR)	1/1/2008	Other Credits—Standard and Simplified Accounts [same as GC-405(OCR)]

* Adopted for mandatory use by all courts.

GC-400(PH)(1)	1/1/2008	Cash Assets on Hand at Beginning of Account Period—Standard and Simplified Accounts *[same as GC-405(PH)(1)]*
GC-400(PH)(2)	1/1/2008	Non-Cash Assets on Hand at Beginning of Account Period—Standard and Simplified Accounts *[same as GC-405(PH)(2)]*
GC-400(SUM)*	1/1/2008	Summary of Account—Standard and Simplified Accounts *[same as GC-405(SUM)*]*
GC-405(A)*	1/1/2008	Schedule A, Receipts—Simplified Account
GC-405(AP)	1/1/2008	Additional Property Received During Period of Account—Standard and Simplified Accounts *[same as GC-400(AP)]*
GC-405(B)	1/1/2015	Schedule B, Gains on Sales—Standard and Simplified Accounts *[same as GC-400(B)]*
GC-405(C)*	1/1/2008	Schedule C, Disbursements—Simplified Account
GC-405(D)	1/1/2015	Schedule D, Losses on Sales—Standard and Simplified Accounts *[same as GC-400(D)]*
GC-405(DIST)	1/1/2008	Distributions to Conservatee or Ward—Standard and Simplified Accounts *[same as GC-400(DIST)]*
GC-405(E)(1)	1/1/2008	Cash Assets on Hand at End of Account Period—Standard and Simplified Accounts *[same as GC-400(E)(1)]*
GC-405(E)(2)	1/1/2008	Non-Cash Assets on Hand at End of Account Period—Standard and Simplified Accounts *[same as GC-400(E)(2)]*
GC-405(F)	1/1/2008	Schedule F, Changes in Form of Assets—Standard and Simplified Accounts *[same as GC-400(F)]*
GC-405(G)	1/1/2008	Schedule G, Liabilities at End of Account Period—Standard and Simplified Accounts *[same as GC-400(G)]*
GC-405(OCH)	1/1/2008	Other Charges—Standard and Simplified Accounts *[same as GC-400(OCH)]*
GC-405(OCR)	1/1/2008	Other Credits—Standard and Simplified Accounts *[same as GC-400(OCR)]*
GC-405(PH)(1)	1/1/2008	Cash Assets on Hand at Beginning of Account Period—Standard and Simplified Accounts *[same as GC-400(PH)(1)]*
GC-405(PH)(2)	1/1/2008	Non-Cash Assets on Hand at Beginning of Account Period—Standard and Simplified Accounts *[same as GC-400(PH)(2)]*
GC-405(SUM)*	1/1/2008	Summary of Account—Standard and Simplified Accounts *[same as GC-400(SUM)*]*
GC-410	1/1/2020	Request and Order for Waiver of Accounting
GC-505	7/1/2007	Forms You Need to Ask the Court to Appoint a Guardian of the Person
GC-505 S	7/1/2007	Forms You Need to Ask the Court to Appoint a Guardian of the Person (Spanish)
GC-510	7/1/2007	What is "Proof of Service" in a Guardianship?
GC-510 S	7/1/2007	What is "Proof of Service" in a Guardianship? (Spanish)

PROOF OF SERVICE

POS-010*	1/1/2007	Proof of Service of Summons
POS-015*	1/1/2005	Notice And Acknowledgment Of Receipt—Civil
POS-020	1/1/2005	Proof Of Personal Service—Civil (Proof of Service) / Information Sheet For Proof Of Personal Service—Civil
POS-020(D)	1/1/2005	Attachment to Proof of Personal Service—Civil (Documents Served) (Proof of Service)
POS-020(P)	1/1/2005	Attachment to Proof of Personal Service—Civil (Persons Served) (Proof of Service)
POS-030	1/1/2005	Proof of Service by First-Class Mail—Civil (Proof of Service) / Information Sheet for Proof of Service by First-Class Mail—Civil
POS-030(D)	1/1/2005	Attachment to Proof of Service by First-Class Mail—Civil (Documents Service) (Proof of Service)
POS-030(P)	1/1/2005	Attachment to Proof of Service by First-Class Mail—Civil (Persons Served) (Proof of Service)
POS-040	1/1/2020	Proof of Service—Civil
POS-040(D)	1/1/2005	Attachment to Proof of Service—Civil (Documents Served)
POS-040(P)	2/1/2017	Attachment to Proof of Service—Civil (Persons Served)
POS-050	2/1/2017	Proof of Electronic Service *[same as EFS-050]*
POS-050(D)	1/1/2010	Attachment to Proof of Electronic Service (Documents Served) *[same as EFS-050(D)]*
POS-050(P)	2/1/2017	Attachment to Proof of Electronic Service (Persons Served) *[same as EFS-050(P)]*

RECEIVERSHIP

RC-200	1/1/2007	Ex Parte Order Appointing Receiver and Order to Show Cause and Temporary Restraining Order—Rents, Issues, and Profits
RC-210	1/1/2007	Order Confirming Appointment of Receiver and Preliminary Injunction—Rents, Issues, and Profits
RC-300	1/1/2007	Order to Show Cause and Temporary Restraining Order—Rents, Issues, and Profits
RC-310	1/1/2007	Order Appointing Receiver After Hearing and Preliminary Injunction—Rents, Issues, and Profits

SAFE AT HOME

SH-001*	9/1/2020	Confidential Information Form Under Code of Civil Procedure Section 367.3
SH-020*	1/1/2021	Motion to Place Documents Under Seal Under Code of Civil Procedure Section 367.3
SH-020-INFO	1/1/2021	Instructions for Motion to Place Documents Under Seal Under Code of Civil Procedure Section 367.3
SH-022*	1/1/2021	Declaration in Support of Motion to Place Documents Under Seal Under Code of Civil Procedure Section 367.3
SH-025*	1/1/2021	Order on Motion to Place Documents Under Seal Under Code of Civil Procedure Section 367.3
SH-030*	1/1/2021	Ex Parte Application for Order Shortening Time for Hearing on Motion to Place Documents Under Seal Under Code of Civil Procedure Section 367.3

---

* Adopted for mandatory use by all courts.

| SH-032* | 1/1/2021 | Declaration Regarding Notice and Service of Ex Parte Application for Order Shortening Time for Hearing on Motion to Place Documents Under Seal Under Code of Civil Procedure Section 367.3 |
| SH-035 | 1/1/2021 | Order on Ex Parte Application for Order Shortening Time for Hearing on Motion to Place Documents Under Seal Under Code of Civil Procedure Section 367.3 |

SCHOOL VIOLENCE PREVENTION

SV-100*	1/1/2018	Petition for Private Postsecondary School Violence Restraining Orders
SV-100-INFO	1/1/2014	How Do I Get an Order to Prohibit Private Postsecondary School Violence? (Private Postsecondary School Violence Prevention)
SV-102*	1/1/2012	*[Revoked]* Confidential CLETS Information (Private Postsecondary School Violence Prevention)
SV-109*	1/1/2012	Notice of Court Hearing (Private Postsecondary School Violence Prevention)
SV-110*	1/1/2017	Temporary Restraining Order (CLETS—TSV)
SV-115*	1/1/2020	Request to Continue Court Hearing (Temporary Restraining Order) (Private Postsecondary School Violence Prevention)
SV-115-INFO	1/1/2020	How to Ask for a New Hearing Date (Private Postsecondary School Violence Prevention)
SV-116*	1/1/2020	Order on Request to Continue Hearing (Temporary Restraining Order) (CLETS—TSV) (Private Postsecondary School Violence Prevention)
SV-120*	1/1/2018	Response to Petition for Private Postsecondary School Violence Restraining Orders
SV-120-INFO	7/1/2014	How Can I Respond to a Petition for Private Postsecondary School Violence Restraining Orders? (Private Postsecondary School Violence Prevention)
SV-130*	1/1/2018	Private Postsecondary School Violence Restraining Order After Hearing (CLETS—SVO)
SV-200	7/1/2014	Proof of Personal Service
SV-200-INFO	1/1/2012	What Is "Proof of Personal Service"? (Private Postsecondary School Violence Prevention)
SV-250	1/1/2012	Proof of Service of Response by Mail (Private Postsecondary School Violence Prevention)
SV-260	1/1/2012	Proof of Service of Order After Hearing by Mail (Private Postsecondary School Violence Prevention)
SV-600*	1/1/2018	Request to Modify/Terminate Private Postsecondary School Violence Restraining Order
SV-610*	1/1/2018	Notice of Hearing on Request to Modify/Terminate Private Postsecondary School Violence Restraining Order
SV-620*	1/1/2018	Response to Request to Modify/Terminate Private Postsecondary School Violence Restraining Order
SV-630*	1/1/2018	Order on Request to Modify/Terminate Private Postsecondary School Violence Restraining Order
SV-700*	1/1/2012	Request to Renew Restraining Order (Private Postsecondary School Violence Prevention)
SV-710*	1/1/2012	Notice of Hearing to Renew Restraining Order
SV-720*	1/1/2012	Response to Request to Renew Restraining Order
SV-730*	1/1/2012	Order Renewing Private Postsecondary School Violence Restraining Order (CLETS)
SV-800	7/1/2014	Proof of Firearms Turned In, Sold, or Stored
SV-800-INFO	7/1/2014	How Do I Turn In, Sell, or Store My Firearms?

SMALL CLAIMS

SC-100*	1/1/2020	Plaintiff's Claim and ORDER to Go to Small Claims Court
SC-100-INFO*	1/1/2020	Information for the Small Claims Plaintiff
SC-100A*	1/1/2017	Other Plaintiffs or Defendants (Attachment to Plaintiff's Claim and ORDER to Go to Small Claims Court)
SC-101*	7/1/2007	Attorney Fee Dispute (After Arbitration) (Attachment to Plaintiff's Claim and ORDER to Go to Small Claims Court)
SC-103	1/1/2006	Fictitious Business Name (Small Claims)
SC-104	1/1/2009	Proof of Service (Small Claims)
SC-104A	1/1/2006	Proof of Mailing (Substituted Service) (Small Claims)
SC-104B	1/1/2011	What Is "Proof of Service"? (Small Claims)
SC-104C	7/1/2017	How to Serve a Business or Public Entity
SC-105	1/1/2007	Request for Court Order and Answer
SC-105A	1/1/2007	Order on Request for Court Order
SC-106	1992	*[Revoked]* Request to Pay Judgment in Installments (Small Claims)
SC-107*	1/1/2000	Small Claims Subpoena for Personal Appearance and Production of Documents at Trial or Hearing and Declaration
SC-108	7/1/2011	Request to Correct or Cancel Judgment and Answer (Small Claims)
SC-108A	1/1/2007	Order on Request to Correct or Cancel Judgment
SC-109	1/1/2007	Authorization to Appear
SC-110	1/1/2004	*[Revoked]* Request to Postpone Small Claims Hearing
SC-111	1/1/2004	*[Revoked]* Order on Request to Postpone Small Claims Hearings
SC-112A	7/1/2010	Proof of Service by Mail (Small Claims)
SC-113A	7/1/2010	Clerk's Certificate of Mailing
SC-114	1/1/2004	Request to Amend Claim Before Hearing (Small Claims)
SC-120*	1/1/2011	Defendant's Claim and ORDER to Go to Small Claims Court (Small Claims)
SC-120A*	1/1/2007	Other Plaintiffs or Defendants (Attachment to Defendant's Claim and ORDER to Go to Small Claims Court)
SC-130*	7/1/2010	Notice of Entry of Judgment (Small Claims)

* Adopted for mandatory use by all courts.

SC-132*	7/1/2010	Attorney-Client Fee Dispute (Attachment to Notice of Entry of Judgment) (Small Claims)
SC-133*	1/1/2011	Judgment Debtor's Statement of Assets (Small Claims)
SC-134*	1/1/2017	Application and Order to Produce Statement of Assets and to Appear for Examination
SC-135	1/1/2007	Notice of Motion to Vacate Judgment and Declaration
SC-140	1/1/2007	Notice of Appeal
SC-145*	1/1/2007	Request to Pay Judgment to Court
SC-150*	7/1/2010	*[Revoked]* Information for the Small Claims Plaintiff
SC-150	7/1/2010	Request to Postpone Trial (Small Claims)
SC-152	7/1/2010	Order on Request to Postpone Trial (Small Claims)
SC-200*	7/1/2010	Notice of Entry of Judgment (Small Claims)
SC-200-INFO	7/1/2010	What to Do After the Court Decides Your Small Claims Case (Small Claims)
SC-200-INFO S	7/1/2010	What to Do After the Court Decides Your Small Claims Case (Small Claims) (Spanish)
SC-202A*	7/1/2010	Decision on Attorney-Client Fee Dispute (Small Claims)
SC-220	7/1/2013	Request to Make Payments (Small Claims)
SC-220-INFO	7/1/2013	Payments in Small Claims Cases (Small Claims)
SC-221	7/1/2013	Response to Request to Make Payments (Small Claims)
SC-222	7/1/2013	Order on Request to Make Payments (Small Claims)
SC-223	7/1/2013	Declaration of Default in Payment of Judgment (Small Claims)
SC-224	7/1/2013	Response to Declaration of Default in Payment of Judgment (Small Claims)
SC-225	7/1/2013	Order on Declaration of Default in Payments (Small Claims)
SC-225A	7/1/2013	Attachment to Order on Declaration of Default in Payments (Small Claims)
SC-290	7/1/2010	Acknowledgment of Satisfaction of Judgment
SC-300	3/15/2019	Petition for Writ (Small Claims)
SC-300-INFO	1/1/2016	Information on Writ Proceedings in Small Claims Cases

SUBPOENA

SUBP-001*	1/1/2007	Civil Subpoena for Personal Appearance at Trial or Hearing
SUBP-002*	1/1/2012	Civil Subpoena (Duces Tecum) for Personal Appearance and Production of Documents, Electronically Stored Information, and Things at Trial or Hearing and Declaration
SUBP-010*	1/1/2012	Deposition Subpoena for Production of Business Records
SUBP-015*	1/1/2009	Deposition Subpoena for Personal Appearance
SUBP-020*	1/1/2009	Deposition Subpoena for Personal Appearance and Production of Documents and Things
SUBP-025*	1/1/2008	Notice to Consumer or Employee and Objection
SUBP-030*	1/1/2010	Application for Discovery Subpoena in Action Pending Outside California
SUBP-035*	1/1/2012	Subpoena for Production of Business Records in Action Pending Outside California
SUBP-040*	1/1/2010	Deposition Subpoena for Personal Appearance in Action Pending Outside California
SUBP-045*	1/1/2012	Deposition Subpoena for Personal Appearance and Production of Documents, Electronically Stored Information, and Things in Action Pending Outside California
SUBP-050*	1/1/2010	Subpoena for Inspection of Premises in Action Pending Outside California

SUMMONS

SUM-100*	7/1/2009	Summons
SUM-110*	7/1/2009	Summons—Cross-Complaint
SUM-120*	7/1/2009	Summons (Joint Debtor)
SUM-130*	9/1/2019	Summons—Unlawful Detainer—Eviction
SUM-140*	7/1/2016	*[Revoked]* Summons—Storage Lien Enforcement
SUM-145*	7/1/2009	Summons—Enforcement of State Housing Law
SUM-200(A)*	1/1/2007	Additional Parties Attachment (Attachment to Summons) *(formerly 982(a)(9)(A))*
SUM-300*	1/1/2007	Declaration of Lost Summons After Service *(formerly 982(a)(12))*

TRAFFIC
Notice to Appear and Related Forms

TR-100*	1/1/2004	Notice of Correction and Proof of Service
TR-106	1/1/2004	Continuation of Notice to Appear
TR-108	1/1/2004	Continuation of Citation
TR-115	6/26/2015	Automated Traffic Enforcement System Notice to Appear
TR-120	6/26/2015	Nontraffic Notice to Appear
TR-130	6/26/2015	Traffic/Nontraffic Notice to Appear
TR-135	6/26/2015	Electronic Traffic/Nontraffic Notice to Appear (4″ format)
TR-145	6/26/2015	Electronic Traffic/Nontraffic Notice to Appear (3″ format)
TR-150	1/1/2009	*[Revoked]* Instructions on Appeal Procedures for Infractions
TR-155	1/1/2009	*[Revoked]* Notice of Appeal (Infraction)
TR-160	1/1/2009	*[Revoked]* Proposed Statement on Appeal (Infraction)
TR-165	1/1/2009	*[Revoked]* Abandonment of Appeal (Infraction)
TR-INST	6/26/2015	Notice to Appear and Related Forms

---

* Adopted for mandatory use by all courts.

TRAFFIC
Traffic Infractions

TR-200*	1/1/1999	Instructions to Defendant
TR-205*	1/1/1999	Request for Trial by Written Declaration
TR-210*	1/1/1999	Notice and Instructions to Arresting Officer
TR-215*	1/1/1999	Decision and Notice of Decision
TR-220*	1/1/1999	Request for New Trial (Trial de Novo)
TR-225*	1/1/1999	Order and Notice to Defendant of New Trial (Trial de Novo)
TR-235*	1/1/2000	Officer's Declaration
TR-300*	1/1/2017	Agreement to Pay and Forfeit Bail in Installments (Vehicle Code, § 40510.5)
TR-300* (online)	1/1/2017	Online Agreement to Pay and Forfeit Bail in Installments (Vehicle Code, § 40510.5)
TR-310*	1/1/2017	Agreement to Pay Traffic Violator School Fees in Installments (Vehicle Code, § 42007)
TR-310* (online)	1/1/2017	Online Agreement to Pay Traffic Violator School Fees in Installments (Vehicle Code, § 42007)
TR-320	4/1/2018	Can't Afford to Pay Fine: Traffic and Other Infractions [same as CR-320]
TR-321	4/1/2018	Can't Afford to Pay Fine: Traffic and Other Infractions (Court Order) [same as CR-321]
TR-500-INFO	9/1/2015	Instructions to Defendant for Remote Video Proceeding
TR-505*	9/1/2015	Notice and Waiver of Rights and Request for Remote Video Arraignment and Trial
TR-510*	9/1/2015	Notice and Waiver of Rights and Request for Remote Video Proceeding

TRANSITIONAL HOUSING MISCONDUCT

TH-100*	9/1/2018	Petition for Order Prohibiting Abuse or Program Misconduct
TH-110*	9/1/2018	Order to Show Cause and Temporary Restraining Order
TH-120*	9/1/2018	Participant's Response to Petition for Order Prohibiting Abuse or Program Misconduct
TH-130*	9/1/2018	Order After Hearing on Petition for Order Prohibiting Abuse or Program Misconduct
TH-140*	9/1/2018	Proof of Personal Service
TH-190	9/1/2018	Restatement of Transitional Housing Misconduct Act (Civil Code section 1954.10 et seq.)
TH-200*	9/1/2018	Instructions for Program Operators (Civil Code section 1954.10 et seq.)
TH-210*	9/1/2018	Instructions for Participants (Civil Code section 1954.10 et seq.)

VEXATIOUS LITIGANTS

VL-100*	9/1/2018	Prefiling Order—Vexatious Litigant [renumbered from MC-700*]
VL-110	9/1/2018	Request to File New Litigation by Vexatious Litigant [renumbered from MC-701]
VL-115	9/1/2018	Order to File New Litigation by Vexatious Litigant [renumbered from MC-702]
VL-120	9/1/2018	Application for Order to Vacate Prefiling Order and Remove Plaintiff/Petitioner From Judicial Council Vexatious Litigant List [renumbered from MC-703]
VL-125	9/1/2018	Order on Application to Vacate Prefiling Order and Remove Plaintiff/Petitioner From Judicial Council Vexatious Litigant List [renumbered from MC-704]

WAGE GARNISHMENT

WG-001*	1/1/2012	Application For Earnings Withholding Order (Wage Garnishment) (formerly 982.5(1))
WG-002*	7/1/2016	Earnings Withholding Order
WG-003*	1/2/2012	Employee Instructions (Wage Garnishment)
WG-004*	1/1/2012	Earnings Withholding Order For Support (Wage Garnishment) (formerly 982.5(3))
WG-005*	9/1/2017	Employer's Return (formerly 982.5(4))
WG-006	1/1/2009	Claim of Exemption (formerly 982.5(5))
WG-007*	1/1/2007	Financial Statement [same as EJ-165*]
WG-008*	1/1/2007	Notice of Filing of Claim of Exemption (formerly 982.5(6))
WG-009*	1/2/2012	Notice of Opposition to Claim of Exemption (Wage Garnishment)
WG-010	1/1/2007	Notice of Hearing on Claim of Exemption [same as EJ-175]
WG-011	1/1/2007	Order Determining Claim of Exemption (formerly 982.5(9))
WG-012	1/1/2012	Notice of Termination or Modification of Earnings Withholding Order (Wage Garnishment) (formerly 982.5(10))
WG-020*	1/1/2007	Application for Earnings Withholding Order for Taxes (State Tax Liability) (formerly 982.5(11))
WG-021*	1/1/2007	Confidential Supplement to Application for Earnings Withholding Order for Taxes (Wage Garnishment—State Tax Liability) (formerly 982.5(11S))
WG-022*	1/1/2007	Earnings Withholding Order for Taxes (Wage Garnishment—State Tax Liability) (formerly 982.5(12))
WG-023*	1/1/2007	Notice of Hearing—Earnings Withholding Order for Taxes (State Tax Liability) (formerly 982.5(13))
WG-024*	1/1/2007	Temporary Earnings Withholding Order for Taxes (State Tax Liability) (formerly 982.5(14))
WG-025*	1/1/2007	Confidential Supplement to Temporary Earnings Withholding Order for Taxes (State Tax Liability) (formerly 982.5(14S))
WG-026*	1/1/2007	Claim of Exemption and Financial Declaration (State Tax Liability) (formerly 982.5(15))
WG-030*	7/1/2016	Earnings Withholding Order for Elder or Dependent Adult Financial Abuse
WG-035*	1/1/2012	Confidential Statement of Judgment Debtor's Social Security Number

* Adopted for mandatory use by all courts.

WORKPLACE VIOLENCE PREVENTION

WV-100*	1/1/2018	Petition for Workplace Violence Restraining Orders
WV-100-INFO	1/1/2014	How Do I Get an Order to Prohibit Workplace Violence? (Workplace Violence Prevention) *(formerly WV-150-INFO*)*
WV-102*	1/1/2012	*[Revoked]* Confidential CLETS Information (Workplace Violence Prevention)
WV-109*	1/1/2012	Notice of Court Hearing (Workplace Violence Prevention)
WV-110*	1/1/2017	Temporary Restraining Order (CLETS—TWH) *(formerly WV-120*)*
WV-115*	1/1/2020	Request to Continue Court Hearing (Temporary Restraining Order)
WV-115-INFO	1/1/2020	How to Ask for a New Hearing Date
WV-116*	1/1/2020	Order on Request to Continue Hearing (Temporary Restraining Order) (CLETS—TWH)
WV-120*	1/1/2018	Response to Petition for Workplace Violence Restraining Orders *(formerly WV-110*)*
WV-120-INFO	7/1/2014	How Can I Respond to a Petition for Workplace Violence Restraining Orders?
WV-130*	1/1/2018	Workplace Violence Restraining Order After Hearing (CLETS—WVO) *(formerly WV-140*)*
WV-131	1/1/2011	*[Renumbered]* Proof of Service by Mail of Completed Response (Workplace Violence)
WV-132	1/1/2011	*[Revoked]* Proof of Service by Personal Delivery of Completed Response (Workplace Violence)
WV-140*	1/1/2011	*[Renumbered]* Order After Hearing on Petition of Employer for Injunction Prohibiting Violence or Threats of Violence Against Employee (CLETS) (Workplace Violence)
WV-145	1/1/2011	*[Renumbered]* Proof of Sale or Turning In of Firearms
WV-150-INFO*	1/1/2011	*[Renumbered]* Instructions for Petitions to Prohibit Workplace Violence
WV-200	7/1/2014	Proof of Personal Service *(formerly WV-130)*
WV-200-INFO	1/1/2012	What Is "Proof of Personal Service"? (Workplace Violence Prevention)
WV-250	1/1/2012	Proof of Service of Response by Mail (Workplace Violence Prevention) *(formerly WV-131)*
WV-260	1/1/2012	Proof of Service of Order After Hearing by Mail
WV-600*	1/1/2018	Request to Modify/Terminate Workplace Violence Restraining Order
WV-610*	1/1/2018	Notice of Hearing on Request to Modify/Terminate Workplace Violence Restraining Order
WV-620*	1/1/2018	Response to Request to Modify/Terminate Workplace Violence Restraining Order
WV-630*	1/1/2018	Order on Request to Modify/Terminate Workplace Violence Restraining Order
WV-700*	1/1/2012	Request to Renew Restraining Order
WV-710*	1/1/2012	Notice of Hearing to Renew Restraining Order
WV-720*	1/1/2012	Response to Request to Renew Restraining Order
WV-730*	1/1/2012	Order Renewing Workplace Violence Restraining Order (CLETS)
WV-800	7/1/2014	Proof of Firearms Turned In, Sold, or Stored *(formerly WV-145)*
WV-800-INFO	7/1/2014	How Do I Turn In, Sell, or Store My Firearms?

---

* Adopted for mandatory use by all courts.

Appendix B
Liability Limits of a Parent or Guardian Having Custody and Control of a Minor for the Torts of a Minor
(Civ. Code, § 1714.1)

Formula

Pursuant to Civil Code section 1714.1, the joint and several liability limit of a parent or guardian having custody and control of a minor under subdivisions (a) and (b) for each tort of the minor shall be computed and adjusted as follows:

$$\text{Adjusted limit} = \left[\frac{\text{Current CCPI} - \text{January 1, 1995, CCPI}}{\text{January 1, 1995, CCPI}} + 1 \right] \times \text{January 1, 1995, limit}$$

Definition

"CCPI" means the California Consumer Price Index, as established by the California Department of Industrial Relations.

July 1, 2019, calculation and adjustment

The joint and several liability of a parent or guardian having custody and control of a minor under Civil Code section 1714.1, subdivision (a) or (b), effective July 1, 2019, shall not exceed $45,000 for each tort.

The calculation is as follows:

$$\$44,968.65 = \left[\frac{272.51 - 151.5}{151.5} + 1 \right] \times \$25,000$$

Under section 1714.1, subdivision (c), the adjusted limit is rounded to the nearest hundred dollars, so the dollar amount of the adjusted limit is rounded to $45,000.

Appendix B amended effective July 1, 2019; adopted effective January 1, 1997; previously amended effective January 1, 1999, January 1, 2001, January 1, 2003, January 1, 2005, January 1, 2007, February 18, 2009, January 1, 2011, July 1, 2013, July 1, 2015, and July 1, 2017.

Appendix C
Guidelines for the Operation of Family Law Information Centers and Family Law Facilitator Offices

(1) *Independence and integrity*

An attorney and other staff working in a family law information center or family law facilitator office should, at all times, uphold the independence and integrity of the center or office in conjunction with its role within the court and the legal system.

(2) *Role as representative of the court*

An attorney and other staff working in a family law information center or family law facilitator office should recognize that they are representatives of the court and, as such, should avoid all acts of impropriety and the appearance of impropriety at all times.

(3) *Impartiality and diligence*

An attorney working in a family law information center or family law facilitator office should perform his or her duties impartially and diligently. Impartiality means delivering services to all eligible litigants in a neutral manner. Diligence requires that the attorney provide the litigants with pertinent information to allow them to bring their matter before the court. This may include appropriate referrals to other resources as well as direct information and assistance at the center or office. The attorney should require similar conduct of all personnel.

(4) *Respect and patience*

An attorney working in a family law information center or family law facilitator office should be aware of the social and economic differences that exist among litigants and maintain patience with and respect for the litigants who seek the services of the center or office. The attorney should require similar conduct of all personnel. However, if a litigant becomes unruly or disruptive, the attorney may ask the litigant to leave the center or office.

(5) *Bias and prejudice*

An attorney working in a family law information center or family law facilitator office should assist the litigants who seek assistance without exhibiting bias or prejudice based on race, sex, religion, national origin, disability, age, sexual orientation, socioeconomic status, or other similar factors, and should require similar conduct of all personnel.

(6) *Competent legal information*

An attorney working in a family law information center or family law facilitator office and his or her staff should provide the litigants who seek assistance with procedural and legal information and education so that the litigants will have increased access to the court. Family law information centers and family law facilitator offices are not intended to replace private counsel.

(7) *Full notification of limits of service*

An attorney working in a family law information center or family law facilitator office should ensure that conspicuous notice is given, as set forth in Family Code section 10013, that no attorney-client relationship exists between the center or office, or its staff, and the family law litigant. The notice should include the advice that the absence of an attorney-client relationship means that communications between the party and the family law information center or family law facilitator office are not privileged and that the services may be provided to the other party. Additionally, the family law information center must use *Family Law Information Center Disclosure* (form FL-945) or provide similar notice. The family law facilitator office must use *Office of the Family Law Facilitator Disclosure* (form FL-940) or provide similar notice of the warnings set forth in Family Code section 10015.

(8) *Public comment*

An attorney working in a family law information center or family law facilitator office and his or her staff must at all times comply with Family Code section 10014, and must not make any public comment about the litigants or about any pending or impending matter in the court.

(9) *Gifts or payments*

An attorney working in a family law information center or family law facilitator office and his or her staff should not accept any gifts, favors, bequests, or loans from the litigants whom they assist, since this may give the appearance of impropriety or partiality—except for nominal gifts such as baked goods, as allowed by local rules.

(10) *Communications with bench officer*

An attorney working in a family law information center or family law facilitator office and his or her staff should avoid all ex parte communications with a bench officer, except as provided in accordance with Family Code section 10005. In addition, an attorney should avoid all communications with a bench officer in which he or she offers an opinion on how the bench officer should rule on a pending case. Communications about purely procedural matters or the functioning of the court are allowed and encouraged.

(11) *Communications with represented litigants*

An attorney working in a family law information center or family law facilitator office and his or her staff should not assist a litigant who is represented by an attorney unless the litigant's attorney consents or the court has referred the litigant for assistance.

Advisory Committee Comment

These guidelines are promulgated as directed by former Family Code section 15010(f). They are intended to guide the attorneys providing assistance in family law information centers and family law facilitator offices created by Family Code sections 10000–10015.

These guidelines are not intended to be exclusive. Attorneys who work in the family law information centers and family law facilitator offices are also bound by the State Bar Act, the Rules of Professional Conduct, local and state court employee rules, and relevant opinions of the California courts to the extent that they apply.

The authorities that govern attorney conduct in California apply to all California attorneys regardless of the capacity in which they are acting in a particular matter. (*Libarian v. State Bar* 25 Cal.2d. 314 (1944).) "Permission" not to comply with these authorities may not be given by the State Bar. (*Sheffield v. State Bar* 22 Cal.2d. 627 (1943).)

Thus, California attorneys, regardless of the capacity in which they are performing in a particular matter, must conform their conduct to the governing California authorities. However, because the disciplinary authorities are activity-specific, not all authorities apply in all instances. For example, a transactional attorney who never appears in court is not likely to be at risk of violating the rules that govern court appearances. The transactional attorney is not immune from those rules; the nature of his or her practice simply minimizes the impact of those rules upon the services he or she performs. Thus, although center and facilitator attorneys will not be immune from the governing authorities, certain rules and requirements will apply more directly to the nature of the services being provided than will others.

Just as the Rules of Professional Conduct are activity-specific in general professional practice, so are center and facilitator office attorneys. Although the Rules of Professional Conduct and related authorities will apply generally, and will apply directly when the attorney is representing clients in an attorney-client relationship, they will not directly be invoked when a center or facilitator attorney provides assistance to a nonclient in a court-based program that does not, by definition, represent "clients."

To the extent that the above-mentioned Family Code sections establish by law that there is no attorney-client relationship or privilege for services provided by a family law information center or family law facilitator office, the Rules of Professional Conduct that specifically address the attorney-client relationship and the conduct of that relationship would not be invoked if the attorney were providing services within the scope of those sections. However, the Rules of Professional Conduct would govern attorneys employed by centers or facilitator offices who also continued to maintain a law practice and worked with actual clients in an attorney-client relationship.

Although center and facilitator office attorneys are not exempt from the Rules of Professional Conduct, the employing court may promulgate guidelines for the services provided by a center or office that are more applicable to the center or office than are some of the Rules of Professional Conduct, however, any such restrictions must still be fully consistent with the Rules of Professional Conduct. The principles set forth in the California Code of Judicial Ethics are often more applicable to the centers and facilitator offices and are consistent with the Rules of Professional Conduct. Those principles form the basis for the guidelines contained in these standards. The court may enforce these guidelines through its employee disciplinary process for court employees. Following are the areas of the Rules of Professional Conduct where these guidelines provide standards that are more applicable to the role of the family law information center or family law facilitator office as an entity of the court.

Rule 2-100 (Communication With a Represented Party)—see proposed guideline 11 (Communication with represented litigants).

Rule 2-400 (Prohibited Discriminatory Conduct in a Law Practice)—see proposed guideline 5 (Bias and prejudice);

Rule 3-110 (Failing to Act Competently)—see proposed guidelines 3 (Impartiality and diligence) and 6 (Competent legal information);

Rule 3-120 (Sexual Relations With Client)—see proposed guideline 2 (Role as representative of the court);

Rule 3-200 (Prohibited Objectives of Employment)—see proposed guideline 2 (Role as representative of the court);

Rule 3-210 (Advising the Violation of Law)—see proposed guideline 2 (Role as representative of the court);

Rule 3-320 (Relationship With Other Party's Lawyer)—see proposed guideline 2 (Role as representative of the court);

Rule 4-300 (Purchasing Property at a Foreclosure or a Sale Subject to Judicial Review)—see proposed guideline 2 (Role as representative of the court);

Rule 4-400 (Gifts From Client)—see proposed guideline 9 (Gifts or payments);

Rule 5-120 (Trial Publicity)—see proposed guideline 8 (Public comment);

Rule 5-220 (Suppression of Evidence)—see proposed guideline 2 (Role as representative of the court);

Rule 5-300 (Contact With Officials)—see proposed guideline 10 (Communications with bench officers);

Rule 5-310 (Prohibited Contact With Witnesses)—see proposed guideline 2 (Role as representative of the court); and

Rule 5-320 (Contact With Jurors)—see proposed guideline 2 (Role as representative of the court).

Appendix D
Judicial Council Governance Policies

APRIL 16, 2020

Judicial Council Governance Policies

The Judicial Council is the policymaking body of the California courts, the largest court system in the nation. Under the leadership of the Chief Justice and in accordance with the California Constitution, the council is responsible for ensuring the consistent, independent, impartial, and accessible administration of justice. Members of the council are appointed by the Chief Justice. Appointees by the State Bar Board of Trustees and both houses of the Legislature also serve as members of the council. Together the members serve to carry out judicial branch goals. Judicial Council staff implements the council's policies, and the goals and priorities of the council are set forth in *Justice in Focus: The Strategic Plan for California's Judicial Branch 2006–2016*:

I. Access, Fairness, and Diversity
II. Independence and Accountability
III. Modernization of Management and Administration
IV. Quality of Justice and Service to the Public
V. Education for Branchwide Professional Excellence
VI. Branchwide Infrastructure for Service Excellence
VII. Adequate, Stable, and Predictable Funding for a Fully Functioning Branch

GOVERNANCE PROCESS

1. Responsibilities of the Council

The council establishes goals and policies for California's judicial branch of government. The council is directly responsible for the following:

a. Establishing broad goals and policies that set the direction and priorities for the continuous improvement of California's system for the administration of justice. These goals and policies include fundamental goals such as promoting public access to the justice system, increasing responsiveness to the needs of court users of diverse backgrounds, and upholding the rule of law and impartiality of judges as constitutional officers.

b. Establishing standards for performance and accountability of the administrative operations and procedures of the branch. These standards address the diverse needs of court users, employ modern management practices that implement and sustain innovative ideas and effective practices, and report on judicial branch performance to the public, Legislature, Governor, and the courts.

c. Developing and maintaining administrative, technological, and physical infrastructures, including court facilities, which enhance accessibility to the courts and support the needs of the people of California and the judicial branch.

d. Taking all appropriate steps to develop and establish the judicial branch's fiscal priorities, secure appropriate funding for the judicial branch, establish fiscal and budget policies for the branch, allocate branch appropriations to the courts and the council, and ensure accountability through reporting on the use of its public resources to the legislative and executive branches of state government and to the public.

e. Sponsoring and taking positions on pending legislation consistent with the council's established goals and priorities to support consistent, effective, statewide programs and policies that provide for the highest quality of administration of justice, and that promote an impartial judiciary.

f. Developing high-quality education and professional development opportunities for all judicial branch personnel to meet public needs and to enhance public trust and confidence in the courts.

g. Communicating with and reporting to the legislative and executive branches of state government to advance judicial branch goals, and account for the use of public funds and resources.

2. Council Policymaking

The Judicial Council establishes judicial branch policy for the improvement of an independent and impartial justice system that meets public needs, and enhances public trust and confidence in the courts. It develops policy in consultation with the people of California, court leadership, judicial officers, Judicial Council advisory bodies, employees in the judicial branch, the State Bar, advocacy groups, the Legislature, the Governor, and other government entities and justice system partners.

The principal focus of the Judicial Council is to establish policies that emphasize long-term strategic leadership and that align with judicial branch goals. Council policymaking is focused on the beneficiaries of the policy, the results to be achieved, the costs to be incurred, and the corresponding judicial branch goals.

To enable the council to make well-informed strategic decisions, all policy proposals submitted for council consideration by internal committees, advisory bodies, the Administrative Director, and staff should address the following:

- Beneficiaries of the policy;
- Results to be achieved;
- Costs to be incurred;
- Each corresponding judicial branch goal, objective, and anticipated outcome;
- Previous council action on the issue or policy;
- Comments from interested parties;
- Analysis of the benefits and risks of the proposals; and
- Analysis of the strengths and weaknesses of alternative options and an explanation of their implications.

3. Maintenance of Governance Policies and Principles

On an annual basis, the chair of the Executive and Planning Committee discusses the governance policies and principles at a council meeting to orient new members and review council governance with continuing members. Every three years, the Judicial Council conducts a review of its governance policies and principles and determines whether any revisions are needed. The Executive and Planning Committee monitors the regular implementation of the governance policies and principles.

In order to ensure that new council members have the knowledge and understanding needed to perform their duties effectively, they are oriented to the council's governance policies and principles as well as the council's history of policymaking on key topics, such as court facilities, fiscal appropriations, and infrastructure initiatives.

4. Council-Staff Relationship

Officially passed motions of the council, and decisions and instructions of the Chief Justice, are binding on the Administrative Director. Decisions or instructions of individual council members or internal and advisory bodies are binding on the Administrative Director if the council or its chair has specifically delegated such exercise of authority.

The Administrative Director has sole authority to assign, supervise, and direct staff. The Administrative Director is responsible for ensuring the completeness and quality of reports and other work product presented to the council. Council members may from time to time request information or assistance from staff, unless in the Director's opinion such requests require an unreasonable amount of staff time or become disruptive. Council members and advisory body members may individually provide information to the Administrative Director on the performance of staff or staff agency to the council.

The Administrative Director, as secretary to the council, may attend and participate in the meetings of each internal committee.

5. Internal Committees

a. Executive and Planning Committee

The Executive and Planning Committee under California Rules of Court, rule 10.11 makes regular reports to the full council on its actions. Its responsibilities include those described below.

Together with the chairs of the other internal committees, the Executive and Planning Committee is responsible for developing and implementing a branchwide plan for general communications between the council and the judicial branch. This responsibility may address such matters as reporting through judicial branch communication channels to the courts and branch stakeholders on Judicial Council meetings and policy actions; communications with the media; communications through Judicial Council members' participation in court site visits, regional meetings, and new judge meetings; and communications from the judicial branch to the Judicial Council through meetings, advisory bodies, public comment processes, and other communication methods.

b. Rules Committee

The Rules [1] Committee under California Rules of Court, rule 10.13 makes regular reports to the full council on its actions. Its responsibilities are described below.

  i. Identifies the need for new rules, standards, and forms;
  ii. Establishes and publishes procedures for the proposal, adoption, and approval of rules of court, forms, and standards of judicial administration that ensure that relevant input from the public is solicited and considered;
  iii. Reviews proposed rules, standards, and forms, and circulates those proposals for public comment in accordance with its procedures and guidelines.
  iv. Provides guidelines for the style and format of rules, forms, and standards and ensures that proposals are consistent with the guidelines;
  v. Ensures that proposals for new or amended rules, standards, and forms do not conflict with statutes or other rules; and
  vi. Determines whether proposals for new or amended rules, standards, or forms have complied with its procedures.

c. Legislation Committee

The [2] **Legislation** Committee under California Rules of Court, rule 10.12 makes regular reports to the full council on its actions. Its responsibilities include those described below.

  The committee represents the Judicial Council's position with other agencies and entities, such as the Legislature, the Governor's Office, the State Bar of California, local government, local bar associations, and other court-related professional associations; reviews and makes recommendations on proposals for Judicial Council-sponsored legislation; reviews pending bills; determines positions consistent with the council's previous policy decisions; and oversees advocacy for those positions.

d. Judicial Council Technology Committee

The Judicial Council Technology Committee under California Rules of Court, rule 10.16 makes regular reports to the full council on its actions. Its responsibilities include those described below.

  The committee oversees the council's policies concerning technology and is responsible in partnership with the courts for coordinating with the Administrative Director and all internal committees, advisory committees, commissions, working groups, task forces, justice partners, and stakeholders on technological issues relating to the branch and the courts. It is responsible for ensuring that council policies are complied with, and that specific projects proceed on schedule and within scope and budget. The committee seeks reports and recommendations from the Administrative Director, the courts, and stakeholders on technology issues. It ensures that technology reports to the council are clear, comprehensive, and provide relevant options so that the council can make effective final technology policy decisions. The committee reports on technology affecting the branch and courts at each Judicial Council meeting.

e. Judicial Branch Budget Committee

The Judicial Branch Budget Committee under California Rules of Court, rule 10.101 makes regular reports to the full council on its actions. Its responsibilities include those described below.

  i. Reviewing budget change proposals for the judicial branch, coordinating these budget change proposals, and ensuring that they are submitted to the council in a timely manner;

  ii. Reviewing and making recommendations on the use of statewide emergency funding for the judicial branch;
  iii. Reviewing and making recommendations on court innovations grant funding;
  iv. Endeavoring to promote the efficient, fiscally prudent, effective, and fair allocation of branch resources so as to advance statewide judicial branch interests; and
  v. Performing such additional tasks as may be assigned to the committee.

f. Litigation Management Committee

The Litigation Management Committee under California Rules of Court, rule 10.14 makes regular reports to the full council on its actions. Its responsibilities include those described below.

  i. The committee oversees litigation and claims against trial and appellate courts, the Judicial Council, and employees of those bodies that seek recovery of $100,000 or more, or raise important policy issues.
  ii. Important policy or court operations issues may include whether to initiate litigation on behalf of a court, when to defend a challenged court practice, or how to resolve disputes where the outcome might have statewide implications.

6. Role of Advisory Committees

Advisory committees under California Rules of Court, rule 10.34(a) are standing committees created by rule of court or the Chief Justice to make recommendations and offer policy alternatives to the Judicial Council for improving the administration of justice within their designated areas of focus by doing the following:

  i. Identifying issues and concerns affecting court administration and recommending solutions to the council;
  ii. Proposing necessary changes to rules, standards, forms, and jury instructions;
  iii. Reviewing pending legislation and making recommendations to the [3] **Legislation** Committee on whether to support or oppose it;
  iv. Recommending new legislation to the council;
  v. Recommending to the council pilot projects and other programs to evaluate new procedures or practices;
  vi. Acting on assignments referred by the council or an internal committee; and
  vii. Making other appropriate recommendations to the council.

APPENDIX

The *Operating Standards for Judicial Council Advisory Bodies* (operating standards) is appended to the *Judicial Council Governance Policies*. The operating standards support the general parameters within which Judicial Council advisory bodies operate under the direction and oversight of the Chief Justice and the Judicial Council. They guide the work of advisory body chairs and Judicial Council staff relative to annual agendas, staffing, committee membership, reporting to the council, and public access.

OPERATING STANDARDS FOR JUDICIAL COUNCIL ADVISORY BODIES

California Rules of Court, rules 10.30-10.34, 10.70, and 10.75 specify the general parameters within which Judicial Council advisory bodies operate under the direction and oversight of the Chief Justice and the Judicial Council.

  • Rule 10.30. Judicial Council advisory bodies
  • Rule 10.31. Advisory committee membership and terms
  • Rule 10.32. Nominations and appointments to advisory committees
  • Rule 10.33. Advisory committee meetings
  • Rule 10.34. Duties and responsibilities of advisory committees
  • Rule 10.70. Task forces, working groups, and other advisory bodies
  • Rule 10.75. Meetings of advisory bodies

The parameters set forth in the rules of court are supported by the following operating standards for Judicial Council advisory bodies. The operating standards guide the work of advisory body chairs and Judicial Council staff relative to annual agendas, staffing, Judicial Council membership, reporting to the council, and public access.

I. Definitions

The following definitions apply for purposes of these operating standards:

1. *Internal committee*
   a. A committee comprised of Judicial Council members.
   b. An "internal oversight committee" is an internal committee to which the Chief Justice has assigned oversight of a specific council advisory body.
2. *Advisory body.* Any multimember body created by the Judicial Council to review issues and report to the council, consistent with rule 10.75 of the California Rules of Court, other than a subcommittee or an internal committee as defined below.
3. *Subcommittee*
   a. A subset of an advisory body.
   b. Typically assists in completing a purpose or task for the parent body and may also advise the parent body.
   c. Two or more advisory bodies may request approval from their internal oversight committee for the establishment of a joint subcommittee.

II. Annual Agendas and Staffing

1. Annual agendas
   a. *Annual agenda template.* An annual agenda is the mechanism by which an advisory body clarifies and documents its plan for addressing an annual scope of work consistent with its charge. It is through this process that advisory bodies receive input, guidance, and delegation from the council in order to provide the necessary information and recommendations to the council to address judicial branch business. Unless otherwise provided for by the assigned internal oversight committee, advisory body annual agendas should be completed using the annual agenda template.
   b. *Agenda planning.* Before developing the proposed annual agenda, the assigned internal oversight committee chair, advisory body chair, office head, and lead staff discuss the work completed during the prior annual agenda period; the potential activities or projects, timelines, and priorities for the upcoming annual agenda period; and Judicial Council staff resource needs. Agendas should be developed based on existing resources.
   c. *Soliciting input from other advisory bodies.* To avoid duplication of effort and ensure the availability of resources, advisory body chairs, office heads, and lead staff should solicit input on activities or projects from affected advisory bodies before or as annual agendas are first drafted. This early collaboration ensures that relevant feedback is received before recommendations are completed and submitted to the council.
   d. *Executive and management review.* Before the proposed final annual agenda is submitted to the assigned internal oversight committee for approval, the heads of all offices that staff advisory bodies meet to review all annual agendas, discuss resource needs, and ensure that the appropriate offices are aware of projects that may impact them. In addition, each office head reviews the proposed final annual agenda with the executive office before internal committee review. The office head discusses any concerns about resource needs with the responsible division chief before the annual agenda meeting. Resource concerns that cannot be resolved by the division chief should be raised with the Chief of Staff and the Administrative Director for further reconciliation with the chair of the appropriate internal oversight committee and for discussion with the advisory body chair.
   e. *Annual agenda meeting.* After consultation with the assigned internal oversight committee chair, the advisory body chair presents the proposed annual agenda to the full internal oversight committee for approval. The lead staff member to the advisory body, the office head, and the division chief also attend this meeting.
   f. *Online posting of approved annual agendas.* Upon completion and the approval of any changes requested by the internal oversight committees, all annual agendas are posted on the Advisory Bodies page of the California Courts website (*www.courts.ca.gov*) under the relevant advisory body link. The advisory body chair should refer members to the approved agenda to guide the work of the group in the coming year.
2. Ongoing communications
3. *Council and advisory body chairs.* The internal oversight committee chair and the advisory body chair should strive to check in over the course of the year to review progress on annual agenda items, resource needs, and other relevant areas.
4. Advisory body chair and staff. The advisory body chair, office head, and lead staff member should be in contact at least twice a year to discuss progress on annual agenda items. In particular, any extraordinary changes in council priorities or additional resource needs that are identified after the internal oversight committee has approved an annual agenda should be discussed and communicated to the Chief of Staff for review with the chair of the assigned internal oversight committee.

Amending Annual Agendas

In the event it is determined that an advisory body's Annual Agenda needs to be updated or changed in the course of the year (for example, to address changes in council priorities or newly enacted laws), the chair of the body may request that the oversight committee amend the advisory body's Annual agenda for this purpose. The oversight committees have approved a process and a form for amending agendas.

5. Staff responsibilities
   a. *Staffing oversight.* The Administrative Director and Chief of Staff have oversight responsibility and authority for directing staff support to the advisory bodies.
   b. *Lead staff.* Each advisory body has a lead staff member assigned to assist the body in meeting its charge and completing the activities and projects identified on the annual agenda. The lead staff member is responsible for keeping his or her office head apprised of the activities of the advisory body, including resource issues. In addition, he or she is responsible for maintaining the accuracy of the advisory body member roster, which should be kept current and consistent between internal and public postings. The lead staff member is also responsible for communicating all membership changes within the advisory body to Judicial Council Support and to the Contact and Position System (CAPS) administrator. The CAPS administrator will ensure that the appropriate judicial experience of each advisory body member is reflected within CAPS, along with the member's correct location, address, phone number, and e-mail address.
   c. *Office heads.* Office heads are required to proactively support the advisory body chairs and lead staff, work with the chairs and lead staff on sensitive issues, and communicate those issues to the responsible division chief.
   d. *General duties.* Judicial Council staff, under rule 10.34(e) of the California Rules of Court, support the planning, coordination, and ongoing implementation of the work of the council's advisory bodies by drafting annual agendas, managing budget and resources, providing legal and policy analysis, organizing and drafting reports, selecting and supervising consultants, providing technical assistance, and assisting chairs in presenting advisory body recommendations to the Judicial Council. Staff also organize meetings, provide information to members and to the public, ensure meeting notices are posted, facilitate advisory body nominations, and coordinate the work of the advisory body with related judicial branch work.
   e. *Alternative analysis/recommendations.* Under rule 10.34(e) of the California Rules of Court, staff may provide independent legal or policy analysis of issues that is different from the advisory body's position, if authorized to do so by the Administrative Director. The decisions or instructions of an advisory body or its chair are not binding on staff except in instances when the council or the Administrative Director has specifically authorized such exercise of authority.
   f. *Addressing resource needs.* Office heads are responsible for ensuring that resource needs are addressed, including discussing those needs with the advisory body chair and the responsible division chief before the annual agenda meeting. Ongoing resource issues brought to the office head's attention that are likely to impede progress or impact the outcome of approved activities or projects should be raised with the Chief of Staff and the Administrative Director for further reconciliation with the chair of the appropriate internal oversight committee and discussion with the advisory body chair. (See Cal. Rules of Court, rule 10.80(d).)

III. Membership and Duration

1. *Composition.* An advisory body and its chair may make recommen-

dations to the Judicial Council and the Executive and Planning Committee about the composition of the advisory body's membership, including nominating members. An advisory body typically has between 12 and 18 members (Cal. Rules of Court, rule 10.31(a)); however, this may vary depending on the charge and the scope of work.

2. *Subcommittees.* An advisory body may propose the establishment of a subcommittee. A proposal for the establishment of a subcommittee should specify:

- The purpose of, or charge for, the new subcommittee;
- Whether standing or ad hoc, and if ad hoc, specify an end date; and
- The timeline for the activity or project.

The chair of a standing subcommittee may request the appointment of a noncommittee member to the subcommittee by completing the form *Request for Appointment to a Subcommittee* and submitting it for consideration to the designated internal oversight committee.[1]

3. *Liaisons.* Standing advisory committees may have liaisons to other advisory bodies to facilitate the accomplishment of their common projects and programs. For example, the Trial Court Presiding Judges Advisory Committee and the Court Executives Advisory Committee have liaisons to other advisory bodies to ensure that the trial court leadership perspective is received in a timely manner on matters under consideration. The liaison process helps to:

- Facilitate an efficient and effective process for advisory bodies to seek and receive input from other advisory bodies that may have an interest in or be affected by its work; and
- Provide an opportunity for liaisons to share input from their respective advisory bodies early in the process on matters being considered by other advisory bodies.

The advisory body chair may determine the selection process for naming a liaison from the advisory body that he or she chairs to another advisory body. Before confirming an appointment, the appointing chair should consult with the chair of the advisory body to which the liaison will be appointed. Where a member of the Trial Court Presiding Judges Advisory Committee or the Court Executives Advisory Committee is a member of another council advisory body, he or she should also serve as the liaison for his or her committee. The appointing advisory body is responsible for costs related to the liaison member fulfilling his or her liaison responsibilities.

4. *Duration.* Sunset dates are required for all advisory bodies other than standing advisory committees. Ad hoc advisory bodies typically are dissolved following the submission and/or consideration of their final reports. The Chief Justice may extend a sunset date.

IV. Meetings

1. *Meeting notification.* Each advisory body's public web page must provide notification of upcoming meetings as well as any meeting materials, consistent with rule 10.75 of the California Rules of Court.

2. *Meeting frequency.* To conserve judicial branch resources, an advisory body may meet in person no more than one time each annual committee cycle unless an internal oversight committee approves otherwise. Consideration should be given to ways to schedule in-person meetings so that same-day travel can be accommodated and overnights avoided unless necessary. If an additional in-person meeting is needed, the responsible office head will review the request with his or her division chief. Final approval of the request will be sought from the assigned internal oversight committee chair in consultation with the Chief of Staff.

3. *Coordination with internal committee schedules.* To ensure the timely submission and review of advisory body recommendations and materials to the council for its consideration, lead staff should coordinate advisory body meetings with the meeting schedule of the internal committee that receives the initial submission.

4. *Minutes.* Following the open meeting guidelines, minutes should contain a brief description of the proposal or other matter considered (e.g., a recommendation that the Judicial Council adopt a rule) and the action taken (e.g., the advisory body recommended that the rule be adopted by the Judicial Council, effective on a particular date). An advisory body may provide more detailed minutes, if necessary.

V. Reports and Recommendations to the Judicial Council

1. *Report writing.* The Judicial Council report writing manual, *The ABC's of 21st Century Judicial Council Report Writing*, specifies the proper format and content standards for all council reports.

2. *Notification of Judicial Council agenda items.* In an effort to assist the Executive and Planning Committee with its agenda-setting responsibilities, Judicial Council staff should submit a draft *Judicial Council Agenda Request* form to Judicial Council Support as early in the process as possible.

3. *Report submission.* Reports to the Judicial Council from an advisory body are first submitted to the Executive and Planning Committee for agenda setting through the approved process and format. Lead staff and report authors should be familiar with and adhere to the chart *JC Report Deadlines and E&P Meeting Dates*,[2] which details a process and timeline that allows the Executive and Planning Committee to consider the readiness and completeness of the report and, if necessary, to ask the advisory body for revisions.

4. *Recommendations.* Reports may reflect an advisory body's recommendations or provide options without a recommendation, allowing the council to weigh the policy considerations in making its decision. The advisory body should carefully consider the recommendations or options that it presents to the council to ensure that they are limited to a manageable number for implementation by the courts or by council staff within reasonable timeframes. This requires regular check-in on scope and expectations with the internal oversight committee chair and executive leadership throughout the process.

5. *Fiscal considerations.* Recommendations or options that may have a significant and unforeseen fiscal impact should be raised with the Administrative Director and the Chief of Staff. The Administrative Director and the Chief of Staff will consult the assigned internal oversight committee chair on financial impacts of concern before the recommendations or options are finalized and the council report is developed. Depending on the outcome of that review, the advisory body may need to conduct additional analysis of the recommendations or options.

VI. Public Access

1. *Rule 10.75.* Public access to advisory body meetings and meeting materials, and meeting minutes as official records, are addressed in rule 10.75 of the California Rules of Court and in the open meeting guidelines. The rule includes a list of advisory bodies that are exempt from the requirements.

2. *Web page content.* The lead staff to each advisory body is responsible for working with web content staff to maintain a public web page with information about the advisory body's charge and its membership and activities.

3. *Member rosters.* Rosters should be accurate and kept current and consistent between internal and public postings.

Appendix D amended effective April 16, 2020; previously amended effective January 1, 2016, and January 1, 2018.

Appendix D. 2020 Deletes. [1] and Projects [2] Policy Coordination and Liaison [3] Policy Coordination and Liaison

---

[1] The form and the accompanying instructions may be accessed on the Judicial Council staff intranet under Reference, Judicial Council & Advisory Bodies, Subcommittee Appointment Process and Request Form.

[2] Posted on the Judicial Council staff intranet under Calendars, JC Report Deadlines.

Appendix E
Guidelines for Determining Financial Eligibility for County Payment of the Cost of Counsel Appointed by the Court in Proceedings Under the Guardianship-Conservatorship Law

1. **Purpose**
2. **Persons responsible for payment of the cost of appointed counsel**
3. **Cost of appointed counsel**
4. **Presumed eligibility for county payment**
5. **Determination of responsible person's obligation for the cost of appointed counsel**
6. **Apportionment**
7. **Private appointed counsel for conservatee under section 1470**
8. **Amount payable by the county**

1. Purpose

These guidelines are adopted to implement Probate Code section 1470(c)(3), which provides that the Judicial Council shall adopt guidelines to assist in determining financial eligibility for county payment of all or part of the reasonable sum fixed by the court for compensation and expenses of counsel appointed by the court under chapter 4 of part 1 of division 4 of the Probate Code.

2. Persons responsible for payment of the cost of appointed counsel

Except to the extent that they are determined to be unable to pay for all or any portion of the cost of appointed counsel under paragraph 5 of these guidelines, the following persons or estates of persons (referred to collectively as the "responsible person") are responsible for the payment of that cost:

A. The estate of the ward or proposed ward in a guardianship proceeding under section 1470;

B. The parent or parents of the ward or proposed ward in a guardianship proceeding under section 1470;

C. The estate of a conservatee or proposed conservatee in a conservatorship proceeding under sections 1470–1472;

D. The conservatee or proposed conservatee, if he or she has no estate, in a conservatorship proceeding under sections 1471–1472;

E. The person alleged to lack legal capacity in a proceeding to authorize a particular transaction in community property under sections 1471–1472, to the extent the court does not order the cost paid from the proceeds of the transaction under section 1472(a)(3); and

F. The health care patient in a proceeding to determine his or her capacity to make a health care decision under sections 1471–1472.

3. Cost of appointed counsel

The cost of appointed counsel is the reasonable sum fixed by the court after the performance of legal services under Probate Code section 1470 or section 1472 for the compensation and expenses of appointed counsel.

4. Presumed eligibility for county payment

Except as provided in paragraph 7, the person responsible for payment of the cost of appointed counsel is presumed to be eligible for payment by the county of that cost if the person satisfies one or more of the following three conditions:

A. The responsible person is eligible for:

(1) Supplemental Security Income (SSI) and State Supplementary Payment (SSP);

(2) Medi-Cal;

(3) General Assistance or General Relief (GA/GR) Program (county general relief);

(4) Cash Assistance Program for [aged, blind, and disabled legal] Immigrants (CAPI);

(5) CalWORKs (California Work Opportunity and Responsibility to Kids) or Tribal (Native American) TANF (Temporary Assistance for Needy Families) grant program;

(6) CalFresh (Supplemental Nutrition Assistance Program (SNAP)) or California Food Assistance Program (CFAP), a California program for immigrants not eligible for federal SNAP; or

(7) In-Home Supportive Services (IHSS);

B. The responsible person's income is 125 percent or less of current federal poverty guidelines, updated periodically in the Federal Register by the United States Department of Health and Human Services; or

C. The responsible person, as individually determined by the court, cannot pay the cost of appointed counsel without using funds that would be normally used to pay for the common necessaries of life for the responsible person and his or her family.

5. Determination of responsible person's obligation for the cost of appointed counsel

If the court finds that the responsible person, including a responsible person described in paragraph 4, can pay all or a portion of the cost of appointed counsel, can pay those costs in installments, or can pay those costs under some other equitable arrangement without using money that normally would pay for the common necessaries of life for the responsible person and the responsible person's family, the court may order the responsible person to pay appointed counsel directly, reimburse the county for the costs of appointed counsel paid by the county, or both, in part or on such other terms as the court determines are fair and reasonable under the circumstances.

6. Apportionment

If the responsible person is the estate of a ward or proposed ward and one or both of his or her parents, the court may allocate the amount determined to be payable by the responsible person under paragraph 5 among them in any proportions the court deems just.

7. Private appointed counsel for conservatee under section 1470

A conservatee or proposed conservatee for whom private counsel is appointed under Probate Code section 1470 is ineligible for payment by the county of any portion of the cost of appointed counsel.

8. Amount payable by the county

Except as provided in paragraph 7, the amount payable by the county for the cost of appointed counsel is all or any part of the cost that the court determines that the responsible person cannot pay under paragraph 5.

Appendix E adopted effective January 1, 2013.

Advisory Committee Comment

The guidelines placed in Appendix E to the California Rules of Court are not rules of court. They are based in part on the conditions for granting an initial court fee waiver under Government Code section 68632(a)–(c). For the purposes of these guidelines as well as of that Government Code section, the term "common necessaries of life" has the same meaning it had in Code of Civil Procedure section 706.051(c)(1) before the amendment of that section effective on January 1, 2012. (Assem. Bill 1388; Stats. 2011, ch. 694, § 1.)

The 2012 amendment of section 706.051(c)(1) completely eliminated "common necessaries of life" from that code section. The deleted phrase referred to an exception to the exemption provided in the section from an earnings withholding order for amounts the debtor can prove are necessary to support himself or herself and his or her family, often referred to as the support exemption. In other words, under former section 706.051(c)(1), the support exemption of section 706.051(b) would not apply to shield the debtor from an earnings withholding order to collect a debt incurred to purchase the "common necessaries of life."

The following appellate cases discussed the meaning of "common necessaries of life" as that phrase was used in section 706.051(c)(1) and predecessor code sections that used the phrase for the same purpose:

- A debt for hospital services to defendant or his family was based on the common necessaries of life. (*J. J. MacIntyre Co. v. Duren* (1981) 118 Cal.App.3d Supp. 16.)
- The performance of legal services and the advancement of costs of litigation giving rise to award to an attorney in marriage dissolution action qualified as "common necessaries of life" for the benefit of the debtor's indigent wife, thereby permitting the attorney to enforce the award by writ of execution on the husband's earnings against his claim of the support exemption. (*In re Marriage of Pallesi* (1977) 73 Cal.App.3d 424.)

- "Common necessaries of life," in former section 690.11 (repealed) exempting debts incurred for common necessaries of life from a statute protecting all of a judgment debtor's earnings from execution or attachment if earnings were necessary for the support of the debtor's family, did not refer to "necessaries" in the broad sense, but meant things that are ordinarily required for everyone's sustenance. (*Ratzlaff v. Portillo* (1971) 14 Cal.App.3d 1013.)
- Attorney's fees former wife incurred in obtaining divorce were not common "necessaries of life" within the meaning of former section 690.11 (repealed). (*Lentfoehr v. Lentfoehr* (1955) 134 Cal.App.2d Supp. 905.)
- "Common necessaries of life," as used in former section 690.11 (repealed), exempting all of the earnings of a debtor if necessary for the use or support of debtor's family residing within the state, except as against the collection of debts incurred by debtor, his wife, or family for common necessaries of life—meant those things that are commonly required by persons for their sustenance regardless of their employment or status. (*Los Angeles Finance Co. v. Flores* (1952) 110 Cal.App.2d Supp. 850.)
- In proceedings supplemental to execution, the debtor was required to pay one-half of a check for $47.50, which was in her possession, and which had been received as salary from the Works Progress Administration, in partial satisfaction of a judgment based on a necessary of life, although money may have been needed by debtor for the support of herself and her family. (*Medical Finance Association v. Short* (1939) 36 Cal.App.2d Supp. 745.)

Appendix F
Guidelines for the Juvenile Dependency Counsel Collections Program (JDCCP)

1. Legal Authority
2. Effective Date
3. Responsible Person—Definition
4. No Liability
5. Determination of Cost of Legal Services
6. Determination of Ability to Pay; Financial Evaluation Officer; Statewide Standard
7. Judicial Proceeding Following Determination of Ability to Reimburse Cost
8. Reevaluation of Ability to Pay
9. Frequency of Determination of Ability to Pay and Assessment
10. Collection Services
11. Recovery of Program Implementation Costs
12. Remittance and Reporting of Collected Revenue
13. Program Data Reporting
14. Allocation of Collected Funds to Trial Courts
15. Technical Assistance

1. Legal Authority

These guidelines are adopted under the authority of section 903.47 of the Welfare and Institutions Code,[1] which mandates that the Judicial Council "establish a program to collect reimbursements from the person liable for the costs of counsel appointed to represent parents or minors pursuant to Section 903.1 in dependency proceedings." (Welf. & Inst. Code, § 903.47(a).) As part of the program, the statute requires the council to "[a]dopt a statewide standard for determining [a responsible person's] ability to pay reimbursements for counsel." This standard must "at a minimum include the family's income, their necessary obligations, the number of people dependent on this income, and the cost-effectiveness of the program." *(Ibid.)* The statute also requires the council to "[a]dopt policies and procedures allowing a court to recover from the money collected the costs associated with implementing the reimbursements program."[2] These policies and procedures must, in turn, "limit the amount of money a court may recover to a reasonable proportion of the reimbursements collected and provide the terms and conditions under which a court may use a third party to collect reimbursements." *(Ibid.)*

Section 903.1 imposes liability on specified persons and estates for the cost of legal services provided to the child and directly to those persons in dependency proceedings. These responsible persons are jointly and severally liable for the cost of the child's representation. If the petition is dismissed at or before the jurisdictional hearing, though, no liability attaches.

Section 904 authorizes the trial court to determine the cost of dependency-related legal services using methods or procedures approved by the Judicial Council.

Under section 903.47(b), the court may designate a court financial evaluation officer (FEO) or, with the consent of the county, a county financial evaluation officer (FEO) to determine a responsible person's ability to pay the cost of court-appointed counsel. The court refers any responsible person to the designated FEO at the close of the dispositional hearing under section 903.45(b) unless that referral would not be cost-effective under section 903.47(a)(1)(A). The FEO then determines the responsible person's ability to pay all or part of the cost of dependency-related legal services under the procedures and within the limits set by section 903.45(b). The statutory scheme, particularly sections 901 and 903, prohibits the assessed amount from exceeding the actual cost of the legal services.

Sections 903.1(c) and 903.47(a)(2) direct each court to deposit collected reimbursements in the same manner as it deposits revenue collected under section 68085.1 of the Government Code. The Judicial Council must then transfer the remitted reimbursements to the Trial Court Trust Fund (TCTF).

Except as otherwise authorized by law, the Judicial Council must allocate the funds collected through the reimbursement program to reduce court-appointed attorney caseloads to the Judicial Council–approved standard. In determining allocations, the council must give priority to courts with the highest attorney caseloads that also demonstrate the ability to immediately improve outcomes for parents and children as the result of lower caseloads.

2. Effective Date

These guidelines are effective for all dependency proceedings filed on or after January 1, 2013. Amendments adopted after that date will take effect as specified by the Judicial Council, but no sooner than 30 days after the council meeting at which they are adopted.

3. Responsible Person—Definition

"Responsible person," as used in these guidelines, refers to the father, mother, spouse, or any other person liable for the support of a child; the estate of that person; or the estate of the child, as made liable under section 903.1(a) for the cost of dependency-related legal services rendered to the child or directly to that person.

4. No Liability

Under section 903.1(b), a responsible person is not liable for, and the court will not seek reimbursement of, the cost of legal services under section 903.1(a) if the dependency petition is dismissed at or before the jurisdictional hearing.

5. Determination of Cost of Legal Services

The court is charged with determining the cost of dependency-related legal services. In doing so, the court may adopt **one** of the three methods in (a)–(c). In no event will the court seek reimbursement of an amount that exceeds the actual cost of legal services already provided to the children and the responsible person in the proceeding. The court may update its determination of the cost of legal services on an annual basis, on the conclusion of the dependency proceedings in the juvenile court, or on the cessation of representation of the child or responsible person.

(a) Actual Cost
The court may determine the actual cost of the legal services provided to a child or responsible person in a dependency proceeding. The court should base this determination on the actual cost incurred per event in the proceeding, per hour billed, or per client represented.

(b) Cost Model
The court may determine the cost of legal services provided to a child or responsible person in a dependency proceeding by applying the Uniform Regional Cost Model available on *jrn.courts.ca.gov* or from *jdccp@jud.ca.gov*. Use of the cost model as described in this section will ensure that the court seeks reimbursement of an amount that most closely approximates, but does not exceed, the actual cost incurred by the court.

(1) *Time Allocated to Each Event per Attorney*
The court will calculate the time allocated to each event in a local dependency proceeding by

(A) Dividing the normative caseload of 141 clients per attorney by the actual caseload reported by the dependency attorneys in the county in which the court sits, and then

(B) Multiplying the result by the number of hours allocated to the type of event in question by the Dependency Counsel Caseload Study.[3]

(2) *Cost of Each Event per Attorney*
The court will then calculate the cost of each type of event by multiplying the time allocated to the event by

---

[1] Except as otherwise specified, all statutory references in these guidelines are to the Welfare and Institutions Code.

[2] This section defines *costs associated with implementing the reimbursements program* as the "court costs of assessing a parent's ability to pay for court-appointed counsel and the costs to collect delinquent reimbursements."

[3] See Center for Families, Children & Cts., Admin. Off. of Cts. Rep., *Court-Appointed Counsel: Caseload Standards, Service Delivery Models, and Contract Administration* (June 23, 2004), p. 3 & appen.

(A) The actual hourly rate billed to the court for the provision of dependency-related legal services, or

(B) The lowest actual hourly rate billed for dependency-related legal services in the region[4] in which the court is located as reported in the most recent survey of those rates, or

(C) The approved hourly rate for the region in which the court is located as provided in the Caseload Funding Model (CFM) approved by the Judicial Council in October 2007 and June 2008.[5]

(3) *Cost of Proceeding per Attorney*

The court will then calculate the cost of the services provided by an attorney in a dependency proceeding by adding together the costs of each event that has occurred in the proceeding at issue.

(c) Flat Rate Fee Structure

The court may adopt a flat rate fee structure for the cost of legal services in a dependency proceeding as long as the fees charged do not exceed the actual cost of the services provided in that proceeding up to and including the date of the determination and assessment.

6. Determination of Ability to Pay; Financial Evaluation Officer; Statewide Standard

(a) Referral for Financial Evaluation

At the close of the dispositional hearing, the court will order any responsible person present at the hearing to appear before a designated financial evaluation officer (FEO) for a determination of the responsible person's ability to pay reimbursement of all or part of the cost of legal services for which he or she is liable under section 903.1(a), unless the court finds that, given the resources of the court, evaluation by an FEO would not be a cost-effective method of determining the responsible person's ability to pay.

(1) *Responsible Person Not Present at Dispositional Hearing*

If a responsible person is not present at the dispositional hearing, the court will issue proper notice and an order for him or her to appear before an FEO for determination of his or her ability to pay reimbursement of all or part of the cost of legal services for which he or she is liable under section 903.1(a) unless the court finds that evaluation by an FEO would not be a cost-effective method of determining the responsible person's ability to pay given the resources of the court.

To issue proper notice to a responsible person not present at the hearing at which appearance for a financial evaluation is ordered, the court should send *Order to Appear for Financial Evaluation* (form JV-131) or the equivalent local form by first-class mail to that person's mailing address of record.

(2) *Alternative Methods*

If the court finds that evaluation by an FEO is not cost-effective, it may take whatever steps it deems cost-effective to determine the responsible person's ability to pay.

(3) *Failure to Appear for Financial Evaluation*

If a responsible person is ordered to appear for financial evaluation, has received proper notice, and fails to appear as ordered, the FEO will recommend that the court order the responsible person to pay the full cost of legal services as determined under section 5 of these guidelines unless the next paragraph applies.

If a responsible person is not present at the hearing at which the order to appear for a financial evaluation is made, has received proper notice and an order to appear, and responds to the order by submitting a declaration that he or she is involuntarily confined and therefore not able to attend or reschedule the evaluation, the FEO or the court may presume that he or she is unable to pay reimbursement and is eligible for a waiver of liability at that time.

(4) *Proper Notice*

Proper notice to a responsible person will contain notice of all of the following:

(A) His or her right to a statement of the costs as soon as it is available;

(B) His or her procedural rights under section 27755 of the Government Code;

(C) The time limit within which his or her appearance is required; and

(D) A warning that if he or she fails to appear before the FEO, the officer will recommend that the court order him or her to pay the full cost of legal services, and that the FEO's recommendation will be a sufficient basis for the court to order payment of an amount up to the full cost.

(b) Financial Evaluation Officer

The court may either designate a court FEO to determine responsible persons' ability to reimburse the cost of legal services or, with the consent of and under terms agreed to by the county, designate a county FEO to determine responsible persons' ability to reimburse the cost of legal services.

(c) Authority of Financial Evaluation Officer

The designated FEO will conduct the evaluation under the procedures outlined in section 903.45(b). The FEO may determine a referred responsible person's ability to pay all or part of the cost of legal services for which he or she is liable, negotiate a plan for reimbursement over a set period of time based on the responsible person's financial condition, enter into an agreement with the responsible person regarding the amount to be reimbursed and the terms of reimbursement, petition the court for an order of reimbursement according to the terms agreed to with the responsible person, and refer the responsible person back to court for a hearing in the event of a lack of agreement.

(d) Standard for Determining Ability to Pay

The FEO will determine the responsible person's ability to reimburse the cost of legal services using the following standard:

(1) *Presumptive Inability to Pay; Waiver*

If a responsible person receives qualifying public benefits or has a household income 125 percent or less of the threshold established by the federal poverty guidelines in effect at the time of the inquiry, then he or she is presumed to be unable to pay reimbursement and is eligible for a waiver of liability.

(A) *Qualifying public benefits* include benefits under any of the programs listed in Government Code section 68632(a).

(2) *Further Inquiry*

If the court has concluded as a matter of policy that further inquiry into the financial condition of persons presumed unable to pay would not be warranted or cost-effective, the inquiry may end at this point with a determination that the person is unable to pay.

If the court has concluded as a matter of policy that further inquiry into the financial condition of persons presumed unable to pay is warranted notwithstanding the presumption, the FEO may proceed to a detailed evaluation under (d)(3).

(3) *Responsible Person's Financial Condition*

The FEO may, at any time following the close of the dispositional hearing, make a detailed evaluation of a referred responsible person's financial condition at that time under section 903.45(b). Based on any relevant information submitted by the responsible person, including but not limited to a completed *Financial Declaration—Juvenile Dependency* (form JV-132) or the equivalent local form, the FEO will assess the responsible person's household income, household needs and obligations (including other court-ordered obligations), and the number of persons dependent on the household income and will determine the person's ability to pay all or part of the cost of legal services without using funds that would normally be used to pay for the common necessaries of life.

When calculating a person's household income, the FEO must exclude from consideration any benefits received from a public assistance program that determines eligibility based on need.[6]

(e) Circumstances Requiring No Petition or Order for Reimbursement

Under section 903.45(b), the FEO may not petition the court to order reimbursement of the cost of legal services, and the court will not so order, if:

(1) The responsible person has been reunified with any of the children under a court order and the FEO determines that requiring repayment would harm his or her ability to support the children;

(2) The responsible person is currently receiving reunification services and the court or the FEO determines that requiring repayment will pose a barrier to reunification; or

---

[4] California trial courts are grouped into four regions based on parity in cost of living, attorney salaries, and other factors among counties in a given region. See Center for Families, Children & Cts., Admin. Off. of Cts. Rep., *DRAFT Pilot Program and Court-Appointed Counsel* (Oct. 26, 2007), pp. 7–8.

[5] See *id.*, at pp. 7–10; Trial Court Budget Working Group Rep., *Court-Appointed Counsel Compensation Model and Workload-Based Funding Methodology* (June 10, 2008).

[6] *In re S.M.* (2012) 209 Cal.App.4th 21, 28–31.

Rules of Court

(3) The court determines that requiring repayment would be unjust under the circumstances of the case.

(f) Amount Assessed

The FEO may, consistent with the responsible person's ability to pay, assess any amount up to the full cost determined under section 5 of these guidelines, and may recommend reimbursement in a single lump sum or in multiple installments over a set period of time.

(g) Agreement; Petition

If the responsible person agrees in writing to the FEO's written determination of the amount that the responsible person is able to reimburse and the terms of reimbursement, the FEO will petition the court for an order requiring the responsible person to reimburse the court in a manner that is reasonable and compatible with the responsible person's financial condition.

(h) Dispute; Referral

If the responsible person disputes his or her liability for the cost of legal services, the amount of that cost, the FEO's determination of his or her ability to reimburse all or part of that cost, or the terms of reimbursement, the FEO will refer the matter, with his or her written determination, back to the juvenile court for a hearing.

7. Judicial Proceeding Following Determination of Ability to Reimburse Cost

On having made a determination of the responsible person's ability to reimburse all or part of the cost of legal services, the FEO will return the matter to the juvenile court as follows:

(a) Agreement; Order

If the responsible person agrees to reimburse the court as recommended by the FEO, the FEO will prepare an agreement to be signed by the responsible person. The agreement will reflect the amount to be reimbursed and the terms under which reimbursement will be paid. The juvenile court may order the responsible person to pay reimbursement under those terms without further notice to the responsible person.

(b) Dispute; Hearing

If the matter is deemed in dispute and the FEO has referred the matter back to the juvenile court under section 6(h), the court will set and conduct a hearing under section 903.45(b).

(c) Judicial Determination

If, at the conclusion of the hearing, the court determines that the responsible person is able to reimburse all or part of the cost of legal services—including the cost of any attorney appointed to represent the responsible person at that hearing—without using funds that would normally be used to pay for the common necessaries of life, the court will set the amount to be reimbursed and order the responsible person to pay that amount to the court in a manner that the court believes reasonable and compatible with the responsible person's financial condition.

8. Reevaluation of Ability to Pay

At any time before reimbursement is complete, a responsible person may petition the court to modify or vacate the reimbursement order based on a change in circumstances affecting his or her ability to pay. The court may deny the petition without a hearing if the petition fails to state a change of circumstances. The court may grant the petition without a hearing if the petition states a change of circumstances and all parties stipulate to the requested modification.

9. Frequency of Determination of Ability to Pay and Assessment

The initial evaluation and determination of a responsible person's ability to pay reimbursement may be conducted at any time following the conclusion of the dispositional hearing. The court may order a reevaluation of a responsible person's financial condition on an annual basis, on the conclusion of the dependency proceedings in the juvenile court, or on the cessation of court-appointed representation of the child or the responsible person.

If the FEO determines on reevaluation that the responsible person is able at that time to pay all or part of the cost of legal services, the FEO may, consistent with the responsible person's ability to pay without using funds that would normally be used to pay for the common necessaries of life, assess an amount up to the full cost, as determined under section 5, of any legal services provided to the child or the responsible person and may recommend reimbursement in a single lump sum or in multiple installments over a set period of time.

10. Collection Services

(a) Court-Based Collection Services

To the extent applicable and consistent with sections 903.1 and 903.47, a court should administer the collection, processing, and deposit of court-ordered reimbursement of the cost of dependency-related legal services under the procedures in policies FIN 10.01 and FIN 10.02 of the *Trial Court Financial Policies and Procedures Manual*.

(b) Outside Collection-Services Providers

When appropriate and consistent with policy FIN 10.01, a court may use an outside collection-services provider.

(1) *Collection Services Provided by County*

If collection services are provided by the county, the agreement should be formalized by a memorandum of understanding (MOU) between the court and county. Judicial Council staff will provide a sample MOU on request. An electronic copy of the MOU, including a scanned copy of the completed signature page, must be sent to *jdccp@jud.ca.gov*.

(2) *Collection Services Provided by Private Vendor*

A court that uses a private collection service should use a vendor that has entered into a master agreement with the Judicial Council to provide comprehensive collection services. A court that uses such a vendor should complete a participation agreement and send it to Judicial Council staff via e-mail to *jdccp@jud.ca.gov*. A court may contract directly with a private vendor only on terms and conditions substantially similar to those set forth in the master agreements for comprehensive collection services available at *jrn.courts.ca.gov/programs/collections/mva.htm*.

(3) *Court Option for Judicial Council Agreement with Collection-Services Provider*

At a court's request, the Judicial Council may directly enter into an MOU with the county or an agreement with a private collection-services vendor for services under this program.

(c) Agreements Between Courts

Nothing in this section is intended to preclude a court or courts from establishing an agreement with another court or courts for one or more courts to perform services under this program on behalf of other courts, or for one or more courts to combine collection efforts under this program.

11. Recovery of Program Implementation Costs

A court may recover, from the money it has collected, its eligible program implementation costs before remitting the balance of the collected funds to the state in the manner required by Government Code section 68085.1. Eligible costs are limited by statute to the cost of determining responsible persons' ability to repay the cost of court-appointed counsel and to the cost of collecting delinquent reimbursements. If a court's eligible costs in any given month exceed the amount of revenue it has collected in that month, the court may carry the excess costs forward within the same fiscal year until sufficient revenue is collected to recover the eligible costs in full. Any program costs recovered by the court must be documented by the court and reported monthly by e-mail to *jdccp@jud.ca.gov* in a format consistent with the Cost Recovery Template available on *jrn.courts.ca.gov* or from *jdccp@jud.ca.gov*.

(a) Delinquent Reimbursement Defined

For purposes of this section, *delinquent reimbursement* means any reimbursement payment not received within one business day of the date it is due.

12. Remittance and Reporting of Collected Revenue

A court will remit collected revenue, less recovered costs, to the state in the same manner as required under Government Code section 68085.1 and will report this revenue on row 130 of *Court Remittance Advice* (form TC-145). The Judicial Council will deposit the revenue received through this program into the Trial Court Trust Fund as required by statute.

(a) Judicial Council Collections Agreement Option

Where the Judicial Council has entered into an MOU or an agreement with a county or a private collection-services vendor under section 10(b)(3) of these guidelines, funds will be remitted directly to the Judicial Council under the terms of the MOU or the agreement.

13. Program Data Reporting

Each court should report JDCCP data to Judicial Council staff to ensure implementation of the Legislature's intent by determining the cost-effectiveness of the program and confirming that efforts to collect reimbursement do not negatively impact reunification; to provide a basis for projecting the amount of future reimbursements; and to evaluate the JDCCP's effectiveness both statewide and at the local level.

(a) Ongoing Reporting Requirement

To support the amount remitted to the Trial Court Trust Fund, each court will report collections data annually on or before September 30, beginning September 30, 2013. The first report should cover the period from January 1, 2013, to June 30, 2013. Each court should submit its completed report attached to an e-mail message to *jdccp@jud.ca.gov*.

(1) *Data Reporting*

Judicial Council staff will provide a reporting template that solicits the following information:

(A) Total number of responsible persons evaluated in the reporting period to determine their ability to pay

(B) Number of persons in (A) found unable to pay

(C) Number of persons in (A) found able to pay but not ordered to pay under section 6(e)

(D) Number of open accounts at the beginning of the reporting period

(E) Dollar amount in open accounts at the beginning of the reporting period

(F) Number of new accounts opened in the reporting period

(G) Dollar amount in accounts opened during the reporting period

(H) Total dollar amount collected from all accounts in the reporting period

(I) Number of accounts closed or discharged in the reporting period

(J) Number of open accounts at the end of the reporting period

(K) Dollar amount in open accounts at the end of the reporting period

(2) *JDCCP Implementation Review*

Within two years of the effective date of these guidelines and thereafter as needed, the Judicial Council will evaluate the progress of the JDCCP's statewide implementation and examine the impact of the program on court workload and finances. For this purpose, Judicial Council staff may survey the courts about their financial evaluation processes, including the time and resources needed to determine responsible persons' ability to pay, the number of such persons evaluated, the results of the evaluations as specified in 6(d)–(g), and the number of judicial hearings necessary under 7(b)–(c).

14. Allocation of Collected Funds to Trial Courts

(a) Eligibility for Allocation

A trial court is eligible to receive an allocation from the funds remitted through the JDCCP for the purpose of reducing its dependency-counsel caseload if it meets the following criteria.

(1) *Participation*

The court has demonstrated its participation in the JDCCP by

(A) adopting a local rule or policy requiring the juvenile court to inquire at or before the close of each dispositional hearing about each responsible person's ability to pay reimbursement and

(B) submitting annual reports under section 13.

(2) *Funding Need*

The court receives a base court-appointed counsel allocation that, viewed as a percentage of the available statewide funding, is less than its percentage share of the statewide court-appointed counsel funding need as estimated by the CFM.[7]

(b) Allocation Methodology

Remitted funds will be allocated annually, as part of the court-appointed counsel budget development process, to each eligible court in an amount equivalent to its need as a percentage of the estimated aggregate funding need of all eligible courts. Any allocation from the remitted funds is separate from, and in addition to, a court's allocation from the statewide court-appointed counsel funding base.

The Judicial Council provides a single funding allocation to the DRAFT program to support court-appointed counsel in participating courts. This funding is managed by the Judicial Council as part of the court-appointed counsel budget development and funding process. Collected reimbursements allocated to the DRAFT program will also be managed by the council through this process.

(c) Review of Determination of Funding Level

A court that believes that the amount of its allocation is due to an error in determining its funding need may request a review of that determination within 90 days. The request should clearly state the nature of the error.

The review will be conducted collaboratively by the court and the Judicial Council.

15. Technical Assistance

Judicial Council staff will provide technical assistance on request to courts that are in the process of implementing the JDCCP or that wish to coordinate collection efforts with other courts. Courts may send requests by e-mail to *jdccp@jud.ca.gov* to receive technical assistance, which can include (but is not limited to) services such as:

(a) Helping a court implement the reimbursement program within its current administrative structure;

(b) Advising a court on the application of the Uniform Cost Model under section 5(b) of these guidelines;

(c) Coordinating a regional reimbursement program among several courts; or

(d) Working with current collection-services providers who have entered into master agreements with the Judicial Council to ensure compliance with the JDCCP reporting requirements.

Appendix F amended effective July 1, 2016; adopted effective January 1, 2013; previously amended effective September 23, 2013, and January 1, 2016.

---

[7] In October 2007, the TCBWG developed and the Judicial Council approved a need-based compensation or caseload funding model (CFM) for court-appointed dependency counsel practicing in courts under the DRAFT program. (See Trial Court Budget Working Group Rep., *supra* note 5.) In June 2008, the council's Executive and Planning Committee extended that methodology to appointed dependency counsel in all juvenile courts statewide. The CFM uses the number of data-supported clients in a county to determine the number of FTE attorneys needed to serve that population at the Judicial Council–approved caseload standard of 188 clients per FTE attorney. (See *id.*, at p. 4.) It then uses cost of living, county counsel salaries, and other economic factors to assign each court to one of four statewide groups. (See *id.*, at p. 5.) To promote equity in attorney compensation, each group of courts is assigned an attorney salary level based on the prevailing county counsel salary range in that group. Each court's appointed-counsel salary needs are determined by multiplying the mid-tier salary level by the number of FTE attorneys needed to serve the client population at the approved caseload. The cost of benefits and overhead, including support staff, are calculated at assigned percentages of the attorney salaries. Adding these elements together yields a precise estimate of the funding needed for a court to ensure competent representation of all parties in juvenile dependency proceedings under sections 317(c) and 317.5, as well as rule 5.660(d) of the California Rules of Court.

Appendix G
Parliamentary Procedures for the Judicial Council of California

Approved by the Judicial Council on December 14, 2012

I. Introduction

These parliamentary procedures are a set of rules for conducting business at Judicial Council meetings.

II. Establishing a Quorum

A quorum is defined as the minimum number of members of the body who must be present at a meeting for business to be legally transacted. The Judicial Council abides by a rule providing that a quorum is one more than half the *voting* members. Because there are 21 voting members on the council, there must be 11 voting members present to legally transact business. Even if the council has a quorum to begin the meeting, it can lose the quorum during the meeting when a member departs. When that occurs, the council loses its ability to transact business until and unless a quorum is reestablished.

III. The Role of the Chair

While all members of the council should know and understand the rules of parliamentary procedure, it is the Chair who is charged with applying the rules in the conduct of the meeting. The Chair, for all intents and purposes, makes the final ruling on the rules every time he or she states an action. In fact, all decisions by the Chair are final unless overruled by the council itself.

Because the Chair conducts the meeting, normally the Chair will play a less active role in the debate and discussion than other members of the council. This does not mean that the Chair should not participate in the debate or discussion. The Chair as a member of the council has the full right to participate in the debate, discussion, and decision making of the council. However, the Chair should generally look to other council members to make or second motions.

IV. Voting Requirement for Judicial Council Action

To take any substantive action, a majority of all voting members of the Judicial Council must vote in favor of the action. (See Gov. Code, § 68508.) Because there are 21 voting members on the council, there must be a quorum of at least 11 members voting to take any action, and a vote on a substantive motion (as defined below) requires 11 affirmative votes to pass.

Advisory members of the council may make or second motions and may fully participate in discussion and debate, but are not counted for purposes of quorum, and may not vote. (See Cal. Rules of Court, rule 10.3(b).)

V. Motions in General

Motions are made in a simple two-step process. First, the Chair should recognize the council member. Second, the member makes a motion by preceding his or her desired approach with the words, "I move ...." A typical motion might be: "I move that we adopt the committee's recommendation."

The Chair usually initiates the motion by doing one of the following:

1. Inviting the council members to make a motion. "A motion at this time would be in order."
2. Suggesting a motion to the members. "A motion would be in order that we adopt the committee's recommendation."
3. Making the motion. As noted, the Chair has every right as a council member to make a motion, but should normally do so only if he or she wishes to make a motion on an item but is convinced that no other member is willing to step forward to do so at a particular time.

After a vote is taken, the Chair should announce the result of the vote as well as the vote count. For example, the Chair might say: "The motion to create a five-member working group to develop parliamentary procedures for the council has passed. The vote was 11 in favor, 9 opposed, and 1 abstention." By announcing the result and the vote count, the Chair clarifies what the council has done for the benefit of the council and the public. Rather than making the announcement, the Chair may ask the Secretary to announce the result of the vote as well as the vote count.

A. Substantive Motions

There are three substantive motions that are the most common and recur often at meetings:

The basic motion. The basic motion is the one that puts forward a decision for the council's consideration. A basic motion might be: "I move that we create a five-member working group to develop parliamentary procedures for the council."

The motion to amend. If a member wants to change a basic motion that is before the body, he or she would move to amend it. A motion to amend might be: "I move that we amend the motion to have a ten-member working group." A motion to amend takes the basic motion that is before the council and seeks to change it in some way. The council would first vote on whether the motion should be amended. If that motion passes, the council would then vote on the motion itself as amended.

The substitute motion. If a member wants to completely do away with the basic motion that is before the council and put a new motion in its place, he or she would move to make a substitute motion. A substitute motion might be: "I move that we impose a moratorium against appointing new working groups."

Motions to amend and substitute motions are often confused. But they are quite different, and their effect (if passed) is also quite different. A motion to amend seeks to retain the basic motion on the floor, but modify it in some way. A substitute motion seeks to throw out the basic motion on the floor and substitute a new and different motion for it. The decision on whether a motion is really a motion to amend or a substitute motion is left to the Chair. So if a member makes what that member calls a motion to amend, but the Chair determines that it is really a substitute motion, the Chair's designation governs.

The basic rule of substantive motions is that they are subject to discussion and debate. Accordingly, basic motions, motions to amend, and substitute motions are all eligible for full discussion by the council. The debate can continue as long as council members wish to discuss an item, subject to the decision of the Chair that it is time to move on and take action.

For a substantive motion to pass, it requires the affirmative concurrence of a majority of voting members of the council. In other words, 11 voting members of the council must vote in favor of a substantive motion for it to pass. An abstention does not constitute a vote in favor of a motion. The order in which various motions are considered is addressed in section VI, Multiple Motions Before the Judicial Council, on pages 5–6.

B. Friendly Amendments

A "friendly amendment" is a practical parliamentary tool that is simple, informal, saves time, and avoids bogging down a meeting with numerous formal motions. It works as follows: During the discussion on a pending motion, it may appear that a change to the motion is desirable or may win support for the motion from some members. When that happens, a member who has the floor may simply say, "I would like to suggest a friendly amendment to the motion." The member suggests the friendly amendment, and if the maker and the person who seconded the motion pending on the floor accept the friendly amendment, that now becomes the pending motion on the floor. If either the maker or the person who seconded rejects the proposed friendly amendment, the proposer can formally move to amend.

C. Procedural Motions

In contrast to the substantive motions described above, which result in the council voting whether to take action, there are several types of procedural motions. These motions differ from substantive motions in both the applicability of the rule of free and open debate on motions and in the number of votes required to pass the motions. The procedural motions, all of which indicate a desire of the council to move on, are *not* debatable. Thus, when the motion is made and seconded, the Chair must immediately call for a vote without debate on the procedural motion.

As for votes on these motions, while substantive motions require the concurrence of 11 voting members, procedural motions require either a majority or a two-thirds vote (depending on the motion) of voting members who are present. For example, if 15 voting members are present, 8 votes are required to pass a motion that requires a majority vote, and 10 votes are required to pass a motion that requires a two-thirds vote. (The counting of votes is discussed in greater detail in section VII, Counting Votes, on pages 7–8.)

Procedural motions that require a **majority vote** include:

Motion to adjourn. This motion, if passed, requires the council to immediately adjourn to its next regularly scheduled meeting. It requires a simple majority vote of those present and voting to pass.

Motion to recess. This motion, if passed, requires the council to immediately take a recess. Normally, the Chair determines the length of the recess, which may be a few minutes or an hour. It requires a simple majority vote of those present and voting to pass.

Motion to fix the time to adjourn. This motion, if passed, requires the council to adjourn the meeting at the specific time set in the motion. For example, the motion might be: "I move we adjourn this meeting at 5 p.m." It requires a simple majority vote of those present and voting to pass.

Motion to table. This motion, if passed, requires discussion of the agenda item to be halted and the agenda item to be placed on "hold." The motion can contain a specific time in which the item can come back to the council: "I move we table this item until our regular meeting in October." Or the motion can contain no specific time for the return of the item, in which case a motion to take the item off the table and bring it back to the council will have to be taken at a future meeting. A motion to table an item (or to bring it back to the council) requires a simple majority vote of those present and voting to pass.

Procedural motions that require a **two-thirds vote** include:

Motion to object to consideration of an item. Normally, such a motion is unnecessary since the objectionable item can be tabled or simply defeated. However, when members of a body do not even want an item on the agenda to be considered, then such a motion is in order. It requires a two-thirds vote of those present and voting to pass.

Motion to limit debate. The most common form of this motion is to say: "I move the previous question" or "I move the question" or "I call the question" or simply "Question." As a practical matter, when a member calls out one of these phrases, the Chair can expedite things by treating it as a "request" rather than as a formal motion. The Chair can then simply inquire, "Is there any further discussion?" If no one wishes to discuss it further, the Chair can proceed to a vote on the underlying matter. On the other hand, if even one council member wishes further discussion and debate on the underlying matter, the Chair must treat the "call for the question" as a motion and proceed accordingly.

When a council member makes such a motion, he or she is really saying, "I've had enough debate. Let's get on with the vote." When such a motion is made, the Chair should ask for a second, stop debate, and vote on the motion to limit debate. Note that a motion to limit debate could include a time limit. For example: "I move we limit debate on this agenda item to 15 minutes." A motion to limit debate requires a two-thirds vote of those present and voting to pass.

D. Motions to Reconsider

There is a special and unique motion that requires a separate explanation: the motion to reconsider. A tenet of parliamentary procedure is finality. After vigorous discussion, debate, and a vote, there must be some closure

to the issue. Thus, after a vote is taken, the matter is deemed closed, subject only to reopening if a proper motion to reconsider is made and passed.

A motion to reconsider is a procedural motion that requires only a majority vote of those voting members who are present to pass, but there are two special rules that apply only to the motion to reconsider.

First is the matter of timing. A motion to reconsider must be made at the meeting at which the item was first voted upon. A motion to reconsider made at a later time is untimely.

Second, a motion to reconsider may be made only by a member who voted *in the majority* on the original motion. If such a member has a change of heart, he or she may make the motion to reconsider. (Any other council member may second the motion.) If a member who voted *in the minority* seeks to make the motion to reconsider, it must be ruled out of order. The purpose of this rule is finality. If a member of the minority could make a motion to reconsider, the item could be brought back to the council again and again, which would defeat the purpose of finality.

If the motion to reconsider passes, then the original matter is back before the body, and a new original motion is in order. The matter may be discussed and debated as if it were on the floor for the first time.

VI. Multiple Motions Before the Judicial Council

There can be up to three motions on the floor at the same time. The Chair can reject a fourth motion until he or she has addressed the three that are on the floor and has resolved them. This rule has practical value. More than three motions on the floor at one time tends to be too confusing and unwieldy for most everyone, including the Chair.

When there are two or three motions on the floor (after motions and seconds) at the same time, the vote should proceed *first* on the *last* motion that was made. So, for example, assume the first motion is a basic motion to appoint a 5-member working group to develop parliamentary procedures for the council. During the discussion of this motion, a member might make a second motion to amend the basic motion so that a 10-member working group would be appointed instead of a 5-member working group. And perhaps, during that discussion, another member makes yet a third motion as a substitute motion to impose a moratorium against appointing new working groups. The proper procedure would be as follows:

First, the Chair would address the third (the last) motion on the floor, the substitute motion. After discussion and debate, a vote would be taken on the third motion. If the substitute motion *passed*, it would be a substitute for the basic motion and would eliminate it. The first motion would be moot, as would the second motion (which sought to amend the first motion), and the action on the agenda item would be completed on the passage by the council of the third motion (the substitute motion). No vote would be taken on the first or second motions.

Second, if the substitute motion failed, the Chair would address the second (now, the last) motion on the floor, the motion to amend. The discussion and debate would focus strictly on the amendment (whether the committee should be 5 members or 10 members). If the motion to amend *passed*, the Chair would now move to consider the main motion (the first motion) *as amended*. If the motion to amend *failed*, the Chair would now move to consider the main motion (the first motion) in its original format, not amended.

VII. Counting Votes

A. Number of Votes Needed to Take Action

As noted above, for substantive motions, a minimum of 11 voting members must be present to constitute a quorum, and a minimum of 11 votes are needed to pass such substantive motions. For procedural motions, a minimum of 11 voting members must be present to constitute a quorum, and there must be either a majority vote or a two-thirds vote of voting members, depending on the motion, to pass such procedural motions.

When a majority vote is needed to pass a motion, one vote more than 50 percent of those voting is required. If a two-thirds vote is needed to pass a motion, there is a formula to determine how many affirmative votes are required. The simple rule of thumb is to count the "no" votes and double that count to determine how many "yes" votes are needed to pass a particular motion. So, for example, if 6 members vote "no," then the "yes" vote of at least 12 members is required to achieve a two-thirds majority vote to pass the motion.

In the event of a tie vote, the motion always fails because an affirmative vote is required to pass any motion. For example, if the vote is 10 in favor and 10 opposed, with 1 member absent, the motion is defeated.

B. Abstentions

Members sometimes prefer to abstain from voting. Members who abstain are counted for purposes of determining whether there is a quorum, but the abstention votes on the motion are treated as if they do not exist. In other words, an abstention is not treated as either a "yes" vote or a "no" vote.

C. Examples

Here are a few examples to illustrate vote-counting under different circumstances:

Majority Vote Counting

Assume that 21 voting members of the council are present to vote on a substantive motion, which requires 11 votes to pass. If the vote on the motion is 11 to 10, the motion passes. If the motion is 10 to 10 with 1 abstention, the motion fails because the abstention is not counted as a "yes" vote.

Assume that 18 members are present and voting on a procedural motion that requires only a majority vote to pass (as opposed to 11 votes). If the vote is 10 to 8, the motion passes. If the vote is 9 to 9, the motion fails. If the vote is 9 to 8 with 1 abstention, the motion fails because 10 votes are required for the motion to pass (one vote more than 50 percent). Once again, the abstention vote is counted only for the purpose of determining quorum, but on the actual vote on the motion, it is as if the abstention vote did not occur.

Two-Thirds Vote Counting

Assume 21 members are present and voting on a motion that requires a two-thirds vote to pass. If the vote is 11 to 10, the motion fails for lack of a two-thirds majority. If the vote is 18 to 3, the motion passes with a clear two-thirds majority. If the vote is 13 to 8, the motion fails. Using the formula discussed above, the "no" votes are counted and doubled to determine whether there are enough "yes" votes to constitute a two-thirds majority. If the vote is 13 to 6 with 2 abstentions, the motion passes because the abstentions are treated as if they don't exist, and with 6 "no" votes, 12 votes are needed to pass the motion. Therefore, the motion passes with 13 votes.

Abstention

To cast an "abstention" vote, a member either votes "abstain" or says "I abstain." However, if a member votes "present," that is also treated as an abstention. The member is essentially saying, "Count me for purposes of a quorum, but my vote on the issue is abstain." In fact, any manifestation of intention to vote neither "yes" nor "no" on the pending motion may be treated by the Chair as an abstention.

Absence

Can a member vote "absent" or "count me as absent?" The ruling on this is up to the Chair. The better approach is for the Chair to count this as a vote to abstain if the person does not actually leave the boardroom. If, however, the member leaves the boardroom and is actually absent, the Chair should count the member as absent. That, of course, may affect the quorum.

VIII. Alternative Methods of Voting

A. Voting by Proxy

Voting by proxy is not permitted. A Judicial Council member, therefore, may not authorize another person to vote on his or her behalf.

B. Attending Meetings and Voting by Telephone or Teleconference

Council members are permitted to attend meetings and vote by telephone or teleconference.

C. Early Voting

On occasion, a voting member of the Judicial Council may be unable to attend a council meeting or must depart before the presentation of a discussion item or the ensuing exchange is completed. Subdivision (c) of rule 10.5 (Notice and agenda of council meeting) defines the term "business meetings" as meetings "at which a majority of voting members are present to discuss and decide matters within the council's jurisdiction." The rule contemplates that members will be present for a discussion of the agenda item. Accordingly, a council member is not permitted to vote before the discussion about the agenda item has ended.

IX. Courtesy and Decorum

The rules of order are meant to create an atmosphere where council members and the public can attend to business efficiently, fairly, and with full participation. At the same time, it is up to the Chair and the council members to maintain common courtesy and decorum. It is always best for only one person at a time to have the floor, and it is always best for every speaker to be first recognized by the Chair before speaking.

The Chair should ensure that discussion and debate of an agenda item focuses on the item and the policy in question. The Chair has the right to cut off discussion that diverges from the agenda item.

Debate and discussion should be focused, but free and open. In the interest of time, the Chair may, however, limit the time allotted to speakers, including council members.

Council members should not interrupt the speaker. There are, however, exceptions. A speaker may be interrupted for the following reasons:

Privilege. The proper interruption would be to say, "Point of privilege." The Chair would then ask the interrupter to "state your point." Appropriate points of privilege relate to anything that would interfere with the normal comfort of the meeting. For example, the room may be too hot or too cold, or a blowing fan might interfere with a person's ability to hear.

Order. The proper interruption would be to say, "Point of order." Again, the Chair would ask the interrupter to "state your point." Appropriate points of order relate to anything that would not be considered appropriate conduct of the meeting, such as the Chair moving on to a vote on a motion that permits debate without allowing that discussion or debate.

Appeal. If the Chair makes a ruling with which a member of the body disagrees, that member may appeal the ruling of the Chair. For example, if the Chair deems a motion to be a substitute motion and a member considers it to be a motion to amend, the member may appeal that ruling. If the motion is seconded and, after debate, it passes by a simple majority vote, the ruling of the Chair is deemed reversed. The motion to appeal the ruling of the Chair is considered a procedural motion.

Call for orders of the day. This is simply another way of saying, "Let's return to the agenda." If a member believes that the council has drifted from the agenda, such a call may be made. It does not require a vote. If the Chair discovers that the agenda has not been followed, the Chair simply reminds the council members to return to the agenda item properly before them. If the Chair fails to do so, the Chair's determination may be appealed.

Withdraw a motion. During debate and discussion of a motion, the maker of the motion on the floor, at any time, may interrupt a speaker to withdraw his or her motion from the floor. The motion is immediately deemed withdrawn, although the Chair may ask the person who seconded the motion if he or she wishes to make the motion, and any other member may make the motion if properly recognized.

X. Recess and Adjournment

Unless there is an objection, the Chair may recess the council meeting for a definite period of time and may adjourn the meeting.

Appendix G adopted effective December 14, 2012.

Appendix H
Amount of Civil Penalty to Cure Alleged Violation of Proposition 65 for Failure to Provide Certain Warnings (Health & Saf. Code, § 26249.7(k))

Formula

Under Health and Safety Code section 26249.7(k), the amount of civil penalty per facility or premises that an alleged violator may agree to pay within 14 days of service of a notice of violation under that section will be computed and adjusted as follows:

$$\text{Adjusted penalty amount} = \left[\frac{\text{annual CCPI (Dec. 2018)} - \text{annual CCPI (Dec. 2013)}}{\text{annual CCPI (Dec. 2013)}} + 1 \right] \times \text{Previous dollar amount}$$

Definition

"CCPI" means the California Consumer Price Index for All Urban Comsumers, as established by the California Department of Industrial Relations.

Calculation and adjustment

Effective April 1, 2019, the amount of civil penalty that an alleged violator may agree to pay within 14 days of service of a notice of violation under Health and Safety Code section 26249.7(k)(2)(B)(ii) is **$565** per facility or premises where the alleged violation occurred.

The calculation is as follows:

$$\$563.92 = \left[\frac{272.51 - 241.623}{241.623} + 1 \right] \times \$500$$

Under Health and Safety Code section 26249.7(k)(2)(B)(ii), the adjusted penalty amount is rounded to the nearest $5, so the dollar amount of the adjusted limit is rounded to $565.

Appendix H adopted effective April 1, 2019.

Appendix I
Emergency Rules Related to COVID-19

[Appendix I amended effective November 13, 2020; adopted effective April 6, 2020; previously amended effective April 17, 2020, April 20, 2020, May 29, 2020, June 20, 2020, and August 13, 2020.]

Emergency rule 1. Unlawful detainers
Emergency rule 2. Judicial foreclosures—suspension of actions
Emergency rule 3. Use of technology for remote appearances
Emergency rule 5. Personal appearance waivers of defendants during health emergency
Emergency rule 6. Emergency orders: juvenile dependency proceedings
Emergency rule 7. Emergency orders: juvenile delinquency proceedings
Emergency rule 8. Emergency orders: temporary restraining or protective orders
Emergency rule 9. Tolling statutes of limitations for civil causes of action
Emergency rule 10. Extensions of time in which to bring a civil action to trial
Emergency rule 13. Effective date for requests to modify support

Emergency rule 1. Unlawful detainers

(a) Application

Notwithstanding any other law, including Code of Civil Procedure sections 1166, 1167, 1169, and 1170.5, this rule applies to all actions for unlawful detainer.

(b) Issuance of summons

A court may not issue a summons on a complaint for unlawful detainer unless the court finds, in its discretion and on the record, that the action is necessary to protect public health and safety.

(c) Entry of default

A court may not enter a default or a default judgment for restitution in an unlawful detainer action for failure of defendant to appear unless the court finds both of the following:

(1) The action is necessary to protect public health and safety; and

(2) The defendant has not appeared in the action within the time provided by law, including by any applicable executive order.

(d) Time for trial

If a defendant has appeared in the action, the court may not set a trial date earlier than 60 days after a request for trial is made unless the court finds that an earlier trial date is necessary to protect public health and safety. Any trial set in an unlawful detainer proceeding as of April 6, 2020 must be continued at least 60 days from the initial date of trial.

(e) Sunset of rule

This rule will remain in effect [1] **through September 1, 2020**, or until amended or repealed by the Judicial Council. **Notwithstanding Code of Civil Procedure section 1170.5 and this subdivision, any trial date set under (d) as of September 1, 2020, will remain as set unless a court otherwise orders.**

(Subd (e) amended effective August 13, 2020; adopted effective April 6, 2020.)

Rule 1(e). 2020 Deletes. [1] until 90 days after the Governor declares that the state of emergency related to the COVID-19 pandemic is lifted
Emergency Rule 1 amended effective August 13, 2000; adopted effective April 6, 2020.

Emergency rule 2. Judicial foreclosures—suspension of actions

Notwithstanding any other law, this rule applies to any action for foreclosure on a mortgage or deed of trust brought under chapter 1, title 10, of part 2 of the Code of Civil Procedure, beginning at section 725a, including any action for a deficiency judgment, and provides that, [1] **through September 1, 2020**, or until this rule is amended or repealed by the Judicial Council:

(1) All such actions are stayed, and the court may take no action and issue no decisions or judgments unless the court finds that action is required to further the public health and safety.

(2) [2] The period for electing or exercising any rights under that chapter, including exercising any right of redemption from a foreclosure sale or petitioning the court in relation to such a right, is extended.
Emergency Rule 2 amended effective August 13, 2020; adopted effective April 6, 2020.

Rule 2. 2020 Deletes. [1] until 90 days after the Governor declares that the state of emergency related to the COVID-19 pandemic is lifted **[2]** Any statute of limitations for filing such an action is tolled. (3)

Advisory Committee Comment

The provision for tolling any applicable statute of limitations, in prior subdivision (2), has been removed as unnecessary because the tolling provisions in emergency rule 9 apply to actions subject to this rule.

Emergency rule 3. Use of technology for remote appearances

(a) Remote appearances

Notwithstanding any other law, in order to protect the health and safety of the public, including court users, both in custody and out of custody defendants, witnesses, court personnel, judicial officers, and others, courts must conduct judicial proceedings and court operations as follows:

(1) Courts may require that judicial proceedings and court operations be conducted remotely.

(2) In criminal proceedings, courts must receive the consent of the defendant to conduct the proceeding remotely and otherwise comply with emergency rule 5. Notwithstanding Penal Code sections 865 and 977 or any other law, the court may conduct any criminal proceeding remotely. As used in this rule, "consent of the defendant" means that the consent of the defendant is required only for the waiver of the defendant's appearance as provided in emergency rule 5. For good cause shown, the court may require any witness to personally appear in a particular proceeding.

(3) Conducting proceedings remotely includes, but is not limited to, the use of video, audio, and telephonic means for remote appearances; the electronic exchange and authentication of documentary evidence; e-filing and e-service; the use of remote interpreting; and the use of remote reporting and electronic recording to make the official record of an action or proceeding.

(b) Sunset of rule

This rule will remain in effect until 90 days after the Governor declares that the state of emergency related to the COVID-19 pandemic is lifted, or until amended or repealed by the Judicial Council.
Emergency Rule 3 adopted effective April 6, 2020.

Emergency rule 4. Emergency Bail Schedule [Repealed]
Emergency Rule 4 repealed effective June 20, 2020; adopted effective April 6, 2020.

2020 Note: Emergency rule 4 was adopted effective April 6, 2020, and repealed effective June 20, 2020. Below is the text of the rule prior to its repeal.
Emergency rule 4. Emergency Bail Schedule
(a) Purpose
Notwithstanding any other law, this rule establishes a statewide Emergency Bail Schedule, which is intended to promulgate uniformity in the handling of certain offenses during the state of emergency related to the COVID-19 pandemic.
(b) Mandatory application
No later than 5 p.m. on April 13, 2020, each superior court must apply the statewide Emergency Bail Schedule:
(1) To every accused person arrested and in pretrial custody.
(2) To every accused person held in pretrial custody.
(c) Setting of bail and exceptions
Under the statewide Emergency Bail Schedule, bail for all misdemeanor and felony offenses must be set at $0, with the exception of only the offenses listed below:
(1) A serious felony, as defined in Penal Code section 1192.7(c), or a violent felony, as defined in Penal Code section 667.5(c);
(2) A felony violation of Penal Code section 69;
(3) A violation of Penal Code section 166(c)(1);
(4) A violation of Penal Code section 136.1 when punishment is imposed under section 136.1(c);
(5) A violation of Penal Code section 262;
(6) A violation of Penal Code sections 243(e)(1) or 273.5;
(7) A violation of Penal Code section 273.6 if the detained person made threats to kill or harm, has engaged in violence against, or has gone to the residence or workplace of, the protected party;
(8) A violation of Penal Code section 422 where the offense is punished as a felony;
(9) A violation of Penal Code section 646.9;
(10) A violation of an offense listed in Penal Code section 290(c);
(11) A violation of Vehicle Code sections 23152 or 23153;
(12) A felony violation of Penal Code section 463; and
(13) A violation of Penal Code section 29800.
(d) Ability to deny bail

Nothing in the Emergency Bail Schedule restricts the ability of the court to deny bail as authorized by article I, section 12, or 28(f)(3) of the California Constitution.

(e) Application of countywide bail schedule

(1) The current countywide bail schedule of each superior court must remain in effect for all offenses listed in exceptions (1) through (13) of the Emergency Bail Schedule, including any count-specific conduct enhancements and any status enhancements.

(2) Each superior court retains the authority to reduce the amount of bail listed in the court's current countywide bail schedule for offenses in exceptions (1) through (13), or for any offenses not in conflict with the Emergency Bail Schedule.

(f) Bail for violations of post-conviction supervision

(1) Under the statewide Emergency Bail Schedule, bail for all violations of misdemeanor probation, whether the arrest is with or without a bench warrant, must be set at $0.

(2) Bail for all violations of felony probation, parole, post-release community supervision, or mandatory supervision, must be set in accord with the statewide Emergency Bail Schedule, or for the bail amount in the court's countywide schedule of bail for charges of conviction listed in exceptions (1) through (13), including any enhancements.

(g) Sunset of rule

This rule will remain in effect until 90 days after the Governor declares that the state of emergency related to the COVID-19 pandemic is lifted, or until amended or repealed by the Judicial Council.

Emergency rule 5. Personal appearance waivers of defendants during health emergency

(a) Application

Notwithstanding any other law, including Penal Code sections 865 and 977, this rule applies to all criminal proceedings except cases alleging murder with special circumstances and cases in which the defendant is currently incarcerated in state prison, as governed by Penal Code section 977.2.

(b) Types of personal appearance waivers

(1) With the consent of the defendant, the court must allow a defendant to waive his or her personal appearance and to appear remotely, either through video or telephonic appearance, when the technology is available.

(2) With the consent of the defendant, the court must allow a defendant to waive his or her appearance and permit counsel to appear on his or her behalf. The court must accept a defendant's waiver of appearance or personal appearance when:

(A) Counsel for the defendant makes an on the record oral representation that counsel has fully discussed the waiver and its implications with the defendant and the defendant has authorized counsel to proceed as counsel represents to the court;

(B) Electronic communication from the defendant as confirmed by defendant's counsel; or

(C) Any other means that ensures the validity of the defendant's waiver.

(c) Consent by the defendant

(1) For purposes of arraignment and entry of a not guilty plea, consent means a knowing, intelligent, and voluntary waiver of the right to appear personally in court. Counsel for the defendant must state on the record at each applicable hearing that counsel is proceeding with the defendant's consent.

(2) For purposes of waiving time for a preliminary hearing, consent also means a knowing, intelligent, and voluntary waiver of the right to hold a preliminary hearing within required time limits specified either in Penal Code section 859b or under emergency orders issued by the Chief Justice and Chair of the Judicial Council.

(3) The court must accept defense counsel's representation that the defendant understands and agrees with waiving any right to appear unless the court has specific concerns in a particular matter about the validity of the waiver.

(d) Appearance through counsel

(1) When counsel appears on behalf of a defendant, courts must allow counsel to do any of the following:

(A) Waive reading and advisement of rights for arraignment.

(B) Enter a plea of not guilty.

(C) Waive time for the preliminary hearing.

(2) For appearances by counsel, including where the defendant is either appearing remotely or has waived his or her appearance and or counsel is appearing by remote access, counsel must confirm to the court at each hearing that the appearance by counsel is made with the consent of the defendant.

(e) Conduct of remote hearings

(1) With the defendant's consent, a defendant may appear remotely for any pretrial criminal proceeding.

(2) Where a defendant appears remotely, counsel may not be required to be personally present with the defendant for any portion of the criminal proceeding provided that the audio and/or video conferencing system or other technology allows for private communication between the defendant and his or her counsel. Any private communication is confidential and privileged under Evidence Code section 952.

(f) Sunset of rule

This rule will remain in effect until 90 days after the Governor declares that the state of emergency related to the COVID-19 pandemic is lifted, or until amended or repealed by the Judicial Council.

Emergency Rule 5 adopted effective April 6, 2020.

Emergency rule 6. Emergency orders: juvenile dependency proceedings

(a) Application

This rule applies to all juvenile dependency proceedings filed or pending until the state of emergency related to the COVID-19 pandemic is lifted.

(b) Essential hearings and orders

The following matters should be prioritized in accordance with existing statutory time requirements.

(1) Protective custody warrants filed under Welfare and Institutions Code section 340.

(2) Detention hearings under Welfare and Institutions Code section 319. The court is required to determine if it is contrary to the child's welfare to remain with the parent, whether reasonable efforts were made to prevent removal, and whether to vest the placing agency with temporary placement and care.

(3) Psychotropic medication applications.

(4) Emergency medical requests.

(5) A petition for reentry of a nonminor dependent.

(6) Welfare and Institutions Code section 388 petitions that require an immediate response based on the health and safety of the child, which should be reviewed for a prima facie showing of change of circumstances sufficient to grant the petition or to set a hearing. The court may extend the final ruling on the petition beyond 30 days.

(c) Foster care hearings and continuances during the state of emergency

(1) A court may hold any proceeding under this rule via remote technology consistent with rule 5.531 and emergency rule 3.

(2) At the beginning of any hearing at which one or more participants appears remotely, the court must admonish all the participants that the proceeding is confidential and of the possible sanctions for violating confidentiality.

(3) The child welfare agency is responsible for notice of remote hearings unless other arrangements have been made with counsel for parents and children. Notice is required for all parties and may include notice by telephone or other electronic means. The notice must also include instructions on how to participate in the court hearing remotely.

(4) Court reports

(A) Attorneys for parents and children must accept service of the court report electronically.

(B) The child welfare agency must ensure that the parent and the child receive a copy of the court report on time.

(C) If a parent or child cannot receive the report electronically, the child welfare agency must deliver a hard copy of the report to the parent and the child on time.

(5) Nothing in this subdivision prohibits the court from making statutorily required findings and orders, by minute order only and without a court reporter, by accepting written stipulations from counsel when appearances are waived if the stipulations are confirmed on the applicable Judicial Council forms or equivalent local court forms.

(6) If a court hearing cannot occur either in the courthouse or remotely, the hearing may be continued up to 60 days, except as otherwise specified.

(A) A dispositional hearing under Welfare and Institutions Code section 360 should not be continued more than 6 months after the detention hearing without review of the child's circumstances. In determining exceptional circumstances that justify holding the dispositional hearing more than 6 months after the child was taken into protective custody, the impact of the state of emergency related to the COVID-19 pandemic must be considered.

i. If the dispositional hearing is continued more than 6 months after the start date of protective custody, a review of the child must be held at the 6-month date. At the review, the court must determine the continued necessity for and appropriateness of the placement; the extent of compliance with the case plan or available services that have been offered; the extent of progress which has been made toward alleviating or mitigating the causes necessitating placement; and the projected likely date by which the child may return home or placed permanently.

ii. The court may continue the matter for a full hearing on all dispositional findings and orders.

(B) A judicial determination of reasonable efforts must be made within 12 months of the date a child enters foster care to maintain a child's federal title IV-E availability. If a permanency hearing is continued beyond the 12-month date, the court must review the case to determine if the agency has made reasonable efforts to return the child home or arrange for the child to be placed permanently. This finding can be made without prejudice and may be reconsidered at a full hearing.

(7) During the state of emergency related to the COVID-19 pandemic, previously authorized visitation must continue, but the child welfare agency is to determine the manner of visitation to ensure that the needs of the family are met. If the child welfare agency changes the manner of visitation for a child and a parent or legal guardian in reunification, or for the child and a sibling(s), or a hearing is pending under Welfare and Institutions Code section 366.26, the child welfare agency must notify the attorneys for the children and parents within 5 court days of the change. All changes in manner of visitation during this time period must be made on a case by case basis, balance the public health directives and best interest of the child, and take into consideration whether in-person visitation may continue to be held safely. Family time is important for child and parent well-being, as well as for efforts toward reunification. Family time is especially important during times of crisis. Visitation may only be suspended if a detriment finding is made in a particular case based on the facts unique to that case. A detriment finding must not be based solely on the existence of the impact of the state of emergency related to the COVID-19 pandemic or related public health directives.

(A) The attorney for the child or parent may ask the juvenile court to review the change in manner of visitation. The child or parent has the burden of showing that the change is not in the best interest of the child or is not based on current public health directives.

(B) A request for the court to review the change in visitation during this time period must be made within 14 court days of the change. In reviewing the change in visitation, the court should take into consideration the factors in (c)(7).

(d) Sunset of rule

This rule will remain in effect until 90 days after the Governor declares that the state of emergency related to the COVID-19 pandemic is lifted, or until amended or repealed by the Judicial Council.

Emergency Rule 6 adopted effective April 6, 2020.

Advisory Committee Comment

When courts are unable to hold regular proceedings because of an emergency that has resulted in an order as authorized under Government Code section 68115, federal timelines do not stop. Circumstances may arise where reunification services to the parent, including visitation, may not occur or be provided. The court must consider the circumstances of the emergency when deciding whether to extend or terminate reunification services and whether services were reasonable given the state of the emergency. (Citations: 42 U.S.C. § 672(a)(1)–(2), (5); 45 CFR § 1355.20; 45 CFR § 1356.21 (b) – (d); 45 C.F.R. § 1356.71(d)(1)(iii); Child Welfare Policy Manual, 8.3A.9 Title IV-E, Foster Care Maintenance Payments Program, Reasonable efforts, Question 2 (www.acf.hhs.gov/cwpm/public_html/programs/cb/laws_policies/laws/cwpm/policy_dsp.jsp?citID=92)]); Letter dated March 27, 2020, from Jerry Milner, Associate Commissioner, Children's Bureau, Administration for Children and Families, U.S. Department of Health and Human Services.)

Emergency rule 7. Emergency orders: juvenile delinquency proceedings

(a) Application

This rule applies to all proceedings in which a petition has been filed under Welfare and Institutions Code section 602 in which a hearing would be statutorily required during the state of emergency related to the COVID-19 pandemic.

(b) Juvenile delinquency hearings and orders during the state of emergency

(1) A hearing on a petition for a child who is in custody under Welfare and Institutions Code section 632 or 636 must be held within the statutory timeframes as modified by an order of the court authorized by Government Code section 68115. The court must determine if it is contrary to the welfare of the child to remain in the home, whether reasonable services to prevent removal occurred, and whether to place temporary placement with the probation agency if the court will be keeping the child detained and out of the home.

(2) If a child is detained in custody and an in-person appearance is not feasible due to the state of emergency, courts must make reasonable efforts to hold any statutorily required hearing for that case via remote appearance within the required statutory time frame and as modified by an order of the court authorized under Government Code section 68115 for that proceeding. If a remote proceeding is not a feasible option for such a case during the state of emergency, the court may continue the case as provided in (d) for the minimum period of time necessary to hold the proceedings.

(3) Without regard to the custodial status of the child, the following hearings should be prioritized during the state of emergency related to the COVID-19 pandemic:

(A) Psychotropic medication applications.

(B) All emergency medical requests.

(C) A petition for reentry of a nonminor dependent.

(D) A hearing on any request for a warrant for a child.

(E) A probable cause determination for a child who has been detained but has not had a detention hearing within the statutory time limits.

(4) Notwithstanding any other law, and except as described in (5), during the state of emergency related to the COVID-19 pandemic, the court may continue for good cause any hearing for a child not detained in custody who is subject to its juvenile delinquency jurisdiction until a date after the state of emergency has been lifted considering the priority for continued hearings in (d).

(5) For children placed in foster care under probation supervision, a judicial determination of reasonable efforts must be made within 12 months of the date the child enters foster care to maintain a child's federal title IV-E availability. If a permanency hearing is continued beyond the 12-month date, the court must nevertheless hold a review to determine if the agency has made reasonable efforts to return the child home or place the child permanently. This finding can be made without prejudice and may be reconsidered at a full hearing.

(c) Proceedings with remote appearances during the state of emergency.

(1) A court may hold any proceeding under this rule via remote technology consistent with rule 5.531 and emergency rule 3.

(2) At the beginning of any hearing conducted with one or more participants appearing remotely, the court must admonish all the participants that the proceeding is confidential and of the possible sanctions for violating confidentiality.

(3) The court is responsible for giving notice of remote hearings, except for notice to a victim, which is the responsibility of the prosecuting attorney or the probation department. Notice is required for all parties and may include notice by telephone or other electronic means. The notice must also include instructions on how to participate in the hearing remotely.

(4) During the state of emergency, the court has broad discretion to take evidence in the manner most compatible with the remote hearing process, including but not limited to taking testimony by written declaration. If counsel for a child or the prosecuting attorney objects to the court's evidentiary procedures, that is a basis for issuing a continuance under (d).

(d) Continuances of hearings during the state of emergency.

Notwithstanding any other law, the court may for good cause continue any hearing other than a detention hearing for a child who is detained in custody. In making this determination, the court must consider the custody status of the child, whether there are evidentiary issues that are contested, and, if so, the ability for those issues to be fairly contested via a remote proceeding.

(e) Extension of time limits under Welfare and Institutions Code section 709

In any case in which a child has been found incompetent under Welfare and Institutions Code section 709 and that child is eligible for remediation services or has been found to require secure detention, any time limits imposed by section 709 for provision of services or for secure detention are tolled for the period of the state of emergency if the court finds that remediation services could not be provided because of the state of emergency.

(f) Sunset of rule

This rule will remain in effect until 90 days after the Governor declares that the state of emergency related to the COVID-19 pandemic is lifted, or until amended or repealed by the Judicial Council.

Emergency Rule 7 adopted effective April 6, 2020.

Advisory Committee Comment

This emergency rule is being adopted in part to ensure that detention hearings for juveniles in delinquency court must be held in a timely manner to ensure that no child is detained who does not need to be detained to protect the child or the community. The statutory scheme for juveniles who come under the jurisdiction of the delinquency court is focused on the rehabilitation of the child and thus makes detention of a child the exceptional practice, rather than the rule. Juvenile courts are able to use their broad discretion under current law to release detained juveniles to protect the health of those juveniles and the health and safety of the others in detention during the current state of emergency related to the COVID-19 pandemic.

Emergency rule 8. Emergency orders: temporary restraining or protective orders

(a) Application

Notwithstanding any other law, this rule applies to any emergency protective order, temporary restraining order, or criminal protective order that was requested, issued, or set to expire during the state of emergency related to the COVID-19 pandemic. This includes requests and orders issued under Family Code sections 6250 or 6300, Code of Civil Procedure sections 527.6, 527.8, or 527.85, Penal Code sections 136.2, 18125 or 18150, or Welfare and Institutions Code sections 213.5, 304, 362.4, or 15657.03, and including any of the foregoing orders issued in connection with an order for modification of a custody or visitation order issued pursuant to a dissolution, legal separation, nullity, or parentage proceeding under Family Code section 6221.

(b) Duration of orders

(1) Any emergency protective order made under Family Code section 6250 that is issued [1] during the state of emergency [2] must remain in effect for up to 30 days from the date of issuance.

(2) Any temporary restraining order or gun violence emergency protective order [3] issued or set to expire during the state of emergency related to the COVID-19 pandemic [4] must [5] **remain in effect** for a period of time that the court determines is sufficient to allow for a hearing on the long-term order to occur, for up to 90 days.

(3) Any criminal protective order, subject to this rule, set to expire during the state of emergency, must be automatically extended for a period of 90 days, or until the matter can be heard, whichever occurs first.

(4) [6] **Upon the filing of a request to renew a** restraining order [7] after hearing [8] that is set to expire during the state of emergency related to the COVID-19 pandemic [9], **the current restraining order after hearing must remain in effect until a hearing on the renewal can occur, for up to 90 days from the date of expiration**.

(Subd (b) amended effective April 20, 2020.)

Rule 8(b). 2020 Deletes. [1] or set to expire [2] , [3] , [4] , [5] be continued [6] Any [7] or protective order [8] , [9] must be automatically extended for up to 90 days from the date of expiration to enable a protected party to seek a renewal of the restraining order

(c) Ex parte requests and requests to renew restraining orders

(1) Courts must provide a means for the filing of ex parte requests for temporary restraining orders **and requests to renew restraining orders**. Courts may do so by providing a physical location, drop box, or, if feasible, through electronic means.

(2) Any ex parte request **and request to renew restraining orders** may be filed using an electronic signature by a party or a party's attorney.

(Subd (c) amended effective April 20, 2020.)

(d) Service of Orders

If a respondent appears at a hearing by video, audio, or telephonically, and the court grants an order, in whole or in part, no further service is required upon the respondent for enforcement of the order, provided that the court follows the requirements of Family Code section 6384.

(e) Entry of orders into California Law Enforcement Telecommunications System

Any orders issued by a court modifying the duration or expiration date of orders subject to this rule, must be transmitted to the Department of Justice through the California Law Enforcement Telecommunications

System (CLETS), as provided in Family Code section 6380, without regard to whether they are issued on Judicial Council forms, or in another format during the state of emergency.

Emergency Rule 8 amended effective April 20, 2020; adopted effective April 6, 2020.

Emergency rule 9. Tolling statutes of limitations for civil causes of action

(a) Tolling statutes of limitations over 180 days

Notwithstanding any other law, the statutes of [1] **limitations and repose** for civil causes of action **that exceed 180 days** are tolled from April 6, 2020, until [2] **October 1, 2020**.

(Subd (a) lettered and amended effective May 29, 2020; adopted effective April 6, 2020.)

Rule 9(a). 2020 Deletes. [1] limitation [2] 90 days after the Governor declares that the state of emergency related to the COVID-19 pandemic is lifted

(b) Tolling statutes of limitations of 180 days or less

Notwithstanding any other law, the statutes of limitations and repose for civil causes of action that are 180 days or less are tolled from April 6, 2020, until August 3, 2020.

(Subd (b) adopted effective May 29, 2020.)

Emergency Rule 9 amended effective May 29, 2020; adopted effective April 6, 2020.

Advisory Committee Comment

Emergency rule 9 is intended to apply broadly to toll any statute of limitations on the filing of a pleading in court asserting a civil cause of action. The term "civil causes of action" includes special proceedings. (See Code Civ. Proc., §§ 312, 363 ["action," as used in title 2 of the code (Of the Time of Commencing Civil Actions), is construed "as including a special proceeding of a civil nature"); special proceedings of a civil nature include all proceedings in title 3 of the code, including mandamus actions under §§ 1085, 1088.5, and 1094.5—all the types of petitions for writ made for California Environmental Quality Act (CEQA) and land use challenges; see also Pub. Resources Code, § 21167(a)–(e) [setting limitations periods for civil "action[s]" under CEQA].)

The rule also applies to statutes of limitations on filing of causes of action in court found in codes other than the Code of Civil Procedure, including the limitations on causes of action found in, for example, the Family Code and Probate Code.

Emergency rule 10. Extensions of time in which to bring a civil action to trial

(a) Extension of five years in which to bring a civil action to trial

Notwithstanding any other law, including Code of Civil Procedure section 583.310, for all civil actions filed on or before April 6, 2020, the time in which to bring the action to trial is extended by six months for a total time of five years and six months.

(b) Extension of three years in which to bring a new trial

Notwithstanding any other law, including Code of Civil Procedure section 583.320, for all civil actions filed on or before April 6, 2020, if a new trial is granted in the action, the three years provided in section 583.320 in which the action must again be brought to trial is extended by six months for a total time of three years and six months. Nothing in this subdivision requires that an action must again be brought to trial before expiration of the time prescribed in (a).

Emergency Rule 10 adopted effective April 6, 2020.

Emergency rule 11. Depositions through remote electronic means [Repealed]

Emergency Rule 11 repealed effective November 13, 2020; adopted effective April 6, 2020.

2020 Note: Emergency rule 11 was adopted effective April 6, 2020, and repealed effective November 13, 2020. Below is the text of the rule prior to its repeal.

Emergency rule 11. Depositions through remote electronic means

(a) Deponents appearing remotely

Notwithstanding any other law, including Code of Civil Procedure section 2025.310(a) and (b), and rule 3.1010(c) and (d), a party or nonparty deponent, at their election or the election of the deposing party, is not required to be present with the deposition officer at the time of the deposition.

(b) Sunset of rule

This rule will remain in effect until 90 days after the Governor declares that the state of emergency related to the COVID-19 pandemic is lifted, or until amended or repealed by the Judicial Council.

Emergency rule 12. Electronic service [Repealed]

Emergency Rule 12 repealed effective November 13, 2020; adopted effective April 17, 2020.

2020 Note: Emergency rule 12 was adopted effective April 17, 2020, and repealed effective November 13, 2020. Below is the text of the rule prior to its repeal.

Emergency rule 12. Electronic service

(a) Application

(1) Notwithstanding any other law, including Code of Civil Procedure section 1010.6, Probate Code section 1215, and rule 2.251, this rule applies in all general civil cases and proceedings under the Family and Probate Codes, unless a court orders otherwise.

(2) Notwithstanding (1), the rule does not apply in cases where parties are already required by court order or local rule to provide or accept notices and documents by electronic service, and is not intended to prohibit electronic service in cases not addressed by this rule.

(b) Required electronic service

(1) A party represented by counsel, who has appeared in an action or proceeding, must accept electronic service of a notice or document that may be served by mail, express mail, overnight delivery, or facsimile transmission. Before first serving a represented party electronically, the serving party must confirm by telephone or email the appropriate electronic service address for counsel being served.

(2) A party represented by counsel must, upon the request of any party who has appeared in an action or proceeding and who provides an electronic service address and a copy of this rule, electronically serve the requesting party with any notice or document that may be served by mail, express mail, overnight delivery, or facsimile transmission.

(c) Permissive electronic service

Electronic service on a self-represented party is permitted only with consent of that party, confirmed in writing. The written consent to accept electronic service may be exchanged electronically.

(d) Time

(1) In general civil cases and proceedings under the Family Code, the provisions of Code of Civil Procedure section 1010.6(a)(4) and (5) apply to electronic service under this rule.

(2) In proceedings under the Probate Code, the provisions of Probate Code section 1215(c)(2) apply to electronic service under this rule.

(e) Confidential documents

Confidential or sealed records electronically served must be served through encrypted methods to ensure that the documents are not improperly disclosed.

(f) Sunset of rule

This rule will remain in effect until 90 days after the Governor declares that the state of emergency related to the COVID-19 pandemic is lifted, or until amended or repealed by the Judicial Council.

Emergency rule 13. Effective date for requests to modify support

(a) Application

Notwithstanding any other law, including Family Code sections 3591, 3603, 3653, and 4333, this rule applies to all requests to modify or terminate child, spousal, partner, or family support. For the purpose of this rule, "request" refers to *Request for Order* (form FL-300), *Notice of Motion (Governmental)* (form FL-680), or other moving papers requesting a modification of support.

(b) Effective date of modification

Except as provided in Family Code section 3653(b), an order modifying or terminating a support order may be made effective as of the date the request and supporting papers are mailed or otherwise served on the other party, or other party's attorney when permitted. Nothing in this rule restricts the court's discretion to order a later effective date.

(c) Service of filed request

If the request and supporting papers that were served have not yet been filed with the court, the moving party must also serve a copy of the request and supporting papers after they have been filed with the court on the other party, or other party's attorney when permitted. If the moving party is the local child support agency and the unfiled request already has a valid court date and time listed, then subsequent service of the request is not required.

(d) Court discretion

Nothing in this rule is meant to limit court discretion or to alter rule 5.92 or 5.260 regarding which moving papers are required to request a modification of support.

(e) Sunset of rule

This rule will remain in effect until 90 days after the Governor declares that the state of emergency related to the COVID-19 pandemic is lifted, or until amended or repealed by the Judicial Council.

Emergency Rule 13 adopted effective April 20, 2020.

SUPPLEMENT TO THE CALIFORNIA RULES OF COURT

California Code of Judicial Ethics

[Adopted by the Supreme Court pursuant to article VI, section 18(m) of the California Constitution]

[Amended by the Supreme Court of California effective July 1, 2020; adopted effective January 15, 1996; previously amended March 4, 1999, December 13, 2000, December 30, 2002, June 18, 2003, December 22, 2003, January 1, 2005, June 1, 2005, July 1, 2006, January 1, 2007, January 1, 2008, April 29, 2009, January 1, 2013, January 21, 2015, August 19, 2015, December 1, 2016, and October 10, 2018]

Preface
Preamble
Terminology
Canon 1. A judge shall uphold the integrity and independence of the judiciary.
Canon 2. A judge shall avoid impropriety and the appearance of impropriety in all of the judge's activities.
Canon 3. A judge shall perform the duties of judicial office impartially, competently, and diligently.
Canon 4. A judge shall so conduct the judge's quasi-judicial and extrajudicial activities as to minimize the risk of conflict with judicial obligations.
Canon 5. A judge or candidate for judicial office shall not engage in political or campaign activity that is inconsistent with the independence, integrity, or impartiality of the judiciary.
Canon 6. Compliance with the Code of Judicial Ethics.

Preface

Formal standards of judicial conduct have existed for more than 65 years. The original Canons of Judicial Ethics promulgated by the American Bar Association were modified and adopted in 1949 for application in California by the Conference of California Judges (now the California Judges Association).

In 1969, the American Bar Association determined that then current needs and problems warranted revision of the canons. In the revision process, a special American Bar Association committee, headed by former California Chief Justice Roger Traynor, sought and considered the views of the bench and bar and other interested persons. The American Bar Association Code of Judicial Conduct was adopted by the House of Delegates of the American Bar Association August 16, 1972.

Effective January 5, 1975, the California Judges Association adopted a new California Code of Judicial Conduct adapted from the American Bar Association 1972 Model Code. The California code was recast in gender-neutral form in 1986.

In 1990, the American Bar Association Model Code was further revised after a lengthy study. The California Judges Association again reviewed the model code and adopted a revised California Code of Judicial Conduct on October 5, 1992.

Proposition 190 (amending Cal. Const., art. VI, §18, subd. (m), operative March 1, 1995) created a new constitutional provision that states, "The Supreme Court shall make rules for the conduct of judges, both on and off the bench, and for judicial candidates in the conduct of their campaigns. These rules shall be referred to as the Code of Judicial Ethics."

The Supreme Court formally adopted the 1992 Code of Judicial Conduct in March 1995, as a transitional measure pending further review.

The Supreme Court formally adopted the Code of Judicial Ethics effective January 15, 1996.

The Supreme Court has formally adopted amendments to the Code of Judicial Ethics on several occasions. The *Advisory Committee Commentary* is published by the Supreme Court Advisory Committee on the Code of Judicial Ethics.

(Preface amended effective August 19, 2015.)

Preamble

Our legal system is based on the principle that an independent, fair, and competent judiciary will interpret and apply the laws that govern us. The role of the judiciary is central to American concepts of justice and the rule of law. Intrinsic to this code are the precepts that judges, individually and collectively, must respect and honor the judicial office as a public trust and must strive to enhance and maintain confidence in our legal system. The judge is an arbiter of facts and law for the resolution of disputes and is a highly visible member of government under the rule of law.

The Code of Judicial Ethics ("code") establishes standards for ethical conduct of judges on and off the bench and for candidates for judicial office.* The code consists of broad declarations called canons, with subparts, and a terminology section. Following many canons is a commentary section prepared by the Supreme Court Advisory Committee on the Code of Judicial Ethics. The commentary, by explanation and example, provides guidance as to the purpose and meaning of the canons. The commentary does not constitute additional rules and should not be so construed. All members of the judiciary must comply with the code. Compliance is required to preserve the integrity* of the bench and to ensure the confidence of the public.

The canons should be read together as a whole, and each provision should be construed in context and consistent with every other provision. They are to be applied in conformance with constitutional requirements, statutes, other court rules, and decisional law. Nothing in the code shall either impair the essential independence* of judges in making judicial decisions or provide a separate basis for civil liability or criminal prosecution.

The code governs the conduct of judges and candidates for judicial

---

* Terms with an asterisk (*) are defined in the Terminology section.

office* and is binding upon them. Whether disciplinary action is appropriate, and the degree of discipline to be imposed, requires a reasoned application of the text and consideration of such factors as the seriousness of the transgression, if there is a pattern of improper activity, and the effect of the improper activity on others or on the judicial system.
(Preamble amended effective August 19, 2015.)

Terminology

Terms explained below are noted with an asterisk (*) in the canons where they appear. In addition, the canons in which these terms appear are cited after the explanation of each term below.

"Candidate for judicial office" is a person seeking election to or retention of a judicial office. A person becomes a candidate for judicial office as soon as he or she makes a public announcement of candidacy, declares or files as a candidate with the election authority, or authorizes solicitation or acceptance of contributions or support. See Preamble and Canons **3B(9) (Commentary)**, 3E(2)(b)(i), 3E(3)(a), 5, 5A, 5A (*Commentary*), 5B(1), 5B(2), 5B(3), 5B(4), 5B (*Commentary*), 5B(4) (*Commentary*) 5C, 5D, and 6E.

"Fiduciary" includes such relationships as executor, administrator, trustee, and guardian. See Canons 3E(5)(d), 4E(1), 4E(2), 4E(3), 4E (*Commentary*), 6B, and 6F (*Commentary*).

"Gender identity" means a person's internal sense of being male, female, a combination of male and female, or neither male nor female. See Canons 2C, 2C (*Commentary*), 3B(5), 3B(6), 3C(1), and 3C(3).

"Gender expression" is the way people communicate or externally express their gender identity to others, through such means as pronouns used, clothing, appearance, and demeanor. See Canons 2C, 2C (*Commentary*), 3B(5), 3B(6), 3C(1), and 3C(3).

"Gift" means anything of value to the extent that consideration of equal or greater value is not received, and includes a rebate or discount in the price of anything of value unless the rebate or discount is made in the regular course of business to members of the public without regard to official status. See Canons 4D(5), 4D(5) (*Commentary*), 4D(6), 4D(6)(a), 4D(6)(b), 4D(6)(b) (*Commentary*), 4D(6)(d), 4D(6)(f), 4D(6)(i), 4D(6)(i) (*Commentary*), 4D(6) and 4D(7) (*Commentary*), 4H (*Commentary*), 5A (*Commentary*), 5B(4) (*Commentary*), 6D(2)(c), and 6D(7).

"Impartial," "impartiality," and "impartially" mean the absence of bias or prejudice in favor of, or against, particular parties or classes of parties, as well as the maintenance of an open mind in considering issues that may come before a judge. See Canons 1, 1 (*Commentary*), 2A, 2 and 2A (*Commentary*), 2B (*Commentary*), 2C (*Commentary*), 3, 3B(9) (*Commentary*), 3B(10) (*Commentary*), 3B(12), 3B(12) (*Commentary*), 3C(1), 3C(5), 3E(4)(b), 3E(4)(c), 4A(1), 4A (*Commentary*), 4C(3)(b) (*Commentary*), 4C(3)(c) (*Commentary*), 4D(1) (*Commentary*), 4D(6)(a) (*Commentary*), 4D(6)(b) (*Commentary*), 4D(6)(g) (*Commentary*), 4D(6)(i) (*Commentary*), 4H (*Commentary*), 5, 5A, 5A (*Commentary*), 5B (*Commentary*), 5B(4) (*Commentary*), 6D(2)(a), and 6D(3)(a)(vii).

"Impending proceeding" is a proceeding or matter that is imminent or expected to occur in the near future. The words "proceeding" and "matter" are used interchangeably, and are intended to have the same meaning. See Canons 2 and 2A (*Commentary*), 3B(7), 3B(7)(a), 3B(9), 3B(9) (*Commentary*), 4H (*Commentary*), and 6D(6). "Pending proceeding" is defined below.

"Impropriety" includes conduct that violates the law, court rules, or provisions of this code, as well as conduct that undermines a judge's independence, integrity, or impartiality. See Canons 2, 2 and 2A (*Commentary*), 2B (*Commentary*), 2C (*Commentary*), 3B(9) (*Commentary*), 4D(1)(b) (*Commentary*), 4D(6)(g) (*Commentary*), 4D(6)(i) (*Commentary*), 4H, and 5.

"Independence" means a judge's freedom from influence or control other than as established by law. See Preamble, Canons 1, 1 (*Commentary*), 2C, 4C(2) (*Commentary*), 4D(6)(a) (*Commentary*), 4D(6)(g) (*Commentary*), 4D(6)(i) (*Commentary*), 4H(3) (*Commentary*), 5, 5A (*Commentary*), 5B (*Commentary*), and 6D(1).

"Integrity" means probity, fairness, honesty, uprightness, and soundness of character. See Preamble, Canons 1, 1 (*Commentary*), 2A, 2 and 2A (*Commentary*), 2B (*Commentary*), 2C (*Commentary*), 3B(9) (*Commentary*), 3C(1), 3C(5), 4D(6)(a) (*Commentary*), 4D(6)(b) (*Commentary*), 4D(6)(g) (*Commentary*), 4D(6)(i) (*Commentary*), 4H (*Commentary*), 5, 5A (*Commentary*), 5B (*Commentary*), and 6D(1).

"Knowingly," "knowledge," "known," and "knows" mean actual knowledge of the fact in question. A person's knowledge may be inferred from circumstances. See Canons 2B(2)(b), 2B(2)(e), 2C (*Commentary*), 3B(2) (*Commentary*), 3B(7)(a), 3B(7)(a) (*Commentary*), 3D(2), 3D(5), 3E(5)(f), 5B(1)(b), 6D(3)(a)(i), 6D(3)(a) (*Commentary*), 6D(4) (*Commentary*), and 6D(5)(a).

"Law" means constitutional provisions, statutes, court rules, and decisional law. See Canons 1 (*Commentary*), 2A, 2C (*Commentary*), 3A, 3B(2), 3B(7), 3B(7)(c), 3B(8), 3B(8) (*Commentary*), 3B(12) (*Commentary*), 3E(1), 4C(3)(c) (*Commentary*), 4F, and 4H.

"Law, the legal system, or the administration of justice." When a judge engages in an activity that relates to the law, the legal system, or the administration of justice, the judge should also consider factors such as whether the activity upholds the integrity, impartiality, and independence of the judiciary (Canons 1 and 2A), whether the activity impairs public confidence in the judiciary (Canon 2), whether the judge is allowing the activity to take precedence over judicial duties (Canon 3A), and whether engaging in the activity would cause the judge to be disqualified (Canon 4A(4)). See Canons 4B (*Commentary*), 4C(1), 4C(1) (*Commentary*), 4C(2), 4C(2) (*Commentary*), 4C(3)(a), 4C(3)(b) (*Commentary*), 4C(3)(d)(ii), 4C(3)(d) (*Commentary*), 4D(6)(d), 4D(6)(e), 5A (*Commentary*), 5D, and 5D (*Commentary*).

"Member of the judge's family" means a spouse, registered domestic partner, child, grandchild, parent, grandparent, or other relative or person with whom the judge maintains a close familial relationship. See Canons 2B(3)(c), 2B (*Commentary*), 4C(3)(d)(i), 4D(1) (*Commentary*), 4D(2), 4D(5) (*Commentary*), 4E(1), and 4G (*Commentary*).

"Member of the judge's family residing in the judge's household" means a spouse or registered domestic partner and those persons who reside in the judge's household and who are relatives of the judge, including relatives by marriage or persons with whom the judge maintains a close familial relationship. See Canons 4D(5), 4D(5) (*Commentary*), 4D(6), 4D(6)(b) (*Commentary*), 4D(6)(f) and 6D(2)(c).

"Nonpublic information" means information that, by law, is not available to the public. Nonpublic information may include, but is not limited to, information that is sealed by statute or court order, impounded, or communicated in camera, and information offered in grand jury proceedings, presentencing reports, dependency cases, or psychiatric reports. Nonpublic information also includes information from affidavits, jury results, or court rulings before it becomes public information. See Canons 3B(11) and 6D(8)(a).

"Pending proceeding" is a proceeding or matter that has commenced. A proceeding continues to be pending through any period during which an appeal may be filed and any appellate process until final disposition. The words "proceeding" and "matter" are used interchangeably, and are intended to have the same meaning. See Canons 2 and 2A (*Commentary*), 2B(3)(a), 3B(7), 3B(9), 3B(9) (*Commentary*), 3E(5)(a), 4H (*Commentary*), and 6D(6). "Impending proceeding" is defined above.

"Political organization" means a political party, political action committee, or other group, the principal purpose of which is to further the election or appointment of candidates to nonjudicial office. See Canon 5A.

"Registered domestic partner" means a person who has registered for domestic partnership pursuant to state law or who is recognized as a domestic partner pursuant to Family Code section 299.2. See Canons 3E(5)(d), 3E(5)(e), 3E(5)(i), 4D(6)(d), 4D(6)(f), 4D(6)(j), 4H(2), 5A (*Commentary*), 6D(3)(a)(v), and 6D(3)(a)(vi).

"Require." Any canon prescribing that a judge "require" certain conduct of others means that a judge is to exercise reasonable direction and control over the conduct of those persons subject to the judge's direction and control. See Canons 3B(3), 3B(4), 3B(6), 3B(8) (*Commentary*), 3B(9), 3C(3), 6D(1), 6D(2)(a), and 6D(6).

"Service organization" includes any organization commonly referred to as a "fraternal organization." See Canons 3E(5)(d), 4C(2) (*Commentary*), 4C(3)(b), 4C(3)(b) (*Commentary*), 4C(3)(d) (*Commentary*), 4D(6)(j), and 6D(2)(b).

"Subordinate judicial officer." A subordinate judicial officer is, for the purposes of this code, a person appointed pursuant to article VI, section 22 of the California Constitution, including, but not limited to, a commissioner, referee, and hearing officer. See Canons 3D(3), 4G (*Commentary*), and 6A.

---

* Terms with an asterisk (*) are defined in the Terminology section.

"Temporary Judge" means an active or inactive member of the bar who, pursuant to article VI, section 21 of the California Constitution, serves or expects to serve as a judge once, sporadically, or regularly on a part-time basis under a separate court appointment for each period of service or for each case heard. See Canons 3E(5)(h), 4C(3)(d)(i), 4C(3)(d) (*Commentary*), 6A, and 6D.

"Third degree of relationship" includes the following persons: great-grandparent, grandparent, parent, uncle, aunt, brother, sister, child, grandchild, great-grandchild, nephew, and niece. See Canons 3E(5)(e), 3E(5)(i), and 6D(3)(a)(v).

(Terminology amended effective July 1, 2020; previously amended effective August 19, 2015, January 21, 2016, and October 10, 2018.)

Canon 1. A judge shall uphold the integrity* and independence* of the judiciary.

An independent, impartial,* and honorable judiciary is indispensable to justice in our society. A judge should participate in establishing, maintaining, and enforcing high standards of conduct, and shall personally observe those standards so that the integrity* and independence* of the judiciary is preserved. The provisions of this code are to be construed and applied to further that objective. A judicial decision or administrative act later determined to be incorrect legally is not itself a violation of this code.

ADVISORY COMMITTEE COMMENTARY: Canon 1

Deference to the judgments and rulings of courts depends upon public confidence in the integrity and independence* of judges. The integrity* and independence* of judges depend in turn upon their acting without fear or favor. Although judges should be independent, they must comply with the law* and the provisions of this code. Public confidence in the impartiality* of the judiciary is maintained by the adherence of each judge to this responsibility. Conversely, violations of this code diminish public confidence in the judiciary and thereby do injury to the system of government under law.*

The basic function of an independent, impartial, and honorable judiciary is to maintain the utmost integrity* in decisionmaking, and this code should be read and interpreted with that function in mind.*

(Canon 1 amended effective August 19, 2015; previously amended effective January 1, 2013.)

Canon 2. A judge shall avoid impropriety* and the appearance of impropriety* in all of the judge's activities.

A. Promoting Public Confidence

A judge shall respect and comply with the law* and shall act at all times in a manner that promotes public confidence in the integrity* and impartiality* of the judiciary. A judge shall not make statements, whether public or nonpublic, that commit the judge with respect to cases, controversies, or issues that are likely to come before the courts or that are inconsistent with the impartial* performance of the adjudicative duties of judicial office.

ADVISORY COMMITTEE COMMENTARY: Canons 2 and 2A

Public confidence in the judiciary is eroded by irresponsible or improper conduct by judges.

A judge must avoid all impropriety and appearance of impropriety.* A judge must expect to be the subject of constant public scrutiny. A judge must therefore accept restrictions on the judge's conduct that might be viewed as burdensome by other members of the community and should do so freely and willingly.*

A judge must exercise caution when engaging in any type of electronic communication, including communication by text or email, or when participating in online social networking sites or otherwise posting material on the Internet, given the accessibility, widespread transmission, and permanence of electronic communications and material posted on the Internet. The same canons that govern a judge's ability to socialize and communicate in person, on paper, or over the telephone apply to electronic communications, including use of the Internet and social networking sites. These canons include, but are not limited to, Canons 2B(2) (lending the prestige of judicial office), 3B(7) (ex parte communications), 3B(9) (public comment about pending or impending proceedings*), 3E(2) (disclosure of information relevant to disqualification), and 4A (conducting extrajudicial activities to avoid casting doubt on the judge's capacity to act impartially,* demeaning the judicial office, or frequent disqualification).*

The prohibition against behaving with impropriety or the appearance of impropriety* applies to both the professional and personal conduct of a judge.*

The test for the appearance of impropriety is whether a person aware of the facts might reasonably entertain a doubt that the judge would be able to act with integrity,* impartiality,* and competence.*

As to membership in organizations that practice invidious discrimination, see Commentary under Canon 2C.

As to judges making statements that commit the judge with respect to cases, controversies, or issues that are likely to come before the courts, see Canon 3B(9) and its commentary concerning comments about a pending proceeding, Canon 3E(3)(a) concerning the disqualification of a judge who makes statements that commit the judge to a particular result, and Canon 5B(1)(a) concerning statements made during an election campaign that commit the candidate to a particular result. In addition, Code of Civil Procedure section 170.2, subdivision (b), provides that, with certain exceptions, a judge is not disqualified on the ground that the judge has, in any capacity, expressed a view on a legal or factual issue presented in the proceeding before the judge.*

(Canon 2A amended effective October 10, 2018; previously amended effective January 1, 2013, and August 19, 2015.)

B. Use of the Prestige of Judicial Office

(1) A judge shall not allow family, social, political, or other relationships to influence the judge's judicial conduct or judgment, nor shall a judge convey or permit others to convey the impression that any individual is in a special position to influence the judge.

(2) A judge shall not lend the prestige of judicial office or use the judicial title in any manner, including any oral or written communication, to advance the pecuniary or personal interests of the judge or others. This canon does not prohibit the following:

(a) A judge may testify as a character witness, provided the judge does so only when subpoenaed.

(b) A judge may, without a subpoena, provide the Commission on Judicial Performance with a written communication containing (i) factual information regarding a matter pending before the commission or (ii) information related to the character of a judge who has a matter pending before the commission, provided that any such factual or character information is based on personal knowledge.* In commission proceedings, a judge shall provide information responsive to a subpoena or when officially requested to do so by the commission.

(c) A judge may provide factual information in State Bar disciplinary proceedings and shall provide information responsive to a subpoena or when officially requested to do so by the State Bar.

(d) A judge may respond to judicial selection inquiries, provide recommendations (including a general character reference relating to the evaluation of persons being considered for a judgeship), and otherwise participate in the process of judicial selection.

(e) A judge may serve as a reference or provide a letter of recommendation only if based on the judge's personal knowledge* of the individual. These written communications may include the judge's title and may be written on stationery that uses the judicial title.

(3) Except as permitted in subdivision (c) or otherwise authorized by law* or these canons:

(a) A judge shall not advance the pecuniary or personal interests of the judge or others by initiating communications with a sentencing judge or a representative of a probation department about a proceeding pending* before the sentencing judge, but may provide information in response to an official request. "Sentencing judge" includes a judge who makes a disposition pursuant to Welfare and Institutions Code section 725.

(b) A judge, other than the judge who presided over the trial of or sentenced the person seeking parole, pardon, or commutation of sentence, shall not initiate communications with the Board of Parole Hearings regarding parole or the Office of the Governor regarding parole, pardon, or commutation of sentence, but may provide these entities with information for the record in response to an official request.

(c) A judge may initiate communications concerning a member of the judge's family* with a representative of a probation department regarding sentencing, the Board of Parole Hearings regarding parole, or the Office of the Governor regarding parole, pardon, or commutation of sentence, provided the judge is not identified as a judge in the communication.

ADVISORY COMMITTEE COMMENTARY: Canon 2B

A strong judicial branch, based on the prestige that comes from effective and ethical performance, is essential to a system of government in which the judiciary functions independently of the executive and legislative branches. A judge should distinguish between proper and improper use of the prestige of office in all of his or her activities.

As to those communications that are permitted under this canon, a judge must keep in mind the general obligations to maintain high standards of conduct as set forth in Canon 1, and to avoid any impropriety or the appearance of impropriety**

---

* Terms with an asterisk (*) are defined in the Terminology section.

as set forth in Canon 2. A judge must also be mindful of Canon 2A, which requires a judge to act at all times in a manner that promotes public confidence in the integrity* and impartiality* of the courts.

A judge must avoid lending the prestige of judicial office for the advancement of the private interests of the judge or others. For example, a judge must not use the judicial position to gain advantage in a civil suit involving a member of the judge's family,* or use his or her position to gain deferential treatment when stopped by a police officer for a traffic offense.

If a judge posts on social networking sites such as Facebook or crowdsourced sites such as Yelp or Trip Advisor, the judge may not lend the prestige of judicial office to advance the pecuniary or personal interests of the judge or others. For example, a judge may not comment on, recommend, or criticize businesses, products, or services on such sites if it is reasonably likely that the judge can be identified as a judge.

See canon 4C(3)(d)(iv) prohibiting the use of the prestige of judicial office for fundraising or membership solicitation, but allowing a judge to be a speaker, guest of honor, or recipient of an award for public or charitable service, provided the judge does not personally solicit funds and complies with Canons 4A(1), (2), (3), and (4).

As to the use of a judge's title to identify a judge's role in the presentation and creation of legal education programs and materials, see Commentary to Canon 4B. In contracts for publication of a judge's writings, a judge should retain control over the advertising, to the extent feasible, to avoid exploitation of the judge's office.

This canon does not afford a judge a privilege against testifying in response to any official summons.

See also Canons 3D(1) and 3D(2) concerning a judge's obligation to take appropriate corrective action regarding other judges who violate any provision of the Code of Judicial Ethics and attorneys who violate any provision of the Rules of Professional Conduct.

Except as set forth in Canon 2B(3)(a), this canon does not preclude consultations among judges. Additional limitations on such consultations among judges are set forth in Canon 3B(7)(a).

(Canon 2B amended effective July 1, 2020; previously amended effective January 1, 2008, January 1, 2013, and August 19, 2015.)

C. Membership in Organizations

A judge shall not hold membership in any organization that practices invidious discrimination on the basis of race, sex, gender, gender identity,* gender expression,* religion, national origin, ethnicity, or sexual orientation.

This canon does not apply to membership in a religious organization.

ADVISORY COMMITTEE COMMENTARY: Canon 2C

Membership by a judge in an organization that practices invidious discrimination on the basis of race, sex, gender, religion, national origin, ethnicity, or sexual orientation gives rise to a perception that the judge's impartiality* is impaired. The code prohibits such membership by judges to preserve the fairness, impartiality,* independence,* and honor of the judiciary, to treat all parties equally under the law,* and to avoid impropriety* and the appearance of impropriety.*

Previously, Canon 2C contained exceptions to this prohibition for membership in religious organizations, membership in an official military organization of the United States and, so long as membership did not violate Canon 4A, membership in a nonprofit youth organization. The exceptions for membership in an official military organization of the United States and nonprofit youth organizations have been eliminated as exceptions to the canon. The exception for membership in religious organizations has been preserved.

Canon 2C refers to the current practices of the organization. Whether an organization practices invidious discrimination is often a complex question to which judges should be sensitive. The answer cannot be determined from a mere examination of an organization's current membership rolls, but rather depends on how the organization selects members and other relevant factors, such as whether the organization is dedicated to the preservation of religious, ethnic, or cultural values of legitimate common interest to its members, or whether it is in fact and effect an intimate, purely private organization whose membership limitations could not be constitutionally prohibited. Absent such factors, an organization is generally said to discriminate invidiously if it arbitrarily excludes from membership on the basis of race, religion, sex, gender, gender identity,* gender expression,* national origin, ethnicity, or sexual orientation persons who would otherwise be admitted to membership.

Although Canon 2C relates only to membership in organizations that invidiously discriminate on the basis of race, sex, gender, gender identity,* gender expression,* religion, national origin, ethnicity, or sexual orientation, a judge's membership in an organization that engages in any discriminatory membership practices prohibited by law* also violates Canon 2 and Canon 2A and gives the appearance of impropriety.* In addition, it would be a violation of Canon 2 and Canon 2A for a judge to arrange a meeting at a club that the judge knows* practices such invidious discrimination or for the judge to use such a club regularly. Moreover, public manifestation by a judge of the judge's knowing* approval of invidious discrimination on any basis gives the appearance of impropriety* under Canon 2 and

diminishes public confidence in the integrity* and impartiality* of the judiciary in violation of Canon 2A.

(Canon 2C amended effective October 10, 2018; previously amended effective June 18, 2003, January 1, 2013, and January 21, 2016.)

Canon 3. A judge shall perform the duties of judicial office impartially,* competently, and diligently.

A. Judicial Duties in General

All of the judicial duties prescribed by law* shall take precedence over all other activities of every judge. In the performance of these duties, the following standards apply.

B. Adjudicative Responsibilities

(1) A judge shall hear and decide all matters assigned to the judge except those in which he or she is disqualified.

ADVISORY COMMITTEE COMMENTARY: Canon 3B(1)

Canon 3B(1) is based upon the affirmative obligation contained in Code of Civil Procedure section 170.

(2) A judge shall be faithful to the law* regardless of partisan interests, public clamor, or fear of criticism, and shall maintain professional competence in the law.*

ADVISORY COMMITTEE COMMENTARY: Canon 3B(2)

Competence in the performance of judicial duties requires the legal knowledge,* skill, thoroughness, and preparation reasonably necessary to perform a judge's responsibilities of judicial office. Canon 1 provides that an incorrect legal ruling is not itself a violation of this code.

(3) A judge shall require* order and decorum in proceedings before the judge.

(4) A judge shall be patient, dignified, and courteous to litigants, jurors, witnesses, lawyers, and others with whom the judge deals in an official capacity, and shall require* similar conduct of lawyers and of all staff and court personnel under the judge's direction and control.

(5) A judge shall perform judicial duties without bias or prejudice. A judge shall not, in the performance of judicial duties, engage in speech, gestures, or other conduct that would reasonably be perceived as (a) bias, prejudice, or harassment, including but not limited to bias, prejudice, or harassment based upon race, sex, gender, gender identity,* gender expression,* religion, national origin, ethnicity, disability, age, sexual orientation, marital status, socioeconomic status, or political affiliation, or (b) sexual harassment.

(6) A judge shall require* lawyers in proceedings before the judge to refrain from (a) manifesting, by words or conduct, bias, prejudice, or harassment based upon race, sex, gender, gender identity,* gender expression,* religion, national origin, ethnicity, disability, age, sexual orientation, marital status, socioeconomic status, or political affiliation, or (b) sexual harassment against parties, witnesses, counsel, or others. This canon does not preclude legitimate advocacy when race, sex, gender, gender identity,* gender expression,* religion, national origin, ethnicity, disability, age, sexual orientation, marital status, socioeconomic status, political affiliation, or other similar factors are issues in the proceeding.

(7) A judge shall accord to every person who has a legal interest in a proceeding, or that person's lawyer, the full right to be heard according to law.* Unless otherwise authorized by law,* a judge shall not independently investigate facts in a proceeding and shall consider only the evidence presented or facts that may be properly judicially noticed. This prohibition extends to information available in all media, including electronic. A judge shall not initiate, permit, or consider ex parte communications, that is, any communications to or from the judge outside the presence of the parties concerning a pending* or impending* proceeding, and shall make reasonable efforts to avoid such communications, except as follows:

(a) Except as stated below, a judge may consult with other judges. A judge presiding over a case shall not engage in discussions about that case with a judge who has previously been disqualified from hearing that case; likewise, a judge who knows* he or she is or would be disqualified from hearing a case shall not discuss that matter with the judge assigned to the case. A judge also shall not engage in discussions with a judge who may participate in appellate review of the matter, nor shall a judge who may participate in appellate review of a matter engage in discussions with the judge presiding over the case.

A judge may consult with court personnel or others authorized by law,* as long as the communication relates to that person's duty to aid the judge in carrying out the judge's adjudicative responsibilities.

---

* Terms with an asterisk (*) are defined in the Terminology section.

In any discussion with judges or court personnel, a judge shall make reasonable efforts to avoid receiving factual information that is not part of the record or an evaluation of that factual information. In such consultations, the judge shall not abrogate the responsibility personally to decide the matter.

For purposes of Canon 3B(7)(a), "court personnel" includes bailiffs, court reporters, court externs, research attorneys, courtroom clerks, and other employees of the court, but does not include the lawyers in a proceeding before a judge, persons who are appointed by the court to serve in some capacity in a proceeding, or employees of other governmental entities, such as lawyers, social workers, or representatives of the probation department.

ADVISORY COMMITTEE COMMENTARY: Canon 3B(7)(a)

Regarding communications between a judge presiding over a matter and a judge of a court with appellate jurisdiction over that matter, see Government Code section 68070.5.

Though a judge may have ex parte discussions with appropriate court personnel, a judge may do so only on matters that are within the proper performance of that person's duties. For example, a bailiff may inform the judge of a threat to the judge or to the safety and security of the courtroom, but may not tell the judge ex parte that a defendant was overheard making an incriminating statement during a court recess. A clerk may point out to the judge a technical defect in a proposed sentence, but may not suggest to the judge that a defendant deserves a certain sentence.

A sentencing judge may not consult ex parte with a representative of the probation department about a matter pending before the sentencing judge.

This canon prohibits a judge who is presiding over a case from discussing that case with another judge who has already been disqualified from hearing that case. A judge also must be careful not to talk to a judge whom the judge knows* would be disqualified from hearing the matter.

(b) A judge may initiate, permit, or consider ex parte communications, where circumstances require, for scheduling, administrative purposes, or emergencies that do not deal with substantive matters provided:

(i) the judge reasonably believes that no party will gain a procedural or tactical advantage as a result of the ex parte communication, and

(ii) the judge makes provision promptly to notify all other parties of the substance of the ex parte communication and allows an opportunity to respond.

(c) A judge may initiate, permit, or consider any ex parte communication when expressly authorized by law* to do so or when authorized to do so by stipulation of the parties.

(d) If a judge receives an unauthorized ex parte communication, the judge shall make provision promptly to notify the parties of the substance of the communication and provide the parties with an opportunity to respond.

ADVISORY COMMITTEE COMMENTARY: Canon 3B(7)

An exception allowing a judge, under certain circumstances, to obtain the advice of a disinterested expert on the law* has been eliminated from Canon 3B(7) because consulting with legal experts outside the presence of the parties is inconsistent with the core tenets of the adversarial system. Therefore, a judge shall not consult with legal experts outside the presence of the parties. Evidence Code section 730 provides for the appointment of an expert if a judge determines that expert testimony is necessary. A court may also invite the filing of amicus curiae briefs.

An exception allowing a judge to confer with the parties separately in an effort to settle the matter before the judge has been moved from this canon to Canon 3B(12).

This canon does not prohibit court personnel from communicating scheduling information or carrying out similar administrative functions.

A judge is statutorily authorized to investigate and consult witnesses informally in small claims cases. Code of Civil Procedure section 116.520, subdivision (c).

(8) A judge shall dispose of all judicial matters fairly, promptly, and efficiently. A judge shall manage the courtroom in a manner that provides all litigants the opportunity to have their matters fairly adjudicated in accordance with the law.*

ADVISORY COMMITTEE COMMENTARY: Canon 3B(8)

The obligation of a judge to dispose of matters promptly and efficiently must not take precedence over the judge's obligation to dispose of the matters fairly and with patience. For example, when a litigant is self-represented, a judge has the discretion to take reasonable steps, appropriate under the circumstances and consistent with the law* and the canons, to enable the litigant to be heard. A judge should monitor and supervise cases so as to reduce or eliminate dilatory practices, avoidable delays, and unnecessary costs.

Prompt disposition of the court's business requires a judge to devote adequate time to judicial duties, to be punctual in attending court and expeditious in determining matters under submission, and to require* that court officials, litigants, and their lawyers cooperate with the judge to those ends.

(9) A judge shall not make any public comment about a pending* or impending* proceeding in any court, and shall not make any nonpublic comment that might substantially interfere with a fair trial or hearing. The judge shall require* similar abstention on the part of staff and court personnel subject to the judge's direction and control. This canon does not prohibit judges from making statements in the course of their official duties or from explaining the procedures of the court, and does not apply to proceedings in which the judge is a litigant in a personal capacity. **In connection with a judicial election or recall campaign, this canon does not prohibit any judge from making a public comment about a pending* proceeding, provided (a) the comment would not reasonably be expected to affect the outcome or impair the fairness of the proceeding, and (b) the comment is about the procedural, factual, or legal basis of a decision about which a judge has been criticized during the election or recall campaign.** Other than cases in which the judge has personally participated, this canon does not prohibit judges from discussing, in legal education programs and materials, cases and issues pending in appellate courts. This educational exemption does not apply to cases over which the judge has presided or to comments or discussions that might interfere with a fair hearing of the case.

ADVISORY COMMITTEE COMMENTARY: Canon 3B(9)

The requirement that judges abstain from public comment regarding a pending* or impending* proceeding continues during any appellate process and until final disposition. A judge shall make reasonable efforts to ascertain whether a case is pending* or impending* before commenting on it. This canon does not prohibit a judge from commenting on proceedings in which the judge is a litigant in a personal capacity, but in cases such as a writ of mandamus where the judge is a litigant in an official capacity, the judge must not comment publicly.

"Making statements in the course of their official duties" and "explaining the procedures of the court" include providing an official transcript or partial official transcript of a court proceeding open to the public and explaining the rules of court and procedures related to a decision rendered by a judge.

The provision allowing a judge to make a public comment about a pending* decision that is the subject of criticism during an election campaign applies to all judicial elections, including recall elections. Depending on the circumstances, the judge should consider whether it may be preferable for a third party, rather than the judge, to respond or issue statements in connection with allegations concerning the decision. For purposes of this provision, a recall campaign begins when a judge is served with a notice of intention to circulate a recall petition (see Elec. Code, § 11006), and a judicial election campaign begins when a judge or candidate for judicial office* files a declaration of intention of candidacy for judicial office (see Elec. Code, § 8023).

Although this canon does not prohibit a judge from commenting on cases that are not pending* or impending* in any court, a judge must be cognizant of the general prohibition in Canon 2 against conduct involving impropriety* or the appearance of impropriety.* A judge should also be aware of the mandate in Canon 2A that a judge must act at all times in a manner that promotes public confidence in the integrity* and impartiality* of the judiciary. In addition, when commenting on a case pursuant to this canon, a judge must maintain the high standards of conduct, as set forth in Canon 1.

Although a judge is permitted to make nonpublic comments about pending* or impending* cases that will not substantially interfere with a fair trial or hearing, the judge should be cautious when making any such comments. There is always a risk that a comment can be misheard, misinterpreted, or repeated. A judge making such a comment must be mindful of the judge's obligation under Canon 2A to act at all times in a manner that promotes public confidence in the integrity* and impartiality* of the judiciary. When a judge makes a nonpublic comment about a case pending* before that judge, the judge must keep an open mind and not form an opinion prematurely or create the appearance of having formed an opinion prematurely.

(10) A judge shall not commend or criticize jurors for their verdict other than in a court order or opinion in a proceeding, but may express appreciation to jurors for their service to the judicial system and the community.

ADVISORY COMMITTEE COMMENTARY: Canon 3B(10)

Commending or criticizing jurors for their verdict may imply a judicial expectation in future cases and may impair a juror's ability to be fair and impartial* in a subsequent case.

(11) A judge shall not disclose or use, for any purpose unrelated to judicial duties, nonpublic information* acquired in a judicial capacity.

---

* Terms with an asterisk (*) are defined in the Terminology section.

(12)   A judge may participate in settlement conferences or in other efforts to resolve matters in dispute, including matters pending before the judge. A judge may, with the express consent of the parties or their lawyers, confer separately with the parties and/or their lawyers during such resolution efforts. At all times during such resolution efforts, a judge shall remain impartial* and shall not engage in conduct that may reasonably be perceived as coercive.

ADVISORY COMMITTEE COMMENTARY: Canon 3B(12)

While the judge plays an important role in overseeing efforts to resolve disputes, including conducting settlement discussions, a judge should be careful that efforts to resolve disputes do not undermine any party's right to be heard according to law.*

The judge should keep in mind the effect that the judge's participation in dispute resolution efforts may have on the judge's impartiality* or the appearance of impartiality* if the case remains with the judge for trial after resolution efforts are unsuccessful. Accordingly, a judge may wish to consider whether: (1) the parties or their counsel have requested or objected to the participation by the trial judge in such discussions; (2) the parties and their counsel are relatively sophisticated in legal matters or the particular legal issues involved in the case; (3) a party is unrepresented; (4) the case will be tried by the judge or a jury; (5) the parties will participate with their counsel in settlement discussions and, if so, the effect of personal contact between the judge and parties; and (6) it is appropriate during the settlement conference for the judge to express an opinion on the merits or worth of the case or express an opinion on the legal issues that the judge may later have to rule upon.

If a judge assigned to preside over a trial believes participation in resolution efforts could influence the judge's decisionmaking during trial, the judge may decline to engage in such efforts.

Where dispute resolution efforts of any type are unsuccessful, the judge should consider whether, due to events that occurred during the resolution efforts, the judge may be disqualified under the law* from presiding over the trial. See, e.g., Code of Civil Procedure section 170.1, subdivision (a)(6)(A).

(Canon 3B amended effective July 1, 2020; previously amended effective December 22, 2003, January 1, 2008, January 1, 2013, August 19, 2015, and October 10, 2018.)

C.   Administrative Responsibilities

(1)   A judge shall diligently discharge the judge's administrative responsibilities impartially,* on the basis of merit, without bias or prejudice, free of conflict of interest, and in a manner that promotes public confidence in the integrity* of the judiciary. A judge shall not, in the performance of administrative duties, engage in speech, gestures, or other conduct that would reasonably be perceived as (a) bias, prejudice, or harassment, including but not limited to bias, prejudice, or harassment based upon race, sex, gender, gender identity,* gender expression,* religion, national origin, ethnicity, disability, age, sexual orientation, marital status, socioeconomic status, or political affiliation, or (b) sexual harassment.

ADVISORY COMMITTEE COMMENTARY: Canon 3C(1)

In considering what constitutes a conflict of interest under this canon, a judge should be informed by Code of Civil Procedure section 170.1, subdivision (a)(6).

(2)   A judge shall maintain professional competence in judicial administration, and shall cooperate with other judges and court officials in the administration of court business.

(3)   A judge shall require* staff and court personnel under the judge's direction and control to observe appropriate standards of conduct and to refrain from (a) manifesting bias, prejudice, or harassment based upon race, sex, gender, gender identity,* gender expression,* religion, national origin, ethnicity, disability, age, sexual orientation, marital status, socioeconomic status, or political affiliation, or (b) sexual harassment in the performance of their official duties.

(4)   A judge with supervisory authority for the judicial performance of other judges shall take reasonable measures to ensure the prompt disposition of matters before them and the proper performance of their other judicial responsibilities.

(5)   A judge shall not make unnecessary court appointments. A judge shall exercise the power of appointment impartially,* on the basis of merit, without bias or prejudice, free of conflict of interest, and in a manner that promotes public confidence in the integrity* of the judiciary. A judge shall avoid nepotism and favoritism. A judge shall not approve compensation of appointees above the reasonable value of services rendered.

ADVISORY COMMITTEE COMMENTARY: Canon 3C(5)

Appointees of a judge include assigned counsel and officials such as referees, commissioners, special masters, receivers, and guardians. Consent by the parties to an appointment or an award of compensation does not relieve the judge of the obligation prescribed by Canon 3C(5).

(Canon 3C amended effective October 10, 2018; previously amended effective December 22, 2003, April 29, 2009, January 1, 2013, and August 19, 2015.)

D.   Disciplinary Responsibilities

(1)   Whenever a judge has reliable information that another judge has violated any provision of the Code of Judicial Ethics, that judge shall take appropriate corrective action, which may include reporting the violation to the appropriate authority. (See Commentary to Canon 3D(2).)

(2)   Whenever a judge has personal knowledge,* or concludes in a judicial decision, that a lawyer has committed misconduct or has violated any provision of the Rules of Professional Conduct, the judge shall take appropriate corrective action, which may include reporting the violation to the appropriate authority.

ADVISORY COMMITTEE COMMENTARY: Canons 3D(1) and 3D(2)

Appropriate corrective action could include direct communication with the judge or lawyer who has committed the violation, writing about the misconduct in a judicial decision, or other direct action, such as a confidential referral to a judicial or lawyer assistance program, or a report of the violation to the presiding judge, appropriate authority, or other agency or body. Judges should note that in addition to the action required by Canon 3D(2), California law imposes additional mandatory reporting requirements to the State Bar on judges regarding lawyer misconduct. See Business and Professions Code sections 6086.7 and 6086.8, subdivision (a), and California Rules of Court, rules 10.609 and 10.1017.

"Appropriate authority" means the authority with responsibility for initiation of the disciplinary process with respect to a violation to be reported.

(3)   A judge shall promptly report in writing to the Commission on Judicial Performance when he or she is charged in court by misdemeanor citation, prosecutorial complaint, information, or indictment with any crime in the United States as specified below. Crimes that must be reported are: (1) all crimes, other than those that would be considered misdemeanors not involving moral turpitude or infractions under California law; and (2) all misdemeanors involving violence (including assaults), the use or possession of controlled substances, the misuse of prescriptions, or the personal use or furnishing of alcohol. A judge also shall promptly report in writing upon conviction of such crimes.

If the judge is a retired judge serving in the **Temporary** Assigned Judges Program, he or she shall promptly report such information in writing to the Chief Justice rather than to the Commission on Judicial Performance. If the judge is a subordinate judicial officer,* he or she shall promptly report such information in writing to both the presiding judge of the court in which the subordinate judicial officer* sits and the Commission on Judicial Performance.

(4)   A judge shall cooperate with judicial and lawyer disciplinary agencies.

ADVISORY COMMITTEE COMMENTARY: Canons 3D(3) and 3D(4)

See Government Code section 68725, which requires judges to cooperate with and give reasonable assistance and information to the Commission on Judicial Performance, and rule 104 of the Rules of the Commission on Judicial Performance, which requires a respondent judge to cooperate with the commission in all proceedings in accordance with section 68725.

(5)   A judge shall not retaliate, directly or indirectly, against a person known* or suspected to have assisted or cooperated with an investigation of a judge or a lawyer.

(Canon 3D amended effective July 1, 2020; adopted effective January 15, 1996; previously amended effective June 19, 1997, March 4, 1999, January 1, 2008, January 1, 2013, August 19, 2015, and October 10, 2018.)

E.   Disqualification and Disclosure

(1)   A judge shall disqualify himself or herself in any proceeding in which disqualification is required by law.*

ADVISORY COMMITTEE COMMENTARY: Canon 3E(1)

The term "proceeding" as used in this canon encompasses prefiling judicial determinations. Thus, if a judge has a disqualifying interest in a matter, the judge is disqualified from taking any action in the matter, even if it predates the actual filing of a case, such as making a probable cause determination, signing a search or arrest warrant, setting bail, or ordering an own recognizance release. Interpreting "proceeding" to include prefiling judicial determinations effectuates the intent of the canon because it assures the parties and the public of the integrity* and fairness of the judicial process.

---

* Terms with an asterisk (*) are defined in the Terminology section.

(2) In all trial court proceedings, a judge shall disclose on the record as follows:

(a) Information relevant to disqualification

A judge shall disclose information that is reasonably relevant to the question of disqualification under Code of Civil Procedure section 170.1, even if the judge believes there is no actual basis for disqualification.

(b) Campaign contributions in trial court elections

(i) Information required to be disclosed

In any matter before a judge who is or was a candidate for judicial office* in a trial court election, the judge shall disclose any contribution or loan of $100 or more from a party, individual lawyer, or law office or firm in that matter as required by this canon, even if the amount of the contribution or loan would not require disqualification. Such disclosure shall consist of the name of the contributor or lender, the amount of each contribution or loan, the cumulative amount of the contributor's contributions or lender's loans, and the date of each contribution or loan. The judge shall make reasonable efforts to obtain current information regarding contributions or loans received by his or her campaign and shall disclose the required information on the record.

(ii) Manner of disclosure

The judge shall ensure that the required information is conveyed on the record to the parties and lawyers appearing in the matter before the judge. The judge has discretion to select the manner of disclosure, but the manner used shall avoid the appearance that the judge is soliciting campaign contributions.

(iii) Timing of disclosure

Disclosure shall be made at the earliest reasonable opportunity after receiving each contribution or loan. The duty commences no later than one week after receipt of the first contribution or loan, and continues for a period of two years after the candidate takes the oath of office, or two years from the date of the contribution or loan, whichever event is later.

ADVISORY COMMITTEE COMMENTARY: Canon 3E(2)(b)

Code of Civil Procedure section 170.1, subdivision (a)(9)(C) requires a judge to "disclose any contribution from a party or lawyer in a matter that is before the court that is required to be reported under subdivision (f) of Section 84211 of the Government Code, even if the amount would not require disqualification under this paragraph." This statute further provides that the "manner of disclosure shall be the same as that provided in Canon 3E of the Code of Judicial Ethics." Canon 3E(2)(b) sets forth the information the judge must disclose, the manner for making such disclosure, and the timing thereof.

"Contribution" includes monetary and in-kind contributions. See Cal. Code Regs., tit. 2, § 18215, subd. (b)(3). See generally Government Code section 84211, subdivision (f).

Disclosure of campaign contributions is intended to provide parties and lawyers appearing before a judge during and after a judicial campaign with easy access to information about campaign contributions that may not require disqualification but could be relevant to the question of disqualification of the judge. The judge is responsible for ensuring that the disclosure is conveyed to the parties and lawyers appearing in the matter. The canon provides that the judge has discretion to select the manner of making the disclosure. The appropriate manner of disclosure will depend on whether all of the parties and lawyers are present in court, whether it is more efficient or practicable given the court's calendar to make a written disclosure, and other relevant circumstances that may affect the ability of the parties and lawyers to access the required information. The following alternatives for disclosure are non-exclusive. If all parties are present in court, the judge may conclude that the most effective and efficient manner of providing disclosure is to state orally the required information on the record in open court. In the alternative, again if all parties are present in court, a judge may determine that it is more appropriate to state orally on the record in open court that parties and lawyers may obtain the required information at an easily accessible location in the courthouse, and provide an opportunity for the parties and lawyers to review the available information. Another alternative, particularly if all or some parties are not present in court, is that the judge may disclose the campaign contribution in a written minute order or in the official court minutes and notify the parties and the lawyers of the written disclosure. See California Supreme Court Committee on Judicial Ethics Opinions, CJEO Formal Opinion No. 2013-002, pp. 7-8. If a party appearing in a matter before the judge is represented by a lawyer, it is sufficient to make the disclosure to the lawyer.

In addition to the disclosure obligations set forth in Canon 3E(2)(b), a judge must, pursuant to Canon 3E(2)(a), disclose on the record any other information that may be relevant to the question of disqualification. As examples, such an obligation may arise as a result of contributions or loans of which the judge is aware made by a party, lawyer, or law office or firm appearing before the judge or a third party in support of the judge or in opposition to the judge's opponent; a

party, lawyer, or law office or firm's relationship to the judge or role in the campaign; or the aggregate contributions or loans from lawyers in one law office or firm.

Canon 3E(2)(b) does not eliminate the obligation of the judge to recuse himself or herself where the nature of the contribution or loan, the extent of the contributor's or lender's involvement in the judicial campaign, the relationship of the contributor or lender, or other circumstance requires recusal under Code of Civil Procedure section 170.1, and particularly section 170.1, subdivision (a)(6)(A).

(3) A judge shall disqualify himself or herself in accordance with the following:

(a) Statements that commit the judge to a particular result

A judge is disqualified if the judge, while a judge or candidate for judicial office,* made a statement, other than in a court proceeding, judicial decision, or opinion, that a person aware of the facts might reasonably believe commits the judge to reach a particular result or rule in a particular way in a proceeding.

(b) Bond ownership

Ownership of a corporate bond issued by a party to a proceeding and having a fair market value exceeding $1,500 is disqualifying. Ownership of a government bond issued by a party to a proceeding is disqualifying only if the outcome of the proceeding could substantially affect the value of the judge's bond. Ownership in a mutual or common investment fund that holds bonds is not a disqualifying financial interest.

ADVISORY COMMITTEE COMMENTARY: Canon 3E(3)(b)

The distinction between corporate and government bonds is consistent with the Political Reform Act (see Gov. Code, § 82034), which requires disclosure of corporate bonds, but not government bonds. Canon 3E(3) is intended to assist judges in complying with Code of Civil Procedure section 170.1, subdivision (a)(3) and Canon 3E(5)(d).

(4) An appellate justice shall disqualify himself or herself in any proceeding if for any reason:

(a) the justice believes his or her recusal would further the interests of justice; or

(b) the justice substantially doubts his or her capacity to be impartial;* or

(c) the circumstances are such that a reasonable person aware of the facts would doubt the justice's ability to be impartial.*

(5) Disqualification of an appellate justice is also required in the following instances:

(a) The appellate justice has served as a lawyer in the pending* proceeding, or has served as a lawyer in any other proceeding involving any of the same parties if that other proceeding related to the same contested issues of fact and law as the present proceeding, or has given advice to any party in the present proceeding upon any issue involved in the proceeding.

ADVISORY COMMITTEE COMMENTARY: Canon 3E(5)(a)

Canon 3E(5)(a) is consistent with Code of Civil Procedure section 170.1, subdivision (a)(2), which addresses disqualification of trial court judges based on prior representation of a party in the proceeding.

(b) Within the last two years, (i) a party to the proceeding, or an officer, director or trustee thereof, either was a client of the justice when the justice was engaged in the private practice of law or was a client of a lawyer with whom the justice was associated in the private practice of law; or (ii) a lawyer in the proceeding was associated with the justice in the private practice of law.

(c) The appellate justice represented a public officer or entity and personally advised or in any way represented that officer or entity concerning the factual or legal issues in the present proceeding in which the public officer or entity now appears.

(d) The appellate justice, his or her spouse or registered domestic partner,* or a minor child residing in the household, has a financial interest or is either a fiduciary* who has a financial interest in the proceeding, or is a director, advisor, or other active participant in the affairs of a party. A financial interest is defined as ownership of more than a 1 percent legal or equitable interest in a party, or a legal or equitable interest in a party of a fair market value exceeding $1,500. Ownership in a mutual or common investment fund that holds securities does not itself constitute a financial interest; holding office in an educational, religious, charitable, service,* or civic organization does not confer a financial interest in the organization's securities; and a proprietary interest of a policyholder in a mutual insurance company or mutual savings associa-

---

* Terms with an asterisk (*) are defined in the Terminology section.

tion or similar interest is not a financial interest unless the outcome of the proceeding could substantially affect the value of the interest. A justice shall make reasonable efforts to keep informed about his or her personal and fiduciary* interests and those of his or her spouse or registered domestic partner* and of minor children living in the household.

(e)(i) The justice or his or her spouse or registered domestic partner,* or a person within the third degree of relationship* to either of them, or the spouse or registered domestic partner* thereof, is a party or an officer, director, or trustee of a party to the proceeding, or

(ii) a lawyer or spouse or registered domestic partner* of a lawyer in the proceeding is the spouse, registered domestic partner,* former spouse, former registered domestic partner,* child, sibling, or parent of the justice or of the justice's spouse or registered domestic partner,* or such a person is associated in the private practice of law with a lawyer in the proceeding.

(f) The justice

(i) served as the judge before whom the proceeding was tried or heard in the lower court,

(ii) has personal knowledge* of disputed evidentiary facts concerning the proceeding, or

(iii) has a personal bias or prejudice concerning a party or a party's lawyer.

(g) A temporary or permanent physical impairment renders the justice unable properly to perceive the evidence or conduct the proceedings.

(h) The justice has a current arrangement concerning prospective employment or other compensated service as a dispute resolution neutral or is participating in, or, within the last two years has participated in, discussions regarding prospective employment or service as a dispute resolution neutral, or has been engaged in such employment or service, and any of the following applies:

(i) The arrangement is, or the prior employment or discussion was, with a party to the proceeding;

(ii) The matter before the justice includes issues relating to the enforcement of either an agreement to submit a dispute to an alternative dispute resolution process or an award or other final decision by a dispute resolution neutral;

(iii) The justice directs the parties to participate in an alternative dispute resolution process in which the dispute resolution neutral will be an individual or entity with whom the justice has the arrangement, has previously been employed or served, or is discussing or has discussed the employment or service; or

(iv) The justice will select a dispute resolution neutral or entity to conduct an alternative dispute resolution process in the matter before the justice, and among those available for selection is an individual or entity with whom the justice has the arrangement, with whom the justice has previously been employed or served, or with whom the justice is discussing or has discussed the employment or service.

For purposes of Canon 3E(5)(h), "participating in discussions" or "has participated in discussions" means that the justice (i) solicited or otherwise indicated an interest in accepting or negotiating possible employment or service as an alternative dispute resolution neutral, or (ii) responded to an unsolicited statement regarding, or an offer of, such employment or service by expressing an interest in that employment or service, making any inquiry regarding the employment or service, or encouraging the person making the statement or offer to provide additional information about that possible employment or service. If a justice's response to an unsolicited statement regarding a question about, or offer of, prospective employment or other compensated service as a dispute resolution neutral is limited to responding negatively, declining the offer, or declining to discuss such employment or service, that response does not constitute participating in discussions.

For purposes of Canon 3E(5)(h), "party" includes the parent, subsidiary, or other legal affiliate of any entity that is a party and is involved in the transaction, contract, or facts that gave rise to the issues subject to the proceeding.

For purposes of Canon 3E(5)(h), "dispute resolution neutral" means an arbitrator, a mediator, a temporary judge* appointed under article VI, section 21 of the California Constitution, a referee appointed under Code of Civil Procedure section 638 or 639, a special master, a neutral evaluator, a settlement officer, or a settlement facilitator.

(i) The justice's spouse or registered domestic partner* a person within the third degree of relationship* to the justice or his or her spouse or registered domestic partner,* or the person's spouse or registered domestic partner,* was a witness in the proceeding.

(j) The justice has received a campaign contribution of $5,000 or more from a party or lawyer in a matter that is before the court, and either of the following applies:

(i) The contribution was received in support of the justice's last election, if the last election was within the last six years; or

(ii) The contribution was received in anticipation of an upcoming election.

Notwithstanding Canon 3E(5)(j), a justice shall disqualify himself or herself based on a contribution of a lesser amount if required by Canon 3E(4).

The disqualification required under Canon 3E(5)(j) may be waived if all parties that did not make the contribution agree to waive the disqualification.

ADVISORY COMMITTEE COMMENTARY: Canon 3E

Canon 3E(1) sets forth the general duty to disqualify applicable to a judge of any court. Sources for determining when recusal or disqualification is appropriate may include the applicable provisions of the Code of Civil Procedure, other provisions of the Code of Judicial Ethics, the Code of Conduct for United States Judges, the American Bar Association's Model Code of Judicial Conduct, and related case law.

The decision whether to disclose information under Canon 3E(2) is a decision based on the facts of the case before the judge. A judge is required to disclose only information that is related to the grounds for disqualification set forth in Code of Civil Procedure section 170.1.

Canon 3E(4) sets forth the general standards for recusal of an appellate justice. The term "appellate justice" includes justices of both the Courts of Appeal and the Supreme Court. Generally, the provisions concerning disqualification of an appellate justice are intended to assist justices in determining whether recusal is appropriate and to inform the public why recusal may occur.

The rule of necessity may override the rule of disqualification. For example, a judge might be required to participate in judicial review of a judicial salary statute, or might be the only judge available in a matter requiring judicial action, such as a hearing on probable cause or a temporary restraining order. In the latter case, the judge must promptly disclose on the record the basis for possible disqualification and use reasonable efforts to transfer the matter to another judge as soon as practicable.

In some instances, membership in certain organizations may have the potential to give an appearance of partiality, although membership in the organization generally may not be barred by Canon 2C, Canon 4, or any other specific canon. A judge holding membership in an organization should disqualify himself or herself whenever doing so would be appropriate in accordance with Canon 3E(1), 3E(4), or 3E(5) or statutory requirements. In addition, in some circumstances, the parties or their lawyers may consider a judge's membership in an organization relevant to the question of disqualification, even if the judge believes there is no actual basis for disqualification. In accordance with this canon, a judge should disclose to the parties his or her membership in an organization, in any proceeding in which that information is reasonably relevant to the question of disqualification under Code of Civil Procedure section 170.1, even if the judge concludes there is no actual basis for disqualification.

(6) It shall not be grounds for disqualification that the justice:

(a) Is or is not a member of a racial, ethnic, religious, sexual, or similar group and the proceeding involves the rights of such a group;

(b) Has in any capacity expressed a view on a legal or factual issue presented in the proceeding, except as provided in Canon 3E(5)(a), (b), or (c);

(c) Has as a lawyer or public official participated in the drafting of laws* or in the effort to pass or defeat laws,* the meaning, effect, or application of which is in issue in the proceeding unless the judge believes that his or her prior involvement was so well known* as to raise a reasonable doubt in the public mind as to his or her capacity to be impartial.*

ADVISORY COMMITTEE COMMENTARY: Canon 3E(6)

Canon 3E(6) is substantively the same as Code of Civil Procedure section 170.2, which pertains to trial court judges.

(Canon 3E amended effective December 1, 2016; adopted effective January 15, 1996; previously amended effective April 15, 1996, June 19, 1997, March 4, 1999, December 13, 2000, June 18, 2003, December 22, 2003, January 1, 2005, January 1, 2007, January 1, 2008, April 29, 2009, January 1, 2013, and August 19, 2015.)

Canon 4. A judge shall so conduct the judge's quasi-judicial and extrajudicial activities as to minimize the risk of conflict with judicial obligations.

A. Extrajudicial Activities in General

---

* Terms with an asterisk (*) are defined in the Terminology section.

A judge shall conduct all of the judge's extrajudicial activities so that they do not

(1) cast reasonable doubt on the judge's capacity to act impartially,*
(2) demean the judicial office,
(3) interfere with the proper performance of judicial duties, or
(4) lead to frequent disqualification of the judge.

ADVISORY COMMITTEE COMMENTARY: Canon 4A

Complete separation of a judge from extrajudicial activities is neither possible nor wise; a judge should not become isolated from the community in which he or she lives. Expressions of bias or prejudice by a judge, even outside the judge's judicial activities, may cast reasonable doubt on the judge's capacity to act impartially as a judge. Expressions that may do so include inappropriate use of humor or the use of demeaning remarks. See Canon 2C and accompanying Commentary.*

Because a judge's judicial duties take precedence over all other activities (see Canon 3A), a judge must avoid extrajudicial activities that might reasonably result in the judge being disqualified.

(Canon 4A amended effective August 19, 2015; previously amended effective January 1, 2013.)

B. Quasi-Judicial and Avocational Activities

A judge may speak, write, lecture, teach, and participate in activities concerning legal and nonlegal subject matters, subject to the requirements of this code.

ADVISORY COMMITTEE COMMENTARY: Canon 4B

As a judicial officer and person specially learned in the law, a judge is in a unique position to contribute to the improvement of the law, the legal system, and the administration of justice,* including revision of substantive and procedural law* and improvement of criminal and juvenile justice. To the extent that time permits, a judge may do so, either independently or through a bar or judicial association or other group dedicated to the improvement of the law.* It may be necessary to promote legal education programs and materials by identifying authors and speakers by judicial title. This is permissible, provided such use of the judicial title does not contravene Canons 2A and 2B.*

Judges are not precluded by their office from engaging in other social, community, and intellectual endeavors so long as they do not interfere with the obligations under Canons 2C and 4A.

(Canon 4B amended effective August 19, 2015; previously amended effective January 1, 2013.)

C. Governmental, Civic, or Charitable Activities

(1) A judge shall not appear at a public hearing or officially consult with an executive or legislative body or public official except on matters concerning the law, the legal system, or the administration of justice,* or in matters involving the judge's private economic or personal interests.

ADVISORY COMMITTEE COMMENTARY: Canon 4C(1)

When deciding whether to appear at a public hearing or to consult with an executive or legislative body or public official on matters concerning the law, the legal system, or the administration of justice, a judge should consider if that conduct would violate any other provisions of this code. For a list of factors to consider, see the explanation of "law, the legal system, or the administration of justice" in the Terminology section. See also Canon 2B regarding the obligation to avoid improper influence.*

(2) A judge shall not accept appointment to a governmental committee or commission or other governmental position that is concerned with issues of fact or policy on matters other than the improvement of the law, the legal system, or the administration of justice.* A judge may, however, serve in the military reserve or represent a national, state, or local government on ceremonial occasions or in connection with historical, educational, or cultural activities.

ADVISORY COMMITTEE COMMENTARY: Canon 4C(2)

Canon 4C(2) prohibits a judge from accepting any governmental position except one relating to the law, legal system, or administration of justice as authorized by Canon 4C(3). The appropriateness of accepting extrajudicial assignments must be assessed in light of the demands on judicial resources and the need to protect the courts from involvement in extrajudicial matters that may prove to be controversial. Judges shall not accept governmental appointments that are likely to interfere with the effectiveness and independence* of the judiciary, or that constitute a public office within the meaning of article VI, section 17 of the California Constitution.*

Canon 4C(2) does not govern a judge's service in a nongovernmental position. See Canon 4C(3) permitting service by a judge with organizations devoted to the improvement of the law, the legal system, or the administration of justice and with educational, religious, charitable, service,* or civic organizations not conducted for profit. For example, service on the board of a public educational institution, other than a law school, would be prohibited under Canon 4C(2), but service on the board of a public law school or any private educational institution would generally be permitted under Canon 4C(3).*

(3) Subject to the following limitations and the other requirements of this code,

(a) a judge may serve as an officer, director, trustee, or nonlegal advisor of an organization or governmental agency devoted to the improvement of the law, the legal system, or the administration of justice* provided that such position does not constitute a public office within the meaning of article VI, section 17 of the California Constitution;

(b) a judge may serve as an officer, director, trustee, or nonlegal advisor of an educational, religious, charitable, service,* or civic organization not conducted for profit;

ADVISORY COMMITTEE COMMENTARY: Canon 4C(3)

Canon 4C(3) does not apply to a judge's service in a governmental position unconnected with the improvement of the law, the legal system, or the administration of justice. See Canon 4C(2).*

Canon 4C(3) uses the phrase, "Subject to the following limitations and the other requirements of this code." As an example of the meaning of the phrase, a judge permitted by Canon 4C(3) to serve on the board of a service organization may be prohibited from such service by Canon 2C or 4A if the institution practices invidious discrimination or if service on the board otherwise casts reasonable doubt on the judge's capacity to act impartially* as a judge.*

Service by a judge on behalf of a civic or charitable organization may be governed by other provisions of Canon 4 in addition to Canon 4C. For example, a judge is prohibited by Canon 4G from serving as a legal advisor to a civic or charitable organization.

Service on the board of a homeowners association or a neighborhood protective group is proper if it is related to the protection of the judge's own economic interests. See Canons 4D(2) and 4D(4). See Canon 2B regarding the obligation to avoid improper use of the prestige of a judge's office.

(c) a judge shall not serve as an officer, director, trustee, or nonlegal advisor if it is likely that the organization

(i) will be engaged in judicial proceedings that would ordinarily come before the judge, or

(ii) will be engaged frequently in adversary proceedings in the court of which the judge is a member or in any court subject to the appellate jurisdiction of the court of which the judge is a member.

ADVISORY COMMITTEE COMMENTARY: Canon 4C(3)(c)

The changing nature of some organizations and of their relationship to the law makes it necessary for the judge regularly to reexamine the activities of each organization with which the judge is affiliated to determine if it is proper for the judge to continue the affiliation. Some organizations regularly engage in litigation to achieve their goals or fulfill their purposes. Judges should avoid a leadership role in such organizations as it could compromise the appearance of impartiality.*

(d) a judge as an officer, director, trustee, nonlegal advisor, or as a member or otherwise

(i) may assist such an organization in planning fundraising and may participate in the management and investment of the organization's funds. However, a judge shall not personally participate in the solicitation of funds or other fundraising activities, except that a judge may privately solicit funds for such an organization from members of the judge's family* or from other judges (excluding court commissioners, referees, [1] court-appointed arbitrators, hearing officers, [2] temporary judges,* **and retired judges who serve in the Temporary Assigned Judges Program, practice law, or provide alternative dispute resolution services**);

(ii) may make recommendations to public and private fund-granting organizations on projects and programs concerning the law, the legal system, or the administration of justice;*

(iii) shall not personally participate in membership solicitation if the solicitation might reasonably be perceived as coercive or if the membership solicitation is essentially a fundraising mechanism, except as permitted in Canon 4C(3)(d)(i);

(iv) shall not permit the use of the prestige of his or her judicial office for fundraising or membership solicitation but may be a speaker, guest of honor, or recipient of an award for public or charitable service provided the judge does not personally solicit funds and complies with Canons 4A(1), (2), (3), and (4).

ADVISORY COMMITTEE COMMENTARY: Canon 4C(3)(d)

A judge may solicit membership or endorse or encourage membership efforts for an organization devoted to the improvement of the law, the legal system, or the administration of justice, or a nonprofit educational, religious, charitable,*

---

* Terms with an asterisk (*) are defined in the Terminology section.

service,* or civic organization as long as the solicitation cannot reasonably be perceived as coercive and is not essentially a fundraising mechanism. Solicitation of funds or memberships for an organization similarly involves the danger that the person solicited will feel obligated to respond favorably if the solicitor is in a position of influence or control. A judge must not engage in direct, individual solicitation of funds or memberships in person, in writing, or by telephone except in the following cases: (1) a judge may solicit other judges (excluding court commissioners, referees, [3] court-appointed arbitrators, hearing officers, [4] temporary judges,* and retired judges who serve in the Temporary Assigned Judges Program, practice law, or provide alternative dispute resolution services) for funds or memberships; (2) a judge may solicit other persons for membership in the organizations described above if neither those persons nor persons with whom they are affiliated are likely ever to appear before the court on which the judge serves; and (3) a judge who is an officer of such an organization may send a general membership solicitation mailing over the judge's signature.

When deciding whether to make recommendations to public and private fund-granting organizations on projects and programs concerning the law, the legal system, or the administration of justice,* a judge should consider whether that conduct would violate any other provision of this code. For a list of factors to consider, see the explanation of "law, the legal system, or the administration of justice" in the Terminology section.

Use of an organization's letterhead for fundraising or membership solicitation does not violate Canon 4C(3)(d), provided the letterhead lists only the judge's name and office or other position in the organization, and designates the judge's judicial title only if other persons whose names appear on the letterhead have comparable designations. In addition, a judge must also make reasonable efforts to ensure that the judge's staff, court officials, and others subject to the judge's direction and control do not solicit funds on the judge's behalf for any purpose, charitable or otherwise.

(e) A judge may encourage lawyers to provide pro bono publico legal services.

ADVISORY COMMITTEE COMMENTARY: Canon 4C(3)(e)

In addition to appointing lawyers to serve as counsel for indigent parties in individual cases, a judge may promote broader access to justice by encouraging lawyers to participate in pro bono publico legal services, as long as the judge does not employ coercion or abuse the prestige of judicial office.

(Canon 4C amended effective July 1, 2020; previously amended effective January 1, 2013, and August 19, 2015.)

Canon 4C. 2020 Deletes. [1] retired judges, [2] and [3] *retired judges,* [4] *and*

D. Financial Activities

(1) A judge shall not engage in financial and business dealings that
(a) may reasonably be perceived to exploit the judge's judicial position, or
(b) involve the judge in frequent transactions or continuing business relationships with lawyers or other persons likely to appear before the court on which the judge serves.

ADVISORY COMMITTEE COMMENTARY: Canon 4D(1)

The Time for Compliance provision of this code (Canon 6F) postpones the time for compliance with certain provisions of this canon in some cases.

A judge must avoid financial and business dealings that involve the judge in frequent transactions or continuing business relationships with persons likely to appear either before the judge personally or before other judges on the judge's court. A judge shall discourage members of the judge's family* from engaging in dealings that would reasonably appear to exploit the judge's judicial position or that would involve family members in frequent transactions or continuing business relationships with persons likely to appear before the judge. This rule is necessary to avoid creating an appearance of exploitation of office or favoritism and to minimize the potential for disqualification.

Participation by a judge in financial and business dealings is subject to the general prohibitions in Canon 4A against activities that tend to reflect adversely on impartiality,* demean the judicial office, or interfere with the proper performance of judicial duties. Such participation is also subject to the general prohibition in Canon 2 against activities involving impropriety* or the appearance of impropriety* and the prohibition in Canon 2B against the misuse of the prestige of judicial office.

In addition, a judge must maintain high standards of conduct in all of the judge's activities, as set forth in Canon 1.

(2) A judge may, subject to the requirements of this code, hold and manage investments of the judge and members of the judge's family,* including real estate, and engage in other remunerative activities. A judge shall not participate in, nor permit the judge's name to be used in connection with, any business venture or commercial advertising that indicates the judge's title or affiliation with the judiciary or otherwise lend the power or prestige of his or her office to promote a business or any commercial venture.

(3) A judge shall not serve as an officer, director, manager, or employee of a business affected with a public interest, including, without limitation, a financial institution, insurance company, or public utility.

ADVISORY COMMITTEE COMMENTARY: Canon 4D(3)

Although participation by a judge in business activities might otherwise be permitted by Canon 4D, a judge may be prohibited from participation by other provisions of this code when, for example, the business entity frequently appears before the judge's court or the participation requires significant time away from judicial duties. Similarly, a judge must avoid participating in any business activity if the judge's participation would involve misuse of the prestige of judicial office. See Canon 2B.

(4) A judge shall manage personal investments and financial activities so as to minimize the necessity for disqualification. As soon as reasonably possible, a judge shall divest himself or herself of investments and other financial interests that would require frequent disqualification.

(5) Under no circumstance shall a judge accept a gift,* bequest, or favor if the donor is a party whose interests have come or are reasonably likely to come before the judge. A judge shall discourage members of the judge's family residing in the judge's household***** from accepting similar benefits from parties who have come or are reasonably likely to come before the judge.

ADVISORY COMMITTEE COMMENTARY: Canon 4D(5)

In addition to the prohibitions set forth in Canon 4D(5) regarding gifts,* other laws* may be applicable to judges, including, for example, Code of Civil Procedure section 170.9 and the Political Reform Act of 1974 (Gov. Code, § 81000 et seq.).

Canon 4D(5) does not apply to contributions to a judge's campaign for judicial office, a matter governed by Canon 5, although such contributions may give rise to an obligation by the judge to disqualify or disclose. See Canon 3E(2)(b) and accompanying Commentary and Code of Civil Procedure section 170.1, subdivision (a)(9).

Because a gift,* bequest, or favor to a member of the judge's family residing in the judge's household* might be viewed as intended to influence the judge, a judge must inform those family members of the relevant ethical constraints upon the judge in this regard and urge them to take these constraints into account when making decisions about accepting such gifts,* bequests, or favors. A judge cannot, however, reasonably be expected to know or control all of the financial or business activities of all family members residing in the judge's household.*

The application of Canon 4D(5) requires recognition that a judge cannot reasonably be expected to anticipate all persons or interests that may come before the court.

(6) A judge shall not accept and shall discourage members of the judge's family residing in the judge's household* from accepting a gift,* bequest, favor, or loan from anyone except as hereinafter set forth. Gifts* that are permitted by Canons 4D(6)(a) through (i) may only be accepted if the gift,* bequest, favor, or loan would neither influence nor reasonably be perceived as intended to influence the judge in the performance of judicial duties:

(a) a gift,* bequest, favor, or loan from a person whose preexisting relationship with the judge would prevent the judge under Canon 3E from hearing a case involving that person;

ADVISORY COMMITTEE COMMENTARY: Canon 4D(6)(a)

Upon appointment or election as a judge or within a reasonable period of time thereafter, a judge may attend an event honoring the judge's appointment or election as a judge provided that (1) the judge would otherwise be disqualified from hearing any matter involving the person or entity holding or funding the event, and (2) a reasonable person would not conclude that attendance at the event undermines the judge's integrity,* impartiality,* or independence.*

(b) a gift* for a special occasion from a relative or friend, if the gift* is fairly commensurate with the occasion and the relationship;

ADVISORY COMMITTEE COMMENTARY: Canon 4D(6)(b)

A gift* to a judge, or to a member of the judge's family residing in the judge's household,* that is excessive in value raises questions about the judge's impartiality* and the integrity* of the judicial office and might require disqualification of the judge where disqualification would not otherwise be required. See, however, Canon 4D(6)(a).

(c) commercial or financial opportunities and benefits, including special pricing and discounts, and loans from lending institutions in their regular course of business, if the same opportunities and benefits or loans are made available on the same terms to similarly situated persons who are not judges;

(d) any gift* incidental to a public testimonial, or educational or resource materials supplied by publishers on a complimentary basis for

---

* Terms with an asterisk (*) are defined in the Terminology section.

official use, **or a discounted or complimentary membership in a bar-related association,** or an invitation to the judge and the judge's spouse or registered domestic partner* or guest to attend a bar-related function or an activity devoted to the improvement of the law, the legal system, or the administration of justice;*

(e) advances or reimbursement for the reasonable cost of travel, transportation, lodging, and subsistence that is directly related to participation in any judicial, educational, civic, or governmental program or bar-related function or activity devoted to the improvement of the law, the legal system, or the administration of justice;*

ADVISORY COMMITTEE COMMENTARY: Canon 4D(6)(e)

Acceptance of an invitation to a law-related function is governed by Canon 4D(6)(d); acceptance of an invitation paid for by an individual lawyer or group of lawyers is governed by Canon 4D(6)(g). See also Canon 4H(2) and accompanying Commentary.

(f) a gift,* award, or benefit incident to the business, profession, or other separate activity of a spouse or registered domestic partner* or other member of the judge's family residing in the judge's household,* including gifts,* awards, and benefits for the use of both the spouse or registered domestic partner* or other family member and the judge;

(g) ordinary social hospitality;

ADVISORY COMMITTEE COMMENTARY: Canon 4D(6)(g)

Although Canon 4D(6)(g) does not preclude ordinary social hospitality, a judge should carefully weigh acceptance of such hospitality to avoid any appearance of impropriety or bias or any appearance that the judge is misusing the prestige of judicial office. See Canons 2 and 2B. A judge should also consider whether acceptance would affect the integrity,* impartiality,* or independence* of the judiciary. See Canon 2A.*

(h) an invitation to the judge and the judge's spouse, registered domestic partner,* or guest to attend an event sponsored by an educational, religious, charitable, service,* or civic organization with which the judge is associated or involved, if the same invitation is offered to persons who are not judges and who are similarly engaged with the organization.

(i) a nominal gift,* provided the gift* is not from a lawyer, law firm, or other person likely to appear before the court on which the judge serves, unless one or more of the exceptions in this canon applies.

ADVISORY COMMITTEE COMMENTARY: Canon 4D(6)(i)

For example, nominal gifts include snacks or a token memento from jurors, keychains or pens provided by vendors at legal conferences, or handicrafts or art projects from students.*

A judge should carefully weigh acceptance of any nominal gift to avoid any appearance of impropriety or bias or any appearance that the judge is misusing the prestige of judicial office. See Canons 2 and 2B. A judge should also consider whether acceptance would affect the integrity,* impartiality,* or independence* of the judiciary. See Canon 2A.*

(7) A judge may accept the following, provided that doing so would neither influence nor reasonably be perceived as intended to influence the judge in the performance of judicial duties:

(a) a scholarship or fellowship awarded on the same terms and based on the same criteria applied to other applicants;

(b) rewards and prizes given to competitors or participants in random drawings, contests, or other events that are open to persons who are not judges.

ADVISORY COMMITTEE COMMENTARY: Canons 4D(6) and 4D(7)

The references to such scholarships, fellowships, rewards, and prizes were moved from Canon 4D(6) to Canon 4D(7) because they are not considered to be gifts under this code, and a judge may accept them.*

(Canon 4D amended effective July 1, 2020; previously amended effective January 1, 2007, January 1, 2013, August 19, 2015, and October 10, 2018.)

E.   Fiduciary* Activities

(1) A judge shall not serve as executor, administrator, or other personal representative, trustee, guardian, attorney in fact, or other fiduciary,* except for the estate, trust, or person of a member of the judge's family,* and then only if such service will not interfere with the proper performance of judicial duties. **A judge may, however, act as a health care representative pursuant to an advance health care directive for a person whose preexisting relationship with the judge would prevent the judge from hearing a case involving that person under Canon 3E(1).**

(2) A judge shall not serve as a fiduciary* if it is likely that the judge as a fiduciary* will be engaged in proceedings that would ordinarily come before the judge, or if the estate, trust, or minor or conservatee will be engaged in contested proceedings in the court on which the judge serves or one under its appellate jurisdiction.

(3) The same restrictions on financial activities that apply to a judge personally also apply to the judge while acting in a fiduciary* capacity.

ADVISORY COMMITTEE COMMENTARY: Canon 4E

The Time for Compliance provision of this code (Canon 6F) postpones the time for compliance with certain provisions of this canon in some cases.

The restrictions imposed by this canon may conflict with the judge's obligation as a fiduciary. For example, a judge shall resign as trustee if detriment to the trust would result from divestiture of trust holdings the retention of which would place the judge in violation of Canon 4D(4).*

(Canon 4E amended effective July 1, 2020; previously amended effective January 1, 2013, and August 19, 2015.)

F.   Service as Arbitrator or Mediator

A judge shall not act as an arbitrator or mediator or otherwise perform judicial functions in a private capacity unless expressly authorized by law.*

ADVISORY COMMITTEE COMMENTARY: Canon 4F

Canon 4F does not prohibit a judge from participating in arbitration, mediation, or settlement conferences performed as part of his or her judicial duties.

(Canon 4F amended effective August 19, 2015.)

G.   Practice of Law

A judge shall not practice law.

ADVISORY COMMITTEE COMMENTARY: Canon 4G

This prohibition refers to the practice of law in a representative capacity and not in a pro se capacity. A judge may act for himself or herself in all legal matters, including matters involving litigation and matters involving appearances before or other dealings with legislative and other governmental bodies. However, in so doing, a judge must not abuse the prestige of office to advance the interests of the judge or member of the judge's family. See Canon 2B.*

This prohibition applies to subordinate judicial officers, magistrates, special masters, and judges of the State Bar Court.*

(Canon 4G amended effective August 19, 2015; previously amended effective January 1, 2005.)

H.   Compensation, Reimbursement, and Honoraria

A judge may receive compensation and reimbursement of expenses as provided by law* for the extrajudicial activities permitted by this code, if the source of such payments does not give the appearance of influencing the judge's performance of judicial duties or otherwise give the appearance of impropriety.*

(1) Compensation shall not exceed a reasonable amount nor shall it exceed what a person who is not a judge would receive for the same activity.

(2) Expense reimbursement shall be limited to the actual cost of travel, food, lodging, and other costs reasonably incurred by the judge and, where appropriate to the occasion, by the judge's spouse, registered domestic partner,* or guest. Any payment in excess of such an amount is compensation.

(3) No judge shall accept any honorarium. "Honorarium" means any payment made in consideration for a speech given, an article published, or attendance at any public or private conference, convention, meeting, social event, meal, or like gathering. "Honorarium" does not include earned income for personal services that are customarily provided in connection with the practice of a bona fide business, trade, or profession, such as teaching or writing for a publisher, and does not include fees or other things of value received pursuant to Penal Code section 94.5 for performance of a marriage. For purposes of this canon, "teaching" includes presentations to impart educational information to lawyers in events qualifying for credit under Minimum Continuing Legal Education, to students in bona fide educational institutions, and to associations or groups of judges.

ADVISORY COMMITTEE COMMENTARY: Canon 4H

Judges should not accept compensation or reimbursement of expenses if acceptance would appear to a reasonable person to undermine the judge's integrity, impartiality,* or independence.**

A judge must assure himself or herself that acceptance of reimbursement or fee waivers would not appear to a reasonable person to undermine the judge's independence, integrity,* or impartiality.* The factors a judge should consider when deciding whether to accept reimbursement or a fee waiver for attendance at a particular activity include whether:*

---

* Terms with an asterisk (*) are defined in the Terminology section.

(a) the sponsor is an accredited educational institution or bar association rather than a trade association or a for-profit entity;

(b) the funding comes largely from numerous contributors rather than from a single entity, and whether the funding is earmarked for programs with specific content;

(c) the content is related or unrelated to the subject matter of a pending* or impending* proceeding before the judge, or to matters that are likely to come before the judge;

(d) the activity is primarily educational rather than recreational, and whether the costs of the event are reasonable and comparable to those associated with similar events sponsored by the judiciary, bar associations, or similar groups;

(e) information concerning the activity and its funding sources is available upon inquiry;

(f) the sponsor or source of funding is generally associated with particular parties or interests currently appearing or likely to appear in the judge's court, thus possibly requiring disqualification of the judge;

(g) differing viewpoints are presented;

(h) a broad range of judicial and nonjudicial participants are invited; or

(i) the program is designed specifically for judges.

Judges should be aware of the statutory limitations on accepting gifts.*

(Canon 4H amended effective October 10, 2018; previously amended effective January 1, 2007, January 1, 2013, and August 19, 2015.)

Canon 5. A judge or candidate for judicial office* shall not engage in political or campaign activity that is inconsistent with the independence,* integrity,* or impartiality* of the judiciary.

Judges and candidates for judicial office* are entitled to entertain their personal views on political questions. They are not required to surrender their rights or opinions as citizens. They shall, however, not engage in political activity that may create the appearance of political bias or impropriety.* Judicial independence,* impartiality,* and integrity* shall dictate the conduct of judges and candidates for judicial office.*

Judges and candidates for judicial office* shall comply with all applicable election, election campaign, and election campaign fundraising laws* and regulations.

ADVISORY COMMITTEE COMMENTARY: Canon 5

The term "political activity" should not be construed so narrowly as to prevent private comment.

(Canon 5 Preface amended effective August 19, 2015; previously amended effective January 1, 2013.)

A. Political Organizations*

Judges and candidates for judicial office* shall not

(1) act as leaders or hold any office in a political organization;*

(2) make speeches for a political organization* or candidate for nonjudicial office, or publicly endorse or publicly oppose a candidate for nonjudicial office; or

(3) personally solicit funds for a political organization* or nonjudicial candidate; or make contributions to a political party or political organization* or to a nonjudicial candidate in excess of $500 in any calendar year per political party or political organization* or candidate, or in excess of an aggregate of $1,000 in any calendar year for all political parties or political organizations* or nonjudicial candidates.

ADVISORY COMMITTEE COMMENTARY: Canon 5A

This provision does not prohibit a judge or a candidate for judicial office from signing a petition to qualify a measure for the ballot, provided the judge does not use his or her official title.*

In judicial elections, judges are neither required to shield themselves from campaign contributions nor are they prohibited from soliciting contributions from anyone, including attorneys. Nevertheless, there are necessary limits on judges facing election if the appearance of impropriety is to be avoided. In soliciting campaign contributions or endorsements, a judge shall not use the prestige of judicial office in a manner that would reasonably be perceived as coercive. See Canons 1, 2, 2A, and 2B. Although it is improper for a judge to receive a gift* from an attorney subject to exceptions noted in Canon 4D(6), a judge's campaign may receive attorney contributions.*

Although attendance at political gatherings is not prohibited, any such attendance should be restricted so that it would not constitute an express public endorsement of a nonjudicial candidate or a measure not affecting the law, the legal system, or the administration of justice otherwise prohibited by this canon.*

Subject to the monetary limitation herein to political contributions, a judge or a candidate for judicial office may purchase tickets for political dinners or other similar dinner functions. Any admission price to such a political dinner or function in excess of the actual cost of the meal will be considered a political contribution.*

The prohibition in Canon 5A(3) does not preclude judges from contributing to a campaign fund for distribution among judges who are candidates for reelection or retention, nor does it apply to contributions to any judge or candidate for judicial office.*

Under this canon, a judge may publicly endorse **or oppose** a candidate for judicial office.* Such [1] **positions** are permitted because judicial officers have a special obligation to uphold the integrity,* impartiality,* and independence* of the judiciary and are in a unique position to know the qualifications necessary to serve as a competent judicial officer.

Although family members of the judge or candidate for judicial office* are not subject to the provisions of this code, a judge or candidate for judicial office* shall not avoid compliance with this code by making contributions through a spouse or registered domestic partner* or other family member.

(Canon 5A amended effective July 1, 2020; previously amended effective January 1, 2007, and August 19, 2015.)

Canon 5A. 2020 Deletes. [1] *endorsements*

B. Conduct During Judicial Campaigns and Appointment Process

(1) A candidate for judicial office* or an applicant seeking appointment to judicial office shall not:

(a) make statements to the electorate or the appointing authority that commit the candidate or the applicant with respect to cases, controversies, or issues that are likely to come before the courts, or

(b) knowingly,* or with reckless disregard for the truth, make false or misleading statements about the identity, qualifications, present position, or any other fact concerning himself or herself or his or her opponent or other applicants.

(2) A candidate for judicial office** shall review and approve the content of all campaign statements and materials produced by the candidate or his or her campaign committee before its dissemination. A candidate shall take appropriate corrective action if the candidate learns of any misrepresentations made in his or her campaign statements or materials. A candidate shall take reasonable measures to prevent any misrepresentations being made in his or her support by third parties. A candidate shall take reasonable measures to ensure that appropriate corrective action is taken if the candidate learns of any misrepresentations being made in his or her support by third parties.

(3) Every candidate for judicial office* shall complete a judicial campaign ethics course approved by the Supreme Court no earlier than one year before or no later than 60 days after the filing of a declaration of intention by the candidate, the formation of a campaign committee, or the receipt of any campaign contribution, whichever is earliest. If a judge appears on the ballot as a result of a petition indicating that a write-in campaign will be conducted for the office, the judge shall complete the course no later than 60 days after receiving notice of the filing of the petition, the formation of a campaign committee, or the receipt of any campaign contribution, whichever is earliest.

Unless a judge forms a campaign committee or solicits or receives campaign contributions, this requirement does not apply to judges who are unopposed for election and will not appear on the ballot. Unless an appellate justice forms a campaign committee or solicits or receives campaign contributions, this requirement does not apply to appellate justices.

ADVISORY COMMITTEE COMMENTARY: Canon 5B

The purpose of Canon 5B is to preserve the integrity of the appointive and elective process for judicial office and to ensure that the public has accurate information about candidates for judicial office.* Compliance with these provisions will enhance the integrity,* impartiality,* and independence* of the judiciary and better inform the public about qualifications of candidates for judicial office.*

This code does not contain the "announce clause" that was the subject of the United States Supreme Court's decision in Republican Party of Minnesota v. White *(2002) 536 U.S. 765. That opinion did not address the "commit clause," which is contained in Canon 5B(1)(a). The phrase "appear to commit" has been deleted because, although candidates for judicial office* cannot promise to take a particular position on cases, controversies, or issues prior to taking the bench and presiding over individual cases, the phrase may have been overinclusive.*

Canon 5B(1)(b) prohibits knowingly making false or misleading statements during an election campaign because doing so would violate Canons 1 and 2A, and may violate other canons.

The time limit for completing a judicial campaign ethics course in Canon 5B(3) is triggered by the earliest of one of the following: the filing of a declaration of intention, the formation of a campaign committee, or the receipt of any campaign contribution. If a judge's name appears on the ballot as a result of a petition indicating that a write-in campaign will be conducted, the time limit for completing the course is triggered by the earliest of one of the following: the notice of the filing of the petition, the formation of a campaign committee, or the receipt of any campaign contribution. A financial contribution by a candidate for judicial office* to his or her own campaign constitutes receipt of a campaign contribution.

(4) In judicial elections, judges may solicit campaign contributions or endorsements for their own campaigns or for other judges and attorneys who are candidates for judicial office.* Judges are permitted to solicit such contributions and endorsements from anyone, including attorneys and other judges, except that a judge shall not solicit campaign contributions or endorsements from California state court commissioners, referees, court-appointed arbitrators, hearing officers, and retired judges serving in the **Temporary** Assigned Judges Program, or from California state court personnel. In soliciting campaign contributions or endorsements, a judge shall not use the prestige of judicial office in a manner that would reasonably be perceived as coercive. See Canons 1, 2, 2A, and 2B.

ADVISORY COMMITTEE COMMENTARY: Canon 5B(4)

Regarding campaign contributions for a judge's own campaign, see Canon 3E(2)(b) and accompanying Commentary addressing disclosure of campaign contributions. See also Code of Civil Procedure section 170.1, subdivision (a)(9), which provides that a judge is disqualified if the judge has received a campaign contribution exceeding $1,500 from a party or an attorney in the proceeding. Although it is improper for a judge to receive a gift* from an attorney subject to exceptions noted in Canon 4D(6), a judge's campaign may receive attorney contributions. **See also Government Code section 8314, which prohibits any elected state or local officer from using public resources, including buildings, telephones, and state-compensated time, for a campaign activity. Under section 8314, subdivision (b)(2), "campaign activity" does not include "the incidental and minimal use of public resources, such as equipment or office space, for campaign purposes, including the referral of unsolicited political mail, telephone calls, and visitors to private political entities."**

Even though it is permissible for a judge to solicit endorsements and campaign funds for attorneys who are candidates for judicial office,* the judge must be cautious. Such solicitation may raise issues of disqualification and disclosure under Code of Civil Procedure section 170.1, subdivision (a), and Canon 3E. Even if the judge is not disqualified, disclosure may be required under Canon 3E(2)(a). For example, a judge who has solicited campaign funds or endorsements for a candidate who is an attorney must consider disclosing that solicitation in all cases in which the attorney candidate appears before the judge. The judge should also consider Canon 4A(1) and Canon 4A(4), which require a judge to conduct extrajudicial activities so they do not cast reasonable doubt on the judge's capacity to act impartially* or lead to frequent disqualification.

"Judicial elections" includes recall elections.

(Canon 5B amended effective July 1, 2020; previously amended effective December 22, 2003, January 1, 2013, August 19, 2015, December 1, 2016, and October 10, 2018.)

C. Speaking at Political Gatherings

Candidates for judicial office* may speak to political gatherings only on their own behalf or on behalf of another candidate for judicial office.*

D. Measures to Improve the Law

A judge or candidate for judicial office* may engage in activity in relation to measures concerning improvement of the law, the legal system, or the administration of justice,* only if the conduct is consistent with this code.

ADVISORY COMMITTEE COMMENTARY: Canon 5D

When deciding whether to engage in activity relating to measures concerning the law, the legal system, or the administration of justice,* such as commenting publicly on ballot measures, a judge must consider whether the conduct would violate any other provisions of this code. See the explanation of "law, the legal system, or the administration of justice" in the Terminology section.

(Canon 5D amended effective August 19, 2015; previously amended effective January 1, 2013.)

Canon 6. Compliance with the Code of Judicial Ethics.

A. Judges

Anyone who is an officer of the state judicial system and who performs judicial functions including, but not limited to, a subordinate judicial officer,* a magistrate, a court-appointed arbitrator, a judge of the State Bar Court, a temporary judge,* or a special master, is a judge within the meaning of this code. All judges shall comply with this code except as provided below.

ADVISORY COMMITTEE COMMENTARY: Canon 6A

*For the purposes of this canon, if a retired judge is serving in the **Temporary** Assigned Judges Program, the judge is considered to "perform judicial functions."*

Because retired judges who are privately retained may perform judicial functions, their conduct while performing those functions should be guided by this code.

(Canon 6A amended effective July 1, 2020; previously amended effective January 1, 2005, January 1, 2013, and August 19, 2015.)

B. Retired Judge Serving in the *Temporary* Assigned Judges Program

A retired judge who has filed an application to serve on assignment, meets the eligibility requirements set by the Chief Justice for service, and has received an acknowledgment of participation in the **Temporary** Assigned Judges Program shall comply with all provisions of this code, except for the following:

4C(2)—Appointment to governmental positions
4E—Fiduciary* activities

(Canon 6B amended effective July 1, 2020; previously amended effective January 1, 2005, and January 1, 2013.)

C. Retired Judge as Arbitrator or Mediator

A retired judge serving in the **Temporary** Assigned Judges Program is not required to comply with Canon 4F of this code relating to serving as an arbitrator or mediator, or performing judicial functions in a private capacity, except as otherwise provided in the *Standards and Guidelines for Judicial Assignments* promulgated by the Chief Justice.

ADVISORY COMMITTEE COMMENTARY: Canon 6C

*Article VI, section 6 of the California Constitution provides that a "retired judge who consents may be assigned to any court" by the Chief Justice. Retired judges who are serving in the **Temporary** Assigned Judges Program pursuant to the above provision are bound by Canon 6B, including the requirement of Canon 4G barring the practice of law. Other provisions of California law,* and standards and guidelines for eligibility and service set by the Chief Justice, further define the limitations on who may serve on assignment.*

(Canon 6C amended effective July 1, 2020; previously amended effective January 1, 2013, and August 19, 2015.)

D. Temporary Judge,* Referee, or Court-Appointed Arbitrator[1]

A temporary judge,* a person serving as a referee pursuant to Code of Civil Procedure section 638 or 639, or a court-appointed arbitrator shall comply only with the following code provisions:

(1) A temporary judge,* a referee, or a court-appointed arbitrator shall comply with Canons 1 [integrity* and independence* of the judiciary], 2A [promoting public confidence], 3B(3) [order and decorum], 3B(4) [patient, dignified, and courteous treatment], 3B(6) [require* lawyers to refrain from manifestations of any form of bias or prejudice], 3D(1) [action regarding misconduct by another judge], and 3D(2) [action regarding misconduct by a lawyer], when the temporary judge,* referee, or court-appointed arbitrator is actually presiding in a proceeding or communicating with the parties, counsel, or staff or court personnel while serving in the capacity of a temporary judge,* referee, or court-appointed arbitrator in the case.

(2) A temporary judge,* referee, or court-appointed arbitrator shall, from the time of notice and acceptance of appointment until termination of the appointment:

(a) Comply with Canons 2B(1) [not allow family or other relationships to influence judicial conduct], 3B(1) [hear and decide all matters unless disqualified], 3B(2) [be faithful to and maintain competence in the law*], 3B(5) [perform judicial duties without bias or prejudice], 3B(7) [accord full right to be heard to those entitled; avoid ex parte communications, except as specified], 3B(8) [dispose of matters fairly and promptly], 3B(12) [remain impartial* and not engage in coercive conduct during efforts to resolve disputes], 3C(1) [discharge administrative responsibilities without bias and with competence and cooperatively], 3C(3) [require* staff and court personnel to observe standards of conduct and refrain from bias and prejudice], and 3C(5) [make only fair, necessary, and appropriate appointments];

(b) Not personally solicit memberships or donations for religious, service,* educational, civic, or charitable organizations from the parties and lawyers appearing before the temporary judge,* referee, or court-appointed arbitrator;

(c) Under no circumstance accept a gift,* bequest, or favor if the donor is a party, person, or entity whose interests are reasonably likely to come before the temporary judge,* referee, or court-appointed arbitrator. A temporary judge,* referee, or court-appointed arbitrator shall discourage members of the judge's family residing in the judge's household*

---

* Terms with an asterisk (*) are defined in the Terminology section.

[1] Reference should be made to relevant commentary to analogous or individual canons cited or described in this canon and appearing elsewhere in this code.

from accepting benefits from parties who are reasonably likely to come before the temporary judge,* referee, or court-appointed arbitrator.

(3) A temporary judge* shall, from the time of notice and acceptance of appointment until termination of the appointment, disqualify himself or herself in any proceeding as follows:

(a) A temporary judge*—other than a temporary judge solely conducting settlement conferences—is disqualified to serve in a proceeding if any one or more of the following are true:

(i) the temporary judge* has personal knowledge* (as defined in Code of Civil Procedure section 170.1, subdivision (a)(1)) of disputed evidentiary facts concerning the proceeding;

(ii) the temporary judge* has served as a lawyer (as defined in Code of Civil Procedure section 170.1, subdivision (a)(2)) in the proceeding;

(iii) the temporary judge,* within the past five years, has given legal advice to, or served as a lawyer (as defined in Code of Civil Procedure section 170.1, subdivision (a)(2)), except that this provision requires disqualification if the temporary judge* represented a party in the past five years rather than the two-year period specified in section 170.1, subdivision (a)(2)) for a party in the present proceeding;

ADVISORY COMMITTEE COMMENTARY: Canon 6D(3)(a)(iii)

The application of Canon 6D(3)(a)(iii), providing that a temporary judge is disqualified if he or she has given legal advice or served as a lawyer for a party to the proceeding in the past five years, may depend on the type of assignment and the amount of time available to investigate whether the temporary judge* has previously represented a party. If time permits, the temporary judge* must conduct such an investigation. Thus, if a temporary judge* is privately compensated by the parties or is presiding over a particular matter known* in advance of the hearing, the temporary judge* is presumed to have adequate time to investigate. If, however, a temporary judge* is assigned to a high volume calendar, such as traffic or small claims, and has not been provided with the names of the parties prior to the assignment, the temporary judge* may rely on his or her memory to determine whether he or she has previously represented a party.*

(iv) the temporary judge* has a financial interest (as defined in Code of Civil Procedure sections 170.1, subdivision (a)(3), and 170.5) in the subject matter in the proceeding or in a party to the proceeding;

(v) the temporary judge,* or the spouse or registered domestic partner* of the temporary judge,* or a person within the third degree of relationship* to either of them, or the spouse or registered domestic partner* of such a person is a party to the proceeding or is an officer, director, or trustee of a party;

(vi) a lawyer or a spouse or registered domestic partner* of a lawyer in the proceeding is the spouse, former spouse, registered domestic partner,* former registered domestic partner,* child, sibling, or parent of the temporary judge* or the temporary judge's spouse or registered domestic partner,* or if such a person is associated in the private practice of law with a lawyer in the proceeding;

(vii) for any reason:

(A) the temporary judge* believes his or her recusal would further the interests of justice;

(B) the temporary judge* believes there is a substantial doubt as to his or her capacity to be impartial;* or

(C) a person aware of the facts might reasonably entertain a doubt that the temporary judge* would be able to be impartial.* Bias or prejudice toward an attorney in the proceeding may be grounds for disqualification; or

(viii) the temporary judge* has received a campaign contribution of $1,500 or more from a party or lawyer in a matter that is before the court and the contribution was received in anticipation of an upcoming election.

(b) A temporary judge* before whom a proceeding was tried or heard is disqualified from participating in any appellate review of that proceeding.

(c) If the temporary judge* has a current arrangement concerning prospective employment or other compensated service as a dispute resolution neutral or is participating in, or, within the last two years has participated in, discussions regarding prospective employment or service as a dispute resolution neutral, or has been engaged in such employment or service, and any of the following applies:

(i) The arrangement or current employment is, or the prior employment or discussion was, with a party to the proceeding;

(ii) The temporary judge* directs the parties to participate in an alternative dispute resolution process in which the dispute resolution neutral will be an individual or entity with whom the temporary judge* has the arrangement, is currently employed or serves, has previously been employed or served, or is discussing or has discussed the employment or service; or

(iii) The temporary judge* will select a dispute resolution neutral or entity to conduct an alternative dispute resolution process in the matter before the temporary judge,* and among those available for selection is an individual or entity with whom the temporary judge* has the arrangement, is currently employed or serves, has previously been employed or served, or is discussing or has discussed the employment or service.

For the purposes of Canon 6D(3)(c), the definitions of "participating in discussions," "has participated in discussions," "party," and "dispute resolution neutral" are set forth in Code of Civil Procedure section 170.1, subdivision (a)(8), except that the words "temporary judge" shall be substituted for the word "judge" in such definitions.

(d) A lawyer is disqualified from serving as a temporary judge* in a family law or unlawful detainer proceeding if in the same type of proceeding:

(i) the lawyer holds himself or herself out to the public as representing exclusively one side; or

(ii) the lawyer represents one side in 90 percent or more of the cases in which he or she appears.

ADVISORY COMMITTEE COMMENTARY: Canon 6D(3)(d)

Under Canon 6D(3)(d), "one side" means a category of persons such as landlords, tenants, or litigants exclusively of one gender.

(4) After a temporary judge* who has determined himself or herself to be disqualified from serving under Canon 6D(3)(a)–(d) has disclosed the basis for his or her disqualification on the record, the parties and their lawyers may agree to waive the disqualification and the temporary judge* may accept the waiver. The temporary judge* shall not seek to induce a waiver and shall avoid any effort to discover which lawyers or parties favored or opposed a waiver.

ADVISORY COMMITTEE COMMENTARY: Canon 6D(4)

Provisions addressing waiver of mandatory disqualifications or limitations, late discovery of grounds for disqualification or limitation, notification of the court when a disqualification or limitation applies, and requests for disqualification by the parties are located in rule 2.818 of the California Rules of Court. Rule 2.818 states that the waiver must be in writing, must recite the basis for the disqualification or limitation, and must state that it was knowingly made. It also states that the waiver is effective only when signed by all parties and their attorneys and filed in the record.*

(5) A temporary judge,* referee, or court-appointed arbitrator shall, from the time of notice and acceptance of appointment until termination of the appointment:

(a) In all proceedings, disclose in writing or on the record information as required by law,* or information that is reasonably relevant to the question of disqualification under Canon 6D(3), including personal or professional relationships known* to the temporary judge,* referee, or court-appointed arbitrator, that he or she or his or her law firm has had with a party, lawyer, or law firm in the current proceeding, even though the temporary judge,* referee, or court-appointed arbitrator concludes that there is no actual basis for disqualification; and

(b) In all proceedings, disclose in writing or on the record membership of the temporary judge,* referee, or court-appointed arbitrator in any organization that practices invidious discrimination on the basis of race, sex, gender, religion, national origin, ethnicity, or sexual orientation, except for membership in a religious organization.

(6) A temporary judge,* referee, or court-appointed arbitrator, from the time of notice and acceptance of appointment until the case is no longer pending in any court, shall not make any public comment about a pending* or impending* proceeding in which the temporary judge,* referee, or court-appointed arbitrator has been engaged, and shall not make any nonpublic comment that might substantially interfere with such proceeding. The temporary judge,* referee, or court-appointed arbitrator shall require* similar abstention on the part of staff and court personnel subject to his or her control. This canon does not prohibit the following:

(a) Statements made in the course of the official duties of the temporary judge,* referee, or court-appointed arbitrator; and

(b) Explanations about the procedures of the court.

(7) From the time of appointment and continuing for two years after the case is no longer pending* in any court, a temporary judge,* referee,

---

* Terms with an asterisk (*) are defined in the Terminology section.

or court-appointed arbitrator shall under no circumstances accept a gift,* bequest, or favor from a party, person, or entity whose interests have come before the temporary judge,* referee, or court-appointed arbitrator in the matter. The temporary judge,* referee, or court-appointed arbitrator shall discourage family members residing in the household of the temporary judge,* referee, or court-appointed arbitrator from accepting any benefits from such parties, persons or entities during the time period stated in this subdivision. The demand for or receipt by a temporary judge,* referee, or court-appointed arbitrator of a fee for his or her services rendered or to be rendered would not be a violation of this canon.

(8)   A temporary judge,* referee, or court-appointed arbitrator shall, from the time of notice and acceptance of appointment and continuing indefinitely after the termination of the appointment:

(a)   Comply with Canon 3B(11) [no disclosure of nonpublic information* acquired in a judicial capacity] (except as required by law*);

(b)   Not commend or criticize jurors sitting in a proceeding before the temporary judge,* referee, or court-appointed arbitrator for their verdict other than in a court order or opinion in such proceeding, but may express appreciation to jurors for their service to the judicial system and the community; and

(c)   Not lend the prestige of judicial office to advance his, her, or another person's pecuniary or personal interests and not use his or her judicial title in any written communication intended to advance his, her, or another person's pecuniary or personal interests, except to show his, her, or another person's qualifications.

(9)(a)   A temporary judge* appointed under rule 2.810 of the California Rules of Court, from the time of the appointment and continuing indefinitely after the termination of the appointment, shall not use his or her title or service as a temporary judge* (1) as a description of the lawyer's current or former principal profession, vocation, or occupation on a ballot designation for judicial or other elected office, (2) in an advertisement about the lawyer's law firm or business, or (3) on a letterhead, business card, or other document that is distributed to the public identifying the lawyer or the lawyer's law firm.

(b)   This canon does not prohibit a temporary judge* appointed under rule 2.810 of the California Rules of Court from using his or her title or service as a temporary judge* on an application to serve as a temporary judge,* including an application in other courts, on an application for employment or for an appointment to a judicial position, on an individual resume or a descriptive statement submitted in connection with an application for employment or for appointment or election to a judicial position, or in response to a request for information about the public service in which the lawyer has engaged.

(10)   A temporary judge,* referee, or court-appointed arbitrator shall comply with Canon 6D(2) until the appointment has been terminated formally or until there is no reasonable probability that the temporary judge,* referee, or court-appointed arbitrator will further participate in the matter. A rebuttable presumption that the appointment has been formally terminated will arise if, within one year from the appointment or from the date of the last hearing scheduled in the matter, whichever is later, neither the appointing court nor counsel for any party in the matter has informed the temporary judge,* referee, or court-appointed arbitrator that the appointment remains in effect.

(11)   A lawyer who has been a temporary judge,* referee, or court-appointed arbitrator in a matter shall not accept any representation relating to the matter without the informed written consent of all parties.

(12)   When by reason of serving as a temporary judge,* referee, or court-appointed arbitrator in a matter, he or she has received confidential information from a party, the person shall not, without the informed written consent of the party, accept employment in another matter in which the confidential information is material.

ADVISORY COMMITTEE COMMENTARY: Canon 6D

Any exceptions to the canons do not excuse a judicial officer's separate statutory duty to disclose information that may result in the judicial officer's recusal or disqualification.

(Canon 6D amended effective December 1, 2016; adopted effective January 15, 1996; previously amended effective April 15, 1996, March 4, 1999, July 1, 2006, January 1, 2007, January 1, 2008, January 1, 2013, August 19, 2015, and January 21, 2016.)

E.   Judicial Candidate

A candidate for judicial office* shall comply with the provisions of Canon 5.

F.   Time for Compliance

A person to whom this code becomes applicable shall comply immediately with all provisions of this code except Canons 4D(4) and 4E and shall comply with Canons 4D(4) and 4E as soon as reasonably possible and in any event within a period of one year.

ADVISORY COMMITTEE COMMENTARY: Canon 6F

If serving as a fiduciary when selected as a judge, a new judge may, notwithstanding the prohibitions in Canon 4E, continue to serve as a fiduciary* but only for that period of time necessary to avoid adverse consequences to the beneficiary of the fiduciary* relationship and in no event longer than one year.*

(Canon 6F amended effective August 19, 2015; previously amended effective January 1, 2013.)

G.   Interim Rule Concerning Subordinate Judicial Officers

(Canon 6G repealed effective June 1, 2005; adopted December 30, 2002.)

H.   Judges on Leave Running for Other Public Office

A judge who is on leave while running for other public office pursuant to article VI, section 17 of the California Constitution shall comply with all provisions of this code, except for the following, insofar as the conduct relates to the campaign for public office for which the judge is on leave:

2B(2)—Lending the prestige of judicial office to advance the judge's personal interest

4C(1)—Appearing at public hearings

5—Engaging in political activity (including soliciting and accepting campaign contributions for the other public office).

ADVISORY COMMITTEE COMMENTARY: Canon 6H

These exceptions are applicable only during the time the judge is on leave while running for other public office. All of the provisions of this code will become applicable at the time a judge resumes his or her position as a judge.

Conduct during elections for judicial office is governed by Canon 5.

(Canon 6H amended effective August 19, 2015; adopted effective January 1, 2005; previously amended effective January 1, 2013.)

SUPREME COURT COMMITTEE ON JUDICIAL ETHICS OPINIONS INTERNAL OPERATING RULES AND PROCEDURES

Pursuant to California Rules of Court, rule 9.80(m), the following are the internal operating rules and procedures of the Supreme Court Committee on Judicial Ethics Opinions. (Adopted by the Committee on Judicial Ethics Opinions on January 6, 2012; approved by the Supreme Court on January 25, 2012.)

Rule 1. Purpose and Scope; Authority; Membership
Rule 2. Definitions
Rule 3. Meetings and Conferences
Rule 4. Referrals to California Judges Association Committee on Judicial Ethics
Rule 5. Confidentiality
Rule 6. Opinion Requests
Rule 7. Consideration of Requests; Response Procedures
Rule 8. Opinion Distribution
Rule 9. California Judges Association

Rule 1.   Purpose and Scope; Authority; Membership

(a) Purpose and scope

The Committee on Judicial Ethics Opinions was established by the Supreme Court to provide judicial ethics advisory opinions on topics of interest to the judiciary, judicial officers, candidates for judicial office, and members of the public. In providing its opinions and advice, the committee acts independently of the Supreme Court, the Commission on Judicial Performance, the Judicial Council, the Administrative Office of the Courts, and all other entities.

The committee will not provide opinions or advice in matters known by a requester or the committee to be the subject of pending litigation or a pending Commission on Judicial Performance or State Bar disciplinary proceeding.

(b) Authority

The committee is authorized by California Rules of Court, rule 9.80, adopted by the Supreme Court, to provide ethics advice to judicial officers

---

* Terms with an asterisk (*) are defined in the Terminology section.

and candidates for judicial office, including formal written opinions, informal written opinions, and oral advice. The committee is also authorized to consider topics for opinions suggested by individuals and entities. California Rules of Court, rule 9.80, and these rules are not intended to prohibit or inhibit individuals from seeking advice from other sources.

The committee is specifically authorized to:

(1) Issue formal written opinions, informal written opinions, and oral advice on proper judicial conduct under the California Code of Judicial Ethics, the California Constitution, statutes, rules of court, and any other applicable authority;

(2) Make recommendations to the Supreme Court for amending the Code of Judicial Ethics, the California Rules of Professional Conduct, or California Rules of Court, rule 9.80;

(3) Make recommendations regarding appropriate subjects for judicial education programs offered by the Center for Judicial Education and Research, the California Judges Association, or other providers.

(4) Make other recommendations to the Supreme Court as deemed appropriate by the committee or as requested by the Court; and

(5) Adopt amendments to these internal operating rules and procedures, subject to approval by the Supreme Court.

(c) Membership

The committee consists of 12 members appointed by the Supreme Court, including at least one justice from a court of appeal and one member who is a subordinate judicial officer employed full-time by a superior court. The remaining members are justices of a court of appeal or judges of a superior court, active or retired. No more than two retired justices or judges may be members of the committee at one time, except if an active justice or judge retires during his or her term, he or she may complete the term. A retired justice or judge committee member may not be an active member of the State Bar of California and may not be engaged in privately compensated dispute resolution activities.

(Adopted by the Committee on Judicial Ethics Opinions on January 6, 2012; approved by the Supreme Court on January 25, 2012.)

Rule 2.   Definitions

The following definitions apply, except where otherwise stated:

(a) "Committee" or "CJEO" means the Supreme Court Committee on Judicial Ethics Opinions.

(b) "Chair" means the member of the committee appointed as the chairperson by the Supreme Court pursuant to California Rules of Court, rule 9.80(g).

(c) "Vice-chair" means the member of the committee appointed as the vice-chairperson by the Supreme Court from the members of the committee pursuant to California Rules of Court, rule 9.80(g).

(d) "Judicial officer" means anyone who is an officer of the state judicial system, who performs judicial functions, and who is bound to comply with the California Code of Judicial Ethics adopted by the Supreme Court pursuant to the California Constitution, article VI, section 18(m).

(e) "Judicial candidate" means a person seeking election to or retention of judicial office by election. A person becomes a candidate for judicial office as soon as he or she makes a public announcement of candidacy, declares or files as a candidate with the election authority, or authorizes solicitation or acceptance of contributions or support. For purposes of these rules, the term "judicial candidate" includes any "candidate" bound to comply with the California Code of Judicial Ethics adopted by the Supreme Court pursuant to the California Constitution, article VI, section 18(m).

(f) "Requester" means an individual or entity who makes a request for an opinion or advice or who suggests a topic for the committee to consider as the subject of a formal opinion.

(g) "Committee counsel" means the legal advisor hired by the committee to serve as its staff and maintain the CJEO legal offices pursuant to these rules and as directed by the committee.

(h) "CJA" means the California Judges Association, a voluntary professional association of the state's judges, and "CJA Ethics Committee" means the California Judges Association Committee on Judicial Ethics.

(i) "CJEO Web site" means *www.JudicialEthicsOpinions.ca.org*, established and maintained by the committee pursuant to California Rules of Court, rule 9.80(n).

(j) "Toll-free CJEO line" means 1-855-854-5366, the toll-free telephone number operated by the committee pursuant to California Rules of Court, rule 9.80(n).

(k) "CJEO e-mail address" means Judicial.Ethics@jud.ca.gov, the e-mail address maintained by the committee pursuant to California Rules of Court, rule 9.80(n).

(l) "CJEO Opinion Request Form" means the form approved by the committee for use in making all requests for opinions, directly available on the CJEO Web site or by mail by calling the toll-free CJEO line.

(m) "CJEO Suggested Topic Form" means the form approved by the committee for use in submitting judicial ethics topics for consideration, directly available on the CJEO Web site or by mail by calling the toll-free CJEO line.

(n) "CJEO Confidentiality Waiver Form" means the form approved by the committee for use when a judicial officer or candidate for judicial office waives confidentiality pursuant to California Rules of Court, rule 9.80(h)(3), and rule 5(b) of these internal operating rules and procedures. This form is directly available on the CJEO Web site or by mail by calling the toll-free CJEO line.

(o) "Disciplinary proceedings" means any formal or informal matters that are being conducted by the Commission on Judicial Performance or the State Bar, including hearings, inquiries, and investigations.

(Adopted by the Committee on Judicial Ethics Opinions on January 6, 2012; approved by the Supreme Court on January 25, 2012.)

Rule 3.   Meetings and Conferences

(a) The chair will call committee meetings as needed, preside over those meetings, appoint subcommittees as needed, and otherwise coordinate the work of the committee. In the absence of the chair, the vice-chair will act as chair and will otherwise perform such duties as assigned by the chair.

(b) The committee should meet in person at least twice a year and, at the discretion of the chair, may confer either in writing, including electronic mail, by telephone, by videoconference, or by other available electronic means as often as needed to conduct committee business and resolve pending opinion requests.

(Adopted by the Committee on Judicial Ethics Opinions on January 6, 2012; approved by the Supreme Court on January 25, 2012.)

Rule 4.   Referrals to California Judges Association Committee on Judicial Ethics

(a) All requests for oral advice will be referred to the California Judges Association Committee on Judicial Ethics, with the following exceptions:

(1) A definitive answer to the request appears to be found in the resolution of an issue by the CJEO in a pending or prior formal or informal opinion;

(2) The requester declines to contact the CJA Judicial Ethics Committee; or

(3) When the request raises an issue that can be resolved by a statute, rule of court, canon, or other source, the committee will inform the requester of the particular source that may resolve the issue but will not provide oral advice. If the cited source does not resolve the issue for the requester, the committee will refer the requester to the CJA Ethics Committee.

(b) At its discretion, the committee will determine whether an exception applies and the oral advice to be given. Both determinations will be made by agreement of no fewer than three committee members who will serve on a rotating basis. Any serving member may request full committee discussion and vote on a determination, to be held at a time and by such means as determined by the chair. Upon such determinations, the chair will assign to one committee member the task of communicating the oral advice to the requester.

(Adopted by the Committee on Judicial Ethics Opinions on January 6, 2012; approved by the Supreme Court on January 25, 2012.)

Rule 5.   Confidentiality

(a) For purposes of this rule, "committee" includes committee members and their staff, committee counsel, and any additional staff hired by the committee.

(b) Pursuant to California Rules of Court, rule 9.80(h), all committee communications are confidential except as described in these rules. To ensure confidentiality, the following apply:

(1) All records of the committee, including all opinions, inquiries, replies, circulated drafts, documents, writings, files, communications with staff, and proceedings of the committee must be maintained as confidential and must not be disclosed outside of the committee unless confidentiality is waived or is otherwise provided for under these rules.

(2) All information electronically gathered by the committee, including on computers and electronic devices, on the CJEO Web site, in the CJEO e-mail accounts, and in the electronic files and e-mail accounts of the committee, must be maintained as confidential using available electronic security applications and other means, including password protections and access restrictions.

(3) The CJEO office, file cabinets, and computers must be maintained using security measures to restrict access and protect confidentiality as provided in these rules.

(4) All communications and documents regarding the opinions and advice of CJA forwarded by CJA to the committee pursuant to CJEO rule 9 are confidential as provided in these rules.

(c) The committee must not disclose outside the committee any confidential information obtained or developed by the committee, including identifying information concerning an individual whose inquiry or conduct has been the subject of any communication.

(d) The committee must not disclose within the committee any identifying information concerning an individual whose inquiry or conduct is the subject of any communication with the committee. In order to fulfill this mandate, the following procedures apply:

(1) Upon receipt of a request for an opinion or advice, committee counsel must assign a number to the request and remove the requester's name and identifying information. The committee members will deliberate and respond to the request under the procedures provided in these rules without identification of the requester.

(2) Any person who learns the identity of the requester through direct contact with the requester or through number assignment and identification removal must maintain the confidentiality of the identifying information of the requester within the committee unless confidentiality is waived or is otherwise provided for under these rules.

(3) If the requester is an entity, such as CJA or the Commission on Judicial Performance, the requester's name need not be removed, but if the request includes identifying information concerning an individual, that information must be removed and maintained as confidential.

(e) A judicial officer or candidate for judicial office may waive confidentiality; any such waiver must be in writing using the CJEO Confidentiality Waiver Form, which is available on the CJEO Web site or by mail by calling the toll-free CJEO line. If the judicial officer or candidate making the request for an opinion or advice waives confidentiality or asserts reliance on an opinion or advice by the committee in judicial or attorney discipline proceedings, such request and opinion or advice no longer are confidential under these rules. Notwithstanding any waiver, committee deliberations and records are confidential.

(Adopted by the Committee on Judicial Ethics Opinions on January 6, 2012; approved by the Supreme Court on January 25, 2012.)

Rule 6.   Opinion Requests

(a) The committee will issue formal written opinions on any subject it deems appropriate. Any person or entity may suggest, in writing, a topic for the committee to consider as the subject of a formal opinion. Topics must be submitted using the CJEO Topic Suggestion Form, which is available on the CJEO Web site or by mail by calling the toll-free CJEO line.

(b) Only judicial officers and candidates for judicial office may request informal written opinions and oral advice.

(c) Any judicial officer or candidate for judicial office may request a formal or informal written opinion from the committee. Requests must be submitted using the CJEO Opinion Request Form, which is available on the CJEO Web site or by mail by calling the toll-free CJEO line. The committee will consider only written requests for formal and informal opinions; the requests must describe the facts and discuss the issues presented in the request. The request should include citation to any constitutional provisions, statutes, rules of court, canons, advisory opinions, case law, or other authorities relevant to the request.

(d) A judicial officer or candidate for judicial office requesting oral advice may communicate in person, in writing (including by electronic mail), or by telephone with committee staff or any member of the committee, who must refer the request to the chair.

(e) A judicial officer or candidate for judicial office requesting an opinion or advice must disclose to the committee whether the issue that is the subject of the request is also the subject of:

(1) Pending litigation;

(2) A pending Commission on Judicial Performance disciplinary proceeding;

(3) A pending State Bar disciplinary proceeding; or

(4) An inquiry to, or an opinion provided by or pending from, the CJA Ethics Committee.

(f) The committee will inform an inquiring judicial officer or candidate for judicial office that he or she must disclose all relevant information as described in these rules and that any opinion or advice issued by the committee will be based on the premise that all relevant information has been disclosed, including whether another inquiry has been made and has been completed or is pending.

(Adopted by the Committee on Judicial Ethics Opinions on January 6, 2012; approved by the Supreme Court on January 25, 2012.)

Rule 7.   Consideration of Requests; Response Procedures

(a) The committee must consider all requests for an opinion. An executive committee consisting of the chair, vice-chair, and two additional members appointed by the chair will review all requests and organize them into two lists comprised of high priority requests and other requests. The executive committee will present both lists to the committee for consideration. The executive committee may perform additional duties as directed by the chair.

(b) The committee will determine whether a request for an opinion should be accepted or declined, and if accepted, whether the committee will provide a formal written opinion, an informal written opinion, oral advice, or any combination of the discretionary options for response provided in these rules. If the committee decides to proceed by way of oral advice, the request shall be referred to the three-member oral advice subcommittee.

(c) Eight members of the committee must vote affirmatively to prepare a formal or informal written opinion. Upon a vote to proceed, the chair will appoint a subcommittee of four members, including at least one court of appeal justice, to analyze the issue and draft an opinion for consideration by the entire committee.

(d) Eight members of the committee must vote affirmatively to adopt a draft formal written opinion drafted by a subcommittee. The draft opinion will be posted and the public will be given notice and an opportunity to comment for at least 45 days on the CJEO Web site, unless the committee in its discretion decides an opinion should be issued in final form in less time or with no prior notice and opportunity to comment. After the public comment period has expired, the committee will decide whether the opinion should be published in its original form, modified, or withdrawn. Eight committee members must vote affirmatively on the final version of the opinion or to withdraw a formal written opinion.

(e) Eight members of the committee must vote affirmatively to adopt an informal written opinion. After the committee adopts an informal written opinion, it will be distributed to the requesting judicial officer or candidate for judicial office by committee counsel.

(Adopted by the Committee on Judicial Ethics Opinions on January 6, 2012; approved by the Supreme Court on January 25, 2012.)

Rule 8.   Opinion Distribution

(a) The committee will, upon final adoption of a formal written opinion, distribute the opinion to all California judicial officers and other interested persons and entities by posting it on the CJEO Web site and by providing copies to the person or entity who requested the opinion. Committee counsel will maintain a list of interested persons and entities who request receipt of distributed CJEO opinions. The committee may withdraw, modify, or supersede an opinion at any time.

(b) The committee will periodically post summaries of its informal written opinions on the CJEO Web site and may, in its discretion, post summaries of its oral advice.

(c) Committee counsel must maintain records of committee determinations and opinions at the CJEO office.

(Adopted by the Committee on Judicial Ethics Opinions on January 6, 2012; approved by the Supreme Court on January 25, 2012.)

Rule 9.   California Judges Association

The CJEO, working with the California Judges Association and its Ethics Committee, will develop procedures for the delivery to CJEO, on a continuing and timely basis, summaries of all "informal responses" issued by CJA. "Informal responses" are the written records maintained by the CJA Ethics Committee that contain a recitation of the oral inquiry and the response. The summaries provided by CJA to CJEO will not include the name of the inquiring judicial officer but will contain: (1) a full description of the inquiry; (2) all of the relevant circumstances; (3) a full description of the answer provided; (4) the reasoning in support of the answer; and (5) any relevant information that would be helpful to CJEO. CJA will begin providing CJEO with summaries on the date of the approval of these rules. After six months of such deliveries, CJEO will evaluate whether the information provided is sufficient to enable it to meet its responsibilities, including determining which topics merit formal written opinions. At that time, CJEO will report to the Supreme Court on its evaluation and may propose any amendments necessary to these rules to reflect the policies and procedures it determines are needed to provide the full scope of service intended by the court. All communications and documents regarding opinions and advice of CJA forwarded by CJA to the committee are confidential.

(Adopted by the Committee on Judicial Ethics Opinions on January 6, 2012; approved by the Supreme Court on January 25, 2012.)

Supreme Court Rules Regarding Electronic Filing

[Amended effective March 18, 2020; adopted effective September 1, 2017; previously amended February 1, 2018, and May 1, 2018.]

Rule 1.   Application; electronic filing system.

These rules govern electronic filing in the Supreme Court under California Rules of Court, rules 8.70 – 8.79. The court's electronic filing system (EFS) is operated by ImageSoft TrueFiling (TrueFiling).
Rule 1 adopted effective September 1, 2017.

Rule 2.   Documents subject to electronic filing.

Rules 3 and 4 identify the documents that must or may be filed electronically in the Supreme Court. **Except as provided in this rule,** no document other than those identified in rules 3 and 4 may be filed electronically in the Supreme Court. **In certain circumstances, including but not limited to natural disasters, public health emergencies, and other situations substantially affecting the court's operations, the Supreme Court may direct the Clerk / Executive Officer of the Supreme Court to accept or require electronic filing of any document and / or to modify the requirements of rule 5 regarding the filing of paper copies. If the court so directs, the Clerk must promptly make reasonable efforts to provide adequate notice to affected parties and counsel, including identifying the type of documents that may or must be electronically filed and the duration of the expanded electronic procedures.**
Rule 2 amended effective March 18, 2020; adopted effective September 1, 2017.

Rule 3.   Mandatory electronic filing.

(a) Documents that attorneys must file electronically

Pursuant to California Rules of Court, rule 8.71, effective September 1, 2017, unless the court grants a motion for an excuse under rule 6, all attorneys representing a party in a matter before the court must file the documents listed in this subdivision electronically through the court's EFS.

(1) *Documents in proceedings under rules 8.495–8.498, 8.500–8.508, 9.13, and 9.60*

All documents filed before the court issues its decision to grant or deny review, including:

(A) Petitions for review; answers, replies;

(B) Applications to permit the filing of a petition, answer, reply, or attachment that exceeds the length limits set by California Rules of Court, rule 8.504(d);

(C) Applications to extend the time to file an answer or reply;

(D) Motions for relief from default for failure to timely file a petition, answer, or reply;

(E) All other applications and motions in these proceedings filed before the court issues its decision to grant or deny review; and

(F) Any correspondence filed in connection with the documents in (A) – (E).

(G) Amicus curiae letters under California Rules of Court, rule 8.500(g) and requests for depublication and related documents under California Rules of Court, rule 8.1125 may be filed electronically on a voluntary basis. (See Rule 4.)

(2) *Documents in proceedings under rules 8.380–8.385*

All documents filed before the court issues an order to show cause or its ruling on the petition, including:

(A) Petitions for writ of habeas corpus; informal responses, replies;

(B) Applications to permit the filing of a petition, informal response, reply, or attachment that exceeds the length limits set by California Rules of Court, rule 8.204(c);

(C) Applications to extend the time to file an informal response or reply;

(D) Motions for relief from default for failure to timely file an informal response, or reply;

(E) All other applications and motions in these proceedings filed before the court issues an order to show cause or its ruling on the petition; and

(F) Any correspondence filed in connection with the documents in (A) – (E).

(3) *Documents in proceedings under rules 8.485–8.486, and 9.13*

All documents filed before the court issues an alternative writ or its ruling on the petition, including:

(A) Petitions; preliminary responses, replies, and accusations against an attorney;

(B) Applications to permit the filing of a petition, preliminary response, reply, or attachment that exceeds the length limits set by California Rules of Court, rule 8.204(c);

(C) Applications to extend the time to file a preliminary response or reply;

(D) Motions for relief from default for failure to timely file a preliminary response, reply, or accusation against an attorney;

(E) All other applications and motions in these proceedings filed before the court issues an alternative writ or its ruling on the petition; and

(F) Any correspondence filed in connection with the documents in (A) – (E).

(4) *Documents in matters arising from a judgment of death*

All documents filed in these matters. For purposes of this subdivision:

(A) Matters arising from a judgment of death include:

(i) Automatic appeals under California Rules of Court, rules 8.600–8.642;

(ii) Habeas corpus proceedings in the court under California Rules of Court, rules 8.380–8.388 that involve a challenge to the validity of the petitioner's death judgment, including proceedings before any referee appointed by the court to conduct a hearing following the court's issuance of an order to show cause; and;

(ii) Other original writ proceedings in the court under California Rules of Court, rules 8.485–8.493 that relate to an automatic appeal or a habeas corpus proceeding challenging the validity of the death judgment, including proceedings on petitions for a writ of mandate under Penal Code section 1405, subdivision (k).

(B) Matters arising from a judgment of death do not include:

(i) Habeas corpus proceedings on petitions challenging only a capital inmate's conditions of confinement; and

(ii) Proceedings under California Rules of Court, rules 8.500–8.552 that relate to an automatic appeal or a habeas corpus proceeding challenging the validity of the death judgment, including petitions for review from lower court decisions regarding Penal Code section 1054.9 motions. These proceedings are governed by subdivision (a)(1) of this rule.

(C) A superior court judge who is appointed by the court as a referee in a proceeding under (A)(ii) is not considered a trial court for purposes of exemption from mandatory e-filing under California Rules of Court, rule 8.71(c).

(3) *Other documents on order of the court*

Any other document on order of the court.

(Subd (a) amended effective May 1, 2018; adopted effective September 1, 2017; previously amended effective February 1, 2018.)

(b) Application to new and pending cases

Electronic filing of the documents listed in (a) is mandatory as of September 1, 2017, including documents filed in cases commenced before that date.

(Subd (b) adopted effective September 1, 2017.)

Rule 3 amended effective May 1, 2018; adopted effective September 1, 2017; previously amended effective February 1, 2018.

Rule 4.   Voluntary electronic filing.

(a) Individuals or entities exempt from mandatory electronic filing

Pursuant to California Rules of Court, rule 8.71(b) and (c), electronic filing is voluntary for:

(1) Self-represented litigants; and

(2) Trial courts.

(Subd (a) adopted effective September 1, 2017.)

(b) Amicus curiae letters and requests for depublication

Amicus curiae letters under California Rules of Court, rule 8.500(g) and requests for depublication and related documents under California Rules of Court, rule 8.1125 may be filed electronically on a voluntary basis.

(Subd (b) relettered from subd (c) effective February 1, 2018; adopted as subd (c) effective September 1, 2017.)

Rule 4 amended effective February 1, 2018; adopted effective September 1, 2017.

Rule 5.   Submission of paper copies of electronically filed documents.

(a) Documents in proceedings under rules 8.380–8.385, 8.485–8.486, 8.495–8.498, 8.500–8.508, 9.13, and 9.60

Unless otherwise ordered by the court:

(1) For each electronically filed document in these proceedings, the filer must also submit to the court one unbound paper copy of the document.

(2) The paper copy must be mailed, delivered to a common carrier, or delivered to the court within two court days after the document is filed electronically with the court. If the filing requests an immediate stay, the paper copy must be delivered to court by the close of business the next court day after the document is filed electronically.

(Subd (a) amended effective May 1, 2018; adopted effective September 1, 2017; previously amended effective February 1, 2018.)

(b) Documents in matters arising from a judgment of death

Unless otherwise ordered by the court:

(1) For each electronically filed document in these matters, the filer must also submit to the court one unbound paper copy of the document.

(2) The paper copy must be mailed, delivered to a common carrier, or delivered to the court within two court days after the document is filed electronically with the court.

(Subd (b) adopted effective September 1, 2017.)

Rule 5 amended effective May 1, 2018; adopted effective September 1, 2017; previously amended effective February 1, 2018.

Rule 6.   Excuse from electronic filing.

(a) Motion requesting excuse

A party wanting to be excused from the requirement to file a document electronically must file a motion in the court requesting to be excused. The motion must comply with California Rules of Court, rule 8.54 and must specify whether the party is requesting to be excused from electronically filing all documents or only a particular document or documents.

(Subd (a) adopted effective September 1, 2017.)

(b) Grounds for excuse

Pursuant to California Rules of Court, rule 8.71(d), the court will grant an excuse on a satisfactory showing that:

(1) The party will suffer undue hardship if required to file electronically;

(2) The party will suffer significant prejudice if required to file electronically; or

(3) It is not feasible for the party to convert a particular document to electronic form by scanning, imaging, or another means.

(Subd (b) adopted effective September 1, 2017.)

Rule 6 adopted effective September 1, 2017.

Rule 7.   Registration of electronic filers.

(a) Obligation to register

Unless the court excuses the filer from this obligation under rule 6, every filer who is required or voluntarily chooses to file a document electronically under these rules must register as a TrueFiling user and obtain a username and password for access to TrueFiling. Registration with and access to the EFS is through the TrueFiling website at https://www.truefiling.com.

(Subd (a) adopted effective September 1, 2017.)

(b) Registered users' responsibilities

A registered TrueFiling user is responsible for all documents filed under the user's registered username and password. The registered user must also comply with the requirements of California Rules of Court, rule 8.32 regarding the duty to provide address and other contact information, and notice of any changes.

(Subd (b) adopted effective September 1, 2017.)

Rule 7 adopted effective September 1, 2017.

Rule 8.   Signatures.

Use of a registered TrueFiling user's username and password to electronically file a document is the equivalent of placing the registered user's electronic signature on the document.

Rule 8 adopted effective September 1, 2017.

Rule 9.   Service.

(a) Electronic service

In addition to the ways identified in California Rules of Court, rule 8.78 that a recipient may agree to accept electronic service, a recipient is deemed to have agreed to electronic service in a matter before this court if the recipient agreed to electronic service in the same matter in the Court of Appeal.

(Subd (a) adopted effective September 1, 2017.)

(b) Service by the court

Documents prepared by the court will be served on EFS users through the EFS or by electronic notification.

(Subd (b) adopted effective September 1, 2017.)

(c) Service of paper copies

When service of a document is required to be made on a person or entity that has not consented to electronic service, the server must comply with California Rules of Court, rule 8.25 regarding service of paper copies.

(Subd (c) adopted effective September 1, 2017.)

Rule 9 adopted effective September 1, 2017.

Rule 10.   Format and size of electronically filed documents.

(a) Format

(1) *Text searchable format*

All documents filed electronically must be in text-searchable PDF (portable document format), or other searchable format approved by the court, while maintaining original document formatting. If an electronic filer must file a document the filer possesses only in paper format, the filer must convert the document to an electronic document that complies with this rule by scanning or other means. It is the filer's responsibility to ensure that any document filed is complete and readable. Except as otherwise specified in this rule, electronically filed documents must comply with the content and form requirements of the California Rules of Court applicable to the particular document, with the exception of those provisions dealing exclusively with requirements for paper documents.

(2) *Pagination*

The page numbering of document filed electronically must comply with California Rules of Court, rule 8.74(b)(3).

(3) *Electronic Bookmarks*

Each document must include in the bookmarks panel of the electronic document a descriptive link (hereafter referred to as an electronic bookmark), to each heading, subheading and to the first page of any component of the document, including any table of contents, table of authorities, petition, verification, points and authorities, declaration, certificate of word count, certificate of interested entities or persons, proof of service, tab, exhibit, or attachment. Each electronic bookmark to a tab, exhibit, or attachment must include the letter or number of the tab, exhibit, or attachment and a description of the tab, exhibit, or attachment.

(Subd (a) adopted effective September 1, 2017.)

(b) Size

(1) An electronic filing may not be larger than 25 megabytes. This rule does not change the length limitations established by the California Rules of Court for petitions, answers, replies, briefs or any other document filed in the court.

(2) If a document exceeds the size limitation in (1), a party must submit the document in multiple files.

(A) These files must be paginated consecutively across all files in the document, including the cover pages required by (B).

(B) Each file must have a cover page that includes the following information:

(i) The total number of files constituting document;

(ii) The number of this file within the document;

(iii) The total number of pages in the document; and

(iv) The page numbers of the document contained in this file.

(C) The cover pages required by (B) must be included in the paper copies of the document submitted to the court under rule 5.

(Subd (b) adopted effective September 1, 2017.)

Rule 10 adopted effective September 1, 2017.

Rule 11. Privacy Protection.

(a) Personal Identifiers

Electronic filers must comply with California Rules of Court, rule 1.201 regarding exclusion or redaction of personal identifiers from all documents filed with the court. Neither TrueFiling nor the Clerk of the Court has any responsibility to review documents for compliance with these requirements.

(Subd (a) adopted effective September 1, 2017.)

(b) Sealed and Confidential Records

Electronic filers must comply with California Rules of Court, rules 8.45–8.47 regarding sealed and confidential records, with the exception of those requirments exclusively applicable to paper filings.

(Subd (b) adopted effective September 1, 2017.)

Rule 11 adopted effective September 1, 2017.

Rule 12. Fees.

(a) Collection of filing fees

For electronic filings, TrueFiling is designated as the court's agent for collection of filing fees required by law and any associated credit card or bank charges or convenience fees.

(Subd (a) adopted effective September 1, 2017.)

(b) Vendor fees

Pursuant to California Rules of Court, rule 8.73 and TrueFiling's contract with the court, in addition the filing fees required by law, TrueFiling will assess fees for each electronic filing in accordance with the schedule posted on the TrueFiling Web site, as approved by the court. These fees will be considered recoverable costs under rule 8.278(d)(1)(D).

(Subd (b) adopted effective September 1, 2017.)

(c) Exemption from vendor fees

The following are exempt from the fees charged for electronic filing under (b):

(1) *Parties with fee waivers*

A party who has been granted a fee waiver by the court who chooses to file documents electronically.

(2) *Government officers and entities*

The persons and entities identified in Government Code section 6103.

(Subd (c) adopted effective September 1, 2017.)

Rule 12 adopted effective September 1, 2017.

Rule 13. Technical Failure of Electronic Filing System.

The court is not responsible for malfunctions or errors occurring in the electronic transmission or receipt of electronically filed documents. The initial point of contact for anyone experiencing difficulty with TrueFiling is the toll-free telephone number posted on the TrueFiling Web site. California Rules of Court, rule 8.77, governs if a filer fails to meet a filing deadline imposed by court order, rule, or statute because of a failure at any point in the electronic transmission and receipt of a document. A motion under California Rules of Court, rule 8.77(d) to accept the document as timely filed must comply with rule 8.54.

Rule 13 adopted effective September 1, 2017.

INTERNAL OPERATING PRACTICES AND PROCEDURES OF THE CALIFORNIA SUPREME COURT

(Revised October 22, 2003, November 24, 2003, August 25, 2004, January 1, 2007, and April 22, 2015)[1]

I. Acting Chief Justice
II. Transfer of Cases
III. Conferences
IV. Conference Memoranda
V. Calendar Sessions for Oral Argument
VI. Calendars and Calendar Memoranda
VII. Submission
VIII. Assignments for Preparation of Opinions
IX. Circulation of Opinions
X. Filing of Opinions
XI. Review of Determinations by the Commission on Judicial Performance
XII. Temporary Absence of Justices
XIII. Disqualification of Justices and Assignment of Court of Appeal Justices
XIV. Applications for Recommendations for Executive Clemency, Habeas Corpus, and Stays
XV. Appointment of Attorneys in Criminal Cases
XVI. Communications From Counsel in Pending Cases
XVII. Suspension of Procedures

The following internal operating practices and procedures are observed by the California Supreme Court in the performance of its duties.[2]

I. ACTING CHIEF JUSTICE

An Acting Chief Justice performs the functions of the Chief Justice when the Chief Justice is absent or unable to participate in a matter. The Chief Justice, pursuant to constitutional authority (Cal. Const., art. VI, § 6), selects on a rotational basis an associate justice to serve as Acting Chief Justice.

II. TRANSFER OF CASES

A. All transfers to the Supreme Court of a cause in a Court of Appeal pursuant to article VI, section 12 of the California Constitution are accomplished by order of the Chief Justice made on a vote of four justices assenting thereto.

B. Unless otherwise ordered by the Chief Justice, all applications for writs of mandate and/or prohibition that have not previously been filed with the proper Court of Appeal are transferred to such court.

III. CONFERENCES

A. Unless otherwise directed by the Chief Justice, regular conferences are held each Wednesday, excluding the Wednesday of regular calendar sessions and the first Wednesday of July and August.

B. Special conferences may be called by the Chief Justice whenever deemed necessary or desirable.

C. Four justices constitute a quorum for any regular or special conference.

D. A judge assigned by the Chief Justice to assist the court, or to act in the place of a regular member of the court who is disqualified or otherwise unable to act, may be counted to obtain a quorum for a conference. A regular member of the court, present at a conference, who is not participating in a particular matter is not counted in determining a quorum for that matter.

E. A justice who has ascertained that he or she will not be present at a conference or will not be participating in a particular matter will notify the

---

[1] These practices and procedures may be amended from time to time, as needed, to facilitate the court's ability to discharge its duties. Amendments are reflected in updated versions of the practices and procedures on the California Courts Web site at <http://www.courtinfo.ca.gov/courts/supreme/iopp.htm>. Section VIII.D was amended October 22, 2003; sections III.E, IX, X, and XII were amended November 24, 2003; sections IV.J and XIII.B were amended August 25, 2004; and, rules references throughout were amended effective January 1, 2007, to reflect the reorganization and renumbering of the California Rules of Court effective on that date.

[2] Various provisions of the California Constitution, codes, and rules of court, as well as numerous provisions of the decisional law, bear on how the court functions. The court's internal operating practices and procedures should be considered in that context.

Chief Justice or the Calendar Coordinator, as specified by sections XII.C and XIII.A. The absent justice may communicate in writing to the Calendar Coordinator his or her votes on some or all of the matters on any given conference, and may be counted to constitute a quorum for each such conference matter on which a vote has been cast.

F. Matters in which time is of the essence may be considered by the court without a formal conference. In such matters, because time is of the essence, an order will be filed as soon as four justices vote for a particular disposition.

IV. Conference Memoranda

A. Unless otherwise directed by the Chief Justice, a conference memorandum is prepared for each petition requiring conference consideration or action.

B. Upon the filing of a petition, motion, or application, the Calendar Coordinator, under the direction of the Chief Justice, assigns it a conference date and refers it to one of the central staffs or a member of the court for preparation of a conference memorandum as follows:

1. Petitions in civil cases, to the civil central staff.

2. Petitions in or derived from criminal cases, other than cases arising from judgments of death, to the criminal central staff.

3. Applications for writs of habeas corpus arising out of criminal proceedings, other than cases arising from judgments of death, to the criminal central staff.

4. Motions in criminal cases arising from judgments of death, to the six associate justices and the Chief Justice, or to the capital central staff.

5. Applications for writs of habeas corpus arising out of judgments of death, to the six associate justices and the Chief Justice, or to the capital central staff.

6. Applications to the Supreme Court pursuant to article V, section 8 of the California Constitution for a recommendation regarding the granting of a pardon or commutation to a person twice convicted of a felony, to the criminal central staff.

7. Petitions for review of State Bar proceedings pursuant to rule 9.13 et seq. of the California Rules of Court, to the civil central staff.

8. All other petitions and applications, to the six associate justices and the Chief Justice in rotation so that, at the end of a given period of time, each justice will have been assigned an equal number of petitions. Petitions for rehearing after decision in the Supreme Court are referred to a justice, other than the author, who concurred in the majority opinion.

C. The recommendation set forth in a conference memorandum will generally be one of the following: (1) "Grant," (2) "Grant and Hold," (3) "Grant and Transfer," (4) "Deny," (5) "Submitted," (6) "Denial Submitted," and (7) "Deny and Depublish." The designation "submitted" is used when the author believes the case warrants special discussion. The designation "denial submitted" is used when the author believes the petition should be denied, but nevertheless believes some ground exists that could arguably justify a grant, or an issue is raised that otherwise warrants discussion by the court. The designation "deny and depublish" is used when the author does not believe the decision warrants review, but nevertheless believes the opinion is potentially misleading and should not be relied on as precedent.

D. The author of the conference memorandum assigns it to either the "A" or the "B" list. Cases assigned to the "A" list include all those in which the recommendation is to grant or take affirmative action of some kind, e.g., "grant and transfer" or "deny and depublish," in which a dissenting opinion has been filed in the Court of Appeal, or in which the author believes denial is appropriate, but that the case poses questions that deserve special attention. Cases assigned to the "B" list concern routine matters, or application of settled law.

E. Conference memoranda are delivered by the author to the Calendar Coordinator for reproduction and distribution to the justices no later than the Tuesday of the week before the conference, thus providing ample time for the justices and their staffs to review the petition and the court's internal memoranda.

F. The court's Calendar Coordinator divides the weekly conference agenda into an "A" and "B" list, based on the designation appearing on each conference memorandum.

G. Matters appearing on the "A" list are called and considered at the conference for which they are scheduled. Before or after a vote is taken, any justice may request that a case be put over to a subsequent conference within the jurisdictional time limit for further study, preparation of a supplemental memorandum, or both. The time within which action thereon must be taken will be extended pursuant to rules 8.264 and 8.500 of the California Rules of Court, if necessary.

H. Matters appearing on the "B" list will be denied in accordance with the recommendation of the memorandum, at the conference at which they are scheduled, unless a justice requests that a case be put over to a subsequent conference within the jurisdictional time limit for further study, preparation of a supplemental memorandum, or both.

I. In any case in which the petition, application, or motion is denied, a justice may request that his or her vote be recorded in the court minutes.

J. When a justice is unavailable or disqualified to participate in a vote on a petition for review or other matter (see, e.g., section XIII.A., *post*), and four justices cannot agree on a disposition, the Chief Justice, pursuant to constitutional authority (Cal. Const., art. VI, § 6), assigns in alphabetical order (except as set forth below) a Court of Appeal justice as a pro tempore justice to participate in the vote on the petition or matter. The assigned justice is furnished all pertinent petitions, motions, applications, answers, briefs, memoranda, and other material. A newly-appointed Court of Appeal justice will be assigned as a pro tempore justice of the Supreme Court only after he or she has served on the Court of Appeal for one year. If a Court of Appeal justice is unable to serve on a particular case, the next justice on the alphabetical list will be assigned, and the Court of Appeal justice who was unable to serve will be assigned in the next case in which a pro tempore appointment is required.

K. Either at the time review is granted, or at any time thereafter, the court may specify which of the issues presented should be briefed and argued.

L. Within 15 days after review is granted in a civil case or a criminal case in which a corporate entity is a party, each party must file a "Certification of Interested Entities or Persons" that lists any persons, associations of persons, firms, partnerships, corporations (including parent and subsidiary corporations) or other entities other than the parties themselves known by the party to have either (i) a financial interest in the subject matter of the controversy or in a party to the proceeding; or (ii) any other kind of interest that could be substantially affected by the outcome of the proceeding. This requirement does not apply to any governmental entity or its agencies. The Clerk's Office shall notify all parties including real parties in interest in writing of this requirement at the time the parties are notified of the court's grant of review.

Revised effective January 1, 2007, and April 22, 2015.

V. Calendar Sessions for Oral Argument

Regular sessions of the court are held each year, on a day or days as determined by the Chief Justice, in San Francisco, Los Angeles, and Sacramento. Special sessions may be held elsewhere by order of the Chief Justice or by order on a vote of four justices assenting thereto.

Unless otherwise ordered by the Chief Justice, the court convenes at 9:00 a.m.

Unless otherwise ordered, only one counsel may be heard for each side. Counsel wishing to divide the time for oral argument must request permission from the Court not later than ten days after the case has been set for oral argument. In no event shall oral argument be divided into segments of less than ten minutes, except that one counsel for the opening side (unless additional counsel are so authorized) may reserve a portion of his or her allotted time for rebuttal.

VI. Calendars and Calendar Memoranda

A. The purpose of the calendar memorandum is to present the facts and legal issues, and to propose a resolution of the legal issues.

B. At the request of the justice preparing a calendar memorandum, or on direction of the Chief Justice, or on the affirmative vote of a majority of the court, the Clerk's Office will request counsel for the parties to be prepared to argue and to submit additional briefs on any points that are deemed omitted or inadequately covered by the briefs or in which the court is particularly interested.

C. In assigning cases for the preparation of calendar memoranda, the Chief Justice takes into account the following considerations, but may depart from these considerations for the purpose of equalizing the workload of the justices or expediting the work of the court:

1. The case is assigned to one of the justices who voted for review. If a case involves substantially the same issues as one already assigned for preparation of a calendar memorandum, it may be assigned to the justice

who has the similar case. Preference in case assignments may be given to a justice who authored the conference memorandum or supplemental conference memorandum on which the petition was granted, unless other factors, such as equalization of workload, suggest a different assignment.

2. Granted petitions in other matters and State Bar proceedings originally referred to the central staffs are generally assigned to the justices in such a manner as to equalize each justice's allotment of cases.

3. Appeals in cases in which the death penalty has been imposed are assigned in rotation as they are filed.

4. When a rehearing has been granted and a supplemental calendar memorandum is needed, the matter will ordinarily be assigned to the justice who prepared the prior opinion if it appears that he or she can present the views of the majority. Otherwise, the case will be assigned to a justice who is able to do so.

D. The court's general procedures for circulation of calendar memoranda, etc., are as follows:

1. The justice to whom a case is assigned prepares and circulates a calendar memorandum within a prescribed time after the filing of the last brief. When the calendar memorandum circulates, the Calendar Coordinator distributes copies of the briefs to each justice. The record remains with the Calendar Coordinator, to be borrowed as needed by a justice or his or her staff.

2. Within a prescribed time after the calendar memorandum circulates, each justice states his or her preliminary response to the calendar memorandum (i.e., that he or she concurs, concurs with reservations, is doubtful, or does not concur). Each justice also indicates whether he or she intends to write a separate concurring or dissenting calendar memorandum in the case. If it appears from the preliminary responses that a majority of the justices concur in the original calendar memorandum, the Chief Justice places the case on a pre-argument conference (§ VI.D.4, *post*). If it appears from the preliminary responses that a majority of the justices will probably not concur in the original calendar memorandum or a modified version of that memorandum, the Chief Justice places the matter on a conference for discussion or reassigns the case.

3. Each justice who wishes to write a concurring or dissenting calendar memorandum does so and circulates that memorandum within a prescribed time after the original calendar memorandum circulates. Soon after any concurring or dissenting calendar memorandum circulates, each justice either confirms his or her agreement with the original calendar memorandum or indicates his or her agreement with the concurring or dissenting calendar memorandum. If the original calendar memorandum thereby loses its tentative majority, the Chief Justice places the matter on a conference for discussion or reassigns the case.

4. The Chief Justice convenes a pre-argument conference at least once each month. The purpose of the conference is to identify those cases that appear ready for oral argument. The Chief Justice constructs the calendars from those cases.

The Chief Justice places on the agenda of the conference any case in which all concurring or dissenting calendar memoranda have circulated and the "majority" calendar memorandum has been approved by at least four justices or is likely to be approved by four justices at the conference. The Chief Justice also includes on the agenda any case in which discussion could facilitate resolution of the issues.

VII. SUBMISSION

A. A cause is submitted when the court has heard oral argument or has approved a waiver of argument and the time has passed for filing all briefs and papers, including any supplementary brief permitted by the court.

B. Submission may be vacated only by an order of the Chief Justice stating in detail the reasons therefor. The order shall provide for prompt resubmission of the cause.

VIII. ASSIGNMENTS FOR PREPARATION OF OPINIONS

A. After argument the Chief Justice convenes a conference to determine whether the calendar memorandum continues to represent the views of a majority of the justices. In light of that discussion, the Chief Justice assigns the case for opinion.

B. The Chief Justice assigns the cases for preparation of opinions in the following manner:

1. If a majority of the justices agree with the disposition suggested in the calendar memorandum, ordinarily the case is assigned to the author of that memorandum.

2. If a majority of the justices disagree with the disposition reached in the memorandum, the case is reassigned to one of the majority.

3. When a case is argued on rehearing, it ordinarily remains with the justice who prepared the prior opinion or the supplemental calendar memorandum if it appears that he or she can express the majority view. If he or she does not agree with the majority view, the case is reassigned to a justice who is a member of the majority.

4. In making assignments pursuant to these guidelines, the Chief Justice takes several considerations into account, including the following: (a) the fair distribution of work among the members of the court; (b) the likelihood that a justice can express the view of the majority of the court in a particular case; (c) the amount of work he or she has done on that case or on the issues involved; and (d) the status of the unfiled cases theretofore assigned to him or her.

C. Every reasonable effort is made by the justices to agree on the substance of opinions, and whenever possible, dissents or special concurrence on minor matters are avoided. When a justice discovers that he or she objects to something in a proposed opinion, he or she will call it to the author's attention. In addition, the objecting justice may prepare and circulate a memorandum setting forth his or her concerns and suggestions for the purpose of giving the author an opportunity to conform to any proposed changes and to remove or meet the objections raised. These practices and filing policies (see § X, *post*) reflect the court's strong preference for assuring that each opinion author be allowed sufficient time to consider the views of every justice before the opinion is released for filing.

D. Unless otherwise ordered by the Chief Justice, all opinions in State Bar and Commission on Judicial Performance cases and all memorandum opinions are issued "By the Court." All other opinions identify the author and the concurring justices unless a majority of the court conclude that because substantial portions of the opinion have been drafted by a number of justices, or for other compelling reasons, the opinion should be issued "By the Court."

E. The rules of the *California Style Manual* are consulted in the preparation of opinions as well as conference and calendar memoranda.

IX. CIRCULATION OF OPINIONS

Within a prescribed time after submission, the justice to whom the case is assigned circulates the proposed majority opinion. Within a prescribed time after the proposed majority opinion circulates, all concurring or dissenting opinions circulate. If the author of the proposed majority opinion wishes to respond by change or by memorandum to any concurring or dissenting opinion, he or she does so promptly after that opinion circulates. The author of the concurring or dissenting opinion thereafter has a prescribed time in which to respond.

All opinions are cite-checked and proofread before circulating. Only copies of an opinion circulate; the original remains in the Calendar Coordination Office. A justice may indicate his or her concurrence in an opinion (including an opinion authored by the justice) by signing the original that is retained in the Calendar Coordination Office or by transmitting to the Calendar Coordinator, by facsimile, a signed copy of the signature page of the opinion, indicating the justice's concurrence. When possible, it is preferred that a justice indicate his or her concurrence by signing the original that is retained in the Calendar Coordination Office.

X. FILING OF OPINIONS

When the circulation process has been completed, the Calendar Coordination Office shall notify the authoring justice of each proposed opinion that the matter appears ready for filing, and shall inquire whether each authoring justice is releasing his or her opinion for filing. When all opinions have been released for filing, the Calendar Coordination Office shall provide for the duplication of the opinion, and shall notify the Clerk of the Court and the Reporter of Decisions of the scheduled filing date. The Clerk of the Court shall file the opinion on the scheduled date at the San Francisco office of the Supreme Court.

Opinions are completed in time for reproduction and filing on a normal opinion-filing day. Unless good cause to vacate submission appears, the opinions are filed on or before the 90th day after submission. Internal circulation of an opinion after the 80th day following submission may result in the inability of the author of the proposed majority or of another timely circulated opinion to afford the views contained in the late circulated opinion full consideration and response. Such late circulated opinions will not be filed until at least 10 days but in no event more than 20 days after the filing of the majority opinion. At any time before the majority or lead opinion is final, the court may modify or grant rehearing pursuant to the applicable rules of court.

XI. REVIEW OF DETERMINATIONS BY THE COMMISSION ON JUDICIAL PERFORMANCE

A petition for review of a determination by the Commission on Judicial Performance to retire, remove, censure, admonish, or disqualify a judge or former judge under subdivision (d) of section 18 of article VI of the California Constitution must address both the appropriateness of review and the merits of the commission's determination. The commission may file a response, and the petitioner a reply, within prescribed times. The petition is assigned by the Calendar Coordinator, under the direction of the Chief Justice, to the civil central staff. When briefing is complete, the staff prepares a conference memorandum in which the recommendation generally will be either to "Deny" or "Retain for Further Consideration." If a majority of the justices vote to "deny," the petition is denied, and an order to that effect is filed forthwith. If a majority vote to "retain for further consideration," the Chief Justice assigns the case to a justice who voted to retain. This justice then prepares a memorandum on the merits, which will serve as a calendar memorandum if an order granting review subsequently is filed. The court's usual procedures for circulation of calendar memoranda then are followed. Once all concurring and dissenting memoranda have circulated, and it appears there is a majority for a particular disposition, the matter is considered at a conference. If a majority vote to deny review, an order to that effect is filed forthwith. If a majority vote to grant review, an order to that effect is filed, and the case is simultaneously set for oral argument at the soonest possible time under the court's usual scheduling rules. Because of the time limitations in subdivision (d) of section 18 of article VI of the California Constitution, continuance of oral argument rarely will be granted. Following oral argument and submission of the cause, the court's usual rules for preparation and circulation of opinions apply.

XII. TEMPORARY ABSENCE OF JUSTICES

A. As soon as a justice knows that he or she will not be attending a conference of the court, he or she will notify the Chief Justice. Any justice who will not be present at conference may communicate his or her votes on any given conference matter as set forth in section III.E. A justice may communicate such votes whether he or she is within or temporarily outside of California. A case may be assigned to a justice for the preparation of a calendar memorandum, under the procedures set forth in section VI, regardless of whether he or she is within or temporarily outside of California at the time the order granting review or issuing a writ or order to show cause is filed.

B. Any justice who is participating in the decision of a case, and who is temporarily outside of California, may communicate his or her concurrence in an opinion (including an opinion authored by that justice) by transmitting to the Calendar Coordinator, by facsimile, a signed copy of the signature page of the opinion, indicating the justice's concurrence, as set forth in section IX. If an opinion is concurred in by four justices, it may be filed as provided above in section X, even though one or more of the concurring justices are temporarily absent from the state and regardless of whether an absent justice is the author of the opinion.

XIII. DISQUALIFICATION OF JUSTICES AND ASSIGNMENT OF COURT OF APPEAL JUSTICES

A. Each justice has a duty to hear and decide all matters coming before the court in the absence of a ground of disqualification. (Cal. Code Jud. Ethics, canon 3B(1).) Although one ground of disqualification is presented when a justice has specified financial interests in a party to a proceeding (id., canon 3E(5)(d)), recusal is not required based on a justice's financial interest in an entity that appears in a proceeding but is not a party (e.g., a nonparty entity or a nonparty member of a nonparty advocacy group that requests publication or depublication of a Court of Appeal opinion, or that writes in support of or in opposition to a petition for review, or that appears in a proceeding as amicus curiae), unless 'the justice believes his or her recusal would further the interests of justice' (id., canon 3E(4)(a)), or 'the justice substantially doubts his or her capacity to be impartial' (id.,

canon 3E(4)(b)), or 'the circumstances are such that a reasonable person aware of the facts would doubt the justice's ability to be impartial' (id., canon 3E(4)(c)). As soon as a justice discovers that he or she is disqualified in any proceeding, he or she will notify the Calendar Coordinator.

B. When it is known after a case is granted but before argument that a justice for any reason is unable to participate in a matter, the Chief Justice pursuant to constitutional authority (Cal. Const., art. VI, § 6) assigns on an alphabetical rotational basis (under the procedure described ante, section IV.J) a Court of Appeal justice to assist the court in place of the nonparticipating justice. The assigned justice is furnished all pertinent petitions, motions, applications, answers, briefs, memoranda, and other material.

C. If an assigned justice has participated in the decision of a case before this court, that justice will also participate in any further proceedings — including requests for modification, petitions for rehearing, and rehearings — until such time as the decision has become final. This procedure is to be followed unless the original assignment was necessitated by the absence of a regular justice of this court, in which event a regular justice, if able to do so, will participate in lieu of the assigned justice in the consideration of any petition for rehearing and, if rehearing is granted, in any subsequent proceeding.

D. If a justice retires before a case in which he or she has heard oral argument is final, he or she may be assigned to continue to participate in the case. When a permanent replacement justice appointed to fill the vacancy created by the retirement of that justice has taken the oath of office, and the opinion has been filed, any petition for rehearing will be acted on by the permanent replacement justice.

Revised effective April 22, 2015.

XIV. APPLICATIONS FOR RECOMMENDATIONS FOR EXECUTIVE CLEMENCY, HABEAS CORPUS, AND STAYS

A. An application for a recommendation for executive clemency comes before this court pursuant to article V, section 8, subdivision (a) of the California Constitution and Penal Code section 4851. When such applications are received by the Clerk's Office, they are given a file number, and the fact that they have been filed is a matter of public record. The papers and documents transmitted to the court by the Governor with the application often contain material that the Governor may have the right to withhold from the public. (See Gov. Code, § 6254, subds. (c), (f), & (l); Civ. Code, § 1798.40, subd. (c).) Accordingly, the court treats these files as confidential and does not make them available to the public.

Applications are denied unless four or more justices vote to recommend that clemency be granted. The Chief Justice informs the Governor by letter of the court's recommendation, and a copy of such letter is included in the court's file and considered a matter of public record. Pursuant to the provisions of Penal Code section 4852, the Clerk transmits the record to the office of the Governor if the court's recommendation is favorable to the applicant. Otherwise, the documents remain in the files of the court. (See Pen. Code, § 4852.)

B. When a defendant in a criminal case files a petition for review after denial without opinion by the Court of Appeal of a petition for prohibition or mandate attacking a Penal Code section 995 or section 1538.5 ruling, the matter will be placed on the agenda of a regular conference and will not be accelerated. Absent extraordinary circumstances, no order staying the trial will issue. If the case goes to trial and the matter becomes moot before the regular conference, the memorandum need only so state, and the petition may then be denied as moot without the necessity of considering its merits.

When the Court of Appeal has denied such a writ petition with opinion, a request to stay the trial pending action by the Supreme Court on the petition for review will be granted when necessary to prevent the matter from becoming moot.

C. When a misdemeanor conviction has become final on appeal or a final contempt order has been filed by a trial court and the defendant or contemner files a petition for review following denial of a timely habeas corpus or certiorari petition by a Court of Appeal or files a timely original petition, a stay of execution of the judgment or order will issue pending determination of the petition. The Chief Justice may condition the stay on the filing of a bond or on the continuation of an appeal bond, if any, if he or she deems it appropriate to do so. If the petition appears to lack merit, however, expedited consideration will be given to deny the petition in preference to releasing an incarcerated petitioner.

D. Pending disposition of a petition for writ of habeas corpus to review an order permitting extradition, the Chief Justice may stay extradition on behalf of the court. If the petition appears to lack merit, however, expedited consideration will be given to deny the petition in preference to staying the extradition proceedings.

E. In cases not covered by subdivisions B and C of this section, and when not precluded by subdivision G of this section, the Chief Justice may, in his or her discretion, grant applications for stays of judicial proceedings or orders pending regular conference consideration of the matters involved.

F. Except as provided in subdivisions B through E of this section and except in emergencies, petitions for habeas corpus, applications for stays of judicial proceedings or orders, and applications for stays of execution are to be resolved at the weekly case conference.

G. Stays governed by special provisions of statutes or rules of court will be issued only in compliance with such provisions. (See, e.g., Pub. Util. Code, §§ 1761–1766; Cal. Rules of Court, rule 8.112.)

H. Applications to stay actions by public agencies or private parties pending consideration of petitions for writs of mandate (i.e., *Emeryville*-type stays [see *People ex rel. S. F. Bay etc. Com. v. Town of Emeryville* (1968) 69 Cal.2d 533]) are to be resolved at the weekly case conference.

I. Upon receipt of a proper notice of bankruptcy relating to a pending petition for review in a creditor's action or an action that would diminish the relevant estate, the court will file an order noting the stay of proceedings and suspending the operation of the applicable rule 8.500 time period. (See 11 U.S.C. § 362(a)(1).) Thereafter, the parties will be directed to file quarterly status reports to apprise the court of the current status of the bankruptcy proceedings. Upon receipt of a proper notice terminating the bankruptcy stay, the court shall enter an order terminating the stay of proceedings and indicating that the applicable time period of rule 8.500(a) shall begin running anew from the date of the order.
Revised effective January 1, 2007.

XV. APPOINTMENT OF ATTORNEYS IN CRIMINAL CASES

A. In criminal matters, upon a verified or certified statement of indigency, the court, acting through the Clerk's Office, will appoint an attorney for a party in the following instances:

1. In a pending case in which the petition for review has been granted;
2. In a pending automatic appeal and/or related state habeas corpus/executive clemency proceedings;
3. In an original proceeding in which an alternative writ or an order to show cause has been issued;
4. In capital cases in the following proceedings:

(a) Proceedings for appellate or other postconviction review of state court judgments in the United States Supreme Court, subject however to the power of that court to appoint counsel therein; and

(b) Conduct of sanity hearings when indicated.

B. At or after the time the court appoints appellate counsel to represent an indigent appellant on direct appeal, the court also shall offer to appoint habeas corpus/executive clemency counsel for each indigent capital appellant. Following that offer, the court shall appoint habeas corpus/executive clemency counsel unless the court finds, after a hearing if necessary (held before a referee appointed by the court), that the appellant rejected the offer with full understanding of the legal consequences of the decision.

C. The court's Automatic Appeals Monitor is responsible for recruiting, evaluating, and recommending the appointment of counsel on behalf of indigent appellants in capital appeals and/or related state habeas corpus/executive clemency proceedings.

D. Counsel in automatic appeals and/or related state habeas corpus/executive clemency proceedings are compensated by one of two alternative methods: Under the "time and costs" method, counsel are compensated on an hourly basis and reimbursed for necessary expenses that were reasonably incurred. The court makes partial payments on counsel's fee claims while these claims are pending full review. Under the alternative optional "fixed fee and expenses" method, counsel are paid a fixed amount at regular stages of a case, according to a predetermined assessment of its difficulty.

E. Habeas corpus petitions in capital cases are governed by the timeliness and compensation standards set out in the "Supreme Court Policies Regarding Cases Arising From Judgments of Death." Habeas corpus counsel appointed in capital cases have the duty to investigate factual and legal grounds for the filing of a petition for a writ of habeas corpus, as delineated in those policies.

XVI. COMMUNICATIONS FROM COUNSEL IN PENDING CASES

Whenever a matter is pending before the court, any communication to the court from counsel is to be addressed to the Clerk's Office, with copies to all counsel.

XVII. SUSPENSION OF PROCEDURES

Whenever exceptional or emergency conditions require speedy action, or whenever there is other good cause for special action regarding any matter, the operation of these procedures may be temporarily suspended by affirmative vote of four justices.

The Chief Justice may extend any applicable time limit (except that stated in section X) on written request by a justice stating good cause and the date by which he or she expects to comply.

SUPREME COURT POLICIES REGARDING CASES ARISING FROM JUDGMENTS OF DEATH

(Adopted by the Supreme Court effective June 6, 1989.)

(Amended effective September 28, 1989, September 19, 1990, January 27, 1992, December 21, 1992, July 29, 1993, December 22, 1993, June 20, 1996, January 22, 1997, January 22, 1998, February 4, 1998, August 23, 2001, December 19, 2001, January 16, 2002, July 17, 2002, July 26, 2002, November 20, 2002, November 30, 2005, and January 1, 2008.)

Stays of execution. Policy Statement 1.
Withdrawal of counsel. Policy Statement 2.
Standards governing filing of habeas corpus petitions and compensation of counsel in relation to such petitions. Policy Statement 3.
Service of process by counsel for defendant. Policy Statement 4.

Policy Statement 1.　Stays of execution.

The court will consider a motion for a stay of execution only if such a motion is made in connection with a petition for a writ of habeas corpus filed in this court, or to permit certiorari review by the United States Supreme Court.
Adopted June 6, 1989.

Policy Statement 2.　Withdrawal of counsel.

In the absence of exceptional circumstances—for example, when an appointed counsel becomes mentally or physically incapacitated—the court will consider a motion to withdraw as attorney of record only if appropriate replacement counsel is ready and willing to accept appointment for the balance of the representation for which the withdrawing attorney has been appointed (i.e., appellate representation, habeas corpus/executive clemency representation, or both).
Adopted June 6, 1989; amended effective Jan. 22, 1998.

Policy Statement 3.　Standards governing filing of habeas corpus petitions and compensation of counsel in relation to such petitions.

The Supreme Court promulgates these standards as a means of implementing the following goals with respect to petitions for writs of habeas corpus relating to capital cases: (i) ensuring that potentially meritorious habeas corpus petitions will be presented to and heard by this court in a timely fashion; (ii) providing appointed counsel some certainty of payment for authorized legal work and investigation expenses; and (iii) providing this court with a means to monitor and regulate expenditure of public funds paid to counsel who seek to investigate and file habeas corpus petitions.

For these reasons, effective June 6, 1989, all petitions for writs of habeas corpus arising from judgments of death, whether the appeals therefrom are pending or previously resolved, are governed by these standards:

1. Timeliness standards

1-1. Appellate counsel in a capital case shall take and maintain detailed, understandable and computerized transcript notes and shall compile and maintain a detailed list of potentially meritorious habeas corpus issues that have come to appellate counsel's attention. In addition, if appellate counsel's appointment does not include habeas corpus representation, until separate counsel is appointed for that purpose, appellate counsel shall preserve evidence that comes to the attention of appellate counsel if that evidence appears relevant to a potential habeas corpus investigation. If separate "post-conviction" habeas corpus/executive clemency counsel (hereafter "habeas corpus" counsel) is appointed, appellate counsel shall deliver to habeas corpus counsel copies of the list of potentially meritorious habeas corpus issues, copies of the transcript notes, and any preserved evidence relevant to a potential habeas corpus investigation, and thereafter shall update the issues list and transcript notes as warranted. Appellate counsel shall consult with and work cooperatively with habeas corpus counsel to facilitate timely investigation, and timely preparation and filing (if warranted) of a habeas corpus petition by habeas corpus counsel.

Habeas corpus counsel in a capital cases shall have a duty to investigate factual and legal grounds for the filing of a petition for a writ of habeas corpus. The duty to investigate is limited to investigating potentially meritorious grounds for relief that come to counsel's attention in the course of reviewing appellate counsel's list of potentially meritorious habeas corpus issues, the transcript notes prepared by appellate counsel, the appellate record, trial counsel's existing case files, and the appellate briefs, and in the course of making reasonable efforts to discuss the case with the defendant, trial counsel and appellate counsel. The duty to investigate does not impose on counsel an obligation to conduct, nor does it authorize the expenditure of public funds for, an unfocused investigation having as its object uncovering all possible factual bases for a collateral attack on the judgment. Instead, counsel has a duty to investigate potential habeas corpus claims only if counsel has become aware of information that might reasonably lead to actual facts supporting a potentially meritorious claim. All petitions for writs of habeas corpus should be filed without substantial delay.

[As amended effective July 29, 1993, and Jan. 22, 1998.]

1-1.1. A petition for a writ of habeas corpus will be presumed to be filed without substantial delay if it is filed within 180 days after the final due date for the filing of appellant's reply brief on the direct appeal or within 36 months after appointment of habeas corpus counsel, whichever is later.

[As amended effective Sept. 19, 1990, Jan. 22, 1998, July 17, 2002, and Nov. 30, 2005.]

1-1.2. A petition filed more than 180 days after the final due date for the filing of appellant's reply brief on the direct appeal, or more than 36 months after appointment of habeas corpus counsel, whichever is later, may establish absence of substantial delay if it alleges with specificity facts showing the petition was filed within a reasonable time after petitioner or counsel (a) knew, or should have known, of facts supporting a claim and (b) became aware, or should have become aware, of the legal basis for the claim.

[As amended effective Sept. 19, 1990, July 29, 1993, Jan. 22, 1998, July 17, 2002, and Nov. 30, 2005.]

Official Note No. 1: The amendments to standards 1-1.1 and 1-1.2, effective July 17, 2002, changing "90 days" to "180 days," shall apply to all petitions for a writ of habeas corpus arising from a judgment of death that were pending before the Supreme Court on July 17, 2002, and to all such petitions filed after that date. *[Note added by Supreme Court order, July 26, 2002.]*

Official Note No. 2: The amendments to standards 1-1.1 and 1-1.2, effective November 30, 2005, changing "24 months" to "36 months," shall apply to all petitions for a writ of habeas corpus arising from a judgment of death that were pending before the Supreme Court on November 30, 2005, and to all such petitions filed after that date. *[Note added by Supreme Court order, Nov. 30, 2005.]*

1-1.3. [Repealed effective Jan. 22, 1998]

1-2. If a petition is filed after substantial delay, the petitioner must demonstrate good cause for the delay. A petitioner may establish good cause by showing particular circumstances sufficient to justify substantial delay.

1-3. Any petition that fails to comply with these requirements may be denied as untimely.

1-4. The court may toll the 180-day period of presumptive timeliness for the filing of a capital-related habeas corpus petition (which begins to run from the final due date to file the appellant's reply brief in the appeal) when it authorizes the appellant to file supplemental briefing. The court will not toll before the 180-day presumptive timeliness period begins to run or after it has finished running.

Ordinarily, the court will toll the 180-day presumptive timeliness period only when the appellant is represented by the same counsel on appeal and also for related habeas corpus/executive clemency proceedings.

If the court determines that it will toll such 180-day presumptive timeliness period, it will so provide in its order authorizing the appellant to file supplemental briefing.

When the court provides for tolling of the 180-day presumptive timeliness period in its order authorizing the appellant to file supplemental briefing, it will determine a reasonable period of time for the appellant to devote to whatever supplemental briefing is authorized, add that period of time to the final due date to file the appellant's reply brief in the appeal, and indicate the new date by which the appellant may file a presumptively timely habeas corpus petition.

Other than under these circumstances, the court will not toll, or otherwise extend, the period in which to file a presumptively timely capital-related habeas corpus petition.

[Standard adopted effective Nov. 20, 2002.]

2. Compensation standards

2-1. This court's appointment of appellate counsel for a person under a sentence of death is for the following: (i) pleadings and proceedings related to preparation and certification of the appellate record; (ii) representation in the direct appeal before the California Supreme Court; (iii) preparation and filing of a petition for a writ of certiorari, or an answer thereto, in the United States Supreme Court and, if certiorari is granted, preparation and filing of a brief or briefs on the merits and preparation and presentation of oral argument; and (iv) representation in the trial court relating to proceedings pursuant to Penal Code section 1193.

This court's appointment of habeas corpus counsel for a person under a sentence of death shall be made simultaneously with appointment of appellate counsel or at the earliest practicable time thereafter. The appointment of habeas corpus counsel is for the following: (i) investigation, and preparation and filing (if warranted), of a habeas corpus petition in the California Supreme Court, including any informal briefing and evidentiary hearing ordered by the court and any petition to exhaust state remedies; (ii) representation in the trial court relating to proceedings pursuant to Penal Code section 1227; and (iii) representation in executive clemency proceedings before the Governor of California.

Absent prior authorization by this court, this court will not compensate counsel for the filing of any other motion, petition, or pleading in any other California or federal court or court of another state. Counsel who seek compensation for representation in another court should secure appointment by, and compensation from, that court.

[As amended effective Dec. 22, 1993, Jan. 22, 1998, and Feb. 4, 1998.]

2-2. Habeas corpus counsel should expeditiously investigate potentially meritorious bases for filing a petition for a writ of habeas corpus. If the timing of separate appointments permits, this investigation should be done concurrently with appellate counsel's review of the appellate record and briefing on appeal, and in any event, in cooperation with appellate counsel.

[As amended effective Dec. 21, 1992, and Jan. 22, 1998.]

2-2.1. In all cases in which counsel was appointed on or after the October 12, 1997, enactment of Senate Bill No. 513 (Stats. 1997, ch. 869), counsel, without prior authorization of the court, may incur expenses up to a total of $25,000 for habeas corpus investigation, and may submit claims to the court for reimbursement up to that amount. Investigative expenses include travel associated with habeas corpus investigation, and services of law clerks, paralegals, and others serving as habeas corpus investigators. The reasonable cost of photocopying defense counsel's trial files is not considered an investigative expense, and will be separately reimbursed. The court will reimburse counsel for expenses up to $25,000 that were reasonably incurred pursuant to the duty to investigate as described in standard 1-1, but it will not authorize counsel to expend, nor will it reimburse counsel for, habeas corpus investigation expenses exceeding $25,000 before the issuance of an order to show cause. This policy applies to both hourly ("time and costs") and fixed fee appointments.

The policy described in the foregoing paragraph shall also apply to those cases in which counsel was appointed prior to October 12, 1997 (the enactment of Sen. Bill No. 513), and in which, by January 22, 1998, the effective date of the above-described policy, the defendant has not filed a habeas corpus petition in this court and no more than 90 days [now 180 days] have passed since the final due date for the filing of the appellant's reply brief on direct appeal.

As to those cases in which, by January 1, 2008 (the effective date of Assem. Bill No. 1248), the defendant has not filed a capital-related habeas corpus petition in this court and the date by which to file a presumptively timely petition has not yet passed, counsel may be reimbursed up to $50,000 for those investigative services and expenses incurred on or after that date. Such investigative funding for expenses incurred after January 1, 2008, also is available in those cases in which a presumptively timely petition has been filed by January 1, 2008, but petitioner's reply to the informal response has not been filed and the time to do so (with any extensions of time) has not passed as of that date.

[As amended effective Jan. 16, 2002, and Jan. 1, 2008; standard adopted effective Jan. 22, 1998.]

2-2.2. In all cases in which counsel was appointed on an hourly basis prior to October 12, 1997, and in which, by January 22, 1998, either a petition for a writ of habeas corpus has been filed in this court, or more than 90 days have passed since the final due date for the filing of the appellant's reply brief on direct appeal, requests by appointed counsel for authorization to incur, and reimbursement of, investigation expenses shall be governed by the following standards (2-2.3 through 2-4.4):

2-2.3. Without prior authorization of the court, counsel may incur expenses up to a total of $3,000 for habeas corpus investigation relating to a death penalty judgment, and may submit claims to the court for reimbursement up to that amount. The court will reimburse counsel for expenses up to $3,000 that were reasonably incurred pursuant to the duty to investigate as described in standard 1-1.

2-2.4. If after incurring $3,000 in investigation expenses (or if $3,000 in reimbursement for investigation funds previously has been granted on behalf of the same defendant/petitioner with regard to the same underlying death penalty judgment), counsel determines it is necessary to incur additional expenses for which he or she plans to seek reimbursement from the court, counsel must seek and obtain prior authorization from the court. As a general rule, the court will *not* reimburse counsel for expenses exceeding $3,000, without prior authorization of the court. Requests by appointed counsel for prior authorization to incur investigation expenses shall be governed by the following standards.

2-3. Counsel shall file with this court a "Confidential request for authorization to incur expenses to investigate potential habeas corpus issues," showing good cause why the request was not filed on or before the date the appellant's opening brief on appeal was filed.

[As amended effective Dec. 21, 1992, and Jan. 22, 1998.]

2-4. The confidential request for authorization to incur expenses shall set out:

2-4.1. The issues to be explored;

2-4.2. Specific facts that suggest there may be an issue of possible merit;

2-4.3. An itemized list of the expenses requested for each issue of the proposed habeas corpus petition; and

2-4.4. (a) An itemized listing of all expenses previously sought from, and/or approved by any court of this state and/or any federal court in connection with any habeas corpus proceeding or investigation concerning the same judgment and petitioner; (b) A statement summarizing the status of any proceeding or investigation in any court of this state and/or any federal court concerning the same judgment and petitioner; and (c) A copy of any related petition previously filed in any trial and/or lower appellate court of this state and/or any federal court concerning the same judgment and petitioner.

[As amended effective Jan. 27, 1992, and Dec. 21, 1992.]

2-5. Counsel generally will not be awarded compensation for fees and expenses relating to matters that are clearly not cognizable in a petition for a writ of habeas corpus.

[As renumbered effective Dec. 21, 1992.]

2-6. When a petition is pending in this court to exhaust claims presented in a federal habeas corpus petition, a request by counsel for investigative funds to bolster or augment claims already presented in the petition normally will be denied absent a showing of strong justification for the request. A request for investigative funds may be granted if the petitioner demonstrates that he or she has timely discovered new and potentially meritorious areas of investigation not previously addressed in the petitioner's federal or state petitions. This has been the internal operating policy of the court since December 16, 1992.

[Standard adopted effective June 20, 1996.]

2-7. Each request for fees relating to a habeas corpus petition must be accompanied by: (a) An itemized listing of all fees previously sought from, and/or approved by any court of this state and/or any federal court in connection with any habeas corpus proceeding or investigation concerning the same judgment and petitioner; (b) A statement summarizing the status of any proceeding or investigation in any court of this state and/or any federal court concerning the same judgment and petitioner; and (c) A copy of any related petition previously filed in any trial and/or lower appellate court of this state and/or any federal court concerning the same judgment and petitioner.

[As renumbered and amended effective Dec. 21, 1992, and as renumbered effective June 20, 1996.]

2-8. In a case in which the court orders an evidentiary hearing, and counsel and the court do not enter into a "fixed fee and expenses agreement" covering the evidentiary hearing (see "Guideline 10" of the "Guidelines for Fixed Fee Appointments, on Optional Basis, to Automatic Appeals and Related Habeas Corpus Proceedings in the California Supreme Court"), requests for reimbursement of necessary and reasonable expenses incurred in preparation for and presentation of the evidentiary hearing shall be governed by the following standards:

2-8.1. Counsel may incur "incidental" expenses (i.e., travel to and from the evidentiary hearing and related hearings before the referee, meals and lodging during the hearing, telephone charges, photocopying, etc.) without prior approval, and the court will reimburse counsel for such itemized, reasonable and necessarily incurred expenses pursuant to the court's "Payment Guidelines for Appointed Counsel Representing Indigent Criminal Appellants in the California Supreme Court," part III ("Necessary Expenses").

2-8.2. Counsel should seek and obtain from this court prior approval for all investigation and witness expenses, including, but not limited to, investigator fees and costs, expert fees and costs, and expert witness fees and costs.

2-8.3. Counsel may submit requests for reimbursement of expenses every 60 days to this court, and will be reimbursed for necessary and reasonable expenses consistently with part III of the "Payment Guidelines," *supra.*

[Standard adopted effective Jan. 22, 1997.]

Policy Statement 4.   Service of process by counsel for defendant.

Consistently with longstanding practice and court policy, except as specified below, counsel for the defendant must serve his or her client, any separate counsel of record in any matter related to the same judgment, counsel of record for every other party, the trial court, the assisting entity or attorney for counsel for the defendant and any separate counsel of record, and trial counsel, with a copy of each motion, request for extension of time, brief, petition or other public document filed in this court or in the trial court on the client's behalf, including any supporting declaration, with attached proof of service. A declaration submitted in support of any motion or request may refer to and incorporate by reference matters set forth in a current "confidential 60-day status report" simultaneously provided only to this court. Counsel also must serve any additional person or entity as requested by this court.

Counsel for the defendant need not serve (1) trial counsel with any matter upon or after the filing in this court of the certified record on appeal; (2) the trial court with any extension-of-time request related to appellate briefing; and (3) the trial court or trial counsel with any matter related to habeas corpus briefing.

If counsel for the defendant elects to serve the defendant personally with the document, counsel may indicate on the proof of service the date by which counsel will so serve the defendant (not to exceed 30 calendar days), and counsel shall thereafter notify the court in writing that the defendant has been served. In the alternative, counsel for the defendant need not serve the defendant with any specific document to be filed if counsel for the defendant attaches to the proof of service for that specific document (1) a declaration by the defendant stating that he or she does not wish to be served with that specific document, and (2) a declaration by counsel for the defendant stating that he or she has described to the defendant the substance and purpose of that specific document.

[Policy amended effective Dec. 19, 2001.]

SUPREME COURT OF CALIFORNIA

Appendix to Supreme Court Policies Regarding Cases Arising From Judgments of Death Concerning Appointed Counsel's Duties

Procedures and policies adopted by the California Supreme Court on August 22, 2001, as amended July 27, 2005, and May 18, 2011, and March 19, 2014

Counsel appointed in capital matters must be familiar with the duties set forth in the timeliness standards and compensation standards contained in the Supreme Court Policies Regarding Cases Arising From Judgments of Death, which are published periodically in Advance Pamphlets of the California Official Reports, in the "Rules" pages, and available on the website www.courts.ca.gov/5641.htm, and in desktop versions of the California Rules of Court. Important aspects of these policies are reiterated below in part I. Counsel is responsible for keeping up to date regarding any amendments to these policies. In addition, counsel must be familiar with the additional duties set forth in part II of this Appendix. For questions regarding the Policies or this Appendix, counsel should contact the court's Capital Appointment Coordinator/Advisor.

I. DUTIES STATED IN THE POLICIES

Appellate counsel in a capital case must take and maintain detailed, understandable, and computerized transcript notes, and must compile and maintain a detailed list of potentially meritorious habeas corpus issues that have come to appellate counsel's attention. Moreover, if appellate counsel's appointment does not include related habeas corpus/executive clemency representation, until separate postconviction habeas corpus/executive clemency counsel ("habeas corpus" counsel) is appointed, appellate counsel must preserve evidence that comes to his or her attention if that evidence appears relevant to a potential habeas corpus investigation. (Supreme Ct. Policies Regarding Cases Arising From Judgments of Death, policy 3, std. 1-1, 1st par.)

After separate habeas corpus counsel is appointed, appellate counsel must deliver to habeas corpus counsel copies of the list of potentially meritorious habeas corpus issues, copies of the transcript notes, and any preserved evidence relevant to a potential habeas corpus investigation, and thereafter must update the "issues list" and the computerized transcript notes as warranted. Moreover, appellate counsel must consult with and work cooperatively with habeas corpus counsel to facilitate a timely investigation, and the timely preparation and filing (if warranted) of a habeas corpus petition by appointed habeas corpus counsel. (Policy 3, std. 1-1, 1st par.)

Appointed appellate counsel's scope of representation includes the preparation and certification of the record on appeal; representation in the direct appeal before the California Supreme Court; preparation and filing of a petition for a writ of certiorari, or an answer thereto, in the United States Supreme Court, and, if certiorari is granted, preparation and filing of a brief or briefs on the merits, and preparation and presentation of oral argument; and representation in the trial court relating to proceedings to set an execution date pursuant to Penal Code section 1193. (Policy 3, std. 2-1, 1st par.)

Appointed habeas corpus counsel's scope of representation includes the investigation, and preparation and filing (if warranted), of a habeas corpus petition in the Supreme Court, including any informal briefing and evidentiary hearing ordered by the court and any petition to exhaust state remedies; representation in the trial court relating to proceedings to set an execution date pursuant to Penal Code section 1227; and representation in executive clemency proceedings before the Governor of California. (Policy 3, std. 2-1, 2d par.)

As noted, habeas corpus counsel in a capital case has a duty to investigate factual and legal grounds for the filing of a petition for a writ of habeas corpus. The duty to investigate is limited to investigating potentially meritorious grounds for relief that come to counsel's attention

in the course of reviewing appellate counsel's list of potentially meritorious habeas corpus issues, the transcript notes prepared by appellate counsel, the appellate record, trial counsel's existing case files, and the appellate briefs, and in the course of making reasonable efforts to discuss the case with the defendant, trial counsel, and appellate counsel. (Policy 3, std. 1-1, 2d par.)

Habeas corpus counsel's duty to investigate does not impose on such counsel an obligation to conduct, nor does it authorize the expenditure of public funds for, an unfocused investigation having as its object uncovering all possible factual bases for a collateral attack on the judgment of death. Instead, habeas corpus counsel has a duty to investigate potential habeas corpus claims only if counsel has become aware of information that might reasonably lead to actual facts supporting a potentially meritorious claim. (Policy 3, std. 1-1, 2d par.) A petition for a writ of habeas corpus will be presumed to be filed without substantial delay if it is filed within 180 days after the final due date for the filing of the appellant's reply brief on the direct appeal, or within 36 months after appointment of habeas corpus counsel, *whichever is later*. (Policy 3, stds. 1-1.1 & 1-1.2, as amended eff. Nov. 30, 2005; see also, *In re Robbins* (1998) 18 Cal.4th 770.)

In the event that more than one counsel is appointed to represent the same defendant jointly, either in a capital appeal, in related habeas corpus/executive clemency proceedings in the Supreme Court or in both classes of proceedings upon an "appellate/habeas corpus" appointment, one such attorney must be designated as lead counsel for each *separate* appointment. Lead counsel is responsible for the overall conduct of the case (i.e., the capital appeal, the related habeas corpus/executive clemency proceedings or, in appellate/habeas corpus representation, both classes of proceedings) and for supervising the work of appointed associate counsel and any nonappointed, supervised counsel. (Cal. Rules of Court, rule 8.605(c)(2); see also, Advisory Com. com. to subd. (c).)

II. ADDITIONAL DUTIES OF APPOINTED COUNSEL

A. Cooperation with Assisting Entity or Counsel

Appellate counsel and habeas corpus counsel also have a duty to cooperate, as a condition of the appointment, with the assisting entity or counsel designated by the Supreme Court to provide outside consultation and resource assistance to appointed counsel. Appointed counsel's cooperation and close working relationship with his or her assisting entity or counsel are important to achieving the common goal of maintaining a high level of legal representation in all capital appeals and related habeas corpus/executive clemency proceedings.

The Supreme Court requires the assisting entity or counsel to report to it periodically and in detail on appointed counsel's case progress. The court places considerable weight on these reports in determining compensation of counsel and whether counsel should be given additional capital case appointments.

Assisting entities that may be designated in this capacity include, as appropriate, the California Appellate Project (CAP) in San Francisco, the Office of the State Public Defender (OSPD), and the Habeas Corpus Resource Center (HCRC). (See Cal. Rules of Court, rule 8.605(c)(5).) In the event the designated assisting entity or counsel has a conflict of interest, the Supreme Court will designate an alternative assisting entity, or an experienced private capital appellate and/or habeas corpus practitioner, as appropriate.

Appointed counsel's obligation to cooperate with other appointed counsel and the assisting entity or counsel includes the following duties:

1. Appellate counsel must promptly make available to the assisting entity or counsel, for review, the above-described computerized transcript notes and detailed list of potentially meritorious habeas corpus issues, as well as a list of potential issues on the direct appeal.
2. Upon a request from the assisting entity or counsel, and after consultation with the Capital Appointment Coordinator/Advisor, appellate counsel must either make a copy of relevant portions of the record available to that entity or counsel for its review, or permit the assisting entity or counsel to photocopy the record.
3. Both appellate and habeas corpus counsel must promptly initiate and maintain communication with the defendant/appellant, trial counsel, and any separately appointed counsel.
4. Both appellate and habeas corpus counsel must review carefully all manuals, newsletters, and other materials distributed by any assist-

ing entity or counsel, and make appropriate use of the resources available in brief and information banks.

5. Unless the Supreme Court advises counsel otherwise, both appellate and habeas corpus counsel are expected to attend post-appointment training programs presented by the assisting entities or counsel.

6. Habeas corpus counsel must submit to the assisting entity or counsel a detailed outline of potential habeas corpus issues to be investigated and a proposed investigation plan, and must conduct a prompt investigation, as described above, of any potentially meritorious habeas corpus issues.

7. Appellate counsel must maintain ongoing consultation with the assisting entity or counsel regarding possible appellate issues; drafts of motions, pleadings, and briefs; and oral argument. The court anticipates that all appointed counsel will participate in a moot court in preparation for oral argument.

8. Both appellate and habeas corpus counsel must consult with the assisting entity or counsel regarding the amount of time appointed counsel plans to spend researching the direct appeal and/or conducting a habeas corpus investigation. In so doing, appointed counsel must consult, and be guided by, the Supreme Court's (a) Policy 3 timeliness standards and compensation standards, referenced above, as well as the court's (b) "time and costs" payment guidelines and (c) "fixed fee" guidelines. The time-and-costs payment guidelines and the fixed fee guidelines are published periodically in Advance Pamphlets of the California Official Reports, in the "Rules" pages, together with the Policies. These and related materials are available on the website www.courts.ca.gov/5641.htm, and in desktop versions of the California Rules of Court. The court's Internal Operating Practices and Procedures are published periodically in Advance Pamphlets of the California Official Reports in the "Rules" pages, and are available on the website www.courts.ca.gov/2007_Supreme_Court_Booklet.pdf, and in desktop versions of the California Rules of Court.

9. Both appellate and habeas corpus counsel must submit drafts of all motions, pleadings, briefs, petitions and replies, investigation plans, etc., to the assisting entity or counsel for review, allowing sufficient time for that review and for incorporating appropriate suggested changes into the final document.

10. Both appellate and habeas corpus counsel must provide the assisting entity or counsel with copies of all court orders, motions, pleadings, briefs, petitions, replies and responses, etc., filed by appointed counsel and by counsel for the respondent.

The Supreme Court anticipates that all appointed counsel will comply with these duties and provide the foregoing level of cooperation with other appointed counsel and with the assisting entity or counsel. The court will consider appointed counsel's cooperation and compliance with these duties in determining counsel's compensation (either fixed fee or time-and-costs) and counsel's suitability for subsequent appointments. Also, unless counsel has substantially complied with these duties, the assisting entity or counsel may be unable to submit the substantial compliance letter required under fixed fee guideline 5 ("Progress Payments").

If appointed counsel, or the assisting entity or counsel, identifies problems in complying with these duties, appointed counsel, or the assisting entity or counsel, should promptly notify the Capital Appointment Coordinator/Advisor.

B. Other Duties of Appointed Counsel Procedures as adopted by the California Supreme Court on August 22, 2001, and amended July 27, 2005, May 18, 2011, and March 19, 2014

1. Contents of Declarations in Support of Extension of Time (EOT) Applications

Any declaration submitted in support of an EOT request must include the following:

a. The original due date for the uncompleted matter for which an EOT is sought; the total amount of time that has elapsed since that date; and the number of prior extensions requested and granted or denied.

b. The number of pages in the record on appeal, as follows: (a) the number of pages in the combined record on appeal, both reporter's and clerk's transcripts, *including* juror questionnaires, and (b) the number of pages in the combined record on appeal, *excluding* the

juror questionnaires. (This information is not required if the EOT request concerns only habeas corpus briefing.)

c. A good faith estimate of the percentage of work accomplished to date, with regard to the uncompleted matter for which an EOT is sought. A good faith estimate of the amount of time required for the remaining work to be done, with regard to the uncompleted matter for which an EOT is sought, and a proposed target date for the filing of that matter.

Pursuant to the court's longstanding practice, extensions of time for briefing in automatic appeals and informal briefing and post-order to show cause briefing in habeas corpus proceedings will be granted in up to 60-day intervals.

2. Confidential Status Report (CSR) of Appointed Counsel and Assisting Entity or Counsel

In accordance with longstanding court practice, until appointed appellate counsel files the appellant's opening brief, and until appointed habeas corpus/executive clemency counsel files a capital-related state habeas corpus petition, a current CSR must be submitted every 60 days. Lead appointed counsel must serve a copy of the CSR on the assisting entity or attorney and on any appointed associate counsel, and must submit proof of service with the report. A CSR submitted by appointed counsel must include the following:

a. Current case status, including a good faith estimate of the percentage of work accomplished to date with regard to each pending uncompleted task.

b. Progress during the last 60 days.

c. Problems and reasons for any delay.

d. Future plans, including a good faith estimate of the amount of time it will take for the remaining work to be done as to each pending uncompleted task, and a proposed target date for completion of each such task.

Whenever appointed appellate counsel has filed a request for an EOT to file the appellant's opening brief or appellant's reply brief, or appointed habeas corpus/executive clemency counsel has filed a request for an EOT to file the reply to an informal response to a petition for a writ of habeas corpus, and the court has subsequently denied that request, appointed counsel must submit to the court and serve upon the assisting entity or attorney a CSR as described above 30 days after the court's order denying the request and every 30 days thereafter until the brief or reply has been filed.

In addition, the assisting entity or attorney must also submit to the court 30 days after the date of the court's order and every 30 days thereafter until the brief or reply is filed a CSR providing the following:

a. The assisting entity's or attorney's assessment of current case status, including a good faith estimate of the percentage of work accomplished to date with regard to each pending uncompleted task.

b. The assisting entity's or attorney's assessment of appointed counsel's progress during the last 30 days.

c. The assisting entity's or attorney's views regarding any problems and the reasons for delay.

d. Future plans and arrangements appointed counsel and the assisting entity or attorney have made, including the assisting entity's or attorney's good faith estimate of the date when the brief or reply will be filed.

The assisting entity or attorney must serve a copy of the CSR on the lead appointed counsel and any appointed associate counsel being assisted, and must submit proof of service with the report.

3. Supplemental Declarations and Confidential Status Reports

As appropriate, counsel of record may be requested to submit a supplemental declaration to establish good cause for any requested EOT. Similarly, appointed counsel, as appropriate, may be requested to submit a supplemental CSR.

4. Certification or Declaration of Contents of Confidential Status Reports are Made Under Penalty of Perjury

In all automatic appeals and capital-related habeas corpus proceedings in which appointed counsel of record is required to submit a periodic CSR, and in all such cases and proceedings in which appointed counsel is not required to submit a CSR but nevertheless chooses to do so, the CSR must contain a certification or declaration under penalty of perjury by lead counsel that the contents of the CSR are true and correct. (Code Civ. Proc., § 2015.5.)

5. *Proof of Service*

In all automatic appeals and capital-related habeas corpus proceedings in which counsel of record is required to provide the court with the original of a proof of service (Policy 4, Supreme Court Policies Regarding Cases Arising From Judgments of Death ["Service of process by counsel for defendant"]), such delivery must be evidenced by a certification or declaration under penalty of perjury. (Code Civ. Proc., § 2015.5.)

PAYMENT GUIDELINES FOR APPOINTED COUNSEL REPRESENTING INDIGENT CRIMINAL APPELLANTS IN THE CALIFORNIA SUPREME COURT

(Revised September 19, 1990, and December 22, 1993)

(Amended effective September 1, 1995, January 1, 1997, July 30, 1997, January 22, 1998, February 4, 1998, January 16, 2002, August 25, 2004, October 1, 2005, November 30, 2005, July 1, 2006, October 1, 2007, July 23, 2008, August 27, 2008, and March 5, 2012)

I. INTRODUCTION

The California Supreme Court determines the compensation of appointed counsel representing indigent criminal appellants. The guidelines set forth below are a general statement of the factors considered by the court in determining appropriate compensation for the time devoted to indigent criminal appeals (and related habeas corpus representation) and the reasonable and necessary expenses incurred by appointed counsel. In reviewing these guidelines, counsel should bear in mind the following:

A. Although most of the guidelines apply routinely, the application of others, such as the reimbursement of travel expenses or of the cost of expert witnesses and investigators, depends on the circumstances of each case.

B. The rates in the guidelines are subject to periodic change. These include the hourly compensation of appointed counsel, mileage and per diem rates for travel, and rates for the reimbursement of the cost of services by others.

C. For the most current information concerning these matters, and the payment guidelines generally, counsel are encouraged to contact the California Appellate Project (CAP). CAP is the appointed counsel administrator that assists private counsel with automatic appeals. CAP's address and telephone number are as follows:

California Appellate Project
101 Second Street, Suite 600
San Francisco, CA 94105
(415) 495-0500

II. REASONABLE COMPENSATION

A. Compensation rate The compensation rate for members of the State Bar of California who are appointed as counsel in indigent criminal appeals is the same allowable-hour rate appointed counsel received or was eligible to receive in the Court of Appeal, except for automatic appeals and/or related habeas corpus/executive clemency proceedings, for which the rate is $145 per allowable hour.

B. "Allowable hours" The compensation rate is multiplied by the number of "allowable hours" of appellate work to determine a reasonable sum for compensation. Benchmarks for "allowable hours" in capital cases (i.e., an estimate of the time an attorney experienced in the handling of criminal appeals might devote to the various stages of capital litigation) are set out below, in part II.*I*.3.

C. Recording of hours Appointed counsel should record the number of hours devoted to the following phases of appellate work:
1. Record review
2. Record correction
3. Motions and applications
4. Sixty-day status reports
5. Researching and writing opening brief
6. Researching and writing reply brief
7. Researching and writing supplemental brief(s)
8. Investigating and writing habeas corpus petition
9. Reply to response(s) to habeas corpus petition
10. Evidentiary hearing
11. Oral argument (includes preparation)
12. Post-oral argument representation
13. Rehearing petition or opposition
14. Certiorari petition or opposition (and briefing and argument in the United States Supreme Court after grant of certiorari; see post, subpart *I*.3.(i))
15. Client communication
16. Travel
17. Other services (specify)

D. Factors considered by the court The following factors are considered by the court in determining the number of allowable hours:
1. Whether the billed hours are within the benchmarks, or whether there exists good cause to depart from the benchmarks.
2. Length of the record.
3. Complexity and novelty of the legal issues.
4. Quality of work.

E. Exceptional procedural matters Counsel should provide the court with an explanation of the time spent on exceptional procedural matters, such as repeated applications for augmentation of the record on appeal.

F. Travel time Travel time will be compensated to the extent that the time could not reasonably be spent working on the case.

G. Circumstances warranting additional compensation If counsel believes there exist extraordinary circumstances that justify compensation beyond that set out in these guidelines, counsel should bring such factors to the attention of the court at the time a claim for payment of compensation and expenses is presented. Counsel's showing of justification should be commensurate with the extent to which he or she seeks to exceed the benchmarks.

H. Submission of payment requests Counsel may submit a request for payment of compensation and expenses every 90 days.

I. Special rules for capital cases The following rules apply to capital cases only:
1. *Delay in certification of record or filing of brief* If delay in the certification of the record on appeal or in the filing of the appellant's opening brief (AOB) is due to a lack of diligence on the part of appointed counsel, payment of compensation will be deferred until the record is certified or the AOB is filed.
2. *Forms and reports* Counsel must submit a cumulative hours compensation form and the most recent status report with every request for payment. The cumulative hours compensation form will be provided by the court or may be obtained from CAP. Counsel should retain a copy of each cumulative hours compensation form submitted. These forms will facilitate completion of the data form for automatic appeals, which must accompany the request for final payment for services rendered in this court. Note that although a request for payment may be submitted every 90 days, a current status report must be submitted every 60 days.
3. *"Allowable hours" benchmarks* The court, after consultation with representatives of a cross-section of the criminal justice bar, has established the following benchmarks for the various stages of capital representation:

(i) APPEAL

Reading the record and producing detailed, understandable and computerized transcript notes:	40 pp./hr.
Record correction:	20–120 hrs.
Client communication:	15–30 hrs.
Appellant's opening brief (AOB):	260–600 hrs.
Appellant's reply brief (ARB):	55–160 hrs.

Oral argument:	40–80 hrs.
Supplemental briefs:	20–80 hrs.
Rehearing petition:	25–75 hrs.
Certiorari petition:	40–75 hrs.

Briefing and argument in the United States Supreme Court after grant of certiorari:

Counsel shall seek compensation for such services from the United States Supreme Court. Should that court deny compensation for such services, this court will authorize reasonable compensation for such services up to a maximum of $6,000.

(ii) HABEAS CORPUS
a. Investigation and Presentation of Petition

(For cases in which appellate counsel also handles habeas corpus responsibilities):
Client communication related to habeas corpus investigation: Up to 60 hours, as follows: Up to 30 hrs. in the first year after appointment; and up to 15 hrs. per year thereafter.

Investigate and present habeas corpus petition:	140–400 hrs.

(For cases in which separate appointed counsel handles habeas corpus responsibilities):
Client communication related to habeas corpus investigation: Up to 70 hours, as follows: Up to 40 hrs. in the first year after appointment; and up to 15 hrs. per year thereafter.

Record review:	50 pp./hr.
Investigate and present habeas corpus petition:	180–500 hrs.
For all cases:	
Informal reply:	50–120 hrs.
Traverse:	50–120 hrs.

b. Habeas Corpus Evidentiary Hearing

Preparation:	150–600 hrs.
Evidentiary hearing:	72–144 hrs.
	(i.e., 3–6 days)
Post-hearing litigation before the referee:	75–125 hrs.

These benchmarks apply collectively to all counsel, appointed and supervised, who are engaged in work related to a habeas corpus evidentiary hearing, and are not multiplied, or otherwise increased, by virtue of the fact that more than one attorney is participating in this work.

c. Post-Hearing Briefs in the Supreme Court

Brief on the merits, response brief, and supplemental brief:	50–150 hrs.

d. Habeas Corpus Proceedings Returnable in Superior Court Following Order to Show Cause on Alleged Mental Retardation of Condemned Inmate

The "allowable hours" benchmark ranges for habeas corpus proceedings after issuance of an order to show cause, including any traverse to the return, and preparation for, or presentation at, an evidentiary hearing, as set forth in Payment Guideline II, subpart *I*.3.(ii), apply to all habeas corpus proceedings following an order to show cause issued by the Supreme Court, including any order to show cause returnable to the superior court regarding a condemned inmate's alleged mental retardation and resulting ineligibility for the death penalty within the meaning of *Atkins v. Virginia* (2002) 536 U.S. 304.

Before requesting compensation from the Supreme Court for attorney fees related to such *Atkins* litigation in superior court, appointed counsel first must obtain the superior court's recommendation for payment of the incurred hours. However, the superior court's recommendation is not binding on the Supreme Court, which will, in all cases, exercise independent review concerning attorney fees recommended for payment by the superior court.

These requirements apply to all such fee requests, for *Atkins* litigation

in superior court, pending before the Supreme Court on or after March 5, 2012.

(iii) EXECUTIVE CLEMENCY

Representation in executive clemency proceedings before the Governor of California:	40–80 hrs.

These benchmarks are guidelines for the expected hours in "typical" cases, and are neither ceilings nor floors for fees in any given case. The court will continue to monitor its fee payment data to determine whether adjustment of the benchmarks is warranted in the future. Counsel is advised to review the benchmarks carefully, and to bear the following in mind throughout the course of representation (i.e., at each "stage" of the litigation):

a. *The "lower range" of the benchmarks* A case that has a relatively short record (i.e., 3,000-6,000 pages), and that raises standard (albeit fact-specific) issues already resolved in prior cases, should generally produce hours near or below the "lower range" of the benchmarks. Based on experience, the court expects a substantial percentage of cases to be completed under the lower range of the benchmarks. Counsel should determine at an early stage of representation whether the case meets the description of a "lower range" case. If counsel has such a case, and submits a fee request substantially exceeding the lower range of the benchmarks for any particular stage of the litigation, he or she must include in each request a detailed explanation of why fees exceeding the lower range of the benchmarks should be awarded. The court will award fees substantially exceeding the appropriate benchmark range only if it is convinced that on the facts of the case, such fees are warranted.

b. *The "upper range" of the benchmarks* Based on experience, the court anticipates a number of cases will produce fee hours at or near the upper range of the benchmarks, and occasionally, over that range. The following important caveats apply in such cases:
The upper range of the benchmarks is generally reserved for those cases with relatively long records (i.e., 10,000 or more pages), *and* that raise novel or difficult issues. The mere fact that the record may be long does *not* indicate that "upper range" or "over-benchmark" hours will be appropriate in any or each stage of the litigation.
If a case does not meet the above description of an "upper range" or "over-benchmark" case, counsel should not expect to receive "upper range" or "over-benchmark" fees. In order to secure such fees in a case not otherwise meeting the above description, counsel must include in the request a detailed explanation of why the fees requested should be awarded. The court will award fees near or exceeding the appropriate benchmark range only if it is convinced that on the facts of the case, such fees are warranted.

4. *Second counsel "override"* In cases in which appointed counsel deems it necessary to associate with second counsel, and the court approves the association, the court may in its discretion, and on a showing of good cause, approve compensation to appointed counsel for hours incurred exceeding the "appeal" through "habeas corpus briefing" benchmarks by 5-15 percent. As a general rule the court will allow the full 15 percent override in cases in which counsel divides the hours fairly evenly for the stage for which fees are sought. If counsel divides the work less evenly, the override will be diminished accordingly. The court will continue to monitor the cases to determine whether the 15 percent ceiling should be increased.

III. NECESSARY EXPENSES

A. Items not qualifying as expenses The hourly fee should cover all overhead related to a case, *including secretarial services, word processing, and the like*. Expenses listed below will be reimbursed to the extent they are itemized, reasonable, and necessarily incurred during the course of the appeal, and otherwise comply with the court's procedures (see below, part III.B). Note that these guidelines apply not only to appointed counsel, but to those persons, including experts and investigators, who assist appointed counsel with the appeal.

B. Prior approval Prior approval is required for extraordinary expenses, such as for out-of-state travel, expert witnesses and investigators. *In capital cases,* expense requests are governed by the court's "Standards

Governing Filing of Habeas Corpus Petitions and Compensation of Counsel in Relation to Such Petitions," published in the Official Reports advance sheet pamphlets. (See *id.*, std. 2-1 et seq.)

C. Reimbursable expenses In general, when making a request for reimbursement, counsel must itemize *all* expenses, and must provide in the request the original receipts for the following: (i) travel expenses (airfare, car rental, hotel bills, etc.) over $47 per day; (ii) telephone and copying expenses over $50 and $100 per month, respectively (see below); and (iii) all other single transactions that exceed $100. Counsel should keep all receipts in the event documentation is later required.

1. *Photocopying* The cost of photocopying will be reimbursed, at not more than 10 cents per page, whether the copying is done inside or outside counsel's office. If counsel represents that photocopying was billed at 10 cents per page or less, receipts will not be required unless the expenses are in excess of $100 per month.

   In addition to investigative expenses as set forth in the "Supreme Court Policies Regarding Cases Arising From Judgments of Death," Policy 3, standard 2-2.1, counsel appointed to handle habeas corpus/executive clemency representation will be reimbursed the reasonable cost of photocopying defense counsel's trial files, at the rate of not more than 10 cents per page, after filing of the certified record on appeal. Counsel must provide a receipt or invoice showing the number of pages copied, and the cost per page. Reimbursement will not be paid for photocopying of items already contained in the record on appeal, such as daily transcripts or exhibits.

2. *Postage and delivery costs* Expenses for express mail/messenger service will be reimbursed only on a showing that use of express mail/messenger service was necessary and reasonable.

3. *Telephone charges* Receipts will not be required unless the expenses are in excess of $50 per month.

4. *Travel expenses*

   a. The court will determine the reasonableness and necessity of travel expenses on a case-by-case basis. Counsel are cautioned that travel expenses are not considered necessary when the purpose of a trip may reasonably be accomplished in another way, such as by telephone or correspondence. Further, counsel should use the least expensive alternative means of travel. For motor vehicles, the mileage rate is the prevailing amount established by the Administrative Office of the Courts.

   b. When travel is required by appointed counsel or a person authorized to assist appointed counsel, reasonable and necessary meals and lodging may be claimed, to the extent allowed under State Board of Control rules. Counsel should contact CAP for further information.

   c. Some of the lesser known provisions of the Board of Control rules are as follows:

   (1) The per diem allowance does not apply for trips of 25 miles or less.

   (2) Lunch is not covered unless the travel period is 24 hours or more.

   (3) The cost of collision coverage in a contract for a rental car is not covered.

5. *Computerized legal research* The reasonable cost of computerized legal research (as opposed to the costs of installation and monthly access fees), when the use is specifically attributable to the case, will be reimbursed to the extent reasonably and necessarily incurred. Counsel must explain in writing the specific nature of the computer expenses (e.g., Shepard's, Autocite, issue searches, etc.), and must explain why computerized research was more efficient than the same research performed "manually."

6. *Services of law clerks, paralegals, and State Bar members*

   a. Counsel shall be reimbursed for the compensation of the following individuals at a rate not to exceed the following:

   (1) Law clerks who are not members of the State Bar of California at $40 per allowable hour.

   (2) Paralegals at $40 per allowable hour.

   (3) Members of the State Bar of California, who are not appointed to the case, at the rate of $98 per allowable hour.

   b. Reimbursement of the compensation for all persons performing legal services, other than appointed counsel, shall be subject to the following conditions:

   (1) In submitting a claim for reimbursement, counsel shall describe with specificity the legal services and number of hours of work performed by each other person so the court can evaluate the reasonableness of the services and expenses as part of appointed counsel's overall claim. *It is expected that the hours devoted to*

legal services by nonappointed counsel, and any "exceptionally high" hours attributed to law clerks and paralegals (i.e., hours exceeding 30 percent of the benchmark hours for appointed counsel for any given stage), *will reduce the hours that appointed counsel will devote to those services.*

(2) Appointed counsel shall not delegate to others those functions that require the ability and experience for which counsel was appointed.

(3) Appointed counsel shall supervise and have full responsibility for the services performed by others.

7. *Services of investigators and experts*

   a. An investigator or expert shall be compensated at a rate not to exceed the maximum rates listed below. Counsel must establish that use of an expert's services is reasonably necessary under the facts of the case. Counsel seeking to use the services of multiple experts relating to a single or common issue must demonstrate a compelling necessity for such use of multiple experts. In addition, counsel must include in the request for reimbursement a representation that the rate requested

   (1) does not exceed the investigator's or expert's customary rates for the services performed, and

   (2) does not exceed local prevailing rates for the services performed.

   b. The maximum rates are as follows

   (1) Investigators, $55-90 per hour.

   (2) Penalty phase consultants, $60-125 per hour.

   (3) Psychiatrists and other medically licensed mental health experts, $200-350 per hour.

   (4) Other forensic experts, $125-225 per hour.

   (5) Psychologists (Ph.D.'s), $150-275 per hour.

   (6) Attorneys serving as experts, $125-145 per hour. (*Note:* Until an order to show cause is issued, *or* the People submit an expert declaration in their informal opposition to a habeas corpus petition, the court will not approve payment for attorney "expert opinion" in the form of declarations, etc.)

   (7) Any expert listed above testifying at a court proceeding, eight times the hourly rate per day or four times the hourly rate per half day.

   c. In exceptional circumstances, when the need for services at a greater rate of compensation is documented and prior authorization is obtained from the Supreme Court, compensation beyond the maximum may be paid.

8. *Proceedings returnable in superior court following order to show cause on alleged mental retardation of condemned inmate*

   In proceedings pending in superior court pursuant to an order to show cause issued by the California Supreme Court, and returnable before the superior court, regarding a condemned inmate's alleged mental retardation and resulting ineligibility for the death penalty within the meaning of *Atkins v. Virginia* (2002) 536 U.S. 304 (see also *In re Hawthorne* (2005) 35 Cal.4th 40), the following practices apply to requests by counsel appointed in the California Supreme Court for the reimbursement of investigation services and expenses incurred in superior court for experts, investigators and law clerks/paralegals:

   a. The superior court in which the *Atkins*-related proceedings are pending makes only a *recommendation* for pre-authorization to incur, and payment of, the expenses of investigators, experts, and other service providers for whom reimbursement is sought by appointed counsel. Thereafter, the Supreme Court independently determines, pursuant to its time-and-costs Payment Guidelines and the Policy 3 compensation standards (see Supreme Ct. Policies Regarding Cases Arising From Judgments of Death), whether the recommended funding is reasonable and, to the extent found reasonable, authorizes appointed counsel to incur such expenses and reimburses appointed counsel, as appropriate.

   This provision will apply to all such funding requests pending before the Supreme Court on or after March 5, 2012.

   b. Appointed counsel may engage experts, investigators and law clerks/paralegals either in the locality where counsel's offices are situated or in the locality where the superior court proceedings are being held, at counsel's option.

   c. The California Supreme Court will pay for investigation services and expenses at the rate prevailing where the services are engaged, if otherwise permissible within the maximum hourly rates and other applicable provisions set forth within these payment guidelines.

IV. FEE AND EXPENSE DISALLOWANCES

The court will provide reasons in writing for fee disallowances of $1,000 or more, and expense disallowances of $500 or more.

V. COURT ACTION UPON NONPERFORMANCE OF WORK, AND REIMBURSEMENT OF FEES UPON AUTHORIZED WITHDRAWAL OF APPOINTED COUNSEL

A. Nonperformance of counsel In the rare circumstance in which appointed counsel ceases work on a case and refuses to complete the work with reasonable diligence, the court has had, and will continue to exercise as appropriate, the following nonexclusive options: The court may enforce its legal rights; the court may refer the matter to the State Bar; and finally, the court may institute contempt proceedings to enforce its orders.

B. Authorized withdrawal of counsel In the event that the court permits appointed counsel to withdraw before completion of counsel's duties in a case, the court will, as appropriate under the circumstances, authorize payment to counsel for legal work completed. Alternatively, the court may, as appropriate under the circumstances, order counsel to reimburse the court for fees paid, less a credit for work performed that is determined by the court to be of value to the court.

Adopted Jan. 1, 1991; amended Dec. 22, 1993; Sept. 1, 1995; Jan. 1, 1997; July 30, 1997; Jan. 22, 1998; Feb. 4, 1998; Jan. 16, 2002; Aug. 25, 2004; Oct. 1, 2005; Nov. 30, 2005; July 1, 2006; Oct. 1, 2007; July 23, 2008; Aug. 27, 2008; Mar. 5, 2012.

GUIDELINES FOR FIXED FEE APPOINTMENTS, ON OPTIONAL BASIS, TO AUTOMATIC APPEALS AND RELATED HABEAS CORPUS PROCEEDINGS IN THE CALIFORNIA SUPREME COURT

(Adopted by the Supreme Court December 14, 1993, effective January 1, 1994)

(Amended effective September 1, 1995, January 1, 1997, January 22, 1997, July 30, 1997, January 22, 1998, February 4, 1998, July 18, 2001, January 16, 2002, March 21, 2002, October 1, 2005, November 30, 2005, July 1, 2006, October 1, 2007, January 1, 2008, and March 5, 2012)

Introduction

Presently, appointed counsel in automatic appeals are compensated on a "time and costs" basis, under the Payment Guidelines for Appointed Counsel Representing Indigent Criminal Appellants in the California Supreme Court (as revised) (hereafter Payment Guidelines). Under the Payment Guidelines, appointed counsel must submit a detailed and lengthy cumulative hours compensation form with every request for payment of fees and reimbursement of expenses. Moreover, "allowable hours" benchmarks limit the fees available for each stage of the capital representation; other provisions limit or exclude reimbursement for expenses. Requests for prior approval of extraordinary expenses are governed by the Supreme Court Policies Regarding Cases Arising From Judgments of Death (as revised).

In an effort to provide appointed counsel in capital cases greater predictability, consistency and control over compensation and expenses, and to reduce administrative burdens on both counsel and the Court, the Court has adopted an optional fixed fee and expenses payment system.

The categories of fixed fees set out below in Guidelines 1, 1.1, and 1.2 establish the compensation and responsibilities of appointed counsel for all services and "incidental expenses" (habeas corpus investigation expenses are separately provided for in Guideline 2):

(1) In cases in which counsel is appointed to represent the defendant both on appeal and in related habeas corpus/executive clemency proceedings, fixed fee compensation is for: (a) the direct appeal, through the filing of a certiorari petition to the United States Supreme Court, or an answer thereto (but not including any briefs or appearances in the United States Supreme Court after grant of certiorari or any briefs or appearances on remand to the California Supreme Court, which work would be compensated under the terms and limitations of the Payment Guidelines); (b) state habeas corpus investigation, and preparation and filing (if warranted) of a state habeas corpus petition and informal reply, and any subsequent habeas corpus petition, including any petition to exhaust state remedies, in the California Supreme Court (but not including any traverse, habeas corpus evidentiary hearing or post-hearing briefs in the California Supreme Court, which work would be compensated under the terms and limitations of the Payment Guidelines); (c) any trial court proceedings under Penal Code sections 1193 and 1227 to set an execution date; and (d) representation in executive clemency proceedings before the Governor of California. (See Cal. Supreme Ct., Policies Regarding Cases Arising From Judgments of Death, *supra*, Compensation Stds., std. 2-1.)

(2) In cases in which counsel is appointed to represent the defendant on appeal only, fixed fee compensation is for: (a) the direct appeal, through the filing of a certiorari petition to the United States Supreme Court, or an answer thereto (but not including any briefs or appearances in the United States Supreme Court after grant of certiorari or any briefs or appearances on remand to the California Supreme Court, which work would be compensated under the terms and limitations of the Payment Guidelines); and (b) any trial court proceedings under Penal Code section 1193 to set an execution date. (See Cal. Supreme Ct., Policies Regarding Cases Arising From Judgments of Death, *supra*, Compensation Stds., std. 2-1.)

(3) In cases in which counsel is appointed to represent the defendant in habeas corpus/executive clemency proceedings only, fixed fee compensation is for: (a) state habeas corpus investigation, and preparation and filing (if warranted) of a state habeas corpus petition and informal reply, and any subsequent habeas corpus petition, including any petition to exhaust state remedies, in the California Supreme Court (but not including any traverse, habeas corpus evidentiary hearing or post-hearing briefs in the California Supreme Court, which work would be compensated under the terms and limitations of the Payment Guidelines); (b) any trial court proceedings under Penal Code section 1227 to set an execution date; and (c) representation in executive clemency proceedings before the Governor of California. (See Cal. Supreme Ct., Policies Regarding Cases Arising From Judgments of Death, *supra*, Compensation Stds., std. 2-1.)

1. Fixed Fee Categories for Cases in Which Counsel Is Appointed to Handle the Appeal and Related Habeas Corpus/Executive Clemency Proceedings

Category I: $160,000

A. An appeal from a judgment based on a guilty plea and penalty phase; or

B. An appeal from a judgment on remand following a reversal limited to penalty.

C. Caveat: An appeal from a judgment on limited remand for a new hearing on the automatic motion to modify the death verdict (Pen. Code, § 190.4, subd. (e)) likely will be valued well below $160,000. (See also Guideline 4 [Case Evaluation], *post*.)

Category II: $231,000

A. An appeal from a judgment on remand following a reversal limited to the special circumstance finding(s) and penalty; or

B. An appeal otherwise in category I(A) or I(B) that presents a more complex case, in the Court's view, by reason of, but not limited to, one or more of the following factors: The combined record on appeal is 4,000 or more pages; there was more than one homicide victim, and the homicides occurred in more than one incident; there were numerous pretrial and/or penalty phase motions; there were multiple defendants and/or appellants; or

C. An initial appeal or an appeal from a judgment on remand following a reversal of guilt, in which the combined record on appeal is under 6,000 pages.

Category III: $283,000

A. An initial appeal or an appeal from a judgment on remand following a reversal of guilt, in which the combined record on appeal is between 6,000 and 12,000 pages; or

B. An appeal otherwise in category II(A) or II(C) that presents a more complex case, in the Court's view, by reason of, but not limited to, one or more of the following factors: The combined record on appeal is 5,000 or more pages; there was more than one homicide victim, and the homicides occurred in more than one incident; there were numerous pretrial and/or penalty phase motions; there were multiple defendants and/or appellants.

Category IV: $322,000

A. An initial appeal or an appeal from a judgment on remand following a reversal of guilt, in which the combined record on appeal is 12,000 or more pages; or

B. An appeal otherwise in category III(A) that presents a more complex case, in the Court's view, by reason of, but not limited to, one or more of the following factors: The combined record on appeal is 10,000 or more pages; there was more than one homicide victim, and the homicides occurred in more than one incident; there were numerous pretrial and/or penalty phase motions; there were multiple defendants and/or appellants.

Category V: $368,000 base fee

Exceptional cases that occur infrequently, involve many victims and incidents, and have a combined record on appeal of 25,000 or more pages. In this category, appointed counsel may present a justification at the outset for a fixed fee higher than the base fee.

1.1. Fixed Fee Categories for Cases in Which Counsel Is Appointed to Handle the Appeal Only

Category I: $65,000

A. An appeal from a judgment based on a guilty plea and penalty phase; or

B. An appeal from a judgment on remand following a reversal limited to penalty.

C. Caveat: An appeal from a judgment on limited remand for a new hearing on the automatic motion to modify the death verdict (Pen. Code, § 190.4, subd. (e)) likely will be valued well below $65,000. (See also Guideline 4 [Case Evaluation], *post*.)

Category II: $136,000

A. An appeal from a judgment on remand following a reversal limited to the special circumstance finding(s) and penalty; or

B. An appeal otherwise in category I(A) or I(B) that presents a more complex case, in the Court's view, by reason of, but not limited to, one or more of the following factors: The combined record on appeal is 4,000 or more pages; there was more than one homicide victim, and the homicides occurred in more than one incident; there were numerous pretrial and/or penalty phase motions; there were multiple defendants and/or appellants; or

C. An initial appeal or an appeal from a judgment on remand following a reversal of guilt, in which the combined record on appeal is under 6,000 pages.

Category III: $178,000

A. An initial appeal or an appeal from a judgment on remand following a reversal of guilt, in which the combined record on appeal is between 6,000 and 12,000 pages; or

B. An appeal otherwise in category II(A) or II(C) that presents a more complex case, in the Court's view, by reason of, but not limited to, one or more of the following factors: The combined record on appeal is 5,000 or more pages; there was more than one homicide victim, and the homicides occurred in more than one incident; there were numerous pretrial and/or penalty phase motions; there were multiple defendants and/or appellants.

Category IV: $219,000

A. An initial appeal or an appeal from a judgment on remand following a reversal of guilt, in which the combined record on appeal is 12,000 or more pages; or

B. An appeal otherwise in category III(A) that presents a more complex case, in the Court's view, by reason of, but not limited to, one or more of the following factors: The combined record on appeal is 10,000 or more pages; there was more than one homicide victim, and the homicides occurred in more than one incident; there were numerous pretrial and/or penalty phase motions; there were multiple defendants and/or appellants.

Category V: $263,000 base fee

Exceptional cases that occur infrequently, involve many victims and incidents, and have a combined record on appeal of 25,000 or more pages.

In this category, appointed counsel may present a justification at the outset for a fixed fee higher than the base fee.

1.2. Fixed Fee Categories for Cases in Which Counsel Is Appointed to Handle Habeas Corpus/Executive Clemency Proceedings Only

Category I: $85,000, plus an additional fixed fee calculated at the rate of $145 for every 50 pages of transcript in the combined record on appeal.

A. Habeas corpus representation related to a case that would fall within Fixed Fee Guideline 1.1, Categories I or II.

B. Habeas corpus representation related to a case that would fall within Fixed Fee Guideline 1.1, Categories III, IV, or V, but that, for case-specific reasons, is of below-average complexity.

Category II: $110,000, plus an additional fixed fee calculated at the rate of $145 for every 50 pages of transcript in the combined record on appeal.

A. Habeas corpus representation related to a case that would fall within Fixed Fee Guideline 1.1, Categories III, IV, or V.

B. Habeas corpus representation related to a case that would fall within Fixed Fee Guideline 1.1, Categories I or II, but that, for case-specific reasons, nevertheless is of average complexity.

Category III: $127,000, plus an additional fixed fee calculated at the rate of $145 for every 50 pages of transcript in the combined record on appeal, for cases of above-average complexity.

For cases of exceptional complexity, appointed counsel may present a justification at the outset for a fixed fee higher than the $127,000 base fee.

1.3. Factors Affecting Fee Categories

The California Supreme Court considers four factors in determining the fee in fixed fee appointments in capital proceedings: *complexity, difficulty, extraordinary costs,* and *time-intensiveness.* The case-specific issues that influence the applicability of these factors often overlap, but examples of such issues include the following:

- Multiple defendants
- Motion for change of venue
- Joint or separate trials with co-defendants
- Multiple homicides or multiple incidents (including multiple victims in separate incidents)
- Mistrials and re-trial(s)
- Substitution of trial counsel; additional trial proceedings or phases (e.g., grand jury, competency phase, sanity phase)
- Multiple special circumstances
- Prior convictions or unadjudicated criminal conduct admitted at penalty phase
- Prosecution's use of informants
- Extensive litigation of the admissibility of evidence
- Forensic testing, analysis, and evidence (e.g., DNA, hair, fingerprint, blood, ballistics) introduced at trial or necessary for habeas investigation
- Mentally ill, mentally impaired, or mentally retarded capital defendants
- Non-English-speaking or foreign national capital defendant
- Non-English-speaking witnesses
- Minimal guilt and/or penalty phase investigation done for trial
- Investigation requirements in multiple locations and/or out of the state or country
- Extended elapsed time since offenses/trial
- Necessity of expert witnesses
- Necessity of using some fees to cover investigative and incidental expenses
- Length of record
- Number of trial witnesses

1.4. Suggested Format and Contents of Fixed Fee Requests

Counsel may submit requests for consideration of a case for a particular fixed fee category. Lengthy letters are not necessary or encouraged. Letters for the most complex cases should not exceed seven pages. A suggested format that will assist the Court in making a fixed fee determination includes the following elements:

Fixed fee request: An opening paragraph stating the fee category and base fee requested, plus additional amounts sought for transcript length and cases of exceptional complexity.

Short summary of the case: This paragraph should not extensively reiterate the facts of the case or the procedural history.

Discussion of the applicability of the four factors to this particular case: An explanation of why the appointed case is particularly complex, difficult, costly, and/or time-intensive.

2. Incidental and Investigative Expenses

All incidental expenses for the direct appeal and habeas corpus/ executive clemency representation are included in the fixed fee. Incidental expenses include photocopying, postage, telephone charges, computerized legal research, travel (other than for habeas corpus investigation) and services of law clerks and paralegals (other than for habeas corpus investigation). In addition to the agreed-upon fixed fee, counsel may also incur up to $25,000 in habeas corpus investigative expenses, without prior Court authorization, subject to the Court's Payment Guidelines, *supra*, part III, subpart C, paragraphs 1-7, inclusive ("Reimbursable expenses"). Investigative expenses include travel associated with habeas corpus investigation, and services of law clerks, paralegals, and others serving as habeas corpus investigators. Counsel will be reimbursed for all such habeas corpus investigative expenses that were reasonably incurred, up to $25,000. The Court will not authorize or reimburse habeas corpus investigative expenses exceeding $25,000 prior to the issuance of an order to show cause.

As to those cases in which, by January 1, 2008 (the effective date of Assem. Bill No. 1248), the defendant has not filed a capital-related habeas corpus petition in this court and the date by which to file a presumptively timely petition has not yet passed, counsel may be reimbursed up to $50,000 for those investigative services and expenses incurred on or after that date. Such investigative funding for expenses incurred after January 1, 2008, also is available in those cases in which a presumptively timely petition has been filed by January 1, 2008, but petitioner's reply to the informal response has not been filed and the time to do so (with any extensions of time) has not passed as of that date. (See also Cal. Supreme Ct., Policies Regarding Cases Arising From Judgments of Death, *supra*, Timeliness Stds., std. 1-1, & Compensation Stds., std. 2-2.1.)

3. Requests for Additional Fees

In extraordinary and unique situations, the Court will entertain requests for additional fees based on exceptional circumstances (e.g., circumstances that were unforeseeable at the time of the appointment of counsel on a fixed fee basis). In such situations, counsel shall have the burden of proof to justify any additional fees.

4. Case Evaluation

There will be agreement on the fixed fee prior to the appointment of counsel. (See also, Guideline 6 [Conversion From Time and Costs Appointment to Fixed Fee], *post*.) Initially, applicant counsel selected to consider an appointment to a specific automatic appeal and/or habeas corpus/executive clemency proceedings will have the option of investigating that case for purposes of proposing a fixed fee pursuant to these alternative guidelines, rather than the traditional time and costs method. At any given time, there will be only one set of applicant counsel investigating a specific automatic appeal and/or habeas corpus/executive clemency proceedings for purposes of a possible appointment. Applicant counsel are encouraged to consult with trial counsel, examine any available transcript "dailies" prepared during the trial or other proceedings, and examine any available materials normally found in the clerk's transcript. Counsel are also encouraged to examine additional materials and information that may be available from the California Appellate Project in San Francisco.

Using these alternative guidelines, applicant counsel opting to be appointed on a fixed fee basis will propose a category and hence a fee for all services and expenses in the case. The Court's concurrence is required for any such appointment.

Discussions with applicant counsel regarding proposals for fixed fee appointments shall be conducted through the Automatic Appeals Monitor.

The fixed fee encompasses counsel's investigative costs in reviewing the case for purposes of considering an appointment. If counsel's proposal for a fixed fee is not accepted by the Court, counsel will not be reimbursed for those investigative costs; however, counsel may request an appointment to that case pursuant to the traditional time and costs method of the Payment Guidelines.

5. Progress Payments

Until appointed appellate counsel files the appellant's opening brief or appointed habeas corpus counsel files a petition, a current status report must be filed every 60 days. Other than reimbursement for habeas corpus investigative expenses, documentation and itemization of hours and expenses by appointed counsel are not required under these alternative fixed fee guidelines.

Counsel appointed for both the direct appeal *and* habeas corpus/ executive clemency proceedings will receive progress payments after specified stages of representation as follows: (i) one-sixth of the fixed amount shortly after counsel is appointed; (ii) one-sixth after counsel (a) submits to the assisting entity or counsel (e.g., the Habeas Corpus Resource Center, the California Appellate Project, or other assisting counsel) detailed, understandable and computerized transcript notes, a list of potentially meritorious habeas corpus issues, and a draft first request for correction of the record (and, if appropriate, any motion for augmentation and/or settled statement), and (b) files this first request; (iii) one-sixth after certification of the record and filing of the record in this court (one-half of this progress payment will be advanced upon request after the trial court's order disposing of the consolidated motion to augment, correct, and settle the record on appeal); (iv) one-sixth after counsel (a) files a confidential declaration that he or she has made reasonable efforts to consult with defendant and trial counsel about potential habeas corpus issues, (b) submits to the assisting entity or counsel a detailed outline of potential habeas corpus issues to be investigated, and (c) files the appellant's opening brief (one-quarter of this progress payment will be advanced upon request after counsel's submission to the assisting entity or counsel of a complete draft of the statement of the case and statement of the facts portion of the appellant's opening brief; one-quarter after submission of a complete draft of the guilt phase and special circumstance issues portion of the appellant's opening brief; and one-quarter after submission of a complete draft of the penalty phase issues portion of the appellant's opening brief [counsel may request these advances before progress payment (iii) has been paid in full]); (v) one-sixth after counsel (a) submits to the assisting entity or counsel a draft reply brief, (b) files a reply brief, and (c) files a confidential declaration that counsel has substantially completed the habeas corpus investigation (to the extent possible given funding provided therefor), and has submitted for review to the assisting entity or counsel a draft habeas corpus petition with necessary exhibits and declarations (or, in the alternative, that counsel has submitted for review to the assisting entity or counsel a draft declaration indicating that all potential leads have been substantially pursued to the extent possible given funding provided therefor, and that it appears that no habeas corpus petition will be filed) (one-half of this progress payment will be advanced upon request after the following: (a) the Attorney General files the respondent's brief, and (b) counsel files a confidential declaration that counsel has completed approximately one-half of the anticipated habeas corpus investigation, and has submitted to the assisting entity or counsel a detailed outline of the remainder of the planned investigation); (vi) one-sixth, less $10,000, after counsel files a habeas corpus petition in this court on behalf of counsel's client, and after oral argument and submission of the matter on the direct appeal (except that if counsel files no petition, counsel must instead file a confidential declaration indicating that all potential leads have been pursued to the extent possible given funding provided therefor, and that no habeas corpus petition will be filed, after which counsel will receive no sixth progress payment, except upon a showing that in view of work performed, full or partial payment is warranted); and finally (vii) the sum of $10,000 after completion of representation in executive clemency proceedings before the Governor of California. With each request for payment except for those set forth above in (i), (vi), and (vii), counsel shall provide to the court a statement from the assisting entity or counsel that counsel's submission to the entity or counsel substantially complies with the conditions set forth for payment.

Counsel appointed for the direct appeal only will receive progress payments after specified stages of representation as follows: (i) one-sixth of the fixed amount shortly after counsel is appointed; (ii) one-sixth after counsel (a) submits to the assisting entity or counsel (e.g., the Habeas Corpus Resource Center, the California Appellate Project, or other assisting counsel) detailed, understandable and computerized transcript notes, and a draft first request for correction of the record (and, if appropriate, any motion for augmentation and/or settled statement), and (b) files this first request; (iii) one-sixth after certification of the record and filing of the record in this court (one-half of this progress payment will be advanced upon request after the trial court's order disposing of the consolidated motion to augment, correct, and settle the record on appeal); (iv) one-sixth after counsel files the appellant's opening brief (one-quarter of this progress payment will be advanced upon request after counsel's submission to the assisting entity or counsel of a complete draft of the statement of the case and statement of the facts portion of the appellant's opening brief; one-quarter after submission of a complete draft of the guilt phase and special circumstance issues portion of the appellant's opening brief; and one-quarter after submission of a complete draft of the penalty phase issues portion of the appellant's opening brief [counsel may request these advances before progress payment (iii) has been paid in full]); (v) one-sixth after counsel (a) submits to the assisting entity or counsel a draft of the appellant's reply brief, and (b) files the reply brief; and (vi) one-sixth after oral argument and submission of the matter on the direct appeal. With each request for payment except for those set forth above in (i) and (vi), counsel shall provide to the court a statement from the assisting entity or counsel that counsel's submission to the entity or counsel substantially complies with the conditions set forth for payment.

Counsel whose appointment is limited to habeas corpus/executive clemency proceedings will receive progress payments after specified stages of representation as follows: (i) one-fifth of the fixed amount shortly after counsel is appointed; (ii) one-fifth after counsel files a confidential declaration that counsel has reviewed the record on appeal and the detailed transcript notes and list of potentially meritorious habeas corpus issues provided by appointed counsel on the direct appeal, has made reasonable efforts to consult with defendant, appellate counsel and trial counsel, and has submitted to the assisting entity or counsel (e.g., the Habeas Corpus Resource Center, the California Appellate Project, or other assisting counsel) a detailed outline of potential habeas corpus issues to be investigated; (iii) one-fifth after counsel files a confidential declaration that counsel has completed approximately one-half of the anticipated habeas corpus investigation, and has submitted to the assisting entity or counsel a detailed outline of the remainder of the planned investigation; (iv) one-fifth after counsel files a confidential declaration that counsel has submitted for review to the assisting entity or counsel a draft habeas corpus petition with necessary exhibits and declarations (or, in the alternative, that counsel has submitted for review to the assisting entity or counsel a draft declaration indicating that all potential leads have been pursued to the extent possible given funding provided therefor, and that no habeas corpus petition will be filed) (one-half of this progress payment will be advanced upon request after counsel files a confidential declaration that counsel has completed the habeas corpus investigation to the extent possible given the funding provided therefor); (v) one-fifth, less $10,000, after counsel files a habeas corpus petition in this court on behalf of his or her client (except that if counsel files no petition, counsel must instead file a confidential declaration indicating that all potential leads have been pursued to the extent possible given funding provided therefor, and that no habeas corpus petition will be filed, after which counsel will receive no fifth progress payment, except upon a showing that in view of work performed, full or partial payment is warranted); and finally (vi) $10,000 after completion of representation in executive clemency proceedings before the Governor of California. With each request for payment except for those set forth above in (i), (v), and (vi), counsel shall provide to the court a statement from the assisting entity or counsel that counsel's submission to the entity or counsel substantially complies with the conditions set forth for payment.

Under limited circumstances (e.g., a delay in the certification of the record not due to a lack of diligence on the part of appointed counsel), the court will authorize partial payments before completion of the relevant stage(s) of representation.

In the event the proceedings terminate prior to the completion of all of the stages set forth in the progress payment schedule (as a result, for example, of the death of the defendant), appointed counsel shall memorialize all work completed and the court shall determine and pay an appropriate sum to compensate counsel for work performed prior to the termination of the proceedings.

6. Conversion From Time and Costs Appointment to Fixed Fee

Counsel appointed to an automatic appeal and/or habeas corpus/executive clemency proceedings under the traditional time and costs basis of the Payment Guidelines are encouraged to consider converting their method of compensation pursuant to this optional, fixed fee payment system. Any such conversion must take into account any payments previously made to counsel, and must be approved by the Court. Ordinarily, conversion will not be approved after the filing of the appellant's opening brief, or, in the case of habeas corpus/executive clemency counsel, after six months following counsel's appointment, whichever is later.

Counsel approved by the Court for an appointment to his/her first automatic appeal and/or habeas corpus/executive clemency proceedings should carefully consider an initial appointment under the time and costs basis of the Payment Guidelines. A conversion to a fixed fee appointment pursuant to these alternative guidelines may be more appropriate after such counsel has become familiar with the case.

7. Second Counsel

The Court encourages association with second counsel. Unlike the procedure under the traditional time and costs appointment scheme of the Payment Guidelines, the fixed fees provided by this optional payment system are intended to adequately compensate appointed counsel and any associate counsel. Hence, the Court will not recognize a "second counsel override" in fixed fee cases.

8. Valuation and Length of Record on Appeal

In determining the length of the combined record on appeal as part of the process whereby a case may be valued within a fixed fee category, the Court will take into consideration whether an unusual proportion of the record is comprised of jury voir dire and/or preliminary hearing transcript. When appropriate, the Court may treat the combined record as having a reduced length. Moreover, consistent with this court's historical practice, when determining the appropriate fixed fee category, the Court will not include, in determining the size of the combined record on appeal, the juror questionnaires completed by actual or prospective jurors.

9. Applicability of Supreme Court Policies Regarding Cases Arising From Judgments of Death

The Supreme Court Policies Regarding Cases Arising From Judgments of Death, as amended, apply to all automatic appeals and habeas corpus/executive clemency proceedings in which counsel has opted for a fixed fee pursuant to these alternative guidelines. However, standard 2-2.2 of the Compensation Standards, through standard 2-4.4 of the Compensation Standards (governing authorization to incur, and reimbursement of, habeas corpus investigation expenses), shall not apply to fixed fee cases.

10. Fixed Legal Fees and Expenses For Evidentiary Hearings

In a case in which the Court orders an evidentiary hearing, counsel may elect to enter a fixed legal fee and expenses agreement covering (i) preparation for the evidentiary hearing, (ii) presentation of the evidentiary hearing, (iii) post-hearing litigation before the referee, and (iv) post-hearing briefs and proceedings in this Court.

(1) Fixed Legal Fee and Expense Categories. The Court and counsel for petitioner will agree to fix legal fees and expenses within one of the following categories.

Each agreement shall specify one fixed dollar sum covering *all* legal fees and *all* expenses—"incidental" and investigative—(e.g., photocopying, postage, telephone charges, travel, computerized legal research,

Rules of Court

services of law clerks and paralegals, services of and witness fees for investigators and experts, and any other witness expenses).

The fixed sum agreement shall also specify separately a dollar amount for the "legal fee component" and the "expenses component" of the fixed sum.

Category A: $68,500 ($60,000 legal fees; $8,500 expenses).

A matter presenting a single issue or limited issues expected to require minimal additional investigation, minimal or no services of experts, and to consume 1-2 hearing days.

Category A(1): $74,000 ($60,000 legal fees; $14,000 expenses)

A matter otherwise within category A, but which is expected to require significant additional investigation and use of experts.

Category B: $108,000 ($94,000 legal fees; $14,000 expenses)

A matter expected to require significant additional investigation and/or significant use of experts, and to consume 3-4 hearing days.

Category B(1): $115,000 ($94,000 legal fees; $21,000 expenses)

A matter otherwise within category B, but which is expected to require substantial additional investigation and use of experts.

Category C: $156,000 ($135,000 legal fees; $21,000 expenses)

A matter expected to require substantial additional investigation and/or services of experts, and to consume 5-6 hearing days.

Category C(1): $165,000 ($135,000 legal fees; $30,000 expenses)

A matter otherwise within category C, but which is expected to require substantial additional investigation and use of experts.

Category D: $202,500 *base sum* ($167,500 base amount for legal fees; $35,000 base amount for expenses)

A matter that is expected to require substantial additional investigation and services of experts, and to consume 7 or more hearing days. In this category, counsel may present justification at the outset for a fixed sum higher than the base amount.

(2) Requests for Additional Legal Fees. In extraordinary and unique situations, the Court will entertain requests for additional fees based on exceptional circumstances, as set out *ante*, Fixed Fee Appointment Guideline 3.

(3) Case Evaluation. A fixed fee and expenses agreement shall be reached within 60 days after the Court issues its order appointing a referee. Discussions with applicant counsel regarding proposals for such an agreement shall be conducted through the Automatic Appeals Monitor.

(4) Fixed Legal Fee and Expense Payments.

Fixed legal fee payments. Counsel shall be entitled to be paid one-fourth of the *legal fee component* of the amount set out in the fixed legal fee and expenses agreement upon the filing of the Court's order making the fixed legal fee and expenses appointment. Thereafter, counsel will receive, on written request (but without the necessity of providing an itemization of hours), a one-fourth progress payment of the legal fee component after (i) the evidentiary hearing commences, (ii) the post-hearing litigation before the referee is completed, and (iii) the post-hearing briefing in this Court is completed. Under limited circumstances (e.g., substantial delay not due to lack of diligence on the part of counsel), the Court will authorize partial payments before completion of the aforementioned stages.

Expense payments. Every 30 days, counsel may request reimbursement from this Court for all necessary and reasonable expenses, up to the amount set out in the fixed legal fee and expenses agreement. Reimbursement shall be governed by and calculated in accordance with the Court's Payment Guidelines, *supra*, part III ("Necessary Expenses").

11. Court Action Upon Nonperformance of Work, and Reimbursement of Fees Upon Authorized Withdrawal of Appointed Counsel

The provisions of "Guideline V" of the "Payment Guidelines for Appointed Counsel Representing Indigent Criminal Appellants in the California Supreme Court" apply as well to counsel appointed on a "fixed fee" basis.

12. Reimbursement for Photocopying Defense Counsel's Trial Files

In addition to investigative expenses as set forth in the "Supreme Court Policies Regarding Cases Arising From Judgments of Death," Policy 3, standard 2-2.1, counsel appointed to handle habeas corpus/executive clemency representation will be reimbursed the reasonable cost of photocopying defense counsel's trial files, at the rate of not more than 10 cents per page, after filing of the certified record on appeal. Counsel must provide a receipt or invoice showing the number of pages copied, and the cost per page. Reimbursement will not be paid for photocopying of items already contained in the record on appeal, such as daily transcripts or exhibits.

Adopted Dec. 14, 1993, effective Jan. 1, 1994; amended Sept. 1, 1995; Jan. 1, 1997; Jan. 22, 1997; July 30, 1997; Jan. 22, 1998; Feb. 4, 1998; Jan. 16, 2002; March 21, 2002; Oct. 1, 2005; Nov. 30, 2005; July 1, 2006; Oct. 1, 2007; Jan. 1, 2008; and Mar. 5, 2012.

GUIDELINES FOR THE COMMISSION ON JUDICIAL APPOINTMENTS

(Adopted by the Commission on Judicial Appointments, effective May 18, 1999; amended effective July 1, 2005, March 1, 2006, February 23, 2007, and November 19, 2007.)

Guideline 1. Definitions; commission headquarters.

(a) **[Definition]** "Nomination" and "nominee" also refer to appointments and appointees, as described in article VI, section 16(d), of the California Constitution.

Adopted effective May 18, 1999.

(b) **[Definition]** "Court days" refer to days on which the California courts are open for official business. Normally, Mondays through Fridays are counted as court days, except for judicial holidays.

Adopted effective May 18, 1999.

(c) **[Commission headquarters]** The headquarters and mailing address of the Commission on Judicial Appointments (commission) are:

Commission on Judicial Appointments
c/o Chief Justice of California
Supreme Court of California
350 McAllister Street
San Francisco, California 94102
Attention: The Secretary to the Commission

The commission's facsimile transmission (fax) number is (415) 865-7181, and its telephone number is (415) 865-7060.

Amended effective February 23, 2007; adopted effective May 18, 1999; previously amended effective March 1, 2006.

Guideline 2. Commission membership (Cal. Const., art. VI, § 7).

The commission consists of the Chief Justice of California, the Attorney General, and the presiding justice of the Court of Appeal of the affected district or, if there are two or more presiding justices, the one who has presided longest or, for a nomination to the Supreme Court, the presiding justice who has presided longest as a presiding justice on any Court of Appeal.

Amended effective July 1, 2005; adopted effective May 18, 1999.

Guideline 3. Commission chairperson.

(a) **[Chairperson]** The Chief Justice (or Acting Chief Justice) shall serve as chairperson of the commission.

Adopted effective May 18, 1999.

(b) [Powers] The chairperson shall preside at the confirmation hearing. The chairperson also is authorized to:

(1) act on behalf of the commission in all matters arising between hearings;

(2) adopt such internal guidelines and order measures as deemed appropriate to implement these guidelines, or for good cause extend or shorten the time periods set forth in these guidelines;

(3) set time limits for the testimony of witnesses;

(4) at the hearing, limit or terminate a witness's testimony for failure to comply with these guidelines;

(5) exclude any person from the hearing who disrupts the proceedings; and

(6) make security arrangements for the confirmation hearing.

Amended effective March 1, 2006; adopted effective May 18, 1999; previously amended effective July 1, 2005.

Guideline 4. Pre-hearing procedures.

(a) [Scheduling, notice, and location of public hearing] The chairperson shall schedule the confirmation hearing within a reasonable time after the nomination and shall issue a press release announcing the time, place, and subject of the hearing.

Adopted effective May 18, 1999.

(b) [Commission on Judicial Nominees Evaluation (Gov. Code, § 12011.5)] The chairperson shall request the Commission on Judicial Nominees Evaluation of the State Bar (JNE) to:

(1) submit to the commission as soon as practicable, but in no event later than the time specified in paragraph (d) of this guideline, its written recommendations to the commission concerning the nominee, and the reasons therefor, and, if specifically requested, all prior JNE recommendations, including the date of evaluation and the court for which the nominee was evaluated; and

(2) designate a representative to testify at the hearing as to the JNE evaluation of the nominee.

Adopted effective May 18, 1999.

(c) [Communications with the commission] All communications regarding a nominee must be made in writing to the commission and/or by testimony at the hearing. Communications regarding a nomination or nominee should be made to the commission as a whole rather than to any commission member individually, and shall be distributed promptly to the members of the commission. Communications may be sent to the commission by United States Mail, overnight delivery, messenger service, or fax, to arrive within the time specified in these guidelines. The commission generally will not formally acknowledge receipt of written presentations concerning a nominee's qualifications. Communications that are received by the commission after the time specified in these guidelines shall be returned to the sender by the secretary to the commission.

Amended effective March 1, 2006; adopted effective May 18, 1999.

(d) [Written presentations and requests to testify; time for submission]

(1) Individuals, including the nominee, who submit a written presentation or request to testify before the commission must identify themselves by name, address, and occupation, and, if applicable, shall identify the name, address, and purpose of any agency or organization for which they are acting in a representative capacity. Telephone numbers and any fax numbers of these individuals and organizations must be included.

(2) Except for the nominee's list of those witnesses whom he or she wishes to testify, as described under paragraph (g), all requests to testify before the commission must be in writing and must specifically state whether the witness will be testifying in support of or in opposition to the nominee, and describe the proposed testimony, its relevance to the nominee's qualifications, and the facts upon which the witness's testimony and opinion will be based. All written presentations or requests to testify must be received by the commission no later than 5:00 p.m. on the fifth court day before the hearing. (For example, if a hearing is to be held on a Monday, the fifth court day before the hearing would be the preceding Monday, unless a judicial holiday falls in between. Each intervening judicial holiday requires an additional court day's notice.)

Amended effective March 1, 2006; adopted effective May 18, 1999; previously amended effective July 1, 2005.

(e) [Permissible testimony] The commission shall review requests to testify and shall permit testimony that is relevant to the nominee's qualifications. Testimony relating to the judicial system generally or to the overall nomination or confirmation process will not be received. Testimony that is unduly cumulative to or repetitive of other testimony may be excluded. A person whose request to testify is denied shall be so informed by the commission as soon as possible before the hearing, by telephone or fax.

Amended effective March 1, 2006; adopted effective May 18, 1999.

(f) [Notice to nominee] The commission promptly shall provide the nominee with a copy of all the written presentations or requests to testify it receives and shall afford the nominee an opportunity to refute, clarify, or comment, either at the hearing or before the hearing in writing, or both. Similarly, if the commission receives any record, public or private, or any other communication relating to the nominee's qualifications, it promptly shall provide the nominee with a copy thereof, and afford the nominee an opportunity to refute, clarify, or comment on that record or communication (consistent with the provisions of Cal. Const. art. VI, § 18.5). All written responses by the nominee must be received by the commission no later than 5:00 p.m. on the third court day before the hearing.

Adopted effective May 18, 1999.

(g) [Nominee's witness list] The nominee shall present the commission with a list of any witnesses he or she wishes to testify at the hearing. This list must include the information required by paragraph (d)(1) and shall be received by the commission no later than 5:00 p.m. on the third court day before the hearing.

Adopted effective May 18, 1999.

(h) [Release of lists of speakers and communications] No later than 2:00 p.m. on the second court day before the scheduled hearing, the commission shall release to the public the following:

(1) the names of witnesses who will testify at the hearing;

(2) the names of any individuals or organizations that have submitted written communications to the commission;

(3) correspondence and public reports received by the commission concerning the nominee's qualifications, including any reports submitted by JNE pursuant to paragraph (b), and the nominee's Personal Data Questionnaire submitted by the Governor to the commission. The commission, however, shall delete any confidential personal information such as an individual's residential address, or Social Security or driver's license number. The written material released shall be made available for copying at the requesting party's expense.

Amended effective July 1, 2005; adopted effective May 18, 1999.

Guideline 5. Hearing procedures.

(a) [Conference] The commission members may confer before the confirmation hearing to consider procedural issues.

Adopted effective May 18, 1999.

(b) [Absence of commission member] Concurrence of at least two commission members present at the hearing is necessary to confirm a nominee. If the Chief Justice is recused or unavailable, the Acting Chief Justice shall serve as the chairperson. If the presiding justice described in Guideline 2 is recused or unavailable, the presiding justice of the affected district who has presided next longest as presiding justice, or, in districts with a single presiding justice, the acting presiding justice, or for a nomination to the Supreme Court, the presiding justice who has presided next longest as presiding justice on any Court of Appeal, shall serve. (See Cal. Const., art. VI, §§ 2, 3, and 7.) A request that a commission member not participate in proceedings of the commission shall be decided by that member alone. The hearing may proceed if two members of the commission are present.

Amended effective July 1, 2005; adopted effective May 18, 1999.

(c) [Witnesses] Witnesses shall be heard in the following order:

(1) witnesses in support of the nominee;

(2) witnesses in opposition to the nominee;

(3) the JNE representative;

(4) the nominee.

Adopted effective May 18, 1999.

(d) [Exhibits and demonstrative evidence] Witnesses must testify orally and have no right to present exhibits or demonstrative evidence at the hearing.

Adopted effective May 18, 1999.

(e) [Record of hearing] The hearing proceedings shall be recorded by audio or video recorder, court reporter, or any other means appropriate for preserving the testimony. A nominee who wishes to make his or her own arrangements to record the hearing by video recorder or other means shall notify the commission in writing. This notice must be received by the commission no later than 5:00 p.m. on the second court day before the hearing.

Adopted effective May 18, 1999.

(f) [Public attendance and broadcasting] The hearing shall be open to the public and to the media. Any request to broadcast, photograph, or record the hearing requires the approval of the chairperson, upon written application received no later than 5:00 p.m. on the second court day before the hearing. The request, as well as the broadcasting, photographing, and recording, shall comply with the provisions of California Rules of Court, rules 1.150 and 2.954, where applicable.

Amended effective November 19, 2007; adopted effective May 18, 1999; previously amended effective July 1, 2005.

(g) [Announcement of decision] The commission may deliberate privately, but shall announce its decision publicly at the hearing, as well as by subsequent news release. If necessary, the hearing may be continued to a future date for further proceedings.

Adopted effective May 18, 1999.

(h) [Official record] The commission's minutes shall be the official record of the hearing.

Adopted effective May 18, 1999.

Guideline 6.   Staff to the commission.

The chairperson of the commission may designate a person to act as secretary to the commission and one or more persons to act as assistant secretaries. The secretary shall maintain custody of the commission's files. The Administrative Office of the Courts, at the chairperson's direction, shall provide additional staff and financial support as necessary to enable the commission to perform its duties.

Adopted effective May 18, 1999.

Guideline 7.   Post-hearing procedures.

(a) [Access to the commission's files] Except as otherwise provided in paragraph (b) of this guideline, after the conclusion of any nomination proceedings of the commission subject to these guidelines, a person, agency, or organization, upon written request to the commission's secretary, may obtain access to the public portions of the commission's files, as defined in guideline 4(h), as well as any transcript of the hearing prepared by a court reporter as a record of those proceedings pursuant to guideline 5(e), for inspection and copying at the requesting party's expense.

(b) [Audio or video recording] Any audio or video recording prepared as a record of the hearing pursuant to guideline 5(e) shall be copyrighted and made available for viewing at a time and location specified by the commission's secretary, but shall not be available for copying by the requesting party unless such copying is authorized by the commission.

Amended effective July 1, 2005; adopted effective May 18, 1999.

Guideline 8.   Publication and distribution of these guidelines.

(a) [Official guidelines] These guidelines for the Commission on Judicial Appointments shall be published by the Reporter of Decisions in the advance pamphlets of the California Official Reports and shall be made available on the judicial branch's Web site (at *www.courtinfo.ca.gov/reference/documents/guidelinescja.pdf*) or by calling the Public Information Office of the Administrative Office of the Courts at (415) 865-7740.

Amended effective November 19, 2007; adopted effective May 18, 1999; previously amended effective July 1, 2005.

(b) [News release] Information regarding access to these guidelines shall accompany each news release announcing a commission hearing.

Adopted effective May 18, 1999.

(c) [Copies] A copy of these guidelines shall be sent to the nominee with the notice of the hearing, and to each designated witness.

Adopted effective May 18, 1999.

LOCAL RULES AND INTERNAL OPERATING PRACTICES AND PROCEDURES OF THE COURTS OF APPEAL

First Appellate District. Rules 1-21; Internal Operating Practices and Procedures.

Second Appellate District. Rules 1-9; Internal Operating Practices and Procedures.

Third Appellate District. Rules 1-6; Internal Operating Practices and Procedures.

Fourth Appellate District. Rules 1-5; Internal Operating Practices and Procedures, Division One; Internal Operating Practices and Procedures, Division Two; Internal Operating Practices and Procedures, Division Three.

Fifth Appellate District. Rules 1-8; Local Court Form; Internal Operating Practices and Procedures.

Sixth Appellate District. Rules 1-4; Internal Operating Practices and Procedures.

FIRST APPELLATE DISTRICT LOCAL RULES

[Adopted effective August 23, 2019]
[Previously adopted effective October 16, 2006; amended effective May 1, 2015, and October 12, 2018; repealed effective August 23, 2019]

Obligation of superior court clerk to prepare and file docketing statements in certain criminal, juvenile, dependency, and family matters. Rule 1.
Extensions of time for superior court clerk or court reporter to prepare transcripts. Rule 2.
Obligation of court reporters to include transcripts of specified proceedings in criminal and juvenile delinquency appeals. Rule 3.
Augmentations of the record. Rule 4.
Parties' stipulation to use original superior court file as the appellate record. Rule 5.
Requests for judicial notice. Rule 6.
Motions to consolidate. Rule 7.
Notification of settlement or basis for early resolution. Rule 8.
Settlement conferences in civil appeals. Rule 9.
Motions for stipulated reversal of judgment. Rule 10.
Extensions of time for filing briefs. Rule 11.
Electronic Filing. Rule 12.
Oral argument. Rule 13.
Oral argument by teleconference. Rule 14.
Focus Letters and Tentative Opinions. Rule 15.
New Authority Prior to Oral Argument. Rule 16.
Electronic Devices in the Courtroom. Rule 17.
Media Coverage of Oral Argument. Rule 18.
Abbreviated Opinions. Rule 19.
Circuit-riding Sessions. Rule 20.
Parties' Obligation to Notify Court of Bankruptcy Stays. Rule 21.
Internal Operating Practices and Procedures.

POLICY OF THE COURT OF APPEAL, FIRST APPELLATE DISTRICT, STATE OF CALIFORNIA ON PUBLIC USE OF ELECTRONIC DEVICES IN THE COURTROOM

The First District adopts the following policy, which allows for restricted public use of electronic devices in the courtroom during oral arguments before the court:

Only counsel and self-represented litigants may use laptop computers and electronic tablets in the courtroom. Such devices may be used only as an aid in presenting oral argument, and may not be used to display demonstrative evidence to the court or for any other purpose. Devices must be silenced and placed in "airplane mode" at all times. No cellular telephones or other electronic devices are permitted in the courtroom, except for assisted listening devices. No audio or video recording or photography is permitted in the courtroom, except in compliance with California Rules of Court, rule 1.150. Failure to comply with these restrictions may result in the violator being removed from the courtroom.

(Adopted effective March 16, 2015)

Rule 1.   Criminal and Juvenile Docketing Statements [Repealed]

Rule 1 adopted, effective October 16, 2006; repealed effective August 23, 2019.

Another Rule 1 follows.

Rule 1.   Obligation of Superior Court Clerk to Prepare and File Docketing Statements in Certain Criminal, Juvenile, Dependency, and Family Matters

(a) [Docketing Statements] In all criminal appeals, juvenile appeals from proceedings arising under Welfare and Institutions Code sections 300, 601, or 602, in all writ proceedings challenging orders entered under

Welfare and Institutions Code sections 366.26 and 366.28, and in proceedings under Family Code section 7800, the clerk of the superior court must, upon the filing of a notice of appeal or notice of intent to file a writ petition, prepare a docketing statement and promptly forward it to this court with (1) the notice of appeal or notice of intent to file a writ petition, and (2) a copy of the abstract of judgment, minutes, or order being appealed or challenged by writ.

(b) [Forms] The following forms of docketing statements shall be used:

(1) Docketing Statement for Criminal Notice of Appeal

(2) Docketing Statement for Juvenile Notice of Appeal and Juvenile Notice of Intent to File Writ Petition

These forms are available on the court's website at: http://www.courts.ca.gov/1954.htm.

(c) [Sanctions] The failure of a superior court clerk to file a docketing statement as required by this rule may result in the imposition of sanctions.

Rule 1 adopted, effective August 23, 2019.

Rule 2.   Mediation in Civil Appeals [Repealed]
Rule 2 adopted, effective October 16, 2006; repealed effective August 23, 2019.

Another Rule 2 follows.

Rule 2.   Extensions of Time for Superior Court Clerk or Court Reporter to Prepare Transcripts

(a) [Extension of Time for Clerk's Transcript] A clerk's request for an extension of time to prepare a clerk's transcript on appeal will not be granted without a showing of good cause.

(b) [Extension of Time for Reporter's Transcript] A court reporter's request for an extension of time to file the reporter's transcript will not be granted without a showing of good cause and the approval of the Presiding Judge, or other duly authorized judge, of the superior court.

(1) Automatic Extension in Certain Criminal Appeals. Court reporters are granted one automatic extension of time of 30 days to prepare and file the reporter's transcript where the defendant appeals from a criminal judgment of conviction after trial. Thus, the reporter's transcript is due within 50 days of the filing of the notice of appeal. (See Cal. Rules of Court, rule 8.336.) This rule does not apply whenever the People appeal, or when a defendant appeals from the following:

- a postjudgment order;
- a judgment entered on a plea of not guilty or nolo contendere;
- a judgment pronounced on resentencing after remand from the appellate court;
- an order revoking probation or a judgment entered after the revocation of probation; and
- an order extending a defendant's term of commitment to a state hospital.

In these cases, the reporter's transcript is due no more than 20 days after the notice of appeal is filed. (See Cal. Rules of Court, rule 8.336(d)(3).)

(2) Automatic Extension in Certain Civil Appeals. Court reporters are granted one automatic extension of time of 30 days to prepare and certify the reporter's transcript where a party appeals from a civil judgment entered after trial by jury or by the court. Thus, the reporter's transcript must be prepared and certified within 60 days after the notice is sent in accordance with California Rules of Court, rule 8.130(d)(2). (See Cal. Rules of Court, rule 8.130(f)(1).) This rule does not apply when a party appeals from the following:

- a postjudgment order;
- a summary judgment;
- a judgment of dismissal after the sustaining of a demurrer without leave to amend;
- a default judgment;
- a judgment of dismissal for failure to proceed in a timely manner;
- any other appealable pretrial order; and
- an order declaring a minor free from the custody and control of his or her parents.

In these cases, the reporter's transcript is due no more than 30 days after the notice is sent in accordance with California Rules of Court, rule 8.130(d)(2). (See Cal. Rules of Court, rule 8.130(f)(1).)

(3) Juvenile Proceedings. Court reporters are not granted an automatic extension of time in appeals and writs from orders or judgments in juvenile proceedings. (Welf. & Inst. Code, §§ 300 et seq., 601, 602.)

In juvenile appeals, the reporter's transcript is due no more than 20 days after the notice of appeal is filed. (See Cal. Rules of Court, rules 8.409(c),

8.416(c)(1).) In juvenile writ proceedings under Welfare and Institutions Code sections 366.26 and 366.28, the reporter's transcript is due 12 calendar days after the notice of intent is filed. (See Cal. Rules of Court, rules 8.450(h)(1), 8.454(h)(1).)

(c) [Reporter Defaults] If a court reporter fails to timely file the reporter's transcript, this court may issue an order directing the court reporter to show cause why he or she should not be declared incompetent to act as an official reporter, under the provisions of section 69944 of the Government Code.

(d) [Sanctions] Sanctions may be imposed upon a clerk who fails to timely file a clerk's transcript, or upon a court reporter who fails to timely file a reporter's transcript. (See Cal. Rules of Court, rule 8.23.)

(e) [Forms] A clerk's request for an extension of time to file a clerk's transcript on appeal shall be substantially in the form of the Clerk's Affidavit and Order for Extension of Time to File Transcript on Appeal. A reporter's request for an extension of time to file the reporter's transcript shall be substantially in the form of the Reporter's Affidavit and Order for Extension of Time to File Transcript on Appeal. These forms are available on the court's website at: http://www.courts.ca.gov/1954.htm.

Rule 2 adopted, effective August 23, 2019.

Rule 3.   Settlement Conferences in Civil Appeals [Repealed]
Rule 3 adopted, effective October 16, 2006; repealed effective August 23, 2019.

Another Rule 3 follows.

Rule 3.   Obligation of Court Reporters to Include Transcripts of Specified Proceedings in Criminal and Juvenile Delinquency Appeals

In addition to the transcripts designated in the California Rules of Court, transcripts of the following proceedings should be included as part of the record in appeals in criminal and juvenile delinquency cases:

(a) [Proceedings on Defense Motions] Reporter's transcripts of the proceedings held on all defense motions that were denied, in whole or in part, including but not limited to the following:

- motions to suppress identification of the defendant;
- motions to suppress evidence;
- motions to exclude evidence of defendant's prior offenses or other conduct;
- motions to suppress defendant's statements (e.g. *Miranda v. Arizona* (1966) 384 U.S. 436);
- motions to permit or preclude impeachment of defendant or witness with prior offenses;
- motions to determine defendant's competence;
- motions for severance or joinder;
- motions to change venue;
- motions for the discovery of police officer records (*Pitchess v. Superior Court* (1974) 11 Cal.3d 531);
- motions for self-representation (*Faretta v. California* (1975) 422 U.S. 806);
- motions in limine;
- motions to terminate or replace defense counsel under *People v. Marsden* (1970) 2 Cal.3d 118. When provided in paper format, an original and two copies of the sealed transcript shall accompany the record upon certification and delivery to this court. When provided in electronic format, a separately saved file containing only the confidential *Marsden* transcript shall be provided. The court will provide appellant's counsel with a copy of the transcript. If appellant raises a *Marsden* issue, a copy of the transcript will then be provided to the Attorney General in the manner prescribed in California Rules of Court, rule 8.47(b)(2).

(b) [Proceedings on Prosecution Motions] Reporter's transcripts of the proceedings held on the following prosecution motions should be included as part of the record when the motion was *granted* in whole or in part:

- motions for joinder;
- motions to impeach the defendant with prior offenses;
- motions for admission of defendant's prior offenses or conduct.

(c) [Revocation of Probation—Plea Proceedings] Transcripts of the hearings held on the following proceedings should be included as part of the record in appeals from decisions to revoke probation:

- the original sentencing proceeding at which probation was imposed;
- the proceedings at the time of entry of a guilty plea or nolo contendere plea if the original judgment of conviction is based on such plea; and

• the proceedings at which probation is revoked and the defendant is sentenced.

(d) [In Camera Hearings] Transcripts of hearings held in camera or under seal shall be transmitted to this court only, and no sealed copies shall be provided to counsel for either party except on application to and approval by this court. When provided in paper format, an original and two copies of the sealed transcript shall accompany the record upon certification and delivery to this court. When provided in electronic format, a separately saved file containing only the confidential transcript shall be provided.

Rule 3 adopted, effective August 23, 2019.

Rule 4. Motions for Stipulated Reversal of Judgment [Repealed]

Rule 4 adopted, effective October 16, 2006; repealed effective August 23, 2019.

Another Rule 4 follows.

Rule 4. Augmentations of the Record

(a) [General Principles] Parties shall limit their augmentation requests to material that was filed or lodged in the trial court. Augmentation cannot be used to add material to the record on appeal that is outside of the superior court's record. (See, e.g., *Vons Companies, Inc. v. Seabest Foods, Inc.* (1996) 14 Cal.4th 434, 444, fn. 3.)

(b) [Items Inadvertently Omitted] If a party realizes that a required or designated item has been omitted from the record, the party shall, in accordance with California Rules of Court, rules 8.155(b), 8.340(c), or 8.410(b)(1), file a notice in the superior court requesting that the item be prepared, certified, and sent to this court. Such a notice should not be filed in this court in the first instance. In criminal and juvenile cases, if a superior court clerk or reporter realizes after a record has been certified that a required or designated item was omitted, the clerk or reporter shall, without the need for a court order, promptly prepare, certify, and send the item to this court in accordance with California Rules of Court, rules 8.340(b) and 8.410(a).

(c) [Time for Seeking Augmentation in this Court] Any motion filed in this court to augment a record shall be submitted on the earliest date practicable. Appellant should file any such request in one motion filed no later than 30 days after the record has been filed in this court, except in certain juvenile dependency appeals or writs that have a shorter deadline. (See Cal. Rules of Court, rules 8.416(d)(2), 8.452(e)(2), 8.456(e)(2).) Respondent should file any such request in one motion made within 30 days of the filing of appellant's opening brief. Thereafter, motions to augment will be considered only upon a showing of good cause.

(1) In cases in which the appellant or petitioner is represented by the First District Appellate Project, any request for an augmentation of the record shall be made within 30 days after the expiration of the 10-day administrative-review period.

(d) [Clerk's Transcript] A motion to augment the clerk's transcript must be accompanied by the proposed augmented document or identify the proposed document with specificity. The record can be augmented only with documents that were filed or lodged in the superior court. A motion to augment shall be accompanied by a declaration stating that the document was so filed or lodged.

(e) [Reporter's Transcript] A motion to augment the reporter's transcript shall identify with specificity the portion of the proceeding sought to be included in the appellate record, the name of the reporter and his or her CSR number if available, and the date or dates of the proceeding. Any such motion shall explain why the transcript may be useful for the appeal. Requests for transcripts of a jury voir dire must be specific and be limited to only the portion of the proceeding that may be useful for the appeal.

(f) [Good Faith Required] Repeated motions to augment are strongly disfavored. A motion to augment shall be made in good faith and shall not be made for the purpose of delay. A motion filed on or close to the date a brief is due may raise an inference that it was filed for the purpose of delay.

Rule 4 adopted, effective August 23, 2019.

Rule 5. Timely Preparation of Clerk's and Reporter's Transcripts [Repealed]

Rule 5 adopted, effective October 16, 2006; repealed effective August 23, 2019.

Another Rule 5 follows.

Rule 5. Parties' Stipulation to Use Original Superior Court File as the Appellate Record

The procedures set forth in California Rules of Court, rule 8.128 allowing the parties to stipulate to using the original superior court file in lieu of the clerk's transcript are approved for use by the superior courts in this district in all civil cases in which the trial court retains no continuing jurisdiction. Any stipulation under this rule shall be substantially in the form of the Stipulation for Use of Original Superior Court File in Lieu of Clerk's Transcript, which is available on the court's website at: http://www.courts.ca.gov/1954.htm.

Rule 5 adopted, effective August 23, 2019.

Rule 6. Contents of Reporter's Transcript in Criminal and Juvenile Delinquency Appeals [Repealed]

Rule 6 adopted, effective October 16, 2006; repealed effective August 23, 2019.

Another Rule 6 follows.

Rule 6. Requests for Judicial Notice

(a) [Form of Request] Requests for judicial notice must comply with California Rules of Court, rule 8.252.

(b) [Deferral of Ruling] If a request for judicial notice is filed at the same time as the moving party's brief, or if the court has deferred ruling on a request for judicial notice, the parties may rely on the item sought to be judicially noticed in their briefs. If the court subsequently denies the request, however, it will not consider any such item in rendering its decision.

Rule 6 adopted, effective August 23, 2019.

Rule 7. Augmentation of Record [Repealed]

Rule 7 adopted, effective October 16, 2006; repealed effective August 23, 2019.

Another Rule 7 follows.

Rule 7. Motions to Consolidate

Motions to consolidate appeals must include a statement indicating whether the other party or parties agree with the proposed consolidation.

Rule 7 adopted, effective August 23, 2019.

Rule 8. Stipulation for Use of Original Superior Court File [Repealed]

Rule 8 adopted, effective October 16, 2006; repealed effective August 23, 2019.

Another Rule 8 follows.

Rule 8. Notification of Settlement or Basis for Early Resolution

Parties shall notify the court as soon as possible when discussions between the parties suggest a reasonable likelihood the case may settle. (See Cal. Rules of Court, rule 8.244.) Likewise, parties shall notify the court as soon as possible if there is any basis for an early dismissal of the appeal. Unless and until the appeal is dismissed, the parties remain obligated to file briefs in a timely fashion and to complete all other tasks that are required by the rules of court. Parties may ask the court that any notice filed under this rule not appear on the public docket.

Rule 8 adopted, effective August 23, 2019.

Rule 9. Judicial Notice Requests [Repealed]

Rule 9 adopted, effective October 16, 2006; repealed effective August 23, 2019.

Another Rule 9 follows.

Rule 9. Settlement Conferences in Civil Appeals

(a) [Application of Rule] This rule applies to all appeals in civil cases except appeals from proceedings under sections 601 and 602 of the Welfare and Institutions Code, appeals arising in proceedings involving jurisdiction over an abused or neglected child or to establish or terminate parental rights, and appeals from original proceedings ancillary to a criminal prosecution.

(b) [Request or Order for Settlement Conference]

(1) A settlement conference will be scheduled if requested in writing by counsel for all parties to the appeal. The request may be made at any time prior to the close of briefing and shall be addressed to the court's Clerk/Executive Officer. A request by counsel for any party that states all other parties join in the request is adequate for this purpose.

(2) At any time during the pendency of an appeal, the panel to which the appeal has been assigned may order a settlement conference even though none was requested.

(3) The pendency of settlement proceedings will not suspend preparation of the appellate record or briefing, unless the court has granted an

extension of time or the parties have stipulated to an extension of time as provided in the California Rules of Court.

(c) [The Settlement Conference]

(1) A justice selected by the court from outside the division to which the appeal is assigned shall preside over the settlement conference. The Settlement Conference Justice will notify the parties of the date and time of the conference. All subsequent communications regarding the settlement conference shall be directed to the Settlement Conference Justice and shall not be entered in the court file. The Settlement Conference Justice may conduct the conference as he or she deems appropriate.

(2) All parties and their counsel of record must attend all settlement conference sessions in person with full settlement authority. If the party is not an individual, a party representative with full authority to settle all appeals and cross-appeals must attend all settlement conference sessions in person, in addition to counsel. If a party has potential insurance coverage applicable to any of the issues in dispute, a representative of each insurance carrier whose policy may apply must also attend all settlement conference sessions in person, with full settlement authority. Any party seeking an exception to these requirements must seek and obtain advance approval by the Settlement Conference Justice. The Settlement Conference Justice may invite participation by any additional person or entity if he or she concludes that such participation would facilitate settlement.

(d) [Implementation of Settlement Agreements] The parties and their counsel shall promptly take the steps necessary to implement the agreements reached at the settlement conference. An appellant who has settled must immediately serve and file a notice of settlement in this court and thereafter seek abandonment or dismissal of the appeal as provided in California Rules of Court, rule 8.244.

(e) [Confidentiality] Except as otherwise required by law, information disclosed to the Settlement Conference Justice, the parties, counsel, or any other participant in the settlement conference shall be confidential and shall not be disclosed to anyone not participating in the settlement conference.

(f) [Appellate Process] Parties and counsel shall comply with all rules applicable to processing appeals while concurrently participating in settlement activities under this rule.

(g) [Sanctions] Monetary sanctions may be imposed by the Settlement Conference Justice or the Administrative Presiding Justice for failure to comply with these rules.

Rule 9 adopted, effective August 23, 2019.

Rule 10.   Filing by Facsimile [Repealed]

Rule 10 adopted, effective October 16, 2006; repealed effective August 23, 2019.

Another Rule 10 follows.

Rule 10.   Motions for Stipulated Reversal of Judgment

A stipulated motion to reverse or vacate a duly entered judgment will be considered only if it satisfies the requirements of Code of Civil Procedure section 128, subdivision (a)(8).

Such a motion must be accompanied by a copy of the judgment and a joint declaration by the parties or their counsel that:

(a) describes the parties and the factual and legal issues presented at trial;

(b) indicates whether the judgment involves important public rights or unfair, illegal or corrupt practices, or torts affecting a significant number of people, or otherwise affects a significant number of people who are not parties to the litigation;

(c) discloses whether the judgment exposes any person who is a state licensee to a possible disciplinary proceeding; and

(d) discloses whether the judgment may have collateral estoppel or other effects in potential future litigation and, if so, whether third parties who might be prejudiced by stipulated reversal of the judgment have received notice of the motion.

Rule 10 adopted, effective August 23, 2019.

Rule 11.   Extensions of Time for Filing Briefs [Repealed]

Rule 11 adopted, effective October 16, 2006; repealed effective August 23, 2019.

Another Rule 11 follows.

Rule 11.   Extensions of Time for Filing Briefs

(a) [Procedure] The deadlines for filing briefs in civil, criminal, and juvenile appeals are specified in the California Rules of Court. In civil cases, the parties may stipulate to extend the time for filing each brief not more than 60 days. In criminal proceedings, extensions of time by

stipulation are not allowed. (See, e.g., Cal. Rules of Court, rule 8.360(c)(4).) Extensions of time will be granted by the court only on a showing of good cause. (See *id.*, rule 8.60(b).) In certain juvenile proceedings, extensions of time may be granted only on an exceptional showing of good cause. (See, e.g., *id.*, rules 8.416(f), 8.450(d), 8.454(d).) The factors the court considers when evaluating whether an applicant for an extension of time has shown good cause or has made an exceptional showing of good cause are identified in California Rules of Court, rule 8.63(b).

An application for an extension of time to file a brief is not necessary, either before or after a default notice is issued under the California Rules of Court, if the brief can be and is filed within the pertinent default period. The clerk shall accept such a brief as timely filed.

(b) [Forms] An application for an extension of time to file a brief shall be substantially in the form of one of the following:

(1) Application for Extension of Time to File Brief (Civil Case) (Judicial Council Forms, form APP-006.)

(2) Application for Extension of Time to File Brief (Criminal Case) (Judicial Council Forms, form CR-126.)

(3) Application for Extension of Time to File Brief (Juvenile Case) (Judicial Council Forms, form JV-816.)

These forms are available on the court's website at: http://www.courts.ca.gov/1954.htm.

(c) [Automatic Extension for Omitted Record] If a party asks the superior court to prepare an omitted part of the record under California Rules of Court, rules 8.155(b), 8.340(b), or 8.410(a), and provides this court with notice of the request, the deadline for filing the party's brief shall be automatically extended by 15 days from the date the omitted part of the record is filed. This extension shall not shorten any other extensions of time that are granted.

Rule 11 adopted, effective August 23, 2019.

Rule 12.   Bankruptcy Stays [Repealed]

Rule 12 adopted, effective October 16, 2006; repealed effective August 23, 2019.

Another Rule 12 follows.

Rule 12.   Electronic Filing

Bookmarking and Pagination

Editor's Note: The document can be found here: https://www.courts.ca.gov/documents/1dca-Local-Rule-12-bookmarks-and-pagination.pdf.

Guide to Creating Electronic Appellate Documents

Editor's Note: The document can be found here: https://www.courts.ca.gov/documents/DCA-Guide-To-Electronic-Appellate-Documents.pdf.

All filings are to be made through the Court's electronic filing system (EFS) operated by ImageSoft TrueFiling (TrueFiling). Use of the EFS system is mandatory for all attorneys filing in this District, unless an exemption is granted, and is voluntary for all self-represented litigants. A filing in electronic format will be accepted in lieu of any paper copies otherwise required under California Rules of Court, rule 8.44, and constitutes the official record of the Court.

(a) [Registration]

(1) Obligation to Register. Each attorney of record in any proceeding in this District is obligated to become an EFS user and obtain a user ID and password for access to the TrueFiling system. Self-represented litigants must register if they wish to e-file. Attorneys and self-represented litigants may register at: https://tf3.truefiling.com/register.

(2) Obligation to Keep Account Information Current. An EFS user is responsible for all documents filed under the user's registered ID and password. Registered users are required to keep their e-mail address current and may update their e-mail address online via the TrueFiling Web site.

(b) [Format]

(1) Documents filed electronically must be in PDF format, or readily capable of conversion to PDF format while maintaining original document formatting by TrueFiling to permit text searches and to facilitate transmission and retrieval. If the filer possesses only a paper copy of a document, it may be scanned to convert it to a searchable PDF format. It is the filer's responsibility to ensure that any document filed is complete and readable. No single document shall exceed a total file size of 25 MB.

(2) Electronic briefs must comply with the content and form requirements of California Rules of Court, rule 8.204, with the exception of those provisions dealing exclusively with requirements for paper. Electronic bookmarks to each topic heading in the text (as listed in the table of

contents) in briefs are required. To the extent reasonably practicable, the court encourages the use of hyperlinks in legal citations to the Westlaw or Lexis legal research database.

(3) Motions, Writs and Other Original Proceedings. All motions, writs and other original proceedings (excluding Judicial Council form pleadings) must include electronic bookmarks to each section heading in the text (as listed in the table of contents), and to the first page of any exhibit(s), with the exhibit number or letter and a description of the exhibit included in the bookmark. All exhibits should be submitted in a single volume if possible, with multiple volumes permitted only to the extent necessary to meet file size limitations in subdivision (b)(1) of this rule. Each page shall be consecutively numbered, starting with the cover page of Volume 1 and ending with the last page of the last volume, including indexes. [Do not use a separate pagination system for indexes within the volumes. The page number does not need to appear on the cover pages and can be suppressed.] Each exhibit volume shall clearly state the volume and page numbers included within that volume and include an index of contents, with a descriptive electronic bookmark including exhibit number or letter, to the first page of each indexed document (e.g., Exhibit 1—First Amended Complaint).

Pleadings and exhibits not properly formatted may be rejected.

(c) [Signatures] A TrueFiling user ID and password is the equivalent of an electronic signature for a registered attorney or party. Any document displaying the symbol "/s/" with the attorney's or party's printed name shall be deemed signed by that attorney/party.

(d) [Trial Court Record]

(1) Appendices, Agreed Statements, and Settled Statements. Parties must submit any appendix filed pursuant to California Rules of Court, rule 8.124, any agreed statement filed pursuant to rule 8.134, or any settled statement filed pursuant to rule 8.137 in electronic form. Appendices should be submitted in a single volume if possible, with multiple volumes permitted only to the extent necessary to meet file size limitations in subdivision (b)(1) of this rule. If multiple volumes are required, they shall be consecutively paginated. Each volume shall clearly state the volume and page numbers included within that volume and include an index of contents, with a descriptive electronic bookmark, to the first page of each indexed document. Appendices exceeding 10 volumes should be delivered to the court on machine readable optical media in lieu of e-filing. A party submitting such an appendix shall file a notice of lodging via TrueFiling.

(2) Administrative Records. In addition to any administrative record provided by the trial court pursuant to California Rules of Court, rule 8.123, the party or parties seeking review must submit a copy of the administrative record in electronic form. An administrative record may be delivered to the court on machine readable optical media in lieu of e-filing.

(3) Reporter's Transcripts. Any party who orders a reporter's transcript of proceedings pursuant to California Rules of Court, rule 8.130, must also request a copy of the transcript in computer-readable format, as provided in Code of Civil Procedure section 271, subdivision (a), and submit an electronic copy to the Court. Should the reporter's transcript exceed the size limitations in subdivision (b)(1) of this rule, a party must either (i) submit the transcript in multiple parts, or (ii) provide the Court with the transcript in digital format on machine readable optical media.

(4) Submissions by the Trial Court.

(i) To the extent that a trial court is able to do so, the court shall submit the clerk's transcript and/or the reporter's transcript(s) in searchable PDF format, either through the TrueFiling system or a court provided portal, in lieu of paper copies otherwise required under the California Rules of Court, and make electronic versions available to parties willing to accept them in lieu of paper copies. One paper copy, in addition to any electronic copy, must be provided to an indigent criminal defendant or his/her counsel. Digital copies of clerk's transcripts and reporter's transcripts must comply with the California Rules of Court.

(ii) Notwithstanding subpart (4)(i) above if, prior to January 1, 2023, a trial court or the court's official reporter or reporter pro tempore lacks the technical ability to use or store a clerk or reporter's transcript in electronic form as prescribed in section 271 of the Code of Civil Procedure and the California Rules of Court, the trial court may provide advance notice of this fact to the Clerk of the Court and may file a paper original of the record or portion of the record that it cannot file electronically. If the proceedings in an action are transcribed by multiple court reporters, those who can deliver transcripts in electronic form must do so, while those who cannot, must notify this court before providing paper copies. All reporters who work on a single action must coordinate with each other to ensure that all transcripts, electronic and paper, are numbered sequentially.

(iii) In the event a paper original of the reporter's transcript is filed with the court and the transcript was produced with computer aided transcription equipment, upon notice by the court made within 120 days of the filing or delivery of the paper transcript, the official reporter or official reporter pro tempore shall provide an electronic copy of the transcript in full text-searchable PDF format.

(e) [Personal Identifiers and Privacy Issues] To protect personal privacy, parties and their attorneys must not include, or must redact where inclusion is necessary, personal identifiers such as social security numbers, driver's license numbers, and financial account numbers from all pleadings and other papers filed in the Court's public file, whether filed in paper or electronic form, unless otherwise provided by law or ordered by the Court. (Cal. Rules of Court, rule 1.201(a).) If an individual's social security number is required in a pleading or other paper filed in the public file, only the last four digits of that number shall be used. If financial account numbers are required in a pleading or other paper filed in the public file, only the last four digits of these numbers shall be used. Particularly sensitive confidential information such as medical records and proprietary or trade secret information should be filed only under seal as required by law or authorized pursuant to the California Rules of Court.

The responsibility for excluding or redacting identifiers from all documents filed with the Court rests solely with the parties and their attorneys. (Cal. Rules of Court, rule 1.201(b).) Neither TrueFiling nor the Clerk of the Court has any responsibility to review pleadings or other papers for compliance.

(f) [Filing Deadlines] Filing documents electronically does not alter any filing deadlines. In order to be timely filed on the day they are due, all electronic transmissions of documents must be completed (i.e., received completely by the Clerk of the Court) prior to midnight. Where a specific time of day is set for filing by Court order or stipulation, the electronic filing shall be completed by that time. Although EFS permits parties to submit documents electronically 24 hours a day, users should be aware that telephone or online assistance may not be available outside of normal Court business hours.

(g) [Completion of Filing] Electronic transmission of a document through TrueFiling in compliance with the California Rules of Court shall, upon confirmed receipt of the entire document by the Clerk of the Court, constitute filing of the document for all purposes.

(h) [Technical Failure/Motions for Late Filing] If a filer fails to meet a filing deadline imposed by Court order, rule, or statute because of a failure at any point in the electronic transmission and receipt of a document, the filer may file the document on paper or electronically as soon thereafter as practicable and accompany the filing with a motion to accept the document as timely filed. For good cause shown, the Court may enter an order permitting the document to be filed nunc pro tunc to the date the filer originally sought to transmit the document electronically.

The Clerk of the Court shall deem the EFS system to be subject to a technical failure whenever the system is unable to accept filings continuously or intermittently over the course of any period of time greater than one hour after 12:00 noon that day. Filings due on the day of a technical failure which were not filed solely due to such technical failure shall be due the next court day. Such delayed filings shall be accompanied by a declaration or affidavit attesting to at least two attempts by the filer to file electronically after 12:00 noon with each attempt at least one hour apart on each day of delay due to such technical failure. The initial point of contact for any practitioner experiencing difficulty filing a document into the EFS system shall be the toll-free number posted on the TrueFiling Web site.

The Court shall not be responsible for malfunction or errors occurring in electronic transmission or receipt of electronically filed documents.

(i) [Manual Filing] An EFS user may be excused from filing a particular document electronically if (1) it is not available in electronic format; (2) it must therefore be scanned to PDF; and (3) the file size of the scanned document exceeds the limit specified on the EFS Web site. Such a document instead shall be manually filed with the Clerk of Court and served upon the parties in accordance with the statutory requirements and the California Rules of Court applicable to service of paper documents. Parties manually filing a document shall file electronically a manual filing notification setting forth the reason why the document cannot be filed electronically.

(j) [Service] Attorneys or self-represented parties who have registered with TrueFiling to participate in EFS consent to service or delivery of all documents by any other party in a case through the system. (Cal. Rules of Court, rule 8.78.) Orders or other documents generated by the Court will be served only through the EFS or by e-mailed notification. Only self-represented litigants who are not registered EFS users will receive manual service or notification by other means.

(k) [Filing fees] TrueFiling is a private vendor under contract with the Court. TrueFiling will assess vendor fees for each filing in accordance with the schedule posted on its website, as approved by the Court. E-filing fees will be considered recoverable costs under California Rules of Court, rule 8.278(d)(1)(D). TrueFiling is designated as the Court's agent for collection of Court imposed fees where required for any filing, and any associated credit card or bank charges or convenience fees (Cal. Rules of Court, rule 8.78; Gov. Code, § 6159).

Self-represented parties are exempt from the requirement of electronic filing. However, should a self-represented party with a fee waiver opt to file documents electronically, that party is exempt from the fees and costs associated with electronic filing. The persons and entities identified in Government Code section 6103 also are exempt from the fees and costs associated with e-filing.

(l) [Exemptions] Self-represented parties may, but are not required to register for electronic filing, but must comply with this rule and the requirements of TrueFiling if they elect to register.

If this rule causes undue hardship or significant prejudice to any party, the party shall lodge the number of paper copies required by the California Rules of Court without regard to electronic filing, plus an additional unbound paper copy in lieu of the electronic copy, accompanied by a declaration setting forth facts that support the claim of hardship. Acceptance of the lodged papers for filing will be subject to further order of the Court. When it is not otherwise feasible for a party to convert a document to electronic form by scanning, imaging or other means, the document may be filed in paper form (Cal. Rules of Court, rule 8.71(g)), together with a declaration setting forth the reasons that electronic filing was not feasible.

(m) [Sanctions for Noncompliance] Failure of counsel to timely register or otherwise comply with EFS filing requirements, unless exempted, shall subject counsel to sanctions as may be imposed by the Court.

Rule 12 adopted, effective August 23, 2019.

Rule 13.   Argument by Teleconference System [Repealed]
Rule 13 adopted, effective October 16, 2006; repealed effective August 23, 2019.

Another Rule 13 follows.

Rule 13.   Oral Argument
(a) [Option to Waive Argument] After a case has been briefed and assigned to a judicial panel for resolution, the parties will be notified that they may elect to waive oral argument. The court attaches no significance to waiving argument, and it understands that oral argument may be unnecessary when the parties' positions have been fully briefed.

(b) [Notice and Procedure] If any party timely elects to proceed with oral argument, the court will notify the parties of the time and date of the argument. The oral argument will be conducted in accordance with the California Rules of Court.

(c) [Time] The amount of time allocated for each side to present oral argument may vary. Normally, the parties should plan on being allocated 15 minutes per side, although the court may expand or shorten this time before or at the oral argument.

(d) [Sharing Argument Time] In cases in which two or more parties have interests that are aligned, i.e., are on the same side, those parties shall confer before the oral argument on how they prefer to share their side's time during the oral argument. Multiple attorneys who share time should avoid repeating arguments made by other attorneys.

(e) [Oral Argument Dates] The court maintains a list of the currently scheduled oral argument dates for each division. The list is available on the court's web site at http://www.courts.ca.gov/11245.htm. The dates on the list are tentative and parties and their counsel should always verify them with the clerk of the division to which a case is assigned.

(f) [Recording of Oral Argument] The court records all oral arguments, including oral arguments presented by telephone conference call. A request for oral argument by telephone will be deemed consent to such recording.

Rule 13 adopted, effective August 23, 2019.

Rule 14.   Circuit Riding Sessions [Repealed]
Rule 14 adopted, effective October 16, 2006; repealed effective August 23, 2019.

Another Rule 14 follows.

Rule 14.   Oral Argument by Teleconference
(a) [Teleconference Availability] Counsel or self-represented litigants may elect to present oral argument by telephone instead of personally appearing in court. Oral arguments by telephone will be heard by the justices while they are in public session in the courtroom.

(b) [Option of Counsel or Party Without Counsel] The decision whether to present oral argument by telephone or in person is within the discretion of counsel or self-represented litigants, except that the court may direct counsel or self-represented litigants to appear in person.

(c) [Election] Counsel or self-represented litigants shall indicate any election to present oral argument by telephone when oral argument is requested. If one party elects to argue by telephone and the other elects to appear in person, the party who elected to argue by telephone may change his or her mind and appear in person, but he or she must promptly inform the divisional deputy clerk and the opposing parties.

(d) [Necessary Information] An election to present oral argument by telephone shall be made in writing and shall contain the following information: (1) the number and title of the case; (2) the name of the person who will present oral argument by telephone; (3) if that person is an attorney, the name of the party whom he or she is representing; and (4) the telephone number to be used for the telephone conference call.

(e) [Fees] No fee shall be charged for an election to present oral argument by telephone that is made by appointed counsel, the Attorney General, counsel representing the state, a county, a municipality or other government agency, or a party whose fees have been waived under California Rules of Court, rule 8.26. In all other cases, a fee of $20 shall be paid by each party who elects to present oral argument by telephone. A check in that amount, payable to the "Clerk, Court of Appeal," shall accompany the party's request for oral argument.

(f) [Notice of Time of Oral Argument] When counsel or parties elect to present oral argument by telephone, the divisional deputy clerk shall provide notice of the date, the approximate time of oral argument, and may indicate the maximum amount of time the court will allow for argument. The deputy clerk will arrange the conference call when the court calls the case for argument. If counsel or a self-represented litigant fails to be available when the case is called, the court may deem oral argument waived.

Rule 14 adopted, effective August 23, 2019.

Rule 15.   Media Coverage of Matters at Oral Argument [Repealed]
Rule 15 adopted, effective October 16, 2006; repealed effective August 23, 2019.

Another Rule 15 follows.

Rule 15.   Focus Letters and Tentative Opinions
(a) [Focus Letters] Panels may issue focus orders or letters in cases scheduled for oral argument. These orders or letters are issued before argument, and they notify the parties about particular issues the panel is interested in discussing.

(b) [Tentative Opinions] Panels may, on occasion and in their sole discretion, issue tentative opinions in cases scheduled for oral argument. Any such tentative opinion will be issued before the argument, and the parties will be notified that the court is prepared to rule along the lines indicated in the tentative opinion. The oral argument will remain calendared unless all parties, within a period designated by the panel, notify the clerk that it is no longer desired.

(1) If all parties notify the clerk that oral argument is no longer desired, the substance of the tentative opinion will be reflected in the court's final opinion, provided however that if, for any reason, the panel subsequently contemplates a substantial change in the analysis or disposition, the parties will be so notified and given the opportunity to request oral argument.

(2) If all parties do not notify the clerk that oral argument is no longer desired, oral argument will proceed as calendared and the views expressed in the tentative opinion will be subject to change.

Rule 15 adopted, effective August 23, 2019.

Rule 16.   Electronic Filing [Repealed]
Rule 16 adopted, effective March 17, 2014; amended, effective May 1, 2015, and October 12, 2018; repealed effective August 23, 2019.

Another Rule 16 follows.

Rule 16.   New Authority Prior to Oral Argument

Parties submitting a letter of new authorities prior to oral argument under California Rules of Court, rule 8.254 must submit the letter when the authorities become available and as far in advance of any scheduled oral argument as possible. No argument or further discussion of those authorities is permitted in the letter.

Rule 16 adopted, effective August 23, 2019.

Rule 17.   Electronic Devices in the Courtroom

Counsel and self-represented litigants may use laptop computers and electronic tablets to aid them in taking notes and presenting oral argument, but they may not use them for any other purpose, including displaying demonstrative evidence. Electronic devices must be silenced at all times. No cellular telephones or other electronic devices are permitted in the courtroom, except for use as assisted-listening devices. No audio or video recording or photography is permitted in the courtroom, except in compliance with California Rule of Court, rule 1.150. Failure to comply with these restrictions may result in the violator being removed from the courtroom.

Rule 17 adopted, effective August 23, 2019.

Rule 18.   Media Coverage of Oral Argument

A request to photograph, record, or broadcast an oral argument must comply with California Rules of Court, rule 1.150 and be approved by written order of the presiding justice of the division to which a case is assigned.

Rule 18 adopted, effective August 23, 2019.

Rule 19.   Abbreviated Opinions

In accordance with Standard 8.1 of the Standards of Judicial Administration, a memorandum or other abbreviated form of opinion may be issued in causes that (1) are determined by a controlling statute not challenged as unconstitutional and not presenting a substantial question of interpretation or application, (2) are determined by a controlling decision that does not require a reexamination or clarification of its principles or holdings, or (3) raise factual issues that are resolved by the substantial-evidence rule.

Rule 19 adopted, effective August 23, 2019.

Rule 20.   Circuit-riding Sessions

The court will conduct its sessions in its courtroom in San Francisco, except that sessions may occasionally be held at educational institutions or elsewhere within the district.

Rule 20 adopted, effective August 23, 2019.

Rule 21.   Parties' Obligation to Notify Court of Bankruptcy Stays

(a) [Conditions for Giving Notice] Any party to a matter pending before this court who is aware of a bankruptcy that could cause or impose a stay of proceedings in this court must promptly give notice of such bankruptcy, as set forth below.

(b) [Procedure for Notice] The notice required by subdivision (a) shall be filed with the court and served on all parties and shall include (1) a copy of the most recent order of the bankruptcy court and of any stay order issued by that court and (2) an explanation of whether a stay order or an automatic stay is in effect and why the stay applies to the pending appeal or writ proceeding. Any party disputing the notifying party's documentation or explanation shall promptly serve and file an opposing statement.

(c) [Status Reports] On the first court days of January, April, July, and October, the debtor or other party for whose benefit a stay of proceedings in this case has been taken must serve and file brief status reports informing the court of the status of the bankruptcy.

(d) [Notice to Proceed] Any party may, at any time, serve and file notice of any circumstances or orders permitting the stay of proceedings in this court to end, including evidence that the bankruptcy stay has been lifted, the bankruptcy proceeding has been dismissed, or the party has obtained relief from the stay.

Rule 21 adopted, effective August 23, 2019.

INTERNAL OPERATING PRACTICES AND PROCEDURES FIRST APPELLATE DISTRICT

(Adopted effective April 2, 2007)

I. INTRODUCTION

A. Purpose and Scope
B. General Information
II. ORGANIZATION OF THE COURT
A. Justices and Staff
B. Clerk/Administrator, Clerk's Office Staff, and Administrative Support Staff
C. Managing Attorney and Central Staff
D. Mediation Program Administrator and Support Staff
III. PROCEDURES FOR PROCESSING CASES
A. Assignment of Cases to Divisions
B. Processing of Appeals
C. Processing of Original Proceedings

I. INTRODUCTION

A. Purpose and Scope

The purpose of this document is to inform members of the bar and other interested persons about the organization of the court and its procedures for processing cases. It is not intended to duplicate the California Rules of Court, the Local Rules of the First Appellate District, or the statutes and constitutional provisions governing the processing of cases.

B. General Information

The court's address is:

California Court of Appeal
First Appellate District
350 McAllister Street
San Francisco, CA 94102

The clerk's office is located on the first floor in Room 1185 and is open to the public from 9 a.m. to 5 p.m., Monday through Friday, exclusive of state holidays. Its internet e-mail address is: first.district@jud.ca.gov

The court's telephone numbers are:

(415) 865-7200 (Clerk's Office)
(415) 865-7209 (Clerk's Office Fax)
(415) 865-7300 (Chambers' Receptionist)
(415) 865-7309 (Reception Fax)

The court's website is:

http://www.courtinfo.ca.gov/courts/
courtsofappeal/1stDistrict/

II. ORGANIZATION OF THE COURT

A. Justices and Staff

The First Appellate District is comprised of five divisions, each consisting of a presiding justice and three associate justices. Each division operates as a separate unit for the purpose of hearing and deciding cases.

The presiding justice of each division convenes conferences and presides at hearings (oral arguments) in the division and has overall responsibility for calendaring cases, managing the caseload of the division, and all other divisional administrative matters. If the presiding justice is absent or disqualified or not a member of the three-justice panel assigned to decide a matter, the presiding justice usually designates the senior associate justice of the division to serve as acting presiding justice. The Chief Justice of California has designated one of the court's presiding justices to serve as its administrative presiding justice, as prescribed in the California Rules of Court.

Each of the court's justices employs a judicial assistant and two chambers attorneys. Some of the court's justices also utilize law student externs to assist in their individual chambers. In addition, each division employs a writ attorney and a divisional attorney, who are selected by the justices of the division and supervised by its presiding justice.

B. Clerk/Administrator, Clerk's Office Staff, and Administrative Support Staff

The court's clerk/administrator is selected by the justices of the court and works under the general direction and supervision of the administrative presiding justice. The clerk/administrator is responsible for planning, organizing, coordinating, and directing the management of the clerk's office and its personnel. The clerk/administrator also supervises the court's administrative support staff. The clerk/administrator is responsible for all nonjudicial support activities, including personnel, budget, technology, and facilities.

C. Managing Attorney and Central Staff

The court's managing attorney is selected by the justices of the court and works under the general direction and supervision of the administrative presiding justice. The managing attorney serves as legal advisor to the court, its justices, and the clerk's office on a variety of issues, including personnel and matters of appellate procedure. The managing attorney also supervises the court's central staff attorneys and judicial assistants.

D. Mediation Program Administrator and Support Staff

The court's mediation program administrator is selected by the administrative presiding justice and works under the general direction and supervision of the administrative presiding justice or a designated supervising justice. The mediation program administrator is responsible for the day-to-day administration of the court's mediation program and supervises its support staff.

III. PROCEDURES FOR PROCESSING CASES

A. Assignment of Cases to Divisions

1. *In General.* Appeals are assigned to a division when the clerk's office receives the notices of appeal from the superior court where they were filed. Writ petitions are assigned to a division when they are filed with the clerk's office. Assignments are made in rotation, without regard to subject matter or complexity. Exceptions to the random assignment procedures are made if multiple appeals or writ petitions arise from the same trial court action or proceeding, in which case later appeals or writ petitions are assigned to the same division to which the first appeal or writ petition was assigned.

2. *Transfer of Cases.* If, subsequent to the initial assignment of an appeal or writ petition to a division, it is determined that it arises from the same trial court action or proceeding as a prior appeal or writ petition, the administrative presiding justice may transfer the later appeal or writ petition to the same division to which the first appeal or writ petition was assigned. If multiple appeals or writ petitions arise from different trial court actions or proceedings, but involve the same parties or co-parties and the same or related subject matter, transaction, or incident, the court may request that the Supreme Court transfer later appeals or writ petitions to the same division to which the first appeal or writ petition was assigned.

B. Processing of Appeals

1. *Assignment of Appeals to Panels.* When an appeal is fully briefed, it is ready for assignment to a panel of three justices for decision. The court maintains a computer-generated list of fully briefed civil appeals and a separate list of fully briefed criminal and juvenile appeals. The appeals are listed in the order in which they became fully briefed. Appeals entitled to priority on calendar are assigned first, followed by non-priority appeals in the order in which they became fully briefed. Appeals are assigned to panels in rotation, equalizing the number of cases in which each justice participates. One of the three justices on the panel is designated as the lead justice for each appeal. Appeals are assigned randomly, without regard to subject matter, except that an appeal may be assigned to the same panel to which a related appeal or writ petition was previously assigned.

2. *Draft Opinions.* After an appeal is assigned to a panel, the lead justice prepares a draft opinion. Although the format may vary somewhat from justice to justice or division to division, the draft opinion generally includes the following information: (1) a statement of the pertinent factual and procedural history of the case; (2) an analysis of each issue necessary to resolve the appeal; and (3) a proposed disposition. The primary purpose of the draft opinion is to provide the panel with all of the relevant information it needs to decide the appeal. Upon completion, the lead justice distributes the draft opinion to the other two justices on the panel for their review. The panel may also meet to discuss the case. Conferencing practices vary from division to division.

3. *Oral Argument and Submission of the Cause.* When an appeal is assigned to a panel of three justices for decision, the court initially notifies the parties that oral argument will be deemed waived unless one of the parties requests oral argument within the time designated in the notice. If the parties request oral argument, or if the court otherwise determines that oral argument would be helpful, the clerk's office then notifies the parties of the date, time, and place of the hearing. A continuance of oral argument will be granted only upon written application and a showing of good cause. Counsel may not stipulate to a continuance. At the conclusion of oral argument, the presiding justice or acting presiding justice will declare the matter submitted, unless submission is deferred pending further briefing.

4. *Preparation and Filing of Opinions.* After oral argument or the waiver of oral argument, the lead justice prepares a final draft of the opinion. If the other two justices on the panel concur in the opinion, they sign it and it is delivered to the clerk's office for filing. If an individual justice does not subscribe to all of the reasoning of an opinion, he or she may file a separate opinion. If the lead justice fails to obtain the concurrence of at least one of the other justices on the panel, the case may be reassigned to one of the other panel members for the preparation of an opinion. An opinion is published if a majority of the justices on the panel certifies it for publication.

5. *Rehearings.* When a petition for rehearing is filed, the clerk's office delivers the petition to the justice who authored the court's opinion. After reviewing the petition and conducting whatever research he or she deems necessary, the authoring justice circulates the petition to the other two justices on the panel with a recommended ruling. Two votes are necessary to grant or deny a petition for rehearing. A petition for rehearing normally will not be granted unless the court has requested an answer. An order granting rehearing vacates the court's original opinion and sets the case for full reconsideration. Generally, the parties have no right to reargue the case; however, the court, in its discretion, may invite either written briefing or oral argument, or both, before resubmitting the matter and filing its new opinion.

C. Processing of Original Proceedings

After a writ petition has been filed, the clerk's office delivers the petition to the writ attorney for the division to which the writ is assigned. Depending upon the nature of the petition and its urgency, the writ attorney may present the petition to a panel of justices shortly after its filing, or may perform extensive research. In appropriate cases, the court may request opposition from the real party or parties in interest. If an opinion is required, the matter is assigned to one of the justices on the writ panel and is thereafter handled much like the court handles an appeal. The specific procedures governing various types of writ petitions are enumerated in the California Rules of Court.

SECOND APPELLATE DISTRICT LOCAL RULES

[Amended effective October 30, 2017; previously amended effective November 19, 2012, December 31, 2012, March 9, 2014, September 1, 2014, March 9, 2015, June 24, 2016, July 15, 2016, and August 26, 2016]

Rule 1.   Contents of reporter's and clerk's transcripts
(a) Criminal and Juvenile Delinquency Appeals

In addition to the normal record prescribed by rules 8.320, and 8.407 of the California Rules of Court, all records in defendants' criminal appeals and minors' juvenile delinquency appeals before the Court of Appeal, Second Appellate District, are hereby augmented under rule 8.340 and 8.410 of the California Rules of Court to include reporter's and clerk's transcripts of the following:

(1) [Jury examination and opening statement]

Except if a conviction was obtained by plea or admission, reporter's transcripts of (a) jury voir dire whenever a motion regarding the composition of the jury or jury panel (for example, a motion under *People v. Wheeler* (1978) 22 Cal.3d 258 [148 Cal.Rptr. 890, 583 P.2d 748]) or a motion for a mistrial was made during the jury voir dire and decided in whole or in part adversely to the defendant; and (b) opening statements.

(2) [Sealed and in camera hearings]

Except if a conviction was obtained by plea or admission, oral proceedings of all sealed and in camera hearings resulting in rulings adverse in whole or in part to the appellant. These transcripts shall be listed in the index to the reporter's transcript, and the original and two copies of the sealed transcripts shall be transmitted to this court in sealed envelopes marked "CONFIDENTIAL—MAY NOT BE EXAMINED WITHOUT COURT ORDER." This court shall provide a copy of the sealed transcripts, other than transcripts of a hearing from which the appellant and defense counsel were excluded, to the appellant's counsel on appeal, upon his or her application. If the appellant raises an issue on appeal relating to the sealed transcripts, copies of transcripts shall then be provided to the Attorney General upon their written request. Unless otherwise ordered by this court, the sealed transcripts of a hearing from which the appellant and defense counsel were excluded may be examined only by a justice of this court personally.

(3) [Waivers of constitutional rights]

Reporter's transcripts of oral proceedings at which the appellant's constitutional rights were waived.

(4) [Guilty or nolo contendere pleas and admissions]

Proceedings at which the appellant moved to withdraw a guilty or nolo contendere plea or a juvenile admission, and proceedings at which sentence or disposition was imposed.

(5) [Pretrial proceedings]

(A) The following pretrial proceedings: (i) proceedings to determine competence of the appellant (Pen. Code, § 1368); and (ii) motions for self-representation (*Faretta* v. *California* (1975) 422 U.S. 806 [95 S.Ct. 2525, 45 L.Ed.2d 562]).

(B) Except if a conviction or sustained petition was obtained by plea or admission, the following pretrial proceedings which were decided in whole or in part adversely to the appellant: (i) motions to suppress identification; (ii) motions to suppress statements of the appellant; (iii) motions to permit or preclude impeachment of the appellant or a witness with prior offenses (*People* v. *Castro* (1985) 38 Cal.3d 301 [211 Cal.Rptr. 719, 696 P.2d 111]); (iv) motions for severance or joinder; (v) motions for change of venue; (vi) motions for discovery of police officer records (*Pitchess* v. *Superior Court* (1974) 11 Cal.3d 531 [113 Cal.Rptr. 897, 522 P.2d 305]); and (vii) *in limine* motions.

(6) [Revocation of probation]

In appeals from revocation of probation: (a) the original sentencing or dispositional proceeding at which probation was imposed; (b) the proceedings at the time of entry of a guilty plea or nolo contendere plea or admission if the original judgment of conviction or sustained petition is based on such plea; and (c) the proceedings at which probation is revoked and the appellant is sentenced or disposition is imposed.

(Adopted Aug. 1, 1992; amended effective July 15, 2016.)

(b) Juvenile dependency

In addition to the normal record prescribed by rules 8.407(a) and (b) of the California Rules of Court, the record in a juvenile *dependency* appeal before the Court of Appeal, Second Appellate District, is hereby augmented under rules 8.155(a), 8.410(b), and 8.416(d) of the California Rules of Court as follows:

(1) In all appeals under Welfare and Institutions Code section 395, subdivision (a) (1), a reporter's transcript of the detention hearing.

(2) For an appeal from an order terminating parental rights under Welfare and Institutions Code section 366.26, except in a case where a notice of intent was previously filed (Welf. & Inst. Code section 366.26 subd. (*l*) (1)), a reporter's transcript of the hearing at which the order setting a section 366.26 hearing was made.

(3) In all appeals under Welfare and Institutions Code section 395, subdivision (a) (1), a clerk's transcript containing the printed ICWA inquiry forms (ICWA 010; ICWA 020); all notices sent to an Indian tribe (ICWA 030); all signed return receipts for the mailing of the ICWA 030 notices; and, all responses from an Indian tribe.

(4) In all appeals under Welfare and Institutions Code section 395, subdivision (a) (1), a reporter's transcript of the oral proceedings for which the minutes indicate that the Indian Child Welfare Act (ICWA) was considered.

(Adopted effective July 15, 2016.)

Rule 1 adopted Aug. 1, 1992; amended Mar. 8, 1993; Jan. 1, 2005; Mar. 20, 2006; Jan. 1, 2007; Apr. 16, 2007; Apr. 27, 2009; July 15, 2016.

Rule 2. Augmentation of record and correction of omissions from record

(a) [Material inadvertently omitted]

Counsel should not file a motion to augment the record when items have been omitted from the designated (civil) or normal (criminal) record on appeal. In those cases counsel should immediately notify the clerk of the superior court, who shall forthwith comply with rule 8.340(b) of the California Rules of Court.

(Adopted Aug. 1, 1992; amended Jan. 1, 2007.)

(b) [When to file motion to augment]

Appellant should file requests for augmentation in one motion within 40 days of the filing of the record or the appointment of counsel. Respondent should file requests for augmentation in one motion made within 30 days of the filing of appellant's opening brief. Thereafter, motions to augment will not be granted except upon a showing of good cause for the delay.

(Adopted Aug. 1, 1992; amended Jan. 1, 2005; Jan. 1, 2007; Dec. 31, 2012.)

(c) [Clerk's transcript]

A motion to augment or correct the clerk's transcript shall be accompanied by the documents requested. If the documents are not provided, the motion must identify them with specificity and contain an explanation for their omission. The motion and the accompanying documents must be served simultaneously on opposing counsel. The requested augmented materials shall have been filed or lodged with the trial court and the declaration shall so state.

(Adopted Aug. 1, 1992.)

(d) [Reporter's transcript]

A motion to augment the reporter's transcript shall identify the portion of the record with specificity, including the reporter's name and the date of the hearing. The motion shall establish with some certainty how the requested materials may be useful on appeal.

(Adopted Aug. 1, 1992.)

(e) [Extensions of time]

The time to perform any act required or permitted by the California Rules of Court will not be automatically extended by the filing of or ruling on a motion to augment. If additional time is needed, counsel may request an extension of time in the motion to augment.

(Adopted Aug. 1, 1992.)

(f) [Good faith required]

A motion to augment shall be made in good faith and shall not be made for the purpose of delay.

(Adopted Aug. 1, 1992.)

(g) [Proposed order]

A motion to augment must be accompanied by a proposed order. The form *Order Re: Augmentation* may be used.

(Adopted Aug. 3, 1998.)

(h) [Attachments]

When more than one document or transcript are attached to or submitted with a motion to augment the record pursuant to California Rules of Court, rule 8.155(a), the pages of the documents and transcripts must be consecutively numbered.

(Adopted Sept. 15, 2003; amended Jan. 1, 2007; Apr. 16, 2007.)

Rule 2 adopted Aug. 1, 1992; amended Aug. 3, 1998; Sept. 15, 2003; Jan. 1, 2005; Jan. 1, 2007; Apr. 16, 2007; Dec. 31, 2012.

Rule 3. Designation of the record in civil appeals under California Rules of Court, rules 8.120, 8.122, and 8.130

(a) [Contents of the notice and designation of record]

The notice to prepare a reporter's transcript and the designation of the contents of a clerk's transcript required to be filed with the clerk of the superior court by the California Rules of Court, rules 8.130, 8.120, and 8.122 shall include the following information:

(1) [Reporter's transcript]

The notice to prepare the reporter's transcript shall state for each oral proceeding to be included in the record (1) the date, (2) the department number, (3) the name of the reporter or electronic recording monitor, and (4) the nature of the proceeding.

(2) [Clerk's transcript]

The designation of the contents of the clerk's transcript shall state for each paper or record to be included (1) the title and (2) the date of filing. For each exhibit to be included in the clerk's transcript, the designation shall include (1) the exhibit number, (2) a brief description, and (3) the admission status.

(Adopted May 17, 1996; amended Jan. 1, 2007; Apr. 16, 2007; Apr. 27, 2009.)

(b) [Form to designate record]

The form *Designation of the Record on Appeal* may be used to designate the record in civil appeals.

(Adopted May 17, 1996.)

(c) [Sanctions]

Failure to comply with this local rule is a failure to properly designate the record under California Rules of Court, rules 8.130, 8.120, and 8.122 and may result in the dismissal of the appeal or the imposition of monetary sanctions.

(Adopted May 17, 1996; amended Jan. 1, 2007; Apr. 27, 2009.)

Rule 3 adopted May 17, 1996; amended Jan. 1, 2007; Apr. 16, 2007; Apr. 27, 2009.

Rule 4.   Proposed orders

Any motion or application filed with this court must be accompanied by a proposed order. Failure to comply with this local rule may result in the denial of the motion or application.

Rule 4 adopted Aug. 3, 1998.

Rule 5.   Requests for Judicial Notice [Repealed]

Rule 5 adopted Apr. 12, 1999; repealed Jan. 1, 2005.

Rule 5.   Extensions of time for filing briefs [Repealed]

Rule 5 adopted effective May 5, 2008; repealed effective June 24, 2016.

Rule 6.   Case Information Statement [Repealed]

Rule 6 adopted Aug. 28, 2000, effective Oct. 30, 2000; repealed Mar. 3, 2003.

Another Rule 6 follows.

Rule 6.   Advance notice of request for immediate relief in juvenile dependency writ petitions

Before filing a petition for extraordinary writ with a request for immediate relief in a juvenile dependency proceeding, the petitioner must use best efforts to provide notice in person, by telephone, by facsimile or by e-mail to all parties at the earliest possible time and, when practical, at least 24 hours before filing. In addition, before filing such a petition, the petitioner must deliver to all parties in person, by facsimile, or by e-mail a copy of the petition. A declaration of notice and delivery, including the date, time, manner, name of the individual notified, any response of the individual notified, and whether any opposition will be filed, or a declaration stating the reasons why notice or delivery could not be accomplished, must accompany the petition. Noncompliance with this rule will not prevent the court from exercising its discretion in the best interest of the child.

Rule 6 adopted Sept. 15, 2003.

Rule 7.   Copies of Briefs, Original Proceedings (Writs), Oppositions or Replies to a Writ Petition Including Any Exhibits or Appendices — Electronic or Paper [Repealed]

Rule 7 adopted Nov. 19, 2012; amended Sept. 1, 2014; Mar. 9, 2015; repealed Oct. 30, 2017.

Rule 8.   Filing of an appeal in a dependency matter by a person who is not the child, parent, guardian or social services agency

In order to comply with Welfare and Institutions Code section 827, an appellant who is not the child, parent, guardian or social services agency must complete and file a JV-570 Judicial Council Form Request for Disclosure of Juvenile Court File (JV-570) as follows:

(1) The JV-570 must be filed in the juvenile court with a timely notice of appeal, or within 10 days after the notice of appeal is filed.

(2) The judge or referee in the dependency case shall rule on the JV-570 within the time limit set forth in Welfare and Institutions Code section 827, subdivision (a) (2) (F).

(3) If the JV-570 is denied, the clerk shall prepare a transcript containing the notice of appeal and the JV-570, the JV-571 [Notice of Request for Disclosure of Juvenile Case File], any JV-572 [Objection to Release of Juvenile Case File] and the JV-573 [Order on Request for Disclosure of Juvenile Case File] and/or JV-574 [Order After Judicial Review].

(4) If the Request is granted in whole or part, the clerk and the reporter shall prepare the record designated and approved by the judge or referee as set forth in the JV-574 Order After Judicial Review.

(5) If the JV-570 is not filed, the superior court clerk must promptly notify the petitioner in writing that if the form is not filed within 15 days after the notice is sent, the reviewing court will dismiss the appeal.

Rule 8 adopted effective July 15, 2016; revised effective August 26, 2016.

Rule 9.   Record in later appeals in the same dependency cases

In a later appeal in a dependency case filed by a party in a prior appeal in the case, the record is augmented with the clerk's and reporter's transcripts in the previous appeal(s), and the record shall be prepared as follows:

(1) A clerk's transcript containing the items listed under California Rules of Court rule 8.407 (a) [normal clerk's transcript] which were filed *after* the judgment or order which was the subject of the prior appeal.

(2) A reporter's transcript of the oral proceedings at any hearing which resulted in the order that is the subject of the later appeal.

Rule 9 adopted effective July 15, 2016.

Policy Statement.   Policy Statement for Voluntary Settlement Conference in Civil Appeals [Repealed]

Policy Statement adopted Feb. 16, 1984; repealed April 22, 2002.

INTERNAL OPERATING PRACTICES AND PROCEDURES
SECOND APPELLATE DISTRICT

(Revised effective September 30, 2016)

Purpose
Organization of the District
Processing of Cases
   Assignment of Cases
   Motions
   Appeals
     Preparation of Bench Memoranda
     Oral Argument
     Determination
     Rehearing
     Publication
   Writ Petitions
Assigned Justices
Externship Program
Settlement/Mediation Program
Local Rules

Purpose

The purpose of this document is to provide members of the bar and other interested persons with general information concerning the organization of the Second Appellate District and its procedures for processing cases.

Organization of the District

The Second Appellate District covers four counties and consists of eight divisions. Each division is a separate court for the purpose of hearing and deciding cases assigned to it. Divisions One through Five, Seven and Eight are located at 300 South Spring Street, Los Angeles, California, 90013 and handle all matters arising from Los Angeles County. Division Six is located at 200 East Santa Clara Street, Ventura, California, 93001 and handles all matters arising from Ventura, Santa Barbara, and San Luis Obispo Counties.

Each division consists of three Associate Justices and a Presiding Justice. The Chief Justice appoints one of the Presiding Justices to serve as Administrative Presiding Justice to perform the duties prescribed in the California Rules of Court.

Each justice maintains a chambers which consists of the justice, judicial attorneys, and a judicial assistant. In addition, each division is assigned other judicial attorneys, including writs attorneys, and other judicial assistants, judicial secretaries, and deputy clerks. A Managing Attorney provides direct assistance to the Administrative Presiding Justice and supervises attorneys and judicial assistants who are not assigned to a particular division. These include the staff responsible for Workers' Compensation matters.

A Clerk/Executive Officer is selected by the justices of the district and works under the general direction and supervision of the Administrative Presiding Justice. The Clerk/Executive Officer is responsible for planning, organizing, coordinating, and directing the management of the clerk's office and its personnel. The Clerk/Executive Officer also supervises the library, administrative, and computer services staffs. The Clerk/Executive Officer is responsible for all district support activities, including personnel, budget, technology, and facilities.

Processing of Cases

Assignment of Cases

Appeals and original proceedings (writ petitions) arising in Ventura, Santa Barbara, and San Luis Obispo Counties are assigned to Division Six. Appeals and writ petitions arising in Los Angeles County are assigned to the divisions in Los Angeles (One through Five, Seven and Eight) on a random, pro rata basis, unless an appeal or writ petition arises from a trial court action or proceeding from which an appeal or writ petition was previously filed in the district. In that case, the appeal or writ petition is generally assigned to the division to which the prior appeal or writ petition was assigned. On occasion and in order to equalize workload, Los Angeles cases may be assigned to Division Six and Division Six cases may be assigned to one of the Los Angeles divisions. Once a case has been assigned to a division it remains in that division for all further proceedings unless the clerk upon direction of the Presiding Justice, requests the Supreme Court or the Administrative Presiding Justice to transfer the case to another division or district, under rule 10.1000 of the California Rules of Court. If two or more justices in a division are recused from a case, the case is to be re-assigned to another division.

Motions

The Presiding Justice of each division determines the manner in which motions are handled within that division. Motions filed before a case is assigned to a division are designated "Division P" motions and are ruled upon by the Administrative Presiding Justice.

Appeals

Preparation of Bench Memoranda

After an appeal has been fully briefed, it is generally assigned on a random, pro rata basis to a three-justice panel. A change in the composition of the panel may be required when, for example, a conflict arises or to accommodate workload imbalances. The case is set for oral argument on an upcoming calendar. Oral argument may be waived by the parties. The court is not obligated to accept a waiver and may ask that the parties appear for oral argument.

The justices on the panel review the briefs and the record. Under the direction of the justices, judicial attorneys generally prepare bench memoranda in anticipation of oral argument. The memoranda discuss the procedural background, facts, and issues in the cases and may recommend various treatments and dispositions. The panel members review the memoranda in preparation for oral argument and the filing of written opinions.

If an issue arises that was not raised by the parties, a letter pursuant to Government Code section 68081 will be sent to the parties requesting briefing. The court may order additional briefing on any issue.

Oral Argument

Each division generally schedules hearings for two days each month and entertains argument on those matters for which oral argument has not been waived by the parties. The manner in which calendars are called and the order in which cases are scheduled for argument differ among the divisions. The composition of the panel assigned to each case is announced at the hearing.

Determination

If the parties have waived oral argument or oral argument does not change the justices' understanding of the case, and all justices on the panel agree with the bench memorandum, it may form the basis of the written opinion to be filed. If oral argument raises additional issues to be considered, or consensus among the panel justices does not exist, the bench memorandum may be altered or discarded and a new memorandum may be circulated. Concurring and dissenting opinions may also be prepared. Unless further briefing is allowed, generally cases are submitted at the close of oral argument. If further briefing is allowed, the date of submission will be ordered by the court.

Rehearing

Timely petitions for rehearing are presented to the court for review. If the court desires opposition, the clerk will be directed to call counsel and request that an answer be filed. In some instances, a modification may be issued and rehearing otherwise denied. Grant of a petition for rehearing may or may not result in a request for further briefing or additional oral argument.

Publication

An opinion or part of an opinion may be published if a majority of the panel rendering the decision determines that it meets the standards for publication contained within the California Rules of Court.

Writ Petitions

Writ petitions are reviewed by the justices of the division to which they are assigned, with the assistance of the division's writs attorneys. Writ petitions that do not seek immediate relief are discussed at periodic writ conferences, usually weekly. If the writ petition seeks immediate relief, a timely determination is made. In appropriate cases, the court may issue a stay or other order to preserve the status quo pending further action. The court may summarily deny a writ petition, either before or after receiving opposition. If a writ petition results in the issuance of an alternative writ or an order to show cause, a written opinion generally results unless the trial court complies with the alternative writ.

Assigned Justices

Upon request, the Chief Justice may assign a judge, retired judge, justice, or retired justice to sit as a justice pro tem in a particular division. Assigned justices assist with the court's workload in various situations, including judicial vacancies and disqualifications.

Externship Program

The Second District maintains a centralized unpaid externship program for law students who participate on a part-time or full-time basis and who may receive law school credit. Externs are recruited or may apply, and those selected are assigned to justices in the various divisions. Once assigned to a justice, externs work under the close supervision of the justice and the justice's staff. Individual justices may accept externship applications in addition to using the district's centralized recruitment and assignment program. Externs have come to the district from law schools throughout the United States.

Settlement/Mediation Program

The Second District participates in a district-wide voluntary settlement/mediation program. A volunteer attorney or mediator presides over the settlement/mediation process. If at any time the parties decide to explore the possibility of settlement/mediation, they should contact the clerk's office.

Local Rules

The Second District has adopted a number of local rules. (See Local Rules of the Second District Court of Appeal.)
Amended Jan. 1, 2007; Jan. 1, 2008; March 2009; Sept. 30, 2016.

THIRD APPELLATE DISTRICT LOCAL RULES

[As amended effective April 10, 2020; adopted effective January 1, 1977, and previously amended May 1, 1982, December 31, 1982, November 10, 1986, September 4, 1989, July 6, 1993; as amended, reorganized, and renumbered effective October 2, 2006; and previously amended March 2, 2007, May 29, 2009, December 2, 2013, September 14, 2015, September 26, 2016, May 26, 2017, December 11, 2017, October 1, 2018, and May 31, 2019]

Mediation in Civil Appeals. Rule 1.
Stipulation for use of original superior court file. Rule 2.
Time for oral argument. Rule 3.
Judicial notice of legislative history materials. Rule 4.
Electronic filing. Rule 5.
Appointed Attorney Deemed to Request a Paper Reporter's Transcript. Rule 6.
Internal Operating Practices and Procedures.

Rule 1. Applicability—Settlement Conference Procedures [Repealed]

Rule 1 adopted Jan. 1, 1977; amended May 1, 1982; Dec. 31, 1982; Nov. 10, 1986; Sept. 4, 1989; repealed eff. Oct. 2, 2006.

Another Rule 1 follows.

Rule 1. Mediation in Civil Appeals

(a) Mediation Program

To enable efficient case management and more expeditious resolution of appeals, the Court of Appeal, Third Appellate District (Court), has a Mediation Program (Program) for all civil appeals not exempt from the

Program. Procedures for mediation and operation of the Program are promulgated by the Court of Appeal Mediation Program Committee (Committee).

(Subd (a) adopted eff. October 2, 2006; amended eff. May 29, 2009; December 2, 2013.)

(b) Program administration

The Program is administered by the Mediation Program Administrator (Administrator) acting under the direction of the Committee and under the supervision of the Administrative Presiding Justice or a designated Supervising Associate Justice (Presiding Justice).

(Subd (b) adopted as part of subd (a) eff. October 2, 2006; relettered to subd (b) & amended eff. May 29, 2009; amended eff. December 2, 2013.)

(c) Civil Appeals exempt from the Program

Any appeal taken from a judgment or order entered in a conservatorship, guardianship, or sterilization proceeding is exempt from the Program.

(Subd (c) adopted as subd (b) eff. October 2, 2006; relettered to subd (c) & amended eff. May 29, 2009; amended eff. December 2, 2013.)

(d) Process prior to referral for assessment

(1) Upon filing a notice of appeal in a civil case not exempt from the Program, the provisions of rules 8.121, 8.124(a)(1), 8.128, and 8.216 of the California Rules of Court, requiring designation of the record, payment of estimated costs of preparation of the record, stipulating to proceeding with the original superior court file, and submission of a proposed briefing schedule, are suspended.

(2) These rules do not prohibit the superior court from collecting its deposit required by section 68926.1 of the Government Code and by rule 8.100(b)(2) of the California Rules of Court.

(3) Upon receiving notice of filing of a civil appeal in a case not exempt from the Program,

(A) The Appellant must file a Civil Case Information Statement form (Form APP-004), as required by rule 8.100(g) of the California Rules of Court, and an Appellant's Civil Appeal Mediation Statement form.

(B) The Respondent must file a Respondent's Civil Appeal Mediation Statement form.

(4) The Appellant's Civil Appeal Mediation Statement form must be served and filed within 15 days after the superior court clerk sends notification of the filing of the notice of appeal. Failure to timely file either the Appellant's Civil Case Information Statement or the Appellant's Civil Appeal Mediation Statement will result in dismissal of the appeal, without prejudice to reinstatement upon a showing of good cause.

(5) The Respondent's Civil Appeal Mediation Statement must be served and filed within 10 days after the Appellant's Civil Appeal Mediation Statement is filed. Failure to timely file a Respondent's Civil Appeal Mediation Statement will result in a Program selection decision without input from the respondent.

(6) Generally, multiple appeals from the same judgment or a related order are assigned the same appellate case number unless the record for the first notice of appeal has already been filed. (See Advisory Committee Comment to Cal. Rules of Court, rule 8.147.) Subsequent appellant's and respondent's Civil Appeal Mediation Statements will not be required when a second or subsequent notice of appeal has been filed within the same appellate case number.

(7) After Respondent's Civil Appeal Mediation Statement has been filed or was due to be filed, the Administrator shall promptly notify the parties whether the appeal has been selected for the Program.

(Subd (d) adopted as subd (c) eff. October 2, 2006; repealed & adopted eff. May 29, 2009; amended eff. December 2, 2013, and May 26, 2017.)

(e) Process for referral, assessment, and selection for the Program

(1) If a civil appeal is not exempt from the Program, the Presiding Justice may refer the appeal to the Administrator for assessment.

(2) Upon referral for assessment, the Administrator will communicate with counsel and/or non-represented parties to assess whether the peal is amenable to mediation. Based on the assessment, the Administrator will recommend to the Presiding Justice whether the appeal should be selected for the Program.

(3) The Presiding Justice will then decide whether to select the appeal for the Program.

(Subd (e) adopted eff. May 29, 2009; amended eff. December 2, 2013.)

(f) Stipulation and order for placement in the Program

(1) A civil appeal exempt from, or not selected for, the Program may nonetheless be placed in the Program by stipulation and order.

(2) If an appeal is exempt from the Program, the stipulation must be served on the superior court and filed with the Court within 30 days after

filing of the notice of appeal. If an appeal was not selected for the Program, the stipulation must be served on the superior court and filed with the Court within 10 days after notification that the appeal was not selected.

(3) The original signature of at least one party must appear on the stipulation filed in the Court. The signatures of the other parties may be in the form of copies of the signed signature page of the stipulation.

(4) Upon receipt of the stipulation by the superior court, the provisions of rules 8.121, 8.124(a)(1), 8.128, and 8.216 of the California Rules of Court, requiring designation of the record, payment of estimated costs of preparation of the record, stipulating to proceeding with the original superior court file, and submission of a proposed briefing schedule, are suspended.

(5) The Court will decide whether to sign the stipulation and order and place the appeal in the Program.

(6) If the appeal is placed in the Program by stipulation and order, suspension of rules 8.121, 8.124(a)(1), 8.128, and 8.216 of the California Rules of Court will remain in effect until completion of mediation.

(7) If the proposed stipulation is not approved by the Court and the appeal is not placed in the Program, the Administrator must notify the parties, the superior court, and the Court, in writing, that suspension of rules 8.121, 8.124(a)(1), 8.128, and 8.216 of the California Rules of Court is terminated.

(Subd (f) adopted as subd (d) eff. October 2, 2006; amended eff. March 2, 2007; relettered to subd (f) & amended eff. May 29, 2009; amended eff. December 2, 2013.)

(g) Process following selection decision and prior to mediation

(1) *Upon selection of an appeal for the Program*

(A) The Court will issue an order directing that the appeal has been selected for the Program.

(B) The Administrator will:

(i) Notify the parties that the appeal will be mediated.

(ii) Assign a mediator to the appeal. The Administrator may replace a selected mediator upon request by a party or the mediator based on good cause.

(iii) Furnish the parties with the name, address, and telephone number of the mediator, and three dates when the mediator is available for the mediation sessions.

(C) Within 10 days after receipt of notice of the dates the mediator is available, the parties must mutually confer and advise the Administrator and the mediator of their scheduling preferences.

(2) *Suspension of rules following selection decision*

(A) If an appeal is selected for the Program, suspension of rules 8.121, 8.124(a)(1), 8.128, and 8.216 of the California Rules of Court will remain in effect until completion of the mediation.

(B) If an appeal is not selected for the Program, the Court will issue an order to this effect and the Administrator must notify the parties and the superior court in writing that suspension of rules 8.121, 8.124(a)(1), 8.128, and 8.216 of the California Rules of Court is terminated. Upon notification by the Court or the Administrator that an appeal was not selected for the Program, the parties' obligation to comply with the requirements of rules 8.121, 8.124(a)(1), 8.128 and 8.216 of the California Rules of Court commences as if notice of appeal was filed on the date specified in the notification.

(Subd (g) adopted as subd (e) eff. October 2, 2006; relettered to subd (g) & amended eff. May 29, 2009; amended eff. December 2, 2013.)

(h) Mediation and mediation preparation

(1) *Costs and fees for mediation preparation and services*

(A) Mediators will not charge the parties any fee for the premediation conference call, the mediator's premediation preparation time, and for the first four hours of the initial mediation session.

(B) Notwithstanding subparagraph (h)(1)(A) above, in exceptional cases, the parties and the mediator may agree before the start of the mediation session, in a writing pursuant to Business and Professions Code section 6148, to a fee to be paid by the parties to the mediator for the mediator's additional preparation time.

(C) Prior to the start of the mediation session, the parties and the mediator may agree, in a writing pursuant to Business and Professions Code section 6148, to a fee to be paid by the parties to the mediator to continue the mediation beyond the initial four hours.

(2) *Continuation of mediation sessions*

For good cause and with approval of the Administrator, the mediator and the parties may continue a mediation session to a date certain.

(3) *Mediator communications with parties and counsel*

(A) The mediator may at any time communicate with any counsel or unrepresented parties with or without notice to the other parties or their counsel.

(B) The mediator may require counsel or unrepresented parties to furnish information, documents, records, or other items specified by the mediator.

(4) *Full authority to settle*

(A) Counsel, parties, and persons with full authority to settle the appeal must personally attend the mediation, unless excused in writing by the mediator for good cause. If any consent to settle is required for any reason, the party or person with that consensual authority must be personally present at the mediation.

(B) If a party has potential insurance coverage applicable to any of the issues in dispute, a representative of each insurance carrier whose policy may apply must attend all mediation sessions in person, with full settlement authority. The party with such potential insurance coverage and that party's counsel shall serve timely notice to each insurance carrier with potential insurance coverage informing the carrier: (i) that appellate mediation has been ordered; (ii) that the carrier must have a representative with full settlement authority attend all mediation sessions in person; and (iii) of the date, time, and place of all mediation sessions. (See *Campagnone v. Enjoyable Pools & Spas Service & Repairs, Inc.* (2008) 163 Cal.App.4th 566.)

(C) The mediator may invite participation by any additional person or entity if the mediator concludes that such participation would facilitate mediation.

(5) *Submission of mediation attendance form*

Prior to the start of mediation, the parties and the mediator shall submit to the Administrator a Mediation Attendance Form, listing all participants in the mediation.

(6) *Completion of mediation*

Within 10 days after completion of mediation, the mediator shall submit to the Administrator a Mediator's Statement notifying the Administrator whether an agreement was reached, and the parties and their counsel must separately complete and submit to the Administrator confidential evaluations of the mediation and the mediator on a form provided by the Administrator.

(7) *Appeal not resolved by mediation*

(A) If completion of mediation does not result in disposition of the appeal, the Administrator must, within 10 days after notice of completion of the mediation, notify the parties, the superior court, and the Court, in writing, that suspension of rules 8.121, 8.124(a)(1), 8.128, and 8.216 of the California Rules of Court is terminated.

(B) The parties' obligation to comply with the requirements of rules 8.121, 8.124(a)(1), 8.128 and 8.216 of the California Rules of Court commences as if notice of appeal was filed on the date specified in the notification.

(8) *Appeal resolved by mediation*

(A) Pursuant to California Rules of Court, rule 8.244(a) and (b), if the mediation results in a disposition of the appeal and the record has not been filed in the Court, the appellant must promptly file a notice of settlement with the Court and, within 45 days thereafter, file an abandonment of the appeal in the superior court.

(B) Pursuant to California Rules of Court, rule 8.244(a) and (c), if the mediation results in a disposition of the appeal and the record has been filed in the Court, the appellant must promptly file a notice of settlement in the Court and must, within 45 days thereafter, serve and file in the Court a request for dismissal of the appeal.

(9) *Confidentiality*

Except as otherwise provided by law, information disclosed to the mediator, the parties, counsel, or any other participant in the mediation including the Administrator, is confidential.

(10) *Ethical Standards*

Mediators must adhere to the rules of conduct for mediators in court-sponsored mediation programs for civil cases, as set forth in the California Code of Civil Procedure and the California Rules of Court.

(11) *Sanctions*

Monetary sanctions may be imposed following a noticed motion by a party seeking sanctions for failure to comply with the rules or upon the Court's own motion.

(Subd (h) adopted as subd (f) eff. October 2, 2006; relettered to subd (h) & amended eff. May 29, 2009; amended eff. December 2, 2013, and May 31, 2019.)

Rule 1 adopted eff. October 2, 2006; amended eff. March 2, 2007; May 29, 2009; December 2, 2013; May 26, 2017; May 31, 2019.

Rule 2.   Notification of Counsel [Repealed]

Rule 2 adopted Jan. 1, 1977; amended May 1, 1982; Dec. 31, 1982; Nov. 10, 1986; repealed eff. Oct. 2, 2006.

Another Rule 2 follows.

Rule 2.   Stipulation for use of original superior court file

Rule 8.128 of the California Rules of Court provides for the use of the original superior court file in lieu of the clerk's transcript on appeal in those civil cases where the parties so stipulate. In accordance with rule 8.128 of the California Rules of Court, the procedure therein is approved for use by the superior courts within this district.

Rule 2 adopted as Rule 22, eff. Sept. 4, 1989; renumbered from rule 22 eff. October 2, 2006; amended eff. March 2, 2007.

Rule 3.   Settlement Conference Statement [Repealed]

Rule 3 adopted Jan. 1, 1977; amended May 1, 1982; Dec. 31, 1982; Nov. 10, 1986; repealed eff. Oct. 2, 2006.

Another Rule 3 follows.

Rule 3.   Time for oral argument

Each side is allowed 15 minutes for oral argument. Where there are more than two parties, a "side" consists of all parties whose interests are not adverse. If there are more than two parties represented by separate counsel who request oral argument, or if counsel for amicus curiae requests oral argument, the court may apportion or expand the time according to the respective interests of the parties and of amicus curiae. Any request for additional time for oral argument must be made by written application submitted to the court within 10 calendar days of the date of the order setting oral argument. The application must be served contemporaneously on all other parties and must specify the amount of time requested and the issues to which additional oral argument will be addressed. When an application is granted, the time allotted to the other side or sides will be similarly enlarged. All parties will be advised of the disposition of any such application prior to hearing.

Rule 3 adopted, eff. April 10, 1998; renumbered from rule 23 eff. October 2, 2006.

Rule 4.   Sanctions and Excuse for Non-Compliance [Repealed]

Rule 4 adopted Jan. 1, 1977; amended May 1, 1982; Dec. 31, 1982; July 6, 1993; repealed eff. Oct. 2, 2006.

Another Rule 4 follows.

Rule 4.   Judicial notice of legislative history materials

A party making a motion to have the Court take judicial notice of legislative history documents must identify each such document as a separate exhibit and must provide legal authority supporting the consideration of each document as cognizable legislative history. (See *Kaufman & Broad Communities, Inc. v. Performance Plastering, Inc.* (2005) 133 Cal.App.4th 26.)

Rule 4 adopted eff. October 2, 2006.

Rule 5.   Court-Ordered Conference [Repealed]

Rule 5 adopted Jan. 1, 1977; amended May 1, 1982; Dec. 31, 1982; Nov. 10, 1986; Sept. 4, 1989; repealed eff. Oct. 2, 2006.

Another Rule 5 follows.

Rule 5.   Electronic Filing.

(a) Definitions

As used in this local rule, unless the context otherwise requires:

(1) "Court" means the Court of Appeal for the Third Appellate District.

(2) "Electronic filing" [1] **and "document" are as defined in rule 8.70(c), California Rules of Court.**

(3) A "file" is a unit of electronic information with a filename.

[2] **(4)** "TrueFiling" is the court's electronic filing portal for registered users.

[3] **(5)** "Registered user" and "registered users" refer to a person or persons registered to use TrueFiling.

[4] **(6)** "EFS" means the court's electronic filing system, which includes, but is not limited to, TrueFiling and the court's file transfer protocol (FTP) server.

[5] **(7)** "EFS user" and "EFS users" refer to a user or users of the court's electronic filing system.

(Subd (a) amended eff. April 10, 2020; previously amended eff. September 26, 2016.)

Rule 5(a). 2020 Deletes. [1] is the electronic transmission to the court of a document in electronic form. (3) A "document" is: (A) Any filing submitted to the court, including but not limited to a brief, a petition, an appendix, or a motion; (B) Any document transmitted by a trial court to the court, including but not limited to a notice or a clerk's or reporter's transcript; or (C) Any writing prepared by the court, including but not limited to an opinion, an order, or a notice. (4) **[2]** (5) **[3]** (6) **[4]** (7) **[5]** (8)

(b) Mandatory electronic filing

[1] Electronic filing is mandatory for all attorneys filing with the court unless an exemption is granted; electronic filing is voluntary for all non-attorney self-represented litigants. [2] **Electronic filers must use the court's EFS**.

(Subd (b) amended eff. April 10, 2020; previously amended eff. September 26, 2016, and December 11, 2017.)

Rule 5(b). 2020 Deletes. [1] Pursuant to the California Rules of Court, the court requires the electronic filing of all documents with the court unless this local rule provides otherwise. **[2]** This local rule applies in all cases, including pending cases in which paper documents have been filed before the effective date of this local rule. Except as provided in this local rule, an electronic filing will be accepted in lieu of any paper copies otherwise required by the California Rules of Court, and constitutes the official record of the court

(c) Registration

(1) *Obligation to Register.* Each attorney in any proceeding in this court is obligated to become a registered user and obtain a username and password for access to TrueFiling unless an exemption is granted. Non-attorney self-represented litigants must become registered users if they wish to file electronically. Attorneys and non-attorney self-represented litigants may become registered users by registering at <http://www.truefiling.com>.

(2) *Responsibility; Obligation to Keep Account Information Current.* A registered user is responsible for all documents filed under the user's registered username and password. The registered user must comply with the requirements of the California Rules of Court.

(Subd (c) amended eff. December 11, 2017; adopted as subd (a) eff. September 14, 2015; previously amended and relettered eff. September 26, 2016.)

(d) [1] Signatures

For registered users, a registered username and password is the equivalent of an electronic signature.

(Subd (d) amended and relettered eff. April 10, 2020; adopted as subd (d) eff. September 14, 2015; previously amended and relettered as subd (f) eff. September 26, 2016.)

Rule 5(d). 2020 Deletes. [1] File Size Limitation; Documents Exceeding Limitation (1) *File Size Limitation.* The file size limitation is 25 megabytes. (2) *Documents Exceeding File Size Limitation.* Any electronic document larger than 25 megabytes must be filed in multiple files, each less than 25 megabytes. (3) *Filing of Document Consisting of More Than Five Files.* (A) *Manual Filing.* When a registered user files an electronic document consisting of more than five files, the document shall not be filed through TrueFiling, but instead shall be filed with the court in electronic format on flash drive, or alternatively on CD (compact disc) or DVD. When a registered user files a flash drive, CD, or DVD with the court, the registered user shall also file, on the same day, a "manual filing notification" in TrueFiling notifying the court and the parties that one or more documents have been filed on flash drive, CD or DVD and explaining the reason for the manual filing. (B) *Naming Convention and Format for Files on Flash Drive, CD, or DVD.* Each file on a flash drive, CD, or DVD shall be separately named so the court and the parties can see the following identifying information without opening the file: (1) the case number, (2) the type of partial document on the file, (3) the page numbers included in the file, and (4) the last name of the filing party. In addition, each file must comply with the format requirements of this local rule. (C) *Manual Service.* The flash drive, CD, or DVD shall be served on the parties in accordance with the applicable requirements and procedures for service of paper documents. **(e) Format** (1) *Text Searchable Format.* All electronic documents must be in electronic text-searchable PDF (portable document format), or other searchable format approved by the court, while maintaining original document formatting. If an EFS user possesses only a paper document, the user must scan the document and convert it to an electronic document complying with this local rule. It is the EFS user's responsibility to ensure that any document filed is complete and readable. Electronically filed documents must comply with the content and form requirements of the California Rules of Court, with the exception of those provisions dealing exclusively with requirements for paper or as otherwise specified in this local rule. (2) *Pagination.* The page numbering of an electronic document must begin with the first page or cover page as page 1 and use only Arabic numerals (e.g., 1, 2, 3) throughout the document. The page number need not appear on the cover page. Briefs may not contain more than one numbering system, e.g., they may not contain Roman numerals for the table of contents and Arabic numerals for the body of the brief. When a document, transcript, or record is filed in both paper format and electronic format, the pagination in both versions must comply with this subparagraph or the party must accurately cite to the correct page for both versions. (3)

Documents Consisting of Multiple Files. A document consisting of multiple files shall: (A) Include on the cover page of each file (i) the file number for that file, (ii) the total number of files for that document, (iii) the page numbers contained in that file, and (iv) the total number of pages for that document. (Example: File 1 of 4, pp. 1–299 of 1198.) (B) Contain its own table(s) and index stating the contents of that file. (C) Be paginated consecutively across all files (e.g., if the first file ends on page 300, the cover of the second file shall be page 301). (4) *Tabs.* Documents shall include tabs to the extent required by the California Rules of Court. A tab shall be a separate page identifying the content following the tab (such as a page stating "Exhibit A"). (5) *Electronic Bookmarks.* An electronic bookmark is a text link that appears in the bookmarks panel of an electronic document. An electronic bookmark is different from a hyperlink. Each document shall include an electronic bookmark to each heading, subheading and component of the document (such as a table of contents, table of authorities, petition, verification, points and authorities, declaration, certificate of word count, certificate of interested entities or persons, or a proof of service if included within the document). Each document shall also include an electronic bookmark to the first page of each tab, exhibit, or attachment, if any. Each bookmark to a tab, exhibit, or attachment shall include the letter or number of the tab, exhibit, or attachment and a description of the tab, exhibit, or attachment. (6) *Hyperlinks.* Hyperlinks are not required. However, if an EFS user elects to include hyperlinks in a document, the hyperlink may be active and should be formatted to standard citation format as provided in the California Rules of Court. (7) *No Color.* Notwithstanding provisions to the contrary in the California Rules of Court, electronic documents shall not have color covers, color signatures, or other color components absent leave of court. This requirement does not apply to the auto-color feature of hyperlinks. **(f)**

(e) Superior Court Record

(1) *Record of Administrative Proceedings.* In addition to any administrative record provided by the trial court pursuant to the California Rules of Court, registered users seeking review of an administrative determination must submit an electronic copy of the administrative record to the court in compliance with [1] **rule 8.74 of** the California Rules of Court **[2]**.

(2) *Reporter's Transcript.* A registered user who orders a reporter's transcript of proceedings must also request a copy of the transcript in electronic format and must submit an electronic copy to the court in compliance with [3] **rule 8.74 of the California Rules of Court.**

(3) *Transmissions by the Superior Court.* The court authorizes and encourages the superior courts within the Third Appellate District to engage in the electronic service and electronic filing of documents, including, but not limited to, the clerk's transcript and reporter's transcripts. **If a superior court transmits an electronic document to the court, it shall also make the electronic document available to the parties.** If a superior court transmits electronic documents to the court in lieu of paper, the court will accept electronic documents complying with the California Rules of Court and this local rule. [4]

(Subd (e) amended and relettered eff. April 10, 2020; adopted as subd (e) eff. September 14, 2015; previously amended and relettered as subd (g) eff. September 26, 2016; previously amended eff. December 11, 2017.)

Rule 5(e). 2020 Deletes. [1] this local rule. (2) *Appendix.* Any appendix filed pursuant to **[2]** must be filed by EFS users in electronic format in compliance with this local rule. (3) **[3]** this local rule. (4) **[4]** A superior court shall transmit electronic documents to the court through the court's FTP server using credentials provided by the court. If a superior court transmits electronic documents to the court, it shall also make the electronic documents available to the parties.

(f) Personal Identifiers and Privacy Issues

To protect personal privacy and other legitimate interests, parties and their attorneys must not include, or must redact where inclusion is necessary, personal identifiers such as Social Security numbers, driver's license numbers, and financial account numbers from all documents filed as part of the court's public record, whether filed in paper or electronic format, unless otherwise provided by law or ordered by the court. If an individual's Social Security number or financial account number is required in a document filed as part of the court's public record, only the last four digits of the number shall be used.

The responsibility for excluding or redacting identifiers from all documents filed with the court rests solely with the parties and their attorneys. Neither TrueFiling nor the Clerk of the Court has any responsibility to review documents for compliance.

(Subd (f) relettered eff. April 10, 2020; adopted as subd (f) eff. September 14, 2015; previously amended and relettered as subd (h) eff. September 26, 2016; previously amended eff. December 11, 2017.)

(g) [1] Filing Deadlines

Electronic filing does not alter any filing deadlines. An electronic filing not completely received by the court by 11:59 p.m. will be deemed to have been received on the next court day. If a specific time of day is set for filing by court order or stipulation, the electronic filing shall be completed by that time. Although the EFS permits users to transmit electronic documents 24 hours a day, EFS users should be aware that telephone or online assistance may not be available outside of normal court business hours, and requests for immediate relief made after the close of the court's normal business hours may not be addressed until the next court day.

(Subd (g) amended and relettered eff. April 10, 2020; adopted as subd (h) eff. September 14, 2015; previously amended and relettered as subd (j) eff. September 26, 2016.)

Rule 5(g).   2020 Deletes. [1] (i) Sealed or Confidential Material Sealed or confidential material may be filed electronically. EFS users must comply with the California Rules of Court pertaining to sealed and confidential material, with the exception of those provisions pertaining exclusively with requirements for paper or as otherwise specified in this local rule. **(j)**

(h) Motion to Accept Filing as Timely Following TrueFiling Technical Failure

If a registered user fails to meet a filing deadline imposed by court order, rule or law because of a TrueFiling failure, the registered user may file the document in electronic or paper format as soon thereafter as practicable and accompany the filing with a motion to accept the document as timely filed. A late submission that missed a jurisdictional deadline will be accepted for filing pursuant to this subparagraph only if the deadline was missed due to a TrueFiling failure. The initial point of contact for anyone experiencing difficulty with TrueFiling shall be the toll-free telephone number posted on the TrueFiling Web site.

The court is not responsible for malfunctions or errors occurring in the electronic transmission or receipt of electronically filed documents.

(Subd (h) relettered eff. April 10, 2020; adopted as subd (i) eff. September 14, 2015; previously amended and relettered as subd (k) eff. September 26, 2016.)

(i) Service

Registration with TrueFiling [1] **manifests affirmative** consent to receive service through the EFS. Documents prepared by the court will be served on EFS users through the EFS or by electronic notification. [2]

(Subd (i) amended and relettered eff. April 10, 2020; adopted as subd (k) eff. September 14, 2015; previously amended and relettered (l) eff. September 26, 2016; previously amended eff. December 11, 2017.)

Rule 5(i).   2020 Deletes. [1] constitutes **[2]** Submission of a petition for review through TrueFiling that is accepted for filing by the Supreme Court constitutes service of a copy of the petition on this court in accordance with the California Rules of Court.

(j) Filing Fees

TrueFiling is operated by a vendor pursuant to a contract with the court. The vendor will assess fees for each electronic filing via TrueFiling in accordance with the schedule posted on the TrueFiling Web site, as approved by the court. TrueFiling fees will be considered recoverable costs under the California Rules of Court. The vendor is designated as the court's agent for collection of court-imposed fees where required for any electronic filing made by registered users, and any associated credit card or bank charges or convenience fees.

If a non-attorney self-represented litigant with a fee waiver chooses to file documents electronically, that litigant is exempt from the fees and costs associated with electronic filing. The persons and entities identified in Government Code section 6103 are also exempt from the fees and costs associated with the EFS.

(Subd (j) relettered eff. April 10, 2020; adopted as subd (l) eff. September 14, 2015; previously amended and relettered as subd (m) eff. September 26, 2016.)

(k) Exemptions

(1) Non-attorney self-represented litigants may, but are not required to, register for electronic filing. Non-attorney self-represented litigants who opt to register for electronic filing must comply with **the California Rules of Court,** this local rule, and the requirements of the EFS.

(2) When it is not feasible for a registered user to convert a document to electronic format [1] **in compliance with rule 8.74 of the California Rules of Court**, the document may be filed in paper format with a declaration setting forth the reason that electronic filing was not feasible.

(3) If the requirements of this local rule cause undue hardship or significant prejudice to any registered user, the registered user may file a motion for an exemption from the requirements of this local rule.

(Subd (k) amended and relettered eff. April 10, 2020; adopted as subd (m) eff. September 14, 2015; previously amended and relettered as subd (n) eff. September 26, 2016; previously amended eff. December 11, 2017.)

Rule 5(k).   2020 Deletes. [1] by scanning, imaging or other means

(*l*) Rejection of an Electronic Filing for Noncompliance

The court will reject an electronic filing if it does not comply with the requirements of **the California Rules of Court and** this local rule.

(Subd (l) amended and relettered eff. April 10, 2020; adopted as subd (n) eff. September 14, 2015; previously amended and relettered as subd (o) eff. September 26, 2016.)

(m) Sanctions for Noncompliance

Failure of counsel to timely register, and failure of any registered user to comply with electronic filing requirements, unless exempted, may be subject to sanctions imposed by the court.

(Subd (m) relettered eff. April 10, 2020; adopted as subd (o) eff. September 14, 2015; previously amended and relettered as subd (p) eff. September 26, 2016.)

(n) Original Documents

The court may scan any paper document into an electronic format, in which case the electronic document will be deemed the original for purposes of the court record.

(Subd (n) relettered eff. April 10, 2020; adopted as subd (q) eff. September 26, 2016.)

(o) Posting and Publication

The Clerk of the Court is directed to post a copy of this local rule on the court's Web site and submit a copy to the Reporter of Decisions for publication.

(Subd (o) relettered eff. April 10, 2020; adopted as subd (p) eff. September 14, 2015; previously amended and relettered as subd (r) eff. September 26, 2016.)
Rule 5 amended eff. April 10, 2020; adopted eff. September 14, 2015; previously amended eff. September 26, 2016, and December 11, 2017.

Rule 6.   Postponement of Briefing [Repealed]

Rule 6 adopted Jan. 1, 1977; amended May 1, 1982; Dec. 31, 1982; Nov. 10, 1986; repealed eff. Oct. 2, 2006.

Another Rule 6 follows.

Rule 6.   Appointed Attorney Deemed to Request a Paper Reporter's Transcript

Prior to January 1, 2023, an appointed attorney is deemed to request, pursuant to Code of Civil Procedure section 271, subdivision (a)(1), that the reporter's transcript be delivered in paper form.
Rule 6 adopted effective October 1, 2018.

Rule 7.   The Settlement Conference [Repealed]

Rule 7 adopted Jan. 1, 1977; amended May 1, 1982; Dec. 31, 1982; repealed eff. Oct. 2, 2006.

Rule 8.   Conference Without Appellate Record [Repealed]

Rule 8 adopted Jan. 1, 1977; amended May 1, 1982; Dec. 31, 1982; Nov. 10, 1986; Sept. 4, 1989; repealed eff. Oct. 2, 2006.

Rule 9.   Exclusion From Conference Requirement [Repealed]

Rule 9 amended Nov. 10, 1986; repealed eff. Oct. 2, 2006.

Rule 10.   Disqualification of Conference Justice [Repealed]

Rule 10 repealed eff. Oct. 2, 2006.

Rule 21.   Tabbing of Exhibits [Repealed]

Rule 21 adopted Jan. 1, 1977; repealed eff. July 6, 1993.

Rule 22.   Stipulation for Use of Original Superior Court File [Renumbered]

Rule 22 adopted Sept. 4, 1989; renumbered to rule 2 eff. Oct. 2, 2006.

Rule 23.   Time for Oral Argument [Renumbered]

Rule 23 adopted Apr. 10, 1998; renumbered to rule 3 eff. Oct. 2, 2006.

Rule 31.   Location of Hearings [Repealed]

Rule 31 repealed eff. Oct. 2, 2006.

INTERNAL OPERATING PRACTICES AND PROCEDURES
THIRD APPELLATE DISTRICT

[Revised effective July 12, 2019; previously amended effective June 24, 2016]

I. INTRODUCTION

The purpose of this publication is to advise the bar and interested members of the public regarding the internal rules and general operating practices of this court. No attempt is made to restate or amplify the California Rules of Court or constitutional provisions and statutes governing the practices and procedures of a Court of Appeal. This publication supersedes previous statements of the court's Internal Operating Practices and Procedures.

II. STRUCTURE OF THE COURT

The Third Appellate District is authorized eleven justices: an administrative presiding justice and ten associate justices.

There are no divisions of this court. The court operates in three-justice panels selected at random on a rotational basis.

The courtroom, judicial offices, and Clerk's Office are located in the Stanley Mosk Library and Courts Building, 914 Capitol Mall, Sacramento, California 95814. The Clerk's Office is located on the fourth floor and is open to the public Monday through Friday, from 8:30 a.m. to 4:30 p.m., except for judicial holidays.

III. FILINGS

All matters are filed with the Clerk's Office. The Clerk's Office processes and files the documents, distributing matters to the court when judicial action is required.

Routine motions or applications, such as requests for extensions of time, are referred to the Administrative Presiding Justice. More substantive motions and extraordinary writ petitions are referred to a three-justice panel.

Generally, upon the completion of briefing, appeals are evaluated and designated for handling by the court based on the number and apparent complexity of the issues raised, the subject matter, and the length of the record. In order to expedite certain proceedings, evaluation of an appeal may be done upon the filing of the last respondent's brief.

IV. ORGANIZATION AND DUTIES OF STAFF ATTORNEYS

Each justice is authorized two staff attorneys who work exclusively for the justice. Some of the justices also utilize law student externs who work under their direct supervision.

In addition, the court maintains a central staff consisting of sixteen attorneys: a managing attorney who directs the work of the staff, four writ attorneys, and eleven other central staff attorneys. The central staff attorneys, including the managing attorney, work under the general supervision of the administrative presiding justice and are responsible to the entire court.

The primary responsibility of staff attorneys assigned to an individual justice is the preparation of memoranda for the appeals that are assigned to the justice's chambers. The attorney studies the record and the briefs, analyzes and researches the legal issues, discusses the issues with the justice, and then prepares a legal memorandum with guidance from the justice. The memorandum is prepared for the exclusive use of the court.

The central staff has two main functions. Central staff writ attorneys study and familiarize themselves with each nonroutine motion, writ petition, and other extraordinary application filed with the court. After analyzing and researching the matter, the writ attorney presents the motion, petition, or application to a three-justice panel of the court for its determination. The other central staff attorneys are assigned appeals that may be authored by any one of the eleven justices. These appeals are concurrently assigned to a central staff attorney and a panel with a designated author-justice. The central staff attorney studies the record and the briefs, analyzes and researches the legal issues, confers with the author-justice, and then prepares a legal memorandum with guidance from the author-justice. The memorandum is prepared for the exclusive use of the court.

V. WRIT PETITIONS, MOTIONS AND OTHER APPLICATIONS

At the weekly writ conference, usually held on Thursdays, a three-justice panel rules on pending writ petitions, nonroutine motions, and other applications. The writ panel varies from week to week, with each justice participating approximately the same number of times during the year as the other justices.

The writ panel considers the parties' written submissions, and central staff writ attorneys make an oral presentation on each matter. The panel discusses each matter and decides what action to take. Unless it summarily denies a writ petition, the panel will issue an alternative writ, an order to show cause, or a writ of review, or the panel will notify the parties that it is considering issuing a peremptory writ in the first instance. If an alternative writ, an order to show cause, or a writ of review is issued, the matter is assigned to one of the justices on the writ panel and is thereafter handled much like the court does with an appeal (see discussion, *post*).

At times, the court is presented with a writ petition, motion, or application that purportedly requires urgent or immediate action. Such matters are promptly assigned to a central staff writ attorney for review. If immediate action is required, a panel of three justices is assembled to hear the matter.

VI. JUDICIAL ASSIGNMENTS IN APPEALS

Assignments of appeals to individual justices are not governed by fixed rules or set formula. Each appeal is evaluated and assigned a weight to reflect its relative complexity. Effort is made to fairly apportion the caseload so that no justice is assigned a disproportionate number of the more difficult or less difficult appeals. Subject matter is not a basis for assignment of an appeal to a particular justice, except that, where a justice has been assigned to the same case in an earlier appeal, a new appeal in that case often will be assigned to the same justice.

The three-justice panels are selected at random in order to vary their composition so that over a period of time each justice will participate with all other members of the court in the multiple combinations possible.

The initial designation of the author of the opinion in an appeal is done on a random basis at the time the case is assigned to chambers or to central staff. Each justice is initially designated to author approximately the same number of opinions that will be authored by each of the other justices during the course of the year. Of course, whether the justice initially designated to author an opinion ultimately does so depends upon whether the justice obtains the concurrence of at least one other member of the panel. If the justice fails to do so, one of the other panel members will take over the responsibility of authoring the opinion of the court.

VII. PREPARATION OF A DRAFT OPINION

A legal memorandum prepared by a staff attorney is submitted to the justice initially designated to author the opinion in the appeal. After examining and evaluating the record, the parties' briefs, and the staff attorney memorandum, and after engaging in any necessary independent research and analysis, the justice prepares a draft opinion for the exclusive use of the court. A copy of the draft opinion, the briefs, and the record are then circulated, in order of seniority, to the other two participating justices. Each of the other participating justices indicates his or her tentative concurrence or dissent, or otherwise recommends changes to the draft opinion. All three justices also indicate their tentative positions on whether the ultimate opinion of the court should be certified for publication. The decision to publish the opinion requires approval by a majority of the three-justice panel.

VIII. ORAL ARGUMENT

When the draft opinion is circulated, each justice assigned to the case indicates whether he or she wants the case calendared for oral argument or whether a waiver of oral argument should be solicited by the court. At the request of one justice, the case will be calendared for oral argument.

If the justices agree to solicit a waiver of oral argument, the Clerk's Office sends the parties a letter indicating that the court is prepared to decide the case without oral argument and that oral argument will be waived unless it is requested by either counsel within ten days. If neither counsel requests oral argument within ten days, the court at that time approves the waiver of oral argument and the matter is deemed submitted for decision.

If either counsel requests oral argument, the case is placed on calendar. Counsel are notified approximately thirty days in advance of the date set for oral argument. With the court's approval, a party may waive its appearance at oral argument requested by another party. Continuances are disfavored and will not be granted in the absence of a showing of unusually compelling circumstances. Oral argument will not be continued by stipulation of parties. The matter is deemed submitted for decision at the conclusion of oral argument or, if supplemental briefing is requested by the court, at the time the last brief is filed.

The panel holds a postargument conference, in most cases on the same day that the case is heard. Often the case is finally decided at this conference, and suggestions may be made to the assigned author concerning the content of the opinion. If there is not agreement at this stage, areas of disagreement may be identified and refined.

An opinion will be filed within ninety days of the date of submission.

IX. CALENDAR

The court sits twelve times a year, once each month. The calendar is usually set to begin on the third Monday or Tuesday of each month and generally lasts for five or six days. Special calendars, although rare, may be held by the court.

Each calendar consists of both civil and criminal appeals and other proceedings ready for decision. The administrative presiding justice is responsible for the final composition of the calendar.

X. FILING OF THE COURT'S DECISION; REHEARING

After oral argument or waiver of oral argument, a final draft opinion is circulated among the participating justices. A justice may indicate conditional approval if certain changes are made or otherwise forward comments on the draft to the author and the other participating justice. If there are to be separate concurring or dissenting opinions, they are circulated in final draft form among the participating justices. At the same time, the panel makes a final decision on publication.

Before the opinion is put in final form for filing, transcript references and citations are verified again.

When the opinion is signed, it is transmitted to the Clerk's Office, where it is filed as a decision and opinion of the court. Counsel of record are sent copies of the opinion on that same day. Copies also are available in the Clerk's Office for the news media and interested members of the public.

For sixty days, the Reporter of Decisions posts published opinions of the Court of Appeal, Third Appellate District, at:

    http://www.courts.ca.gov/opinions-slip.htm?Courts=C

Unpublished opinions of the court are posted for sixty days at http://www.courts.ca.gov/opinions-nonpub.htm?Courts=C

Timely petitions for rehearing are immediately presented to the author of the opinion and the other panel members for review. If the petition lacks merit, it is denied. In some cases, the opinion may be modified and rehearing otherwise denied. The granting of a petition for rehearing may or may not result in a request by the court for additional briefing or oral argument.

XI. MEDIATION OF CIVIL APPEALS

In October 2006, the court initiated a mediation program for civil appeals governed by its Local Rule 1.

Revised effective July 12, 2019; previously amended effective June 24, 2016.

FOURTH APPELLATE DISTRICT
LOCAL RULES

[Amended effective February 23, 2019; previously amended January 1, 2007, November 9, 2007, August 13, 2010, July 1, 2015, April 1, 2016, and January 3, 2017]

Writ proceedings. Rule 1.
Covers on documents filed with the court. Rule 2.
Stipulation for use of original superior court file. Rule 3.
Civil settlement conference procedures (Division Two only). Rule 4.
Reporter's transcripts in felony appeals. Rule 5.
Internal Operating Practices and Procedures for the Fourth Appellate District, Division One.
Internal Operating Practices and Procedures Fourth Appellate District, Division Two.
Internal Operating Practices and Procedures Fourth Appellate District, Division Three.

Rule 1.   Service of Writ Petitions Requesting Immediate Relief [Repealed]
Rule 1 adopted Sept. 9, 1996; repealed Oct. 29, 2004.

    Another Rule 1 follows.

Rule 1.   Writ Proceedings
(a) [Request for immediate stay] A request that an immediate stay be issued or other immediate relief be granted is to be served on the respondent and each real party in interest by (1) personal delivery or (2) an expeditious method consented to in advance by the party served. If the respondent or any real party in interest is not served personally or by an expeditious method consented to in advance by the party served, the court will not act on the request for five days, except to deny it summarily, absent a showing of good cause. The document cover must state conspicuously "STAY REQUESTED" or "IMMEDIATE RELIEF REQUESTED" or words of similar effect.

The court may issue a stay or other order necessary to preserve the status quo or the court's jurisdiction without opposition. However, a request for immediate relief, other than a stay or other order necessary to preserve the status quo or the court's jurisdiction, will not be granted unless the court has received an unsolicited opposition or, alternatively, has requested opposition.

(Subd (a) amended, eff. Aug. 13, 2010; adopted, eff. Oct. 29, 2004.)

(b) [Preliminary opposition] In an extraordinary proceeding involving a petition for writ of mandate, certiorari or prohibition pursuant to California Rules of Court, rules 8.485-8.493, the real party in interest need not file a preliminary opposition as provided in rule 8.487(a) unless requested to do so by the court. Except as provided in subdivision (a) of this rule, the court will not take any action on a writ petition, other than to summarily deny it, without first giving the real party in interest an opportunity to respond.

(Subd (b) adopted, eff. Aug. 13, 2010.)
Rule 1 amended, eff. Aug. 13, 2010; adopted, eff. Oct. 29, 2004.

Rule 2.   Covers on Documents Filed With the Court
The court will not accept for filing any document that has a plastic or acetate cover or does not conform strictly to rules 8.144 and 8.204 of the California Rules of Court.

Rule 2 amended, eff. Jan. 1, 2007; adopted, eff. Oct. 2, 1983; and previously amended, eff. Oct. 29, 2004.

Rule 3.   Petitions for Extraordinary Writs (Division One Only) [Repealed]
Rule 3 adopted Aug. 10, 1982; repealed Oct. 29, 2004.

    Another Rule 3 follows.

Rule 3.   Stipulation for Use of Original Superior Court File
Rule 8.128 of the California Rules of Court provides for the use of the original superior court file in lieu of the clerk's transcript on appeal in those civil cases where the parties so stipulate. In accordance with rule 8.128 of the California Rules of Court, the procedure therein is approved for use by the superior courts within this district unless the Court of Appeal orders otherwise in a particular case.

Rule 3 amended, eff. Jan. 1, 2007; former rule 10 adopted, eff. April 26, 1992; and renumbered, eff. Oct. 29, 2004.

Rule 4.   Civil Settlement Conference Procedures (Division Two Only)
(a) [Application of rule] This rule is adopted pursuant to rule 8.248, California Rules of Court, and shall apply to all civil cases except appeals from proceedings under sections 300, 601, and 602 of the Welfare and Institutions Code, appeals from proceedings under sections 221 and 232 of the Civil Code, and appeals from original proceedings ancillary to a criminal prosecution.

(Amended, eff. Jan. 1, 2007; adopted, eff. Oct. 13, 1992; and previously amended, eff. Oct. 29, 2004.)

(b) [Notice of availability of conference] Upon receipt of notice of the filing of a notice of appeal, the clerk of this court shall mail a copy of this rule to counsel for all parties.

(Adopted, eff. Oct. 13, 1992.)

(c) [General settlement conference procedure]

(1) The presiding justice may schedule a settlement conference and order the parties' attendance at any time during the pendency of an appeal.

(2) Written notice of the date and time of the settlement conference will be given by the court.

(3) Immediately upon accepting a case for the settlement conference procedure, all further proceedings, including the filing of briefs, shall be suspended until further order of the court. However, this rule shall not suspend preparation of the appellate record unless a specific order is issued directing suspension of record preparation.

(Adopted, eff. Oct. 13, 1992.)

(d) [Prebriefing settlement conference procedure and sanctions]

(1) A request for a settlement conference to be held prior to completion of briefing shall be served and filed within 30 days from the date of

mailing of the notice specified in subdivision (b). Opposition to a request for a settlement conference must be served and filed within 15 days after the request's filing date.

(2) If the court orders a settlement conference prior to the completion of briefing, the parties shall each serve and file an original and one copy of a settlement conference statement at least 15 days before the settlement conference. The parties may file by the same date a joint settlement conference statement in lieu of separate statements. Failure to timely serve and file a settlement conference statement complying with this rule may result in the imposition of sanctions including dismissal of the appeal. Every settlement conference statement shall contain the following:

(A) The trial court name and case title and number;

(B) The name of the judge who rendered the judgment or order appealed and the date of its entry;

(C) The date the notice of appeal was filed;

(D) The names, address, and telephone numbers of counsel for all parties to the appeal;

(E) A brief description of the judgment or order appealed;

(F) A concise statement of the case, including a brief procedural history and all facts material to consideration of the issues presented; and,

(G) The issues expected to be raised in the briefs.

(Amended, eff. Oct. 29, 2004; adopted, eff. Oct. 13, 1992.)

(e) [Postbriefing settlement conference procedure and sanctions] After briefing is completed, the court may request the parties to provide information helpful to the court in deciding whether to order the parties to participate in a settlement conference. The parties shall complete all post-briefing settlement conference questionnaires and respond to all confidential settlement conference inquiries within 15 days of mailing by the clerk of the court. Failure to timely respond to a settlement conference inquiry or questionnaire may result in the imposition of sanctions including dismissal of the appeal.

(Amended, eff. Jan. 1, 2007; adopted, eff. Oct. 13, 1992.)

(f) [Settlement conference and sanctions]

(1) The court shall maintain a list of attorneys who have developed expertise in specified areas of law, are generally respected in the legal community, and are willing to mediate settlement conferences at this court. These attorneys shall be designated as settlement conference mediators and preside over every settlement conference unless otherwise ordered. A justice or assigned justice may be designated as a settlement conference mediator and preside over a settlement conference if so ordered.

(2) The mediator presiding over a settlement conference may in his or her discretion continue it from time to time to allow for further negotiation.

(3) Counsel for every party to the appeal and their clients shall attend any settlement conference. Failure to attend a settlement conference may result in the imposition of sanctions against any party or counsel, including dismissal.

(4) The settlement conference mediator may invite parties to the action who are not parties to the appeal, or any person who has an interest in the action, to attend the settlement conference if it appears to the mediator that their presence may facilitate settlement of the case. Any party to the appeal may serve and file a written request for the attendance of such a party or person at least 15 days before the settlement conference.

(5) Counsel shall confer with their clients in advance and be thoroughly familiar with the case and prepared to present their contentions in detail.

(6) The presiding justice, a justice designated by the presiding justice, or the settlement conference mediator may excuse a client's personal attendance upon request and a showing that hardship or unusual circumstances make the client's attendance impossible or impractical. If personal attendance is excused, counsel either shall have obtained full authority to agree to a settlement that binds the client or the client shall be available for consultation by telephone.

(7) Where settlement cannot be reached, partial settlement will be sought. Any settlement shall be reduced to writing and signed by counsel. After a complete settlement has been agreed to in writing, the parties shall promptly file a stipulation to dismiss the appeal on the ground that the case has been settled. The stipulation shall specify the allocation of costs on appeal and state whether the remittitur is to issue immediately.

(Amended, eff. Jan. 1, 2007; adopted, eff. Oct. 13, 1992.)

(g) [Disqualification of settlement conference justice]

(1) A justice or assigned justice who participates in a settlement conference that does not result in complete settlement shall not thereafter participate in any way in the consideration or disposition of the case on its merits.

(2) A justice or assigned justice of the court will not be disqualified to participate in the consideration or disposition of a case on its merits because he or she has ruled on a request for a settlement conference, ordered that a settlement conference be held, signed orders granting relief from default for an act required by a party under this rule, extended or shortened any time period specified in this rule, or otherwise signed an order concerning a procedural aspect of the settlement conference process. Only mediating a settlement conference shall disqualify a justice from consideration or disposition of the case on its merits.

(Adopted, eff. Oct. 13, 1992.)
Rule 4 amended, eff. Jan. 1, 2007; adopted, eff. Oct. 13, 1992; and previously amended, eff. Oct. 29, 2004.

Rule 5.   Payment of Filing Fee in Civil Appeals [Repealed]

Rule 5 adopted, eff. Oct. 5, 1984; repealed, eff. Sept. 9, 1996.

Rule 5.   Filing by Facsimile [Repealed]

Rule 5 adopted, eff. Nov. 9, 2007; repealed, eff. April 3, 2013.

Rule 5.   Electronic Filing (Division One Only) [Repealed]

Rule 5 adopted, eff. July 1, 2015; repealed, eff. April 1, 2016.

Rule 5.   Electronic Filing (Division One Only) [Repealed]

Rule 5 adopted, eff. April 1, 2016; repealed, eff. Jan. 3, 2017.

2017 Note: Misc. Order No. 010317 provided the effective date for Local Rule 5's repeal: "Local Rule 5 of the Fourth District is repealed effective January 3, 2017."

Another Rule 5 follows.

Rule 5.   Reporter's Transcripts in Felony Appeals

(a) Except as provided in (b), defendant's counsel is deemed to have requested under Code of Civil Procedure section 271(a)(1) that his or her copy of the reporter's transcript be delivered in paper form.

(Adopted, eff. February 23, 2018.)

(b) Within 15 days after the notice of appeal is filed, defendant's counsel, or, if the defendant is not yet represented by appellate counsel, the district appellate project, may serve the lead court reporter and the superior court with a request that defendant's counsel's copy of the reporter's transcript be delivered in electronic form.

(Adopted, eff. February 23, 2018.)
Rule 5 adopted, eff. February 23, 2018.

Rule 6.   Writ Petitions: Supporting Records and Stay Requests [Repealed]

Rule 6 adopted, eff. May 18, 1987; repealed, eff. Sept. 9, 1996.

Rule 7.   Civil Settlement Conference Procedures (Division Three Only) [Repealed]

Rule 7 adopted, eff. Sept. 14, 1989; repealed, eff. Dec. 1, 2003.

Rule 8.   Attachments to Briefs (Division One Only) [Repealed]

Rule 8 adopted, eff. April 2, 1990; repealed, eff. Oct. 29, 2004.

Rule 9.   Civil Docketing Statement; Form [Repealed]

Rule 9 adopted, eff. Jan. 3, 1997; repealed, eff. March 10, 2003.

Rule 10.   Stipulation for Use of Original Superior Court File [Renumbered]

Rule 10 adopted, eff. April 26, 1992; renumbered to rule 3, eff. Oct. 29, 2004.

INTERNAL OPERATING PRACTICES AND PROCEDURES
FOR THE FOURTH APPELLATE DISTRICT, DIVISION ONE

(Revised effective January 27, 2012; September 19, 2014; June 1, 2017; March 1, 2019)

I. INTRODUCTION

  A. Purpose

  B. Organization of the District

  C. Justices and Judicial Staff

  D. Clerk/Executive Officer, Clerk's Office Staff and Administrative Support Staff

  E. Managing Attorney and Central Staff

  F. The Clerk's Office

I. INTRODUCTION

A. Purpose

The purpose of this document is to provide members of the bar and other interested persons with general information concerning the organization of the Fourth Appellate District, Division One and its procedures for processing cases. It is not intended to duplicate the California Rules of Court, the Local Rules of the Fourth Appellate District, or the statutes and constitutional provisions governing the processing of cases. This document describes the internal operating practices and procedures of Division One for review of appeals and original proceedings. This publication supersedes previous statements of the court's Internal Operating Practices and Procedures.

B. Organization of the District

The Court of Appeal for the Fourth Appellate District consists of three divisions. Division One, which generally hears appeals in cases from San Diego and Imperial Counties, is located in San Diego. Division Two, which generally hears appeals in cases from Riverside, San Bernardino and Inyo Counties, is located in Riverside. Division Three, which generally hears appeals in cases from Orange County, is located in Santa Ana. Cases filed in one division may be transferred to another division to equalize the workload of the three courts.

The courtroom and Office of the Clerk are located at 750 B Street, Suite 300, San Diego, California 92101.

C. Justices and Judicial Staff

Each division consists of associate justices and a presiding justice. The Chief Justice appoints one of the presiding justices to serve as administrative presiding justice to perform the duties prescribed in the California Rules of Court, rule 10.1004. Division One has 10 justices. Each justice maintains a chamber which consists of the justice, judicial attorneys, and a judicial assistant. The court also has a central staff consisting of judicial attorneys, including writs attorneys, and other judicial assistants who work for each of the justices on a rotating basis.

D. Clerk/Executive Officer, Clerk's Office Staff and Administrative Support Staff

A clerk/executive officer is selected by the presiding justices of the district and works under the general direction and supervision of the administrative presiding justice. The clerk/executive officer is responsible for planning, organizing, coordinating and directing the management of the clerk's office and all nonjudicial support activities as prescribed in the California Rules of Court, rule 10.1020. The clerk/executive officer is responsible for all district support activities, including personnel, budget, technology, and facilities.

E. Managing Attorney and Central Staff

The court's managing attorney is selected by the justices of the court and works under the general direction and supervision of the administrative presiding justice. The managing attorney serves as legal advisor to the court, its justices, and the clerk's office on a variety of issues, including matters of appellate procedure. The managing attorney also supervises the court's central staff attorneys and judicial assistants who are not assigned to a particular chambers.

F. The Clerk's Office

Each appeal or writ petition filed in Division One is assigned a six-digit identification number that is preceded by a "D" (e.g., D000000). A digit deputy is assigned two of the numbers from zero to nine and is responsible for processing all filings in cases that end in either of those numbers. (For example, the digit deputy that is assigned the numbers "1" and "2" is responsible for processing all filings in cases that have a number ending in a "1" or a "2".) Thus, parties or practitioners seeking information or assistance in their cases should ask to speak with the appropriate digit deputy, unless the case has been placed on a court calendar, in which case they should speak to the calendaring clerk.

II. THE WORK OF THE COURT

A. Original Proceedings (Writs)

Writs are reviewed and decided by a panel of three justices, the composition of which rotates on a monthly basis. The clerk's office forwards all writ petitions to the writ department, which is staffed by central staff attorneys. The supervising writ attorney reviews each petition to determine its urgency. If an immediate stay or other form of urgent action appears to be necessary, a writ attorney may orally present the petition to the writ panel; otherwise, petitions are generally processed in order of their filing, subject to adjustments for impending hearing or trial dates. Normally, a writ attorney reviews the petition without waiting for a response, although one may be solicited; the attorney thereafter prepares a written memorandum evaluating the petition and circulates it to the writ panel.

After a writ petition is presented (whether orally or in writing), the justices on the writ panel may:

(1) request a response;

(2) deny the petition (regardless of whether a response has been requested or filed);

(3) issue a peremptory writ in the first instance without oral argument, but only after a response has been requested or filed and the parties have been notified in writing, of its possible issuance; or

(4) issue an alternative writ or order to show cause.

It is the court's practice to request an initial response to a petition before issuing an alternative writ or an order to show cause. If the panel issues an alternative writ or an order to show cause, the real party in interest is given an opportunity to file a formal response and the cause will be placed on calendar. Generally, the writ attorney who presented the petition to the writ panel assists the lead justice in drafting the opinion when the court issues a peremptory writ in the first instance. When the panel has issued an alternative writ or an order to show cause, the matter is assigned to the lead justice's chambers for the drafting of the opinion.

B. Appeals

1. Case Screening

In civil cases, the California Rules of Court require an appellant to file a Civil Case Information Statement (Cal. Rules of Court, rule 8.100(g)), which is reviewed by a central staff attorney to determine if there is any issue regarding the timeliness of the appeal or the appealability of the challenged judgment or order, whether the case is entitled to calendar priority, whether there has been a previous writ or appeal in the same case or in a closely related case, and whether the appeal is affected by a pending bankruptcy. It is the court's practice to grant priority on its own motion to matters involving child custody or visitation.

In all appeals, after the respondent's brief is filed or the time for filing such a brief has run in a case, the managing attorney or a designated staff attorney screens the case and estimates the amount of time that the preparation of a draft opinion is likely to take.

Criminal appeals involving issues that can be resolved with little difficulty based upon well-established law and that do not present a likelihood of dispute as to how the law applies to the facts are designated as "by the court" ("BC") cases. In criminal appeals in which the appellant's counsel is unable to discern any reasonably arguable issues to raise, the court must independently review the record in accordance with *People v. Wende* (1979) 25 Cal.3d 436 and are accordingly designated as "*Wende*" appeals.

All other appeals are assigned a numerical value based on the likely amount of time to research the case. These assigned "weights" are used in assigning cases to chambers and to central staff, to balance workloads throughout the court.

2. *Case Assignment/Processing*

BCs, *Wende*s, juvenile dependency cases and cases weighted 10 or higher are generally assigned by the managing attorney to central staff attorneys for processing. Priority is given to cases as required by law and, within the priority classification on a first-in, first-out basis. These cases are assigned randomly, in rotation, to a lead justice, who supervises the preparation of a draft opinion.

All other types of appeals are usually assigned by the managing attorney to a lead justice's chambers. Absent unusual circumstances, these assignments are made on a random basis to the justices. The internal procedures for assigning cases to chambers attorneys and for preparing draft opinions varies from one chambers to another.

3. *Oral Argument*

Once a draft opinion has been prepared in a case, its path is determined by whether a party or parties have requested oral argument. In cases where oral argument is waived, the draft opinion is circulated in order of seniority to the other justices assigned to the panel for that case, for their review.

In cases for which oral argument is requested, the draft opinion is placed in a calendar book. The calendar book contains the draft opinions for those cases on which the justice is participating. The justices hear oral argument and then confer immediately after argument takes place.

Oral argument is generally held during the second full week of the month, although occasionally cases are calendared for argument at other times, if necessitated by urgency or other good cause. Argument is limited to 15 minutes per side, unless the court grants a party's advance written request for more time pursuant to Miscellaneous Order 061218.

4. *Submission of Cases*

Cases that are orally argued are normally submitted at the conclusion of argument. Where oral argument is waived, the case is submitted at the conclusion of the argument calendar for the month to which it is assigned. Submission of the case triggers the 90-day rule for the filing of the opinion. (Cal. Const., art. VI, § 19.)

C. Filing of the Court's Decision; Rehearing

1. *Signed Opinions*

Unless the two other participating justices disagree with the disposition proposed by the assigned author, the justice assigned will prepare the majority opinion. When a proposed majority opinion has been drafted, it is circulated to the other participating justices. They indicate approval, disapproval, or proposed changes. Differences of opinion as to the language of the opinion or the ultimate disposition of the case may be taken up in conference. The opinion may then be modified in a manner acceptable to the justices. If two justices agree, a written opinion is filed.

2. *Concurring or Dissenting Opinions*

Where a difference of opinion exists among the justices participating in a case, a justice who agrees with the result reached but not with the reasoning of the majority may write a separate concurring opinion or may merely indicate concurrence only in the judgment reached by the majority. Likewise, a justice who disagrees with the result reached by the majority may write a dissenting opinion. Each panel member has a full opportunity to consider the views of associates prior to the completion and filing of the opinion.

3. *Publication of Opinions*

A decision of the court is not published in the official reports unless it is certified for publication by a majority of the participating justices. The criteria for publication and publication requests are set forth in rules 8.1105 and 8.1120, respectively, of the California Rules of Court.

4. *Rehearing*

The procedure for filing a petition for rehearing is governed by rule 8.268 of the California Rules of Court. When a petition for rehearing is filed, the petition is routed to the justice who authored the opinion with copies to the participating justices. The authoring justice reviews the petition, and then indicates whether he or she votes to grant or deny the petition. The petition, along with any staff memorandum, is then circulated to the other two justices on the panel for their decisions. Two votes are necessary to grant or deny a petition for rehearing.

D. Posting of Opinions

For 60 days, the Reporter of Decisions posts published opinions of the Court of Appeal at: http://www.courts.ca.gov/opinions-slip.htm?Courts=D

Unpublished opinions of the court are posted for 60 days at http://www.courts. ca.gov/opinions-nonpub.htm?Courts=D

E. Motions

Routine applications and motions are reviewed and ruled on by the Presiding or Acting Presiding Justice. Dispositive motions, such as motions to dismiss an appeal, are ruled on by a panel of three justices. Requests for extensions of time to file briefs or other papers are ruled on by the Presiding Justice. Motions in writ proceedings are not held for opposition absent a request by the parties.

III. SETTLEMENT CONFERENCES

The general information packet sent to parties at the commencement of the appeal includes guidelines for the settlement program and an appellate settlement request form. The program is voluntary and available at the request of both parties or, should there be more than two parties, at the request of any two opposing parties. The request for a settlement conference may be made as soon as the notice of appeal is filed, and settlement proceedings may commence before briefing but, in any event, the request must be received no later than 30 days after the filing of the last brief. The request normally does not affect or extend the normal briefing schedule. In selecting the justice to participate in the settlement conference, the presiding justice considers any request by the parties for a particular justice. If settlement efforts prove unsuccessful, the settlement justice recuses from hearing the appeal in the case and all settlement papers are maintained as strictly confidential, kept separate from the appellate record and not considered by the attorneys or justices assigned to work on the appeal.

IV. EXTERN PROGRAM

The court has an unpaid extern program for select law school students three times a year (fall, spring and summer sessions). Each justice who participates in the program selects the extern who will work for him or her, usually for 20 to 40 hours per week during the session. A central staff attorney supervises the program, which includes a general orientation about the court and its work, a series of substantive and procedural law lectures, and monthly group meetings. Once assigned to a justice, externs work under the close supervision of the justice and the justice's staff. Students who participate in the extern program as part of their school's extern/clinic program may earn course credit for their work at the court.

V. LOCAL RULES

The Fourth District has adopted a number of local rules. (See Local Rules of the Fourth District Court of Appeal.)

(Adopted Sept. 1, 2004; amended Jan. 1, 2005; Jan. 1, 2007; Jan. 1, 2008; Feb. 15, 2010; Jan. 27, 2012; Sept. 19, 2014; June 1, 2017; Mar. 1, 2019.)

INTERNAL OPERATING PRACTICES AND PROCEDURES
FOURTH APPELLATE DISTRICT, DIVISION TWO

(March 2005 Revision)

SECTION I. INTRODUCTION
SECTION II. THE COURT
SECTION III. ORIGINAL PROCEEDINGS
SECTION IV. CIVIL CASE INFORMATION STATEMENT
SECTION V. CIVIL APPELLATE SETTLEMENT PROGRAM
SECTION VI. EXTENSIONS TO FILE BRIEFS
SECTION VII. CASE ASSIGNMENT
SECTION VIII. TENTATIVE OPINIONS AND ORAL ARGUMENT
SECTION IX. FILING OPINIONS
SECTION X. PRESIDING JUSTICE
SECTION XI. STAFF

SECTION I. INTRODUCTION

To implement the rules governing appellate court procedure, each district and division of the Court of Appeal has developed local customs and practices that may be similar to or different from other districts and divisions. This statement of the internal operating procedures and practices describes the more important customs of this court. The purpose of the statement is to inform the public and the bar of the general manner in which this court conducts its business.

SECTION II. THE COURT

Division Two of the Fourth District is located in Riverside and operates with almost complete autonomy from Division One located in San Diego and Division Three located in Santa Ana. Under the supervision of the Administrative Presiding Justice of the Fourth District, a clerk/administrator plans, organizes, coordinates, and manages the budget, personnel, facilities, and non-judicial activities of the district as a whole. Under the supervision of the Presiding Justice of each division (the Administrative Presiding Justice is also the Presiding Justice of Division One), an assistant clerk administrator is responsible for assisting the clerk/administrator in managing personnel and non-judicial programs within organizational and policy confines of an appellate court. In Divisions Two and Three the assistant clerk/administrator has total responsibility for all administrative activities of the division.

Division Two currently has seven justices including a presiding justice and six associate justices. Division Two handles all appellate matters arising in Inyo, Riverside, and San Bernardino Counties. Division One handles all appellate matters arising in San Diego and Imperial Counties. Division Three handles all appellate matters arising in Orange County. Additionally, cases originating in one division may be transferred to another division by the Administrative Presiding Justice if required because of recusals or decision of an earlier case by a different division. (See Cal. Rules of Court, rule 47.1(b).)

SECTION III. ORIGINAL PROCEEDINGS

Original proceedings are assigned to panels of three justices selected each month by a rotation distinct from the rotation from which panel assignments are made for appeals. Three writ attorneys assist the justices by preparing written summaries. The justices review the summaries and meet informally or formally as necessary to decide the case.

More urgent writ matters, including those requesting immediate stays, are the subject of immediate action by the justices facilitated by oral summaries by writ attorneys. If an alternative writ or order to show cause is issued, the issuing justice normally prepares the tentative opinion (see Section VIII., below) with the assistance of the writ attorney who prepared the summary.

SECTION IV. CIVIL CASE INFORMATION STATEMENT

California Rules of Court, rule 1(f), requires the filing of a civil case information statement in the Court of Appeal with a copy of the judgment or order appealed in all civil appeals within 10 days after the clerk mails the notice to do so and the required form. Under the supervision of the Presiding Justice, a central staff attorney reviews the civil case information statement to determine the appealability of the ruling designated in the notice of appeal, the timeliness of its filing, consolidation with other related appeals, and the apparent appellate case title and parties.

This court uses the civil case information statement to implement this court's policy to honor its jurisdictional limitations. Thus, this court will not construe a nonappealable ruling to include language of judgment or dismissal, or allow the appellant to belatedly obtain an appealable ruling, to "save" an appeal. (See *Shpiller v. Harry C's Redlands* (1993) 13 Cal.App.4th 1177, 1179-1181; *Passavanti v. Williams* (1990) 225 Cal.App.3d 1602, 1608-1610.) This court also uses the civil case information statement to initially screen cases for the court's settlement program. (See Section V., below.)

SECTION V. CIVIL APPELLATE SETTLEMENT PROGRAM

Division Two of the Fourth District began its civil appellate settlement program using volunteer attorney mediators in June 1991, the first program of its kind in California. The program helped dramatically in reducing backlog by freeing justices to work on cases that could not be settled. The program received the 1997 Kleps Award for court administration. Approximately 70 volunteer attorney mediators are now approaching 600 cases settled with the value of these settlements nearing an estimated 400 million dollars. This division has a population-to-justice ratio of 540,000 to 1 (compared to the First District's 280,000 to 1) and includes the fastest growing two-county area in California. The resulting increase in case filings now makes the settlement program more necessary than ever.

Volunteer attorney mediators chosen and scheduled by the Presiding Justice in cooperation with the court's settlement coordinator conduct most of the settlement conferences for civil appeals. On occasion, justices also act as mediators in selected cases. The volunteer mediators are experienced and respected attorneys from Riverside and San Bernardino Counties who are assigned cases for settlement according to their areas of expertise. The Presiding Justice selects cases for settlement based on settlement conference information forms filed by counsel and the availability of an appropriate mediator. Once a case has been selected by the court for settlement proceedings, participation is mandatory.

Settlement conferences may be held either before or after briefing is completed. Postbriefing settlement conferences were the rule when the court was using the program to reduce its backlog in the early and mid-1990's, but since the court has eliminated its backlog, prebriefing conferences are the rule and postbriefing conferences rare and generally discouraged. When cases are selected for a prebriefing settlement conference, generally the court permits a record produced by the superior court to be filed but stays filing of the briefs. Parties file a settlement conference statement within 10 days after notice that the case has been selected. Settlement conferences are held over a period of time before settlement is achieved or determined not to be possible. All documents relating to settlement proceedings are retained in a separate, confidential file for the case, and the proceedings and results are confidential and not revealed to the panel that decides the case if settlement is not achieved. Postbriefing settlement cases that do not settle are given priority over other civil cases. Court of Appeal, Fourth District, Division Two, Local Rules of Court, rule 4 authorizes the program.

SECTION VI. EXTENSIONS TO FILE BRIEFS

Extensions to file briefs are granted or denied based on the factors listed in California Rules of Court, rule 45.5(b). When further extensions on the usual grounds (the existence of other time limited commitments, the size of the record and number and complexity of the issues, and planned vacations) are no longer appropriate, counsel is so notified in an order granting the last extension on the usual grounds. Thereafter, no extensions will be granted except upon other factors listed in rule 45.5(b). If a further extension is obtained on one or more of those grounds, counsel is again notified that no further extensions will be granted on the usual grounds or the grounds stated in the application. A request for an extension on an excluded ground will be denied, and the clerk directed to issue a notice of default in failing to timely file the brief. (Cal. Rules of Court, rule 17(a)(1), (2).)

SECTION VII. CASE ASSIGNMENT

When a case is ready for assignment, the record is checked to see if any justice was involved in trial court proceedings or for other reasons should not be involved in deciding the case. The court under the supervision of the Presiding Justice maintains a confidential recusal list, which is reviewed prior to final case assignment. Cases are divided into five categories: unusually difficult chambers cases, chambers cases, "fast track" dependency cases (Cal. Rules of Court, rule 37.4(a)(1)(A)), dependency writs reviewing orders setting a hearing under Welfare and Institutions Code section 336.26 (Cal. Rules of Court, rules 38-38.1), and central staff cases. The cases are randomly assigned to a justice as author, and those in the categories of the unusually difficult, "fast track" dependency, and rules 38-38.1 writs are assigned by a rotation. Assignments to authors are usually made weekly, except the "fast track" cases and rules 38-38.1 writs are assigned immediately. When the author has prepared the tentative opinion (see Section VIII, below), the case is randomly assigned to a panel.

SECTION VIII. TENTATIVE OPINIONS AND ORAL ARGUMENT

A tentative opinion is the preliminary draft of the court's decision prepared by the author and reviewed by the panel members. The author circulates the tentative opinion with a cover sheet to the other two justices and notes a recommendation for or against oral argument. The two panel justices consider the briefs and record and note on the cover sheet their preliminary responses and evaluation of the need for oral argument.

Depending on the author's and panel justices' evaluation of the need for oral argument, one of two notices regarding oral argument is mailed to counsel with the tentative opinion. The first notice invites participation in oral argument and informs counsel that a notice will be mailed at least 30 days in advance of the date and time of oral argument. The second notice informs counsel that, while "[t]he court is not unalterably bound by the tentative opinion and is willing to amend or discard the tentative opinion if counsel's arguments persuade the court that the tentative opinion is incorrect in any way," "*at present, in this case the court believes that the record and briefs thoroughly present the facts and legal arguments such that the court is prepared to rule as set forth in the tentative opinion without oral argument.*" The notice advises the parties that oral argument will be deemed waived unless the clerk of the court receives a request for oral argument on the form attached to the notice on or before 12 days after the date of the notice.

Oral argument is held on the first Tuesday and Wednesday of each month, with slight adjustments occasionally made for holidays. If a party requests oral argument or the justices have decided that oral argument would be helpful, the clerk prepares the calendar and mails it to counsel at least 30 days in advance of the hearing. Two or three weeks before oral argument, the justices discuss the cases set for oral argument at a calendar conference.

SECTION IX. FILING OPINIONS

After oral argument, or waiver of oral argument, authors and panel justices develop the tentative opinions and preliminary responses into the opinions, concurrences, and dissents filed as the final decisions. If oral argument is deemed waived in a case, the opinion is circulated for signature to the other panel members as soon as it is signed by the author. The opinion is filed as soon as it is signed by all members of the panel. The sooner oral argument is waived, the sooner the opinion is filed, so that opinions in waived cases tend to be filed more quickly than cases in which oral argument is held. The additional time required to file opinions in orally argued cases results from the time it takes to schedule oral argument and/or from continuances requested by counsel or required by the absence of one of the panel members.

Argued cases are deemed submitted on the date of oral argument, and the opinions are generally filed within the same month.

SECTION X. PRESIDING JUSTICE

In addition to the regular duties of an associate justice, the Presiding Justice handles the administrative operation of the court including the functions designated in California Rules of Court, rule 77. In so doing, the Presiding Justice performs a number of tasks essential to the functioning of the court. These include without limitation policymaking, personnel, budgeting, oversight of facilities, grounds, furnishings, and equipment, case assignment, calendar preparation, backlog management, decision of all motions and applications until the case is assigned to an author, opinions in all criminal cases in which appellants file briefs under *People v. Wende* (1979) 25 Cal.3d 436, appointments of counsel, supervision of, and selection of cases for, the settlement program, and supervision of the central staff and clerk's office. Staff assist in these tasks when necessary in the Presiding Justice's discretion.

SECTION XI. STAFF

This division currently has 24 attorneys. Fourteen of these positions are chambers attorneys hired by the individual justices. The remaining 10 attorneys form the central staff consisting of one managing (formerly principal) attorney, one senior attorney acting as an assistant managing attorney, three writ attorneys, and five other central staff attorneys who primarily research and draft opinions. All central staff attorneys are under the supervision of the Presiding Justice, who assigns each attorney to a particular justice to research and draft opinions.

The clerk's office includes an assistant clerk/administrator, a number of deputy clerks, and other supporting clerical personnel. A settlement coordinator manages the volunteer attorney mediator settlement conference program. A systems administrator and an assistant maintain the court's computer systems. A librarian organizes and updates a central library, distributes materials to the justices' and attorneys' libraries, assists justices and attorneys with legal research, and prepares a library budget for approval by the Presiding Justice. There are also 10 judicial assistants employed by the court, who facilitate case flow in and out of the chambers and perform secretarial services for the justices and attorneys.

INTERNAL OPERATING PRACTICES AND PROCEDURES
FOURTH APPELLATE DISTRICT, DIVISION THREE

(Revised effective January 1, 2008)

SECTION I. INTRODUCTION
SECTION II. STRUCTURE OF COURT AND ORGANIZATION OF STAFF
SECTION III. PROCEDURES FOR PROCESSING CASES
  A. Appeals
  B. Original Proceedings
  C. Motions
  D. Filings by Facsimile, E-mail or Other Electronic Means
SECTION IV. JUDICIAL SETTLEMENT PROGRAM
  A. Purpose and Structure
  B. Filings
  C. Location and Telephone
  D. Settlement Conference Information Forms (SCIF's)
  E. Settlement Conferences
  F. "Workout" Conferences
  G. Private Mediations
  H. Stays; Tolling
  I. Disqualification
  J. Sanctions
SECTION V. SETTLEMENT NOTICES & STIPULATIONS
  A. Notice of Settlements
  B. Stipulated Requests for Dismissal
  C. Stipulated Requests for Reversal (Code Civ. Proc., §128, subd. (a)(8))
SECTION VI. ETHICAL SCREENS

SECTION I. INTRODUCTION

This document describes the general internal operating practices and procedures of this court. These practices and procedures supplement the statutes and rules of court that otherwise govern the court's business.

SECTION II. STRUCTURE OF COURT AND ORGANIZATION OF STAFF

Division Three of the Fourth Appellate District is currently authorized eight justices — a presiding justice and seven associate justices. The Chairperson of the Judicial Council periodically assigns pro tem justices to assist the court.

Each justice's staff consists of two or three judicial attorneys and a judicial assistant. The managing appellate court attorney supervises a separate central staff. The managing appellate court attorney and central staff work under the direction and supervision of the presiding justice. They review original proceedings, motions, and extension requests, act as counsel for the clerk's office, and assist in the evaluation of cases. Many of the justices also utilize law student externs who may receive academic credit, without pay, while working at the court.

The assistant clerk/administrator supervises the court's administrative staff under the direction of the presiding justice. The court's administrative staff consists of deputy clerks, librarian, court systems administrators, and office assistants.

SECTION III. PROCEDURES FOR PROCESSING CASES

A. Appeals.

1. When an appeal is fully briefed, the clerk's office sends out a notice to the parties who have appeared to give them an opportunity to request oral argument. (Cal. Rules of Court, rule 8.220(a).) Cases are generally scheduled for oral argument in order of the requests. Statutory priorities are enforced, and parties claiming calendar preference must promptly serve and file a motion for preference. (Cal. Rules of Court, rule 8.240.) Non-oral argument cases are similarly assigned in order based on the date oral argument is waived. Panels, including a justice tentatively designated to author the opinion, are generally assigned on a random rotating basis, subject to the presiding justice's responsibility to ensure that the court's resources are allocated in an effective and efficient manner to fairly and expeditiously resolve disputes, and to promote access to justice for all members of the public. (Cal. Rules of Court, rule 10.603(a).).

2. A confidential written summary is prepared by the authoring justice and provided to each panel member prior to oral argument. The panel may conference on a case before argument and always conferences after oral argument is completed. Thereafter, a proposed final opinion circulates among the panel members for comments and/or approval. Proposed opinions for cases in which oral argument has been waived generally circulate among panel members without a formal conference. All cases may routinely be discussed among the justices and staff members informally on an as-needed basis.

3. All requests for continuances of oral argument must be in writing and contain a particularized showing of compelling circumstances. The written request must inform the court of opposing counsel's position regarding any continuance. No request will be forwarded to the presiding justice until the court is made aware of opposing counsel's position. Counsel's stipulation to continue oral argument is not sufficient in the absence of a showing of compelling cause.

4. Any post-briefing citation of additional authorities must be made by letter to the court, without further legal argument, and served upon opposing counsel. The court retains discretion to strike or disregard late-filed or untimely citations of authority as they deprive the court and opposing counsel of sufficient opportunity to prepare for oral argument.

5. The court offers remote video appearances for oral argument on criminal matters, allowing counsel to appear via video from Division One in San Diego.

B. Original Proceedings.

1. The presiding justice assigns on a quarterly basis three justices to serve as the court's writ panel for a three-month period. The writ panel members also rule on motions requiring a three-judge panel.

2. The clerk's office notifies the managing appellate court attorney when an original proceeding is filed. The managing appellate court attorney determines the urgency of the relief sought. The matter is calendared for the weekly writ panel conference if court action is not required before then. Impromptu writ conferences are held when court action is required earlier. The managing appellate court attorney and central staff attorneys prepare written summaries of original proceedings which are provided to the writ panel members before their weekly conference.

C. Motions.

1. The court's practice is to hold motions on appeals (Cal. Rules of Court, rule 8.54) in the clerk's office until (1) an opposition has been served and filed, or (2) the time has passed to serve and file an opposition, whichever is earlier. To expedite the processing of an unopposed motion, the moving party should file a stipulation of nonopposition from other counsel.

2. Motions in writ proceedings are not generally held for opposition absent a request by the parties.

D. Filings by Facsimile, E-mail or Other Electronic Means

The court does not accept filings by facsimile, e-mail or other electronic means unless specifically authorized by court order or court rule. Local Rule 5 provides for a voluntary fax filing pilot project throughout the Fourth Appellate District for specified documents, but not briefs.

SECTION IV. JUDICIAL SETTLEMENT PROGRAM

A. Purpose and Structure.

1. The court has established a judicial settlement program to mediate appellate disputes, and, where appropriate, to establish briefing schedules, to simplify appellate issues, and to address procedural concerns. The court encourages appellate mediations and settlement conferences, and will make its resources available to parties who attempt in good faith to resolve a dispute on appeal.

2. The judicial settlement program is directed by the presiding justice, who appoints a supervising judicial attorney to administer the program and to conduct settlement conferences. In addition, a senior clerk schedules the settlement conferences and provides an interface between the public and the court.

B. Filings.

All papers pertaining to the judicial settlement program should be filed with the clerk's office at the courthouse, located at 925 No. Spurgeon Street, or mailed to the court at the following address:

California Court of Appeal
Fourth Appellate District, Division Three
P.O. Box 22055
Santa Ana, CA 92702
Attn: Judicial Settlement Program

These papers ordinarily are retained separately from the other documents filed on appeal, and, where appropriate, are confidential and for the purposes of the Judicial Settlement Program only.

C. Location and Telephone.

1. The judicial settlement program is physically housed in the Civic Center Professional Plaza, about one-half mile from the Spurgeon Street courthouse. The street address is:

Civic Center Professional Plaza
500 West Santa Ana Blvd., Room 400
Santa Ana, CA 92701

2. The telephone number is (714) 564-3600. The fax number is (714) 567-6060. Callers also may use the court's general telephone number: (714) 558-6777.

D. Settlement Conference Information Forms (SCIF's).

1. The presiding justice may order any pending civil appeal to be scheduled for a settlement conference pursuant to the California Rules of Court, rule 8.248. This decision is based upon the court's review of Settlement Conference Information Forms (SCIF), which are prepared by the parties and filed with the court. Preference is given to any stipulated requests for a settlement conference.

2. Request or stipulation for SCIF orders should be made in writing, directed to the Judicial Settlement Program. Requests may be made in confidence.

E. Settlement Conferences.

1. TIMING. Settlement conferences may be ordered before, during or after briefing. The court generally does not schedule a conference after an appeal has been set for oral argument except for good cause. The court tries to accommodate stipulations for specific day or dates. Parties may ascertain available settlement conference dates by telephoning the settlement conference clerk.

2. SETTLEMENT CONFERENCE OFFICER. The presiding justice appoints the person who conducts the settlement conference. In addition to the supervising attorney who manages the judicial settlement program, the settlement conference officer may be an individual justice, assigned pro tem justice, or other judicial attorney.

3. PERSONAL ATTENDANCE. Unless otherwise specified, all parties and their counsel must attend any settlement conference in person, and must have full settlement authority. Attendance by counsel claiming settlement authority is not sufficient. Any exceptions must be approved in advance by the court.

a. INSTITUTIONAL LITIGANTS. If the party is not an individual, then a party representative with full authority to settle must personally attend all settlement conferences in person, in addition to counsel.

b. INSURANCE. If a party has potential insurance coverage applicable to any of the issues in dispute, a representative of each insurance carrier whose policy may apply also must personally attend all settlement conferences, with full settlement authority.

c. TELEPHONIC APPEARANCES. The court prefers in-person settlement conferences and does not ordinarily grant requests for telephonic appearances. Parties who desire to participate by telephone must promptly serve and file a written request at least five court days before any settlement conference explaining why the attendee's personal presence is impossible or impracticable.

4. ADDITIONAL PARTICIPANTS. The court may order other necessary persons (whether or not a party to the appeal) to personally attend settlement conferences. In addition, the conference officer may invite parties to the action who are not parties to the appeal, or any person or entity having interest in the action, to attend. Any party may serve and file a written request for the attendance of such a party or person at least five

court days before any settlement conference. No other person may attend a settlement conference without the permission of the conference officer.

5. SETTLEMENT BRIEFS. If a settlement conference is held before appellate briefing or record preparation, the conference officer may direct that the parties provide settlement conference briefs, or other appropriate documents, to facilitate a meaningful and productive settlement conference.

6. PRE-CONFERENCE PREPARATION. Counsel should confer with their clients in advance of any settlement conference and be thoroughly familiar with the case and prepared to present their contentions in detail. Counsel should review their SCIFs for completeness and accuracy and promptly notify the conference officer of any material changes or omissions at least three court days before the settlement conference.

7. LOCATION. Settlement conferences generally are held at the court's settlement conference facilities. (See IVC, above for address.) Settlement conferences also may be held at the Spurgeon Street courthouse. Participants should carefully check the notice of a settlement conference for the correct location.

8. DURATION. Participants should be prepared to remain for the duration of the day, or until dismissed by the conference officer. No person who has been ordered to appear may leave without permission of the conference officer. At the conclusion of a prehearing conference, the conference officer may continue the conference to another date to allow for further discussions.

9. CONTINUANCES. Parties who seek to continue a settlement conference should attempt to do so by stipulation, with a mutually agreeable alternative date. Any request for continuances should be made in writing, with reasons stated, and served and filed at least five court days before the conference. Continuances are not granted, except for good cause.

10. EX PARTE COMMUNICATIONS. The conference officer may communicate with any of the parties or their counsel with or without notice to the other parties or their counsel.

11. CONFIDENTIALITY. All discussions and information imparted during the settlement conference are confidential, and the conference officer cannot testify about them.

F. "Workout" Conferences.

The presiding justice may order that a prehearing "workout" conference be held for any of the following purposes: (1) to simplify issues on appeal, (2) to establish a briefing schedule, (3) to address procedural questions, issues or outstanding motions or applications, (4) to lay the groundwork for a future settlement conference, (5) to facilitate ongoing settlement discussions, (6) to monitor the progress of a pending settlement or private mediation, or (7) for any other reason or reasons. Unlike settlement conferences, workout conferences are conducted either in person or by telephone. Generally, only counsel, not clients, participate in "workout" conferences.

G. Private Mediations.

The presiding justice entertains stipulated requests to stay of appellate proceedings to allow private mediations. Stay requests shall not exceed 60 days except for good cause. Any such stipulated request shall specify the identity of the mediator, the scheduled day or dates for mediation, and any other pertinent factors.

H. Stays; Tolling.

Appeals are not automatically stayed merely because parties are ordered to prepare a SCIF, or to choose dates for a settlement conference. The tolling provisions for briefs (Cal. Rules of Court, rule 8.248(d)) commence to run only when the court mails notice of a settlement conference for a specific date and time. Record preparation is not automatically stayed without a court order. The court's policy is to conduct settlement conferences as expeditiously as possible, and to issue a rule 8.248(d) notice lifting any stay or tolling order within 90 days from the date of the notice of the settlement conference.

I. Disqualification.

Disqualification of justices is governed by the Canon 3E of the California Code of Judicial Ethics. Justices are not disqualified to hear appeals merely because they rule on settlement conference requests or sign orders pertaining to procedural aspects of the settlement conference

process. If appeals do not settle, neither the conference officer nor any other court personnel present at a conference will participate further in the determination of the appeal on the merits. (Cal. Rules of Court, rule 8.248(c)(2).)

J. Sanctions.

The judicial settlement program shall not be employed by any party in bad faith or for purposes of delay. The court may impose sanctions for (1) failure to appear at a prehearing (settlement) conference, (2) failure to participate in good faith in the judicial settlement program, or to cooperate in good faith with the conference officer, or (3) failure to comply with a court order or court rule. Sanctions may include monetary awards, or, in the case of an appellant's failure to comply, dismissal of the appeal.

SECTION V. SETTLEMENT NOTICES & STIPULATIONS

A. Notice of Settlements.

The settling appellants shall immediately serve and file notices of settlement of any pending civil appeal, and telephone the court if the case has been calendared for oral argument. (See Cal. Rules of Court, rule 8.244(a) for other requirements concerning notice of settlements.) Settling appellants also should e-mail or telephone the settlement conference clerk if the appeal has been placed in the judicial settlement program.

B. Stipulated Requests for Dismissal.

Counsel should promptly serve and file stipulated requests for dismissal because of settlements. The stipulation should specify the allocation of costs on appeal and whether the remittitur is to issue immediately. (Cal. Rules of Court, rule 8.244(c).)

C. Stipulated Requests for Reversal. (Code Civ. Proc., §128, subd. (a)(8).)

Stipulated requests for a reversal of the judgment ordinarily are heard by the writ panel, unless the appeal already has been assigned to a panel for decision.

1. GOOD CAUSE. The parties must provide a sufficient showing to satisfy the statutory criteria in Code of Civil Procedure section 128, subdivision (a)(8). A copy of the judgment shall accompany the motion.

2. JOINT DECLARATION. The motion shall include a joint declaration of counsel that (1) describes the parties and the factual and legal issues presented at trial; (2) indicates whether the judgment involves important public rights or unfair, illegal or corrupt practices, or torts affecting a significant number of persons, or otherwise affects the public or a significant number of persons not parties to the litigation (if the judgment is against a state licensee, the declaration must also disclose whether it exposes such person to any possible disciplinary proceeding); (3) discloses whether the judgment sought to be reversed may have collateral estoppel or other effects in potential future litigation and, if so, whether any third parties who might be prejudiced by stipulated reversal of the judgment have received notice of the motion and (4) discloses whether the judgment involves discretionary determinations by the trial court that cannot be reversed by stipulation of the parties alone without independent appellate review (see, e.g., *Garabedian v. Los Angeles Cellular Telephone Co.* (2004) 118 Cal.App.4th 123; *Stewart v. Stewart* (1955) 130 Cal.App.2d 186, 193.)

3. NOTICE TO PARTY. The joint declaration shall include a certification that a copy of the stipulation and joint declaration has been delivered to the client. The certification need not include the address of the party notified. In a class action, the copy required need be delivered to only one represented party.

SECTION VI. ETHICAL SCREENS

The court maintains an ethical screening process for its judicial attorneys, judicial assistants, clerks, externs and other staff members in order to maintain and preserve public confidence in the judicial system. The purpose of this process is to inform the justices at the earliest possible opportunity of any circumstances of an actual or potential conflict of interest involving a court staff member that could give rise to the need for an ethical screen. If applicable, the ethical screen is promptly implemented.

(Amended Apr. 14, 2004; Mar. 1, 2005; Jan. 1, 2007; Jan. 1, 2008.)

FIFTH APPELLATE DISTRICT
LOCAL RULES

[As amended effective June 5, 2017; adopted, effective July 1, 1981; and previously amended February 25, 1983, February 8, 1985, October 2, 1992, November 15, 1993, June 25, 1999, August 25, 2003, January 1, 2007, August 17, 2007, September 1, 2011, February 10, 2012, November 1, 2012, December 1, 2014, May 11, 2015, February 19, 2016, and August 1, 2016.]

Order Regarding Penal Code section 4019 Amendment Supplemental Briefing

February 11, 2010

In pending appeals in which an appellant arguably is entitled to additional presentence custody credits under the January 25, 2010 amendments to Penal Code section 4019, the court will deem the following issues raised without additional briefing:

(1) Under amended Penal Code section 4019, appellant is entitled to recalculation of presentence work and custody credits;

(2) To hold otherwise would violate equal protection principles.

This order applies to all appeals. If the court deems supplemental briefing necessary from either the appellant or the respondent, it will request a letter brief from counsel.

JAMES A. ARDAIZ, P.J.

Order Regarding Supplemental Briefing
February 21, 2007

In cases remanded from the United States Supreme Court for further consideration in light of *Cunningham v. California* (2007) 549 U.S. __ [127 S.Ct. 856, 2007 U.S. Lexis 1324]:

(1) Within 30 days after of the order remanding the case to the Court of Appeal for further proceedings, appellant may serve and file a supplemental opening brief in the Court of Appeal. Within 30 days after such a brief is filed, the respondent may serve and file a supplemental responding brief.

(2) Supplemental briefs must be limited to matters arising after the previous Court of Appeal decision in the cause.

JAMES A. ARDAIZ, P.J.

Amended Order Regarding Cunningham Briefing
February 16, 2007

If the appellant has raised an issue challenging the imposition of the upper term, in reliance on *Blakely v. Washington* (2004) 542 U.S. 296 or *Apprendi v. New Jersey* (2000) 530 U.S. 466, it shall be deemed that the appellant is also relying on *Cunningham v. California* (2007) 549 U.S. __ [127 S.Ct. 856, 2007 U.S. LEXIS 1324].

If the court deems supplemental briefing necessary from either the appellant or the respondent to address related issues such as forfeiture, waiver, prejudice, etc., it will request a letter brief from counsel. Any request to file supplemental briefing will be considered on a case-by-case basis.

JAMES A. ARDAIZ, P.J.

Rule 1. Circuit-Riding Sessions [Repealed]
Rule 1 adopted July 1, 1981; repealed Aug. 25, 2003.

Another Rule 1 follows.

Rule 1. Augmentation of Record and Correction of Omissions from Record

(a) [Material inadvertently omitted] Counsel should not file a motion to augment the record when items have been omitted from the normal (criminal) record on appeal. In those cases counsel should immediately notify the clerk of the superior court, who shall comply with rule 8.155(b) of the California Rules of Court.

(b) [When to file motion to augment] Appellant should file requests for augmentation in one motion within 40 days of the filing of the record. Respondent should file requests for augmentation in one motion made within 30 days of the filing of appellant's opening brief. Thereafter, motions to augment will not be granted except upon a showing of good cause for the delay.

(c) [Clerk's transcript] A motion to augment or correct the clerk's transcript shall be accompanied either by certified copies of the documents requested, or, if the documents are not provided, the motion must identify them with specificity and contain an explanation for their omission. When submitting an electronic motion to augment or correct the clerk's transcript, a party must electronically submit the documents requested as a separate .pdf file at the same time as the motion and ensure the documents are formatted in compliance with this court's Local Rule 8. When electronically submitting a motion to augment or correct the clerk's transcript, a party may exceed the 300-page limit, contained in California Rules of Court, rules 8.124(d)(1) and 8.144(c)(1), as long as the file size is 25 megabytes or smaller.

(d) [Reporter's transcript] A motion to augment the reporter's transcript shall identify the portion of the record with specificity, including the reporter's name and the date of the hearing. The motion shall establish with some certainty how the requested materials may be useful on appeal.

(e) [Extension of time] The time to perform any act required or permitted by the California Rules of Court will not be automatically extended in civil cases by the filing of or ruling on a motion to augment. If additional time is needed, counsel may request an extension of time in the motion to augment.

(f) [Good faith required] A motion to augment shall be made in good faith and shall not be made for the purpose of delay.

Rule 1 adopted Nov. 15, 1993; renumbered from Rule 2 Aug. 25, 2003; amended Jan. 1, 2007; Aug. 17, 2007; Feb. 19, 2016.

Rule 2. Settlement Conferences in Civil Appeals [Repealed]
Rule 2 adopted Jan. 28, 1982; repealed Sept. 1, 2011.

Another Rule 2 follows.

Rule 2. Mediation Program for Civil Appeals

The Court has established a Judicial Mediation Program to assist parties to resolve appellate disputes in civil cases the Court finds suitable.

(a) Rule application: This rule applies to all civil appeals except those under Welfare and Institutions Code sections 300, 601, and 602 and Family Code section 7802, appeals in conservatorship and guardianship matters, and appeals from original proceedings ancillary to a criminal prosecution.

(Subd (a) adopted effective Sept. 1, 2011.)

(b) Questionnaire: When a notice of appeal is filed in any civil case to which this rule applies, the Clerk will promptly mail or e-mail to appellant and respondent instructions for the filing of the non-confidential Civil Appeal Case Screening Questionnaire. [Downloadable form available on the Court's website http://www.courts.ca.gov/5dca.htm.] Within 10 calendar days after the Clerk mails or e-mails instructions regarding the Civil Appeal Case Screening Questionnaire, each party must complete, sign, and serve the Questionnaire, and file it electronically.

The Questionnaire will assist the Court in selecting a case for mediation with a sitting Justice of this Court. The Court will select a case promptly after the Questionnaire is submitted and before the parties have incurred the expense of record preparation and appellate briefing. The Court recognizes the parties are asked to prepare the Questionnaire very early in the appellate process and may not be able to identify all appellate contentions. The Court will not deem an omission to be a waiver or forfeiture of any claim on appeal.

Failure to return the Questionnaire timely on appellant's part may result in dismissal of the appeal, without prejudice to reinstatement on a showing of good cause, or in imposition of monetary sanctions pursuant to subdivision (e).

Failure to return the Questionnaire timely on respondent's part may result in the appeal being considered for mediation suitability without input from respondent, or in imposition of monetary sanctions pursuant to subdivision (e).

(Subd (b) amended effective Feb. 19, 2016; adopted effective Sept. 1, 2011; previously amended Feb. 10, 2012.)

(c) Mediation/Settlement Process:

(1) Effective upon the filing of any civil notice of appeal to which the rule applies, the provisions of rules 8.121, 8.124 and 8.216 of the

California Rules of Court requiring designation of the record, payment of estimated costs for preparation of the record, and submission of a proposed briefing schedule are suspended, pending the Court's decision to select or not select the civil appeal for mediation.

These rules do not prohibit the superior court from collecting the deposit required by Government Code section 68926.1 and by California Rules of Court, rule 8.100(b)(2).

(2) Within 14 calendar days after the Court receives the Civil Appeal Case Screening Questionnaires, it will notify the parties in writing, by telephone, or by e-mail whether the Court has or has not selected the civil appeal for mediation. If a civil appeal is selected for mediation, the Court's Mediation Coordinator will provide the parties with three dates on which the Justice is available for the mediation session. At the same time, the Court will furnish the Justice mediator with copies of the Civil Appeal Case Screening Questionnaires. Within 14 calendar days after receipt of the dates the Justice mediator is available, the parties must advise the Court's Mediation Coordinator of their scheduling preferences. The Justice mediator will promptly select the date for the mediation session and the Mediation Coordinator will notify the parties by e-mail.

If a civil appeal is selected for mediation, suspension of rules 8.121, 8.124, and 8.216 of the California Rules of Court will remain in effect until the mediation process is complete.

If a civil appeal is not selected for mediation, the Court will notify the parties and the superior court, in writing, that the suspension of rules 8.121, 8.124, and 8.216 of the California Rules of Court is terminated. The parties must comply with the requirements of rules 8.121, 8.124, and 8.216 as if the notice of appeal had been filed on the date specified in the Court's notice.

If a civil appeal is not selected for mediation, the parties may thereafter electronically file a stipulation for entry into the mediation program. The Court will promptly decide whether or not to accept the case into the mediation program and the Mediation Coordinator will notify the parties of the Court's decision.

(3) The Justice mediator may, for good cause, continue a mediation session to a date certain. The Justice may also continue the mediation from time-to-time to allow further opportunity for negotiation and agreement.

(4) The parties shall submit in writing, directly to the Justice mediator, a CONFIDENTIAL Mediation Statement at least seven (7) calendar days before the scheduled mediation. The statement shall provide:

(A) The names of parties and their attorneys.

(B) A statement regarding the existence of any applicable insurance, and, if so, the identity of the carrier, the amount of the applicable insurance policy limits, and the nature of any insurance coverage disputes/issues.

(C) A statement indicating whether or not a board, council or other committee must approve any settlement, and, if so, the identity of that body.

(D) The identification of any person not named as a party whose consent is necessary to achieve settlement.

(E) The dates and results of prior arbitration, mediation, and most recent settlement discussions.

(F) The dates and amounts of any Code of Civil Procedure section 998 offers.

(G) A statement identifying and discussing in detail all facts and law pertinent to the issues of liability and damages involved in the case as to that party.

(H) An itemization of all economic and noneconomic damages claimed by the plaintiff.

(I) A description of any liens and their amounts.

(J) A statement whether there is any claim for recovery of attorney's fees, and, if so, the amount incurred to date.

(K) A statement of any additional information that might assist the Justice mediator.

(5) All parties and their counsel of record must attend all mediation sessions in person and with full settlement authority. If a party is not an individual, then a party representative with full authority to settle all appeals and cross-appeals must attend all mediation sessions in person, in addition to counsel. If a party has potential insurance coverage applicable to any of the issues in dispute, a representative of each insurance carrier whose policy may apply also must attend all mediation sessions in person, with full settlement authority. Any exception to this requirement must be approved in writing by the Justice mediator. The Justice mediator may invite participation by any additional person or entity if the mediator concludes that such participation would facilitate mediation.

(6) If completion of mediation does not result in disposition of the appeal, the Court will immediately notify the parties and the superior court in writing or e-mail that suspension of rules 8.121, 8.124, and 8.216 of the California Rules of Court is terminated. The parties must comply with the requirements of rules 8.121, 8.124, and 8.216 as if the notice of appeal had been filed on the date specified in the Court's notice.

(Subd (c) amended effective Feb. 19, 2016; adopted effective Sept. 1, 2011; previously amended effective Feb. 10, 2012.)

(d) Confidentiality: Except as otherwise required by law, information disclosed to the Justice mediator, the parties, counsel, or any other participant in the mediation, or in the Mediation Statement, is confidential and must not be disclosed to anyone not participating in the program. The parties are required to sign a confidentiality agreement in a form designated by the Court.

(Subd (d) adopted effective Sept. 1, 2011.)

(e) Sanctions: Monetary sanctions may be imposed following an electronically filed noticed motion by a party seeking sanctions for failure to comply with the rules or on the Court's own motion. Any date selected for a motion for sanctions must be cleared in advance with the Court's Mediation Coordinator at 5DC_Mediation@jud.ca.gov.

(Subd (e) amended effective Feb. 19, 2016; adopted effective Sept. 1, 2011.)

(f) Disqualification of *Justice Mediator*: Any Justice who participates in a mediation shall not thereafter participate in the consideration or disposition of the appeal on its merits.

(Subd (f) amended effective Feb. 19, 2016; adopted effective Sept. 1, 2011.)
Rule 2 amended effective Feb. 19, 2016; adopted effective Sept. 1, 2011; former rule 2, Settlement Conferences in Civil Appeals, repealed effective Sept. 1, 2011; previously amended effective Feb. 10, 2012.

Rule 3. Stipulation for Use of Original Superior Court File [Repealed]

Rule 3 adopted Dec. 29, 1989; repealed Aug. 25, 2003.

Another Rule 3 follows.

Rule 3. Writ Petitions: Supporting Records and Stay Requests

(a) [Information Sheet] All petitions for extraordinary writs, other than habeas corpus, shall be accompanied by a properly completed face sheet, the *Appellate Court Writ Petition Information Sheet.* This form is available through TrueFiling on the Court's website and from the clerk of the court.

(Subd (a) amended effective Aug. 1, 2016; previously amended Nov. 1, 2012 and May 11, 2015.)

(b) [Required Exhibits] A petition for an extraordinary writ that seeks review of a trial court ruling shall be accompanied by the following:

(1) a copy of the order or judgment from which relief is sought;

(2) copies of all documents submitted to the trial court supporting and opposing petitioner's position; and

(3) a transcript of the proceedings leading to the order or judgment below, or if a transcript is unnecessary or unavailable, a declaration by counsel (i) explaining why a transcript is unnecessary or unavailable and (ii) fairly summarizing the proceedings, including arguments by counsel and the basis of the trial court's decision, if stated.

(Subd (b) amended effective Nov. 1, 2012.)

(c) [Copies of Filed Documents] A party who electronically files any petition, answer, opposition, reply, or other response to a petition, including any supporting documents, according to the requirements of Local Rule 8, is exempt from submitting copies of such documents. A self-represented party may electronically file such documents according to the requirements of Local Rule 8, but is not required to do so.

Otherwise and in lieu of the requirements contained in California Rules of Court, rule 8.44(b)(3) and (5), a party who files a petition, answer, opposition, reply, or other response to a petition, including any supporting documents, in paper form shall file an original and one paper copy that is unbound, printed on white paper and does not contain tabs or a red cover.

A self-represented person who files a petition for writ of habeas corpus is only required to file the original petition.

(Subd (c) amended effective Aug. 1, 2016; adopted effective Nov. 1, 2012; previously amended May 11, 2015.)

(d) [Stay Request] A petitioner who requests an immediate stay shall explain in the petition the reasons for the urgency and set forth all relevant time constraints. If a petitioner does not submit the required record and explanations or does not present facts sufficient to excuse the failure to submit them, the Court may summarily deny the stay request.

(Subd (d) amended effective Aug. 1, 2016; previously amended Nov. 1, 2012.)
Rule 3 adopted Nov. 15, 1993; amended and renumbered from Rule 5 Aug. 25, 2003; amended effective Nov. 1, 2012; May 11, 2015; Aug. 1, 2016.

Rule 4. Settlement Conferences in Civil Appeals [Renumbered]

Rule 4 adopted Jan. 28, 1985; renumbered to Rule 2 Aug. 25, 2003.

Another Rule 4 follows.

Rule 4. Telephonic Oral Argument

Telephonic oral argument is available to all parties.

Telephonic Oral Argument Procedures

1. A party who requests oral argument must return to the court a questionnaire designating the time requested. The questionnaire must designate the attorney arguing the case, if the party is represented by counsel, or the name(s) of the litigant(s) who will appear if the party is self-represented.

2. The process for appearing telephonically for oral argument is described on the court's website.

3. A party, if self-represented, or a party's designated counsel is expected to be available during the time oral argument has been scheduled and until such time as it has been completed.

Failure to be available to participate in telephonic oral argument, once requested, will be treated in the same manner as a failure to personally appear for scheduled oral argument.

4. Parties are encouraged to use a landline telephone for telephonic oral argument because landlines typically facilitate better two-way communication. If a party must use a cellular phone, pausing occasionally during the argument is critical to allow the Justices to ask questions.

5. Any deviation by appointed or retained counsel from these procedures shall not be permitted except by express prior approval of the court.
Rule 4 adopted Nov. 15, 1993; renumbered from Rule 6 Aug. 25, 2003; amended Aug. 17, 2007; June 5, 2017.

Rule 5. Writ Petitions: Supporting Records and Stay Requests [Renumbered]

Rule 5 adopted Nov. 15, 1993; renumbered to Rule 3 Aug. 25, 2003.

Rule 5. Stipulation for Use of Original Superior Court File [Repealed]

Rule 5 adopted Oct. 16, 2006; repealed Aug. 1, 2016.

Rule 6. The Teleconference Oral Argument Option [Renumbered]

Rule 6 adopted Nov. 15, 1993; renumbered to Rule 4 Aug. 25, 2003.

Rule 7. Record Preparation in Juvenile Appeals and Writs

(a) [Application]

This rule applies to record preparation in:

(1) Appeals from judgments or appealable orders in:

(A) Cases under Welfare and Institutions Code sections 300, 601, and 602; and

(B) Actions to free a child from parental custody and control under Family Code section 7800 et seq.; and

(2) Writ petitions under Welfare and Institutions Code sections 366.26 and 366.28.

(Subd (a) adopted effective Dec. 1, 2014.)

(b) [Sending the Record]

Within 20 days after a notice of appeal or notice of intent is filed, the clerk of the superior court shall send, by the most expeditious method, the original record to this court, noting the sending date on each original.

In appeals, copies of the record shall be sent at the same time to counsel pursuant to California Rules of Court, rules 8.409(e)(1)(B), (e)(2) and 8.416(c)(2)(B), (c)(3), as applicable.

In writ proceedings under Welfare and Institutions Code sections 366.26 and 366.28, copies of the record shall be sent at the same time to counsel or any unrepresented party pursuant to California Rules of Court, rules 8.450(i)(2) and 8.454(i)(2), as applicable.

(Subd (b) adopted effective Dec. 1, 2014.)

(c) [Enforcement]

In the event this court does not receive the original record within 23 calendar days after a notice of appeal or notice of intent is filed, this court shall issue an order directed to the superior court executive officer to deliver the original transcripts to this court within 2 court days. If the superior court executive officer does not comply with this court's order, an order to show cause may issue.

(Subd (c) adopted effective Dec. 1, 2014.)
Rule 7 adopted Dec. 1, 2014.

Rule 8. Electronic Filing

Pursuant to California Rules of Court, rule 8.70, the Court will require all filings in this District be made through the Court's electronic filing system (EFS) operated by ImageSoft TrueFiling (TrueFiling). Use of the EFS system is mandatory for all attorneys filing in this District, unless an exemption is granted, and is voluntary for all self-represented litigants. A filing in electronic format will be accepted in lieu of any paper copies otherwise required under California Rules of Court, rule 8.44 and constitutes the official record of the Court.

(a) [Registration]

(1) Obligation to Register. Each attorney of record in any proceeding in this District is obligated to become an EFS user and obtain a user ID and password for access to the TrueFiling system. Self-represented litigants must register if they wish to e-file. Attorneys and self-represented litigants may register at: https://www.truefiling.com/_layouts/ElectronicFile.Main/SignUp.aspx

(2) Obligation to Keep Account Information Current. An EFS user is responsible for all documents filed under the user's registered ID and password. Registered users are required to keep their e-mail address current and may update their e-mail address online via the TrueFiling Web site. The user also must comply with the requirements of California Rules of Court, rule 8.32.

(Subd (a) amended effective May 11, 2015; adopted effective Dec. 1, 2014.)

(b) [Format]

Documents filed electronically must be in PDF format, or readily capable of conversion to PDF format while maintaining original document formatting by TrueFiling to permit text searches and to facilitate transmission and retrieval. If the filer possesses only a paper copy of a document, it may be scanned to convert it to a searchable PDF format. It is the filer's responsibility to ensure that any document filed is complete and readable. No single document shall exceed a total file size of 25 MB.

Briefs must comply with the content and form requirements of California Rules of Court, rule 8.204, with the exception of those provisions dealing exclusively with requirements for paper. The table of contents for each brief shall include electronic bookmarks to each heading in the text. All original proceedings must include electronic bookmarks from the table of contents for each hearing in the text, and to the first page of any exhibit(s), with a description of the exhibit included in the bookmark.

(Subd (b) amended effective May 11, 2015; adopted effective Dec. 1, 2014.)

(c) [Signatures]

A TrueFiling user ID and password is the equivalent of an electronic signature for a registered attorney or party. Any document displaying the symbol "/s/" with the attorney's or party's printed name shall be deemed signed by that attorney/party.

(Subd (c) adopted effective Dec. 1, 2014.)

(d) [Trial Court Record]

(1) Appendices, Agreed Statements, and Settled Statements. Parties must submit any appendix filed pursuant to California Rules of Court, rule 8.124, any agreed statement filed pursuant to California Rules of Court, rule 8.134, or any settled statement filed pursuant to California Rules of Court, rule 8.137 in electronic form. Each part of the record submitted in any appendix shall clearly state the volume and page numbers included within that part and include an index of contents, with a descriptive electronic bookmark to the first page of each indexed document.

(2) Administrative Records. In addition to any administrative record provided by the trial court pursuant to California Rules of Court, rule 8.123, the party or parties seeking review of a board case under California Rules of Court, rule 8.498(b) must submit a copy of the administrative record in electronic form.

(3) Reporter's Transcripts. Any party who orders a reporter's transcript of proceedings pursuant to California Rules of Court, rule 8.130 must also request a copy of the transcript in computer-readable format, as provided in California Rules of Court, rule 8.130(f)(4), and submit an electronic copy to the Court.

(Subd (d) amended effective May 11, 2015; adopted effective Dec. 1, 2014.)

(e) [Personal Identifiers and Privacy Issues]

To protect personal privacy, parties and their attorneys must not include, or must redact where inclusion is necessary, personal identifiers such as social security numbers, driver's license numbers, and financial account numbers from all pleadings and other papers filed in the Court's public file, whether filed in paper or electronic form, unless otherwise provided by law or ordered by the Court. (California Rules of Court, rule 1.20(b).) If an individual's social security number is required in a pleading or other paper filed in the public file, only the last four digits of that number shall be used. If financial account numbers are required in a pleading or other paper filed in the public file, only the last four digits of these numbers shall be used.

The responsibility for excluding or redacting identifiers from all documents filed with the Court rests solely with the parties and their attorneys. (California Rules of Court, rule 1.20(b)(3).) Neither TrueFiling nor the Clerk of the Court has any responsibility to review pleadings or other papers for compliance.

(Subd (e) amended effective May 11, 2015; adopted effective Dec. 1, 2014.)

(f) [Sealed or Confidential Material]

All filers must comply with California Rules of Court, rules 8.46 and 8.47 pertaining to sealed and confidential material.

(Subd (f) adopted effective May 11, 2015.)

(g) [Filing Deadlines]

Filing documents electronically does not alter any filing deadlines. In order to be timely filed on the day they are due, all electronic transmissions of documents must be completed (i.e., received completely by the Clerk of the Court) prior to midnight. Where a specific time of day is set for filing by Court order or stipulation, the electronic filing shall be completed by that time. Although EFS permits parties to submit documents electronically 24 hours a day, users should be aware that telephone or online EFS assistance may not be available outside of normal Court business hours.

(Subd (g) repealed, amended and relettered from subd (f) effective May 11, 2015; adopted effective Dec. 1, 2014.)

(h) [Technical Failure/Motions for Late Filing]

If a filer fails to meet a filing deadline imposed by Court order, rule, or statute because of a failure at any point in the electronic transmission and receipt of a document, the filer may file the document as soon thereafter as practicable and accompany the filing with a motion to accept the document as timely filed. (See Cal. Rules of Court, rule 8.54(a)(1)&(2).)

The Clerk of the Court shall deem the EFS system to be subject to a technical failure whenever the system is unable to accept filings continuously or intermittently over the course of any period of time greater than one hour after 12:00 noon that day. Filings due on the day of a technical failure which were not filed solely due to such technical failure shall be due the next court day. The initial point of contact for any practitioner experiencing difficulty filing a document into the EFS system shall be the toll-free number posted on the TrueFiling Web site.

The Court shall not be responsible for malfunction or errors occurring in electronic transmission or receipt of electronically filed documents.

(Subd (h) amended effective May 11, 2015; adopted effective Dec. 1, 2014.)

(i) [Service]

An attorney's registration with TrueFiling to participate in EFS constitutes consent to service or delivery of all documents by any other party in a case through the system. (California Rules of Court, rule 8.71.)

(Subd (i) repealed, amended and relettered from subd (j) effective May 11, 2015; adopted effective Dec. 1, 2014.)

(j) [Filing Fees]

TrueFiling is a private vendor under contract with the Court. TrueFiling will assess vendor fees for each filing in accordance with the schedule posted on its Web site, as approved by the Court. e-Filing fees will be considered recoverable costs under California Rules of Court, rule 8.278(d)(1)(D). TrueFiling is designated as the Court's agent for collection of Court imposed fees where required for any filing, and any associated credit card or bank charges or convenience fees (California Rules of Court, rule 8.78; Gov. Code, § 6159).

Should a self-represented party with a fee waiver opt to file documents electronically, that party is exempt from the fees and costs associated with electronic filing. The persons and entities identified in Government Code section 6103 also are exempt from the fees and costs associated with e-Filing.

(Subd (j) amended and relettered from subd (k) effective May 11, 2015; adopted effective Dec. 1, 2014.)

(k) [Exemptions]

Self-represented parties may, but are not required to register for electronic filing, but must comply with this rule and the requirements of TrueFiling if they elect to register.

If electronic filing and/or service causes undue hardship or significant prejudice to any party, the party may file a motion for an exemption from the requirements of this rule. (See Cal. Rules of Court, rule 8.54(a)(1)&(2).) When it is not otherwise feasible for a party to convert a document to electronic form by scanning, imaging or other means, the document may be filed in paper form (California Rules of Court, rule 8.73(c)), together with a declaration setting forth the reasons that electronic filing was not feasible.

(Subd (k) amended and relettered from subd (l) effective May 11, 2015; adopted effective Dec. 1, 2014.)

(l) [Sanctions for Noncompliance]

Failure of counsel to timely register or otherwise comply with EFS filing requirements, unless exempted, shall subject counsel to sanctions as may be imposed by the Court.

(Subd (l) relettered from subd (m) effective May 11, 2015; adopted effective Dec. 1, 2014.)

Rule 8 amended effective May 11, 2015; adopted Dec. 1, 2014.

Local Court Form.   Appellate Court Writ Petition Information Sheet

By order dated November 23, 1982, all petitions for extraordinary writs, other than habeas corpus, shall be accompanied by a properly completed face sheet, the *Appellate Court Writ Petition Information Sheet*. This form is available from the clerk of the court, and also is available on the court Web site.

Local Court Form amended Aug. 25, 2003; amended Aug. 17, 2007.

INTERNAL OPERATING PRACTICES AND PROCEDURES
FIFTH APPELLATE DISTRICT

(Adopted August 1993, revised February 2005, January 1, 2007)

I. INTRODUCTION

The purpose of this memorandum is to acquaint the bar and litigants with the general internal operating procedures of this court. It does not duplicate the California Rules of Court nor the statutes that govern the processes of the Courts of Appeal.

II. STRUCTURE OF COURT AND ORGANIZATION OF STAFF

The court is currently authorized ten judges — a presiding justice and nine associate justices.

The court is not divided into divisions and normally operates with three panels. The justices are rotated among the panels each month so that over time each justice will sit an equal number of times with every other justice on the court.

Each justice is authorized two staff attorneys. In addition, the court has a central staff consisting of experienced attorneys who write draft opinions in cases that are screened for routine disposition. The court also employs experienced writ and motion attorneys. The central staff and writ and motion attorneys work under the direction and supervision of the presiding justice.

III. PRACTICES AFFECTING THE DECISIONAL PROCESS

The workload of the court is divided into six principal categories: regular appeals (those not screened for routine disposition treatment); routine disposition appeals; writs; motions; petitions for rehearing and applications for publication; and settlement conferences in civil cases.

A. Regular Appeals.

When the appellant's reply brief has been filed or the time for filing that brief has passed, the case is ready for disposition by written opinion. The cases are placed on the ready list in the order in which they become ready and are set in that order absent a granted motion to advance or a statutory priority. Although the clerk attempts to note those cases that are entitled to statutory priority, counsel is advised to remind the court of any particular case that is entitled to priority.

When placed on the ready list, the managing attorney screens all cases under the supervision of the presiding justice. Those cases subject to routine disposition in accordance with the procedure described below are so designated on the list of ready cases. The balance of the cases are designated as regular appeals.

During the last two weeks of each month the managing attorney under the supervision of the presiding justice prepares a list of the cases to be set on the regular calendar in the third following month. For example, cases to be set in April are selected in the last two weeks of January. In order to equalize the workload among the justices, the managing attorney assigns a weight to all cases according to degree of difficulty. Consistent with the goal of achieving an equal caseload for each justice, and absent a compelling reason to the contrary, the cases are then assigned at random to the individual justices for authorship. The total weight of the cases assigned to each justice is approximately equal. Two other justices from the same panel are assigned to participate in deciding each case. The cases are then calendared for oral argument, and notices of the settings are sent to the attorneys of record. The court does not look with favor upon requests for continuance of the hearing date and will normally refuse to grant a continuance unless a request is received within five days of the time the notice is sent and good cause is shown for the continuance.

If oral argument is requested, counsel may utilize the telephonic oral argument option which is available in this court (Oral argument by telephone option — see Section IV, post.)

When a case is calendared for oral argument, one of the staff attorneys for the justice to whom the case is assigned prepares a memorandum of facts and law in that case. Memoranda in all cases are normally completed during the month following the setting. For example, memoranda for cases calendared for April are completed in February. When completed, the memorandum is distributed to the three justices assigned to decide the case. The authoring justice will normally prepare a proposed opinion in each case to be distributed to the other two justices assigned to that case prior to the pre-argument conference which is held shortly before the date set for oral argument. Each of the justices will have read the briefs, as much of the record as they deem necessary, the case memorandum and the proposed opinion, if any, prior to the pre-argument conference.

Well in advance of oral argument, each case is reviewed by the court to determine if the issues can be narrowed or if the court will accept waiver of oral argument. In the former case, the court may advise counsel by letter of the particular issues upon which the court would like to hear oral argument. In the latter case, the court will advise counsel by letter that it is willing to accept a waiver of oral argument.

As a result of the court's preparation for oral argument, the justices are thoroughly familiar with the facts and issues before oral argument commences. The court normally asks questions of counsel during oral argument in an effort to pinpoint those issues that are particularly troublesome, to clear up any areas of confusion or uncertainty, and to further narrow the issues. Occasionally, supplementary briefing is permitted or requested. Otherwise, cases are submitted for decision at the conclusion of oral argument. (See Cal. Rules of Court, rule 8.256(d).)

After argument, the participating justices hold a post-argument conference. Thereafter, the authoring justice circulates a draft opinion to the other justices on the panel for their concurrence or dissent. In the event a majority of the justices do not eventually concur in the opinion of the justice to whom the case was assigned for authorship, a non-concurring justice prepares the majority opinion.

Discussion as to whether an opinion qualifies for full or partial publication under California Rules of Court, rules 8.1105 or 8.1110, normally occurs at the pre and post-oral argument conferences, though the question remains open until the opinion becomes final.

If oral argument is waived, the case is ordered removed from the calendar and submitted for decision. The opinion may be filed any time thereafter. The decisional process is substantially the same as that outlined above except for the pre-oral argument conference.

B. Routine Dispositions.

A routine disposition is a case on appeal which raises no new or novel questions of law, is not of wide public interest, and can be disposed of by the application of settled principles of law to the facts. The draft opinion is written by an experienced attorney assigned to the central staff or by a justice.

The court is sensitive to the concern that the judicial input into this type of case may be diluted and therefore carefully supervises these cases. First, the presiding justice supervises the initial selection of the case for treatment as a routine disposition. Second, a panel of three justices is selected at random to participate on the case. Third, in each case a lead justice will read the briefs, the record where indicated, and approve or disapprove the draft opinion in writing. If the lead justice approves the draft opinion either as written or with changes, the two other justices must read and approve the opinion in writing. Fourth, if any justice so requests, a conference will be held among the justices and the author of the draft opinion. If, after a conference, any justice is of the opinion the case is inappropriate for routine disposition treatment, its designation as a regular appeal is restored and the case is processed in accordance with the procedure for regular appeals.

Last, when a draft opinion is approved by the justices, counsel are sent a letter indicating the court is willing to accept waiver of oral argument. Counsel are free to request oral argument and, if requested, the case is then placed on the oral argument calendar. Oral argument is requested in only a small percentage of these cases.

Appointed counsel are advised that the court will consider the extent to which requested oral argument was a reasonable consideration by counsel and the extent to which such argument, if presented, adds to or enhances the arguments presented in the briefs in evaluating compensation claimed for preparation time and travel time. If oral argument is requested, counsel should consider utilizing the telephonic oral argument option, which is available in this court. (See Section IV, post.)

If oral argument is waived or if oral argument is requested, after argument and post-argument conference, the opinion as written or as modified may be filed either as a signed opinion or as an unsigned per curiam opinion. In the latter case, the participating justices' names appear at the bottom of the first page.

C. Writs.

The term "writs" as used here includes the traditional writs (mandamus, prohibition, certiorari, supersedeas, habeas corpus, error coram vobis), also writs of review, petitions in Workers' Compensation Appeals Board cases, Agricultural Labor Relations Board matters, Public Employment Relations Board, Alcoholic Beverage Control Board, and Public Utilities Commission cases.

The court has two writ panels of three justices each, the membership of which is rotated among all the justices from month to month. Writs are assigned to the panels so as to approximately equalize the workload. Writ conferences are held by each panel at least once per week, usually on Thursday mornings.

When a writ petition is filed, copies are distributed to the writ attorneys who, under the supervision of the presiding justice, assign them to the panels. A memorandum is prepared in each case by the writ attorney and delivered to each justice on the assigned panel prior to the writ conference. Emergency writs, usually involving a request for a stay of a proceeding in the trial court, are by necessity considered and disposed of as required by the particular circumstances, the constraints of time involved, and other court business. Other than issuance of a temporary stay order, writs will not be issued prior to the receipt of a response from parties who would be adversely affected or unless such parties inform the court that no response will be filed. A petition for a writ may be denied without a response being filed.

If it appears the matter is one in which relief may be appropriate but a peremptory grant would be inappropriate, an order to show cause or alternative writ is issued and the case may be calendared for oral argument. The case is then handled in accordance with the procedure for regular appeals.

Occasionally, if the issuance of a peremptory writ in the first instance has been prayed, and the facts are clear, and the case has been fully briefed and nothing would be added by oral argument, relief by way of peremptory writ may be granted without the issuance of an order to show cause or alternative writ. In these cases, a short opinion or a written order with reasons stated will be filed. Summary denials are more frequent, in which event, the law of the case doctrine does not apply. (See *Kowis v. Howard* (1992) 3 Cal.4th 888.)

California Rules of Court, rule 8.452 writ petitions taken from orders setting a hearing under Welfare and Institutions Code section 366.26 are handled on the writ calendar. Such cases, generated by the filing of a notice of intent to file a writ petition are distributed to a central staff attorney specializing in juvenile dependency law and rule 8.452 writ practice. The central staff attorney works under the supervision of the presiding justice and assigns such cases to panels on a rotating basis. Once the time passes under rule 8.452 for the filing of a response to such a writ petition, the central staff attorney prepares an Order to Show Cause setting the case for oral argument with the proviso that, in the event the parties do not advise this court of their desire to orally argue the case within seven days' time, the matter will be submitted. Thereafter, the central staff attorney prepares a memorandum, which in most cases addresses the merits of the writ petition, and delivers the memorandum to each justice on the assigned panel prior to the writ conference. The case is then handled in accordance with the procedure for routine dispositions.

Petitions for review of Agricultural Labor Relations Board decisions, of orders and awards of the Workers' Compensation Appeals Board, the Public Employment Relations Board, the Public Utilities Commission, and the Alcoholic Beverage Control Board, and review of decisions of appellate divisions of superior courts pursuant to California Rules of Court, rule 8.1002, are handled on the writ calendar. If a petition for review is granted, or the certification under rule 8.1005 is accepted, the case is set for oral argument after briefing is completed. The case is then disposed of in accordance with the procedure for handling regular appeals.

D. Motions.

Non-routine motions and applications, including applications for bail, are processed in accordance with the procedure for handling writs.

Applications in routine matters (see Cal. Rules of Court, rules 8.50, 8.57), including motions to augment or correct the record, requests for extensions of time, and disciplinary proceedings against attorneys and court reporters for failure to timely file briefs and records, are normally disposed of by the presiding justice with the assistance of a writ attorney.

E. Petitions for Rehearing and Applications for Publication.

Petitions for rehearing and applications for publication are assigned for disposition to the same panel members who participated in the initial opinion.

F. Settlement Conferences in Civil Cases.

Upon stipulation of all parties to a civil case pending in the court or on the presiding justice's own motion, a settlement conference will be calendared and held pursuant to California Rules of Court, rule 8.284. Notice of availability of a settlement conference is sent to counsel at the time the record on appeal is filed. For further details, see local rule 2 on settlement conferences in civil appeals, a copy of which will be furnished upon request.

IV. TELEPHONIC ORAL ARGUMENT OPTION

The court has in place a teleconferencing system that allows up to five attorneys in different offices to present their argument over the telephone in a single case. Attorneys selecting this option remains in their office until the clerk notifies them that their case has been called. The attorneys will then come on the line and are part of a telephone conference call. The system broadcasts the attorney's voice over the courtroom public address system as well as to other counsel appearing by telephone. The justices are convened in open court and speak into microphones which broadcast into court and through the telephone system. Counsel can hear each other and the court. The system allows one or more attorneys to appear in court and argue while other counsel listen and present their argument over the telephone. The argument is tape-recorded just as if all attorneys were present in court.

The teleconferencing option was implemented to accommodate counsel's time and to provide a significant cost savings to clients and the state by eliminating travel time and costs, as well as time spent waiting for a case to be called. Retained counsel selecting the telephonic oral argument receive a nominal billing from the court following the argument to cover the cost of the conference call and administrative time involved.

Details of the practices and procedures related to the telephonic oral argument option are available from the clerk upon request and may be found in the California Rules of Court, Local Rules of the Courts of Appeal.

V. PRELIMINARY REVIEW OF APPELLANT'S OPENING BRIEF IN CIVIL CASES

The court presumes that briefs filed by counsel will comply with applicable standards. (See Cal. Rules of Court, rule 8.204 [Contents and form of briefs]). Unfortunately, many briefs do not. This adds to the court's workload and delays resolution of appeals.

Therefore, in civil appeals in this court:

(1.) After appellant's opening brief is filed, the managing attorney reviews the brief for basic compliance with pertinent rules, statutes, and case law. The review is non-substantive; the court does not engage in advocacy for the parties.

(2.) Should the brief fail to comply with minimum standards, the court may strike or return the brief and give counsel the opportunity to file an adequate brief within a specified time.

(3.) Should a subsequent brief continue to fail minimum standards, the court may dismiss the appeal without further notice. (*In re S.C.* (2006) 138 Cal.App. 4th 396, 406-407.)

The same standards apply to briefs filed by pro se appellants. A party proceeding inpropria persona is treated like any other party and is entitled to the same, but no greater consideration than other litigants and attorneys. A propria persona litigant is held to the same rules of procedure as an attorney. (*First American Title Co. v. Mirzaian* (2003) 108 Cal.App.4th 956, 958, fn. 1.)

(Amended Jan. 1, 2007.)

SIXTH APPELLATE DISTRICT LOCAL RULES

(Amended effective October 26, 2020; revised effective January 16, 2016; amended effective June 5, 2017; February 13, 2018; April 16, 2018)

Mediation. Rule 1.
Electronic filing. Rule 2.
Reporter's transcripts in felony appeals — Exception to California Code of Civil Procedure section 271(a). Rule 3.
Establishing appellate jurisdiction, civil case information statement, required attachments. Rule 4.

POLICY REGARDING *IN RE PHOENIX H.* BRIEFS IN LIGHT OF NEW EFILING REQUIREMENT

Effective immediately, the Sixth District Court of Appeal will no longer require compliance with California Rules of Court, rule 8.360 (a) for briefs filed Pursuant to *In re Phoenix H.* (2009) 47 Cal.4th 835. Court-appointed counsel should now submit a *Phoenix H.* brief in letter format when court-appointed counsel find no arguable issue to be pursued on appeal. All letter briefs filed pursuant to *In re Phoenix H.* shall be electronically filed. All other procedures and requirements associated with *Phoenix H.* briefs shall remain unchanged.

Dated: May 10, 2012

Conrad L. Rushing P.J.

Rule 1.   Location of Court Hearings [Repealed]
Rule 1 adopted Aug. 16, 1985; repealed Dec. 20, 2006.

Another Rule 1 follows.

Rule 1.   Mediation

  (a) [Application of rule]   This rule is adopted pursuant to rule 8.248, California Rules of Court, and shall apply to all civil appeals filed in the Sixth District Court of Appeal.

(Subd (a) adopted effective February 5, 2010.)

  (b) [Purpose of Mediation Program]   To aid the expeditious and just resolution of civil appeals, the Court of Appeal for the Sixth District has established a mediation Program ("Program"). The Program shall be administered by the Administrative Presiding Justice or a designated Supervising Justice, and their designated staff.

(Subd (b) amended effective April 16, 2018; adopted effective February 5, 2010.)

  (c) [Scope of Mediation Program]   At the court's discretion, any civil appeal may be placed in the Program upon the agreement of all parties to the appeal. The Court may, at its discretion, remove an appeal from the Program.

(Subd (c) amended effective April 16, 2018; adopted effective February 5, 2010.)

(d) [Mediators]

1. The court shall maintain a list of attorneys who have developed expertise in specified areas of law, are generally respected in the legal community, and are willing to mediate cases at this court. These attorneys shall be designated as mediators and preside over mediations conducted within the scope of the Program.

2. A justice or assigned justice of this court may, at the court's discretion, be designated as a mediator and preside over a mediation. A justice or assigned justice who participates in a mediation that does not result in complete settlement shall not thereafter participate in any way in the consideration or disposition of the case on its merits.

3. A justice or assigned justice of the court will not be disqualified to participate in the consideration or disposition of a case on its merits because he or she has ruled on a request for a mediation, ordered that a mediation be held, signed orders granting relief from default for an act required under this rule, extended or shortened any time period specified in this rule, or otherwise signed an order concerning a procedural aspect of the mediation process.

(Subd (d) amended effective June 11, 2010; adopted effective February 5, 2010.)

(e) [General Mediation Program Procedure]

1. All parties in a civil appeal shall file a Mediation Statement Form within 15 days of the date the Clerk of this court sends notice that the court has received the notice of appeal. Each party shall also serve a copy of their completed Mediation Statement Form on all other parties.

2. The Mediation Statement Form shall be transmitted by the Clerk to the Program and shall not be entered into the court file.

3. Within 15 days of receipt of the Mediation Statement Forms, the court shall notify the parties when a case is selected for mediation and furnish the name, address and telephone number of the mediator selected for the mediation. The court shall provide three possible dates for mediation.

4. The parties shall meet and confer to agree on the date of mediation, and inform the court within 5 days of the date selected for mediation. The court will issue written notice of the date and time of the mediation. The mediator, with the approval of the Court, may, for good cause, postpone or continue a mediation session to a date certain.

5. The Court may replace a selected mediator upon written request by a party supported by a showing of good cause or upon request of the mediator.

6. Immediately upon acceptance of a case into the Program, all further proceedings, including the filing of briefs, shall be suspended for 90 days. However, this rule shall not suspend preparation of the appellate record unless a specific order is issued directing suspension of record preparation. Upon the expiration of the stay, the appeal shall be reinstated to active status on the court's docket. Any request for further stay shall be granted only upon written application to the court and only upon a showing of good cause.

7. Mediation services shall be furnished by the Court without fee to the parties for up to a total of 4 hours. Any further mediation services shall be at the discretion of the mediator, on such terms as the mediator and the parties may agree upon, and consistent with the provisions of this rule.

(Subd (e) amended effective April 16, 2018; adopted effective February 5, 2010; previously amended effective June 11, 2010.)

(f) [Mediation Hearing and Sanctions]

1. All parties and their counsel of record must attend all mediation sessions in person with full settlement authority. If the party is not an individual, then a party representative with full authority to settle all appeals and cross-appeals must attend all mediation sessions in person, in addition to counsel. If a party has potential insurance coverage applicable to any of the issues in dispute, a representative of each insurance carrier whose policy may apply must also attend all mediation sessions in person, with full settlement authority. Any exception to this requirement must be approved in writing by the Court. Failure to attend may result in the imposition of sanctions against any party or counsel, up to and including immediate termination from the Program or dismissal of the appeal.

2. The mediator may invite parties to the action who are not parties to the appeal, or any person who has an interest in the action, to attend the mediation if it appears to the mediator that their presence may facilitate settlement of the case. Any party to the appeal may serve and file a written request for the attendance of such a party or person at least 15 days before the mediation.

3. Counsel shall confer with their clients in advance and be thoroughly familiar with the case and prepared to present their contentions in detail.

4. The presiding justice, a justice designated by the presiding justice, or the mediator may excuse a client's personal attendance upon request and a showing that hardship or unusual circumstances make the client's attendance impossible or impractical. If personal attendance is excused, counsel either shall have obtained full authority to agree to a settlement that binds the client or the client shall be available for consultation by telephone.

5. The mediator may require parties or their counsel to furnish information, documents, records or other items specified by the mediator.

(Subd (f) amended effective April 16, 2018; adopted effective February 5, 2010; previously amended effective June 11, 2010.)

(g) [Post Mediation Procedure]

1. No later than 10 days after completion of mediation, the mediator shall submit to the Court a Mediation Attendance Form, listing all participants in the mediation, and a brief summary of the procedural outcome of the mediation.

2. Each party and their counsel shall separately complete and submit to the Court evaluations of the mediation and the mediator on a form provided by the Court.

3. The parties and their counsel shall promptly take the steps necessary to implement the agreements reached in mediation. An appellant who has settled must immediately serve and file a notice of settlement in the Court of Appeal and, thereafter, must seek abandonment or dismissal of the appeal as provided in the California Rules of Court. The notice of settlement shall specify the allocation of costs on appeal and state whether the remittitur is to issue immediately.

4. Upon receiving notification that no agreement was reached at mediation, this court will immediately vacate the stay and reinstate the appeal to active status on the court's docket.

(Subd (g) adopted effective February 5, 2010.)

(h) [Confidentiality] Except as otherwise required by law, information disclosed to the mediator, the parties, counsel, or any other participant in the mediation, shall be confidential and shall not be disclosed to anyone not participating in the mediation Program.

(Subd (h) adopted effective February 5, 2010.)

(i) [Ethical Standards] Mediators shall adhere to the Rules of Conduct for Mediators in Court-Connected Mediation Programs for Civil Cases set forth in the California Rules of Court.

(Subd (i) adopted effective February 5, 2010.)

(j) [Appellate Process] Parties and counsel shall comply with all rules applicable to processing appeals while concurrently participating in the mediation Program.

(Subd (j) adopted effective February 5, 2010.)

(k) [Sanctions] Monetary sanctions may be imposed by the Administrative Presiding Justice or Supervising Justice for failure to comply with these rules.

(Subd (k) adopted effective February 5, 2010.)

Rule 1 reinstated effective November 13, 2013; suspended effective April 2, 2013; amended effective June 11, 2010; April 16, 2018; adopted effective February 5, 2010; former Rule 1 repealed effective March 2, 2007.

2013 Note: The Publisher received the following court order dated April 2, 2013 through November 12, 2013, "IT IS HEREBY ORDERED that the Mediation Program pursuant to Local Rule 1 is suspended."

Rule 2. Electronic Filing

Pursuant to California Rules of Court, rule 8.72, the Court of Appeal for the Sixth Appellate District (court) adopts the following requirements for electronic filing in this district. To the extent any portion of these requirements conflict with California Rules of Court, rules 8.70 – 8.79, these requirements govern.

a. Registration.

1. Obligation to Register. The court's electronic filing system (EFS) is operated by ImageSoft, Inc. (ImageSoft), and may be accessed via the TrueFiling portal (TrueFiling). In order to access TrueFiling, each attorney of record in any proceeding pending in this court is obligated to become an EFS user and obtain a username and password. Self-represented litigants must register if they wish to file electronically. Attorneys and self-represented litigants may register at www.truefiling.com.

2. Obligation to Keep Account Information Current. Registered users are required to keep their e-mail addresses current and must update their

e-mail addresses online via the TrueFiling web site. Updating TrueFiling does not relieve the user of the notice of change requirements in California Rules of Court, rule 8.32, subdivision (b).

b. Format.

1. Form of Documents. An EFS user is responsible for all documents filed under the user's registered username and password. All documents filed electronically must be in electronic text-searchable portable document format (PDF) while maintaining original document formatting. If an EFS user possesses only a paper document, the user must scan the document and convert it to an electronic text-searchable PDF. It is the filer's responsibility to ensure that any document filed is complete and readable. Electronically filed briefs must comply with the content and form requirements of California Rules of Court, rule 8.204, with the exception of those provisions specifying requirements for the use of paper, or as otherwise specified in this rule.

2. Pagination of Documents. Document pages must be consecutively numbered using only the Arabic numbering system, beginning with the number 1 on the cover page of the document. When a document is filed in both paper format and electronic format, the pagination must comply with this subparagraph.

3. Electronic Bookmarks. An electronic bookmark in a PDF document is an electronic tab created by a user to allow quick access to the bookmarked part of the document. Electronic bookmarks are required to be included with all electronic briefs, all appendixes, and all writ proceedings. Electronic bookmarks may be included with motions but are not required. In addition to requiring bookmarks, this rule allows hyperlinks. The electronic bookmark must include a brief description of the bookmarked item.

i. Each electronic brief shall include electronic bookmarks to the following: each heading and subheading, table of contents, table of authorities, certificate of word count, certificate of interested persons or entities, proof of service, and any attachment or exhibit included with the brief.

ii. Any appendix filed electronically pursuant to subparagraph (e) of this rule shall have a separate electronic bookmark to the table of contents and to the first page of each separate exhibit and attachment. Any exhibit or attachment included within an exhibit or attachment shall be separately bookmarked. (E.g., if an exhibit consists of a declaration containing multiple exhibits, each should be separately bookmarked.)

iii. All writ proceedings must include the electronic bookmarks required for electronic briefs listed above and also must include electronic bookmarks to the petition, points and authorities, and verification. All supporting documents must include the electronic bookmarks required for an appendix listed above.

c. Size. The file size limitation is 25 megabytes. If a filing exceeds the file size limitation, a party must submit the filing in multiple parts.

d. Paper Copies. An unbound paper copy of all electronically filed briefs, writ petitions, and documentation submitted in support of a writ petition must be lodged in this court within two days of the electronic filing. If the submission requests an immediate stay, the paper copy must be lodged in this court by the next court day.

e. Record on Appeal and Writ Proceedings.

1. Appendix. Parties must submit any appendix filed pursuant to California Rules of Court, rule 8.124 or 8.486 in electronic format. Each part of the appendix shall comply with the format, pagination and bookmark requirements enumerated in subparagraph (b) of this rule. If submitted in multiple parts, the cover of each part of the record submitted in any appendix or exhibit volume shall clearly state the volume and page numbers included within that part, and include an index of contents.

2. Administrative Record. In addition to any administrative record provided by the trial court pursuant to California Rules of Court, rule 8.123, the party or parties seeking review of an administrative determination must submit a copy of the administrative record as an electronic text-searchable PDF. An administrative record may be delivered to the court on CD, DVD, or flash drive.

3. Reporter's Transcript. Any party who orders a reporter's transcript of proceedings pursuant to California Rules of Court, rule 8.130, must also request a copy of the transcript in electronic format, as provided in California Rules of Court, rule 8.130(f)(4), and must submit an electronic copy to the court.

f. Personal Identifiers and Privacy Issues. To protect personal privacy, parties and their attorneys must not include, or must redact where inclusion is necessary, personal identifiers such as social security num-

bers, driver's license numbers, and financial account numbers from all pleadings and other papers filed in the court's public file, whether filed in paper or electronic format, unless otherwise provided by law or ordered by the court. (Cal. Rules of Court, rule 1.201.) If an individual's social security number is required in a pleading or other paper filed in the public file, only the last four digits of that number shall be used. If financial account numbers are required in a pleading or other paper filed in the public file, only the last four digits of these numbers shall be used.

The responsibility for excluding or redacting identifiers from all documents filed with the court rests solely with the parties and their attorneys. (Cal. Rules of Court, rule 1.201(b).) Neither ImageSoft nor the Clerk of the Court has any responsibility to review pleadings or other papers for compliance.

g. Sealed or Confidential Material. All filers must comply with rules 8.45 – 8.47 of the California Rules of Court pertaining to sealed and confidential material.

h. Filing Deadlines. Consistent with rule 8.77(c), filing documents electronically does not alter any filing deadlines.

i. Motion to Accept Filing as Timely Following TrueFiling Technical Failure. If a filer fails to meet a filing deadline imposed by court order, rule or law because of a failure of the EFS, the filer may file a paper or electronic document as soon thereafter as practicable and accompany the filing with a motion to accept the document as timely filed pursuant to rule 8.77(d).

j. Service. An attorney's registration with TrueFiling to participate in the EFS constitutes consent to service or delivery of all documents by any other party in a case through the system. (Cal. Rules of Court, rule 8.78.) Orders or other documents generated by the court will be served only through the EFS or by e-mailed notification. Only those exempted from the EFS pursuant to subparagraph (l) will receive manual service or notification by other means.

k. Filing Fees. ImageSoft is a private vendor under contract with the court. ImageSoft will assess EFS fees for each filing in accordance with the schedule posted on the TrueFiling web site, as approved by the court. EFS fees will be considered recoverable costs under California Rules of Court, rule 8.278(d)(1)(D). ImageSoft is designated as the court's agent for collection of court-imposed fees where required for any filing, and any associated credit card or bank charges or convenience fees (Cal. Rules of Court, rule 8.76; Gov. Code, § 6159).

If a party with a fee waiver chooses to file documents electronically, that party is exempt from the fees and costs associated with electronic filing. The persons and entities identified in Government Code section 6103 are also exempt from the fees and costs associated with the EFS.

l. Exemptions.

1. Self-represented parties are exempt from mandatory electronic filing. Self-represented parties may register for electronic filing. Self-represented parties who opt to register for electronic filing must comply with this rule and the requirements of TrueFiling.

2. Upon a showing of good cause, the court may allow an exemption from all or some of the requirements of this rule, pursuant to rule 8.71.

If an exemption is granted, the paper documents shall be filed and served upon the parties in accordance with all statutory requirements and the California Rules of Court applicable to paper documents.

m. Rejection of Electronic Filing for Noncompliance. The court will reject an electronic filing if it does not comply with the requirements of this rule pursuant rule 8.77(b).

n. Sanctions for Noncompliance. Failure of counsel to timely register, and failure of any registered user to comply with EFS filing requirements, unless exempted, may be subject to sanctions imposed by the court.

o. Posting and Publication. The Clerk of the Court is directed to post a copy of this rule on the court's web site pursuant to California Rules of Court, rule 8.72(a), and to submit a copy to the Reporter of Decisions for publication pursuant to California Rules of Court, rule 10.1030(a).

Rule 2 amended effective April 16, 2018; adopted effective January 16, 2016; previously amended effective June 5, 2017.

Rule 3. Reporter's Transcripts in Felony Appeals — Exception to California Code of Civil Procedure section 271(a)

a. Effective February 13, 2018, except as provided in subsection (b) below, counsel for a defendant in a felony appeal shall be deemed to have requested that his or her copy of the reporter's transcript be delivered in paper form pursuant to Code of Civil Procedure section 271(a)(1).

(Adopted, effective February 13, 2018.)

b. Notwithstanding the exception set forth in subsection (a) above, defendant's counsel, or, if the defendant is not yet represented by appellate counsel, the district appellate project, may request that his or her copy of the reporter's transcript be delivered in electronic form as provided in California Code of Civil Procedure section 271(a) by serving the lead court reporter and the superior court with a written request within 15 days after the notice of appeal is filed.

(Adopted, effective February 13, 2018.)

Rule 3 adopted effective February 13, 2018.

Rule 4. Establishing Appellate Jurisdiction, Civil Case Information Statement, Required Attachments

(a) An appellant filing a completed *Civil Case Information Statement* (Form APP-004) in this District pursuant to California Rules of Court, rule 8.100, subdivision (g), must attach the following documents:

(1) A copy of the judgment or order being appealed, including:

(A) A judgment of dismissal, if the appeal challenges a judgment entered after:

i. an order granting summary judgment, or

ii. an order sustaining a demurrer without leave to amend, or

iii. an order granting judgment on the pleadings;

(B) If appealing an order made after judgment (Code of Civ. Proc. §904.1, subd. (a)(2)), a copy of the final judgment or order of dismissal that predated the order being appealed (see Code Civ. Proc., §§ 577, 581d);

(2) A copy of the proof of service from the clerk of the superior court or any party's notice of entry of the order or judgment being appealed; or if neither the clerk of the superior court nor any party served a proof of service or notice of entry, a statement under penalty of perjury that no such document exists;

(3) If claiming an extension of time to file the appeal pursuant to California Rules of Court, rule 8.108, subdivision (b), (c), (d) or (e), a copy of the trial court's order granting or denying the applicable motion;

(4) The proof of service or notice of entry of any order listed in (3); or, if neither the clerk of the superior court nor any party served a proof of service or notice of entry, a statement under penalty of perjury stating that no such document exists;

(5) Any additional documents that may be necessary to establish appellate jurisdiction pursuant to Code of Civil Procedure section 904.1 and California Rules of Court, rules 8.104 and 8.108.

(Adopted, effective October 26, 2020.)

(b) If appellant fails to comply with this rule, or if the court requires additional documents to verify appellate jurisdiction, the court will notify the appellant in writing of any omission or additional request. If any requested document is unavailable or does not exist, appellant shall so notify the court in writing with a statement under penalty of perjury stating why the document(s) cannot be provided. If appellant fails to comply with the court's request within the specified time, the court may, on its own motion or upon motion of any party, dismiss the appeal.

(Adopted, effective October 26, 2020.)

Rule 4 adopted effective October 26, 2020.

INTERNAL OPERATING PRACTICES AND PROCEDURES
SIXTH APPELLATE DISTRICT

(Revised effective January 1, 2009)

Introduction

The purpose of this document is to acquaint the bar and interested members of the public with the general operating practices of the Court of Appeal, Sixth Appellate District.

The internal procedures of the Court of Appeal are largely governed by the California Constitution, statutes, and the appellate rules adopted by the Judicial Council. The Court of Appeal may adopt and publish its own rules that do not conflict with a statute or rule adopted by the Judicial Council.

I. STRUCTURE OF THE COURT AND ORGANIZATION OF STAFF

A. JUSTICES

The court has seven authorized judicial positions, consisting of a presiding justice and six associate justices.

The Chief Justice, as Chairperson of the Judicial Council, may assign a retired justice or judge, or an active trial court judge to serve temporarily on a Court of Appeal. Justices pro tem may be assigned (1) when there is a judicial vacancy, or (2) when a Court of Appeal justice is absent or unable to serve, or is disqualified in a given case, or (3) when the court needs assistance in reducing a backlog of cases.

Justices sit in panels of three that change periodically.

The courtroom and office of the clerk of the court are located in the Comerica Bank building at 333 West Santa Clara Street, Suite 1060, San Jose, California 95113.

B. PRESIDING JUSTICE

The presiding justice convenes conferences and presides at hearings (oral argument) when he or she is a member of the three-justice panel assigned to hear a case. The presiding justice has specific authority under rule 10.1012 of the California Rules of Court to grant or deny applications and to extend time for filing of records and briefs on appeal. The rule also gives the presiding justice limited authority to dismiss an appeal for noncompliance with the Rules of Court and to grant relief from default. The presiding justice also has overall responsibility for the calendaring of cases, the management of the caseload within the district, and the scheduling of oral arguments.

If the presiding justice is absent or disqualified, or not a member of the three-justice panel that is to decide a matter, the presiding justice designates the senior associate justice to serve as acting presiding justice.

C. CLERK/ADMINISTRATOR

The Clerk/Administrator is responsible for maintaining the court's public records and files and for advising litigants, counsel, and the public of the status of matters before the court.

Appointed by the court, the clerk assists in the preparation of the court's calendar, dockets its cases, and supervises other administrative functions required for the court's operation. The clerk is aided by an assistant clerk/administrator, six deputy clerks and a support staff.

D. RESEARCH ATTORNEYS

1. Attorneys Assigned to Justices

Each justice is currently authorized to employ two permanent research attorneys.

Research attorneys employed by or assigned to a justice work primarily on appeals assigned to the justice. The attorney's work involves legal research, examination of the trial court record, conferring with the justices assigned to the case, and preparing written memoranda and draft opinions.

2. Writ Attorneys

The court is currently authorized to employ two writ attorneys who assist the court in reviewing petitions for various writs, such as mandate, prohibition, certiorari or review, habeas corpus, and error coram vobis.

3. Central Staff

In addition to the writ attorneys and research attorneys assigned to justices, the court employs a staff of several senior research attorneys. This staff is known as the "central staff" because it provides research and analysis assistance for the justices of the court. Central staff attorneys are assigned to individual justices by the court and provide the same research and assistance required of the justices' permanent research staff.

4. Externs

The Sixth Appellate District cooperates with law schools in enabling law students to earn academic credits by working one semester, without pay, performing research for individual justices. These law students are selected and supervised by individual justices.

E. LAW LIBRARIAN

The court's law library collection of approximately 30,000 volumes is maintained by a professional Law Librarian. The collection includes the latest technological developments in legal research such as: a wide variety of CD-ROM's on the Local Area Network (LAN); access to various online research services including the Internet; and a selection of microforms, audio tapes and video tapes, in addition to the books. The Law Librarian is also responsible for keeping current on technology and legal trends, which affords the court staff the opportunity to do efficient and effective research on all issues before the court.

F. JUDICIAL ASSISTANTS TO APPELLATE COURT JUSTICES

Each justice is authorized to employ one judicial assistant who is responsible for the timely processing of the justice's opinions, including circulating draft opinions for review by other members of the panel, typing judicial correspondence, cite-checking and shepardizing draft opinions, and delivering opinions to the clerk for filing. The court employs other secretarial support staff as needed.

II. PROCESSING APPEALS

A. In General

When a criminal or civil appeal is fully briefed, it is identified on a computer-generated list indicating the case is ready for analysis and decision. The appeals are considered by the court after they are fully briefed. Decisions may be made and the opinions filed in a different order depending on factors such as the complexity of the litigation and whether oral argument is requested. The California Constitution requires the filing of a written opinion in every appeal.

1. Assignment of Cases

Assignment of cases to individual justices is generally made by rotation from the list of ready cases. The justice assigned to a particular case then has lead or primary responsibility for that case in the course of conference discussions, research and preparation of the opinion.

2. Preliminary Case Conferences

In the course of preparing an opinion, conferences are held at the request of the author or other panel members. In difficult or complex cases, more than one conference may be held. Conferences are generally not held in cases involving routine issues.

3. Oral Argument

When a case is ready for possible argument, the clerk will write and ask the parties whether they desire to exercise their right to appear personally for oral argument or to argue by teleconference. [The Sixth District Court of Appeal Teleconferencing Oral Argument Procedures Manual is available from the clerk's office upon request.] If oral argument is requested, the case is placed on an oral argument calendar.

After the case is scheduled for oral argument, any party or counsel for a party may contact the clerk's office and be informed of the names of the justices assigned to the case.

The order in which cases are to be argued is determined by the presiding justice. Because of the considerable investment of court time and resources necessary to prepare a case for oral argument, continuances are disfavored and will be granted only on a showing of good cause. Oral argument will not be continued by stipulation of counsel absent a showing of good cause. If no appearance is made, the case may be ordered submitted.

The order and the time allotted for counsel to make their presentations are specified in rule 8.256 of the California Rules of Court.

In most instances, the presiding justice will inform counsel at the beginning of each session that the court has reviewed the briefs and is familiar with the facts and issues. The court requests that counsel not merely reiterate the argument contained in his or her brief. Oral argument is generally most helpful and effective when reasonably brief and when counsel focuses on the decisive issues, succinctly clarifies the facts as they relate to a given issue, or clarifies the holding or reasoning of potentially applicable or controlling authority.

The court disfavors the submission of untimely citations of authority as it deprives the court and opposing counsel of sufficient opportunity to prepare for oral argument. The court retains discretion to strike or disregard such citations.

When oral argument has concluded in a given case, the justice presiding will declare the cause submitted, unless submission has been deferred for additional briefing.

4. Post-Oral Argument Conference

A post-oral argument conference is held in which the justices again discuss the case and finally determine the decision to be reached.

B. Preparation and Filing of Opinions

1. Signed Opinions

Unless the two other participating justices disagree with the disposition proposed by the assigned author, the justice assigned will prepare the majority opinion. When a proposed majority opinion has been drafted, it is circulated to the other participating justices. They indicate approval, disapproval, or proposed changes. Differences of opinion as to the language of the opinion or the ultimate disposition of the case may be taken up in conference. The opinion may then be modified in a manner acceptable to the justices. If two justices agree, a written opinion is filed.

2. Concurring or Dissenting Opinions

Where a difference of opinion exists among the justices participating in a case, a justice who agrees with the result reached but not with the reasoning of the majority may write a separate concurring opinion, or may merely indicate concurrence only in the judgment reached by the majority. Likewise, a justice who disagrees with the result reached by the majority may write a dissenting opinion. Each panel member has a full opportunity to consider the views of associates prior to the completion and filing of the opinion.

3. Publication of Opinions

A decision of the court is not published in the official reports unless it is certified for publication by a majority of the participating justices. The criteria for publication and publication requests are set forth in rules 8.1105 and 8.1120, respectively, of the California Rules of Court.

C. Rehearings

The procedure for filing a petition for rehearing is governed by rule 8.268 of the California Rules of Court. When a petition for rehearing is filed, the petition is routed to the justice who authored the opinion with copies to the participating justices. The authoring justice reviews the petition, and then indicates whether he or she votes to grant or deny the petition. The petition, along with any staff memorandum, is then circulated to the other two justices on the panel for their decisions. Two votes are necessary to grant or deny a petition for rehearing.

D. Original and Discretionary Proceedings

Petitions for writ of mandate, prohibition, certiorari, and habeas corpus, statutory review petitions, other miscellaneous applications to the original jurisdiction of the court, and applications for supersedeas or other relief pending appeal under Code of Civil Procedure section 923 or other statutory provisions are normally handled independently of the court's appellate caseload.

In original proceedings the court expects counsel to comply with the provisions of rules 8.486–8.488 of the California Rules of Court and all applicable time limitations, to explain any substantial delay in seeking relief in matters to which specific time limits do not apply, and to lodge with the court (and serve on adverse parties) a properly organized and indexed record sufficient to permit informed review. Any request for a stay of proceedings must be clearly labeled as such (Cal. Rules of Court, rule 8.116), and circumstances that require expedited consideration should be clearly identified in the petition or application and noted on its cover.

Counsel should advise the clerk of the next trial court date at the time the petition or application is filed.

Parties to statutory writ review proceedings should comply with applicable briefing schedules (for example, Cal. Rules of Court, rules 8.495(b), 8.498(c)). The court will strictly apply those schedules, absent a timely application for exception supported by a showing of good cause.

In habeas corpus matters, the court in appropriate cases will request an informal response and provide for a reply to the response under rule 8.385(b) of the California Rules of Court.

In other original proceedings it is the court's policy not to grant affirmative relief (beyond a temporary stay) without first giving adverse parties an opportunity to submit a memorandum of points and authorities in opposition. Opposition need not be submitted in these matters unless expressly requested by the court. If requested, opposition must be submitted on or before the date stated in the request, unless an extension is obtained before that date.

Original proceedings are referred to the writ attorney for initial review. The writ attorney thereafter communicates with the court concerning the matter. The court will conduct a writ conference and meet specially when necessary. All written submissions by any party, and any written staff memoranda, are distributed to and reviewed by all participating justices.

If affirmative relief is to be granted, the Sixth District will issue an alternative writ of mandate or prohibition, which directs the relief prayed for in the petition or, in the alternative, that the respondent appear and show cause why the relief should not be granted. An order to show cause may be issued without the alternative writ. In limited circumstances, the court may issue a peremptory writ in the first instance without allowing oral argument.

Counsel seeking writ relief should carefully review the "Sixth District Court of Appeal Outline on Original Proceedings and Relief Ancillary to Appeal," which is available on request from the clerk's office or available for download in .pdf or .doc format from the court's website.

E. Communications with Counsel or Parties

Except in oral argument, the justices do not communicate directly with counsel or parties concerning pending cases. Any necessary communications are handled by the clerk.

Attorneys employed by the court do not communicate with counsel or parties concerning pending cases.

F. Settlement

The parties must immediately notify the court of the settlement of any pending case (Cal. Rules of Court, rule 8.244).

Upon the request of all parties to a pending case, the court will schedule and conduct a settlement conference. The conference will be conducted before a justice of the court or an assigned judge. The settlement conference must be attended by the parties unless counsel or another authorized representative in attendance have full authority to settle.

No justice conducting a settlement conference will participate in deciding the case or discuss the case with any justice deciding the case if the case is not settled.

(Amended Jan. 1, 2007; Jan. 1, 2008; Jan. 1, 2009.)

CALIFORNIA RULES OF PROFESSIONAL CONDUCT

2021 EDITION

Rules of Professional Conduct adopted by the Board of Trustees of the State Bar and approved by the Supreme Court with revisions operative June 1, 2020. Prior version adopted by the Board of Governors of the State Bar and approved by the Supreme Court operative May 27, 1989.

Rules of Professional Conduct promulgated by the Board of Trustees of the State Bar and approved by the Supreme Court with amendments current through November 22, 2020.

Rules of Professional Conduct are reprinted with permission from the State Bar of California. No part of this work may be reproduced, stored in a retrieval system, or transmitted in any medium without prior written permission of the State Bar of California.

Table Showing Changes Approved by the Supreme Court
From November 21, 2019 Through November 22, 2020

Rule	Effect	Date
1.16[5]	Amended	June 1, 2020
3.8[7]	Amended	June 1, 2020

Cross-Reference Chart of the Current California Rules to the New Rules
Sorted by the Current California Rule Number

Current Rules of Professional Conduct *Operative until October 31, 2018* (Rule Number and Title)	New Rules of Professional Conduct *Effective on November 1, 2018* (Rule Number and Title)
1-100(A) [Rules of Professional Conduct, in General]	1.0 Purpose and Function of the Rules of Professional Conduct
1-100(B)	1.0.1 Terminology
1-100(D)	8.5 Disciplinary Authority; Choice of Law
1-110 Disciplinary Authority of the State Bar	8.1.1 Compliance with Conditions of Discipline and Agreements in Lieu of Discipline
1-120 Assisting, Soliciting, or Inducing Violations	8.4 Misconduct
1-200 False Statement Regarding Admission to the State Bar	8.1 False Statement Regarding Application for Admission to Practice Law
1-300 Unauthorized Practice of Law	5.5 Unauthorized Practice of Law; Multijurisdictional Practice of Law
1-310 Forming a Partnership With a Non-Lawyer	5.4 Financial and Similar Arrangements with Nonlawyers
1-311 Employment of Disbarred, Suspended, Resigned, or Involuntarily Inactive Members	5.3.1 Employment of Disbarred, Suspended, Resigned, or Involuntarily Inactive Lawyer
1-320(A)	5.4 Financial and Similar Arrangements with Nonlawyers
1-320(A)(4) & (B)-(C) [Financial Arrangements With Non-Lawyer]	7.2(b) Advertising
1-400 Advertising and Solicitation	7.1 Communications Concerning a Lawyer's Services 7.2 Advertising 7.3 Solicitation of Clients 7.4 Communication of Fields of Practice and Specialization 7.5 Firm Names and Trade Names
1-500 Agreements Restricting a Member's Practice	5.6 Restrictions on a Lawyer's Right to Practice
1-600 Legal Service Programs	5.4 Financial and Similar Arrangements with Nonlawyers
1-650 Limited Legal Service Programs	6.5 Limited Legal Services Programs
1-700 Member as Candidate for Judicial Office	8.2 Judicial Officials
1-710 Member as Temporary Judge, Referee, or Court-Appointed Arbitrator	2.4.1 Lawyer as Temporary Judge, Referee, or Court-Appointed Arbitrator
2-100 Communication With a Represented Party	4.2 Communication with a Represented Person
2-200(A) Financial Arrangements Among Lawyers	1.5.1 Fee Divisions Among Lawyers
2-200(B)	7.2(b) Advertising
2-300 Sale or Purchase of a Law Practice of a Member, Living or Deceased	1.17 Sale of a Law Practice
2-400 Prohibited Discriminatory Conduct in a Law Practice	8.4.1 Prohibited Discrimination, Harassment and Retaliation
3-100 Confidential Information of a Client	1.6 Confidential Information of a Client
3-110 Failing to Act Competently	1.1 Competence
3-110(B)	1.3 Diligence
3-110, Discussion ¶.1	5.1 Responsibilities of Managerial and Supervisory Lawyers 5.2 Responsibilities of a Subordinate Lawyer 5.3 Responsibilities Regarding Nonlawyer Assistants
3-120 Sexual Relations With Client	1.8.10 Sexual Relations with Current Client

Current Rules of Professional Conduct *Operative until October 31, 2018* (Rule Number and Title)	New Rules of Professional Conduct *Effective on November 1, 2018* (Rule Number and Title)
3-200 Prohibited Objectives of Employment	3.1 Meritorious Claims and Contentions
3-210 Advising the Violation of Law	1.2.1 Advising or Assisting the Violation of Law
3-300 Avoiding Interests Adverse to a Client	1.8.1 Business Transactions with a Client and Pecuniary Interests Adverse to the Client
3-310(B), (C) Avoiding the Representation of Adverse Interests	1.7 Conflict of Interest: Current Clients
3-310(D)	1.8.7 Aggregate Settlements
3-310(E)	1.9 Duties To Former Clients
3-310(F)	1.8.6 Compensation from One Other than Client
3-320 Relationship With Other Party's Lawyer	1.7(c)(2) Conflict of Interest: Current Clients
3-400 Limiting Liability to Client	1.8.8 Limiting Liability to Client
3-410 Disclosure of Professional Liability Insurance	1.4.2 Disclosure of Professional Liability Insurance
3-500 Communication	1.4 Communication with Clients
3-510 Communication of Settlement Offer	1.4.1 Communication of Settlement Offers
3-600 Organization as Client	1.13 Organization as Client
3-700 Termination of Employment	1.16 Declining or Terminating Representation
4-100 Preserving Identity of Funds and Property of a Client	1.15 Safekeeping Funds and Property of Clients and Other Persons
4-200 Fees for Legal Services	1.5 Fees for Legal Services
4-210 Payment of Personal or Business Expenses Incurred by or for a Client	1.8.5 Payment of Personal or Business Expenses Incurred by or for a Client
4-300 Purchasing Property at a Foreclosure or a Sale Subject to Judicial Review	1.8.9 Purchasing Property at a Foreclosure or a Sale Subject to Judicial Review
4-400 Gifts From Client	1.8.3 Gifts from Client
5-100 Threatening Criminal, Administrative, or Disciplinary Charges	3.10 Threatening Criminal, Administrative, or Disciplinary Charges
5-110 Performing the Duty of Member in Government Service (**Note:** Rule 5-110 recently was revised effective November 2, 2017.)	3.8 Special Responsibilities of a Prosecutor
5-120 Trial Publicity	3.6 Trial Publicity
5-200(A)–(D) Trial Conduct	3.3 Candor Toward the Tribunal
5-200(E) Trial Conduct	3.4 Fairness to Opposing Party and Counsel
5-210 Member as Witness	3.7 Lawyer as Witness
5-220 Suppression of Evidence (**Note:** Rule 5-220 recently was revised effective May 1, 2017.)	3.4 Fairness to Opposing Party and Counsel (**Note:** See also Rule 3.8(d) regarding the duties of a prosecutor.)
5-300 Contact With Officials	3.5 Contact with Judges, Officials, Employees, and Jurors
5-310 Prohibited Contact With Witnesses	3.4 Fairness to Opposing Party and Counsel
5-320 Contact With Jurors	3.5 Contact with Judges, Officials, Employees, and Jurors

New Rules With No California Counterpart

---

[1] But see Bus. & Prof. Code § 6068(e).
[2] But see current rule 3-600(D) regarding similar duties in an organizational context.

Cross-Reference Chart of the New Rules to the Current California Rules
Sorted by the New Rule Number

New Rules of Professional Conduct
Effective on November 1, 2018
(Rule Number and Title)

Current Rules of Professional Conduct
Operative until October 31, 2018
(Rule Number and Title)

New Rules of Professional Conduct	Current Rules of Professional Conduct
1.0 Purpose and Function of the Rules of Professional Conduct	1-100 Rules of Professional Conduct, in General
1.0.1 Terminology	1-100(B)
1.1 Competence	3-110 Failing to Act Competently
1.2 Scope of Representation and Allocation of Authority	No California Rule Counterpart
1.2.1 Advising or Assisting the Violation of Law	3-210 Advising the Violation of Law
1.3 Diligence	3-110(B)[3]
1.4 Communication with Clients	3-500 Communication
1.4.1 Communication of Settlement Offers	3-510 Communication of Settlement Offer
1.4.2 Disclosure of Professional Liability Insurance	3-410 Disclosure of Professional Liability Insurance
1.5 Fees for Legal Services	4-200 Fees for Legal Services
1.5.1 Fee Divisions Among Lawyers	2-200 Financial Arrangements Among Lawyers
1.6 Confidential Information of a Client	3-100 Confidential Information of a Client
1.7 Conflict of Interest: Current Clients	3-310(B),(C) [Avoiding the Representation of Adverse Interests] 3-320 Relationship With Other Party's Lawyer
1.8.1 Business Transactions with a Client and Pecuniary Interests Adverse to the Client	3-300 Avoiding Interests Adverse to a Client
1.8.2 Use of Current Client's Information	No California Rule Counterpart[4]
1.8.3 Gifts from Client	4-400 Gifts From Client
1.8.5 Payment of Personal or Business Expenses Incurred by or for a Client	4-210 Payment of Personal or Business Expenses Incurred by or for a Client
1.8.6 Compensation from One Other than Client	3-310(F)
1.8.7 Aggregate Settlements	3-310(D)
1.8.8 Limiting Liability to Client	3-400 Limiting Liability to Client
1.8.9 Purchasing Property at a Foreclosure or a Sale Subject to Judicial Review	4-300 Purchasing Property at a Foreclosure or a Sale Subject to Judicial Review
1.8.10 Sexual Relations with Current Client	3-120 Sexual Relations With Client
1.8.11 Imputation of Prohibitions Under Rules 1.8.1 to 1.8.9	No California Rule Counterpart
1.9 Duties To Former Clients	3-310(E)
1.10 Imputation of Conflicts of Interest: General Rule	No California Rule Counterpart
1.11 Special Conflicts of Interest for Former and Current Government Officials and Employees	No California Rule Counterpart
1.12 Former Judge, Arbitrator, Mediator or Other Third-Party Neutral	No California Rule Counterpart
1.13 Organization as Client	3-600 Organization as Client
1.14 [Reserved][5]	
1.15 Safekeeping Funds and Property of Clients and Other Persons	4-100 Preserving Identity of Funds and Property of a Client
1.16 Declining or Terminating Representation	3-700 Termination of Employment
1.17 Sale of a Law Practice	2-300 Sale or Purchase of a Law Practice of a Member, Living or Deceased
1.18 Duties To Prospective Client	No California Rule Counterpart

New Rules of Professional Conduct *Effective on November 1, 2018* (Rule Number and Title)	Current Rules of Professional Conduct *Operative until October 31, 2018* (Rule Number and Title)
	1-400 Advertising and Solicitation 2-200 Financial Arrangements Among Lawyers
7.3 Solicitation of Clients	1-400 Advertising and Solicitation
7.4 Communication of Fields of Practice and Specialization	1-400 Advertising and Solicitation
7.5 Firm Names and Trade Names	1-400 Advertising and Solicitation
7.6 [Reserved][9]	
8.1 False Statement Regarding Application for Admission to Practice Law	1-200 False Statement Regarding Admission to the State Bar
8.1.1 Compliance with Conditions of Discipline and Agreements in Lieu of Discipline	1-110 Disciplinary Authority of the State Bar
8.2 Judicial Officials	1-700 Member as Candidate for Judicial Office
8.3 [Reserved][10]	
8.4 Misconduct	1-120 Assisting, Soliciting, or Inducing Violations
8.4.1 Prohibited Discrimination, Harassment and Retaliation	2-400 Prohibited Discriminatory Conduct in a Law Practice
8.5 Disciplinary Authority; Choice of Law	1-100(D) Rules of Professional Conduct, in General

---

[3] Rule 3-110(B) provides:

(B) For purposes of this rule, "competence" in any legal service shall mean to apply the 1) *diligence*, 2) learning and skill, and 3) mental, emotional, and physical ability reasonably necessary for the performance of such service. (Emphasis added.)

[4] But see Cal. Bus. & Prof. Code § 6068(e)(1).
[5] ABA Model Rule 1.14 ("Client With Diminished Capacity") has not been adopted in California.
[6] ABA Model Rule 2.3 ("Evaluation For Use By Third Persons") has not been adopted in California.
[7] But see rule 3-110, Discussion ¶.1.
[8] But see rule 3-110, Discussion ¶.1.
[9] ABA Model Rule 7.6 ("Political Contributions To Obtain Legal Engagements Or Appointments By Judges") has not been adopted in California.
[10] ABA Model Rule 8.3 ("Reporting Professional Misconduct") has not been adopted in California.

Cross-Reference Chart of the New Rules to the Current ABA Model Rules
Sorted by the New Rule Number

New Rules of Professional Conduct *Effective on November 1, 2018* (Rule Number and Title)	Current ABA Model Rules (Rule Number and Title)
1.0 Purpose and Function of the Rules of Professional Conduct	Preamble and Scope
1.0.1 Terminology	1.0 Terminology
1.1 Competence	1.1 Competence
1.2 Scope of Representation and Allocation of Authority	1.2(a)-(c) Scope of Representation and Allocation of Authority Between Client and Lawyer
1.2.1 Advising or Assisting the Violation of Law	8.4(a)
1.3 Diligence	1.3 Diligence
1.4 Communication with Clients	1.4 Communications
1.4.1 Communication of Settlement Offers	No ABA Model Rule Counterpart[11]
1.4.2 Disclosure of Professional Liability Insurance	No ABA Model Rule Counterpart[12]
1.5 Fees for Legal Services	1.5 Fees
1.5.1 Fee Divisions Among Lawyers	1.5(e)
1.6 Confidential Information of a Client	1.6 Confidentiality of Information
1.7 Conflict of Interest: Current Clients	1.7 Conflict of Interest: Current Clients
	1.8 Conflict of Interest: Current Clients: Specific Rules[13]
1.8.1 Business Transactions with a Client and Pecuniary Interests Adverse to the Client	1.8(a)
1.8.2 Use of Current Client's Information	1.8(b)
1.8.3 Gifts from Client	1.8(c)
No New Rule Counterpart	1.8(d) [Acquisition of client's literary or media rights]
1.8.5 Payment of Personal or Business Expenses Incurred by or for a Client	1.8(e)
1.8.6 Compensation from One Other than Client	1.8(f)
1.8.7 Aggregate Settlements	1.8(g)
1.8.8 Limiting Liability to Client	1.8(h)
No New Rule Counterpart	1.8(i)
1.8.9 Purchasing Property at a Foreclosure or a Sale Subject to Judicial Review[14]	No ABA Model Rule Counterpart
1.8.10 Sexual Relations with Current Client	1.8(j)
1.8.11 Imputation of Prohibitions Under Rules 1.8.1 to 1.8.9	1.8(k)
1.9 Duties to Former Clients	1.9 Duties to Former Clients
1.10 Imputation of Conflicts of Interest: General Rule	1.10 Imputation of Conflicts of Interest: General Rule
1.11 Special Conflicts of Interest for Former and Current Government Officials and Employees	1.11 Special Conflicts of Interest for Former and Current Government Officers and Employees
1.12 Former Judge, Arbitrator, Mediator or Other Third-Party Neutral	1.12 Former Judge, Arbitrator, Mediator or Other Third-Party Neutral
1.13 Organization as Client	1.13 Organization as Client
No New Rule Counterpart	1.14 Client with Diminished Capacity
1.15 Safekeeping Funds and Property of Clients and Other Persons	1.15 Safekeeping Property

New Rules of Professional Conduct *Effective on November 1, 2018* (Rule Number and Title)	Current ABA Model Rules (Rule Number and Title)
7.2 Advertising	7.2 Advertising
7.3 Solicitation of Clients	7.3 Solicitation of Clients
7.4 Communication of Fields of Practice and Specialization	7.4 Communication of Fields of Practice and Specialization
7.5 Firm Names and Trade Names	7.5 Firm Names and Letterhead
No New Rule Counterpart	7.6 Political Contributions to Obtain Legal Engagements or Appointments by Judges
8.1 False Statement Regarding Application for Admission to Practice Law	8.1 Bar Admission and Disciplinary Matters
8.1.1 Compliance with Conditions of Discipline and Agreements in Lieu of Discipline	No ABA Model Rule Counterpart
8.2 Judicial Officials	8.2 Judicial and Legal Officials
No New Rule Counterpart	8.3 Reporting Professional Misconduct
8.4 Misconduct	8.4 Misconduct
8.4.1 Prohibited Discrimination, Harassment and Retaliation	8.4(g)
8.5 Disciplinary Authority; Choice of Law	8.5 Disciplinary Authority; Choice of Law

Rules of Conduct

---

[11] But see Model Rule 1.4, Cmt. [2].

[12] Although there is no counterpart to new rule 1.4.2 in the ABA Model Rules of Professional Conduct, there is an ABA Model Court Rule on Insurance Disclosure. See http://www.americanbar.org/content/dam/aba/migrated/cpr/clientpro/ Model_Rule_InsuranceDisclosure.authcheckdam.pdf [Last accessed 3/15/17].

[13] Model Rule 1.8 is a collection of 11 rules that regulate specific conflicts involving current clients. Each rule is assigned a separate paragraph letter but is untitled.

[14] Although new rule 1.8.9 is not a direct counterpart to Model Rule 1.8(i), it has been assigned the number 1.8.9. Model Rule 1.8(i) provides:

  (i) A lawyer shall not acquire a proprietary interest in the cause of action or subject matter of litigation the lawyer is conducting for a client, except that the lawyer may:
  (1) acquire a lien authorized by law to secure the lawyer's fee or expenses; and
  (2) contract with a client for a reasonable contingent fee in a civil case.

[15] There is no ABA Model Rule 2.2. Although the original Model Rules (1983) included Model Rule 2.2 ("Intermediary"), that rule was rejected by the ABA in 2002 and deleted.

[16] But see Rule 1.0, Cmt. [5].

CONTENTS

Rules

RULES OF PROFESSIONAL CONDUCT

Rules of Conduct

CALIFORNIA RULES OF PROFESSIONAL CONDUCT

Purpose and Function of the Rules of Professional Conduct. Rule 1.0. Terminology. Rule 1.0.1.

Rule 1.0   Purpose and Function of the Rules of Professional Conduct

(a)   Purpose.

The following rules are intended to regulate professional conduct of lawyers through discipline. They have been adopted by the Board of Trustees of the State Bar of California and approved by the Supreme Court of California pursuant to Business and Professions Code sections 6076 and 6077 to protect the public, the courts, and the legal profession; protect the integrity of the legal system; and promote the administration of justice and confidence in the legal profession. These rules together with any standards adopted by the Board of Trustees pursuant to these rules shall be binding upon all lawyers.

(b)   Function.

(1)   A willful violation of any of these rules is a basis for discipline.

(2)   The prohibition of certain conduct in these rules is not exclusive. Lawyers are also bound by applicable law including the State Bar Act (Bus. & Prof. Code, § 6000 et seq.) and opinions of California courts.

(3)   A violation of a rule does not itself give rise to a cause of action for damages caused by failure to comply with the rule. Nothing in these rules or the Comments to the rules is intended to enlarge or to restrict the law regarding the liability of lawyers to others.

(c)   Purpose of Comments.

The comments are not a basis for imposing discipline but are intended only to provide guidance for interpreting and practicing in compliance with the rules.

(d)   These rules may be cited and referred to as the "California Rules of Professional Conduct."

Comment

[1]   The Rules of Professional Conduct are intended to establish the standards for lawyers for purposes of discipline. (See *Ames v. State Bar* (1973) 8 Cal.3d 910, 917 [106 Cal.Rptr. 489].) Therefore, failure to comply with an obligation or prohibition imposed by a rule is a basis for invoking the disciplinary process. Because the rules are not designed to be a basis for civil liability, a violation of a rule does not itself give rise to a cause of action for enforcement of a rule or for damages caused by failure to comply with the rule. (*Stanley v. Richmond* (1995) 35 Cal.App.4th 1070, 1097 [41 Cal.Rptr.2d 768].) Nevertheless, a lawyer's violation of a rule may be evidence of breach of a lawyer's fiduciary or other substantive legal duty in a non-disciplinary context. (*Ibid.*; see also *Mirabito v. Liccardo* (1992) 4 Cal.App.4th 41, 44 [5 Cal.Rptr.2d 571].) A violation of a rule may have other non-disciplinary consequences. (See, e.g., *Fletcher v. Davis* (2004) 33 Cal.4th 61, 71-72 [14 Cal.Rptr.3d 58] [enforcement of attorney's lien]; *Chambers v. Kay* (2002) 29 Cal.4th 142, 161 [126 Cal.Rptr.2d 536] [enforcement of fee sharing agreement].)

[2]   While the rules are intended to regulate professional conduct of lawyers, a violation of a rule can occur when a lawyer is not practicing law or acting in a professional capacity.

[3]   A willful violation of a rule does not require that the lawyer intend to violate the rule. (*Phillips v. State Bar* (1989) 49 Cal.3d 944, 952 [264 Cal.Rptr. 346]; and see Bus. & Prof. Code, § 6077.)

[4]   In addition to the authorities identified in paragraph (b)(2), opinions of ethics committees in California, although not binding, should be consulted for guidance on proper professional conduct. Ethics opinions and rules and standards promulgated by other jurisdictions and bar associations may also be considered.

[5]   The disciplinary standards created by these rules are not intended to address all aspects of a lawyer's professional obligations. A lawyer, as a member of the legal profession, is a representative and advisor of clients, an officer of the legal system and a public citizen having special responsibilities for the quality of justice. A lawyer should be aware of deficiencies in the administration of justice and of the fact that the poor, and sometimes persons* who are not poor cannot afford adequate legal assistance. Therefore, all lawyers are encouraged to devote professional time and resources and use civic influence to ensure equal access to the system of justice for those who because of economic or social barriers cannot afford or secure adequate legal counsel. In meeting this responsibility of the profession, every lawyer should aspire to render at least fifty hours of pro bono publico legal services per year. The lawyer should aim to provide a substantial* majority of such hours to indigent individuals or to nonprofit organizations with a primary purpose of providing services to the poor or on behalf of the poor or disadvantaged. Lawyers may also provide financial support to organizations providing free legal services. (See Bus. & Prof. Code, § 6073.)

(Adopted Sept. 26, 2018, eff. Nov. 1, 2018.)

Rule 1.0.1   Terminology

(a)   "Belief" or "believes" means that the person* involved actually supposes the fact in question to be true. A person's* belief may be inferred from circumstances.

(b)   [Reserved]

(c)   "Firm" or "law firm" means a law partnership; a professional law corporation; a lawyer acting as a sole proprietorship; an association authorized to practice law; or lawyers employed in a legal services organization or in the legal department, division or office of a corporation, of a government organization, or of another organization.

(d)   "Fraud" or "fraudulent" means conduct that is fraudulent under the law of the applicable jurisdiction and has a purpose to deceive.

(e)   "Informed consent" means a person's* agreement to a proposed course of conduct after the lawyer has communicated and explained (i) the relevant circumstances and (ii) the material risks, including any actual and reasonably* foreseeable adverse consequences of the proposed course of conduct.

(e-1)   "Informed written consent" means that the disclosures and the consent required by paragraph (e) must be in writing.*

(f)   "Knowingly," "known," or "knows" means actual knowledge of the fact in question. A person's* knowledge may be inferred from circumstances.

(g)   "Partner" means a member of a partnership, a shareholder in a law firm* organized as a professional corporation, or a member of an association authorized to practice law.

(g-1)   "Person" has the meaning stated in Evidence Code section 175.

(h)   "Reasonable" or "reasonably" when used in relation to conduct by a lawyer means the conduct of a reasonably prudent and competent lawyer.

(i)   "Reasonable belief" or "reasonably believes" when used in reference to a lawyer means that the lawyer believes the matter in question and that the circumstances are such that the belief is reasonable.

(j)   "Reasonably should know" when used in reference to a lawyer means that a lawyer of reasonable prudence and competence would ascertain the matter in question.

(k)   "Screened" means the isolation of a lawyer from any participation in a matter, including the timely imposition of procedures within a law firm* that are adequate under the circumstances (i) to protect information that the isolated lawyer is obligated to protect under these rules or other law; and (ii) to protect against other law firm* lawyers and nonlawyer personnel communicating with the lawyer with respect to the matter.

(*l*)   "Substantial" when used in reference to degree or extent means a material matter of clear and weighty importance.

(m)   "Tribunal" means: (i) a court, an arbitrator, an administrative law judge, or an administrative body acting in an adjudicative capacity and authorized to make a decision that can be binding on the parties involved; or (ii) a special master or other person* to whom a court refers one or more issues and whose decision or recommendation can be binding on the parties if approved by the court.

(n)   "Writing" or "written" has the meaning stated in Evidence Code section 250. A "signed" writing includes an electronic sound, symbol, or process attached to or logically associated with a writing and executed, inserted, or adopted by or at the direction of a person* with the intent to sign the writing.

Comment

Firm or Law Firm*

---

* An asterisk (*) identifies a word or phrase defined in the terminology rule, rule 1.0.1.

[1] Practitioners who share office space and occasionally consult or assist each other ordinarily would not be regarded as constituting a law firm.* However, if they present themselves to the public in a way that suggests that they are a law firm* or conduct themselves as a law firm,* they may be regarded as a law firm* for purposes of these rules. The terms of any formal agreement between associated lawyers are relevant in determining whether they are a firm,* as is the fact that they have mutual access to information concerning the clients they serve.

[2] The term "of counsel" implies that the lawyer so designated has a relationship with the law firm,* other than as a partner* or associate, or officer or shareholder, that is close, personal, continuous, and regular. Whether a lawyer who is denominated as "of counsel" or by a similar term should be deemed a member of a law firm* for purposes of these rules will also depend on the specific facts. (Compare *People ex rel. Department of Corporations v. Speedee Oil Change Systems, Inc.* (1999) 20 Cal.4th 1135 [86 Cal.Rptr.2d 816] with *Chambers v. Kay* (2002) 29 Cal.4th 142 [126 Cal.Rptr.2d 536].)

*Fraud**

[3] When the terms "fraud"* or "fraudulent"* are used in these rules, it is not necessary that anyone has suffered damages or relied on the misrepresentation or failure to inform because requiring the proof of those elements of fraud* would impede the purpose of certain rules to prevent fraud* or avoid a lawyer assisting in the perpetration of a fraud,* or otherwise frustrate the imposition of discipline on lawyers who engage in fraudulent* conduct. The term "fraud"* or "fraudulent"* when used in these rules does not include merely negligent misrepresentation or negligent failure to apprise another of relevant information.

Informed Consent and Informed Written Consent**

[4] The communication necessary to obtain informed consent* or informed written consent* will vary according to the rule involved and the circumstances giving rise to the need to obtain consent.

*Screened**

[5] The purpose of screening* is to assure the affected client, former client, or prospective client that confidential information known* by the personally prohibited lawyer is neither disclosed to other law firm* lawyers or nonlawyer personnel nor used to the detriment of the person* to whom the duty of confidentiality is owed. The personally prohibited lawyer shall acknowledge the obligation not to communicate with any of the other lawyers and nonlawyer personnel in the law firm* with respect to the matter. Similarly, other lawyers and nonlawyer personnel in the law firm* who are working on the matter promptly shall be informed that the screening* is in place and that they may not communicate with the personally prohibited lawyer with respect to the matter. Additional screening* measures that are appropriate for the particular matter will depend on the circumstances. To implement, reinforce and remind all affected law firm* personnel of the presence of the screening,* it may be appropriate for the law firm* to undertake such procedures as a written* undertaking by the personally prohibited lawyer to avoid any communication with other law firm* personnel and any contact with any law firm* files or other materials relating to the matter, written* notice and instructions to all other law firm* personnel forbidding any communication with the personally prohibited lawyer relating to the matter, denial of access by that lawyer to law firm* files or other materials relating to the matter, and periodic reminders of the screen* to the personally prohibited lawyer and all other law firm* personnel.

[6] In order to be effective, screening* measures must be implemented as soon as practical after a lawyer or law firm* knows* or reasonably should know* that there is a need for screening.*

(Adopted Sept. 26, 2018, eff. Nov. 1, 2018.)

CHAPTER 1
LAWYER-CLIENT RELATIONSHIP

Rule 1.1   Competence

(a)   A lawyer shall not intentionally, recklessly, with gross negligence, or repeatedly fail to perform legal services with competence.

(b)   For purposes of this rule, "competence" in any legal service shall mean to apply the (i) learning and skill, and (ii) mental, emotional, and physical ability reasonably* necessary for the performance of such service.

(c)   If a lawyer does not have sufficient learning and skill when the legal services are undertaken, the lawyer nonetheless may provide competent representation by (i) associating with or, where appropriate, professionally consulting another lawyer whom the lawyer reasonably believes* to be competent, (ii) acquiring sufficient learning and skill before performance is required, or (iii) referring the matter to another lawyer whom the lawyer reasonably believes* to be competent.

(d)   In an emergency a lawyer may give advice or assistance in a matter in which the lawyer does not have the skill ordinarily required if referral to, or association or consultation with, another lawyer would be impractical. Assistance in an emergency must be limited to that reasonably* necessary in the circumstances.

Comment

[1] This rule addresses only a lawyer's responsibility for his or her own professional competence. See rules 5.1 and 5.3 with respect to a lawyer's disciplinary responsibility for supervising subordinate lawyers and nonlawyers.

[2] See rule 1.3 with respect to a lawyer's duty to act with reasonable* diligence.

(Adopted Sept. 26, 2018, eff. Nov. 1, 2018.)

Rule 1.2   Scope of Representation and Allocation of Authority

(a)   Subject to rule 1.2.1, a lawyer shall abide by a client's decisions concerning the objectives of representation and, as required by rule 1.4, shall reasonably* consult with the client as to the means by which they are to be pursued. Subject to Business and Professions Code section 6068, subdivision (e)(1) and rule 1.6, a lawyer may take such action on behalf of the client as is impliedly authorized to carry out the representation. A lawyer shall abide by a client's decision whether to settle a matter. Except as otherwise provided by law in a criminal case, the lawyer shall abide by the client's decision, after consultation with the lawyer, as to a plea to be entered, whether to waive jury trial and whether the client will testify.

(b)   A lawyer may limit the scope of the representation if the limitation is reasonable* under the circumstances, is not otherwise prohibited by law, and the client gives informed consent.*

Comment

Allocation of Authority between Client and Lawyer

[1] Paragraph (a) confers upon the client the ultimate authority to determine the purposes to be served by legal representation, within the limits imposed by law and the lawyer's professional obligations. (See, e.g., Cal. Const., art. I, § 16; Pen. Code, § 1018.) A lawyer retained to represent a client is authorized to act on behalf of the client, such as in procedural matters and in making certain tactical decisions. A lawyer is not authorized merely by virtue of the lawyer's retention to impair the client's substantive rights or the client's claim itself. (*Blanton v. Womancare, Inc.* (1985) 38 Cal.3d 396, 404 [212 Cal.Rptr. 151, 156].)

[2] At the outset of, or during a representation, the client may authorize the lawyer to take specific action on the client's behalf without further consultation. Absent a material change in circumstances and subject to rule 1.4, a lawyer may rely on such an advance authorization. The client may revoke such authority at any time.

Independence from Client's Views or Activities

[3] A lawyer's representation of a client, including representation by appointment, does not constitute an endorsement of the client's political, economic, social or moral views or activities.

Agreements Limiting Scope of Representation

---

* An asterisk (*) identifies a word or phrase defined in the terminology rule, rule 1.0.1.

[4] All agreements concerning a lawyer's representation of a client must accord with the Rules of Professional Conduct and other law. (See, e.g., rules 1.1, 1.8.1, 5.6; see also Cal. Rules of Court, rules 3.35-3.37 [limited scope rules applicable in civil matters generally], 5.425 [limited scope rule applicable in family law matters].)

(Adopted Sept. 26, 2018, eff. Nov. 1, 2018.)

Rule 1.2.1   Advising or Assisting the Violation of Law

(a) A lawyer shall not counsel a client to engage, or assist a client in conduct that the lawyer knows* is criminal, fraudulent,* or a violation of any law, rule, or ruling of a tribunal.*

(b) Notwithstanding paragraph (a), a lawyer may:

(1) discuss the legal consequences of any proposed course of conduct with a client; and

(2) counsel or assist a client to make a good faith effort to determine the validity, scope, meaning, or application of a law, rule, or ruling of a tribunal.*

Comment

[1] There is a critical distinction under this rule between presenting an analysis of legal aspects of questionable conduct and recommending the means by which a crime or fraud* might be committed with impunity. The fact that a client uses a lawyer's advice in a course of action that is criminal or fraudulent* does not of itself make a lawyer a party to the course of action.

[2] Paragraphs (a) and (b) apply whether or not the client's conduct has already begun and is continuing. In complying with this rule, a lawyer shall not violate the lawyer's duty under Business and Professions Code section 6068, subdivision (a) to uphold the Constitution and laws of the United States and California or the duty of confidentiality as provided in Business and Professions Code section 6068, subdivision (e)(1) and rule 1.6. In some cases, the lawyer's response is limited to the lawyer's right and, where appropriate, duty to resign or withdraw in accordance with rules 1.13 and 1.16.

[3] Paragraph (b) authorizes a lawyer to advise a client in good faith regarding the validity, scope, meaning or application of a law, rule, or ruling of a tribunal* or of the meaning placed upon it by governmental authorities, and of potential consequences to disobedience of the law, rule, or ruling of a tribunal* that the lawyer concludes in good faith to be invalid, as well as legal procedures that may be invoked to obtain a determination of invalidity.

[4] Paragraph (b) also authorizes a lawyer to advise a client on the consequences of violating a law, rule, or ruling of a tribunal* that the client does not contend is unenforceable or unjust in itself, as a means of protesting a law or policy the client finds objectionable. For example, a lawyer may properly advise a client about the consequences of blocking the entrance to a public building as a means of protesting a law or policy the client believes* to be unjust or invalid.

[5] If a lawyer comes to know* or reasonably should know* that a client expects assistance not permitted by these rules or other law or if the lawyer intends to act contrary to the client's instructions, the lawyer must advise the client regarding the limitations on the lawyer's conduct. (See rule 1.4(a)(4).)

[6] Paragraph (b) permits a lawyer to advise a client regarding the validity, scope, and meaning of California laws that might conflict with federal or tribal law. In the event of such a conflict, the lawyer may assist a client in drafting or administering, or interpreting or complying with, California laws, including statutes, regulations, orders, and other state or local provisions, even if the client's actions might violate the conflicting federal or tribal law. If California law conflicts with federal or tribal law, the lawyer must inform the client about related federal or tribal law and policy and under certain circumstances may also be required to provide legal advice to the client regarding the conflict (see rules 1.1 and 1.4).

(Adopted Sept. 26, 2018, eff. Nov. 1, 2018.)

Rule 1.3   Diligence

(a) A lawyer shall not intentionally, repeatedly, recklessly or with gross negligence fail to act with reasonable diligence in representing a client.

(b) For purposes of this rule, "reasonable diligence" shall mean that a lawyer acts with commitment and dedication to the interests of the client and does not neglect or disregard, or unduly delay a legal matter entrusted to the lawyer.

Comment

[1] This rule addresses only a lawyer's responsibility for his or her own professional diligence. See rules 5.1 and 5.3 with respect to a lawyer's disciplinary responsibility for supervising subordinate lawyers and nonlawyers.

[2] See rule 1.1 with respect to a lawyer's duty to perform legal services with competence.

(Adopted Sept. 26, 2018, eff. Nov. 1, 2018.)

Rule 1.4   Communication with Clients

(a) A lawyer shall:

(1) promptly inform the client of any decision or circumstance with respect to which disclosure or the client's informed consent* is required by these rules or the State Bar Act;

(2) reasonably* consult with the client about the means by which to accomplish the client's objectives in the representation;

(3) keep the client reasonably* informed about significant developments relating to the representation, including promptly complying with reasonable* requests for information and copies of significant documents when necessary to keep the client so informed; and

(4) advise the client about any relevant limitation on the lawyer's conduct when the lawyer knows* that the client expects assistance not permitted by the Rules of Professional Conduct or other law.

(b) A lawyer shall explain a matter to the extent reasonably* necessary to permit the client to make informed decisions regarding the representation.

(c) A lawyer may delay transmission of information to a client if the lawyer reasonably believes* that the client would be likely to react in a way that may cause imminent harm to the client or others.

(d) A lawyer's obligation under this rule to provide information and documents is subject to any applicable protective order, non-disclosure agreement, or limitation under statutory or decisional law.

Comment

[1] A lawyer will not be subject to discipline under paragraph (a)(3) of this rule for failing to communicate insignificant or irrelevant information. (See Bus. & Prof. Code, § 6068, subd. (m).) Whether a particular development is significant will generally depend on the surrounding facts and circumstances.

[2] A lawyer may comply with paragraph (a)(3) by providing to the client copies of significant documents by electronic or other means. This rule does not prohibit a lawyer from seeking recovery of the lawyer's expense in any subsequent legal proceeding.

[3] Paragraph (c) applies during a representation and does not alter the obligations applicable at termination of a representation. (See rule 1.16(e)(1).)

[4] This rule is not intended to create, augment, diminish, or eliminate any application of the work product rule. The obligation of the lawyer to provide work product to the client shall be governed by relevant statutory and decisional law.

(Adopted Sept. 26, 2018, eff. Nov. 1, 2018.)

Rule 1.4.1   Communication of Settlement Offers

(a) A lawyer shall promptly communicate to the lawyer's client:

(1) all terms and conditions of a proposed plea bargain or other dispositive offer made to the client in a criminal matter; and

(2) all amounts, terms, and conditions of any written* offer of settlement made to the client in all other matters.

(b) As used in this rule, "client" includes a person* who possesses the authority to accept an offer of settlement or plea, or, in a class action, all the named representatives of the class.

Comment An oral offer of settlement made to the client in a civil matter must also be communicated if it is a "significant development" under rule 1.4.

(Adopted Sept. 26, 2018, eff. Nov. 1, 2018.)

Rule 1.4.2   Disclosure of Professional Liability Insurance

(a) A lawyer who knows* or reasonably should know* that the lawyer does not have professional liability insurance shall inform a client in writing,* at the time of the client's engagement of the lawyer, that the lawyer does not have professional liability insurance.

(b) If notice under paragraph (a) has not been provided at the time of a client's engagement of the lawyer, the lawyer shall inform the client in writing* within thirty days of the date the lawyer knows* or reasonably should know* that the lawyer no longer has professional liability insurance during the representation of the client.

(c) This rule does not apply to:

(1) a lawyer who knows* or reasonably should know* at the time of the client's engagement of the lawyer that the lawyer's legal representation of the client in the matter will not exceed four hours; provided that if the representation subsequently exceeds four hours, the lawyer must comply with paragraphs (a) and (b);

(2) a lawyer who is employed as a government lawyer or in-house counsel when that lawyer is representing or providing legal advice to a client in that capacity;

(3) a lawyer who is rendering legal services in an emergency to avoid foreseeable prejudice to the rights or interests of the client;

Rules of Conduct

(4) a lawyer who has previously advised the client in writing* under paragraph (a) or (b) that the lawyer does not have professional liability insurance.

Comment

[1] The disclosure obligation imposed by paragraph (a) applies with respect to new clients and new engagements with returning clients.

[2] A lawyer may use the following language in making the disclosure required by paragraph (a), and may include that language in a written* fee agreement with the client or in a separate writing:

"Pursuant to rule 1.4.2 of the California Rules of Professional Conduct, I am informing you in writing that I do not have professional liability insurance."

[3] A lawyer may use the following language in making the disclosure required by paragraph (b):

"Pursuant to rule 1.4.2 of the California Rules of Professional Conduct, I am informing you in writing that I no longer have professional liability insurance."

[4] The exception in paragraph (c)(2) for government lawyers and in-house counsels is limited to situations involving direct employment and representation, and does not, for example, apply to outside counsel for a private or governmental entity, or to counsel retained by an insurer to represent an insured. If a lawyer is employed by and provides legal services directly for a private entity or a federal, state or local governmental entity, that entity is presumed to know* whether the lawyer is or is not covered by professional liability insurance.

(Adopted Sept. 26, 2018, eff. Nov. 1, 2018.)

Rule 1.5   Fees for Legal Services

(a) A lawyer shall not make an agreement for, charge, or collect an unconscionable or illegal fee.

(b) Unconscionability of a fee shall be determined on the basis of all the facts and circumstances existing at the time the agreement is entered into except where the parties contemplate that the fee will be affected by later events. The factors to be considered in determining the unconscionability of a fee include without limitation the following:

(1) whether the lawyer engaged in fraud* or overreaching in negotiating or setting the fee;

(2) whether the lawyer has failed to disclose material facts;

(3) the amount of the fee in proportion to the value of the services performed;

(4) the relative sophistication of the lawyer and the client;

(5) the novelty and difficulty of the questions involved, and the skill requisite to perform the legal service properly;

(6) the likelihood, if apparent to the client, that the acceptance of the particular employment will preclude other employment by the lawyer;

(7) the amount involved and the results obtained;

(8) the time limitations imposed by the client or by the circumstances;

(9) the nature and length of the professional relationship with the client;

(10) the experience, reputation, and ability of the lawyer or lawyers performing the services;

(11) whether the fee is fixed or contingent;

(12) the time and labor required; and

(13) whether the client gave informed consent* to the fee.

(c) A lawyer shall not make an agreement for, charge, or collect:

(1) any fee in a family law matter, the payment or amount of which is contingent upon the securing of a dissolution or declaration of nullity of a marriage or upon the amount of spousal or child support, or property settlement in lieu thereof; or

(2) a contingent fee for representing a defendant in a criminal case.

(d) A lawyer may make an agreement for, charge, or collect a fee that is denominated as "earned on receipt" or "non-refundable," or in similar terms, only if the fee is a true retainer and the client agrees in writing* after disclosure that the client will not be entitled to a refund of all or part of the fee charged. A true retainer is a fee that a client pays to a lawyer to ensure the lawyer's availability to the client during a specified period or on a specified matter, but not to any extent as compensation for legal services performed or to be performed.

(e) A lawyer may make an agreement for, charge, or collect a flat fee for specified legal services. A flat fee is a fixed amount that constitutes complete payment for the performance of described services regardless of the amount of work ultimately involved, and which may be paid in whole or in part in advance of the lawyer providing those services.

Comment

Prohibited Contingent Fees

[1] Paragraph (c)(1) does not preclude a contract for a contingent fee for legal representation in connection with the recovery of post-judgment balances due under child or spousal support or other financial orders.

Payment of Fees in Advance of Services

[2] Rule 1.15(a) and (b) govern whether a lawyer must deposit in a trust account a fee paid in advance.

[3] When a lawyer-client relationship terminates, the lawyer must refund the unearned portion of a fee. (See rule 1.16(e)(2).)

Division of Fee

[4] A division of fees among lawyers is governed by rule 1.5.1.

Written* Fee Agreements

[5] Some fee agreements must be in writing* to be enforceable. (See, e.g., Bus. & Prof. Code, §§ 6147 and 6148.)

(Adopted Sept. 26, 2018, eff. Nov. 1, 2018.)

Rule 1.5.1   Fee Divisions Among Lawyers

(a) Lawyers who are not in the same law firm* shall not divide a fee for legal services unless:

(1) the lawyers enter into a written* agreement to divide the fee;

(2) the client has consented in writing,* either at the time the lawyers enter into the agreement to divide the fee or as soon thereafter as reasonably* practicable, after a full written* disclosure to the client of: (i) the fact that a division of fees will be made; (ii) the identity of the lawyers or law firms* that are parties to the division; and (iii) the terms of the division; and

(3) the total fee charged by all lawyers is not increased solely by reason of the agreement to divide fees.

(b) This rule does not apply to a division of fees pursuant to court order.

Comment

The writing* requirements of paragraphs (a)(1) and (a)(2) may be satisfied by one or more writings.*

(Adopted Sept. 26, 2018, eff. Nov. 1, 2018.)

Rule 1.6   Confidential Information of a Client

(a) A lawyer shall not reveal information protected from disclosure by Business and Professions Code section 6068, subdivision (e)(1) unless the client gives informed consent,* or the disclosure is permitted by paragraph (b) of this rule.

(b) A lawyer may, but is not required to, reveal information protected by Business and Professions Code section 6068, subdivision (e)(1) to the extent that the lawyer reasonably believes* the disclosure is necessary to prevent a criminal act that the lawyer reasonably believes* is likely to result in death of, or substantial* bodily harm to, an individual, as provided in paragraph (c).

(c) Before revealing information protected by Business and Professions Code section 6068, subdivision (e)(1) to prevent a criminal act as provided in paragraph (b), a lawyer shall, if reasonable* under the circumstances:

(1) make a good faith effort to persuade the client: (i) not to commit or to continue the criminal act; or (ii) to pursue a course of conduct that will prevent the threatened death or substantial* bodily harm; or do both (i) and (ii); and

(2) inform the client, at an appropriate time, of the lawyer's ability or decision to reveal information protected by Business and Professions Code section 6068, subdivision (e)(1) as provided in paragraph (b).

(d) In revealing information protected by Business and Professions Code section 6068, subdivision (e)(1) as provided in paragraph (b), the lawyer's disclosure must be no more than is necessary to prevent the criminal act, given the information known* to the lawyer at the time of the disclosure.

(e) A lawyer who does not reveal information permitted by paragraph (b) does not violate this rule.

Comment

Duty of confidentiality

[1] Paragraph (a) relates to a lawyer's obligations under Business and Professions Code section 6068, subdivision (e)(1), which provides it is a duty of a lawyer: "To maintain inviolate the confidence, and at every peril to himself or herself to preserve the secrets, of his or her client." A lawyer's duty to preserve the confidentiality of client information involves public policies of paramount importance. (*In Re Jordan* (1974) 12 Cal.3d 575, 580 [116 Cal.Rptr. 371].) Preserving the confidentiality of client information contributes to the trust that is the hallmark of

---

* An asterisk (*) identifies a word or phrase defined in the terminology rule, rule 1.0.1.

the lawyer-client relationship. The client is thereby encouraged to seek legal assistance and to communicate fully and frankly with the lawyer even as to embarrassing or detrimental subjects. The lawyer needs this information to represent the client effectively and, if necessary, to advise the client to refrain from wrongful conduct. Almost without exception, clients come to lawyers in order to determine their rights and what is, in the complex of laws and regulations, deemed to be legal and correct. Based upon experience, lawyers know* that almost all clients follow the advice given, and the law is upheld. Paragraph (a) thus recognizes a fundamental principle in the lawyer-client relationship, that, in the absence of the client's informed consent,* a lawyer must not reveal information protected by Business and Professions Code section 6068, subdivision (e)(1). (See, e.g., *Commercial Standard Title Co. v. Superior Court* (1979) 92 Cal.App.3d 934, 945 [155 Cal.Rptr.393].)

Lawyer-client confidentiality encompasses the lawyer-client privilege, the work-product doctrine and ethical standards of confidentiality

[2] The principle of lawyer-client confidentiality applies to information a lawyer acquires by virtue of the representation, whatever its source, and encompasses matters communicated in confidence by the client, and therefore protected by the lawyer-client privilege, matters protected by the work product doctrine, and matters protected under ethical standards of confidentiality, all as established in law, rule and policy. (See *In the Matter of Johnson* (Rev. Dept. 2000) 4 Cal. State Bar Ct. Rptr. 179; *Goldstein v. Lees* (1975) 46 Cal.App.3d 614, 621 [120 Cal.Rptr. 253].) The lawyer-client privilege and work-product doctrine apply in judicial and other proceedings in which a lawyer may be called as a witness or be otherwise compelled to produce evidence concerning a client. A lawyer's ethical duty of confidentiality is not so limited in its scope of protection for the lawyer-client relationship of trust and prevents a lawyer from revealing the client's information even when not subjected to such compulsion. Thus, a lawyer may not reveal such information except with the informed consent* of the client or as authorized or required by the State Bar Act, these rules, or other law.

Narrow exception to duty of confidentiality under this rule

[3] Notwithstanding the important public policies promoted by lawyers adhering to the core duty of confidentiality, the overriding value of life permits disclosures otherwise prohibited by Business and Professions Code section 6068, subdivision (e)(1). Paragraph (b) is based on Business and Professions Code section 6068, subdivision (e)(2), which narrowly permits a lawyer to disclose information protected by Business and Professions Code section 6068, subdivision (e)(1) even without client consent. Evidence Code section 956.5, which relates to the evidentiary lawyer-client privilege, sets forth a similar express exception. Although a lawyer is not permitted to reveal information protected by section 6068, subdivision (e)(1) concerning a client's past, completed criminal acts, the policy favoring the preservation of human life that underlies this exception to the duty of confidentiality and the evidentiary privilege permits disclosure to prevent a future or ongoing criminal act.

Lawyer not subject to discipline for revealing information protected by Business and Professions Code section 6068, subdivision (e)(1) as permitted under this rule

[4] Paragraph (b) reflects a balancing between the interests of preserving client confidentiality and of preventing a criminal act that a lawyer reasonably believes* is likely to result in death or substantial* bodily harm to an individual. A lawyer who reveals information protected by Business and Professions Code section 6068, subdivision (e)(1) as permitted under this rule is not subject to discipline.

No duty to reveal information protected by Business and Professions Code section 6068, subdivision (e)(1)

[5] Neither Business and Professions Code section 6068, subdivision (e)(2) nor paragraph (b) imposes an affirmative obligation on a lawyer to reveal information protected by Business and Professions Code section 6068, subdivision (e)(1) in order to prevent harm. A lawyer may decide not to reveal such information. Whether a lawyer chooses to reveal information protected by section 6068, subdivision (e)(1) as permitted under this rule is a matter for the individual lawyer to decide, based on all the facts and circumstances, such as those discussed in Comment [6] of this rule.

Whether to reveal information protected by Business and Professions Code section 6068, subdivision (e) as permitted under paragraph (b)

[6] Disclosure permitted under paragraph (b) is ordinarily a last resort, when no other available action is reasonably* likely to prevent the criminal act. Prior to revealing information protected by Business and Professions Code section 6068, subdivision (e)(1) as permitted by paragraph (b), the lawyer must, if reasonable* under the circumstances, make a good faith effort to persuade the client to take steps to avoid the criminal act or threatened harm. Among the factors to be considered in determining whether to disclose information protected by section 6068, subdivision (e)(1) are the following:

  (1) the amount of time that the lawyer has to make a decision about disclosure;

  (2) whether the client or a third-party has made similar threats before and whether they have ever acted or attempted to act upon them;

  (3) whether the lawyer believes* the lawyer's efforts to persuade the client or a third person* not to engage in the criminal conduct have or have not been successful;

  (4) the extent of adverse effect to the client's rights under the Fifth, Sixth and Fourteenth Amendments of the United States Constitution and analogous rights and privacy rights under Article I of the Constitution of the State of California that may result from disclosure contemplated by the lawyer;

  (5) the extent of other adverse effects to the client that may result from disclosure contemplated by the lawyer; and

  (6) the nature and extent of information that must be disclosed to prevent the criminal act or threatened harm.

A lawyer may also consider whether the prospective harm to the victim or victims is imminent in deciding whether to disclose the information protected by section 6068, subdivision (e)(1). However, the imminence of the harm is not a prerequisite to disclosure and a lawyer may disclose the information protected by section 6068, subdivision (e)(1) without waiting until immediately before the harm is likely to occur.

Whether to counsel client or third person not to commit a criminal act reasonably* likely to result in death or substantial* bodily harm*

[7] Paragraph (c)(1) provides that before a lawyer may reveal information protected by Business and Professions Code section 6068, subdivision (e)(1), the lawyer must, if reasonable* under the circumstances, make a good faith effort to persuade the client not to commit or to continue the criminal act, or to persuade the client to otherwise pursue a course of conduct that will prevent the threatened death or substantial* bodily harm, including persuading the client to take action to prevent a third person* from committing or continuing a criminal act. If necessary, the client may be persuaded to do both. The interests protected by such counseling are the client's interests in limiting disclosure of information protected by section 6068, subdivision (e) and in taking responsible action to deal with situations attributable to the client. If a client, whether in response to the lawyer's counseling or otherwise, takes corrective action — such as by ceasing the client's own criminal act or by dissuading a third person* from committing or continuing a criminal act before harm is caused — the option for permissive disclosure by the lawyer would cease because the threat posed by the criminal act would no longer be present. When the actor is a nonclient or when the act is deliberate or malicious, the lawyer who contemplates making adverse disclosure of protected information may reasonably* conclude that the compelling interests of the lawyer or others in their own personal safety preclude personal contact with the actor. Before counseling an actor who is a nonclient, the lawyer should, if reasonable* under the circumstances, first advise the client of the lawyer's intended course of action. If a client or another person* has already acted but the intended harm has not yet occurred, the lawyer should consider, if reasonable* under the circumstances, efforts to persuade the client or third person* to warn the victim or consider other appropriate action to prevent the harm. Even when the lawyer has concluded that paragraph (b) does not permit the lawyer to reveal information protected by section 6068, subdivision (e)(1), the lawyer nevertheless is permitted to counsel the client as to why it may be in the client's best interest to consent to the attorney's disclosure of that information.

Disclosure of information protected by Business and Professions Code section 6068, subdivision (e)(1) must be no more than is reasonably necessary to prevent the criminal act*

[8] Paragraph (d) requires that disclosure of information protected by Business and Professions Code section 6068, subdivision (e) as permitted by paragraph (b), when made, must be no more extensive than is necessary to prevent the criminal act. Disclosure should allow access to the information to only those persons* who the lawyer reasonably believes* can act to prevent the harm. Under some circumstances, a lawyer may determine that the best course to pursue is to make an anonymous disclosure to the potential victim or relevant law-enforcement authorities. What particular measures are reasonable* depends on the circumstances known* to the lawyer. Relevant circumstances include the time available, whether the victim might be unaware of the threat, the lawyer's prior course of dealings with the client, and the extent of the adverse effect on the client that may result from the disclosure contemplated by the lawyer.

Informing client pursuant to paragraph (c)(2) of lawyer's ability or decision to reveal information protected by Business and Professions Code section 6068, subdivision (e)(1)

[9] A lawyer is required to keep a client reasonably* informed about significant developments regarding the representation. (See rule 1.4; Bus. & Prof. Code, § 6068, subd. (m).) Paragraph (c)(2), however, recognizes that under certain circumstances, informing a client of the lawyer's ability or decision to reveal information protected by section 6068, subdivision (e)(1) as permitted in paragraph (b) would likely increase the risk of death or substantial* bodily harm, not only to the originally-intended victims of the criminal act, but also to the client or members of the client's family, or to the lawyer or the lawyer's family or associates. Therefore, paragraph (c)(2) requires a lawyer to inform the client of the lawyer's ability or decision to reveal information protected by section 6068, subdivision (e)(1) as permitted in paragraph (b) only if it is reasonable* to do so under the circumstances. Paragraph (c)(2) further recognizes that the appropriate time for the lawyer to inform the client may vary depending upon the circumstances. (See Comment [10] of this rule.) Among the factors to be considered in determining an appropriate time, if any, to inform a client are:

---

* An asterisk (*) identifies a word or phrase defined in the terminology rule, rule 1.0.1.

(1) whether the client is an experienced user of legal services;

(2) the frequency of the lawyer's contact with the client;

(3) the nature and length of the professional relationship with the client;

(4) whether the lawyer and client have discussed the lawyer's duty of confidentiality or any exceptions to that duty;

(5) the likelihood that the client's matter will involve information within paragraph (b);

(6) the lawyer's belief,* if applicable, that so informing the client is likely to increase the likelihood that a criminal act likely to result in the death of, or substantial* bodily harm to, an individual; and

(7) the lawyer's belief,* if applicable, that good faith efforts to persuade a client not to act on a threat have failed.

Avoiding a chilling effect on the lawyer-client relationship

[10] The foregoing flexible approach to the lawyer's informing a client of his or her ability or decision to reveal information protected by Business and Professions Code section 6068, subdivision (e)(1) recognizes the concern that informing a client about limits on confidentiality may have a chilling effect on client communication. (See Comment [1].) To avoid that chilling effect, one lawyer may choose to inform the client of the lawyer's ability to reveal information protected by section 6068, subdivision (e)(1) as early as the outset of the representation, while another lawyer may choose to inform a client only at a point when that client has imparted information that comes within paragraph (b), or even choose not to inform a client until such time as the lawyer attempts to counsel the client as contemplated in Comment [7]. In each situation, the lawyer will have satisfied the lawyer's obligation under paragraph (c)(2), and will not be subject to discipline.

Informing client that disclosure has been made; termination of the lawyer-client relationship

[11] When a lawyer has revealed information protected by Business and Professions Code section 6068, subdivision (e) as permitted in paragraph (b), in all but extraordinary cases the relationship between lawyer and client that is based on trust and confidence will have deteriorated so as to make the lawyer's representation of the client impossible. Therefore, when the relationship has deteriorated because of the lawyer's disclosure, the lawyer is required to seek to withdraw from the representation, unless the client has given informed consent* to the lawyer's continued representation. The lawyer normally must inform the client of the fact of the lawyer's disclosure. If the lawyer has a compelling interest in not informing the client, such as to protect the lawyer, the lawyer's family or a third person* from the risk of death or substantial* bodily harm, the lawyer must withdraw from the representation. (See rule 1.16.)

Other consequences of the lawyer's disclosure

[12] Depending upon the circumstances of a lawyer's disclosure of information protected by Business and Professions Code section 6068, subdivision (e)(1) as permitted by this rule, there may be other important issues that a lawyer must address. For example, a lawyer who is likely to testify as a witness in a matter involving a client must comply with rule 3.7. Similarly, the lawyer must also consider his or her duties of loyalty and competence. (See rules 1.7 and 1.1.)

Other exceptions to confidentiality under California law

[13] This rule is not intended to augment, diminish, or preclude any other exceptions to the duty to preserve information protected by Business and Professions Code section 6068, subdivision (e)(1) recognized under California law.

(*Adopted Sept. 26, 2018, eff. Nov. 1, 2018.*)

Rule 1.7   Conflict of Interest: Current Clients

(a) A lawyer shall not, without informed written consent* from each client and compliance with paragraph (d), represent a client if the representation is directly adverse to another client in the same or a separate matter.

(b) A lawyer shall not, without informed written consent* from each affected client and compliance with paragraph (d), represent a client if there is a significant risk the lawyer's representation of the client will be materially limited by the lawyer's responsibilities to or relationships with another client, a former client or a third person,* or by the lawyer's own interests.

(c) Even when a significant risk requiring a lawyer to comply with paragraph (b) is not present, a lawyer shall not represent a client without written* disclosure of the relationship to the client and compliance with paragraph (d) where:

(1) the lawyer has, or knows* that another lawyer in the lawyer's firm* has, a legal, business, financial, professional, or personal relationship with or responsibility to a party or witness in the same matter; or

(2) the lawyer knows* or reasonably should know* that another party's lawyer is a spouse, parent, child, or sibling of the lawyer, lives with the lawyer, is a client of the lawyer or another lawyer in the lawyer's firm,* or has an intimate personal relationship with the lawyer.

(d) Representation is permitted under this rule only if the lawyer complies with paragraphs (a), (b), and (c), and:

(1) the lawyer reasonably believes* that the lawyer will be able to provide competent and diligent representation to each affected client;

(2) the representation is not prohibited by law; and

(3) the representation does not involve the assertion of a claim by one client against another client represented by the lawyer in the same litigation or other proceeding before a tribunal.

(e) For purposes of this rule, "matter" includes any judicial or other proceeding, application, request for a ruling or other determination, contract, transaction, claim, controversy, investigation, charge, accusation, arrest, or other deliberation, decision, or action that is focused on the interests of specific persons,* or a discrete and identifiable class of persons.*

Comment

[1] Loyalty and independent judgment are essential elements in the lawyer's relationship to a client. The duty of undivided loyalty to a current client prohibits undertaking representation directly adverse to that client without that client's informed written consent.* Thus, absent consent, a lawyer may not act as an advocate in one matter against a person* the lawyer represents in some other matter, even when the matters are wholly unrelated. (See *Flatt v. Superior Court* (1994) 9 Cal.4th 275 [36 Cal.Rptr.2d 537].) A directly adverse conflict under paragraph (a) can arise in a number of ways, for example, when: (i) a lawyer accepts representation of more than one client in a matter in which the interests of the clients actually conflict; (ii) a lawyer, while representing a client, accepts in another matter the representation of a person* who, in the first matter, is directly adverse to the lawyer's client; or (iii) a lawyer accepts representation of a person* in a matter in which an opposing party is a client of the lawyer or the lawyer's law firm.* Similarly, direct adversity can arise when a lawyer cross-examines a non-party witness who is the lawyer's client in another matter, if the examination is likely to harm or embarrass the witness. On the other hand, simultaneous representation in unrelated matters of clients whose interests are only economically adverse, such as representation of competing economic enterprises in unrelated litigation, does not ordinarily constitute a conflict of interest and thus may not require informed written consent* of the respective clients.

[2] Paragraphs (a) and (b) apply to all types of legal representations, including the concurrent representation of multiple parties in litigation or in a single transaction or in some other common enterprise or legal relationship. Examples of the latter include the formation of a partnership for several partners* or a corporation for several shareholders, the preparation of a pre-nuptial agreement, or joint or reciprocal wills for a husband and wife, or the resolution of an "uncontested" marital dissolution. If a lawyer initially represents multiple clients with the informed written consent* as required under paragraph (b), and circumstances later develop indicating that direct adversity exists between the clients, the lawyer must obtain further informed written consent* of the clients under paragraph (a).

[3] In *State Farm Mutual Automobile Insurance Company v. Federal Insurance Company* (1999) 72 Cal.App.4th 1422 [86 Cal.Rptr.2d 20], the court held that paragraph (C)(3) of predecessor rule 3-310 was violated when a lawyer, retained by an insurer to defend one suit, and while that suit was still pending, filed a direct action against the same insurer in an unrelated action without securing the insurer's consent. Notwithstanding *State Farm*, paragraph (a) does not apply with respect to the relationship between an insurer and a lawyer when, in each matter, the insurer's interest is only as an indemnity provider and not as a direct party to the action.

[4] Even where there is no direct adversity, a conflict of interest requiring informed written consent* under paragraph (b) exists if there is a significant risk that a lawyer's ability to consider, recommend or carry out an appropriate course of action for the client will be materially limited as a result of the lawyer's other responsibilities, interests, or relationships, whether legal, business, financial, professional, or personal. For example, a lawyer's obligations to two or more clients in the same matter, such as several individuals seeking to form a joint venture, may materially limit the lawyer's ability to recommend or advocate all possible positions that each might take because of the lawyer's duty of loyalty to the other clients. The risk is that the lawyer may not be able to offer alternatives that would otherwise be available to each of the clients. The mere possibility of subsequent harm does not itself require disclosure and informed written consent.* The critical questions are the likelihood that a difference in interests exists or will eventuate and, if it does, whether it will materially interfere with the lawyer's independent professional judgment in considering alternatives or foreclose courses of action that reasonably* should be pursued on behalf of each client. The risk that the lawyer's representation may be materially limited may also arise from present or past relationships between the lawyer, or another member of the lawyer's firm*, with a party, a witness, or another person* who may be affected substantially by the resolution of the matter.

[5] Paragraph (c) requires written* disclosure of any of the specified relationships even if there is not a significant risk the relationship will materially limit the lawyer's representation of the client. However, if the particular circumstances present a significant risk the relationship will materially limit the lawyer's

representation of the client, informed written consent* is required under paragraph (b).

[6] Ordinarily paragraphs (a) and (b) will not require informed written consent* simply because a lawyer takes inconsistent legal positions in different tribunals* at different times on behalf of different clients. Advocating a legal position on behalf of a client that might create precedent adverse to the interests of another client represented by a lawyer in an unrelated matter is not sufficient, standing alone, to create a conflict of interest requiring informed written consent.* Informed written consent* may be required, however, if there is a significant risk that: (i) the lawyer may temper the lawyer's advocacy on behalf of one client out of concern about creating precedent adverse to the interest of another client; or (ii) the lawyer's action on behalf of one client will materially limit the lawyer's effectiveness in representing another client in a different case, for example, when a decision favoring one client will create a precedent likely to seriously weaken the position taken on behalf of the other client. Factors relevant in determining whether the clients' informed written consent* is required include: the courts and jurisdictions where the different cases are pending, whether a ruling in one case would have a precedential effect on the other case, whether the legal question is substantive or procedural, the temporal relationship between the matters, the significance of the legal question to the immediate and long-term interests of the clients involved, and the clients' reasonable* expectations in retaining the lawyer.

[7] Other rules and laws may preclude the disclosures necessary to obtain the informed written consent* or provide the information required to permit representation under this rule. (See, e.g., Bus. & Prof. Code, § 6068, subd. (e)(1) and rule 1.6.) If such disclosure is precluded, representation subject to paragraph (a), (b), or (c) of this rule is likewise precluded.

[8] Paragraph (d) imposes conditions that must be satisfied even if informed written consent* is obtained as required by paragraphs (a) or (b) or the lawyer has informed the client in writing* as required by paragraph (c). There are some matters in which the conflicts are such that even informed written consent* may not suffice to permit representation. (See *Woods v. Superior Court* (1983) 149 Cal.App.3d 931 [197 Cal.Rptr. 185]; *Klemm v. Superior Court* (1977) 75 Cal.App.3d 893 [142 Cal.Rptr. 509]; *Ishmael v. Millington* (1966) 241 Cal.App.2d 520 [50 Cal.Rptr. 592].)

[9] This rule does not preclude an informed written consent* to a future conflict in compliance with applicable case law. The effectiveness of an advance consent is generally determined by the extent to which the client reasonably* understands the material risks that the consent entails. The more comprehensive the explanation of the types of future representations that might arise and the actual and reasonably* foreseeable adverse consequences to the client of those representations, the greater the likelihood that the client will have the requisite understanding. The experience and sophistication of the client giving consent, as well as whether the client is independently represented in connection with giving consent, are also relevant in determining whether the client reasonably* understands the risks involved in giving consent. An advance consent cannot be effective if the circumstances that materialize in the future make the conflict nonconsentable under paragraph (d). A lawyer who obtains from a client an advance consent that complies with this rule will have all the duties of a lawyer to that client except as expressly limited by the consent. A lawyer cannot obtain an advance consent to incompetent representation. (See rule 1.8.8.)

[10] A material change in circumstances relevant to application of this rule may trigger a requirement to make new disclosures and, where applicable, obtain new informed written consents.* In the absence of such consents, depending on the circumstances, the lawyer may have the option to withdraw from one or more of the representations in order to avoid the conflict. The lawyer must seek court approval where necessary and take steps to minimize harm to the clients. See rule 1.16. The lawyer must continue to protect the confidences of the clients from whose representation the lawyer has withdrawn. (See rule 1.9(c).)

[11] For special rules governing membership in a legal service organization, see rule 6.3; and for work in conjunction with certain limited legal services programs, see rule 6.5.

(Adopted Sept. 26, 2018, eff. Nov. 1, 2018.)

Rule 1.8.1   Business Transactions with a Client and Pecuniary Interests Adverse to a Client

A lawyer shall not enter into a business transaction with a client, or knowingly* acquire an ownership, possessory, security or other pecuniary interest adverse to a client, unless each of the following requirements has been satisfied:

(a)   the transaction or acquisition and its terms are fair and reasonable* to the client and the terms and the lawyer's role in the transaction or acquisition are fully disclosed and transmitted in writing* to the client in a manner that should reasonably* have been understood by the client;

(b)   the client either is represented in the transaction or acquisition by an independent lawyer of the client's choice or the client is advised in writing* to seek the advice of an independent lawyer of the client's choice and is given a reasonable* opportunity to seek that advice; and

(c)   the client thereafter provides informed written consent* to the terms of the transaction or acquisition, and to the lawyer's role in it.

Comment

[1] A lawyer has an "other pecuniary interest adverse to a client" within the meaning of this rule when the lawyer possesses a legal right to significantly impair or prejudice the client's rights or interests without court action. (See *Fletcher v. Davis* (2004) 33 Cal.4th 61, 68 [14 Cal.Rptr.3d 58]; see also Bus. & Prof. Code, § 6175.3 [Sale of financial products to elder or dependent adult clients; Disclosure]; Fam. Code, §§ 2033-2034 [Attorney lien on community real property].) However, this rule does not apply to a charging lien given to secure payment of a contingency fee. (See *Plummer v. Day/Eisenberg, LLP* (2010) 184 Cal.App.4th 38 [108 Cal.Rptr.3d 455].)

[2] For purposes of this rule, factors that can be considered in determining whether a lawyer is independent include whether the lawyer: (i) has a financial interest in the transaction or acquisition; and (ii) has a close legal, business, financial, professional or personal relationship with the lawyer seeking the client's consent.

[3] Fairness and reasonableness under paragraph (a) are measured at the time of the transaction or acquisition based on the facts that then exist.

[4] In some circumstances, this rule may apply to a transaction entered into with a former client. (Compare *Hunniecutt v. State Bar* (1988) 44 Cal.3d 362, 370-71 ["[W]hen an attorney enters into a transaction with a former client regarding a fund which resulted from the attorney's representation, it is reasonable to examine the relationship between the parties for indications of special trust resulting therefrom. We conclude that if there is evidence that the client placed his trust in the attorney because of the representation, an attorney-client relationship exists for the purposes of [the predecessor rule] even if the representation has otherwise ended [and] It appears that [the client] became a target of [the lawyer's] solicitation because he knew, through his representation of her, that she had recently received the settlement fund [and the court also found the client to be unsophisticated]."] with *Wallis v. State Bar* (1942) 21 Cal.2d 322 [finding lawyer not subject to discipline for entering into business transaction with a former client where the former client was a sophisticated businesswoman who had actively negotiated for terms she thought desirable, and the transaction was not connected with the matter on which the lawyer previously represented her].)

[5] This rule does not apply to the agreement by which the lawyer is retained by the client, unless the agreement confers on the lawyer an ownership, possessory, security, or other pecuniary interest adverse to the client. Such an agreement is governed, in part, by rule 1.5. This rule also does not apply to an agreement to advance to or deposit with a lawyer a sum to be applied to fees, or costs or other expenses, to be incurred in the future. Such agreements are governed, in part, by rules 1.5 and 1.15.

[6] This rule does not apply: (i) where a lawyer and client each make an investment on terms offered by a third person* to the general public or a significant portion thereof; or (ii) to standard commercial transactions for products or services that a lawyer acquires from a client on the same terms that the client generally markets them to others, where the lawyer has no advantage in dealing with the client.

(Adopted Sept. 26, 2018, eff. Nov. 1, 2018.)

Rule 1.8.2   Use of Current Client's Information

A lawyer shall not use a client's information protected by Business and Professions Code section 6068, subdivision (e)(1) to the disadvantage of the client unless the client gives informed consent,* except as permitted by these rules or the State Bar Act.

Comment

A lawyer violates the duty of loyalty by using information protected by Business and Professions Code section 6068, subdivision (e)(1) to the disadvantage of a current client.

(Adopted Sept. 26, 2018, eff. Nov. 1, 2018.)

Rule 1.8.3   Gifts from Client

(a)   A lawyer shall not:

(1)   solicit a client to make a substantial* gift, including a testamentary gift, to the lawyer or a person* related to the lawyer, unless the lawyer or other recipient of the gift is related to the client, or

(2)   prepare on behalf of a client an instrument giving the lawyer or a person* related to the lawyer any substantial* gift, unless (i) the lawyer or other recipient of the gift is related to the client, or (ii) the client has been advised by an independent lawyer who has provided a certificate of independent review that complies with the requirements of Probate Code section 21384.

(b)   For purposes of this rule, related persons* include a person* who is "related by blood or affinity" as that term is defined in California Probate Code section 21374, subdivision (a).

Rules of Conduct

Comment

[1] A lawyer or a person* related to a lawyer may accept a gift from the lawyer's client, subject to general standards of fairness and absence of undue influence. A lawyer also does not violate this rule merely by engaging in conduct that might result in a client making a gift, such as by sending the client a wedding announcement. Discipline is appropriate where impermissible influence occurs. (See *Magee v. State Bar* (1962) 58 Cal.2d 423 [24 Cal.Rptr. 839].)

[2] This rule does not prohibit a lawyer from seeking to have the lawyer or a partner* or associate of the lawyer named as executor of the client's estate or to another potentially lucrative fiduciary position. Such appointments, however, will be subject to rule 1.7(b) and (c).

(Adopted Sept. 26, 2018, eff. Nov. 1, 2018.)

Rule 1.8.4   [Reserved]

Rule 1.8.5   Payment of Personal or Business Expenses Incurred by or for a Client

(a)   A lawyer shall not directly or indirectly pay or agree to pay, guarantee, or represent that the lawyer or lawyer's law firm* will pay the personal or business expenses of a prospective or existing client.

(b)   Notwithstanding paragraph (a), a lawyer may:

(1)   pay or agree to pay such expenses to third persons,* from funds collected or to be collected for the client as a result of the representation, with the consent of the client;

(2)   after the lawyer is retained by the client, agree to lend money to the client based on the client's written* promise to repay the loan, provided the lawyer complies with rules 1.7(b), 1.7(c), and 1.8.1 before making the loan or agreeing to do so;

(3)   advance the costs of prosecuting or defending a claim or action, or of otherwise protecting or promoting the client's interests, the repayment of which may be contingent on the outcome of the matter; and

(4)   pay the costs of prosecuting or defending a claim or action, or of otherwise protecting or promoting the interests of an indigent person* in a matter in which the lawyer represents the client.

(c)   "Costs" within the meaning of paragraphs (b)(3) and (b)(4) are not limited to those costs that are taxable or recoverable under any applicable statute or rule of court but may include any reasonable* expenses of litigation, including court costs, and reasonable* expenses in preparing for litigation or in providing other legal services to the client.

(d)   Nothing in this rule shall be deemed to limit the application of rule 1.8.9.

(Adopted Sept. 26, 2018, eff. Nov. 1, 2018.)

Rule 1.8.6   Compensation from One Other than Client

A lawyer shall not enter into an agreement for, charge, or accept compensation for representing a client from one other than the client unless:

(a)   there is no interference with the lawyer's independent professional judgment or with the lawyer-client relationship;

(b)   information is protected as required by Business and Professions Code section 6068, subdivision (e)(1) and rule 1.6; and

(c)   the lawyer obtains the client's informed written consent* at or before the time the lawyer has entered into the agreement for, charged, or accepted the compensation, or as soon thereafter as reasonably* practicable, provided that no disclosure or consent is required if:

(1)   nondisclosure or the compensation is otherwise authorized by law or a court order; or

(2)   the lawyer is rendering legal services on behalf of any public agency or nonprofit organization that provides legal services to other public agencies or the public.

Comment

[1] A lawyer's responsibilities in a matter are owed only to the client except where the lawyer also represents the payor in the same matter. With respect to the lawyer's additional duties when representing both the client and the payor in the same matter, see rule 1.7.

[2] A lawyer who is exempt from disclosure and consent requirements under paragraph (c) nevertheless must comply with paragraphs (a) and (b).

[3] This rule is not intended to abrogate existing relationships between insurers and insureds whereby the insurer has the contractual right to unilaterally select counsel for the insured, where there is no conflict of interest. (See *San Diego Navy Federal Credit Union v. Cumis Insurance Society* (1984) 162 Cal.App.3d 358 [208 Cal.Rptr. 494].).

[4] In some limited circumstances, a lawyer might not be able to obtain client consent before the lawyer has entered into an agreement for, charged, or accepted compensation, as required by this rule. This might happen, for example, when a lawyer is retained or paid by a family member on behalf of an incarcerated client or in certain commercial settings, such as when a lawyer is retained by a creditors' committee involved in a corporate debt restructuring and agrees to be compensated for any services to be provided to other similarly situated creditors who have not yet been identified. In such limited situations, paragraph (c) permits the lawyer to comply with this rule as soon thereafter as is reasonably* practicable.

[5] This rule is not intended to alter or diminish a lawyer's obligations under rule 5.4(c).

(Adopted Sept. 26, 2018, eff. Nov. 1, 2018.)

Rule 1.8.7   Aggregate Settlements

(a)   A lawyer who represents two or more clients shall not enter into an aggregate settlement of the claims of or against the clients, or in a criminal case an aggregate agreement as to guilty or nolo contendere pleas, unless each client gives informed written consent.* The lawyer's disclosure shall include the existence and nature of all the claims or pleas involved and of the participation of each person* in the settlement.

(b)   This rule does not apply to class action settlements subject to court approval.

(Adopted Sept. 26, 2018, eff. Nov. 1, 2018.)

Rule 1.8.8   Limiting Liability to Client

A lawyer shall not:

(a)   Contract with a client prospectively limiting the lawyer's liability to the client for the lawyer's professional malpractice; or

(b)   Settle a claim or potential claim for the lawyer's liability to a client or former client for the lawyer's professional malpractice, unless the client or former client is either:

(1)   represented by an independent lawyer concerning the settlement; or

(2)   advised in writing* by the lawyer to seek the advice of an independent lawyer of the client's choice regarding the settlement and given a reasonable* opportunity to seek that advice.

Comment

[1] Paragraph (b) does not absolve the lawyer of the obligation to comply with other law. (See, e.g., Bus. & Prof. Code, § 6090.5.)

[2] This rule does not apply to customary qualifications and limitations in legal opinions and memoranda, nor does it prevent a lawyer from reasonably* limiting the scope of the lawyer's representation. (See rule 1.2(b).)

(Adopted Sept. 26, 2018, eff. Nov. 1, 2018.)

Rule 1.8.9   Purchasing Property at a Foreclosure or a Sale Subject to Judicial Review

(a)   A lawyer shall not directly or indirectly purchase property at a probate, foreclosure, receiver's, trustee's, or judicial sale in an action or proceeding in which such lawyer or any lawyer affiliated by reason of personal, business, or professional relationship with that lawyer or with that lawyer's law firm* is acting as a lawyer for a party or as executor, receiver, trustee, administrator, guardian, or conservator.

(b)   A lawyer shall not represent the seller at a probate, foreclosure, receiver, trustee, or judicial sale in an action or proceeding in which the purchaser is a spouse or relative of the lawyer or of another lawyer in the lawyer's law firm* or is an employee of the lawyer or the lawyer's law firm.*

(c)   This rule does not prohibit a lawyer's participation in transactions that are specifically authorized by and comply with Probate Code sections 9880 through 9885, but such transactions remain subject to the provisions of rules 1.8.1 and 1.7.

Comment

A lawyer may lawfully participate in a transaction involving a probate proceeding which concerns a client by following the process described in Probate Code sections 9880-9885. These provisions, which permit what would otherwise be impermissible self-dealing by specific submissions to and approval by the courts, must be strictly followed in order to avoid violation of this rule.

(Adopted Sept. 26, 2018, eff. Nov. 1, 2018.)

Rule 1.8.10   Sexual Relations with Current Client

(a)   A lawyer shall not engage in sexual relations with a current client who is not the lawyer's spouse or registered domestic partner, unless a consensual sexual relationship existed between them when the lawyer-client relationship commenced.

---

* An asterisk (*) identifies a word or phrase defined in the terminology rule, rule 1.0.1.

(b) For purposes of this rule, "sexual relations" means sexual intercourse or the touching of an intimate part of another person* for the purpose of sexual arousal, gratification, or abuse.

(c) If a person* other than the client alleges a violation of this rule, no Notice of Disciplinary Charges may be filed by the State Bar against a lawyer under this rule until the State Bar has attempted to obtain the client's statement regarding, and has considered, whether the client would be unduly burdened by further investigation or a charge.

Comment

[1] Although this rule does not apply to a consensual sexual relationship that exists when a lawyer-client relationship commences, the lawyer nevertheless must comply with all other applicable rules. (See, e.g., rules 1.1, 1.7, and 2.1.)

[2] When the client is an organization, this rule applies to a lawyer for the organization (whether inside counsel or outside counsel) who has sexual relations with a constituent of the organization who supervises, directs or regularly consults with that lawyer concerning the organization's legal matters. (See rule 1.13.)

[3] Business and Professions Code section 6106.9, including the requirement that the complaint be verified, applies to charges under subdivision (a) of that section. This rule and the statute impose different obligations.

(Adopted Sept. 26, 2018, eff. Nov. 1, 2018.)

Rule 1.8.11   Imputation of Prohibitions Under Rules 1.8.1 to 1.8.9

While lawyers are associated in a law firm,* a prohibition in rules 1.8.1 through 1.8.9 that applies to any one of them shall apply to all of them.

Comment

A prohibition on conduct by an individual lawyer in rules 1.8.1 through 1.8.9 also applies to all lawyers associated in a law firm* with the personally prohibited lawyer. For example, one lawyer in a law firm* may not enter into a business transaction with a client of another lawyer associated in the law firm* without complying with rule 1.8.1, even if the first lawyer is not personally involved in the representation of the client. This rule does not apply to rule 1.8.10 since the prohibition in that rule is personal and is not applied to associated lawyers.

(Adopted Sept. 26, 2018, eff. Nov. 1, 2018.)

Rule 1.9   Duties to Former Clients

(a) A lawyer who has formerly represented a client in a matter shall not thereafter represent another person* in the same or a substantially related matter in which that person's* interests are materially adverse to the interests of the former client unless the former client gives informed written consent.*

(b) A lawyer shall not knowingly* represent a person* in the same or a substantially related matter in which a firm* with which the lawyer formerly was associated had previously represented a client

(1) whose interests are materially adverse to that person;* and

(2) about whom the lawyer had acquired information protected by Business and Professions Code section 6068, subdivision (e) and rules 1.6 and 1.9(c) that is material to the matter;

unless the former client gives informed written consent.*

(c) A lawyer who has formerly represented a client in a matter or whose present or former firm* has formerly represented a client in a matter shall not thereafter:

(1) use information protected by Business and Professions Code section 6068, subdivision (e) and rule 1.6 acquired by virtue of the representation of the former client to the disadvantage of the former client except as these rules or the State Bar Act would permit with respect to a current client, or when the information has become generally known;* or

(2) reveal information protected by Business and Professions Code section 6068, subdivision (e) and rule 1.6 acquired by virtue of the representation of the former client except as these rules or the State Bar Act permit with respect to a current client.

Comment

[1] After termination of a lawyer-client relationship, the lawyer owes two duties to a former client. The lawyer may not (i) do anything that will injuriously affect the former client in any matter in which the lawyer represented the former client, or (ii) at any time use against the former client knowledge or information acquired by virtue of the previous relationship. (See *Oasis West Realty, LLC v. Goldman* (2011) 51 Cal.4th 811 [124 Cal.Rptr.3d 256]; *Wutchumna Water Co. v. Bailey* (1932) 216 Cal. 564 [15 P.2d 505].) For example, (i) a lawyer could not properly seek to rescind on behalf of a new client a contract drafted on behalf of the former client and (ii) a lawyer who has prosecuted an accused person* could not represent the accused in a subsequent civil action against the government concerning the same matter. (See also Bus. & Prof. Code, § 6131; 18 U.S.C. § 207(a).) These

duties exist to preserve a client's trust in the lawyer and to encourage the client's candor in communications with the lawyer.

[2] For what constitutes a "matter" for purposes of this rule, see rule 1.7(e).

[3] Two matters are "the same or substantially related" for purposes of this rule if they involve a substantial* risk of a violation of one of the two duties to a former client described above in Comment [1]. For example, this will occur: (i) if the matters involve the same transaction or legal dispute or other work performed by the lawyer for the former client; or (ii) if the lawyer normally would have obtained information in the prior representation that is protected by Business and Professions Code section 6068, subdivision (e) and rule 1.6, and the lawyer would be expected to use or disclose that information in the subsequent representation because it is material to the subsequent representation.

[4] Paragraph (b) addresses a lawyer's duties to a client who has become a former client because the lawyer no longer is associated with the law firm* that represents or represented the client. In that situation, the lawyer has a conflict of interest only when the lawyer involved has actual knowledge of information protected by Business and Professions Code section 6068, subdivision (e) and rules 1.6 and 1.9(c). Thus, if a lawyer while with one firm* acquired no knowledge or information relating to a particular client of the firm,* and that lawyer later joined another firm,* neither the lawyer individually nor lawyers in the second firm* would violate this rule by representing another client in the same or a related matter even though the interests of the two clients conflict. See rule 1.10(b) for the restrictions on lawyers in a firm* once a lawyer has terminated association with the firm.*

[5] The fact that information can be discovered in a public record does not, by itself, render that information generally known* under paragraph (c). (See, e.g., *In the Matter of Johnson* (Review Dept. 2000) 4 Cal. State Bar Ct. Rptr. 179.)

[6] With regard to the effectiveness of an advance consent, see rule 1.7, Comment [9]. With regard to imputation of conflicts to lawyers in a firm* with which a lawyer is or was formerly associated, see rule 1.10. Current and former government lawyers must comply with this rule to the extent required by rule 1.11.

(Adopted Sept. 26, 2018, eff. Nov. 1, 2018.)

Rule 1.10   Imputation of Conflicts of Interest: General Rule

(a) While lawyers are associated in a firm,* none of them shall knowingly* represent a client when any one of them practicing alone would be prohibited from doing so by rules 1.7 or 1.9, unless

(1) the prohibition is based on a personal interest of the prohibited lawyer and does not present a significant risk of materially limiting the representation of the client by the remaining lawyers in the firm;* or

(2) the prohibition is based upon rule 1.9(a) or (b) and arises out of the prohibited lawyer's association with a prior firm,* and

(i) the prohibited lawyer did not substantially participate in the same or a substantially related matter;

(ii) the prohibited lawyer is timely screened* from any participation in the matter and is apportioned no part of the fee therefrom; and

(iii) written* notice is promptly given to any affected former client to enable the former client to ascertain compliance with the provisions of this rule, which shall include a description of the screening* procedures employed; and an agreement by the firm* to respond promptly to any written* inquiries or objections by the former client about the screening* procedures.

(b) When a lawyer has terminated an association with a firm,* the firm* is not prohibited from thereafter representing a person* with interests materially adverse to those of a client represented by the formerly associated lawyer and not currently represented by the firm,* unless:

(1) the matter is the same or substantially related to that in which the formerly associated lawyer represented the client; and

(2) any lawyer remaining in the firm* has information protected by Business and Professions Code section 6068, subdivision (e) and rules 1.6 and 1.9(c) that is material to the matter.

(c) A prohibition under this rule may be waived by each affected client under the conditions stated in rule 1.7.

(d) The imputation of a conflict of interest to lawyers associated in a firm* with former or current government lawyers is governed by rule 1.11.

Comment

[1] In determining whether a prohibited lawyer's previously participation was substantial,* a number of factors should be considered, such as the lawyer's level of responsibility in the prior matter, the duration of the lawyer's participation, the extent to which the lawyer advised or had personal contact with the former client, and the extent to which the lawyer was exposed to confidential information of the former client likely to be material in the current matter.

---

* An asterisk (*) identifies a word or phrase defined in the terminology rule, rule 1.0.1.

[2] Paragraph (a) does not prohibit representation by others in the law firm* where the person* prohibited from involvement in a matter is a nonlawyer, such as a paralegal or legal secretary. Nor does paragraph (a) prohibit representation if the lawyer is prohibited from acting because of events before the person* became a lawyer, for example, work that the person* did as a law student. Such persons,* however, ordinarily must be screened* from any personal participation in the matter. (See rules 1.0.1(k) and 5.3.)

[3] Paragraph (a)(2)(ii) does not prohibit the screened* lawyer from receiving a salary or partnership share established by prior independent agreement, but that lawyer may not receive compensation directly related to the matter in which the lawyer is prohibited.

[4] Where a lawyer is prohibited from engaging in certain transactions under rules 1.8.1 through 1.8.9, rule 1.8.11, and not this rule, determines whether that prohibition also applies to other lawyers associated in a firm* with the personally prohibited lawyer.

[5] The responsibilities of managerial and supervisory lawyers prescribed by rules 5.1 and 5.3 apply to screening* arrangements implemented under this rule.

[6] Standards for disqualification, and whether in a particular matter (1) a lawyer's conflict is imputed to other lawyers in the same firm,* or (2) the use of a timely screen* is effective to avoid that imputation, are also the subject of statutes and case law. (See, e.g., Code Civ. Proc., § 128, subd. (a)(5); Pen. Code, § 1424; *In re Charlisse C.* (2008) 45 Cal.4th 145 [84 Cal.Rptr.3d 597]; *Rhaburn v. Superior Court* (2006) 140 Cal.App.4th 1566 [45 Cal.Rptr.3d 464]; *Kirk v. First American Title Ins. Co.* (2010) 183 Cal.App.4th 776 [108 Cal.Rptr.3d 620].)

(Adopted Sept. 26, 2018, eff. Nov. 1, 2018.)

Rule 1.11   Special Conflicts of Interest for Former and Current Government Officials and Employees

(a)   Except as law may otherwise expressly permit, a lawyer who has formerly served as a public official or employee of the government:

(1)   is subject to rule 1.9(c); and

(2)   shall not otherwise represent a client in connection with a matter in which the lawyer participated personally and substantially as a public official or employee, unless the appropriate government agency gives its informed written consent* to the representation. This paragraph shall not apply to matters governed by rule 1.12(a).

(b)   When a lawyer is prohibited from representation under paragraph (a), no lawyer in a firm* with which that lawyer is associated may knowingly* undertake or continue representation in such a matter unless:

(1)   the personally prohibited lawyer is timely screened* from any participation in the matter and is apportioned no part of the fee therefrom; and

(2)   written* notice is promptly given to the appropriate government agency to enable it to ascertain compliance with the provisions of this rule.

(c)   Except as law may otherwise expressly permit, a lawyer who was a public official or employee and, during that employment, acquired information that the lawyer knows* is confidential government information about a person,* may not represent a private client whose interests are adverse to that person* in a matter in which the information could be used to the material disadvantage of that person.* As used in this rule, the term "confidential government information" means information that has been obtained under governmental authority, that, at the time this rule is applied, the government is prohibited by law from disclosing to the public, or has a legal privilege not to disclose, and that is not otherwise available to the public. A firm* with which that lawyer is associated may undertake or continue representation in the matter only if the personally prohibited lawyer is timely screened* from any participation in the matter and is apportioned no part of the fee therefrom.

(d)   Except as law may otherwise expressly permit, a lawyer currently serving as a public official or employee:

(1)   is subject to rules 1.7 and 1.9; and

(2)   shall not:

(i)   participate in a matter in which the lawyer participated personally and substantially while in private practice or nongovernmental employment, unless the appropriate government agency gives its informed written consent;* or

(ii)   negotiate for private employment with any person* who is involved as a party, or as a lawyer for a party, or with a law firm* for a party, in a matter in which the lawyer is participating personally and substantially, except that a lawyer serving as a law clerk to a judge, other adjudicative officer or arbitrator may negotiate for private employment as permitted by rule 1.12(b) and subject to the conditions stated in rule 1.12(b).

Comment

[1]   Rule 1.10 is not applicable to the conflicts of interest addressed by this rule.

[2]   For what constitutes a "matter" for purposes of this rule, see rule 1.7(e).

[3]   Paragraphs (a)(2) and (d)(2) apply regardless of whether a lawyer is adverse to a former client. Both provisions apply when the former public official or employee of the government has personally and substantially participated in the matter. Personal participation includes both direct participation and the supervision of a subordinate's participation. Substantial* participation requires that the lawyer's involvement be of significance to the matter. Participation may be substantial* even though it is not determinative of the outcome of a particular matter. However, it requires more than official responsibility, knowledge, perfunctory involvement, or involvement on an administrative or peripheral issue. A finding of substantiality should be based not only on the effort devoted to the matter, but also on the importance of the effort. Personal and substantial* participation may occur when, for example, a lawyer participates through decision, approval, disapproval, recommendation, investigation or the rendering of advice in a particular matter.

[4]   By requiring a former government lawyer to comply with rule 1.9(c), paragraph (a)(1) protects information obtained while working for the government to the same extent as information learned while representing a private client. This provision applies regardless of whether the lawyer was working in a "legal" capacity. Thus, information learned by the lawyer while in public service in an administrative, policy, or advisory position also is covered by paragraph (a)(1).

[5]   Paragraph (c) operates only when the lawyer in question has actual knowledge of the information; it does not operate with respect to information that merely could be imputed to the lawyer.

[6]   When a lawyer has been employed by one government agency and then moves to a second government agency, it may be appropriate to treat that second agency as another client for purposes of this rule, as when a lawyer is employed by a city and subsequently is employed by a federal agency. Because conflicts of interest are governed by paragraphs (a) and (b), the latter agency is required to screen* the lawyer. Whether two government agencies should be regarded as the same or different clients for conflict of interest purposes is beyond the scope of these rules. (See rule 1.13, Comment [6]; see also *Civil Service Commission v. Superior Court* (1984) 163 Cal.App.3d 70, 76-78 [209 Cal.Rptr. 159].)

[7]   Paragraphs (b) and (c) do not prohibit a lawyer from receiving a salary or partnership share established by prior independent agreement, but that lawyer may not receive compensation directly relating the lawyer's compensation to the fee in the matter in which the lawyer is personally prohibited from participating.

[8]   Paragraphs (a) and (d) do not prohibit a lawyer from jointly representing a private party and a government agency when doing so is permitted by rule 1.7 and is not otherwise prohibited by law.

[9]   A lawyer serving as a public official or employee of the government may participate in a matter in which the lawyer participated substantially while in private practice or non-governmental employment only if: (i) the government agency gives its informed written consent* as required by paragraph (d)(2)(i); and (ii) the former client gives its informed written consent* as required by rule 1.9, to which the lawyer is subject by paragraph (d)(1).

[10]   This rule is not intended to address whether in a particular matter: (i) a lawyer's conflict under paragraph (d) will be imputed to other lawyers serving in the same governmental agency; or (ii) the use of a timely screen* will avoid that imputation. The imputation and screening* rules for lawyers moving from private practice into government service under paragraph (d) are left to be addressed by case law and its development. (See *City & County of San Francisco v. Cobra Solutions, Inc.* (2006) 38 Cal.4th 839, 847, 851-54 [43 Cal.Rptr.3d 776]; *City of Santa Barbara v. Superior Court* (2004) 122 Cal.App.4th 17, 26-27 [18 Cal.Rptr.3d 403].) Regarding the standards for recusals of prosecutors in criminal matters, see Penal Code section 1424; *Haraguchi v. Superior Court* (2008) 43 Cal.4th 706, 711-20 [76 Cal.Rptr.3d 250]; and *Hollywood v. Superior Court* (2008) 43 Cal.4th 721, 727-35 [76 Cal.Rptr.3d 264]. Concerning prohibitions against former prosecutors participating in matters in which they served or participated in as prosecutor, see, e.g., Business and Professions Code section 6131 and 18 United States Code section 207(a).

(Adopted Sept. 26, 2018, eff. Nov. 1, 2018.)

Rule 1.12   Former Judge, Arbitrator, Mediator, or Other Third-Party Neutral

(a)   Except as stated in paragraph (d), a lawyer shall not represent anyone in connection with a matter in which the lawyer participated personally and substantially as a judge or other adjudicative officer, judicial staff attorney or law clerk to such a person* or as an arbitrator, mediator, or other third-party neutral, unless all parties to the proceeding give informed written consent.*

(b)   A lawyer shall not seek employment from any person* who is involved as a party or as a lawyer for a party, or with a law firm* for a party, in a matter in which the lawyer is participating personally and substantially as a judge or other adjudicative officer or as an arbitrator, mediator, or other third party neutral. A lawyer serving as a judicial staff attorney or

---

* An asterisk (*) identifies a word or phrase defined in the terminology rule, rule 1.0.1.

law clerk to a judge or other adjudicative officer may seek employment from a party, or with a lawyer or a law firm* for a party, in a matter in which the staff attorney or clerk is participating personally and substantially, but only with the approval of the court.

(c)   If a lawyer is prohibited from representation by paragraph (a), other lawyers in a firm* with which that lawyer is associated may knowingly* undertake or continue representation in the matter only if:

(1)   the prohibition does not arise from the lawyer's service as a mediator or settlement judge;

(2)   the prohibited lawyer is timely screened* from any participation in the matter and is apportioned no part of the fee therefrom; and

(3)   written* notice is promptly given to the parties and any appropriate tribunal* to enable them to ascertain compliance with the provisions of this rule.

(d)   An arbitrator selected as a partisan of a party in a multimember arbitration panel is not prohibited from subsequently representing that party.

Comment

[1]   Paragraphs (a) and (b) apply when a former judge or other adjudicative officer, or a judicial staff attorney or law clerk to such a person,* or an arbitrator, mediator, or other third-party neutral, has personally and substantially participated in the matter. Personal participation includes both direct participation and the supervision of a subordinate's participation, as may occur in a chambers with several staff attorneys or law clerks. Substantial* participation requires that the lawyer's involvement was of significance to the matter. Participation may be substantial* even though it was not determinative of the outcome of a particular case or matter. A finding of substantiality should be based not only on the effort devoted to the matter, but also on the importance of the effort. Personal and substantial* participation may occur when, for example, the lawyer participated through decision, recommendation, or the rendering of advice on a particular case or matter. However, a judge who was a member of a multi-member court, and thereafter left judicial office to practice law, is not prohibited from representing a client in a matter pending in the court, but in which the former judge did not participate, or acquire material confidential information. The fact that a former judge exercised administrative responsibility in a court also does not prevent the former judge from acting as a lawyer in a matter where the judge had previously exercised remote or incidental administrative responsibility that did not affect the merits, such as uncontested procedural duties typically performed by a presiding or supervising judge or justice. The term "adjudicative officer" includes such officials as judges pro tempore, referees, and special masters.

[2]   Other law or codes of ethics governing third-party neutrals may impose more stringent standards of personal or imputed disqualification. (See rule 2.4.)

[3]   Paragraph (c)(2) does not prohibit the screened* lawyer from receiving a salary or partnership share established by prior independent agreement, but that lawyer may not receive compensation directly related to the matter in which the lawyer is personally prohibited from participating.

(Adopted Sept. 26, 2018, eff. Nov. 1, 2018.)

Rule 1.13   Organization as Client

(a)   A lawyer employed or retained by an organization shall conform his or her representation to the concept that the client is the organization itself, acting through its duly authorized directors, officers, employees, members, shareholders, or other constituents overseeing the particular engagement.

(b)   If a lawyer representing an organization knows* that a constituent is acting, intends to act or refuses to act in a matter related to the representation in a manner that the lawyer knows* or reasonably should know* is (i) a violation of a legal obligation to the organization or a violation of law reasonably* imputable to the organization, and (ii) likely to result in substantial* injury to the organization, the lawyer shall proceed as is reasonably* necessary in the best lawful interest of the organization. Unless the lawyer reasonably believes* that it is not necessary in the best lawful interest of the organization to do so, the lawyer shall refer the matter to higher authority in the organization, including, if warranted by the circumstances, to the highest authority that can act on behalf of the organization as determined by applicable law.

(c)   In taking any action pursuant to paragraph (b), the lawyer shall not reveal information protected by Business and Professions Code section 6068, subdivision (e).

(d)   If, despite the lawyer's actions in accordance with paragraph (b), the highest authority that can act on behalf of the organization insists upon action, or fails to act, in a manner that is a violation of a legal obligation to the organization or a violation of law reasonably* imputable to the

organization, and is likely to result in substantial* injury to the organization, the lawyer shall continue to proceed as is reasonably* necessary in the best lawful interests of the organization. The lawyer's response may include the lawyer's right and, where appropriate, duty to resign or withdraw in accordance with rule 1.16.

(e)   A lawyer who reasonably believes* that he or she has been discharged because of the lawyer's actions taken pursuant to paragraph (b), or who resigns or withdraws under circumstances described in paragraph (d), shall proceed as the lawyer reasonably believes* necessary to assure that the organization's highest authority is informed of the lawyer's discharge, resignation, or withdrawal.

(f)   In dealing with an organization's constituents, a lawyer representing the organization shall explain the identity of the lawyer's client whenever the lawyer knows* or reasonably should know* that the organization's interests are adverse to those of the constituent(s) with whom the lawyer is dealing.

(g)   A lawyer representing an organization may also represent any of its constituents, subject to the provisions of rules 1.7, 1.8.2, 1.8.6, and 1.8.7. If the organization's consent to the dual representation is required by any of these rules, the consent shall be given by an appropriate official, constituent, or body of the organization other than the individual who is to be represented, or by the shareholders.

Comment

The Entity as the Client

[1]   This rule applies to all forms of private, public and governmental organizations. (See Comment [6].) An organizational client can only act through individuals who are authorized to conduct its affairs. The identity of an organization's constituents will depend on its form, structure, and chosen terminology. For example, in the case of a corporation, constituents include officers, directors, employees and shareholders. In the case of other organizational forms, constituents include the equivalents of officers, directors, employees, and shareholders. For purposes of this rule, any agent or fiduciary authorized to act on behalf of an organization is a constituent of the organization.

[2]   A lawyer ordinarily must accept decisions an organization's constituents make on behalf of the organization, even if the lawyer questions their utility or prudence. It is not within the lawyer's province to make decisions on behalf of the organization concerning policy and operations, including ones entailing serious risk. A lawyer, however, has a duty to inform the client of significant developments related to the representation under Business and Professions Code section 6068, subdivision (m) and rule 1.4. Even when a lawyer is not obligated to proceed in accordance with paragraph (b), the lawyer may refer to higher authority, including the organization's highest authority, matters that the lawyer reasonably believes* are sufficiently important to refer in the best interest of the organization subject to Business and Professions Code section 6068, subdivision (e) and rule 1.6.

[3]   Paragraph (b) distinguishes between knowledge of the conduct and knowledge of the consequences of that conduct. When a lawyer knows* of the conduct, the lawyer's obligations under paragraph (b) are triggered when the lawyer knows* or reasonably should know* that the conduct is (i) a violation of a legal obligation to the organization, or a violation of law reasonably* imputable to the organization, and (ii) likely to result in substantial* injury to the organization.

[4]   In determining how to proceed under paragraph (b), the lawyer should consider the seriousness of the violation and its potential consequences, the responsibility in the organization and the apparent motivation of the person* involved, the policies of the organization concerning such matters, and any other relevant considerations. Ordinarily, referral to a higher authority would be necessary. In some circumstances, however, the lawyer may ask the constituent to reconsider the matter. For example, if the circumstances involve a constituent's innocent misunderstanding of law and subsequent acceptance of the lawyer's advice, the lawyer may reasonably* conclude that the best interest of the organization does not require that the matter be referred to higher authority. If a constituent persists in conduct contrary to the lawyer's advice, it will be necessary for the lawyer to take steps to have the matter reviewed by a higher authority in the organization. If the matter is of sufficient seriousness and importance or urgency to the organization, referral to higher authority in the organization may be necessary even if the lawyer has not communicated with the constituent. For the responsibility of a subordinate lawyer in representing an organization, see rule 5.2.

[5]   In determining how to proceed in the best lawful interests of the organization, a lawyer should consider the extent to which the organization should be informed of the circumstances, the actions taken by the organization with respect to the matter and the direction the lawyer has received from the organizational client.

Governmental Organizations

[6]   It is beyond the scope of this rule to define precisely the identity of the client and the lawyer's obligations when representing a governmental agency. Although in some circumstances the client may be a specific agency, it may also be a branch

Rules of Conduct

of government or the government as a whole. In a matter involving the conduct of government officials, a government lawyer may have authority under applicable law to question such conduct more extensively than that of a lawyer for a private organization in similar circumstances. Duties of lawyers employed by the government or lawyers in military service may be defined by statutes and regulations. In addition, a governmental organization may establish internal organizational rules and procedures that identify an official, agency, organization, or other person* to serve as the designated recipient of whistle-blower reports from the organization's lawyers, consistent with Business and Professions Code section 6068, subdivision (e) and rule 1.6. This rule is not intended to limit that authority.

(Adopted Sept. 26, 2018, eff. Nov. 1, 2018.)

Rule 1.14   [Reserved]

Rule 1.15   Safekeeping Funds and Property of Clients and Other Persons*

(a)   All funds received or held by a lawyer or law firm* for the benefit of a client, or other person* to whom the lawyer owes a contractual, statutory, or other legal duty, including advances for fees, costs and expenses, shall be deposited in one or more identifiable bank accounts labeled "Trust Account" or words of similar import, maintained in the State of California, or, with written* consent of the client, in any other jurisdiction where there is a substantial* relationship between the client or the client's business and the other jurisdiction.

(b)   Notwithstanding paragraph (a), a flat fee paid in advance for legal services may be deposited in a lawyer's or law firm's operating account, provided:

(1)   the lawyer or law firm* discloses to the client in writing* (i) that the client has a right under paragraph (a) to require that the flat fee be deposited in an identified trust account until the fee is earned, and (ii) that the client is entitled to a refund of any amount of the fee that has not been earned in the event the representation is terminated or the services for which the fee has been paid are not completed; and

(2)   if the flat fee exceeds $1,000.00, the client's agreement to deposit the flat fee in the lawyer's operating account and the disclosures required by paragraph (b)(1) are set forth in a writing* signed by the client.

(c)   Funds belonging to the lawyer or the law firm* shall not be deposited or otherwise commingled with funds held in a trust account except:

(1)   funds reasonably* sufficient to pay bank charges; and

(2)   funds belonging in part to a client or other person* and in part presently or potentially to the lawyer or the law firm,* in which case the portion belonging to the lawyer or law firm* must be withdrawn at the earliest reasonable* time after the lawyer or law firm's interest in that portion becomes fixed. However, if a client or other person* disputes the lawyer or law firm's right to receive a portion of trust funds, the disputed portion shall not be withdrawn until the dispute is finally resolved.

(d)   A lawyer shall:

(1)   promptly notify a client or other person* of the receipt of funds, securities, or other property in which the lawyer knows* or reasonably should know* the client or other person* has an interest;

(2)   identify and label securities and properties of a client or other person* promptly upon receipt and place them in a safe deposit box or other place of safekeeping as soon as practicable;

(3)   maintain complete records of all funds, securities, and other property of a client or other person* coming into the possession of the lawyer or law firm;*

(4)   promptly account in writing* to the client or other person* for whom the lawyer holds funds or property;

(5)   preserve records of all funds and property held by a lawyer or law firm* under this rule for a period of no less than five years after final appropriate distribution of such funds or property;

(6)   comply with any order for an audit of such records issued pursuant to the Rules of Procedure of the State Bar; and

(7)   promptly distribute, as requested by the client or other person,* any undisputed funds or property in the possession of the lawyer or law firm* that the client or other person* is entitled to receive.

(e)   The Board of Trustees of the State Bar shall have the authority to formulate and adopt standards as to what "records" shall be maintained by lawyers and law firms* in accordance with paragraph (d)(3). The standards formulated and adopted by the Board, as from time to time amended, shall be effective and binding on all lawyers.

Standards:

Pursuant to this rule, the Board of Trustees of the State Bar adopted the following standards, effective November 1, 2018, as to what "records" shall be maintained by lawyers and law firms* in accordance with paragraph (d)(3).

(1)   A lawyer shall, from the date of receipt of funds of the client or other person* through the period ending five years from the date of appropriate disbursement of such funds, maintain:

(a)   a written* ledger for each client or other person* on whose behalf funds are held that sets forth:

(i)   the name of such client or other person;*

(ii)   the date, amount and source of all funds received on behalf of such client or other person;*

(iii)   the date, amount, payee and purpose of each disbursement made on behalf of such client or other person;* and

(iv)   the current balance for such client or other person;*

(b)   a written* journal for each bank account that sets forth:

(i)   the name of such account;

(ii)   the date, amount and client or other person* affected by each debit and credit; and

(iii)   the current balance in such account;

(c)   all bank statements and cancelled checks for each bank account; and

(d)   each monthly reconciliation (balancing) of (a), (b), and (c).

(2)   A lawyer shall, from the date of receipt of all securities and other properties held for the benefit of client or other person* through the period ending five years from the date of appropriate disbursement of such securities and other properties, maintain a written* journal that specifies:

(a)   each item of security and property held;

(b)   the person* on whose behalf the security or property is held;

(c)   the date of receipt of the security or property;

(d)   the date of distribution of the security or property; and

(e)   person* to whom the security or property was distributed.

Comment

[1]   Whether a lawyer owes a contractual, statutory or other legal duty under paragraph (a) to hold funds on behalf of a person* other than a client in situations where client funds are subject to a third-party lien will depend on the relationship between the lawyer and the third-party, whether the lawyer has assumed a contractual obligation to the third person* and whether the lawyer has an independent obligation to honor the lien under a statute or other law. In certain circumstances, a lawyer may be civilly liable when the lawyer has notice of a lien and disburses funds in contravention of the lien. (See *Kaiser Foundation Health Plan, Inc. v. Aguiluz* (1996) 47 Cal.App.4th 302 [54 Cal.Rptr.2d 665].) However, civil liability by itself does not establish a violation of this rule. (Compare *Johnstone v. State Bar of California* (1966) 64 Cal.2d 153, 155-156 [49 Cal.Rptr. 97] [" 'When an attorney assumes a fiduciary relationship and violates his duty in a manner that would justify disciplinary action if the relationship had been that of attorney and client, he may properly be disciplined for his misconduct.' "] with *Crooks v. State Bar* (1970) 3 Cal.3d 346, 358 [90 Cal.Rptr. 600] [lawyer who agrees to act as escrow or stakeholder for a client and a third-party owes a duty to the nonclient with regard to held funds].)

[2]   As used in this rule, "advances for fees" means a payment intended by the client as an advance payment for some or all of the services that the lawyer is expected to perform on the client's behalf. With respect to the difference between a true retainer and a flat fee, which is one type of advance fee, see rule 1.5(d) and (e). Subject to rule 1.5, a lawyer or law firm* may enter into an agreement that defines when or how an advance fee is earned and may be withdrawn from the client trust account.

[3]   Absent written* disclosure and the client's agreement in a writing* signed by the client as provided in paragraph (b), a lawyer must deposit a flat fee paid in advance of legal services in the lawyer's trust account. Paragraph (b) does not apply to advance payment for costs and expenses. Paragraph (b) does not alter the lawyer's obligations under paragraph (d) or the lawyer's burden to establish that the fee has been earned.

(Adopted Sept. 26, 2018, eff. Nov. 1, 2018.)

Rule 1.16   Declining or Terminating Representation

(a)   Except as stated in paragraph (c), a lawyer shall not represent a client or, where representation has commenced, shall withdraw from the representation of a client if:

(1)   the lawyer knows* or reasonably should know* that the client is bringing an action, conducting a defense, asserting a position in litigation, or taking an appeal, without probable cause and for the purpose of harassing or maliciously injuring any person;*

---

* An asterisk (*) identifies a word or phrase defined in the terminology rule, rule 1.0.1.

(2) the lawyer knows* or reasonably should know* that the representation will result in violation of these rules or of the State Bar Act;

(3) the lawyer's mental or physical condition renders it unreasonably difficult to carry out the representation effectively; or

(4) the client discharges the lawyer.

(b) Except as stated in paragraph (c), a lawyer may withdraw from representing a client if:

(1) the client insists upon presenting a claim or defense in litigation, or asserting a position or making a demand in a non-litigation matter, that is not warranted under existing law and cannot be supported by good faith argument for an extension, modification, or reversal of existing law;

(2) the client either seeks to pursue a criminal or fraudulent* course of conduct or has used the lawyer's services to advance a course of conduct that the lawyer reasonably believes* was a crime or fraud;*

(3) the client insists that the lawyer pursue a course of conduct that is criminal or fraudulent;*

(4) the client by other conduct renders it unreasonably difficult for the lawyer to carry out the representation effectively;

(5) the client breaches a material term of an agreement with, or obligation, to the lawyer relating to the representation, and the lawyer has given the client a reasonable* warning after the breach that the lawyer will withdraw unless the client fulfills the agreement or performs the obligation;

(6) the client knowingly* and freely assents to termination of the representation;

(7) the inability to work with co-counsel indicates that the best interests of the client likely will be served by withdrawal;

(8) the lawyer's mental or physical condition renders it difficult for the lawyer to carry out the representation effectively;

(9) a continuation of the representation is likely to result in a violation of these rules or the State Bar Act; or

(10) the lawyer believes* in good faith, in a proceeding pending before a tribunal,* that the tribunal* will find the existence of other good cause for withdrawal.

(c) If permission for termination of a representation is required by the rules of a tribunal,* a lawyer shall not terminate a representation before that tribunal* without its permission.

(d) A lawyer shall not terminate a representation until the lawyer has taken reasonable* steps to avoid reasonably* foreseeable prejudice to the rights of the client, such as giving the client sufficient notice to permit the client to retain other counsel, and complying with paragraph (e).

(e) Upon the termination of a representation for any reason:

(1) subject to any applicable protective order, non-disclosure agreement, statute or regulation, the lawyer promptly shall release to the client, at the request of the client, all client materials and property. "Client materials and property" includes correspondence, pleadings, deposition transcripts, experts' reports and other writings,* exhibits, and physical evidence, whether in tangible, electronic or other form, and other items reasonably* necessary to the client's representation, whether the client has paid for them or not; and

(2) the lawyer promptly shall refund any part of a fee or expense paid in advance that the lawyer has not earned or incurred. This provision is not applicable to a true retainer fee paid solely for the purpose of ensuring the availability of the lawyer for the matter.

Comment

[1] This rule applies, without limitation, to a sale of a law practice under rule 1.17. A lawyer can be subject to discipline for improperly threatening to terminate a representation. (See *In the Matter of Shalant* (Review Dept. 2005) 4 Cal. State Bar Ct. Rptr. 829, 837.)

[2] When a lawyer withdraws from the representation of a client in a particular matter under paragraph (a) or (b), the lawyer might not be obligated to withdraw from the representation of the same client in other matters. For example, a lawyer might be obligated under paragraph (a)(1) to withdraw from representing a client because the lawyer has a conflict of interest under rule 1.7, but that conflict might not arise in other representations of the client.

[3] Withdrawal under paragraph (a)(1) is not mandated where a lawyer for the defendant in a criminal proceeding, or the respondent in a proceeding that could result in incarceration, or involuntary commitment or confinement, defends the proceeding by requiring that every element of the case be established. (See rule 3.1(b).)

[4] Lawyers must comply with their obligations to their clients under Business and Professions Code section 6068, subdivision (e) and rule 1.6, and to the courts under rule 3.3 when seeking permission to withdraw under paragraph (c). If a tribunal* denies a lawyer permission to withdraw, the lawyer is obligated to comply with the tribunal's* order. (See Bus. & Prof. Code, §§ 6068, subd. (b) and 6103.) This duty applies even if the lawyer sought permission to withdraw because of a conflict of interest. Regarding withdrawal from limited scope representations that involve court appearances, compliance with applicable California Rules of Court concerning limited scope representation satisfies paragraph (c).

[5] Statutes may prohibit a lawyer from releasing information in the client materials and property under certain circumstances. (See, e.g., Pen. Code, §§ 1054.2 and 1054.10.) A lawyer in certain criminal matters may be required to retain a copy of a former client's file for the term of his or her imprisonment. (See, Pen. Code, § 1054.9.)

[6] Paragraph (e)(1) does not prohibit a lawyer from making, at the lawyer's own expense, and retaining copies of papers released to the client, or to prohibit a claim for the recovery of the lawyer's expense in any subsequent legal proceeding.

(Amended Apr. 23, 2020, eff. June 1, 2020; Adopted Sept. 26, 2018, eff. Nov. 1, 2018.)

Rule 1.17 Sale of a Law Practice

All or substantially* all of the law practice of a lawyer, living or deceased, including goodwill, may be sold to another lawyer or law firm* subject to all the following conditions:

(a) Fees charged to clients shall not be increased solely by reason of the sale.

(b) If the sale contemplates the transfer of responsibility for work not yet completed or responsibility for client files or information protected by Business and Professions Code section 6068, subdivision (e)(1), then;

(1) if the seller is deceased, or has a conservator or other person* acting in a representative capacity, and no lawyer has been appointed to act for the seller pursuant to Business and Professions Code section 6180.5, then prior to the transfer;

(i) the purchaser shall cause a written* notice to be given to each client whose matter is included in the sale, stating that the interest in the law practice is being transferred to the purchaser; that the client has the right to retain other counsel; that the client may take possession of any client materials and property, as required by rule 1.16(e)(1); and that if no response is received to the notice within 90 days after it is sent, or if the client's rights would be prejudiced by a failure of the purchaser to act during that time, the purchaser may act on behalf of the client until otherwise notified by the client, and

(ii) the purchaser shall obtain the written* consent of the client. If reasonable* efforts have been made to locate the client and no response to the paragraph (b)(1)(i) notice is received within 90 days, consent shall be presumed until otherwise notified by the client.

(2) in all other circumstances, not less than 90 days prior to the transfer;

(i) the seller, or the lawyer appointed to act for the seller pursuant to Business and Professions Code section 6180.5, shall cause a written* notice to be given to each client whose matter is included in the sale, stating that the interest in the law practice is being transferred to the purchaser; that the client has the right to retain other counsel; that the client may take possession of any client materials and property, as required by rule 1.16(e)(1); and that if no response is received to the notice within 90 days after it is sent, or if the client's rights would be prejudiced by a failure of the purchaser to act during that time, the purchaser may act on behalf of the client until otherwise notified by the client, and

(ii) the seller, or the lawyer appointed to act for the seller pursuant to Business and Professions Code section 6180.5, shall obtain the written* consent of the client prior to the transfer. If reasonable* efforts have been made to locate the client and no response to the paragraph (b)(2)(i) notice is received within 90 days, consent shall be presumed until otherwise notified by the client.

(c) If substitution is required by the rules of a tribunal* in which a matter is pending, all steps necessary to substitute a lawyer shall be taken.

(d) The purchaser shall comply with the applicable requirements of rules 1.7 and 1.9.

(e) Confidential information shall not be disclosed to a nonlawyer in connection with a sale under this rule.

(f) This rule does not apply to the admission to or retirement from a law firm,* retirement plans and similar arrangements, or sale of tangible assets of a law practice.

---

* An asterisk (*) identifies a word or phrase defined in the terminology rule, rule 1.0.1.

Comment

[1] The requirement that the sale be of "all or substantially* all of the law practice of a lawyer" prohibits the sale of only a field or area of practice or the seller's practice in a geographical area or in a particular jurisdiction. The prohibition against the sale of less than all or substantially* all of a practice protects those clients whose matters are less lucrative and who might find it difficult to secure other counsel if a sale could be limited to substantial* fee-generating matters. The purchasers are required to undertake all client matters sold in the transaction, subject to client consent. This requirement is satisfied, however, even if a purchaser is unable to undertake a particular client matter because of a conflict of interest.

[2] Under paragraph (a), the purchaser must honor existing arrangements between the seller and the client as to fees and scope of work and the sale may not be financed by increasing fees charged for client matters transferred through the sale. However, fee increases or other changes to the fee arrangements might be justified by other factors, such as modifications of the purchaser's responsibilities, the passage of time, or reasonable* costs that were not addressed in the original agreement. Any such modifications must comply with rules 1.4 and 1.5 and other relevant provisions of these rules and the State Bar Act.

[3] Transfer of individual client matters, where permitted, is governed by rule 1.5.1. Payment of a fee to a nonlawyer broker for arranging the sale or purchase of a law practice is governed by rule 5.4(a).

(Adopted Sept. 26, 2018, eff. Nov. 1, 2018.)

Rule 1.18 Duties to Prospective Client

(a) A person* who, directly or through an authorized representative, consults a lawyer for the purpose of retaining the lawyer or securing legal service or advice from the lawyer in the lawyer's professional capacity, is a prospective client.

(b) Even when no lawyer-client relationship ensues, a lawyer who has communicated with a prospective client shall not use or reveal information protected by Business and Professions Code section 6068, subdivision (e) and rule 1.6 that the lawyer learned as a result of the consultation, except as rule 1.9 would permit with respect to information of a former client.

(c) A lawyer subject to paragraph (b) shall not represent a client with interests materially adverse to those of a prospective client in the same or a substantially related matter if the lawyer received from the prospective client information protected by Business and Professions Code section 6068, subdivision (e) and rule 1.6 that is material to the matter, except as provided in paragraph (d). If a lawyer is prohibited from representation under this paragraph, no lawyer in a firm* with which that lawyer is associated may knowingly* undertake or continue representation in such a matter, except as provided in paragraph (d).

(d) When the lawyer has received information that prohibits representation as provided in paragraph (c), representation of the affected client is permissible if:

(1) both the affected client and the prospective client have given informed written consent,* or

(2) the lawyer who received the information took reasonable* measures to avoid exposure to more information than was reasonably* necessary to determine whether to represent the prospective client; and

(i) the prohibited lawyer is timely screened* from any participation in the matter and is apportioned no part of the fee therefrom; and

(ii) written* notice is promptly given to the prospective client to enable the prospective client to ascertain compliance with the provisions of this rule.

Comment

[1] As used in this rule, a prospective client includes a person's* authorized representative. A lawyer's discussions with a prospective client can be limited in time and depth and leave both the prospective client and the lawyer free, and sometimes required, to proceed no further. Although a prospective client's information is protected by Business and Professions Code section 6068, subdivision (e) and rule 1.6 the same as that of a client, in limited circumstances provided under paragraph (d), a law firm* is permitted to accept or continue representation of a client with interests adverse to the prospective client. This rule is not intended to limit the application of Evidence Code section 951 (defining "client" within the meaning of the Evidence Code).

[2] Not all persons* who communicate information to a lawyer are entitled to protection under this rule. A person* who by any means communicates information unilaterally to a lawyer, without reasonable* expectation that the lawyer is willing to discuss the possibility of forming a lawyer-client relationship or provide legal advice is not a "prospective client" within the meaning of paragraph (a). In addition, a person* who discloses information to a lawyer after the lawyer has stated his or her unwillingness or inability to consult with the person* (*People v. Gionis* (1995) 9 Cal.4th 1196 [40 Cal.Rptr.2d 456]), or who communicates information to a lawyer without a good faith intention to seek legal advice or representation, is not a prospective client within the meaning of paragraph (a).

[3] In order to avoid acquiring information from a prospective client that would prohibit representation as provided in paragraph (c), a lawyer considering whether or not to undertake a new matter must limit the initial interview to only such information as reasonably* appears necessary for that purpose.

[4] Under paragraph (c), the prohibition in this rule is imputed to other lawyers in a law firm* as provided in rule 1.10. However, under paragraph (d)(1), the consequences of imputation may be avoided if the informed written consent* of both the prospective and affected clients is obtained. (See rule 1.0.1(e-1) [informed written consent].) In the alternative, imputation may be avoided if the conditions of paragraph (d)(2) are met and all prohibited lawyers are timely screened* and written* notice is promptly given to the prospective client. Paragraph (d)(2)(i) does not prohibit the screened* lawyer from receiving a salary or partnership share established by prior independent agreement, but that lawyer may not receive compensation directly related to the matter in which the lawyer is prohibited.

[5] Notice under paragraph (d)(2)(ii) must include a general description of the subject matter about which the lawyer was consulted, and the screening* procedures employed.

(Adopted Sept. 26, 2018, eff. Nov. 1, 2018.)

CHAPTER 2
COUNSELOR

Rule 2.1 Advisor

In representing a client, a lawyer shall exercise independent professional judgment and render candid advice.

Comment

[1] A lawyer ordinarily has no duty to initiate investigation of a client's affairs or to give advice that the client has indicated is unwanted, but a lawyer may initiate advice to a client when doing so appears to be in the client's interest.

[2] This rule does not preclude a lawyer who renders advice from referring to considerations other than the law, such as moral, economic, social and political factors that may be relevant to the client's situation.

(Adopted Sept. 26, 2018, eff. Nov. 1, 2018.)

Rule 2.2 [Reserved]

Rule 2.3 [Reserved]

Rule 2.4 Lawyer as Third-Party Neutral

(a) A lawyer serves as a third-party neutral when the lawyer assists two or more persons* who are not clients of the lawyer to reach a resolution of a dispute, or other matter, that has arisen between them. Service as a third-party neutral may include service as an arbitrator, a mediator or in such other capacity as will enable the lawyer to assist the parties to resolve the matter.

(b) A lawyer serving as a third-party neutral shall inform unrepresented parties that the lawyer is not representing them. When the lawyer knows* or reasonably should know* that a party does not understand the lawyer's role in the matter, the lawyer shall explain the difference between the lawyer's role as a third-party neutral and a lawyer's role as one who represents a client.

Comment

[1] In serving as a third-party neutral, the lawyer may be subject to court rules or other law that apply either to third-party neutrals generally or to lawyers serving as third-party neutrals. Lawyer neutrals may also be subject to various codes of ethics, such as the Judicial Council Standards for Mediators in Court Connected Mediation Programs or the Judicial Council Ethics Standards for Neutral Arbitrators in Contractual Arbitration.

[2] A lawyer who serves as a third-party neutral subsequently may be asked to serve as a lawyer representing a client in the same matter. The conflicts of interest that arise for both the individual lawyer and the lawyer's law firm* are addressed in rule 1.12.

[3] This rule is not intended to apply to temporary judges, referees or court-appointed arbitrators. (See rule 2.4.1.)

(Adopted Sept. 26, 2018, eff. Nov. 1, 2018.)

---

* An asterisk (*) identifies a word or phrase defined in the terminology rule, rule 1.0.1.

Rule 2.4.1   Lawyer as Temporary Judge, Referee, or Court-Appointed Arbitrator

A lawyer who is serving as a temporary judge, referee, or court-appointed arbitrator, and is subject to canon 6D of the California Code of Judicial Ethics, shall comply with the terms of that canon.

Comment

[1]   This rule is intended to permit the State Bar to discipline lawyers who violate applicable portions of the California Code of Judicial Ethics while acting in a judicial capacity pursuant to an order or appointment by a court.

[2]   This rule is not intended to apply to a lawyer serving as a third-party neutral in a mediation or a settlement conference, or as a neutral arbitrator pursuant to an arbitration agreement. (See rule 2.4.)

(Adopted Sept. 26, 2018, eff. Nov. 1, 2018.)

CHAPTER 3
ADVOCATE

Rule 3.1   Meritorious Claims and Contentions

(a)   A lawyer shall not:

(1)   bring or continue an action, conduct a defense, assert a position in litigation, or take an appeal, without probable cause and for the purpose of harassing or maliciously injuring any person;* or

(2)   present a claim or defense in litigation that is not warranted under existing law, unless it can be supported by a good faith argument for an extension, modification, or reversal of the existing law.

(b)   A lawyer for the defendant in a criminal proceeding, or the respondent in a proceeding that could result in incarceration, or involuntary commitment or confinement, may nevertheless defend the proceeding by requiring that every element of the case be established.

(Adopted Sept. 26, 2018, eff. Nov. 1, 2018.)

Rule 3.2   Delay of Litigation

In representing a client, a lawyer shall not use means that have no substantial* purpose other than to delay or prolong the proceeding or to cause needless expense.

Comment

See rule 1.3 with respect to a lawyer's duty to act with reasonable* diligence and rule 3.1(b) with respect to a lawyer's representation of a defendant in a criminal proceeding. See also Business and Professions Code section 6128, subdivision (b).

(Adopted Sept. 26, 2018, eff. Nov. 1, 2018.)

Rule 3.3   Candor Toward the Tribunal*

(a)   A lawyer shall not:

(1)   knowingly* make a false statement of fact or law to a tribunal* or fail to correct a false statement of material fact or law previously made to the tribunal* by the lawyer;

(2)   fail to disclose to the tribunal* legal authority in the controlling jurisdiction known* to the lawyer to be directly adverse to the position of the client and not disclosed by opposing counsel, or knowingly* misquote to a tribunal* the language of a book, statute, decision or other authority; or

(3)   offer evidence that the lawyer knows* to be false. If a lawyer, the lawyer's client, or a witness called by the lawyer, has offered material evidence, and the lawyer comes to know* of its falsity, the lawyer shall take reasonable* remedial measures, including, if necessary, disclosure to the tribunal,* unless disclosure is prohibited by Business and Professions Code section 6068, subdivision (e) and rule 1.6. A lawyer may refuse to offer evidence, other than the testimony of a defendant in a criminal matter, that the lawyer reasonably believes* is false.

(b)   A lawyer who represents a client in a proceeding before a tribunal* and who knows* that a person* intends to engage, is engaging or has engaged in criminal or fraudulent* conduct related to the proceeding shall take reasonable* remedial measures to the extent

permitted by Business and Professions Code section 6068, subdivision (e) and rule 1.6.

(c)   The duties stated in paragraphs (a) and (b) continue to the conclusion of the proceeding.

(d)   In an ex parte proceeding where notice to the opposing party in the proceeding is not required or given and the opposing party is not present, a lawyer shall inform the tribunal* of all material facts known* to the lawyer that will enable the tribunal* to make an informed decision, whether or not the facts are adverse to the position of the client.

Comment

[1]   This rule governs the conduct of a lawyer in proceedings of a tribunal,* including ancillary proceedings such as a deposition conducted pursuant to a tribunal's* authority. See rule 1.0.1(m) for the definition of "tribunal."

[2]   The prohibition in paragraph (a)(1) against making false statements of law or failing to correct a material misstatement of law includes citing as authority a decision that has been overruled or a statute that has been repealed or declared unconstitutional, or failing to correct such a citation previously made to the tribunal* by the lawyer.

Legal Argument

[3]   Legal authority in the controlling jurisdiction may include legal authority outside the jurisdiction in which the tribunal* sits, such as a federal statute or case that is determinative of an issue in a state court proceeding or a Supreme Court decision that is binding on a lower court.

[4]   The duties stated in paragraphs (a) and (b) apply to all lawyers, including defense counsel in criminal cases. If a lawyer knows* that a client intends to testify falsely or wants the lawyer to introduce false evidence, the lawyer should seek to persuade the client that the evidence should not be offered and, if unsuccessful, must refuse to offer the false evidence. If a criminal defendant insists on testifying, and the lawyer knows* that the testimony will be false, the lawyer may offer the testimony in a narrative form if the lawyer made reasonable* efforts to dissuade the client from the unlawful course of conduct and the lawyer has sought permission from the court to withdraw as required by rule 1.16. (See, e.g., *People v. Johnson* (1998) 62 Cal.App.4th 608 [72 Cal.Rptr.2d 805]; *People v. Jennings* (1999) 70 Cal.App.4th 899 [83 Cal.Rptr.2d 33].) The obligations of a lawyer under these rules and the State Bar Act are subordinate to applicable constitutional provisions.

Remedial Measures

[5]   Reasonable* remedial measures under paragraphs (a)(3) and (b) refer to measures that are available under these rules and the State Bar Act, and which a reasonable* lawyer would consider appropriate under the circumstances to comply with the lawyer's duty of candor to the tribunal.* (See, e.g., rules 1.2.1, 1.4(a)(4), 1.16(a), 8.4; Bus. & Prof. Code, §§ 6068, subd. (d), 6128.) Remedial measures also include explaining to the client the lawyer's obligations under this rule and, where applicable, the reasons for the lawyer's decision to seek permission from the tribunal* to withdraw, and remonstrating further with the client to take corrective action that would eliminate the need for the lawyer to withdraw. If the client is an organization, the lawyer should also consider the provisions of rule 1.13. Remedial measures do not include disclosure of client confidential information, which the lawyer is required to protect under Business and Professions Code section 6068, subdivision (e) and rule 1.6.

Duration of Obligation

[6]   A proceeding has concluded within the meaning of this rule when a final judgment in the proceeding has been affirmed on appeal or the time for review has passed. A prosecutor may have obligations that go beyond the scope of this rule. (See, e.g., rule 3.8(f) and (g).)

Ex Parte Communications

[7]   Paragraph (d) does not apply to ex parte communications that are not otherwise prohibited by law or the tribunal.*

Withdrawal

[8]   A lawyer's compliance with the duty of candor imposed by this rule does not require that the lawyer withdraw from the representation. The lawyer may, however, be required by rule 1.16 to seek permission of the tribunal* to withdraw if the lawyer's compliance with this rule results in a deterioration of the lawyer-client relationship such that the lawyer can no longer competently and diligently represent the client, or where continued employment will result in a violation of these rules. A lawyer must comply with Business and Professions Code section 6068, subdivision (e) and rule 1.6 with respect to a request to withdraw that is premised on a client's misconduct.

[9]   In addition to this rule, lawyers remain bound by Business and Professions Code sections 6068, subdivision (d) and 6106.

(Adopted Sept. 26, 2018, eff. Nov. 1, 2018.)

Rule 3.4   Fairness to Opposing Party and Counsel

A lawyer shall not:

(a)   unlawfully obstruct another party's access to evidence, including a witness, or unlawfully alter, destroy or conceal a document or other material having potential evidentiary value. A lawyer shall not counsel or assist another person* to do any such act;

---

* An asterisk (*) identifies a word or phrase defined in the terminology rule, rule 1.0.1.

(b) suppress any evidence that the lawyer or the lawyer's client has a legal obligation to reveal or to produce;

(c) falsify evidence, counsel or assist a witness to testify falsely, or offer an inducement to a witness that is prohibited by law;

(d) directly or indirectly pay, offer to pay, or acquiesce in the payment of compensation to a witness contingent upon the content of the witness's testimony or the outcome of the case. Except where prohibited by law, a lawyer may advance, guarantee, or acquiesce in the payment of:

(1) expenses reasonably* incurred by a witness in attending or testifying;

(2) reasonable* compensation to a witness for loss of time in attending or testifying; or

(3) a reasonable* fee for the professional services of an expert witness;

(e) advise or directly or indirectly cause a person* to secrete himself or herself or to leave the jurisdiction of a tribunal* for the purpose of making that person* unavailable as a witness therein;

(f) knowingly* disobey an obligation under the rules of a tribunal* except for an open refusal based on an assertion that no valid obligation exists; or

(g) in trial, assert personal knowledge of facts in issue except when testifying as a witness, or state a personal opinion as to the guilt or innocence of an accused.

Comment

[1] Paragraph (a) applies to evidentiary material generally, including computerized information. It is a criminal offense to destroy material for purpose of impairing its availability in a pending proceeding or one whose commencement can be foreseen. (See, e.g., Pen. Code, § 135; 18 U.S.C. §§ 1501-1520.) Falsifying evidence is also generally a criminal offense. (See, e.g., Pen. Code, § 132; 18 U.S.C. § 1519.) Applicable law may permit a lawyer to take temporary possession of physical evidence of client crimes for the purpose of conducting a limited examination that will not alter or destroy material characteristics of the evidence. Applicable law may require a lawyer to turn evidence over to the police or other prosecuting authorities, depending on the circumstances. (See *People v. Lee* (1970) 3 Cal.App.3d 514, 526 [83 Cal.Rptr. 715]; *People v. Meredith* (1981) 29 Cal.3d 682 [175 Cal.Rptr. 612].)

[2] A violation of a civil or criminal discovery rule or statute does not by itself establish a violation of this rule. See rule 3.8 for special disclosure responsibilities of a prosecutor.

(Adopted Sept. 26, 2018, eff. Nov. 1, 2018.)

Rule 3.5 Contact with Judges, Officials, Employees, and Jurors

(a) Except as permitted by statute, an applicable code of judicial ethics or code of judicial conduct, or standards governing employees of a tribunal,* a lawyer shall not directly or indirectly give or lend anything of value to a judge, official, or employee of a tribunal.* This rule does not prohibit a lawyer from contributing to the campaign fund of a judge or judicial officer running for election or confirmation pursuant to applicable law pertaining to such contributions.

(b) Unless permitted to do so by law, an applicable code of judicial ethics or code of judicial conduct, a rule or ruling of a tribunal,* or a court order, a lawyer shall not directly or indirectly communicate with or argue to a judge or judicial officer upon the merits of a contested matter pending before the judge or judicial officer, except:

(1) in open court;

(2) with the consent of all other counsel and any unrepresented parties in the matter;

(3) in the presence of all other counsel and any unrepresented parties in the matter;

(4) in writing* with a copy thereof furnished to all other counsel and any unrepresented parties in the matter; or

(5) in ex parte matters.

(c) As used in this rule, "judge" and "judicial officer" shall also include: (i) administrative law judges; (ii) neutral arbitrators; (iii) State Bar Court judges; (iv) members of an administrative body acting in an adjudicative capacity; and (v) law clerks, research attorneys, or other court personnel who participate in the decision-making process, including referees, special masters, or other persons* to whom a court refers one or more issues and whose decision or recommendation can be binding on the parties if approved by the court.

(d) A lawyer connected with a case shall not communicate directly or indirectly with anyone the lawyer knows* to be a member of the venire from which the jury will be selected for trial of that case.

(e) During trial, a lawyer connected with the case shall not communicate directly or indirectly with any juror.

(f) During trial, a lawyer who is not connected with the case shall not communicate directly or indirectly concerning the case with anyone the lawyer knows* is a juror in the case.

(g) After discharge of the jury from further consideration of a case a lawyer shall not communicate directly or indirectly with a juror if:

(1) the communication is prohibited by law or court order;

(2) the juror has made known* to the lawyer a desire not to communicate; or

(3) the communication involves misrepresentation, coercion, or duress, or is intended to harass or embarrass the juror or to influence the juror's actions in future jury service.

(h) A lawyer shall not directly or indirectly conduct an out of court investigation of a person* who is either a member of a venire or a juror in a manner likely to influence the state of mind of such person* in connection with present or future jury service.

(i) All restrictions imposed by this rule also apply to communications with, or investigations of, members of the family of a person* who is either a member of a venire or a juror.

(j) A lawyer shall reveal promptly to the court improper conduct by a person* who is either a member of a venire or a juror, or by another toward a person* who is either a member of a venire or a juror or a member of his or her family, of which the lawyer has knowledge.

(k) This rule does not prohibit a lawyer from communicating with persons* who are members of a venire or jurors as a part of the official proceedings.

(*l*) For purposes of this rule, "juror" means any empaneled, discharged, or excused juror.

Comment

[1] An applicable code of judicial ethics or code of judicial conduct under this rule includes the California Code of Judicial Ethics and the Code of Conduct for United States Judges. Regarding employees of a tribunal* not subject to judicial ethics or conduct codes, applicable standards include the Code of Ethics for the Court Employees of California and 5 United States Code section 7353 (Gifts to Federal employees). The statutes applicable to adjudicatory proceedings of state agencies generally are contained in the Administrative Procedure Act (Gov. Code, § 11340 et seq.; see Gov. Code, § 11370 [listing statutes with the act].) State and local agencies also may adopt their own regulations and rules governing communications with members or employees of a tribunal.*

[2] For guidance on permissible communications with a juror in a criminal action after discharge of the jury, see Code of Civil Procedure section 206.

[3] It is improper for a lawyer to communicate with a juror who has been removed, discharged, or excused from an empaneled jury, regardless of whether notice is given to other counsel, until such time as the entire jury has been discharged from further service or unless the communication is part of the official proceedings of the case.

(Adopted Sept. 26, 2018, eff. Nov. 1, 2018.)

Rule 3.6 Trial Publicity

(a) A lawyer who is participating or has participated in the investigation or litigation of a matter shall not make an extrajudicial statement that the lawyer knows* or reasonably should know* will (i) be disseminated by means of public communication and (ii) have a substantial* likelihood of materially prejudicing an adjudicative proceeding in the matter.

(b) Notwithstanding paragraph (a), but only to the extent permitted by Business and Professions Code section 6068, subdivision (e) and rule 1.6, lawyer may state:

(1) the claim, offense or defense involved and, except when prohibited by law, the identity of the persons* involved;

(2) information contained in a public record;

(3) that an investigation of a matter is in progress;

(4) the scheduling or result of any step in litigation;

(5) a request for assistance in obtaining evidence and information necessary thereto;

(6) a warning of danger concerning the behavior of a person* involved, when there is reason to believe* that there exists the likelihood of substantial* harm to an individual or to the public but only to the extent

---

* An asterisk (*) identifies a word or phrase defined in the terminology rule, rule 1.0.1.

that dissemination by public communication is reasonably* necessary to protect the individual or the public; and

(7)   in a criminal case, in addition to paragraphs (1) through (6):

(i)   the identity, general area of residence, and occupation of the accused;

(ii)   if the accused has not been apprehended, the information necessary to aid in apprehension of that person;*

(iii)   the fact, time, and place of arrest; and

(iv)   the identity of investigating and arresting officers or agencies and the length of the investigation.

(c)   Notwithstanding paragraph (a), a lawyer may make a statement that a reasonable* lawyer would believe* is required to protect a client from the substantial* undue prejudicial effect of recent publicity not initiated by the lawyer or the lawyer's client. A statement made pursuant to this paragraph shall be limited to such information as is necessary to mitigate the recent adverse publicity.

(d)   No lawyer associated in a law firm* or government agency with a lawyer subject to paragraph (a) shall make a statement prohibited by paragraph (a).

Comment

[1] Whether an extrajudicial statement violates this rule depends on many factors, including: (i) whether the extrajudicial statement presents information clearly inadmissible as evidence in the matter for the purpose of proving or disproving a material fact in issue; (ii) whether the extrajudicial statement presents information the lawyer knows* is false, deceptive, or the use of which would violate Business and Professions Code section 6068, subdivision (d) or rule 3.3; (iii) whether the extrajudicial statement violates a lawful "gag" order, or protective order, statute, rule of court, or special rule of confidentiality, for example, in juvenile, domestic, mental disability, and certain criminal proceedings, (see Bus. & Prof. Code, § 6068, subd. (a) and rule 3.4(f), which require compliance with such obligations); and (iv) the timing of the statement.

[2] This rule applies to prosecutors and criminal defense counsel. See rule 3.8(e) for additional duties of prosecutors in connection with extrajudicial statements about criminal proceedings.

(Adopted Sept. 26, 2018, eff. Nov. 1, 2018.)

Rule 3.7   Lawyer as Witness

(a)   A lawyer shall not act as an advocate in a trial in which the lawyer is likely to be a witness unless:

(1)   the lawyer's testimony relates to an uncontested issue or matter;

(2)   the lawyer's testimony relates to the nature and value of legal services rendered in the case; or

(3)   the lawyer has obtained informed written consent* from the client. If the lawyer represents the People or a governmental entity, the consent shall be obtained from the head of the office or a designee of the head of the office by which the lawyer is employed.

(b)   A lawyer may act as advocate in a trial in which another lawyer in the lawyer's firm* is likely to be called as a witness unless precluded from doing so by rule 1.7 or rule 1.9.

Comment

[1] This rule applies to a trial before a jury, judge, administrative law judge or arbitrator. This rule does not apply to other adversarial proceedings. This rule also does not apply in non-adversarial proceedings, as where a lawyer testifies on behalf of a client in a hearing before a legislative body.

[2] A lawyer's obligation to obtain informed written consent* may be satisfied when the lawyer makes the required disclosure, and the client gives informed consent* on the record in court before a licensed court reporter or court recorder who prepares a transcript or recording of the disclosure and consent. See definition of "written" in rule 1.0.1(n).

[3] Notwithstanding a client's informed written consent,* courts retain discretion to take action, up to and including disqualification of a lawyer who seeks to both testify and serve as an advocate, to protect the trier of fact from being misled or the opposing party from being prejudiced. (See, e.g., *Lyle v. Superior Court* (1981) 122 Cal.App.3d 470 [175 Cal.Rptr. 918].)

(Adopted Sept. 26, 2018, eff. Nov. 1, 2018.)

Rule 3.8   Special Responsibilities of a Prosecutor

The prosecutor in a criminal case shall:

(a)   not institute or continue to prosecute a charge that the prosecutor knows* is not supported by probable cause;

(b)   make reasonable* efforts to assure that the accused has been advised of the right to, and the procedure for obtaining, counsel and has been given reasonable* opportunity to obtain counsel;

(c)   not seek to obtain from an unrepresented accused a waiver of important pretrial rights unless the tribunal* has approved the appearance of the accused in propria persona;

(d)   make timely disclosure to the defense of all evidence or information known* to the prosecutor that the prosecutor knows* or reasonably should know* tends to negate the guilt of the accused, mitigate the offense, or mitigate the sentence, except when the prosecutor is relieved of this responsibility by a protective order of the tribunal;* and

(e)   exercise reasonable* care to prevent persons* under the supervision or direction of the prosecutor, including investigators, law enforcement personnel, employees or other persons* assisting or associated with the prosecutor in a criminal case from making an extrajudicial statement that the prosecutor would be prohibited from making under rule 3.6.

(f)   When a prosecutor knows* of new, credible and material evidence creating a reasonable* likelihood that a convicted defendant did not commit an offense of which the defendant was convicted, the prosecutor shall:

(1)   promptly disclose that evidence to an appropriate court or authority, and

(2)   if the conviction was obtained in the prosecutor's jurisdiction,

(i)   promptly disclose that evidence to the defendant unless a court authorizes delay, and

(ii)   undertake further investigation, or make reasonable* efforts to cause an investigation, to determine whether the defendant was convicted of an offense that the defendant did not commit.

(g)   When a prosecutor knows* of clear and convincing evidence establishing that a defendant in the prosecutor's jurisdiction was convicted of an offense that the defendant did not commit, the prosecutor shall seek to remedy the conviction.

Comment

[1] A prosecutor has the responsibility of a minister of justice and not simply that of an advocate. This responsibility carries with it specific obligations to see that the defendant is accorded procedural justice, that guilt is decided upon the basis of sufficient evidence, and that special precautions are taken to prevent and to rectify the conviction of innocent persons.* This rule is intended to achieve those results. All lawyers in government service remain bound by rules 3.1 and 3.4.

[2] Paragraph (c) does not forbid the lawful questioning of an uncharged suspect who has knowingly* waived the right to counsel and the right to remain silent. Paragraph (c) also does not forbid prosecutors from seeking from an unrepresented accused a reasonable* waiver of time for initial appearance or preliminary hearing as a means of facilitating the accused's voluntary cooperation in an ongoing law enforcement investigation.

[3] The disclosure obligations in paragraph (d) are not limited to evidence or information that is material as defined by *Brady v. Maryland* (1963) 373 U.S. 83 [83 S.Ct. 1194] and its progeny. For example, these obligations include, at a minimum, the duty to disclose impeachment evidence or information that a prosecutor knows* or reasonably should know* casts significant doubt on the accuracy or admissibility of witness testimony on which the prosecution intends to rely. Paragraph (d) does not require disclosure of information protected from disclosure by federal or California laws and rules, as interpreted by case law or court orders. Nothing in this rule is intended to be applied in a manner inconsistent with statutory and constitutional provisions governing discovery in California courts. A disclosure's timeliness will vary with the circumstances, and paragraph (d) is not intended to impose timing requirements different from those established by statutes, procedural rules, court orders, and case law interpreting those authorities and the California and federal constitutions.

[4] The exception in paragraph (d) recognizes that a prosecutor may seek an appropriate protective order from the tribunal* if disclosure of information to the defense could result in substantial* harm to an individual or to the public interest.

[5] Paragraph (e) supplements rule 3.6, which prohibits extrajudicial statements that have a substantial* likelihood of prejudicing an adjudicatory proceeding. Paragraph (e) is not intended to restrict the statements which a prosecutor may make which comply with rule 3.6(b) or 3.6(c).

[6] Prosecutors have a duty to supervise the work of subordinate lawyers and nonlawyer employees or agents. (See rules 5.1 and 5.3.) Ordinarily, the reasonable* care standard of paragraph (e) will be satisfied if the prosecutor issues the appropriate cautions to law enforcement personnel and other relevant individuals.

[7] When a prosecutor knows* of new, credible and material evidence creating a reasonable* likelihood that a person* outside the prosecutor's jurisdiction was convicted of a crime that the person* did not commit, paragraph (f) requires prompt disclosure to the court or other appropriate authority, such as the chief prosecutor of the jurisdiction where the conviction occurred. If the conviction was obtained in the prosecutor's jurisdiction, paragraph (f) requires the prosecutor to examine the evidence and undertake further investigation to determine whether the defendant is in fact innocent or make reasonable* efforts to cause another appropriate authority

---

* An asterisk (*) identifies a word or phrase defined in the terminology rule, rule 1.0.1.

to undertake the necessary investigation, and to promptly disclose the evidence to the court and, absent court authorized delay, to the defendant. Disclosure to a represented defendant must be made through the defendant's counsel, and, in the case of an unrepresented defendant, would ordinarily be accompanied by a request to a court for the appointment of counsel to assist the defendant in taking such legal measures as may be appropriate. (See rule 4.2.) Statutes may require a prosecutor to preserve certain types of evidence in criminal matters. (See Pen. Code, §§ 1417.1-1417.9.) In addition, prosecutors must obey file preservation orders concerning rights of discovery guaranteed by the Constitution and statutory provisions. (See People v. Superior Court (Morales) (2017) 2 Cal.5th 523 [213 Cal.Rptr.3d 581]; Shorts v. Superior Court (2018) 24 Cal.App.5th 709 [234 Cal.Rptr.3d 392].)

[8] Under paragraph (g), once the prosecutor knows* of clear and convincing evidence that the defendant was convicted of an offense that the defendant did not commit, the prosecutor must seek to remedy the conviction. Depending upon the circumstances, steps to remedy the conviction could include disclosure of the evidence to the defendant, requesting that the court appoint counsel for an unrepresented indigent defendant and, where appropriate, notifying the court that the prosecutor has knowledge that the defendant did not commit the offense of which the defendant was convicted.

[9] A prosecutor's independent judgment, made in good faith, that the new evidence is not of such nature as to trigger the obligations of paragraphs (f) and (g), though subsequently determined to have been erroneous, does not constitute a violation of this rule.

(Amended Apr. 23, 2020, eff. June 1, 2020; Adopted Sept. 26, 2018, eff. Nov. 1, 2018.)

Rule 3.9   Advocate in Nonadjudicative Proceedings

A lawyer representing a client before a legislative body or administrative agency in connection with a pending nonadjudicative matter or proceeding shall disclose that the appearance is in a representative capacity, except when the lawyer seeks information from an agency that is available to the public.

Comment

This rule only applies when a lawyer represents a client in connection with an official hearing or meeting of a governmental agency or a legislative body to which the lawyer or the lawyer's client is presenting evidence or argument. It does not apply to representation of a client in a negotiation or other bilateral transaction with a governmental agency or in connection with an application for a license or other privilege or the client's compliance with generally applicable reporting requirements, such as the filing of income-tax returns. This rule also does not apply to the representation of a client in connection with an investigation or examination of the client's affairs conducted by government investigators or examiners. Representation in such matters is governed by rules 4.1 through 4.4. This rule does not require a lawyer to disclose a client's identity.

(Adopted Sept. 26, 2018, eff. Nov. 1, 2018.)

Rule 3.10   Threatening Criminal, Administrative, or Disciplinary Charges

(a)   A lawyer shall not threaten to present criminal, administrative, or disciplinary charges to obtain an advantage in a civil dispute.

(b)   As used in paragraph (a) of this rule, the term "administrative charges" means the filing or lodging of a complaint with any governmental organization that may order or recommend the loss or suspension of a license, or may impose or recommend the imposition of a fine, pecuniary sanction, or other sanction of a quasi-criminal nature but does not include filing charges with an administrative entity required by law as a condition precedent to maintaining a civil action.

(c)   As used in this rule, the term "civil dispute" means a controversy or potential controversy over the rights and duties of two or more persons* under civil law, whether or not an action has been commenced, and includes an administrative proceeding of a quasi-civil nature pending before a federal, state, or local governmental entity.

Comment

[1] Paragraph (a) does not prohibit a statement by a lawyer that the lawyer will present criminal, administrative, or disciplinary charges, unless the statement is made to obtain an advantage in a civil dispute. For example, if a lawyer believes* in good faith that the conduct of the opposing lawyer or party violates criminal or other laws, the lawyer may state that if the conduct continues the lawyer will report it to criminal or administrative authorities. On the other hand, a lawyer could not state or imply that a criminal or administrative action will be pursued unless the opposing party agrees to settle the civil dispute.

[2] This rule does not apply to a threat to bring a civil action. It also does not prohibit actually presenting criminal, administrative or disciplinary charges, even if doing so creates an advantage in a civil dispute. Whether a lawyer's statement

violates this rule depends on the specific facts. (See, e.g., *Crane v. State Bar* (1981) 30 Cal.3d 117 [177 Cal.Rptr. 670].) A statement that the lawyer will pursue "all available legal remedies," or words of similar import, does not by itself violate this rule.

[3] This rule does not apply to: (i) a threat to initiate contempt proceedings for a failure to comply with a court order; or (ii) the offer of a civil compromise in accordance with a statute such as Penal Code sections 1377 and 1378.

[4] This rule does not prohibit a government lawyer from offering a global settlement or release-dismissal agreement in connection with related criminal, civil or administrative matters. The government lawyer must have probable cause for initiating or continuing criminal charges. (See rule 3.8(a).)

[5] As used in paragraph (b), "governmental organizations" includes any federal, state, local, and foreign governmental organizations. Paragraph (b) exempts the threat of filing an administrative charge that is a prerequisite to filing a civil complaint on the same transaction or occurrence.

(Adopted Sept. 26, 2018, eff. Nov. 1, 2018.)

CHAPTER 4
TRANSACTIONS WITH PERSONS* OTHER THAN CLIENTS

Truthfulness in Statements to Others. Rule 4.1.
Communication with a Represented Person. Rule 4.2.
Communicating with an Unrepresented Person. Rule 4.3.
Duties Concerning Inadvertently Transmitted Writings. Rule 4.4.

Rule 4.1   Truthfulness in Statements to Others

In the course of representing a client a lawyer shall not knowingly:*

(a)   make a false statement of material fact or law to a third person;* or

(b)   fail to disclose a material fact to a third person* when disclosure is necessary to avoid assisting a criminal or fraudulent* act by a client, unless disclosure is prohibited by Business and Professions Code section 6068, subdivision (e)(1) or rule 1.6.

Comment

[1] A lawyer is required to be truthful when dealing with others on a client's behalf, but generally has no affirmative duty to inform an opposing party of relevant facts. A misrepresentation can occur if the lawyer incorporates or affirms the truth of a statement of another person* that the lawyer knows* is false. However, in drafting an agreement or other document on behalf of a client, a lawyer does not necessarily affirm or vouch for the truthfulness of representations made by the client in the agreement or document. A nondisclosure can be the equivalent of a false statement of material fact or law under paragraph (a) where a lawyer makes a partially true but misleading material statement or material omission. In addition to this rule, lawyers remain bound by Business and Professions Code section 6106 and rule 8.4.

[2] This rule refers to statements of fact. Whether a particular statement should be regarded as one of fact can depend on the circumstances. For example, in negotiation, certain types of statements ordinarily are not taken as statements of material fact. Estimates of price or value placed on the subject of a transaction and a party's intentions as to an acceptable settlement of a claim are ordinarily in this category, and so is the existence of an undisclosed principal except where nondisclosure of the principal would constitute fraud.*

[3] Under rule 1.2.1, a lawyer is prohibited from counseling or assisting a client in conduct that the lawyer knows* is criminal or fraudulent.* See rule 1.4(a)(4) regarding a lawyer's obligation to consult with the client about limitations on the lawyer's conduct. In some circumstances, a lawyer can avoid assisting a client's crime or fraud* by withdrawing from the representation in compliance with rule 1.16.

[4] Regarding a lawyer's involvement in lawful covert activity in the investigation of violations of law, see rule 8.4, Comment [5].

(Adopted Sept. 26, 2018, eff. Nov. 1, 2018.)

Rule 4.2   Communication with a Represented Person*

(a)   In representing a client, a lawyer shall not communicate directly or indirectly about the subject of the representation with a person* the lawyer knows* to be represented by another lawyer in the matter, unless the lawyer has the consent of the other lawyer.

(b)   In the case of a represented corporation, partnership, association, or other private or governmental organization, this rule prohibits communications with:

(1)   A current officer, director, partner,*or managing agent of the organization; or

(2)   A current employee, member, agent, or other constituent of the organization, if the subject of the communication is any act or omission of such person* in connection with the matter which may be binding upon or imputed to the organization for purposes of civil or criminal liability.

---

* An asterisk (*) identifies a word or phrase defined in the terminology rule, rule 1.0.1.

(c)   This rule shall not prohibit:

(1)   communications with a public official, board, committee, or body; or

(2)   communications otherwise authorized by law or a court order.

(d)   For purposes of this rule:

(1)   "Managing agent" means an employee, member, agent, or other constituent of an organization with substantial* discretionary authority over decisions that determine organizational policy.

(2)   "Public official" means a public officer of the United States government, or of a state, county, city, town, political subdivision, or other governmental organization, with the comparable decision-making authority and responsibilities as the organizational constituents described in paragraph (b)(1).

Comment

[1] This rule applies even though the represented person* initiates or consents to the communication. A lawyer must immediately terminate communication with a person* if, after commencing communication, the lawyer learns that the person* is one with whom communication is not permitted by this rule.

[2] "Subject of the representation," "matter," and "person" are not limited to a litigation context. This rule applies to communications with any person,* whether or not a party to a formal adjudicative proceeding, contract, or negotiation, who is represented by counsel concerning the matter to which the communication relates.

[3] The prohibition against communicating "indirectly" with a person* represented by counsel in paragraph (a) is intended to address situations where a lawyer seeks to communicate with a represented person* through an intermediary such as an agent, investigator or the lawyer's client. This rule, however, does not prevent represented persons* from communicating directly with one another with respect to the subject of the representation, nor does it prohibit a lawyer from advising a client concerning such a communication. A lawyer may also advise a client not to accept or engage in such communications. The rule also does not prohibit a lawyer who is a party to a legal matter from communicating on his or her own behalf with a represented person* in that matter.

[4] This rule does not prohibit communications with a represented person* concerning matters outside the representation. Similarly, a lawyer who knows* that a person* is being provided with limited scope representation is not prohibited from communicating with that person* with respect to matters that are outside the scope of the limited representation. (See, e.g., Cal. Rules of Court, rules 3.35 – 3.37, 5.425 [Limited Scope Representation].)

[5] This rule does not prohibit communications initiated by a represented person* seeking advice or representation from an independent lawyer of the person's* choice.

[6] If a current constituent of the organization is represented in the matter by his or her own counsel, the consent by that counsel to a communication is sufficient for purposes of this rule.

[7] This rule applies to all forms of governmental and private organizations, such as cities, counties, corporations, partnerships, limited liability companies, and unincorporated associations. When a lawyer communicates on behalf of a client with a governmental organization, or certain employees, members, agents, or other constituents of a governmental organization, however, special considerations exist as a result of the right to petition conferred by the First Amendment of the United States Constitution and article I, section 3 of the California Constitution. Paragraph (c)(1) recognizes these special considerations by generally exempting from application of this rule communications with public boards, committees, and bodies, and with public officials as defined in paragraph (d)(2) of this rule. Communications with a governmental organization constituent who is not a public official, however, will remain subject to this rule when the lawyer knows* the governmental organization is represented in the matter and the communication with that constituent falls within paragraph (b)(2).

[8] Paragraph (c)(2) recognizes that statutory schemes, case law, and court orders may authorize communications between a lawyer and a person* that would otherwise be subject to this rule. Examples of such statutory schemes include those protecting the right of employees to organize and engage in collective bargaining, employee health and safety, and equal employment opportunity. The law also recognizes that prosecutors and other government lawyers are authorized to contact represented persons,* either directly or through investigative agents and informants, in the context of investigative activities, as limited by relevant federal and state constitutions, statutes, rules, and case law. (See, e.g., *United States v. Carona* (9th Cir. 2011) 630 F.3d 917; *United States v. Talao* (9th Cir. 2000) 222 F.3d 1133.) The rule is not intended to preclude communications with represented persons* in the course of such legitimate investigative activities as authorized by law. This rule also is not intended to preclude communications with represented persons* in the course of legitimate investigative activities engaged in, directly or indirectly, by lawyers representing persons* whom the government has accused of or is investigating for crimes, to the extent those investigative activities are authorized by law.

[9] A lawyer who communicates with a represented person* pursuant to paragraph (c) is subject to other restrictions in communicating with the person.* (See, e.g. Bus. & Prof. Code, § 6106; *Snider v. Superior Court* (2003) 113 Cal.App.4th 1187, 1213 [7 Cal.Rptr.3d 119]; *In the Matter of Dale* (2005) 4 Cal. State Bar Ct. Rptr. 798.)

(Adopted Sept. 26, 2018, eff. Nov. 1, 2018.)

Rule 4.3   Communicating with an Unrepresented Person*

(a)   In communicating on behalf of a client with a person* who is not represented by counsel, a lawyer shall not state or imply that the lawyer is disinterested. When the lawyer knows* or reasonably should know* that the unrepresented person* incorrectly believes* the lawyer is disinterested in the matter, the lawyer shall make reasonable* efforts to correct the misunderstanding. If the lawyer knows* or reasonably should know* that the interests of the unrepresented person* are in conflict with the interests of the client, the lawyer shall not give legal advice to that person,* except that the lawyer may, but is not required to, advise the person* to secure counsel.

(b)   In communicating on behalf of a client with a person* who is not represented by counsel, a lawyer shall not seek to obtain privileged or other confidential information the lawyer knows* or reasonably should know* the person* may not reveal without violating a duty to another or which the lawyer is not otherwise entitled to receive.

Comment

[1] This rule is intended to protect unrepresented persons,* whatever their interests, from being misled when communicating with a lawyer who is acting for a client.

[2] Paragraph (a) distinguishes between situations in which a lawyer knows* or reasonably should know* that the interests of an unrepresented person* are in conflict with the interests of the lawyer's client and situations in which the lawyer does not. In the former situation, the possibility that the lawyer will compromise the unrepresented person's* interests is so great that the rule prohibits the giving of any legal advice, apart from the advice to obtain counsel. A lawyer does not give legal advice merely by stating a legal position on behalf of the lawyer's client. This rule does not prohibit a lawyer from negotiating the terms of a transaction or settling a dispute with an unrepresented person.* So long as the lawyer discloses that the lawyer represents an adverse party and not the person,* the lawyer may inform the person* of the terms on which the lawyer's client will enter into the agreement or settle the matter, prepare documents that require the person's* signature, and explain the lawyer's own view of the meaning of the document and the underlying legal obligations.

[3] Regarding a lawyer's involvement in lawful covert activity in the investigation of violations of law, see rule 8.4, Comment [5].

(Adopted Sept. 26, 2018, eff. Nov. 1, 2018.)

Rule 4.4   Duties Concerning Inadvertently Transmitted Writings*

Where it is reasonably* apparent to a lawyer who receives a writing* relating to a lawyer's representation of a client that the writing* was inadvertently sent or produced, and the lawyer knows* or reasonably should know* that the writing* is privileged or subject to the work product doctrine, the lawyer shall:

(a)   refrain from examining the writing* any more than is necessary to determine that it is privileged or subject to the work product doctrine, and

(b)   promptly notify the sender.

Comment

[1] If a lawyer determines this rule applies to a transmitted writing,* the lawyer should return the writing* to the sender, seek to reach agreement with the sender regarding the disposition of the writing,* or seek guidance from a tribunal.* (See *Rico v. Mitsubishi* (2007) 42 Cal.4th 807, 817 [68 Cal.Rptr.3d 758].) In providing notice required by this rule, the lawyer shall comply with rule 4.2.

[2] This rule does not address the legal duties of a lawyer who receives a writing* that the lawyer knows* or reasonably should know* may have been inappropriately disclosed by the sending person.* (See *Clark v. Superior Court* (2011) 196 Cal.App.4th 37 [125 Cal.Rptr.3d 361].)

(Adopted Sept. 26, 2018, eff. Nov. 1, 2018.)

CHAPTER 5
LAW FIRMS* AND ASSOCIATIONS

Responsibilities of Managerial and Supervisory Lawyers. Rule 5.1.
Responsibilities of a Subordinate Lawyer. Rule 5.2.
Responsibilities Regarding Nonlawyer Assistants. Rule 5.3.
Employment of Disbarred, Suspended, Resigned, or Involuntarily Inactive Lawyer. Rule 5.3.1.

---

* An asterisk (*) identifies a word or phrase defined in the terminology rule, rule 1.0.1.

Financial and Similar Arrangements with Nonlawyers. Rule 5.4.
Unauthorized Practice of Law; Multijurisdictional Practice of Law. Rule 5.5.
Restrictions on a Lawyer's Right to Practice. Rule 5.6.

Rule 5.1   Responsibilities of Managerial and Supervisory Lawyers

(a)   A lawyer who individually or together with other lawyers possesses managerial authority in a law firm,* shall make reasonable* efforts to ensure that the firm* has in effect measures giving reasonable* assurance that all lawyers in the firm* comply with these rules and the State Bar Act.

(b)   A lawyer having direct supervisory authority over another lawyer, whether or not a member or employee of the same law firm,* shall make reasonable* efforts to ensure that the other lawyer complies with these rules and the State Bar Act.

(c)   A lawyer shall be responsible for another lawyer's violation of these rules and the State Bar Act if:

(1)   the lawyer orders or, with knowledge of the relevant facts and of the specific conduct, ratifies the conduct involved; or

(2)   the lawyer, individually or together with other lawyers, possesses managerial authority in the law firm* in which the other lawyer practices, or has direct supervisory authority over the other lawyer, whether or not a member or employee of the same law firm,* and knows* of the conduct at a time when its consequences can be avoided or mitigated but fails to take reasonable* remedial action.

Comment
Paragraph (a) – Duties Of Managerial Lawyers To Reasonably* Assure Compliance with the Rules

[1] Paragraph (a) requires lawyers with managerial authority within a law firm* to make reasonable* efforts to establish internal policies and procedures designed, for example, to detect and resolve conflicts of interest, identify dates by which actions must be taken in pending matters, account for client funds and property, and ensure that inexperienced lawyers are properly supervised.

[2] Whether particular measures or efforts satisfy the requirements of paragraph (a) might depend upon the law firm's structure and the nature of its practice, including the size of the law firm,* whether it has more than one office location or practices in more than one jurisdiction, or whether the firm* or its partners* engage in any ancillary business.

[3] A partner,* shareholder or other lawyer in a law firm* who has intermediate managerial responsibilities satisfies paragraph (a) if the law firm* has a designated managing lawyer charged with that responsibility, or a management committee or other body that has appropriate managerial authority and is charged with that responsibility. For example, the managing lawyer of an office of a multi-office law firm* would not necessarily be required to promulgate firm-wide policies intended to reasonably* assure that the law firm's lawyers comply with the rules or State Bar Act. However, a lawyer remains responsible to take corrective steps if the lawyer knows* or reasonably should know* that the delegated body or person* is not providing or implementing measures as required by this rule.

[4] Paragraph (a) also requires managerial lawyers to make reasonable* efforts to assure that other lawyers in an agency or department comply with these rules and the State Bar Act. This rule contemplates, for example, the creation and implementation of reasonable* guidelines relating to the assignment of cases and the distribution of workload among lawyers in a public sector legal agency or other legal department. (See, e.g., State Bar of California, Guidelines on Indigent Defense Services Delivery Systems (2006).)

Paragraph (b) – Duties of Supervisory Lawyers
[5] Whether a lawyer has direct supervisory authority over another lawyer in particular circumstances is a question of fact.

Paragraph (c) – Responsibility for Another's Lawyer's Violation
[6] The appropriateness of remedial action under paragraph (c)(2) would depend on the nature and seriousness of the misconduct and the nature and immediacy of its harm. A managerial or supervisory lawyer must intervene to prevent avoidable consequences of misconduct if the lawyer knows* that the misconduct occurred.

[7] A supervisory lawyer violates paragraph (b) by failing to make the efforts required under that paragraph, even if the lawyer does not violate paragraph (c) by knowingly* directing or ratifying the conduct, or where feasible, failing to take reasonable* remedial action.

[8] Paragraphs (a), (b), and (c) create independent bases for discipline. This rule does not impose vicarious responsibility on a lawyer for the acts of another lawyer who is in or outside the law firm.* Apart from paragraph (c) of this rule and rule 8.4(a), a lawyer does not have disciplinary liability for the conduct of a partner,* associate, or subordinate lawyer. The question of whether a lawyer can be liable civilly or criminally for another lawyer's conduct is beyond the scope of these rules.

(Adopted Sept. 26, 2018, eff. Nov. 1, 2018.)

Rule 5.2   Responsibilities of a Subordinate Lawyer

(a)   A lawyer shall comply with these rules and the State Bar Act notwithstanding that the lawyer acts at the direction of another lawyer or other person.*

(b)   A subordinate lawyer does not violate these rules or the State Bar Act if that lawyer acts in accordance with a supervisory lawyer's reasonable* resolution of an arguable question of professional duty.

Comment
When lawyers in a supervisor-subordinate relationship encounter a matter involving professional judgment as to the lawyers' responsibilities under these rules or the State Bar Act and the question can reasonably* be answered only one way, the duty of both lawyers is clear and they are equally responsible for fulfilling it. Accordingly, the subordinate lawyer must comply with his or her obligations under paragraph (a). If the question reasonably* can be answered more than one way, the supervisory lawyer may assume responsibility for determining which of the reasonable* alternatives to select, and the subordinate may be guided accordingly. If the subordinate lawyer believes* that the supervisor's proposed resolution of the question of professional duty would result in a violation of these rules or the State Bar Act, the subordinate is obligated to communicate his or her professional judgment regarding the matter to the supervisory lawyer.

(Adopted Sept. 26, 2018, eff. Nov. 1, 2018.)

Rule 5.3   Responsibilities Regarding Nonlawyer Assistants

With respect to a nonlawyer employed or retained by or associated with a lawyer:

(a)   a lawyer who individually or together with other lawyers possesses managerial authority in a law firm,* shall make reasonable* efforts to ensure that the firm* has in effect measures giving reasonable* assurance that the nonlawyer's conduct is compatible with the professional obligations of the lawyer;

(b)   a lawyer having direct supervisory authority over the nonlawyer, whether or not an employee of the same law firm,* shall make reasonable* efforts to ensure that the person's* conduct is compatible with the professional obligations of the lawyer; and

(c)   a lawyer shall be responsible for conduct of such a person* that would be a violation of these rules or the State Bar Act if engaged in by a lawyer if:

(1)   the lawyer orders or, with knowledge of the relevant facts and of the specific conduct, ratifies the conduct involved; or

(2)   the lawyer, individually or together with other lawyers, possesses managerial authority in the law firm* in which the person* is employed, or has direct supervisory authority over the person,* whether or not an employee of the same law firm,* and knows* of the conduct at a time when its consequences can be avoided or mitigated but fails to take reasonable* remedial action.

Comment
Lawyers often utilize nonlawyer personnel, including secretaries, investigators, law student interns, and paraprofessionals. Such assistants, whether employees or independent contractors, act for the lawyer in rendition of the lawyer's professional services. A lawyer must give such assistants appropriate instruction and supervision concerning all ethical aspects of their employment. The measures employed in instructing and supervising nonlawyers should take account of the fact that they might not have legal training.

(Adopted Sept. 26, 2018, eff. Nov. 1, 2018.)

Rule 5.3.1   Employment of Disbarred, Suspended, Resigned, or Involuntarily Inactive Lawyer

(a)   For purposes of this rule:

(1)   "Employ" means to engage the services of another, including employees, agents, independent contractors and consultants, regardless of whether any compensation is paid;

(2)   "Member" means a member of the State Bar of California;

(3)   "Involuntarily inactive member" means a member who is ineligible to practice law as a result of action taken pursuant to Business and Professions Code sections 6007, 6203, subdivision (d)(1), or California Rules of Court, rule 9.31(d);

(4)   "Resigned member" means a member who has resigned from the State Bar while disciplinary charges are pending; and

(5)   "Ineligible person" means a member whose current status with the State Bar of California is disbarred, suspended, resigned, or involuntarily inactive.

(b)   A lawyer shall not employ, associate in practice with, or assist a person* the lawyer knows* or reasonably should know* is an ineligible person to perform the following on behalf of the lawyer's client:

---
* An asterisk (*) identifies a word or phrase defined in the terminology rule, rule 1.0.1.

(1)   Render legal consultation or advice to the client;

(2)   Appear on behalf of a client in any hearing or proceeding or before any judicial officer, arbitrator, mediator, court, public agency, referee, magistrate, commissioner, or hearing officer;

(3)   Appear as a representative of the client at a deposition or other discovery matter;

(4)   Negotiate or transact any matter for or on behalf of the client with third parties;

(5)   Receive, disburse or otherwise handle the client's funds; or

(6)   Engage in activities that constitute the practice of law.

(c)   A lawyer may employ, associate in practice with, or assist an ineligible person to perform research, drafting or clerical activities, including but not limited to:

(1)   Legal work of a preparatory nature, such as legal research, the assemblage of data and other necessary information, drafting of pleadings, briefs, and other similar documents;

(2)   Direct communication with the client or third parties regarding matters such as scheduling, billing, updates, confirmation of receipt or sending of correspondence and messages; or

(3)   Accompanying an active lawyer in attending a deposition or other discovery matter for the limited purpose of providing clerical assistance to the active lawyer who will appear as the representative of the client.

(d)   Prior to or at the time of employing, associating in practice with, or assisting a person* the lawyer knows* or reasonably should know* is an ineligible person, the lawyer shall serve upon the State Bar written* notice of the employment, including a full description of such person's current bar status. The written* notice shall also list the activities prohibited in paragraph (b) and state that the ineligible person will not perform such activities. The lawyer shall serve similar written* notice upon each client on whose specific matter such person* will work, prior to or at the time of employing, associating with, or assisting such person* to work on the client's specific matter. The lawyer shall obtain proof of service of the client's written* notice and shall retain such proof and a true and correct copy of the client's written* notice for two years following termination of the lawyer's employment by the client.

(e)   A lawyer may, without client or State Bar notification, employ, associate in practice with, or assist an ineligible person whose sole function is to perform office physical plant or equipment maintenance, courier or delivery services, catering, reception, typing or transcription, or other similar support activities.

(f)   When the lawyer no longer employs, associates in practice with, or assists the ineligible person, the lawyer shall promptly serve upon the State Bar written* notice of the termination.

Comment

If the client is an organization, the lawyer shall serve the notice required by paragraph (d) on its highest authorized officer, employee, or constituent overseeing the particular engagement. (See rule 1.13.)

(Adopted Sept. 26, 2018, eff. Nov. 1, 2018.)

Rule 5.4   Financial and Similar Arrangements with Nonlawyers

(a)   A lawyer or law firm* shall not share legal fees directly or indirectly with a nonlawyer or with an organization that is not authorized to practice law, except that:

(1)   an agreement by a lawyer with the lawyer's firm,* partner,* or associate may provide for the payment of money or other consideration over a reasonable* period of time after the lawyer's death, to the lawyer's estate or to one or more specified persons;*

(2)   a lawyer purchasing the practice of a deceased, disabled or disappeared lawyer may pay the agreed-upon purchase price, pursuant to rule 1.17, to the lawyer's estate or other representative;

(3)   a lawyer or law firm* may include nonlawyer employees in a compensation or retirement plan, even though the plan is based in whole or in part on a profit-sharing arrangement, provided the plan does not otherwise violate these rules or the State Bar Act;

(4)   a lawyer or law firm* may pay a prescribed registration, referral, or other fee to a lawyer referral service established, sponsored and operated in accordance with the State Bar of California's Minimum Standards for Lawyer Referral Services; or

(5)   a lawyer or law firm* may share with or pay a court-awarded legal fee to a nonprofit organization that employed, retained or recommended employment of the lawyer or law firm* in the matter.

(b)   A lawyer shall not form a partnership or other organization with a nonlawyer if any of the activities of the partnership or other organization consist of the practice of law.

(c)   A lawyer shall not permit a person* who recommends, employs, or pays the lawyer to render legal services for another to direct or regulate the lawyer's independent professional judgment or interfere with the lawyer-client relationship in rendering legal services.

(d)   A lawyer shall not practice with or in the form of a professional corporation or other organization authorized to practice law for a profit if:

(1)   a nonlawyer owns any interest in it, except that a fiduciary representative of a lawyer's estate may hold the lawyer's stock or other interest for a reasonable* time during administration;

(2)   a nonlawyer is a director or officer of the corporation or occupies a position of similar responsibility in any other form of organization; or

(3)   a nonlawyer has the right or authority to direct or control the lawyer's independent professional judgment.

(e)   The Board of Trustees of the State Bar shall formulate and adopt Minimum Standards for Lawyer Referral Services, which, as from time to time amended, shall be binding on lawyers. A lawyer shall not accept a referral from, or otherwise participate in, a lawyer referral service unless it complies with such Minimum Standards for Lawyer Referral Services.

(f)   A lawyer shall not practice with or in the form of a nonprofit legal aid, mutual benefit or advocacy group if the nonprofit organization allows any third person* to interfere with the lawyer's independent professional judgment, or with the lawyer-client relationship, or allows or aids any person* to practice law in violation of these rules or the State Bar Act.

Comment

[1]   Paragraph (a) does not prohibit a lawyer or law firm* from paying a bonus to or otherwise compensating a nonlawyer employee from general revenues received for legal services, provided the arrangement does not interfere with the independent professional judgment of the lawyer or lawyers in the firm* and does not violate these rules or the State Bar Act. However, a nonlawyer employee's bonus or other form of compensation may not be based on a percentage or share of fees in specific cases or legal matters.

[2]   Paragraph (a) also does not prohibit payment to a nonlawyer third-party for goods and services provided to a lawyer or law firm;* however, the compensation to a nonlawyer third-party may not be determined as a percentage or share of the lawyer's or law firm's overall revenues or tied to fees in particular cases or legal matters. A lawyer may pay to a nonlawyer third-party, such as a collection agency, a percentage of past due or delinquent fees in concluded matters that the third-party collects on the lawyer's behalf.

[3]   Paragraph (a)(5) permits a lawyer to share with or pay court-awarded legal fees to nonprofit legal aid, mutual benefit, and advocacy groups that are not engaged in the unauthorized practice of law. (See *Frye v. Tenderloin Housing Clinic, Inc.* (2006) 38 Cal.4th 23 [40 Cal.Rptr.3d 221]; see also rule 6.3.) Regarding a lawyer's contribution of legal fees to a legal services organization, see rule 1.0, Comment [5] on financial support for programs providing pro bono legal services.

[4]   This rule is not intended to affect case law regarding the relationship between insurers and lawyers providing legal services to insureds. (See, e.g., *Gafcon, Inc. v. Ponsor Associates* (2002) 98 Cal.App.4th 1388 [120 Cal.Rptr.2d 392].)

[5]   Paragraph (c) is not intended to alter or diminish a lawyer's obligations under rule 1.8.6 (Compensation from One Other than Client).

(Adopted Sept. 26, 2018, eff. Nov. 1, 2018.)

Rule 5.5   Unauthorized Practice of Law; Multijurisdictional Practice of Law

(a)   A lawyer admitted to practice law in California shall not:

(1)   practice law in a jurisdiction where to do so would be in violation of regulations of the profession in that jurisdiction; or

(2)   knowingly* assist a person* in the unauthorized practice of law in that jurisdiction.

(b)   A lawyer who is not admitted to practice law in California shall not:

(1)   except as authorized by these rules or other law, establish or maintain a resident office or other systematic or continuous presence in California for the practice of law; or

(2)   hold out to the public or otherwise represent that the lawyer is admitted to practice law in California.

Comment

Paragraph (b)(1) prohibits lawyers from practicing law in California unless otherwise entitled to practice law in this state by court rule or other law. (See, e.g., Bus. & Prof. Code, § 6125 et seq.; see also Cal. Rules of Court, rules 9.40 [counsel

---

* An asterisk (*) identifies a word or phrase defined in the terminology rule, rule 1.0.1.

Rules of Conduct

pro hac vice], 9.41 [appearances by military counsel], 9.42 [certified law students], 9.43 [out-of-state attorney arbitration counsel program], 9.44 [registered foreign legal consultant], 9.45 [registered legal services attorneys], 9.46 [registered in-house counsel], 9.47 [attorneys practicing temporarily in California as part of litigation], 9.48 [non-litigating attorneys temporarily in California to provide legal services].)

(Adopted Sept. 26, 2018, eff. Nov. 1, 2018.)

Rule 5.6   Restrictions on a Lawyer's Right to Practice

(a) Unless authorized by law, a lawyer shall not participate in offering or making:

(1) a partnership, shareholders, operating, employment, or other similar type of agreement that restricts the right of a lawyer to practice after termination of the relationship, except an agreement that concerns benefits upon retirement; or

(2) an agreement that imposes a restriction on a lawyer's right to practice in connection with a settlement of a client controversy, or otherwise.

(b) A lawyer shall not participate in offering or making an agreement which precludes the reporting of a violation of these rules.

(c) This rule does not prohibit an agreement that is authorized by Business and Professions Code sections 6092.5, subdivision (i) or 6093.

Comment

[1] Concerning the application of paragraph (a)(1), see Business and Professions Code section 16602; *Howard v. Babcock* (1993) 6 Cal.4th 409, 425 [25 Cal.Rptr.2d 80].

[2] Paragraph (a)(2) prohibits a lawyer from offering or agreeing not to represent other persons* in connection with settling a claim on behalf of a client.

[3] This rule does not prohibit restrictions that may be included in the terms of the sale of a law practice pursuant to rule 1.17.

(Adopted Sept. 26, 2018, eff. Nov. 1, 2018.)

Rule 5.7   [Reserved]

CHAPTER 6
PUBLIC SERVICE

Membership in Legal Services Organization. Rule 6.3.
Limited Legal Services Programs. Rule 6.5.

Rule 6.1   [Reserved]

Rule 6.2   [Reserved]

Rule 6.3   Membership in Legal Services Organization

A lawyer may serve as a director, officer or member of a legal services organization, apart from the law firm* in which the lawyer practices, notwithstanding that the organization serves persons* having interests adverse to a client of the lawyer. The lawyer shall not knowingly* participate in a decision or action of the organization:

(a) if participating in the decision or action would be incompatible with the lawyer's obligations to a client under Business and Professions Code section 6068, subdivision (e)(1) or rules 1.6(a), 1.7, 1.9, or 1.18; or

(b) where the decision or action could have a material adverse effect on the representation of a client of the organization whose interests are adverse to a client of the lawyer.

Comment

Lawyers should support and participate in legal service organizations. A lawyer who is an officer or a member of such an organization does not thereby have a lawyer-client relationship with persons* served by the organization. However, there is potential conflict between the interests of such persons* and the interests of the lawyer's clients. If the possibility of such conflict disqualified a lawyer from serving on the board of a legal services organization, the profession's involvement in such organizations would be severely curtailed.

(Adopted Sept. 26, 2018, eff. Nov. 1, 2018.)

Rule 6.4   [Reserved]

Rule 6.5   Limited Legal Services Programs

(a) A lawyer who, under the auspices of a program sponsored by a court, government agency, bar association, law school, or nonprofit organization, provides short-term limited legal services to a client without expectation by either the lawyer or the client that the lawyer will provide continuing representation in the matter:

(1) is subject to rules 1.7 and 1.9(a) only if the lawyer knows* that the representation of the client involves a conflict of interest; and

(2) is subject to rule 1.10 only if the lawyer knows* that another lawyer associated with the lawyer in a law firm* is prohibited from representation by rule 1.7 or 1.9(a) with respect to the matter.

(b) Except as provided in paragraph (a)(2), rule 1.10 is inapplicable to a representation governed by this rule.

(c) The personal disqualification of a lawyer participating in the program will not be imputed to other lawyers participating in the program.

Comment

[1] Courts, government agencies, bar associations, law schools and various nonprofit organizations have established programs through which lawyers provide short-term limited legal services — such as advice or the completion of legal forms that will assist persons* in addressing their legal problems without further representation by a lawyer. In these programs, such as legal-advice hotlines, advice-only clinics or pro se counseling programs, whenever a lawyer-client relationship is established, there is no expectation that the lawyer's representation of the client will continue beyond that limited consultation. Such programs are normally operated under circumstances in which it is not feasible for a lawyer to systematically screen* for conflicts of interest as is generally required before undertaking a representation.

[2] A lawyer who provides short-term limited legal services pursuant to this rule must secure the client's informed consent* to the limited scope of the representation. (See rule 1.2(b).) If a short-term limited representation would not be reasonable* under the circumstances, the lawyer may offer advice to the client but must also advise the client of the need for further assistance of counsel. Except as provided in this rule, these rules and the State Bar Act, including the lawyer's duty of confidentiality under Business and Professions Code section 6068, subdivision (e)(1) and rules 1.6 and 1.9, are applicable to the limited representation.

[3] A lawyer who is representing a client in the circumstances addressed by this rule ordinarily is not able to check systematically for conflicts of interest. Therefore, paragraph (a)(1) requires compliance with rules 1.7 and 1.9(a) only if the lawyer knows* that the representation presents a conflict of interest for the lawyer. In addition, paragraph (a)(2) imputes conflicts of interest to the lawyer only if the lawyer knows* that another lawyer in the lawyer's law firm* would be disqualified under rules 1.7 or 1.9(a).

[4] Because the limited nature of the services significantly reduces the risk of conflicts of interest with other matters being handled by the lawyer's law firm,* paragraph (b) provides that imputed conflicts of interest are inapplicable to a representation governed by this rule except as provided by paragraph (a)(2). Paragraph (a)(2) imputes conflicts of interest to the participating lawyer when the lawyer knows* that any lawyer in the lawyer's firm* would be disqualified under rules 1.7 or 1.9(a). By virtue of paragraph (b), moreover, a lawyer's participation in a short-term limited legal services program will not be imputed to the lawyer's law firm* or preclude the lawyer's law firm* from undertaking or continuing the representation of a client with interests adverse to a client being represented under the program's auspices. Nor will the personal disqualification of a lawyer participating in the program be imputed to other lawyers participating in the program.

[5] If, after commencing a short-term limited representation in accordance with this rule, a lawyer undertakes to represent the client in the matter on an ongoing basis, rules 1.7, 1.9(a), and 1.10 become applicable.

(Adopted Sept. 26, 2018, eff. Nov. 1, 2018.)

CHAPTER 7
INFORMATION ABOUT LEGAL SERVICES

Communications Concerning a Lawyer's Services. Rule 7.1.
Advertising. Rule 7.2.
Solicitation of Clients. Rule 7.3.
Communication of Fields of Practice and Specialization. Rule 7.4.
Firm Names and Trade Names. Rule 7.5.

Rule 7.1   Communications Concerning a Lawyer's Services

(a) A lawyer shall not make a false or misleading communication about the lawyer or the lawyer's services. A communication is false or misleading if it contains a material misrepresentation of fact or law, or omits a fact necessary to make the communication considered as a whole not materially misleading.

(b) The Board of Trustees of the State Bar may formulate and adopt standards as to communications that will be presumed to violate rule 7.1, 7.2, 7.3, 7.4 or 7.5. The standards shall only be used as presumptions affecting the burden of proof in disciplinary proceedings involving alleged violations of these rules. "Presumption affecting the burden of proof"

---

* An asterisk (*) identifies a word or phrase defined in the terminology rule, rule 1.0.1.

means that presumption defined in Evidence Code sections 605 and 606. Such standards formulated and adopted by the Board, as from time to time amended, shall be effective and binding on all lawyers.

Comment

[1] This rule governs all communications of any type whatsoever about the lawyer or the lawyer's services, including advertising permitted by rule 7.2. A communication includes any message or offer made by or on behalf of a lawyer concerning the availability for professional employment of a lawyer or a lawyer's law firm* directed to any person.*

[2] A communication that contains an express guarantee or warranty of the result of a particular representation is a false or misleading communication under this rule. (See also Bus. & Prof. Code, § 6157.2, subd. (a).)

[3] This rule prohibits truthful statements that are misleading. A truthful statement is misleading if it omits a fact necessary to make the lawyer's communication considered as a whole not materially misleading. A truthful statement is also misleading if it is presented in a manner that creates a substantial* likelihood that it will lead a reasonable* person* to formulate a specific conclusion about the lawyer or the lawyer's services for which there is no reasonable* factual foundation. Any communication that states or implies "no fee without recovery" is also misleading unless the communication also expressly discloses whether or not the client will be liable for costs.

[4] A communication that truthfully reports a lawyer's achievements on behalf of clients or former clients, or a testimonial about or endorsement of the lawyer, may be misleading if presented so as to lead a reasonable* person* to form an unjustified expectation that the same results could be obtained for other clients in similar matters without reference to the specific factual and legal circumstances of each client's case. Similarly, an unsubstantiated comparison of the lawyer's services or fees with the services or fees of other lawyers may be misleading if presented with such specificity as would lead a reasonable* person* to conclude that the comparison can be substantiated. An appropriate disclaimer or qualifying language often avoids creating unjustified expectations.

[5] This rule prohibits a lawyer from making a communication that states or implies that the lawyer is able to provide legal services in a language other than English unless the lawyer can actually provide legal services in that language or the communication also states in the language of the communication the employment title of the person* who speaks such language.

[6] Rules 7.1 through 7.5 are not the sole basis for regulating communications concerning a lawyer's services. (See, e.g., Bus. & Prof. Code, §§ 6150–6159.2, 17000 et seq.) Other state or federal laws may also apply.

(Adopted Sept. 26, 2018, eff. Nov. 1, 2018.)

Rule 7.2   Advertising

(a)   Subject to the requirements of rules 7.1 and 7.3, a lawyer may advertise services through any written,* recorded or electronic means of communication, including public media.

(b)   A lawyer shall not compensate, promise or give anything of value to a person* for the purpose of recommending or securing the services of the lawyer or the lawyer's law firm,* except that a lawyer may:

(1)   pay the reasonable* costs of advertisements or communications permitted by this rule;

(2)   pay the usual charges of a legal services plan or a qualified lawyer referral service. A qualified lawyer referral service is a lawyer referral service established, sponsored and operated in accordance with the State Bar of California's Minimum Standards for a Lawyer Referral Service in California;

(3)   pay for a law practice in accordance with rule 1.17;

(4)   refer clients to another lawyer or a nonlawyer professional pursuant to an arrangement not otherwise prohibited under these Rules or the State Bar Act that provides for the other person* to refer clients or customers to the lawyer, if:

(i)   the reciprocal referral arrangement is not exclusive; and

(ii)   the client is informed of the existence and nature of the arrangement;

(5)   offer or give a gift or gratuity to a person* having made a recommendation resulting in the employment of the lawyer or the lawyer's law firm,* provided that the gift or gratuity was not offered or given in consideration of any promise, agreement, or understanding that such a gift or gratuity would be forthcoming or that referrals would be made or encouraged in the future.

(c)   Any communication made pursuant to this rule shall include the name and address of at least one lawyer or law firm* responsible for its content.

Comment

[1] This rule permits public dissemination of accurate information concerning a lawyer and the lawyer's services, including for example, the lawyer's name or firm* name, the lawyer's contact information; the kinds of services the lawyer will undertake; the basis on which the lawyer's fees are determined, including prices for specific services and payment and credit arrangements; a lawyer's foreign language ability; names of references and, with their consent, names of clients regularly represented; and other information that might invite the attention of those seeking legal assistance. This rule, however, prohibits the dissemination of false or misleading information, for example, an advertisement that sets forth a specific fee or range of fees for a particular service where, in fact, the lawyer charges or intends to charge a greater fee than that stated in the advertisement.

[2] Neither this rule nor rule 7.3 prohibits communications authorized by law, such as court-approved class action notices.

Paying Others to Recommend a Lawyer

[3] Paragraph (b)(1) permits a lawyer to compensate employees, agents, and vendors who are engaged to provide marketing or client-development services, such as publicists, public-relations personnel, business-development staff, and website designers. See rule 5.3 for the duties of lawyers and law firms* with respect to supervising the conduct of nonlawyers who prepare marketing materials and provide client development services.

[4] Paragraph (b)(4) permits a lawyer to make referrals to another lawyer or nonlawyer professional, in return for the undertaking of that person* to refer clients or customers to the lawyer. Such reciprocal referral arrangements must not interfere with the lawyer's professional judgment as to making referrals or as to providing substantive legal services. (See rules 2.1 and 5.4(c).) Conflicts of interest created by arrangements made pursuant to paragraph (b)(4) are governed by rule 1.7. A division of fees between or among lawyers not in the same law firm* is governed by rule 1.5.1.

(Adopted Sept. 26, 2018, eff. Nov. 1, 2018.)

Rule 7.3   Solicitation of Clients

(a)   A lawyer shall not by in-person, live telephone or real-time electronic contact solicit professional employment when a significant motive for doing so is the lawyer's pecuniary gain, unless the person* contacted:

(1)   is a lawyer; or

(2)   has a family, close personal, or prior professional relationship with the lawyer.

(b)   A lawyer shall not solicit professional employment by written,* recorded or electronic communication or by in-person, telephone or real-time electronic contact even when not otherwise prohibited by paragraph (a), if:

(1)   the person* being solicited has made known* to the lawyer a desire not to be solicited by the lawyer; or

(2)   the solicitation is transmitted in any manner which involves intrusion, coercion, duress or harassment.

(c)   Every written,* recorded or electronic communication from a lawyer soliciting professional employment from any person* known* to be in need of legal services in a particular matter shall include the word "Advertisement" or words of similar import on the outside envelope, if any, and at the beginning and ending of any recorded or electronic communication, unless the recipient of the communication is a person* specified in paragraphs (a)(1) or (a)(2), or unless it is apparent from the context that the communication is an advertisement.

(d)   Notwithstanding the prohibitions in paragraph (a), a lawyer may participate with a prepaid or group legal service plan operated by an organization not owned or directed by the lawyer that uses in-person, live telephone or real-time electronic contact to solicit memberships or subscriptions for the plan from persons* who are not known* to need legal services in a particular matter covered by the plan.

(e)   As used in this rule, the terms "solicitation" and "solicit" refer to an oral or written* targeted communication initiated by or on behalf of the lawyer that is directed to a specific person* and that offers to provide, or can reasonably* be understood as offering to provide, legal services.

Comment

[1] A lawyer's communication does not constitute a solicitation if it is directed to the general public, such as through a billboard, an Internet banner advertisement, a website or a television commercial, or if it is in response to a request for information or is automatically generated in response to Internet searches.

[2] Paragraph (a) does not apply to situations in which the lawyer is motivated by considerations other than the lawyer's pecuniary gain. Therefore, paragraph (a) does not prohibit a lawyer from participating in constitutionally protected activities of bona fide public or charitable legal-service organizations, or bona fide political, social, civic, fraternal, employee or trade organizations whose purposes include

---

* An asterisk (*) identifies a word or phrase defined in the terminology rule, rule 1.0.1.

providing or recommending legal services to its members or beneficiaries. (See, e.g., *In re Primus* (1978) 436 U.S. 412 [98 S.Ct. 1893].)

[3] This rule does not prohibit a lawyer from contacting representatives of organizations or groups that may be interested in establishing a bona fide group or prepaid legal plan for their members, insureds, beneficiaries or other third parties for the purpose of informing such entities of the availability of and details concerning the plan or arrangement which the lawyer or lawyer's firm* is willing to offer.

[4] Lawyers who participate in a legal service plan as permitted under paragraph (d) must comply with rules 7.1, 7.2, and 7.3(b). (See also rules 5.4 and 8.4(a).)

(Adopted Sept. 26, 2018, eff. Nov. 1, 2018.)

Rule 7.4   Communication of Fields of Practice and Specialization

(a) A lawyer shall not state that the lawyer is a certified specialist in a particular field of law, unless:

(1) the lawyer is currently certified as a specialist by the Board of Legal Specialization, or any other entity accredited by the State Bar to designate specialists pursuant to standards adopted by the Board of Trustees; and

(2) the name of the certifying organization is clearly identified in the communication.

(b) Notwithstanding paragraph (a), a lawyer may communicate the fact that the lawyer does or does not practice in particular fields of law. A lawyer may also communicate that his or her practice specializes in, is limited to, or is concentrated in a particular field of law, subject to the requirements of rule 7.1.

(Adopted Sept. 26, 2018, eff. Nov. 1, 2018.)

Rule 7.5   Firm* Names and Trade Names

(a) A lawyer shall not use a firm* name, trade name or other professional designation that violates rule 7.1.

(b) A lawyer in private practice shall not use a firm* name, trade name or other professional designation that states or implies a relationship with a government agency or with a public or charitable legal services organization, or otherwise violates rule 7.1.

(c) A lawyer shall not state or imply that the lawyer practices in or has a professional relationship with a law firm* or other organization unless that is the fact.

Comment
The term "other professional designation" includes, but is not limited to, logos, letterheads, URLs, and signature blocks.

(Adopted Sept. 26, 2018, eff. Nov. 1, 2018.)

Rule 7.6   [Reserved]

CHAPTER 8
MAINTAINING THE INTEGRITY OF THE PROFESSION

False Statement Regarding Application for Admission to Practice Law. Rule 8.1.

Compliance with Conditions of Discipline and Agreements in Lieu of Discipline. Rule 8.1.1.

Judicial Officials. Rule 8.2.

Misconduct. Rule 8.4.

Prohibited Discrimination, Harassment and Retaliation. Rule 8.4.1.

Disciplinary Authority; Choice of Law. Rule 8.5.

Rule 8.1   False Statement Regarding Application for Admission to Practice Law

(a) An applicant for admission to practice law shall not, in connection with that person's* own application for admission, make a statement of material fact that the lawyer knows* to be false, or make such a statement with reckless disregard as to its truth or falsity.

(b) A lawyer shall not, in connection with another person's* application for admission to practice law, make a statement of material fact that the lawyer knows* to be false.

(c) An applicant for admission to practice law, or a lawyer in connection with an application for admission, shall not fail to disclose a fact necessary to correct a statement known* by the applicant or the lawyer to have created a material misapprehension in the matter, except that this rule does not authorize disclosure of information protected by Business and Professions Code section 6068, subdivision (e) and rule 1.6.

(d) As used in this rule, "admission to practice law" includes admission or readmission to membership in the State Bar; reinstatement to active membership in the State Bar; and any similar process relating to admission or certification to practice law in California or elsewhere.

Comment
[1] A person* who makes a false statement in connection with that person's* own application for admission to practice law may be subject to discipline under this rule after that person* has been admitted. (See, e.g., *In re Gossage* (2000) 23 Cal.4th 1080 [99 Cal.Rptr.2d 130].)

[2] A lawyer's duties with respect to a *pro hac vice* application or other application to a court for admission to practice law are governed by rule 3.3.

[3] A lawyer representing an applicant for admission to practice law is governed by the rules applicable to the lawyer-client relationship, including Business and Professions Code section 6068, subdivision (e)(1) and rule 1.6. A lawyer representing a lawyer who is the subject of a disciplinary proceeding is not governed by this rule but is subject to the requirements of rule 3.3.

(Adopted Sept. 26, 2018, eff. Nov. 1, 2018.)

Rule 8.1.1   Compliance with Conditions of Discipline and Agreements in Lieu of Discipline

A lawyer shall comply with the terms and conditions attached to any agreement in lieu of discipline, any public or private reproval, or to other discipline administered by the State Bar pursuant to Business and Professions Code sections 6077 and 6078 and California Rules of Court, rule 9.19.

Comment
Other provisions also require a lawyer to comply with agreements in lieu of discipline and conditions of discipline. (See, e.g., Bus. & Prof. Code, § 6068, subds. (k), (*l*).)

(Adopted Sept. 26, 2018, eff. Nov. 1, 2018.)

Rule 8.2   Judicial Officials

(a) A lawyer shall not make a statement of fact that the lawyer knows* to be false or with reckless disregard as to its truth or falsity concerning the qualifications or integrity of a judge or judicial officer, or of a candidate for election or appointment to judicial office.

(b) A lawyer who is a candidate for judicial office in California shall comply with canon 5 of the California Code of Judicial Ethics. For purposes of this rule, "candidate for judicial office" means a lawyer seeking judicial office by election. The determination of when a lawyer is a candidate for judicial office by election is defined in the terminology section of the California Code of Judicial Ethics. A lawyer's duty to comply with this rule shall end when the lawyer announces withdrawal of the lawyer's candidacy or when the results of the election are final, whichever occurs first.

(c) A lawyer who seeks appointment to judicial office shall comply with canon 5B(1) of the California Code of Judicial Ethics. A lawyer becomes an applicant seeking judicial office by appointment at the time of first submission of an application or personal data questionnaire to the appointing authority. A lawyer's duty to comply with this rule shall end when the lawyer advises the appointing authority of the withdrawal of the lawyer's application.

Comment
To maintain the fair and independent administration of justice, lawyers should defend judges and courts unjustly criticized. Lawyers also are obligated to maintain the respect due to the courts of justice and judicial officers. (See Bus. & Prof. Code, § 6068, subd. (b).)

(Adopted Sept. 26, 2018, eff. Nov. 1, 2018.)

Rule 8.3   [Reserved]

Rule 8.4   Misconduct

It is professional misconduct for a lawyer to:

(a) violate these rules or the State Bar Act, knowingly* assist, solicit, or induce another to do so, or do so through the acts of another;

(b) commit a criminal act that reflects adversely on the lawyer's honesty, trustworthiness, or fitness as a lawyer in other respects;

(c) engage in conduct involving dishonesty, fraud,* deceit, or reckless or intentional misrepresentation;

(d) engage in conduct that is prejudicial to the administration of justice;

(e) state or imply an ability to influence improperly a government agency or official, or to achieve results by means that violate these rules, the State Bar Act, or other law; or

---

* An asterisk (*) identifies a word or phrase defined in the terminology rule, rule 1.0.1.

(f)　knowingly* assist, solicit, or induce a judge or judicial officer in conduct that is a violation of an applicable code of judicial ethics or code of judicial conduct, or other law. For purposes of this rule, "judge" and "judicial officer" have the same meaning as in rule 3.5(c).

Comment

[1]　A violation of this rule can occur when a lawyer is acting in propria persona or when a lawyer is not practicing law or acting in a professional capacity.

[2]　Paragraph (a) does not prohibit a lawyer from advising a client concerning action the client is legally entitled to take.

[3]　A lawyer may be disciplined for criminal acts as set forth in Business and Professions Code sections 6101 et seq., or if the criminal act constitutes "other misconduct warranting discipline" as defined by California Supreme Court case law. (See *In re Kelley* (1990) 52 Cal.3d 487 [276 Cal.Rptr. 375].)

[4]　A lawyer may be disciplined under Business and Professions Code section 6106 for acts involving moral turpitude, dishonesty, or corruption, whether intentional, reckless, or grossly negligent.

[5]　Paragraph (c) does not apply where a lawyer advises clients or others about, or supervises, lawful covert activity in the investigation of violations of civil or criminal law or constitutional rights, provided the lawyer's conduct is otherwise in compliance with these rules and the State Bar Act.

[6]　This rule does not prohibit those activities of a particular lawyer that are protected by the First Amendment to the United States Constitution or by Article I, section 2 of the California Constitution.

(Adopted Sept. 26, 2018, eff. Nov. 1, 2018.)

Rule 8.4.1　Prohibited Discrimination, Harassment and Retaliation

(a)　In representing a client, or in terminating or refusing to accept the representation of any client, a lawyer shall not:

(1)　unlawfully harass or unlawfully discriminate against persons* on the basis of any protected characteristic; or

(2)　unlawfully retaliate against persons.*

(b)　In relation to a law firm's operations, a lawyer shall not:

(1)　on the basis of any protected characteristic,

(i)　unlawfully discriminate or knowingly* permit unlawful discrimination;

(ii)　unlawfully harass or knowingly* permit the unlawful harassment of an employee, an applicant, an unpaid intern or volunteer, or a person* providing services pursuant to a contract; or

(iii)　unlawfully refuse to hire or employ a person*, or refuse to select a person* for a training program leading to employment, or bar or discharge a person* from employment or from a training program leading to employment, or discriminate against a person* in compensation or in terms, conditions, or privileges of employment; or

(2)　unlawfully retaliate against persons.*

(c)　For purposes of this rule:

(1)　"protected characteristic" means race, religious creed, color, national origin, ancestry, physical disability, mental disability, medical condition, genetic information, marital status, sex, gender, gender identity, gender expression, sexual orientation, age, military and veteran status, or other category of discrimination prohibited by applicable law, whether the category is actual or perceived;

(2)　"knowingly permit" means to fail to advocate corrective action where the lawyer knows* of a discriminatory policy or practice that results in the unlawful discrimination or harassment prohibited by paragraph (b);

(3)　"unlawfully" and "unlawful" shall be determined by reference to applicable state and federal statutes and decisions making unlawful discrimination or harassment in employment and in offering goods and services to the public; and

(4)　"retaliate" means to take adverse action against a person* because that person* has (i) opposed, or (ii) pursued, participated in, or assisted any action alleging, any conduct prohibited by paragraphs (a)(1) or (b)(1) of this rule.

(d)　A lawyer who is the subject of a State Bar investigation or State Bar Court proceeding alleging a violation of this rule shall promptly notify the State Bar of any criminal, civil, or administrative action premised, whether in whole or part, on the same conduct that is the subject of the State Bar investigation or State Bar Court proceeding.

(e)　Upon being issued a notice of a disciplinary charge under this rule, a lawyer shall:

(1)　if the notice is of a disciplinary charge under paragraph (a) of this rule, provide a copy of the notice to the California Department of Fair Employment and Housing and the United States Department of Justice, Coordination and Review Section; or

(2)　if the notice is of a disciplinary charge under paragraph (b) of this rule, provide a copy of the notice to the California Department of Fair Employment and Housing and the United States Equal Employment Opportunity Commission.

(f)　This rule shall not preclude a lawyer from:

(1)　representing a client alleged to have engaged in unlawful discrimination, harassment, or retaliation;

(2)　declining or withdrawing from a representation as required or permitted by rule 1.16; or

(3)　providing advice and engaging in advocacy as otherwise required or permitted by these rules and the State Bar Act.

Comment

[1]　Conduct that violates this rule undermines confidence in the legal profession and our legal system and is contrary to the fundamental principle that all people are created equal. A lawyer may not engage in such conduct through the acts of another. (See rule 8.4(a).) In relation to a law firm's operations, this rule imposes on all law firm* lawyers the responsibility to advocate corrective action to address known* harassing or discriminatory conduct by the firm* or any of its other lawyers or nonlawyer personnel. Law firm* management and supervisorial lawyers retain their separate responsibility under rules 5.1 and 5.3. Neither this rule nor rule 5.1 or 5.3 imposes on the alleged victim of any conduct prohibited by this rule any responsibility to advocate corrective action.

[2]　The conduct prohibited by paragraph (a) includes the conduct of a lawyer in a proceeding before a judicial officer. (See Cal. Code Jud. Ethics, canon 3B(6) ["A judge shall require lawyers in proceedings before the judge to refrain from manifesting, by words or conduct, bias or prejudice based upon race, sex, gender, religion, national origin, ethnicity, disability, age, sexual orientation, marital status, socioeconomic status, or political affiliation against parties, witnesses, counsel, or others."].) A lawyer does not violate paragraph (a) by referring to any particular status or group when the reference is relevant to factual or legal issues or arguments in the representation. While both the parties and the court retain discretion to refer such conduct to the State Bar, a court's finding that peremptory challenges were exercised on a discriminatory basis does not alone establish a violation of paragraph (a).

[3]　A lawyer does not violate this rule by limiting the scope or subject matter of the lawyer's practice or by limiting the lawyer's practice to members of underserved populations. A lawyer also does not violate this rule by otherwise restricting who will be accepted as clients for advocacy-based reasons, as required or permitted by these rules or other law.

[4]　This rule does not apply to conduct protected by the First Amendment to the United States Constitution or by Article I, section 2 of the California Constitution.

[5]　What constitutes a failure to advocate corrective action under paragraph (c)(2) will depend on the nature and seriousness of the discriminatory policy or practice, the extent to which the lawyer knows* of unlawful discrimination or harassment resulting from that policy or practice, and the nature of the lawyer's relationship to the lawyer or law firm* implementing that policy or practice. For example, a law firm* non-management and non-supervisorial lawyer who becomes aware that the law firm* is engaging in a discriminatory hiring practice may advocate corrective action by bringing that discriminatory practice to the attention of a law firm* management lawyer who would have responsibility under rule 5.1 or 5.3 to take reasonable* remedial action upon becoming aware of a violation of this rule.

[6]　Paragraph (d) ensures that the State Bar and the State Bar Court will be provided with information regarding related proceedings that may be relevant in determining whether a State Bar investigation or a State Bar Court proceeding relating to a violation of this rule should be abated.

[7]　Paragraph (e) recognizes the public policy served by enforcement of laws and regulations prohibiting unlawful discrimination, by ensuring that the state and federal agencies with primary responsibility for coordinating the enforcement of those laws and regulations is provided with notice of any allegation of unlawful discrimination, harassment, or retaliation by a lawyer that the State Bar finds has sufficient merit to warrant issuance of a notice of a disciplinary charge.

[8]　This rule permits the imposition of discipline for conduct that would not necessarily result in the award of a remedy in a civil or administrative proceeding if such proceeding were filed.

[9]　A disciplinary investigation or proceeding for conduct coming within this rule may also be initiated and maintained if such conduct warrants discipline under California Business and Professions Code sections 6106 and 6068, the California Supreme Court's inherent authority to impose discipline, or other disciplinary standard.

(Adopted Sept. 26, 2018, eff. Nov. 1, 2018.)

Rule 8.5　Disciplinary Authority; Choice of Law

(a)　Disciplinary Authority.

---

* An asterisk (*) identifies a word or phrase defined in the terminology rule, rule 1.0.1.

A lawyer admitted to practice in California is subject to the disciplinary authority of California, regardless of where the lawyer's conduct occurs. A lawyer not admitted in California is also subject to the disciplinary authority of California if the lawyer provides or offers to provide any legal services in California. A lawyer may be subject to the disciplinary authority of both California and another jurisdiction for the same conduct.

(b)   Choice of Law.

In any exercise of the disciplinary authority of California, the rules of professional conduct to be applied shall be as follows:

(1)   for conduct in connection with a matter pending before a tribunal,* the rules of the jurisdiction in which the tribunal* sits, unless the rules of the tribunal* provide otherwise; and

(2)   for any other conduct, the rules of the jurisdiction in which the lawyer's conduct occurred, or, if the predominant effect of the conduct is in a different jurisdiction, the rules of that jurisdiction shall be applied to the conduct. A lawyer shall not be subject to discipline if the lawyer's conduct conforms to the rules of a jurisdiction in which the lawyer reasonably believes* the predominant effect of the lawyer's conduct will occur.

Comment

Disciplinary Authority

The conduct of a lawyer admitted to practice in California is subject to the disciplinary authority of California. (See Bus. & Prof. Code, §§ 6077, 6100.) Extension of the disciplinary authority of California to other lawyers who provide or offer to provide legal services in California is for the protection of the residents of California. A lawyer disciplined by a disciplinary authority in another jurisdiction may be subject to discipline in California for the same conduct. (See, e.g., § 6049.1.)

(Adopted Sept. 26, 2018, eff. Nov. 1, 2018.)

* An asterisk (*) identifies a word or phrase defined in the terminology rule, rule 1.0.1.

RULES AND POLICY DECLARATIONS OF THE COMMISSION ON JUDICIAL PERFORMANCE

2021 EDITION

The Rules of the Commission on Judicial Performance were adopted at the commission's October 22-23, 1996 meeting. The rules are effective December 1, 1996, and supersede Rules 901–922 of the Rules of Court.

The Policy Declarations of the Commission on Judicial Performance were approved by the commission on May 28, 1997.

The Rules and Policy Declarations of the Commission on Judicial Performance promulgated and adopted by the commission with amendments from November 21, 2019 through November 22, 2020.

The Rules of the Commission on Judicial Performance were last amended October 9, 2020. The Policy Declarations of the Commission on Judicial Performance were last amended July 1, 2020.

RULES AND POLICY DECLARATIONS OF THE COMMISSION ON JUDICIAL PERFORMANCE

2021 EDITION

The Rules of the Commission on Judicial Performance were adopted at the commission's October 22-23, 1994, meeting. The rules are effective December 1, 1996, and supersede Rules 901–922 and the Rules of Court.

The 2016 edition of the Rules of Judicial Performance were approved by the commission on March 9, 1996.

The Rules and Policy Declarations of the Commission on Judicial Performance promulgated and adopted by the commission at which are supplemental/overruled 21 to 2019 through November 2, 2020.

The Rules of the Commission on Judicial Performance were last amended October 9, 2020. The Policy Declarations of the Commission on Judicial Performance were last amended July 1, 2020.

PREFACE

From 1961 to 1994, the Judicial Council was responsible for promulgating rules of procedure for the Commission on Judicial Performance. The Judicial Council adopted rules 901–922 of the Rules of Court as rules for the censure, removal, retirement or private admonishment of judges.

Since its early history, the commission has deliberated on and recorded in its minutes its resolutions regarding significant policy issues. These resolutions address areas not detailed in its governing provisions (California Constitution, Rules of Court, and Government Code) including internal organization and management, staff functions, and implementation of the rules and statutes regarding formal proceedings and disability matters. In 1984, the commission collected the statements of existing policy in a single, amendable document entitled Policy Declarations of the Commission on Judicial Performance.

Proposition 190, approved by California voters in the November 1994 general election, took effect March 1, 1995. One of the most significant changes implemented by Proposition 190 was a change in authority for promulgating rules regarding commission procedures and confidentiality. The commission now has the authority to promulgate its own rules.

In April 1995, the commission adopted rules 901–922 of the Rules of Court as interim rules pending a comprehensive review of the rules. The commission also adopted Policy Declarations 1.1 through 4.4, amended rule 917 to require a vote of six members of the commission, and adopted transitional Rules 1, 2 and 3. The commission adopted two new rules, Rules 120 and 127, as interim rules in May 1996.

At its October 22-23, 1996 meeting, the commission adopted the Rules of the Commission on Judicial Performance. The commission Rules took effect December 1, 1996 and replaced rules 901–918 and 922 of the Rules of Court and transitional Rules 1, 2 and 3. Rules 919, 920 and 921 concern Supreme Court review of commission determinations and were not reviewed by the commission.

The Policy Declarations of the Commission on Judicial Performance were approved by the commission on May 28, 1997.

Table Showing Changes Promulgated by the Commission on Judicial Performance
From November 21, 2019 Through November 22, 2020

Rule	Effect	Date
102	Amended	Jan. 29, 2020
116	Amended	June 26, 2019
122	Amended	July 1, 2020
125	Amended	Oct. 9, 2020
128	Amended	Oct. 9, 2020
129	Amended	Oct. 9, 2020
138	Amended	Oct. 9, 2020

Policy Declaration	Effect	Date
3.5	Amended	July 1, 2020

Rules of Jud Perf

RULES OF THE COMMISSION ON JUDICIAL PERFORMANCE

Rule 101. Interested Party.

Judges who are members of the commission or of the Supreme Court may not participate as such in any commission proceedings involving themselves.

Adopted Oct. 24, 1996, effective Dec. 1, 1996.

Rule 102. Confidentiality and Disclosure.

(a) (Scope of rule) Except as provided in this rule, all papers filed with and proceedings before the commission shall be confidential. Nothing in this rule prohibits the respondent judge or anyone other than a commission member or member of commission staff from making statements regarding the judge's conduct underlying a complaint or proceeding.

(b) (Disclosure after institution of formal proceedings) When the commission institutes formal proceedings, the following shall not be confidential:

(1) The notice of formal proceedings and all subsequent papers filed with the commission and the special masters, all stipulations entered, all findings of fact and conclusions of law made by the special masters and by the commission, and all determinations of removal, censure and public admonishment made by the commission;

(2) The formal hearing before the special masters and the appearance before the commission.

(c) (Explanatory statements) The commission may issue explanatory statements under article VI, section 18(k) of the California Constitution.

(d) (Submission of proposed statement of clarification and correction regarding commission proceedings by judge) Notwithstanding rule 102(a), if public reports concerning a commission proceeding result in substantial unfairness to the judge involved in the proceeding, including unfairness resulting from reports which are false or materially misleading or inaccurate, the involved judge may submit a proposed statement of clarification and correction to the commission and request its issuance. The commission shall either issue the requested statement, advise the judge in writing that it declines to issue the requested statement, or issue a modified statement.

(e) (Disclosure to complainant) Upon completion of an investigation or proceeding, the commission shall disclose to the person complaining against the judge that the commission (1) has found no basis for action against the judge or determined not to proceed further in this matter, (2) has taken an appropriate corrective action, the nature of which shall not be disclosed, or (3) has publicly admonished, censured, removed, or retired the judge, or has found the person unfit to serve as a subordinate judicial officer. Where a matter is referred to the commission by a presiding judge or other public official in his or her official capacity, disclosure under this subdivision concerning that matter shall be made to the individual serving in that office at the time the matter is concluded. The name of the judge shall not be used in any written communication to the complainant, unless formal proceedings have been instituted or unless the complainant is a presiding judge or other public official in his or her official capacity. Written communications in which the judge's name is not used shall include the date of the complaint as a cross-reference.

(f) (Public safety) When the commission receives information concerning a threat to the safety of any person or persons, information concerning such a threat may be provided to the person threatened, to persons or organizations responsible for the safety of the person threatened, and to law enforcement and/or any appropriate prosecutorial agency.

(g) (Disclosure of information to prosecuting authorities) The commission may release to prosecuting authorities at any time information which reveals possible criminal conduct by the judge or former judge or by any other individual or entity.

(h) (Disclosure of records to public entity upon request or consent of judge) If a judge or former judge requests or consents to release of commission records to a public entity, the commission may release that judge's records.

(i) (Disclosure of records of disciplinary action to appointing authorities) The commission shall, upon request, provide to the Governor of any State of the Union, the President of the United States, or the Commission on Judicial Appointments the text of any private admonishment or advisory letter issued after March 1, 1995 or any other disciplinary action together with any information that the commission deems necessary to a full understanding of the commission's action, with respect to any applicant under consideration for any judicial appointment, provided that:

(1) The request is in writing; and

(2) Any information released to the appointing authority is simultaneously provided to the applicant.

All information disclosed to appointing authorities under this subdivision remains privileged and confidential. Private admonishments and advisory letters issued before March 1, 1995 shall only be disclosed under this section with the judge's written consent.

(j) (Disclosure of information regarding pending proceedings to appointing authorities) The commission may, upon request, in the interest of justice or to maintain public confidence in the administration of justice, provide to the Governor of any State of the Union, the President of the United States, the Commission on Judicial Appointments, or any other state or federal authorities responsible for judicial appointments information concerning any pending investigation or proceeding with respect to any applicant under consideration for any judicial appointment, provided that:

(1) The request is in writing; and

(2) Any information released to the appointing authority is simultaneously provided to the applicant.

If a disclosure about a pending matter is made and that matter subsequently is closed by the commission without discipline being imposed, disclosure of the latter fact shall be made promptly to the appointing authority and the judge.

All information disclosed to appointing authorities under this subdivision remains privileged and confidential.

(k) (Disclosure of information to the State Bar upon retirement or resignation) If a judge retires or resigns from office or if a subordinate judicial officer retires, resigns or is terminated from employment after a complaint is filed with the commission, or if a complaint is filed with the commission after the retirement, resignation or termination, the commission may, in the interest of justice or to maintain public confidence in the administration of justice, release information concerning the complaint, investigation and proceedings to the State Bar, provided that the commission has commenced a preliminary investigation or other proceeding and the judge or subordinate judicial officer has had an opportunity to respond to the commission's inquiry or preliminary investigation letter.

(*l*) (Disclosure of information about subordinate judicial officers to presiding judges) The commission may release to a presiding judge or his or her designee information concerning a complaint, investigation or disposition involving a subordinate judicial officer, including the name of the subordinate judicial officer, consistent with the commission's jurisdiction under article VI, section 18.1 of the California Constitution.

(m) (Disclosure of information regarding disciplinary action and pending proceedings to the Chief Justice) With respect to any judge who is under consideration for judicial assignment following retirement or resignation, or is sitting on assignment, the commission may, upon the request of the Chief Justice of California and with the consent of that judge, in the interest of justice or to maintain public confidence in the administration of justice, provide the Chief Justice information concerning any record of disciplinary action or any pending investigation or proceeding with respect to that judge, provided that:

(1) The request and consent are in writing;

(2) If the disclosure involves a pending investigation or proceeding, the judge has had an opportunity to respond to the pending investigation or proceeding; and

(3) Any information released to the Chief Justice is simultaneously provided to the judge seeking assignment.

If the disclosure involves disciplinary action, the commission may include any information the commission deems necessary to a full understanding of its action.

If a disclosure about a pending matter is made and that matter subsequently is closed by the commission without discipline being imposed, disclosure of the latter fact shall be made promptly to the Chief Justice and the judge.

All information disclosed to the Chief Justice under this subdivision remains privileged and confidential.

(n) (Disclosure of information to presiding judges about possible lack of capacity or other inability to perform) The commission may release to a presiding judge or his or her designee information concerning an investigation involving possible lack of capacity or other inability to perform judicial duties on the part of a judge of that court, except that no confidential medical information concerning the judge may be released.

(o) (Disclosure of closing to judge who provides information to the commission) Upon completion of the commission's review of a complaint or an investigation, the commission may notify a judge who is the subject of a complaint and has voluntarily provided information to the commission concerning the complaint, that the commission has found no basis for action against the judge or determined not to proceed further in the matter. The notification shall be in writing.

(p) (Disclosure of information to regulatory agencies) The commission may in the interest of justice, to protect the public, or to maintain public confidence in the administration of justice, release to a federal, state or local regulatory agency information which reveals a possible violation of a law or regulation within the agency's jurisdiction by a judge, former judge, subordinate judicial officer or former subordinate judicial officer, provided the commission has commenced a preliminary investigation.

In the event information is revealed under this subsection, the agency must be admonished that the fact that the commission has undertaken an investigation of the judge must remain confidential unless formal proceedings have been instituted.

(q) (Disclosure of information to mentor judge) When a judge has agreed to participate in a mentoring program, the commission may provide the mentor judge with the specifications of the allegations before the commission, any materials concerning the allegations the commission deems relevant and necessary for the mentor to perform his or her services, and any prior discipline, including private discipline, imposed on the judge for similar misconduct. The mentor judge will not be given the complaint or witness statements, but may be given a summary of information provided in the complaint and witness statements.

If a judge who participated in mentoring is found to have engaged in subsequent misconduct, any resulting discipline, including public discipline, on the subsequent matter may include a discussion of the prior matter that was the subject of the mentoring and that the judge participated in mentoring.

The provision of subsection (q) of rule 102 shall take effect June 29, 2016, and shall be operative until [1] **December 31, 2022**, unless after review, it is reenacted by the commission.

(r) (Disclosure to California State Auditor) The commission shall provide to the California State Auditor, or an authorized employee of the Auditor, access to confidential commission records pursuant to the provisions of Government Code sections 8545.1 and 8545.2 in connection with an audit mandated by statute or requested by the California State Legislature. This subdivision applies to confidential records in the commission's possession prior to the enactment of subdivision (r) of rule 102.

Adopted Oct. 24, 1996, effective Dec. 1, 1996; amended Oct. 8, 1998, Feb. 11, 1999; interim amendment May 9, 2001; amended Jan. 29, 2003; amended and interim amendment Aug. 26, 2004; amended Oct. 25, 2005, May 23, 2007, Jan. 28, 2009, Mar. 23, 2011, May 13, 2015; interim amendment June 29, 2016, Mar. 28, 2018; amended Sept. 20, 2018; interim amendment Jan. 29, 2020.

Rule 102.   2020 Deletes. [1] June 28, 2020

Rule 103.   Protection From Liability for Statements.

The making of statements to the commission, the filing of papers with or the giving of testimony before the commission, or before the masters appointed by the Supreme Court pursuant to rule 121, shall not give rise to civil liability for the person engaged in such acts. This privilege extends to any motions or petitions filed in the Supreme Court, as well as papers filed in connection therewith. No other publication of such statements, papers or proceedings shall be so privileged.

Adopted Oct. 24, 1996, effective Dec. 1, 1996.

Rule 104.   Duty to Cooperate; Response by Respondent Judge.

(a) A respondent judge shall cooperate with the commission in all proceedings in accordance with Government Code section 68725. The judge's cooperation or lack of cooperation may be considered by the commission in determining the appropriate disciplinary sanction or disposition as well as further proceedings to be taken by the commission but may not be considered in making evidentiary determinations.

(b) A respondent judge shall, within the time limits set forth in rules 110(a) and 111(a), respond to the merits of a staff inquiry letter or preliminary investigation letter.

(c) A respondent judge shall, within the time limits set forth in rule 119(b), file an answer to a notice of formal proceedings which comports with the requirements set forth in rule 119(c).

(d) A respondent judge shall file all other responses and documents required in commission proceedings within such reasonable time as the commission may prescribe, and shall comply with all other requirements of commission proceedings, including the discovery requirements set forth in rule 122.

(e) In accordance with California Evidence Code section 913, no inference shall be drawn as to any matter in issue or to the credibility of the judge based on a refusal to respond as required by this rule or to respond to a question at a hearing under rule 123 when such refusal is based on the exercise of the privilege against self-incrimination or of any other Evidence Code privilege or of any other privilege recognized by law.

Adopted Oct. 24, 1996, effective Dec. 1, 1996; amended Oct. 25, 2005.

Rule 105.   Medical Examination.

A judge shall, upon a finding of good cause by seven members of the commission and within such reasonable time as the commission may prescribe, submit to a medical examination ordered by the commission. The examination must be limited to the conditions stated in the finding of good cause. No examination by a specialist in psychiatry may be required without the consent of the judge.

Adopted Oct. 24, 1996, effective Dec. 1, 1996.

Rule 106.   Judge's Representation by Counsel.

A judge may be represented by counsel in all commission proceedings. The written communications of counsel shall be deemed to be the written communications of the judge. Counsel has the authority to bind the judge as to all matters except a stipulation as to discipline.

Any paper filed with the commission and any written statement made to the commission or to its staff must be signed by the judge or the judge's counsel. A stipulation as to discipline must be signed by the judge. The signing of any document or statement warrants that the signer has personal knowledge of the matter contained in the document or statement or has investigated the matter and has a good faith belief in the accuracy of the representations contained in the document or statement.

This rule applies to the filing of responses to staff inquiry letters and preliminary investigation letters under rules 110 and 111, to the filing of answers in formal proceedings under rule 119, and to all other filings with the commission and the masters and all other correspondence with the commission.

Adopted Oct. 24, 1996, effective Dec. 1, 1996.

Rule 107.   Notice Requirements.

(a)   (Notices of staff inquiry, preliminary investigation, tentative private admonishment, and tentative public admonishment)   All notices of a staff inquiry, preliminary investigation, or tentative private admonishment or public admonishment shall be sent to a judge at chambers or at his or her residence unless otherwise requested, and a copy thereof shall be mailed to counsel of record. If a judge does not occupy chambers and his or her place of residence is unknown, the notice shall be sent to the judge's last known address. If the notice relates to a staff inquiry, the notice shall be given by first-class mail. If the notice relates to a preliminary investigation or tentative private admonishment or public admonishment, the notice shall be given by prepaid (1) certified mail return receipt requested, or (2) overnight mail delivery with a proof of delivery service, or (3) personal service with proof of service. If the judge's last known address is outside of the United States, service shall be made by recorded delivery. Envelopes containing such notices shall be marked "personal and confidential"; the inscription "Commission on Judicial Performance" shall not be used on the envelopes. In the event of service by certified or recorded mail, service is complete at the time of mailing.

(b)   (Service of notice of formal proceedings, other notices and correspondence in connection with formal proceedings)   After institution of formal proceedings, the service of the notice of formal proceedings shall be made as set forth in rule 118, and the giving of notice or sending of other correspondence in connection with the formal proceedings shall be accomplished as set forth in rule 126.

Adopted Oct. 24, 1996, effective Dec. 1, 1996; amended Oct. 25, 2005, June 26, 2019.

Rule 108.   Extensions of Time.

(a)   (Extensions for response to staff inquiry letters)   A judge may, upon submission of a written request for extension to the chairperson prior to the expiration of time for filing a response to a staff inquiry letter under rule 110, obtain a 30-day extension of time for filing the response to the staff inquiry letter.

(b)   (Extensions for response to preliminary investigation letter and for answer to notice of formal proceedings)   Upon a showing of good cause submitted by the judge, the chairperson may extend the time for filing a response to a preliminary investigation letter under rule 111 or for filing an answer to a notice of formal proceedings.

(c)   (Extension of time for commencing hearing before the special masters)   In order to maintain public confidence in the integrity of the judiciary and protect the welfare of the public, all hearings before the special masters shall be heard at the earliest possible time after the issuance under rule 118 of the notice of formal proceedings. In accordance

with this policy, extensions of time for commencing a hearing before the special masters are disfavored. The chairperson of the commission or the presiding master may extend the time for commencing a hearing before the special masters upon a showing of good cause, supported by declaration detailing specific facts showing that a continuance is necessary. Good cause does not include the ordinary press of business.

(d)   (Extension of time for filing report of the masters)   The chairperson may, upon request of the masters, extend the time for the filing of the report of the masters under rule 129.

(e)   (Other extensions of time)   Any other or further extension of time, other than to demand an appearance before the commission to object to a private or public admonishment pursuant to rule 114(b) or 116(b), or to demand formal proceedings pursuant to rule 114(c) or 116(c), may be granted by the chairperson only upon a showing of good cause.

(f)   (Alternative authority)   The chairperson may delegate his or her authority under this rule to another member, and the commission may designate any member to act instead of the chairperson.

Adopted Oct. 24, 1996, effective Dec. 1, 1996; amended Oct. 8, 1998, Jan. 26, 2000, Oct. 25, 2005; interim amendment Jan. 31, 2007; amended May 23, 2007, Jan. 28, 2009, Oct. 19, 2011.

Rule 109.   Commencement of Commission Action.

(a)   (Receipt of written statement)   Upon receiving a written statement alleging facts indicating that a judge is guilty of willful misconduct in office, persistent failure or inability to perform the duties of office, habitual intemperance in the use of intoxicants or drugs, or conduct prejudicial to the administration of justice that brings the judicial office into disrepute, or that the judge has a disability that seriously interferes with the performance of the duties of office and is or is likely to become permanent, or that the judge has engaged in an improper action or a dereliction of duty, the commission may:

(1)   In an appropriate case, determine that the statement is obviously unfounded or frivolous and dismiss the proceeding;

(2)   If the statement is not obviously unfounded or frivolous, make a staff inquiry to determine whether sufficient facts exist to warrant a preliminary investigation; or

(3)   If sufficient facts are determined in the course of a staff inquiry or otherwise, make a preliminary investigation to determine whether formal proceedings should be instituted and a hearing held.

(b)   (Staff inquiry or preliminary investigation on commission's own motion)   The commission may make a staff inquiry or preliminary investigation on the basis of information received by the commission not contained in a written report indicating that a judge is guilty of willful misconduct in office, persistent failure or inability to perform the duties of office, habitual intemperance in the use of intoxicants or drugs, or conduct prejudicial to the administration of justice that brings the judicial office into disrepute, or that the judge has a disability that seriously interferes with the performance of the duties of office and is or is likely to become permanent, or that the judge has engaged in an improper action or a dereliction of duty.

(c)   (Staff inquiry or preliminary investigation of subordinate judicial officers)   The commission may make a staff inquiry or a preliminary investigation of a subordinate judicial officer whenever:

(1)   The commission receives from a complainant a written request within 30 days after the date of mailing of notice to the complainant by the local court of the disposition of a complaint against a subordinate judicial officer, and the commission concludes that the local court may have abused its discretion in its disposition of such complaint;

(2)   The commission receives from a local court a request that the commission investigate or adjudicate a complaint against a subordinate judicial officer;

(3)   The commission receives from a local court information that a complaint resulted in the written reprimand, suspension, or removal of the subordinate judicial officer; or

(4)   The commission receives from a local court information that a subordinate judicial officer resigned while an investigation was pending and before a final decision was made by the local court.

(5)   The commission receives a complaint concerning a subordinate judicial officer who resigned or retired before the local court received the complaint.

Subsection (c) applies only to complaints about a subordinate judicial officer received in the local court on or after June 3, 1998; subdivision (1) of subsection (c) applies only in cases in which the complainant was apprised by the local court of the 30-day time limit for seeking review by the commission.

(d) (Notification of disposition at the judge's request) Upon request from a judge who is the subject of a complaint before the commission, the commission shall notify the judge in writing of the disposition of the complaint if:

(1) The judge's request to the commission specifically describes the underlying incident giving rise to the complaint;

(2) The pendency of the complaint has become generally known to the public; or

(3) The judge has received written notice of the complaint from someone who is not associated with the commission.

Adopted Oct. 24, 1996, effective Dec. 1, 1996; amended Oct. 8, 1998; interim amendment Feb. 11, 1999; amended Jan. 29, 2003, Oct. 25, 2005, Mar. 23, 2011.

Rule 110.   Staff Inquiry; Advisory Letter after Staff Inquiry.

(a) (Notice prior to issuance of advisory letter) If the commission makes a staff inquiry, the judge shall be notified of the inquiry and the nature of the charge, before the commission issues an advisory letter. The respondent judge so notified shall be afforded a reasonable opportunity in the course of the inquiry to present such matters as the judge may choose. A reasonable time for a judge to respond to an inquiry letter shall be 20 days from the date the letter was mailed to the judge unless the time is extended pursuant to rule 108.

(b) (Staff inquiry letter) A staff inquiry letter shall include specification of the allegations, including, to the extent possible: the date of the conduct; the location where the conduct occurred; and, if applicable, the name(s) of the case(s) or identification of the court proceeding(s) in relation to which the conduct occurred. If the inquiry concerns statements made by or to the judge, the letter shall include the text or summaries of the comments.

(c) (Termination of staff inquiry) If the staff inquiry does not disclose sufficient cause to warrant issuance of a confidential advisory letter or further proceedings, the commission shall terminate the staff inquiry and notify the judge in writing of such action if the judge was notified of the staff inquiry pursuant to subdivision (a).

(d) (Advisory letter) At any time after notice of a staff inquiry and a reasonable opportunity to respond has been given to the judge, the commission may determine that the judge's conduct does not constitute a basis for further proceedings and issue a confidential advisory letter to the judge.

Adopted Oct. 24, 1996, effective Dec. 1, 1996; amended May 8, 2013.

Rule 111.   Preliminary Investigation.

(a) (Notice) If the commission commences a preliminary investigation, the judge shall be notified of the investigation and the nature of the charge, and shall be afforded a reasonable opportunity in the course of the preliminary investigation to present such matters as the judge may choose. A reasonable time for a judge to respond to a preliminary investigation letter shall be 20 days from the date the letter was mailed to the judge unless the time is extended pursuant to rule 108.

(b) (Preliminary investigation letter) A preliminary investigation letter shall include specification of the allegations, including, to the extent possible: the date of the conduct; the location where the conduct occurred; and, if applicable, the name(s) of the case(s) or identification of the court proceeding(s) in relation to which the conduct occurred. If the investigation concerns statements made by or to the judge, the letter shall include the text or summaries of the comments.

(c) (Termination of investigation) If the preliminary investigation does not disclose sufficient cause to warrant further proceedings, the commission shall terminate the investigation and notify the judge in writing.

(d) (Advisory letter) At any time after notice of a preliminary investigation and a reasonable opportunity to respond has been given to the judge, the commission may determine that the judge's conduct does not constitute a basis for further proceedings and may terminate the investigation by issuing a confidential advisory letter to the judge.

Adopted Oct. 24, 1996, effective Dec. 1, 1996; amended May 8, 2013.

Rule 111.4.   Legal Error.

Discipline, including an advisory letter, shall not be imposed for mere legal error without more. However, a judge who commits legal error which, in addition, clearly and convincingly reflects bad faith, bias, abuse of authority, disregard for fundamental rights, intentional disregard of the law, or any purpose other than the faithful discharge of judicial duty is subject to investigation and discipline.

Adopted May 8, 2013.

Rule 111.5.   Correction of Advisory Letter.

A judge who receives an advisory letter under either rule 110(d) or rule 111(d) may, within 30 days of the mailing thereof, apply to the commission for correction of an error of fact or law or both. The application shall be determined by the commission without an appearance by the judge before the commission unless the commission determines otherwise. Factual representations or information, including documents, letters, or witness statements, will be considered only if the factual information is relevant to the question of whether the advisory letter contains an error of fact.

Adopted Oct. 25, 2005; interim amendment Mar. 23, 2011; amended Oct. 19, 2011, May 8, 2013.

Rule 112.   Monitoring.

The commission may defer termination of a preliminary investigation for a period not to exceed two years for observation and review of a judge's conduct. The judge shall be advised in writing of the type of behavior for which the judge is being monitored. (Such disclosure shall not limit the commission's consideration of misconduct involving other types of behavior which may be observed or reported during the period of monitoring.)

Adopted Oct. 24, 1996, effective Dec. 1, 1996.

Rule 113.   Notice of Tentative Private Admonishment.

If after a preliminary investigation the commission determines that there is good cause for a private admonishment, the commission may issue a notice of tentative private admonishment to the judge by certified mail. The notice shall include a statement of facts and the reasons for the proposed admonishment. The notice shall also contain an advisement as to the judge's options under rule 114. The notice may cite any discipline that was imposed on the judge prior to issuance of the notice.

Adopted Oct. 24, 1996, effective Dec. 1, 1996; amended Feb. 11, 1999, May 23, 2007, June 26, 2019.

Rule 114.   Private Admonishment Procedure.

A judge who receives a notice of tentative private admonishment pursuant to rule 113 has the following options:

(a) (Acceptance of private admonishment) The judge may choose not to object to the tentative private admonishment. If the judge does not demand formal proceedings or an appearance before the commission to object to the tentative private admonishment within 30 days after the mailing of a notice of tentative private admonishment, the admonishment becomes effective.

(b) (Appearance before the commission) The judge may, within 30 days of the mailing of a notice of tentative private admonishment, file with the commission a written demand for an appearance before the commission to object to the tentative private admonishment, and waive the right to formal proceedings under rule 118 and to review by the Supreme Court. A judge who demands an appearance before the commission shall, within 30 days of the mailing of the notice of tentative private admonishment, submit a written statement of the basis of the judge's objections to the tentative admonishment.

After the time set for the appearance before the commission, the commission may:

(1) Close the matter without disciplinary action;

(2) Close the matter with a confidential advisory letter; or

(3) Issue a private admonishment.

If the commission determines to issue discipline after an appearance under this rule, it may in its final decision modify the notice in response to the judge's written objections and any oral presentation.

An appearance before the commission under this rule is not an evidentiary hearing. Factual representations or information, including documents, letters, or witness statements, not previously presented to the commission during the preliminary investigation will not be considered unless it is shown that the new factual information is either: (1) (a) material to the question of whether the judge engaged in misconduct or the appropriate level of discipline, and (b) could not have been discovered and presented to the commission with reasonable diligence during the preliminary investigation, (2) offered to correct an error of fact in the notice of tentative private admonishment, or (3) necessary to prevent a miscarriage of justice.

To be considered under this rule, new factual information must be presented at the time the judge submits written objections to the tentative admonishment. When newly presented factual information meets the criteria for consideration under this rule, the commission may investigate the new information before proceeding with its disposition pursuant to the appearance process. If this investigation discloses information of possible other misconduct, that information will not be considered in the disposition of the pending notice of tentative private admonishment but may be the subject of a new staff inquiry or preliminary investigation.

(c) **(Formal proceedings)**   The judge may, within 30 days of the mailing of a notice of tentative private admonishment, file with the commission a demand for formal proceedings pursuant to rule 118.

(d) **(Extensions of time)**   The 30 days provided to demand formal proceedings or an appearance before the commission to object to a tentative private admonishment pursuant to subdivisions (b) and (c) may not be extended. The time for filing a written statement of the judge's objections to the tentative admonishment pursuant to subdivision (b) may be extended by the chairperson or the chairperson's designee upon a showing of good cause, if the judge has, within 30 days of the mailing of a notice of tentative private admonishment, filed a demand for an appearance with a personal waiver of the right to formal proceedings and to review by the Supreme Court.

Adopted Oct. 24, 1996, effective Dec. 1, 1996; amended Jan. 29, 2003, Oct. 25, 2005, Jan. 31, 2007, Jan. 28, 2009; interim amendment Mar. 23, 2011; amended Oct. 19, 2011, May 8, 2013, June 26, 2019.

Rule 115.   Notice of Tentative Public Admonishment.

If the commission determines following a preliminary investigation that there is good cause for public discipline, the commission may issue a notice of tentative public admonishment to the judge by certified mail. The notice shall include a statement of facts and the reasons for the proposed admonishment. The notice shall also contain an advisement as to the judge's options under rule 116. The notice may cite any discipline that was imposed on the judge prior to issuance of the notice.

Adopted Oct. 24, 1996, effective Dec. 1, 1996; amended Feb. 11, 1999, May 23, 2007, June 26, 2019.

Rule 116.   Public Admonishment Procedure.

A judge who receives a notice of [1] **tentative** public admonishment pursuant to rule 115 has the following options:

(a) **(Acceptance of public admonishment)**   The judge may choose not to object to the [2] **tentative** public admonishment. If the judge does not demand formal proceedings or an appearance before the commission to object to the [3] **tentative** public admonishment within 30 days after the mailing of a notice of [4] **tentative** public admonishment, the admonishment becomes effective.

(b) **(Appearance before the commission)**   The judge may, within 30 days of the mailing of a notice of [5] **tentative** public admonishment, file with the commission a written demand for an appearance before the commission to object to the [6] **tentative** public admonishment, and waive the right to formal proceedings under rule 118 and to review by the Supreme Court. A judge who demands an appearance before the commission shall, within 30 days of the mailing of the notice of [7] **tentative** public admonishment, submit a written statement of the basis of the judge's objections to the [8] **tentative** admonishment.

After the time set for the appearance before the commission, the commission may:

(1)   Close the matter without disciplinary action;

(2)   Close the matter with a confidential advisory letter;

(3)   Issue a private admonishment; or

(4)   Issue a public admonishment.

If the commission determines to issue discipline after an appearance under this rule, it may in its final decision modify the notice in response to the judge's written objections and any oral presentation.

[9] **In** appearance before the commission under this rule is not an evidentiary hearing. Factual representations or information, including documents, letters, or witness statements, not previously presented to the commission during the preliminary investigation will not be considered unless it is shown that the new factual information is either: (1) (a) material to the question of whether the judge engaged in misconduct or the appropriate level of discipline, and (b) could not have been discovered and presented to the commission with reasonable diligence during the

preliminary investigation, (2) offered to correct an error of fact in the notice of [10] **tentative** public admonishment, or (3) necessary to prevent a miscarriage of justice.

To be considered under this rule, new factual information must be presented at the time the judge submits written objections to the [11] **tentative** admonishment. When newly presented factual information meets the criteria for consideration under this rule, the commission may investigate the new information before proceeding with its disposition pursuant to the appearance process. If this investigation discloses information of possible other misconduct, that information will not be considered in the disposition of the pending notice of [12] **tentative** public admonishment but may be the subject of a new staff inquiry or preliminary investigation.

(c) **(Formal proceedings)**   The judge may, within 30 days of the mailing of a notice of [13] **tentative** public admonishment, file with the commission a demand for formal proceedings pursuant to rule 118.

(d) **(Extensions of time)**   The 30 days provided to demand formal proceedings or an appearance before the commission to object to [14] **a tentative** public admonishment pursuant to subdivisions (b) and (c) may not be extended. The time for filing a written statement of the judge's objections to the [15] **tentative** admonishment pursuant to subdivision (b) may be extended by the chairperson or the chairperson's designee upon a showing of good cause, if the judge has, within 30 days of the mailing of a notice of [16] **tentative** public admonishment, filed a demand for an appearance with a personal waiver of the right to formal proceedings and to review by the Supreme Court.

Adopted Oct. 24, 1996, effective Dec. 1, 1996; amended Jan. 29, 2003, Oct. 25, 2005, Jan. 28, 2009; interim amendment Mar. 23, 2011; amended Oct. 19, 2011, May 8, 2013, June 26, 2019.

Rule 116.   2020 Deletes. [1] intended [2] intended [3] intended [4] intended [5] intended [6] intended [7] intended [8] proposed [9] An [10] intended [11] proposed [12] intended [13] intended [14] an intended [15] intended [16] intended

Rule 116.5.   Negotiated Settlement During Preliminary Investigation.

At any time during a preliminary investigation or an admonishment proceeding under rules 113-116, the commission may authorize legal staff or other designated attorney to negotiate with the judge a resolution of any matter at issue. The judge may also initiate settlement discussions with legal staff or other designated attorney. A proposed resolution agreed to by the judge and legal staff or other designated attorney shall be jointly submitted to the commission, which may accept it, reject it or return it to the judge and legal staff or other designated attorney to consider modifications to it. No agreement between the judge and legal staff or other designated attorney is binding unless approved by the commission. A settlement proposal rejected by the commission cannot be used against the judge in any proceedings. After formal proceedings are instituted, settlement negotiations are governed by rule 127.

Adopted May 23, 2007; amended June 28, 2017.

Rule 117.   Records Disposition Program.

The commission shall adopt a records disposition program designed to dispose of records of complaints against a judge. The commission's records disposition program shall be consistent with constitutional language and case law and shall be published in the Policy Declarations of the Commission on Judicial Performance.

Adopted Oct. 24, 1996, effective Dec. 1, 1996; amended Jan. 31, 2018.

Rule 118.   Notice of Formal Proceedings.

(a) **(Issuance of notice)**   After the preliminary investigation has been completed, if the commission concludes that formal proceedings should be instituted, the commission shall without delay issue a written notice to the judge advising the judge of the institution of formal proceedings to inquire into the charges against the judge. Such proceedings shall be entitled:

"BEFORE THE COMMISSION ON JUDICIAL PERFORMANCE Inquiry Concerning Judge _____, No. _____."

(b) **(Content of notice)**   The notice shall specify in ordinary and concise language the charges against the judge and the alleged facts upon which such charges are based, and shall advise the judge of the duty to file a written answer to the charges within 20 days after service of the notice upon the judge.

(c) **(Service of notice)**   After a notice of formal proceedings is signed by the chairperson of the commission, the chairperson's designee or other member designated by the commission, the notice shall be served by personal service of a copy thereof on the judge, unless the judge personally or through counsel waives personal service and consents to service by mail. If there is no consent to service by mail and it appears to the chairperson of the commission upon affidavit that, after reasonable effort for a period of 10 days, personal service could not be had, service may be made upon the judge by mailing, by prepaid certified mail, copies of the notice addressed to the judge at the judge's chambers and last known residence. In the event of service by certified mail, service is complete at the time of mailing.

(d) **(Public announcement)** Not less than five days after service of the notice of formal proceedings as set forth above, the commission shall issue a public announcement advising that formal proceedings have been instituted, and shall make public the notice of formal proceedings. The public announcement shall set forth the date the judge's answer to the notice of formal proceedings is due, and shall indicate that the answer to the notice of formal proceedings will be made public.

Adopted Oct. 24, 1996, effective Dec. 1, 1996; amended Feb. 11, 1999, Oct. 25, 2005, Oct. 17, 2007.

Rule 119. Answer.

(a) **(Pleadings and motions)** The notice of formal proceedings and answer shall constitute the pleadings. No further pleadings shall be filed and no motion or demurrer shall be filed against any of the pleadings.

(b) **(Filing of answer)** Within 20 days after service of the notice of formal proceedings the judge shall serve, in accordance with rule 119.5, and file with the commission an answer, which shall be verified and shall conform in style to subdivision (b) of rule 8.204 of the California Rules of Court. The chairperson, the chairperson's designee or other member designated by the commission may grant an extension of time only upon timely written request establishing good cause for an extension of time.

(c) **(Content of answer)** The answer shall be as complete and straightforward as the information reasonably available to the respondent judge permits. The answer shall (1) admit each allegation which is true, (2) deny each allegation which is untrue, and (3) specify each allegation as to the truth of which the judge lacks sufficient information or knowledge. If a respondent judge gives lack of information or knowledge as a reason for a failure to admit or deny any allegation, the respondent judge shall state in the answer that a reasonable inquiry concerning the matter in the particular allegation has been made, and that the information known or readily obtainable is insufficient to enable the respondent judge to admit or deny the matter.

Adopted Oct. 24, 1996, effective Dec. 1, 1996; amended Jan. 26, 2000, Jan. 29, 2003, Jan. 31, 2007.

Rule 119.5. Filing with the Commission During Formal Proceedings.

(a) **(Procedures for filing)** After the institution of formal proceedings, all briefs and other papers to be filed with the commission shall be delivered to the commission office during regular business hours by hand delivery or by mail, or electronic or facsimile transmission as provided in this rule, and shall be accompanied by a proof of service of the document upon the other party or parties, and upon the special masters if they have been appointed in the matter. This includes documents submitted in conjunction with a hearing before the special masters, other than exhibits to be admitted at the hearing. Exhibits admitted at a hearing before the masters shall be transmitted to the commission office pursuant to rule 125.5. A document is filed with the commission when the original is stamped or otherwise marked "filed" with the date. The commission's agent for purposes of filing documents after institution of formal proceedings is the Legal Advisor to Commissioners or the Legal Advisor's designee. A filing may be evidenced by a conformed copy of the cover page of each document submitted for filing.

(b) **(Facsimile filing)** Facsimile filing means the transmission of a document by facsimile, directed to the Legal Advisor to Commissioners or the Legal Advisor's designee.

(c) **(Electronic filing)** Electronic filing means the transmission of a document by electronic service to the electronic address of the commission, directed to the Legal Advisor to Commissioners or the Legal Advisor's designee. The electronic address for filing pursuant to these rules is filings@cjp.ca.gov.

(d) **(Conditions for facsimile and electronic filing)** After the institution of formal proceedings, parties or non-parties pursuant to rule 131 may file documents with the commission electronically or by facsimile, subject to the following conditions:

(1) Original paper documents, with any required signatures, shall be delivered to the commission office by mail or hand delivery within five calendar days of the facsimile or electronic filing, and shall be accompanied by proof of service.

(2) A document transmitted electronically or by facsimile shall be deemed filed on the date received, or the next business day if received on a non-business day or after 5:00 p.m., provided the original paper document is received pursuant to subsection (1) of this subdivision.

(3) The document shall be considered filed, for purposes of filing deadlines and the time to respond under these rules, at the time it is received electronically or by facsimile by the commission as set forth in subsection (2) of this subdivision.

(4) Upon receipt of a facsimile or electronically filed document, the commission shall promptly send the filer confirmation that the document was received.

(e) **(Signatures)** When the document to be filed requires the signature of any person, the document shall be deemed to have been signed by that person if filed electronically or by facsimile.

(f) **(Electronic and facsimile service)** After the institution of formal proceedings, documents may be served by electronic means or by facsimile on another party, a party's attorney, or the special masters when the party, attorney, or special master has agreed to accept electronic service and/or facsimile service, provided the documents have been submitted to the commission office at the same time by the same method of service with the original to be submitted in accordance with subdivision (d), subsection (1).

Adopted Feb. 11, 1999; amended Oct. 25, 2005; interim amendment Jan. 31, 2007; amended May 23, 2007; interim amendment Oct. 17, 2012; amended May 8, 2013.

Rule 120. Disqualification.

(a) **(Disqualification upon determination to remove, retire or bar from assignments)** If the commission determines that a judge should be removed or retired from office, the commission will, in its order of removal or retirement, also order pursuant to article VI, section 18(b) of the California Constitution that the judge be disqualified from acting as a judge, without loss of salary, until the commission's determination becomes final or until any decision by the Supreme Court on any petition for review becomes final. If the commission determines to censure and bar a former judge from receiving assignments, the commission will, in its order of censure, also order that the judge be barred from receiving assignments until the commission's determination becomes final or until any decision by the Supreme Court on any petition for review becomes final.

(b) **(Disqualification upon notice of formal proceedings)** Before the commission has reached a determination regarding removal or retirement of a judge, the commission may temporarily disqualify a judge without loss of salary upon notice of formal proceedings pursuant to article VI, section 18(b) of the California Constitution if the commission determines that there is substantial evidence that the continued service of the judge poses a threat of serious harm to the public or to the administration of justice.

If good cause for disqualification is apparent, the commission may issue a notice of intention to temporarily disqualify the judge along with a notice of formal proceedings. Subsequent to the filing of a notice of formal proceedings, the examiner may file with the commission a motion to temporarily disqualify the judge. The commission's notice of intention to disqualify or the examiner's motion to disqualify shall be by personal service or service upon the judge's counsel. If such service cannot be effectuated, service shall be by prepaid certified mail upon the judge at his or her chambers and last known residence. If service is by mail, the notice shall be accompanied by an affidavit or certificate of mailing and an affidavit shall be filed regarding the inability to effectuate personal service or service upon counsel.

The judge shall have an opportunity to respond in writing within 10 days of receipt of the commission's notice of intention to disqualify or the examiner's motion to disqualify, or within 15 days after the mailing of the notice, whichever occurs first. The time for filing a response shall not be subject to extension under rule 108. The judge's response may include points and authorities in support of any legal arguments, and may include verified statements, other testimony, medical or other expert reports and any other evidence in opposition to the facts on which the commission's notice of intention to disqualify or the examiner's motion to disqualify is based. Upon the filing of a response or expiration of time for filing a response, the commission may issue an order of temporary disqualification.

(c) **(Accelerated disposition of charges)** In cases in which a judge is temporarily disqualified under rule 120(b) the disposition of the charges in the notice of formal proceedings shall be accelerated and the formal proceedings shall proceed without appreciable delay. In such cases, the commission may reduce the number of days provided in rules 122, 129, and 130 for the filing of papers in connection with the formal proceedings.

(d) **(Duration of temporary disqualification)** An order for temporary disqualification of a judge under subdivision (b) of this rule shall remain in effect until further order of the commission or until the pending formal proceedings have been concluded by the commission.

Adopted Oct. 24, 1996, effective Dec. 1, 1996; amended Oct. 8, 1998, Feb. 11, 1999, June 28, 2017.

Rule 120.5.   Suspension; Termination of Suspension; Removal of Suspended Judge.

(a) **(Felony)** When the commission receives proof that a judge has pled guilty or no contest to, or has been found guilty of, a felony under California or federal law, the commission shall promptly issue an order suspending the judge from office without salary.

(b) **(Crime punishable as a felony or that involves moral turpitude)** When the commission receives proof that a judge has pled guilty or no contest to, or has been found guilty of, a crime that is not a felony under California or federal law but is punishable as a felony under that law or involves moral turpitude under that law, the commission shall promptly issue a notice of intention to suspend the judge without salary in accordance with subdivision (e) of this rule.

(c) **(Reversal of conviction)** If a judge is suspended by reason of article VI, section 18, subdivision (c) of the California Constitution, and the commission receives proof that the conviction has been reversed, the commission shall promptly issue a notice of intention to terminate the suspension in accordance with subdivision (e) of this rule.

(d) **(Finality of conviction)** If a judge is suspended by reason of article VI, section 18, subdivision (c) of the California Constitution, and the commission receives proof that the conviction is final, the commission shall promptly issue a notice of intention to remove the judge from office in accordance with subdivision (e) of this rule.

(e) **(Notice)** Any notice issued pursuant to this rule shall be in accordance with the following:

(1) The notice shall be given to the judge or judge's counsel and to the examiner or other attorney designated by the commission to receive notice in the matter.

(2) The notice shall be by personal service or service upon the judge's counsel. If such service cannot be effectuated, service shall be by prepaid certified mail upon the judge at his or her chambers and last known residence. If service is by mail, the notice shall be accompanied by an affidavit or certificate of mailing and an affidavit shall be filed regarding the inability to effectuate personal service or service upon counsel. If the service is by certified mail, service is complete at the time of mailing.

(3) The judge shall have an opportunity to respond in writing within 10 days of receipt by the judge of a notice of intended suspension under subdivision (b) or a notice of intended removal under subdivision (d), or within 15 days after the mailing of the notice, whichever occurs first. Within five days after receipt of the judge's response, or within 20 days of the mailing of the notice if no response is filed, whichever occurs first, the examiner or other attorney designated by the commission may present points and authorities respecting the notice and in reply to any response. The commission may request additional briefing. Extensions of time under this subdivision are disfavored and will be granted only upon a specific and affirmative showing of good cause. Good cause does not include ordinary press of business.

(4) The examiner or other attorney designated by the commission shall have an opportunity to respond in writing within 10 days of receipt of a notice of intended termination of suspension under subdivision (c). Within five days after receipt of the response of the examiner or other attorney designated by the commission, or within 15 days of the mailing of the notice if no response is filed, whichever occurs first, the judge may present points and authorities respecting the notice and in reply to any

response. The commission may request additional briefing. Extensions of time under this subdivision are disfavored and will be granted only upon a specific and affirmative showing of good cause. Good cause does not include ordinary press of business.

(5) Upon receipt of the points and authorities or reply or the expiration of the time for the filing thereof, whichever occurs first, or upon receipt of any additional briefs as may be requested by the commission, the commission shall promptly issue its order if it concludes that the relevant standards specified in article VI, section 18, subdivision (c) of the California Constitution have been met.

Adopted Oct. 25, 2005; amended Jan. 31, 2007.

Rule 121.   Setting for Hearing Before Commission or Masters.

(a) **(Time for setting for hearing)** On filing or on expiration of the time for filing an answer, the commission shall set the matter for hearing.

(b) **(Appointment of special masters or master)** Unless the commission determines to hold the hearing before itself, the commission may request the Supreme Court to appoint three special masters to hear and take evidence in the matter, and to report to the commission. On a vote of seven members of the commission and with the consent of the judge involved, the commission may request the Supreme Court to appoint one special master in place of three special masters. Consent of the judge shall be defined as (1) written agreement by the judge or counsel of record, or (2) failure to object in writing within 30 days of notice of the commission's intention to request the appointment of one special master.

(c) **(Requirements for special masters)** Special masters shall be judges. When there are three special masters, not more than two of them may be retired judges from courts of record.

(d) **(Notice to respondent judge of appointment of special masters and examiner)** Upon appointment of special masters or a single special master by the Supreme Court and appointment of an examiner by the commission, the respondent judge shall be given notice of the orders appointing the masters and the examiner, and the examiner shall be given notice of the order appointing the special masters.

(e) **(Notice of hearing)** The commission shall set a time and place for hearing before itself or before the masters and shall give notice by mail confirming the date and place of the hearing to the judge and the examiner at least 20 days before the hearing.

Adopted Oct. 24, 1996, effective Dec. 1, 1996.

Rule 122.   Discovery Procedures.

(a) **(Exclusive procedures)** The procedures in this rule shall constitute the exclusive procedures for discovery. Discovery may be obtained only after a written notice of formal proceedings is issued.

(b) **(Applicability to both parties)** The examiner and the judge are each entitled to discovery from the other in accordance with these procedures.

(c) **(Initial discovery provided by trial counsel)** At the time of service of the notice of formal proceedings, the judge shall be provided copies of all documents and other information specified in rule 122(e) which is not privileged and is in the possession of the commission. Such information shall be made available at the commission offices. Alternatively, if a judge requests that the materials be sent to a specific address, the commission shall provide the judge with copies of said documents and information at that address.

(d) **(Discovery requests)** Discovery requests may be made in writing at any time after the filing of the notice of formal proceedings. All requests for discovery must be made in writing to the opposing side within 30 days after service of the answer to the written notice of formal proceedings or within 30 days after service of the written notice of formal proceedings if no answer has yet been filed, or within 15 days after service of any amendment to the notice.

(e) **(Inspection and copying)** The following items may be inspected or copied by the side requesting discovery:

(1) The names, and if known, the business addresses and business telephone numbers of persons the opposing side then intends to call as witnesses at the hearing;

(2) The names, and if known, the business addresses and business telephone numbers of those persons who may be able to provide substantial material information favorable to the judge. Substantial material information favorable to the judge is evidence bearing directly on

the truth of the charges **or** relevant to the credibility of a witness intended to be called;

(3) All statements about the subject matter of the proceedings, including any impeaching evidence, made by any witness then intended to be called by either side;

(4) All statements about the subject matter of the proceedings made by a person named or described in the notice, or amendment to the notice, other than the judge when it is claimed that an act or omission of the judge as to the person described is a basis for the formal proceeding;

(5) All investigative reports made by or on behalf of the commission, the examiner, or the judge, about the subject matter of the proceeding;

(6) All writings, including reports of mental, physical, and blood examinations, then intended to be offered in evidence by the opposing side;

(7) All physical items of evidence then intended to be offered in evidence;

(8) All writings or physical items of evidence which would be admissible in evidence at the hearing.

(f) **(Compliance with request)** If either side receives a written request for discovery in accordance with these procedures, the side receiving the request shall have a continuing duty to provide discovery of items listed in the request until proceedings before the masters are concluded. When a written request for discovery is made in accordance with these rules, discovery shall be provided within a reasonable time after any discoverable items become known to the side obligated to provide discovery.

(g) **(Depositions)** After the filing of the notice of formal proceedings, depositions shall be allowed as provided in this subdivision. The party requesting the deposition shall bear all costs for service of process, reporter, transcripts and facility usage, and in the case of a videotaped deposition to perpetuate testimony under subpart (1), all direct costs incurred in videotaping the deposition.

(1) **(Depositions to perpetuate testimony)** The commission or the special masters shall order the taking of the deposition of any person upon a showing by the side requesting the deposition that the proposed deponent is a material witness who is unable or cannot be compelled to attend the hearing. If a deposition is ordered, the procedures stated in Government Code section 68753 shall be followed. Depositions to perpetuate testimony may be videotaped.

(2) **(Discovery depositions)** In addition to depositions to perpetuate testimony provided for under subpart (1) of this subdivision, discovery depositions are permitted as provided in this subpart (2). Discovery depositions may not be videotaped.

a. The judge shall have the right to take depositions of up to four material witnesses, and the examiner shall have the right to take depositions of the judge and up to three other material witnesses. Depositions of commission members or staff are not permitted. Bench officers, other than the respondent judge, and court staff shall be afforded counsel for the deposition, upon request, by the Judicial Council.

b. If the examiner and judge stipulate in writing that a deposition may be taken as a matter of right under subpart (a), the commission shall issue a subpoena for such deposition. If the examiner and judge are unable to agree that a witness is material, or unable to agree concerning the manner, time and place of a deposition, the party seeking the deposition may file a request for deposition subpoena with the commission. Objections shall be filed within five days of filing the request. The commission may place restrictions or conditions on the manner, time and place of any deposition.

c. Each deposition upon oral examination is limited to one day of seven hours. Any objection during a deposition upon oral examination must be stated concisely and in a non-argumentative and non-suggestive manner. A person may instruct a deponent not to answer only when necessary to preserve a privilege, to enforce a limitation directed by the commission, or to present a motion to the commission that the deposition is being conducted in bad faith or in such manner unreasonably to annoy, embarrass or oppress the deponent or party.

d. Depositions shall be completed 30 days prior to the hearing, unless a cut-off time otherwise is set by the commission or by stipulation of the examiner and the judge.

e. Any motion under this subpart (2) shall be presented to the commission. The commission may designate the chairperson or the chairperson's designee to perform all or any part of its duties under this subdivision. If special masters have been appointed pursuant to rule 121,

subdivision (b), the chairperson may designate one or more of them to perform all or any part of the commission's duties under this subpart.

(h) **(Subpoenas for the production of documents)** After the filing of the notice of formal proceedings, subpoenas for the production of documents by nonparties shall be allowed as provided in this subdivision. The party requesting the subpoena shall bear all costs for service of process of the subpoena on a nonparty.

(1) The parties shall have the right to the issuance of up to four subpoenas for the production of documents to nonparties, subject to the requirements of this rule. The parties may seek more than four subpoenas only upon a showing of good cause for the issuance of the additional subpoena(s). Subpoenas issued to commission members or staff under this rule are not permitted. Commission files and records are not subject to a subpoena for production of documents.

(2) If the examiner and judge stipulate in writing that a subpoena for the production of documents may issue, the commission shall issue the subpoena. If the examiner and judge are unable to agree to the issuance of a particular subpoena, the party seeking the subpoena may file an application for the issuance of that subpoena with the commission. The application shall be made on a form provided by the commission and shall include a declaration from the party or the party's attorney establishing good cause and including (a) an itemization, with reasonable particularity, of each document requested, (b) facts establishing why each document is relevant to the issues raised in the formal proceeding, and (c) facts establishing that the witness has the documents requested in the witness's custody or control. A copy of the proposed subpoena shall be attached to the application. The application must be served on the other party. Upon a finding of good cause based on the foregoing factors, the chairperson of the commission, the chairperson's designee, or the special masters may issue the subpoena.

Objections to an application for a subpoena for the production of documents shall be filed within seven days of the filing of the application. The commission or the special masters may place restrictions or conditions on the manner, time, and place of the document production.

(3) Applications for subpoenas for the production of documents shall be made in sufficient time for service of the subpoena and the production of documents to be completed 30 days prior to the hearing, unless a later cut-off time otherwise is set by the commission or by stipulation of the examiner and the judge.

(4) If an application for a subpoena seeks documents that are personal records as defined by Code of Civil Procedure section 1985.3, or employment records as defined by Code of Civil Procedure section 1985.6, the application shall include a "notice of privacy rights" advising the individual whose records are sought of the subpoena and of the individual's right to object within seven days of receipt of the notice. The notice of privacy rights shall state that the documents sought may be protected by a right to privacy; that any objection to the subpoena may be filed with the commission, with copies sent to the examiner and the respondent, within seven days of receipt of the notice; and that if the party seeking the documents will not agree to cancel or limit the subpoena, an attorney should be consulted about the recipient's privacy rights. If the subpoena is issued, the subpoena, accompanied by the notice of privacy rights, shall first be served on the individual whose records are sought by the subpoena. The notice of privacy rights must be personally served or acknowledged in writing by the individual upon whom the notice was served. A proof of service, or a written acknowledgment of receipt, shall be filed with the commission. The recipient of a notice of privacy rights has seven days to file an objection. If no objection is filed by the individual within seven days, the subpoena may be served on the nonparty custodian of the individual's records.

(5) Documents shall be produced within 15 days of service of the subpoena, unless an objection has been filed with the commission. If an objection is filed, no documents that are the subject of the objection shall be produced in response to a subpoena until the objection has been considered by the chairperson of the commission or an appropriate designee has considered the objection and ordered the documents to be produced. Unless otherwise directed by the commission, copies of any documents produced in response to a subpoena issued pursuant to this rule shall be provided to the opposing party within seven days of the party's receipt of the documents.

(6) Any motions under this subdivision shall be presented to the chairperson. The commission may designate the commission or the special masters to perform all or any part of the chairperson's duties under this subdivision.

(i)   (**Failure to comply with discovery request**)   If any party fails to comply with a discovery request as authorized by these procedures, the items withheld shall be suppressed or, if the items have been admitted into evidence, shall be stricken from the record. If testimony is elicited during direct examination and the side eliciting the testimony withheld any statement of the testifying witness in violation of these discovery procedures, the testimony shall be ordered stricken from the record. Upon a showing of good cause for failure to comply with a discovery request, the commission, master, or masters may admit the items withheld or direct examination testimony of a witness whose statement was withheld upon condition that the side against whom the evidence is sought to be admitted is granted a reasonable continuance to prepare against the evidence, or may order the items or testimony suppressed or stricken from the record. The commission may, upon review of any hearing, order any evidence stricken from the record for violation of a valid discovery request if the evidence could have been ordered stricken by the masters for violation of a valid discovery request.

(j)   (**Applicable privileges**)   Nothing in these procedures shall authorize the discovery of any writing or thing which is privileged from disclosure by law or is otherwise protected or made confidential as the work product of the attorney, including memoranda by commission staff and examiners. Statements of any witness interviewed by the examiner, by any investigators for either side, by the judge, or by the judge's attorney shall not be protected as work product.

(k)   (**Definition of statement**)   For purposes of these procedures, "statement" shall mean either (1) a written statement prepared by or at the direction of the declarant or signed by the declarant, or (2) an oral statement of the declarant which has been recorded stenographically, mechanically, or electronically, or which has been videotaped, transcribed, or summarized in writing.

(l)   (**Return of discovery, continued confidentiality of discovery**)   Upon the completion or termination of commission proceedings, the respondent judge shall return to the commission all materials provided to the judge under this rule that have not become part of the public record. All items provided in discovery pursuant to this rule remain confidential under rule 102 until and unless those items become part of the public record.

(m)   (**Protective orders**)   The commission or the masters may, upon application supported by a showing of good cause, issue protective orders to the extent necessary to maintain in effect such privileges and other protections as are otherwise provided by law.

Adopted Oct. 24, 1996, effective Dec. 1, 1996; amended Jan. 29, 2003, Oct. 17, 2007, Mar. 23, 2011, Dec. 5, 2012, June 28, 2017, June 26, 2019, July 1, 2020.

Rule 123.   Hearing.

(a)   (**Hearing without answer or appearance by judge**)   At the time and place set for hearing, the commission, or the masters when the hearing is before masters, shall proceed with the hearing whether or not the judge has filed an answer or appears at the hearing. The examiner shall present the case in support of the charges in the notice of formal proceedings.

(b)   (**Consideration of failure to answer, appear, or respond to questions**)   The failure of the judge to answer the charges or to appear at the hearing shall not, standing alone, be taken as evidence of the truth of the facts alleged to constitute grounds for censure, removal, retirement or public or private admonishment. In accordance with California Evidence Code section 413, in reviewing the evidence and facts in the case against the judge, the commission and the masters may consider the judge's failure to explain or deny evidence or facts in the case or any willful suppression of evidence if that is the case, unless the failure or suppression is due to the judge's exercise of any legally recognized privilege. A lack of cooperation by the judge may be considered by the commission under rule 104.

(c)   (**Reporting of hearing**)   A verbatim record shall be made of the proceedings at the hearing.

(d)   (**Number of commission members at hearing**)   When the hearing is before the commission, not fewer than six members shall be present when the evidence is produced.

Adopted Oct. 24, 1996, effective Dec. 1, 1996; amended Oct. 25, 2005.

Rule 124.   Media at Hearing.

All applications for film or electronic coverage of hearings in formal proceedings are to be submitted to the commission a reasonable time prior to the commencement of the hearing. The commission shall promptly inform the respondent judge of any requests for film or electronic coverage of the hearing. Applications for film or electronic coverage of the hearing are to be decided by the chairperson of the commission or the chairperson's designee after conferring with the masters or presiding master, if masters have been appointed.

Adopted Oct. 24, 1996, effective Dec. 1, 1996.

Rule 125.   Evidence.

(a)   (**Applicable law and agreed statement**)   The California Evidence Code shall be applicable to all hearings before the commission or masters. Oral evidence shall be taken only on oath or affirmation. The examiner or the judge may propose to the other party an agreed statement in place of all or a part of the testimony. An agreed statement shall not foreclose argument to the commission or masters.

(b)   (**Prior disciplinary action**)   Any prior disciplinary action may be received in evidence to prove that conduct is persistent or habitual or to determine what action should be taken regarding discipline. Prior disciplinary action includes any disciplinary action which is in effect before the conclusion of a commission proceeding, including review by the Supreme Court.

(c)   (**Settlement discussions**)   **Evidence of any settlement offer made by the judge, the examiner, or the commission to resolve any or all of the charges against the judge, or of any written or oral statements made during settlement discussions between the judge and the examiner or commission staff, shall be inadmissible in all public proceedings before the commission or masters. Nothing in this rule shall limit the admissibility, during formal proceedings, of the written responses of the judge or the judge's counsel to preliminary investigation or staff inquiry letters.**

Adopted Oct. 24, 1996, effective Dec. 1, 1996; amended Oct. 9, 2020.

Rule 125.5.   Exhibits at Hearing.

Original exhibits admitted at a hearing before the special masters shall be transmitted by the masters to the commission office at the completion of the evidentiary portion of the hearing, unless the masters determine that there is reason to retain the original exhibit or exhibits to assist in the preparation of their report to the commission. Any original exhibits retained by the masters shall be transmitted to the commission at or before the time the report of the masters is submitted to the commission.

Adopted as interim rule Jan. 31, 2007; adopted May 23, 2007.

Rule 126.   Procedural Rights of Judge in Formal Proceedings.

(a)   (**Enumeration of rights, subpoenas**)   When formal proceedings have been instituted, a judge shall have the right and reasonable opportunity to defend against the charges by the introduction of evidence, to be represented by counsel, and to examine and cross-examine witnesses. The judge shall have the right to the issuance of subpoenas for attendance of witnesses to testify or produce books, papers, and other evidentiary matter. The judge shall also have the right to the issuance of subpoenas for the production of documents, as set forth in rule 122. Subpoenas are to be issued by the chairperson of the commission, the chairperson's designee, or the special masters. Subpoenas addressed to the commission or its staff may only be obtained from the special masters upon a showing of good cause with notice to the commission.

(b)   (**Transcripts**)   When a transcript of the testimony has been prepared at the expense of the commission, a copy thereof shall, upon request, be available for use by the judge and his counsel in connection with the proceedings at the judge's expense, or the judge may arrange to procure a copy from the reporter at the judge's expense. The judge shall have the right, without any order or approval, to have all or any portion of the testimony in the proceedings transcribed at the judge's expense.

(c)   (**Manner of service**)   Subject to rule 118(c), concerning service of a notice of formal proceedings, all notices and correspondence in connection with formal proceedings shall be sent to the judge's chambers, unless otherwise requested, and a copy thereof shall be mailed to counsel of record.

(d)   (**Appointment of conservator**)   If the judge is adjudged to be of unsound mind or incompetent, or if it appears to the commission at any time during the proceedings that the judge is not competent to act for himself or herself, the commission may petition a court of competent jurisdiction for the appointment of a conservator unless the judge has a conservator who will represent the judge. If a conservator is or has been appointed for a judge, the conservator may claim and exercise any right and privilege and make any defense for the judge with the same force and effect as if claimed, exercised, or made by the judge, if competent, and whenever these rules provide for serving, giving notice or sending any matter to the judge, such notice or matter shall be served, given, or sent to the conservator.

Adopted Oct. 24, 1996, effective Dec. 1, 1996; amended Jan. 31, 2007, May 23, 2007, June 28, 2017, June 26, 2019.

Rule 127.   Discipline by Consent.

(a)   **(Negotiations)**   Either respondent or the examiner may initiate negotiations on discipline by consent. Both the examiner and respondent must agree to any proposed disposition before submission to the commission. No agreement between the examiner and respondent is binding until approved by the commission.

(b)   **(Submission to commission)**   At any time after the initiation of formal charges and before final disposition, the respondent may agree with the examiner that the respondent shall admit to any or all of the charges in exchange for a stated sanction. The agreement shall be submitted to the commission, which shall accept or reject the agreement.

(c)   **(Rejection of agreement)**   If the stated sanction is rejected by the commission, the admission shall be withdrawn and cannot be used against the respondent in any proceedings.

(d)   **(Affidavit of consent)**   A respondent who consents to a stated sanction shall personally execute an affidavit stating that:

(1)   The respondent consents to the sanction;

(2)   The consent is freely and voluntarily rendered;

(3)   The respondent admits the truth of the charges as alleged; and

(4)   The respondent waives review by the Supreme Court.

Adopted Oct. 24, 1996, effective Dec. 1, 1996.

Rule 128.   Amendments to Notice or Answer; Dismissals.

(a)   **(Amendments)**   The commission, at any time prior to its determination, may allow or require amendments to the notice of formal proceedings and may allow amendments to the answer. During the evidentiary hearing, the special masters may allow amendments to the notice to conform to proof. If a motion to amend the notice to set forth additional facts not presented at the hearing is made during the evidentiary hearing, the chairperson of the commission, or the chairperson's designee, shall determine whether the motion shall be determined by the full commission or the special masters. In case such an amendment is made, the judge shall be given reasonable time both to answer the amendment and to prepare and present his or her defense against the matters charged thereby.

(b)   **(Dismissals by examiner)**   At any time after the filing of formal charges and before final disposition, where exigent circumstances prevent consideration by the full commission, the examiner, with the concurrence of the director–chief counsel and the chairperson, may dismiss any charge from the notice of formal proceedings, if it appears that the available evidence is insufficient to sustain the charge or that dismissal is otherwise in the interest of justice, and such dismissal is not tantamount to dismissal of the proceedings as a whole.

(c)   **(Dismissals by special masters)   The special masters may not dismiss any charge contained in the notice of formal proceedings.**

Adopted Oct. 24, 1996, effective Dec. 1, 1996; amended June 26, 2019, Oct. 9, 2020.

Rule 129.   Report of Masters.

(a)   **(Transcript)**   Upon the completion of **the presentation of evidence at** a hearing before the masters, a transcript of the hearing shall be promptly prepared and submitted to the Legal Advisor**,** who shall promptly mail a copy to each of the special masters, the examiner and the respondent judge.

(b)   **(Submission of proposed findings of fact and conclusions of law)**   Unless the masters specify an earlier date, the examiner and the respondent judge shall submit to the masters proposed findings of fact and conclusions of law, with citations to the transcript and exhibits, no later than 30 days after mailing of the [1] transcript **described in rule 129(a)**. Submission to the masters shall occur by a delivery method that results in actual receipt by them of the documents on or before the specified due date for submission. The masters may waive the submission of such proposed findings and conclusions.

(c)   **(Preparation of report of masters)**   Within 45 days after mailing of the [2] transcript **described in rule 129(a)** or within 15 days after submission of the parties' proposed findings of fact and conclusions of law, whichever occurs later, the masters shall submit a report to the commission. Prior to the submission of their report, the masters may require such additional briefing and argument by the examiner and the respondent judge as the masters may desire. Upon request of the presiding master, the chair of the commission or the chair's designee may grant additional time for the submission of the report of the masters to the commission.

(d)   **(Content of report of masters)**   The report of the masters shall contain findings of fact and conclusions of law, along with an analysis of the evidence and reasons for the findings and conclusions, but shall not contain a recommendation as to discipline.

(e)   **(Copy of report to judge and examiner)**   Upon receiving the report of the masters, the commission shall promptly mail a copy to the judge and the examiner.

Adopted Oct. 24, 1996, effective Dec. 1, 1996; amended Jan. 29, 2003, Oct. 25, 2005, Mar. 23, 2011, Oct. 9, 2020.

Rule 129.   2020 Deletes. [1] hearing [2] hearing

Rule 130.   Briefs to the Commission.

(a)   **(Filing of opening briefs)**   Within 15 days after the date of mailing of the copy of the masters' report to the judge as reflected on the proof of service by mail, the examiner or the judge may file with the commission opening briefs which may consist of objections to the report of the special masters and points and authorities concerning the issues in the matter, including the issue of sanctions. Objections to the masters' report and all factual statements shall be specific and shall be supported by reference to the book and page number of the record. Briefs shall conform in style to subdivision (b) of rule 8.204 of the California Rules of Court, shall follow the length limitations set forth in subdivision (c) of rule 8.204 of the California Rules of Court, and, when filed by the examiner, a copy shall be sent by first-class mail to the judge.

(b)   **(Response to briefs)**   Within 10 days after the filing of opening briefs, the examiner or the judge may file with the commission a response.

Adopted Oct. 24, 1996, effective Dec. 1, 1996; amended Jan. 29, 2003, Jan. 31, 2007, Mar. 23, 2011.

Rule 131.   Participation by Non-Parties.

Briefs of amicus curiae will be considered by the commission if they present legal issues or represent perspectives not otherwise presented or represented by the parties. An amicus curiae brief may not be used to present inadmissible or non-admitted evidentiary materials to the commission.

A brief of an amicus curiae may be filed only if accompanied by the written consent of all parties, or upon a motion demonstrating to the chairperson of the commission or the chairperson's designee that the filing of the brief would be helpful to the commission in the resolution of the pending matter. When consent to the filing of a brief of an amicus curiae is refused by a party to the case, a motion for leave to file the brief, accompanied by the proposed brief, may be presented to the chairperson or the chairperson's designee. The motion shall concisely state the nature of the applicant's interest and set forth facts or questions of law that have not been, or reasons for believing that they will not be, presented by the parties and their relevancy to the disposition of the case. The motion may be in letter form but may not exceed four pages. The commission shall forward copies of any such motion and proposed brief to both the examiner and the judge.

The cover of the amicus brief must identify the party supported, and the brief shall not exceed 50 pages in length. Evidentiary references shall include citation to the record before the commission.

An amicus brief shall be submitted or filed within the time limits prescribed for the party that the brief supports. No reply briefs or briefs of an amicus curiae in support of reconsideration shall be received.

Any brief of an amicus curiae that fails to comply with this rule will not be considered by the commission.

Adopted Oct. 24, 1996, effective Dec. 1, 1996.

Rule 132.   Appearance Before Commission.

Upon receipt of the masters' report and any objections, the commission shall give the judge and the examiner an opportunity to be heard orally before the commission, and written notice of the time and place of such hearing shall be mailed to the judge, at least 10 days prior thereto.

Adopted Oct. 24, 1996, effective Dec. 1, 1996.

Rule 133. Hearing Additional Evidence.

(a) The commission may order a hearing for the taking of additional evidence at any time while the matter is pending before it. The order shall set the time and place of hearing and shall indicate the matters on which the evidence is to be taken. A copy of such order shall be sent by mail to the judge at least 10 days prior to the date of hearing.

(b) In any case in which masters have been appointed, the hearing of additional evidence may be before such masters or before the commission, and the proceedings therein shall be in conformance with the provisions of rules 121 to 130, inclusive.

Adopted Oct. 24, 1996, effective Dec. 1, 1996; amended Jan. 29, 2003.

Rule 134. Commission Vote.

The commission may privately or publicly admonish, censure, remove or retire a judge, or find a person unfit to serve as a subordinate judicial officer. The affirmative vote of six members of the commission who have considered the record and report of the masters and who were present at any oral hearing as provided in rule 132 or, when the hearing was before the commission without masters, of six members of the commission who have considered the record, and at least four of whom were present when the evidence was produced, is required for a private or public admonishment, censure, removal or retirement of a judge, or a finding that a person is unfit to serve as a subordinate judicial officer, or for dismissal of the proceedings.

Adopted Oct. 24, 1996, effective Dec. 1, 1996; amended Oct. 8, 1998, Feb. 11, 1999, Jan. 29, 2003.

Rule 134.5. Rule of Necessity.

A commission member shall not be subject to disqualification based on an actual or potential conflict of interest if his or her disqualification would prevent the existence of a quorum. This rule does not apply if a quorum can be convened with members who are not actually present. The basis of the commission member's actual or potential conflict and the reason the member's participation was necessary shall be recorded in the minutes and included in any resulting discipline.

Adopted May 23, 2007.

Rule 135. Record of Commission Proceedings.

The commission shall maintain records of all actions taken by the commission concerning a judge. Notice of any disciplinary determination and notice of any disqualification under article VI, section 18(b) of the California Constitution shall be mailed to the judge. In all formal proceedings, the commission shall prepare a transcript of the testimony and of all proceedings and shall make written findings of fact and conclusions of law.

Adopted Oct. 24, 1996, effective Dec. 1, 1996.

Rule 136. Finality.

A commission determination to impose discipline upon a judge following formal proceedings under rule 118 shall become final 30 days after the date of the order regarding the disciplinary determination.

Adopted Oct. 24, 1996, effective Dec. 1, 1996.

Rule 137. Retroactivity.

Those cases in which formal proceedings have been instituted on or before February 28, 1995 will be governed by the provisions of article VI, section 18 of the California Constitution which are operative and in effect as of February 28, 1995. Those cases in which formal proceedings are instituted on or after March 1, 1995 will be governed by the provisions of article VI, section 18 of the California Constitution operative as of March 1, 1995.

Adopted Oct. 24, 1996, effective Dec. 1, 1996.

Rule 138. Definitions.

In these rules, unless the context or subject matter otherwise requires:

(a) "Commission" means the Commission on Judicial Performance.

(b) "Judge" means a judge of any court of this state or a retired judge who has elected to serve on senior judge status or former judge as provided in California Constitution, article VI, section 18(d). For purposes of these rules, "judge" also means a court commissioner or referee, included as subordinate judicial officers in the commission's jurisdiction under California Constitution, article VI, section 18.1.

(c) "Chairperson" includes the acting chairperson.

(d) "Masters" means the special master or special masters appointed by the Supreme Court upon request of the commission.

(e) "Presiding master" means the master so designated by the Supreme Court or, if no designation is made, the judge selected by the panel.

(f) "Examiner" means the counsel designated by the commission to gather and present evidence before the masters or commission with respect to the charges against a judge.

(g) "Shall" is mandatory and "may" is permissive.

(h) "Mail" and "mailed" include ordinary mail, **email,** and personal delivery.

(i) "Filing" means delivering to commission staff at the commission office during regular business hours. A filing may be evidenced by a conformed copy of the cover page of each document submitted for filing. To be filed, a document must be accompanied by a proof of service of the document upon the other party or parties.

Adopted Oct. 24, 1996, effective Dec. 1, 1996; amended Oct. 8, 1998, Feb. 11, 1999, Oct. 9, 2020.

Rules of Jud Perf

POLICY DECLARATIONS OF THE COMMISSION ON JUDICIAL PERFORMANCE

PREAMBLE

In consideration of the need for both uniformity and continuity of procedure and equitable, expeditious resolution of recurrent and detailed issues of procedure, the commission has authorized the formulation of the following policy declarations detailing commission policies, procedures and practices. These policy declarations are to reflect internal procedural detail neither duplicative of nor inconsistent with constitutional mandate or statutes or commission rules. These policy declarations are based upon concepts of utility, experience, and fair hearing of matters before the commission.

Rules referred to in the policy declarations are Rules of the Commission on Judicial Performance.

TITLE

These policy declarations shall be known and may be cited as the Policy Declarations of the Commission on Judicial Performance.

DIVISION I
COMPLAINTS AND INVESTIGATIONS

Anonymous complaints. Policy Declaration 1.1.
Reconsideration of complaints closed upon initial review. Policy Declaration 1.1.5.
Staff inquiries. Policy Declaration 1.2.
Staff inquiry letters. Policy Declaration 1.3.
Preliminary investigations. Policy Declaration 1.4.
Preliminary investigation letters. Policy Declaration 1.5.
Authorization for staff inquiries and preliminary investigations between meetings. Policy Declaration 1.6.
Authorization for supplemental staff inquiry and preliminary investigation letters between meetings. Policy Declaration 1.6.5.
Staff inquiry and preliminary investigation letters not authorized or determined not to be warranted. Policy Declaration 1.7.
Cases removed from active calendar. Policy Declaration 1.8.
Admonishments to persons giving interviews and statements. Policy Declaration 1.9.
Consent, preservation of witness interviews and statements. Policy Declaration 1.10.
Independent record of witness statements. Policy Declaration 1.11.
Investigation subpoenas. Policy Declaration 1.12.
Witness statements under oath. Policy Declaration 1.13.
Submission of character letters. Policy Declaration 1.14.

Policy Declaration 1.1. Anonymous Complaints.

Staff will evaluate anonymous complaints for merit; if a complaint is deemed sufficiently meritorious, it will be placed on the oversight agenda for consideration by the commission as to whether or not it should be docketed.

Approved May 28, 1997.

Policy Declaration 1.1.5. Reconsideration of Complaints Closed Upon Initial Review.

If a matter is closed by the commission at initial review because a complaint does not state sufficient facts or information to establish a prima facie case of misconduct, the complainant shall be informed that if further new information is provided, it will be reviewed and, if sufficient, the complaint will be reconsidered.

Approved June 28, 2017.

Policy Declaration 1.2. Staff Inquiries.

The staff inquiry is one of the commission's two levels of investigation. A staff inquiry may, but need not, precede a preliminary investigation. The purpose of a staff inquiry is to determine whether sufficient facts exist to warrant a preliminary investigation.

At the conclusion of a staff inquiry the commission may take any of the following actions:
(1) Close the matter;
(2) Authorize a preliminary investigation; or
(3) Issue an advisory letter.

A judge must receive an inquiry letter and be afforded an opportunity to respond before an advisory letter may issue.

Approved May 28, 1997.

Policy Declaration 1.3. Staff Inquiry Letters.

An inquiry letter includes specification of the allegations and may include: the date of the conduct; the location(s) where the conduct occurred; if applicable, the name(s) of the case(s) or identification of the court proceeding(s) in relation to which the conduct occurred. If the inquiry concerns statements made by or to the judge, the letter may also include the text or summaries of the comments.

The purpose of the inquiry letter is to afford the judge an opportunity to provide such matters as the judge may choose, including information about the factual aspects of the allegations and other relevant comment.

Approved May 28, 1997.

Policy Declaration 1.4. Preliminary Investigations.

The preliminary investigation is the second of the commission's two levels of investigation. A preliminary investigation may follow a staff inquiry or may be instituted without a staff inquiry having been conducted. Where the allegations, if true, would warrant consideration of commission action greater than issuance of an advisory letter or when the use of investigation subpoenas and more formal investigative procedures are contemplated, the commission may commence with a preliminary investigation. The purpose of a preliminary investigation is to determine whether formal proceedings should be instituted and a hearing held.

At the conclusion of a preliminary investigation, or at the conclusion of a period of monitoring under rule 112, the commission may take any of the following actions:
(1) Close the matter;
(2) Issue an advisory letter;
(3) Issue a notice of tentative private admonishment or notice of tentative public admonishment; or
(4) Institute formal proceedings.

A judge must receive an inquiry letter and be afforded an opportunity to respond before an advisory letter may issue. A judge must receive a preliminary investigation letter and be afforded an opportunity to respond before a notice of tentative private admonishment or notice of tentative public admonishment may issue or formal proceedings may be instituted.

Approved May 28, 1997; amended June 26, 2019.

Policy Declaration 1.5. Preliminary Investigation Letters.

A preliminary investigation letter provides the judge notice of the investigation and the nature of the charge under review and may include: the date of the conduct; the location(s) where the conduct occurred; if applicable, the name of the case(s) or identification of the court proceeding(s) in relation to which the conduct occurred. If the investigation concerns statements made by or to the judge, the letter may also include the text or summaries of the comments.

The purpose of the preliminary investigation letter is to afford the judge an opportunity to provide such matters as the judge may choose including information about the factual aspects of the allegations and other relevant comment.

Approved May 28, 1997.

Policy Declaration 1.6.   Authorization for Staff Inquiries and Preliminary Investigations Between Meetings.

In instances where a matter comes to the attention of the commission between meetings, which on its face appears to warrant a staff inquiry or a preliminary investigation and there has already been direct communication with the subject judge or other exigent circumstances exist, an effort should be made, whenever possible, to poll all of the commission members for authorization of a staff inquiry or preliminary investigation. If, in the discretion of the chairperson or acting chairperson, polling all of the members is not feasible, the chairperson or acting chairperson may authorize the staff inquiry or preliminary investigation. When a staff inquiry or preliminary investigation is authorized without a poll of the members, the members shall be promptly notified of the action taken.

Approved May 28, 1997.

Policy Declaration 1.6.5.   Authorization for Supplemental Staff Inquiry and Preliminary Investigation Letters Between Meetings.

When a judge's response to a staff inquiry or preliminary investigation letter fails to respond to an allegation in the letter or reveals additional instances or a variation of the same conduct that is the subject of the commission's investigation, the chairperson or acting chairperson may authorize staff to send a supplemental letter to obtain the judge's explanation concerning the omitted, additional or variation of the allegations.

Approved Feb. 1, 2017.

Policy Declaration 1.7.   Staff Inquiry and Preliminary Investigation Letters Not Authorized or Determined Not to Be Warranted.

At the time a staff inquiry or preliminary investigation is authorized by the commission, the authorization may or may not include writing the judge a letter, in addition to other investigation. If information acquired during the inquiry or preliminary investigation establishes that there is no basis for further proceedings, the inquiry or preliminary investigation may be closed without the judge being contacted. An inquiry or preliminary investigation letter authorized by the commission need not be sent if information obtained by staff before the letter is sent shows that the letter may not be warranted.

Approved May 28, 1997.

Policy Declaration 1.8.   Cases Removed From Active Calendar.

The commission may defer its consideration of a pending staff inquiry or preliminary investigation and direct that the matter be removed from the commission's active calendar. Circumstances which may warrant deferral in the commission's consideration of a matter include: when the case from which the complaint arose is still pending before the judge; when an appeal or ancillary proceeding is pending in which factual issues or claims relevant to the complaint are to be resolved; when criminal or other proceedings involving the judge are pending. In appropriate cases, the complainant may be notified that the commission has deferred action on the complaint.

When a matter is removed from the commission's active calendar, it shall be placed on the commission agenda at every meeting, and subject to active consideration at the discretion of the commission.

Approved May 28, 1997; amended Mar. 22, 2017.

Policy Declaration 1.9.   Admonishments to Persons Giving Interviews and Statements.

In the course of a staff inquiry or preliminary investigation, persons questioned or interviewed to ascertain the validity of allegations shall be admonished that the inquiry or investigation is confidential under the California Constitution and Commission Rules. When it appears that there may be use of the elicited information in connection with possible testimony or discovery, the person providing the information shall be so advised.

Approved May 28, 1997.

Policy Declaration 1.10.   Consent, Preservation of Witness Interviews and Statements.

Consent to mechanical recording may be obtained from interviewees. Statements and interviews may be transcribed and preserved, and may be submitted to interviewees for signature and verification.

Approved May 28, 1997.

Policy Declaration 1.11.   Independent Record of Witness Statements.

Where a witness statement or interview is not transcribed or recorded, it is not to be conveyed, commented upon or otherwise communicated to the commission by commission staff unless an independent memorialization of the statement has been prepared by staff (a writing other than a case memorandum or report from staff to the commission).

Approved May 28, 1997.

Policy Declaration 1.12.   Investigation Subpoenas.

Commission investigation subpoenas may issue upon application to the commission chairperson, vice-chairperson or the designee of either, stating the name, address and title, if any, of the person from whom information is sought, and whether or not a statement under oath is to be taken.

Approved May 28, 1997.

Policy Declaration 1.13.   Witness Statements Under Oath.

When the statement of a witness is taken under oath pursuant to Government Code section 68750, the witness may be given an opportunity to review and make corrections to the transcript of the witness's testimony at the office of the court reporter before whom the statement was taken. A copy of the statement shall not otherwise be furnished to the witness unless formal proceedings are instituted in the matter in which the testimony was given and the witness's statement is discoverable under rule 122.

Approved June 25, 1998.

Policy Declaration 1.14.   Submission of Character Letters.

(1)   Written communications submitted during staff inquiry or preliminary investigation

During a staff inquiry or preliminary investigation, written communications containing information related to the character of a judge who has a matter pending before the commission may be submitted to the commission. Such written communications must be delivered to the commission office, and shall not be delivered to individual commission members.

In determining the weight to be given to written character references, the commission may consider, but is not limited to, the following list of factors:

(a)   The length of time the author of the written communication has known the judge, and the nature and extent of the author's contact with the judge;

(b)   Whether the character reference is submitted in the form of a declaration signed under penalty of perjury; and

(c)   Whether the information provided by a person other than a judge or subordinate judicial officer is based on personal knowledge.

Pursuant to canon 2B, character references submitted by judges or subordinate judicial officers must be based on personal knowledge.

(2)   Written communications submitted after the initiation of formal proceedings

After the initiation of formal proceedings, written communications related to the character of the respondent judge may only be submitted by stipulation of the parties at the hearing held pursuant to rule 123 or rule 133. After the completion of the evidentiary hearing pursuant to rule 123 or 133, such communications shall not be accepted by the commission.

Approved May 22, 2008.

DIVISION II
DISCIPLINE, APPEARANCES AND FORMAL PROCEEDINGS

Opposition to tentative private and tentative public admonishments; statement of objections and appearance. Policy Declaration 2.1.

Limitation on requests for correction of advisory letters. **Policy Declaration 2.1.5.**

Date of hearing. **Policy Declaration 2.2.**

Prehearing proceedings. **Policy Declaration 2.3.**

Deposition transcripts taken pursuant to Rule 122(g). **Policy Declaration 2.3.5.**

Agreed statement and discipline by consent. **Policy Declaration 2.4.**

Order barring assignments to former judges. **Policy Declaration 2.5.**

Modification of decision following formal proceedings. **Policy Declaration 2.6.**

Citation of commission decisions. **Policy Declaration 2.7.**

Policy Declaration 2.1. Opposition to Tentative Private and Tentative Public Admonishments; Statement of Objections and Appearance.

An appearance before the commission to object to the imposition of a tentative private admonishment under rule 114, or to object to the imposition of a tentative public admonishment under rule 116, means an opportunity for a judge to informally object to the imposition of an admonishment in argument before the commission based on the proceedings which resulted in the issuance of a notice of tentative admonishment and the judge's statement of objections.

A judge's demand for an appearance after notice of tentative private admonishment under rule 114, or notice of tentative public admonishment under rule 116, shall include a written statement of the basis of the judge's objections to the tentative admonishment. The appearance before the commission will be scheduled after receipt of the judge's demand for appearance and statement of objections. The commission may request further briefing.

At the appearance before the commission, the judge may appear with or without counsel. The appearance is not an evidentiary hearing and there is no testimony by witnesses. Argument shall be limited to oral presentation not to exceed thirty (30) minutes by the judge and thirty (30) minutes by trial counsel or other attorney designated by the commission to present argument in support of the admonishment.

Approved May 28, 1997; amended Oct. 6, 2009, Oct. 19, 2011, June 26, 2019.

Policy Declaration 2.1.5. Limitation on Requests for Correction of Advisory Letters.

Applications pursuant to rule 111.5 are limited to requests for correction of errors of fact or law or both. Rule 111.5 applications are not intended to provide an opportunity to present arguments and facts previously presented to the commission in response to the staff inquiry or preliminary investigation.

Approved June 30, 2010.

Policy Declaration 2.2. Date of Hearing.

Absent unusual circumstances, the evidentiary hearing on the charges set forth in a notice of formal proceedings shall be set to commence two to four months following the issuance under rule 118 of the notice of formal proceedings.

Approved May 28, 1997; amended Aug. 26, 2004.

Policy Declaration 2.3. Prehearing Proceedings.

The commission or the special masters may require prehearing status statements, briefs or conferences (either by telephone or in person), or require any other appropriate prehearing proceeding. The purpose of such prehearing proceedings is to provide the commission or the special masters with pertinent information for prehearing and to ensure that the hearing proceeds efficiently. The masters may issue appropriate prehearing orders and may determine whether any such order needs be in writing.

Approved May 28, 1997; amended Aug. 26, 2004.

Policy Declaration 2.3.5. Deposition Transcripts Taken Pursuant to Rule 122(g).

The following procedures apply to the transcription of depositions taken pursuant to rule 122(g):

(1) The party noticing the deposition shall arrange for a court reporter.

(2) The party noticing the deposition shall bear the cost of the transcription.

(3) The court reporter shall send written notice to the deponent, the judge, and the examiner when the original transcript of the deposition is available.

(4) The court reporter shall certify on the transcript of the deposition that the deponent was duly sworn and that the transcript is a true record of the testimony given.

(5) The original transcript shall be transmitted to the party noticing the deposition, at that party's expense. The other party and the deponent may obtain a copy of the transcript from the court reporter upon request and at the expense of that party or deponent.

(6) A copy of the transcript shall not be filed with the commission unless admitted at a hearing held pursuant to rule 123 or rule 133, or as an exhibit to a motion filed with the commission or the special masters.

Approved Jan. 30, 2013.

Policy Declaration 2.4. Agreed Statement and Discipline by Consent.

An agreed statement under rule 125(a) may be offered by the respondent judge and the examiner in place of all or part of the evidence after institution of formal proceedings. An agreement between the respondent judge and the examiner for discipline by consent under rule 127 may be submitted to the commission after institution of formal proceedings. The examiner is responsible for handling negotiations with the respondent judge or respondent judge's counsel concerning agreed statements and agreements for discipline by consent.

Approved May 28, 1997.

Policy Declaration 2.5. Order Barring Assignments to Former Judges.

If the commission determines to bar a former judge from receiving an assignment, appointment to or reference of work from any California state court, pursuant to article VI, section 18(d) of the California Constitution, the order barring the judge from receiving assignments will be included in the commission's order of censure.

Notice of an order barring a former judge from receiving assignments shall be given to the Chief Justice and to the Administrative Office of the Courts for distribution to the presiding judges of the state courts.

Approved June 25, 1998.

Policy Declaration 2.6. Modification of Decision Following Formal Proceedings.

At any time before a commission determination to impose discipline upon a judge following formal proceedings becomes final under rule 136, the commission may modify the order regarding the disciplinary determination to eliminate any erroneous statement of fact or law in the order.

Adopted June 29, 2005.

Policy Declaration 2.7. Citation of Commission Decisions.

Citations to commission decisions following formal proceedings should be to the CJP Supplement to the Official California Reports in the following form: Inquiry Concerning _____ (year) (volume) Cal.4th CJP Supp. (page). Citations to public decisions not reported in the Official California Reports should be in the following form: [Censure/Censure and Bar/Public Admonishment] of Judge _____ (year) (page).

Approved June 30, 2010.

DIVISION III
COMMISSION ADMINISTRATION

Policy Declaration 3.1. Setting Regular and Special Meetings.

(1) Before the end of each calendar year, staff will propose a choice of dates for each meeting for the next calendar year. At its March

Rules of Jud Perf

organizational meeting, the commission will approve the meeting dates for the remainder of the year.

(2) A special meeting shall be called (a) upon not less than five (5) days notice by the chairperson or acting chairperson, or (b) upon notice of request of not less than four (4) members.

Approved May 28, 1997.

Policy Declaration 3.2. Organizational Meeting; Election of Chairperson and Vice-Chairperson.

At its March meeting each year, the commission shall organize itself for the conduct of business for the ensuing year and shall select a chairperson and vice-chairperson.

Approved May 28, 1997.

Policy Declaration 3.3. Preparation of Annual Report.

At the end of each calendar year, staff will prepare a draft annual report for circulation to the commission or such members as the commission delegates for review of the draft report. After the draft report is reviewed and suggestions made, staff will revise the draft report in accordance therewith and will submit the report in final form to the chairperson for approval for publication within the first quarter of the calendar year.

Approved May 28, 1997; amended Feb. 11, 1999.

Policy Declaration 3.4. Availability of Commission Rules and Policy Declarations.

The rules and policy declarations of the commission will be published by the commission and distributed to the public upon request. The commission's rules and policy declarations are also to be published, to the extent possible, in legal publications including the California Official Reports Advance Sheets and other legal publications and on-line services.

Approved May 28, 1997; amended Feb. 11, 1999.

Policy Declaration 3.5. Review of Commission Rules, Proposed Changes.

(1) Biennial Rules Review

Every two years, in even-numbered years, the commission shall review its rules, and any rule enactments, amendments or repeals proposed by commission members or staff, or third parties. Proposed changes to the rules by commission members or staff, or third parties which are received by the commission other than during its biennial rules review may be considered by the commission and either deferred to the next review of the rules or, in the commission's discretion, acted upon prior to the next biennial rules review pursuant to the procedures specified in this policy declaration.

(2) Submission of Rule Proposals

Proposed rules, amendments and repeals must be submitted in writing to the commission's office and include a statement of the specific purpose of the proposed rule, amendment or repeal and explain how the proposal would achieve the intended purpose. The commission or a designated member of staff may, in writing, solicit further information or clarification from the proponent of the rule, amendment or repeal.

(3) Public Comment

All rule proposals submitted to the commission pursuant to subdivision (2) or by a member of the commission or commission staff shall be reviewed by the commission or the commission's rules committee. If, after review, the commission is considering the adoption of a proposed rule or amendment or the repeal of an existing rule, the proposal must be circulated for public comment. The invitation to comment shall include the express language of the proposal or proposed change and an explanation of the reason for the proposed change. There shall be a 60-day comment period, the expiration of which shall be noticed in the invitation to comment. The time to comment may be shortened to 30 days or extended to 90 days for good cause. Within 30 days after the expiration of the initial comment period, responses to comments submitted during the initial comment period may be submitted. The period to respond to comments may be shortened for good cause. All comments and responses shall be submitted in writing. The commission shall not consider any further comments or input after the expiration of the comment and response periods.

The commission may determine that exigent circumstances require it to adopt, amend, or suspend a rule on an interim basis without first circulating it for public comment. Before the rule is enacted, amended or repealed on a permanent basis, it shall be circulated for public comment according to the provisions of this policy declaration.

The commission may correct inadvertent, non-substantive errors in commission rules without circulating the revision for public comment and issuing a public report.

(4) Commission Action on Proposal

As soon as feasible after the expiration of the comment and response periods, the commission shall review and consider all written comments and responses received and vote to adopt, modify, or reject the proposal. The commission may modify the proposed rule or amendment in view of the comments received and other considerations without seeking further public comment, unless the modification results in a significant change to the substance of the proposal. The adoption, amendment, or repeal of a rule becomes effective as of the date of the commission's action, unless otherwise specified.

(5) Public Report

A final public report shall be issued as promptly as possible after the commission votes to adopt, reject or modify the proposed rule. The report shall include the express language of the rule or amendment adopted by the commission and the language of any rule that was repealed by the commission. The report shall include a summary of any written comment submitted during the comment and response periods together with an explanation of why a change was made to accommodate the comment or the reasons for making no change. The commission may respond to repetitive comments as a group or summarily dismiss irrelevant comments.

(6) Public File

The commission shall maintain a public rules file. The file shall include copies of any rule proposals submitted to the commission pursuant to this policy declaration, written correspondence with proponents of a rule amendment, the invitation to comment circulated by the commission, any comments received during the public comment and response periods, the final public report, and any external reports, studies or documentary evidence relied on by the commission in reaching its determination on a proposed rule, amendment or repeal. Confidential information included in a public comment shall be redacted from the copy placed in the public file. Copies of any materials contained in the public file shall be provided to any member of the public upon request, subject to a reasonable administrative fee.

Approved May 28, 1997; amended Feb. 4, 2004, Dec. 5, 2013, July 11, 2018, July 1, 2020.

Policy Declaration 3.6. Policy Declarations.

When there is commission approval for staff to draft a policy declaration, any proposed enactment, amendment or repeal shall be submitted to each commission member for consideration at a duly convened meeting of the commission at which a vote thereon is taken. The commission may have the proposed enactment, amendment or repeal reviewed by the rules committee prior to a vote by the commission.

Approved May 28, 1997; amended Jan. 30, 2013.

Policy Declaration 3.7. Staff Authorization for Announcements Between Meetings.

When the director believes an announcement pursuant to California Constitution, article VI, section 18(k) or pursuant to rule 102(c) is appropriate between meetings in a particular proceeding, the director shall so advise the chairperson or acting chairperson. An effort should be made, whenever possible, to poll all of the members for authorization of the announcement. If, in the discretion of the chairperson or acting chairperson, polling all of the members is not feasible, the chairperson or acting chairperson may authorize the announcement. When an announcement is authorized without a poll of the members, the members shall be promptly notified of the action taken.

Approved May 28, 1997.

Policy Declaration 3.7.5. Announcement at Conclusion of Previously-Announced Investigation.

When the commission has issued a public statement announcing or confirming that a matter is under investigation pursuant to article VI, section 18(k) or pursuant to rule 102(c), at the conclusion of the investigation, the commission shall issue a public statement indicating that the previously-announced investigation has been completed. If the matter has been concluded by the commission, the announcement shall so state. If the commission has instituted formal proceedings, the announcement shall so state, and the announcement may include an explanation of formal proceedings.

Approved Feb. 11, 1999.

Policy Declaration 3.8. Duties of Trial Counsel.

Trial counsel shall serve as examiner in formal proceedings instituted by the commission and shall represent the commission in litigation before the California Supreme Court and other courts when directed to do so by the commission. Trial counsel shall serve under the direction of the commission's director-chief counsel.

Approved May 28, 1997.

Policy Declaration 3.9. Legal Advisor to Commissioners.

The commission has established the position of legal advisor to commissioners and shall designate an attorney to serve in that capacity. The legal advisor reports directly to the commission and shall assist the commission in its adjudicatory function, including in its consideration and adjudication of matters in which formal proceedings have been instituted and matters in which judges demand an appearance before the commission to object to a tentative private admonishment or a tentative public admonishment.

The legal advisor shall not participate in the investigation of complaints or prosecution of charges against judges. If the legal advisor previously participated in an investigation or adversarial proceeding in another capacity as an attorney for the commission, he or she shall not assist the commission in its deliberations or adjudication of that matter absent a written waiver by the judge.

The legal advisor shall present to the commission proposals for disposition of matters in which formal proceedings have been instituted which have been jointly offered by trial counsel and the judge or judge's counsel. After institution of formal proceedings, the legal advisor shall be responsible for requesting the appointment of special masters by the Supreme Court and shall serve as the commission's liaison to special masters appointed in formal proceedings.

The legal advisor shall perform such additional duties as may be assigned by the commission that do not require or cause the legal advisor to participate in the commission's investigatory or prosecutorial functions.

Approved May 28, 1997; amended Aug. 26, 2004, Oct. 19, 2011, June 26, 2019.

Policy Declaration 3.10. Records Disposition Policy.

At the beginning of each calendar year, the commission shall destroy all files which did not result in an advisory letter, public or private admonishment, public reproval, censure, removal or involuntary retirement, resignation or retirement with proceedings pending, or finding that a person was unfit to serve as a subordinate judicial officer as follows:

(1) Files involving complaints against municipal or superior court judges dated or docketed by the commission in the thirteenth year prior to the new calendar year; and

(2) Files involving complaints against appellate or Supreme Court justices dated or docketed by the commission in the nineteenth year prior to the new calendar year; and

(3) Files involving complaints against subordinate judicial officers dated or docketed by the commission in the thirteenth year prior to the new calendar year.

Approved May 28, 1997; amended Feb. 11, 1999.

Policy Declaration 3.11. Biennial Adjustment of Gift Limitation Amount.

(1) Code of Civil Procedure section 170.9(a) limits to $250 the total value of gifts that an individual judge may accept from any single source in any calendar year. Section 170.9(d) requires that the commission adjust that amount biennially to reflect changes in the Consumer Price Index, rounded to the nearest $10. Since section 170.9(d) took effect January 1, 1995, an adjustment must be made in subsequent odd-numbered years (commencing in 1997).

(2) The adjusted gift limitation amount shall apply as of January 1 of the year in which the adjustment is announced and shall remain in effect until January 1 of the next odd-numbered year.

(3) The adjusted gift limitation amount shall be calculated by the commission as follows:

(a) The base dollar amount ($250) shall be increased or decreased by the percentage change in the annual average California Consumer Price Index (CCPI) for all urban consumers from the base year (1994) to the end of the calendar year immediately preceding the year of adjustment.

(b) Formula: The base dollar amount ($250) is multiplied by a fraction whose numerator is the annual average CCPI for the even-numbered year preceding the year of adjustment and whose denominator is the 1994 annual average CCPI (151.5). The resulting dollar amount is rounded to the nearest $10, unless that amounts ends in the numeral five with no cents, in which case it is not rounded in either direction.

Approved May 28, 1997.

Policy Declaration 3.12. Extensions of Time.

Unnecessary delay in commission proceedings is incompatible with the commission's mandate to protect the public and the judiciary in general. Accordingly, extensions of time are disfavored.

Approved Aug. 26, 2004.

Policy Declaration 3.13. Procedures and Standards for Staff Recusal.

(1) The chairperson of the commission or the chairperson's designee shall be informed if any member of legal staff, the director, or the legal advisor has any possible conflicts of interest involving either a case assigned to him or her or any other case pending before the commission and of information that might be considered relevant to the question of disqualification, even if the attorney believes there is no actual basis for disqualification.

(2) The chairperson or the chairperson's designee shall make a determination as to whether the attorney shall be recused or other action taken. The commission shall be appraised at each meeting of any conflicts or potential conflicts brought to the attention of the chairperson. The commission may overrule or modify any resolution of a conflict by the chairperson.

(3) An attorney shall be recused under the following circumstances:

(a) The attorney in the course of a previous representation of a client has received confidential information that has any relevance to a commission investigation;

(b) The attorney has personal knowledge of disputed evidentiary facts concerning the proceedings;

(c) The attorney has a current personal, financial, or professional relationship with the judge, the judge's counsel, or the complainant;

(d) The attorney has a previous personal, financial, or professional relationship with the judge, the judge's counsel, or the complainant which casts a substantial doubt on the attorney's ability to be impartial;

(e) The attorney's spouse or partner has a personal, financial, or professional relationship with the judge, the judge's counsel, or the complainant which casts a substantial doubt on the attorney's ability to be impartial;

(f) Where a reasonable person aware of the facts would entertain a substantial doubt that the attorney would be impartial.

(4) In the event an attorney other than the director is recused, the recused attorney shall not review any materials concerning the matter or discuss the matter with commission staff. The recusal shall be noted prominently in the file and commission staff shall be directed not to circulate any materials concerning the matter to the recused attorney, not to consult with the recused attorney concerning the matter and not to discuss the matter in the presence of the recused attorney. The entire legal staff need not be recused from the matter unless the commission determines that the recused attorney's conflict casts a substantial doubt on the ability of the entire staff to be impartial. The recusal of the attorney shall be noted in the commission's minutes.

(5) In the event the director is recused, the entire legal staff, excluding the legal advisor, shall be recused. The commission may obtain outside counsel to handle intake, investigation, and any further proceedings involving the case, including acting as media contact, without consultation with the director or legal staff. The recusal of the director shall be noted in the commission's minutes.

(6) In the case of a recusal of the legal advisor or trial counsel, the commission may designate a member of legal staff or obtain outside counsel to advise the commission or act as examiner.

Approved June 30, 2010.

Policy Declaration 3.14. Certification Applications: Confidentiality.

The commission shall treat as confidential any information which is presented to the commission by a former judge or justice for certification to administer oaths or affirmations pursuant to Code of Civil Procedure Section 2093 and Government Code Section 1225 for retirement purposes, except the fact that a certification is in effect may be revealed.

Approved Dec. 1, 2015.

DIVISION IV
DISCLOSURE OF INFORMATION

Public safety. Policy Declaration 4.1.

Disclosure of information to prosecuting authorities. Policy Declaration 4.2.

Disclosure of disciplinary records to public entity upon request/with consent of judge. Policy Declaration 4.3.

Disclosure of records of disciplinary action to appointing authorities. Policy Declaration 4.4.

Disclosure of information regarding pending proceedings to appointing authorities. Policy Declaration 4.5.

Limitation on disclosure to appointing authorities—Complaints not yet reviewed by the commission. Policy Declaration 4.5.5.

Disclosure of information to public entities upon retirement or resignation. Policy Declaration 4.6.

Policy Declaration 4.1.   Public Safety.

The disclosure of information concerning a threat to public safety under rule 102(f) may be made by the chairperson, the director or the designee of either.

Approved May 28, 1997.

Policy Declaration 4.2.   Disclosure of Information to Prosecuting Authorities.

When, in the course of evaluating complaints or conducting investigations, commission staff acquires information revealing possible criminal conduct by a judge, former judge or by any other individual or entity, such information shall be brought to the attention of the commission at the earliest possible opportunity for consideration of a referral of the information to prosecuting authorities. Such a referral requires a vote of a majority of the commission members.

Approved May 28, 1997.

Policy Declaration 4.3.   Disclosure of Disciplinary Records to Public Entity Upon Request/With Consent of Judge.

When a judge requests or consents to the release of commission records of disciplinary action under rule 102(h), the judge's request must be made in writing to the commission office. If the judge is consenting to a request by a public entity for records of disciplinary action, the judge's written consent and a copy of the entity's request must be received by the commission office. Copies of any information released to the public entity shall be provided simultaneously to the judge requesting or consenting to the release of records.

Approved May 28, 1997.

Policy Declaration 4.4.   Disclosure of Records of Disciplinary Action to Appointing Authorities.

Requests by an appointing authority for records of disciplinary action pursuant to California Constitution, article VI, section 18.5 or rule 102(i) must be made in writing to the commission office. Copies of any information provided to the appointing authority shall be provided simultaneously to the applicant judge.

Approved May 28, 1997.

Policy Declaration 4.5.   Disclosure of Information Regarding Pending Proceedings to Appointing Authorities.

Requests by an appointing authority for information regarding pending investigations or proceedings pursuant to rule 102(j) must be made in writing to the commission office. Copies of any information provided to the appointing authority shall be provided simultaneously to the applicant judge.

Approved May 28, 1997.

Policy Declaration 4.5.5.   Limitation on Disclosure to Appointing Authorities—Complaints Not Yet Reviewed by the Commission.

When responding to a request for information regarding pending investigations from appointing authorities (rule 102(j)), the director-chief counsel shall state that the commission's discretionary authority to release information concerning pending investigations does not encompass comment on any complaint that may have been received by the commission and has not yet been reviewed by the commission to determine whether or not to authorize an investigation or whether any such complaint exists.

Approved Mar. 13, 2002.

Policy Declaration 4.6.   Disclosure of Information to Public Entities Upon Retirement or Resignation.

The release of information to a public entity following a judge's retirement or resignation, pursuant to rule 102(k), requires a vote of a majority of the commission members. The commission may, in its discretion, notify the judge that such disclosure is being made. Copies of any information being disclosed to the public entity may, in the commission's discretion, be made available to the judge who has retired or resigned.

Approved May 28, 1997; amended Jan. 29, 2003.

DIVISION V
DISABILITY RETIREMENT APPLICATIONS

Disability applications: confidentiality. Policy Declaration 5.1.

Disability applications: medical consultants. Policy Declaration 5.2.

Reexamination of judges retired for disability. Policy Declaration 5.3.

Procedure in disability retirement matters. Policy Declaration 5.4.

Disability applications: burden of proof. Policy Declaration 5.5.

Procedure in restoration to capacity matters. Policy Declaration 5.6.

Policy Declaration 5.1.   Disability Applications: Confidentiality.

The commission shall treat as confidential any information which is presented to the commission by a judge for retirement purposes, except as follows:

(1)   The fact and date that an application has been filed and has been approved or rejected or remains pending may be revealed.

(2)   If the Judges' Retirement System (JRS) submits a written request for information concerning a particular disability retirement application pursuant to Government Code section 75080(d) or 75580(a), the commission shall provide to JRS any information that the commission deems necessary to a full understanding of the commission's action, in furtherance of the statutory scheme embodied in articles 3 and 4 of the Judges' Retirement Law and articles 4 and 6 of the Judges' Retirement System II (JRS II). The commission shall furnish the judge in question with a copy of any documents provided to JRS. All information released under this section shall remain confidential and privileged.

Approved May 28, 1997; amended June 21, 2000, Aug. 26, 2004, Jan. 30, 2013.

Policy Declaration 5.2.   Disability Applications: Medical Consultants.

The commission may arrange with the University of California Medical Centers and/or other qualified medical practitioners for medical consultants to provide independent medical examinations for disability retirement applicants, to assist the commission as necessary in evaluating disability retirement applications under Government Code sections 75060 and 75560.1, making findings under policy declaration 5.4(4) in order to facilitate implementation of Government Code sections 75080(d) and 75580(a), and/or reevaluating the medical status of a judge retired on disability under Government Code sections 75060.6 and 75560.6.

Approved May 28, 1997; amended June 21, 2000, Jan. 30, 2013.

Policy Declaration 5.3.   Reexamination of Judges Retired for Disability.

When approving a request for disability retirement, the commission shall decide on a case-by-case basis whether and when the judge shall be required to be reexamined pursuant to Government Code section 75060.6 or 75560.6. Notwithstanding such decision, a judge retired for disability may be required to undergo reexamination pursuant to Government Code section 75060.6 or 75560.6.

Approved May 28, 1997; amended Jan. 30, 2013.

Policy Declaration 5.4.   Procedure in Disability Retirement Matters.

(1)   An application for disability retirement must include: a consent to disability retirement, executed by the judge or, in an application by a JRS II judge, a family member or legal representative acting on behalf of the judge pursuant to Government Code section 75560.1(a), and a medical certificate of disability, executed under penalty of perjury by a licensed physician. To complete the application, the commission ordinarily will require a medical report prepared by that physician in support of certification, which shall include a statement specifying the nature of the judicial duties that cannot be efficiently discharged due to the judge's disability, and all pertinent medical documentation.

A judge seeking the disability retirement allowance provided under Government Code section 75560.4(b) must inform the commission in the judge's consent to disability retirement that the judge is seeking a determination by the commission whether the disability is predominantly a result of injury arising out of and in the course of judicial service. The commission will not make a determination whether the injury is predominantly a result of injury arising out of and in the course of judicial service if the judge is entitled to 65 percent of the judge's final compensation on the effective date of the disability retirement under Government Code section 75560.4(a).

(2)   When a judge submits an application for disability retirement, the commission will advise the judge if the certifying physician's report or other medical documentation supporting the application is inadequate, and will give the judge thirty (30) days to supply more complete data. The judge shall cooperate in obtaining any medical/psychiatric records the commission or the special master needs in evaluating the judge's disability application.

(3)   Following receipt of a complete application, the commission may request review of medical reports and documents by independent consultants and/or medical examiners. One or more independent medical examinations and/or additional medical information may be requested within one hundred twenty (120) days of the first commission meeting after receipt of complete medical records. This time may be extended for good cause. If an independent medical examination is conducted, the commission will provide a copy of the examiner's report to the judge. If the examiner concludes that the judge suffers from a disability that precludes the efficient discharge of judicial duties and is permanent or likely to become so, the examiner's report shall include a statement specifying the nature of the judicial duties that cannot be efficiently discharged due to the disability.

If the judge has informed the commission that the judge is seeking a disability retirement allowance pursuant to Government Code section 75560.4(b), the examiner's report shall also set forth the examiner's opinion whether the disability is predominantly a result of injury arising out of and in the course of judicial service and the basis for that opinion.

(4)   Within sixty (60) days of the first commission meeting after receipt of all reports by consultants and medical examiners, the commission will: approve the application, or tentatively deny it, or extend its time to act on the application for good cause, "good cause" to include circumstances in which the judge's condition cannot yet be deemed permanent or likely to become so, within the meaning of Government Code section 75060 or 75560.1. If the commission extends its time to act, notice of such extension shall be provided to the judge.

(5)   If the commission approves the application, the commission will refer the application to the Chief Justice. If the Chief Justice approves the application, the Judges' Retirement System will be informed that the disability application has been approved. The commission may also prepare a statement of findings specifying the nature of the judicial duties that cannot be efficiently discharged due to the disability.

(6)   If the commission tentatively denies the application, or approves the application but tentatively determines that the disability is not predominantly a result of injury arising out of and in the course of judicial service, the commission will within thirty (30) days issue a tentative decision setting forth the reasons for the denial. The tentative decision will be provided to the judge upon issuance.

(7)   If the commission approves the disability application, but tentatively determines that the disability is not predominantly a result of injury arising out of and in the course of judicial service, the commission will refer the application to the Chief Justice. If the Chief Justice approves the application, Judges' Retirement System will be informed that the disability application has been approved, subject to a pending determination whether or not the disability is predominantly a result of injury arising out of and in the course of judicial service.

(8)   A tentative denial of the disability application or a determination that the disability is not predominantly a result of injury arising out of and in the course of judicial service becomes final thirty (30) days after issuance unless, within thirty (30) days of the tentative denial, or tentative determination, the judge (1) files a request to submit additional information to the commission, or (2) files a request for an evidentiary hearing to contest the tentative denial or tentative determination. A request to submit additional information shall explain the relevance of the additional information to the commission's determination(s). A request for an

evidentiary hearing shall specify the factual and legal issues to be contested at the evidentiary hearing.

(9)   If a judge's request to submit additional information is granted, the commission shall reconsider the tentative denial of the application or tentative work-related determination based on the new information submitted. Within sixty (60) days of the first commission meeting after receipt of the new information, the commission shall make a decision approving the application and referring it to the Chief Justice, or denying the application, and, if requested, shall make a determination either that the disability is work-related or is not work-related and advise the Judges' Retirement System.

(10)   Within thirty (30) days of the first commission meeting after a judge requests an evidentiary hearing, the commission will appoint a special master authorized to take evidence on the matter, and to report to the commission. The proceedings before the special master are not a de novo review of the basis for the commission's tentative denial of the disability application or tentative determination regarding work-relatedness. The special master's report to the commission shall contain proposed findings of fact and conclusions of law on the issues specified in the judge's request for an evidentiary hearing and on any other issues raised by the parties during the proceedings, as deemed relevant by the special master.

(11)   Upon appointment, the special master shall be given a copy of the judge's application for disability retirement, the commission's tentative denial of the application or tentative determination that the disability is not predominantly a result of injury arising out of and in the course of judicial service, and any medical and/or psychiatric reports considered by the commission. These documents may be considered by the special master in reaching proposed findings and conclusions.

(12)   The special master may require briefing from the parties before and after the evidentiary hearing. The judge and the examiner shall submit a list of witnesses and exhibits to be presented at the evidentiary hearing within ten days prior to the hearing, unless otherwise specified by the special master.

(13)   The California Evidence Code shall be applicable to an evidentiary hearing before a special master held pursuant to policy declaration 5.4(6).

(14)   Within one hundred twenty (120) days after the appointment of a special master, the master will refer the matter back to the commission with a report containing proposed findings, unless the special master requests and is granted an extension of time from the chairperson or another member designated by the chairperson or the commission.

(15)   Within sixty (60) days of the first commission meeting following such referral, the commission will make a decision approving the application and referring it to the Chief Justice or denying the application and advising the Chief Justice, or, pursuant to Government Code section 75560.4(b), determining either that the disability is predominantly a result of injury arising out of and in the course of judicial service or that it is not such an injury and advising Judges' Retirement System.

Approved May 28, 1997; amended June 21, 2000, Jan. 30, 2013, Mar. 22, 2017.

Policy Declaration 5.5.   Disability Applications: Burden of Proof.

Unless Government Code section 75062, 75063, or 75064, 75562, 75563 or 75564 applies, a judge seeking disability retirement must establish by a preponderance of the evidence that the judge is eligible for disability retirement under section 75560 or 75560.1 and that the judge is unable to discharge efficiently the duties of judicial office by reason of mental or physical disability that is or is likely to become permanent. A judge seeking benefits under section 75560.4(b) must establish by a preponderance of the evidence that the disability is predominantly a result of injury arising out of and in the course of judicial service.

Approved May 28, 1997; amended Jan. 30, 2013, Feb. 1, 2017.

Policy Declaration 5.6.   Procedure in Restoration to Capacity Matters.

(1)   An application for restoration to capacity must be in writing, executed by the judge, and be accompanied by one or more medical reports sufficient to establish that the judge is no longer mentally or physically incapacitated and is capable of discharging efficiently the duties of judicial office.

(2)   When a judge submits an application for restoration to capacity, the commission will advise the judge if the certifying physician's report

or other medical documentation supporting the application is inadequate, and will give the judge thirty (30) days to supply more complete data.

(3) Following receipt of a complete application, the commission may request review of medical reports and documents by independent consultants and/or medical examiners. One or more independent medical examinations may be requested within one hundred twenty (120) days of the first commission meeting after receipt of complete medical records. This time may be extended for good cause. If an independent medical examination is conducted, the commission will provide a copy of the examiner's report to the judge.

(4) Within sixty (60) days of the first commission meeting after receipt of all reports by consultants and medical examiners, the commission will either approve the application or tentatively deny it.

(5) If the commission tentatively denies the application, the commission will within thirty (30) days issue a tentative decision setting forth the reasons for the denial. The tentative decision will be provided to the judge upon issuance.

(6) A tentative denial becomes final thirty (30) days after issuance unless, within thirty (30) days of the tentative denial, the judge files a request to present additional evidence. Within thirty (30) days of the first commission meeting after such filing, the commission will appoint a special master authorized to take evidence, obtain additional medical information, and take any other steps the special master deems necessary to resolve the matter.

(7) Within one hundred eighty (180) days after the appointment of a special master, the master will refer the matter back to the commission with a report containing proposed findings.

(8) Within ninety (90) days of the first commission meeting following such referral, the commission will make a decision either approving the application for restoration to capacity or denying it.

Approved May 28, 1997.

DIVISION VI
CODE OF ETHICS FOR COMMISSION MEMBERS

Recusal. Policy Declaration 6.1.
Confidentiality. Policy Declaration 6.2.
Ex parte contacts. Policy Declaration 6.3.
Judicial election activities. Policy Declaration 6.4.
Impropriety and appearance of impropriety. Policy Declaration 6.5.

Preface

As the agency charged with enforcing standards of judicial conduct in order to maintain the integrity and independence of the judiciary, the California Commission on Judicial Performance (commission) recognizes the importance of observing high standards of ethical conduct in the performance of its responsibilities. The Code of Ethics (Code) set forth in these policy declarations describes ethical standards expected of a commission member. The Code does not confer any substantive or procedural due process rights other than those provided by law, or create a separate basis for civil liability or criminal prosecution.

For purposes of this Code, the judge who is the subject of a complaint, an investigation, or formal proceedings before the commission shall be referred to as the "subject judge."

Adopted Jan. 31, 2007; amended Dec. 13, 2007.

Policy Declaration 6.1.   Recusal.

(1) A commission member shall recuse himself or herself if:

(a) The member does not think he or she is able to act fairly and impartially in a matter;

(b) The member or an immediate family member is the subject of the investigation;

(c) The member served as a lawyer in any proceedings that are the subject of the investigation;

(d) The member has a case pending before the subject judge either as a litigant or in the member's capacity as a lawyer;

(e) A lawyer with whom the member practices is involved in the complaint;

(f) The member has a bias or prejudice for or against the subject judge; or

(g) A reasonable person aware of the facts would entertain a substantial doubt that the member would be able to be impartial.

(2) If a member determines to recuse himself or herself:

(a) The member shall recuse himself or herself promptly;

(b) The recused member may, but is not required to, state the reason(s) for his or her recusal;

(c) The recused member shall leave the room, not comment further or otherwise participate in the commission's consideration of the matter from which the member is recused; and

(d) The recused member shall not receive further written materials on the matter from which the member is recused while the matter is pending before the commission.

Adopted Jan. 31, 2007; amended Jan. 30, 2013.

Policy Declaration 6.2.   Confidentiality.

(1) Confidentiality shall be maintained with regard to all new, pending, and closed matters pursuant to rule 102 and other applicable legal requirements.

(2) Members shall ensure that all confidential documents are secured. When the members are notified in writing (e.g., through the meeting minutes) that documents in selected matters may be discarded, members who choose to discard such documents shall ensure that they are destroyed. Members who choose to retain such documents shall ensure that they are secured.

(3) A member shall not use or disclose, for any purpose unrelated to commission duties, non-public or confidential information acquired in his or her capacity as a commission member.

Adopted Jan. 31, 2007.

Policy Declaration 6.3.   Ex Parte Contacts.

(1) A member shall not initiate, permit, or consider ex parte communications regarding a matter pending or impending before the commission, other than authorized communications with other commission members and staff.

(2) If a member is contacted about a new or pending matter by a subject judge, a judge's attorney or other agent, or a subject judge's family or friends, the member shall not discuss the matter, but may refer the person to the director-chief counsel.

(3) If a member is contacted by a complainant, witness, or potential witness about a new, pending, or closed matter, the member shall not discuss the matter, but may refer the person to the director-chief counsel. Correspondence from complainants about commission business shall be referred to the director-chief counsel for acknowledgement and disposition.

(4) After the initiation of formal proceedings, commission members shall not initiate communications with or receive communications from the director-chief counsel, investigative staff, or trial counsel concerning the matter except as provided by commission rules or stipulation of all parties in the proceeding.

Adopted Jan. 31, 2007; amended Dec. 13, 2007.

Policy Declaration 6.4.   Judicial Election Activities.

(1) A member of the commission shall not publicly support or oppose a candidate for election to judicial office in California while a member of the commission. For purposes of this guideline, both incumbent judges and attorneys seeking election to a judicial position are considered candidates for judicial office.

(2) A member of the commission shall not personally contribute funds directly to any candidate for election to judicial office in California while a member of the commission. If a commission member is a member of a partnership or professional corporation that contributes funds to candidates for judicial office in California, the commission member should not participate in such contribution decisions. If a commission member is assessed a portion of any contribution made to a candidate for judicial office by the member's firm, the commission member's recusal from matters involving the judge may be appropriate under some circumstances. In assessing whether to recuse, relevant factors include: whether the amount of money assessed from the commission member is de minimis (less than $10), whether the commission member's name is included in the firm name, the number of other partners in the member's firm, and the total number of judges in the county in which the judicial candidate was elected.

(3) A member of the commission who is also a member of the board of an organization which is involved in judicial election activities in California should exercise caution over his or her participation in such activities. A member of the commission should not participate in the organization's endorsements of or opposition to specific judicial candidates in California. Ideally, any publication of the organization's endorse-

ment of or opposition to specific judicial candidates would state that the commission member on the board of the organization had not participated in the endorsement or opposition. In some instances, depending on the size of the organization, its purpose and its activities, the commission member should consider resigning from the organization's board if an appearance of conflict of interest or other impropriety cannot otherwise be avoided.

Adopted Jan. 31, 2007; amended Mar. 28, 2018.

Policy Declaration 6.5.   Impropriety and Appearance of Impropriety.

(1)   A member shall not lend the prestige of his or her commission office to advance his or her private interests or the interests of others; nor shall the member convey or permit others to convey the impression that they are in a special position to influence the commission.

(2)   A member shall not be swayed by partisan interests, public clamor, or fear of criticism with respect to the conduct of commission business.

(3)   In conducting commission business, a member shall refrain from manifesting by word or action bias or prejudice based on race, sex, religion, national origin, disability, age, sexual orientation or socio-economic status against parties, witnesses, counsel, or others.

Adopted Jan. 31, 2007.

DIVISION VII
DISCIPLINE

Policy Declaration 7.1.   Non-Exclusive Factors Relevant to Sanctions.

The following non-exclusive factors may be relevant in considering the appropriate discipline to be ordered. Because each case is considered on its own facts, the applicability and weight given to any factor is within the discretion of the commission.

(1)   Characteristics of Misconduct:

(a)   The number of acts of misconduct;

(b)   The nature and seriousness of the misconduct;

(c)   Whether the misconduct occurred in the judge's official capacity or in the judge's private life;

(d)   Whether the misconduct involved dishonesty or lack of integrity;

(e)   Whether the misconduct was intentional, premeditated, negligent, or spontaneous;

(f)   The nature and extent to which the misconduct has been injurious to other persons;

(g)   Whether the judge was motivated by a desire to satisfy a personal or venal interest, vindictiveness, or an interest in justice, or compassion;

(h)   Whether the misconduct undermines the integrity of the judiciary, respect for the judiciary or the administration of justice;

(i)   Whether the misconduct involves unequal application of justice on the basis of such considerations as race, ethnicity or national origin, gender, sexual orientation, or religion.

(2)   Service and Demeanor of the Judge:

(a)   Whether the judge has acknowledged the acts occurred and has shown an appreciation of the impropriety of his or her acts;

(b)   Whether the judge cooperated fully and honestly in the commission proceedings;

(c)   Whether the judge has evidenced an effort to change or modify the conduct;

(d)   The judge's length of service in a judicial capacity;

(e)   Whether there has been prior disciplinary action concerning the judge;

(f)   Whether there are exceptional personal circumstances that warrant consideration;

(g)   The judge's reputation for administering his or her judicial duties in a fair, impartial, and dignified manner and for making positive contributions to the court or community.

Approved Oct. 22, 2008.

INDEX

CIVIL CODE

CODE OF CIVIL PROCEDURE

EVIDENCE CODE

FAMILY CODE

PROBATE CODE

RULES OF COURT

RULES OF PROFESSIONAL CONDUCT

RULES OF COMMISSION ON JUDICIAL PERFORMANCE

GOVERNMENT CODE [ADMINISTRATIVE PROCEDURE ACT,

GOVERNMENT CLAIMS ACT & MISCELLANEOUS FEE PROVISIONS]

ABBREVIATIONS

CC .... Civil Code
CCP .... Code of Civil Procedure
Ev .... Evidence Code
Fam .... Family Code
Gov .... Government Code
Pro .... Probate Code
JudPerR .... Rules of Commission on Judicial Performance
JudPerPolicy .... Policy Declarations of the Commission on Judicial Performance
ProfC .... Rules of Professional Conduct
CRC .... Rules of Court
CRCAppx .... Rules of Court Appendix
CRCSupp .... Rules of Court Supplement
CRC ArbEthicsStand .... Rules of Court Ethics Standards for Neutral Arbitrators in Contractual Arbitration
CRC JudAdminStand .... Rules of Court Standards of Judicial Administration
CRCSupp JudEthicsCanon .... Code of Judicial Ethics

INDEX
TO THE
CIVIL, CIVIL PROCEDURE,
EVIDENCE, FAMILY, PROBATE CODES,
RULES OF COURT, RULES OF PROFESSIONAL CONDUCT,
RULES OF COMMISSION ON JUDICIAL PERFORMANCE,
GOVERNMENT CODE [ADMINISTRATIVE PROCEDURE ACT,
GOVERNMENT CLAIMS ACT & MISCELLANEOUS FEE PROVISIONS]

Abbreviations used in references are listed in Table of Abbreviations on facing page.

A

Index

ACTIONS—Cont.

Privacy—Cont.

Photographs, films, etc., exposing intimate body parts or sexual acts of another without permission, distribution

Actions for injunctions, damages, etc   CC §1708.85

Confidential information form   CRCAppx A

Real estate transfer disclosure statements

Actions, claims for damages, etc   CC §1102.6

Rental passenger vehicle transactions

Actions for violation of provisions   CC §1939.25

School grounds

Force, threat or other obstruction of access to facility

Damages or injunctions, actions to enforce provisions   CC §1708.9

Sexual exploitation

Commercial sexual exploitation, minor or nonminor dependent victims   CC §3345.1

Sexually explicit depiction of individual, creation or disclosure

Cause of action   CC §1708.86

Sexual orientation violence   CC §52.45

Small claims court (See **SMALL CLAIMS COURTS**)

Spousal support, action to enforce right to   Fam §4303

Stay of proceedings

Notice of stay, filing of   CRC 3.650

Student borrower bill of rights

Enforcement of compliance with rights   CC §1788.103

Subcutaneous implanting of identification device, requiring of another   CC §52.7

Summary adjudication as to   CCP §437c

Survival of actions (See **SURVIVAL OF ACTIONS**)

Time for commencing actions (See **STATUTES OF LIMITATION**)

Transfer of actions (See **TRANSFER OF ACTIONS**)

Types of actions   CCP §24

Unclaimed deposits and payments, controller bringing up actions on   CCP §1572

Unlimited civil cases

Appellate forms   CRCAppx A

Usury

Payment of illegal interest

Rights of person paying   CC §1916.12-3

Vexatious litigants (See **VEXATIOUS LITIGANTS**)

Video recordings of dead bodies, use in civil proceedings   CCP §129

Witnesses

Preservation of evidence or perpetuation of testimony prior to filing action   CCP §§2035.010 to 2035.060

ACTORS AND ACTRESSES

Child performers

Extras, background performers, etc

Trusts for percentage of earnings, exceptions to requirements   Fam §6752

Employer and employee

Commercial online entertainment employment service providers

Age information of subscribers, restriction on disclosure   CC §1798.83.5

Injunctive relief, applicability of   CCP §526

Minor's contracts for artistic services   Fam §§6750 to 6753

ACTORS FUND OF AMERICA

Minors, employment

Arts, entertainment, and professional sports, contracts for employment in

Trust for portion of gross earnings, fund's duties as to   Fam §6752

ACTS (See **CITATION OF ACTS**)

ACTS OF GOD (See **NATURAL CATASTROPHES**)

ACUPUNCTURISTS

Discovery of records of health care professional review committees   Ev §1157

Monetary liability of   CC §43.7

ADDING MACHINES

Serial number destroyed or altered prior to sale   CC §1710.1

ADDITIONAL WRITS OF ATTACHMENT (See **ATTACHMENT**)

ADDRESS

Adoption proceedings, address information of birth parent in (See **ADOPTION**)

Adoption proceedings, address of birth parents   Fam §§8702, 8703, 8818, 8819

Apartment building owner, notice of address of   CC §§1962, 1962.5

Appellate rules, superior court appeals

Address of record

Notice of change   CRC 8.816

ADDRESS—Cont.

Change of address

Appeals

Electronic filing, when required   CRCSupp 1st AppDist

Service and filing notice of change   CRC 8.32

Conservators

Residence of conservatee   CRC 7.1063

Credit card issuers

Notice to cardholder   CC §1799.1b

Verification of change of address for offeree or cardholder   CC §1747.06

Earnings assignment for support   Fam §5237

Electronic filing and service rules

Change of electronic service address   CRC 2.251

Guardian and ward

Ward's residence, change   CRC 7.1013

Service and filing of notice of   CRC 2.200

Telephone accounts

Notice to account holder   CC §1799.1b

Confidentiality

Reproductive health care service providers

Address confidentiality for reproductive health care service providers, employees, volunteers and patients   Gov §§6215 to 6218.5

Victims of certain crimes   Gov §§6205 to 6211

Actions, confidentiality requirements for protected persons in civil proceeding   CCP §367.3

Judicial council forms   CRCAppx A

Name change proceedings under address confidentiality program   CRC 2.575 to 2.577

Credit card issuers

Change of address requests

Notice to cardholder   CC §1799.1b

Verification of change of address for offeree or cardholder   CC §1747.06

Domestic violence

Emergency protective orders

Prohibition on obtaining address or location of protected person   Fam §6252.5

Ex parte protective orders

Prohibition on obtaining address or location of protected person   Fam §6322.7

Protection order, address of applicant for   Fam §6225

Electronic filing and service rules

Change of electronic service address   CRC 2.251

Executor residing out of state as required to furnish address   Pro §8573

Family rules

Default

Service address requirement   CRC 5.402

Identity theft

Credit reports

Verification of addresses by users of credit reports   CC §1785.20.3

Information Practices Act (See **INFORMATION PRACTICES ACT**)

Intangible personalty escheated, determining address of owner of   CCP §1510

Juror personal information (See **JURY**)

Letters correctly addressed and posted presumed to be received   Ev §641

Marriage licenses

Options for address   Fam §§351.5, 351.6

Money orders, determining address of purchaser of   CCP §§1511, 1513, 1542, 1581

Sex offenses, exclusion as evidence of address and telephone number of victims of   Ev §352.1

Telephone accounts

Change of address requests

Notice to account holder   CC §1799.1b

Traveler's checks, determining address of purchaser of   CCP §§1511, 1513, 1542, 1581

Trial court rules

Attorneys, address

Papers, first page format and content   CRC 2.111

Service and filing notice of change of party or attorney address   CRC 2.200

Unknown address

Family rules

Service of process by publication or posting   CRC 5.72

Missing persons (See **MISSING PERSONS**)

Service of papers (See **SERVICE OF PAPERS**)

ADEQUATE REMEDY AT LAW

Injunction in absence of   CC §3422, CCP §526

Specific performance of   CC §3387

ADJACENT COUNTIES

Small claims court advisory services   CCP §116.940

Index

Index

Index

ADMINISTRATIVE ADJUDICATION—Cont.

Precedent decisions   Gov §11425.60

Prehearing conferences

    Generally   Gov §11511.5

    Public meeting requirement, exception to   Gov §11425.20

Presiding officers

    Bad faith or frivolous tactics, authority to award expenses for   Gov §11455.30

    Cross-examination in informal hearings, actions concerning use of   Gov §11445.50

    Disqualification

        Generally   Gov §11425.40

        Prohibited communications, receipt of   Gov §11430.60

    Eligibility   Gov §11425.30

    Ethics, Administrative Adjudication Code of   Gov §§11475 to 11475.70

    Exclusion of evidence, authority for   Gov §11513

    Informal hearings, regulation of   Gov §11445.40

    Prohibited communications   Gov §§11430.10 to 11430.80

    Subpoena powers   Gov §§11450.20, 11450.30

Prevailing law   Gov §11415.20

Privileged communications, generally (See **PRIVILEGED COMMUNICATIONS**)

Probation   Gov §11519

Prohibited communications   Gov §§11430.10 to 11430.80

Quash subpoena, motion to   Gov §11450.30

Quasi-public entity, applicability of administrative adjudication provisions to   Gov §11410.60

Reconsideration of decision

    Generally   Gov §11521

    Judicial review, effect of failure to request agency reconsideration on   Gov §11523

Record of proceedings

    Converted proceeding, use of original record in   Gov §11470.30

    Decision based on   Gov §11517

    Emergency decision   Gov §11460.70

    Formal hearing   Gov §11512

    Judicial review, preparation of record for   CCP §§1094.5, 1094.6, Gov §11523

    Public record   Gov §11517

Regulatory agencies subject to formal hearing provisions   Gov §11501

Reinstatement of license, petition for   Gov §11522

Request for hearing by respondent   Gov §11505

Response to accusation

    Generally   Gov §11506

    Amended or supplemental accusation, response to   Gov §11507

    Failure to file notice of defense, effect of   Gov §11520

    Objection to   Gov §11506

    Request for hearing   Gov §§11505, 11506

Response to district statement of reduction in force

    Generally   Gov §11506

    Amended or supplemental statement, response   Gov §11507

    Objection to   Gov §11506

    Request for hearing   Gov §11506

Restitution   Gov §11519

Sanctions

    Bad faith or frivolous action causing delay, award of expenses for   Gov §11455.30

    Contempt sanction (See within this heading, **"Contempt sanction"**)

    Settlement including   Gov §11415.60

Service of papers

    Accusations, service of   Gov §11505

    Corrected decision   Gov §11518.5

    Decision   Gov §11518

    Discovery, motion or petition to compel   Gov §11507.7

    Mail, service by

        Generally   Gov §11440.20

        Subpoenas   Gov §11450.20

    Manner of   Gov §11440.20

    Statement of issues, service of   Gov §11504

    Subpoenas   Gov §11450.20

    Written notice in lieu of subpoena   Gov §11450.50

Settlement

    Conference   Gov §11511.7

    Decision by   Gov §11415.60

    License, timing of settlement of proceeding involving   Gov §11415.60

    Public hearing requirement, applicability of   Gov §11425.20

    Sanctions included in   Gov §11415.60

Sexual harassment, assault or battery, evidence in proceedings alleging   Gov §11440.40

Statements

    Factual basis for decision   Gov §11425.50

ADMINISTRATIVE ADJUDICATION—Cont.

Statements—Cont.

    License or privilege action, statement of issues in   Gov §11504

        Procedural requirements for accusations, applicability   Gov §§11504, 11504.5

    Respondent, statement to   Gov §11505

Stay of execution

    Generally   Gov §11519

    Pending judicial review   CCP §1094.5

Subpoenas

    Applicability of procedures   Gov §11450.05

    Issuance of   Gov §§11450.10, 11450.20

    Mileage and fees of witness   Gov §11450.40

    Objection to   Gov §11450.30

    Presiding officers, subpoena powers of   Gov §§11450.20, 11450.30

    Quash, motion to   Gov §11450.30

    Satisfaction of subpoena duces tecum   Gov §11450.10

    Service of   Gov §11450.20

    Written notice in lieu of   Gov §11450.50

Supplemental accusations, filing of   Gov §11507

Supplemental district statement of reduction in force   Gov §11507

Sympathy expressed to accident victim or family

    Evidentiary effect   Gov §11440.45

Telephone, television or electronic means

    Hearings, generally   Gov §§11425.20, 11440.30

    Prehearing conference conducted by   Gov §11511.5

    Settlement conference conducted by   Gov §11511.7

Television (See within this heading, **"Telephone, television or electronic means"**)

Temporary decision

    Emergency decisions generally (See within this heading, **"Emergency decisions"**)

Time

    Hearing   Gov §11508

Translators (See within this heading, **"Language assistance"**)

Vacate decision, motion to   Gov §11520

Verification

    Accusations, verification of   Gov §11503

    Statement of issues, verification of   Gov §11504

Voting by agency members

    Adjudicatory proceedings, voting on decisions in   Gov §11517

    Mail, voting by   Gov §11526

Waiver of rights, generally   Gov §11415.40

Witnesses

    Deposition of   Gov §11511

    Examination

        Generally   Gov §11513

        Affiants, cross-examination of   Gov §11514

    Exchange of witness lists at prehearing conference   Gov §11511.5

    Mileage and fees   Gov §11450.40

    Oaths generally (See within this heading, **"Oaths"**)

Written decision   Gov §11425.50

ADMINISTRATIVE CODE (See **ADMINISTRATIVE PROCEDURE ACT**)

ADMINISTRATIVE LAW

Generally (See **ADMINISTRATIVE PROCEDURE ACT**)

Adjudicative proceedings (See **ADMINISTRATIVE ADJUDICATION**)

Environmental quality act

    Petitions under environmental quality act, civil rules governing   CRC 3.1365, 3.2200 to 3.2237

ADMINISTRATIVE OFFICE OF THE COURTS (See **JUDICIAL COUNCIL**)

ADMINISTRATIVE PRESIDING JUSTICE

Appellate rules, supreme court and courts of appeal (See **APPELLATE RULES, SUPREME COURT AND COURTS OF APPEAL**)

Superior courts

    Presiding judge (See **SUPERIOR COURTS**)

ADMINISTRATIVE PROCEDURE ACT

Adjudicative proceedings (See **ADMINISTRATIVE ADJUDICATION**)

Administrative Code (See within this heading, **"Code of Regulations"**)

Administrative Code Supplement (See within this heading, **"Regulatory Code Supplement"**)

Administrative law judges

    Adjudicative proceedings (See **ADMINISTRATIVE ADJUDICATION**)

    Appointment of   Gov §§11370.3, 11502

Administrative Notice Register (See within this heading, **"Regulatory Notice Register"**)

Index

Index

Index

ADOPTION—Cont.

Visitation rights

Deceased parent, effect of adoption on visitation rights of relatives of   Fam §3102

Kinship adoption agreements   CRC 5.451

Postadoption contact agreement with birth parent   Fam §8616.5

Readoption in state of child originally adopted in foreign country

Separated siblings, visitation   Fam §8920

Waiver of right to revoke consent   Fam §8814.5

Will, adopted persons included in class for disposition under   Pro §21115

ADR PROGRAMS (See ALTERNATIVE DISPUTE RESOLUTION)

ADULT

Adoption of (See **ADOPTION**)

Child support for adult children (See **CHILD SUPPORT**)

ADULT-ORIENTED BUSINESSES

Human trafficking or slavery

Signs, businesses required to post notice concerning relief from slavery or human trafficking   CC §52.6

ADULT SCHOOLS (See SCHOOLS; UNIVERSITIES AND COLLEGES)

AD VALOREM TAX (See TAXATION)

ADVANCEMENTS

Ademption distinguished   Pro §6409

Death of recipient prior to distribution   Pro §6409

Hearings for   Pro §11640

ADVANCES

Loans (See **PREPAYMENTS**)

ADVERSE PARTY

Authentication of document   Ev §1414

Hearsay declarant, examination of   Ev §1203

Opinion evidence, examination of   Ev §804

Witnesses (See **WITNESSES**)

ADVERSE POSSESSION (See also QUIETING TITLE)

Absence of written instrument or judgment, extent of possession in   CCP §324

Actual continued occupation under claim of title not founded on written instrument or judgment   CCP §324

Alienation pending suit for possession   CCP §747

Claim of title

Founded on written instrument or judgment   CCP §§322, 323

Not founded on written instrument or judgment   CCP §§324, 325

Complaint in quieting title action specifying   CCP §761.020

Continued occupation and possession under claim of title based on written instrument or judgment   CCP §§322, 323

Cultivation of land

Not founded on written instrument or judgment, adverse possession by person claiming title   CCP §325

Sufficiency of possession, use and inclosure for claim based on written instrument, judgment   CCP §323

Damages for withholding property   CCP §§740, 741

Death of adverse possessor   CCP §327

Description of property in complaint   CCP §455

Disabilities tolling statute   CCP §328

Entry upon real estate deemed sufficient or valid as claim   CCP §320

Fences   CCP §§323, 325

Five years

Cessation of disability, commencement of action or making defense on   CCP §328

Continued occupation and possession under claim of title based on written instrument or judgment   CCP §322

Entry upon real estate deemed sufficient or valid as claim   CCP §320

Mortgaged premises, adverse possession of   CCP §346

Not founded on written instrument or judgment, adverse possession by person claiming title   CCP §325

Seisin or possession within five years of commencement of action   CCP §§318, 319

Subordinate occupation presumption   CCP §321

Tenant, adverse possession by   CCP §326

Imprisonment tolling statute   CCP §328

Improvement of land

Not founded on written instrument or judgment, adverse possession by person claiming title   CCP §325

Sufficiency of possession, use and inclosure for claim based on written instrument, judgment   CCP §323

ADVERSE POSSESSION—Cont.

Inclosure of land

Not founded on written instrument or judgment, adverse possession by person claiming title   CCP §325

Sufficiency of possession, use and inclosure for claim based on written instrument, judgment   CCP §323

Legal capacity lacking

Tolling of statute   CCP §328

Minority tolling statute   CCP §328

Mortgaged premises, adverse possession of   CCP §346

Mortgage, effect on   CC §2921

Occupancy

Actual continued occupation under claim of title not founded on written instrument or judgment   CCP §324

Continued occupation and possession under claim of title based on written instrument or judgment   CCP §§322, 323

Subordination to legal title, presumption of   CCP §321

Presumptions

Continued occupation and possession under claim of title based on written instrument or judgment   CCP §322

Subordinate occupation presumption   CCP §321

Tenant, adverse possession by   CCP §326

Public improvement liens, effect of   CCP §§801.1 to 801.15

Seisin or possession within five years of commencement of action   CCP §§318, 319

Statutes of limitation

Disabilities tolling statute   CCP §328

Five years (See within this heading, **"Five years"**)

Legal capacity lacking

Tolling of statute   CCP §328

Subordinate occupation presumption   CCP §321

Sufficiency of possession, use and inclosure for claim based on written instrument, judgment   CCP §323

Taxes levied and assessed upon land, payment of   CCP §325

Tenant, adverse possession by   CCP §326

Title to real property

Claim of title   CCP §§322 to 325

Seisin or possession within five years of commencement of action arising out of   CCP §319

Subordination to legal title, presumption of   CCP §321

Transfer of property   CC §1047

Venue in action for recovery of real property   CCP §392

ADVERTISING

Adoptions (See **ADOPTION**)

Asian language contracts, regulating advertising as to   CC §1632

Attorney professional conduct   ProfC 7.2

Communications about lawyer's services generally   ProfC 7.1 to 7.5

Solicitation of clients   ProfC 7.3

Auctions   CC §1812.607

Automobile leases   CC §§2985.71, 2989.4

Campaign advertising (See **CANDIDATES FOR OFFICE**)

Consumer protection in   CC §1770

Dating services   CC §1694.4

Debt collectors advertising name of debtor   CC §1788.12

Deceased personality's name, voice, signature, photograph, or likeness, unauthorized use of   CC §3344.1

Deceptive advertising prohibited   CC §1770

Discount buying services   CC §1812.120

Employment agencies, advertising practices of   CC §1812.508

Employment counseling services, advertising requirements for   CC §1812.513

Enforcement of judgments (See **ENFORCEMENT OF JUDGMENTS**)

Floating homes and floating home marinas (See **FLOATING HOMES**)

Grey market goods, advertising requirements for   CC §1797.82

Invoice or statement of account due, restrictions on solicitations resembling   CC §1716

Job listing services, advertising requirements of   CC §1812.520

Judges

Name

Use in advertising   CRCSupp JudEthicsCanon 4

Levied property, advertising sale of   CCP §701.545

Membership camping contract, advertisements for   CC §1812.301

Mobilehomes, sale or rent of   CC §§798.70, 799.1.5

Name used without authorization   CC §§3344, 3344.1

Nurses' registries, advertising by   CC §1812.533

Photograph used without authorization   CC §§3344, 3344.1

Political advertising, sale of items involving   CC §1739.1

Realty sale signs   CC §§712, 713

Rental passenger vehicle transactions

Quotes and additional mandatory charges

Disclaimers   CC §1939.19

Index

AGE—Cont.

Adult, age of   Fam §§6501, 6502
Burden of proof to establish age of accused   CRC 4.116
Discrimination
     Judicial ethics code
         Administrative responsibilities of judge, impartial discharge CRCSupp JudEthicsCanon 3
         Attorneys, judges to require to refrain from manifesting   CRCSupp JudEthicsCanon 3
         Bias, prejudice or harassment in performance of judicial duties CRCSupp JudEthicsCanon 3
         Court personnel and staff under direction of judge, standards of conduct enforced by judge   CRCSupp JudEthicsCanon 3
Domestic partners
     Age requirement   Fam §297
         Younger than minimum age, order of court granting permission   Fam §297.1
Entertainment industry
     Commercial online entertainment employment service providers
         Age information of subscribers, restriction on disclosure   CC §1798.83.5
Housing discrimination
     Age discrimination in housing, generally   CC §51.2
     Mobilehome parks (See **MOBILEHOMES**)
     Senior citizen housing, requirements for (See **SENIOR CITIZENS**)
Marriage, capacity to consent to   Fam §301
Minor, age of   Fam §§6500, 6502
Preference, motion for   CCP §36
Sale of age-restricted products
     Verification of age for sale of age-restricted products   CC §1798.99.1
Senior citizens (See **SENIOR CITIZENS**)
Spousal support   Fam §4320

AGED PERSONS (See SENIOR CITIZENS)

AGENCIES FOR ADOPTIONS (See ADOPTION)

AGENCY

Actual agency   CC §§2298, 2299
Administration of estates (See **ADMINISTRATION OF ESTATES**)
Arbitration award against principal affecting surety   CC §2855
Art dealer as agent of artist   CC §1738.6
Attorney in fact (See **POWER OF ATTORNEY**)
Auctioneer, agency relationship of   CC §§2362, 2363
Authority of agent   CC §§2019, 2304, 2305, 2315 to 2326, 2330 to 2339
Automobile sales, agency loan financing   CC §2983.4
Bills and notes (See **BILLS AND NOTES**)
Brokers (See **BROKERS**)
Business management by   CC §2319
Challenge of juror for implied bias, relationships giving rise to   CCP §229
Consideration requirements   CC §2308
Corporations (See **CORPORATE OFFICERS AND EMPLOYEES**)
Damages for breach of warranty of authority of   CC §3318
Death terminating   CC §§2355, 2356
Defined   CC §2295
Delegation of authority   CC §§2304, 2349 to 2351
Discretionary powers   CC §2320
Eligibility of agency   CC §2296
Extinguishment of   CC §§2355, 2356
Factors, agency relationship of   CC §§2367 to 2369
General terms, authority in   CC §§2321, 2322
Incapacity of parties   CC §§2355, 2356
Indemnity contracts covering agency   CC §2775
Information to agent   CC §2020
Mechanics' liens
     Scope of agency and authority of agents   CC §8066
Negligence   CC §§2338, 2339
Notes (See **BILLS AND NOTES**)
Oral authorization for   CC §2309
Ostensible agents   CC §§2298, 2300, 2317
Parol, authority granted by   CC §2309
Payment, authority to receive   CC §§2325, 2326
Personal liability of agency   CC §2343
Power of attorney (See **POWER OF ATTORNEY**)
Ratification of acts   CC §§2307, 2310 to 2314
Real estate brokers (See **BROKERS**)
Real property
     Agency listings for transfer of property   CC §§1086 to 1089.5
Referees, disqualification of   CCP §641
Representations by   CC §2319

AGENCY—Cont.

Revocation of authority   CC §2356
Sale of realty (See **VENDOR AND PURCHASER**)
Scope of authority, acts within   CC §§2330, 2343
Special agents   CC §2297
Special terms, authority in   CC §2321
Statute of frauds   CC §1624, CCP §1971
Subagents   CC §2022
Termination of   CC §§2355, 2356
Third parties, transactions with   CC §§2342 to 2345
Undisclosed principal   CC §2336

AGING DEPARTMENT

Supportive care pilot projects
     Medical information disclosures   CC §56.10

AGISTER'S LIENS (See PASTURES)

AGISTMENT (See PASTURES)

AGREED CASE

Appeals   CCP §1140
Applicable cases   CCP §1138
Enforcement of judgment   CCP §1140
Entry in judgment roll   CCP §1139
Family rules
     Rescheduling hearings
         Written agreements to reschedule   CRC 5.95
Hearing and determination   CCP §1138
Submission of   CCP §1138
Summary judgment   CCP §437c

AGREED STATEMENT

Appellate rules, superior court appeals
     Limited civil cases in appellate division
         Record on appeal   CRC 8.836
Appellate rules, supreme court and courts of appeal (See **APPELLATE RULES, SUPREME COURT AND COURTS OF APPEAL**)

AGRICULTURAL LABOR RELATIONS BOARD

Judicial review of ALRB orders   CRC 8.728

AGRICULTURE (See FARMS AND FARMERS)

AID FOR DEPENDENT CHILDREN (See CHILD SUPPORT)

AIDING AND ABETTING

Attorney-client privilege, applicability of   Ev §956
Identification of person aiding in crime, admissibility of hearsay evidence concerning   Ev §1238
Physician's services aiding in commission of crime, absence of privilege where Ev §997
Privilege claim in obtaining services of lawyer to aid in commission of crime   Ev §§956, 981
Psychotherapist's services aiding in commission of crime, absence of privilege where   Ev §1018

AIDS (See ACQUIRED IMMUNE DEFICIENCY SYNDROME (AIDS))

AIR

Appurtenance   CC §662
Easement rights to   CC §801
Realty including airspace   CC §659

AIR CONDITIONING

Construction defects, actions for
     Actionable defects   CC §896
Home improvement goods and services   CC §1689.8
Landlord terminating   CC §789.3

AIRCRAFT AND AVIATION (See also AIRPORTS)

Blind persons having equal access rights to   CC §§54.1, 54.3, 54.4, 55
     Construction or application of provisions in issue, solicitor general notified CC §55.2
Disabled persons having equal access rights to   CC §§54.1, 54.3, 54.4, 55
     Construction or application of provisions in issue, solicitor general notified CC §55.2
Drones   Gov §§853 to 853.5
     Emergency response
         Drones or unmanned aircraft systems damaged by emergency responder, immunity from liability for damage to drone interfering with emergency response   CC §43.101

Index

AIRCRAFT AND AVIATION—Cont.

Guide dogs permitted aboard   CC §§54.2, 54.3
  Construction or application of provisions in issue, solicitor general notified   CC §55.2

Liens
  Assignment of   CCP §1208.63
  Federal statutes, applicability of   CCP §1208.70
  Fraud, loss by   CCP §§1208.64, 1208.69
  Notice of   CCP §1208.62
  Repairs   CCP §1208.61
  Sale to satisfy   CCP §§1208.65 to 1208.68
  Storage   CCP §1208.61

Retail installment sales of aircraft   CC §1801.4

Terrorism
  September 11, 2001 terrorist attacks
    Statute of limitations on actions   CCP §340.10

Unmanned aircraft
  Emergency response
    Drones or unmanned aircraft systems damaged by emergency responder, immunity from liability for damage to drone interfering with emergency response   CC §43.101

Unruh Act, exclusion of aircraft sales from   CC §1801.4

AIR FORCE (See **MILITARY**)

AIRPLANES (See **AIRCRAFT AND AVIATION**)

AIR POLLUTION (See **ENVIRONMENTAL HAZARDS**)

AIRPORTS (See also **AIRCRAFT AND AVIATION**)

Eminent domain   CCP §§1240.110, 1240.125

Human trafficking
  Signs, businesses required to post notice concerning relief from slavery or human trafficking   CC §52.6

Indemnity contract for construction of   CC §2783

Nuisance, actions to abate   CCP §§731a, 731b

Real Estate Transfer Disclosure Statements, form of
  Proximity of airport, localities adopting different or additional disclosure   CC §1102.6a

Slavery
  Signs, businesses required to post notice concerning relief from slavery or human trafficking   CC §52.6

AIR QUALITY (See **ENVIRONMENTAL HAZARDS**)

AIR RESOURCES BOARD

Gasoline stations, emission standards for   CC §1952.8

ALAMEDA COUNTY

Unlawful detainer actions
  Controlled substances as nuisance
    Pilot program   CC §3486.5

ALARMS (See **BURGLAR ALARMS**)

ALCOHOLIC BEVERAGES

Abuse (See **SUBSTANCE ABUSE**)

Commercial motor vehicle employer for vehicle accident caused by intoxicated employee, damages recoverable from   CC §3333.7

Custody of children
  Drug or alcohol abuse as custody determination factor
    Testing for alcohol or controlled substance use ordered by court   Fam §3041.5

Decedent's estate, filing tax claims against   Pro §§9200 to 9205

Guardian and ward, custody of child
  Drug or alcohol abuse as custody determination factor
    Testing for alcohol or controlled substance use ordered by court   Fam §3041.5

Human trafficking
  Signs, businesses required to post notice concerning relief from slavery or human trafficking   CC §52.6

Ignition interlock orders   CRC 4.325

Marriage license denied to persons under influence of   Fam §352

On-sale licenses
  Human trafficking
    Signs, businesses required to post notice concerning relief from slavery or human trafficking   CC §52.6

Public nuisances, attorney's fees recoverable for enjoining unlawful sales or distribution of alcoholic liquor as   CC §3496

Rape, use to accomplish
  Statute of limitations on sexual assault damages   CCP §340.16

ALCOHOLIC BEVERAGES—Cont.

Satisfaction of judgment, interest in alcoholic beverage license applied to   CCP §708.630

Slavery
  Signs, businesses required to post notice concerning relief from slavery or human trafficking   CC §52.6

Social host's liability to third parties after serving   CC §1714

Third party liability of social host after serving   CC §1714

Voidable transactions provisions, applicability to sale of wine   CC §3440

ALCOHOLISM (See **SUBSTANCE ABUSE**)

ALE (See **ALCOHOLIC BEVERAGES**)

ALIAS WRITS

Attachments writs   CCP §482.090

ALIENATION OF AFFECTION

Generally   CC §43.5

Foster parent, action against   CC §43.56

ALIENATION, RESTRAINTS ON (See **PERPETUITIES AND RESTRAINTS ON ALIENATION**)

ALIENS

Attorneys
  Registered foreign legal consultants admitted to practice as attorney   CRC 9.44
    Fingerprinting of special admission attorneys   CRC 9.9.5

Child custody
  Immigration status, effect   Fam §3040

Children and minors
  Actions for damages
    Discovery into immigration status prohibited   CC §3339.5
    Immigration status irrelevant   CC §3339.5

Citizenship (See **CITIENSHIP**)

Contracts
  Local government or law enforcement agency contracts to detain noncitizens for civil immigration custody
    Prohibition   CC §1670.9

Damages
  Children and minors
    Immigration status irrelevant   CC §3339.5
  Civil rights enforcement, irrelevance of immigration status   CC §3339

Death of foreign citizen, notice of   Pro §8113

Discrimination prohibited   CC §51

Forcible entry and detainer
  Immigration or citizenship status irrelevant to issue of liability or remedy   CC §3339.10

Foreign legal consultants   CRC 9.44
  Fingerprinting of special admission attorneys   CRC 9.9.5

Inheritance by alien   Pro §6411

Jury service, exceptions to eligibility for   CCP §203

Landlord and tenant
  Immigration or citizenship status of persons
    Actions to recover possession, restrictions on landlord actions based in immigration or citizenship status   CCP §1161.4
    Definition of immigration or citizenship status   CC §1940.05
    Involuntary quit by tenant, restrictions on landlord actions based in immigration or citizenship status   CCP §1161.4
    Prohibited acts based on   CC §§1940.3, 1940.35
    Retaliation against tenant by reporting or threatening to report to immigration authorities   CC §1942.5
    Unduly influencing tenant to vacate by threating disclosures relating to immigration or citizenship status   CC §1940.2

Ownership of land by   CC §671

ALIMONY (See **SPOUSAL SUPPORT**)

ALLEGATIONS (See **PLEADINGS**)

ALTERATION OF CLOTHING (See **TAILORS**)

ALTERATION OF INSTRUMENTS (See **MODIFICATION**)

ALTERNATE JURORS (See **JURY**)

ALTERNATIVE DISPUTE RESOLUTION

Administration of ADR program by trial court   CRC 10.780 to 10.783

ADR committee
  Administration of program   CRC 10.783

ADR program information, court to furnish   CRC 10.781

ALTERNATIVE DISPUTE RESOLUTION—Cont.
Attorney professional conduct
    Former judges, arbitrators, mediators, etc, restrictions on representation of clients   ProfC 1.12
    Service by attorney as third-party neutral   ProfC 2.4
Civil action mediation program   CRC 3.890 to 3.898
Civil rules
    Information package
        Papers to be filed   CRC 3.221
Committee
    ADR committee
        Administration of program   CRC 10.783
Common interest developments
    Associations and members, disputes between   CC §§5900 to 5920 (See **COMMON INTEREST DEVELOPMENTS**)
    Generally   CC §§5925 to 5965 (See **COMMON INTEREST DEVELOPMENTS**)
Construction defects, actions for
    Prelitigation procedures generally   CC §§910 to 938 (See **CONSTRUCTION DEFECTS, ACTIONS FOR**)
Coordination by trial courts   CRC JudAdminStand 10.70
Court officers and employees
    Labor relations
        Submission for dispute resolution   CRC 10.659
Criteria for referring cases to dispute resolution providers   CRC JudAdminStand 10.72
Definitions   CRC 3.800
Family law
    Mediators and evaluators
        Ex parte communications   Fam §216
Forms
    Judicial council legal forms   CRCAppx A
Informational statements to parties
    Papers to be filed   CRC 3.221
Judges
    Employment or prospective employment as a dispute resolution neutral as basis for disqualification of judges   CCP §§170.1, 1281.9
Judicial administration standards
    Committees to oversee ADR programs   CRC JudAdminStand 10.71
    Coordination of ADR programs, judicial council guidelines   CRC JudAdminStand 10.70
    Criteria for referring cases to ADR providers, judicial council guidelines   CRC JudAdminStand 10.72
Judicial arbitration   CRC 3.810 to 3.830
Mediation Act   CRC 3.890 to 3.898
Mediators standards of conduct
    Ethical standards for conduct of mediators   CRC 3.850 to 3.860
        Complaints about court-program mediators   CRC 3.865 to 3.872
Neutrals, list of   CRC 10.781
Plaintiff, ADR information provided   CRC 3.221
Privilege to serve as neutral   CRC 10.781
Programs   CCP §1775
    Administrative adjudication (See **ADMINISTRATIVE ADJUDICATION**)
    Arbitration (See **ARBITRATION**)
    Common interest developments (See **COMMON INTEREST DEVELOPMENTS**)
    Eminent domain proceedings postponed for ADR purposes   CCP §1250.430
    Hazardous releases, procedures for resolving liability for (See **ENVIRONMENTAL HAZARDS**)
    Information   CRC 3.221
    Judicial administration standards (See **JUDICIAL ADMINISTRATION STANDARDS**)
    Judicial arbitration (See **JUDICIAL ARBITRATION**)
    Mediation (See **MEDIATION**)
    Trial court administration   CRC 10.780 to 10.783
        ADR committee   CRC 10.783
        ADR program administrator   CRC 10.783
        Applicability of rules   CRC 10.780
        Information reporting   CRC 10.782
        Neutrals, listing   CRC 10.781
        Privilege to serve as neutral   CRC 10.781
Settlement and compromise
    Notice to neutral of settlement of case   CRC 3.1385
Stipulation to ADR
    Form   CRC 3.221

ALTERNATIVE WRITS
Court commissioner's powers to hear and determine   CCP §259

ALZHEIMER'S DISEASE
Neurocognitive disorders
    Major neurocognitive disorder conservatorships   Pro §2356.5

AMBASSADORS
Affidavits taken before   CCP §2014
Signature of secretary on documents presumed to be genuine   Ev §§1454, 1530

AMBER ALERT
Rental passenger vehicle transactions
    Electronic surveillance technology
        Exceptions to restrictions on use   CC §1939.23

AMBIGUITIES (See **CERTAINTY**)

AMBULANCES
Public health and safety labor or service providers
    Logo or identifying mark of public agency, display   CC §3273

AMENDMENTS
Administrative regulations (See **ADMINISTRATIVE PROCEDURE ACT**)
Bill of Rights
    Fourth Amendment (See **SEARCH AND SEIZURE**)
Common interest developments, amended declaration for (See **COMMON INTEREST DEVELOPMENTS**)
Complaints (See **COMPLAINTS**)
Contempt proceedings, rules to amend affidavit or statement of facts in   CCP §1211.5
Decedent's estate, amendment of creditors' claims filed against   Pro §9104
Eminent domain action, pleading amendments in   CCP §1250.340
Judge's removal or censure, amendment to pleadings in proceedings for   JudPerR 128
Mobilehome park rules   CC §798.25
Personal data records   CC §§1798.22, 1798.26
Pleadings (See **PLEADINGS**)
Premarital agreements   Fam §1614
Pretrial conference orders   CCP §576
Small claims actions (See **SMALL CLAIMS COURTS**)
State agency regulations, amendment procedure for (See **ADMINISTRATIVE PROCEDURE ACT**)

AMERICAN INDIANS (See **NATIVE AMERICANS**)

AMERICAN RED CROSS
Adoption proceedings, absence of adoptive parent serving in Red Cross   Fam §8613

AMERICANS WITH DISABILITIES ACT COMPLIANCE
Civil rights violation, ADA violation as
    Construction or application of provisions in issue
        Solicitor general notified   CC §51.1
Courts   CRC 1.100
Interrogation of hard of hearing, use of interpreter   Ev §754
Transportation, equal access to
    Construction or application of provisions in issue, solicitor general notified   CC §55.2

AMICUS CURIAE
Appellate rules, supreme court and courts of appeal
    Certiorari, mandate and prohibition
        Attorney general and other amicus briefs   CRC 8.487
    Death penalty
        Habeas corpus, appeals from superior court decisions in habeas cases involving death penalty   CRC 8.396
Briefs   CRC 8.200
    Appellate rules, supreme court and courts of appeal
        Habeas corpus, appeals from superior court decisions in habeas cases involving death penalty   CRC 8.396
    Attorney general's amicus brief   CRC 8.200
    Capital cases   CRC 8.630
    Criminal appeals   CRC 8.360
    Juvenile case appeals   CRC 8.412
Filing of documents
    Number   CRC 8.44
Judges, proceedings against   JudPerR 131
Supreme court
    Filing briefs in   CRC 8.520
    Oral argument   CRC 8.524
        Habeas corpus   CRC 8.386
    Review of amicus curiae letters   CRC 8.500

AMMUNITION
Firearms and other weapons (See **FIREARMS AND OTHER WEAPONS**)

AMOUNT IN CONTROVERSY
Attachment (See **ATTACHMENT**)

Index

Index

APPEALS—Cont.

Costs

    Frivolous appeals   CCP §907

    Recovery of costs on appeal   CCP §1034

    Supreme Court and Courts of Appeal, rules on appeal to (See **APPELLATE RULES, SUPREME COURT AND COURTS OF APPEAL**)

Courts of Appeal

    Generally (See **COURTS OF APPEAL**)

    Appellate rules, supreme court and courts of appeal   CRC 8.1 to 8.642 (See **APPELLATE RULES, SUPREME COURT AND COURTS OF APPEAL**)

Death penalty cases (See **CAPITAL PUNISHMENT**)

Demurrer sustained without leave to amend   CCP §472c

Dismissal

    Generally   CCP §913

    Superior court, rules on appeal to

        Abandonment and dismissal (See **APPELLATE RULES, SUPERIOR COURT APPEALS**)

    Supreme Court and Courts of Appeal, rules on appeal to (See **APPELLATE RULES, SUPREME COURT AND COURTS OF APPEAL**)

Disregard of nonprejudicial error   CCP §475

Entering judgment of reviewing court in records of trial court   CCP §912

Exceptions, orders and rulings reserved without   CCP §647

Executors and administrators, orders concerning (See **EXECUTORS AND ADMINISTRATORS**)

Family Code, general provision concerning appealable orders under   CCP §904.1

Findings contrary to or in addition to those of trial court   CCP §909

Forcible entry and detainer   CCP §§1176, 1178

Frivolous appeals   CCP §907

Guardian and ward, orders concerning (See **GUARDIAN AND WARD**)

Injunctions   CCP §§904.1, 904.2

Interlocutory judgments

    Generally   CCP §§904.1, 904.2

    Special defense, separate trial of   CCP §597

Irrigation, mandamus affecting   CCP §1110a

Justice courts (See **JUSTICE COURTS**)

Juvenile appeals (See **JUVENILE COURTS**)

Juvenile rules

    Representation of child on appeal   CRC 5.661

Modification of judgment (See **MODIFICATION OF JUDGMENT**)

Monetary sanctions against party or attorney, appeal of   CCP §904.1

New trial motion   CCP §657

Nonjury trials   CCP §909

Notice of appeal

    Indigent appeal   CCP §936.1

    Small claims court (See **SMALL CLAIMS COURTS**)

    Superior court, appellate rules (See **APPELLATE RULES, SUPERIOR COURT APPEALS**)

    Supreme court and courts of appeal, appellate rules (See **APPELLATE RULES, SUPREME COURT AND COURTS OF APPEAL**)

    Withdrawal of legal service agency attorney for indigent client, effect on time limitations of   CCP §285.3

Notwithstanding verdict, motion for judgment   CCP §629

Parties to action   CCP §902

Perpetuation of testimony pending appeal   CCP §§2036.010 to 2036.050

Power of attorney, orders concerning   Pro §§1302, 1302.5, 1310

Powers of reviewing court   CCP §906

Prejudicial error required for reversal   CCP §475

Public improvement assessments, appeal of judgment in action contesting validity of   CCP §329.5

Quash, motion to   CCP §§904.1 to 904.2

Record on appeal

    Death of reporter as preventing preparation of   CCP §914

    Felony case, preparation of record for   CCP §269

    Loss or destruction of   CCP §1953.06

    Superior courts, appellate rules (See **APPELLATE RULES, SUPERIOR COURT APPEALS**)

    Supreme court and courts of appeal, appellate rules (See **APPELLATE RULES, SUPREME COURT AND COURTS OF APPEAL**)

Rehearings

    Superior courts, appellate rules (See **APPELLATE RULES, SUPERIOR COURT APPEALS**)

    Supreme court and courts of appeal, appellate rules (See **APPELLATE RULES, SUPREME COURT AND COURTS OF APPEAL**)

Reversal of judgment (See **REVERSAL OF JUDGMENT**)

Rules of court

    Superior court, appellate division proceedings   CRC 8.800 to 8.936 (See **APPELLATE RULES, SUPERIOR COURT APPEALS**)

    Supreme court and courts of appeal, appellate rules   CRC 8.1 to 8.642 (See **APPELLATE RULES, SUPREME COURT AND COURTS OF APPEAL**)

Small claims court (See **SMALL CLAIMS COURTS**)

APPEALS—Cont.

Statute of limitation extended where judgment for plaintiff reversed on appeal   CCP §355

Striking of pleading as issue on appeal   CCP §472c

Summary judgment proceeding, review of determination in   CCP §437c

Superior courts

    Appellate division

        Generally (See **APPELLATE DIVISION OF SUPERIOR COURT**)

        Proceedings in appellate division   CRC 8.800 to 8.936 (See **APPELLATE RULES, SUPERIOR COURT APPEALS**)

Support proceedings, appeal of judgment in   Fam §3554

Supreme court (California)

    Generally (See **SUPREME COURT, CALIFORNIA**)

    Appellate rules, supreme court and courts of appeal   CRC 8.1 to 8.642 (See **APPELLATE RULES, SUPREME COURT AND COURTS OF APPEAL**)

Termination of parental rights   Fam §§7893 to 7895

Trusts, orders concerning (See **TRUSTS**)

Unlawful detainer actions   CCP §§1176, 1178

Validation proceedings   CCP §870

Water supply, mandamus affecting   CCP §1110a

Will probate, orders concerning (See **WILL PROBATE**)

Witnesses

    Perpetuation of testimony pending appeal   CCP §§2036.010 to 2036.050

APPEARANCE

Generally   CCP §1014

Adoption proceedings (See **ADOPTION**)

Answer, appearance by filing   CCP §1014

Arbitration proceedings (See **ARBITRATION**)

Attorney, appearance through

    Waiver of personal appearance

        COVID-19, emergency rule   CRCAppx I Emer Rule 5

Child support

    Show cause orders   Fam §17404.1

    Title IV-D support actions

        Telephone appearances   CRC 3.670, 5.324

Citation to appear (See **CITATION TO APPEAR**)

Conservatee   CCP §372

Criminal cases

    Traffic offenses

        Bail, when deposit required   CRC 4.105

        Notice to appear forms   CRC 4.103

Death penalty

    Lists of appearances, exhibits and motions   CRCAppx A

    Pretrial proceedings   CRC 4.119

    Trial, additional requirements   CRC 4.230

Discovery

    Interstate and international depositions and discovery act

        Choice of law to resolve disputes, appearance fees   CCP §2029.610

Dissolution of marriage (See **DISSOLUTION OF MARRIAGE**)

Enforcement of judgments (See **ENFORCEMENT OF JUDGMENTS**)

Ex parte proceedings

    Generally (See **EX PARTE PROCEDURE**)

Family centered case resolution orders

    Without appearance   CRC 5.83

Family rules   CRC 5.62

    Emergency or ex parte orders, requests

        Appearance at hearing   CRC 5.169

    General appearance, effect   CRC 5.68

    Telephone appearance   CRC 5.9

Guardians ad litem

    Pseudonym, appointment under

        Leave to appear under pseudonym, ex parte request   CCP §372.5

Inconvenient forum, effect of general appearance on motion to stay or dismiss on grounds of   CCP §410.30

Indian child welfare act involuntary placements

    Tribal appearance by telephone or other remote means   CRC 5.482

Judges, proceedings against   JudPerR 114, 116, 123

Jurisdiction, motion to quash service of summons for lack of   Fam §2012

Juvenile rules

    Telephone appearances   CRC 5.531

        Nonminor dependents, retention of jurisdiction   CRC 5.900

Juvenile wardship proceedings

    Remote appearances

        COVID-19, emergency rule   CRCAppx I Emer Rule 7

Legal capacity lacking   CCP §372

Mediation sessions   CRC 3.894

Military counsel, appearance by   CRC 9.41

Index

Index

Index

Index

Index

Index

Index

ARBITRATION—Cont.

Joinder of parties   CCP §1281.2

Judges, service as arbitrators   CRCSupp JudEthicsCanons 3 to 6

Judicial Arbitration   CRC 3.810 to 3.830 (See **JUDICIAL ARBITRATION**)

Jurisdiction   CCP §§86, 116.220, 1292.4 to 1293

Labor and labor unions

    Collective bargaining agreement, representation by non-attorney in arbitration arising under   CCP §1282.4

    Firefighters and law enforcement officers (See within this heading, **"Firefighters and law enforcement officers"**)

Law and motion proceedings

    Motions concerning arbitration   CRC 3.1330

Leases, violation of   CC §§1942.1, 1942.5

Medical malpractice (See **MALPRACTICE**)

Motor vehicle warranties, actions involving   CC §1793.22

Nonresident attorneys, representation in arbitration proceedings by   CCP §1282.4, CRC 9.43

Notice

    Correction of award, prospective   CCP §1286.8

    Hearing   CCP §1282.2

    Motor vehicle warranties, actions involving   CC §1793.22

    Petition   CCP §1290.4

    Vacation of award, prospective   CCP §1286.4

Oaths   CCP §1282.8

Objections and exceptions

    Award in arbitration, objection to   CCP §§1283.8, 1284

    Judicial arbitration   CCP §1141.15

Offer to compromise, costs chargeable against party refusing   CCP §998

Other states, representation in arbitration proceedings by attorneys from   CCP §1282.4, CRC 9.43

Out-of-state attorney arbitration counsel   CRC 9.43

Petitions

    Compelling arbitration (See within this heading, **"Compelling arbitration"**)

    Consolidation of proceedings   CCP §1281.3

    Correction of awards (See within this heading, **"Correction of awards"**)

    General provisions   CCP §§1290 to 1293.2

    Jurisdiction   CCP §§86, 1292.4 to 1293

    Notice of hearing   CCP §1290.4

    Service   CCP §§1290.4, 1290.6, 1290.8

    Stay of proceedings (See within this heading, **"Stay of proceedings"**)

    Summary hearings   CCP §1290.2

    To compel arbitration   CRC 3.1330

    Vacation of awards (See within this heading, **"Vacation of awards"**)

    Venue   CCP §§1292, 1292.2

Physicians and surgeons (See **PHYSICIANS AND SURGEONS**)

Pretrial arbitration (See **JUDICIAL ARBITRATION**)

Principal, surety affected by award against   CC §2855

Priority of proceedings   CCP §1291.2

Private arbitration companies

    Disclosures   CCP §1281.96

Provisional remedies, party's rights under arbitration agreement on filing for   CCP §1281.8

Public agency, construction contract with   CC §1670, CCP §1296

Real estate contracts, arbitration of (See **REAL ESTATE CONTRACT ARBITRATION**)

Receiver, party's rights under arbitration agreement on appointment of   CCP §1281.8

Reports

    Data collection and reports available to public   CCP §1281.96

Request to arbitrate pursuant to written agreement   CCP §1281.1

Rules of court arbitration (See **JUDICIAL ARBITRATION**)

Separate proceedings   CCP §1281.3

Service

    Awards   CCP §1283.6

    Petitions   CCP §1290.4

    Responses   CCP §§1290.6, 1290.8

    Witnesses, list of   CCP §1282.2

Settlements

    Notice to neutral of settlement of case   CRC 3.1385

Small claims jurisdiction to confirm, correct or vacate award   CCP §116.220

Stay of proceedings

    Generally   CCP §1281.4

    Arbitration agreement provisions set forth in petition for   CRC 3.1330

    Construction lien claim, effect of filing application for   CCP §1281.5

    Jurisdiction   CCP §1292.8

    Pending actions, effect of   CCP §1281.2

    Provisional remedies, effect of filing for   CCP §1281.8

Submission of controversy to arbitration, party's request for   CCP §1281.1

Subpoenas   CCP §1282.6

Subpoenas duces tecum   CCP §1282.6

Surety, effect of award against principal on   CC §2855

ARBITRATION—Cont.

Telephone, appearance by

    Fees   CCP §367.6

    Hearing on status of arbitration or mediation   CCP §367.5

Time for proceedings   CCP §1283.8

    Tolling by filing of civil action   CCP §1281.12

Transcripts

    Certified shorthand reporters

        Party's right   CCP §1282.5

Uninsured motorist cases

    Differential case management rules, applicability   CRC 3.712

    Rules for arbitration of   Gov §68609.5

Vacation of awards

    Generally   CCP §§1285, 1286

    Contents of petition   CCP §§1285.4, 1285.8

    Dismissal of proceedings   CCP §§1286, 1287.2

    Grounds   CCP §1286.2

    Judicial arbitration   CCP §1141.22, CRC 3.828

    Notice requirement   CCP §1286.4

    Rehearing before new arbitrators   CCP §1287

    Requisites   CCP §1286.4

    Response to petition   CCP §§1285.2, 1285.6, 1285.8

    Small claims action for attorney fee award   CCP §116.220

    Time limits for serving and filing of papers   CCP §§1288 to 1288.8

    Unconfirmed and unvacated awards, effect of   CCP §1287.6

Venue of proceedings   CCP §§1292, 1292.2

Waiver of arbitration

    Construction lien claim, effect of filing application for   CCP §1281.5

    Provisional remedies, effect of filing for   CCP §1281.8

Warranties on motor vehicles, actions involving   CC §1793.22

Witnesses

    Generally   CCP §1282.2

    Fees of   CCP §1283.2

    List of   CCP §1282.2

    Subpoenas for attendance of   CCP §1282.6

Writ of possession, party's rights under arbitration agreement on filing for   CCP §1281.8

Wrongful death action   CCP §1283.1

ARBITRATORS

Affiliations, disclosure of   CCP §1281.95

Appointment   CCP §1281.6

Attorney professional conduct

    Former judges, arbitrators, mediators, etc

        Restrictions on representation of clients   ProfC 1.12

    Service as temporary judge, referee or court-appointed arbitrator, applicability of judicial ethics canon 6D   ProfC 2.4.1

    Service by attorney as third-party neutral   ProfC 2.4

Co-arbitrators, authority of   CCP §1282

Conflicts of interest

    Disclosures by and disqualification of arbitrators   CCP §§1281.9 to 1281.95

    Judges' employment or prospective employment as a dispute resolution neutral as basis for disqualification of judges   CCP §§170.1, 1281.9

Consumer arbitration

    Definition of consumer arbitration

        Arbitrators, ethics standards for neutral arbitrators   CRC ArbEthicsStand 2

    Disclosures by arbitrator

        Openness to offers of employment or professional relationship   CRC ArbEthicsStand 7

        Provider organizations administering arbitration   CRC ArbEthicsStand 8

    Disqualification

        Financial interests of private arbitration companies in consumer arbitrations   CCP §1281.92

Contracts

    Ethics standards for neutral arbitrators   CRC ArbEthicsStand 1 to CRC ArbEthicsStand 17

Corruption of   CCP §1286.2

Court-appointed arbitrators, compliance with Code of Judicial Ethics   CRCSupp JudEthicsCanon 6

Disciplinary action

    Ethics standards

        Disclosures   CRC ArbEthicsStand 7

Discovery, power to compel   CCP §1283.05

Discrimination, prohibition against in court appointments   CRC 10.611, CRC JudAdminStand 10.21

Disqualification   CCP §§1281.9, 1281.91, 1281.95

    Financial interests of private arbitration companies in consumer arbitrations   CCP §1281.92

ARBITRATORS—Cont.
Disqualification —Cont.
　Judges' employment or prospective employment as a dispute resolution
　　neutral as basis for disqualification of judges　CCP §§170.1, 1281.9
Ethics standards　CCP §1281.85, CRC ArbEthicsStand 1 to CRC ArbEthicsStand
　17
　Applicability of provisions　CRC ArbEthicsStand 3
　Bequests
　　Refusal　CRC ArbEthicsStand 11
　Compensation　CRC ArbEthicsStand 16
　Conducting proceedings　CRC ArbEthicsStand 13
　Confidentiality　CRC ArbEthicsStand 15
　Construction of provisions　CRC ArbEthicsStand 1
　Consumer arbitrations done by provider organizations, disclosures　CRC
　　ArbEthicsStand 8
　Contents of rules of court　CRC 1.4
　Continuing duty to disclose　CRC ArbEthicsStand 7
　Definitions　CRC ArbEthicsStand 2
　Disclosures　CRC ArbEthicsStand 7
　　Consumer arbitrations done by provider organizations　CRC ArbEth-
　　　icsStand 8
　　Duty of arbitrator as to matters disclosed　CRC ArbEthicsStand 8
　Disqualification　CRC ArbEthicsStand 10
　Duration of ethical duty　CRC ArbEthicsStand 4
　Effective date　CRC ArbEthicsStand 3
　Ex parte communications　CRC ArbEthicsStand 14
　Fairness of process　CRC ArbEthicsStand 5
　Favors
　　Refusal　CRC ArbEthicsStand 11
　Future professional relationships
　　Duties and limitations　CRC ArbEthicsStand 12
　Gifts
　　Refusal　CRC ArbEthicsStand 11
　Integrity of process　CRC ArbEthicsStand 5
　Intent of provisions　CRC ArbEthicsStand 1
　Judges as private arbitrators　CRCSupp JudEthicsCanon 4
　Marketing　CRC ArbEthicsStand 17
　Purpose of provisions　CRC ArbEthicsStand 1
　Refusal of appointment
　　When required　CRC ArbEthicsStand 6
　Soliciting business　CRC ArbEthicsStand 17
　Time for disclosure　CRC ArbEthicsStand 7
Ex parte communications with
　Judicial arbitration　CRC 3.820
Immunity from civil liability　CCP §1297.119
Intervenors　CCP §1281.2
Judge serving as
　Employment or prospective employment as a dispute resolution neutral as
　　basis for disqualification of judges　CCP §§170.1, 1281.9
Judicial arbitration (See **JUDICIAL ARBITRATION**)
Misconduct of　CCP §1286.2
Neutral arbitrators, authority of　CCP §§1282 to 1282.8
Postponement of hearings　CCP §1286.2
Pretrial arbitration (See **JUDICIAL ARBITRATION**)
Qualifications　CCP §1281.6
Reports
　Data collection and reports available to public　CCP §1281.96
Standards for neutral arbitrators
　Ethics standards for neutral arbitrators　CRC ArbEthicsStand 1 to CRC
　　ArbEthicsStand 17
Unanimous agreement　CCP §1282

ARCHITECTS
Bond required to secure costs in action against　CCP §1029.5
Certificate of merit in negligence action against　CCP §§411.35, 430.10
Construction defects, actions for　CC §§895 to 945.5 (See **CONSTRUCTION
　DEFECTS, ACTIONS FOR**)
Design professionals' liens　CC §§8300 to 8319 (See **LIENS**)
Indemnity against loss from design defects　CC §§2783, 2784
　Public agencies, contracts with　CC §2782.8
Latent deficiencies in planning or construction of improvement to real property,
　statute of limitation for damages from　CCP §337.15
Late payment penalty in lieu of interest, contract provision for　CC §3319
Liens　CC §§8300 to 8319 (See **LIENS**)
Mechanics' liens　CC §§8000 to 9566 (See **MECHANICS' LIENS**)
Patent deficiencies in planning or construction of improvement to real property,
　statute of limitation for injury or death from　CCP §337.1
Public agencies, payment schedule for　CC §3320
Stipulated judgments in construction defect actions　CCP §664.7
Subcontractor design professionals, payments to　CC §3321
Withholding disputed amount　CC §§3320, 3321

AREIAS CREDIT CARD FULL DISCLOSURE ACT　CC §§1748.10,
　1748.11

AREIAS RETAIL INSTALLMENT ACCOUNT FULL DISCLOSURE ACT
　CC §§1810.20, 1810.21

AREIAS-ROBBINS CHARGE CARD FULL DISCLOSURE ACT　CC
　§§1748.20 to 1748.23

ARGUMENT AND COMMENT OF COUNSEL
Appellate division of superior court
　Transfer from division to court of appeals
　　Issues to be considered　CRC 8.1012
Appellate rules, superior court appeals
　Oral argument　CRC 8.885
　　Applicability of provisions　CRC 8.880
　　Infraction case appeals　CRC 8.929
Closing argument (See **CLOSING ARGUMENT**)
Court reporters to take down all arguments of prosecuting attorney　CCP §269
Judgment by stipulation　CCP §665
Order of proceedings　CCP §607
Rules on appeal
　Supreme court and courts of appeal (See **APPELLATE RULES, SU-
　　PREME COURT AND COURTS OF APPEAL**)

ARMED FORCES (See **MILITARY**)

ARMENIA
Limitations period for action by Armenian genocide victims
　Banks and other financial institutions　CCP §354.45
　Insurers, actions against　CCP §354.4

ARRAIGNMENT　CRC 4.100
Court reporters to take down all arraignments, pleas and sentences in felony cases
　CCP §269
Criminal case management, trial courts　CRC 10.951
Hearsay evidence, sufficient cause based upon　Ev §1203.1
Judicial holiday, proceedings on　CCP §134
Time for arraignment　CRC 4.110

ARREST
Bench warrants to secure attendance of witnesses　CCP §§1993, 1994
　Fee for processing civil warrant　Gov §26744.5
　Release of arrested witness　CCP §1993.1
　　Failure of released witness to appear　CCP §1993.2
Booking
　Commercial use of booking photographs　CC §1798.91.1
Children and minors
　Dependency proceedings　CRC 5.526
　Sealing arrest records of juvenile delinquents
　　Order on prosecutor request for access　CRCAppx A
　　Prosecuting attorney request to access sealed juvenile case files　CRC
　　　5.860
Claims against law enforcement officers (See **CLAIMS AGAINST PUBLIC
　ENTITIES AND EMPLOYEES**)
Contempt proceedings　CCP §§1212, 1214, 1220
Courthouses
　Civil arrest at courthouse
　　Judicial officer's power to protect privilege from civil arrest at court
　　　house　CCP §177
　　Restrictions on arrest at courthouse of person attending court proceed-
　　　ing or attending to legal business in courthouse　CC §43.54
Credit reporting (See **CREDIT REPORTING**)
Debt collectors threatening　CC §1788.10
Dogs used in police or military work, injuries inflicted by　CC §§3342, 3342.5
Employment investigations, notification of subsequent arrests
　Attorneys, fingerprinting　CRC 9.9.5
Examination proceedings for purposes of enforcement of judgments, failure to
　appear at　CCP §708.170
Informer, disclosure of　Ev §1042
Marital privilege
　Knowledge of prior arrest　Ev §972
Presumption of official duty regularly performed　Ev §664
Sealing and destruction of arrest records
　Judicial council legal forms　CRCAppx A
　Juvenile records
　　Order on prosecutor request for access　CRCAppx A
　　Prosecuting attorney request to access sealed juvenile case files　CRC
　　　5.860
Sheriff's fees for serving bench warrants　Gov §26744

Index

Index

Index

Index

ATTORNEY GENERAL—Cont.

Appellate rules, supreme court and courts of appeal—Cont.

Certification of state-law questions to California supreme court by federal appellate courts, notice to attorney general   CRC 8.548

Certiorari, mandate and prohibition

Amicus brief of attorney general and others   CRC 8.487

California coastal act

Civil actions to enforce provisions

Fees and costs for attorney general   CCP §1021.8

Change of venue of actions by or against state   CCP §401

Charitable trusts, supervision of trustees

Civil actions to enforce provisions

Fees and costs for attorney general   CCP §1021.8

Civil rights violation, bringing action for   CC §§52, 52.1

Construction or application of civil rights provisions in issue, solicitor general notified   CC §51.1

Fees and costs for attorney general   CCP §1021.8

Constitutional challenge to state law, Attorney General's intervention in appeal of   CCP §§664.5, 902.1

Consumer privacy rights

Actions for damages, injunctions, declaratory relief, etc

Notice to attorney general of action   CC §1798.150

Businesses, service providers, contractors, etc, violation

Actions for injunctions, civil penalties, etc, by attorney general   CC §1798.199.90

Rulemaking to implement provisions   CC §1798.185

California privacy protection agency takeover of rulemaking responsibility   CC §1798.199.40

Containers, fair packaging and labeling

Civil actions to enforce provisions

Fees and costs for attorney general   CCP §1021.8

Data broker registration

Information provided for registration   CC §1798.99.82

Access by public to information filed   CC §1798.99.84

Disabled persons access, actions to enforce

Fees and costs for attorney general   CCP §1021.8

Electronic court records, remote access

Government entities, access by

List of government entities which may be authorized to receive access   CRC 2.540

Electronic recording delivery systems

Evaluation of system   Gov §27398

Monitoring system   Gov §27396

Regulation and oversight costs

County responsibility for attorney general regulation and oversight   Gov §27397

Rulemaking to implement provisions   Gov §27393

System certification

Required   Gov §27392

Voidable transactions

Action for relief   Gov §27396

Eminent domain summons served on   CCP §1250.140

Environmental protection

Civil actions to enforce provisions

Fees and costs for attorney general   CCP §1021.8

Pollution action, Attorney General to be provided copy of pleading by party filing   CCP §388

Escheat (See **ESCHEAT**)

False claims actions

Filing records under seal   CRC 2.570 to 2.573

Felon's story, action regarding proceeds from sale of   CC §2225

Firefighting liability

Civil actions to enforce provisions

Fees and costs for attorney general   CCP §1021.8

Fish and wildlife laws

Civil actions to enforce provisions

Fees and costs for attorney general   CCP §1021.8

Gang database removal, appeal proceedings

Order to remove name

Service on attorney general   CRC 3.2300

Hazardous substances, underground storage

Civil actions to enforce provisions

Fees and costs for attorney general   CCP §1021.8

Housing discrimination

Civil actions to enforce provisions

Fees and costs for attorney general   CCP §1021.8

Immigration consultants

Civil actions to enforce provisions

Fees and costs for attorney general   CCP §1021.8

Information Practices Act, obtaining injunctive relief under   CC §1798.47

ATTORNEY GENERAL—Cont.

Interstate family support

Duties of state officials, compelling performance   Fam §5700.308

Labor disputes, action for violence during   CC §52

Marital status, action for denial of credit because of   CC §§1812.32, 1812.33

Police officers (See **LAW ENFORCEMENT OFFICERS**)

Quo warranto proceedings brought by   CCP §803

San Francisco Bay conservation and development commission

Civil actions to enforce provisions

Fees and costs for attorney general   CCP §1021.8

Small claims advisory committee, composition of   CCP §116.950

Smokeless tobacco nonsale distribution

Civil actions to enforce provisions

Fees and costs for attorney general   CCP §1021.8

Smoking, tobacco sales and distribution

Civil actions to enforce provisions

Fees and costs for attorney general   CCP §1021.8

Solicitor general

Civil rights actions

Construction or application of civil rights provisions in issue, solicitor general notified   CC §51.1

Disabled, blind, deaf, etc., equal access provisions

Construction of application of provisions in issue, solicitor general notified   CC §55.2

Terrorism

September 11, 2001 terrorist attacks

Identification of participants and conspirators   CCP §340.10

Trusts (See **TRUSTS**)

Unclaimed deposits and payments   CCP §§1574, 1575

Unruh Civil Rights Act, bringing action under   CC §52

Water, federal water pollution control act enforcement

Civil actions to enforce provisions

Fees and costs for attorney general   CCP §1021.8

Water, unauthorized diversion or use

Civil actions to enforce provisions

Fees and costs for attorney general   CCP §1021.8

Water, waste or unreasonable use

Civil actions to enforce provisions

Fees and costs for attorney general   CCP §1021.8

Water, water quality enforcement

Civil actions to enforce provisions

Fees and costs for attorney general   CCP §1021.8

Water, water rights enforcement

Civil actions to enforce provisions

Fees and costs for attorney general   CCP §1021.8

Will probate proceedings, notice of   Pro §§1209, 8111

ATTORNEY IN FACT (See **POWER OF ATTORNEY**)

ATTORNEY PROFESSIONAL CONDUCT   ProfC 1.0 to 8.5

Admission to practice

False statements regarding application for admission   ProfC 8.1

Advertising   ProfC 7.2

Solicitation of clients   ProfC 7.3

Advising client to or assisting client to violate law   ProfC 1.2.1

Advocacy role   ProfC 3.1 to 3.10

Aggregate settlements involving multiple clients   ProfC 1.8.7

Law firms

Imputation to all members of firm of violations of certain provisions   ProfC 1.8.11

Allocation between attorney and client of authority   ProfC 1.2

Associations

Law firms and associations generally   ProfC 5.1 to 5.6

Organization or entity as client   ProfC 1.13

Business expenses incurred by or for client

Law firms

Imputation to all members of firm of violations of certain provisions   ProfC 1.8.11

Restrictions on attorney payment of client's business or personal expenses   ProfC 1.8.5

Business transactions with clients   ProfC 1.8.1

Law firms

Imputation to all members of firm of violations of certain provisions   ProfC 1.8.11

Candid advice   ProfC 2.1

Candor towards the tribunal   ProfC 3.3

Client-lawyer relationship   ProfC 1.0 to 1.18

Comments to rules

Purpose of official comments   ProfC 1.0

Communications concerning lawyer's services   ProfC 7.1

Index

ATTORNEYS—Cont.

Continuance of trial, agreement on   CCP §595.2

Continuing legal education

    Delinquency cases

        Training of attorneys representing children in delinquency cases   CRC 5.664

    Discipline   CRC 9.31

    Noncompliance

        Inactive status

            Expungement of record of inactive enrollment   CRC 9.31

Coordination proceedings   CRC 3.550

Counsel pro hac vice   CRC 9.40

County counsel (See **COUNTY COUNSEL**)

Court's assumption of jurisdiction over practice

    Extension of limitations period   CCP §353.1

    Relief from judgment or other proceedings   CCP §473.1

Criminal history information records

    Fingerprinting of attorneys

        Active licensed attorneys   CRC 9.9.5

        Foreign countries, active attorneys residing in   CRC 9.9.5

        Inactive status prior to becoming active status   CRC 9.9.5

        Special admissions attorneys   CRC 9.9.5

    Subsequent arrest notifications

        Fingerprinting of attorneys   CRC 9.9.5

Cross complaint served on   CCP §428.60

Custody of children (See **CUSTODY OF CHILDREN**)

Damages, liability of legal professional societies for   CC §§43.7, 43.95

Death of attorney

    New attorney appointed by client on death of attorney   CCP §286

    Practice administrator appointed by personal representative on death of attorney   Pro §§9764, 17200

Death of client, availability of attorney-client privilege following   Ev §957

Death penalty

    Appointed counsel

        Appellate counsel appointments   CRC 8.605

        Appellate counsel qualifications   CRC 8.605

        Habeas counsel appointments   CRC 8.605

        Habeas counsel qualifications   CRC 8.652

    Habeas corpus

        Attorney appointments for death penalty cases   CRC 4.561

Debt collection, false representations in   CC §§1788.13, 1788.16

Decedents' estates

    Probate attorneys

        Education requirements   CRC 10.478

        Qualifications   CRC 10.776, 10.777

Delaying tactics, assessment against attorney of expenses and attorney fees incurred as result of (See **SANCTIONS**)

Deliberation and verdict, post-trial discussions with jurors regarding   CCP §206

Dependent children

    Collection for reimbursement of appointed attorneys

        Guidelines for juvenile dependency counsel collections program   CR-CAppx F

    Guardian ad litem

        Child abuse and treatment act (CAPTA) guardians ad litem   CRC 5.662

    Legal costs, liability for

        Juvenile dependency counsel collections program, guidelines   CR-CAppx F

Depositions

    Subpoenas

        Issuance by attorney of record   CCP §2020.210

Deposit of estate-planning documents with attorney (See **TRUSTS; WILLS**)

Disability of attorney, appointment of practice administrator in event of   Pro §§2468, 17200

Disability of plaintiff tolling statute of limitation for legal malpractice actions   CCP §340.6

Discipline

    Attorney discipline generally (See **ATTORNEY DISCIPLINE**)

    Rules of professional conduct generally (See **ATTORNEY PROFESSIONAL CONDUCT**)

Discovery (See **DISCOVERY**)

Discrimination

    Court appointment   CRC 10.611, CRC JudAdminStand 10.21

Dismissal, consent of or notice to attorney of   CCP §581

Disqualification of judges (See **JUDGES, DISQUALIFICATION OF**)

Domestic violence

    Appointment of attorney in domestic violence proceedings   Fam §6340

    Victim representatives   Fam §6228

Donative transfers

    Presumption of fraud or undue influence

        Duties of counsel   Pro §21384

ATTORNEYS—Cont.

Electronic court records

    Remote access

        Parties, designees, attorneys, court-appointed persons or persons working in legal organization or qualified legal services project, access by   CRC 2.515 to 2.528

Electronic filing and service rules

    Fees

        Sanctions for attorney's failure to pay provider fees   CCP §411.20.5

Emancipation of children (See **EMANCIPATION OF MINORS**)

Enforcement of judgments (See **ENFORCEMENT OF JUDGMENTS**)

Executors and administrators (See **EXECUTORS AND ADMINISTRATORS**)

Ex parte proceedings

    Identification of attorney or party   CRC 3.1202

Extension of time

    Court's assumption of jurisdiction over practice   CCP §353.1

    Legislature, time extension for attorneys attending   CCP §1054.1

Family law facilitators, minimum standards   CRC 5.430

Family law proceedings

    Appointment by court

        Applicable guidelines for appointment   CRC JudAdminStand 5.30

        Compensation of court-appointed attorneys   CRC JudAdminStand 5.30

    Limited scope representation   CRC 5.425

    Service of papers on attorney of record   Fam §215

    Title IV-D support enforcement

        Attorney of record in support actions   CRC 5.320

Fax transmissions, attorney-client privilege for   Ev §952

Fees (See **ATTORNEY'S FEES**)

Fingerprinting

    Active licensed attorneys   CRC 9.9.5

    Foreign countries, active attorney residing in   CRC 9.9.5

    Inactive status attorneys prior to becoming active status   CRC 9.9.5

    Special admissions attorneys   CRC 9.9.5

Foreign countries, licensed attorneys residing in

    Fingerprinting   CRC 9.9.5

Foreign legal consultants   CRC 9.44

    Fingerprinting of special admission attorneys   CRC 9.9.5

Frivolous actions, assessment against attorney of expenses and attorney fees incurred as result of (See **SANCTIONS**)

Guardianship (See **GUARDIAN AND WARD**)

Habeas corpus

    Attorney appointments

        Death penalty cases   CRC 4.561, 8.391

    Attorney qualifications

        Death penalty cases   CRC 4.562, 8.391, 8.652

    Ineffective assistance

        Death penalty cases, appeals from superior court habeas proceedings   CRC 8.397

    Petitions filed by attorneys   CRC 8.384

Health care provider's negligence, noncompliance with notice requirement for commencement of action for   CCP §365

Incompetent representation

    Attorney misconduct triggering notification to state bar

        Appellate justice's duties   CRC 10.1017

        Trial judge duties   CRC 10.609

Indigent persons (See **INDIGENT PERSONS**)

Ineffective assistance

    Habeas corpus, capital cases

        Appeals from superior court decisions in habeas cases involving death penalty   CRC 8.397

In-house counsel

    Registered in-house counsel   CRC 9.46

        Fingerprinting of special admission attorneys   CRC 9.9.5

Inspection of records by (See **INSPECTION**)

Insurance (See **INSURANCE**)

Interest on lawyers trust accounts (IOLTA)

    Unclaimed property

        Administration of funds escheated from IOLTA accounts   CCP §1564.5

International wills, authorized persons re   Pro §§6388, 6389

Interstate family support

    Private counsel authorized   Fam §5700.309

Judge advocate, appearance in state court   CRC 9.41

Judges

    Practice of law   CRCSupp JudEthicsCanons 3, 4

    Temporary judges

        Appointment of attorney as temporary judge   CRC 2.810, 2.812

Judges' right to representation in proceedings for censure, removal or admonishment   JudPerR 106, 126

Judicial arbitration proceedings   CRC 3.821

Index

Index

AUTOMOBILES—Cont.

Warranty—Cont.

Military

Motor vehicle purchased in US, applicability of California warranty provisions   CC §1791.8

Sale of personal information, opting out

Information shared between new vehicle dealer and manufacturer for warranty or recall purposes   CC §1798.145

Used vehicles

Buy-here-pay-here dealers' obligations   CC §1795.51

Weight

Administrative regulations

Vehicle weight impacts and ability of manufacturers and operators to comply with weight laws   Gov §11343.3

Written declaration, trial by for infractions offenses   CRC 4.210

AUTOMOBILE SALES FINANCE   CC §2982.5

Buy-here-pay-here dealers

Obligations of dealers   CC §2983.37

Contracts

Electric vehicle charging stations included in contract

Disclosures   CC §2982.11

Dealers

Buy-here-pay-here dealers

Obligations of dealers   CC §2983.37

Disclosures

Electric vehicle charging stations included in contract   CC §2982.11

Electric vehicles

Charging stations included in contract

Disclosures   CC §2982.11

Finance charge   CC §§2981, 2981.7, 2981.8, 2982, 2982.8

AUTOMOBILE THEFT

Keys left in parked vehicle, liability affected by   CC §1630.5

Limitation on liability, effect of signs stating   CC §1630

Parking facility, liability of   CC §1630.5

AUTOPSIES

Child victims

Sealing autopsy report and evidence   CCP §130

Restriction on reproducing photograph or video taken in course of   CCP §129

AVIATION (See **AIRCRAFT AND AVIATION**)

AVOIDANCE

Voidable transactions   CC §3439.07

AWARDS

Attorneys' fees (See **ATTORNEY'S FEES**)

International commercial arbitration awards (See **INTERNATIONAL COMMERCIAL ARBITRATION AND CONCILIATION**)

Judicial arbitration awards (See **JUDICIAL ARBITRATION**)

Non-judicial arbitration awards (See **ARBITRATION**)

B

BABYSITTING AND BABYSITTERS (See **CHILD CARE**)

BACKGROUND

Expert witnesses   Ev §802

BAD CHECKS (See **CHECKS**)

BAD FAITH

Award of expenses and attorney's fees incurred as result of bad-faith actions or tactics (See **SANCTIONS**)

Landlord, bad faith retention of deposits by   CC §1950.7

Powers of attorney

Bad faith of attorney in fact   Pro §§4231, 4231.5

Small claims court judgment, award of attorney's fees on appeal from   CCP §116.790

Summary judgment motion support or opposition presented in bad faith   CCP §437c

BAGGAGE

Bus, liability for loss by operator of   CC §2205

Common carriers liens for fares   CC §2191

Delivery requirements   CC §2183

Foreclosure of deposit liens   CC §1857

Free carriage of   CC §§2180, 2181

Higher value declaration   CC §§2177, 2205

BAGGAGE—Cont.

Hotel, apartment, lodging or hospital, limitation of action for recovery or conversion of personal property left at   CCP §341a

Hotel keeper's lien on   CC §1861

Lien for rent   CC §§1861, 1861a

Limitation on liability

Carrier's liability   CC §§2178, 2182

Innkeeper's liability   CC §1859

Notice of valuable goods   CC §2177

Place for carrying   CC §2183

Tagging requirements   CC §2205

BAIL

Amount of bail

Jury trial, request for as affecting amount   CRC 4.101

Schedules   CRC 4.102

Appeal, bail pending   CRC 8.312

Finality of court of appeals ruling on bail   CRC 8.366

Boating violations

Bail schedule   CRC 4.102

Business licensing violations, bail schedule   CRC 4.102

Check, payment by means of   CRC 10.821

Contempt proceedings   CCP §§1213, 1215, 1216

Fish and game violations, bail schedule   CRC 4.102

Forestry violations, bail schedule   CRC 4.102

Jury trial request, effect of   CRC 4.101

Parks and recreation violations, bail schedule   CRC 4.102

Payment   CRC 10.821

Public utilities violations, bail schedule   CRC 4.102

Reduction of bail

Pending appeal   CRC 8.312

Schedules   CRC 4.102

Uniform Bail and Penalty Schedules   CRC 4.102

BAILIFFS

Appointment   CRCSupp JudEthicsCanon 3

Juvenile court proceedings   CRC 5.530

BAILMENT

Automobiles (See **AUTOMOBILES**)

Death of party to   CC §1934

Default on obligations by lessor   CC §1957

Delivery of property under   CC §1955

Demand for return of property loaned   CC §1894

Deposits (See **DEPOSITS**)

Enforcement of judgments (See **ENFORCEMENT OF JUDGMENTS**)

Expenses and upkeep   CC §§1956, 2078

Fitness requirement of property held under   CC §1955

Gratuitous bailee   CC §§1505, 2078

Hiring contracts   CC §§1925 to 1935

Indemnity requirements   CC §§1893, 1894

Loss from early termination of   CC §§1894, 1935

Negligence   CC §§1888, 1928, 2078

Notice of expenditures   CC §1957

Offer of contract   CC §1503

Place for redelivery of property held under   CC §§1896, 1958

Possession, transfer of   CC §1925

Quiet enjoyment, right of   CC §1955

Repairs   CC §§1889, 1929

Return of bailed property   CC §1958

Termination of agreement   CC §§1894 to 1896, 1931 to 1934

Use, bailment for   CC §§1884 to 1896

Vessels held under charter-party agreement   CC §1959

BALLOON PAYMENTS (See **TRUST DEEDS AND MORTGAGES**)

BALLOT MEASURES

Precedence to cases involving certification of   CCP §35

BANK ACCOUNTS

Community property accounts of spouses

Statutory language for creating particular types of accounts   Pro §5203

Electronic transactions

Exceptions to applicability of electronic transactions provisions   CC §1633.3

Joint accounts

Excess withdrawal by party

Claim for recovery   Pro §5301

Proportional ownership interest in other parties   Pro §5301

Pay-on-death accounts

Excess withdrawal by party

Claim for recovery   Pro §5301

Index

BARBERING AND COSMETOLOGY
Gender
>> Prohibition against charging different price for services of similar or like kind based solely on   CC §51.6
>> Small business gender discrimination in pricing services compliance act   CC §§55.61 to 55.63

BAR EXAMINATION
Analysis of validity of examination   CRC 9.6
Committee of Bar Examiners
> Appointments   CRC 9.4
> Duties as to bar examination   CRC 9.6
> Nominations   CRC 9.4
> Rules adopted by committee and approved by trustees
>> Supreme court review and approval   CRC 9.5
Supreme court
> Approval by supreme court   CRC 9.6

BARLEY
Crusher, lien for use of   CC §3061
Storage regulations after sale of   CC §§1880 to 1881.2

BARS (See COCKTAIL LOUNGES)

BASTARDS (See PARENT AND CHILD)

BATTERED WOMAN OR INTIMATE PARTNER BATTERING EFFECTS
Admissibility of expert testimony of   Ev §1107
Child victims, 12 or older
> Medical care and treatment
>> Consent   Fam §6930
Domestic violence generally (See DOMESTIC VIOLENCE)
Mitigation of circumstances   CRC 4.423

BATTERY (See ASSAULT AND BATTERY)

BB DEVICES
Sale to minor
> Verification of age for sale of age-restricted products   CC §1798.99.1

BEACHES
Public entity's liability for   Gov §831.21
Public use of private land   CC §1009

BEAUTY SALONS (See BARBERING AND COSMETOLOGY)

BED AND BREAKFAST LODGING
Human trafficking or slavery
> Signs, businesses required to post notice concerning relief from slavery or human trafficking   CC §52.6

BED BUG INFESTATIONS
Landlord and tenant   CC §§1954.600 to §CC 1954.605
> Current infestation
>> Showing, renting or leasing of premises prohibited   CC §1954.602
> Information on bed bugs provided to prospective tenants   CC §1954.603
> Inspections
>> Entry by landlord to inspect   CC §1954.604
>> Findings, notice to tenant   CC §1954.605
> Legislative findings and intent   CC §1954.600
> Notice by tenant of suspected infestation
>> Retaliatory eviction or other retaliatory actions, prohibitions   CC §1942.5
> Pest control operators
>> Defined   CC §1954.601

BEEF (See LIVESTOCK)

BEER (See ALCOHOLIC BEVERAGES)

BENEFICIARIES
Life insurance (See LIFE INSURANCE)
Power of attorney (See POWER OF ATTORNEY)
Trusts (See TRUSTS)
Wills (See WILLS)

BEST AND SECONDARY EVIDENCE
Generally   Ev §§1520 to 1522
Business records, admissibility of (See BUSINESS RECORDS)
Certified copies   Ev §1531
Computer information, printed representations of (See COMPUTERS)
Deeds   Ev §§1600 to 1605

BEST AND SECONDARY EVIDENCE—Cont.
Duplicate defined   Ev §260
Lost or destroyed original, secondary evidence of contents of   Ev §§1523, 1551
Microphotographed files, records, photographs, etc., in custody of criminal justice agency
> Reproductions, admissibility   Ev §1550.1
Numerous accounts or writings, admissibility of oral evidence representing   Ev §1523
Official records   Ev §§1530 to 1532
Oral evidence, admissibility of   Ev §1523
Original defined   Ev §255

BEST INTEREST OF CHILD (See CUSTODY OF CHILDREN)

BEVERAGES (See ALCOHOLIC BEVERAGES)

BEYOND REASONABLE DOUBT
Criminal proceedings   Ev §§501, 502
Presumptions, effect on   Ev §607
Requirement for burden of proof   Ev §115
Sterilization proceedings, findings in   Pro §1958

BIAS AND PREJUDICE
Court commissioners, disqualification of   CCP §170.6
Disqualification of judges (See JUDGES, DISQUALIFICATION OF)
Disregard of nonprejudicial error   CCP §475
Evidence excluded for creating   Ev §352
Judges   CRCSupp JudEthicsCanons 3, 4 (See JUDGES)
Judicial administration standards
> Appointments by court, nondiscrimination in   CRC JudAdminStand 10.21
> Duty of court to prevent bias   CRC JudAdminStand 10.20
Jury
> Civil cases, judicial administration standards   CRC JudAdminStand 3.25
> Peremptory challenge to juror based on bias   CCP §§231.5, 231.7
> Voir dire examination calculated to discover   CCP §222.5
Petit jurors
> Civil cases, judicial administration standards   CRC JudAdminStand 3.25
Pleadings and proof, material variance in   CCP §469
Presumption against prejudice   CCP §475
Referees, disqualification of   CCP §§170.6, 639, 641

BIBLE
Ancestry, family entries as evidence   Ev §1312

BICYCLES
Common carriers transporting   CC §2181
Electric bicycles
> Shared mobility devices   CC §2505
Serial numbers destroyed or altered prior to sale   CC §1710.1
Shared mobility devices   CC §2505

BIDS AND BIDDING (See also AUCTIONS)
Administration of estates (See ADMINISTRATION OF ESTATES)
Enforcement of judgments (See ENFORCEMENT OF JUDGMENTS)
Homestead exemption, effect of bids failing to exceed amount of   CCP §704.800
Leases on city property   CC §719
Mortgages, sales under   CC §§2924g, 2924h
> Prospective owner-occupant as bidder   CC §2924m
Partition sales   CCP §873.680

BIFURCATION
Family law rules (See FAMILY RULES)
Motion of court for   CCP §§597, 597.5
New trial motion following bifurcated trial   CRC 3.1591
Statement of decision   CRC 3.1591

BIGAMY
Spousal testimony in bigamy proceedings, admissibility of   Ev §§972, 985

BILLBOARDS (See SIGNS AND BILLBOARDS)

BILLING COMPANIES
Medical claims, release of information for   CC §56.16

BILLING CYCLE (See RETAIL INSTALLMENT SALES)

BILL OF EXCEPTIONS
Extensions of time   CCP §§1054, 1054.1
New trial, loss as grounds for   CCP §663.1

BILL OF LADING
Apportionment of freightage under   CC §2140

BILL OF LADING—Cont.
Limitation on liability   CC §2176

BILL OF PARTICULARS
Demand and response
    Limitation on papers filed   CRC 3.250

BILL OF RIGHTS
Fourth Amendment (See **SEARCH AND SEIZURE**)

BILL OF SALE
Generally   CC §1053
Cancellation   CC §1058
Consignment (See **COMMON CARRIERS**)
Constructive delivery   CC §1059
Delivery   CC §§1054 to 1056, 1059
Escrow, transfer through   CC §§1057, 1057.5
Grain sold by bill of sale without delivery   CC §§1880.3 to 1880.6, 1880.8, 1880.9
Hearsay rule affecting admissibility of statements in   Ev §1330
Mining machinery   CC §1631
Redelivery   CC §1058
Unclaimed property, controller executing bills of sale for   CCP §1376
Vessels   CC §1135

BILLS AND NOTES
Accrual of interest on promissory note secured by trust deed   CC §2948.5
Administrator executing notes   Pro §§9805, 9806
Attachment (See **ATTACHMENT**)
Common carrier's liability for transporting   CC §2200
Dance studio, defenses on notes given for lessons by   CC §1812.55
Discount buying services   CC §1812.113
Executors executing notes   Pro §§9805, 9806
Guardianship (See **GUARDIAN AND WARD**)
Health studio fees, defenses against holders of notes given for   CC §1812.87
Joinder of parties, costs in absence of   CCP §1022
Nonprobate transfers (See **NONPROBATE TRANSFERS**)
Possession of note as presumption of payment   Ev §634
Retail installment sales notes, defenses against holders of   CC §1810.7
Seller assisted marketing plan   CC §1812.210
Trust deeds and mortgages, notes secured by (See **TRUST DEEDS AND MORTGAGES**)
Unsolicited goods, billing statements sent for   CC §§1584.5, 1584.6
Variable interest note, requirements of notice for   CC §1916.5

BILLS OF EXCHANGE
Generally (See **NEGOTIABLE INSTRUMENTS**)
Checks (See **CHECKS**)
Joinder of parties, costs in absence of   CCP §1022

BINDING
Attorney's authority to bind client   CCP §283

BINS
Grain storage after sale, regulation of   CC §§1880 to 1881.2

BIRTH
Adoption proceedings (See **ADOPTION**)
Bible entries as evidence   Ev §1312
Certificates of birth (See **BIRTH CERTIFICATES**)
Church records as evidence   Ev §1315
Community reputation concerning   Ev §1314
Declarant unavailable, admissibility of statement of   Ev §1310
Family friends, statements concerning birth by   Ev §1311
Genetic defects, failure of parent to abort on discovery of   CC §43.6
Neighbor's testimony concerning   Ev §1314
Paternity suits (See **PATERNITY**)
Records as proof of   Ev §1281
Relative's statements concerning   Ev §1311
Reputation among family members concerning   Ev §1313
Statutes of limitation for personal injuries to minor sustained during birth   CCP §340.4

BIRTH CERTIFICATES
Adoption proceedings (See **ADOPTION**)
Evidence concerning family history   Ev §§1315, 1316
Forms
    Judicial council legal forms   CRCAppx A
Parentage, voluntary declarations   Fam §§7570 to 7581
    Challenge to declaration
        New certificates, issuance in light of ruling   Fam §7578
Recordation of (See **RECORDS AND RECORDING**)

BIRTH CONTROL
Abortion (See **ABORTIONS**)
Sterilization (See **STERILIZATION**)

BIRTH NAME
Dissolution and annulment proceedings, restoration of former name in   Fam §§2080 to 2082, 2401
Refusal to do business with person due to use of birth name   CCP §1279.6

BIRTH PARENTS (See **ADOPTION**)

BLACKLISTING
Civil rights protection
    Construction or application of provisions in issue, solicitor general notified   CC §51.1

BLIND PERSONS
Administrative procedure act
    Visual or communication disability
        Narrative description of proposed regulation upon request   Gov §11346.6
Commercial and industrial common interest developments
    Disabled access
        Modification of separate interests   CC §6714
Definition of visually impaired   CC §54.6
Discrimination (See **DISCRIMINATION**)
Equal access to public facilities   CC §§54, 54.1, 54.3, 54.4, 55
    Construction or application of provisions in issue, solicitor general notified   CC §55.2
Guide dogs for (See **DOGS**)
Housing, denial of   CC §54.1
    Construction or application of provisions in issue, solicitor general notified   CC §55.2
Injunctions for violation of equal rights   CC §55
Jury (See **JURY**)
Negligence, failure to use white cane or guide dog as not constituting   CC §54.4
Privacy
    Touch screen devices for self-service check-in at hotels or transportation facilities   CC §54.9
Public restrooms, right to use of   CC §55
Telephone facilities, use of   CC §54.1
    Construction or application of provisions in issue, solicitor general notified   CC §55.2
Touch screen devices
    Self-service check-in at hotels or passenger transportation facilities   CC §54.9
Visually impaired defined   CC §54.6
White cane
    Day set aside for   CC §54.5
    Negligence in failure to use   CC §54.4

BLOCKED ACCOUNTS
Conservators and guardians, reduction of surety bond amount required for   Pro §2328
Executors and administrators, reduction of surety bond amount required for   Pro §8483

BLOOD TESTS
Admissibility of evidence from   Ev §712
Adoption
    DNA testing (See **ADOPTION**)
Parentage
    Genetic testing to determine parentage   Fam §§7550 to 7562 (See **PATERNITY**)

BLUE LAWS (See **SUNDAYS**)

BLUNT WRAPS
Minors
    Verification of age for sale of age-restricted products   CC §1798.99.1

BOARDING FACILITIES AND STABLES
Statutes of limitation for injury to animal   CCP §340

BOARDINGHOUSES
Blind persons   CC §§54.1, 54.3, 54.4, 55
    Construction or application of provisions in issue, solicitor general notified   CC §55.2
Demolition
    Notice of application to demolish   CC §1940.6
Disabled persons   CC §§54.1, 54.3, 54.4, 55
    Construction or application of provisions in issue, solicitor general notified   CC §55.2

BOARDINGHOUSES—Cont.
Forcible entry statute, protection under   CCP §1159
Guide dogs permitted in   CC §§54.2, 54.3
    Construction or application of provisions in issue, solicitor general notified   CC §55.2
Liens   CC §§1861 to 1861.28
Loss of property, liability of housekeeper for   CC §§1859, 1860
Monthly tenancy presumed   CC §1944
Occupancy, right to   CC §1940.1
Rent control ordinances, effect of substantial compliance with   CC §1947.7
Statute of limitation for recovery or conversion of personal property left at   CCP §341a
Tenants, classification as   CC §1940
Termination, notice of   CC §1946.5

BOARD OF SUPERVISORS (See SUPERVISORS)

BOARDS
Agricultural Labor Relations Board, judicial review of decisions   CRC 8.728
Public Employment Relations Board, judicial review of decisions   CRC 8.728
Service of process on   CCP §416.50
Validation proceedings   CCP §§860 to 870
Workers' Compensation Appeals Board, judicial review of decisions   CRC 8.720

BOATING TRAILS
Closure of   CCP §731.5

BOATS (See VESSELS)

BODYWORKERS
Human trafficking or slavery
    Signs, businesses required to post notice concerning relief from slavery or human trafficking   CC §52.6

BOGUS CHECKS (See CHECKS)

BOLTS
Fixtures attached to real property by   CC §660

BOMB SHELTERS
Personal injury liability of governmental agency to parties using   CC §1714.5

BONA FIDE PURCHASERS
Art works sold by dealer to   CC §1738.7
Home equity sales contracts   CC §1695.12
Nonprobate transfers to former spouse   Pro §5044
Partition sales   CCP §873.690
Voidable transactions   CC §3439.08

BONDING COMPANY (See SURETYSHIP, BONDS AND UNDERTAKINGS)

BONDS
Adoption facilitators   Fam §8636
    Registration process   Fam §8632.5
Appeal bonds   CCP §§917.9 to 922
Appellate rules, superior court appeals
    Costs
        Recoverable costs   CRC 8.891
Attachment (See ATTACHMENT)
Child custody
    Orders
        Risk of abduction findings and preventative measures   Fam §3048
Claims against public entities and employees, requirement for bonds to pay   Gov §§975.2 to 978.8
Common interest developments
    Directors, officers and employees
        Association to maintain fidelity bond coverage for directors, officers and employees   CC §5806
Conservators   CRC 7.207
Corporate sureties, prerequisites to acceptance of   CRC 3.1130
Decedents' estates (See ADMINISTRATION OF ESTATES)
Defined   CCP §349.2
Enforcement of bond
    Deposit in lieu of bond
        Collection, sale, etc, to enforce liability   CCP §995.760
Enforcement of judgments (See ENFORCEMENT OF JUDGMENTS)
Fax filing and service
    Excluded documents and papers from   CRC 2.300
Fidelity bonds (See SURETYSHIP, BONDS AND UNDERTAKINGS)
Guardians   CRC 7.207
Injunctions (See INJUNCTIONS)

BONDS—Cont.
Law and motion rules
    Acceptance of corporate sureties, prerequisites to   CRC 3.1130
Mechanics' liens   CC §§8150 to 8154, 8424 (See MECHANICS' LIENS)
Official bonds (See BONDS OF PUBLIC OFFICIALS)
Partition sale proceeds invested in government obligations   CCP §873.810
Payment bonds (See PAYMENT BONDS)
Power of attorney, statutory form   Pro §4453
Preliminary injunction, bond requirements   CRC 3.1150
Principal and income allocations   CC §§731 to 731.15, Pro §16357
Public officials (See BONDS OF PUBLIC OFFICIALS)
Receivers (See RECEIVERS AND RECEIVERSHIP)
Statutes of limitation
    California-issued bonds
        No limitation   CCP §348.5
    Contesting validity of bonds   CCP §349.2
    Corporate bonds, notes or debentures, action upon   CCP §336a
    Exception to limitation   CCP §337.6
    General obligation bonds, action upon   CCP §§337.5, 337.6
    State bonds, action on   CCP §337.5
Surety bonds (See SURETYSHIP, BONDS AND UNDERTAKINGS)
Trust administration, allocation of principal and income during   Pro §16357
Validation
    Authorization and existence of bonds, dates of   CCP §864
    Procedure for validation   CCP §349.4
    Statute of limitation contesting validity of bonds   CCP §349.2
    Taxes pledged for bond payments by agency other than agency imposing tax, notice requirements concerning   CCP §870.5
Vexatious litigants   CCP §§391 to 391.8
Voidable transactions, undertaking and action to set aside   CC §§3445 to 3449
Withdrawal of bond   CRC 3.1130
Wrongfully enjoining public improvement or utility, damages for   CCP §526b

BONDS OF PUBLIC OFFICIALS
Generally   CCP §§995.810 to 995.850
Commissioner handling property or money   CCP §571
Court reporter taking down and transcribing at cost of county   CCP §274a
Indemnity rights, bond as basis for   CCP §1055
Referee handling property or money   CCP §571
Statute of limitation upon bond of public official   CCP §338

BONUSES
Attachments, exemption from   CCP §487.020

BOOK ACCOUNTS
Attorney's fees in action on book accounts, recovery of   CC §1717.5
Defined   CCP §337a

BOOKING PHOTOGRAPHS
Commercial use of booking photographs   CC §1798.91.1

BOOKKEEPING (See ACCOUNTS AND ACCOUNTING)

BOOKS (See also LITERARY PROPERTY)
Admissibility of statements in   Ev §§1340, 1341
Assignment for benefit of creditors, property exempt from   CCP §1801
Bible, evidence of ancestry   Ev §1312
County recorder's books   CC §1171
Infringement, action for   CCP §429.30
Judges' writings, Code of Judicial Ethics provisions concerning   CRCSupp JudEthicsCanons 2, 4
Law books, presumptions of accuracy of   Ev §645
Presumptions of printing or publishing of   Ev §644
Privacy
    Reader privacy act   CC §§1798.90, 1798.90.05
Trial publicity
    Court proceedings, restrictions on media coverage of   CRC 1.150

BOTTOMRY
Discharge provisions applicable to mortgages, exception to   CC §2942
Lien statutes applicable to   CC §2877
Priority rule, exception from   CC §2897

BOULEVARDS (See STREETS AND HIGHWAYS)

BOUNDARIES
Adjoining landowners   CC §§829 to 835
Burden of proof in dispute involving state   Ev §523
Cities (See CITIES AND MUNICIPALITIES)
Common interest developments   CC §4220
Condominiums   CC §§783, 4220

BROKERS—Cont.

Buyer's agents

Disclosure

Acknowledgment of receipt of disclosure form   CC §2079.14

Duties   CC §2079.14

Commercial real property

Duties owed to prospective purchaser

Definition of commercial real property   CC §2079.13

Compensation of agent not determinative of relationship   CC §2079.19

Confidential information

Dual agency or representation

Restrictions on disclosure of confidential information   CC §2079.21

Construction trucking services brokers

Transportation charges, payment   CC §3322

Contract modification to agency relationship permitted   CC §2079.23

Definitions   CC §§1086, 2079.13

Disclosure requirements   CC §§1102 to 1103.15

Agency   CC §§2079.12 to 2079.25

Acknowledgment of receipt of disclosure form   CC §2079.14

AIDS, disclosures regarding prior occupant afflicted with   CC §1710.2

Amendment of disclosure   CC §§1102.9, 1103.9

Applicability of requirements   CC §§1089, 1102, 1102.18, 1103, 1103.15, 2079.25

Death of prior occupant occurring within three years, disclosures regarding   CC §1710.2

Delivery of disclosure statements   CC §§1102.3, 1102.12, 1103.3, 1103.10, 1103.12

Earthquake hazard   CC §§1103 to 1103.15

Consumer information handbooks   CC §§2079.8, 2079.9, 2079.11

Environmental hazards, complying with requirements to inform transferee of   CC §§2079.7, 2079.11

Errors or omissions, liability for   CC §§1102.4, 1102.5, 1103.4

Explosive munitions in neighborhood area, written notice of   CC §1102.15

Fire hazard disclosure   CC §§1103 to 1103.15

Flood hazard disclosure   CC §§1103 to 1103.15

Forms

General form of transfer disclosure statement   CC §1102.6

Local requirements, disclosure statement reflecting   CC §1102.6a

Natural hazards, disclosure concerning   CC §1103.2

Home energy ratings, information regarding   CC §2079.10

Industrial use zoning   CC §1102.17

Inspection of property, duty to disclose findings concerning   CC §2079

Legislative intent   CC §1102.1

Mello-Roos Community Facilities Act, disclosure regarding special tax liens on transfer of property pursuant to   CC §1102.6b

Mobilehome sales   CC §§1102 to 1102.18

Natural hazard disclosure statements   CC §§1103 to 1103.15

Other laws, effect   CC §1103.8

Registered sex offenders, notification concerning statewide database of locations of   CC §2079.10a

Taxation

Supplemental property tax bills   CC §1102.6c

Transfer fees, property subject to   CC §1102.6e

Water conservation   CC §2079.10

Plumbing retrofits, disclosures as to noncompliant plumbing fixtures   CC §1102.155

Window security bars and safety release mechanism   CC §1102.16

Dual agency   CC §§2079.21, 2079.22

Duties owed to prospective purchasers

Associate real estate licensee's duty equivalent to that owed by broker   CC §2079.13

Disclosure requirements (See within this heading, "**Disclosure requirements**")

Real estate agency relationship, disclosure regarding   CC §§2079.12 to 2079.25

Earthquake hazards (See within this heading, "**Disclosure requirements**")

Environmental hazards, complying with requirements to inform transferee of   CC §§2079.7, 2079.11

Executors employing brokers for sale of estate assets (See **ADMINISTRATION OF ESTATES**)

Explosive munitions in neighborhood area, disclosure of   CC §1102.15

Fire hazard, disclosure of   CC §§1103 to 1103.15

Flood hazard, disclosure of   CC §§1103 to 1103.15

Home energy ratings, disclosure of information regarding   CC §2079.10

Home improvement financing, unfair trade practice constituted by mortgage broker negotiating through contractor to arrange terms of   CC §1770

Industrial use zoning, disclosure of   CC §1102.17

Inspection of residential property

Generally   CC §2079

Buyer's duty of reasonable care, effect of   CC §2079.5

Disclosure of inspection, form of   CC §§1102.6, 1102.6a

BROKERS—Cont.

Inspection of residential property—Cont.

Inaccessible areas or unaffected units, liability for   CC §2079.3

Lease transactions, applicability of article to   CC §2079.1

New subdivisions, duty to inspect inapplicable to   CC §2079.6

Standard of care for   CC §2079.2

Statute of limitations for breach of duty   CC §2079.4

Late payment charges   CC §2954.4

Listing agents

Agency relationship, required disclosure regarding   CC §§2079.12 to 2079.25

Compensation   CC §2079.19

Multiple listing service   CC §§1086 to 1089.5

Loans arranged or made by brokers, exemption from usury laws for   CC §1916.1

Mello-Roos Community Facilities Act, disclosure regarding special tax liens on transfer of property pursuant to   CC §1102.6b

Membership camping contract brokers   CC §1812.314

Multiple listing services   CC §§1086 to 1089.5

New subdivisions, broker's duty to inspect residential property inapplicable to   CC §2079.6

Partition referees contracting with   CCP §873.110

Peer review societies, immunity of   CC §43.91

Privileged communications, professional societies protected under   CC §43.91

Professional societies, liability of   CC §43.91

Real Estate Transfer Disclosures

Statements, form   CC §§1102.6, 1102.6a

Taxation

Supplemental property tax bills   CC §1102.6c

Record retention for listings   CC §1088

Registered sex offenders, notification concerning statewide database of locations of   CC §2079.10a

Securities broker-dealer, contract formation by electronic submission of application to   CC §1633

Seller's agents

Acknowledgment of receipt of disclosure form   CC §2079.14

Buyer's agents, seller's agent acting as   CC §2079.22

Contents of required disclosure regarding agency relationship   CC §2079.16

Definitions   CC §2079.13

Delivery of required disclosure regarding agency relationship   CC §2079.14

Disclosure as to status as seller's agent or as dual agent   CC §2079.17

Sexual harassment, civil action for

Construction or application of provisions in issue, solicitor general notified   CC §51.1

Statute of limitation for breach of duty to inspect property   CC §2079.1

Transient occupancy in common interest developments, apartment buildings or single-family homes, recordkeeping required for accepting reservations or money for   CC §1864

Usury laws, exemption from   CC §1916.1

Water conservation disclosure requirements   CC §2079.10

Plumbing retrofits, disclosures as to noncompliant plumbing fixtures   CC §1102.155

Window security bars and safety release mechanism, disclosure of   CC §1102.16

Written contracts for employment of   CC §1624

BROTHERS AND SISTERS

Administrators, priority for serving as   Pro §8461

Adoption proceedings (See **ADOPTION**)

Inheritance by   Pro §§6402, 6402.5

Visitation rights of   Fam §3102

BUCKER

Lien   CC §§3065 to 3065c

BUDGETS, COURT

Judicial Administration Rules (See **JUDICIAL ADMINISTRATION RULES**)

BUDGETS, STATE

Consumer privacy rights

California privacy protection agency

Appropriations to fund agency   CC §1798.199.95

BUILDING AND LOAN ASSOCIATIONS (See **SAVINGS AND LOANS**)

BUILDING CODES

Inspection warrants to determine violations   CCP §1822.50

BUILDING CONSTRUCTION

Arbitration

Lien claim as affecting arbitration rights   CCP §1281.5

Index

BUILDING CONSTRUCTION—Cont.

Arbitration—Cont.

    Out-of-state arbitration, invalidity of contract provision requiring   CCP §410.42

    Public contracts   CC §1670, CCP §§1281.5, 1296

Bond required to secure costs in action against designers   CCP §1029.5

Burden of proving necessity for zoning ordinances limiting   Ev §669.5

Common interest developments (See **COMMON INTEREST DEVELOPMENTS**)

Construction defects, action for (See **CONSTRUCTION DEFECTS, ACTIONS FOR**)

Construction trucking services brokers

    Transportation charges, payment   CC §3322

Contractors (See **BUILDING CONTRACTORS**)

Covenants prohibiting prefabricated modular homes, validity of   CC §714.5

Damages for intentional destruction of property under construction   CC §1721

Defects in construction

    Actions for construction defects   CC §§895 to 945.5 (See **CONSTRUCTION DEFECTS, ACTIONS FOR**)

Good faith improver of property of another (See **GOOD FAITH IMPROVER**)

Indemnity agreements   CC §§2782 to 2784

    January 1, 2013, contracts on or after   CC §2782.05

    Subcontractor's defense or indemnity obligation   CC §2782.05

    Void or unenforceable provisions, insertion   CC §2782.05

Injunction, security for costs incurred as result of delay   CCP §§529.1, 529.2

Insurance

    Wrap-up insurance covering, indemnity agreements   CC §2782.9

        Private residential improvements   CC §2782.95

        Public works   CC §2782.96

Latent deficiencies in planning or construction, limitation of actions for damages for   CCP §337.15

Mechanics' liens (See **MECHANICS' LIENS**)

Notice of pendency of action to declare building uninhabitable   CCP §405.7

Out-of-state arbitration or litigation of disputes, invalidity of contract provision requiring   CCP §410.42

Patent deficiencies in planning or construction, limitation of actions for injury or death from   CCP §337.1

Prefabricated modular homes, validity of covenants prohibiting   CC §714.5

Public contracts and works (See **PUBLIC CONTRACTS AND WORKS**)

Residential building permits

    Quality reviewers

        Immunity from liability   CC §43.99

Residential construction, indemnity agreements   CC §2782

    Wrap-up insurance policies applicable   CC §2782.9

        Private residential improvement covered   CC §2782.95

Small business action, costs in   CCP §1028.5

Statutes of limitation

    Latent deficiencies in planning or construction, damages for   CCP §337.15

    Patent deficiencies in planning or construction, injury or death from   CCP §337.1

Stipulated judgments in construction defect actions   CCP §664.7

Subdivisions (See **SUBDIVISIONS**)

Substantial completion for purposes of running of limitations period   CCP §§337.1, 337.15

BUILDING CONTRACTORS

Arbitration

    Lien claim as affecting arbitration rights   CCP §1281.5

    Out-of-state arbitration, invalidity of contract provisions requiring   CCP §410.42

    Public contracts   CC §1670, CCP §§1281.5, 1296

Bonds

    Injunction, motion for security re   CCP §529.1

Common interest developments (See **COMMON INTEREST DEVELOPMENTS**)

Construction defects, actions for   CC §§895 to 945.5 (See **CONSTRUCTION DEFECTS, ACTIONS FOR**)

Excavation (See **EXCAVATIONS**)

Indemnity agreements   CC §§2782 to 2784

Mechanics' liens (See **MECHANICS' LIENS**)

Out-of-state arbitration or litigation of disputes, invalidity of contract provisions requiring   CCP §410.42

Public contracts and works (See **PUBLIC CONTRACTS AND WORKS**)

Release from liability, agreements for   CC §2782.5

Residential construction

    Indemnity agreements   CC §2782

Service and repair contracts

    Commencement of work

        Effect on contract   CC §1689.15

    Rescission   CC §1689.15

Support from adjacent land   CC §832

BUILDING INSPECTORS

Witnesses, subpoenaed as   Gov §§68097.1, 68907.2

BUILDING PERMITS

Burden of proving necessity for zoning ordinances limiting   Ev §669.5

Mechanics' liens

    Requirements   CC §8172

BUILDINGS

Generally   CC §660

Bins (See **BINS**)

Condominiums (See **COMMON INTEREST DEVELOPMENTS**)

Elevators (See **ELEVATORS**)

Life tenant's duty to repair   CC §840

Prefabricated modular homes, validity of covenants prohibiting   CC §714.5

Public buildings (See **PUBLIC BUILDINGS**)

Solar energy systems (See **SOLAR ENERGY**)

Walls (See **WALLS**)

Windows (See **WINDOWS**)

BUILDING STANDARDS

Accessibility standards

    Construction-related accessibility claims   CC §§55.3 to 55.57 (See **CONSTRUCTION-RELATED ACCESSIBILITY CLAIMS**)

Inspections

    Exterior elevated elements

        Landlord entry of building to comply with provisions   CC §1954

Regulations (See **ADMINISTRATIVE PROCEDURE ACT**)

BULK SALES

Storage of grain after sale in bulk   CC §§1880 to 1881.2

Voidable transactions (See **VOIDABLE TRANSACTIONS**)

Wage claims, preference for   CCP §1205

BUNGALOW COURT

Limitation of actions for recovery or conversion of personal property left at   CCP §341a

BURDEN OF GOING FORWARD

Generally   Ev §§550, 630

Definition   Ev §110

Mechanics' liens

    Release of property from claim of lien

        Hearing   CC §8488

Official records, presumptions of existence of   Ev §1530

Presumptions affecting   Ev §§603, 604, 630

BURDEN OF PRODUCING EVIDENCE (See **BURDEN OF GOING FORWARD**)

BURDEN OF PROOF

Generally   Ev §§500, 520 to 522

Age of accused person   CRC 4.116

Attachments   CCP §482.100

Beyond reasonable doubt (See **BEYOND REASONABLE DOUBT**)

Boundary dispute involving state   Ev §523

Clear and convincing evidence (See **CLEAR AND CONVINCING EVIDENCE**)

Confidential communication, claim for   Ev §917

Contract consideration   CC §1615

Criminal proceedings   Ev §501

Definition   Ev §115

Degree of proof required in proceedings   Ev §115

Enforcement of judgment, third party claim of ownership or security interest in property subject to   CCP §720.360

Equalization, state board

    Evasion or fraud cases, penalty sought   Ev §524

Foreign country judgments   CCP §1715

Good faith improver   CCP §871.3

Grants of land involving state, dispute over   Ev §523

Housing limits, proving necessity for zoning ordinances setting   Ev §669.5

Interstate family support

    Contest of validity or enforcement of registered order

        Defenses and burdens of proof applicable   Fam §5700.607

Jury instructions   Ev §502

Mechanic's liens

    Public works

        Summary proceeding for release of funds   CC §9410

    Release of property from claim of lien

        Hearing   CC §8488

Missing person, presumption of death of   Ev §667

C

CABLE TELEVISION COMPANIES
Cancellation of utility, cable, etc, services on behalf of deceased person
In-person cancellation not to be required   Pro §217
Service or repairs during specified time period where subscriber's presence required, liability for failure to provide   CC §1722

CABS (See **TAXIS**)

CADAVERS (See **DEAD BODIES**)

CALAMITIES (See **EMERGENCIES**)

CALENDAR
Appeals
Superior court appeals
Oral argument   CRC 8.885
Supreme court and courts of appeal cases (See **APPELLATE RULES, SUPREME COURT AND COURTS OF APPEAL**)
Coordination of actions, standards for   CCP §404.1
Court calendars (See **COURT CALENDARS**)
Judicial holidays, effect of   CCP §136
Preference in setting for trial or hearing (See **PRIORITIES AND PREFERENCES**)
Pretrial arbitration, trial de novo after   CCP §1141.20
Superior courts (See **SUPERIOR COURTS**)

CALIFORNIA COASTAL ACT
Attorney general, civil actions to enforce provisions
Fees and costs for attorney general   CCP §1021.8

CALIFORNIA CONSERVATORSHIP JURISDICTION ACT
Interstate jurisdiction, transfer and recognition   Pro §§1980 to 2033 (See **CONSERVATORS**)

CALIFORNIA CONSUMER PRIVACY ACT OF 2018   CC §§1798.100 to 1798.199.100

CALIFORNIA FAMILY SUPPORT COUNCIL
Child support, reporting of delinquencies for   Fam §§4700, 4701

CALIFORNIA FORECLOSURE PREVENTION ACT   CC §2924

CALIFORNIA HEALTH BENEFIT EXCHANGE
Adoption
Health insurance
Notice of reduced-cost options through California health benefit exchange or no-cost Medi-Cal   Fam §8613.7
Annulment of marriage
Health insurance
Notice of reduced-cost options through California health benefit exchange or no-cost Medi-Cal   Fam §2024.7
Divorce
Health insurance
Notice of reduced-cost options through California health benefit exchange or no-cost Medi-Cal   Fam §2024.7
Legal separation
Health insurance
Notice of reduced-cost options through California health benefit exchange or no-cost Medi-Cal   Fam §2024.7

CALIFORNIA-MADE
Made in California program
Unfair competition or deceptive trade practices   CC §1770

CALIFORNIA NATIONAL GUARD
Immunity of public entity for injury arising from action of   Gov §816

CALIFORNIA PARENT LOCATOR SERVICE
Earnings assignment for support, whereabouts of obligor unknown   Fam §5280

CALIFORNIA PRIVACY PROTECTION AGENCY   CC §§1798.199.10 to 1798.199.100 (See **CONSUMER PRIVACY RIGHTS**)

CALIFORNIA RESEARCH BUREAU
Frivolous actions
Motions for sanctions, etc
Copy of motion to bureau   CCP §128.5
Unlawful detainer actions
Reports to bureau
Controlled substances as nuisance   CC §§3486, 3486.5

CALIFORNIA RESEARCH BUREAU—Cont.
Unlawful detainer actions—Cont.
Reports to bureau —Cont.
Firearms or weapons as nuisance   CC §3485

CALIFORNIA RULES OF COURT
Rules applicable to all courts   CRC 1.1 to 1.201 (See **RULES OF COURT**)

CALIFORNIA STATE UNIVERSITY
Claims against public entities and employees
Payments by trustees   Gov §935.9
Presentation of claims
Applicable provisions   Gov §905.9
Trustees' actions on claims   Gov §912.5
Construction-related accessibility claims
Attorney prelitigation letter to education entities   CC §54.27
Social security numbers
Public posting or display
Implementation of provisions   CC §1798.85
Unclaimed property
Disposition   CC §2080.8
Claim not required for controller to transfer property to state or local agencies   CCP §1540

CALIFORNIA STATUTORY WILL (See **WILLS**)

CALLING CARDS
Gift certificate provisions inapplicable   CC §1749.45

CALWORKS
Child support
Local child support agencies
Assigned support payments made for CalWORKs recipients, notice   Fam §17504.1
Duties for CalWORKs cases   Fam §3680.5

CAMPAIGN BUTTONS
Sale of   CC §1739.1

CAMPERS
Mobilehomes (See **MOBILEHOMES**)
Recreational vehicles (See **RECREATIONAL VEHICLES**)

CAMPING
Liability of owner for recreational land   CC §846
Membership camping contracts   CC §§1812.300 to 1812.309
Waiver of protections   CC §1812.316
Special occupancy parks
Danger imminent, requiring guests to move   CC §1867
Eviction of overstaying guests   CC §1866
Minors
Conditions for minors staying   CC §1866

CANADA
Domestic violence protective orders, recognition and enforcement   Fam §§6450 to 6460

CANALS
Public liability for injury caused by condition of   Gov §831.8

CANCELLATION OF ASSESSMENT
Public improvement assessment, action to determine adverse interests in real property arising out of   CCP §801.15

CANCELLATION OF INSTRUMENTS
Action for   CC §§3412 to 3415
Credit cards   CC §1747.85
Dance studio contracts   CC §1812.54
Discount buying services contracts   CC §1812.118
Electronic transaction, notice of right to cancel   CC §1633.16
Health studio contracts   CC §§1812.85, 1812.89
Home equity sales contracts (See **HOME EQUITY SALES CONTRACTS**)
Home solicitation sales contracts (See **HOME SOLICITATION SALES CONTRACTS**)
Intent to cancel contract   CC §1699
Membership camping contracts   CC §§1812.303, 1812.304, 1812.314
Mortgage foreclosure consultants contract   CC §§2945.2, 2945.3
Parties bound by   CC §1700
Private child support collectors   Fam §5613
Notice of cancellation form   Fam §5611
Seller assisted marketing plans   CC §§1812.208, 1812.209, 1812.215
Seminar sales solicitation contracts (See **SEMINAR SALES SOLICITATION CONTRACTS**)

CANDIDATES FOR OFFICE
Advertising, superimposition of photographs
    Precedence of proceedings involving elections   CCP §35
Damages for misleading advertising
    Candidate's cause of action based on false depiction of representations of
        official public documents   CC §3344.6
    Unauthorized signatures in campaign advertisements, action for damages for
        CC §3344.5
Precedence to cases involving elections proceedings (See **ELECTIONS AND
ELECTIONS PROCEEDINGS**)
Radio or television broadcast libelous to character of candidate   CC §48.5
Shortening of time to respond to complaint in action for libel alleged to have
    occurred during election campaign   CCP §460.7
Unauthorized signatures in campaign advertisements, action for damages for   CC
    §3344.5

CANONS OF JUDICIAL ETHICS (See **JUDGES**)

CAPACITY
Contracts (See **CONTRACTS AND AGREEMENTS**)
Due Process in Competence Determinations Act   Pro §§810, 813, 1801, 1881,
    3201, 3204, 3208, 3208.5
Emancipated minors   Fam §7050
Judicial determinations, generally   Pro §§810 to 813
Marriage (See **MARRIAGE**)
Medical decisions (See **MEDICAL TREATMENT**)
Standing to sue (See **CAPACITY TO SUE**)
Wills, capacity to make   Pro §§810 to 812, 6100, 6100.5

CAPACITY TO SUE
Contract made for benefit of another   CCP §369
Decedent's estate, personal representative to (See **EXECUTORS AND ADMIN-
ISTRATORS**)
De facto parents   CRC 5.534
Emancipated minors   Fam §7050
Executors and administrators (See **EXECUTORS AND ADMINISTRATORS**)
Limited conservatees   Pro §1872
Married persons   CCP §370
Objection to complaint or cross-complaint, lack of capacity as grounds for   CCP
    §430.10
Parents maintaining action for injury of child   CCP §376
Partners and partnerships   CCP §369.5
Third party beneficiary contracts   CCP §369
Unincorporated associations   CCP §369.5

CAPITAL PUNISHMENT
Appeals   CRC 8.601 to 8.652
    Automatic appeals
        Supreme court, automatic appeal to   CRC 8.603
    Briefs   CRC 8.630, 8.631
    Decision, filing, finality and modification
        Applicability   CRC 8.642
    Exhibits
        Transmission of exhibits in death penalty appeals   CRC 8.634
    Extension of time limit
        Electronic filing, when required   CRCSupp 1st AppDist
    Judgment
        Copies, distribution   CRC 8.603
    Oral argument   CRC 8.638
    Record on appeal   CRC 8.608 to 8.622
        Accuracy of trial record on appeal, certification   CRC 8.622
        Augmenting record in supreme court   CRC 8.634
        Completeness of record on appeal, certification   CRC 8.619
        Confidential records   CRC 8.610
        Contents   CRC 8.610
        Extensions of time   CRC 8.608
        Juror-identifying information   CRC 8.610, 8.611
        Preliminary proceedings, preparing and certifying record   CRC 8.613
        Sealed record   CRC 8.610
        Supervision of preparation of record   CRC 8.608
        Transcripts, delivery date   CRC 8.608
        Trial record   CRC 8.616 to 8.622
    Rehearings
        Applicable provisions   CRC 8.642
    Remittitur   CRC 8.642
    Submission of cause   CRC 8.638
    Supreme court, practices and policies   CRCSupp SuprCtPract
    Transcripts
        Notice to prepare   CRC 8.613
Appearance
    Lists of appearances, exhibits and motions   CRCAppx A
        Pretrial proceedings   CRC 4.119

CAPITAL PUNISHMENT—Cont.
Appearance—Cont.
    Lists of appearances, exhibits and motions —Cont.
        Trial, additional requirements   CRC 4.230
Attorneys for capital cases   CRC 4.561, 4.562
    Appeals, appointments   CRC 8.605
    Appeals, qualifications   CRC 8.605
    Appointed counsel
        Appellate counsel appointments   CRC 8.605
        Appellate counsel qualifications   CRC 8.605
        Declaration of counsel for appointment, form   CRCAppx A
        Habeas counsel appointments   CRC 8.605
        Habeas counsel qualifications   CRC 8.652
        Trial counsel qualifications   CRC 4.117
    Compensation   CRCSupp SupCtPolicy
    Habeas corpus proceedings (See **HABEAS CORPUS**)
    Habeas counsel, appointments   CRC 8.605
    Habeas counsel, qualifications   CRC 8.652
    Record on appeal
        Preliminary proceedings   CRC 8.613
    Supreme court
        Habeas corpus petitions, compensation of attorneys   CRCSupp
            FixedFeeAppoint
        Withdrawal of counsel   CRCSupp FixedFeeAppoint
    Withdrawal from representation   CRCSupp SupCtPolicy
Checklist   CRCAppx A
    Pretrial proceedings   CRC 4.119
    Trial, additional requirements   CRC 4.230
Electronic recordings presented or offered into evidence
    Pretrial proceedings   CRC 4.119
    Trial, additional requirements   CRC 4.230
Evidence
    Electronic recordings presented or offered into evidence
        Pretrial proceedings   CRC 4.119
        Trial, additional requirements   CRC 4.230
Execution
    Date for   CRC 4.315
Exhibits
    Lists of appearances, exhibits and motions   CRCAppx A
        Pretrial proceedings   CRC 4.119
        Trial, additional requirements   CRC 4.230
Fixed fee guidelines for appointed counsel in automatic appeals   CRCSupp
    FixedFeeAppoint
Habeas corpus
    Appointment of counsel   CRC 8.605
    Compensation of attorney   CRCSupp SupCtPolicy
    Death penalty-related proceedings in superior court   CRC 4.560 to 4.577
        Appeals from superior court decisions in habeas cases involving death
            penalty   CRC 8.390 to 8.398
    Duty to investigate, attorney's   CRCSupp SupCtPolicy
    Fixed fee guidelines for appointed counsel in automatic appeals and related
        habeas corpus proceedings   CRCSupp FixedFeeAppoint
    Forms, judicial council   CRCAppx A
    Qualifications of counsel   CRC 8.652
    Supreme court policies   CRCSupp SupCtPolicy
    Time for filing   CRCSupp SupCtPolicy
Indigents, Supreme Court guidelines for compensating counsel appointed for
    CRCSupp PayGuideAppoint
Judges
    Education of judicial branch
        Additional education recommendations for certain judicial assignments
            CRC 10.469
Jury instructions
    Lists of appearances, exhibits, motions and jury instructions   CRCAppx A
        Trial, additional requirements   CRC 4.230
Jury selection in death penalty cases (See **JURY**)
Justices
    Education of judicial branch
        Additional education recommendations for certain judicial assignments
            CRC 10.469
Motions
    Lists of appearances, exhibits and motions   CRCAppx A
        Pretrial proceedings   CRC 4.119
        Trial, additional requirements   CRC 4.230
Policies of Supreme Court   CRCSupp SupCtPolicy
Pretrial proceedings   CRC 4.119
Procedure in capital cases
    Pretrial proceedings   CRC 4.119
    Trial
        Additional requirements in capital cases   CRC 4.230

CHARACTER AND REPUTATION—Cont.

Credibility, attack on
Generally   Ev §§780, 785, 786, 790
Felony convictions   Ev §788
Previous consistent statements   Ev §791
Religious beliefs   Ev §789
Sexual assault victim, procedures regarding   Ev §§782, 783
Specific instances of conduct   Ev §787
Criminal cases
Generally   Ev §1102
Conduct of victim   Ev §§782, 1103
Conviction of crime   Ev §788
Sexual assault (See within this heading, **"Sexually oriented offenses"**)
Family history, reputation among other family members concerning   Ev §1313
History of community as evidence   Ev §1320
Information Practices Act, protection under   CC §1798.38
Judges
Testimony by   CRCSupp JudEthicsCanon 2
Professional persons, investigation of   CC §§43.7, 43.8
Sexually oriented offenses
Administrative adjudication proceedings alleging sexual harassment, assault or battery   Gov §11440.40
Commission of other sexual offense, admissibility of evidence of   Ev §1108
Conduct of victim, admissibility of evidence regarding   Ev §§1103, 1106
Credibility of victim, procedures for attacking   Ev §§782, 783
Time of particular character trait, proof of   Ev §1324

CHARGE CARDS (See CREDIT CARDS)

CHARGE TO JURY (See JURY)

CHARITABLE ORGANIZATIONS

Exemption for purposes of enforcement of judgments of aid from   CCP §704.170
Eyeglasses
Immunity from liability
Nonprofit charitable organization and volunteer eye care professionals donating screening, eyeglasses, etc   CC §1714.26
Fine prints sale, charities exempt from disclosure requirements for   CC §1742.6
Judges
Office of judge in organization not a financial interest for purposes of disqualification   CCP §170.5
Participation in charitable activities   CRCSupp JudEthicsCanon 4
Nonprofit corporations (See **NONPROFIT CORPORATIONS AND ASSOCIATIONS**)
Trusts for charitable purposes (See **TRUSTS**)
Uniform prudent management of institutional funds act   Pro §§18501 to 18510 (See **INSTITUTIONAL FUNDS MANAGEMENT**)
Vision screenings, eyeglasses, etc
Immunity from liability
Nonprofit charitable organization and volunteer eye care professionals donating screening, eyeglasses, etc   CC §1714.26

CHARITABLE TRUSTS (See TRUSTS)

CHARTERED CITIES

Assessment against real property for public improvements, time limit for contesting validity of   CCP §329.5

CHARTERED COUNTIES (See COUNTIES)

CHARTERS

Vessels held under   CC §1959

CHASTITY

Slander by imputing absence of   CC §46

CHATTEL MORTGAGES (See also CONDITIONAL SALES; SECURED TRANSACTIONS)

Administrators executing   Pro §9805
Apartment housekeeper's lien subordinate to rights under   CC §1861a
Attachment (See **ATTACHMENT**)
Automobiles (See **AUTOMOBILES**)
Decedents' estates, securing credit sale of personalty of   Pro §§10257, 10258
Enforcement of judgments (See **ENFORCEMENT OF JUDGMENTS**)
Executors executing   Pro §9805
Foreclosure, stay of proceedings   CCP §917.2

CHECK CASHERS

Amount cashed for person during year requiring report to IRS   CC §1789.30
Deferred deposit of personal check, agreement for   CC §1789.35
Defined   CC §1789.31

CHECK CASHERS—Cont.

Fines for operating without permit   CC §1789.37
Government checks, limitations on fees charged for cashing   CC §1789.35
Identification   CC §1789.35
Payroll checks, limitations on fees charged for cashing   CC §1789.35
Penalties for operating without permit   CC §1789.37
Permit, application procedures for   CC §1789.37
Personal checks, terms for cashing   CC §1789.35
Posting of fee schedules   CC §§1789.30, 1789.32
Registration of check cashers with Department of Justice   CC §1789.37
Remedies and damages against check cashers   CC §1789.35
Unfair business practices related to posting of information   CC §1789.32
Waiver of protections   CC §1789.38

CHECKS

Accord and satisfaction, effect of check payments of disputed amounts for purposes of   CC §1526
Attachment of   CCP §486.060
Bad checks
Filing fees, consequences of paying with bad check   CCP §411.20
Liability for making   CC §1719
Check cashers (See **CHECK CASHERS**)
Court clerks, checks for making payments to   CCP §411.20, CRC 8.100, 10.821
Underpayment   CCP §411.21
Credit card issuer extending credit to cardholder by means of preprinted check or draft, required disclosures by   CC §1748.9
Credit card number as identification for negotiable instruments, use of   CC §1725
Debit cards, cardholder's liability for unauthorized use
Waiver of protections
Void   CC §1748.32
Demand for payment following dishonor   CC §1719
Dissemination of information regarding consumer checking accounts, liability for   CC §1785.5
Forged or raised check, limitation of action for payment of   CCP §340
Good faith dispute requirement for stop payments   CC §1719
"Insufficient funds" defined   CC §1719
Presumption of evidence for check payments in dispute   Ev §670
Protective order's effect on amount of   CCP §486.060
Stop payments, notice requirements and damages for   CC §1719
Traveler's checks (See **TRAVELER'S CHECKS**)
Treble damages for making bad checks   CC §1719

CHICKENS (See POULTRY)

CHIEF JUSTICE

Appellate duties and powers of (See **APPELLATE RULES, SUPREME COURT AND COURTS OF APPEAL**)
Education of judicial branch
Additional education recommendations for certain judicial assignments   CRC 10.469
Duties of chief judge   CRC 10.452

CHIEF OF POLICE (See LAW ENFORCEMENT OFFICERS)

CHILD ABDUCTION (See CUSTODY OF CHILDREN)

CHILD ABUSE

Character of defendant, admission of other-acts evidence to establish
Previous child abuse   Ev §1109
Custody and visitation, effect of child abuse conviction on   Fam §3030
Domestic Violence Protection Act, protection against child abuse and abduction under (See **DOMESTIC VIOLENCE**)
Government tort liability
Childhood sexual abuse damage claims   Gov §831.8
Hearsay rule, exceptions to   Ev §§1228, 1253, 1293, 1360
Libel and slander action by person accused of   CC §48.7
Mediators, continuing education of   Fam §1816
Medical diagnosis or treatment, admissibility of statements made for purposes of   Ev §1253
Parental control, grounds in actions to declare child free from   Fam §§7820 to 7827
Privileged communications between sexual assault victim and counselor
Name change proceedings under address confidentiality program   CRC 2.575 to 2.577
Reliability of minor's statement, determination of   Ev §1360
Reports
Human trafficking victim-caseworker privilege
Duty to report not diminished by provisions   Ev §1038.3
Resource guidelines for court practice   CRC JudAdminStand 5.45

Index

CITY ATTORNEYS—Cont.

Dog bites, actions pertaining to   CC §3342.5

Electronic court records, remote access

    Government entities, access by

        List of government entities which may be authorized to receive access   CRC 2.540

Unruh Civil Rights Act, bringing action under   CC §52

CITY CLERK

Acknowledgment of instruments   CC §1181

CIVIC ORGANIZATIONS

Judge's office in organization not a financial interest for purposes of disqualification   CCP §170.5

CIVIL ACTION MEDIATION (See MEDIATION)

CIVIL ACTIONS

Actions generally (See **ACTIONS**)

Commencement of actions (See **COMMENCEMENT OF ACTIONS**)

Coordination of actions (See **COORDINATION OF ACTIONS**)

Economic litigation procedures (See **ECONOMIC LITIGATION PROCE-DURES**)

Generally (See **ACTIONS**)

Law and motion proceedings   CRC 3.1100 to 3.1372 (See **LAW AND MOTION PROCEEDINGS**)

Limitation of actions (See **STATUTES OF LIMITATION**)

Limited civil cases (See **LIMITED CIVIL CASES**)

Parties (See **PARTIES**)

Pleadings (See **PLEADINGS**)

Time for commencing actions (See **STATUTES OF LIMITATION**)

Vexatious litigants (See **VEXATIOUS LITIGANTS**)

CIVIL ACTIVE LIST

Superior courts (See **SUPERIOR COURTS**)

CIVIL COMMITMENT

Appeals

    Notice of appeal

        Form, judicial council   CRCAppx A

    Order of civil commitment, appeal from   CRC 8.483

CIVIL DISCOVERY ACT   CCP §§2016.010 to 2036.050

CIVIL HARASSMENT (See HARASSMENT)

CIVIL PROCEDURE

Citation of code   CCP §19

Construing Code of Civil Procedure (See **CONSTRUCTION AND INTERPRE-TATION**)

Effective date of Code of Civil Procedure   CCP §2

Judicial officers   CCP §§165 to 187

Jurors and court commissioners   CCP §§190 to 259

Ministerial officers and powers   CCP §§262 to 286

Organization and jurisdiction of courts   CCP §§33 to 153

Preliminary provisions   CCP §§2 to 32

Title and division of Code of Civil Procedure   CCP §1

CIVIL RIGHTS (See DISCRIMINATION)

CIVIL RULES   CRC 3.1 to 3.2237

Alternative dispute resolution   CRC 3.800 to 3.878, 3.890 to 3.898

    Definitions   CRC 3.800

    Information package

        Papers to be filed   CRC 3.221

    Judicial arbitration   CRC 3.810 to 3.830

    Mediation

        Applicability of provisions   CRC 3.835

        Civil action mediation   CRC 3.890 to 3.898

        Complaints about court-program mediators   CRC 3.865 to 3.872

        Reports or statements of mediator   CRC 3.845

        Standards of conduct for mediators   CRC 3.850 to 3.860

Appearances

    Telephone appearances   CRC 3.670

Applicability of rules   CRC 3.10

Arbitration

    Case management conference

        Determination as to arbitration   CRC 3.722

        Telephone appearance at case management conferences   CRC 3.670

    Judicial arbitration   CRC 3.810 to 3.830

Assignment of judges

    Case management   CRC 3.734

CIVIL RULES—Cont.

Attorneys' fees   CRC 3.1702

Attorneys, limited scope representation   CRC 3.35 to 3.37

    Applicability of provisions   CRC 3.35

    Definition of limited scope representation   CRC 3.35

    Noticed representation

        Providing notice   CRC 3.36

        Relief as attorney, request   CRC 3.36

        Types of limited scope representation   CRC 3.35

    Undisclosed representation

        Attorneys' fees sought   CRC 3.37

        Drafting or other preparation of court documents   CRC 3.37

        Types of limited scope representation   CRC 3.35

Bifurcated trials

    Statement of decision, judgment and motion for new trial following   CRC 3.1591

Case management   CRC 3.700 to 3.771

    Additional case management conferences   CRC 3.723

    Alternative dispute resolution

        Initial conference, determination as to ADR   CRC 3.722

        Stipulation   CRC 3.726

        Telephone appearance at case management conferences   CRC 3.670

    Applicability of case management rules   CRC 3.720

    Assignment of judges   CRC 3.734

    Class actions   CRC 3.760 to 3.771

    Collections cases   CRC 3.740, 3.741

        Civil case cover sheet to be checked   CRC 3.740

        Default judgment, time for   CRC 3.740

        Definitions   CRC 3.740

        Failure to serve in timely manner   CRC 3.740

        Settlement   CRC 3.741

        Time for service of complaint   CRC 3.740

    Complex cases   CRC 3.750, 3.751

        Judicial administration standards   CRC JudAdminStand 3.10

    Conferences   CRC 3.722

        Additional case management conferences   CRC 3.723

        Applicability of case management rules when conference set   CRC 3.720

        Class actions   CRC 3.762

        Complex cases   CRC 3.750

        Judicial arbitration   CRC 3.812

        Subjects considered at conferences   CRC 3.727

        Telephone appearance at case management conferences   CRC 3.670

    Differential case management   CRC 3.710 to 3.715

    Environmental quality act

        Petitions under environmental quality act, civil rules governing   CRC 3.2220

    Forms

        Judicial council legal forms   CRCAppx A

    Initial conference   CRC 3.722

        Complex cases   CRC 3.750

        Telephone appearance at case management conferences   CRC 3.670

    Joint case management statement   CRC 3.725

    Judge assignment   CRC 3.734

    Meet and confer

        Complex cases   CRC 3.750

        Duty to meet and confer   CRC 3.724

        Judicial council legal forms   CRCAppx A

    Orders

        Appearance at conference not required for order   CRC 3.722

        Contents of case management order   CRC 3.728

        Controlling effect of order   CRC 3.730

    Review of case

        Time for review   CRC 3.721

    Scope and purpose of case management rules   CRC 3.700

    Short cause cases   CRC 3.735

    Statement   CRC 3.725

    Suspension of case management rules for certain cases   CRC 3.720

    Trial date

        Setting   CRC 3.729

Class actions

    Case management   CRC 3.760 to 3.771

        Certifying or decertifying class, motions   CRC 3.764

        Class notices   CRC 3.766

        Complaint form   CRC 3.761

        Conducting class action, orders   CRC 3.767

        Conferences   CRC 3.762

        Discovery   CRC 3.768

        Dismissal of action   CRC 3.770

        Governing rules   CRC 3.760

        Judgments   CRC 3.771

Index

Index

Index

CLAIMS AGAINST PUBLIC ENTITIES AND EMPLOYEES—Cont.

Prompt payment provisions
Late payments generally (See within this heading, **"Late payment by state agencies"**)

Proximate cause of injury, liability of public entity where employee is   Gov §815.2

Public entities, presentation of claims for inverse condemnation against   Gov §905.1

Public health or disease prevention acts, injury resulting from decision about   Gov §855.4

Public property
Generally   Gov §835
Attorney's fees in recreational user's action against public entity, administrative claim for recovery of   CC §846.1
Authorized entry on property, liability for   Gov §821.8
Beaches deemed in natural unimproved condition   Gov §831.21
Court's determination that condition not dangerous   Gov §830.2
Definition of dangerous condition   Gov §835.2
Definitions involving dangerous condition of   Gov §830
Emotional distress resulting from land failure of unimproved public property   Gov §831.25
Hazardous recreational activity, liability for injury to participant or spectator in   Gov §831.7
Impending peril, liability for activities to abate an   Gov §§865 to 867
Legislative declarations and public access programs, liability for   Gov §831.5
Natural condition of unimproved public property, liability for   Gov §§831.2, 831.21
Notice of dangerous condition, definition of   Gov §§835.2, 840.4
Plan, design, construction or improvement of public property, injury caused by   Gov §830.7
Public employees, liability of   Gov §§840 to 840.2
Reasonableness of act or omission causing dangerous condition, effect of   Gov §§835.4, 840.6
Res ipsa loquitur doctrine, applicability of   Gov §830.5
Safety improvements by special assessment districts not constituting   Gov §830.1
Schools (See within this heading, **"Schools"**)
Signs or roadway markings, failure to provide   Gov §830.4
Streets and highways (See within this heading, **"Streets and highways"**)
Traffic signals (See within this heading, **"Traffic signals"**)

Punitive damages   Gov §818
Indemnification of public employees   Gov §825

Real property
Public property generally (See within this heading, **"Public property"**)

Recreational property, liability for injuries on unpaved roads or trails providing access to   Gov §831.4

Refusal of public entity to defend action against employee   Gov §995.2

Reimbursement of state employee for costs of defense   Gov §955.3

Rejected claim, reexamination of   Gov §913.2

Reservoir, liability for injury caused by condition of   Gov §831.8

Res ipsa loquitur doctrine   Gov §830.5

Roads (See within this heading, **"Streets and highways"**)

Safety improvements by special assessment districts not constituting public property   Gov §830.1

Scene of accident, discretion of law enforcement officer to leave   Gov §820.25

Schools
Asbestos exposure, liability of school district for   Gov §905.5
Controlled substances violation, liability of schools for publication or reports or photographs of persons convicted of   Gov §818.7
Prohibition on submission of claims by school district   Gov §905.3
Publications of school, liability for   Gov §818.7
Unsold school lands, liability for injuries on   Gov §831.6

Secretary of State, actions involving   Gov §§960.3, 960.4

Service of summons
Order allowing service on Secretary of State   Gov §960.3
Registry of Public Agencies, service in conformity with statement in   Gov §960.8
Required filings concerning public agency, service in absence of   Gov §960.2
State, service in action against   Gov §955.4

Sexual battery, liability for   Gov §815.3

Signature on claim   Gov §910.2

Signs (See within this heading, **"Traffic signals"**)

Signs or roadway markings, failure to provide   Gov §830.4

Small claims court advisors, immunity for   CCP §116.940, Gov §818.9

Social workers and child protection workers, extent of civil immunity of   Gov §820.21

State, claims against
Presentation of claims   Gov §§905.2, 910.8, 911

State Controller (See within this heading, **"Controller"**)

CLAIMS AGAINST PUBLIC ENTITIES AND EMPLOYEES—Cont.

State defined   Gov §§900.6, 940.6

Statutes of limitation for actions against peace officer, criminal charges tolling   Gov §945.3

Statutory liability of public entities   Gov §815

Streets and highways
Grading or maintenance of road, liability for injury caused by   Gov §831.3
Traffic signals (See within this heading, **"Traffic signals"**)
Unpaved roads or trails providing access to unimproved property, liability for   Gov §831.4
Weather conditions, liability for effect of   Gov §831

Submerged lands, liability for injuries on portions of   Gov §831.6

Suits (See within this heading, **"Actions"**)

Summons, service
Judicial branch entities, service on   Gov §955.9

Survivors of law enforcement officer slain in line of duty as immune from liability for officer's actions in line of duty   Gov §823

Tax law administration, liability for   Gov §§860 to 860.4

Theft of money from employee's official custody, liability for   Gov §822

Third persons, liability of employee for acts or omissions of   Gov §820.8

Tidelands, liability for injuries on portions of   Gov §831.6

Time limits on presentation of claim   Gov §911.2

Tort liability under agreements between public entities   Gov §§895 to 895.8

Traffic signals
Generally   Gov §830.4
Dangerous conditions, failure to provide traffic or warning signals of   Gov §830.8
Emergency vehicle, liability for operation of traffic signals controlled by   Gov §830.9

Transportation Department
Controller's duty to draw warrant for claims against   Gov §965.2
Payment of claims by department   Gov §935.7

Trial court employees, claims affecting   Gov §811.9

United States Treasurer, issuance of warrant payable to   Gov §926.8

Unpaved roads or trails providing access to unimproved property, liability for   Gov §831.4

Untimely filed claim, notice of   Gov §911.3

Venue
City, county or agency's action against State, venue in   Gov §955.3
Death or injury to person or property within State, venue in action for   Gov §955.2
Relief from bar to suit for failure to present timely claim, venue in action for   Gov §946.6
State, venue in action for claims against   Gov §§955, 955.2, 955.3

Vicarious liability of local public officials   Gov §820.9

Victim compensation and government claims board
Claims for consideration by board   Gov §905.3

Volcanic prediction, immunity from liability for   Gov §955.1

Waiver of defense as to sufficiency of claim   Gov §911

Water Resources, actions arising out of work of Department of   Gov §956

Weather conditions, liability for effect on streets and highways of   Gov §831

Witness, conditions under which public entity may indemnify or defend   Gov §995.9

Workers' compensation provisions, no implied repeal of   Gov §814.2

CLASS ACTIONS

Authorizing provision   CCP §382

Case management   CRC 3.760 to 3.771
Certification or decertification of class
Motion   CRC 3.764
Order   CRC 3.765
Complaint form   CRC 3.761
Conducting class action, orders   CRC 3.767
Conferences   CRC 3.762
Order upon conclusion of conference   CRC 3.763
Telephone appearance at case management conferences   CRC 3.670
Discovery from unnamed class members   CRC 3.768
Dismissal of action   CRC 3.770
Governing rules   CRC 3.760
Judgments   CRC 3.771
Judicial council legal forms   CRCAppx A
Notices
Class members, notice to   CRC 3.766
Settlement of class actions   CRC 3.769

Certification or decertification of class
Motion   CRC 3.764
Order   CRC 3.765

Complex litigation defined   CRC 3.400

Conducting class action
Orders   CRC 3.767

Index

Index

COMMON CARRIERS—Cont.
Passengers—Cont.
　　Fare, payment of　CC §§2173, 2187 to 2191
　　Free carriage of baggage for　CC §§2180, 2181
　　Overcrowding prohibited　CC §§2102, 2184, 2185
　　Payment of fare by　CC §§2173, 2187 to 2191
　　Rules of conduct, obedience to　CC §2186
　　Seats required　CC §2185
Perishables, sale of　CC §2204
Preferential treatment　CC §§2170, 2171
Priority in transportation by　CC §§2170, 2171
Railroads (See **RAILROADS**)
Service rendered in carriage of freight　CC §2203
Shipping instructions, compliance with　CC §2115
Space flight liability and immunity　CC §§2210 to 2212
　　Definitions　CC §2210
　　Entity liability　CC §2212
　　Warning and acknowledgment statements　CC §2211
Speed of vehicle, requirements for　CC §2104
Standard of care required
　　Negligence generally (See within this heading, **"Negligence"**)
Storage or rental equipment charges from delay caused by consignor or consignee, liability for　CC §§2197, 2197.5
Street railways (See **STREET RAILWAYS**)
Telephones and telegraphs (See **TELEPHONES AND TELEGRAPHS**)
Time schedule requirements　CC §§2170, 2172
Treatment of passengers　CC §2103
Unclaimed property, sale of　CC §§2081 to 2081.4
Valuable goods, liability for loss of　CC §§2177, 2200
Vessels (See **VESSELS**)
Weight certification, carrier's lien for fines resulting from owner's false　CC §§2144, 3051.6

COMMON INTEREST DEVELOPMENTS　CC §§4000 to 6150
Accessory dwelling units
　　Construction or use on single-family residential lot
　　　　Restrictions prohibited　CC §4751
Access to separate interest
　　Barring access to separate interest　CC §4510
Accounts and accounting
　　Budgets (See within this heading, **"Budget of association"**)
　　Finances
　　　　Large transfers, board approval　CC §5502
　　　　Monthly review by board　CC §5500
　　　　Review by board　CC §§5500 to 5502
　　　　Satisfaction of review requirements　CC §5501
　　Financial documents
　　　　Availability of financial statement, notice　CC §5320
　　　　Budgets (See within this heading, **"Budget of association"**)
　　　　Review of financial statement　CC §5305
　　Managing agent, disposition of association funds by　CC §5380
Actions　CC §§5975 to 5986
　　Alternative dispute resolution　CC §§5925 to 5965
　　Comparative fault reducing damage recovery　CC §5985
　　Covenants and restrictions, enforcement　CC §5975
　　Declarants, developers or builders, legal proceedings against
　　　　Governing documents not to restrict　CC §5986
　　　　Limitations of actions not extended　CC §5986
　　Notice to owners　CC §6150
　　Standing of association　CC §5980
Agent for receipt of payments
　　Record notice of agent　CC §4210
Agents, managing　CC §§5375 to 5385
Agriculture
　　Personal agriculture by homeowner
　　　　Unreasonable restrictions in governing documents, void　CC §4750
Airport influence areas
　　Disclosure requirements
　　　　Special disclosures in declaration　CC §4255
Alternative dispute resolution　CC §§5925 to 5965
　　Assessment liens
　　　　Pre-lien dispute resolution　CC §5670
　　Definitions　CC §5925
　　Developer, action against　CC §6000
　　Dispute resolution for disputes between association and member generally　CC §§5900 to 5920
　　Enforcement action
　　　　Certificates required at commencement　CC §5950
　　　　Costs and fees, effect of refusal to engage in dispute resolution　CC §5960
　　　　Defined　CC §5925

COMMON INTEREST DEVELOPMENTS—Cont.
Alternative dispute resolution —Cont.
　　Enforcement action—Cont.
　　　　Filing preceded by attempt at dispute resolution　CC §5930
　　　　Reference to dispute resolution after filing　CC §5955
　　　Evidence code applicability　CC §5940
　　　Filing enforcement action preceded by attempt at dispute resolution　CC §5930
　　　Foreclosure　CC §5705
　　　Reference to dispute resolution after filing of enforcement action　CC §5955
　　　Request for resolution
　　　　Contents　CC §5935
　　　　Service　CC §5935
　　　Summary to members of provisions　CC §5965
　　　　Dispute resolution for disputes between association and member, content of summary　CC §5920
　　　Time to complete dispute resolution　CC §5940
　　　Tolling statute of limitations　CC §5945
Amendment of declaration
　　Authorized　CC §4260
　　Extension of term of declaration　CC §4265
　　Judicial authorization of amendment　CC §4275
　　Procedure for amendment　CC §4270
American flag display
　　Restrictions on limitations, prohibitions　CC §4705
Annual policy statement　CC §5310
　　Alternative dispute resolution
　　　　Summary to members of provisions　CC §§5920, 5965
　　Availability, notice　CC §5320
　　Collection of assessment
　　　　Statement of collection procedure included in policy statement　CC §5730
　　Defined　CC §4078
Annual reports　CC §§5300 to 5320
　　Annual policy statement　CC §5310
　　　　Availability, notice　CC §5320
　　Budget
　　　　Annual budget report　CC §5300
　　　　Availability, notice　CC §5320
　　Financial statement
　　　　Review　CC §5305
Applicability of provisions
　　Prospective application　CC §4010
Arbitration (See within this heading, **"Alternative dispute resolution"**)
Architectural review and decisionmaking
　　Improvements to separate interests
　　　　Standards when review required　CC §4765
Articles of incorporation, requirements for　CC §4280
　　Bylaws
　　　　Consistency with articles and declaration　CC §4205
　　Consistency with declaration　CC §4205
　　Governing documents defined to include declarations, bylaws, etc　CC §4150
　　Operating rules
　　　　Consistency with declaration, articles and bylaws　CC §4205
Artificial turf
　　Architectural guidelines not to prohibit　CC §4735
Assembly by and communication among owners, guests, residents, etc
　　Permitted activities　CC §4515
Assessments　CC §§5600 to 5740
　　Alternative dispute resolution for assessment disputes
　　　　Operating rules changes, types of rules to which provisions applicable　CC §4355
　　Approvals　CC §5605
　　　　Emergency exception to requirements　CC §5610
　　Assignment or pledge of right to collect　CC §5735
　　Collection process　CC §§5700 to 5740
　　　　Applicability of provisions　CC §5740
　　　　Assignment or pledge of right to collect　CC §5735
　　　　Common area damage, limitation on foreclosure for penalties or damages　CC §5725
　　　　Foreclosure, decisionmaking　CC §5705
　　　　Limitation on foreclosure　CC §5720
　　　　Manner of enforcing lien　CC §5700
　　　　Redemption after trustee sale　CC §5715
　　　　Sale under foreclosure　CC §5710
　　　　Statement of collection procedure　CC §5730
　　Debt of owner　CC §5650
　　Delinquent assessments
　　　　Costs recovery　CC §5650

Index

COMMON INTEREST DEVELOPMENTS—Cont.

Repair of premises—Cont.
    Termite work   CC §4780
        Temporary relocation for pest control work   CC §4785

Reports
    Annual reports   CC §§5300 to 5320

Reserve accounts, statement of
    Definition of reserve accounts   CC §4177
    Requirements
        Definition of reserve account requirements   CC §4178

Reserve funds   CC §§5510 to 5520
    Assessment and reserve funding disclosure   CC §5570
    Litigation
        Use for litigation   CC §5520
    Planning   CC §§5550 to 5580
        Assessment and reserve funding disclosure   CC §5570
        Community service organization report   CC §5580
        Contents of reserve funding plan   CC §5560
        Exterior elevated elements, visual inspection   CC §5551
        Inspection of premises and components   CC §5550
        Study of reserve needs   CC §5550
        Summary of association reserves   CC §5565
    Temporary transfer of reserve funds   CC §5515
    Use of reserve funds   CC §5510

Roofs
    Fire retardant roof coverings
        Restrictions on limitations, prohibitions   CC §4720

Rules
    Operating rules   CC §§4340 to 4370

Sale of interest
    Restrictions on owner's marketing of interest   CC §4730

San Francisco Bay conservation and development commission jurisdiction
    Disclosure requirements
        Special disclosures in declaration   CC §4255

Satellite dish restrictions
    Restrictions on limitations, prohibitions   CC §4725

Senior citizen housing developments, generally   CC §§51.2 to 51.4

Separate interests
    Access to separate interest   CC §4510
    Assessments
        Levy on separate interests within development, when permitted   CC §5625
    Defined   CC §4185
    Improvements to separate interests   CC §4760
        Architectural review and decisionmaking, standards when required   CC §4765
    Maintenance   CC §4775
    Modification   CC §§4760, 4765
    Operating rules, changes
        Types of rules to which provisions applicable   CC §4355
    Pest control
        Notice of pesticide application when not applied by licensed pest control operator   CC §4777
    Protected uses of separate interests   CC §§4700 to 4753
    Religious items displayed on dwelling entry
        Governing documents not to restrict   CC §4706
    Transfer disclosures   CC §4535
        Enforcement of disclosure requirements   CC §4540
    Transfers   CC §§4625 to 4650

Settlement agreement with builder, disclosure to association members concerning   CC §6100

Signs
    For sale signs on property
        Provisions outside of common interest development law limiting association's regulation of member's separate interest   CC §4700
    Noncommercial signs, posters, flags or banners
        Restrictions on limitations, prohibitions   CC §4710

Small claims courts
    Appearance
        Associations managing development   CCP §116.540

Solar energy systems installed in common areas, restrictions on   CC §714.1
    Approvals
        Determinations of applications   CC §714

Solar energy systems, restrictions on installation
    Common areas, exclusive use grants   CC §4600
    Protected uses of separate interests
        Solar energy systems on multifamily common area roofs   CC §4746
    Provisions outside of common interest development law limiting association's regulation of member's separate interest   CC §4700

COMMON INTEREST DEVELOPMENTS—Cont.

Statutes of limitation
    Alternative dispute resolution
        Tolling statute of limitations   CC §5945
    Declarants, developers or builders, legal proceedings against
        Limitations of actions not extended   CC §5986
    Notice requirements for actions against developer, effect of   CC §§6000, 6150

Stock cooperatives
    Common interest development defined to include stock cooperatives   CC §4100
    Defined   CC §4190
    Transfer of separate interest   CC §4640

Telephone wiring, access to
    Communications wiring access   CC §4790

Television antennas, restrictions on installation or use of
    Restrictions on limitations, prohibitions   CC §4725

Temporary relocation for pest control work
    Termite work   CC §4785

Termite damage, liability for   CC §4780
    Temporary removal of occupant   CC §4785

Tort action (See within this heading, **"Damages, action for"**)

Tort liability based on interest in common area   CC §5805

Transfer of interests
    Billing disclosures
        Form   CC §4528
        Information provided by association   CC §4530
    Disclosures   CC §§4525 to 4545 (See within this heading, **"Disclosure requirements"**)
    Exclusive use of common area, granting
        Action for declaratory or equitable relief to enforce procedure   CC §4605
        Restrictions on granting   CC §4600
    Fees
        Exemption from transfer fee limitations   CC §4580
        Permitted fees   CC §4575
    Lien for work performed in project
        Restrictions on transfer   CC §4615
    Partition of condominium   CC §4610
    Restricting marketing of owner's interest   CC §4730
    Restrictions on transfer   CC §§4600 to 4605
    Separate interests   CC §§4625 to 4650
        Community apartment projects   CC §4625
        Condominium projects   CC §4630
        Disclosures   CC §4535
        Enforcement of disclosure requirements   CC §4540
        Exclusive use common areas   CC §4645
        Planned developments   CC §4635
        Severability of interests   CC §4650
        Stock cooperatives   CC §4640
    Title to property transferred in violation of provisions   CC §4545

Transient occupancy in dwelling unit of common interest development, record-keeping requirements for person accepting reservations or money for   CC §1864

Trust deeds and mortgages
    Redemption
        Foreclosure by association for nonpayment of assessments   CCP §729.035

Trust fund account for association funds
    Managing agent's duties as to   CC §5380

United States flag
    Display
        Restrictions on limitations, prohibitions   CC §4705

Video or television antennas, restrictions on installation or use of
    Restrictions on limitations, prohibitions   CC §4725

Volunteer officer or director, limited liability of   CC §5800

Water use
    Artificial turf
        Restrictions on water efficiency measures prohibited   CC §4735
    Low water-using plants
        Restrictions on water efficiency measures prohibited   CC §4735

Zones and zoning ordinances
    Local zoning ordinances, interpretation of   CC §4020

COMMON LAW

Applicability of common-law rule construing code   CCP §4
Change of name   CCP §1279.5
Civil Code, effect on   CC §§4, 5
Rule against perpetuities, validity of   Pro §21201
Rule of decision in courts   CC §22.2
Trusts, applicability of common law to   Pro §15002

Index

Index

Index

Index

Index

Index

Index

CORPORATE SHARES AND SHAREHOLDERS—Cont.
Briefs, certificates in interested entities or persons   CRC 8.208, 8.361, 8.488
    Electronic filing, when required   CRCSupp 1st AppDist
Broker-dealer, contract formation by electronic submission of application to   CC §1633
Conservators (See **CONSERVATORS**)
Decedent's estate
    Administration of estates (See **ADMINISTRATION OF ESTATES**)
    Registration in beneficiary form   Pro §§5500 to 5512
    Stock bonus or employee savings plan, nonprobate transfer of   Pro §§6321 to 6330
    Trusts (See **TRUSTS**)
Dividends
    Escheat to state   CCP §1516
    Principal and income allocations   CC §731.07, Pro §16350
Electronic submission of application to securities broker-dealer, contract formation by   CC §1633
Emancipated minor holding stock   Fam §7052
Employee benefit plan including stock options   Fam §80
Employee savings plan or stock bonus, nonprobate transfer of   Pro §§6321 to 6330
Enforcement of judgments (See **ENFORCEMENT OF JUDGMENTS**)
Gifts to minors (See **UNIFORM TRANSFERS TO MINORS ACT**)
Jurisdiction over trustees and stockholders of corporation forfeiting charter   CCP §410.60
Marital status, denial of credit because of   CC §1812.32
Minors, transfers to (See **UNIFORM TRANSFERS TO MINORS ACT**)
Partition sales of securities   CCP §873.660
Power of attorney, statutory form   Pro §4453
Principal and income allocations   CC §731.07, Pro §16350
Proxies, estate representative exercising (See **EXECUTORS AND ADMINISTRATORS**)
Receivers depositing   CCP §568.1
Statute of limitation against shareholders to recover penalty or forfeiture or enforce liability   CCP §359
Stay of order to inspect books   CCP §917.8
Trusts (See **TRUSTS**)
Uniform TOD Security Registration Act   Pro §§5500 to 5512
Uniform Transfers to Minors Act (See **UNIFORM TRANSFERS TO MINORS ACT**)

CORPORATIONS
Acknowledgment of instruments   CC §§1185, 1190, 1190.1
Administrators (See **EXECUTORS AND ADMINISTRATORS**)
Admitted surety insurer (See **SURETYSHIP, BONDS AND UNDERTAKINGS**)
Agents (See **CORPORATE OFFICERS AND EMPLOYEES**)
Appellate rules, supreme court and courts of appeal
    Briefs
       Certificates in interested entities or persons   CRC 8.361, 8.488, CRCSupp 1st AppDist
Attachments, corporate assets subject to   CCP §487.010
Attorney professional conduct
    Organization or entity as client   ProfC 1.13
Attorneys
    Registered in-house counsel   CRC 9.46
       Fingerprinting of special admission attorneys   CRC 9.9.5
Bonds (See **BONDS**)
Common interest developments (See **COMMON INTEREST DEVELOPMENTS**)
Depositions, procedure for
    Economic litigation procedures   CCP §94
    Notice of deposition
       Description of matters on which examination requested   CCP §2025.230
Directors and officers
    Briefs, certificates of interested entities or persons   CRC 8.208, 8.361, 8.488
       Electronic filing, when required   CRCSupp 1st AppDist
    Judges, service as directors or officers   CRCSupp JudEthicsCanon 4
Dissolution (See **CORPORATE DISSOLUTION**)
Eminent domain, officers giving evidence on valuation for   Ev §813
Enforcement of judgments (See **ENFORCEMENT OF JUDGMENTS**)
Executors (See **EXECUTORS AND ADMINISTRATORS**)
Filing of instruments
    Identity theft in business entity filings   CC §§1798.200 to 1798.202
Foreign corporations (See **FOREIGN CORPORATIONS**)
Forfeiture of charter or right to do business
    Jurisdiction over trustees and stockholders   CCP §410.60
    Service of process on corporation   CCP §416.20
Health care providers, access to medical information maintained by corporation deemed as   CC §§56.06, 56.07

CORPORATIONS—Cont.
Identity theft in business entity filings   CC §§1798.200 to 1798.202
Inclusions in definition   CCP §17
In-house counsel
    Registered in-house counsel   CRC 9.46
       Fingerprinting of special admission attorneys   CRC 9.9.5
Injunctions suspending business of   CCP §531
Jurisdiction when charter is forfeited   CCP §410.60
Marital status, denial of credit because of   CC §1812.32
Medical information corporations, access to medical records maintained by   CC §§56.06, 56.07
Municipal corporations (See **CITIES AND MUNICIPALITIES**)
Nonprofit corporations (See **NONPROFIT CORPORATIONS AND ASSOCIATIONS**)
Person defined to include   CCP §17
Pleadings verification by   CCP §446
Process
    Default against corporation   CCP §412.30
    Designated agent receiving service of   CCP §416.10
    Forfeit of charter or right to do business   CCP §416.20
    Manner of service of business organizations
       Leaving summons and complaint at office, mailing copy   CCP §415.95
    Notice   CCP §412.30
    Officer receiving service of   CCP §416.10
    Trustee of corporation, service on   CCP §416.20
Public trail, enjoining closure of   CCP §731.5
Registered in-house counsel   CRC 9.46
    Fingerprinting of special admission attorneys   CRC 9.9.5
Seal, affixed   CC §1628
Service of process
    Process generally (See within this heading, **"Process"**)
Statutes of limitation
    Corporate bonds, notes or debentures, actions upon   CCP §336a
    Directors or shareholders, actions against   CCP §359
    Dissolved corporation, action to set aside any action taken by trustees of   CCP §341
Stock (See **CORPORATE SHARES AND SHAREHOLDERS**)
Surety capacity (See **SURETYSHIP, BONDS AND UNDERTAKINGS**)
Tax liens and other federal liens, filing of notice of   CCP §2101
Venue in actions against   CCP §395.5
Verifications of pleadings   CCP §446

CORPORATIONS SOLE
Attorney professional conduct
    Organization or entity as client   ProfC 1.13

CORPSES (See **DEAD BODIES**)

CORRECTIONS OF ERRORS
Appellate rules
    Superior court appeals (See **APPELLATE RULES, SUPERIOR COURT APPEALS**)
    Supreme court and courts of appeal (See **APPELLATE RULES, SUPREME COURT AND COURTS OF APPEAL**)
Information Practices Act (See **INFORMATION PRACTICES ACT**)
Libel by newspaper or radio, correction demand to avoid   CC §48a

CORRESPONDENCE (See **LETTERS**)

COSMETICS
Animal testing to develop or manufacture   CC §1834.9.5

COSMETOLOGY (See **BARBERING AND COSMETOLOGY**)

COSTA-HAWKINS RENTAL HOUSING ACT   CC §§1954.50 to 1954.53

COSTS (See also **COMPENSATION; FEES**)
Generally   CCP §§1032, 1033, 1033.5
Administration of decedents' estates
    Generally (See **ADMINISTRATION OF ESTATES**)
    Claims against decedents' estates (See **CLAIMS AGAINST ESTATES**)
Administrative law and procedure
    Adjudicative proceedings (See **ADMINISTRATIVE ADJUDICATION**)
    Economic impact of regulation, assessment of (See **ADMINISTRATIVE PROCEDURE ACT**)
Annulment of marriage   Fam §§270 to 274, 2010, 2030 to 2034, 2255
    Financial need basis   CRC 5.427
Appeals
    Certiorari, mandate and prohibition
       Award and recovery of costs   CRC 8.493
    Superior court appeals (See **APPELLATE RULES, SUPERIOR COURT APPEALS**)
    Supreme court and courts of appeal (See **APPELLATE RULES, SUPERIOR COURT APPEALS**)
Arbitration (See **ARBITRATION**)

Index

COURTS OF APPEAL—Cont.

Libel or slander actions by person holding elective office or by candidate, preference to   CCP §44

Local rules of court (See **APPELLATE RULES, SUPREME COURT AND COURTS OF APPEAL**)

Managing attorneys

Education of judicial branch

Minimum education requirements for managing attorneys, supervisors, etc   CRC 10.472

New trial, authority to direct   CCP §43

Original writs, procedural rules

Habeas corpus   CRC 8.380 to 8.398

Mandate, certiorari and prohibition in supreme court or court of appeal   CRC 8.485 to 8.493

Environmental quality act cases under public resources code   CRC 8.703

Presiding justices and acting presiding justices

Administrative presiding justices

Education of judicial officers, duties of administrative presiding justices   CRC 10.452

Probate proceedings, preference to   CCP §44

Public Employment Relations Board, judicial review of decisions   CRC 8.728

Records

Public access to judicial administrative records   CRC 10.500

Rehearings   CRC 8.268

Habeas corpus   CRC 8.387

Satisfaction of judgment, justice's power to take and certify acknowledgment of   CCP §179

Statutory powers, listing of   CCP §128

Supervisors

Education of judicial branch

Minimum education requirements for managing attorneys, supervisors, etc   CRC 10.472

Support staff ethics program   CRC JudAdminStand 10.16

Time

Appellate rules (See **APPELLATE RULES, SUPREME COURT AND COURTS OF APPEAL**)

Transact business at any time, courts may   CCP §41

Transfer of cause   CRC 10.1000

Wrong court, appeal or petition filed in   CCP §396

Travel expense reimbursement for judicial officers and employees   CRC 10.106

Vacancy in office of all or any justices, effect on proceedings of   CCP §184

COURT TECHNOLOGY

Indexes, automated maintenance   CRC 10.851

Judicial Branch Statistical Information System (JBSIS)   CRC 10.400

Trial court automation   CRC 10.870

COVENANTS AND CONDITIONS

Adjacent property   CC §§1469, 1470

Apportionment   CC §§1467, 1469

Appurtenances   CC §1460

Breach, liability for   CC §1466

Commercial and industrial common interest developments

Restrictive covenants   CC §6606

Common interest developments   CC §5975

Unlawful restrictive covenants, deletion   CC §4225

Consent for transfer   CC §1457

Conservation easements

Forest health maintenance and improvement

Landowner responsibility as part of easement management plan   CC §815.11

Contracts (See **CONTRACTS AND AGREEMENTS**)

Creation, time of   CC §749

Defined   CC §1462

Discriminatory restrictions   CC §§53, 782, 782.5

Common interest developments

Unlawful restrictive covenants, deletion   CC §4225

Environmental covenants   CC §1471

Hazardous materials, lands containing   CC §1471

Implied from deed   CC §1113

Leases   CC §§1469, 1470

Parties bound by   CC §1465

Prefabricated modular homes, validity of covenants restricting use of   CC §714.5

Quiet enjoyment   CC §1463

Racial covenants   CC §§53, 782, 782.5

Common interest developments

Unlawful restrictive covenants, deletion   CC §4225

Recordation   CC §1468

Repairs   CC §1468

Restrictions defined   CC §784

COVENANTS AND CONDITIONS—Cont.

Restrictive covenants

Commercial and industrial common interest developments   CC §6606

Running with land   CC §§1460 to 1463

Satellite dishes in common interest developments

Restrictions on limitations, prohibitions   CC §4725

Solar energy systems, invalidity of covenants prohibiting use of   CC §714

Successive owners bound by   CC §1468

Taxes, payment of   CC §1468

COVENANTS NOT TO SUE

Contribution among joint tortfeasors, effect on   CCP §877

COVID-19

Appellate rules, supreme court and courts of appeal

E-filing in supreme court and courts of appeal

Documents subject to e-filing in Supreme Court, modifications in light of emergencies   CRCSupp SuprCtE-file 2

Tolling or extension of time for public health emergencies   CRC 8.66

Continuances in civil cases

Cases extended pursuant to state of emergency   CCP §599

Deeds of trust and mortgages

Small landlord and homeowner relief act   CC §§3273.01 to 3273.16

Emergency rules related to COVID-19   CRCAppx I Emer Rules 1 to 13

Landlord and tenant

COVID-19 tenant relief act of 2020   CCP §§1179.01 to 1179.07

Damages owed by landlord for certain violations, effect of declaration of COVID-19 financial distress   CC §789.4

Mortgages

Small landlord and homeowner relief act   CC §§3273.01 to 3273.16

Small claims courts

Jurisdiction for action to recover COVID-19 rental debt   CCP §116.223

CPR (See **CARDIOPULMONARY RESUSCITATION**)

CREDIBILITY (See **WITNESSES**)

CREDIT

Attorneys' fees in action for denial of credit

Marital status, action for denial because of   CC §1812.34

Reasons for denial, action for failure to state   CC §1787.3

Childbearing age affecting extension of   CC §1812.30

Conditional sales (See **CONDITIONAL SALES**)

Consumer protection (See **CONSUMER PROTECTION**)

Cosigner's liability   CC §§1799.90 to 1799.103

Costs in action for denial of credit because of marital status   CC §1812.34

Debt collectors affecting   CC §§1788.20 to 1788.22

Definition   CC §1812.30

Denial   CC §§1787.1 to 1787.3

Waiver of protections   CC §1787.4

Electronic fund transfers   CC §1747.02, 1747.03

Fines and penalties for denial of credit because of marital status   CC §1812.33

Grey market goods, buyer's right to credit on return of   CC §1797.85

Injunctions against denial of credit because of marital status   CC §§1812.32, 1812.33

Marital status of applicant, discrimination because of   CC §§1812.30 to 1812.35

Notice of denial   CC §§1787.1 to 1787.3

Waiver of protections   CC §1787.4

Partition sales on credit   CCP §873.630

Reasons for denial, disclosure of   CC §§1787.1 to 1787.3

Waiver of protections   CC §1787.4

Retail installment sales (See **RETAIL INSTALLMENT SALES**)

Separate accounts, applications by married persons for   CC §1812.30

Services organizations (See **CREDIT SERVICES ORGANIATIONS**)

Statute of limitation for denial of credit because of marital status   CC §1812.35

Women, transactions involving   CC §§1812.30 to 1812.35

CREDIT CARDS

Generally   CC §§1747 to 1748.95

Account numbers printed on receipts, restrictions concerning   CC §1747.09

Activation process   CC §1747.05

Address change for offeree or cardholder

Notice to cardholder of request   CC §1799.1b

Verification by issuer   CC §1747.06

Annual statement of finance charges at cardholder request   CC §1748.5

Appellate rules, supreme court and courts of appeal

E-filing in supreme court and courts of appeal

Fees for filing, methods of payment   CRC 8.76

Billing errors

Correction of   CC §§1747.50 to 1747.65

Defined   CC §1747.02

Index

Index

Index

CUSTODY OF CHILDREN—Cont.

More than 2 parents

Allocation of custody and visitation based on best interests of child   Fam §3040

Murder of one parent by other, custody and visitation determinations following   Fam §3030

Native Americans

Abandoned children

Transfer by parent of care, custody and control to Indian custodian as not constituting abandonment   Fam §7822

Alcohol or drug abuse as custody determination factor   Fam §3041

Applicability of California provisions   Fam §177

Applicability of Indian Child Welfare act   Pro §1459.5

Indian Child Welfare Act, compliance with   Fam §§170 to 185, 3041

Forms, judicial council   CRCAppx A

Involuntary placements   CRC 5.480 to 5.488 (See **INDIAN CHILD WELFARE ACT INVOLUNTARY PLACEMENTS**)

Interstate compact on placement of children

Applicability to Indian children   Fam §7907.3

Legislative findings and intent   Fam §175, Pro §1459

Nonminor dependents, retention of jurisdiction

Request for court to resume jurisdiction   CRC 5.906

Status review hearings   CRC 5.903

Notice   Fam §180

Returning physical custody of Indian child, ex parte hearings

Forms, judicial council   CRCAppx A

Temporary custody of Indian child, agreement   CRCAppx A

Termination of parental rights   Fam §7892.5

Tribe of child

Consideration of connection to tribal community   Fam §170

Determination   Pro §1449

Participation by tribe in proceedings   Fam §185

Uniform Child Custody Jurisdiction and Enforcement Act, applicability of   Fam §3404

Nonparent, custody awarded to   Fam §§3040, 3041

Notice

Change of residence of child   Fam §3024

Indian child custody proceedings   Fam §180

Risk of abduction findings and preventative measures   Fam §3048

Uniform Child Custody Jurisdiction and Enforcement Act, notice requirements under   Fam §§3408, 3425

Orders

Generally   Fam §3022

Ex parte orders   Fam §§3062 to 3064

Mediation of existing order   Fam §3173

Modification (See within this heading, **"Modification of orders"**)

Risk of abduction findings and preventative measures   Fam §3048

Show cause orders

Compensation for failure to exercise visitation or custody rights   Fam §3028

Temporary custody   Fam §3062

Statement explaining basis of court decision   Fam §3022.3

Temporary restraining orders   Fam §§2040, 2041

Removal of child from state   Fam §3063

Other states (See **UNIFORM CHILD CUSTODY JURISDICTION AND ENFORCEMENT ACT**)

Paternity at issue   Fam §3172

Petition for grandparental visitation   Fam §§3103, 3104

Preference in award of custody   Fam §3040

Presumption of joint custody   Fam §3080

Priority on calendar

Trial on issue of custody   Fam §3023

Uniform Child Custody Jurisdiction and Enforcement Act, challenge to jurisdiction under   Fam §3407

Probation officers making investigations   Fam §§3110 to 3116

Pro per court documents, interactive computer system authorized to prepare standardized   CCP §1062.20

Property of child, parent's control over   Fam §7502

Protective custody warrant for unlawfully detained or concealed child   Fam §3134.5

Psychological evaluation of child involved in custody or visitation proceedings

Confidentiality   Fam §3025.5

Public assistance eligibility, specifying primary parent for   Fam §3086

Public policy   Fam §3020

Reconsideration of custody order based on false accusations of abuse   Fam §3022.5

Records

Parental access to records   Fam §3025

Supervised visitation records   CRC JudAdminStand 5.20

CUSTODY OF CHILDREN—Cont.

Records—Cont.

Uniform Child Custody Jurisdiction and Enforcement Act, requirements under (See **UNIFORM CHILD CUSTODY JURISDICTION AND ENFORCEMENT ACT**)

Registered sex offenders, denial of custody and visitation to   Fam §3030

Removal of child from state   Fam §§233, 2030, 3063, 3064

Reports

Child protective services agencies, release of reports of   Fam §3152

Custody evaluations   CRC 5.220, Fam §3111

Residence of child

Absence or relocation of parent from family residence as consideration for court in awarding custody or visitation   Fam §3046

Military deployment   Fam §3047

Notice to other parent of change of child's residence   Fam §3024

Right of custodial parent to change child's residence   Fam §7501

Sale of family home to be deferred, request of custodial parent for   Fam §§3800 to 3810

Sanctions for false accusation of child abuse or neglect   Fam §3027.1

School records, access to   Fam §3025

Separate trial on issue of custody   Fam §3023

Sex offenders

Household membership of or permitting contact by registered sex offender   Fam §3030

Modification or termination of custody upon commission of offense requiring registration by custodian or person residing with   Fam §3030.5

Sexual abuse

Child abuse or neglect generally (See within this heading, **"Child abuse or neglect"**)

Show cause orders

Compensation for failure to exercise visitation or custody rights   Fam §3028

Temporary custody   Fam §3062

Siblings, visitation rights of   Fam §3102

Sole legal custody defined   Fam §3006

Sole physical custody

Defined   Fam §3007

Missing party or child, action to locate   Fam §3133

Spousal support, denial of   Fam §4321

Statement explaining basis of court decision   Fam §3022.3

Stay of execution of judgment affecting custody   CCP §917.7

Stepparent's visitation rights   Fam §§3101, 3171, 3176, 3185

Substance abuse

Best interest of child, factor in determining   Fam §3011

Determining factor in custody

Testing for alcohol or controlled substance use ordered by court   Fam §3041.5

Termination of parental rights

Circumstances where proceedings may be brought   Fam §7824

Supervised visitation and exchange programs   CRC JudAdminStand 5.20, Fam §§3200 to 3204

Administration of programs

Definitions   Fam §3201.5

Compliance with provisions   Fam §3202

Grant funds

Administration   Fam §3204

Providers, standards   Fam §3200.5

Declaration of provider, form   CRCAppx A

Temporary custody

Agreement, custody awarded in accordance with   Fam §3061

Ex parte orders   Fam §§3062 to 3064

Military deployment, duty, etc

Effect on custody orders of temporary deployment, duty, etc   Fam §3047

Petition for   Fam §3060

Uniform Parentage Act   Fam §7604

Temporary guardian appointment as affecting visitation rights   Pro §2250

Temporary restraining orders

Generally   Fam §§2040, 2041

Removal of child from state   Fam §3063

Termination of parental rights (See **TERMINATION OF PARENTAL RIGHTS**)

Thwarting other parent's visitation or custody rights   Fam §3028

Transfer of causes

Retention of jurisdiction to issue protective orders   CCP §399

Subsequent to final judgment   CCP §397.5

Time frames for transferring jurisdiction

Family law actions or proceedings   CRC 5.97

Translators for child custody proceedings, public provision of   Fam §3032

Uniform Child Custody Jurisdiction and Enforcement Act (See **UNIFORM CHILD CUSTODY JURISDICTION AND ENFORCEMENT ACT**)

Uniform Parentage Act   Fam §§7604, 7637

D

Index

Index

DATA BROKER REGISTRATION—Cont.
Requirement of registration   CC §1798.99.82

DATA PROCESSING (See **COMPUTERS**)

DATA SECURITY BREACH NOTICE
Customer records   CC §1798.82
Information practices   CC §1788.61

DATING SERVICES
Cancellation of agreement
    Buyer's right to cancel   CC §1694.1
        Noncompliance with statute, cancellation for   CC §1694.2
Damages recoverable   CC §1694.4
Death or disability of buyer, effect of   CC §1694.3
Defined   CC §1694
False and misleading advertisement, liability for   CC §1694.4
Installment payments
    Generally   CC §1694.2
    Refund or credit, buyer's right to   CC §1694.4
Online dating services
    Cancellation of agreement
        Method of cancellation   CC §1694.1
        Notice of right to cancel   CC §1694.2
    Dating safety awareness information
        Access   CC §1694.3
    Defined   CC §1694
    Reporting behavior of other users
        Providing mechanism for reporting by service   CC §1694.3
    Written contract requirement   CC §1694.2
Refund or credit of payments, buyer's right to   CC §1694.4
Relocation of buyer's residence, effect of   CC §1694.3
Terms of agreement   CC §1694.2
Void and unenforceable contracts, grounds for   CC §1694.4

DATING VIOLENCE
Victim service providers, personal information protection   CC §§1798.79.8 to 1798.79.95
    Definitions   CC §1798.79.8
    Disclosing personal information
        Grants, requiring disclosure as condition   CC §1798.79.9
        Injunctions to prevent   CC §1798.79.95
        Prohibited   CC §1798.79.9

DAVIS-STIRLING COMMON INTEREST DEVELOPMENT ACT
Common interest developments generally   CC §§4000 to 6150 (See **COMMON INTEREST DEVELOPMENTS**)

DAYCARE (See **CHILD CARE**)

DEAD BODIES
Juries of inquest (See **JURIES OF INQUEST**)
Restriction on reproducing photograph or video taken at scene of death or in course of postmortem examination or autopsy   CCP §129

DEADLOCK OF JURY
Discharge   CCP §616

DEAD MAN'S STATUTE   Ev §1261

DEAF AND HARD OF HEARING PERSONS
Access to public facilities   CC §54.1
    Construction or application of provisions in issue, solicitor general notified   CC §55.2
Administrative adjudicative proceeding, interpreters in   Gov §11435.10
Assistive listening systems in judicial proceedings   CC §54.8
Commercial and industrial common interest developments
    Disabled access
        Modification of separate interests   CC §6714
Court personnel, disabled, reasonable accommodation for   CRC JudAdminStand 10.25
Courts, access rights   CC §54.8
Criminal cases
    Admissibility of oral or written statements by deaf or hard-of-hearing persons in   Ev §754
Defined   CC §54.8, Ev §754
Interpreters
    Appointment by court or parties   Ev §754
    Assistive listening systems in judicial proceedings   CC §54.8
    Certification programs for interpreters, guidelines for   CRC 2.892
    Court-appointed interpreters for   Ev §754
    Generally (See **TRANSLATORS AND INTERPRETERS**)

DEAF AND HARD OF HEARING PERSONS—Cont.
Interpreters—Cont.
    Guidelines   Ev §754
    Jurors, interpreters for   CCP §224
    Privileged communication, effect of interpreter's presence during   Ev §754.5
Jury (See **JURY**)
Jury service
    Eligibility for   CCP §§203, 228
    Sign language interpreters and other assistance   CC §54.8, CCP §224
Mobilehome parks, restrictions as to signal dogs in   CC §798.33
Privileged communications   Ev §754.5
    Effect of interpreter's presence during   Ev §754.5
Signal dogs, right to   CC §54.2
Speech-to-text equipment
    Court, access rights   CC §54.8
Telephone facilities, use of   CC §54.1
    Construction or application of provisions in issue, solicitor general notified   CC §55.2

DEALERS
Art dealers (See **ART DEALERS**)
Autographed sports memorabilia, sale of   CC §1739.7
Automobile manufacturers, transporters, dealers and sales professionals
    Restitution, licensee ordered to pay
        Effect of order for restitution   Gov §11519.1
Fair dealership law   CC §§80 to 86

DEATH
Administration of estates (See **ADMINISTRATION OF ESTATES**)
Administrator (See **EXECUTORS AND ADMINISTRATORS**)
Advancement, death of heir after receipt of   Pro §6409
Adverse possessor, death of   CCP §327
Advertising, unauthorized use of name or likeness of deceased personality in   CC §3344.1
Agency, termination of   CC §§2355, 2356
Annulment when spouse that was believed dead is living   Fam §2210
Appeal, right of   CCP §903
Attachment (See **ATTACHMENT**)
Attorneys (See **ATTORNEYS**)
Bailment, death of party to   CC §1934
Bank accounts, effect of death on multiple-party   Pro §§5302, 5405
Bible entries as evidence   Ev §1312
Cancellation of utility, cable, etc, services on behalf of deceased person
    In-person cancellation not to be required   Pro §217
Capital punishment (See **CAPITAL PUNISHMENT**)
Certificates
    Evidence of family history   Ev §§1315, 1316
    Forms
        Judicial council legal forms   CRCAppx A
    International wills   Pro §6389
    Records and recordings (See **RECORDS AND RECORDING**)
Child support terminated on death of child   Fam §2023
Child victims
    Sealing autopsy report and evidence   CCP §130
Church records as evidence of   Ev §1315
Common accident causing (See **SIMULTANEOUS DEATH**)
Community reputation concerning   Ev §1314
Conservators
    Generally (See **CONSERVATORS**)
    Notice of death of conservatee   Pro §2361
Contracts (See **CONTRACTS AND AGREEMENTS**)
Convalescent home contract, death of patient terminating   CC §1934.5
Court reporter's death, effect of   CCP §§657.1, 914
Damages (See **DAMAGES**)
Dance studio contract, refund under   CC §1812.57
Dating service contracts, payment liability under   CC §1694.3
Dissolution of marriage (See **DISSOLUTION OF MARRIAGE**)
Enforcement of judgments (See **ENFORCEMENT OF JUDGMENTS**)
Estates (See **DECEDENTS' ESTATES**)
Executor (See **EXECUTORS AND ADMINISTRATORS**)
Fact of death (See **FACT OF DEATH**)
Family friends, statements concerning death by   Ev §1311
Gang-related crime, decedent's sworn statement concerning (See **GANG VIO-LENCE**)
Gifts in view of death
    Creditors, recovery of property for benefit of   Pro §5705
    Defined   Pro §§5700, 5702
    Governing law   Pro §5701
    Presumption of   Pro §5703

Index

Index

DECLARATIONS—Cont.

Economic litigation provision for use of declaration in lieu of direct testimony
    CCP §98

Emancipation of minors (See **EMANCIPATION OF MINORS**)

Homesteads (See **HOMESTEADS**)

Identity of judgment debtor, declaration under penalty of perjury executed by judgment creditor as to   CCP §680.135

Judicial officer's power to take and certify   CCP §179

Legal separation, assets and liabilities disclosure required for   Fam §§2100 to 2113

Mortgages, satisfaction of   CC §2941.7

Oath defined to include declaration   CCP §17

Part offered in evidence   Ev §356

Penalty of perjury, declaration of written instrument executed under   CCP §2015.5

Property   Fam §2330.5

Property declarations defined   Fam §115

Small claims court (See **SMALL CLAIMS COURTS**)

Survival of actions, execution of supporting declaration in (See **SURVIVAL OF ACTIONS**)

Trust deeds, satisfaction of   CC §2941.7

Written instrument executed under penalty of perjury, declaration of   CCP §2015.5

DECLARATORY JUDGMENTS

Administrative law
    Action for declaratory relief (See **ADMINISTRATIVE PROCEDURE ACT**)
    Adjudication proceeding, declaratory decision in (See **ADMINISTRATIVE ADJUDICATION**)

Common interest developments
    Board meetings
        Actions for declaratory or equitable relief to enforce provisions   CC §4955
    Member elections
        Action for declaratory or equitable relief to enforce   CC §5145

Consumer privacy rights
    Actions for damages, injunctions, declaratory relief, etc
        Security practices and procedures not in place   CC §1798.150

Contracts, determining rights under   CCP §1060

Cross-complaint provisions, applicability of   CCP §426.60

Cumulative remedies   CCP §1062

Deeds, determining rights under   CCP §1060

Health care providers, insurer of   CCP §1062.5

Identity theft, declaratory relief in actions involving   CC §1798.93

Income tax liability of nonresident   CCP §1060.5

Limited civil cases, unavailability of declaratory relief in   CCP §580

Necessary relief   CCP §1061

Parks, purpose in taking for   CCP §1240.700

Precedence over other matters   CCP §1062.3

Professional liability insurer's liability   CCP §1062.5

Rivers, determining natural flow of   CCP §1060

Will probate
    Construction of writing   CCP §1060
    No contest clauses, declaratory relief   Pro §§21320 to 21322

DECREES (See **JUDGMENTS**)

DEDICATION

Decedent's estate, property of   Pro §§9900, 9901

Prescriptive use   CC §§813, 1007

Public land, private property used as   CC §1009

Quieting title action, effect on   CCP §§771.010, 771.020

Title held under   CC §670

Trust property   Pro §16230

DEEDS (See also **COVENANTS AND CONDITIONS**)

Acknowledgments
    Superior court fees, specified services   Gov §70626

Administrators of decedents' estates (See **EXECUTORS AND ADMINISTRATORS**)

Adverse possession by person claiming title founded on written instrument   CCP §§322, 323

Advertising for sale, restrictions on   CC §712

Boundary determination   CCP §2077

Commercial and industrial common interest developments
    Liberal construction   CC §6602
    Physical boundaries prevail over description in deed, plan, etc   CC §6604

Conclusive against grantor   CC §1107

Conflicting clauses   CC §1070

Consolidation of   CC §1093

DEEDS (—Cont.

Construction of   CC §§1066 to 1070, CCP §2077

Copies, admissibility of   Ev §§1600 to 1605

Declaratory judgments determining rights under   CCP §1060

Delivery   CC §§1054 to 1056, 1059, 1627

Description   CCP §2077

Executors of decedents' estates (See **EXECUTORS AND ADMINISTRATORS**)

Fee-simple title presumed   CC §1105

Form for transfer   CC §1092

Hearsay rule affecting admissibility of statements in   Ev §1330

Highways, deed for land bordering   CC §1112

Implied covenants   CC §1113

Inheritance, use of words of   CC §1072

Mortgage, deed shown as   CC §§2925, 2950

Names
    Changed by grantee   CC §1096
    Unnamed party as grantee   CC §1085

Partition action   CCP §873.230

Presumptions of authenticity   Ev §643

Privileged communications in determining validity of   Ev §§959 to 961, 1002, 1003, 1021, 1022

Quiet enjoyment under   CC §1463

Quitclaim deeds (See **QUITCLAIM DEEDS**)

Recording (See **RECORDS AND RECORDING**)

Redelivery   CC §1058

Revocable transfer on death deeds   Pro §§5600 to 5696 (See **TRANSFER ON DEATH DEEDS**)

Sheriff's deed (See **ENFORCEMENT OF JUDGMENTS**)

Statute of limitation   CC §1067

Title to   CC §994

Transfer on death deeds   Pro §§5600 to 5696 (See **TRANSFER ON DEATH DEEDS**)

Trust deeds and mortgages (See **TRUST DEEDS AND MORTGAGES**)

Unclaimed property, controller executing deeds for   CCP §1376

DEEDS OF TRUST (See **TRUST DEEDS AND MORTGAGES**)

DEEPFAKES

Sexually explicit depiction of individual, creation or disclosure
    Actions for damages   CC §1708.86

DEFACEMENT OF PROPERTY

Art works, defacement of   CC §987

Parent's liability for acts of minor children   CC §1714.1

DEFAMATION (See **LIBEL AND SLANDER**)

DEFAULT JUDGMENTS   CCP §585, CRC 3.110

Administrative adjudication, default by respondent in   Gov §11520

Affidavits
    Civil Code provisions, stating action not subject to   CCP §585.5
    Copy of application mailed to defendant, stating that   CCP §587
    Evidence presented by   CCP §585

Answers to complaint   CCP §§585, 586

Application for entry of default   CCP §§585 to 587

Associations   CCP §412.30

Attorney's fees   CCP §585
    Fee schedules   CRC 3.1800

Case management
    Collections cases
        Time for default judgment   CRC 3.740

Child support proceedings (See **CHILD SUPPORT**)

Complaint
    Conformity to pleadings   CCP §580
    Defined   CCP §587.5
    Failure to respond   CCP §§585, 586, CRC 3.110

Conformity to pleadings   CCP §580

Contracts   CCP §§585, 585.5

Corporations   CCP §412.30

Costs   CRC 3.1700

Court reporter's fees   Gov §69949

Damages
    Determination of damages   CCP §585
    Reservation of right to seek punitive damages on default   CCP §§425.12, 425.115

Definitions   CCP §587.5

Demurrer to complaint   CCP §§585, 586

Destroyed land records relief law proceedings   CCP §751.14

Disallowed before expiration of time to respond   CCP §418.10

Dismissal, motions for   CCP §§585, 586

Dissolution of marriage (See **DISSOLUTION OF MARRIAGE**)

Index

DEFINITIONS—Cont.

CASp
 Construction-related accessibility claims, compliance with standards   CC §55.52

Catalog sale   CC §1791

Catalogue of electronic communications
 Fiduciary access to digital assets   Pro §871

CCPI
 Children and minors, calculations for imputed liability for willful misconduct of minor   CRCAppx B

Central authority
 Intercountry adoptions   Fam §8900.5
 Interstate family support
  Convention support proceedings   Fam §5700.701

Certificate
 Appellate briefs, certificate of interested entities or persons   CRC 8.208

Certificate of authenticity   CC §1740

Certificate of missing status   Pro §3700

Certified access specialist
 Construction-related accessibility claims, compliance with standards   CC §55.52

Certified interpreter
 Interpreters, appointment in court proceedings   CRC 2.893

Certiorari writ   CCP §1067

Chair
 Judges, committee on judicial ethics opinions   CRCSupp JudEthicsOpinionsIOP 2
 Judicial council advisory bodies, meetings   CRC 10.75

Chairperson
 Judicial performance commission rules   JudPerR 138

Challenge   CCP §225

Charge card   CC §1748.21

Charged
 Sentencing rules, determinate sentencing   CRC 4.405

Charged-off consumer debt
 Fair debt buying practices   CC §1788.50

Charges
 Mobilehome parks, management approval of mobilehome purchaser   CC §798.74

Charging stations
 Commercial lease restrictions   CC §1952.7
 Lessee installation, landlord approval   CC §1947.6

Charitable interest
 Trust decanting, uniform act   Pro §19502

Charitable organization
 Trust decanting, uniform act   Pro §19502

Charitable purpose
 Uniform prudent management of institutional funds act   Pro §18502

Charitable remainder trust   Pro §16061.7

Charitable trust   Pro §16100

Charter party   CC §1959

Chattel interests   CC §765

Chattel paper   CCP §§481.040, 680.140

Chattels real   CC §765

Check cashers   CC §1789.31

Chief administrative officer
 Postsecondary educational institutions, protection orders against violence threatened on campus or facility   CCP §527.85

Chief justice
 Rules of court   CRC 1.6

Chief trial counsel
 Attorneys, judges and law practice, rules governing   CRC 9.1

Child   Pro §26
 Interstate compact on placement of children   CRC 5.616
 Interstate family support   Fam §5700.102
 Juvenile rules   CRC 5.502
 Uniform Parentage Act, vacation or setting aside of judgment   Fam §7645

Child abuse
 Criminal action, evidence   Ev §1109

Child abuse prevention and treatment act (CAPTA) guardian ad litem for child subject to juvenile dependency petition
 Juvenile rules   CRC 5.502

Child custody evaluation
 Child custody evaluators, qualifications for appointment   CRC 5.225
 Court-ordered child custody evaluation   CRC 5.220

Child custody evaluators   CRC 5.225
 Court-ordered child custody evaluation   CRC 5.220

Child for whom support may be ordered   Fam §58

Childhood sexual assault   CCP §340.1

Child support   CCP §680.145

Child support delinquency   Fam §17450

DEFINITIONS—Cont.

Child support obligee   Fam §4550

Child support order
 Interstate family support   Fam §5700.102

Chose in action   CC §953

Circumstances in aggravation
 Sentencing rules, determinate sentencing   CRC 4.405

Circumstances in mitigation
 Sentencing rules, determinate sentencing   CRC 4.405

Civil action   CCP §30, Ev §120

Civil action for injury or illness based upon exposure to a hazardous material or toxic substance
 Statutes of limitation   CCP §340.8

Civil action or proceeding
 Tribal court civil money judgment act   CCP §1732

Civil case
 Appellate rules, superior court appeals   CRC 8.803
 Rules of court   CRC 1.6

Civil petitions
 Rules of court   CRC 1.6

CJA
 Judges, committee on judicial ethics opinions   CRCSupp JudEthicsOpinionsIOP 2
 Probate cases, education of judges and subordinate judicial officers regularly assigned to   CRC 10.468

CJEO
 Judges, committee on judicial ethics opinions   CRCSupp JudEthicsOpinionsIOP 2

CJEO confidentiality waiver form
 Judges, committee on judicial ethics opinions   CRCSupp JudEthicsOpinionsIOP 2

CJEO email address
 Judges, committee on judicial ethics opinions   CRCSupp JudEthicsOpinionsIOP 2

CJEO opinion request form
 Judges, committee on judicial ethics opinions   CRCSupp JudEthicsOpinionsIOP 2

CJEO suggested topic form
 Judges, committee on judicial ethics opinions   CRCSupp JudEthicsOpinionsIOP 2

CJEO web site
 Judges, committee on judicial ethics opinions   CRCSupp JudEthicsOpinionsIOP 2

CJER
 Education of personnel responsible for probate cases   CRC 10.478
 Probate cases, education of judges and subordinate judicial officers regularly assigned to   CRC 10.468

Claimant
 Construction defects, actions for   CC §895
 Family rules, joinder of parties   CRC 5.24
 Mechanics' liens   CC §8004

Claims
 Claims against estates   Pro §19000
 Undisputed claims, penalty against state for failure to pay   Gov §927.2
 Voidable transactions   CC §3439.01

Class of internet content, application, service or device
 Net neutrality   CC §3100

Claws
 Landlord and tenant, requiring declawing or devocalizing animals as condition of occupancy   CC §1942.7

Clear and conspicuous
 Direct marketing, medical information used for   CC §1798.91

Clergy   Ev §1030

Clerk
 Civil rules, coordination of complex actions   CRC 3.501
 Juvenile rules   CRC 5.502

Client   Ev §951
 Attorney referral service-client privilege   Ev §965
 Discovery, attorney work product   CCP §2018.010

Close of business
 Electronic filing and service rules   CRC 2.250

Close of escrow
 Construction defects, actions for   CC §895

Clotheslines
 Common interest developments, governing document restrictions   CC §4753
 Tenant use of clothesline or drying rack in private areas   CC §1940.20

Clothing   CC §1791

Cohabitant   CC §51.3, Fam §6209
 Donative transfers   Pro §21364

Collateral   CC §1799.100

Index

Index

DEFINITIONS—Cont.

Employ
    Attorney professional conduct
        Law firm employment of disbarred, suspended, resigned or involuntarily inactive lawyers   ProfC 5.3.1

Employee   CCP §706.011
    Arbitration   CCP §1280
    Postsecondary educational institutions, protection orders against violence threatened on campus or facility   CCP §527.85
    Subpoena duces tecum for employment records   CCP §1985.6
    Workplace violence, protection orders   CCP §527.8

Employee benefit plan   Pro §266

Employee pension benefit plan   Fam §80

Employees who regularly have contact with customers
    Customer records, disclosure of personal information   CC §1798.83

Employer   Fam §5210
    Postsecondary educational institutions, protection orders against violence threatened on campus or facility   CCP §527.85
    Workplace violence, protection orders   CCP §527.8

Employment agencies   CC §1812.501

Employment counseling services   CC §1812.501

Employment records
    Subpoena duces tecum for employment records   CCP §1985.6

Encrypted
    Customer records, computerized personal information   CC §1798.82
    Information practices, breach of security system   CC §1798.29

Encryption key
    Customer records, computerized personal information   CC §1798.82
    Information practices, breach of security system   CC §1798.29

Encumbered property   Pro §10320

Encumbrance   CC §1114

Endanger
    Confidentiality of medical information   CC §56.05

Endowment funds
    Uniform prudent management of institutional funds act   Pro §18502

End users
    Net neutrality   CC §3100

Enforcement action
    Common interest developments, alternative dispute resolution   CC §5925

Enforcement of judgments   CCP §§680.110 to 680.380

Engage in the business
    Student borrower bill of rights   CC §1788.100

Enhanced association records
    Common interest developments, fiscal matters   CC §5200

Enhancement
    Sentencing rules, determinate sentencing   CRC 4.405

Enrollee
    Confidentiality of medical information   CC §56.05

Enterprise service offering
    Net neutrality   CC §3100

Entitled person   CC §2943
    Equity lines of credit, suspending and closing line on borrower's instruction   CC §2943.1

Entity
    Appellate briefs, certificate of interested entities or persons   CRC 8.208
    Principal and income act, allocation of receipts from entity   Pro §16350
    Quieting title   CCP §765.010

Environmental leadership development project
    Appellate review of CEQA cases   CRC 8.700
    Petitions under environmental quality act, civil rules governing   CRC 3.2220

Epinephrine auto-injectors
    Immunity from liability for administration   CC §1714.23

Equity   CCP §680.190

Equity lines of credit
    Suspending and closing line on borrower's instruction   CC §2943.1

Equity purchaser   CC §1695.1

Equity seller   CC §1695.1

Escheat   CCP §1300

Escrow   CC §1057
    Escrow agent rating services   CC §1785.28

Escrow agent
    Escrow agent rating services   CC §1785.28

Escrow agent rating services   CC §1785.28

Escrow service
    Buyer's choice act   CC §1103.22

Established business relationship
    Customer records, disclosure of personal information   CC §1798.83

Estate   Pro §353
    Guardians and conservators of the estate   Pro §2400
    Inventory and accounts of guardians and conservators   Pro §2600

DEFINITIONS—Cont.

Estate plan of conservatee   Pro §2586

Estimated time for repair
    Rental passenger vehicle transactions   CC §1939.01

Estimated time for replacement
    Rental passenger vehicle transactions   CC §1939.01

Ethnic or racial group
    Genetic testing to determine parentage   Fam §7550.5

Evaluation
    Child custody, domestic violence protocol for family court services   CRC 5.215
    Court-ordered child custody evaluation   CRC 5.220

Evidence-based practices
    Sentencing rules, determinate sentencing   CRC 4.405

Evidentiary hearing
    Habeas corpus   CRC 4.545

Examiner
    Judicial performance commission rules   JudPerR 138

Exception   CCP §646

Exclusive use common area
    Commercial and industrial common interest developments   CC §6550

Excused jurors   CCP §194

Executed contract   CC §1661

Execution of instruments   CCP §1933

Executor   Pro §6203

Executory contract   CC §1661

Exemplary damages   CC §48a

Exempted providers
    Intercountry adoptions   Fam §8900.5

Expanded distributive discretion
    Trust decanting, uniform act   Pro §19502

Ex parte communication
    Child custody, ex parte communications   CRC 5.235
    Probate proceedings, rule governing ex parte communications   CRC 7.10

Expedited jury trial   CCP §630.01, CRC 3.1545

Expenses
    Civil rules, coordination of complex actions   CRC 3.501

Expert witnesses
    Groundwater rights actions   CCP §832

Expiration of rental restriction
    Rent setting and limitations   CC §1947.13

Express consent
    Rental-purchase contracts   CC §1812.622

Express contracts   CC §1620

Express warranty   CC §1791.2

Extended family member
    Indian children   Fam §170

Exterior elevated elements
    Common interest developments, financial reserve planning   CC §5551

Facility
    Force, threat or other obstruction of access to facility   CC §1708.9

Factors   CC §§2026, 2367

Failure to appear
    Infractions, failure to appear or failure to pay for notice to appear   CRC 4.106

Failure to maintain
    Foreclosure, maintaining vacant residential property   CC §2929.3

Failure to pay
    Infractions, failure to appear or failure to pay for notice to appear   CRC 4.106

Family allowance   Pro §38

Family centered case resolution conference   CRC 5.83

Family centered case resolution process   CRC 5.83

Family code
    Family rules   CRC 5.2

Family court services
    Child custody, domestic violence protocol for family court services   CRC 5.215

Family of absentee   Pro §3700

Family support   Fam §92

Farm machinery   CC §1718

Farm products   CCP §481.110

Fax
    Fax filing and service   CRC 2.301
    Levying officer electronic transactions act   CCP §263.1

Fax filing   CRC 2.301

Fax filing agency
    Fax filing and service   CRC 2.301

Fax machine
    Fax filing and service   CRC 2.301
    Levying officer electronic transactions act   CCP §263.1

Index

Index

Index

Index

DEFINITIONS—Cont.

Reasonably should know
 Attorney professional conduct   ProfC 1.0.1
Receivables   CCP §1800
Received by a state agency
 Claims against public entities and employees, late payment   Gov §927.2
Receiving court
 Probation, out-of-county transfers   CRC 4.530
Reciprocal assignment orders
 Trial court management   CRC 10.630
Recognized employee organization
 Labor relations of court employees   CRC 10.652
Record
 Canadian domestic violence protection orders, recognition and enforcement   Fam §6451
 Commercial real property tenancies, disposition of property remaining upon termination   CC §1993
 Conservators, interstate jurisdiction, transfer and recognition   Pro §1982
 Customer record, disposition   CC §1798.80
 Fiduciary access to digital assets   Pro §871
 Interstate family support   Fam §5700.102
 Landlord and tenant, abandoned personal property disposition   CC §1980
 Levying officer electronic transactions act   CCP §263.1
 Name change proceedings under address confidentiality program   CRC 2.575
 Protected consumer security freezes   CC §1785.11.9
 Sealed and confidential records, appellate rules for supreme court and courts of appeal   CRC 8.45
 Trial court rules, sealed records   CRC 2.550
 Uniform prudent management of institutional funds act   Pro §18502
 Voidable transactions   CC §3439.01
Recorded
 Transfer on death deeds   Pro §5612
Recordings
 Court proceedings, photographing, recording and broadcasting   CRC 1.150
Record on appeal
 Juvenile case appeals, confidentiality   CRC 8.401
Record on writ petition
 Juvenile case appeals, confidentiality   CRC 8.401
Record owners   CCP §1255.450
Records in the juvenile case file
 Juvenile case appeals, confidentiality   CRC 8.401
Recreational vehicle parks   CC §§799.29, 799.30
Recreational vehicles
 Special occupancy parks   CC §1866
Recross-examination   Ev §763
Redacted version
 Sealed and confidential records, appellate rules for supreme court and courts of appeal   CRC 8.45
Redirect examination   Ev §762
Reel
 Records of court proceedings, electronic   CRC 2.952
Refund
 Consumer refunds offered by prepaid debit card   CC §1748.40
Regional court interpreter coordinator
 Court interpreters, cross-assignments   CRC 10.762
Register
 Interstate family support   Fam §5700.102
 TOD security registration act   Pro §5501
Registered domestic partner
 Judicial ethics code   CRCSupp JudEthicsTerminology
Registered interpreter
 Interpreters, appointment in court proceedings   CRC 2.893
Registered process server   CCP §§481.205, 680.330
Registering entity
 TOD security registration act   Pro §5501
Registering tribunal
 Interstate family support   Fam §5700.102
Regular filing hours
 Electronic filing and service rules   CRC 2.250
Regular grand jury
 Demographic data on regular grand jurors   CRC 10.625
Regularly assigned to hear probate proceedings
 Probate cases, education of judges and subordinate judicial officers regularly assigned to   CRC 10.468
Regulation   Gov §§11342, 11342.600
Regulation Z
 Automobile sales finance   CC §2981
Related by blood or affinity
 Donative transfers   Pro §21374

DEFINITIONS—Cont.

Related cases
 Civil rules   CRC 3.300
 Family rules, coordination of court resources   CRC 5.440
Related cause of action   CCP §426.10
Relationship index
 Genetic testing to determine parentage   Fam §7550.5
Relative
 Juvenile rules   CRC 5.502
Relative caregiver   Fam §17550
Release
 Deeds of trust and mortgages, secured party access to inspect for environmental damage   CC §2929.5
 Receivers   CCP §564
Relevant evidence   Ev §210
Religion
 Discrimination   CC §51
Religious items
 Religious items displayed on dwelling entry, property owner restrictions   CC §1940.45
Remainder   CC §769
Remainderman   CC §731.03
Remand
 Civil rules, coordination of complex actions   CRC 3.501
Remote access
 Electronic court records   CRC 2.502
Remote-computing services
 Fiduciary access to digital assets   Pro §871
Remotely
 Radio frequency identification (RFID) to remotely read identification document without knowledge or consent   CC §1798.795
Remote technical assistance
 Rental-purchase contracts   CC §1812.622
Remote video proceedings
 Criminal rules, remote video proceedings for trial of traffic infractions   CRC 4.220
Removal
 Juvenile rules   CRC 5.502
Rental agreement
 Landlord and tenant, water service in multifamily residential rental buildings   CC §1954.202
Rental company
 Rental passenger vehicle transactions   CC §1939.01
Rental payment
 COVID-19 tenant relief act of 2020   CCP §1179.02
Rental-purchase agreement   CC §1812.622
Renter
 Rental passenger vehicle transactions   CC §1939.01
Renting
 Landlord and tenant, water service in multifamily residential rental buildings   CC §1954.202
Rent skimming   CC §890
Repair service facility   CC §1791
Representation
 Autographed memorabilia   CC §1739.7
Representative
 Protected consumer security freezes   CC §1785.11.9
Representative of the news media
 Court records, public access   CRC 10.500
Representative of victim
 Domestic violence, access to reports   Fam §6228
Requester
 Judges, committee on judicial ethics opinions   CRCSupp JudEthicsOpinionsIOP 2
Request for hearing
 Family rules, interstate income withholding orders   CRC 5.335
Request for review
 Gang database removal, appeal proceedings   CRC 3.2300
Request regarding resuscitative measures   Pro §4780
Require
 Judicial ethics code   CRCSupp JudEthicsTerminology
Require, coerce or compel
 Subcutaneous implanting of identification device, requiring of another   CC §52.7
Required payment approval date
 Claims against public entities and employees, late payment   Gov §927.2
Reschedule the hearing
 Family rules   CRC 5.2
Research
 Consumer privacy rights   CC §1798.140

Index

DEFINITIONS—Cont.
Security credentials—Cont.
Information practices, breach of security system   CC §1798.29
Security features
Connected devices, security   CC §1798.91.05
Security freezes   CC §1785.11.2
Protected consumer security freezes   CC §1785.11.9
Security interests   CCP §§680.360, 1800
Security testing
Electronic recording delivery systems   Gov §27390
Self-represented
Electronic filing and service rules   CRC 2.250
Sell
Consumer privacy rights   CC §1798.140
Real estate brokers and sales persons   CC §2079.13
Seller
Automobile sales finance   CC §2981
Buyer's choice act   CC §1103.22
Seller assisted marketing plan   CC §1812.201
Seller's agent
Real estate brokers and sales persons   CC §2079.13
Selling
Consumer privacy rights   CC §1798.140
Seminar solicitation sales contracts   CC §1689.24
Senior citizen
Deeds of trust and mortgages, modification or workout plan to avoid foreclosure   CC §2944.8
Home solicitation sales contracts   CC §1689.5
Seminar solicitation sales contracts   CC §1689.24
Senior citizen housing developments   CC §51.3
Sensitive personal information
Consumer privacy rights   CC §1798.140
Sensitive services
Confidentiality of medical information   CC §56.05
Sentence choice
Sentencing rules, determinate sentencing   CRC 4.405
Separate fund
Principal and income act   Pro §§16361, 16361.1
Separate interest
Commercial and industrial common interest developments   CC §6564
Separate property   Fam §§130, 770, 2502, 3515
Separate residential units
Mechanics' liens   CC §8448
Serve and file
Civil rules, coordination of complex actions   CRC 3.501
Rules applicable to all courts   CRC 1.21
Service
Appellate rules, superior court appeals   CRC 8.803
Cancellation of utility, cable, etc, services on behalf of deceased person   Pro §217
Consumer privacy rights   CC §1798.140
Home solicitation sales contracts   CC §1689.5
Mortgage foreclosure consultants   CC §2945.1
Rules of court   CRC 1.6
Service bulletins   CC §1795.90
Service by fax
Fax filing and service   CRC 2.301
Service contract   CC §1791
Automobile sales finance   CC §2981
Service contract administrator
Consumer warranty protection   CC §1791
Service contract seller
Consumer warranty protection   CC §1791
Service member
Attorney practice, registered military spouse attorneys   CRC 9.41.1
Service organizations
Judicial ethics code   CRCSupp JudEthicsTerminology
Service provider
Consumer privacy rights   CC §1798.140
Service provider for disabled juror   CCP §224
Servicing
Student borrower bill of rights   CC §1788.100
Servient tenement   CC §803
Settlement services
Family rules, settlement service providers   CRC 5.420
Settlor
Trust decanting, uniform act   Pro §19502
Several ownership   CC §681
Sex
Discrimination   CC §51

DEFINITIONS—Cont.
Sex, race, color, religion, ancestry, national origin, disability, medical condition, , genetic information, marital status or sexual orientation
Discrimination   CC §51
Sexual assault
Actions for damages   CCP §340.16
Contempt, enforcement against victims for refusal to testify   CCP §1219
Settlement of employment disputes   CCP §1002.5
Sexual battery   CC §1708.5
Sexual conduct
Sexually explicit depiction of individual, actions for damages   CC §1708.86
Sexual contact   CC §43.93
Sexual harassment
Settlement of employment disputes   CCP §1002.5
Sexually explicit material
Sexually explicit depiction of individual, actions for damages   CC §1708.86
Sexual orientation
Discrimination   CC §51
Sexual orientation violence
Unruh civil rights act   CC §52.45
Sexual relations
Attorney professional conduct   ProfC 1.8.10
Shall
Judicial performance commission rules   JudPerR 138
Share
Consumer privacy rights   CC §1798.140
Shared
Consumer privacy rights   CC §1798.140
Shared appreciation loans   CC §1917
Shared mobility device   CC §2505
Shared mobility service provider   CC §2505
Sharing
Consumer privacy rights   CC §1798.140
Sheriff   CCP §17
Rules of court   CRC 1.6
Short cause cases
Civil rules, case management   CRC 3.735
Short-pay agreements
Mortgages and deeds of trust   CC §2943
Short-pay demand statements
Mortgages and deeds of trust   CC §2943
Short-pay requests
Mortgages and deeds of trust   CC §2943
Sibling
Adoption, sibling contact information requests   CRC 5.460
Adoption, visitation with adopted siblings   Fam §8920
Sibling group
Juvenile rules   CRC 5.502
Side
Civil rules, coordination of complex actions   CRC 3.501
Sign
Voidable transactions   CC §3439.01
Signatures   CCP §17
Signed
Attorney professional conduct   ProfC 1.0.1
Common interest developments, member elections   CC §5130
Significant-connection state
Conservators, interstate jurisdiction, transfer and recognition   Pro §1991
Significant personal relationship
Arbitrators, ethics standards for neutral arbitrators   CRC ArbEthicsStand 2
Simple-interest basis
Automobile sales finance   CC §2981
Single-family, owner-occupied dwelling   CC §2954.4
Single-family residential property
Real estate brokers and salespersons   CC §2079.13
Single-family residential real property
Real estate brokers and salespersons   CC §2079.13
Water conserving plumbing retrofits   CC §1101.3
Sister state judgment   CCP §1710.10
Site
Construction-related accessibility claims, compliance with standards   CC §55.52
Mechanics' liens   CC §8040
Special occupancy parks   CC §1866
Site improvement
Mechanics' liens   CC §8042
Slander   CC §46
Sliding scale recovery agreements   CCP §877.5

Index

Index

Index

Index

DESTRUCTION OF INSTRUMENTS AND RECORDS—Cont.
Oral evidence of contents of destroyed writing, admissibility of   Ev §1523
Parties bound by   CC §1700
Photographic copies as evidence   Ev §1551
Restoration, action for   CC §3415
Secondary evidence of contents of destroyed writing   Ev §§1523, 1551
Superior court records destroyed   CRC 10.855, 10.856
Trust documents deposited with attorney (See **TRUSTS**)
Wills (See **WILLS**)

DESTRUCTION OF PROPERTY
Art works, defacement of   CC §987
Construction, damages for intentional destruction of property under   CC §1721
Escheated property   CCP §1379
Ex parte order enjoining   Fam §6320
    California law enforcement telecommunications (CLETS) information form, confidentiality and use of information   CRC 1.51, CRCAppx A
Sale of realty, risk of loss under contract for   CC §1662

DETAINER
Forcible entry and detainer (See **FORCIBLE ENTRY AND DETAINER**)
Unlawful detainer (See **UNLAWFUL DETAINER**)

DETENTION
Child custody
    Electronic testimony or participation allowed in cases of   Fam §3012

DETERMINABLE ESTATES   CC §§739 to 742

DETINUE
Statute of limitation   CCP §338

DETRIMENT
Damage award, effect on   CC §§3282, 3304 to 3318

DEVALUATION OF CURRENCY
Loan repayment, effect on   CC §1913

DEVELOPERS (See **BUILDING CONSTRUCTION**)

DEVELOPMENTALLY DISABLED PERSONS
Adoption of (See **ADOPTION**)
Conservatorship for (See **CONSERVATORS**)
Criminal offenders
    Judicial commitment
        Appeal from order of civil commitment   CRC 8.483
Defined   Pro §1420
Guardianship for (See **GUARDIAN AND WARD**)
Housing discrimination against disabled persons
    Construction or application of provisions in issue, solicitor general notified   CC §55.2
Information Practices Act, disclosure to patients' rights protection agency under   CC §1798.24b
Judicial commitment
    Appeal from order of civil commitment   CRC 8.483
Juvenile court, inquiry into mental health of child before   CRC 5.643
    Competence of minor subject to juvenile proceedings, doubt as to
        Evaluation of competence   CRC 5.645
Payments pursuant to compromise or judgment for minor or person with disability
    Trusts, payment into   CRC JudAdminStand 7.10
Rape victim incapable of giving consent due to illness, proof that
    Statute of limitations on sexual assault damages   CCP §340.16
Special needs trusts (See **SPECIAL NEEDS TRUSTS**)
Sterilization proceedings (See **STERILIZATION**)
Termination of parental rights, parent declared developmentally disabled or mentally ill
    Circumstances where proceedings may be brought   Fam §7826

DEVELOPMENTAL SERVICES DEPARTMENT
Conservatorship proceedings involving state hospital patient, notice of   Pro §§1461, 1461.4, 1822
Guardianship proceedings involving state hospital patient, notice of   Pro §§1461, 1461.4, 1511
Special needs trust for minor or person with disability, notice of   Pro §§3602, 3605, 3611
    Definition of person with disability   Pro §3603
    Express consent of protected person to court orders, when required   Pro §3613

DEVISEES (See **WILLS**)

DIES, MOLDS AND FORMS
Ownership of   CC §1140

DIETITIANS
Review committees, liability of   CC §§43.7, 43.8

DIFFERENTIAL CASE MANAGEMENT (See **CIVIL RULES**)

DIFFERENTIAL CASE MANAGEMENT RULES (See **TRIAL COURT DELAY REDUCTION**)

DIGITAL ASSETS, FIDUCIARY ACCESS   Pro §§870 to 884 (See **FIDUCIARY ACCESS TO DIGITAL ASSETS**)

DINING FACILITIES (See **RESTAURANTS**)

DIPLOMATS
Ambassadors (See **AMBASSADORS**)
Consuls (See **CONSULS AND CONSULATES**)

DIRECTED VERDICT (See **VERDICT**)

DIRECT EXAMINATION
Adverse party called as witness   Ev §776
Court control over interrogation of witnesses   Ev §765
Definition   CCP §2005, Ev §760
Documents   Ev §768
Expert witnesses   Ev §732
Inconsistent statements by witnesses (See **WITNESSES**)
Leading questions   Ev §§764, 767
Redirect examination (See **REDIRECT EXAMINATION**)
Refreshing memory, witness' use of writings for   Ev §771
Responsive answers from witnesses   Ev §766

DIRECTORIES
Admissibility of   Ev §1340

DIRECTORS
Corporate directors (See **CORPORATE OFFICERS AND EMPLOYEES**)

DISABILITIES, GENERALLY (See **DISABLED PERSONS**)

DISABILITY BENEFITS
Assignment for benefit of creditors, property exempt from   CCP §1801
Exempt property for purposes of enforcement of judgments   CCP §704.130

DISABLED PERSONS
Accessibility of buildings and facilities
    Attorney general, civil actions to enforce
        Fees and costs for attorney general   CCP §1021.8
        Construction or application of provisions in issue, solicitor general notified   CC §55.2
    Construction-related accessibility claims   CC §§55.3 to 55.57, CRCAppx A (See **CONSTRUCTION-RELATED ACCESSIBILITY CLAIMS**)
Accommodations requested of courts, requirements for   CRC 1.100
    Forms
        Judicial council forms   CRCAppx A
Administrative procedure act
    Visual or communication disability
        Narrative description of proposed regulation upon request   Gov §11346.6
Adoption (See **ADOPTION**)
Attorney's disability, appointment of practice administrator in event of   Pro §§2468, 17200
Attorney's performance of professional services, plaintiff's disability tolling statute of limitation for actions arising out of   CCP §340.6
Blindness (See **BLIND PERSONS**)
Building access
    Construction or application of provisions in issue, solicitor general notified   CC §55.2
Commercial and industrial common interest developments
    Disabled access
        Modification of separate interests   CC §6714
Compromise and settlement
    Court approval of compromise
        Appellate court opinions, privacy protection as to use of names in opinions   CRC 8.90
        Forms, use of judicial council forms   CRC 7.101
        Notice of settlement   CRC 3.1385
    Electronic court records
        Courthouse electronic access   CRC 2.503
Construction-related accessibility claims   CC §§55.3 to 55.57 (See **CONSTRUCTION-RELATED ACCESSIBILITY CLAIMS**)
Consumer protection provisions, remedies for disabled persons under   CC §§1780, 3345

Index

DISCLOSURE—Cont.

Inspection of residential property, disclosure to prospective buyer required following   CC §2079

International commercial arbitration and conciliation (See **INTERNATIONAL COMMERCIAL ARBITRATION AND CONCILIATION**)

Investigative consumer reporting agencies (See **INVESTIGATIVE CONSUMER REPORTING AGENCIES**)

Mediation
    Standards of conduct for mediators
        Complaints about mediator conduct, disclosures concerning proceedings   CRC 3.860

Medical records (See **MEDICAL RECORDS**)

Membership camping contracts   CC §1812.302

Mobilehomes (See **MOBILEHOMES**)

Natural hazards, real estate sales   CC §§1103 to 1103.15

Personal records (See **INFORMATION PRACTICES ACT**)

Privileged communications (See **PRIVILEGED COMMUNICATIONS**)

Public guardians, duty to disclose property information to   Pro §2901

Public policy affecting   Ev §§1040 to 1042

Real estate transfer disclosure statements (See **VENDOR AND PURCHASER**)

Renegotiable interest rates   CC §1916.8

Rental-purchase contracts, Karnette Rental-Purchase Act for   CC §§1812.620 to 1812.650

Sale or other transfer of real estate
    AIDS disclosures   CC §1710.2
    Amendment of disclosure   CC §§1102.9, 1103.9
    Applicability of requirements   CC §§1102, 1102.18, 1103.15
    Completion of duty to disclose   CC §1103.5
    Delivery of disclosure statements   CC §§1102.2, 1102.3, 1103.3
    Energy rating   CC §2079.10
    Errors or omissions, liability   CC §§1102.4, 1102.5, 1103.4
    Exempt transactions   CC §1103.1
    Fire hazard severity zone
        High or very high fire hazard severity zone, documentation of compliance with firebreak, vegetation management, etc, requirements   CC §1102.19
        High or very high fire hazard severity zone, notice by seller to buyer   CC §1102.6f
    Form for disclosure statement
        Local requirements, form of statement reflecting   CC §1102.6a
    Forms
        Natural hazards, disclosure concerning   CC §1103.2
    Legislative intent   CC §1102.1
    Mello-Roos Community Facilities Act, disclosure regarding special tax liens on transfer of property pursuant to   CC §1102.6b
    Other laws, effect   CC §1103.8
    Residential property   CC §§1102 to 1103.15
    Taxation
        Supplemental property tax bills   CC §1102.6c
    Water conservation programs   CC §2079.10
    Water conserving plumbing retrofits
        Disclosures as to noncompliant plumbing fixtures   CC §1102.155

Seller assisted marketing plans   CC §§1812.203, 1812.205, 1812.206

Seminar sales contracts, disclosure requirement in   CC §1689.21

Sex offenses
    Disclosure requirements for transactions involving sex offenders   CC §2079.10a

Shared appreciation loans (See **SHARED APPRECIATION LOANS**)

Sliding scale recovery agreement between joint tortfeasors   CCP §877.5

Social security numbers, prohibiting posting or display to general public of   CC §1798.85
    Financial institutions, continued use   CC §1786.60
    Waiver of protections   CC §1798.86

Transfer or sale of residential property, disclosure statements involving (See **VENDOR AND PURCHASER**)

Trust deeds and mortgages (See **TRUST DEEDS AND MORTGAGES**)

Unemployment insurance administration, information obtained through   Ev §1040

Vendor and purchaser (See **VENDOR AND PURCHASER**)

Waiver of privilege   Ev §919

Wheelchairs offered for sale or lease, defects in returned   CC §1793.025

DISCOUNTS

Credit card, discount for purchase by means other than   CC §§1748, 1748.1

Discount buying services contracts   CC §§1812.100 to 1812.129

Supermarket club cards (See **GROCERY STORES**)

DISCOVERY   CRC 3.1000, 3.1010

Abuse of discovery process, sanctions for (See **DISCOVERY ABUSES, SANCTIONS FOR**)

Accounting companies disclosing information during   CC §1799.1

DISCOVERY—Cont.

Actions
    Defined   CCP §2016.020

Administration of estates
    Conveyance or transfer of property claimed by decedent or other person   Pro §851.1
    Law and motion rules
        Applicable to discovery proceedings in probate   CRC 3.1100

Administrative adjudication (See **ADMINISTRATIVE ADJUDICATION**)

Aliens
    Children and minors
        Discovery into immigration status prohibited   CC §3339.5

Appeals
    Discovery pending appeal
        Perpetuation of testimony or preservation of information pending appeal   CCP §§2036.010 to 2036.050
    Interstate and international depositions and discovery act
        Choice of law to resolve disputes, appeal for extraordinary writ   CCP §2029.650

Arbitration   CCP §1283.05
    Judicial arbitration (See **JUDICIAL ARBITRATION**)

Attachment order, discovery by plaintiff allowed pursuant to   CCP §485.230

Attorney work product   CCP §§2018.010 to 2018.080
    Breach of attorney-client relationship   CCP §2018.080
    Clients
        Defined   CCP §2018.010
    Construction of provisions to restate existing law   CCP §2018.040
    Crime or fraud, participation by attorney
        No protection of work product   CCP §2018.050
    Deposition on written question
        Objection to question based on work product   CCP §2028.050
    Disciplinary proceedings of state bar   CCP §2018.070
    Electronically stored information (ESI)
        Applicable rules   CCP §2020.220
        Subpoenas, applicability of privilege   CCP §1985.8
    In camera hearings   CCP §2018.060
    Inspection demands for electronically stored information
        Privilege claimed or attorney work product protection requested   CCP §2031.285
    Mental examinations, discovery procedure for
        Reports of examination, waiver of work product privilege   CCP §§2032.610, 2032.630
    Physical examinations, discovery procedure for
        Reports of examination, waiver of work product privilege   CCP §§2032.610, 2032.630
    Policy of state   CCP §2018.020
    When discoverable   CCP §2018.030

Boundary dispute involving state, disclosure of written evidence in   CCP §2031.510

Censure, removal or admonishment of judges (See **JUDGES**)

Child support (See **CHILD SUPPORT**)

Chiropractic review boards, exemption of records of   Ev §1157

Civil discovery act   CCP §§2016.010 to 2036.050
    Short title of provisions   CCP §2016.010

Class actions   CRC 3.768

Conduct of discovery
    Civil rules   CRC 3.1010

Contempt   CCP §1991.1

Continuance of trial proceedings includes   CCP §595.1

Coordinated actions   CRC 3.541

Copies
    Demand for inspection, copying, testing or sampling
        Inspection demands generally   CCP §§2031.010 to 2031.510 (See **INSPECTION DEMANDS**)

Courts
    Defined   CCP §2016.020

Custodial officer's personnel records   Ev §§1043 to 1047

Dead bodies
    Video recordings or photographs of dead bodies taken by coroners   CCP §129

Declaration for additional discovery
    Limitation on papers filed   CRC 3.250

Definitions   CCP §2016.020

Demand for inspection of documents, tangible things, land or other property (See **INSPECTION DEMANDS**)

Dental committee records subject to discovery   Ev §§1156, 1157

Dental hygienist review committee records exempt from   Ev §1157

Dependent adults
    Elder abuse and dependent adult civil protection act   CCP §§2017.310, 2017.320

Index

Index

DISTRICTS—Cont.

Reorganization

Contesting reorganization, limitation of actions for   CCP §349.1

Validation procedure   CCP §349.4

School districts (See **SCHOOL DISTRICTS**)

Service of process on   CCP §416.50

Statutes of limitation

Boundaries, actions to contest change of   CCP §349.1

Contesting formation, dissolution, consolidation or change of organization   CCP §349.1

Unclaimed deposits and payments escheated   CCP §1519

Unclaimed property, disposition of   CC §2080.6

Validation proceedings   CCP §§860 to 870

Venue in actions by or against   CCP §394

DIVERSION OF CRIMINAL DEFENDANTS

Juvenile wardship proceedings

Diversion services

Sealing of records upon satisfactory completion of informal supervision, diversion, etc   CRC 5.850

Mental disorders, individuals with

Pretrial diversion   CRC 4.130

Traffic violators   CRC 4.104

DIVIDENDS

Corporate shareholders (See **CORPORATE SHARES AND SHAREHOLDERS**)

Income of property   CC §748

DIVISION OF CODES (See **TITLES AND DIVISION OF CODES**)

DIVISION OF MARITAL PROPERTY (See **COMMUNITY PROPERTY; DISSOLUTION OF MARRIAGE**)

DIVORCE (See **DISSOLUTION OF MARRIAGE**)

DMV (See **MOTOR VEHICLES DEPARTMENT**)

DNA TESTING

Genetic information generally (See **GENETIC INFORMATION**)

Parentage

Genetic testing to determine parentage   Fam §§7550 to 7562 (See **PATERNITY**)

DOCKS (See **WHARVES**)

DOCTORS

Generally (See **PHYSICIANS AND SURGEONS**)

Chiropractors (See **CHIROPRACTORS**)

Dentists (See **DENTISTS**)

Opticians and optometrists (See **OPTICIANS AND OPTOMETRISTS**)

Osteopaths (See **OSTEOPATHS**)

Podiatry and podiatrists (See **PODIATRY AND PODIATRISTS**)

Psychotherapists (See **PSYCHOTHERAPISTS**)

Veterinarians (See **VETERINARIANS AND VETERINARY TECHNICIANS**)

DOCUMENTARY EVIDENCE

Ancient documents, admissibility of   Ev §1331

Arbitration proceedings

Judicial arbitration   CRC 3.823

Attorney-client privilege applicable in determining validity of   Ev §§959 to 961

Authentication   Ev §§403, 1400 to 1454

Best and secondary evidence (See **BEST AND SECONDARY EVIDENCE**)

Business records (See **BUSINESS RECORDS**)

Cancellation of instruments (See **CANCELLATION OF INSTRUMENTS**)

Certificates (See **CERTIFICATES AND CERTIFICATION**)

Contracts (See **CONTRACTS AND AGREEMENTS**)

Copies (See **BEST AND SECONDARY EVIDENCE**)

Duplicate defined   Ev §260

Examination as to contents of documents   Ev §768

Exhibits (See **EXHIBITS**)

Hearsay rule, writing previously made by witness as admissible under   Ev §1237

Inspection demands during discovery (See **INSPECTION DEMANDS**)

Literary property (See **LITERARY PROPERTY**)

Lost instruments (See **LOST INSTRUMENTS**)

Medical records (See **MEDICAL RECORDS**)

Newspapers and periodicals, presumption regarding publications purporting to be   Ev §645.1

Original defined   Ev §255

Part of writing offered, entire instrument examined   Ev §356

Petitions (See **PETITIONS**)

DOCUMENTARY EVIDENCE—Cont.

Presumptions

Authenticity   Ev §643

Date   Ev §640

Newspapers and periodicals, publications purporting to be   Ev §645.1

Truth of recitals in   Ev §622

Privilege claims concerning attested documents   Ev §§959, 1002, 1003, 1021, 1022

Refreshing memory, witness' use of writings for   Ev §771

Statute of frauds (See **STATUTE OF FRAUDS**)

DOCUMENTARY FILMS

Animals depicted in   CC §3508

DOCUMENTARY TRANSFER TAX

Records and recording

Fees

Effect of tax on additional fees   Gov §27388

DOCUMENTS AND PAPERS

Abbreviations in legal papers   CCP §186

Best evidence (See **BEST AND SECONDARY EVIDENCE**)

Change of venue, transfer of pleadings and papers on   CCP §399

Claims against decedent's estate based on written instruments, filing requirements for   Pro §9152

Common carrier's liability for   CC §2200

Common interest developments (See **COMMON INTEREST DEVELOPMENTS**)

Deposit of estate-planning documents with attorney (See **TRUSTS; WILLS**)

Destruction (See **DESTRUCTION OF INSTRUMENTS AND RECORDS**)

English language, papers and proceedings to be in   CCP §185

Evidence (See **DOCUMENTARY EVIDENCE**)

Fact of death (See **FACT OF DEATH**)

FAX filing of legal documents (See **FAX FILING AND SERVICE**)

Inspection of documents and things (See **INSPECTION DEMANDS**)

Jury taking into jury room   CCP §612

Medical records (See **MEDICAL RECORDS**)

Numerals in legal papers   CCP §186

Privacy protection   CRC 1.20

Records and recordings (See **RECORDS AND RECORDING**)

Recycled paper (See **RECYCLED PRODUCTS**)

Request for production of (See **INSPECTION DEMANDS**)

Seal of court, documents requiring   CCP §153

Service of (See **SERVICE OF PAPERS**)

Superior court fees

Hearings, filing motion, application or paper filed which would require   Gov §70617

Superior court rules (See **SUPERIOR COURTS**)

DOGS

Biting dogs

Duty of owner to protect others from   CC §3342.5

Liability of owner   CC §3342

Claims against public entities and employees

Dog parks owned or operated by public entity

Death or injury caused by actions of dog, immunity of public entity   Gov §831.7.5

Damages

Animals, injury to   CC §3341

Biting by dogs   CC §3342

Dangerous and vicious

Forms

Judicial council legal forms   CRCAppx A

Liability of owner   CC §§3341 to 3342.5

Licensing and regulation

Judicial council legal forms   CRCAppx A

Deaf persons, signal dogs for   CC §§54.1, 54.2

Construction or application of provisions in issue, solicitor general notified   CC §55.2

Discrimination

Law enforcement officers, firefighters, or search and rescue dog handlers serving outside jurisdiction

Lodging, eating, or transportation, prohibition on discrimination   CC §54.25

Fighting

Property used for dog or cock fighting as nuisance   CC §3482.8

Unlawful detainer actions   CCP §1161

Firefighters

Assignment of firefighter to canine unit serving outside jurisdiction

Prohibition on discrimination in lodging, eating, or transportation due to dog   CC §54.25

Guide dogs (See within this heading, **"Seeing eye dogs"**)

Index

Index

Index

EASEMENTS—Cont.

Rents, right of collecting CC §§802, 808
Repair, duty of CC §845
Restrictions defined CC §784
Right of way
    Generally CC §§801, 802
    Repairs CC §845
Riparian rights CC §801
Servient tenement defined CC §803
Snow removal CC §845
Solar easements CC §§801, 801.5
Sports, using land for CC §801
Statute of frauds CC §1624, CCP §1971
Streets CC §802
Termination CC §811
Timber, taking of CC §§801, 802
Tolls, right to collect CC §802
Vested estate, easement in CC §§804, 805
Walls, use of CC §801
Waste, easement affecting right to prevent CC §808
Water CC §§801, 802

EAVESDROPPING AND WIRETAPPING

Dissolution of marriage proceedings, inadmissibility of evidence in Fam §2022

E-BOOKS

Privacy
    Reader privacy act CC §§1798.90, 1798.90.05

ECOLOGY (See ENVIRONMENTAL HAZARDS)

ECONOMIC LITIGATION PROCEDURES

Affidavit or declaration, prepared testimony by CCP §98
Appeal, right to CCP §100
Applicability of economic litigation provisions CCP §91
Applicability of law for civil actions generally CCP §90
Case questionnaires CCP §93
Conclusive effect of judgment or final order CCP §99
Discovery
    Additional discovery, motion or stipulation for CCP §95
    Case questionnaire CCP §93
    Permissible forms of discovery CCP §94
    Request for statement identifying witnesses and evidence CCP §96
    Sanctions for failure to respond to case questionnaire CCP §93
Exclusion of evidence or witnesses not included in statement CCP §97
Forms
    Case questionnaires CCP §93
    Request for statement identifying witnesses and evidence CCP §96
Permissible pleadings and motions CCP §92
Prepared testimony by affidavit or declaration CCP §98
Request for statement identifying witnesses and evidence CCP §96
Sanctions for failure to respond to case questionnaire CCP §93
Withdrawal of action from economic litigation requirements CCP §91

ECONOMIC STATUS

Jury service exemption not allowed based on CCP §204

ECONOMY AND EFFICIENCY

Separate trial of issues CCP §598

EDITORS

Contempt charge for refusal to reveal source of information Ev §1070

EDUCATION

Child custody mediators and investigators, continuing education requirements for Fam §3165
Community property rights regarding (See COMMUNITY PROPERTY)
Conciliation Court counselors, continuing education programs Fam §1816
Conservators
    Appointment of person to make educational decisions for minor Pro §2662
    Court staff Pro §1456
    Non-professional conservators or guardians, educational program Pro §1457
Expert witnesses, qualification of Ev §§720, 801
Guardianships
    Appointment of person to make educational decisions for minor Pro §2662
    Court staff Pro §1456
    Non-professional conservators or guardians, educational program Pro §1457
Judges
    Domestic violence issues CRC 10.464

EDUCATION—Cont.

Judges—Cont.
    Family law matters CRC 10.463, CRC JudAdminStand 5.30
    Judicial branch education generally CRC 10.451 to 10.491
    Probate cases, judges and subordinate judicial officers regularly assigned to CRC 10.468
        Domestic violence issues CRC 10.464
    Temporary judges
        Training programs CRC 2.813
    Trial Court Delay Reduction Act, training program under Gov §68610
Judicial officers' education (See JUDGES)
Law students (See LAW STUDENTS)
Spousal support, consideration of education and training of supported spouse Fam §4320

EDUCATIONAL DEBT COLLECTION PRACTICES CC §§1788.90 to 1788.93

Definitions CC §1788.92
Legislative findings and intent CC §1788.91
Prohibited debt collection practices by schools CC §1788.93
Short title of act CC §1788.90
Transcript used as leverage to collect debt, prohibition CC §1788.93

EDUCATIONAL ORGANIZATIONS

Judge's office in organization not a financial interest for purposes of disqualification CCP §170.5

EFFECTIVE DATES

Code of Civil Procedure CCP §2

E-FILING

Appellate rules, supreme court and courts of appeal
    E-filing in supreme court and courts of appeal CRC 8.70 to 8.79
        Supreme court-specific rules CRCSupp SuprCtE-file 1 to CRCSupp SuprCtE-file 13
Electronic filing and service generally CCP §1010.6, CRC 2.250 to 2.261 (See ELECTRONIC FILING AND SERVICE)

EGG DONATION FOR FERTILITY TREATMENTS

Parent-child relationship, effect on Fam §7613

EGRESS (See ACCESS)

ELDER ABUSE (See SENIOR CITIZENS)

ELDERLY PERSONS (See SENIOR CITIZENS)

ELECTION OF RIGHTS OR REMEDIES

Judicial arbitration, election for (See JUDICIAL ARBITRATION)
Small claims court advisory services, election with respect to CCP §116.940

ELECTION OF SURVIVING SPOUSE

Small estates without administration (See SMALL ESTATES WITHOUT ADMINISTRATION)
Will, election to take against (See WILLS)

ELECTIONS AND ELECTIONS PROCEEDINGS

Campaign funds
    Judges, contributions by CRCSupp JudEthicsCanon 5
Campaigns
    Judges, political activities by CRCSupp JudEthicsCanon 5
Candidates for office (See CANDIDATES FOR OFFICE)
Conservatee's right to vote Pro §§1865, 1910
Judicial elections
    Campaign contributions
        Disclosures CRCSupp JudEthicsCanon 3
        Disqualification from case, contribution as grounds CCP §170.1
    Code of judicial ethics
        Disclosures of campaign contributions CRCSupp JudEthicsCanon 3
        Leave, applicability of code to judge on leave to pursue election to other office CRCSupp JudEthicsCanon 6
    Ethical obligations of candidates CRCSupp JudEthicsCanon 6
    Judicial performance, commission on
        Ethics code for commission members JudPerPolicy 6.4
    Political activities by judges CRCSupp JudEthicsCanon 5
Mobilehomes
    Signs, placement of
        Political campaign signs CC §§798.51, 799.10
Political vote, evidentiary privilege to refuse disclosure of Ev §1050
Precedence
    Certification of ballot measures, cases involving CCP §35
    Certification of candidates, cases involving CCP §35

Index

Index

Index

Index

Index

Index

Index

Index

Index

Index

Index

Index

Index

FARMS AND FARMERS—Cont.

Common interest developments

    Personal agriculture by homeowner

        Unreasonable restrictions in governing documents, void   CC §4750

Dairies (See **DAIRIES AND DAIRY PRODUCTS**)

Disclosures incident to residential land transfers

    Right to farm notice   CC §1103.4

Eminent domain   CCP §1263.250

Enforcement of judgments (See **ENFORCEMENT OF JUDGMENTS**)

Fixtures, farm products as   CC §660

Irrigation (See **IRRIGATION**)

Landlord and tenant

    Personal agriculture by tenant   CC §1940.10

Lease restrictions   CC §717

Liens by farm workers   CC §§3061 to 3061.6

Nuisances

    Agricultural activities and operations in general, exclusion of   CC §3482.5

    Agricultural processing facilities, exclusion of   CC §3482.6

Owner's immunity for injury to person invited on premises to glean farm products for charitable purposes   CC §846.2

Repair of farm machinery, invoice requirements for   CC §1718

Right to farm

    Disclosures incident to residential land transfers   CC §1103.4

Small business action, costs in   CCP §1028.5

FAST TRACK RULES OF COURT (See **TRIAL COURT DELAY REDUCTION**)

FAX FILING AND SERVICE   CRC 2.300 to 2.306

Certification of documents and papers for court filing   CRC 2.303

Confidentiality requirements   CRC 2.303

    Juvenile court   CRC 5.522

Court proceedings and documents and papers subject to   CRC 2.300

Cover sheet   CRC 2.304

    Juvenile court   CRC 5.522

Credit card payment of fax filing charges   CCP §1010.5, CRC 2.304

Definitions   CRC 2.301

Direct filing   CRC 2.304

    Fees

        Courts, authority to set fees for products or services   CRC 10.815

Errors in fax transmission when unknown to sending party, effect of   CRC 2.304

Excluded documents and papers from   CRC 2.300

Fax filing agency

    Defined   CRC 2.301

    Duties of   CRC 2.303

Fees

    Accounts for filing fees   CRC 2.304

    Courts, authority to set fees for products or services   CRC 10.815

    Credit or debit card payments   CRC 2.304

1st Appellate District local rules   CRCSupp 1st AppDist

Inspection rights of other party to original signed document   CRC 2.305

Judicial Council to adopt rules governing filing of papers by facsimile transmission   CCP §1010.5

Judicial performance, commission on

    Censure, removal, admonishment or retirement of judges

        Filing with Commission   JudPerR 119.5

Juvenile court   CRC 5.522

Levying officer electronic transactions act   CCP §§263 to 263.7

Methods of filing   CCP §1013

    Direct filing   CRC 2.304

    Fax filing agency

        Defined   CRC 2.301

        Duties   CRC 2.303

Motion for order nunc pro tunc as judicial remedy for failure to file caused by errors unknown to sending party   CRC 2.304

Original document, sending party in possession or control of   CRC 2.305

Papers, form or format

    Documents for faxing to comply with provisions   CRC 2.302

Presumption of filing   CRC 2.304

Proof of service   CRC 2.306

Service, generally   CCP §1013, CRC 2.306

Service lists   CRC 2.306

Signature requirement   CRC 2.305

    Juvenile court   CRC 5.522

Small claims courts

    Claims, fax filing   CCP §116.320

FAX NUMBER

Change of number

    Service and filing notice of change   CRC 2.200

        Appeals   CRC 8.32, 8.816

FEDERAL COURTS

Automobile lease action previously filed in   CC §2989

Certification of state-law questions to California Supreme Court by federal appellate courts   CRC 8.548

Injunctions against proceedings in   CC §3423

Judicial notice of rules prescribed by   Ev §451

Notice of pendency of action on real property, applicability of state law in U.S district courts for filing of   CCP §405.5

Statutes of limitation upon judgment or decree of   CCP §337.5

Time for response after remand from   CCP §430.90

FEDERAL ENCLAVES

Appropriation of water originating in   CC §1422

Real property law of state, applicability of   CC §755

FEDERAL GOVERNMENT (See **UNITED STATES**)

FEDERAL LIEN REGISTRATION ACT   CCP §§2100 to 2107

Fees for recording under act   Gov §27388.1

FEEBLE MINDED PERSONS (See **DEVELOPMENTALLY DISABLED PERSONS**)

FEED YARDS

Liens   CC §3051

FEES (See also **COMPENSATION; COSTS**)

Administrative adjudication (See **ADMINISTRATIVE ADJUDICATION**)

Administrators (See **EXECUTORS AND ADMINISTRATORS**)

Admitted surety insurer (See **SURETYSHIP, BONDS AND UNDERTAKINGS**)

Adoption (See **ADOPTION**)

Answers

    Filing fees (See **ANSWERS**)

Appellate rules, superior court appeals

    Costs

        Recoverable costs   CRC 8.891

    Limited civil cases in appellate division

        Notice of appeal   CRC 8.821

Appellate rules, supreme court and courts of appeal (See **APPELLATE RULES, SUPREME COURT AND COURTS OF APPEAL**)

Arbitration (See **ARBITRATION**)

Arrest

    Witnesses, arrest on bench warrant

        Fee for processing civil warrant   Gov §26744.5

Attachment (See **ATTACHMENT**)

Attorney general

    Civil actions enforcing public rights   CCP §1021.8

Attorneys' fees (See **ATTORNEY'S FEES**)

Burden of proof

    Evasion or fraud cases   Ev §524

Change of venue   CCP §399

Check for fees returned unpaid   CCP §411.20

Checks, court fees paid by   CCP §411.20

    Underpayment   CCP §411.21

Claims against public entities and employees

    State, claims against

        Filing fees   Gov §905.2

Clerks of court (See **CLERKS OF COURT**)

Complaints

    Filing generally (See **COMPLAINTS**)

Complex litigation

    Designation fee   Gov §70616

        Permissible additional fees   Gov §70603

Conciliation court proceedings, filing of petition   Fam §1835

Confession of judgments   CCP §1134

Confidential marriages, application for approval of notaries to authorize   Fam §536

Conservatorships (See **CONSERVATORS**)

Conveyances

    Transfer fees   CC §§1098, 1098.5

        Disclosures as to fees   CC §1102.6e

County clerks (See **CLERKS OF COURT**)

County recorders (See **RECORDS AND RECORDING**)

Court reporters (See **COURT REPORTERS**)

Credit card or debit card payments   CRC 3.100

Credit reports (See **CREDIT REPORTING**)

Debit card payments   CRC 3.100

Debt collectors   CC §1788.14

Depositions (See **DEPOSITIONS**)

Dissolution of marriage (See **DISSOLUTION OF MARRIAGE**)

Domestic violence protective orders, filing fees for (See **DOMESTIC VIOLENCE**)

Index

FOREST FIRE PREVENTION AND CONTROL
Realty located in forest fire hazard area, disclosure to purchaser   CC §§1103 to 1103.15

FORESTRY
Appropriation of water originating in national forest   CC §1422
Conservation easements
    Forest health maintenance and improvement
        Landowner responsibility as part of easement management plan   CC §815.11
Fines and penalties
    Bail schedule   CRC 4.102
Forestry and fire protection department
    Donations of apparatus to volunteer fire departments
        Immunity from liability   CC §1714.11
Logs and timbers (See **LOGS AND TIMBER**)

FORESTRY AND FIRE PROTECTION DEPARTMENT
Bail and penalty schedules for violating forestry regulations   CRC 4.102

FORFEITURES   CC §3275
Bail (See **BAIL**)
Corporate charter or right to do business (See **CORPORATIONS**)
Enforcement restrictions   CC §3369
Future interest defeated by   CC §741
Judicial council, budgeting responsibilities
    Fee, fine and forfeiture revenue
        New revenue, allocation   CRC 10.105
Leases (See **UNLAWFUL DETAINER**)
Liens, property subject to   CC §2889
Oil and gas liens on leasehold estates   CCP §1203.55
Statutes of limitation
    Action upon statute for forfeiture   CCP §340
    Against officer to recover damages for seizure of property for statutory forfeiture   CCP §340
    Corporation, actions against directors, shareholders or members of   CCP §359
Venue in actions for recovery of   CCP §393

FORGERY
Statutes of limitation for payment of forged or raised check   CCP §340
Trust deeds (See **TRUST DEEDS AND MORTGAGES**)

FORMA PAUPERIS
Application to proceed in forma pauperis
    Waiver of fees and costs
        Application   CRC 3.50 to 3.58 (See **CIVIL RULES**)
        Bench warrants to secure attendance of witnesses, applicability of waiver   Gov §26744.5
        Generally   Gov §§68630 to 68641 (See **INDIGENT PERSONS**)

FORMATION (See **PUBLIC ENTITIES**)

FORMER ADJUDICATION (See **RES JUDICATA**)

FORMER NAME
Change of name, right at common law to   CCP §1279.5
Women using   CCP §1279.5

FORMER TESTIMONY
Admissibility of   Ev §§1290 to 1293

FORMS
Acknowledgments (See **ACKNOWLEDGMENTS**)
Administration of estates (See **ADMINISTRATION OF ESTATES**)
Adoption (See **ADOPTION**)
Alternative dispute resolution
    Judicial council legal forms   CRCAppx A
Annulment of marriage
    Judicial council legal forms   CRCAppx A
Appearances
    Notice to appear forms
        Judicial council legal forms   CRCAppx A
Appellate forms
    Judicial council legal forms   CRCAppx A
Approved forms, use of (See **JUDICIAL COUNCIL**)
Attorney in fact (See **POWER OF ATTORNEY**)
Automobiles (See **AUTOMOBILES**)
Bonds by party to action   CCP §995.330
Case management
    Judicial council legal forms   CRCAppx A

FORMS—Cont.
Case questionnaires under economic litigation provisions for limited civil cases, responsibility for development of   CCP §93
Child custody and visitation
    Judicial council legal forms   CRCAppx A
Child support
    Case registry forms   CRC 5.330
    Government support enforcement services
        Judicial council legal forms   CRCAppx A
Civil rules
    Waiver of fees and costs, application
        Forms for application   CRC 3.51
        Judicial council legal forms   CRCAppx A
Claim and delivery
    Generally (See **CLAIM AND DELIVERY**)
    Judicial council legal forms   CRCAppx A
Claims against estates (See **CLAIMS AGAINST ESTATES**)
Conciliation court, caption of petition filed in   Fam §1832
Construction-related accessibility claims
    Judicial council legal forms   CRCAppx A
Criminal law and procedure
    Judicial council legal forms   CRCAppx A
Decedent's estates
    Judicial council legal forms   CRCAppx A
    Notice to creditors to file claims against   Pro §9052
Deeds   CC §1092
Delinquent children
    Judicial council legal forms   CRCAppx A
Dependent child of court proceedings
    Judicial council legal forms   CRCAppx A
Destroyed land records relief law proceedings   CCP §§751.05, 751.23
Discovery
    Judicial council legal forms   CRCAppx A
Dissolution of marriage proceedings, forms of notice to insurance carriers in   Fam §§2050, 2051
Divorce
    Judicial council legal forms   CRCAppx A
Domestic violence
    Forms approved by Judicial Council
        List of judicial council legal forms   CRCAppx A
Donative transfers
    Presumption of fraud or undue influence
        Certificate of independent review   Pro §21384
Economic litigation procedures (See **ECONOMIC LITIGATION PROCE-DURES**)
Elder abuse and neglect
    Judicial council legal forms   CRCAppx A
Electronic filing and service rules
    Judicial council forms   CRCAppx A
    Modification of judicial council forms   CRC 2.261
Emancipation of children (See **EMANCIPATION OF MINORS**)
Emergency protective orders
    Judicial council legal forms   CRCAppx A
Eminent domain valuation statements   CCP §1258.210
Enforcement of judgments (See **ENFORCEMENT OF JUDGMENTS**)
Executors and administrators (See **EXECUTORS AND ADMINISTRATORS**)
Family law proceedings (See **FAMILY RULES**)
Fax filing of legal documents (See **FAX FILING AND SERVICE**)
Fees
    Courts, authority to set fees for products or services   CRC 10.815
Forma pauperis, application for fee and cost waivers
    Forms for application   CRC 3.51
        Judicial council legal forms   CRCAppx A
Garnishment (See **GARNISHMENT**)
Grain sold in bulk, form of notice of   CC §1880.7
Guardian and ward (See **GUARDIAN AND WARD**)
Handwritten or handprinted forms   CRC 2.135
Harassment
    Judicial council legal forms   CRCAppx A
Home solicitation contract, cancellation of   CC §1689.7
Ignition interlock devices
    Judicial council legal forms   CRCAppx A
Insurers notified in dissolution of marriage proceedings   Fam §§2050, 2051
Interpreters
    Judicial council legal forms   CRCAppx A
Interrogatories
    Form interrogatories
        List of judicial council legal forms   CRCAppx A
Judge, peremptory challenge of   CCP §170.6
Judgments
    Judicial council legal forms   CRCAppx A

Index

G

GAMBLING
Inspection warrants, authorization for   CCP §1822.60
Native Americans
Injunction to protect gaming rights   CCP §1811
Public nuisance, attorney's fees recoverable for enjoining use of building for illegal gambling as   CC §3496

GANG VIOLENCE
Decedent's sworn statement
Administration and certification of oath   Ev §1231.2
Admissibility under hearsay rule, generally   Ev §1231
Jury instructions concerning unavailability of witness   Ev §1231.4
Notice of intent to offer statement, requirement for   Ev §1231.1
Peace officer testifying concerning statement, qualifications of   Ev §1231.3
Injunction for relief from   CCP §527.7
Shared gang databases
Appeal of designation
Proceedings for review   CRC 3.2300

GARAGES (See PARKING FACILITIES)

GARBAGE
Leases premises, disposal of garbage from   CC §§1941.1, 1941.2

GARNISHMENT
Accounting report from levying officer   CCP §706.026
Applicable law governing   CCP §706.020
Application for earnings withholding order
Generally   CCP §706.102
Contents of   CCP §706.121
Process server, application for issuance of withholding order by   CCP §706.108
Child support
Earnings assignment for support (See EARNINGS ASSIGNMENT FOR SUPPORT)
Priority of withholding orders   CCP §706.030
Withholding order for support (See within this heading, "Withholding order for support")
Consumer Credit Protection Act of 1968 affecting   CCP §706.151
Costs
Court order or memorandum of costs allowing additional costs as part of   CCP §685.090
Final earnings withholding order to collect unsatisfied costs and interests   CCP §706.028
Court order for withholding order against earnings of spouse   CCP §706.109
Creation of lien on earnings   CCP §706.029
Definitions   CCP §706.011
Dismissal of employee, restrictions on   Pro §3088
Disposable earnings
Defined   CCP §706.011
Maximum amount of disposable earnings   CCP §706.050
Distribution when levy less than wage claims   CCP §1208
Duration of lien on earnings   CCP §706.029
Duties and instruction of employers
Generally   CCP §§706.022, 706.104
Form of instructions   CCP §706.127
General requirements for service of documents on employer   CCP §706.103
Violation of employer, failure to withhold or pay over constituting   CCP §§706.152 to 706.154
Duties of levying officer   CCP §706.026
Earnings assignment for support (See EARNINGS ASSIGNMENT FOR SUPPORT)
Earnings withholding order
Amount required from employer to satisfy   CCP §706.024
Application for (See within this heading, "Application for earnings withholding order")
Contents of   CCP §706.125
Costs and interest, judgment creditor seeking additional earnings withholding order for   CCP §706.028
Deduction for employer from payments under order   CCP §706.034
Earnings assignment for support, priority of   CCP §706.031
Elder and dependent adult abuse cases
Judicial council forms   CRCAppx A
Exemptions generally (See within this heading, "Exemptions")
Interest not collected, final earnings withholding order for   CCP §706.028
Levy of execution effective on service of   CCP §706.021
Lien upon earnings, creation and duration of   CCP §706.029
Multiple orders, effect of service of   CCP §706.023

GARNISHMENT—Cont.
Earnings withholding order—Cont.
Notice to employer
Generally   CCP §706.024
Contents of   CCP §706.122
Satisfaction of judgment   CCP §706.027
Return of order
By employer to levying officer   CCP §706.032
Contents of employer's return   CCP §706.126
Supplemental return by levying officer   CCP §706.033
Return of writ of execution, effect on   CCP §699.560
Service and issuance of orders and exemption claims   CCP §§706.101 to 706.109
State taxes (See within this heading, "Tax liability")
Support, withholding order for (See within this heading, "Withholding order for support")
Termination of order
Employment termination of judgment debtor, effect of   CCP §706.032
Order or assignment with higher priority, earnings of judgment debtor subject to   CCP §706.032
Satisfaction of judgment   CCP §706.027
Supplemental return by levying officer   CCP §706.033
Elder or dependent adult financial abuse
Earnings withholding orders
Defined   CCP §706.011
Priorities   CCP §706.023, CRCAppx A
Equitable division of judgment debtor's earnings, motion for   CCP §706.052
Exemptions
Attorneys' fees for certain purposes not subject to exemption   CCP §706.051
Judgment debtor's exemption claim, contents of   CCP §706.123
Office of levying officer, prescribed forms available at   CCP §706.129
Opposition to exemption claim, contents of notice of   CCP §706.128
Personal services, unavailability of exemption   CCP §706.051
Procedure for claim of   CCP §706.105
Support of debtor or family, earnings necessary for   CCP §706.051
Tax orders from state, unavailability of exemption   CCP §706.051
Time for service of notice of hearing for claim of exemption   CCP §1005
Withholding order for support, earnings exempt from   CCP §706.052
Financial statement of judgment debtor
Contents of   CCP §706.124
Office of levying officer, prescribed forms available at   CCP §706.129
Findings, requirement for   CCP §706.106
Foreign-money claims   CCP §676.11
Forms
Generally   CCP §706.120
Application for issuance of earnings withholding order   CCP §706.121
General contents of earnings withholding order   CCP §706.125
Instructions to employer   CCP §706.127
Judgment debtor's exemption claim, contents of   CCP §706.123
Judicial Council forms, prescribed usage of   CCP §706.120
List of judicial council legal forms   CRCAppx A
Return of employer   CCP §706.126
State tax liability, forms for collection of   CCP §706.081
Inapplicable provisions   CCP §684.310
Interest accrued, final earnings withholding order for   CCP §706.028
Jeopardy withholding order for taxes   CCP §706.078
Judicial Council forms, prescribed usage of   CCP §706.120
Labor claims against garnishee, priority and processing of   CCP §§1206 to 1208
Levy of execution upon earnings of employee made by service of earnings withholding order   CCP §706.021
Lien on earnings, creation and duration of   CCP §706.029
Memorandum of garnishee
Request, service and contents of   CCP §§488.610, 701.030
Third party, liability of   CCP §§488.620, 701.035
Multiple withholding orders, service on employer of   CCP §706.023
Notices
Earnings withholding order (See within this heading, "Earnings withholding order")
Exemption, contents of notice of opposition to claim of   CCP §706.128
Taxes, issuance of withholding order for   CCP §706.072
Time for service of notice of hearing for claim of exemption   CCP §1005
Payment of withheld wages to levying officer   CCP §§706.025, 706.026
Preference to wage claims   CCP §1206
Priorities
Earnings assignment order for support, priority over any earnings withholding order of   CCP §706.031
Labor claims against garnishee   CCP §§1206 to 1208
Withholding order for support, priority over other earnings withholding orders of   CCP §706.030

Index

Index

HALF-BLOOD

Inheritance by kindred of   Pro §6406

HANDICAPPED PERSONS (See DISABLED PERSONS)

HANDWRITING

Authentication of document   Ev §§1415 to 1419
Controlling words   CCP §1862
Holographic wills   Pro §6111
Proof of execution of instruments   CC §1198
Will admitted to probate on proof of   Pro §§8220, 8221

HANG GLIDING

Landowner's liability for injuries from   CC §846

HARASSMENT   CRC 3.1160

Appellate court opinions
    Privacy, use of names in opinions   CRC 8.90
Attorney professional conduct
    Prohibited discrimination, harassment and retaliation   ProfC 8.4.1
Conservators
    Petitions
        Unmeritorious petitions intended to annoy or harass   Pro §1970
Courts
    Workplace conduct policies
        Courts' duties   CRC 10.351
COVID-19, emergency rule   CRCAppx I Emer Rule 8
Debt collectors, harassment by   CC §1788.11
Domestic violence (See DOMESTIC VIOLENCE)
Forms
    Judicial council legal forms   CRCAppx A
Guardian ad litem for minor seeking injunction against harassment or violence   CCP §§372, 374
    Appearance of minor under 12 to request or oppose temporary order   Fam §6229
Injunctive relief   CRC 3.1160
    Address or location of complaining party or family, prohibition on enjoined party from obtaining   CCP §527.10
    California law enforcement telecommunications (CLETS) information form, confidentiality and use of information   CRC 1.51, CRCAppx A
    COVID-19, emergency rule   CRCAppx I Emer Rule 8
    Dependency proceeding
        Firearm relinquishment procedures   CRC 5.495
        Forms for firearm relinquishment   CRCAppx A
    Firearm relinquishment and disposition   CCP §527.9
        Dependency proceeding   CRC 5.495
        Forms for firearm relinquishment   CRCAppx A
    Minor's appearance in proceedings to enjoin harassment or violence   CCP §§372, 374, 374.5
        Appearance of minor under 12 to request or oppose temporary order   Fam §6229
    Minor's information confidentiality, request in civil harassment proceedings   CRC 3.1161, CRCAppx A
        Release of minor's confidential information   CRC 3.1161
    Petition for
        Memorandum in support of petition not required   CRC 3.1114
    Requests for protective orders   CRC 3.1160
    Translation of court orders into languages other than English   CCP §185
Judicial administration rules
    Workplace conduct policies
        Courts' duties   CRC 10.351
Landlord and tenant
    Immigration or citizenship status of tenant, occupant, etc
        Disclosures to immigration authorities with intent to intimidate or harass   CC §1940.35
Mail harassment protective orders
    Denial of petition for ex parte order, reasons to be provided   Fam §6320.5
Minors
    Appearance in proceedings to enjoin harassment or violence
        Appearance of minor under 12 to request or oppose temporary order   Fam §6229
    Privacy protection
        Forms, judicial council   CRCAppx A
Minor's appearance in proceedings to enjoin harassment or violence   CCP §§372, 374, 374.5
Phone harassment protective orders
    Denial of petition for ex parte order, reasons to be provided   Fam §6320.5
Protective orders   CCP §527.6
    Address or location of complaining party or family, prohibition on enjoined party from obtaining   CCP §527.10

HARASSMENT—Cont.
Protective orders —Cont.
    California law enforcement telecommunications (CLETS) information form, confidentiality and use of information   CRC 1.51, CRCAppx A
    COVID-19, emergency rule   CRCAppx I Emer Rule 8
    Denial of petition for ex parte order, reasons to be provided   Fam §6320.5
    Firearm relinquishment and disposition   CCP §527.9
        Forms for firearm relinquishment   CRCAppx A
        Procedures   CRC 4.700, 5.495
    Forms
        Judicial council legal forms   CRCAppx A
    Minor's information confidentiality, request in civil harassment proceedings   CRC 3.1161, CRCAppx A
        Release of minor's confidential information   CRC 3.1161
    Requests for protective orders   CRC 3.1160
Public officials, liability for harassment by   Gov §815.3
Sexual harassment (See SEXUAL HARASSMENT)
Small claims court judgment, award of attorney's fees on appeal from   CCP §116.790
Vexatious litigants   CCP §391.7
Witnesses protected from   Ev §765
Workplace harassment or discrimination
    Restrictions on nondisclosure agreements (NDAs) in certain cases   CCP §1001
Workplace Violence Safety Act
    COVID-19, emergency rule   CRCAppx I Emer Rule 8

HARBORS

Leasing of   CC §718

HARD-OF-HEARING PERSONS (See DEAF AND HARD OF HEARING PERSONS)

HARDSHIP

Child support (See CHILD SUPPORT)
Jury service, grounds for exemption from   CCP §204

HASTINGS COLLEGE OF LAW

Eminent domain taking by   CCP §1245.210

HATE CRIMES

Civil rights violations
    Construction or application of civil rights provisions in issue, solicitor general notified   CC §51.1
Misdemeanor hate crimes
    Sentencing considerations   CRC 4.330
Sentencing   CRC 4.427
    Aggravating circumstances   CRC 4.421
    Misdemeanor hate crimes, sentencing considerations   CRC 4.330
Violence
    Freedom from violence
        Waiver of right to freedom from violence, coerced or involuntary   CC §51.7

HAZARDOUS SUBSTANCES

Emergency response
    Public health and safety labor or service providers
        Logo or identifying mark of public agency, display   CC §3273
Enforcement of standards and regulations
    Civil actions   CCP §338.1
Exposure to hazardous materials or toxic substances
    Statutes of limitation   CCP §340.8
Underground storage
    Attorney general, civil actions to enforce provisions
        Fees and costs for attorney general   CCP §1021.8

HEALTH

Hearsay testimony showing   Ev §§1250 to 1252
Information Practices Act, information furnished under   CC §1798.24
Public health
    Medical information disclosures by providers
        Disease prevention or control   CC §56.10
Spousal support   Fam §4320

HEALTH, ACCIDENT, AND DISABILITY INSURANCE

Adoption
    Notice of reduced-cost options through California health benefit exchange or no-cost Medi-Cal
        Court notice to petitioners for adoption   Fam §8613.7
Advance health care directive as prerequisite for issuance of policy, prohibition on   Pro §4677

Index

IDENTITY THEFT—Cont.
Business entity filings —Cont.
  Order for alleged perpetrator to show cause
    Contents of orders　CC §1798.202
    Findings　CC §1798.202
    Form　CRCAppx A
    Hearing on petition　CC §1798.202
    Petition　CC §1798.201
Certificate of Identity: Judicial Determination of Factual Innocence (CR-150) forms, access to　CRC 4.601
Change of address requests
  Credit card issuers and telephone account businesses
    Notice to customer of requests　CC §1799.1b
Collection agencies
  Duties upon notice from victim of identity theft　CC §1788.18
Common interest developments
  Record inspection
    Withholding or redacting information from records　CC §5215
Consumer credit reporting, security alerts or security freezes for (See **CREDIT REPORTING**)
Continuing jurisdiction of action　CC §1798.95
Credit card application using person's name by unauthorized person　CC §1748.95
Credit reports
  Address verification by users of credit reports　CC §1785.20.3
  Blocking access to fraudulent data　CC §1785.15
  Fees for security freezes for victims prohibited　CC §1785.15
  Security alerts or freezes　CC §§1785.11.1 to 1785.11.11
  Victims to be provided information as to statutory rights　CC §1785.15.3
Debt collectors
  Duties upon notice from victim of identity theft　CC §1788.18
Definitions　CC §1798.92
Escrow agent rating service
  Personally identifiable information, safeguarding　CC §§1785.28, 1785.28.6
Joinder of claimants against victim of identity theft　CC §1798.94
Perpetrator of identity theft, claimant's rights and remedies against　CC §1798.97
Process and service of process
  Levying officer electronic transactions act
    Identifiers, exclusion or redaction　CCP §263.7
Radio frequency identification (RFID)
  Use to remotely read identification document without knowledge or consent　CC §1798.79
    Definitions　CC §1798.795
Social security number confidentiality　CC §§1798.85 to 1798.89
Statute of limitations　CC §1798.96
Victim service providers, personal information protection　CC §§1798.79.8 to 1798.79.95

IGNITION INTERLOCK DEVICES
Forms
  Judicial council legal forms　CRCAppx A
Orders, guidelines　CRC 4.325

ILLEGITIMATE CHILDREN (See **PARENT AND CHILD; PATERNITY**)

ILLNESS
Child support, illness of obligor　Fam §4726
Contagious diseases (See **CONTAGIOUS DISEASES**)
Contempt, effect on person under arrest for　CCP §1221
Cotrustee, illness as grounds for incapacity of　Pro §15622
Genetic information generally (See **GENETIC INFORMATION**)
Inspection warrants for purposes of eradication of (See **INSPECTION WARRANTS**)
Juror, procedure in event of illness of　CCP §233
Last illness (See **LAST ILLNESS**)
Preference, motion for　CCP §36
Telegrams, priority for transmitting　CC §2207
Witnesses unavailable due to　Ev §240

IMMATERIAL ALLEGATIONS
Defined　CCP §431.10

IMMIGRATION
Child custody
  Effect of immigration status　Fam §3040
  Special immigrant juvenile status　CCP §155
    Nonprofit charitable corporations, guardianship of minor with special immigrant juvenile status　Pro §2104.1

IMMIGRATION—Cont.
Consultants
  Attorney general, civil actions to enforce provisions
    Fees and costs for attorney general　CCP §1021.8
  Foreign legal consultants　CRC 9.44
Contracts
  Local government or law enforcement agency contracts to detain noncitizens for civil immigration custody
    Prohibition　CC §1670.9
Criminal law and procedure
  Disclosure of immigration status in open court　Ev §351.4
Damages
  Children and minors
    Immigration status irrelevant　CC §3339.5
Disclosure in open court of immigration status
  Civil actions　Ev §351.3
  Criminal cases　Ev §351.4
Discrimination prohibited　CC §51
Evidence of immigration status
  Disclosure in open court
    Civil actions　Ev §351.3
  Tort or wrongful death cases
    Inadmissibility　Ev §351.2
Family rules
  Request for orders
    Special immigrant juvenile findings, request　CRC 5.130
Forcible entry and detainer
  Immigration or citizenship status irrelevant to issue of liability or remedy　CC §3339.10
Guardianships
  Special immigrant juvenile status
    Appointment of guardians　Pro §1510.1
    Findings　CRC 7.1020
Interpreters
  Juveniles
    Determination of special immigrant juvenile status　Ev §757
Juvenile courts
  Special immigrant juvenile status
    Findings　CRCAppx A
    Guardianships by nonprofit charitable corporation　Pro §2104.1
    Interpreters in proceedings to determine special immigrant juvenile status　Ev §757
    Request for orders, family rules　CRC 5.130
Juvenile status
  Special immigrant juvenile status　CCP §155
    Forms, judicial council　CRCAppx A
    Guardianships by nonprofit charitable corporation　Pro §2104.1
    Request for orders, family rules　CRC 5.130
Landlord and tenant
  Immigration or citizenship status of persons
    Actions to recover possession, restrictions on landlord actions based in immigration or citizenship status　CCP §1161.4
    Definition of immigration or citizenship status　CC §1940.05
    Involuntary quit by tenant, restrictions on landlord actions based in immigration or citizenship status　CCP §1161.4
    Prohibited acts based on　CC §§1940.3, 1940.35
    Retaliation against tenant by reporting or threatening to report to immigration authorities　CC §1942.5
    Unduly influencing tenant to vacate by threating disclosures relating to immigration or citizenship status　CC §1940.2
Minors
  Actions for damages
    Discovery into immigration status prohibited　CC §3339.5
    Immigration status irrelevant　CC §3339.5
Superior court
  Jurisdiction
    Child custody, etc, determinations　CCP §155
Torts
  Evidence of immigration status
    Inadmissibility of evidence in tort or wrongful death cases　Ev §351.2
Wages, hours and working conditions
  Deductions from wages for costs of transport to US
    Void contracts　CC §1670.7
Wrongful death
  Evidence of immigration status
    Inadmissibility of evidence in tort or wrongful death cases　Ev §351.2

IMMIGRATION CONSULTANTS
Foreign legal consultants
  Fingerprinting of special admission attorneys　CRC 9.9.5

IMPROVEMENTS—Cont.
Support from adjacent property for CC §832
Surveyors (See **SURVEYS AND SURVEYORS**)
Taxation (See **TAXATION**)
Trust property Pro §16229

IMPUTED NEGLIGENCE (See **NEGLIGENCE**)

INADVERTENCE (See **MISTAKE**)

IN CAMERA PROCEEDINGS
Sealed records CRC 2.585

INCARCERATION
Jury summons, failure to respond to CCP §209

INCEST
Annulment of marriage Fam §2200
Aunts and nephews, invalidity of marriage between Fam §2200
Siblings, invalidity of marriage between Fam §2200
Uncles and nieces, invalidity of marriage between Fam §2200

INCOME
Accumulations CC §§722 to 726
Blind persons, income considered when renting housing accommodations to CC §§54.1, 54.3, 54.4, 55
Decedent's estate (See **ADMINISTRATION OF ESTATES**)
Disabled persons, income considered when renting housing accommodations to CC §§54.1, 54.3, 54.4, 55
Family law matters, income and expense declaration defined Fam §95
Support proceedings, income and expense declarations in (See **CHILD SUPPORT; SPOUSAL SUPPORT**)
Trust income (See **TRUSTS**)
Unclaimed property fund, separate accounts in CCP §1319
Will (See **WILLS**)

INCOME AND EXPENSE DECLARATION
Child support (See **CHILD SUPPORT**)
Spousal support (See **SPOUSAL SUPPORT**)

INCOME TAX
Child support (See **CHILD SUPPORT**)
Community property
 Joint income tax liability Fam §2628
Decedent's estate, tax claims against Pro §§9200 to 9205
Declaratory judgments in action by nonresident CCP §1060.5
Dissolution of marriage
 Division of community property Fam §2628
Liens by federal government, Uniform Registration Act for CCP §§2100 to 2107
 Fees for recording under act Gov §27388.1
Power of attorney, powers under statutory form of Pro §4463
Public entity's liability for tax law administration Gov §§860 to 860.4
Returns
 Child support delinquency
  Use of return data to collect delinquency Fam §17452
Support proceedings Fam §§3552, 3665, 3667, 4320

INCOMPETENCE (See **MENTAL DISABILITY**)

INCONSISTENT STATEMENTS (See **WITNESSES**)

INCONVENIENCE
Damages recoverable for CC §3333.2

INCONVENIENT FORUM
Generally CCP §§410.30, 410.40
Choice of law (See **CHOICE OF LAW**)
Stay or dismissal of action, motion for CCP §§410.30, 418.10
Tribal court civil money judgment act
 Objections
  Grounds for objection CCP §1737
Uniform Child Custody Jurisdiction and Enforcement Act, inconvenient forum determination under Fam §3427

INCORPORATION BY REFERENCE
Arbitration statutes CCP §1283.1
Fictitious mortgage or trust deed, provisions of CC §2952
Will construction (See **WILL CONSTRUCTION**)

INCRIMINATION (See **SELF-INCRIMINATION**)

INDECENCY AND OBSCENITY
Children and minors
 Offenses against
  Statute of limitations on sexual assault damages CCP §340.16
 Settlement of civil cases
  Confidentiality agreements, restrictions CCP §1002
Debt collectors using obscene language CC §1788.11
Public nuisance, attorney's fees recoverable for enjoining commercial sale or distribution of obscene matter as CC §3496

INDEMNITY
Acceptance of contract CC §2795
Agents covered by CC §2775
Attorneys' fees CCP §1021.6
Bailment, loss from property held under CC §§1893, 1894
Borrowed property, defects in CC §1893
Cartage contracts CC §2784.5
Claims against public entities and employees (See **CLAIMS AGAINST PUBLIC ENTITIES AND EMPLOYEES**)
Community property as consideration for indemnity contract Fam §782
Conditional liability CC §§2806 to 2808
Construction contracts CC §§2782 to 2784
 January 1, 2013, contracts on or after CC §2782.05
 Subcontractor's defense or indemnity obligation CC §2782.05
 Void or unenforceable provisions, insertion CC §2782.05
Costs of action CC §2778, CCP §1038
Damages, reimbursement for CC §2779
Defined CC §2772
Deposits, requirements for CC §1833
Design professionals
 Public agencies, contracts with CC §2782.8
Engineers (See **ENGINEERING**)
Good faith of settlement, contest of CCP §877.6
Hauling contracts CC §2784.5
Hazardous materials identification, indemnity agreements concerning CC §2782.6
Health care service plan, prohibition against indemnification by health care provider for breach of duty by CC §3428
Hospitals, public
 Medical or mental facilities (See **CLAIMS AGAINST PUBLIC ENTITIES AND EMPLOYEES**)
Interpretation of contract CC §§2778, 2782
Joint and several liability CC §2777
Joint tortfeasors, effect of settlement by one of CCP §877.6
Judgment admissible from earlier action Ev §1301
Judicial administration rules
 Contracts with courts CRC 10.203
Latent deficiencies in planning or construction of improvement to real property, limitation of actions for damages for CCP §337.15
Multiple tortfeasors, effect of settlement by one of CCP §877.6
Negligence CC §2784.5
Notices
 Attorneys' fees in indemnity action CCP §1021.6
 Default notice CC §§2807, 2808
Past conduct CC §2774
Public employees, indemnification of (See **PUBLIC OFFICERS AND EMPLOYEES**)
Public officer bonds (See **BONDS OF PUBLIC OFFICIALS**)
Public works
 Wrap-up insurance, construction contracts CC §2782.96
Repairs, contract for CC §2783
Residential construction contracts CC §2782
 Wrap-up insurance, construction contracts CC §2782.9
  Private residential improvement covered CC §2782.95
Retail installment sales financed by third-party loans CC §1801.6
Retail seller's right against manufacturer CC §1792
Rules of construction of indemnity agreements CC §2778
Spouse's act of negligence causing injury to other spouse Fam §782
Trucking contracts CC §2784.5
Two or more persons covered by CC §2776
Unclaimed deposits and payments escheated, indemnity of holder of CCP §1561
Unclaimed property, delivery of CCP §1321
Unlawful conduct, exclusion of CC §2773
Willful misconduct CC §2784.5
Witness, public entity defending or indemnifying Gov §995.9
Wrap-up insurance, construction contracts
 Public works CC §2782.96
 Residential construction CC §2782.9
  Private residential improvements CC §2782.95

INDEPENDENT ADMINISTRATION OF ESTATES ACT
Actions not requiring court supervision Pro §§10550 to 10564

Index

INSPECTION DEMANDS—Cont.

Boundary of land granted by state
    Duty to disclose   CCP §2031.510

Civil rules
    Limitation on papers filed   CRC 3.250

Complete or partial compliance with demand
    Statement as to   CCP §2031.220

Contents of demand   CCP §2031.030

Defendants
    Making demand at any time   CCP §2031.020

Documents produced to respond
    Form   CCP §2031.280
    Organization   CCP §2031.280

Economic litigation provisions for limited civil cases, permissible forms of discovery under   CCP §94

Electronically stored information (ESI)   CCP §2031.010
    Form of information, specifying   CCP §2031.030
    Objections   CCP §2031.240
    Privilege claimed or attorney work product protection requested   CCP §2031.285
    Protective orders   CCP §2031.060
    Response, form of information furnished   CCP §2031.280
    Sanctions for failure to provide, circumstances avoiding   CCP §§2031.300, 2031.320
    Unreasonably inaccessible
        Burden of proof   CCP §2031.060
        Compelling discovery despite burden of providing   CCP §2031.310
        Details as to inaccessible information as part of response   CCP §2031.210

Extension of time to serve response   CCP §2031.270

Failure to serve timely response   CCP §2031.300

Fax filing, inspection of original signed document where subject of   CRC 2.305

Format of demand   CCP §2031.030

Identification by set and number   CCP §2031.030, CRC 3.1000, 3.1345
    Response to demand   CCP §2031.210

Inability to comply   CCP §2031.230

Land patents or grants
    Duty to disclose   CCP §2031.510

Limitation on papers filed   CRC 3.250

Methods of discovery   CCP §§2019.010, 2031.010

Motion to compel
    Response to demand   CCP §2031.300
        Failure to permit inspection in accord with demand   CCP §2031.320
        Further response, motion to compel   CCP §2031.310
    Separate document setting forth item to which further response, answer or production is requested   CRC 3.1345

Numbering demands   CCP §2031.030

Objections
    Response to demand
        Statement regarding demands objectionable in whole or in part   CCP §2031.240

Partial compliance with demand
    Statement as to   CCP §2031.220

Plaintiffs
    When plaintiff may make demand   CCP §2031.020

Privileges
    Electronically stored information
        Privilege claimed or attorney work product protection requested   CCP §2031.285

Protective orders and sanctions   CCP §2031.060

Response to demand   CCP §§2031.210 to 2031.320
    Attorney work product claimed
        Electronically stored information   CCP §2031.285
    Complete or partial compliance with demand
        Statement as to   CCP §2031.220
    Contents   CCP §2031.210
    Documents produced to respond
        Form   CCP §2031.280
        Organization   CCP §2031.280
    Failure to permit inspection in accord with demand   CCP §2031.320
    Further response
        Motion to compel further response   CCP §2031.310, CRC 3.1345
    Identification and sequence of responses   CRC 3.1000
    Inability to comply   CCP §2031.230
    Motion to compel   CCP §2031.300, CRC 3.1345
    Objections
        Statement regarding demands objectionable in whole or in part   CCP §2031.240
    Privilege claimed
        Electronically stored information   CCP §2031.285
    Retention of demand, proof of service and response   CCP §2031.290

INSPECTION DEMANDS—Cont.

Response to demand —Cont.
    Separate response   CCP §2031.210
    Signature   CCP §2031.250
    Time to serve response   CCP §2031.260
        Extension of time to serve response   CCP §2031.270
        Failure to serve timely response   CCP §2031.300

Retention of demand, proof of service and response   CCP §2031.290

Right to discovery by   CCP §2031.010

Sanctions
    Protective orders
        Unsuccessfully making or opposing motion for protective order   CCP §2031.060
    Response to demand
        Failure to file timely response   CCP §2031.300
        Failure to permit inspection in accord with demand   CCP §2031.320
        Further response, motion to compel   CCP §2031.310

Sequence of responses   CRC 3.1000

Service of demand   CCP §2031.040
    Retention of demand, proof of service and response   CCP §2031.290

Signature
    Response to demand   CCP §2031.250

Supplemental inspection demands   CCP §2031.050, CRC 3.1000

Time to serve response   CCP §2031.260
    Extension of time to serve response   CCP §2031.270
    Failure to serve timely response   CCP §2031.300

Unlawful detainer
    Time to serve response   CCP §2031.260
    When demand may be made   CCP §2031.020

INSPECTION WARRANTS

Affidavit for   CCP §1822.51

Aquaculture, warrant for inspection of storage location of   CCP §1822.58

Authorized or required by state or local law or regulation, order to conduct inspection   CCP §1822.50

Cause, determination for   CCP §§1822.51 to 1822.54

Defined   CCP §1822.50

Description requirements
    Generally   CCP §1822.54
    Geographical area description requirements   CCP §1822.59

Gambling Control, warrant for inspection by   CCP §1822.60

Refusal to permit inspection   CCP §1822.57

Time of service   CCP §§1822.55, 1822.56

INSTALLMENTS

Costs and filing fees
    Indigent persons
        Rules allowing installment payment   Gov §68640

Dating services (See **DATING SERVICES**)

Infractions   CRC 4.108
    Failure to pay or make payment under installment payment plan   CRC 4.106

Judgments (See **JUDGMENTS**)

Land sales contracts (See **REAL PROPERTY SALES CONTRACTS**)

Retail installment sales (See **RETAIL INSTALLMENT SALES**)

Weight loss program (See **WEIGHT LOSS PROGRAMS**)

INSTANT MESSAGING

Statute of frauds
    Insufficiency of text message or instant message format communications to constitute contract to convey realty   CC §1624

INSTITUTIONAL FUNDS MANAGEMENT   Pro §§18501 to 18510

Accumulations   Pro §18504

Applicability of provisions   Pro §18508

Appropriations   Pro §18504

Citation of provisions   Pro §18501

Compliance with provisions   Pro §18507

Considerations in managing and investing funds   Pro §18503

Definitions   Pro §18502

Delegation of management or investment function   Pro §18505

Effective date of provisions   Pro §18508

Electronic signatures in global and national commerce act
    Effect of provisions on federal act   Pro §18509

Investments
    Considerations in managing and investing funds   Pro §18503
    Delegation of management or investment function   Pro §18505

Restrictions in gift instruments
    Release   Pro §18506

Uniform construction of provisions   Pro §18510

Uniform prudent management of institutional funds act   Pro §§18501 to 18510

Index

INTESTATE SUCCESSION—Cont.
Severance of matters associated with proceedings and actions under Probate Code   Pro §801
Simultaneous death (See **SIMULTANEOUS DEATH**)
Sisters, inheritance by   Pro §§6402, 6402.5
Stepparents
    Adoption by stepparents   Fam §9004, Pro §6451
    Establishing parent-child relationship in absence of adoption   Pro §6454
Surviving spouse, rights of   Pro §§6401 to 6402.5
Time period required for heirs to survive decedent   Pro §6403
Two lines of blood, persons related to decedent through   Pro §6413
Undue influence
    Definition of undue influence   Pro §86
Uniform Parentage Act governing determination of natural parent and child relationship   Pro §6453

INTIMATE PARTNER BATTERING EFFECTS
Expert testimony   Ev §1107

INTIMIDATION
Civil rights, deprivation by
    Waiver of right to freedom from violence, coerced or involuntary   CC §51.7
Health care facilities
    Intimidation
        Force, threat or other obstruction of access to health facilities or school grounds   CC §1708.9
Landlord and tenant
    Immigration or citizenship status of tenant, occupant, etc
        Disclosures to immigration authorities with intent to intimidate or harass   CC §1940.35
Sexual orientation, intimidation based on
    Waiver of right to freedom from violence, coerced or involuntary   CC §51.7

INTOXICATED PERSONS (See **SUBSTANCE ABUSE**)

INTOXICATING BEVERAGES (See **ALCOHOLIC BEVERAGES**)

INVASION OF PRIVACY
Generally   CC §1798.53
Advertising, unauthorized use of name or likeness in   CC §§3344, 3344.1
Assault with intent to capture visual image or sound recording   CC §1708.8
Constructive invasion of privacy   CC §1708.8
Credit reporting (See **CREDIT REPORTING**)
Damages
    Advertising, unauthorized use of name or likeness in   CC §§3344, 3344.1
    Information Practices Act   CC §1798.53
    Visual image or sound recording or other physical impression of plaintiff engaged in personal or familial activity, attempt to capture   CC §1708.8
Eavesdropping and wiretapping (See **EAVESDROPPING AND WIRETAPPING**)
False imprisonment with intent to capture visual image or sound recording   CC §1708.8
Information Practices Act (See **INFORMATION PRACTICES ACT**)
Personal information, protection for (See **INFORMATION PRACTICES ACT**)
Photographs (See within this heading, "**Visual images and sound recordings**")
Public employees, liability of   CC §1798.53
Right of protection from   CC §43
Sound recordings
    Generally (See within this heading, "**Visual images and sound recordings**")
    Eavesdropping and wiretapping (See **EAVESDROPPING AND WIRETAPPING**)
Visual images and sound recordings
    Advertising, unauthorized use of name or likeness in   CC §§3344, 3344.1
    Exposing intimate body parts or sexual acts of another without permission, distribution of photos, etc
        Actions for injunctions, damages, etc   CC §1708.85
        Confidential information form   CRCAppx A
    Personal or familial activity, attempt to capture visual image or sound recording or other physical impression of plaintiff engaged in   CC §1708.8

INVENTIONS (See **PATENT OF INVENTION**)

INVENTORY
Administration of decedents' estates
    Generally (See **ADMINISTRATION OF ESTATES**)
    Small estates without administration (See **SMALL ESTATES WITHOUT ADMINISTRATION**)
Attachment (See **ATTACHMENT**)

INVENTORY—Cont.
Claim and delivery   CCP §511.050
Conservators (See **CONSERVATORS**)
Family allowance payments, effect on   Pro §6541
Guardianship (See **GUARDIAN AND WARD**)
Homesteads, filing inventory affecting possession of   Pro §§6510, 6520
Life tenant furnishing inventory to personal representative   Pro §11752
Receiver's inventory, law and motion rule of court regarding   CRC 3.1181
Small estates without administration (See **SMALL ESTATES WITHOUT ADMINISTRATION**)
Veterans Administration, notice requirement for   Pro §1461.5

INVERSE CONDEMNATION (See **EMINENT DOMAIN**)

INVESTIGATIONS
Adoption proceedings (See **ADOPTION**)
Agencies (See **INVESTIGATIVE CONSUMER REPORTING AGENCIES**)
Child custody proceedings (See **CUSTODY OF CHILDREN**)
Conservators (See **CONSERVATORS**)
Credit report disputes   CC §1785.25
Guardianship (See **GUARDIAN AND WARD**)
Judges
    Facts of case   CRCSupp JudEthicsCanon 3
Missing person, administrator of estate seeking   Pro §12406
Sterilization proceedings   Pro §1955
Surveyors investigating boundaries   CC §846.5
Termination of parental rights   Fam §§7850 to 7852

INVESTIGATIVE CONSUMER REPORTING AGENCIES
Access to report, consumer's   CC §1786.11
Accuracy of information supplied, procedures to ensure   CC §1786.20
Adverse information
    Disclosure to consumer of   CC §§1786.10, 1786.28
    Subsequent reports, inclusion of adverse information in   CC §1786.30
Arrest information, restrictions on disclosure of   CC §1786.18
Attorney-client privilege
    Law not changed by provisions   CC §1786.55
Attorneys' fees, action for   CC §1786.50
Bankruptcy information, restrictions on   CC §1785.18
Certification of users' lawful purpose and compliance with relevant requirements, requirement for   CC §1786.20
Charges to consumer   CC §§1786.22, 1786.26
Citations of statutes affecting   CC §1786.1
Codes explained   CC §1786.22
Conditions for procuring report   CC §1786.16
Consumer privacy rights
    Relation between records of agencies and obligations imposed under consumer privacy provisions   CC §1798.145
Consumer reports
    Personal information protection
        Software updates and other measures by consumer credit reporting agencies to address security vulnerability   CC §1798.81.6
Conviction of crime, restrictions on disclosure of   CC §1786.18
Corrected records   CC §1786.24
Costs, action for   CC §1786.50
Court order, furnishing of report in compliance with   CC §1786.12
Damages action   CC §1786.50
Definitions   CC §1786.2
Deletion of information   CC §1786.24
Disclosures by reporting entities not using agencies   CC §1786.53
Disputed information   CC §1786.24
Employers gathering information without use of agencies   CC §1786.55
Federal statutes, action under   CC §1786.52
Fees charged to consumers   CC §§1786.22, 1786.26
Furnishing of report, circumstances warranting   CC §§1786.12, 1786.14
Governmental agencies, information to   CC §1786.14
Identification of prospective users   CC §§1786.20, 1786.22
Indictment information, restrictions on   CC §1786.18
Inspection of files by consumers   CC §§1786.10, 1786.22
Insurance denials based on information reported by agency
    Information given to rejected applicant   CC §1786.40
Invasion of privacy action   CC §1786.52
Libel and slander action   CC §1786.52
Medical information   CC §§1786.2, 1786.12
New investigations   CC §1786.24
Notice
    Disputed information, notices in connection with   CC §1786.24
    Procuring of report, notice to consumer of   CC §1786.16
    Rights and obligations of recipient of report, notice of   CC §1786.29
Old information   CC §1786.18

Index

Index

Index

Index

Index

Index

Index

Index

JURIES OF INQUEST
Defined   CCP §194
Function of   CCP §236
Selection, compensation and obligation   CCP §235
Types of juries   CCP §193
Witness fees   Gov §68095

JURISDICTION
Administration of estates (See **ADMINISTRATION OF ESTATES**)
Adoption   Fam §§8714, 9210
    Interstate adoptions   Fam §9212
Amount in controversy (See **AMOUNT IN CONTROVERSY**)
Annulment   Fam §§2010 to 2013
    Same sex marriages
        Residence requirements   Fam §2320
Answer alleging lack of   CCP §430.10
Appearance (See **APPEARANCE**)
Arbitration proceedings   CCP §§86, 1292.4 to 1293
Assisted reproduction
    Gestational carriers, agreements   Fam §7620
Attorney's practice, court's assumption of jurisdiction over (See **ATTORNEYS**)
Cause, jurisdiction over   CCP §1917
Certiorari   CCP §1068
Change of names   CCP §1275
Child custody
    Exclusive jurisdiction of juvenile court   CRC 5.510
    Generally (See **CUSTODY OF CHILDREN**)
Child support
    Interstate family support   Fam §§5700.201 to 5700.211
Child support proceedings (See **CHILD SUPPORT**)
Choice of law (See **CHOICE OF LAW**)
Civil rights actions   CC §52.2
Community property (See **COMMUNITY PROPERTY**)
Conciliation court proceedings (See **CONCILIATION COURTS**)
Conservators
    California conservatorship jurisdiction act
        Judicial council legal forms   CRCAppx A
    Generally (See **CONSERVATORS**)
    Interstate jurisdiction, transfer and recognition
        Generally   Pro §§1980 to 2033 (See **CONSERVATORS**)
        Judicial council legal forms   CRCAppx A
Constitution   CCP §410.10
Continuing jurisdiction   CCP §410.50
Contract, persons liable on   CCP §410.70
Coordination of actions   CRC 3.540 to 3.545
Corporations forfeiting charter, jurisdiction over trustees and stockholders of   CCP §410.60
Courts of appeal, original jurisdiction
    Habeas corpus   CRC 8.380 to 8.398
    Mandate, certiorari and prohibition in supreme court or court of appeal   CRC 8.485 to 8.493
Custody of children (See **CUSTODY OF CHILDREN**)
Defined as to court authority   CCP §410.10
Demurrer alleging lack of   CCP §430.10
Destroyed land records relief law proceedings   CCP §751.11
Dissolution of marriage (See **DISSOLUTION OF MARRIAGE**)
Earthquakes, boundary reestablishment after   CCP §751.55
Eminent domain action   CCP §1250.010
Enforcement of judgments (See **ENFORCEMENT OF JUDGMENTS**)
Escheat (See **ESCHEAT**)
Family law   Fam §200
Foreign country judgments
    Personal jurisdiction lacking
        Circumstances allowing for recognition   CCP §1717
Forum non conveniens (See **INCONVENIENT FORUM**)
Guardianship (See **GUARDIAN AND WARD**)
Habeas corpus proceedings   CRC 4.551
Impeachment of record for absence of   CCP §1916
Implied powers to effectuate conferred powers   CCP §187
Inconvenient forum doctrine (See **INCONVENIENT FORUM**)
Information Practices Act, proceedings under   CC §1798.49
International commercial arbitration and conciliation (See **INTERNATIONAL COMMERCIAL ARBITRATION AND CONCILIATION**)
Interstate family support   Fam §§5700.201 to 5700.211
Judges   Pro §800
Judge's power to act, effect of proceedings for disqualification on   CCP §170.4
Judgment on the pleadings, jurisdiction as basis of motion for   CCP §438
Juvenile courts, exclusive jurisdiction of   CRC 5.510, 5.620
    Harassment or domestic violence proceedings brought against or initiated by minor, jurisdiction over   CCP §374.5

JURISDICTION—Cont.
Juvenile courts, exclusive jurisdiction of —Cont.
    Termination of juvenile court jurisdiction
        Nonminor dependents or wards in foster care   CRC 5.555
Labor disputes, limitation on enjoining acts relating to   CCP §527.3
Legal separation   Fam §§2010 to 2013
    Same sex marriages
        Residence requirements   Fam §2320
Limited civil cases
    Generally   CCP §85
    Amount in controversy   CCP §85
    Jurisdictional classification defined   CCP §32.5
    Long-Term Care, Health, Safety and Security Act, jurisdiction in actions brought pursuant to   CCP §86.1
    Original jurisdiction   CCP §86
    Reclassification generally (See within this heading, **"Reclassification of action"**)
    Small claims division   CCP §87
    Statutes relating to court's authority in limited and unlimited civil cases   CCP §89
    Unlimited civil case defined   CCP §88
Mandate
    Writs of mandate, certiorari and prohibition in supreme court or court of appeal   CCP §1085, CRC 8.485 to 8.493
Missing persons' estate, administration of   Pro §12403
Motions   CCP §1004
Motion to quash service of summons on ground of lack of   CCP §418.10, Fam §2012
Nazi regime, actions by victims of (See **NAI GERMANY**)
Objection to jurisdiction   CCP §§418.10, 418.11
Other states (See **OTHER STATES**)
Over parties
    Extends from service through subsequent proceedings   CCP §410.50
    Record, jurisdiction sufficient to sustain   CCP §1917
Particular persons, jurisdiction over
    Contract, persons liable on   CCP §410.70
    Trustees and stockholders of corporation forfeiting charter   CCP §410.60
Parties
    Extension of jurisdiction over parties from service to subsequent proceedings   CCP §410.50
    Record, jurisdiction sufficient to sustain   CCP §1917
Partition (See **PARTITION**)
Paternity actions
    Juvenile court jurisdiction   CRC 5.510
Power of attorney, jurisdiction in actions involving (See **POWER OF ATTORNEY**)
Presumption of lawful exercise of   Ev §666
Prohibition writs   CCP §1103
Property settlement   Fam §§2010 to 2013
Public administrators   Pro §7601
Quieting title action   CCP §760.040
Reclassification of action
    Appearance, filing for reclassification constituting   CCP §1014
    Applicability of reclassification provisions   CCP §403.010
    Commencement of reclassified action, deemed time of   CCP §403.070
    Fees   CCP §§403.050 to 403.060
    Procedure for reclassifying actions   CCP §§403.020 to 403.040
    Review of reclassification order, writ of mandate for   CCP §403.080
    Rules for reclassification, Judicial Council's authority to prescribe   CCP §403.090
Related causes of action   CCP §§426.30, 426.40
Severance of trial or action   CRC 3.529
Simultaneous death, establishment of   Pro §232
Small claims court (See **SMALL CLAIMS COURTS**)
Spousal support proceedings (See **SPOUSAL SUPPORT**)
Sufficiency of jurisdiction to sustain record   CCP §1917
Superior courts   CCP §86
    Appellate division jurisdiction on appeal   CCP §77
    Child custody and care determinations
        Immigration and nationality act decisions   CCP §155
    Limited civil cases   CCP §§85 to 89
Support proceedings   Fam §§2010 to 2013
    Child support (See **CHILD SUPPORT**)
    Spousal support (See **SPOUSAL SUPPORT**)
Surety bonds, jurisdiction for enforcement of liability on   CCP §§996.420, 996.430
Tribal court civil money judgment act
    Objections
        Grounds for objection   CCP §1737
Trusts (See **TRUSTS**)

Index

Index

Index

Index

K

L

Index

LANDLORD AND TENANT—Cont.

Water service in multifamily residential rental buildings —Cont.

    Repairs—Cont.

        Fixtures   CC §1954.210

        Water-saving devices   CC §1954.210

    Shutting off of or other interference with water service by landlord

        Prohibition   CC §1954.213

    Submeters   CC §1954.203

        Disclosures to tenants   CC §1954.204

        Entry by landlord to install, repair, etc   CC §1954.211

        Final reading and billing   CC §1954.207

        Information as to maintenance   CC §1954.209

        Initial reading and billing   CC §1954.207

        Maintenance   CC §1954.209

        Monthly reading unavailable, calculations for billing   CC §1954.212

        Portion of unit's usage metered, applicability of provisions   CC §1954.217

        When required   CC §1954.219

    Waiver of provisions prohibited   CC §1954.215

Withdrawal of property from rental market

    Termination of tenancy

        Year's continuous, lawful occupation, no-fault just cause for termination   CC §1946.2

LAND SALES CONTRACTS (See **REAL PROPERTY SALES CONTRACTS**)

LANDSCAPERS

Bond required to secure costs in action against   CCP §1029.5

Water conservation

    Commercial and industrial common interest developments

        Water-efficient landscaping, protected interest   CC §6712

    Common interest developments

        Artificial turf, architectural guidelines not to prohibit   CC §4735

        Low water-using plants, architectural guidelines not to prohibit   CC §4735

LAND SURVEYORS

Design professionals' liens   CC §§8300 to 8319 (See **LIENS**)

Generally (See **SURVEYS AND SURVEYORS**)

LAND TITLES (See **TITLE AND OWNERSHIP**)

LANGUAGE

Descriptions (See **DESCRIPTIONS**)

English (See **ENGLISH LANGUAGE**)

Home solicitation sales contracts

    Cancellation

        Notice of right to cancel in contract in same language as language of negotiation   CC §1689.7

International commercial arbitration and conciliation   CCP §§1297.221 to 1297.224

Spanish (See **SPANISH**)

Translators (See **TRANSLATORS AND INTERPRETERS**)

LARCENY (See **THEFT**)

LAST DAY

Computation of time in which act provided by law is to be done   CCP §12

LAST ILLNESS

Community property, last illness expense liability of   Pro §11446

Conservatorship, last illness expense liability of   Pro §2631

Guardianship, last illness expense liability of   Pro §2631

Priority for payment of last illness expenses by decedent's estate   Pro §§11420, 11421

Trust estate of deceased settlor, claim for last illness expenses against   Pro §19326

LATENT DEFECTS

Statutes of limitation on actions for damages for deficiencies in planning or construction of improvement to real property   CCP §337.15

LATERAL SUPPORT FROM ADJOINING PROPERTY

Right to   CC §832

LAUNDRIES

Gender

    Prohibition against charging different price for services of similar or like kind based solely on   CC §51.6

    Small business gender discrimination in pricing services compliance act   CC §§55.61 to 55.63

LAUNDRIES—Cont.

Lien for services of   CC §§3051, 3066

LAW

Generally   CCP §1895

Constitution and statutes, law expressed by   CC §22.1

Organic law   CCP §1897

Unwritten law   CCP §§1895, 1899

Written laws   CCP §1896

LAW AND FACT QUESTIONS (See **QUESTIONS OF LAW OR FACT**)

LAW AND MOTION PROCEEDINGS   CRC 3.1100 to 3.1372

Administrative mandate cases, lodging of record in   CRC 3.1140

Advancing case set for trial

    Motion or application to advance, specially set or reset   CRC 3.1335

Amended pleadings   CRC 3.1324

Appendices

    Papers, etc, in support of motion   CRC 3.1112

Applicability   CRC 3.1100, 3.1103

Arbitration, motions concerning   CRC 3.1330

Attachments to notice of motion   CRC 3.1113

Attorneys

    Relief as counsel, motion for   CRC 3.1362

Binding together of document with exhibits   CRC 3.1110

Bonds and undertakings   CRC 3.1130

Captions

    Declaration or affidavit   CRC 3.1115

    Demurrers   CRC 3.1320

Case citation format

    Memorandum in support of motion   CRC 3.1113

Change of venue, motion for   CRC 3.1326

Civil petitions

    Emancipation of minors   CRC 3.1370

    Environmental quality act   CRC 3.1365

    Military service

        Financial obligations during service, relief   CRC 3.1372

Clerk, material lodged with   CRC 3.1302

Combined summons and complaint regarding parental obligations   CRC 5.325

Continuance, motion for   CRC 3.1332

Copies of authorities   CRC 3.1113

Counsel, motion to be relieved as   CRC 3.1362

Date, time and location of hearing, papers to specify   CRC 3.1110

Declarations in support of motion   CRC 3.1112

Definitions and construction   CRC 3.1103

Demurrers   CRC 3.1320

Depositions

    Use as exhibits   CRC 3.1116

Determination of submitted matters, notice of   CRC 3.1109

Discovery   CRC 3.1100

Dismissal of actions

    Delay in prosecution   CRC 3.1342

    Motions to dismiss   CRC 3.1340

Driving license suspension, stay of   CRC 3.1142

Emancipation of minors   CRC 3.1370

Environmental quality act   CRC 3.1365

    Petitions under environmental quality act   CRC 3.2200 to 3.2237

Evidence at hearings   CRC 3.1306

Exhibits

    Format for submission   CRC 3.1110

    Papers, etc, in support of motion   CRC 3.1112

    References   CRC 3.1113

Ex parte applications and orders   CRC 3.1200 to 3.1207

Foreign language, translation of exhibits written in   CRC 3.1110

Format and filing of papers   CRC 3.1110 to 3.1116

General format requirements   CRC 3.1110

Hearings   CRC 3.1304, 3.1306

    Telephone appearance at law and motion hearings   CRC 3.670

Injunctions   CRC 3.1150 to 3.1161

In limine motions

    Format of motion papers   CRC 3.1112

Judicial notice of material   CRC 3.1306

Late filing of papers   CRC 3.1300

Length of memorandum in support of motion   CRC 3.1113

Lien on cause of action, motion to grant   CRC 3.1360

Memorandum in support of motion   CRC 3.1113

    Summary judgment or adjudication   CRC 3.1350

    When memorandum not required   CRC 3.1114

Military service

    Financial obligations during service, relief   CRC 3.1372

LICENSES AND PERMITS—Cont.

Membership camping facility, disclosure of operating license for   CC §1812.302

Mobilehome parks, change of use of   CC §798.56

Mortgage foreclosure consultants, licensing requirements for   CC §2945.11

Professional license applicant, disclosure of information about   CC §1798.61

Professional licensing boards, communication of information to   CC §§43.8, 43.96

Radio frequency identification (RFID)
Use to remotely read identification document without knowledge or consent   CC §1798.79
Definitions   CC §1798.795

Recording or registering licenses and certificates, fees for   Gov §26851
Superior court fees, specified services   Gov §70626

State agencies, adjudicatory proceedings of (See **ADMINISTRATIVE ADJUDICATION**)

Support obligation, suspension or denial of licenses and permits for noncompliance with   Fam §§17520, 17521

Surety bonds (See **SURETYSHIP, BONDS AND UNDERTAKINGS**)

Unlicensed person, action for injury caused by   CCP §1029.8

LICENSES IN REALTY

Personal injury   CC §846

LIE DETECTOR (See **POLYGRAPH**)

LIENS

Absence of recordation of, certification   CCP §2103

Administration of decedents' estates
Generally (See **ADMINISTRATION OF ESTATES**)
Claims against decedents' estates (See **CLAIMS AGAINST ESTATES**)

After-acquired property covered by   CC §2883

Aircraft and aviation (See **AIRCRAFT AND AVIATION**)

Alternative lien-sale procedure for charges not exceeding $150   CC §3052b

Animals   CCP §1208.5

Apartment housekeeper's lien   CC §1861a

Artisans' liens   CC §§3051, 3051a

Assignment for benefit of creditors (See **ASSIGNMENT FOR BENEFIT OF CREDITORS**)

Attachment (See **ATTACHMENT**)

Auctioned items, disclosure of liens on   CC §1812.607

Automobiles (See **AUTOMOBILES**)

Bankers' liens   CC §3054

Bankruptcy affecting   CCP §§493.030 to 493.050

Blanket encumbrances, required notice to purchaser or lessee of   CC §1133

Blanket liens, priority of   CC §2899

Boarding houses   CC §§1861 to 1861.28

Bottomry lien regulations applicable to   CC §2877

Breeders' liens   CC §§3062 to 3064.1

Carriers' liens (See **COMMON CARRIERS**)

Cause of action, lien on   CRC 3.1360

Child support (See **CHILD SUPPORT**)

Civil rules
Waiver of fees
Amount of lien   CRC 3.57

Claims against decedents' estates (See **CLAIMS AGAINST ESTATES**)

Cleaners' lien   CC §3066

Commercial and industrial common interest developments
Assessments
Common areas, damage   CC §6824
Contents   CC §6814
Enforcement of lien   CC §6820
Governing documents, no lien for noncompliance   CC §6824
Noncompliance with procedures for liens   CC §6819
Pre-lien notice to owner   CC §6812
Priority   CC §6816
Release of lien   CC §6818
Sale to enforce lien   CC §§6820, 6822
Scope of liens   CC §6658

Common carriers' liens (See **COMMON CARRIERS**)

Common interest developments
Condominiums, contractor's lien
Transfer restrictions   CC §4615
Generally (See **COMMON INTEREST DEVELOPMENTS**)

Concurrent liens, priority between   CC §2899

Construction liens   CC §§8000 to 9566 (See **MECHANICS' LIENS**)

Contract, creation by   CC §2881

Conversion extinguishing   CC §2910

Damages for conversion   CC §3338

Defined   CC §2872, CCP §1180

Deposits (See **DEPOSITS**)

LIENS—Cont.

Design professionals' liens   CC §§8300 to 8319
Availability of other remedies   CC §8314
Conditions for lien   CC §8304
Conversion to mechanics lien   CC §8319
Creation of lien   CC §§8302, 8306
Definition of design professional   CC §8300
Expiration   CC §8306
Mechanics' liens
Relationship between different lien provisions   CC §8310
Priority of lien   CC §8316
Provisions of part applicable   CC §8308
Recordation   CC §8306
Time to record   CC §8312
Residences
Single-family owner-occupied residence, applicability of provisions   CC §8318

Disclosures on purchase money liens on residential property   CC §§2956 to 2967

Discriminatory clauses in lien instruments, prohibition against   CC §§53, 782

Earnings assignment for support   Fam §5242

Eminent domain (See **EMINENT DOMAIN**)

Enforcement of judgments (See **ENFORCEMENT OF JUDGMENTS**)

Expenditures concerning lien, recovery of   CC §2892

Factors   CC §3053

Family law attorney's real property lien   Fam §§2033, 2034

Family support
Judgments, abstract of
Digital form of lien record   Fam §17523.5

Farm workers, liens by   CC §§3061 to 3061.6

Federal Lien Registration Act   CCP §§2100 to 2107
Fees for recording under act   Gov §27388.1

Fixtures   CC §1013.5

Floating homes (See **FLOATING HOMES**)

Foreclosure
Generally   CCP §726
Apartment housekeepers' lien   CC §1861a
Appraisal on   CCP §726
Attorneys' fees   CCP §730
Boarding housekeeper's liens   CC §1861
Deficiency judgments   CCP §726
Deposit, lien for   CC §1857
Hospital liens   CC §1862.5
Hotelkeeper's liens   CC §1861
Judgments   CCP §726
Mortgage foreclosure prevention   CC §2924
Nuisance property
Abatement assessment or lien, maximum amount   CC §2929.45
Partial sales   CCP §728
Stay of proceedings   CCP §917.2
Surplus on   CCP §727

Forfeiture agreement, validity of   CC §2889

Forms
Service dealer lien notice   CC §3052.5
Wages, liens securing   CC §§3061.5, 3061.6

Future act secured by   CC §2884

Garnishment proceedings (See **GARNISHMENT**)

General liens defined   CC §§2873, 2874

Harvester's liens   CC §§3061.5, 3061.6

Health care liens   CC §3040

Home equity loans   CC §§2970 to 2971

Homesteads (See **HOMESTEADS**)

Horses (See **HORSES**)

Hospital liens (See **HOSPITALS**)

Implied obligations   CC §2890

Improvements (See **IMPROVEMENTS**)

Income tax (federal), registration act for   CCP §§2100 to 2107
Fees for recording under act   Gov §27388.1

Indigent persons
Waiver of fees
Amount of lien   CRC 3.57

Inferior liens
Dwelling, lienholder served with notice of removal of occupant from   CCP §700.080
Mobilehomes (See **MOBILEHOMES**)
Priorities   CC §§2897 to 2899
Redemption   CC §2904

Information Practices Act, disclosure under   CC §1798.67

Jewelers' liens   CC §3052a

Judgment liens (See **JUDGMENTS**)

Index

Index

LOW INCOME HOUSING—Cont.
Injunctions against projects CCP §529.2

LUGGAGE (See BAGGAGE)

LUMBER (See LOGS AND TIMBER)

LUNACY (See MENTAL DISABILITY)

LUNCHROOMS (See RESTAURANTS)

LUXURY CRUISERS (See VESSELS)

M

MACHINERY
Eminent domain compensation for CCP §§1263.205, 1263.620
Mining machinery, records of sale of CC §1631

MADE IN CALIFORNIA PROGRAM
Unfair competition or deceptive trade practices CC §1770

MAGAZINES (See NEWSPAPERS AND MAGAZINES)

MAGISTRATES
Judicial ethics, code of
  Applicability CRCSupp JudEthicsCanon 6
Marriage ceremony Fam §400

MAGNETIC RECORD DEVICES (See RECORDING OF SOUND)

MAIDEN NAME
Refusal to do business with person using CCP §1279.6

MAIDS (See PERSONAL SERVICES)

MAIL AND MAILING
Administration of decedents' estates (See ADMINISTRATION OF ESTATES)
Administrative adjudicative proceedings (See ADMINISTRATIVE ADJUDICATION)
Authentication of document Ev §1420
Automobile repossession notice, regulating mailing of CC §§2982, 2983.2, 2983.3
Certified mail
  Electronic service not authorized when certified or registered mail required CCP §1020
  Probate proceedings, sufficiency of notice in Pro §5
  Registered mail, certified mail in lieu of CC §17, CCP §11
Conservatorship proceedings Pro §1467
Credit reports, copy of CC §1785.15
Defined CCP §116.130
Dies, molds and forms, notice of termination of customer's title to CC §1140
Eminent domain taking notice CCP §1245.235
Enforcement of judgments (See ENFORCEMENT OF JUDGMENTS)
Executor as nonresident, mailing process to Pro §§8574, 8575
Express mail
  Summary judgment, notice of motion
    Time limits, effect of express or other overnight mail delivery CCP §437c
Fees
  Courts, authority to set fees for products or services CRC 10.815
Filing fees
  Notice of return of check for CCP §411.20
  Underpayment, notice CCP §411.21
Groundwater rights actions
  Notice of complaint CCP §835
Guardianship proceedings Pro §1467
Hospital lien notice transmitted by CC §3045.3
Jury summons CCP §208
Landlord and tenant
  Locking mail receptacles
    Untenantable if lacking CC §1941.1
  Notifying tenant of sale of building by CC §1950.5
Lease notices (See LEASES)
Mechanic's lien, notice of
  Method of giving CC §8106
  Notice of cessation or completion
    Copy to be mailed to person giving preliminary notice by county clerk CC §8214
    Requirements when notice mailed CC §8110
Merchandise offered to consumers CC §§1584.5, 1584.6

MAIL AND MAILING—Cont.
Missing person, notice of administration of estate of Pro §12405
Motion, service by mail of notices of (See MOTIONS)
Notice of pendency, service of CCP §§405.22, 405.23
Presumption of receipt of letters correctly addressed and posted Ev §641
Probate proceedings
  Delivery of notice
    Methods Pro §1215
Proof of service by mail CCP §1013a
Public entities and employees, manner of mailing claim against Gov §915.2
Registered mail, certified mail in lieu of CC §17, CCP §11
  Electronic service not authorized when certified or registered mail required CCP §1020
Sale by (See MAIL ORDER SALES)
Service of process (See PROCESS AND SERVICE OF PROCESS)
Small claims court (See SMALL CLAIMS COURTS)
Social security numbers
  Visible display on mail CC §1786.60
Tax lien, notice to state tax debtor of CC §2885
Trial notice served through CCP §594
Unconditional gifts CC §§1584.5, 1584.6
Unlawful detainer process, service of CCP §415.45
Unsolicited goods sent by CC §§1584.5, 1584.6
Will probate proceedings (See WILL PROBATE)

MAILING LISTS
Information Practices Act (See INFORMATION PRACTICES ACT)
Jurors, sources for selection of CCP §197

MAIL ORDER SALES
Assistive devices CC §1793.02
Autographed memorabilia, sale of CC §1739.7
Fine prints, sale of CC §§1742 to 1744
Place of business defined CC §1791
Retail installment sales provisions applicable CC §1803.8
Unsolicited goods sent by CC §§1584.5, 1584.6
Warranties CC §1792.4

MAINTENANCE
Recordkeeping (See RECORDS AND RECORDING)
Repairs (See REPAIRS)
Spousal support (See SPOUSAL SUPPORT)

MAJORITY
Joint authority, effect of grant of CCP §15

MAJORITY OF WARD (See GUARDIAN AND WARD)

MALFEASANCE
Jury service, exceptions to eligibility for CCP §203
Notary public, statutes of limitation on actions upon bond of CCP §338

MALICE
Construction, damages for malicious destruction of property under CC §3294
Damages awarded CC §3294
Exemplary damages for CC §3294
Libel and slander CC §§47, 48, 48a

MALICIOUS PROSECUTION (See VEXATIOUS LITIGANTS)

MALPRACTICE
Arbitration
  Health care providers
    General arbitration provisions inapplicable CCP §§1281.2, 1281.3
Architects (See ARCHITECTS)
Attorney professional conduct
  Communications with clients
    Malpractice insurance lacking, duty to inform client ProfC 1.4.2
  Limitation of attorney liability to client
    Prohibitions ProfC 1.8.8
Attorneys
  Action for wrongful act or omission arising in performance of professional services CCP §340.6
  Referrals by professional society, immunity from liability for CC §43.95
Damages
  Health care providers (See within this heading, "Health care providers")
  Unlicensed person, treble damages for injury caused by CCP §1029.8
Engineers (See ENGINEERING)
Health care providers
  Arbitration
    General arbitration provisions inapplicable CCP §§1281.2, 1281.3
    Medical services contract, arbitration provision in CCP §1295

Index

Index

Index

Index

MEDICAL RECORDS—Cont.

Disclosure—Cont.

    Genetic characteristics, test results for   CC §56.17

    Health care providers and contractors, disclosure by   CC §§56.10 to 56.16, 56.35 to 56.37, 56.101, 56.104

    Health care service plans, disclosure by   CC §§56.10 to 56.17, 56.35 to 56.37, 56.101, 56.104

    HIV status of workers, limited confidentiality of   CC §56.31

    Information Practices Act (See **INFORMATION PRACTICES ACT**)

    Insurance underwriters   CC §56.265

    Liability for wrongful disclosure   CC §§56.35 to 56.37

    Marketing

        Defined   CC §56.05

        Disclosure of information for use in marketing   CC §56.10

    Medical information corporation, disclosure by   CC §56.06

    Misdemeanor, violations as   CC §56.36

    Pharmaceutical company requiring disclosure as condition of receiving pharmaceuticals   CC §56.102

    Physician-patient privilege, effect of disclosure on   Ev §1156

    Psychotherapy, authorized disclosure concerning   CC §56.104, Ev §1158

    Third party administrators, disclosure by   CC §56.26

Discovery procedure (See **DISCOVERY**)

Electronic medical records

    Attorney inspection of records

        Requirements for situations where records kept electronically   Ev §1158

    System requirements   CC §56.101

Employers, disclosure by   CC §§56.20 to 56.25, 56.27

Fines for wrongful disclosure   CC §56.36

Forensic pathologists

    Disclosure of medical records to coroners, medical examiners or forensic pathologists   CC §56.10

Forms

    Authorization for release   Ev §1158

Genetic characteristics, disclosure of test results for   CC §56.17

Health Care Decisions Law (See **HEALTH CARE DECISIONS LAW**)

Health care providers and contractors, disclosure by   CC §§56.10 to 56.16, 56.35 to 56.37, 56.101, 56.104

Health care service plans, disclosure by   CC §§56.10 to 56.17, 56.35 to 56.37, 56.101, 56.104

HIV status of workers, limited confidentiality of   CC §56.31

Information Practices Act (See **INFORMATION PRACTICES ACT**)

Information Practices Act, protection under   CC §§56.29, 1798.3

Inspection by authorized attorney   CCP §1985.7, Ev §1158

Insurance companies' access to   CC §§56.10, 56.27

Insurance underwriters, restrictions on   CC §56.265

Investigative agencies having medical information   CC §§1786.2, 1786.12

Medical examiners

    Disclosure of medical records to coroners, medical examiners or forensic pathologists   CC §56.10

Medical information corporations, access to medical information maintained by   CC §§56.06, 56.07

Minors, disclosure of mental health records of

    Removal from physical custody of parent or guardian, protection of mental health records from release   CC §56.106

Noncustodial parent's right to   Fam §3025

Parent's right to access records of child   Fam §3025

Penalties for wrongful disclosure   CC §56.36

Physician-patient privilege, effect of disclosure on   Ev §1156

Police officers   Ev §1044

Psychotherapy, authorized disclosure concerning   CC §56.104, Ev §1158

Release, requirements for   CC §§56.101, 56.104, 56 to 56.37

    Employer release   CC §56.21

Review committees, admissibility of research findings of   Ev §§1156, 1156.1

Third party administrators, use and disclosure by   CC §56.26

Wrongful disclosure

    Disclosure generally (See within this heading, **"Disclosure"**)

MEDICAL SOCIETIES (See **PROFESSIONAL SOCIETIES**)

MEDICAL TREATMENT

Capacity determinations

    Conservators   Pro §§1880 to 1898, 2354, 2355

    Health care decisions for adult with conservator   Pro §§3200 to 3212

    Judicial determinations, generally   Pro §§810 to 813, 3200 to 3212

    Primary physician making capacity determinations under Health Care Decisions Law   Pro §4658

MEDICAL TREATMENT—Cont.

Capacity to consent to medical treatment, generally   Pro §813

Conservatorship (See **CONSERVATORS**)

Emergencies (See **EMERGENCIES**)

Guardian and ward (See **GUARDIAN AND WARD**)

Health Care Decisions Law (See **HEALTH CARE DECISIONS LAW**)

Health care power of attorney (See **POWER OF ATTORNEY**)

Health care providers (See **HEALTH CARE PROVIDERS**)

Health care service plans (See **HEALTH CARE SERVICE PLANS**)

Hospitals (See **HOSPITALS**)

Malpractice (See **MALPRACTICE**)

Medical records (See **MEDICAL RECORDS**)

Minors (See **MINORS**)

Power of attorney for health care (See **POWER OF ATTORNEY**)

Prohibited treatment involving adult patient without conservator   Pro §3211

Prosthetics (See **PROSTHETICS**)

Psychotropic medication to major neurocognitive conservatees   Pro §2356.5

Spiritual means of treatment, right to choose   Pro §3212

Sterilization (See **STERILIZATION**)

MEDICINES (See **PHARMACISTS AND PHARMACIES**)

MEET-AND-CONFER REQUIREMENT

Civil rules

    Case management   CRC 3.724

        Complex cases   CRC 3.750

        Telephone appearance at case management conferences   CRC 3.670

    Forms

        Judicial council legal forms   CRCAppx A

Common interest developments

    Dispute resolution for disputes between association and member

        Meet and confer procedure   CC §5915

Demurrer

    Forms

        Judicial council legal forms   CRCAppx A

    Prerequisite to filing demurrer   CCP §430.41

Family rules

    Request for orders   CRC 5.98

MEETINGS

Common interest developments (See **COMMON INTEREST DEVELOP-MENTS**)

Demonstrations (See **DEMONSTRATIONS, PARADES AND MEETINGS**)

Libel and slander action, public meetings privileged from   CC §47

Mobilehome tenants (See **MOBILEHOMES**)

Public entities

    Participation by public

        Decisions and pending opportunities for public participation link on homepage   Gov §§11364, 11365

Quorum (See **QUORUM**)

MEMBERS

Associations and clubs (See **ASSOCIATIONS**)

Camping contracts, regulation of membership   CC §§1812.300 to 1812.309

Discount buying services   CC §§1812.100 to 1812.129

MEMORABILIA

Autographed memorabilia   CC §1739.7

MEMORANDUM

Costs (See **COSTS**)

Enforcement of judgments (See **ENFORCEMENT OF JUDGMENTS**)

Garnishment memorandum (See **GARNISHMENT**)

Points and authorities (See **POINTS AND AUTHORITIES**)

MENACE (See also **DURESS**)

Contracts, consent for   CC §§1567, 1570

Debt collection by use of   CC §1788.10

Forcible detainer   CCP §1160

Rescission of contract because of   CC §1689

Wills, general discussion of effect on   Pro §6104

MENTAL DISABILITY (See also **MENTAL HOSPITALS**)

Administrators (See **EXECUTORS AND ADMINISTRATORS**)

Adoption (See **ADOPTION**)

Adverse possession, disabilities tolling statutes of limitation on actions for   CCP §328

Annulment, grounds for   Fam §2210

MENTAL EXAMINATIONS—Cont.
Economic litigation provisions for limited civil cases, permissible forms of discovery under   CCP §94
Judges, proceedings for removal of   JudPerR 105
Sterilization proceedings   Pro §1955

MENTAL FUNCTIONS
Judicial determination regarding capacity to perform specific acts   Pro §§810 to 813

MENTAL HEALTH DEPARTMENT
Special needs trust for minor or person with disability, notice of
    Definition of person with disability   Pro §3603
    Express consent of protected person to court orders, when required   Pro §3613

MENTAL HEALTH PRACTITIONERS (See **PSYCHOTHERAPISTS**)

MENTAL HOSPITALS (See also **MENTAL DISABILITY**)
Admissibility of hospital records   Ev §§1156.1, 1157.6
Child support
    Suspension of orders or judgments for incarcerated or involuntarily institutionalized   Fam §4007.5
Claims against public entities and employees (See **CLAIMS AGAINST PUBLIC ENTITIES AND EMPLOYEES**)
Conservatee, mental health facility placement of   Pro §2356
Convulsive therapy, consent required for treatment of minor using   Fam §6924
Escheat of patient's assets   CCP §1447
Psychosurgery, consent required for treatment of minor using   Fam §6924
Restoration to capacity (See **MENTAL DISABILITY**)
Review committees, admissibility of research findings of   Ev §1156.1
Sexual battery against medically incapacitated patients
    Statute of limitations on sexual assault damages   CCP §340.16
Sheriff's fees for transporting patients to   Gov §26749
Statutes of limitation for recovery or conversion of personal property left at   CCP §341a
Ward, mental health facility placement of   Pro §2356

MENTAL ILLNESS (See **MENTAL DISABILITY**)

MENTALLY DISORDERED OFFENDERS
Commitment
    Appeal from order of civil commitment   CRC 8.483

MENTALLY DISORDERED SEX OFFENDERS
Commitments to nonpenal institutions   CRC 4.300
    Appeal of commitment order
        Procedure for appeal from order of civil commitment   CRC 8.483
Maximum term of commitment   CRC 4.453

MENTALLY RETARDED PERSONS (See **DEVELOPMENTALLY DISABLED PERSONS**)

MERCHANDISE
Clubs for sale of   CC §§1584.5, 1584.6
Unsolicited goods   CC §§1584.5, 1584.6

MERCHANTABILITY
Warranty of   CC §1791.1

MERCHANTS (See **STORES AND STOREKEEPERS**)

MERGER
Civil and criminal actions, merger of   CCP §32

MERITORIOUS CAUSE OF ACTION
Architect, engineer or surveyor, certificate of merit requirement in action based on professional negligence of   CCP §§411.35, 430.10
Sexual abuse of minor, certificate of merit requirement in action for   CCP §340.1
Summary judgment motion where action is without merit or defense   CCP §437c
Vexatious litigant defined   CCP §391

MESNE PROFITS
Statutes of limitation   CCP §336

MESOTHELIOMA
Depositions
    Time limits for witness examination
        Actions involving mesothelioma or silicosis   CCP §2025.295

MIA-POWS (See **MILITARY**)

MICROFICHE
Fees
    Courts, authority to set fees for products or services   CRC 10.815

MICROFILM
Business records for evidence   Ev §1550
Certified copies of documents recorded on   CCP §1985
Conciliation court records and documents   Fam §1819
Indexes accessible by   CRC 10.851
Judgments recorded on   CCP §668.5
Lost or destroyed writings   Ev §1551

MIDWIVES
Communications to review committees, etc
    Immunity for communications in aid of evaluation   CC §43.8
Professional standards committees
    Discovery of proceedings, limitation   Ev §1157
    Immunity from liability   CC §43.7

MILEAGE
Depositions (See **DEPOSITIONS**)
Subpoena duces tecum, mileage costs for   Ev §1563

MILITARY
Absentees
    Fiduciaries substituted during wartime (See **FIDUCIARIES' WARTIME SUBSTITUTION LAW**)
    Missing persons generally (See within this heading, "**Missing persons**")
Acknowledgment of instruments   CC §1183.5
Adoption proceedings, absence of adoptive parent serving in military   Fam §8613
Annulment of marriage or legal separation, waiver of respondent's filing fees in action for   Gov §70673
Attack shelters, governmental liability   CC §1714.5
Attorney practice
    Registered military spouse attorney   CRC 9.41.1
Attorney representation by military counsel   CRC 9.41
Child support
    Arrears collection
        Compromise of arrears program   Fam §17560
    Modification of support
        Active duty   Fam §§3651, 3653
        Government support enforcement services   Fam §17440
Consumer warranty protection
    Motor vehicle purchased in US   CC §1791.8
Custody of children
    Absence or relocation of parent from family residence as consideration for court in awarding custody or visitation
        Active service in military   Fam §3047
Discharge from service records, waiver of recording fees for   Gov §27381
Dissolution of marriage or legal separation, waiver of respondent's filing fees in action for   Gov §70673
Dogs used in police work, injuries inflicted by   CC §§3342, 3342.5
Escheated property, military awards and decorations
    Separate notice for savings bonds, war bonds and military awards   CCP §1531.6
Family support
    Modification of support
        Active duty   Fam §§3651, 3653
Fiduciaries substituted during wartime (See **FIDUCIARIES' WARTIME SUBSTITUTION LAW**)
Financial obligations during service, relief
    Petitions for relief   CRC 3.1372
Forms   CRCAppx A
Infants (See **PARENT AND CHILD**)
Investigative agencies, military identification card as identification   CC §1786.22
Judge advocate, appearance in state court   CRC 9.41
Judges   CRCSupp JudEthicsCanon 2
Landlord and tenant
    Deposits, limitations for military service members   CC §1950.5
Marriage
    Overseas personnel
        Attorney-in-fact, appearance on behalf of personnel stationed overseas to solemnize marriage   Fam §420
Minor's enlistment in armed forces   Fam §6950
Missing persons
    Generally   Pro §3700
    Agency, revocation of   CC §2357
    Fiduciaries substituted during wartime (See **FIDUCIARIES' WARTIME SUBSTITUTION LAW**)
    Judicial proceedings to set aside personal property of   Pro §§3701 to 3708

Index

MUTUAL SAVINGS ASSOCIATIONS

Disqualification of judges, proprietary interest of depositor as financial interest for purposes of   CCP §170.5

MUTUAL WILLS   Pro §21700

N

NAILS

Fixtures attached to real property with   CC §660

NAMEPLATES

Manufacturer's nameplate removed from articles   CC §1710.1

NAMES

Adoption proceedings (See **ADOPTION**)

Advertising, unauthorized use of name or likeness in   CC §§3344, 3344.1

Annulment, restoration of former name in proceedings for   Fam §§2080 to 2082

Attorney professional conduct

    Firm names and trade names   ProfC 7.5

Change of (See **CHANGE OF NAMES**)

Commercial blockage tort, pseudonyms used in civil proceedings for   CC §3427.3

Complaint, names of parties in title   CCP §422.40

Deeds (See **DEEDS**)

Dissolution of marriage, restoration of former name in proceedings for   Fam §2401

Doe defendants, generally (See **UNKNOWN PERSONS**)

Fictitious names (See **FICTITIOUS NAMES**)

Guardians ad litem

    Pseudonym, appointment under   CCP §372.5

Invasion of privacy, unauthorized use of name or likeness in advertising as   CC §§3344, 3344.1

Judgment lien on property of misidentified owner, release of   CCP §§697.410, 697.660

Juror personal information (See **JURY**)

Owner of property (See **TITLE AND OWNERSHIP**)

Pleadings, amendment of   CCP §473

Prohibition against refusal to engage in business with person using birth or former name regardless of marital status   CCP §1279.6

Restoration of former name   Fam §§2080 to 2082, 2401

Small claims court (See **SMALL CLAIMS COURTS**)

True name of defendant designated as unknown, amendment to add   CCP §474

NARCOTICS AND DANGEROUS DRUGS

Abuse of (See **SUBSTANCE ABUSE**)

Custody of children

    Substance abuse as custody determining factor

        Testing for alcohol or controlled substance use ordered by court   Fam §3041.5

Guardian and ward, custody of child

    Substance abuse as custody determining factor

        Testing for alcohol or controlled substance use ordered by court   Fam §3041.5

Marriage license denied to persons under influence of   Fam §352

Mobilehome tenancy terminated for conviction of use on premises   CC §798.56

Nuisance actions (See **NUISANCES**)

Pharmacists and pharmacies (See **PHARMACISTS AND PHARMACIES**)

Secure drug take-back bins

    Liability of collector, limitation   CC §1714.24

Unlawful detainer proceedings based on tenant's drug-selling on premises   CCP §1161

    Nuisance, termination of leases for   CC §§3486, 3486.5

NATIONAL BANKS (See **BANKS AND BANKING**)

NATIONAL INFLUENZA PROGRAM

Public entity or employee participating in program, immunity of   Gov §856.6

NATIONAL ORIGIN

Adoption proceedings, prohibited discrimination in   Fam §8708

Discrimination   CC §§51 to 53

    Judicial ethics code

        Administrative responsibilities of judge, impartial discharge   CRCSupp JudEthicsCanon 3

        Attorneys, judges to require to refrain from manifesting   CRCSupp JudEthicsCanon 3

        Court personnel and staff under direction of judge, standards of conduct enforced by judge   CRCSupp JudEthicsCanon 3

        Membership in discriminatory organizations   CRCSupp JudEthicsCanon 2

NATIONAL ORIGIN—Cont.

Equal protection

    Political structure equal protection   CC §53.7

Foster care placement   Fam §7950

Jury service exemption not allowed based on   CCP §204

Political structure equal protection   CC §53.7

NATIONAL PARKS

Appropriation of water originating in   CC §1422

NATIVE AMERICANS

Abandoned children

    Transfer by parent of care, custody and control to Indian custodian as not constituting abandonment   Fam §7822

Adoption (See **ADOPTION**)

Child custody

    Temporary custody of Indian child, agreement   CRCAppx A

Child support

    Title IV-D support actions

        Transfer of title IV-D cases from tribal court   CRC 5.372

        Transfer of title IV-D cases to tribal court   CRC 5.372

Conservation easements held by tribes   CC §815.3

Conservatorship proceedings for Indian children

    Applicability of Indian Child Welfare Act   Pro §1459.5

    Attorneys

        Inability to afford counsel   Pro §1474

    Interstate jurisdiction, transfer and recognition

        Generally   Pro §§1980 to 2033

        Judicial council legal forms   CRCAppx A

        Provisions specific to federally recognized Indian tribes   Pro §§2031 to 2033

    Involuntary placements

        Indian Child Welfare Act, rules governing   CRC 5.480 to 5.487 (See **INDIAN CHILD WELFARE ACT INVOLUNTARY PLACEMENTS**)

    Legislative findings and intent   Pro §1459

    Notice

        Indian children as proposed conservatee   Pro §1460.2

    Registration and recognition of orders from other states

        Tribal courts (California tribes), applicability of provisions   Pro §2019

    Transfers of conservatorships

        Tribal courts (California tribes), transfers to or from   Pro §2003

    Tribal membership of conservatee

        Petition, contents   Pro §§1821, 1826

Custody of children (See **CUSTODY OF CHILDREN**)

Dependency matters

    Appearances

        Telephone or computerized remote appearances by tribe   CRC 5.531

    Detention hearing

        Active efforts   CRC 5.678

        Evidence required for detention of Indian child   CRC 5.676

        Findings necessary to detain   CRC 5.674, 5.678

        Placement preferences   CRC 5.678

    Emergency removal

        Hearing for return of custody when emergency ends   CRC 5.678

    Generally (See **DEPENDENT CHILDREN**)

    Inquiry as to Indian status at first appearance   CRC 5.668

    Intake process

        Purposes of intake process   CRC 5.510

    Notice under Indian Child Welfare Act   CRC 5.725

    Orders

        Judicial council form   CRCAppx A

    Placement under Indian Child Welfare Act   CRC 5.565, 5.570

        Out-of-county placements   CRC 5.614, CRCAppx A

        Rules governing involuntary placements   CRC 5.480 to 5.488 (See **INDIAN CHILD WELFARE ACT INVOLUNTARY PLACEMENTS**)

    Reunification services, requirement

        Termination of reunification services, findings   CRC 5.570

    Telephone or computerized remote appearances by tribe   CRC 5.531

    Termination of juvenile court jurisdiction

        Nonminor dependents or wards in foster care   CRC 5.555

    Tribal rights in   CRC 5.534

    Tribal information form   CRCAppx A

Divorces, validity of   Fam §295

Electronic court records, remote access

    Government entities, access by

        List of government entities which may be authorized to receive access   CRC 2.540

NEW TRIAL—Cont.
Court reporter
    Death or disability, effect   CCP §§657.1, 914
    Hearings on new trial motion, transcripts   CCP §660
Courts of appeal authorized to direct   CCP §43
Damages
    Excessive or inadequate damages   CCP §662.5
    Grounds for new trial   CCP §657
    Reduction of   CCP §662.5
Death or disability of court reporter as grounds for   CCP §§657.1, 914
Defined   CCP §656
Denial of motion, extension of time for appeal   CRC 8.108
Discretion abuse as ground for   CCP §657
Dismissal actions regarding   CCP §583.320
Dismissal for delay in prosecution following granting of new trial motion
    COVID-19, emergency rule   CRCAppx I Emer Rule 10
Dissolution of marriage (See **DISSOLUTION OF MARRIAGE**)
Environmental quality act
    Jobs and economic improvement through environmental leadership act of 2011
        Appellate review of CEQA cases   CRC 8.702
    Sacramento downtown arena project, CEQA challenges
        Appellate review of CEQA cases   CRC 8.702
Evidence
    Grounds for new trial   CCP §657
    Motions, evidence supporting   CCP §660
Expedited jury trials
    Permissible grounds   CCP §630.09
    Waiver of motions concerning amount of damages   CCP §630.08
Extensions of time   CCP §§659, 659a
Fire destroying bill of exceptions   CCP §663.1
Grounds for   CCP §657
Hearings   CCP §§660, 663.2
Judicial arbitration (See **JUDICIAL ARBITRATION**)
Jury misconduct as grounds for new trial   CCP §657
Law errors as grounds for   CCP §657
Mandamus   CCP §1092
Mandatory time to bring action to trial
    Generally   CCP §583.320
    Computation of   CCP §583.340
    Extension of time   CCP §§583.330, 583.350
    Failure to obtain action within time limit, effect of   CCP §583.360
Mediation, new trial on grounds of irregular reference to   CCP §1775.12, Ev §1128
Motion for new trial
    Affidavit in support of new trial motion   CCP §659a
    Bifurcated trial, motion following   CRC 3.1591
    Evidence considered on   CCP §660
    Hearings on   CCP §§660, 663.2
    Memorandum in support of   CRC 3.1600
    Notice of   CCP §659
    Ruling on motion, alternatives   CCP §662
    Time for filing   CCP §659
    Trial judge determining   CCP §661
Natural catastrophe destroying bill of exceptions   CCP §663.1
Newly-discovered evidence as ground for   CCP §657
Nonjury cases   CCP §662
Reporter
    Death or disability of court reporter, effect of   CCP §§657.1, 914
    Hearings on new trial motion, use of transcripts at   CCP §660
Reviewing court's authority to order new trial   CCP §906
Ruling on motion, alternatives   CCP §662
Service of papers
    Motion for new trial   CCP §659
    Supporting affidavit for new trial   CCP §659a
Special proceedings   CCP §1110
Supreme Court authorized to direct   CCP §43
Surprise as grounds for   CCP §657
Time
    Vacation of judgment
        Notice of motion, time for   CCP §663a
        Ruling on motion, time for   CCP §663a
Trial court rules
    Notice of intention to move for
        Memorandum in support of   CRC 3.1600
Unlawful detainer   CCP §1178
Will probate proceedings   Pro §7220

NEXT BUSINESS DAY
Extension of time to next day which is not a holiday   CCP §12a
Postponing performance from holiday to   CCP §13

NIGHT SESSIONS
Small claims court sessions   CCP §116.250

911 EMERGENCY LINE
Immunity from liability, telecommunications services providing   CC §1714.55

99-YEAR LEASE
Validity of   CC §§718, 718f

NO CONTEST CLAUSES (See **WILL PROBATE**)

NOISE
Eminent domain to prevent noise pollution, taking for   CCP §1240.110
Shooting range exemption from liability for noise pollution   CC §3482.1

NOLO CONTENDERE PLEAS
Appealability of conviction   CRC 8.304
Appellate rules, supreme court and courts of appeal
    Appeal after plea of nolo contendere   CRC 8.304
Certificate of probable cause for appeal   CRC 8.304
Certification for superior court sentencing following plea of   CRC 4.114
Judgment based on plea of nolo contendere, admissibility of   Ev §1300
Punishment
    Specification in plea   CRC 4.412
Report to Justice Department concerning nolo contendere plea   CRC 4.320
Setting date for sentencing and reference of case to probation officer   CRC 4.114

NOMINAL DAMAGES   CC §3360

NON-DOMICILIARIES
Jury service, exceptions to eligibility for   CCP §203

NONJUDICIAL REMEDIES
Administrative hearings, procedure for (See **ADMINISTRATIVE ADJUDICATION**)
Arbitration (See **ARBITRATION**)

NONJURY TRIALS
Appeals   CCP §909
Default judgments   CCP §636
Evidence   CCP §631.8
Fact issues   CCP §592
Liability issue, trial of   CCP §598
Motion for judgment in   CCP §631.8
New trial, motion for   CCP §661
Order of   CCP §631.7
Rebuttal of evidence after motion for judgment   CCP §631.8
Rendition of judgment   CCP §636
Statement of decision   CCP §632
Waiver of jury trial   CCP §631
Witnesses, rehabilitation of   CCP §631.8

NONMARITAL RELATIONSHIPS (See **COHABITATION**)

NONNEGOTIABLE INSTRUMENTS
Endorsement of   CC §1459
Transfer of   CC §955

NONPROBATE TRANSFERS
Community property
    Execution of provision for nonprobate transfer without consent of spouse, validity of   Pro §5020
    Fraud, undue influence, duress or mistake, validity of consent procured by   Pro §5015
    Holder of community property under nonprobate instrument, effect on   Pro §5012
    Limitations on parties' community property rights   Pro §5011
    Modification of provision for nonprobate transfer   Pro §5023
    Revocation of consent
        Generally   Pro §5030
        Holder's authority to transfer property, effect on   Pro §5031
        Manner of revocation   Pro §5031
        Passage of property after   Pro §5032
    Right of survivorship without administration pursuant to terms of written instrument   CC §682.1
    Scope of law   Pro §5014
    Set-aside proceeding for nonprobate transfer   Pro §5021
    Transmutation of consenting spouse's interest, effect of spousal consent on   Fam §853, Pro §5022
    Waiver of surviving spouse's rights, effect on   Pro §5013
    Written consent, written joinder by parties to provisions of instrument interpreted as   Pro §5010

Index

NURSING HOMES—Cont.
Sexual battery against incapacitated person
    Statute of limitations on sexual assault damages   CCP §340.16
Statutes of limitation for recovery or conversion of personal property left at   CCP §341a

O

OAKLAND, CITY OF
Unlawful detainer actions
    Controlled substances as nuisance
        Pilot program   CC §3486.5
    Firearms or weapons as nuisances
        Applicability of provisions   CC §3485

OATHS
Generally   CCP §§2015.6, 2093 to 2094
Administrative Procedure Act (See **ADMINISTRATIVE PROCEDURE ACT**)
Administrators (See **EXECUTORS AND ADMINISTRATORS**)
Arbitration   CCP §1282.8
    Judicial arbitration   CRC 3.824
Attachment (See **ATTACHMENT**)
Claims and delivery possession writ, application for   CCP §512.010
County recorder's fees for administering or certifying   Gov §27379
Declaration or certification of written instrument executed under penalty of perjury   CCP §2015.5
Dependent persons   Ev §710
Depositions
    Oath of deponent   CCP §2025.330
Executors (See **EXECUTORS AND ADMINISTRATORS**)
Form of   CCP §2094
Inclusions in definition   CCP §17
Innkeeper's liens, writ of possession on   CC §1861.5
Judges
    Temporary judges   CRC 2.814
        Request by parties for temporary judge   CRC 2.831
Jurors, oath sworn by   CCP §232
Jury commissioner's power to administer   CCP §196
Manner of administering oath or affirmation   CCP §2094
Parties administering   CCP §2093
Penalty of perjury, declaration or certification of written instrument executed under   CCP §2015.5
Power of court to administer   CCP §128
Power of judge to administer   CCP §177
Proofs of execution of instruments, officers administering oaths for   CC §1201
Public guardians appointed as guardian or conservator, oaths required for   Pro §2922
Receivers, faithful performance of   CCP §567
Shorthand reporters at deposition proceedings, oaths administered by   CCP §2093
State agency proceedings (See **ADMINISTRATIVE PROCEDURE ACT**)
Statutory requirement   Ev §710
Temporary restraining order, certification of attempt to notify party of   CCP §527
Translators and interpreters in court proceedings   Ev §751
Witnesses   Ev §710

OATS
Storage regulations after sale of   CC §§1880 to 1881.2

OBJECTIONS AND EXCEPTIONS
Administrators of decedents' estates (See **EXECUTORS AND ADMINISTRATORS**)
Answers, objection to allegations in   CCP §430.20
Appealable orders deemed excepted to   CCP §647
Arbitration (See **ARBITRATION**)
Blood test, submission of evidence on technique of taking   Ev §712
Complaints, objection to allegations in   CCP §§430.10, 430.30
Conservatorship proceedings (See **CONSERVATORS**)
Court reporters to take down all objections and exceptions made   CCP §269
Cross-complaints, objection to allegations in   CCP §§430.10, 430.30
Demurrers (See **DEMURRERS**)
Economic litigation provision excluding evidence or witness not included in statement   CCP §97
Eminent domain, objections to right to take in   CCP §§1250.350 to 1250.370, 1260.110, 1260.120
Enforcement of judgments (See **ENFORCEMENT OF JUDGMENTS**)
Evidence erroneously admitted   Ev §353
Exception defined   CCP §646
Executors of decedents' estates (See **EXECUTORS AND ADMINISTRATORS**)
Guardian and ward (See **GUARDIAN AND WARD**)

OBJECTIONS AND EXCEPTIONS—Cont.
Interlocutory orders deemed excepted to   CCP §647
Judges (See **JUDGES**)
Judicial arbitration, exceptions to   CCP §§1141.13, 1141.15
Jurisdiction, objection to   CCP §§418.10, 418.11
Orders and rulings, exceptions to   CCP §§646, 647
Pleadings, objections to   CCP §§430.10 to 430.80
Referee's statement of decision   CCP §645
Reversed without exceptions, orders and rulings   CCP §647
Sterilization proceedings, objections by party to be sterilized in   Pro §1958
Striking out or refusing to strike out pleading   CCP §647
Summary judgment hearing, waiver of objections not raised in   CCP §437c
Superior courts (See **SUPERIOR COURTS**)
Surety and fidelity bonds (See **SURETYSHIP, BONDS AND UNDERTAKINGS**)
Time to except   CCP §646
Verdicts deemed excepted to   CCP §647

OBLIGATIONS
Abstaining from injuring person or property of another   CC §1708
Civil actions, obligations as basis for   CCP §26

OBSCENITY AND INDECENCY (See **INDECENCY AND OBSCENITY**)

OCCUPANCY (See **ADVERSE POSSESSION**)

OCCUPATION
Jury service exemption not allowed based on   CCP §204

OFFAL (See **GARBAGE**)

OFFENSES (See **CRIMINAL ACTIONS AND PROCEEDINGS**)

OFFER
Contracts (See **CONTRACTS AND AGREEMENTS**)
Settlement offers (See **SETTLEMENT AND COMPROMISE**)
Tender, refused offer as   CCP §2074

OFFICE
Service of process at office of person being served   CCP §415.20

OFFICE OF ADMINISTRATIVE LAW (See **ADMINISTRATIVE PROCEDURE ACT**)

OFFICE OF INFORMATION PRACTICES (See **INFORMATION PRACTICES ACT**)

OFFICERS
Police officers (See **LAW ENFORCEMENT OFFICERS**)
Probation officers (See **PROBATION OFFICERS AND DEPUTIES**)
Public officers and employees (See **PUBLIC OFFICERS AND EMPLOYEES**)

OFFICIAL BONDS (See **BONDS OF PUBLIC OFFICIALS**)

OIL AND GAS
Administration of estates (See **ADMINISTRATION OF ESTATES**)
Discharge or leaking, absolute liability for damages caused by pipeline   CC §3333.5
Indemnity coverage for construction, repair, renovation, maintenance or demolition of lines   CC §2783
Injunctions, secondary recovery operations   CCP §731c
Liens
    Assignments of   CCP §1203.64
    Bonds for release of   CCP §1203.60
    Citation of statute   CCP §1203.50
    Drilling defined   CCP §1203.51
    Enforcement of   CCP §1203.61
    Forfeiture of leasehold estates   CCP §1203.55
    Labor liens, preference of   CCP §1203.57
    Notice of lien claims   CCP §1203.59
    Owner defined   CCP §1203.51
    Parties entitled to   CCP §1203.52
    Perfection of   CCP §1203.65
    Personal action for debt, right to   CCP §1203.62
    Priority   CCP §1203.56
    Record of   CCP §1203.58
    Services defined   CCP §1203.51
    Statutory construction   CCP §1203.66
    Subcontractor's liens   CCP §1203.54
    Time of   CCP §1203.53
    Waiver of   CCP §1203.63
Mineral rights (See **MINERALS AND MINERAL RIGHTS**)

Index

Index

Index

Index

Index

POLYGRAPH

Exclusion of polygraph evidence   Ev §351.1

POOLS

Juror pools (See **JURY**)

POOR PERSONS (See **INDIGENT PERSONS**)

POPULAR NAMES OF ACTS (See **CITATION OF ACTS**)

PORCELAIN PAINTING

Fine art, defined as   CC §997

PORTER-COLOGNE WATER QUALITY CONTROL ACT

Limitation of actions   CCP §338

POSSESSION

Action to recover for   CC §§3375, 3379, 3380

Administrator having right of   Pro §§9650, 9651

Adverse possession (See **ADVERSE POSSESSION**)

Attachment (See **ATTACHMENT**)

Bailment contract, transfer under   CC §1925

Bonds

     Corporate executors, bond requirements for   Pro §301

     Trust companies   Pro §301

Claim and delivery (See **CLAIM AND DELIVERY**)

Contempt for re-entry after removal from   CCP §1210

Damages for wrongful possession   CC §§3334 to 3336

Domestic violence protective orders determining   Fam §6324

Easement, rights under   CC §810

Eminent domain

     Orders for possession

         After judgment   CCP §§1268.210 to 1268.240

         Prior to judgment   CCP §§1255.410 to 1255.480

Enforcement of judgments (See **ENFORCEMENT OF JUDGMENTS**)

Executor having right of   Pro §§9650, 9651

Future time, possession at   CC §767

Homestead   Pro §6520

Innkeeper's lien   CC §§1861 to 1861.28

Judgment granting recovery of   CCP §667

Lien dependent on possession   CC §§2913, 3051

Lost property, liability and duties of finder of   CC §2080

Mobilehomes, writ of possession for   CCP §§515.010, 515.020

Mortgages (See **TRUST DEEDS AND MORTGAGES**)

Ouster, cotenant's right to establish   CC §843

Ownership presumed from   Ev §637

Quieting title (See **QUIETING TITLE**)

Receivers   CCP §568

Recovery of real property, seisin or possession within five years of commencement of action for   CCP §318

Renewal of lease presumed   CC §1945

Retail installment sales, finance charge assessed after buyer's possession of goods   CC §§1805.6, 1810.10

Risk of loss under sales contract after transfer of   CC §1662

Room, tenant's right to possession of   CC §1950

Special administrators having possession of estate assets   Pro §8544

Specific relief, award of   CC §3367

Stay of judgment for delivery of   CCP §917.4

Third party claim of right of possession of property levied upon   CCP §§720.110 to 720.170

Title to real property, seisin or possession within five years of commencement of action arising out of   CCP §319

Unlawful detainer (See **UNLAWFUL DETAINER**)

Voidable transaction presumed in absence of   CC §3440

Wills (See **WILLS**)

POSSIBILITY OF REVERTER

Conveyances   CC §1045

POSTADOPTION CONTACT AGREEMENTS   CRC 5.451, Fam §§8616.5, 8714, 8714.5

POSTAL SERVICE (See **MAIL AND MAILING**)

POSTERS

Political posters, sale of   CC §1739.1

POSTHUMOUS CHILDREN

Conception after death of decedent

     Heirs, identity and distributions   Pro §§249.5 to 249.8

         Early distribution, petition for   Pro §249.8

         Effect on distribution   Pro §249.6

POSTHUMOUS CHILDREN—Cont.

Conception after death of decedent—Cont.

     Heirs, identity and distributions —Cont.

         Failure to provide timely notice   Pro §249.7

     Intestate descent   Pro §6453

     Presumption of birth during lifetime of decedent   Pro §249.5

Future interests   CC §§698, 739

Intestate descent   Pro §§240, 6407

POSTING

Administration of estates (See **ADMINISTRATION OF ESTATES**)

Apartment house owner, posting notice of   CC §1962.5

Decedents' estates (See **ADMINISTRATION OF ESTATES**)

Destroyed land records relief law proceedings, service in   CCP §751.08

Earthquakes, boundary reestablishment after   CCP §751.54

Electronic court records

     Privacy policy, posting   CRC 2.504

Enforcement of judgments (See **ENFORCEMENT OF JUDGMENTS**)

Grain sold in bulk, posting notice of   CC §1880.7

Hotel rights, notice of   CC §1863

Human trafficking

     Businesses required to post notice concerning relief from slavery or human trafficking   CC §52.6

Letters of administration, notice of hearing for   Pro §8003

Mobilehome parks

     Mobilehome assistance center

         Signs, posting by housing and community development department   CC §798.29

Parking facilities' limitation of liability, posting contract for   CC §1630

Process (See **PROCESS AND SERVICE OF PROCESS**)

Quieting title action   CCP §763.020

Unlawful detainer actions, service in   CCP §415.45

POSTMORTEM EXAMINATIONS

Restriction on reproducing photograph or video taken in course of   CCP §129

POSTPONEMENT

Continuances (See **CONTINUANCES**)

Holiday postponing performance of act required by law or contract   CCP §13

Small claims court (See **SMALL CLAIMS COURTS**)

POSTRELEASE COMMUNITY SUPERVISION

Jury service

     Felons currently on parole, probation, etc

         Ineligibility to serve as juror   CCP §203

Revocation

     Sentencing upon revocation   CRC 4.435

Revocation procedure

     Supervising agency reports as to compliance with provisions   CRC 4.541

Risk/needs assessment, court use in sentencing   CRC JudAdminStand 4.35

POSTSECONDARY EDUCATION

Debt collection

     Educational debt collection practices   CC §§1788.90 to 1788.93

         Definitions   CC §1788.92

         Legislative findings and intent   CC §1788.91

         Prohibited debt collection practices by schools   CC §1788.93

         Short title of act   CC §1788.90

         Transcript used as leverage to collect debt, prohibition   CC §1788.93

Students

     Violence threatened on campus or facility

         Orders against violence threatened on campus or facility   CRCAppx I Emer Rule 8

Violence threatened on campus or facility

     Orders against violence threatened on campus or facility

         COVID-19, emergency rule   CRCAppx I Emer Rule 8

POST-TRAUMATIC STRESS DISORDER (PTSD)

Veterans in need of services

     Sentence and punishment, alternate commitment for combat veterans

         Orders for dismissal, judicial council legal forms   CRCAppx A

POULTRY

Dogs injuring   CC §3341

Statute of limitation against veterinarians or persons boarding or feeding   CCP §340

POUR-OVER PROVISIONS

Life insurance   Pro §§6321 to 6330

Trusts (See **TRUSTS**)

Wills (See **WILLS**)

POWER OF ATTORNEY—Cont.

Incorporation of powers by reference to other statutes, grant of authority by Pro §4263

Instructions of principal, duty to follow Pro §4234

Insurance

Medical insurance conditioned on execution of durable power of attorney for health care, prohibition on Pro §4677

Statutory form power of attorney, powers under Pro §4457

Intentional wrongdoing of attorney in fact Pro §4231.5

Judges, service as attorney in fact CRCSupp JudEthicsCanon 4

Judicial intervention, exercise of power of attorney free of Pro §4500

Jurisdiction

Generally Pro §§4520 to 4522

Health care power of attorney, actions involving Pro §§4760 to 4762

Jury trial, unavailability of

Generally Pro §4504

Health care power of attorney Pro §4754

Legal separation from principal by attorney in fact, effect of Pro §3722

Legal sufficiency of power of attorney, requirements for Pro §4121

Liability of third person acting in reliance on power of attorney Pro §4303

Limitation in power of attorney

Generally Pro §§4101, 4262

Health care power of attorney

Express statement in power of attorney, limitation by Pro §§4681, 4753

Statutory limitation on consent in behalf of principal Pro §4652

Judicial proceedings, authority in Pro §§4502, 4503

Loans

Authority to perform act regarding Pro §4264

Financial institution not required to make loan where no prior relationship with principal Pro §4310

Marriage

Military personnel

Overseas personnel

Attorney-in-fact, appearance on behalf of personnel stationed overseas to solemnize marriage Fam §420

Mechanical acts, power of attorney in fact to delegate authority for Pro §4205

Medical treatment (See within this heading, **"Health care power of attorney"**)

Mercy killing Pro §4653

Military missing persons Pro §§3720 to 3722

Missing persons Pro §§3720 to 3722

Modification

Generally Pro §4150

Durable power of attorney Pro §4206

Mortgages, execution of CC §§2933, 2945.4

Multiple-party accounts Pro §5204

Murder, actions under durable power of attorney for health care considered as Pro §4743

Nondurable power of attorney, termination of authority of attorney in fact under Pro §4155

Other jurisdiction, execution of health care power of attorney in Pro §4053

Personal and family maintenance, powers under statutory form power of attorney regarding Pro §4460

Petitions

Capacity to file Pro §4540

Commencement of proceedings under Pro §4542

Dismissal of Pro §4543

Health care power of attorney Pro §§4765 to 4770

Limiting authority for Pro §4503

Notice of time and place of hearings regarding petitions Pro §4544

Purpose of petition regarding power of attorney Pro §4541

Printed form of durable power of attorney Pro §4102

Recordation of revocation of power of attorney CC §1216

Records of transactions, duty to maintain Pro §4236

Redesignation of attorney in fact Pro §4207

Reference in law, effect of Pro §4052

Refusal to engage in transaction with attorney in fact, right of third person for Pro §4309

Remarriage to former spouse, revival of designation on Pro §4154

Restrictions on limiting application of Pro §4101

Resuscitative measures, request regarding Pro §§4780 to 4786

Retirement plan transactions, powers under statutory form power of attorney regarding Pro §4462

Revocation

Generally Pro §4151

Attorney in fact, authority of Pro §4153

Fiduciary or conservator's power to revoke or amend durable power of attorney Pro §4206

Health care power of attorney Pro §§4695 to 4698

Recordation of revocation of power of attorney CC §1216

Separate and distinct, duty to keep principal's property as Pro §4233

POWER OF ATTORNEY—Cont.

Short form power of attorney, validity of Pro §4409

Sole interest of principal, duty of attorney in fact to act in Pro §4232

Special power of attorney applicable to transactions with financial organizations Pro §5204

Special skills, duty of attorney in fact to apply Pro §4237

Springing power of attorney

Contingency, designation of person with power to determine event of Pro §4129

Defined Pro §4030

Standard of care in dealing with principal's property Pro §§4231, 4231.5

Statutes governing CC §2400

Statutory form power of attorney

Generally Pro §§4400, 4401

Applicability of provisions Pro §4407

Attorney's fees in action to compel honoring of authority under Pro §4406

Beneficiaries

Powers of agent as to Pro §4458

Claims and litigation, powers regarding Pro §4459

Commodity and option transactions, powers regarding Pro §4454

Estate transactions

Powers of agent as to Pro §4458

Event or contingency, effectiveness on occurrence of Pro §4405

Execution, powers unaffected by location of Pro §4464

Express grant of power required Pro §4465

Family maintenance, powers under statutory form power of attorney regarding Pro §4460

Financial institutions, powers regarding Pro §4455

Governmental programs, powers regarding Pro §4461

Health care powers generally (See within this heading, **"Health care power of attorney"**)

Initialing line providing for all listed powers in Pro §4403

Insurance and annuity transactions, powers granted to agent Pro §4457

Legal sufficiency of Pro §4402

Location of property, powers unaffected by Pro §4464

Express grant of power required Pro §4465

Particular subject granted to agent, powers regarding Pro §4459

Personal and family maintenance, powers regarding Pro §4460

Personal property, powers regarding Pro §§4452 to 4454

Real property transactions, powers regarding Pro §4451

Retirement plan transactions, powers regarding Pro §4462

Short form power of attorney, validity of Pro §4409

Stock and bond transactions, powers regarding Pro §4453

Tax matters, powers regarding Pro §4463

Time interest in acquired, powers unaffected by Pro §4464

Express grant of power required Pro §4465

Trusts, modification or revocation

Powers of agent as to Pro §4458

Stay on appeal Pro §1310

Stock and bond transactions, statutory form power of attorney regarding Pro §4453

Successor attorneys in fact, designation of one or more Pro §4203

Survivorship interest, authority to perform act regarding Pro §4264

Tax matters, powers under statutory form power of attorney regarding Pro §4463

Termination

Generally Pro §4152

Death or incapacity of principal, effect of third person acting without knowledge of Pro §4304

Delivery of property and records on termination of authority, duty for Pro §4238

Dissolution of marriage or legal separation as grounds for Pro §§3722, 4154

Health care power of attorney

Revocation of advance directive, termination by Pro §§4695 to 4698

Nondurable power of attorney, termination of authority of attorney in fact under Pro §4155

Revocation generally (See within this heading, **"Revocation"**)

Third persons

Affidavit regarding good faith action without knowledge of death or incapacity of principal Pro §4305

Attorney's fees generally (See within this heading, **"Attorney's fees"**)

Bank not required to open deposit account where no previous relationship with principal Pro §4310

Death or incapacity of principal, effect of third person acting without knowledge of Pro §4304

Employees, effect of power of attorney on third person conducting activities through Pro §4308

Identification of attorney in fact, right to require Pro §4302

Liability of third person acting in reliance on power of attorney Pro §4303

Refusal of third person to accept authority of attorney in fact Pro §4306

POWER OF ATTORNEY—Cont.
Third persons—Cont.
Refusal to engage in transaction with attorney in fact, right of third person for   Pro §4309
Rights and privileges accorded by   Pro §4300
Specific authorization, actions by third persons without regard to   Pro §4301
Statutory form power of attorney, compelling third person to honor authority under   Pro §4406
Transfer of property   CC §1095
Trusts
General authority to perform act regarding   Pro §4264
Statutory form power of attorney, powers under   Pro §4458
Undue influence or financial abuse of elder or dependent adult to take, conceal, etc., property of principal
Liability of attorney in fact for attorney fees   Pro §4231.5
Uniform statutory form power of attorney (See within this heading, "Statutory form power of attorney")
Venue
Generally   Pro §4523
Health care power of attorney   Pro §4763
Will, authority to act regarding   Pro §4265
Witnesses
Generally   Pro §4122
Health care, witnesses to durable power of attorney for   Pro §4674

POWER OF SALE (See TRUST DEEDS AND MORTGAGES)

POWER OF TERMINATION (See TITLE AND OWNERSHIP)

POWERS
Executors, testator limiting administrative powers of   Pro §12206
Judges (See JUDGES)
Judicial arbitrators   CCP §1141.19
Receivers   CCP §568

POWS (See MILITARY)

PRACTICE ADMINISTRATORS (See ATTORNEYS)

PRACTICE OF LAW (See ATTORNEYS)

PRECEDENCE (See PRIORITIES AND PREFERENCES)

PREEXISTING DEBT
Promise to pay as admissible evidence of   Ev §1152

PREFABRICATED HOUSING (See MANUFACTURED HOMES)

PREFERENCES (See PRIORITIES AND PREFERENCES)

PREFILING ORDERS
Vexatious litigants subject to   CCP §391.7
Vacating prefiling order and removing name from list   CCP §391.8

PREGNANCY
Abortion (See ABORTIONS)
Assisted reproduction
Consent required for   Fam §7613
Parentage of child conceived by   Fam §7613
Forms for assisted reproduction   Fam §7613.5
Birth (See BIRTH)
Birth control
Abortion (See ABORTIONS)
Sterilization (See STERILIZATION)
Minors
Consent to medical care   Fam §6925
Requests by minor to marry or establish domestic partnership
Waiting period after order granting request not required in cases of pregnancy   CRC 5.448
Parentage
Voluntary declaration   Fam §§7570 to 7581

PREJUDICE (See BIAS AND PREJUDICE)

PRELIMINARY EXAMINATION OR HEARING
Disposition of cases prior to, procedures for   CRC 10.953
Readiness conferences (See SUPERIOR COURTS)

PRELIMINARY FACT
Admissibility, preliminary fact proved for purpose of   Ev §§400 to 405

PRELIMINARY INJUNCTIONS (See INJUNCTIONS)

PRELIMINARY INVESTIGATION (See JUDGES)

PRELIMINARY PROVISIONS
Code of Civil Procedure   CCP §§2 to 32

PREMARITAL AGREEMENTS
Uniform premarital agreement act (See PROPERTY SETTLEMENT AGREEMENTS)

PREMISES LIABILITY
Common interest development, liability based on interest in common area   CC §5805
Farm owner's immunity for injury to person invited on premises to glean farm products for charitable purposes   CC §846.2
Felony, immunity of landowner for personal injuries to person committing   CC §847
Judicial Council to develop and approve forms   CCP §425.12
Public property (See CLAIMS AGAINST PUBLIC ENTITIES AND EMPLOYEES)
Recreational users
Generally   CC §846
Attorney's fees in recreational user's action against public entity or private owner contractually related to public or nonprofit agency, administrative claim for recovery of   CC §846.1

PREMIUM COUPONS
Gift certificates, expiration dates
Bankruptcy of issuer, duty to honor   CC §1749.6
Waiver of protections   CC §1749.51

PRE-NUPS (PREMARITAL AGREEMENTS)
Premarital agreements   Fam §§1600 to 1620

PREPAID CALLING CARDS
Gift certificate provisions inapplicable   CC §1749.45

PREPAID DEBIT CARDS
Consumer refunds offered by prepaid debit card
Alternative method of receiving refund required to be offered   CC §1748.41
Definitions   CC §1748.40

PREPAYMENTS
Automobiles purchased under conditional sales contract   CC §2982
Real property sales contracts, right under   CC §2985.6
Single family dwellings, prepayment charges on loans secured by mortgage or deed of trust   CC §2954.9
Trust deeds and mortgages (See TRUST DEEDS AND MORTGAGES)

PREPONDERANCE OF EVIDENCE
Burden of proof required in proceedings except where higher degree of proof otherwise required by law   Ev §115
Jury instructions on   Ev §502
Sentencing procedure, applicability to   CRC 4.420

PRESCRIPTIONS
Default judgment for recovery of realty   CCP §585
Easements   CC §§813, 1008
Medical information disclosures
Minors
Coordination of health care services and treatment   CC §56.103
Nuisances, prescriptive rights for   CC §3490
Opioid antagonists   CC §1714.22
Psychotropic medication
Juvenile rules
Release of psychotropic medication prescription information to medical board, authorization   CRC 5.642
Public easement on private land   CC §813
Secure drug take-back bins
Liability of collector, limitation   CC §1714.24
Take-back bins
Secure drug take-back bins
Liability of collector, limitation   CC §1714.24
Title by   CC §§813, 1007 to 1009

PRESERVATION OF INTEREST
Easements (See EASEMENTS)
Mineral rights (See MINERALS AND MINERAL RIGHTS)
Records and recordings (See RECORDS AND RECORDING)

PRESIDING JUDGES (See JUDGES)

PRESUMED FATHER (See PATERNITY)

PRETRIAL CONFERENCES—Cont.
Coordinated actions   CRC 3.541
Criminal cases
    Readiness conference   CRC 4.112
Expedited jury trials   CRC 3.1548
Family centered case resolution conferences   CRC 5.83
Initial case management conference   CRC 3.722
    Complex cases   CRC 3.750
    Environmental quality act
        Petitions under environmental quality act, civil rules governing   CRC 3.2226
    Telephone appearance at case management conferences   CRC 3.670
Judge allowing amended order   CCP §576
Judicial arbitration   CCP §1141.16, CRC 3.812
Judicial Council rules authorized   CCP §575
Management of trial, judge's responsibilities   CRC JudAdminStand 2.20
Mediation, mandatory   CCP §1734
Postponement of   CCP §595.1
Superior courts (See **SUPERIOR COURTS**)
Telephone appearances   CRC 3.670, CRC JudAdminStand 10.21
Trial date
    Setting trial date   CRC 3.729
        Telephone appearances   CCP §§367.5, 367.6
Voir dire
    Pre-voir dire conference in criminal cases   CRC 4.200

PRETRIAL DIVERSION OF MISDEMEANOR OFFENDERS
Mental disorders, individuals with
    Mental competency proceedings   CRC 4.130

PREVENTION OF DOMESTIC VIOLENCE (See **DOMESTIC VIOLENCE**)

PREVENTIVE RELIEF
Generally   CC §§3368, 3369
Injunctions (See **INJUNCTIONS**)

PREVIOUS WILLS (See **WILLS**)

PRICE
Gender, prohibition against charging different price for services of similar or like kind based solely on   CC §51.6
Partition sales   CCP §873.710
Real property (See **VENDOR AND PURCHASER**)
Scanners
    Automatic checkout systems   CC §§7100 to 7106
Unassembled furniture, advertising price for   CC §1770

PRICE DISCRIMINATION BASED ON GENDER
Small business gender discrimination in pricing services compliance act   CC §§55.61 to 55.63

PRIESTS (See **CLERGYPERSONS**)

PRIMA FACIE EVIDENCE
Generally   Ev §602
Transcripts as prima facie evidence of testimony and proceedings   CCP §273

PRINCIPAL AND AGENT (See **AGENCY**)

PRINCIPAL AND INCOME
Legal Estates Principal and Income Law (See **LEGAL ESTATES PRINCIPAL AND INCOME LAW**)
Trusts (See **TRUSTS**)

PRINTERS AND PRINTING
Administrative Procedure Act, official publications under (See **ADMINISTRATIVE PROCEDURE ACT**)
Affidavit of printer as evidence of publication   CCP §2010
Presumptions of printing of books   Ev §644
Type size (See **TYPE SIZE**)
Writing defined to include printing   CCP §17
Written part of document controlling   CCP §1862

PRIOR CONVICTIONS (See **CONVICTION OF CRIME**)

PRIOR INCONSISTENT STATEMENTS (See **WITNESSES**)

PRIORITIES AND PREFERENCES
Administration of estates
    Abatement of bequests (See **ADMINISTRATION OF ESTATES**)
    Claims against estates, payment of   Pro §§11420, 11421
    Executors and administrators (See **EXECUTORS AND ADMINISTRATORS**)
Adoption placement preference rules (See **ADOPTION**)

PRIORITIES AND PREFERENCES—Cont.
Affidavit in support of motion for preference   CCP §36.5
Appeal, motion for calendar preference   CRC 8.240
Arbitration proceedings   CCP §1291
Assignment for benefit of creditors (See **ASSIGNMENT FOR BENEFIT OF CREDITORS**)
Attachment (See **ATTACHMENT**)
Child support (See **CHILD SUPPORT**)
Commission of felony, precedence where damages caused during   CCP §37
Common carriers   CC §§2170, 2171
Concurrent liens   CC §2899
Continuances, effect of grant of motion for preference on   CCP §36
Custody proceedings (See **CUSTODY OF CHILDREN**)
Debt payments   CC §3432
Decedents' estates
    Abatement of bequests (See **ADMINISTRATION OF ESTATES**)
    Claims against estates, payment of   Pro §§11420, 11421
    Executors and administrators (See **EXECUTORS AND ADMINISTRATORS**)
Declaratory relief   CCP §1062.3
Earnings assignment for support (See **EARNINGS ASSIGNMENT FOR SUPPORT**)
Elections proceedings, precedence to cases involving   CCP §§35, 44
Eminent domain proceedings   CCP §1260.010
Enforcement of judgments (See **ENFORCEMENT OF JUDGMENTS**)
Family law rules (See **FAMILY RULES**)
First in time   CC §2897
Foster care placement (See **FOSTER CARE HOMES**)
Garnishment claims (See **GARNISHMENT**)
Illness or condition raising substantial medical doubt of survival of party   CCP §36
Interests of justice served by granting preference, discretion of court to grant motion where   CCP §36
Issues, order of trial of   CCP §598
Juvenile appeals, priority of   CCP §45
Landlord, deposits by tenant to   CC §1950.7
Libel, action for   CCP §460.5
Liens (See **LIENS**)
Livestock service liens   CC §3080.01
Mechanics' liens   CC §§8450 to 8458
    Public works, stop payment notices   CC §9456
Messages transmitted by carriers   CC §§2207 to 2209
Mortgage liens (See **TRUST DEEDS AND MORTGAGES**)
Nonjury trials, priority of   CCP §598
Oil and gas liens   CCP §§1203.56, 1203.57
Over age of 70 years, motion for preference of party who is   CCP §36
Parental rights of alleged father, action to terminate   Fam §7667
Partition (See **PARTITION**)
Preliminary injunctions granted without notice, precedence to hearing on   CCP §527
Purchase money mortgage or trust deed   CC §2898
Recording instruments   CC §1214
Related cases   CRC 3.300
Satisfaction of money judgments, priorities for crediting money received in   CCP §§695.220, 695.221
Setting for trial   CCP §36
Settlement in good faith, review of determination of   CCP §877.6
Slander, action for   CCP §460.5
Subordinate liens   CC §2899
Termination of parental rights, proceedings for   Fam §7870
Transportation of persons or goods   CC §§2170, 2171
Under age of 14, preference in wrongful death or personal injury action to party   CCP §36
Unlawful detainer cases   CCP §1179a
Validation proceedings   CCP §867
Wage assignment for support, priority of   CCP §706.031
Wage claims, preference to   CCP §§1204 to 1208

PRISONERS (See also **IMPRISONMENT**)
Acknowledgments
    Identification   CC §1185
Adverse possession, disabilities tolling statute of limitation in actions for   CCP §328
Appellate rules, superior court appeals
    Filing
        Timeliness of documents mailed from custodial institutions   CRC 8.817
Appellate rules, supreme court and courts of appeal
    Filing
        Timeliness   CRC 8.25

Index

Index

Index

Index

Index

Index

Index

PUBLIC ADMINISTRATORS—Cont.

Burial instructions, search for   Pro §7602
Claims against estates, payment of   Pro §7662
Compensation
    Generally   Pro §7622
    Additional compensation   Pro §7623
    Attorney for public administrator, services of   Pro §7622
    Small estates, compensation for summary disposition of   Pro §7666
Continuing education   Pro §7605
Convalescent hospitals' duty to notify public administrator of death of patient
    Pro §7600.5
Costs of estate administration
    Generally   Pro §7621
    Small estates, summary disposition of   Pro §§7662, 13114
    Subsequent personal representative, costs recoverable on appointment of
      Pro §7604
Delivery of decedent's tangible personal property to surviving spouse   Pro §330
Deposit of funds
    Generally   Pro §7640
    County treasurer, funds deposited with   Pro §7643
    Interest on money deposited   Pro §7642
    State treasurer, deposit with   Pro §7644
    Unclaimed deposits   Pro §§7624, 7643, 7644, 7663
    Withdrawal by public administrator for estate administration   Pro §7641
Electronic court records, remote access
    Government entities, access by   CRC 2.540
English language, judicial proceedings preserved and published in   CCP §185
Escheat of assets held by   CCP §1449, Pro §§7643, 7644
Fees
    Additional compensation   Pro §7623
    Costs and expenses for small estate administration   Pro §§7662, 13114
    Probate proceedings, filing fees payable by public administrator as petitioner
      in   Gov §70659
Final distribution of estate, money remaining after   Pro §§7624, 7663
Financial institutions
    Surrender of decedent's property to public administrator   Pro §7603
    Unclaimed money deposited by public administrator, distribution of   Pro
      §7644
Funds, refusal to surrender   Pro §7624
Funeral director's duty to notify public administrator of unclaimed body   Pro
    §7600.6
Funeral instructions, search for   Pro §7602
Hospitals' duty to notify public administrator of death of patient   Pro §7600.5
Interest on money deposited, disposition of   Pro §7642
Jurisdiction of   Pro §7601
Letters issued to   Pro §7621
Petition for appointment as personal representative   Pro §7620
Possession and control of decedent's property subject to loss or waste   Pro
    §§7601, 7602
Priority of appointment   Pro §8461
Probate proceedings, filing fees payable by public administrator as petitioner in
    Gov §70659
Public employees' duty to notify public administrator of decedent's property
    subject to loss or waste   Pro §7600
Safe deposit box of decedent, right to access to   Pro §7603
Savings and loans
    Surrender of decedent's property to public administrator   Pro §7603
    Unclaimed money deposited by public administrator, distribution   Pro
      §7644
Small claims court law and procedures, publications describing   CCP §116.930
Small estates, summary disposition of (See **SMALL ESTATES WITHOUT**
    ADMINISTRATION)
State treasurer, deposit of unclaimed funds with   Pro §7644
Stranger, administering estate of   Pro §§7600.5, 7601
Summary disposition of small estates (See **SMALL ESTATES WITHOUT**
    ADMINISTRATION)
Surety
    Bonds   Pro §7621
      Liability on bond   Pro §7624
Trustees
    Public administrators as trustees   Pro §15660.5
      Compensation   Pro §15688
Unclaimed property, disposition of   Pro §§7624, 7643, 7644, 7663
Waste, prevention of   Pro §§7601, 7602
Wills, search for   Pro §7602
Withdrawal of money deposited by public administrator for estate administration
    Pro §7641
Written certifications, collection of property by   Pro §7603

PUBLIC ASSISTANCE (See WELFARE)

PUBLICATION

Administration of estates (See **ADMINISTRATION OF ESTATES**)
Administrative Procedure Act (See **ADMINISTRATIVE PROCEDURE ACT**)
Affidavit, proof by   CCP §2010
Appellate opinions, publication of (See **APPELLATE RULES, SUPREME**
    COURT AND COURTS OF APPEAL)
Change of name proceedings, publication requirement in   CCP §1277
Claims against decedent's estate, notice for filing   Pro §9001
Contempt charge for refusing to reveal source of information   Ev §1070
Continuous defamatory publication, shortening time to respond for   CCP §460.5
Decedents' estates (See **ADMINISTRATION OF ESTATES**)
Default judgment after service by   CCP §585
Destroyed land records relief law proceedings, service in   CCP §751.06
Earthquakes, boundary reestablishment after   CCP §751.54
Eminent domain summons served by   CCP §1250.125
Enforcement of judgments (See **ENFORCEMENT OF JUDGMENTS**)
Escheat (See **ESCHEAT**)
Lease of city property, notice of   CC §719
Libel and slander (See **LIBEL AND SLANDER**)
Liens by service dealers   CC §3052.5
Local rules   CCP §575.1
Lost property, notice of   CC §§2080.3 to 2080.8
Newspapers (See **NEWSPAPERS AND MAGAZINES**)
Opinions (See **PUBLICATION OF OPINIONS**)
Partition action, Service of process in   CCP §§872.310 to 872.330
Presumptions of publication of books   Ev §644
Process (See **PROCESS AND SERVICE OF PROCESS**)
Quieting title action, service in   CCP §§763.010 to 763.040
Sale and leaseback, notices required   CC §3440
Service dealers' liens   CC §3052.5
Service of process (See **PROCESS AND SERVICE OF PROCESS**)
Sexually explicit depiction of individual, creation or disclosure
    Actions for damages   CC §1708.86
Trust deed or mortgage, notice of sale under power of sale in   CC §2924f
Type size requirements   CCP §1019
Unclaimed deposits and payments escheated, publication of notices of   CCP
    §1531
Unclaimed property, notice for   CC §§2080.3, 2080.4
Unknown persons' funds, notice of   CCP §570
Validation proceedings, summons in   CCP §861
Voidable transactions, publication of notice of intended transfer   CC §3440
Will probate (See **WILL PROBATE**)

PUBLICATION OF OPINIONS   CRC 8.1100 to 8.1125

Assignments for preparation of opinions   CRCSupp SupCtIOPP VIII
Authority for rules governing   CRC 8.1100
Circulation of opinions   CRCSupp SupCtIOPP IX
Citation   CRC 8.1115
Computer-based source of decisional law   CRC 8.1115
Depublication   CRC 8.1125
Dismissal after supreme court grant of review   CRC 8.528
Filing of opinions   CRCSupp SupCtIOPP X
Memorandum opinions by courts of appeal   CRC JudAdminStand 8.1
Partial publication   CRC 8.1110
Publication and depublication orders by Supreme Court   CRC 8.1105
Request for depublication of published opinion   CRC 8.1125
Request for publication of unpublished opinion   CRC 8.1120
Review of published opinion granted   CRC 8.1115
Standards for publication   CRC 8.1105
Unpublished opinions
    Citation   CRC 8.1115
    Effect   CRC 8.1115
    Request for publication of unpublished opinion   CRC 8.1120

PUBLIC AUCTIONS (See AUCTIONS)

PUBLIC BENEFIT CORPORATIONS, NONPROFIT

Attorney professional conduct
    Organization or entity as client   ProfC 1.13

PUBLIC BENEFIT TRUST FUND

Creation   CC §3294.5
Punitive damage awards
    Allocation of punitive damage awards to fund   CC §3294.5

PUBLIC BUILDINGS

Accessibility of buildings and facilities
    Attorney general, civil actions to enforce
      Fees and costs for attorney general   CCP §1021.8
Blind persons having equal rights to use of   CC §§54, 54.3, 54.4, 55
    Construction or application of provisions in issue, solicitor general notified
      CC §55.2

PUBLIC OFFICERS AND EMPLOYEES—Cont.

Presumptions

     Due care, statutory violation as failure to exercise   Ev §669.1

     Official duty regularly performed   Ev §664

Probation officers and deputies (See **PROBATION OFFICERS AND DEPUTIES**)

Promotion in employment, information concerning   CC §1798.38

Psychotherapists, employees functioning as   Ev §1010

Public administrators (See **PUBLIC ADMINISTRATORS**)

Public defender in conservatorship proceedings   Pro §§1471, 1472

Public Employment Relations Board, judicial review of decisions   CRC 8.728

Public guardians (See **PUBLIC GUARDIANS**)

Quieting title to improperly encumbered property of public officer or employee, proceedings for   CCP §§765.010 to 765.060

   Counsel for officer or employee supplied by employer   CCP §765.060

   Financial institution claims

     Applicability of provisions   CCP §765.050

   Order striking lien or encumbrance   CCP §765.030

   Penalty for filing for lien or encumbrance designed to hinder or harass   CCP §765.040

   Petition to strike lien or incumbrance   CCP §765.010

     Affidavit in support of petition   CCP §765.020

       Contents   CCP §765.020

   Prohibition on filing lawsuit, lien, etc, to harass or hinder officers and employees   CCP §765.010

Quo warranto   CCP §§802 to 811, 917.8

Rape committed by public official by threatening to use authority

   Statute of limitations on sexual assault damages   CCP §340.16

Referee (See **REFEREES**)

Sealed documents presumed to be genuine   Ev §1452

Seal of (See **SEAL**)

Secretary of State (See **SECRETARY OF STATE**)

Sexual acts performed under threat by person claiming to be

   Statute of limitations

     Civil damages   CCP §340.16

Sexual harassment, civil action for

   Elected officials   CC §51.9

Sheriff (See **SHERIFF**)

Signatures presumed to be genuine   Ev §§1453, 1454, 1530

Supervisors (See **SUPERVISORS**)

Surveyor general   Ev §1605

Tenure (See **TERMS OF OFFICE**)

Tort Claims Act (See **CLAIMS AGAINST PUBLIC ENTITIES AND EMPLOYEES**)

Treasurer (See **TREASURER**)

Undertakings

   Exemption from bond requirement in actions or proceedings   CCP §995.220

   Indemnity rights, bond as basis   CCP §1055

   Official bonds generally (See **BONDS OF PUBLIC OFFICIALS**)

Usurpation of office   CCP §§802 to 811, 917.8

Venue in actions against   CCP §393

Witnesses, compensation of public employee as   Gov §68097.2

PUBLIC OFFICES

Holiday for purposes of computing time if public office closed   CCP §12b

Quo warranto   CCP §§802 to 811, 917.8

Usurpation of office   CCP §§802 to 811, 917.8

PUBLIC POLICY

Acceleration of loan provisions, waiver of   CC §2924.6

Automobile leases   CC §2988

Conservation easements   CC §815

Credit reports   CC §1785.1

Custody of children   Fam §3020

Dance studio contracts, regulation of   CC §1812.50

Disclosure of public information   Ev §§1040 to 1042

Discount buying services contracts   CC §1812.127

Exemptions from enforcement of judgments, waiver of   CCP §703.040

Health studio services contracts   CC §1812.80

Jury service and selection   CCP §191

Layaway provisions, buyer waiving   CC §1749.2

Retail installment sales provisions, waiver of   CC §1801

Seller assisted marketing plans, regulation of   CC §1812.200

Warranties on consumer goods, waiver of   CC §1790.1

PUBLIC RESTROOMS

Disabled persons' right to use of   CC §55

PUBLIC SAFETY EMPLOYEES

Contempt orders, stay of execution of   CCP §128

PUBLIC SALES (See **AUCTIONS**)

PUBLIC SITTINGS

Court sittings   CCP §124

PUBLIC TRAILS

Enjoining closure of   CCP §731.5

PUBLIC TRANSPORTATION (See **COMMON CARRIERS**)

PUBLIC UTILITIES

Bail and penalty schedules for misdemeanor cases involving   CRC 4.102

Cancellation of utility, cable, etc, services on behalf of deceased person

   In-person cancellation not to be required   Pro §217

Consumer's personal records, subpoena of   CCP §1985.3

Damages

   Diversion or tampering with gas or electric utility services, action for   CC §§1882 to 1882.6

   Repairs or service during specified time period where subscriber's presence required, failure to provide   CC §1722

Diversion of gas or electricity, damages for   CC §§1882 to 1882.6

Electricity (See **ELECTRICITY AND ELECTRIC COMPANIES**)

Eminent domain (See **EMINENT DOMAIN**)

Fines and penalties

   Bail schedule   CRC 4.102

Gas companies (See **GAS COMPANIES**)

Jurors, source for selection of   CCP §197

Landlord and tenant (See **LANDLORD AND TENANT**)

Mineral rights owner, notice of intent to enter on land for excavation by   CC §848

Mobilehome parks (See **MOBILEHOMES**)

Penalty schedules for misdemeanor cases involving   CRC 4.102

Pipeline corporation's absolute liability for damages caused by discharge or leaking   CC §3333.5

Repairs or service during specified time period where subscriber's presence required, liability for failure to provide   CC §1722

Wrongfully enjoining public improvement or utility, damages for   CCP §526b

PUBLIC UTILITIES COMMISSION

Administrative Procedure Act, applicability of rulemaking provisions of   Gov §11351

Judicial review of decisions   CRC 8.724

   Procedural provisions   CRC 8.724

   Supreme Court review   CRC 8.724

Petition for review   CRC 8.724

PUBLIC WATER SYSTEMS

Groundwater rights actions

   Definition of public water systems   CCP §832

PUBLIC WORKS

Generally (See **PUBLIC CONTRACTS AND WORKS**)

Mechanics' liens   CC §§9000 to 9566 (See **MECHANICS' LIENS**)

PUBLIC WORKS DEPARTMENT

Eminent domain taking by   CCP §1245.210

PUERTO RICO

Acknowledgment of instruments   CC §1183.5

PUNITIVE DAMAGES

Exemplary damages (See **DAMAGES**)

PURCHASER OF REALTY (See **VENDOR AND PURCHASER**)

PURCHASER'S LIEN

Generally   CC §§3048, 3050

PUTATIVE SPOUSE

Generally   Fam §§2251, 2252

Defined   CCP §377.60

Wrongful death actions, assertion of   CCP §377.60

Q

QUALIFICATIONS

Congress of United States (See **CONGRESS**)

Jurors (See **JURY**)

Personal sureties, affidavit of qualifications by   CCP §995.520

Small claims advisors   CCP §116.920

Witnesses   Ev §§700, 701

QUARRIES

Tenant's use of quarries   CC §819

Index

Index

Index

RECORDS AND RECORDING—Cont.

Trial court records
    Electronic trial court records   CRC 2.500 to 2.545
Trial courts   CRC 2.400, CRC JudAdminStand 10.17
Truncation of social security numbers, program for
    Generally   Gov §§27300 to 27307 (See **SOCIAL SECURITY**)
Trust deeds (See **TRUST DEEDS AND MORTGAGES**)
Trusts   Pro §15210
    Certification of trust   Pro §18100.5
    Change of trustee, recordation of affidavit   Pro §§18105 to 18108
Typewritten copies   Gov §27361.7
Unclaimed deposits and payments, controller examining records of   CCP §1571
Unexercised options (See **TITLE AND OWNERSHIP**)
Validity of unrecorded instruments   CC §1217
Vessels, transfers of   CC §1173
Vexatious litigants subject to prefiling orders, records of   CCP §391.7
    Vacating prefiling order and removing name from list   CCP §391.8
Voidable transactions, notice of transfer as affecting claim of   CC §3440
Water appropriation   CC §§1415, 1421
Wills, recordation requirements for   Pro §8225

RECOVERY OF PROPERTY

Claim and delivery (See **CLAIM AND DELIVERY**)
Real property, recovery of (See **REAL PROPERTY**)

RECREATIONAL VEHICLE PARKS

Abandoned possessions, disposition of   CC §799.75
Attorney's fees awarded to prevailing party in actions involving   CC §799.78
Citation of Act   CC §799.20
Defaulting occupant
    Abandoned possessions, disposition of   CC §799.75
    Defined   CC §799.22
    Liens for charges due   CC §799.75
    Nonmotorized vehicle, removal of   CC §799.56
    Physically incapacitated occupant, removal of vehicle belonging to   CC §799.56
    Reasonable and ordinary care in removing vehicle to storage area, management's duty of   CC §799.59
    Service of notice   CC §799.56
    72-hour notice
        Statement required concerning removal and storage of vehicle   CC §799.57
        Written notice requirement prior to removal of vehicle   CC §799.55
    Sheriff or police, removal of vehicle by   CC §799.58
    Special occupancy parks
        Eviction of overstaying guests   CC §1866
Defaulting resident
    Abandoned possessions, disposition of   CC §799.75
    Defined   CC §799.23
    Eviction of   CC §799.71
    Liens for charges due   CC §799.75
    Termination or refusal to renew right of occupancy, grounds for management's right of   CC §799.70
Defaulting tenant
    Abandoned possessions, disposition of   CC §799.75
    Defined   CC §799.24
    Eviction of   CC §799.67
    Liens for charges due   CC §799.75
    Nonpayment of rent or other charges, termination by management for   CC §799.65
    Refusal to renew right of occupancy other than nonpayment of rent or other charges, grounds for termination by management by   CC §799.66
Definitions   CC §§799.20 to 799.32
Disabled occupant, removal of vehicle belonging to   CC §799.56
Eviction from park
    Defaulting tenants generally (See within this heading, **"Defaulting tenant"**)
    Occupant, eviction of   CC §799.67
    Resident   CC §799.71
    Tenant   CC §799.67
Fines and penalties against park management for violation of statute   CC §799.79
General provisions   CC §§799.40 to 799.46
Guests defined   CC §799.25
Liens for charges due   CC §799.75
Manufactured homes, provisions governing recreational vehicles as inapplicable to   CC §799.41
Mobilehomes, provisions governing recreational vehicles as inapplicable to   CC §799.41
Nonmotorized vehicle, removal of   CC §799.56
Notices
    72-hour notice for removal of vehicle
        Statement concerning removal and storage of vehicle   CC §799.57

RECREATIONAL VEHICLE PARKS—Cont.

Notices—Cont.
    72-hour notice for removal of vehicle —Cont.
        Written notice requirement before removal   CC §799.55
    Termination
        Defaulting residents   CC §799.70
        Defaulting tenants generally (See within this heading, **"Defaulting tenant"**)
Physically incapacitated occupant in default, removal of vehicle belonging to   CC §799.56
Registration agreement
    Form and content of   CC §799.43
    Occupancy in excess of 30 consecutive days, validity of rental agreements for   CC §799.45
    Park rules and regulations, furnishing copy of   CC §799.44
    Waiver of tenant's rights in rental agreement prohibited   CC §799.46
Remedial statutory rights as cumulative to other relief available to parties   CC §799.40
Removal of vehicle
    Defaulting occupant
        Generally (See within this heading, **"Defaulting occupant"**)
    Defaulting resident   CC §799.71
    Defaulting tenant   CC §799.67
    Sign posted at park entrance warning of removal of vehicle for nonpayment, requirement of   CC §799.46
72-hour notice
    Statement required in 72-hour notice concerning removal and storage of vehicle   CC §799.57
    Written notice requirement before removal of vehicle   CC §799.55
Special occupancy parks
    Danger imminent, requiring guests to move   CC §1867
    Eviction of overstaying guests   CC §1866
    Minors
        Conditions for minors staying   CC §1866
Termination
    Defaulting resident   CC §799.70
    Defaulting tenant
        Generally (See within this heading, **"Defaulting tenant"**)
Waiver of tenant's rights in rental agreement, prohibition against   CC §799.42

RECREATIONAL VEHICLES (See also **MOBILEHOMES**)

Alteration of new vehicles into housecars, effect on warranties upon   CC §1793.05
Recreational vehicle parks (See **RECREATIONAL VEHICLE PARKS**)
Warranties on new vehicles altered into house cars   CC §1793.05

RECREATION AREAS

Camps (See **CAMPING**)
Caves (See **CAVES**)
Easement holder's liability   CC §846
Eminent domain (See **EMINENT DOMAIN**)
Landowner's liability for recreation activities   CC §846
Parks (See **PARKS AND PLAYGROUNDS**)
Public entity's liability for injuries on unpaved roads or trails providing access to   Gov §831.4

RECROSS EXAMINATION (See **CROSS-EXAMINATION**)

RECUSAL OF JUDGES

Disqualification (See **JUDGES, DISQUALIFICATION OF**)

RECYCLED PRODUCTS

Appeals
    Transcripts   CRC 8.144
Fire hydrants or fire department corrections
    Damages for wrongful possession by junk dealers or recyclers   CC §3336.5
Judicial Council policy regarding waste reduction and recycling programs for local courts   CRC JudAdminStand 10.55
Trial court rules
    Forms   CRC 2.131

RED CROSS (See **AMERICAN RED CROSS**)

REDELIVERY

Conveyances   CC §1058

REDEMPTION

Enforcement of judgments (See **ENFORCEMENT OF JUDGMENTS**)
Execution sales   CCP §701.680
Liens (See **LIENS**)
Mortgages (See **TRUST DEEDS AND MORTGAGES**)

Index

REQUEST FOR ADMISSION—Cont.
Response to request   CCP §§2033.210 to 2033.300
  Amendment of response   CCP §2033.300
  Completeness   CCP §2033.220
  Failure to timely serve response   CCP §2033.280
  Format of response   CCP §2033.210
  Further response
    Motion to compel   CCP §2033.290
  Motion to deem matters admitted   CCP §2033.280
  Objections   CCP §2033.230
  Reasonable inquiry to formulate response   CCP §2033.220
  Retention   CCP §2033.270
  Signature   CCP §2033.240
  Time for service of response   CCP §2033.250
    Extension of time for response   CCP §2033.260
  Withdrawal of admission   CCP §2033.300
  Written response   CCP §2033.210
Restriction to combining other discovery methods with   CCP §2033.010
Retention of request, proof of service, and response   CCP §2033.270
Sanctions
  Generally (See **DISCOVERY**)
  Protective orders
    Unsuccessfully making or opposing motion for protective order   CCP §2033.080
  Response to request
    Failure to timely respond   CCP §2033.280
    Further response, failure to provide   CCP §2033.290
Scope   CCP §2033.010
Service of request   CCP §2033.070
  Retention of request, proof of service, and response   CCP §2033.270
Signature of response   CCP §2033.240
Style of request   CCP §2033.060
Time for service of response   CCP §2033.250
  Extension of time for response   CCP §2033.260
Time limitations for   CCP §2033.020
Unlawful detainer
  Time for service of process   CCP §2033.250
  Time limitations for   CCP §2033.020
Withdrawal of admission   CCP §2033.300

REQUEST FOR PRODUCTION (See INSPECTION DEMANDS)

REQUEST FOR STATEMENT OF DAMAGES   CCP §§425.11, 425.12

REQUESTS FOR ADMISSIONS
Civil rules
  Limitation on papers filed   CRC 3.250
Form requests for admissions
  List of judicial council legal forms   CRCAppx A
Identification   CRC 3.1000, 3.1345
Limitation on papers filed   CRC 3.250
Motion to compel
  Separate document setting forth item to which further response, answer or production is requested   CRC 3.1345
Objections to
  Limitations on papers filed   CRC 3.250
Response to request
  Further response
    Motion to compel   CRC 3.1345
  Identification and sequence of responses   CRC 3.1000
  Limitations on papers filed   CRC 3.250
Sequence of responses   CRC 3.1000
Supplemental and further discovery, format of   CRC 3.1000

RESCISSION
Generally (See **CONTRACTS AND AGREEMENTS**)
Adoption agency, relinquishment of child to   Fam §8700
  Revocation of right to relinquish, waiver   Fam §8700.5
Adoption facilitators
  Enforcement of provisions   Fam §8638
Agency, rescinding ratification of acts of   CC §2314
Contracts (See **CONTRACTS AND AGREEMENTS**)
Emancipation of minors, declaration of   Fam §§7130, 7132 to 7135
Health studio services contracts
  Cancellation of   CC §§1812.85, 1812.89
Home solicitation sales contracts
  Cancellation   CC §§1689.6, 1689.9
    Notice of right to cancel in contract   CC §1689.7
    Service and repair project contracts   CC §1689.15
Small claims court jurisdiction to grant equitable relief in lieu of or in addition to money damages   CCP §116.220
Trust deeds (See **TRUST DEEDS AND MORTGAGES**)

RESCUE WORKERS
Anaphylaxis
  Epinephrine auto-injector administration for first aid
    Immunity from civil liability of lay rescuers, prehospital emergency medical care providers or authorized entities   CC §1714.23
Public health and safety labor or service providers
  Logo or identifying mark of public agency, display   CC §3273

RESEARCH
Animal shelter sign stating use of animals for   CC §1834.7
Hospital mortality studies, admissibility of   Ev §§1156, 1156.1
Medical information disclosed for purposes of   CC §§56.15, 56.16

RESERVE POLICE OFFICERS (See LAW ENFORCEMENT OFFICERS)

RESERVOIRS (See DAMS)

RES GESTAE
Hearsay evidence, admissibility of   Ev §§1240, 1241

RESIDENCE
Assignment for benefit of creditors, property exempt from   CCP §1801
Children and minors   CRC 5.510
  Parent subject to juvenile proceedings, notice of address   CRC 5.534
Conservatee, restrictions on changing residence of   Pro §§2253, 2254, 2352
  Least restrictive appropriate residence   Pro §2352.5
Conveyance of residential property (See **CONVEYANCES**)
Custody of children (See **CUSTODY OF CHILDREN**)
Debt collectors and   CC §1788.15
Deferred sale of family home, request of custodial parent for   Fam §§3800 to 3810
Dissolution of marriage   Fam §§2320 to 2322
Domicile (See **DOMICILE**)
Excluding party from dwelling   Fam §§5552, 6321, 6340
Executors (See **EXECUTORS AND ADMINISTRATORS**)
Guardian subject to juvenile proceedings, notice of address   CRC 5.534
Legal separation proceeding   Fam §2321
Missing person's estate, jurisdiction for administration of   Pro §12403
Parent's right to determine residence of minor child   Fam §7501
Parent subject to juvenile proceedings, notice of address   CRC 5.534
Referees   CCP §640
Same sex marriage
  Dissolution of marriage, annulment or legal separation   Fam §2320
Senior citizen housing developments, generally   CC §§51.2 to 51.4
Small claims court hearing, effect of residence of defendant on scheduling case for   CCP §116.330
Support, duty of   Fam §3550
Transfer of causes
  Family Law Act proceedings, subsequent to final judgment   CCP §397.5
  Retention of jurisdiction to issue protective orders   CCP §399
  Time frames for transferring jurisdiction
    Family law actions or proceedings   CRC 5.97
Transfer of residential property (See **CONVEYANCES**)
Venue in county of residence of defendant   CCP §395
Ward, guardian establishing residence of   Pro §2352

RESIDENTIAL HOTELS (See HOTELS AND MOTELS)

RESIDUAL RIGHTS
Artworks, residual rights of artist in   CC §986
Unclaimed residuals, escheat of   CCP §§1501, 1521

RESIDUARY CLAUSE (See WILLS)

RESIGNATION
Guardianship (See **GUARDIAN AND WARD**)
Personal representative of decedent's estate   Pro §§8520 to 8525
Trustees (See **TRUSTS**)

RES IPSA LOQUITUR
Certificate of meritorious cause   CCP §411.35
Presumptions   Ev §646
Public property, applicability to dangerous condition of   Gov §830.5

RES JUDICATA   CCP §§1908 to 1911
Credit reports   CC §1785.34
Foreign judgments   CCP §§1913, 1914
Investigative agencies   CC §1786.52
Separate trial of special defense   CCP §597
Uniform Child Custody Jurisdiction and Enforcement Act, effect of custody determinations under   Fam §3406
Unpublished opinion, reliance on   CRC 8.1115

Index

Index

Index

SALE OF REALTY—Cont.

Judgment lien on real property, effect on   CCP §697.390

Judicial officer's power to take and certify proof and acknowledgment of conveyance   CCP §179

Karnette Rental-Purchase Act for rental-purchase contracts   CC §§1812.620 to 1812.650

Notice of pendency of action (See **PENDENCY OF ACTIONS**)

Rental-purchase contracts, Karnette Rental-Purchase Act for   CC §§1812.620 to 1812.650

Sheriff, conveyances on sale of real estate by   CCP §262.4

Text message or instant message format communications, insufficiency to constitute contract to convey realty   CC §1624

SALES

Abandoned property of tenant, landlord selling   CC §1988

Administration of estates (See **ADMINISTRATION OF ESTATES**)

Aerosol paint containers

   Verification of age for sale of age-restricted products   CC §1798.99.1

Aircraft liens, satisfaction of   CCP §§1208.65 to 1208.68

Artworks, residual rights of artist in   CC §986

"As is" sales   CC §§1790 to 1795.8

Attachment (See **ATTACHMENT**)

Auctions (See **AUCTIONS**)

Autographed memorabilia, sale   CC §1739.7

Automobile manufacturers, transporters, dealers and sales professionals

   Restitution, licensee ordered to pay

      Effect of order for restitution   Gov §11519.1

Automobiles (See **AUTOMOBILES**)

Bill of sale (See **BILL OF SALE**)

Birth name use   CCP §1279.6

Bonds, procedure for validation of authorization, issuance, sale or exchange of   CCP §349.4

Bulk sales (See **BULK SALES**)

Catalogs (See **MAIL ORDER SALES**)

Child support, sale of assets deposited to secure future payment   Fam §§4616, 4630 to 4632

Clubs for periodic sale   CC §§1584.5, 1584.6

Commingling of goods   CC §1497

Community property (See **COMMUNITY PROPERTY**)

Conditional sales (See **CONDITIONAL SALES**)

Confession of judgments for debts arising from   CCP §1132

Conservators (See **CONSERVATORS**)

Consumer protection (See **CONSUMER PROTECTION**)

Credit cards (See **CREDIT CARDS**)

Damages (See **DAMAGES**)

Delivery of merchandise purchased under retail sales contract within specified 4-hour period   CC §1722

Delivery requirements   CC §1496

Deposits (See **DEPOSITS**)

Discount buying services   CC §§1812.100 to 1812.129

Door-to-door sales (See **HOME SOLICITATION SALES CONTRACTS**)

Electronic commercial services (See **ELECTRONIC COMMERCIAL SERVICES**)

Enforcement of judgments (See **ENFORCEMENT OF JUDGMENTS**)

Factors, sale of property by   CC §§2027 to 2030

Family use, warranty of goods sold for   CC §§1790 to 1795.8

Felon's story, trust established for proceeds from sale of   CC §2225

Fine prints, regulating sale of   CC §§1740 to 1745.5

Fitness warranty   CC §1791.1

Grey market goods (See **GREY MARKET GOODS**)

Guardianship (See **GUARDIAN AND WARD**)

Home solicitation sales contracts (See **HOME SOLICITATION SALES CONTRACTS**)

Homesteads, sale of (See **HOMESTEADS**)

Independent Administration of Estates Act, sale of property under (See **INDEPENDENT ADMINISTRATION OF ESTATES ACT**)

Innkeeper's lien   CC §§1861.19, 1861.24

Installments (See **RETAIL INSTALLMENT SALES**)

Judicial sales (See **ENFORCEMENT OF JUDGMENTS**)

Landlord and tenant

   Commercial real property tenancies

      Disposition of property remaining upon termination, public sale   CC §1993.07

Liens (See **LIENS**)

Livestock service liens, sale under   CC §§3080.02 to 3080.22

Lost property not claimed   CC §§2080.4 to 2080.8

Mail order sales (See **MAIL ORDER SALES**)

Marketplace sales and sellers

   Commercial relationships, terms and conditions   CC §1749.7

Membership camping contracts   CC §§1812.300 to 1812.309

Merchandise sales by clubs   CC §§1584.5, 1584.6

SALES—Cont.

Merchantability, warranty of   CC §1791.1

Mining machinery   CC §1631

Mixing of goods   CC §1497

Mobilehomes (See **MOBILEHOMES**)

Nonconforming goods, notice of   CC §1793.1

Order of sale

   Superior court fees, specified services   Gov §70626

Paintings, resale of   CC §986

Partition (See **PARTITION**)

Periodic ordering of merchandise   CC §§1584.5, 1584.6

Political items   CC §§1739 to 1739.4

Products liability (See **PRODUCTS LIABILITY**)

Real property (See **SALE OF REALTY; VENDOR AND PURCHASER**)

Receivers selling personal property   CCP §568.5

Rental-purchase contracts, Karnette Rental-Purchase Act   CC §§1812.620 to 1812.650

Repairs for goods sold under warranty   CC §§1793.1 to 1795.8

Retail installment sales (See **RETAIL INSTALLMENT SALES**)

Serial number destroyed or altered prior to   CC §1710.1

Social security numbers

   Prohibition of sale, advertising for sale or offering for sale of number of another   CC §1798.85

Spray paint containers

   Verification of age for sale of age-restricted products   CC §1798.99.1

Stay of proceedings pending appeal   CCP §§917.2, 917.4

Tax (See **SALES AND USE TAX**)

Trust deeds (See **TRUST DEEDS AND MORTGAGES**)

Trusts (See **TRUSTS**)

Unclaimed property (See **UNCLAIMED PROPERTY**)

Unsolicited goods   CC §§1584.5, 1584.6

Warranties (See **WARRANTIES**)

Wholesale sales representatives (See **WHOLESALE SALES REPRESENTATIVES**)

SALES AND USE TAX

Automobile sales warranties, manufacturer's reimbursement for sales or use tax refunded to new buyer for restitution under   CC §1793.25

Decedent's estate, tax claims against   Pro §§9200 to 9205

Schedules for reimbursement of retail sales tax   CC §1656.1

SAME SEX MARRIAGE BAN

Recognition of certain same sex marriages contracted in other jurisdictions

   Dissolution, annulment or legal separation of recognized same sex marriages, jurisdiction   Fam §2010

      Residence requirements   Fam §2320

Repeal   Fam §300

SANCTIONS

Administrative adjudication (See **ADMINISTRATIVE ADJUDICATION**)

Appeal as frivolous action or tactic, sanction based on   CCP §907, CRC 8.276

Appeal of sanction orders or judgments   CCP §904.1

Appellate rules, superior court appeals   CRC 8.891

   Infraction case appeals

      Record on appeal, failure to procure   CRC 8.924

   Limited civil cases in appellate division

      Record on appeal, failure to procure   CRC 8.842

   Misdemeanor appeals

      Record on appeal, failure to procure   CRC 8.874

Appellate rules, supreme court and courts of appeal

   Briefs

      Failure to file brief   CRC 8.220

   Certiorari, mandate and prohibition   CRC 8.492

   Frivolous actions or tactics   CRC 8.276

      Criminal appeals   CRC 8.366

   Grounds for sanctions   CRC 8.276

      Criminal appeals   CRC 8.366

   Procedure   CRC 8.276

      Criminal appeals   CRC 8.366

   Record on appeal

      Failure of party to procure   CRC 8.140

Bad faith actions (See within this heading, **"Frivolous actions or delaying tactics"**)

Case questionnaires under economic litigation provisions for limited civil cases, failure to answer or obey order compelling response to   CCP §93

Child abuse or neglect, false accusations of   Fam §3027.1

Child support, incomplete and inaccurate income and expense declarations   Fam §3667

Delay, appeal taken for purposes of   CRC 8.276

Discovery abuse (See **DISCOVERY ABUSES, SANCTIONS FOR**)

Index

Index

Index

Index

Index

SHEEP
Dogs injuring   CC §3341

SHELLEY'S CASE
Heirs of body, remainder limited to   CC §§779, 780

SHELTER, ANIMAL (See **ANIMALS**)

SHERIFF
Attachment (See **ATTACHMENT**)
Bench warrants, fees for service and execution of   Gov §26744
Certificate
    Generally   CCP §§2015.3, 2015.5
    Redemption, certificate or deed of   Gov §26740
Contempt   CCP §1209
Conveyances on sale of real estate by sheriff   CCP §262.4
Court operations costs, salaries and benefits included as   CRC 10.810
Deeds on sale of real estate by (See **ENFORCEMENT OF JUDGMENTS**)
Deposits in court, sheriff receiving   CCP §574
Electronic court records, remote access
    Government entities, access by
        List of government entities which may be authorized to receive access   CRC 2.540
Enforcement of judgments (See **ENFORCEMENT OF JUDGMENTS**)
Execution of process
    Directions of party re   CCP §262
    Liability of sheriff for   CCP §262
    New county, effect of creation of   CCP §262.11
    Party to action, execution of process where sheriff is   CCP §§262.6, 262.8
    Regular on its face, sheriff to execute process   CCP §262.1
    Successors in office, execution by   CCP §262.3
Fees   Gov §26720.9
    Generally   Gov §26720
    Attachment (See **ATTACHMENT**)
    Bench warrants, service and execution of   Gov §26744
    Collection
        Generally   Gov §26720
        Additional fees collectible   Gov §§26746, 26748
    Conducting or postponing property sales, fees for   Gov §26730
    Copy fees   Gov §26727
    Deed of sale, execution and delivery of   Gov §26741
    Earnings withholding orders, fee for serving   Gov §26750
    Emergency protective orders   Gov §26721
    Eviction   Gov §26733.5
    Execution, writ of (See **ENFORCEMENT OF JUDGMENTS**)
    Indigent party, waiver of fee for   Gov §26720.5
    In forma pauperis, waiver of fee where   Gov §26720.5
    Insane persons transported to state hospital   Gov §26749
    Jury summons, fee for   Gov §26745
    Mental hospitals, transportation of insane persons to   Gov §26749
    Other instruments, executing and delivering of   Gov §26742
    Possession, writ of (See **ENFORCEMENT OF JUDGMENTS**)
    Prisoners, transportation of
        To county jail   Gov §26747
        To state prison   Gov §26749
    Property keeper fee
        Generally   Gov §26726
        Additional fees, collection of   Gov §26748
    Real property, writs on   Gov §§26725, 26725.1, 26726
    Redemption, execution and delivery of certificate of   Gov §26740
    Repossessed automobiles, notice of   Gov §26751
    Safe deposit box, opening   Gov §26723
    Sale, writ of (See **ENFORCEMENT OF JUDGMENTS**)
    Service of process   Gov §26720.9
        Generally   Gov §26721
        Cancellation of service, fee charged for   Gov §26736
        Copy of service, fee for   Gov §26727
        Earnings withholding orders   Gov §26750
        Emergency protective orders   Gov §26721
        Forced sale of personal property, fee for notice of   Gov §§26728, 26728.1
        Indigent party, fee waived for   Gov §26720.5
        Not found returns, fee for   Gov §26738
        Publication, fee for notice of   Gov §§26729, 26732
        Real property, writs related to   Gov §§26725, 26725.1
        Superior court summons   Gov §26721.2
        Unlawful detainer action   Gov §26721.1
    Superior court summons   Gov §26721.2
    Wage garnishment orders, fees for service of   Gov §26750
    Witnesses, subpoena of   Gov §26743

SHERIFF—Cont.
Inclusions in definition   CCP §17
Inquest jury (See **JURIES OF INQUEST**)
Interested persons, process shown to   CCP §262.2
Levying officer electronic transactions act   CCP §§263 to 263.7
Lost property, duties as to   CC §§2080.1 to 2080.5
Marriage
    Local government officials, authority to solemnize   Fam §400
Motor vehicle certificate of correction, special county fund for fees collected by sheriff's inspection for proof of   Gov §26746.1
Prisoners, fee for transporting
    To county jail   Gov §26747
    To state prison   Gov §26749
Process
    Service
        Fees (See within this heading, **"Fees"**)
        Subpoenas   CCP §1988, Gov §26743
Property keeper fee   Gov §26746
    Additional fees, collection   Gov §26748
Redemption, execution and delivery of certificate of   Gov §26740
Salaries and benefits as court operations costs   CRC 10.810
Sales by sheriff (See **ENFORCEMENT OF JUDGMENTS**)
Service of papers on   CCP §262.5
Service of process
    Action against sheriff   CCP §262.7
    Fees (See within this heading, **"Fees"**)
    Levying officer electronic transactions act   CCP §§263 to 263.7
        Citation of provisions   CCP §263
        Definitions   CCP §263.1
        Electronic records as substitute for paper   CCP §§263.1, 263.4
        Execution writs, retention of original or electronic copy   CCP §263.6
        Facsimile transmissions   CCP §§263.1, 263.3
        Identifiers, exclusion or redaction   CCP §263.7
        Information processing systems   CCP §§263.1, 263.2
        Legislative intent   CCP §263
        Technical problems, effect on filing day   CCP §263.2
    Subpoenas, service of
        Concealed witness   CCP §1988
        Fees for service   Gov §26743
Special sheriff's fund
    Allocation of sheriff's fees collected to   Gov §26731
    Motor vehicle certificate of correction, deposit of fees collected from sheriff's inspection for   Gov §26746.1
Statute of limitation against   CCP §339
Subpoenas
    Concealed witness, service by sheriff on   CCP §1988
    Fees for service of   Gov §26743
Successors in office, execution of process by   CCP §262.3
Wage garnishment orders, fees for service of   Gov §26750
Warrants (See **ARREST**)
Witnesses, sheriffs as (See **WITNESSES**)

SHIPMENT
Bill of lading (See **BILL OF LADING**)
Common carriers (See **COMMON CARRIERS**)

SHIPS (See **VESSELS**)

SHOOTING RANGES
Noise pollution liability, exemption from   CC §3482.1

SHOP BOOK RULE (See **BOOK ACCOUNTS**)

SHORT CAUSES
Case management   CRC 3.735

SHORTENING TIME
Administration of decedents' estates (See **ADMINISTRATION OF ESTATES**)
Appellate court rules   CRC 8.68
    Superior court appeals   CRC 8.813
Complex case coordination   CRC 3.503
Continuous defamatory publication, shortening time to respond for   CCP §460.5
Election campaign, shortening of time to respond to complaint in action for libel alleged to have occurred during   CCP §460.7
Enforcement of judgments (See **ENFORCEMENT OF JUDGMENTS**)
Law and motion rule   CRC 3.1300
Rules of court   CRC 1.10
Will probate proceedings, shortening time for giving notice in   Pro §1203

SHORTHAND REPORTERS
Oath at deposition proceedings, administration of   CCP §2093

SHOTGUNS (See **FIREARMS AND OTHER WEAPONS**)

Index

SNOW

Easements, snow removal from right-of-way on   CC §845

Water appropriation construction, effect of snow on completion of   CC §1416

SNOWMOBILES

Landowner liability for snowmobilers   CC §846

SNUFF FILMS   CC §§3504 to 3508.2

SOCIAL HOSTS

Alcoholic beverages, liability after serving   CC §1714

SOCIAL MEDIA

Judicial ethics code

    Public confidence in judiciary

        Electronic communications, care in using   CRCSupp JudEthicsCanon 2

SOCIAL SECURITY

Abstracts of judgment requiring Social Security number   CCP §674

Annulment of marriage proceedings

    Social security numbers

        Redaction from documents to ensure privacy   Fam §2024.5

Assignment for benefit of creditors, property exempt from   CCP §1801

Child support payment made by government pursuant to   Fam §4504

Confidentiality

    Financial institutions, continued use   CC §1786.60

    Social security numbers

        Businesses   CC §1798.85

        Financial institutions, continued use   CC §1786.60

        Redaction from documents to ensure privacy   Fam §2024.5

        Truncation program   Gov §§27300 to 27307

        Untruncated social security numbers, filing documents that will be public containing   CC §1798.89

        Waiver of protections   CC §1798.86

Dissolution of marriage proceedings   Fam §2337

    Social security numbers

        Redaction from documents to ensure privacy   Fam §2024.5

Earnings, Social Security payments as   CC §1812.30

Enforcement of judgments, payments for (See **ENFORCEMENT OF JUDGMENTS**)

Financial institutions

    Continued use   CC §1786.60

Investigative agencies, Social Security number as identification   CC §1786.22

Legal separation proceedings

    Social security numbers

        Redaction from documents to ensure privacy   Fam §2024.5

Malpractice suits against physicians, evidence in   CC §3333.1

Prohibiting posting or display to general public of social security numbers   CC §1798.85

    Waiver of protections   CC §1798.86

Sale of social security numbers

    Prohibition of sale, advertising for sale or offering for sale of number of another   CC §1798.85

Truncation of social security numbers, program for   Gov §§27300 to 27307

    County recorder

        Due diligence   Gov §27302

        Duties   Gov §27301

        Implementation of provisions, powers as to   Gov §27307

    DD214 official record

        Copy upon request, criteria   Gov §27303.5

    Definitions   Gov §27300

    Establishment of program   Gov §27301

    Funding of program   Gov §§27304, 27361

    Legislature, report to   Gov §27305

    Public record version of official records   Gov §27301

        Disclosures   Gov §27303

SOCIAL SERVICES DEPARTMENT

Adoption proceedings (See **ADOPTION**)

Deceptive practice of charging unreasonable fees to assist applicants for public social services   CC §1770

    Treble damages   CC §1780

Enforcement of judgment, filing with department for   CCP §§708.730, 708.740

Medical information, release of   CC §56.25

Unreasonable fees to assist applicants for public social services

    Deceptive practices   CC §1770

    Treble damages   CC §1780

SOCIAL WORKERS

Discovery of records of health care professional review committees   Ev §1157

SOCIAL WORKERS—Cont.

Juvenile rules

    Removal of juvenile from home

        Family finding and notice performed by social worker or probation officer   CRC 5.637

Privileged communications (See **PRIVILEGED COMMUNICATIONS**)

Psychotherapists, psychiatric social workers as   Ev §1010

Removal of juvenile from home

    Family finding and notice performed by social worker or probation officer   CRC 5.637

Sexual harassment, civil action for

    Construction or application of provisions in issue, solicitor general notified   CC §51.1

SODOMY (See **SEX OFFENSES**)

SOFTWARE (See **COMPUTERS**)

SOIL

Real property, part of   CC §659

SOLAR ENERGY

Common interest developments, restrictions in   CC §714.1

    Approvals

        Determinations of applications   CC §714

    Common areas, exclusive use grants   CC §4600

    Protected uses of separate interests

        Solar energy systems on multifamily common area roofs   CC §4746

        Provisions outside of common interest development law limiting association's regulation of member's separate interest   CC §4700

Covenants prohibiting use of solar energy systems, invalidity of   CC §714

Easements   CC §§801, 801.5

SOLDIERS (See **MILITARY**)

SOLE PROXIMATE CAUSE (See **PROXIMATE CAUSE**)

SOLICITATION

Advertising (See **ADVERTISING**)

Arbitrators

    Ethics standards

        Soliciting business   CRC ArbEthicsStand 17

Attorney professional conduct

    Clients, solicitation of   ProfC 7.3

Home solicitation sales contracts (See **HOME SOLICITATION SALES CONTRACTS**)

Mediation

    Standards of conduct for mediators

        Marketing   CRC 3.858

Murder

    Attempting or soliciting murder of spouse

        Damages for injuries to married person   Fam §782.5

        Spousal support, denial   Fam §4324

Seminar sales solicitation contracts (See **SEMINAR SALES SOLICITATION CONTRACTS**)

Telemarketing

    Unlawfulness of contracts generated by unlawful telemarketing   CC §1670.6

Transient occupancy in common interest developments, apartment buildings or single-family homes, recordkeeping required for accepting reservations or money for   CC §1864

SOLID WASTE RECOVERY AND RECYCLING

Fire hydrants or fire department corrections

    Damages for wrongful possession by junk dealers or recyclers   CC §3336.5

SONG-BEVERLY CONSUMER WARRANTY ACT   CC §§1790 to 1795.8 (See **WARRANTIES**)

SONG-BEVERLY CREDIT CARD ACT   CC §§1747 to 1748.95 (See **CREDIT CARDS**)

SORGHUM

Storage regulations after sale of   CC §§1880 to 1881.2

SOUND RECORDINGS (See **RECORDING OF SOUND**)

SOURCE OF INFORMATION (See **INFORMATION PRACTICES ACT**)

SOVEREIGN IMMUNITY (See **CLAIMS AGAINST PUBLIC ENTITIES AND EMPLOYEES**)

Index

SPOUSAL SUPPORT—Cont.

Obligor   Fam §3550

Orders

Generally   Fam §§4330 to 4338

Defined   Fam §155

Modification (See within this heading, **"Modification"**)

Retroactivity of   Fam §4333

Subsequent orders, rights with respect to   Fam §3604

Temporary support (See within this heading, **"Temporary support"**)

Vocational training consultant, examination by   Fam §4331

Parent Locator Service and Central Registry   Fam §17506

Pendente lite support (See within this heading, **"Temporary support"**)

Pilot projects (See **FAMILY LAW PILOT PROJECTS**)

Presumption of duration of marriage   Fam §4336

Probate proceedings

Power of appointment, claims against powerholder's property subject to   Pro §684

Property settlement agreements, support provisions severable from   Fam §§3590 to 3593

Public entity's obligation to judgment debtor, application to satisfaction on money judgment of   CCP §§708.710 to 708.795

Putative spouse   Fam §2254

Quasi-community property liable for   Fam §4338

Reconciliation of parties, effect of   Fam §3602

Relief from judgment or order   Fam §§2120 to 2129, 3690 to 3693, 17432

Remarriage, effect of   Fam §4337

Residence of obligor   Fam §3550

Satisfaction of money judgment for support, crediting of   CCP §695.221

Security for payment   Fam §4339

Self-help materials   Fam §291

Self-supporting within reasonable time, goal that recipient become   Fam §§4320, 4330

Separate property   Fam §§915, 4301, 4320 to 4322, 4338

Separation agreement, provisions for support in   Fam §3580

Software used to determine support amount   Fam §3830

Standard of living   Fam §§4320, 4330, 4332

Summary dissolution of marriage, effect of judgment of   Fam §2404

Support factors

Judicial Council forms   CRCAppx A

Support order defined   Fam §155

Surviving spouse (See within this heading, **"Death of party"**)

Tax consequences of   Fam §4320

Tax returns of parties   Fam §§3552, 3665, 3667

Temporary support

Generally   Fam §3600

Termination of   Fam §§3601, 3603

Transfer of venue, determining support issues prior to determination of motion for   CCP §§396b, 397

Termination

Generally   Fam §§3650 to 3654

Admissibility of income and benefit information provided by employer   Ev §1567

Changed circumstances   Fam §4336

Contingent period of time, support for   Fam §4334

Discovery procedures   Fam §§3660 to 3668

Effective dates for termination and requests for termination   CRCAppx I Emer Rule 13

Relief from support judgment or order   Fam §§2120 to 2129, 3690 to 3693, 17432

Retroactivity of   Fam §3653

Support agreement, authority to terminate   Fam §3591

Temporary support   Fam §§3601, 3603

Transfer of venue, determining support issues prior to determination of motion for   CCP §§396b, 397

Trust to provide for support   Fam §4360

Unemployment periods of spouse devoting time to domestic duties   Fam §4320

Vocational training   Fam §§4320, 4331

Welfare recipients, enforcement in behalf of   Fam §4351

Workers' compensation temporary disability benefits in satisfaction of support judgment, assignment of   CCP §704.160

SPOUSES (See **HUSBAND AND WIFE**)

SPRAY PAINT CONTAINERS

Minors, sale to

Verification of age for sale of age-restricted products   CC §1798.99.1

SPRINGING POWER OF ATTORNEY (See **POWER OF ATTORNEY**)

SPRINGING USE   CC §773

STABLES (See **BOARDING FACILITIES AND STABLES**)

STADIUMS AND ARENAS

Sacramento downtown arena

Petitions under environmental quality act, civil rules governing

Sacramento downtown arena project, CEQA challenges   CRC 3.2220 to 3.2237

STAINED GLASS ARTISTRY

Fine art, defined as   CC §997

STAIRWAYS

Landlord's duty to repair   CC §1941.1

STALKING

Access to domestic violence incident reports   Fam §6228

Address confidentiality for victims

Actions, confidentiality requirements for protected persons in civil proceeding   CCP §367.3

Judicial council forms   CRCAppx A

Name change proceedings under address confidentiality program   CRC 2.575 to 2.577

Damages   CC §1708.7

Ex parte order enjoining   Fam §§6274, 6320

California law enforcement telecommunications (CLETS) information form, confidentiality and use of information   CRC 1.51, CRCAppx A

Denial of petition for ex parte order, reasons to be provided   Fam §6320.5

Injunctions

COVID-19, emergency rule   CRCAppx I Emer Rule 8

Dependency proceeding

Firearm relinquishment procedures   CRC 5.495

Forms for firearm relinquishment   CRCAppx A

Ex parte order enjoining

Denial of petition for ex parte order, reasons to be provided   Fam §6320.5

Landlord and tenant

Termination of tenancy

Victims of domestic violence, sexual assault or stalking   CC §1946.7, CCP §1161.3

Unlawful detainer proceedings, nuisance committed by tenant as grounds

Presumption of nuisance   CCP §1161

Restrictions on termination of tenancy   CC §1946.7, CCP §1161.3

Name change to avoid stalking   CCP §1277

Postsecondary educational institutions

Injunction against violence threatened on campus or facility

Judicial council legal forms   CRCAppx A

Orders against violence threatened on campus or facility

COVID-19, emergency rule   CRCAppx I Emer Rule 8

Prostitution, evidence

Extortion, serious felony, assault, domestic violence, human trafficking, sexual battery or stalking, victims or witnesses

Inadmissibility of evidence of prostitution in prosecution for prostitution   Ev §1162

Protective orders

Address or location of complaining party or family, prohibition on enjoined party from obtaining   CCP §527.10

California law enforcement telecommunications (CLETS) information form, confidentiality and use of information   CRC 1.51, CRCAppx A

COVID-19, emergency rule   CRCAppx I Emer Rule 8

Firearm relinquishment and disposition

Forms for firearm relinquishment   CRCAppx A

Procedures   CRC 4.700, 5.495

Name change proceedings under address confidentiality program   CRC 2.575 to 2.577

Requests for protective orders   CRC 3.1160

Waiver of fees   CCP §527.6

Public records

Address confidentiality for victims

Actions, confidentiality requirements for protected persons in civil proceeding   CCP §367.3

Judicial council forms   CRCAppx A

Name change proceedings under address confidentiality program   CRC 2.575 to 2.577

Universities and colleges

Injunction against violence threatened on campus or facility

Requests for protective orders   CRC 3.1160

Protection orders against violence threatened on campus or facility   CCP §527.85

California law enforcement telecommunications (CLETS) information form, confidentiality and use of information   CRC 1.51, CRCAppx A

Memorandum in support of petition not required   CRC 3.1114

Index

Index

Index

Index

Index

Index

Index

SURVIVORSHIP
Attorney in fact, authority of   Pro §4264
Deposits delivered to survivor   CC §1828
Marital deduction gifts, survivorship requirements for   Pro §21525
Right of survivorship (See **RIGHT OF SURVIVORSHIP**)

SUSPENSION
Attorney's suspension, appointment of new attorney on   CCP §286
Conservators (See **CONSERVATORS**)
Driving privilege (See **AUTOMOBILES**)
Executors and administrators (See **EXECUTORS AND ADMINISTRATORS**)
Guardians (See **GUARDIAN AND WARD**)
Notaries public, registration of   Fam §535

SUSTAINABLE GROUNDWATER MANAGEMENT ACT
Groundwater rights actions
   Definitions of sustainable groundwater management act   CCP §832

SWEARING (See **OATHS**)

SYPHILIS
Minor's consent to treatment   Fam §6926

T

TAGALOG
Contracts in Chinese, Tagalog, Vietnamese or Korean languages   CC §1632
Gender tax repeal act preventing charging different prices for services of similar or like kind based on gender
   Consumer affairs department pamphlet for affected businesses and other notice of requirements of provisions   CC §51.63
   Licensing authority notice of provisions to licensee upon issuance or renewal   CC §51.6
Mortgages of residential property, foreign language summaries of terms   CC §1632.5

TAGS
Baggage, tagging requirements for   CC §2205

TAILORS
Gender, prohibition against charging different price for services of similar or like kind based solely on   CC §51.6
Small business gender discrimination in pricing services compliance act   CC §§55.61 to 55.63

TAKING (See **EMINENT DOMAIN**)

TANGIBLE THINGS, INSPECTION OF (See **INSPECTION DEMANDS**)

TANNING FACILITIES
Minors
   Verification of age for sale of age-restricted products   CC §1798.99.1

TAX ASSESSMENTS (See **TAXATION**)

TAXATION
Assessments
   Adverse interests in real property arising out of public improvement assessment, action to determine   CCP §§801.1 to 801.15
   Adverse possession, payment of taxes to establish   CCP §325
   Auction of land subject to assessment lien, time limit for public official's   CCP §330
   Chartered city, action to contest validity of levy by   CCP §329.5
   Condemnation proceedings, assessment liens in   CCP §§1250.250, 1265.250
   Covenants requiring payment of   CC §1468
   Definition of encumbrance   CC §1114
   Eminent domain proceedings
      Basis for value of property, tax assessments establishing   Ev §822
      Encumbered by tax lien, acquisition of property   CCP §§1250.250, 1265.250
   Environmental constraints on use of land, consideration of
      Greenway easements as enforceable restriction   CC §816.66
   Life tenant to pay   CC §840
   Mello-Roos Community Facilities Act, disclosure regarding special tax liens on transfer of property pursuant to   CC §1102.6b
   Quieting title to real property subject to public improvement assessment, action to   CCP §§801.1 to 801.15
   Restricted property valuations
      Greenway easements as enforceable restriction   CC §816.66

TAXATION—Cont.
Assessments—Cont.
   Special assessment liens
      Eminent domain, encumbered property acquired by   CCP §1265.250
      Mello-Roos Community Facilities Act, disclosure regarding special tax liens on transfer of property pursuant to   CC §1102.6b
      Statute of limitation for bringing action to challenge validity of levy   CCP §338
   Statutes of limitation
      Chartered city, action to contest validity of levy by   CCP §329.5
      Special assessment, action challenging validity of   CCP §338
      Street improvement assessment, action on lien securing   CCP §329
   Street improvement assessment, action on lien securing   CCP §329
   Supplemental property tax bills
      Disclosures upon transfer of real property   CC §1102.6c
Auction of land subject to assessment lien, time limit for public official's   CCP §330
Child support (See **CHILD SUPPORT**)
Claims against decedents' estates   Pro §§9200 to 9205
Costs, motion to tax (See **COSTS**)
Disclosure of information
   By bookkeeping services   CC §1799.1a
   By Franchise Tax Board   CC §1798.28
Dissolution of marriage proceedings   Fam §2337
Distribution of estates, payment of taxes prior to   Pro §9650
Eminent domain (See **EMINENT DOMAIN**)
Enforcement of judgments (See **ENFORCEMENT OF JUDGMENTS**)
Estate tax (See **ESTATE TAX**)
Foreign country judgments
   Applicability of provisions   CCP §1715
Garnishment proceedings (See **GARNISHMENT**)
Generation-skipping transfer tax (See **GENERATION-SKIPPING TRANSFER TAX**)
Impound accounts (See **IMPOUND ACCOUNTS**)
Income tax (See **INCOME TAX**)
Inheritance tax (See **INHERITANCE TAX**)
Internal revenue department
   Estate tax (See **ESTATE TAX**)
   Income tax (See **INCOME TAX**)
   Marital deduction gifts (See **MARITAL DEDUCTION GIFTS**)
   Will construction, application of Internal Revenue Code provisions to (See **WILL CONSTRUCTION**)
Liens
   Assessments generally (See within this heading, **"Assessments"**)
   Credit reports (See **CREDIT REPORTING**)
   Federal tax lien registration   CCP §§2100 to 2107
      Fees for recording under act   Gov §27388.1
   State tax lien, notice of   CC §2885
Mello-Roos Community Facilities Act, disclosure regarding special tax liens on transfer of property pursuant to   CC §1102.6b
Mine co-owners failing to pay   CCP §§853 to 859
Mortgages (See **TRUST DEEDS AND MORTGAGES**)
Motion to tax costs (See **COSTS**)
Postponed property taxes, notice of default on property subject to lien for   CC §2924b
Power of attorney, powers under statutory form of   Pro §4463
Principal and income allocations   CC §731.14, Pro §§6371, 6374, 6375
Public entity's liability for tax law administration   Gov §§860 to 860.4
Quiet title to real property subject to public improvement assessment, action to   CCP §§801.1 to 801.15
Real property sales contract, payments received under   CC §2985.4
Sales tax (See **SALES AND USE TAX**)
Special assessments
   Assessments generally (See within this heading, **"Assessments"**)
Statutes of limitation on actions based on assessments (See within this heading, **"Assessments"**)
Trust decanting, uniform act
   Exercise of decanting power
      Tax-related limitations   Pro §19519
Trust deeds (See **TRUST DEEDS AND MORTGAGES**)
Trusts (See **TRUSTS**)
Unclaimed property fund appropriations for payment   CCP §1325
Validation proceedings on bonds for which tax revenue has been pledged by agency other than agency imposing tax, notice requirements for   CCP §870.5

TAX COLLECTOR
Limitation of actions to recover goods seized by   CCP §341

TAXING COSTS (See **COSTS**)

Index

Index

THREATS—Cont.

Rape accomplished by threat of future retaliation
  Statute of limitations
    Civil damages   CCP §340.16
Schools
  Force, threat or other obstruction of access to health facilities or school grounds   CC §1708.9
  Grounds, threats to commit violence using firearm or deadly weapon on   CC §48.8
Sodomy perpetrated by
  Statute of limitations
    Civil damages   CCP §340.16
Stalking
  Name change proceedings under address confidentiality program   CRC 2.575 to 2.577

THREE MONTHS (See STATUTES OF LIMITATION)

THREE YEARS (See STATUTES OF LIMITATION)

THRESHING MACHINES

Lien for use of   CC §3061

TICKETS

Common carrier limiting liability by provisions in   CC §2176
Railroads (See **RAILROADS**)
Vessels (See **VESSELS**)

TIDELANDS

Eminent domain, taking for   CCP §1240.110
Highwater mark as boundary   CCP §2077
Leasing of   CC §718
Ownership of   CC §670
Public entity's liability for injury on   Gov §831.6
Public lands, private property used as   CC §1009
Title to
  Border land   CC §830
  State   CC §670

TIMBER (See LOGS AND TIMBER)

TIME

Administration of decedents' estates
  Generally (See **ADMINISTRATION OF ESTATES**)
  Claims against decedents' estates (See **CLAIMS AGAINST ESTATES**)
Administrative law and procedure
  Adjudicative proceedings (See **ADMINISTRATIVE ADJUDICATION**)
  Rulemaking and regulation (See **ADMINISTRATIVE PROCEDURE ACT**)
Annulment proceedings, time for filing responsive pleading   Fam §2020
Appellate rules
  Superior court appeals
    Extensions of time (See **APPELLATE RULES, SUPERIOR COURT APPEALS**)
    Supreme court and courts of appeal (See **APPELLATE RULES, SUPREME COURT AND COURTS OF APPEAL**)
Appropriation of waters, time for completion of work for   CC §1416
Arbitration awards   CCP §1283.8
Attachment (See **ATTACHMENT**)
Attorneys (See **ATTORNEYS**)
Blood test, submission of affidavit stating technique in taking   Ev §712
Change of venue, time to file petition for writ of mandate on grant or denial of motion for   CCP §400
Civil Code takes effect   CC §2
Claim and delivery, return of possession writs to court   CCP §514.040
Claims against decedents' estates (See **CLAIMS AGAINST ESTATES**)
Commencing actions, time for (See **STATUTES OF LIMITATION**)
Common carriers, time schedules required for   CC §§2170, 2172
Community property, valuation of   Fam §2552
Computation of time
  Holidays (See **HOLIDAYS**)
  Limitation of actions (See **STATUTES OF LIMITATION**)
Conciliation court hearings   Fam §1837
Consent for contract agreement, time for   CC §1583
Courts of appeal (See **COURTS OF APPEAL**)
Cross-complaints (See **CROSS-COMPLAINTS**)
Custody investigation, time for filing reports of   Fam §3111
Default judgments (See **DEFAULT JUDGMENTS**)
Demurrers   CCP §§430.40, 432.10, 471.5, 472a, 472b
Discovery
  Saturday, Sunday or holiday, deadline falling on   CCP §2016.060
Dismissal of action (See **DISMISSAL**)
Disqualification of judges (See **JUDGES, DISQUALIFICATION OF**)

TIME—Cont.

Dissolution of marriage proceedings, time for filing responsive pleadings   Fam §2020
Effect of codes   CC §23
Enforcement of judgments (See **ENFORCEMENT OF JUDGMENTS**)
Enjoyment of real property   CC §707
Environmental quality act
  Petitions under environmental quality act, civil rules governing
    Extensions of time   CRC 3.2221
Evidence excluded on undue consumption of   Ev §352
Exceptions   CCP §646
Extensions of time (See **EXTENSIONS OF TIME**)
Family law rules (See **FAMILY RULES**)
Forms, molds and dies, notice of termination of customer's title to   CC §1140
Groundwater rights actions
  Notice of complaint   CCP §835
Harassment, duration of protection order   CCP §527.6
  COVID-19, emergency rule   CRCAppx I Emer Rule 8
Health care provider's professional negligence, notice of intention to commence action based on   CCP §364
Information Practices Act (See **INFORMATION PRACTICES ACT**)
Judges (See **JUDGES**)
Judgments, entry of   CCP §664
Judicial arbitration (See **JUDICIAL ARBITRATION**)
Jury instructions, time for decision on proposed   CCP §607a
Jury summons, time for mailing   CCP §208
Last day to perform act before hearing date
  Computation   CCP §12c
Limitation of actions (See **STATUTES OF LIMITATION**)
Mandamus   CCP §§1094.6, 1108
Mechanics' liens (See **MECHANICS' LIENS**)
Missing persons (See **MISSING PERSONS**)
Mistake, inadvertence, surprise or excusable neglect, time to apply for relief from judgment based on   CCP §473
Molds, forms and dies, notice of termination of customer's title to   CC §1140
Motion, service of notice of   CCP §§1005, 1013
Motions to strike   CRC 3.1322
Motor vehicle warranties, actions involving   CC §1793.22
New trial motion   CCP §§659, 659a, 661
Notices served by mail   CCP §1013
Oil and gas liens, duration of   CCP §1203.53
Pending litigation (See **PENDENCY OF ACTIONS**)
Process (See **PROCESS AND SERVICE OF PROCESS**)
Protective orders, expiration of   CCP §486.090
Receiver, hearing on order to show cause re ex parte appointment of   CRC 3.1176
Referee's report of statement of decision, filing of   CCP §643
Rent, payment of   CC §1947
Rules of court
  Computation of time   CRC 1.10
  Extending or shortening time   CRC 1.10
    Trial court rules   CRC 2.20
Service of process (See **PROCESS AND SERVICE OF PROCESS**)
Service of summons (See **PROCESS AND SERVICE OF PROCESS**)
Setting for trial (See **TRIAL**)
Settlements
  Request for additional time to complete   CRC 3.1385
Shortened time (See **SHORTENING TIME**)
Small claims court (See **SMALL CLAIMS COURTS**)
Stay of enforcement of judgment, duration of   CCP §918
Subpoena duces tecum, delivery pursuant to   Ev §1560
Summary dissolution of marriage, time for entry of judgment in   Fam §2403
Summary judgments, motion for   CCP §437c
Summons, service of (See **PROCESS AND SERVICE OF PROCESS**)
Sundays and holidays in time computation   CC §§10, 12, 12a
Superior courts (See **SUPERIOR COURTS**)
Supreme Court (See **SUPREME COURT, CALIFORNIA**)
Surety bonds (See **SURETYSHIP, BONDS AND UNDERTAKINGS**)
Temporary restraining orders, day upon which order is made returnable   CCP §527
Termination of parental rights, hearings   Fam §7870
Trial court rules
  Extension of time
    Application for order to extend time   CRC 2.20
Uniform Transfers to Minors Act (See **UNIFORM TRANSFERS TO MINORS ACT**)
Unlawful detainer (See **UNLAWFUL DETAINER**)
Vacate judgment
  Ruling on motion   CCP §663a

Index

Index

Index

Index

Index

Index

Index

Index

Index

Index

Index

UNIVERSITIES AND COLLEGES—Cont.
Violence
> Protection orders against violence threatened on campus or facility   CCP §527.85
>> California law enforcement telecommunications (CLETS) information form, confidentiality and use of information   CRC 1.51, CRCAppx A
>> COVID-19, emergency rule   CRCAppx I Emer Rule 8
>> Judicial council legal forms   CRCAppx A
>> Memorandum in support of petition not required   CRC 3.1114
>> Requests for protective orders   CRC 3.1160

UNIVERSITY OF CALIFORNIA
Asbestos claims against   Gov §905.6
Attachment proceedings   CCP §481.200
Claim and delivery   CCP §511.100
Construction of actions against   Gov §943
Construction-related accessibility claims
> Attorney prelitigation letter to education entities   CC §54.27
Eminent domain taking by   CCP §1245.210
Information Practices Act, disclosures under   CC §1798.24
Physician employed by or with privileges at university facility
> Statute of limitations on sexual assault or other inappropriate action by physician   CCP §340.16
Service of process on regents of   CCP §416.50
Sexual assault
> Statute of limitations on sexual assault or other inappropriate action by physician employed by or with privileges at university facility   CCP §340.16
Social security numbers
> Public posting or display
>> Implementation of provisions   CC §1798.85
Unclaimed property, disposition of   CC §2080.8
> Claim not required for controller to transfer property to state or local agencies   CCP §1540

UNIVERSITY OF SOUTHERN CALIFORNIA
Student health center
> Sexual assault
>> Actions claiming damages for sexual assault at student health center, revival when otherwise barred by statute of limitations   CCP §340.16

UNKNOWN CLAIMS
Release affecting   CC §1542

UNKNOWN PERSONS (See also **MISSING PERSONS**)
Adoption proceedings
> Termination of unknown biological father's parental rights   Fam §7665
Amendment to add true name of defendant designated as unknown   CCP §474
Complaint   CCP §474
Death of unknown person, giving notice of   Pro §7600.5
Default judgments   CCP §474
Distributee under decedent's estate, whereabouts unknown for   Pro §11603
Eminent domain proceedings   CCP §1260.240
Guardian ad litem appointed for   CCP §373.5
Lost property, unknown owners of   CC §2080.1
Mortgagee   CC §2941.7
Partition (See **PARTITION**)
Publication of notice of funds by receiver   CCP §570
Public improvement assessments, actions to determine adverse interests in real property arising out of   CCP §§801.4, 801.9, 801.10
Quieting title action, defendant in   CCP §§762.020, 762.060, 762.070
Receivers holding funds of   CCP §570
Trust deed, obligor under   CC §2941.7
Unclaimed property (See **UNCLAIMED PROPERTY**)

UNLAWFUL DETAINER (See also **FORCIBLE ENTRY AND DETAINER**)
Access to court records, restrictions on   CCP §1161.2
> COVID-19 rental debt recovery actions   CCP §1161.2.5
>> Superior court fees
>>> Permissible additional fees   Gov §70603
Acts constituting   CCP §§1161, 1161a
Affirmative defense of habitability, effect of   CCP §1174.2
Answer or demurrer
> Generally   CCP §1170
> Forms
>> Judicial council legal forms   CRCAppx A
> Time for   CCP §§1167, 1167.3
Appeals
> Generally   CCP §§1176, 1178

UNLAWFUL DETAINER—Cont.
Appeals—Cont.
> New trial   CCP §1178
> Stay of execution pending   CCP §1176
Attachment, writ of   CCP §483.020
Claim of right to possession
> Claim of occupant   CCP §1174.25
> Form   CCP §1174.3
> Objection to enforcement of judgment against occupant by filing   CCP §1174.3
> Prejudgment claim of right to possession, service on occupant of   CCP §415.46
Commercial real property, unlawful detainer of   CCP §1161.1
Commercial tenants
> Notice to quit   CCP §1162
Complaints
> Generally   CCP §§425.12, 1166
> Amendment of   CC §1952.3, CCP §1173
> Contents of   CCP §1166
> Immediate possession on filing   CCP §1166a
> Judicial Council development and approval of pleading forms   CCP §425.12
> Possession no longer in issue   CC §1952.3
> Verification of   CCP §1166
Conditional sales contract, holding over after sale pursuant to default provisions of   CCP §1161a
Controlled substances, use by tenants
> Nuisances involving controlled substances   CC §3486.5
Costs
> Award to prevailing party   CCP §1174.2
> Default judgment, costs on   CCP §1169
> Nuisances
>> Controlled substances activities   CC §§3486, 3486.5
>> Weapons or ammunition on real property   CC §3485
> Rent default as basis of unlawful detainer complaint
>> Untenantable dwellings, landlord liability for costs and attorney fees   CCP §1174.21
> Supplemental costs bill, filing of   CCP §1034.5, CRC 3.2000
> Warranty of habitability as affirmative defense, award of costs in action involving   CCP §1174.2
Court records, restricted access to   CCP §1161.2
> COVID-19 rental debt recovery actions   CCP §1161.2.5
> Superior court fees
>> Permissible additional fees   Gov §70603
COVID-19
> Emergency rule   CRCAppx I Emer Rule 1
> Financial distress, declaration
>> Damages owed by landlord for certain violations, effect of declaration   CC §789.4
> Judicial council form   CRCAppx A
> Rental debt recovery actions
>> Access to case records   CCP §1161.2.5
> Tenant relief act of 2020   CCP §§1179.01 to 1179.07
>> Agreements purporting to waive statutory provisions   CCP §1179.06
>> Cover sheet for unlawful detainer actions   CCP §1179.01.5
>> Definitions   CCP §§1179.02, 1179.02.5
>> Findings required for determination of unlawful detainer   CCP §1179.03.5
>> High-income tenants   CCP §1179.02.5
>> Legislative intent   CCP §1179.01.5
>> Local provisions to protect tenants from eviction, requirements   CCP §1179.05
>> Notice demanding payment of COVID-19 rental debt   CCP §1179.03
>> Notice from landlord for tenants defaulting on one or more rental payments   CCP §1179.04
>> Prohibited actions by courts   CCP §1179.01.5
>> Sunset of statutory provisions   CCP §1179.07
>> Title of chapter   CCP §1179.01
Credit reporting (See **CREDIT REPORTING**)
Cumulative remedies   CC §1952
Damages
> Generally   CCP §1174
> Possession, damages after delivery of   CC §1952.3
> Treble damages   CCP §735
Deed of receiver or levying officer, service or exhibition of   CCP §1162a
Default judgments   CCP §1169
Defaults
> COVID-19
>> Emergency rule   CRCAppx I Emer Rule 1
>> Financial distress, declaration   CRCAppx A
>> Tenant relief act of 2020   CCP §§1179.01 to 1179.07

Index

Index

VIRGIN ISLANDS
Acknowledgment of instruments   CC §1183.5

VISION SCREENING
Immunity from liability
  Nonprofit charitable organization and volunteer eye care professionals donating screening, eyeglasses, etc   CC §1714.26

VISITATION RIGHTS   CRC 5.695
Appointment of attorney for child   CRC 5.240 to 5.242, Fam §§3114, 3150 to 3153
Child custody proceedings, visitation in   CRC 5.695
Custody of children (See **CUSTODY OF CHILDREN**)
Dependent children
  Detained child, visitation with   CRC 5.670
  Grandparents' visitation rights   CRC 5.695
  Parents' or guardians' visitation rights   CRC 5.695
  Sibling visitation   CRC 5.670
Family reunification services, visitation orders   CRC 5.695
Forms
  Judicial council legal forms   CRCAppx A
Guardianships
  Jurisdiction   Pro §2205
  Venue, multiple counties with pending proceedings   Pro §2204
    Communications between/among courts involved with custody, visitation and guardianship involving ward   CRC 7.1014
    Ward's participation and testimony in probate guardianship proceedings   CRC 7.1016
Juvenile court, exclusive jurisdiction of   CRC 5.510
  Termination of jurisdiction
    Orders as to custody or visitation   CRC 5.700
Modification of orders
  Domestic violence prevention act proceedings   CRC 5.381
Reasons for no or for supervised visitation
  Form   CRCAppx A
Supervised visitation
  Reasons for no or for supervised visitation
    Form   CRCAppx A
Supervised visitation, child abuse and neglect cases   CRC JudAdminStand 5.20

VISUALLY HANDICAPPED PERSONS (See **BLIND PERSONS**)

VITAL STATISTICS
Birth (See **BIRTH**)
Records admissible in evidence   Ev §§1281 to 1283

VOCATIONAL TRAINING
Spousal support, order for examination by vocational training consultant   Fam §4331

VOICES
Invasion of privacy, unauthorized use of voice in advertising as   CC §§3344, 3344.1

VOIDABLE TRANSACTIONS   CC §§1227, 3439 to 3439.14, 3440, 3440.3
Actual intent to hinder, delay or defraud creditors   CC §3439.04
Agency, application of rules relating to law of   CC §3439.12
Antecedent debt, property received to secure   CC §3439.03
Assignee of assignment for benefit of creditors, rights and remedies   CC §3439.07
Attachment against asset transferred or its proceeds   CC §3439.07
Avoidance of obligation as remedy   CC §3439.07
Bona fide purchasers as affected by   CC §3439.08
Bond in action to set aside   CC §§3445 to 3449
Cause of action, when extinguished   CC §3439.09
Citation of act   CC §3439
Coercion, application of rules as to effect of   CC §3439.12
Consideration   CC §§3439.03, 3439.04
  Value given   CC §3439.04
Construction of statute   CC §§3439.12, 3440.9
Damages, recovery of   CC §3439.08
Debts, fraudulent incurring of   CC §§3439.04, 3439.05
Decedent's estate, recovering property for creditors of   Pro §9653
Definitions   CC §§3439.01, 3445
Defraud or delay creditors, transaction made with intent to   CC §3439.04
Delivery requirements   CC §3440
Discount buying organization officer   CC §1812.106
Duress, application of rules   CC §3439.12
Equity rules, application   CC §3439.12
Execution
  Property, execution on   CC §3439.07

VOIDABLE TRANSACTIONS—Cont.
Exemptions
  Generally   CC §§3440.1, 3440.2
  Secured party, interest from transferee or successor acquired by   CC §3440.5
Former law, transfers made under   CC §3439.14
Fraud, application of rules   CC §3439.12
Good faith takers for value   CC §3439.08
Hinder creditors, transaction made with intent to   CC §3439.04
Injunctive relief   CC §3439.07
Innocent purchasers
  Delivery, purchase of personal property without   CC §§3440.3, 3440.4
  Real property   CC §§1227, 1228
  Remedies of creditors   CC §3439.07
  Rights of good faith purchasers   CC §§3439.08, 3440.4
Insolvency
  Application of rules   CC §3439.12
  Defined   CC §3439.02
  Partnership, determination of insolvency of   CC §3439.02
  Transaction resulting in, as fraudulent   CC §3439.05
Intent to defraud   CC §3439.04
Law merchant, application   CC §3439.12
Limitation of actions   CC §3439.09
Marital property, fraudulent transmutation of   Fam §851
Multiple-party accounts law, effect   Pro §5202
Nonvoidable transfers or obligations   CC §3439.08
Notices requirements   CC §§1228, 3440.1
Obligations
  Fraudulently incurred   CC §§3439.04, 3439.05
  Nonvoidable   CC §3439.08
  When incurred   CC §3439.06
Partnership, insolvency of   CC §3439.02
Possession not transferred   CC §3440
Principal and agent, application of law   CC §3439.12
Purchasers' rights
  Good faith purchasers
    Innocent purchasers generally (See within this heading, **"Innocent purchasers"**)
  Secured party, interest from transferee or successor acquired by   CC §3440.5
Purpose of provisions   CC §3439.13
Receivers
  Actions for vacation   CCP §564
  Appointment   CC §3439.07
Remedies of creditors   CC §3439.07
Retroactive nature of Uniform Voidable Transactions Act   CC §3439.14
Secured party, interest from transferee or successor acquired by   CC §3440.5
Small estate dispositions without administration   Pro §§13100 to 13117
Statutes of limitation
  Personal property, transfers involving   CC §3440.6
  Uniform Voidable Transactions Act, action under   CC §3439.09
Subsequent transferees for value   CC §3439.08
Time of transfer of property, determination   CC §3439.06
Transfers
  Nonvoidable   CC §3439.08
  Rights of transferees   CC §3439.08
  When made   CC §3439.06
Trust beneficiary's disclaimer of interest, effect   Pro §283
Undertaking   CC §§3445 to 3449
  Amount   CC §3448
  Condition   CC §3447
  Effect   CC §3446
  Effective date   CC §3449
Uniform act   CC §§3439 to 3439.14
Value, when given   CC §3439.03
Water supply property
  Personal property conveyed without delivery
    Exception to provisions   CC §3440.1

VOID FILING
Check for filing fees
  Returned unpaid   CCP §411.20
  Underpayment   CCP §411.21

VOID OR VOIDABLE MARRIAGES (See **ANNULMENT; MARRIAGE**)

VOIR DIRE (See **JURY**)

VOLCANIC ACTIVITY
State's immunity from liability for prediction of   Gov §955.1

VOLUNTARY MANSLAUGHTER (See **MANSLAUGHTER**)

VOLUNTEERS

Court-appointed special advocates (CASA)
    Appointment of volunteers   CRC 5.655
    Oath   CRC 5.655
    Prohibited activities   CRC 5.655
    Removal, resignation or termination   CRC 5.655
    Screening of volunteers   CRC 5.655
    Supervision, support, etc   CRC 5.655
    Training   CRC 5.655
Small claims advisors   CCP §116.940
Vision screening
    Immunity from liability
        Nonprofit charitable organization and volunteer eye care professionals donating screening, eyeglasses, etc   CC §1714.26

VOTER REGISTRATION

Jurors, list of registered voters as source for selection of   CCP §197
Precedence to cases involving elections proceedings   CCP §35

VOTES AND VOTING

Administrative adjudicative proceedings (See **ADMINISTRATIVE ADJUDICATION**)
Conservatee's right to vote   Pro §§1823, 1828, 1851
Elections (See **ELECTIONS AND ELECTIONS PROCEEDINGS**)
Initiative and referendum
    Tax limitation initiative (See **TAXATION**)
Judges participating in political activities, Code of Judicial Ethics provisions regarding   CRCSupp JudEthicsCanon 5
Recall of elective officer (See **RECALL**)

VOTING TRUSTS

Participation in voting trusts by trustee   Pro §16237

VOUCHERS

Administration of estates (See **ADMINISTRATION OF ESTATES**)
Claims against decedent's estate, vouchers filed in support of   Pro §9151

W

WAGE ASSIGNMENTS FOR SUPPORT (See **EARNINGS ASSIGNMENT FOR SUPPORT**)

WAGERING (See **GAMBLING**)

WAGES (See **SALARIES AND WAGES**)

WAIVER

Acceleration of loan provisions, waiver of   CC §2924.6
Administration of decedents' estates (See **ADMINISTRATION OF ESTATES**)
Administrative adjudication provisions, waiver of rights under   Gov §11415.40
Adoption proceedings, waiver of confidentiality in   Fam §§9204, 9205
    Sibling contact
        Request for sibling contact information   CRC 5.460
Adoption, waiver of right to revoke consent to   Fam §8814.5
Alteration of instruments affecting   CC §1698
Appearances
    Personal appearance waivers
        COVID-19, emergency rule   CRCAppx I Emer Rule 5
Arbitration, waiver of (See **ARBITRATION**)
Artists waiving rights to art dealers   CC §1738.8
Assistive devices, warranty on sale of   CC §1793.02
Attachment proceedings, waiver of defense in   CCP §484.110
Attorney-client privilege   Ev §912
Automobile conditional sales contract, prohibited provision in   CC §2983.7
Claim and delivery possession writs   CCP §512.100
Claims against decedent's estate, effect of personal representative waiving defects in filing   Pro §9154
Clergyman-penitent privilege   Ev §912
Confession of judgment, attorneys advising defendant of waiver of rights in   CCP §1132
Conservators
    Accounting
        Order waiving accounting   CRC 7.575
Consumer credit organization, waiver of rights by buyer using   CC §1789.19
Consumer goods or services, contract for sale or lease
    Statements by consumer about seller, lessor, goods or services
        Prohibited contract provisions   CC §§1670.8, 1670.8.5
Consumer privacy rights
    Waiver or limitation of consumer rights
        Contracts or agreements void   CC §1798.192
Contract rights   CC §3268

WAIVER—Cont.
Court fees and costs
    Bench warrants to secure attendance of witnesses, applicability of waiver   Gov §26744.5
    Civil rules governing waiver of fees and costs   CRC 3.50 to 3.58
    Court reporters
        Request for reporter if granted fee waiver   CRC 2.956
    Economically unable to pay   Gov §§68630 to 68641
    Forms, judicial council   CRCAppx A
Court reporters
    Request for reporter if granted fee waiver
        Judicial council form   CRCAppx A
Criminal conduct
    Contract or settlement waiving right to testify concerning criminal conduct or sexual harassment   CC §1670.11
Dance studio contracts, provisions regulating   CC §1812.61
Demurrer (See **DEMURRERS**)
Disability insurance provisions, effect of waiver of   CC §1812.408
Disclaimer of estate interest, waiver of right to file   Pro §284
Domestic violence counselor-victim privilege   Ev §912
Enforcement of judgments (See **ENFORCEMENT OF JUDGMENTS**)
Floating homes and floating home marinas (See **FLOATING HOMES**)
Foster care
    Specialty mental health services
        Judicial council legal forms   CRCAppx A
        Presumptive transfer of responsibility for services upon change of child placement, proceedings upon request for waiver   CRC 5.647
Guardianships
    Accounting
        Order waiving accounting   CRC 7.575
Health studio services contracts, effect of buyer waiving rights under   CC §1812.93
Home equity sales contracts   CC §1695.10
Indigent persons (See **INDIGENT PERSONS**)
Innkeeper's lien, writ of possession on   CC §1861.13
Interest   CC §3290
Judges, waiver of disqualification of   CCP §1170.3
Jury trial   CCP §631
Landlord and tenant
    Rent increase limitations for residential real property
        Void nature of waiver   CC §1947.12
    Water service in multifamily residential rental buildings
        Waiver of provisions prohibited   CC §1954.215
Layaway provisions, buyer waiving   CC §1749.2
Leases (See **LEASES**)
Limitation, statutes of   CCP §360.5
Livestock service liens, sale under   CC §3080.08
Marital privilege   Ev §§912, 973
Merchantability warranty   CC §1792.3
Mobilehomes (See **MOBILEHOMES**)
Mortgage foreclosure consultant provisions   CC §2945.5
Mortgages, rights under statute governing   CC §2953
Net neutrality
    Barring waiver of provisions   CC §3104
Objections to pleadings   CCP §430.80
Oil and gas liens   CCP §1203.63
Oral argument   CRC 8.885
Pension claimants, affidavit fees waived for   Gov §26858
Physician-patient privilege   Ev §912
Privileged communication   Ev §§912, 919
Psychotherapist-patient privilege   Ev §912
Realty sales contract waiving provisions of Subdivision Map Act   CC §2985.51
Rental passenger vehicle transactions
    Damage waivers   CC §1939.09
        Defined   CC §1939.01
        Purchase of damage waiver or optional insurance, prohibited practices to induce   CC §1939.13
    Provisions of chapter, restrictions on waiver   CC §1939.29
Retail installment sales provisions   CC §1801.1
Seller assisted marketing plans, rights of purchaser   CC §1812.216
Sexual harassment
    Contract or settlement waiving right to testify concerning criminal conduct or sexual harassment   CC §1670.11
Small claims court (See **SMALL CLAIMS COURTS**)
Statutes of limitation   CCP §360.5
Subrogation, guarantor waiving rights of   CC §2856
Sureties and suretyship (See **SURETYSHIP, BONDS AND UNDERTAKINGS**)
Surviving spouse, rights of (See **SURVIVING SPOUSE**)
Tender, objection to   CCP §2076
Title, effect on marketability of   CC §880.030
Trust deeds, rights under statute governing   CC §2953

Index

Index

Index

Index